POLITICAL PARTIES OF THE WORLD

Other current affairs reference titles from John Harper Publishing include:

Border and Territorial Disputes of the World
The Council of the European Union
Directory of European Union Political Parties
The European Commission
The European Courts
The European Parliament
Revolutionary and Dissident Movements of the World
Trade Unions of the World
Treaties and Alliances of the World

POLITICAL PARTIES
OF THE WORLD

6th edition

Edited by Bogdan Szajkowski

JOHN HARPER
PUBLISHING

Political Parties of the World, 6th edition

Published by John Harper Publishing
Editorial enquiries: John Harper Publishing, 27 Palace Gates Road, London N22 7BW, UK. Email: jhpublish@aol.com
Sales enquiries: Extenza-Turpin, Stratton Business Park, Pegasus Drive, Biggleswade, SG18 8QB,
UK. Email: books@extenza-turpin.com

Distributed exclusively in the United States and Canada, and non-exclusively outside North America, by Gale Group Inc.,
27500 Drake Rd., Farmington Hills, Michigan 48331, USA

1st edition (1980), Longman Group UK Ltd
2nd edition (1984), Longman Group UK Ltd
3rd edition (1988), Longman Group UK Ltd
4th edition (1996), Cartermill International Ltd
5th edition (2002), John Harper Publishing

This edition first published 2005
© John Harper Publishing 2005
ISBN 0-9543811-4-9

Printed in Great Britain by the Cromwell Press

Table of Contents

Preface

The relentless expansion of the universe of political parties is reflected in the continuing increase in the size of successive volumes of *Political Parties of the World*, this sixth edition being over 20 per cent greater in extent than the fifth edition, published three years ago. The early editions of the book, published from 1980 onwards, captured the worldwide increase in party numbers generated by the decolonization of the 1960s and 1970s. Nonetheless, in the 1980s, the Soviet Union and the eight communist countries of Eastern Europe were single-party states and the single ruling party model also prevailed in many former colonies. In the early 1990s a further huge wave of party formation was triggered by the collapse of communism in the Soviet Union and Eastern Europe: that region has broken into 27 countries, mostly with vigorous party systems and accounting for several hundred party entries in the present volume. The dramatic shift was mirrored in much of Africa, where multi-partyism made rapid strides in the early 1990s, while former authoritarian regimes in Latin America also adopted pluralist models.

There has been no further "big bang" since the early 1990s, but the forces unleashed in previous decades continue to be felt – there is a continuing churn as new parties emerge, are tested, grow, fragment or perish, and many of the currently most significant parties in the former one-party states are of very recent formation, with many of those that were prominent in the early days of democratization having fallen by the wayside. Furthermore, the conventional shorthand that placed most parties on a well-understood left-right continuum increasingly fails to characterize large numbers of parties. Issues of national, regional, ethnic and religious identity are seemingly to the fore, while even well-established party systems are being strained by the emergence of parties around issues, such as integration in the European Union or cultural identity in the face of in-flows of different population groups, that have moved from the fringe to the mainstream.

As with previous editions, illegal, guerrilla and terrorist movements have not usually been included: these are dealt with in the Publishers' periodically updated companion volume, *Revolutionary and Dissident Movements of the World*, published most recently in 2004. Some exceptions continue to be made on a case-by-case basis, however, in respect of certain countries where the exercise of political power is particularly fluid, where such banned organizations exercise de facto political power in part of the national territory, or where exclusion would otherwise render understanding of the overall political situation impossible. Defunct parties are not normally described except in the context of the historical antecedents of existing parties, other than for a limited number of parties that have folded very recently. As previously, more significant parties are listed first, in alphabetical order according to the English language version of their name, while minor parties follow separately under the designation "Other Parties" – the distinction is inevitably to some degree arbitrary and is made purely for ease of reference.

The team of contributors involved in this new edition was the largest ever. The Editor and Publishers are indebted to them for their efforts, and details of the contributors are given in the pages following.

THE CONTRIBUTORS

Shirin Akiner (Central Asian Republics) is Lecturer in Central Asian Studies at the School of Oriental and African Studies, University of London, and an Associate Fellow of the Royal Institute of International Affairs, London. She has published widely on such topics as Islam, ethnicity, political change and security challenges in Central Asia.

Joseph Ayee (Ghana) is Professor of Political Science and Public Administration and Dean, Faculty of Social Studies, University of Ghana, Legon, Ghana, and has published extensively on decentralization, elections, privatization, the civil service and related topics.

Matthias Basedau (Botswana, Chad, Malawi, Namibia) is a Research Fellow at the Institute of African Affairs in Hamburg, Germany. He specializes in political parties in Africa, the political role of the military, strategic resources in sub-Saharan Africa, conditions for democracy in Africa, electoral systems, fraud and electoral engineering.

Florian Bieber (Bosnia, Serbia & Montenegro) is a senior non-resident research associate of the European Centre for Minority Issues, based in Belgrade and a recurrent visiting professor at the Central European University, Budapest. He also teaches the Regional Masters Program for Democracy and Human Rights, Sarajevo.

Tor Bjørklund (Norway) is Professor in Comparative Politics at the Department of Political Science, University of Oslo. He has published several books and numerous articles about elections, referendums and public opinion. His PhD dissertation was about nationwide referendums in Norway.

Duncan Brown (Bulgaria) is a PhD candidate at Keele University, UK, completing a thesis on the development of the Union of Democratic Forces in Bulgaria.

Martin Bull (Italy & San Marino, with James Newell) is Professor of Politics and Associate Dean for Research at the University of Salford, with research interests and publications in Italian and comparative politics. He is co-editor of the journal *Modern Italy*.

Julia Buxton (Venezuela) is a Senior Research Fellow at the Centre for International Cooperation and Security, Department of Peace Studies, Bradford University, and the author of *The Failure of Political Reform in Venezuela* (Ashgate, Basingstoke 2001).

Ladislav Cabada (Czech Republic) is the Head of the Department of Political Science and International Relations at the Faculty of Human Studies, University of West Bohemia, Pilsen. His publications include *Intellectuals and the Idea of Communism in Czech lands 1900-1939* (Prague, ISE 2000), *Czech Party System 1890-1939* (Pilsen, UWB Press 2000), *Contemporary Questions of Central European Politics* (editor, Dobra Voda, Ales Cenek 2002), *Europeanisation of National Political Parties* (co-editor with Alenka Krasovec, Dobra Voda, Ales Cenek 2004), *Political System of Republic of Slovenia*.

Peter Calvert (Argentina, Bolivia, Colombia, Ecuador, Mexico, Panama, Paraguay, Peru, Uruguay) is Emeritus Professor of Comparative and International Politics, University of Southampton. His most recent publications include (with Susan Calvert) *Politics and Society in the Third World* (2nd edn, 2001); *Comparative Politics: an Introduction* (2002); and (co-edited with Peter Burnell) *Civil Society in Democratization* (2004).

William Case (Malaysia) teaches in the Department of International Business and Asian Studies at Griffith University, Brisbane, Australia. He has taught at the MARA University of Technology in Shah Alam, Malaysia and held visiting research positions at the University of Malaya and the National University of Malaysia.

Peter Clegg (Caribbean States, Costa Rica, El Salvador,

Honduras and Nicaragua) is Lecturer in Politics at the University of the West of England, Bristol. His publications are in the area of Caribbean politics, trade and international relations and he is a member of the Caribbean Board, which provides the British government with independent advice on UK–Caribbean matters.

Charles A. Coppel (Indonesia) is a Principal Fellow in History at the University of Melbourne, where he has taught and researched for 30 years, specializing in the modern history of Indonesia and its ethnic Chinese minority. His publications include *Indonesian Chinese in Crisis* (1983) and *Studying Ethnic Chinese in Indonesia* (2002), and he is editor of the forthcoming *Violent Conflicts in Indonesia*.

Cátia Míriam Costa (Cape Verde) has degrees in International Relations and African Studies. Her specialization is the social and political situation of the former Portuguese colonies.

Tim Curtis (Bhutan, India, Maldives, Nepal, Pakistan, Sri Lanka) is a staff writer on Asian affairs for the current affairs journal *Keesing's Record of World Events*.

Zhidas Daskalovski (Macedonia) gained his PhD in 2003 in the Political Science Department at the Central European University in Budapest. He has published a number of scholarly articles on the Southeast European region.

José Lino de Souza (Benin, Burkina, Togo, with Sylvain Zinsou) is Administrative Assistant at the Regional Bureau of the Konrad Adenauer Foundation, Cotonou, Benin.

Gero Erdmann (Tanzania, Zambia) is a Senior Research Fellow at the Berlin office of the Institute of African Affairs (Hamburg) and a lecturer in political science. His current research focus is on democratization and political parties in several African countries.

Jocelyn Evans (France) is Senior Lecturer in Politics at the University of Salford. He is the author of *Voters and Voting: an Introduction* (Sage, 2004) and the editor of *The French Party System* (Manchester UP, 2003), as well as articles on French politics in *Electoral Studies*, *Revue Française de Science Politique*, *Revue Politique et Parlementaire* and *French Politics*.

Helga Fleischhacker (Gambia) holds degrees in Political Science (Ludwig-Maximilians-Universität, München) and Public Administration (Deutsche Hochschule für Verwaltungswissenschaft, Speyer). She was a research fellow and PhD candidate in Heidelberg, her thesis focusing on political parties in Africa. She is currently working as a institution building project manager in Iraq.

Vincent Foucher (Senegal) holds a PhD from the School of Oriental and African Studies, University of London; he did his research on separatism in Casamance (south Senegal). He currently is a researcher at the Centre d'Etudes d'Afrique Noire in Bordeaux (France).

Robert Funk (Chile) is Latin American Analyst with Enterprise LSE Ltd. His current research focuses on political learning and democratization in the Southern Cone.

John Gledhill (Moldova and Romania) is a PhD candidate in Comparative Government at Georgetown University. His current research focuses on the relationship between political violence and regime transition. His recent articles on Romanian history and politics have appeared in *East European Politics and Societies* and *National Identities*.

Geoffrey C. Gunn (East Timor) is Professor of International Relations in the Faculty of Economics, Nagasaki University. He is the author of several books on East Timor including *East Timor and the United Nations: The Case for Intervention* (Trenton, N.J., Red Sea Press, 1997). In 2000 he worked as a consultant to the UNTAET mission in East Timor; returning in 2003, he worked as history consultant to the Commission on Reception, Truth and Reconciliation for East Timor.

F. J. Harper (UK, USA, various Asian) is a writer and publisher on world affairs and politics.

Dragutin Hedl (Croatia) is a journalist who has written on Balkan politics for many international news magazines and held editorial positions on leading Croatian newspapers, including editor in-chief of *Glas Slavonje*. He is the editor of *Feral Tribune*.

Steve Hewitt (Canada) is a Lecturer in the Department of American and Canadian Studies at the University of Birmingham, UK. He is the author, with Reg Whitaker, of *Canada and the Cold War* (James Lorimer, 2003) and of *Spying 101: The RCMP's Secret Activities at Canadian Universities, 1917-1997* (University of Toronto Press, 2002).

A.V.M. Horton (Brunei) is an honorary fellow of the Centre for South-East Asian Studies, University of Hull.

Olexander Hryb (Ukraine) is a BBC World Service radio producer. Born in Lviv (Ukraine), he completed his doctoral studies at the Graduate School for Social Research (Polish Academy of Science) and the University of Sussex. He has published on Eastern European nationalism, Cossack revival, and media in Ukraine.

Derek S. Hutcheson (Russia) is a British Academy Postdoctoral Fellow in the Department of Politics, University of Glasgow. He is the author of *Political Parties in the Russian Regions* (London/New York: RoutledgeCurzon, 2003) and co-editor (with Elena A. Korosteleva) of *The Quality of Democracy in Post-Communist Europe* (London: Routledge, 2005 – forthcoming).

Francis Jacobs (Ireland, Appendix B – Pan-European Political Groupings) is currently the Head of Unit on the staff of the European Parliament's Committee on Environment, Public Health and Food Safety. He has written and lectured extensively on different aspects of European Union politics and is on the editorial board of the journal *Party Politics*; his publications include (with Richard Corbett and Michael Shackleton) *The European Parliament*, now in its 5th edition (John Harper Publishing, 2003).

Lawrence Joffe (Algeria, Bahrain, Egypt, Israel, Jordan, Kuwait, Lebanon, Libya, Mauritania, Morocco, Palestine, Western Sahara, Yemen) is a writer on Middle Eastern affairs, contributing to a range of newspapers and magazines. His publications include *Keesing's Guide to the Middle East Peace Process* (1997).

Maria D'Alva Kinzo (Brazil) is Professor of Political Science at the Universidade de São Paulo, Brazil. She has published widely on political parties, elections and democratization in Brazil, including the books *Legal Opposition Politics under Authoritarian Rule in Brazil* (Basingstoke, 1988), *Radiografia do Quadro Partidário Brasileiro* (São Paulo, 1993) and *Brazil since 1985: Economy, Polity and Society* (London, 2003).

Lubomir Kopecek (Slovakia) is Assistant Professor of Political Science in the Faculty of Social Studies, Masaryk University, Brno, Czech Republic. His main fields of research and publication are comparative politics and parties and party systems in post-communist countries and he is managing editor of the electronic journal *Central European Political Studies Review* (www.iips.cz/seps).

Elena A. Korosteleva (Belarus), formerly British Academy Research Fellow at Glasgow University, is now Lecturer at the Department of International Politics, University of Wales, Aberystwyth. Her recent publications include *The Quality of Democracy in Post-Communist Europe* (Cass, 2004, with Derek Hutcheson) and *Postcommunist Belarus* (Rowman & Littlefield, 2004, with Stephen White).

Baz Lecocq (Mali, Niger) studied African History at Leiden University; he gained his PhD in 2002 with a thesis on the Tuareg rebellions in Mali and is now researching at the Zentrum Moderner Orient in Berlin. He is particularly interested in the contemporary political history of the francophone countries of the Sahel and the Maghreb and has published articles on Tuareg Society and politics in Mali.

Charles Lees (Germany) is Lecturer in Politics at the University of Sheffield and Academic Fellow at the Sussex European

Institute, University of Sussex. He is also Editor of the PSA journal *Politics*, Managing Editor of *Journal of Common market Studies*, and co-Editor of the Manchester University Press series *Issues in German Politics*. Recent publications include *Bundestagswahl 2002: the Battle of the Candidates*, Frank Cass 2004 (with Thomas Saalfeld, eds.); *Social Democracy: Global and National Perspectives*, Palgrave, 2001 (with L. Martell *et al* (eds.)); and *The Red-Green Coalition in Germany: Politics, Personalities and Power*, Manchester University Press, 2000.

Kurt Richard Luther (Austria) is Senior Lecturer at Keele University, Convenor of the Keele European Parties Research Unit (KEPRU) and of the Parties Standing Group of the European Consortium for Political Research. His publications include the co-edited volumes *Party Elites in Divided Societies: Political Parties in Consociational Democracy* (Routledge 1999) and *Political Parties in the New Europe: Political and Analytical Challenges* (Oxford University Press, 2002). He is currently working on a major comparative project on the "Europeanization of National Parties" in the EU.

Colin Mackerras (China) is Foundation Professor in China Studies at Griffith University in Queensland, Australia. He has published numerous books and articles on Chinese history and contemporary China, especially its minority nationalities and theatre, his most recent book being *China's Ethnic Minorities and Globalisation* published by RoutledgeCurzon, London and New York, 2003.

José M. Magone (Portugal, Spain) is Senior Lecturer in European Politics in the Department of Politics and International Studies at the University of Hull (UK). Among his publications are *Contemporary Spanish Politics* (2004) and *The Developing Place of Portugal in the European Union*.

Andrew Mango (Turkey), formerly Head of BBC South European and French Language Services, is the author of *Ataturk*, a biography of the founder of modern Turkey (1999, new edition 2004) and of *The Turks Today* (2004), both published by John Murray in London. His study of terrorism in Turkey will appear in 2005.

David Scott Mathieson (Myanmar) is a doctoral student at the Australian National University. He has written on Burmese political economy and the civil war and his current research is on the economics of conflict in modern Burma.

Ronald J May (Papua New Guinea, Philippines) is a Senior Fellow, Research School of Pacific and Asian Studies, and convenor of the Centre for Conflict and Post-Conflict Studies, Asia Pacific, at the Australian National University. He has written extensively on topics including the Philippines, Papua New Guinea, and ethnicity.

Nadia Milanova (Afghanistan, Armenia, Azerbaijan, Georgia) is Programme Director for the non-governmental organization Human Rights Without Frontiers International and a former head of the Prague office of the OSCE Secretariat. She holds a PhD from the University of Exeter for a thesis on the conflict over Nagorno Karabakh and the conflict resolution activities of the OSCE.

Raymond Miller (New Zealand) is a Senior Lecturer in the Department of Political Studies, University of Auckland, where he teaches and researches in New Zealand and comparative politics. He has authored, co-authored or edited five books, including *New Zealand Politics in Transition* and *New Zealand Government and Politics*, both of which were published by Oxford University Press.

Frank Mols (Netherlands, Suriname) is currently working towards his PhD at the Centre for European Studies, University of Exeter (UK). His research interests include nationalism, stateless nations, separatism and international cooperation and integration.

James Newell (Italy & San Marino, with Martin Bull) is Reader in Politics at the University of Salford. His research interests lie mainly in the field of Italian politics on which he has published a number of books and articles, and he is co-editor of the European Consortium for Political Research's journal of the political science profession, *European Political Science*.

Alvaro Nobrega (Guinea-Bissau) is Lecturer at the Instituto Superior de Ciências Sociais e Politicas of the Universidade Técnica de Lisboa, Portugal. Author of the book *The Struggle for power in Guinea Bissau*, he was recently an EU election monitor in Bissau.

Alfred Oehlers (Singapore) is an Associate Professor in Economics in the Faculty of Business, Auckland University of Technology, New Zealand. His teaching and research focus on the political economy of development in East and Southeast Asia.

Roderick Pace (Malta) is Lecturer in International Relations and European Studies at the University of Malta and Director of the European Documentation and Research Centre (EDRC). His main research interests and publications focus on EU-Malta relations, the Euro-Mediterranean Partnership and small states in international relations and in the EU. His most recent work is *Micro State Security in Global System: EU-Malta Relations* (Midsea Books, Malta, 2001).

Despina Papadimitriou (Greece) is a Lecturer in History at Panteion University, Greece. Her main research interests include political conservatism, fascism and extremism, and mass ideological thought.

Robert G. Patman (Djibouti, Eritrea, Ethiopia, Somalia) is an Associate Professor in the Department of Political Studies at the University of Otago, New Zealand, and Director of the Master of International Studies programme. His research interests centre on international relations, the Horn of Africa, the ending of the Cold War and the relationship between order and justice in a globalizing world. His publications include *The Soviet Union in the Horn of Africa: the Diplomacy of Intervention and Disengagement* (Cambridge: Cambridge University Press, 1990), *Security in a Post-Cold War World* (Basingstoke: Macmillan, 1999; New York: St Martin's Press, 1999) and *Universal Human Rights?* (Basingstoke: Macmillan, 2000; New York: St Martin's Press, 2000).

Charlie Pericleous (Cyprus) is a doctoral candidate in International Relations at the University of Southampton, with a special interest in territorial disputes and counter-terrorist policies in the European Union.

Philippe Poirier (Luxembourg) was awarded a PhD in political science from the University of Rennes I in 2002 for a thesis on extreme right parties in Europe. He is currently a researcher and lecturer in politics at the Faculty of Humanities of the New University of Luxembourg.

Vesa Puuronen (Finland) is the Programme Manager in the Karelian Institute of the University of Joensuu. The main focus of his research has been right-wing extremism and political socialization of young people in Russia and in Finland and he has published on these topics in both English and Finnish.

Steven Ratuva (Pacific Island States) is a visiting fellow at the Australian National University and also a fellow at the Pacific Institute of Advanced Studies for Governance and Development at the University of the South Pacific in Fiji. His areas of research and publications are state-civil relations, ethnic politics, security, conflict resolution, post-colonial development and affirmative action.

Petra Roter (Slovenia) earned her PhD from the University of Cambridge. She is currently an Assistant Professor of International Relations at the University of Ljubljana, Slovenia, and a Research Fellow at the Ljubljana-based Centre of International Relations.

Kelvin Rowley (Cambodia) is Senior Lecturer in Politics in the Faculty of Life and Social Sciences, Swinburne University of Technology, Hawthorn, Australia. He is co-author of *Red Brotherhood at War: Vietnam, Cambodia and Laos Since 1975* (2nd ed, 1990), "The Making of the Royal Government of Cambodia" in Viberto Selochan and Carlyle A Thayer (eds) *Bringing Democracy to Cambodia* (1996), and "Second Life, Second Death: The Khmer Rouge Since 1978" in Susan Cook (ed), *Genocide in Cambodia and Rwanda: New Perspectives* (2004).

Marcel Rutten (Kenya) is Head of the Economy, Ecology and Exclusion research group of the African Studies Centre, Leiden, Netherlands. He was staff co-ordinator of the Election Observation Centre during Kenya's 1997 general elections and international observer during the 2002 elections. His publications include *Out for the Count — The 1997 General Elections and Prospects for Democracy in Kenya* (with A. Mazrui and F. Grignon) (2001) and *Selling Wealth to Buy Poverty* (1992).

D. J. Sagar (various African) is a writer on international affairs and a former Deputy Editor of *Keesing's Record of World Events*.

Abbas William Samii (Iran) is the Regional Analysis Coordinator for Southwest Asia and the Middle East at Radio Free Europe/Radio Liberty, and a recent Osher Fellow at the Hoover Institution. He edits an analytical weekly entitled RFE/RL *Iran Report* (www.rferl.org/reports/iran-report), and his research articles have been published in *Middle East Journal*, *Middle East Policy*, and elsewhere.

Ana Margarida Sousa Santos (Mozambique, Sao Tome) has a Bachelors degree in Anthropology and a Masters degree in African Studies from the Instituto Superior de Ciencias Sociais e Politicas, in Lisbon. She is now doing an MPhil in Social Anthropology at the Institute of Social and Cultural Anthropology in Oxford, looking at issues of identity and territory in Mozambique.

Steve Saxonberg (Sweden) is Associate Professor of Political Science at Uppsala University and Dalarna University College, both in Sweden. His recent books include *The Fall: A Comparative Study of the End of Communism in Czechoslovakia, East Germany, Hungary and Poland* (Harwood Academic/Routledge: Amsterdam/London 2001) and *The Czech Republic Before a New Millennium: Politics, Parties and Gender* (East European Monographs: Boulder, 2003).

Nicolas Schmitt (Switzerland) is Fellow Researcher at the Institute of Federalism of the University of Fribourg, Switzerland, and Editor of the *Bulletin de Legislation*. He is a former Secretary-Treasurer of the International Association of Federal Studies, a member of the Swiss Group of Election Observers and a member of the IPSA Research Committee on Comparative Federalism and Federations. He has published extensively on the Swiss political system.

Ibrahim J. Al-Sharifi (Oman, Qatar, Saudi Arabia, UAE), a former officer of the Kuwaiti Armed Forces, graduated from the Maxwell Air University in Alabama, USA and subsequently received his doctorate in Public Administration from the University of Exeter in the United Kingdom. He is a prolific writer on contemporary Arab affairs and has published several books in Arabic.

Rachel Sieder (Guatemala) is Senior Lecturer in Politics at the Institute for the Study of the Americas, School of Advanced Study, University of London. Her research has focused on indigenous rights and legal reform in Latin America. Her most recent book is *Multiculturalism in Latin America: Indigenous Rights, Diversity and Democracy* (Palgrave Macmillan, 2003).

Roger Southall (Lesotho, South Africa) is Distinguished Research Fellow, Democracy and Governance, Human Sciences Research Council, Pretoria, South Africa. He was formerly Professor of Political Studies at Rhodes University, having previously taught in universities in Lesotho, Canada and the UK. He has published widely on African, particularly southern African, topics.

Gareth Stansfield (Iraq) is Lecturer in Middle East Politics at the Institute of Arab and Islamic Studies at the University of Exeter, and Associate Fellow on the Middle East Programme at the Royal Institute of International Affairs, London. He specializes principally on Iraqi and Kurdish politics. His recent publications include *Iraqi Kurdistan: Political Development and Emergent Democracy* (London: RoutledgeCurzon, 2003), and *The Future of Iraq: Dictatorship, Democracy or Division?* (co-authored with Liam Anderson. New York: Palgrave Macmillan, 2004).

J. A. A. Stockwin (Japan) retired in September 2003 as Nissan Professor of Modern Japanese Studies and Director of the Nissan Institute of Japanese Studies, at the University of Oxford, and is an Emeritus Fellow of St Antony's College. Among other works on Japanese politics he is author of *Governing Japan* (1999) and *Dictionary of the Modern Politics of Japan* (2003).

Anders Strindberg (Syria) is a correspondent for *Jane's Intelligence Review* and a fellow in the Center for Strategic Studies and Research, Damascus University, Syria.

Martin Stuart-Fox (Laos) is Professor of History at the University of Queensland. As a former correspondent for United Press International, he covered the Vietnam War for three years from both Laos and Vietnam. He has written six books and numerous articles on Lao history and politics.

Bogdan Szajkowski (Albania, Andorra, Estonia, Hungary, Latvia, Liechtenstein, Lithuania, Poland, Vatican) is Professor of Pan-European Politics at the University of Exeter, UK and Professor of Politics in the Institute of Political Science, University of Szczecin, Poland. He has authored and/or edited nearly 50 books and has published numerous monographs, book chapters, working papers and articles in international journals. His publications have appeared in Arabic, English, French, Polish, Portuguese and Russian. His current research and teaching interests concentrate on political, ethnic, religious and social conflicts and the implications of these for international society and its institutions and organizations. He is also particularly interested in Euro-Arab dialogue and the relationship between the EU and its neighbourhood. He has worked with various international institutions and organizations and is a regular broadcaster on radio and television and a producer of several television documentaries.

Florence Terranova (Belgium, Denmark, Iceland, Monaco, Tunisia) graduated in political and administrative sciences at Mons and subsequently obtained a Master of Business Administration at the University of Antwerp and a PhD in political science at the University of Exeter, UK. She is currently assistant researcher and director of a Local Development Agency (Hainaut-Belgium).

Carlyle A. Thayer (Vietnam) is Professor of Politics and Foundation Director of the University of New South Wales Defence Studies Forum at the Australian Defence Force Academy in Canberra.

Jeanne Maddox Toungara (Côte d'Ivoire) is Associate Professor of History at Howard University, where she teaches courses on African history and the African Diaspora. Her research interests focus on political culture, gender and history among the peoples of West Africa, especially in Côte d'Ivoire, and she is preparing a new edition of the *Historical Dictionary of Côte d'Ivoire* for Scarecrow Press.

Rae Wear (Australia) teaches Australian politics at the University of Queensland. Her publications on Australian state and federal politics include *Johannes Bjelke-Petersen: the Lord's Premier* (2002).

Sylvain Zinsou (Benin, Burkina, Togo, with José Lino de Souza) is Programme Officer at the Regional Bureau of the Konrad Adenauer Foundation, Cotonou, Benin

Afghanistan

Capital: Kabul
Population: 21,500,000 (2000E)

The Islamic State of Afghanistan was proclaimed in April 1992 as successor to the Soviet-backed regime of President Mohammed Najibullah, which had been overthrown by opposition *mujaheddin* ("holy warriors") following the end of the 1979-89 Soviet military intervention. Following further conflict, the Taliban militia took power in Kabul in September 1996, and in October 1997 proclaimed the Islamic Emirate of Afghanistan. Forces of the deposed government of President Burhanuddin Rabbani had meanwhile established the United National Islamic Front for the Salvation of Afghanistan (UNIFSA). The Islamic State of Afghanistan (with UNIFSA "Northern Alliance" forces holding some northern areas) retained the recognition of the UN and much of the international community, while the Taliban consolidated de facto control of most of the country, including the capital. Continuing sporadic conflict was given impetus by the ethnic hostility of minority northern Uzbeks and Tajiks to the (majority) Pushtun-dominated Taliban.

Following the terrorist attacks in New York and Washington on Sept. 11, 2001, the USA charged the Taliban regime with providing shelter to Osama bin Laden, regarded as the instigator of the attacks. After a period of unsuccessful pressure on the Taliban to surrender Bin Laden, the USA commenced overt military operations in support of the Northern Alliance on Oct. 7. Parallel efforts (involving the UN and also Pakistan, previously the Taliban's principal sponsor) were also underway to prepare for the creation of a government of national unity, representative of the various ethnic groups. The fall of Kabul to the Northern Alliance was reported on Nov. 13.

On Nov. 27, 2001, major Afghan factions opposed to the Taliban met in Bonn under international auspices to agree on a process to restore stability and governance to the country. The main terms in the resultant Bonn Agreement were the establishment of an Interim Authority; the convening of an Emergency *Loya Jirga* (Grand Assembly) within six months of the establishment of the Interim Authority, to decide on a Transitional Authority; the convening of a Constitutional *Loya Jirga* within eighteen months of the establishment of the Transitional Authority in order to adopt a new constitution for Afghanistan; and the establishment of a Constitutional Commission within two months of the commencement of the Transitional Administration to draft the constitution.

In June 2002, the Emergency *Loya Jirga* established a Transitional Administration to govern until elections could be held. The arrangements for the *Loya Jirga* were designed to enable a broad-based representation. Seats were reserved for women, refugees, displaced persons, nomads, businessmen, intellectuals and religious scholars. In addition to the 11% of seats reserved for women, 40 women were elected in the regional contests. The Emergency *Loya Jirga* concluded on June 19 with the inauguration of Hamid Karzai as President of Afghanistan (Afghan Transitional Administration Chairman).

In October 2002, President Karzai appointed a Constitutional Drafting Committee, chaired by Vice-President Shahrani, to draft a constitution. In April 2003, the Drafting Committee submitted a preliminary proposal to a 35-member Constitutional Review Commission, appointed by presidential decree the same month. Following discussions between President Karzai, the National Security Council and the Constitutional Drafting Committee, a final draft was published on Nov. 3, 2003.

The Constitutional *Loya Jirga*, which was convened on Dec.14, 2003, comprised 500 delegates. Of these, 344 were elected on a provincial basis by 16,000 registered district representatives from the Emergency *Loya Jirga*. An additional 106 were allocated for election of special-category representatives, including women, refugees in Pakistan and Iran, internally displaced people, Kuchis (nomads), Hindus, and Sikhs. The President appointed the remaining 50 delegates with legal or constitutional expertise. The new constitution was agreed on Jan. 4, 2004. The constitution establishes a presidential system of government with all Afghans being equal before the law. There are to be two houses of parliament: a directly elected lower house or *Wolesi Jirga* (house of people); and an upper house or *Meshrano Jirga* (house of elders). The President will have the right to appoint ministers and other key officials. The human rights and gender provisions are an improvement on the 1964 constitution. A minimum number of seats for women are guaranteed in both houses. There are also provisions for minority languages and the rights of the Shia minority.

The last general elections were held in 1988. Under the terms of the 2001 Bonn Agreement, elections were due to take place by June 2004. They were first scheduled for June 2004 but had to be postponed for security reasons. On March 28, 2004, President Karzai announced that elections would take place in September 2004. On July 9, the elections were further postponed – the presidential ballot was re-scheduled for Oct. 9, 2004, and the parliamentary elections were deferred until April or May of 2005.

On May 26, 2004, Karzai signed a new election law, the first one in the post-war period. The new election law guarantees the vote to every citizen aged 18 and over, and outlines the composition of Afghanistan's bicameral parliament. Seats in the lower house will be allocated on the basis of results at the polls. Each province will be granted seats in proportion to its population. For the upper house, one-third will be appointed by city councils, one-third by district councils, and the rest by the President. A presidential candidate can win by a simple majority. Candidates for the presidency should each put forward the names of two vice presidents. The new law also limits the duration of the election campaign to 30 days with campaigning set to end 48 hours prior to the beginning of elections. The ratification of the new election law came at a time when the signing of a power-sharing agreement between President Karzai and leaders of the Northern Alliance was reported, under which the latter pledged not to field a candidate against Karzai in return for top government positions.

To ensure the rights of political parties and independent candidates, the Interior Ministry had issued a conduct code to the country's governors and security commanders. The code forbids the use of state resources to support or criticize parties or candidates. It also warns against voter intimidation and harrassment of journalists covering the elections.

Despite these measures, insecurity, factionalism, warlordism, and voter intimidation remained major concerns ahead of elections. In April 2004 Karzai visited the southern city of Kandahar, a former Taliban stronghold, calling on its members to participate in the upcoming elections. Some Taliban members had earlier threatened to disrupt elections and Karzai had embarked on negotiations with less radical Taliban members.

The first law on political parties was passed on Sept. 8, 2003. Under the 1964 constitution, which was in effect at the time of the adoption of the new constitution, political parties were not recognized. Under the new law, registration is to be denied to parties which pursue objectives opposed to the principles of Islam, use force or propagate the use of force, incite to ethnic, racial, religious or sectional violence, threaten the rights and freedom of individuals or intentionally disrupt public order, have military organizations or affiliations with armed forces, or receive funds from foreign sources. 700 members are required for a political party to be registered.

On Aug. 25, 2003, after a discussion under the leadership of Chief Justice Mawlawi Fazl Hadi Shinwari, the Afghan Supreme Court unanimously decided to ban the activities of the newly formed United National Party (UNP). The new party was established by supporters of the former Afghan communist party, the People's Democratic Party of Afghanistan. The decision was based on a recent verdict issued by the Ulama Council of Afghanistan, which stipulated that any political party that had a history of anti-Islamic activities or had adopted anti-Islamic policies should not be allowed to function in Afghanistan, as was stipulated in the new election law adopted a few days after the Supreme Court decision.

Some 70 political parties, including both *mujaheddin* factions and non-militarized parties established after the collapse of the Taliban, applied for registration at the Office for Coordination and Registration of Political Parties and Social Organizations at the Justice Ministry. By the end of September 2004, 35 had been accredited. At the end of August 2004, the number of registered voters in Afghanistan stood at 10,353,380, of whom 58.6% were men and 41.4% women. Though the main voter-registration process was scheduled to end on Aug. 15, the UN-led Joint Electoral Management Body continued to register voters until August 20 in seven provinces in the south and southeastern parts of the country.

On Aug. 11, 2004, the Afghan/UN Joint Electoral Management Body (JEMB) announced that 18 eligible candidates, representing different ethnic and factional interests, had successfully registered as presidential candidates for the Oct. 9 elections. These included Hamid Karzai (independent), supported by Afghan Nation (also known as the Afghan Social Democratic Party), National Solidarity Movement of Afghanistan, Republican Party, National United Party of Afghanistan, Islamic Justice Party of Afghanistan, and Youth National Solidarity Party of Afghanistan; Mohammad Yunus Qanuni of the National Movement of Afghanistan, a former Education and Interior Minister; Abdul Rashid Dostum, an ethnic Uzbek militia commander, running as an independent but leader of the National Islamic Movement of Afghanistan; Mohammad Mohaqeq, an ethnic Hazara candidate running as an independent but party leader of the Islamic Unity Party of the People of Afghanistan; Abdul Latif Pedram, running as the candidate of the recently established National Congress Party of Afghanistan; Homayun Shah Asefi, running as an independent, but closely identified with the National Unity Movement; Mohammad Mahfuz Nedayi, independent; Sayyed Eshaq Gailani, candidate of the National Solidarity Movement of Afghanistan; Abdul Satar Sitar, independent; Abdul Hafez Mansur, running as independent but a member of Burhanuddin Rabbani's Islamic Society of Afghanistan; Gholam Faruq Nejrabi, candidate of the Afghanistan Independence Party; Ahmad Shah Ahmadzai, running as an independent but a member of the conservative Islamic Call Organization of Afghanistan; Abdul Hasib Aryan, independent; Wakil Mangal, independent; Abdul Hadi Khalilzai, independent; Mohammad Ebrahim Rashid, independent; Sayyed Abdul Hadi Dabir, independent. Mas'uda Jalal, independent, was the only woman running for president.

There were allegations that the UN-Afghan election board violated the election law by allowing private militia commanders to compete. The law on political parties passed in September 2003 stipulated that political parties must not "have military organizations or affiliations with armed forces". Protests were filed against Dostum as well as against Karzai's running mate Mohammad Karim Khalili, and the ethnic Hazara candidate Mohammad Mohaqeq. In August 2004, 14 presidential candidates called for Karzai's resignation as chairman of the Transitional Administration to be able to run in the presidential elections. On Oct. 6, two candidates, Sayyed Eshaq Gailani and Abdul Hasib Aryan, announced their plans to withdraw from the elections.

Despite security concerns, the Oct. 9 presidential elections proceeded smoothly and without any major incidents. About eight million Afghans cast ballots. The validity of the vote was, however, challenged over allegations of fraud due to the flawed system of indelible ink supposed to prevent multiple casting of ballots. On election day, halfway through the vote, 15 candidates announced their plans to boycott the elections. Four days later, most of them withdrew from the boycott, including Hamid Karzai's main opponent, Yunus Qanuni. After delays caused by inquiries into allegations of voting irregularities, Hamid Karzai was declared the winner, with 55% of the vote on November 3. Yunus Qanuni came second with 16%, Mohammad Mohaqeq third with 12% and Abdul Rashid Dostum fourth with 10%.

Afghanistan Independence Party
Hizb-e Istiqlal-e Afghanistan
Leadership: Faruq Nejrabi

The leader of the Afghanistan Independence Party was a presidential candidate in October 2004, running on a platform which criticized the foreign presence in the country and the Transitional Administration. However, Faruq Nejrabi was one of the four candidates who did not join the August call for Karzai to resign his Transitional Administration chairmanship to run in the presidential elections.

Afghan Nation (Afghan Social Democratic Party)
Afghan Mellat
Leadership. Anwar al-Haq Ahadi

The Transitional Administration registered the Afghan Social Democratic Party officially on May 16, 2004. The party congress in 1995 elected as its president Dr. Anwar al-Haq Ahadi, a political science professor at Providence College, Rhode Island. He is currently Governor of Afghanistan's Central Bank. In late September, the party announced its backing for Hamid Karzai in the October 2004 presidential contest.

Islamic Movement of Afghanistan
Harakat-e Islami-ye Afghanistan
Leadership. Mohammad Assef Mohseni

This is a Shia movement with a predominantly Pashtun membership led by Ayatollah Mohammad Assef Mohseni. It was one of the 13 organizations which made up the United National and Islamic Front for the Salvation of Afghanistan (UNIFSA), known as the Northern Alliance. In meetings with members of the Constitutional Drafting Committee, Mohseni sought the inclusion in the new constitution of the Shia Ja'fari school as an official sect. The 1964 Afghan constitution had a special reference to the Sunni Hanafi school of jurisprudence. For the new constitution, Mohseni had proposed two formulas – either mentioning Islam and the Islamic sects or just mentioning Islam without referring to any sects. The final constitution adopted on Jan. 4, 2004, contains a reference to Islam with no mention of any sects.

Islamic Unity Party of Afghanistan
Hizb-e Wahdat-e Islami-ye Afghanistan
Leadership. Mohammad Karim Khalili

Hizb-e Wahdat is the main party representing Afghanistan's Shia minority and is led by Mohammad Karim Khalili, deputy of Afghan Transitional Administration Chairman Hamid Karzai. In the run-up to the October 2004 presidential elections, Karzai named Khalili as his choice for the post of second vice president.

Islamic Unity Party of the People of Afghanistan
Hizb-e Wahdat-e Islami-ye Mardum-e Afghanistan
Leadership. Mohammad Mohaqeq

Islamic Unity Party of the People of Afghanistan is a Shi'a party which arose from a split with the Islamic Unity Party of Afghanistan. It is led by Mohammad Mohaqeq, an ethnic Hazara, who draws his primary support from Hazaras in central Afghanistan. He served as Planning Minister in the Transitional Administration. On Feb. 25, 2004, Mohaqeq announced his decision to run for President as an independent candidate. In March 2004, there were conflicting reports as to why Mohaqeq had left his post as Planning Minister. He claimed to have been dismissed by Hamid Karzai after a dispute over division of responsibilities within the government, while a spokesman for the Afghan leader claimed that Mohaqeq resigned.

National Congress Party of Afghanistan
Hizb-e Kongra-ye Melli-ye Afghanistan
Leadership. Abdul Latif Pedram

The National Congress Party of Afghanistan is a newly established political formation under the leadership of Abdul Latif Pedram, an ethnic Tajik returning from exile. He was the party's candidate in the October 2004 presidential elections, though for some time his candidacy was threatened with disqualification for allegedly making anti-Islamic remarks. In late August, Pedram spearheaded the initial call by a majority of the candidates for Hamid Karzai to step down from his Transitional Administration chairmanship in order to run for the presidency.

National Islamic Movement of Afghanistan
Hizb-e Junbish-e Melli-ye Afghanistan
Leadership. Abdul Rashid Dostum

Before the Taliban came to power, the National Islamic Movement of Afghanistan controlled a number of northern provinces. Its leader, Abdul Rashid Dostum, an ethnic Uzbek, has had a career as a militia commander for two decades. He backed the US-led military operations to oust the Taliban in 2001. He was appointed as security advisor to the Transitional Administration Chairman Karzai. In the October 2004 presidential elections, Dostum ran as an inde-pendent candidate despite his leadership of the National Islamic Movement of Afghanistan. His candidacy was challenged on the basis of the political parties' law stipulating that political parties must not "have military organizations or affiliations with armed forces". By early August, the Joint Electoral Management Body (JEMB) had received more than 50 complaints or legal challenges to Dostum's candidacy based on accusations of criminal or other misconduct.

National Solidarity Movement of Afghanistan
Nahzat-e Hambastagi-ye Melli-ye Afghanistan
Leadership. Sayyed Eshaq Gailani

The National Solidarity Movement of Afghanistan is led by Sayyed Eshaq Gailani, former *mujahedin* and member of one of the country's most influential religious families. Gailani is a monarchist who advocates a major role for ex-king Zaher Shah. He was one of the successfully registered presidential candidates in 2004, but on Oct. 6 announced his withdrawal.

National Unity Party
Tahrik-e Wahdat-e Melli
Leadership. Sultan Mahmud Ghazi

The National Unity Party was launched on Aug. 9, 2003, by Sultan Mahmud Ghazi, a first cousin of the former Afghan king, Mohammed Zaher Shah. The party's platform calls for a return to constitutional monarchy. The party was inaugurated on the same day Zaher Shah returned to Kabul from France after a period of medical treatment. 2,000 supporters urged him to take a leadership role in the government. The former king, however, issued a communiqué to distance himself from the newly established National Unity Party.

Republican Party of Afghanistan
Hizb-e Jamhuri Khwahan-e
Leadership. Sebghatullah Sanjar

The Kabul-based Republican Party of Afghanistan was the first to be registered. It is led by Sebghatullah Sanjar, a former member of the Emergency *Loya Jirga* Commission. The party decided not to nominate a candidate for the 2004 presidential elections and in August announced its support for the candidacy of incumbent Hamid Karzai.

Albania

Capital: Tirana
Population: 3,592,900 (2004)

Albania was the last nation in Eastern Europe to undertake the transition from totalitarianism to democracy after more than four decades of particularly oppressive and xenophobic communist rule by the Party of Labour of Albania (APL). The period of transition proved difficult as successive governments tried to deal with high unemployment, a dilapidated infrastructure, organized crime and widespread gangsterism. Though ethnically homogenous (over 90% Albanian), the country is linguistically and culturally divided into southern Tosks, currently dominant demographically and politically, and northern Ghegs. Some 70% of the country's population are Muslims (Sunni or Bektashi), 20% Greek Orthodox and 10% Roman Catholic. Religion was banned in Albania in 1967 and the country declared "the first atheist state in the world".

In December 1990 the regime bowed to popular pressure and allowed the formation of political parties to compete with the ruling communists. The first party to emerge, the Democratic Party (DP), was formed by a group of students and intellectuals at Tirana University, only a day after the announcement of the legalization of other political parties. Most of the new party's senior members had to resign from the communist party in order to start the job of making Albania a multi-party state. Between December 1990 and March 1991 five political parties were created reflecting the emerging social and political differentiation of the country. Their membership, although growing steadily, as well as their social base, were, however very fragile reflecting the limited financial, physical and manpower resources. Electoral legislation adopted in February 1991 banned "extremist" parties and those based exclusively in ethnic minorities.

The first multi-party elections, in which eleven parties and organizations registered their candidates, were held on March 31, 1991. The APL won a two-thirds majority in the People's Assembly (169 seats) by capturing almost all the seats in the rural areas where over 70% of the country's population live. On the other hand the newly created DP received overwhelming support in the cities, winning 75 of the 250 seats. Five of the remaining seats were won by the political organization of ethnic Greeks, OMONIA, and one by the communist affiliated Democratic Front.

The new People's Assembly on April 30, 1991, approved an interim constitution and proclaimed Albania a Republic, replacing the Socialist People's Republic of Albania. It elected the leader of the APL, Ramiz Alia, as the President of the Republic despite the fact that he failed to be elected to the Assembly. The new government, sworn in in early May, was headed by the pro-reform APL economist, Fatos Nano. His government was brought down by general strike a month later and replaced by coalition government – "government of personalities" – led by Ylli Bufi. On June 11, 1991 the congress of the Albanian Party of Labour approved fundamental changes to the party's structure and the ideology. The APL was renamed the *Partia Socialiste ë Shqipërisë* (Socialist Party of Albania, SP) and Fatos Nano was elected President of the Managing Committee.

The Bufi government survived with considerable difficulties until December 1991 when the chairman of the Democratic Party, Sali Berisha, announced the party's withdrawal from the coalition. A caretaker administration was appointed and continued until the general elections in March 1992.

In the elections the DP won a landslide victory, 62.08% of the votes, which gave it 92 seats in the 140-seat parliament, just one short of a two-thirds majority. The SP gained 38 seats, the Social Democratic Party 7 and the Human Rights Union Party 2. The electoral law prevented parties such as OMONIA who campaigned on "ethnic principles" from participating in the elections. Therefore OMONIA and a smaller party, Prespa, representing Albania's tiny Macedonian population both put forward their candidates in the list of Human Rights Union Party, a party that was created only a month before the elections.

On April 4, 1992, Ramiz Alia announced his decision to resign from the post of President. Five days later, the then leader of the DP, Sali Berisha, was elected by a large majority as the President of the country. The new Prime Minister, Aleksander Meksi of the DP, faced mounting problems of falling industrial and agricultural production, a high level of unemployment and breakdown of state authority. The problems were further aggravated by Sali Berisha who consolidated a considerable amount of power around him and fractured the Democratic Party. Under Berisha, Albania was governed by an increasingly authoritarian regime without any separation of powers and with no respect for the opposition and minorities.

In November 1994 the DP government organized a referendum on the first post-communist constitution which contained provisions for a further increase in the powers of the President, especially over the judiciary and the media. The final result of the referendum was an overwhelming anti-government vote, a vote of no confidence for the DP and particularly Berisha.

In the parliamentary elections held in May 1996 the DP claimed an overwhelming victory and emerged with control of 122 out of 140 seats. This election was characterized by blatant ballot-rigging, intimidation, and in some instances open violence against opposition candidates and supporters. The result of the elections was accompanied by riots in Tirana which subsequently exploded into violent rebellion that engulfed the country for several months. The spark that set off the country's crisis was the collapse of the pyramid schemes in which Albanians had invested an estimated $1.5 billion. But the underlying reason was Berisha's disregard for the rule of law and a persistent pattern of human rights violations by the government The Berisha administration tolerated the pyramid investment scams and even encouraged people to invest, despite warnings from the international financial institutions. Tens of thousands of Albanians lost their entire savings. The old north-south tension re-emerged with the southern Tosks rioting against the northern Gegs' rule symbolised by Berisha. In March 1997 southern Albania was out of control. In a pattern repeated in a large number of southern towns, the rebels broke into military armouries and seized large quantities of guns, ammunition and grenades. An estimated 550,000 weapons (mostly Kalashnikov AK-47 assault rifles) were looted from military depots (by 2003 only 36% of the weapons had been recovered). In some towns, members of the police and the army (many of whom were victims of the collapsed pyramid schemes) sided with the rebels and voluntarily handed over their weapons. Order was only restored following the deployment of an Italian-led multinational protection force.

A snap election was called on June 29, 1997, in which the Socialist Party won a two-thirds majority in the Assembly. Berisha resigned after the elections and the parliament elected Rexhep Mejdani as President, who later appointed Fatos Nano as Prime Minister, both SP members. The task faced by the new five-party coalition government was particularly difficult as it had to re-impose the rule of law, fight against the black economy, and clean up the financial mess in order to attract international donors and investors.

Finally on Nov. 27, 1998, a new democratic constitution was overwhelmingly approved by popular referendum. Under the constitution the supreme political authority is vested in the *Kuvendi i Republikës së Shqipërisë* (Assembly of the Republic of Albania), the unicameral legislature, whose 140 members are elected for a four-year term. The President is elected by the Assembly for a five-year term once renewable; the Assembly also approves the Prime Minister and Council of Ministers designated by the President.

The current Electoral Code envisages the use of a mixed first-past-the-post and proportional voting system that combines elements from various European countries. It provides for the use of two ballots, one for the single-member zone in which the voter resides, the other for the party lists on the national level. Article 64 of the 1998 Constitution states that the Assembly of the Republic of Albania consists of 140 deputies, 100 elected in single-member zones and remaining 40 – called "compensatory seats" – distributed among the registered parties and coalitions proportionally, according their showing in the national vote. To be involved in the allocation of the 40 "compensatory" mandates, parties must receive at least 2.5% (and coalitions at least 4%) of the valid votes. For instance, if a particular party or coalition won 50% of the national vote but only 40 directly elected seats, they would receive an additional 30 compensatory seats, bringing their total number of seats to 70, or 50% of the parliament's 140 seats. If, however, they won 70 directly elected seats, and 50% of the national vote, they would not receive any compensatory seats, because their total number of seats would already correspond to their percentage of the national vote.

The Electoral Code provides for multiple rounds of voting. A subsequent round is held a fortnight after the previous one. A second round of voting is required in each single member constituency where no candidate receives an absolute majority. In cases of adjudicated complains the Central Electoral Commission may order the holding of subsequent rounds in electoral districts (zones) or individual polling stations until it is satisfied with the result.

In the parliamentary elections held in June and July 2001, 28 political parties and coalitions took part. An important feature of the contest was the decision of the SP to break with the Alliance for the State, the governing coalition between 1997-2001. In addition to the SP, the Alliance had also included the Social Democratic Party (SDP), the Human Rights Union Party (HRUP), the Agrarian Party (AP), and the Democratic Alliance Party (PAD), and contested the elections alone. Without SP support, smaller parties from that coalition faced the likelihood of losing their seats in parliament and their government posts. The DP formed an electoral alliance, the Union for Victory (UfV), which also included the Republican Party (PR), the National Front Party (PBK), the Movement of Legality Party (PLL), and the Liberal Democratic Union (PBD). The Democratic Party once again fought the campaign under the leadership of Sali Berisha, the disgraced former President. This time he re-emerged as a more softly spoken, more reasonable leader. Following a split in the DP at the beginning of 2001, some of its MPs formed the New Democratic Party (NDP) under the leadership of Genc Pollo, and the new party contested the election as an alternative to both the SP and DP.

The Socialist Party won 73 seats in the legislature, against 46 for the Union for Victory led by the Democratic Party. The remaining 21 seats were allocated among five small parties – New Democratic Party, 6; Social Democratic Party, 4; Human Rights Union Party, 3; Agrarian Party, 3; Democratic Alliance Party, 3; independents, 2. Each of these gained the necessary 2.5% of votes while two independent candidates won direct mandates. The Union for Victory gained a considerably higher percentage of votes cast than of seats won.

Albanian electoral politics has traditionally involved a sharp north-south divide, and the 2001 results reflected this division. Almost 3 million of the Albanian population of 3.5 million lives in the south of the country. The opposition DP scored a virtual sweep of northern constituencies while the SP, as usual, did well in southern districts. Voters in both halves of the country cast their ballots for more of the same on the local scene – in the north for continued regional DP predominance, in the south for leaving uninterrupted leadership networks.

Following the elections political feuding virtually paralysed the Albanian government until the middle of 2002 when the European Parliament brokered an agreement between the main political parties which led to the election, in June 2002, of 73-year-old retired army general Alfred Moisiu as the consensus choice for President. After a long period of confrontation, the country entered a phase of political dialogue. The opposition Democratic Party ended its boycott of local government institutions and began to work with the ruling Socialist Party. In August 2002 parliament voted in a new Socialist-led government with the SP chairman, Fatos Nano, as Prime Minister for a third time. By early 2003, however, this unusual consensus appeared to have unravelled and Albania returned to its usual fractured politics. Demonstrations were held in February 2004 by the opposition parties and non-governmental organizations. Dissatisfaction over issues such as corruption, conflicts over high prices, poverty and human trafficking, brought an estimated 50,000 people to the streets of Tirana on Feb. 21, 2004, calling for the resignation of Prime Minister Fatos Nano. The Socialist Party urged the opposition to stop calling for early elections and instead join efforts to integrate Albania into the European Union and NATO.

European integration has been the utmost priority of all Albanian governments since 1991 and it is also one of the few issues the ruling Socialist and Democratic Party in opposition agree upon. Despite the fact that membership of the EU is still far away, many European leaders have reiterated that Albania belongs to Europe and will sooner or later be accepted as a full-time member.

Agrarian Party of Albania (AP)
Partia Agrare e Shqipërisë (PASh)
Address. Rruga "Budi" 6, Tirana
Telephone. 355-4-237-109
Leadership. Lufter Xhuveli (president)
The party was founded before the first multi-parliamentary elections in 1991. Despite the fact that an overwhelming majority of the Albanian population live in the countryside it has managed to establish only a limited support from the rural population. In the June–July 2001 parliamentary elections it won 2.6% of the popular vote and secured 3 seats in the Assembly.

Democratic Alliance Party
Partia Aleanca Demokratike (PAD)
Address. Rruga "Murat Toptani" 10, Tirana
Telephone. 355-4-251-958
Fax. 355-4-251-958
Email. axhaxhiu@yahoomail.com
Leadership. Neritan Ceka (chairman)
The party was founded in October 1992 by dissident members of the then ruling Democratic Party opposed to the "autocratic rule" of President Berisha who accused it of having pro-Serbian tendencies. It campaigned with its own list in the 1997 Assembly elections, winning two seats and subsequently joined the centre-left ruling coalition headed by the Socialist Party. It improved its results in 2001, gaining 2.4% of the vote and winning three seats. During the elections the PAD, although running independently, was allied to the SP and in several crucial constituencies where they supported each other. Since then it has split in two main factions.

Democratic Party of Albania (DP)
Partia Demokratike të Shqipërisë (PDSh)

Address. Rruga Punetoret e Rilindjes, Tirana
Telephone. 355-4-228-091
Fax. 355-4-223-525
Email. chairman-office@pdalbania.org
Website. www.albania.co.uk/dp
Leadership. Sali Berisha (president)

The Democratic Party of Albania was founded on Dec. 12, 1990, immediately after the mass student demonstrations in Tirana, only a day after the legalization of non-communist organizations. It was launched by a group of intellectuals and students at Tirana University which included Dr Sali Berisha, a cardilogist; Dr Gramoz Pashko, an economist; Azem Hajdari, a student activist; Dr Eduard Selami, a professor of the philosophy of aesthetics; and Arben Imami, a professor of drama. It was the first opposition party to be registered on Dec. 17.

With little financial and material resources the DP struggled to build membership and its infrastructure. In February 1991 it claimed a membership of 60,000. By the time of the first parliamentary elections in March 1991, barely three months after its foundation the DP managed to establish branches in both the northern (Gegs areas) and southern (Tosk areas) parts of the country thus becoming a genuinely national party.

In the first multi-party elections in March 1991, the DP won 75 of the 250 seats in the People's Assembly. A year later, during in the second parliamentary elections in March it increased its representation to 92 in the 140-seat assembly and became the main party in the first post-war non-communist government. Its chairman Sali Berisha was elected the President of Albania in April 1992

However, at the end of 1991 serious policy differences over the party's continuous participation in the Bufi National Stability Government marked the beginning of a series of splits in the DP ranks. In July 1992 several of its prominent members, including Gramoz Pashko, were expelled from the party and formed the Albanian Democratic Alliance Party. Another split occurred in August 1993 when two prominent members of a right-wing faction, known as *Balli Kombëter*, were dismissed from its ranks. This led in March 1994 to the formation of the Democratic Party of the Right.

During the period 1993-94 the DP-led government became increasingly authoritarian and consequently the party's popularity and popular support declined dramatically. The rejection of a new constitution backed by the DP in a popular referendum on Nov. 6, 1994, represented another major setback for the party, which was accused of seeking to increase presidential powers at the expense of the People's Assembly. President Berisha responded by carrying out a major government reshuffle in December, as a result of which he lost the support of DP's coalition partners, the Republican Party (PRSh) and the the Social Democratic Party. At a special DP conference in March 1995, the party's chairman, Eduard Selami, was dismissed as after he opposed Berisha's plan to hold another referendum on a new draft constitution. He was replaced by Tritan Shehu and the party launched its election campaign on a platform of lower taxes and more privatization. The following month Selami and seven others were ousted from the party's National Steering Council.

The party claimed to have won 122 of the 140 seats in the May–June 1996 parliamentary elections – a poll marked by electoral fraud and intimidation and condemned by international observers. In 1996 the DP effectively lost control over the government and country with the outbreak of mass riots following the collapse of the pyramid schemes in which tens of thousands of Albanians lost their entire savings. In snap elections on June 29, 1997, in which the DP led the Union for Democracy, it gained 25.7% of the vote and won 28 seats. Sali Berisha resigned as Albania's President and the party went into opposition.

The DP boycotted the parliament after one of its MPs was shot in September 1997. The boycott lasted for nearly two years other than for some short intervals of participation. The assassination of Azem Hajdari, a senior party official, in September 1998 produced a new crisis during which Sali Berisha and the DP were accused of attempting to seize government institutions by force. New internal strains developed after Berisha called on party supporters to boycott a constitutional referendum in November 1998.

In September 1999 the parliamentary leader of the DP Genc Pollo called on the centre-right opposition parties to unite under DP leadership. However, at a party congress the following month Pollo failed to unseat Berisha, who was re-elected as chairman of the party unopposed following a purge of several senior moderate party officials.

The DP suffered another electoral loss in local elections in October 2000, winning only about a third of the vote and losing control of Tirana's local government to the Socialist Party. The DP contested the mid-2001 parliamentary elections leading a coalition of small right wing parties. It won 42 seats, but remained in opposition.

After it fell from power in 1997 the DP boycotted the political process and lost touch with much of the electorate. Its membership base has declined dramatically.

Human Rights Union Party (HRUP)
Partia Bashkimi për të Drejtat e Njeriut (PMDN)

Address. Bulevardi "Bajram Curru" 32, Tirana 1
Telephone. +355-4-377-92
Fax. +355-4-377-92
Email. edoules@yahoo.com.uk
Leadership. Vangjel Dule (chairman)

The PMDN was officially registered on Feb. 24, 1992, principally to represent Albania's ethnic Greek population, which constitutes around 3% of the country's population and is concentrated mainly in the hillside villages of southern Albania, an area known to Greeks as Northern Epirus (a name widely believed by Albanians to disguise irredentist claims). The region, which borders the Greek province of Southern Epirus, was incorporated into the modern Albanian state in 1925. The launching of the PMDN followed the enactment of a new electoral law which banned the formation of parties on ethnic principles. The law prevented the participation in the 1992 election of Albania's biggest minority organization, the Democratic Union of the Greek Minority (OMONIA). In the March 1991 elections OMONIA won five seats and became the third largest political party with a reported membership of 60,000. The decision to ban OMONIA appears to be closely linked to the deteriorating Albanian-Greek state relations at that time, which resulted in a series of border clashes and the flight of many ethnic Greeks from Albania to Greece.

In the March 1992 parliamentary elections, OMONIA included its candidates on the PMDN list. The new party won two of the 140 seats with 2.9% of the first-round vote. During 1994 Albanian-Greek relations deteriorated further when two Albanian conscripts were killed in a cross-border raid on a military training camp. The attack was blamed by Tirana on ethnic Greek separatist gunmen. In the wake of the attack the Albanian army quickly dismissed its last ethnic Greek officer. He joined a multitude of other ethnic Greeks sacked from the civil service or barred from senior posts in private companies. Subsequently Albania announced the trial of six ethnic Greeks for spying. On May 26, 1994, Albania arrested more than 50 ethnic Greek politicians, intellectuals and journalists (mostly in the southern Albanian town of Dervitsani), members of OMONIA (including its chairman, Theodhori Bezhani) on suspicion of "anti-state" activities, including the possession of arms and espionage. Five were convicted in September 1994 on treason and other charges. By early 1995, however, all five had been released, as the Albanian government sought to accommodate ethnic Greek grievances.

In the 1996 elections the PMDN won three seats, and in 1997 four, when it was allocated one portfolio in the socialist-led coalition government. In the June 2001 parliamentary elections the party received 2.6% of the vote and secured 3 members of the assembly. The party is comparatively strong at a local level, ranking in third place in terms of elected officials and fourth in terms of percentage of votes.

Liberal Democratic Union
Bashkimi Liberal Demokrat (PBD)
Leadership. Teodor Laco (president)
The PBD is a small conservative party and is part of the opposition bloc. In the 2001 elections it was part of the Union for Victory (*Bashkimi për Fitoren)* coalition led by the DP, which received 37.1% of the vote and 46 members of parliament.

Movement of Legality Party
Partia Lëvizja e Legalitetit (PLL)
Address. Rr. P. Shkurti pall. 5/1, Tirana
Website. www.french-market.com/albania/defaultpll.htm
Leadership. Guri Durollari (chairman)
The Movement of Legality Party is the political arm of the monarchist movement founded in 1943 to support the unsuccessful attempt of the self-proclaimed King Zog (deposed in 1939) to regain the throne. Albania's monarchy was abolished by the Communists in 1946. The PLL supports the restoration of the royal family now headed by Zog's only son, Leka Zogu, who was crowned king in Paris in 1961 after the death of his father. Leka briefly visited Albania in November 1993 to participate in the Movement's 50th anniversary celebrations. He flew to Tirana from Jordan on a private plane lent by his friend, King Hussein. Upon arrival, he was asked to leave because his passport gave his occupation as "King of the Albanians". He was bluntly told that he would only be re-admitted if he was in possession of an ordinary citizen's passport and deported the following morning. He returned again in April 1997 following the period of anarchy "to share the suffering" of the Albanian people and successfully called for a referendum on whether the monarchy should be restored. The non-biding referendum was held simultaneously with the third round of the parliamentary elections on June 29, 1997. The restoration call was rejected by 66.7% of the electorate, but never accepted by Leka's supporters. During the campaign Leka Zogu held a rally of armed supporters at which one person was shot dead; he was later convicted *in absentia* of trying to organize a coup attempt but early in 2002 was granted an amnesty for charges relating to the possession of weapons.

In June 2002 Leka Zogu returned to live in Albania after 63 years of exile. When he arrived, 84 weapons, including nine Kalashnikovs, were confiscated from his entourage. In February 2003, Leka and his family were issued with diplomatic passports. Subsequently the government has made efforts to reintegrate the former royal family into post-communist Albanian society. Discussions are taking place about the status of the royal family with a view to granting it a special position and authorizing a return of its property. Leka lives in one of his father's old villas in the centre of Tirana and makes occasional pronouncements on the injustice of the division of the Albanian nation into multiple states. His main support base remains his family's traditional homeland in the Mati Valley, together with the area around the southeastern town of Pogradec.

The PLL refused to participate in the 1992 parliamentary elections on the grounds that republicanism as a political system in Albania was a foregone conclusion. However, during the 1992 local elections a handful of its candidates were elected to district and communal councils. In the 1997 parliamentary election, the PLL won two seats in the Assembly as part of the Union for Democracy coalition headed by the DP. In the 2001 parliamentary elections the PLL was also part of the Union for Victory coalition headed by the Democratic Party.

The Movement has only narrow and very small support inside Albania. It does, however, have some support among the Albanian expatriate community in Europe and the United States.

New Democratic Party (NDP)
Partia Demokrate (PD (R))
Address. Rruga "Myslim Shyri", 47, Tirana, Albania
Telephone. 355-42-69-107
Fax. 355-42-69-110
Email. pdlr@sanz.net
Leadership. Genc Pollo (president)
The New Democratic Party, also known as the Reformed Democratic Party or Democrat Party, was founded in February 2001 by several MPs following a split in the parliamentary Democratic Party. It held its first Congress in February 2002. It contested the June 2001 parliamentary election under the leadership of Genc Pollo, as an alternative to both the SP and DP, and won 6 seats. It emerged as Albanian's third political force.

Party of the Albanian National Front
Partia Balli Kombëtar Shqiptar (PBK)
Telephone. +355 4 830 29 77
Fax. +355 4 830 29 77
Website. http://ballikombit.albanet.org/
Leadership. Abaz Ermenji (leader)
The PBK is one of the oldest parties in the country. A right-wing, nationalist party it claims its origins in the anti-communist and anti-fascist resistance during World War II. It was revived in 1991. Abaz Ermenji, its leader, returned to Albania in October 1995 after 49 years of exile. In the 2001 parliamentary elections the PBK was part of the Union for Victory coalition headed by the Democratic Party. The participation in the coalition led to major disagreements within the PBK as a result of which several prominent members left the party.

Republican Party of Albania
Partia Republikane ë Shqipërisë (PR)
Address. Rruga "Sami Frasheri", Tirana
Telephone. +355-4-237-242
Fax. +355-4-237-242
Email. f-mediu@icc-al.or
Leadership. Fatmir Mediu
Founded in January 1991 with support from the Italian Republican Party, the PR has its main power base in southern Albania. Until 1992 the Republicans appeared to have adopted a rather cautious wait-and-see attitude. After the 1992 parliamentary elections, in which they won one seat, the PR joined the Democratic Party-dominated government with one minister (Transport) and two deputy ministers. The PR held its first congress in June 1992 during which major divisions within the party emerged that subsequently led to splits and the creation of two small parties – the right-wing Republican Party and the Party of Republican Alliance. In the mid-2001 Assembly elections the PR was part of the Union for Victory alliance headed by the Democratic Party. The party often acts as a strong supporter of the Democratic Party.

Social Democratic Party
Partia Social Demokrate (PSD)

Address. "Sheshi Austria", Tirana
Telephone. +355-4-226-540
Fax. +355-4-227-485
Leadership. Skender Gjinushi (president)

The PSD, established in March 1991, traces its origins to the pre-communist workers' parties. Founded on a democratic socialist platform it won seven Assembly seats in the March 1992 elections and subsequently joined the coalition government headed by the Democratic Party of Albania, providing two junor ministers, but withdrew from the coalition in 1994. The PSD failed to secure a mandate in the elections of May 1996, which were generally recognized as fraudulent, and in December 1996 joined the "Forum for Democracy" which included the Albanian Socialist Party. In the 1997 parliamentary elections the PSD won eight seats in alliance with the SP and formed part of the coalition government. In the 2001 parliamentary elections it received 3.6% of the votes and secured only 4 seats in the Assembly. The PSD maintains close contacts with some of the new independent trade unions. The party favours economic reforms linked to a social programme. Its leader, Skender Gjinushi, is a former Minister of Education.

The PSD claims a membership of about 20,000 and it is a full member of the Socialist International.

Socialist Party of Albania (SP)
Partia Socialiste ë Shqipërisë (PSSh)

Address. Rruga "4 Shkurti", n.1, Tirana
Telephone. +355-4-228-432
Fax. +355-4-228-384
Email. international_spa@yahoo.com
Leadership. Fatos Nano (chairman)

The Socialist Party is the sucessor of Party of Labour of Albania (ALP) which itself descended from the Albanian Communist Party (ACP) (founded on Nov. 8, 1941). The ACP was established when two agents of the Yugoslav Communist Party (YCP), on instruction from Belgrade, convened a meeting of twenty delegates which elected the party's Central Committee headed by a former school teacher, Enver Hoxha. The party, which was in fact no more than an off-shoot of the YCP until 1948, operated under the "guidance" of Josip Broz – Tito. Like its Yugoslav counterpart, the Albanian communists dominated the nationalist movement. The Anti-Fascist National Liberation Council, under their control, in October 1944 transformed itself into the Provisional Democratic Government of Albania, with Enver Hoxha as its Prime Minister. The ACP was renamed the Albanian Party of Labour in September 1948 and purged of Yugoslav supporters.

Following the Soviet-Yugoslav split in June 1948, the APL became dominated by the Communist Party of the Soviet Union (CPSU) and followed religiously the Soviet pattern of development. The relations between the two parties prospered till the 20th Congress of the CPSU in February 1956. The strong denunciation, at the Congress, of Stalin and Stalinism disturbed the Albanian leadership and Enver Hoxha who supported both vigorously. Next, the APL began to consolidate its ties with the Chinese Communist Party (CCP), which also opposed de-Stalinization. From 1961 to 1977 the APL copied the Chinese model. In 1966 Enver Hoxha initiated the Albanian Cultural Revolution aimed to "preserve Marxist-Leninist purity in all aspects of Albanian life". The special relationship with the CCP came to end after the reconciliation between China and the United States, the downfall of the Gang of Four and rehabilitation of Deng Xiaoping. In 1978 China announced the ending, with immediate effect, of all aid and all civilian and military credits to Albania and the withdrawal of all Chinese specialists.

With the ending of the Chinese phase the APL became isolated. Hoxha, who regarded himself as the only true Marxist-Leninist in the world, embarked on a policy of self-reliance. His ideologically inspired fantasies reduced the country to ruin. Hoxha died in 1985 and the APL and country's leadership was taken over by his chosen successor, Ramiz Alia. He wanted to preserve the essential elements, if not the violent excesses, of the rigid Stalinist system. The initial changes he made in 1990 were clearly forced upon him the dismantling of communism throughout Eastern Europe and the disastrous state of the country's economy. Alia's attempts at controlled change led quickly to a social and political explosion beyond the control of the APL.

Perhaps one of the most difficult and decisive points in the history of the APL was its 10th Congress held between June 11-13, 1991. The Congress approved the main points of the party's policies; political pluralism, support for agricultural co-operatives, "property pluralism" but with state control of land and natural resources, and help for the Albanians in Kosovo. At the same time it attacked some of the cornerstones of the past policies of the regime under Enver Hoxha and the former leader personally. To mark the APL's final parting with its Stalinist past, the Congress also decided to change the party's name to the Socialist Party of Albania (SP), and alter its leadership structure. Alia surrundered the party leadership in favour of Fatos Nano, but he remained the President of the Republic.

The party won the first multi-party parliamentary elections in 1991 with 169 of the 250 seats in the People's Assembly. Popular demonstrations forced President Ramiz Alia to appoint a "non-partisan" government led by Ylli Bufi of the SP. The new government included representatives of opposition parties. Continuing protests forced the Socialist Party to give up the premiership in December 1991. The SP was heavily defeated in the 1992 parliamentary elections by the Democratic Party and went into opposition. During 1993 and 1994 the party was shaken by a series of arrests and trials of the former members of the communist establishment. In July 1993, its chairman Fatos Nano, was arrested and charged with corruption during his term as Prime Minister from April to June 1991. His parliamentary immunity was withdrawn the following month. Nano, who was alleged to have appropriated $8 million, declared his innocence, claiming that his arrest and subsequent trial was politically motivated. In protest the Socialist Party MPs boycotted parliament for two months (July-August 1993). After his arrest a mass rally attended by some 20,000 people was held in Tirana demanding new elections. He was convicted on April 3, 1994 of misappropriating state funds, dereliction of duty and falsifying official documents, and sentenced to 12 years' imprisonment. No evidence that Nano benefited directly from the alleged fraud was offered in court. Despite his conviction Nano remained SP chairman, with deputy chairman Servent Pellumbi becoming acting chairman. Nano led the Socialist Party from prison until his release in spring 1997.

During 1993 several former high ranking party officials were arrested including former President Ramiz Alia, and were charged with violation of citizens' rights while in office and in July 1994 sentenced to several years of imprisonment.

In November 1995 the SP deputies were among those who unsuccessfully opposed legislation requiring senior public officials to be screened for their activities in the communist era. Under this so-called Genocide Act, a number of proposed SP candidates were barred from contesting the 1996 legislative elections that were widely regarded as riddled with fraud and intimidation. The party boycotted the second round and was credited with only 10 seats when the official results were published.

In early 1997 the SP led popular opposition to the subsequent DP-led government, assisted by popular general outrage after the collapse of pyramid savings schemes in 1997. In March 1997 the SP joined a "government of reconciliation" headed by Bashkim Fino and was boosted by the release of Nano on a presidential pardon. In the June-July 1997 parliamentary elections the party won 52.8% of the popular vote and returned to power with 101 of the 155 seats. In July 1997, Rexhep Meidani, the then secretary general of the SP replaced Sali Berisha as President of the Republic. Fatos Nano was appointed Prime Minister leading a five-party coalition government.

In September 1998, Nano was replaced as Prime Minister by Pandeli Majko. Intra-party feuds caused Nano to resign as the party's chairman in January 1999. He was, however, re-elected to that post in October 1999 by a narrow majority and his challenger, Majko resigned as Prime Minister. Majko was replaced by deputy Prime Minister Ilir Meta.

In October 2000 the SP received substantial backing in local elections, winning over 50% of the popular vote and 252 out of 398 local authorities, including Tirana, hitherto a DP stronghold.

In the June-July 2001 parliamentary elections the Socialist Party secured 42% of the poplar vote and won 73 of the 140 seats. Since the election, however, internal party disputes have dominated Albanian political life. After the re-election of Nano at the party Congress in December 2003, his opponents founded a new political movement named the Socialist Movement for Integration, led by Meta. Ten other deputies joined the movement. The aim is to set up a new party, if Fatos Nano does not resign both as Prime Minister and party leader, and if the party does not democratize. This party will be based on social democratic values and will include the one member one vote principle.

The disintegration of the socialist majority might lead to a strengthened call for early elections. Long-term implications could be the further weakening of the polarized political situation, perhaps eventually ending the bi-polar system consisting of the Socialist Party and the Democratic Party.

The SP is a member of the Socialist International.

Other Parties

Christian Democratic Party (*Partia Demokristiane e Shqipërisë*, PDK); the party is based on the Catholic areas of northern Albania and is rather small in terms of its membership and electoral support.
Address. Rr. Dëshmorët e Shkurtit, Tirana
Telephone. +355-42 30042
Fax. +355-42 33024
Leadership. Zef Bushati

The Greens (*Te Gjelberit*), founded on Sept. 1, 2001, in Tirana as a new political party on the initiative of a group of young intellectuals and students concerned with ecological issues. In the local elections of October 2003, the Albanian Greens for the first time participated in elections wining two local council seats.
Address. Bajram Curri Boulevard, Pall.31, No.1, Apt.4., Tirana
Telephone. +355 4 266 809
Fax. +355 4 266 809
Email. albgreens@yahoo.com
Website. www.tegjelberit.8k.com/
Leadership. Edlir Petanaj (chairman)

Group of Reformist Democrats, led by Leonard Ndoka.

Labour Party of Albania (*Partia e Punës e Shqipërisë*). This Marxist-Leninist party claims to be the direct successor of the Albanian Communist Party, founded in Tirana, on Nov. 8, 1941, by Enver Hoxha, and re-named as the Labour Party of Albania in November 1948. Following the demise of communism in the country, in December 1991, a group of hardline communists opposed to the policies of the reformed Albanian Socialist Party formed the Albanian Communist Party, which produced a political platform for the 1992 parliamentary elections. In the summer of 1992 the Albanian parliament imposed a ban on the activities of the Albanian Communist Party and on the formation in the future of similar organizations. The ban was lifted in June 1992. The current party emerged as a result of the merger of several communist and Marxist-Leninist groups and fringe organizations between 1998-2000. The name Labour Party of Albania was adopted on June 30, 2000.
Website. http://www.ppsh.org/

Party of National Unity (*Partia Bashkimi Kombëtare Shqipërisë*, PUK). The Party of National Unity is a pan-Albanian nationalist organization which also operates in Kosovo. Its aim is to bring about the re-unification of lands inhabited by Albanians.
Leadership. Idajet Bequiri (president)

Algeria

Capital: Algiers
Population: 32,818,500 (July 2003E)

The Democratic and Popular Republic of Algeria, under an amendment to its 1976 constitution adopted in September 1989, moved from the status of one-party state in which the National Liberation Front (FLN) was the "vanguard, leadership and organization of the people with the aim of building socialism" to being a qualified multi-party democracy. By Dec. 31, 1990, over 50 legal parties existed; a new party law was enacted in March 1997. The constitution also provides for an executive President, who is directly elected by universal suffrage of those aged at least 18 for a renewable five-year term and who appoints and presides over a Council of Ministers. Presidential candidates must be over 40, Muslim, and of Algerian nationality by birth.

After a hiatus following the cancellation of the second round of parliamentary elections in January 1992 because of the imminent victory of the Islamic Salvation Front (*Front Islamique du Salut*, FIS), a new parliamentary structure approved in a constitutional referendum in November 1996 provides for a bicameral Parliament (*Barlaman*) consisting of (i) an upper Council of the Nation (*Majlis al-Oumma*) of 144 members, of whom one-third are appointed by the President and two-thirds indirectly elected for six-year terms by a college of local government representatives; and (ii) a lower National People's Assembly (*Majlis Ech Chaabi al-Watani*) of 380 members (eight representing Algerians abroad), directly elected for a five-year term by proportional representation from party lists. The 1996 constitutional referendum also approved the proscription of political parties based on religion, language, gender or region.

Assembly elections on June 5, 1997, resulted as follows: National Democratic Rally (RND) 156 seats (36.3% of the vote); Movement of Society for Peace (MSP) 69 (16.0%); Party of the National Liberation Front (FLN, *Hizb Jabha al Tahrir al Watani*) 62 (15.3%); Renaissance Movement (*Nahda*) 34 (9.4%); Socialist Forces Front - FFS 20 (4.8%); Rally for Culture and Democracy - RCD 19 (4.6%); Workers'

Party (*Parti du Travailleurs* - PT) 4 (2.0%); Progressive Republican Party 3 (0.7%); Union for Democracy and Liberties 1 (0.5%); Social Liberal Party 1 (0.4%); independents 11 (4.9%). Critics ascribed RND's victory to rigging.

The RND took control of 55% of councils in local elections in November 1997. It went on to win most of the indirectly elected seats in the Council of the Nation, in December 1997 (the RND got 80 seats, FLN 10, FFS 4, and MSP 2). In controversial presidential elections on April 15, 1999, Abdelaziz Bouteflika of the FLN, who was supported by the military and also by the RND, the MSP and *Nahda*, was declared the winner with 73.8% of the vote. However, the withdrawal of the six other candidates shortly before polling (though their names appeared on ballot papers) tainted the result. Similarly, the opposition claimed that the vote had been rigged and that the turnout had been drastically lower than the official figure of 60.9%. In October 1999 a national referendum approved President Bouteflika's 'civil concord' with FIS and its allies.

New elections to the National People's Assembly were held on May 30, 2002. These were only the second held in 10 years, though the turnout was a low 46.2%, reflecting enduring popular dissatisfaction with the political system. The results were as follows: FLN 199 seats (34.3% of the vote); Movement for National Reform (*el-Islah*) 43 (9.5%); RND 47 (8.2%); MSP 38 (7.0%); Workers' Party (PT) 21 (3.3%); Algerian National Front (FNA) 8 (1.6%); Renaissance Movement 1 (0.6%); Party of Algerian Renewal (PRA) 1 (0.3%); Movement of National Understanding 1 (0.2%); independents 30 (4.9%). Most significant was the collapse of the RND, and the revival of the FLN. The elections were boycotted by the FFS, RCD, PT and Rally for Culture and Democracy (MDA).

Some commentators deem elections for town and district councils to be more relevant, in terms of real autonomous power, than national assembly elections. Such local elections – the third since the constitution introduced a multi-party system in 1989 – were held on Oct. 11, 2002. These polls yielded impressive gains for the FLN, largely at the expense of the RND although smaller parties did well, too. Turnout, however, was just 50%, and that was excluding a boycott in Berber areas where just 2% of the electorate voted. After the October elections, a major schism developed between President Bouteflika and Prime Minister Ali Benflis, head of the FLN. Bouteflika sacked Benflis in mid-2003, replacing him as Prime Minister with the presumably more loyal Ahmed Ouyahia, head of the RND. Unsurprisingly, critics of the regime pointed out the undemocratic nature of this change, given the RND's weaker showing vis-à-a vis the FLN in the two elections of 2002.

The Islamic Salvation Front remains illegal, despite the release from house arrest and imprisonment of its leader and deputy leader in July 2003. Presidential elections were announced for April 8, 2004, amidst initial reports that the powerful Algerian army had begun to withdraw support from incumbent President Bouteflika, international criticism of the likely lack of transparency of the elections, and warnings from the Berber population that they would boycott the polls. In the event Bouteflika was re-elected with 85.0% of the vote; former Prime Minister and current head of the FLN, Ali Benflis took 6.4%; and Abdallah Djaballah of the Movement of National Reform (*El-Islah*) came

third with 5.0%. Certain FLN members preferred Bouteflika to their own official nominee, Benflis, resulting in a serious split within the ruling party.

Algeria's problems include unemployment at 30%; lack of political accountability; corruption; behind-the-scenes domination by the military; and Berber unrest in Kabylia since early 2001. Most of all, Algeria still suffers from a clandestine 'civil war' between the security forces and radical Islamist militias that since 1992 has claimed perhaps as many as 150,000 lives, although the extent of the killings has declined since 2002. In addition individual Algerian migrants in European cities have been associated with *Al Qaeda* and similar groups, especially since Sept. 11, 2001 – though proof of direct contacts with Algerian groups often proves illusory.

Algerian National Front
Front National de la Algérie
Leadership. Moussa Touati
Founded and led by Moussa Touati, the FNA won eight seats on 1.6% of the popular vote (with 120,830 ballots cast) in the May 2002 assembly elections. It accused the National Liberation Front (FLN) of monopolizing ballot boxes in the district of El Bayadh during the local elections in October 2002, though the FNA's natural nationalist inclinations puts it in the same camp as the FLN. The party shares its name with a nationalist organization active in the 1950s. The Algerian newspaper, *L'Actualité*, reported that the FNA was gaining ground amongst younger, educated voters. In 2003 Touati predicted that the replacement of Prime Minister Benflis by Ahmed Ouyahia would change nothing in Algeria.

Islamic Salvation Front
Front Islamique du Salut (FIS)
Website. www.fisalgeria.org
Leadership. Abassi Madani (president); Ali Belhadj (vice-president); Anouar Haddam (spokesman in exile)
Formed from student and other Islamist groups dating from the early 1970s, the FIS obtained official recognition in February 1989 amid a rising tide of opposition to the government of the National Liberation Front (FLN).

In municipal elections in June 1990 FIS candidates took 55% of the popular vote, winning control of 853 municipalities and 32 out of 48 provinces. Serious clashes between FIS supporters and the security forces resulted, in June 1991, in the postponement of Assembly elections and the arrest of hundreds of FIS activists, including Abassi Madani and Ali Belhadj. Divisions between moderates and extremists in the remaining leadership resulted in the former prevailing in their view that the FIS should contest the elections, set for December 1991, and call off street demonstrations.

Led in the elections by Abdelkader Hachani and presenting candidates for all 430 seats, the FIS took a commanding lead in the first-round voting, winning 188 seats outright (and 47.5% of the vote). With the FIS poised to secure a substantial overall majority in the second round, Hachani made it clear that an FIS government would seek an early presidential election and, "should that be the people's demand", embark upon constitutional reform; he gave no specific commitment to the multi-party system, but stressed that Islamicization would be pursued by legal means.

Hachani and Rabeh Kebir were among several FIS leaders arrested in January 1992 following the cancellation of the second electoral round and the military's effective assumption of power. Upon petition by the High State Council, the FIS was banned by a court ruling in March 1992 (upheld by the Supreme Court in April) on the grounds that it had violated the 1989 law prohibiting a religious basis for parties. In a major clamp-down on FIS activists, many thousands were arrested and detained in desert concentration camps. FIS moderates, committed to non-violence, sought political accommodation with the regime (and the FIS leadership denied any involvement in the assassination of head of state Mohammed Boudiaf in June 1992); but the initiative passed increasingly to radical splinter-groups favouring armed struggle, notably to the Armed Islamic Group (GIA). In July 1992 both Madani and Belhadj were sentenced to 12 years' imprisonment after being convicted on insurgency charges. The following month Kebir escaped from detention and was later granted political asylum in Germany, together with Ossama Madani, son of Abbasi. In September 1993 the German authorities refused an Algerian extradition request for these two, who had both been sentenced to death *in absentia* for their alleged part in a bomb attack at Algiers airport in August 1992.

In 1993–94 attacks on security personnel and foreign nationals mounted, as did arrests and executions of FIS militants, bringing the country to a state of virtual civil war. In February 1994 the new Zéroual government released two senior FIS figures in an effort to promote political talks; but a subsequent unofficial dialogue involving FIS representatives produced no agreement. In September Madani and Belhadj were transferred from prison to house arrest in a regime move to promote further dialogue; when this did not occur, both were reimprisoned in November. The release of the two FIS leaders was the main demand of the hijackers of a French airliner at Algiers in December; presumed to be members of the GIA, all four hijackers were killed by French security forces at Marseilles. The episode generated press speculation on whether the GIA and the official armed wing of the FIS, called the Islamic Salvation Army (AIS), had merged. French sources put the death toll in Algeria's internal conflict in 1994 at some 40,000, the majority of them civilians.

In January 1995 the FIS was represented at a conference of Algerian opposition parties held in Rome, but a draft peace plan drawn up on that occasion found little favour with the Algerian government. The following month several prominent FIS members were among many killed when the Algerian security forces put down a revolt by Islamist prisoners at the Serkadji prison in Algiers. Talks between FIS leaders and the government were initiated in April 1995, initially in secret, but broke down in July, with the government claiming that the FIS had entered new conditions at a late stage and had refused to give a commitment to pluralist democracy. Having again been released to house arrest during the talks, Madani and Belhadj were again returned to prison when the talks failed. The FIS boycotted the November 1995 presidential elections, claiming after the result was declared that the turnout had been only about 30% rather the 75% cited by the Algerian authorities. Growing divisions in the Islamist opposition were highlighted in December 1995 by the execution by a GIA firing squad of two aides of the FIS leader who had criticized the GIA's campaign of violence.

In April 1997 the FIS participated in a Madrid meeting of opposition parties which called for the opening of a peace dialogue. The FIS urged a boycott of the June 1997 parliamentary elections, following which Madani and Hachami were conditionally released from prison in July in a gesture of conciliation by the new government headed by the National Democratic Rally (RND). Although secret negotiations made little immediate progress, and Madani was returned to house arrest in October, the AIS declared a unilateral truce from Oct. 1, 1997. In March 1998 FIS spokesman Anouar Haddam was sentenced to death *in absentia* for his alleged involvement in various killings.

However, instead of calling for a boycott, as before, FIS

discreetly backed Ahmed Taleb Ibrahimi – a past minister, and son of the president of the pre-independence Islam Reform movement – as its preferred candidate in the April 1999 presidential elections. Its executive committee, based abroad, officially endorsed him just before polling day. Ibrahimi campaigned on a platform of "national reconciliation"; but he and six other candidates withdrew on the eve of the election, citing gross irregularities, and thus allowing Abdelaziz Bouteflika to win without opposition.

In April 1999 newly-elected President Bouteflika declared that the FIS would not be re-legalized, although former FIS members would be allowed to join legal parties. In June the AIS announced the permanent ending of its armed struggle, reportedly being joined by some 1,000 GIA defectors (although GIA violence continued), while the approval of Bouteflika's new "civil concord" in a referendum in October 1999 generated new hopes for peace. Despite the assassination of Hachami in Algiers in November, in January 2000 the AIS announced that it would disband. Reports suggested that former AIS activists would join government forces in fighting the GIA and other militant groups. One of the most extreme of the latter is the Salafist Group for Conversion and Combat (GSPC), which some analysts suggest takes orders from *Al-Qaeda*.

After some initial confusion, the President granted a blanket pardon to all former AIS members. With the FIS remaining banned, many Front members joined the new Wafa party, although in November 2000 the Interior Minister refused to to authorize legal recognition for the new formation, after considering the matter for several months. On July 2, 2003, FIS leader Abbas Madani was released from house arrest and his deputy, Ali Belhadj, from prison in the town of Blida, south of Algiers. Both men had served their 1991 sentences to the day. Neither man was allowed to express political views in private or public. Belhadj refused to accept government strictures, and was barred from leaving the country. However, Madani did formally accept the strictures, and paid visits to other Arab states. On Jan. 15 he launched a new peace plan, dubbed the "popular national initiative", in Doha. It invited Algerians to redress their "deteriorating situation", and called for a state that "guarantees freedoms in the framework of Islamic principles". Algiers was angry when Saudi King Fahd invited Madani to a reception in early February for the Muslim feast of Eid al-Adha. This they interpreted as Madani flouting the terms of his signed agreement; the incident also revived old fears of the Algerian establishment about FIS links to Saudi Wahabi-style Islam.

Movement for the Defence of Democracy in Algeria
Le Mouvement pour la Démocratie en Algérie (MDA)
Leadership. Ahmed Ben Bella (president)

Ben Bella, one of the nine *chefs historique* who founded the National Liberation Front (FLN) in 1954, and the first president of an independent Algeria, until he was deposed in 1965, launched *Le Mouvement pour la Démocratie en Algérie* (MDA) on May 29, 1984, in Lausanne, Switzerland. Ben Bella had been exiled to France in 1981, and then to Switzerland in 1983, having been imprisoned in Algeria from 1965 to 1981. Ben Bella and his former ally and foe, Hocine Aït Ahmed, leader of the Socialist Forces Front, had created the International Islamic Commission for Human Rights in London, in 1981. During his prison years, Ben Bella had begun to incorporate Islamic elements into his philosophy of anti-imperialism and radical socialism; these views were reflected in the MDA manifesto.

Ben Bella returned to Algeria on September 27, 1990, to contest the nation's first multiparty elections as an alternative to the Islamist FIS and ruling FLN, but it did poorly at the polls. Ben Bella condemned the military takeover of January 1992, and called for the relegalization of FIS, while criticizing Islamic militants who turned to violence. His MDA spearheaded the San Egido Rome Platform for restoring Algerian democracy; Ben Bella and his deputy, Khaled Bensmain, co-signed the final declaration on Jan. 13, 1995. The MDA boycotted the November 1996 constitutional referendum and threatened to oppose the 1997 elections rather than amend articles 3 and 6 of its electoral platform, as ordered by the government. Article 6 spoke of "the defense and growth of Islam, the religion of the State and of the people." Human Rights Watch protested the government's decision. The MDA was subsequently banned on June 12, 1997, along with six other parties.

Ben Bella heads several NGOs, including the Democratic Revolutionary Arab Dialogue Forum, a leftist pan-Arab group. Since the late 1990s he has campaigned against globalization, US foreign policy and ecological devastation. Arguably the MDA has suffered from its veteran leader's preference for international and regional issues.

Movement of National Reform
El-Islah
Leadership. Sheikh Abdallah Djaballah
This Islamist party was formed when Sheikh Abdallah Djaballah was dismissed as leader of the Renaissance Movement, *Nahda*, in January 1999. The cause of the split was Djaballah's opposition to Nahda's support for Bouteflika's candidacy in that year's presidential elections. Many analysts say that the new party is ideologically close to the still-banned Islamic Salvation Front (FIS). However, as of October 2002, total support for all Islamist parties, including *El-Islah*, totalled some two million votes in local elections, or half of what FIS had scored in 1990.

El-Islah surprised many when it took second place in the May 2002 elections, winning 9.5% of votes and 45 seats. This result forced the RND into third place in terms of votes cast, although the RND did win two more seats than *El-Islah* in the Assembly. The new party also overwhelmed its former parent party, *Nahda*, which won only a single seat; and it overtook the pro-government Islamist Movement of Society for Peace (MSP) to become the leading Islamist party in the Assembly. Again, *El-Islah* was the only Islamist party to do well in the October 2002 local elections, winning 39 town councils. About a million Algerians voted for the party, twice the number for *Nahda*. According to a Human Rights Watch report, *El-Islah*, together with the secular Workers Party, distinguished themselves in pressing for information on the thousands of "disappearances" since violence first erupted in 1992.

In February 2003 Djaballah announced that he would stand in presidential elections, scheduled for April 8, 2004, against the incumbent, President Bouteflika, and Ali Benflis of the FLN. At the time he vowed to campaign on support for a "holy war" against US forces in Iraq; a year later he was concentrating more on domestic grievances. His party won public affection when it set up camps to help people rendered homeless after the devastating earthquake that hit Algeria in May 2003. However, Djaballah came only third behind Bouteflika and Benflis in the presidential poll. To counter Djaballah's support among 'moderate' Islamists, Bouteflika courted *zaouia,* or popular indigenous Muslim folk fraternities (more militant Islamists, inspired by Wahhabi or Salafi doctrines, condemn *zaouia* as non-Islamic).

Movement of Society for Peace
Harakat Moudjtamaa as-Silm
Mouvement de la Société pour la Paix (MSP)
Address. 63 rue Ali Haddad, El Mouradia, Algiers
Telephone. (213–2) 272572
Fax. (213–2) 675024

Email. info@hms-algeria.net
Website. www.hms-algeria.net
Leadership. Sheikh Mahfoud Nahnah (president); Magharia Mohamed (vice-president for political relations); Farid Hebbaz (vice-president for co-ordination)
This moderate Islamist party was formed in 1990 as the Movement for an Islamic Society (*Hamas*), being unrelated to the Palestinian movement with the same acronym. Declaring its opposition to the radicalism of the Islamic Salvation Front (FIS), it advocates the gradual creation of an Islamic state and respect for individual liberties and the democratic process. Many of its followers came from a charitable and preaching organization, *El-Islah Oual Ershad* (Association for Reform and Guidance) that Sheikh Nahnah had created after the riots of October 1988.

The party failed to win a seat in the first round of the December 1991 Assembly elections. It subsequently supported the regime's anti-fundamentalist campaign, and was the only significant party to participate in the "national consensus conference" convened by the government in January 1994. Sheikh Mahfoud Nahnah was a candidate in the November 1995 presidential elections, coming in second place with 25.4% of the vote. After the result was declared, Sheikh Nahnah asserted that 4 million names added to the electoral register since 1991 could not be justified by population growth; he also claimed that his supporters and monitors had been intimidated by the authorities. Nevertheless, in January 1996 *Hamas* accepted two portfolios in a government reshuffle announced by President Liamine Zéroual.

The party renamed itself the MSP in light of the November 1996 referendum decision proscribing religious identification for parties. This did not stop Sheikh Nahnah from condemning Kabyle Berber rebels, who he said "opposed the Arab-Islamic heritage of Algeria". In the June 1997 parliamentary elections the MSP took second place, with 69 of the 380 seats and 16% of the vote. Nahnah claimed that the polling had been rigged and that the MSP had won 100 fewer seats than its real entitlement. The party nevertheless entered a new coalition government headed by the National Democratic Rally (RND), seeking to rally moderate Islamist opinion against the extremists. In the December 1997 indirect elections to the Council of the Nation the MSP took only two of the 96 elective seats.

After Sheikh Nahnah had been barred from standing in the April 1999 presidential elections (because he had not proved that he had participated in Algeria's war of independence), the MSP backed the successful candidacy of the Abdelaziz Bouteflika of the National Liberation Front (FLN) and was again included in the subsequent government. The party supported Bouteflika's "civil concord" peace plan approved by referendum in November 1999. The MSP dropped from 69 seats to 38 on 7.0% of the vote in the May 2002 Assembly elections. This made it the fourth largest party in the legislature, but placed it well behind Sheikh Djaballah's Movement of National Reform (*El-Islah*), which henceforth became the leading legal Islamist group in Algeria.

National Democratic Rally
Rassemblement National pour la Démocratie (RND
Address. c/o Barlaman, Algiers
Leadership. Ahmed Ouyahia (secretary-general)
The creation of the RND was announced in March 1997 by supporters of then President Liamine Zéroual with the aim of providing a vehicle for the ruling establishment in the June 1997 parliamentary elections. The trade union leader, Abdelhak Benhamouda, had begun creating the party earlier that year, but was assassinated on Jan. 27, 1997.

The RND succeeds an earlier abortive attempt to create a "party of government", the National Patriotic Rally, in June 1992. The new party, with Abdelkader Bensalah as its general secretary, declared itself to be in favour of political democracy, social justice and modernization of the economy by privatization. It also vowed to crush the "extremism" of the Islamic Salvation Front (FIS) and other Islamist groups. In the June 1997 elections the RND became substantially the largest Assembly party, winning 156 of the 380 seats with 36.3% of the vote, although its success was tainted by charges of vote rigging and electoral fraud. Critics also drew attention to the menacing presence of 300,000 soldiers and policemen who "looked after" 37,000 polling stations; they said that the RND's power derived from ties to the administration, rather than any genuine popular appeal.

The party thereupon formed a coalition government headed by Ahmed Ouyahia which included the National Liberation Front (FLN) and the Movement of Society for Peace (MSP). Partially to allay growing public criticism, the RND-led government attempted to broker a ceasefire with FIS-AIS. In local elections held in November 1997, the RND took control of 55% of the local councils – again, to considerable public protest at alleged vote-rigging. And on Dec. 25, 1997, the RND won 80 of 97 of the indirectly elected seats in the Council of the Nation, in December 1997.

At the first RND congress in April 1998 Tahar Benbaibeche was confirmed as secretary-general heading a 15-member national bureau. However, Benbaibeche's resistance to RND endorsement of the army-backed presidential candidacy of Abdelaziz Bouteflika (FLN) precipitated his dismissal in January 1999 and replacement by Ouyahia (who had vacated the premiership the previous month). Following Bouteflika's controversial victory in the April 1999 presidential elections, the RND continued to be the leading component in the government coalition, which was extended to the Renaissance Movement (*Nahda*). The RND gave strong backing to Bouteflika's "civil concord" peace plan approved by referendum in on Sept. 16, 1999. Yet a non-party Prime Minister, Ahmed Benbitour, was appointed to head the new multi-party government, on Dec. 24, 1999.

The RND won 47 seats in the May 2002 elections, making it the second-placed party in the Algerian assembly – though well behind the victorious and resuscitated FLN. Analysts blamed its poor showing on voter dissatisfaction with its record in town and city councils; and the allegedly fraudelent nature of its 1997 victory, the result, it is claimed, of Bouteflika's gerrymandering of local government structures. Furthermore, in terms of votes cast, the RND came third behind the FLN and the Islamist Movement for National Reform (*El-Islah*).

In May 2003 the RND leader, Ahmed Ouyahia, was named as Algeria's new Prime Minister, replacing the ousted Ali Benflis of FLN. Ouyahia, a good debater favoured by the military, was earlier Prime Minister from Dec. 31, 1995, to Dec. 15, 1998. During this period he had presided over a stringent economic 'structural adjustment programme'. Ouyahia enthusiastically supported Bouteflika's victorious presidential candidacy in 2004, and promised major economic changes to follow in the post-election government. These included a hydrocarbon bill designed to attract investors following the privatization of Algeria's state oil companies and ambitious plans for the diversification of the national economy for the future, when oil eventually runs out. Abdelkader Bensalah, RND's first leader, is currently President of the Council of the Nation.

National Liberation Front
Hizb Jabha al-Tahrir al-Watani
Parti du Front de Libération Nationale (FLN)
Address. 7 rue du Stade, Hydra, Algiers
Telephone. (213–2) 592149
Fax. (213–2) 591732
Website. http://www.pfln.org.dz/

Leadership. Ali Benflis (secretary-general)
The FLN was founded at Cairo in November 1954 under the leadership of Ahmed Ben Bella and other nationalists as an anti-colonialist, socialist, non-aligned, pan-Arabist and pro-Islam movement dedicated to ending French rule. After achieving independence and coming to power in 1962, it experienced internal strife in which Ben Bella was initially victorious but which eventually resulted in his replacement in July 1965 by Col. Houari Boumedienne, who held the government and party leadership until his death in December 1978. The FLN was then reorganized and given a new statute at its fourth congress in January 1979, at which Chadli Bendjedid was elected party leader and designated as sole candidate for the presidency in elections the following month. Re-elected unopposed in January 1984, Bendjedid embarked upon a programme of economic reform, emphasizing "pragmatic" socialism and the virtues of the private enterprise, to the chagrin of the FLN's socialist old guard. Following anti-FLN riots in late 1978, he also sought to democratize political structures, to which end the posts of head of state and party leader were made incompatible by decision of an FLN congress in November. Bendjedid was succeeded as FLN secretary-general by his brother-in-law, Abdelhamid Mehri, and himself took the new post of party president.

The move to multi-party democracy in 1989 revealed the extent of popular discontent with the FLN, which suffered a serious rebuff in local elections in June 1990 marking the emergence of the fundamentalist Islamic Salvation Front (FIS) as a major force. Subsequent anti-government demonstrations resulted in the formation in June 1991 of the first post-independence government not dominated by the FLN, Bendjedid resigning as party president the same month. In Assembly elections in December 1991 the FLN trailed a poor third in the first-round voting despite putting up 429 candidates, after which the military intervened to prevent a likely FIS victory in the second round and Bendjedid resigned as President. A five-member Higher State Council took over government in January 1992, under Mohammed Boudiaf, a 'pragmatist' venerated for his role as military leader of the war of independence. Boudiaf imposed a state of emergency and launched an anti-corruption campaign, but was assassinated on June 29, 1992.

Although the new regime included many figures associated with the years of FLN rule, the party itself effectively went into opposition, joining other parties in calling for a transitional government of national unity and condemning the use of military courts to enforce emergency regulations banning fundamentalist political activity. It also declined to join a regime-sponsored National Patriotic Rally, announced in June 1992 as a new "foundation" for political co-operation; for its pains the FLN was dispossessed of its state-owned properties, including its party headquarters in Algiers. In March 1994 the FLN joined other parties in opening a dialogue with the new Zéroual government, while in January 1995 Mehri attended the Rome conference of Algerian opposition parties at which a peace plan was drawn up, although without substantive effect. A member of the FLN central committee, Ahmed Kasmi, was found beheaded in February 1995, apparently the victim of Islamic militants. The FLN joined the opposition parties' boycott of the November 1995 presidential elections, after which Mehri called on the government to enter into real dialogue with the FIS.

However, some considered Mehri as being too conciliatory to the Islamists, and on Jan. 4, 1996, the more hard-line Boualem Benhamouda replaced Mehri as FLN general secretary. The FLN participated in the June 1997 parliamentary elections, coming in third place with 62 of the 380 seats and 15.3% of the popular vote. The party gained control of 20%

of local councils in November 1997, by contrast with the RND's 55%; and in the December indirect elections to the Council of the Nation it took 10 of the 96 elective seats (while the RND won 80).

FLN participation in the new coalition government headed by the National Democratic Rally (RND) precipitated divisions between party "reformists", led by former Prime Minister Mouloud Hamrouche, who favoured accommodation with the FIS, and the "old guard" leadership of Boualem Benhamouda, who asserted his authority at an FLN congress in March 1998. With military backing, the FLN nominated former Foreign Minister Abdelaziz Bouteflika as its candidate for the April 1999 presidential elections, while Hamrouche entered the contest as the nominee of a new alliance of six parties called the Group of National Forces (GFN). Bouteflika was also backed by the RND, the Movement of Society for Peace (MSP) and the Renaissance Movement (*Nahda*) and was controversially elected with 73.8% of the vote, after the other candidates had withdrawn shortly before polling.

The FLN continued to participate in the government, backing Bouteflika's "civil concord" peace plan approved by referendum in September 1999. In February 2001 a new party called the Rally for National Concord (RCN) was launched to provide a broader political base for the President. Meanwhile on Sept. 20, 2001, Ali Benflis, Algeria's Prime Minister since Aug. 27, 2000, replaced Benhamouda as FLN secretary-general. Benhamouda formally nominated Benflis as his successor. Benflis, born in 1944, is a lawyer who became Justice Minister, and joined the FLN political bureau in 1989.

The FLN came first in the May 2002 national assembly elections, significantly increasing its tally of seats from 62 to 199, and gaining 35.52% of votes cast. It thus overwhelmed the previous top-ranked party, the RND, which, according to the online journal, *Algeria Interface*, had a "disastrous record in town and city councils". Benflis formed a new FLN-led government on June 17, 2002. The FLN also won at the RND's expense in October local elections, gaining control of 668 out of 1,541 town councils, and 43 of 48 district councils.

However, Benflis broke with his former mentor, Bouteflika, and was dismissed as Prime Minister in May 2003. Benflis subsequently announced he would stand against Bouteflika in the presidential elections scheduled for April 8, 2004. Meanwhile, rebel elements in the FLN took out lawsuits against Benflis's candidacy, resulting in the FLN being temporarily frozen by the courts. This situaton appeared to undermine hopes of a Benflis victory, and in the election he came a poor second with only 6.4% of the vote.

The FLN has openly accused Bouteflika of suppressing parties and the independent press, and of using state funds to get re-elected. In February 2004 Benflis helped to create an "anti-fraud front", called the Group of 10.

Progressive Republican Party
Parti Républicain Progressif (PRP)

Address. 10 rue Ouahrani Abou-Mediêne, Cité Seddikia, Oran
Telephone. (213–5) 357936
Leadership. Slimane Cherif (secretary-general)
The moderate PRP was established as a legal party in 1990 under the leadership of Khadir Driss, who led the party till at least 1999. In June 1997 parliamentary elections the PRP won three seats with 0.7% of the national vote.

Rally for Culture and Democracy
Rassemblement pour la Culture et la Démocratie (RCD)

Address. 87 rue Didouche Mourad, Algiers
Telephone. (213–2) 738487
Fax. (213–2) 738472
Email. rcd@rcd-dz.org
Website. www.rcd-dz.org
www.rcd.asso.fr
Leadership. Saïd Sadi (president)
Based in the Berber community, the secular RCD was formed in February 1989 on a platform of "economic centralism" and official recognition of the Berber language, Tamazight. It took third place in the June 1990 local elections (which were boycotted by the rival Berber-based Socialist Forces Front), winning 5.7% of the vote and majorities in 87 municipalities and the province of Tizi Ouzou. In the December 1991 Assembly elections, however, none of its 300 candidates were elected in the first round. The RCD joined other mainstream parties in opposing the military-led regime installed in January 1992, launching the broad-based Movement for the Republic (MPR) in November 1993 to rally support, until Liamine Zéroual's accession to the presidency in January 1994 heralded a more conciliatory government stance, enabling political dialogue to commence in March.

Saïd Sadi, a trained psychiatrist, and at the time RCD secretary-general, was a candidate in the November 1995 presidential elections, winning 9.3% of the vote. During the 1980s he had been the chief representative of the then clandestine FFS in the Kabylie province, and fought for Tamazight and democratic rights (which resulted in two years' harsh imprisonment). Over time Sadi adopted a more ethnically centred policy and a fiercer antipathy to Islamists than the FFS showed. In the June 1997 parliamentary elections the RCD won 19 of the 380 seats (and 4.6% of the national vote), including 15 of the 24 Algiers seats, but it claimed that it had been particularly damaged by electoral fraud. The party therefore organized large protest demonstrations in Algiers, and boycotted the December 1997 elections to the new Council of the Nation – where one leading RCD figure, the former human rights campaigner, Aït Larbi Mokrane, had been appointed earlier that year. After the second RCD congress in February 1998 had elected Sadi as party president, the RCD announced in February 1999 that it would boycott the forthcoming presidential elections.

The RCD joined Algeria's coalition government in July 2000; it left in May 2001, in the wake of police versus Berber clashes in Kabyle district. Bouteflika promised to accord 'national' status to Tamazight, and passed a constitutional revision to this effect in January 2002. Still, Berbers queried the government's sincerity, citing continuing police repression in Kabyle, and the RCD boycotted the May 2002 elections. The RCD called for a boycott in Kabyle during October 2002 local elections, though its success backfired somewhat, when the rival FFS increased its representation there at the RCD's expense.

Sadi came fourth in the April 2004 presidential polls, taking 1.9% of the vote.

Rally for National Concord
Rassemblement pour la Concorde Nationale (RCN)

Address. c/o Barlaman, Algiers
Leadership. Larbi Belkheir (honorary president)
The RCN was launched in February 2001 with the stated aim of providing "a popular base" for President Bouteflika, who had been a member of the National Liberation Front (FLN) when he was elected in 1999. Sid Ahmed Abachi was the RCN's first chairman, and retired Gen. Mohammed Attaïlia its founder. Claiming to represent over 7,000 national and local associations, the RCN undertook to support the President against those trying to obstruct his national reconciliation programme, and against the "forces of sedition".

In 2002 the RCN appointed an old revolutionary hero, Gen. Larbi Belkheir, as its honorary president. In December 1991 Gen. Larbi and then Defence Minister Khaled Nezzar had forced President Chadli Benjedid to resign. According to *Algeria Interface*, writing in 2001, Nezzar and Belkheir have been "for the last 20 years the all-powerful duo behind the decision-makers in the army establishment".

The party failed to make its presence felt overtly in the elections of 2002. Nonetheless, the RCN still wields influence as a voice for the generals. In June 2003 Attaïlia announced at a conference in Zeralda that the RCN had gathered 100,000 petitions in support of Bouteflika's candidacy. At the same event, the RCN tried to relaunch itself as a proper political party with a programme and constitution.

It seems the RCN remains caught up in rivalry amongst the generals. In 1999 Belkheir had restrained his close colleague, Nezzar, when the latter criticized Bouteflika that year. More recently, Attaïlia has attacked Nezzar for dishonouring the army in controversial memoirs that Nezzar published in 2000. These memoirs had spoken of army coups, massacres, torture and political appointments. Before the 2004 poll, there were rumours that the military would not support Bouteflika; conceivably the RCN's recent actions are an attempt to prove otherwise.

Renaissance Movement
Harakat al-Nahda (Nahda)
Mouvement de la Renaissance (MR)

Address. 4 ave des Ecoles, Place des Martyrs, Algiers
Telephone. (213–2) 667666
Fax. (213–2) 667666
Leadership. Lahib Adami (secretary-general)

This moderate Islamist party sprang from a Constantine University movement of the 1970s and was called the Islamic Renaissance Movement until early 1997, when it dropped the "Islamic" descriptor to conform with the new constitutional ban on parties of religious orientation. It was unsuccessful in the December 1991 Assembly elections and subsequently declared itself in favour of dialogue to bring about a national consensus, being boosted by the government as an alternative to the extremist Islamic Salvation Front (FIS). Its leader participated in a conference of Algerian opposition parties held in Rome in January 1995 and endorsed a resultant draft peace agreement, but this text did not impress the regime in Algiers.

Nahda joined other opposition parties in boycotting the November 1995 presidential elections, but participated in the June 1997 parliamentary elections, winning 34 of the 380 seats and 9.4% of the vote. It opted not to participate in the subsequent coalition government headed by the National Democratic Rally (RND), following which internal divisions developed between long-time *Nahda* leader Sheikh Abdallah Djaballah and secretary-general Lahib Adami over whether the party should back government candidate Abdelaziz Bouteflika of the National Liberation Front (FLN) in the April 1999 presidential elections. The outcome was the dismissal of Djaballah as leader in January 1999 (and his formation of the breakaway Movement of National Reform), whereupon the rump *Nahda* supported Bouteflika in his successful but highly controversial candidacy. *Nahda* was subsequently included in a new coalition headed by the RND. Evidently voters punished the MR for its connivance with the Bouteflika government at the May 2002 polls, giving it just one seat on less than 1% of votes cast.

Socialist Forces Front
Front des Forces Socialistes (FFS)

Address. 56 ave Souidani Boudjemaa, 16000 Algiers
Telephone. (213–2) 593313
Fax. (213–2) 591145
Email. ffs.idf@wanadoo.fr
Website. www.f-f-s.com
Leadership. Hocine Aït Ahmed (president); Ahmed Djeddaï

(first secretary)

Originally founded in September 1963 and revived and legalized in November 1989 after 14 years of clandestine existence, the FFS espoused democratic socialist principles as contrasted with the state centralism of the then ruling National Liberation Front (FLN). Its founder and leader, Hocine Aït Ahmed, is one of the surviving *neuf historiques* who launched the Algerian war of independence against France in November 1954. Following independence in 1962, he instigated an unsuccessful Berber revolt against the Ben Bella government in 1963. Arrested in October 1964, Aït Ahmed was sentenced to death in April 1964 (the sentence being commuted to life imprisonment) but escaped abroad in May 1966.

Between 1966 and 1980 he ran the FFS as an opposition movement based in exile, with an extensive network amongst Kabyle (Berber) labour migrants in France, and an underground network in Kabylia as well. By 1978 the FFS had formally adopted the Berber language claim as a matter of democratic principle. Its key representative in Kabylia during the unrest in that province in 1980 was Saïd Sadi, who by 1989 deserted the FFS to found the rival and more decidedly ethnically based Rally for Culture and Democracy. Despite their mutual antipathy, the FFS and the RCD have jointly backed the Berber Cultural Movement (MCB; also called Amazigh Cultural Movement).

After Aït Ahmed had returned to Algeria from Switzerland in December 1989, the FFS held its first post-legalization congress in March 1991. After an abortive attempt to create a broad coalition to oppose the Islamic Salvation Front (FIS), and after declining to contest the 1990 local and regional elections, the FFS emerged as the leading non-Islamist party in the first round of Assembly elections in December 1991. It put up 317 candidates and won 25 seats outright with 15% of the vote on a platform advocating a mixed economy, regional autonomy and recognition of the Berber language. By contrast, the ruling FLN gained only 16 seats. Having ruled out a second-round alliance with either the FLN or the FIS, Ahmed strongly criticized the subsequent military intervention and returned to exile in Switzerland.

Calling for a government of national unity and an end to anti-FIS repression, the FFS rejected affiliation with the National Patriotic Rally launched by the government in June 1992 and also boycotted the "national consensus conference" convened in January 1994. Nevertheless, having urged moderate army elements to join with the democratic opposition, the FFS responded to the conciliatory overtures of the new Zéroual government in March 1994, while insisting that political dialogue must result in a resumption of multi-party democracy. In January 1995 Aït Ahmed attended the Rome conference of Algerian opposition parties at which a putative peace plan was formulated. Following its rejection by the government, the FFS was one of several opposition parties that boycotted the November 1995 presidential elections. Aït Ahmed returned to Algeria in March 1996 to attend the second FFS congress, at which he was elected party president (having hitherto been secretary-general) and which appealed for national dialogue to achieve civil peace.

In January 1997 Aït Ahmed criticized government policy of promoting the creation of local anti-Islamist militias, contending that they were involved in smuggling, organized crime and vendettas between families and clans. In the June 1997 parliamentary elections the FFS took fifth place (just ahead of the rival Berber-based Rally for Culture and Democracy), winning 20 of the 380 seats and 4.8% of the vote. It thereafter remained in opposition to the new government headed by the National Democratic Rally (RND), urging it to move towards legalization of the FIS. In the December 1997 indirect elections to the Council of the

Nation it took four of the 96 elective seats.

A special FFS congress in February 1999 nominated Aït Ahmed as the party's candidate for the presidential elections in April; however, together with other opposition candidates he withdrew shortly before polling day in protest at the military 'rigging the ballot' in favour of Abdelaziz Bouteflika of the National Liberation Front (FLN). Even so, 3.19 % of voters still cast their ballots for Aït Ahmed, formally placing him second to Bouteflika. The third FFS congress in May 2000 reaffirmed the party's opposition to Bouteflika's "civil concord" peace plan approved by referendum in September 1999, calling instead the election of a constituent assembly to bring about genuine "democratic alternance".

The FFS led large protest marches, even in Algiers, after the Kabyle violence of early 2001. It boycotted the May 2002 assembly elections, along with three other parties. It did contest the local elections of October 2002, and increased the number of municipalities under its control, yet received 150,000 fewer votes than in previous local polls, because of a 98% boycott of the elections in the Kabylia region.

In late 2002, Ahmed Djeddaï, a young doctor from eastern Algeria, was the first national secretary of the FFS. A fierce critic of military domination, he said le pouvoir had "privatized the state, and led it to the brink of chaos". In September 2002 he faced protests by militant FFS supporters demanding a poll boycott in local elections. By June 2003, Djoudi Mameri was described as FFS national secretary, with Djeddaï as his colleague. Aït Ahmed has increasingly delegated activities to these younger men.

The FFS claims more support outside its Kabyle Berber homeland than does the RCD, partly because of its stance on one truly national issue, namely, its principled opposition to military interference in politics. It boasts a membership of 30,000 and belongs to the Socialist International. Nonetheless, it is said to lack support amongst disenchanted youth, and within Kabyle faces powerful opposition from popular local community-based committees, called 'arush.

Workers' Party
Parti des Travailleurs (PT)
Address. 2 rue Belkheir Belkacemi, Hassan Badi, El Harrach, Algiers
Telephone. (213–2) 753637
Fax. (213–2) 753698
Website. www.multimania.com/tribune
Leadership. Louisa Hanoun (president)
The leftist PT arose out of the illegal Trotskyist Social Workers Organization (OST) and became a recognized party in in 1989. Its long-term president and spokesperson is Louisa Hanoun. A law graduate and women's rights campaigner who was imprisoned in 1981-4, she helped found the Association for the Equality of Men and Women Before the Law in 1984, and became its president. Though decidedly secular in her views, Hanoun demanded the release of Islamist leaders imprisoned since June 1991, and encouraged comprehensive dialogue with the FIS. By contrast with the Rally for Culture and Democracy (RCD) and certain army factions, the PT does not favour "eradicating" Islamists.

Hanoun represented the PT at the Rome conference of opposition parties in January 1995. The party won four seats, including Hanoun, in the June 1997 parliamentary election with 2% of the national vote. PT assembly representatives won praise for highlighting workers' rights and the fate of the thousands of missing (presumed captured or killed by militias or security forces). In January 1999 the PT central committee nominated Hanoun as their candidate for the April 1999 presidential elections, but she was barred from standing because she could not provide the required 75,000 signatures of support.

Possibly as a result of the PT's creditable performance in the assembly, it more than quintupled its tally of seats to 21 and won 3.3% of the popular vote, becoming, in Hugh Roberts' words, Algeria's "leading secular-democratic party". On Feb. 20, 2004, Hanoun announced that she would contest the presidential elections in April. The national council of the PT, meeting in Zeralda, near Algiers, backed Hanoun and this time claimed to have gathered 92,000 signatures in support of her candidacy. Hanoun became the first woman to stand for President in Algerian history, taking 1.0% of the vote

Other Parties

The large number of legal minor parties in Algeria was reduced by an announcement by the authorities in May 1998 that 30 parties had been banned for failing to meet new rules pertaining to such organizations, including a provision that a party must have at least 2,500 individual members. Below are three groups whose current status is questionable.

Not mentioned in this list are such entities as the Islamic Salvation Army (AIS), regarded as the armed wing of FIS; the Armed Islamic Group (GIA); and the *Al-Qaeda*-connected Salafist Group for Preaching and Combat (GSPC). The AIS, GIA and GSPC are all essentially extra-legal militias or terrorist groups, and therefore not political parties in their own right, although some do have links to established parties.

Likewise, the list excludes pressure groups that play a crucial role in the battle for civil liberties and against military domination of politics. Premier amongst these is the Algerian League for the Defence of Human Rights (*Ligue algérienne pour la défense des droits de l'homme* – LADDH) under the leadership of the veteran Maître Ali Yahia Abdenour. Also worth mentioning are the National Association for Families of the Disappeared (ANFD); the Citizens' Movement (*Le Mouvement des Citoyens* – MDC) under Saïd Khélil; and Youth Action Rally (*Rassemblement Action Jeunesse* – RAJ) led by Hakim Addad, amongst others.

Democratic Social Movement (*Mouvement Démocratique et Social,* MDS), launched in October 1999 as successor to the Challenge (*Ettahaddi*) movement, itself created in January 1993 as successor to the Socialist Vanguard Party (*Parti de l'Avant-Garde Socialiste*, PAGS), itself descended from the Algerian Communist Party (CPA) founded in the 1930s. *Ettahaddi* boycotted the the 1997 parliamentary and 1999 presidential elections, its conversion into the MDS signifying a renewed commitment to the democratic process and the mixed economy, as well as opposition to any compromise with Islamic extremism. Its leader, Al-Hashemi Cherif, is a Berber veteran of the fight against the French; he became a Communist and leading trade unionist, and by 1991 keenly supported the cancellation of elections after the FIS victory. Cherif's ferocious opposition to Islamists may explain an attempt on his life in 1994.
Address. 67 blvd Krim Belkacem, Algiers
Telephone. (213–2) 420336
Fax. (213–2) 429723
Email. mds@mds.pol.dz
Website. www.mds.pol.dz
Leadership. Al-Hashemi Cherif (secretary-general)

Group of 10, founded in February 2004, is a self-styled "anti-fraud" front of ten parties that demanded free and fair presidential elections in April. Its strongest figure is Ali Benflis, head of the FLN. The Group of 10 echoes similar ad hoc unions in the past; to some such alliances presage an eventual potential coalition of parties that may one day coalesce to form a government to challenge the power of the military in Algerian politics.

Wafa Party, founded in early 2000 mainly by former members of the banned Islamic Salvation Front (FIS) following the Bouteflika presidency's new accommodation with the FIS. Bouteflika had accepted that FIS activists could join other legal parties. *Wafa* is a conservative movement; its name stands for "Movement for Loyalty and Justice". The party arose out of the April 1999 campaign of presidential candidate, Ahmed Taleb Ibrahim. Ibrahim made Belaid Mohand-Oussaid the party spokesman. Better known as Mohamed Said, Mohand-Oussaid is a Berber, a former pan-Arabist activist and a retired anchorman on Algerian television. He was director of the Ministry of Information when Ibrahim was its minister, in 1970. When Ibrahim became Foreign Minister, he made Said an ambassador to the Gulf. Said is now general secretary of *Wafa*. Like his mentor and party president, Ibrahim, Said seeks to present an acceptable, establishment veneer to a party that many secularists fear is an extremist Islamist reincarnation of FIS. In November 2000 the Interior Ministry refused Ibrahim's application to register his party. Many Islamists interpreted this rejection as a sign of the bankrupcy of the recently passed law on civil concord; and the GIA and similarly radical groups used the refusal of *Wafa's* party licence as a pretext for hugely escalating violence.

Andorra

Capital: Andorra la Vella
Population: 69,865 (2004E)

The origins of the Principality of Andorra go back to 1278 when an independent feudal state ruled by two co-Princes, the Count of Foix (later the head of state of France) and the Bishop of Urgel (in Spain), was created. A parliament, but without real powers, was created in 1419 and general male suffrage was introduced in 1866. Andorra effectively gained independence on May 4, 1993, with the entry into force of its first written constitution, adopted by referendum on March 14. The sovereignty hitherto vested in the President of the French Republic and the Bishop of Urgel as co-Princes was transferred to the "parliamentary co-principality" of Andorra. The co-Princes were retained with the status of a single constitutional monarch, with much reduced powers, and were still represented by their respective Permanent Delegates, and locally by the *Veguer de França* and the *Veguer Episcopal*.

The unicameral legislature, the 28-member General Council of the Valleys (*Consell General de las Valls d'Andorra*), is elected for a four-year term by universal franchise of Andorran citizens aged 18 and over, 14 members being elected on a national list system and two each from the seven constituent parishes. Most residents are ineligible to vote, being French or Spanish nationals. The General Council, under the new dispensation, selects the Head of Government (*Cap del Govern*) who presides over an Executive Council or Cabinet (*Govern d'Andorra*); neither the Head of Government nor the ministers may be members of the General Council.

Political parties were legalized by the 1993 constitution, which also formalized trade union and civil rights and the separation of the judiciary from the executive and legislative branches. Various ad hoc groupings had contested earlier elections, and the General Council balloting on Dec. 12, 1993, marked the development of these groups into political parties.

In elections to the General Council on March 4, 2001, the Liberal Party of Andorra won 15 seats (with 46.1% of the vote), the Social Democratic Party 6 (30.0%), the Democratic Party 5 (23.8%) and the Lauredian Union 2.

Democratic Party
Partit Demòcrata (PD)
Address. c/o Consell General, Casa de la Vall, Andorra la Vella
Leadership. Lluís Viu Torres (chairman); Josep Garrallà Rossell (chairman of parliamentary group)
The PD was formed prior to the 2001 General Council elections as the successor principally to the centre-right National Democratic Grouping (*Agrupament Nacional Democratica*, AND) and was also joined by the Union of the People of Ordino (*Unió del Poble d'Ordino*, UPd'O).

The AND had been founded in 1979 by Oscar Ribas Reig, who presided over the Executive Council in 1982-84 and 1990-94, latterly for a ten-month period as the first Head of Government under the 1993 constitution. Modernizing reforms introduced under Ribas Reig included the abolition of capital punishment, implementation of the new constitution, a customs union with the European Union and admission to the United Nations in July 1993. More controversially, he proposed to widen indirect taxation beyond sales to cover banking, insurance and other sectors to finance infrastructural development, and it was on this issue that his government fell in November 1994. However, two AND members who helped to vote in the successor government headed by the Liberal Party of Andorra (PLA) did so only on condition that it agreed to implement a broadly similar budget. In the February 1997 General Council elections, the AND slipped from eight to six seats and remained in opposition to a further administration headed by the PLA.

The UPd'O had been based in the constituency parish of Ordino, from which it had elected two representatives in the February 1997 elections, both of whom joined the PLA parliamentary group.

In the March 2001 General Council elections the new PD won a disappointing five seats (and remained in opposition), with a national vote share of 23.8%.

Lauredian Union
Unió Laurediana (UL)
Address. c/o Consell General, Casa de la Vall, Andorra la Vella
Leadership. Marc Pintat Forné (leader)
Based in the parish of Sant Julià de Lòria, the UL was part of the victorious list of the Liberal Party of Andorra (PLA) in the 1997 General Council elections. Standing in its own right in the March 2001 contest, it won the two parish seats for Sant Julià de Lòria, its two elected members joining the PLA parliamentary group.

Liberal Party of Andorra
Partit Liberal d'Andorra (PLA)
Address. Edif. Elan 1°/4a, Avda. del Fener 11, Andorra la Vella
Telephone. (376) 869708
Fax. (376) 869728
Email. pla@andorra.ad
Website. www.partitliberal.ad
Leadership. Marc Forné Molné (president); Antoni Martí Petit (chairman of parliamentary group); Estanislau Sangrà Cardona (secretary-general)
Granted legal status in July 1992, the PLA is a centre-right formation advocating deregulation of the economy and greater openness to foreign investment.

In the December 1993 elections the PLA secured five

seats on the General Council in its own right, with 22 per cent of the national vote, while four allied independents were elected from two parish constituencies. The Liberal group voted against the nomination of Oscar Ribas Reig of the National Democratic Grouping (AND) as Head of Government in January 1994. When Ribas Reig's coalition partners in New Democracy withdrew their backing for budget proposals in November 1994, PLA leader Marc Forné Molné garnered sufficient votes from other parties (including two from AND) to form a new administration with six other Liberal members and three non-party ministers.

In the February 1997 elections the PLA formed the core of the Liberal Union (*Uniò Liberal*) alliance, which included *Unitat i Renovació* in the parish of Canillo, an independent Liberal grouping in La Massana and the Lauredian Union in Sant Julià de Lòria. The alliance won a total of 16 seats (with 42.3% of the national vote) and the Liberal group in the General Council was also joined by the two representatives of the Union of the People of Ordino. Forné Molné was accordingly confirmed as Head of Government with a substantially improved majority. He continued in office after the March 2001 General Council elections, in which the PLA won 15 seats in its own right with a 46.1% national vote share, its parliamentary group being increased to 17 by the adhesion of the two elected Lauredian Union (UL) councillors.

The PLA has been a member of the Liberal International since 1994 and became a full member of the European Liberal, Democratic and Reformist (ELDR) organization in June 2001.

Social Democratic Party
Partit Socialdemòcrata (PS)
Address. c/Verge del Pilar 5, 3r/1a, Andorra la Vella
Telephone. (376) 820320
Fax. (376) 867979
Email. ps@andorra.ad
Leadership. Albert Salvadó Miras (president); Jaume Bartumeu Cassany (chairman of parliamentary group & secretary-general)

The centre-left PS was founded in 2000, partly on the basis of the New Democracy (*Nova Democracia*, ND) grouping, which had won five seats in the 1993 General Council elections and two in 1997. The PS also attracted most of the National Democratic Initiative (*Iniciatíva Democratica Nacional*, IDN), which had also won two seats in the 1997 elections. The new party performed creditably in its first General Council elections in March 2001, winning six seats with a 30% share of the national vote, but remained in opposition to the Liberal Party of Andorra.

The PS is a consultative member of the Socialist International.

Angola

Capital: Luanda
Population: 13,100,000

Angola achieved independence from Portugal in November 1975 as the People's Republic of Angola, with the Popular Movement for the Liberation of Angola (MPLA) becoming the sole ruling party in Luanda. By early 1976 the MPLA government, assisted by Cuban military forces, had established control over most of Angola, although the competing Union for the Total Independence of Angola (UNITA), backed by South Africa and the USA, remained active in the south. Following the signature in December 1988 of the Brazzaville Agreement, providing for the

withdrawal of Cuban and South African troops, the MPLA in December 1990 abandoned Marxism-Leninism and embraced "democratic socialism". The Lisbon Accord of May 1991 provided for an end to the civil war with UNITA and for reform of the political structure, including the introduction of a multi-party system. Under constitutional amendments adopted in August 1992, the country was renamed the Republic of Angola and provision made for a "semi-presidential" system headed by an executive President, directly elected for a five-year term in two rounds of voting, who appoints a Prime Minister. Legislative authority is vested in a National Assembly (*Assembléia Nacional*) elected for a four-year term by universal adult suffrage and proportional representation, with 130 members being returned nationally, 90 from provincial constituencies and possibly three by Angolans living abroad.

A law enacted in May 1991 specifies that political parties "must be national in character and scope". Specifically prohibited are parties that "are local and regional in character; foster tribalism, racism, regionalism or other forms of discrimination against citizens or affect national unity and territorial integrity; use or propose the use of violence to pursue their aims . . . adopt a uniform for their members or possess clandestine parallel structures; use military, para-military or militarized organization; [or] are subordinate to the policy of foreign governments, bodies or parties". The 1991 law also makes provision for registered parties to receive state financial assistance on the basis of their support in the most recent general election and the number of candidates presented.

Multi-party elections to the new National Assembly on Sept. 29-30, 1992, produced the following results: MPLA 129 seats (53.7% of the national vote), UNITA 70 (34.1%), Social Renewal Party 6 (2.3%), National Front for the Liberation of Angola 5 (2.4%), Liberal Democratic Party 3 (2.4%), Democratic Renewal Party 1 (0.9%), Democratic Alliance of Angola 1 (0.9%), Social Democratic Party 1 (0.8%), Party of the Alliance of Angolan Youth, Workers and Peasants 1 (0.4%), Angola Democratic Forum 1 (0.3%), Democratic Party for Progress–Angolan National Alliance 1 (0.3%), Angolan National Democratic Party 1 (0.3%). By agreement of the parties, the three seats reserved for Angolans abroad were not filled. In concurrent presidential elections, incumbent José Eduardo dos Santos (MPLA) won 49.6% of the first-round vote, just short of the 50% needed to make a second round unnecessary, although this was not held. A newly-appointed transitional government headed by the MPLA included representatives of four smaller parties, while posts were also allocated to UNITA. The latter nevertheless disputed the official election results and resumed military activities. Direct negotiations between the two sides opened in Lusaka in November 1993 after UNITA had declared its acceptance of the September 1992 election outcome. This process yielded the signature of a ceasefire and power-sharing agreement in the Zambian capital on Nov. 20, 1994.

Shortly before the expiry of its four-year term, the Assembly on Nov. 13, 1996, adopted a constitutional amendment extending its mandate for up to four years. In April 1997 UNITA representatives at last took up their Assembly seats and their posts in a "government of national unity and reconciliation". However, as warfare in the country intensified, the government in January 1999 formally repudiated the Lusaka Agreement. Although President dos Santos promised in March 2000 that presidential and Assembly elections would be held in 2001, continuing hostilities forced the abandonment of this plan, the mandate of the Assembly being extended indefinitely on Oct. 17, 2000. The leader of UNITA, Jonas Savimbi, was killed by government forces in an ambush on Feb. 20, 2002. Savimbi's death came in the context of imminent military defeat for UNITA and shortly afterwards there began a genuine process of disarmament and demobilization, as set down in a Memorandum of Understanding signed on April 2, 2002. As of mid-2004 most analysts were agreed that there was little likelihood of a resumption of hostilities in Angola. In early 2004 the government indicated that national elections were likely to be held in 2006.

Angolan Democratic Forum
Fórum Democrático Angolano (FDA)
Address. c/o Assembléia Nacional, Luanda
Leadership. Jorge Rebelo Pinto Chicoti
The conservative FDA was registered in 1992 and won one seat in the National Assembly in elections held that year.

Angolan National Democratic Party
Partido Nacional Democrático Angolano (PNDA)
Address. c/o Assembléia Nacional, Luanda
Leadership. Pedro Joao Antonio
The PNDA was founded (as the Angolan National Democratic Convention) in 1991 and went on to win one seat in the National Assembly in elections held in September 1992.

Democratic Alliance of Angola
Aliança Democrática de Angola (AD)
Address. c/o Assembléia Nacional, Luanda
Leadership. Simba da Costa
The AD was created by a number of opposition parties prior to the September 1992 legislative elections. The party won one seat in the elections.

Democratic Party for Progress–Angolan National Alliance
Partido Democrático para Progreso/Aliança Nacional Angolano (PDP-ANA)
Address. c/o Assembléia Nacional, Luanda
Leadership. (vacant)
The conservative PDP-ANA won one seat in the National Assembly in the last elections held in September 1992. Mfulumpinga Lando Victor, the party leader, was shot dead by unidentified gunmen in Luanda in July 2004.

Democratic Renewal Party
Partido Renovador Democrático (PRD)
Address. c/o Assembléia Nacional, Luanda
Leadership. Luís da Silva dos Passos
The centrist PRD was founded by surviving dissidents of the ruling Popular Movement for the Liberation of Angola (MPLA) who staged an abortive coup in 1977. The party won one seat in the National Assembly in the last elections held in September 1992.

Liberal Democratic Party of Angola
Partido Liberal Democrático de Angola, PLDA
A centrist pro-democracy formation which won three Assembly seats in the 1992 elections with 2.4% of the vote, although the PLDA leader came tenth in the presidential contest with only 0.3%. The PLDA is a member of the Liberal International.
Address. Rua Che Guevara 181, Luanda
Email. pld@ebonet.net
Leadership. Analia de Victoria Pereira Simea (president)

National Front for the Liberation of Angola
Frente Nacional de Libertação de Angola (FNLA)
Address. c/o Assembléia Nacional, Luanda
Email. fnla@ifrance.com
Website. www.fnla-angola.org/
Leadership. Holden Roberto (faction leader); Ngola Kabango (secretary-general of Roberto faction); Lucas Ngonda (faction leader); Francisco Mendes (secretary-general of Ngonda faction)
The FNLA was founded in March 1962 as a merger of the *União das Populações de Angola* (UPA) led by Holden Roberto and the *Partido Democrático Angolano* (PDA), two northern nationalist movements which had launched an anti-Portuguese peasants' revolt the previous year. Based in what was then Zaïre and backed by President Mobutu (Roberto's brother-in-law), the FNLA the following month formed the "revolutionary Angolan government-in-exile" (GRAE), with Roberto as prime minister. Although vigorously anti-communist, the FNLA secured the backing of China, which switched its support from the pro-Soviet Popular Movement for the Liberation of Angola (MPLA) in December 1962; it was also at various times aided by South Africa and the USA. In 1966 it was weakened by the formation of the breakaway National Union for the Total Independence of Angola (UNITA), but it subsequently allied itself with UNITA in a pre-independence struggle for supremacy with the MPLA, interspersed with the signature of abortive "unity" pacts with the latter.

Following the left-wing military coup in Lisbon in April 1974, Portugal signed ceasefire agreements with the FNLA and UNITA, but a powerful pro-Soviet faction of the new Portuguese regime favoured the MPLA. In January 1975 all three Angolan movements received OAU recognition and formed a transitional government, but hostilities between them resumed almost immediately, with the FNLA–UNITA alliance receiving active military support from South Africa. On the MPLA's declaration of an independent People's Republic of Angola in November 1975, the FNLA and UNITA declared a rival Democratic Republic. However, following the withdrawal of South African forces in early 1976, Cuban-backed MPLA troops established control of most of Angola, driving FNLA forces into Zaïre and winning a decisive victory over them at Kifangondo in November 1977. The FNLA then ceased to be a significant force and President Mobutu transferred Zaïrean support to UNITA, which continued to resist the MPLA in the south. Expelled from Zaïre in 1979 (and subsequently from Senegal and Gabon), Roberto was eventually granted asylum in France.

Following the signature of the May 1991 Lisbon Accord between the MPLA government and UNITA, Roberto returned to Angola at the end of August and announced his candidacy for the presidency in the planned multi-party elections. After some dispute over whether it had a military wing (possession of which was supposed to disqualify parties), the FNLA was registered as a political party and in October 1991 joined the pro-democracy National Opposition Council. In the September 1992 elections Roberto came fourth in the first-round presidential balloting, with 2.1% of the vote, while the FNLA won five of the 220 seats in the new National Assembly.

Although the FNLA was named as a member of the "unity" government announced in December 1992, it subsequently played no part in the governance of the country and did not figure in the further "national reconciliation" government announced in April 1997. It thereafter maintained outspoken opposition to the MPLA regime from its overseas headquarters in Paris, although internal divisions became apparent in Angola between the Roberto leadership and a group led by Lucas Ngonda favouring accommodation with the government. A congress convened by Ngonda's faction in

February 1999 at which he was elected FNLA president was followed by another in May at which Roberto's leadership was reaffirmed. Efforts to reconcile the two FNLA factions began shortly afterwards and culminated in a meeting in April 2004 between Roberto and Ngonda. In August the two factions agreed to hold a reconciliation congress in October.

National Union for the Total Independence of Angola
União Nacional para a Independência Total de Angola
(UNITA)

Address. c/o Assembléia Nacional, Luanda

Leadership. Isaias Samakuva (president); Ernesto Mulato (vice-president); Mario Miguel Vatuva (secretary-general)

UNITA was founded in March 1966 by a breakaway faction of the National Front for the Liberation of Angola (FNLA) consisting mainly of elements of the former *União das Populações de Angola* (UPA) led by Jonas Savimbi, who had resigned as foreign minister in the FNLA-sponsored "revolutionary Angolan government-in-exile" (GRAE) in July 1964. Based in the Ovimbundu and Chokwe tribes of central and southern Angola, UNITA had Maoist ideological roots but moved to an anti-leftist stance as it adopted a policy of co-operation with the Portuguese authorities against the dominant Soviet-backed Movement for the Liberation of Angola (MPLA). After the left-wing military coup in Lisbon in April 1974, UNITA signed a separate ceasefire agreement with Portugal in June. In 1975, following the collapse of an OAU-sponsored transitional government of all three liberation movements, UNITA forces, allied with the FNLA, came increasingly into conflict with the MPLA, receiving substantial military support from South Africa. According to later South African accounts, the 2,000 South African troops sent into Angola could have taken the whole country by late 1975 had not Savimbi insisted that he wanted control only of areas of UNITA support in the interests of reaching a settlement with the MPLA.

Following the declaration of the independent People's Republic of Angola by the MPLA in November 1975, Cuban-supported government troops launched an offensive against the FNLA and UNITA, whose capacity to resist was seriously weakened by the withdrawal of South African forces across the Namibian border early in 1976. By late February UNITA had been forced to vacate all its positions and to resort to guerrilla warfare in the bush. A UNITA congress at Cuanza (central Angola) in May 1976 called for intensified armed struggle "against the regime imposed by the Cubans and Russians" and approved a reorganization of UNITA structures, including the creation of an armed people's militia. Subsequent clashes between UNITA and forces of the MPLA led to widespread losses and chaotic conditions, especially in the south. From 1982 onwards UNITA attacks were increasingly directed at economic targets, including the Benguela railway from the coast to what was then Zaïre; abduction of foreign specialists and their families also become a regular UNITA practice. In September 1985 the South African government admitted that it had provided military and humanitarian aid to UNITA for a number of years with the aim of halting "Marxist infiltration and expansionism". In mid-1985 the US Congress voted to repeal the 1976 Clarke Amendment which had prohibited US financial or military aid for UNITA.

After military setbacks for UNITA and South African forces in early 1988, UNITA came under further pressure later that year when it was agreed that South African and Cuban forces would be withdrawn from Angola as part of the Namibian peace settlement. The MPLA–PT government showed its willingness to negotiate by releasing 700 UNITA detainees in June 1988 and by conceding UNITA's demand for multi-partyism (as endorsed by an MPLA–PT congress in December 1990). Talks in Lisbon resulted in the signature

in May 1991 of the Estoril Accord providing for a ceasefire, demobilization of forces and democratic elections. Savimbi returned to Luanda in September 1991 and in December UNITA published an election manifesto identifying the economic upliftment of the people as a central aim. In early 1992 UNITA was damaged by the defection of two senior members, amid charge and counter-charge cataloguing nefarious activities on both sides. Tending to sour UNITA–US relations, the episode deprived UNITA of support in Cabinda (where the defectors came from) and narrowed its ethnic base to the Ovimbundu in the south.

In the September 1992 Assembly elections UNITA came a poor second to the MPLA, winning only 70 of the 220 seats; but Savimbi did better in the simultaneous presidential poll, taking 40.1% of the first-round vote and helping to deny President dos Santos of the MPLA an outright majority, although no second round was held. Despite the verdict of international observers that the polling had been fair in the main, UNITA alleged widespread fraud in both contests and ordered its troops, most of whom had evaded demobilization, to resume armed struggle. The naming of a "unity" government in December 1992 with one cabinet and five other posts reserved for UNITA did not resolve the crisis. Conflict of unprecedented ferocity ensued, with UNITA making major advances not only in the south but also in central and northern Angola. It continued unabated after the opening of peace talks in Lusaka in November 1993 on the basis that UNITA would accept the 1992 election results. Factors impelling UNITA to negotiate included the USA's decision to recognize the MPLA government in May 1993 (implying the end of US backing for UNITA) and the imposition of a mandatory UN oil and arms embargo against UNITA in September. Factors encouraging it to continue fighting included the temporary weakness of Angolan government forces, many of which had been demobilized under the 1991 accord.

Despite continued fighting between UNITA and government forces, the Lusaka talks on power-sharing made headway in mid-1994, as UNITA suffered serious military reverses. A ceasefire and power-sharing agreement was at last signed in Lusaka on Nov. 20, 1994, but Savimbi signalled his displeasure with continued advances by government forces by leaving the signature to the then UNITA secretary-general, Gen. Eugénio Manuvakola. Amidst efforts by UN mediators to consolidate the Lusaka agreement, a UNITA congress at Bailundo (in Huambo province) in February 1995 was marked by serious divisions between those favouring the accord and hardliners. On Savimbi's proposal, delegates voted to accept the agreement; but a senior UNITA defector, Col. Isaac Zabarra, claimed subsequently that Savimbi in reality opposed the Lusaka accord and had instructed his military leaders to use the ceasefire to reorganize UNITA forces. According to Col. Zabarra, several UNITA leaders identified with the peace process were under detention, including Gen. Manuvakola. At the Bailundo congress, the latter was replaced as UNITA secretary-general by Gen. Paulo Lukamba ("Gen. Gato").

Savimbi had talks with President dos Santos in Lusaka in June 1995 and again in Gabon in August, reportedly agreeing in principal to accept a vice-presidency in the government and to implement the other power-sharing clauses of the November 1994 accord. However, the MPLA regime's insistence on the prior disarming of UNITA guerrillas and their confinement to barracks pending the creation of a national army remained a major obstacle to implementation of the accord.

In April 1997 four UNITA ministers and seven deputy ministers at last took up their designated posts in a government of national unity and reconciliation, while UNITA National Assembly representatives took their seats in the National Assembly. However, Savimbi refused not only to become a Vice-President but even to attend the new government's inauguration, as UNITA and Angolan government forces fought a proxy war in Zaïre, the former backing President Mobutu in his efforts to retain power and the latter the rebels led by Laurent Kabila. Kabila's victory in what became the Democratic Republic of the Congo was a setback for UNITA, although its capability as a fighting force in Angola appeared to be little affected, despite the imposition of UN sanctions on UNITA from October 1997.

In Luanda a split developed in late 1997 between pro-Savimbi and anti-Savimbi UNITA factions, the latter headed by former secretary-general Gen. Manuvakola and backed by the MPLA. After most pro-Savimbi UNITA officials had fled the capital in July 1998, the following month UNITA members were suspended from the Assembly, as the MPLA-led regime sought to promote the pro-peace UNITA–Renewal faction. Savimbi dismissed as "irrelevant" the activities of the breakaway faction, which held what it described as the ninth UNITA congress in Luanda in January 1999. Most UNITA Assembly members refused to join UNITA–Renewal, notably parliamentary leader Abel Chivukuvuku.

UNITA's apparent responsibility for the downing of two UN planes in December 1998 and January 1999, with the loss of 23 lives, sharpened UN condemnation of the movement's perceived unwillingness to end the civil war, although the MPLA-led government was also blamed. In July 1999 the UN launched an investigation into UNITA involvement in the illegal diamond trade, as UNITA forces were accused of massacring 50 women and children in the southern village of Sachitembo. Military reverses for UNITA in late 1999 continued in early 2000, but a UNITA counter-offensive in eastern Angola in April 2000 was attributed to the movement's receipt of new weaponry despite the UN sanctions.

Jonas Savimbi was killed by government forces in an ambush in the eastern province of Moxico in February 2002. Savimbi's death (as well as that of other prominent UNITA leaders including his second-in-command, Gen. Antonio Dembo) came in the context of the prospect of imminent military defeat for UNITA. Less than two months after Savimbi's death, UNITA and the government signed a memorandum of understanding which covered all aspects of a military nature necessary for a peaceful resolution to the conflict. Following the signing of the memorandum, UNITA embarked on a process of disarmament and demobilization. Whilst the process had not been fully completed as of mid-2004, analysts agreed that there was little likelihood of a resumption of hostilities in Angola.

The death of Savimbi also facilitated the reunification of UNITA, which officially occurred in July 2002 with the resignation of Eugénio Ngolo Manuvakola as president of the UNITA-Renewal faction. Under the leadership of secretary-general Gen. Paulo Lukamba ("Gen. Gato"), the unified UNITA embarked on an internal reorganization process, nominating a standing commission and a political committee to replace the interim "management commission" that assumed the leadership of the movement in the immediate aftermath of Savimbi's death. In June 2003 UNITA held a national congress and Gen. Gato, who favoured close co-operation with the government, failed to win the support of the party to replace Savimbi. Instead, delegates elected Isaias Samakuva, who favoured building a broad-based opposition with other parties, as the new leader.

Party of the Alliance of Angolan Youth, Workers and Peasants
Partido da Aliança da Juventude, Operários e Campesinos de Angola (PAJOCA)
Address. c/o Assembléia Nacional, Luanda
Leadership. Alexandre Sebastião André
The extreme left PAJOCA won one seat in the National

Assembly in the last elections held in September 1992.

Popular Movement for the Liberation of Angola
Movimento Popular de Libertação de Angola (MPLA)
Address. c/o Assembléia Nacional, Luanda
Leadership. José Eduardo dos Santos (president); Antonio Pitra Costa Neto (deputy president); Gen. Juliao Mateus Paulo ("Dino Matross") (secretary-general)
The MPLA was founded in 1956 as a merger of two nationalist movements, the *Partido da Luta Unida dos Africanos de Angola* and the (Communist) *Movimento para a Independencia de Angola*, initially under the leadership of Mário de Andrade and, from 1962, that of Agostinho Neto. Backed by the USSR, it played a leading part in the struggle against Portuguese rule, sometimes in collaboration but usually in conflict with the two other nationalist movements, the National Front for the Liberation of Angola (FNLA) and the National Union for the Total Independence of Angola (UNITA). On Portugal's transference of sovereignty to "the Angolan people" in November 1975, the MPLA proclaimed the People's Republic of Angola in Luanda, with Neto as President and of Lopo do Nascimento as Prime Minister, and secured recognition from many states (although not the USA). By February 1976 the MPLA government, assisted by Cuban forces, was in control of the greater part of the country, although UNITA continued to conduct military operations in the south.

Pre-independence dissension within the MPLA resurfaced in 1976, when Andrade and other leaders of his *Revolte Activa* faction were arrested; the following year another dissident faction attempted a coup in Luanda. At its first congress in December 1977 the MPLA restructured itself as a Marxist-Leninist "vanguard of the proletariat" and added the suffix Party of Labour (*Partido de Trabalho*, PT) to its title to signify its claim to unite the working and intellectual classes. Further internal divisions in 1978 resulted in the abolition of the post of Prime Minister in December 1978 and the dismissal of do Nascimento and other ministers. Neto died in Moscow in September 1979 and was succeeded as President and party leader by José Eduardo dos Santos, whose preference for a negotiated settlement with UNITA and rapprochement with the West was resisted by the hardline pro-Soviet faction. At the second party congress in December 1985 the MPLA–PT central committee was enlarged to give the President's supporters a majority, three veteran hardliners being dropped from the resultant political bureau.

The third congress in December 1990 ratified a central committee recommendation that Angola should "evolve towards a multi-party system", dos Santos acknowledging that the collapse of communism in Eastern Europe indicated a need for democratic reform and that collectivist policies had failed. The congress approved the jettisoning of Marxist-Leninist ideology, which was to be replaced by a commitment to "democratic socialism", including a free enterprise economy and protection of private property and foreign investment. Under the May 1991 Lisbon Accord with the UNITA, the MPLA–PT government made provision for the legalization of competing parties and for multi-party elections. These changes were approved by a special MPLA–PT congress in May 1992, when reformers secured the enlargement of the central committee from 180 to 193 members and the election to it of representatives of the business community, intellectuals and some former dissidents.

Elections in September 1992 resulted in the MPLA–PT winning a decisive majority in the new National Assembly, while dos Santos took a commanding 49.6% in the first round of simultaneous presidential balloting. UNITA's rejection of the results and resumption of armed struggle meant that the second presidential round could not be held. A new "unity" government appointed in December 1992 was dominated by the MPLA–PT but included nominees of four small parties as well as, notionally, UNITA representatives. In 1993 MPLA–PT hardliners regained some influence with criticism of the dos Santos leadership for precipitate army demobilization under the Lisbon Accord, to the advantage of UNITA in the renewed civil war. By then the MPLA had officially dropped the Party of Labour suffix to demonstrate its inclusive aspirations and commitment to democratic socialism.

In May 1993 the USA at last recognized the MPLA-led government, signalling an end to its support for UNITA, which in November indicated its acceptance of the September 1992 election results. Peace talks then resumed in Lusaka between the government and UNITA on an agenda which included power-sharing at national and provincial level. After intensified conflict from mid-1994, a ceasefire and power-sharing agreement was signed in the Zambian capital on Nov. 20, 1994, as government forces made important advances against UNITA. A year later, however, the agreement remained unimplemented, despite two face-to-face meetings between dos Santos and UNITA leader Jonas Savimbi in June and August 1995, principally because of the difficulty of arranging for the disarming of guerrilla forces.

Although UNITA representatives at last took up posts in a government of national unity in Luanda in April 1997, the MPLA continued to be in open conflict with UNITA in the country. After the government had effectively severed relations with the Savimbi UNITA leadership in August 1998, opponents of the peace process gained the ascendancy at the fourth MPLA congress held in December 1998, when João Lorenço was elected secretary-general in place of do Nascimento, hitherto regarded as likely successor to the ailing dos Santos. In January 1999 the MPLA-led government formally repudiated the Lusaka peace agreement and accorded exclusive recognition to the anti-Savimbi National Union for the Total Independence of Angola–Renewal. Having already voted a four-year extension of the parliamentary mandate in November 1996, the MPLA-dominated Assembly in October 2000 approved an indefinite extension, as plans for presidential and Assembly elections in 2001 were abandoned amid undiminished hostilities between government and UNITA forces. With the death of Savimbi in February 2002, renewed peace negotiations began and within two months a memorandum of understanding had been signed which provided for the disarmament and demobilization of UNITA. National elections scheduled to be held in 2006 constitute the next, crucial, stage of the national reconciliation process

The MPLA held its fifth congress in Luanda in December 2003. President dos Santos was re-elected as party president and Antonio Pitra Costa Neto, the Minister of Public Administration, Employment, and Social Welfare and a leading technocrat, was elected to the new post of party deputy president. The biggest surprise was the election of Gen. Juliao Mateus Paulo ("Dino Matross"), a veteran of the liberation struggle against Portugal, as the new secretary-general. Dino Matross replaced João Lourenco, who had previously been touted as a possible successor to President dos Santos. Lourenco's removal followed allegations of poor organization within the party.

The MPLA is an observer member of the Socialist International.

Social Democrat Party
Partido Social-Democrata (PSD)
Address. c/o Assembléia Nacional, Luanda
Leadership. Bengue Pedro Joao
Formed in 1991, the party's leader, Bengue Pedro Joao, was placed seventh in presidential elections held the following year. The party won one seat in the National Assembly in elections held at the same time.

Social Renewal Party
Partido de Renovação Social (PRS)
Address. c/o Assembléia Nacional, Luanda
Leadership. Eduardo Kwangana (leader)
The centrist PRS was formed in 1991. The party won six National Assembly seats in the last elections held in September 1992.

Other Parties

Angolan Democratic Party (*Partido Democrático Angolana*, PDA), founded in 1992 and opposed both the ruling Popular Movement for the Liberation of Angola (MPLA) and the opposition National Union for the Total Independence of Angola (UNITA). PDA leader Antonio Alberto Neto was placed third in the 1992 presidential election, but the party failed to gain representation in the National Assembly.
Leadership. Antonio Alberto Neto (leader)

Angolan Democratic Liberal Party (*Partido Democrático Liberal Angolan*, PDLA), founded in 1991, but failed to win a seat in National Assembly elections held the following year.
Leadership. Honorato Lando (leader)

Angolan Liberal Party (*Partido Angolano Liberal*, PAL)
Leadership. Manuel Francisco Lulo (leader)

Angolan Social Democratic Party (*Partido Social Democratico de Angola*, PSDA)
Leadership. Andre Milton Kilandamoko

Democratic Civilian Opposition (*Oposicao Democrática de Civil*), opposition alliance founded in 1994 that included the National Ecological Party of Angola, the National Union for Democracy, the Movement of Defense of the Interests of Angola-Conscience Party and the National Democratic Convention of Angola.

Movement of Defense of the Interests of Angola-Conscience Party (*Movimento de Defesa dos Interesses de Angola-Partido Consciencia*), member of the Democratic Civilian Opposition.
Leadership. Isidoro Klala (leader)

National Ecological Party of Angola (*Partido Nacional Ecologico de Angola*, PNEA), green party formed in 1989 and member of the Democratic Civilian Opposition.
Leadership. Sukawa Dizizeko Ricardo (leader)

National Democratic Convention of Angola (*Convencao Nacional Democrata de Angola*, CNDA), member of the Democratic Civilian Opposition.
Leadership. Paulino Pinto Joao (leader)

National Democratic Union of Angola (*União Democrática National de Angola*, UDNA), founded by exiles in London in the 1980s, registered in Angola in 1999. Espousing the political principles of Montesquieu, the party is associated with the International Democrat Union through the Democrat Union of Africa.
Leadership. Francisco J. Pedro Kizadilamba (president)

National Union for Democracy (*União Nacional para Democracia*), member of the Democratic Civilian Opposition.
Leadership. Sebastiao Rogerio Suzama (leader)

Party of Solidarity in the Conscience of Angola (*Partido de Solidariedade na Consciência de Angola*, PSCA)
Leadership. Fernendo Dombassi Quiessa (leader)

Party for the Support of Democracy and Progress in Angola (*Partido de Apoio Democratico e Progresso de Angola*, PADPA)
Leadership. Carlos Leitao (leader)

Republican Party of Angola (*Partido Republicano de Angola*, PreA), founded in 1997 in opposition to the dos Santos government headed by the Popular Movement for the Liberation of Angola, accusing it of war crimes, institutional corruption, nepotism and denial of free speech.
Address. C.P. 3626, Luanda
Telephone. (244–2) 347739
Email. preasecretariadogeral_org@yahoo.com
Leadership. Carlos Contreiras (president)

United Independent Union of Democratic Parties (*União Independente Unida de Partidos Democráticos*, UIUPD), formed in June 2000 as a coalition of five parties not represented in the National Assembly.
Leadership. José Julia (leader)

Cabinda Movements

Various movements and factions seeking separate independence for Cabinda—an oil-rich coastal enclave which is not contiguous with Angola proper, being bordered by Congo and the Democratic Republic of the Congo (formerly Zaïre)—are descended from the **Front for the Liberation of the Enclave of Cabinda** (*Frente para a Libertação do Enclave de Cabinda*, FLEC), which was founded in 1963. Encouraged by the Portuguese colonial authorities as an ally of sorts against the Popular Movement for the Liberation of Angola (MPLA), FLEC refused to co-operate with other nationalist movements and rejected the claim of the MPLA government installed in Luanda at independence in November 1975 that Cabinda was part of Angola. Forced on the defensive by Cuban-supported government troops, FLEC was also weakened in the late 1970s by internal divisions which resulted in the creation of several factions. Two of these declared "independent" governments in Cabinda and one claimed in 1979 to control 30% of Cabindan territory. Guerrilla action by the FLEC factions was sporadic in the 1980s, being usually directed at state oil installations and similar targets. In 2001 the government appealed to FLEC separatists to end hostilities so that a peaceful solution could be found, but in the event talks failed to take place. The death of Jonas Savimbi, leader of the National Union for the Total Independence of Angola (UNITA), in February 2002 led directly to a renewed government offensive against the separatists, taking advantage of the freeing up of military resources previously used in combating UNITA.

Antigua and Barbuda

Capital: St John's
Population: 68,000 (2003E)

Antigua and Barbuda became internally self-governing in 1967 and independent from the United Kingdom in 1981. The head of state is the British sovereign, represented by a Governor-General who is appointed on the advice of the Antiguan Prime Minister. Legislative power is vested in a bicameral parliament, which comprises an upper 17-member appointed Senate, and a House of Representatives. The House consists of 17 members that are directly elected for up to five years, one ex-officio member and a speaker. The Prime Minister and Cabinet are responsi-ble to parliament and are appointed to office by the Governor-General acting upon its advice. Barbuda, the smaller of the country's two inhabited constituent islands, maintains a considerable degree of control over its local affairs.

Elections to the House of Representatives on March 23, 2004, resulted in a historic victory for the opposition United Progressive Party (UPP) led by Baldwin Spencer. The UPP won 12 seats and 55.3% of the popular vote, while the governing Antigua Labour Party (ALP), which had been in power for the previous 28 years, won four seats and 41.8% of the vote. The poll in the single Barbuda seat ended in a tie with the Barbuda People's Movement (BPM) and the Barbuda People's Movement for Change (BPMC) each winning 400 votes. The ballot was subsequently re-run on April 16, with the BPM gaining victory.

In the Barbuda Council elections held on March 23, 2001, the Barbuda People's Movement (BPM) won all five seats.

Antigua Labour Party (ALP)
Address. St Mary's Street, St John's
Telephone. (1-268) 462-2235
Leadership. Lester Bird (party leader); Robin Yearwood (parliamentary leader)
Long affiliated with the Antigua Trades and Labour Union (of which Vere Bird, Prime Minister and ALP leader until 1994, was a founder member), the domestically conservative ALP was continuously in power in the colony from 1946 to 1971. Returned to office in 1976, the ALP remained the ruling party until the March 2004 general election. From 1994 to 2004 Vere Bird's son, Lester Bird was both party and parliamentary leader. The standing of Prime Minister Bird's government, however, was undermined by a number of scandals. Most significantly was the publication of a report, in August 2002, by the public enquiry established to consider allegations of fraud concerning the country's Medical Benefits Scheme (MBS). It stated that several former ministers and MBS senior employees had benefited illegally from the scheme's funds.

The problems for the ALP government continued into 2003 when ALP legislator Sherfield Bowen filed a motion of no confidence on June 12 alleging corruption and lack of transparency in Prime Minister Bird's administration. Although the motion was not put to a vote, the government almost collapsed five days later after four parliamentary representatives, including Bowen, resigned from the ALP. A crisis was only averted when one of the ALP MPs withdrew his resignation, thereby restoring the government's parliamentary majority. Subsequently, the Public Works and Junior Finance Minister Senator Asot Michael resigned on June 19, after other members of the administration threatened to leave their posts unless Michael departed the government. It was alleged that ALP ministers were unhappy that Prime Minister Bird had conferred on Michael so much responsibility, given that he was an unelected member of parliament. In a further development the main opposition United Progressive Party (UPP) filed an unsuccessful motion of no confidence in the Bird administration in November. The UPP alleged that two government ministers received "substantial sums of money" from Texan billionaire Allen Stanford in respect of a controversial land swap deal involving the government and Stanford. The party's standing in the country was further damaged by the deteriorating state of public finances, which forced the late payment of government salaries. The result was a series of industrial disputes involving air-traffic controllers, teachers, public works staff, and agricultural workers in the latter part of 2003.

The general election held in March 2004 clearly indicated the population's dissatisfaction with the ALP government under the leadership of Lester Bird. The party lost eight of its parliamentary representatives, with Prime Minister Bird failing to retain his seat. This brought to a close almost three decades of unbroken ALP rule, and ended the Bird family's dynastic control over the country. The day after the election, Robin Yearwood, the former public utilities minister in the previous Bird administration was sworn in as parliamentary leader of the ALP. Lester Bird remained as ALP party leader.

United Progressive Party (UPP)

Address. c/o House of Representatives, St John's
Email. upp@candw.ag
Leadership. Baldwin Spencer (leader); George Daniel (chairman)

The UPP was formed in early 1992 by the merger of the Antigua Caribbean Liberation Movement (founded in 1977 as a "new left" organization), the Progressive Labour Movement (established in 1970, and the ruling party from 1971 to 1976), and the United National Democratic Party (a formation identified with business and professional interests, which arose from the merger of the small United People's Movement and National Democratic Party in 1986).

In the 1994 general election the UPP was runner-up with five of the 17 lower house seats, winning nearly 44% of the vote. It slipped to four seats in the 1999 election, despite increasing its share of the vote. Although the veracity of the election was placed in doubt, the UPP accepted the results, but threatened to boycott the next election unless reforms of the electoral system were implemented. The House of Representatives passed the necessary reforms in 2003. In the build up to the March 2004 general election the UPP showed a new professionalism and under Baldwin Spencer's leadership the party was seen as a viable alternative government. The party put forward a manifesto, entitled "Agenda for Change", that contained a number of social and poverty relief programmes, as well as measures to promote judicial and constitutional reform. These proposals, together with widespread public disenchantment with the ALP government, allowed the UPP to gain a clear victory at the polls, winning 12 seats in the House. Baldwin Spencer, therefore, became the third Prime Minister of Antigua and Barbuda since independence in 1981.

Other Parties

Barbuda People's Movement (BPM) campaigns for greater autonomy for Barbuda. It controls the local Barbuda Council, and has won the single Barbudan seat in the House of Representatives in recent general elections. The victorious BPM candidate in the 2004 general election, Trevor Walker, was appointed to the cabinet of Baldwin Spencer. This was the first occasion since independence that the representative for Barbuda had been included in the government.

Barbuda People's Movement for Change (BPMC) was established in 2003 after internal tensions within the Barbuda People's Movement. Arthur Nibbs, leader of the BPMC, left the BPM after falling out with BPM leader Hilbourne Frank over the nature of the relationship between Barbuda and the central government in Antigua. Nibbs called for a closer relationship between the two island governments, and aligned his party to Lester Bird's ALP. In 2004, Nibbs stood as the BPMC's candidate for the Barbuda seat in the general election, but lost the re-run ballot.

Organisation for National Development (OND), formed in early 2003 by three former UUP members who believed that the party was not a credible alternative to the ALP government. The main platform of the OND is to promote "integrity, honesty, probity, transparency, honour and humility" in government, after what the party sees as the years of corruption and mismanagement under the ALP. However, the party decided not to contest the March 2004 elections, saying that it did not have the financial resources or the candidates to undertake an effective campaign.

Argentina

Capital: Buenos Aires
Population: 36,223,947 (2001 census)

Upon returning to civilian rule in 1983 following seven years of military rule by successive juntas, most of the constitutional structure of 1853 was restored. The Republic is composed of an autonomous Federal District, 23 provinces and the National Territory of Tierra del Fuego. Each province has its own elected governor and legislature, concerned with all matters not delegated to the federal government. A new constitution entered into effect on Aug. 24, 1994, under which the President, hitherto appointed by an electoral college, is directly elected for a four-year term (reduced from the six years allowed under the 1853 constitution) with re-election allowed for only one consecutive term. Run-off elections for the presidential and vice-presidential posts take place unless a candidate obtains 45% of the vote (or 40% with a 10% advantage over the second-placed candidate). The new constitution also allows for an autonomous government for the capital, Buenos Aires, with a directly-elected mayor. As previously, in the absence of the President, the president of the Senate assumes the presidency. The cabinet is appointed by the President, who exercises executive power and is head of state.

The federal legislature consists of a Chamber of Deputies of 257 members elected for four-year terms with half of the seats renewable every two years, and a 72-member Senate. Until 2001, two senators were nominated by the legislature of each of the 23 provinces for nine-year terms (one-third of the seats being renewable every three years), and a third senator was directly elected from each province. Under new arrangements introduced in 2001, all senators are now directly elected, so in that year only all 72 seats were up for election.

The late 1990s were a period of retreat for the Peronist Justicialist Party (PJ), which had retained control of the presidency and the Chamber of Deputies in the presidential and legislative elections of May 14, 1995. In the congressional elections of Oct. 26, 1997, in which 127 of the 257 seats in the Chamber of Deputies were at stake, the opposition Alliance (*Alianza*), a coalition of the centre-left Radical Civic Union (UCR) and the Front for a Country in Solidarity (FREPASO) secured 45.6% of the popular vote compared with the 36.1 percent secured by the PJ. Although the PJ secured 118 seats as against the *Alianza*'s 110, the balance of power shifted to the *Alianza* and smaller provincial parties (which collectively held 29 seats).

In the presidential election of Oct. 24, 1999, Fernando de la Rúa, the *Alianza* candidate, defeated former Vice-President Eduardo Duhalde of the PJ, thus ending a decade of Peronist domination of the presidency. De la Rúa and his FREPASO running-mate, Carlos "Chacho" Alvarez, secured 48.5% of the popular vote against 38.1% for Duhalde. Domingo Cavallo of the right-wing Action for the Republic (AR) won 10.1% of the popular vote. In simultaneous legislative elections, in which 130 of the 257 seats in the Chamber of Deputies were contested, the *Alianza* won 63 seats, increasing its representation in the Chamber to 127 seats—two seats short of an overall majority. The PJ secured 50 seats, increasing its strength to 101 seats and the Action for the Republic won 9 seats, increasing its representation to 12 seats. However in the mid-term elections of October 2001, in which 127 of the 257 seats in the Chamber were contested, the PJ came back strongly to win 66 seats, or 116 seats overall, while the *Alianza* won only 35, cutting their representation to 88 (UCR 71, Frepaso 17). The AR took 8 seats, increasing their representation further to 17. All 72 seats in the Senate were renewed, giving the PJ 40, UCR 24, Frepaso 1, AR 1 and others 6.

In the presidential election of April 27, 2003, two PJ candidates confronted one another. However, Néstor Carlos Kirchner Ostoic (PJ), of the Front for Victory (*Frente para la Victoria*) faction of the PJ, backed by President Duhalde, obtained 22% of the votes cast and was declared the winner following the withdrawal of former President Carlos Saúl Menem, who had run as candidate of the Front for Liberty (*Frente por la Libertad*), but obtained only 19.4%.

In concurrent congressional elections, the PJ consolidated their dominant position, holding 134 of the 257 seats in the Chamber. The second party in the Chamber is the Radical Civic Union (UCR) and there is a long tail of minor parties, with some 39 formations in all represented in the Chamber in mid-2004, of which 22 had only one seat each.

Action for the Republic – New Direction
Acción por la República – Nueva Dirigencia (AR-ND)

Address. Congreso de la Nación, 1835–1849 Buenos Aires 1089

Telephone. (54–11) 4502–6800

Website. www.ar-partido.com.ar

Leadership. César Albrisi (president of AR); Alfredo José Castañón (secretary-general); Domingo Cavallo (1999 presidential candidate); Gustavo Béliz (leader of ND).

The centre-right AR was established in April 1997 by Domingo Cavallo, the former Economy Minister (1991-96) who had been responsible for the successful Convertibility Plan, as a vehicle to support his bid for a congressional seat in the October 1997 legislative elections and for a possible candidacy in the 1999 presidential elections. In the 1997 elections the party secured three seats. In the presidential election of 1999 Cavallo secured 10.1% of the popular vote, while in the simultaneous legislative elections the AR increased its representation from nine seats to 12. Cavallo joined the *Alianza* government as Economy Minister in March 2001 but was unable to repeat his former success and was forced to flee on the resignation of President de la Rúa in December 2000. In 2003 the party elected only one deputy.

Affirmation for a Republic of Equals
Afirmación para una República Igualitaria (ARI)

Address. Casa de la Militancia, Abasto y Once, Buenos Aires

Website. www.elisacarrio.com.ar

Leadership. Elisa María Avelina Carrió (2003 presidential candidate)

This is a progressive party, founded in 2001. ARI held 11 seats in the Chamber following the 2003 elections, when its candidate, Elisa Carrió, obtained 14.1% of the votes cast for President.

Alliance for Work, Justice and Education
Alianza para el Trabajo, la Justicia y la Educacion (ATJE)

Address. Congreso de la Nación, 1835–1849 Buenos Aires 1089

Leadership. Carlos "Chacho" Alvarez (1999 vice-presidential candidate)

A coalition formed in 1997 between the Radical Civic Union and the Front for a Country in Solidarity (FREPASO), the ATJE or *Alianza* was successful in electing its presidential candidate, Fernando de la Rúa, in 1999 and in obtaining a working majority in Congress. The *Alianza* survived the resignation of de la Rúa in 2001 but lost ground substantially in the elections of 2003.

Christian Democratic Party of Argentina
Partido Demócrata Cristiano de Argentina (PDCA)

Address. Combate de los Pozos 1055, Buenos Aires C1222AAK

Telephone. (54–11) 4304–2915

Fax. (54–11) 4306–8242

Email. juntanacional@dc.org.ar

Website. www.dc.org.ar

Leadership. Eduardo Cúneo (president); Gerardo Marturet (secretary-general)

Dating from 1954, the PDCA was one of the five small parties in the *Multipartidaria* democratic movement whose PDCA presidential candidate won 0.3% of the national vote in the October 1983 elections and obtained one seat in the Chamber of Deputies. A rapprochement with the Peronist Justicialist Party (PJ) in 1984 led to a conflict in the party which caused a majority of the centre-left Humanism and Liberation faction to split away and join the Intransigent Party (PI). In the congressional elections of September 1987, the party received only 0.2% of the national vote despite greater unity within the party. To improve their electoral chances the PDCA joined the FREJUPO electoral alliance supporting the Peronists' presidential candidate Carlos Saúl Menem, who won the election on May 14, 1989. The Christian Democrats' support was rewarded with the appointment as Social Security Minister of António Erman González, who in December 1989 was transferred to the important Economy Ministry. The PDCA withdrew from the FREJUPO alliance in October 1990 in protest against Gonzalez' economic measures.

The PDCA fought the 1997 legislative and 1999 legislative and presidential elections as part of Front for a Country in Solidarity (FREPASO), the coalition of centre-left parties of which it had been a founder member of in 1994. The party secured just one seat in the 1999 elections. At a party convention in November 2000, the PDCA decided to withdraw from the *Alianza* of FREPASO and the Radical Civic Union (UCR) in protest at the economic policy of the *Alianza* government, and was unrepresented in Congress following the 2003 elections.

The PDC is affiliated to the Christian Democrat International and the Christian Democrat Organization of America.

Front for a Country in Solidarity
Frente País Solidario (FREPASO)

Address. Congreso de la Nación, 1835-1849 Buenos Aires 1089

Telephone. (54-11) 4370-7100

Email. frepaso@sion.com

Website. www.frepaso.org.ar

Leadership. Carlos "Chacho" Alvarez (1999 *Alianza* vice-presidential candidate); Dario Pedro Alessandro (congressional president)

FREPASO was launched in late 1994 as a moderate left

coalition designed to link the Broad Front (FG) with the Christian Democratic Party (PDC), Open Politics for Social Integrity (PAIS) and Socialist Unity (US). It includes a number of independent communists and socialists. FREPASO as a whole secured 26 seats in the simultaneous legislative elections, leaving the Front third overall. On May 17, 1995, FREPASO came into being as a permanent structure.

A coalition arrangement, the *Alianza para el Trabajo, la Justicia y la Educacion* (ATJE) between FREPASO and the Radical Civic Union (UCR) brought electoral success to both parties in the legislative elections of 1997 and the presidential and legislative elections of 1999. In the 1997 legislative elections the UCR-FREPASO *Alianza* secured 110 seats based upon 45.6% of the popular vote. In the 1999 presidential elections Carlos "Chacho" Alvarez, the FREPASO running mate of Fernando de la Rúa, was elected Vice-Ppresident and, in simultaneous legislative elections in which 130 of the 257 seats in the Chamber of Deputies were at stake, FREPASO secured 36 seats.

The UCR-FREPASO *Alianza*, however, came under the twin stresses of a corruption scandal, which prompted Alvarez's resignation from government in October 2000 in protest at de la Rúa's retention of two ministers implicated in the scandal and FREPASO displeasure at austerity measures announced by the government in late 2000 and the first few months of 2001. Although FREPASO had not officially withdrawn its support from the *Alianza*, as many as 14 deputies had expressed their intention to withdraw their support from the government by the end of April 2001, and the FREPASO Minister of Welfare Marcos Makon and the FREPASO Chief of Staff to the President, Ricardo Mitre, resigned from the government in March 2001 in protest at proposed cuts in public spending. The last FREPASO minister, Juan Pablo Cafiero, resigned from the government in October 2001, shortly before its collapse. In the 2001 legislative elections the party had won one seat in the Senate and 17 seats in the Chamber of Deputies. It retained its Senate seat but declined to five seats in the Chamber following the 2003 elections, when the *Frente Grande* elected one Senator and one deputy.

Intransigent Party
Partido Intransigente (PI)

Address. Riobamba 482, 1025 Buenos Aires
Website. www.pi.org.ar
Leadership. Gustavo Cardesa (president); Jorge Drkos (secretary)

The PI originated in a left-of-centre split from the Radical Civic Union (UCR) in 1956 and the formation of the UCR *Intransigente* (UCRI) in 1957, which changed its name to Intransigent Party in 1972 after the rival People's UCR had won the exclusive right to the UCR title. For the presidential elections of 1973 the party joined forces with the Communist Party of Argentina (PCA) and two other small parties and fielded Oscar Alende as their candidate, who, however, polled only 7.4% of the vote. Following the coup of 1976 the PI was banned and many activists were imprisoned and tortured.

In the first presidential election following Argentina's return to democracy, in October 1983 Alende, with Lisandro Viale as his running-mate, came third but won only 2.3% of the valid vote. With its support waning, the PI joined the FREJUPO alliance backing the Peronist Justicialist Party (PJ) candidate, Carlos Saúl Menem, for the May 1989 elections. Menem won the presidency with a majority in the electoral college (48.5% of the national vote). The PI left FREJUPO in October 1990 in protest at the government's economic policies. It won one chamber seat in 1993 and none in 1995. In the congressional elections held in October 1997 the party secured just one seat, which it retained in the 1999 and 2003 elections.

Justicialist Party
Partido Justicialista (PJ–Peronist)

Address. Matheu 128, 1082 Buenos Aires
Telephone. (54–11) 4952–4555
Fax. (54–11) 4954–2421
Email. bpj@hcdn.gov.ar
Website. www.pj.org.ar
Leadership. Carlos Saúl Menem (president); Rubén Marín (first vice-president); Carlos Reutemann (second vice-president); Eduardo Duhalde (President 2001-03); Humberto Jesús Roggero (congressional president); Eduardo Bauzá (secretary-general)

Founded in 1945, the PJ is populist in outlook, encompassing groups from the far right to the far left. Formerly the Justicialist Nationalist Movement (*Movimiento Nacionalista Justicialista,* MNJ) the PJ grew out of the nationalist *Peronista* movement led by Lt.-Gen. Juan Domingo Perón Sosa during his 1946-55 presidency. Perón returned to power in 1973 after he was deposed by a military coup in 1955 but died in the following year and was succeeded by his Vice-President, his wife María Estela ('Isabel') Martínez de Perón, whose government was overthrown by the armed forces in March 1976.

In the October 1983 elections which followed the Falklands/Malvinas war and the collapse of the military regime, the Peronists lost to the Radical Civic Union (UCR) in both the presidential and congressional elections but beat the UCR in the provincial governorship elections. The party, with Isabel Perón as its figurehead, obtained 40.5% of the vote, which translated into 111 seats in Congress, while its presidential candidate – Italo Luder – came second (with 40.2% of the vote) to Raul Alfonsín Foulkes of the UCR. This defeat resulted in a long period of internal turmoil which split the Peronist movement into two main rival factions with parallel leaderships: the right-wing *oficialistas* (official wing) and the *renovadores* (renovator wing). A party congress in July 1985, intended to reunite the party, resulted in an *oficialista* takeover of the party machinery. All *oficialista* candidates were confirmed for the forthcoming congressional elections because of a boycott by the left wing, which subsequently put forward alternative candidates under the name of the *Frente Renovador* (Renovation Front), led by Antonio Cafiero. Neither the official PJ, which fought the election as the leading party in the FREJULI alliance, nor the Renovation Front did well, overall PJ representation in the congress being reduced by 10 seats.

Despite further splits within the two factions in 1986, which produced four distinct PJ blocs in Congress, the Peronists began to gain in popularity. Benefiting from widespread discontent with the UCR government's austerity measures and its lenient treatment of the army, the PJ won the highest number of votes (41.5%) in the September 1987 congressional elections and narrowed the gap between the PJ and UCR representation in Congress. As well as increasing their congressional seats to 105, the PJ won 16 provincial governorships, including that of the crucial province of Buenos Aires. With the general election of 1989 in view, the PJ regrouped. Isabel Perón was finally replaced as the party's president and a leadership comprising *oficialistas, renovadores* and the Federalism and Liberation faction, linked to Carlos Saúl Menem, was elected. Small left-wing and right-wing factions were ignored and Herminio Iglesias' right-wing group, which had contested the elections separately as the October 17 Party, was expelled in December 1987.

The modern PJ became defined from 1989 when Menem gained the leadership of the party and the nation. The dominant *menemista* faction, promoting a free-market economy and privatization, moved the party sharply to the right.

Menem took office in July 1989 and struggled with a fundamentally destabilized economy with policies as diverse as rationing, an expansion of the state privatization programme, and large reductions in the workforce of the state iron and steel plants. Although Menem largely continued his UCR predecessor's policy of leniency towards the military, measures such as an amnesty for crimes perpetrated during the so-called "dirty war" of 1976-83 could not prevent increasingly vocal discontent over army low pay and lack of status.

The PJ's electoral performance between 1989 and 1997 was a strong one, and Menem himself overcame a long period of unpopularity in his party for his perceived abandonment of Peronism. In congressional and gubernatorial elections held in August, September, October and December 1991, the PJ increased its seats in the Chamber of Deputies from 112 to 119, and won the governorships of 14 provinces. The Peronists won the Chamber elections (for 127 seats) in October 1993, increasing their total number of seats to 125; this total was further raised, to 137 seats, in the elections (for 130 seats) in May 1995, when they also took nine of the 14 provincial governorships at stake. The Peronists had won 136 seats in the elections held in April 1994 to the new 305-member Constituent Assembly, which was responsible for drawing up a new constitution.

Menem was re-elected President in May 1995 with 49.8% of the vote and was sworn into office on July 8 along with the majority of the previous cabinet. In a Senate election for the federal district of Buenos Aires in October 1995 the PJ won only 22.6% of the vote, against 45.7% for the centre-left Front for a Country in Solidarity (FREPASO) coalition and 24.3% for the UCR. Nevertheless, the Peronists held power in 14 of the 23 provinces following provincial elections staged between July and October 1995.

The party's electoral success came to an end in the October 1997 congressional elections, in which 127 of the 257 seats in the Chamber of Deputies were contested. The PJ secured 36.1% of the popular vote compared with the 45.6% won by the *Alianza*. The PJ's representation in the Chamber was reduced to 118 compared with the *Alianza*'s 110, leaving the balance of power in the hands of the *Alianza* and smaller parties which collectively held 29 seats. The defeat was ascribed to public concern at rising unemployment and the imposition of orthodox economic policies.

In the presidential election on Oct. 24, 1999, a decade of Peronist rule was ended when Eduardo Duhalde, the PJ candidate, was defeated by Fernando de la Rúa of the opposition *Alianza*. De la Rúa and his FREPASO running-mate, Carlos "Chacho" Alvarez, secured 48.5% of the popular vote compared with Duhalde's 38.1%. In simultaneous legislative elections, in which 127 of the 257 seats in the Chamber of Deputies were at stake, the PJ won 50 (with 33.7% of the vote), so that its representation fell to 101 seats.

In opposition, the PJ experienced the familiar problem of internal dissension, much of it generated by the wish of former President Menem, whom many blamed for the state of the economy, to justify his past record by securing re-election to a third term. The party's difficulties increased in May 2001 when Menem was subpoenaed by a federal judge to testify in an investigation of illegal arms supplies to Croatia and Ecuador during his presidency. However by August the country was in a state of economic crisis so serious that the electorate gave the PJ a working majority in Congress. Consequently when in December rioting forced President de la Rúa to resign, it was former Vice-President Eduardo Duhalde who was chosen by Congress to serve as interim President.

Three factions within the party contested the April 27, 2003, presidential elections, in which Néstor Carlos Kirchner Ostoic, of the Victory Front (*Frente para la Victoria*) supported by President Duhalde, narrowly defeated Carlos Saul Menem, of the Liberty Front (*Frente por la Libertad*), supported by the Union of the Democratic Centre party. A second round was scheduled to be held on May 18, but when on May 14 polls showed that Kirchner was set to gain some 63% of the expected vote, Menem withdrew, successfully denying his rival the legitimacy of a popular mandate. As a result of congressional elections in 2003, the PJ consolidated its dominance of the Chamber of Deputies, holding 134 of the 257 seats.

The PJ is a member of the International Democrat Union, the Christian Democrat International and the Christian Democrat Organization of America.

Popular Movement Front
Frente Movimiento Popular (FMP)
Emerged from the 2003 elections with six seats in the Chamber of Deputies.

Popular Socialist Party
Partido Socialista Popular (PSP)
Address. Entre Rios 1018 1080 Buenos Aires
Telephone. (54–11) 4304–0644
Website. www.psp.org.ar
Email. pspcn@abaconet.com.ar
Leadership. Ruben Giustiniani; Guillermo Estévez Boero; Edgardo Rossi
Affiliated to the Socialist International, the party was founded at the return of civilian government in 1982. It later joined the Broad Front which was the basis of the Front for a Country in Solidarity (FREPASO) coalition and as part of the *Alianza* contested the 1999 elections. In 2003 it merged with the *Partido Socialista Demócrata* to form the Socialist Party.

Progressive Democratic Party
Partido Democrata Progresista (PDP)
Address. Chile 1934, 1227 Buenos Aires
Email. bdprogresista@hcdn.gov.ar
Leadership. Rafael Martínez Raymonda (president), Alberto Adolfo Natale (congressional president)
The PDP participated in the 1980 talks with the military regime negotiating the normalization of political activities and in August of the same year it joined the Union of the Democratic Centre (UCeDe). In the presidential elections of 1983, however, the party's then leader, Rafael Martinez, stood as candidate of the Democratic Socialist Alliance against the UCeDe's Alvaro Alsogaray and obtained 0.3% of the vote. The PDP contested the partial congressional elections of 1985 as a separate party and gained one seat in the Chamber of Deputies. In the elections of September 1987 the party's share of the national vote was 1.3% and it increased its representation in the Chamber to two seats. The PDP thereafter joined forces again with the UCeDe and in the May 1989 presidential elections, in which Alberto Natale was running-mate to the UCeDe's Alvaro Alsogaray, who came third with 6.4% of the vote. The party won three lower house seats in 1995, two on a joint ticket with the Corrientes Liberal Party (PLC). One PDP candidate secured election to the Chamber of Deputies in the legislative elections of 1997, to be joined by two others in the elections of 1999. The party declined to one seat in the Chamber in the 2003 elections.

Radical Civic Union
Unión Civica Radical (UCR)
Address. Alsina 1786, 1088 Buenos Aires
Telephone. (54–11) 449–0036
Email. info@ucr.org.ar
Website. www.ucr.org.ar
Leadership. Fernando de la Rúa (president); Horacio Francisco Pernasetti (congressional president)
As Argentina's largest centrist/moderate left party, the UCR

has been the dominant mainstream opposition to the Peronist Justicialist Party (PJ). The party was founded by Leandro N. Alem in 1890, when the radical faction split away from the mainstream Civic Union and led an unsuccessful revolt against the Conservative government. One of the party's main demands was the enfranchisement of all adult male Argentines, and it did not participate in any elections until 1912, when that demand was met. In 1916 the UCR formed its first government and remained in power until 1930, when President Hipólito Yrigoyen, nephew of Alem, was ousted by a military coup. After losing both the 1945 and the 1951 elections to the Peronists, the UCR suffered internal problems which culminated in a dramatic split in 1956, caused by the nomination as the UCR's presidential candidate of Arturo Frondizi of the Intransigent faction, who was favourable to some co-operation with the Peronists. Frondizi became the candidate of the newly-formed UCR *Intransigente* (UCRI, later the Intransigent Party) and, with assistance from the Peronists, won the presidency in 1958.

The conservative wing of the party, led by the former UCR presidential candidate Ricardo Balbín, formed the People's UCR (UCR *del Pueblo*, UCRP) in 1956, which was to become the official UCR in 1972, when a court ruling awarded it the sole right to the name. The UCRP supported the military coup against Frondizi in 1962 and in the subsequent elections of 1963 the UCRP's candidate, Arturo Umberto Illía, was elected President. He was himself overthrown in 1966 in another military coup which was supported by the UCRI. Balbín stood again in the 1973 presidential elections for the now renamed UCR and was heavily defeated by Peronists in both the April and September polls.

In 1981 the UCR helped to form a five-party democratic alliance opposed to the latest military junta (in power since 1976), which called for the restoration of democracy. Following the deposition of the military regime in 1982, UCR candidate Raul Alfonsín Foulkes won a major victory in presidential elections in October 1983. He took 317 of the 600 seats in the electoral college, which gave him 51.8% of the electoral college vote. The UCR also won a majority of Chamber of Deputies seats (129 out of 256) but only 16 of the 48 Senate seats and seven of the 24 provincial governorships, including Buenos Aires.

Inaugurated in December 1983, Alfonsín proceeded to make good his election promises of reorganizing the armed forces and putting an end to the cycle of political instability and military intervention. Over half the military high command was forced into retirement and members of the military juntas since 1976 were prosecuted for murder, torture and abduction, some being sent to prison. However, after uprisings in a number of army garrisons in April 1987 and amid persistent rumours of an impending coup, Alfonsín introduced the law of "Due Obedience", dropping all prosecutions against lower-ranking army and police officers indicted for human rights violations. Further military uprisings by officers demanding greater army spending and an extension of the military amnesty to higher-ranking officers nevertheless followed in January and December 1988, followed in January 1989 by an incident, thought to have been provoked by the armed forces, in which a left-wing group attacked La Tablada barracks in order to suppress a rumoured military coup.

Spiralling inflation and a highly unstable economy forced Alfonsín to relinquish power to Carlos Menem of the PJ in July 1989, five months before the expiry of his presidential mandate. Two months earlier Menem had comfortably won presidential elections in which the defeated UCR candidate was Eduardo César Angeloz. The UCR became the main opposition party, and in February 1990 Angeloz refused an invitation from President Menem to join his cabinet. Instead, he called for all political parties to sign a pact under which a plan for effective government would be drawn up to preserve and consolidate democracy in an extreme social and economic crisis. Such proposals, and the UCR's criticism of government policies did not improve the party's electoral performance. In the 1991 mid-term elections the UCR lost five Chamber seats, its strength thus falling to 85 seats, while in the gubernatorial elections the UCR retained only three governorships.

One of the victims of this poor showing was Alfonsín himself, who, following strong criticism from within the UCR, resigned the party leadership in mid-November 1991. Upon his resignation, Alfonsín announced the formation of an internal faction within the UCR, the Movement for Social Democracy (*Movimiento por la Democracia Social*, MDS), which called for the defence of traditional UCR democratic principles. The eventual outcome was his re-election as party leader by an overwhelming majority in November 1993. In the 1995 presidential elections, the party's nominee, Horatio Massacesi, came a disappointing third with 17.1% of the vote. However, in legislative balloting the UCR retained the second highest Chamber representation with 69 seats.

The UCR contested the 1997 legislative elections in an alliance (*Alianza*) with the Front for a Country in Solidarity (FREPASO) which won 45.6% of the popular vote against the 36.1% for the PJ. Although the PJ secured 118 seats compared with the *Alianza*'s 110, the balance of power shifted to the *Alianza* and smaller provincial parties which collectively held 29 seats. In the October 1999 presidential elections, Fernando de la Rúa, the *Alianza* candidate, defeated Eduardo Duhalde of the PJ, thus ending a decade of Peronist domination of the presidency. De la Rúa and his FREPASO running-mate, Carlos "Chacho" Alvarez, took 48.5% of the popular vote against 38.1% for Duhalde. In simultaneous legislative elections, in which 127 of the 257 Chamber seats were contested, the *Alianza* won 63 seats, increasing its representation in the Chamber to 127 seats, two seats short of an overall majority.

In 2000 the government of President de la Rúa, and the stability of the UCR-FREPASO *Alianza*, were shaken by a corruption scandal in which ministers were accused of having bribed legislators in order to secure the enactment of labour reform. However it was a new collapse in confidence in the economy that began in late 2000 that eventually forced the resignation of President de la Rúa in December 2001. The party seemed so discredited that two of its presidential candidates chose to run in 2003 as independents. However Ricardo López Murphy, who had served as Minister of Defence and, briefly, as Economy Minister under de la Rúa, came a creditable third with 16.35% of the votes cast, while the party retained its position as the second-largest in both the Senate and the Chamber of Deputies, though with only 15 seats in the former and 46 in the latter.

Socialist Party
Partido Socialista (PS)
Address. Hipólito Yrigoyen 1708 5° Oficina 509 (C1089AAH) - Capital Federal
Tel. 4379-5875
Website. www.psdcapital.org
Leadership. Alfredo Bravo (congressional president); Sen. Rubén Héctor Giustiniani

This party was formed in 2003 by amalgamation of the *Partido Socialist Demócrata* (PSD) and the *Partido Socialista Popular* (PSP). The leftist PSD had four seats in the Chamber of Deputies in the 1999-2003 legislature, two of whom had first been elected in 1997 and two in 1999. The party had fought the 1997 and 1999 legislative elections as part of the Front for a Country in Solidarity (FR EPASO) coalition. At the 2003 elections the party's candidate for president, Alfredo Bravo, obtained only 1.1% of the vote but the party held one seat in the Senate and five seats in the Chamber.

Union of the Democratic Centre
Unión del Centro Democratico (UCeDe)

Address. Av. R. S. Peña 628, P.I Of.2, 1008 Buenos Aires
Email. bucd@hcdn.gov.ar
Leadership. Alvaro Alsogaray (president)

More right-wing than centrist, the UCeDe is a conservative party standing for a free market economy and a reduced public sector. Originally a coalition of eight small centre-right parties, the UCeDe was formed in 1980 under the leadership of Alvaro Alsogaray, who had held an important position in the post-1976 military government. In the October 1983 elections the party won only two seats in the Chamber of Deputies, Alsogaray receiving only 0.3% of the presidential vote. In order to improve its chances in the Federal Capital of Buenos Aires in the November 1985 elections, the UCeDe formed the "Popular Centrist Alliance" coalition with the Capital Democratic Party (PDC) and Federalist Centre Party (PFC). The vote for the alliance increased to 3.5% of the national vote.

Although Alsogaray was elected as the UCeDe presidential candidate in June 1988, the party leadership at the same time decided to support the campaign of the Peronist Justicialist Party (PJ), hoping thereby to raise the UCeDe's profile. This strategy led to the party polling 9.5% of the national vote, giving the UCeDe nine seats out of the 127 up for election in the May 1989 elections. In the presidential election, Alsogaray came third with 6.4% of the vote.

The party's share of the legislative vote was 3.0% in 1995. However with the accession of President Menem, the party was invited to participate in government, a cabinet position going to Alsogaray's daughter, María Julia Alsogaray. The UCeDe supported the unsuccessful candidature of Menem in the presidential election of 2003, holding only one seat in the Chamber following the 2003 elections.

Other Parties

Buenos Aires Popular Front (*Frente Popular Bonaerense, FrePoBo*), vehicle for the candidature of the former *carapintada*, Aldo Rico, for governor of the Province of Buenos Aires in 2003; won four seats in the Chamber of Deputies and now has five representatives.

Civic Front of Jujuy (*Frente Cívico Jujeño*, FCJ), provincial party in the northern state of Jujuy, represented by one Senator in 2003.
Address. Hipólito Yrigoyen 1708 5° Of.502 (C1089AAH), Capital Federal
Telephone. 4959-3000 Interno 3508/09/10
Leadership. Sen. Lylia Mónica Arancio de Beller

Communist Party of Argentina (*Partido Comunista de la Argentina*, PCA), founded in 1918 and in long-term decline from its early importance. The party has no parliamentary representation and has supported the United Left (*Izquierda Unida*) alliance, which held one seat in the Chamber as a result of the 2003 elections.
Address. Av. Entre Rios 1033, 1080 Buenos Aires
Telephone. (54–11) 4304-0066
Email. central@pca.org.ar
Website. www.pca.org.ar

Compromise for Change (*Compromiso para Cambio,* Cp/C), elected two deputies in the 2003 elections.

Corrientes Liberal Party (*Liberal de Corrientes*, LdC), provincial conservative party, returned one deputy to the Chamber in 1997, unrepresented after 2003 elections.
Email. blcorrientes@hcdn.gov.ar
Leadership. Luis María Díaz Colodrero (president)

Corrientes Self-Government Party (*Autonomista de Corrientes*, AdC), based in the province of Corrientes, elected one candidate to the Chamber of Deputies in 1999, but was unrepresented in 2003.
Email. bacorrientes@hcdn.gov.ar
Leadership. Ismael Ramón Cortinas (president)

Federalist Unity Party (*Partido Unidad Federalista*, PAUFE), local party of Province of Buenos Aires, elected three deputies in 2003 and in 2004 has five representatives.
Leadership. Luis Alberto Patti

Fuerza Porteña (FP), local party in the Federal Capital, elected two deputies in 2003.

Mendoza Democratic Party (Partido *Demócrata [Mendoza]*, PD), based in the province of Mendoza, returned two deputies to the Chamber in 1997 and a third in 1999, but retained only one in 2003.
Email. bdmendoza@hcdn.gov.ar
Leadership. Carlos Mario Balter (president)

New Party (*Partido Nuevo,* PN), returned two deputies to the Chamber in 1997 and another in 1999. In 2003 it was represented by one Senator and one deputy.
Address. Hipólito Yrigoyen 1849 3° Of.52 "D" (C1089AAH)
Telephone. 4959-3000 Internos 1375/76/77/78
Email. bfrepanu@hcdn.gov.ar
Leadership. Sen. Carlos Alberto Rossi (president), Catalina Méndez de Medina Lareu

New Party of Buenos Aires (*Partido Nuevo de Buenos Aires,* PNBA), elected two deputies to Congress in 2003.

New Party [Córdoba] (*Partido Nuevo,* PN), Córdoba provincial party, returned three deputies in 2003.

Party of the Democratic Revolution (*Partido de la Revolución Democrática,* PRD), progressive party, elected one deputy in 2003.

Popular Fueguino Movement (*Movimiento Popular Fueguino*, MPF or MoPoF), provincial party in the Province of Tierra del Fuego, returned one deputy to the Chamber in 1997. In gubernatorial elections in July 2004 MoPoF obtained 18% of the votes cast.
Email. bmpfueguino@hcdn.gov.ar
Leadership. Ernesto Adrián Löffler (president)

Popular Neuquino Movement (*Movimiento Popular Neuquino*, MPN), provincial party, founded in 1961 when Peronism was banned. It returned one deputy to the Chamber in 1997 and another in 1999. In 2003 it elected two Senators and four deputies.
Address. Hipólito Yrigoyen 1708 4° Oficina 409 (C1089AAH) Capital Federal
Telephone. 4959-3000 Interno 3456
Website. www.mpn.org.ar
Leadership. Sen. Pedro Salvatori (president)

Radical Party of Río Negro (*Radical Rionegrino*, RR), provincial party in the province of Río Negro, represented by one Senator in 2003 but unrepresented in the Chamber of Deputies.
Address. Hipólito Yrigoyen 1708 5° Of.505 (C1089AAH)
Telephone. 4959-3000 Interno 3529/30
Leadership. Sen. Luis Alberto Falcó

Republican Force (*Fuerza Republicana,* FR), an authoritarian right-wing party; founded in 1989 but confined to the north-western province of Tucumán, the FR had links with the previous military regime. It increased its seats in the Chamber of Deputies from two to four in the October 1991 mid-term elections, went on to win three lower house seats in October 1993, adding another in 1995. It kept only two seats in the legislative elections of 1997 but won a third in 1999. It returned two Senators and four deputies to the Chamber in the 2003 elections.

Address. Hipólito Yrigoyen 1760 4° Oficina 411 (C1089AAH), Capital Federal
Telephone. 4959-3000 Interno 3472/73
Email. bfrepublicana@hcdn.gov.ar
Leadership. Sen. Ricardo Argentino Bussi (president)

Salta Renewal Party (*Partido Renovador de Salta*, PRS), provincial party which returned one deputy to the Chamber in 1997 and a second in 1999, and retained both seats in 2003. It is also represented by one Senator.

Address. Hipólito Yrigoyen 1768 5° Oficina 511 (C1089AAH), Capital Federal
Telephone. 4959-3000 Interno 3569 al 72
Email. brsalta@hcdn.gov.ar
Leadership. Ricardo Gómez Diez (president)

San Juan Bloc (*Bloquista de San Juan*, BSJ), populist provincial party which emerged in the province of San Juan in the 1920s as an offshoot of Radicalism. Elected one deputy to the Chamber in 1999, but was unrepresented in 2003.

Email. bbsanjuan@hcdn.gov.ar
Leadership. Julio César Conca (president)

Self-determination and Liberty (*Autodeterminación y Libertad*, AL), elected four deputies in 2003.

Social and Civic Front of Catamarca (*Frente Civico y Social de Catamarca*, FCSC), Catamarca provincial party, returned one deputy to the Chamber of Deputies in 1997 and two in 1999. In 2003 it elected two Senators and retained its two seats in the Chamber.

Address. Hipólito Yrigoyen 1849 3° Oficina 75 (C1089AAI), Capital Federal
Telephone. 4959-3000 Interno 1396/97
Email. bfcsocial@hcdn.gov.ar
Leadership. Simón Fermín Guadalupe Hernández (president), Sen. María Teresita Colombo

Armenia

Capital: Yerevan
Population: 3,300,000 (2004E)

The former Soviet republic of Armenia declared independence as the Republic of Armenia in August 1990 and became a sovereign member of the Commonwealth of Independent States (CIS) on the latter's creation in December 1991. Independent Armenia retained its Soviet-era constitution, with some adjustments to cater for a multi-party system, until the approval of a new constitution in a referendum on July 5, 1995. The constitution establishes a democratic "presidential" system. Directly elected for a five-year term, the executive President appoints the Prime Minister and other ministers and may dissolve the National Assembly and call new elections. Legislative authority is vested in the unicameral National Assembly (*Azgayin Zhoghov*), whose 131 members are elected for a four-year term by universal adult suffrage, 56 by majority voting in single-

member constituencies and 75 by proportional representation from national lists of parties obtaining at least 5% of the vote.

In presidential elections on February 19 and March 5, 2003, non-party candidate Robert Kocharian was elected with 67.5% of the second-round vote against 32.5% for Stepan Demirchian of the People's Party of Armenia.

Legislative elections were held on May 25, 2003. In the national proportional list election, five parties and one electoral bloc passed the threshold of 5% of votes. The distribution of the 75 seats filled by the proportionate system is as follows: Republican Party of Armenia 23 seats (23.5% of the proportional vote), Justice Alliance Bloc 14 (13.7%), *Orinats Yerkir* (Rule of Law Country) 12 (12.4%), Armenian Revolutionary Federation (*Dashnak*) 11 (11.4%), National Unity Party 9 (8.8%), and United Labour Party 6 (5.7%). Of the 56 majoritarian constituencies, 37 seats were won by citizens' initiatives rather than by parties. The Republican Party of Armenia received 10 seats, *Orinats Yerkir* 7, Hanrapetutiun (Republic) Party (part of Justice Alliance) 1, and Pan-Armenian Workers' Party 1.

Under the National Assembly's rules of procedure, the parties and blocs that won representation by the proportional list system constitute parliamentary "factions" and no other factions may be formed. Deputies elected by the majoritarian system may affiliate to one of the factions by the latter's consent. Only 14 seats remained unaffiliated. The composition of the factions confirmed that many non-partisan candidates who won in majoritarian constituencies had a political party affiliation. The 131 seats of the National Assembly are distributed by faction/deputies' group as follows: Republican Party faction 40 seats, *Orinats Yerkir* faction 19, Justice Alliance faction 15, Armenian Revolutionary Federation faction seats 11, National Unity Party faction 9 seats, United Labour Party faction 6, "People's Deputy" group 17, and unaffiliated 14.

Armenian Revolutionary Federation
Hai Heghapokhakan Dashnaktsutiune (HHD/Dashnak)
Address. P.O. Box 123, Yerevan 375010
Telephone. (374–2) 535623
Fax. (374-2) 531362
Email. buro@arf.arm
Website. www.arf.am
Leadership. Hrand Margaryan (chairman of world bureau); Armen Rustamyan (political representative of the ARF executive council); Giro Manoyan (executive director); Levon Mkrtchyan (chairman, parliamentary faction)
Dating from 1890, *Dashnak* was the ruling party in pre-Soviet independent Armenia (1918-20) and retained a large following in the Armenian diaspora after it had been outlawed by the Bolsheviks in 1920. Re-established in 1990 as a nationalist opposition party of socialist orientation (and also calling itself the Armenian Socialist Party), *Dashnak* put up the actor Sos Sargsyan in the October 1991 presidential election but received only 4% of the vote. The party became a fierce critic of the conduct of the war in Nagorno-Karabakh by the government of the Pan-Armenian National Movement (HHSh), which claimed in response that *Dashnak* leaders in exile had co-operated with the Soviet security authorities. *Dashnak* parliamentary leader Gagik Ovanessian was expelled from the party in June 1994 for publicly criticizing its "Bolshevik" methods.

In late December 1994 the *Dashnak* was "temporarily suspended" by presidential decree, on the grounds that it had allegedly engaged in terrorism, political assassination and drug-trafficking. It therefore did not participate as a party in the July 1995 legislative elections, although party members stood in many constituencies and one was elected. Some 30 *Dashnak* activists were put on trial in March 1996 charged with involvement in an alleged coup attempt during the elections, those receiving prison sentences including chairman Vahan Hovhannisyan and executive council member Hrand Margaryan. However, they were all released in February 1998 when the ban on the party was lifted, a week after the resignation of President Ter-Petrosyan (HHSh).

Dashnak backed the successful candidacy of Robert Kocharian (non-party) in the March 1998 presidential elections, following which Hovhannisyan became a presidential adviser and the party obtained two ministerial portfolios in the new government. In the May 1999 Assembly elections *Dashnak* achieved third place with nine of the 131 seats and 7.8% of the proportional vote, subsequently obtaining one portfolio in the new government coalition.

Dashnak held its 28th world congress in Tsaghkadzor in February 2000 (its first in Armenia since 1919), electing Margaryan as chairman of the party's world executive bureau and establishing the party's head office in Yerevan. The Armenian executive subsequently appointed Armen Rustamyan as the principal *Dashnak* representative in Armenia. In June 2001 *Dashnak* again warned that it would oppose any government concessions on the Nagorno-Karabakh issue that it considered to be a danger to national unity.

The 29th congress was held in February 2004 and was attended by representatives from Armenia and Nagorno Karabakh as well as by delegates representating the party's structures in 30 countries. The speeches focused on issues concerning the Armenian genocide, Armenian-Turkish relations, and the Armenian-populated region of Javakheti in Georgia.

Dashnak is a consultative member of the Socialist International (having joined the pre-World War I Second International in 1907).

Democratic Party of Armenia
Hayastani Demokratakan Kusaktutyun (HDK)
Address. 14 Koryun Street, Yerevan
Telephone. (374–2) 525273
Fax. (374–2) 525273
Leadership. Aram G. Sarkisian (chairman)
The HDK was established in late 1991 as the would-be successor to the former ruling Communist Party of Armenia (HKK), which was suspended in September 1991 after having secured the second-largest number of seats in the 1990 legislative elections. Many senior Communists switched allegiance to the ruling Pan-Armenian National Movement (HHSh) rather than to the HDK, which was also weakened by the revival of the HKK in 1994. In the 1995 legislative elections the HDK took only 1.8% of the vote and failed to win representation.

The resignation of President Ter-Petrosyan (HHSh) in February 1998 produced a partial revival for the HDK, whose chairman became a foreign policy adviser to the new non-party President, Robert Kocharian. In the May 1999 Assembly elections the HDK won one seat and 1% of the proportional vote.

In the 2003 Assembly elections, HDK participated as one of the constituent parties of the Justice Alliance.

Hanrapetutiun (Republic) Party
Address. Mashtosti Ave. 37, apt.30, Yerevan
Telephone. (374) 538634
Leadership. Aram Sargsian
In February 2001, former Prime Minister Aram Sargsian and the former mayor of Yerevan, Albert Bazeyan, announced their intention of forming a new "conservative opposition organization". Both Sargsian and Bazeyan had quit the Republican Party of Armenia (HHK). In a statement released

on Feb. 6, 2001, they accused the party of diverging from the principles of its founder, Sargsian's brother Vazgen, murdered in the parliamentary shootings in 1999. Other disaffected HHK members also joined the new Hanrapetutiun (Republic) Party. In September 2001, Hanrapetutiun, together with the People's Party of Armenia and the National Accord Party, announced their intention of beginning impeachment proceedings against President Robert Kocharian, whom they accused of violating the constitution.

In February 2003, Aram Sargsian announced in a televized speech that he was withdrawing his candidacy in the presidential elections in favour of the People's Party of Armenia (HZhK) chairman, Stepan Demirchian, and appealed to his supporters and members of his party to campaign on behalf of Demirchian. Sargsian said his decision was tantamount to the creation of a new electoral alliance between Hanrapetutiun and the HZhK and a bid to revive the defunct *Miasnutiun* bloc that won a majority in the 1999 parliamentary elections. Following the election of Robert Kocharian as President, Sargsian, among other opposition leaders, argued in favor of boycotting the parliamentary elections to protest the presumed falsification of the presidential ballot.

In March 2003, Hanrapetutiun (Republic) Party entered into a coalition with a dozen other opposition parties in the Justice Alliance, which received 13.6% of the vote in the May elections.

In April 2004, Aram Sargsian, alongside the HZhK leader Demirchian, spearheaded a protest campaign agaisnt the policies of the President and the government.

Justice Alliance
Ardarutiun
Justice Alliance unites several political parties under the leadership of Stepan Demirchian (HZhK). The most important parties in the bloc are the Armenian People's Party (HZhK), formerly part of the Unity bloc; the National Democratic Union (AzhM) led by Vazgen Manoukian; the National Democratic Party (AzhK) led by Sharvash Kocharian; the National Democratic Alliance (AzhD) led by Arshak Sadoyan; the Armenian Democratic Party (HDK) led by Aram G. Sarkisian; and the Constitutional Rights Union, formerly part of the Right and Accord Bloc.

In the aftermath of the 2003 presidential elections, the opposition parties grouped around the defeated presidential candidate Stepan Demirchian. The alliance agreed on a single list of candidates. Stepan Demirchian, Hanrapetutiun (Republic) party leader Aram Sargsian, and two former presidential candidates defeated in the February first round of voting – Vazgen Manoukian and Aram Karapetian – topped the electoral slate.

Justice Alliance is the main opposition group in the Parliament which has rejected as fraudulent the official vote results of the 2003 elections. They considered boycotting the parliament but finally decided to accept the 14 parliamentary seats which they got as a result of winning 13.7% of votes. In March 2004, the Justice Alliance led by Stepan Demirchian and the National Unity Party of Artashes Geghamian launched a protest campaign designed to force President Robert Kocharian's resignation. The opposition characterized Kocharian's administration as illegitimate and protested against its refusal to organize a nationwide referendum on the government's performance, which had been recommended by the Constitutional Court in a ruling dated April 16, 2003.

National Democratic Alliance (AZhD)
Leadership. Arshak Sadoyan
The National Democratic Alliance was founded in April 2001 by a dissident faction of the National Democratic Union of Armenia (AZhM) who had opposed the AzhM's

support for the post-1999 government headed by the Republican Party of Armenia. In June 2001, Arshak Sadoyan called for the state to retain a majority stake in the energy and other strategic industries.

AzhD was part of Justice Alliance in the 2003 Assembly elections.

National Democratic Party (AZhK)

Leadership. Sharvash Kocharian

The National Democratic Party was founded in February 2001 by a dissident faction of the National Democratic Union of Armenia (AZhM), which opposed the AZhM support for the post-1999 government headed by the Republican Party of Armenia. AzhK was part of the Justice Alliance in the 2003 Assembly elections.

National Democratic Union of Armenia
Azgayin Zhoghorvrdavarakan Miutyun (AZhM)

Address. 12 Abovian Street, Yerevan
Telephone. (374–2) 523412
Fax. (374–2) 563188
Leadership. Vazgen Manoukian (chairman)

The centre-right AZhM was formed by Vazgen Manukian following his resignation as Prime Minister in September 1991, when he also left the then ruling Pan-Armenian National Movement (HHSh). In mid-1994 the AZhM organized demonstrations against the HHSh government in Yerevan. The party won 7.5% of the vote and five Assembly seats in the 1995 Assembly elections, while in the September 1996 presidential contest Manoukian was runner-up with 41.3% of the vote, subsequently claiming that the result had been rigged.

Manukian stood again in the March 1998 presidential elections, being eliminated in the first round with 12.2% of the vote. Having failed to find alliance partners for the May 1999 Assembly elections, the AZhM slipped to 5.2% of the vote but increased its representation to six seats. Although critical of the presidency of Robert Kocharian, the party accepted a ministerial post in February 2000. In September 2000 Manukian ruled out entering an alliance with the main ruling Republican Party of Armenia or any other formation, although at an AZhM congress in December he favoured qualified co-operation with the Kocharian presidency, thereby coming under criticism from party members who advocated a return to outright opposition. The AZhM was weakened in early 2001 when several senior members, including Shavarsh Kocharian and Arshak Sadoyan, resigned from the party expressing disagreement with its participation in the government.

In the Assembly elections of 2003, AZhM was one of the constituent parties of the Justice Alliance alongside the parties established by dissidents that splintered from its ranks – the National Democratic Party (AzhK) led by Sharvash Kocharian, and the National Democratic Alliance (AzhD) led by Arshak Sadoyan.

National Unity Party (AMK)

Telephone. (374–2) 530 351
Leadership. Artashes Geghamian (chairman); Alexan Karapetian (deputy chairman)

The National Unity Party was founded in April 1997 by its leader Artashes Geghamian, who headed the "Right and Unity" faction of the Parliament elected in 1999. Following these elections, Geghamian became increasingly critical of successive governments headed by the centre-right Republican Party of Armenia. Geghamian argued that far greater state involvement was needed to overcome Armenia's economic crisis.

In the presidential elections in 2003, Artashes Geghamian was the third main contender, receiving nearly 18% of the votes in the first round. In the 2003 Assembly elections, the party received 8.8% of the votes and gained 9 parliamentary seats. In March 2004, Geghamian signalled his support for the Justice Alliance, hitherto his rival, in staging protests to force the resignation of President Robert Kocharian.

Orinats Yerkir
Rule of Law Country Party

Address. 2 Arshakuniatis Street, Yerevan
Telephone. (374–2) 563584
Leadership. Artur Baghdasaryan (chairman)

Launched in March 1998, the right-wing *Orinats Yerkir* backed the successful presidential candidacy of Robert Kocharian (non-party), subsequently becoming a core supporter of the new President. In the May 1999 Assembly elections the party took fifth place in the proportional section, with 5.3% of the vote, and obtained six of the 131 seats. In the 2003 Assembly elections, the party came third with 12.4% of the proportional vote, receiving seven of the parliamentary seats. Twelve more deputies elected by the majoritarian system joined the *Orinats Yerkir* faction.

Pan Armenian Workers' Party

The Pan Armenian Workers' Party received one of the 56 National Assembly seats allocated by majority voting in single-member constituencies in the 2003 elections.

People's Party of Armenia
Hayastani Zhoghovrdakan Kusaktsutyun (HZhK)

Address. 24 Moskovian Street, Yerevan
Telephone. (374–2) 581577
Leadership. Stepan Demirchian (chairman)

The HZhK held its foundation congress in Yerevan in February 1999, proclaiming a commitment to "democratic and popular socialism" and to reversing post-Soviet "deindustrialization". The party had been launched in 1998 by Karen Demirchian on the strength of his support in the March 1998 presidential elections, when he had been runner-up to Robert Kocharian (non-party) with 30.7% in the first round and 40.5% in the second. Karen Demirchian had been first secretary of the then ruling Communist Party of Armenia from 1974 until his dismissal in 1988 for failing to clamp down on Armenian nationalism.

The HZhK contested the May 1999 Assembly elections in an alliance with the Republican Party of Armenia (HHK) called the Unity Bloc (*Miasnutiun*), which dominated the contest by winning 55 of the 131 seats and 41.7% of the proportional vote. While the then HHK leader became Prime Minister, Karen Demirchian was elected Speaker of the new Assembly. However, in October 1999 he was one of eight political leaders, including the Prime Minister, slain by intruding gunmen during an Assembly debate. He was succeeded as HZhK chairman in December by his younger son, Stepan Demirchian, while Armen Khachatrian of the HZhK became Speaker.

Although Stepan Demirchian initially pledged the HZhK's continued participation in the Unity Bloc, his criticism of government policies intensified following the appointment of HHK chairman Andranik Margarian as Prime Minister in May 2000. In the following year, the Unity Bloc experienced internal discord, as a result of which in September 2001 the HZhK announced an end to the coalition and called for new parliamentary elections. In its statement, HZhK accused Prime Minister Andranic Margarian of using the HHK as a vehicle to maintain President Robert Kocharian's hold on power in the government.

In the 2003 presidential elections Stepan Demirchian was the main contender for the post against the incumbent President. In the second round of voting, he received 32.5% of votes. After the defeat, the main opposition parties grouped around the presidential candidate in the Justice

Alliance, which agreed on a single list of candidates for the May 2003 Assembly elections.

Republican Party of Armenia
Hayastani Hanrapetakan Kusaktsutyun (HHK)
Address. 23 Toumanian Street, Yerevan
Telephone. (374–2) 580031
Fax. (374–2) 581259
Website. www.hkk.am
Leadership. Andranik Margarian (chairman); Tigran Torosian and Razmik Zohrabian (deputy chairmen).
The centre-right HHK was relaunched in mid-1998 as a merger of the Yerkrapah Union of Veterans (of the Nagorno-Karabakh war) and the original HHK, which had been founded in May 1991 by a moderate faction of the National Self-Determination Union and had been part of the victorious Republic Bloc in the 1995 Assembly elections. Yerkrapah leader and then Defence Minister Vazgen Sarkisian was elected chairman of the new HHK, which espoused free market economic policies.

The HHK stood in the May 1999 Assembly elections in an alliance with the left-leaning People's Party of Armenia (HZhK) called the Unity Bloc (*Miasnutiun*), which dominated the contest by winning 55 of the 131 seats and 41.7% of the proportional vote. As leader of the stronger partner, Vazgen Sarkisian became Prime Minister of a government in which smaller parties were also represented. However, in October 1999 he was one of eight political leaders assassinated by gunmen who invaded an Assembly debate. He was succeeded as Prime Minister by his younger brother, Aram Sargsian, and as HHK chairman by Andranik Margarian.

In May 2000 Aram Sargsian was dismissed as Prime Minister by President Kocharian and replaced by Margarian, who was quickly faced with dissidence from the HHK's Yerkrapah wing, which formed a separate Assembly group (*Hayastan*) strongly critical of President Kocharian. Also undermining the *Miasnutiun* alliance in late 2000 was the increasing disaffection of the HZhK. In February 2001 Aram Sargsian resigned from the HHK and announced his intention to form a new "conservative opposition" party, together with Albert Bazeyan, the former mayor of Yerevan, and the *Hayastan* faction. A statement from Aram Sargsian and Albert Bazeyan accused Margarian of becoming "the appendage of a vicious government" and showing "total neglect of the rule of law".

In the 2003 presidential elections, the HHK supported the incumbent President Robert Kocharian. In the parliamentary elections in May 2003, HHK emerged in first place with 23.5% of the proportional vote.

United Labour Party (MAK)
Telephone. (374-9) 425-504
Leadership. Gurgen Arsenian (chairman)
The United Labour Party was founded in September 2002 by Gurgen Arsenian, a wealthy entrepreneur. The new party delivered the biggest election surprise in the May 2003 polls when it cleared the 5% of the vote threshold and won 6 out of 131 parliamentary seats. Arsenian is known for his staunch support for President Kocharian and was accused by the Armenian opposition of buying his party's way into the legislature.

Australia

Capital: Canberra, ACT
Population: 20,194, 000

The Commonwealth of Australia is a parliamentary democracy with the British monarch as non-executive head of state, represented by a locally nominated Governor-General. Australia comprises six states, each with its own directly-elected assembly with extensive powers, and two territories. There is a bicameral federal Parliament. The membership of the Senate is currently fixed at 76 – 12 members from each state, directly elected for a six-year term (with half the seats renewed at three-year intervals), and two members each from the Northern Territory and the Australian Capital Territory (ACT), directly elected for three-year terms. The members of the House of Representatives – currently totaling 150 – serve a three-year term. Either the House or both chambers may be dissolved early by the Governor-General, whose powers are by convention exercised in accordance with the advice of the Australian government.

Elections to the House, and to most state lower chambers, use the alternative vote system in single-member constituencies; those to the Senate, the Tasmanian lower house and the ACT Legislative Assembly, use proportional representation in multi-seat constituencies. Federal and state elections are on the basis of universal and (with some exceptions) compulsory suffrage. The Governor-General appoints the Prime Minister, who is normally the majority leader in the federal House of Representatives, and who exercises executive power along with a cabinet drawn from and answerable to Parliament; broadly similar arrangements apply at state level, each state having its own constitution and a government led by a state premier.

The activities of political parties are regulated principally by the Commonwealth Electoral Act and the Australian Electoral Commission. On the recommendation of an all-party parliamentary committee in 1994, the Act was amended to increase public funding of parties, also imposing stricter requirements to disclose donations to party funds. Federal funds are allocated to those registered parties and independent candidates obtaining at least 4% of state or territory formal first-preference votes in elections for either the federal House of Representatives or the Senate. Under half-yearly indexing in line with the consumer price index, the rate per first-preference vote was set at 194.37 cents for the 2004 federal election.

After winning five general elections in a row, the Australian Labor Party (ALP) lost power on March 2, 1996, to the Liberal-National Party coalition. The coalition was returned to office in 1998, 2001, and again in 2004 at an election held on Oct. 9, which resulted in a swing to the government. By Oct. 15, 2004, it was clear that the Australian Labor Party had won 57 House of Representatives seats (with 38.04% of first-preference votes), the Liberal Party of Australia 72 (40.56%), the National Party 12 (5.91%), independents 3, and Country Liberal–The Territory Party 1, with 5 seats at this point undecided. Until June 30, 2005, the composition of the upper house remains Liberal Party of Australia 31, ALP 28, Australian Democrats 7, the National Party 3, Australian Greens 2, One Nation 1, Country Liberal–The Territory Party 1, independents 3. At the end of June 2005 the composition of the Senate will change to reflect the 2004 elections for 40 of the 76 Senate seats. It appears likely that the coalition will then control the Senate.

Five states have bicameral legislatures, whereas Queensland, the Northern Territory and the ACT have single-chamber assemblies.

New South Wales. Australia's most populous state has a 93-member Legislative Assembly and an upper Legislative Council with 60 members. Assembly elections are held at maximum intervals of four years, a quarter of Council seats being also renewed at each election. In elections on March 22, 2003, the ALP retained power with 55 Assembly seats, to 32 for the Liberal-National coalition and six independents.

Queensland. The Legislative Assembly's 89 members represent single-seat constituencies and are elected for three-year terms. In elections held on Feb. 7, 2004, the Labor government was returned, with the ALP winning 63 seats, the Nationals 15, Liberal Party 5, independents 5, and One Nation 1.

South Australia. The House of Assembly has 47 members, serving a four-year term, and the Legislative Council has 22 members serving an eight-year term with half being elected at each general election. In elections on Feb. 9, 2002, there was a change of government with the ALP winning office with the support of an independent. Labor won 23 Assembly seats, the Liberals 20, independents 3 and National Party 1. In early 2003 one Labor member defected to the Australian Greens but this did not alter the balance of power.

Tasmania. Australia's island state has five constituencies, each returning five members for a four-year term in the House of Assembly. The 15-member Legislative Council is directly elected, each member serving for six years with 3 or 2 members elected in alternate years. In elections on July 20, 2002, the ALP was returned to office with 14 seats. The Liberal Party won 7 seats and the Tasmanian Greens 4.

Victoria. The 88 members of the Legislative Assembly are elected every three years, along with half of the 44 Legislative Council members, who serve a six-year term. In elections on Nov. 30, 2002, the Labor Party was returned to office with an increased majority. The ALP won 62 seats, the Liberal Party 17, the National Party 7 and independents 2.

Western Australia. The Legislative Assembly, with 57 members, is subject to election every four years. The Legislative Council's 34 members are elected from six electoral regions for a four year fixed term. In Assembly elections on Feb. 10, 2001, a strong vote (although no seats) for One Nation resulted in the incumbent Liberal-National coalition losing power to the ALP, which won 32 seats, while the Liberals won 16, the National Party 5 and independents 4.

Australian Capital Territory. The 17-member Legislative Assembly is elected using the Hare-Clark voting method for a fixed three-year term. An election was held on October 16, 2004. As of October 19, the Labour Party appeared likely to win 9 or 10 seats giving it government in its own right, the Liberal Party 6 or 7 and the Greens 1.

Northern Territory. The sparsely-populated NT's unicameral Legislative Assembly has 25 members directly elected under a two-party preferred vote system. In elections on Aug. 18, 2001, the Country Liberal Party lost office to the ALP which won 13 seats to the Country Liberals' 10 and independents 2. In a referendum held simultaneously with the federal elections on Oct. 3, 1998, NT voters rejected a government offer of statehood.

Australian Democrats

Address. PO Box 5089, Kingston, ACT 2604
Telephone. (+61–2) 6273–1059
Fax. (+61–2) 6273–1251
Email. inquiries@democrats.org.au
Website. www.democrats.org.au
Leadership. Andrew Bartlett (leader); Nina Burridge (national president); Jason Wood (national secretary).
Founded in May 1977 by former Liberal Party cabinet minister Donald L. (Don) Chipp, by a merger of the Australia Party and the New Liberal Movement, the Democrats (as the party is informally known) pursue a centre-left agenda. The party emphasizes its independence from business and organized labour as well as environmental, social justice and civil liberties issues.

The Democrats have never won a seat in the House of Representatives, but under proportional representation have been represented in the Senate continuously since 1977. In 1997 the Democrats' parliamentary leader Cheryl Kernot defected to the ALP, ushering in a period of instability within the party. In the October 2004 federal elections their share of the vote dropped to 1.18% in elections to the House, a fall of over four percentage points, while in elections to the Senate they faced a swing of more than 6% and failed to win any seats, leaving the party with 4 senators in the new parliament. Former leader Meg Lees, who resigned from the Democrats to sit as an independent in July 2002 and then as a member of the Australian Progressive Alliance from April 2003, failed in her bid to retain her Senate seat as an Alliance candidate.

Australian Greens

Address. GPO Box 1108, Canberra, ACT 2601
Telephone (+61-2) 6162 0036
Fax. (+61-2) 6247 6455
Email. frontdesk@greens.org.au
Website. www.greens.org.au
Leadership. Stewart Jackson (national convenor); Carol Berry (national secretary)
The Australian Greens were established in August 1992 as the federal co-ordinating body for numerous state, territorial and local ecologist parties. All state parties belong to the national confederation, with The Greens (WA) joining in October 2003. The movement drew many adherents from the Nuclear Disarmament Party, which had been launched by Australian Labor Party (ALP) dissidents in 1984. Although the Greens do not formally have a national leader, Senator Robert (Bob) Brown is often described in those terms by the Australian media.

The Greens won 6.89% of the House of Representatives vote in the October 2004 elections and 7.46% of the Senate vote. It is unclear if this will be sufficient to increase their Senate representation from the current two senators. They won their first House of Representatives seat in a by-election in 2002 but lost it to Labor in the October 2004 federal elections. On occasions, they have influenced the programmes of other parties, most recently the ALP.

Australian Labor Party (ALP)

Address. 2 Centenary House, 19 National Circuit, Barton, ACT 2600
Telephone. (+61–2) 6120-0800
Fax. (+61–2) 6120-0801
Email. info@cbr.alp.org.au
Website. www.alp.org.au
Leadership. Mark Latham (leader); Jennifer (Jenny) Macklin (deputy leader); Greg Sword (national president); Tim Gartrell (national secretary)
Founded in 1901 as the political arm of the trade union movement (with which it retains close links) the social democratic ALP is Australia's oldest national political party, and since 1922 the only one to have held power other than in coalition. It first formed a government in 1904.

The party was seriously affected by ideological divisions during the Cold War and was out of office from 1949 until 1972 when, under the leadership of Gough Whitlam, it returned to government. The Whitlam administration oversaw an ambitious policy reform programme, established diplomatic ties with China and lowered the voting age to 18. It was forced to an early election in 1974 which it won with a reduced majority but its failure to secure a Senate majority in May 1974 brought on a constitutional crisis, culminating in Governor-General John Kerr's controversial intervention to dismiss the Whitlam government in November 1975.

The ALP lost the following month's general elections.

The ALP recovered some ground in the October 1980 elections under the leadership of William (Bill) Hayden, who later became Governor-General of Australia. His successor was Robert (Bob) Hawke, former president of the Australian Council of Trade Unions who led the party to successive election victories in 1983, 1984, 1987 and 1990. Under Hawke's leadership the ALP discarded many of its traditional commitments and pursued economic policies such as deregulation, privatization and cutting tariffs. During 1991 Hawke's leadership was twice challenged by the federal Treasurer, Paul Keating. Succeeding at the second attempt in December, Keating took over as Prime Minister at a time of considerable economic difficulties but in March 1993 elections the government won a fifth consecutive term, winning 80 seats for a lower house majority of 13.

Keating continued Hawke's economic policy direction and also developed a range of what he called "big picture issues" including settler relations with indigenous Australians, Australia's relationship with Asia, multiculturalism, and turning Australia into a republic. His vision on these issues, however, did not enthuse voters sufficiently for Labor to win a sixth term in the March 1996 elections, when it retained only 49 seats (on a 38.8% first-preference vote share) and went into opposition. Keating resigned as ALP leader immediately after the contest and was succeeded by Kim Beazley, the former Deputy Prime Minister.

The ALP recovered some ground in the October 1998 national elections, winning 67 seats, 40% of first-preference votes, and a majority of two-party-preferred votes, but remained in opposition. In a constitutional referendum in November 1999 the change to a republic advocated by the ALP and some Coalition parliamentarians was rejected, in part because the model proposed was unpopular among many republicans who voted against it.

The ALP was defeated again in November 2001, unable to match the government's electoral support, which had soared as a result of its tough stance on asylum seekers and its response to the September 11 terrorist attacks on the United States. Labor won 65 seats with 37.84% of first preference votes. After the election, Kim Beazley stood down as party leader, to be replaced by Simon Crean. After failing to maintain the support of party members, Crean was replaced by Mark Latham on Dec. 2, 2003. Latham led the party to another defeat in elections held on Oct. 9, 2004, when it won 38.04% of first preference votes and (as of Oct. 15) had won 57 seats, with 5 seats still undecided at that point.

Despite losing the last four federal elections and appearing at federal level to be a party unsure of what it stands for, as of October 2004 the ALP held power in every state and territory.

The ALP is believed to have about 50,000 members. It has adopted affirmative action policies and is currently officially committed to a target of having at least 40% women parliamentarians at federal and state levels. There is an autonomous Young Labor Association. The ALP is affiliated to the Socialist International and the Socialist International Asia Pacific Committee.

Country Liberal Party–The Territory Party (CLP)

Address. PO Box 4194, Darwin, NT 0801
Telephone. (+61–8) 8981–8986
Fax. (+61–8) 8981–4226
Email. ntclp@bigpond.com
Website. www.clp.org.au
Leadership. Terry Mills (leader); Paul Bunker (president); Charlie Taylor (general secretary)
Conservative in outlook and closely aligned to the federal Liberal and National Parties of Australia, the CLP governed the Northern Territory (NT) from the first territorial legisla-

tive election in 1974 until 2001, when it lost to the ALP. After the elections held in October 2004 the party is represented federally by one senator and one member of the House of Representatives.

The party is a strong promoter of regional development and an advocate of statehood for the Northern Territory, which was, however, rejected in a referendum held simultaneously with the October 1998 federal elections.

Liberal Party of Australia

Address. PO Box E13, Kingston, ACT 2604
Telephone. (+61–2) 6273–2564
Fax. (+61–2) 6273–1534
Email. libadm@liberal.org.au
Website. www.liberal.org.au
Leadership. John W. Howard (leader); Shane Stone (federal president)
The Liberal Party (as it is invariably called) has been, since its foundation by Sir Robert Gordon Menzies in October 1944, the main anti-socialist party in Australia, representing views ranging from the centre to the conservative right. Its core values are support for free enterprise and individual initiative, for the family and for "a common set of Australian values". It opposes state ownership of other than essential public services and advocates neo-liberal economic policies, including rewarding enterprise through low levels of personal taxation.

The party originated in succession to the United Australia Party, which merged with other forces opposed to the Australian Labor Party (ALP). The Liberals went into coalition with the (then) Country Party to form a federal government in 1949 and the party then remained in office until 1972, when the ALP returned to power. Invited by the Governor-General to form a minority government in November 1975, Liberal leader Malcolm Fraser secured a majority for the coalition in elections in December, and retained office in 1977 and 1980. Returned to opposition by the March 1983 elections, the Liberals subsequently underwent an intricate series of leadership changes. Andrew Peacock, who took over as leader after the 1983 defeat, was replaced by John Howard in September 1985. The coalition with the National Party (the former Country Party) temporarily collapsed in 1987. Following the July 1987 federal election, in which the Liberals lost two seats in the House to hold 45, Peacock was appointed Howard's deputy, eventually ousting him and being reappointed leader in May 1989. But when the 1990 election saw the opposition fail to overturn Labor's majority, Peacock again resigned, to be succeeded by Dr John R. Hewson. Unpopular budget measures proposed by Hewson, including a 15% goods and services tax (GST) and cutbacks in the welfare state, were seen as contributing to the opposition's failure to oust an embattled Labor government in 1993, and Howard made another, unsuccessful bid for the Liberal leadership. Hewson stepped down in May 1994, to be succeeded by Alexander Downer. However, after eight months in the post, during which he secured the abandonment of the GST plan but got into political difficulties on other issues, Downer gave up the Liberal leadership in January 1995. Howard was elected unopposed to the post, completing his comeback at a time of auspicious opinion poll ratings for the opposition.

The Liberals expressed reservations about the ALP's proposal to abolish the monarchy, although the issue caused some friction with the firmly monarchist National Party and some Liberal republicans. The outcome was a Liberal pledge to convene a "people's convention" to consider the constitutional options before any decision was taken. Howard declared, on resuming the leadership, that the Liberals were opposed to tax increases and favoured reductions in public expenditure, this platform taking the party to a sweeping victory in the March 1996 general elections (with 75 seats on a 38.69% first-preference vote share), after which Howard formed a coalition government with the National Party.

The Liberal–National government came under challenge in 1997 from the new One Nation party, which attracted considerable support from conservative voters for its anti-immigration and pro-protection policies, which Howard was accused of not attacking sufficiently vigorously. Nevertheless, the coalition retained power in the October 1998 federal elections, in which Liberal representation in the lower house fell to 64 seats on the strength of a 34.1% first-preference vote share. Howard therefore continued as Prime Minister and played an important role in the November 1999 referendum rejection of an Australian republic by opposing the abolition of the monarchical system.

The Howard government was returned again in elections held in November 2001. The Liberal party won 68 seats and its partner, the National Party, 13. The government won domestic support, and international condemnation, for its refusal to allow asylum seekers rescued from their sinking vessel by the Norwegian freighter, the *Tampa*, to land on Australian soil. The September 11 terrorist attacks on the United States and subsequent commitment of Australian troops to the Persian Gulf and Afghanistan strengthened the vote for the government. In its third term, the Howard government remained strongly supportive of President Bush, commiting Australian troops to the war in Iraq. The Howard government was returned for a fourth term in elections held on Oct. 9, 2004, when it increased its representation in both houses of parliament. The Liberals won 40.56% of the first preference vote and increased their seats to 72, with 4 still undecided as of Oct. 13. The coalition was also poised to win a majority in the Senate, providing it with the assurance that its legislation would be passed in both houses from July 1, 2005.

The Liberal Party claims a membership of 80,000 and is structured in seven autonomous state and territory divisions (the exception being the Northern Territory, where it is associated with the Country Liberal Party).

The Liberal Party is affiliated to the International Democrat Union and the Pacific Democrat Union.

National Party of Australia (The Nationals)

Address. PO Box 6190, Kingston, ACT 2604
Telephone. (+61–2) 6273–3822
Fax. (+61–2) 6273–1745
Email. federal@nationalparty.org
Website. www.nationalparty.org
Leadership. John Anderson (leader); Mark Vaile (deputy leader); Helen Dickie (federal president); John Sharp (federal secretary)

A conservative force traditionally identified with rural interests, the Nationals emerged in 1920 under the original title of the Country Party from various state farmers' organizations. It was both a regional and sectional party, vigorously defending rural interests. Its electoral appeal has been based on defending free enterprise (but simultaneously arguing for government financial support for farmers), family values, national security and national economic development while emphasizing the concerns of people outside the relatively populous south-eastern coastal areas.

The party has participated in many federal coalition governments with the Liberal Party of Australia, although the two conservative parties have differences in emphasis, in geographical spread and on policy matters and electoral strategy. The Nationals have shown a strong ideological commitment to the preservation of the monarchy, on which the Liberals have been divided, and the parties have sometimes disagreed on whether they should refrain from contesting each other's safe seats. The Country Party entered a fed-

eral coalition pact with the Liberals in 1949 and, as the junior partner, shared power with it until 1972. After changing its name to the National Country Party in 1974, it returned to federal office, again in partnership with the Liberals, from 1975 to 1983. By the time it reverted to opposition it had become the National Party. In October 2003 the party opted for a change to the Nationals.

The Nationals' strongest base is in Queensland, where the state government was led for nearly two decades by the controversial right-winger Sir Johannes Bjelke-Petersen; he resigned in December 1987 after failing in a bid to take over the party's federal leadership and after damaging revelations of government corruption. At national level, the party lost two seats in the June 1987 election, leaving it with 19 members in the House, but picked up a sixth Senate seat. Leader Ian Sinclair was replaced by Charles Blunt, who lost his seat in the party's election disaster of 1990 and was succeeded by Tim Fischer. Left with only 14 seats in the House, the party was severely dented by the findings of an official inquiry into corruption in the Queensland state administration. Over 200 officials and businessmen, Bjelke-Petersen included, faced criminal charges.

The fifth successive federal election victory of the Australian Labor Party (ALP) in 1993 heightened the National Party's differences with the Liberals, leading to demands for an increased share of shadow cabinet portfolios for the smaller party. These problems were overcome, however, and the Nationals participated in the defeat of the ALP in the March 1996 federal elections, again becoming the junior government partner with the Liberals. In 1997 the National Party came under challenge from the new Queensland-based One Nation party, which attracted considerable support in rural areas for its anti-immigration and pro-protection policies. In the Queensland state election in June 1998 One Nation successes resulted in the National-Liberal government being replaced by an ALP administration.

Nevertheless, the federal Liberal-National coalition retained power in the October 1998 national elections, in which the Nationals lost only two of their 18 seats, on a first-preference vote share cut from 8.2% to 5.6%. In July 1999 Tim Fischer resigned as party leader and Deputy Prime Minister, being succeeded in both posts by deputy leader John Anderson, who retained ministerial responsibility for transport and regional services.

In November 1999 the Nationals helped to secure a decisive referendum decision against abolishing the monarchical system and moving to a republic. In February 2001 the party failed to regain power in Queensland, again being defeated by the ALP, in part because of a strong vote for One Nation. In the federal election held on Nov. 10, 2001, the Liberal-National coalition was returned to office, winning 13 House of Representatives seats with a small increase in its primary vote to 5.61%. Although the party's primary vote increased slightly in the October 2004 federal election to 5.91%, it may have lost a seat, giving it 12 in the new parliament. In the earlier 2004 Queensland state election, with One Nation all but disappearing, the Nationals performed poorly, losing to the ALP.

At 100,000, the Nationals have the highest membership of any Australian party. This, however, has not stopped its slow electoral decline and failure to recapture the votes lost to One Nation.

One Nation

Address. PO Box 428, Ipswich, Queensland 4305
Telephone. (+61–7) 3281–0077
Fax. (+61–7) 3281–0899
Email. onenation@gil.com.au
Website. www.onenation.com.au
Leadership. Niel Russell-Taylor (national president);

Patricia Buckham (national secretary)

One Nation was launched in March 1997 by Pauline Hanson, a former fish-and-chip shop proprietor who had been elected to the federal House of Representatives as an independent from Queensland in March 1996 and had gained national prominence for her outspoken populist views. The party has called for curbs on immigration from Asia, cuts in what it regards as disproportionately large welfare provision for Aborigines and the reversal of recent court decisions establishing the land title rights of the Aboriginal people. It also advocates tariff barriers to protect Australian enterprises from "unfair" foreign competition.

Drawing particular support from relatively disadvantaged rural voters, One Nation stunned the established parties by winning 23% of first-preference votes in the Queensland state elections in June 1998, thereby taking 11 of the 89 seats. In the federal elections in October 1998, however, it failed to win a single lower house seat (Hanson narrowly losing hers), despite taking 8.4% of first preferences, and returned only a single member to the Senate.

In early 1999, 10 of the 11 One Nation members of the Queensland legislature left the party and one resigned his seat in protest against the party's "autocratic and undemocratic structure". In August 1999 the Queensland Supreme Court ruled that One Nation's registration as a political party had been "induced by fraud and misrepresentation". In January 2000 the police raided One Nation offices in Queensland and New South Wales and seized hundreds of documents relating to the party's membership and finances. Two state One Nation branches subsequently lost their registered status, and the party appeared to be on a downward spiral. However, in state elections in Queensland and Western Australia in February 2001 One Nation bounced back, winning around 9% of the vote (and three seats in Queensland), effectively ensuring ALP victories in each state by taking votes from the Liberal and National parties.

The party's state successes were not repeated federally. In the November 2001 elections the party's vote was halved to 4.34% of first preference votes. After the election, Pauline Hanson announced her retirement from active involvement with One Nation, but re-emerged to stand for a New South Wales Legislative Council seat as an independent in the March 2003 election. She was unsuccessful, and further misfortune followed when in August 2003 she was jailed for three years after being found guilty of fraudulently registering a party and improperly claiming almost $500,000 from the Queensland Electoral Commission. She was held in a high-security jail until her conviction was overturned by the Queensland Court of Appeal in November 2003. Despite protestations that she would never return to politics, she unsuccessfully contested a Queensland Senate seat as an independent in the October 2004 federal election. Her former party continued its decline, taking only 1.16% of the first preference vote in the House of Representatives, and losing the party's only senator with a first preference vote of 1.7%.

Other Parties

Australian Republican Movement (ARM), a non-partisan organization, rather than a political party, formed to advance the campaign for the removal of the British monarchy from the Australian constitution.
Address. PO Box A870, Sydney South, NSW 1235
Telephone. (+61–2) 9267–8022
Fax. (+61–2) 9267–8155
Email. republic@ozemail.com.au
Website. www.republic.org.au
Leadership. John Warhurst (chairman); James Terrie (national director)

Christian Democratic Party (CDP), also known as the Fred Nile Group after its leader, promotes Christian values in parliament and evaluates all legislation on biblical principles. It won 0.62% of the national vote in the October 2004 federal lower house elections and has two members in the New South Wales upper chamber.
Address. PO Box 141, Sydney, NSW 2001
Telephone. (+ 61-2) 9645-9092
Fax. (+61-2) 9645-9093
Website. www.christiandemocratic.org.au
Leadership. Rev. Fred Nile (national president)

Citizens Electoral Council of Australia (CEC) was established in Queensland in 1988 and is affiliated with the United States based LaRouche movement. The well-funded CEC won 0.35% of the House of Representatives vote in the 2004 federal election.
Address. PO Box 376, Coburg, Vic, 3058
Telephone. (+61-3) 9354-0544
Fax. (+61-3) 9354 0166
Email cec@cecaust.com.au
Website. www.cecaust.com.au
Leadership. Craig Isherwood (national secretary)

Family First was founded in 2001 and is closely associated with the evangelical Christian movement, especially the Assemblies of God, a rapidly growing Pentecostal church. In 2002 the party won a seat in the South Australian Legislative Council. In the 2004 federal election the party won 1.96% of first preference votes in the lower house and 1.77% in the Senate, where because of preference didtrubutions the party appears likely to win two senate seats.
Address. PO Box 1042, Campbelltown, SA, 5074
Telephone. (+61-8 8368 6112)
Fax. (+61-8 8266 4069)
Email. admin@familyfirst.org.au
Website familyfirst.org.au
Leadership. Andrea Mason (federal party leader)

Shooters' Party, seeking to represent the rights of law-abiding firearms owners, it has one representative, John Tingle in the New South Wales upper house.
Address. PO Box 376, Baulkham Hills, NSW 1755
Telephone. (+61–2) 9686–2396
Fax. (+61–2) 9686–2396
Email. chairman@shootersparty.org.au
Website. www.shootersparty.org.au
Leadership. David Leyonjelm (chairman)

Austria

Capital: Vienna
Population: 8,174,762 (2004E)

First founded in 1919 following the demise of the Austro-Hungarian Empire in World War I, the Republic of Austria was re-established after World War II and obtained international recognition as a "sovereign, independent and democratic state" under the Austrian State Treaty signed on May 15, 1955, by Austria, France, the UK, the USA and the USSR.

The Austrian constitution provides for a parliamentary system of government based on elections by secret ballot and by "free, equal and universal suffrage"; as amended in 1945, it proscribes any attempt to revive the pre-war Nazi Party. There is a bicameral parliament consisting of a 183-member lower house called the National Council (*Nationalrat*) and an upper house called the Federal Council (*Bundesrat*), which in mid-2004 had 62 members. Together, they form the Federal Assembly (*Bundesversammlung*). The *Nationalrat* is elected for a four-year term under a highly proportional representation system (subject to a minimum requirement of 4% of the national vote) by all citizens over 18 years of age. Members of the *Bundesrat* are elected for from four to six years by the legislatures of the nine Austrian provinces (*Länder*), each of which has an elected assembly (*Landtag*). The President of the Republic (*Bundespräsident*) is elected for a six-year term (to a maximum of two consecutive terms) by universal suffrage, the functions of the post being mainly ceremonial but including the appointment of the Federal Chancellor (*Bundeskanzler*) as head of government, who recommends ministerial appointments for confirmation by the President. Each member of the government must enjoy the confidence of a majority of members of the *Nationalrat*. Austria joined what became the European Union on Jan. 1, 1995, and as of 2004 elects 18 (hitherto 21) members to the European Parliament.

Under the Parties Financing Act of 1975, parties represented in the *Nationalrat* are granted federal budget support (for publicity and campaigning) in the form of a basic sum and additional amounts in proportion to the number of votes received in the previous election, subject to at least 1% of the valid votes being obtained. Parties also receive state contributions to their national and European Parliament election expenses. The total such support paid in 2002 was €25,840,000 (ca. $31,810,000), dropping to an estimated €14,380,000 (ca. $17,710,000) in 2003, when no national election was held. Of this funding, the total available to the Social Democratic Party of Austria (SPÖ), for example, was €8,950,000 in 2002 and an estimated €5,240,000 in 2003. Separate state assistance is available to research foundations linked to the parties, totalling an estimated €9,140,000 in 2003, of which, for example, the SPÖ-linked Karl Renner Institute received €3,050,000.

Elections to the *Nationalrat* on Nov. 24, 2002, resulted as follows: Austrian People's Party (ÖVP) 79 seats (with 42.3% of the vote), Social Democratic Party of Austria (SPÖ) 69 (36.5%), Freedom Party of Austria (FPÖ) 18 (10.0%), The Greens–Green Alternative 17 (9.5%). In presidential elections on April 25, 2004, former SPÖ *Nationalrat* President, Heinz Fischer, defeated ÖVP Foreign Minister Benita Ferrero-Waldner by 52.4% to 47.6% of the vote.

In the European Parliament elections held on June 13, 2004, the opposition Social Democrats performed marginally better than Chancellor Wolfgang Schüssel's conservative People's Party. Very significant, however, were the losses suffered by the far-right Freedom Party. Its share of the vote slumped dramatically from 23.4% in the last election to 6.4%, losing the party four of the five seats it had previously held. The other surprise of the contest was the success of a list fielded by independent candidate Hans-Peter Martin, an MEP who had waged an anti-fraud campaign after being kicked out of his party for exposing what he saw as expenses abuses by his European colleagues. On a turnout of 42.44% the SPÖ, with 33.4% of the vote, won 7 seats (+1); the ÖVP (32.7% of the vote) won 6 seats; the GA (12.7% of the vote) won 2 seats; Hans-Peter Martin (Independent anti-fraud list, 14.0% of the vote) won 2 seats (+2); and the FPÖ 1 seat (-4).

Austrian People's Party
Österreichische Volkspartei (ÖVP)

Address. Lichtenfelsgasse 7, A–1010 Vienna
Telephone. (43–1) 401–260
Fax. (43–1) 4012–6000
Email. info@oevp.at
Website. www.oevp.at
Leadership. Wolfgang Schüssel (chairman); Wilhelm Molterer (parliamentary group leader); Andreas Khol (*Nationalrat* President); Reinhold Lopatka (general secretary)

Founded in 1945 from pre-war Christian democratic groups, the ÖVP was the leading government party from 1945-66, in coalition with what later became the Social Democratic Party of Austria (SPÖ). In sole power from 1966, the ÖVP was narrowly defeated by the SPÖ in the 1970 election, after which it was in opposition for 16 years. Although it lost ground in the 1986 election, simultaneous SPÖ losses dictated the formation of the first of a series of ÖVP-SPÖ "grand coalitions" that were to rule the country until 1999, with the ÖVP as junior partner. Earlier in 1986, the ÖVP had become enmeshed in public controversy over Kurt Waldheim, whose election as President with ÖVP backing was accompanied by claims that as a German Army officer he had at least been fully aware of Nazi atrocities in the Balkans during World War II.

Waldheim's successor as President, Thomas Klestil, was elected in 1992 as the ÖVP-backed nominee. But other elections in the early 1990s showed falling support for the ÖVP, mainly to the benefit of the Freedom Party of Austria (FPÖ). In the October 1994 federal election, the ÖVP slumped from 60 to 52 seats and to a low of 27.7% of the vote. Given their determination to exclude the FPÖ from government, the ÖVP and SPÖ both felt obliged to resurrect their coalition. Vice-Chancellor Erhard Busek later paid the price of the ÖVP's election setbacks, being replaced in April 1995 as party chair and Vice-Chancellor by Wolfgang Schüssel.

The SPÖ-ÖVP coalition unexpectedly collapsed in October 1995 over budget policy differences. To general surprise, the ÖVP emerged from the election of Dec. 17 with slightly higher representation of 53 seats, on a vote share of 28.3%, and in March 1996 entered a further coalition headed by the SPÖ. In Austria's first direct Euro-elections in October 1996 the ÖVP headed the poll with 29.6% and seven seats, following which Klestil was re-elected as President in April 1997 with ÖVP backing. Strains arose in the coalition in March 1998 when the SPÖ insisted on maintaining Austria's neutrality, whereas the ÖVP favoured a commitment to NATO membership. In the June 1999 Euro-elections the ÖVP slipped to second place behind the SPÖ in percentage terms, although it improved to 30.6% of the vote and again won seven seats.

The governmental dominance of the SPÖ, combined with the electoral rise of the FPÖ, culminated in the ÖVP being reduced, very narrowly in terms of the popular vote, to third-party status in the October 1999 national elections. Although it retained 52 seats, its vote share was a post-war low of 26.9%. Schüssel initially announced the party would go into opposition, but in February 2000 formed a controversial coalition with the FPÖ, whose presence in Austria's government caused the EU to impose diplomatic sanctions on Austria. Schüssel stood his ground, however, and the sanctions were eventually lifted in September 2000.

Schüssel's leadership of his party was greatly strengthened and the ÖVP reinvigorated by the sanctions, the ÖVP's reacquisition of the chancellorship (last held in 1970) and by the manifest success of his strategy of co-opting and thus demystifying the FPÖ. At the Styrian provincial election of October 2000, the party gained 11 percentage points, winning 47.3% of the vote and an absolute majority of seats. At the general election of Nov. 24, 2002 – held early because of the 'Knittelfeld' crisis within the FPÖ – the ÖVP experienced the greatest ever increase in an Austrian party's share of the vote. With 42.3% and 79 seats it also came ahead of the SPÖ for the first time since 1966. At provincial elections in March 2003, the ÖVP retained the governorships of Lower Austria, where its historic absolute majority of the vote was restored, and of Tyrol, where it obtained an absolute majority of seats.

Thereafter, however, the ÖVP lost electoral ground, largely because of squabbling within its coalition partner and the unpopularity of the government's policies of economic retrenchment, privatization and welfare state reform. In September 2003 it retained the Upper Austrian governorship, despite a small reduction in its share of the vote at the *Landtag* election. In March 2004, however, an analogous decline in Salzburg resulted in the ÖVP's first ever loss of the governorship of that *Land*, whilst in Carinthia the party suffered a virtual halving (to 11.6%) of its vote and has been replaced by the SPÖ as the FPÖ's partner in the *Land* government. In view of these setbacks, Schüssel's leadership of his party has come under renewed internal criticism.

Claiming a membership of c.300,000, the ÖVP is affiliated to the International Democrat Union and the Christian Democrat International. The party's six representatives in the European Parliament sit in the European People's Party/European Democrats group.

Freedom Party of Austria
Freiheitliche Partei Österreichs (FPÖ)

Address. Theobaldgasse 19, A-1060 Vienna
Telephone. (43–1) 512–3535
Fax. (43–1) 512–3539
Email. bgst@fpoe.at
Website. www.fpoe.or.at
Leadership. Ursula Haubner (chairperson); Heinz-Christian Strache and Günther Steinkellner (deputy chairpersons); Herbert Scheibner (parliamentary group leader); Uwe Scheuch (general secretary)

Often described by the international media as far-right or even "neo-Nazi" because of its historical antecedents, opposition to immigration and other populist policies, the FPÖ vigorously rejects such descriptions. It was formed in 1956 as a merger of three right-wing formations, notably the League of Independents, which had won 14 lower house seats in 1953 on a platform of opposition to the post-war system of Proporz, under which state jobs and resources were largely shared out between the two main parties. Initially supported by many former Nazis, the FPÖ remained for many beyond the political pale and languished at around 6-7% of the vote. From the late 1960s, Friedrich Peter (FPÖ leader from 1958-78) sought to modernise the party's programmatic profile and membership. In 1983 the FPÖ won 5% of the vote and 12 seats under the liberal leadership of Norbert Steger and joined a coalition government with what later became the Social Democratic Party of Austria (SPÖ). This alienated the party's traditionally protest-oriented and right-wing grass-root activists and weakened it in the polls. The ensuing intra-party conflict culminated in Steger being replaced by youthful populist Jörg Haider in September 1986, whereupon the SPÖ unilaterally terminated the coalition.

At the November 1986 election the FPÖ almost doubled its vote share to 9.7% on a populist platform including opposition to party clientelism. In 1989 Haider became governor of the southern province of Carinthia in a coalition between the FPÖ and the Austrian People's Party (ÖVP), but was obliged to resign two years later after asserting in a *Landtag* debate that "an orderly employment policy was carried out in the Third Reich, which the government in Vienna cannot manage". Further honing its populist message, the FPÖ

increased its vote to 16.6% at the 1990 federal election and thereafter made a series of major gains in provincial elections. Haider replaced the FPÖ's traditionally strong support for European integration with opposition to European Union membership, but failed to prevent the electorate voting decisively in favour in June 1994. After registering a further advance in the Vorarlberg provincial election in September 1994, the FPÖ's share of the vote rose to 22.6% (and 42 seats) in the October federal elections.

Caught off guard by the sudden collapse of the federal SPÖ-ÖVP coalition in October 1995, the FPÖ slipped to 40 seats and 21.9% at December's snap election. Yet the re-establishment of the SPÖ-ÖVP coalition gave the party renewed momentum at Austria's first direct Euro-elections of October 1996, at which it won 27.5% of the vote and six seats. Its subsequent provincial election successes featured a 42% vote share in Carinthia in March 1999, as a result of which Haider again became provincial governor (in coalition with the SPÖ and the ÖVP).

In the June 1999 Euro-elections the FPÖ fell back to 23.5% and five seats. But Haider achieved a major advance in the October federal election, his party's 26.9% vote share being slightly greater than the ÖVP's and giving it 52 *Nationalrat* seats, the same number as the ÖVP. The eventual outcome in February 2000 was the formation of a highly controversial ÖVP–FPÖ coalition in which the FPÖ took half of the ministerial posts, although the coalition agreement contained none of the FPÖ's more radical policies. Haider himself not only did not figure in the new ministerial team but also bowed out as FPÖ chairman, being succeeded by the new Vice-Chancellor, Susanne Riess-Passer. He nevertheless remained effective leader of the party.

Soon after the diplomatic sanctions imposed on Austria because of the FPÖ's entry into government were lifted in September 2000, the party started to experience the political consequences of its abrupt transition from strident populist protest to incumbency. From late 2000 onwards, it lost substantial ground at virtually all elections, including in Vienna in March 2001 (minus 8 percentage points and 8 seats). Haider blamed the party's participation in a federal government which "needed to show more concern for the common people". The gulf between the FPÖ's government team and its uncompromising grass-roots (egged on by Haider, who was then still a member of the coalition committee) grew. Divisions crystallized in particular around various government policies that were at odds with the party's longstanding populist message. These included the decision to fund interceptor fighters and delay tax reductions at a time of welfare cuts; the government's acceptance of EU enlargement eastwards despite concerns over the Czech Republic's refusal to rescind the Benes decrees (enacted after World War II to expropriate the Sudetenland Germans) or close down a nuclear plant that the FPÖ and many others argued was unsafe; and what the party grass-roots regarded as wholly inadequate safeguards against post-enlargement migration of eastern European workers.

Added to such substantive concerns were petty jealousies, political rivalries and a patent inability to recruit and retain competent ministers. The outcome was a public and highly dramatic process of political self-destruction that peaked in the so-called "Knittelfeld rebellion" of September 2002, which saw Ries-Passer's leadership team resign its government and party offices because it was unable to convince the grass-roots of the need to compromise. Schüssel called early elections for November 2002, at which the FPÖ crashed to 10% of the vote and 18 seats. Though the coalition was eventually reformed, the FPÖ received only three seats in cabinet and has since suffered further electoral setbacks, the last being at the Euro-elections of June 2004, when it could muster only 6.3% of the vote and one seat. By contrast, at the Carinthian *Landtag* elections of March 2004, Haider not only retained the governorship, but marginally increased his party's share of the vote (to 42.4%).

Though Haider remained the power behind the throne, the FPÖ has formally had four leaders since September 2002: Herbert Scheibner, former Infrastructure Minister Matthias Reichhold, Social Affairs Minister Herbert Haupt and, since July 3, 2004, Haider's sister, Ursula Haubner, who was elected at an extraordinary party congress. She took over an organizationally weak and demoralized party that had lost more than half of its state funding. Persistent calls for party unity notwithstanding, it appeared likely in mid-2004 that the internal disputes would continue.

In mid-2004, the FPÖ headed the Carinthia government, but only participated in one other provincial administration: that of Vorarlberg (in coalition with the ÖVP). It was reluctant to disclose its membership figures, which have presumably dropped from the 2000 level of 51,296. The FPÖ does not belong to a transnational party federation and its single MEP is part of the "unattached" contingent.

The Greens–Green Alternative
Die Grünen–Die Grüne Alternativen (GA)
Address. Lindengasse 40, A–1070 Vienna
Telephone. (43–1) 5212–5201
Fax. (43–1) 526–9110
Email. bundesbuero@gruene.at
Website. www.gruene.at
Leadership. Alexander Van der Bellen (spokesperson and parliamentary group leader); Eva Glawischnig (deputy spokesperson); Madeleine Petrovic (deputy spokesperson and leader of Lower Austrian *Landtag* group); Michaela Sbury (business manager)

The GA was formed in 1987 as a union of three alternative groupings which had won a total of eight seats in the 1986 federal election, although the conservative United Greens of Austria subsequently opted to retain their organizational independence. Its component groups had already become influential through campaigning on environmental issues, their biggest success being the referendum decision in 1978 not to proceed with the commissioning of the country's first nuclear power station at Zwentendorf. As a parliamentary party, the GA has not only sought to bring environmental concerns to the forefront of economic and industrial decision-making but has also pressed for the dismantling of the Proporz system whereby the two main post-war parties have shared out the top posts in government bodies and nationalized industries. Compared to many Green parties abroad, the GA's policy profile is relatively moderate and its leader enjoys very high public approval ratings.

The GA increased its representation to 10 seats in the 1990 federal election and thereafter unsuccessfully opposed the government's policy of joining the European Union. In the October 1994 federal elections the formation advanced to 7% of the national vote, giving it 13 seats, but it fell back to 4.8% and nine seats in the December 1995 elections. In Austria's first direct elections to the European Parliament in October 1996, the GA improved to 6.8%, which gave it one seat. It doubled this tally to two seats in the June 1999 Euro-elections (with 9.2% of the vote) and then advanced to 14 *Nationalrat* seats in the October 1999 federal elections (with 7.4% of the vote). The party's growing success continued at the general election of November 2002 (9.5% and 17 seats) and the Euro-election of June 2004 (12.75% and two seats). A key consequence of the GA's enhanced electoral strength has been the perception that it may soon enter national government. Until the end of the 2002 campaign, this seemed most likely to be in coalition with the SPÖ. Yet, to the surprise of many, the GA was invited by Chancellor Schüssel to post-election discussions about a possible coalition with the ÖVP and that option has remained a topic of conversation ever since.

At provincial level the GA was in mid-2004 represented in all nine of Austria's *Landtage*. Its share of the vote is greatest in urban Vienna (12.5% in March 2001) and in Tyrol (15.6% in 2003), where transit traffic constitutes a major political theme. The GA passed a political milestone in December 2003, when following its strong showing at the Upper Austrian *Landtag* election of September 2003 it entered a provincial government for the first time. The fact that its partner was the ÖVP significantly weakens the arguments of those who seek to portray the GA as a peripheral party lacking governmental potential.

Claiming an individual membership of 3,000 as well as many affiliated groups, the GA is a member of the European Federation of Green Parties. Its two representatives in the European Parliament sit in the Greens/European Free Alliance group.

Social Democratic Party ofAustria
Sozialdemokratische Partei Österreichs (SPÖ)
Address. Löwelstrasse 18, A–1014 Vienna
Telephone. (43–1) 53427
Fax. (43–1) 535–9683
Email. international@spoe.or.at
Website. www.spoe.at
Leadership. Alfred Gusenbauer (chairman and parliamentary party leader); Josef Cap (executive parliamentary party leader); Doris Bures & Norbert Darabos (party managers)

The SPÖ is descended from the 1874 Social Democratic Workers' Party, which advocated social revolution and the transformation of the Austro-Hungarian Empire into a federation of co-existing nations. It developed a mass party organization and became the largest parliamentary party on the strength of universal male franchise, but had no direct political influence before World War I. On the establishment of the Austrian Republic in 1919 it was briefly in government under Karl Renner, but went into opposition in 1920, formally remaining committed to "Austro-Marxism" and to resorting to armed struggle if the bourgeoisie sought to resist social revolution. In the early 1930s, the pro-fascist Dollfus government adopted authoritarian methods, dissolving the *Nationalrat* in March 1933 and introducing rule by decree. The party's paramilitary Republican Defence League, itself already banned, responded by mounting an uprising in Vienna in February 1934, but was quickly defeated. Following the proclamation of a quasi-fascist constitution three months later, the party went underground and participated with other democratic forces in anti-fascist resistance until German forces occupied Austria in 1938.

On the re-establishment of the Republic in 1945, the SPÖ adopted a pro-Western stance and participated in an all-party coalition government including the Communist Party of Austria. From November 1947, however, it became the junior partner in a two-party coalition with the Austrian People's Party (ÖVP) that endured until 1966, when the SPÖ went into opposition. In 1970 it returned to power as the sole governing party under the leadership of Bruno Kreisky, forming a minority government until 1971, when it gained an absolute *Nationalrat* majority it retained in the 1975 and 1979 elections. A party congress in 1978 renounced public ownership as a necessary requirement of democratic socialism.

Losing its overall majority in the 1983 election, the SPÖ formed a coalition with the Freedom Party of Austria (FPÖ) and Kreisky handed over the government and party leadership to Fred Sinowatz. The day after the SPÖ's candidate failed to win the presidential election in June 1986, Sinowatz resigned and was succeeded as Chancellor by Franz Vranitzky, who in September 1986 terminated the coalition because of the FPÖ's move to the right. Having lost ground sharply in November elections, the SPÖ formed a "grand coalition" with the ÖVP in January 1987, under Vranitzky's chancellorship. Later that year an SPÖ congress gave qualified support to the government's privatization programme.

The SPÖ-ÖVP coalition was maintained after the October 1990 elections, in which the SPÖ remained the largest party. In 1991 the party renamed itself "Social Democratic" rather than "Socialist", retaining the SPÖ abbreviation. The government's key external policy of EC/EU membership was endorsed by the electorate in June 1994 by a 2:1 majority. In the October 1994 federal elections, the SPÖ vote slipped to a new post-war low of 35.2% and the party opted to continue its coalition with the ÖVP. In October 1995, however, the coalition collapsed over budget policy differences, with the result that new elections were held in December. Against most predictions, Vranitzky led the SPÖ to a significant electoral recovery, yielding 71 seats and 38.1% of the vote. In March 1996 he was appointed to a fifth term as Chancellor, heading a further coalition between the SPÖ and the ÖVP.

Austria's first direct elections to the European Parliament in October 1996 produced a slump in SPÖ support, to 29.2% and six seats. In January 1997 Vranitzky resigned as Chancellor, a week after the SPÖ had pushed through the controversial privatization of the Creditanstalt, the country's second-largest bank. The architect of the privatization, Finance Minister Viktor Klima, succeeded him as Chancellor and, in April 1997, as SPÖ chairman. Subsequent regional elections showed an erosion of SPÖ support, which recovered only to 31.7% in the June 1999 European Parliament elections, in which the party increased from six to seven seats.

The October 1999 parliamentary elections produced a setback for both federal coalition parties, the SPÖ falling to 33.2% and 65 seats. As leader of still the largest party, Klima was asked to form a new government, but this attempt failed and the SPÖ went into opposition to a controversial new coalition of the ÖVP and the FPÖ. Klima resigned as party chairman in February 2000 and was succeeded by Alfred Gusenbauer. He inherited a party in considerable debt, shell-shocked at being catapulted into opposition – a role the SPÖ had only experienced for four of the preceding 55 years – and at risk of severe internal conflict over policy. During the early months of his leadership, Austria's political agenda was dominated by the sanctions imposed upon the government by the remaining members of the EU, making it all but impossible for Gusenbauer to focus public attention on issues he thought might help his party, including, for example, the government's unpopular economic retrenchment policies.

Yet the SPÖ's electoral fortunes did revive, first at Vienna's 2001 provincial election, where the party won 47% of the vote and 50 (of 100) seats. In the November 2002 general election the party came second with 69 seats (36.5% of the vote); at the presidential election of April 2004 its candidate won by 52% to 48%; and in the EU elections of June 2004 it increased its share of the vote by four percentage points to 33% and took seven of the 18 seats. The SPÖ also made advances at all provincial elections held between 2001 and mid-2004. Increases ranged from 3 to 13 percentage points (Lower Austria in March 2003 and Salzburg in March 2004 respectively). In mid-2004, the SPÖ held the governorships of Vienna (in coalition with the ÖVP), of Burgenland (in coalition with the ÖVP and FPÖ) and – for the first time ever – that of Salzburg (in coalition with the ÖVP). It also participated in the governments of the other six provinces.

Though he managed to somewhat reduce the intra-party influence of the SPÖ's trade union wing, by mid-2004 Gusenbauer had not realized his ambition to radically overhaul the party's cumbersome apparatus. Nor had he been able to capitalize fully on the frequent crises within and between the governing parties. Moreover, the post-2002 election coalition discussions between the ÖVP and GA mean the latter could in principle coalesce with the ÖVP, which in turn means that even if the SPÖ were to emerge from a subsequent general election as the strongest party, it could potentially still find itself relegated to an opposition role.

In mid-2004, the SPÖ's membership was about 360,000 (down from a high of 721,262 in 1979). The SPÖ is a founder member of the Socialist International and its seven representatives in the European Parliament are members of the Party of European Socialists group.

Other Parties

Communist Party of Austria (*Kommunistische Partei Österreichs, KPÖ*), founded by pro-Soviet Social Democrats in 1919. In government from 1945-47 and represented in the lower house until 1959; it was until the 1990s reputedly one of the richest Austrian parties on the strength of industrial holdings acquired under the post-war Soviet occupation. In late 2003, it finally lost a lengthy legal battle to control the assets of the former East German company Novum and found itself in severe financial straits. It took only 0.3% of the vote in 1994 parliamentary elections, improving to 0.48% in 1999 and 0.56% in 2002.
Address. Drechslergasse. 42, A–1140 Vienna
Telephone. (43–1) 503–6580 0
Fax. (43–1) 503–411/499
Email. kpoe@magnet.at
Website. www.kpoe.at
Leadership. Walter Baier (chairman)

Hans-Peter Martin List – For Real Control in Brussels (*Liste Dr Hans-Peter Martin – Für echte Kontrolle in Brüssel* (HPM)), launched in May 2004, the HPM List won 14% of the vote and two seats at the 2004 European Parliament elections. Having achieved Europe-wide publicity for his attacks on fellow MEPs' alleged abuse of the European Parliament's lax regulations on travel expenses, Hans-Peter Martin fought the elections on a ticket opposing EU waste and corruption. His success owed much to the support of the tabloid *Kronenzeitung*, Austria's largest circulation newspaper. An author and former *Spiegel* journalist, Martin had headed the SPÖ list at the 1999 European elections, but soon broke with his delegation and the party. Though it has suggested it might contest Austria's next general election, in July 2004 it remained unclear whether the HPM List would turn out to be just a flash party.
Address. Böcklinstraße 90, A–1020 Vienna
Telephone. (43) 664201 80 37
Fax. (43–1) 503 06 67 20
Email. office@hpm.net
Website. www.hpmartin.net
Leadership. Hans-Peter Martin (party leader)

Liberal Forum (LIF, *Die Liberalen*), launched in February 1993 by five *Nationalrat* deputies of the Freedom Party of Austria (FPÖ) who disagreed with Haider's anti-EU and anti-foreigner stance and were led by Heide Schmidt. Given the prevailing mood of anti-party scepticism, the LIF eschewed the label "party" and terms its members "partners". It sought to position itself as market oriented and libertarian and in June 1996 became a full member of the Liberal International.

The LIF achieved successes in the federal elections of October 1994 (5.7% and 11 seats) and December 1995 (5.7% and 10 seats), as well as at the October 1996 European

Parliament elections (4.3% and one seat). However, its failure to surmount the 4% barrier at any subsequent national election means it no longer has *Nationalrat* or European Parliament seats. Though it won representation in the *Landtage* of Lower Austria (1993), Styria (1995) and Vienna (1996), it has since failed to get elected to any provincial parliament. These failures unleashed severe internal conflict regarding the leadership of Schmidt, who resigned in 2000, and the relative significance of social and economic liberalism. In October 2002, the LIF obtained only 0.98% of the general election vote.

Address. Dürrergasse 6/10, A–1060 Vienna

Telephone. (43–1) 503 06 67

Fax. (43–1) 503 06 67 20

Email. office@lif.at

Website. www.liberale.at

Leadership. Alexander Tach (party spokesperson)

Azerbaijan

Capital: Baku
Population: 7,868,385 (2004E)

The Azerbaijan Republic declared independence from the USSR in August 1991, becoming a sovereign member of the Commonwealth of Independent States (CIS) created on the dissolution of the USSR in December 1991. Interim constitutional arrangements based on the 1978 Soviet-era text applied until the adoption of a new constitution in November 1995, providing for an executive President, who is directly elected by universal adult suffrage for a five-year term and who appoints the Prime Minister and other ministers. Legislative authority is vested in a 125-seat National Assembly (*Milli Majlis*), also elected for a five-year term, with 100 members being returned from single-member constituencies by simple majority and 25 proportionally from party lists which obtain at least 6% of the national vote.

Since independence Azerbaijan has moved to a limited multi-party system, qualified by the exigencies of hostilities with Armenia over Nagorno Karabakh, internal political conflict and the continuing preponderance of former Communists in the state bureaucracy. Stringent registration requirements for Assembly elections held on Nov. 12 and 26, 1995, and Feb. 4, 1996, resulted in only eight parties being deemed eligible to stand (and about a dozen being deemed ineligible), with the consequence that a UN/OSCE monitoring mission subsequently concluded that the elections, producing an overwhelming majority for the ruling New Azerbaijan Party (YAP), had not been conducted fairly.

Similar criticism was directed at the conduct of presidential elections held on Oct. 11, 1998, in which Heydar Aliyev (YAP) was re-elected with an official tally of 76.1% of the vote against five other candidates. International pressure resulted in a last-minute relaxation of registration requirements for Assembly elections held on Nov. 5, 2000, in which 12 parties and one bloc were allowed to stand, although the process was again strongly criticized by both the domestic opposition and international observers. The results were annulled in 11 electoral districts, where further polling took place on Jan. 7, 2001. According to the official results, the YAP won 75 seats (with 62.5% of the proportional vote), the Azerbaijan Popular Front 6 (10.9%), the Civic Unity Party 3 (6.4%), the Azerbaijan Communist Party 2 (6.3%), New Equality Party (*Musavat*) 2 (4.9%), the Azerbaijan National Independence Party (AMIP-Istiqlal) 2 (3.9%), other parties 5 and independents 29 (one seat being unfilled). The two AMIP-Istiqlal deputies were subsequently expelled from the party.

In August 2003, Ilham Aliyev, son of President Heydar Aliyev, was named Prime Minister by presidential decree. On August 4, after limited debate, the parliament approved the appointment by a 101-1 vote. Opposition MPs boycotted the vote and Isa Gambar, head of the *Musavat* party, denounced the appointment as "usurpation of power".

The presidential elections in October 2003 exacerbated the internal political conflicts. In June 2003, the ruling YAP named the incumbent President Aliyev as its candidate despite his deteriorating health. On Oct. 2, just two weeks before the election day, he withdrew his candidacy in favor of his son, Ilham Aliyev, who had earlier been nominated as a candidate by a citizens' initiative group.

There was a lengthy but ultimately unsuccessful process among opposition parties to reach agreement on a single presidential candidate. In September, two opposition parties agreed on a single presidential candidate when the supreme council of the reformist wing of the divided Azerbaijan Popular Front (AKXC) decided to support the Azerbaijan National Independence Party (AMIP) chairman, Etibar Mamedov – the Azerbaijan Popular Front reformist faction chairman, Ali Kerimov, withdrawing his candidacy. The Azerbaijan Democratic Party (ADP) leader Rasul Guliyev, who was denied registration as a candidate, endorsed *Musavat* candidate Isa Gambar.

Presidential elections were held on Oct. 16, 2003. Ilham Aliyev was credited with 76.84% of the vote, with his nearest contender Isa Gambar taking 13.97%. All other candidates were below 3%, except for Lala Shovket Gadjieva, former chairwoman of the Liberal Party of Azerbaijan, with 3.62%.

The elections were marred by widespread voting irregularities including ballot box stuffing, multiple voting, and intimidation of voters and election observers. Opposition leaders denounced the results as falsified. On the election night, violence erupted in front of the Musavat headquarters. Demonstrations were followed by a wave of detentions of over 600 people. The OSCE Election Report concluded that the arrests constituted a general crackdown on some opposition parties. Several leaders of opposition parties were among those detained. While *Musavat* and ADP activists appeared to be the primary targets, AMIP, Azerbaijan Popular Front and Liberal Party supporters were also detained. In a series of trials held in the first months of 2004, over 30 detainees were sentenced to to prison terms of three to six years under Art. 220, para. 1 (participation in mass disorders) and Art. 315, para. 2 (resistance to authority representatives) of Azerbaijan's Criminal Code.

Seven prominent opposition figures – Musavat deputy chairmen Arif Hadjili and Ibrahim Ibrahimli, People's Party chairman Panakh Huseinov, Umid party Chairman Igbal Agazade, ADP secretary general Sardar Djalaloglu, Etimad Asadov, chaiman of the Society of Handicapped Veterans of the Karabakh war, and Rauf Arifoglu, editor of the opposition paper *Yeni Musavat* – were also arrested and held in custody from October 2003 on charges of involvement in the Baku clashes following the disputed presidential ballot. The preliminary hearing of their trial started on May 7, 2004.

Azerbaijan Communist Party
Azerbaycan Kommunist Partiyasi (AKP)

Address. 29 Hussein Javid Prospekti, Room 637te, Baku
Telephone. (994–12) 380151
Leadership. Ramiz Ahmedov (chairman)

The AKP governed the republic during the Soviet era, latterly under the hardline rule of Ayaz Mutalibov. In elections to the 360-member Azerbaijan Supreme Soviet in September-October 1990, the AKP won 280 of the 340 seats contested (with 78% of the vote) and Mutalibov was re-elected President unopposed in post-independence direct elections in September 1991 which were boycotted by the opposition parties. Following military setbacks in Nagorno Karabakh, Mutalibov was forced to resign in March 1992 and fled to Russia after a shortlived return to power in May (for which alleged coup attempt criminal charges were later preferred against him). The AKP was effectively suspended under the subsequent government of the Azerbaijan Popular Front, which replaced the Supreme Soviet with an interim 50-member National Assembly dominated by Azerbaijan Popular Front members. Nevertheless, party members remained preponderant in the state bureaucracy and former AKP deputies continued to regard the 1990 Supreme Soviet as the legitimate legislative body.

In November 1993 an attempt was made to relaunch the party as the Azerbaijan United Communist Party (AVKP), the aim being to rally the opposition to the government of Heydar Aliyev of the New Azerbaijan Party (YAP). On Sept. 1, 1995, the Supreme Court banned the AVKP in light of Justice Ministry allegations that the party had engaged in anti-state activities by advocating union with other ex-Soviet republics. On Sept. 19, however, the Court reversed its decision, which it described as "groundless and illegal", thus enabling the party to contest legislative elections in November 1995, although it failed to win representation.

Divisions in Communist ranks resulted in the effective relaunching of the AKP as a registered party for the October 1998 presidential elections, although candidate Firudin Hasanov received only 0.9% of the vote. Whereas the AVKP was renamed the Azerbaijan Communist Workers' Party in August 2000, the rump AKP achieved registration for the November 2000 Assembly elections. It was allocated two seats, being officially credited with having just surmounted the 6% barrier to representation in the proportional section.

Azerbaijan Democratic Party
Azerbaycan Democrat Partiyasi (ADP)

Leadership. Rasul Guliyev & Ilyas Ismailov (co-chairmen); Sardar Jalaloglu (secretary-general)

The current Azerbaijan Democratic Party was founded in 1998 and is led by former Speaker of Parliament and exiled politician, Rasul Guliyev. He had resigned from his position in 1996 and sought exile in the United States, facing embezzlement charges in Azerbaijan. ADP achieved official registration in February 2000 but was initially excluded from the Assembly elections in the same year. The Central Election Commission accepted the ADP's list for the proportional system only after international organizations intervened. The party won only 1.1% of the proportional vote and no seats.

In June 2003, the ADP nominated Rasul Guliyev as its candidate for the upcoming presidential elections. His application was rejected by the Central Election Committee (CEC) since he was the holder of a green card. The case was appealed to the Supreme Court, which upheld the CEC's decision.

In the run-up to the 2003 presidential elections, ADP participated in meetings of opposition leaders to discuss possibility of nominating a single candidate. A week before the elections, the ADP chairman Rasul Guliyev endorsed *Musavat* party candidate Isa Gambar.

Azerbaijan National Independence Party
Azerbaycan Milli Istiqlal Partiyasi (AMIP–Istiqlal)

Address. 179 Azadliq Prospect, 370087 Baku
Telephone. (994–12) 622917
Fax. (994–12) 980098
Email. nipa@azeri.com
Website. www.amip.azeri.com
Leadership. Etibar Mamedov (chairman)

The right-wing AMIP was founded in July 1992 by Etibar Mamedov, who had been a prominent leader of the then ruling Azerbaijan Popular Front but had defected in light of resistance to his hardline nationalist approach to the Nagorno-Karabakh conflict with Armenia. Mamedov had been an initial candidate for the June 1992 presidential election but had withdrawn, claiming that the arrangements favoured the Azerbaijan Popular Front candidate. He found no more acceptance of his line from Heydar Aliyev of the New Azerbaijan Party (YAP) when the latter came to power in June 1993 and refused a post in the Aliyev government.

The AMIP was officially stated to have won three seats in the November 1995 Assembly elections on the basis of a national vote share of 9%. The party gravitated thereafter to an outright opposition stance, highlighted by Mamedov's candidacy in the controversial October 1998 presidential elections, in which he was runner-up to President Aliyev with 11.8% of the vote (and later failed in a legal challenge to the outcome). In April 1999 the AMIP parliamentary deputies joined a new opposition Democratic Bloc, as the party participated in broader opposition fronts such as the Movement for Democracy and the National Resistance Movement. Having boycotted the December 1999 local elections, in April 2000 the AMIP entered into a bilateral co-operation pact with the Azerbaijan Democratic Party (ADP).

Registered for the November 2000 legislative elections, the AMIP was stated to have polled well below the 6% threshold for seats in the proportional section. Two candidates elected on the AMIP ticket in constituency seats were quickly expelled from the party. Mamedov joined in opposition demands for the elections to be annulled because of widespread gerrymandering by the government.

On June 8, 2003, more than 4,000 delegates to the eighth congress of the party nominated Etibar Mamedov as AMIP's candidate for the presidential elections. Mamedov particpated in talks with other opposition leaders on nominating a single candidate. In September, AMIP and the Azerbaijan Popular Front signed an agreement "on coalition in the presidential elections", under which Azerbaijan Popular Front activists would vote for AMIP's candidate. However, Etibar Mamedov came in fourth position with only 2.92 % of the vote.

AMIP was admitted to the International Democrat Union in September 1999.

Azerbaijan Popular Front Party
Azerbaycani Xalq Cabhasi Partiyasi (AXCP)

Address. 1 Injasanat Street, 370000 Baku
Telephone. (994–12) 921483
Fax. (994–12) 989004
Leadership. Ali Kerimov (leader of "reformist" faction); Mirmahmud Fattaev (leader of "conservative" faction)

The Azerbaijan Popular Front Party was founded in 1989 under the leadership of Abulfaz Elchibey (then a teacher of oriental philosophy) as a broad-based opposition movement calling for reform of the then Communist-run political system. The movement took a broadly pan-Turkic line, supporting nationalist calls for the acquisition of Azeri-populated areas of northern Iran. In January 1990 Popular Front members were among 150 people killed by the security forces in Baku and elsewhere in disturbances arising from anti-

Armenian demonstrations. Allowed to contest the Supreme Soviet elections of September–October 1990, the Popular Front-led opposition won only 45 of the 360 seats (with a vote share of 12.5%). Together with other opposition parties, the Popular Front boycotted the direct presidential election held in September 1991 but subsequently brought about the resignation of President Mutalibov in March 1992. In a further presidential election in June 1992, Elchibey was returned with 59.4% of the vote against four other candidates.

In government, the Popular Front blocked ratification of Azerbaijan's CIS membership but came under increasing pressure from opposition groups, notably the New Azerbaijan Party led by Heydar Aliyev and the forces of Col. Surat Guseinov. Replaced as head of state by Aliyev in June 1993, Elchibey fled to Nakhichevan and disputed the official results of an August referendum (boycotted by the Popular Front) in which only 2% of voters were said to have expressed confidence in Elchibey. Aliyev secured popular endorsement as President in September 1993, in direct elections that were also boycotted by the Popular Front. The authorities subsequently launched a crackdown against the party, raiding its headquarters in Baku in February 1994 and arresting 100 supporters for "resisting the police". Popular Front leaders claimed that weapons said to have been found at the building had been planted by the police. Nevertheless, the Popular Front was able in 1994-95 to command substantial popular support for its opposition to the Aliyev government's policy of seeking a Nagorno-Karabakh settlement via close relations with Russia.

In May 1995 Elchibey repeated the Popular Front call for the creation of a "greater Azerbaijan", to include the estimated 15 million ethnic Azeris inhabiting northern Iran (twice as many as the entire population of Azerbaijan proper). The Iranian authorities responded by cutting off electricity supplies to Elchibey's stronghold of Nakhichevan. In the same month Shahmerdan Jafarov, a Popular Front deputy, was stripped of his parliamentary immunity and accused of setting up illegal armed groups in Nakhichevan, where Elchibey's residence was reportedly surrounded by government troops. On June 17 Jafarov was shot in a clash in the enclave, subsequently dying of his injuries, while in October 1995 former Foreign Minister Tofik Gasymov was arrested and charged with involvement in a coup attempt earlier in the year.

In the November 1995 Assembly elections the Popular Front was officially credited with winning three proportional seats on the basis of a national vote share of 10%, taking a fourth seat in balloting for unfilled seats in February 1996. Proceedings against Popular Front members early in 1996 included the sentencing to death *in absentia* of former Defence Minister Rakhim Gaziyev for treason, although his sentence was commuted to life imprisonment on his extradition from Moscow to Baku in April. Some Popular Front leaders were released under a presidential amnesty in July 1996 and in October 1997 Elchibey returned to Baku after four years in internal exile.

The Popular Front opted not to participate in the October 1998 presidential election, following which Elchibey was put on trial for insulting the head of state. That the proceedings were called off in February 1999 on the initiative of President Aliyev was widely attributed to international pressure. Thereafter the Popular Front continued to be the leading component in various opposition fronts and in local elections in December 1999 won 754 seats out of about 10,000 at issue. However, the party became riven by internal divisions which led to an open split in August 2000, coinciding with the death of Elchibey in Turkey from cancer. A "reformist" faction led by former Popular Front deputy chairman Ali Kerimov favoured some accommodation with the regime, while the "conservative" wing led by Mirmahmud Fattaev maintained an uncompromising line.

The Fattaev faction of the Azerbaijan Popular Front was barred from presenting candidates in the November 2000 Assembly elections, instead forming an alliance with *Musavat*. The Kerimov faction of the Popular Front was allowed to stand, being credited with 10.8% of the vote in the proportional section and six seats (including one won in re-runs for 11 seats in early January 2001). In the wake of the balloting both factions joined in opposition condemnations of its validity. In mid-January 2001 the Kerimov Azerbaijan Popular Front announced jointly with the Civic Unity Party that its deputies would participate in the work of the new Assembly, but in order to campaign for new elections.

The split in the Azerbaijan Popular Front caused a split in the oppositiion Democratic Congress, an umbrella organization of 10 political parties. The two party wings affiliated with rival opposition alignments: the "reformists" with the Azerbaijan National Independence Party (AMIP) and the "conservatives" with *Musavat* and Azerbaijan Democratic Party.

In early 2002, the two wings of the divided Azerbaijan Popular Front issued statements proposing their reunification but prospects remained remote. In April 2002, at a meeting of the supreme council of the reformist wing, Gudrad Gasankuliev was expelled for his attempts to reconcile the two factions. Subsequently, he tried to forge a third Azerbaijan Popular Front Party when some 400 former members of both the "conservative" and the "reformist" wings gathered in Baku on Aug. 18, 2002. Delegates to the congress adopted a new party programme and statutes and elected a chairman and a governing council. The new party formally applied to register with the Minister of Justice. Other opposition parties continued to regard the Gudrad Gasankuliev group with suspicion and hostility. On Aug. 9, leaders of 15 political parties, including both Azerbaijan Popular Front wings, *Musavat*, Azerbaijan National Independence Party, the Azerbaijan Democratic Party, and the Civic Unity Party signed a statement affirming that the congress convened by Gasankuliev had nothing in common with Azerbaijan Popular Front. They further accused the authorities of using Gasankuliev and his supporters in a bid to further divide the opposition camp.

In the run-up to the 2003 presidential elections, the "reformist" wing nominated its chairman Ali Kerimov as presidential candidate. In a bid to forge a united opposition coalition, Kerimov had offered to withdraw his candidacy provide that his party, Azerbaijan National Independence Party (AMIP), the Azerbaijan Democratic Party and *Musavat* reached agreement on backing a single opposition candidate.

In September 2003, the "reformist" wing of the Popular Front decided to support the candidacy of AMIP chairman Etibar Mamedov and Kerimov withdrew his candidacy. Kerimov and Mamedov signed a formal agreement, under which the Azerbaijan Popular Front would be entitled to nominate the Prime Minister if Mamedov was elected President. No other opposition parties joined their election coalition.

Civic Unity Party
Address. c/o Milli Majlis, 2 Mehti Hussein, Baku
Leadership. Sabir Hajiev (secretary general)
The Civic Unity Party was established in April 2000 as the political vehicle of ex-President Ayaz Mutalibov, the former leader of the Azerbaijan Communist Party who had lived in exile in Moscow since May 1992. The party was among the first to be registered for the November 2000 Assembly elections, which it contested as the leading component of the Democratic Azerbaijan bloc, also including the groupings Courage (*Geyryat*) led by Ashraf Mekhtiev, Education (*Maarifchilik*) led by Mahmed Hanifa Musayev and Honour (*Namus*) led by Togrul Ibragimli. It was officially stated to

have just surmounted the 6% barrier to representation in the proportional section of the balloting and was allocated three seats.

Mutalibov was formally elected chairman at the party's second congress in December 2000 and declared his intention to contest the presidential elections due in 2003. In mid-January 2001, the Civic Unity Party announced jointly with the "reformist" wing of the Azerbaijan Popular Front that its deputies would participate in the work of the new Assembly in order to campaign for new elections.

In the summer of 2002, the National Security Ministry released a statement claiming that Ayaz Mutalibov planned to overthrow the leadership. The Civic Unity Party secretary general Sabir Hajiev and Mutalibov himself issued statements denying the claims. Five Mutalibov supporters were put on trial charged with planning a coup d'état.

On Aug. 8, 2003, the Civic Unity Party held an emergency congress and adopted a decision to merge with the Social Democratic Party of Azerbaijan (SDPA). At a congress on Aug. 27, the SDPA elected Ayaz Mutalibov as its co-chairman alongside Araz Alizade. The merger of the Civic Unity Party and the SDPA became possible after the supreme council of the Civic Unity Party expelled its secretary-general, Sabir Hajiev, and five other members for their opposition to the ongoing negotiations. Mutalibov stated that the unification with the Social Democratic Party of Azerbaijan was prompted by the repeated refusal of the Justice Ministry to register the Civic Union Party, but Sabir Hajiev announced that the party would continue to function under its own name.

Ayaz Mutalibov was denied registration as an SDPA presidential candidate and the party did not participate in the 2003 elections.

Liberal Party of Azerbaijan

The Liberal Party was founded in June 1995 and since then has been one of the major opposition parties in the country. Prof. Lala Shovket Gajieva headed the party until her resignation in 2003, paving the way for her participation in the presidency contest, in which she won 3.62% of the vote. In 1993, she resigned from the post of state secretary to protest the policies of then President Elchibey and had established a reputation as an opposition party leader. In 1998, the Liberal Party boycotted the presidential elections to protest against the election law.

New Azerbaijan Party
Yeni Azerbaycan Partiyasi (YAP)

Address. 6 Landau Street, 370073 Baku
Telephone. (994–12) 393875
Leadership. Ilham Aliyev (chairman); Ali Ahmedov (secretary-general)

The YAP was founded by Heydar Aliyev in September 1992 as an alternative to the then ruling Azerbaijan Popular Front following his exclusion from the June 1992 presidential election because he was over a newly-decreed age limit of 65. At the time he held the presidency of the Azerbaijani enclave of Nakhichevan and had previously been a politburo member of the Soviet Communist Party and first secretary of the party in Azerbaijan (from 1969); he had also served as a Soviet deputy premier until being dismissed by Mikhail Gorbachev in 1987 for alleged corruption. Returning to Nakhichevan, he had become chairman of its Supreme Soviet in September 1991 and had conducted an independent foreign policy for the enclave, signing a cease-fire with Armenia and developing relations with Russia, Turkey and Iran. The new party pledged itself to the defence of the rights of all individuals, regardless of nationality, and the creation of a law-based state.

Aliyev used the YAP to rally opposition to the Azerbaijan

Popular Front government of Abulfaz Elchibey, who was deposed in June 1993 with assistance from Col. Surat Guseinov, a former wool merchant who had recently been dismissed as commander of Azerbaijani forces in Nagorno-Karabakh. Elected interim head of state, Aliyev appointed Col. Guseinov as Prime Minister and received popular endorsement of sorts in a presidential election in October 1993 (for which the 65-year age limit was rescinded), being credited with 98.8% of the vote against two other candidates, neither of whom represented major opposition parties. Meanwhile, at Aliyev's urging in September, parliamentary approval had at last been given to Azerbaijan's membership of the CIS. The new government launched a crackdown against the Azerbaijan Popular Front, while Aliyev moved to improve Azerbaijan's regional relations and sought a settlement of the conflict with Armenia involving the deployment of Turkish troops in Nagorno-Karabakh and the return of a limited Russian military presence in Azerbaijan proper.

In a further power struggle in October 1994, Col. Guseinov was dismissed as Prime Minister and replaced by Fuad Kuliyev. The YAP regime accused Col. Guseinov of treasonable activities, reportedly in connivance with opposition groups and the Russian authorities. The episode therefore marked a distinct cooling between the YAP government and Moscow. In the November 1995 legislative elections (completed in February 1996) the YAP formed a front with the Azerbaijan Independent Democratic Party, the Motherland Party and United Azerbaijan, being credited with 62% of the national vote in its own right and winning an overwhelming majority of Assembly seats when pro-government independents were included in the tally.

Firmly entrenched in power, Aliyev secured a predictable victory in the October 1998 presidential elections as the YAP candidate, being credited with 76.1% of the vote against five other contenders. International bodies criticized widespread irregularities in the polling, the official result of which was rejected by the opposition parties. Aliyev nevertheless reappointed Artur Rasizade as Prime Minister of a YAP-dominated government and in December 1999 was re-elected YAP chairman at the party's first congress. Five deputy chairmen also elected included the President's son, Ilham Aliyev, whom the YAP newspaper had described as his natural successor because his "genetic code does not belong to an ordinary person".

Ilham Aliyev headed the YAP list for the proportional section of legislative elections held in November 2000 and January 2001. Amid opposition cries of widespread fraud, the ruling party won another commanding majority of 75 seats (with 62.5% of the proportional vote) and could also expect backing from most of the 29 "independents" also elected.

Despite Heydar Aliyev's deteriorating health, YAP nominated him as its 2003 presidential candidate. At the same time, his son Ilham Aliyev, the YAP first deputy secretary, was also a candidate backed by a citizens' initiative group from Nakhichevan. For several months, both father and son were running for the presidency. On Oct. 2, just two weeks before the election day, Heydar Aliyev withdrew his candidacy in favour of his son, who received 76.8% of the vote.

New Equality Party
Yeni Musavat Partiyasi (YMP-Musavat)
Musavat

Address. 37 Azerbaijan Prospekt, 370001 Baku
Telephone. (994–12) 981870
Fax. (994–12) 983166
Leadership. Isa Gambar (chairman); Vergun Ayub (secretary-general)

The YMP (usually referred to as *Musavat*) was founded in June 1992, indirectly descending from the pre-Soviet *Musavat* nationalists, of moderate Islamic, pan-Turkic orientation. It was closely allied with the Azerbaijan Popular

Front under the 1992–93 government, when party leader Gambar was president of the interim National Assembly. The party came into sharp conflict with the succeeding government of Heydar Aliyev of the New Azerbaijan Party and won only one seat in the legislative elections held in November 1995 and February 1996. In December 1997 *Musavat* was temporarily weakened by the formation of the breakaway National Congress Party by dissidents who objected to Gambar's leadership style.

Musavat boycotted the October 1998 presidential election but participated in local elections in December 1999, winning 618 of some 10,000 seats at issue. In February 2000 *Musavat*'s Baku headquarters were ransacked by around 100 armed men from Nakhichevan who reportedly objected to recent coverage of the enclave in *Yeni Musavat* (the party's newspaper), although some observers saw the government's hand in the action. Initially refused registration for the November 2000 Assembly elections, as a result of international pressure *Musavat* was in the end allowed to present candidates and won two constituency seats (having taken only 4.9% of the vote in the proportional section). The party subsequently joined with other opposition formations in condemning the balloting as fraudulent and immediately expelled a newly-elected *Musavat* deputy who had disregarded the party's boycott of the new Assembly.

For the 2003 presidential elections, *Musavat* nominated Isa Gambar as its presidential candidate. Subsequently, *Musavat* and three more opposition parties – the Azerbaijan Popular Front Party (reformist faction led by Ali Kerimov), the Azerbaijan National Independence Party and the Azerbaijan Democratic Party (ADP) – agreed to participate in the elections with a common candidate for the ballot but agreed to withhold the name until the time of registration. This agreement did not come to fruition as the Azerbaijan Popular Front Party/reformist faction and the Azerbaijan National Independence Party joined forces behind Etibar Mamedov, and the Azerbaijan Democratic Party chairman Rasul Guliyev endorsed *Musavat* candidate Isa Gambar one week before the elections. Despite *Musavat*'s popularity, Isa Gambar received only 14% of the vote, which dealt a major blow to Azerbaijan's main opposition party leaders. Despite reports of voting irregularities and fraud, the voting results were officially endorsed. Disappointed *Musavat* supporters staged demonstrations leading to clashes with the police and arrests. Arrests spread across the country and for a several days hundreds of opposition leaders were detained. Regional branches of *Musavat* and coalition partner ADP were targeted. On Oct. 24, the Baku municipal council demanded that *Musavat* vacate its headquarters and the Baku District Court upheld the eviction.

Three of Isa Gambar's associates – *Musavat* deputy chairmen Arif Hadjili and Ibrahim Ibrahimli, and Rauf Arifoglu, editor of the opposition paper "*Yeni Musavat*" – were arrested in October 2003 in the wake of the presidential elections. The preliminary hearing of their trial started in May 2004.

Social Democratic Party of Azerbaijan (SDPA)

Address. 28 May str., Baku
Telephone. (994–12) 983378; 938148
Leadership. Ayaz Mutalibov & Araz Alizade (co-chairmen)
Founded in 1989 by Araz Alizade with most members coming from the Popular Front, the Social Democratic Party was the first non-Communist party to be officially registered. In August 2003 the SDPA elected former Civic Unity Party leader and Soviet era President Ayaz Mutalibov as its co-chairman alongside Araz Alizade. Mutalibov was denied registration as an SDPA presidential candidate, however, and the party did not participate in the 2003 elections. Co-chairman Araz Alizade called for a boycott of the elections.

SDPA has observer status with the Socialist International.

Party Groupings

Democratic Congress. The Azerbaijan political landscape is largely characterized by attempts at forging alignments, which are generally short-lived and ineffective. The most prominent was the Democratic Congress uniting 10 opposition parties. In August 2000, the formation split into two factions – reformist and conservative – duplicating a similar rift in the Azerbaijan Popular Front Party.

In October 2001, *Musavat* party chairman Isa Gambar, who headed the Democratic Congress, called on opposition leaders to adopt four principles: holding a summit of party leaders, concluding an agreement on cooperation, creating a permanent opposition alignment, and agreeing on a single candidacy for the 2003 presidential elections. Many opposition leaders voiced their disagreement with the last point.

Two weeks later, the leader of the reformist wing of the Azerbaijan Popular Front Party, Ali Kerimov, signed a cooperation agreement with Etibar Mamedov, chairman of the Azerbaijan National Independence Party. The small Taraggi Party also signed the agreement. The common platform they adopted included several points – coordination of activities, approval of a single position, adoption of unified policies with regard to other political parties, refraining from mutual criticism, and approval of a single presidential candidate.

Musavat chairman Isa Gambar made his alignment with the new bloc conditional on the approval of a single presidential candidate. There were attempts at rapprochement between *Musavat* and Kerimov's wing of the Azerbaijan Popular Front Party, which were unsuccessful.

United Opposition Movement. The *Musavat* party and the "conservative" wing of the Azerbaijan Popular Front Party, alongside the Azerbaijan Democratic Party and some 20 other political parties, joined forces in a new United Opposition Movement created on Jan. 10, 2002, in Baku. The new political formation pledged to work for the replacement of the administration by "a legitimate government".

NAGORNO-KARABAKH

Legally part of Azerbaijan, the Armenian-populated enclave of Nagorno-Karabakh made a unilateral declaration of independence in 1996 and has since adopted all the appurtenances of statehood with president, parliament and the normal range of ministries and departments of state. Presidential and legislative elections, which have both been held, have been declared illegal by the Azerbaijani authorities.

The president is elected for a five-year term. The incumbent president was first elected in November 1997 in succession to Robert Kocharian after the latter had been appointed Prime Minister of Armenia. Arkady Ghukasyan was re-elected by 88.4 % of the vote in August 2002.

The National Assembly (*Azgayin Zhogov*) has 33 members, elected for a five-year term in single-seat constituencies. Three political parties and a group of non-partisans were allotted Assembly seats following elections in June 2000.

Armenakan Party (AP), won one out of 33 seats.

Armenian Revolutionary Federation (*Hai Heghapokhakan Dashnaktsutiune, HHD/Dashnak*), Nagorno-Karabakh wing of the Armenian party, won nine out of 33 seats.

Democratic Artsakh Party (ZhAM), supportive of "President" Arkady Gukasyan, headed the poll in the 2000 elections, winning 13 of the 33 seats.

Bahamas

Capital: Nassau
Population: 297,500 (2003E)

The Bahamas gained independence from the United Kingdom in 1973 after two centuries of colonial rule. The head of state is the British sovereign, represented by a Governor-General, and the head of government is the Prime Minister. Legislative power is vested in a bicameral parliament consisting of a 40-member House of Assembly elected for five years by universal adult suffrage and an appointed 16-member Senate. A general election held on May 2, 2002, resulted in the opposition Progressive Liberal Party (PLP) gaining a convincing victory and putting an end to 10 years in opposition for the party. The PLP won 29 seats compared with four in the 1997 election, while the ruling Free National Movement (FNM) saw its representation drop from 35 seats to just seven. Independents won the remaining four seats, three of which are former members of the FNM and one is a former member of the PLP. Over 90% of the electorate participated in the election.

Free National Movement (FNM)

Address. Mackey Street, PO Box N-10713, Nassau
Telephone. (1-242) 393-7853
Fax. (1-242) 393-7914
Email. fnm@coralwave.com
Website. www.freenationalmovement.org
Leadership. Orville "Tommy" Turnquest (leader)
The conservative FNM was founded in the early 1970s by Kendal Isaacs as a merger of the United Bahamian Party and an anti-independence dissident faction of the Progressive Liberal Party (PLP). Reconstituted in 1979 as the Free National Democratic Movement, the organization absorbed defectors from the now-defunct Bahamian Democratic and the Social Democratic Party, and was recognized as the official opposition in 1981 (subsequently reverting to the name FNM).

In the 1992 elections the FNM ended the PLP's long reign in power by winning 33 seats out of 49 in the House of Assembly (later being awarded an additional seat) and formed a new government under the premiership of Hubert Ingraham. The FNM retained power in the March 1997 general elections, winning 34 seats in an Assembly reduced to 40 members. The FNM began to lose support, however, in late 2000 when it introduced tighter regulation of the offshore financial sector to control money laundering. The position of the party was not helped by a divisive succession struggle in August 2001, which saw "Tommy" Turnquest become leader-designate. The authority of the FNM was further undermined when it was defeated in a referendum in February 2002 over five proposed constitutional amendments. In the general election held in May 2002, the FNM suffered a crushing defeat, with only Ingraham and one other FNM cabinet minister retaining their seats. The FNM's effectiveness as an opposition has been seriously weakened with Turnquest now sitting in the Senate, rather than the House of Assembly.

Progressive Liberal Party (PLP)

Address. PO Box N-547, Nassau
Telephone. (1-242) 325-5492
Website. www.progressiveliberalparty.com
Leadership. Perry G. Christie (leader); Raynard S. Rigby (chairman)
The centrist PLP was founded in 1953 as a mainly Black-supported party. A leading proponent of Bahamian independence and aspiring to overturn White economic dominance of the islands, the party came to power in 1967 and took the Bahamas to independence in 1973 under the premiership of Sir Lynden Pindling. Having won five successive general elections on a platform of economic self-reliance and greater government involvement in a mixed economy, the PLP lost power dramatically in 1992, after allegations were made linking the Prime Minister with Colombian drug lords.

The PLP suffered a further bad defeat in the March 1997 Assembly elections, winning only six seats out of 40, although its share of the vote in the constituency-based system was 42 percent. Pindling retired from politics in July 1997 and was succeeded as leader by Perry Christie. In the general election held in May 2002, the PLP gained victory, ending 10 years in opposition for the party. Incoming Prime Minister Christie promised to govern with "clean hands", a reference to the PLP's campaign allegations of government corruption. In addition, Christie wanted to blunt FNM charges that leading figures in his party were still involved with organized crime, particularly drug trafficking. Since returning to power the PLP has toned down its hostility towards foreign investors, with the party continuing the privatization programme started by the previous FNM administration. The party, however, retains a belief that the state should have an active role in economic development.

Bahrain

Capital: Manama
Population: 663,000 (2004E)

The State of Bahrain, fully independent since 1971 having previously been a British protected state, is a monarchy whose Emir governs through an appointed Cabinet. As in the other Gulf Co-operation Council states, political parties are banned in Bahrain by law. However, in Bahrain various "societies" exist that have some of the characteristics of political parties.

The 1973 constitution provided for a National Assembly consisting of the Cabinet and 30 other members to be elected by popular vote. Elections were held in 1974. However, the National Assembly was dissolved in August 1975 for being "dominated by ideas alien to the society and values of Bahrain". In January 1993 the Emir appointed a 40-member Consultative Council (*Majlis al-Shura*) with limited law-making authority of its own.

Denied legal political parties, opponents of the Emir expressed themselves via clandestine groups, mainly based in the majority Shia Muslim community. A notable Shia cleric and critic of the ruling family, Sheikh Ali Salman, was arrested on Dec. 5, 1994, and expelled to London in January 1995. Others joined him there after the government suppressed Shia unrest, which began with a mass petition and later included bomb attacks. London-based opposition groups include the Islamically oriented Bahrain Freedom Movement (BFM). In June 1996 the Emirate accused Iran of fomenting uprisings through a group called *Hizballah*-Bahrain. It recalled its ambassador to Tehran and arrested some 1,600 people.

In March 1999 Sheikh Hamad ibn Issa Al Khalifa succeeded his father as Emir of Bahrain, and in October 2000 announced a new National Charter of Action. The Charter outlined four main political reforms: the creation of bicameral parliament with an upper house of appointed members and a lower house with elected members; the creation of an independent judicial system; the granting of full suffrage to male and female citizens; and the transformation into a constitutional monarchy, with the Emir (Prince) as King.

The charter received 98% approval in a national referendum held on Feb. 14-15, 2001, and 289 political prisoners were released. Women voted for the first time, and even London-based oppositionists supported the reforms. Later in the year Bahrain ended its ban (imposed in 1984) on Sheikh Issa Qasim's Islamic Awareness Society. The state also pardoned nearly 900 opponents, and freed BFM leader, Sheikh Abdul Amir al-Jamri, after three years under house arrest. In July 2001 Islamists, mostly Shias, formed a loose umbrella group, the *Al-Wefaq* National Islamic Society (also called the Islamic National Accord Association, INAA), led by Sheikh Salman. In October 2001 the King was quoted as saying that "should the next parliament allow the creation of political parties in Bahrain, we will not object, but at the same time we will not encourage anything that will lead to divisions within the country".

Two rounds of parliamentary elections were held in October 2002, resulting in the election of an assembly dominated by independents and moderate Sunni Islamists, with turnout put at 51%. Bahrain's Western allies, the USA and UK, welcomed the elections as a sign that conservative Gulf states could embrace democratization, and even incorporate Islamist trends, without destablizing or radicalizing their societies. *Al-Wefaq*, however, boycotted the poll, alleging that it was designed to perpetuate Sunni minority domination as the King still retained control over the dominant Consultative Council. *Al-Wefaq* was joined in the boycott by the leftist National Democratic Action Society (NDAS), led by Abdulrahman al-No'aimi, the pan-Arab Nationalist Democratic Rally, and the Shia Islamic Action Association. Certain Islamists also opposed the poll because it granted the suffrage to women. The Shia boycott resulted in a preponderance of Sunni representatives.

On Jan. 21, 2004, Bahraini MP Farid Ghazni tabled a motion to interrogate three ministers about alleged irregularities in the management of pension funds. Ghazni and 16 fellow MPs together constituted a parliamentary panel of inquiry. If ministers were found to have flouted the law, said Ghazni, there could be a vote of no-confidence in the government. This was the first time assembly members had directly challenged the government since the October 2002 elections.

Bangladesh

Capital: Dhaka
Population: 129,000,000 (2000E)

The People's Republic of Bangladesh achieved sovereignty in 1971, having previously formed the eastern part of Pakistan (which had become independent from Britain in 1947). After a brief period of parliamentary democracy until August 1975, the country was then ruled by a series of military dictatorships, albeit with increasing scope for party activity, until Lt.-Gen. (retd.) Hussain Mohammed Ershad was finally forced to resign in December 1990. Under amendments to the 1972 constitution approved by referendum in September 1991, full legislative authority was restored to the unicameral National Parliament (*Jatiya*

Sangsad) of 330 members elected for a five-year term. Of these, 300 are returned from individual constituencies by universal suffrage of those aged 18 and over, and can be of either sex, and the other 30 are women elected by the directly elected members. The country's President is elected by the *Jatiya Sangsad*, also for a five-year term, and has largely ceremonial powers. Executive power is vested in the Prime Minister and Council of Ministers, formally appointed by the President but responsible to the *Jatiya Sangsad*.

In February 1991 general elections to the *Jatiya Sangsad* resulted in victory for the Bangladesh Nationalist Party (BNP) with the Awami League in second place. After a long political crisis, general elections on Feb. 15, 1996, were boycotted by the main opposition parties and resulted in the ruling BNP winning an overwhelming majority. Amid continuing deadlock, the new BNP government resigned at the end of March 1996, a neutral caretaker Prime Minister being appointed pending new elections later that year. These resulted in the Awami League taking 176 of the 330 seats, with the BNP taking second place with 116. The Awami League's leader, Sheikh Hasina Wazed, formed a new government, initially with the support of the National Party, which had come third with 33 seats. In 1998 the National Party split and its majority joined the BNP-led opposition in walking out of parliament and launching a civil disobedience campaign to force an early general election. However, the government served its full term and resigned in favour of another neutral caretaker Prime Minister on July 12, 2001.

A general election on Oct. 1, 2001, resulted in a close contest in terms of the share of the vote between the Awami League and the BNP, but with the BNP winning three times as many seats, enabling it to form a government in coalition with the Bangladesh Islamic Assembly (*Jamaat-e-Islami*, JIB) and two smaller parties. The results of the 300 directly elected seats were as follows: BNP 198 seats (42.7% of the vote); Awami League 63 (40.1%); Bangladesh Islamic Assembly 17 (4.3%), National Party (*Jatiya Dal*–Ershad) 14 (7.2%); others 8 (5.6%).

Bangladesh Awami League (AL)
Address. 23 Bangabandha Avenue, Dhaka
Website. www.albd.org
Leadership. Sheikh Hasina Wazed (president); Abdul Jalil (general secretary)
The AL was founded in 1949 as the Awami (i.e. People's) Muslim League by left-wing Bengali nationalists opposed to the right-wing orientation of the Muslim League after the 1947 partition. It headed coalition governments in East Pakistan in 1956–58 and was concurrently represented in the central government, although it was weakened by secession of pro-Soviet elements in 1957. In elections held in 1970 the AL won 151 of the 153 East Pakistan seats in the central parliament on a pro-independence and secular platform. Led by Sheikh Mujibur Rahman, it then brought about the secession of what was renamed Bangladesh, assisted by the Indian Army, and became the ruling party on the establishment of the new state in 1971. In 1972 the AL underwent a split when young advocates of "scientific socialism" broke away to form the National Socialist Party. In January 1975 Sheikh Mujib introduced a presidential form of government and moved to a one-party system by creating the Bangladesh Peasants' and Workers' Awami League, within which all existing parties were required to operate. However, Sheikh Mujib was overthrown and killed by the military in August 1975, the AL being temporarily banned.

Resuming activity under the leadership of Sheikh Hasina (Mujib's daughter), the AL headed the Democratic United Front coalition which backed the candidacy of Gen. Mohammed Ataul Ghani Osmani in the June 1978 presidential election, won by Gen. Ziaur (Zia) Rahman of what became the Bangladesh Nationalist Party (BNP). In the 1979 parliamentary elections the AL won 40 of the 300 elective seats, while in the November 1981 presidential contest the AL candidate, Kamal Hossain, was officially credited with 25.4% of the vote in a disputed result. Following Lt.-Gen. Ershad's seizure of power in March 1982, the AL was prominent in demanding a return to democracy, forming a 15-party left-wing alliance, which in September 1983 joined the BNP and its allies in creating the Movement for the Restoration of Democracy (MRD). Leftist elements of the AL broke away in July 1983 to form the Peasants' and Workers' Awami League (which was reintegrated with the parent party in 1991).

MRD pressure produced a partial resumption of legal party activity from January 1986 and the calling of parliamentary elections for May 1986. But the MRD parties were divided on whether adequate concessions had been made, with the result that the BNP and its allies boycotted the poll whereas the AL and seven associated parties opted to participate, being credited with 76 of the 300 elective seats in disputed results. AL and other opposition members boycotted the opening of parliament in July in protest at the slow progress of democratization, setting up a "people's parliament", of which Sheikh Hasina was elected leader. Both the AL and the BNP boycotted the October 1986 presidential contest, after which efforts by the Ershad government to entice the AL to attend parliament were eventually rebuffed.

The AL was then a leading organizer of a series of mass demonstrations and strikes demanding Ershad's resignation, culminating in the "siege of Dhaka" of November 1987, when over two million opposition supporters sought to immobilize government activity in the capital, Sheikh Hasina being briefly held under house arrest as a result. Both main MRD parties declined to participate in the March 1988 parliamentary elections. Renewed opposition demonstrations from October 1990 yielded the departure of Ershad in December and the holding of parliamentary elections in February 1991, when the AL came a poor second to the BNP in terms of seats although with a similar percentage share of the popular vote.

In December 1994 the AL began a boycott of parliament intended to force the government's resignation. Although this action was declared unconstitutional by the High Court, in January 1995 Sheikh Hasina called the boycott "irrevocable" and the AL thereafter stepped up its campaign of strikes and other actions aimed at forcing new elections under a caretaker government. Elections eventually held in February 1996 were boycotted by the AL and the other main opposition parties, with the result that new elections were held in June. These resulted in the AL taking the largest number of seats, enabling Sheikh Hasina to form a coalition government that included the National Party. However, in 1998 the BNP and other opposition parties (including a section of the National Party) walked out of parliament to orchestrate a campaign of civil disobedience, similar to that led by the Awami League in 1994 and aimed at forcing another early general election. This failed, but the AL lost the election of October 2001, declining to 63 of the 300 directly elected seats although only 2.6 percentage points behind the BNP in the popular vote.

Bitter political rhetoric continued after the election. AL officials accused the government of being behind those responsible for a grenade attack on Aug. 21, 2004, at a political rally being held by Sheikh Hasina in which 20 were killed, including the party's women's affairs secretary, Ivy Rahman. Sheikh Hasina stated that "hundreds" of AL supporters had been killed or tortured by the BNP-led government since 2001 and that the Aug. 21 attack was a continuation of this policy. The AL maintains an essentially secular posture, accusing the Bangladesh Islamic Assembly, the BNP's Islamist partner in government, of misinterpreting Islam.

Bangladesh Islamic Assembly
Jamaat-e-Islami Bangladesh (JIB)

Address. 505 Elephant Road, Bara Maghbazar, Dhaka 1217
Website. www.jamaat-e-islami.org
Leadership. Maulana Motiur Rahman Nizami (leader); Ali Ahsan Mohammad Mojahid (secretary general)

The Islamist *Jamaat* was originally founded in 1941 under the British Raj and opposed the creation of a separate Muslim state as being contrary to the principles of Islam. It combined this line with pronounced anti-Hindu and anti-Indian attitudes. After the 1947 partition its main strength was in West Pakistan, but its leader Gholam Azam built up a considerable following in East Pakistan. Opposed to the secular socialism and Bengali nationalism of the Awami League (AL), the *Jamaat* campaigned against the Bangladesh independence movement in 1970–71. On the creation of the new state, the party was banned and Azam was deprived of his citizenship for alleged collaboration with Pakistan.

Following the overthrow of the AL government by the military in 1975, the *Jamaat* regained legal status in 1977 within the Islamic Democratic League, but was weakened in 1978 when its dominant liberal wing joined the new Bangladesh Nationalist Party. The party's fundamentalist wing responded by relaunching the *Jamaat* in May 1979 under the leadership of Abbas Ali Khan as proxy for Azam, who had returned from exile. After the March 1982 military coup, the *Jamaat* maintained its distance from the main opposition alliances, although it made similar demands that the Ershad regime should restore democracy. In the May 1986 parliamentary elections *Jamaat* candidates were returned in 10 of the 300 elective seats.

The resignation of Ershad in December 1990 served to sharpen the *Jamaat*'s Islamist profile, which in the 1991 parliamentary elections yielded 18 elective seats and, by dint of post-election co-operation with the BNP, two of the 30 seats reserved for women. In December 1991 Azam was elected to resume the party leadership, even though his lack of Bangladeshi citizenship made this technically illegal. Popular pressure then mounted, led by the AL, for Azam to be brought to trial for crimes allegedly committed during the 1970–71 independence struggle. Such demands were resisted by the BNP government, which accepted a High Court ruling in April 1993 that Azam should be granted citizenship (this being upheld by the Supreme Court in June 1994).

In 1994 the *Jamaat* was prominent in the fundamentalist campaign against the Bangladeshi writer Taslima Nasreen. In 1995 the party participated in AL-led strikes and civil disobedience aimed at forcing the government's resignation. With other opposition parties it boycotted elections held in February 1996 but it won three seats in re-run elections later that year. However, and in spite of the resulting change of government, the *Jamaat* continued to line up with the parliamentary opposition: this time, from 1998, joining the BNP in a civil disobedience campaign against the AL's administration. From this time, too, it stepped up its fundamentalist activities, protesting against judicial secularism and against the influence of foreign (western) non-governmental organizations in the country.

In late 2000 Gholam Azam was replaced as party leader by another cleric, Maulana Nizami, who was also accused by opponents of complicity in war crimes by Pakistan in 1971. Allied with the BNP, the *Jamaat* took 17 of the elective seats in the October 2001 election on a 4.3% share of the vote, with most of its seats being won in the Khulna (7 seats with

11% of the vote) and Rajshahi (6 seats with 6.8% of the vote) divisions; in contrast, it won no seats, with only 0.8% of the vote, in the Dhaka division. It has subsequently participated in the BNP-led government, with *Jamaat* leader Nizami being Minister of Industry.

Bangladesh Nationalist Party (BNP)
Bangladesh Jatiyatabadi Dal (BJD)

Address. Sattar House, 19/A Road No. 16, Dhanmondi R/A, Dhaka 9

Website. www.bnpbd.com

Leadership. Begum Khaleda Zia Rahman (chairperson)

The centre-right BNP was launched in September 1978 by the then President, Gen. Ziaur (Zia) Rahman, on the basis of the Nationalist Front which had successfully campaigned for his election in June 1978. In the parliamentary elections of February 1979 the BNP obtained 49% of the vote and two-thirds of the seats on a platform of inscribing Islam into the constitution and pursuing social justice rather than social-ism. Martial law and the state of emergency were lifted in the course of 1979, and the BNP attracted various defectors from other parties. President Zia was assassinated in May 1981 in an apparent coup attempt and was succeeded by Vice-President Abdus Sattar, senior BNP vice-chair, who secured a popular mandate in presidential elections in November 1981. On Lt.-Gen. Ershad's seizure of power in March 1982 the BNP went into opposition, joining with the Awami League (AL) and other parties in creating the Movement for the Restoration of Democracy (MRD) in September 1983. In January 1984 Begum Khaleda, the late President's widow, succeeded Sattar as leader of the main BNP (the party having in 1983 suffered defections by ele-ments opposed to confrontation with the Ershad regime).

MRD pressure produced a partial resumption of legal party activity from January 1986 and the calling of parlia-mentary elections for May 1986. But the MRD parties were divided on whether adequate concessions had been made, with the result that the BNP and its allies boycotted the poll whereas the AL and its major allies opted to participate. MRD co-operation resumed after the legislative elections and both the BNP and the AL boycotted the October 1986 presidential contest. The BNP was then involved in demon-strations and strikes demanding Ershad's resignation, Begum Khaleda being briefly held under house arrest as a result. Both main MRD parties declined to participate in the March 1988 parliamentary elections, after which the BNP was again distracted by internal factionalism.

Renewed opposition demonstrations from October 1990 yielded the departure of Ershad in December. In parliamen-tary elections in February 1991 the BNP ended up with a comfortable majority of seats (although it took only some 35% of the popular vote) and Begum Khaleda was sworn in as the country's first woman Prime Minister. In October 1991 the BNP nominee, Abdur Rahman Biswas, was elected President by the new *Jatiya Sangsad*. In government, the BNP dropped its previous aim of restoring presidential gov-ernment but found itself in renewed conflict with the AL, now the main opposition party.

From May 1994 the BNP government faced an opposi-tion boycott of parliament and other protest action aimed at forcing early general elections. Amid mounting pressure, Begum Khaleda in September 1995 offered to hold talks with the opposition parties, while rejecting their demand for a caretaker government. As civil disturbances continued, President Biswas in November 1995 announced the dissolu-tion of parliament, preparatory to general elections that were eventually held in February 1996. With the main opposition parties boycotting the poll, the BNP won almost all the elec-tive seats and formed a new government under Begum Khaleda. However, amid undiminished civil disobedience by

the opposition, the BNP leader resigned at the end of March, giving way to a neutral caretaker Prime Minister until new elections in June, in which the BNP was decisively defeated. Restive in opposition, in 1998 Begum Khaleda walked out of parliament and launched her own civil disobedience cam-paign against the new AL government. In the October 2001 election the BNP regained power, taking 198 of the 300 directly elected seats on a 42.7% vote share.

National Party
Jatiya Dal

Address. 104 Road No. 3, Dhanmondi R/A, Dhaka 9

Website. www.jatiyaparty.org

Leadership. Lt.-Gen. (retd.) Mohammad Ershad (leader)

The *Jatiya Dal* was launched in January 1986 as a political base for Lt.-Gen. Ershad, who had seized power in March 1982, and succeeded an earlier National Front of pro-Ershad formations headed by the People's Party (*Jana Dal*). The new formation, which was joined by all the then government ministers, advocated national unity on the basis of independ-ence and sovereignty, faith in Islam, nationalism, democracy and social progress. In the May 1986 parliamentary elections the *Jatiya Dal* won 180 of the 300 elective seats. In September 1986 Ershad was elected as party chair (having resigned as Army Chief of Staff) and the following month was returned as President with 83.6% of the vote in a presi-dential election boycotted by the main opposition parties.

Having gained an even bigger majority (251 elective seats) in the March 1988 parliamentary elections, which were also boycotted by the opposition, the *Jatiya Dal* government was gradually paralyzed by renewed popular agitation. Shunned by opposition leaders and in the end deserted by the military establishment, Ershad resigned in December 1990 and was later arrested, put on trial and convicted, together with several close associates. The *Jatiya Dal* continued under new leader-ship, which in January 1991 "begged forgiveness" from the people for the Ershad years. In the February 1991 parliamen-tary elections, the party won 35 of the 300 elective seats, with some 10% of the popular vote, and became part of the oppo-sition to the new Bangladesh Nationalist Party (BNP) govern-ment. In September 1993 a pro-Ershad faction of the party formed the National Party (Nationalist), which quickly estab-lished overall control of the party.

In 1994-95 the *Jatiya Dal* participated in the opposition campaign to force the resignation of the Zia government and the calling of new elections. Having joined the opposition boycott of the February 1996 elections, the *Jatiya Dal* took 33 seats in the re-run elections later that year. It then joined a coalition government headed by the Awami League, report-edly in return for a promise that Ershad would be released on parole, which he was soon afterwards. Ershad's decision to accept office generated some internal dissent and provoked the resignation from the party of its former parliamentary leader, Moudad Ahmed. However, in 1998, Ershad led his (majority) faction of the party away from the AL government benches, joining an opposition "walk out" from parliament led by the BNP. He also co-operated with the BNP in its civil disobedience campaign against the new AL government. In May 2001, however, he abandoned his alliance with the BNP and his faction won 14 seats in the October 2001 elections; all 14 seats were won in the Rajshahi Division, where the *Jatiya Dal*-Ershad took 15.1% of the vote. A faction known as the *Jatiya Dal*-Naziur, allied with the BNP, won 4 seats and joined the government.

Other Parties

Bangladesh Peasants' and Workers' People's League (*Bangladesh Krishak Sramik Janata League*, BKSJL), won one seat in the 2001 elections.

Communist Party of Bangladesh (CPB), founded in 1948 as the East Pakistan section of the Communist Party of Pakistan (CPP), itself an offshoot of the Communist Party of India. In East Pakistan the pro-Soviet wing in 1968 formed an independent party, which was renamed the CPB on the creation of Bangladesh in 1971. Following the exit of President Ershad in December 1990 and the restoration of parliamentary democracy, the CPB won five of the 300 elective seats in the 1991 parliamentary elections. Meanwhile, the collapse of communism in Europe had inspired new thinking in the party leadership, with the party leader advocating the abandonment of Marxism-Leninism but being opposed by a majority of the CPB central committee. Eventually, in June 1993, the Manik faction broke away, later joining the new People's Forum, while in April 1994 the rump CPB became a component of the Left Democratic Front. The CPB put up 64 candidates in the 2001 elections, without success, winning 0.1% of the vote. It participates in the alliance of eleven parties that replaced the Left Democratic Front. Various small factions and offshoots of the main party continue to exist, none of electoral significance.

Islamic Unity Front (*Islami Oikya Jote*, IOJ), established by seven Islamist parties in 1990 to create a unified Islamic movement; won one seat in 1996 and two in 2001. Supports the BNP-led government.

National Party–Mangur (*Jatiya Dal*-Mangur); splinter from the main National Party; won one seat in 2001.

National Party–Naziur (*Jatiya Dal*-Naziur); splinter from the main pro-Ershad National Party; won four seats in the 2001 election and supports the BNP government.

National Socialist Party (*Jatiya Samajtantrik Dal*, JSD), originally founded in 1972 by left-wing Awami League dissidents, including Abdul Rab and Shajahan Siraj. The JSD gained an urban following for its militant opposition to the AL government and was banned in 1975 after its armed wing, called the Revolutionary People's Army, had allegedly attempted to seize power. It welcomed the military coup of August 1975 and played a prominent role in elevating Gen. Ziaur (Zia) Rahman to power later that year. Nevertheless, Gen. Zia disowned the JSD, whose leaders were arrested and brought to trial in 1976 on sedition charges, one being executed. In later years it suffered numerous splits, and the JSD name is used by various factions. The JSD (Rab), formed in January 1984 by Abdul Rab, put up 76 candidates in the 2001 elections, taking 0.21% of the vote. Another faction, the JSD (Inu) is led by Hasanul Huq Inu.

People's Forum (PF) (*Gano Forum*). The PF was founded in August 1993 by a dissident faction of the Awami League (AL) led by Kamal Hossain, who had been the first Law Minister of independent Bangladesh, the framer of its constitution and later Foreign Minister in the 1971–75 AL government. It advocated "violence-free politics, economic progress at the grass-roots and basic amenities for all". Influential PF recruits included Saifuddin Ahmed Manik, who had vacated the leadership of the Communist Party of Bangladesh after failing to persuade it to renounce Marxism-Leninism. The PF also included the faction of the National Socialist Party led by Shajahan Siraj. However, it failed to win any seats in the 1996 elections. The party put up 17 candidates, winning 0.015% of the vote, in the 2001 elections. It is in opposition to the current BNP-led government and part of the current broad left 11-party alliance.
Leader. Kamal Hossain

Workers' Party of Bangladesh; left-wing opposition party. It put up 32 candidates in the 2001 elections but won only 0.07% of the vote.

Barbados

Capital: Bridgetown
Population: 277,000 (2003E)

Barbados gained its independence from the United Kingdom in 1966. The head of state is the British sovereign, represented by a Governor-General, with the head of government being the Prime Minister. There is a bicameral parliament (with colonial era origins dating back to 1639), consisting of a 30-member House of Assembly and an appointed 21-member Senate. Elections to the House are on the Westminster model, with MPs elected for five-year terms by universal adult suffrage on the first past the post single-member constituency system.

In the most recent general election, held on May 21, 2003, the Barbados Labour Party (BLP) (in office since 1994) was re-elected, winning 23 of the House of Assembly seats with 56% of the popular vote, while the Democratic Labour Party (DLP) took seven seats and 44% of the vote. However, only 56.7% of eligible voters cast ballots – the lowest turnout since the country gained its independence. Barbados has a tradition of political stability and the BLP and DLP have been the two main parties since independence, sharing considerable ideological common ground. With no real ideological differences separating the parties, rivalry centres on personalities and political competence.

Barbados Labour Party (BLP)
Address. Grantley Adams House, 111 Roebuck Street, Bridgetown
Telephone. (1-246) 429–1990
Email. hq@blp.org.bb
Website. www.blp.org.bb
Leadership. Owen Arthur (chairman and political leader); Mia Amor Mottley (general secretary)
Founded in 1938, the moderate social democratic BLP held office in the pre-independence period from 1951 to 1961 under the leadership of Sir Grantley Adams. It then went into opposition until the 1976 elections when, led by J.M.G. (Tom) Adams (Sir Grantley's son), it was returned to power. The party was affected by factional splits after Tom Adams's death in 1985 and was defeated heavily in the polls the following year. It then remained in opposition until a general election in September 1994 when, under the leadership of Owen Arthur, it won 19 of the then 28 House of Assembly seats with just over 48% of the votes cast.

In the January 1999 elections the government ran on its success with the economy, with a campaign slogan of "one good term deserves another". It won 26 of the 28 House seats (the biggest ever victory in a Barbados election), taking 65% of the vote. The BLP retained its coherence and direction during its second term, despite a serious economic downturn and a number of financial scandals. In the elections of May 2003 the BLP retained power by promising to make "Every Bajan A Winner". A relatively weak and divided opposition also helped the BLP to remain in office.

The BLP is a member party of the Socialist International.

Democratic Labour Party (DLP)
Address. George Street, Belleville, St Michael

Telephone. (1-246) 429-3104
Fax. (1-246) 427-0548
Email. dlp@sunbeach.net
Website. www.dlpbarbados.org
Leadership. Clyde Mascoll (leader and party president); David Estwick (general secretary)

Dissident members of the Barbados Labour Party (BLP), led by Errol Barrow, formed the DLP in 1955. It was seen as standing somewhat to the left of the BLP and has traditionally been strongest among the urban electorate. Between 1961 and 1976 it was the governing party (during which time it led Barbados to independence), but then spent the following ten years in opposition before returning to power in the 1986 elections. The party leader and Prime Minister, Errol Barrow, died in 1987 and was succeeded by Erskine Sandiford. The party won the 1991 elections, but suffered a resounding defeat in the September 1994 polls (called early by Sandiford in response to an internal DLP revolt). David Thompson assumed leadership of the party, whose parliamentary strength fell to eight seats.

In the January 1999 election campaign the DLP charged that under the BLP lower and middle-income people had been excluded from increasing prosperity, and crime had increased, but it suffered a sweeping defeat, retaining only two seats (one of them Thompson's). Thompson remained as leader until September 2001, when a poor showing in a parliamentary by-election prompted his resignation. The departure of Thompson placed the DLP in a difficult position, as the only other MP, Denis Kellman, had fallen out with Thompson some months before. A leadership election was then held in November 2001, in an attempt to resolve the impasse between the two elected DLP MPs. The result was that Clyde Mascoll, an appointed member of the Senate, took control of the DLP. In the build-up to the May 2003 general election, Mascoll fought a strong campaign, focusing on the BLP's alleged mismanagement of public funds used for capital projects. Despite a third heavy electoral defeat the DLP emerged as a more united and effective opposition. In August 2003 the leadership position of Mascoll (now an MP) was reinforced when he was overwhelmingly re-elected by the DLP's rank and file.

National Democratic Party (NDP)

Address. c/o Dr Haynes, Delaware Clinic, Jemmott's Lane, St Michael
Leadership. Richard Haynes

Formed in February 1989 under the leadership of Richard (Richie) Haynes, a former Finance Minister, following his resignation and that of three other MPs from the then ruling Democratic Labour Party. The party lost its four seats in the 1991 elections, but regained one (won by Haynes), taking nearly 13% of the vote, in the 1994 polls. In the 1999 and 2003 elections, however, the NDP did not put up candidates, with Haynes calling on his supporters to vote for the BLP, saying that it had implemented NDP policies.

Belarus

Capital: Minsk
Population: 10,200,000 (2004)

The Soviet Socialist Republic of Byelorussia declared independence from the USSR on Aug. 25, 1991. It adopted the name of the Republic of Belarus the following month and became a founder and a sovereign member of the Commonwealth of Independent States (CIS) in December 1991, on the demise of the USSR. The ruling republican Communist Party was suspend-

ed four days after the declaration of independence, and, on its subsequent revival in December 1991 (registered May 1992), appeared to have lost the allegiance of most of the Soviet-era personnel who remained in control of government and state structures. A new constitution was approved in March 1994, which provided for a 260-member Supreme Council to be the highest representative and sole legislative body of state power elected every four years. It instituted the post of President of the Republic as Head of State and Government and the commander-in-chief of the armed forces, elected by universal adult suffrage for a five-year term (once renewable). The constitution gave the President extensive powers, including the right to set up and abolish ministries and to appoint and dismiss, with the consent of the Supreme Council, the Prime Minister, his deputies, and members of the Cabinet.

The first presidential elections were held in June-July 1994, and an independent candidate, Alyaksandr Lukashenka, was elected in the second round with 81.7% of the vote. He soon drafted controversial amendments to the constitution, which enabled him to assume power over the legislature, and which were approved by 87% of elegible voters at a referendum in November 1996. As a consequence, the President was granted the right to appoint and control members of legislative, judicial and executive bodies at all levels. Under the same referendum Lukashenka's five-year tenure in office was extended by two years to 2001.

In 1996, on the President's initiative, the legislature was reorganised into the bicameral National Assembly, consisting of an upper Council of the Republic (*Savet Respubliki*) of 64 members (56 indirectly elected by regional councils and eight appointed by the President) and the 110-member House of Representatives members (*Palata Pradstaunikou*) directly elected with a majority required on the first ballot in a turnout of over 50% of eligible votes. If no candidate obtained a majority, a second and final ballot would be held with the turnout threshold set at of 25%.

The legitimacy of the new legislature and the expansion of the President's authority were strongly opposed by parties dominant in the previous unicameral Supreme Council. This laid the foundation for the growth of a strong political divide between the opposition activists and the protagonists of Lukashenka's rule.

The next elections to the House of Representatives were held on Oct. 15 and 29, 2000 (with re-runs held in 13 constituencies on March 18 and April 1, 2001). They resulted in opposition parties obtaining no seats and pro-presidential parties all but three of the 110 seats. The results of the elections were not recognized by the European Union and the United States. The OSCE election observers reported that the required 50% threshold was not met in more than a third of the constituencies. They also established strong evidence that the nationwide turnout was about 40%, rather than the 60% claimed, and documented 80 different methods employed to manipulate the vote count. The OSCE declared that these elections "were neither free, fair, nor democratic" and that "the Thirteenth Supreme Soviet, (the parliament elected in 1995) ...should continue to be accepted by the international community as the legitimate parliament of Belarus".

The presidential election held on Sept. 9, 2001, was won by Lukashenka with 75.62% of the vote. Official results gave the chairman of the Belarusan Trade Union Federation, Uladzimir Hancharyk, 15.39%, and the leader of the Liberal Democratic Party, Siarhiej

Hajdulievich, 2.48%. Lukashenka declared that he had won an "elegant victory", but Hancharyk disputed the official results, claiming that he had received 40% of the vote and Lukashenka 44%. In such a case, according to Article 79 of the Electoral Code, a run-off between the two should have taken place. The United States and countries of the European Union chose to ignore Lukashenka's second inauguration ceremony in Minsk, declaring the elections neither free nor fair. The OSCE Limited Election Observation Mission concluded that "the entire 2001 presidential election process has been marked by grave flaws and consistent interference by Belarusian authorities". According to the OSCE the election process "failed to meet the OSCE commitments for democratic elections".

One important aspect of the regime's control has been its ruling that requires all political parties, trade unions and NGOs to register and periodically re-register with the Ministry of Justice. With each re-registration more restrictions are imposed on these organizations and fewer organizations are able to function legally.

There are at present 18 registered political parties. The Party of the Belarusan Popular Front, the Party of Communists (Belaruskaya) and the Liberal Democratic Party remain the largest political organizations, whose reported memberships exceed 5000 supporters and which have regional and local branches throughout Belarus.

On Oct. 17, 2004, Belarusian citizens went to the polls to elect a new parliament, and to vote in a referendum whether or not to allow the incumbent President to participate in future presidential elections and on eliminating the existing constitutional limit on two presidential terms in office. According to official reports, the turnout for the elections and referendum was 90.14% and 90.28% respectively (beer and sausages were provided to voters in polling stations at cut-rate prices) and 79.42% voted to allow Lukashenka to run again - in effect, removing limitations on his tenure in office.

After two rounds of parliamentary elections (Oct. 17 and 27) 109 deputies out of 110 were elected to the House of Representatives including only 12 representatives of political parties: eight from the Belarusan Communist Party (KPB), three from the Agrarian Party (APB), and one Liberal Democrat. None of the opposition candidates was elected. Some were intimidated from the start including situations when lives of their close kin were put at risk; many were refused registration beforehand or discriminated against during the election campaign following the President's orders "to eliminate and spread the ashes of both internal and external opposition in the country".

The OSCE, which refused to monitor the referendum, issued strong criticism of the election stating that: "The Belarusian authorities failed ... to ensure the fundamental commitment - that the will of the people serves a basis for the authority of government - could be fulfilled. The dominant influence of the State administration was apparent throughout the organisation of the election process, and at all levels of the election administration. In this regard, it is of great concern that during the election campaign period, President Alexander Lukashenko made a statement affirming that the Constitution and laws of the Republic of Belarus have 'elements of authoritarianism'".

Liberal Democratic Party of Belarus
Liberal'na-Demakratychnaya Partyya Belarusi (LDPB)

Address. 22 Platonava Street, Minsk 220071
Telephone. (375–17) 2318047; 231-6331
Website. www.ldbsm.narod.ru
Leadership. Syargey Gaydukevich (chairman)

The right-wing pan-Slavic LDPD is the Belarusan fraternal party of the Liberal Democratic Party of Russia and therefore advocates close links with Russia. However, with the latter's decline in Russia, the LDPB began to distance itself from its parent organization in a more liberal nationalist direction. It was established at the regional level in 1991 but was not registered until 1994, and has a personalized style of politics based upon its leader Syargey Gaydukevich. The LDPB has been working on developing its regional network in Belarus, and has a reported membership of 17,637 supporters. Gaydukevich himself jokes that it could have been more, if more drink had been provided. In September 1998 the LDPB was a founder member of the pro-Lukashenka Belarusan People's Patriotic Union, grouping some 30 conservative parties which backed the proposed Belarus-Russian union treaty, including the Belarus Popular Party and Communist Party of Belarus. The party won one seat in the October 2000 legislative elections.

Party of the Belarusan Popular Front
Partyya Belaruskaga Narodnaga Frontu (Party BNF)

Address. 8 Varvasheni Street, Minsk 220005
Telephone. (375-17) 284–5012
Email. bpf@bpf.minsk.by
Website. pages.prodigy.net/dr_fission/bpf/
Leadership. Vintsuk Vyachorka (chairman)

As a political movement, the Belarusan Popular Front was launched in June 1989 at a conference held in Vilnius (Lithuania) of representatives of groups and organizations united by the belief that Belarus should be governed by its own independent authorities rather than by Moscow. The then Communist Party regime had refused to allow the conference to be held in the republic and had denounced its organizers as "chauvinists". The elected party leader at the Vilnius session was Zyanon Paznyak, an archaeologist who in 1988 had published evidence of mass graves found at Kurapaty, near Minsk, on the site of a detention/execution camp established on Stalin's orders in 1937. The BNF had originally organized itself as an all-inclusive political movement, extending its appeal beyond the core nationalist constituency, and positioning itself as an umbrella movement for all democratic forces.

The BNF as a party was established on May 30, 1993, at the third congress of the movement, and registered in December of the following year. Officially the party and the movement were separate organizations; however, in practice their organizational structures (leadership and core membership) largely coincided, which was a cause of a conflict leading to a formal split in 1999.

In January 1990 Belarusan replaced Russian as the official language, and BNF candidates were allowed to run in the April 1990 Supreme Soviet elections. However, the entrenched Communist Party won a large majority, and the BNF was confined to 27 seats in the 360-member legislature. Thereafter, the BNF sought to accelerate the government's hesitant moves to assert sovereignty and was strongly critical of its initial support for the attempted coup by hardliners in Moscow in August 1991. It therefore welcomed the resultant downfall of the Minsk conservatives and the advent of the Shushkevich government, supporting the latter's declaration of independence in August. But the simultaneous suspension of the Communist Party deprived the opposition of a valuable target: although effectively a continuation of the previous regime, the new government could depict itself as independent.

The BNF opposed the constitution introduced in March 1994, on the grounds that a democratic parliament had not yet been elected. It also opposed the treaty on monetary union with Russia signed by the government in April and Belarusan participation in the CIS security pact. In the direct presidential elections of June-July 1994, Paznyak stood as the BNF candidate but received only 13.5% of the first-round vote and was eliminated. In the second round, BNF support swung overwhelmingly behind Alyaksandr Lukashenka as apparently being the more reformist of the two candidates on offer.

Opposed to the government's policy of close integration with Russia, the BNF won no seats in the 1995 parliamentary elections. Following the signature of a treaty of union between Belarus and Russia in April 1996, BNF leaders came under pressure from the authorities for organizing protests against constitutional amendments tabled by the government to significantly increase presidential powers. The approval of the amendments by 70.5% on a turnout of 84% in a referendum in November 1996 was rejected as invalid by the BNF.

After 1995 the party divided into two factions. The dominant radical wing was headed by Paznyak, and pursued extreme nationalist policies offering no compromise towards any political forces that favoured a closer association with Russia. The liberal wing, headed by Vintsuk Vyachorka, retained the original policy of compromise and cooperation with other political forces.

The political impasse continued over the next four years, during which time the BNF was at the core of regular opposition demonstrations. In May 1999 the BNF was the principal organizer of "alternative" presidential elections, which unofficially yielded a two-thirds majority for Paznyak (although the exercise was called off before the results were declared). Thereafter the government combined repression of the BNF leaders and other opponents with periodic attempts, under pressure from Western governments, to initiate a dialogue with the opposition, although with no substantive outcome.

The sixth BNF congress held in Minsk in August 1999 featured deep divisions between critics of Paznyak's leadership in exile and his supporters. The following month the latter minority faction broke away to form the Conservative Christian Party, of which Paznyak was declared leader, while Vyachorka was elected chairman of the party (subsequently renamed as the Party of BNF, registered in April 2000) with reported membership over 5,200 supporters.

On the OSCE Advisory and Monitoring Group's initiative, a coordinating council (KRDS) of opposition groups was formed in 1999 to unite BNF and other parties. This action failed to propagate the 1999 alternative presidential elections, and instead led to the boycott of the October 2000 legislative elections. The BNF formed part of the anti-Lukashenka "For a New Belarus" front in the September 2001 presidential elections.

As a pluralist organization which includes a strong Christian democratic current, the BNF is affiliated to the Christian Democrat International.

Party of Communists of Belarus
Partyya Kamunistay Belaruskaya (PKB)

Address. 24-2-17 V. Kharuzhay Street, Minsk 220013
Telephone. (375–17) 232–2573
Leadership. Syargey Kalyakin (chairman)

The Soviet-era Communist Party had originated as a regional committee of the Russian Social Democratic Labour Party (formed in 1904) covering both Belarus and Lithuania. Established as the ruling Communist Party of the Soviet Socialist Republic of Byelorussia in 1920, the party suffered heavily during Stalin's terror of the 1930s, when almost all of its leaders were liquidated and party membership fell by more than half. Enlarged by Soviet territorial acquisitions from Poland in World War II, the Byelorussian SSR was given UN membership in 1945 but its ruling party and government remained wholly subservient to Moscow.

From mid-1989 the republican leadership came under official Soviet criticism for lacking "tolerance...and readiness to make compromises". It therefore allowed candidates of the opposition BNF to contest the April 1990 Supreme Soviet elections, correctly calculating that its control of the levers of power would ensure a decisive Communist victory. But the conservative Minsk leadership miscalculated when it backed the abortive coup by hardliners in Moscow in August 1991. In the immediate aftermath, the hardline Chairman of the Supreme Soviet (head of state), Nikalay Dzemyantsey, was replaced by the reformist Stanislau Shushkevich; independence from the USSR was declared; the first secretary of the republican Communist Party, Anatol Malafeeu, resigned from the Soviet politburo; and the party itself was suspended and its property nationalized.

The new Communist Party was launched in December 1991, and officially registered in May 1992 as the Party of Communists Belarusslaya (PKB). However, only a few regarded it as a true successor to the Communist Party in Belarus. Despite a smear campaign against the former Communist Party, and the fact that some distinguished politicians, like Shushkevich (parliament's chairman) and Vyacheslau Kebich (Prime Minister) publicly left the KPB in 1991, the government and the legislature continued to be under the control of people appointed or previously elected as Communists. The re-legalization of the Communist Party in February 1993 did little to clarify true allegiance, in part because government members preferred to retain the "independent" label. In May 1993 at a joint Congress the two parties – PKB and restored KPB – united and were named after the officially registered PKB. There was, however, an internal leadership dispute: in addition to the party led by Syargey Kalyakin and Uladzimir Novikau, another faction emerged under the leadership of Viktar Chykin, who in October 1993 founded the Movement for Democracy, Social Progress and Justice as a merger of seven hardline communist groups.

Having embraced the concept of multi-partyism, the PKB contested the June–July 1994 presidential elections in its own right, with Vasil Novikau as candidate. Its problem was that voters had other "establishment" candidates to choose from, including Kebich and Shushkevich, both standing as independents. The result of the first round was last place out of six candidates for Novikau, who managed only 4.5% of the vote. But forecasts that "*nomenklatura* power" would ensure victory for Kebich proved wide of the mark: relegated to a poor second place in the first round, he was heavily defeated in the second by another independent, Alyaksandr Lukashenka, a moderate conservative who in his parliamentary role as anti-corruption supremo had played a key role in the ousting of Shushkevich from the Speaker position in 1993. The PKB's stronger organization enabled it to become the largest formal party in the 1995 legislative elections, in which it won 42 seats, and the third strongest faction (43 members) in parliament.

As a result of internal frictions following the dissolution of the Supreme Soviet in 1996, the party formally split, and a conservative-communist splinter organization (the KPB) emerged. Led by Chykin, 24 members of the KPB joined the 1997 House of Representatives. Many regional and local organizations ceased their activities at the beginning of 1998. On registration in 1999, the original PKB reported a total membership of 7878, with 19 urban, 119 regional and 534 local organizations in operation.

Having established leadership of the rump KPB, Chykin in September 1998 became executive secretary of the pro-Lukashenka Belarusan People's Patriotic Union, grouping some 30 conservative parties which backed the proposed Belarus–Russian union treaty. This party failed to pass the registration procedure imposed by the President in 1999. The rump KPB now led by Valeryi Zakharchanka obtained six seats in the October 2000 legislative elections.

Other Parties

Agrarian Party of Belarus (*Agrarnaya Partyya Belarusi*, APB). Founded in June 1992, the APB provides a national political framework for agrarian interests associated with the communist-era agricultural system, being opposed in particular to the restoration of individual peasant ownership of the land. Its membership grew from 250 to reportedly over 12,000 party activists in 1995. The party emerged as a powerful agrarian party in the 1995 legislative elections, winning 33 out of 260 seats, and forming the second largest faction with 45 members in parliament. In January 1996 the APB leader, Syamion Sharetsky, was elected to the chairmanship of the then unicameral legislature. With the 1996 crisis the party split, and ceased to exist. Soon after, on the president's initiative, the party reinvented itself under the leadership of Mikhail Shymansky, chief editor of pro-government newspaper *Narodnaya Gazeta* (registered in 1999). The APB won five out of 110 lower house seats in the October 2000 legislative elections. After 1999 its membership was reported to be above 1,000.
Address. 31-110 Zakharova Street, Minsk 220073
Telephone. (375–17) 231-0945
Leadership. Mikhail Shymansky (chairman)

Belarusan Communist Party (*Kamunistychnaia Partyia Belarusi*), founded in 1996, re-registered in 1999.
Address. 21 Checheryna Street, Minsk, 220029
Telephone. (375 17) 239-4311, 239-4888
Leadership. Valeryi Zakharchanka

Belarusan Ecological Green Party "BEZ" (*Belaruskaia Ekalagichnaia Partyia Zialionykh* "BEZ"), founded in 1998 as a merger of the Ecological and Green parties, which had each won one seat in the 1995 legislative elections.
Address. 33 Zakhodniaia Street, Homel 246027
Telephone. (375-232) 279-3220
Leadership. Mikola Kartash

Belarusan Green Party (*Belaruskaia Partyia Zialenykh*), founded in 1994, re-registered in 1999.
Address. 6 Brestskaia Street, Homel 246023
Telephone. (375 232) 479696
Leadership. Aleg Gramyka

Belarusan Party of Labour (*Belaruskaia Partyia Pratsy*, BPP). The BPP, founded in 1993 and registered in 1995, represents the interests of the official trade unions in parliament. The party pursues the traditions and principles of the international social democratic and labour movements, and has been led by the party chairman, Aliaksandr Bukchvostau, since 1996. The party is based on a modest network of regional political clubs, which are governed by the Regional Association of the BPP. The party was relatively effective in its negotiations with the authorities until 1999, when a presidential decree brought an end to the existing system of trade unions based on the payment of dues and allocation of bonuses. The party consequently suffered a considerable decline in membership. At present it remains Minsk-based and moderately anti-Lukashenka, and takes part together with *Narodnaya Hramada* in the activities of the Coordinating Council of Democratic Forces (KRDS).
Address. 21-3 Kazintsa Street, Minsk 220099
Telephone. (375 17) 223-8204, 222-0450

Belarusan Party of Labour and Justice (*Respublikanskaya Partyia Pratsy i Spravyadlivastsi*, RPPS), founded in 1993, won one seat in the 1995 legislative elections and two in 2000.
Address. 7 Amuratarskaya Street, Minsk 220004
Telephone. (375–17) 237–8725, 221-4350
Leadership. Viktar Sakalou (deputy chairman)

Belarusan Patriotic Party (*Belaruskaia Patryiatychnaia Partyia*), founded in 1994, and re-registered in 1999.
Address. 7-107 Papanina Street, Minsk, 220089.
Telephone. (375 17) 226-3260, 274-6495
Leadership. Mikola Ulakhovich

Belarusan Social Democratic Hramada (*Belaruskaia Satsyial-Demakratychnaia Hramada*), founded in 1998, and registered in 1999.
Address. 8-52 Drazda Street, Minsk, 220035
Telephone. (375 17) 226-7078
Leadership. Stanislau Shushkevich

Belarusan Social Democratic Party "People's Assembly" (*Satsiyal–Demakratychnaya Partyya Belarusi "Narodnaya Hramada"*, SDPB/Hramada). The SDPB was founded in 1991 as a latter-day renaissance of the Revolutionary *Hramada* (Assembly) Party (founded in 1903), which spearheaded the early movement for the creation of a Belarusan state but was outlawed following the declaration of the Soviet Socialist Republic in January 1919. The revived party, also known as the *Hramada*, was originally formed as a merger of former CPB and BNF members, and even supported its own candidate, Stanislau Shushkevich, in the 1994 presidential election, in opposition to Paznyak. This action led to internal frictions and a change of leadership within the party in 1995. Mykola Statkevich, an engineer and leader of the Belarusan Assembly of Armed Forces, which had been banned in 1993, became party chairman, and its policies began to drift to the left, aiming to create a wide social democratic coalition. In 1995 it was joined by part of the Party of Popular Accord (PNZ), Party of Common Sense (PZS) and Party of All-Belarus Unity (PVES), having formed a Social Democratic Union (CDC) for the election campaign. It subsequently won two seats and later formed an 18-member strong parliamentary group "Union of Labour". However, in January 1997 the former part of PNS left the CDC to form its own party, the Belarusan Social Democratic Party of Popular Accord (SDPNZ), under the leadership of Leanid Sechka. In Septmber that year the CDC finally split in two: the BSDP NG, with a centre-left orientation, led by Statkevich, and the Belarusan Social Democratic Hramada (BSDG), with a rightist orientation, led by Shushkevich. After 1998 the Statkevich party continued its independent strategy against the joint agreement of all oppositional parties, and unlike them did not boycott the 2000 parliamentary election. In 2001 a new fraction emerged under the leadership of Alyaksey Karol', who disapproved of Statkevich's policy of participation in the 2000 parliamentary elections. Along with Stanislau Shushkevich (BSDG) and Valyantsina Palevikova (former Nadzeya), Karol' formed a new United Social Democratic Party in 2002, which has not yet been registered by the Ministry of Justice.

The SDPB/*Hramada* is an observer member of the Socialist International.
Address. 153-2-107 Skaryny Avenue, Minsk 220114
Telephone. (375–17) 269–4774, 263-3748
Website. www.sdpb.net
Leadership. Mykola Statkevich (chairman)

Belarusan Social-Sports Party (*Belaruskaia Satsyal-spartyynaia Partyia*), founded in 1994, and re-registered in 1999.
Address. 77a-3, Kalinoyskaga Street, Minsk
Telephone. (375-17) 222-6412
Leadership. Uladzimir Aleksandrovich

Belarusan Women's Political Party–Hope (*Belaruskaya Partyya Zhanchyn "Nadzeia"*). The Women's Party "Hope" was first registered in 1994. The then party leader, Valyantsina Palevikova, had maintained very close links with the official trade unions led by Uladzimir Hancharyk, and was his campaign manager during the 2001 presidential election. The party does not have an ideological mission statement, and focuses on helping families, women and children. In August 2002, at a special convention of the party, Valyantsina Palevikova was replaced by Valyantsina Matusevich. According to Matusevich, the convention was intended to reanimate Hope and prevent it from disappearing from the political map of Belarus, as a result of its announced merger with the two social democratic parties, splinter BSDP/*Hramada* and BSDG. The merger took place on Aug. 24, 2002, on the initiative of the BSDP/*Hramada* splinter organization led by Alyaksey Karol and Stanislau Shushkevich, and a new United Social Democratic Party was launched, but not (yet) registered.
Address. 21-1 Kazintsa Street, Minsk 220099
Telephone. (375–17) 236-1843, 223-8653
Website. www.nadzeya.org
Leadership. Valyantsina Matusevich (chairwoman)

Conservative Christian Party (*Kanservatyuna Khrystsiyanskaia Partyia*, KKP), founded in 1999 as a splinter of the BNF.
Address. 8 Varvasheni Street, Minsk 220005
Telephone. (375-17) 284-5012
Website. www.bpfs.boom.ru
Leadership. Zyanon Paznyak (chairman)

Republican Party (*Respublikanskaia Partyia*), founded in 1994, and re-registered in 1999.
Address. 34 Prytytskaga Street, Minsk 220050.
Telephone. (375-17) 223-9783, 224-9037
Leadership. Uladzimir Belazor (chairman)

Social Democratic Party of Popular Accord (*Satsiyal-Demakratychnaya Partyya Narodnay Zgody*, SDPNZ). The SDPNZ dates as such from 1997, when the Party of Popular Accord (PNZ) adopted the Social Democratic rubric. The PNZ was founded in 1992 as a technocratic party emphasizing the need for economic reform, independent of the competing pro-democracy and conservative alliances. Although it backed the BNF candidate in the 1994 presidential elections, in 1995 it partly merged with the *Hramada*, led by Leanid Sechka. Its former leader, Henadz Karpenka (died in 1999) joined the United Civic Party. The PNZ won eight of the declared seats in the 1995 legislative elections and joined an 18-member strong parliamentary group "The Union of Labour". After splitting with the *Hramada* in 1996, it was subsequently re-founded in 1997 as the SDPNZ, led by Sechka. Its 7 members joined the 1997 House of Representatives, on Lukashenka's initiative. The SDPNZ won one seat in the October 2000 legislative elections.
Address. 10 Karl Marx Street, Minsk 220050
Telephone. (375–17) 222-3833, 222-6928
Leadership. Syargey Ermak (first deputy)

United Civic Party of Belarus (*Abyadnanaya Grazhdanskaya Partyya Belarusi*, AGP). The AGP, the leading liberal conservative party of Belarus, was established in October 1995 as a result of the merger of two like-minded parties – the United Democratic Party (formed in 1990) and the Civic Party (formed in 1994). It stands for an independent sovereign Belarus based upon human rights, democratic forms of government, private property, free enterprise and a market economy. Among its policy priorities are the introduction of a mixed electoral system, direct election of the heads of local administration, the replacement of Lukashenka, and eventual membership of the European Union. Up to spring 2000 Stanislau Bahdankevich, a former professor and ex-chairman of the National Bank, was party chairman. The party leadership also included Aliaksandr Dabravol'sky, Vasil' Shlyndikau, a former MP and businessman, Henadz Karpenka, former leader of PNZ, and Anatol' Lyabedzka, a former deputy and chairman of the Association of Young Politicians, who in 1999 succeeded to the position of chairman. The party claims to have 4,500 members and branches in 6 regions, 28 towns and 66 districts. It also has an established partnership with the British Conservative Party, the Polish Union of Freedom, Russia's Union of Right Forces, and Reforms and Order in Ukraine. It is a member of the European Democrat Union
Address. 22-38 V. Kharuzhay Street, Minsk 220123
Telephone. (375-17) 237-7009
Website. www.ucpb.org
Leadership. Anatol' Lyabedzka (chairman)

Belgium

Capital: Brussels
Population: 10,348,276 (2004E)

The Kingdom of Belgium is a constitutional monarchy with a parliamentary democracy in which two distinct party systems co-exist based on the country's linguistic communities, Flemish in the North and French-speaking in the South. The constitutional monarch, as head of state, has limited powers, with central executive authority residing in the Prime Minister and the Council of Ministers being responsible to a federal bicameral legislature. The federal parliament has a lower and a upper chamber; the Chamber of People's Representatives (*Chambre des Représentants* or *Kamer van Volksvertegen-woordigers*) with 150 members elected directly and the Senate (*Sénat/Senaat*) with 71 members (40 elected directly and the remainder co-opted and/or representative of federal entities). Both chambers have virtually equal powers and are elected for a four-year term by universal compulsory suffrage of those aged 18 and over according to a system of proportional representation. Belgium was a founder member of the European Union and elects 24 members to the European Parliament.

From 1970, several packages of constitutional reforms have led to the transfer of substantial competencies to regions and communities. Since 1993 (July 14), the country has been officially divided into three territorial regions (Flanders, Wallonia and Brussels-Capital, which has a bilingual status) and three linguistic and cultural communities (Flemish, French and German). Each region has received economic and social competencies (e.g. territorial development, transport, environment, housing, etc.) and got a distinct government emanating from a directly elected council (118 members for the Flemish Parliament, 75 for the Walloon and the Brussels parliaments). While each community has in theory its own council and government, the Flemish Council is identical to the Flemish Parliament, while the French Community council is indirectly constituted by the 75 Walloon regional deputies and 19 deputies of the Brussels Parliament. The German community has a council with 25 members elected directly. A direct consequence of the 1993 reform is the organization of distinct elections at the federal and regional levels; every four years at the federal and every five years at the regional level.

Between 1999 and 2004, other amendments were made to the electoral law: introduction of the 5% threshold, the obligation to include 50% of women on electoral lists, extension of electoral constituencies. Each party receives a public subsidy (€125,000, plus €1.25 for each vote). According to a 1999 law, a party can be deprived of this subsidy when it does not respect human rights and civil liberties. During the same period, several parties changed their denomination in order to reposition themselves on the political scene (see below).

After the defeat of the Christian Democrats at the 1999 federal elections, Guy Verhofstadt, Flemish Liberal (VLD), became the Prime Minister of a coalition between the Socialist, Liberal and Green families of the North and the South. The simultaneity of federal and regional elections led to a political symmetry at the various levels of power. Elections to the federal parliament held on May 18, 2003, resulted as follows: Flemish Liberals and Democrats 25 seats (15.4% of the national vote), Flemish Socialist Party/Spirit 23 (14.9%), Flemish Christian Democratic Party 21 (13.3%), Flemish Bloc 18 (11.6%), French-speaking Reform Movement 24 (11.4%), French-speaking Humanist Democratic Centre 8 (5.5%), French-speaking Green Party 4 (3.1%), New Flemish Alliance 1 (3.1%), National Front 1 (1.5%). As a result of the 2003 elections, Verhofstadt arranged a second coalition between the Socialists and Liberals without the Greens.

The 2004 regional elections led to a differentiated and asymmetric situation. In the Flemish region, the Christian Democrats won back their status of the leading party and took over the formation of the new government in a difficult context where the far right Flemish Bloc became the second political group at the Flemish parliament. Ultimately, an agreement between the five traditional Flemish parties (VLD, CD&V, NVA, SPA and Spirit) was reached. In Wallonia, the Socialist Party, winner of the elections, reshaped the governmental coalition by choosing another main partner than the Liberals, the former French-speaking Christian Democrats (CDH). The situation was repeated in Brussels where the French-speaking Socialists formed a new government with CDH, the French-speaking Greens, the Flemish Socialist Party, the Flemish Christian Democrats and Liberals.

The European Parliament elections held on June 13, 2004, resulted in the following outcome: Christian Democratic and Flemish Party/National Free Alliance (CDV/NVA) – 17.4% of the vote – 4 seats (+1); Flemish Bloc – 14.3% of the vote – 3 seats (+1); Flemish Liberals and Democrats – 13.6% of the vote – 3 seats; Socialist Party – 13.5% of the vote – 4 seats (+1); Social Progressive Alternative+SPIRIT – 11% of the vote – 3 seats (+1); Reformist Movement – 10.3% of the vote – 3 seats; Humanist Democratic Centre – 5.7% of the vote – 1 seat (+1); Greens – 4.9% of the vote – 1 seat (-1); Ecologist Party – 3.7% of the vote – 1 seat (-2); Christian Social Party–European People's Party CSP-EVP – 0.2% of the vote – 1 seat. The CSP-EVP won the seat reserved for a representative of the German speaking minority. Turnout in a country which has compulsory voting was

90.08%, the highest in the EU.

Christian Democratic and Flemish Party
Christen-Democratic and Vlaams (CD&V)

Address. Wetstraat 89, B-1040 Brussels
Telephone. (32-2) 238-38011
Fax. (32–2) 238-3871
Email. webmaster@cdenv.be
Website. www.cdenv.be
*Leadership.*Yves Leterme; Pieter Demeester (secretary general)

Historically descended from the *Katholieke Vlaamse Volkspartij*, which was the Flemish wing of the pre-war Belgian Catholic Party, the CVP was created in 1945 as the Flemish counterpart of the French-speaking Christian Social Party (PSC), initially within a single party structure. It has always drawn its electorate from Flemish Catholic workers and farmers (via the powerful "Boerenbond", the Flemish farmers' association). From 1947 the CVP/PSC participated in successive coalition governments, except for the period 1954–58. By the mid-1960s the CVP and the PSC had effectively become separate parties, the former considerably larger than the latter in terms of electoral support. Consistently the strongest single parliamentary party, the CVP provided the Prime Minister in coalitions, with the Socialists and the Democratic Front of French-Speakers of Brussels in 1979–80; with the Socialists and Liberals briefly in 1980; with the Socialists in 1980–81; with the Liberals in 1981–88; with the Socialists and the People's Union in 1988–91; and with the Socialists in 1992-99.

In the November 1991 Chamber elections the CVP's representation fell from 43 to 39 seats out of 212 and its share of the vote from 19.5% to 16.7%. After 13 years of almost continuous incumbency as CVP Prime Minister, Wilfried Martens gave way to Jean-Luc Dehaene in the government formed in March 1992. In the June 1994 European Parliament elections the party took 17% of the vote (compared with 21.1% in 1989) and four of the 25 Belgian seats. In further Chamber elections in May 1995 the CVP unexpectedly increased its vote share to 17.2%, winning 29 out of 150 seats, so that Dehaene remained head of a federal coalition with the Socialists. In simultaneous elections for the 118-member Flemish regional council the CVP won a plurality of 35 seats (with 26.8% of the vote), providing the minister-president of Flanders in the person of Luc van den Brande, who headed a coalition with the Flemish Socialists.

From 1996 the CVP shared in the Dehaene coalition's deep unpopularity over official mishandling of a gruesome paedophile case, amidst widespread protest against expenditure cuts introduced to enable Belgium to qualify for the single European currency. On the eve of the June 1999 general, regional and European elections, moreover, two major food safety scares proved to be the death-knell for the government. Support for the CVP fell to 14.1% in the Chamber elections (22 seats) relegating it to second place behind the Flemish Liberals and Democrats (VLD), with the result that the party went into opposition for the first time since 1958 together with the French-speaking Democrats. The CVP also lost ground in the Flemish regional council elections (taking 22.1% of the vote and 28 seats) and was obliged to surrender the post of minister-president to the VLD. The period of opposition led CVP leaders to question the main objectives of the party and its positioning regarding several key issues such as the pursuit of the reform of the State and the future of the Flemish region.

Renamed as CD&V in 2001 in order to emphasise its Flemish and Christian identity, the party began a campaign of renewal in the 2003 and 2004 elections. In 2003 after modest results in the federal elections, Yves Leterme replaced Stefaan de Clerq as leader of the party and signed an electoral pact with the New Flemish Alliance (NVA), a small nationalist party created after the dismissal of the *Volksunie* (see below). The combined CD&V–NVA took over the position of the leading Flemish party (35 seats, with 26.09% of the vote) and Yves Leterme formed the new regional government. At the European election, CD&V-NVA won back a seat lost in 1999 (giving it four in total) and increased its share of the vote to 17.43%.

The CD&V is a member of the Christian Democrat International and the European Union of Christian Democrats. Its four representatives in the European Parliament sit in the European People's Party/European Democrats group.

Democratic Front of French-Speakers
Front Démocratique des Francophones (FDF)

Address. Chaussée de Charleroi 127, B–1060 Brussels
Telephone. (32–2) 538–8320
Fax. (32-2) 539–3650
Email. fdf@fdf.be
Website. www.fdf.be
Leadership. Olivier Maingain (president); Daniel Bacquelaine (chairman in federal Chamber)

Founded in May 1964 with the aim of preserving the French character of the Belgian capital, the FDF incorporated various militant francophone groupings of Brussels. Its three Chamber seats in the 1965 elections were increased to 10 by 1977, after which it joined a coalition government with the Christian Socials and Socialists and assisted with the enactment of the 1978 Egmont Pact on regional devolution. Under the plan, Brussels was to become a separate (bilingual) region, i.e. not included in surrounding Flanders as some Flemish nationalists had demanded. Having risen to 11 seats in 1978, the FDF went into opposition again from 1980 and slipped to six seats in 1981. Two of these deputies defected to the Walloon Socialist Party in March 1985 and the FDF was reduced to three seats in the October 1985 elections, retaining them in 1987 and 1991.

The FDF retained representation in the May 1995 Chamber elections by virtue of an alliance with the Liberal Reformist Party (PRL). In simultaneous elections, the PRL/FDF alliance became the largest bloc in the Brussels regional council, winning 28 of the 75 seats (with 35% of the vote), and the second largest in the Walloon regional council, with 19 of the 75 seats and a 23.7% vote share. The FDF was allocated one portfolio in the six-party Brussels regional government.

The PRL–FDF alliance was maintained in the June 1999 elections, retaining 18 federal Chamber seats on a slightly reduced vote share of 10.1%, improving to 21 seats (24.7% of the vote) in the Walloon regional council and slipping to 27 seats (34.4%) in the Brussels regional council. In the simultaneous European Parliament elections the FDF was allied with both the PRL and the Citizens' Movement for Change (MCC), the joint list winning three seats on a 10% vote share. The FDF received no portfolios in the new federal government which included the PRL, but was represented at the French-speaking community and the Brussels region.

On March 2, 2002, the logic of alliance between the FDF and the Liberals was pushed further with the creation of the Reform Movement (MR). In the May 2003 elections the joint list consolidated its position of second most important French-speaking party in the federal parliament with 24 seats (11.4%) just behind the Socialists. First among political groups at the Brussels region and the French community level in 1999, the FDF and MR encountered a setback at the 2004 regional elections where they lost two seats (from 27 to 25) and the presidency of the region. While being relegated to the opposition, FDF continues its political fight for the defence of French-speaking interests and against the nationalist and extremist parties present in the Brussels region.

Ecologist Party
Ecologistes Confédérés pour l'Organisation de Luttes Originales (ECOLO)

Address. Espace « Kegeljan » 52 rue Marlagane B-5000 Namur
Telephone. (32–81) 227–871
Fax. (32–81) 230–603
Email. info@ecolo.be
Website. www.ecolo.be
Leadership. Jean-Michel Javaux, Isabelle Durant and Claude Brouir (federal secretaries)

Originally founded in 1978 by Walloon environmentalists, ECOLO was reorganized for the 1981 elections, in which it co-operated with the Flemish Live Differently (AGALEV) grouping and won two Chamber seats. Having established a significant local government presence, ECOLO increased its Chamber tally to five seats in 1985 (standing independently), but slipped back to three seats in 1987. The November 1991 elections brought a major advance, to 10 seats out of 212, with 5.1% of the vote, double the party's 1987 share. In the June 1994 European Parliament elections ECOLO won 4.8% of the national vote and one seat, compared with 6.3% and two seats in 1989. Its share in the May 1995 Chamber elections fell back to 4.0%, giving it six of the 150 seats, while in simultaneous regional polling it won eight and seven seats respectively on the 75-member Walloon and Brussels regional councils (with 10.4% and 9.0% of the vote respectively).

ECOLO resumed its electoral advance in the June 1999 federal, regional and European elections. Its representation in the federal Chamber almost doubled to 11 seats (from a vote share of 7.3%); it won 14 seats in both the Walloon and Brussels councils (with 18.2% and 18.3% respectively); it again took three seats on the 25-member council of the German-speaking community (with 12.7% of the vote); and it increased its European Parliament representation to three seats (with 8.4% of the vote). In July 1999 ECOLO joined a new federal coalition headed by the Flemish Liberals and Democrats, Isabelle Durant being appointed Deputy Prime Minister and Minister for Mobility and Transport. The ECOLO and AGALEV members in the federal Chamber formed a single group under the chairmanship of Jef Tavernier.

With this first participation in the federal and regional governments, the Green family had to consolidate its presence at each level of power in the perspective of the next elections. The pre-electoral context of 2003 was however not favourable to green ideas (a law against tobacco advertising resulting in the cancellation of the F1 Belgian race, controversy around night flights above Brussels, etc.). One week before the election, the French-Speaking Green ministers chose to resign from the federal government. The defeat proved severe; from 7.3% of the vote and 11 seats in 1999, ECOLO declined to 4 seats at the Federal Parliament. One year later, the same situation was repeated at the regional level but produced two different outcomes: ECOLO was ejected from the Walloon and French-speaking coalition (declining from 14 to 3 seats) while it remained a partner in the new Brussels government with one minister (Evelyne Huytebroeck – energy & transport) despite poor results (from 14 to 7 seats). Between the two elections, the party renewed its leadership and performed its *mea culpa* on past controversies. The next electoral battles will be determining for the existence of the party itself which has been considerably deprived of resources after the severe blow of 2003.

ECOLO is a member of the European Federation of Green Parties. Its sole representative in the European Parliament sits in the newly-created European Green Party.

Flemish Bloc
Vlaams Blok (VB)

Address. Madouplein 8 bus 9, B–1210 Brussels
Telephone. (32–2) 219–6009
Fax. (32–2) 217–1958
Email. vlblok@vlaams-blok.be
Website. www.vlaams-blok.be
Leadership. Frank Vanhecke (president); Karel Dillen (founder and honorary president); Luc Van Nieuwenhuysen (vice-president); Gerolf Annemans (chairman in federal Chamber); Filip Dewinter (chairman in Flemish council)
Described as a far right party, controversy around the origins of the Flemish Bloc remains persistent. Considered by some observers to be the heir of the fascist and wartime collaborationist party *Vlaams Nationaal Verbond* (VNV) created in 1933, a movement led in the 1950s by Karel Dillen promoted ultra-nationalist ideas and the defence of Flemish interests. The Flemish Bloc was created in December 1978 from the alliance between the Flemish People's Party, established in 1977 by Lode Claes following a split in the People's Union (VU), and the Flemish National Party, led by Karel Dillen and also founded in 1977. Having won one seat in that contest, the two parties formally merged under Dillen's leadership in May 1979 on a platform of opposition to the 1978 Egmont Pact on devolution on the grounds that it demanded too many concessions by the Flemish. Having increased its Chamber tally to two seats in 1987, the Bloc experienced a surge of support in the 1990s on a platform which now emphasized opposition to immigration. In the November 1991 elections the Bloc's representation in the Chamber increased to 12 seats and its vote share to 6.6%, ahead of the VU, for long the main vehicle of Flemish nationalism. During the campaign brown-shirted VB militants were involved in numerous violent incidents involving foreigners.

In the June 1994 European Parliament elections the Bloc won two seats and increased its vote to 7.8% (from 4.1% in 1989) on a platform which combined anti-immigration policies with opposition to the Maastricht process of European union. It made further advances in local elections in October 1994, winning representation in 82 of the 308 municipal councils and a total of 202 seats nationally. The Bloc headed the poll in Antwerp, winning 29% of the vote and 18 of the 55 seats, but its leader in the city, Filip Dewinter, was excluded from the mayorship by a combination of the other parties represented. The VB again registered 7.8% of the national vote in the May 1995 Chamber elections, giving it 11 out of 150 seats, while in simultaneous polling for the 118-member Flemish regional council it won 15 seats with a 12.3% vote share.

The VB made a further advance in the June 1999 federal, regional and European elections, winning 15 seats in the federal Chamber (with 9.9% of the vote) and 20 seats on the Flemish regional council (with 15.5% of the vote), also retaining two European Parliament seats (on an increased vote share of 9.4%). In local elections in October 2000 the VB registered major gains in several cities, winning 33% of the vote in Antwerp and consolidating its position as the largest party on the city council, although it remained in opposition because none of the main parties would form a coalition with it. The policy of the *cordon sanitaire* was also maintained at the federal and regional governments despite the growth of the VB's vote. In 2003, the Bloc increased its number of seats in the federal parliament (from 15 to 18 with 11.6% of the votes) and formed with the French-speaking National, the third political family of the country behind the traditional groups and ahead of the Greens.

Firmly opposed by other political parties, the Bloc faced severe opposition from anti-racism groups and the national Centre for Equal Opportunities. As a result, associations (*De Vlaamse Concentratie, De Nationalistische Vorminginstituut* and *De Nationalist Omroepstichting*) linked to the party were declared guilty of using racist propaganda against immigrants in March 2004. While the affair occurred shortly before the regional ballot, it did not seem to influence the Bloc electorate. As the second political force in the Flemish region after the elections (increasing from 22 to 32 seats, which represents 25.15% of the Flemish vote), the party remains in opposition in the regional assembly after the formation of a coalition among the other Flemish parties.

The VB's three representatives in the European Parliament are among the "unattached" contingent. The party claims a membership of about 25,000.

Flemish Liberals and Democrats–Citizens' Party
Vlaamse Liberalen en Demokraten (VLD)–Partij van de Burger

Address. Melsensstraat 34, B–1000 Brussels
Telephone. (32–2) 549–0020
Fax. (32–2) 512–6025
Email. vld@vld.be
Website. www.vld.be
Leadership. Bart Somers (president); Hendrik Daems (chairman in federal Chamber); De Cock Lieve (secretary-general)
The VLD is descended from the historic Belgian Liberal Party, which was founded in 1846 as the country's earliest political formation. It was in power in 1857–70 and 1878–84 but was then overtaken on the left by the new Belgian Labour Party, becoming the country's third political force behind the Catholics and Socialists. Having participated in a succession of coalitions after World War II, notably the 1954–58 Socialist-Liberal government, the Liberal Party was reconstituted in 1961 as the Party of Liberty and Progress (PLP). In 1970 the Flemish wing (*Partij voor Vrijheid en Vooruitgang*, PVV) became an autonomous formation, leaving the PLP as a Walloon party. Having participated in various coalitions in the 1970s, both the PVV and its Walloon counterpart, by now called the Liberal Reformist Party (PRL), were in government with the Christian People's and Christian Social parties in 1981–88, being regarded as the right-wing component of the coalition. In the November 1991 general elections the opposition PVV increased its Chamber representation from 25 to 26 seats out of 212 and its vote share from 11.5% to 11.9%.

In November 1992, in a move to broaden its support base, the PVV switched to its current VLD designation, also using the sub-title Party of Citizens (*Partij van de Burger*). In the June 1994 European Parliament elections the VLD took 11.4% of the vote and three of the 25 Belgian seats, against 10.6% and two seats for the PVV in 1989. In municipal and provincial elections in October 1994 the VLD replaced the Flemish Socialists as the second-largest party in Flanders. It made a further advance in the May 1995 Chamber elections, winning 21 of the 150 seats with 13.1% of the vote, but not enough to oust the incumbent coalition. In simultaneous regional polling the VLD consolidated its position as second party in Flanders, winning 26 of the 118 seats in the Flemish regional council. In light of the party's relatively disappointing performance, Guy Verhofstadt resigned as leader and was succeeded in September 1995 by Herman de Croo.

Verhofstadt resumed the VLD presidency in 1997 and led the party to a significant advance in the June 1999 federal, regional and European elections, assisted by the deep unpopularity of the incumbent government. The party's representation in the federal Chamber increased to 23 seats (from a vote share of 14.3%); its seat tally in the Flemish regional council improved to 27 (with 22% of the vote); and it again won three

European Parliament seats (with an increased vote share of 13.6%). In July 1999 Verhofstadt became Prime Minister of a new federal coalition which also included the PRL, the two Socialist parties, and the Green parties Ecolo and Agalev.

Most popular Flemish party in the period 1999-2003, VLD won the next (2003) federal elections and a new coalition headed by Verhofstadt was established between the Liberals and Socialists. The relatively favourable situation of the party was threatened in early 2004 mainly due to the question of the right to vote of non-Europeans at local elections (law passed by the federal parliament on Feb. 19). The absence of consensus within the party (Karel de Gucht, president of the party, threatened to leave the government) and a Flemish public opinion mostly against the legislation dealt a serious blow to the party of the Prime Minister. A direct sanction of the electorate came at the following regional elections where the VLD lost its status of first Flemish party (losing 2 seats) and the presidency of the region. For this election, the VLD had concluded an electoral pact with *Vivant* (Alive) in Brussels and Flanders. VLD-*Vivant* won 4 seats in the Brussels Council and 25 in the Flemish region.

Claiming a membership of 80,000, the VLD is a member party of the Liberal International. Its 3 representatives in the European Parliament sit in the European Liberal, Democratic and Reformist group.

Green! (former Live Differently - AGALEV)
Groen!
Address. Serg. De Bruynestraat 78-82, B–1070 Anderlecht
Telephone. (32–2) 219–1919
Fax. (32–2) 223–1090
Email. info@groen.be
Website. www.groen.be
Leadership. Vera Dua (leader of the party); Johan Hamels (secretary of the party)

This Flemish environmentalist formation (formerly known as *Anders Gaan Leven* – Live Differently, AGALEV) won two Chamber seats in the 1981 elections standing jointly with the Walloon Ecologist Party (ECOLO). Established as an independent party in 1982, AGALEV increased its representation to four seats in 1985, six in 1987 and seven in November 1991, when its share of the poll was 4.9%. In the June 1994 European Parliament elections, it retained one seat with 6.7% of the vote (as against 7.6% in 1989), while in the May 1995 Chamber elections it slipped to 4.4% of the national vote, winning five out of 150 seats. In simultaneous regional balloting, AGALEV took 7.1% of the vote in Flanders, winning seven of the 118 regional council seats.

AGALEV resumed its electoral advance in the June 1999 federal, regional and European elections. Its representation in the federal Chamber almost doubled to nine seats (with a vote share of 7.0%); it won 12 seats in the Flemish regional council (with 11.6% of the vote); and a joint list of AGALEV and the Flemish Socialist Party (SP) won two seats on the Brussels regional council (with 3.1% of the vote). In the simultaneous European Parliament elections AGALEV improved from one to two seats (with 7.5% of the vote). In July 1999 AGALEV joined a new federal coalition headed by the Flemish Liberals and Democrats, Magda Aelvoet being appointed Minister of Consumer Protection, Public Health and Environment. The AGALEV and ECOLO members in the federal Chamber formed a single group.

The 2003 elections resulted in a very severe defeat for AGALEV. The party lost all its deputies in the federal Chamber and as a result most of its financing. The post-election period proved stressful, and several leaders of the movement sought an alliance with the Flemish Socialists. The party was renamed *"Groen!"* (Green) as the first step towards the redefinition of the party's message. However, the change of leaders and political slogan cost the party 6 of its

12 seats in the Flemish regional parliament at the 2004 elections. The party won one seat in the June 2004 European Parliament elections.

Groen! is a member of the European Federation of Green Parties. Its sole representative in the European Parliament sits in the new European Green Party.

Humanist Democratic Centre (former Christian Social Party)
Centre Démocrate Humaniste (CDH)
Address. Rue des Deux Églises 41/45, B–1040 Brussels
Telephone. (32–2) 238–0111
Fax. (32–2) 238–0129
Email. info@lecdh.be
Website. www.lecdh.be
Leadership. Joëlle Milquet (president); Melchior Wathelet (chairman in federal Chamber); Benoît Lutgen (secretary general)

The PSC has its historical origins in the Catholic Union, one of several such organizations set up in Belgium in the 19th century. It is directly descended from the Belgian Catholic Party (PCB) created in 1936 and more specifically from the *Parti Catholique Social* (PCS), the PCB's French-speaking section. As the country's strongest party, the PCB took part in coalition governments before and during World War II, the PCS providing Belgium's wartime Prime Minister. At Christmas 1945 the PCB was reconstituted, the PCS becoming the PSC and the Flemish wing becoming the Christian People's Party (CVP), at that stage within one overall party structure. Having confirmed its dominant position in the 1946 elections, the joint party entered a coalition with the Socialists in 1947. Thereafter the PSC/CVP tandem participated continuously in the central government until 1999, except for the period 1954–58.

From the mid-1960s the PSC and CVP effectively became two separate parties, the former becoming substantially the smaller of the two. The PSC has therefore been a junior partner in recent coalitions headed by the CVP, with the Socialists and the Democratic Front of French-Speakers of Brussels in 1979–80; with the Socialists and Liberals briefly in 1980; with the Socialists in 1980–81; with the Liberals in 1981–88; with the Socialists and the People's Union in 1988–91; and with the Socialists from 1992. In the November 1991 Chamber elections PSC representation slipped from 19 to 18 seats out of 212 and its vote share from 8% to 7.8%. In the June 1994 European Parliament elections the PSC retained two of the 25 Belgian seats but its vote share fell to 6.9% from 8.1% in 1989. This setback coincided with disclosures of financial corruption in the Brussels section of the party. Nevertheless, in the May 1995 Chamber elections the PSC retained a 7.7% vote share, winning 12 of the 150 seats, and took third place in the simultaneous elections to the Walloon regional council, with 16 of the 75 seats and 21.6% of the vote. Thereafter, in addition to remaining in the federal coalition, the PSC also maintained its coalition with the Walloon Socialists in the regional government of Wallonia.

In simultaneous federal, regional and European elections held in June 1999, support for the PSC fell to 6.1% in the Chamber elections and its representation to 10 seats, with the result that the party went into federal opposition for the first time since 1958. In the Walloon regional elections the PSC fell to 17.1% of the vote and 14 seats and likewise vacated the regional government. In the Euro-elections, PSC declined to 4.9% of the vote and its representation from two seats to one. The PSC leadership subsequently passed from Philippe Maystadt to Joëlle Milquet and the party relaunched itself as the "New" PSC.

However, the 1999 defeat and the severe loss of representation led the party to undertake a profound reform which, unlike its Flemish counterpart, implied putting aside the

Christian religious reference. The renewal of personalities within the party and the opening towards civil society laid the basis of a new movement which claims to be centrist. This internal reform did not significantly impact on the results of the federal elections of 2003 where the party barely consolidated the results of June 1999 (8 seats). At the 2004 regional elections, the results indicated a slight progression of the party (+0.5%), which has been chosen by the Socialists as sole partner of a coalition government in the Walloon region and the French-Community. The single representative of CDH in the European Parliament sits in the European People's Party/European Democrats group.

Liberal Reformist Party
Parti Réformateur Libéral (PRL)

The PRL was descended from the historic Belgian Liberal Party and its successors (see Flemish Liberals and Democrats–Citizens' Party entry); the French-speaking PRL came into being in June 1979 as a merger of the Party of Reforms and Liberty of Wallonia (PRLW) and the Brussels Liberal Party. Of these, the PRLW had been formed in November 1976 as successor to the Party of Liberty and Progress (*Parti de la Liberté et du Progrès*, PLP), which had continued as the main Walloon Liberal party after the Flemish wing had become a separate formation in 1970, later becoming the Flemish Liberals and Democrats (VLD). The Brussels Liberals had adopted the party's historic name in June 1974 as successor to the distinct Liberal Democrat and Pluralist Party (PLDP) founded in January 1973. The PLP and the successor PRL (with the Flemish Liberals, who were consistently the stronger) participated in various coalitions, most recently with the Christian People's Party and the Christian Social Party in 1981–88, being regarded as the coalition's right-wing component.

In the November 1991 general elections, the opposition PRL's representation in the Chamber fell from 23 to 20 seats out of 212 and its vote share from 9.4% to 8.2%. In the June 1994 European Parliament elections the PRL won 9.0% of the vote and three seats compared with 8.7% and two seats in 1989. For the May 1995 Chamber elections the PRL presented a joint list with the Democratic Front of French-Speakers (FDF) of Brussels, winning 18 out of 150 seats on a 10.3% vote share. In simultaneous elections, the PRL/FDF alliance became the largest bloc in the Brussels regional council, winning 28 of the 75 seats (with 35% of the vote), and the second largest in the Walloon regional council, with 19 of the 75 seats and a 23.7% vote share. The PRL was allocated two portfolios in the six-party Brussels regional government.

The PRL–FDF alliance was maintained in the June 1999 elections, retaining 18 federal Chamber seats on a slightly reduced vote of 10.1%, improving to 21 seats (24.7% of the vote) in the Walloon regional council and slipping to 27 seats (34.4%) in the Brussels regional council. In the simultaneous European Parliament elections the PRL was allied with both the FDF and the Citizens' Movement for Change (MCC), the joint list winning three seats on a 10% vote share. In July 1999 the PRL joined a new federal coalition headed by the VLD, while the party also provided the minister-presidents of the new Brussels regional and French-speaking community governments, respectively Jacques Simonet and Hervé Hasquin.

Since 2002, the PRL has been merged with three other parties (the PFF – the German branch of the PRL; the Democratic Front of French-Speakers (FDF); and the MCC) within the **Reform Movement** (MR).

National Front
Front National (FN)

Address. Clos du Parnasse 12/8, B–1050 Brussels
Telephone/Fax. (32–2) 511–7577

Email. fn@frontnational.be
Website. www.frontnational.be
Leadership. Daniel Féret (president); Guy Hance & Alain Sadaune (vice-presidents); Jacqueline Merveille (secretary-general)

The extreme right-wing FN, modelled on the National Front of France, was founded in 1983 on a platform of opposition to non-white immigration. Based mainly in the French-speaking community, it achieved a breakthrough in the November 1991 elections, winning one Chamber seat with 1.1% of the vote. A further advance came in the June 1994 European Parliament elections, when it took 2.9% of the vote and one of the 25 Belgian seats. In October 1994 the FN leadership announced the expulsion of a member who had been shown on television desecrating a Jewish grave. In local elections the same month the party doubled its share of the vote in Wallonia compared with the previous contest in 1988. In the May 1995 Chamber elections the NF advanced to 2.3% of the national vote, winning two seats, while in simultaneous regional balloting it won six seats on the 75-member Brussels regional council (with 7.5% of the vote) and two seats in Wallonia (with 5.2% of the vote).

The FN lost ground in the June 1999 elections, winning only one Chamber seat (with 1.5% of the vote), two on the Brussels regional council (with 2.6%) and one in Wallonia (with 4.0%).

Unlike its Flemish counterpart, which concentrates a lot of resources on advertising its ideology (tracts, attendance of political programs on TV), the FN remains absent from the public scene. Despite this situation, the party achieved a consolidation of its position in the Walloon region at the 2003 elections. In the regional ballot of June 2004, it increased its number of deputies from one to four. No FN members represent the party at the European Parliament.

New Flemish Alliance (former Volksunie, People's Alliance)
Niew-Vlaamse Alliantie

Address. Barrikadenplein 12, B–1000 Brussels
Telephone. (32–2) 219–4930
Fax. (32–2) 217–3510
Email. info@n-va.be
Website. www.n-va.be
Leadership. Koen Kennis (president); Piet de Zaeger (secretary-general)

The *Volksunie* (People's Alliance, VU) was founded in December 1954 as a nationalist party seeking autonomy for Flanders on a "socially progressive, tolerant, modern and forward-looking" platform. It made a breakthrough in the 1965 Chamber elections, winning 12 seats, which it increased to 20 in 1969 and to 22 in 1974. It fell back to 20 seats in 1977, in which year it entered government for the first time, in coalition with the Christian Socials, Socialists and Democratic Front of French-Speakers (FDF) of Brussels, with the task of enacting regional devolution plans. Enshrined in the 1978 Egmont Pact, these were opposed by many VU militants as being inimical to Flemish interests, the result being the secession of a VU faction which later became part of the Flemish Bloc (VB). The VU retained only 14 seats in the December 1978 elections and reverted to opposition status. Rebuilding its strength, it won 20 seats in 1981 but slipped again in 1985 to 16. Having again won 16 seats in the December 1987 elections, it accepted participation in a coalition with the Christian Socials and Socialists formed in March 1988 but withdrew in September 1991 over an arms export controversy.

In the November 1991 elections the VU retained only 10 seats (and 5.9% of the vote), being overtaken by the VB. In the June 1994 European Parliament elections it slipped to 4.4% of the vote, from 5.4% in 1989, while retaining one seat. The

May 1995 Chamber elections yielded a further setback for the VU, which fell to 4.7% of the national vote and five seats (out of 150). In simultaneous regional elections it won 9% of the vote in Flanders and nine of the 118 regional council seats, while in Brussels it won one seat and was allocated one portfolio in the six-party Brussels regional government.

The VU gained ground in the June 1999 national, regional and European elections, winning eight federal Chamber seats (with 5.6% of the vote) and 11 on the Flemish regional council in an alliance with the Complete Democracy for the 21st Century (ID21) grouping (with 9.3%), although it lost its single seat on the Brussels regional council. In the simultaneous European elections the VU-ID21 advanced to two seats on the strength of a 7.6% vote share.

In 2000 the VU became divided over the leadership's support for federal government plans for further constitutional reform under which responsibility for trade policy and agriculture would pass to the regions. In early 2001 Patrik Vankrunkelsven was succeeded as VU chairman by Fons Borginon, although the party continued to support the changes. In May 2001 the VU Interior Minister in the Flemish regional government, Johan Sauwens, was forced to resign over his attendance at a meeting of former Belgian members of Hitler's *Waffen SS*.

The internal quarrels about the evolution of constitutional reform led to the split of VU into two new parties: NVA (New Flemish Alliance) and Spirit. Led in the first instance by Geert Bourgeois, NVA sought to represent the Flemish nationalist legacy and position itself in favour of the creation of a Flemish Republic. In the 2003 elections however, the party got only one seat in the federal parliament. The strategy of NVA was then to conclude an agreement with the Christian Democrats in order to create a new moderate nationalist and Flemish cartel. At the 2004 election, the combined NVA-CD&V became the leading political movement in Flanders. Geert Bourgeois is the current Flemish minister of international relations.

Reform Movement
Mouvement Reformateur (MR)

Address. Rue de Naples 41, B–1050 Brussels
Telephone. (32–2) 500–3511
Fax. (32–2) 500–3500
Email. mr@mr.be
Website. www.mr.be
Leadership. Antoine Duquesne (president); D. Bacquelaine (chairman in federal Chamber); Jacques Simonet (secretary-general)

The Reform Movement was formed in 2002 by the Liberal Reformist Party (*Parti Réformateur Libéral*, PRL), the Party of Liberty and Progress (*Partei für Freiheit und Fortschritt*, PFF), the Democratic Front of French-Speakers (FDF), and the Citizens' Movement for Change (MCC). The leading party in Brussels and second in Wallonia, MR confirmed its good results at the 2003 elections (+ 1.3% vote share and + 6 seats). The participation of the MR in the federal government crystallized around Louis Michel, former leader of the PRL and a popular Minister of Foreign Affairs. In early 2004, the resignation of Daniel Ducarme, president of the MR, for tax fraud and the replacement of several ministers at the Brussels region and French-speaking community levels had an impact on the electoral campaign. The MR lost its first position in Brussels (- 2 seats) and was relegated to opposition while losing the presidency to the Socialists. In the Walloon region, the MR was not able to consolidate its position (- 1 seat) and returned to opposition after five years of coalition with the Socialists.

The three MR members of the European Parliament sit in the European Liberal, Democratic and Reformist group.

Socialist Party
Parti Socialiste (PS)

Address. Blvd de l'Empereur 13, B–1000 Brussels
Telephone. (32–2) 548-3211
Fax. (32–2) 548-3380
Email. info@ps.be
Website. www.ps.be
Leadership. Elio Di Rupo (president); Christie Morreale, Maurice Bayenet & Philippe Moureaux (vice-presidents); Thierry Giet (chairman in federal Chamber); Jean-Pol Baras (secretary general)

Dating as a separate French-speaking party from October 1978, the PS is descended from the Belgian Labour Party (POB) founded in April 1885 with its base in industrial Wallonia and its support in organized labour. After obtaining universal male suffrage through a general strike, the POB was well-represented in the Chamber from 1894 and was admitted to the government-in-exile formed at Le Havre (France) in 1915 during World War I. In 1938 Paul-Henri Spaak became Belgium's first POB Prime Minister, but the German occupation of Belgium in 1940 forced the party underground under the leadership of Achille van Acker. Reconstituted in 1944 as the Belgian Socialist Party, with direct membership rather than group affiliation, it took part in post-war coalition governments until 1949 and again (with the Liberals) in 1954–58. Thereafter it was in coalition with the Christian Socials in 1961–66 and 1968–72; with the Christian Socials and Liberals in 1973–74; and with the Christian Socials, the Democratic Front of French-Speakers (FDF) and the People's Union (VU) in 1977–78. In October 1978 the Socialists emulated the other main Belgian political formations by formalizing the separation of their Flemish and French-speaking wings into autonomous parties, respectively the PS and the SP (see next entry).

Both the PS and the SP participated in coalitions with the Christian Socials and the FDF in 1979–80; with the Christian Socials and Liberals briefly in 1980; and with the Christian Socials in 1980–81. Both parties were then in opposition until, having become the largest lower house force in the December 1987 elections (for the first time since 1936), they joined a coalition with the Christian Socials and the VU in March 1988. Following the VU's withdrawal in September 1991, both Socialist parties lost ground in Chamber elections the following month (the PS falling from 40 to 35 seats out of 212 on a vote share of 15.6%) and joined a new coalition with the two Christian Social parties in March 1992. Concurrently, the PS also headed the regional governments of Wallonia and Brussels, championing the channelling of redevelopment resources to French-speaking areas and the maintenance of a large nationalized sector.

The murder in Liège in July 1991 of André Cools (a former PS Deputy Prime Minister) led eventually to the uncovering of the Agusta scandal, involving allegations of financial corruption in the party leadership in connection with a 1988 government contract for military helicopters awarded to an Italian firm. In January 1994 the disclosures resulted in the resignations of Guy Coëme (as federal Deputy Prime Minister), Guy Spitaels (as minister-president of Wallonia) and Guy Mathot (as interior minister of Wallonia), although all three denied any impropriety and the main focus of investigations was on the SP rather than the PS. In European Parliament elections in June 1994, the PS vote share slipped to 11.3% (from 14.5% in 1989 and 13.6% in the 1991 national balloting), so that it won only three of the 25 Belgian seats.

The May 1995 elections demonstrated the party's resilience, the PS winning 21 out of 150 seats on an 11.9% vote share and remaining a member of the federal centre-left coalition headed by the Christian People's Party. In simultaneous regional elections the PS remained by far the strongest party in Wallonia, taking 30 of the 75 regional council seats with a 35.2% vote share, so that the party retained the leadership of the regional government. In the Brussels region the PS won 21.4% and 17 seats out of 75, enabling Charles Picqué of the PS to remain head of government in charge of a six-party administration.

Corruption allegations continued to dog the PS in the late 1990s, the party's headquarters being raided by the police in January 1997 after new evidence had emerged about financial contributions in return for government contracts. Having resigned as president of the Walloon regional assembly in February, Spitaels was indicted the following month on charges arising from the affair (which he denied). His trial and that of other PS and SP figures opened in September 1998 and resulted in December 1998 in all being found guilty and given suspended prison sentences.

The PS shared in the ruling coalition's general unpopularity in the June 1999 elections, being reduced to 19 seats in the federal Chamber (with 10.1% of the vote), to 25 seats in the Walloon regional council (with 29.5%) and to 13 seats on the Brussels regional council (with 16.0%). In simultaneous European Parliament elections the PS retained three seats but its vote share slipped to 9.6%. In July 1999 the PS entered a new federal coalition, this time headed by the Flemish Liberals and Democrats and also including the two Green parties. The party also retained the leadership of the Walloon regional government, with Jean-Claude Van Cauwenberghe.

In May 2003, the French-speaking Socialists increased their seats from 19 to 25 at the federal parliament and resumed their collaboration with the Liberals and the Flemish Socialists without the Greens. One year later, the PS became the first party in the Brussels (33.35% with 35 seats) and Wallonia (36.91% with 34 seats) regional councils. The comfortable status of being the leading French-speaking party allowed the PS to form and head new coalitions for the Brussels and Walloon regions. As a new main political player, Elio Di Rupo chose to work with the Humanist Democratic Centre (CDH), excluding the Liberals from a second legislature. In Brussels, the situation was repeated when the PS headed by Charles Picqué formed a new coalition with their Flemish counterpart, the CDH, the CD&V, ECOLO and the VLD.

The PS is a full member party of the Socialist International. Its two European Parliament representatives sit in the Party of European Socialists group.

Social Progressive Alternative (former Flemish Socialist Party)
Sociaal Progressief Alternatief
Address. Grasmarkt, 105 B–1000 Brussels
Telephone. (32–2) 552–0219
Fax. (32–2) 552–0226
Email. info@s-p-a.be
Website. www.s-p-a.be
Leadership. Steve Stevaert (chairman); Dirk Van Der Maelen (chairman in federal Chamber); Alain André (national secretary)
As the Flemish section of the post-war Belgian Socialist Party, the SP had its origins in the *Belgische Werklieden Partij* founded in October 1885 as the Flemish wing of the Belgian Labour Party; it became an autonomous party on the formal separation of the two Socialist wings in October 1978. Before and subsequently it participated in all the central coalition governments of which the Walloon PS was a member (see previous entry). Having formally renounced Marxism and class struggle in 1980, the SP became more "social democratic" in orientation than its Walloon counterpart, distancing itself in particular from the pro-nationalization line of the latter. For long the weaker of the two parties

electorally, the SP maintained its Chamber representation at 32 seats out of 212 in December 1987 but fell back to 28 seats in November 1991. In the June 1994 European Parliament elections the SP retained three Belgian seats but its vote share slipped to 10.8%, from 12.4% in the 1989 Euro-elections and 12.0% in the 1991 national poll.

Following the appointment of Willy Claes (then SP Deputy Premier and Foreign Minister) to the post of NATO secretary-general in October 1994, Frank Vandenbroucke replaced him in the government and was succeeded as SP chair by Louis Tobback, hitherto Interior Minister. In March 1995 Vandenbroucke became the most senior casualty to date of the Agusta bribery scandal, resigning from the government after admitting that in 1991 he knew that the party held a large sum of undeclared money in a bank safe deposit. Also implicated was Claes, who as Economic Affairs Minister in 1988 had been closely involved in the helicopter contract at the centre of the bribery allegations. Despite these difficulties, the SP advanced to 12.6% in the May 1995 general elections (ahead of the Walloon Socialists), winning 20 of the 150 Chamber seats. In the simultaneous regional polling, it took 25 of the 118 Flemish council seats (with a 19.4% vote share) and continued to participate in the Flanders government, while winning two seats on the Brussels regional council (with 2.4%)

In October 1995 Claes was obliged to resign his NATO post when the Belgian parliament voted in favour of his being brought to trial. Court proceedings opened in September 1998 and resulted in December in Claes and 12 other defendants being found guilty of corruption and given suspended prison sentences.

The SP shared in the ruling coalition's general unpopularity in the June 1999 elections, being reduced to 14 seats in the federal Chamber (with 9.6% of the vote) and to 19 seats in the Flemish regional council (with 15.0%), while retaining two seats on the Brussels regional council on a joint list with Live Differently (AGALEV) which took 3.1% of the vote. In simultaneous European Parliament elections the SP lost one of its three seats on a reduced vote share of 8.8%. In July 1999 the SP entered a new federal coalition, this time headed by the Flemish Liberals and Democrats and also including the two Green parties. The party also provided the new minister-president of the German-speaking community (Karl-Heinz Lambertz), having won four of the 25 council seats with a 15.0% vote share.

The arrival of Steve Stevaert as new president of the movement contributed to increasing the popularity of the party in Flanders. A former mayor of Hasselt, where he led various successful urban policies, Stevaert set up a renewed team and was able to secure an electoral alliance with SPIRIT. The cartel got 23 seats (14.9%) at the federal elections of May 2003 and Stevaert was voted the most popular politician in the north of the country. In 2004, the cartel increased its number of seats from 19 to 25 (19.66%) in the Flemish parliament and is a partner in the new regional government. In Brussels, the cartel got 3 seats.

Claiming a membership of 76,000, the PS is a full member party of the Socialist International. Its three European Parliament representatives sit in the Party of European Socialists group.

SPIRIT
Address. Woeringenstraat 19-21, B–1000 Brussels
Telephone. (32–2) 513–2063
Fax. (32–2) 512–8575
Email. info@meerspirit.be
Website. www.meerspirit.be
Leadership. Geert Lambert (president), Stefan Walgraeve (deputy president), Peter Van Hoof (secretary general)
Descended from the former *Volksunie* (see New Flemish

Alliance), the fraction led by Bert Anciaux joined the Flemish Socialists in order to create a new cartel SPA-SPIR-IT. This was very successful for the Socialists, the alliance winning 23 seats in the federal parliament in the elections of 2003, a gain of nine. As a result of the election, the leader of the party, Bert Anciaux, became a government minister. This alliance was resumed in the 2004 regional elections where the cartel increased its number of seats to 25 (+6). The party has no representatives at the European Parliament.

Other Parties

Many minor parties contested the June 2003 and 2004 elections at federal, regional or European level. The following list focuses on the better-supported groupings.

Alive (*Vivant*), Originally a French-speaking formation created by the businessman Roland Duchâtelet, *Vivant* urges abolition of taxes and social charges on the workplace and a big increase in VAT to compensate; it won 130,703 votes (2.1%) in 1999 federal Chamber elections (but no seats) and one seat on Brussels regional council (with 1.5%). In the 2003 federal elections, *Vivant* got 81,338 votes; it formed an electoral alliance with VLD in the regional ballot of 2004.
Address. Blvd du Midi 25–27, 4ème étage, B–1000 Brussels
Telephone. (32–2) 513–0888
Fax. (32–2) 502–0107
Email. info@vivant.org
Website. www.vivant.org
Leadership. Dirk Vangossum

Christian Social Party (*Christlisch Soziale Partei*, CSP), the Christian Social party of Belgium's small German-speaking minority, secured one seat in the 1994 and 1999 European Parliament elections (with only 0.2% of the overall vote), on the ticket of the (Flemish) Christian People's Party; the CSP MEP sits in the European People's Party/European Democrats group.
Leadership. Mathieu Grosch (president)

Christian Democrats French-Speakers Party (*Chrétiens Démocrates Francophones, CDF)*, was founded in 2002 by dissidents from the newly-created Humanist Democratic Centre (created from the Christian Social Party) who rejected the removal of the Christian reference. The party got no seats in the 2003 elections.
Address. Square Joséphine-Charlotte 12, B–1120 Brussels
Telephone. (32–2) 763-0601
Fax. (32–2) 770-8379
Website. www.cdf-info.be
Leadership. Michel Van Den Abbeele

Citizens' Movement for Change (*Mouvement des Citoyens pour le Changement*, MCC), founded in 1998 by Gérard Deprez on the strength of public outrage at official mishandling of the Dutroux paedophile controversy; allied with Liberal Reformist Party and Democratic Front of French-Speakers in the 1999 national, regional and European elections, it secured four representatives in the various assemblies, Deprez being elected to the European Parliament and chosing to join the European People's Party/European Democrats group. MCC joined the Reform Movement (MR) in 2002.
Address. Rue de la Vallée, 50 B–1000 Brussels
Telephone. (32–2) 642-2999
Fax. (32–2) 642-2999
Email. info@lemcc.be
Website. www.lemcc.be/
Leadership. Nathalie de T'serclaes (president)

Communist Party (*Parti Communiste*, PC), French-speaking formation (autonomous since 1992) descended from the historic Belgian Communist Party (PCB/KPB); founded in 1921, powerful after World War II on a pro-Soviet tack but in decline since the mid-1950s; unrepresented in the Chamber since 1985, has renounced Marxism-Leninism in favour of socialist democracy.
Address. Rue Rouppe 4, B–1000 Brussels
Telephone. (32–2) 548–0290
Fax. (32–2) 548–0295
Leadership. Pierre Beauvois (president)

Communist Party (*Parti Kommunistische, KP*), Flemish formation (autonomous since 1992) descended from the historic Belgian Communist Party (PCB/KPB) founded in 1921 (see previous entry).
Address. Galgenberg 29, B–9000 Ghent
Telephone. (32–9) 225–4584
Fax. (32–9) 233–5678
Email. kp@democratisch-links.be
Website. www.democratisch-links.be

New Front of Belgium (*Front Nouveau de Belgique/Front Nieuw België*, FNB), a "democratic nationalist party", founded in 1997; won one seat on Brussels regional council in June 1999 with 1.3% of the vote, but only 0.4% in federal Chamber elections and 0.6% in Walloon regional council elections (and no seats).
Address. Rue de la Cambre 336, B–1200 Brussels
Telephone/Fax. (32–2) 770–8866
Website. www.fnb.to
Leadership. Marguerite Bastien

Party of Belgian German-Speakers (*Partei der Deutschsprachigen Belgier*, PDB), founded in 1971 to campaign for equal rights for the German-speaking minority; won three seats in 1999 elections for German-speaking community council.
Address. Kaperberg 6, B–4700 Eupen
Telephone. (32–87) 555–987
Fax. (32–87) 555–984
Email. guido.breuer@skynet.be
Website. users.skynet.be/pdb
Leadership. Guido Breuer

Walloon Party (*Parti Wallon*, PW), left-wing nationalist party advocating a socialist Wallonia, founded in 1985 as a merger of the *Rassemblement Wallon* (RW) and other radical Walloon groups under the leadership of Jean-Claude Piccin. Founded in 1968, the RW had participated in a coalition government with the Christian Socials and Liberals in 1974–77, helping to secure the passage of the Egmont Pact on devolution; but it had been weakened by defections of moderates to what became the Liberal Reformist Party. Whereas the RW won two Chamber seats in the 1981 elections on a joint list with the Democratic Front of French-Speakers, in 1985 the PW failed to gain representation and was no more successful in subsequent electoral contests, winning only 0.2% in the 1999 federal Chamber elections. In 1999, a merger between RW, ADW (Walloon Democratic Alliance) and MRWF (Movement for the return to France) led to the creation of the RWF (*Rassemblement Wallonie-France*).
Address. BP 28 - B–1050 Ixelles
Email. rwf@rwf.be
Website. www.rwf.be
Leadership. Paul-Henri Gendebien

Workers' Party of Belgium (*Partij van de Arbeid van België/Parti du Travail de Belgique,* PvdA/PTB) founded in 1979 in opposition to the reformism of the Communist

Party; part of the All Power to the Workers (*Alle Macht Aan de Arbeiders*, AMADA) movement in the 1979 Euro-elections, unsuccessful then and subsequently in securing representation; won 0.5% of the vote in the 1995 and 1999 federal Chamber elections.
Address. Lemonnierlaan 171/2, B–1000 Brussels
Telephone. (32–2) 513–7760
Fax. (32–2) 513–9831
Email. ptb@ptb.be
Website. www.ptb.be
Leadership. Ludo Martens

Belize

Capital: Belmopan
Population: 266,500 (2003E)

Belize became independent within the British Commonwealth on September 21, 1981. A Legislative Assembly has been in existence since 1935 and was given responsibility for internal self-government under the former constitution of 1954. Under the 1981 constitution the head of state is the British monarch, represented by a Governor-General. The head of government is the Prime Minister. The Governor-General formally appoints the Prime Minister, who is the leader of the party able to command a parliamentary majority. There is a bicameral National Assembly, comprising an appointed nine-member Senate and a House of Representatives with 29 elected members. Belize uses the first-past-the-post electoral system, with successful candidates requiring a simple majority in one of the single-member constituencies. The National Assembly sits for a five-year term subject to dissolution.

In a general election held on March 5, 2003, the People's United Party was re-elected with 53.3% of the vote and 22 seats in the new House, while the United Democratic Party took 45.6% of the vote and seven seats.

People's United Party (PUP)
Address. 3 Queen Street, Belize City
Telephone. (501) 224-5886
Fax. (501) 223-3476
Website. www.pupbelize.org
Leadership. Said Musa (leader)
Founded in 1950, the centrist PUP has traditionally drawn more of its support from Catholics, Indians and Spanish-speakers than from the black population. The party was founded as a reformist party motivated by co-operatist ideas and supported by the General Workers' Union and the Roman Catholic Church. It campaigned for independence from Britain, a position that helped it win a comprehensive victory in the 1954 general election, following which (under the leadership of George C. Price from 1956) it remained the leading party through to independence in 1981.

In the first post-independence election in 1984, however, the PUP won only seven seats in the enlarged 28-member House. The party returned to power in the 1989 general election, when it won 15 seats, narrowly defeating the UDP, which took 13. During Price's post-1989 term of office the country identified itself more closely with the region, being accepted as a member of the Organization of American States (OAS) in January 1991. In September 1991 diplomatic relations were established with neighbouring Guatemala, which had long claimed sovereignty over the country.

In an early general election called by Price in June 1993, the PUP was unexpectedly defeated, retaining only 13 seats against 16 for the UDP. Price resigned as leader in

October 1996 and was succeeded by Said Musa, a lawyer and hitherto PUP chairman. In the August 1998 legislative elections, the PUP benefited from the relatively poor performance of the Belizean economy, the introduction of an unpopular business tax by the UDP government and the widespread perception that inquiries into corruption allegations against leading PUP figures were politically motivated. Following his decisive victory by 26 seats to only three for the UDP, Musa was sworn in as Prime Minister. During Musa's first term in office the government faced a number of domestic difficulties. The most serious came in September 2002 after grave allegations of fraud and corruption were made against the Immigration and Nationality Department and their passports-for-sale programme. The revelations cost the Minister of Police and Immigration his post, while the director of immigration was suspended. Despite this Musa was reelected for another five-year term in May 2003, and thus became the first Prime Minister to serve two consecutive terms in office since the nation gained independence.

United Democratic Party (UDP)
Address. South End Bel-China Bridge, PO Box 1898, Belize City
Telephone. (501) 227-2576
Fax. (501) 227-6441
E-mail. info@udp.org.bz
Website. www.udp.org.bz
Leadership. Dean Barrow (leader); Douglas Singh (chairman)
Founded in September 1973, the conservative UDP has a predominantly black (Creole) ethnic base but also claims to have support from the Mayan and Mestizo communities.

The UDP was created by the fusion of the previous National Independence Party, Liberal Party and People's Development Movement as a right-wing opposition to the dominant People's United Party (PUP). In the 1979 general election, it won 46.8% of the vote and five seats on the basis of a campaign charging that the PUP government was influenced by communism. The party opposed early independence from Britain in view of Guatemala's territorial claim on Belize.

Manuel Esquivel became leader of the UDP in 1982 and led the party to power in 1984. However, in September 1989 the UDP lost office to the PUP. In September 1991 Belize established diplomatic relations with Guatemala and the party leadership's support for this resulted in some dissidents breaking away in February 1992 to launch the National Alliance for Belizean Rights (NABR). The UDP unexpectedly returned to power in the June 1993 general elections, winning 16 of the 29 seats.

In the August 1998 general election the party slumped to only three seats, although taking 39.1% of the vote. Having lost his own seat, Esquivel resigned as party leader and was succeeded by Dean Barrow as interim party leader. At the party's national convention in October 1999, Barrow was unanimously elected as leader of the party. Despite campaigning on a strong anti-corruption platform and a pledge to "repair Belize's social compass, rescue her economy and reinvigorate her democracy", the DLP only slightly increased its parliamentary representation after the May 2003 general election. However, the party received a boost in late October 2003, after winning the parliamentary seat of Cayo South from the PUP in a by-election.

The UDP is affiliated to the Caribbean Democrat Union.

Other parties

National Alliance for Belizean Rights (NABR)
Founded in February 1992 by former United Democratic Party (UDP) members disaffected by maritime concessions to Guatemala (resulting in the conclusion of a non-

aggression pact between the two countries in April 1993). Although a splinter group of the UDP, the NABR campaigned with the parent party in the 1993 elections and was subsequently included in the UDP government. In the 1998 and 2003 general elections the NABR did not stand for parliament. The party does, however, participate in the National Advisory Commission (NAC) set up by the government to coordinate a united national front in the face of Guatemala's revival of its territorial claims.

Address. 27 South Street, Belize City
Telephone. (501) 207-2843
Fax. (501) 227–4274
Coordinator. Emma Boiton

Benin

Capital: Porto Novo
Population: 6,400,000 (2000E)

Benin achieved independence from France in 1960 as Dahomey, was renamed the People's Republic of Benin in 1972 and became the Republic of Benin in 1990. The People's Republic was proclaimed following a military coup led by Mathieu Kérékou, who installed a Marxist-Leninist regime with the People's Revolutionary Party of Benin (PRPB) as the sole ruling party. The Republic of Benin was proclaimed under new constitutional arrangements approved by referendum on Dec. 2, 1990, and providing for multi-party democracy (the PRPB having dissolved itself in April). The executive President, who appoints the Council of Ministers, is directly elected for a five-year term. Legislative authority is vested in a unicameral National Assembly (*Assemblée Nationale*) of 83 members, which is elected for a four-year term according to a department-based system of proportional representation and which may not be dissolved by the President.

Presidential elections held in 1991 were won by Nicéphore Soglo (backed by a coalition of parties), who defeated Gen. Kérékou (standing without party attribution). The following year President Soglo became identified with the new Benin Revival (*La Renaissance du Bénin*) party. Elections to the National Assembly in March and May 1995 resulted in Benin Revival and its allies becoming the largest bloc with 28 seats, although the other 55 seats went to nine anti-Soglo parties. In subsequent presidential elections in March 1996, President Soglo was defeated in the second round by Kérékou.

In further legislative elections on March 30, 1999, Benin Revival won 27 seats, the Party of Democratic Renewal (PRD) 11, the Action Front for Renewal and Development (FARD-Alafia) 10, the Social Democratic Party (PSD) 9 and the African Movement for Democracy and Progress (MADEP) 6. Eleven other parties won 20 seats between them. Presidential elections on March 4 and 22, 2001, were contested by 17 candidates. In the second round, boycotted by second-placed Soglo and third-placed Adrien Houngbedji (of the PRD) amid claims of election irregularities, Kérékou was re-elected with 84% of the vote.

For the December 2002 local elections, President Kérékou grouped all the parties supporting him into the **Union for the Future of Benin** (*Union pour le Bénin du Futur* – UBF); the alliance scored well in the local elections and was relaunched for the March 2003 legislative elections. The alliance, led by Amoussou

Bruno, president of the Social Democratic Party (PSD), was composed of over 50 parties and various political movements of which the most important were: the Action Front for Renewal and Development (*Front d'Action pour le Renouveau et le Développement* – Fard Alafia), the African Congress for Renewal (*Congrès Africain pour le Renouveau* – Car Dunya), the Social Democratic Party (*Parti Social Démocrate* – PSD), the Alliance for Democracy and Progress (*Alliance pour la Démocratie et le Progrès* – ADP), the Union for Labour and Democracy (*Union pour le Travail et la Démocratie* – UTD), the Patriotic Union for Labour (*Union Patriotique pour le Travail* – UPT), the Beninist Party of Revolution (*Parti Béniniste de la Révolution* – PBR), the Action Front for Economic and Social Development (*Front d'Action pour le Développement Economique et Social* – FADES), and the National Together Party (*Parti National Ensemble* – PNE). The alliance won 31 seats to become the largest group at the Assembly but internal dissensions resulted in it soon splitting into three groups in the Assembly.

The March 2003 elections also saw the emergence of the **Key Alliance** (*Alliance Clef*), composed of the Movement for the People's Alternative (*Mouvement pour l'Alternative du Peuple*, MAP), the 30th April Movement (*Mouvement du 30 Avril*, M 30.4) and some political leaders. The Key Alliance created a major stir by winning five seats. Two seats were won by a grouping allying the Movement for Development through Culture (*Mouvement pour le Développement par la Culture*, MDC), the Party of Salvation (*Parti du Salut*, PS) and the People's Convention for Progress (*Convention du Peuple pour le Progrès*, CPP). Two seats were also won by the **New Alliance** (*La Nouvelle Alliance* – LNA) composed of the Democratic Party of Benin (*Parti Démocratique du Bénin*, PDB) and the Union for Progress and Democracy (*Union pour le Progrès et la Démocratie*, UPD-Gamessu).

Action Front for Renewal and Development
Front d'Action pour le Renouveau et le Développement (FARD-Alafia)
Address. BP 925 Cotonou
Leadership. Jérôme Sacca Kina
Proclaiming itself to be a party of national unity on its foundation in 1994 by five opposition deputies, the FARD-Alafia formed part of the anti-Soglo group of parties in the 1995 Assembly elections, in which it won 14 seats. In the legislative elections in March 1999, the party lost four of its seats but remained the third largest group in the Assembly. It contested the 2003 legislative elections as a component party of the Union for the Future of Benin (UBF).

African Movement for Democracy and Progress
Mouvement Africain pour le Démocratie et le Progrès (MADEP)
Leadership. Séfou Fagbohoun
This party won six seats in the 1999 Assembly elections. Its leader, a very rich and influential businessman, is popular among the Yoruba and Nagot ethnic groups. The party won nine seats in the 2003 assembly elections. The general secretary of the party and Minister of Foreign Affairs, Idji Kolawole, had been appointed president of the National Assembly for a four-year term.

Benin Revival
La Renaissance du Bénin (RB)
Address. BP 2205 Cotonou
Leadership. Nicéphore Soglo (president); Rosine Soglo
The formation of Benin Revival was announced in March

1992 by President Soglo's wife, Rosine Soglo, and was intended as a new political base for the President, who had been elected in March 1991 with the backing of the Union for the Triumph of Democratic Renewal (*Union pour la Triomphe du Renouveau Démocratique*, UTRD). A former World Bank official, Soglo had been named Prime Minister in February 1990 by a National Conference charged with establishing a new political structure for Benin. After heading the first-round balloting in the subsequent presidential contest, Soglo had secured a decisive 68% advantage over President Kérékou in the second, thus becoming the first successful challenger to an incumbent head of state in black continental Africa.

The three component parties of the UTRD were the Democratic Union of Progressive Forces (UDFP) led by Timothée Adanlin, the Movement for Democracy and Social Progress (MDPS) led by Joseph Marcelin Degbe and the Union for Freedom and Development (ULD) led by Marius Francisco. In the February 1991 Assembly elections the UTRD had become the largest grouping with 12 of the then 64 seats, the UTRD contingent forming the nucleus of the broader Renewal (*Renouveau*) Group which by mid-1992 numbered 34 deputies and thus gave the government a working majority. In July 1993 President Soglo effectively assumed the leadership of Benin Revival, saying that he would "come down into the political arena" and promote the new formation as a "catalyst" for the country's emerging democracy. His decision contributed to strains within the presidential coalition in the Assembly, where 15 members of the Renewal Group defected in October 1993, claiming that they had been "marginalized" by the President. Later the same month, however, 11 pro-Soglo parties and associations, including the UTRD rump (but not Benin Revival), formed the African Rally for Progress and Solidarity (RAPS), thus restoring the government's Assembly majority.

Further strains were apparent in September 1994, when President Soglo declared his intention to introduce the latest budget by decree, thus ignoring parliamentary opposition to the measure. In October 1994 Benin Revival absorbed the small Pan-African Union for Democracy and Solidarity (*Union Panafricaine pour la Démocratie et la Solidarité*, UPDS). But presidential efforts to elevate Benin Revival into the dominant party were confounded by voters in the 1995 Assembly elections, in which it won only 21 of the 83 seats (and its allies a further seven), while anti-Soglo parties aggregated 55 seats. In July 1995 Benin Revival was formally joined by a majority of the RAPS leadership.

In that he also held French citizenship, Soglo's quest for a second term in the 1996 presidential elections appeared at first to be ruled out by the passage in September 1995 of a law barring anyone with dual nationality from standing. In the event, he entered the contest in March 1996 and was unexpectedly defeated in the second round by the resurrected Gen. Kérékou, who had retained powerful support in the state bureaucracy. Having at first complained of electoral fraud, Soglo accepted the voters' verdict on April 2.

In legislative elections in March 1999, Benin Revival increased its representation to 27 seats, so remaining the largest single party in the Assembly. Soglo stood again for the presidency in elections in March 2001, gaining 29% of the votes to Gen. Kérékou's 47% in the first round. However, he boycotted the second round (as did the third-placed Party of Democratic Renewal candidate), claiming that there had been electoral irregularities, although his allegations were not upheld by the Constitutional Court.

In the March 2003 legislative elections the party won 15 seats. This poor result was attributed to a crisis that had developed within the party concerning the issue of the leading role of the President's wife, Rosine Soglo.

Party of Democratic Renewal
Parti du Renouveau Démocratique (PRD)

Address. c/o Assemblée Nationale, BP 371, Porto Novo
Leadership. Adrien Houngbedji
Website. www.prd-bj.net

The PRD contested the February 1991 Assembly elections in an alliance with the National Party for Democracy and Development which came in second place, although together they won only nine of the 64 seats. Party leader Adrien Houngbedji was subsequently elected president of the National Assembly, despite not having the backing of the then President Soglo. In the 1995 Assembly elections the PRD headed the victorious group of anti-Soglo parties, winning 18 of the 83 seats in its own right. In that he also held French citizenship, Houngbedji's candidacy for the 1996 presidential election appeared to be blocked by the passage of a law in September 1995 banning anyone with dual nationality from standing for the presidency. However, he did stand, taking third place with 17% of the vote in the first round on March 3 and subsequently announcing his support for Gen. Kérékou in the second.

In the March 1999 legislative elections, the PRD emerged as the second largest party again, but with a lower tally of 11 seats. Houngbedji contested the first round of the March 2001 presidential poll, winning 12% of the vote. But he refused to enter the second round run-off against Gen. Kérékou following the withdrawal of Soglo, the second-placed candidate, on the grounds of electoral irregularities.

In the March 2003 legislative elections the party took 11 seats. In June 2003 the party left the opposition to join Kérékou's group.

Social Democratic Party
Parti Social-Démocrate (PSD)

Address. BP 04–0772 Cotonou
Leadership. Bruno Amoussou

The PSD was formed on the introduction of multi-partyism in 1990 and presented candidates in the November 1990 local elections. It contested the February 1991 Assembly elections in alliance with the National Union for Solidarity and Progress, registering a joint tally of eight of the 64 seats. It retained eight seats in the 1995 elections (out of 83), forming part of the victorious group of anti-Soglo parties. In the 1999 legislative poll, the PSD increased its representation to nine seats. Despite having come only fourth in the first ballot of the March 2001 presidential elections (mirroring his performance in the 1996 poll), party leader Amoussou contested the second round run-off against Gen. Kérékou following the withdrawal of the second- and third-placed candidates amid allegations of electoral irregularities. However, he gained only 16% of the vote.

The PSD is component party of the Union for the Future of Benin (UBF) and is affiliated to the Socialist International as a consultative member.

Other Parties

Alliance of Progressive Forces (*Alliance des Forces du Progrès*, AFP), won one seat in the 2003 Assembly elections
Leadership Valentin Houdé

Communist Party of Benin (*Parti Communiste de Benin*, PCB), granted legal registration in September 1993, being the successor to the Dahomey Communist Party (PCD) founded in 1977 in opposition to the brand of Marxism-Leninism propagated by Kérékou regime. The PCD had boycotted the 1990 negotiations on transition to multi-partyism, most of its leaders remaining in exile. By 1993, however, many had returned to Benin and, undeterred by the demise of communism elsewhere in the world, had reconstituted the

party under the PCB rubric. The party won one seat in the 1995 Assembly elections, on a platform of opposition to President Soglo, but ceased to be represented in 1999. The party split into two with the formation of the Communist Marxist-Leninist Party of Benin (*Parti Communiste Marxiste-Leniniste du Bénin* – PCLMP) led by Magloire Gnanssounou, a well-known Beninese lawyer.
Address. BP 2582 Cotonou
Leadership. Pascal Fantondji (first secretary)

Democratic Party of Benin (*Parti Démocratique du Bénin,* PDB), registered in October 1996, secured one seat in the 1999 Assembly elections. For the March 2003 legislative elections the party united with the New Alliance (*La Nouvelle Alliance*, LNA)
Address. BP 407 Cotonou
Leadership. Soule Dankoro

Impulse for Progress and Democracy (*Impulsion pour le Progrès et la Démocratie, IPD*), won two Assembly seats in 1995 as part of the anti-Soglo opposition, increasing its representation (as Alliance IPD) to four seats in March 1999. It secured two seats in the March 2003 Assembly elections.

Movement for Democracy and Solidarity (*Mouvement pour la Démocratie et la Solidarité*, MDS*)* gained one seat in the March 2003 Assembly elections
Leadership. Sacca Fikara

National Together Party (*Parti National Ensemble*), gained one Assembly seat in the 1999 elections. The party did not take part in the March 2003 legislative elections.

Party of Salvation (*Parti du Salut*, PS), won one seat in the 1999 Assembly elections. For the March 2003 legislative election, the party formed an alliance with the MDC and the CPP.
Leadership. Damien Alahassa

Rally for Democracy and Panafricanism (*Rassemblement pour la Démocratie et le Panafricanisme*, RDP), founded in mid-1994 by a faction of the Pan-African Union of Democracy and Solidarity that opposed the latter's merger with the Benin Revival. It won one seat in both the 1999 and 2003 Assembly elections.
Address. BP 03–4073 Cotonou
Leadership. Dominique Houngninou

Star Alliance (*Alliance Étoile*), won four seats in the 1999 Assembly elections and three seats in the March 2003 elections.

Bhutan

Capital: Thimphu
Population: 2,202,000 (2002E)

The Kingdom of Bhutan is an hereditary monarchy in which power is shared between the King (assisted by a Royal Advisory Council), the Council of Ministers, the *Tsogdu* (Nationa l Assembly) and the monastic head of Bhutan's Buddhist priesthood. The Council of Ministers is appointed by the King and may be dismissed by him with the consent of the National Assembly, which was established in 1953 as the principal legislative body. The unicameral National Assembly has 154 members, of whom 105 are directly elected on a non-partisan basis, 12 represent religious bodies, and 37 are appointed by the King to rep-

resent various interests.

There are no legal political parties, with opposition to the government primarily based in a combination of dissident members of the Drukpa ethnic majority and minority ethnic Nepali groups exiled in Nepal or India, including the Druk National Congress (DNC). King Jigme Singye Wangchuk inaugurated on Nov. 30, 2001, the drafting of a written constitution for the Kingdom of Bhutan. The constitutional committee, which was headed by Chief Justice Lyonpo Sonam Tobgye, presented a draft constitution to the King on Dec. 9, 2002, but no details were released. The King had said that the purpose of the constitution was to ensure the security and sovereignty of the nation and to establish a democratic system of governance. It was reported in October 2002 that the committee had held prolonged discussions on the concept of political parties, but there was no indication of their outcome. There were apparently no further developments until it was reported in September 2003 that on a state visit to India the King had requested Indian expertise in assisting the drafting of a constitution for Bhutan

The chief exiled illegal political parties are the Bhutan People's Party (BPP), led by Teknath Rizal, a former Cabinet minister, and the Druk National Congress (DNC), led by Rongthong Kinley Dorji. These groups not only campaign for multi-party democracy but also champion the right of return of about 118,000 ethnic Nepalese (*Lhotshampas*) refugees in Nepal who were expelled or fled from southern Bhutan in the early 1990s. Teknath Rizal, who had himself been imprisoned for "antinational activities" in Bhutan in 1989-99, in September 2003 formed the Human Rights Council of Bhutan (HRCB) as an umbrella organization for refugee and human rights groups.

Bolivia

Capital: La Paz
Population: 8,400,000 (2002E)

Bolivia claimed independence from Spain in 1825 and its first constitution was written in November 1826. From World War II until the 1990s the leading political formation was the Nationalist Revolutionary Movement (MNR) under its veteran leader, Victor Paz Estenssoro, who first came to power in the popular revolution of 1952. Bolivia was subsequently under the rule of military juntas almost continuously between 1964 and 1982, when it was returned to civilian rule under President Hernán Siles Zuazo.

The present constitution dates from 1947 and was revived after a coup in 1964. Executive power is vested in the President, who appoints the Cabinet, the nine departmental prefects and the country's diplomatic representatives, and nominates archbishops and bishops. The bicameral Congress comprises a 27-seat Senate and a 130-seat Chamber of Deputies. The President is elected by direct suffrage for a five-year term (four years until 1997) and is not eligible to serve two consecutive terms. If no candidate emerges from the election with an absolute majority the newly-elected Congress appoints a President. Senators (three for each of the nine provinces) and deputies are elected by proportional representation, also for a five-year term. There has been universal suffrage in Bolivia since the 1952 popular uprising and voting is compulsory.

Bolivia has a highly fragmented party system characterized by frequent splits, personalism and populism. In the first round of the 1997 presidential elections, no candidate received a majority of the popular vote. Gen. (retd.) Hugo Bánzer Suárez of the Nationalist Democratic Action (ADN) won a congressional run-off vote on Aug. 5, 1997, after forming a "mega-coalition" with the Movement of the Revolutionary Left (MIR), Civic Solidarity Union (UCS), Conscience of the Fatherland (Condepa), New Republican Force (NFR) and the Christian Democratic Party (PDC). In concurrent congressional elections, the ADN-led coalition won an overwhelming majority in both the Chamber of Deputies and the Senate.

President Bánzer resigned because of illness in August 2001 and was succeeded by Vice-President Jorge Fernando Quiroga Ramírez. In the presidential election held on June 30, 2002, former head of state Gonzálo Sánchez de Lozada of the MNR won 22.5% of the votes. Unexpectedly, Evo Morales, of the Movement towards Socialism (*Movimiento al Socialismo*, MAS) came a strong second, with 20.9%, but under the Constitution the decision went to the newly-elected Congress, which chose Sánchez de Lozada by 84 votes to 43. However following violent demonstrations against his policies, President Sánchez de Lozada was forced to resign on Oct. 17, 2003, and was succeeded by his Vice President, Juan Carlos Meza Gisbert.

Bolivian Communist Party
Partido Comunista de Bolivia (PCB)
Address. c/o Camara de Diputados, La Paz
Leadership. Marcos Domic (secretary-general); Simón Reyes Rivera (first secretary)
Founded in 1950 by dissident members of the Party of the Revolutionary Left (PIR) youth section, the PCB attained legal status after the 1952 revolution. Its line was orthodox communist before the collapse of the Soviet Union, since when internal disputes have plagued the party.

The party at first supported the government of the Nationalist Revolutionary Movement (MNR) but soon became critical of its effective one-party rule and stood against it in the general elections of 1956, in alliance with the PIR, winning only 1.5% of the vote. In 1960, when the PCB contested an election by itself for the only time in its history, the party found support among only 1% of the voters. In 1965 the PCB split into pro-Soviet and pro-Chinese factions and both were banned in 1967 even though their involvement with the guerrillas of Che Guevara's National Liberation Army, then attempting to ignite a domestic revolution, was limited to some pro-Soviet PCB youth section members who were subsequently expelled. Although the ban was later lifted, the PCB was again driven underground during the Bánzer military regime of 1971 to 1978.

Under new leadership, the PCB fought the 1985 general elections in the United People's Front alliance with the Revolutionary Party of the National Left (PRIN) and two dissident factions of the Movement of the Revolutionary Left (MIR), which won four congressional seats. In September 1988 it became a founder member of the United Left (IU), within which it has contested subsequent elections.

Christian Democratic Party
Partido Demócrata Cristiano (PDC)
Address. Casilla 4345, La Paz
Telephone. (591–2) 32–1918
Fax. (591–2) 32–8475
Leadership. Benjamín Miguel Harb (president); José Roberto Castro (secretary-general)
The PDC is a centre-left Roman Catholic grouping that was founded by Remo di Natale in 1954 as the Social Christian

Party, taking its present name at its 1964 congress.

In the 1962 partial elections PDC leader Benjamin Miguel obtained the party's first congressional seat. Although it boycotted the 1966 general elections called by the military junta, the following year the PDC accepted the labour portfolio, which it resigned when President René Barrientos sent in the army to quell protesting miners. The PDC opposed all subsequent military regimes, which eventually led to the exile of both Miguel and the party's organizing secretary, Felix Vargas, from 1974 until 1978. In the 1979 elections the PDC, in an alliance with the Nationalist Revolutionary Movement (MNR) and three minor parties, won nine seats in the Chamber of Deputies and three in the Senate. It was given a cabinet post after democracy was restored in October 1982.

In the 1985 elections the PDC's presidential candidate, Luis Ossio Sanjines, won only 1.4% of the vote, while the party's representation in Congress dwindled to three seats. In the run-up to the May 1989 elections, the PDC tried to negotiate an alliance with the left-wing Movement of the Revolutionary Left (MIR). When the talks broke down in January 1989, it agreed to join forces with the right-wing Nationalist Democratic Action (ADN), Ossio Sanjines becoming Gen. Hugo Bánzer's running-mate in his successful candidacy in the May 1989 presidential elections. In August 1989 Ossio Sanjines accordingly became Vice-President of the new Patriotic Accord (AP) coalition government.

Having contested the 1993 elections within the AP, in 1997 the PDC campaigned as a member of the "mega-coalition" which supported Bánzer's successful presidential candidacy, but failed to win any congressional seats then or in 2003.

The PDC is an affiliate of the Christian Democrat International and of the Christian Democrat Organization of America (ODCA).

Civic Solidarity Union
Union Civica Solidaridad (UCS)
Address. Calle Mercado 1064, La Paz
Telephone. (591–2) 36–0297
Fax. (591–2) 37–2200
Leadership. Max (Johnny) Fernández Rojas
An offshoot of the National Civic Union (*Union Civica Nacional*, UCN), the UCS was founded in 1988 as a vehicle for the presidential campaign of Johnny Fernández. He won a surprising third place in the May 1989 election with 22.8% of the vote but his candidacy was subsequently nullified by the Electoral Court after he was found to have forged 40,000 of the 60,000 votes he received. He nevertheless announced his candidature for the 1993 presidential elections, in which he polled 13.1% of the votes cast.

Following the 1993 elections, in which Gonzalo Sánchez de Lozada of the Nationalist Revolutionary Movement (MNR) won the presidency, the UCS, with 21 seats in the Chamber of Deputies, was invited to be one of three parties in a new government coalition with the MNR and the Free Bolivia Movement (MBL). In the 1997 presidential election the party ran its own candidate, Ivo Kuljis, who obtained 16% of the votes cast. In the concurrent congressional elections the party again won 21 seats in the Chamber and increased its representation from one to two in the Senate. It thereafter formed part of a coalition government headed by Nationalist Democratic Action (ADN).

Kuljis subsequently left the party to form the Unity and Progress Movement (MUP). The party unsuccessfully contested the mayoralty of La Paz in 1999 with Moisés Jarmusz as its candidate. In 2003 it obtained five seats in the Chamber of Deputies.

Conscience of the Fatherland
Conciencia de Patria (Condepa)

Address. c/o Camara de Diputados, La Paz

Leadership. Remedios Loza Alvarado (president)

The centre-left Condepa was founded in 1988 by a well-known singer and broadcaster, Carlos Palenque. In the May 1989 general elections, Condepa won nine seats in the Chamber of Deputies and two in the Senate. During the presidential run-off in the Congress in August, the party threw its support behind Jaime Paz Zamora, candidate of the Movement of the Revolutionary Left (MIR), but the party remained in opposition to the subsequent Patriotic Accord (AP) government. In the municipal elections of December 1991, Condepa candidate Julio Mantilla Cuéllar was elected mayor of La Paz with 26.4% of the vote, and the party also won the major neighbouring city of El Alto with 34% of the vote, the results representing the party's most significant achievement to date. Mantilla pledged to use his office to bring justice to the poorest sectors of the population.

Condepa was placed fourth in the 1993 legislative balloting, winning 14 seats overall. Palenque died in March 1997 and was succeeded as Condepa leader by Remedios Loza, who in June 1997 became the first female Indian to run for the presidency, winning 16% of the vote. As a member of the "mega-coalition" led by Gen. (retd.) Hugo Bánzer Suárez of the Nationalist Democratic Action (ADN), Condepa increased its strength to 17 seats in the Chamber of Deputies and won three in the Senate. The party was included in the resultant ruling coalition headed by the ADN, but was dropped from the government in August 1998 because of its internal divisions. The Condepa candidate, Jorge Dockweiler, polled 5.4% of the votes for the mayoralty of La Paz in 1999. The party failed to win any seats in the congressional elections of 2003.

Free Bolivia Movement
Movimiento Bolivia Libre (MBL)

Address. Edificio Camiri, Oficina 201, Calle Comercio 972 esq., Yamacocha Casilla 10382, La Paz

Telephone. (591–2) 34–0257

Fax. (591–2) 39–2242

Website. www.bolivian.com/mbl

Leadership. Antonio Aranibar Quiroga (president)

This nominally left-wing party was founded in 1985 by the then secretary-general of the main Movement of the Revolutionary Left (MIR), Antonio Aranibar Quiroga, after he and a left-wing section of the MIR split away in protest against participation in the government of Hernán Siles Zuazo of the Leftist Nationalist Revolutionary Movement (MNRI). Aranibar fought the 1985 election as the presidential candidate of the left-wing People's United Front alliance and won 2.2% of the vote, while the alliance obtained four seats in Congress.

The municipal elections of 1987 showed an increase in the MBL's support, the party winning in Bolivia's legal capital Sucre and coming second in Cochabamba. In 1988 its electoral success brought the MBL to the leadership of the newly-formed United Left (IU), as whose candidate Aranibar contested the May 1989 presidential elections but won a negligible percentage of the vote. In February 1990 the MBL left the IU alliance and was subsequently prominent in protracted opposition dialogue with the Patriotic Accord (AP) government over such issues as the independence of the Supreme Court and the establishment of a new electoral system presided over by a impartial electoral court.

In the 1993 presidential election Aranibar polled 5.1% of the vote and his party won seven seats in the Chamber of Deputies. In the June 1997 elections, the MBL's representation fell to four seats. Its candidate, Hernán Zenteno, gained only just over 1% of the votes in municipal elections in La

Paz in 1999. However in the 2003 elections it ran in alliance with the MNR and regained ground.

Indigenous Pachakuti Movement
Movimiento Indigena Pachakuti (MIP)

Leadership. Felipe ("Mallku") Quispe (president)

Founded in November 2000 as one of several formations aiming to represent Amerindians, and led by the president of the CSUTCB peasant organization. In the 2002 elections, its presidential candidate, Felipe Quispe, obtained 6.1% of the vote and the party won six seats in the Chamber of Deputies.

Movement of the Revolutionary Left
Movimiento de la Izquierda Revolucionaria (MIR)

Address. Calle Ingavi 600, Casilla de Correo 7397, La Paz

Telephone. (591–2) 31–0416

Fax. (591–2) 40–6455

Email. mir@ceibo.entelnet.bo

Website. www.cibergallo.com

Leadership. Jaime Paz Zamora (president), Oscar Eid Franco (secretary general)

Founded in 1971, the MIR professes to be left-wing but in power has usually proved to be conservative. Having its main power base in the liberal urban middle class, the party was formed in opposition to the 1971 military coup as a merger of small left-wing groups and young Christian democrats. It drew considerable support from the radical student movement and was linked to the insurgent National Liberation Army (ELN) in the early years of the military dictatorship of Gen. Hugo Bánzer Suárez (1971-78).

The MIR gradually moved away from its Marxist roots but nevertheless remained in strong opposition to the military regime, which continued to persecute and imprison members of the party, among them Bánzer's future political ally, Jaime Paz Zamora. The party contested the elections of 1978, 1979 and 1980 as part of an alliance led by the Leftist Nationalist Revolutionary Movement (MNRI) with Paz Zamora as running-mate of the victorious but ill-fated MNRI leader, Hernán Siles Zuazo, in 1979 and 1980. Paz Zamora came third with 8.8% of the vote in the July 1985 presidential contest and in the simultaneous congressional elections the depleted MIR won 16 seats. When Congress had to vote in the second round of the presidential elections, the MIR joined with other centre-left parties in electing the presidential runner-up, Victor Paz Estenssoro of the Nationalist Revolutionary Movement (MNR), in preference to ex-dictator Bánzer.

Having failed to form an alliance with the Christian Democratic Party, the MIR contested the May 1989 elections alone, winning 41 congressional seats. In the presidential race Paz Zamora was placed a close third with 19.6% of the vote. In the absence of a conclusive winner, the runner-up, Gen. Bánzer, withdrew and switched the 46 congressional votes of the Nationalist Democratic Action (ADN) to Paz Zamora, who in August was duly elected President by Congress. The price exacted for this support was the necessity for the MIR to share power with the ADN in the Patriotic Accord (AP). In an August 1991 major cabinet reshuffle, three MIR ministerial posts were allocated to members of the MIR-New Majority (MIR–NM) faction, which, due to the domination of the ADN, had previously been circumspect in its support for the MIR's involvement in the AP coalition. In March 1992, however, the MIR–NM confirmed its support for Bánzer as AP candidate in the 1993 presidential elections.

After persistent criticism of his presidency, Paz Zamora entered into "permanent" retirement in March 1994, but returned less than eight months later following the arrest on drugs charges of the party's secretary-general, Oscar Eid Franco. In the June 1997 presidential elections Paz Zamora came third with 16.7% of the votes cast and his party won 25 seats in the Chamber and six in the Senate. The party was included in the resultant ruling coalition government headed by the ADN. The MIR candidate, Jorge Torres, obtained 15.9% of the votes in municipal elections in La Paz in 1999, by which time the party was officially calling itself the MIR–NM. In the 2003 elections Paz Zamora obtained 16.3% of the votes cast for the presidency and the party won five seats in the Senate and 26 in the Chamber, to make it the third-largest party in each house.

The party is a member of the Socialist International.

Movement towards Socialism – Popular Instrument for Solidarity with the People
Movimiento al Socialismo – Instrumento Popular para Solidaridad con el Pueblo (MAS, MAS-IPSP)
Address. c/o Camara de Diputados, La Paz
Leadership. Evo Morales
Founded in 1987, and originally known as Assembly for the Peoples' Sovereignty (*Asamblea por la Soberania de los Pueblos*, ASP), this leftist nationalist party led by Evo Morales contested the 1997 elections as part of the United Left (IU). In the presidential elections of June 2003 the MAS candidate, Morales, spokesperson of the country's peasant coca growers, came second. In the concurrent legislative elections the party won 8 seats in the Senate and 27 seats in the Chamber of Deputies, making it the second-largest party in both houses.

Nationalist Democratic Action
Accion Democrática Nacionalista (ADN)
Address. c/o Camara de Diputados, La Paz
Website. www.bolivian.com/adn
Leadership. Jorge Fernando Quiroga Ramírez (leader, former President of the Republic); Ronald Maclean (2002 presidential candidate)
The ADN was formed as a vehicle for Gen. (retd.) Hugo Bánzer Suárez – who had ruled as dictator after seizing power in a coup in August 1971 until himself being overthrown in November 1978 – for the July 1979 general elections, in which he came third with 14.9% of the vote. In the 1980 general election his share of the vote increased slightly to 16.9% and the ADN won 30 congressional seats, which were finally taken up when Congress was recalled in September 1982. The ADN initially supported the July 1980 coup led by Gen. Luis García Meza, but in April 1981 this backing was withdrawn. A month later Bánzer was arrested on a charge of plotting a counter-coup.

The general elections of July 1985 resulted in Bánzer winning the largest share of the vote (28.6%) in the presidential contest, while the ADN obtained 51 seats in Congress. However, because no presidential candidate had obtained a clear majority, a centre-left alliance in Congress elected Victor Paz Estenssoro of the Nationalist Revolutionary Movement (MNR) as President. For the May 1989 elections the ADN entered into an alliance with the Christian Democratic Party (PDC). Bánzer, the alliance's joint candidate, won 22.7% of the vote in the presidential contest and was narrowly outpolled for second place by the MNR candidate, Gonzalo Sánchez de Lozada. Personal dislike between the two candidates precluded an ADN–MNR pact and ensured that neither was elected President by Congress, which opted for Jaime Paz Zamora of the Movement of the Revolutionary Left (MIR). The resultant Patriotic Accord (AP) coalition government led by the ADN and the MIR assumed power in August 1989. In return for the presidency, Jaime Paz Zamora awarded the ADN 10 out of 18 ministerial posts, including the most important portfolios of finance, defence and foreign affairs. Bánzer personally took the chairmanship of the Political Council of Convergence

and National Unity, a post which gave him effective control over government policy.

In March 1992 MIR leaders ratified Bánzer as the AP's 1993 presidential candidate. However, although the AP secured 43 seats in the Chamber of Deputies and eight in the Senate, Bánzer himself could only manage second place in the presidential elections, victory going to Sánchez de Lozada of the MNR. The AP was consequently dissolved in August 1993, with Bánzer resigning as ADN leader in November. In February 1995, however, Bánzer changed his mind, returning to leadership of the ADN.

In August 1997 Bánzer again became President, having headed the popular polling in June with 22.3% of the vote and securing election in a congressional vote with the support of an ADN-headed "mega-coalition" which included the MIR, Conscience of the Fatherland (Condepa) and the Civic Solidarity Union. In the June 1997 congressional elections the ADN headed the poll, winning 33 Chamber seats and 13 in the Senate. The party was therefore dominant in the resultant coalition government.

In August 2001, announcing that he was suffering from cancer, Bánzer resigned both the state presidency and the party leadership, and was succeeded in both by his Vice President, Jorge Fernando Quiroga Ramírez. In the 2002 elections however the ADN won only one seat in the Senate and four in the Chamber; Bánzer died on May 5, 2002.

The ADN is an associate member of the International Democrat Union.

Nationalist Revolutionary Movement
Movimiento Nacionalista Revolucionario (MNR)
Address. Calle Nicolás Acosta 574, La Paz
Telephone. (591–2) 249–0748
Fax. (591–2) 249–0009
Email. mnr2002@ceibo.entelnet.bo
Website. www.bolivian.com/mnr
Leadership. Gonzalo Sánchez de Lozada (President of the Republic), Carlos Sánchez Berzain (secretary general)
The MNR was founded in 1941 and over the decades has spawned various factions with suffixes in their title, reflecting internal party divisions. Most recently, the main party current was known as the Historic Nationalist Revolutionary Movement (MNHR). The MNR's founders included Victor Paz Estenssoro, the left-wing Hernán Siles Zuazo and the fascist sympathizer Carlos Montenegro. The party's original policies reflected Paz Estenssoro's World War II attempt to combine the nationalist developmentalist ideas of the American Popular Revolutionary Alliance Party (APRA) of Peru with those of European fascism, as enunciated by Italian dictator Benito Mussolini. The MNR first participated in government from 1943 under President Gualberto Villaroel.

When the military overthrew Villaroel in 1946, numerous MNR leaders were killed or exiled. Paz Estenssoro fought the 1951 elections from exile as the MNR's presidential candidate and won the highest vote, although not an outright majority. The incumbent President handed power to a military junta which, less than a year later, was toppled by an MNR-led popular uprising, known thereafter as the 1952 Revolution, assisted by the police and tin miners. Paz Estenssoro was allowed to return from Argentina and was appointed President in April 1952.

Paz Estenssoro's coalition government with the Labour Party introduced a number of progressive reforms, including the nationalization of the mines, agrarian reform and the enfranchisement of illiterates. The MNR remained in power for two more terms, with Siles Zuazo taking the presidency in 1956 and Paz Estenssoro being elected President again in 1960. In November 1964, following widespread strikes and disorder, Paz Estenssoro was overthrown and forced into exile by his Vice-President, Air Force Gen. René Barrientos Ortuño, who took power with the assistance of the army. The MNR was thrown into disarray and only re-emerged onto the political scene in 1971 as supporters of the military coup of Gen. Hugo Bánzer Suárez (Nationalist Democratic Action, ADN). Since then its main tendency has been centre-right.

The MNR participated in Bánzer's government until 1974, when it was expelled for protesting that the promised process of democratization had not begun. By then, the left wing of the party, led by Siles Zuazo, had broken away and formed the Leftist Nationalist Revolutionary Movement (MNRI), to which Paz Estenssoro's faction, the MNRH, came second in the 1979 and 1980 presidential elections. Paz Estenssoro was beaten by Siles in both elections, winning 35.9% and 20.1% of the vote respectively. The MNRH, however, won 44 seats in the Congress in 1979.

Following another period of military government (1980-82) and three years of opposition to an MNRI government, Paz Estenssoro once again made a bid for the presidency. In the June 1985 elections he obtained 26.4% of the vote, 2.2% less than Bánzer of the ADN. However, in a run-off congressional vote in August 1985, the centre-left parties added their votes to those of the 59 MNRH congressmen and brought Paz Estenssoro to power again. He quickly introduced a strict austerity programme to reduce rampant inflation, a policy persisted with despite the collapse of the international tin market in late 1985.

Faced with general labour unrest, Paz Estenssoro found greater common ground with the right-wing ADN than with his erstwhile supporters of the centre-left. A "pact for democracy" between the MNRH and the ADN was duly signed in October 1985. In the municipal elections of December 1987 the MNRH polled poorly, amid widespread discontent with the government. This was further fuelled by the US-assisted anti-drug programme, which threatened the livelihood of many peasant coca growers, whose numbers had been swollen by unemployed miners. Nevertheless, in the May 1989 general elections the MNRH presidential candidate, Gonzalo Sánchez de Lozada (formerly Minister of Planning), headed the popular poll with 23.1% of the vote. A run-off election in the newly-elected Congress, in which the MNRH had 49 seats, did not produce a renewal of the pact with the ADN. Personal animosity between Sánchez de Lozada and ADN leader Bánzer resulted in the ADN switching its support to Jaime Paz Zamora of the Movement of the Revolutionary Left (MIR), who was elected President.

Three months after the election of Paz Zamora as President, the 84-year-old Paz Estenssoro announced his desire to resign the MNR leadership. At the next party congress in mid-1990 the decision was formalized and Sánchez de Lozada was elected as his successor, although in 1992 he briefly stood down following a death threat from an MNR congressional deputy. In the June 1993 elections Sánchez de Lozada again defeated Bánzer, winning 33.8% of the popular vote and this time obtained congressional endorsement as President, with Víctor Hugo Cárdenas Conde of the Tupaq Katari Revolutionary Movement–Liberation (MRTK-L) becoming Vice-President. In the simultaneous legislative balloting the MNR/MRTK-L alliance raised its representation to 69 out of 157 seats, thus confirming the MNR's status as the dominant ruling party.

In the June 1997 presidential elections, the MNR candidate, Juan Carlos Durán Saucedo, came a poor second, winning only 17.7% of the vote, while in the concurrent congressional elections the party's representation was cut to 26 seats in the Chamber of Deputies and three in the Senate. The MNR's Guido Capra came second with 16% of the votes cast for the mayoralty of La Paz in 1999, whereas Percy Fernández of the MNR was an easy winner in Santa Cruz de la Sierra.

Paz Estenssoro died in June 2001 at the age of 93. In the presidential election of June 2002, the MNR candidate, Gonzalo Sánchez de Lozada, gained the largest percentage of the vote (22.5%) and was later (Aug. 4) chosen by Congress to serve as President. In the concurrent legislative elections the party won 11 seats in the Senate and 36 seats in the Chamber of Deputies, making it the largest party in each house. In the face of massive hostile demonstrations involving farmers, miners, indigenous people and trade unionists, resulting in some 70 deaths, Sánchez de Lozada lost the support of the ruling coalition and stood down as President on Oct. 17, 2003, being succeeded by Vice President Juan Carlos Meza Gisbert.

Socialist Party
Partido Socialista (PS)
Leadership. Jerjes Justiniano
Founded in 1989 as the Socialist Vanguard of Bolivia (VSB), it secured only 1.4% of the vote in the 1997 elections and subsequently changed its name. In the 2002 elections it obtained only 0.7% of the vote but won one seat in the Chamber of Deputies.

Tupaq Katari Revolutionary Movement–Liberation
Movimiento Revolucionario Tupaq Katari–Liberación (MRTK-L)
Address. Avda. Baptista 939, Casilla 9133, La Paz
Telephone. (591–2) 35–4784
Leadership. Victor Hugo Cárdenas Conde (president); Norberto Pérez Hidalgo (secretary general)
A splinter group of the *indigenista* and peasant-oriented Tupaq Katari Revolutionary Movement (MRTK) founded in 1978, the MRTK-L outpolled its weak parent party in 1985, winning two congressional seats, both of which were subsequently lost in 1989. In the June 1993 presidential elections the MRTK-L leader, Victor Cárdenas, was the running-mate of Gonzalo Sánchez de Lozada of the Nationalist Revolutionary Movement (MNR), which was seeking to broaden its popular appeal. They were successful and the party has since then run in alliance with the MNR.

United Left
Izquierda Unida (IU)
Address. c/o Camara de Diputados, La Paz
Leadership. Marcos Domic (Bolivian Communist Party)
The IU alliance was formed for the 1989 elections following the demise of the previous leftist coalition, the United People's Front (*Frente del Pueblo Unido*, FPU). The IU fielded the Free Bolivia Movement (MBL) leader, Antonio Aranibar Quiroga, as its presidential candidate with Walter Delgadillo of the Patriotic Alliance (AP) as his running mate. The IU won 12 congressional seats, a poor result compared with that achieved by its component parties in the 1985 elections, as Aranibar won a negligible percentage of the total vote. In the municipal elections of December 1989 the IU maintained the MBL's hold on power in the judicial capital, Sucre. Two months later, however, the MBL left the alliance, leaving it in a state of disarray.

The IU put forward Ramiro Velasco of the Socialist Party-One as its presidential candidate in the 1993 election, at which it polled less than 1% of the vote and lost all 10 of its legislative seats. In 1997 it supported the successful presidential candidature of Hugo Bánzer of the Nationalist Democratic Action (ADN) and won four seats in the Chamber of Deputies, which it failed to hold in 2002.

Other Parties

April 9 Revolutionary Vanguard (*Vanguardia Revolucionaria 9 de Abril*, VR-9), obtained 17% of the vote in municipal elections in Sucre in 1999.

Address. Avda. 6 de Agosto 2170, Casilla 5810, La Paz
Telephone. (591–2) 32–0311
Fax. (591–2) 39–1439
Leadership. Dr Carlos Serrate Reich (president)

Left Revolutionary Front (*Frente Revolucionario de Izquierda*, FRI), formed by a splinter group of the Movement of the Revolutionary Left (MIR) prior to the 1985 elections, in which it was allied with the Nationalist Revolutionary Movement (MNR), gaining the Senate presidency for then leader Oscar Zamora Medinacelli. He achieved similar success in 1989 by backing the MIR–ADN coalition which yielded him the job of labour minister in the government of his nephew, Jaime Paz Zamora. In August 1991, the FRI joined the Patriotic Accord government and he re-obtained the Labour portfolio in an August 1991 reshuffle. This post he resigned in 1992 to accept the vice-presidential position in the unsuccessful presidential campaign ticket of the ADN's Hugo Bánzer, the former military dictator. The party contested the 1997 elections as part of the United Left (IU).
Leadership. Mónica Medina (president)

Leftist Nationalist Revolutionary Movement (*Movimiento Nacionalista Revolucionario de Izquierda*, MNRI), founded after the left wing of the Nationalist Revolutionary Movement (MNR) split away in the early 1970s. Led by MNR founding member and former President (1956–60) Hernán Siles Zuazo, the MNRI was the leading force of the Popular Democratic Unity (UDP) alliance in the 1978 elections. Siles Zuazo won both the 1979 and the 1980 presidential elections with 36% and 38.7% of the vote, but each time was prevented from taking power by a military coup. In October 1982 he was finally allowed to return from his Peruvian exile and take office. His UDP government rapidly lost support from the left, the unions and the peasantry as it failed to implement social reforms. The 1985 elections resulted in the heavy defeat of the MNRI presidential candidate, Roberto Jordan Pando, who received a mere 4.8% of the vote, with the party obtaining only eight seats in the Congress. The MNRI proceeded to split into a number of factions, including the centre-right *Movimiento Nacionalista Revolucionario–Vanguardia Revolucionaria 9 de Abril* (MNR-V) and the Leftist Nationalist Revolutionist Movement–One (MNRI-l), each of which subsequently campaigned separately with little electoral success.

National Leftist Revolutionary Party (*Partido Revolucionario de Izquierda Nacionalista*, PRIN), founded in 1964 as a splinter from the Nationalist Revolutionary Movement (MNR), representing the Miners' Federation (FSTMB) and the Bolivian Workers' Federation (COB). It currently has no seats in Congress.
Address. Calle Colón 693, La Paz
Leadership. Juan Lechín Oquendo (president)

Nationalist Katarista Movement (*Movimiento Katarista Nacionalista*, MKN), emerged among the Aymara Indians in the early 1970s. Indigenist and pluri-national, it was named in memory of Tupaj Katari, an Aymara leader who led an anti-colonial uprising in 1781. The MKN is the present name of the rump of the Tupaq Katari Revolutionary Movement (*Movimiento Revolucionario Tupaj Katari*, MRTK), following the secession of the Tupaq Katari Revolutionary Movement–Liberation (MRTK-L) in 1985. It polled 12,627 votes in the 1993 legislative elections but won no seats. Other factions include the Front of Katarista Unity (FULKA) led by Genaro Flores and Katarismo National Unity (KND) led by Felipe Kittelson.
Leadership. Fernando Untoja

New Bolivia Nationalist Front (*Frente Nacionalista Nueva Bolivia*, FNNB), founded in May 2001 by prominent businessman Nicolas Valdivia Almanza to support his intended candidacy in the 2002 presidential elections.
Leadership. Nicolas Valdivia Almanza (president)

New Republican Force (*Nueva Fuerza Republicana*, NFR), supported the successful candidacy of Gen. Hugo Bánzer of the Nationalist Democratic Action (ADN) in the 1997 presidential elections; holds no seats in Congress and in the 1999 municipal elections its candidate for mayor of La Paz, Gregorio Lanza, obtained only 1.4% of the vote. The party was expelled from the government coalition in February 2000 when leader Reyes Villa opposed an increase in water rates in Cochabamba, where he was mayor.
Leadership. Manfred Reyes Villa (president)

Popular Patriotic Movement (*Movimiento Popular Patriótico*, MPP), led by a former member of Conscience of the Fatherland (Condepa), who secured less than 1% of the vote in the 1999 municipal elections.
Leadership. Julio Mantilla Cuellar (president)

Revival Axis (*Eje Pachakuti*, EJE), indigenous socialist party standing for independence and multiculturalism. It polled 18,176 votes and elected one deputy in the 1993 legislative elections.
Leadership. Ramiro Barrenechea Zambrana (president)

Revolutionary Workers' Party–Masses (*Partido Obrero Revolucionario–Masas*, POR–Masas), Trotskyist party with limited support and three prominent internal factions, founded as the Revolutionary Workers' Party (POR) in 1934; affiliate of the Fourth International. It did not contest the 1997 elections.
Leadership. Guillermo Lora Escobar (president)

Bosnia and Herzegovina

Capital: Sarajevo
Population: 3,800,000 (2000E)

The Republic of Bosnia & Herzegovina declared its independence from the Socialist Federal Republic of Yugoslavia (SFRY) in March 1992 and was admitted to the UN in May 1992. Its pre-independence ethnic composition by main group was 44% Muslim (or Bosniak, a term officially adopted in 1994), 31% Serb and 17% Croat, a mixture which precipitated a bloody conflict from 1992-95 (Bosniaks and Croats having supported independence in a 1991 referendum while the majority of Serbs opposed it). Bosnian Serbs, with support from Serbia and the Serb controlled Yugoslav National Army, during 1992 seized large swathes of territory, ethnically cleansed non-Serbs (leading to the largest refugee crisis in Europe since World War II) and proclaimed their intention to incorporate the land they controlled in a "Greater Serbia". In 1993 a separate war between Croats and Muslims broke out in parts of the remaining territories, which was resolved with US mediation in March 1994, when the Federation of Bosnia-Herzegovina was established on the Muslim and Croat controlled territories.

A shift in the military balance, assisted by US-led air attacks that forced Serb forces to abandon their three-year long siege of Sarajevo, paved the way to the ending of military conflict through the Dayton Agreement of November 1995. The Agreement specified that Bosnia and Herzegovina would remain a single sovereignty but would consist of two entities, namely the Federation of Bosnia and Herzegovina (comprising 51% of the country's territory) and the Serb Republic (*Republika Srpska*, RS) (comprising 49%). The Agreement made provision for the return of all refugees as a precondition for reconstruction and redevelopment, a process which is still underway.

The administration of Bosnia and Herzegovina has some aspects of an international protectorate. The High Representative (HR), an international official nominated by the countries and organizations gathered in the Peace Implementation Council (PIC), has wide-ranging powers, including the ability to dismiss elect-ed and appointed officials and the right to pass deci-sions and laws. The HR, a position currently held by Paddy Ashdown, has been a key actor in Bosnia. The international community also maintains a military (NATO-led SFOR stabilization force) presence in the country. Bosnian politics are additionally affected by the operations of the International Tribunal for War Crimes in former Yugoslavia, established by the UN in 1993 and based in The Hague, which has resulted in the indictment and in some cases arrest of prominent (primarily Serb) political leaders.

Under the remarkably complex Dayton structure, the central government is primarily responsible for for-eign relations, trade and customs, monetary policy and communications. It is headed by (i) a three-person Presidency – one Bosniak and one Croat (elected in the Federation) and one Serb (elected in the Serb Republic) – elected for four-year terms, and (ii) a Council of Ministers, headed by a Premier. The Council of Ministers is responsible to a bicameral Parliament (*Skupstina*), consisting of (i) an upper 15-member House of Peoples (*Dom naroda*) indirectly elected for a four-year term by the legislatures of the entities (5 Bosniaks and 5 Croats from the Federation of Bosnia & Herzegovina and 5 Serbs from the Serb Republic), and (ii) a 42-member House of Representatives (*Zastupnicki Dom*) directly elected for a four-year term from each entity (28 from the Federation and 14 from the Serb Republic).

The Federation of Bosnia & Herzegovina is headed by a President and two Vice-Presidents, elected by the Federation's legislature for four-year terms and drawn alternately from the three communities. The Federation's President, with the agreement of the Vice-Presidents, nominates the Federation Prime Minister and Council of Ministers for endorsement by the bicameral legislature, consisting of an indirectly-elect-ed upper House of Peoples of 58 members, of whom 17 have to be Croats, Bosniaks and Serbs and 7 "Others" (minorities and others not identifying with one of the three nations) and a directly-elected House of Representatives of 98 members (with a minimum of 4 seats from each of the three constituent peoples).

The Serb Republic is headed by a President and two Vice-Presidents, who are directly elected for a four-year term. The Prime Minister and Council of Ministers are nominated by the President for approval by the directly-elected unicameral 83-member People's Assembly (with a minimum of 4 seats from each of the three constitutent peoples). All elections until 2002, which took place generally at two-year intervals, were organized and ver-ified by the Organization for Security and Co-operation in Europe (OSCE).

The state (union) presidency, elected in Oct. 5, 2002, includes members of all three nationalist parties: Dragan Covic (Croatian Democratic Union, HDZ), who won 61.5% of the vote for Croat candidates,

Sulejman Tihic (Party of Democratic Action, SDA), winning 37.2% of the Bosniak vote, and Mirko Sarovic (Serb Democratic Party, SDS) with 35.5% of the Serb vote. Sarovic was forced to resign in April 2003 over an arms smuggling scandal and was replaced by Borislav Paravac (SDS).

In the union parliamentary elections held at the same time, the nationalist parties SDA, HDZ and SDS re-gained the dominance they had temporarily lost to a coalition of moderate parties in power in 2001-02. In the Federation (for the seats in the union House of Representatives), the SDA gained 32.4% of the vote (9 seats), the HDZ 15.9% (5 seats), the Party for Bosnia and Herzegovina (SBiH) 16.2% (5 seats), the Social Democratic Party (SDP) 15.7% (4 seats), with smaller parties winning a further five seats. For the seats reserved for the Serb Republic, the SDS gained 33.7% (5 seats), the Party of Independent Social Democrats (SNSD) 22.4% (3 seats), Party of Democratic Progress (PDP) 10.4% (2 seats), the SDA 7.3% (1) seat and other parties another 3 seats.

The results of the elections in the two entities mir-rored the results at the union level. In the RS presiden-tial vote, Dragan Cavic (SDS), proved victorious with 35.9% of the vote. In compliance with the recent con-stitutional changes, one Croat (Ivan Tomljenovic, SDP) and one Bosniak (Adil Osmanovic, SDA) Vice-President were also elected. In the Serb National Assembly, the SDS remained the dominant party, with 26 seats. The other larger parties are the SNSD (19 seats) and the PDP (9 seats). The election results in the Federation testified to the reestablished dominance of the nationalist parties and the fragmentation among more moderate parties. A total of 18 parties gained representation in the House of Representatives, with the HDZ and the SDA taking 48 of the 98 seats.

BOSNIAK PARTIES

Bosnian Party
Bosanska Stranka (BOSS)
Address. Stari Grad 9, Tuzla
Telephone. (387–35) 251035
Fax. (387–35) 251035
Website. www.trazim.com/BOSS
Email. boss.bh@delta.com.ba
Leadership. Mirnes Ajanovic (chairman)
BOSS, which is mainly Bosniak based, took three seats in the Federation lower house October 2002 elections.

Bosnian-Herzegovinian Patriotic Party
Bosanskohercegovacka Patriotska Stranka (BPS)
Address. Husrefa Redzica 4, Sarajevo
Telephone. (387–33) 216-881
Fax. (387–33) 216-881
Leadership. Sefer Halilovic (chairman)
Led by a war-time Chief of Staff of the B–H Army in 1992–93, and supported mostly by Bosniak immigrants from Sandjak (south Serbia/north Montenegro). In the October 2002 elections the BPS won one seat in the union parlia-ment's lower house and in the Federation lower house. Halilovic was indicted at The Hague in September 2001 and voluntarily surrendered to the tribunal. The High Representative prevented Halilovic from taking office as minister following the indictment, but Halilovic continued to head the party.

Democratic People's Union
Demokratska Narodna Zajednica (DNZ)
Address. Sulejmana Topica 7, Velika Kladusa

Telephone. (387–37) 770-407
Fax. (387–37) 770-307
Email. dnzbih@bih.net.ba
Website. www.dnz-cazin.co.ba
Leadership. Fikret Abdic (chairman)
The DNZ, established in 1996, is the dominant party in the isolated north-west Bosnia Muslim-inhabited region of Velika Kladusa, but has no support outside that area. Its founder and leader, Fikret Abdic, was a local political strongman and entrepreneur in the Yugoslav period. He won the largest number of votes in elections to the collegial presidency in 1990 as a candidate of the Party of Democratic Action (SDA) but was subsequently passed over by the SDA in favour of Alija Izetbegovic in making its nomination for the president of the republic. During the Bosnian war, Abdic in 1993 established the "autonomous province of Western Bosnia", reaching an accommodation with Serb forces that brought him into bitter conflict with the Bosnian army.

Abdic won second place in the Muslim section in the September 1998 elections to the collective presidency, but with only 6.2% of the Muslim vote. Abdic has since been sentenced in Croatia for war crimes. In the 2002 elections the DNZ took one seat in the union lower house and two in the Federation lower house.

Party of Democratic Action
Stranka Demokratske Akcije (SDA)
Address. Mehmeda Spahe 14, Sarajevo
Telephone. (387–33) 472 192
Fax. (387–33) 650 429
Email. sda@bih.net.ba
Website. www.sda.ba
Leadership. Sulejman Tihic (chairman)
The SDA is a nationalist Muslim party founded in May 1990. It became the largest Assembly party in elections in November–December 1990, with party leader Alija Izetbegovic also becoming President of the republic and then leading it to the declaration of independence from Yugoslavia in March 1992 and through the war period. In the first post-Dayton elections (September 1996) the SDA maintained its hold on the Muslim vote. Izetbegovic was elected as the Muslim representative on the collective presidency, with over 80% of the Muslim vote, while the SDA won 19 of the 42 seats in the lower house of the union legislature and 78 of 140 seats in the Muslim-Croat Federation lower house. Edem Bicakcic of the SDA accordingly became Federation Prime Minister.

In the September 1998 elections the SDA participated in a coalition including the Party for Bosnia and Herzegovina (SBiH). Izetbegovic, as the candidate for the Coalition for a Single and Democratic Bosnia & Herzegovina (KCD), was re-elected to the collective presidency with 86.8% of the Muslim vote (and about 32% nationally). Although the KCD won only 17 seats in the union lower house and 68 in the Federation lower house, Bicakcic continued as Federation Prime Minister (but was later disqualified from any public office by the High Representative).

In mid-1999 the SDA was threatened with sanctions by the Office of the High Representative for its alleged failure to implement local power-sharing accords. The Federation President, Ejup Ganic of the SDA, was expelled from the party in May for refusing to resign over the SDA's poor showing in local elections the previous month. Standing on its own in the November 2000 legislative elections, the SDA won only eight of the union lower house seats and only 38 in the Federation lower house, being challenged in both legislatures by the multi-ethnic Social Democratic Party (SDP). Prior to the elections, Izetbegovic retired as a member of the union collective presidency (being succeeded by Halid Genjac of the SDA), although he continued as SDA chairman until October 2001. Izetbegovic's successor Tihic narrowly won the elections for the Bosniak presidency member in the October 2002 elections of Haris Silajdzic of the Party for Bosnia and Herzegovina (SBiH).

The party won 32.7% of the votes and 32 seats in the Federation's lower house in October 2002 and subsequently formed a coalition with the Party for Bosnia and Herzegovina (SBiH), Croat Democratic Union (HDZ), Serb Democratic Party (SDS) and the Party for Democratic Progress (PDP) at the union-level.

Party for Bosnia and Herzegovina
Stranka za Bosnu i Hercegovinu (SBiH)
Address. Marsala Tita 7A, Sarajevo
Telephone. (387–33) 214-417
Fax. (387–33) 214-417
Email. zabih@zabih.ba
Website. www.zabih.ba
Leadership. Safet Halilovic (president)
The SBiH is a centrist party aiming to rally moderate non-sectarian opinion, but having mainly Bosniak support. It was founded in April 1996 by Haris Silajdzic, who had resigned as Prime Minister of the Bosnian government in January over what he saw as Islamic fundamentalist tendencies in the dominant Party of Democratic Action (SDA). In the first post-Dayton elections in September 1996, Silajdzic came second in the contest for the Muslim member of the collective presidency and he was then one of the two union Prime Ministers from December 1996 until the move to a single Prime Minister in June 2000. The SBiH contested the September 1998 elections within the SDA-led Coalition for a Single and Democratic Bosnia and Herzegovina (KCD).

Standing alone in the November 2000 elections, the SBiH won five union lower house seats and 21 in the Federation lower house. It subsequently formed a coalition with the Social Democratic Party (SDP) and a number of smaller parties in the Alliance for Change which governed in the Federation and at the union level in 2001-02. After the break-up of the coalition, the SBiH ran alone in 2002, winning 5 seats in the union lower house and 15 in the Federation lower house. The party later joined the coalition of nationalist parties at the union and Federation level.

CROAT PARTIES

Croatian Christian Democratic Union
Hrvatska Krscanska Demokratska Unija (HKDU)
Address. Kulina Bana bb., Tomislavgrad
Telephone. (387–34) 34 352 051
Email. hkdubih@tel.net.ba
Website. www.posluh.hr/hkdu-bih
Leadership. Mijo Ivancic-Lonic (chairman)
Affiliated to the Christian Democrat International, the HKDU in October 2002 won one seat in the House of Representatives of the Bosnian-Croat Federation.

Croatian Democratic Union
Hrvatska Demokratska Zajednica (HDZ)
Address. Kneza Domagoja bb, Mostar
Telephone. (387–36) 314-686
Fax. (387–36) 322-799
Leadership. Barisa Colak (president)
Email. hdzbih@hdzbih.org
Web. www.hdzbih.org
The HDZ, a nationalist Croat party with close links to the Bosnian Catholic hierarchy, was launched in Bosnia-Herzegovina in August 1990, partly on the initiative of the then ruling Croatian Democratic Union in Croatia. In the pre-independence Assembly elections of November–December

1990 it took most of the ethnic Croat vote. The party withdrew from the central government at the height of the Bosnian war in 1993 and became the main proponent of the breakaway Croatian Republic of Herceg-Bosna in the western Herzegovina region. This precipitated a Croat-Muslim war, during which the HDZ and Croat Defense Council (HVO) lines of responsibility intermingled (later leading to the indictment at The Hague of the wartime HDZ President Dario Kordic for war crimes).

International pressure on Zagreb, however, resulted in HDZ participation in the March 1994 agreement to end the Croat–Muslim conflict and set up a (Muslim–Croat) Federation of Bosnia & Herzegovina in the territory not under Bosnian Serb control. The moderate Kresimir Zubak became Federation President in May 1994. After protracted resistance by hardline Croats, Zubak in August 1996 signed an agreement for the abolition of Herceg-Bosna and full Croat participation in the Federation. In the first post-Dayton elections (September 1996), Zubak was elected as the Croat member of the union collective presidency with overwhelming support from Croat voters, whilst the HDZ won seven of 42 seats in the all-Bosnia House of Representatives and 35 of 140 in the Federation lower house.

The election of Croat nationalist Ante Jelavic as HDZ chairman in May 1998 precipitated the exit of Zubak and his supporters, who formed the New Croatian Initiative (NHI), while the OSCE banned some HDZ candidates from running in the September 1998 elections because of their close links with Croatia. Nevertheless, the HDZ remained dominant among Croat voters. In early 2001, the HDZ initiated the establishment of parallel structures for a form of Croat self-government in Herzegovina, defying the international community and resulting in the dismissal in March 2001 of the chairman of the HDZ, Ante Jelavic, from his post as Croat member of the presidency. He was arrested, together with other high-ranking HDZ officials, in 2004 for corruption and abuse of funds. Although having abandoned the effort to create an alternative autonomy, the party remains torn between a more radical and a moderate wing. In October 2002, the HDZ gained 16 seats of 98 in the Federation lower house and 5 in the union lower house.

Croatian Party of Rights
Hrvatska Stranka Prava (HSP)
Address. Fra Petra Bakule 2, Ljubuški
Telephone. (387–39)831-917
Fax. (387–39)831-917
Website. www.hsp-bih.org
Leadership. Zdravko Hrstic (chairman)
The ultra-nationalist HSP believes in the unification of Bosnia and Herzegovina with Croatia. It denies the existence of a distinct Bosniak nation. In the November 2000 and October 2002 elections it gained one seat in the Federation House of Representatives. Like all other Croat parties in Bosnia, except the New Croatian Initiative (NHI), it has a sister party in Croatia.

Croatian Peasant Party
Hrvatska Seljacka Stranka (HSS)
Address. Radiceva 4, Sarajevo
Telephone. (387-33) 441-897
Email. info@hssbih.co.ba
Website. www.hssbih.co.ba
Leadership. Marko Tadic (president)
The moderate HSS is the counterpart in Bosnia & Herzegovina of the Croatian Peasant Party in Croatia. It won one seat in the Federation lower house in the November 2000 and October 2002 elections.

New Croatian Initiative
Nova Hrvatska Inicijativa (NHI)
Address. Sime Milutinovica 2/II, Sarajevo
Telephone. (387-33) 214-602
Fax. (387-33) 214-603
Email. nhi@nhi.ba
Leadership. Kresimir Zubak (chairman)
The moderate NHI was launched in June 1998 by Kresimir Zubak, then the Croat member of the union collective presidency, who had broken with the dominant Croatian Democratic Union (HDZ) after hardliner Ante Jelavic had replaced him as HDZ leader the previous month. It won one seat in the union lower house and two in the Federation lower house in the elections in November 2000 and in October 2002. The party participated in the Alliance for Change government of moderate parties in power in the Federation and at the union level 2001-2002. It is a member of the Christian Democrat International.

SERB PARTIES

Alliance of Independent Social Democrats
Savez Nezavisnih Socijaldemokrata (SNSD)
Address. Petra Kocica 5, Banja Luka
Telephone. (387–51) 318-492
Fax. (387–51) 318-495
Email. kontakt@snsd.org
Web. www.snsd.org
Leadership. Milorad Dodik (chairman)
The SNSD was founded in March 1996. It won two RS Assembly seats in November 1997, following which party leader Milorad Dodik became RS Prime Minister in January 1998, heading a non-partisan administration and moving the seat of government from the Pale stronghold of the hardline Serb Democratic Party (SDS) to Banja Luka. In early 1999 Dodik, with Western support, successfully resisted efforts by RS President Nikola Poplasen of the ultra-nationalist Serb Radical Party (SRS) to replace him as Prime Minister. In elections in November 2000 Dodik came a poor second in the contest for the RS presidency. Although the SNSD improved its representation in the RS Assembly to 11 seats (and also won one in the Federation lower house), Dodik was succeeded as RS Prime Minister by Mladen Ivanic of the Party of Democratic Progress. In 2002, the party gained 21.8% of the vote and 19 seats in the RS Assembly, making it the strongest opposition party. While formally espousing a social democratic program, the party has been driven by its president and did not hesitate to adopt nationalist positions.

Democratic Party
Demokratska Stranka (DS)
Address. Kneza Milosa 28, Bijeljina
Telephone. (387-55) 201-951
Fax. (387-55) 201 951
Leadership. Dragomir Dumic
This small nationalist party gained one seat in the RS assembly in 2002.

Democratic People's Alliance
Demokratski Narodni Savez (DNS)
Address. Aleja Svetog Save 20, Banja Luka
Telephone. (387–51) 219-020
Fax. (387–51) 219-033
Website. www.dnsrs.org
Leadership. Marko Pavic (president)
The DNS was launched in July 2000 as a breakaway from the Serb People's Alliance–Biljana Plavsic (SNS–BP) and won three seats in the November 2000 and the October 2002 elections for the RS Assembly.

Party of Democratic Progress
Partija Demokratskog Progresa (PDP)

Address. Majke Marije i brace Mazar br. 52, 51000 Banja Luka
Telephone. (387–51) 218-115
Fax. (387–51) 218-078
Email.pdp@blic.net
Website. www.pdp-rs.org
Leadership. Mladen Ivanic (president)

The PDP was launched in September 1999 by economist Mladen Ivanic. In November 2000 it took 11 of the 83 seats in the RS Assembly. Ivanic became Serb Republic Prime Minister in January 2001 at the head of a loose coalition which included the Socialist Party of the Serb Republic, one Muslim and one member of the Serb Democratic Party (SDS). After the 2002 elections, where the PDP gained 9 seats in the RS Assembly, Ivanic took office as Foreign Minister of Bosnia. The party portrays itself as reformist, but has worked closely with the SDS and endorsed some of its Serbian nationalist positions.

Pensioners' Party of the Serb Republic
Penzionerska Stranka Republike Srpske (PSRS)

Address. Grcka 19, Banja Luka
Telephone. (387–51)) 213-198
Fax. (387–51)) 213-198
Leadership. Stojan Bogosavac (chairman)

Promotes the interests of pensioners and won one seat in the November 2000 elections to the RS Assembly.

Serb Democratic Party
Srpska Demokratska Stranka (SDS)

Address. Magistralni put bb, Pale
Telephone. (387–65) 690-510
Fax. (387–51) 217-640

The SDS was launched in July 1990 as the political voice of Bosnian Serb nationalism and secured most of the ethnic Serb vote in the November–December 1990 elections. It joined a post-election coalition with the (Muslim) Party of Democratic Action (SDA) and the Croatian Democratic Union (HDZ), arguing that Bosnia & Herzegovina should remain within a federal Yugoslavia. When the government opted for independence, the SDS withdrew from the Assembly in Sarajevo and in March 1992 led the proclamation of the Serb Republic of Bosnia & Herzegovina in Serb-controlled territory, with its own assembly at Pale. The SDS leadership was thereafter prominent in the prosecution of the war against the Bosnian republic.

Under the leadership of Radovan Karadzic, the SDS secured the Bosnian Serbs' rejection of successive international peace plans, on the grounds that they involved the surrender of too much Serb-controlled territory and did not guarantee sovereignty for a Bosnian Serb entity. The SDS leadership came under increasing Yugoslav and international pressure in 1995 to accept a settlement preserving the nominal sovereignty of Bosnia–Herzegovina and reducing the Bosnian Serbs' effective control to around half of the state's territory. In consequence, serious divisions became apparent in the SDS. In April 1995 Karadzic was named as a suspected war criminal by the UN War Crimes Tribunal at The Hague. Under the US-brokered peace agreement concluded at Dayton, Ohio, in November 1995, indicted war criminals were specifically excluded from standing for office in post-settlement political structures. Bowing to international pressure, Karadzic relinquished the RS presidency and the SDS leadership to Biljana Plavsic in mid-1996, but remained very much in control behind the scenes.

The SDS maintained its hold on the Serb vote in the first post-Dayton elections in September 1996. Hardliner Momcilo Krajisnik was elected as the Serb member of the

new collective presidency of Bosnia–Herzegovina, while Plavsic was elected as RS President. Plavsic quickly came into conflict with Karadzic and was expelled by the SDS in July 1997, subsequently forming what became the Serb People's Union–Biljana Plavsic (SNS–BP). In further RS elections in November 1997 the SDS was reduced to 24 seats, with the result that Gojko Kliskovic (SDS) was succeeded as RS Prime Minister by Western-backed moderate Milorad Dodik of the Party of Independent Social Democrats (SNSD).

In June 1998 hardliner Dragan Kalinic became SDS chairman and in the September 1998 elections for the RS presidency the SDS backed Nikola Poplasen of the ultra-nationalist Serb Radical Party (SRS), ensuring his easy victory over Plavsic. The SDS lost ground in legislative elections, however, and Krajisnik failed to secure re-election as the Serb member of the union collective presidency. The SDS staged a recovery in the November 2000 elections, securing the election of Mirko Sarovic as RS President with 50.1% of the vote and taking 31 seats in the 83-member RS Assembly. From its restored dominance, the SDS agreed in January 2001 to support a new RS government headed by Mladen Ivanic of the Party of Democratic Progress, who appointed one SDS minister to his "non-partisan" administration despite Western opposition to SDS participation. The SDS managed to increase its strength in the 2002 elections, gaining the Serb seat of the union presidency and the Serb Republic presidency and emerging as strongest party with 31.2% of the vote and 26 seats in the RS assembly. The entire party leadership resigned in 2004 over the dismissal of Sarovic from all party offices – a year after he had been forced to resign from his position as Serb presidency member. In the largest dismissal since the end of the war, the High Representative dismissed some 60 officials in the Serb Republic in July 2004, including many high ranking SDS officials. He furthermore dismissed Dragan Kalanic as party president (and president of parliament) and banned him from all political offices. Meanwhile Karadzic remained at large, reportedly in Bosnian Serb-controlled territory, despite various efforts by SFOR to detain him.

Serb Patriot Party
Srpska Patriotska Stranka (SPAS)

Address. Dragana Bubica 19D, Banja Luka
Telephone. (381-66) 306-125
Fax. (381-51) 306-250
Leadership. Slavko Zupljanin

The radical nationalist party SPAS gained one seat in the National Assembly of the RS in the elections in October 2002.

Serb People's Alliance
Srpski Narodni Savez (SNS)

Address. Krarjiskih brigada 61, Banja Luka
Telephone. (387–51) 219-469
Fax. (387–51) 217-416
Leadership. Branislav Lolic (chairperson)

The SNS was launched in September 1997 by Biljana Plavsic, who had been elected as President of the Serb Republic (RS) in September 1996 as the candidate of the Serb Democratic Party (SDS). Plavsic, a wartime hardliner who subsequently adopted a more moderate position, was expelled from the SDS when she acted to dissolve the SDS-dominated RS Assembly in July 1997. New RS Assembly elections were held in November 1997 and resulted in the SNS winning 15 of the 83 seats, mainly at the expense of the SDS. Plavsic was therefore able to appoint a "non-partisan" RS government headed by Milorad Dodik of the Party of Independent Social Democrats (SNSD) and to move the seat of government from Pale to Banja Luka.

In the September 1998 elections Plavsic was defeated in the RS presidential contest by Nikola Poplasen of the ultra-nationalist Serb Radical Party (SRS), who was backed by the SDS, and in the RS Assembly elections SNS representation was reduced to 12 seats. In June 2000 the party split, with Dragan Kostic forming the breakaway Democratic People's Alliance. Plavsic surrendered to the Hague war crimes tribunal following her indictment in January 2001. After pleading guilty, she was sentenced to 11 years in prison. In October 2002, the party won one seat in the RS Assembly. The party has become politically irrelevant since then.

Serb Radical Alliance "Dr. Vojislav Seselj"
Srpski radikalni savez "Dr.Vojislav Seselj"

Address. Karadjordjeva 27, Bijeljina
Telephone. (387-55) 203-948
Fax. (055) 203-948
Leadership. Ognjen Tadic (general secretary)
This small radical nationalist group from the eastern Serb Republic gained one seat in the RS parliament in the 2002 elections. The party split off from the SRS.

Serb Radical Party of the Serb Republic
Srpska Radikalna Stranka Republike Srpske (SRS)

Address. Vidovdanska broj 53, Banja Luka
Telephone. (387-51) 219-428
Fax. (387-51) 219-428
Leadership. Milanko Mihajlica (chairman)
The ultra-nationalist SRS originated as the Bosnian Serb wing of the Serb Radical Party in Serbia. It opposed the 1995 Dayton Agreement ending the war. In the September 1998 elections, SRS leader Nikola Poplasen, to Western dismay, won the RS presidency, running with the backing of the Serb Democratic Party (SDS). Poplasen's subsequent effort to install a new RS Prime Minister, in place of Milorad Dodik of the moderate Party of Independent Social Democrats (SNSD), led the High Representative to dismiss him as President in March 1999 for "abuse of power". Poplasen's unwillingness to depart produced a political impasse, with his Vice-President, Mirko Sarovic (SDS), also considered unacceptable. The party was banned by the OSCE in April 2000 for being chaired by Poplasen. The ban was lifted for the 2002 elections, when the party, running separately, gained 4.4% of the vote and 4 seats in the Serb Assembly.

Socialist Party of the Serb Republic
Socijalisticka Partija Republike Srpske (SPRS)

Address. Bana Lazarevica 7, Banja Luka
Telephone. (387-51) 308-839
Fax. (381-51) 308-839
Leadership. Zivko Radisic (chairman)
The SPRS was founded in 1993 as effectively the Bosnian Serb wing of the then ruling Socialist Party of Serbia (Yugoslavia) of Slobodan Milosevic. In the post-Dayton period it opposed the dominant Serb Democratic Party (SDS) then led by Radovan Karadzic, in line with Belgrade's increasing disenchantment with the latter's hardline opposition to the Dayton Agreement. In September 1998 party chairman Radisic, running as the candidate of the moderate Accord (*Sloga*) alliance, won election as the Serb member of the union collective presidency. The SPRS withdrew from the *Sloga* alliance ruling coalition in January 2000. However, the SPRS ministers remained in the government, and in March a dissident SPRS faction opposed to the withdrawal broke away to form the Democratic Socialist Party (DSP).

In the November 2000 elections, the rump SPRS was damaged by the impact of the new DSP, its representation falling to four seats in the RS Assembly and to one in the all-Bosnia lower house. In 2002, the party won three seats in the RS Assembly.

Multi-ethnic Parties

Civic Democratic Party
Gradjanska Demokratska Stranka (GDS)

Address. Marsala Tita 9A/V, Sarajevo
Telephone. (387-33) 213-435
Fax. (387-33) 213-435
Leadership. Ibrahim Spahic (president)
The GDS, which has mainly Bosniak support, won one seat in the Federation lower house in the November 2000 and October 2002 elections.

Liberal Democratic Party
Liberalna Demokratska Stranka (LDS)

Address. Marsala Tita 9A/III, Sarajevo 71000
Telephone. (387-33) 664-540
Email. centrala@liberali.ba
Website. www.liberali.ba
Leadership. Rasim Kadic (president)
An affiliate of the Liberal International, LDS support comes mainly from non-sectarian Muslim voters and it won one seat in the Federation lower house in the November 2000 and October 2002 elections.

Social Democratic Party of Bosnia & Herzegovina
Socijaldemokratska Partija Bosne i Hercegovine (SDP)

Address. Alipasina 41, Sarajevo
Telephone. (387-33) 663-753 *Fax*. (387-33) 213-675
Website. www.sdp-bih.org.ba
Leadership. Zlatko Lagumdzija (chairman); Karlo Filipovic (general secretary)
The SDP (or SDPBiH) was created by merger in February 1999 of the Social Democrats of Bosnia & Herzegovina (SDBiH) and the Democratic Party of Socialists (DSS), formerly the Union of Bosnian Social Democrats (ZSDB) under the leadership of Selim Beslagic, the Muslim mayor of Tuzla. Affiliated to the Socialist International (which had pressed for the merger), the SDP aims to be a social democratic party on the West European model, favouring a regulated market economy and opposing ethnic nationalism.

Between them the SDBiH and DSS in the September 1998 elections won six seats in the union lower house and 25 in the Federation lower house. In the November 2000 elections, however, the new SDP did better than its predecessor parties had separately, winning nine of the 42 seats in the union lower house, and second place in the Federation lower house, with 37 of the 140 seats. The party also won four seats in the Serb Republic Assembly. While deriving particular support from Bosniaks disaffected from the nationalist Party of Democratic Action (SDA), as well as from Bosnians of mixed ethnic background, the party has emphasized its inter-ethnic character in the composition of its lists. The party formed the government between 2001 and 2002 with the Party for Bosnia and Herzegovina (SBiH) and other small parties. After the break-up of the coalition, the party lost considerable support in the parliamentary elections of October 2002, winning 15.6% of the votes and 15 seats in lower house of the Federation parliament. Some members subsequently left the party and founded the Social Democratic Union of Bosnia and Herzegovina, blaming the authoritarian style of the party president for the party's defeat.

Botswana

Capital: Gaborone
Population: 1,680,863 (2001)

The Republic of Botswana became independent from

Britain in 1966, Sir Seretse Khama becoming its first President. Under its 1966 constitution, executive power is vested in the President as head of state, elected for a renewable five-year term by an absolute majority of the elected members of the National Assembly, which has legislative authority. Under a constitutional amendment adopted in 1997 (but not retrospectively applicable to the then current incumbent), no person may serve more than two presidential terms. The President appoints a Vice-President from among the members of the Assembly as well the members of the Cabinet, over which he presides. The Vice-President succeeds to the presidency in the event of the resignation or death in office of the President.

The National Assembly, also having a term of five years, consists of 40 members directly elected from single-member constituencies by universal suffrage of those aged 18 and over, as well as four members chosen by the elected Assembly members (from a list of eight submitted by the President) and three ex-officio members (the Speaker, the non-voting Attorney-General and the President). A second chamber, a 15-member House of Chiefs, composed of representatives of the principal Tswana groups, considers draft legislation on constitutional or chieftaincy matters (but has no veto) and may make representations to the President on tribal matters. Due to the Tswana bias in its composition the constitutional provisions for the House of Chiefs came under pressure from minority groups. Plans for a ethnically balanced reform, however, met resistance from traditional groups and currently are being revised.

Elections in Botswana, regularly held under free and fair conditions, have been dominated by the Botswana Democratic Party (BDP), winning an absolute majority of seats in all post-independence elections. The opposition parties, although gaining ground in the popular vote since the early 1990s, have suffered from serious factionalism that has minimized their prospect of winning a parliamentary majority in the first-past-the-post electoral system. Several attempts to unite the opposition failed during the 1990s. In elections for the elective seats in the National Assembly on Oct. 16, 1999, the BDP won 33 (with 54.34% of the vote), the Botswana National Front (BNF) 6 (24.67%) and the Botswana Congress Party (BCP) one (11.31%). Festus Mogae, who had succeeded to the presidency in April 1998 on the resignation of Sir Ketumile Masire (who himself succeeded Khama in 1980), began his first full term as President of Botswana on Oct. 20, 1999, when he was elected by the members of the new National Assembly. In September 2004, President Mogae dissolved Parliament in order to prepare general elections which were set for Oct. 30. There is little doubt that the BDP will win a sound majority.

Botswana Congress Party (BCP)

Address. POB 2918, Gaborone
Leadership. Otlaadisa Koosaletse (president)
The BCP was formed in July 1998 following a split in the Botswana National Front (BNF) at an acrimonious BNF party congress in April 1998 that reflected long standing dissatisfaction with BNF's leadership. BCP's founder, Michael Dingake, had served as deputy leader of the BNF. The BCP (with 11 members in the National Assembly) superseded the BNF as the official opposition party for the remainder of the current term of the Assembly. In the 1999 Assembly elections, however, the BCP won only one seat (though 11.31% of the vote), Dingake being among its defeated candidates.

Dingake withdrew from active politics on the party's congress in July 2001 and was replaced as party president by Otlaadisa Koosaletse. Efforts to unite with the Botswana Alliance Movement (BAM) proved unsuccessful the same year. BCP refused to join the electoral alliance formed by BNF, BAM, and the Botswana People's Party (BPP) in September 2003. The BCP portrays itself as a social democratic party.

Botswana Democratic Party (BDP)

Address. POB 28, Gaborone
Telephone. (267) 352564
Fax. (267) 313911
Leadership. Festus Gontebanye Mogae (president); Ian Seretse Khama (chairman); Daniel Kwelagobe (secretary-general)
The BDP was founded in 1962 as the Bechuanaland Democratic Party, adopting its present name in 1965, when it won a decisive majority in pre-independence elections. Favoured by the British colonial authorities and white residents for its relative moderation, the party led Botswana to independence in September 1966, its then leader, Sir Seretse Khama, becoming President. Pursuing conservative domestic policies and adopting a pragmatic line externally (notably in regard to South Africa), the BDP was returned to power with further large majorities in the 1969, 1974 and 1979 elections.

On Khama's death in 1980, he was succeeded as President and party leader by Vice-President Quett (later Ketumile) Masire. The BDP won further landslide victories in the 1984 and 1989 elections but faced increasing popular unrest in the early 1990s as well as opposition charges of graft and corruption. In March 1992 the report of a commission of inquiry into land allocations resulted in the resignations of Peter S. Mmusi as Vice-President and of Daniel Kwelagobe as Agriculture Minister, both men also losing their senior party posts. However, at a BDP congress in June 1993 Mmusi and Kwelagobe were elected party chairman and secretary-general respectively, while some senior cabinet ministers failed to secure election to the BDP central committee. Thereafter, tensions increased between the Mmusi/Kwelagobe faction (the "Small Two") and a group of technocrats led by Foreign Secretary Lt.-Gen. Mompati Merafhe (the "Big Five"). This at least partly reflected a struggle for the succession to the ailing Masire.

The BDP retained an overall majority in the October 1994 Assembly elections, but its support – mainly concentrated in the rural areas – slipped sharply to 53.1% (from 64.8% in 1989) and several cabinet ministers lost their seats. Mmusi died during the election campaign. The new Assembly re-elected Masire as President, while the post-election government included Kwelagobe as Minister of Works, Transport and Communications. In July 1995 the Presidential Affairs and Public Administration Minister, Pontashego Kedikilwe, long standing ally to Kwelagobe, was elected as BDP chairman. Festus Mogae, who had served as Vice-President since 1992, automatically succeeded Masire as President (for the remainder of the current term) when Masire retired from politics at the end of March 1998. Mogae also became BDP party president.

The BDP won 33 seats (with 57.2% of the vote) in the October 1999 Assembly elections. The Assembly subsequently elected Mogae to the Presidency in his own right. President Mogae appointed Lt.-Gen. Seretse Ian Khama, former commander of the Botswana Defence Force and son of Botswana's first President, as his Vice-President. This move led to a regrouping of the factions in the party, with Khama gaining ground versus the old guard led by Kedikilwe and Kwelagobe, in his effort to succeed Mogae who is expected to step down some time after the elections in 2004. At the party congress in Ghanzi in July 2003 the Khama faction gained a sweeping victory over Kedikilwe and his allies. Khama replaced Kedikilwe as party chairman while Mogae, rather sympathizing with Khama, retained the supreme post of party president. Only Kwelagobe managed to keep his post as secretary general.

The BDP is associated with the International Democrat Union through the Democrat Union of Africa.

Botswana National Front (BNF)

Address. POB 1720, Gaborone
Telephone. (267) 351789
Leadership. Otsweletse Moupo (president); Akanyang Magama (secretary-general)

The left-leaning BNF was established shortly before independence in 1966 by opposition elements seeking to provide an alternative to the dominant BDP. It won three Assembly seats in 1969, two in 1974 and 1979 and four in 1984, this last tally increasing to seven by late 1985 as a result of a by-election victory and two BDP defections. In 1989 the BNF fell back to three elective seats, although its share of the vote increased from 20.4% in 1984 to 26.9%. Based in the urban and semi-urban areas, the BNF had a Marxist orientation in the 1980s – its "philosopher king" Kenneth Koma was educated in Eastern Europe – but moved to a social democratic stance after the 1989 elections (in 1995 BNF's "social democratic prorgamme" was approved by the party's congress). In 1991 the BNF joined other opposition groups in the Botswana People's Progressive Front (BPPF), which called for the creation of an all-party commission to supervise the next elections, claiming that the previous contest had been rigged.

In 1993, however, dissension developed within the BPPF over whether the alliance should boycott the next elections if its demands for electoral reform were not met. In the event, the BNF contested the October 1994 elections in its own right, substantially increasing its vote share (to 37.7%) and winning 13 elective seats, including all four in Gaborone. In July 1998 its Assembly representation was reduced to two when 11 of its deputies formed the BCP. In February 1999 the BNF helped form the Botswana Alliance Movement (BAM), this also comprising several smaller opposition parties, but left only two months later.

In the elections the same year the BNF won 26% of the vote (compared with the BCP's 11.9%) and, with six seats, regained its former status of official opposition party in the National Assembly. However, new factionalism fuelled by Koma's erratic leadership style, brought another split to the party. Kenneth Koma's "party liners" were defeated by Otsweletse Moupo's "concerned group" at the party congress in November 2001. Allegations of vote rigging and suspension of party liners by the new leadership – amongst them Koma himself – eventually resulted in the breakaway and foundation of the New Democratic Front (NDF) in March 2003. In September 2003 the BNF, BAM, and BPP, formed an electoral alliance for the general elections in 2004. The BNF also embraces three smaller parties, the Botswana Labour Party (BLP), **Botswana Workers' Front** (BWF) and **United Socialist Party** (USP), as group members.

The BNF is an observer member of the Socialist International.

Other Parties

Botswana Alliance Movement (BAM). BAM registered officially as a political party in February 2003. BAM was originally formed as an electoral alliance of five independent opposition parties in February 1999 comprising its initiator, the BNF (including its three group members BLP, USP, and BWF), the Independence Freedom Party (IFP), the

United Action Party (UAP), the BPP, and the Botswana Progressive Union (BPU). However, the BNF left BAM in April 1999. The BPU also withdrew from the fold on the eve of the elections in October 1999 and BAM gained no seats, with only 4.7% of the vote. In August 2000 BPP's withdrawal meant a further weakening and resulted in legal action by the BPP because of the contested use of party symbols. In 2001 negotiations between BAM and BCP failed to produce a more comprehensive alliance. Similar efforts, however, proved to be successful in September 2003, when BAM formed an electoral alliance with its former members BNF and BPP in order to avoid fielding competing candidates in the single-member constituencies in the 2004 elections.
Leadership. Ephraim Lepetu Setshwaelo

Botswana People's Party (BPP). The BPP was formed in 1962 as a strongly anti-colonialist grouping with strongholds in the Northeast in Kalanga country. Until 1984 BPP gained rather marginal representation in the National Assembly (up to three seats and 14.2% of the vote). After being reduced to 4.1% of the popular vote in 1994 the BPP joined BAM in 1999 but left the unsuccessful alliance in August 2000, accusing BAM of the unlawful use of its party symbols. In August 2003 the long standing party president Motlatsi Molapisi was replaced by Bernard Balikani. Only one month later BPP joined an electoral alliance with the BNF and BAM for the elections in 2004.
Leadership. Bernard Balikani (president), Keorapetse Mafa (secretary general).

Botswana Progressive Union (BPU), was formed by the former BDP assistant minister Daniel Kwele in 1982. The BPU unsuccessfully contested three subsequent elections and failed to participate in the 1999 elections after withdrawing at the last minute from BAM, which it helped form in April 1999.

Botswana Worker's Front (BWF), was formed in April 1993 by Shawn Nthaile as another splinter group of the BNF and registered as a political party in September 1993. It contested the general elections in 1994 as part of the short-lived United Democratic Front, an opposition umbrella organisation formed by BWF, Social Democratic Party (SDP) and Mels Movement of Botswana (MELS). In 1999 BWF contested the elections as a group member of the BNF.

Independence Freedom Party (IFP), formed through a merger between the Botswana Freedom Party and the Botswana Independence Party in April 1993. The IFP contested the 1994 elections unsuccessfully and formed the BAM together with other parties in 1999, this being transformed into a fully-fledged political party in 2003.

Mels Movement of Botswana (MELS). Emerging from a student study group at the University of Botswana, MELS registered as a political party in October 1997. MELS had been part of the short-lived opposition umbrella organisation UDF that obtained only 0.3% of the vote share in the elections in 1994. Strongly attached to scientific socialism and the teachings of Marx, Engels, Lenin, and Stalin (MELS), MELS gained only 22 votes in the 1999 elections.
Leadership. Themba Joina (president)

New Democratic Front (NDF). The NDF is a breakaway from the BNF and consists mostly of members of the "party line" faction in BNF. However, neither the ageing Kenneth Koma nor his would-be successor Peter Woto (who failed to be elected BNF president in 2001), became the leader, but attorney Dick Bayford. The NDF registered as a political party in March 2003 and has – according to official statements – a social democratic to socialist ideology. *Leadership*. Dick Bayford (president); Philipp Monowe (secretary general)

Social Democratic Party (SDP), another breakaway from the BNF, was led by the BNF veteran Mareldi Giddie. In the run-up to the 1994 elections the SDP joined the now defunct UDF together with MELS and BWF in an alliance that gathered only 0.3% of the popular vote. In 1999 the SDP failed to contest the legislative elections.

United Action Party (UAP), also known as "Bosele", was founded by Ephraim Lepetu Setshwaelo in 1997. The UAP allied with other opposition parties in BAM in 1999. The transformation of BAM into a political party in 2003 ended UAP's existence as an independent party.

United Socialist Party (USP), also known by the acronym PUSO, was formed in April 1994 as a splinter group of the BNF and registered as a political party in May 1994. The USP believes in a socialist ideology whereby the state controls the means of production. In 1999 USP reconciled with the BNF and joined the latter in the form of a group membership. USP's leader Nehemia Modubule, MP for Lobatse, became offical leader of the opposition after Kenneth Koma left the BNF in March 2003.
Leadership: Nehemia Modubule

Brazil

Capital: Brasília
Population: 174,632,960 (2002E)

The Federative Republic of Brazil became independent from Portugal in 1822 and a federal republic in 1889. It comprises 26 states and a federal district (Brasília). National legislative authority rests with the bicameral National Congress, comprising a 513-member Chamber of Deputies which is directly elected every four years by a system of proportional representation, and an 81-member Federal Senate whose members are elected for eight-year terms at four-year intervals for, alternately, one-third and two-thirds of the members. Congressional elections are by universal and compulsory adult suffrage. Executive power is exercised by the President who appoints and leads the Cabinet. A new constitution entered into effect on Oct. 6, 1988, and removed many of the restrictions imposed under military rule between 1964 and 1985. The presidential term is four years and incumbents may be reelected for one additional, consecutive term, following a 1997 constitutional amendment.

Each state has its own government, with a structure that mirrors the federal level, enjoying all the powers (defined in its own constitution) which are not specifically reserved for the federal government or assigned to the municipal councils. The head of the state executive is the Governor, elected by direct popular vote under the federal constitution. The one-chamber state legislature is a State Assembly. The state judiciary follows the federal pattern and has its jurisdiction defined so as to avoid any conflict or superimposition with the federal courts.

In October 2002 elections the left-wing Workers' Party (PT) won the presidential elections for the first time. It also gained the largest number of seats in the Chamber of Deputies (91) and 14 in the Senate. In contrast to the preceding elections of 1994 and 1998, in

which Fernando Henrique Cardoso was victorious in the first round, the 2002 presidential contest was characterized by a tight race between four candidates: José Serra of the Brazilian Social Democratic Party (PSDB), the government candidate, Anthony Garotinho of the Brazilian Socialist Party (PSB), Ciro Gomes of the Popular Socialist Party (PPS) and Luiz Inácio Lula da Silva, the PT candidate. Lula (as he is universally known) was the candidate of a coalition that included its traditional ally, the leftist Communist Party of Brazil (PC do B), and the right-wing Liberal Party (PL). The subsequent run-off election was contested by Lula (PT) and Serra (PSDB). The former was backed by a much wider alliance which included the PSB, PPS, Democratic Labour Party (PDT), Brazilian Labour Party (PTB) and Green Party (PV), apart from the above-mentioned parties. The latter candidate was supported by an alliance that included the Party of the Brazilian Democratic Movement (PMDB), the Liberal Front Party (PFL) and the Progressive Brazilian Party (PPB) (now called the Progressive Party or PP). Lula and his running-mate, vice-presidential candidate José Alencar (PL), won the second-round election with 61.3% of the vote. Since the elections Lula has also brought the PMDB into a cabinet-based governing alliance.

Brazilian Labour Party
Partido Trabalhista Brasileiro (PTB)
Address. SLCN 303 Bloco C, Sala 105, Brasília-DF 70735-530
Telephone. (55-61) 327 6144/6010
Fax. (55–61) 327 8657
Email. ptb@org.br
Website. www.ptb.org.br
Leadership. Roberto Jefferson (president); Duciomar Costa (Senate leader); José Múcio Monteiro (Chamber leader)
Founded in 1980, the centre-right PTB is a direct successor of the pre-1965 Brazilian Labour Party founded in the 1940s by former President Getúlio Vargas. It elected 31 deputies in the 1998 elections and was part of the governmental alliance that supported President Cardoso after his first election in 1994. In 2002 the PTB elected 26 deputies and three senators. It supported Lula in the second-round election and is a member of the current government coalition.

Brazilian Social Democratic Party
Partido da Social Democracia Brasileira (PSDB)
Address. Avenida L2 Sul, Quadra 607, Edificio Metrópolis, Brasília-DF 70200-670
Telephone. (55–61) 424-0500
Fax. (55–61) 424 0519
Email. tucano@psdb.org.br
Website. www.psdb.org.br
Leadership. Fernando Henrique Cardoso (honorary president); José Serra (president); Arthur Virgílio (Senate leader); Custódio Mattos (Chamber leader)
The centre-left PSDB was founded in June 1988 with a manifesto advocating social justice, economic development, land reform and environmental protection. It also called for the establishment of a parliamentary system within four years. The party was broadly modelled on the European social democratic tradition, although it had no organized working-class support. It is strong in the state of São Paulo and other states of the south-east as well as in the north-eastern state of Ceará.

The PSDB was formed by dissident members of the Party of the Brazilian Democratic Movement (PMDB) opposed to President Sarney's retention of the presidential system and his determination not to shorten his term of office. The catalyst, however, was the unsuccessful challenge by Mario Covas, PMDB leader in the Constituent

Assembly, for the PMDB leadership. The new party also attracted defectors from the PFL, the PSB and the PTB. Soon after its formation the PSDB became the third largest party in Congress, with eight senators and 60 deputies. In 1994 the party joined the PFL, the PTB and the PL in supporting the successful presidential campaign of its leader, Fernando Henrique Cardoso. During Cardoso's two terms in office (1995-2002) the party moved to the centre of the political spectrum, supporting the President's programme of economic modernization (market opening and privatization). Cardoso's electoral successes benefited the PSDB, which in the 1998 elections won 99 seats in the Chamber of Deputies and 16 seats in the Senate, making it the second largest party in Congress, behind the PFL. In 2002 the PSDB elected 71 deputies, 11 senators and seven governorships, becoming – together with the PFL – the opposition to the Lula administration.

The PSDB is an observer member of the Christian Democrat Organization of America (ODCA).

Brazilian Socialist Party
Partido Socialista Brasileiro (PSB)
Address. SCLN 304, Bloco 'A', Entrada 63, Sobreloja, Brasília-DF 70736-510
Telephone. (55–61) 327 6405/5096
Fax. (55–61) 327 6405/5096
Email. psb@psbnacional.org.br
Website. www.psbnacional.org.br
Leadership. Miguel Arraes de Alencar (president); João Capiberibe (Senate leader); Renato Casagrande (Chamber leader)
Founded in 1986, the PSB is an independent leftist party whose lineage goes back to the PSB of the 1946-65 period. The party managed to send only one deputy and two senators to Congress in the elections of November 1986. However, in the 1990s the party established itself as part of the left-wing opposition and increased its representation in the Chamber of Deputies to 11 seats in 1990 and 15 in 1994.In the 1995-2002 period the party was in opposition to the government of President Cardoso. In 1998 the PSB supported the presidential candidacy of Luís Inácio (Lula) da Silva of the Workers' Party, winning 19 seats in the Chamber of Deputies. In 2002 the PSB won 22 seats in the Chamber of Deputies and 4 seats in the Senate. Currently it is part of the government coalition.

Communist Party of Brazil
Partido Comunista do Brasil (PCdoB)
Address. Alameda Sarutaiá 185, Jardim Paulista, São Paulo-SP 01403–010
Telephone. (55–11) 3054 1808
Fax. (55–11) 3051 7738
Email. cno@pcdob.org.br
Website. www.pcdob.org.br
Leadership. José Renato Rabelo (president); Renildo Calheiros (Chamber leader)
The PCdoB originated in a Maoist faction within the Brazilian Communist Party (PCB, now the Popular Socialist Party, PPS). It split away from the PCB in 1962 and set up as a separate party under the PCB's original name after the Communist Party had abandoned internationalism. Banned as soon as it was founded, the PCdoB worked within what became the Party of the Brazilian Democratic Movement, the official opposition party. After the death of Mao and the arrest of the "Gang of Four" in 1976, the PCdoB turned away from China and became pro-Albanian. An official amnesty in 1979 allowed the party to operate more openly, although it remained officially illegal until June 1985.

Following the defeat of the Workers' Party (PT) candidate, Lula da Silva, in the 1989 presidential elections, the PCdoB again campaigned by itself in the 1990 congressional elections and won five seats in the Chamber. It gave further backing to Lula in the 1994 and 1998 presidential elections. As part of a left-wing opposition bloc, the PCdoB strongly opposed the policies of President Cardoso of the Brazilian Social Democratic Party (1995-2002). The party won ten Chamber seats in 1994, seven in 1998 and 12 in 2002. Currently it is a member of the Lula coalition government.

Democratic Labour Party
Partido Democrático Trabalhista (PDT)
Address. Av. Marechal Câmara 160, Edificio Orly, Sala 418, Rio de Janeiro-RJ 20020-080
Telephone. (55–21) 2262–8834 or 2533 1535
Fax. (55–21) 2262–8834
Email. pdtconta@abeunet.com.br
Website. www.pdt.org.br
Leadership. Carlos Roberto Lupi (president); Jefferson Peres (Senate leader); Hélio de Oliveira Santos (Chamber leader)
Founded by Leonel Brizola (who died in June 2004), Doutel de Andrade (party vice-president until his death in January 1991) and other exiled members of the old Brazilian Labour Party (PTB) after their return to Brazil under the 1979 amnesty, the party had to adopt its current name after a dissident group won a court case over the old party name in 1980. The PDT had the support of ten deputies from the start and in the general election of 1982 it increased its representation to 24 deputies and one senator thus forming the largest labour bloc in Congress. Although the party had thrown its weight behind Tancredo Neves, the victorious Democratic Alliance candidate in the 1985 presidential elections, it was one of the few parties to take an early stand against the economic policies of his running-mate and replacement, President Sarney. This unpopular stand, however, was vindicated in 1988, when, following social and industrial tensions, the PDT made major gains in the November municipal elections at the expense of the ruling Party of the Brazilian Democratic Movement (PMDB). In the first round of the1989 presidential election Brizola came very close to the two frontrunners, Lula da Silva of the Workers' Party and Fernando Collor de Mello of the National Reconstruction Party (the latter going on to win the run-off election). The PDT did well in the October 1990 congressional and gubernatorial elections, increasing its representation in the Chamber of Deputies from 24 to 46 seats and thus becoming the third largest party. However, Brizola's personalist style of leadership alienated voters and led to prominent politicians leaving the party. Brizola went on to stand as the PDT presidential candidate in 1994, coming in fifth place with a poor 2.6% of the vote and 34 seats in the Chamber.

In 1998 the PDT supported the further presidential candidacy of Lula da Silva, with Brizola running as vice-president. However, its share of congressional votes continued to decline and the party won only 25 seats in the Chamber and two seats in the Senate. It thereafter maintained strong opposition to the presidency of Fernando Henrique Cardoso of the Brazilian Social Democratic Party. In 2002 the tendency of decline continued and the PDT elected only 21 deputies, but in the Senate the party won five seats, three more than the last election.

The party is a full member of the Socialist International.

Liberal Front Party
Partido da Frente Liberal (PFL)
Address. Senado Federal, Anexo I, 26º andar, sala 2602 Brasília-DF 70165–900
Telephone. (55–61) 311–4305/ 4307/ 1609
Fax. (55–61) 224–1912
Email. delegadonacional@pfl.org.br
Website. www.pfl.org.br
Leadership. Jorge Konder Bornhausen (president); José Carlos

Aleluia (Chamber leader); José Agripino (Senate leader)

The centre-right PFL has its traditional stronghold in the underdeveloped north-east of the country and has been accused of appealing to traditional political practices such as patronage to gather electoral support. The party was founded in 1984 and was formed by the liberal faction of the right-wing Social Democratic Party (PDS) following disagreements over the appointment of Paulo Salim Maluf as the party's candidate for the 1985 presidential elections. The PFL became Brazil's third largest party in parliament almost overnight, with José Sarney (president of the military's official party ARENA, 1970-79, and president of the PDS, 1979-84) and the Brazilian Vice-President Aureliano Chaves among its leaders, and 72 deputies and 12 senators having sworn allegiance to the party. Although the PFL was not officially a legal political party until June 1985, it nevertheless formed a democratic alliance with the Party of the Brazilian Democratic Movement (PMDB) in order to contest the indirect presidential elections of January 1985, which were won by Tancredo Neves and José Sarney, as presidential and vice-presidential opposition candidates. The PMDB's Tancredo Neves died before taking office and José Sarney ended up assuming the presidency, and affiliating to the PMDB, despite the fact he had been the PFL's candidate. In September 1987 the PFL officially withdrew from the Democratic Alliance, claiming that it was too dominated by the PMDB, although some PFL members retained their cabinet and other government posts.

In 1989, in the first presidential elections held after redemocratization, the PFL ran Sarney's Mines and Energy Minister, Aureliano Chaves, as its candidate: he obtained only a small percentage of the valid votes. In the elections of the following year, however, his party won the highest number of state governors' posts and again proved to be the second most popular party, winning 92 seats in the Chamber of Deputies. The PFL supported the successful presidential candidacies of Fernando Henrique Cardoso of the Brazilian Social Democratic Party in 1994 and 1998 and was a key member of Cardoso's government coalition. In 1998 the PFL became the largest party in Congress, electing 106 deputies and 20 senators. In the 2002 presidential contest the PFL did not formally support any candidate in the first round. In the run-off, however, it allied with the PSDB candidate – José Serra – against Lula. In that year the PFL won 84 seats in the Chamber of Deputies, 19 seats in the Senate and four governorships.

Liberal Party
Partido Liberal (PL)

Address. SCN-Qd.2, Bloco D, Sala 601a-606a, Asa Norte, Brasília-DF 70712-930

Telephone. (55–61) 3202-9922

Fax. (55–61) 3202 9911 ext. 203

Email. pl@pl.org.br

Website. www.pl.org.br

Leadership. Valdemar Costa Neto (president); Magno Malta (Senate leader); Sandro Mabel (Chamber leader)

Founded in 1985, the centre-right PL secured seven seats in the Chamber of Deputies and one Senate seat in the 1989 elections, bring ing this number up to 15 in the 1990 elections. As a small party the PL stands for the country's small businesses and supports free enterprise and fair wages for all. In 1994 the party supported the successful presidential candidacy of Fernando Henrique Cardoso of the Brazilian Social Democratic Party. In 1998 it moved to the opposition, supporting the left-of-centre presidential candidacy of Ciro Gomes. In that year's parliamentary election the PL won 12 seats in the Chamber of Deputies. In 2002 the PL continued its opposition stance, forming an alliance with the PT, through which it won the position of vice-president. That year the PL won 26 seats in the Chamber of Deputies and three in the Senate.

Party of the Brazilian Democratic Movement
Partido do Movimento Democrático Brasiliero (PMDB)

Address. Câmara dos Deputados, Edificio Principal, Sala T4, Brasília-DF 70160–900

Telephone/fax. (55–61) 215 9211/ 9209/ 9206

Email. pmdbl@pmdb.org.br

Website. www.pmdb.org.br

Leadership. Michel Temer (president); Renan Calheiros (Senate leader); José Borba (Chamber leader); José Sarney (president of the Senate)

The centrist PMDB is the successor to the Brazilian Democratic Movement (MDB) created in 1966 as a legal outlet of opposition to the military regime of the time. Renamed the PMDB in 1979, the party played an important role in the process of transition to democracy in the late 1970s and early 1980s. Its campaign for democratization attracted support from a wide section of society, ranging from left-wing forces, such as the illegal Communist Party (now the Popular Socialist Party) and trade unions, to moderate conservatives.

In November 1986 the PMDB became the most powerful party in Brazil, with 22 governorships, 260 out of 487 seats in the Chamber of Deputies and 46 out of 72 seats in the Senate, and thus also dominated the Constituent Assembly which President Sarney established in February 1987 to draft the 1988 constitution. However, by September 1987, with the economy in turmoil, an agrarian reform plan held in disrepute and a raging controversy regarding the length of Sarney's presidential mandate, the PMDB-led Democratic Alliance was dissolved. Sarney agreed to hand over power in March 1990 and in September 1988 endorsed the bid of the PMDB's Ulysses Guimarães to become his successor.

In the 1990s the PMDB became an electoral machine with very little internal discipline or ideological coherence. The party also became tainted by allegations of corruption against several of its leaders. In March 1991 the 20-year party leadership of Guimarães finally ended, when he was defeated in a party election by the former governor of São Paulo, Orestes Quercia. In October the following year Guimarães was killed in a helicopter crash. In 1994 Quercia himself was forced to resign amid allegations of corruption.

As the largest component of the coalition supporting the presidential candidacy of Fernando Henrique Cardoso of the Brazilian Social Democratic Party (PSDB) in 1994, the PMDB won 107 seats in the Chamber of Deputies, 22 seats in the Senate and nine of the 26 governorships. In the 1998 congressional elections, however, the PMDB came third behind the Liberal Front Party and the PSDB, securing 82 seats in the Chamber and 27 in the Senate. In 2002 the PMDB won 74 seats in the Chamber of Deputies, 19 in the Senate and five governorships. In the presidential election this party allied with the PSDB in support of José Serra, who was defeated by Lula. Following the inauguration of the Lula administration, the PMDB joined the coalition government.

Popular Socialist Party
Partido Popular Socialista (PPS)

Address. SCS Quadra 7, Bloco A, Edificio Executive Tower, sala 826-28, Brasília-DF 70307-901

Telephone. (55–61) 223 0623 or 323 2723/2923

Fax. (55–61) 323 3623

Email. pps23@pps.com.br

Website. www.pps.org.br

Leadership. Roberto Freire (President and Chamber leader); Mozarildo Cavalcante (Senate leader); Júlio Delgado (Chamber leader); Euzébio Diniz (secretary-general)

Originally founded in 1922 as the Communist Party of

Brazil, the party was renamed as the PPS in January 1992 under the leadership of Roberto Freire. It supported the liberation of the former Soviet Union, describing Marxism-Leninism as "corruption by Stalin of the thoughts of Marx, Engels and Lenin". In 1992 the party opted for the pursuit of socialism through democratic means, effectively becoming a moderate left-of-centre organization. The PPS mainly campaigns for job creation, the abolition of "unproductive landholdings" and the autonomy of Amazonia.

In 1998 the PPS, in alliance with the small Liberal Party, supported the presidential candidacy of Ciro Gomes, a dissident of the Brazilian Social Democratic Party and former governor of Ceará. Gomes did well in the presidential election, polling almost 11% of the votes, but his popularity did not help the PPS, which won only three seats in the Chamber of Deputies. In 2002 Gomes contested the presidential election with the support of two other parties, the Democratic Labour Party (PDT) and the Brazilian Labour Party (PTB). He came out of the polls in fourth position. Ciro Gomes and his party supported Lula's candidacy in the second-run election and is a member of the current coalition government. In the same elections, the PPS enlarged its representation, gaining 15 seats in the Chamber of Deputies and one senatorial seat, and elected two state governors.

Progressive Party
Partido Progressista (PP)
Address. Anexo I do Senado Federal, 17 Andar, Brasília-DF, 70165–900
Telephone. (55–61) 311–3041
Fax. (55–61) 311 3984 or 223 2255
Website. www.pp.org.br
Leadership. Paulo Salim Maluf (honorary president); Pedro Corrêa (president); Pedro Henry (Chamber leader); Javier Arenas (general secretary)

A centre-right party based in Brazil's south and south-east, the PP was formed in 1993 as a merger of the Social Democratic Party (PDS) and the Christian Democratic Party (PDC). Since its origins – it emerged from the pro-military Arena, and was renamed the PDS after democratization – what is now the PP has changed its denomination several times and has undergone multiple splits as well as mergers with other parties. Although not an original member of the coalition supporting the successful presidential candidacy of Fernando Henrique Cardoso of the Brazilian Social Democratic Party in 1994, the PP later joined the government alliance.

The party had depended heavily on the political popularity of its leader, the former governor of São Paulo, Paulo Salim Maluf, who has recently been replaced in the party's leadership due to his declining popularity. In the 1998 elections the PP won 60 seats in the Chamber of Deputies and five in the Senate, making it the fourth largest party in Congress. In the 2002 elections the PP supported the government candidate José Serra. In that election the PP had its representation reduced to 49 seats in the Chamber of Deputies, elected only one Senator and no state governors. It is currently part of the government coalition.

Workers' Party
Partido dos Trabalhadores (PT)
Address. Rua Silveira Martins, 132, Centro, São Paulo-SP 01019-000
Telephone. (55–11) 2343 1327 or 3243 1332
Fax. (55–11) 3243 1335
Email. snc@pt.org.br
Website. www.pt.org.br
Leadership. Luíz Inácio Lula da Silva (honorary president); José Genoíno (president); Jorge Bittar (general secretary); Ideli Salvatti (Senate leader); Arlindo Chinaglia (Chamber leader); João Paulo Cunha (president of the Chamber)

The PT was founded by the leader of the powerful United Confederation of Workers (CUT), Luíz Inácio Lula da Silva (known universally as Lula), Jacó Bitar and Airton Soares and emerged from the growing São Paulo *autêntico* independent trade union movement in the late 1970s. The party also received strong support from the progressive branch of the Catholic Church and members of small left-wing groups as well as from previous supporters of the former Brazilian Labour Party (PTB), which had backed Presidents Vargas and Kubitschek in the 1950s. The PT has a diverse base of support, from organized urban industrial workers (especially those affiliated to the CUT), public sector unions, rural movements and social justice movements linked to the Catholic Church.

In its first congressional elections in 1982, the PT received only six seats in the Chamber of Deputies. The more open elections of 1986 gave the party 19 seats in the Chamber. However, opposition to President Sarney's austerity measures and support for the strikes and demonstrations called by the CUT greatly broadened the PT's electoral appeal. This became evident in the municipal elections of 1988 when the PT won control of 36 important towns and Luiza Erundina da Souza became mayor of São Paulo, a city then of 9.5 million inhabitants. In the presidential election of November 1989, the PT formed a Popular Front with the Brazilian Socialist Party (PSB), the Communist Party of Brazil (PCdoB) and other left-wing parties. In the second-round, the PT's candidate, Lula, came a close second to Fernando Collor de Mello.

In the 1990s the party underwent a progressive change of identity, abandoning its radical socialist proposals in favour of a more moderate programme aimed at appealing to wider sections of the electorate. In both the 1994 and 1998 presidential elections Lula da Silva came second to Fernando Henrique Cardoso of the Brazilian Social Democratic Party (PSDB), with 27% and 31.7% of the popular vote respectively. In the 1998 congressional elections the PT won 58 seats in the Chamber of Deputies and seven in the Senate. It acted as the main opposition party to the Cardoso administration.

In 2002 the PT won the presidential election with Lula reaping 61.3% of the vote in the run-off. It gained 91 seats in the Chamber of Deputies, 14 seats in the Senate and three governorships. Given Brazil's highly fragmented party system and the need for strong parliamentary support, the PT built a wide and heterogeneous coalition government that includes not only those parties that had formed the electoral alliance in the first-round (the PC do B and the PL) and in the second-round presidential elections (the PSB, PPS, PDT, PTB and the PV), but also other parties that had supported the previous government and its presidential candidate (namely the PMDB and the PP).

Other Parties

Another seven parties also won representation in the 2002 congressional elections, as follows:

Christian Social Democrat Party (*Partido Social Democrata Cristão*), which won one seat in the Chamber in 2002. This is the new incarnation of the Christian Democrat Party (*Partido Democrata Cristão*), which won five seats in the Chamber in 1986 and 22 in 1990.
Address. Avenida Padre Pereira de Andrade 758, Jardim Boaçava, São Paulo- SP 15469-000
Telephone. (55-11) 3022 7161/ 8881
Fax. (55-11) 3022 2181
Email. psdc@psdc.org.br

Website. www.psdc.org.br
Leadership. José Maria Eymael

Christian Social Party *(Partido Social Cristão,* PSC), a centrist formation which won two seats in the Chamber of Deputies in the 1998 and one in the 2002 elections.
Address. R. Pouso Alegre 1390, Floresta, Belo Horizonte–MG, 31015-030
Telephone. (55–31) 3467–1390
Fax. (55-31) 3467–6522
Email. psc@psc.org.br
Website. www.psc.org.br
Leadership. Vítor Jorge Abdala Nósseis (president); Amarildo Martins da Silva (Chamber leader)

Green Party *(Partido Verde)*, a small ecologist party which won one seat in the Chamber of Deputies in 1998 and five in 2002.
Address. Rua dos Pinheiros 812, Pinheiros, São Paulo-SP 05422–001
Telephone. (55–11) 3083–1722
Fax. (55–11) 3083 1062
Email. pv@pv.org.br
Website. www.partidoverde.org.br
Leadership. José Luiz de França Penna (president); José Sarney Filho (Chamber leader)

National Mobilization Party *(Partido da Mobilização Nacional,* PMN), won two Chamber seats in 1998 and one in 2002 elections.
Address. Rua Martins Fontes 197 3° andar, Conjunto 32, São Paulo-SP 01050-906
Telephone. (55–11) 3214 4261/4280
Fax. (55-11) 3120 2669
Email. pmn.sp@ig.com.br
Website. www.pmn.org.br
Leadership. Oscar Noronha Filho (president)

National Order Reconstruction Party *(Partido da Reedificaço da Ordem Nacional,* PRONA), a far-right party at the service of its populist leader, Enéas Carneiro, which won two Chamber seats in 1998 and six seats in the 2002 elections.
Address. (55-61) SCN Quadra 1, Bloco E, No 50, Sala 114, Edificio Central Park, Asa Norte, Brasília - DF 70710-500
Telephone. (55–61) 3964 5656
Fax. (55-61) 3864 5656
Email. prona@prona.org.br
Website. www.prona.org.br
Leadership. Enéas Carneiro (president)

Social Democratic Party *(Partido Social Democrático,* PSD), won three seats in the Chamber in 1998 and four in the 2002 elections. It subsequently merged with the Democratic Labour Party (PTB).

Social Labour Party *(Partido Social Trabalhista,* PST), small right-wing party which won one Chamber seat in 1998 and three in the 2002 elections. It subsequently merged with the Liberal Party (PL).

Social Liberal Party *(Partido Social Liberal,* PSL), won one Chamber seat in both the 1998 and 2002 elections.
Address. SCS, Quadra 1, Bloco E, Sala 1004 BSB Edificio Ceará, DF 70303-900
Telephone. (55–61) 322 1721 or 9643 4695
Fax. (55-61) 322 1721
Leadership. Luciano Caldas Bivar (president)

Brunei Darussalam

Capital: Bandar Seri Begawan
Population: 332,844 (2001 census)

The Sultanate of Brunei, having been a British protectorate since 1888, became internally self-governing in 1959 and fully independent in 1984. Under the 1959 constitution, supreme executive authority was vested in the Sultan. He is formally assisted by a Council of Cabinet Ministers, a Privy Council and a Religious Council. However, the Legislative Council (*Majlis Mesyuarat Negeri*) – non-elective since 1970 – was abolished shortly after full independence. Since then there has been little meaningful political party activity under an absolute monarchy which has codified its principles in a state ideology called "Malay Islamic Monarchy" (MIB), with major emphasis on the tenets of conservative Islam. In September 2004, however, the Legislative Council convened for the first time in two decades and the Sultan signed a new constitution providing for the restoration of limited elections. Under the new constitution the Legislative Council would have up to 45 members (not including the Speaker), 15 of whom would be elected with the remainder appointed by the Sultan, and would have only an advisory role. No date was set for elections.

The Sultans (Omar Ali Saifuddin III until 1967, followed by his son Hassanal Bolkiah) have ruled substantially by decree since December 1962. In that month, the left-wing nationalist Brunei People's Party (PRB), which had won all the elective seats in the first elections in August 1962 on a platform of opposition to merger with Malaysia, staged a revolt, believing that the Sultan and the British were preparing to impose merger. The revolt was put down by British forces, and the party was banned under a State of Emergency which has been in force continuously since then. After new elections in 1965, but still without responsible government, a People's Independence Front was formed as an amalgamation of all existing political formations, with a view to pressing the British for democracy and independence. But this move was partly diverted by Sultan Omar's abdication. By the time of independence in 1984, party politics had been moribund for 18 years, during which a neo-monarchical polity was consolidated, funded by astronomical oil wealth.

Brunei was proclaimed to be "democratic" under its 1984 independence declaration, following which some political association was allowed. Two new parties were granted registration: the Brunei National Democratic Party (PKDB) in 1985 and the Brunei National Solidarity Party (PPKB) in 1986. In March 1988, however, the government announced that it had dissolved the PKDB, while the PPKB became moribund until resurfacing in the 1990s. A further political party, *Parti Kesedaran Rakyat* (PAKAR), or People's Awareness Party, was founded in 2000 but has remained nearly invisible.

Brunei National Solidarity Party
Partai Perpaduan Kebangsa'an Brunei (PPKB)
Leadership. Mohamad Hatta bin Zainal Abidin (president)
The PPKB was established in 1985 under the leadership of Jumat bin Idris and Mohamad Hatta bin Zainal Abidin, as a breakaway from the Brunei National Democratic Party (*Partai Kebangsa'an Demokratik Brunei*, PKDB), which had originally been led by Abdul Latif bin Abdul Hamid and Abdul Latif bin Chuchu.

The PKDB had proclaimed itself as a party of "Brunei Malays" connoting almost any indigenous Muslim. The PKDB leaders were arrested in January 1988, the party being banned shortly afterwards (and Latif bin Abdul Hamid dying in 1990). The grounds given for the ban were that the party had breached its terms of registration by opening connections with a foreign organization, the Pacific Democratic Union (of regional centre-right parties).

The PPKB invited membership from all indigenous Bruneians, regardless of religion but was restricted by the ban on government officials joining political parties. Its lack of success in recruiting members resulted in de-registration but it re-emerged in February 1995 when it was allowed to hold its first national assembly. Its president, former PKDB leader Abdul Latif bin Chuchu, soon resigned under government pressure. The party subsequently revived with Mohamad Hatta bin Zainal Abidin (who had been its first secretary-general in 1985) as its new president. The party now expressed support for the government's determination to investigate the Amedeo scandal, centring on the affairs of the over-stretched conglomerate of Prince Jefri, who was simultaneously director of the Brunei Investment Agency (BIA). This "revival" of the party, with leave to direct critical if oblique attention towards a member of the royal family, prompted speculation as to inter-factional intrigue within the Palace, as also at the time of the original breakaway from the PKDB.

Following Prince Jefri's dismissl from the BIA (in July 1998), Mohamed Hatta bin Zainal Abidin came under fierce criticism from government sources, prompting speculation that the brief period of "openness" had passed with the weathering of the crisis.

The PPKB held further assemblies in February 2000 and October 2001, with Hatta being re-elected party president on the latter occasion. A message of condolence was addressed to the US embassy in Bandar Seri Begawan following Sept. 11, and in the wake of the 2002 Bali bombing, Hatta denounced Prime Minister John Howard for appearing to imply that Australia was prepared to act against terrorists in neighbouring Asian countries. The party in December 2003 suggested an annual day of recognition for patriotic figures similar to the existing *Hari Guru* awards for teachers and *Tokoh Hijrah* awards for Islamic religious figures. In October 2002 the party's deputy president, Osman Omar, 59, resigned from the party in order to concentrate on his business empire.

Brunei People's Party
Partai Rakyat Brunei (PRB)

Leadership. Ahmad Azahari bin Mahmud; Zaini bin Ahmad

This left-wing nationalist party, long since banned, won all the elective seats in the first elections in August 1962 on a platform of opposition to merger with Malaysia. Believing that the Sultan and the British were prepared to impose merger, it staged an unsuccessful revolt in December 1962 and was banned. Azahari then spent most of his life in Indonesia until his death in Bogor on May 30, 2002. Zaini escaped from detention in 1973 and fled to Malaysia, but returned some time in the early 1990s to make his peace with the Sultan; after a further period of imprisonment without trial, he was released in July 1996 and now lives at liberty in his homeland. Another former PRB stalwart, Muhammad Yassin Affendy bin Abdul Rahman, who played a pivotal role in the 1962 revolt and escaped to Malaysia with Zaini in 1973, returned to Bandar Seri Begawan in 1997. He was set free in August 1999 after taking an oath of loyalty to the Sultan. To all intents and purposes the PRB has long since been defunct.

People's Awareness Party
Parti Kesedaran Rakyat (PAKAR)

The *Parti Kesedaran Rakyat* (with *pakar* meaning "expert" or "specialist") was founded on May 9, 2000. It gives support to the Sultan, while criticizing administrative shortcomings, but has been largely dormant. In mid-September 2004 PAKAR was threatened with de-registration because of its alleged failure to provide details of its leadership, membership and meetings.

Bulgaria

Capital: Sofia
Population: 7,977,646 (2001 Census)

The Republic of Bulgaria became a multi-party parliamentary democracy in November 1990, replacing the People's Republic which had existed since the Bulgarian Communist Party (BCP) came to power after World War II. Under a new constitution formally effective since July 1991 and declaring Bulgaria to be a "democratic, constitutional and welfare state", the President is directly elected (with a Vice-President) for a five-year term and nominates the Prime Minister and Council of Ministers for parliamentary endorsement.

Legislative authority is vested in a unicameral National Assembly (*Narodno Subranie*), whose 240 members are elected for a four-year term by universal suffrage of those aged 18 and over. Elections are held under a system of proportional representation, the threshold for representation being 4% of the national vote. The 1991 constitution guarantees freedom of political activity with the exception of parties with separatist aims or likely to promote ethnic or religious divisions.

After a series of short-lived elected governments, or non-elected 'governments of experts' the Bulgarian Socialist Party (BSP) won a general election in 1994 with 43.5% of the vote against SDS's 23.5%. In presidential elections on Oct. 27 and Nov. 3, 1996, Petar Stoyanov of the Union of Democratic Forces (SDS) was the victor in the second round with 59.7% of the votes cast, defeating the candidate of the BSP. An economic crisis and popular unrest forced the calling of an early general election in April 1997 which gave an overall majority of 127 seats to the SDS-led coalition, the United Democratic Forces (ODS). This government became the first post-1989 government to complete its mandated four years in office.

In the next Assembly elections on June 17, 2001, however, the new National Movement Simeon II (NDSV), headed by the former Bulgarian monarch, came to power by winning 120 seats (with 42.7% of the vote). The ODS took 51 (18.8%), the Coalition for Bulgaria (headed by the BSP) 48 (17.2%) and the party representing the country's Turkish minority, the Movement for Rights and Freedoms (DPS), 21 (7.5%). Lacking an outright majority in parliament, NDSV governs in coalition with the DPS.

Presidential elections on Nov. 11 and 18, 2001, brought a further upset with the election of Bulgaria's first elected BSP President, Georgi Purvanov. Despite being supported by both the ODS and NDSV, the incumbent, Petar Stoyanov, was narrowly defeated in the first round, Purvanov taking 36.37% and Stoyanov 34.94% of the vote, with 19% going to a former SDS Minister, Bogomil Bonev. Turnout in the first round being less than 50%, the contest went to a second round which was decisively won by Purvanov (54% of the vote) in an election marred by poor turnout (42% in the first round and 55% in the second). Local elections in 2003, also on a low turnout of 47%, reversed the results of the general election, the BSP taking 33%

of the vote, SDS 21% and NDSV and the DPS equal on 10%.

Bulgarian Agrarian National Union
Bulgarski Zemedelski Naroden Sayuz (BZNS)

Address. 1 Vrabcha Street, Sofia 1000 (BZNS)/ 2nd Floor, 4A Slaveikov Square, Sofia (BZNS-NS)

Telephone. (359–2) 986-28-34 (BZNS/ (359–2) 987-05-77 (BZNS-NS)

Website. www.bzns-ns.bg (BZNS-NS)

Leadership. Petko Iliev (chairperson of BZNS); Liuben Bozhilov (chairperson, BZNS-NP); Anastasia Dimitrova-Moser (chairperson, BZNS-NS)

The many current incarnations of BZNS (ten contested the 2003 local elections) are successor parties to the historical BZNS founded in 1899. A peasant party promulgating the co-operative ideals of rural life as an exemplar for national development, BZNS was in power from 1920 under its charismatic leader Alexander Stamboliiski, until being overthrown by a right-wing coup in 1923. Stamboliiski was assassinated during the coup and BZNS subsequently split into right- and left-wing parties. During World War II leftwing BZNS elements participated in the Fatherland Front led by the Bulgarian Communist Party (BCP), which came to power in 1944 after the ejection of German forces by the Red Army. The anti-Communist wing of the party, led by Nikola Petkov, joined the opposition grouping for the October 1946 elections, which were won decisively by the Fatherland Front. Petkov was hanged for alleged treason in September 1947. The Fatherland Front BZNS faction, uniquely among the Fatherland Front member parties, was allowed to co-exist with the BCP, allowing the People's Republic therefore to be seen, nominally at least, as a coalition of anti-fascist forces. BZNS was always represented in the National Assembly (with about a quarter of the seats) as well as in successive governments (usually holding the agriculture portfolio). The party had no record of ever contesting BCP decisions, and its vetted membership was limited to 120,000.

Following the resignation of the long-standing Communist leader, Todor Zhivkov, in November 1989, BZNS asserted its independence from the BCP by replacing its long-time leader (and Deputy Premier), Petur Tanchev, and by refusing to participate in the BSP government of February 1990. Meanwhile, the party's anti-communist faction was reconstituted as the Bulgarian Agrarian National Union-Nikola Petkov (BZNS–NP) led by Milan Drenchev. Advocating democracy and a market economy based on private agriculture, BZNS–NP became a component of the opposition Union of Democratic Forces (SDS) and figured in the SDS list of candidates for the June 1990 Assembly elections. BZNS won 16 of the 400 seats in those elections and in December 1990 joined a national unity coalition with the Bulgarian Socialist Party (the former BCP) and elements of the SDS. In early 1991 a faction of the BZNS–NP reunited with BZNS to form BZNS–United for the October 1991 elections, while the bulk of the remaining BZNS–NP opted to stand independently of the SDS. Neither party gained 4% of the vote.

Despite attempts at reconciliation between the various BZNS parties further splits occurred, and by 1994 there were three separate Agrarian parties with a national base and many more active regionally. In February 1992 Drenchev was replaced as BZNS–NP leader by Anastasia Dimitrova-Moser, who advocated co-operation with the SDS minority government then in office. The following month the BZNS–NP faction which had remained in the SDS opted to set up its own organization within the SDS, while most of the BZNS–United became the Bulgarian Agrarian National Union–Alexander Stamboliiski (BZNS-AS). Dimitrova-Moser's faction (BZNS-NS) contested the December 1994 Assembly elections within the People's Union (*Narodni*

Soiuz, NS) an alliance with the Democratic Party (DP), which won 18 of the 240 seats. The remainder of the BZNS-NP participated in the defeated SDS electoral front and the BNZS-AS was part of the victorious BSP-led alliance.

Both BZNS–NP and BZNS-NS backed the successful SDS candidacy of Petar Stoyanov in the autumn 1996 presidential elections, in which Todor Kavaldzhiev, a BZNS-NP representative, became Vice-President. Thereafter Dimitrova-Moser's BZNS-NS became part of the United Democratic Forces (ODS) coalition, with the result that the two anti-BSP Agrarian factions were part of the victorious United Democratic Forces (ODS) alliance headed by the SDS in the April 1997 Assembly elections, taking about a dozen seats between them. Strains quickly developed, however, and in October 1999 Vice-President Kavaldzhiev complained that BZNS was being sidelined by the other coalition partners, while in January 2001 two BZNS deputies withdrew from the SDS Assembly group.

Dimitrova-Moser's BZNS-NS took part in the ODS coalition for the general election of June 2001, but following the coalition's defeat by the National Movement Simeon II, expressed dissatisfaction with the "unequal partnership" with SDS, citing it as one of the reasons for the ODS defeat. It threatened to withdraw from the ODS parliamentary group in January 2002, but following a redrawing of the agreement between the parties in March remained in the ODS parliamentary group. BZNS-NS has functioned as an independent parliamentary force, though voting on the whole with SDS in the *Subranie*. BZNS-NP has remained inside SDS while BZNS-NS contested the 2003 municipal elections in coalition with Gergiovden. Following a split in SDS in March 2004, BZNS-NS formed a new parliamentary group with the Democratic Party.

BZNS-NS is affiliated to the Christian Democrat International and is an associate of the European People's Party (EPP).

Bulgarian Agrarian National Union–Alexander Stamboliiski
Bulgarski Zemedelski Naroden Soiuz–Alexander Stamboliiski (BZNS–AS)

Address. Entrance B, 5th Floor, 29 Ivan Vasov Street, Sofia

Telephone. (359-2) 980-77-20

Leadership. Svetoslav Shivarov

The BZNS-AS designation was adopted by factions of the Bulgarian Agrarian National Union (BZNS) favouring alliance with the Bulgarian Socialist Party (BSP) rather than the centre-right SDS. The BSP/BZNS-AS ticket (which included the Ecoglasnost Political Club) won a decisive victory in the December 1994 Assembly elections, following which two BZNS–AS ministers were included in the BSP-led government formed in January 1995.

In the autumn 1996 presidential elections the BZNS–AS backed the defeated BSP candidate, while in the April 1997 Assembly elections it was part of the defeated BSP coalition. Opposition to the party's link with the BSP culminated in mid-2000 in the withdrawal from the alliance of a majority BZNS–AS faction which opposed the BSP's support for EU and NATO membership. One faction, BZNS-AS 1899, remained part of the BSP's Coalition for Bulgaria in the 2001 elections.

Bulgarian Social Democratic Party
Bulgarska Sotsialdemokraticheska Partia (BSDP)

Address. (Dertliev faction) Floor 5, 19 Boulevard Kniaz Alexander Dondukov-Korsakov, 1504 Sofia

Telephone. (359–2) 988-05-91

Website. www.bsdp.bg

Leadership. Petur Agov (chairman); Stefan Radoslavov (general secretary)

Address. (SDS faction) 37 Exzarh Josif Street, Sofia 1000
Telephone (359-2) 88 319 748
Website. www.bsdp.net
E-mail. president@bsdp.net
Leadership. Georgi Anastasov (president)

The BSDP traces its descent from the historic BSDP founded in 1891 and more especially from the non-revolutionary "broad" party resulting from the secession in 1903 of the "narrow" revolutionary wing which became the Bulgarian Communist Party in 1919. The BSDP opposed right-wing regimes of the inter-war period. During World War II left-wing Social Democrats joined the Communist-dominated Fatherland Front while an opposition faction, the Workers' Social Democratic Party (United) joined the opposition. Following the declaration of a People's Republic in December 1947, the BSDP was merged with the Communist Party in 1948 (although it was never formally banned). Over the next four decades exiles kept the party alive as the Socialist Party, which was re-established in Bulgaria in 1989 under the leadership of Petur Dertliev, a veteran of the pre-1948 party and a former political prisoner.

In March 1990 the party reverted to the historic BSDP title in view of the imminent decision of the Communist Party to rename itself the Bulgarian Socialist Party (BSP). As a member of the opposition Union of Democratic Forces (SDS), the BSDP took 29 of the 144 seats won by the SDS in the June 1990 Assembly elections. The following month Dertliev was the initial SDS candidate for the presidency but withdrew to allow SDS chair Zhelyu Zhelev to be appointed unopposed after six rounds of voting in the National Assembly. The BSDP supported the decision of some SDS elements to participate in the government of Dimitur Popov in December 1990 but thereafter came into increasing conflict with the SDS pro-market wing. Whereas the latter advocated full-scale economic liberalization, the BSDP favoured a welfare market economy (including private, co-operative and state sectors) and argued that privatised industries should become co-operatives where possible. In the October 1991 Assembly elections it formed one of the SDS splinter groups, SDS-Centre, but failed to gain 4% of the vote.

The BSDP backed Zhelev's successful candidacy in the first direct presidential elections in 1992 and thereafter sided with the President in his developing conflict with the SDS minority government. Following the appointment of a non-party "government of experts" in December 1992, the BSDP warned that it marked a reassertion of Communist influence. In March 1993, seeking to establish a credible third force between the BSP and an SDS seen as moving to the right, the BSDP launched the Bulgarian Social Democratic Union, which the following month was enlarged into a Council of Co-operation of centre-left parties, two of them with Assembly representation. Further alliance building by the BSDP resulted in the formation of the Democratic Alternative for the Republic (which included the Green Party) for the December 1994 Assembly elections, but its vote share of 3.8% was below the 4% minimum required for representation. An extraordinary BSDP congress in April 1995 endorsed the established line of seeking an alliance of all social democratic forces, rejecting a minority argument that the party should federate with the ruling BSP.

The BSDP supported the successful SDS candidate in the autumn 1996 presidential elections and contested the April 1997 Assembly elections as part of ODS. However, left-inclined BSDP elements opposed the party's centrist orientation, with the result that in late 1998 the party split into a pro-SDS faction and an anti-SDS majority faction led by Dertliev. In January 2001 Dertliev took the majority faction into a New Left alliance headed by the BSP, while the minority BSDP remained within the SDS fold. In the event, both factions were on the losing side in the June 2001 Assembly

elections, which were won by the new National Movement Simeon II. Dertliev died in November 2001 and was succeeded by Petur Agov. A feud between the two wings of the BSDP over which has the right to the BSDP name has continued unabated since the split and is currently the subject of a long-running and inconclusive court case. For the 2003 regional elections the SDS faction was registered as the Party of Bulgarian Social Democrats.

The BSDP is a full member party of the Socialist International.

Bulgarian Socialist Party
Bulgarska Sotsialisticheska Partia (BSP)

Address. 20 Positano Street, Sofia 1000
Telephone. (359–2) 989–2010
Fax. (359–2) 980–5219
Email. bsp@bsp.bg
Website. www.bsp.bg
Leadership. Sergei Stanishev (chairman)

The BSP dates from April 1990, when the then ruling Bulgarian Communist Party (BCP) changed its name, abandoned Marxism-Leninism (although not Marxist theory) and embraced democratic socialism. The BCP traced its descent from the Bulgarian Social Democratic Party (BSDP), founded in 1891, which in 1903 split into left-wing "narrow" and non-revolutionary "broad" parties. The BCP as such dated from 1919, when the pro-Bolshevik "narrow" party became a founder member of the Third International (Comintern), later organizing armed opposition to right-wing regimes of the inter-war period and renaming itself the Workers' Party in 1927. Finally banned in 1934, the party was for a decade based in Moscow, where many of its exiled leaders were executed in Stalin's purges.

During World War II (in which Bulgaria was allied with Nazi Germany until mid-1944) the party played a leading role in the anti-Nazi resistance, its activities being directed by Georgi Dimitrov, Bulgarian secretary-general of the Comintern. In September 1944 with the support of the Soviet Union, the Communist-dominated Fatherland Front (FF), including left-wing Agrarians and Social Democrats, took power in Sofia. In the post-war period the Communists consolidated their position, Dimitrov becoming Prime Minister after the October 1946 elections and a People's Republic being declared in December 1947. In 1948 the rump of the BSDP was merged with the Workers' Party, the resultant formation readopting the BCP rubric. It thus effectively became the sole ruling party, although the Bulgarian Agrarian National Union (BZNS) remained a component of the Front, the smaller members of which were dissolved in 1949.

On Dimitrov's death in 1949 the BCP leadership passed to Vulko Chervenkov, but he was replaced in 1954 by Todor Zhivkov after being accused of fostering a personality cult. Under Zhivkov's long rule Bulgaria remained closely aligned with the USSR and participated in the 1968 Soviet-led intervention in Czechoslovakia, at one stage proposing that Bulgaria should become a constituent republic of the USSR. In 1971 Zhivkov added the post of head of state to his BCP leadership and subsequently appeared to be grooming his daughter Liudmila for the succession, until her sudden death in 1981. At the 13th BCP congress in April 1986 he announced a reform programme reflecting the Gorbachev *glasnost* and *perestroika* initiatives in the USSR; but reform proved difficult to accomplish because of party in-fighting between reformers and the "Konsumativno" who stood for the preservation of the *status quo*. In November 1989, Zhivkov was replaced as BCP leader and head of state by one of the principal reformers, Petur Mladenov. A purge of Zhivkov and his supporters followed, accompanied by denunciations of 35 years of "feudal, repressive, corrupt and incompetent" government.

The BCP's "leading role" in society and the state was ended by constitutional amendments enacted in January 1990, following which an extraordinary party congress on Jan. 30-Feb.2 renounced "democratic centralism", replaced the BCP central committee with a supreme council and its politburo and secretariat with a presidium, and opted for a "socially-oriented market economy". Three principal factions emerged from the 1990 BCP Congress, which were to remain dominant in the years that followed. A Union of Social Democracy (USD), whose principal figure was the former Prime Minister Andrei Lukanov, promoted democratic socialism and a social market economy based largely on the then existent property relationship. The Marxist Platform (MP) led by Alexander Lilov promoted the central role of the state, renationalization and a redistribution of national wealth, promulgating "post-communist" Marxism. The third "technocratic" centre-left wing consisted of former Komsomol members led by the 1994 Prime Minister, Zhan Videnov and functioned pragmatically as an arbitrator between the two other factions. In keeping with a pledge to separate state and party functions, the party leadership passed to Alexander Lilov (a prominent BCP reformer of the Zhivkov era), with Mladenov remaining head of state. Later in February 1990, paradoxically, the BCP was obliged to form the first openly all-Communist government in Bulgaria's history when BZNS, now asserting its independence, opted to go into opposition and the new Union of Democratic Forces (SDS) refused to join a national unity coalition. In April 1990, following a ballot of party members, the BCP officially renamed itself the BSP. In multiparty elections in June the BSP, against the East European trend, was returned to power with 211 of the 400 seats and Andrei Lukanov became Prime Minister. Although the SDS did well in Sofia and other cities, the ruling party's organizational strength in rural areas proved the decisive factor in returning it to power.

In July 1990 Mladenov resigned as head of state, to be replaced in August by SDS leader Zhelyu Zhelev, after disclosures about his role in the suppression of anti-government demonstrations in December 1989. Faced with sometimes violent street protests, a significant drop in BSP membership and an increasingly bitter division between the social democratic and Marxist factions, in December 1990 Lukanov resigned from the premiership, and was replaced by an interim coalition government led by the non-party Sofia lawyer Dimitur Popov, which included ministers from the BSP, BZNS and, SDS. Following the adoption of a new democratic constitution in July 1991, this division was to widen further over the alleged support of elements of the Marxist faction for the plotters of the August 1991 coup attempt in Moscow. In further elections in October 1991 the BSP was allied with eight small parties and organizations ranging from the centre left to the nationalist Fatherland Party of Labour. Its sometimes tenuous unity was preserved by an election programme emphasizing "civil order, social justice and democracy" without providing specific definitions. It was narrowly defeated by the SDS and therefore went into opposition for first time since 1944. The election loss further exacerbated internal tensions and unity was only preserved by the election of Zhan Videnov as leader in December 1991, who advocated a "modern left socialist party". The BSP also suffered a narrow defeat in the presidential election of January 1992, its preferred candidate securing 46.5% of the second-round vote.

After a collapse of the SDS government in September 1992, no party was able to form an administration, and, in the dire economic circumstance of the time, none wished for an election. It fell to President Zhelev to nominate his economic adviser Liuben Berov to head a nominally non-party "government of experts" which nevertheless was substantially influenced by the BSP (although a faction led by former leader Lilov voted against the Berov government) in an unofficial alliance with the DPS. By mid-1993 the BSP was again the largest Assembly party, because of resignations from the SDS parliamentary group. Dissent rumbled on in the party, however. The choice of Videnov as leader had been seen as a victory for the MP and the social democrat faction retaliated by launching an Alliance for Social Democracy in 1991 (later in 1993 the Civic Alliance for the Republic) as a rallying point for their cause.

At the 1994 party congress, Videnov had secured his leadership enough to persuade the party to adopt a united programme, "Renovating Democratic Socialism", which envisaged the creation of a social market economy in which the state had a permanent guiding role and private and state forms of ownership were to be treated equally. Thus, after the resignation of the Berov government in September 1994, the BSP pushed for new elections. These were held in December, the BSP being allied principally with the Bulgarian Agrarian National Union–Alexander Stamboliiski and Ecoglasnost. The outcome was an overall Assembly majority for the BSP-led list and the formation of a coalition government in January 1995 under the premiership of Videnov. In local elections in October-November 1995 the BSP consolidated its position as the strongest party, winning 41% of the first-round vote in its own right.

The Videnov government, however, proved incapable of economic management, and was accused of corruption, particularly in relation to the conduct of privatisation deals, and by late 1996 had precipitated an economic crisis. In the autumn 1996 presidential elections the BSP sought to attract centrist support by nominating a senior USD figure, Georgi Pirinski (then Foreign Minister), but he was ruled ineligible because he had been born in the USA. The BSP replacement was Culture Minister Ivan Marazov, who stood on the "Together for Bulgaria" label but who was defeated by Petar Stoyanov (SDS) in the second voting round in early November on a 60%-40% split. This defeat, nationwide demonstrations over food shortages and the drastic fall in the value of the lev forced Videnov to resign as both Prime Minister and BSP chairman, being replaced in the latter capacity by Georgi Purvanov in December 1996. Despite opposition from the BSP, President Stoyanov installed a caretaker administration and called early Assembly elections in April 1997. The BSP ran as leader of the Democratic Left alliance (again including BZNS and Ecoglasnost factions) but was heavily defeated by the SDS-led United Democratic Forces (ODS), the BSP-led alliance being reduced to 58 seats and 22% of the vote.

In opposition, the BSP in December 1998 formed the Social Democracy Union with other left-wing forces, while also establishing an alliance with the Euro-Left Coalition with a view to broadening its popular base for the 2001 Assembly elections. In mid-2000 the pro-BSP faction of the BZNS broke into two groups, the main one withdrawing from the alliance in opposition to the BSP's support for NATO and EU membership. In January 2001 the BSP launched another alliance of left-wing parties, the New Left, which was committed to "the values of modern social democracy and the European left".

The BSP and its allies adopted another title, Coalition for Bulgaria, for the general election of June 2001. The election though was won by the newly-formed National Movement Simeon II and the BSP-led alliance gained only 48 seats and 17.2% of the vote. After the elections, Purvanov accepted "full responsibility" for his party's defeat but received a vote of confidence from its executive council. Purvanov was the party's somewhat surprising choice for presidential candidate in Presidential elections in October 2001, winning in the second round against the incumbent, Petar Stoyanov, with 54% of the vote. Following his election as President, Purvanov was replaced as BSP leader by Sergei Stanishev, a youthful Moscow and English educated centre-leftist. In his first leader's address to a BSP congress in 2002, he emphasized the need to recast the party as a competent alternative to the rightist governments of SDS and NDSV, and present an alternative statist solution to the economic problems facing the country.

Simeon's decision to appoint two former BSP mayors as ministers in the NDSV cabinet raised tensions within the party over the degree of co-operation between the two parties. Stanishev, however, firmly ruled out the possibility of any official or unofficial alliance, stating that the ministers concerned would have to choose between the principles of the left or loyalty to the premier, and he has demonstrated this in parliament with an almost constant record of opposition to government initiatives. One of these ministers, the Minister for Regional Development, Kostadin Paskalev, resigned in October 2002, but the other, Minister of State Administration Dimitur Kalchev, remains. The process begun in 1998 of forming a left-wing bloc was accelerated in February 2002 with the announcement that the partners in the Coalition for Bulgaria would begin a process of organizational unification, leading to a merger within two years. The BSP won a majority of votes, 33% of the total, and mayoral candidates in the 2003 local elections, leading to speculation that they would be in a strong position to form the next government.

The BSP is a Consultative Member of the Socialist International.

Democrats for a Strong Bulgaria
Demokrati za Silna Bulgaria
Address. 5th Floor, 10A Graf Ignatiev Street, Sofia
Telephone. (359–2) 980-53-34
Fax. (359–2) 987-17-51
Website. www.dsp.bg
E-mail. mediacentre@dsp.bg
Leadership. Ivan Kostov (President)
The Democrats for a Strong Bulgaria (DSB) were formed in March 2004 from a defecting faction of SDS. Led by SDS's former leader and Prime Minister between 1997 and 2001, Ivan Kostov, DSB leads a parliamentary group called the United Democratic Forces consisting of 28 of SDS's 42 former parliamentary deputies. The party has in the main attracted the right-wing of SDS and its political stance, calling for strong government and decommunisation, reflects this.

Democratic Party
Demokraticheska Partia (DP)
Address. 61 Hristo Botev, Sofia 1303
Telephone. (359–2) 930-80-30
Fax. (359–2) 930-80-31
Website. www.demparty.org
Leadership. Alexander Pramatarski (chairman)
Successor party to the conservative party of the same name founded in 1896, the DP was revived in 1989 and joined the opposition Union of Democratic Forces (SDS). Following the SDS victory in the October 1991 elections, DP leader Stefan Savov was elected president of the National Assembly. However, shortly before the fall of the minority SDS government, he resigned from the Assembly post in September 1992, after being named in a censure motion tabled by the opposition Bulgarian Socialist Party and supported by some SDS dissidents. For the December 1994 Assembly elections the DP broke with the SDS, forming the People's Union with a faction of the Bulgarian Agrarian National Union. The alliance took third place, with 18 of the 240 seats and a vote share of 6.5%.

The DP backed the winning SDS candidate, Petar

Stoyanov, in the autumn 1996 presidential elections and subsequently rejoined the SDS-led alliance, called the United Democratic Forces (ODS). In April 1997 it shared in the landslide victory of the ODS in Assembly elections, taking seven of the 134 seats won by the alliance. Savov died in January 2000 and was succeeded as DP leader by Alexander Pramatarski. The DP was part of the defeated ODS coalition in the June 2001 Assembly elections and, as with BZNS-NU, expressed dissatisfaction after the election with the "unequal partnership" of ODS. The DP took part in restructuring discussions with SDS in March 2002, following the threat by BZNS-NU to withdraw from the ODS parliamentary group and opted to remain within the group. The party fought the 2003 local elections in a coalition with Gergiovden and BZNU-NS and, after the fragmentation of SDS in March 2004, its two parliamentary representatives joined a new parliamentary group with BZNS-NS.

The DP is affiliated to both the International Democrat Union and the Christian Democrat International and is an associate member of the European People's Party (EPP).

Movement for Rights and Freedoms
Dvizhenie za Prava i Svobodi (DPS)
Address. 45A Bul. Aleksander Stamboliiski, 1301 Sofia
Telephone. (359–2) 986-44-54
Website. www.dps.bg
Email. dogan@dps.bg
Leadership. Ahmed Dogan (president); Kasim Dal (vice-president)
The DPS was founded in January 1990 based mainly in the Muslim ethnic Turkish community, forming some 10% of Bulgaria's population. The campaign of compulsory assimilation undertaken in the 1980s by the Zhivkov regime, resulting in the flight of many ethnic Turks to Turkey and elsewhere, formed the background to the DPS's aims, which included full political, cultural and religious rights but excluded any fundamentalist or separatist objectives. In the June 1990 Assembly elections the DPS won 23 of the 400 seats at issue with 6% of the national vote. From December 1990 it participated in a national unity coalition under a non-party Prime Minister, together with the dominant Bulgarian Socialist Party (BSP) and the Union of Democratic Forces (SDS). In further elections in October 1991 it improved its position, winning 24 of 240 seats with 7.6% of the vote.

From November 1991 the DPS gave crucial parliamentary backing to a minority SDS administration, being rewarded with the lifting of a ban on optional Turkish-language instruction in secondary schools. But the SDS government's subsequent pro-market policies affected the DPS's Turkish constituency disproportionately, and it withdrew its support in September 1992, thereby precipitating the government's fall in October. After the BSP had failed to fill the political vacuum, the DPS successfully nominated a non-party Prime Minister (Liuben Berov) to head a "government of experts" which included semi-official DPS representation. In the Assembly vote to endorse the new government in December 1992, the DPS was supported by most BSP deputies and by some SDS dissidents. In 1993 the DPS backed the Berov government but was weakened by internal dissension and by continuing emigration of ethnic Turks. In March 1994, after Berov had suffered a heart attack, the DPS Deputy Premier, Evgeni Matinchev (an ethnic Bulgarian), became acting Prime Minister. In May 1994 the DPS successfully opposed the ailing Berov's proposal to appoint a BSP member as Economy Minister.

Weakened by the launching of at least two breakaway parties in 1994, the DPS slipped to 5.4% of the vote and 15 seats out of 240 in the December 1994 elections, therefore reverting to opposition status. It won 8.2% of the vote in municipal elections in October 1995. The DPS backed the successful candidacy of Petar Stoyanov of the SDS in the autumn 1996 presidential elections.

Prior to April 1997 Assembly elections, a majority decision by the DPS not to join the SDS-led United Democratic Forces (ODS) caused a pro-SDS faction to form the breakaway National Movement for Rights and Freedoms. For the elections the rump DPS headed the Union for National Salvation (ONS), including the Green Party and the New Choice Union, which won 19 seats on a 7.6% vote share. In opposition, the DPS in July 1998 participated in the launching of the four-party Liberal Democratic Alliance, while in January 2000 the Party of Democratic Change (PDP), one of the 1994 breakaway groups, rejoined the DPS.

The DPS contested the June 2001 Assembly elections at the head of an alliance which included the Liberal Union and the Euro-Roma formation. Notwithstanding predictions that the emigration of ethnic Turks to Turkey had reduced the level of natural DPS support, the alliance won 7.4% of the national vote and 21 seats. Recapitulating the power-broking role it had with the 1991 SDS government, the DPS joined a coalition government headed by the new National Movement Simeon II. One of its parliamentary representatives, Mehmed Dikme, became a vice-premier and Minister of Agriculture in the new cabinet. The DPS supported Purvanov's campaign for the presidency in 2001 and in some other respects has taken a different line from NDSV, using its pivotal role to promote its own interests. This became particularly apparent over discussions about the privatization of the Bulgarian tobacco industry, a major plank of NDSV's economic strategy, over which the DPS, whose members form the majority of the country's tobacco-growers, was able to exert considerable influence. The DPS's electoral standing has remained relatively stable since 2001, while its partner's has fallen drastically and it is to be expected that the DPS will use this and the resignations from NDSV to its advantage in the future. Despite retaining a 10% standing in the local elections of 2003, the party is entering a period of potential uncertainty. With the election of 15 Bulgarians to its Central Council in 2003, it signalled a move away from its ethnic background to a new and as yet undefined national role. In addition, Ahmed Dogan, the DPS's leader since its foundation, announced in March 2003 that he would relinquish the leadership in 2004.

New Time Party
Partia "Novoto Vreme"
Address. 7A 6th September Street, Sofia
Telephone. (359–2) 980-23-76
Fax. (359–2) 980-68-46
Website. www.novotovreme.bg
Email. party@novotovreme.bg
Leadership. Emil Koshlukov (President)
The New Time parliamentary group was formed in March 2004 by what had been called a "discussion group" of 10 parliamentary deputies within NDSV, concerned by the quality of Simeon's leadership and a perceived lack of openness in the party. Further defections raised the number of New Time Parliamentary deputies to 13 by July 2004, when it was transformed into a political party. The leader of the new party is Emil Koshlukov, a former SDS activist and deputy turned NDSV deputy.

National Movement Simeon II
Natsionalno Dvizhenie Simeon Vtori (NDSV)
Address. 23 Vrabcha Street, Sofia 1000
Telephone. (359- 2) 980-38-08
Fax. (359-2) 980-38-07
Website. www.ndsv.bg
Email. ndsv@ndsv.bg, centrala@ndsv.bg
Leadership. Simeon Saxe-Coburg-Gotha (chairman);

Plamen Panayotov (parliamentary leader)
The NDSV was launched in April 2001 to rally anti-government opinion around the person of Simeon Saxe-Coburg-Gotha, who as Tsar Simeon II had lost the Bulgarian throne in 1946 at the age of nine and had later become a successful businessman in exile in Spain. He stressed that his movement was not seeking the restoration of the monarchy, instead setting out an 800-day programme to eradicate government corruption, to improve living standards and to create a healthy market economy to enable Bulgaria to become a member of the European Union.

The origins of the movement lie in a programme of annual conferences inaugurated by Prime Minister Kostov, called the Bulgarian Easter initiative, which aimed to draw on the expertise of Western-educated professional Bulgarians living abroad. Many of these professionals, however, opted to form their own party with Simeon. On its formation NDSV attracted many disaffected SDS members and previously non-politically active professionals in Bulgaria. NDSV applied for registration as a political party in April 2001 but was refused because of irregularities in its application. It therefore resorted to forming an alliance with two small already-registered parties (the Movement for National Revival *Oborishte* led by Tosho Peikov and the Bulgarian Women's Party led by Vesela Draganova), campaigning under the name NDSV. Despite finally registering as a unitary party in February 2002, it remains a somewhat uneasy coalition between these four groups.

In the July 2001 Assembly elections, NDSV won 120 of the 240 seats with a vote share of 42.7%. Two similarly-named parties unconnected to NDSV, the Simeon II Coalition and the National Union for Tsar Simeon II, obtained 5% of the vote between them, leading to speculation that confusion over the names had robbed NDSV of an absolute majority in the *Subranie*.

Simeon himself did not stand for election to the Assembly, but was not barred from becoming Prime Minister under the Bulgarian constitution. With no absolute majority, NDSV was forced to negotiate a coalition agreement with another party and after some indecision, formed a coalition government with DPS (21 seats in the *Subranie*). Replicating the experience of the previous SDS government, NDSV has recorded some successes in foreign policy, notably Bulgaria's invitation to join NATO and the publication of a "road map" to EU membership by the European Commission, but has fallen prey to domestic discontent. From an initial 70% approval rating at election time, Simeon's standing had fallen to 30% by early 2003, with most observers citing Simeon's personal aloofness and his ministers' lack of political experience as the principal reasons for this decline. In the local elections of October 2003, NDSV failed to win any of the major municipal mayorships, winning only 6% of council seats and an overall vote of 10%. The government's political difficulties and tensions within NDSV have also taken their toll on the parliamentary party, from which 19 representatives have resigned at different times in the last three years, 13 of them to form a new parliamentary group, the New Time.

Union of Democratic Forces
Soiuz na Demokratichnite Sili (SDS)
Address. 134 Rakovski Street, Sofia 1000
Telephone. (359–2) 986-50-08
Fax. (359–2) 981–0522
Email. iac@sds.bg
Website. www.sds.bg
Leadership. Nadezhda Mihailova (chairman and parliamentary leader); Ivan Ivanov (secretary-general)
The SDS was established in December 1989 by 10 fledgling pro-democracy movements – Podkrepa (Support) trade

unions federation (formed in February 1989 by Konstantin Trenchev); the Ecoglasnost environmentalist movement; Citizens' Initiative (GI); the "Nikola Petkov" faction of the Bulgarian Agrarian National Union (BZNS); the Bulgarian Social Democratic Party (BSDP); the Independent Association for the Defence of Human Rights in Bulgaria, led by Ilya Minev; the Club of Persons Illegally Repressed Since 1945, led by Dimitur Bakalov; the Committee for Religious Rights, Freedom of Conscience and Spiritual Values, led by Father Hristofor Subev; the Federation of Clubs for Democracy, led by Petko Simeonov (later founder of the Liberal Party); and the Federation of Independent Student Societies. In the period up to the June 1990 elections the SDS was also joined by the Radical Democratic Party (RDP); what became the United Christian Democratic Centre (OHZ); the Democratic Party (DP); the Christian Democratic Union (HDS); and the Alternative Social–Liberal Party (ASP). The Bulgarian Democratic Forum (BDF) and the Republican Party (RP) became observer members of the SDS.

Chaired by Zhelyu Zhelev (a dissident philosophy professor of the Zhivkov era), the SDS entered into round-table talks with the ruling Bulgarian Communist Party (BCP) in January 1990, first on ethnic Turkish rights (which the SDS supported) and then on the country's political future. The agreement between the SDS and the BSP emerging from the Round Table Talks was that the SDS should be allowed to publish a newspaper (*Demokratsia*) and that an election to be held in June 1990 should elect a Grand National Assembly (GNA), the purpose of which was to design a new constitution. In the run-up to the elections, SDS, hampered by organizational immaturity, ran a negative campaign, more effective at gaining international than domestic support, and was defeated decisively by the then renamed BCP, the Bulgarian Socialist Party (BSP), a result accepted by the SDS despite a widespread belief within the movement that the BSP had engineered substantial ballot-rigging.

The period of the GNA saw increasing tension within the movement and a developing division between what became known as the "light" and "dark" blue factions (blue being the colour of the SDS ballot paper). The leadership of the movement consisted of an uneasy mix of moderates, mostly centre-left intellectuals (the light blues) and radicals (the dark blues). While the movement remained united after the election, it was only the need to confront the BSP as a united force that kept it so. The dark blue faction viewed the BSP-dominated GNA as incapable of passing a genuinely democratic constitution while the more liberal light blues were willing to co-operate with the BSP within the GNA. Two incidents particularly incensed the dark blues. In February 1991, the SDS's then leader, Petur Beron, was forced to resign after disclosures that he had been an employee of the State Security Services. Secondly, 1991 negotiations to replace the 1967 treaty of mutual assistance with the Soviet Union were conducted without the participation of the parliament or the respective parliamentary commissions. When the conditions of the new prospective treaty, which included a clause precluding the signatories from joining any alliance that could be directed against either side, came to light in May 1991, it resulted generally in an increasing polarization of the parties in the GNA and an increased militancy of the radical faction within the SDS. A refusal by the dark blue faction to ratify the new constitution, which was passed in the parliament by the combined vote of the BSP, the MRF and light blue SDS deputies, led to a split in the movement. As a result, the light blue faction was expelled from the SDS and formed two light blue offshoot parties: SDS-Centre, headed by the main BSDP and including the Alternative Socialist Association and factions of the DP and Ecoglasnost; and SDS-Liberal, including the Green Party, the OHZ, a faction of the DP and the Federation of Clubs for

Democracy. The dark blue faction, comprising the ASP, the BDF, two dissident factions of the BSDP, the GI, the main DP, part of the Ecoglasnost movement, the RDP, the RP and the UDC, retained the movement's headquarters and organizational structures and fought and won the 1991 election as the SDS.

After the defections and splits of the period of the GNA, the SDS in government under its leader Filip Dimitrov was a considerably less faction-ridden force than it had been previously. Reflecting its dark blue origins, the highest stated priority of the new government was to "complete the decommunisation of the country". Decommunisation took the form of agricultural decollectivization, restitution of land and property to pre-communist owners, prosecution of former communist leaders and the introduction of the controversial Panev Law, a measure to bar from civil service or academic posts former members of the BCP. This policy of "restitution first" took precedence over economic and political reform and brought it into conflict with the trade unions, in particular Podkrepa, which resigned from SDS, and President Zhelev, who accused it, in a groundbreaking speech in August 1992, of "being at war with everyone". The SDS's narrow win in the 1991 election had forced it into a governing coalition with the largely ethnic Turkish party, the Movement for Rights and Freedoms (DPS). In protest at the SDS's refusal to consult the DPS, especially over the issue of agricultural decollectivisation which affected the Turkish community disproportionately, the DPS voted with the BSP to pass a vote of no confidence in the SDS government in October 1992, forcing the Dimitrov government's resignation.

After this the movement further radicalised, many in the movement interpreting its deposition as the result of BSP machinations. In consequence, Liuben Berov's nominally all-party "government of responsibility" which replaced the Dimitrov government, voted in by the BSP and 20 light blue deputies, was seen as a tool of the BSP. Zhelev's support for the Berov government led to SDS demonstrations against him and accusations that he was participating in the "recommunisation" of the country. In consequence, there was substantial support among the smaller organisations of the SDS, mostly unrepresented in the *Subranie*, for a boycott of parliament. This led to the creation of two loci of power and influence within the movement, the SDS's parliamentary group in which the larger parties were strongly represented and the Union's headquarters, dominated by the smaller formations. The struggle between the two resulted in the expulsion in 1994 of 32 SDS deputies who voted with the Berov government and triggered the defection of a large party, the Democratic Party, in June of that year. In September they formed the New Union for Democracy.

Defeat in the elections of December 1994, in which the movement secured only 69 of the 240 seats and 24% of the vote against the BSP's 43%, further exacerbated internal tensions and triggered another round of defections and expulsions, including a wholesale dismissal of headquarters staff. Soon afterwards Dimitrov was replaced as SDS leader by Ivan Kostov (a former Finance Minister), who moulded the unwieldy coalition into a unitary nominally Christian Democrat political party (registered in February 1997). Having failed to secure the passage of a motion of no confidence in the government in September 1995 (although it attracted 102 votes), the SDS won 24.7% of the first-round vote in municipal elections the following month.

Public dissatisfaction with the BSP-led government facilitated a comeback for the SDS in the autumn 1996 presidential elections, in which SDS candidate Petar Stoyanov, a relatively unknown lawyer, was elected with just under 60% of the vote in the second round. He eventually succeeded in calling early Assembly elections for April 1997, in which the SDS, heading an alliance called the United Democratic Forces (ODS) with the Democratic Party and BZNS-NS, won 137 of the 240 seats. Kostov became the new Prime Minister, heading an SDS-led government.

The ODS government served the full four-year parliamentary term (the first government to do so since 1989) and was regarded as having brought a degree of economic stability to the country and substantially improving relations with the EU and NATO. However, persistent allegations of corruption and the government's inability to raise living standards made it domestically unpopular and it lost the June 2001 Assembly elections to the new National Movement Simeon II, retaining only 51 seats with 18.2% of the national vote. Kostov accepted responsibility for the defeat and was succeeded as SDS leader by the party secretary, Ekaterina Mihailova. She was replaced as leader by the former Foreign Minister, Nadezhda Mihailova (no relation), at a party congress in February 2002. Defeat in the 2001 elections had two consequences for ODS. Firstly it weakened the coalition between SDS, the Democratic Party and BZNS-NS, with both of SDS's coalition partners demanding a more equal relationship with SDS. Despite signing a new coalition agreement in early 2002, BZNS-NS and the Democratic Party announced that they would run separately for the local elections in 2003. Secondly, tensions within the party prior to the election resulted in the formation of two new offshoot parties (in late 2000 one offshoot party, the Civic Party, had already been founded by a former Minister of the Interior, Bogomil Bonev); in November 2001 the mayor of Sofia, Stefan Sofianski, a former Prime Minister and leader of SDS's United Christian Democrat Centre, formed the Union of Free Democrats and in December 2001 former SDS deputy leader, Evgeni Bakardzhiev, formed the Bulgarian Democratic Union /radicals.

After these defections SDS remained relatively stable until the local elections in 2003, although tension remained between Mihailova and Ivan Kostov, who had retained his position on the party's National Executive Committee and therefore considerable influence in the party. This tension came to a head after the party's disappointing showing in the 2003 local elections, compounded by an unsuccessful attempt by Mihailova to challenge the popular incumbent mayor, Stefan Sofianski, as SDS candidate for the mayorship of Sofia. SDS took 21% of the popular vote and retained only Plovdiv of the larger municipal mayorships, losing much of the ground it had made up in the 1999 local elections. This failure and SDS's perceived inability under her leadership to capitalise on the unpopularity of the NDSV government, prompted Kostov and 28 SDS deputies to announce the formation of a new party, Democrats for a Strong Bulgaria, in March 2004, reducing SDS's parliamentary strength to 14 deputies.

Other Parties

Bulgarian Democratic Union/radicals (BDU/r). A right-wing party formed by former deputy leader of SDS, Evgeni Bakardzhiev, in December 2001. Bakardzhiev was elected as an ODS deputy in 2001 and retains his parliamentary seat, currently the party's only parliamentary representative.
Address. 1 Vrabcha Street, Sofia 1000
Telephone. (359–2) 986-13-63
Website. www.bdsradikali.bg
Leadership. Evgeni Bakardzhiev (president)

Bulgarian National Radical Party (*Bulgarska Natsionalna Radikalna Partia*, BNRP). Nationalist party which won 1.1% of the vote in the 1991 elections, falling to 0.1% in June 2001 contest.
Address. 14 St. Ivan Rilski Street, 1000 Sofia
Telephone. (359-2) 51-44-67
Leadership. Ivan Georgiev (chairman)

Bulgarian Social Democracy. Formerly the Euro-Left Coalition (*Koalitsia Evrolevitsa*), a pro-EU formation launched in February 1997 by two left-leaning parties, including the Civic Union of the Republic led by Alexander Tomov and some dissident deputies of the Bulgarian Socialist Party (BSP); it won 14 seats with 5.6% of the vote in April 1997 Assembly elections. The grouping in December 1998 reached agreement with the BSP on the creation of a broad left-wing front for the June 2001 elections, but a faction called the Bulgarian Euro-Left stood independently and won 1% of the vote. The party is an observer member of the Socialist International.
Address. 7 Suborna Street, Sofia 1000
Telephone. (359–2) 980-99-43
Leadership: Alexander Tomov (chairman)

Democratic Party of Justice in the Republic of Bulgaria (*Demokraticheska Partia na Spravedlivostta v Republika Bulgariya*, DPSRP). Founded in 1994 as a breakaway of the ethnic Turkish Movement for Rights and Freedoms, led initially by Chief Mufti Nedim Gendzhev; won only 0.3% in June 2001 Assembly elections.
Address. 1st Floor, 27 Blvd. Maria Louisa, Sofia 1000
Telephone. (359–2) 980-71-11
Leadership. Ali Ibrahimov (chairman)

Euroroma (*Evroroma*). Formed in December 1998 as an association representing 20 Roma organizations under the chairmanship of a Euroleft deputy and former trade union leader, Tsvetelin Kunchev, Euroroma stood as a political party in the 2001 elections in coalition with the DPS. None of its representatives took seats in parliament but, standing alone in the 2003 local elections, it took 33 council seats.
Address. Apartment 97, 18th Floor, 58a Chekhov Street, Iztok District, Izgrev, Sofia
Telephone. (359–2) 870-43-72
Leadership. Tsvetelin Kunchev (chairman)

Georgi Ganchev Bloc (*Georgi Ganchev Blok*, GGB). Created in March 2000 as successor to the Bulgarian Business Bloc (BBB), which had been founded in November 1990 by leading businessman Valentin Mollov as a right-wing, pro-market formation advocating the conversion of Bulgaria into a tariff- and tax-free zone so that it could act as a conduit for commerce between the former Soviet republics and the West. It won 1.3% of the vote (and no seats) in the 1991 elections but began to attract growing support under the new leadership of the charismatic Georgi Ganchev, a former fencing champion whose accounts of a colourful past attracted much media publicity. In the December 1994 Assembly elections the BBB broke through to representation, winning 4.7% of the vote and 13 of the 240 Assembly seats. In the first voting round of the 1996 presidential elections Ganchev attracted an impressive 21.9%, taking third place. In the April 1997 Assembly elections the BBB improved slightly to 4.9% of the vote but its representation fell to 12 seats. By September 1997 two expulsions and a resignation from the BBB Assembly group had reduced its size to below the 10 deputies required to qualify for status as a parliamentary group. Its relaunch as the GGB failed to arrest the decline, the party winning only 0.4% of the vote (and no seats) in the June 2001 Assembly elections. A dissident faction of GGB relaunched the BBB for the 2003 local elections, with however only the GBB winning council seats and then only four in total.
Address. 13 Shipka Street, Oborishte, Sofia 1504 (GGB)/14 Kitna Prolet Street, Bankia (BBB)
Telephone. (359–2) 944-61-28 (GGB)/ 99-76-205 (BBB)
Leadership. Georgi Ganchev (president, GGB); Hristo Ivanov (president, BBB)

Gergiovden. Movement formed in 1996 by two former political satirists, which claims to represent an "anti-party" vote. After failed discussions with the DPS, fought the 2001 Assembly elections in coalition with VMRO and the 2003 local elections with BZNS-NS, gaining 1.9% of the vote.

Address. Entrance A3, NDK, 1 Bulgaria Square, Sofia 1414
Telephone. (359-2) 916-63-19
Leadership. Stanimir Zashev

Green Party (*Zelena Partia*, ZP). Derives from the Ecoglasnost Movement of anti-communist environmentalists which played a key role in bringing an end to one-party Bulgarian communism in 1989-90 as part of the Union of Democratic Forces (SDS). The party left SDS in 1991, standing unsuccessfully in the 1991 and 1994 elections in coalition with other smaller parties. In 1997 it became part of the Alliance for National Salvation coalition with the DPS, taking two seats in parliament. These were lost in the 2001 elections for which it stood in coalition with Ecoglasnost and, standing independently in the 2003 local elections, it gained only 18 council seats and less than 1% of its potential vote

Address. 30 Pavele Street, Sofia 1000
Telephone. (359-2) 987-69-24
Website. www.greenparty.bg
Email. green@mail.bol.bg
Leadership. Aleksandur Karakachanov

Internal Macedonian Revolutionary Organization (*Vutreshna Makedonska Revolutsionerna Organizatsia*, VMRO). Bulgarian offshoot of the Macedonian nationalist movement of the same name, in its pre-communist manifestation it represented Macedonian separatist ambitions. Reforming after 1989 it initially claimed to represent Bulgarian citizens of Macedonian origin, but is now a right-of-centre party, the mantle of Macedonian nationalism having passed to a number of other legal and illegal similarly-named groups. VMRO won two Assembly seats in the 1997 Assembly elections within ODS; it contested the June 2001 elections in alliance with the Gergiovden movement, winning 3.6% of the vote, thus failing to surmount the 4% threshold. In the 2003 local elections it also gained about 3% of the vote and 25 local council seats.

Address. 5 Pirotska Street, 1301 Sofia
Telephone. 980-25-82
Fax.. 980-25-83
Website. www.vmro.org
Email. vmro@vmro.org
Leadership. Krasimir Karakachanov (chairman)

National Movement for Tsar Simeon II, a party which won 1.7% in June 2001 Assembly elections, apparently attracting votes intended for the victorious National Movement Simeon II.

Political Club Ecoglasnost (*Politicheski Klub Ekoglasnost*) The Ecoglasnost dissident movement was formed by anti-communist environmentalists in April 1989 under the leadership of the zoologist Petur Beron and the actor Petur Slabakov. Ecoglasnost was the principal organizer of the popular demonstrations which surrounded the downfall of Todor Zhivkov in November 1989 and became a leading component of the opposition Union of Democratic Forces (SDS). On the election of Zhelyu Zhelev as President in July 1990, Beron succeeded him as SDS chair but was forced to resign in December by disclosures about his past role as a government informer. His successor, Filip Dimitrov, was also from Ecoglasnost and led the SDS to a narrow victory in the October 1991 Assembly elections, becoming Prime Minister

of an SDS minority government. In those elections, a radical Ecoglasnost faction, taking the name Green Party, presented a separate SDS-Liberal list with other left-of-centre groups but failed to secure representation.

Following the fall of the Dimitrov government in October 1992, Ecoglasnost became concerned at the rightward drift of the SDS. Some elements moved to centre-left alliances initiated by the Bulgarian Social Democratic Party, while the main faction opted for alignment with the Bulgarian Socialist Party (BSP) for the December 1994 elections. It was therefore on the winning side and was allocated the environment portfolio in the resultant BSP-led government. In the April Assembly 1997 elections, however, Ecoglasnost shared in the defeat of the BSP-led Democratic Left alliance, while in the June 2001 elections Ecoglasnost elements also participated in the equally unsuccessful BSP-led Coalition for Bulgaria.

Address. 8th Floor, Entrance D, Block 240, Geo Milev, Sofia 1111
Telephone. (359-2) 73-00-11
Leadership. Stefan Gaitandzhiev

Radical Democratic Party (*Radikalna Demokraticheska Partia*, RDP). Descended from a pre-war party, revived in 1989 and a participant in the Union of Democratic Forces in recent elections, member of the Liberal International.

Address. 3rd Floor, 1 Hristo Velchev Street, Sofia, 1000
Telephone/Fax. (359-2) 986-12-00
Website. www.rdp-bg.org
Email. rdp-bg@online.bg
Leadership. Zahari Petrov (president)

Simeon II Coalition, a party which won 3.4% in June 2001 Assembly elections, apparently attracting votes intended for the victorious National Movement Simeon II.

Union of Free Democrats (*Soiuz na Svobodnite Demokrati*, SSD). Formed in November 2001 by the mayor of Sofia, Stefan Sofianski, the party is a breakaway faction of SDS. Sofianski, a former Prime Minister, was the leader and a founding member of United Christian Democrat Centre, a member of SDS, and the new party's programme reflects these origins. Sofianski, as an SSD candidate, retained the mayorship of Sofia in the 2003 local elections and the party gained council seats in 11 of the other 30 electoral regions.

Address. 91 Boulevard 'Vasil Levski' Sofia 1000
Telephone. (359-2) 989-59-99
Website. www.ssd.bg
Leader. Stefan Sofianski

United Bloc of Labor (*Obedinen Blok na Truda*, OBT). Formed in May 1997 as an offshoot of the BSP, OBT describes itself as Gaullist type of party with social-democratic leanings and claims 5000 members. Since its formation, it has been led by its founder, Professor Krusto Petkov, a former director of the Institute of Sociology of the Bulgarian Academy of Sciences. It participated in the 2001 elections in the BSP's Coalition for Bulgaria and, standing alone in the 2003 local elections, gained 42 council seats. In March 2004 it announced that it had formed a coalition claiming to consist of 40,000 members, the Bulgarian Republican Bloc, with a small BZNS party and a DPS breakaway party, the National Movement for Rights and Freedoms.

Address. 136b Tsar Boris the Second Street, Sofia 1618
Telephone. (359–2) 955-43-66
Leadership. Krusto Petkov (chairman)

Burkina Faso

Capital: Ouagadougou
Population: 11,950,000 (2000E)

Burkina Faso achieved independence from France in August 1960 and was called Upper Volta until August 1984. After 20 years of alternating parliamentary and military rule, a military coup in 1980 led to the installation of a radical left-wing regime by Capt. Thomas Sankara, who was overthrown (and killed) in a further coup in 1987 led by Capt. Blaise Compaoré at the head of an army faction called the Popular Front. Following the African trend, the government brought military rule to an end in June 1991 on the approval by referendum (and immediate promulgation) of a new constitution providing for multi-party democracy. Under its terms, an executive President is directly elected for a seven-year term by universal adult suffrage in two rounds of voting if no candidate secures an absolute majority in the first. The President appoints the Prime Minister and Council of Ministers subject to parliamentary approval. Legislative authority resides in the Assembly of People's Deputies (*Assemblée des Députés Populaires*), which is popularly elected for a five-year term on a constituency basis. The Assembly has 111 members (increased from 107 by a constitutional amendment adopted in Jan. 1997).

Presidential elections on Dec. 1, 1991, were boycotted by the opposition parties, with the result that Compaoré was elected unopposed in a turnout of only 28%. Assembly elections on May 24, 1992, resulted in victory for Compaoré's Organization for Popular Democracy-Labour Movement (ODP-MT), which won 78 seats, and several smaller allied parties in the Popular Front. In 1996 the ODT-MT was superseded by the pro-Compaoré Congress for Democracy and Progress (CDP), which was returned to power in the next Assembly elections on May 11, 1997, with 97 seats initially, and another four following a further round of voting in June. The Party for Democracy and Progress took six seats, the African Democratic Rally two, and the Alliance for Democracy and Federation two.

The presidential elections on Nov. 15, 1998, returned Compaoré for another seven-year term with over 87% of the vote, although several opposition parties again boycotted the poll. Prime Minister Kadre Desiré Ouedraogo resigned in November 2000, to be replaced by Paramanga Ernest Yonli presiding over a government with representatives from 10 political parties, including some opposition groupings. Assembly elections in May 2002 resulted in the Congress for Democracy and Progress remaining the largest party with 57 seats. An alliance of the African Democratic Rally and the Alliance for Democracy and Federation came in second place with 17 seats.

African Democratic Rally
Rassemblement Démocratique Africain (RDA)
Address. BP 347, Ouagadougou
Leadership. Gérard Kango Ouedraogo (secretary-general)
The RDA is descended from the nationalist movement of the same name founded in 1946 to promote independence in French West Africa, its local branch, the Voltaic Democratic Union (UDV), becoming the dominant party in the two decades after independence in 1960. Revived in 1991, the RDA selected Gérard Kango Ouedraogo (a former Prime Minister) as its presidential candidate, but in the event the party joined the general opposition boycott of the December 1991 election. It participated in the May 1992 Assembly elections, achieving third place with six seats, and subsequently secured one portfolio in the broad coalition government appointed in June. In the May 1997 legislative elections the RDA retained two seats, while in the 1998 presidential poll its candidate, Frédéric Guirma, took third place but with less than 6% of the vote. In the May 2002 Assembly elections the party formed an alliance with the Alliance for Democracy and Federation (ADF) and together they gained 17 seats.

African Party for Independence
Parti Africain pour l'Indépendence (PAI)
Address. 01 BP 1035, Ouagadougou 01
Leadership. Philippe Ouedraogo (secretary-general)
The PAI was active as a pro-Soviet Marxist party in the 1970s but was banned following the 1983 Sankara coup. Following the 1987 Compaoré coup, it became a component of the ruling umbrella Popular Front (FP). It backed Compaoré's candidacy in the December 1991 presidential poll and won two seats in the May 1992 Assembly elections. The party was unsuccessful in the 1997 polls, but obtained representation in the government appointed at the end of 2000. In the May 2002 Assembly elections the party secured five seats.

Alliance for Democracy and Federation
Alliance pour la Démocratie et la Fédération (ADF)
Address. BP 1943, Ouagadougou
Leadership. Herman Yaméogo
The ADF was launched in December 1990, its leader (son of a President deposed in 1966) having in 1978 founded the opposition National Union for the Defence of Democracy (UNDD). He later became leader of the Movement of Progressive Democrats (MDP) but broke away to form the ADF after the MDP had been expelled from the ruling umbrella Popular Front in June 1990 because of his alleged "irresponsible" behaviour. In February 1991 the ADF issued a joint statement with the Alliance for Democracy and Social Development calling for a transitional government and the exclusion of the ruling Popular Front parties from elections. Yaméogo was appointed Agriculture Minister in June 1991 but he and two other ADF ministers resigned in August in protest against the slow pace of democratization. The ADF boycotted the December 1991 presidential election but Yaméogo again accepted a cabinet post in February 1992. The party won four seats in the May 1992 Assembly elections but lost two in the May 1997 polls, although it obtained representation in the government formed in late 2000.

In the May 2002 Assembly elections the party formed an alliance with the African Democratic Rally (RDA) and together they gained 17 seats. However, in 2003 the ADF/RDA split into two groups in the Assembly. Nine members left the party to form the National Union for Democracy and Development (*Union Nationale pour la Démocratie et le Développement*, UNDD) leaving the ADF/RDA with eight members in parliament.

Alliance for Liberty and Progress
Alliance pour la Liberté et le Progrès (APL)
The party gained one seat in the May 2002 Assembly elections.

Coalition of Democratic Forces
Coalition des Forces Démocratiques (CFD)
A coalition formed on the occasion of the May 2002 Assembly Elections. It was composed of the Union of Greens for the Development of Burkina (*Union des Verts du Burkina*, UVDB), the Front of Refusal (*Front du Refus*, FR), the Union for Democracy and Federation (*Union pour la Démocratie et la Fédération*, UDF), the Liberal Union for

Democracy (*Union des Libéraux pour la Démocratie*, ULD), the Convention for Democracy and Federation (*Convention pour la Démocratie et la Fédération*), the Movement for Tolerance and Progress (*Mouvement pour la Tolérance et le Progrès*, MTP) and the Alliance for Progress and Liberty (*Alliance pour le Progrès et la Liberté*, APL). This coalition won five seats in the May 2002 elections.

Congress for Democracy and Progress
Congrès pour la Démocratie et le Progrès (CDP)

Address. c/o Assemblée des Députés, Ouagadougou
Leadership. Roch Marc Christian Kaboré (president)
Website. www.cdp.bf

The CDP was created early in 1996 as a merger of President Compaoré's Organization for Popular Democracy-Labour Movement (ODP-MT) and some 10 other pro-regime parties. The ODP-MT had been created in April 1989 by a merger of the Burkinabe Union of Communists (UCB) and a faction of the Union of Communist Struggles (ULC), from which the UCB had previously split. It was intended originally to provide a single-party base for the Compaoré regime by unifying "all political tendencies in the country" and became the leading component of the pro-Compaoré Popular Front (*Front Populaire*, FP), first created in October 1987 and reorganized in 1991. Meanwhile, the first ODP-MT secretary-general, Clément Ouedraogo (former UCB leader), had been dismissed in April 1990 for "serious failures of principle and party policy". At a congress in March 1991, the ODP-MT formally renounced Marxism-Leninism and embraced a free enterprise, pro-Western philosophy, while remaining unenthusiastic about multi-party politics.

Asserting its autonomy and dominance within the FP, the ODP-MT backed Compaoré's (uncontested) presidential candidacy in December 1991 and in May 1992 unexpectedly won a large majority in Assembly elections (which were condemned as fraudulent by the opposition parties). The ODP-MT was the leading party in the post-election coalition government headed by Youssouf Ouedraogo, which included six other parties, several of them outside the FP. In March 1994 Ouedraogo was replaced by Roch Marc Christian Kaboré after failing to reach a wage agreement with the trade unions in the wake of the devaluation of the CFA franc. In January 1995 the leader of the ODP-MT youth wing, Moumouni Ouedraogo, was killed in disturbances preceding local elections the following month.

On the creation of the CDP in February 1996, Kaboré was replaced as Prime Minister by Kadre Desiré Ouedraogo, who remained in office until November 2000, when he was replaced by Paramanga Ernest Yonli. During Kaboré's premiership, the CDP won the May 1997 legislative elections with a massive majority, taking 101 of the 111 Assembly seats, and President Compaoré was returned to office in the November 1998 poll. In the May 2002 Assembly elections the party once more showed its strength by winning 57 seats.

Democrats and Independent Progressives Union
Union des Démocrates et Progressistes Indépendants (UDPI)

Leadership. Joseph Somda

The party was founded in 1994 and won one seat in the May 2002 Assembly elections.

Movement for Progress and Tolerance
Mouvement pour le Progrès et la Tolérance (MPT)

Leadership. Noyabtigungu Congo Kabore

Founded as an "anti-imperialist and nationalist/progressive" party, the MPT has been more prepared for co-operation with the Compaoré regime than other opposition parties and obtained representation in the government formed in November 2000. The party entered the Coalition of Democratic Forces to participate in the May 2002 Assembly elections but won no seats.

National Convention of the Patriotic Democrats
Convention Nationale des Democrates Patriotes (CNDP)

Leadership. Alfred Kaboré

The party won two seats in the May 2002 Assembly elections.

Panafrican Sankarist Convention
Convention des Partis Sankaristes (CPS)

Leadership. Ernest Nongma Ouedraogo

The CPS was established in 1999 to pursue the leftist policies of the 1983-87 Sankara regime. It obtained representation in the government formed in November 2000. In the May 2002 Assembly elections the party won three seats.

Party for Democracy and Progress
Parti pour la Démocratie et le Progrès (PDP)

Address. BP 606, Ouagadougou
Telephone. (226) 362190
Fax. (226) 362902
Leadership. Joseph Ki-Zerbo

The PDP came into being as a result of a power struggle in the National Convention of Progressive Patriots-Social Democratic Party (CNPP-PSD) in 1993. Prof. Ki-Zerbo had been placed fourth in presidential elections in 1978 as candidate of what became the socialist-oriented Voltaic Progressive Front (FVP), which was banned after the 1980 Sankara coup. On the restoration of multi-partyism in 1991, Ki-Zerbo returned to Burkina Faso and became associated with the CNPP-PSD, heading the allied Union of Independent Social Democrats (*Union des Sociaux-Démocrates Indépendants*, USDI) in the May 1992 Assembly elections, in which it won one seat.

Ki-Zerbo broke with the CNPP-PSD following the retirement of its leader in May 1993, complaining of the "suspicion, internal quarrels and absence of motivation" generated by the resultant succession struggle. His new PDP was formally constituted at a congress in April 1994, when it claimed to have the support of nine of the 13 CNPP-PSD/USDI deputies and thus to be the second strongest party in the Assembly. In the May 1997 legislative elections, the PDP won six seats to become the second largest party and the main opposition in the Assembly.

The PDP inherited the FVP's membership of the Socialist International. In 1999 the party merged with the Socialist Party (PS), and in the May 2002 Assembly elections the PDP/PS party won 10 seats to become the third largest party in the Assembly.

Party for Democracy and Socialism
Parti pour la Démocratie et le Socialisme (PDS)

Leadership. Joseph Ki-Zerbo

Founded in May 2000, the party won two seats in the May 2002 Assembly Elections.

Party of the National Revival
Parti de la Renaissance Nationale (PAREN)

Leadership. Laurent Bado

This party was founded on Sept. 8, 1999, and won four seats in the May 2002 Assembly elections.

Patriotic Front for Change
Front Patriotique pour le Changement (FPC)

Leadership. Tahirou Zon

The party gained one seat in the May 2002 Assembly elections.

Union of Greens for the Development of Burkina
Union des Verts pour le Développement du Burkina
(UVDB)
Leadership. Ram Ouedraogo
The party was founded in 1991 and its leader was the first declared candidate for the December 1991 presidential election, although he later withdrew along with all other opposition nominees. In the 1998 presidential poll (again subject to opposition boycotts), Ouedraogo came second to the incumbent, Blaise Compaoré, but with only 6.6% of the vote. The party obtained representation in the government formed in November 2000. The party entered the Coalition of the Democratic Forces to participate in the May 2002 Assembly elections.

Union for Revival/Sankarist Movement
Union pour la Renaissance/Mouvement Sankariste
(UNIR/MS)
Leadership. Bénéwendé Stanislas Sankara
This party was founded in November 2000 and won three seats in the May 2002 Assembly elections.

Burundi

Capital: Bujumbura
Population: 7,100,000 (2002E)

Burundi was granted independence as a monarchy in 1962, having previously been administered by Belgium since the termination of German rule during World War I, first under a League of Nations mandate and from 1946 as a UN trusteeship. The overthrow of the monarchy in 1966 and the declaration of the Republic of Burundi was followed, from 1976, by a series of military regimes and one-party government. After a coup in 1987, Maj. Pierre Buyoya, of the minority Tutsis, came to power. Buyoya published a National Unity Charter in May 1990, under which Burundi moved to civilian rule and "controlled" multi-partyism. However, the period of transition only served to unleash conflict between the majority Hutu ethnic group and the minority Tutsis who had traditionally exercised dominance. Presidential elections held in June 1993 resulted in victory for Melchior Ndadaye (a Hutu) and subsequent legislative elections were won by the (Hutu) Burundi Front for Democracy (FRODEBU), marking an end to centuries of rule by the Tutsi minority.

President Ndadaye was killed in an attempted coup by militant Hutu dissidents in October 1993 and he was succeeded in January 1994 by Cyprien Ntaryamira, a Hutu and a member of FRODEBU. Three months later Ntaryamira himself died in an unexplained air crash near Kigali (together with the President of Rwanda) and was succeeded by another Hutu and FRODEBU member, Sylvestre Ntibantunganya.

From 1994 Hutu guerrillas groups launched a campaign against the Tutsi-dominated armed forces. Mounting insecurity culminated in a further military coup in July 1996 that brought Buyoya back to power. Buyoya tried to form an ethnically mixed government and announced a three-year transition to civil rule, initiating a "national debate". This led by mid-1998 to a partnership agreement between the executive and the FRODEBU-dominated National Assembly, and the adoption of a new transitional constitution. This enlarged the National Assembly to 121 members; FRODEBU remained the dominant party, although a small number of seats were held by the (Tutsi) Union

for National Progress (UPRONA). Buyoya was officially sworn in as President (head of state and government) in June 1998.

Peace talks facilitated by former South African President Nelson Mandela resulted in the signing in July 2001 of the Arusha power-sharing agreement designed to end the civil war. Under the terms of the agreement, a new transitional government was formed in November 2001, composed of members of both the Tutsi and Hutu ethnic groups. It was agreed that President Buyoya would hold the presidency for a term limited to only 18-months at the start of a three-year transitional period. The transition was relatively orderly and in April 2003 Domitien Ndayizeye, a leader of the FRODEBU, replaced Buyoya as President. However, Hutu rebel opposition to the Arusha peace process – and in particular to Tutsi control of the armed forces – continued, led by hardline factions of the two main militias, the National Council for the Defence of Democracy/Forces for the Defence of Democracy (CNDD-FDD) and the Palipehutu-Forces for National Liberation (Palipehutu-FNL). In mid-November 2003 President Ndayizeye and Pierre Nkurunziza, leader of the dominant faction of the CNDD-FDD, signed a comprehensive peace agreement and CNDD-FDD members were incorporated into a new Cabinet. In January 2004 President Ndayizeye held talks in the Netherlands with the leadership of the Palipehutu-FNL, the only main Hutu rebel faction still offering armed opposition to the government.

Alliance for the Rule of Law and Economic Development
Alliance Nationale pour le Droit et le Développement (ANADDE)
Leadership. Ignace Bankamwabo
Pro-Tutsi party registered in 1992 and signatory of the July 2001 peace agreement. Party representative Alphonse Barancira was appointed as Minister of Institutional Reforms, Human Rights and Relations with Parliament in the transitional government formed in November 2001. Barancira was not reappointed in the new Cabinet formed in November 2003, but party member Antoine Butoyi was appointed as Minister for Mobilisation of Peace and National Reconciliation.

Alliance of Valiant People
Alliance des Vaillants (AV-INTWARI)
Leadership. André Nkundikije
Pro-Tutsi party registered in 1996 and signatory of July 2001 peace agreement. Party leader Nkundikije was appointed as Minister of Development Planning and Reconstruction in the transitional government formed in November 2001. In July 2002 Nkundikije was shifted to the Energy and Mines portfolio, a post he retained in the November 2003 reshuffle.

Burundi-African Alliance for Salvation
Alliance Burundo-Africaine pour le Salut (ABASA)
Leadership. Térence Nsanze (external wing); Serge Mukamarakiza (internal wing)
Pro-Tutsi party registered in 1993 and signatory of July 2001 peace agreement. Party member Edouard Kadigiri was appointed as Minister of Finance in the transitional government formed in November 2001. He was replaced in January 2003 by another party member, Athanase Gahunhu.

Burundi Front for Democracy
Front pour la Démocratie au Burundi (FRODEBU)
Leadership. Jean Minani (president)
FRODEBU began as an informal alliance of Hutu-dominat-

ed opposition groups which campaigned for a "no" vote in the March 1992 constitutional referendum on the grounds that the Buyoya regime had refused to convene a full national conference to agree the transition to multi-partyism. Following the promulgation of the new constitution, FRODEBU registered as a political party, containing both Hutus and Tutsis. The first round of presidential elections in June 1993, resulted in an outright victory for Melchior Ndadaye, the FRODEBU leader, who easily defeated the incumbent Buyoya, of the Union for National Progress (UPRONA). In Assembly elections also held in June 1993, FRODEBU won 65 of the 81 seats. The accession to power of Ndadaye, a member of the majority Hutu ethnic group, marked an interruption of centuries of rule by the Tutsi minority, although UPRONA members were allocated the premiership and six portfolios in the post-election coalition government. Ndadaye was killed in an attempted coup by militant Hutu dissidents in October 1993 and was succeeded in January 1994 by Cyprien Ntaryamira (FRODEBU), also a Hutu, who likewise appointed a Tutsi (and UPRONA member) as Prime Minister of a broad coalition government charged with promoting inter-ethnic peace. Nevertheless, some FRODEBU leaders were implicated in Hutu revenge attacks on Tutsis.

In April 1994 Ntaryamira himself died in an unexplained air crash near Kigali (together with the President of Rwanda) and was succeeded by Sylvestre Ntibantunganya (FRODEBU), a Hutu, who was formally endorsed by the National Assembly in September 1994. Immediately prior to his endorsement, FRODEBU signed the "convention of government" providing for power-sharing with other parties. Following Ntibantunganya's inauguration in October, a new government included representatives of FRODEBU (the dominant party), UPRONA (which continued to hold the premiership) and five other parties. Subsequent strains between the main coalition partners were partially resolved in January 1995 by the election of Léonce Ngendakumana of FRODEBU as Assembly Speaker with UPRONA support, while the controversial original nominee for the post, Jean Minani, became FRODEBU president in place of President Ntibantunganya.

FRODEBU continued to participate in the new power-sharing government installed in March 1995, holding 10 portfolios. In May President Ntibantunganya rejected suggestions that the territories of Burundi and Rwanda should be reorganized into ethnically pure Hutu and Tutsi states. The following month he was rebuffed by his own FRODEBU Assembly deputies when he sought approval to rule by decree, amid a serious deterioration in the internal security situation. In September 1995 FRODEBU and other "presidential bloc" ministers, calling themselves the Force for Democratic Change (*Force pour le Changement Démocratique*, FCD), issued a statement criticizing the UPRONA Interior Minister for having rejected an assertion by the US ambassador to Burundi that the security situation caused him "deep concern". The same statement accused the Interior Minister of refusing to apply the law on political parties and of failing to take action to curb the continuing violence.

Upon the resumption of executive power by Maj. Buyoya in July 1996 and subsequent dialogue with the FRODEBU-dominated National Assembly, transitional constitutional measures were adopted, including the appointment in mid-1998 of a FRODEBU representative, Frederic Bamvuginyumvira, as one of two vice-presidents. Under the terms of the July 2001 Arusha peace agreement signed by FRODEBU and the other main political parties and groups—although not the two main Hutu rebel factions—FRODEBU held 14 posts in a new transitional government formed some three months later. The predominantly Tutsi UPRONA also held 14 posts in the new Cabinet. In January 2002 FRODEBU leader Jean Minani was elected as Speaker of the transitional Assembly, easily defeating his only rival, Augustin Nzojibwami, leader of a rival faction of FRODEBU. Nzojibwami responded by leaving FRODEBU and forming a rival Hutu-dominated party, the Party for Democracy and Reconciliation. In April 2003 Maj Buyoya handed the presidency of Burundi to leading FRODEBU member, and former Vice-President, Domitien Ndayizeye, as provided for under the Arusha peace deal. Ndayizeye pushed ahead with the peace process and had by March 2004 brought all but one of the Hutu rebel factions into his government.

G-7

Loose coalition formed by majority Hutu or exclusively Hutu parties. Members are: Burundi Front for Democracy; National Council for the Defence of Democracy; Palipehutu-Forces for National Liberation; National Liberation Front; People's Party; Rally for the Burundi People; and the Liberal Party.

G-8

Loose coalition incorporating the smaller Tutsi-majority parties. Members are: Party for National Redress; People's Reconciliation Party; Alliance of Valiant People; Burundi-African Alliance for Salvation; Social Democratic Party; Guarantor of the Freedom of Speech in Burundi; Alliance for the Rule of Law and Economic Development; and the Workers' Independent Party.

Guarantor of the Freedom of Speech in Burundi
Inkinzo y'Igambo Ry'abarundi (INKINZO)
Leadership. Alphonse Rugumbarara (president)
Pro-Tutsi party registered in 1993 and signatory of July 2001 peace agreement. Party representative Francoise Ngendahayo was appointed as Minister of Reintegration and Resettlement of Displaced Persons and Repatriates in the transitional government formed in November 2001 and retained the post in the new Cabinet formed in November 2003.

Liberal Party
Parti Libéral (PL)
Leadership. Gaëtan Nikobamye
Pro-Hutu party registered in 1992 and signatory of the July 2001 peace agreement. Party leader Nikobamye was appointed as Minister of Territorial Development, Environment and Tourism in the transitional government formed in November 2001. The party had no representative in the new Cabinet formed in November 2003.

National Council for the Defence of Democracy/Forces for the Defence of Democracy
Conseil national pour la défense de la démocratie/Forces pour la défense de la démocratie(CNDD-FDD)
Leadership: Col Jean-Bosco Ndayikengurukiye (faction leader); Pierre Nkurunziza (faction leader).
Hutu militia group. During 2002 the government signed ceasefire agreements with both CNDD-FDD factions, firstly, in October, with the faction led by Ndayikengurukiye (the so-called Jean-Bosco faction) and secondly, in December, with the faction led by Nkurunziza. The groundwork for peace had been laid in July 2001 when Hutu and Tutsi representatives agreed to share power in an interim administration. However, the ceasefire agreement with the dominant Nkurunziza faction was shortlived and FDD fighters under Nkurunziza's control launched a series of attacks on Bujumbura in mid-April 2003. The attacks were launched to coincide with the implementation of the 2001 Arusha peace accords, under the terms of which President Buyoya (a Tutsi) had agreed to hand over the presidency over to Domitien Ndayizeye, a leading member of the main Hutu political

party, the Front for Democracy in Burundi (FRODEBU) in late April. The handover went ahead as planned, despite continued attacks by fighters loyal to Nkurunziza, who had said that he would suspend attacks only if the Tutsi-led army disarmed. A new Cabinet appointed by President Ndayizeye in May included a member of the Jean-Bosco faction of the CNDD-FDD, namely Gaspar Kobako, Minister of Public Works and Equipment. In November 2003 Nkurunziza's dominant faction of the CNDD-FDD signed a comprehensive peace agreement with the government and a number of CNDD-FDD members were brought into the Cabinet. Furthermore, in January 2004 President Ndayizeye signed a decree establishing a new integrated national command of the national army – some 40% of the new command was composed of CNDD-FDD members.

National Liberation Front
Front pour la libération nationale (Frolina)
Leadership. Joseph Karumba (chairman).
Small but long-established Hutu rebel group which accepted the terms of the July 2001 peace accords and in May 2003 entered the government of President Ndayizeye.

Palipehutu-Forces for National Liberation
Parti pour la libération du peuple hutu (Palipehutu)- Forces nationales de libération (Palipehutu-FNL)
Leadership. Agathon Rwasa (faction leader); Alain Mugabarabona (faction leader).
Sole Hutu rebel faction still offering armed opposition to the government. President Ndayizeye held talks with Palipehutu-FNL leaders in the Netherlands in January 2004. After the talks the President said that "some progress" had been made and that the two sides had agreed to meet again "to exchange ideas".

Party for National Redress
Parti pour le Redressement National (PARENA)
Leadership. Jean-Baptiste Bagaza
Pro-Tutsi party registered in 1994 and signatory of July 2001 peace agreement. The party's leader, former President Jean-Baptiste Bagaza (1976-87), was placed under house arrest in November 2002 accused of drawing up a plan to "destabilise the country". He was released in April 2003 and the following month the government lifted suspension measures imposed on PARENA at the time of Bagaza's detention.

People's Party
Parti du Peuple (PP)
Leadership. Shadrack Niyonkuru (external wing); Séverin Ndikumugongo (internal wing)
Pro-Hutu party, registered in 1992 and signatory of the July 2001 peace agreement. Party representative Séverin Ndikumugongo was appointed as Minister of Transport, Posts and Telecommunications in the transitional government formed in November 2001 and retained the post in the new Cabinet formed in November 2003.

People's Reconciliation Party
Parti pour la Réconciliation du Peuple (PRP)
Leadership. Mathias Hitimana
Pro-Tutsi party, registered in 1992 initially as the *Parti Royaliste parlementaire*, and signatory of July 2001 peace agreement. Party leader Hitimana was appointed Minister of Energy and Mines in the transitional government formed in November 2001. He was dismissed from the government in July 2002, reportedly because he was suspected of financing and arming extremist Tutsi militia in the mid-1990s. Another party member, Deogratias Rusengwamihigo, was appointed as Minister of Institutional Reforms, Human Rights and Relations with Parliament in the Cabinet formed in November 2003.

Rally for Democracy and Economic and Social Development
Ralliement pour la Démocratie et le Développement Economique et Social (RADDES)
Leadership. Joseph Nzeyimana
Pro-Tutsi party registered in 1992 and signatory of July 2001 peace agreement. Party representative Dismas Nditabiriye was appointed as Minister of Labour and Social Security in the transitional government formed in November 2001; he retained in the post in the government formed in November 2003.

Rally for the Burundi People
Rassemblement du Peuple Burundais (RPB)
Leadership. Balthazar Bigirimana (external wing); Philippe Nzobonariba (internal wing)
Pro-Hutu party registered in 1992 and signatory of July 2001 peace agreement. The party held two posts in the transitional government formed in November 2001 (party leader Bigirimana as Minister of Public Works and Equipment and Barnabe Muteragiranwa as Minister of Youth, Sports and Culture). Muteragiranwa retained his post in the new Cabinet formed in November 2003.

Social Democratic Party
Parti Social-Démocrate (PSD)
Leadership. Godefroy Hakizimana
Pro-Tutsi party registered in 1993 and signatory of July 2001 peace agreement. Party leader Hakizimana was appointed as Minister of Handicrafts, Vocational Training and Adult Literacy in the transitional government formed in November 2001 and retained the post in the new Cabinet formed in November 2003.

Union for National Progress
Union pour le Progrès National (UPRONA)
Address. BP 1810, Bujumbura
Leadership. Luc Rukingama (president)
Founded in 1959 by Prince Louis Rwagasore, the predominantly Tutsi UPRONA has over the years undergone various adjustments in its French title, although all have retained the UPRONA acronym. It was in the forefront of the struggle against Belgian rule, winning an overwhelming majority in Assembly elections in 1961 (after which Prince Rwagasore was assassinated) and leading Burundi to full independence as a monarchy the following year. Having retained its majority in the 1965 Assembly elections (and lost two more Prime Ministers by assassination), UPRONA was proclaimed the sole ruling party on the overthrow of the (Tutsi) monarchy by the Tutsi-dominated army in 1966, whereupon Michel Micombero was installed as President. He was ousted in 1976 by Col. Jean-Baptiste Bagaza (a Tutsi), who declared the Second Republic and reorganized UPRONA as the ruling party. At its first congress in December 1979 UPRONA adopted a new charter and statutes, defining the party as a democratic centralist organization dedicated to the struggle against exploitation and imperialism and in favour of self-reliance, the preservation of national culture, and co-operation in community development.

A new constitution for Burundi, drafted by the UPRONA central committee and providing for a return to civilian rule, secured referendum approval in November 1981. In August 1984 Bagaza was re-elected President as the UPRONA (and only) candidate, but in September 1987 he was overthrown (while out of the country) by a military coup led by Maj. Pierre Buyoya, another Tutsi and a then little-known UPRONA central committee member. Although Buyoya dismissed the incumbent UPRONA central committee, he was backed by the party's national secretariat, which was instructed to establish a new structure for UPRONA. Full party activity was resumed in 1989 (after a spate of Tutsi-Hutu conflict), with Nicolas Mayugi (a Buyoya nominee and a Hutu) as UPRONA secretary-general. Under a National Unity Charter published by Buyoya in May 1990, the UPRONA central committee in December 1990 took over the functions of the Military Committee for National Salvation.

Having at that stage shown a preference for "democracy within the single party", Buyoya in May 1991 declared his support for a measure of pluralism, which was enshrined in the new constitution adopted in March 1992. At an extraordinary congress the same month UPRONA delegates elected a new 90-member central committee and also endorsed Mayugi as party president in succession to Buyoya (who stood down in accordance with the new constitution). That Mayugi and a majority of the new central committee were Hutus (despite UPRONA's membership being 90% Tutsi) reflected the regime's sensitivity to charges that it was dominated by the minority Tutsis.

The stratagem did not help Buyoya in the presidential elections of June 1993, when he was defeated outright in the first round by the Hutu candidate of the Burundi Front for Democracy (FRODEBU). UPRONA was also decisively defeated in Assembly elections later the same month, winning only 16 of the 81 seats, after which the party complained of "ethnic manipulation" by FRODEBU. Nevertheless, UPRONA accepted representation in the post-election government, the premiership going to Sylvie Kinigi, a Tutsi and former UPRONA member, who became Burundi's first woman Prime Minister. Following the murder of President Ndadaye in October 1993, UPRONA again charged FRODEBU leaders of fomenting anti-Tutsi violence but accepted participation in a broad coalition government formed in February 1994 and headed by UPRONA member Anatole Kanyenkiko, a Tutsi.

The death of President Ntaryamira in April 1994 gave rise to fears of a tribal bloodbath on the Rwandan scale, to avert which UPRONA eventually co-operated in the elevation to the presidency of the FRODEBU Speaker of the National Assembly, a Hutu, and continued to participate in the coalition government. The initial UPRONA candidate for the presidency had been Charles Mukasi, who replaced Mayugi as party president. UPRONA was a signatory of the September 1994 "convention of government" providing for power-sharing between the main parties. Following the parliamentary confirmation of the FRODEBU President in September 1994, UPRONA was the second-strongest party in the new broad coalition appointed in October, with Kanyenkiko continuing as Prime Minister. However, the latter was expelled from UPRONA in January 1995 (for having dismissed two UPRONA ministers at the President's behest) and was eventually replaced by Antoine Nduwayo after UPRONA had mounted anti-Kanyenkiko demonstrations.

In June 1995 most UPRONA Assembly deputies supported the President's unsuccessful request to be allowed to rule by decree. The following month UPRONA unsuccessfully demanded the dissolution of the Assembly and new elections, claiming that many FRODEBU deputies had fled the country. In September Nduwayo and the UPRONA Interior Minister, Gabriel Sinarinzi, came under attack from FRODEBU and other members of the government for downplaying the extent of violence in Burundi and for allegedly resisting multi-party democracy. He was dismissed from the government in October 1995.

Amid increasing insecurity and ethnic violence, the military again seized power in July 1996 under Maj. Buyoya, who subsequently negotiated a partnership agreement with the FRODEBU-dominated National Assembly. Buyoya was officially sworn in as President (head of state and government) in June 1998, and Mathias Sinamenye of UPRONA assumed one of two new vice-presidential posts.

Under the terms of the July 2001 Arusha peace agreement signed by UPRONA and the other main political parties and groups – although not the two main Hutu rebel factions – UPRONA held 14 posts in the newly installed transitional government. The predominantly Hutu FRODEBU also held 14 posts in the new Cabinet. In April 2003 Maj Buyoya handed the presidency of Burundi to leading FRODEBU member, and former Vice-President, Domitien Ndayizeye, as provided for under the Arusha peace deal. The orderly transfer of power from a Tutsi to a Hutu President was hailed by the international community. However, ethnic Hutu rebels dismissed Ndayizeye as a "figurehead", claiming that real power continued to be held by the Tutsi-controlled army. Nonetheless, Ndayizeye pushed ahead with the peace process and had as of March 2004 brought all but one of the Hutu rebel factions into his government.

Workers' Independent Party
Parti Indépendant des Travailleurs (PIT)
Leadership. Nicéphore Ndimurukundo
Pro-Tutsi party registered in 1993 and signatory of July 2001 peace agreement. Party representative Genevieve Sindabizera was appointed as Minister in the Office of the President (in charge of AIDS control) in the transitional government formed in November 2001. The party had no representative in the new Cabinet formed in November 2003.

Other parties

Burundian Communist Party (*Parti Communiste Burundais* (PCB))
Leadership. Ernest Bategere
Formed in 1998.

Liberal Alliance for Development (*Alliance Libérale pour le Développement* (ALD))
Leadership. Joseph Ntidendereza
Formed in September 2002 by Joseph Ntidendereza, hitherto a leader of a faction of the Liberal Party.

National Consensus Party
Parti pour la Concorde Nationale (PACONA)
Leadership. Jean-Bosco Ndayizambaye
Formed in February 2004 by Jean-Bosco Ndayizambaye, hitherto vice chairman of the pro-Tutsi Workers' Independent Party. Ndayizambaye said that PACONA's objectives were based on "justice, reconciliation and development".

National Resistance Movement for the Rehabilitation of the Citizen (*Mouvement de Rassemblement pour la Réhabilitation du Citoyen* (MRC-Rurenzangemero Party))
Leadership. Lt-Col Epitace Bayaganakandi
Registered in November 2002 and led by former Interior and Public Security Minister Lt-Col Epitace Bayaganakandi

New Alliance for Democracy and Development (*Nouvelle Alliance pour la Démocratie et le Développement* (NADD))
Leadership. Jean-Paul Burafuta
Formed in September 2002.

Party for Justice and Development (*Parti pour la Justice et le Développement* (Pajude-Intazimiza))
Leadership. Pascal Nkunzumwami
Constituent assembly held in July 2002.

Party for the Non-Violent Society (*Parti pour une Société Non-Violente* (Sonovi-Ruremesha))
Leadership. Deogratias Ndayishimiye
Pro-Tutsi party formed in December 2002.

Party for Democracy and Reconciliation (*Parti pour la*

Démocratie et la Reconciliation (Sangwe-Pader))
Leadership. Augustin Nzojibwami
Formed by Augustin Nzojibwami, hitherto a leader of a faction of the pro-Hutu Front for Democracy in Burundi, in May 2002.

Union for Peace and Development
Leadership. Freddy Feruvi
Formed in September 2002.

Cambodia

Capital: Phnom Penh
Population: 13,125,000 (2003E)

Cambodia achieved its independence in 1953 when the French transferred most political authority from their colonial officials to King Norodom Sihanouk, whom they had placed on the throne in 1941. The Geneva Conference of 1954 decided that nation-wide, internationally-supervised elections should be held within two years to choose new governments for the former colonies of French Indochina, and the Cambodian elections were held in 1955. Sihanouk abdicated the throne in favour of his father and formed a political party, *Sangkum Reastr Niyum* (People's Socialist Community), to contest the elections. In an election characterized by frequent intimidation, the *Sangkum* decisively defeated its main rival, the Democrat Party. Prince Sihanouk dominated Cambodian politics for the next 15 years. Sihanouk pursued a policy of non-alignment, which became increasingly difficult to sustain as the war in neighbouring Vietnam escalated in the 1960s. Sihanouk was deposed in 1970 by General Lon Nol and Prince Sirik Matik, who took Cambodia into the Vietnam War in the US side. Sihanouk joined with local communist insurgents, known as the *Khmer Rouge* (KR), to fight the Lon Nol regime with the backing of the Chinese and Vietnamese communists. In response, Lon Nol abolished the monarchy and proclaimed a Khmer Republic.

In 1975 the Lon Nol government collapsed, and the country was taken over by a government which was nominally a royalist-communist coalition. However real power lay with the KR leaders, above all Pol Pot. They forcibly evacuated the urban population to the countryside, implemented a harsh program of agrarian communism, and carried out a series of purges against their enemies, their allies, and dissidents in their own ranks. Following the proclamation of a Democratic Kampuchea (DK) government in early 1976, Sihanouk resigned as head of state and was replaced by Khieu Samphan. Sihanouk was kept under house arrest in the Royal Palace.

In 1977-78 the DK government launched a series of attacks on Vietnam, and was overthrown by a Vietnamese invasion in 1979. Cambodian Communist opponents of the Pol Pot regime who had fled to Vietnam established a provisional government in Phnom Penh. In 1981 this became the People's Republic of Kampuchea (PRK), led by the Kampuchean People's Revolutionary Party (KPRP). In 1982 the KR joined with royalists and the Khmer People's National Liberation Front (KPNLF) to form the Coalition Government of Democratic Kampuchea (CGDK), which Prince Sihanouk headed. The CGDK enjoyed UN recognition and waged a guerrilla war against the PRK government and the Vietnamese army in Cambodia from the Thai border.

Initially, the Vietnamese bore the brunt of fighting against the CGDK. From 1981 they gradually withdrew, shifting responsibility for national security to the PRK. The Vietnamese completed their withdrawal in September 1989.

Attempts to achieve a political settlement began with negotiations between Sihanouk and the PRK Prime Minister, Hun Sen, in 1987, and culminated in the four-party Paris Agreement of October 1991. The PRK renamed itself the State of Cambodia (SoC) in 1989, and the KPRP was renamed the Cambodian People's Party (CPP) in the wake of the Paris Agreement. Under the terms of that agreement, a United Nations Transitional Authority in Cambodia (UNTAC) oversaw Cambodia until UN-organized elections were held in May 1993 and a new government was formed in October 1993. Until the formation of that government, each of the contending factions administered the areas they controlled separately. Each group was supposed to submit to UN supervision, and disarm. The KR (now calling themselves the Party of Democratic Kampuchea, PDK, with Khieu Samphan as their main public spokesman) refused to do this, and boycotted the 1993 elections.

UNTAC proceeded with the elections nonetheless. This was not Cambodia's first experience with elections. That began in 1947, under the French, and each regime since has held them, even Pol Pot's DK. But Cambodian elections were mostly devices to boost the legitimacy of those in power, rather than a means of choosing leaders, settling disputes between them, or making them accountable to the people. However the 1993 elections, like those of 1955, involved a real contest for power. They also involved a significantly new electoral system. The Paris Agreement replaced single-member district electorates with multi-member provincial electorates, and required a two-thirds majority to form a government. This system was designed to force the leading party into co-operation with its rivals. It has been retained after the 1993 elections.

The 1993 elections resulted in the royalist party, the United National Front for an Independent, Neutral, Peaceful and Co-operative Cambodia (FUNCINPEC), headed by Prince Norodom Rannaridh, winning 58 of the 120 seats in the Constituent Assembly (with 45.5% of the vote). The CPP won 51 seats (with 38.2% of the vote). A third party, the Buddhist Liberal Democratic Party (BLDP), won 10 seats (with 3.8% of the vote), and one seat went to a group called *Moulinaka* (with 1.4% of the vote). After a period of maneuvering and instability, a coalition government of FUNCINPEC, the CPP and the two smaller parties was formed. A new constitution was promulgated restoring the monarchy as the constitutional head of a pluralistic, liberal and democratic political system. Sihanouk returned to the throne, but with little of the power, he had enjoyed before 1970. The Constituent Assembly transformed itself into a National Assembly and on Oct. 29, 1993, proclaimed a new government, the Royal Government of Cambodia (RGC), with Prince Rannaridh and Hun Sen respectively as the First and Second Prime Minister.

This unusual arrangement reflected the fact that the RGC was built around the co-operation of FUNCINPEC and the CPP, but Rannaridh and Hun Sen competed for power and patronage. Hun Sen soon proved to be the most effective in this, FUNCINPEC was riven by factional rivalries, and Rannaridh became increasingly resentful. Tensions between the two leaders were exacerbated by disagreements over how to deal with the KR.

The KR denounced the "two-headed" government as another puppet of the Vietnamese and continued their insurgency. However, in 1996 one of the top KR leaders, Ieng Sary, surrendered to the government in return for an amnesty. He chose to negotiate with Hun Sen rather than Rannaridh. Following this, Rannaridh pursued an agreement with the remaining KR, if they removed Pol Pot. In 1997 Pol Pot's own lieutenants deposed him and Rannaridh's military chief, Nhek Bun Chhay, negotiated a political and military alliance between FUNCINPEC and the KR against the CPP. This was immediately followed by two days of intense fighting between military and police forces loyal to Rannaridh and Nhek Bun Chhay on the one side and to Hun Sen on the other. Rannaridh and other opponents of Hun Sen fled the country on the eve of the fighting. Meanwhile the KR imploded. Most of the remaining leaders, including Khieu Samphan, defected to the government, along with most of the movement's followers. Only a couple of hundred continued their insurgency. Pol Pot died in 1998, and the leader of the remaining KR remnants, Ta Mok, was captured in 1999. The PDK ceased to exist.

Hun Sen stressed that elections would go ahead in 1998 as scheduled, but initially insisted that the 'criminal' Rannaridh would not be allowed to return. Under considerable international pressure he relented, and Rannaridh was amnestied. Rannaridh returned to assume the leadership of FUNCINPEC for the election campaign.

In the elections of July 26, 1998, voters chose a 122-member National Assembly. This time the CPP came out in front of FUNCINPEC, winning 64 seats (with 41.4% of the vote), against 43 (with 31.7% of the vote) for FUNCINPEC. The third party voted in was the Sam Rainsy Party (SRP), which won 15 seats (with 14.3% of the vote). Rannaridh and Sam Rainsy challenged the legitimacy of these results, and called their followers out to demonstrate against Hun Sen and to call for new elections. Violent clashes between pro- and anti-Hun Sen demonstrators followed. This crisis was resolved in November 1998 by an agreement between the CPP and FUNCINPEC providing for a new coalition government headed by Hun Sen.

It also created an unelected upper house, the Senate. Chea Sim of the CPP became chair of the Senate and Rannaridh took his previous position as chair of the National Assembly. In this way, a prestigious but powerless position was created to accommodate the Prince, and more legislative posts were created for the party leaders to allocate to their followers. In March 1999 the National Assembly created a Senate of 61 members, of whom 57 were appointed on a proportional basis by the parties in the Assembly, two were elected by the lower house and two were chosen by the king. Following this, FUNCINPEC adopted a policy of four C's – coalition, co-operation and competition without confrontation.

Long-delayed elections for local government were held on Feb. 3, 2002. These were supposed to bring about a decentralization of power, with voters electing 1,621 communal governments in rural and urban districts across the country. In practice, little changed. Ministerial bureaucracies which centralized power in Phnom Penh, still largely controlled the new commune governments. The elections ended the monopoly of power enjoyed by the CPP at this level of government since the 1980s, but the party remained very solidly entrenched. The CPP won 68% of the available places, FUNCINPEC 20%, and the SRP won 12%. This gave effective control of the great majority of communes to the CPP, but it entered into power sharing arrangements with the other two major parties.

The pattern was broadly similar in the national elections of July 27, 2003. A report by the UN special envoy for human rights in Cambodia concluded that, while the elections were flawed by intimidation and lax law enforcement, they were generally conducted in a peaceful and order manner. They were better organized and more peaceful than either those of 1993 or 1998. There were 123 seats in the new National Assembly, of which the CPP won 73 (with 47.4% of the vote), FUNCINPEC 26 (with 20.8% of the vote) and the SRP 24 (with 21.9% of the vote). This involved a significant deviation from proportionality in favour of the CPP. This was mainly at the expense of the numerous minor parties who won some votes but gained no representation, rather than at the expense of the CPP's major-party rivals.

The main loser since 1998 has been FUNCINPEC. The party was still divided, and there was much dissatisfaction with Rannaridh's leadership. After the 2003 elections there were public calls from within royalist ranks for his resignation. But FUNCINPEC had no obvious alternative leader. While the CPP has undoubtedly benefited from FUNCINPEC's decline, the principal beneficiary has been Sam Rainsy. However Rainsy's achievements still fell short of his ambitions. Before the 2003 elections, he was predicting the SRP would win as much as 40% of the vote; in the event, it achieved only half that.

Once again, the elections were followed by a political crisis. When the National Election Commission announced the count, Rannaridh and Rainsy both claimed improprieties. After investigation, the NEC rejected all their complaints. This did not resolve the crisis. While the CPP had a majority in the new National Assembly, under the 1993 constitution still it needed a two-thirds majority to form a government. For this, Hun Sen needed either the support of either FUNCINPEC or the SRP.

Neither party was forthcoming with this. Rannaridh and Rainsy formed a 'Union of Democrats' which offered to join a coalition with the CPP provided Hun Sen stand down. The CPP insisted that, as he had led his party to a convincing electoral victory, Hun Sen had the right to head the new government. He continued to enjoy the support not only of his party, and a simple parliamentary majority. He also had the support of the government and the bureaucracy, including the military and the police. This time neither Rannaridh nor Rainsy made any substantial effort to mobilize their supporters for street confrontations with pro-Hun Sen forces. But they continued to demand his resignation as a precondition for forming a government.

In March 2004 Rannaridh and Hun Sen agreed in principle to form a coalition, but the details were not finalized until July. Hun Sen became Prime Minister and Rannaridh became Chair of the National Assembly. The agreement was achieved by expanding the number of ministerial posts, and thus the patronage powers of both leaders. The SRP was excluded from this agreement.

Hun Sen has served as Cambodia's Prime Minister since 1985. Once derided as a puppet of the Vietnamese, he has kept his party in government through the often-turbulent transformation of Cambodia from a beleaguered communist one-party state into a post-communist semi-democracy.

Cambodian People's Party (CPP)
Kanakpak Pracheachon Kampuchea
Address. 203 Norodom Blvd, Phnom Penh
Telephone. +855 23 215 801
Fax. +855 23 215 801
Email. cpp@thecpp.org
Website. www.thecpp.org
Leadership. Chea Sim (chairman); Hun Sen (vice-chairman); Heng Samrin (honorary chairman).
Membership. The CPP claimed to have four million members in 2003.

The CPP was launched in October 1991 as a non-communist successor to the Kampuchean People's Revolutionary Party (KPRP), the ruling party in Phnom Penh. The KPRP was descended from the Indo-Chinese Communist Party founded by Ho Chi Minh in 1930, which had divided into separate parties for Cambodia, Laos and Vietnam in 1951. Following the end of French rule, the KPRP conducted open, peaceful opposition to the Sihanouk government through the Pracheachon (People's Party), but its position in Cambodian politics was marginal.

In 1960 the PRPK was taken over by Paris-educated intellectuals led by Pol Pot (then known by his real name, Saloth Sar) and Ieng Sary. They renamed the party the Communist Party of Kampuchea (CPK), adopted an ultra-secretive leadership style and, influenced by Maoist ideas, attempted to launch a guerilla insurgency. Sihanouk called the insurgents the *Khmer Rouge* (KR). In 1970, following Sihanouk's overthrow, they joined with his followers in opposition to the Lon Nol regime. From 1973 Pol Pot began purging pro-Vietnamese elements from the CP. Following the fall of the Lon Nol regime in 1975, the Pol Pot faction took power in Phnom Penh. The obsession with secrecy remained strong, and not until September 1977 was it officially confirmed that the CPK, with Pol Pot at the helm, was the ruling party.

In 1978, Cambodian communists opposed to the Pol Pot leadership formed the Kampuchean National United Front for National Salvation (KNUFNS) to overthrow the DK regime. The KNUFNS came to power when the Vietnamese overthrew the Pol Pot regime in January 1979. A 'reorganization' congress in Phnom Penh renounced Pol Pot's CPK, resurrected the KPRP, and elected a new leadership with Pen Sovan as general secretary. Under the 1981 constitution, the KPRP was the sole legal party and the leading force of the Kampuchean United Front for National Construction and Defence (KUFNCD), the successor to the KNUFNS. In December 1981, following an internal power struggle, Heng Samrin replaced Pen Sovan as KPRP general secretary.

After the Paris Peace Agreement in October 1991, the KPRP changed its name to the Cambodian People's Party (CPP), and formally embraced multi-party democracy. The CPP renounced Marxism-Leninism, and reorganized itself as a catch-all mass party rather than a revolutionary vanguard party. It set out to encourage as many people as possible to become members. Chea Sim, President of the National Assembly, replaced Heng Samrin as party leader, and Hun Sen served as deputy leader. Heng Samrin became the party's honorary chair. In the 1993 election campaign the party took pride in its record in the 1980s, stressing that it had saved the nation from the Pol Pot regime, and claimed that in the future only it could protect the nation from the return of the KR.

The CPP took half the ministerial posts in the government formed after the 1993 elections. Observers detected factional tensions between Chea Sim and Hun Sen. Sar Kheng, a nephew of Chea Sim's, became Minister of the Interior, and was seen as a potential rival to Hun Sen. But the party maintained its unity and Hun Sen's dominance was consolidated in the post-election competition with Prince Rannaridh over the

spoils of office, and in the violent 1997 confrontation with the supporters of Rannaridh and Nhek Bun Chhay.

Since then the CPP oligarchy has remained highly stable. The appeals by Rannaridh and Rainsy after the 2003 election for a government without Hun Sen were presumably aimed at those in the CPP unhappy with his dominance of the party and government. Their failure has only confirmed that dominance.

Sam Rainsy Party (SRP)
Kanakpak Sam Rainsy
Address. 71 Sotheros Road, Phnom Penh
Telephone. +855 23 217452/+855 23 211 336
Fax. +855 23 217452
Email. samrainsy@samrainsyparty.org/
srphqpp@forum.org.kh
Website. www.samrainsyparty.org
Leadership. Sam Rainsy (chair); Kong Korm (vice-chair)
Membership. The SRP claimed to have 540,000 members in 2003.

The Sam Rainsy Party was launched in March 1998. Its Cambodian-born, French-educated founder is the son of a Cambodian politician exiled by Sihanouk in the 1950s. Sam Rainsy returned to Phnom Penh as a FUNCINPEC candidate after the 1991 peace agreement, and became Minister of Finance in the 1993 coalition government. He quickly attracted a popular following, and alienated members of the government, with outspoken denunciations of corruption and calls for strict transparency and accountability in government.

In 1994, Rannaridh dismissed Rainsy from his government post, expelled him from FUNCINPEC, and stripped him of his post in the National Assembly. Rainsy then formed the Khmer Nation Party (KNP), and continued to make strident denunciations of Cambodian politicians, especially Hun Sen and Rannaridh. In March 1997, a grenade attack on a KNP rally outside the National Assembly in March 1997 killed 16 people and injured over 200. Rainsy blamed Hun Sen for this atrocity.

On the eve of the violent confrontation of July 1997, Rainsy fled the country and called for international intervention against Hun Sen. In his absence, his deputy Kong Money took over the KNP presidency, and refused to stand down when Rainsy returned. Rainsy then formed the SRP to run in the 1998 elections.

Rainsy's campaign was vituperative, attacking the CPP for corruption and violence, and appealing to racial nationalism with attacks on the Vietnamese as *youns* ("savages"). The SRP won 15 seats in the elections. Rainsy joined Rannaridh in challenging the election results. When the US launched missile attacks against alleged *Al-Qaeda* targets in Chad and Afghanistan, he called for similar attacks against Hun Sen's home. He conceded defeat in November 1998, but refused to join in the Rannaridh-Hun Sen coalition government, declaring that he would have no part of this "mafia government."

Over the next few years, Rainsy continued to be a persistent critic of the government. But he moderated his tone, and admitted that his rhetoric had on occasion been "over the top". This new stance of persistent but restrained opposition has paid off. In the commune elections of 2002 and the national elections of 2003, the SRP won over a significant part of FUNCINPEC's constituency.

United National Front for an Independent, Neutral, Peaceful and Co-operative Cambodia
Front Uni National, pour un Cambodge Indépendant, Neutre, Pacifique et Coopérative (FUNCINPEC)
Address. 11 Motha Vithei Preah Monivong (93), PO Box 1444 Sankat Srah Chak, Khan Daun Penh, Phnom Penh
Telephone. +855 23 428 864/+855 23 426521

Fax. +855 23 218547
Email. funcipec@funcinpec.org
Website. www.funcinpec.org
Leadership. Prince Norodom Ranariddh (president); Prince Norodom Sirivuth (secretary-general); Nhek Bun Chhay (deputy secretary-general)
Membership. FUNCINPEC claimed to have two million members in 2003.

FUNCINPEC was launched in March 1982 by Prince Sihanouk as the political wing of the Sihanoukist National Army (ANS), then fighting against the Vietnamese and the PRK as part of the CGDK. It drew on Sihanouk's royal mystique and nostalgia for the relatively prosperous and peaceful Sangkum era. In 1990, the CGDK and the SoC agreed to form a Supreme National Council (SNC) representing Cambodia's four main parties at that time (the PRPK, FUNCINPEC, the PDK, and the BLDP). Prince Sihanouk agreed to become chair of the SNC. To ensure that he carried out this role in a neutral manner, Sihanouk resigned as FUNCINPEC leader. A FUNCINPEC special congress in February 1992 elected Prince Norodom Ranaridh as his successor.

FUNCINPEC came to Phnom Penh under the terms of the Paris Peace Agreement of October 1991, and campaigned throughout the country in the 1993 elections. Hun Sen sought to negotiate a pre-election coalition with FUNCINPEC, but Rannaridh refused. He hoped to win enough votes to govern in his own right. His campaign stressed two themes: anti-Vietnamese nationalism, and the claim that only royal leadership could reconcile the opposing sides in Cambodia's divided politics. This campaign was successful, and FUNCINPEC became the largest party in the new National Assembly. However FUNCINPEC lacked the numbers to form a government in its own right. As a result, the new government was a FUNCINPEC-CPP coalition, with a few posts for minor parties.

Ranariddh became First Prime Minister in October 1993, with Hun Sen as Second Prime Minister. From late 1994 to mid-1997, the relationship between Rannaridh and Hun Sen steadily deteriorated and FUNCINPEC became increasingly divided. When Rannaridh expelled Sam Rainsy, the FUNCINPEC Foreign Minister, Prince Sirivuth, resigned in solidarity. Accused of plotting the assassination of Hun Sen, he went into exile in 1995.

At a FUNCINPEC Congress in March 1996, Rannaridh sought to strengthen his position by demanding that Hun Sen give more positions to his supporters, and threatened to pull FUNCINPEC out of the government if he refused. Hun Sen did refuse, and challenged Rannaridh to quit. The Prince was unwilling to do so. FUNCINPEC splintered further, into as many as eight separate parties. These included the National Unity Party led by Toan Chhay (governor of Siem Reap), the New Society Party led by Loy Sim Chheang, the Khmer Citizen Party led by Nguon Souer and the Khmer Unity Party led by Khieu Rada.

In the wake of this debacle, Rannaridh turned increasingly to the sections of FUNCINPEC most opposed to the CPP, the military commanders who had served on the Thai border in the 1980s. Under their influence, he moved towards recreating a military alliance with the KR and towards a showdown with Hun Sen. Tensions escalated rapidly, coming to a head in July 1997. Rannaridh fled into exile on the eve of the confrontation, and Hun Sen's supporters quickly defeated the FUNCINPEC hard-liners. In the wake of these events, the remaining FUNCINPEC members of the National Assembly elected Ung Huot as their leader.

The RGC allowed Ranariddh back into Cambodia after being charged with smuggling and co-operating with an illegal organization (the KR), being found guilty, and being amnestied by King Sihanouk. Rannaridh reassumed the leadership of FUNCINPEC. He brought its warring factions

back together, and led the party to second place in the 1998 elections. In his campaign he denounced the Vietnamese, and accused the CPP of being their puppet. Ung Huot, now an outcast within FUNCINPEC, formed his own party (*Reastr Niyum*) but was not re-elected to the National Assembly.

In November 1998 Rannaridh agreed to a new FUNCINPEC-CPP coalition government. Hun Sen agreed to an amnesty for those who engaged in rebellion against the RGC since 1993, including Prince Sirivuth and Nhek Bun Chhay. Rannaridh made Sirivuth FUNCINPEC's general-secretary, and Nhek Bun Chhay was elected to the National Assembly as a FUNCINPEC candidate in 2003.

The coalition government formed in 1998 continued to work reasonably smoothly through to the 2003 elections. FUNCINPEC ministers co-operated with their CPP counterparts under Hun Sen's leadership. The party remained divided into groups strongly opposed to the CPP and those who favoured working with it, while Rannaridh tried to keep the party unified with his 4 C's policy. But Rannaridh's government post was largely symbolic, and his power very limited. Frustrated supporters, particularly those most opposed to the CPP, accused him of being a weak leader. In the elections of 2003, many of them switched their support to Sam Rainsy, and FUNCINPEC fell to third place among Cambodia's political parties.

Other Parties

The 2003 elections were contested by a total of 23 parties. None beyond the three already discussed are of great significance in contemporary Cambodian politics. However the following are worth mention for the historical role of their leaders.

Buddhist Liberal Democratic Party (BLDP) *(Kanakpak Preacheathippatai Serei Preah Puthasasna)*. The BLDP was founded by Son Sann in 1992 as the successor to the Khmer People's National Liberation Front (KPNLF). Son Sann, who served as an administrator under the French and Sihanouk regimes (and briefly held the office of Prime Minister under Sihanouk) launched the KPNLF in 1979 as a non-communist resistance force, and it was the principal heir of Lon Nol's republic. In the 1980s it played an important role on the Thai border, and was seen by some observers as the strongest force for liberal democracy in Cambodian politics.

However in the 1993 election Son Sann's rhetoric emphasized anti-Vietnamese racist nationalism. The BLDP won few seats, but was still included in the new coalition government. The party soon split into pro- and anti-CPP factions, with Son Sann leading the latter group. In July 1995, the BLDP replaced him as leader with Ieng Mouli. Son Sann quit the BLDP and formed the Grandfather Son Sann Party (*Kanakpak Ta Son Sann*), hoping to benefit from traditional respect for age and venerability in Cambodian society. Both parties failed to win a seat in the National Assembly in the 1998 elections, and were dissolved. Son Sann died in December 2000 at the age of 89.

Norodom Chakkrapong Cambodian Soul Party *(Norodom Chakkrapong Proleung Khmer)*. This party was formed to contest the 2003 national elections. Prince Norodom Chakkrapong was the military commander of the Sihanoukist National Army (ANS) on the Thai border in the 1980s. He was deeply upset when he was passed over in favour of Prince Rannaridh for the political leadership of FUNCINPEC in 1992. His first response was to attempt to join the KR; when they refused to accept him, he defected to the Phnom Penh government. The CPP leaders welcomed him into their party and appointed him as a Vice-Premier in the government.

After the 1993 elections, realizing the animosity between Rannaridh and Chakkrapong, the CPP dropped Chakkrapong from its list of candidates for the National Assembly. He then launched a secessionist movement in Cambodia's eastern provinces (in Sihanouk's name). This collapsed when Hun Sen toured the region, a CPP stronghold, appealing to provincial leaders not to support it. Over the next year, Chakkrapong repeatedly denounced the Rannaridh-Hun Sen coalition government for its alleged incompetence. After being involved in an unsuccessful military coup he went into exile in 1994.

Chakkrapong returned to Phnom Penh under the amnesty following the 1998 elections. Disenchanted with FUNCINPEC under Rannaridh, he founded his own party to promote "true Sihanoukism." The party won only 1.1 % of the vote.
Leadership. Prince Norodom Chakkrapong (president), General Toan Chay (vice president), Lim Sopheap (vice president), Peou Sithik (general secretary)
Address. 61 Street 294, Sangkath Boeung Keng Kang 1, Khann Chamkar Mon, Phnom Penh
Telephone. +855 23 212597
Fax.+855 23 212597
Email. ncpp@bigpond.com.kh
Website. www.ncppk.org

Cameroon

Capital: Yaoundé
Population: 15,500,000 (2002E)

French-administered (East) Cameroon achieved independence in 1960 and the following year was united with the southern part of British-administered (West) Cameroon, both areas having been under German colonial rule until World War I. A one-party state established in 1966 under the National Cameroon Union, renamed the Cameroon People's Democratic Movement (CPDM) in 1985, gave way to a multi-party system in 1990.

Under its 1972 constitution as amended, the Republic of Cameroon has an executive President who is elected for a seven-year term (once renewable) by universal suffrage of those aged 20 and over, requiring only a relative majority in a single voting round. The President is head of state and government, appointing the Prime Minister and other members of the government. There is a National Assembly (Assemblée Nationale) of 180 members directly elected by proportional representation for a five-year term. Legislation to establish a second parliamentary chamber, the Senate (Sénat), was enacted in 1996 without specifying any timetable for the implementation of bicameralism (which was still awaited in 2003). Under laws enacted in 1990-91, political parties may not be based on regional or tribal support and may not form coalitions for electoral purposes. Registered parties are eligible for financial support from state funds for their electoral campaigns.

National Assembly elections held between June and September 2002 resulted as follows: CPDM 149 seats, Social Democratic Front (SDF) 22, Democratic Union of Cameroon (UDC) 5, Union of the Peoples of Cameroon (UPC) 3, National Union for Democracy and Progress (UNDP) 1. The elections were denounced as flawed by many opposition politicians and church leaders. A presidential election held in October 1997, was won by Paul Biya of the CPDM, this being his fourth consecutive victory, but the first since the introduction of a constitutional amendment limiting future Presidents to a maximum of two terms. The 1997 presidential election was also contested by candidates from six minor parties, who received in aggregate 7.4% of the votes cast (the election having been boycotted by the main opposition parties).

Cameroon People's Democratic Movement (CPDM)
Rassemblement Démocratique du Peuple Camerounais (RDPC)
Address. BP 867, Yaoundé
Telephone. (237) 23–27–40
Website. www.rdpcpdm.cm
Leadership. Paul Biya (president); Joseph Charles Doumba (secretary-general)
The CPDM is the successor, created in March 1985, to the Cameroon National Union (UNC), which was established as the sole ruling party in 1966 as a merger of the francophone Cameroon Union (UC) and five other parties, including three of anglophone identity. The UC had taken Cameroon to independence in 1960 under the leadership of Ahmadou Ahidjo (a Muslim), whose post-1966 one-party UNC government claimed credit for economic advances. When Ahidjo unexpectedly resigned in November 1982, he was succeeded as President and party leader by Paul Biya (a Christian), who had held the premiership since 1975. After surviving coup attempts in 1983 and 1984, Biya was confirmed in office in an April 1988 one-party presidential election (officially with 100% of the vote). Meanwhile, the UNC had renamed itself the CPDM, against strong internal opposition from the party's anglophone wing.

From mid-1990 the CPDM government accepted opposition demands for a transition to multi-party democracy, although Biya refused to convene a sovereign national conference on political change. In Assembly elections in March 1992 the CPDM maintained its dominance, although its 88-seat tally was short of an overall majority. The CPDM benefited from a boycott by some opposition parties and from its following in the francophone Christian south, but gained little support in the anglophone west or the Muslim north. In the October 1992 presidential election, Biya as CPDM candidate won a narrow victory over the nominee of the Social Democratic Front, which made vigorous allegations of electoral fraud. In November 1992 the post-April coalition government of the CPDM and the small Movement for the Defence of the Republic was expanded to include the other two parties represented in the Assembly. In 1993–94 the government came under persistent pressure from the political opposition and also faced growing secessionist tendencies in anglophone areas. It was reported in September 1994 that an assassination plot against President Biya had been foiled the previous May.

A presidential election held in October 1997 (and boycotted by the principal opposition parties) resulted in the re-election of Biya with 92.6% of the recorded vote for a seven-year term. In legislative elections held in June 2002 (and completed in September 2002) the CPDM won 149 of 180 seats, up from 116 seats in the previous election held in 1997. The CPDM held virtually all the posts in the Cabinet appointed in August 2002 (the exceptions being appointees from the National Union for Democracy and Progress and the Union of the Peoples of Cameroon).

Democratic Union of Cameroon
Union Démocratique du Cameroun (UDC)
Address. BP 1638, Yaoundé
Leadership. Adamou Ndam Njoya (president)
The UDC achieved legal status in April 1991, its president having been a senior minister under the pre-1982 Ahidjo regime. Together with the Social Democratic Front (SDF), it headed the boycott of the March 1992 Assembly elections by

some opposition parties on the grounds that the electoral arrangements gave an unfair advantage to the ruling Cameroon People's Democratic Movement. It changed tack for the October 1992 presidential poll, in which Ndam Njoya came in fourth place with 3.6% of the votes cast. Thereafter strains developed between the UDC and the SDF: in January 1993 the UDC vice-president, Benjamin Menga, was fatally injured in an attack in which the SDF was implicated. The UDC won 5 seats in the May 1997 legislative elections. It boycotted the October 1997 presidential election in protest at the Government's failure to establish an independent electoral commission. The party retained its five seats in the legislature in elections held between July and September 2002. All of the seats were in Noun, the home district of Ndam Njoya.

National Union for Democracy and Progress
Union Nationale pour la Démocratie et le Progrès
(UNDP)

Address. BP 656, Douala

Leadership. Maigari Bello Bouba (chairman)

The UNDP was founded in 1991 mainly by supporters of ex-President Ahidjo and was based in the Muslim community (forming 22% of the population). In early 1992 its first leader, Samuel Eboua, was displaced by Bello Bouba, who had been Prime Minister in 1982–83 following Ahidjo's resignation but had later been implicated in an alleged plot to restore Ahidjo. Having initially decided to boycott the March 1992 Assembly elections, the UNDP changed its mind and proceeded to win 68 of the 180 seats at issue, only 20 seats behind the ruling Cameroon People's Democratic Movement (CPDM). In the October 1992 presidential election the UNDP leader came in third place with 19.2% of the vote and afterwards joined the leader of the Social Democratic Front in challenging the validity of the official results. Nevertheless, in November 1992 the UNDP accepted participation in a coalition government of all four Assembly parties under the leadership of the CPDM.

The basic impasse persisted in subsequent years. In November 1994 UNDP deputies launched a boycott of the Assembly in protest against the arrest of some 30 party activists four months earlier. The party called off the boycott the following month (without securing the release of its members), but a presidential initiative to achieve reconciliation quickly collapsed when the UNDP and other parties refused to participate in a "constitutional consultative committee". The UNDP won 13 seats in the May 1997 Assembly elections, but boycotted the October 1997 presidential election in protest at the Government's failure to establish an independent electoral commission. Three UNDP members (including party chairman Bello Bouba) were appointed to Cabinet positions in December 1997. The party managed to win only one seat in legislative elections held between June and September 2002. Bello Bouba retained his post (Minister of State for Trade and Industrial Development) in the new Cabinet appointed in August 2002.

Social Democratic Front (SDF)

Address. PO Box 490, Bamenda

Telephone. (237) 36–39–49

Fax. (237) 36–29–91

Website. www.sdfparty.org

Leadership. John Fru Ndi (chairman); Tazoacha Asonganyi (secretary-general)

Founded in early 1990, the SDF gained legal recognition in March 1991 after a year in which its anti-government rallies had frequently been subject to official repression. Based in the English-speaking north and west, the SDF opted to boycott the May 1992 Assembly elections but changed its line for the October 1992 presidential contest. Standing as the SDF candidate, party chairman John Fru Ndi attracted support from anglophone and francophone voters, winning 36% of the popular vote and thus coming a close second to incumbent Paul Biya of the Cameroon People's Democratic Movement (CPDM). Supported by many foreign observers, the SDF claimed that the presidential poll had been fraudulent, but its petition was rejected by the Supreme Court. In November 1992 the SDF refused to join a new CPDM-led coalition government, calling instead for the convening of an all-party national conference on the country's political future. It then initiated the formation of a 10-party opposition alliance called the Union for Change (*Union pour le Change*), with Fru Ndi as its leader, which launched a campaign of popular protests against the Biya government. The latter responded in March 1993 by banning demonstrations involving "a risk of violence" and by arresting over 100 opposition activists.

In June 1993 Fru Ndi refused to participate in a government-proposed "grand national debate" on constitutional reform, the idea of which generated some dissension within the SDF between moderates and radicals. An SDF congress in August 1993 endorsed the moderates' call for acceptance of the 1992 election results and participation in constitutional talks; but renewed harassment of Fru Ndi (who briefly took refuge in the Netherlands embassy in November 1993) reopened the government-opposition divide. In May 1994 Siga Asanga was suspended as SDF secretary-general for making unauthorized contact with the government on possible SDF participation in a national unity coalition. He subsequently left the party to form the Social Democratic Movement. In July 1994 the SDF reacted to a major Cabinet reshuffle by repeating its call for a sovereign national conference and for an interim government involving "all the nation's active political forces".

The SDF participated in the May 1997 Assembly elections, winning 43 seats, but boycotted the October 1997 presidential election in protest against the government's failure to set up an independent electoral commission. In February 1998 (after the reported failure of talks with the CPDM on possible SDF participation in a coalition government) the SDF announced its intention to form a "common opposition front" with the Democratic Union of Cameroon. A party congress in April 1999 re-elected Fru Ndi as party chairman (in a contested election) and voted not to enter into dialogue with the government until an independent electoral commission was established in Cameroon. The party contested legislative elections held between June and September 2002, but managed to win only 22 seats, compared to 43 seats in the previous election. Despite the losses the party remained in firm control of the English-speaking North West Province, where 19 of its candidates won seats. In August 2002 dissident members of the party, led by former deputy chairman Maidadi Saidou Yaha, formed a new party, the Alliance of Progressive Forces. The dissidents had resigned from the SDF citing Fru Ndi's "autocratic management" of the party.

The SDF is a member of the Socialist International.

Union of the Peoples of Cameroon
Union des Populations du Cameroun (UPC)

Addresses. Ntumazah faction: BP 8647, Douala. Kodock faction: c/o Assemblée Nationale, Yaoundé.

Leadership. Ndeh Ntumazah & Augustin Frederic Kodock (leaders of rival factions)

The UPC was founded in the late 1940s as a Marxist-Leninist party opposed to French rule, under which it was banned in 1955. Relegalized at independence in 1960, it won 22 seats in the 1961 Assembly elections but became split into pro-Soviet and Maoist factions, both of which went underground in armed opposition to the one-party regime created in 1966. By 1970 the UPC insurgency had been largely suppressed, party leader Ernest Ouandié being executed in January 1971 after being convicted of "attempted revolution". Led by Ngouo Woungly-Massaga, the UPC survived in exile (based in Paris) and regained legal status in February 1991 as a social democratic formation. Meanwhile, Woungly-Massaga had left the UPC to form the People's Solidarity Party, after failing to persuade his colleagues to join an anti-Biya united front and being accused by them of abuse of office. The leadership passed to Ndeh Ntumazah, a UPC founder, who led half the party into a boycott of the March 1992 Assembly elections, while the other half followed Augustin Frederic Kodock (UPC secretary-general) in putting up candidates, 18 of whom were elected. The split in the party deepened when Kodock alienated many of his colleagues by accepting a ministerial post in the coalition government formed in November 1992.

In 1996 Kodock was dismissed from party office. He subsequently formed a rival UPC faction with himself as leader, this being often referred to as the UPC(K) to distinguish it from the UPC(N) of Ntumazah (although both factions claimed to be entitled to unqualified use of the original party name). A member of the UPC(K) faction won one seat in the May 1997 legislative elections. A UPC candidate, Henri Hogbe Nlend, won 2.5% of the vote in the October 1997 presidential election and subsequently accepted a ministerial post in December 1997. The UPC(K) contested Assembly elections held between June and September 2002 and won three seats. The faction joined the government formed by Biya's ruling Cameroon People's Democratic Movement (CPDM) in August 2002: Kodock was appointed as Minister of State for Agriculture.

Other Parties

Dozens of other parties have been legalized in Cameroon since 1991. The listing below focuses on those for which there is evidence of recent political activity.

Action for Meritocracy and Equal Opportunity Party (AMEC), whose leader received less than 1% of the vote in the 1997 presidential election.
Leadership. Joachim Tabi Owono

Alliance of Progressive Forces (AFP), formed in mid-2002 by dissident members of the opposition Social Democratic Front (SDF) who decided to form their own party citing the "autocratic management" of SDF leader John Fru Ndi. The founding members of the party included Maidadi Saidou Yaya, the former deputy chairman of the SDF, Evariste Okusi Foto, Samuel Swinko, and Yves Epata.

Cameroon Anglophone Movement (CAM), originally a pro-federalist movement, has more recently supported separatist demands for the establishment of an independent republic in predominantly anglophone provinces of Cameroon.
Leadership. Vishe Fai (secretary-general)

Democratic Progressive Party of Cameroon (*Parti Démocratique et Progressif du Cameroun*, PDPC), an observer member of the Christian Democrat International.
Address. BP 6589, Yaoundé
Leadership. François Mama Etogo

Democratic Rally of People without Frontiers (*Rassemblement Démocratique du Peuple sans Frontières*, RDPF), founded in 1997. Its candidate received less than 1% of the vote in the 1997 presidential election.
Leadership. Antoine Demannu

Integral Democracy of Cameroon (*Démocratie Intégrale du Cameroun*, DIC), legalized in February 1991. Its leader received less than 1% of the vote in the 1997 presidential election.
Address. BP 8647, Douala
Leadership. Gustave Essaka

Liberal Democratic Alliance (LDA), anglophone grouping launched in 1993 to campaign for speedier constitutional reform.
Leadership. Henri Fossung

People's Solidarity Party (*Parti de la Solidarité du Peuple*, PSP), founded by Ngouo Woungly-Massaga in 1991 following his break with the Union of the Peoples of Cameroon, presented 25 candidates in March 1992 elections, without success.

Popular Development Party (*Parti Populaire pour le Développement*, PPD), founded in 1997. Its candidate received 1.2% of the vote in the 1997 presidential election.
Leadership. Albert Dzongang

Progressive Movement (*Mouvement Progressif*, MP), legalized in August 1991, in January 1994 joined opposition front with Social Democratic Party of Cameroon, Social Movement for New Democracy and other groups.
Address. BP 2500, Douala
Leadership. Jean-Jacques Ekindi

Social Democratic Movement (SDM), founded in 1995 by a former secretary-general of the Social Democratic Front following a split in that party.
Leadership. Siga Asanga

Social Democratic Party of Cameroon (*Parti Social-Démocrate du Cameroun*, PSDC), legalized in December 1991, in January 1994 joined opposition front with Progressive Movement, Social Movement for New Democracy and other groups.
Leadership. Jean-Michel Tekam

Social Movement for New Democracy (*Mouvement Social pour la Nouvelle Démocratie*, MSND), founded in 1991 by a former Bar Association president who was active in the early pro-democracy movement and served a prison term in 1990; in January 1994 joined opposition front with Progressive Movement, Social Democratic Party of Cameroon and other groups.
Address. BP 1641, Douala
Leadership. Yondo Mandengue Black

Social Programme for Liberty and Democracy (*Programme Sociale pour la Liberté et la Démocratie*, PSLD), an opposition party whose leader was arrested in February 1995.
Leadership. Massok Mboua

Southern Cameroons National Council (SCNC), a separatist movement established in 1995 to campaign for the establishment of an independent republic in anglophone Cameroon. The SCNC proclaimed the establishment of a "Federal Republic of Southern Cameroon" in December 1999, and in April 2000 named a judge, Frederick Ebong Alobwede, as the president of the self-styled republic.
Leadership. Sam Ekontang Elad (chairman)

Union of Democratic Forces of Cameroon (*Union des Forces Démocratiques du Cameroun*, UFDC), legalized in March 1991 but boycotted March 1992 Assembly elections

in protest against electoral law banning party alliances; the party's leader was detained in November 1992 for alleged anti-government activities.

Address. BP 7190, Yaoundé

Leadership. Victorin Hameni Bialeu

Union of the Forces of Progress (UFP) was formed in June 2003 by the merger of four opposition parties, the Movement for the Liberalization and the Development of Cameroon (MLDC), the Alliance of the Patriotic Forces (AFP), the Movement for the Defence of Republic (MDR) and the Movement for Democracy and Progress (MDP). Marcel Yondo, hitherto national president of the MLDC, was elected as secretary-general of the UFP.

Canada

Capital: Ottawa
Population: 31,082,000 (2001E)

The Dominion of Canada is a member of the Commonwealth with the British sovereign as head of state represented by a Governor-General. The Governor-General formally appoints the Prime Minister (the head of government) and, on the latter's recommendation, the members of the Cabinet. The federal legislature (Parliament) comprises a Senate of 105 members and a House of Commons of 308 members. The House of Commons is elected (on the Westminster model) for a period of up to five years by universal adult suffrage under the first past the post system in single-member constituencies (ridings). Appointment of Senators is controlled by the Prime Minister and follows party lines. Canada comprises 10 provinces and (since the creation of the territory of Nunavut, with 25,000 mainly Inuit inhabitants, in April 1999) three territories. There is considerable decentralization of authority to the provincial governments, with the territories having lesser powers.

Political parties exist at both federal and provincial levels and one provincial party, the Quebec separatist *Parti Québécois* (PQ), has had particular significance in the development of Canadian politics. Elections Canada is the agency responsible for the registration of parties and conduct of elections at federal level. To achieve registration at federal level a party must endorse a candidate in at least 50 electoral districts in a general election. There is no limit on the amount that may be contributed to a candidate or political party, although donations from foreign sources are prohibited. However, the names of persons or organizations making contributions above $200 to a party or candidate must be disclosed. In addition, there are limits on spending by parties and candidates, varying by riding, and detailed restrictions on campaign activities. There are also relatively low ceilings on "third-party" advertising by individuals or organizations in support of candidates, in part to prevent circumvention of the limits on party spending. Candidates elected or receiving at least 15% of the vote in their riding, and parties receiving at least 2% of the votes cast nationally or 5% of the votes in the ridings where they present candidates, are entitled to reimbursement of (respectively) 50% and 22.5% of election expenses. Legislation and agencies regulating the registration of political parties and their finances also exist at provincial level.

In the most recent federal general election, held on June 28, 2004, the centrist Liberal Party of Canada (LPC), in office since 1993, retained power, albeit in the form of a minority instead of a majority government, winning 135 of the 308 seats in the House of Commons and 36.7% of the popular vote. The Conservative Party of Canada, a merger between the Canadian Alliance Party and the Progressive Conservative Party of Canada, won 99 seats with 29.6% of the vote, the separatist *Bloc Québécois* (BQ), with candidates only in Quebec, won 54 (12.4%), and the democratic socialist New Democratic Party (NDP) 19 (15.7%). One independent, a former Canadian Alliance Member of Parliament, was elected in British Columbia. Several other registered parties, with the Green Party of Canada leading the way, took a fraction of 5.5% of the vote and won no seats.

The results underscored the deep divisions between the different regions of Canada, showing fault-lines between east and west and between Quebec and the rest of the country. The Conservative Party, campaigning on a programme of opposition to "big government" in Ottawa, won 68 of the 92 available seats in the four western provinces of Manitoba, Saskatchewan, Alberta and British Columbia. It also made inroads in the province of Ontario but continuing Liberal strength in that province plus provinces to the east ensured its minority victory. In mainly French-speaking Quebec (the second most populous province) the separatist BQ gained votes and seats at the expense of the Liberals while the other parties were shut out. Although the Quebec electorate narrowly rejected independence in a referendum in October 1995 this remains a goal of the BQ and the *Parti Québécois* (PQ). However, the cause of separatism received a blow on April 14, 2003, when the PQ were defeated by the federalist and provincial version of the Liberal Party under the leadership of the former leader of the federal Progressive Conservatives, Jean Charest.

At provincial level the relative strength of the various parties does not overlap in a clear way with electoral performance at federal level. Although a Liberal Party controls the provincial government of British Columbia, it represents an amalgamation of right-wing interests and shares only a name with the federal party which came a distant second to the Conservative Party in the June 2004 federal election in British Columbia. Although the right-wing Conservative Party won 13 of the 14 seats in Saskatchewan in the June 2004 federal elections, the left-of-centre NDP, which was shut out in the province in the federal election for the first time since the 1960s, controls the provincial government.

Seats in the provincial legislatures were distributed as follows as a result of the most recent elections (the months of which are shown in parentheses): *Alberta* (March 2001) – PCP 74, LPC 7, NDP 2; *British Columbia* (May 2001) – LPC 77, NDP 2; *Manitoba* (June 2003) – NDP 35, PCP 20, LPC 2; *New Brunswick* (June 2003) – PCP 28, LPC 26, NDP 1; *Newfoundland and Labrador* (October 2003) – LPC 34, PCP 12, NDP 2; *Nova Scotia* (August 2003) – PCP 25, NDP 15, LPC 12; *Ontario* (October 2003) – LPC 72, PCP 24, NDP 7; *Prince Edward Island* (September 2003) – PCP 23, LPC 4; *Quebec* (April 2003) – LPC 76, PQ 45, *Action démocratique du Québec* (ADQ) 4; *Saskatchewan* (November 2003) – NDP 30, Saskatchewan Party (SP) 28.

Under a consensus-style system elections in the territories of *Nunavut* and the *Northwest Territories* in February 2004 and December 2003 respectively resulted in all of the seats being won by independents.

The new parlamentarians then selected the premier and cabinet by secret ballot. Elections to the *Yukon* legislature in November 2002 resulted in the Yukon Party winning 12 seats, the NDP 5 seats, and the LPC one.

Canada evidences the decline in voter participation seen in other developed countries. Turnout was 60.5% in the 2004 general election, compared with 61.2% in 2000, 67.0% in 1997, 69.6% in 1993 and 75.3% in 1988.

Bloc Québécois (BQ)
(Quebec Bloc)

Address. 3750 Crémazie Blvd. East, Suite 307, Montreal, Quebec, H2A 1B6
Telephone. (1–514) 526–3000
Fax. (1–514) 526–2868
Email. info@bloc.org
Website. www.blocquequebecois.org
Leadership. Gilles Duceppe (leader)

The BQ was founded under the leadership of Lucien Bouchard in 1991 as the federal voice of Quebec separatism, committed to the achievement of sovereignty for the predominantly French-speaking province. It won 54 of the 295 seats in the House of Commons in the federal elections of October 1993, becoming the second largest party and the official opposition despite having seats in only one province. In support of the provincial *Parti Québécois* (PQ), Bouchard campaigned intensively in the run-up to the October 1995 referendum on independence, which was lost only by the narrowest of margins. In the wake of the referendum, Bouchard became Premier of Quebec in January 1996, having been elected unopposed as leader of the PQ. In the June 1997 federal elections the BQ again came first in Quebec, winning 44 seats, although it lost its position as the official opposition in Ottawa to the Reform Party.

In the November 2000 federal election the BQ won fewer votes in Quebec than the Liberals, but emerged with 38 seats to the Liberals' 36, and came third nationally. During the campaign, BQ leader Gilles Duceppe emphasized the central importance of achieving sovereignty, although in September 2000 Bouchard had said "we sense a great fatigue on this issue". The BQ considers itself to be "Quebec's representative to Canada" and on the international stage and says that it will cease to exist when Quebec has achieved its independence. It won 54 seats in the June 2004 federal election, again coming third nationally.

Canadian Reform Conservative Alliance Party

Ceased to exist as of December 2003.

Registered as the Canadian Reform Conservative Alliance, the Canadian Alliance was formed in March 2000 as the outcome of a two-year process aimed at unifying the right against the ruling Liberal Party of Canada (LPC) at federal level. The Alliance failed to unseat the LPC in the November 2000 federal election, but consolidated its status as the main opposition party.

The roots of the Alliance lay in the mix of western populist neo-conservative politics and hostility to the federal government, seen as dominated by the eastern provinces of Ontario and Quebec, that had led to the formation in 1987 of the Reform Party (RP) under the leadership of Preston Manning. The RP had itself been in a populist tradition exemplified by Alberta's Social Credit Party, for which Preston Manning's father, Ernest Manning, had been premier of Alberta from 1943-68. The RP opposed bilingualism and multiculturalism, also advocating fiscal reform, a reduction in immigration and decreased powers for the federal government. In the 1993 federal general election it won 18% of the vote (predominantly in western Canada), giving it 52 seats in the House of Commons. It thus became the main voice of the right, eclipsing the party of traditional moderate conservatism, the Progressive Conservative Party (PCP).

In the 1997 general election the RP retained its position as the principal opposition party, but won all of its 60 seats in just four western provinces (Manitoba, Saskatchewan, Alberta and British Columbia). In that contest the RP and the PCP in aggregate polled a similar proportion of the total vote to the Liberals, but under the first-past-the-post system won only half as many seats. This stimulated a drive, led by Manning, to create a unified conservative movement that could achieve success on a fully national basis, initially known as the "United Alternative". In March 2000 the RP voted to fold the party into what had become known as the Canadian Alliance, but in July 2000 Alberta Treasurer Stockwell Day defeated Manning in a membership ballot for leadership of the Alliance.

The Alliance ran in the November 2000 federal election on a platform that called for the downsizing of federal government, a single rate of taxation and mandatory balanced budgets. Other Alliance themes included the need for reform of the appointed, patronage-based Senate, extension of direct democracy through means such as initiative and recall and referenda, and an end to affirmative action and discriminatory quotas and other policies seen as unfairly assisting minorities. However, the PCP declined to ally itself with the Alliance, which won only six seats more than had the RP in 1997. While it won by a wide margin in Alberta, Saskatchewan and British Columbia, it failed to make any breakthrough in the eastern provinces. It took only two seats (of 103) in Ontario (although with 23.6% of the vote) and none in the Atlantic provinces, where the Progressive Conservatives remained the principal opposition to the Liberals.

In May 2001 a number of Alliance members in the Commons, dissatisfied with Day's leadership, announced that they would caucus separately, while remaining in the party. Day criticized those in the party who, he said, wished it to be a "regional splinter". On July 17, 2001, he announced that in view of the "deep divisions" that had developed in the Alliance he had called on the party's national council to initiate a leadership election. In that subsequent election Day was easily defeated by Stephen Harper, a former party MP. Harper subsequently was elected to the House of Commons in a Calgary area seat.

In October 2003 the leader of the Alliance Party reached an agreement with the leader of the Progressive Conservative Party, pending approval by the members of the respective parties, to merge their two parties into a new entity to be called the Conservative Party of Canada. This vote occurred in December 2003 and with the approval of the members of the two parties, the old parties ceased to exist.

Conservative Party of Canada

Address. 1720-130 Albert Street, Ottawa, Ontario, K1P 5G4
Telephone. (613) 755–2000
Fax. (613) 755–2001
Website. www.conservative.ca
Leadership. Stephen Harper (leader); Don Plett (interim president)

The Conservative Party of Canada was created in December 2003 when members of the Progressive Conservative Party and the Canadian Reform Conservative Alliance Party (see also separate entries) voted to merge their respective parties to create a new political entity. In many respects this represented a takeover of the old Conservative Party by the Alliance in an effort to end the splitting of the right-wing vote that had aided the Liberals in winning three straight federal elections. Some traditional Progressive Conservatives, often nicknamed "Red Tories," including former party leader

Joe Clark, refused to join the new party. The new political entity held a leadership race in early 2004 and Stephen Harper, the last leader of the Alliance Party, won the race to become the new party's first leader. In the June 2004 election he led the party to a solid second place finish although some were disappointed with the result as during the campaign some polls suggested the possibility of the Conservatives winning more seats than the Liberals.

Liberal Party of Canada (LPC)

Address. 81 Metcalfe Street, Suite 400, Ottawa, Ontario, K1P 6M8

Telephone. (1–613) 237–0740

Fax. (1–613) 235–7208

Website. www.liberal.ca

Leadership. Paul Martin (leader); Mike Eizenga (president); Steven MacKinnon (national director)

Founded in 1867, the Liberal Party was the ruling party in Canada for the greater part of the 20th century. It has had only eight leaders since 1887, reflecting the party's long-term stability. It is preeminently the party of national unity, resisting the forces of regional separatism threatening to tear Canada apart, which it counters with an emphasis on multiculturalism and respect for minorities. In respect of the problem of Quebec it has sought to steer a difficult course aimed at heading off separatist sentiment by accommodating many of the demands of the francophone majority in Quebec while attempting not to alienate the anglophone majority in the rest of Canada, many of whom believe Quebec enjoys preferential treatment.The Liberal Party favours free markets tempered by a social welfare system closer to Western European models than that of the USA.

In recent decades, the Liberals were returned to office under the leadership of Pierre Trudeau at federal general elections in 1968, 1972, 1974, and again in 1980, following a brief minority Progressive Conservative Party (PCP) administration. However, in 1984, in the face of increasing unpopularity, Trudeau resigned and the party was decisively beaten at the polls by the PCP, which then retained power until 1993. In the October 1993 election the Liberals returned to office, winning 177 seats under Jean Chrétien (party leader since 1990), who went on to lead the successful campaign by pro-federalists against separatism in the October 1995 Quebec referendum.

The Chrétien government was re-elected in June 1997 (when it won 155 seats with 38.5% of the vote) and again in November 2000 (when it won 172 seats and 40.8% of the vote). However, although the Liberals (unlike any other party) won seats and took at least 20% of the vote in every province in the 2000 election, they were heavily defeated by the right-wing Canadian Alliance in the western provinces of British Columbia, Alberta and Saskatchewan. Of the Liberals' successful candidates, 100 were elected in the single province of Ontario, where the Liberals won all but three of the seats. The Liberals had claimed during the campaign that the Canadian Alliance programme would lead to the disintegration of a unified country, survival of the fittest, tax cuts for the rich and the introduction of two-tier health care. The Liberals positioned themselves as champions of federalism and moderation, encouraging free markets while preserving Canada's traditional welfare state.

Despite the Liberals' victory at federal level in three successive elections, prior to April 2003, when the party won the Quebec provincial election, they held power in only two provinces, British Columbia and Newfoundland and Labrador. In addition, despite Chrétien's electoral success he faced pressure from within the party to retire. Heeding that pressure, he announced in August 2002 that he would retire in February 2004. A leadership convention was called for the fall of 2003 with former Minister of Finance Paul

Martin emerging as the new party leader. Under Martin's leadership, the party won 135 seats in the June 2004 federal election and was able to form a minority government.

The party is affiliated to the Liberal International.

New Democratic Party (NDP)

Address. 85 Albert St., Suite 802, Ottawa, Ontario, K1P 6A4

Telephone. (1–613) 236–3613

Fax. (1–613) 230–9950

Email. ndpadmin@fed.ndp.ca

Website. www.ndp.ca

Leadership. Jack Layton (leader); Dave MacKinnon (president)

Established in 1961, the democratic socialist NDP was the third main party at federal level behind the Liberal Party of Canada (LPC) and the Progressive Conservative Party (PCP) until the 1993 general election, when it slipped to fifth in terms of vote share (6.6%) and retained only nine of the 43 seats in the House of Commons which it had won in the 1988 polling. In 1997 it won 21 seats with 11.0% of the vote, but in the November 2000 general election it subsided to 13 seats, taking 8.5% of the vote. In the June 2004 general election it recovered ground to take 19 seats, with 15.7% of the vote, leaving it in fourth place nationally.

The NDP nationally has not succeeded in displacing the Liberals as the principal anti-conservative party. The NDP's vote is comparatively scattered geographically (other than for having virtually no presence in Quebec), a weakness given that Canadian politics have become highly polarized regionally and legislators are elected on the first past the post system. However, it has had more success at provincial than at federal level, including holding office in the most populous province, Ontario, in 1990-95. In provincial elections in 2003 the NDP remained the largest party in both Manitoba and Saskatchewan (the latter in particular being a traditional NDP stronghold). It lost power to the Liberals in a landslide in British Columbia in May 2001.

The NDP is supported by the Canadian Labour Congress, the national federation of trade unions. The NDP's campaign in the November 2000 elections focused on what it saw as the threat to replace Medicare with US-style two-tier health care. Following its poor performance at the polls it initiated a review of its policy positions. In June 2002 the party's leader Alexa McDonough resigned. At the January 2003 leadership convention Jack Layton, a Toronto city councillor with no experience of federal politics, won the party's leadership in a surprisingly easy fashion.

The NDP is a member party of the Socialist International.

Parti Québécois (PQ)
Quebec Party

Address. 1200 av. Papineau, Suite 150, Montreal, Quebec, H2K 4R5

Telephone. (1–514) 526–0020

Fax. (1–514) 526–0272

Email. info@pq.org

Website. www.partiquebecois.org

Leadership. Bernard Landry (leader)

Founded in 1968 by René Lévesque, the separatist PQ was the governing party in the province of Quebec from 1976 to 1985 and its strength was reflected in a range of measures to consolidate and promote the French linguistic and cultural identity of the province. The vigorous enforcement of these measures precipitated the departure from the province of many from the anglophone community. However, the PQ failed in a referendum in 1980 to obtain a mandate to negotiate "sovereignty-association" with the federal government, and was subsequently weakened by divisions between moderate and hardline party factions over the separatist issue.

In December 1985 the PQ was ousted by the Liberal

Party of Canada, which retained office until the provincial elections in September 1994, in which the PQ, under the leadership of Jacques Parizeau, won a comfortable majority of seats (although only by a margin of 44.7% to 44.3% of the vote). A new referendum on independence for Quebec took place in October 1995, resulting in a very narrow victory for the opponents of separation. Factors in the result included the potential loss of subsidies from the rest of Canada. Parizeau subsequently resigned and was replaced in January 1996 as PQ leader and Quebec Premier by Lucien Bouchard, the leader of the *Bloc Québécois* in Ottawa. Following the referendum defeat the PQ focused on issues such as Quebec's public finances, health and education, while proposing to hold a further referendum when circumstances were deemed favourable. Hardline separatists continued to press for early action to secure independence and further legislation to enforce the use of French. The PQ retained power in provincial elections in November 1998, winning 76 of the 125 seats. In January 2001 Bouchard announced he would stand down as party leader and Premier of Quebec, saying that "the results of my work are not very convincing" and that he wished to hand over to someone who could renew the fight for sovereignty. He was succeeded in March 2001 by Bernard Landry, formerly the Deputy Premier and Finance Minister.

In early 2003, while ahead in the opinion polls, Landry called a provincial election for April 14, 2003. Electoral fortunes quickly turned against the PQ and the party was soundly defeated by the provincial Liberal Party. Although initially hinting at resignation, Landry later promised to remain party leader until the PQ's next major policy convention.

Progressive Conservative Party (PCP)

Ceased to exist at federal level as of December 2003.
The PCP (referred to as the Conservatives or Tories), with a history dating back to 1854, was historically (with the Liberal Party of Canada) one of the two major Canadian national parties, although it more commonly constituted the opposition than the government. It was essentially a moderate and traditionalist conservative party which proved resistant to the populist, radical, anti-government and evangelical Christian streams of thought that have influenced most right-of-centre North American parties in recent times.

The period from 1963 to 1984 was spent almost entirely in opposition to Liberal administrations, although a minority PCP government was briefly in power under Joe Clark from May 1979 until its collapse nine months later. Under the leadership (from June 1983) of Brian Mulroney, the party won the 1984 federal election by a substantial majority. Having retained power in the 1988 elections, PCP popularity diminished to an unprecedented level in the face of economic recession and the rise of the neo-conservative western-based Reform Party, and the party was decimated in the October 1993 federal polls, retaining only two seats. Kim Campbell, who had replaced Mulroney in June 1993 to become Canada's first woman Prime Minister, subsequently resigned and was replaced by Jean Charest, a strong federalist.

In the 1997 election the PCP won 20 seats but its eclipse in the western region was confirmed, the party taking no seats at all in Saskatchewan, Alberta and British Columbia, where the Reform Party won a total of 57 seats. In April 1998 Charest stood down and former Prime Minister Joe Clark returned to public life to be elected leader in November 1998. However, the November 2000 election repeated the 1997 pattern with the Canadian Alliance (the successor to the Reform Party) almost totally shutting the PCP out of the west, although Clark was elected as the sole PCP member from Alberta. The PCP remained the main

challenger to the Liberals only in the Atlantic provinces of Newfoundland and Labrador, Prince Edward Island, Nova Scotia and New Brunswick, prompting comment that it had become an "Atlantic rump".

Following the 2000 election Clark charged that the Canadian Alliance had "played to prejudice" and that the PCP, which had "founded the country" would be "here for centuries to come". In June 2001, however, he announced a series of round tables with other parties to try to build a coalition to oppose the dominance of the Liberals. Critics unhappy at Clark's efforts placed increasing pressure on him to retire. In August 2002 he announced his resignation and called for a party leadership convention. This was held at the end of May 2003 and resulted in the election of thirty-seven-year-old lawyer and MP Peter MacKay as the new party leader. In gaining the leadership MacKay was forced to rely on the support of David Orchard, a left-of-centre leadership contender and a strong opponent of Canada's free trade agreement with the United States. Two of the conditions for Orchard's support were that MacKay would oppose any merger talks with the Canadian Alliance Party and hold a review of the free trade agreement. In late 2003, however, MacKay broke his agreement and engaged in merger talks. An agreement was reached and ratified by the membership of the two parties. The result was the merger of the two parties into the new Conservative Party of Canada. Some Progressive Conservatives, including former party leader Joe Clark, rejected the merger and refused to join the new party.

Despite the Progressive Conservative Party of Canada ceasing to exist at the federal level, as of July 2004 it remained in government in five provinces, these being Alberta (where it won 74 of the 83 seats in March 2001 provincial elections despite having taken only 13.5% of the vote and one seat in the November 2000 federal elections), New Brunswick, Nova Scotia, Prince Edward Island and Ontario.

The party is affiliated to the International Democrat Union.

Other Parties

Action démocratique du Québec (ADQ) (Democratic Action of Quebec), launched in 1993 by former members of the Liberal Party of Canada; backed the unsuccessful separatist cause in the 1995 referendum; won one seat in the provincial general election of November 1998 and four in that of April 2003 (taking 18% of the vote), having called for a moratorium on constitutional referenda and for economic deregulation to energize the Quebec economy.
Address. 5115 rue de Gaspé, Bureau 420, Montreal, Quebec, H2T 3B7
Telephone. (1–514) 270–4413
Fax. (1–514) 270–4469
Email. adq@adq.qc.ca
Website. www.adq.qc.ca
Leadership: Mario Dumont

Alberta Independence Party, founded in January 2001 ahead of provincial elections in which it won 7,400 votes; calls for provincial autonomy, the "preservation of Western culture", smaller government, and direct democracy.
Telephone. (1–403) 254–1419
Website. www.albertaindependence.com
Leadership. Cory Morgan (interim leader)

Canadian Action Party, founded in 1997 by Paul T. Hellyer (a minister in the Trudeau government in the 1960s); argues that Canada must "reclaim its sovereignty" in the face of "corporate rule" and absorption by the US and calls for abrogation of the Canada–US Free Trade Agreement and

NAFTA; took less than 0.1% of the vote in the June 2004 general election.

Address. 99 Atlantic Avenue, Suite 302, Toronto, Ontario, M6K 3J8

Telephone. (1–416) 535–4144

Fax. (1–416) 535–6325

Email. info@canadianactionparty.ca

Website. www.canadianactionparty.ca

Leadership. Connie Fogal

Christian Heritage Party of Canada (CHP), bases its principles on "Biblical ethics"; has a mainly conservative agenda but says it is "falsely tagged" as part of the "religious right". Captured 0.3% of the popular vote in the June 2004 general election.

Address. Heritage Place, 155 Queen Street, Suite 200, Ottawa, Ontario, K1P 6L1

Telephone. (1–819) 669–0673

Fax. (1–819) 669–6498

Email. edchp@ottawa.com

Website. www.chp.ca

Leadership. Ron Gray (national leader)

Communist Party of Canada, founded 1921 and historically an orthodox pro-Soviet party. Coinciding with the disintegration of the Soviet Union a reform group briefly came to prominence but was denounced as petty bourgeois reformists and purged in 1992 by Marxist-Leninist traditionalists; took less than 0.1% of the vote in the June 2004 general election.

Address. 290A Danforth Avenue, Toronto, Ontario, M4K 1N6

Telephone. (1–416) 469–2446

Fax. (1–416) 469–4063

Email. pvoice@web.net

Website. www.communist-party.ca

Leadership. Miguel Figueroa

Communist Party of Canada (Marxist-Leninist), founded in 1970 in succession to "The Internationalists"; took 0.1% of the vote in the June 2004 general election.

Address. 396 Cooper Street, Suite 200, Ottawa, Ontario K2P 2H7

Telephone. (1–613) 565–6446

Email. office@cpcml.ca

Website. www.cpcml.ca

Leadership. Sandra Smith (national leader)

Equality Party, Quebec-based party which believes that the English-speaking minority in Quebec is denied the protections given to the French-speaking minority elsewhere in Canada. It argues that if Quebec unilaterally breaks away from the rest of Canada it would have to be partitioned to protect those of its communities that wished to remain in Canada.

Address. PO Box 21, NDG Station, Montreal, Quebec, H3A 3P4

Telephone. (1–514) 488–7586

Fax. (1–514) 488–7306

E-mail. canadian@equality.qc.ca

Website. www.equality.qc.ca

Leadership. Vacant (leader Keith Henderson resigned after April 2003 election)

Green Party of Canada, federal organization of Green parties formed at provincial level from 1983, influenced by developments in Western Europe. The Greens have been unable to gain legislative representation at federal or provincial level under the first-past-the-post system and are campaigning for proportional representation. The Green move-

ment scored its most substantial success to date when, although it took no seats, the Green Party of British Columbia won 12.4% of the vote in provincial elections on May 16, 2001. Then in the June 2004 general election it took 4.3% of the vote.

Address. 244 Gerrard Street East, Toronto, Ontario, M5A 2G2

Telephone. (1–416) 929–2397

Fax. (1–416) 929–7709

Email. info@green.ca

Website. www.green.ca

Leadership. Jim Harris

Libertarian Party of Canada, small group that opposes government restrictions on personal freedom; its leader was imprisoned in November 2000 as an outcome of his persistent refusal to wear a car seat belt. It took under 0.1% of the vote in the June 2004 general election.

Address. 1843 Ste. Marie, Embrun, Ontario, K0A 1W0

Phone. (1–613) 443 5423

Website. www.libertarian.ca

Leadership. Jean-Serge Brisson

Marijuana Party, became a registered party in November 2000, immediately prior to the federal general election in which it took 0.5% of the vote. Its share of the vote fell to 0.3% in June 2004. It campaigns on a single issue: the legalization of marijuana.

Address. PO 361, Station "C", Montreal, Quebec, H2L 4K3

Telephone. (1–514) 528–1768

Email. info@marijuanaparty.org

Website. www.marijuanaparty.org

Leadership. Marc-Boris St-Maurice (leader)

Saskatchewan Party (SP), founded in August 1997 and led by former Reform Party agriculture spokesman Elwin Hermanson. In the September 1999 provincial general election it won more votes than the New Democratic Party but fewer seats, with the NDP subsequently forming a coalition with the three Liberals elected. In the 2003 election, it slipped back as the NDP won more votes and formed a slim majority government. It opposes what it sees as the big government and high taxation policies of the NDP and calls for direct accountability of members of the legislature to the electors through recall.

Address. PO Box 546, Regina, Saskatchewan, S4P 3A2

Telephone. (1–306) 359–1638

Fax. (1–306) 359–9832

Email. skparty@sk.sympatico.ca

Website. www.saskparty.com

Leadership. Brad Wall (leader)

Western Canada Concept, founded by Douglas Christie in 1980, advocating an independent nation of Western Canada. It calls for the introduction of referendum, initiative and recall to make politicians accountable, mandatory balanced budgets, and an end to immigration. It emphasizes individualism, Christian values and the English language as unifying forces.

Address. Box 143, 255 Menzies Street, Victoria, British Columbia, V8W 2G6

Telephone. (1–250) 727–3438

Fax. (1–250) 479–3294

Website. www.westcan.org

Leadership. Douglas Christie (leader)

Yukon Party (YP), believes in self-sufficiency and fiscal responsibility for the Yukon territory and advocates that north of latitude 60° should be a zone without gun controls. It won seven of the 17 seats in the Yukon legislature in elections in October 1992 and formed a minority administration that held office until 1996 when the New Democratic Party came to power. The YP won only one seat in elections in April 2000 in which the Liberals came to power for the first time in Yukon, but in November 2002 elections recovered to take 12 of the 18 seats.

Address. Box 31113, Whitehorse, Yukon, Y1A 5P7
Telephone. (1–867) 668–6505
Fax. (1–867) 667–7660
Email. yukonparty@mailcity.com
Leadership. Dennis Fentie (leader)

Cape Verde

Capital: Praia
Population: 450,000 (2003)

The Republic of Cape Verde achieved independence from Portugal in 1975 and had a one-party system under what became the African Party for the Independence of Cape Verde (PAICV) until moving to multi-partyism under legislation enacted in September 1990. The 1980 constitution as amended in 1990 provides for an executive President who appoints the government and who is directly elected for a five-year term by universal suffrage of those aged 18 and over. Legislative authority is vested in a unicameral National People's Assembly (*Assembleia Nacional Popular*) of 72 members, who are directly elected for a five-year term from 21 multi-member constituencies.

National Assembly elections were held in early 1991, the decisive victory of the Movement for Democracy (MPD) marking the first ever constitutional transfer of power to an opposition party in West Africa. In the next Assembly elections held on Dec. 17, 1995, the MPD comfortably retained power winning 50 seats and 61.3% of the vote; the PAICV won 21 and 29.7% and the Democratic Convergence Party 1 and 6.7%. In a presidential election on Feb. 18, 1996, the MPD candidate, António Mascarenhas Monteiro, was re-elected unopposed, having in 1991 defeated the then incumbent PAICV nominee by 73.5% to 26.5%.

In early 2001 the PAICV were returned to power after a ten-year absence. In the legislative elections on Jan. 14, the party gained 40 of the 72 seats, while the MPD took 30 and the Democratic Alliance for Change 2. In the presidential poll held over two rounds on Feb. 11 and 25, 2001, PAICV candidate Pedro Verona Rodrigues Pires very narrowly defeated Carlos Alberto Wahnon de Carvalho Veiga of the MPD.

African Party for the Independence of Cape Verde
Partido Africano da Independência de Cabo Verde (PAICV)
Address. CP 22, Praia, Santiago
Telephone. (238) 612136
Fax. (238) 615239
Website. www.paicv.org
Leadership. José Maria Neves (president)
The PAICV originated as the islands' branch of the African Party for the Independence of Guinea and Cape Verde (PAIGC), which had been founded by Amilcar Cabral in 1956 to oppose Portuguese colonial rule. The PAIGC led both Guinea-Bissau and Cape Verde to independence in 1974-75, becoming the sole ruling party in each. Following the November 1980 coup in Guinea-Bissau, the Cape Verde party reconstituted itself as the PAICV in January 1981,

under the leadership of President Arístides Maria Pereira.

Under the 1980 constitution the PAICV was defined as the leading force in society and nominated all candidates in legislative elections. However, an extraordinary PAICV congress in February 1990 endorsed constitutional changes providing for the introduction of a multi-party system, to herald which Pereira resigned as party general secretary in July and was replaced the following month by Gen. Pedro Verona Rodrigues Pires, the Prime Minister since 1975. In multi-party elections in January 1991 the PAICV was heavily defeated by the opposition Movement for Democracy (MPD), winning only a third of the popular vote and only 23 of the 79 seats. The following month Pereira, standing effectively as the PAICV candidate, went down to an even heavier defeat in presidential balloting, managing only just over a quarter of the vote.

In opposition for the first time, the PAICV underwent some internal strains and suffered a further rebuff in local elections in December 1991. In August 1993 a party congress elected Pires to the newly-created post of president, while Arístides Lima, the PAICV leader in the Assembly, took the vacated job of general secretary.

Having been defeated again in the December 1995 Assembly elections (taking only 21 of 72 seats), the PAICV returned to office in early 2001, securing an overall majority with 40 seats in the legislative polling, and a narrow victory in the presidential elections. PAICV candidate Pires (who had relinquished the party presidency to José Maria Neves) defeated his MPD rival in the second round of voting by just 17 votes. Neves was appointed as Prime Minister of the new PAICV government.

The PAICV is a full member of the Socialist International.

Democratic Alliance for Change
Aliança Democrática para a Mudança (ADM)
Address. c/o Assembleia Nacional Popular, Praia, Santiago
Leadership. Eurico Correia Monteiro (president)
The ADM was founded in 2000 as an alliance of the Democratic Convergence Party (PCD), the Party of Labour and Solidarity (PTS) and the Cape Verde Independence and Democratic Union (UCID). In the January 2001 Assembly elections, the ADM won only two seats with 6.1% of the vote.

Democratic Convergence Party
Partido da Convergência Democrática (PCD)
Address. c/o Assembleia Nacional Popular, Praia, Santiago
Leadership. Eurico Correia Monteiro (president)
Founded in 1994 by dissidents of the Movement for Democracy, the centrist PCD won only one seat in the December 1995 legislative elections, with 6.7% of the popular vote. It contested the January 2001 Assembly elections as part of the Democratic Alliance for Change (ADM), whereas in the following month's presidential poll the party nominated Jorge Carlos de Almeida Fonseca, who won 3.9% of the vote.

Movement for Democracy
Movimento para Democracia (MPD)
Address. c/o Assembleia Nacional Popular, Praia, Santiago
Leadership. Agostinho Lopes (president)
The MPD was founded by Lisbon-based exiles who in April 1990 issued a manifesto demanding the introduction of multi-party democracy and a free enterprise economy. The concurrent move of the ruling African Party for the Independence of Cape Verde (PAICV) in that direction enabled the MPD leaders to return to Praia and to negotiate on a timetable for elections with the government. In mid-1990 the MPD signed a co-operation agreement with the

Cape Verde Independent and Democratic Union in an attempt to extend its influence throughout the islands.

In the Assembly contest in January 1991 the MPD registered a landslide victory, winning 56 of the 79 seats and nearly two-thirds of the popular vote. In presidential balloting the following month, moreover, the MPD candidate and then leader, António Mascarenhas Monteiro (a former PAICV member), overwhelmingly defeated the PAICV incumbent, winning nearly three-quarters of the vote. The resultant MPD government under the premiership of Carlos Veiga quickly experienced tensions between radical and more cautious reformers. The dismissal of Jorge Carlos Fonseca as Foreign Minister in March 1993 intensified internal divisions, which erupted in February 1994 when the reappointment of Veiga as MPD chairman provoked the resignations of several leading party members. Nevertheless, the MPD won a further convincing victory in legislative elections in December 1995, while President Monteiro was re-elected unopposed in February 1996.

In the legislative elections on Jan. 14, 2001, the MPD lost 20 of its seats and its share of the vote fell to about 40%, so relinquishing power back to the PAICV. Having resigned as Prime Minister in July 2000 in order to contest the presidential elections in February 2001, Veiga was marginally beaten by PAICV candidate Pires over two rounds of voting.

Other Parties

Cape Verde Independent and Democratic Union (*União Caboverdiana Independente e Democrática*, UCID), founded in 1974 by exiles opposed to the government of the African Party for the Independence of Cape Verde (PAICV), registered in 1991; allied with the Movement for Democracy in the 1990s, it was part of the Democratic Alliance for Change (ADM) in the January 2001 elections.
Leadership. Manuel Rodrigues (president)

Democratic Renovation Party (*Partido da Renovação Democrática,* PRD), contested the January 2001 Assembly elections, attracting just over 3% of the vote but gaining no seats.
Leadership. Simão Monteiro (interim president)

Party of Labour and Solidarity (*Partido de Trabalho e Solidariedade*, PTS), founded in 1998 and formed part of the Democratic Alliance for Change (ADM) in the January 2001 Assembly elections.
Leadership. Isaías Rodrigues (president)

Social Democratic Party (*Partido Social Democrático,* PSD), founded in 1992. It has failed to win any representation in Assembly elections, gaining less than 0.5% of the vote in January 2001.
Leadership. João Alem (president)

Central African Republic

Capital: Bangui
Population: 3,800,000

The Central African Republic (CAR) became independent from France in 1960 and a one-party state from 1962. Military rule was imposed in 1966 by Col. Jean-Bedel Bokassa, who created the Central African Empire in 1977 but was deposed in 1979 by ex-President David Dacko, who revived the CAR. Military rule under Gen. André Kolingba from 1981 gave way in 1986 to a semi-civilian one-party regime

under Kolingba's Central African Democratic Rally (RDC), which in turn gave way to multi-party democracy in 1991. Under a new constitution introduced in January 1995, the previous "semi-presidential" arrangements gave way to a fully presidential system in which the President, directly elected for a six-year term (renewable once), was to "embody and symbolize national unity" and was empowered to give policy direction to the Prime Minister. The latter is responsible to a National Assembly (Assemblée Nationale), with 109 members (increased from 85 for the 1998 polls) directly elected for a five-year term by universal adult suffrage in two rounds of voting. The 1995 constitution also provided for the establishment of directly-elected regional assemblies.

Assembly elections held between August and October 1993 and in November-December 1998 led in each case to the Central African People's Liberation Party (MLPC), led by Ange-Félix Patassé, becoming the largest single party but without an overall majority. Patassé's government had to rely on a number of smaller coalition partners and independent candidates. The RDC, with ex-President Kolingba as chairman, remained the strongest opposition party. Presidential elections held in August-September 1993 resulted in victory for Patassé. The country experienced a series of army mutinies in 1996-97, with the mutineers seeking to force Patassé to step down. The instability necessitated intervention by French troops and the deployment of a United Nations peacekeeping force which oversaw the presidential poll in September 1999 in which Patassé was returned to power, defeating Kolingba and Dacko.

After a further period of instability, Patassé was deposed in March 2003 in a coup, staged while he was visiting Niger, led by Gen. François Bozize, a former armed forces chief of staff. Bozize dissolved the National Assembly, suspended the constitution and appointed as Prime Minister Abel Goumba, veteran leader of the FPP. In May 2003 he established a 98-member National Transition Council to serve as an advisory and lawmaking body during a transitional period that was to last between 18 and 30 months.

Alliance for Democracy and Progress
Alliance pour la Démocratie et le Progrès (ADP)
The ADP was launched in 1991 and became a founder member of the opposition Consultative Group of Democratic Forces (CFD) headed by the Patriotic Front for Progress. The ADP suffered a setback in October 1992 when its first leader, Jean-Claude Conjugo, was killed by security forces during a trade union demonstration. In March 1993 the party expelled its first general secretary, Tehakpa Mbrede, when he accepted a ministerial post under the Kolingba regime. In the 1993 presidential elections the ADP supported the unsuccessful CFD candidate, while the simultaneous legislative elections gave the ADP six of the 85 seats. In October 1993 the ADP broke with the CFD by accepting representation in a coalition government headed by the Central African People's Liberation Movement. In the 1998 elections, the ADP secured five seats in the enlarged 109-member Assembly.

Central African Democratic Rally
Rassemblement Démocratique Centrafricain (RDC)
Leadership. André Dieudonné Kolingba (leader)
Founded in May 1986 as the sole ruling party of the regime of Gen. Kolingba, who had come to power in a bloodless military coup in 1981, the RDC held its inaugural congress in February 1987. Launched as the country moved to semi-civilian rule, the RDC was intended to represent all political

and social tendencies except those seeking "to impose a totalitarian doctrine". The RDC provided the only authorized candidates in elections held in July 1987. The RDC at first resisted the post-1989 world trend against one-party regimes, but in April 1991 President Kolingba announced his conversion to multi-partyism and his party followed suit. At an extraordinary party congress in August 1991, he resigned as RDC leader with the aim of "putting himself above all political parties". Thereafter Kolingba and the RDC resisted opposition demands for a sovereign national conference and instead promoted the idea of a "grand national debate", which was boycotted by most other parties when it was held in mid-1992. The first attempt to hold democratic elections, in October 1992, was aborted by the authorities, reportedly with the opposition well ahead of the RDC.

In the first round of rescheduled presidential elections in August 1993, Kolingba trailed in a poor fourth place as the RDC candidate, winning only 12.1% of the vote and therefore being eliminated. Attempts by him to suppress the results were successfully resisted by the opposition, so that the RDC was obliged to hand over power to the Central African People's Liberation Movement (MLPC) after the second round in September. In simultaneous Assembly elections the RDC also polled weakly, winning only 13 of the 85 seats, although this tally made it the second strongest party after the MLPC. Having resumed effective leadership of the RDC, Kolingba was stripped of his military rank in March 1994, under a 1985 law (which he had signed as President) banning army officers from participating in elections or holding public office. This move, and the concurrent arrest of two senior RDC members on charges of "creating pockets of social tension", caused Kolingba to declare that democracy had been dangerously derailed.

In the 1998 legislative elections the RDC, although again emerging the second strongest party, won only 20 of 109 seats in the Assembly. Kolingba similarly failed in his bid to secure the presidency in September 1999, trailing the incumbent Patassé with only 19.4% of the vote. Kolingba claimed responsibility for a failed coup attempt in May 2001, but the RDC never endorsed his action. Nevertheless, its activities were suspended for several months by the Ministry of the Interior. There were reports in the aftermath of the coup attempt that members of Kolingba's ethnic group, the Yakoma from the south of the country, had been targeted for reprisal attacks by militias made up of members of President Patassé's predominantly northern Kaba ethnic group. Kolingba himself fled to Uganda and in August 2002 he was amongst 22 people sentenced to death in absentia for their part in the failed coup.

Following the seizure of power by Gen. Bozize in March 2003, Bozize stated that Kolingba's security would be guaranteed if he returned from exile. Following an amnesty granted to all May 2001 coup convicts by Bozize, Kolingba and thousands of other exiles returned home in the latter half of 2003. At a reconciliation conference held in October 2003, Kolingba apologised for the errors of his government during his 12-year rule and for his role in the May 2001 failed coup attempt.

Central African People's Liberation Movement
Mouvement pour la Libération du Peuple Centrafricain (MLPC)
Leadership. Ange-Félix Patassé (president-in-exile); Francis Albert Oukanga (secretary-general)
The MLPC was founded in Paris in mid-1979 by exiles led by Patassé, who as Bokassa's Prime Minister from September 1976 had overseen the creation of the Central African Empire in December 1976. Dismissed in July 1978 and forced to flee the country, he had then disclosed details of the barbarism and corruption of the Bokassa regime. The

MLPC opposed the succeeding Dacko government established in September 1979 and Patassé, who returned to Bangui, spent a year in prison for "fomenting unrest", emerging to take second place in the March 1981 presidential election. Again forced into exile in April 1982 (this time in Togo), Patassé was ousted as MLPC leader in September 1983 by a majority that favoured a leftist orientation and alliance with what became the Patriotic Front for Progress (FPP). The new leadership involved the MLPC in attempts to overthrow the Kolingba regime, but Patassé regained control by the time of the transition to multi-partyism, securing legalization for the MLPC in September 1991.

As MLPC presidential candidate, Patassé was well-placed in the first round of October 1992 elections, which were aborted by the authorities. In February 1993 Patassé accepted membership of a government-appointed transitional legislature but in April the MLPC refused to join a coalition administration. Concurrently, the MLPC leader dismissed as "slander" public allegations by the FPP leader that Patassé had links with international diamond merchants and right-wing mercenary groups. In resumed elections in August-September 1993, Patassé headed the field in the first ballot (with 37.3% of the vote) and won the run-off (with 52.5%) against the FPP leader. In simultaneous Assembly elections the MLPC became substantially the strongest party, although its 34 seats out of 85 left it without an overall majority. It therefore formed a coalition government, under the premiership of Jean-Luc Mandaba (MLPC vice-president), with the Liberal Democratic Party, the Alliance for Democracy and Progress and the six Assembly supporters of ex-President David Dacko (later organized as the Movement for Democracy and Development).

President Patassé's powers were significantly enhanced under the new constitution introduced in January 1995 following approval in a referendum the previous month. In April 1995 Mandaba was forced to resign as Prime Minister after more than half the Assembly deputies had signed a no-confidence motion tabled by his own MLPC and citing government corruption, maladministration and lack of consultation. He was succeeded by Gabriel Koyambounou, a technocrat close to the President, at the head of a new government coalition of the "presidential majority" parties.

The MLPC retained power after the legislative elections of 1998 (winning 47 of the 109 Assembly seats) and the presidential contest in September 1999 (in which Patassé was re-elected with 51.6% of the vote). Patassé was deposed in March 2003 in a coup led by Gen. François Bozize, a former armed forces chief of staff. Bozize carried out his coup while Patassé was attending a conference in Niger. He attempted to return to Bangui, but his aircraft came under fire and he was forced to fly to Cameroon where he joined other members of his government who had fled the country. Patassé later went into exile in Togo. With Patassé's departure the MLPC divided into two factions – one composed of exiles headed by the former President and one based in Bangui. Leading members of the latter faction included party deputy chairman Hugues Dobozendi and secretary-general Francis Albert Ouakanga. Two MLPC members remained in the Cabinet.

Civic Forum
Forum Civique (FC)
Leadership. Gen. (retd.) Timothée Malendoma (president)
The FC was one of many newly-founded parties which in late 1991 joined the opposition Consultative Group of Democratic Forces (CFD) headed by the Patriotic Front for Progress. Its CFD membership was suspended in August 1992, however, when it opted to participate in the "grand national debate" convened by the then Kolingba government. Its relations with the CFD worsened in December 1992 when

Malendoma was appointed Prime Minister, although they recovered somewhat in February 1993 when the FC leader was dismissed by Kolingba for "blocking the democratic process". Malendoma won only 2% of the vote in the presidential election first round in August 1993, while the FC secured only one of the 85 Assembly seats in concurrent legislative elections. In the Assembly elections in November-December 1998, the FC retained its one seat.

Democratic Forum for Modernity
Forum Démocratique pour la Modernité (FODEM)
The FODEM secured two seats in the 1998 legislative elections, but party leader Charles Massi gained only 1.3% of the vote in the presidential poll in September 1999. Following Gen. André Kolingba's failed coup attempt in May 2001, Massi fled to Paris and in March 2002 he created a new party, the Front for the Restoration of National Unity and Democracy. FODEM remained legal.

Front for the Restoration of National Unity and Democracy
Front pour la restauration de l'unité nationale et de la démocratie (FRUD)
Leadership. Charles Massi (leader)
FRUD was formed in Paris by Massi, hitherto leader of the Democratic Forum for Modernity, who had fled the CAR in the aftermath of Gen. André Kolingba's failed coup attempt in May 2001. Massi formed the new party along with a mutineer from 1996, Isidore Dokodo. In August 2002 Massi, alongside Kolingba and others, was sentenced to death in absentia. Following the seizure of power by Gen. Bozize in March 2003, Massi was given an amnesty. He returned to Bangui and was appointed as a member of Bozize's National Transition Council

Liberal Democratic Party
Parti Libéral-Démocrate (PLD)
Leadership. Nestor Kombo-Naguemon (president)
The PLD was launched amid the transition to multi-partyism in 1991-92. Advocating a deregulated market economy, the party won seven of the 85 Assembly seats in the 1993 legislative elections and accepted representation in the coalition government formed in October 1993 under the leadership of the Central African People's Liberation Movement. The PLD retained only two seats in the 1998 legislative elections. The party was represented in April 2001 in the MLPC-led government under premier Martin Ziguélé, who was replaced by leader of the Patriotic Front for Progress Abel Goumba in the aftermath of the March 2003 coup which toppled the regime of President Ange-Félix Patassé.

Movement for Democracy and Development
Mouvement pour la Démocratie et le Développement (MDD)
The MDD was launched in January 1994 by ex-President David Dacko, who had led the CAR to independence in 1960 and had established one-party rule in 1962 through the Movement for the Social Evolution of Black Africa (MESAN). He was overthrown in 1966 by his cousin, Col. Jean-Bedel Bokassa, who appropriated MESAN as his political vehicle and placed it under new management. In 1976 Dacko accepted appointment as a special adviser to Bokassa, shortly before the latter's controversial self-elevation to the status of Emperor, but in 1979, with the assistance of French paratroopers, led the ousting of Bokassa and the re-establishment of the republic. Installed as President again, Dacko in March 1980 founded the Central African Democratic Union (UDC) as the sole ruling party, but later accepted multi-party competition under a new constitution promulgated in February 1981.

Declared the victor in disputed presidential elections in March 1981, Dacko was overthrown six months later by Gen. André Kolingba and thereafter was a key figure in the exiled anti-Kolingba opposition. Returning to the CAR on the introduction of multi-partyism, Dacko held aloof from party identification, standing as an independent in the August 1993 first round of presidential elections, in which he was placed third with 20.1% of the vote. In the concurrent Assembly elections, nominally independent candidates identified with Dacko won six of the 85 seats and in October 1993 became part of a coalition headed by the Central African People's Liberation Movement. The subsequent creation of the MDD was intended to provide a party framework for the pro-Dacko element of the new government.

The MDD secured eight seats in the 1998 legislative elections, but Dacko came a distant third in the September 1999 presidential poll with 11.1% of the vote. Dacko died on Nov. 20, 2003, having a month earlier taken part in a reconciliation conference with Prime Minister Abel Goumba and other former opponents.

National Convention
Convention National (CN)
The CD was founded in October 1991, immediately becoming a founder member of the opposition Consultative Group of Democratic Forces (CFD) headed by the Patriotic Front for Progress (FPP). It backed the unsuccessful CFD/FPP candidate in the August–September 1993 presidential election, while winning three of the 85 seats in simultaneous Assembly elections. The CN failed to win any seats in the 1998 legislative elections. Nonetheless, it was represented in April 2001 in the MLPC-led government under Prime Minister Martin Ziguélé, who was replaced by FPP leader Abel Goumba in the aftermath of the March 2003 coup which overthrew the regime of President Ange-Félix Patassé.

Party of National Unity
Parti de l'Unité Nationale (PUN)
Leadership. Jean-Paul Ngoupande
The PUN gained three seats in the Assembly elections in late 1998, and party leader Ngoupande (who had been Prime Minister from June 1996-January 1997) contested the September 1999 presidential poll, attracting 3.1% of the vote to take sixth place. Although it was repeatedly accused of siding with rebels, the PUN was represented in April 2001 in the MLPC-led government under premier Martin Ziguélé, who was replaced by the leader of the Patriotic Front for Progress, Abel Goumba, in the aftermath of the March 2003 coup which toppled the regime of President Ange-Félix Patassé.

Patriotic Front for Progress
Front Patriotique pour le Progrès (FPP)
Address. BP 259, Bangui
Telephone. (236-61) 5223
Leadership. Abel Goumba (president); Patrice Endjimoungou (secretary-general)
The FPP was launched in 1981 as the (Congo-based) Ubangi Patriotic Front-Labour Party after veteran anti-Bokassa campaigner Goumba had broken with the post-Bokassa Dacko government. During the late 1980s the party co-operated closely with the Central African People's Liberation Movement (MLPC) when the latter was under left-wing leadership. It also forged links with the European democratic left, becoming an affiliate of the Socialist International. The party obtained legal recognition as the FPP in August 1991, but not before Goumba had spent six months in prison for participating in an unauthorized opposition attempt to initiate a national conference on political reform. In late 1991 the FPP took the lead in the formation of the Consultative Group of Democratic Forces (CFD), with 13 other parties and six trade

unions, which refused to participate in a "grand national debate" proposed by President Kolingba.

Standing as the CFD candidate in the October 1992 presidential elections, Goumba was reported to be leading the first-round count when the elections were aborted. In February 1993 Goumba accepted membership of a government-appointed transitional legislature, but the CFD formations refused to join a coalition administration. When the electoral process was resumed in August 1993, Goumba took second place in the first round of presidential balloting, winning 21.7% of the vote. He therefore went forward to the second round in September but was defeated by the MLPC candidate by 52.5% to 45.6%. In simultaneous legislative elections, the FPP won seven of the 85 seats in its own right. After the elections the CFD was weakened by the decision of the Alliance for Democracy and Progress to join an MLPC-led coalition government. Nevertheless, the FPP became an active focus of opposition to the new Patassé administration, opposing the move to a presidential constitution in January 1995.

In the 1998 legislative polling, the FPP retained its seven-seat representation in the enlarged 109-member Assembly. Goumba stood again for the presidency in September 1999, achieving fourth place with 6% of the vote. After Patassé was deposed in March 2003 in a coup led by Gen. François Bozize Goumba was appointed as the new Prime Minister.

The party has observer status within the Socialist International.

Social Democratic Party
Parti Social-Démocrate (PSD)

Leadership. Enoch Dérant Lakoué (president)
Founded in 1991, the PSD distanced itself from the main anti-Kolingba opposition, favouring instead an accommodation with the then ruling Central African Democratic Rally (RDC). The PSD leader was a candidate in the aborted October 1992 presidential election and in February 1993 accepted President Kolingba's invitation to become Prime Minister. However, he failed in his quest to bring other major opposition parties into the government, his role in which precipitated wholesale defections from the PSD. Standing again for the presidency, Lakoué obtained only 2.4% of the vote in the August 1993 first round, while in Assembly elections the PSD took three of the 85 seats. Thereafter it formed part of the opposition to the new Patassé administration.

The PSD increased its representation in the Assembly to six seats in the 1998 legislative elections, but Lakoué managed to attract only 1.3% of the vote in the September 1999 presidential poll. The party was represented in April 2001 in the MLPC-led government under premier Martin Ziguélé, who was replaced by leader of the Patriotic Front for Progress, Abel Goumba, in the aftermath of the March 2003 coup which overthrew the regime of President Ange-Félix Patassé.

Chad

Capital: N'Djaména
Population: 8,420,000 (2000E)

The Republic of Chad achieved independence from France in 1960 and became a one-party state in 1962 under N'garta Tombalbaye's Chadian Progressive Party. Tombalbaye's overthrow in 1975 ushered in a lengthy north-south civil war and a series of shortlived regimes, leading to the seizure of power by the Patriotic Salvation Movement (MPS) led by Col. Idriss Déby in late 1990. In October 1991 the new regime agreed to legitimize political parties that renounced "intolerance, tribalism, regionalism, religious discrimination and violence". In

April 1993 a sovereign national conference planned for a transition to multi-party democracy. Déby remained head of state, but the conference itself elected a transitional Prime Minister and a 57-member Higher Transitional Council (Conseil Supérieur de Transition) pending general elections. Initially, transition was to last a year but 12-month extensions were decreed in April 1994 and May 1995.

In light of continuing rebel activity by numerous rebel groups (so called politico-military movements), the government established a National Reconciliation Committee in May 1994 to serve as a framework for the achievement of peace. In November 1995 a timetable was published scheduling presidential and legislative elections. Signed by the government and 13 opposition parties on March 9, 1996, the so-called Franceville Accord advocated a new constitution modeled on that of France. A national referendum approved the Accord in a 63.5% vote on March 31.

This paved the way for two-stage National Assembly elections in January and February 1997, which resulted in a small but absolute majority – 63 out of 125 seats – for the President's party, the MPS. To foster national reconciliation, two opposition parties, the National Union for Democracy and Renewal (UNDR) and the Union for Democracy and the Republic (UDR), joined the MPS in government. Nonetheless, clashes in southern Chad continued between rebels and the army in late 1997, but were (temporarily) ended by a peace agreement in May 1998 (and re-erupted in 2000). The same year a new uprising started in the north, the *Mouvement pour la Démocratie et la justice au Tchad* (MDJT). A peace agreement in early 2002 and the death of its leader in September 2002 seemed to pave the way for a peaceful solution, but hardline factions continued the armed struggle.

Presidential elections on May 20, 2001, saw Idriss Déby returned to office on a high turnout. He won 63.2% of the vote in the first round, compared with 16.1% for his nearest rival, Ngarlejy Yorongar. Allegations of fraud led to the detention of all six losing candidates, and heralded suppression of press and public protest. Parliamentary elections, originally planned for 2001, were postponed to April 2002. Under contested conditions – the European Union criticised in particular the delimitation process and two major opposition parties boycotted the elections – the MPS swept the polls by gaining a large majority in the National Assembly.

There is a multitude of political parties and political organizations in Chad (some 60 in mid-2003), often commanding only short lived and limited support. Although opposition parties, civic organizations and armed rebel groups have been banding together in coalitions in recent years, such as the 13-member Coordinated Armed Movements and Political Parties of the Opposition (CMAP) in late 1999, the 35-member Vital Forces of Chad in late 2000, and the six-member Convention for Democratic Alternation (CAD) in April 2003, they pose a minor threat to Déby's rule. Due to personal ambitions or cooption by the government, defections and factionalism are rife and opposition coalitions lack substantial coherence. This applies in particular to the numerous armed rebel groups, the so called politico-military movements, that have been playing a significant role in Chadian politics for decades, notably the *Front de Libération National du Tchad* (FROLINAT). FROLINAT factions ruled parts of the country from 1979 country until 1990 when then President Hissène Habré was overthrown by

Déby. Since 1998, the main politico-military movement has been the MDJT. In many cases the politico-military movements portray themselves as political parties, were originally political parties or intend to turn (or have indeed turned) into political parties once their political demands are met. The following groupings only include legal political organizations that have been operating mainly peacefully in recent years.

Federation, Action Front for the Renewal / Federation Party
Fédération, Action pour le renouveau (FAR)/ Parti Fédération
Address. POB 4197, N'Djaména
Telephone. 51-91-12
Fax. 51-78-60
E-mail. yorongar@intnet.td
Leadership. Ngarlejy Yorongar
FAR is a strongly anti-Déby group, originally named *Front des Forces d'Action pour la République* (FFAR) and also known as *Front d'Action pour la République*. In 1996 party leader Yorongar, a Southern Christian, led a campaign against alleged kickbacks that the government was receiving from the Elf petroleum company. The party won a single seat in the 1997 assembly elections. In the 2001 presidential elections, however, Yorongar garnered more than 16% of the votes in a run-off with Déby, gaining national prominence through his uncompromising criticism of the Déby government. Yorongar accused the government of electoral fraud; his subsequent detention aroused international protest. In the 2002 legislative elections FAR came third as the strongest opposition party in the National Assembly, winning nine seats. Yorongar is a pronounced critic of the handling of oil production in southern Chad (that started in mid-2003), where he comes from. In distinct contrast to other opposition parties FAR has an ideological agenda. FAR strongly advocates federalism and formed a parliamentary caucus together with two opposition deputies in May 2002.

National Rally for Democracy and Progress
Rassemblement National pour la Démocratie et le Progrès (RNDP)
Leadership. Delwa Kassiré Koumakoyé (president)
The RNDP, also called *Viva*, was founded in early 1992. Its French-educated legally-trained leader became spokesman of the National Co-ordination of the Opposition (CNO) created in May 1992, but later gravitated towards the ruling Patriotic Salvation Movement (MPS). He failed in a bid to become chairman of the sovereign national conference convened in January 1993. In June 1993 Koumakoyé accepted the post of Justice Minister in a transitional coalition government and in November was elevated to the premiership. His main stated aims were the further demobilization of armed forces, a social pact with the trade unions, the preparation of elections and reconciliation with unreconciled rebel movements.

In April 1995, however, he was dismissed by decision of the legislative Higher National Council, apparently at the instigation of President Déby. Koumakoyé condemned what he termed the government's "drift towards totalitarianism and dictatorship". In 1996 he spent three months in jail on charges of illegal possession of arms. Koumakouye nonetheless participated in the 1996 presidential elections, but performed poorly with only 2.2% of the votes cast. Similarly, the RNDP failed to secure seats in the National Assembly in 1997. Koumakoyé contested the 2001 presidential election, but received little support beyond his southern stronghold of Tandjilé. Original plans to boycott the legislative elections in 2002 were cancelled and the RNDP's participation resulted in its winning five seats.

National Union for Democracy and Renewal
Union Nationale pour la Démocratie et le Renouvellement (UNDR)
Leadership. Saleh Kebzabo
The UNDR won 15 seats out of 125 in the National Assembly elections in 1997, making it the third strongest party in Chad after the MPS and URD. Its leader, Saleh Kebzabo, is a former news agency director and journalist whose stronghold lies in the south of Chad. In September 1995 he was arrested and charged with making illegal contacts with rebel groups. Formerly an opposition grouping (Kebzabo took 8.6% of the votes cast in the first round of the presidential elections in 1996), after 1997 the UNDR rallied to support President Déby. Kebzabo entered the cabinet as Minister for Mining.

In May 1998 he returned to opposition with two other ministers from his party, and in 1999 led a campaign against restrictions on press freedom. Kebzabo returned to government as agriculture minister in 2000, but lost this post in a cabinet reshuffle in April 2001 after he had announced his intention to contest the presidential elections the same year. However, Kebzabo came a poor third behind the winner, Déby, and runner-up, Ngarlejy Yorongar. Protesting against the conditions in which the elections were held and their aftermath, the UNDR planned to boycott the legislative elections in 2002 together with other opposition parties. Nevertheless the UNDR participated in the elections, but was reduced to five seats.

Patriotic Salvation Movement
Mouvement Patriotique du Salut (MPS)
Leadership. Idriss Déby (president)
The MPS was founded in March 1990 by Sudan-based and Libyan-backed opponents of the regime of Hissène Habré. The MPS leader, a northern Muslim from the Zagahwa tribe, was formerly a top adviser to the French-backed Habré, who had held power in Chad since 1982. He then led forces against pro-Libyan troops in the east. Déby participated in a coup attempt in April 1989, and was the only one of the three principals to escape when it failed. At first the MPS included Déby's April 1 Action (*Action du 1 April*) based in the Zagahwa and Hadjerai tribes of central Chad, the southern-based Movement for Chadian National Salvation (*Mouvement pour le Salut National du Tchad*, MOSANAT), and remnants of the Chadian Armed Forces (*Forces Armées Tchadiennes*, FAT).

The MPS then launched a major offensive against the Habré government which brought it to power in N'Djaména, and Déby to the presidency, in December 1990. The MPS emphasized political reconciliation, and attracted the allegiance of other groups, including the Chadian People's Revolution (*Révolution du Peuple Tchadienne*, RPT) led by Adoum Togoi (later MDJT) and a faction of the FROLINAT. Internal strains were highlighted by the arrest in October 1991 of MPS vice-president Maldom Baba Abbas for an alleged coup attempt, but he was later rehabilitated.

From May 1992 President Déby expanded the political basis of the government to include several new parties, notably Chadian Action for Unity and Socialism (ACTUS), the National Alliance for Development (AND), the National Rally for Democracy and Progress (RNDP), the *Rassemblement du Peuple Tchadien* (RPT), the Union for Democracy and Progress (UDP), the Union for Democracy and the Republic (UDR), the Union for Renewal and Democracy (URD) and the *Union des Forces Démocratiques* (UFD). In January 1993 the President hosted a sovereign national conference on the country's political future. He ensured that some 75% of the delegates (representing 66 parties and organizations) were MPS supporters. In April 1993 it adopted a transitional charter which left Déby as the head of state and commander-in-chief. However, the conference elected the Prime Minister (initially, Fidèle Moungar of ACTUS) and an interim legislature, pending multi-party general elections. These were delayed by internal strife until January-February 1997, when the MPS achieved a bare absolute majority with a tally of 63 seats in the 125-seat national assembly.

Idriss Déby was reelected as president in May 2001 by 63.2% of the votes cast in the first round. Subsequently, benefiting from irregularities, the MPS swept the 2002 legislative elections, but thereafter had to deal with factionalist infighting between pro-Déby conservatives and reformers who seek an end to Déby's presidency after his constitutional maximum of two terms. The planned MPS party congress had to be postponed twice and was finally held in mid November 2003, after leading reformers such as former Prime Minister Haroun Kabadi and Mahamat Ali Abdallah were removed from the cabinet in late June. The 500 congress delegates opted for a revision of the consitution in order to allow Déby a third term as president.

Rally for Democracy and Progress
Rassemblement pour la Démocratie et le Progrès (RDP)
Leadership. Lol Mahamat Choua (president)
The RDP was launched in December 1991 under the leadership of Lol Mahamat Choua (mayor of N'Djaména). In 1979, as head of a FROLINAT offshoot group, he had briefly been President of an abortive national unity government. He later held ministerial office under the post-1982 Habré regime. Strong in the Kanem tribe around Lake Chad, the RDP came under heavy pressure from the security forces for its alleged involvement in the Kanem-backed coup attempt of January 1992. The party was nevertheless one of the first to be legalized in March 1992 and in May joined the *Coordination Nationale d' Opposition* (CNO). It participated in the sovereign national conference of January-April 1993. Its leader was elected chairman of the interim legislature pending general elections. When the initial transitional period of 12 months was extended by a further year in April 1994, Choua complained that the Déby government had failed to make adequate preparations for democratic elections. Ousted from the CST chairmanship in October 1994, he claimed that the government had ordered the assassination of two RDP journalists and had arrested a dozen other RDP members.

Choua came a distant fifth in the first round of the 1996 presidential elections. The RDP won three seats in the 1997 elections and joined the pro-Déby camp afterwards. The RDP supported Déby in the 2001 presidential elections and was rewarded with two cabinet minister posts in Déby's government. The RDP came a distant second in the legislative elections in April 2002, securing 12 seats in the National Assembly. On Nov. 10, 2003, however, the RDP joined ranks with 19 opposition parties when it signed a memorandum demanding a better organization of the elections in the country. On Nov. 17, 2003, Choua and two RDP ministers announced their intention to leave the government because of the MPS's move to seek a – hitherto unconstitutional – third term for Déby.

Union for Renewal and Democracy
Union pour le Renouveau et la Démocratie (URD)
Address. BP 92, N'Djaména
Telephone. 51-44-23
Fax. 51-44-87
Leadership. Wadal Abdelkader Kamougué (president)
Founded in March 1992 and legalized two months later, the URD consisted of supporters of Lt.-Gen. Kamougue. He was born in Gabon to parents from the Mbaye ethnic group, from the south of Chad. First appointed a minister in 1975, he had

commanded anti-Habré forces in southern Chad in the 1980s and had been a vice-president of the Libyan-backed Gouvernement d'Union Nationale de Transition (GUNT). Kamougué founded the *Mouvement pour la Révolution Populaire* (MRP) in the late 1980s, but abandoned his creation to form the URD. Following the sovereign national conference held in early 1993, he was in April 1993 appointed Minister of Civil Service and Labour but was dismissed in May 1994 in the wake of a strike by civil servants.

Kamougué contested the 1996 presidential elections, and came second to the winner, Idriss Déby, with 28.4% of the vote, thus making him the strongest southern politician. In the general elections of early 1997, the URD came second to the ruling MPS, with a tally of 29 seats. It initially joined in a national coalition government, but subsequently distanced itself from Idriss Déby. In May 2001 Kamougue came a poor fourth in presidential polls, with just over 6.0% of the votes cast. After initial plans to boycott the elections jointly with other major opposition parties were cancelled, the URD participated in the 2002 legislative elections but was reduced to three seats.

Other Parties

Action for the Renewal of Chad (*Action pour le Renouvellement du Tchad*, ART), failed to win a seat in the legislative elections in 1997. As a pro-Déby party, however, the ART gained two seats in the National Assembly in 2002.

Chadian Action for Unity and Socialism (*Action Tchadienne pour l'Unité et le Socialisme*, ACTUS), originated as a faction of the Transitional Government of National Unity (GUNT), which had been created in 1979 to unite the forces of Hissène Habré and Goukouni Oueddei but disintegrated in 1980. In 1990 ACTUS backed the successful offensive against the Habré regime by the MPS led by Idriss Déby. After Déby assumed power in December 1990, ACTUS reemerged as a distinct formation under Fidèle Moungar, a prominent surgeon. In April 1993 Moungar was elected Prime Minister by the sovereign national conference which planned the transition to multi-party elections. In October 1993, however, he was forced to resign after the transitional legislature had passed a no-confidence motion, apparently inspired by Déby. ACTUS took one seat in the 1997 elections. In December 1999 it joined 12 other parties in a coalition grouping called the Coordinated Armed Movements and Political Parties of the Opposition (CMAP). ACTUS did not contest the 2001 presidential elections but retained one seat in the legislative elections in 2002. ACTUS joined the profederation parliamentary caucus formed by FAR in June 2002. *Leadership.* Fidèle Moungar (president)

Chadian Social Democratic Party (*Parti Social-Démocrate du Tchad*, PSDT), a southern-based movement led by Niabe Romain, a businessman. It unsuccessfully contested the legislative elections in 1997 but gained a single seat in the legislative elections in 2002.

Convention for Democracy and the Federation (*Convention pour la Démocratie et la Fédération*, CDF). Founded in 2000 the CDF supports the establishment of a federal state. The CDF gained two seats in the National Assembly in the 2002 elections. The CDF joined the pro-federation caucus formed by FAR in May 2002.

Convention for Democratic Alternation (*Convention pour l'alternance démocratique*, CAD). *Leadership.* Jean Bawoyeu Alingué (speaker). The CAD was formed in April 2003 by six minor opposition parties including the Party for Freedom and Development (PLD) and the Union for

Democracy and the Republic (UDR). The CAD aims at fighting electoral fraud and a peaceful change of power. In September 2003 the CAD issued a memorandum demanding public information on president Déby's allegedly poor health. On Nov. 10, 2003, the CDA participated in a another memorandum issued by 20 opposition parties that demanded free and fair elections.

Coordinated Armed Movements and Political Parties of the Opposition (*La Coordination des mouvements armés et partis politiques de l'opposition*, CMAP), The CMAP was founded in December 1999 in Benin as an umbrella for 13 opposition groups from Chad. Antoine Bangui, a former minister, ambassador, and Chad representative to UNESCO became the president of its council. He also leads one of the constituent parties, the *Front Extérieur pour la Rénovation* (FER). The other 12 parties included a faction of the former ruling party FROLINAT, headed by Goukouni Queddei, a national president from 1979-1982, the Action for Unity and Socialism (ACTUS), and the National Front of Chad Renewed (FNTR). In early 2002, at a congress in Paris, the CMAP was shaken by infighting. Bangui and Queddei apparently left the group, Bourkine Louise Ngaradoum becoming interim president. The CMAP's future is currently uncertain.

Movement for Democracy in Chad (*Mouvement pour la Démocratie au Tchad*, MPDT), contested unsuccessfully the 1997 legislative elections but won a single seat in 2002.

National Alliance for Development (*Alliance Nationale pour le Développement*, AND), also known as *Alliance Nationale pour la Démocratie et le Développement* (ANDD) is led by Salibou Garba. It was one of a number of parties formed in early 1992 on the fringes of the ruling Patriotic Salvation Movement (MPS). The Prime Minister appointed in May 1992, Joseph Yodemane, was at first described as being close to the AND, while one of his ministers, Nabia Ndali, was an actual party member. However, Ndali resigned in July 1992 as a result of a dispute between AND leaders and Yodemane. The AND attracted 1.9% of the votes cast in the second round of the 1997 elections for the National Assembly, winning one seat, which it retained in the 2002 legislative elections.

National Front of Chad Renewed (*Front National du Tchad Rénové*, FNTR). *Leadership*. Ahmat Yacoub (secretary-general). Based in central-eastern Chad, the rebel *Front National du Tchad* (FNT) under Alarit Bachar signed a peace agreement with the Déby government in October 1992 providing for its political and military integration into national structures. However, most FNT elements continued military activities, stepping them up in 1994. Bachar disowned a further ceasefire agreement signed with the government by a renegade faction in October 1994. The FNT reconstituted itself as the FNTR in April 1996, in Brussels. Under its new leader, Ahmat Yacoub, the FNTR was committed to a social democracy and opposed tribalism, regionalism and corruption. FNTR joined the Co-ordinated Armed Movements and Political Parties of the Opposition (CMAP) opposition alliance in December 1999. The FNTR gave up the armed struggle and declared itself to be a fully fledged political party in mid-2002.

Party for Freedom and Development (*Parti pour la Liberté et le Développement*, PLD), founded in late 1993 by Ibn Oumar Mahamat Saleh and Paul Saradori, following the former's dismissal in May as Minister of Planning and Co-operation, advocating the "rehabilitation" of Chad. The party won three seats in the 1997 elections. It joined the MPS government afterwards, but all three PLD ministers were sacked when Saleh announced his plans to stand for the presidential elections in 2001. Saleh came fifth with 2.9% of the popular vote. The PLD was one of two parties that actually did not participate the parliamentary elections in April 2002 after the major opposition parties had announced plans to jointly boycott the legislative elections after the contested conditions of the presidential race in 2001. In April 2003 the PLD helped form the opposition coalition Convention for Democratic Alternation (CAD).

Rally of Chadian Democratic Forces (*Rassemblement des Forces Démocratiques du Tchad*, RFDT), allied to the MPS and President Déby, and secured two seats in the National Assembly in 2002, after having failed to win a seat in 1997.

Union for Democracy and the Republic (*Union pour la Démocratie et la République*, UDR). *Leadership*. Jean Bawoyeu Alingué. The UDR was still awaiting official recognition when, in March 1992, it elected Jean Bawoyeu Alingué as its president on his appointment as Prime Minister by President Déby of the Patriotic Salvation Movement. The UDR leader ceased to be Prime Minister in May 1992, although the party remained in government. In April 1995 the UDR regained the premiership in the person of Keibla Djimasta. Alingué came a distant fourth in the first round of the presidential elections in 1996, but the UDR won four seats in the 1997 elections, and initially backed the MPS government. Returned to the oppositions ranks, the UDR's presidential candidate in May 2001 Alingué attracted only 2.2% of the popular vote. The legislative elections in April 2001 were boycotted by the UDR, protesting electoral malpractice during the presidential elections the year before. The UDR joined the CAD opposition coalition in April 2003, Alingué becoming its speaker.

Vital Forces of Chad (*Les Forces Vives du Tchad*). A loose grouping of some 35 political parties, civic organizations and politico-military movements which was formed in late 2002. Members are almost all political parties opposed to the Déby government, such as the ATD, the AND, the FAR, the PLD, the ACTUS, the UDR, the URD, the UNDR and the (Viva-)RNDP. The Vital Forces of Chad have failed to pose a substantial challenge to the Déby government. In early 2002, plans to jointly boycott the 2002 legislative elections failed when several parties opted to participate in the elections.

Chile

Capital: Santiago
Population: 15,116,435 (2002E)

The Republic of Chile won its independence in 1818. Prior to a right-wing military coup led by Gen. Augusto Pinochet Ugarte in September 1973, Chile had been a parliamentary democracy with an executive President and a National Congress elected by universal adult suffrage. After the coup, absolute power rested with the military junta, and increasingly with Pinochet, who in June 1974 was designated Supreme Chief of State, and in December, President of the Republic (although he did not formally assume that title until March 1981). The junta proclaimed various "constitutional acts" in 1976 purporting to establish an "authoritarian democracy", with executive and legislative authority vested in the President and the junta, assisted by a Cabinet.

In accordance with the March 1981 constitution, as amended and approved by referendum in July 1980, Chile is a democratic republic; executive power lies with the President, who is directly elected for a six-year term. Legislative power is held by a bicameral National Congress, comprised of a 48-member Senate serving an eight-year term (of whom 38 members are elected and nine are designated, while one former President of the Republic sits as a lifetime senator) and a 120-member Chamber of Deputies elected for a four-year term. A binomial electoral system requires that parties present lists of two candidates per constituency. When a list attains over twice the number of votes of its nearest rival, it wins both seats. If it fails to do so, one of its candidates is elected together with one from the next most popular list.

This electoral system, together with other measures and bodies such as the National Security Council, the Constitutional Tribunal, and the presence of designated senators comprise "authoritarian enclaves" which have prevented a full redemocratization of the political system.

In a plebiscite held on Oct. 5, 1988, a majority of nearly 55% voted against Pinochet remaining in office for a further eight years upon the expiry of his term in 1990. In the resulting presidential elections held on Dec. 14, 1989, Patricio Aylwin Azócar of the Christian Democratic Party (PDC), representing a 17-party Coalition of Parties for Democracy (CPD), was the clear winner. He took office on March 11, 1990. Since then the CPD has retained control of the presidency with the election in December 1993 of Eduardo Frei Ruíz-Tagle of the PDC and Ricardo Lagos Escobar, of the Socialist Party of Chile, on Jan. 16, 2000 (by a vote of 51.3% in a run-off election). In congressional elections on Dec. 16, 2001, the CPD parties won 62 of the 120 seats in the Chamber of Deputies.

Alliance for Chile
Alianza por Chile (ApC)
Leadership. Joaquín Lavín Infante (1999 presidential candidate)

The ApC is the latest incarnation of the coalition of right-wing parties, previously known as the Union for Chile (*Unión por Chile*, UpC). In the December 1999 presidential elections, the Alliance backed the candidacy of Joaquín Lavín Infante of the Independent Democratic Union (UDI), whose narrow defeat in the run-off polling in January 2000 confirmed the ApC parties as the effective opposition in Chile.

The ApC constituent parties are the UDI, National Renewal (RN) and the Party of the South (*Partído del Sur*).

Christian Democratic Party
Partido Democrata Cristiana (PDC)
Address. Alameda B. O'Higgins 1460, Santiago
Telephone. (+56–2) 757-4400
Website. www.pdc.cl
Email. info@pdc.cl
Leadership. Adolfo Zaldívar Larraín (president)

The PDC was created in July 1957 as a merger of the National Falange (founded in 1934) and the majority faction of the Social Christian Conservative Party. The party's then leader, Eduardo Frei Montalva, came third in the presidential elections of 1958. The party built up its support in rural areas, especially through illegal rural unions. In 1961 the PDC became the largest party in Congress and remained so under the 1970-73 Allende government, to which it formed an effective and vigourous opposition.

The 1973 military coup was welcomed by many within the PDC. However, the party's support for the junta diminished as evidence emerged of human rights abuses and as Gen. Pinochet developed his own political agenda. In 1977 the PDC was banned, along with all other parties.

In August 1983 the party founded the Democratic

Alliance (AD), a centre-left grouping which superseded the *Multipartidaria* alliance formed only months earlier. In 1986 the party announced its acceptance of the military's 1980 constitution as an instrumental strategy for overthrowing the Pinochet regime. At the same time it became the main force in the AD's campaign for free elections and was a signatory to the National Accord, an opposition document outlining the agenda for a transition to democracy.

Patricio Aylwin Azócar, the party leader, became the spokesman for a 13-party opposition alliance that successfully campaigned against the extension of Pinochet's term as President, an issue submitted to a plebiscite in October 1988. The popular support, energy and enthusiasm generated by the "no" vote was harnessed to establish the Coalition of Parties for Democracy (CPD), a 17-member electoral alliance led by the Christian Democrats. In July 1989 the CPD parties agreed to support Aylwin as the main opposition presidential candidate. His campaign programme included pledges to investigate human rights abuses, improve education and health care and increase the minimum wage within the context of a sound economic programme designed to boost exports and control inflation. In the December 1989 elections, Aylwin was elected President with 55.2% of the valid votes and the PDC became the largest party in Congress.

Having won a third of the available votes in the 1992 municipal elections, the PDC provided the successful presidential candidate in the December 1993 elections, Eduardo Frei Ruíz-Tagle. However, in the primaries for the 1999 presidential elections the PDC candidate, Andrés Zaldívar, lost to the candidate of the Socialist Party of Chile (a CPD member), Ricardo Lagos Escobar, who was elected in January 2000. The primaries initiated a period of decline for the PDC, which the party's current president, Adolfo Zaldívar, has attempted to reverse by moving the party to the right. As a result of the 2001 parliamentary elections, it now has 22 seats in the Chamber of Deputies and 12 in the Senate.

The PDC is an affiliate of the Christian Democrat International and the Christian Democrat Organization of America (ODCA).

Coalition of Parties for Democracy
Concertación de los Partidos por la Democracia (CPD)
Leadership. Ricardo Lagos Escobar (President of the Republic)

The centre-left CPD alliance was founded in its present form in November 1988, arising out of the Democratic Alliance led by the Christian Democratic Party (PDC) and the "Command for the No Vote" opposition alliance which successfully campaigned to prevent Gen. Pinochet from extending his presidential term of office beyond 1990, a view subsequently endorsed in a plebiscite held in October 1988. The other main members of the CPD are the Socialist Party of Chile (PS), the Party for Democracy (PPD) and the Radical Social Democratic Party.

In order not to fragment the pro-democracy vote in the December 1989 presidential elections, the CPD's 17 member parties officially decided in July 1989 to back Patricio Aylwin Azócar, who was already the PDC candidate. After his inauguration in March 1990, President Aylwin formed a CPD coalition government with cabinet posts allocated to the main alliance parties proportionate to their representation in Congress. The new President had the difficult task of implementing the coalition's election promises while adopting a conciliatory approach towards the military and the two main right-wing parties.

The CPD repeated its 1989 success in the December 1993 presidential elections, securing victory for Eduardo Frei Ruíz-Tagle (PDC), the son of an earlier Christian Democratic President. In 1999, however, the leadership of the CPD shifted to the Socialists and the PPD, with the election of Ricardo Lagos Escóbar (PPD) as the coalition's presidential candidate. Lagos effectively tied with his opponent in the first round of the December 1999 elections, but narrowly won the second round in January 2000 with 51.3% of the vote. Inter-party tensions and several corruption scandals have strained relations between the main parties of the CPD, but the coalition remains committed to putting forward a single candidate for the 2005 presidential elections.

Communist Party of Chile
Partido Comunista de Chile (PCCh)
Address. San Pablo 2271, Santiago
Telephone. (+56-2) 724164
Website. www.pcchile.cl
Email. www@pcchile.cl
Leadership. Gladys Marín (president)
Formed by Luis Emilio Recabarren as the Socialist Workers' Party, the Communist Party adopted its present name in 1922, the year it joined the Third International (Comintern). The party contested the 1949 general election, obtaining six seats in the Chamber under the name National Democratic Front, which it retained until the PCCh was legalized in 1958. Joining forces with the Socialist Party (PS) in 1952, it supported the unsuccessful presidential campaign of Salvador Allende and continued to do so in the elections of 1958, 1964 and 1970, when Allende was elected. The party's representation in the lower house rose throughout the 1960s. By the time it was invited into the Allende government in 1970, the PCCh was one of the largest Communist parties outside the Eastern bloc.

The PCCh was banned following the September 1973 military coup and many of its leaders and activists were imprisoned. Some leaders, including the party's longstanding secretary-general, Luís Corvalán, were sent into exile in 1976. Like other Marxist parties, the PCCh was not permitted to register in 1987 and for the December 1989 elections the party relied on the support of the Christian Democrat-led Coalition for Democracy (CPD) and on PCCh-sponsored lists in exchange for the Communists' support elsewhere. Relations with other opposition parties, however, were strained because of the attempted assassination of General Pinochet in 1986, which the party supported. In January 1990, however, the PCCh finally renounced its policy of violent struggle by declaring that it had severed all links with the Manuel Rodríguez Patriotic Front (*Frente Patriotica Manuel Rodríguez,* FPMR), an active left-wing guerrilla group.

In the 1989 elections PCCh candidates won a total of 300,000 votes, but largely due to the binomial electoral system the party gained no seats in Congress. Despite regularly polling about 5% of the vote, the PCCh remains unrepresented in parliament. In the December 1999 presidential elections Gladys Marín garnered only 3.2 % of the vote.

Independent Democratic Union
Union Democrática Independiente (UDI)
Address. Suecia 286, Providencia, Santiago
Telephone. (+56-2) 244-2331
Fax. (+56-2) 233-6189
Website. www. udi.cl
Email. udi@udi.cl
Leadership. Jovino Novoa Vásquez (president)
The right-wing UDI was founded in the early 1980s under the leadership of Jaime Guzmán. Its original platform included the creation of a nominal parliament in order to counteract growing popular demands for a transition to democracy, thereby ensuring the continuation of the military's political legacy. The UDI merged with two other groups to form the National Renewal (PR) party in 1987, but was expelled in April 1988. It supported Gen. Pinochet's attempt to extend his presidency, voted down in the October 1988 plebiscite. The party then attempted to distance itself

from the military regime by backing the presidential candidacy of Hernán Buechi, the Finance Minister and an independent right-wing technocrat, who came second in the December 1989 elections.

The UDI was dealt a serious blow in April 1991 when its president, Jaime Guzmán, was assassinated by left-wing terrorists. However, in recent years it has become the principal right-wing party and is now the largest single party in Congress. In 2001 it took 35 seats in the Chamber of Deputies and 11 seats in the Senate. In the first round of presidential elections in December 1999, its candidate, Joaquín Lavín Infante, the former mayor of a prosperous Santiago suburb, came close to defeating the candidate of the Coalition of Parties for Democracy, winning 47.5% of the vote, thereby forcing a run-off election, which he narrowly lost (by a margin of 2.6%). Since then UDI has made major gains in municipal elections and in 2000 Lavín was elected mayor of Santiago. It is widely expected that Lavín will again represent the parties of the right in the 2005 presidential elections.

National Renewal
Renovacion Nacional (RN)
Address. Antonio Varas 454, Providencia, Santiago
Telephone. (+56-2) 373-8740
Fax. (+56-2) 373 8709
Website. www.rn.cl
Email. rn@rn.cl
Leadership. Sergio Diez Urzúa (president)
The right-wing RN was founded in 1987 as a merger of the National Union, the National Labour Front and the Independent Democratic Union (UDI, which was expelled a year later). The RN campaigned in the 1989 elections as the party that would protect the 1980 constitution installed by the Pinochet military regime but subsequently it distanced itself from the regime. Following the October 1988 plebiscite rejection of an extension of Pinochet's presidency, the party tried to project a moderate image by declaring itself willing to negotiate with the pro-democracy movement. In early 1989 the RN put pressure on Pinochet to consider the constitutional reform proposals put forward by the Coalition of Parties for Democracy (CPD).

In recent years the RN's alliance with the Independent Democratic Union (UDI) has been strained by personal and political differences and the party which was once the principal representative of the Chilean right has been significantly weakened.

Following the 2001 parliamentary elections the RN has 18 seats in the Chamber of Deputies and 7 seats in the Senate.

Party for Democracy
Partido por la Democracia (PPD)
Address. Erasmo Escala 2154, Santiago
Telephone. (+56–2) 671–5830
Website. www.ppd.cl
Email. informaciones@ppd.cl
Leadership. Víctor Barrueto (president)
The PPD was founded in December 1987 by Ricardo Lagos Escobar as a political vehicle of the then illegal Socialist Party of Chile (PS), in which all PPD members and leaders retained their membership. The party supported the "no" campaign leading up to the October 1988 plebiscite and was a member of the Coalition of Parties for Democracy (CPD) from its inception in November 1988. After the CPD victory in the December 1989 general election, the PPD became a major player in Congress. Following the 2001 parliamentary elections it has 20 seats in the Chamber of Deputies and 2 Senators. Its greatest political success to date has been the election of its founder, Ricardo Lagos, to the presidency in January 2000.

The PPD is a member of the Socialist International.

Radical Social Democratic Party
Partido Radical Social Democráta (PRSD)

Address. Miraflores 495, Santiago
Telephone. (+56–2) 639–1053
Website. www.partidoradical.cl
Email. partido@partidoradical.cl
Leadership. Enrique Silva Cimma (president)

The PRSD was originally founded in 1863 as the Radical Party (*Partido Radical,* PR) and is the country's oldest existing party. It was Chile's main progressive party around the turn of the last century and was in government from 1938 to 1952. The party lost power following bitter factional fights and subsequent division. It held some ministerial posts in the National Party government of Jorge Alessandri (1958-64). In 1969, after the defection of its right-wing faction to Alessandri's camp, it joined the broad Popular Unity (UP) alliance backing the presidential candidacy of Salvador Allende of the Socialist Party of Chile, Radicals holding important portfolios in the 1970-73 Allende government.

Following the overthrow of Allende in September 1973, the party shared in the military's repression of the UP parties and other democratic elements. In the 1980s the Radical Party became an influential force in the Coalition of Parties for Democracy (CPD). Having polled very poorly in the 1993 elections, the party adopted its present name. In the 1997 congressional elections it won four seats in the Chamber of Deputies. As a result of the 2001 elections the party has five Deputies.

The PRSD is a member of the Socialist International.

Socialist Party of Chile
Partido Socialista de Chile (PS or PSCh)

Address. Paris 873, Santiago
Telephone. (+56–2) 630-6900
Website. www.pschile.cl
Email. pschile@terra.cl
Leadership. Gonzalo Martner (president)

The centre-left PS is one of Chile's oldest political parties. It was founded in 1933 by a merger of six parties which had supported the Socialist Republic proclaimed by Col. Marmaduke Grove, which lasted for 13 days. The PS won 19 seats in the Chamber of Deputies in the 1937 elections as part of a left-wing Popular Front alliance. After several conflicts with the Communist Party of Chile (PCCh), the PS suffered a major split in 1948. A reunited party under the leadership of Saldavor Allende Gossens joined the Popular Unity (UP) alliance in 1969. With Allende as its candidate, the UP won the 1970 presidential elections, the PS receiving 22.8% of the overall UP vote.

Allende's reforms included the full nationalization of the copper industry, a price freeze and an increase in wages. Holding four ministerial posts, the Socialists were initially the most radical force in the Allende government, supporting land and factory seizures, but then increasingly called for moderation, as the government faced increasing opposition. Dogged by spiralling inflation, a US embargo, economic sabotage by the business sector and pressure from the army, the Allende government made increasing concessions to the right and in late 1972 included members of the military in the cabinet. This did not prevent a military coup in September 1973, in which Allende lost his life and many PS leaders were killed, imprisoned, tortured or exiled.

The party fragmented thereafter, undergoing an intense period of introspection and renovation. For the December 1989 presidential elections the main PS faction joined the Coalition of Parties for Democracy (CPD) supporting the victorious campaign of Patricio Aylwin Azócar of the Christian Democratic Party (PDC). As a result the PS obtained cabinet representation under Aylwin's presidency and that of his PDC successor, Eduardo Frei Ruíz-Tagle.

Together with its allies in the Party for Democracy (PPD), the PS effectively led the CPD alliance in the December 1999 presidential elections, in which the CPD candidate was Ricardo Lagos Escobar, a member of both the PDD and the PS. The narrow 51.3% to 48.7% victory of Lagos in the run-off voting in January 2000 re-established the PS as one of the dominant forces in Chilean politics. Following the 2001 parliamentary elections the PS has 10 seats in the Chamber of Deputies and 5 seats in the Senate.

The PS is a member of the Socialist International.

Other Parties

Humanist Party (*Partido Humanista,* PH), left-leaning "alternative" and pro-environment formation founded in 1984, a member of the Humanist International. Its presidential candidates won 1.2% in 1993 and 0.5% in 1999.
Address. Alameda 129, 4° piso, Santiago.
Tel. (+56-2) 632-6787
Email. phchile@ctcinternet.cl
Leadership. Efrén Osorio

Liberal Party (*Partido Liberal,* PL), founded in 1998 by centrist dissidents.
Address. Eduardo de la Barra 1384, Providencia
Tel. (+56-2) 335-5233
Fax. (+56-2) 233-2750
Website. www.partidoliberal.cl
Leadership. José Ducci (president)

Party of the South (*Partido del Sur,* PdS), regional right-wing party.

Progressive Central-Central Union (*Union de Centro-Centro Progresista,* UCCP), populist party which won one Chamber seat in 1997 on the "Chile 2000" ticket, supplementing its single seat in the Senate. It was represented in the 1999 presidential elections by Arturo Frei Bolívar, who had left the ruling Christian Democratic Party in protest over the arrest of Gen. Pinochet in London and who took only 0.4% of the vote.

China

Capital: Beijing
Population: 1,265,830,000 (2000 census)

The People's Republic of China (PRC) was proclaimed in 1949 on the victory of Mao Zedong's Communist Party of China (CPC) in a long civil war with Chiang Kai-shek's Nationalists. The first three PRC constitutions were promulgated in 1954, 1975 and 1978, the second and third specifically enshrining the leading role of the CPC. The 1982 constitution, the PRC's fourth and currently in force, describes China as "a socialist state under the people's democratic dictatorship led by the working class". It makes no reference to the role of the CPC in its main articles, although its preamble asserts that the Chinese people are "under the leadership of the CPC and the guidance of Marxism-Leninism and Mao Zedong Thought", with "Deng Xiaoping Theory" being added through an amendment approved in March 1999. The preamble also makes reference to "a broad patriotic united front" headed by the CPC and "composed of democratic parties and people's organizations", eight such parties being in nominal existence within this front, which is manifest in the China People's Political Consultative Conference (CPPCC).

Legislative authority is vested in the unicameral National People's Congress (Quanguo Renmin Daibiao Dahui), whose members are indirectly elected for a five-year term by the people's congresses of China's 22 provinces, five autonomous regions and four municipalities (themselves elected by all citizens aged 18 and over) and by the People's Liberation Army (PLA). All these candidates are approved by the CPC but are not necessarily party members. In addition delegates are selected from the newly created Special Administrative Regions of Hong Kong and Macau. The National People's Congress (NPC) meets annually, legislative authority being exercised in the interim by a Standing Committee elected by the NPC, which also elects the President and Vice-President of the PRC for a concurrent five-year term. All effective power, however, resides in the leadership bodies of the CPC. Since the sixth NPC elected in 1983, the size of this body has been just short of 3,000. The tenth NPC opened on March 5, 2003, with 2,983 deputies.

Communist Party of China (CPC)
Zhongguo Gongchan Dang

Address. CPC Central Committee, Beijing

Leadership (Politburo Standing Committee elected November 2002, listed by order of rank, with year of birth). Hu Jintao, 1942 (general secretary), Wu Bangguo, 1941, Wen Jiabao, 1942, Jia Qinglin, 1940, Zeng Qinghong, 1939, Huang Ju, 1938, Wu Guanzheng, 1938, Li Changchun, 1944, and Luo Gan, 1935.

According to its authorized history, the CPC was founded in July 1921 at a congress in Shanghai attended by a dozen delegates (among them Mao Zedong) from Marxist groups with a total membership of 57. Independent accounts say that the inaugural congress took place a year earlier but was expunged from later official histories because one of the founders (Zhang Shenfu) was rapidly expelled from the party. The accounts agree that Chen Duxiu became general secretary of the new party. The CPC's first programme advocated "science and democracy", the nurturing of Chinese culture and the abolition of feudalism. Party membership rose to 1,000 by 1925 and to 58,000 by 1927. Among its sources of support was the patriotic May 4 Movement, which had originated in Chinese outrage at the 1919 transfer of the leased port of Qingdao from Germany to Japan.

Inspired by the 1917 Bolshevik revolution in Russia, the CPC followed Soviet instructions to co-operate with the Nationalist government (headed by Chiang Kai-shek from 1925) and to infiltrate the ruling *Kuomintang* (KMT) party organization. Mao Zedong was elected a politburo member in 1924 and took charge of the CPC peasant department in 1926. He placed great emphasis on the role of the peasantry as a revolutionary class, giving much less focus to the industrial working classes than traditional Marxists.

In 1927 Chiang broke with his increasingly numerous CPC allies in Shanghai. A period of confusion followed, in which Chen Duxiu was replaced as CPC general secretary by Qu Qiubai and then by Li Lisan. Mao was sent to Hunan to organize a peasant revolt, but the "autumn harvest uprising" was a failure and Mao lost his seat on the politburo. He and about 1,000 followers nevertheless set up headquarters in mountains on the Hunan-Jiangxi border, where he was joined in 1928 by Zhu De, who was to become the outstanding Communist military leader of the revolutionary period. From this base the Communists took control of most of Jiangxi and of large parts of Hunan and Fujian, where a Chinese Soviet Republic (CSR) was established in 1931 under the leadership of Mao and Zhu De. Meanwhile, Li Lisan had been removed from the CPC leadership in 1930 and Mao's belief in the revolutionary potential of the peasantry had begun to gain acceptance.

The CPC central committee, which had been operating underground in Shanghai, joined Mao in Jiangxi in 1931, after which the CSR declared war on Japan in light of its invasion of Manchuria. Policy differences resulted in Mao's removal from his military and political posts in 1932-4, as KMT forces mounted a series of offensives against the Communists. The fifth such onslaught, involving some 900,000 troops, compelled the Communists to evacuate Jiangxi in October 1934 and to start out on their Long March to the remote north-west. During the march a conference at Zunyi (Guizhou province) in January 1935 elected Mao as chairman of the CPC military affairs committee (and thus effective party leader) and Zhang Wentian as general secretary. After a 6,000-mile trek, only 4,000 of the 86,000 people who had set out on the Long March reached Shaanxi and established a headquarters at Yan'an.

In 1937, following a revolt among his own followers, Chiang Kai-shek entered into an alliance with the Communists to resist Japanese aggression. This broke down in the early 1940s, when KMT troops began attacking CPC units. From then on Chiang combined passive resistance to the Japanese with military operations against the Communists, who by 1944 were holding down two-thirds of the Japanese occupation forces. By 1945 the Communists controlled a large area of rural northern China and had some 900,000 regulars and over 2 million militia under arms, facing 4 million KMT troops holding all the main towns.

The seventh CPC congress, held in Yan'an in 1945, elected Mao as central committee chairman, adopted a new constitution embracing Mao Zedong Thought and noted that party membership had risen to 1,210,000. Under Moscow's instruction to come to terms with the KMT, Mao solicited US support for the formation of a post-war coalition government, but Chiang had Washington's ear. Renewed civil war broke out in 1946. Numerical superiority gave the KMT the advantage at first, but the tide turned in 1948 and Communist forces gained control of most of China in 1949. The People's Republic of China (PRC) was established in Beijing on Oct. 1, 1949, with Mao as Chairman (President) and Zhou Enlai as Prime Minister of a nominal coalition government that included some small non-communist parties (see below).

The new regime was confronted by an economy ruined by years of war, its problems soon being exacerbated by China's involvement in the Korean War of 1950-53. Communist China was therefore dependent for some years on Soviet economic and military aid, its first five-year plan (1953-57) being concentrated on the development of heavy industry. From 1955, however, Mao set out to develop a distinctively Chinese form of socialism, pushing through the collectivization of agriculture in 1955 and the transfer of private enterprises to joint state-private ownership in 1956. Following Khrushchev's denunciation of Stalin at the 20th Soviet party congress in 1956, the eighth CPC congress the same year approved the deletion of references to Mao Zedong Thought from the party constitution. It also revived the post of general secretary (vacant since 1937), to which Deng Xiaoping was elected, and created a new five-member standing committee of the CPC politburo (the first members being Mao, Deng, Zhu, Liu Shaoqi and Chen Yun). Party membership was reported to the congress as 10,734,384. Mao had by then enunciated the slogan "Let 100 flowers bloom, let 100 schools of thought contend", which he developed in 1957 by launching a "rectification campaign" in which the people were encouraged to criticize government and party officials. The response was so great that the campaign was changed into one against "rightists" (defined as critics of the regime). The non-communist ministers were dropped from the government.

In 1958 the CPC launched China on the Great Leap Forward, a grandiose attempt to develop Chinese socialism at high speed. Industrial and agricultural targets were repeatedly raised, agricultural co-operatives were grouped into large communes that also undertook small-scale manufacturing, and over 2 million "backyard furnaces" were set up for the local production of iron and steel. This policy quickly led to economic and political crisis. A CPC central committee meeting in December 1958 adopted a critical resolution and Mao was forced to yield the PRC chairmanship to Liu Shaoqi in April 1959.

A concurrent deterioration in relations with the USSR, mainly over ideological questions but also involving territorial and national issues, resulted in the termination of Soviet aid in 1960 and the onset of the Sino-Soviet dispute. This became official when the CPC broke off relations with the Soviet Communist Party in 1966, after which the only ruling Communist party to back China was that of Albania. Meanwhile, a series of disastrous harvests, as well as human errors, had caused mass starvation and had impelled Deng and Liu not only to allow peasants to cultivate private plots but also to introduce bonuses and incentives in the industrial sector.

Regarding such policies as leading to a restoration of capitalism, or at least to Soviet-style revisionism, Mao in 1962 enunciated the slogan "Never forget the class struggle". He was supported by Marshal Lin Biao, the Minister of National Defence, who promoted the study of Mao Zedong Thought in the army and in 1964 published a compendium of the leader's ideas in *Mao Zhuxi yulu* (*Quotations from Chairman Mao*), usually known simply as the *Little Red Book*. Opposition in the CPC leadership remained strong, however, and in October 1965 Mao moved from Beijing to Shanghai, where he set up his base for the campaign that became known as the Cultural Revolution. With army backing, he forced the CPC politburo, meeting in Shanghai on May 16, 1966, to issue a circular calling for a purge of "those who have sneaked into the party, the government, the army and various spheres of culture".

Demonstrations against such elements began at Beijing University later in May 1966, followed by the formation of Red Guard units of students and schoolchildren, who terrorized those suspected of bourgeois tendencies. Returning to Beijing, Mao presided over a CPC central committee meeting on Aug. 1-12, 1966, which issued instructions for the conduct of the Cultural Revolution. On Aug. 18 Mao and Marshal Lin (by now second in the party hierarchy) reviewed a parade of more than a million Red Guards in the capital. They received support from Zhou, who nevertheless endeavoured to moderate the excesses into which the Cultural Revolution quickly descended.

Having generated much public uneasiness, in 1967 the Red Guards were replaced as the main agents of the Cultural Revolution by the Revolutionary Rebels, consisting of adult workers. Pitched battles between rival factions followed in many parts of China, producing a state of virtual anarchy and obliging Mao to fall back on the support of the army. The party and government disintegrated, as almost all the leading members came under attack and were replaced. The most virulent campaign was directed against Liu Shaoqi (the "number one capitalist roader"), who was removed from the chairmanship of the PRC in 1968 (the post being left vacant), expelled from the party and put in prison, where he died in November 1969. Also purged was Deng Xiaoping ("number two capitalist roader"), whose post of general secretary was abolished by the 9th CPC congress in 1969. At that congress Marshal Lin became Mao's designated successor, Mao Zedong Thought was reinstated in the party constitution and a new politburo was elected, dominated by Lin's military associates and recently-promoted politicians.

The new leadership was soon split over foreign policy, however. In the light of a deepening Sino-Soviet rift, Mao and Zhou favoured détente with the USA, but this policy was opposed by Lin, whose supporters began to plan a coup. After the announcement in July 1971 that US President Nixon would visit China in 1972, Mao again withdrew to Shanghai to rally support. When he returned to Beijing, Lin fled the country in September 1971 and was killed when his plane crashed or was shot down in Mongolia, whereupon his supporters on the CPC politburo were arrested.

Mao's failing health in his last years obliged him to live in seclusion. He presided over the 10th CPC congress in 1973 but apparently took no part in its deliberations. These ushered in a new power struggle between the moderates, led by Zhou, and the extremist "gang of four" politburo members headed by Mao's fourth wife, former actress Jiang Qing, who had the advantage of being able to claim that Mao supported them. Zhou secured the rehabilitation of many of those disgraced during the Cultural Revolution, including Deng, who became a Deputy Premier in 1973 and was readmitted to the CPC politburo in 1974. Zhou died in January 1976, however, and was succeeded as Prime Minister by Hua Guofeng, who took an anti-moderate line, assisted by serious disturbances in Beijing on April 5, 1976, that were labelled "counter-revolutionary". Later that month Deng was again removed from all his offices, accused of being an "unrepentant capitalist roader".

Following Mao's death in September 1976 (at the age of 82), Hua Guofeng took over as CPC chairman (and chairman of the central military commission) and turned against the radicals. The "gang of four" and their supporters were arrested in October 1976 on charges of plotting to seize power and in July 1977 Deng was again rehabilitated to his former party and government posts. A massive campaign was launched against the alleged misdeeds of the "gang of four", of whom Jiang Qing and one other were, in 1981, sentenced to death and the other two to long prison sentences, as were six former associates of Lin Biao. (The executions were not carried out, and Jiang committed suicide in 1991.)

Under Deng's influence, the theories and practices of the Great Leap Forward and the Cultural Revolution were gradually abandoned and earlier critiques of revisionism were admitted to be incorrect. The communes were dismantled and land was allocated to households on a contract basis. Central economic planning was relaxed and wages were related more closely to output. The formation of small private enterprises was encouraged and former capitalists' confiscated property was restored to them. Loans were accepted from external sources and foreign investment in joint enterprises was permitted. However, Deng defined the limits to change in his Four Principles of early 1979, requiring China to keep to the socialist road, uphold the people's democratic dictatorship, maintain the CPC's leading role and stay true to Marxism-Leninism and Mao Zedong Thought. Thus Deng broke with the radical pro-democracy April 5 movement (named after the 1976 clashes in Beijing), the better to deal with opposition to his reforms from the politburo conservatives headed by Hua.

The power struggle between Hua and Deng culminated in the former's replacement as Prime Minister in September 1980 and as CPC chairman in June 1981, respectively by Zhao Ziyang and Hu Yaobang, both Deng associates who had been disgraced during the Cultural Revolution. In the reform period since 1978, Deng never served as CPC general secretary, or as president of the PRC or as prime minister, but is still rightly regarded as the architect of reform. He did serve as a member of the CPC politburo standing committee from 1982 to 1987 and chairman of the powerful CPC central military commission from 1983 to 1989. In this phase some 100,000 people disgraced after 1957 were rehabilitated, many of them posthumously (including Liu Shaoqi), and a 1981 central committee resolution condemned most of Mao's post-1957 policies, while conceding that his contribution had outweighed his mistakes. The 12th CPC congress in September 1982 abolished the post of party chairman, Hu being elected to the strengthened post of general secretary (which had been revived in 1980), while Hua was excluded from the new politburo. A revised CPC constitution retained the reference to Mao Zedong Thought, but defined it as representing the distilled wisdom of the party rather than a programme of action. Under the new PRC constitution adopted in December 1982, Li Xiannian (a former close associate of Zhou) was elected to the restored post of President of China in June 1983.

There followed an extensive reorganization and relative rejuvenation of party and government bodies, with many of the "old guard" figures being replaced by supporters of Deng's pragmatic policies. The economy embarked on a phase of rapid expansion (growing at nearly 10% a year through the 1980s) and its integration into the world system gathered pace. This process was boosted by the signature in September 1984 of an agreement with Britain under which Hong Kong would revert to Chinese sovereignty in 1997 but retain its existing capitalist system for at least 50 years thereafter. Nevertheless, greater reliance on market forces led to increased corruption among party cadres, which in turn aroused popular discontent over the slow pace of political liberalization. Pro-democracy student demonstrations in several cities began in late 1986 and were stamped out only after some delay. Hu Yaobang was forced to resign as CPC general secretary in January 1987, being accused by Deng and others of excessive leniency to the demonstrators, and was replaced by Zhao Ziyang, who embarked on a campaign against "bourgeois liberalization".

Zhao was formally confirmed in office at the 13th CPC congress in October-November 1987, when Deng stood down from the politburo's standing committee while retaining the chairmanship of the central military commission. Endeavouring to attune his policies to Deng's thinking, Zhao pushed ahead with economic reform, proposing in mid-1988 that state price controls should be abolished within five years. Although this reform was quickly postponed (so that Zhao was left isolated), popular pressure for political reform, led by intellectuals and focusing on official corruption and rapidly rising prices, gathered impetus in late 1988 and early 1989.

The sudden death in April 1989 of Hu Yaobang, shortly after he had delivered an impassioned critique of government policy to the CPC politburo, gave renewed impetus to the pro-democracy movement. Demonstrations in Beijing's Tiananmen Square sparked similar protest rallies in other cities, gathering strength in mid-May during an historic visit to Beijing by Mikhail Gorbachev to mark the normalization of Sino-Soviet relations. For the demonstrators, mostly students but also including workers and intellectuals, Gorbachev's reformist policies in the USSR merited emulation. Zhao favoured a conciliatory approach but lost the argument to the hardliners led by Prime Minister Li Peng. On June 3-4 army units were sent in to clear the square, this being accomplished in bloody fighting which left up to 1,000 demonstrators dead and many thousands injured. Similar crackdowns followed in other parts of China, although on a less violent scale. In the inevitable conservative backlash, Zhao and his supporters were ejected from their politburo and other party posts, the position of CPC general secretary going to Jiang Zemin, hitherto party secretary in Shanghai. He joined a politburo standing committee enlarged to six members, whose dominant figure at that time was Li Peng. Also in the conservative camp was Yang Shangkun, a politburo member who had been elected President of the PRC in April 1988 in succession to Li Xiannian.

On Nov. 9, 1989, Deng Xiaoping finally vacated the chairmanship of the central military commission at a CPC central committee meeting, being replaced by Jiang Zemin.

But Deng remained the effective leader of the regime as China's "elder statesman", issuing instructions that economic reform should be suspended and an austerity drive launched to curb inflation. In mid-1990 fears of an economic downturn led to a resumption of economic reform, while in 1991 some Zhao supporters were rehabilitated. In January and February 1992, Deng Xiaoping made a high-profile visit to several major cities of the south, signalling a strong revival of reform policies. Nevertheless, on the third anniversary of the Tiananmen Square massacre in June 1992, new regulations were published which placed even tighter restrictions on demonstrations. A 1992 codification of Deng's speeches asserted that the response to the "turmoil" of June 1989 had been correct. Differences persisted, however, as highlighted by the contrast in May-June 1992 between Li Peng's further warning against "bourgeois liberalization" and Jiang Zemin's criticism of "leftists" for using revolutionary slogans to "confuse the people".

The 14th CPC congress, held in October 1992, was told that party membership stood at around 52 million and elected a central committee (of 189 full and 130 alternate members) on which nearly half the members were new. Jiang was re-elected CPC general secretary (and chairman of the central military commission) and three of the other six members of the standing committee were also re-elected, although a majority of the other politburo members were also new, most of them Dengists. Features of the changes included the demotion of both President Yang and his half-brother, Yang Baibing, who had been prominent Dengists but were reportedly seen as an alternative power centre, and the inclusion of only one army representative (Gen. Liu Huaqing) on the new politburo.

At the eighth National People's Congress (NPC) in March 1993, the first session elected Jiang as President of the PRC in succession to Yang Shangkun. It also re-elected Li Peng as Prime Minister, although an unprecedented 330 votes were cast against him, indicating strong underlying disapproval of his role in the 1989 events. Jiang thus became the first Chinese leader since Hua Guofeng (in the immediate post-Mao period) to hold the three top posts of party leader, chairmanship of the central military commission and head of state or government. However, despite being designated "core leader", he remained in the shadow of Deng until the latter's death in February 1997. The broad Dengist line of economic liberalization combined with political conservatism continued to deliver success in terms of economic expansion: according to the IMF in March 1993, China had become the world's third-largest economy after the USA and Japan on the basis of purchasing power parity. Nevertheless, concern about inflation and other negative phenomena continued to generate strains within the leadership, highlighted by regular switches of economic policy priorities.

A CPC central committee session in November 1993 adopted a new blueprint for what was termed a "socialist market economic system" and appeared to mark a crucial victory for those favouring rapid economic change. In April 1994, however, there was a renewed crackdown on prominent dissidents in the run-up to the anniversary of the 1989 events. A session of the CPC central committee in September 1994 resolved that the "extensive and profound social change currently taking place in China" required the party "to do better in upholding and improving democratic centralism". In May 1995 Jiang launched a campaign against high-level corruption, requiring all state and party officials (and their children in some cases) to declare their incomes from all sources. At the same time, the *People's Daily* (organ of the CPC) began citing the teachings of Confucius – once denounced by the Communists as the creator of Chinese feudalism – on the need for social and political harmony.

At the 15th congress of the CPC, held in September 1997, Jiang Zemin was re-elected general secretary. At the next session of the NPC (March 1998) Zhu Rongji was elected Prime Minister in place of Li Peng (who became chairman of the NPC), whilst a representative of the next generation of party officials, Hu Jintao, was elected Vice-President of the country. In 1999 he also became deputy chairman of the central military commission. This made him Jiang's likely successor.

The 15th party congress was told that CPC membership had risen to 58 million, one-fifth being women and 22.4% aged under 35. A rise in the educational level of the membership was also apparent: 43.4% had at least graduated from senior high school and almost 18% were university graduates. At the same time, the central committee was becoming more "technocratic": 92% had university degrees (44% in engineering). The new generation of politicians coming to the fore were expected to compose a majority of the politburo after the next congress in 2002.

The run-up to the 2002 congress saw new thinking on the position of the CPC in society. In February 2000 Jiang Zemin launched the concept of the "three represents", i.e. the party should represent the advanced forces of production, the forward direction of advanced culture and the fundamental interests of the majority of the Chinese people. In mid-2001 he went a step further by changing party rules so that entrepreneurs could become CPC members, although old-style Maoists derided this. There were calls in some quarters for competitive elections for party posts.

In 2001 the NPC approved the tenth five-year plan for the economy covering the period 2001-05. This envisaged an average annual growth rate of 7% as compared with the 8.3% achieved between 1996 and 2000. Yet despite the optimism of these figures, society was becoming more turbulent. Tides of migrants flocked to and between cities, while peasants continued to mount sporadic demonstrations over difficult living conditions and "exploitation" by officials. Large numbers of workers in loss-making state-owned enterprises faced unemployment, and public opinion became increasingly exercised by growing social and geographical inequality and by increasing levels of crime and corruption. The party responded by stepping up campaigns against official corruption (a former provincial governor and Vice-Chairman of the NPC, Cheng Kejie, being executed in September 2000) and against crime in general (Amnesty International calculating that the PRC now carries out more judicial executions than the rest of the world combined), as well by launching a programme to "open up" the western part of the country. It also cracked down brutally on real or perceived opponents.

At the turn of the century, the CPC leadership was also concerned by the rise of the quasi-religious Falun Gong movement, which organized a demonstration of over 10,000 people outside the central leadership compound in Beijing in April 1999. This took the regime entirely by surprise. The subsequent investigation further unsettled the leadership by revealing that senior officials in the government and the army were members of the sect. Even though the Falun Gong were no contender for political power, their stubborn persistence in continuing to organize demonstrations despite persecution served as a reminder that alternative ideas were challenging the legitimacy of CPC leadership.

At the end of 2001, China joined the World Trade Organization (WTO). The resulting acceleration of relaxations on trade barriers with the outside world propelled China even further into engagement with the world economy. Although this benefits China in many ways, it also means that some industries have been unable to compete with outside counterparts, one result being a growth in unemployment. The period following China's accession to the WTO saw major strikes and other industrial disputes, which the CPC suppressed. In May 2003, two labour leaders from strikes in the first half of 2002 were sentenced to prison terms.

On Sept. 2, 2002, the *People's Daily* announced figures for

the CPC applying to June. Total membership was 66,355,000, of whom 17.5%, or 11,598,000, were women, and 14,800,000, or 22.3%, were aged 35 or less. Workers, farmers, fishermen and rural enterprise labourers accounted for 29,913,000 members, that is 45.1%, while cadres, entrepreneurs, managers, members of the army and armed police were 14,112,000, or 21.3%. Those with senior secondary education and above were 52.5% of the total, while those with university or tertiary specialist education accounted for 23.2% of the total. The proportion of women had shrunk since 1992, but the CPC was better educated than ever before, and the category "entrepreneurs" was included for the first time.

The 16th CPC Congress of November 2002 brought in an almost completely new leadership, headed by Hu Jintao, who had joined the politburo standing committee in 1992. At the 10th NPC in March 2003, Hu Jintao replaced Jiang Zemin as PRC president, while Wen Jiabao became Prime Minister in succession to Zhu Rongji.

This was the first time the CPC had undergone a major leadership change without a major political upheaval. At the same time, Jiang Zemin retained his position as chairman of the CPC's central military commission, and thus was able to continue to exert influence. The 16th CPC Congress also changed the party's Constitution to include Jiang Zemin's concept of the "three represents". The new Constitution praised Jiang Zemin's thirteen years of leadership and made the CPC "the vanguard of the Chinese people" as well as of the working class, thus moving towards being a party of the whole people and changing its nature significantly.

The first major test facing the new Hu Jintao leadership was the outbreak of an unknown virus in China called the "severe acute respiratory syndrome" (SARS). Initially the government was defensive, trying to play down the seriousness of the issues such an outbreak posed. However, in April 2003 it changed direction, dismissing two senior officials, including the Minister of Health, and taking other drastic measures to halt the disease, such as closing campuses and cancelling the May Day week-long holiday for that year to prevent people travelling and spreading the disease. Late in June 2003, the World Health Organization lifted its travel ban on Beijing, thus declaring that China had beaten the SARS virus, at least for the time being.

Other Parties

Eight other "democratic" parties are permitted to exist in China on the basis of participation in a "united front" with the CPC. Officially they are recognized as having co-operated with the CPC in the "war of resistance" against Japan (1937-45) and in the "war of liberation" against the *Kuomintang* (KMT), and as having played a role, as members of the China People's Political Consultative Conference (CPPCC), in the formulation of the first PRC constitution. Not allowed to operate during the Cultural Revolution, these essentially powerless parties re-emerged in the late 1970s. They are customarily allocated about 7% of the seats in the National People's Congress.

China Association for Promoting Democracy (*Zhongguo Minzhu Cujin Hui*), founded in December 1945 to represent literary, cultural and educational personnel, emphasizes the importance of education in building a socialist society, running over 230 schools. In July 2004, the Association claimed over 84,000 members.
Address. 98 Xinanli Guloufangzhuangchang, 100009 Beijing
Website. http://www.mj.org.cn
Leadership. Xu Jialu (chairman)

China Democratic League (*Zhongguo Minzhu Tongmeng*), founded in 1941 as the League of Democratic Parties and

Organizations of China to unite intellectuals against the KMT, membership (about 130,000 in November 2002) drawn from scientific, educational and cultural intellectuals.
Address. 1 Beixing Dongchang Hutong, 100006 Beijing
Leadership. Ding Shisun (chairman)

China National Democratic Construction Association (*Zhongguo Minzhu Jianguo Hui*), founded in 1945, membership (nearly 70,000 late in 2002) is drawn from industrialists and businessmen, promotes contact with overseas Chinese.
Address. 93 Beiheyan Dajie, 100006 Beijing
Leadership. Cheng Siwei (chairman)

China Party for Public Interests (*Zhongguo Zhi Gong Dang*), founded in San Francisco in 1925, descended from 19th-century secret society for overseas Chinese, advocates "reform and construction under the banner of socialism and patriotism". There were more than 15,000 members in November 2002, most of them returned overseas Chinese and their relatives, experts, scholars and representative personages with overseas connections.
Leadership. Luo Haocai (chairman)

Chinese Peasants' and Workers' Democratic Party (*Zhongguo Nonggong Minzhu Dang*), descended from pre-war movement of anti-Chiang Kai-shek Nationalists who abandoned the objective of a bourgeois republic in 1935 and joined forces with the Communist Party of China. Adopted present name in 1947. In November 2002 there were more than 65,000 members; most of them work in the fields of public health, culture and education, science and technology.
Leadership. Jiang Zhenghua (chairman)

Chinese Revolutionary Committee of the Kuomintang (*Zhongguo Guomindang Geming Weiyuanhui*). Founded in 1948 in Hong Kong by notional KMT members opposed to Chiang Kai-shek, "carrying forward Dr Sun Yat-sen's patriotic and revolutionary spirit" by seeking the "peaceful reunification of the motherland"; membership (over 53,000 in November 2002) is drawn from health, finance, culture and education sectors.
Leadership. He Luli (chair)

September 3 Society (*Jiu San Xuehui*), founded in 1944 in Sichuan as the Democracy and Science Forum, renamed to commemorate the date of the Japanese surrender in 1945, membership drawn from scientists and technologists.
Leadership. Wu Jieping (chairman)

Taiwan Democratic Self-Government League (*Taiwan Minzhu Zizhi Tongmeng*), founded in 1947 by pro-PRC Chinese from Taiwan, promotes contacts with Taiwan to further the goal of reunification.
Leadership. Zhang Kehui (chairman)

Pro-democracy activists failed in 1998 in several attempts to register the **Chinese Democracy Party**. Three leaders of the party –Wang Youcai, Xu Wenli and Qin Yongmin – received lengthy prison sentences and many activists were detained.

HONG KONG SPECIAL ADMINISTRATIVE REGION

Population: 6,708,389 (2001 census)

The former British colony of Hong Kong returned to Chinese sovereignty on July 1, 1997, to become a special administrative region (SAR) of the People's Republic under the basic principle of "one country, two systems" guaranteed for 50 years. In April 1990, China's NPC adopted the Basic Law of the Hong Kong SAR, which enshrined the "one country, two systems" principles.

After the British and Chinese governments signed the 1984 Joint Declaration providing for the reversion, they had agreed to allow election instead of selection of some members to the Legislative Council (LegCo), but they had argued over the precise figures. Changes introduced by the last UK Governor were bitterly opposed in Beijing, which responded with a plan for an alternative Provisional Legislative Council (PLC). Immediately after the transfer of sovereignty, the new SAR Chief Executive, Tung Chee-hwa, dissolved LegCo and replaced it with the PLC. This laid down the detailed framework for implementing the Basic Law for the SAR that had previously been promulgated in Beijing and then it arranged for elections to a restored LegCo in May 1998 for a two-year term. New elections were held in September 2000. Voter turnout was 53% in 1998 but only 43% in 2000.

LegCo has 60 members, of whom 30 are elected directly from geographical constituencies, 24 elected from functional constituencies and six chosen indirectly by the 800 directly-elected representatives on the Election Committee. The Basic Law states that all LegCo seats will be directly elected at an indeterminate date in the future. Since 1997 Hong Kong has sent 36 delegates to the National People's Congress in Beijing.

Elections for district councils in 1999 saw a turnout of 36%, but this rose to 44% in the district council elections of November 2003. The elections saw strong swings against pro-Beijing parties and towards the democratic parties. Protests late in 2002 and a mass demonstration of some half a million people in July 2003 resulted in the withdrawal of a security law the government had proposed.

These protests signalled a steep decline in the popularity of Tung Chee-hwa's government. A demonstration in July 2004 over the government's decision to postpone fully democratic elections in Hong Kong attracted far fewer people than its 2003 counterpart, but was still very large in scale. The pro-government parties did unexpectedly well in the September 2004 LegCo elections, winning 12 of the 30 directly elected geographical constituencies (up from 7). The pro-democracy parties won the remaining 18 seats (up from 17), but though they won 60% of the popular vote, opinion polls had predicted a considerably better performance.

Citizens' Party (CP)
Address. Room 319, 88 Commercial Building, 28-34 Wing Lok Street, Sheung Wan
Telephone. (+852) 2893-0029
Fax. (+852) 2147-5796
Email. enquiry@citizensparty.org
Website. www.citizensparty.org
Leadership. Alex Chan (chairman)
Formed in May 1997 by Christine Loh, the CP proclaims a belief in liberal democratic values and openness. Loh was the only CP candidate who won a seat in LegCo in 1998 (having been an independent member in 1995). In the summer of 2000 she announced that she would not contest the next round of LegCo elections and would instead concentrate on political activity outside. In 2001 Alex Chan succeeded her as party chairman.

Democratic Alliance for the Betterment of Hong Kong (DABHK
Address. 12/F, 83 King's Road, North Point
Telephone. (+852) 2528-0136
Fax. (+852) 2528-4339

Email. info@dab.org.hk
Website. www.dab.org.hk
Leadership. Ma Lik (chairman)

Founded in July 1992, its main orientation has been to co-operate with the mainland authorities in looking after the interests of the people of Hong Kong. As the disputes between London and Beijing became embittered, it picked up support by encouraging moderation, whilst occasionally standing up to Beijing. In 1995 it won six LegCo seats and was rewarded with 42 seats on the PLC. Since 1997 it has made great efforts to collaborate with the government on day-to-day issues and in June 2003 claimed 2,073 members. In 1998 it gained 10 seats with around 25% of the vote and in 2000 11 seats with around 35%, though one seat was later lost in a by-election. In the district council elections of 1999 it won 83 seats, but only 62 in those of 2003, triggering the resignation of founding chairman Jasper Tsang both from leadership in his party and from the Executive Council, a chamber of appointed advisers to Hong Kong chief executive Tung Chee-Hwa. It did unexpectedly well in the September 2004 LegCo elections, and became the biggest political party in the LegCo with 25 out of the total 60 seats, including 8 of the 30 directly elected geographical constituencies.

Democratic Party (DP)

Address. 4/F Hanley House, 776-8 Nathan Road, Kowloon
Telephone. (+852) 2397-7033
Fax. (+852) 2397-8998
Email. dphk@dphk.org
Website. www.dphk.org
Leadership. Yeung Sum (chairman); Martin Lee (one of two vice-chairmen)

Founded originally in 1991 as the United Democrats of Hong Kong, this party took its present name in 1994. It gained 12 out of 18 geographical seats in the 1991 elections and 19 out of 20 in 1995. It has consistently pushed for full democracy in Hong Kong and the observance of human rights on the mainland. This has led it into regular clashes with Beijing. Its leaders mounted a symbolic demonstration against the dissolution of LegCo in July 1997 and it refused to co-operate with the PLC. In 1998 it won in nine out of 20 geographical constituencies and in four functional ones with 43% of the vote, making it the largest party in LegCo. In 2000 this slipped to just under 35% and 12 seats. It was the main beneficiary of the anti-government swing in the district council elections of November 2003, winning 93 councillor seats. In January 2004 it claimed 598 members. However, its performance in the September 2004 LegCo elections was disappointing. It won only 12 out of the 60 seats, including 7 of the 30 directly elected geographical constituencies, becoming the third largest party in the LegCo.

The Frontier

Address. Flat B, 9/F, 557-9 Nathan Road, Yaumati, Kowloon
Telephone. (+852) 2524-9899
Fax. (+852) 2524-5310
Leadership. Emily Lau Wai-hing

Founded in 1996 by the current unofficial leader, Emily Lau Wai-hing, and two other members of LegCo, this formation was the most intransigent critic of London and Beijing over the handover of power. More loosely organized and rejecting the designation of a party as such, it has limited funds. It has sought to play a moral role in Hong Kong society by defending human rights, chiefly through operating in other environments than LegCo. Nevertheless, it won three geographical constituencies there in 1998 and two in 2000.

Hong Kong Progressive Alliance

Address. 11/F, 1 Lockhart Road, Central
Telephone. (+852) 2377-3030

Fax. (+852) 2377-2211
Website. www.hkpa.org.hk
Leadership. Ambrose Lau Hon-chuen (chairman)

Formed in 1994 by Ambrose Lau Hon-chuen, on encouragement from mainland officials who felt that the Democratic Alliance for the Betterment of Hong Kong was too independent-minded, it has stayed closer to the line from Beijing. It gained three seats in 1995 and subsequently was rewarded with the largest proportion of seats (47) on the PLC. In 1998 it gained a total of five seats, though none were directly elected.

Liberal Party

Address. 7/F, Printing House, 6 Duddell Street, Central
Telephone. (+852) 2869-6833
Fax. (+852) 2533-4238
Leadership. James Tien Pei-chun (chairman)

Founded in July 1993, this party is most associated with the interests of business. In the 1991 LegCo it had 15 seats. Subsequently its status declined as it was squeezed on the one side by the rise of more overtly pro-mainland parties and on the other by the success of the Democratic Party, which took up traditional "liberal" values such as human rights and the rule of law. In 1995 and 1998 it won 10 seats, falling to eight in 2000, but none of these were directly elected. The party strongly opposes proposals to abolish the functional constituencies.

MACAU SPECIAL ADMINISTRATIVE REGION

Population: 448,500 (2003E)

Macau followed Hong Kong in returning to Chinese sovereignty in December 1999 as a special administrative region (SAR) of the People's Republic under the same basic principle of "one country, two systems" guaranteed for 50 years. Like Hong Kong, the Macau SAR has a Legislative Council (LegCo). In pre-reversion elections in September 1996, eight out of the 23 members were elected by popular vote by proportional representation, eight were elected indirectly and seven were appointed by the Chief Executive. In new elections on Sept. 23, 2001, 10 members were directly elected from among 15 groups and 10 were elected indirectly from functional constituencies representing 625 registered business, labour and community organizations, while a further seven continued to be appointed by the Chief Executive.

There are no political parties as such in Macau, but 12 civic groups put forward lists of candidates for direct election in 1996. The results, amidst widespread suspicions of vote-buying were as follows: *Associação Promotora para a Economia de Macau* 2 seats, *União Promotora para o Progresso* 2, *Convergencia para o Desenvolvimento* 1, *União Geral para o Desenvolvimento de Macau* 1, *União para o Desenvolvimento* 1, *Associação de Novo Macau Democratico* 1. Macau has yet to see ardent pro-democracy movements, as exist in Hong Kong. The main issues in elections tend to be economic development, health care, education and bureaucratic administration.

Colombia

Capital: Santafé de Bogotá
Population: 42,310,775 (2004E)

The territory of Colombia gained independence from Spain in 1819 after liberation by the forces of Simón Bolívar and, after several boundary changes, became an independent Republic in 1886. Colombian politics have long been dominated by the Liberal Party (PLC) and the Conservative Party, now called the Social Conservative Party (PSC), both of which were founded in the 1840s. Colombia's only military government of the twentieth century was overthrown in 1958, when the two rival parties joined forces and formed a National Front coalition government which lasted from 1958 until 1974. Under the terms of the 1991 constitution, executive authority is vested in the President, who is elected directly for a four-year term by direct universal suffrage and may not serve a second consecutive term. A Vice-President, Fiscal General, and Defender of the People assist the President in policy-making. The President is also assisted by a Cabinet, which he appoints.

Legislative power is vested in a bicameral Congress, consisting of a 102-seat Senate and a 161-seat House of Representatives. Members of Congress cannot hold any other public post. A system of proportional representation operates for the election of members of both houses, who are also elected for a four-year period. The Senate has 99 nationally elected members; indigenous people in specific regions have two appointed senators selected in special elections and one elected senator. Each of the 23 departments, four intendencies and five commissaries (32 in all) elects two members of the House of Representatives and further seats are allotted to each state on the basis of population. Governors are elected directly in the 27 departments and intendencies. All Colombian citizens aged 18 or over are eligible to vote, except members of the armed forces on active service, the national police and people who have been deprived of their political rights. Women obtained the vote in 1957. The indigenous population enjoys judicial autonomy in minor internal disputes within certain recognized territories.

Legislative elections held on March 8, 1998, took place against the backdrop of a violent guerrilla offensive in the country, as left-wing rebels continued to oppose government security forces in the country's nearly 30-year-old civil war. Final results gave the PLC a renewed clear majority in both chambers, and in presidential elections held on May 31 and June 21, 1998, the PSC candidate, Andrés Pastrana Arango, polled 50.6% of the vote, defeating the candidate of the ruling PLC, Horacio Serpa Uribe, who won 46.5% of the vote. The legislative elections of March 10, 2002, were characterized by apathy and widespread abstention. In the new Senate the Liberals gained seats, the results being: PLC 28, PSC 13, Coalition Party 6, National Movement 6; the balance of power being held by no less than 38 minor parties which gained at least one of the 49 remaining seats. Seats in the 161-seat Chamber of Deputies followed a similar pattern, the PLC winning only 54 seats and the PSC 21. In the first round of the presidential elections held on May 26, 2002, Alvaro Uribe Velez, running as candidate of the right-wing Colombia First (*Primero Colombia*) coalition, secured 53.04% of the votes to secure an unprecedented outright win. The official candidate of the outgoing PLC, Horacio Serpa Uribe, obtained only 31.72%. The PSC candidate, Juan Camilo Restrepo, had withdrawn after the legislative elections and the party then endorsed Uribe. On June 11 the PLC agreed to support the new government, ensuring it a large majority in both houses of Congress.

Liberal Party of Colombia
Partido Liberal Colombiano (PLC)

Address. Avenida Caracas No.36–01, Santafé de Bogotá, DC
Telephone. (57–1) 288-1138, 287-9809
Fax. (57–1) 287–9740
Email. prensa@partidoliberal.org.co
Website. www.partidoliberal.org.co
Leadership. Joaquin José Vives (president); Piedad Córdoba (co-director); Juan Pablo Camacho (vice-president); Eduardo Verano de la Rosa (secretary-general)

Founded in the 1840s, the progressive centrist PLC has been a mainstay of the country's political history, standing in recent times for free enterprise and privatization, improved living standards and combating drug-trafficking. The party emerged from the rise of the American-born Spanish middle-classes influenced by European republican and radical utopian ideas. Although its major founding forces were the political discussion clubs which opposed Simón Bolívar, the PLC's classic liberal reforms, such as the abolition of slavery, reduction of church power, decentralization of government, an end to state monopolies and the introduction of freedom of the press, were inspired by the earlier independence movement.

In the mid-1950s the PLC and the Conservative Party of Colombia (PCC) agreed on a power-sharing arrangement whereby the presidency would be held by each party in rotation and cabinet posts divided equally between them. This National Front agreement was approved by a referendum in December 1957, and in the subsequent elections the Liberal candidate (and former President), Lleras Camargo, became the first National Front President. Even though the parity agreement officially expired in 1974, the Liberals, who won the elections of 1974 and 1978, continued to award half the cabinet portfolios to Conservatives.

Successive Liberal governments proved largely ineffective against the illegal drugs trade and the escalating violence, which in 1988 alone saw an estimated 18,000 political and drug-cartel-related killings. In the political turmoil of 1989 leading PLC members were among victims of the growing spate of assassinations of politicians. Nevertheless, in the March 1990 poll the PLC increased its representation in the Senate to 72 seats and in the House of Representatives to 120. The victory was crowned in the presidential election of May 1990, which PLC candidate César Gaviria Trujillo won with 47% of the vote.

President Gaviria's inauguration pledge to continue his predecessor's campaign against "narco-terrorism", but not his policy of extraditing drug traffickers, soon came to fruition. He issued a decree offering drug barons, who called themselves the *extraditables*, a guarantee that they would not be extradited to the USA if they surrendered to the authorities. Although this was generally seen as a concession to the Medellín cartel, the deal was followed by the surrender of several major drug traffickers and an end to all-out war between the government and the drug cartels. This in turn had the desired effect of stabilizing the country for economic growth. At the end of 1991 Gaviria announced major investment in infrastructure to assist this trend. The PLC government also continued the peace initiatives with the country's guerrilla groups, so that by the time of the opening of the Constitutional Assembly in February 1991 peace agreements with some groups had been signed.

The resignation of Alfonso Lopez Michelsen as PLC leader in April 1992 ushered in a period of internal strife within the party that forced four successive factional leadership changes in a four-month period. Coming from the party's left-wing faction, the PLC's 1994 presidential candidate, Ernesto Samper Pizano, narrowly defeated the PSC contender. The Liberals were also successful in legislative elections held in the same year, retaining congressional majorities with 89 seats in the Chamber of Representatives and 52 seats in the Senate. The PLC retained its control of Congress in the 1998 legislative elections, but the defeat of PLC candidate Horacio Serpa Uribe in the subsequent presidential elections ended 12 years of Liberal rule.

Following PLC criticism of his proposal for a referendum on rooting out corruption from the political system, President Pastrana reshuffled his government in July 2000, bringing in two members of the PLC (Juan Manuel Santos Calderón as Finance Minister and Consuelo Araújo Noguera as Culture Minister). However, then PLC leader Serpa Uribe insisted that the new Liberal ministers were acting in a "personal capacity" and denied that a coalition government had been formed. The Liberals performed well in departmental and municipal elections held in October 2000, securing 15 out of 30 governorships in contention and winning control of 13 out of 30 departmental capitals (including Medellín). They gained congressional seats in the 2002 elections, but lost the presidency to Alvaro Uribe Velez of the Colombia First coalition.

The PLC is a full member of the Socialist International.

Social Conservative Party of Colombia/Conservative Party of Colombia
Partido Social Conservador (PSC)/Partido Conservador Colombiano (PCC)

Address. Avenida 22 No.37–09, La Soledad, Santafé de Bogotá, DC
Telephone. (57–1) 369–0011, 369-0289, 369-0076
Fax. (57–1) 369–0187
Email. secretaria@partidoconservador.com
Website. www.partidoconservador.com.co
Leadership. Carlos Holguín Sardi (president); Jorge Sedano (secretary-general)

The PCC was founded in 1849. The party stands for law and order and traditional religious values, its doctrine being based upon the encyclicals of the Roman Catholic Church. The PCC was founded by Mariano Ospina Rodriguez, a leading member of the conservative Popular Societies, and supporters of President Jose Ignacio Marquez (1837-42). The party drew its members and leaders chiefly from the landed classes and business. It originally stood for protectionism and a centralized state controlled by the traditional elite, their power being legitimized by the Roman Catholic Church which was given an important role in society.

Belisario Betancur of the PCC was inaugurated as President in August 1982 and his administration, hampered by a Congress dominated by the Liberal Party of Colombia (PLC), still managed to pass a variety of social and economic reforms. In November 1982, in an attempt to bring about peace, Betancur announced an amnesty for the country's guerrilla groups and in mid-1984 secured agreement for a year-long ceasefire with the three main groups. However, this first step towards reconciliation was quickly overshadowed by an escalating war with the powerful drug cartels. After the murder of Justice Minister Rodrigo Lara Bonilla in May 1984, Betancur imposed a state of siege and in November of the following year, with the internal situation rapidly deteriorating, he declared a state of economic and social emergency. In the subsequent congressional elections of March 1986, and the presidential elections in the following May, the PCC was defeated by its old rival, the PLC, its seats in the Senate being reduced to 45 and in the House of Representatives to 82. In 1987 it changed its name to the Social Conservative Party (PSC) for electoral purposes.

In late May 1988 the former PCC presidential candidate, Alvaro Gomez Hurtado, was abducted by the M19 guerrilla group for two months, which caused widespread protests against the government and demands for his release. Gomez broke with the PSC in 1990 to form the National Salvation Movement (MSN), a move that greatly damaged the Conservatives. In the congressional elections of March 1990, the PSC again came second to the PLC, and in the presidential elections in May Rodrigo Lloreda Caicedo of the PSC finished only fourth with 12.2% of the vote. In 1994, moreover, the PSC's presidential candidate, Andrés Pastrana Arango, lost to Ernesto Samper of the PLC, although by less than 1% of the vote in the second round. The party had again been defeated by the PLC in the earlier legislative elections (taking 56 seats in the House of Representatives and 21 in the Senate).

The PSC returned to power in the mid-1998 presidential poll, with Andrés Pastrana defeating the PLC candidate in the run-off. A few months earlier, however, the PLC had managed to retain a narrow overall majority in both houses of Congress. The elections had been marred by guerrilla attacks aimed at disrupting polling, with some 250,000 troops and police being deployed to ensure the safety of voters. The PSC suffered a severe setback, however, in departmental and municipal elections held in October 2000, winning control of just two departmental capitals and failing to win a single governorship. The elections were marked by a considerable degree of violence and intimidation, including the kidnapping of seven congressmen by the United Self Defence Forces of Colombia (AUC), a right-wing paramilitary organization, and the assassination of dozens of local candidates across the country by both leftist and right-wing groups. In 2002 its presidential candidate Juan Camilo Restrepo, withdrew and the party endorsed the candidature of Alvaro Uribe Velez, running as candidate of the right-wing Colombia First.

The PSC is a member of the Christian Democrat International, the Christian Democrat Organization of America (ODCA) and the International Democrat Union.

Other Parties

Citizen Convergence (*Convergencia Ciudadana*, CC) won one seat in the Senate and two in the Chamber of Deputies in 2002.

Coalition (*Coalición*, C), won six seats in the Senate and 11 in the Chamber of Deputies in 2002.

Colombia for Ever (*Colombia Siempre*, CS) won two seats in the Senate and three in the Chamber of Deputies in 2002.

Colombian Communal and Community Political Movement (*Movimiento Político Comunal y Comunidad Colombiano*, MPCCC) won two seats in the Chamber of Deputies in 2002.

Democratic Alliance–April 19 Movement (*Alianza Democratica–Movimiento 19 de Abril*, AD-M19). This left-wing party and former guerrilla group dates from 1973. The M19 had been formed by National Popular Alliance (ANAPO) supporters as the party's armed wing in reaction to the disputed April 19, 1970, election results. The group's ideology was originally an amalgam of Marxism-Leninism and the radical liberal ideas of Jorge Eliecer Graitan (assassinated 1948), which attracted dissident members of the Revolutionary Armed Forces of Colombia (FARC) guerrilla group to M19. As its first public act, M19 seized Simón Bolívar's sword and spurs in January 1974. ANAPO, which had shifted to the right, disassociated itself from M19 soon after.

Specializing in kidnappings and sabotage of multinational companies, M19 started its guerrilla activity in 1976 with the abduction and killing of a trade union leader whom M19 suspected of having links with the CIA. In early 1982 the guerrillas suffered heavy losses in counterinsurgency operations and clashes with the new right-wing paramilitary group Death to Kidnappers (MAS). In August 1984, M19, by now Colombia's most prominent guerrilla group, announced its intention to become a political party. In May 1988 M19, in an attempt to force the government to hold peace talks, kidnapped the presidential candidate of the Conservative Party of Colombia (PSC), Alvaro Gomez Hurtado. Partly as a result of this action, the government put forward a new peace plan the following September. The M19 called a unilateral ceasefire, and negotiations began in January 1989. An agreement with the government on reintegration of the M19 into civilian life was signed two months later and in October the M19 was constituted as a political party – incorporating a number of other left-wing groups. In March 1990 the guerrillas signed a final peace treaty with the government and surrendered their arms. In exchange the government guaranteed the M19 a general amnesty, full political participation in elections and the holding of a referendum on the question of a new constitution.

In April 1990 the M19 leader and presidential candidate for the newly-formed Democratic Alliance M19 (AD-M19) Carlos Pizarro Leongomez was gunned down, at the instigation, it was thought, of the Medellín drugs cartel. He was replaced as candidate in the May presidential elections by Antonio Navarro Wolff, who came third with 12.6% of the vote. The M19 won the majority of the 19 seats secured by the AD-M19 in the Constitutional Assembly also elected, and as the largest opposition block made an important contribution to the drawing-up of the constitution which came into effect in July 1991. However, in the municipal elections of March 1992 the party suffered big losses, especially in the capital, Santafé de Bogotá.

In the March 1994 legislative elections the party saw its representation fall sharply, to only two seats in the House of Representatives and one in the Senate. In the first round of presidential balloting in May 1994, Navarro Wolff (who had served as Health Minister in the early 1990s) was again well beaten with a meagre 3.8% of the vote. Subsequently, a dissident faction, led by Carlos Alonso Lucio, a former guerrilla commando, split away from the main party. The party failed to make any impact in the 1998 legislative and presidential elections, although it retained a small presence in the House of Representatives. The AD-M19 is an observer member of the Socialist International.
Address. Transversal 28, No. 37–78, Santafé de Bogotá
Telephone. (157–1) 348–9436
Leadership. Antonio Navarro Wolff (president)

Democratic Progress (*Progresismo Democrático*, MPD) won one seat in the Senate and two in the Chamber of Deputies in 2002.

Green Oxygen Party (*Partido Verde Oxigeno*) obtained 0.5% of the vote in 2002 for its presidential candidate, Ingrid Betancourt Pulecio, but was unrepresented in Congress.

Independent Conservative Movement (*Movimiento Conservatismo Independiente*, MCI), won one seat in the Chamber of Deputies in 2002.

Independents Front of Hope (*Independientes Frente de Esperanza*, FE), won one Senate seat in 1998 and held it in 2002.

Indigenous Authorities of Colombia (*Autoridades Indigenas de Colombia*, AICO), won one Senate seat in 1998 and in 2002 won one seat in each House.

Let's Go Colombia (*Partido Vanguardia Moral y Social – Vamos Colombia*, VC), won one Senate seat in 1998 and one seat in each House in 2002.

Liberal Opening (*Apertura Liberal*, AL) won 5 seats in the Chamber of Deputies in 2002.

Movement C4 (*Comp. Cív. Cristiano Com. Movimiento C4,* MC4), won one Senate seat in 1998 and held it in 2002.

National Movement (*Movimiento Nacional*, MN) won six seats in the Senate and one in the Chamber of Deputies in 2002.

Movement Social Indigenous Alliance (*Movimiento Alianza Social Indigena'as*, MASI), won two Senate seats in 1998 but retained only one in 2002.

National Conservative Movement (*Movimiento Nacional Conservador*, MNC), increased its number of seats in the Senate from one in 1991 to eight in 1998, but was unrepresented in the 2002 Congress.
Address. Carrera 16, No. 33–24, Santafé de Bogotá
Telephone. (57–1) 245 4418
Fax. (57–1) 284 8529
Leadership. Juan Pablo Cepera Marquez

National Popular Alliance (*Alianza Nacional Popular*, ANAPO). ANAPO was formally inaugurated in 1971 by Gen. Gustavo Rojas Pinilla, who had been President in 1953-57, and his daughter, Maria Eugenia Rojas de Moreno Diaz. From the outset ANAPO campaigned for a "Colombian socialism" on a Christian social basis. In 1975 Rojas de Moreno assumed the leadership of the party on the death of her father. Under her leadership ANAPO gradually lost influence, its various factions failing to achieve significant results in subsequent elections. In the 2002 legislative elections the party won only one seat in the Senate, that of its leader.
Address. Carrera 18, No. 33–95, Santafé de Bogotá
Telephone. (57–1) 287–7050
Fax. (57–1) 245–3138
Leadership. Senator Maria Eugenia Rojas de Moreno Díaz (president)

National Progressive Movement (*Movimiento Nacional Progresista*, MNP), won two Senate seats in the 1998 legislative elections, and one seat in the Senate and one in the Chamber of Deputies in 2002.
Address. Carrera 10, No. 19-45, Bogota
Telephone. (57-1) 286 7517
Fax. (57-1) 341 9368
Leadership. Eduardo Aismak Leon Beltran

National Salvation Movement (*Movimiento de Salvacion Nacional*, MSN). Founded in 1990 by a splinter group of the Conservative Party of Colombia (PSC) led by Alvaro Gomez Hurtado, who had been PCC presidential candidate in 1974 and 1986 and who came second in 1990 with some 24%, almost twice the PSC vote. The MSN played a significant legislative role in the early 1990s, but after the assassination of Gomez Hurtado in 1995 declined in importance, retaining only one seat in the Senate in 1998. It won one seat in the Senate and two in the Chamber of Deputies in 2002.

New Democratic Force (*Nueva Fuerza Democratica*, NFD), a conservative party that won one Senate seat in 1998, and in 2002 one seat in each House.

New Liberalism (*Nuevo Liberalismo*, NL), a left-wing Liberal group which won two seats in each House in 2002.

Popular Civic Convergence (*Convergencia Popular Civica*, CPC) won one seat in the Senate and four in the Chamber of Deputies in 2002.

Popular Integration Movement (*Movimiento Integración Popular*, MIP) won four seats in the Senate and two in the Chamber of Deputies in 2002.

Popular Will Movement (*Movimiento Voluntad Popular*, MVP) won one seat in the Senate and two in the Chamber of Deputies in 2002.

Progressive Force (*Fuerza Progresista*, FP) won one seat in the Senate and two in the Chamber of Deputies in 2002.

Radical Change (*Cambio Radical*, CR), won two seats in the Senate and seven in the Chamber of Deputies in 2002.

Regional Integration Movement (*Movimiento Integración Regional*, MIR) won two seats in the Chamber of Deputies in 2002.

Republican Movement (*Movimiento Republicana*, MR) won one seat in the Senate and two in the Chamber of Deputies in 2002.

Social and Political Front (*Frente Social y Político*, FSP) won one seat in the Senate and two in the Chamber of Deputies in 2002.

Team Colombia (*Equipo Colombia*, EC), won three seats in the Senate and four in the Chamber of Deputies in 2002.

United Popular Movement (*Movimiento Popular Unido*, MPU) won two seats in each House in 2002.

Unionist Movement (*Movimiento Unionista*, MU) won one seat in the Senate and two in the Chamber of Deputies in 2002.

Comoros

Capital: Moroni
Population: 586,000

The Comoros, comprising Grande Comore (Njazidja), Anjouan (Nzwani) and Mohéli (Mwali), achieved independence from France in 1975, although neighbouring Mayotte chose to remain under French administration. Politically, the Comoros have been very unstable, enduring over 20 coups or attempted coups since independence, instigated mainly by groups based abroad, particularly in France. Increasing political instability and violence arose from 1997 as the islands of Anjouan and Mohéli sought to secede from the Comoros, and then in November 1998 President Mohamed Taki Abdoulkarim – elected in 1996 – died in office. In April 1999, the military seized power from interim President Tajiddine Ben Said Massounde in a bloodless coup led by army chief of staff Col. Azali Assoumani, who became head of state. The Federal Assembly (the unicameral legislature) was dissolved and the 1996 constitution suspended.

Col. Assoumani sought to resolve the secessionist crisis through a confederal arrangement. Consequently, in February 2001 the Fomboni accord on national reconciliation was signed by representatives of the military government and the three islands. The accord provided for the preparation of a new constitution envisaging greater autonomy, under which each island would have its own President and legislative assembly while respecting the unity and territorial integrity of the Comoros state. There would also be a rotating union President (initially from Grande Comore) and a union legislature comprising appointed and directly elected members. The

new constitution was approved in a national referendum in December 2001.

Presidential elections for the autonomous islands of Anjouan and Mohéli were held in March 2002. Col. Mohamed Bacar secured the Anjouan poll outright, while Mohamed Said Fazal won the runoff election for the Mohéli presidency in early April. Voting for the union presidency took place in March and April. Despite a boycott of the second round of voting by two of the three candidates due to allegations of irregularities, Col. Assoumani's victory was confirmed in early May. In Grande Comore, Abdou Soule Elbak was elected President in a second round of voting in mid-May, defeating the official candidate put forward by Col. Assoumani.

Elections were held in March 2004 for assemblies on each of the three islands. Candidates supporting Col. Assoumani suffered a serious defeat. Those supporting the presidents of the three islands won a majority of seats in their respective assemblies. Elections to the Federal Assembly, the unicameral legislature of the union of Comoros, were held in April. The Assembly had 33 seats, 18 elected directly in single seat constituencies and 15 representatives of the three islands. Of the 18 seats decided by direct universal suffrage, six were won by members of the Convention for the Renewal of the Comoros (CRC), which supported Col. Assoumani, while the remaining 12 seats were won by opponents of Assoumani – 11 from the coalition of the three presidents of the islands (the Camp of the Autonomous Islands), and one from the Islands' Fraternity and Unity Party (CHUMA).

Camp of the Autonomous Islands
Camp des Iles Autonomes (CdIA)
The CdIA is a not a formal party, but a coalition of opposition parties and groups organized by the presidents of the three federated islands and opposed to President Assoumani. On Ngazidja, the CdIA is called *Mdjidjengo* (Autonomy). In elections to the Federal Assembly, the unicameral legislature, held in April 2004, the CdIA was extremely successful, winning all the seats in Anjouan and Mohéli and six of nine seats in Assoumani's home base of Grande Comore. Since the CdIA controlled the legislatures of all three of the semi-autonomous islands that make up Comoros, the majority of the 15 Assembly members subsequently chosen by them also opposed Assoumani.

Convention for the Renewal of the Comoros
Convention pour le Renouveau des Comores (CRC)
Leadership. Col. Azali Assoumani.
The CRC is the party of Col. Azali Assoumani, who took control of the country in a coup in April 1999. In elections to the Federal Assembly, the unicameral legislature, held in April 2004, the CRC was heavily defeated, winning no seats in Anjouan and Mohéli and only six of nine seats in Assoumani's home base of Grande Comore. Since the opposition, loosely grouped together as the Camp of the Autonomous Islands, controlled the legislatures of all three of the semi-autonomous islands that made up Comoros, the majority of the 15 Assembly members chosen by them also opposed Assoumani.

Forum for National Recovery
Forum pour le Redressement National (FRN)
Leadership. Abbas Djoussouf, Saïd Hassan Saïd Hachim
The FRN was created as an opposition alliance in January 1994, a month after Assembly elections in which the presidential Rally for Democracy and Renewal (RDR) had won a substantial majority. Five of the FRN parties had hitherto comprised the National Union for Democracy and Progress (*Union*

Nationale pour la Démocratie et le Progrès, UNDP), namely: the opposition rump of the Comoran Union for Progress (*Union Comorienne pour le Progrès*, UCP/UDZIMA) led by Omar Tamou; the Movement for Renovation and Democratic Action (*Mouvement pour la Rénovation et l'Action Démocratique*, MOURAD) led by Abdou Issa; the National Union for Democracy in the Comoros (UNDC) led by Mohamed Taki Abdoulkarim (who later broke away from the FRN); the Rally for Change and Democracy (*Rassemblement pour le Changement et la Démocratie*, RACHADE) led by Saïd Ali Youssouf; and the Socialist Party of the Comoros (*Parti Socialiste des Comores*, PASOCO) led by Ali Idarousse.

The UCP/UDZIMA had been founded as the sole government party in 1982 under President Ahmed Abdullah Abderrahman and had been inherited in 1989 by his successor, Saïd Mohamed Djohar. Having backed the latter's successful re-election campaign in 1990, the party became increasingly estranged from Djohar and went into opposition in 1991 in protest against the formation of a coalition government as a prelude to the move to multi-partyism. The UCP/UDZIMA participated in the national conference of early 1992 but opposed the resultant constitution and did not contest the October 1992 Assembly elections, in part because its leaders had been implicated in a coup attempt the previous month.

Of the other FRN participants, RACHADE was founded in December 1990 by UDC/UDZIMA dissidents, joined the coalition government formed in 1992 and approved the new constitution, although it later called for President Djohar's resignation. The PCDP also derived from the UDC/UDZIMA, Ali Mroudjae having held high government office under both Abdullah and Djohar; standing for his new party in the March 1990 presidential elections, Mroudjae came fourth and in 1991 took the PCDP into the opposition camp. The FPC leader had also contested the 1990 presidential elections, subsequently joining the transitional government of 1992 and backing the new constitution, as did the FDC, whose leader had previously been imprisoned for alleged involvement in a 1985 coup attempt and had also stood for the presidency in 1990. The MDP also backed the 1992 constitution and joined the interim government, its leader having been another unsuccessful presidential contender in 1990; it polled strongly in the November 1992 Assembly elections and was the largest single party at the dissolution in June 1993. The Islamist PSN won one seat in the 1992 elections and became alienated from Djohar by the growing influence of the President's son-in-law, Mohamed Saïd Abdullah M'Changama.

The UNDC-led alliance won 18 of the 42 Assembly seats in the December 1993 Assembly elections, the official outcome of which was described as a "masquerade" by the opposition. Contesting the results and the resultant appointment of an RDR Prime Minister, the opposition parties nevertheless acknowledged that their divisions had assisted what they described as Djohar's "political coup" and the "brutal interruption of the transition to democracy". They therefore agreed in January 1994 to form the FRN as a focus of joint opposition.

Following an abortive coup by rebel soldiers and mercenaries in September 1995, the FRN accepted representation in a new "unity" government announced in early November. However, in presidential elections in March 1996 Abbas Djoussouf, as FRN candidate, was easily defeated by Taki Abdoulkarim of the UNDC. The FRN opposed the new constitution approved in October 1996 following a referendum, and boycotted the legislative elections the following December.

After President Taki's death in office in November 1998, his interim replacement appointed a coalition government led by the FRN (with six Cabinet seats and Djoussouf as Prime Minister), but this was deposed by the military coup in April 1999.

Islands' Fraternity and Unity Party
Chama cha Upvamodja na Mugnagna wa Massiwa (CHUMA)
Leadership. Prince Saïd Ali Kemal (president); Sy Mohamed Nacer-Eddine (secretary-general)

CHUMA was founded in the late 1980s as an anti-Abdullah "patriotic alliance" of exiled groups under the leadership of Kemal, grandson of the last Sultan of the Comoros. He took third place in the first round of the March 1990 presidential elections (with 13.7% of the vote) and backed Djohar in the second, being rewarded with a cabinet post. CHUMA was also a member of the interim government formed in 1992 and endorsed the new constitution. Party leader Kemal contested the first round of elections for the president of the new union in March 2002, winning over 10% of the vote, against almost 40% for the incumbent, Col. Azali Assoumani. Kemal boycotted the second round of voting in April, after he and a third candidate, Col. Mahamoud Mradabi, called for a postponement of the election to permit voter lists to be updated. CHUMA contested the elections to the Federal Assembly held in April 2004 and won one seat.

National Front for Justice
Front National pour la Justice (FNJ)
Leadership. Ahmed Abdallah Mohamed, Ahmed Aboubacar, Soidiki M'Bapandza

An Islamist formation, the FNJ won three seats in the Federal Assembly in the December 1996 elections, so qualifying as the opposition to the National Rally for Development.

National Rally for Development
Rassemblement National pour le Développement (RND)
Leadership. Ali Bazi Selim (chairman)

The RND was formally established in October 1996. A pro-presidential grouping, it was formed by the merger of most of the parties which had supported Mohamed Taki Abdoulkarim in the second round of the presidential elections the previous March, including the National Union for Democracy in the Comoros (*Union Nationale pour la Démocratie aux Comores*, UNDC). In the legislative polling in December 1996, the RND won 39 of the 43 Assembly seats (many of which were unopposed due to an opposition boycott). President Taki died in office in November 1998. His interim replacement appointed a coalition government, including four RND Cabinet members, but this was deposed by the military in April 1999.

Rally for Democracy and Renewal
Rassemblement pour la Démocratie et le Renouveau (RDR)
Leadership. Mohamed Abdou Madi (secretary-general)

The RDR was created immediately prior to the December 1993 elections as a political vehicle for President Djohar. The latter had come to power in 1989 following the assassination of President Ahmed Abdullah Abderrahman and had inherited the latter's one-party regime of the Comoran Union for Progress (UCP/UDZIMA). He had nevertheless permitted opposition candidates to contest the March 1990 presidential elections, in which he was the comfortable second-round victor with the official backing of the UCP/UDZIMA. On the formal move to multi-partyism in 1991-92, the UCP/UDZIMA ceased to be the government party. In Assembly elections in November 1992 Djohar backed the Union for Democracy and Development but there was no clear overall majority.

After a period of political instability, the President dissolved the Assembly in June 1993 and new elections were eventually held in December. For these the RDR was created as a merger of the *Mwangaza* party (headed by the President's controversial son-in-law, Mohamed Saïd Abdullah M'Changama) and dissident groups of other parties. The outcome was an RDR victory, which was hotly contested by what became the opposition Forum for National Recovery (FRN), and the appointment of the RDR secretary-general as Prime Minister in January 1994. In major government changes in October 1994, however, Mohamed Abdou Madi was replaced as Prime Minister by Halifa Houmadi, amid dissension within the RDR over privatization plans supported by the former but opposed by M'Changama. Houmadi was replaced in April 1995 by Caabi el-Yachroutou Mohamed, a former Finance Minister.

In late September 1995 the Comoros experienced its 17th coup attempt since independence, when a group of rebel soldiers backed by foreign mercenaries seized power in Moroni and held it until being overcome early in October by forces sent in by France. Restored to office, President Djohar proceeded to form a "unity" government headed by the RDR but including representatives of the FRN. This lasted until a presidential election in March 1996 was won by the candidate of the National Union for Democracy in the Comoros (Forum for National Recovery).

Democratic Republic of the Congo

Capital: Kinshasa
Population: 51,600,000

The Democratic Republic of the Congo (DRC, known as Zaïre from 1971-97) achieved independence from Belgium in 1960. Mobutu Sese Seko, who took power in a military coup in 1965, was President from 1970–97, ruling through the Popular Movement of the Revolution (MPR), which was the sole legal party until 1990, when the introduction of a multi-party system was announced. After 1990, however, there was persistent political conflict between Mobutu and opposition groups who organized a National Conference that for a time appointed its own rival "Cabinet".

In the wake of the 1994 Rwanda genocide, long-standing ethnic tensions between Tutsi and Hutu inhabitants in the east of the country worsened. In October 1996 the Tutsi *Banyamulenge*, led by Laurent-Désiré Kabila, and other rebel groups formed the Alliance of Democratic Forces for the Liberation of the Congo (AFDL) and began a revolt against the Mobutu regime. The AFDL made dramatic military gains against the Zaïrean army, entering the capital Kinshasa in May 1997. Mobutu fled to Morocco (where he subsequently died) and Kabila declared himself President, head of both state and government.

Progress towards political reform and the holding of fresh elections, scheduled for April 1999, was derailed by renewed conflict and regional intervention from mid-1998. As Kabila's relations with his former Ugandan and Rwandan backers deteriorated, he ordered all foreign troops to leave. However, anti-Kabila Congolese rebels, now supported by Uganda and Rwanda, began to take control of large areas of the east and north of the country from August 1998. Meanwhile, Zimbabwe, Angola and Namibia intervened on Kabila's behalf. The Lusaka ceasefire agreement, setting out a framework for national dialogue and reconciliation, was signed in the autumn of 1999, but never came into real effect. In January 2001, when the political situation was at a complete impasse, Kabila was assassinated by one of his bodyguards. When his son Joseph Kabila took over as President he quickly implemented a number of political reforms, including the lifting of the restrictions on party political activity maintained by his father, and undertook to press ahead with the peace process.

In February 2002 an Inter-Congolese National Dialogue opened in Sun City, South Africa, with the objective of laying the basis of a future political transition and involving the government, rebel movements, civil society and representatives of political parties. The dialogue ended in April 2003 with the signing of a peace agreement which provided for a two-year transitional period during which President Kabila would be supported by four Vice Presidents – two drawn from the main rebel groups, the Rwandan-backed, Goma-based Congolese Rally for Democracy (RCD-Goma) and the Ugandan-backed Movement for the Liberation of Congo (MLC), one from Kabila's government and one from the unarmed political opposition. In July 2003 the new transitional government was sworn in. A transitional bicameral legislature, comprising a 500-member Chamber of Representatives and a 120-member Senate, appointed in August comprised representatives of the former Kabila government, the main rebel groups, the political non-armed opposition and civil society. Elections were due to be held by mid-2005. In September 2003 the Interior Ministry announced that former rebel groups had been authorized to function as political parties in the run-up to the elections.

Alliance of Democratic Forces for the Liberation of the Congo
Alliance des Forces Démocratiques pour la Libération du Congo (AFDL)
Address. c/o President's Office, Mont Ngaliema, Kinshasa
Leadership. Joseph Kabila (leader)
The AFDL was formed under the leadership of Laurent-Désiré Kabila by anti-Mobutu rebels in October 1996. The AFDL was a coalition of four opposition political parties: Kabila's own Revolutionary Party of the People (*Parti Révolutionnaire du Peuple*, PRP), originally formed in 1967 as a Marxist party; the National Resistance Council (*Conseil Nationale de la Résistance*, CNR), led by André Kissasse-Ngandu and made up of fighters from east Kasai province; the Revolutionary Movement for the Liberation of Congo-Zaïre (*Mouvement Révolutionaire pour la Liberation du Congo-Zaïre*, RMLC), led by Mosasa Minitaga and composed of tribes from around the Bukavu area; and the Democratic Alliance of the People (*Alliance Démocratique des Peuples*, ADP), led by Deogratias Bugera, made up of Tutsis from north and south Kivu provinces. Kabila claimed the presidency in May 1997 on Mobutu's flight abroad and formed a new administration. In early 1999 he announced that the ADFL was to be dissolved and local People's Power Committees created. The unstable internal security situation, however, undermined progress towards political reform, and then in January 2001 Kabila was assassinated. He was replaced as head of state and government by his son, Joseph, who also took over the leadership of the AFDL.

Democratic and Social Christian Party
Parti Démocrate et Social Chrétien (PDSC)
Leadership. André Boboliko Lokanga (chairman)
The PDSC was founded in 1990, achieved legal status the following year, and joined the anti-Mobutu opposition grouping, the Sacred Union of the Radical Opposition. The party is an affiliate of the Christian Democrat International.

Political Forces of the Conclave
Forces Politiques du Conclave (FPC)
Established in 1993, the FPC was an alliance of pro-Mobutu groups, led by the Popular Movement of the Revolution. In January 1994 the major constituent parties of the FPC and the opposition Sacred Union of the Radical Opposition (with the exception of the Union for Democracy and Social

Progress) signed an agreement to form a government of national reconciliation. In June 1995 political consensus was reached between the FPC and the opposition resulting in the extension of the period of national transition by two years.

Sacred Union of the Radical Opposition
Union Sacrée de l'Opposition Radicale (USOR)

The USOR developed in the course of 1991 as an umbrella group of organizations opposed to the Mobutu regime. Originally drawing on the ranks of the Union for Democracy and Social Progress, the Union of Federalists and Independent Republicans (which was subsequently expelled) and the Democratic and Social Christian Party, the USOR linked some 130 anti-Mobutu movements and factions. The existence within the transitional legislature of an expanded radical opposition grouping, known as the Sacred Union of the Radical Opposition and its Allies (USORAL), was announced in late 1994.

Union for Democracy and Social Progress
Union pour la Démocratie et le Progrès Social (UDPS)

Leadership. Etienne Tshisekedi wa Malumba

The UDPS emerged in the early 1980s as an attempt to establish an opposition party within Zaïre to counter the "arbitrary rule" of the Mobutu regime. Various of its members suffered consequent arrest and imprisonment, and serious splits in its leadership were subsequently reported. The party was legalized in 1991. The UDPS leader, Etienne Tshisekedi, was elected Prime Minister in August 1992 by the national conference, but the legitimacy of his government was resisted by President Mobutu who, in early 1993, appointed a rival administration, so heightening the political impasse. The UDPS did not sign the agreement in January 1994 on the formation of a government of national reconciliation.

The UDPS is associated with the International Democrat Union through the Democrat Union of Africa.

Union of Federalists and Independent Republicans
Union des Fédéralistes et Républicains Indépendants (UFERI)

Leadership. Jean Nguza Karl-I-Bond (leader)

Founded in 1990 and seeking autonomy for Shaba/Katanga province, the UFERI was initially one of the most prominent groups in the Sacred Union of the Radical Opposition. However, after party leader Nguza Karl-I-Bond had controversially accepted nomination by President Mobutu for the post of Prime Minister in November 1991, the UFERI was expelled from the Sacred Union coalition.

Former Rebel Groups

Congolese Rally for Democracy–Goma
Rassemblement congolais pour la démocratie–Goma (RCD–Goma)

Leadership. Azarias Ruberwa Manywa

The RCD–Goma is the main faction of the Congolese Rally for Democracy, the other two smaller factions being the Congolese Rally for Democracy–Liberation Movement and the Congolese Rally for Democracy–National. Based in Goma and backed by Rwanda, the faction was a signatory to the April 2003 peace accord and the leader, Azarias Ruberwa, was appointed as a Vice President in the transitional government formed in July 2003. The faction was also given control of a number of ministries, most crucially that of Defence (Jean-Pierre Ondekane) and, like the Ugandan-backed Movement for the Liberation of Congo, was appointed to 116 seats in the transitional bicameral legislature (94 members in the lower house and 22 in the upper).

Congolese Rally for Democracy–Liberation Movement
Rassemblement congolais pour la démocratie–mouvement de libération (RCD-ML)

Leadership. Mbusa Nyamwisi.

Based in Kisangani, and therefore sometimes known as RCD–Kisangani, the RCD–ML was originally led by Ernest Wamba di Wamba, who was overthrown by Mbusa Nyamwisi. The RCD–ML was originally backed by Uganda, but in late 2000 it went over to the government side, prompting clashes with the Ugandan-backed Movement for the Liberation of Congo (MLC). Nyamwisi was appointed as Minister of Regional Co-operation in the transitional government formed in July 2003 and the faction has 19 seats in the transitional bicameral legislature appointed in August 2003 (15 in the lower chamber and four in the upper).

Congolese Rally for Democracy–National
Rassemblement congolais pour la démocratie–nacional (RCD-N)

Leadership. Roger Lumbala

The RCD–N is a Ugandan-backed faction of the Congolese Rally for Democracy that was allied during the civil war with the Movement for the Liberation of Congo. The faction, based in Isiro, Orientale Province, was a signatory to the April 2003 peace accord. The leader, Roger Lumbala, was appointed as Minister of External Trade in the transitional government formed in July 2003 and the faction has seven seats in the transitional bicameral legislature appointed in August 2003 (five in the lower chamber and two in the upper). On a number of occasions during 2003 the faction was accused of carrying out a series of massacres, targeting mainly the Pygmies in north-eastern Ituri and Nord-Kivu provinces.

Movement for the Liberation of Congo
Mouvement pour la libération du Congo (MLC)

Leadership. Jean-Pierre Bemba

The MLC is a Ugandan-backed rebel group formed by Kinshasa businessman, Jean-Pierre Bemba, and based in the north-western province of Equateur, bordering the Central African Republic. Although Bemba did not sign the April 2003 peace accord, citing ill health, he took up the post of Vice President in the transitional government formed in July. MLC members were also given high-profile Cabinet posts (Foreign Affairs and Planning) and 116 seats in the transitional legislature (94 in the lower house and 22 in the upper).

Other Parties

The following parties were amongst the signatories to the April 2003 peace agreement:

Christian Social Democratic Party (*Parti Démocratique Social Chretienne*, PDSC). The party's leader, André Bo-Boliko, is a member of the transitional Chamber of Representatives.

Collective of the Democratic Opposition (*Collectif de l'Opposition Démocratique Plurielle*, CODEP)
Leadership. Raymond Tshibanda N'tunga

Collective of the Parties of Consistency (*Collectif des Partis de Constance*, COPACO). Christophe Tshimanga, the leader, is a member of the transitional Chamber of Representatives.

Collective of the Progressive Radicals and Allies (*Collectif Progressite Radical et Alliés*, CPRAL)
Leadership. Alphonse Lupumba

Democratic Federalist Christians (*Démocratiques Chrétiens Federalistes*, DCF). The leader, Venant Tshipasa Vangi Sivavi, was appointed as Minister of Land Affairs in the transitional government formed in July 2003.

Forces of New Ideas for Unification and Solidarity (*Forces Novatrices pour l'Union et la Solidarité*, FONUS). The leader was appointed as Minister of Transport in the transitional government formed in July 2003.
Leadership. Joseph Olenghankoy

Forces of the Future (*Forces du futur*). The party leader was appointed as a Vice President in the transitional government formed in July 2003.
Leadership. Arthur Z'Ahidi Ngoma

Front for the Pursuit of Democracy (*Front pour la Survie de la Démocratie*, FSD)
The party leader was appointed as Minister of Mines in the transitional government formed in July 2003.
Leadership. Eugène Diomi Ndongala Nzomambu

Front for the Unified Non-armed Opposition (*Front Uni de l'Opposition Non-Armée*, FRUONAR). The leader, Cyprien Rwakabuba Shinga, is a member of the transitional Senate.

Grouping of the Progressive Political Parties (*Regroupement des Partis Politiques Progressistes*, RPPP)
Leadership. Bembe Majimo Bathy

Movement of Congolese Nationalists–Lumumba (**MNC/L**). The leader, François Lumumba, is a member of the transitional Chamber of Representatives.

Patriotic Front (*Front Patriotique*, FP)
Leadership. Kabamba Mbwebwe

Party of Unified Lumumbists (*Parti Lumumbist Unifié*, PALU)
Leadership. Antoine Gizenga

Popular Movement for the Revolution (*Mouvement Populaire de la Révolution*, MPR–Fait Privé). The MPR was launched in 1967 by President Mobutu Sese Seko, advocating national unity and African socialism, and opposing tribalism. As the main vehicle of the Mobutu regime, it became the sole legal political party in 1969 and, until political liberalization in 1990, party membership was deemed to be acquired automatically by all Zaïreans at birth. President Mobutu was deposed in May 1997, fleeing to Morocco where he subsequently died. Catherine Nzuzi wa Mbombo Tshianga, the party leader, was appointed as Minister of Solidarity and Humanitarian Affairs in the transitional government formed in July 2003.
Leadership. Catherine Nzuzi wa Mbombo Tshianga

Progressive Lumumbiste Movement (*Mouvement Lumumbiste Progressiste*, MLP)
Leadership. Franck Diongo Shamba

Non-Parliamentary Opposition Group (*Groupe Non-Parlementaire de l'Opposition*, GNPO)
Leadership. Dénis Katalay

Regrouping of the Congolese Opposition (*Regroupement de l'Opposition Congolaise*, ROC). The party leader was appointed as Minister of Social Affairs in the transitional government formed in July 2003.
Leadership. Ingele Ifoto

Regrouping of the Moderate Opposition (*Regroupement de l'Opposition Modérée*, ROM). The leader is a member of the transitional Chamber of Representatives.
Leadership. Patrice-Aimé Sesanga

Solidarity Movement for Democracy and Development (*Mouvement de Solidarité pour la Démocratie et le Développement*, MSDD). The leader is a member of the transitional Chamber of Representatives.
Leadership. Christophe Lutundula Apala

Union of Democratic Opposition of Congo (*Union de l'Opposition Démocratique du Congo*, UODC)
Leadership. Binda Phumu

Union of Federal Nationalists of the Congo (*Union des Nationalistes Federaliste du Congo*, UNAFEC). The party leader was appointed as Minister of Justice in the transitional government formed in July 2003.
Leadership. Kisimba Ngoy Ndalawe

Congo

Capital: Brazzaville
Population: 3,7000,000

Three years after independence from France in 1960, the Congo became a one-party state under a Marxist-Leninist National Movement of the Revolution (*Mouvement national de la révolution*, MNR). Following a military coup in 1968 led by Capt. Marien Ngoubai, the MNR was superseded by the Congolese Party of Labour (*Parti Congolais du Travail*, PCT) as the sole ruling party, and the country was renamed (in 1970) the People's Republic of the Congo (although it reverted to the name Republic of Congo in 1991).

Factional rivalries within the PCT during the 1970s were reflected in the assassination of Ngoubai in 1977 and the replacement of his successor, Jacques-Joachim Yhombi-Opango, only two years later by Denis Sassou-Nguesso. A new constitution approved in 1979 provided for a popularly elected legislature, consisting of candidates nominated by the PCT. Sassou-Nguesso remained the country's dominant political figure throughout the 1980s, but in 1990, under popular pressure, the PCT gave in to demands for political change and a transition to multi-partyism. A referendum in March 1992 gave overwhelming approval to a revised constitution recognizing a multi-party state. Presidential elections in August 1992 saw the defeat of the incumbent Sassou-Nguesso by Pascal Lissouba, leader of the Pan-African Union for Social Democracy (*Union Panafricaine pour la Démocratie Sociale*, UPADS).

Legislative elections in 1993, giving pro-Lissouba parties a majority, provoked armed skirmishes between rival militias which quickly escalated into open civil war from June 1993 in the run-up to presidential elections. Confrontation was centred in the capital, Brazzaville, which was divided into zones occupied by militias backing the three leading figures: the Cocoye forces loyal to President Lissouba; the Cobras loyal to former President Sassou-Nguesso; and the Ninjas supporting Bernard Kolelas of the Congolese Movement for Democracy and Integral Development (*Mouvement Congolais pour la Démocratie et le Développement Intégral*, MCDDI). Lissouba appointed Kolelas as Prime Minister in August 1997, and their joint forces appeared to be making gains until Angola intervened in support of Sassou-Nguesso, who proclaimed himself President in October 1997. The previous elected legislature was dissolved and replaced in January 1998 by a 75-member National Transitional Council, appointed by the President.

A new constitution, providing for a directly elected presidency with executive powers and a seven-year mandate and a bicameral legislature, was approved overwhelmingly by national referendum in January 2002. However, the referendum was boycotted by opposition parties, which claimed that the National Electoral Commission overseeing voting was made up almost entirely of allies of Sassou-Nguesso. Presidential elections were held in March 2002, in which Sassou-Nguesso won close to 90% of the vote amid further claims of vote rigging. In two rounds of legislative elections for the new 137-member National Assembly (Assemblée Nationale, the lower house of the bicameral legislature) held in May and June 2002, Sassou-Nguesso's PCT won 53 seats, while a further 30 went to parties allied with the PCT. Elections to the 66-member Senate (Sénat) held in July resulted similarly in a majority for the President and his allies.

Congolese Labour Party
Parti Congolais du Travail (PCT)

Leadership. Gen. Denis Sassou-Nguesso (president); Léon Zokoni (secretary-general)

The PCT was launched in 1969 as the sole ruling party of the military regime of Capt. Marien Ngouabi, replacing the National Movement of the Revolution. Forming Africa's first Marxist-Leninist government, the party was riven by factional struggle in the 1970s: among several purges, one in 1972 ousted Ambroise Noumazalaye as first secretary and resulted in him being condemned to death, although he was later amnestied. The PCT establishment took a back seat to the military regime of 1977-79, but was then instrumental in the replacement of Gen. Jacques-Joachim Yhombi-Opango by Col. (as he then was) Sassou-Nguesso, who was elected party chairman and thus head of state at an extraordinary congress in March 1979. Victims of a purge of "leftists" in 1984 included Jean-Pierre Thystère-Tchikaya, who was subsequently condemned for involvement in bomb attacks but amnestied in 1988. Yhombi-Opango was later to found the Rally for Democracy and Development (RDD) and Thystère-Tchikaya the Rally for Democracy and Social Progress (RDPS).

In mid-1990 the PCT opened the way for President Sassou-Nguesso's decision of October that year to accede to pressure for a transition to multi-partyism. In December 1990 a PCT congress opted to abandon Marxism-Leninism and to embrace democratic socialism; it also reinstated Noumazalaye, who was elected to the new post of secretary-general. In early 1991 the party participated in the national conference which drafted a new constitution, although a hardline PCT faction bitterly criticized the surrender of authority to the conference and the resultant transitional government. From mid-1991 the latter took steps to remove PCT cadres from their entrenched position in the state bureaucracy, some prominent members being convicted of corruption. Paradoxically, the PCT's surrender of power meant that popular discontent now focused as much on the transitional government as on President Sassou-Nguesso and the former ruling party. Nevertheless, in the mid-1992 elections the PCT came in third place, with 19 Assembly and three Senate seats, while Gen. Sassou-Nguesso also took third place in the first round of the August 1992 presidential elections (with 16.9% of the vote) and was therefore eliminated. Accepting his defeat "with serenity", Sassou-Nguesso endorsed the successful candidacy of Pascal Lissouba of the

Pan-African Union for Social Democracy (UPADS) in the second round and the PCT accepted membership of a post-election coalition government dominated by the UPADS.

Reports that a formal PCT/UPADS alliance had been agreed proved to be exaggerated, however. In late October 1992 the PCT deputies combined with those of the Union for Democratic Renewal (URD) to defeat the government on a no-confidence motion, as a result of which President Lissouba dissolved the Assembly and called new elections. In December 1992 both the PCT and the URD were included in an interim national unity government, which kept the peace until the elections began in May 1993. But opposition charges of electoral fraud in the first round of voting, and a joint PCT/URD boycott of the second round in June, were accompanied by escalating violence. Rejecting the official results giving the UPADS and its allies a comfortable overall Assembly majority, the PCT/URD axis refused to recognize the new UPADS-dominated Cabinet headed by Yhombi-Opango (RDD) and named a parallel government headed by Thystère-Tchikaya (RDPS). Growing civil unrest, featuring bloody clashes between government and opposition militias in Brazzaville and elsewhere, was stemmed by a Gabonese-brokered accord concluded in August 1993 under which the disputed elections were re-run in 11 constituencies in October. Seven of these contests were won by the opposition (so that the PCT's final tally was 15 seats and one pro-PCT independent), but the UPADS and its allies still had an overall Assembly majority.

Further fighting ensued, especially around the PCT/URD stronghold of Bacongo in south Brazzaville, until the signature of a precarious ceasefire at the end of January 1994. The following month an international panel ruled that a further nine 1993 election results were invalid, but the government took no immediate steps to hold re-run contests. Nor was there was much progress in disarming the contending party militias, among which Sassou-Nguesso's so-called "Cobras" (including many former presidential guards) achieved particular notoriety. Amid continuing violence, the PCT in September 1994 announced the formation of a new opposition alliance called the United Democratic Forces (FDU), which subsequently changed its name to the Democratic and Patriotic Forces (FDP).

Civil unrest involving clashes between government forces and the opposition militias, including the Cobras, simmered throughout 1995 and 1996, culminating in civil war from June 1997. Sassou-Nguesso emerged as the dominant political figure, deposing the Lissouba regime and assuming the presidency in October 1997. The legislature was dissolved and Sassou-Nguesso appointed a 75-member National Transitional Council pending the approval of a new constitution and the organisation of fresh elections. Fresh fighting broke out in the Pool region around Brazzaville in late 1998 and continued for a year until a peace agreement was reached between the Sassou-Nguesso regime and opposing militias.

Presidential elections held in March 2002 resulted in an overwhelming victory for Sassou-Nguesso, who won 89.41% of the vote, easily defeating six rival candidates. However, the main opposition candidate, André Milongo of the Union for Democracy and the Republic (UDR), had withdrawn from the contest during campaigning after claiming that "fraud is the national sport of Congo" and accusing Sassou-Nguesso of rigging the poll. In two round of elections for the new 137-member National Assembly held in May and June 2002, the PCT won 53 seats, while a further 30 went to parties in the PCT-supported FDP or to individuals supporting Sassou-Nguesso and the PCT. Senate elections held in July resulted similarly in a majority for the PCT and its allies.

Congolese Movement for Democracy and Integral Development
Mouvement Congolais pour la Démocratie et le Développement Intégral (MCDDI)

Website. www.mcddi.org

Leadership. Bernard Kolelas (leader-in-exile); Michel Mampouya (leader in Congo)

Founded in 1990, the centre-right MCDDI was a member of the broad Forces of Change coalition which spearheaded the transition to multi-partyism in 1991, Bernard Kolelas becoming an adviser to the Prime Minister of the resultant transitional government. In the mid-1992 legislative elections, the MCDDI became the second-strongest party, with 29 Assembly and 13 Senate seats. In the August 1992 presidential contest, Kolelas likewise took second place in the first voting round (with 22.9% of the vote), thus going on to the run-off, in which he was defeated by Pascal Lissouba of the Pan-African Union for Social Democracy (UPADS) by 61.3% to 38.7%. The MCDDI had meanwhile formed the seven-party Union for Democratic Renewal (URD), which opted to oppose the new UPADS-dominated government and procured an alliance with the former ruling Congolese Labour Party (PCT) for this purpose. Having brought down the government in October 1992, both the MCDDI-led URD and the PCT joined an interim national unity government formed in December 1992 pending new Assembly elections. These began in May 1993, but Kolelas claimed that "monstrous irregularities" had been perpetrated by the government in the first voting round and led an opposition boycott of the second in June. After Kolelas had urged the army to intervene to restore law and order (without result), the MCDDI/URD boycotted the new Assembly and participated in the formation of an alternative government to oppose the new UPADS-dominated coalition. The immediate crisis was partially resolved by an electoral re-run in 11 constituencies in October 1993, as a result of which the final MCDDI tally in the 125-member Assembly was 28 seats (out of 56 held by the opposition parties).

Clashes between government forces and militiamen of the URD/PCT axis intensified in late 1993 and early 1994, until the signature of a ceasefire agreement in late January 1994 by UPADS and MCDDI representatives brought some respite. In July 1994 popular anti-government feeling in Brazzaville was demonstrated by the election of Kolelas as the capital's mayor. But the incipient accommodation between the MCDDI/URD and the UPADS-led government was consolidated in January 1995 when the URD accepted representation in a new coalition, thus apparently breaking with the PCT. The MCDDI's strong support in the capital was demonstrated in by-elections in May 1995; but the party was weakened the same month by a split that yielded the creation of the Party for Unity, Work and Progress. The MCDDI continued to co-operate with the UPADS in the coalition formed in September 1996.

As the country subsided into civil war from mid-1997, Kolelas, backed by the Ninja militia, was appointed in August as Prime Minister by President Lissouba. However, his appointment was short-lived as the government was deposed by PCT leader Sassou-Nguesso and his forces in October 1997. Kolelas and Lissouba both fled the country into exile. Kolelas, based in Washington DC, was sentenced to death in absentia in May 2000 after being found guilty of a range of crimes. In the aftermath of the March 2002 presidential election, won by Sassou-Nguesso, fresh fighting broke out between the Ninjas and government forces in the volatile south-western Pool region. In March 2003 the government signed peace agreements with the Ninjas and a number of rebels were subsequently integrated into the national army. However, Sassou-Nguesso refused demands to offer Kolelas an amnesty and he

remained in exile as of mid-2004. Michel Mampouya leads a faction of the MCDDI in the Congo which accepts the rule of Sassou-Nguesso.

Congolese Renewal Party
Parti Congolaise du Renouvellement (PCR)

Leadership. Grégoire Lefouaba (president)

The PCR was founded in late 1992 by Grégoire Lefouaba, who had previously been a member of the Congolese Labour Party. Forming part of the Presidential Tendency alliance in the mid-1993 Assembly elections, the party won two seats in its own right. The PCR was a member of the Convention for Democracy and Salvation (CODESA) formed in March 2002 as an opposition umbrella group to contest the May-June 2002 legislative elections.

Convention for the Democratic Alternative
Convention pour l'Alternative Démocratique (CAD)

Leadership. Leon Alfred Opimba

Member of the ruling Democratic and Patriotic Forces (FDP) alliance, dominated by President Sassou-Nguesso Congolese Labour Party (PCT). The leader served as a minister in the late 1990s.

Convention for Democracy and Salvation
Convention pour la Démocratie et le Salut (CODESA)

Leadership. André Milongo

CODESA was founded in March 2002 as an umbrella group of some 16 opposition parties to contest the May-June 2002 legislative elections. The loose coalition was led by André Milongo, leader of the Union for Democracy and the Republic (UDR). CODESA's poor performance in the election was blamed by opposition leaders on widespread electoral malpractice carried out by the regime of President Sassou-Nguesso.

Democratic and Patriotic Forces
Forces Démocratiques et Patriotiques (FDP)

Leadership. Gen. Denis Sassou-Nguesso (PCT); Leon Alfred Opimba (CAD); Nicéphore Fyla (PLR); Pierre N'Ze (UNDP); Mathias Dzon (UPRN); Gabriel Bokilo (URN)

The FDP was launched as the United Democratic Forces (*Forces Démocratiques Unies*, FDU) in September 1994 as an opposition alliance of six parties headed by the Congolese Labour Party (PCT) and including the Convention for the Democratic Alternative (CAD), the Liberal Republican Party (PLR), the National Union for Democracy and Progress (UNDP), the Patriotic Union for National Reconstruction (UPRN) and the Union for National Recovery (URN). The leadership came mainly from northern Congo, in contrast to the central and southern provenance of the Union for Democratic Renewal (URD), then the FDP's ally in opposition to the government headed by President Lissouba's Pan-African Union for Social Democracy (UPADS). In January 1995 the FDP parties refused to participate in a new UPADS-led coalition, whereas the URD accepted representation. In October 1997 the PCT leader, Sassou-Nguesso, deposed the elected Lissouba regime and assumed the presidency. The FDP supported Sassou-Nguesso's successful candidacy in the March 2002 presidential elections. In legislative elections held shortly afterwards, FDP-allied parties won 83 of the 137 National Assembly seats contested.

Liberal Republican Party
Parti Libéral Républicain (PLR)

Leadership. Nicéphore Fyla

Member of the ruling Democratic and Patriotic Forces (FDP) alliance, dominated by President Sassou-Nguesso Congolese Labour Party (PCT).

National Union for Democracy and Progress
Union Nationale pour la Démocratie et le Progrès (UNDP)

Leadership. Pierre N'Ze

Founded in 1990, the UNDP was prominent in the early pro-democracy movement, but lost support to the Pan-African Union for Social Democracy, and joined the Democratic and Patriotic Forces (FDP) alliance, dominated by President Sassou-Nguesso's Congolese Labour Party (PCT).

Pan-African Union for Social Democracy
Union Panafricaine pour la Démocratie Sociale (UPADS)

Leadership. Pascal Lissouba (leader-in-exile); Martin Mberi (leader in Congo)

The left-of-centre UPADS emerged from the opposition National Alliance for Democracy, formed in July 1991, and contested the 1992 elections in its own right, having attracted defectors from other parties. Its leader, Pascal Lissouba, had served as Prime Minister in 1963-66 and had narrowly failed to be elected head of the transitional government formed in mid-1991 as a result of the national conference. The UPADS became the largest party in the legislative elections of June-July 1992, winning 39 Assembly and 23 Senate seats. Lissouba then won the presidential elections of August 1992, heading the first-round vote with 35.9% and taking 61.3% of the second-round vote, thanks in part to being endorsed by the outgoing President, Denis Sassou-Nguesso of the Congolese Labour Party (PCT). The UPADS/PCT axis did not last long, as the PCT formed an opposition alliance with the Union for Democratic Renewal (URD). The post-election UPADS-dominated coalition government lost a vote confidence at the end of October 1992, whereupon President Lissouba dissolved the Assembly the following month and called new elections.

A national unity government appointed in December 1992, including both the PCT and the URD, kept the peace until the elections began in May 1993. But opposition charges of electoral fraud in the first round of voting, and a joint PCT/URD boycott of the second round in June, were accompanied by escalating violence. On the strength of official results giving the UPADS and its allies a comfortable overall Assembly majority, Lissouba appointed a UPADS-dominated government headed by the leader of the Rally for Democracy and Development (RDD). It faced a parallel government named by the PCT/URD and growing disorder, as government forces and opposition militias fought regular battles in Brazzaville and elsewhere. Under a Gabonese-brokered accord concluded in August 1993, re-run elections were held in 11 constituencies in October, seven being won by the opposition. This outcome still left the UPADS and its allies with an overall Assembly majority of 65 seats. Further bloody clashes ensued, until the signature of a precarious ceasefire at the end of January 1994.

The UPADS remained the dominant formation in a new coalition formed in January 1995 (again under the premiership of the RDD leader) and succeeded in persuading the URD to break with the PCT (by now heading the United Democratic Forces) by accepting ministerial representation. Immediately after the new government formation, however, 12 UPADS Assembly deputies resigned from the party, complaining that they had been marginalized.

In September 1996 a new government was appointed, headed by Charles David Ganao (of the Union of Democratic Forces) and including the Congolese Movement for Democracy and Integral Development and the Rally for Democracy and Social Progress as well as UPADS. However, continuing civil unrest intensified in mid-1997 culminating in the overthrow of the government by PCT leader Sassou-Nguesso and his militia in October 1997. Lissouba, whose Cocoye militia had fought alongside the Ninja militia of Congolese Movement for Democracy and Integral Development (MCDDI) leader Bernard Kolelas, against Sassou-Nguesso, fled into exile in London. Lissouba was sentenced in absentia to 30 years' imprisonment in January 2002. Martin Mberi leads a faction of the UPADS in the Congo which accepts the rule of Sassou-Nguesso. Mberi served as Minister of Transport and Civil Aviation in the Cabinet formed by Sassou-Nguesso in late 1997, but failed to retain his post in the government formed in the aftermath of the 2002 presidential and legislative election.

Party for Unity, Work and Progress
Parti pour l'Unité, le Travail et le Progrès (PUTP)

Leadership. Didier Sengha

The PUTP was launched in May 1995 by a dissident faction of the Congolese Movement for Democracy and Integral Development (MCDDI), the breakaway party's leader, Didier Sengha, claiming that the MCDDI had ceased to care about "democracy, freedom, equity, legality and fraternity". The MCDDI leader, Bernard Kolelas, responded by accusing Sengha of financial misappropriation and embezzlement. The PUTP supports the regime of President Sassou-Nguesso.

Patriotic Union for National Reconstruction
Union Patriotique pour la Réconstruction Nationale (UPRN)

Leadership. Mathias Dzon

The UPRN was formed prior to the 1993 Assembly elections as a party at that stage independent of both the government and the opposition alliances. It won one seat in that contest and in September 1994 joined the opposition Democratic and Patriotic Forces (FDP) alliance headed by the Congolese Labour Party (PCT). The return to power of the PCT leader Denis Sassou-Nguesso in 1997 brought the UPRN into the government and party leader Mathias Dzon served for a time as Minister of Finance and Budget.

Rally for Democracy and Development
Rassemblement pour la Démocratie et le Développement (RDD)

Leadership. Gen. Jacques-Joachim Yhombi-Opango; Saturnin Okabe (chairman)

The RDD was founded in 1990 as a political vehicle for Gen. Yhombi-Opango, who had become President of a military government in 1977 but had been ousted in 1979 and expelled from the then ruling Congolese Labour Party. The RDD was at first an influential element in the broad Forces of Change alliance, which dominated the transitional government formed after the 1991 national conference. But by April 1992 the party was openly criticizing the Prime Minister for alleged misuse of public funds for electoral purposes. In the mid-1992 Assembly elections the RDD won five seats and thereafter aligned itself with the opposition to the newly-dominant Pan-African Union for Social Democracy (UPADS). However, in further Assembly elections in mid-1993 the RDD formed part of the UPADS-led Presidential Tendency alliance, winning six seats in its own right, whereupon Gen. Yhombi-Opango accepted appointment as Prime Minister in a new coalition government. In January 1995 he was reappointed as head of a broader coalition, still dominated by the UPADS but also including the Union for Democratic Renewal, but resigned the premiership in August 1996.

With the outbreak of civil war in mid-1997, Yhombi-Opango rallied behind President Pascal Lissouba (the UPADS leader) against former President Denis Sassou-Nguesso. With the latter's eventual victory, Yhombi-Opango went into exile in France. However, in July 2004 Yhombi-Opango met with visiting President Sassou-Nguesso in Paris and was reported to have pledged to support his government.

Rally for Democracy and Social Progress
Rassemblement pour la Démocratie et le Progrès Social (RDPS)

Leadership. Jean-Pierre Thystère-Tchicaya

The RDPS was founded in 1990 by Thystère-Tchicaya, once an ideologist of the former ruling Congolese Labour Party (PCT), before being purged as a "leftist" in 1984. It won nine Assembly and five Senate seats in the mid-1992 elections, although Thystère-Tchikaya came a poor fifth in the first round of presidential elections in August, winning only 5.9% of the vote. The party was thereafter a member of the opposition Union for Democratic Renewal (URD) led by the Congolese Movement for Democracy and Integral Development, whose post-election axis with the PCT resulted in the fall in late October of the coalition government dominated by the Pan-African Union for Social Democracy (UPADS). The RDPS participated in the opposition boycott of the second round of new Assembly elections in June 1993, when Thystère-Tchicaya was named as head of a parallel government set up by the URD and the PCT. Following electoral re-runs in 11 constituencies in October 1993, the RDPS tally in the Assembly was 10 seats. As a constituent party of the Union for Democratic Renewal (URD), the RDPS lined up initially in opposition to the UPADS-dominated Lissouba administration. But in January 1995 the URD accepted representation in a new coalition government headed by the UPADS, and similarly participated with the UPADS in subsequent administrations from September 1996 until Sassou-Nguesso's assumption of power in October 1997. Despite his support for Lissouba, Thystère-Tchicaya remained in the Congo following Sassou-Nguesso's victory in the 1997 civil war. He was subsequently elected as president of the National Assembly, a post he continued to hold as of mid-2004.

Union for Democracy and the Republic
Union pour la Démocratie et la République (UDR)

Leadership. André Milongo

The UDR was founded in 1992 by Milongo (a former World Bank official), who in June 1991 had been elected transitional Prime Minister by the national conference convened to determine the country's constitutional future. He had then represented the broad coalition of pro-democracy parties called the Forces of Change (FDC), which designation was used by him in the 1992 legislative and presidential elections, although by then many of its original components were in open opposition to his government. In the legislative elections of June-July 1991, the FDC failed to win a seat in the Assembly and won only one in the Senate. In the August 1992 presidential elections, Milongo came in fourth place in the first round, with 10.2% of the vote. Launched after his electoral failure, the UDR gave broad support to President Pascal Lissouba and the new government dominated by his Pan-African Union for Social Democracy (UPADS), without becoming a member of the Presidential Tendency coalition. In the 1993 Assembly elections, the UDR was at first credited with six seats on the strength of the disputed balloting of May-June, but its tally fell to two seats as a result of the re-runs in 11 constituencies in October. By the latter date, however, Milongo had been elected president of the Assembly, but he was eventually replaced by Jean-Pierre Thystère-Tchicaya, leader of the Rally for Democracy and Social Progress (RDPS)

Milongo was chosen as the main opposition candidate to challenge then incumbent, Denis Sassou-Nguesso, in the March 2002 presidential elections. However, he withdrew before the start of polling, alleging widespread electoral malpractice. At the same time, Milongo formed an opposition umbrella group – the Convention for Democracy and Salvation (CODESA) – to contest the May-June 2002 leg-

islative elections, but it was easily defeated by Sassou-Nguesso's ruling Congolese Labour Party (PCT). Again, Milongo accused Sassou-Nguesso and the PCT of cheating.

Union for Democratic Renewal
Union pour le Renouveau Démocratique (URD)

The centre-right URD was created at the time of the mid-1992 elections as an alliance of seven parties, notably the Congolese Movement for Democracy and Integral Development (MCDDI) and the Rally for Democracy and Social Progress (RDPS), both with their main strength in central and southern Congo. Joining a post-election opposition axis with the former ruling Congolese Labour Party (PCT), the URD helped to bring about the fall in late October 1992 of the coalition government dominated by the Pan-African Union for Social Democracy (UPADS). It became a member of the interim national unity government formed in December 1992 but again came into conflict with the UPADS-dominated administration of President Pascal Lissouba when new elections were held. Claiming that the first round of voting in May 1993 had featured massive electoral fraud by the authorities, the URD and the PCT boycotted the second round in June and set up their own parallel government under the premiership of RDPS leader Jean-Pierre Thystère-Tchicaya, amid a descent into bloody civil conflict.

The impasse was partially resolved by repeat elections in 11 constituencies in October 1993, seven of them won by the opposition. As a result, however, the UPADS and its allies still had an overall majority in the 125-member Assembly and the opposition parties 56 seats, of which the URD parties held 40 (including two won by candidates standing under the URD rubric rather than for constituent parties). Further serious violence between government forces and the URD/PCT axis in late 1993 and early 1994 was temporarily stemmed by a cease-fire agreement of late January. The URD also welcomed the finding of an international panel in February 1994 that the 1993 election results were invalid in a further nine seats, although its demand for re-runs met with no immediate response from the UPADS-dominated government. However, little progress was subsequently made in disarming the opposing militias, that of the URD being concentrated in the south Brazzaville stronghold of MCDDI leader Bernard Kolelas, who was elected mayor of the capital in July 1994.

The URD at first aligned itself with the opposition United Democratic Forces (FDU) launched in September 1994 under the leadership of the PCT; but in January 1995 it broke with the FDU by accepting representation in a new coalition government headed by the UPADS. It similarly participated with UPADS in subsequent administrations from September 1996 until Sassou-Nguesso's assumption of power in October 1997.

Union for National Recovery
Union pour le Rétablissement National (URN)

Leadership. Gabriel Bokilo

Member of the ruling Democratic and Patriotic Forces (FDP) alliance, dominated by President Sassou-Nguesso Congolese Labour Party (PCT).

Other Parties, Alliances and Militias

The main three militias, linked to the political factions, operating in the Congo since the 1997 civil war were as follows: (i) the Cocoye forces loyal to former President Pascal Lissouba, leader of the Pan-African Union for Social Democracy (UPADS); (ii) the Ninja militia of Bernard Kolelas, leader of the Congolese Movement for Democracy and Integral Development; and the Cobra militia of the current President, Denis Sassou–Nguesso, leader of the Congolese Labour Party.

Citizens' Rally (*Rassemblement des Citoyens, RC*), founded in March 1998.
Leadership. Claude Alphonse Silou

Movement for Democracy and Solidarity (*Mouvement pour la Démocratie et la Solidarité, MDS*), a member party of the Christian Democrat International.
Leadership. Paul Kaya

Union for Congolese Democracy (*Union pour la Démocratie Congolaise*, UDC). The formation of the UDC was announced in November 1989 in neighbouring Côte d'Ivoire, where its founder, Sylvain Bemba, a former government official and associate of President Fulbert Youlou (1960–63), had been in exile for some 25 years. It was one of the first groups to challenge the one-party rule of the Congolese Labour Party and joined the National Alliance for Democracy, becoming closely aligned with the Pan-African Union for Social Democracy (UPADS). As part of the UPADS-led Presidential Tendency alliance in the mid-1993 Assembly elections, the UDC won one seat in its own right.
Leadership. Félix Makosso (chairman)

Union for Development and Social Progress (*Union pour le Développement et le Progrès Social*, UDPS), formed prior to the mid-1993 Assembly elections by a dissident group, headed by trade union leader Boukamba-Yangouma, of the Union for Social Progress and Democracy. As part of the Presidential Tendency alliance in those elections, it won one seat in its own right.
Leadership. Jean-Michel Boukamba-Yangouma (president)

Union for Social Progress and Democracy (*Union pour le Progrès Social et la Démocratie, UPSD*), founded in 1991 by former prominent members of the Congolese Labour Party, joined the opposition National Alliance for Democracy, won two Assembly seats in the 1992 elections, thereafter gravitating to the anti-Lissouba opposition, weakened by the formation of the splinter Union for Development and Social Progress, failed to win representation in the 1993 and 2002 elections. Party leader Poungui was Prime Minister in 1985–89.
Leadership. Ange-Édouard Poungui

Union of Democratic Forces (*Union des Forces Démocratiques*, UFD), grouping a number of parties, the UFD formed part of the Presidential Tendency alliance in the mid-1993 Assembly elections, in which it won three seats in its own right. The UFD's David Charles Ganao was an unsuccessful contender for the Assembly presidency, despite receiving opposition backing because of his reputed political objectivity. He subsequently served as Prime Minister of a coalition government under President Lissouba from September 1996 to mid-1997.
Leadership. Sebastian Ebao (chairman)

Costa Rica

Capital: San José
Population: 3,956,500 (2004E)

Costa Rica gained independence from Spain in 1821 and was a member of the United Provinces of Central America until 1838. Following civil war in 1948 a new constitution was promulgated and the army was disbanded, boosting the country's claim to be the longest established democracy in Latin America. A social democratic political tradition, represented by the National Liberation Party (PLN) dominated politics until the late 1970s, when the more conservative Social Christian Unity Party (PUSC) developed a strong following in the country. More recently, the rise of the Citizens' Action Party (PAC), an offshoot of the PLN, has challenged the two-party system, reflecting the growing public mistrust of the state, and a disconnection between voters and the two main political parties.

Under the 1949 constitution, a unicameral Legislative Assembly is made up of 57 members. Executive power rests with the President, who appoints a Cabinet. The President is elected directly by universal adult suffrage for a four-year non-renewable term. However, since a constitutional change in April 2003 overturning an outright ban on re-election, a President can be re-elected eight years after leaving office. Members of the Legislative Assembly are elected by proportional representation for the same period to coincide with the presidential term. It is possible for one party to control the executive branch and for the legislature to be controlled by another party. This was the case following the 1958 and 1966 elections. Since 1994 the party holding the presidency has been forced to strike deals to maintain leadership of the legislature. Voting is compulsory for all men and women, but the level of abstentions is high, reaching record levels in the 2002 elections when almost 40% of voters stayed away.

Abel Pacheco de la Espriella of the PUSC won the presidency in 2002 gaining 58.0% of the vote in the country's first ever second-round election. Simultaneous elections to the Legislative Assembly resulted as follows: PUSC 19 seats (with 29.8% of the vote), PLN 17 (27.1%), PAC 14 (21.9%), Libertarian Movement Party 6 (9.3%), Costa Rican Renewal Party 1 (3.6%). The outcome created the most politically divided legislature in modern history.

Citizens' Action Party
Partido Acción Ciudadana (PAC)
Address. Sede San José, San Pedro de Montes de Oca, de Ferreterias el Mar
Telephone. (506) 281-2727
Email. amontoya.amnet.co.cr
Website. www.pac.or.cr
Leadership. Ottón Solís Fallas
The party was established in January 2001 and is led by former National Liberation Party (PLN) backbencher Ottón Solís Fallas. Solís enjoys the support of Margarita Penón, former first lady and presidential candidate of the PLN, and Alberto Cañas, a well-known intellectual and one of the last surviving founders of the PLN. The PAC campaigns against corruption in public life and opposes economic neo-liberalism. In the presidential election of February 2002 Solis won 26.2% of the vote, forcing the candidates from the two main parties into a run-off for the first time; in simultaneous parliamentary elections the PAC won 21.9% of the vote and 14 seats. Since the elections the party's popularity has held steady. The PAC has tended to oppose policies advocated by President Pacheco.

In the mayoral elections of December 2002 and January 2003 the PAC did not perform well but this was due in part to the party having no nationwide organization. A more serious development came in February 2003 when eight of the 14 PAC legislators decided to leave the party following a dispute with Solís over the interpretation of the party's Ethical Code. The eight deputies resigned from the party and formed the Patriotic Parliamentary Bloc (*Bloque Patriótico Parlamentario*). Two of the legislators then returned to the PAC in March, giving the PAC a total of eight seats in the Assembly.

Costa Rican Renewal Party
Partido Renovación Costarricense (PRC)
Address. c/o Asamblea Legislativa, 1000 San José
Leadership. Justo Orozco Alvarez

Formed in 1995, the PRC stresses the importance of values in society, claiming to be a party of "God, the nation and the family". Its programme defends the right to work and to enjoy the fruits of that labour, advocating that support should be given to small and medium-sized enterprises and that provision of social security must be balanced with productivity of the economy. The party won one seat and 3.6% of the vote in the 2002 legislative elections, while in the simultaneous presidential contest the party's candidate, Justo Orozco Alvarez, took 1.1% of the vote.

Libertarian Movement Party
Partido Movimiento Libertario (PML)
Address. c/o Asamblea Legislativa, 1000 San José
Email. otto@libertario.org
Leadership. Otto Guevara Guth (president)

Founded in 1995 the PML advocates material and spiritual well being, and seeks a "moral revolution". Standing on a political programme combining anti-inflation measures, reducing the size of the state and more police on the beat with more popular participation in politics, the party won six seats in the 2002 elections. Otto Guevara, meanwhile, won 1.7% in the first round of the presidential elections held in February 2002.

National Liberation Party
Partido de Liberación Nacional (PLN)
Address. Sabana Oeste, San José
Telephone. (506) 232-5133
Fax. (506) 296-0916
Leadership. Oscar Arias Sánchez

Founded in October 1951, the PLN is nominally social democratic though has been relatively conservative in office. The successor to the Social Democratic Party (PSD) founded in 1948, the PLN was formed around José "Pepe" Figueres Ferrer, who promised socio-economic reforms, restructuring of the government and better management of the state-run sector. The party lost the presidential elections in 1958 but regained the presidency in 1962 and held it from 1970-78, 1982-90 and 1994-98. Until recently the PLN had had near continuous control of the Legislative Assembly (the exception being 1978-82). The nomination of Oscar Arias Sánchez as presidential candidate in 1986 marked a rupture with the old guard in the party who had a conservative pro-USA foreign policy and were hostile to the Sandinistas in Nicaragua. Arias gained international status for his Central American peace plan and received the Nobel Peace Prize in 1987. Domestically, however, the effects of foreign debt and pressure for economic restructuring, including the privatization of the state sector and banking reform, saw the PLN's moderate social democratic wing squeezed. Drug-related scandals involving prominent party figures, including Daniel Oduber Quirós, party president between 1974-79, damaged the PLN's image and the shift in policy failed to restore it. The party's conservative candidate for the 1990 presidential elections, Carlos Manuel Castillo, was defeated and, symbolic of the end of PLN domination, long-time party leader José Figueres Ferrer died later that year.

The 1990s saw the emergence of an alternative grouping to the PLN's old-style statists and market orientated pragmatists, consisting of a new generation of technocrats aiming to fuse the two traditions. The divisions that resulted, however, engendered a prolonged crisis within the party. The PLN's situation was further clouded after 1998 as former President Oscar Arias Sánchez sought constitutional changes, which would have allowed him to run for the presidency in 2002.

As it turned out, the National Assembly by a substantial majority rejected the amendments as proposed by Otto Guevara Guth of the Libertarian Movement Party, which would have made this possible. As a result, defeated 1998 candidate José Miguel Corrales Bolaño emerged as joint front-runner for the PLN nomination, along with Rolando Araya Monge. In the end, Corrales graciously accepted Araya's victory after an internal party election, and the PLN appeared to have re-established unity. However, any appearance of harmony was soon shattered with the defection of Ottón Solís Fallas and a number of other PLN members to form the Citizens' Action Party (PAC) in 2001. The electoral consequences of the defections and the party's inability to agree on a shared position concerning privatization and the role of the state, contributed to its poor showing in the 2002 elections. In the aftermath of defeat, former President Arias took the reins of the PLN in an attempt to reinvigorate the party, and to consolidate his position as front-runner for the party's nomination for the 2006 presidential election.

The PLN is a member party of the Socialist International.

Social Christian Unity Party
Partido Unidad Social Cristiana (PUSC)
Address. Apartada 725-1007, Centro Colón, San José
Telephone. (506) 234-8395
Fax. (506) 234-8683
Email. partidounidad@racsa.co.cr
Website. www.partidounidadsocialcristiana.com
Leadership. Lorena Vásquez Badilla (president); Abel Pacheco de la Espriella (party leader)

The right-wing Christian democratic PUSC was originally formed in 1978 as the four-party Unity (*Unidad*) alliance of the Christian Democratic Party (PDC, founded in 1962), the Calderonist Republican Party (PRC, founded in 1970), the Popular Union Party (PUP, founded in 1974) and the Democratic Renewal Party (PRD, founded in 1971). The coalition combined the right-wing republican tradition of ex-President Rafael Angel Calderón Guardia (1942-44) and the conservatism of the "coffee barons" with the guiding principles of Christian democracy. The *Unidad* presidential candidate, Rodrigo Carazo Odio, was successful in the 1978 election and the alliance took 28 seats in the Assembly, one short of an absolute majority. Carazo's government clashed with the trade unions and cooled relations with Cuba and Sandinista Nicaragua. In 1982 the *Unidad* candidate, Rafael Angel Calderón Fournier, lost the presidential election and the party's strength in the Assembly was reduced to 18 seats. In the following year the PUSC title was adopted by the alliance.

In 1986 the PUSC's Calderón, standing on a platform that advocated opposition to agrarian reform, cuts in public spending and the privatization of state assets, came second in the presidential race to the candidate of the National Liberation Party (PLN); but the party increased its number of seats in the Assembly. In opposition, the PUSC pressed for the breaking of diplomatic relations with Nicaragua, tax reforms and increased law and order. Calderón finally gained the presidency in February 1990, and the party a majority in the Assembly, promising more moderate economic measures and new social packages for the majority of the population. Instead, the government implemented drastic IMF-approved economic shock measures in June 1990, provoking widespread opposition, particularly from public sector trade unions. Government attempts to form a social pact with the trade unions and business sector failed, as did its attempt to gain public acceptance for a plan to deal with poverty.

As President Calderón's popularity plummeted, many PUSC officials and representatives in the Assembly publicly criticized the government's emphasis on economic readjustment as "excessive" and argued that more pressing social problems were being neglected. Nevertheless, the conditions for a third phase of the government's economic structural readjustment policies were finalized with the IMF in early 1992. The result was that in a close election contest in February 1994, Miguel Angel Rodríguez of the PUSC lost in the presidential race to the PLN candidate by 47.5% to 49.6% of the vote, while PUSC representation in the Assembly fell to 25 seats. However, indicative of the genuinely two-party nature of Costa Rican democracy in the 1990s, the PUSC returned to power in February 1998, winning the presidency and a majority of seats in the Assembly. The selection of a 2002 presidential candidate by the PLN was bitter and divisive. In February 2001 former President Calderón (1990-94) accused leading contender Abel Pacheco of emotional instability, triggering much insult slinging and allegations of fraud. In the event, 67-year-old Pacheco beat off the challenge of the slightly younger Rodolfo Méndez Mata with a landslide victory. Pacheco subsequently won the 2002 presidential election – the first time that the PUSC has succeeded itself in the presidency. The PUSC retained its position as the largest party in the legislature, but lost its overall majority.

During 2003 Pacheco's popularity declined. This was due to a belief on the part of the electorate that the government was not doing enough to improve the performance of the economy. The government, however, was constrained in its actions because of the protracted policymaking process, owing to the tradition of consensus politics in Costa Rica and exacerbated by the government's minority position in the Assembly. Pacheco was forced to negotiate short-term alliances between party blocs in order to pass legislation. However, the government was unable to win sufficient parliamentary support for a key piece of its programme – the fiscal reform bill. The legislation was first introduced in early 2003, and included significant changes to income tax, the introduction of VAT to replace the sales tax, and a series of new tax administration measures, but was blocked through 2003 and into 2004. In May 2004, an under-pressure Pacheco called on the Legislative Assembly to stop obstructing the bill, warning that a failure to implement this legislation would impact negatively on the country's economic and social outlook.

President Pacheco's problems were not solely confined to parliament. Over the course of 2003 workers from the energy and telecommunications sectors coordinated strikes against the government's privatization plans for the industries. The situation was aggravated when schoolteachers withdrew their labour to express dissatisfaction over the late payment of their salaries. The unrest precipitated the resignation of three government ministers. Pacheco's room for manoeuvre was further constrained by the growing influence of the "old guard" within the PUSC, such as former presidents Miguel Angel Rodriguez (1998-2002) and Rafael Angel Calderon (1990-94), in shaping government policy.

The PUSC is a member of the Christian Democrat International and of the Christian Democrat Organization of America.

Other Parties

Agricultural Labour Action Party (*Partido Acción Laborista Agricola*, PALA). Formed in the late 1980s, PALA is a provincial party, being based in Alajuela. Its programme seeks a recognition of the still predominantly agrarian nature of Costa Rican society and therefore of the importance of Costa Rica's *campesino* population. The party favours various reforms to social security provision to better suit the needs of rural workers and is against large government subsidies for agriculture, contending that they tend only to benefit a small number of large producers. The party won one

seat the 1998 legislative elections, but failed to win any in 2002 gaining only 0.72% of the vote.
Address. c/o Asamblea Legislativa, 1000 San José
Leadership. Carlos Alberto Solis Blanco

Democratic Force Party (*Partido Fuerza Democrática*, PFD). Having originated in the run-up to the 1994 elections as an alliance of mainly left-wing parties, the PFD is against the neo-liberal economic model and in favour of social solidarity. The party campaigns for social justice, workers' rights, a reduction in indirect taxes and regulation of the cost of basic public services such as electricity. It campaigns against tax evasion and other forms of corruption. The party won two Assembly seats in both 1994 and 1998 (and 5.3% of the vote on the latter occasion), but failed to gain any parliamentary representation in 2002 winning only 2.0% of the vote. The loss of parliamentary representation was caused by a damaging internal power struggle, which discredited the party.
Address. c/o Asamblea Legislativa, 1000 San José
Leadership. José Nunez

National Integration Party (*Partido de Integración Nacional*, PIN). The PIN calls for the promotion of small business, better provision for children and senior citizens, provincial autonomy, and resistance to privatization in order to allow longer-range planning. The PIN won one seat in the 1998 legislative elections, but lost it four years later, gaining only 1.7% of the vote. Party leader Walter Muñoz Céspedes took 0.41% of the vote in the presidential contest held in 2002.
Address. c/o Asamblea Legislativa, 1000 San José
Leadership. Walter Muñoz Céspedes (president)

Côte d'Ivoire

Capital: Yamoussoukro
Population: 16,300,000 (2001E)

The Republic of Côte d'Ivoire achieved independence from France in 1960 and was then a de facto one-party state under President Félix Houphouët-Boigny and his Democratic Party of Côte d'Ivoire (*Parti Démocratique de la Côte d'Ivoire*, PDCI or PDCI-RDA) until 1990, when a multi-party system was introduced. Executive power is vested in the President, who is directly elected by universal adult suffrage of those aged 21 and over for a renewable five-year term (limited to two terms under the Constitution of the Second Republic, enacted by Law No. 2000-513, Aug. 1, 2000) and who appoints the Prime Minister and Council of Ministers. A controversial electoral code enacted in December 1994 required all future presidential candidates to be Ivoirian by birth and born of parents also Ivoirian by birth, never to have renounced Ivoirian citizenship and to have resided in the country for a minimum of ten years (continuously for the five years preceding elections). Legislative authority is vested in a unicameral National Assembly (*Assemblée Nationale*) of 225 members (increased from 175 for the December 2000–January 2001 elections), who are elected on a constituency basis, also for a five-year term.

The official results of presidential elections held on Oct. 22, 1995 (but boycotted by most opposition parties), showed a turnout of less than 50% and a victory for incumbent Henri Konan Bédié (Hophouët-Boigny's successor) of the PDCI, who was credited with 95.3% of the vote. Assembly elections on Nov. 26, 1995, resulted in an overwhelming number of seats for the PDCI. On Dec. 24, 1999, 40 years of civilian rule came to an abrupt end as a military coup led by junior officers ousted the Bédié regime. General Robert Guëi formed an interim government – the National Committee of Public Safety (*Comité National de Salut Public*), pledged to end the xenophobia against Northerners and Burkinabé that had characterized Bédié's rule, promised an early return to democracy, and endorsed the referendum for a new constitution held on July 23, 2000.

In early October 2000 the Constitutional Chamber of the Supreme Court ruled that only five of the 19 originally nominated candidates for presidential elections later that month were eligible to stand. The main exclusions were Alassane Ouattara, the leader of the Rally of Republicans (RDR) (on nationality grounds) and PDCI candidate Claude Bombet, whose parties jointly represented some two-thirds of the electorate. The Oct. 22 polling was fought chiefly between Gen. Guëi and the Ivoirian Popular Front (FPI) leader, Laurent Gbagbo. Guëi's attempt to claim victory led to a popular uprising by disgruntled opposition supporters who successfully ousted Guëi and his forces from power. The National Electoral Commission subsequently declared Gbagbo the winner with 60% of the votes cast by just over one-third of the electorate. Further violence between FPI and RDR followers ensued in late October before Ouattara acknowledged Gbagbo's election victory and his new civilian administration.

Legislative elections were held on Dec. 10, 2000, and Jan. 14, 2001, again in controversial circumstances as Ouattara was once more disqualified from standing by the Supreme Court, resulting in a divisive RDR boycott of the polls. In the final results the FPI took 96 seats and the PDCI 94, with the remainder shared between minor parties and independent candidates. Municipal elections held peacefully on March 25, 2001, reflected a more realistic distribution of party support by number of districts won: RDR 63, PDCI-RDA 60, Independents 38, FPI 33. Only 30% of the electorate voted in the peaceful turnout on July 7, 2002, for the *Conseils Généraux,* departmental representatives (58), that yielded somewhat different results: FPI 18, PDCI 18, RDR 10, Union for Democracy and Peace in Côte d'Ivoire (UDPCI) 4, Independents 5, and 3 coalition seats – FPI/PDCI.

A partially successful coup on Sept. 19, 2002, seriously challenged Gbagbo's executive powers, resulted in the occupation of half of the country from Yamoussoukro northward by mutineers, and brought about endless rounds of negotiations involving the international commu nity, ECOWAS, and African heads of state. Gbagbo, accused of allowing paramilitary forces and death squads free rein to persecute opposition members and foreigners in the aftermath of his ascendance to the presidency, had ignored and never followed up on recommendations of the 2001 Forum for national reconciliation chaired by Seydou Diarra that shed light on the December 1999 coup, flaws in the October 2000 presidential elections, and conflicts between the principal party leaders – Gbagbo, Ouattara, Guëi, and Bédié. Direct military intervention by the French (*Opération Licorne*, involving 4,000 troops) and later ECOWAS (1,500 troops) enforced, sometimes with difficulty, a cease fire and held back excessive violence in the occupied North; in the government-controlled South they played a daily

peacekeeping role between dissidents and Gbagbo supporters and facilitated the repatriation of over 16,000 French residents. The rebel forces organized regionally as the Patriotic Movement of Côte d'Ivoire (MPCI, the largest group), the Popular Ivoirian Movement of the Great West (MPIGO), and the Movement for Justice and Peace (MJP) and there were regular attacks by insurgents spilling over the western border from Liberia.

Refusing to comply with efforts, led by Presidents Abdoulaye Wade (Senegal), John Kufuor (Ghana) and Gnassingbé Eyadema (Togo), in October and November 2000 to resolve the conflict, Gbagbo reluctantly agreed to the terms of a negotiated peace at a French-sponsored roundtable attended by 32 delegates representing both government and opposition parties and rebel forces, held at Linas-Marcoussis (near Paris) from Jan. 15- 23, 2003. The proposed settlement or Marcoussis Accord was signed on Jan. 24, 2003, and endorsed by African heads of state and leaders of the international community. Côte d'Ivoire's civil war, aggravated by instability in Liberia and Sierra Leone, has elicited fears throughout the international community for the stability and economic security of the entire West African region.

The agreement required the establishment of a reconciliation government, the reintegration of rebels, the elimination of the *Carte de sejour* (residency cards), constitutional revisions regarding eligibility for the presidency (Article 35) and requirements for citizenship, revision of rights of succession and access to land policies, among others. The African heads of state went a step further, proposing that Gbagbo select as Prime Minister Seydou Diarra, a former ambassador and head of government under Guëi, and naming an international monitoring group to provide oversight for implementation of reforms. Incited by Gbagbo's reversal of his support for the Marcoussis Accord, protests led by youthful FPI supporters against the French and the peace proposal resulted in violent clashes with the French 43rd Infantry Batallion of the Navy (BIMa) protecting the airport. Ultimately, Gbagbo conceded and by March 2003 Diarra named a government consisting of 41 members representing both the political parties and the rebel factions: FPI 10, PDCI-RDA 7, RDR 7, MPCI 7, UDPCI 2, Ivoirian Workers' Party PIT 2, Movement of Forces for the Future (MFA) 1, Democratic Citizens' Union (UDCY) 1, MJP 1, MPIGO 1. The former rebels still occupying the northern half of the country are now called the *Forces Nouvelles*, their reintegration troubled by a refusal to disarm and resentment on behalf of loyalists. The fragile government fell into disarray when Gbagbo named Ministers of Security and Defence without consulting oppositions leaders. Scheduled peaceful protests in March 2004 turned violent when Gbagbo refused to approve the marches and his loyalist troops attempted to restore order. The opposition parties insist on full implementation of the Marcoussis Accord and several meetings have taken place in Accra with African heads of state to reconcile differences between Gbagbo, the *Forces Nouvelles*, and opposition parties.

Democratic Party of Côte d'Ivoire
Parti Démocratique de la Côte d'Ivoire (PDCI) (PDCI-RDA)

Address. c/o Assemblée Nationale, Abidjan
Leadership. Henri Konan Bédié (president); Alphonse Djédjé Mady (secretary-general)
The PDCI was founded in 1946 as the local section of the

pro-independence movement of French West Africa called the African Democratic Rally (*Rassemblement Démocratique Africain*, RDA), which designation is still a suffix of the PDCI's full official title. The party's Ivoirian founder, Félix Houphouët-Boigny, sat in the French National Assembly from 1946 to 1959 (also holding ministerial office during this period), before returning home to lead Côte d'Ivoire to independence in 1960. For the next 30 years the PDCI was the only authorized party, although a one-party system was never formalized by law. Every five years a PDCI congress would draw up a list of Assembly candidates for endorsement by the electorate and would also renominate Houphouët-Boigny as the sole presidential candidate. By 1990 he had served six consecutive terms and was Africa's longest-serving head of state, running an administration committed to a free enterprise system, open access for Western capitalists and close relations with France (which remained Côte d'Ivoire's financial and military guarantor).

Bowing to a new wind of change in black Africa, Houphouët-Boigny in May 1990 publicly endorsed a transition to multi-partyism. The change was approved by a PDCI congress in October 1990, when changes in the party's structure were also agreed, including the revival of the post of secretary-general (abolished in 1980) and the creation of an 80-member central committee with executive responsibilities. The congress also again endorsed Houphouët-Boigny as the PDCI candidate in the presidential election due later that month, resisting internal pressure from the party's "new guard" for the nomination of Henri Konan Bédié, who as Assembly president was next in line to the President under a 1985 constitutional amendment. Houphouët-Boigny was duly re-elected with nearly 82% of the popular vote (according to official figures), defeating a candidate of the Ivoirian Popular Front (FPI), who claimed that the elections had been fraudulent. In multi-party Assembly elections in November 1990, the PDCI swept to a landslide victory, winning 163 of the 175 seats, although again the results were disputed by the FPI. The PDCI therefore remained in power, despite a sharp deterioration in economic and social conditions since the late 1980s.

The move to multi-partyism served to reveal long-suppressed tribal divisions within the PDCI, reflecting broader tensions between Côte d'Ivoire's predominantly Muslim north and the Christian south of Houphouët-Boigny. The election of Laurent Dona-Fologo as party secretary-general in April 1991 was in line with the President's ruling that the post should be held by someone not from his own ethnic background. Nevertheless, tension increased between heir apparent Konan Bédié (a southerner) and then Prime Minister Alassane Ouattara (a northern Muslim), being sharpened by the death of Houphouët-Boigny in December 1993. An attempt by Ouattara to assume supreme power (with army backing) was successfully resisted by Bédié (with French backing), who proceeded to appoint a new Prime Minister and was succeeded as Assembly president by Charles Donwahi of the PDCI. Thereafter, the PDCI government resisted calls from some opposition parties for a national conference to determine the country's future political structure.

In April 1994 President Konan Bédié was unanimously elected PDCI chairman, thus ensuring his candidacy for the ruling party in the 1995 presidential elections. The following month Ouattara resigned from the PDCI and subsequently became identified with the breakaway Rally of Republicans (RDR). Assisted by the enactment in December 1994 of new presidential qualifications that effectively barred Ouattara from being able to stand, Konan Bédié won 95.3% of the vote in the presidential elections of October 1995, his only opponent being a candidate of the Ivoirian Workers' Party. The following month the PDCI retained its overwhelming majority in the Assembly.

In the wake of serious civil unrest, 40 years of PDCI rule was brought to an end in December 1999 as President Konan Bédié was deposed by Gen. Robert Guëi in a military coup. Under subsequent plans for a return to representative government, presidential elections were scheduled for the autumn of 2000. Claude Bombet was selected as the PDCI candidate, but he was declared ineligible by the Supreme Court, prompting a PDCI boycott of the Oct. 22 polling. Gen. Guëi's attempt to rig the result led to a popular uprising in support of the FPI candidate, who was subsequently declared the winner. In the legislative elections in December 2000–January 2001, the PDCI won 94 of the 225 seats, making it the second largest party in the Assembly, just behind the FPI. Bédié overcame a challenge by Laurent Dona Fologo to regain control of the party at the eleventh PDCI Congress, in April 2002, winning 82% of the vote.

The PDCI is associated with the International Democrat Union through the Democrat Union of Africa.

Ivoirian Popular Front
Front Populaire Ivoirien (FPI)
Address. c/o Assemblée Nationale, Abidjan
Website. www.fpi.ci
Leadership. Laurent Gbagbo (chairman); Abou Dramane Sangare (secretary-general)

The FPI was founded in France in 1982 by the then exiled Laurent Gbagbo (a history professor), who was granted an amnesty on his return in September 1988 but was harassed by the authorities in his moves to establish the party in Côte d'Ivoire. At its founding (illegal) congress in November 1989, the FPI committed itself to a mixed economy with a private sector emphasis, thus placing itself to the left of the ruling Democratic Party of Côte d'Ivoire (PDCI). Legalized in May 1990, the FPI became the acknowledged leader of an opposition coalition which included the Ivoirian Workers' Party, the Ivoirian Socialist Party and the Union of Social Democrats. This coalition endorsed Gbagbo's candidature for the October 1990 presidential elections, as agreed the previous month by the first legal FPI congress. But sparse finance and organization compared with the resources of the PDCI contributed to Gbagbo's heavy defeat, the official results showing support of less than 18% for the FPI candidate. This outcome was hotly disputed by the FPI, which also denounced alleged government fraud in Assembly elections the following month, when the FPI was awarded only nine of the 175 seats. Its support in that contest came mainly from the north-east of the country and from the more affluent districts of Abidjan.

Amid growing popular unrest in 1991, the FPI declined to endorse a call by other opposition parties for a national conference to determine the future political structure; instead, it demanded the outright resignation of President Houphouët-Boigny and announced a campaign of civil disobedience. Arrested in February 1992 amid anti-government demonstrations in Abidjan, Gbagbo and his chief lieutenant, Mollé Mollé, were sentenced the following month to two years' imprisonment, but were amnestied in July 1992 on the recommendation of the President. In October 1992 the FPI launched a new attack on the government for its failure to deal with the deteriorating economic and social situation; but it remained outside an opposition front of 15 other parties formed in December 1992. In the prelude to the death of Houphouët-Boigny in December 1993, the FPI publicly backed the Assembly president, Henri Konan Bédié (PDCI), for the succession as provided for under constitutional law. However, when newly-installed President Konan Bédié failed to offer Gbagbo the premiership, the FPI rejected his proposal that it should join a coalition with the PDCI and returned to opposition mode, although it did not join the Group for Solidarity formed by 19 opposition parties in April 1994.

In December 1994 Gbagbo was endorsed as the FPI candidate in the 1995 presidential elections, but the party subsequently decided to boycott the contest. The FPI assailed the new presidential qualifications code as being "xenophobic and dangerous", joining with the Rally of Republicans in mounting anti-government demonstrations. In June 1995 an FPI leader, Abou Dramane Sangare, was beaten by police while in the office of the Security Minister; the same month the pro-FPI weekly *La Patrie* was suspended for three months and two of its journalists were sent to prison after being convicted of conspiring to give offence to the President. Having not contested the October 1995 presidential contest, the FPI won 12 seats in the following month's Assembly elections.

A military coup brought an end to the PDCI government of President Konan Bédié in December 1999 following serious civil unrest. Under subsequent plans for a return to representative government, presidential elections were scheduled for the autumn of 2000. Gbagbo was again selected as the FPI candidate, his eligibility to stand being approved (unlike other leading opposition figures) by the Supreme Court. After a successful popular uprising by FPI supporters against the attempt by the incumbent, Gen. Guëi, to manipulate the results of the Oct. 22 polling, Gbagbo was declared the winner with about 60% of the vote by the National Electoral Commission. Despite further street violence, Gbagbo's victory was subsequently acknowledged by the other main parties and he nominated a new government. In the legislative elections in December 2000–January 2001, which were boycotted the Rally of Republicans (RDR), the FPI won 96 of the 225 seats making it the largest party in the Assembly, just ahead of the PDCI; it received 10 posts in the 41-member government appointed in March 2003.

Strongly based in the trade union movement, the FPI is a member of the Socialist International.

Ivoirian Workers' Party
Parti Ivorien des Travailleurs (PIT)
Address. c/o Assemblée Nationale, Abidjan
Leadership. Francis Wodié (secretary general)
The left-of-centre PIT achieved legalization in May 1990 and joined a pro-democracy opposition alliance headed by the Ivoirian Popular Front (FPI), backing the latter's unsuccessful candidate in the October 1992 presidential elections. In Assembly elections the following month the PIT was the only opposition party apart from the FPI to gain representation, Wodié winning a seat in the affluent Cocody suburb of Abidjan. Three PIT leaders were among those sentenced to prison terms in March 1992 for their participation in anti-government demonstrations the previous month, although all the detainees were amnestied four months later. Thereafter the PIT and the FPI drifted apart, with the latter declining to endorse the former's demand for a fullscale national conference to decide the country's future political system.

In December 1992 the PIT joined with 14 other opposition parties (excluding the FPI) in an alliance called the Union of Democratic Forces. Shortly before President Houphouët-Boigny's death in December 1993, the PIT and five other parties called for the creation of a transitional all-party government. Wodié was the only opposition candidate in the October 1995 presidential election, being credited with 3.8% of the vote. He also contested the October 2000 presidential poll, attracting 5.7% of the vote. In the subsequent legislative elections in December 2000–January 2001, the PIT won four seats.

Rally of Republicans
Rassemblement des Républicains (RDR)
Leadership. Alassane Ouattara (president); Henriette Diabate (secretary-general)

The RDR was formally launched in October 1994 by a dissident faction of the ruling Democratic Party of Côte d'Ivoire (PDCI) consisting mainly of "old guard" elements. Claiming to have the support of 31 Assembly deputies, the new party was joined by several former PDCI ministers. Its posters featured pictures of Alassane Ouattara, the former (northern Muslim) Prime Minister who had resigned from the PDCI in May 1994 six months after losing the power struggle for the succession to President Houphouët-Boigny. Ouattara had then taken up a post with the IMF in Washington and was thought likely to be the RDR candidate in the 1995 presidential elections. However, he was effectively barred from standing because his previous alleged citizenship of Burkina Faso and overseas residence ran foul of a new qualifications code enacted in December 1994 by the PDCI Assembly majority. In the run-up to the elections, the RDR took a prominent role in anti-government demonstrations, calling in particular for the electoral code to be rescinded. Having not contested the October 1995 presidential elections, the RDR won 13 seats out of 175 in the following month's balloting for the Assembly.

From August 1999 violent clashes between the security forces and RDR supporters led to the arrest and detention of RDR leaders, including secretary-general Henriette Diabate. On Dec. 24, 1999, 40 years of civilian rule in Côte d'Ivoire came to an end as a military coup led by Gen. Robert Guëi ousted the PDCI regime. Under subsequent plans for a return to representative government, presidential elections were scheduled for the autumn of 2000. In early October 2000 the Constitutional Chamber of the Supreme Court ruled Ouattara was ineligible to stand, again on nationality grounds. RDR supporters boycotted the Oct. 22 poll, and later clashed with Ivoirian Popular Front (FPI) followers whose leader successfully claimed victory against the incumbent, Gen. Guëi, after a popular uprising. Ouattara recognized the FPI's presidential victory, but was again disqualified from standing in the December 2000–January 2001 legislative polling by the Supreme Court, prompting a further RDR electoral boycott. Its claims to represent a national constituency were confirmed in the municipal elections of 2001, although repression of northerners and Muslims by the Gbagbo regime has attracted disproportionate numbers to the RDR.

Union for Democracy and Peace in Côte d'Ivoire (UDPCI)
Leadership. Paul Yao Akoto (vice president); Salif Alassane N'Diaye (secretary-general). Founded in February 2001 by Gen. Guëi, and seeking to liberalize the economy, attract foreign investment and promote regional co-operation, the party emerged in the centre-western region. Attracting ten former PDCI ministers and a large cohort of regional educated elites, the UDPCI had by July 2002 gained the status of the nation's fourth largest party, just months prior to Guëi's untimely and violent death in the Sept. 19, 2002 coup. Former Minister Balla Këita followed Akoto as secretary-general from May 2002 until his assassination in exile in Burkina Faso on Aug. 1, 2002.

Croatia

Capital: Zagreb
Population: 4,437,460 (2001 census)

The Republic of Croatia declared independence from the Socialist Federal Republic of Yugoslavia in June 1991 and was admitted to UN membership in May 1992. Meanwhile, hostilities between Croatian forces and the Serb-dominated Yugoslav Federal Army had resulted in the declaration of what became the Republic of Serbian Krajina in Serb-populated areas of Croatia. The pre-independence ethnic composition of the republic was Croats 74.6% and Serbs 11.3%, with Muslims, Slovenes, Hungarians, Italians and Czechs forming small locally-significant other minorities. A census conducted in early 2001 showed that the ethnic Serb minority had fallen to only 4.54% of the population.

The 1990 constitution provided for a presidential form of government, with the President as head of the executive branch. However, under amendments approved in November 2000, Croatia moved to a system of parliamentary democracy under which the Prime Minister and Cabinet became fully accountable to the legislature, which could only be dissolved by the President on its recommendation. The President nevertheless retained substantial powers in the foreign and security policy spheres and continued to be directly elected for a five-year term. Legislative authority is vested in the Parliament (*Sabor*), which under the constitutional amendments promulgated in March 2001 became unicameral (having previously consisted of an upper Chamber of Districts and a lower Chamber of Representatives). The legislature has up to 152 members elected for a four-year term, 140 by proportional representation from multi-member constituencies, up to four to represent Croatians abroad and eight to represent ethnic minorities.

Under legislation first enacted in 1993, state financial support is available to all parties represented in the *Sabor* in proportion to their number of members, the current arrangements specifying that the total sum available in a given year is equivalent to 0.056% of central state expenditure in the previous year. The total sum available to the parties in 2000 was 19.2 million kunas (about $2.4 million).

The most recent legislative elections were held on Nov. 23, 2003. Voting took place in 12 electoral units – 10 that each had about the same number of voters, and two special ones: one for the Croatian diaspora and another for national minorities. The Croatian Democratic Union (HDZ) won the biggest number of seats in the Parliament (62 plus four from the diaspora list). The Social Democratic Party (SDP) received 36 seats; the Croatian People's Party (HNS) 10; the Croatian Peasant Party (HSS) 10; the Croatian Party of Rights (HSP) 8; the Istrian Democratic Assembly (IDS) 4; three seats each were won by the Croatian Party of Pensioners (HSU) and Libra; the Croatian Social Liberal Party (HSLS) and Liberal Party (LS) won two each; one seat each was won by the Littoral and Highland Region Alliance (PGC), the Democratic Centre (DC) and the Croatian Democratic Peasant Party (HDSS). Two other parties gained representation in Parliament – the Independent Democratic Serbian Party (SDSS) won three seats and the Party of Democratic Action of Croatia (SDAH) won one. Their representatives were elected from a special minority list, based on special rights that are enjoyed by the minorities in Croatia.

After the election a coalition was formed by the HDZ, HSLS and DC, and the HSU and the national minorities gave their support to the Government led by the HDZ. Croatia is thus de facto run by a minority government.

In presidential elections on Jan. 24 and Feb. 7, 2000, the HNS candidate, Stjepan Mesic, headed the first round with 41.1%, against 27.7% for Drazen Budisa of the HSLS (and backed by the SPH) and

22.5% for Mate Granic of the HDZ, who was therefore eliminated. In the second round Mesic defeated Budisa by 56% to 44%.

Croatian Democratic Peasant Party
Hrvatska Demokratska Seljacka Stranka (HDSS)
Address. Strossmayerova 9, 40000 Cakovec
Telephone and fax. (385-4) 036440
Leadership. Ivan Martan (president)
The founding assembly of the Croatian Democratic Peasant Party was held in Zagreb on Sept. 18, 1994. The HDSS offers a programme that orients the party toward the centre-right, with an emphasis on the market economy, free enterprise and the development of family-owned businesses. It won one seat in the November 2003 legislative elections.

Croatian Democratic Union
Hrvatska Demokratska Zajednica (HDZ)
Address. Trg Zrtava fasizma 4, 11000 Zagreb
Telephone. (385–1) 455–3000
Fax. (385–1) 455–2600
Email. hdz@hdz.hr
Website. www.hdz.hr
Leadership. Ivo Sanader (president); Jadranka Kosor (vice president), Luka Bebic (parliamentary group chairman); Branko Vukelic (secretary-general)
Formally launched in June 1989 in opposition to the then communist regime, the HDZ spearheaded the drive both to multi-party democracy and to independence from the Yugoslav federation. A nationalist party, it was joined by many of the elite of the Yugoslav regime, although its leader Franjo Tudjman himself, a history professor with a military background, had been a prominent dissident in the 1970s and 1980s. Contesting the 1990 multi-party elections on a pro-autonomy platform, the HDZ won a landslide parliamentary majority, by virtue of which Tudjman was elected President in May 1990 by vote of the deputies. The HDZ government secured a 94% pro-independence verdict in a referendum in May 1991 and declared Croatia's independence the following month. In further elections in August 1992, the HDZ retained an overall parliamentary majority and Tudjman was directly re-elected President with 56.7% of the popular vote. Thereafter, the HDZ government was riven by dissension about how to deal with the civil war in neighbouring Bosnia & Herzegovina; also controversial was its maintenance of much of the communist-era panoply of central economic control, despite the party's claim to be of the centre-right. Nevertheless, the HDZ in February 1993 won 37 of the 63 elective seats in the upper house, thereafter accepting the small Croatian Peasant Party (HSS) into the government.

In October 1993 a special HDZ congress approved a new party programme espousing Christian democracy, describing the HDZ as the guarantor of Croatian independence and defining the liberation of Serb-held Croatian territory as the government's most important task. In addition to re-electing Tudjman as party president, the congress elected the hardline nationalist Defence Minister, Gojko Susak, as vice-president but also, on Tudjman's urging, replaced some other hardliners with moderates on the HDZ presidium. But the impact of this move was diminished by Tudjman's proposal that Jasenovac in southern (Serb-held) Croatia, site of the camp where the wartime pro-Nazi *Ustasa* regime had exterminated Serbs, Jews and Gypsies, should also commemorate "all the victims of communism" (including *Ustasa* officials executed after the war) as well as the Croatian dead in the 1991 war with Serbia. In February 1994 President Tudjman publicly apologized for having, in an earlier book, doubted the veracity of received accounts of the Nazi extermination of Jews during World War II; the following month he also apologized for the role of the *Ustasa* regime in such extermination.

In April 1994 the HDZ was weakened by the formation of the breakaway Croatian Independent Democrats by liberal elements which favoured alliance with the Muslims of Bosnia & Herzegovina against the Serbs and also objected to Tudjman's dictatorial tendencies. Further internal conflict was evident in the resignations of two prominent HDZ hardliners in September 1994, Vladimir Seks (as Deputy Prime Minister) and Branimir Glavas (as party chairman in Osijek), in what appeared to be the start of a purge of the party's radical right wing. Nevertheless, Seks's popularity among HDZ deputies was demonstrated the following month when he was elected HDZ leader in the lower house. Buoyed by Croat military successes against the Serbs, the HDZ retained an overall majority in lower house elections in October 1995, although short of the two-thirds majority required for constitutional amendments and with a vote share of 45.2%. The party also retained its majority in the upper house in April 1997, following which Tudjman was re-elected President two months later with 61.4% of the vote.

In the late 1990s, as Tudjman's health deteriorated, the HDZ became increasingly divided between hardliners and moderates, amidst rising popular discontent with economic and social conditions. Following Tudjman's death in December 1999, the HDZ was heavily defeated in Assembly elections in early January 2000, retaining only 40 of the 151 seats (with 26.7% of the vote) and going into opposition to a centre-left government headed by the Social Democratic Party of Croatia. In presidential elections in late January, moreover, outgoing Deputy Premier and Foreign Minister Mate Granic failed to overcome the HDZ's new unpopularity, despite resigning his party offices on the eve of polling, and was eliminated in the first round with only 22.5% of the vote.

In unaccustomed opposition, the HDZ was further weakened by an exodus of leading members, including Granic in March 2000, as evidence began to emerge of extensive corruption under the Tudjman regime. In April 2000 the party presidency was conferred on Ivo Sanader, reputedly a moderate nationalist, who set as his first objective the restoration of the HDZ's public image. In November 2000 HDZ deputies unsuccessfully opposed the conversion of Croatia into a parliamentary democracy.

At the seventh party convention in April 2002, Ivo Sanader was once again elected president of the party. The convention ended with the victory of the moderate faction. Ivic Pasalic, the representative of the hard-core nationalistic faction of the HDZ, was defeated in the party's presidential elections by a small margin. Pasalic and some of his supporters were subsequently expelled from the party. Ivic Pasalic then founded his own political party, the Croatian Bloc. Some radicals, such as Seks and Glavas, remained by Sanader's side. Ivo Sanader managed to consolidate his party before the elections in November 2003 and bring it back to power. He improved relations with national minorities, particularly the Serbian one, and set achieving Croatian membership of the European Union by 2007 as the primary goal of his government.

Claiming a membership of over 400,000, the HDZ is affiliated to the Christian Democrat International and has observer status in the European People's Party and European Democrat Union.

Croatian Liberal Democrats–LIBRA
Stranka Liberalnih Demokrata–LIBRA

Address. Teslina 8, 10000 Zagreb
Telephone. (385–1) 481–4365
Fax. (385–1) 481–4368
Email. libra@libra.hr
Website. www.libra.hr

Leadership. Jozo Rados (president and parliamentary group chairman); Zrinjka Glovacki-Bernardi and Milka Blagdan (deputy presidents); Mladen Ruzman (secretary general)

The Croatian Liberal Democrats–LIBRA was founded in September 2002 by a large number of Croatian Social Liberal Party (HSLS) members who had left that party. Ten HSLS representatives in the Parliament switched to LIBRA, which enabled the survival of the government coalition that came to power at the elections of 2000. LIBRA is a left-of-centre party that advocates basic liberal principles: equal treatment for all citizens under law, a multi-party parliamentary system, division of the government into three branches, freedom of the economy, social dialogue and religious freedoms. It won three seats in the November 2003 legislative elections.

Croatian Party of Pensioners
Hrvatska Stranka Umirovljenika (HSU)

Address. Frankopanska 7/I, 10000 Zagreb
Telephone. (385-1) 4840058
Fax. (385-1) 14815324
Email. strankahsu@hsu.hr
Website. www.hsu.hr

Leadership. Vladimir Jordan (president); Josip Sudec (parliamentary group chairman)

The Croatian Party of Pensioners was founded on April 24, 1996. The goal of the party is to protect the interests of Croatian pensioners, without any political orientation. In the parliamentary elections of 2000, the HSU list received 53,000 votes, which was not enough to meet the election threshold, but was the best election result of any party not represented in Parliament. In the elections of November 2003 three members of the party were for the first time elected to Parliament.

Croatian Party of Rights
Hrvatska Stranka Prava (HSP)

Address. Primorska 5, 10000 Zagreb
Telephone. (385–1) 377–8016
Fax. (385–1) 377–8736
Email. hsp@hsp.hr
Website. www.hsp.hr

Leadership. Anto Djapic (president), Miroslav Rozic (parliamentary group chairman); Vlado Jukic (secretary-general)

Descended indirectly from a pre-war nationalist party of the same name, the far-right HSP was founded in February 1990 by Dobroslav Paraga and had considerable support among Croats outside Croatia. It advocates "national-state sovereignty throughout the whole of [Croatia's] historical and ethnic space", which has been taken to imply a territorial claim not just to the Croat-populated areas of Bosnia-Herzegovina but to the whole of that state. To these ends, the party formed a military wing called the Croatian Defence Association (*Hrvatski Obrambeni Savez*, HOS), which became heavily involved on the Croat side in inter-ethnic conflict in Bosnia (and was seen by many as the modern counterpart of the wartime pro-fascist *Ustasa* movement). The party won five lower house seats in the August 1992 elections and Paraga came fourth in the concurrent presidential contest, winning 5.4% of the national vote. It failed to win a seat in the February 1993 upper house elections, after which Paraga and three other HSP leaders were charged with terrorism and inciting forcible changes to the constitutional order. The government also applied to the Constitutional Court for a ban on the HSP.

In July 1993 Zagreb police evicted the party from its headquarters in the capital, on the grounds that its occupation of the state-owned building since 1991 was illegal. Steps were also taken by the authorities to curtail the independence of the HOS by integrating its forces into units controlled by the Defence Ministry. Meanwhile, Paraga had come under criticism for his leadership, this resulting in his being replaced by Boris Kandare at an extraordinary congress in September 1993, when a new main committee was elected as the party's governing body. Having been acquitted of the charges against him in November 1993, Paraga proceeded to form the new Croatian Party of Rights 1861. In the October 1995 lower house elections the HSP just surmounted the 5% representation threshold winning five seats.

In the January 2000 parliamentary elections the HSP was allied with the Croatian Christian Democratic Union (HKDU), their joint list winning 5.2% and five seats, four of which went to the HSP. In the presidential elections later the same month HSP-HKDU candidate Anto Djapic took only 1.8% of the first-round vote. In the November 2003 legislative elections, however, the HSP increased its total of seats to eight.

Croatian Peasant Party
Hrvatska Seljacka Stranka (HSS)
Address. Ulica Kralja Zvonimira 17, 10000 Zagreb
Telephone. (385–1) 455–3624
Fax. (385–1) 455–3631
Email. hss-sredisnjica@hss.hr and hss@hss.hr
Website. www.hss.hr
Leadership. Zlatko Tomcic (president and parliamentary group chairman); Ljubica Lalic (deputy president); Stanko Grcic (general secretary)
The HSS is descended from a co-operative party founded by the Radic brothers in 1904, which became a standard-bearer of Croat nationalism in inter-war Yugoslavia but was suppressed by the wartime pro-Nazi *Ustasa* regime in Croatia. Revived in November 1989 and committed to pacifism, local democracy, privatization and rural co-operatives, the HSS won three seats in the August 1992 lower house elections and five in the February 1993 upper house balloting. It then effectively entered a coalition with the then ruling Croatian Democratic Union (HDZ). On succeeding Drago Stipac as HSS president in December 1994, however, Zlatko Tomcic vacated his post as Minister of Urban Planning, Housing and Construction. In the October 1995 lower house elections the HSS won 10 seats as part of the opposition Joint List (ZL) bloc.

In the January 2000 lower house elections the HSS was again part of the ZL, which included the Istrian Democratic Assembly, the Liberal Party and the Croatian People's Party (HNS). The HSS took 16 of the 25 seats won by the alliance and obtained two portfolios (including agriculture) in the new centre-left coalition government headed by the Social Democratic Party of Croatia. In addition, Tomcic was elected president of the new chamber. In presidential elections in January-February 2000 the HSS backed the successful candidacy of Stjepan Mesic of the HNS. Zlatko Tomcic was once again elected president at the party convention in December 2002 and the party won ten seats in the November 2003 elections, going into opposition.

Croatian People's Party
Hrvatska Narodna Stranka (HNS)
Address. Tomiceva 2, 10000 Zagreb
Telephone. (385–1) 487–7000
Fax. (385–1) 487–7009
Email. hns@hns.hr
Website. www.hns.hr
Leadership. Vesna Pusic (president); Radimir Cacic (president of board); Savka Dabcevic-Kucar (honorary president); Dragutin Lesar (parliamentary group chairman); Srecko Ferencak (general secretary)
The HNS was founded in October 1990, although its core leadership had formed a coherent dissident group since the attempt in 1970–71 to liberalize the then ruling League of Communists of Croatia. It advocated "modernity" in politi-

cal and economic structures, private enterprise, regionalism and the creation of a "civil society", and drew considerable support from ethnic Serbs. On its creation, it attracted the backing of five Assembly deputies elected under other labels in 1990 and in the August 1992 elections it won six lower house seats, while its president came third in the concurrent presidential contest with 6% of the national vote. In the February 1993 upper house elections the HNS won one of the elective seats. For the October 1995 lower house elections it was part of the centre-right Joint List (ZL) bloc, winning two seats.

The HNS retained its two lower house seats in the January 2000 parliamentary elections, again standing as part of the ZL, which included the Croatian Peasant Party, the Istrian Democratic Assembly and the Liberal Party. One HNS minister was appointed to the resultant centre-left government headed by the Social Democratic Party of Croatia. The HNS also secured the election of its vice-chairman, Stjepan Mesic, as President of Croatia in the subsequent presidential elections, in which he stood as the HNS/ZL candidate. Against most initial predictions, Mesic led in the first round with 41.1% of the vote and was elected in the second with 56%. The HNS took 10 seats in the November 2003 parliamentary elections.

Croatian Social Liberal Party
Hrvatska Socijalno Liberalna Stranka (HSLS)
Address. Trg Nikole Subica Zrinskog 17/1, 10000 Zagreb
Telephone. (385–1) 481–0401
Fax. (385–1) 481–0404
Email. hsls@hsls.hr
Website. www.hsls.hr
Leadership. Ivan Cehok (president); Zrinka Radnic (secretary-general)
The HSLS was founded in May 1989 as a liberal party on the classic European model, emphasizing the "democratic and European tradition and orientation of Croatia". Having made little impact in the 1990 pre-independence elections, it became the second-strongest party in the lower house elections of August 1992, winning 14 seats, while its president took second place in the simultaneous presidential contest with 21.9% of the national vote. In the February 1993 upper house elections, the party won 16 of the 63 elective seats. Opposed to the government of the Croatian Democratic Union (HDZ), the HSLS participated in an opposition boycott of parliament from May to September 1994 in protest against irregularities in the election of new presidents of the two houses in the wake of the formation of the Croatian Independent Democrats. In the October 1995 lower house elections the party took 11.6% of the vote and 12 seats, confirming its status as the strongest single opposition party.

For the January 2000 Assembly elections, the HSLS was allied with the Social Democratic Party of Croatia (SPH), together with two small regional formations, and won 24 seats in the anti-HDZ victory. The party was allocated six portfolios in the resultant six-party coalition government headed by the SPH. In the presidential elections three weeks later HSLS chairman Drazen Budisa, backed by the SPH, took second place in the first round with 27.7% of the vote and therefore contested the second round in early February, but was defeated by the candidate of the Croatian People's Party (HNS) by 44% to 56%.

In June 2002 the HSLS left the coalition. This was a result of its dissatisfaction with the attitude of the government towards the International Criminal Tribunal for the former Yugoslavia at the Hague, although officially the HSLS stated that the reason for its break with the coalition had to do with the way the government dealt with foreign affairs. Subsequently, there were splits in the higher ranks of the party, and some important members were expelled. These members then founded their own party, LIBRA. The departure of the HSLS from the left-of-centre coalition signaled the party's shift to the right, and its views gradually grew more similar to those held by the HDZ. The HSLS took two seats in the November 2003 legislative elections and joined the HDZ in government.

Claiming a membership of 15,000, the HSLS is a member of the Liberal International and an associate member of the European Liberal, Democratic and Reformist (ELDR) organization.

Democratic Centre
Demokratski Centar

Address. Ilica 48, 10000 Zagreb
Telephone. (385–1) 483–1111
Fax. (385–1) 481–483-1045
Email. demokratski-centar@demokratski-centar.hr
Website. www.demokratski-centar.hr
Leadership. Vesna Skare-Ozbolt (president); Dubravko Mateljan (secretary general)

The Democratic Centre (DC) is a party of the centre, founded in April 2002 by several HDZ members who had left that party. The leader of the DC is Mate Granic, the former Minister of Foreign Affairs, who did not share the right-wing views of the HDZ. The Democratic Centre is a modern European national party that advocates safeguarding the values and traditions of the Republic of Croatia. The party is represented by one member of Parliament.

Independent Democratic Serbian Party
Samostalna Demokratska Srpska Stranka (SDSS)

Address. Radnicki dom (3. floor), Borovo naselje, 32010 Vukovar
Telephone/Fax. +38532423211
Email. ivanasdss@yahoo.com
Website. www.sdss.hr
Leadership. Vojislav Stanimirovic (president and parliamentary group chairman)

The party was formed in 1997, in order to organize the Serbs from the region of the Croatian Podunavlje, who had until then been living in the self-proclaimed Republic of Serbian Krajina. The SDSS in a Serbian national party of liberal and social democratic orientation. During the process of the peaceful reintegration of this area, led by the temporary administration of the United Nations, the SDSS strove to protect the human, political and national rights of the Serbs and to ensure they remained in Croatia.

Istrian Democratic Assembly
Istarski Demokratski Sabor (IDS)
Sieta Democratica Istriana (SDI)

Address. Splitska 3, 52100 Pula
Telephone. (385–52) 380 183
Fax. (385–52) 223 316
Website. www.ids-ddi.com
Email. ids-ddi@pu.htnet.hr
Leadership. Ivan Jakovcic (president); Damir Kajin (parliamentary group chairman)

The centre-right IDS confines its activities to the Istrian region, where it represents the aspirations of ethnic Italians and other minorities, advocating the creation of a "trans-border" Istria encompassing Croatian, Slovenian and Italian areas. It has been especially exercised by Croatian-Slovenian border definition issues and by the Croatian-Italian dispute over compensation for Italians who left Yugoslavia in the wake of the Istrian territorial gains by the latter after World War II.

In the August 1992 lower house elections, the IDS was allied with Dalmatian Action and the Rijeka Democratic League in a regionalist front, winning four of the six seats

taken by the alliance. In the February 1993 upper house elections the IDS won one elective seat and was allocated two more under the President's prerogative. In the same month it won 72% of the Istrian vote in local elections. In the October 1995 lower house elections it formed part of the centre-right Joint List bloc (ZL), winning four seats.

The IDS remained part of the ZL alliance in the January 2000 lower house elections, winning four of the ZL's 25 seats. The party subsequently joined the new government headed by the Social Democratic Party of Croatia (SPH), its chairman becoming Minister for European Integration. In June 2001, however, the party withdrew from the ruling coalition, complaining that the government was almost as hostile to regional autonomy as the previous Tudjman regime had been. It again won four seats in the 2003 parliamentary elections.

Liberal Party
Liberalna Stranka (LS)

Address. Ilica 16/I, 10000 Zagreb
Telephone. (385–1) 483–3896
Fax. (385–1) 483–3799
Email. liberali@globalnet.hr
Website. www.liberali.hr
Leadership. Ivo Banac (leader); Karl Gorinsek (secretary general)

The centrist LS was founded in February 1998 by unsuccessful 1997 presidential candidate Vlado Gotovac after he had been ousted from the leadership of the Croatian Social Liberal Party (HSLS). In the January 2000 parliamentary elections the party was part of the Joint List (ZL) alliance headed by the Croatian Peasant Party, obtaining two seats and one ministerial post in the resultant six-party coalition government headed by the Social Democratic Party of Croatia (SPH). At the party's second congress in October 2000, Zlatko Kramaric was elected LS chairman in succession to Gotovac, who died two months later. At the election convention in January 2003, Ivo Banac became the party leader, and the LS again won two seats in the 2003 parliamentary elections.

Claiming a membership of 4,500, the LS is a member of the Liberal International and an associate member of the European Liberal, Democratic and Reformist (ELDR) organization.

Littoral and Highland Region Alliance
Primorsko Goranski Savez (PGS)

Address. Ciottina 19, 51000 Rijeka
Telephone. (385–51) 335359
Fax. (385–51) 213 867
Email. pgs@kvarner.net
Website. www.pgs.hr
Leadership. Nikola Ivanic (president). Zoran Dragicevic (secretary)

The PGS was established in September 1996 as the successor to the Rijeka Democratic League (*Rijecki Demokratski Savez*, RDS), which had been founded in 1990 as a pro-market left-of-centre formation based in the ethnic Italian population of Rijeka to articulate issues of cultural expression, minority rights and education. The RDS had contested the August 1992 lower house elections in a regionalist alliance with Dalmatian Action and the Istrian Democratic Assembly, winning one of the six seats accruing to that alliance. It retained representation in the October 1995 elections.

The change of name to the PGS reflected the party's aspiration to broaden its base beyond its ethnic Italian base in the city of Rijeka and surrounding area. In the January 2000 lower house elections the PGS was part of the victorious alliance headed by the Social Democratic Party of Croatia (SPH), obtaining two seats. However, the resultant SPH-led government's declared commitment to regional autonomy and minority rights came under question within the PGS. In the parliamentary elections of 2003, the party won only one seat in the Parliament, and formed a coalition with the HNS in its election unit.

Party of Democratic Action of Croatia
Stranka Demokratske Akcije Hrvatske (SDAH)
Address. Mandalicina 17, 10000 Zagreb
Telephone. (385–1) 3772212
Fax. (385–1) 3771288
Email. sdah@sdah.hr
Website. www.sdah.hr
Leadership. Semso Tankovic (president)
The Party of Democratic Action of Croatia was founded on June 20, 1990 and is a sister party of the Party of Democratic Action in Bosnia. Its most important goals are to affirm and defend the national identity of the Bosnian nation and to preserve Bosnia and Herzegovina and to defend the political, social, economic, cultural and national rights of Bosnians in Croatia.

Social Democratic Party of Croatia (SDP)
Socijaldemokratska Partija Hrvatske (SPH)
Address. Trg Iblerov 9, 10000 Zagreb
Telephone. (385–1) 455–2055
Fax. (385–1) 455–2842
Email. sdp@sdp.hr
Website. www.sdp.hr
Leadership. Ivica Racan (president and parliamentary group chairman); Zeljka Antunovic (deputy president); Igor Dragovan (secretary general)
The SDP/SPH is descended from the Croatian Communist Party (created in 1937 when Yugoslavia's Communist movement was reorganized by Josip Broz Tito) and from the succeeding League of Communists of Yugoslavia (LCY), created as the ruling party in 1952. Croatian elements were prominent in periodic attempts to liberalize and reform the LCY regime from within; but in the post-1989 move to independence and multi-partyism the Croatian LCY was rapidly sidelined by the rise of the new Croatian Democratic Union (HDZ). Seen as tainted with "Yugoslavism", the LCY lost much of its membership to the HDZ and other parties, failing to stem the outflow by changing its name to Party of Democratic Reform (SDP) and committing itself to democratic socialism and a market economy. In the 1990 pre-independence elections, the SDP trailed a poor second to the HDZ, winning 75 of the 349 legislative seats in its own right and a further 16 on joint lists with other parties. In further changes in 1991, the SPH title was adopted (the SDP rubric being temporarily retained as a suffix) and the party deferred to pro-independence sentiment by acknowledging Croatia as the "national state of the Croatian people", while stressing the need to accommodate non-Croat groups.

Advocating economic modernization combined with preservation of a welfare state, the SPH-SDP was reduced to 11 seats in the August 1992 lower house elections and failed to secure representation in its own right in the February 1993 upper house balloting, although it was allocated one seat by virtue of a pact with the Croatian Social Liberal Party (HSLS). It performed better in the October 1995 lower house elections, winning nearly 9% of the vote and 10 seats, while in the June 1997 presidential elections SDP candidate Zdravko Tomac took second place with 21% of the vote.

Following the death of President Tudjman of the HDZ in December 1999, the SPH contested the January 2000 Assembly elections in tandem with the HSLS and two small regional formations. It became the dominant party by winning 44 of the 71 seats won by the alliance (on a 38.7% vote share) and formed a six-party centre-left coalition government head-ed by SPH chairman Ivica Racan. In immediately succeeding presidential elections, the SPH backed the HSLS candidate in both voting rounds, but applauded the eventual victory of Stjepan Mesic of the Croatian People's Party, which was a member of the new ruling coalition. The party fell back to second place in the November 2003 legislative elections, with 36 seats, and lost office to an HDZ-led government.

The SDP is a member party of the Socialist International.

Cuba

Capital: Havana
Population: 11,300,000 (2003E)

The Republic of Cuba, ceded by Spain to the United States following the Spanish-American war of 1898, became independent in 1902. Under the 1976 constitution (as modified in 1993) executive authority resides with the President of the Council of State, Fidel Castro Ruz, who has held power since January 1959 (following the revolutionary overthrow of the Batista regime). Nominal legislative authority is vested in the unicameral National Assembly of People's Power (*Asamblea Nacional del Poder Popular,* ANPP), which sits for a five-year term, holds twice-yearly ordinary sessions and elects a Council of State to represent it in the interim. Executive and administrative authority is held by a Council of Ministers, which is appointed by the ANPP upon the recommendation of the President. The majority of office-holders are members of the Communist Party of Cuba (PCC), the only authorized political party.

Direct elections to the ANPP were held in January 2003. Only candidates nominated by the PCC were permitted to contest the election. Figures released by the National Electoral Commission showed that all 601 PCC candidates for the 601 posts obtained the necessary 50% of the votes to be elected. The turnout amongst the 8.2 million registered voters was officially put at 96.14%.

In addition to the national political institutions Cuba has an extensive system of provincial, municipal and local assemblies. There are 14 provincial assemblies and in the last elections held at the same time as the National Assembly vote, all 1,199 candidates, who ran unopposed, were elected. 169 municipal assemblies also exist, together with a large number of People's Councils, the latter being a new tier of government introduced as part of the constitutional changes in 1993.

Communist Party of Cuba
Partido Comunista de Cuba (PCC)
Address. c/o National Assembly of People's Power, Havana
Website. www.pcc.cu
Leadership. Fidel Castro Ruz (first secretary); Raúl Castro Ruz (second secretary)
The PCC was founded in 1961 as the Integrated Revolutionary Organizations (*Organizaciones Revolucionarias Integradas,* ORI), a coalition of the political and military groupings which had defeated the Batista dictatorship in the revolution of 1956-59. The components were Castro's rural guerrilla army, the July 26 Movement (*Movimiento 26 de Julio*); the communist Popular Socialist Party (*Partido Socialista Popular,* PSP); and the Revolutionary Directorate (*Directorio Revolucionario,* DR). No other political organizations were permitted to function after 1961. The ORI was transformed into the United Party of the Cuban Socialist Revolution in 1962, and adopted its

present name in 1965. The PCC has more than 770,000 members, more than one in six of the population aged between 15 and 65.

The first PCC congress, held in 1975, approved a party constitution and programme, and the special status of the party as the leading force of society and the state was enshrined in the 1976 constitution. The second congress was held in 1980 and the third in 1986, at which time major changes in structure and personnel were approved. At its fourth congress in 1991, the PCC endorsed direct election to the ANPP, abolished the party secretariat, approved a substantially restructured politburo and removed the requirement that party members must be atheists. The fifth congress, held in 1997, adopted a cautious programme, which re-emphasized the need for political stability. The politburo was reduced from 26 to 24 members and reshuffled, while a new generation of politicians gained access to the upper levels of government, including a number of economic modernizers.

There has been an increased emphasis more generally on the role of youth in national political life in recent years. This was in response to heightened levels of dissatisfaction on the part of the younger generation during the economic slump of the 1990s. Further, as Castro gets older (he reached 78 in August 2004), there has been an attempt to infuse the party and the government with a new generation of activists and policy practitioners. Castro continues to play a central role in overseeing party business and government policy, but there are indications that he has delegated greater responsibility to a group of political figures around him. The internal dynamics of the PCC government were highlighted starkly in November 2003 when a number of senior officials in the largest state-run tourism organization in Cuba, Cubanacan, were dismissed and placed under house arrest on suspicion of corruption. It was alleged that million of dollars had been misappropriated from Cubanacan's hotel, restaurant and travel agency businesses. However, the Cuban authorities subsequently denied that the senior officials from Cubanacan had been arrested or were under investigation for embezzlement or fraud. Rather, it was claimed that they had committed "grave errors in their management duties". In an attempt to restore confidence in Cubanacan and in the important tourism sector more generally, the government replaced Ibrahim Ferradaz as Cuba's Tourism Minister in February 2004.

The PCC's position and legitimacy in Cuban politics was challenged during 2002 and 2003 by the activities of the All United opposition group and its Valera Project – a petition to bring about political change through a referendum. In May 2002, the organizers of the project presented more than 11,000 signatures to the National Assembly calling for a referendum on civil and political reform. The official response to the Valera Project was swift and overwhelming. On June 18, 2002, the PCC government announced that nearly 99% of the country's voters had signed a counter petition supporting constitutional amendments that would prevent reforms to the country's political, economic and social system. The announcement was then followed by a Special Session of the National Assembly on June 26, 2002, which amended the Constitution to make socialism irrevocable. Then on Jan. 24, 2003, the legislature officially invalidated the Valera Project's attempt to hold a referendum on political and economic reforms. The reaction of the Cuban authorities increased in severity during March and April 2003 when 75 pro-democracy and human rights activists were arrested, charged and convicted for "mercenary activities and other acts against the independence and territorial integrity of the Cuban state". Many of the people arrested had links to the Valera Project and were given the harshest sentences.

Illegal Opposition Groups

All United (*Todos Unidos*). Under the leadership of Oswaldo Payá Sardiñas and his Cuban Liberation Movement, a number of internal opposition groups came together to form the "All United" movement in November 1999. The group's primary function was to oversee the Valera Project – a petition to bring about changes to society through a referendum. The project was established in March 2001 and named after Felix Valera, a 19th century Cuban priest who called for Cuba's independence from Spain. It was based on a provision in the Cuban Constitution (Article 88) that allows for citizens to introduce legislative initiatives to be decided by national referendum when accompanied by the signatures of at least 10,000 registered voters. The project proposed five reforms: democratic elections, free speech, free enterprise, free assembly and freedom for political prisoners. In May 2002, the organizers of the project, led by Payá, presented more than 11,000 signatures to the National Assembly calling for a referendum on civil and political reform. The initiators of the project received a boost later in the month when former US President Jimmy Carter on a visit to Cuba made direct reference to Valera, and stated that Cuba should allow democratic changes and grant basic political freedoms. However, the Cuban government responded by invalidating the Valera Project's attempt to hold a referendum on political and economic reforms, and later by arresting, charging and imprisoning 75 pro-democracy and human rights activists. Many of the people arrested had links to the Valera Project and were given the harshest sentences. Oswaldo Payá was not arrested, due to his high international profile after receiving the European Parliament's Andrei Sakharov Prize for Freedom of Thought in December 2002. Despite being under constant surveillance, the recipient of threats and the subject of harassment, Payá presented a second petition to parliament in October 2003. The petition signed by over 14,000 people, called for a referendum on freedom of expression and an amnesty for political prisoners. In December 2003 Payá launched a new campaign setting out plans for a peaceful transition to democracy. *Leadership*. Oswaldo Payá Sardiñas

Assembly to Promote Civil Society in Cuba (*Asamblea para Promover la Sociedad Civil en Cuba*). Martha Beatriz and colleagues from the Cuban Institute of Independent Economists established the Assembly in March 2002. The Assembly, which consists of more than 250 organizations but excluding Valera Project supporters, has not met as a single entity. However, the Assembly has undertaken a number of initiatives in support of its aims that include: a reinstatement of civil society, the education of the citizenry in the principles of democracy, the development of a non-violent civil struggle movement, and the building of a self-renewing pluralist and participative democratic process. In October 2002, for example, the Assembly called for all dissident groups to participate in a campaign to promote the Universal Declaration of Human Rights, in order to inform people of their rights and to highlight violations by the Cuban authorities. However, as with Valera Project participants, the Cuban authorities incarcerated Martha Beatriz and other leading figures of the Assembly in 2003. Beatriz is now serving a 20-year sentence, while the activities of the Assembly to Promote Civil Society in Cuba have been curtailed severely. *Leadership*. Martha Beatriz Rogue Cabello

Cuban Socialist Democratic Current (*Corriente Socialista Democrática Cubana*, CSDC). The CSDC was established in 1992 and is committed to national independence, popular sovereignty, political pluralism, a mixed economy, social justice, and respect for fundamental human rights and freedoms. The CSDC publishes a newsletter, "Nueva Izquierda" (New Leftwing), devoted to political and economic news and analysis.

Address. 5430 W. 7th Ave., Hialeah, FL 33012, USA
Email. micael@netzero.net
Website. www.corriente.org
Leadership. Manuel Cuesta Morúa (secretary-general)

Christian Liberation Movement (*Movimiento Cristiano Liberación,* MCL). Founded in 1989 by Oswaldo Payá Sardiñas and members of the Christian Club for Cuban Political Thought. The Movement's objectives include national dialogue with the participation of all popular sectors, freedom of expression and association and to ward off civil war, foreign intervention and state repression. Most particularly the MCL and Oswaldo Payá have been at the forefront of the Valera Project. The MCL is affiliated with All United and the Christian Democrat and People's Parties International.

Address. Calle Peñón no. 221, Cerro, Ciudad de la Habana
Email. Mclpaya2@compuserve.com
Website. www.mclpaya.org
Leadership. Oswaldo Payá Sardiñas

Democratic Solidarity Party (*Partido Solidaridad Democrática,* PSD). The Democratic Solidarity Party was established in December 1993, and has since campaigned for a plebiscite and a non-violent progression towards democracy. In 1998, for example, the party called on internal opposition groups and government representatives to engage in nation-wide dialogue – their inspiration coming from Pope John Paul's message of solidarity and reconciliation during his visit to Cuba in May of that year. More recently, the PSD has been involved in the discussions surrounding the various projects and proposals to further democracy in the country. In particular, the party has been supportive of the work undertaken by the Assembly to Promote Civil Society in Cuba. The PSD is an observer member of the Liberal International.

Address. PO Box 310063, Miami, FL 33131, USA
Telephone. (305) 408-2659
Email. gladyperez@aol.com
Website. www.ccsi.com/~ams/psd/psd.htm
Leadership. Fernando Sánchez Lopez (president)

Liberal Democratic Party (*Partido Liberal Democrático,* PLD). Founded in 1991, its objective is to push for a democratic transition and the safeguarding of the rule of law in Cuba. The party is affiliated to All United and is a member of the Liberal International.

Address. Vista Hermosa no. 608, 5to Piso, Apt. K, entre Santa Ana y Concepción, Cerro, Ciudad de la Habana
Leadership. Osvaldo Alfonso Valdes (president)

Social Democratic Party of Cuba (*Partido Social Democrata de Cuba, PSC*). Vladimiro Roca, a former member of the Communist Party and of the Cuban Armed Forces, established the party in July 1996. Roca had become disillusioned with Castro's regime, chose to renounce his ties to the administration and began to speak out against government policies. Notwithstanding, the party's objectives are quite conservative in outlook. The underlying belief is that with state repression, the lack of freedom and the government's attempts to perpetuate itself in power, the goals of any centre-left movement must be relatively limited. In particular, the party emphasises its support for self-employed workers, farmers and small producers to be able to invest in the national economy and develop their own businesses in the service and manufacturing sectors. In more recent years, the Social Democratic Party has become affiliated to the "All United" movement, although their limited scope of ambition remains. Despite this Roca is one of the most prominent leaders of the internal opposition, having been imprisoned for co-authoring "The Homeland Belongs to Us All". The book, a socio-economic critique of a Cuban Communist Party manifesto, was published in 1997. Two weeks after publication Roca and his co-authors were arrested and subsequently imprisoned. Roca received a five-year sentence and he served four of those years in solitary confinement.

Address. Calle 36 no.105, Nuevo Vedado, Ciudad de la Habana, C. P. 1060
Telephone. (7) 8818203
Email. Infopsc@psccuba.org
Website. www.pscuba.org
Leadership. Vladimiro Roca Antunes

Cyprus

Capital: Nicosia
Population: 930,000 (2004E, including TRNC)

The Republic of Cyprus achieved independence from the UK in 1960 on the basis of a constitution that involved power sharing between the majority Greek Cypriots and the minority Turkish Cypriots. Guaranteed by the UK, Greece and Turkey, this arrangement broke down by 1964, amid an escalation of inter-communal conflict. In 1974 the territorial division between the two communities was solidified by the military intervention of Turkey, whose forces facilitated the effective partition of the island into a Greek Cypriot sector and what in 1983 became the Turkish Republic of Northern Cyprus (TRNC). The TRNC's self-proclaimed "independence" in about 40% of the island's area has been recognized only by Turkey.

UN-sponsored peace talks are aimed at producing a federal settlement, which preserves Cyprus as one sovereign state. UN Secretary-General Kofi Annan tabled a comprehesive settlement plan in November 2002, but after many rounds of negotiations agreement could not be reached. Following the Turkish Cypriot parliamentary elections in December 2003, UN-sponsored intercommunal talks resumed in February 2004. Lack of progress in the talks led to Annan finalizing a settlement plan, which was put to simultaneous referenda in both parts of Cyprus on April 24, 2004, a week before Cyprus' accession to the European Union (EU) on May 1. The Greek Cypriot community overwhelmingly rejected the settlement plan, with 75.8% voting against, whilst 64.9% of the Turkish Cypriot community voted in favour of the plan to reunite the island. This failure to agree on a settlement plan resulted in only the Greek-controlled south of Cyprus joining the EU on May 1.

Under the 1960 constitution, which the Greek Cypriots continue to observe where possible, the Republic of Cyprus has an executive President, who is directly elected for a five-year term by compulsory universal suffrage of those aged 18 and over, and who appoints the government. Legislative authority is vested in a unicameral House of Representatives (*Vouli Antiprosópon* in Greek, *Temsilciler Meclisi* in Turkish), which theoretically has 80 members elected for a five-year term by proportional representation, 56 by the Greek Cypriot community and 24 by the Turkish Cypriots. Since 1964, however, the Turkish Cypriot community has declined to participate in these arrangements and has set up its own political structures (see separate section below). Three representatives are elected by the Armenian, Maronite and Latin religious communities and have a consultative role in the House.

The total government grant allocated for political parties in 2004 was CY£1,156,000. An equal amount of CY£40,000 is allocated as a basic grant to all political parties without exception. An amount of CY£16,000 is allocated to political parties to cover their contributions towards the respective political parties of the EU. The remaining balance of CY£1,180,000 is distributed proportionally according to the results of the last parliamentary elections.

Elections on May 27, 2001, for the 56 Greek Cypriot seats in the House of Representatives resulted as follows: Progressive Party of the Working People (AKEL) 20 (with 34.7% of the vote), Democratic Rally (DISY) 19 (34.0%), Democratic Party (DIKO) 9 (14.8%), Movement of Social Democrats (KISOS) 4 (6.5%), New Horizons (NEO) 1 (3.0%), United Democrats (EDI) 1 (3.7%), Fighting Democratic Movement (ADIK) 1 (2.2%), Cyprus Green Party 1 (2.0%). In Greek Cypriot presidential elections held on Feb. 8 and 15, 1998, Glafcos Clerides (DISY) was re-elected for a second five-year term with 40.1% in the first voting round and 50.8% in the second.

Presidential elections took place on Feb. 16, 2003. Tassos Papadopoulos (DIKO) supported by AKEL, KISOS and the Ecological Environmental Movement, became the fifth President of the Republic since independence in 1960 with 213,353 votes or 51.51% of the valid votes. Glafcos Clerides (DISY, supported by EDI and ADIK), gained 160,274 votes or 38.8%, Alecos Markides (KEA) 27,404 or 6.62% and Nicos Koutsou (NEO) 8,771 or 2.12%.

Cyprus joined the EU on May 1, 2004, as a divided island and on June 13 the first European parliamentary elections were held in the Republic of Cyprus only. In a turnout of 71.19% Cypriot voters showed continuing strong support for the rejection of the Annan plan for the reunification of the island. Four of the six seats allocated to Cyprus were won by parties opposed to reunification: Democratic Party – 17.1% of votes (1 seat); Progressive Party of the Working People – 27.9% (2 seats); For Europe party – 10.8% (1 seat). The Democratic Rally, which supported the Annan plan, won 28.2% of the votes (2 seats).

Democratic Party
Dimokratiko Komma (DIKO)
Address. 50 Grivas Dighenis Ave, 1687 Nicosia; PO Box 23979, 1080 Nicosia
Telephone. (357) 2287-3800
Fax. (357) 2287-3801
Email. diko@diko.org.cy
Website. www.diko.org.cy
Leadership. Tassos Papadopoulos (president; President of the Republic of Cyprus); Nicos Cleanthous (vice-president & parliamentary spokesman); Vassilis Palmas (general secretary)

DIKO was founded in May 1976 as the Democratic Front, a centre-right alliance supporting President Makarios's policy of "long-term struggle" against the Turkish occupation of northern Cyprus. It became the largest party in the 1976 parliamentary elections, winning 21 of the 35 available seats in a pro-Makarios alliance which included the (communist) Progressive Party of the Working People (AKEL) and the EDEK Socialist Party, which later became the Movement of Social Democrats (KISOS). Having succeeded Makarios as President on the latter's death in August 1977, then DIKO leader Spyros Kyprianou was elected unopposed in his own

right in January 1978 and re-elected in February 1983, when he received 56.5% of the first-round vote.

Meanwhile, DIKO had been weakened by defections and its parliamentary representation had slumped to eight seats in the 1981 elections (held by proportional representation), when its vote share was 19.5%. Kyprianou nevertheless retained the reins of power, supported by AKEL until the latter ended the alliance in late 1984 because it objected to the President's alleged intransigence in inter-communal talks. In early elections in December 1985 DIKO increased its vote share to 27.7% and its seat total to 16 in a House enlarged to 56 Greek Cypriot members. But Kyprianou failed to obtain a third presidential term in February 1988, receiving only 27.3% in the first round of voting and being eliminated.

DIKO mounted strong opposition to the policies of the new AKEL-endorsed independent President, George Vassiliou, particularly his handling of the inter-communal talks. It was strengthened in 1989 when it absorbed the small Centre Union party led by Tassos Papadopoulos. Nevertheless, in parliamentary elections in May 1991 DIKO remained the third party, falling to 11 seats and 19.5% of the vote. Thereafter it formed a tactical alliance with the EDEK Socialists to oppose the 1992 UN plan for Cyprus, claiming that it formalized the island's partition. In the February 1993 presidential elections, DIKO and EDEK presented a joint candidate, Paschalis Paschalides, who obtained only 18.6% of the first-round vote and was eliminated. In the second round, official DIKO support was given to Glafcos Clerides of the Democratic Rally (DISY), who won a narrow victory over Vassiliou. In return for this support, President Clerides included five DIKO ministers in the new 11-member government.

DIKO slipped further to 10 seats and 16.4% of the vote in the May 1996 elections, following which Kyprianou was elected president of the House of Representatives, the second highest post in the state hierarchy. The February 1998 presidential elections occasioned serious divisions within the party, which officially joined with AKEL to back the independent candidacy of George Iacovou, whereas a minority faction supported the candidacy of DIKO deputy chairman Alexis Galanos. Galanos obtained only 4% of the first-round vote, in which Iacovou headed the field with 40.6%; but Galanos' endorsement of Clerides in the second round was sufficient to give the incumbent a second term by a narrow margin. Rewarded with a presidential advisory post, Galanos subsequently formed the Eurodemocratic Renewal Party, while other DIKO rebels were appointed to a new "national unity government".

The rump DIKO formed part of the opposition in the second Clerides presidency, articulating criticism in particular of the President's handling of the continuing impasse on the Cyprus problem. In October 2000 Kyprianou was succeeded as DIKO chairman by Papadopoulos, an outspoken critic of the government's conduct of UN talks on Cyprus. In the May 2001 parliamentary elections, however, DIKO continued its downward trend, falling to nine seats with 14.8% of the vote. The party then backed the successful candidacy of the AKEL leader to succeed Kyprianou as president of the House of Representatives.

The alliance with AKEL was maintained and ensured the victory of DIKO president Tassos Papadopoulos in the Feb.16, 2003, presidential elections. Tassos Papadopoulos was elected on a platform of criticism of Clerides' handling of the settlement talks, in particular opposition to certain settlement terms and concessions given to Turkish Cypriots. The Council of Ministers which took office in March 2003 saw DIKO members appointed to three ministries. After initial consideration of the settlement plan tabled by the UN Secretary-General on March 31, 2004, President Papadoupolos, in a televised address, successfully urged Greek Cypriot voters to reject the UN plan in the April 24 referendum. President Papadopoulos objected to several revisions in the settlement plan, namely those restricting the number of Greek Cypriot refugees allowed to return to the north and the continued presence of Turkish military forces on the island.

Democratic Rally
Dimokratikos Synagermos (DISY)
Address. 25 Pindarou Street,1061 Nicosia; PO Box 25305, 1308 Nicosia
Telephone. (357) 2288–3000
Fax. (357) 2275–2751
Email. disy@disy.org.cy
Website. www.disy.org.cy
Leadership. Nicos Anastasiades (president); Averof Neophytou (deputy president); Demetris Syllouris (parliamentary spokesman); George Liveras (director-general)
DISY was founded in 1976 by Glafcos Clerides as a conservative, pro-Western union of elements of the former Progressive Front and United and Democratic National parties. As president of the House of Representatives, Clerides had previously been acting President of Cyprus in the wake of the right-wing coup and the resultant Turkish invasion of mid-1974, until the return of Archbishop Makarios as head of state in December 1974. The new party won 27.5% of the vote in the 1976 parliamentary elections but failed to obtain a seat because of the constituency-based system then in force. In that contest DISY condemned the victorious alliance of the centre-right Democratic Party (DIKO), the left-wing Progressive Party of the Working People (AKEL) and the EDEK Socialists (later the Movement of Social Democrats) as being communist-inspired.

Held under a proportional system, the 1981 parliamentary elections gave DISY 32% of the vote and 12 of the 35 available seats, while the 1983 presidential balloting resulted in Clerides winning 34% in the first round and being defeated by the DIKO incumbent, Spyros Kyprianou. During 1985 DISY attacked President Kyprianou for his alleged intransigence in the UN-sponsored negotiations on the status of Cyprus, combining with AKEL to force early parliamentary elections in December 1985. These resulted in DISY supplanting AKEL as the largest single party, its support increasing from 31.9% in 1981 to 33.6%, which gave it 19 seats in a House enlarged to 56 Greek Cypriot members.

In the presidential election of February 1988, Clerides was again defeated, winning 48.4% of the second-round vote against the victorious AKEL-supported independent candidate, George Vassiliou. In parliamentary elections in May 1991 DISY's share of the vote, on a joint list with the small Liberal Party (KTP), rose to 35.8%, which yielded 20 seats (of which one went to the KTP). Thereafter, DISY gave broad support to President Vassiliou's conduct of the intercommunal talks, including his acceptance of a new UN plan tabled in 1992 demarcating Greek Cypriot and Turkish Cypriot areas of administration in a federal state, whereas DIKO and EDEK contended that the plan would entrench the island's partition. In the February 1993 presidential elections, however, Clerides astutely distanced himself from the UN plan and emerged as the unexpected victor against Vassiliou, his narrow 50.3% winning margin in the second round being in part due to the transfer to him of DIKO and EDEK voting support. Six DISY and five DIKO ministers were included in the new government appointed by President Clerides, who stood down as DISY leader in light of his election. In further talks, Clerides reverted to broad acceptance of the UN plan and sought to use his longstanding personal relationship with the Turkish Cypriot leader, Rauf Denktash, to expedite a settlement, although to no avail as at mid-2001.

DISY remained the strongest party in the May 1996 elections, winning 20 seats in its own right with 34.5% of the vote. In the February 1998 presidential elections Clerides came second in the first round (with 40.1%), behind an independent candidate backed by AKEL and most of DIKO, but narrowly secured re-election in the second round (with 50.8%) by dint of attracting dissident DIKO support. He then formed a "national unity government" which included DISY, EDEK, Liberal and rebel DIKO members as well as what became the United Democrats (EDI). However, EDEK withdrew its two ministers in January 1999 in protest against Clerides' decision to abandon a controversial plan to deploy Russian-made surface-to-air missiles in Cyprus. In August 1999 allegations of improper ministerial participation in the 1999 stock market boom prompted the resignation of two DISY ministers.

In parliamentary elections in May 2001, DISY lost its position as the largest party, slipping to 19 seats and 34.0% of the vote. When the new House convened in June, DISY leader Nicos Anastasiades was defeated by the AKEL leader in a contest for the vacant presidency of the legislature. In the presidential elections of February 2003, Glafcos Clerides was supported by DISY and sought re-election for a limited third term of 16 months to ensure Cyprus' accession to the European Union and negotiate a political settlement. However, the incumbent Clerides was defeated by Tassos Papadopoulos, who received 51.51% of the vote compared to Clerides' 38.8%. On May 25, 2003, Nicos Anastasiades was re-elected as president of DISY defeating former Foreign Minister Ioannis Kasoulides by 55% to 45% in a ballot of party members.

Having an official membership of 30,000, DISY is affiliated to the European People's Party as well as to the International Democrat Union and the European Democrat Union.

Ecological-Environmental Movement–The Cyprus Green Party
Kinima Ekologon Perivallontiston–To Prasino Komma tis Kyprou
Address. 169 Athalassas Ave, Flat 303, 2024 Strovolos; PO Box 29682, 1722 Nicosia
Telephone. (357) 2251–8787
Fax. (357) 2251–2710
Email. greenpar@cytanet.com.cy
Website. www.cyprus-green-party.org
Leadership. George Perdikis (general secretary); Savvas Philippou (deputy general secretary)
Officially called the Ecologist and Environmentalist Movement, the Greens were launched as a national political movement shortly before the May 1996 parliamentary elections, in which they won a 1% vote share and therefore failed to gain representation. In the late 1990s the party achieved a higher profile as environmental issues came to the fore, notably over its campaign for the preservation of the unique Akamas peninsula as a haven for rare flora and fauna. In the May 2001 elections the Greens advanced to 2% of the vote and therefore obtained one seat in the new House.

The movement is administered by a 11-member political committee and a 56 member Pancyprian Coordination Committee. The Cyprus Greens are part of the European Federation of Green Parties.

Eurodemocratic Renewal Party
Komma Evrodimokratikis Ananeosis (KEA)
Address. 3 Theokritou Street, Office 3, 1060 Nicosia
Telephone. (357) 2243–1625
Fax. (357) 2243–2627
Leadership. Antonis Paschalides (president)
The KEA was founded in October 1998 by former House of Representatives president Alexis Galanos, who had broken with the Democratic Party (DIKO) before the February 1998 presidential elections because he disagreed with DIKO's

decision to back the (ultimately unsuccessful) independent candidacy of George Iacovou. Galanos had himself obtained 4% in the first round of that contest, the switch of his dissident DIKO support contributing to the victory of incumbent Glafcos Clerides of the Democratic Rally (DISY) in the second round.

The KEA contested the May 2001 parliamentary elections in alliance with the Movement of Social Democrats (KISOS) but failed to secure representation.

Fighting Democratic Movement
Agonistiko Dimocratico Kinima (ADIK)
Address. 80 Arch. Makariou III Street, Flat 401, 1077 Nicosia; P.O.Box 16095, 2085 Nicosia
Telephone. (357) 2276-5353,
Fax. (357) 2237-5737
*Email.*adhk@spidernet.com.cy
Website. www.adik.org.cy
Leadership. Dinos Michaelides (president); Edwin Josephides (vice president); Yiannis Papadopoulos (general secretary); Andreas Papamiltiades (general organizing secretary)
ADIK was launched by Dinos Michaelides following his resignation as Interior Minister in March 1999 amidst allegations of corruption (of which he was later substantially cleared). Michaelides had previously been a member of the Democratic Party (DIKO), but had been among the DIKO dissidents who refused to follow the party's decision to back the (ultimately unsuccessful) independent candidacy of George Iacovou in the February 1998 presidential elections. In the May 2001 parliamentary elections ADIK obtained 2.2% of the vote and one seat, Michaelides being returned in the Limassol district.

Movement of Social Democrats–EDEK
Kinima Socialdimokraton (KISOS)
Address. 40 Byron Ave, 1096 Nicosia; PO Box 21064, 1501 Nicosia
Telephone. (357) 2267–0121, 2267-8617
Fax. (357) 2267–8894
Email. socialdimokrates@cytanet.com.cy
Website. www.kisos.org
Leadership. Yiannakis Omirou (president); Kyriacos Mavronicolas (deputy president) Marinos Sizopoulos (first vice president); Sofoklis Sofokleous (second vice president); Vassos Lyssarides (life honorary president)
KISOS was launched in February 2000 as a merger of the Unified Democratic Union of Cyprus (EDEK Socialist Party) and smaller centre-left groups, its declared aim being to spearhead the process of Cyprus' integration into the European Union and to build a classic European social democratic party in Cyprus.

Founded in 1969 by Vassos Lyssarides, EDEK contested the 1970 parliamentary elections as the Democratic Centre Union, winning two seats. In the early 1970s it opposed both Greek interference in Cyprus and the Turkish invasion of the island of 1974, which some of its members actively resisted. It supported the return to power of President Makarios in late 1974 and in the 1976 elections participated in a pro-Makarios alliance with the centre-right Democratic Party (DIKO) and the left-wing Progressive Party of the Working People (AKEL), winning four seats. It fell back to three seats in 1981 campaigning independently, and in the 1983 presidential election Lyssarides, presented as the candidate of the broader National Salvation Front, took third place with 9.5% of the vote, despite having withdrawn from the contest at the last minute. EDEK increased its House representation to six seats in the 1985 elections, winning 11.1% of the vote, being at that time broadly supportive of President Kyprianou's tough line in the Cyprus inter-communal talks.

Lyssarides stood again in the February 1988 presidential

elections but was eliminated in the first round, with only 9.2% of the vote. In the second round EDEK transferred its support to the AKEL-backed independent candidate, George Vassiliou, who was elected by a narrow margin. But EDEK quickly came to oppose President Vassiliou's more accommodating line in the inter-communal talks, making common cause on this issue with DIKO against AKEL and the conservative Democratic Rally (DISY). In the May 1991 parliamentary elections EDEK won 10.9% of the vote and seven seats. Thereafter it mounted strong opposition, with DIKO, to Vassiliou's acceptance of the UN plan demarcating Greek Cypriot and Turkish Cypriot areas of administration in a federal Cyprus, claiming that the proposals amounted to partition of the island.

In the February 1993 presidential elections, EDEK and DIKO presented a joint candidate, Paschalis Paschalides, who obtained only 18.6% in the first round and was eliminated. In the second round, EDEK gave its support to Glafcos Clerides of DISY, who was narrowly victorious over Vassiliou. In the May 1996 legislative elections EDEK fell back to five seats with 8.1% of the vote. Lyssarides stood for the third time in the February 1998 presidential elections, being eliminated in the first round with 10.6% of the vote. Although EDEK did not formally back Clerides in the second round, his narrow victory was followed by the appointment of a "national unity government" in which EDEK took two portfolios.

Increasingly unhappy with Clerides' conduct of foreign policy, EDEK withdrew from the government in January 1999 in protest against the President's decision to abandon a controversial plan to deploy Russian-made surface-to-air missiles in Cyprus. It thereafter became an opposition party, maintaining this stance after the creation in February 2000 of KISOS, of which Lyssarides was elected president. Subsequent moves towards a merger between KISOS and the United Democrats proved abortive.

In the May 2001 parliamentary elections, KISOS fell back to four seats and 6.5% of the vote, whereupon Lyssarides tendered his resignation as leader. He was succeeded in July by Yiannakis Omirou. In the February 2003 presidential elections, DISY's decision to support Clerides forced KISOS leader Yiannakis Omirou (who had previouly enjoyed DISY support) to withdraw from the race. Following the presidential elections in February 2003, in which KISOS supported the successful candidate Tassos Papadopoulos (DIKO), the new Council of Ministers (which took office in March 2003) contained two KISOS members. In June 2003, a KISOS congress decided to return to the old EDEK title, therefore renaming the party the Movement of Social Democrats–EDEK.

EDEK is a member party of the Socialist International.

New Horizons
Neoi Orizontes (NEO)
Address. 3 Trikoupi Street, 1015 Nicosia; PO Box 22496, 1522 Nicosia
Telephone. (357) 2276–1476
Fax. (357) 2276–1144
Email. neo@logos.cy.net
Website. www.neoiorizontes.org
www.neo.org.cy, www.koutsou.com
Leadership. Nicos Koutsou (president); Stratos Panayides (deputy president); Stelios Americanos (first vice president); Yiannis Kozakos (general secretary)
The right-wing NEO was founded in early 1996 by elements close to the Greek Orthodox Church. Its platform on the Cyprus question differed from those of other parties in that, while they all accepted the concept of a federal Cyprus, the NEO argued in favour of a unitary state and a single government. It failed to gain representation in the May 1996 elec-

tions, taking only 1.7% of the vote, but in May 2001 obtained one seat on the strength of a 3% vote share.

Progressive Party of the Working People
Anorthotiko Komma Ergazomenou Laou (AKEL)
Address. 4. Ezekias Papaioannou Street, 1075 Nicosia
Telephone. (357) 2276–1121
Fax. (357) 2276–1574
Email. k.e.akel@cytanet.com.cy
Website. www.akel.org.cy
Leadership. Demetris Christofias (general secretary, president of the House of Representatives); Nicos Katsourides (parliamentary leader)

AKEL is directly descended from the Communist Party of Cyprus, which held its first congress in 1926 but was declared illegal by the British authorities amid the political and social unrest of 1931. Reconstituted as AKEL in 1941, the party emerged after the war as an orthodox pro-Soviet Marxist-Leninist formation and was again banned by the British in 1955. Legalized again in December 1959, it consolidated its dominant position in the trade union movement after independence in 1960. In the 1976 parliamentary elections it was part of a victorious alliance with the (centre-right) Democratic Party (DIKO) and the EDEK Socialists (later the Movement of Social Democrats).

Following the death of President Makarios in 1977, AKEL gave general backing to the new government of President Spyros Kyprianou (DIKO) and headed the poll in the 1981 parliamentary elections, winning 32.8% of the vote and 12 of the 35 seats then available. The alliance with DIKO was terminated by AKEL in December 1984 on the grounds that the President was showing insufficient flexibility in inter-communal talks with the Turkish Cypriots. In the December 1985 parliamentary elections AKEL slipped to third place, winning 27.4% and 15 seats in a House enlarged to 56 Greek Cypriot members.

For the February 1988 presidential elections AKEL opted to endorse an independent candidate, George Vassiliou, who was elected in the second round by a narrow 51.6% margin over Glafcos Clerides of the Democratic Rally (DISY), receiving support from EDEK and many DIKO voters. In early 1990 AKEL appeared to be weakened by the formation of the breakaway Democratic Socialist Reform Movement (ADISOK), when the leadership declined to revise the party's Marxist-Leninist principles and mode of operation. However, the collapse of communism elsewhere in Europe and the demise of the Soviet Union in 1991, although regretted by AKEL hardliners, inevitably brought the party onto a democratic socialist path.

In the May 1991 parliamentary elections, AKEL increased its vote share to 30.6% and its representation to 18 seats (while ADISOK won none). AKEL again endorsed Vassiliou in the February 1993 presidential elections, but the opposition of DIKO and EDEK to his handling of the national question resulted in their supporters swinging behind Clerides (DISY) in the second round, in which Vassiliou was defeated by a 50.3% to 49.7% margin. Later in the year the ex-President launched the Movement of Free Democrats, but this centre-left formation, which later became the United Democrats when it merged with ADISOK, was seen as more of a threat to DIKO and EDEK than to AKEL.

AKEL gained ground in the May 1996 parliamentary elections, winning 19 seats and 33% of the vote, but failed in its aim of overtaking DISY as the largest party. In the February 1998 presidential elections, AKEL joined with DIKO to back the independent candidacy of George Iacovou, who led the first-round vote with 40.6% but was narrowly defeated by incumbent Clerides in the second round. AKEL maintained its opposition stance and was rewarded in the May 2001 parliamentary elections by overtaking DISY as

the largest single party with 20 of the 56 seats on a 34.7% vote share.

An immediate benefit was the election in June 2001 of AKEL leader Demetris Christofias as the new president of the House of Representatives (the second highest post in the state hierarchy), with support from DIKO deputies. This was seen as indicating the likely constellation of political forces in the presidential elections due in 2003. Indeed the election of Tassos Papadopoulos (DIKO) on Feb.16, 2003, with the support of AKEL resulted in AKEL making up a significant component of the Council of Ministers which took office on March 3, 2003. AKEL entered the government for the first time with four ministries. In the debate following the presentation of the UN settlement plan on March 31, 2004, AKEL withdrew its support for the plan before the April 24 referendum, citing inadequate UN guarantees that Turkish military forces would be removed following reunification. AKEL's proposals to delay the referendum were quashed.

United Democrats
Enomeni Dimokrates (EDI)
Address. 8 Iassonos Street, 1082 Nicosia; PO Box 23494, 1683 Nicosia
Telephone. (357) 2266–3030
Fax. (357) 2266–4747
Email. edicy@spidernet.com.cy
Website. www.edi.org.cy
Leadership. George Vassiliou (president); Michalis Papapetrou (deputy president); George Christofides (first vice president); Costas Themistocleous (general secretary)

The centre-left EDI was created in December 1996 as a merger of the Movement of Free Democrats (KED) and the Democratic Socialist Reform Movement (ADISOK), which had been founded in 1990 by an anti-communist faction of the Progressive Party of the Working People (AKEL).

The KED had been launched in April 1993 by ex-President Vassiliou following his unexpected failure to secure a second term in the February 1993 presidential elections. A wealthy businessman, he had been elected to the presidency in 1988 as an independent candidate with the backing of AKEL, which had again supported him in 1993. The KED was described as a centre-left formation which aimed to contribute to "the struggle of our people to solve the national problem" and to promote the admission of Cyprus to the European Union.

The KED won 5.1% of the vote and two seats in the May 1996 parliamentary elections, these going to Vassiliou and his wife Androulla. The formation then reached agreement to merge with ADISOK to create the EDI, of which Vassiliou was elected president at the founding conference in December 1996. However, the new movement made little subsequent progress in its declared aim of becoming the dominant centre-left party in Cyprus.

In the February 1998 presidential elections Vassiliou obtained only 3% of the first-round vote, following which the party joined a "national unity government" and Vassiliou was appointed as Cyprus' chief negotiator on European Union accession. In the May 2001 parliamentary elections EDI obtained only 2.2% of the vote and one seat (retained by Androulla Vassiliou). In April 2002 George Vassiliou (then Cyprus' chief EU negotiator) was re-elected unopposed as president of the EDI; also re-elected was deputy president Michalis Papapetrou.

TURKISH REPUBLIC OF NORTHERN CYPRUS (TRNC)

The "independent" TRNC was proclaimed in November 1983 as successor to the Turkish Federated State of Cyprus (TFSC), itself created in February

1975 as successor to the Turkish Cypriot Autonomous Administration dating from December 1968. Under its 1985 constitution, the TRNC has an executive President directly elected for a five-year term by universal adult suffrage and a 50-member Assembly of the Republic (*Cumhuriyet Meclisi*), also elected for a five-year term by proportional representation of parties winning at least 5% of the vote. Assembly elections on Dec. 6, 1998, resulted as follows: National Unity Party (UBP) 24 seats (with 40.3% of the vote), Democratic Party 13 (22.6%), Communal Liberation Party 7 (15.4%), Republican Turkish Party 6 (13.4%). In the first round of presidential elections on April 15, 2000, Rauf Denktash (standing as an independent) obtained 43.7% of the vote and was declared elected by default after the withdrawal from the second round of the UBP runner-up.

Elections for the 50 seats in the Assembly took place on Dec. 14, 2003. The Republican Turkish Party (CTP) gained 35.2% of the vote and 19 seats. The National Unity Party (UBP) gained 32.9 % of the vote and 18 seats. The Peace and Democracy Movement (BDH) gained 13.1% of the vote and 6 seats. The Democratic Party (DP) took 12.9% of the vote and 7 seats. In addition, the National Peace Party (MBP) gained 3.2%, the Solution and EU Party (CABP) 2.0%, the Cyprus Justice Party (KAP) 0.6%, but none gained the minimum 5% to gain a seat in the House of Representatives. A coalition government of the CTP and DP was formed in early January 2004.

Only Turkey has recognized the TRNC. The Greek Cypriot government regards the TRNC government and Assembly as illegal, although it accepts the legitimacy of the political parties operating in the Turkish Cypriot sector. Under the TRNC's 2003 budget, a total of 1,233,000,000,000 TL (Turkish lira) was allocated in financial support for the parties represented in the Assembly in proportion to their number of seats.

Communal Liberation Party
Toplumcu Kurtulus Partisi (TKP)
Address. 13 Mahmut Pasa Street, Lefkosa/Nicosia
Telephone. (90–392) 2272555
Leadership. Hüseyin Angolemli (leader)
The left-of-centre TKP (sometimes known as the Socialist Salvation Party) was founded in 1976 with the support of then Turkish Cypriot leader Fazil Küçük and espoused the principles of Mustapha Kemal Atatürk, founder of the modern Turkish state. It won six Assembly seats in 1976 and 13 in 1981. In the latter year the TKP presidential candidate, Ziya Rizki, came second with 30.4% of the vote. The party fell back to 10 seats in the June 1985 Assembly elections (winning 16% of the vote) and its presidential candidate, Alpay Durduran, came third with 9.2% of the vote. It then joined a coalition government with the National Unity Party (UBP), but withdrew in August 1986 amid differences on economic policy.

In 1989 the TKP absorbed the Progressive People's Party (AHP), itself the product of a 1986 merger between the Democratic People's Party (DHP) and the Communal Endeavour Party (TAP). Of these ingredients, the DHP had been founded in 1979 by two former UBP Prime Ministers, Nejat Könük and Osman Örek, of whom the former had in 1983–85, by then an independent, again been Prime Minister of a coalition government. The centre-right TAP had been founded in 1984, and neither it nor the DHP had won representation in the 1985 Assembly elections.

In the 1990 elections the TKP's seat tally slipped to seven. In those of December 1993, which it contested as part of the Democratic Struggle alliance with the Republican

Turkish Party and the New Dawn Party, it declined further to five seats. In the first round of TRNC presidential elections in April 1995, TKP leader Mustafa Akinci came in fourth place with 14.2% of the vote. By then the party had become the most "moderate" of the main TRNC parties on the Cyprus issue, favouring a federal solution which preserves Cyprus as a single sovereignty and the island's entry into the European Union, even without Turkey's accession.

The TKP advanced to seven seats and 15.4% of the vote in the December 1998 legislative elections, becoming in January 1999 the junior partner in a coalition government headed by the UBP. The party strongly supported the UN-sponsored "proximity" talks with the Greek Cypriots that opened in December 1999. In the April 2000 presidential elections, however, Akinci won only 11.7% of the first-round vote. The Turkish Cypriot withdrawal from the UN talks in November 2000 exposed the TKP's differences with the UBP, which favoured separate sovereignty for the TRNC. In May 2001 the TKP was abruptly ejected from the government and replaced by the Democratic Party. Former TKP leader Mustafa Akinci went onto form an alliance of centre left parties named the Peace and Democracy Movement (BDH). The TKP was a member of the Peace and Democracy Movement (BDH) in the December 2003 parliamentary elections, in which the movement gained 13.1% of the vote and 6 seats.

Democratic Party
Demokrat Partisi (DP)
Address. 10 Mersin Street, Lefkosa/Nicosia
Telephone. (90–542) 8576000
Fax. (90–392) 2287130
Email. yenidem@kktc.net
Leadership. Serdar Denktash (leader); Hursit Eminer (general secretary)
The DP was launched in mid-1992 by a dissident faction of the National Unity Party (UBP) which advocated a more conciliatory line in the inter-communal talks than that favoured by the then UBP Prime Minister, Dervis Eroglu. Backed by President Denktash (formerly a UBP member), the new party had the support of 10 of the 45 UBP Assembly deputies elected in 1990–91. In October 1992 it was formally joined by Denktash, who was precluded by the constitution from leading a political party or submitting to party discipline.

In the December 1993 Assembly elections, the DP came close to supplanting the UBP as the leading party, winning 15 of the 50 seats against 17 for the UBP. The then DP leader, Hakki Atun, was appointed Prime Minister of a majority coalition government embracing the Republican Turkish Party (CTP). The coalition policy agreement, while not following a pro-partition line, offered little accommodation on the Cyprus question, favouring joint sovereignty and a rotational presidency. The DP backed Denktash's successful re-election bid in April 1995, after which Atun was reappointed to the premiership of a further DP/CTP coalition.

In May 1996 Atun was replaced as DP leader by Serdar Denktash, son of the TRNC President, following which the coalition with the CTP was ended in July 1996 and replaced the following month by a UBP/DP government in which Serdar Denktash became Deputy Prime Minister. Despite absorbing part of the small Free Democratic Party in September 1998, in legislative elections in December the DP slipped to 13 seats (with 22.6% of the vote) and went into opposition to a coalition of the UBP and the Communal Liberation Party (TKP). The DP backed Rauf Denktash's successful re-election bid in April 2000, following which internal divisions resulted in Serdar Denktash being succeeded as party leader by Salih Cosar in November 2000. In June 2001 the DP replaced the TKP as the UBP's coalition partner. Serdar Denktash returned as DP leader in December 2002.

Following the December 2003 parliamentary elections in

which the DP received 12.9% of the votes and 7 seats, the DP formed a coalition government with the Republican Turkish Party (CTP). The DP were allocated four ministries, including the foreign ministry, which gives the DP a key role in UN settlement negotiations. In the new coalition DP leader Serdar Denktash continues his role as Deputy Prime Minister of the TRNC, in addition to leading the foreign ministry. The decision by TRNC President Rauf Denktash to boycott the second phase of UN peace talks in March 2004 resulted in Serdar Denktash, along with TRNC Prime Minister Ali Talat, leading the Turkish Cypriot delegation in Switzerland.

National Peace Party
Milliyetçi Baris Partisi (MBP)
Leadership Ertugrul Hasipoglu
Telephone. (90-392) 2273141
Three smaller parties from the right of the political spectrum entered the December 2003 parliamentary elections on a single ticket under the title of National Peace Party (MBP). These parties included Our Party (BP) led by Okyay Sadikoglu, which believes that the Annan Plan can be accepted when certain conditions are met, the National Justice Party (MAP) led by Ali Gorgun, which is strongly critical of the Annan plan and the Justice and Peace Party (ABP) led by the Hasipoglu brothers, which is also critical of the Annan plan, but is in favour of a comprehensive solution. The parties had believed working together under a single banner would provide a greater chance of earning the 5% of the vote necessary to receive a seat in the parliament. However, the coalition of parties received only 3.2% in the December 2003 elections and therefore no seat.

National Unity Party
Ulusal Birlik Partisi (UBP)
Address. 9 Atatürk Meydani, Lefkosa/Nicosia
Telephone. (90–392) 2283669
Fax. (90-392) 2279252
Leadership. Dervis Eroglu (leader); Suha Turkoz (general secretary)
Email. ubp@kibris.net
The centre-right UBP was founded in 1976 by Rauf Denktash, leader of the Turkish Cypriot community, and had its origins in an earlier National Solidarity (UD) movement. Espousing the political principles of Mustapha Kemal Atatürk, founder of the modern Turkish state, the party won three-quarters of the seats in the 1976 Turkish Cypriot Assembly elections. Its then general secretary, Nejat Konuk, became the first Prime Minister of the Turkish Federated State of Cyprus (TFSC), but resigned in March 1978, as did his successor, Osman Örek. Both participated in the formation of the breakaway Democratic People's Party, which later became part of the Communal Liberation Party (TKP). Having been formally elected to the Turkish Cypriot presidency in 1976, Denktash was re-elected in 1981 as the UBP candidate with 51.8% of the vote. In the 1981 Assembly elections, the UBP was reduced to 18 deputies but remained the largest party and in August 1981 formed a new government, which fell on a no-confidence vote in December 1981, whereafter the UBP formed a coalition with two other parties.

Following the declaration of the TRNC in November 1983, the UBP continued as the main ruling party and increased its representation to 24 seats out of 50 in the June 1985 elections, with 37% of the vote. In the same month, Denktash was re-elected to the TRNC presidency as the UBP candidate, with 70.5% of the vote. A new coalition government between the UBP and the TKP broke down when the latter withdrew in August 1986, to be replaced by the New Dawn Party. Standing this time as an independent, Denktash was in April 1990 re-elected TRNC President with 66.7% of

the vote. In the May 1990 Assembly elections, the UBP won an absolute majority of 34 of the 50 seats, increasing this tally to 45 in by-elections in October 1991.

Strains then intensified between Denktash and the UBP Prime Minister, Dervis Eroglu, with the latter advocating the formal partition of Cyprus on the basis of the existing territorial division, whereas the President then favoured further exploration of a bicommunal solution in UN-sponsored talks. This divergence resulted in July 1992 in the formation of the breakaway pro-Denktash Democratic Party (DP), which included 10 former UBP deputies. The rump UBP, following Eroglu's pro-partition line, remained the largest single party in the early Assembly elections of December 1993, but with only 17 seats (and 29.6% of the vote) it was unable to prevent the formation of a coalition of the DP and the Republican Turkish Party (CTP).

Eroglu came in second place in the first round of TRNC presidential elections in April 1995 (winning 24.2% of the vote), but was easily defeated in the second by Denktash. In August 1996 Eroglu returned to the premiership, heading a coalition of the UBP and the DP. In the December 1998 legislative elections the UBP advanced to 24 seats (with 40.3% of the vote), so that Eroglu continued as Prime Minister, although the TKP replaced the DP as the UBP's junior coalition. In the April 2000 presidential elections Eroglu again came second with 30.1% of the first-round vote, helping to deny Denktash an outright majority, but he withdrew from the second round in protest against voting irregularities.

Having given qualified support to President Denktash's participation in UN-sponsored "proximity" talks from November 1999, the UBP strongly backed the decision to withdraw from the talks in November 2000. Increasing strains with the pro-settlement TKP impelled the UBP to terminate the coalition in May 2001 and the following month to form a new coalition with the DP, with Eroglu continuing as Prime Minister. The UBP was the second most successful party in the December 2003 parliamentary elections gaining 32.9 % of the vote and 18 seats in the Assembly.

Peace and Democracy Movement
Baris ve Demokrasi Hareketi (BDH)
Leadership. Mustafa Akinci
Telephone.(90-392) 2280108
Email. bdh@kktc.net
The Peace and Democracy Movement founded in 2003 is an alliance of smaller left-wing parties and unions. The BDH is critical of the current regime and believes the TRNC is not a true democracy. The BDH wants to reach a solution through the Annan plan. The alliance gained 13.1% of the vote and 6 seats in the December 2003 parliamentary elections. The alliance includes the Communal Liberation Party, the Socialist Party of Cyprus and the United Cyprus Party.

Republican Turkish Party–Allied Forces
Cumhuriyetçi Türk Partisi (CTP-BG)
Address. 99A Sehit Salahi Street, Lefkosa/Nicosia
Telephone. (90–392) 2273300
Fax. (90–392) 2281914
Email. ctp@ctpkibris.org
Website. www.ctpkibris.org
Leadership. Mehmet Ali Talat (chairman); Mustafa Ferdi Soyer (general secretary)
The CTP was founded in 1970 by Ahmed Mithat Berberoghlou as a Marxist-Leninist formation espousing anti-imperialism, non-alignment and a settlement of the Cyprus question "on the basis of top-level agreements between the leaders of the two communities". In 1973 Berberoghlou stood unsuccessfully against Rauf Denktash, then of the National Unity Party (UBP), for the vice-presidency of (then undivided) Cyprus. He also contested the 1976 presidential election in

the TFSR, again losing to Denktash, while the CTP won only two out of 40 Assembly seats.

Under the new leadership of Özker Özgür, the party increased its representation to six seats in 1981, when the CTP leader came in third place in the presidential elections with 12.8% of the vote. In the June 1985 presidential contest, Özgür improved to second place with 18.4% of the vote, while in Assembly elections the same month the CTP won 12 out of 50 seats with 21% of the vote. In 1988 the CTP's financial viability came under serious threat when a TRNC court awarded President Denktash over £100,000 in damages for an alleged libel in the party newspaper. The CTP did not contest the April 1990 presidential election, while in the May 1990 Assembly balloting it won only seven seats, standing as part of the Democratic Struggle alliance with the Communal Liberation Party and the New Dawn Party.

Having eschewed Marxism-Leninism in favour of democratic socialism, the CTP recovered in the December 1993 Assembly elections, winning 13 seats standing in its own right. It subsequently entered a coalition government led by the recently-formed pro-Denktash Democratic Party (DP). Özgür took third place in the April 1995 presidential elections (winning 18.9% of the vote), whereafter the CTP joined a new coalition government with the DP. This alliance collapsed in November 1995 when President Denktash vetoed two CTP-approved cabinet changes, but was re-established the following month. In January 1996 Özgür was ousted as CTP leader by Mehmet Ali Talat, who in July 1996 took the party into opposition.

The CTP fell back to six seats (and 13.4% of the vote) in the December 1998 legislative elections, remaining in opposition. In the April 2000 presidential elections Talat came fourth in the first round with 10% of the vote. The CTP-BG gained the most votes in the December 2003 parliamentary elections with 35.2% of the vote and 19 seats. In early January 2004, the CTP-BG formed a coalition government with the Democratic Party (DP). CTP-BG chairman Mehmet Ali Talat became Prime Minister and the party gained six ministries, including the important finance ministry. The CTP-BG/DP coalition have 26 deputies in the 50-seat parliament. In March 2004, TRNC Prime Minister Mehmet Ali Talat and Deputy Prime Minister Serdar Denktash led the Turkish Cypriot delegation for the second phase of UN settlement talks in Switzerland, following President Denktash's decision to boycott the talks. Although Rauf Denktash strongly opposed the UN settlement plan, Prime Minister Ali Talat and the CTP-BG supported the UN plan in the April 24 referendum, when it received 64.9% backing in the TRNC.

Solution and EU Party
Çözüm ve AB Partisi (ÇABP)
Leadership Ali Erel
Telephone. (90-533) 8640848
Ali Erel, head of the Chamber of Commerce, leads the Solution and European Union Party. The party, formed in 2003, represents Turkish Cypriot manufacturers and other business interests that hope to take advantage of trade opportunties offered by EU accession. The party support the adoption of the Annan plan. The party won 2% of the votes in December 2003 elections but no seats.

Other Parties

Freedom and Justice Party, right-wing formation launched in August 2000, apparently as successor to the Unity and Sovereignty Party (*Birlik ve Egemenlik Partisi*, BEP) founded in 1990.
Leadership. Arif Salih Kirdag (chairman)

Cyprus Justice Party (*Kibris Adalet Partisi*, KAP), conserva-

tive party formed in June 2003. Promotes national unity and the continuation of the TRNC's sovereignty. Received 0.6% of the vote in the December 2003 parliamentary elections.
Leadership. Oguz Kaleioglu.
Telephone.(90-392) 2289731
Website. www.kibrisadaletpartisi.com
Email. k.ap@mynet.com

Liberal Party (*Liberal Partisi*, LP), launched in January 2001 as an alternative to "the dirty atmosphere, degenerated cadres and cliques" of the existing parties.
Leadership. Kemal Bolayir (chairman)

Nationalist Justice Party (*Midiyetçi Adalet Partisi, MAP*), right-wing pro-Turkey party founded in 1991, formed part of the unsuccessful National Struggle Party (MMP) alliance in the 1993 Assembly elections. Following the 1998 elections it was joined by Kenan Akin, a Turkish settler who had been elected to the Assembly for the Democratic Party. The party took part in the December 2003 parliamentary elections under the banner of the National Peace Party (MBP) coalition.
Leadership. Ali Gorgun
Telephone. (90-392) 2276190

National Revival Party (*Ulusal Dirilis Partisi*, UDP), nationalist formation founded in 1997 by Enver Emin, a former general secretary of the National Unity Party who in 1994 had launched the breakaway National Birth Party and who in 1996 had taken the latter into the Democratic Party, from which he had broken within a year. The UDP won 4.6% in the December 1998 Assembly elections.
Address. 10 Mersin Street, Lefkosa/Nicosia
Leadership. Enver Emin (chairman)

New Dawn Party (*Yeni Dogus Partisi*, YDP), centre-right formation originally founded in 1984 and mainly representing Turkish settlers. It won four Assembly seats in 1985 and joined a coalition with the National Unity Party in 1986; declined to one seat in 1990 (within the opposition Democratic Struggle alliance) and failed to secure representation in 1993, whereupon it merged with the Democratic Party until being revived in 1997.

New Democracy Party, centre-right grouping founded in December 2000.
Leadership. Esref Düsenkalkar, Çetin Atalay

Our Party, Islamist grouping founded in 1998, won 1.2% in the December 1998 Assembly elections. The party took part in the National Peace Party (MBP) coalition in the December 2003 parliamentary elections but received no seat.
Leadership. Ökyay Sadikoglu, Seyh Nasim Kibrisi

Patriotic Unity Movement (*Yurtsever Birlik Hareketi*, YBH), left-wing formation established in 1998 as successor to the New Cyprus Party (YKP), which had been founded in 1989 by Alpay Durduran, the 1985 presidential candidate of the Communal Liberation Party who won 1.8% of the first-round vote in the 1995 presidential contest. The YBH was also joined by Özker Özgür, former leader of the Republican Turkish Party. Advocating a federal settlement for Cyprus and opposing separate sovereignty or union with Turkey, the YBH won only 2.5% in the December 1998 Assembly elections. In the April 2000 presidential contest, YBH candidate Arif Hasan Tahsin took 2.6% of the first-round vote. The YBH did not stand in the December 2003 parliamentary elections declaring the elections illegal due to the increased number of Turkish settlers in Northern Cyprus.
Address. 10 Mersin Street, Lefkosa/Nicosia
Telephone. (90–392) 2274917

Fax. (90–392) 2288931
Email. ybh@north-cyprus.net
Leadership. Alpay Durduran, Rasih Keskiner (general secretary)

Socialist Party of Cyprus (*Kibris Sosialist Partisi*, KSP), founded in 2002 and took part in the 2003 elections as part of the Peace and Democracy Movement (BDH).
Leadership. Mehmet Suleymanoglou.
Website. www.st-cyprus.co.uk.
Email. kibris_sosyalist_partisi@yahoo.

United Cyprus Party (*Birlesik Kibris Partisi*, BKP), founded in 2002 and a member of the Peace and Democracy Movement in the 2003 elections.
Leadership. Izzet Izcan.
Website. www.birlesikkibris.com.
Email. bkp@birlesikkibris.com

Czech Republic

Capital: Prague
Population: 10,305,976 (2003)

The Czech Republic became independent on Jan. 1, 1993, as a result of the dissolution of the Czech and Slovak Federative Republic, which had been under Communist rule (under various names) from 1948 to 1989 and had then become a multi-party democracy. Under the Czech constitution of December 1992, legislative power is vested in a bicameral Parliament of the Czech Republic (*Parlament Ceske Republiky*), of which the lower house is the 200-member Chamber of Deputies (*Snemovna Poslancu*), elected by proportional representation for a four-year term by universal suffrage of those aged 18 and over. The threshold for representation is 5% of the national vote for single parties, 10% for coalitions of two parties, 15% for coalitions of three parties and 20% for coalitions of four or more parties. Under constitutional implementing legislation enacted in September 1995, there is also an 81-member Senate (*Senat*) as the upper house, whose members are directly elected from single-member constituencies for a six-year term, with one third being renewed every two years (although all 81 were elected in the inaugural poll in 1996). Executive power is vested primarily in the Council of Ministers responsible to parliament, although considerable authority resides in the President, who is elected for a five-year term by the members of the legislature.

Under the 1991 Law on Political Parties as subsequently amended, state financial support is available to each party which obtains at least 1.5% of the national vote, the current rates being a basic annual subsidy of CzK6 million plus CzK200,000 for each 0.1% of the party's vote. A further CzK900,000 is payable to parties for each seat obtained in either chamber of the national legislature, while CzK250,000 is payable for each seat won in regional assemblies.

To assure the transition to separate sovereignty, the National Council elected in the Czech Lands on June 5–6, 1992, under the federation became the Chamber of Deputies of the independent Czech Republic. The first post-separation elections were held on May 31–June 1, 1996, the second on June 19–20, 1998, and the third on June 14-15, 2002, the last of these resulting as follows: Czech Social Democratic Party (CSSD) 70 seats (30.2% of the vote); Civic Democratic Party (ODS) 58

(24.5%); Communist Party of Bohemia and Moravia (KSCM) 41 (18.5%); Coalition (Christian Democratic Union–Czechoslovak People's Party (KDU-CSL), Freedom Union–Democratic Union (US-DEU)) 31 (14.3%).

Partial elections to the Senate on Oct. 25-26, 2002 (in November 2003 two seats were re-elected, when two senators became members of the Constitutional Court) resulted in its full composition becoming: ODS 26 seats, independents 22, KDU–CSL 14, CSSD 7, US 6, KSCM 3, Civic Democratic Alliance (ODA) 1, Association of Independent Candidates (SNK) 1, Movement for Concordant Developmment of Communes and Cities (HNHRM, a local group backing only one candidate) 1.

Following its accession to the European Union on May 1, 2004, the Czech Republic elected 24 members of the European Parliament in elections held in June 2004.

Christian Democratic Union–Czechoslovak People's Party
Krestansko-demokraticka Unie-Ceskoslovenska Strana Lidova (KDU-CSL)
Address. Karlovo nam. 5, 12 801 Prague 2
Telephone. (+420) 224 914 793
Email. info@kdu.cz
Website. www.kdu.cz
Leadership. Miroslav Kalousek (chairman); Jan Kasal (first deputy chairman); Jaromir Talír (Chamber group chairman); Josef Kana (Senate group chairman); Petr Rybar (secretary-general)
The KDU-CSL is descended from the Czechoslovak People's Party founded in 1918 as the new state's main Catholic formation and represented in most inter-war governments until it was dissolved in late 1938 in the aftermath of the Munich crisis. Revived as a component of the Communist-dominated National Front in 1945, the People's Party was allowed to continue in existence as a Front party after the Communists took sole power in 1948. From late 1989 it sought to free itself from its recent history as a satellite of the outgoing Communist regime, undertaking personnel and policy changes designed to re-establish itself as an independent pro-democracy formation. Having joined the broad-based coalition government appointed in December 1989, the People's Party in June 1990 removed Josef Bartoncik as party chairman amid allegations that he had been secret police informer. The party contested the elections of the same month in an alliance with other groups allied as the Christian and Democratic Union, which won nine of the 101 Czech seats in the federal lower house (with 8.7% of the vote), six of the 75 Czech seats in the federal upper house (with 8.8% of the vote) and 19 seats in the 200-member Czech National Council (with 8.4% of the vote).

Included in the post-1990 Czech coalition government, the Christian and Democratic Union was weakened in late 1991 by the departure of the Christian Democratic Party (KDS) to form an alliance with the new Civic Democratic Party (ODS). In April 1992 the remaining constituents officially became the KDU-CSL, which in the June 1992 elections won 15 seats in the Czech National Council (with 6.3% of the vote) as well as seven and six of the Czech seats in the federal lower and upper houses respectively. The party became a member of the ODS-led Czech coalition government which took the republic to independence in January 1993, after which it no longer advocated autonomy for Moravia, where it had its strongest popular support. A hankering after old borders is apparent in the party's retention of "Czechoslovak" in its sub-title.

Following the separation, the KDU-CSL became an advocate of the social free-market economy and Czech membership of Western economic and security structures. In late 1995 its parliamentary party was strengthened by the defection to it of five KDS deputies opposed to their party's decision to merge with the ODS. In the 1996 lower house elections the KDU-CSL won 18 seats on a vote share of 8.1% and was included in another ODS-led government, now with minority status. However, political and economic difficulties in 1997 impelled the KDU-CSL and the other junior coalition party (ODA) to withdraw in November 1997, causing the government's resignation, following which the party was represented in a transitional administration pending new elections.

In the early lower house elections in June 1998, the KDU-CSL advanced to 20 seats and 9% of the vote, but went into opposition to a minority government headed by the Czech Social Democratic Party. In June 1999 long-serving party chairman Josef Lux was succeeded by Jan Kasal, who took the KDU-CSL into an opposition Coalition of Four with the Freedom Union (US), the Civic Democratic Alliance and the Democratic Union, which planned to present joint candidates and prospective ministers in the 2002 elections. In the November 2000 partial Senate elections the KDU-CSL advanced strongly within the opposition alliance, becoming the second largest party with 21 of the 81 seats.

In January 2001 KDU-CSL deputy chairman Cyril Svoboda was unexpectedly elected leader of the Coalition of Four, ahead of the party's official candidate, Jaroslav Kopriva. Two months later Svoboda resigned from the post, in protest against the inclusion in the Coalition's shadow cabinet of a former KDU-CSL vice-minister (Miroslav Kalousek) with a dubious past, and was replaced by the then US leader. The consequent turmoil within the KDU-CSL resulted in Svoboda ousting Kasal as party chairman in May 2001. At the beginning of 2002 the KDU-CSL increased the pressure on its three partners in the Coalition to join together (a coalition with four members must obtain 20% of votes, a coalition with two parties only 10%). The Freedom Union and Democratic Union combined to create the Freedom Union–Democratic Union (US-DEU) as the second member of the Coalition; the Civic Democratic Alliance (ODA) was excluded from the Coalition because of financial troubles from the past. The Coalition did not succeed in the parliamentary elections in June 2002 winning only 14.3% of votes and 31 seats in the Chamber of Deputies – 21 of the deputies being members of the KDU-CSL.

After the elections the KDU-CSL became a member of the CSSD-led left-oriented government coalition with three members; the Freedom Union–Democratic Union was also included in the government, but the Coalition split. In the period between the elections of 2002 and the KDU-CSL Congress in November 2003 internal criticism of the party leadership under Cyril Svoboda grew. The main critic emerged as Miroslav Kalousek, who prefered more right-wing policies then the party leadership. At the KDU-CSL Congress in November 2003 Kalousek was elected as the new party chair and the KDU-CSL declared its right-wing affiliation and possible co-operation in particular with the Civic Democratic Party. In the elections to the European Parliament in June 2004 the party won 2 seats with almost 10% of the vote.

Having an official membership of 55,000, the KDU-CSL is an affiliate of the Christian Democrat International and an associate member of the European People's Party.

Civic Democratic Party
Obcanska Demokraticka Strana (ODS)
Address. Snemovni 177/3, 11 800 Prague 1
Telephone. (+420) 257 534 920
Fax. (+420) 257 530 378
Email. hk@ods.cz

Website. www.ods.cz
Leadership. Mirek Topolanek (chairman); Jan Zahradil (first deputy chairman); Vlastimil Tlusty (Chamber group chairman); Jiri Liska (Senate group chairman)

The ODS came into being in early 1991 as a result of a split in the original pro-democracy Civic Forum (*Obcanske Forum*, OF), which had been launched in November 1989 by various anti-communist groups, notably the Charter 77 movement, under the acknowledged leadership of dissident playwright Vaclav Havel. Together with its Slovak counterpart Public against Violence (*Verejnost proti nasiliu*), the OF had then brought about the "velvet revolution", quickly forcing the regime to give up sole state power. In December 1989 Havel had been elected President by a federal parliament still dominated by Communists, while the OF itself had triumphed in the Czech Lands in the June 1990 Czechoslovak elections, winning 68 of the 101 Czech seats in the 150-member federal lower house (with 53.2% of the Czech vote) and 127 of the 200 seats in the Czech National Council (with 49.5% of the vote). It had then entered a federal coalition government with other pro-democracy parties (in which Klaus became Finance Minister) and had headed the Czech government in the person of Petr Pithart. In October 1990 Klaus had been elected as first official chairman of the OF, announcing his intention to steer the movement to the right.

Once in power, the OF had experienced the inevitable internal strains between its disparate components. In February 1991 Klaus and his supporters formally launched the ODS, while elements preferring the maintenance of a broad-based movement converted the OF into the Civic Movement (*Obcanske Hnuti*), which later became the Free Democrats, which in turn became the Free Democrats–Liberal National Social Party (SD-LSNS). A third OF breakaway party was the Civic Democratic Alliance (ODA). The ODS quickly built a strong organization and concluded an electoral alliance with the Christian Democratic Party (KDS). In the June 1992 elections the ODS/KDS combination became the leading formation both at federal level (with 48 of the 99 Czech seats in the lower house and 33.9% of the Czech vote) and in the Czech National Council (with 76 of the 200 seats and 29.7% of the vote). The resultant Czech-Slovak federal coalition was headed by Jan Strasky (ODS), while Klaus preferred to take the Czech premiership at the head of a coalition of the ODS, the KDS, the ODA and the Christian Democratic Union-Czechoslovak People's Party (KDU-CSL).

In dominant governmental authority, the ODS moved swiftly to implement its programme of economic reform, including wholesale privatization of the state sector, especially in the Czech Lands. But its main immediate concern was the constitutional question and in particular the gulf between the Slovak demand for sovereignty within a federation and the Czech government view that preservation of the federation only made sense if it had a real role. Opinion polls at that stage showed that a majority of both Czechs and Slovaks favoured a continued federal structure. But the failure of Vaclav Havel to secure re-election as President in July 1992, due to Slovak opposition in the federal legislature, served to harden attitudes. The upshot, probably desired more by the Czechs than by the Slovaks, was a formal separation as from the beginning of 1993, when the Czech coalition headed by the ODS became the government of the independent Czech Republic, with Klaus as Prime Minister.

In January 1993 Havel was elected President of the new Republic on the proposal of the ODS and its government allies, although foreign policy differences between the (non-party) head of state and the ODS emerged subsequently. Whereas the former promoted the Visegrad Group (with Hungary, Poland and Slovakia) as a Central European framework of economic reform and progress, the Klaus government saw speedy integration with Western economic and security structures as the priority. In 1994–95 the Klaus government remained the most stable in ex-communist Europe. In local elections in November 1994 the ODS headed the poll, with 28.7% of the vote.

In November 1995 the ODS voted in favour of a formal merger with the KDS (under the ODS party name), although the decision of half of the 10-strong KDS parliamentary party to join the KDU-CSL rather than the ODS reduced the impact of the merger. The KDS had originated in the mid-1980s as an unofficial ecumenical Christian group calling for party pluralism and had been established as a distinct political party in December 1989. It espoused family values and strong local government, opposed abortion and easy divorce, and favoured a market economy and integration with Western Europe. At first a component of the broad pro-democracy Civic Forum (OF), the KDS had left the OF to contest the June 1990 elections within the broader Christian and Democratic Union. Included in the post-election Czech government headed by the OF, the KDS had opted in late 1991 to form an electoral alliance with the new ODS, while its erstwhile partners had later become the KDU-CSL. Having won 10 seats in the 1992 Czech National Council elections, the KDS had been included in the consequent Czech coalition headed by the ODS.

Despite the merger with the KDS, the ODS lost ground in the 1996 lower house elections, winning only 68 seats on a 29.6% vote share. Klaus was nevertheless reappointed Prime Minister of a further coalition with the KDU-CSL and the ODA, now with minority status and dependent on the qualified external support of the Czech Social Democratic Party (CSSD). Mounting difficulties in 1997, including a major financial crisis in May and allegations that the ODS had accepted illegal funding, led to the resignation of the Klaus government in November.

Although Havel secured parliamentary re-election as President in January 1998 on the proposal of the ODS, divisions in the party resulted in the creation of the breakaway Freedom Union (US) and a sharp decline in ODS membership. In early lower house elections in June 1998 the ODS slipped to 63 seats and 27.7% of the vote, being overtaken by the CSSD. It opted thereafter to enter into a so-called "opposition agreement" under which it undertook to give external support to the resultant CSSD minority government, thus ending its previous centre-right alliance. In partial Senate elections in November 2000 the ODS won eight seats (its representation in the 81-member upper chamber falling to 22), while in simultaneous regional elections its vote share fell to 23.8%.

In March 2001 the ODS and the CSSD government agreed to continue the "opposition agreement" until the parliamentary elections due in 2002. The following month, however, Klaus criticized newly-elected CSSD chairman Vladimir Spidla as being "too left-wing" and warned that the ODS would terminate the agreement if the CSSD replaced Milos Zeman as Prime Minister. In the June 2002 elections the ODS won 24.5% of votes and 58 seats in the Chamber of Deputies and became the strongest opposition party. The election result was understood as a failure, since the party remained in opposition for the second electoral term.

In December 2002 at the ODS Congress Vaclav Klaus decided to leave the position of party chairman. Congress elected Mirek Topolanek as the new chairman. Klaus became honorary chairman of the ODS and in February 2003 he was elected as the President of the Czech Republic. In all public opinion polls in 2003 the ODS got the biggest support. In the elections to the European Parliament of June 2004 the ODS came first with 30% of the vote, taking 9 of the 24 seats.

Having an official membership of 28,000, the ODS is affiliated to the International Democrat Union and the European Democrat Union.

Communist Party of Bohemia and Moravia
Komunisticka Strana Cech a Moravy (KSCM)

Address. Politickych Veznu 9, 11 121 Prague 1
Telephone. (+420) 222 897 111
Fax. (+420) 222 897 207
Email. tiskove.oddeleni@kscm.cz
Website. www.kscm.cz
Leadership. Miroslav Grebenicek (chair of central committee); Vlastimil Balin (first deputy chair of central committee); Pavel Kovacik (Chamber group chairman)

Founded under its present name in March 1990, the KSCM is directly descended from the Communist Party of Czechoslovakia (KSC), which was founded in 1921 by the pro-Bolshevik wing of the Czech Social Democratic Party (CSSD). The KSC won nearly a million votes in the 1925 elections and was the only East European communist party to retain legal status in the 1930s, under the leadership of Klement Gottwald. It was eventually banned, as a gesture of appeasement to Nazi Germany, in the authoritarian aftermath of the 1938 Munich agreement, its leaders mostly taking refuge in Moscow. They returned at the end of World War II in the wake of the victorious Red Army as the dominant element of a National Front of democratic parties and in the 1946 elections became the largest party in the Czech Lands and the second strongest in Slovakia. Gottwald became Prime Minister and Communists thereafter used their control of the security apparatus to eliminate serious opposition to the party's designs. A government crisis of February 1948 enabled it to assume sole power, although most other Front parties were allowed to remain in existence in a subservient role throughout the subsequent 40 years of Communist rule (the exception being the Social Democrats, who were obliged to merge with the KSC). Elections in May 1948 were held on the basis of a single National Front list controlled by the Communists, after which Gottwald took over the Czechoslovak presidency.

Purges of the KSC leadership in 1951 in the wake of the Soviet–Yugoslav breach led to show trials and the execution of 11 prominent Communists in 1952, among them Rudolf Slansky, who had succeeded President Gottwald as party leader. They had been found guilty of being "Trotskyist-Titoist-Zionist-bourgeois-nationalist traitors". Following Gottwald's sudden death in 1953 (from pneumonia contracted at Stalin's funeral in Moscow), Antonin Novotny was elected to the revived post of party leader and later became President. Nikita Khrushchev's denunciation of Stalin in 1956 resulted in the rehabilitation of most of those executed in Czechoslovakia in 1952 (posthumously) and also of those imprisoned in that era, including Gustav Husak. But no serious attempt was made to introduce political reform, pressure for which grew in the 1960s within and outside the party. Major economic reforms in 1967, largely inspired by Prof. Ota Sik, were aimed at decentralization and the creation of a "socialist market economy" but failed to stem the tide in favour of change. In January 1968 Novotny was replaced as KSC leader by Alexander Dubcek and as President by Gen. Ludvik Svoboda. Hitherto Slovak Communist leader, Dubcek initiated what turned out to be the short-lived Prague Spring.

In April 1968 the KSC central committee elected a new presidium dominated by reformers and also adopted an "action programme" promising democratization of the government system (although not party pluralism), freedom of assembly, the press, foreign travel and religion, curbs on the security police, rehabilitation of previous purge victims, and autonomy for Slovakia. Inevitably, this policy of "socialism with a human face" seriously alarmed the Soviet leadership and its Warsaw Pact satellites. Increasing pressure on the Prague reformers culminated in the military occupation of Czechoslovakia in August 1968 by forces of the USSR, East Germany, Poland, Hungary and Bulgaria (although not of Romania), on the stated grounds that they had been invited in by KSC leaders, including Husak, who believed that the reform movement was out of control. Dubcek and his immediate supporters were taken to Moscow as prisoners. They were quickly released on the insistence of President Svoboda, but the reform movement was effectively over. After anti-Soviet riots in early 1969, Gustav Husak replaced Dubcek as party leader and initiated a major purge of reformist elements which reduced KSC membership from 1,600,000 to 1,100,000. Those expelled from the party included Dubcek and other leaders of the Prague Spring.

Over the following two decades, Husak combined rigorous pro-Soviet orthodoxy and repression of political dissidents with a measure of economic liberalization. Having become President in 1975, Husak in December 1987 surrendered the party leadership to Milos Jakes, another political hardliner. But the post-1985 reform programme of Mikhail Gorbachev in the USSR had its inevitable impact in Czechoslovakia, with the complication that the party leadership could not easily subscribe to reforms which they had been brought into power to eradicate. The upshot was that the Communist regime crumbled with remarkable rapidity following the opening of the Berlin Wall in early November 1989, amid an upsurge of massive popular protest. At the end of November Jakes was replaced as KSC leader by Karel Urbanek and the following month Husak resigned as President, having sworn in the first government with a non-Communist majority for over four decades, although it was led by a KSC member. After Dubcek had been elected chairman of the Federal Assembly (as a co-opted member), Husak was succeeded by the dissident playwright Vaclav Havel, who was elected head of state by a parliament still dominated by KSC deputies. In late December 1989 an extraordinary KSC congress elected Ladislav Adamec to the new post of party chairman and issued a public apology for the party's past actions.

The Czech component of the KSC responded to events by relaunching itself as the KSCM in March 1990, with Jiri Svoboda as leader and with a socialist rather than a Marxist-Leninist orientation. Hitherto, the KSC had embraced the Communist Party of Slovakia but had had no Czech counterpart to that organization. In the June 1990 multi-party elections, the Czech Communists took second place in the Czech National Council, winning 32 of the 200 seats with 13.2% of the vote; they were also runners-up in the Czech balloting for the Federal Assembly, winning 15 of the 101 Czech lower house seats (with 13.5% of the vote) and 12 of the 75 Czech upper house seats (with 13.8%). The Communists then went into opposition for the first time since 1945, amid a continuing exodus of party members. In October 1990 the KSCM declared itself independent of the federal KSC, shortly before the passage of a law requiring the KSC to hand over to the government all of its assets at end-1989. In mid-1991 the KSC was officially dissolved, but both the KSCM and its Slovak counterpart remained "Czechoslovak" in orientation.

In the June 1992 elections, the KSCM headed the Left Block Party, which included the Democratic Left Movement, the Left Alliance and the Movement for Social Justice. The Block won 35 of the 200 Czech National Council seats (with 14.1% of the vote) as well as 19 of the 99 Czech seats in the federal lower house and 15 of the 75 Czech seats in the upper house. Still in opposition, the KSCM mounted ultimately abortive resistance to the dissolution of the federation. Following the creation of the independent Czech Republic in January 1993, the party experienced much internal strife, including the resignation of Svoboda as leader over the

rejection of his proposal to drop "Communist" from the party's title. He was replaced in June 1993 by the conservative Miroslav Grebenicek, whose election precipitated the formation of the breakaway Democratic Left Party. A further split in December 1993 resulted in the creation of the Left Block. These secessions meant that the KSCM had lost the majority of its deputies elected in 1992; it had also ceased to be supported by the former party newspaper *Rude Pravo*, which now favoured the Social Democrats (and later dropped "*Rude*", meaning "Red", from it masthead). The official party newspaper became the *Halo noviny*.

The KSCM nevertheless retained substantial core membership and organizational strength, as well as a significant public following for its advocacy of a "socialist market economy" based on economic democracy and co-operatives and for its opposition to NATO membership and to absorption into the "German sphere of influence". In local elections in November 1994 it won 13.4% of the overall vote. In the 1996 parliamentary elections it took 10.3% of the national vote and 22 lower house seats, effectively becoming the main opposition to a further coalition headed by the Civic Democratic Party, given that the Czech Social Democratic Party (CSSD) agreed to give the new government qualified support. In the January 1998 parliamentary election for the presidency, KSCM candidate Stanislav Fischer, an astrophysicist, failed to progress to the second round against incumbent Vaclav Havel.

In April 1998 the KSCM joined the far-right Association for the Republic–Czechoslovak Republican Party in voting against NATO membership in the decisive parliamentary division on the Czech Republic's accession. In the early June 1998 elections the KSCM advanced marginally to 24 lower house seats on an 11% vote share, remaining in opposition, now to a minority government of the CSSD. In regional elections in November 2000 the KSCM advanced strongly to 21% of the vote.

A major success for the KSCM came in the parliamentary elections of June 2002, when the party won 18.5% of votes and 41 seats in the Chamber of Deputies. The influence of the party continued to increase thereafter, since the left-wing government had only a one- seat majority and the government often looked for support from the KSCM. President Vaclav Klaus also accepts the KSCM as a partner in negotiations whereas former President Vaclav Havel boycotted the party. In the elections to the European Parliament in June 2004 the KSCM got more than 20% of the vote and 6 of 24 seats.

The KSCM has officialy 130,000 members. The party is not included in any European party federation.

Czech Social Democratic Party
Ceska Strana Socialne Demokraticka (CSSD)
Address. Hybernska 7, 110 00 Prague 1
Telephone. (+420) 296 522 111
Email. info@socdem.cz
Website. www.cssd.cz

Leadership. Stanislav Gross (acting chairman); Petr Ibl (Chamber group chairman); Petr Smutny (Senate group chairman)

Founded in 1878 as an autonomous section of the Austrian labour movement, the CSSD became an independent party in 1911. Following the creation of Czechoslovakia after World War I, it won 25.7% of the vote in the 1920 elections (an inter-war record) but was weakened by the exodus of its pro-Bolshevik wing in 1921. Strongly supportive of the post-1918 political system (and a member of various coalitions), in 1938 the party was obliged to become part of the newly-created National Labour Party under the post-Munich system of "authoritarian democracy". Following the further dismantling of Czechoslovakia by Hitler in March 1939, the party went underground. It was a member of the government-in-exile in London during World War II, after which it participated in the Communist-dominated National Front, winning 37 of the 231 Czech seats in the May 1946 elections. The Social Democrats then came under mounting pressure from the Communists, who used the state security apparatus in a campaign to eliminate their main political rivals. Following a political crisis in February 1948, the CSSD was forced to merge with the Communist Party and thereafter maintained its existence in exile.

Following the collapse of Communist rule in late 1989, the CSSD was officially re-established in Czechoslovakia in March 1990, aspiring at that stage to be a "Czechoslovak" party appealing to both Czechs and Slovaks. It failed to secure representation in the June 1990 elections, after which its Czech and Slovak wings in effect became separate parties, although "Czechoslovak" remained its official descriptor. In the June 1992 elections the CSSD won 16 seats in the 200-member Czech National Council (with 6.5% of the vote) and also secured representation in the Czech sections of both federal houses. It then mounted strong opposition to the proposed "velvet divorce" between Czechs and Slovaks, arguing in favour of a "confederal union", but eventually accepted the inevitability of the separation which duly came into effect at the beginning of 1993. At its first post-independence congress in February 1993, the party formally renamed itself the "Czech" SSD and elected a new leadership under Milos Zeman. He declared his aim as being to provide a left-wing alternative to the neo-conservatism of the government in power, while at the same time ruling out co-operation with the Communist Party of Bohemia and Moravia.

The CSSD made a major advance in the 1996 parliamentary elections, winning 61 of the 200 lower house seats on a 26.4% vote share and becoming the second strongest party. It opted to give qualified external support to a new centre-right coalition headed by the Civic Democratic Party (ODS), on the basis that privatization of the transport and energy sectors would be halted and that a Social Democrat would become chairman of the new lower house. Following the resignation of the government in November 1997, the CSSD became the largest single party in early elections in June 1998, winning 74 of the lower house seats with 32.3% of the vote. Zeman therefore formed a minority CSSD government, which was given external support by the ODS under a so-called "opposition agreement".

In March 1999 the Zeman government took the Czech Republic into NATO and in December secured official candidate status for European Union accession. It also continued the previous government's pro-market liberalization policies, although a deteriorating economic situation eroded its support, as did allegations of illicit CSSD party financing. In partial Senate elections in November 2000 the CSSD won only one seat (its representation in the 81-member upper chamber falling to 15), while in simultaneous regional elections its vote slumped to 14.7%.

In April 2001 Zeman vacated the party chairmanship and was succeeded by Vladimir Spidla, who distanced himself from the agreement with the ODS, arguing that the CSSD should be "free and without commitment" in the parliamentary elections due in 2002. Zeman continued as Prime Minister, having been persuaded to remain in office by an ODS threat to withdraw its support if he were replaced by Spidla, who was regarded as too left-wing. Nevertheless, after the June 2002 parliamentary elections the CSSD stayed the strongest Czech political party, with 30.2% of the vote and 70 seats in the Chamber of Deputies. Vladimir Spidla became the new Prime Minister of the centre-left government coalition, in which the Christian Democratic Union–Czechoslovak People's Party and Freedom Union–Democratic Union also participate. The government completed the Czech path towards EU entry with a success-

ful referendum on accession in June 2003.

However, the position of the government and the CSSD as its biggest party was not very stable. Budget deficits from the period of Milos Zeman's government continued and the government was pushed to apply reforms that had a negative impact on many CSSD supporters. In partial Senate elections in November 2002 the CSSD lost 8 seats (its representation in the 81-member upper chamber falling to 7). In the second presidential election the CSSD did not support the former chairman Milos Zeman and in the third round the former chairman of the Civic Democratic Party Vaclav Klaus was elected. After the elections to the European Parliament in June 2004, when the CSSD got less then 9% of votes and won only 2 of the 24 seats, party and government leader Spidla resigned from both posts and was replaced by the new Prime Minister and acting party chairman Stanislav Gross.

Having an official membership of 28,000, the CSSD is a member party of the Socialist International.

Freedom Union–Democratic Union
Unie Svobody–Demokraticka unie (US-DEU)

Address. Malostranske nam. 266/5, 11800 Prague 1
Telephone. (+420) 257 011 411
Fax. (+420) 257 530 102
Email. info@unie.cz
Website. www.unie.cz
Leadership. Pavel Nemec (chairman); Svatopluk Karasek (first deputy chairman); Karel Kuhnl (chairman of Chamber group); Jan Hadrava (Senate group chairman)

The centre-right US was established in January 1998 by a breakaway group of the Civic Democratic Party (ODS). Divisions within the ODS had intensified following the resignation in November 1997 of the government led by Vaclav Klaus, whose abrasive leadership style impelled a faction led by former Interior Minister Jan Ruml to form the new party. The new party attracted the support of 30 of the 69 ODS lower house deputies, including two of the ODS ministers in the post-Klaus interim government, who had accepted portfolios in defiance of a party instruction not to participate. Next to the former ODS members also politicians from local politics (especially from Eastern Bohemia) participated strongly in the process of building new party; later the "former-ODS" wing overruled the party.

In early lower house elections in June 1998, the US retained 19 seats, with an 8.6% vote share, and went into opposition to a minority government of the Czech Social Democratic Party backed externally by the ODS. In opposition, the US in September 1999 formed a Coalition of Four with the Civic Democratic Alliance (ODA), the Christian Democratic Union–Czechoslovak People's Party (KDU-CSL) and the Democratic Union (DEU), announcing that the alliance would present a joint list of candidates and prospective ministerial team in the 2002 elections. In February 2000 Ruml was succeeded as party chairman by Karel Kuhnl, a former Trade and Industry Minister. In the November 2000 partial Senate elections the US advanced strongly within the opposition alliance, becoming the third largest party with 18 of the 81 seats.

As serious strains developed in the Coalition of Four, Kuhnl was elected leader of the alliance in March 2001 to replace the original KDU-CSL holder of the post. He therefore stood down as US chairman, being succeeded in June by Hana Marvanova, who became the first woman to lead a major Czech party. At the beginning of 2002 the US fused with another member of the Coalition – the Democratic Union (DEU). The right-wing DEU was founded in June 1994, backed by the *Cesky Denik* newspaper. It was critical of the then ruling Civic Democratic Party (ODS) for emphasizing economic reform at the expense of law and order and was described by ODS Prime Minister Klaus as "a party of fundamentalist anti-Bolsheviks with no positive programme". The party won 2.8% of the vote and no lower house seats in 1996, although it returned one member to the Senate. In the 1998 lower house elections it again failed to secure representation, its vote falling to 1.4%. In September 1999 the DEU joined the Coalition of Four opposition alliance. After joining the US and building the Freedom Union-Democratic Union (US-DEU) former chairman of DEU Ratibor Majzlik became one of the deputy chairmen in the party.

In the parliamentary elections of June 2002 the Coalition got only 14.3% of votes and 31 seats in the Chamber of Deputies. The US-DEU was represented only by 8 deputies and it was unable by itself to establish an independent Chamber group (for which at least 10 members are needed), going on to establish this with the support of two independent deputies from the Coalition list, that were connected with the second member of the Coalition, KDU-CSL. Both parties became members of the CSSD-led left-of-centre government coalition, but the Coalition split after the partial Senate elections in November 2002, when the US-DEU (and also KDU-CSL) lost ground badly. The consequence of this electoral failure was the resignation of the chairperson Hana Marvanova. In January 2003, Petr Mares was elected as the new chairman of US-DEU. In every public opinion poll since the parliamentary election in June 2002 the US-DEU has had under 5% support. This was reflected in the elections to the European Parliament in June 2004, when the US-DEU got only 1.6% of votes and no seats. After the elections the party leader Petr Mares resigned and Pavel Nemec was elected as the new chairman.

Claiming a membership of 2,500, the US is an associate member of the European People's Party (EPP).

Other Parties

Association of Independent Candidates (*Sdruzeni nezavislych kandidati*, SNK), originating in August 2000. The reason for its creation was an electoral law applying to elections to newly established regional chambers, that prohibited the candidacy of independent candidates. SNK was established as an umbrella for independent candidates. In the regional elections on Nov. 10, 2000, SNK candidates got more than 5% of votes (the legal threshold) in three regions – 12.9% in Vysocina (Jihlava), 10.6% in South Bohemia (Ceske Budejovice), and 5.5% in Northern Moravia (Ostrava). Partial Senate elections were also held in November 2000 and were a big success for independent candidates (6 being elected from 27 seats contested). These results led to the idea of converting the umbrella into a political movement, which was implemented on Nov. 10, 2001, when the Association of Independent Candidates was established with the authorities. The movement declares itself not to be right, centrist or left but seeks to give to the voters the opportunity not to vote for political parties, but for independent candidates and professionals.

As a result of the partial Senate elections in November 2002 the number of independents in the 81-member upper chamber grew to 22.. Five independent members of the Senate decided to establish a Senate group. In every public opinion poll since the beginning of 2003 the SNK got more then 5% support and in the June 2004 European elections a coalition with the European Democrats got more than 11% of the vote and 3 of 24 seats.

Address. Husova 1312/7, 586 01 Jihlava
Telephone. (+420) 567 308 907
Email. kancelar@snk.cz
Website. www.snk.cz
Leadership. Ivo Petrov (chairman); Zdenka Markova (first deputy chairman); Helena Rognerova (Senate group chairperson)

Civic Democratic Alliance (*Obcanska Demokraticka Aliance*, ODA). The conservative ODA was launched in December 1989 and contested the June 1990 multi-party elections as part of the victorious Civic Forum (*Obcanske Forum*, OF), becoming a member of both the federal and the Czech republican governments. Set up as an independent party on the fracturing of the OF in early 1991, the ODA contested the June 1992 elections its own right, winning 14 of the 200 Czech National Council seats (with 5.9% of the vote) but none in either house of the Federal Assembly. As a member of the subsequent Czech coalition government headed by the Civic Democratic Party (ODS), it supported the creation of a separate Czech Republic from January 1993. Its pro-market policy line was very similar to that of the ODS, the main differentiation lying in its greater emphasis on regional self-government and on the need for a reduction of the state's role.

Under the leadership of Jan Kalvoda, the ODA won 13 lower house seats in the mid-1996 elections, on a 6.4% vote share, and continued as a government coalition partner. But both the government and the ODA became increasingly beset by scandal, as the country experienced a major financial crisis. Kalvoda resigned as Deputy Prime Minister in December 1996 over a claim that he had pretended to have a doctorate and was succeeded as party chairman in March 1997 by Michael Zantovsky, a former ambassador to the USA and spokesman for President Havel. Internal divisions intensified, however, with the result that Zantovsky stood down in November 1997, as the withdrawal of the ODA from the government forced its resignation and the calling of early elections, pending which the ODA participated in a caretaker administration.

The next ODA chairman, Deputy Premier Jiri Skalicky, lasted only until February 1998, when he was forced to resign from the government and the party leadership by allegations of illegal party funding, being replaced as ODA chairman by Daniel Kroupa. Meanwhile, the defection of a group of dissidents in January had further weakened the ODA, which opted not to contest the June 1998 lower house elections, instead urging its supporters to vote for other centre-right parties. The party nevertheless continued to be represented in the Senate, where Kroupa chaired a joint group of the ODA and the Freedom Union (US).

In September 1999 the ODA joined an opposition Coalition of Four with the US, the Christian Democratic Union-Czechoslovak People's Party (KDU-CSL) and the Democratic Union (DEU), which planned to present joint candidates and prospective ministers in the 2002 elections. In June 2001 Zantovsky returned to the ODA chairmanship, being elected unopposed by a party conference after Kroupa and another contender had withdrawn their candidacies.

At the beginning of 2002 the other members of the Coalition asked ODA to solve its financial problems from the past and later excluded ODA from the Coalition. In the parliamentary elections of June 2002 ODA got only 0.5% of the vote. The majority of known politicians and also members subsequently left the party. The ODA lost real political influence, although it still has two members in the Senate.

The ODA is a member of the International Democrat Union and since 2001 also an associate member of European Liberal, Democratic and Radical Party.
Address. Stefanikova 21, 150 00 Prague 5
Telephone/Fax. (+420) 257 327 072
Email. oda@oda.cz
Website. www.oda.cz
Leadership. Jirina Novakova (chairperson)

Conservative Party (*Konzervativni strana*, KS), established on the basis of the former Conservative Consensus Party, a right-wing faction of Civic Democratic Alliance.

Address. Rimska 678/26, 120 00 Prague 2
Telephone. (+420) 222 518 030
Fax. (+420) 222 518 031
Email. konzervativnistrana@skos.cz
Website. www.konzervativnistrana.cz
Leadership. Jan Fort

Czech Right (*Ceska Pravice,* CP), far-right party founded in 1993.
Address. Slavojova 9, 128 00 Prage 2
Telephone. (+420) 222 936 232
Email. cp-praha@ceskapavice.cz
Website. www.ceskapravice.cz
Leadership. Milan Simkanic

European Democrats (*Evropsti demokrate*, ED), centre-right political party established by the former Civic Democratic Party member and Prague Lord Mayor Jan Kasl in 2002. The party is based on the big cities, especially on Prague. The European elections of June 2004 proved a big success for the party when, in an electoral coalition with the Association of Independent Candidates (SNK), the party got more than 11% of the vote and 3 of 24 seats.
Address. Vaclavske namesti 835/15, 110 00 Prague 1
Telephone/Fax. (+420) 224 217 787
Website. www.edomkrate.cz
Leadership. Jan Kasl

Green Party (*Strana Zelenych,* SZ), founded in 1989 and prominent in the "velvet revolution", but failed to win representation in the 1990 elections, and so for the 1992 elections joined the broader Liberal Social Union (LSU), which won 16 seats in the Czech National Council. The SZ opposed the conversion of the LSU into a unitary party and reverted to independent status in November 1993, but was barred from the 1996 elections because it could not pay the required deposits. The party is a member of the European Federation of Green Parties. In the parliamentary election 2002 the SZ got 2.4% of votes.
Address. Postovska 455/8, 602 00 Brno
Telephone. (+420) 542 214 269
Fax. (+420) 542 214 271
Email. info@stranazelenych.cz
Website. www.zeleni.net
Leadership. Jan Beranek

Hope (*Nadeje*), centrist party established in 2001 on the basis of the former student movement from the year 1989. In the parliamentary elections of June 2002 it got 0.6% of votes.
Address. Na porici 1041/2, 110 00 Prague 1
Telephone/Fax. (+420) 224 872 010
Email. kancelar@strana-nadeje.cz
Website. www.strana-nadeje.cz
Leadership. Monika Pajerova

Moravian Democratic Party (*Moravska demokraticka strana*, MDS), founded in Brno in 1997 as a merger of the Bohemian–Moravian Centre Union (CMUS) and the Moravian National Party (MNS); argues that Moravians should be defined as a separate ethnic group. In the parliamentary elections 2002 the MDS got 0.3% of votes.
Address. Slavickova 10, 638 00 Brno
Leadership. Ivan Drimal

Party of Democratic Socialism (*Strana Demokratického Socialismu,* SDS), formed in 1998 as a merger of the Left Bloc and the Democratic Left Party. In the parliamentary elections of 2002 the SDS got less than 0.01% of the votes.
Address. Jeremenkova 753/88, 140 00 Prague 4
Telephone/Fax. (+420) 272 103 270

Email. secret@sds.cz
Website. www.sds.cz
Leadership. Milan Neubert

Party for a Secure Life (*Strana za Zivotni Jistoty,* DZJ), founded in December 1989 as Pensioners for a Secure Life to promote the interests of pensioners in the post-communist era, obtained 3.8% of the vote in the 1992 Czech National Council elections, 3.1% in 1996, 3.1% in 1998 and 0.9% in 2002
Address. Sudomerska 32, 130 00 Prague 3
Telephone. (+420) 222 723 688
Fax. (+420) 222 729 785
Email. szj@volnz.cz
Website. www.szj.cz
Leadership. Marcela Kozerova

Republican Movement (*Republikani Miroslava Sladka,* RMS). The far-right populist RMS is directly descended from the Association for the Republic–Czechoslovak Republican Party (SPR-RSC), which was founded in February 1990 and subsequently campaigned for economic protectionism, drastic cuts in the state bureaucracy, military neutrality, non-participation in international organizations such as the IMF, rejection of restitution claims by Sudeten Germans expelled after World War II, measures against "unadaptable" minorities such as Gypsies and the reintroduction of capital punishment.

Obtaining its main support in northern Bohemia, the SPR-RSC won 14 seats in the 200-member Czech National Council in June 1992 (with 6% of the vote); it also secured representation in both houses of the then Federal Assembly. At that stage the SPR-RSC supported the preservation of Czechoslovakia and urged the recovery of the country's original 1918 borders, i.e. including Transcarpathian Ruthenia, which was annexed by the USSR in 1945 and today forms part of Ukraine. Following the inauguration of the independent Czech Republic in January 1993, the party experienced serious dissension within its parliamentary group, whose membership had fallen to six deputies by mid-1995 as a result of defections. Some of these were to the Patriotic Republican Party launched in August 1995. In December 1995 party leader Miroslav Sladek received a suspended prison sentence for an assault on a policeman. In the 1996 lower house elections, however, the SPR-RSC staged a recovery, winning 18 seats with 8% of the vote.

Sladek was again arrested in January 1998 for failing to appear in court on charges of inciting racial hatred, his sojourn in prison coinciding with his candidacy for the Czech presidency, in which he failed to progress to the second round of the parliamentary vote against incumbent Vaclav Havel. He was quickly acquitted on the incitement charges, but failed in a challenge to the validity of the presidential election. In May 1998 a physical attack on Sladek by Gypsies, over a speech with critical references to Gypsy lifestyle, sparked violent protests by party supporters. The SPR-RSC subsequently supported a plan by a Czech town – which was eventually abandoned – to build a wall around a Gypsy neighbourhood to protect other citizens against their alleged criminality.

In the June 1998 lower house elections, the SPR-RSC fell back to 3.9% of the vote and so failed to retain representation. In December 1999 the party was widely condemned for publishing a list of "Jews and Jewish half-breeds" in the political hierarchy. Having lost the state subsidy paid to represented parties, the SPR-RSC was declared bankrupt in early 2001, following which the RMS was launched by Sladek as the successor party. In the parliamentary elections of June 2002 the RMS won 1% of the vote.
Address. Kubanky 6, 644 00 Brno
Leadership. Miroslav Sladek (chairman)

Right Block *(Pravy blok*, PB*)*, right-wing political party established in 1996. In the parliamentary elections in 2002 the PB got 0.6% of votes.
Address. Zitna 606/29
Telephone. (+420) 605 230 238
Fax. (+420) 224 254 407
Email. pravyblok@pravyblok.cz
Website. www.pravyblok.cz
Leadership. Petr Cibulka

Romany Civic Initiative *(Romska Obcanska Iniciativa,* ROI), a party promoting the interests of Gypsies in the Czech Republic. In the parliamentary elections of June 2002 the ROI got less than 0.01% of votes.

Way of Change *(Cesta zmeny*, CZ*)*, was established in 2001 as a centrist political party with a liberal background. In the parliamentary elections of June 2002 the CZ got 0.3% of the vote.
Address. Svedska 22, 150 00 Praha 5
Telephone. (+420) 257 116 235
Fax. (+420) 257 116 252
Email. info@cestazmeny.cz
Website. www.cestazmeny.cz
Leadership. Jiri Lobkowicz

Denmark

Capital: Copenhagen
Population: 5,397,640 (2004E)

Under its 1953 constitution the Kingdom of Denmark is a democratic, multi-party constitutional monarchy in which legislative power is vested in the unicameral *Folketing*, whose members are elected under a highly complex proportional system for a four-year term (subject to dissolution) by universal suffrage of those aged 18 years and above. Of the 179 *Folketing* members, 135 are elected by proportional representation in 17 metropolitan districts, with 40 additional seats being divided to achieve overall proportionality among parties that have secured at least 2% of the vote nationally. In addition, the Faroe Islands and Greenland are allotted two representatives each (see separate sections below).

Public financial support for Danish parties falls into two categories. (1) Under Promulgation Act No 704 of Aug. 21, 1995, state funding is available (*a*) to parties represented in the *Folketing* in approximate proportion to their number of seats, and (*b*) to party organizations and independent candidates contesting national, regional or local elections on the basis of the number of votes received in the previous election (subject to a minimum requirement of 1,000 votes). Parties must not use income from one category of subsidy for expenditure in the other. The total amount available in this category in 2001 was Dkr77.5 million (about $9 million). (2) Under the rules of the *Folketing* as amended in December 1996, each party group is supported in its parliamentary work by (a) a basic payment, set at Dkr225,610 per month as from April 1, 2001, (*b*) an additional payment for each member of the group, set at Dkr35,323 per month as from April 1, 2001 (except that only a third of this sum, Dkr11,774, is payable where a group member is Speaker of the *Folketing* or a government minister). The total amount available under this category in 2001 was Dkr97.8 million (about $11 million).

Elections for the 175 metropolitan *Folketing* seats on Nov. 20, 2001 produced the following results: Liberal Party (*Venstre*) 56 seats (with 31.3% of the vote), Social Democratic Party 52 (29.1%), Danish People's Party 22 (12.0%), Conservative People's Party 16 (9.1%), Socialist People's Party 12 (6.4%), Radical Liberal Party 9 (5.2%), Red-Green Unity List 4 (2.4%), Christian People's Party 4 (2.3%). Excluded from the *Folketing* were the Centre Democrats and the Progress Party with 1.8% and 0.6% respectively. The two parties of the Faroes to win a seat each were the Union Party (*Sambandspartiet*) and the Republican Party; in the Greenland election, the Socialist Party (*Inuit Ataqatigiit*) and the Forward party (*Siumut*), each won a seat.

Denmark joined what became the European Union on Jan. 1, 1973, and elects 14 representatives to the European Parliament. Despite Denmark's strong tradition of euroscepticism, the European Parliament (EP) elections held on June 13, 2004, handed a clear victory to the Social Democrats, who are supporters of EU integration. The SD increased its number of seats from 2 to 5. Besides the Social Democratic Party seven other parties represent Denmark in the European Parliament: Liberal Party 3 seats; Radical Liberal Party 1; People's Movement against the European Union 1; Socialist People's Party 1; Danish People's Party 1; June Movement 1; and Conservative People's Party 1 seat. The result of the EP elections was seen in part as a backlash against the ruling Liberal Party's support for the war against Iraq. The party saw its score decline to 19.4% against 23.4% in 1999.

Christian Democrats (former Christian People's Party) Kristendemokraterne (KD) (former Kristeligt Folkeparti, KrF)
Address. Allegade 24A/1, DK-2000 Frederiksberg
Telephone. (0045–33) 277–810
Fax. (0045–33) 213–116
Email. kd@kd.dk
Website. www.kd.dk
Leadership. Marianne Karlsmose (leader); Mogens Nørgård Pedersen (parliamentary group chairman); Børge Klit Johansen (secretary-general)
The Christian People's Party (KrF) was founded in April 1970 as an inter-denominational formation of Christian groups opposed to abortion on demand, pornography and the permissive society in general. The party achieved representation in the *Folketing* for the first time in 1973, winning seven seats and 4.0% of the vote. It advanced to nine seats and 5.3% in 1975 but lost ground in subsequent elections, taking only four seats and 2.3% in 1981. In September 1982 it was allocated two portfolios in a centre-right coalition headed by the Conservative People's Party (KFP), but left the government after the 1988 elections, in which it just attained the 2% minimum required for representation and retained four seats. It again won four seats in the 1990 contest (on a 2.3% vote share) and in January 1993 was allocated two portfolios in a centre-left coalition headed by the Social Democratic Party.

The KrF slipped to 1.1% in the June 1994 European Parliament elections (insufficient for representation) and took only 1.8% in the September 1994 national elections, thus exiting from both the *Folketing* and the government. The party recovered to 2.5% in the March 1998 general election, enough to re-enter the *Folketing* with four seats. Although in opposition, the KrF was part of the broad coalition which attempted to secure referendum approval in September 2000 for Danish membership of the euro single currency, the outcome being a decisive "no" vote by the electorate. In the 2001 elections, the KrF retained its four seats in the *Folketing*. In 2003, party leader Marianne Karlsmose sought to give the party a sharper profile and increase the party's links to the broader Christian democratic movement. At the party's congress that same year, this resulted in the party changing its name to the Christian Democrats (*Kristendemokraterne* – KD).

Claiming a membership of 6,500, the KD is affiliated to the Christian Democrat International and the European People's Party.

Conservative People's Party
Det Konservative Folkeparti (KFP)

Address. Nyhavn 4, DK-1051 Copenhagen K
Telephone. (0045–33) 134–140
Fax. (0045–33) 933–773
Email. info@konservative.dk
Website. www.konservative.dk
Leadership. Bendt Bendtsen (leader); Knud Erik Kirkegaard (parliamentary group chairman); Morten Bangsgaard (secretary-general)

The KFP was founded in February 1916 by progressive elements of the old *Hoejre* (Right) grouping that had been represented in the *Folketing* since 1849 but had lost its traditional dominance with the rise of the Liberal Party (*Venstre*) and the Social Democratic Party (SD). The new party abandoned the reactionary stance of the old *Hoejre*, adopting a programme featuring support for proportional representation and social reform. It provided parliamentary support for three *Venstre* governments in the 1920s but was in opposition from 1929 until joining a national unity coalition during World War II. After the war it maintained its pre-war electoral strength of 16–20% in most elections up to 1971 before falling to under 10% in the 1970s (and to a low of 5.5% and only 10 seats in 1975). It was in opposition to centre-left coalitions or minority SD governments for most of the period to 1982, the exceptional years being 1950–53, when it governed with the *Venstre*, and 1968–71, when it was in coalition with the Radical Liberal Party (RV) and the *Venstre*. The KFP strongly backed Denmark's entry into the European Community in 1973 and also remained a staunch supporter of Danish membership of NATO.

Under the leadership of Poul Schlüter, the KFP recovered to 12.5% and 22 seats at the 1979 elections and to 14.5% and 26 seats in 1981, with the result that in September 1982 Schlüter became the first Conservative Prime Minister since 1901, heading a four-party centre-right coalition with the *Venstre*, the Centre Democrats (CD) and the Christian People's Party. Committed to reducing the role of the state, the Schlüter government was to remain in office for more than a decade, albeit with changes in its party composition in 1988 and 1990. A further KFP advance to a high of 23.4% and 42 seats in 1984 was followed by a decline to 20.8% and 38 seats in 1987 and to 19.3% and 35 seats in the 1988 snap elections, called by Schlüter after the government had been defeated on an opposition motion that visiting warships should be informed of Denmark's nuclear weapons ban. He was nevertheless able to form a new minority government, this time consisting of the KFP, the *Venstre* and the RV. The KFP fell back to 16.0% and 30 in the December 1990 elections, after which Schlüter was obliged to form a minority two-party coalition with the *Venstre* because the other centre-right parties declined to participate. In June 1992 the government was severely embarrassed when Danish voters disregarded its advice by narrowly rejecting the Maastricht Treaty on European Union.

The KFP participated in the seven-party "national compromise" of October 1992 establishing the terms of joint support for the Maastricht Treaty in a further referendum. Before it could be held, the "Tamilgate" scandal, relating to

the exclusion of relatives of Tamil refugees in the late 1980s, unexpectedly brought about the downfall of the Schlüter government in January 1993 and the installation of a majority coalition (the first since 1971) headed by the SD. In opposition, the KFP in September 1993 elected Hans Engell, a former Defence and Justice Minister, to succeed Schlüter as party chair. The party won 17.7% of the vote in the June 1994 European balloting, increasing its representation from two to three seats. It slipped to 15.0% percent and 27 seats in the September 1994 national elections, remaining in opposition.

Engell was obliged to resign as KFP chair in February 1997 after being involved in a car accident and being found to be over the legal alcohol limit; he was replaced by Per Stig Møller (a former Environment Minister). The March 1998 general election resulted in a major setback for the party, which declined to 8.9% of the vote and 16 seats, losing votes to the new Danish People's Party in particular. Møller was subsequently succeeded as party leader by Bendt Bendtsen. In the June 1999 European Parliament elections the KFP lost two of its three seats, winning only 8.6% of the vote. Although in opposition, the CD was part of the broad coalition which attempted to secure referendum approval in September 2000 for Danish membership of the euro single currency, the outcome being a decisive "no" vote by the electorate.

In the November 2001 general election the party did not improve on the 16 seats won in 1998, but this was enough for it to join the Liberal Party (taking first place in the election with 56 seats) in forming a minority government, with the support of the Danish People's Party (22 seats). The KFP has thereby again become a major political factor in Denmark, with KFP leader Bendt Bendtsen being appointed as Minister of Economic and Business Affairs as well as Deputy Prime Minister and the KFP taking charge of the ministries of Foreign Affairs, Justice, Culture, Transport and Social Affairs.

Claiming a membership of 25,000, the KFP is a member of the International Democrat Union and the European Democrat Union. Its European Parliament representative sits in the European People's Party/European Democrats group.

Danish People's Party
Dansk Folkeparti (DF)

Address. Christiansborg, DK-1240 Copenhagen K
Leadership. Pia Kjærsgaard (leader); Kristian Thulesen Dahl (parliamentary group chairman); Steen Thomsen (secretary-general)
Telephone. (0045–33) 375–199
Fax. (0045–33) 375–191
Email. df@ft.dk
Website. www.danskfolkeparti.dk

The DF was launched in October 1995 by four disaffected deputies of the right-wing Progress Party (FP), including Pia Kjærsgaard, who had been ousted as FP leader earlier in the year. The DF espoused the same policies as the FP but was regarded as being to the right of the parent party. Its overall objective is "to re-establish Denmark's independence and freedom to ensure the survival of the Danish nation and the Danish monarchy"; it opposes in particular the development of Denmark into a multi-ethnic society through immigration. It is also opposed to membership of the European Union (EU), arguing that European cooperation should be limited to free trade and protection of common natural assets.

After winning 6.8% of the vote in the November 1997 local elections, in its first general election in March 1998 the DF easily outpolled the rump FP, winning 13 seats with a 7.4% vote share. It unsuccessfully opposed approval of the EU's Amsterdam Treaty in the May 1998 referendum, taking some comfort from the size (44.9%) of the "no" vote. In the

June 1999 European Parliament elections the DF won 5.8% of the vote and one of Denmark's 16 seats. Kjærsgaard was subsequently the effective leader of the successful campaign against Danish membership of the euro single currency, which was decisively rejected by the electorate in a referendum in September 2000.

In the 2001 general election, the DF was the big winner, taking 22 seats and becoming the third party in Denmark after the Liberal Party and the Social Democratic Party, only six years after being founded. The DF has achieved an important role in Danish politics, supporting the existing government of the Liberal Party and Conservative People's Party, without actually being a part of the government, and being decisive in establishing a majority in the passing of legislative proposals and political measures.

The party has a membership of 4,000. Its representative in the European Parliament sits in the Union for a Europe of Nations group.

Liberal Party
Venstre (V)

Address. Søllerødvej 30, DK-2840 Holte
Telephone. (0045–45) 802–233
Fax. (0045–45) 803–830
Email. venstre@venstre.dk
Website. www.venstre.dk
Leadership. Anders Fogh Rasmussen (leader); Erik Larsen (parliamentary group chairman); Jens Skipper Rasmussen (secretary-general)

The *Venstre* (literally "Left", although the party has long opted for the rubric "Liberal") was founded in June 1870 as Denmark's first organized party, derived from the Friends of the Peasants (*Bondevennerne*) and drawing its main support from small independent farmers (and later from sections of the urban middle class) opposed to the conservatism and political hegemony of the old *Hoejre* (Right), forerunner of the present-day Conservative People's Party (KFP). It became dominant in the then lower house by the 1880s but remained in opposition due to *Hoejre* control of the upper house. In 1901, however, what was then called the *Venstre* Reform Party formed a majority government under Johan Henrik Deuntzer, who was succeeded as Prime Minister by Jens Christian Christensen in 1905. The party was weakened in the latter year by the formation of the breakaway Radical Liberal Party (RV) but recovered partially in 1910 when it reunited with the small Moderate *Venstre* faction under the simple title *Venstre*. The party remained dominant until the 1924 elections, when it was replaced as Denmark's leading political formation by the Social Democratic Party (SD), although it was again in power in 1926–29.

In opposition through the 1930s, *Venstre* experienced electoral decline, to 17.8% of the vote in 1935 compared with a high of 47.9% in 1903. After participating in the World War II national unity government, it rose to 23.4% in 1945 and formed a minority government under Knut Kristensen. Despite improving to 28.0% in 1947, *Venstre* went into opposition until 1950, when it formed a coalition with the KFP under the premiership of Erik Eriksen, who oversaw the introduction of the 1953 constitution. It then remained in opposition for 15 years, during which it support declined from 25.1% in 1957 to 18.5% in 1968, when it entered a centre-right coalition with the RV and KFP. This coalition lasted until 1971, but the watershed December 1973 elections, yielding fragmentation of the party structure (and only 22 seats for the *Venstre* on a 12.3% vote share), resulted in a highly minority *Venstre* government under Poul Hartling. Despite almost doubling its support to 23.3% and 42 seats in 1975, the *Venstre* went into opposition and slumped to 12.0% and 21 seats at the 1977 elections.

In August 1978 the *Venstre* entered its first-ever formal peace-time coalition with the SD, but this collapsed a year later, precipitating elections in which the *Venstre* obtained 12.5% and 22 seats. Having slipped to 11.3% and 21 seats in the 1981 elections, in September 1982 it joined a four-party centre-right government headed by Poul Schlüter of the KFP and also including the Centre Democrats (CD) and the Christian People's Party (KrFP). The KFP/*Venstre* tandem was to survive for over a decade, creating an all-time longevity record for a non-socialist government, although the CD and KrFP were replaced by the RV in 1998–90, after which the KFP and the *Venstre* formed a two-party coalition that lasted until January 1993. During this period *Venstre* electoral support improved to 12.1% and 22 seats in 1984, slipped to 10.5% and 19 seats in 1987, rose to 11.8% and 22 seats in 1988 and rose again to 15.8% and 29 seats in 1990.

As a pro-European party, the *Venstre* shared in the Schlüter government's embarrassment over the electorate's rejection of the EU's Maastricht Treaty in June 1992. In October 1992 it participated in the seven-party "national compromise" establishing the terms of joint support for the treaty in a second referendum. Before it was held, the Schlüter government resigned in January 1993 over the "Tamilgate" affair, so that the *Venstre* returned to opposition. Under the new leadership of Uffe Ellemann-Jensen (former Foreign Minister), the party headed the poll in the June 1994 European Parliament elections, winning 19.0% and four of Denmark's 16 seats. In September 1994 it was the principal victor in general elections, receiving its highest vote share (23.3%) for two decades and 42 seats. During the campaign Ellemann-Jensen controversially proposed the formation of a centre-right coalition that would for the first time include the populist Progress Party. In the event, the party continued in opposition to another SD-led government.

Venstre repeated its 1994 success in the March 1998 national elections, again winning 42 seats with a slightly higher vote share of 24.0%. It remained in opposition, while giving strong backing to the SD-led government's successful advocacy of a "yes" vote in the May 1998 referendum on the EU's Amsterdam Treaty. In the June 1999 European Parliament elections *Venstre* headed the poll with 23.3%, increasing its representation from four to five seats. Although in opposition, *Venstre* was part of the broad coalition which attempted to secure referendum approval in September 2000 for Danish membership of the euro single currency, the outcome being a decisive "no" vote by the electorate.

Anders Fogh Rasmussen and *Venstre*'s breakthrough came in the general election of November 2001, where the party became Denmark's largest with 31.3% of the votes and 56 seats, allowing it to form a new centre-right government with the Conservative People's Party, after ten years of Social Democratic rule. Denmark held the presidency of the EU Council in July-December 2002 and Rasmussen and his government played a major role in the historic task of completing the accession negotiations with the ten candidate countries to enter the European Union in May 2003.

Claiming a membership of some 84,000, the *Venstre* is a member party of the Liberal International. Its representatives in the European Parliament sit in the European Liberal, Democratic and Reformist (ELDR) group.

Progress Party
Fremskridtspartiet (FrP)

Address. Postboks 180, DK-2630 Taastrup
Telephone. (0045–70) 262–027
Fax. (0045–70) 262–327
Email. frp@frp.dk
Website. www.frp.dk
Leadership. Jørn Herkild (chairman)

The FrP was launched in August 1972 by Mogens Glistrup,

a tax lawyer, who advocated the abolition of income tax, the dismissal of most civil servants and a major reduction of the state's role in the economy. The resultant increase in consumer demand would, he envisaged, yield more revenue from value-added tax (VAT), sufficient to cover drastically reduced government expenditure. More idiosyncratically, he also urged the abolition of Denmark's defence forces and the replacement of the Defence Ministry by a telephone answering machine giving the message "we surrender" in Russian. The party caught a populist tide in the watershed 1973 general elections, contributing to the fragmentation of the party system by winning 28 seats and 15.9% of the vote, so that it became the second strongest party in the *Folketing*. It fell back to 24 seats and 13.6% in 1975, recovered to 26 seats and 14.6% in 1977 and then declined progressively to 20 seats (11.0%) in 1979, 16 seats (8.9%) in 1981 and six seats (3.6%) in 1984.

Meanwhile, Glistrup's parliamentary immunity was regularly suspended so that he could face charges of tax fraud in what turned out to be the longest trial in Danish history. Finally convicted in 1983 and sentenced to three years' imprisonment, he was expelled from the *Folketing*, re-elected in the 1984 elections (on temporary release from prison) and again expelled soon afterwards and returned to prison (from which was released in March 1985). Meanwhile, the FrP's slump in the 1984 elections had exacerbated internal party dissension over his leadership style, resulting in the election of a new leadership under Pia Kjærsgaard and the moderation of the FrP's more controversial policies. In particular, it now endorsed Denmark's continued membership of NATO and the preservation of the welfare state. On the other hand, it took a strong anti-immigration stance, seeking to articulate growing public concern on the issue.

The FrP advanced slightly in the 1987 elections (to nine seats and 4.8%), before becoming the main victor in the 1988 poll (rising to 16 seats and 9.0%). It fell back to 12 seats and 6.4% in the 1990 contest, prior to which Glistrup was expelled from the FrP *Folketing* group for indiscipline and subsequently suspended from party membership. The FrP was the only parliamentary party that opposed Danish ratification of the EU's Maastricht Treaty in both the 1992 and the 1993 referendums, its lack of Euro-enthusiasm producing a slump in its vote to 2.9% in the June 1994 European Parliament elections. It recovered its 1990 share of 6.4% in the September 1994 national elections, although its representation slipped to 11 seats. During the campaign the Liberal Party leader caused controversy by publicly envisaging the formal inclusion of the FrP in a future centre-right coalition.

Internal divisions in the FrP in 1995 resulted in the ousting of Pia Kjærsgaard as leader and her replacement by Kirsten Jacobsen, following which a dissident faction including four FrP deputies broke away to form the Danish People's Party (DF). The result was that the FrP's vote slumped to 2.4% in the March 1998 general elections and its representation to four seats. In October 1999, however, the four FrP deputies, including Jacobsen, resigned from the party after an FrP congress had voted for the readmission of Glistrup. The four deputies formed the Freedom 2000 grouping in the *Folketing*, so that the FrP was left without parliamentary representation and was therefore required to re-register with the Interior Ministry if it wished to contest the next general elections.

In the general elections of 2001, the FrP lost its place in the *Folketing*, winning a mere 0.6% of the votes, considerably below the minimum limit of 2%.

Radical Liberal Party
Det Radikale Venstre (RV)

Address. Christiansborg, DK-1240 Copenhagen K
Telephone. (0045–33) 374–747

Fax. (0045–33) 137–251
Email. radikale@radikale.dk
Website. www.drv.dk
Leadership. Søren Bald (chairman); Elisabeth Arnold (parliamentary group chairman); Anders Kloppenborg (secretary-general)

Preferring to be known in English by the title "Social Liberal Party", the RV dates from 1905 as a left-wing splinter group of the historic Liberal Party (*Venstre*) inspired by the example of the Radical Party of France. Its original Odense Programme called for Danish neutrality in war, constitutional reform (including universal adult suffrage), a secret ballot, democratic local elections, provision for referendums on major issues, progressive taxation and land reform. Progress towards these aims was achieved by all-RV governments that held office in 1909–10 and 1913–20 (under the premiership of Carl Theodor Zahle, and more especially by the 1929–40 coalition between the RV and the now dominant Social Democratic Party (SD). Having participated in the World War II national unity government and the post-war all-party administration, the RV returned to coalition with the SD in 1957–64 (with the Single-Tax Party participating in 1957–60). During this period the party share of the vote rose from 8.1% in 1945 to 8.6% in 1953 but slipped to 5.3% by 1964, in which year it won only 10 *Folketing* seats out of 175.

Having recovered to 7.3% and 13 seats in 1967, the RV made a major advance in January 1968, to 15.0% and 27 seats, under the leadership of Hilmar Baunsgaard, who became Prime Minister of a non-socialist coalition that also included the *Venstre* and the Conservative People's Party (KFP). This lasted until 1971, when the RV slipped to a vote share of 14.3% (retaining 27 seats) and went into opposition; the next three elections also yielded major setbacks, to 11.2% and 20 seats in 1973, 7.1% and 13 seats in 1975, and 3.6% and six seats in 1977. Recovering to 5.4% and 10 seats in 1979, the RV slipped to 5.1% and nine seats in 1981 and remained outside the KFP-led centre-right coalition formed in September 1982. It improved to 5.5% and 10 seats in 1984 and to 6.2% and 11 seats in 1987, after which contest RV leader Niels Helveg Petersen rebuffed the SD's attempt to form a centre-left coalition and thereafter gave external support to a further cent re-right government.

Having slipped to 5.6% and 10 seats in the 1988 elections, the RV accepted five cabinet posts in a new KFP-led coalition, but withdrew from participation in 1990 over its opposition to the latest austerity budget. In the December 1990 elections it slumped to a post-war low of 3.5% and seven seats, but nevertheless entered the SD-led centre-left coalition formed in January 1993, receiving three portfolios. In the June 1994 European Parliament balloting, the RV was the only government party to increase its vote share, to 8.5% (yielding one of the 16 seats). In the September 1994 national elections it scored 4.6% and increased its seat total to eight, thereafter joining another SD-led coalition that also included the Centre Democrats (CD).

Following the exit of the CD in December 1996, the RV became the SD's only formal coalition partner. In the March 1998 national elections the RV lost some ground, winning seven seats on a 3.9% vote share. It nevertheless continued as the junior coalition party, receiving four portfolios out of 20 in the new SD-led minority government. In the June 1999 European Parliament elections the RV improved to 9.1% of the vote while again winning one seat.

The RV was part of the broad government/opposition coalition which attempted to secure referendum approval in September 2000 for Danish membership of the euro single currency, the outcome being a decisive "no" vote by the electorate. In somewhat belated acceptance of a share of responsibility for the defeat, RV Foreign Minister Niels Helveg Petersen resigned in December 2000. With the victory of the

Liberal-Conservative coalition in the November 2001 general election, and the consequent fall of the SD-RV coalition, the RV (which won 5.2% of the vote and nine seats) joined the opposition.

Claiming a membership of 6,000, the RV is a member party of the Liberal International. Its representative in the European Parliament sits in the European Liberal, Democratic and Reformist (ELDR) group.

Red–Green Unity List
Enhedslisten-de Roed-Groenne (ELRG)

Address. Studiestræde 24, DK-1455 Copenhagen K
Telephone. (0045–33) 933–324
Fax. (0045–33) 320–372
Email. enhedslisten@enhedslisten.dk
Website. www.enhedslisten.dk
Leadership. 21-member collective; Søren Kolstrup (parliamentary group chairperson); Keld Albrechtsen (secretary)

The ELRG was established in 1989 as an alliance of three parties of leftist and/or environmentalist orientation. Strongly opposed to Danish membership of NATO and the European Community (later Union), it was part of the campaign against Danish ratification of the Maastricht Treaty (successful in Denmark's first referendum in June 1992, but unsuccessful in the second in May 1993). It achieved a breakthrough in the September 1994 general elections, winning 3.1% of the vote and six seats. Thereafter, its external support was important for the survival of the centre-left coalition government headed by the Social Democratic Party (SD), notably in the passage of the 1997 budget.

The ELRG lost ground in the March 1998 national elections, slipping to 2.7% of the vote and five seats. It continued thereafter to give qualified external support to a new SD-led minority government, but was part of the left-right coalition which campaigned successfully against Danish membership of the euro in the September 2000 referendum.

In the general elections of 2001, the ELRG lost still more ground, winning a mere 2.4% of the vote (dangerously close to the minimum limit of 2%) and slipping back to four seats.

Social Democratic Party
Socialdemokratiet (SD)

Address. Danasvej 7, DK-1910 Frederiksberg C
Telephone. (0045–72) 300–800
Fax. (0045–72) 300–850
Email. partikontoret@net.dialog.dk
Website. www.socialdemokratiet.dk
Leadership. Mogens Lykketoft (chairman); Lotte Bundsgaard & Bent Hansen (deputy chairpersons); Pia Gjellerup (parliamentary group chairperson); Jens Christiansen (general secretary)

Founded in 1871 to represent the emerging industrial working class, the SD first won seats in the *Folketing* in 1884 and in 1913–20 supported a minority government of the Radical Liberal Party (RV). It became the strongest parliamentary party (with 55 out of 148 seats) in 1924, in which year it formed its first government under the premiership of Thorvald Stauning. In opposition from 1926, the party returned to government in 1929 under Stauning, who headed a coalition with the RV until the German occupation in May 1940 and thereafter, until his death in May 1942, a national unity government. Having achieved its its highest voting support to date in the 1931 elections (46.1%), the SD was instrumental in the 1930s in introducing advanced welfare state legislation and other social reforms on the Scandinavian model.

The SD continued to be the dominant party after World War II, although it has never won an overall majority and has averaged about a third of the vote in recent elections. Stauning's successor as Prime Minister and SD leader,

Vilhelm Buhl, headed the immediate post-war all-party coalition formed in May 1945, but the party lost support in the October 1945 elections and went into opposition. Talks with the Danish Communists on the creation of a broad Labour Party came to nothing. The SD returned to power in November 1947 as a minority government under Hans Hedtoft until his death in January 1955 and then under Hans Christian Hansen. In May 1957 the SD formed a majority coalition with the RV and the Single-Tax Party, under the premiership of Hansen until his death in February 1960 and then under Viggo Kampmann. After improving to 42.1% and 76 seats in the November 1960 elections (its best post-war result), the party formed a two-party coalition with the RV, under Kampmann until he was succeeded as party leader and Prime Minister by Jens Otto Krag in September 1962.

Krag reverted to a minority SD government after the September 1964 elections (in which the party slipped to 41.9% but retained 76 seats); however, after losing ground in the next two elections, the party was in opposition from January 1968 until, following SD gains in the September 1971 elections (to 37.3% and 70 seats), Krag was able to form a new minority government the following month. Immediately after the October 1972 referendum decision in favour of European Community membership, Krag unexpectedly resigned in January 1973 and was succeeded by trade union leader Anker Jørgensen. Later that year the SD was weakened by the formation of the Centre Democrats by a right-wing splinter group which claimed that the party was moving too far to the left. Heavy SD losses in the December 1973 elections (to 25.6% and 46 seats, its worst result in half a century) sent the party into opposition; but a partial recovery in the January 1975 contest (to 30.0% and 53 seats) resulted in an SD minority government under Jørgensen. Following a further SD recovery in the February 1977 elections (to 37.0% and 65 seats), Jørgensen in August 1978 negotiated the SD's first-ever formal coalition with the *Venstre* Liberals in peace-time. However, after another SD advance in the September 1979 elections (to 38.3% and 68 seats), Jørgensen formed an SD minority government.

The SD suffered a setback in the 1981 elections, falling to 59 seats and 32.9% of the vote. It nevertheless remained in office until September 1982, when Jørgensen resigned and was replaced by Denmark's first Prime Minister from the Conservative People's Party since 1901. The SD lost further ground at the January 1984 and September 1987 elections (to 56 seats and 31.6%, then to 54 seats and 29.3%), by which time the party had experienced its longest period of opposition since the 1920s. After unsuccessfully seeking to form a coalition with the RV and the Socialist People's Party (SFPP), Jørgensen resigned as SD chair after the 1987 elections and was succeeded (in November 1987) by Svend Auken. But a lacklustre SD performance in further elections in May 1988 (in which it slipped to 55 seats and 29.9%) kept the party in opposition. It improved sharply at the next contest in December 1990 (to 69 seats and 37.4%), but remained in opposition, with the eventual result that in April 1992 Auken was replaced as party chair by Poul Nyrup Rasmussen. Two months later the SD shared in the general embarrassment of the pro-European government parties when Danish voters narrowly rejected the Maastricht Treaty of the European Union (EU).

The SD participated in the seven-party "national compromise" of October 1992 establishing the terms of joint support for the Maastricht Treaty in a further referendum. Before it could be held, the "Tamilgate" scandal unexpectedly brought about the downfall of the centre-right coalition in January 1993 and the installation of a majority coalition (the first since 1971) headed by the SD and including the RV, the Centre Democrats (CD) and the Christian People's Party. The Maastricht Treaty was duly approved at the second time of asking in May 1993, but a significant minority of SD activists and voters remained in the "no" camp. The party's continuing difficulties over the EU were apparent in the June 1994 European Parliament elections, when the SD managed only 15.8% of the vote and three of the 16 Danish seats. In the September 1994 national elections, however, the party recovered to 34.6%, yielding 62 seats and enabling Rasmussen to form a three-party minority coalition with the RV and the CD.

The CD's resignation from the government in December 1996, in protest against an agreement between Rasmussen and the Socialist People's Party and the Red–Green Unity List ensuring passage of the 1997 budget, reduced the ruling coalition to two parties. Although it lost ground in the November 1997 local elections, in the March 1998 national elections the SD unexpectedly increased its vote share to 35.9% and its representation to 63 seats. Rasmussen accordingly formed another minority government in coalition with the RV. In the June 1999 European Parliament elections the SD posted its customary poor performance in such contests, again winning only three seats (with a 16.5% vote share).

Intense debate within the SD on whether Denmark should enter the single European currency eventually resulted in a majority decision in favour at the party's 2000 congress. Many SD supporters remained opposed, however, and contributed to the decisive majority against in the September 2000 referendum. Continuing in office despite this major setback, Rasmussen in December 2000 appointed five new ministers, including three relatively unknown Social Democrats, in an attempt to rejuvenate his government.

In the general election of November 2001, the SD lost its status as Denmark's strongest party, a position it had enjoyed in every national election from 1924 through to 1998. SD was displaced by *Venstre*, the Liberal Party, which won 56 seats agaist SD's 52 and ended the SD's reign as leader of either a majority or minority government since 1992.

In August 2002, party leader Rasmussen launched a renewal of the party image, omitting to involve his right hand man, Mogens Lykketoft. Lykketoft had had an important role in Rasmussen's appointment as party leader in the early 1990s, had been his Finance Minister and later Minister of Foreign Affairs, and had been Rasmussen's closest political advisor. Rasmussen's renewal plan resulted in divisions within the party, and Lykketoft, not wanting to be a part of it, limited himself to retaining his position as spokesman for the party. The crisis ended at the SD's congress in December 2002, where Lykketoft was appointed as new party leader, as he was considered to be the right man to reunite the party.

Claiming a membership of 100,000, the SD is a member party of the Socialist International. Its representatives in the European Parliament sit in the Party of European Socialists group.

Socialist People's Party
Socialistisk Folkeparti (SFP)

Address. Christiansborg, DK–1240 Copenhagen K
Telephone. (0045–33) 374–444
Fax. (0045–33) 327–248
Email. sf@sf.dk
Website. www.sf.dk
Leadership. Holger K. Nielsen (chairman); Trine Bendix Knudsen (deputy chairperson); Aage Frandsen (parliamentary group chairman); Turid Leirvoll (secretary-general)
The SFP was founded in November 1958 by a dissident faction of the Communist Party of Denmark (DKP) led by former DKP chair Aksel Larsen, following the latter's expulsion from the party for praising Titoism in Yugoslavia and criticizing the Soviet Union's suppression of the 1956 Hungarian Uprising. The new party advocated left-wing socialism inde-

pendent of the Soviet Union, unilateral disarmament, Nordic co-operation, and opposition to NATO and to Danish accession to the European Community (EC).

The SFP won 11 seats and 6.1% of the vote at its first elections in 1960, fell back slightly in 1964 but advanced to 20 seats and 10.9% in 1966. Apart from the 1971 contest, the next five elections brought a gradual decline for the SFP, to a low of six seats and 3.9% in 1977, in part because of competition from the new Left Socialists party, founded by SFP dissidents in 1967. In 1972 the SFP took a leading role in the unsuccessful "no" campaign in the Danish referendum on EC entry, acting in this as on other issues as an unofficial left wing of the Social Democratic Party (SD). During the 1970s the SFP usually gave external support to the SD-led minority governments characteristic of the decade.

The four elections from 1979 yielded an SFP resurgence, to an all-time high of 27 seats and 14.6% in 1987, when it was the only party to make significant gains and became the third-strongest parliamentary party. It remained in opposition to the Schlüter centre-right government and lost ground in the 1988 contest, falling to 24 seats and 13.0% of the vote. SD gains in the 1990 elections further reduced the SFP tally, to 15 seats and 8.3%. The party campaigned on the "no" side in the June 1992 referendum in which Danish voters narrowly rejected the Maastricht Treaty of what became the European Union (EU), although it no longer advocated Denmark's withdrawal. In October 1992, after some agonizing, the KFP joined the seven-party "national compromise" setting new terms for approval of the treaty, which was given by voters at the second time of asking in May 1993.

In June 1994 the SFP won 8.6% of the vote in European Parliament elections, thus retaining the one seat it won in 1989. It declined to 13 seats and 7.3% in the September 1994 general elections, partly because of a rise in support for the new Red-Green Unity List (ELRG), thereafter pledging conditional support for the reconstituted SD-led coalition. This support proved crucial in 1996 over the passage of the disputed 1997 budget, on the basis of a deal between the SD, the SFP and the ELGR which gave the two non-governmental parties a promise of increased social spending.

The SFP again won 13 seats in the March 1998 national elections, with a slightly increased vote share of 7.6%. and continued to give qualified support to another SD-led government. In the June 1999 European Parliament elections it retained its single seat with 7.1% of the vote. In 2000 the SFP was part of the left-right coalition which campaigned successfully against Danish membership of the euro in the September 2000 referendum.

The party slipped back slightly in the general election of November 2001, with a vote share of 6.4% and 12 seats. It joined the SD in the opposition to the new government.

With an official membership of 8,000, the SFP is a member of the New European Left Forum (NELF). Its European Parliament representative sits in the European United Left/Nordic Green Left group.

Other Parties and Movements

Communist Party of Denmark (*Danmarks Kommunistiske Parti*, DKP). Founded in 1919 and represented in the *Folketing* from 1932. It participated in the immediate postwar coalition government, winning 18 seats in 1945 but declined steadily thereafter to nil in 1960, having been weakened by the formation of the Socialist People's Party. It reentered the *Folketing* in 1973 with six seats, rising to seven in 1975 and 1977, but has been unrepresented since 1979.
Address. Studiesstræde 24/1, DK-1455 Copenhagen K
Telephone. (0045–33) 916–644
Fax. (0045–33) 320–372
Email. dkp@dkp.dk

Website. www.dkp.dk
Leadership. Mogens Høver (chairman)

Communist Party of Denmark/Marxist-Leninist (*Danmarks Kommunistiske Parti/Marxister-Leninister*, DKP/ML), formerly pro-Albanian formation.
Address. Griffenfeldsgade 26, DK-2200 Copenhagen N
Telephone. (0045–31) 356–069
Fax. (0045–35) 372–039
Email. dkp-ml@dkp-ml.dk
Website. www.dkp-ml.dk
Leadership. Jørgen Petersen

Danish Centre Party (*Dansk Center Parti,* DCP), deceptively named anti-immigration formation established in 1992, advocating a complete embargo on immigration and admittance of refugees.
Address. PB 150, DK-2880 Bagsværd
Telephone/Fax. (0045–44) 972–738
Email. dcp@post7.tele.dk
Website. home7.inet.tele.dk/dcp
Leadership. Per W. Johansson (chairman)

Freedom 2000
Frihed 2000
Freedom 2000 was launched in late 1999 by the remaining four deputies of the populist Progress Party (FP) following the decision of an FP congress to readmit controversial original FP leader Mogens Glistrup. The new grouping was active in the successful campaign against Danish membership of the euro single currency in the September 2000 referendum.
Address. Christiansborg, 1240 Copenhagen K
Telephone. (0045–33) 373–860
Fax. (0045–33) 151–399
Email. frihed@ft.dk
Leadership. Kirsten Jacobsen

Green Party (*Partiet de Grønne*), sub-titled Realistic-Ecological Alternative (*Oekoloisk-Realistik Alternativ*), founded in 1983, has remained small because of the strong environmentalist current in several mainstream parties and also because of the recent success of the Red–Green Unity List; affiliated to the European Federation of Green Parties.
Address. Westend 15 st.th, DK-1661, Copenhagen V
Telephone. (0045–33) 253–339
Email. grondebat@groenne.dk
Website. www.groenne.dk
Leadership. Anders Wamsler & Jean Thierry

June Movement (*Junibevægelsen,* JB)*,* anti-EU formation named after the month of the initial Danish referendum rejection of the Maastricht Treaty; won 15.2% and two seats in the 1994 elections to the European Parliament, improving to 16.1% and three seats in the 1999 contest on a platform of vigorous opposition to any attempt to take Denmark into the single European currency; its MEPs sat in the Europe of Democracies and Diversities group at Strasbourg. It retained one seat in the European Parliament in the June 2004 elections.
Address. Kronprinsensgade 2, DK-1114 Copenhagen K
Telephone. (0045–33) 930–046
Fax. (0045–33) 933–067
Email. jb@junibevaegelsen.dk
Website. www.j.dk
Leadership. Jens-Peter Bonde

Left Socialist Party (*Venstresocialisterne,* VS), founded in December 1967 by left-wing dissidents of the Socialist People's Party (SFP), won four *Folketing* seats in 1968, lost them in 1971, regained them in 1975, reached high point of six seats in 1979, falling to five in 1981 and 1984, but weakened thereafter by factionalism and retro-defections to the SFP; unrepresented in the national parliament since 1987, much of its support having switched to the Red-Green Unity List (with which it has allied in elections.)
Address. Solidaritetshuset, Griffenfeldsgade 41, DK-2200 Copenhagen N
Telephone/Fax. (0045–35) 350–608
Email. vs@venstresocialisterne.dk
Website. www.venstresocialisterne.dk

People's Movement against the European Union (*Folkebevægelsen mod EF-Unionen*), founded to articulate rank-and-file anti-European feeling in officially pro-European parties, won 18.9% and four seats in the 1989 European Parliament elections, falling to 10.3% and two seats in 1994 (when it faced competition from the June Movement) and to 7.3% and one seat in 1999, its MEP sitting in the Europe of Democracies and Diversities group. It retained its European Parliament seat in the 2004 elections.
Address. Sigurdsgade 39A, DK-2200 Copenhagen N
Telephone. (0045–35) 821–800
Fax. (0045–35) 821–806
Email. folkebevaegelsen@folkebevaegelsen.dk
Website. www.folkebevaegelsen.dk
Leadership. Poul Gerhard Kristiansen

Schleswig Party (*Schleswigsche Partei/Slesvigsk Parti*), founded in August 1920 following the incorporation of former northern German Schleswig into Denmark; representing the German minority, it had one *Folketing* seat until 1964 and again in 1973–79, latterly in alliance with the Centre Democrats.
Address. Vestergade 30, DK-6200 Åbenrå
Telephone (0045–74) 623–833
Fax. (0045–74) 627–939
Email. sp@bdn.dk
Website. www.schleswigsche-partei.dk
Leadership. Gerhard Mammen (chairman)

Single-Tax Party, also known as the Justice Party of Denmark (*Danmarks Retsforbund*), founded in 1919 to propagate the theories of US economist Henry George, won between two and four *Folketing* seats in 1930s and 1940s, rising to 12 in 1950 but falling unevenly to nil in 1960, following participation in a coalition government headed by the Social Democratic Party from 1957; re-entered *Folketing* in 1973 with five seats, lost them all in 1975, won six seats in 1977 and five in 1979, but has been unrepresented since 1981.
Address. Lyngbyvej 42, DK-2100 Copenhagen Ø
Telephone. (0045–39) 204–488
Fax. (0045–39) 204–450
Email. sekretariat@retsforbundet.dk
Website. www.retsforbundet.dk
Leadership. Mette Langdal Kristiansen (chairman)

Socialist Workers' Party (*Socialistisk Arbejderparti,* SAP), far-left grouping which has made little electoral impact in Danish politics.
Address. Studiestræde 24, o.g. 1.sal, DK-1455 Copenhagen K
Telephone. (0045–33) 337–948
Fax. (0045–33) 330–317
Email. sap@sap-fi.dk
Website. www.sap-fi.dk

Union Opposers Democratic Renewal (*Unionsmodstanderne* Demokratisk Fornyelse, *DF*), electoral alliance of various left-wing and centrist groups opposed to membership of the European Union; won only 0.3% of the vote in 1998 general elections. Have an electoral cooperation with the Green Party, which they call the Green Democrats (website : www.groennedemokrater.dk).

Address. Askevej 16, DK-3630 Jægerspris
Telephone/Fax. (0045–47) 500–692
Email. udf@demokratisk-fornyelse.dk
Website. www.demokratiskfornyelse.dk

DANISH DEPENDENCIES

FAROE ISLANDS

Capital: Tórshavn
Population: 46,000 (2000E)

Under the 1993 Danish constitution the Faroe Islands are an internally self-governing part of the Kingdom of Denmark, whose government retains responsibility for their foreign affairs, defence, judiciary and monetary affairs. Executive power is formally vested in the Danish monarch, who is represented in Tórshavn by a High Commissioner, but actual authority for Faroese affairs (including fisheries) is exercised by a government (*Landsstyret* or *Landsstyrid*) headed by a Chief Minister (*Løgmadur* or *Lagmand*). Legislative authority is vested in a Faroes parliament (*Lagting* or *Løgting*), 27 of whose seats are filled by direct proportional election under universal adult suffrage and up to five more by distribution to party lists under an equalization system. Two representatives from the Faroes are elected to the *Folketing* in Copenhagen in Danish national elections. The Faroe Islands remained outside the European Community (later Union) when Denmark joined in 1973 but later signed a special trade agreement with the grouping.

Elections to the *Løgting* on April 30, 2002, resulted as follows: Union Party 8 seats (with 26.0% of the vote), Republican Party 8 (23.7%), Social Democratic Party 7 (20.9%), People's Party 7 (20.8%), Self-Government Party 1 (4.4%), Centre Party 1 (4.2%). The November 2001 general elections to the Danish *Folketing* in the Faroes resulted in the Union and Republican parties winning a seat each.

Centre Party
Midflokkurin (Mfl)
Address. PO Box 3237, 110 Tórshavn
Email. midflokk@post.olivant.fo
Website. www.midflokkurin.fo
Leadership. Tordur Niclasen (chairman)
The Mfl was founded in 1991 in opposition to the then coalition government of the Social Democratic and People's parties. It won two seats out of 32 in the July 1994 election (and continued in opposition) but failed to retain representation in the 1998 polling. In 2002 it regained a seat in the Løgting, with 4.2% of the votes, and joined the People's, Republican and Self-Government parties in the government.

Christian People's Party/Faroes Progressive and Fishing Industry Party
Kristiligi Fólkaflokkurin/Framburds– og Fiskivinnuflokkurin (KF/FFF)
Address. Brekku 5, 700 Klaksvík
Telephone. (00298) 457–580
Fax. (00298) 457–581
Leadership. Rev. Niels Pauli Danielsen (chairman)
The KF/FFF was formed prior to the 1978 elections as an alliance of the centrist Progressive Party (which had been in coalition government in 1963–66) and centre-oriented fish-ing industry elements. Favouring increased self-government for the Faroes, it won two seats in 1978, 1980 and 1984, subsequently entering a centre-left coalition headed by the Social Democratic Party. It again won two seats in 1988, switching to the resultant centre-right coalition headed by the People's Party, but withdrawing in June 1989. It retained two seats in the 1990 and 1994 elections, but failed to win representation in both 1998 and 2002.

People's Party
Fólkaflokkurin (Fkfl)
Address. Jónas Broncksgøta 29, 100 Tórshavn
Email. xa@folkaflokkurin.fo
Website. folkaflokkurin.fo
Leadership. Anfinn Kallsberg (parliamentary leader); Óli Breckmann (chairman)
The moderate conservative and pro-autonomy Fkfl was founded in 1940 as a merger of a right-wing faction of the Self-Government Party (Sjfl) and the small Commerce Party (*Vinnuflokkur*). It first entered a coalition government in 1950, with the Union Party (Sbfl) until 1954 and thereafter with the Sjfl until 1958. In 1963–66 its then leader, Jógvan Sundstein, headed a coalition with the Republican Party (Tjfl), the Christian People's Party/Progressive and Fishing Industry Party (KF/FFF) and the Sjfl. The party was again in opposition from 1966 to 1974, when it joined a centre-left coalition with the Social Democratic Party (Jvfl) and the Tjfl, this alliance being continued after the 1978 election. In 1981 it entered a centre-right coalition with Sbfl and the Sjfl, becoming the second strongest parliamentary party in the 1984 elections with seven seats, but nevertheless going into opposition.

The Fkfl became the strongest party, with eight seats, in the 1988 election, after which Sundstein formed a centre-right coalition with the Tjfl, the Sjfl and the KF/FFF. This gave way to a Fkfl/Tjfl/Sbfl governing alliance in mid-1989, but the Fkfl's two new partners withdrew support in October 1990, precipitating an early election the following month in which the Fkfl slipped to seven seats. In January 1991 the party became the junior partner in a coalition with the Jvfl but withdrew in April 1993 over a fisheries policy disagreement. It declined to six seats in the July 1994 election, after which it remained in opposition.

The Fkfl again won one of the two Faroes seats in the Danish elections of March 1998, its deputy (Óli Breckmann) joining the metropolitan Liberal Party (*Venstre*) parliamentary group. In the April 1998 Faroes elections, the Fkfl advanced to eight seats with 21.3% of the vote. Accordingly, Anfinn Kallsberg of the Fkfl became Chief Minister of a coalition which also included the Tjfl and the Sjfl.

In February 2001 the Kallsberg government announced that it would call a referendum in May to seek popular endorsement for its plan to phase out the need for Danish subsidies over a 10-year period with a view to holding a further referendum in 2012 on declaring full independence. However, in the face of metropolitan displeasure, Kallsberg's Fkfl quickly withdrew its support for the plan, provoking a coalition crisis which was uneasily resolved in March by an agreement not to proceed with the referendum but to concentrate instead on laying the economic foundations of full sovereignty.

In the 2002 election, the Fkfl slipped back to 7 seats, with 20.8% of the votes, and was only the third-strongest party. However, it remained in the goverment, again forming an alliance with the Republican and Self-Government parties. A new member joined this alliance, to make it a coalition of four: the small Centre Party.

The Fkfl is affiliated to the International Democrat Union.

Republican Party
Tjódveldisflokkurin (Tjfl)

Address. N. Finsensgøta 16, Postrúm 143, 110 Tórshavn
Telephone. (00298) 312–200
Fax. (00298) 312–262
Email. loysing@post.olivant.fo
Website. www.tjodveldi.fo
Leadership. Høgni Hoydal (chairman)

The *Tjódveldisflokkurin,* meaning literally "Party for People's Government", was founded in 1948 as a left-wing party advocating secession from Denmark, citing as justification a 1946 plebiscite in which 48.7% had voted for independence and 47.2% for home rule under Danish sovereignty. Having won two seats in 1950, it improved sharply to six in 1954 and subsequently participated in centre-left coalitions in 1963–66, 1974–80 and 1985–88. It again won six seats in the 1988 election and joined a coalition headed by the People's Party (Fkfl), but this finally collapsed in October 1990.

The Tjfl fell back to four seats in the November 1990 election and was in opposition until joining a coalition headed by the Social Democratic Party in April 1993. It again won four seats in the July 1994 election, after which it went into opposition. It returned to government after advancing to eight seats (with 23.8% of the vote) in the April 1998 elections, joining a coalition headed by the Fkfl and also including the Self-Government Party.

The Tjfl was the prime mover of the Kallsberg government's announcement in February 2001 that a referendum would be held in May on its plan to phase out dependence on Danish subsidies over a 10-year period and to hold a full independence referendum in 2012. It was therefore greatly displeased when Kallsberg's Fkfl quickly backed away from the plan, although it eventually agreed to remain in the coalition on the basis of an agreement to shelve the speedy referendum plan and to concentrate instead on laying the economic foundations of full sovereignty.

The party one of the two seats in the *Folketing* in the Danish elections of November 2001. In the 2002 Faroes election, the Tjfl repeated the result of 1998, again winning eight seats (23.7% of the vote). The governing coalition of 1998 stayed in power, with the addition of the small Centre Party (one seat).

Self-Government Party
Sjálvstyrisflokkurin (Sjfl)

Address. Postboks 131, FO-600 Saltangará
Email. post@sjalvstyrisflokkurin.fo
Website. www.sjalvstyrisflokkurin.fo
Leadership. Helena Dam A. Neystabø (chairperson)

Also known in English as the Home-Rule Party, the Sjfl was founded in 1906 by the poet Joannes Patursson to campaign for real powers for the Faroes parliament (which then had a consultative role) and the preservation of the Faroese language. Opposing the pro-Danish line of the Union Party (Sbfl), it won 51.7% of the popular vote in 1916 (but not a parliamentary majority) and 49.8% in 1918, when it obtained an absolute majority of seats for the first (and so far only) time. Following the defection of its left wing to the Social Democratic Party (Jvfl) in 1928, a right-wing faction broke away in 1940 to join the People's Party (Fkfl), leaving the rump Sjfl as a centrist party. Having fallen to 16.7% and four seats in 1940, the Sjfl was unrepresented from 1943 to 1946, when it regained two seats in an electoral alliance with the Jvfl.

From the granting of home rule to the Faroes in 1948, the party was a partner in coalition governments in 1948–50 and 1954–75 and was then opposition until until January 1981, when it joined a centre-right coalition with the Union Party (Sbfl) and the Fkfl. Having slipped to one seat in 1966, the

Sjfl recovered to two in 1974 and went up to three in 1980. After losing one seat in the 1984 election (on a slightly higher vote share), it entered a centre-left coalition headed by the Jvfl. After retaining two seats in the November 1988 election, it joined a centre-right coalition headed by the Fkfl but withdrew in June 1989. In early elections in November 1990 it moved back to three seats but remained in opposition until April 1993, when it joined another centre-left coalition.

The Sjfl slipped back to two seats in July 1994 (with 5.6% of the vote) but nevertheless joined a four-party coalition headed by the Sbfl. It continued in government after the April 1998 elections, in which it again won two seats (with 7.7% of the vote), joining a three-party coalition headed by the Fkfl and also including the Tjfl.

The Sjfl strongly backed the Kallsberg government's announcement in February 2001 that a referendum would be held in May on its plan to phase out dependence on Danish subsidies over a 10-year period and to hold a full independence referendum in 2012. It was therefore strongly critical of Kallsberg's Fkfl when it quickly reneged on the plan, although it agreed to remain in the coalition on the basis of an agreement to shelve the referendum plan and to concentrate instead on laying the economic foundations of full sovereignty.

The party once more slipped back to one seat (4.4% of the vote) in the 2002 elections, but remained in government, again in alliance with the Fkfl and the Tjfl, with the addition of the Centre Party.

Social Democratic Party
Javnadarflokkurin (Jvfl)

Address. Áarvegur 2, Postboks 208, FO-100 Tórshavn
Telephone. (00298) 312–493
Fax. (00298) 319–397
Email. hps@hagstova.fo
Website. www.javnadarflokkurin.fo
Leadership. Jóannes Eidesgaard (chairman); Eydolvur Dimon (secretary-general)

Its Faroese title meaning "Equality Party", the Jvfl dates from 1925 and first gained representation in 1928, when it was strengthened by the adhesion of a splinter group of the Self-Government Party (Sjfl). After making a breakthrough to six seats in 1936, it was a member of the first home rule government in 1948–50 and in 1958 became the strongest parliamentary party, winning eight seats out of 30 and forming a coalition with the Sjfl and the Union Party (Sbfl) under the premiership of Peter Mohr Dam. It was to retain a narrow plurality until 1978, although 27.6% was its highest vote share. In opposition from 1962, the Jvfl returned to government in 1966 and was continuously in office until 1980, providing the Chief Minister in 1966–68 and in 1970–80, latterly in the person of Atli Dam. After four years in opposition, the Jvfl again became the largest party in 1984, with eight seats out of 32, enabling Atli Dam to form a centre-left coalition with the Sjfl, the Republican Party (Tjfl) and the Christian People's Party/Progressive and Fishing Industry Party (KF/FFF).

A shift to the right in the 1988 election reduced the Jvfl to seven seats and consigned it to opposition. An early election in November 1990 restored the Jvfl to plurality status, with 10 seats, so that in January 1991 Atli Dam formed a two-party coalition with the People's Party (Fkfl). In April 1993 Atli Dam was succeeded as Jvfl leader and Chief Minister by Marita Petersen, but in October 1993 the Fkfl withdrew from the government and was replaced by the Tjfl and the Sjfl. In the July 1994 election the Jvfl went down to a heavy defeat, winning only five seats (and 15.4% of the vote), partly because of competition from the new Workers' Front (Vf). It nevertheless joined a new coalition headed by the Sbfl and including the Sjfl and the Vf.

The Jvfl went into opposition after the April 1998 elections, despite increasing its representation to seven seats on a 21.9% vote share. In the previous month's Danish elections, the Jvfl had won one of the two Faroes seats in the metropolitan legislature, although its representative (Jóannes Eidesgaard) did not formally join the Danish Social Democratic Party group. However, in the 2001 Danish elections it lost its seat in the *Folketing*, and in the Faroe elections of 2002 it retained seven seats (with 20.9% of the votes), but remained in the opposition.

The party has a membership of 1,800.

Union Party
Sambandsflokkurin (Sbfl)

Address. Gongin 10, PO Box 1340, FO-110 Tórshavn
Telephone. (00298) 318–870
Fax. (00298) 318–910
Email. samband@post.olivant.fo
Leadership. Lisbeth L. Petersen (chairperson)
The conservative Sbfl was founded in 1906 in support of the maintenance of close relations between the islands and the Danish Crown and therefore in opposition in particular to the Self-Government Party (Sjfl). It won 62.4% of the vote in its first election in 1906 and 73.3% in 1910, remaining the majority parliamentary party until 1918, when it was overtaken by the Sjfl. It recovered its dominance in the 1920s, but the advent of the Social Democratic Party (Jvfl) in 1925 heralded increasing fragmentation of the party structure. In 1936 the Sbfl vote dropped sharply to 33.6% and since 1943 the party has never exceeded a 30% share. Following the introduction of home rule in 1948, the Sbfl provided the Faroes' Chief Minister until 1958: Andreas Samuelsen headed a coalition of the Jvfl and the Sjfl in 1948-50, while Kristian Djurhuus led one with the People's Party (Fkfl) in 1950–54 and another with the Fkfl and the Sjfl in 1954–58. It continued in government in 1958–62, but went into opposition after the 1962 election, in which it won only six seats and 20.5% of the vote.

Although it remained at six seats in the 1966 election, it entered a coalition with the Jvfl and the Sjfl that lasted until 1974, with then party leader Pauli Ellefsen holding the premiership in 1968–70. Having slipped to five seats and 19.1% in the 1974 election, the Sbfl won a narrow plurality in 1978 (eight seats and 26.3% of the vote) but remained in opposition. It retained eight seats on a 23.9% vote share in the 1980 contest, following which Ellefsen formed a coalition with the Fkfl and the Sjfl that lasted until 1984. In the latter year it slipped to seven seats (and 21.2%) and reverted to opposition status, subsequently registering an identical electoral result in 1988. In June 1989 the Sbfl joined a coalition headed by the Fkfl and including the Republican Party (Tjfl), but this collapsed in October 1990, causing an early election the following month in which the Sbfl won six seats.

After four years in opposition, the Sbfl became the largest party in the July 1994 election, with eight seats, and subsequently formed a coalition with the Jvfl, the Sjfl and the new Workers' Front under the premiership of Sbfl leader Edmund Jønsen. The Sbfl again won one of the two Faroes seats in the March 1998 Danish elections, its deputy opting to join the Conservative People's Party parliamentary group in Copenhagen. In the April 1998 Faroes polling, the Sbfl fell back to six seats (with 18.0% of the vote) and returned to opposition status. In March 2001 Jønsen was replaced as party leader by Lisbeth L. Petersen, a former mayor of Tórshavn.

In the 2001 Danish elections the Sbfl repeated the performance of 1998, retaining its seat in the *Folketing*, and the party was the strongest party after the Faroe elections of 2002, winnng eight seats (with 26.0% of the votes). Despite this, the party remained in opposition.

Workers' Front
Verkmannafylkingin (Vf)

Address. Árvegur, PO Box 208, 110 Tórshavn
Leadership. Óli Jacobsen (chair)
The Vf was founded in 1994 by left-wing dissidents of the Social Democratic Party (Jvfl) in alliance with some trade union leaders unhappy with the recent performance of the Jvfl in government. In its first election in July 1994 the Vf won three seats (from 9.5% of the vote) and obtained one portfolio in a coalition government headed by the right-wing Union Party and also including the Jvfl and the Self-Government Party. Its government role ended at the April 1998 election, in which it slumped to 0.8% of the vote and no seats.

GREENLAND

Capital: Nuuk (Godthaab)
Population: 56,000 (2000E)

The Arctic island of Greenland is a part of the Kingdom of Denmark but has had internal self-government since May 1979, as approved by referendum in January 1979 by 70.1% of participating voters. Greenland accordingly has its own 31-member parliament (*Landsting*), which is popularly elected by proportional representation, and a government (*Landsstyre*) with responsibility for internal economic and social affairs, while the Danish government retains responsibility for foreign affairs, defence and monetary policy. Greenland entered the European Community (later Union) in 1973 as part of Denmark, but withdrew with effect from Feb. 1, 1985, on the strength of a local referendum decision against membership in February 1982.

Elections to the *Landsting* on Dec. 3, 2002, resulted as follows: Forward (*Siumut*) 10 seats (with 28.7% of the vote), Eskimo Community (*Inuit Ataqatigiit*) 8 (25.5%), Community Party (*Atassut*) 7 (20.4%), Democrats 5 (15.6%), Independents (*Katusseqatigiit*) 1 (5.3%). The 2001 elections to the Danish *Folketing* in Greenland resulted in the *Siumut* and *Inuit Ataqatigiit* parties winning a seat each.

Centre Party
Akulliit Partiiat (AP)

Address. PO Box 456, 3900 Nuuk
Leadership. Bjarne Kreutzmann (chairman)
The liberal pro-market AP was formed prior to the 1991 Greenland election, in which it won two seats in the *Landsting*. It retained two seats in the March 1995 election and remained in opposition. It failed to gain representation in both the 1999 and 2002 elections.

Community Party
Atassut

Address. PO Box 399, 3900 Nuuk
Telephone. (00299) 323–366
Fax. (00299) 325–840
Email. atassut@greennet.gl
Website. www.atassut.gl
Leadership. Augusta Salling (chairperson); Finn Karlsen (political vice-chairman); Ellen Christoffersen (organization vice-chairman)
Describing itself as "Greenland's liberal party", the centrist *Atassut* was founded in 1978 and achieved official status as a political party in 1981 under the leadership of Lars Chemnitz, who was chair of the pre-autonomy Greenland council. In the April 1979 election preceding the move to autonomy it was defeated by the Forward (*Siumut*) party and went into opposition, from where it campaigned in favour of

Greenland remaining in the European Community in the 1982 referendum—unsuccessfully as it turned out. *Atassut* retained opposition status after the 1983 election despite winning a larger popular vote than Forward, which got the same number of seats. Chemnitz resigned the party leadership in March 1984 and *Atassut* lost ground in the June 1984 election, therefore remaining in opposition.

In the May 1987 election *Atassut* again overtook *Siumut* in popular vote terms but won the same number of seats (11) and therefore continued in opposition. Its status was not changed by the 1991 contest, in which it fell back to eight seats, but in March 1995 *Atassut* won 25.3% of the vote and 10 seats (out of 31) and accepted participation in a coalition headed by *Siumut*. However, *Atassut* slipped back to eight seats (and 25.3% of the vote) in the February 1999 *Landsting* elections, going into opposition to a coalition of *Siumut* and the Eskimo Community. Again in the 2002 elections, *Atassut* slipped further back to 7 seats (20.4% of the vote) and remained in the opposition.

Atassut has consistently returned one of Greenland's two members of the *Folketing* in Copenhagen, where its deputy usually sits in the parliamentary group of the Danish Liberal Party (*Venstre*).

Eskimo Community
Inuit Ataqatigiit (IA)
Address. PO Box 321, 3900 Nuuk
Telephone. (00299) 323702
Fax. (00299) 323232
Email. inuit.ataqatigiit@greennet.gl
Website. www.ia.gl
Leadership. Josef Motzfeldt (chairman)
The IA was founded in 1978 by a group of Marxist-Leninists who had been active in the Young Greenland Council in Copenhagen and who opposed the home rule arrangements then being negotiated, advocating instead Greenland's "total independence from the capitalist colonial power". The new party also urged that Greenland citizenship should be restricted to those with at least one Eskimo parent and that the US military base at Thule should be closed. Having failed to persuade Greenlanders to vote against home rule in the January 1979 referendum, the IA failed to obtain representation in the April 1979 election, but was on the winning side in the 1982 referendum in which Greenlanders voted to leave the European Community. Having effectively absorbed the small Wage-Earners' Party (*Sulissartut*), the IA won two seats in the 1983 Greenland election. It increased to three seats in the next contest in 1984, when it joined a coalition government headed by the Forward (*Siumut*) party.

The coalition collapsed in March 1987 after the then IA leader, Aqqaluk Lynge, had accused the *Siumut* Chief Minister of being "totally passive" in the face of the US government's enhancement of the Thule base. Having improved to four seats in the resultant May 1987 election, the IA joined another coalition with *Siumut* with increased ministerial responsibilities, but again withdrew in 1988. The IA moved up to five seats in the March 1991 election and again formed a coalition with *Siumut*, under a new Chief Minister. In the March 1995 election the IA made further progress, to six seats (out of 31) and 20.3% of the vote, but went into opposition after failing to persuade *Siumut* to take up its revived demand for complete independence for Greenland.

The IA gained further ground in the February 1999 *Landsting* election, winning seven seats and a vote share of 20.3%. Having moderated its pro-independence line, it joined a coalition government with *Siumut*, receiving two portfolios out of seven as well as the presidency of the *Landsting*.

In the 2001 Danish election, the IA won a seat in the *Folketing* and in the 2002 *Landsting* elections, it was the sec-

ond-strongest party with eight seats and 25.5% of the vote. It once again joined *Siumut* in a two-party government coalition.

Forward
Siumut
Address. PO Box 357, 3900 Nuuk
Telephone. (00299) 322–077
Fax. (00299) 322–319
Email. siumut@greennet.gl
Website. www.siumut.gl
Leadership. Jonathan Motzfeldt (chairman); Vittus Qujaukitsoq (secretary)
The socialist *Siumut* party was founded in July 1977, derived from earlier pro-autonomy groups and the political review *Siumut*. Having supported the autonomy arrangements approved by referendum in January 1979, *Siumut* won an absolute majority of 13 seats (out of 21) in the April 1979 election and formed Greenland's first home rule government under the premiership of Jonathan Motzfeldt. Opposed to Greenland's membership of the European Community, *Siumut* campaigned successfully for a vote in favour of withdrawal in the 1982 referendum.

In the April 1983 election the party slipped to 11 seats (out of 24) but continued as a minority government until another election in June 1984, when it again won 11 seats (out of 25) and formed a majority coalition with the small Eskimo Community (IA). The coalition collapsed in March 1987, amid dissension over the status of the US military base at Thule, and *Siumut* retained 11 seats (out of 27) in the resultant May 1987 election, whereupon Motzfeldt sought to negotiate a "grand coalition" with the Community (*Atassut*) party. This provoked opposition from within *Siumut*, the eventual outcome being a further left-wing coalition with the IA.

Triggered by allegations of corruption among government ministers, an early election in May 1991 resulted in *Siumut* again winning 11 seats (out of 27) and forming a new coalition with the IA, although Motzfeldt was obliged, in view of the scandal, to vacate the premiership and *Siumut* leadership in favour of Lars Emil Johansen. In the next election in March 1995 *Siumut* won 38.5% of the vote and 12 seats (out of 31), but attempts to reconstitute the *Siumut*/IA combination foundered on the IA's revived demand for complete independence for Greenland. The outcome was the formation of a "grand coalition" between *Siumut* and *Atassut* committed to maintaining Greenland's autonomous status.

Motzfeldt regained the *Siumut* leadership and the premiership in September 1997 when Johansen accepted appointment as deputy director of the state fisheries company. In the February 1999 *Landsting* election *Siumut* slipped to 11 seats and 35.3% of the vote. It nevertheless formed a coalition government with the IA (the latter having moderated its pro-independence aim) under the continued premiership of Motzfeldt.

Siumut won a seat in the *Folketing* in the 2001 Danish election (its deputy usually sits in the parliamentary group of the Danish Social Democratic Party), and in the 2002 *Landsting* elections it was the strongest party with ten seats and 28.7% of the vote. It retained its position as leader of a two-party government coalition with the Eskimo Community.

Independents
Kattusseqatigiit
Address. c/o Landsting, 3900 Nuuk
Leadership. Anthon Frederiksen (chairman)
This pro-business and anti-independence grouping of independents won 12.3% of the vote and four seats (out of 31) in the February 1999 *Landsting* election, following which it formed part of the parliamentary opposition. In 2002 election it slipped back to one seat (5.3% of the vote) and remained in the opposition.

Djibouti

Capital: Djibouti
Population: 702,000 (UN, 2003)

The French Territory of the Afars and the Issas became the Republic of Djibouti in 1977. The country has a largely Muslim population with two main ethnic groups, the Issa of Somali origin and the Afar of Ethiopian origin. After independence, Djibouti was left with a government which initially tried to maintain a balance between the two groups. However, by 1981, the country's first President, Hassan Gouled Aptidon, installed an authoritarian one-party state dominated by his own Issa community. The Popular Rally for Progress (RPP) was the ruling party, but Afar resentment erupted into a civil war in the early 1990s.

Under pressure from France, President Gouled introduced a limited multi-party system in 1992. A total of four parties were allowed to compete for the 65-member Chamber of Deputies, although in the December 1992 poll only three were registered, one of which, the National Democratic Party, withdrew before balloting began. The rebels from the Afar party, the Front for the Restoration of Unity and Democracy (FRUD), were not allowed to participate. As a result, Gouled's RPP eclipsed its only rival, the Party of Democratic Renewal (PDR) and took all 65 seats. The civil war continued. It largely ended in 1994 with a power-sharing deal which brought the main faction of FRUD into government. In legislative elections in December 1997, the RPP in alliance with the FRUD won all 65 seats with 78.6% of the vote. The opposition Party of Democratic Renewal (PRD) and the National Democratic Party fielded candidates but failed to gain representation.

In the presidential election in April 1999, Ismail Omar Guelleh of the RPP succeeded his uncle, Hassan Gouled Aptidon, and was elected as Djibouti's second president. Meanwhile, a radical splinter faction of the FRUD that had continued to fight President Gouled's government, signed a peace deal with the government of President Guelleh in 2000.

The 1992 law limiting competition with the ruling party expired in September 2002, opening the way for Djibouti's first full multi-party election since independence. In January 2003, a coalition of parties supporting President Guelleh, the Union for a Presidential Majority (UMP), a coalition that included RPP, FRUD, PPSD and PND, defeated an opposition group of parties, the Union for a Democratic Alternative (UAD), a coalition that encompassed the ARD, MRDD, UDJ and PDD. The UMP gained 62.7% of the votes cast while the opposition took 37.3%.

Under Djibouti's winner-takes-all electoral system, the party that obtains a majority in a constituency wins all of its parliamentary seats. So while the UAD won more than one-third of the vote in 2003, it failed to win any of the 65 seats in the assembly. However, according to the leader of the UAD, Ahmed Dini, this alliance was the victim of fraud rather than just an unfair electoral system. A dozen foreign observers monitored the election and seemed to uphold some complaints of disenfranchisement in what was otherwise a smoothly run election.

The 2003 election also marked, for the first time, the election of women to Djibouti's national assembly. This followed enactment of a law forcing political parties to put forward female candidates.

Thus, in the space of 27 years of independence, Djibouti has evolved from a one-party state to a fledgling multi-party democracy. However, a range of factors could in the future weaken or strengthen recent political trends. On the one hand, the resumption of ethnic strife cannot be completely ruled out. While a number of Afars currently hold cabinet posts, it is clear that the Issas dominate the government, civil service and the ruling party. This is a situation that continues to breed resentment and political competition between the Somali Issas and the Afars.

On the other hand, Djibouti continues to strengthen its ties with key Western countries. Bordering Eritrea, Ethiopia and Somalia in the troubled Horn of Africa, Djibouti commands an important geo-strategic position. It overlooks the busy sea lanes where the Red Sea, the Gulf of Aden and the Indian Ocean converge. Moreover, since the 1998-2000 border war between Ethiopia and Eritrea, the country's capital, Djibouti city, has become a major transshipment point for goods entering or leaving landlocked Ethiopia. It not only hosts some 2,700 troops from the former colonial power, France, but, following the terrorist attacks of September 11, provides a military base for 900 US troops. According to President Guelleh, the expanded foreign presence in Djibouti has generated considerable economic benefits for his small country. He will be reluctant, therefore, to jeopardise Djibouti's economic gains by appearing to take actions which, in the eyes of the USA and France, could undermine the country's new political direction.

Front for the Restoration of Unity and Democracy
Front pour la Restauration de l'Unité et de la Démocratie (FRUD)

Address. c/o Chambre des Députés, Djibouti
Leadership. Ali Mohamed Daoud (president); Ahmed Ougoureh Kifleh Ahmed (secretary-general)

The FRUD was formed in 1991 by the merger of three Afar groups: Action for the Revision of Order in Djibouti (*Action pour la Révision de l'Ordre à Djibouti*, AROD), the Front for the Restoration of Right and Equality (*Front pour la Restauration du Droit et l'Egalité*, FRDE) and the Djibouti Patriotic Resistance Front (*Front de la Résistance Patriotique de Djibouti*, FRPD). Advocating fair representation in government of Djibouti's different ethnic groups, the FRUD began an armed insurgency against the regime in late 1991.

Factional divisions in the organization led in the first half of 1994 to the emergence of a new leadership, under Ali Mohamed Daoud, favouring negotiations with the government to end the civil war. This culminated in a peace agreement in December 1994, providing for an immediate ceasefire and revision of the constitution and of electoral lists before the next elections. It also provided for an alliance between the FRUD led by Daoud and the ruling Popular Rally for Progress. The agreement, which led to the inclusion of two FRUD members in the government in 1995, was condemned by the faction of the ousted former FRUD leader, Ahmed Dini Ahmed, as a "betrayal" of the organization's aims. In April 1997, the pro-government faction of the FRUD convened its first party conference. Confirming its earlier power sharing agreement, it contested the December elections of that year with the RPP; it secured 11 of the 65 alliance seats and participated in the new government. The FRUD armed wing, which had split from the main party in 1994 and had launched a series of military attacks against the regime, signed a peace agreement with the government on May 12, 2001, apparently marking the end of Djibouti's civil war. In the 2003 elections the FRUD formed part of the pro-government Union for a Presidential Majority.

Party of Democratic Renewal
Parti du Renouveau Démocratique (PRD)

Address. BP 2198, Djibouti

Leadership. Abdullahi Hamareiteh (president); Maki Houmed Gaba (secretary-general)

The PRD was formed in September 1992 to succeed the Movement for Peace and Reconciliation, which had been launched six months earlier by Mohamed Djama Elabe. Advocating the establishment of democratic parliamentary government, the PRD was the only opposition party to take part in the 1992 legislative elections, but was not awarded any seats despite being credited with about a quarter of the vote. Djama Elabe was the runner-up in the 1993 presidential election, with a 22% share of the poll.

Hamareiteh was elected as the party's new president in May 1997 to succeed Djama Elabe, who had died in late 1996. The PRD failed to secure any seats in the December 1997 elections, although it polled around 19% of the vote. In 1999, the PRD backed the unsuccessful candidate of a coalition of opposition factions (Moussa Ahmed Idriss) in the presidential elections. The editor-in-chief of the party journal *Le Renouveau*, Daher Ahmed Farah, who had entered politics in 1992 and was a founding member of the PRD, was sentenced to six months imprisonment in October 1999 for "spreading false news".

Popular Rally for Progress
Rassemblement Populaire pour le Progrès (RPP)

Address. c/o Chambre des Députés, Djibouti

Leadership. Ismael Omar Guelleh (chairman)

The RPP was set up in 1979, its main component being the African People's League for Independence (*Ligue Populaire Africaine pour l'Indépendance*, LPAI), which was a primarily Issa-supported organization prior to the country's accession to independence in 1977. The RPP was the ruling party under the single-party system from 1981, and was the first political group to be legalized under the pluralist constitution of 1992. Maintaining its grip on political power, the party took all the seats in the December 1992 elections to the Chamber of Deputies, and in the following year Hassan Gouled Aptidon was re-elected President of the Republic for a third six-year term.

In December 1994 the RPP signed a peace agreement with the Front for the Restoration of Unity and Democracy (FRUD). The party retained power in the 1997 parliamentary elections, winning 54 of the 65 alliance seats and forming a coalition government with the FRUD. In February 1999 Gouled Aptidon announced his intention to retire from politics. The party named his nephew and chief of staff, Guelleh, as its presidential candidate for the April elections, and he was returned in the poll with a 74.1% share of the vote. Guelleh has favoured continuing Djibouti's traditionally strong ties with France and has played an important role in trying to reconcile the different factions in neighbouring Somalia.

National Democratic Party
Parti National Democratique (PND)

Leadership. Aden Robleh Awaleh (chairman)

The PND was founded in 1992 by Aden Robleh Awaleh, a former cabinet minister and vice-president of the ruling Popular Rally for Progress (RPR) who, from exile, was active in anti-government groupings from 1986. The PND withdrew from the December 1992 legislative elections and subsequently appealed for the formation of a transitional government of national unity to supervise the implementation of democratic reforms. Robleh Awaleh came third in the May 1993 presidential election, attracting about 12% of the vote. In November 1995 he received a one-month suspended prison sentence for illegally organizing an opposition demonstration.

The PND participated, but failed to secure representation, in the 1997 legislative elections. Its presidential candidate, Moussa Ahmed Idriss (representing an opposition coalition which included the Party of Democratic Renewal (PRD) and the Dini faction of the Front for the Restoration of Unity and Democracy), stood alone against Guelleh of the RPR in the April 1999 presidential elections. He was defeated, attracting 25% of the vote. In the 2003 elections the PND formed part of the Union for a Presidential Majority.

Other Parties and Groups

Alliance for Democracy (ARD), established in 2002; member of the Union for a Democratic Alternative in the 2003 elections.
Leadership. Ahmed Dini Ahmed

Centrist and Democratic Reforms Party (*Parti Centriste et des Réformes Démocratiques*, PCRD), formed in late 1993 by a breakaway faction of the Front for the Restoration of Unity and Democracy.
Leadership. Hassan Abdallah Watta (chairman)

Djibouti Democratic Union (*Union Démocratique Djiboutienne*, UDD), primarily Gadabursi (ethnic) party formed in January 1992.
Leadership. Mahdi Ibrahim God

Djibouti Development Party (PDD), established in 2002; member of the Union for a Democratic Alternative in the 2003 elections.
Leadership. Mohamed Daoud Chehem

Front for the Liberation of the Somali Coast (*Front pour la Libération de la Côte des Somalis*, FLCS), an Issa-supported group, urging that Djibouti be incorporated into a greater Somalia.
Leadership. Abdallah Waberi Khalif (chairman)

Group for Democracy and the Republic (*Groupe pour la Démocratie et la République*, GDR), formed in 1996 by a dissident faction of the Popular Rally for Progress (RPP) which included 13 of the 65 members of the chamber of deputies. Party leader Bahdon Farah had opposed the 1994 peace agreement with the Front for the Restoration of Unity and Democracy and the faction of the RPP supporting Ismael Omar Guelleh's candidacy for the presidency. He was dismissed from his positions as Minister of Justice and Islamic affairs and member of the RPP's executive committee, and was sentenced to six months imprisonment in 1996 for "insulting the head of state".
Leadership. Moumin Bahdon Farah

Movement for the Democratic Revival and Development (MRDD), established in 2002; member of the Union for a Democratic Alternative in the 2003 elections.
Leadership. Daher Ahmed Farah

Movement for Unity and Democracy (*Mouvement pour l'Unité et la Démocratie,* MUD), launched in 1990 campaigning in favour of a pluralist democratic system. The party leader was an unsuccessful candidate in the 1993 presidential election, taking fourth place.
Leadership. Mohammed Moussa Ali Tourtour

Peoples Social Democratic Party (PPSD), established in 2002; part of the Union for a Presidential Majority in the 2003 elections.
Leadership. Moumin Bahdon Farah

Union for Justice and Democracy (UDJ), established in 2002; member of the Union for a Democratic Alternative in the 2003 elections.

Dominica

Capital: Roseau
Population: 70,000 (2003E)

The Commonwealth of Dominica gained its independence from the United Kingdom as a republic in 1978. The head of state is the President, who is elected by Parliament for not more than two five-year terms in office. The head of government is the Prime Minister. The legislature is the unicameral House of Assembly. Its 32 members comprise 21 members elected for five-year terms in single seat constituencies on the first past the post system, nine appointed senators, the Speaker and one ex-officio member.

There are three political parties, the Dominica Freedom Party (DFP), the Dominica Labour Party (DLP) and the United Workers' Party (UWP), each of which has had a period in government since independence. The DFP was in office from 1980-95, but lost power to the UWP in the June 1995 election. Further elections on January 31, 2000, resulted in the DLP winning 10 seats with 43.1 percent of the vote, the UWP nine seats (43.3 percent) and the DFP two seats (13.6 percent). The following month the DLP formed a coalition government (the first since the establishment of ministerial government in 1956) with the DFP. Turnout in the election was 60.2 percent.

Dominica Freedom Party (DFP)
Address. 37 Great George Street, Roseau
Telephone. (1-767) 448-2104
Fax. (1-767) 448-1795
Email. dominicafree@hotmail.com
Leadership. Charles Savarin (leader)
The conservative DFP came to power, under the forceful leadership of its founder (later Dame) Eugenia Charles, the first woman Prime Minister in the Caribbean, in an overwhelming election victory in 1980 after a period of national political crisis following independence in 1978. The party then retained office, although with decreasing electoral majorities, until the June 1995 election (at which Charles retired from political life), when it won only five seats despite coming first in the popular vote.

The DFP took only two seats in the January 2000 election and entered a coalition government as minority partner with the DLP, its one-time bitter rival. However, the DFP presence in the coalition and the governing coalition itself was weakened in November 2002 when Freedom Party MP Frederick Baron withdrew his support from the government. In justifying the move Brown cited a loss of confidence in Prime Minister Pierre Charles' handling of the economy. Brown's decision left the government with a majority of one seat. Former diplomat Charles Savarin has led the DFP since 1996. It is a member of the Caribbean Democrat Union.

Dominica Labour Party (DLP)
Address. 64 Cork Street, Roseau
Telephone/Fax. (1-767) 448-8511
Email. jillian_charles@hotmail.com
Leadership. Roosevelt Skerrit (leader)
The centre-left (and formerly left wing) DLP was in office at independence in 1978 but was subsequently weakened by internal schisms and lost power to the conservative DFP in

1980. In 1981 the Dominican Defence Force was disbanded after being implicated in a plot by supporters of former DLP Prime Minister Patrick John to overthrow the government. John was himself convicted in 1986 for his involvement and served a prison term before being released in 1990 and returning to political life.

The DLP retained a minority position in successive elections from 1985 until January 2000, when it won the largest number of seats (10 of the 21) although polling slightly fewer votes than the governing UWP, which took nine seats. DLP campaign themes in the 2000 election included criticism of the UWP government for corruption and alleged sale of passports to Mafia figures taking advantage of Dominica's lax financial regulation. A new government was formed under DLP leader (1992-2000) Roosevelt (Rosie) Douglas. The new government had the support of the two members of the DFP, although the parties had in earlier decades been bitterly opposed.

However, Douglas died in office on October 1, 2000, and was succeeded as Prime Minister and party leader by Pierre Charles. Under Charles' leadership, the DLP/DFP governing coalition was placed under severe strain because of political infighting and a worsening economic situation that required a series of unpopular austerity measures. The government's weakness was further exacerbated after Prime Minister Charles suffered a number of serious health scares during 2003. On Jan. 6, 2004, Charles died of heart failure, the second time in less than four years that a Dominican prime minister had died in office. Charles' replacement as Prime Minister and leader of the DLP was Roosevelt Skerrit, the Education, Sports and Youth Affairs Minister in the previous government, and at 31 the country's youngest-ever Prime Minister. A new cabinet was sworn in on Jan. 9, with the most controversial appointment being Ambrose George as Minister of Agriculture and the Environment, who subsequently also gained the DLP deputy leadership. George had previously served as Finance Minister in the Charles administration, but was dismissed in 2001 following a money laundering scandal. The DLP was given a boost in early April 2004 when the party easily retained the parliamentary seat left vacant after the death of Pierre Charles.

The DLP is a consultative member of the Socialist International.

United Workers' Party (UWP)
Address. 47 Cork Street, Roseau
Telephone. (1-767) 448-5051
Fax. (1-767) 449-8448
Email. uwp@cwdom.dm
Website. www.unitedworkersparty.com
Leadership. Edison James (leader); Ron Green (president)
The UWP was established in 1988 and became the official opposition following the 1990 election when it came second to the DFP, winning six seats in the House of Assembly. In the June 1995 election the UWP won 11 of the 21 elected seats (although polling fewer votes than the DFP) and formed the government with Edison James, a former leader of the banana growers' association, becoming Prime Minister. Under James the government sought to reduce Dominica's dependence on agriculture, especially bananas, and to promote financial services, although the pursuit of this policy led to allegations of abuse of Dominica's light regulatory regime by criminals engaged in money laundering.

In the January 2000 elections, despite increasing its share of the vote, the UWP won only nine seats and lost office to a coalition of the DLP and the DFP. Since losing power the UWP has undertaken an active process of opposition both inside and outside of parliament. The party has been particularly aggressive in denouncing the government's economic austerity measures, and has organized repeated demonstrations against them. However, the UWP's record in government has also been questioned after allegations of financial mismanagement and corruption were made against it.

Dominican Republic

Capital: Santo Domingo
Population: 8,715,000 (2003E)

A Spanish colony until 1821, the Dominican Republic was subjugated in 1822 by neighbouring Haiti before achieving its independence in 1844. Having been occupied by the United States from 1916 to 1924, the country was then dominated by General Rafael Trujillo from 1930, when he overthrew the elected President, until his assassination in 1961. The United States again intervened militarily in 1965 to suppress a popular rebellion against a regime that had assumed power following a military coup in 1963. In 1966, following fresh elections, a new constitution was promulgated. Under its provisions, legislative power is exercised by a bicameral Congress of the Republic (*Congreso de la República*) consisting of a 32-member Senate (*Senado*) and a 150-member Chamber of Deputies (*Cámara de Diputados*). Members of both houses are elected for four years by universal adult suffrage. Executive power lies with the President, who is also elected by direct popular vote for four years.

In presidential elections held on May 16, 2004, former President Leonel Fernández Reyna of the Dominican Liberation Party (PLD) secured a clear victory, gaining 57.1% of the vote, defeating President Hipólito Mejía Domínguez of the Dominican Revolutionary Party (PRD) and Eduardo Estrella of the Social Christian Reformist Party (PRSC). Despite the fact that all three leading presidential candidates signed a pact opposing the use of violence in the electoral campaign, several incidents of unrest were reported, and at least seven people were killed. Legislative elections held on May 16, 2002, saw the PRD gain the most votes, retaining a majority of seats in the Senate, but losing its majority in the Chamber of Deputies. The PLD and the PRSC took the other seats.

Dominican Liberation Party
Partido de la Liberación Dominicana (PLD)
Address. Avenida Independencia 401, Santo Domingo
Telephone. (1-809) 685-3540
Fax. (1-809) 687-5569)
Website. www.pld.org
Leadership. Leonel Fernández Reyna (leader); Reinaldo Pared Pérez (secretary-general)
Juan Bosch Gaviño, the founder of the Dominican Revolutionary Party (PRD), led a breakaway group from that party to form the left-wing PLD during the 1974 election campaign. The PLD secured congressional representation in all elections from 1982, although in May 1994 it retained only 13 of the 44 seats in the Chamber of Deputies that it had won in the 1990 polling. An earlier serious factional split in 1992 had resulted in the defection of a large number of left-wing party members who subsequently formed the Alliance for Democracy (APD). As the PLD presidential candidate, Bosch came third in the 1978, 1982 and 1986 elections, before running a very close second to incumbent President Balaguer in 1990. Having then come a distant third in the 1994 polling, he resigned as PLD president.

Bosch's replacement, Leonel Fernández, proved more successful, wining a narrow victory against the PRD candidate in the 1996 presidential elections. The party's success was short-lived, however, since it lost heavily to the PRD in legislative and municipal elections held in May 1998. The defeat hinted at difficulties for Fernández in maintaining his presidential hold, and the party chose to select another candidate, Danilo Medina Sánchez, to contest the May 2000 presidential election. The change had little effect and the PRD candidate defeated Medina Sánchez. In the 2002 legislative and municipal elections, the party again faired poorly, unable to capitalize on public disappointment at the PRD's record in government. In a successful attempt to regain electoral credibility, the PLD looked to former President Leonel Fernández for leadership. On June 29, 2003, Fernández won the right to lead the PLD in the presidential election the following May. In the build-up to his election victory Fernández issued a five-point election manifesto, which pledged to consolidate democratic governance, restore economic stability, increase productivity and competitiveness, and improve levels of social equity.

Dominican Revolutionary Party
Partido Revolucionario Dominicano (PRD)
Address. Avda. Bolívar, Casi esquina Dr Delgado, Santo Domingo
Telephone. (1–809) 688–9735
Fax. (1–809) 688–2753
Email. prd@partidos.com
Website. www.prd.partidos.com
Leadership. Hipólito Mejía Domínguez (leader)
The left-of-centre PRD was founded in 1939 by Juan Bosch Gaviño who, having been in exile throughout the Trujillo dictatorship, returned to win the presidential election in 1962. He was deposed in a military coup in mid-1963, and in 1965 the PRD led an insurrection against the new regime that resulted in armed intervention by the USA. Having lost the subsequent elections in 1966 to the Social Christian Reformist Party (PRSC), the PRD remained in opposition for the following 12 years. During that period Bosch resigned to form the Dominican Liberation Party (PLD).

In 1978 the PRD candidate, Silvestre Antonio Guzmán Fernández, became President in the country's first peaceful and constitutional transfer of power. His party colleague, Jorge Salvador Blanco, was elected his successor in 1982 when the party also secured an absolute majority in both houses of Congress. During the Blanco regime the PRD experienced internal divisions between a pro-government bloc and rival centre-right and centre-left factions, led respectively by Jacobo Majluta Azar and José Fransisco Peña Gómez. Majluta registered his faction of the PRD (the Liberal Party for Restructuring, PLE) as a separate political party in 1985, but nevertheless secured the PRD's nomination as presidential candidate in the 1986 contest (which he lost), while Peña Gómez succeeded him as PRD president.

In 1994 a revived PRD, in coalition with the Democratic Unity (UD), won 15 seats in the Senate and 57 in the Chamber of Deputies. Peña Gómez took second place by a very narrow margin in the presidential race, which prompted accusations by the PRD of widespread irregularities and led to the party boycotting Congress from August 1994. In the presidential elections of 1996 the PLD candidate, Leonel Fernández, narrowly defeated Peña Gómez, making his third bid for the presidency.

In May 1998 the PRD swept to victory in legislative and municipal elections, despite the death of Peña Gómez a week before polling. Under new leader Hipólito Mejía Domínguez, the party won 83 seats in the newly enlarged 150-seat Chamber of Deputies and 24 seats in the 30-member Senate. The PRD also took control of some 90% of the country's municipalities, including the capital, Santa

Domingo. Mejía Domínguez went on to win the presidential elections of May 2000, as candidate of the PRD and six small allied parties. Despite his winning less than an absolute majority in the first round of voting, his two challengers from the PLD and the PRSC withdrew from the race, making a second round unnecessary.

During the campaign Mejía promised wide-ranging political and economic reform, including large-scale public investment in infrastructure and social programmes. However, the country's economic performance and social conditions did not improve during Mejía's first two years in office. These failings, together with serious accusations of government corruption, resulted in periodic outbreaks of civil unrest and violence. Despite this disappointing record the PRD nonetheless remained the largest party in Congress after mid-term elections in May 2002. The party retained its majority in the Senate and although losing its majority in the lower house remained the largest party. The PRD also won 104 of 125 municipalities in local polls. However, the government's position came under increasing pressure during 2003, not helped by serious divisions over who should be the PRD's presidential candidate for the 2004 elections.

Although having previously ruled out re-election, President Mejía announced on April 27, 2003, that he would indeed run for a second term. His decision, however, was extremely controversial and unpopular within the PRD with many members criticizing his decision, accusing him of breaking his word and destroying the democratic tradition of the party. Further, as the one-term presidential limit was only abolished in 2002, some party activists questioned the legitimacy of Mejía's change of heart, arguing that he was elected under a constitution that prohibited re-election, and therefore he was still bound by that constitution. As an indication of the PRD's divisions over this issue, the PRD's president Hatuey Decamps and Vice President Milagros Ortiz Bosch, together with five other PRD members, made clear their intention to run in the party's presidential primary election. In an attempt to settle the issue a non-binding plebiscite was undertaken in October 2003 to gauge the opinion of the party's grassroots about whether Mejía should offer himself as the party's presidential candidate. The result was an overwhelming no, with over 90% of PRD members voting against Mejía's re-election bid. Despite such a result the President insisted on continuing his campaign for a second term.

As a consequence deep fissures opened up within the PRD. In December 2003, a PRD convention was held to select a presidential candidate; this resulted in victory for Hatuey Decamps, but was subsequently declared invalid by the Central Electoral Board. The party held a second convention on Jan. 18, 2004, which overwhelmingly backed the nomination of Hipólito Mejía. However, other factions of the governing party rejected the results of this convention as invalid. Nevertheless, Mejía was officially pronounced as the PRD's presidential candidate on Jan. 31. The tensions within the party were further exacerbated with the dismissal of Decamps as president of the PRD for not supporting Mejía's candidature.

The countrywide standing of President Mejía and the PRD more generally was not helped by a worsening economic crisis affecting the country. In 2003 and the early part of 2004 the peso's value against the US dollar declined dramatically, inflation rose steadily, and there were persistent power shortages. The poor economic situation precipitated growing civil unrest. On Nov. 11, 2003, at least eight people, including one policeman, were killed during violent clashes between anti-government protesters and security forces. The protest coincided with a 24-hour general strike. A two-day national strike followed at the end of January 2004, with associated violence leading to six deaths, more than 60 injuries, and over 400 arrests. The economic crisis afflicting

the country was a decisive factor in Mejía's defeat in the presidential election held in May 2004.

The PRD has been a member of the Socialist International since 1966.

Social Christian Reformist Party
Partido Reformista Social Cristiano (PRSC)

Address. Avenida San Cristobal, Ensanche, La Fe, Apdo 1332, Santo Domingo
Telephone. (1-809) 682-9581
Fax. (1-809) 567-6033
Leadership. Donald Reid Cabral (president); Federicdo Antun (secretary-general)

Joaquín Balaguer, who had been Vice-President and then President of the Republic (under the Trujillo dictatorship) between 1957 and 1962, founded the centre-right PRSC in 1964. He returned to presidential office in elections in 1966 (after the US military intervention of 1965), in which the PRSC also won a majority of seats in both houses of the new National Congress. Balaguer served three consecutive terms until his electoral defeat in 1978, when the PRSC became the main opposition party to the Dominican Revolutionary Party (PRD). Having lost the 1982 elections, Balaguer narrowly regained the presidency and the PRSC won control of both congressional houses in the 1986 polls. In 1990 Balaguer retained office but the PRSC lost its majority in the Chamber of Deputies.

While most elections since the 1960s had been marked by accusations of fraud, the outcome in May 1994 sparked a political crisis. In the presidential poll Balaguer was awarded a disputed victory by a margin of less than 1% over his PRD rival. Under the terms of an accord signed by all major parties in August 1994 to end the crisis, a fresh presidential election was to be held in November 1995 (subsequently rescheduled for May 1996 despite the opposition of the PRD) and re-election of a President to a consecutive term would be prohibited. With Balaguer barred from standing again, the PRSC nominated Jacinto Peynado as its presidential candidate. In the first round of the election in May 1996 Peynado trailed in third place with less than 18% of the vote and was eliminated from the second round run-off held at the end of June.

The PRSC, under Balaguer, was the main loser in the 1998 legislative elections, winning only two senate seats and 17 seats in the Chamber of Deputies. However, Balaguer, who was personally close to Hipólito Mejía, supported the PRD government in return for specific favours, either in the form of posts in the state apparatus, or through the de facto granting of immunity from prosecution for irregularities committed under previous PRSC administrations. The party's electoral decline continued in the May 2000 presidential election when Balaguer finished third, winning less than 25% of the vote. Former Foreign Minister Donald Reid Cabral then replaced Balaguer as party president.

In the 2002 legislative elections the PRSC strengthened its position, winning enough seats to prevent the PRD from retaining a majority in the Chamber of Deputies, but maintained its support for the government after being offered the presidency of the lower house. Despite an upturn in electoral fortunes the PRSC was undermined by a bitter leadership struggle, which came to a head in March 2003 when the party selected its candidate for the presidential election due in May 2004 – Eduardo Estrella won a narrow victory (52% to 48%) over Jacinto Peynado, but Peynado refused to concede defeat, citing fraud. Following an internal investigation, the PRSC officially declared Estrella to be its candidate. Peynado appealed against the decision, but in June the Central Electoral Board ruled in favour of Estrella and registered him as the PRSC's candidate. Despite the ruling, divisions persisted within the party in the run-up to the election, and this contributed to Estrella's poor showing in the presidential election held in May 2004.

The PRSC is affiliated to the Christian Democrat International and the International Democrat Union.

East Timor (Timor-Leste)

Capital: Dili
Population: 850,000 (2001E)

First contacted by Portuguese seafarers in the sixteenth century, the island of Timor came to be divided between Dutch and Portuguese spheres of influence. Dili, the modern capital of East Timor, was only founded in 1769, following the transfer of power eastward from the enclave territory of Oecusse-Ambeno. Long ruled from Goa or Macau, Portuguese Timor was established as a separate colony in 1896.

In May 1974 the new leftist government in Portugal announced that it would free all of its colonies. Portugal's decolonization project in East Timor, however, was interrupted on Aug. 10, 1975, by an Indonesian-backed coup d'état spearheaded by the Timorese Democratic Union (UDT). In the ensuing civil war the Revolutionary Front of Independent East Timor (Fretilin) took control of the capital, Dili, and unilaterally declared independence on Nov. 28, 1975. Fearing the establishment of a Southeast Asia "Cuba," Washington endorsed the full-scale invasion of East Timor, which occurred one day after a meeting in Jakarta on Dec. 6, 1975, between Indonesian President Suharto and visiting US President Gerald Ford and Secretary of State Henry Kissinger.

Although the Indonesian invasion and occupation of East Timor was condemned as illegal in a total of ten UN General Assembly and Security Council resolutions passed between 1975 and 1982, Indonesia ruled the territory as its 27th province. Though this annexation was never recognized internationally (Australia was an exception), neither did the international community impose sanctions upon Indonesia. Nevertheless, media exposure of the Dili massacre of Nov. 12, 1991, along with the award of the 1996 Nobel Peace Prize to Bishop Ximenes Belo and José Ramos-Horta, drew international attention to grave human rights abuses committed during the two decades of military occupation. While the armed wing of Fretilin also continued a policy of armed struggle to the end, retribution by the Indonesian armed forces led to the loss of between one quarter and one-third of the civilian population.

After the collapse of the Suharto regime in Indonesia in May 1998, President B.J. Habibie unexpectedly declared his willingness to allow a referendum in East Timor on its status. Although twice postponed owing to Indonesian-backed militia violence, the referendum held under UN auspices on Aug. 30, 1999, resulted in a 78.5% majority vote for independence. Defeat for the pro-integrationists triggered violent attacks on pro-independence supporters by militias and their Indonesia military backers, leading to massive population dislocation, thousands of deaths, and the destruction of some 70% of infrastructure. On Sept. 15, 1999, the UN Security Council authorized a multinational intervention force to restore security, to facilitate emergency humanitarian assistance, and to oversee the departure of remaining Indonesian occupation forces. The outcome was reluctantly approved by the Indonesian House of Representatives on Oct. 20, 1999, and the province was transferred to a UN-backed interim administration.

On Aug. 30, 2001, 91% of eligible voters took part in elections to a Constituent Assembly of 88 members, of whom 75 were elected by proportional representation from national party lists and 13 from single-member constituencies corresponding to East Timor's 13 districts. Of the 16 parties which contested the elections, Fretilin won 55 seats (with 57.4% of the vote), the Democratic Party 7 (8.7%), the Social Democratic Party 6 (8.2%) and the Timorese Social Democratic Association 6 (7.8%), while five parties won two seats each and three parties one seat each. Fretilin thus fell just short of the two-thirds majority that would have enabled it to adopt a new constitution without other support. Following much debate and even controversy, especially at Fretilin's guiding hand, the constitution was drafted and duly ratified in the run-up to the much-anticipated independence celebrations. In presidential elections on April 14, 2002, the historic (though no longer current) leader of Fretilin, José Alexandre (Xanana) Gusmão, was elected (non-executive) President with 82.7% of the vote, his only opponent being Francisco Xavier do Amaral. On May 15, 2002, the UN flag was lowered in East Timor – although a scaled-back assistance mission remains – and replaced by the flag of the independent Democratic Republic of Timor-Leste, this also becoming the 191st member of the UN General Assembly.

Following an electoral census conducted in mid-2004 East Timor prepared for its first local elections to be held at the end of 2004. Timorese will vote for chiefs in 433 communal regions as well as some 2,300 village leaders

Democratic Party
Partido Democrático (PD)
Address. Rua Democracia No.1, Pantai Kelapa, Dili
Leadership. Fernando de Araujo
The PD was founded in early 2001 by a number of former activists in various student circles in Java and Bali as well as by some who had returned from abroad after the departure of Indonesian forces. Fernando de Araujo, founder of Renetil, an underground student organization, was a close confidant of José Xanana Gusmão in Cipinang prison in Jakarta. It won seven seats in the August 2001 elections to the Constituent Assembly. PD's appeal is with youth, especially those educated by Indonesia.

Revolutionary Front of Independent East Timor
Frente Revolucionária do Timor-Leste Independente (Fretilin)
Address. Rua dos Martires do Patria, West Dili
Leadership. Francisco Guterres-Lu Olo (president); Mari Alkatiri (secretary-general)
Fretilin was established in 1974 with a radical Marxist programme of social reform and created its own armed wing (Falintil). Its victory in the civil war following Portugal's withdrawal in 1974 provoked Indonesian intervention and the annexation of East Timor. Fretilin then led the resistance to Indonesian occupation, but from 1987 it moved towards a more inclusive strategy of national unity under its then leader, José Xanana Gusmão. After his capture by the Indonesian authorities in 1992, a number of groups broke away from Fretilin.

In April 1998 Fretilin joined with other pro-independence groups to form the National Council for Timorese Resistance (CNRT), of which Gusmão (then still in prison, but later released) was named president and Ramos-Horta vice-president. Following the collapse of the Suharto regime in May 1998, Fretilin spearheaded the campaign which produced an overwhelming pro-independence referendum vote in August 1999 followed by Indonesia's withdrawal. From July 2000 Fretilin representatives joined a joint UN-Timorese interim administration, Ramos-Horta becoming Foreign Minister in October. But it also became clear at the August 2000 CNRT Congress held in Dili that Gusmão and Ramos-Horta had broken with Fretilin.

With the conflict over, Fretilin turned to building up its party membership, claiming 150,000 members by mid-2001. Standing on a programme that called for democracy, pluralism and mutual toleration, Fretilin confirmed its political dominance in the August 2001 Constituent Assembly elections by winning 55 of the 88 seats.

Social Democratic Party
Partido Social Democrata (PSD)
Address. Apartado 312 Correios de Dili, Dili
Leadership. Mario Vargas Carrascalão
The PSD was launched in September 2000 at a founding conference attended by former members of the Timorese Democratic Union (UDT) and also by José Alexandre (Xanana) Gusmão, the former leader of the Revolutionary Front of Independent East Timor (Fretilin). The party projects itself as a moderate, centrist alternative to Fretilin and the UDT and argues that East Timor needs effective administration rather than mass movements. In fact, the appeal of this party is restricted by its urban middle-class bias and lack of rural networks. Advocating a government of national unity, the PSD won six Constituent Assembly seats in the August 2001 elections.

Timorese Democratic Union
União Democrática Timorense (UDT)
Address. Palapago Rua da India, Dili
Email. laclubar@iinet.net.au
Website. www.fitini.net/apps/lusonews/udt2
Leadership. João Viegas Carrascalão
Founded in 1974, the UDT originally consisted of former Portuguese colonial officials and members of local elites favouring looser ties with Portugal and eventual independence. Although strongly anti-communist, it joined with the Marxist-oriented Revolutionary Front of Independent East Timor (Fretilin) to oppose integration with Indonesia. It later split with Fretilin and was forced to operate abroad during the 25-year Indonesian occupation.

In April 1998 the UDT joined with Fretilin and other pro-independence groups to form the National Council for Timorese Resistance (CNRT), which campaigned successfully for the withdrawal of the Indonesians. In the 2001 Constituent Assembly elections, it advocated a centralized, presidential system with election of local administrators and a role for village elders in solving local problems according to customary law. Having suffered a number of defections to the Social Democratic Party, the UDT won only two seats in August 2001.

Timorese Nationalist Party
Partido Nacionalista Timorense (PNT)
Address. Matadouro – Petamakan, Dili
Leadership. Alianca Araujo
Founded in July 1999 by Abilio Araujo, the expelled former Revolutionary Front of Independent East Timor (Fretilin) president-turned-businessman, the PNT originally favoured the continuation of Indonesian status for East Timor, with broad autonomy to run its own affairs, although it accepted the overwhelming pro-independence verdict of the August 1999 referendum. In the August 2001 elections it won two seats in the Constituent Assembly.

Timorese Social Democratic Association
Associação Social-Democrata Timorense (ASDT)
Address. Avenida Direitos Humanos Lecidere, Dili
Leadership. Francisco Xavier do Amaral
The ASDT leader, Francisco Xavier do Amaral, was a founding figure in the Revolutionary Front of Independent East Timor (Fretilin) and was briefly President of East Timor in 1975. Eventually expelled from the Fretilin leadership after disagreements over tactics, he was later captured by the Indonesians and spent 22 years in jail. In the August 2001 Constituent Assembly elections, the ASDT campaigned using the old Fretilin flag to win support in the countryside, especially in the highland districts of Aileu, Manufahi, and Same. It obtained six seats. With the enthusiastic backing of the Mambae-speaking people, do Amaral contested the post of President in elections held on April 14, 2002. Losing with only 17.31% of the vote to the popular Xanana Gusmão, the two embraced as compatriots rather than rivals in a non-conflictual poll in which party preferences were largely subordinated to personalities.

Other Parties

Association of Timorese Heroes (*Klibur Oan Timor Asuwain*, KOTA), originally established in 1974 as the Popular Association of Monarchists of Timor, whose leader at first accepted integration into Indonesia. Reconstituted in 2000, KOTA stands for traditional Timorese values and is primarily an association of traditional monarchical families, although it accepts universal human rights and a multi-party democracy. It won two seats in August 2001.
Leadership. Leao Pedro dos Reis

Christian Democratic Party (*Partido Democrata Cristão*, PDC), established in August 2000 after a split in the Timor Christian Democratic Party. It won two seats in August 2001.
Leadership. Antonio Ximenes

Liberal Party (*Partai Liberal*, PL), won one seat in August 2001.
Leadership. Armando Jose-Dourado da Silva

Timor Christian Democratic Party (*Partido Democrata-Cristão de Timor*, UDC/PDC*)*, a combination of two Christian parties which have co-operated, split and recombined since their founding in 2000. It won one seat in August 2001.
Leadership. Vicente da Silva Guterres

Timor People's Party (*Partido do Povo do Timor*, PPT), established in May 2000 with some support from local monarchical families and also local pro-Indonesian militias seeking East Timor's return to Indonesia. It won two seats in August 2001.
Leadership. Jacob Xavier

Timor Socialist Party (*Partido Socialista de Timor*, PST), founded in the 1990s by a student-based splinter group of the Revolutionary Front of Independent East Timor (Fretilin). The PSI advocates a socialist, classless society, it won one seat in 2001.
Leadership. Avelino Coelho da Silva

Ecuador

Capital: Quito
Population: 13,212,742 (2004E)

The Republic of Ecuador achieved independence from Spain in 1822 as part of Gran Colombia and became a separate republic in 1830. Its first 120 years were marked by frequent changes of government, particularly the period from 1925 to 1948, during which 22 heads of state held office. In 1963 the Liberal government of President José María Velasco Ibarra was toppled by a military coup. Velasco was reinstalled in 1968 for a fifth term and from 1970 assumed dictatorial powers. He was ousted by the military in 1972 and a civilian democratic government was not restored until 1979.

Under the 1979 constitution Ecuador has an executive President. The President is directly elected, together with a Vice-President, for a four-year term and is precluded from seeking re-election. If no candidate wins an absolute majority, there follows a run-off election between the two best-placed candidates. The President appoints the Cabinet and the governors of Ecuador's 20 provinces, including the Galapagos Islands. Legislative power is exercised by the unicameral National Congress (*Congreso Nacional*), which is elected for a four-year term on a national basis. It sits for a 60-day period from Aug. 10 of every year, although special sessions may be called. Congress is required by the constitution to set up four full-time legislative commissions to consider draft laws when the House is in recess. Under a set of new electoral rules approved in 1998, the number of seats in the Congress was increased from 82 to 121 and mid-term elections were abolished.

Presidential elections held in May and July 1996 were won by Abdalá Bucaram Ortiz of the populist Ecuadorian Roldosist Party (PRE). After only nine months in power, however, Bucaram was removed from office by the National Congress on grounds of mental incapacity. Fabián Alarcon Rivera, hitherto President of Congress, was appointed by the National Congress as interim President for an 18-month period. In fresh elections held on May 31 and July 12, 1998, Quito mayor Jamil Mahuad Witt of the centre-left Popular Democracy (DP) was elected as the new President. In the midst of a prolonged economic and political crisis, and after repeated calls for his resignation, President Mahuad was ousted in a bloodless coup in January 2000. After an unsuccessful attempt at installing a civilian-military junta, Mahuad was replaced by Vice-President Gustavo Noboa Bejarano. In elections held in October 2002, strong indigenous support from the Pachakutik Plurinational United Movement–New Country (MUPP-NP) helped Lucio Edwin Gutiérrez Borbua of the *Partido Sociedad Patriótica 21 de Enero* (Party of Patriotic 21 January Society, PSP) – the man who ousted Mahuad – win 58.7% of the vote in a run-off election with Alvaro Noboa Pontón of the Renewal Party of National Action (PRIAN) and take office as President in 2003.

Alfarist Radical Front
Frente Radical Alfarista (FRA)
Address. c/o Congreso Nacional, Palacio Legislativo, Piedrahita y 6 de Diciembre, Quito
Leadership. Fabián Alarcón Rivera (leader)
Founded in 1972 by dissidents from the Radical Liberal Party (PLR), the centre-left FRA was named after the leader of the 1895 Liberal Revolution, Eloy Alfaro. Although the party is small (it won only two seats in the 1998 legislative elections), it has played a major role in Ecuadorian politics in recent years. In February 1997 the party's leader and the then Speaker of the National Congress, Fabián Alarcón Rivera, was appointed as interim President for an 18-month period after President Bucaram was declared unfit to serve.

Democratic Left
Partido Izquierda Democrática (ID)
Address. Polonia 161, entre Vancouver y Eloy Alfaro, Quito
Telephone. (593–2) 564436
Fax. (593–2) 569295
Leadership. Rodrigo Borja Cevallos (leader)
Founded in 1970, the ID is a social democratic party in orientation but in office has proved to be rather conservative and neo-liberal in its economic policies. The party was formed by a faction of the Radical Liberal Party (PLR) led by Rodrigo Borja Cevallos, together with some independents and dissident members of the Ecuadorian Socialist Party (PSE).

The ID broke the long-standing rightist monopoly of power when in 1988 Borja won the presidential election and the party gained the largest number of seats in Congress. Borja's first task was to deal with Ecuador's economic problems, which he did by implementing highly unpopular austerity measures. Although modest in comparison to economic shock therapy in other Latin American countries, they lost the ID the 1990 mid-term legislative elections. In 1991 the party absorbed the left-wing *Alfaro Vive, Carajo!* (AVC) guerrilla group. The ID's candidate in the 1992 presidential poll, former Congress Speaker Raul Baca Carbo, had close links with the unpopular Borja government and consequently came a poor fourth.

The party again performed badly in the 1996 elections, making little progress in the presidential poll and winning only three legislative seats. However, it enjoyed an upsurge in support in the 1998 poll, when Borja Cevallos stood as the party's candidate and finished third, gaining over 16% of the vote. In the legislative elections the party won 17 seats. In regional and local elections held in May 2000, the ID candidate, Gen. (retd) Francisco Moncayo Gallegos, was the winner in the contest for the mayoralty of Quito. An ID Congress member, Moncayo was alleged to have been instrumental in the January 2000 coup against President Mahuad. However, he enjoyed great popularity as a result of his role in the brief war with Peru. In the 2002 presidential elections, the ID candidate, Rodrigo Borja Cevallos, came fourth with 14% of the votes and the party won 13 seats in Congress.

The ID is a member party of the Socialist International.

Democratic Popular Movement
Movimiento Popular Democrático (MPD)
Address. c/o Congreso Nacional, Palacio Legislativo, Piedrahita y 6 de Diciembre, Quito
Leadership. Maria Eugenia Lima Garzón (1998 presidential candidate)
The leftist MPD has had some limited electoral success, winning a small number of legislative seats (two in the 1998 elections) and fielding candidates in the presidential contests. In the 1998 presidential election, the MPD candidate, Maria Eugenia Lima Garzón, was eliminated in the first round of voting, gaining 2.4% of the vote.

Jaime Hurtado González, the party's founder and leader, and presidential candidate in the 1980s, was assassinated outside the National Congress building in Quito in February 1999. One of those arrested after the killing was reported to have claimed that the assassination had been ordered by right-wing Colombian paramilitaries in reprisal for Hurtado's alleged support for left-wing Colombian guerrillas. In the 2002 elections the party won three seats in Congress.

Ecuadorian Conservative Party
Partido Conservador Ecuatoriano (PCE)
Address. Wilson 578, Quito
Telephone. (593–2) 505061
Leadership. Sexto Durán-Ballén Córdovez (leader)

Dating from 1855, the right-wing PCE is Ecuador's oldest extant political party. It was founded by Gabriel García Moreno, who was assassinated in 1875 after ruling the country as a dictator for 15 years. The party has traditionally represented the country's oligarchy, the church and the army, and its ideology has remained basically unchanged despite major reorganizations, most recently in 1995, when it incorporated the Republican Unity Party (PUR) led by Sexto Durán-Ballén, who had served as President from 1992 to 1996. With the incorporation of the PUR, Durán-Ballén became the leader of the PCE, but the party's fortunes diminished and it managed to win only two seats in the 1996 and the 1998 legislative elections, and failed to win any in 2002.

Ecuadorian Roldosist Party
Partido Roldosista Ecuatoriano (PRE)

Address. c/o Congreso Nacional, Palacio Legislativo, Piedrahita y 6 de Diciembre, Quito
Leadership. Abdalá Bucaram Ortiz

The PRE was founded in 1982 by former Olympic hurdler Abdalá Bucaram Ortiz and was named after his brother-in-law, Jaime Roldos Aguilera, who served as President from 1979 until his death in 1981. The party started as a movement within Roldos's Concentration of Popular Forces (PCD), but registered as a party in its own right after Roldos's death.

The PRE's strong opposition to the post-1988 Borja government of the Democratic Left (ID) paid dividends in the 1990 legislative elections, in which the PRE increased its representation to 13 seats. The party joined forces with the Social Christian Party (PSC) and, as the dominant congressional bloc, caused the Borja government serious problems. Bucaram was selected as PRE candidate for the May 1992 presidential election, despite fears that his past adverse comments about the army might result in a military coup if he were elected. In the event, he came third with 20.7% of the vote and the party won 13 seats in the accompanying congressional elections.

The 1996 presidential election was notable for Bucaram's populist campaigning style. Bucaram, who eventually won the election in a second round of voting, adopted the nickname *El Loco* ("madman") and campaigned under the slogan "Vote for the madman, vote for the clown". He made numerous populist pledges, including the provision of low-cost housing to 200,000 poor families and the extension of social security benefits to poor peasant families. However, once in power, Bucaram adopted unpopular free-market policies designed to tackle the country's large budget deficit, including rises of up to 300% in basic utility prices. Charges of political nepotism and allegations of gross corruption fuelled cross-party demands for Bucaram's resignation and culminated in violent nationwide strikes and protests in early 1997. In February 1997 the National Congress declared Bucaram unfit to remain in office and he left the country, accusing the military of intervening to oust him.

The PRE initially nominated Marco Proaño as its next presidential candidate, but a party convention in Panama in January 1998 opted for the exiled Bucaram. His stand-in in the elections in mid-1998 was Alvaro Noboa Pontón, who came second in the first round with 26.5% of the vote and lost the run-off to Jamil Mahuad Witt of the Popular Democracy (DP). In concurrent legislative elections the PRE won 22 seats, becoming the third largest party in Congress. Following the ousting of President Mahuad in a military coup in January 2000, his successor Gustavo Noboa Bejarano (DP) appointed a government which included members of the PRE and the Social Christian Party (PSC). In the presidential elections in October, the party's candidate, Jacobo Bucaram Ortiz, came fifth with 11.9% of the vote and his party won 15 seats in Congress.

Pachakutik Plurinational United Movement–New Country
Movimiento Unidad Plurinacional Pachakutik–Nuevo País (MUPP-NP)

Address. Lugo E13-04 y Pasaje 1, Sector La Floresta, Quito
Telefax. (593-2) 560422 / (593-3) 277054 / (593-3) 277259
Email. info@pachakutik.org
Website. pachakutik.org.ec
Leadership. Freddy Ehlers Zurita (president)

The MUPP-NP is an indigenist, anti-establishment formation founded in 1996 by television journalist Freddy Ehlers, who contested the 1996 presidential elections on an environmentalist and anti-corruption platform and came third in the first round with 21% of the vote. In the concurrent congressional elections his movement won eight seats. In the mid-1998 elections Ehlers slipped to fourth place in the presidential contest with 14.3% and the MUPP-NP to six congressional seats. However with strong support from the indigenous community the party supported the successful candidature of Lucio Edwin Gutiérrez Borbua in 2002 and forms part of the ruling coalition; in the congressional elections it won 5 seats on its own, 6 in coalition with the PSP, 2 in coalition with the PS-FA and 1 with the MCNP.

Popular Democracy–Christian Democratic Union
Democracia Popular–Unión Demócrata Cristiana (DP-UDC or DP)

Address. C/ Pradera n. 30–58 y San Salvador, Casilla 17–012300, Quito
Telephone. (593–2) 900968
Fax. (593–2) 555567
Email. dp@interactive.net.ec
Leadership. Ramiro Rivera-Molina (president); Pedro Salas Montalvo (secretary-general)

The centre-left DP has consistently campaigned on the issues of communal socialism, democracy and Latin American nationalism. The party had its origins in the Christian Democratic Party (PDC), formed in 1964, which merged with the progressive faction of the Ecuadorian Conservative Party (PCE) led by Julio César Trujillo to form the DP in 1978.

In 1979 Osvaldo Hurtado Larrea (formerly PDC leader) was elected Vice-President to President Jaime Roldós Aguilera of the Concentration of Popular Forces (CFP) and assumed the presidency after the latter's death in a plane crash in 1981. Hurtado's DP government became unpopular with the left for his policy of reducing state spending and for austerity measures introduced in 1983, but also with the right, which opposed any state intervention in the running of the economy. DP presidential candidate Trujillo was accordingly defeated in the 1984 elections.

Having backed the successful presidential candidate of the Democratic Left (ID) in 1988, the DP withdrew from the alliance in late 1989, following disagreements over vegetable oil price rises imposed by the government. This decision saved the DP from suffering the fate of the ID (whose seats were nearly halved) in the 1990 mid-term congressional elections, in which the party retained its seven seats. In the 1992 elections, however, DP presidential candidate Vladimiro Alvarez Grau received a negligible vote and the party's representation was reduced to five seats (which fell to four in the 1994 legislative polls).

The DP performed better in 1996, when it won 12 seats in the legislature and its candidate in the presidential poll, Rodrigo Paz, gained 13.5% of the total vote. This advance led on to a major success in the mid-1998 elections, in which the DP candidate, Quito mayor Jamil Mahuad Witt, won the presidential poll (with 35.3% in the first round and 51.3% in the second) and the party gained the largest number of seats (33) in the National Congress. However, triumph soon turned to disaster for the party. In the midst of a prolonged economic and political crisis, and after repeated calls for his resignation, Mahuad was ousted in a bloodless coup in January 2000 and replaced by Vice-President Alvaro Noboa Ponton of the PRE. In 2002 the DP-UDC won only four seats in Congress.

The DP is a member of the Christian Democrat International and the Christian Democrat Organization of America.

Renewal Party of National Action
Partido Renovador de Acción Nacional (PRIAN)
This is a personalist party founded in 2002 to serve as a vehicle for the presidential candidature of Alvaro Fernando Noboa Pontón, a wealthy banana-grower and exporter who was candidate for the PRE in 1998. At his second attempt, he came second in the first round of presidential elections in 2002 with 17.4% of the vote, but was defeated in the run-off election by Col. Edwin Gutiérrez. In the concurrent congressional elections the party won 10 seats.
Address. Malecón 512 y Tomás Martínez, Guayaquil
Website. www.prian.org.ec
Leadership. Alvaro Noboa Pontón (2002 presidential candidate)

Social Christian Party
Partido Social Cristiano (PSC)
Address. Carrion 548 y Reina Victoria, Casilla 9454, Quito
Telephone. (593–2) 568560
Fax. (593–2) 568562
Leadership. Jaime Nebot Saadi (president)
The PSC was formed in 1951 (as the Social Christian Movement) to support Camilo Ponce Enríquez, who went on to serve as President in 1956-60. The party adopted its present name in 1967 and continued to operate during the 1972-79 military dictatorship, but went through a period of crisis after Ponce's death in 1976. In the 1988 elections the PSC's presidential candidate, Sexto Durán-Ballén, came third with around 15% of the vote and the party was reduced to only six deputies in the National Congress. (Durán-Ballén went on to form the Republican Unity Party, which was eventually incorporated into the Ecuadorian Conservative Party, and served as President from 1992 to 1996.)

The party had more success in the June 1990 mid-term elections, winning 16 seats, making it the largest party in Congress. The PSC then entered into a parliamentary alliance with the Ecuadorian Roldosist Party (PRE), establishing joint control of Congress. Jaime Nebot Saadi was the PSC presidential candidate in the 1992 elections, coming second to Durán-Ballén in the first round with 26.2% of the vote before losing the run-off. In the simultaneous congressional elections the PSC won 21 seats, making it the largest party bloc.

The PSC was again the only conspicuous winner in the 1994 polls with 26 seats, which increased to 27 in 1996, eight more than its nearest rival, the PRE. However, Nebot Saadi was less successful in the 1996 presidential poll, again losing over two rounds, this time to the PRE's Abdalá Bucaram Ortiz. In the run-up to the 1998 presidential elections Nebot Saadi announced that he would not contest the poll, in which the party did not present a candidate. Despite Nebot Saadi's withdrawal, the PSC performed well in the congressional elections, winning 28 seats, only five less than the Popular Democracy (DP), the overall winner. Initially the party offered support to President Mahuad Witt (DP), but in March 1999 it announced its refusal to endorse the President's controversial austerity programme and eventually backed the campaign against him. Following the ousting of President Mahuad in a military coup in January 2000, replacement Gustavo Noboa Bejarano appointed a government which included PSC representatives. In the 2002 presidential elections the PSC candidate, Antonio Xavier Neira Menendez, came fifth with 12.2% of the votes but the party only won two seats in the new Congress.

Other Parties and Movements

Confederation of Ecuadorian Indigenous Nationalities (*Confederación de Nacionalidades Indígenas del Ecuador*, CONAIE), the country's main indigenous peoples' organization. It has campaigned for the return of traditional community-held lands, the payment by oil companies of compensation to tribes for environmental damage and for the recognition of Quechua as an official Ecuadorian language. In January 2000 CONAIE played a key role in the ousting of President Jamil Mahuad Witt (Popular Democracy) by mobilizing thousands of Indians who, with the acquiescence of the army, occupied Quito and other provincial capitals. In early 2001 CONAIE, alongside trade unions and civic groups, organized a "great national mobilization" which secured a reversal in government policy on fuel taxation. In turn this mobilization played a large part in the success of the Pachakutik Plurinational United Movement–New Country (MUPP-NP) in 2002.
Address. Av Granados 2553 y 6 de Diciembre, Casilla 17-17-1235, Quito.
Tel. (5932) 248930
Fax. (5932) 442271
Email. ccc@conaie.ec
Website. conaie.nativeweb.org
Leadership. Luis Macas (president)

Independent Movement for an Authentic Republic (*Movimiento Independiente para una República Auténtica*, MIRA), created in 1996 by Rosalía Arteaga, who in 1996-97 served as Vice-President under President Bucaram Ortiz of the Ecuadorian Roldosist Party. During the turmoil which accompanied Bucaram's downfall in early 1997, Arteaga briefly held the presidency for a few days, before it passed to Congress Speaker Fabián Alarcon Rivera. One of two women who contested the 1998 presidential election, Arteaga came fifth with only 5.2%, while MIRA failed to win any congressional seats.
Leadership. Rosalía Arteaga Serrano de Fernández de Córdova

Movement of Citizen Forces (*Movimiento Fuerza Ciudadana*, MFE), a liberal party founded in 1995, contested the 1998 legislative election as the Movement of Ecuadorian Forces but failed to win a seat. The party was accorded observer status of the Liberal International at the organization's 2000 congress in Ottawa, but though still active failed to win a seat in Congress in 2002.
Address. Luis Urdaneta 204 y Cordova, Guayaquil
Telephone. (593–4) 568863
Fax. (593–4) 5666291
Email. info@fuerzaecuador.org
Website. www.fuerzaecuador.org
Leadership. Humberto X. Mata (president); Ivan Baquizero (secretary-general)

Egypt

Capital: Cairo
Population: 70,300,000 (2003E)

The Arab Republic of Egypt achieved full independence in 1936, initially as a monarchy, which was overthrown in 1952. There were several experiments with single-party structures, the last and most durable being the Arab Socialist Union (ASU), effectively a platform for the late President Gamal Abdel Nasser. Under Nasser's successor, Anwar Sadat, a limited multi-party system evolved from 1976 which has been dominated by the National Democratic Party (NDP). Under the 1971 constitution, legislative power is exercised by the unicameral People's Assembly (*Majlis al-Shaab*) of 444 elective and 10 appointed members, which is elected for a five-year term by universal adult suffrage (of those aged 18 years and over). The Assembly nominates the President, who is confirmed by popular referendum for a six-year term. The President then appoints a Council of Ministers. In addition, there is an advisory Consultative Council (*Shura*). Two-thirds of its 210 members are popularly elected; the rest are appointed by the President.

According to the Political Parties Law (No. 40 of 1977), prospective parties must apply to a semi-governmental Political Parties Committee for a licence. If turned down – as has happened in all but seven cases since 1977 – they can appeal to a special court. Grounds for declining a licence include abuse of religious issues, and duplication of other parties' policies. In the view of Nabil Abdel-Fattah, an expert at the *Al-Ahram* Centre for Political and Strategic Studies, "the Egyptian legal system has managed to disfigure the political parties". Excluded groups, like Nasserists, Islamists and Marxists, he argues, have used existing political parties as vehicles of convenience, with little consideration to their platforms. In practice, independent MPs find it difficult to get their voices heard in the assembly; hence the attraction of affiliating to an existing party.

Since coming to power in October 1981, following the assassination of President Anwar Sadat, Mohammed Hosni Mubarak has spoken of his commitment to democracy. He has also sought to increase the status of the NDP. Critics believe that the latter aim constricts the former; to them, the Emergency Law, instituted since 1981 and repeatedly renewed ever since, limits the rights of all other parties. Tellingly, Mubarak turned to the parties for support after a flurry of terrorist attacks in 1994; he promptly called a National Dialogue Conference to restore "national unity".

A list system was instituted for elections in 1987, though the government reverted to a system based on individual candidacy in 1995. Thus parties were only allowed a loosely defined "co-ordinating" role regarding the choice of candidates and constituencies. In elections to the People's Assembly on Nov. 29 and Dec. 6, 1995, the NDP was officially stated to have won 317 of the 444 elective seats, "independents" 114, the New *Wafd* Party 6, the National Progressive Unionist Party 5, the Liberal Socialist Party 1 and the Nasserite Party 1. Of the 114 "independent" deputies, 99 quickly declared their allegiance to the NDP. A further 10 members of the Assembly were appointed by the President.

In a national referendum on Oct. 4, 1993, Hosni Mubarak of the NDP, the sole candidate, was endorsed for a third six-year presidential term by 94.9% of valid votes cast. Extra-parliamentary critics, however, drew attention to alleged vote-rigging by forces loyal to the NDP. In October-November 2000, following an even larger presidential victory in 1999, Egypt held People's Assembly elections in which the NDP won a commanding 353 seats. Another 35 "independents" subsequently joined the party in the Assembly. The New *Wafd* Party, National Progressive Unionist Party and Nasserites won seven, six and three seats respectively.

A low turnout was reported.

However, the NDP's victory came only after initial reports of significant opposition gains, subsequently denied by the government. There were allegations of irregularities, despite the presence of judges inside polling stations for the first time. Protests continued into 2001, especially after the widespread arrest of Islamist candidates in April, prior to the *Shura* Council elections of May. As of January 2004, and following by-elections, deaths, resignations and realignments, the NDP held 410 seats. President Mubarak is due to complete his fourth consecutive six-year term in October 2005. Meanwhile, in February 2000 the Assembly had passed a bill to renew the 20-year state of emergency from June 2000, for a further three years. It was renewed once more in February 2003.

In June 2003 the People's Assembly passed landmark bills to abolish the much-criticized State Security Courts and create a National Council for Human Rights. Fathi Surour, the long-serving Speaker of the People's Assembly, promised that the new council would directly examine citizens' complaints of rights abuses, and would consider all new legislation concerning human rights. Opposition politicians nonetheless decried the decision to place the body under the purview of the *Shura* Council, and not the People's Assembly. They said that two bodies that already operate under the *Shura* Council – the Higher Political Parties Council and the Higher Press Council – were notorious for curtailing political and press freedom.

On Dec. 24, 2003, four political parties – the New *Wafd*, Communist, National Progressive Unionist and Nasserite Democrat – launched a petition together with six NGOs to attain sweeping economic and constitutional reforms and political freedom. Meanwhile, overpopulation, widespread penury (economists estimate that 40% of Egyptians live below the poverty line), economic stagnation and anger at US policies in the region, all contribute to dissatisfaction with the ruling NDP.

Arab Socialist Egypt Party

Leadership. Wahid el-Uqsuri (secretary-general)
The party was founded in 1976 by then Prime Minister Mamdouh Salem, following Egypt's switch to a multi-party system. Known simply as *Misr* (Egypt) it won that year's election to become the ruling party. However, the ASEP collapsed after July 1978, when President Sadat established the National Democratic Party, and ASEP members flocked to the new entity. However, three of the 30 members of the ASEP political bureau – Mamdouh Salem, Abdel-Azim Abul-Atta and Gamal el-Din Rabie – and some 800 other members rejected the enforced merger with the NDP. They won their case in 1985, effectively re-establishing the ASEP on a platform of free speech and popular will. The NDP filed a counter-suit against *Misr's* re-creation, but a court granted recognition to the *Misr* Party in 1991.

Financially bereft after the legal battles, *Misr* aimed for Egyptian revival based on identifying "seven categories of ignorance". Rabie attended the National Dialogue Conference in 1994, and the party claimed to field 26 party candidates in the 1995 election, plus a further 41 as independents. Egypt's Political Parties Committee froze the party in November 2001 after severe internal disputes split the ASEP. Party secretary-general, Wahid el-Uqsuri, had rejected chairman Rabie's decision to appoint three renegades from the New *Wafd* Party as the ASEP's representatives in the Assembly. The three MPs – Ayman Nour, Mohamed Farid Hassanein and Seif Mahmoud – were expelled from the NWP in March and June 2001. There were allegations that Nour had bribed Rabie to gain acceptance of the renegades as MPs for the ASEP. If, however, a court overturns the earlier verdict, the ASEP may automatically have three MPs, despite failing to field a single candidate in the 2000 elections.

Labour Party
Hizb al-Amal al-Ishtiraki

Address. 313 Port Said Street, Sayyida Zeinab, Cairo
Telephone. (20–2) 390–9261
Fax. (20–2) 390–0283
Leadership. Magdi Hussain (secretary-general), Abdel-Hamid Barakat(deputy secretary-general)
The LP was officially organized in November 1978 by Agriculture Minister Ibrahim Shukri to provide "loyal and constructive opposition", to the ruling National Democratic Party (NDP). Osama El-Ghazali Harb of the *Al Ahram* newspaper affirms that Shukri did so with the full approval of then President Anwar Sadat. In 1950 Shukri, a member of the Young Egypt Party, had become the first socialist MP ever elected to the Egyptian parliament. In 1978 his new party was called the Socialist Labour Party, but later dropped the term "socialist". Hilmi Murad later became LP secretary general, and then by 1995, its deputy chairman. He had helped revive the New *Wafd* Party in 1978, but a year later left it for Labour. Murad had been Egypt's Education Minister in 1969, though was fired the following year after criticizing then President Gamal Abdel Nasser.

While affirming the need for Islamic precepts to serve as the basis of Egyptian legislation, the party advocated a democratic regime with a proper welfare system, and more equal sharing of wealth between urban and rural areas. Although the largest opposition party after the 1979 elections, the LP lost ground to the benefit of the New *Wafd* Party in the early 1980s, failing to secure any elective Assembly seats in May 1984.

At that juncture Adel Hussain joined the party and encouraged a more Islamic agenda. A former Communist (imprisoned during 1953-6 and 1959-64) turned Islamist theorist and author, his views angered resident LP Marxists and Nasserists. By 1987 the party had begun to abandon its support for a stronger Arab League, and pan-Arabism, in favour of pan-Islamic ties. In the 1987 elections it campaigned under the slogan, "Islam is the Solution", and joined an alliance that became the principal opposition force. In 1995 party chairman Shukri claimed that in 1987 the New *Wafd* had originally agreed to such a broad-based bloc, as proposed by Shukri, but then declined. In the event the LP, the Liberal Socialist Party (LSP), and others produced a joint list which unofficially included candidates of the formally proscribed Muslim Brotherhood. All told, the list won 60 seats (20 of which the LP held in its own right).

The LP boycotted the 1990 Assembly election, claiming that President Mubarak's government was insufficiently committed to democracy, although eight party members reportedly contested and won seats as independents. In the build-up to the 1991 Gulf war, Labour was a vocal critic of the government's alignment with the US-led coalition against Iraq. This campaign led to judicial action against party members for inciting unrest. Anti-government articles in the party newspaper in 1993-94 led to the brief detention of several LP members and accusations of defamation against the party chairman, Shukri. At the same time, the LP opposes Islamic militancy, along with emergency regulations and government-favoured land and cement 'mafias'. In Harb's view, the LP's main problem has always been "the ambiguity of its ideological framework", and its alliance with the Muslim Brotherhood was bound to lead to rivalry.

Amidst growing restraints on forces both liberal and Islamist, the LP was formally suspended in May 2000, by the administrative court responsible for political parties. Secretary-general Adel Hussain was charged with "working against national unity". Simultaneously, Ahmed Idris and Hamdi Ahmed claimed to have toppled the venerable Shukri as party boss. Evidently, Shukri had struck a 'secret deal' with the state, to replace Islamist influences, restore its original socialist line and exclude Hussein from leading posts, in exchange for reconciliation, and presumably re-legitimizing the party. Shukri also seemed willing to counter-balance Muslim Brotherhood influence by courting former Nasserists.

Adel Hussain died in March 2001, after which his younger brother, Magdi Hussain, was named as the LP secretary-general. Apart from the bi-quarterly *Manbar el-Sharq* Labour also publishes the influential and controversial bi-weekly, *Al-Shaab* (The People), which is often the target of official anger. *Al-Shaab* was accused of libelling Deputy Prime Minister Youssef Wali on charges of corruption and importing "carcinogenic chemicals". In April 2000 Magdi Hussain was sentenced to two years' imprisonment and a fine for the libel.

A final decision on the fate of both Labour and its organ, *Al-Shaab*, is scheduled for April 2004. Though still banned in its press version, *Al-Shaab* has moved online with Magdi Hussain as editor-in-chief. Meanwhile, LP deputy secretary-general Abdel-Hamid Barakat fears that the party will never be re-legalized, because "it would make the US mad", and because curbing the LP silences "the annoying Islamist voice, which continues to expose the government's poor performance and policies".

Liberal Socialist Party (LSP)
Hizb al-Ahrar al-Ishtiraki

Address. c/o Majlis al-Shaab, Cairo
Leadership (still unresolved following the death of former leader Mustapha Kamal Murad in 1998)
A small party that emerged in 1976 from the right wing of the then ruling Arab Socialist Union, the LSP promotes private enterprise within the Egyptian economy, and backed the Camp David Accords with Israel. The party also supports an independent free press, broader labour rights, and *sharia* as the basis of the constitution. LSP representation in the People's Assembly fell progressively from 12 seats to none in elections between 1976 and 1984, as voters saw little difference between its platform and the NDP's. It then allied itself with the stronger Labour Party (LP) – which also unofficially included the Muslim Brotherhood (MB) – and saw three of its Assembly candidates elected in 1987. However, the move towards Islamist platforms antagonized liberals, who began deserting to the New *Wafd* Party. The LSP boycotted polls in 1990, and subsequently discontinued its alliance with Labour and the MB. It won one seat in the 1995 Assembly elections, and one in 2000. The party publishes one daily, *Al-Ahrar*, and two weeklies, *Al-Haquiqa* and *Al-Nour*.

National Democratic Party (NDP)
Hizb al-Wataniyh al-Dimuqratiyah

Address. Corniche al-Nil Street, Cairo
Telephone. (20–2) 575–7450
Fax. (20–2) 360–7681
Leadership. Mohammed Hosni Mubarak (chairman); Dr Yusuf Amin Wali (deputy secretary-general)
The NDP was organized by President Anwar Sadat in July 1978 as the party of government in succession to the Arab Socialist Union (ASU). The latter party, seen as the creature of the late President Nasser, had been dissolved in 1977. Its three constituent "forums", representing left, right and centre, were incorporated into the NDP in October 1978. That same month Sadat instituted a National Development Bank to finance the NDP's various development projects. The new party, which derived its legacy from the long defunct National Party founded in 1907, was to be a broad-based centrist force favouring a mixed economy. In terms of for-

eign policy, the NDP places a high premium on Egypt's relations with the USA, and supports President Mubarak as a peace broker between Israel and the Palestinians.

The NDP confirmed its dominance with an overwhelming majority at the 1979 Assembly elections and in all subsequent polls, though the opposition claims the electoral system is biased in its favour. After Sadat's assassination in October 1981, Vice-President Hosni Mubarak became president of both the country and the ruling party. Twice the NDP was ruled to have abused the constitution, via its slate system of elections, in 1987 and 1990, and on both occasions the Assembly had to be dissolved. Mubarak has won four consecutive presidential elections, most recently in 1999, by overwhelming majorities. Critics have accused NDP representatives of being supine and rubber-stamping executive decisions, although legislators have played a role in unearthing corruption and highlighting social problems.

After the October-November 2000 Assembly elections, the NDP was announced to have won 353 seats, up from 318 previously. A further 35 "independents" later joined the NDP. Widespread protests erupted following allegations of rigged polls. Initially numerous candidates from the NDP's official list had apparently suffered defeat. Some reports suggested the party's "lowest ever share of seats"; only "corrective" recounts and run-off polls, claimed opponents, explained the magnitude of the NDP's victory. Human rights groups and Egyptian lawyers criticized security forces for bullying voters into supporting the NDP. Mubarak was blamed for curtailing non-NDP campaigning; banning critical publications; and arresting several candidates. The NDP for its part claimed the elections were the "cleanest yet".

In 2001 Gamal Mubarak, an investment banker and son of the President, began recruiting youth for the NDP, prompting rumours that he was being groomed to succeed his father. In September 2002 he became Secretary for NDP Policy, and three youthful allies, Ahmed Ezz, Hossam Badrawi and Hossam Ahmed, took over other party committees and secretariats. In 2003 Gamal Mubarak demanded better human rights laws, and this led to the NDP proposing two landmark bills which the People's Assembly passed in June. Legislators voted to abolish the much-criticized State Security Courts, and create a National Council for Human Rights. Nonetheless, in July 2003 Salam Ahmed Salama, a columnist for Egypt's leading and usually pro-government *Al Ahram* newspaper, accused the NDP of blocking reforms to the 1971 national constitution. He called the NDP "devoid of innovative ideas", and blamed it for fostering political apathy, confusion and uncertainty. Possibly in response to such charges, the September 2003 NDP conference adopted a package of policies to ease restrictions on parties and trade unions, entitled "New Thinking: the Rights of the Citizen". The document bore the imprimatur of Gamal Mubarak, who has close ties to reformers in the British Labour Party, like Peter Mandelson. Critics said New Thinking meant little as long as the emergency law applied; the NDP overwhelmingly supported the law's renewal in February 2003.

In late 2003 President Mubarak denied rumours that his son would succeed him, either as party leader or head of state. Subsequently the *Middle East Times*, an Egyptian newspaper, quoted the political analyst and dissident, Saad Eddin Ibrahim, who predicted that, following Egyptian custom, a military figure – in his view, intelligence chief, Gen. Omar Suleiman – would serve as president for six years with Gamal Mubarak as his deputy.

In November 2003 17 MPs, all NDP members, were forced to resign when it was revealed that they had evaded military service, thereby nullifying their original candidacies. Earlier, in February 2002, two NDP MPs from Fayum were found guilty of theft and forgery, and were sentenced to 15 and five years in prison respectively.

As of January 2004, the NDP held 410 seats in the 454-member National Assembly. The NDP is an affiliate of the Socialist International, and it publishes two weekly newspapers, *Mayo* and Islamic *Iowa*.

National Progressive Unionist Party (NPUP)
Hizb al-Tagammu al-Wataniyah al-Taqaddumi al-Wahdawi

Address. 1 Karim al-Dawla Street, Talaat Harb, Cairo
Telephone. (20–2) 575–9281
Fax. (20–2) 578–6298
Leadership. Rifaat El Said (secretary-general)

The NPUP, popularly known simply as *Tagammu*, was created in 1976 by chairman Khaled Mohieddin from the left-wing component of the Arab Socialist Union. It advocated state ownership of industry and the exclusion of foreign investment. The NPUP claims to have suffered harassment by the government, particularly in the late 1970s because of its antipathy (alone among the main parties) towards the Egyptian-Israeli peace process. Having failed to win any seats in the elections of 1979, 1984 and 1987, the party shunned the electoral boycott by other opposition parties in 1990, and secured six seats in the Assembly. Increasingly, *Tagammu* portrayed itself as an umbrella coalition of Nasserists, Marxists and Arab nationalists; by the same token it suffers from factionalism as different trends jostle for supremacy. Since the collapse of East European Communism, the NPUP has embraced democratic values, though it still opposes privatization and has called for the return to a national command economy.

The NPUP led domestic opposition to the decision to participate in the US-led coalition that fought Iraq in the 1991 Gulf war. The party blamed NDP economic policies for causing unemployment, and opposed the passage of legislation in 1992 aimed primarily at combating Islamic fundamentalists, which gave the authorities greater internal security powers (in addition to those under emergency laws in force since 1981). The NPUP won five seats in the 1995 legislative elections, and six in the 2000 elections. NPUP politburo chief, Dr El Said, formerly spent 14 years as a political prisoner, but is currently a member of the Shura Council. The party fielded women and Copts amongst its 40 candidates.

New Wafd Party (NWP)
Hizb al-Wafd al-Gadid

Address. 1 Bolis Hanna Street, Dokki, Cairo
Telephone. (20–2) 348–0830
Fax. (20–2) 360–2007
Website. www.alwafd.org
Leadership. Naaman Gomaa (chairman)

The original *Wafd* (Delegation) had been a popular liberal and nationalist movement in the 1920s, and was pivotal in the early years of Egyptian independence, after 1936. However, it was banned after the 1952 revolution, despite its opposition to the now deposed King Farouk, because of its association with British interests. The *Wafd* re-emerged as the NWP in February 1978 under its veteran leader, Mohammed Fouad Serageddin. In 1981 he led opposition to Egypt's peace treaty with Israel, called for a stronger multi-party system, and stressed human rights and recognition of Egypt's multiple Arab, Islamic and African identities.

After a prolonged legal struggle the NWP won the right to contest Assembly elections in October 1983. In alliance with a number of Islamic groups, notably the Muslim Brotherhood, the NWP won 58 seats with 15 per cent of the vote in May 1984. It thus became the only opposition party with parliamentary representation. Although strengthened by absorbing the small National Front Party led by Mahmoud al-Qadi, the NWP lost 23 of its seats in the 1987 election. Much of its support siphoned away when the Muslim

Brotherhood switched sides to entere a de facto coalition with the Labour Party (LP) and Liberal Socialist Party (LSP). Together with other opposition parties that favoured constitutional reform, the NWP boycotted the 1990 Assembly elections, although party members who ran as independents retained at least 14 seats.

The NWP was the only opposition party to support President Mubarak's commitment of troops to Saudi Arabia during the Gulf crisis of 1990-91, a position which prompted widespread internal dissension and the defection of an influential member, Naaman Gomaa. The party was officially credited with six seats in the Assembly elections of late 1995. Deserters decreased the tally to four in 1997. Increasingly, the NWP acquired an Islamist tinge and criticized governmental corruption. It suppports free enterprize and freedom of expression, and has called for the President to be elected by direct ballot, rather than by referendum. In foreign affairs, the NWP backs Arab unity and Palestinian rights.

Serageddin said the government had rigged the 1995 elections, undermined peaceful opposition, and thereby had lent succour to militant foes like the Islamic Group. Within the party, a new generation chafed at the NWP's "ossified" ancient leadership. Some even deserted to the NDP in local elections. Gomaa was subsequently rehabilitated, and in August 2000, following Serageddin's death at 91, he defeated the latter's brother, deputy party leader and reputed Mubarak ally, Yassin Serageddin, to became head of the NWP.

Gomaa's triumph raised hopes that he would rehabilitate the party. But with little time to plan a decisive campaign, his party gained just seven seats in the election of 2000 (reduced to six by late 2003). Even so, the NWP was again Egypt's largest opposition party. Internal divisions continued, however: in March and June 2001 Gomaa expelled three NWP MPs – Ayman Nour, Mohamed Farid Hassanein and Seif Mahmoud – for opposing his policies (see Egypt Arab Socialist Party). The Muslim Brotherhood accused the NWP of acting in cahoots with the ruling NDP, especially in colluding in electoral misdeeds. Nonetheless, the NWP itself boycotted a by-election on Dec. 25, 2003, citing attempts by the NDP to 'control' the constituencies.

Other Parties

Centre Party (*Al Wasat*), led by Abul Ella Madi, launched in early 1996 by a youthful faction of the Muslim Brotherhood. It included some Christian Copts as well as Muslims. Governmental refusal to recognize the party was seen as a favour to ageing Brotherhood leaders.

Committee for the Defence of Democracy, a coalition of opposition figures and human rights activists that in December 2002 launched a campaign against emergency laws. These regulations were introduced in 1967 and have been reimposed continually since October 1981. The committee includes members of the New *Wafd* Party.

Democratic People's Party, founded in 1990, and ratified in 1992, but denied a licence and largely inactive since then. Its leader was Anwar Afifi.

Democratic Unionist Party, founded in 1990 and led by Idrul Moneim Tork. The DUP supports economic development and personal rights, as well as a freer Egyptian foreign policy, though the party has been denied a licence.

Egypt the Motherland (*Misr Al Um*), or Egypt Mother Party, was founded in early 2004 and accepted for registration. It seeks to restore Egypt's pharaonic heritage and opposes Islamism, Nasserism and "years of failure of the Arab nationalism project", according to a founding member,

Talaat Radwan. The party wants to drop the word "Arab" from Egypt's official title, and wishes to introduce study of indigenous Egyptian languages, Coptic and Hieroglyphics, in Egyptian schools. Its constitution calls for equal rights for all and a new national flag.

One of the party's leaders is the lawyer and former Liberal Party member, Sami Harak. Another founding member and co-leader Mohsen Lutfi, explained the party's stance: "We are Egyptians... The Arabs are our friends and neighbors and we have common destiny, but we are not Arabs." *Misr Al Um* calls for an "equal footing" with Israel, and endorses the right of Iraqi and Palestinian peoples to "liberate their soil". It also wants to repeal the totalitarian heritage and endorses fully democratic elected governments. However, other secularists have lampooned their efforts; Jamal Badawi, writing in the New *Wafd* Party organ, *Al-Wafd*, accused *Misr Al Um* of fearing political Islam, hence their attempt to target Arabs instead, and "bunch the Arabs together with the foreign forces which occupied Egypt".

Egyptian Green Party, founded in 1990, enjoys little of the support of its European ecologist allies. In September 1993 it named Kamal Kira as leader. It has run numerous local anti-pollution and anti-smoking campaigns. The party supports the "academic and scientific handling of problems". Yet it is split between those, like its founding chairman, Hassan Ragab, who stress ecological issues above all else, and those, like Kira, who see the environment as just one plank of its platform, alongside social issues. Abdul Moneim El-Aasar was once director-general of the Greens, whose weekly paper is *Al-Khodr* (The Green).

Egyptian Organization for Human Rights, though not a political party per se, places a vital role in advocating greater freedom for political parties. The EOHR joined *Tagammu* and New *Wafd* in opposing a new bill regulating the activities of NGOs, passed on June 3, 2002. Its secretary-general, Hafez Abu Saada, praised the two human rights bills of June 2003 as a "good step, but not enough". It continually calls for the rescinding of Egypt's Emergency Law.

Nasserite Democratic Arab Party, led by Diaeddin Dawood, was founded in 1992, and has experienced a revival in recent years. In 2000 the party won three seats, compared with one seat won under the former leadership of Farid Abdel Karim in 1995. A Nasserite group failed to gain legal recognition in 1990 because it allegedly advocated a return to totalitarianism. However, in late 2000 the NDAP exploited nostalgia for the old hero of pan-Arabism, and seemed to provide a home for those who distrust both Israel and Islamic militants in equal measure. The party virulently opposes what it sees as US imperialism and globalization, and remains extremely anti-Zionist. In economic terms, it prefers a central state-run economy. It publishes the weekly *Al-Arabi*.

The Nation Party (*Al Ummah*) was founded in June 1983, after its creator, the veteran politician and author of many books on the interpretation of dreams, Haj Ahmed El-Sabahi, won a lawsuit in an administrative court. Sabahi was and possibly still is a member of Egypt's *Shura* Council. After losing an expensive lawsuit against the government in the late 1990s, he set up the El-Sabahi Effendi International Centre internet site, which for a fee offered users astrological and psychiatric interpretations. *Umma* seeks to "revive Egyptian identity", partially by re-introducing the wearing of the *tarboush* head covering. In 1995 *Umma* promised to field 70 candidates in December elections, but won no seats. It publishes a weekly newspaper, *Al-Ummah*, and has advocated "Islamicization as remedy to all ailments".

National Accord Party, founded in March 2000, the first new party to win a licence in 22 years and providing a home for malcontents from other opposition parties.

Solidarity Party (*Al Takaful*) – sometimes translated as "Mutual Support" – the party was founded in 1995, but denied a licence. Led by Dr Usama Mohammed Shaltout, it advocated a "solidarity tax" on the wealthy only, instead of an income tax on workers or civil servants, so as to provide food, clothing and housing for poorer Egyptians. Shaltout also wants Sunnis and Shias to unite in one group, followed by all of "humanity embracing a single religion".

Young Egypt Party (*Misr Al Fattah*) derives its name from Arab nationalists of the late 19th century, and the radical party established in 1936 by Ahmed Hussain, elder brother of Adel Hussain (see Labour Party). *Misr Al Fattah* had changed its name to the *Misr* Socialist Party by 1948, when Ibrahim Shukri, a leader of the 1935 student revolt against British occupation, became its deputy chairman. The party was dissolved in 1953, along with all other parties.

When YEP stalwart, Shukri, set up and became chairman of the (Socialist) Labour Party, in 1978, many saw it as the YEP's natural successor. However, in 1990 Aliedin Saleh, Mahmoud El-Meligi and Ibrahim Zeidan left Labour to re-establish the YEP. Since then 12 rivals challenged Saleh's leadership, which led to intricate legal battles and the freezing of the party's activities until the crisis was resolved. In 1995 Saleh claimed an affinity with the thought of Libyan leader, Moamer al Kadhafi, and his party opposes the USA, Israel and Arab monarchies.

Illegal Groups

Dignity (*Al-Karama*) consists of prominent left-leaning nationalists, like Essam al-Islambouli. Its application for a license was turned down in March 2002 by the relevant administrative court.

Egyptian Communist Party (*Hizb al-Shuyui al-Misri*), has been banned since 1925, subsequently experiencing numerous ideological schisms and breakaways which have yielded many splinter groups.

Holy War (*Jihad*), a secret organization of militant Muslims who split from the Muslim Brotherhood in the late 1970s because of the latter's objection to the use of violence. The group was blamed for the assassination of President Sadat in 1981. In 1998 the group allied itself to the terrorist cell network headed by the renegade Afghan-based Saudi, Osama bin Laden. But this move generated a split between more cautious figures, and the group's leader, Dr Ayman al-Zawahiri, one of Bin Laden's closest colleague. *Jihad* figures were accused of involvement in the bombing of US embassies in east Africa, in August 1998. *Jihad* reputedly lacks the mass support of the Islamic Group. Its political offshoot, the *Sharia* (Islamic Law) Party, has yet to be recognized.

Islamic Group (*Al-Gamaa Al-Islamiyya*), emerged in the 1970s as the student wing of the Muslim Brotherhood, subsequently breaking away and aligning (until the mid-1980s) with Holy War (*Jihad*) in seeking to overthrow the government. A loose-knit, but very militant umbrella organization for many smaller groups (technically, *Gamaa* means groups, not group), it has been accused of spearheading attacks on the security forces, government officials and tourists since 1992. Militants affiliated with the group were blamed for 900 deaths from 1992-95. The spiritual leader of the Islamic Group is believed to be Sheikh Omar Abdel Rahman, a blind theologian. Egyptian authorities still seek his extradition

from detention in the United States, where he was charged with being behind the bombing of the World Trade Centre in 1993. In June 1994 it claimed responsibility for a failed attempt on the life of President Mubarak in Addis Ababa and in November 1997 *Gamaa* was blamed for a massacre of 57 tourists in Luxor.

However, in March 1998 its leaders announced a truce in their six-year terror campaign, following a concerted government campaign to arrest members and freeze its assets, and an earlier such declaration, in July 1997, that the Mubarak regime initially mistrusted. Later in 1998, party officials tried to distance themselves from the Saudi-born terrorist chief, Osama bin Laden, with whom they had formerly associated. *Gamaa* now backs the Islamist Reform Party, but it lacks official recognition.

Between 2000 and 2003, the governemnt released up to 1,000 Gamaa members, out of a total of 15,000 Islamists thought to sit in Egyptian prisons. In July 2003 *Gamaa* leader, Karam Zohdi, then 51, shocked many supporters when he told a London-based Arabic daily that terror was wrong, Sadat was a "martyr", and Muslim youth should shun *Al-Qaeda*. Foreign-based militants once associated with *Gamaa*, including London's Sheikh Abu Hamza al-Masri, fiercely criticized amelioratory statements by *Gamaa* leaders. But analysts felt their criticisms may backfire and merely bolster *Gamaa* domestically. Diaa Rashwan, respected political researcher from the *Al Ahram* Centre for Political Studies, noted that *Gamaa's* centralized organizational structure resembles those of leftist parties, and insulates it from the splits which have blighted other *jihadi* organizations.

Muslim Brotherhood (*Ikhwan al-Muslimin*)
Website. www.ummah.org.uk/ikhwan
Established in 1928 to promote the creation of a pan-Arab Islamic state, and declared an illegal organization in 1954. Nasser executed its leading ideologist, Sayid Qutb, in the 1960s. Sadat, however, nurtured unofficial ties with the movement and, although still technically banned, the Brotherhood has enjoyed de facto recognition since entering into coalition politics under President Mubarak. It secured indirect Assembly representation in 1984 by running a number of its candidates under New Wafd Party auspices, and in the 1987 elections it joined forces with the Labour Party (then Socialist Labour Party) and Liberal Socialist Party, winning 37 of the coalition's 60 seats.

The Brotherhood boycotted the 1990 elections along with other opposition parties, but is still thought to have the largest following and financial resources among Egypt's Islamic organizations, despite the emergence of more radical groups, like the Islamic Group (*Gamaa*) and Holy War (*Jihad*). It has 5,000 local offices throughout Egypt, has much influence over professional syndicates, and runs extensive charity and finance networks. Nonetheless, in 1995 fears at Islamic unrest inspired an unexpected crackdown on even the moderate *Ikhwan*, who for some 25 years had eschewed violence. That year, most members of the MB *Shura* Council were arrested when they met. Frustrated at domination by an ageing *ulama* (Muslim priesthood) many prominent younger Brothers resigned en masse in 1996.

Seventeen MB-affiliated independent candidates won seats in the October 2000 national elections, making it the largest (albeit unofficial) opposition bloc in parliament. However, in June 2002, 22 men stood trial in a state security court on charges of belonging to the MB and of plotting to seize power in Egypt; another 60 mid-ranking MB officials were arrested on similar charges in 2003. One MB-affiliated MP, Gamal Hishmet – hailed by the *New York Times* as "the modern face of Egypt's Muslim Brotherhood", and a champion of the fight against official corruption – was forced into a by-election in January 2003. When his New

Wafd Party opponent, Khairi Kaleg, won that poll by an unlikely margin, Hishmet protested police intimidation of voters, a charge backed by foreign diplomats and observers. In 2002 there were similar accusations of persecution of MB supporters in controversial by-elections.

Maamoun al-Hudaiby, the MB spiritual guide, toned down his opposition to the US-led war on Iraq in March 2003. He advocated *jihad* (righteous struggle) through giving money, food and medical aid to Iraq, rather than overt combat against US forces, who are military allies of the Egyptian Army. Hudaiby also reiterated MB support for multi-party democracy, which evidently contradicts notions that the MB means dictatorship by clergy when it speaks of "an Islamic state" as its ultimate goal. Hudaiby's views were seen as insuring against further government crackdowns on the MB. Many observers speculate that if legalized, the MB would win genuinely free and fair general elections in Egypt.

The movement's current spiritual leader is Mohammad Mahdi Akef. He was elected in a secret ballot to the post by the group's guidance committee on Jan. 15, 2004, and received nine votes to six against. This mode was unprecedented, as all earlier elections had been by public referendum. Akef, 76, had joined the MB in 1948 and was previously its liason official with the Muslim world. Interviewed after becoming the group's chief 'guide', Akef said the MB was ready to set up a political party, as soon as the government gave it the green light. Meanwhile he said the MB was prepared to "cooperate on common goals" with secular parties.

Akef succeeded Maamoun al-Hudaiby when the latter died aged 83 on Jan. 9, 2004. The charismatic Hudaiby had been secretary-general and chief public spokesman; he stood for elections to the district of Doqqi and Agouza in 2000, but failed to win, claiming polling irregularities. His predecessor was Mustafa Masshur, who died in November 2002. Masshur in turn had become leader when Hamid Abu al-Nasr died in January 1996. It remains to be seen whether the educated, younger generation of MB leaders – led by Essam al-Arrian, Hilmi Gazzar and Abdel-Moneim Abdel-Fatouh – will remain content to take orders from old guard figures who came to the fore in the 1940s.

Reform Party (*Al-Islah*) supported by Islamic Group members who now claim to favour democratic change. *Islah* favours free election of the President, and election by religious scholars (and not the state) of the Sheikh of Al Azhar, in Cairo, the senior religious authority in Sunni Islam. Its founding member is Gamal Sultan. The party applied for a licence in 1998, but this was denied; a resubmittal in 2002 was also denied on the grounds that the party was "not distinguished" by unique points in its political platform.

El Salvador

Capital: San Salvador
Population: 6,587,500 (2004E)

The Republic of El Salvador was ruled by Spain until 1821 and gained full independence in 1839. Throughout its history, military dictatorships have often either ruled directly or dominated the civilian administrations nominally in power, frequently intervening in the electoral process to choose a President suitable to the requirements of the current dictatorship and of the country's powerful oligarchy.

Under the 1983 constitution, legislative power is vested in a unicameral Legislative Assembly (*Asamblea Legislativa*), enlarged to 84 seats in 1991. Executive power rests with the President, who appoints the Council of Ministers and is assisted by a Vice President. Every two years the legislature appoints three substitute Vice-Presidents to assume the presidency in the case of the Vice-President being unable to do so. The President and Vice-President are elected nationally by universal adult suffrage for a five-year term and may not stand for immediate re-election. The members of the Legislative Assembly are elected for three-year terms. Suffrage is universal for nationals over 18 years of age, except for members of the armed forces, who are not permitted to vote. Elections are regulated by the electoral law of 1961, which established the Electoral Council as a supervisory body for all elections.

The most recent presidential elections held on March 21, 2004, resulted in a clear victory for Antonio Elías Saca of the Nationalist Republican Alliance (ARENA). In the Legislative Assembly elections held on March 15, 2003, however, ARENA had lost ground to the Farabundo Marti National Liberation Front (FMLN). ARENA won 27 seats compared to the FMLN's 31. The National Conciliation Party (PCN) won 16 seats, the United Democratic Centre (CDU) 5, the Christian Democratic Party (PDC) 4, and a coalition of the PDC, Social Democratic Party (PSD) and Renewal Movement (PMR) the remaining one seat.

Christian Democratic Party
Partido Demócrata Cristiano (PDC)
Address. 3ra Calle Poniente No.924, San Salvador
Telephone. (503) 281-9251
Fax. (503) 281-9271
Leadership. Rodolfo Parker

Founded in 1960 by José Napoleón Duarte, the PDC originally claimed to be seeking a "third way" between capitalism and communism. However, years of co-habitation with the military during the 1980s shifted the party to the right, especially in the late 1980s, when it called for the "re-privatization" of the economy.

Although the PDC contested legislative and presidential elections in 1964 and 1967 respectively, it was not until the 1970s that it made a significant political impact. In 1972 and 1977 the PDC led an opposition electoral alliance, the National Opposition Union (UNO), backing Duarte's candidacy for the presidency. Duarte was elected President in 1972 but was forced to flee the country following a military coup. He returned from exile in 1979 to join the "government junta" formed after the overthrow of the Romero military regime and in December was appointed President, the first civilian to hold the post in almost 50 years.

The PDC participated in two more national junta governments until 1982, relying on a tacit pact with the military. Right-wing parties controlled the legislature following the 1982 elections, but the PDC's 24 seats legitimized its participation in a government of national unity. Duarte's victory in the presidential elections of March 1984 was widely believed to have been reliant on US assistance. The outcome, however, ensured that the existing "unity Cabinet" was replaced by a PDC one. The party consolidated its hold on power in the March 1985 elections in which it won 33 Assembly seats and gained control of the majority of local councils.

The Duarte government was involved in intermittent efforts to negotiate a peace settlement with the Farabundo Marti National Liberation Front (FMLN), but was constrained by hardliners in the military high command opposed to any major concessions. It retained the support of the US administration under President Ronald Reagan, whose aid financed the quadrupling of the army and an intensification of the civil war against the guerrillas. A serious political split over the PDC presidential nomination for the 1989 elections debilitated the party and led to the PDC's loss of control of the Legislative Assembly in 1988, when it won only 25 seats.

Fidel Chávez Mena then shifted the party appreciably to the right by advocating liberal economic policies, but was comfortably defeated in the first round of the 1989 presidential elections by Alfredo Cristiani Burkard of the Republican Nationalist Alliance (ARENA). In elections to an enlarged 84-seat Assembly in March 1991, the PDC won 26 seats, coming second to ARENA. In the run-up to the 1994 presidential elections there were two leading PDC factions sparring for the party's nomination, which eventually went again to Chávez Mena rather than his main rival, Abraham Rodríguez. However, the PDC candidate finished third in the national poll, while the battle between the two competing factions finally came to a head with dissident *abrahamistas* (supporters of Rodríguez) breaking away to form the Renewal Social Christian Movement.

Support for the PDC has dwindled in recent years. The party won only seven Assembly seats in 1997, six in March 2000, and slipped further to five seats in 2003 (one of which was gained in coalition with the Social Democratic Party and the Renewal Movement). Likewise, PDC presidential candidates did very badly in the 1999 and 2004 elections, despite linking up with the United Democratic Centre (CDU) in the latter contest. Although the PDC still maintains several dozen mayoralties it is no longer a significant electoral force.

The PDC is affiliated to the Christian Democrat International and the Christian Democrat Organization of America.

Farabundo Marti National Liberation Front
Frente Farabundo Martí para la Liberación Nacional (FMLN)

Address. 27 Calle Poniente 1316, San Salvador
Telephone. (503) 226-7138
Fax. (503) 226-5236
Email. fmlncp@integra.com.sv
Website. www.fmln.org.sv
Leadership. Salvador Sánchez Cerén (coordinator general)
Founded in 1980, the FMLN took its name from a communist leader of a 1932 peasant revolt and was originally a hard left guerrilla organization with the Democratic Revolutionary Front (FDR) as its political arm. FMLN guerrillas launched a general offensive in January 1981, during which they secured strongholds in many areas. However, from the mid-1980s onwards, the FMLN was almost as active on the diplomatic front as it was militarily, proposing various power-sharing solutions to end the civil war. The FMLN sought to make the country ungovernable so long as the ruling Nationalist Republican Alliance (ARENA) resisted a negotiated settlement. To this end it launched large-scale military offensives in May and November 1990, both of which penetrated into the capital, San Salvador, to strengthen its position in UN-sponsored peace talks with the government. A peace agreement was signed in January 1992. Then, in May 1992, the FMLN announced that it intended to form itself into a political party. The Supreme Electoral Court recognized the party in December 1992, by which time the leadership had effectively abandoned the FMLN's original Marxist-Leninist orientation and embraced democratic socialism.

At its first national convention in September 1993, the FMLN endorsed Rubén Ignacio Zamora Rivas of the Democratic Convergence (CD) – later part of the United Democratic Centre – as its 1994 presidential candidate. In the event, Zamora came second, with some 26% of the vote, while in its first legislative elections in March 1994 the FMLN won 21 seats (against ARENA's 39). The candidacy of Zamora exacerbated already existing internal tensions, and in December 1994 a majority of two of the FMLN's constituent groups left the Front to form the Democratic Party.

In the 1997 legislative elections the FMLN improved to 27 seats (compared with 28 for ARENA), also winning 100 of the 262 municipalities it contested, including San Salvador. The party suffered a setback in the March 1999 presidential election when its candidate Facundo Guardado gained only 29% of the vote in losing to Francisco Flores of ARENA (52%).

The FMLN had greater success in legislative elections in March 2000, winning 31 seats (against ARENA's 29) with 35% of the vote. The Front was helped by a pre-election promise made by the new FMLN mayor of San Salvador, Hector Silva, to co-operate with business and avoid new taxes. However, despite gaining the largest number of seats in the Assembly, the Front remained in opposition because of ARENA's ability to forge an alliance with other right-wing parties. In addition, a further bout of political infighting weakened the party's parliamentary standing in 2001, when the orthodox Marxist wing of the party gained control of the party's leadership. In response six dissident legislators from the moderate reform wing refused to follow the party line, and in 2002 the six were thrown out of the party. Although one of the dissidents subsequently returned to the FMLN fold, the remaining five sealed the break in April 2002, registering the Renewal Movement as a new party.

Despite this setback the FMLN managed to win back the seats lost after the defections in the 2003 legislative elections to bring its total back to 31. The party then established an ad hoc alliance with the National Conciliation Party (PNC) in an attempt to debilitate the government ahead of the presidential vote. Despite this strategy the FMLN suffered another crushing defeat in the 2004 presidential election. The FMLN candidate, Schafik Handal, a hardline former secretary general of the Salvadorian Communist Party, was defeated by a 21 percentage-point margin. In the aftermath a number of leading reformers within the FMLN demanded that Schafik and his central committee colleagues should resign. They wanted to make the party more democratic, make a decisive break from its guerrilla past and offer more realistic policies for the middle class.

Nationalist Republican Alliance
Alianza Republicana Nacionalista (ARENA)

Address. Prolongación Cl Arce No. 2429. Ent 45 y 47 Av. Nte. San Salvador
Telephone. (503) 260-4400
Fax. (503) 260-1371
Email. comunicaciones@arena.co.sv
Website. www.arena.com.sv
Leadership. Alfredo Cristiani Burkard (president)
Roberto D'Aubuisson Arrieta, a former major and once head of the intelligence section of the notoriously brutal National Guard, founded ARENA in 1981. This complemented his involvement during the 1970s in the National Democratic Organization (Orden), a mass-based paramilitary organization said to be linked to the security forces and the White Warriors Union, one of several right-wing death squads.

ARENA quickly became a leading political force, winning 19 seats in the 1982 elections to the legislature, of which D'Aubuisson was elected president. D'Aubuisson was accused of personally organizing political killings from an office in the Assembly, the most notorious being the assassination in March 1980 of Monsignor Oscar Arnulfo Romero, Archbishop of San Salvador and a fierce critic of state violence.

Having been shunned by the 1977-81 US Democratic administration of Jimmy Carter, D'Aubuisson was rehabilitated by the succeeding Republican administration of Ronald Reagan as part of its anti-communist Cold War stance towards Central America. However, D'Aubuisson's continued association with the death squads meant that the USA did not endorse his candidacy for President in 1984 but instead supported, and some said "engineered", the victory of José Napoleón Duarte of the Christian Democratic Party. The defeat provoked the first split in ARENA, D'Aubuisson's vice-presidential running mate Hugo Barrera forming a breakaway party in May 1985.

Eager for increased influence and respectability, ARENA's September 1985 national general assembly accepted D'Aubuisson's resignation as secretary-general and elected him as honorary life president. Under the new leadership of Alfredo Cristiani Burkard, ARENA presented a more moderate image, especially to the USA, and won the 1988 presidential elections on a programme that offered the prospect of national reconciliation. In the March 1991 legislative elections, the party lost its overall majority in the Legislative Assembly; although it remained the country's largest party, the result encouraged moderate elements to pursue a course of political consensus. Tentative peace negotiations with the Farabundo Marti National Liberation Front (FMLN), which hardline elements in both the army and ARENA tried to sabotage, began in April 1990 under UN auspices; a peace treaty was formally signed in January 1992 and a ceasefire established in February 1992. Before dying of throat cancer in February 1992, D'Aubuisson adopted an increasingly "pragmatic" approach to the peace process and was judged to have played a crucial role behind the scenes in keeping ARENA's most fundamentalist anti-communist factions in line behind Cristiani.

The party's legislative representation was unchanged in 1994, when ARENA candidate Armando Calderón Sol was the comfortable victor in presidential elections. In 1997 ARENA lost considerable ground to the FMLN and only managed to defeat it in legislative elections by a margin of one seat. The party retained the presidency in March 1999, when Francisco Guillermo Flores Pérez easily defeated the FMLN candidate with 51.4% of the vote. However, ARENA faced further difficulties in the 2000 legislative elections, winning 29 seats against 31 for the FMLN. The party lost some popular support because of fears about rising crime and its continued espousal of free-market policies. Despite losing first place to the FMLN in the poll, ARENA managed to retain control of the Assembly through the support of other right-wing parties. Nevertheless the election results gave rise to a rapid shift in party and government policy. In the immediate aftermath of the poll, the Flores administration announced a succession of populist measures to mark its last year in office, and modified its hardline position on a number of controversial issues, such as healthcare reform. At the same time the process of party modernization undertaken by Flores came under severe criticism from the traditional wing of the party. Modernization had diluted the party's original strong nationalist platform and marginalized the role of many long-time ARENA militants whose participation in the party dated from the civil war. In their place, a new class of leader drawn from the private sector came to the fore.

The Assembly elections in 2003 again saw ARENA lose ground to the FMLN, and without the support of the National Conciliation Party (PCN) the parliament became more hostile to the government's legislative programme. Despite this setback ARENA won a convincing victory in the presidential election held in March 2004 with its candidate Antonio Elías Saca, a young media magnate. It was the fourth successive presidential victory for ARENA. Saca undertook an effective negative campaign that portrayed the FMLN candidate as representing a return to times of division, civil war, and fractious relations with the USA. Indeed, the Bush administration made clear its preference for Saca, and warned against an FMLN victory. The result meant that El Salvador kept its small contingent of troops in Iraq and would continue to follow a liberal market economic policy. These include dollarization, privatization and support for the Central American Free Trade Agreement. ARENA also hoped that the Saca's clear presidential victory, which left the opposition in disarray, would help him to exploit their weakness to his legislative advantage.

National Conciliation Party
Partido de Conciliación Nacional (PCN)
Address. 15 Av. Nte y 3a Cl Pte. No. 244, San Salvador
Telephone. (503) 221-3752
Leadership. Ciro Cruz Zepeda Peña (president)
The direct successor of the Revolutionary Party of Democratic Unification, the right-wing PCN was founded in 1961 as a social reform party and was in power from 1961 to 1979 until a coup overthrew President Carlos Humberto Romero in October 1979. The party was then a vehicle for a succession of fraudulently elected military Presidents, supported by the elite families, and also used patronage to maintain the loyalty of civilian officials.

In the 1982 elections the PCN obtained 14 seats in the 60-seat Constituent Assembly and received four Cabinet posts in a government of national unity, despite the party's strong anti-reformist bias and remaining close ties with the military. The party, however, split in the same year, with its right wing, including nine Assembly delegates, forming the Authentic Institutional Party (PAISA). In 1985, the PCN, as a junior partner in an alliance with the Nationalist Republican Alliance (ARENA) party, won 12 seats in the 1985 elections, a short-lived partnership ending when the party expelled three leaders who had colluded with the ARENA to get the elections declared void.

In 1987, in an attempt at political rehabilitation, the PCN claimed to have rediscovered its "social democratic" roots and opposed the Christian Democrat Party (PDC) government's austerity package, including a war tax. The manoeuvre produced scant reward, the party winning only seven seats in the March 1988 legislative elections and its candidate in the 1989 presidential election received a modest 4.9% of the vote. In July 1989 the party temporarily joined an alliance with the PDC and the Democratic Convergence (CD), claiming to be interested in promoting dialogue with the Farabundo Marti National Liberation Front (FMLN).

In the lead-up to the March 1991 legislative elections, the PCN had clear problems deciding where to locate itself on the political spectrum, one leader claiming that the party was "to the left of ARENA and to the right of the PDC". It chose not to ally itself with ARENA and came third after the PDC, winning 9% of the vote and nine seats. In 1994, despite having developed links with ARENA, support for the PCN slumped and it won only four seats in the Assembly. The party's performance improved in 1997, when it won 11 seats, which increased to 14 in 2000, making it the third most powerful force in the legislature. The upward trend in parliamentary representation continued in 2003 with the PCN gaining a further two seats. After the elections relations between the PCN and ARENA deteriorated, leading to a break-up of the informal coalition that had given the government a working majority in the Assembly. Subsequently the PCN's legislative activity tended to be based on clientist rather than ideological considerations. In exchange for greater representation on legislative committees, for example, the right-wing PCN sided with the left-wing FMLN on several issues. In the presidential contests the PCN won less than 4% of the vote in both 1999 and 2004.

United Democratic Centre
Centro Demócratico Unido (CDU)
Address. c/o Asamblea Legislativa, Palacio Legislativo, Centro de Gobierno, AP 2682 San Salvador
Leadership. Rubén Ignacio Zamora Rivas (secretary general)
The moderate social democratic CDU was formed prior to the

1999 presidential election through a merger of the Democratic Convergence (CD), the Social Democrat Party (PSD) and the Popular Laborist Party (PPL). The CD, founded in 1987 as an umbrella organisation of Marxist parties and professional and labour organizations, made up the bulk of the newly formed CDU. In the 1999 presidential election, the CDU's candidate (and former CD leader), Rubén Ignacio Zamora Rivas, finished third with 7.4% of the vote. The party won three Assembly seats in the 2000 elections, and five in the elections held three years later. In the build up to the presidential contest of 2004 the CDU put forward Héctor Silva Argüello as a joint candidate with the Christian Democratic Party (PDC). Silva was a popular former FMLN mayor of San Salvador in 1997-2003. A respected centrist politician, he broke away from the FMLN is late 2002, and a won a legislative seat with the CDU in the March 2003 elections. Despite his personal standing Silva gained only 3.9% of the vote in the presidential election.

Other Parties

National Action Party (*Partido Accion Nacional,* PAN) won 3.7% of the vote and two Assembly seats in the March 2000 elections, but gained only 1.0% of the vote in the elections held in 2003, losing both of its seats.
Leadership. Gustavo Rogelio Salinas (secretary-general)

Renewal Movement (*Movimiento Renovador*, PMR), derived from a 2002 moderate breakaway group of the Farabundo Marti National Liberation Front (FMLN). Five legislators were thrown out of the FMLN and established the PMR in response. In the 2003 Assembly elections the party won 1.9% of the vote and no seats. However, the PMR did pick up one seat in coalition with the Christian Democratic and Social Democratic Parties.

Social Democratic Party (*Partido Social Demócrata*, PSD) was originally established in 1987 but was shorn of most of its members after the formation of the United Democratic Centre (CDU) prior to the 1999 presidential election. However, a number of members unhappy about the merger with the Democratic Convergence (CD) and the Popular Laborist Party (PPL) retained the PSD name. The party contested the 2003 Assembly elections but gained only 0.7% of the vote and no seats. However, the PSD did pick up one seat in coalition with the Christian Democratic Party (PDC) and the Renewal Movement (PMR).
Leadership. Juan Medrano

Equatorial Guinea

Capital: Malabo
Population: 481,400 (2002E)

The Republic of Equatorial Guinea won independence from Spain in 1968. The current President, Brig.-Gen. Teodoro Obiang Nguema Mbasogo, seized power from the dictatorship of Francisco Macias Nguema in a coup in 1979. Ruling through a Supreme Military Council, the regime banned all political parties until 1987, when Obiang Nguema announced the formation of a single "party of government", the Democratic Party of Equatorial Guinea (PDGE). Constitutional amendments, approved by referendum in 1982, extended the President's term of office for a further seven years, and provided for the holding of presidential and legislative elections in a gradual transition from military to civilian rule. A new constitution, providing for the introduction of multiparty politics, was adopted by referendum in 1991. It provided for the separation of powers between the President and Prime Minister and also provided for a unicameral legislature (the House of People's Representatives) of 80 members who are directly elected for a five-year term by universal adult suffrage.

Obiang Nguema was first elected (unopposed) as President in 1989 and subsequently secured re-election in February 1996 and December 2002. His most recent victory (with 99.5% of the vote) was marred by irregularities, prompting opposition parties to withdraw their candidates some two hours after voting had started. Legislative elections held in March 1999 gave the PDGE an overwhelming majority, with opposition parties winning only five of the 80 seats. The opposition parties protested during the campaign against electoral irregularities and refused to take up their new seats in the legislature, calling for the results to be annulled.

Democratic Party of Equatorial Guinea
Partido Democrático de Guinea Ecuatorial (PDGE)
Address. c/o Cámara de Representantes del Pueblo, Malabo
Leadership. Brig.-Gen. Teodoro Obiang Nguema Mbasogo (chairman); Filberto Ntutumu Nguema (secretary-general)
The PDGE was launched as the sole legal political party by President Obiang Nguema in October 1987. Shortly afterwards, a law was passed requiring all wage earners and public employees to contribute 3% of their income to the new government party. In response to increasing pressure for greater pluralism, party delegates at an extraordinary congress in August 1991 urged the regime to establish a framework for the legalization of other political parties. A new constitution, approved in November 1991, abolished the PDGE's sole party status and legislation permitting the formation of other parties, although very restrictive in its application, was adopted in early 1992.

The party maintained its dominance in the legislative elections in November 1993, taking 68 of the 80 seats, and was the only party represented in the government appointed the following month. In October 1994 two prominent members of the PDGE resigned from the party in protest against the government's alleged human rights violations and its obstruction of the democratic process. The official results giving the PDGE victory in the September 1995 municipal elections were contested by the opposition, as was the official outcome of the presidential elections in February 1996 and December 2002 giving Obiang Nguema over 99% of the vote.

In April 1997 the government and 13 opposition parties agreed a new national pact for holding elections which provided for the creation of a multiparty electoral commission and an observance commission to monitor compliance. However, the March 1999 legislative elections were held amid opposition claims that the government did not abide by the provisions, that its candidates were arrested and harassed and that electoral malpractice was rife. The PDGE increased its parliamentary majority by seven seats, claiming 85.5% of the vote. It also won power in all 30 municipal councils in May 2000, according to official results of the elections which were marked by a low voter turn-out following a boycott call by the opposition parties.

Popular Union
Unión Popular (UP)
Address. C/Kenia s/n Apdo. 587, Malabo
Leadership. Andrés-Moisés Mba Ada (leader); Fabian Nsue Nguema (secretary-general).
The UP was legally recognized in 1992. As a member of the Joint Opposition Platform (POC, formed in 1992 but dissolved in 1996), it boycotted the November 1993 legislative elections but participated in the March 1999 poll, securing

four seats with 6.45% of the vote. The UP rejected the election results, alleging irregularities in procedure; it refused to join the new administration, although some dissident members did. The party also boycotted the December 2002 presidential election, although again dissident members were rewarded with positions within the government, most notably parliamentary faction leader Jeremias Ondo Ngomo, who was appointed Deputy Prime Minister in charge of Social Affairs and Human Rights. Earlier, in August 2002, party secretary-general Fabian Nsue Nguema had been sentenced to one year in prison after being found guilty of insulting President Obiang Nguema

The UP has observer status with the Christian Democrat International.

Social Democratic Convergence
Convergencia para la Democracia Social (CPDS)

Address. C/ Tres de Agosto, 72, 2° 1 Malabo

Telephone/Fax. 240 92013

Website. www.cpds-gq.org

Leadership. Placido Miko Abogo (secretary-general); Santiago Obama Ndong (president)

The CPDS was formed in 1984 in Paris by two opposition groups, of which the Democratic Movement for the Liberation of Equatorial Guinea (*Reunión Democrática para la Liberación de Guinea Ecuatorial*, RDLGE), led by Manuel Rubén Ndongo, had in March 1983 announced the creation of a provisional government-in-exile. The CPDS was active within Equatorial Guinea from 1991 onwards in pressing for democratization, and was legally recognized in February 1993. The party did not join the boycott of the November 1993 elections and secured six seats in the House of People's Representatives.

In the 1999 legislative elections, the CPDS retained only a single seat with 5.3% of the vote. With other opposition parties, it formally demanded the annulment of the poll and refused to take up its seat alleging fraud during the voting. Party secretary-general Miko Abogo also complained that there were insufficient numbers of international observers to monitor polling procedures. The party did not participate in the municipal elections in 2000 nor the presidential poll of December 2002.

In June 2002 Miko Abogo was among some 70 opposition figures imprisoned for their alleged involvement in a failed coup attempt in 1997. Miko Abogo was sentenced to 14 years' imprisonment, but, along with many other political prisoners, was pardoned by President Obiang Nguema in August 2003.

The CPDS is a full member of the Socialist International.

Other Parties

Democratic National Union (*Unión Democrática Nacional*, UDENA), pro-government party, leader serves as adviser to President Obiang Nguema. Affiliated to the Liberal International.

Leadership. Pedro Cristino Bueriberi Bokesa

Liberal Democratic Convention (*Conventión Liberal Democrática*, CLD), in coalition with ruling Democratic Party of Equatorial Guinea. The party president serves in government as Minister-Delegate for Press, Radio and Television.

Leadership. Alphonso Nsue Mokuy (president)

Liberal Party (*Partido Liberal*, PL), pro-government party, leader serves as adviser to President Obiang Nguema.

Leadership. Antonio Nkulu Asumu.

Party of the Social Democratic Coalition (*Partido de la Coalición Social Demócrata*, PCSD), pro-government party,

leader serves as Minister-Delegate for Planning and Economic Development.

Leadership. Buenaventura Monsuy Asumu.

Progressive Alliance (*Alianza Progresista*, AP), pro-government party, leader serves as adviser to President Obiang Nguema.

Leadership. Carmelo Mba Bakale

Progressive Democratic Alliance (Alianza *Democrática y Progresista,* ADP), pro-government party, leader serves as Minister-Delegate for Communications and Transport.

Leadership. Francisco Mba Olo Bahamonde.

Social Democratic and Popular Convergence (*Convergencia Social Democrática y Popular*, CSDP), pro-government party, leader serves as Minister-Delegate for Justice.

Leadership. Secundino Oyono Awong.

Social Democratic Party (*Partido Socialdemócrata*, PSD), pro-government party, leader serves as Secretary of State for Energy.

Leadership. Francisco Mabale Nseng.

Social Democratic Union (*Unión Democrática y Social*, UDS), pro-government party, leader serves in government as Minister of State in charge of Industry, Commerce and Small Business Promotion.

Leadership. Carmelo Modu Acuse Bindang (secretary-general).

Socialist Party of Equatorial Guinea (*Partido Socialista de Guinea Ecuatorial*, PSGE), pro-government party, leader serves as Minister-Delegate for Health and Social Welfare.

Leadership. Tomas Mechebe Fernandez Galilea.

Banned parties and groups

Progress Party of Equatorial Guinea (*Partido del Progreso de Guinea Ecuatorial*, PPGE), declared illegal in 1997 following allegations of a planned coup in which party leader Severo Mota Nsa was implicated. The PPGE is an affiliate of the Christian Democrat International.

National Resistance of Equatorial Guinea (*Resistencia Nacional de Guinea Ecuatorial*, RENAGE), Spanish-based opposition umbrella organisation that includes amongst its members: the Independent Union of Democrats (*Unión de Demócratas Independientes*); the Movement for the Self-determination of the Island of Bioko (*Movimiento para la Autodeterminación de la Isla de Bioko*); the Union for Democracy and Social Development (*Unión para la Democracia y el Desarollo Social*); the non-parliamentary wing of the Popular Union (*Unión Popular*); and the Republican Democratic Forces (*Fuerza Demócrata Republicana*).

Eritrea

Capital: Asmara

Population: 4,100,000 (UN, 2003)

A former Italian colony, Eritrea was a British protectorate from 1941 to 1952, when it became federated with Ethiopia by a decision of the United Nations. It was annexed by Ethiopia in 1962. That action violated the terms of the UN-sponsored federation arrangement and triggered an armed rebellion by secessionist forces in Eritrea. Nearly three decades later, the Eritrean insurgency played a key part in the toppling of Mengistu Haile Mariam's Marxist dictatorship in Addis Ababa in May 1991.

Initially after Mengistu's collapse, Eritrea functioned as an autonomous region with the Eritrean People's Liberation Front (EPLF), now the People's Front for Democracy and Justice (PFDJ), establishing a provisional government. The Republic of Eritrea was declared in May 1993 following a UN-supervised referendum.

A transitional government led by Isayas Afewerki, the leader of the PFDJ, was established to administer the country for a maximum of four years pending the drafting of a constitution and multi-party elections. Legislative power was vested in a unicameral National Assembly, comprising 75 members of the central committee of the PFDJ, plus (from March 1994) an equal number of members elected by PFDJ regional committees. The National Assembly elected the President, who was in turn its Chairman. Executive power was vested in a State Council appointed and chaired by the President.

In May 1997 a Constituent Assembly, comprising the 150 members of the current National Assembly and 377 representatives of regional assemblies and Eritreans living outside the country, adopted a draft constitution. Under this a President would be popularly elected for a maximum of two five-year terms, while a popularly elected legislature would have powers to revoke the President's mandate by a two-thirds majority vote. Political "pluralism" was authorized on a "conditional" basis with a view to holding elections (and thereby bringing the new constitution into force) in 1998. Pending the elections, legislative power was vested in a transitional National Assembly comprising the 75 members of the PDFJ central committee, 60 regional members of the former Constituent Assembly and 15 representatives of Eritreans living outside the country. The presidency and the executive continued to function on the basis of existing transitional arrangements.

However, the holding of general elections in 1998 was postponed by the outbreak of a two-year border war with Ethiopia, and it was not until October 2000 that the transitional National Assembly set a new target date of December 2001 for the elections. Regulations governing political parties were to be drafted by a committee of the transitional National Assembly. In the meantime, President Afewerki continued to govern by proclamation, unrestrained by a transitional national assembly that met infrequently.

The slow pace of reform in Eritrea led to growing political discontent. In October 2000, 13 academics and professionals sent the President a letter suggesting a "critical review" of post-independence development. President Afewerki met with the group but rejected its criticism. In February 2001, the President removed the Minister of Local Government, Mohammed Sherifo, after he questioned country's leadership and requested meetings of the PFJD's central and national councils, which had met only twice during the war with Ethiopia.

Criticism of presidential rule gathered momentum in May 2001 when 15 of the 75-member central council of the PFDJ published an open letter demanding reforms. This letter urged full application of the constitution, multi-party elections, abolition of the non-judicial Special Court, and other reforms. Among the signatories were the former Defence Minister, Mesfin Hagos, other prominent former ministers and ambassadors, and three generals.

In September 2001, the Afewerki government instituted a political crackdown. It arrested 11 of the 15 dissidents that had signed the May protest letter. Only three who were abroad for medical or business reasons and one who had retracted his signature avoided arrest. All of those arrested were held without charge at an unknown location. At the same time, the Eritrean government shut down the independent press and arrested its reporters and editors. Again, they were held incommunicado and without charge. As a result, Eritrea became the only African country to have no privately-owned news media. In subsequent weeks, the government arrested other individuals, including two Eritrean employees of the US Embassy in Asmara.

Despite stinging criticisms from the US State Department, the EU and organizations like Amnesty International and Reporters Without Borders, President Afewerki's government made no apologies for its repressive actions. The political reformers were described as "traitors" who engaged in acts that "jeopardized the nation's sovereignty" and the government also implied that some of the detainees were CIA agents.

In late January 2002, the PFDJ-dominated National Assembly met for the first time in 18 months and decided not to allow the creation of political parties in Eritrea, at least for the near future. That decision did not provoke a visible domestic reaction. In an interview with the *Atlantic Monthly* journal in April 2003, President Aferwerki said that given Eritrea had nine language groups and two religions "we will have to manage the creation of political parties, so that they don't become means of religious and ethnic division, like in Ivory Coast or Nigeria".

While the recent political clampdown in Eritrea is having a negative impact on aid from the international community, political pressures to liberalize in Eritrea could be offset by new strategic imperatives after the events of September 11. The Pentagon is interested in military bases in places like Assab and Massawa, but it is believed that the State Department remains opposed until President Afewerki meets US demands on human rights and political pluralism.

People's Front for Democracy and Justice (PFDJ)

Address. PO Box 1081, Asmara

Leadership. Isayas Afewerki (chairman); Gen. Alamin Mohamed Said (secretary-general)

The PFDJ's predecessor, the Eritrean People's Liberation Front (EPLF), was originally founded in 1970 as a left-wing breakaway group from the traditionalist Eritrean Liberation Front, in pursuit of Eritrean independence. It latterly moved away from a Marxist stance. For much of its pre-independence existence the EPLF controlled large areas of the Eritrean countryside. By 1989 it claimed to control 90% of the province, completing its dominance thereafter with the fall of the Mengistu regime in 1991. The EPLF converted itself from a national liberation movement into a political party, taking the PFDJ designation, at a congress in February 1994. The 75 members of the central committee of the PFDJ constituted the core membership of the transitional National Assembly set up to exercise legislative power pending the finalization of a timetable for holding multi-party elections. The transitional legislature was responsible for electing the President of Eritrea (an office held by Isayas Afewerki throughout the transitional period).

Other Groups

Democratic Movement for the Liberation of Eritrea (DMLE), an organization opposed to the People's Front for Democracy and Justice (PFDJ).

Leadership. Hamid Turky

Eritrean Islamic Jihad (EIJ), a radical opposition group. *Leadership.* Sheikh Mohamed Arafa

Eritrean Liberation Front (ELF), mainly Muslim and formed in the late 1950s to pursue Eritrean autonomy. It initiated anti-Ethiopian guerrilla activity in the early 1960s, but its influence later declined as it was increasingly marginalized by the breakaway Eritrean People's Liberation Front (which later became the People's Front for Democracy and Justice). Now split into numerous factions, the ELF opposed the PDFJ transitional government of Eritrea.

Eritrean People's Liberation Front Democratic Party (EPLFDP) is the first opposition organization to be created from the membership of the PFDJ party that now rules Eritrea. Established in January 2002 with a statement on the internet, the EPLFDP aims to protest at President Afewerki's authoritarian rule. It believed that one of its founding members is the former Defence Minister, Mesfin Hagos.

Estonia

Capital: Tallinn
Population: 1,356,045 (2003)

The full sovereignty of the Republic of Estonia was declared on Aug. 20, 1991 (and recognized by the USSR State Council on Sept. 6, 1991), following the Estonian legislature's repudiation in March 1990 of the absorption of Estonia by the USSR in August 1940. A new constitution approved by referendum in June 1992 provided for a parliamentary system combined with a strong presidency. The President is elected for a five-year term by secret ballot of members of the legislature. In the absence of the required two-thirds majority after three voting rounds, the President is elected by a special assembly of parliamentary deputies and local council representatives. The President nominates the Prime Minister, who forms the Council of Ministers. The government must command the support of the 101-member unicameral Parliament (*Riigikogu*), itself popularly elected for a four-year term by a system of proportional representation of parties which obtain at least 5% of the vote. Under constitutional amendments adopted in November 1998, parties may not contest elections in alliances, although joint lists of candidates are permissible. The franchise is vested in those possessing Estonian citizenship.

In the third parliamentary elections since independence, held on March 7, 1999, the Estonian Centre Party (EKe) won 28 seats (with 23.4% of the vote), Fatherland Union (IML) 18 seats (16.1%), Estonian Reform Party (ER) 18 seats (15.9%), Moderates 17 seats (15.2%), Estonian Coalition Party (EK) 7 seats (7.6%), Estonian Rural People's Party (EME) 7 seats (7.3%), and United People's Party of Estonia (EÜR) 6 seats (6.1%). Mart Laar (Fatherland Union) became the Prime Minister and headed Estonia's reformist three-party, centre-right coalition. While his government's performance was quite impressive in foreign affairs and in continuing reforms, his overconfident political style spoiled relations with the coalition partners. He resigned on Jan. 10, 2002, and another right-of-centre coalition headed by the Reform Party under Prime Minister Siim Kallas governed Estonia until March 2003.

The March 3, 2003, elections produced the following results: Estonian Centre Party 25.4% of the vote,

28 seats; Union for the Republic–Res Publica 24.6%, 28 seats; Estonian Reform Party 17.7%, 19 seats; Estonian People's Union 13%, 13 seats; Pro Patria–Fatherland Union 7.3%, 7 seats; Moderates 7%, 6 seats; United People's Party of Estonia 2.2%, no seats; Estonia Christian Party 1.1%, no seats.

Overall, centre-right parties won 60 seats in parliament, with left-oriented parties winning just 41. The Estonian President, Arnold Ruutel, found himself in the difficult position of having to choose which of the two parties that won an equal number of seats could form the next government, both parties having ruled out a coalition with the other. After extensive consultations Union for the Republic-Res Publica formed the government with the support of Estonian Reform Party and Estonian People's Union.

Estonia became a member of the European Union on May 1, 2004, and on June 13, 2004, Estonians elected their six representatives to the European Parliament. Estonia's 14-month-old centre-right coalition government was sidelined as the pro-EU Social Democratic Party (the re-named Moderates) seized three of the country's six seats with 36.8% of the vote. The Centre Party secured 17.5% of the vote – 1 seat; Estonian Reform Party 12.2% – 1 seat; and Fatherland Union 10.5% – 1 seat. The turnout was the third lowest in the EU with just 26.7% of the country's more than 874,000 eligible voters casting ballots.

Estonian Centre Party
Eesti Keskerakond (EKe)
Address. PO Box 3737, Tallinn 10158
Telephone. (372–6) 273460
Fax. (372–6) 273461
Email. keskerakond@keskerakond.ee
Website. www.keskerakond.ee
Leadership. Edgar Savisaar (chairman); Toomas Varek (parliamentary group chairman); Küllo Arjakas (secretary-general)

The populist EKe was founded on Oct. 12 1991, being an offshoot of the Estonian Popular Front (*Eestimaa Rahvarinne*, ER) which had spearheaded the post-1988 independence movement but had split into various parties after independence was achieved. As ER leader, Edgar Savisaar had been Prime Minister from April 1990 to January 1992, having previously been chairman of the Estonian branch of the Soviet-era Planning Committee (Gosplan). The EKe used the ER designation in the September 1992 parliamentary and presidential elections, winning 15 seats (with 12.2% of the vote) and achieving third place (with 23.7%) for its presidential candidate, Rein Taagepera, in the popular balloting which then applied. The EKe absorbed the Estonian Entrepreneurs' Party (*Eesti Ettevtjate Erakond*, EEE) prior to the March 1995 parliamentary elections, in which it won 16 seats with 14.2% of the vote. In April 1995 it joined a coalition government with the Coalition and Rural People's Union (headed by the Estonian Coalition Party, EK), Savisaar becoming Minister of Internal Affairs.

The dismissal of Savisaar in October 1995 for alleged involvement in phone-tapping (of which he was later cleared) resulted in the collapse of the government and the exclusion of the EKe from the succeeding coalition. Savisaar was replaced as EKe leader by Andra Veidemann and announced his retirement from politics. In early 1996, however, he became leader of an anti-Veidemann faction and was re-elected leader of the party in March. Veidemann and her supporters responded by forming the breakaway Progressive Party (AP), which was joined by seven of the 16 EKe deputies.

Having absorbed the small Green Party in June 1998, the EKe entered into talks with the Estonian Rural People's Party (EME) on a ruling coalition after the March 1999 parliamentary elections. Campaigning on a populist platform designed to appeal to voters disenchanted with the free-market economy, the EKe advanced strongly to become the largest party 28 seats and 23.4% of the vote). However, the fact that the EME won only seven seats meant that an EKe-EME government was not feasible. The EKe therefore continued in opposition to a precarious coalition led by the Fatherland Union (IL). In the March 3, 2003, parliamentary elections the party won 25.4% of the vote – 28 seats.

In August 2001 the Liberal International announced that it had rejected the EKe's application for membership on the grounds that the conduct of Savisaar "does not always conform to liberal principles". On June 13, 2004, Edgar Savisaar was elected a member of the European Parliament, the EKe having secured one of the six seats alocated to Estonia on a 17.5% share of the vote.

Estonian Coalition Party
Eesti Koonderakond (EK)

Address. Tulika 19, Tallinn 10613
Telephone. (372–6) 505113
Fax. (372–6) 505114
Email. koondera@delfi.ee
Website. www.koonderakond.ee
Leadership. Märt Kubo (chairman); Mart Siimann (parliamentary group chairman); Juhan Hindov (secretary-general)
The centrist urban-based EK was founded in December 1991, its then effective leader, Tiit Vähi, becoming caretaker Prime Minister in January 1992. In the September 1992 parliamentary elections the party was part of the nationalist Secure Home coalition, which formed the main parliamentary opposition until 1995. The EK headed the Coalition and Rural People's Union (KMÜ) in the March 1995 parliamentary elections, winning 18 of the alliance's 41 seats. The following month Vähi became Prime Minister of a coalition government between the KMÜ and the Estonian Centre Party (EKe).

A government crisis in October 1995 resulted in the departure of the EKe and its replacement by the Estonian Reform Party (ER), under the continued premiership of Vähi. He remained in office after the ER also withdrew from the government in November 1996, but finally resigned in February 1997. He was succeeded as Prime Minister and EK chairman by Märt Siimann, who led the party to a major defeat in the March 1999 parliamentary elections. The EK won only seven seats (with 7.6% of the vote) and went into opposition. In May 1999 Siimann was replaced as party chairman by Märt Kubo, who faced falling support for a party which appeared to have failed to reconcile its broadly pro-market line with its caution on the dismantling of the state-controlled economy.

With a membership of just over 1,000, the EK is a member of the Liberal International.

Estonian People's Union
Eestimaa Rahvaliit (ERL)

Address. Marja 4d, Tallinn 10617
Telephone. (372–6) 112909
Fax. (372–6) 112908
Email. erl@erl.ee
Website. www.erl.ee
Leadership. Villu Reiljan (chairman); Arnold Rüütel (honorary chairman); Mai Treial & Ants Kaarma (deputy chairpersons); Lea Kiivit (secretary-general)
The ERL was founded in June 2000 as a merger of the Estonian Rural People's Party (EME), the country's largest agrarian formation, with the small Estonian Rural Union (EM) and the Estonian Pensioners' and Families' League (EPPL). These three parties had each gained representation in the 1995 parliamentary elections as components of the victorious Coalition and Rural People's Union (KMÜ), but only the EME had continued to be represented after the 1999 elections.

The EME was founded in September 1994 on the initiative of Arnold Rüütel, who as Chairman of the Estonian Supreme Soviet had supported moves to throw off Soviet rule and had become independent Estonia's first head of state. Rüütel had subsequently headed the popular poll in the September 1992 presidential elections as the Secure Home candidate, winning 42.2% of the vote, but had been narrowly defeated in the decisive legislative balloting. The EME formed the KMÜ alliance with the Estonian Coalition Party (EK) for the 1995 elections, bringing agrarian support to the alliance. Having won nine seats, it joined a coalition government headed by the EK. In February 1996 the EME was weakened by two defections from its parliamentary group, but it made its presence felt in government by opposing what it regarded as over-hasty pro-market reforms. In the run-up to the March 1999 elections the EME and the Estonian Centre Party (EKe) drew up plans to form a post-election government. However, despite the EKe's major advance, the EME retained only seven seats (with 7.3% of the vote), so that an EKe-EME coalition was not feasible.

Founded in March 1991, the EM had contested the 1992 parliamentary elections as part of the Secure Home coalition and had won eight seats in the 1995 elections as part of the KMÜ. The EPPL was derived from the Estonian Democratic Justice Union/Pensioners' League (EDO/PÜ) and had won six seats in 1995.

A congress of the new ERL in Tallinn in June 2001 elected honorary chairman Rüütel as the party's candidate in the forthcoming presidential elections. ERL chairman Villu Reiljan, a former Environment Minister, directed fierce criticism at the government headed by the Fatherland Union, calling for its resignation.

In the March 2003 parliamentary elections the party won 13% of the vote and 13 seats and joined the coalition government led by Prime Minister Juhan Parts.

Estonian Reform Party
Eesti Reformierakond (ER)

Address. Tõnismägi 3a-15, Tallinn 10119
Telephone. (372–6) 408740
Email. info@reform.ee
Website. www.reform.ee
Leadership. Siim Kallas (chairman); Toomas Savi (parliamentary group chairman); Eero Tohver (secretary-general)
The centre-right pro-market ER was launched by Siim Kallas in late 1994 after he had helped, as president of the Bank of Estonia, to bring about the downfall of Prime Minister Mart Laar (of the Pro Patria National Coalition, later the Fatherland Union) but had then failed to secure parliamentary endorsement as Laar's successor in the premiership. The ER incorporated the Estonian Liberal Democratic Party (*Eesti Liberaaldemokraatlik Partei*, ELDP) led by Paul-Eerik Rummo, which had contested the 1992 elections as part of the winning Pro Patria coalition but had withdrawn from the latter in June 1994 in protest against Maar's leadership style.

Using the unofficial designation "Liberals", the ER took second place in the March 1995 parliamentary elections, winning 19 seats and 16.2% of the vote. Having thus effectively become leader of the opposition, Kallas resigned from his central bank post. Six months later, in November 1995, he became Deputy Premier and Foreign Minister when the ER joined a new government coalition headed by the Estonian Coalition Party and including five other ER ministers. In late 1996, however, the ER left the government, while continuing to give it qualified external support.

In the March 1999 parliamentary elections the ER

slipped to 18 seats with 15.9% of the vote. It nevertheless joined a centre-right coalition headed by the Fatherland Union in which Kallas obtained the finance portfolio and four other ER ministers were appointed. Despite an ongoing court case against him over alleged financial impropriety, Kallas was re-elected ER chairman in May 1999. He was again re-elected in May 2001, at a party congress which also elected ER parliamentary group chairman Toomas Vilosius as the party's candidate in the forthcoming presidential elections. In the March 2003 parliamentary elections the party won 17.7% of the vote and 19 seats in parliament and joined the coalition government led by Prime Minister Juhan Parts. In the June 13, 2004, elections to the European Parlaiment the ER won 12.2% of the national vote and secured one of the six seats alocated to Estonia.

With an official membership of some 2,000, the ER is a member of the Liberal International.

Estonian Social Democratic Labour Party
Eesti Sotsiaalemokraatlik Tööpartei (ESDT)
Address. PO Box 4102, Tallinn 10111
Telephone. (372–6) 493965
Fax. (372–6) 472147
Email. esdtp@hot.ee
Website. www.esdtp.ee/
Leadership. Tiit Toomsalu (chairman)
The ESDT was founded on Nov. 28, 1992 as the Estonian Democratic Labour Party (EDT) by elements of the former ruling Estonian Communist Party, now proclaiming a democratic socialist orientation. Having unsuccessfully contested the 1995 elections within the Justice (*Öiglus*) alliance, the EDT became the ESDT in December 1997. In the March 1999 parliamentary elections it won two seats on the list of the United People's Party of Estonia (EÜRP). However, in the March 2, 2003, elections it secured only 0.4% of the votes and won no seats.

Fatherland Union–Pro Patria
Isamaaliit (IML)
Address. Endla 4a/VI Korrus, Tallinn 10142
Telephone. (372–6) 263325
Fax. (372–6) 263324
Email. isamaaliit@isamaaliit.ee
Website. www.isamaaliit.ee
Leadership. Tunne Kelam (chairman)
The centre-right IML was founded in December 1995 as a merger of the Fatherland (or "Pro Patria") National Coalition (*Rahvuslik Koonderakond Isamaa*, RKI) and the Estonian National Independence Party (*Eesti Rahvusliku Sötumatuse Partei*, ERSP). Then the dominant government formations, these two parties had contested the March 1995 elections in alliance but had retained only eight seats with 7.9% of the vote, thereafter going into opposition.

The RKI had been formed in early 1992 as an alliance of several Christian democratic and other centre-right parties seeking to make a decisive break with the Soviet era. Led by Mart Laar, it won an indecisive plurality of 29 seats in the September 1992 elections (with 22% of the vote), its deputies combining the following month with those of the ERSP and others to elect Lennart Meri as President despite his having come second in the popular balloting with 29.8% of the vote. Laar then engineered the conversion of the RKI into a unitary formation and was named to head a coalition government. But he was eventually ousted as Prime Minister in September 1994, in part because of his self-confessed "dictatorial" methods.

The ERSP had been founded in August 1988, being then the only organized non-communist party in the whole of the USSR. Although centrist in orientation, it was consistently more anti-communist than other pro-independence formations,

declining to participate in the 1990 Estonian Supreme Soviet elections and instead organizing the alternative "Congress of Estonia". Following independence in 1991, the ERSP became Estonia's strongest party, but was eclipsed by the RKI in the September 1992 elections, when the then ERSP chair, Lagle Parek, took fourth place in the presidential contest with only 4.3% of the vote. Thereafter the ERSP became a junior coalition partner in the government headed by the RKI.

In the March 1999 parliamentary elections the IML took second place, winning 18 seats with 16.1% of the vote. The resultant constellation of forces meant that Laar was able to form a three-party centre-right coalition with the Moderates and the Estonian Reform Party, the new government commanding 53 of the 101 parliamentary seats. In April 2001 an IML congress elected Peeter Tulviste, chairman of the Tartu city council, as the party's candidate in the forthcoming presidential elections.

In the March 2003 parliamentary elections the party won 7.3% of the vote and 7 seats, while in the June 2004 elections to the European Parlaiment the ER won 10.5% of the national vote and secured one of the six seats alocated to Estonia.

The IML is a member of the International Democrat Union and the Christian Democrat International.

Social Democratic Party (former Moderates)
Sotsiaaldemokraatlik Erakond (SDE) (former Mõõdukad)
Address. Asukoht: Pärnu mnt. 41 a, 10119 Tallinn
Telephone. (372–6) 44 0071
Fax. (372–6) 44 0071
Email. kantselei@sotsdem.ee
Website. www.sotsdem.ee/sotsdem/
Leadership. Andres Tarand (chairman); Tõnu Köiv (secretary-general)
The Moderates (*Mõõdukad*) was launched in 1990 as an electoral alliance of the Estonian Rural Centre Party (EMK) and the Estonian Social Democratic Party (ESDP). The EMK had been founded in 1990 to represent small farmers who favoured transition to a market economy and the restoration of pre-war property rights. Re-established in 1990, the ESDP was descended from the historic Social Democratic Party founded in 1905 (when Estonia was part of the Russian Empire) and was maintained in exile during the post-1945 Soviet era.

The alliance won 12 seats in the 1992 parliamentary elections, becoming a member of the resultant government headed by the Pro Patria National Coalition (later the Fatherland Union). It was therefore closely associated with the radical pro-market policies pursued by the 1992-95 government and with resultant rising unemployment and high inflation. Its punishment in the March 1995 elections, in which it was endorsed by then Prime Minister Andres Tarand (EMK), was a slump to only six seats in aggregate (with 6% of the vote). The response of the partners was to merge under the *Mõõdukad* title in April 1996, with Tarand becoming chairman.

In the March 1999 parliamentary elections the Moderates recovered strongly to 17 seats on a 15.2% vote share, becoming the progressive wing of a new centre-right coalition government headed by the Fatherland Union and also including the Estonian Reform Party. Having failed to obtain the premiership, Tarand became chairman of the coalition's co-ordinating council. In May 1999 the Moderates absorbed the People's Party (*Rahvaerakond*), which had been formed in 1998 as a merger of the Estonian Farmers' Party (ETRE) and the right-wing Republican and Conservative People's Party (*Parempoolsed*).

In the March 2003 parliamentary elections the party won 7% of the vote and 6 seats. On Feb. 7, 2004, the party changed its name to the Social Democratic Party

(*Sotsiaaldemokraatlik Erakond*). In the June 13, 2004, elections to the European Parliament the Social Democratic Party won 36.8% of the national vote on a pro-EU platform and secured three of the six seats alocated to Estonia.

The party inherited the ESDP's full membership of the Socialist International.

Union for the Republic–Res Publica
Ühendus Vabariigi Eest–Res Publica
Address. Narva rd. 7, Tallinn 10117
Telephone. (372–6) 109 244
Fax. (372–6) 109 243
Email. tallinn@respublika.ee
Website. www.respublica.ee
Leadership. Juhan Parts (chairman)
Res Publica claims to be the oldest political organization in Estonia, having been established on Aug. 18, 1989, in Tallinn as the Union for the Republic, a club for young political enthusiasts. In March 1999 two of its members were elected to the *Riigikogu* on the lists of the Reform Party and the Pro Patria Union. In the local elections of November 1999 it secured the election of 30 councillors, including the mayor of Central Tallinn. The Union was transformed into a political party on Dec. 8, 2001, and Rein Taagepera elected its first chairperson. He was replaced at the party's second general meeting on Aug. 24, 2002, by Juhan Parts, the former Auditor General. In the parliamentary elections on March 2, 2003, Res Publica won 24.6% of the vote and 28 seats in the *Riigikogu* and subsequently Juhan Parts formed a coalition government that also includes the Estonian Reform Party and Estonian People's Party.

The party promotes what it calls a compassionate conservative programme – traditional cultural and moral values, high ethical standards, clean government, a low tax burden, limited state interference in entrepreneurial activities and a stable economic environment. It maintains that the state's task is not to redistribute the wealth of its citizens, but to provide all job-seekers with skills and training opportunities for them to begin creating wealth of their own. In the March 2003 parliamentary elections Res Publica campaigned on an anti-crime, anti-corruption platform, and was one the harshest critics of the Centre Party and its controversial leader Edgar Savisaar.

At the end of March 2004, Res Publica claimed a membership of 5,028.

United People's Party of Estonia
Eestimaa Ühendatud Rahvapartei (EÜRP)
Address. Estonia pst 3/5, Tallinn 10143
Email. eurp@stv.ee
Website. www.stv.ee/~eurp
Leadership. Viktor Andreyev (chairman)
The EÜRP is the main party of the estimated 30% of Estonia's population who were, or are descended from, Soviet-era settlers, mainly from Russia. For the 1995 parliamentary elections the EÜRP joined with the Russian Party of Estonia (VEE) and the Russian Unity Party (RUP) in the Our Home is Estonia (*Meie Kodu on Eestimaa*, MKE) alliance. This strongly opposed the 1993 Estonian citizenship law defining ethnic Russians and other Soviet-era settlers as foreigners and setting exacting conditions for their naturalization. The fact that only Estonian citizens were entitled to vote resulted in the alliance obtaining only 5.9% of the vote and six seats. The resultant parliamentary group was called the Russian Faction, which quickly split into at least two sub-factions and was dissolved in December 1996, before being revived in June 1998.

The EÜRP contested the March 1999 parliamentary elections in a bloc with the RUP and the (ex-Communist) Estonian Social Democratic Labour Party (ESDT), the outcome again

being six seats (on a 6.1% vote share). The personality clashes that had kept the VEE out of the bloc appeared to be resolved later in 1999. In May 2000 the EÜRP parliamentary faction outraged most Estonian parties by signing a co-operation agreement with the Fatherland–All Russia group in the Russian *Duma*, confirming among other things the parties' joint opposition to Estonian membership of NATO.

In the March 2003 parliamentary elections the party won just 2.2% of the vote and no seats in parliament.

Other Parties

Estonian Blue Party (*Eesti Sinine Erakond,* ESE), also known as the Democrats, unsuccessful in the 1995 and 1999 elections, winning 1.6% in the latter contest.
Leadership. Neeme Kuningas

Estonian Christian People's Party (*Eesti Kristlik Rahvapartei*, EKRP), Christian democratic formation which won 2.4% of the vote in the March 1999 parliamentary elections. In the March 2003 parliamentary elections the party won just 1.1% of the vote and no seats in parliament.
Address. Nava 51, Tallinn 10152
Telephone. (372–6) 688490
Fax. (372–6) 688491
Email. ekrp@ekrp.ee
Website. www.ekrp.ee/

Estonian Greens (*Eesti Rohelised,* ER), founded in 1991, won one legislative seat in 1992, but failed to win representation in 1995 as part of the Fourth Force (*Neljas Jud*, NJ) coalition with the Estonian Royalist Party.
Leadership. Jüri Liim

Estonian Home (*Eesti Kodu*), formed part of the unsuccessful right-wing alliance Better Estonia and Estonian Citizens (*Parem Eesti ja Eesti Kodanik*) in the 1995 elections.
Leadership. Kalju Poldvere (chairman)

Estonian Indepedence Party *(Eesti Iseseisvus Partei)*
Website. www.iseseisvuspartei.ee

Estonian Liberal-Democratic State Party (*Eesti Liberaal-Demokraatlik Riigipartei*)
Website. www.hot.ee/eldrpa/

Estonian National Party (*Eesti Rahvuslik Erakond*), formed part of the unsuccessful right-wing alliance Better Estonia and Estonian Citizens (*Parem Eesti ja Eesti Kodanik*) in the 1995 elections.
Leadership. Elmut Laane (chairman)

Estonian National Progressive Party (*Eesti Rahvuslik Eduerakond*), formed part of the unsuccessful right-wing alliance Better Estonia and Estonian Citizens (*Parem Eesti ja Eesti Kodanik*) in the 1995 elections.
Leadership. Ants Erm (chairman)

Estonian National Protection Party (*Eesti Rahva Jäägerpartei*), formed part of the unsuccessful right-wing alliance Better Estonia and Estonian Citizens (*Parem Eesti ja Eesti Kodanik*) in the 1995 elections.
Leadership. Asso Kommer (chairman)

Estonian People's Radical Party (*Eestimaalaste Radikaalne Erakond*).
Address. Jaama 1a, Tallinn, 11615
Telephone. (372–6) 555 077
Email. radikaalid@hot.ee
Website. www.radikaalid.ee

Estonian Royalist Party (*Eesti Rojalistlik Partei*, ERP), founded in 1989, won eight legislative seats in 1992 but lost them all in 1995 standing as part of the Fourth Force (*Neljas Jud*, NJ) alliance with the Estonian Greens. Seeking a candidate to head an Estonian constitutional monarchy, the party at one stage proposed Prince Edward of England, before endorsing a Swedish prince with better credentials.
Address. PO Box 300, Tartu 2400
Telephone. (372–7) 432986
Fax. (372–7) 431466
Leadership. Kalle Kulbok (chairman)

Farmers' Assembly (*Põllumeeste Kogu*, PK), founded in 1992, was a component of the victorious Coalition and Rural People's Union in the March 1995 elections, in which its candidates stood under the banner of the Estonian Rural People's Party, with which it formed a joint parliamentary group. In February 1996, however, the two PK deputies withdrew their support from the government (effectively becoming independents) on the grounds that it had given insufficient attention to the needs of farmers. The PK won only 0.5% of the vote in the 1999 parliamentary elections.
Address. PO Box 543, Tallinn 10111
Leadership. Eldur Parder

National Conservative Party/Farmers Assembly, formed in August 2002 by dissendent members of Res Publica and Pro Patria Union, the party aims to increase the the country's birth rate, encourage family values and preserve the Estonian language. It advocates direct elections for the President, police chiefs and judges. It claims membership of 1,700.
Leadership. Mart Helme (chairma), Andres Herkel (deputy chairman).

Party for Legal Justice (*Õigusliku Tasakaalu Erakond*, OTE), contested the 1995 elections within the unsuccessful Justice (*Õiglus*) alliance, which also included what became the Estonian Social Democratic Labour Party.
Address. Nunne 8, Tallinn 10111
Leadership. Peeter Tedre (chairman)

Progressive Party (*Arengupartei*, AP), launched in May 1996 by a dissident faction of the Estonian Centre Party (EKe) led by Andra Veidemann, who had replaced Edgar Savisaar as EKe leader in October 1995 on the party's exit from government. She had then faced internal opposition orchestrated by Savisaar, who had been re-elected EKe leader in March 1996, whereupon she and six other EKe deputies founded the AP, which was identified as being to the right of the parent party. It joined the ruling coalition led by the Estonian Coalition Party. Facing the probable loss of their seats, Veidemann and the other AP deputies opted for inclusion on the list of the Estonian Rural People's Party (later the Estonian People's Union) in the March 1999 parliamentary elections, and were promptly expelled from the AP, which won only 0.4% of the vote.

Republican Party (*Vabariiklik Partei*)
Address. Kuperjanovi 56-5, 50409 Tartu
Telephone. +3725214512
Email. Leping.Vp@mail.ee
Website. www.vabariiklikpartei.ee/
Leadership. Kristijan-Olari Leping

Russian Party of Estonia (*Vene Erakond Eestis*, VEE), seeking to represent Estonia's substantial ethnic Russian minority, won 2% of the vote in the 1999 parliamentary elections.
Leadership. Nikolai Maspanov (chairman)

Russian Unity Party (RUP), contested the 1999 parliamentary elections in alliance with the United People's Party of Estonia.
Leadership. Igor Sedashev (chairman)

Ethiopia

Capital: Addis Ababa
Population: 70.7 million (UN, 2003)

The Federal Democratic Republic of Ethiopia is located in the Horn of Africa and is bordered on the north and northeast by Eritrea, on the east by Djibouti and Somalia, on the south by Kenya, and on the west and southwest by Sudan. The country has a highly diverse population. Most of its people speak a Semitic or Cushitic language. The Oromo, Amhara, and Tigreans comprise more than 75% of the population, but there are more than 80 different ethnic groups within Ethiopia.

Ethiopia is the oldest independent country in Africa and was an absolute monarchy before 1935, when it was invaded and occupied by Italy. The Emperor Haile Selassie I was restored to his throne by the British army in 1941. He embarked on a modernization programme during the post-war period, and in 1955 the Emperor established a legislature with a lower house elected by universal suffrage. However, despite establishing some of the institutional features of a democratic state, Haile Selassie retained political power in his own hands and certainly remained the real ruler of the country.

After a period of civil unrest which began in February 1974, the aging Haile Selassie was deposed on Sept. 12, 1974, and a provisional administrative council of soldiers, known as the Derg ("committee") seized power from the emperor and installed a government which was socialist in name and military in style. Lt. Col. Mengistu Haile Mariam assumed power as head of state and Derg chairman in February 1977, after having his two predecessors killed.

Mengistu's years in office were marked by a totalitarian-style government and the country's massive militarization, financed by the Soviet Union and the Eastern Bloc, and assisted by Cuba. From 1977 through early 1978 thousands of suspected enemies of the Derg were tortured and/or killed in a purge called the "red terror." Communism was officially adopted during the late 1970s and early 1980s with the promulgation of a Soviet-style constitution, rule through a politburo, and the creation of the Workers' Party of Ethiopia (WPE) in 1984.

The nationalization of agriculture and endless wars with secessionist groups in the northern regions of Tigre and Eritrea led to famine in the 1980s, and in May 1991 the Mengistu regime, deprived of Soviet aid, collapsed. The Ethiopian People's Revolutionary Democratic Front (EPRDF), a coalition of ethnically based opposition movements, came to power and Meles Zenawi became acting Prime Minister in July 1991. At the same time, Ethiopia recognised the independence of Eritrea.

Interim President Meles Zenawi and members of the Transitional Government of Ethiopia (TGE) pledged to oversee the formation of a multi-party democracy. The election for a 547-member constituent assembly was held in June 1994, and this assembly adopted the constitution of the Federal Democratic Republic in December 1994.

The new constitution divided Ethiopia into nine ethnically-based states, each with a popularly elected legislature, and established a system of national government centred on a bicameral federal parliament. This comprises a directly elected House of People's Representatives with a maximum of 550 members and an upper House of the Federation whose members are elected by the state legislatures. The maximum interval between legislative elections is five years.

The federal President (ceremonial head of state) is elected by a two-thirds majority of both houses of the federal parliament for a six-year term (renewable once); candidates are nominated by the House of People's Representatives. A presidential candidate who is a member of parliament must resign from parliament if elected President. The federal Prime Minister (leader of the majority party in the House of People's Representatives) is head of the executive branch, chairman of the Council of Ministers and commander-in-chief of the armed forces.

Elections for Ethiopia's first popularly chosen national parliament and regional legislatures were held in May and June 1995. Most opposition parties chose to boycott these elections. That ensured a landslide victory for the EPRDF. In August 1995, the Federal Republic of Ethiopia was proclaimed. While the introduction of Ethiopia's new constitutional structures stimulated the formation of new political parties and facilitated the beginnings of freer political debate in the country, a brutal 1998-2000 border war with Eritrea, in which tens of thousands died, created a sense of political crisis in the country and put something of a brake on its democratic development.

The two countries signed a peace agreement in December 2000, but final demarcation of the boundary is currently on hold due to Ethiopian objections to the findings of an independent international commission in 2002 which require Addis Ababa to surrender sensitive territory to Eritrea. At present, the United Nations Mission in Ethiopia and Eritrea (UNMEE), a 4,200 strong peacekeeping force, patrols a 25-kilometer-wide Temporary Security Zone (TSZ) between the countries, but the situation remains extremely tense.

Meanwhile in May 2000, Ethiopia's general elections were characterized by massive fraud, irregularities and violence. More than 50 political parties took part, including 23 opposition parties. The Meles Zenawi government barred interntional election observers but permitted over 1,500 national election observers, including those from the Ethiopian Human Rights Council, to operate.

According to a report by Amnesty International on the 2000 elections, there "were numerous complaints by opposition parties of repression and intimidation during voter registration and campaigning, particularly in the southern region. The All-Amhara People's Organization and several southern opposition parties, including the Southern Peoples' Democratic Congress, complained of supporters being beaten and detained, offices closed, candidates prevented from registering and supporters dismissed from government employment."

The elections resulted in the ruling EPRDF getting 88% of the seats in parliament. Out of a total of 547 seats, the opposition parties won only 13 seats (2%). Parties affiliated with the EPRDF and a few independent candidates took the rest of the seats. The next general elections in Ethiopia to elect members of the national parliament are due to be held in May 2005.

Recent trends in Ethiopia suggest it would be unwise to assume that these elections will be run in a fair and free fashion. Writing in January 2004, a commentator in the privately-owned *Addis Tribune* newspaper noted that "the EPRDF government has flirted with the ballot by letting itself go through the motions of elections...However, previous experience in these elections shows a ruling party thinking along the lines of [Robert] Mugabe's ZANU-PF, reacting with force whenever the ballot threatens to end its grip on power."

Certainly, the Ethiopian government has continued to deny its citizens' basic human rights and to repress opposition parties. Although Ethiopia's 1994 constitution (article 55, sections 22-23) requires parliament to establish a Human Rights Commission and an Ombudsman, neither exists despite repeated pledges by parliamentary leaders, beginning in 2001, that appointments would "soon" be made. A 1999 broadcasting law was intended to end the EPRDF government's monopoly of radio and television stations, but no licenses have ever been issued and the only non-government radio station is actually owned by the ruling party. Radio is a crucial source of information for much of Ethiopia's rural, often illiterate, population.

Provincial authorities, including local leaders of political parties allied with the ruling coalition, the EPRDF, are often implicated in physical assaults on supporters of registered opposition parties. For example, in 2002, such attacks accounted for the deaths of 15 political demonstrators in Awassa and 128 political protestors in Tepi. There was also a police crackdown against members of two opposition parties, the All-Amhara People's Organization (AAPO) and the Ethiopians' Democratic Party (EDP). Over four hundred AAPO members were arrested between April and June. Many of those taken into custody were candidates in local elections. Over one hundred EDP members were arrested

Major foreign aid donors like the EU and the USA have generally done little to correct these abuses. To some degree, these donors have been pre-occupied by the threat of famine in Ethiopia, the possibility of a renewed Ethiopia-Eritrea war, and, in the case of the USA, the perceived need for Addis Ababa's close cooperation in the new "war on terrorism". In 2003, the US military, operating out of its base in Djibouti, trained an Ethiopian army division in counter-terrorism.

The following list is a selection of the parties, groupings and resistance movements that are of some continuing significance in Ethiopian national politics.

All Amhara People's Organization (AAPO)
Address. c/o House of People's Representatives, Addis Ababa
Leadership. Kegnazmatch Neguea Tibeb
The AAPO was established in 1991 to defend the rights of the Amhara people, which it believed were best served by a unitary Ethiopian state rather than the federation advocated by the Ethiopian People's Revolutionary Democratic Front (and implemented in the 1995 constitution). The AAPO's then leader was jailed from 1994 to 1998, having been convicted of incitement to armed insurrection for making statements which he claimed were within his right to free speech. The AAPO boycotted the 1995 federal elections but contested those of 2000 in order to retain its party registration (which would otherwise have been withdrawn). It fielded 17 candidates for the House of People's Representatives and won one seat in Addis Ababa.

Amhara National Democratic Movement (ANDM)
Address. c/o House of People's Representatives, Addis Ababa

Leadership. Adisu Legese (secretary-general)

Amhara National Democratic Movement is the name adopted in 1994 by the former Ethiopian People's Democratic Movement (EPDM), founded in 1980. The EPDM was one of the two original components of the Ethiopian People's Revolutionary Democratic Front (EPRDF) set up in May 1988, its forces having emerged as a military element in the anti-Mengistu insurgency in the mid-1980s, particularly in Wollo province. The party's change of name in 1994 reflected its standing as the EPRDF constituent party in areas of predominantly Amharic ethnicity. In the 2000 federal elections the ANDM fielded candidates for 134 of the 138 seats allocated to Amhara state in the House of People's Representatives. All 134 candidates were elected. The party also won 11 seats in Addis Ababa.

Council of Alternative Forces for Peace and Democracy in Ethiopia (CAFPDE)

Address. c/o House of People's Representatives, Addis Ababa

Leadership. Beyene Petros (chairman)

The CAFPDE was formed in 1993 but was unable to contest the 1995 elections because it was not granted official registration until mid-1996. Chaired by Beyene Petros and including his Southern Ethiopia People's Democratic Coalition among its constituent groupings, it sought to bring together political parties and organizations based on a variety of interests, as well as bodies representing professional groups, to campaign on a pro-human rights and economic liberalization agenda. Originally comprising 30 organizations and groupings, the CAFPDE was reduced to a coalition of five small groupings following a split in December 1999. Beyene Petros successfully contested the 2000 federal elections as a CAFPDE candidate in a constituency where a new election was held on June 25 after annulment of the May 14 result by the National Electoral Board (which had upheld claims that the conduct of the May elections in this and 13 other southern Ethiopian constituencies was "undemocratic and not free"). No other CAFPDE candidates were elected (although several other members of parties in the coalition were elected to represent their own parties).

Ethiopian Democratic Party (EDP)

Address. c/o House of People's Representatives, Addis Ababa

Leadership. Lidetu Ayalew (secretary-general)

The EDP was formed in 1998 following a split in the All Amhara People's Organization. It fielded 15 candidates for the federal House of People's Representatives in May 2000, winning two seats in Addis Ababa. Its policies included land reforms to benefit peasant farmers. EDP party members (including candidates in current local government elections) were among those targeted by the security forces in May 2001 in a campaign against "political activists" following the violent suppression of student demonstrations in Addis Ababa.

Ethiopian People's Revolutionary Democratic Front (EPRDF)

Address. c/o House of People's Representatives, Addis Ababa

Leadership. Meles Zenawi (chairman)

The EPRDF was set up in May 1988 at the initiative of the Tigre People's Liberation Front (TPLF), in alliance with the Ethiopian People's Democratic Movement (later renamed the Amhara National Democratic Movement, ANDM). The EPRDF's third full member was the Oromo People's Democratic Organization (OPDO), a party formed on the initiative of the TPLF in 1990 after the Oromo Liberation Front (OLF) had refused to join the EPRDF. Although the

TPLF had long subscribed to Marxist-Leninist ideology, an EPRDF congress in early 1991 endorsed an expansion of private enterprise and the introduction of market mechanisms in small-scale agriculture. While advocating a united federal Ethiopia, the congress also accepted Eritrea's right to self-determination.

In military co-operation with the OLF and the Eritrean People's Liberation Front (which subsequently set up the first government of independent Eritrea, renaming itself the People's Front for Democracy and Justice), the EPRDF led the march on Addis Adaba which toppled the Mengistu regime in May 1991. Meles Zenawi became interim President of the transitional government which oversaw the drafting and introduction of a new federal constitution. Already the largest grouping in the interim Council of Representatives formed in July 1991 (where its member parties had 32 of the 87 seats), the EPRDF created an extensive network of affiliated parties and groupings throughout most of Ethiopia. In November 1993 a total of 17 EPRDF affiliates in southern Ethiopia formed the Southern Ethiopian People's Democratic Front (SEPDF), which became the EPRDF's fourth full member.

The EPRDF and its affiliates won an overwhelming majority when elections were held under a new federal constitution in 1995, easily retaining power in 2000. The numbers of federal seats won by each full member of the EPRDF in the 2000 legislative elections were TPLF 40, SEPDF 114, ANDM 145 and OPDO 182. Within the EPRDF's general council (the highest policy-making body) each full member has a fixed entitlement of 20 seats.

The long tradition of TPLF dominance within the EPRDF appeared to be under threat in early 2001 when Meles Zenawi's leadership was challenged by a dissident faction of the TPLF central committee. According to some reports from Ethiopia, leaders of the SEPDF, ANDM and OPDO did not come out in support of Meles Zenawi until it was clear that his faction had prevailed within his own party. According to political analysts, Ethiopia's 1998-2000 border war with Eritrea had reinforced cross-party Ethiopian nationalist sentiments within the EPRDF, a development which tended to undermine the TPLF's influence in joint policy-making forums.

Hadiya National Democratic Organization (HNDO)

Address. c/o House of People's Representatives, Addis Ababa

Leadership. Beyene Petros (president)

The HNDO, founded in 1991, is a regionally-based party associated with several wider alliances promoted by its leader, Beyene Petros (a professor at Addis Ababa university). His outspoken criticisms of government encroachments on human rights and political freedoms made him one of the most prominent opposition figures in Ethiopian parliamentary politics in 2001. The HNDO won 5 seats in the federal House of People's Representatives in 2000, although Beyene Petros himself stood in a neighbouring constituency as a candidate of the Council of Alternative Forces for Peace and Democracy in Ethiopia. All the HNDO deputies were, like Beyene Petros himself, returned in new elections held on June 25 after the annulment of the May 14 results by the National Electoral Board.

Oromo Liberation Front (OLF)

Leadership. Daoud Ibsa Gudina (chairman)

Formed in 1975, the OLF operated through different branches with little central leadership, making a minor contribution to the military struggle against the Mengistu regime compared with the contributions of Eritrean forces or the Tigre People's Liberation Front (TPLF). Mutual antipathy between the OLF and TPLF led to the creation, under the latter's auspices, of the

207

rival Oromo People's Democratic Organization (OPDO) in 1990. Initially committed to an independent Oromo state, the OLF said in June 1991 that it would support substantial regional autonomy within a federal Ethiopia, and in August 1991 it accepted four ministerial posts in the transitional government headed by Meles Zenawi of the Ethiopian People's Revolutionary Democratic Front (EPRDF).

Clashes between members of the OLF and members of OPDO (an EPRDF member-party) during the run-up to elections led to a final break with the EPRDF in 1992, after which the OLF went into armed opposition to the Government, carrying out low-level guerrilla operations and advocating boycotts of all elections. The OLF also clashed with rival Oromo rebel groups (some of which had come into being through splits in the OLF).

In July 2000 the OLF held a meeting with three other groups (United Oromo Liberation Front, Oromo Liberation Council and Islamic Front for the Liberation of Oromia) to discuss joint action against the Ethiopian Government, which had ignored a peace proposal put forward by the OLF in February 2000.

Oromo National Congress (ONC)

Address. c/o House of People's Representatives, Addis Ababa

Leadership. Merera Gudina (president)

The ONC, founded in 1996 by a member of Addis Ababa university's political science faculty, exists to oppose the Oromo People's Democratic Organization through legitimate electoral channels (in contrast to the armed opposition of the Oromo Liberation Front and other resistance movements, which the ONC condemns). It fielded 36 candidates in the 2000 federal elections and won one seat in the federal House of People's Representatives.

Oromo People's Democratic Organization (OPDO)

Address. c/o House of People's Representatives, Addis Ababa

Leadership. Kuma Demeksa (secretary-general)

The OPDO was set up in 1990 under the direction of the Tigre People's Liberation Front (TPLF) as the Oromo ethnic element in the Ethiopian People's Revolutionary Democratic Front (EPRDF). Its creation was regarded as a hostile act by the major Oromo organization active at that time, the Oromo Liberation Front (OLF), which had itself refused to join the EPRDF. A member of the OPDO, Negasso Gidado, was elected President (ceremonial head of state) of Ethiopia in August 1995. In the 2000 elections to the federal House of People's Representatives the OPDO won a total of 182 seats, including 173 of the 178 federal seats in Oromia state.

Somali People's Democratic Party (SPDP)

Address. c/o House of People's Representatives, Addis Ababa

Leadership. Mahmud Dirir Gidi (chairman)

The SPDP, a party supportive of the ruling Ethiopian People's Revolutionary Democratic Front and represented in the federal government, was formed in 1998 through the merger of the Ogaden National Liberation Front and the Ethiopian Somali Democratic League (an 11-party alliance). In the 2000 elections in the Somali state of Ethiopia, the SPDP won 19 of the state's 23 seats in the federal House of People's Representatives (the remaining four going to independents) and 148 of the 168 seats in the State Council.

Southern Ethiopia People's Democratic Coalition (SEPDC)

Address. c/o House of People's Representatives, Addis Ababa

Leadership. Beyene Petros (chairman)

The SEPDC was founded in 1992 as a multi-party coalition under the leadership of Beyene Petros, president of the Hadiya National Democratic Organization. Having attained a peak membership of 14 parties, it split in 1993, retaining as members several parties which were prepared to accept exclusion from the transitional Council of Representatives over a current political dispute. Strongly critical of the EPRDF government's record in office (and of the authorities' conduct of the elections), the SEPDC won three seats in the federal House of People's Representatives in 2000.

Southern Ethiopian People's Democratic Front (SEDPF)

Address. c/o House of People's Representatives, Addis Ababa

Leadership. Abate Kisho (secretary-general)

The SEPDF was created in November 1993 on the initiative of the Ethiopian People's Revolutionary Democratic Front (EPRDF) to provide a joint platform within the EPRDF for a number of small parties representing different groups in the ethnically diverse south of Ethiopia. In terms of the state boundaries adopted in 1995, the SEPDF's heartland is the Southern Nations, Nationalities and Peoples (SNNP) state, the federation's third most populous state after Oromia and Amhara. Each of 17 parties or groupings of parties within the SEPDF contests elections under its own name as the local representative of the EPRDF line on core policy issues. There is an SEPDF parliamentary group in the federal legislature and an SEPDF party hierarchy whose senior figures participate in EPRDF decision-making. In the 2000 federal elections SEPDF member parties won 112 of the SNNP state's 123 seats in the House of People's Representatives, plus two of the Addis Ababa seats. Several of the smallest SEPDF member-parties (e.g. the Konso People's Democratic Organization) won one seat each, having each fielded one candidate. The largest component of the SEPDF (the Walayta, Gamo-Gofa, Dawro and Konta Peoples' Democratic Organization) fielded 33 candidates and won 30 seats.

Tigre People's Liberation Front (TPLF)

Leadership. Meles Zenawi (chairman)

Originally formed as a Marxist-Leninist party in 1975, the TPLF pursued a separatist goal for Tigre Province until the late 1980s. It then moderated its ideological stance and its objective became an overall change of regime in a federally structured Ethiopia. Having achieved dominance over Tigre province through its military insurgency, the TPLF initiated the establishment of the Ethiopian People's Revolutionary Democratic Front in 1988, precipitating the overthrow of the Mengistu regime in May 1991 and the assumption of power in the name of the EPRDF by TPLF chairman, Meles Zenawi. As the leader of the EPRDF (the majority group in the House of People's Representatives), Meles Zenawi became the first federal Prime Minister (executive head of government) under the new constitution introduced in 1995. He was reappointed to the premiership after the legislative elections of 2000. Although the TPLF (with 40 federal seats in 2000, including all 38 in Tigre state) is the EPRDF component with the smallest parliamentary group, it has always been the dominant political force within the wider grouping.

A major split occurred in the TPLF's central committee in early 2001 after a "hard-line" faction led by the party's deputy chairman, Tewolde Wolde-Mariam, accused Meles Zenawi and his closest advisers of embracing capitalist values, kowtowing to the USA and abandoning the TPLF's original aim of creating a "popular revolutionary democracy". Meles Zenawi was also attacked for the terms on which a border war with Eritrea had been ended in late 2000 (and in particular for agreeing to the deployment of UN peace-keepers). Tewolde Wolde-Mariam and 11 other dissident members of the 30-member TPLF central committee were expelled from the party after they refused to appear at an EPRDF general council meeting in March 2001 to explain their views (for which they had already been suspended from the TPLF). Nine of the dissidents were subsequently deprived of their parliamentary seats (on the basis of voters' petitions to the National Electoral Board) and by-elections were ordered to be held in July 2001.

Fiji

Capital: Suva
Population: 790,000 (2000E)

Formerly a British colony, Fiji became an independent state within the Commonwealth in 1970. The moderate Alliance Party, defending the constitutional and legal rights of the indigenous Fijian (Melanesian – Polynesian) population, ruled the country from independence until its defeat in the general election of April 1987 (after which it effectively ceased to operate). A new government was formed from a coalition of the Fiji Labour Party (FLP) and the National Federation Party (NFP), which largely drew support from the population of Indian descent. In May 1987 a military coup was staged by Lt.-Col. Sitiveni Rabuka. Although civilian government was subsequently restored with the establishment of an interim administration, Rabuka staged a second coup in September 1987. The following month he announced that the 1970 constitution had been revoked and declared Fiji a republic. The British sovereign ceased to be the head of state upon the resignation of the Governor-General, and Fiji's membership of the Commonwealth lapsed. The country was returned nominally to civilian rule in December 1987 when the former Governor-General accepted the presidency of the republic and a Fijian-dominated Cabinet (including Rabuka as Minister for Home Affairs) was appointed.

A new constitution, promulgated in 1990, guaranteed the political dominance of the indigenous Fijian community within a bicameral parliament. In 1995, however, a Constitutional Review Commission (CRC) was set up, the eventual result being the 1997 constitution, which prescribes a parliamentary structure and electoral system properly reflecting the multi-ethnic nature of Fijian society. It provides for a bicameral Parliament consisting of (i) a 32-member Senate (*Seniti*), appointed by the President on the recommendation of the Great Council of Chiefs and the political parties, with 23 seats being reserved for ethnic Fijians and nine for Indians and other groups; and (ii) a 71-member House of Representatives (*Vale*) elected for a five-year term. The House has 46 "communal" seats (23 reserved for indigenous Fijians, 19 for Indo-Fijians, three for other ethnic groups and one for the inhabitants of Rotuma) and 25 seats "open" to all races but filled from single-member constituencies. The head of state is the President, who is appointed by the Great Council of Chiefs for a five-year term. The head of government is the Prime Minister, who is appointed by the President subject to parliamentary approval and who himself appoints the Cabinet.

The 1999 general elections brought the FLP back to office in a coalition with two indigenous Fijian parties which was headed by Mahendra Chaudhry, who thus became the first Fijian Prime Minister of Indian descent. In May 2000 the Chaudhry government was overthrown in a civilian coup led by George Speight,

who claimed that indigenous Fijian interests were under threat. Two months later the army intervened to install an interim administration headed by Laisenia Qarase of the new National Unity Party (SDL). General elections on Aug. 25 and Sept. 2, 2001, were contested by some 20 parties and resulted in the SDL becoming the largest party in the House of Representatives with 31 seats. The FLP won 27 seats, the Conservative Alliance (MV) 6, the New Labour Unity Party (NLUP) 2, the National Federation Party (NFP) 1, the United General Party (UGP) 1 and independents 2. The resultant government was a coalition headed by the SDL and including the MV and a member of the NLUP. The seat won by the NFP was disputed by the FLP and after a recount in 2002 the FLP candidate won. This brought their total to 28 seats. In August 2004 one of the members of the MV was imprisoned along with other people including the Vice President for their part in the 2000 coup. This automatically made his parliamentary seat vacant thus reducing the total number of MV seats to 5.

Conservative Alliance
Matanitu Vanua (MV)
Address. PO Box 1694, Nasea Labasa
Telephone. (679) 362560
Leadership. Rakuita Vakalalabure (leader)
The MV consists of supporters of the May 2000 coup. Amongst its members are coup leader George Speight and several others who had been imprisoned with him on Nukulau island, off Suva, due to their involvement. The party has an extremist nationalist ideology that indigenous Fijians must have total control of political power. It advocates amendment of the 1997 constitution to provide more protection for indigenous Fijian rights. Its supporters are largely rural people from Tailevu and Cakaudrove provinces.

The MV won six seats in the 2001 elections, its successful candidates including Speight. The party was included in the new coalition government, being allocated two ministerial posts.

Fiji Labour Party (FLP)
Address. PO Box 2162, Suva
Telephone. (679) 308602
Fax. (679) 307829
Leadership. Mahendra Chaudhry (general secretary)
The FLP was formed in 1985 as a multi-racial party, although it has drawn most of its support from the Indo-Fijian community. It came to power briefly, in coalition with the National Federation Party (NFP), in the April 1987 general elections, but this government was overthrown the following month in a military coup. In 1991 the FLP broke with the NFP over the former's decision (which was ultimately reversed) to boycott the 1992 general elections. Of the 13 (Indian-reserved) seats gained by the FLP in the 1992 elections, only seven were retained in the balloting in February 1994.

In the May 1999 general elections the FLP won all the Indian seats (open and communal) and an overall total of 34 out of 71 seats in the House of Representatives. This enabled the FLP to form the new government in a coalition arrangement which included the Fijian Association Party and the General Voters' Party, with Mahendra Chaudhry becoming Fiji's first Indo-Fijian Prime Minister. He was quickly accused of pro-Indian nepotism and of being anti-Fijian in his policies. In May 2000 the government was overthrown in a Fijian nationalist civilian coup, Chaudhry being among those held hostage for nearly two months. Following his release and the installation of an interim government, Chaudhry insisted that he was the legal Prime Minister. He obtained an Appeal Court ruling to that effect in March 2001 and was reinstated, but was immediately dismissed by the President so that new elections could be held.

In the election run-up the FLP experienced internal divisions, resulting in the departure of deputy party leader Tupeni Baba to form the New Labour Unity Party. In the August-September 2001 balloting the FLP fell back to 27 seats and became the principal opposition to a coalition government headed by the National Unity Party (SDL), after the SDL had refused to entertain the FLP's conditions for joining the government. The FLP subsequently challenged the constitutional legitimacy of the new government in court.

The FLP is a consultative member of the Socialist International.

National Federation Party (NFP)
Address. PO Box 4399, Samabula, Suva
Telephone. (679) 385916
Fax. (679) 381991
Leadership. Attar Singh (leader)
Formed in the 1960s, the NFP is the oldest political party in Fiji, deriving its support predominantly from the Indo-Fijian community. It was the main opposition party following independence in 1970, but came to power in a coalition with the Fiji Labour Party (FLP) following the April 1987 elections. The new government was promptly ousted in a military coup the following month. The alliance with the FLP ended in 1991 when the NFP voted not to join the FLP in its decision (which was subsequently reversed) to boycott the 1992 general elections. Having won 14 of the 27 seats reserved for Indo-Fijians in that election, the NFP increased its representation to 20 seats in the February 1994 polling.

In the 1999 elections the NFP failed to win representation, losing all of its seats to Labour, with the result that then leader Jai Ram Reddy resigned. The party regained a single seat in the 2001 elections, opting to be part of the opposition despite being approached to join the new coalition headed by the National Unity Party. Following an election recount the NFP lost their single seat to the FLP.

National Unity Party
Soqosoqo Duavata ni Lewenivanua (SDL)
Address. 28 Tuisowaqa Road, Namadi Heights, Suva
Telephone. (679) 314609
Fax. (679) 314491
Leadership. Laisenia Qarase (leader)
The SDL was formed in May 2001 by members of the interim government installed under the premiership of Laisenia Qarase, after the eventually abortive coup by indigenous Fijian militants in May 2000. The party has a multi-racial stance with considerable support amongst business people of all ethnic groups, while also aiming to promote the business interests of indigenous Fijians. Although a new party, the SDL attracted impressive support in the August-September 2001 elections, especially among indigenous Fijians, winning 31 seats to become the largest in parliament.

Qarase was sworn in as Prime Minister on Sept. 9, 2001, at the head of a 20-member Cabinet which included 15 SDL members, two from the Conservative Alliance, one from the New Labour Unity Party and two independents. The new coalition was predominantly drawn from indigenous Fijians, whilst the opposition led by the Fiji Labour Party was mainly Indo-Fijian.

New Labour Unity Party (NLUP)
Address. PO Box 1258, Suva
Telephone. (679) 370511
Fax. (679) 370511
Leadership. Tupeni Baba (leader)
Formed in April 2001, the NLUP is a breakaway from the

Fiji Labour Party (FLP) by a faction which had been dissatisfied with the leadership style of Labour leader Mahendra Chaudhry. The party has a multi-racial base and believes in national unification of all ethnic groups through dialogue. Its significant Indian and Fijian following yielded two seats in the 2001 elections, although party leader Tupeni Baba failed to be re-elected. One of the victorious NLUP candidates accepted a post in the new government headed by the National Unity Party, whereas the other decided not to. This caused friction within the party, the member who joined the government being threatened with expulsion from the party.

United General Party (UGP)
Address. PO Box 9403, Nadi Airport
Telephone. (679) 312866
Fax. (679) 303052
Leadership. Mick Beddoes (leader)
The UGP is a breakaway from the General Voters' Party (GVP), representing "general" voters from ethnic groups other than indigenous Fijians and Indo-Fijians (i.e. Europeans, Chinese and various Pacific islanders). Whereas the GVP failed to win representation in the 2001 elections, the UGP gained one seat and became part of the opposition.

Other Parties

Fijian Association Party (FAP), formed prior to the 1994 elections by a breakaway faction of the Fijian Political Party (SVT). It was part of the ruling coalition headed by the Fiji Labour Party after the 1999 elections, but was weakened by a split. The rump FAP had no success in the 2001 elections, party leader and former Deputy Premier Kuini Speed losing her seat.
Address. PO Box 633, Suva
Telephone/Fax. (679) 307282
Leadership. Kuini Speed

Fijian Political Party (*Soqosoqo ni Vakavulewa ni Taukei, SVT*), launched in 1991 with the aim of uniting indigenous Fijians, headed in the 1990s by Sitiveni Rabuka, who had led two military coups in 1987. The party won majorities in the 1992 and 1994 elections, forming coalition governments under Rabuka's premiership. It was in opposition from the 1999 elections until the May 2000 coup, being weakened subsequently by the defection of a faction to the National Unity Party. The failure of the rump SVT in the 2001 elections was attributed to indigenous Fijians' rejection of its "moderate" multi-racialism.
Address. PO Box 2259, Suva
Telephone. (679) 308300
Fax. (679) 300717
Leadership. Filipe Bole

General Voters' Party (GVP), formed in 1990, representing those not belonging to either the indigenous Fijian or ethnic Indian communities (i.e. Europeans, Chinese and Pacific islanders). It won five seats in the 1992 elections (and four in 1994), participating in a government led by the Fijian Political Party until withdrawing in 1995. It again held office following the 1999 elections until the May 2000 coup. Weakened by breakaways such as that producing the United General Party, it failed to win any seats in the 2001 elections.
Address. PO Box 482, Government Buildings, Suva
Telephone. (679) 305811
Fax. (679) 314095
Leadership. John Sanday

Nationalist Vanua Tako Lavo Party (NVTLP), a revamped version of the original Fijian Nationalist Party, which used to advocate the repatriation of Indo-Fijians to India. The

NVTLP won a seat in a 1997 by-election and two seats in the 1999 elections. It broke up into factions over the 2000 coup, some supporting it and others not, and failed to win representation in 2001.

Address. PO Box 323, Suva

Leadership. Watisoni Butadroka

Party of National Unity (PANU), formed in 1998, with a multi-racial philosophy, based in western Fiji. It was set up by western chiefs unhappy with the distribution of state resources to the area producing the large sugar and tourism revenues. Presenting a similar programme to Protector of Fiji, it was unsuccessful in the 2001 elections.

Address. PO Box 4106, Lautoka

Telephone. (679) 665559

Leadership. Meli Bogileka

Protector of Fiji (*Bai Kei Viti,* BKV), formed in early 2001, dominated by indigenous Fijians from the western part of Fiji, for whom it advocates a fair distribution of resources. Despite having some high-profile political figures, it won no seats in 2001.

Address. PO Box 7260, Lautoka

Telephone. (679) 668859

Leadership. Tevita Momoidonu & Apisai Tora

Finland

Capital: Helsinki
Population: 5,206,295 (2003)

The Republic of Finland is a democratic parliamentary state with a President elected for a six-year term by universal adult suffrage in two rounds of voting if no candidate obtains an absolute majority in the first round. According to a new constitution in effect from 2000, the executive power of the President has been reduced and the executive power of the government led by the Prime Minister has been increased. The President leads foreign affairs in co-operation with the government and can dissolve the parliament in agreement with and on the initiative of the Prime Minister. Finland has a 200-member unicameral parliament (*Eduskunta*) elected for a four year-term by general elections. Parliamentary elections are held under a system of proportional representation in 15 electoral districts, with the number of seats being allocated according to the most recent population census figures. One of the electoral districts is formed by the autonomous Åland Islands (inhabited mainly by ethnic Swedes), which has one MP in the Finnish Parliament.

The state contributes to the financing of the national and international activities of political parties represented in the parliament in proportion to their number of seats. In 2001 the total amount available was FMk64.2 million (about $10.3 million), of which, for example, the Finnish Social Democratic Party was allocated FMk17.9 million (about $2.6 million).

Parliamentary elections on March 16, 2003, resulted as follows: Centre Party of Finland 55 seats (with 24.7% of the votes), Finnish Social Democratic Party 53 seats (24.3%), National Coalition 40 (18.5%), Left Alliance 19 (9.9%), Green Union 14 (8.0%), Swedish People's Party 9 (4.6%), Finnish Christian Democrat Party (former Finnish Christian Union) 7 (5.3 %), True Finns Party 3 (1.6%).

Presidential elections held on Jan. 16 and Feb. 6, 2000, resulted in the candidate of the Finnish Social

Democratic Party, Tarja Halonen, being elected with 51.6% of the second-round vote. She is Finland's first female head of state.

Finland joined the European Union on Jan. 1, 1995, electing 16 (from 2004, 14) members of the European Parliament. In the elections to the European Parliament held on June 13, 2004, the results were: National Coalition 23.7% of the votes and 4 seats; Centre Party of Finland 23.3% (4 seats); Finish Social Democratic Party 21.1% (3 seats); Green Union 10.4% (1 seat); Left Alliance 9.1% (1 seat); Swedish People's Party 5.7% (1 seat).

Centre Party of Finland
Suomen Keskusta (KESK)

Address. Apollonkatu 11 a, 00100 Helsinki

Telephone. (09) 751 44 200

Fax. (09) 751 44 230

Email. puoluetoimisto@keskusta.fi

Website. www.keskusta.fi

Leadership. Matti Vanhanen (chairman); Timo Kalli (parliamentary group chairman); Eero Lankia (secretary-general)

The Centre Party was founded in 1906 as the Agrarian Union, committed to improving the lot of Finland's large rural population and also to national independence, social justice and democracy. Its chief ideologue was Santeri Alkio (1862–1930), who wrote the first detailed Agrarian programme. Following Finland's declaration of independence in 1917, the Agrarians were part of the successful opposition to right-wing attempts to install a monarchy, while welcoming the victory of the anti-socialist Whites in the 1918 civil war. On the declaration of a republic in 1919, the party increased its electoral support to 19.7% and began its long career in government. Of the 69 governments formed since independence, until 2004, 52 have included the Agrarian/Centre Party, which has provided the Prime Minister on 23 occasions, as well as three Presidents, namely Lauri Kristian Relander (1925–32), Kyösti Kallio (1937–40) and Urho Kekkonen (1956–81).

The Agrarians reached an inter-war electoral peak of 27.3% in 1930, but were usually the second party after the Finnish Social Democratic Party (SDP), with which they formed a "red-green" coalition from 1937. The Agrarians subsequently shared government responsibility for Finland's hostilities with the USSR in 1939–40 and 1941–44, resulting in the loss of a tenth of Finnish territory. Under the leadership of V.J. Sukselainen, the party took 21.4% of the vote in the 1945 elections and became the third largest party in the Parliament. Rising to 24.2% in 1948, it became the largest parliamentary party and retained this status in the 1951 and 1954 elections. Kekkonen was the Prime Minister in five out of the seven governments formed between 1950 and 1956. Elected President in 1956, he was to complete four consecutive terms before resigning during his fifth (in October 1981) because of ill-health. His main contribution in the foreign policy sphere was to refine the so-called "Paasikivi-Kekkonen line", involving preferential relations with the USSR in the context of neutrality and non-alignment. By this strategy, he hoped to secure the return of the Finnish territories ceded during World War II, but faced a firm Soviet refusal to consider territorial change.

The Agrarians fell back to third position in the 1958 elections and were weakened by the formation in 1959 of the Finnish Rural Party (SMP) by populist Agrarian politicians (at present True Finns Party). They nevertheless continued to play a pivotal role in successive coalitions and in 1962 recovered a Parliament plurality, winning 53 seats and 23.0% of the vote. In November 1963 Ahti Karjalainen (Agrarian) formed the first non-socialist government since World War II, the other participants being the conservative National

Coalition (KOK), together with what became the Liberal People's Party (LKP) and the Swedish People's Party (RKP/SFP). It resigned the following month and was eventually succeeded in September 1964 by one of the same party composition but headed by the Agrarian leader, Johannes Virolainen. In 1965 the Agrarians followed the Scandinavian trend by changing their name to Centre Party, aiming to broaden their support beyond the declining rural population. In the 1966 elections, however, the party slipped to 49 seats and 21.2% and joined a centre-left coalition headed by the SDP. Because of competition from the SMP, KESK lost further ground in the next two elections, falling to 37 seats and 17.1% in 1970 and to 35 seats and 16.4% in 1972. Karjalainen was nevertheless again Prime Minister in 1970-71 and the party participated in subsequent centre-left combinations.

Having recovered to 39 seats and 17.6% in 1975, KESK provided the Prime Minister (Martti Miettunen) of centre-left coalitions in office until 1977, when it switched to a subordinate ministerial role. It slipped back to 36 seats and 17.3% in the 1979 elections (which it fought in alliance with the LKP), thereafter participating in SDP-led coalitions until 1987. In 1980 Paavo Väyrynen was elected KESK chairman at the age of 34. In 1982 the LKP became a constituent organization of KESK, which inched up to 38 seats and 17.6% in the 1983 elections. In 1986 the LKP reverted to independent status; but its support remained with KESK, which improved to 40 seats and 17.6% (again) in the 1987 elections, after which the party had the unusual experience of being in opposition for a whole parliamentary term. Its reward in the 1991 elections was a surge to a plurality of 55 seats and 24.8%, enabling it to form a centre-right coalition with KOK, the RKP/SFP and the Finnish Christian Union (SKL), with new KESK leader Esko Aho (37) becoming the youngest Prime Minister in Finnish history.

Contending with deepening economic recession, the Aho government also faced opposition within the coalition parties on its aim of accession to the European Union (EU), not least within KESK itself. An additional farm support package served to defuse opposition to the entry terms in KESK rural ranks, and accession was duly approved in the October 1994 referendum, although not before the anti-EU SKL had withdrawn from the coalition. Meanwhile, former KESK leader Väyrynen had been placed third in the first round of presidential elections in January 1994, winning 19.5% of the vote. In the March 1995 legislative elections, moreover, KESK was the main loser, falling to 44 seats and 19.9%, and went into opposition to a five-party coalition headed by the SDP.

KESK made a comeback in the October 1996 European Parliament elections, heading the poll with 24.4% (which gave it four of Finland's 16 seats) on a platform of opposition to further European integration. In the March 1999 national elections KESK advanced to 48 seats (on a 22.4% vote share) but remained in opposition to another SDP-led coalition. In the June 1999 European Parliament elections KESK slipped to 21.3% of the vote but again won four seats.

Standing as the KESK candidate in the January–February 2000 presidential elections, Aho came second in the first round with 34.4% of the vote, but was narrowly defeated by the SDP nominee Tarja Halonen in the second in a 48.4% to 51.6% split.

Anneli Jäätteenmäki took over from Esko Aho as party chair in 2002 and in the general election on March 16, 2003, KESK again became the largest party with 55 seats in the parliament. Jäätteenmäki, as the first Finnish woman Prime Minister, formed a red-green coalition government. Jäätteenmäki's premiership proved short, as she was forced to resign at the end of June 2003 after only three months. Jäätteenmäki was accused of having used secret foreign pol-

icy documents concerning Finland's attitude to the USA in the run-up to the war in Iraq in her electoral campaign. She was succeeded as Prime Minister by Matti Vanhanen, also KESK.

With an official membership of over 200,000, KESK is an affiliate of the Liberal International. Its European Parliament representatives sit in the European Liberal, Democratic and Reformist group.

Finnish Christian Democrats (former Finnish Christian Union)
Suomen Kristillisdemokraatit (KD) (former Suomen Kristillinen Liitto, SKL)

Address. Karjalankatu 2 C 7th floor, 00520 Helsinki
Telephone. +358 9 348 822 00
Fax. +358 9 348 822 28
Email. kd@kristillisdemokraatit.fi
Website. www.kristillisdemokraatit.fi
Leadership. C.P. Bjarne Kallis (chairman); Päivi Räsänen (parliamentary group chairman); Annika Kokko (secretary)
The KD, the former Finnish Christian Union (SKL), is an evangelical party founded in 1958 to propagate Christian values in public life and to resist secularization. It won its first parliamentary seat in 1970 on a 1.1% vote share, advancing to four seats and 2.5% in 1972 and to nine seats and 3.3% in 1975, when it benefited from the electoral slump of the Finnish Rural Party (SMP, now True Finns Party). After SKL candidate Raino Westerholm had won a respectable 9% of the vote in the 1978 presidential elections, the party retained nine seats on a 4.8% vote share in the 1979 parliament elections. It slipped back to three seats and 3.0% in 1983, while in 1987 its reduced share of 2.6% gave it five seats on the strength of local electoral alliances with the Centre Party of Finland (KESK) and the Liberal People's Party (LKP). It advanced again in 1991, to eight seats and 3.1%, and opted for its first taste of government, joining a non-socialist coalition headed by KESK and including the conservative National Coalition and the Swedish People's Party.

Opposed to Finnish accession to the European Union (as supported by its coalition partners), the SKL withdrew from the government in June 1994. In the March 1995 general election the SKL slipped to seven seats and 3.0% of the vote, remaining in opposition and subsequently losing one deputy to KESK. It revived to 10 seats and 4.2% in the March 1999 elections, but again continued in opposition. A vote share of 2.4% in the June 1999 European Parliament elections gave the SKL one seat. In the parliamentary elections of March 2003 the Christian Democrats won 5.9% of the vote and 7 seats.

With an official membership of 13,000, the KD is affiliated to the Christian Democrat International. Its representative in the European Parliament sits in the European People's Party/European Democrats group.

Finnish Social Democratic Party
Suomen Sosiaalidemokraattinen Puolue (SDP)

Address. Saariniemenkatu 6, 00530 Helsinki
Telephone. (358-9) 478–988
Fax. (358-9) 712–752
Email. palaute@sdp.fi
Website. www.sdp.fi
Leadership. Paavo Lipponen (chairman); Tarja Filatov & Säde Tahvanainen (deputy chairpersons); Jouni Backman (parliamentary group chairman); Eero Heinäluoma (general secretary)
The party was founded in 1899 as the Finnish Workers' Party to represent the growing ranks of organized labour as well as landless labourers, adopting its present name in 1903, when Finland was still part of the Russian Empire. The advent of universal suffrage in 1906 enabled the SDP to become the

largest parliamentary party (with 37% of the vote in that year), but its reforms were blocked by the Tsar. Following Finland's declaration of independence in 1917, radical Social Democrats fought on the losing Red side in the 1918 civil war (and later founded the Finnish Communist Party), whereas the non-revolutionary majority led by Vainö Tanner made its peace with the victorious Whites and embarked on a reformist path in the Finnish Republic declared in 1919. Despite electoral competition from Communist-front formations and the powerful Agrarians, the Social Democrats were usually the strongest party in the inter-war period, but managed only one period of minority government (in 1926–27) before entering a "red-green" coalition with the Agrarians in 1937. The SDP vote rose to 39.8% in 1939, whereupon Tanner not only backed Finland's losing popular cause in the 1939–40 Winter War with the USSR but also supported Finnish participation in Nazi Germany's invasion of the USSR in 1941 with the aim of recovering lost territory. The SDP leadership rejected adhesion to the Communist-led Finnish People's Democratic League (SKDL) formed in 1944, but many pro-Soviet party sections joined the new organization. Finland's defeat in 1944, combined with post-war Soviet regional ascendancy, resulted in Tanner being imprisoned in 1946–48 as a war criminal.

Having won only 25.1% of the vote in the 1945 elections, the SDP remained in a coalition government with the SKDL and the Agrarians (later called the Centre Party, KESK), but internal strife between pro-Soviet left and anti-communist right was to fester for more than two decades. With its vote share remaining stable at around 26% in successive elections, the party participated in coalition governments in 1951 and 1954–57, the latter a centre-left combination with the Agrarians. In the 1956 presidential elections Karl-August Fagerholm of the SDP was narrowly defeated by Urho Kekkonen (Agrarian). In 1957 Fagerholm was also defeated (by one vote) for the SDP chair, the winner being rehabilitated Tanner, whose return provoked a new phase of internal party strife. In the 1958 elections the SDP lost its customary status as the biggest parliamentary party (and declined further in 1962). In 1959 left-wingers broke away to form what became the Social Democratic League of Workers and Smallholders (TPSL), which won seven seats in the 1966 election in alliance with the SKDL. But the same contest yielded a major recovery for the SDP to 27.2% of the vote, well ahead of its rivals. Moreover, the TPSL failed to win seats in the 1970 and 1972 contests, while successive SDP-led centre-left coalitions – under Rafael Paasio (who had succeeded the 82-year-old Tanner as party leader in 1963), Mauno Koivisto and Kalevi Sorsa – confirmed the ascendancy of the SDP's moderate wing. The party headed the poll in all four elections of the 1970s, but had fallen to 23.9% of the vote by 1979.

In January 1982 Koivisto was elected President of Finland as the SDP candidate and a new centre-left coalition was formed under Sorsa as the Prime Minister. A strong SDP advance in the 1983 elections, to 26.7%, enabled Sorsa to form another government embracing KESK, the Finnish Rural Party (SMP, now the True Finns Party) and the Swedish People's Party (RKP/SFP). The March 1987 elections produced a setback for the SDP, to 24.1% and 56 seats, only just ahead of the conservative National Coalition (KOK), which became the lead party in a new coalition surprisingly including the SDP. At the 34th SDP congress in June 1987 Sorsa was succeeded as party chairman by Pertti Paasio (son of Rafael). The same congress adopted a new programme which defined the party's six central aims as being a world of cooperation, peace and freedom; coexistence with nature; the transfer of power from capital owners to working people; a shift from representative democracy to "an active civil state"; a culturally equal society; and a vig-

orous process of social reform. In February 1988 President Koivisto was elected to a second six-year term as candidate of the SDP.

The March 1991 elections ended a quarter-century of continuous SDP government office, the party slipping to 22.1% and 48 seats and going into opposition to a centre-right coalition. Having replaced Paasio as SDP chairman in November 1991, Ulf Sundqvist himself resigned the leadership in February 1993 over allegations of financial impropriety in his previous post as executive director of the STS-Bank. He was succeeded by Paavo Lipponen, who steered the party into supporting Finnish accession to the European Union in the October 1994 referendum, although rank-and-file SDP opposition was considerable. In March 1995 Lipponen led the party to a major victory in parliamentary elections, its vote share rising to 28.3%, which yielded 63 seats out of 200. In April 1995 Lipponen formed a five-party "rainbow" coalition that included KOK, the RKP/SFP, the Left Alliance and the Green Union. Meanwhile, in Finland's first direct presidential elections in February 1994, SDP candidate Martti Ahtisaari had won a second-round victory with 53.9% of the vote, having headed the first-round voting with 25.9%.

In the first direct Finnish elections to the European Parliament in October 1996, the SDP fell back to 21.5% of the vote and four of the 16 seats, appearing to be damaged by the government's decision to take Finland into the EU's exchange rate mechanism. Further buffeted by events, the party recovered only slightly in the March 1999 national elections, to a 22.9% vote share and 51 seats, 12 less than in 1995. It nevertheless remained the largest party, forming a new coalition government of the same parties with Lipponen continuing as Prime Minister. In the June 1999 Euro-elections the SDP was relegated to third place, with only 17.8% of the vote and three seats.

The SDP nominated Foreign Minister Tarja Halonen as its candidate in the January–February 2000 presidential elections. She headed the first-round voting with 40% and narrowly triumphed in the second with 51.6%, becoming Finland's first female head of state. In the parliamentary elections of March 2003 the SDP was supported by 24.3% of the voters, making the party the second largest in the Finnish Parliament with 53 MPs.

With a membership of 50,000, the SDP is a member of the Socialist International. Its representatives in the European Parliament sit in the Party of European Socialists group.

Green Union
Vihreä Liitto (VL or VIHR)
Address. Osoite: Fredrikinkatu 33, 3rd floor , 0020 Helsinki
Telephone. (358–9) 5860 4160
Fax. (358–9) 5860 4161
Email. vihreat@vihrealiitto.fi
Website. www.vihrealiitto.fi
Leadership. Osmo Soininvaara (chairman); Satu Hassi (parliamentary group chairman); Ari Heikkinen (secretary)

The VL was formed in February 1987 as a cooperative body for various existing local and national environmentalist organizations, the latter including the Green Parliamentary Group (*Vihreä Eduskuntaryhmä*), which had won two seats in 1983. Presenting a mainstream environmentalist platform, the Greens increased to four seats in the March 1987 elections and to 10 in March 1991. They fell back to nine seats on a 6.5% vote share in March 1995 but nevertheless took ministerial office for the first time the following month, when Pekka Haavisto became Environment Minister in a five-party "rainbow" coalition headed by the Finnish Social Democratic Party (SDP).

Bolstered by its government status and despite being fundamentally "Eurosceptic", the VL advanced to 7.6% in the

October 1996 direct elections to the European Parliament, taking one of the 16 seats. In the March 1999 national elections it won 7.5% of the vote and 11 seats, subsequently joining a new SDP-led coalition in which it took two portfolios. In the June 1999 European Parliament elections the VL made a major advance to 13.4% of the vote and two seats. In the first round of presidential elections in January 2000, however, VL candidate Heidi Hautala, a member of the European Parliament, came in fifth place with only 3.3% of the vote. In the March 2003 parliamentary election the party was supported by 8.0% of the voters and got 14 MPs.

The VL is affiliated to the European Federation of Green Parties. Its two members of the European Parliament sit in the Greens/European Free Alliance group.

Left Alliance
Vasemmistoliitto (VAS)
Vänsterförbundet

Address. Viherniemenkatu 5 A, 2nd floor, 00530 Helsinki
Telephone. (358–9) 774–741
Fax. (358–9) 7747–4200
Email. vas@vasemmistoliitto.fi
Website. www.vasemmistoliitto.fi
Leadership. Suvi-Anne Siimes (chairperson); Martti Korhonen (parliamentary group chairman); Aulis Ruuth (secretary)

VAS was launched in April 1990 at a Helsinki congress of representatives of the leading Communist and left-socialist groups, who took cognizance of the collapse of East European socialism then in progress. Following the congress, the Finnish Communist Party (SKP) and its electoral front organization, the Finnish People's Democratic League (*Suomen Kansan Demokraattinen Liitto*, SKDL), voted to disband in favour of the new party, which adopted a left-socialist programme and declared its opposition to Finnish membership of the European Community, later Union (EC/EU), as favoured by most other parties.

The SKP had been founded in 1918 by the left wing of the Finnish Social Democratic Party (SDP) but remained banned until 1944, when Finland was for the second time in five years militarily defeated by the USSR. The SKDL was created in 1944 by communists and left wing socialists. SKDL won 23.5% of the vote in 1945, becoming the largest parliamentary party in 1958-62 and participating in various centre-left coalitions until 1982. Meanwhile, the SKP had in 1969 split into majority "revisionist" and minority "Stalinist" wings, the latter being formally ousted from the party in 1984 and two years later launching Democratic Alternative (*Demokraattinen Vaihtoehto*, DEVA) electoral front, which achieved little more than to weaken the SKDL, whose electoral support slumped to 9.4% in 1987 against 4.2% for DEVA.

In its first general elections in March 1991, VAS won 10.2% of the vote and 19 seats, thereafter forming part of the opposition to the 1991–95 centre-right government. It was prominent in the unsuccessful "no" campaign in the October 1994 referendum on EU accession, acting as a focus for considerable anti-EU sentiment among SDP activists. In a substantial swing to the left in the March 1995 parliamentary elections, VAS advanced to 11.2% and 22 seats, subsequently being allocated two minister posts in a five-party "rainbow" coalition headed by the SDP and also including the conservative National Coalition, the Swedish People's Party and the Green Union.

The VAS won 10.5% of the vote and two seats in the European Parliament elections in October 1996. In the March 1999 national elections it took 10.9% of the vote, slipping to 20 seats. It nevertheless continued in a new SDP-led coalition of the same composition. In the June 1999 European Parliament elections the VAS slipped to 9.1% and

was reduced to one seat. In the March 2003 national elections VAS was supported by 9.9% of the voters and obtained 19 seats in parliament.

The VAS has a membership of 11,000 and is a member of the New European Left Forum (NELF). Its representative in the European Parliament sits in the European United Left/Nordic Green Left group.

National Coalition
Kansallinen Kokoomus (KOK)

Address. Pohjoinen Rautatiekatu 21 B, 00100 Helsinki
Telephone. 358-9-0207 488 488
Fax. 358-9-0207 488 505
Email. info@kokoomus.fi
Website. www.kokoomus.fi
Leadership. Ville Itälä (chairman); Ben Zyskowicz (parliamentary group chairman); Heikki A. Ollila (secretary-general)

The moderate conservative KOK was founded in December 1918 following the victory of the anti-socialist Whites in the civil war. Although monarchist in sympathy, the new party reconciled itself with the republic declared in 1919 and participated in several inter-war coalitions, averaging around 15% of the vote. In the early 1930s it gravitated towards the semi-fascist Lapua rural movement, but KOK leader J.K. Paasikivi later broke with the far right. KOK and participated in all five governments in office from 1939 to 1944 (providing the Prime Minister on two occasions) and thus shared responsibility for the conduct of the 1939–40 Winter War against the USSR and for Finland's participation in Nazi Germany's invasion of the USSR in 1941.

KOK was in opposition to successive centre-left coalitions from 1944 to 1958, its vote share fluctuating from a high of 17.3% in 1948 to a low of 12.8% in 1954. On the other hand, Paasikivi served in the powerful post of President from 1946 to 1956 and was instrumental in establishing a consensus on Finland's post-war policy of good relations with the USSR – this being continued by his successor, Urho Kekkonen, of what became the Centre Party (KESK), and therefore becoming known as the "Paasikivi-Kekkonen line". Between 1958 and 1966 KOK participated in several coalition governments, including the first completely non-socialist administration since the war, formed in 1963 and headed by KESK. Having slipped to 13.8% in the 1966 elections, KOK reverted to opposition status and was to remain out of office for over two decades. Under the successive chairmanships of Juha Rihtniemi (1965-71) and Harri Holkeri (1971-79), the party moved to a more centrist position, notably by endorsing the "Paasikivi-Kekkonen line". One consequence was the departure of traditionalist elements in 1973 to join the Constitutional Party of the Right. But KOK compensated by attracting additional support in the centre, rising steadily to 22.1% of the vote in 1983 and establishing itself as the second strongest party after the Finnish Social Democratic Party (SDP).

KOK made another advance in the 1987 elections (to 23.1% and 53 seats) and proceeded to form a four-party coalition with the SDP, the Swedish People's Party (RKP/SFP) and the Finnish Rural Party (SMP, later True Finns Party), with Holkeri becoming Finland's first KOK Prime Minister since 1944. The coalition was weakened by the withdrawal of the SMP in August 1990 and also faced sharply deteriorating economic conditions. In the March 1991 elections KOK slipped to 19.3% and 40 seats (the third largest contingent) and was obliged to accept a subordinate role in a four-party non-socialist coalition headed by KESK and also including the RKP/SFP and the Finnish Christian Union (SKL). In presidential elections in January 1994 the KOK candidate, Raimo Ilaskivi, came in fourth place in the first round with 15.2% of the vote. KOK strongly backed Finland's accession to the European Union, although internal strains were apparent when Deputy Prime Minister Pertti Salolainen resigned as KOK chairman in June 1994 after some party members had criticised his role in the accession negotiations.

The general elections of March 1995 brought a further setback to KOK, which fell to 17.9% and 39 seats. It nevertheless opted to join a "rainbow" coalition headed by the SDP and also including the RKP/SFP, the Left Alliance and the Green Union. The party advanced to 20.2% of the vote and four seats in the October 1996 European Parliament elections and to 21.0% and 46 seats in the March 1999 national elections, after which it joined another SDP-led coalition government. In the June 1999 European Parliament elections KOK won 25.3% of the vote, retaining its four seats. In the first round of presidential elections in January 2000, KOK candidate Riitta Uosukainen, the parliamentary Speaker, came in third place with 12.8% of the vote. In parliamentary elections in March 2003 KOK obtained 40 seats with 18.5% of the vote.

With a membership of 40,000, KOK is affiliated to the Christian Democrat International and the International Democrat Union. Its representatives in the European Parliament are members of the European People's Party/European Democrats group.

Swedish People's Party
Svenska Folkpartiet (SFP)
Ruotsalainen Kansanpuolue (RKP)

Address. Simonsgatan 8 A, PB 430, 00101 Helsingfors
Fax. 358-9-693 1968
Telephone. 358-9-693 070
Email. info@sfp.fi
Website. www.sfp.fi
Leadership. Jan-Erik Enestam (chairman); Christina Gestrin (parliamentary group chairman); Berth Sundström (secretary)

The RKP/SFP was founded in 1906, when Finland was still a duchy of the Russian Empire, to represent the political and social interests of the ethnic Swedish population, which was then economically dominant. Being ethnically based, the party has traditionally encompassed a wide spectrum of ideological preferences, although it is usually characterized as centrist with progressive leanings. Its share of the overall vote has shown a gradual decline over recent decades (from 8.4% in 1945 to 4.6 % in 2003), in line with the falling proportion of ethnic Swedes in the population. Also its representation in the Parliament has decreased (the 2003 tally being 9 seats, compared with a high of 15 in 1951). The RKP/SFP's parliamentary contingent customarily includes the single deputy returned by the ethnic Swedish inhabitants of the autonomous Åland Islands, where the main local parties, modelled on those of Sweden, form the Ålands Coalition for Finnish national elections.

The RKP/SFP has been in government more often than it has been in opposition, having participated in about two-thirds of all Finnish coalitions formed since 1906, including centre-left, centre-right and ideologically-mixed combinations. The pattern after 1945 was RKP/SFP participation in successive centre-left coalitions headed by the Finnish Social Democratic Party (SDP) or the Centre Party (KESK), although in 1963–66 it was a member of the first entirely non-socialist governments since the war. Subsequent centre-left combinations also included the RKP/SFP as a pivotal member, while in 1987 it joined a four-party coalition headed by the conservative National Coalition (KOK) and also including the SDP and the Finnish Rural Party (SMP, now True Finns Party). Having slipped from 13 to 12 seats in the 1991 elections, the RKP/SFP joined another non-socialist coalition, this time headed by KESK and including KOK and the Finnish Christian Union.

For the January–February 1994 presidential elections the RKP/SFP candidate was Defence Minister Elisabeth Rehn, who surprised many (given her Swedish ethnicity and gender) by taking second place in the first round, with 22% of the vote. Going forward to the second round, she was defeated by the SDP candidate but got 46.1% of the vote. The RKP/SFP supported Finland's accession to the European Union (as approved in the October 1994 referendum) and was allocated one of Finland's 16 seats in the European Parliament. Having retained 12 seats in the March 1995 parliamentary elections, it accepted two minister posts in a five-party "rainbow" coalition headed by the SDP and also including KOK, the Left Alliance and the Green Union.

In the October 1996 direct elections to the European Parliament the RKP/SFP retained its single seat with 5.8% of the vote. In the March 1999 national elections it won 12 seats (with 5.1% of the vote) and opted to join another five-party coalition headed by the SDP. In the June 1999 European Parliament elections it advanced to 6.8%, retaining its single seat. Rehn was again the party's candidate in the January–February 2000 presidential elections, but this time she managed only fourth place in the first round with 7.9% of the vote. In the parliamentary elections of March 2003 RKP/SFP won 9 seats while in the June 2004 European elections it lost its only seat.

With a membership of 32,000, the RKP/SFP is affiliated to both the International Democrat Union and the Liberal International.

True Finns Party
Perussuomalaiset (PS)

Address. Mannerheimintie 40B, 00100 Helsinki
Telephone. (358–9) 454 0411
Fax. (358–9) 454 0466
Email. timo.soini@eduskunta.fi
Website. www.perussuomalaiset.fi/
Leadership. Timo Soini (chairman); Hannu Purho (secretary)

The PS was founded prior to the 1999 elections as successor to the Finnish Rural Party (SMP), following serious internal disputes in the latter. The SMP had been derived from the Finnish Smallholders' Party, which was launched in 1959 by a populist faction of what later became the Centre Party of Finland (KESK). Led by the charismatic Veikko Vennamo, the breakaway party took an anti-establishment "Poujadist" line, defending the rights of "forgotten Finland" and claiming that the parent party and all other old parties have neglected the interests of small farmers and small businessmen. Renamed the SMP after obtaining negligible support in the 1962 and 1966 elections, the party came to prominence in 1968 when Vennamo won over 11% in challenging incumbent Urho Kekkonen (KESK) for the presidency. It achieved a breakthrough in the 1970 parliamentary elections, winning 10.5% and 18 seats (mainly as the expense of KESK), and retained 18 seats in 1972, although it support slipped to 9.2%.

The SMP was then weakened by splits arising from criticism of Vennamo's authoritarian leadership style and right-wing opposition to his willingness to co-operate with parties of the left. In the 1975 elections the rump SMP slumped to two seats and 3.6%, recovering only partially to seven seats and 4.5% in 1979, in which year Vennamo stood down as leader and was succeeded by his son Pekka. The 1983 elections yielded another breakthrough for the SMP, which won 17 seats and 9.7% of the vote and thereafter entered government for the first time as part of a coalition headed by the Finnish Social Democratic Party (SDP) and including KESK and the Swedish People's Party (RKP/SFP). In the 1984 municipal elections the SMP obtained over 600 council seats.

The SMP fell back to nine seats and 6.3% in the 1987 elections but nevertheless joined a four-party coalition headed by the conservative National Coalition and including the SDP and the RKP/SFP. It withdrew from the coalition in August 1990 in protest against new pension proposals, but lost further support to a resurgent KESK in the 1991 elections, falling to seven seats and 4.8% and remaining outside the resultant non-socialist coalition headed by KESK. Having been part of the unsuccessful opposition to Finnish accession to the European Union, the SMP almost disappeared from the parliament in the March 1995 elections, winning only one seat on a 1.3% vote share. A period of internal division followed, culminating in the creation of PS as the successor party. In the March 1999 elections the PS just managed to retain one seat, winning only 1% of the vote. The same percentage was obtained by PS candidate Ilkka Hakalehto in the first round of the 2000 presidential elections. In the parliamentary elections of March 2003 PS managed to increase the number of its MPs to three with 1.6% of the vote after mounting a right-wing anti-immigrant campaign.

Other Parties

Communist Workers' Party (*Kommunistinen Työväenpuolue*, KTP), founded in 1988 by a Stalinist faction of the Democratic Alternative (later part of the Left Alliance). It contested the 1991, 1995 and 1999 elections under the slogan "For Peace and Socialism", winning 0.2% and 0.1% of the vote respectively. In the 2003 elections the KTP got no MPs with 0.1% of the vote.
Address. PL 93, Vantaa
Telephone. (358-9) 857-1022
Fax. (358-9) 857-3097
Email. ktp@kaapeli.fi
Website. www.kaapeli.fi
Leadership. Hannu Harju (chairman); Hannu Tuominen (general secretary)

Ecological Party (*Ekologinen Puolue*, EP). Founded in 1990 as a populist formation aiming to provide a "non-ideological" alternative to the left-leaning Green Union; failed to win representation in the 1991 parliamentary elections, but secured one seat on a 0.3% vote share in March 1995, losing it in 1999 with only 0.4%. The party did not participate in the 2003 elections.
Address. Mannerheimintie 40A, 00100 Helsinki
Telephone. (358–9) 432–3566
Fax. (358–9) 432–2717
Leadership. Pertti (Veltto) Virtanen (chairman)

Finnish Communist Party (*Suomen Kommunistinen Puolue*, SKP). Re-launched in 1997 as self-declared successor to the historic SKP, in opposition to the participation of the Left Alliance in a "neo-liberal" government; won 0.8% of the vote in both the 1995 and 1999 elections; contested the 1996 Euro-elections on joint list with the Communist Workers' Party and other leftist groups. In the parliamentary elections of March 2003 the party got 0.8% of the vote.
Address. Petter Wetterintie 1A, 6 krs, 00810 Helsinki
Telephone. (358–9) 7743 8150
Fax. (358–9) 7743 8160
Email. skp@skp.fi
Website. www.skp.fi
Leadership. Yrjö Hakanen (chairman); Arto Viitaniemi (general secretary)

Finnish Pensioners' Party (*Suomen Eläkeläisten Puolue*, SEP), launched in 1986 but had minimal electoral impact, winning 0.1% of the vote in 1995 and 0.2% in 1999.
Leadership. Erkki Pulli & Saara Mölsä

League for a Free Finland (*Vapaan Suomen Liitto*, VSL), right-wing nationalist formation which won 1% of the vote in 1995 and 0.4% in 1999.

Pensioners for the People (*Elakeläiset Kansan Asialla*, EKA), senior citizens' grouping, won only 0.2% of the vote in the 1999 and 2003 elections.

Reform Group (*Remonttiryhma*, REM), launched in 1997 by veteran trade union activist and member of parliament Risto Kuisma, who defected from the Finnish Social Democratic Party and initially joined the Young Finns but soon accused the latter of elitism and founded his own party. Describing itself as "the movement of people who want change", the REM stands for full employment and a radical reduction in income tax. In the March 1999 parliamentary elections it won 1.1% of the vote and one seat. The party's only MP rejoined the SDP in 2001.
Address. Mannerheimintie 40A, 00100 Helsinki
Telephone. (358–9) 414–3352
Fax. (358–9) 645–379
Email. risto.kuisma@eduskunta.fi
Leadership. Risto Kuisma (chairman); Seija Lahti (secretary)

France

Capital: Paris
Population: 59,303,800 (2004E)

The French Republic has one of the world's most developed multi-party systems that is perpetually fluid but essentially unchanging in its broad ideological structure. Under the 1982 constitution of the Fifth Republic as amended, an executive President, who appoints the Prime Minister, is elected by universal suffrage of citizens above the age of 18 years, the requirement being an absolute majority of the votes cast either in the first round of voting or, if necessary, in a second. In September 2000 referendum approval was given to a reduction of the presidential term from seven to five years with effect from the 2002 elections. Legislative authority is vested in a bicameral Parliament (*Parlement*) consisting of (i) a 321-seat Senate (*Sénat*) whose members are currently indirectly elected for a nine-year term (a third being renewed every three years), 309 by electoral colleges of national and local elected representatives in the metropolitan and overseas departments/territories and 12 by the *Conseil Supérieur des Français de l'Étranger* to represent French citizens living abroad; and (ii) a 577-member National Assembly (*Assemblée Nationale*) directly elected for a maximum five-year term by universal adult suffrage. For the March 1986 Assembly elections the then Socialist-led government introduced a system of department-based proportional representation for the first time under the Fifth Republic; however, the incoming centre-right administration enacted legislation providing for a return to the previous system of majority voting in two rounds in single-member constituencies. France was a founder member of what is now the European Union and elects 78 members to the European Parliament.

Under laws enacted in March 1988 and January 1990, state funding is payable to (i) political parties with parliamentary representation, in proportion to the size of their respective groups; (ii) all accredited presidential candidates (with the two reaching the second round receiving additional sums), according to a complex formula for the reimbursement of varying proportions of the ceilings set for campaign expenses; and (iii) Assembly election candidates who receive at least 5% of the first-round vote, at a rate equivalent to 10% of the applicable expenses ceilings.

National Assembly elections held on June 9 and 16, 2002, resulted as follows: Union for a Presidential Majority (UMP, now the Union for a Popular Movement) 357 (with 33.3% of the first-round vote), Socialist Party (PS) 140 seats (24.1%), Union for French Democracy (UDF) 29 (4.9%), French Communist Party (PCF) 21 (4.8%), Left Radical Party (PRG) 7 (1.5%), various Greens 3 (5.7%), Rally for France (RPF) 2 (0.4%), Movement for France (0.8%) 1, various left 6 (1.1%), various right 9 (3.7%), regionalists 1 (0.3%) independents and others 1 (4.0%).

Presidential elections on April 21 and May 5, 2002, resulted in Jacques Chirac of the RPR-UMP being elected in the second round with 82.2% of the votes cast, against 17.8% for the National Front (FN) candidate, Jean-Marie Le Pen.

France held elections to the European Parliament on June 13, 2004. In a turnout of 43.1% the elections produced the following results: Socialist Party won 28.9% of the votes and gained 31 (+9) of the country's 78 seats; Union for a Popular Movement 16.6%, 17 seats (+5); Union for French Democracy 11.9%, 11 seats (+2); National Front 9.8%, 7 seats (+2); The Greens 7.4%, 6 seats (-3); Movement for France 7.6%, 3 seats (-10); French Communist Party 5.2%, 3 seats (-3).

French Communist Party
Parti Communiste Français (PCF)
Address. 2 place du Colonel Fabien, 75019 Paris
Telephone. (33–1) 4040–1212
Fax. (33–1) 4040–1356
Email. pcf@pcf.fr
Website. www.pcf.fr
Leadership. Robert Hue (president); Marie-George Buffet (national secretary)

The PCF came into being in December 1920 when a majority of delegates at the Tours congress of the Socialist Party (then the SFIO) voted to join the Soviet-run Communist International (Comintern), whereas the anti-Bolshevik minority opted to maintain the SFIO. From 1921 to 1933 the PCF pursued a hardline policy of class war and opposition to all "bourgeois" parties, including the SFIO. From 1934, however, it gave priority to the struggle against fascism and supported (without joining) the 1936–38 Popular Front government headed by the Socialists. The PCF approved the August 1939 non-aggression pact between Nazi Germany and the USSR, but reverted to anti-fascist mode following the German invasion of the USSR in June 1941, its activists subsequently playing a prominent role in the French Resistance. The party joined the post-liberation government formed by Gen. de Gaulle in 1944, although it was denied any powerful portfolios. With the onset of the Cold War, it was excluded from the 1947 government headed by Paul Ramadier (SFIO) and was to remain in opposition for 34 years.

Strongly based in the General Confederation of Labour (the largest trade union body), the PCF outvoted the SFIO in most elections under the Fourth Republic, winning 25–29% of the vote. Having opposed the creation of the Fifth Republic in 1958, the PCF saw its vote fall to 18.9% in Assembly elections later that year but recovered to 20–22% in the contests of the 1960s and 1970s. In December 1966 the then PCF leader, Waldeck Rochet, signed an agreement with the Socialist-led Federation of the Democratic and Socialist Left (FGDS) providing for reciprocal voting support in the March 1967 Assembly elections. The arrange-

ment resulted in PCF representation almost doubling, to 73 seats, although this tally was reduced to 34 in elections held in June 1968 in the aftermath of the "May events" that nearly toppled President de Gaulle. The PCF repudiated the Soviet-led military intervention that suppressed the 1968 "Prague Spring" in Czechoslovakia, although it remained in most respects an orthodox Marxist–Leninist party aligned to Moscow and opposed to French membership of NATO and the European Community. In 1969 the Communist presidential candidate, Jacques Duclos, came third in the first round, with 21.3% of the vote.

Following the election of François Mitterrand as leader of the new Socialist Party (PS) in 1971, the following year the PCF signed a common programme with the PS and the Left Radical Movement (MRG), now the Left Radical Party. The union yielded major left-wing gains in the March 1973 Assembly elections, which restored Communist representation to 73 seats. From 1974, however, serious strains developed within the alliance, not least because the steady growth of PS strength was viewed by the PCF as imperilling the union's equilibrium and as encouraging the Socialists to revert to a centre-left strategy. At its 22nd congress in February 1976 the PCF repudiated the thesis of the dictatorship of the proletariat and came out in favour of a specifically French model of socialism. The party nevertheless kept its distance from the revisionist "Eurocommunist" line then being advanced by the Italian Communists. Mainly because of PS and MRG resistance to further PCF nationalization proposals, no agreement was reached on a revised common programme for the March 1978 Assembly elections, in which the PCF presented its own manifesto. Second-round reciprocal support nevertheless applied, with the result that the PCF rose to 86 seats amid a left-wing advance that fell short of an overall majority.

The PCF candidate in the watershed May 1981 presidential elections was the then party leader, Georges Marchais, who obtained 15.4% of the first-round vote, whereafter the PCF swung behind Mitterrand in the second round and contributed to the PS leader's victory. In the resultant Assembly elections of June 1981, second-round support arrangements among the left-wing parties yielded most benefit to the Socialists, who won an absolute majority, while the PCF fell to 44 seats. The French Communists nevertheless entered government for the first time since 1947, obtaining four portfolios in the new PS-led administration. But strains quickly developed between the PS and PCF in government, notably over the latter's refusal to condemn the imposition of martial law in Poland and its opposition to the deployment of new US nuclear missiles in Europe. In the European Parliament elections of June 1984 the PCF took only 11.2% of the vote, less than in any national election since 1932. When Laurent Fabius of the PS formed a new government in July 1984, the Communists refused to participate, on the grounds that he was equivocal on giving priority to economic expansion and job-creation. In September 1984 the PCF deputies broke with the PS-led Assembly majority and voted against the government for the first time in the budget debate of December 1984.

At the PCF congress of February 1985 the party leadership under Marchais firmly resisted the demand of a "renovator" group for changes in policy and for greater internal party democracy. The Assembly elections of March 1986 produced a further setback for the PCF, which slipped to 35 seats and 9.8% of the vote, in part because some of its working-class support in city suburbs with a high immigrant population switched to the far-right National Front (FN). Further internal strains and defections served to harden the Marchais line, which prevailed at the PCF conference in Nanterre in June 1987, when hardliner André Lajoinie was adopted as PCF presidential candidate. Prior to its 26th congress in

December 1987, the PCF central committee expelled Pierre Juquin for having announced his presidential candidacy as a Communist "renovator". In the first round of the April–May 1988 presidential contest that saw the re-election of Mitterrand, Lajoinie recorded the PCF's lowest-ever national vote share (6.8%), while Juquin got 2.1%. In the June 1988 Assembly elections the PCF recovered somewhat to 11.3% in the first round, but slipped to representation of 27 seats.

Still resisting pressure for change in the PCF, Marchais responded to the collapse of East European communism in 1989-90 and of the USSR in 1991 by claiming that he had been "duped" by his erstwhile comrades in that part of the world. The party suffered a further setback, to 9.2% of the first-round vote, in the March 1993 Assembly elections which brought the right back to governmental power, but displayed resilience in its strongholds by retaining 23 seats. Avowedly because of ill-health, Marchais formally vacated the PCF leadership at the party's 28th congress in January 1994 and was succeeded by Robert Hue, who was assigned the title "national secretary" as part of a decision to abandon "democratic centralism" in party decision-making. The Communist list won only 6.9% of the vote in the June 1994 European Parliament elections (and seven of the 87 French seats). In the April–May 1995 presidential elections, Hue took fifth place in the first round with 8.6% of the vote, whereupon the PCF backed the unsuccessful candidacy of Lionel Jospin (PS) in the second round.

In a high-profile Assembly by-election for a Marseilles constituency in October 1996, the PCF candidate defeated an FN challenge on the strength of second-round backing from centre-left parties. For the mid-1997 Assembly elections the PCF issued a joint declaration of policy objectives with the PS, but the two parties confined their electoral cooperation to mutual second-round support. The PCF shared in the victory of the left, winning 38 seats and a first-round vote share of 9.9%, and subsequently accepting portfolios in a Socialist-led coalition government. In the June 1999 European Parliament elections the PCF list slipped to six seats on a vote share of 6.8%, two of the elected candidates being "independents".

In 2000 the PCF became caught up in the wave of corruption allegations buffeting French parties, being accused of benefiting from the system of kickbacks for public contracts allegedly run by the Rally for the Republic (RPR-UMP) in Paris when Jacques Chirac was mayor in 1977–95. In October 2000, moreover, Hue and 19 others went on trial in Paris on charges related to an alleged slush fund operated by the PCF in the early 1990s. Hue denied the charges, contending that the party had always been entirely financed by members' dues, levies on PCF parliamentarians' salaries and May Day sales of lilies of the valley (the party's official flower). In late October 2000 the trial was adjourned *sine die* after defence lawyers had challenged the impartiality of the judge.

The PCF fared badly in countrywide local council elections in March 2001, losing many seats and being ousted from control in about a dozen of its former strongholds. Calls for withdrawal from the government in advance of the 2002 elections were resisted by the leadership, which saw no alternative to continued co-operation with the PS. Hue fared equally badly at the 2002 presidential elections, winning only 3.4% of the vote, behind the Trotskyist candidates, although the party revived slightly in the ensuing general election with 4.7% of the vote. In May 2004, prior to the European elections, the PCF formed a new transnational party, the "European Left", with 14 other European left-wing parties, confirming the party's new outward looking reformist stance on Europe. However, in the June elections, the PCF lost four of its six seats, although this was partially due to the reduction in the number of French seats in the European Parliament. In the regional elections, it managed

to hold on to one council presidency.

The PCF members of the European Parliament sit in the European United Left/Nordic Green Left group. The party is a member of the New European Left Forum (NELF).

The Greens
Les Verts
Address. 247, rue du Faubourg St-Martin, 75010 Paris
Telephone. (33–1) 5319–5319
Fax. (33–1) 5319–0393
Email. verts@les-verts.org
Website. www.les-verts.org
Leadership. Gilles Lemaire (national secretary); Noël Mamère (2002 presidential candidate); Marie-Hélène Aubert, Yves Contassot, Mireille Ferri & Yann Wehrling (spokespersons)

The Greens were organized as a unified mainstream environmentalist party in January 1984, officially embracing the suffix Ecologist Confederation–Ecologist Party (*Confédération Écologiste–Parti Écologiste*). This cumbersome nomenclature reflected the complexities of the movement's evolution since it fielded René Dumont for the presidency in 1974 and received 1.3% of the first-round vote. In the 1978 Assembly elections the earlier movement presented 200 candidates under the banner *Écologie 78*, winning 2.1% of the vote, while the *Écologie Europe* list took 4.4% in the 1979 European Parliament elections. Encouraged by that relative success, the movement in February 1980 joined with other groups to create the *Mouvement d'Écologie Politique* (MEP), which in 1981 backed the presidential candidacy of Brice Lalonde, then leader of Friends of the Earth and later founder of Ecology Generation (GE). As Ecology Today (*Aujourd'hui l'Ecologie*), the MEP presented 82 candidates in the 1981 Assembly elections, winning 1.2% of the first-round vote (and no seats). In November 1982 the MEP became a political party called *Les Verts-Parti Écologiste* (VPE), which won some 6% of the overall vote in the 1983 municipal elections and elected several dozen councillors. The adoption of the longer title referred to above occurred at a Clichy congress (in January 1984) which achieved a merger of the VPE with various other environmentalist group.

Standing as *Les Verts-Europe Écologie*, the formation again failed to win representation in the 1984 European Parliament elections, when its vote fell to 3.4%, and was no more successful in the 1986 Assembly elections, when it managed only 1.1% of the first-round vote. Subsequent internal divisions were reflected in the rejection by a Paris general assembly in September 1986 of a policy paper presented by the movement's four spokesmen urging rapprochement with like-minded groups. Four new spokesmen were elected from among the "fundamentalist" wing, one of whom, Antoine Waechter, stood in the 1988 presidential elections, winning 3.8% of the first-round vote. The Greens declined to present official candidates for the June 1988 Assembly elections in protest against the return to constituency-based polling as opposed to the proportional system used in 1986. Returning to the electoral fray, they polled strongly in the 1989 European Parliament elections on a joint list with other groups, winning 10.6% of the vote and nine seats.

The 1993 Assembly elections yielded a 4% first-round vote for the Greens but no seats, despite an agreement with the GE not to run competing candidates. At their annual conference in November 1993 the Greens moved sharply to the left, electing Dominique Voynet as 1995 presidential candidate, while the disaffected Waechter later broke away to form the Independent Ecological Movement. Standing separately in the 1994 European Parliament elections, neither the Greens nor the GE gained sufficient support to win seats. Standing as the sole Green candidate in the 1995 presidential contest, Voynet was placed eighth of nine candidates, with 3.3% of the vote.

For the mid-1997 Assembly elections the Greens presented 455 candidates, 29 of whom were backed by the Socialist Party (PS) while the Greens agreed to support PS candidates in 70 constituencies. The outcome was a breakthrough for the Greens, to seven Assembly seats on the strength of a first-round vote of 6.8% achieved in alliance with other groups. The Greens thereupon joined the new PS-led coalition government, in which Voynet became Minister of the Environment. Its Assembly deputies joined the Radical, Citizen and Green group headed by the Left Radical Party. In the June 1999 European Parliament elections the Greens advanced strongly to 9.7% of the vote, taking nine of the 87 French seats, the leader of the list being the 1968-vintage revolutionary Daniel Cohn-Bendit.

In the March 2001 municipal and local council elections, the Greens played a key role in securing the election of the PS candidate as mayor of Paris, their 12.3% share of the first-round vote being swung behind the Socialists in the second round. In June 2001 the party selected Alain Lipietz, a former Maoist, as its candidate in the 2002 presidential elections. The following month Voynet left the government to take over the party leadership, being replaced as Environment Minister by Yves Cochet, a former Green MEP. In October 2001 the controversial Lipietz was dropped as presidential candidate and replaced by Noël Mamère, a profitable strategy which won the Green candidate 5.31% of the vote, the highest ever for a Green presidential candidate. The legislative score in 2002 saw a slight fall to 4.51% in the 555 constituencies where they stood, somewhat of a disappointment, especially in the 57 seats reserved for them in the left –wing coalition – only three won their seats. The left-wing revival in the 2004 regional and European elections saw a return to form for the Greens with 7.4% of the vote and 7 seats.

The French Greens are affiliated to the European Federation of Green Parties. Their representatives in the European Parliament sit in the Greens/European Free Alliance group.

Hunting, Fishing, Nature, Traditions
Chasse, Pêche, Nature, Traditions (CPNT)

Address. 245 blvd de la Paix, 64000 Pau
Telephone. (33–5) 5914–7171
Fax. (33–5) 5914–7172
Email. cpnt@cpnt.asso.fr
Website. www.cpnt.asso.fr
Leadership. Jean Saint-Josse (president); Michel Raymond (secretary-general)

The CPNT movement advocates the protection and furtherance of traditional countryside pursuits and maintenance of the rural way of life and values. Opposed to further European integration, it contested the 1994 European Parliament elections without success (taking 3.9% of the vote), but made a breakthrough in the 1999 contest, winning 6.8% and six seats. In the 2002 presidential elections, the party fielded Saint-Josse as its candidate, winning 4.3% of the first-round vote. However, the limits of the party's national base meant that it could only muster 1.7% of the vote in the legislative elections. In the 2004 European Parliament elections the party lost all six of its seats.

Left Radical Party
Parti Radical de Gauche (PRG)

Address. 13 rue Duroc Paris
Telephone. (33–1) 4566–6768
Fax. (33–1) 4566–4793
Email. prg-nat@club-internet.fr
Website. www.planeteradicale.org
Leadership. Jean-Michel Baylet (president); Christiane Taubira (vice-president); Elisabeth Boyer (secretary general);

Roger-Gérard Schwartzenberg (Assembly group chairman)
The PRG is the current rubric of what was the Left Radical Movement (MRG) until 1996, following a succession of name changes that were disputed in the courts. The MRG had originated in July 1972 as a left-wing faction of the historic Radical Party which endorsed the common programme issued the previous month by the Socialist Party (PS) and the French Communist Party (PCF), whereas the Radical majority then led by Jean-Jacques Servan-Schreiber declined to join the new Union of the Left. Initially organized as the Radical-Socialist Study and Action Group, the left-wing faction was expelled in October 1972 and contested the March 1973 Assembly elections on a joint list with the PS called the *Union de la Gauche Socialiste et Démocrate*, taking 11 of the 100 seats won by the alliance. The faction formally constituted itself as the MRG in December 1973 under the presidency of Robert Fabre, taking as its watchword the famous Radical slogan *"Pas d'ennemi à gauche"* ("No enemy to the left").

In contentious negotiations on revision of the common programme for the March 1978 Assembly elections, the MRG caused the first formal breakdown of talks in September 1977, when Fabre rejected the extensive nationalization programme demanded by the PCF. In the 1988 elections the MRG presented its own policy platform which differed from those of the PS and PCF in important respects; but the electoral alliance with the PS was maintained, and reciprocal support arrangements between the PS/MRG and the PCF again came into play in the second round. The result was that the MRG took 10 of the 113 seats won by the PS/MRG alliance. Immediately after the polling, Fabre repudiated the original common programme of the left and resigned the MRG presidency. He was succeeded by Michel Crépeau, who favoured the continuation of left-wing union, whereas the MRG right advocated reversion to a centre-left orientation and eventually, for the most part, rejoined the parent Radical Party or other centre-left groupings.

Crépeau stood as the MRG candidate in the first round of the 1981 presidential elections, winning only 2.2% of the vote. In the second round the MRG backed François Mitterrand of the PS, whose victory resulted in the appointment of a left-wing government in which Crépeau obtained a ministerial portfolio. In the June 1981 Assembly elections the MRG increased its seat tally to 14 by virtue of a further alliance with the victorious PS. Thereafter, the MRG participated in the PS-led government throughout its five-year tenure, while regularly seeking to assert its distinct political identity. In the 1984 European Parliament elections, for example, it was the principal component of a centre-left/ecological list called *Entente Radicale Écologiste pour les États-Unis d'Europe*, which secured 3.3% of the vote and no seats. The MRG also contested the 1986 Assembly elections in its own right (the move to proportional representation obviating the need for a joint list with the PS), but mustered only 0.4% of the total vote and two seats. The party nevertheless maintained a significant presence in local and regional government.

In opposition in 1986–88, the MRG experienced much internal agonizing about whether to maintain its leftward orientation or to turn to the centre. In the event, it was again allied with the PS in the 1988 Assembly elections held after the re-election of Mitterrand to the presidency. With majority voting by constituency having been reinstated, the MRG obtained nine seats and was allocated three ministerial posts in the resultant PS-led coalition. It remained in government for the next five years, but had little success in its attempts to build a "second force" within the then "presidential majority". In the March 1993 Assembly elections the MRG shared in the heavy defeat of its Socialist allies, although left-wing voting discipline and the MRG's resilience in its remaining strongholds enabled the party to retain six seats with a first-round vote share of 0.9%.

Again in opposition, the MRG was temporarily strengthened by the adhesion of controversial businessman Bernard Tapie, who had served two brief spells as a minister in 1992-93 and had been elected as a "presidential majority" candidate in the 1993 Assembly elections. In the June 1994 European Parliament elections Tapie headed the MRG's *Énergie Radical* list, which won 13 seats on an impressive vote share of 12.1%, while the PS under the new leadership of Michel Rocard performed so badly that Rocard had to resign. Having backed Rocard's efforts to build a broader social democratic party, the MRG was much less enthusiastic about his left-wing successor, Henri Emmanuelli, and initially announced that its leader, Jean-François Hory, would contest the 1995 presidential elections with the aim of rallying the centre-left opposition. In the event, the selection of Lionel Jospin as the PS candidate served to restore the PS/MRG axis, in that Hory withdrew his candidacy and the MRG contributed to Jospin's powerful, albeit losing, performance in the presidential contest. Shortly after the second-round polling (in May 1995), the MRG's "Tapie era" finally ended when the former tycoon (by now bankrupt) was sentenced to a prison term after being convicted of attempted match-fixing when he owned Marseilles football club.

Hory resigned as MRG president in October 1995 and was succeeded by Jean-Michel Baylet in January 1996, when a party congress also elected six vice-presidents. These included the former Socialist minister, Bernard Kouchner, whose Reunite (*Réunir*) grouping, founded in November 1994, was merged into the MRG. With a view to sharpening its public image, the party decided to adopt the one-word title "Radical" for campaigning purposes, thereby creating much scope for confusion as between it and the historic Radical Party. In March 1996 a Paris court ordered it to revert to the MRG name within four months. It then opted for the title "Radical Socialist Party" (PRS), under which name it won 12 seats in the mid-1997 Assembly elections in alliance in many constituencies with the PS. In then joined the new PS-led coalition government, receiving one portfolio.

The party was subsequently told by a court that its PRS title was also unlawful because of potential confusion, so that in January 1998 it almost reverted to its original name by becoming the "Left Radical Party" (PRG). In the June 1999 European Parliament elections the party was part of a joint list with the PS and the Citizens' Movement (MRC), the list heading the poll with 22% of the vote and 22 seats, of which the PRG took two.

In 2002, the party fielded a presidential candidate for the first time – France's first black female candidate, and the party's current vice-president Christiane Taubira, also a Walawari deputy in French Guiana. As one of the "plural left" candidates, however, her securing 2.1% of the vote contributed to the defeat of Lionel Jospin of the Socialist Party and consequently received some negative attention in the left-wing press. The party remained a marginal force in the legislative elections, with 1.6% of the vote. In the 2004 European elections, the party fielded independent lists in three regions. However, since the defeat of 2002, the party has generally fallen back into line behind its Socialist allies, a strategy from which it has profited, particularly in the left's strong showing in the 2004 regional elections.

National Centre of Independents and Peasants
Centre National des Indépendants et Paysans (CNIP)
Address. 6 rue Quentin Beauchart, 75008 Paris
Telephone. (33–1) 4723–4700
Fax. (33–1) 4723–4703
Email. contact@cni.asso.fr
Website. www.cni.asso.fr
Leadership. Annick du Roscoat (president); Bernard Beaudet (secretary-general)

The CNIP is derived from the *Centre National des Indépendants* (CNI), which was formed in July 1948 on the initiative of Roger Duchet and René Coty and quickly succeeded in federating most independent parliamentarians of the moderate right. The CNI became the CNIP in January 1949 when it absorbed the small peasant-based *Parti Républicaine de la Liberté*. Between 1951 and 1962 the CNIP took part in various coalition governments, with party members Antoine Pinay being Prime Minister in 1952 and Coty serving as President in 1952–59. In July 1954 the CNIP was joined by Gaullist dissidents of the *Action Républicaine et Sociale* who had supported the Pinay government. In 1958 the CNIP supported the return to power of Gen. de Gaulle and the creation of the Fifth Republic, reaching its electoral peak in the November 1958 Assembly elections, in which it won 22% of the vote and 132 seats. One of these was filled by Jean-Marie Le Pen, who was later to become leader of the far-right National Front (FN).

The CNIP's influence declined in the 1960s. Deeply divided over de Gaulle's policy of withdrawal from Algeria, it finally broke with him in October 1962. In Assembly elections the following month it lost almost all its representation, as its outgoing deputies either were defeated or transferred to the "majority" camp as Independent Republicans (later the nucleus of the Republican Party, now Liberal Democracy). In 1967–68 the CNIP was in alliance with Jean Lecanuet's *Centre Démocrate*, but proposals for a formal merger came to nothing. Although nominally an opposition leader during this period, CNIP honorary president Pinay declined invitations to stand against de Gaulle and Georges Pompidou in the presidential elections of 1965 and 1969 respectively. In 1974 the CNIP supported the successful presidential candidacy of Valéry Giscard d'Estaing (Independent Republican) and thereafter became one of the four main parties of the "presidential majority", being represented from 1976 in successive governments headed by Raymond Barre.

The CNIP contested the March 1978 Assembly elections in alliance with other non-Gaullist "majority" parties (winning nine seats), although it did not join the Union for French Democracy formed on the eve of the poll. Having backed Giscard d'Estaing's unsuccessful re-election bid in 1981, the CNIP was reduced to five seats by the Socialist landslide in the June 1981 Assembly elections, despite an electoral pact with the other centre-right parties. Another pact for the 1986 Assembly elections brought the CNIP a similar level of representation as a component of the victorious centre-right front, although its influence was further eroded by the Socialist victory in the 1988 presidential and Assembly elections. Through this period the CNIP maintained a significance presence in the Senate, where its representatives sat in broader centre-right groups. Continuance of the relationship in the 1993 Assembly elections was impaired by the CNIP's public support for the anti-immigration policies of the FN. However, both in that contest and in the 1997 Assembly elections successful "various right" candidates included a number of CNIP adherents.

In the 2002 presidential elections, the CNIP declared its support for the candidacy of Jacques Chirac and in October signed a declaration of assocation with the UMP, as part of its explicit move to place itself in the Republican right camp. Thus, whilst remaining officially independent, the CNIP now forms part of the right-wing umbrella, on its rural/petit bourgeois flank.

National Front
Front National (FN)
Address. 4 rue Vauguyon, 92210 Saint Cloud
Telephone. (33–1) 4112–1000
Fax. (33–1) 4112–1086
Email. internet@frontnational.com

Website. www.frontnational.com

Leadership. Jean-Marie Le Pen (president); Marine Le Pen (vice-president); Jean-Claude Martínez (vice-president); Carl Lang (secretary-general)

The right-wing populist FN was founded in October 1972 on an anti-immigration, law and order, and strongly pro-market platform, bringing together various groups and personalities of the far right. The party has consistently denied that it is racist, pointing to the presence of French Afro-Caribbeans in its ranks and claiming that it welcomes non-whites provided they fully embrace French culture and civilization. Its founder and leader, Le Pen, had served in the elite Parachute Regiment and had been a National Assembly deputy in 1956–62, initially as a member of the *Union de Défense des Commerçants et Artisans* (UDCA) led by Pierre Poujade and later under the auspices of the National Centre of Independents and Peasants (CNIP), and had been closely identified with the *Algérie Française* movement. The FN made little impact in the 1970s, winning only 2.5% of the vote in the 1973 Assembly elections and 3% in 1978, while Le Pen took only 0.7% in the first round of the 1974 presidential contest and was unable to stand in 1981 because he could not obtain the required sponsorship of at least 500 national or local elected representatives.

The return to national power of the left in 1981 and increasing public concern about immigration yielded a surge of support for the FN, which successfully repackaged itself as a legitimate force on the right of the centre-right opposition. This approach brought the first far-right electoral success in 25 years when, in the March 1983 municipal elections, an FN candidate was returned to one of the new district councils in the Paris region, while later in the year the then FN secretary-general, Jean-Pierre Stirbois, won 16.7% of the first-round vote in a local by-election in Dreux, thus bringing about a second-round alliance between the FN and the Gaullist Rally for the Republic (RPR-UMP). The FN's major breakthrough came in the European Parliament elections of June 1984, when to the surprise of many observers it won 10.9% of the French vote and 10 seats. In the March 1985 regional elections it slipped to 8.7% of the first-round vote, and was weakend in late 1985 by a split which produced the rival *Front d'Opposition Nationale*. However, in the March 1986 Assembly elections (held under proportional representation), it secured 35 of the 577 seats, winning some 2.7 million votes (9.7%), many of them in working-class areas of high immigrant population where previously the French Communist Party (PCF) had held sway. As a result of simultaneous regional elections, several RPR regional presidents were elected or re-elected with FN support.

Although the FN initially decided to support Jacques Chirac (then RPR Prime Minister) in the 1988 presidential elections, in May 1986 it withdrew its backing because of Chirac's insistence on abandoning proportional representation for Assembly elections. In January 1987 Le Pen announced his own presidential candidacy, thereby generating dissension within the RPR between those who rejected any co-operation with the far right and those who recognized that the centre-right candidate might need FN backing in the second round. In September 1987 Le Pen caused a major controversy when he publicly referred to Nazi extermination camps as a "detail" of the history of World War II, although he later expressed regret for the remark. The episode did him little damage in the 1988 presidential elections, in which he took fourth place in the first round with 14.4% of the vote (and declined to give endorsement to Chirac in the second). However, in Assembly elections in June 1988 (for which constituency-based majority voting again applied), the FN lost all but one of its seats despite achieving a first-round vote share of 9.7%. The successful FN candidate was Yann Piat (in the Var), but she was expelled from the FN in

October 1988, whereafter she joined the Republican Party (and was assassinated in 1994).

The FN regained an Assembly seat in a by-election for Dreux in December 1989, when Marie-France Stirbois (widow of Jean-Pierre, who had died in a car crash in November 1988) won 61.3% of the second-round vote. Le Pen acclaimed the result as demonstrating public support for the FN's opposition to immigration and to "French decadence", and called for the repatriation of all foreigners who had come to France since 1974. While not opposing French membership of the European Union (EU), the FN strongly endorsed the old Gaullist concept of a "Europe of nation states" and therefore was part of the opposition to the EU's Maastricht Treaty on ever closer union, which obtained wafer-thin referendum endorsement by French voters in September 1992. In the March 1993 Assembly elections, the FN failed to win representation, despite a national first-round vote share of 12.4% and an election campaign in which the "respectable" centre-right parties took up many of the FN's concerns about immigration and the rule of law.

In the June 1994 European Parliament elections the FN slipped back to 10.5% (winning 11 of the 87 French seats). In the 1995 presidential elections, however, Le Pen took fourth place in the first round with an all-time FN electoral high of 15.0% (4,573,202 votes). He again declined to give endorsement to Chirac of the RPR in the second round, announcing that he would cast a blank ballot in protest against "a detestable choice between two left-wing candidates". The FN continued its advance in municipal elections in June 1995, trebling its complement of councillors to 1,075 and winning control of three substantial southern towns (Toulon, Orange and Marignane). According to a post-election statement by Le Pen, the FN would apply "national preference" in the municipalities under its control, so that immigrants and foreigners would no longer get equal treatment in the allocation of subsidized housing, welfare benefits and public-sector jobs.

In February 1997 the FN narrowly won a high-profile mayoral by-election in Vitrolles, near Marseilles, and the following month gained more publicity when its 10th congress in Strasbourg attracted a major protest demonstration backed by the Socialist Party (PS) and the PCF. In the mid-1997 National Assembly elections the NF advanced to 14.9% of the first-round vote, but returned only one deputy (from Toulon). It lost even this seat in a May 1998 by-election (called because the NF deputy had infringed party finance rules in the 1997 contest) and failed to regain it in a further by-election in September 1998 (called because of ballot irregularities in the first). There was evidence in these and other electoral contests that moderate conservative voters were prepared to combine with the left in unofficial "republican fronts" to defeat the FN.

In November 1998 a Versailles appeal court disqualified Le Pen from elective office for a year and confirmed a suspended three-month sentence imposed on the FN leader for assaulting a PS candidate in the 1997 Assembly elections. The affair contributed to deepening internal divisions, which came to a head in January 1999 when deputy leader and chief ideologue Bruno Mégret was elected leader of the "National Front–National Movement" (FN-*Mouvement National*, FN-MN) at a conference held in Marignane after some 17,000 of the 40,000 FN members had signed a petition in favour of a leadership election. Le Pen boycotted the conference and also dismissed Mégret's claim that he now led the authentic FN. The dispute between the two was about political strategy rather than ideology, in that Le Pen opposed any alliances with other parties, whereas Mégret favoured pragmatic electoral pacts with centre-right formations. Le Pen appeared to be losing the struggle when in March 1999 the influential FN mayor of Toulon declared his support for Mégret. However, in May a Paris court banned the Mégret faction from "usurping" the FN name and logo, with the result that it assumed the title National Republican Movement (MNR) and Le Pen continued as leader of the FN.

Headed by Le Pen, the FN list in the June 1999 European Parliament elections easily outpolled the MNR, although it took only 5.7% of the vote and elected five MEPs, who were numbered among the "unattached" contingent when the new Parliament assembled. In February 2000 Le Pen's disqualification from public office was at last applied to his seat on the Provence-Alpes-Côte d'Azur regional council, while two months later the French government banned him from sitting in the European Parliament. Le Pen lost appeals against this decision in October 2000, whereupon European Parliament president Nicole Fontaine (France) ordered his exclusion. In January 2001, however, the European Court of Justice ruled that Fontaine had acted illegally in relying on French legal decisions to exclude Le Pen, who therefore regained his seat.

The FN suffered a major setback in the March 2001 local council elections, losing control of Toulon and surrendering many seats to centre-right/left second-round alliances. Nevertheless, in June 2001 Le Pen confirmed that he would contest the 2002 presidential elections and that the FN would field candidates for all 577 seats in the subsequent National Assembly elections.

Le Pen's second place, and victory over the Socialist candidate Lionel Jospin, in the 2002 presidential election first round was regarded as a political earthquake in France. His 17.2% share of the vote, his highest to date, showed that the party and candidate, despite being shaken by the split with Mégret's MNR, could still mobilise its increasingly stable electorate. In the second round run-off against Jacques Chirac, Le Pen's share of the vote remained essentially stable (18.1%) after massive mobilisation on the street and in the press against him. Similarly, the party dropped back to 11.4% in the subsequent legislative elections, unable to capitalise further on its presidential success, and equally challenged by a newly cohesive moderate right-wing party, the Union for a Presidential Majority, making explicit reference to their candidate's presidential landslide.

The departure of Mégret in 1999 has not marked the end of power struggles within the FN. Increasingly present on the public stage both next to and independently of her father, Marine Le Pen is now seen by her father, if not other party apparatchiks, as his likely successor. In 2003 at the party congress in Nice, she was elected to the post of vice-president, and in the 2004 elections to the European Parliament won one of the FN's seven seats as head of the Ile-de France list. Other pretenders to the FN throne, for instance the general delegate and former secretary general Bruno Gollnisch, look unlikely to accept her political primacy in the future, however.

National Republican Movement
Mouvement National Républicain (MNR)

Address. 15 rue de Cronstadt, 75015 Paris
Telephone. (33–1) 5656–6434
Fax. (33–1) 5656–5247
Email. m-n-r@m-n-r.com
Website. www.m-n-r.com
Leadership. Bruno Mégret (president); Yves Dupont (vice-president); Bertrand Robert (vice-president); Annick Martin (secretary-general)

The MNR was founded in 1999 by a dissident faction of the radical right-wing National Front (FN) led by Bruno Mégret, the FN deputy leader and chief ideologue, who had come into serious conflict with FN leader Jean-Marie Le Pen over political strategy. Whereas Le Pen opposed any alliances between the FN and other parties, Mégret favoured pragmatic electoral pacts with centre-right formations. After some

17,000 of the 40,000 FN members had signed a petition in favour of a leadership election conference, and Le Pen had opted to ignore the petition, a conference of the dissident faction in Marignane in January 1999 elected Mégret as leader of the "National Front–National Movement". Having boycotted the conference, Le Pen dismissed Mégret's claim that he now led the authentic FN.

The breakaway party was strengthened when in March 1999 the influential FN mayor of Toulon declared his support for it. However, in May a Paris court banned the Mégret faction from "usurping" the FN name and logo, with the result that it assumed the title National Republican Movement (MNR). In the June 1999 European Parliament elections the Mégret list was easily outpolled by the rump FN, winning only 3.3% of the vote and no seats.

The party and its leader have continued with similarly marginal results in the 2002 presidential (2.4%) and legislative (1.1%) elections. His wife Catherine's loss of the Vitrolles mayorship in 2002 marked the disppearance of the MNR's last bastion. Mégret's suspended sentence of a year for misuse of public funds in 2004 has not helped the party consolidate its image as one fighting against elite corruption. The subsequent nullification of Mégret's European candidacy and the party's meagre 0.3% of the Euro-vote in June 2004 suggest that the party's future is less than assured.

Rally for France and the Independence of Europe
Rassemblement pour la France et l'Indépendance de l'Europe (RPF-IE)

Address. 120 ave Charles de Gaulle, 92200 Neuilly-sur-Seine Cedex
Telephone. (33–1) 7292–0503
Fax. (33–1) 7292–0513
Email. infos@charles-pasqua.com
Website. www.rpf-ie.org
Leadership. Charles Pasqua (president): François Asselineau (spokesperson)

Opposed to further European integration, the RPF-IE was formally established as a political party in November 1999, following the success of the RPF-IE list in the June 1999 European Parliament elections. It united the Rally for France (RPF), launched by former Gaullist Interior Minister Charles Pasqua in June 1998 as a breakaway from the Rally for the Republic (RPR-UMP), and the Movement for France (*Mouvement pour la France*, MPF) led by Philippe de Villiers.

The MPF had been formed in November 1994 as the successor to The Other Europe (*L'Autre Europe*), which had been created to contest the June 1994 European Parliament elections, principally on the initiative of the French-British financier, Sir James Goldsmith. Opposed to the Maastricht process of closer EU economic and monetary union, it also condemned the 1993 GATT world trade liberalization agreement, arguing that Western Europe needed to protect its industry and employment levels from Asian competition based on cheap labour. In the 1994 European poll, The Other Europe list obtained 12.4% of the vote and 13 of the 87 French seats. In the 1995 presidential elections, MPF leader de Villiers (a former member of the Union for French Democracy) was placed seventh out of nine first-round candidates, winning 4.7% of the vote.

In the June 1999 Euro-elections the RPF-IE list took second place, ahead of the RPR, winning 13.1% of the vote and 13 seats on a platform of opposition to further European integration and enlargement. In late 1999 the new formation numbered five Assembly members and six senators among its adherents. By mid-2000, however, policy and personal differences between Pasqua and de Villiers had caused the withdrawal of the latter, who in January 2001 told magistrates investigating an arms trafficking affair that Pasqua had received illegal funds via the company at the centre of the scandal. On being placed under criminal investigation in April 2001, Pasqua dismissed the allegations as "trumped-up rubbish" and as "an attempt to destabilize democracy". However, in the 2002 presidential race, he was unable to stand as he intended due to his failure to collect the requisite 500 signatures. In the ensuing legislative elections, the party won only 0.37% of the vote, taking two seats

By October of the same year, the party had allowed its members to hold dual membership of the UMP. Given its small number of activists, it has only been able to field a small number of regional and European lists in the 2004 elections, losing all 13 of its seats in the European Parliament with just 1.7% of the vote.

Republican and Citizens Movement
Mouvement Républicain et Citoyen (MRC)
Address. 9 rue du Faubourg-Poissonnière, 75009 Paris
Telephone. (33–1) 4483–8300
Fax. (33–1) 4483–8320
Email. contact@mrc-france.org
Website. mrc-france.org
Leadership. Jean-Pierre Chevènement (president); Jean-Luc Laurent (first secretary)
What became the MRC was launched in 1993 under the name of the Citizens' Movement (*Mouvement des Citoyens*, MDC) by former Socialist Party (PS) minister Jean-Pierre Chevènement on a platform of opposition to the Maastricht Treaty and further European integration. In the 1994 European Parliament elections Chevènement headed the "Alternative Politics" (*L'Autre Politique*) list, winning 2.5% of the vote and no seats. Having won a National Assembly by-election in December 1995, the MDC contested the mid-1997 Assembly elections in alliance with the PS, winning seven seats in its own right and subsequently joining the new PS-led coalition government, in which Chevènement became Interior Minister (and stood down from the MDC leadership). The MDC deputies in the Assembly joined the Radical, Citizen and Green group headed by the Left Radical Party (PRG), while in the Senate the MDC secretary-general, Paul Loridant, sat in the Communist, Republican and Citizen group headed by the French Communist Party. The MDC was part of the PS-headed list for the June 1999 European Parliament elections (with the PRG), taking two of the 22 seats won by the list.

Chevènement got into difficulties in May 2000 when he criticized German proposals for a federal Europe by contending that Germany had "an ethnic concept of nationhood", was still aspiring to creating "a Germanic Holy Roman Empire" and had still not recovered from "the aberration of Nazism". In August 2000 he resigned from the government (for the third time in his political career) in protest against a new plan for Corsican autonomy, claiming in May 2001, when it was adopted by the National Assembly, that the plan was "a time-bomb" which would lead to the "territorial fragmentation" of France.

His strong Jacobin republicanism led him to field himself as a presidential candidate in 2002, using the classic "neither left nor right" formula as a republican centrist. To this end, the MDC was used as a pole around which to affiliate a number of ideologically disparate groupuscules to support his candidacy, under the Republican Pole (PoR) banner. In polls preceding the elections, he looked a likely third-place candidate for the first round, but as the election approached, his ratings slid dramatically with voters more convinced by ideological allegiance to clear left-wing or right-wing candidates. His final score of 5.4%, however, was sufficient for him to be particularly vilified by the left as having lost Lionel Jospin the key votes which allowed Jean-Marie Le Pen to overtake him. The vilification was particularly strong given his former ministerial position in a left-wing govern-

ment, and despite his receiving strong support from many former right-wing voters, including voters who would have chosen Charles Pasqua of the RPF-IE, had he been able to stand.

In an attempt to cement unity, the MDC was officially dissolved on May 12 and the PoR given party status. However, in the subsequent legislative elections, the Republican Pole was abandoned by the majority of its electorate, and won only 1.25% of the national vote, and a number of members left the party to set up the Association for a Republican Left. The party again officially changed its name to the Republican and Citizens Movement on Jan. 26, 2003, but in subsequent elections, the PoR has still been the label under which the party stands together with other members such as the Gaullist Union for a Republican France, the Union of Young Republicans and the Union of Radical Republicans. In elections in 2004, its results have been very marginal and generally only feature under the "other votes" category in reported figures.

Together with the PS and PRG members, the MDC representatives in the European Parliament sit in the Party of European Socialists group. The party is a member of the New European Left Forum (NELF).

Socialist Party
Parti Socialiste (PS)
Address. 10 rue de Solférino, 75333 Paris 07
Telephone. (33–1) 4556–7700
Fax. (33–1) 4705–1578
Email. infops@parti-socialiste.fr
Website. www.parti-socialiste.fr
Leadership. François Hollande (first secretary)
The party was founded in April 1905 as the French Section of the Workers' International (*Section Française de l'Internationale Ouvrière*, SFIO), being a merger of the Socialist Party of France (inspired by Jules Guesde) and the French Socialist Party (led by Jean Jaurès). The SFIO sought to rally pre-1914 labour opposition to war within the Second International, but a majority of the party regarded World War I as one of French national defence (one notable exception being Jaurès, who was assassinated in July 1914 by a nationalist fanatic). At its December 1920 congress in Tours the SFIO was split when a majority of delegates voted for membership of the Communist International (Comintern) and thus founded the French Communist Party (PCF), while the minority maintained the SFIO as a non-revolutionary party. Having supported Radical Party administrations from 1924, the SFIO became the largest party in the 1936 elections under the leadership of Léon Blum, who formed a Popular Front government with the Radicals, supported externally by the PCF. In opposition from 1938, the "reconstituted" SFIO went underground following the French surrender to Nazi Germany in 1940; it played an active part in the resistamce and also participated in the Algiers Committee set up by Gen. Charles de Gaulle as leader of the Free French.

Following the liberation of France in 1944, the SFIO joined a provisional government headed by de Gaulle, becoming the third largest Assembly party in the 1945 elections with 139 seats, behind the PCF and the (Christian democratic) Popular Republican Movement, and retaining this ranking in both 1946 elections, although its representation fell to 93 seats. Eschewing alliance with the PCF in favour of centre-left cooperation, the SFIO headed the first two Fourth Republic governments (under Blum in 1946–47 and Paul Ramadier in 1947), instituting an extensive nationalization programme. In 1947 Vincent Auriol of the SFIO was elected President of France, and in the 1951 Assembly elections the SFIO recovered to 104 seats. Although it fell back to 95 seats in the 1956 elections, in 1956–57 the then SFIO leader, Guy Mollet, was Prime Minister of the Fourth

Republic's longest-lasting government, playing a major role in the creation of the European Economic Community. However, internal dissension and defections over the role of the Mollet government in the 1956 Suez crisis and over the SFIO's support for the retention of French sovereignty in Algeria were intensified by the participation of Mollet and other SFIO ministers in the national unity government formed by de Gaulle on the collapse of the Fourth Republic in mid-1958. In Assembly elections in November 1958 the SFIO slumped to 40 seats, following which the party leadership supported the installation of de Gaulle as President of the Fifth Republic. The SFIO nevertheless refused to participate in the Gaullist-led government formed in January 1959 and was to remain in opposition for over two decades.

Having recovered somewhat to 66 seats in the 1962 Assembly elections, the SFIO in September 1965 joined with the Radicals and the small Convention of Republican Institutions (CIR) to form the Federation of the Democratic and Socialist Left (*Fédération de la Gauche Démocratique et Socialiste*, FGDS). Elected president of the FGDS was the CIR leader, François Mitterrand, who as leader of the former Democratic and Social Union of the Resistance (*Union Démocratique et Sociale de la Résistance*, UDSR) had participated in successive Fourth Republic governments and had opposed Gen. de Gaulle's return to power in 1958. As candidate of the FGDS, and supported by the PCF and other left-wing formations, Mitterrand took de Gaulle to the second round in the 1965 presidential elections (held by direct suffrage), winning 44.8% of the vote. In the 1967 Assembly elections the FGDS benefited from a second-round support pact with the PCF, winning a total of 121 seats. However, in further elections held in June 1968 in the wake of the May "events" the FGDS retained only 57 seats, amid a landslide to the Gaullists. This defeat heightened disagreements among the FGDS constituent groupings, in light of which Mitterrand resigned from the presidency in November 1968, shortly before the Radicals decided against joining a unified party based on the FGDS.

Notwithstanding the effective collapse of the FGDS, the SFIO pursued the goal of a broader "new" socialist party on the basis of a merger with Mitterrand's CIR and the Union of Clubs for the Renewal of the Left (*Union des Clubs pour le Renouveau de la Gauche*, UCRG). On the eve of the May 1969 presidential elections an intended founding congress of the new party was held at Alfortville, but the CIR refused to back the presidential candidacy of SFIO right-winger Gaston Defferre (mayor of Marseilles), who went on to score an ignominious 5% of the vote in the first round. Subsequently, the CIR did not participate when a new Socialist Party was proclaimed at the Issy-les-Moulineaux congress of July 1969, as a merger of the SFIO and the UCRG, whose leader, Alain Savary, was elected PS first secretary (and Mollet bowed out after 23 years as SFIO leader). However, renewed efforts to bring the CIR into the new party reached a successful conclusion in June 1971 with the holding of a "congress of socialist unity" at Epinay, with Mitterrand being elected first secretary of the enlarged PS.

Under Mitterrand's leadership, the PS adopted a strategy of "union of the left", signing a common programme with the PCF and the Left Radical Movement (MRG) (Left Radical Party) in June 1972 which featured wide-ranging nationalization plans. On the basis of the programme, the left made major gains in the Assembly elections of March 1973, when the PS and the MRG (standing as the Union of the Socialist and Democratic Left) jointly returned 102 deputies, including 89 Socialists. The following year Mitterrand contested presidential elections as the agreed candidate of virtually the entire left in both rounds of voting, but was narrowly defeated by Valéry Giscard d'Estaing (Independent Republican) in the second round, receiving 49.2% of the vote. In 1975 the PS was further enlarged when it was joined by the minority wing of the Unified Socialist Party (*Parti Socialiste Unifié*, PSU) led by Michel Rocard and also by a "third component" consisting mainly of affiliated members of the Socialist-led CFDT trade union federation. However, the steady growth of PS strength engendered serious strains in the party's alliance with the PCF, culminating in the failure of the left to agree on a revised common programme for the March 1978 Assembly elections. In that contest reciprocal support arrangements were operated by the left-wing parties in the second round, but the PS tally of 103 seats (plus 10 for the MRG) was disappointing, even though the PS could claim to have become the strongest single party with around 23% of the first-round vote.

Standing as the PS candidate in the May 1981 presidential elections, Mitterrand obtained 25.9% in the first round, which was also contested by PCF and MRG candidates; backed by the entire left in the second round, he defeated incumbent Giscard d'Estaing by 51.8% to 48.2%, thus becoming President at his third attempt. Assembly elections in June 1981 gave the Socialists their first-ever absolute majority, of 285 seats out of 491. The new PS-led government, which included MRG and PCF ministers, was headed by Pierre Mauroy, while Lionel Jospin succeeded Mitterrand as PS first secretary. The Mauroy government proceeded to implement extensive nationalization measures, but was quickly obliged to abandon plans for state-led economic expansion in the interests of containing inflation and preventing currency depreciation. The PCF withdrew from the government in July 1984 when Mauroy was replaced as Prime Minister by Laurent Fabius, who faced considerable unrest in the party and country over the government's switch to orthodox economic policies. In the Assembly elections of March 1986 (held under proportional representation) the PS lost its absolute majority, although it remained the largest party with 206 seats and 31.6% of the vote. It accordingly went into opposition to a centre-right coalition headed by Jacques Chirac of the (Gaullist) Rally for the Republic (RPR-UMP), with whom President Mitterrand was obliged to govern in uneasy political "cohabitation".

In opposition, the PS undertook a reassessment of its economic policies, including its traditional commitment to state ownership, and advocated a broad alliance of "progressive" forces against the centre-right. But the party's relations with the PCF remained badly strained, not least because of the growing influence of the "moderate" PS faction led by Rocard, who favoured realignment towards the centre. In the 1988 presidential elections Mitterrand was opposed in the first round by two Communist candidates (one official) as well as by Chirac for the RPR and Raymond Barre for the centrist Union for French Democracy (UDF, Union for French Democracy). He headed the poll with 34.1% of the vote, whereupon all the left-wing parties backed him in the second round, in which he easily defeated Chirac by 54.01% to 45.98%. In new Assembly elections in June 1988 (for which constituency-based majority voting was reinstated), the PS increased its representation to 260 seats out of 577, short of an overall majority but sufficient to underpin a PS-led government headed by Rocard that included the MRG and independent centrists. Immediately after the presidential contest, former Prime Minister Mauroy succeeded Jospin as PS first secretary.

Legislative setbacks and disagreements with Mitterrand provoked Rocard's resignation in May 1991 and his replacement by Édith Cresson (PS), who became France's first woman Prime Minister. She failed to stem plummeting support for the government and was replaced in April 1992 by Pierre Bérégovoy, a Mitterrand loyalist and hitherto Finance Minister. In January 1992, moreover, former Prime Minister Fabius, also a Mitterrand loyalist, was elected to succeed

Mauroy as PS first secretary, following an extraordinary party congress in December 1991 at which delegates had accepted that only free-market policies could achieve economic growth. The Bérégovoy government had some success in restoring stability, and in September 1992 secured referendum approval of the controversial Maastricht Treaty on European union, albeit by a very narrow majority. But public disquiet at continuing economic recession was aggravated by a series of corruption and other scandals involving prominent PS politicians.

The PS went down to a widely-predicted heavy defeat in the March 1993 Assembly elections, retaining only 54 seats on a 17.6% first-round vote share and going into opposition to another "cohabitation" government of the centre-right. In the immediate aftermath, Rocard took over the PS leadership from Fabius and embarked upon an attempt to convert the party into a broader-based social democratic formation oriented towards the centre. However, unresolved internal party divisions contributed to a poor performance in the June 1994 European Parliament elections, in which the PS list managed only 14.5% (and 15 of the 87 French seats), compared with 23.6% in the 1989 contest. Rocard immediately resigned as party leader and was succeeded by Henri Emmanuelli, a former National Assembly president identified with the traditional PS left. Straitened financial circumstances were highlighted by the sale of the PS headquarters building in Paris, while the implication of PS officials in further corruption cases added to the party's problems in the run-up to the 1995 presidential elections.

An attempt to draft the outgoing president of the European Commission, Jacques Delors, as the PS presidential candidate was rebuffed by Delors himself in December 1994. In February 1995 a special PS congress in Paris endorsed former party leader Jospin as presidential candidate, on the basis of a primary election among party members in which the former Education Minister had easily defeated Emmanuelli, winning 66% of the votes. Closely supported by Delors, Jospin confounded the pundits by mounting an impressive presidential campaign and heading the first-round voting in April 1995, with 23.3% of the vote. He was defeated by Chirac of the RPR in the second round, but his tally of 47.4% as the candidate of the left served to restore Socialist morale after two years of turmoil. In June 1995 Jospin replaced Emmanuelli as PS first secretary and declared his intention to carry out a complete reform of party structures and policies before the next Assembly elections. The previous month Emmanuelli had received a suspended one-year prison sentence for receiving illicit campaign contributions as PS treasurer in the 1980s. Seven months after leaving office, Mitterrand died in January 1996 at the age of 79.

In late 1996 the PS national council decided that women candidates would be presented in at least 30% of constituencies in the next Assembly elections. In April 1997 the PS issued a joint declaration with the PCF setting a 35-hour week (with no loss of wages) and a halt to major privatizations as central objectives of a left-wing government, although the two parties made no formal electoral pact. In contrast, the PS entered into agreements with both the Left Radicals and the Greens not to oppose a number of their candidates in the first round of voting. The outcome of the polling in May-June 1997 gave the PS a large relative majority of 241 seats (on a first-round vote share of 23.5%) and the left as a whole an overall majority. Facing a period of "cohabitation" with the Chirac presidency, Jospin formed a coalition government dominated by the PS and also including the PCF, the Greens, the Left Radicals and the Citizens' Movement (MDC) led by former PS minister Jean-Pierre Chevènement.

From January 1998 the Elf-Aquitaine affair, centring on financial corruption allegations against former PS Foreign Minister Roland Dumas (then the president of the Constitutional Council), caused increasing embarrassment for the party. The PS-led government, and Jospin in particular, nevertheless retained a high popularity rating, despite continuing high unemployment, as it implemented key policies such as the 35-hour week. The PS and its allies outpolled the centre-right in regional elections in March 1998, and the following month the government secured parliamentary approval for French entry into the single European currency, relying on centre-right votes to counter PCF and MDC opposition. In May 1998 PS candidate Odette Casanova narrowly prevented the far-right National Front (FN) from regaining its single Assembly seat in Toulon, on the strength of second-round support from the centre-right parties. She repeated the feat in September 1998 when the by-election had to be re-run.

The PS contested the June 1999 European Parliament elections in alliance with the Left Radicals and the MDC, their joint list heading the poll with 22% of the vote and 22 of the 87 French seats, of which the PS took 18. For the elections the PS had subscribed to a joint manifesto of EU Socialist parties which had sought to bridge the gap between the pro-market "third way" line of the British Labour Party and the continental preference for the social market economy. In a speech to EU Socialists in October 1999, however, Jospin distanced the PS from the Anglo-Saxon model, asserting that "the market economy does not find harmony of its own accord" and that "it needs rules".

In 2000 the PS was tarnished by new disclosures about its involvement in corrupt party funding in Paris allegedly orchestrated by the RPR when Chirac was mayor in 1977–95. It also faced the embarrassment in early 2001 of the trial of Dumas, his former mistress and five others in the Elf corruption case, which exposed some of the web of illegal payments by the company at home and abroad, notably under the Mitterrand presidency and often at his instigation. The trial did not prevent a PS senator, Bertrand Delanoë, being elected mayor of Paris in local elections in March 2001, bringing the left to power in the capital for the first time since the 1871 Commune. But the PS and the other government parties fared poorly elsewhere in the country, being outvoted by the centre-right parties by 46.9% to 44.9%, while several PS ministers failed in mayoral candidacies.

The conviction of Dumas and four other defendants in the Elf trial in May 2001 led to further difficulties for the PS. On bail pending his appeal, Dumas the following month told the press that two senior ministers in the current government, Foreign Minister Hubert Védrine and Employment and Solidarity Minister Elisabeth Guigou, had been complicit, as Mitterrand aides in the 1990s, in Elf's illicit payments practices. Both ministers denied any impropriety. Also in June 2001, Prime Minister Jospin was forced to admit that he had been a committed Trotskyist before joining the PS in 1971, although he did not respond to press claims that he had been an "entryist" and had remained a member of what became the International Communist Party (PCI) at least until the mid-1970s. Jospin had previously denied reports of his radical past, so that his image of integrity suffered a blow in advance of his candidacy in the 2002 presidential elections.

However, the result of the 2002 presidential election cannot be ascribed to this factor alone. The presence of a large number of minor left-wing candidates, a strong showing by the extreme left and a combination of diffidence and overconfidence amongst normally reliable Socialist voters, saw Jospin relegated to third place in the first round (15.9% of the vote) and consequently eliminated from the run-off by Jean-Marie Le Pen of the National Front. Jospin's immediate acceptance of all responsibility for the fiasco and withdrawal from French political life did little to help the Socialist

Party regroup with its left coalition allies, particularly given the animosity shown by many Socialists towards the Left Radicals and the Republican Pole (see Republican and Citizens Movement) for their part in Jospin's defeat. Unsurprisingly, the left was soundly defeated in the legislative elections by the Union for a Presidential Majority (UMP), with the Socialists winning only 24.3% of the vote. In the months that followed the defeat, the party seemed unable to find a replacement for Jospin around whom to group, and the former members of the left governing coalition, in particular the Greens, seemed reluctant to renew a close relationship with the party.

In the 2004 regional elections, however, the party profited from the unpopularity of the Raffarin government to win 22 of the 26 regional council presidencies, a strong turnaround given the situation of two years earlier. Similarly, in the European elections, Socialists accounted for 28.9% of the vote and 31 MEPs, almost twice the UMP tranche. The party still has some way to go to ensure success in the 2007 presidential and legislative races. François Hollande and his wife Ségolène Royal, the Socialist "ruling family", both have strong media profiles and political ambitions, but they are not alone – Dominique Strauss-Kahn, the former Finance Minister, has been rehabilitated since his corruption indictment and presents a popular and charismatic alternative. Laurent Fabius, similarly renewed since the contaminated blood scandal, is also an able politician, and has Prime Ministerial experience, even if he lacks the charm of his colleagues. Such divisions are common to all major French parties, but the Socialists have an interest in reconciling these competing factions to provide a winning presidential candidate at the next election.

The PS is a member party of the Socialist International. Its representatives in the European Parliament sit in the Party of European Socialists group.

Union for French Democracy
Union pour la Démocratie Française (UDF)
Address. 33bis rue de l'Université, 75014 Paris
Telephone. (33–1) 5359–2000
Fax. (33–1) 5359–2059
Email. internet@udf.org
Website. www.udf.org
Leadership. François Bayrou (president); Jean Arthuis (vice-president); Bernard Bosson (vice-president); André Santini (vice-president)

The "New" UDF (subsequently returning to its original name) was launched in 1999 following a UDF congress decision in November 1998 that the UDF constituent parties would formally combine into a unified organization and therefore cease to exist independently. The centre-right UDF had been created in February 1978 as an electoral alliance of the non-Gaullist "majority" (i.e. then ruling) parties, namely (i) what was then called the Republican Party (PR), which in 1997 became Liberal Democracy and in May 1998 left the UDF; (ii) the Radical Party; (iii) what was then called the Centre of Social Democrats (CDS) and in 1995 become the Democratic Force (FD); (iv) what later became the Social Democratic Party (PSD); and (v) the *Clubs Perspectives et Réalités*, which in 1995 became the Popular Party for French Democracy (PPDF).

Of the original UDF components, the **Radical Party** was by far the oldest, having been founded in 1901 from pre-existing Radical groups sharing a commitment to anti-clericalism and the separation of Church and State. Its full title, rarely used under the Fifth Republic, was Radical Republican and Radical-Socialist Party (*Parti Républicain Radical et Radical-Socialiste*, PRRRS), reflecting the Radicals' history as the mainstay of the Third Republic (1871–1940) and their frequent cooperation with the left-

wing parties under both the Third and Fourth Republics. The party was also often referred to as the *Parti Valoisien* after its headquarters address in Paris, from where it provided many Prime Ministers up to and after World War I, including Georges Clemenceau in 1906–09 and 1917–19. Its celebrated slogan was "*Pas d'ennemi à gauche*" ("No enemy to the left"), on which basis it participated in the anti-fascist Popular Front government formed in 1936 under the leadership of what was then the SFIO and much later became the Socialist Party (PS). Despite a post-war electoral decline, the Radicals remained a focal point in the frequent coalition building of the Fourth Republic until its demise in 1958, providing the Prime Ministers of no less than 12 governments.

Traditionally eschewing rigid structures, the Radical Party suffered a series of splits in 1954–56, when Pierre Mendès-France moved the party to the left and tried to impose more internal discipline. By late 1958 Mendès-France and his left-wing followers had become the minority and subsequently broke away to participate in the formation of the Unified Socialist Party (PSU), part of which later joined the PS. During the first decade of the Fifth Republic (1958–68) the rump Radicals under the leadership of René Billères participated in moves towards union of the non-Communist left, joining the Federation of the Democratic and Socialist Left (FGDS) in 1965 and participating in the FGDS advance in the 1967 Assembly elections. After the May 1968 political and social crisis, however, Maurice Faure moved the party back to a centrist posture, which was consolidated following the election of Jean-Jacques Servan-Schreiber to the party presidency in 1971. The Radical majority's refusal to subscribe to a new union of the left involving the Socialists and the French Communist Party (PCF) caused the exit of the left-wing minority in 1972 to form what became the Left Radical Movement (MRG), now called the Left Radical Party (PRG).

In the 1974 presidential elections the Radicals backed the successful candidacy of Valéry Giscard d'Estaing (Independent Republican), but only after the first round and in return for specific policy commitments. Under the Giscard d'Estaing presidency the Radicals were included in successive centre-right coalitions, although their initial return to government was controversial: appointed Minister of Reforms, Servan-Schreiber was dismissed within a fortnight for criticizing the proposed resumption of French nuclear tests in the Pacific. Pursuing attempts to forge greater unity among the smaller centrist and centre-left parties, the Radicals in July 1977 absorbed the Movement of Social Liberals (*Mouvement des Sociaux Libéraux*, MSL), which had been formed earlier in the year by Gaullist dissidents led by Olivier Stirn.

The forerunner of the **Democratic Force** (*Force Démocrate*, FD) was the centrist, Christian democratic and pro-European Centre of Social Democrats (*Centre des Sociaux Démocrates*, CSD) founded in May 1976, although its constituent elements had their roots in a 19th-century movement aimed at reconciling Catholics with the Third Republic (1871–1940). After World War II these forces were represented by the Popular Republican Movement (*Mouvement Républicain Populaire*, MRP) led by Georges Bidault and other wartime resistance leaders, which was the strongest parliamentary party until the 1951 elections and took part in most Fourth Republic governments until its demise in 1958. Bidault was himself Prime Minister in 1946 and 1949–50; other MRP premiers were Robert Schuman (1947–48) and Pierre Pflimlin (1958). The immediate antecedents of the CDS were the Democratic Centre (*Centre Démocrate*, CD) and the Democracy and Progress Centre (*Centre Démocratie et Progrès*, CDP), both of which emerged under the Fifth Republic.

The CD had been launched in March 1966 by Jean

Lecanuet, who had scored 15.9% in the 1965 presidential elections. In the 1969 contest most CD elements had backed Alain Poher (who received 23.3% in the first round and 41.8% in the second), although some had supported the successful Gaullist candidate, Georges Pompidou, thus abandoning the previous centrist policy of acting as a balancing force between the right-wing "majority" parties and the left-wing opposition. The CDP had been founded after the 1969 elections by centrist supporters of President Pompidou, notably Jacques Duhamel, Joseph Fontanet and René Pleven. In the 1973 Assembly elections the CD and the CDP had returned 24 and 34 deputies respectively, the former as part of the Reformers' Movement (created in 1971 by various centrist groups then outside the government "majority") and the latter in alliance with the ruling Gaullists and Independent Republicans. In the first round of the 1974 presidential elections the CDP had supported Jacques Chaban-Delmas (Gaullist) and the CD Giscard d'Estaing, but both parties had contributed to the victory of the latter in the second round. Both parties had joined the resultant centre-right government headed by Jacques Chirac and had been prominent in further moves towards greater cohesion of the centre, notably the six-party Federation of Reformers created in June 1975, prior to the launching of the CDS in May 1976 under the presidency of Lecanuet.

The forerunner of the **Popular Party for French Democracy** (*Parti Populaire pour la Démocratie Française*, PPDF) was the Perspectives and Realities Clubs (*Clubs Perspectives et Réalités*, CPR) grouping founded in 1965 by Jean-Pierre Fourcade, which had acted as a think tank for the UDF as a whole, providing a political home for centrist intellectuals reluctant to join a traditional political party. Many of its leading members were associated with the Republican Party component of the UDF (Liberal Democracy), notably its chair from 1982 to 1984, Jean-François Deniau, who had been a minister and European commissioner under the Giscard d'Estaing presidency (1974–81). Having lost the French presidency in 1981, Giscard d'Estaing himself took the chairmanship of the CPR until 1989.

The **Social Democratic Party** (*Parti Social-Démocrate*, PSD) had been established in December 1973 as the Movement of Democratic Socialists of France (*Mouvement des Démocrates Socialistes de France*, MDSF) by a faction of the PS opposed to the common programme issued by the PS and PCF in 1972. Claiming to enshrine the authentic socialist tradition of Jean Jaurès and Léon Blum, the MDSF advocated centrist unity and joined both the Reformers' Movement and the Federation of Reformers in the mid-1970s. The first MDSF vice-president, Émile Muller, won 0.7% of the vote in the first round of the 1974 presidential elections, whereafter the MDSF backed the successful candidacy of Giscard d'Estaing in the second. The MDSF transformed itself into the PSD in October 1982, at the same time absorbing some other social democratic elements.

The decision of the above parties to create the Union for French Democracy (*Union pour la Démocratie Française*, UDF) a month before the March 1978 Assembly elections was inspired in part by the decision of the (Gaullist) RPR to withdraw from first-round electoral pacts with the PR and CDS on the grounds that negotiation by these two parties of separate first-round agreements with the Radicals (the most left-wing of the "majority" parties) had violated the terms of the RPR/PR/CDS agreement. The UDF was backed from the outset by President Giscard d'Estaing (after whose 1977 book *Démocratie Française* the alliance was named) and by his Prime Minister, Raymond Barre. Its creation therefore heightened tensions between the Giscardian and Gaullist wings of the "majority", the former viewing it as an attempt to engineer electoral superiority. In the 1978 elections the UDF parties won increased aggregate representation of 124

seats (compared with 154 for the RPR), assisted by the operation of reciprocal voting support arrangements with the RPR in the second round. The elected UDF deputies included 71 from the PR, 35 from the CDS, seven Radicals and four from the MDSF. Immediately after polling the UDF council formally elevated the alliance to the status of a federation of its constituent parties, under the presidency of Jean Lecanuet (leader of the CDS). In the June 1979 elections to the European Parliament the strongly pro-European UDF list (*Union pour la France en Europe*) came top of the poll with 27.6%.

The UDF was the mainstay of Giscard d'Estaing's bid for a second presidential term in 1981 as a "citizen-candidate" rather than as the nominee of any party. Following his narrow second-round defeat by François Mitterrand (PS), the UDF formed an electoral alliance with the RPR for the June 1981 Assembly elections, called the *Union pour la Majorité Nouvelle* (UMN) and providing for single first-round candidates in 385 of the 474 metropolitan constituencies as well as reciprocal voting support for the best-placed second-round candidate in the others. The UDF nevertheless shared in the rout of the centre-right by the PS, winning 19.2% of the first-round vote and retaining only 63 Assembly seats, of which the PR took 32, the CDS 25 and the Radicals two. It therefore went into opposition for the next five years, the UMN alliance lapsing in 1983.

In April 1985 the UDF signed a new cooperation agreement with the RPR, with which it drew up a joint manifesto for the March 1986 Assembly elections (in which proportional representation applied). Presenting some candidates jointly with the RPR and others in its own right, the UDF played its part in the defeat of the PS-led government, increasing its representation to 131 seats out 577, the PR remaining the strongest UDF component with 59 seats. In the succeeding centre-right coalition headed by the RPR, the UDF parties received 17 ministerial posts out of 41. But the fragility of the ruling coalition became apparent in 1987 when the PR leader, François Léotard, announced that he would not support the RPR leader (and Prime Minister), Jacques Chirac, in the first round of the 1988 presidential elections. When it was announced in September 1987 that Barre (a centrist without formal party affiliation) would be a candidate, the PR and other UDF components declared their support for him. In the event, Barre came in third place in the first round in April 1988 with 16.5% of the vote, whereupon the UDF gave second-round support to Chirac in his unsuccessful attempt to deny Mitterrand a second term.

New Assembly elections held in June 1988 (by constituency-based majority voting) were contested by the UDF in an alliance with the RPR called the *Union du Rassemblement et du Centre* (URC). The centre-right parties lost their majority but the UDF showed resilience, for the first time returning more deputies (129) than the RPR (127), the UDF contingent including 58 PR, 49 CDS, three Radical and three PSD deputies. Immediately after the elections Giscard d'Estaing replaced Lecanuet as president of the UDF. In opposition over the next five years, most of the UDF contested the 1989 European elections on a joint list with the RPR (winning 28.9% of the vote and 26 seats), whilst the CDS presented an independent list which took 8.4% and seven seats. In June 1990 the UDF and RPR announced the creation of the *Union pour la France* (UPF), amid much talk about the need for a unified party. In reality, the UDF and the RPR continued their long struggle for supremacy on the centre-right, with the added ingredient of resumed rivalry between Giscard d'Estaing and Chirac. Also divisive was the Maastricht Treaty on European union, which was fully supported by the UDF, whereas important sections of the RPR campaigned for a "no" vote in the September 1992 referendum that yielded a narrow majority for French ratification.

As widely anticipated, the Assembly elections of March 1993 produced a landslide victory for the UDF/RPR alliance, which won 80% of the seats on a 40% first-round vote share. Crucially, the RPR emerged with 247 of the 577 seats, against 213 for the UDF parties, thus effectively dashing Giscard d'Estaing's further presidential ambitions. The PR remained dominant in the UDF elected contingent, taking 104 seats compared with 57 for the CDS (which had declined to give automatic support to better-placed centre-right candidates in the second round). The UDF parties were allocated important portfolios in the new "cohabitation" government headed by Edouard Balladur of the RPR, and in the European Parliament elections of June 1994 Giscard d'Estaing headed another joint UDF/RPR list (this time including the CDS), which slipped to 25.6%, giving it 28 seats.

The UDF was weakened by a series of corruption scandals which yielded the resignations of several ministers in 1994, with the result that both Giscard d'Estaing and Barre announced that they would not stand in the 1995 presidential elections. In the absence of a candidate from their own ranks, most UDF components initially supported Balladur as the more centrist of the two RPR contenders. After Balladur had been eliminated in the first round, however, the UDF officially swung behind the victorious candidacy of Chirac in the second, being rewarded with a strong ministerial presence in the resultant centre-right government headed by Alain Juppé of the RPR. In an apparent reconciliation of their longstanding personal rivalry, Giscard d'Estaing was invited to give "elder statesman" advice to the newly-installed President Chirac.

In July 1995 the CPR grouping converted itself into the PPDF under the leadership of Hervé de Charette and Jean-Pierre Raffarin, while in November 1995 the CDS became the FD under the leadership of François Bayrou. Both new creations remained under the UDF umbrella.

Giscard d'Estaing stood down as UDF leader in March 1996 (to devote himself to founding a centrist think tank) and indicated his preference that the succession should go to Alain Madelin (then of the PPDF, formerly a vice-president of the PR and subsequently leader of Liberal Democracy), who had the previous August been dismissed as Economy and Finance Minister after failing to persuade Prime Minister Juppé of the need for drastic measures to curb the budget deficit. However, UDF constituents preferred the PR leader, François Léotard, who secured 57.4% of delegates' votes at a national council meeting in Lyon. Thereafter, the growing influence of the far-right National Front (FN) became an increasingly divisive issue, with some UDF elements being prepared to support left-wing candidates to defeat the FN, while the UDF leadership declined to give specific endorsement to anti-FN "republican fronts".

The UDF shared in the defeat of the centre-right in the mid-1997 Assembly elections, its aggregate representation falling to 108 seats following a first-round vote share of only 14.2%. Consigned to opposition, the UDF also lost ground in the March 1998 regional elections, following which five UDF politicians were elected as regional assembly presidents on the strength of FN support. Two of these subsequently stood down under pressure, but the other three were expelled from the UDF, with the result that one of them, Charles Millon, launched what later became the Liberal Christian Right. In May 1998 the UDF and the RPR set up the "Alliance" as a joint umbrella organization, whereupon Liberal Democracy (successor to the PR) formally withdrew from the UDF and opted instead to become an autonomous component of the Alliance.

Mired in a party financing scandal, Léotard was in September 1998 succeeded as president of the UDF by François Bayrou, leader of Democratic Force (now the largest UDF component). At a congress in Lille in November 1998 the remaining UDF formations decided that they would cease to have separate existences and would instead combine into a unitary party. Bayrou resisted RPR pressure for another joint list for the June 1999 Euro-elections, opting for a separate UDF slate, which took 9.3% of the vote and only nine seats. The UDF then resorted in the short term to the time-honoured marketing stratagem of adding "New" to its title, so that it became "*La Nouvelle* UDF".

Memories of old scandals were revived in March 2000 when three former ministers, Pierre Méhaignerie, Jacques Barrot and Bernard Bosson, were fined and give suspended prison sentences after being convicted of illegal funding of the CDS (before it became the FD). Evidence also emerged in 2000 that the old UDF had been implicated in the system of kickbacks for public contracts allegedly run by the RPR in Paris when Chirac was mayor in 1977–95. Nevertheless, the combined forces of the UDF and the RPR outpolled the ruling coalition parties in the March 2001 local council elections, winning 46.9% of the first-round vote. At the same time, UDF parliamentary forces maintained their independence of the RPR by ensuring the passage in April 2001 of a government proposal that the 2002 presidential elections should precede Assembly elections rather then follow them, thereby (it was thought) likely reducing Chirac's chances of being re-elected.

In the 2002 presidential race, Bayrou scored a respectable 6.95% of the first-round vote, even against a UDF splinter candidate Christine Boutin (1.2%), but this was overshadowed by Chirac's call for the creation of a united centre-right party, the Union for a Presidential Majority. On April 25, the majority of UDF deputies decamped to the UMP, leaving only a core of support for Bayrou's intention of remaining an independent force. In the subsequent legislative elections, the party won 29 seats, just sufficient to form its own parliamentary group. Since then, the party and its leaders have striven valiantly to retain autonomy from the UMP. At the end of 2003, the party leadership decided to field separate lists in the 2004 regional elections, a strategy which whilst ensuring that it won no regional presidencies, at least also ensured that it was not tarnished by the electoral disaster which befell the governing UMP, which lost control of all councils which it had held. Thus, in the 2004 elections the party won a very creditable 11.95% of the vote and 11 seats overall, just 5% behind the UMP.

The UDF is a member of the International Democrat Union and the European Democrat Union; through the FD it is also affiliated to the Christian Democrat International. The UDF members of the European Parliament sit in the European People's Party group.

Union for a Popular Movement (former Union for a Presidential Majority)
Union pour un Mouvement Populaire (former Union pour une Majorité Présidentielle) (UMP)

Address. 55, rue La Boétie 75384 Paris Cedex 08

Telephone. (33–1) 4076–6000

Website. www.u-m-p.org

Leadership. Alain Juppé (president); Jean-Claude Gaudin (vice-president); Philippe Douste-Blazy (general secretary)

The UMP (sometimes also referred in English as Union for a People's Movement) represents the most recent attempt by politicians on the right to form a cohesive single party able to monopolise the (moderate) right-wing vote in presidential and legislative elections. Originally designed as a vehicle for providing the returned presidential incumbent Jacques Chirac with a legislative majority in 2002, the UMP built upon the former *Association des Amis de Jacques Chirac*, a presidential rallying organization headed by Bernard Pons, and the organizational ideas of three young right-wing deputies, Renaud Dutreuil (Union for French Democracy,

UDF), Dominique Bussereau (UDF) and Hervé Gaynard (Rally for the Republic, RPR). The initial organization, *Alternance 2002*, provided a joint text for presidential campaign strategy and the future of the right in France, and included a number of influential regional politicians, including Jean-Pierre Raffarin, the future Premier, and Alain Juppé, former Premier and the mayor of Bordeaux. Renamed *Union en Mouvement* (UEM) in April 2001, it rapidly became associated with Juppé as Chirac's closest ally, and intended to provide a rehabilitation for the unpopular years of his premiership (1993–1997).

The plans were unpopular with many of the RPR, including its general secretary Michèle Alliot-Marie and some of Chirac's own allies, such as Michel Debré, and also with the other right-wing parties which it threatened. Younger members of the RPR, however, saw it as a useful new platform for their own ambitions, including Philippe Douste-Blazy, the current general secretary, and Nicolas Sarkozy, the future Minister of the Interior and 2007 presidential hopeful in his own right. After the first round of the 2002 presidential elections, the disarray of the left and the powerful performance of Jean-Marie Le Pen, the need for right-wing unity was pushed strongly by the UEM, which was dissolved to give way to the UMP, initially organized around the RPR and other right-wing deputies in the legislature.

Three principal components make up the UMP – the old Gaullist Rally for the Republic (RPR); the free-market oriented Liberal Democracy (DL); and the majority of the UDF (although this party remains a significant independent party in its own right).

Although established under its present name in December 1976, the broadly conservative **Rally for the Republic** (RPR, *Rallie pour la République*) was directly descended from the *Rassemblement du Peuple Français* (RPF) established in April 1947 by Gen. Charles de Gaulle, who had been head of the London-based Free French forces during World War II and then Prime Minister of the first post-liberation government (1944–46). Formed with the central objective of returning de Gaulle to power, the RPF became the strongest Assembly party in 1951 (with 118 seats), but was weakened in 1952 by the creation of the dissident *Action Républicaine et Sociale* (ARS). When members of the rump RPF accepted ministerial posts in 1953, de Gaulle severed his links with the party, which was dissolved as a parliamentary group. Gaullist deputies then created the *Union des Républicains d'Action Sociale* (URAS), which became the *Centre National des Républicains Sociaux* (CNRS) in February 1954. Following de Gaulle's return to power in mid-1958 amid the collapse of the Fourth Republic, the movement was reconstituted for the November 1958 Assembly elections as the *Union pour la Nouvelle République* (UNR), which won a plurality of 188 seats. Inducted as President of the Fifth Republic in January 1959, de Gaulle appointed Michel Debré (UNR) as his Prime Minister.

Under the right-oriented Debré premiership a left-wing Gaullist faction formed the *Union Démocratique du Travail* (UDT), which was reunited with the UNR following the replacement of Debré by the technocratic Georges Pompidou in April 1962. In the November 1962 Assembly elections the UNR-UDT increased its dominance by winning 219 seats. In December 1965 de Gaulle won popular election for a second presidential term, comfortably defeating left-wing candidate François Mitterrand in the second round with 55.2% of the vote. For the March 1976 Assembly elections the UNR-UDT adopted the title *Union des Démocrates pour la Cinquième République* (UDCR), which slipped to 200 seats and henceforth relied on Valéry Giscard d'Estaing's Independent Republicans for a parliamentary majority. In November 1967 the UDCR title was formally adopted by the party, which at the same time absorbed a faction of the (Christian democrat-

ic) *Mouvement Républicain Populaire* (MRP) and other groups further to the left. In the wake of the May 1968 national crisis, the Gaullists registered a landslide victory in Assembly elections in June, winning 292 seats under the designation *Union pour la Défense de la République* and continuing in office under the reformist premiership of Maurice Couve de Murville. The new parliamentary group preferred the slightly different title *Union des Démocrates pour la République* (UDR), which was subsequently applied to the party as a whole.

De Gaulle resigned in April 1969 after unexpectedly being denied referendum approval of constitutional and regional reform proposals. He was succeeded in June elections by Pompidou, who won a comfortable 57.6% victory over a centrist candidate in the second round. The new Gaullist Prime Minister was Jacques Chaban-Delmas, seen as representative of the UDR's modernist wing, but corruption charges and other difficulties resulted in his replacement by the orthodox Pierre Messmer in July 1972. In the Assembly elections of March 1973 the UDR slumped to 183 seats, but Messmer continued as Prime Minister at the head of a coalition with centrist parties. Pompidou's death in office in April 1974 precipitated presidential elections in May, when Chaban-Delmas as the UDR candidate was eliminated in the first round (with only 14.6% of the vote). Many Gaullist voters preferred the more dynamic Giscard d'Estaing (Independent Republican), who won a narrow second-round victory over Mitterrand and proceeded to appoint Jacques Chirac (UDR) to head a government with strong centrist representation. Increasing strains between President and Prime Minister yielded Chirac's resignation in August 1976, whereupon the Gaullists ceased to hold the premiership but continued as part of the ruling coalition. In December 1976 Chirac engineered the conversion of the UDR into the RPR, which became his power base in increasingly acrimonious competition between the Gaullist and Giscardian wings of the "majority". In March 1977 Chirac was elected mayor of Paris, defeating the centrist candidate backed by the President.

After Chirac had failed to create a "majority" alliance for the March 1978 Assembly elections, the RPR slipped to 154 seats, against 124 for the new Union for French Democracy (UDF), grouping the Giscardian centrist parties (Union for French Democracy, UDF). In the June 1979 European Parliament elections the RPR list (called *Défense des Intérêts de la France*, reflecting traditional Gaullist doubts about the European idea) managed only 16.3% (and fourth place) as against the UDF's 27.6%. In the 1981 presidential elections, moreover, Chirac took a poor third place in the first round (with 18% of the vote) and was eliminated; although he said that he would personally vote for Giscard d'Estaing in the second round in May, his failure to urge RPR supporters to do likewise was seen as contributing to the incumbent's narrow defeat by Mitterrand. In the resultant Assembly elections in June the RPR shared in the centre-right's decimation by the Socialist Party (PS), slumping to 88 seats notwithstanding the presentation of single centre-right candidates in over three-quarters of the metropolitan constituencies under the banner of the *Union pour la Majorité Nouvelle* (UMN).

In opposition from 1981 to 1986, the RPR launched an internal modernization and rejuvenation programme, with Chirac bringing forward a new generation of leaders more favourable to European integration and more in tune with the changing social composition of France. On the basis of a declaration signed in April 1985, the RPR and the UDF presented a joint manifesto in the March 1986 Assembly elections as well as single candidates for many seats. In the resultant centre-right victory, the RPR emerged with 155 deputies in the new 577-seat Assembly elected by proportional representation, ahead of the UDF, so that Chirac was again appointed Prime Minister of a coalition government in which the RPR held 21 posts and the UDF parties 17. During the ensuing two years of "cohabitation" between a Socialist President and a Gaullist Prime Minister, the RPR experienced internal divisions about how to respond to the growing strength of the far-right National Front (FN) led by Jean-Marie Le Pen, with some Gaullists rejecting any links with the FN and others arguing that the party could not be ignored, especially since the FN was making inroads into RPR support. The debate intensified in January 1987 when Le Pen announced his own candidacy in the 1988 presidential elections, having previously indicated that the FN would support Chirac. After some equivocation, the RPR leader announced in May 1987 that there would be no national alliance between the RPR and the FN, while not prohibiting the informal RPR/FN voting co-operation that was already a factor in some localities and regions.

In his second tilt at the presidency in April-May 1988, Chirac took second place in the first round (with 19.9% of the vote) and thus went forward to the second against Mitterrand, losing to the incumbent by 45.98% to 54.02%. The relatively wide margin of the RPR candidate's defeat was attributed in part to the refusal of Le Pen to instruct his four million first-round supporters to vote for Chirac in the second. Assembly elections in June 1988 (held by constituency-based majority voting) were contested by the RPR in an alliance with the UDF called the *Union du Rassemblement et du Centre* (URC), but not only did the centre-right parties lose their majority but also the RPR for the first time returned fewer deputies (127) than the UDF (129). In opposition over the next five years, the RPR and UDF contested the 1989 European Parliament on a joint list (winning 28.9% of the vote) and in June 1990 announced the creation of yet another alliance, called the *Union pour la France* (UPF), amid much talk about the need for a unified party in the next legislative elections and a single presidential candidate. In reality, the RPR and the UDF continued their long struggle for supremacy on the centre-right, with the added spice of resumed personal rivalry between Chirac and Giscard d'Estaing. Also divisive in this period was the Maastricht Treaty on European union, which was supported wholeheartedly by the UDF, whereas important sections of the RPR (although not Chirac himself) campaigned for a "no" vote in the September 1992 referendum that yielded a very narrow majority for French ratification.

As widely forecast, the Assembly elections of March 1993 produced a landslide victory for the RPR/UDF alliance, which won 80% of the seats on a 39.5% first-round vote share. Crucially, the RPR emerged with 247 of the 577 seats (and 20.4% of the first-round vote), against 213 (and 19.1%) for the UDF parties, so that Chirac was able to nominate the new Prime Minister. His choice fell on Edouard Balladur, a former RPR Finance Minister and supposedly a Chirac loyalist, who was charged with running the government while the RPR leader concentrated on mounting a third attempt on the presidency. A leading RPR campaigner against the Maastricht Treaty, Philippe Séguin, was elected president of the National Assembly in April 1993. In the event, Balladur became so popular as Prime Minister that he was persuaded to renege on a pledge not to enter the presidential race. The upshot was that both Chirac and Balladur contested the 1995 elections, with the latter securing backing from within the UDF (which did not put up a candidate). Meanwhile, the RPR/UDF alliance was maintained for the June 1994 European Parliament elections, in which their combined vote slipped to 25.6%, yielding 28 of the 87 French seats.

After a slow start, Chirac's campaigning skills and command of the powerful RPR party machine, plus a late-breaking phone-tapping scandal in which Balladur was implicat-

ed, took the RPR leader to second place in the first round of the presidential balloting in April 1995 (with 20.8% of the vote), behind the Socialist candidate but ahead of Balladur (18.6%). Chirac therefore went into the second round in May and was at last victorious with 52.6% of the vote, despite again being denied second-round endorsement by the FN. Pledging himself to restoring "social cohesion", Chirac named Foreign Minister Alain Juppé (who had been the new President's campaign manager in his role as RPR secretary-general) to head a new coalition government maintaining approximate balance between the RPR and the UDF. At a party congress in October 1995 Juppé was formally elected to the RPR presidency in succession to Chirac, receiving 93% of the ballots in an uncontested election.

Damaged by corruption allegations in 1996, the RPR also experienced internal divisions on how the party should respond to the growing strength of the FN. Although the RPR leadership opposed any political cooperation with the FN, it declined to give formal backing to anti-FN "republican fronts" with the centre and left, despite narrowly defeating the FN in a mayoral by-election in Dreux in November 1996 on the strength of left-wing support. In an Assembly by-election in Vitrolles, near Marseilles, in February 1997 Juppé urged first-round RPR voters "to face up to their responsibilities" in the second, but the contest was won by the FN candidate. Meanwhile, an RPR national council meeting had approved an age-limit of 75 years for candidates in the next Assembly elections and of 70 thereafter; it had also declared its opposition to French-style "multiple mandates" often held by politicians and decided that in future party list elections at least one-third of RPR candidates with a chance of being elected would be women.

Despite the Juppé government's unpopularity, Chirac unexpectedly called early Assembly elections for May-June 1997. A general rout for the centre-right, in which the RPR slumped to 134 seats and a first-round vote share of 15.7%, resulted in Chirac having to accept "cohabitation" with a Socialist-led government. It also resulted in Juppé's immediate resignation as RPR president, in which post he was succeeded by Séguin at a special party congress in July. Séguin declared that the RPR should neither demonize the FN nor form tactical alliances with it, but should rather seek to appeal to most FN voters who were "neither fascists nor opposed to democracy". In regional elections in March 1998 the RPR/UDF were again outpolled by the left, though only narrowly. An injunction from both the RPR and UDF leaderships that their regional parties should not make deals with the FN to secure regional presidencies was observed by RPR federations (but not by the UDF).

Having failed to persuade a party conference that the RPR should shorten its name to "*Le Rassemblement*", Séguin was buffeted in early 1998 by further corruption cases involving RPR politicians in Paris and elsewhere. In April 1998 dissident RPR members of the Paris city council launched the PARIS formation, in protest against the alleged corruption of the RPR administration. In the same month RPR members of the Assembly staged a surprise walk-out before a vote to approve French participation in the single European currency (euro), contending that their action did not indicate disapproval of the euro but opposition to the government's economic policies. In May 1998 RPR and UDF agreed to form a loose umbrella organization called the "Alliance". However, the RPR was weakened in June 1998 by the launching of a new movement by former Gaullist Interior Minister Charles Pasqua opposed to further European integration and enlargement. In February 1999 efforts by Séguin to persuade the UDF as a whole to present a joint list under his leadership in the forthcoming Euro-elections came to nought, amid much acrimony on both sides. In April 1999 Séguin unexpectedly resigned as RPR president, claiming that his authority had been undermined by Chirac. RPR secretary-general Nicolas Sarkozy became acting president and led the party in the June 1999 Euroelections, in which the RPR presented a joint list with former UDF component Liberal Democracy (DL) which also included Civil Society and Ecology Generation. The list was relegated to third place with 12.8% of the vote and 12 of the 87 seats (of which the RPR took six), being outpolled by Pasqua's new Rally for France and the Independence of Europe (RPF-IE).

Sarkozy immediately resigned as RPR acting president and in September 1999 also vacated the post of secretary-general, asserting that he would not seek the party presidency. A divisive leadership contest resulted in the election in early December of former Sports Minister Michèle Alliot-Marie as RPR president. A pro-European, Alliot-Marie easily defeated Chirac-backed candidate Jean-Paul Delevoye in the runoff balloting, to become the first woman leader of a major French party.

Alliot-Marie immediately faced a deluge of new evidence about a system of kickbacks for public contracts allegedly run by the RPR in Paris when Chirac was mayor in 1977–95 and about vote-rigging and other illegal practices under his successor, Jean Tiberi, aided and abetted by his redoubtable wife, Xavière Tiberi. As investigations ground on, Jean Tiberi was expelled from the RPR in October 2000 for refusing to accept the nomination of party elder Philippe Séguin as the RPR mayoral candidate in Paris. He took his revenge in the March 2001 municipal elections, running as an independent and winning 14% of the first-round vote, thus reducing Séguin to 26% and second place against the PS candidate. Although Tiberi gave unenthusiastic backing to Séguin in the second round, the PS candidate triumphed and the right lost control of the capital for the first time since 1871. In the rest of the country, however, the RPR and its allies in what was now the UDF polled strongly, obtaining 46.9% of the first-round vote against 44.9% for the ruling coalition parties and winning control of 318 of the 583 larger towns, a net gain of 40.

The Paris corruption scandal deepened in April 2001 when the investigating magistrate concluded that there was plausible evidence of Chirac's past involvement in illegal activities and, in view of the President's immunity from prosecution in the courts, invited parliament to institute impeachment proceedings. Chirac continued to make robust denials of any wrongdoing, but came under further intense pressure in June 2001 over new disclosures about large cash payments made by him in 1992–95 for holidays for himself and members of his family. The President again denied any impropriety and claimed that the PS and its supporters in the judiciary were seeking to damage his prospects of re-election in 2002.

The liberal conservative **Liberal Democracy (DL)** was launched following the mid-1997 Assembly elections as successor to the Republican Party (*Parti Républicain*, PR), adopting the suffix "Independent Republicans and Republicans". The PR had been formed in May 1977 as a merger of the National Federation of Independent Republicans (*Fédération Nationale des Républicains Indépendants*, FNRI), the Social and Liberal Generation (*Génération Sociale et Libérale*, GSL), Act for the Future (*Agir pour l'Avenir*) and various support committees which had backed Valéry Giscard d'Estaing in his successful bid for the presidency in 1974. The PR's social liberal and strongly pro-European orientation was closely based on the theses advanced by Giscard d'Estaing in his 1977 book *Démocratie Française*.

The FNRI had been established in June 1966 by Giscard d'Estaing as leader of a modernizing faction that had broken away from the National Centre of Independents and Peasants (CNIP) in 1962 in order to be able to criticize government policy while remaining part of the ruling "majority". On founding the FNRI Giscard d'Estaing himself left the government of Georges Pompidou (although other FNRI representatives continued to participate) and led the new party to significant advances in the 1967 and 1968 Assembly elections (to 42 and 61 seats respectively) on the basis of his celebrated "*oui, mais*" ("yes, but") line of qualified support for the Gaullist-led government. In April 1969 Giscard d'Estaing effectively supported the winning "no" side in the constitutional referendum which yielded the resignation of President de Gaulle, whereupon the FNRI backed the victorious Pompidou in the June 1969 presidential elections. The FNRI leader then resumed his former post as Economy and Finance Minister, retaining it in successive Gaullist-led governments under the Pompidou presidency, while the FNRI slipped to 55 seats in the 1973 Assembly elections.

Following Pompidou's death in office in April 1974, Giscard d'Estaing was elected President in May as candidate of the FNRI and other centrist formations, taking second place in the first round (with 32.9% of the vote) and winning a narrow 50.7% victory in the run-off against François Mitterrand of the Socialist Party (PS). He proceeded to appoint Jacques Chirac (Gaullist) to head a government with strong centrist representation, including his principal FNRI lieutenant, Michel Poniatowski, at the powerful Interior Ministry. Growing strains between the Giscardian and Gaullist wings of the "majority" from 1975 resulted in Chirac's resignation in August 1976 and his replacement by a non-Gaullist (Raymond Barre), whereafter Chirac relaunched the Gaullist party as the Rally for the Republic (RPR). The superior organization of the new RPR over the FNRI and other centrist parties (and the challenge to presidential authority which the RPR represented) was highlighted in March 1977 when Chirac defeated a candidate backed by the President in elections for the important post of mayor of Paris.

Seeking to build an effective counterweight to the RPR for the 1978 Assembly elections, the new PR participated in the formation of the broader Union for French Democracy (UDF), winning 71 of the 124 UDF seats. PR representatives took prominent portfolios in the reconstituted Barre government, but suffered from association with scandals such as the De Broglie affair. In 1981 the PR and the rest of the UDF endorsed Giscard d'Estaing's re-election bid, although the President chose to stand as a "citizen-candidate" without specific party attribution. Following his narrow defeat by Mitterrand in the second round, the PR shared in the decimation of the UDF in the June 1981 Assembly elections, retaining only 32 seats. After five years in opposition, however, the PR shared in the centre-right's victory in the March 1986 Assembly elections, winning 59 seats in its own right and accordingly taking a prominent role in the resultant centre-right "cohabitation" government headed by Chirac of the RPR.

In mid-1987 the then PR president and government minister, François Léotard, disappointed Chirac by announcing that the PR would not support the RPR leader in the first round of the 1988 presidential elections, but rather would put up its own candidate. After speculation that Léotard would run himself, in September 1987 the PR gave its backing to Barre (not a PR member). However, the former Prime Minister managed only third place in the first round of voting in April 1988 (with 16.5%) and was eliminated, whereafter the PR backed Chirac in his losing contest with Mitterrand in the second round. In the June 1988 Assembly elections the PR shared in the defeat of the centre-right alliance, although its individual seat tally of 58 out of 129 for the UDF showed electoral resilience. The PR was then in opposition for five years, during which it established itself as the organizational core of UDF, although the traditional reluctance of the centrist parties to develop party structures outside parliament continued to be apparent.

In the landslide victory of the RPR/UDF alliance in the March 1993 Assembly elections, the PR took 104 of the 213 seats won by the UDF and was accordingly allocated important portfolios in the new centre-right "cohabitation" government headed by Edouard Balladur of the RPR. The PR was subsequently tainted by a series of corruption scandals that necessitated the resignations of several of its ministers, including in October 1994 the then PR president Gérard Longuet, amid allegations of irregular party financing activities. The February 1994 murder of PR deputy Yann Piat (once a member of the far-right National Front) added to the party's poor public image. The decision of Giscard d'Estaing (by now heading the UDF) not to contest the 1995 presidential elections deprived the PR of its obvious candidate, with the result that the party opted for Balladur as the more centrist of the two RPR contenders. After Balladur had been eliminated in the first round, the PR supported the victorious candidacy of Chirac in the second, being rewarded with a strong ministerial presence in the resultant centre-right government. In June 1995 François Léotard was elected to resume the PR presidency in succession to Longuet.

The PR shared in the defeat of the centre-right in the mid-1997 Assembly elections, whereupon the party converted itself into the DL under the leadership of former Finance Minister Alain Madelin, embracing a more free-market economic policy. In the new Assembly the 44-strong Liberal Democracy and Independents group was separate from the UDF. In May 1998 a DL convention decided that the party should formally withdraw from the UDF and instead become an autonomous component of the "Alliance" umbrella organization which the RPR and UDF had created that month (Union for French Democracy). In the June 1999 European Parliament elections the DL opted to stand on a joint list with the RPR and other groups, but the result was a disappointing third place yielding 12.8% of the vote and 12 seats, of which the DL took four.

Alain Madelin secured 3.96% of the vote in the 2002 presidential elections and, despite the formation of the UMP subsequent to Jacques Chirac's victory, refused immediate absorption into the new right-wing party. However, with only 0.24% of the legislative vote six weeks later, the party's position was unviable at the national level and the inevitable merger with the UMP occurred. Within this organization, Alain Madelin has since organized his own faction dedicated to the promotion of free market economic ideas against more traditionally statist Gaullists.

The victory of the UMP at the 2002 legislative elections has ensured the short-term survival of the newly formed umbrella party. However, the party's success in the elections was as much due to the left's disarray as to any widespread support for the UMP, and indeed since 2002 the party's incumbency has been rocked by internal dissent, scandal and electoral decline. The two Raffarin governments have enjoyed a modicum of success in the area of law-and-order and decentralization, but the economic record has been weak, its policy proposals diluted and hesitant, and the divisions between ideological streams in the party (particularly between former UDF and RPR factions) have drawn attention to what voters perceive as a lack of direction in governmental policy. The creation in April 2004 of political factions within the party was intended to defuse potentially conflictual situations between such groups, but may serve to widen divisions in the future, particularly in the personality politics of presidential campaigns.

In February 2004 the general secretary of the party, Alain Juppé, received a blow to his rehabilitation with his 18-month suspended sentence for illegal party fund-raising. Despite losing his political rights, he has remained general secretary of the party with the support of the President, but the return of the spectre of corruption to haunt mainstream politicians cannot help in their quest to remobilise and raise the confidence of the French electorate.

Electorally, the party has suffered blows in both the regional and European elections of 2004. In the former, the party received only 21.7% of the vote, winning only a single regional presidency out of 26. In the European elections, the UMP managed only 16.6% of the vote and 17 seats at the European Parliament, another heavy decline from the national results of 2002. In both cases, voter apathy undoubtedly hit the right-wing badly, but the victory of the left suggests that dissatisfaction with the immobilist Raffarin governments is equally, if not more, to blame.

The UMP's representatives in the European Parliament sit in the European People's Party (Christian Democrats) group.

Workers' Struggle
Lutte Ouvrière (LO)
Address. BP 233, 75865 Paris 18

Leadership. Arlette Laguiller (spokesperson)

Descended from a Trotskyist group which in 1940 rejected membership of the French Committees for the Fourth International, the LO was founded in June 1968 as the direct successor to *Voix Ouvrière* following the banning of the latter and other student-based Trotskyist organizations in the wake of the May 1968 "events". It contested the 1973 Assembly elections jointly with the Communist League (itself later succeeded by the Revolutionary Communist League, LCR), but the two groups put up separate candidates in the 1974 presidential elections, in which Arlette Laguiller of the LO won 2.3% in the first round. Having failed to return any of its 470 candidates in the 1978 Assembly elections on a platform that featured robust condemnation of the common programme of the mainstream left, the LO reverted to alliance with the LCR for the 1979 European Parliament elections, their joint list (*Pour les États-Unis Socialistes d'Europe*) winning 3.1% of the vote but no seats.

Laguiller again won 2.3% in the first round of the 1981 presidential contest and all 158 LO candidates were again unsuccessful in the ensuing Assembly elections. Standing on its own, the LO slipped to 2.1% in the 1984 Euro-elections, while Laguiller managed only 1.99% in the first round of the 1988 presidential contest and her party failed to win representation in either the 1988 or the 1993 Assembly elections. In her fourth presidential bid in 1995, however, Laguiller had her best result to date, winning 1,616,566 votes (5.3%) in the first round. The LO again won no seats in the mid-1997 Assembly elections, its candidates being credited with about 2% of the first-round vote.

For the June 1999 European Parliament elections the LO entered into a new alliance with the LCR on a platform of opposition to a "capitalist Europe" and in favour of a "Europe for workers". Headed by Laguiller, the joint list achieved an electoral breakthrough, winning 5.2% of the vote and five seats, three of which were taken by the LO. In June 2001 Laguiller was named as the LO candidate for the 2002 presidential elections, which would be her fifth campaign. The perceived monotony of the mainstream candidates for younger voters saw her 2002 vote rise to 5.8% in the first round, even with competition from the charismatic Olivier Besancenot of the Revolutionary Communist League. Controversially, she refused to advise her supporters which of the candidates (Chirac or Le Pen) to pick in the second round. In the 2002 legislative elections, her party only managed 1.2% of the vote, a more reliable indicator of national support for the party as opposed to the candidate herself. The joint lists presented with LCR in the 2004 regional and European elections secured 4.6% and 2.7% of the vote respectively.

Other National Parties

Association for a Republican Left (*Association pour une Gauche Républicaine*), splinter group from Republican and Citizens' Movement in 2002, with very marginal electoral presence to date.
Leadership. Jean-Pierre Michel (president); Pierre Pertus (general secretary)
Address. 32 rue des Ormeaux, 70400 Héricourt
Telephone. (33-6)0825–1117
Email. info@a-g-r.com

Bonapartist Party (*Parti Bonapartiste*, PB), founded in 1993 to promote the ideas and achievements of Emperor Napoleon Bonaparte.
Leadership. Emmanuel Johans

Citizenship, Action and Participation for the 21ˢᵗ Century (*Citoyenneté Action et Participation pour le XXIème Siècle*, CAP21), founded in 1996 as independent, right-wing oriented ecologist movement.
Address. 40 rue Monceau, 75008 Paris
Telephone. (33–1) 4562–2221
Website. www.cap21.net
Leadership. Corinne Lepage (president); Eric Delhaye (spokesperson)

Ecology Generation (*Génération Écologie*, GE), established in 1990 by Brice Lalonde, a presidential candidate for Friends of the Earth (*Amis de la Terre*) and other groups in 1981 (when he received 3.9% of the first-round vote) and subsequently Environment Minister in the 1991–92 government led by Édith Cresson of the Socialist Party (PS). Then more sympathetic to the Socialists than the rival Greens, the GE nonetheless refused to enter the subsequent Bérégovoy administration headed by the PS. The GE won 7% of the vote at the March 1992 regional elections, before slipping to less than 1% in the 1993 Assembly elections, despite a reciprocal support agreement with the Greens. Contesting the June 1994 European Parliament poll as an independent list, the GE recovered to just over 2% of the vote, without winning a seat. Following the victory of Jacques Chirac of the Rally for the Republic (RPR-UMP) in the April-May 1995 presidential elections, a former GE member, Corinne Lepage, accepted appointment as Environment Minister in the new centre-right government. In the mid-1997 Assembly elections the GE again failed to win representation, but in the June 1999 European Parliament elections the GE won one seat on the list headed by the RPR, its representative joining the European People's Party/European Democrats group. In September 2002, Brice Lalonde resigned from the party, ceding the presidency to France Gamerre.
Address. 22 rue Daguerre, 75014 Paris
Telephone. (33–1) 4427–1166
Fax. (33–1) 4327–0555
Leadership. France Gamerre (president)

Federalist Party (*Parti Fédéraliste*, PF), advocates creation of a federal European state.
Address. 18 place du 8 Septembre, BP 76222, 25015 Besançon 6
Telephone/Fax. (33–3) 8121–3233
Email. pfed.allen@wanadoo.fr
Website. www.dalmatia.net/parti-federaliste
Leadership. Jean-Philippe Allenbach

Federation for a New Solidarity (*Fédération pour une Nouvelle Solidarité*, FNS), a rightist formation derived from the European Labour Party (*Parti Ouvrier Européen*, POE), created by Argentine-born Jacques Chéminade to support his candidacy in the 1995 presidential elections, in which he finished last of nine first-round candidates, with only 0.3% of the vote.
Leadership. Jacques Chéminade

Forum of Social Republicans (*Forum des Républicains Sociaux*, FRS), created in 2001 as presidential campaign vehicle for Christine Boutin, and subsequently cooperating with Union for a Popular Movement.
Address. 17, boulevard Raspail, 75007 Paris
Telephone. (33–1) 4439–2002
Fax. (33–1) 4436–2018
Email. contac@frs-online.org
Leadership. Christine Boutin (president); Gilles Romain-Desfosses (general secretary)

French and European Nationalist Party (*Parti Nationaliste Français et Européen*, PNFE), a far-right group.
Leadership. Claude Cornilleau

French Nationalist Party (*Parti Nationaliste Français*, PNF), far-right grouping formed in 1983 by a faction of the National Front opposed to the leadership of Jean-Marie Le Pen.

French Royalist Movement (*Mouvement Royaliste Français*, MRF), anti-left grouping aiming to restore a French monarchy.
Leadership. Jean de Beauregard

Independent Ecological Movement (*Mouvement Ecologiste Indépendant*, MEI), formed by Antoine Waechter, the 1988 presidential candidate of the Greens, from which he broke away in 1993; critical of the Greens' participation in the post-1997 government headed by the Socialist Party; Waechter headed an MEI list for the 1999 European Parliament elections which obtained 267,853 votes (1.5%) without winning a seat. The party continues to contest elections, but with only marginal results.
Address. 7 rue du Vertbois, 75003 Paris
Telephone. (33–1) 4027–8536
Fax. (33–1) 4027–8544
Website. www.mei-fr.org
Email. contact@mei-fr.org
Leadership. Antoine Waechter

Liberal Christian Right (*Droite Libérale Chrétienne*, DLC), led by former Defence Minister Charles Millon. Launched at a Paris conference in November 1999 on the basis of "The Right" (*La Droite*) created by Millon in April 1998 following his expulsion from the UDF (Union for French Democracy) for having accepted National Front (FN) support to secure re-election as president of the Rhône-Alpes regional council. Claiming a membership of 20,000, the DLC aspires to become the French equivalent of Germany's Christian Democratic/Social Union (CDU/CSU). In November 2002, the party associated itself with the UMP. In September 2003, Millon was named ambassador for food and agriculture to the UN by Jean-Pierre Raffarin. At the same time, the party group in the Rhône-Alpes regional council was absorbed by the UMP. The DLC is consequently currently "in hibernation".
Address. 21 rue de Bourgogne, 75007 Paris
Telephone. (33–1) 5359–5300
Email. La-Droite@wanadoo.fr
Website. www.la-droite.org
Leadership. Charles Millon (president)

National Restoration (*Restauration Nationale*, RN), right-wing pro-monarchy formation supporting the claim of the Count of Paris, weakened in 1971 by a breakaway that led to

the creation of New Royalist Action.
Leadership. Guy Steinbach (president)

New Royalist Action (*Nouvelle Action Royaliste*, NAR), founded in 1971 as a splinter group of National Restoration, advocating the restoration of a progressive monarchy.
Address. 17 rue des Petits-Champs, 75001 Paris
Telephone. (33–1) 4297–4257
Leadership. Bertrand Renouvin & Yvan Aumont

Red and Green Alternatives (*Alternatifs Rouge et Verte*, ARV). Founded in November 1989 as a merger of the rump Unified Socialist Party (*Parti Socialiste Unifié*, PSU) and the New Left (*Nouvelle Gauche*, NG), espousing anarcho-syndicalism, internationalism, environmentalism and feminism; dating from 1960, the PSU had remained in existence as a minority faction led by Michel Rocard had joined the Socialist Party in 1975, while the NG had been joined in 1987 by an expelled "renovator" of the French Communist Party, Pierre Juquin, who won 2.1% in the 1988 presidential elections.
Address. 40 rue de Malte, 75011 Paris
Telephone. (33–1) 4357–4480
Fax. (33–1) 4357–6450
Email. alternatifs@wanadoo.fr
Website. perso.wanadoo.fr/alternatifs

Revolutionary Communist League (*Ligue Communiste Révolutionnaire*, LCR), a Trotskyist party founded in 1973 as successor to the Communist League, as whose candidate Alain Krivine won 1.1% of the vote in the 1969 presidential elections; contested Assembly and European elections of the 1970s in alliance with the Workers' Struggle (LO), which became the stronger of the two. Krivine on his own won 0.4% in the 1974 presidential contest, while in 1988 the LCR backed Pierre Juquin of the New Left (which later joined the Red and Green Alternative). Having contributed to LO leader Arlette Laguiller's 5.3% first-round vote in the 1995 presidential elections, the LCR joined with the LO in the June 1999 Euro-elections, their joint list winning 5.2% and five seats, Krivine being elected as one of two successful LCR candidates, who joined the European United Left/Nordic Green Left group. In the 2002 presidential election, the young Olivier Besancenot won 4.3% of the first-round vote from young left-wing voters who found him more appealing than the older leftist candidates. However in the legislative elections, the party could only manage 1.3% of the vote. In November 2003 the party congress voted to form an alliance with Workers' Struggle to consolidate the anti-capitalist left. This strategy has borne some fruit, with votes of 4.6% and 2.6% in the regional and European elections of 2004, respectively.
Address. 2 rue Richard Lenoir, 93198 Montreuil
Telephone. (33–1) 4870–4230
Fax. (33–1) 4859–2328
Website. www-lcr-rouge.org
Email. redaction@lcr-rouge.org
Leadership. Alain Krivine; Olivier Besancenot; Roseline Vachetta

The Right to Hunt (*Droit de Chasse*), splinter party from Hunting, Fishing, Nature, Traditions formed in April 2001 in the South of France.
Address. 26, avenue de la République, 13111 Coudoux
Telephone. (33–6) 1905–3092
Email. droit-de-chasse@wanadoo.fr
Leadership. Franck Vidal (president); Hubert Fayard (general secretary); Thierry Maille (vice-president)

Workers' Party (*Parti des Travailleurs*, PT), extreme left-wing grouping. Its presidential candidate, Daniel Gluckstein, received 0.5% of the vote in 2002.

Address. 87 rue du Faubourg Saint-Denis, 75010 Paris
Telephone. (33–1) 4801–8829
Email. parti-des-travailleurs@wanadoo.fr
Leadership. Yannick Giou

Regional Parties

ALSACE-LORRAINE

Alsace-Lorraine National Forum (*Nationalforum Elsass-Lothringen/Forum Nationaliste d'Alsace-Lorraine*), based in the German-speaking population of Alsace-Lorraine.
Email. geraldmueller@nfel.org
Website. www.geocities.com/~bfel
Leadership. Gerald Müller

Union of the Alsatian People (*Union du Peuple Alsacien/Elsass Volksunion*, UPA/EVU), political movement favouring autonomy for Alsace within the European Union.
Address. BP 75, 67402 Illkirch Graffenstaden
Fax. (33–3) 8907–9024
Website. www.multimania.com/elsassnet

BRITTANY

Breton Democratic Union (*Unvaniezh Demokratel Breizh/Union Démocratique Bretonne*, UDB), left-oriented party founded in 1964 in quest of complete autonomy for Brittany in the French Republic and European Union by non-violent means; has obtained representation on most main city councils in Brittany, including Nantes, Rennes, Lorient and Saint-Malo, but remains a regional minority party; a member of Democratic Party of the Peoples of Europe–European Free Alliance.
Address. BP 203, 56102 Lorient, Brittany
Telephone/Fax. (33–2) 9784–8523
Email. udbbzh@voila.fr
Website. www.geocities.com/CapitolHill/2177
Leadership. Christian Guyonvarc'h

Party for the Organization of a Free Brittany (*Parti pour l'Organisation d'une Bretagne Libre*, POBL), proclaiming "the inalienable right of the Breton people freely to rule itself and to become independent again".
Address. BP 4518, 22045 Saint-Brieuc 2

CORSICA

Corsican Nation (*Corsica Nazione*, CN), electoral coalition of nationalist movements, with linked trade union and social organizations, which claims to have won around 20% of vote in recent Corsican regional elections; highly critical of Corsican autonomy plan adopted by French National Assembly in May 2001.
Address. c/o Assemblée de Corse, BP 215, 20187 Ajaccio Cedex 1
Website. www.corsica-nazione.com
Email. corsica-nazione@corsica-nazione.com
Leadership. P. Andreucci

Independence (*Indipendenza*), separatist political formation founded in May 2001 from a merger of *A Cuncolta Indipendentista*, the political wing of the banned Front for the National Liberation of Corsica–Historic Wing (FLNC-CH), with three other hardline groups (*Corsica Viva, Associu per a Suvranita* and *U Collettivu Naziunale*). Although *A Cuncolta* had been weakened by the arrest of several leaders in 1996–97 on terrorism charges, the FLNC-CH was believed to have become the largest faction of the FLNC following the latter's signature of a ceasefire in December

1999. The new Independence grouping declared that nationalist violence "is given legitimacy by the aggressive line taken by the French state" and vowed to contest the next Corsican elections within the Corsican Nation alliance on a platform of opposition to the autonomy plan approved by the French National Assembly in May 2001.

National Presence (*Presenza Naziunale*), nationalist formation, whose leader François Santoni in July 2001 called for the release of all Corsican political prisoners held on mainland France and for an alternative to the "government lies" enshrined in the autonomy plan for the island. In August 2001 Santoni was murdered in Corsica by unidentified gunmen.

Union of the Corsican People (*Unione di u Populu Corsu*, UPC), legal pro-autonomy party which has obtained minority representation in the Corsican regional assembly, sometimes in alliance with more militant nationalist groups.
Address. BP 165, 20293 Bastia, Corsica
Telephone. (33–4) 9532–2787
Fax. (33–4) 9531–6490

NORMANDY

Normandy Movement (*Mouvement Normand*, MN), formation advocating a self-governing Normandy within the European Union.
Address. Le Gab, Les Bruyères, 27290 Écaquelon
Website. perso.wanadoo.fr/unite.normande/
Email. mouvement.normand@wanadoo.fr

Party for Independent Normandy (*Parti pour la Normandie Indépendante*, PNI), seeks an independent Normandy with its political capital at Caen, its industrial capital at Le Havre and its military capital at Cherbourg, to which end it has set up a "provisional government".
Website. www.multimania.com/pni
Email. vivapni@lycos.fr
Leadership. Jér/emy Lefèvre & Sylvain Bion

OCCITANIA

Occitania Party (*Partit Occitan*, POC), founded in Toulouse in 1987 to seek "self-government" for the region of southern France where Occitan is spoken; won up to 1.8% of the vote in southern constituencies in 1997 Assembly elections.
Address. Sant Ostian, 43260 St Julien Chapteuil
Telephone/Fax. (33–4) 7157–6413
Email. poc@multimania.com/poc
Website. partitoccitan.org
Leadership. Gustave Alirol

SAVOY

Savoy League (*Ligue Savoisienne/Liga de Saboya*, LS), founded in 1995 with aim of reversing French annexation of Savoy in 1860 and re-establishing it as a sovereign independent state; its secretary-general is a regional concillor.
Address. 2 ave de la Mavéria, 74940 Annecy le Vieux, Savoy
Telephone. (33–4) 5009–8713
Fax. (33–4) 5009–9580
Website. http://www.ligue.savoie.com/
Email. ligue@savoie.com
Leadership. Patrice Abeille (secretary-general)

OVERSEAS DEPARTMENTS

Under decentralization legislation enacted in 1982 by the then Socialist-led government in Paris, the four French overseas departments (*départements d'outre-mer*, DOM) of

French Guiana, Guadeloupe, Martinique and Réunion each have the additional status of a region of France. Each therefore has a regional council (*conseil régional*) that is directly elected for a six-year term from party lists by proportional representation and has increased powers as compared with the previous indirectly-elected bodies. At the same time, the traditional departmental council (*conseil général*) remained in being in each overseas department, these bodies also being directly elected for a six-year term but by majority voting over two rounds in constituent cantons. Each overseas department elects representatives to the National Assembly and the Senate in Paris according to the procedures applicable in metropolitan France (the precise number depending on size of population) and the DOM electorates also participate in French elections to the European Parliament. Political parties active in the overseas departments include local sections of metropolitan parties as well as a number of formations specific to particular departments.

French Guiana

Situated on the northern South American littoral between Suriname and Brazil, French Guiana (*capital*: Cayenne; *population*: 155,000) has been under French control since the 17th century and a recognized French possession since 1817, being accorded departmental status in 1946. Elections to the 31-member regional council in 2004, resulted as follows: Guianese Socialist Party 17 seats, Guianese Democratic Forces 7, Union for a Popular Movement 7.

Guianese Democratic Forces (*Forces Démocratiques Guyanaises*, FDG), founded in 1989 by a dissident faction of the Guianese Socialist Party, became second-largest party in the regional council in 1992 but lost ground sharply in May 1998, though Othily was re-elected to the French Senate in September 1998.
Leadership. Georges Othily

Guianese Socialist Party (*Parti Socialiste Guyanais*, PSG), founded in 1956, consistently the strongest party in the department, for long led by Elie Castor; once officially the departmental section of the metropolitan Socialist Party, now autonomous and supportive of autonomy for French Guiana leading to full independence; won 16 regional council seats in 1992, subsequently providing the presidents of both the regional council and the general council, although it lost its National Assembly seat to an independent leftist in 1993; slipped to 11 regional council seats in March 1998 and to five out of 19 departmental council seats, Karam being nevertheless re-elected to the council presidency, whereas Stéphan Phinéra-Horth of the PSG lost the departmental council presidency. As with its former metropolitan partner, it experienced a renaissance in the 2004 elections.
Address. 1 cité Césaire, Cayenne
Leadership. Antoine Karam

Union for a Popular Movement (*Union pour un Mouvement Populaire*, UMP), departmental section of the metropolitan UMP, which won an Assembly seat in 2002.
Address. 84 ave Léopold Héder, Cayenne
Leadership. Roland Ho-Wen-Sze

Walawari, left-wing movement emphasizing non-French aspects of departmental society, won two regional council seats in 1998. In 2002, Christiane Taubira, the former *Parti Radical de Gauche* presidential candidate, won an Assembly seat.
Leadership. Christiane Taubira

Guadeloupe

A group of islands located in the Caribbean south-east of Puerto Rico, Guadeloupe (*capital*: Basse-Terre; *population*: 430,000) has been a French possession since the 17th century and was annexed in 1815. Elections to the 41-member regional council in 2004 resulted as follows: Guadeloupe Progressive Democrat–Socialist Party Alliance (PPDG-PS) 28 seats, Union for a Popular Movement (UMP) 13 seats.

Guadeloupe Communist Party (*Parti Communiste Guadeloupéen,* PCG), founded in 1944 as the departmental section of the French Communist Party, became independent in 1958, for long favoured retention of departmental status, moved to cautious support for eventual independence in the 1980s as it steadily lost former electoral dominance; weakened by the formation of the Guadeloupe Progressive Democratic Party, it managed only fifth place in the 1992 regional council elections with three seats and slipped to two in 1998 and none in 2004.
Address. 119 rue Vatable, Pointe-à-Pitre
Leadership. Christian Céleste

Guadeloupe Progressive Democratic Party (*Parti Progressiste Démocratique Guadeloupéen,* PPDG), founded in 1991 by dissident members of the Guadeloupe Communist Party (PCG) and others, outpolled the PCG in the 1992 regional council elections but took only fourth place; despite retaining a National Assembly seat in mid-1997, it lost its representation in the regional council in 1998, although Lubeth was elected president of the departmental council.
Leadership. Marcellin Lubeth & Ernest Moutoussamy

Socialist Party (*Parti Socialiste,* PS), departmental federation of the metropolitan party, held the presidency of the regional council from 1986, but was split into two factions for the 1992 elections, the main party winning nine seats and a dissident group led by Dominique Larifla seven; went into regional council opposition after the December 1993 re-run election, but returned one National Assembly deputy (out of four) in March 1993 and retained its dominance of the general council in March 1994 elections; won 12 seats in the 1998 regional council elections and an overwhelming majority in 2002.
Address. rés. Collinette 801, Grand Camp, Les Abymes
Leadership. Victorin Lurel

Union for a Popular Movement (*Union pour un Mouvement Populaire,* UMP), departmental federation of the metropolitan party, supportive of French status, suffered electorally from the defection of the RPR regional council president to the Union for French Democracy in 1986 (Union for French Democracy), but recovered in 1992 as the leading component of the Guadeloupe Objective (OG) alliance, which won a narrow overall majority in re-run elections in January 1993, although the party took only one of Guadeloupe's four National Assembly seats in 1993 and 1997; the RPR-led OG won an overall majority of 25 regional council seats in March 1998, Michaux-Chevry being re-elected council president.
Address. 1 rue Baudot, Basse-Terre
Leadership. Lucette Michaux-Chevry & Aldo Blaise

Union for French Democracy (*Union pour la Démocratie Française,* UDF), departmental section of the centre-right metropolitan formation; after serious strains in the 1980s it resumed alliance with the Rally for the Republic for the 1992 regional council elections, participating in the eventual victory of the Guadeloupe Objective alliance and its further triumph in 1998.
Leadership. Marcel Esdras

Martinique

Located in the Caribbean, Martinique (*capital*: Fort-de-France; *population*: 400,000) came under French control in the 17th century and was annexed in 1790, achieving departmental status in 1946. Elections to the 41-member regional council in 2004 resulted as follows: Independent Martinique Movement 28, Martinique Progressive Party 9, Union for a Popular Movement 4.

Independent Martinique Movement (*Mouvement Indépendantiste Martiniquais,* MIM), pro-independence formation that once aimed to seize power through revolution, obtained increasing support through the 1980s, taking second place in the 1992 regional council election campaigning as the Martinique Patriots (*Patriotes Martiniquais*); after Marie-Jeanne had been returned to the French National Assembly in 1997, the MIM headed the poll with 13 seats in 1998 regional council elections, Marie-Jeanne being elected president. In 2002 the party won one of the four Martinique Assembly seats. In 2004, the party increased its share to 28 seats.
Address. Mairie de Rivière-Pilote, Martinique
Leadership. Alfred Marie-Jeanne

Martinique Communist Party (*Parti Communiste Martiniquais,* PCM), founded in 1957 when the departmental federation of the French Communist Party split and the socialist pro-autonomy Martinique Progressive Party (PPM) was formed; the PCM itself later favoured autonomy, especially after its pro-independence wing broke away in 1984; from 1974 co-operated with the PPM and other left-wing parties, often in government in the department; shared in the electoral decline of French communism in the 1980s, taking fourth place in the 1992 regional council election standing as For a Martinique of Labour; left-wing voting discipline secured the election of Émile Capgras of the PCM as council president, but he lost the post following the further PCM decline in the 1998 regional elections. There were no signs of recovery in 2004.
Address. rue Émile Zola, Fort-de-France
Leadership. Georges Erichot

Martinique Forces of Progress (*Forces Martiniquaises de Progrès,* FMP), successor to the departmental federation of the centre-left metropolitan Union for French Democracy (UDF); as the UDF, had been junior partner to the Rally for the Republic (RPR-UMP), their combined forces consistently proving inferior to those of the Martinique left, as after the 1992 regional council elections, in which the RPR/UDF Union for a Martinique of Progress list won the most seats but remained in opposition; the UDF took one of the four Martinique seats in the 1993 French National Assembly elections but lost it in 1997, before winning five seats in the March 1998 regional council elections.

Martinique Progressive Party (*Parti Progressiste Martinique,* PPM), founded in 1957 by a splinter group of the Martinique Communist Party, eventually overtaking the parent party, Césaire being elected president of the first directly-elected regional council in 1983, retaining the post in 1986; dissension between the PPM pro-autonomy and pro-independence wings weakened the party thereafter, third place being achieved in the 1992 regional council elections; won one of Martinique's four National Assembly seats in 1993 and 1997, as well as holding both departmental seats in French Senate; slipped to seven seats in 1998 regional council elections, but Claude Lise of the PPM was re-elected president of departmental council; in 2002 Camille Darsières was elected to the National Assembly; and the

party enjoyed a slight increase in 2004 to 9 seats.
Address. rue André Aliker, Fort-de-France
Leadership. Aimé Césaire & Camille Darsières

Martinique Socialist Party (*Parti Martiniquais Socialiste,* PMS), won three seats in 1998 regional council elections.
Leadership. Louis Joseph Dogué & Ernest Wan Ajouhu

Martinique Liberal Movement (*Mouvement Libéral Martiniquais,* MLM) won a seat in the 2002 Assembly elections.
Leadership. Philippe Petit.

Socialist Federation of Martinique (*Fédération Socialiste de Martinique,* FSM), departmental section of the metropolitan Socialist Party, but consistently surpassed electorally by other left-wing parties, securing a poor fifth place for its New Socialist Generation list in the 1992 regional contest and declining further in 1998.
Address. cité la Meynard, 97200 Fort-de-France
Leadership. Jean Crusol

Union for a Popular Movement (*Union pour un Mouvement Populaire,* UMP), departmental federation of the metropolitan party and of similar conservative persuasion, formerly the strongest single party in Martinique but usually in opposition to left-wing alliances; allied with the Union for French Democracy (UDF) in the 1992 regional council elections, their Union for a Martinique of Progress list winning a substantial plurality, although not enough to obtain the council presidency; won two of the department's four National Assembly seats in 1993 and 1997 but slipped to six seats in the 1998 regional council elections standing independently of the UDF (Martinique Forces of Progress). In 2004, it slipped further to only four seats.
Leadership. Anicet Turinay

Réunion

The Indian Ocean island of Réunion (*capital*: Saint-Denis; *population*: 700,000) has been a French possession since the 17th century and an overseas department since 1946. Elections to the 45-member regional council in 2004 resulted as follows: Union for French Democracy 11 seats, Réunion Communist Party 27, Socialist Party 7.

FreeDOM, led by Camille Sudre (formerly a member of the Socialist Party) and Marguerite (Margie) Sudre, pro-autonomy but conservative movement whose use of English in its title has raised eyebrows in Paris; polled strongly in the 1991 general council and 1992 regional council elections, Camille Sudre (a medical doctor and well-known pirate broadcaster) being elected president of the latter body but later being obliged to face new elections in 1993 because of illegal broadcasts; again returned as the largest single party, FreeDOM secured the election of Margie Sudre (wife of Camille) as regional council president, to which post she added that of metropolitan State Secretary for Francophone Affairs following the advent of a centre-right government in Paris in 1995; in some disarray after the defeat of the metropolitan centre-right in mid-1997, FreeDOM candidates retained only five seats in the 1998 regional council elections.
Leadership. Camille Sudre & Marguerite (Margie) Sudre

Union for French Democracy (*Union pour la Démocratie Française,* UDF), departmental section of the centre-right metropolitan formation, favouring retention of French status, has been allied with the larger Rally for the Republic (RPR-

UMP) in recent elections; won eight regional council seats in March 1998, when Poudroux was elected president of the departmental council with some left-wing support.
Leadership. Gilbert Gérard & Jean-Luc Poudroux

Union for a Popular Movement (*Union pour un Mouvement Populaire,* UMP), departmental section of the conservative metropolitan party, favouring retention of French status, for long the leading electoral formation in alliance with what became the Union for French Democracy (UDF), but in local opposition in the 1980s to the combined forces of the left; lost ground in the 1992 and 1993 regional council elections to the new FreeDOM movement, and to the left in the 1994 general council elections; returned one of Réunion's five National Assembly deputies in 1993 and 1997; won four regional council seats in 1998.
Address. BP 11, 97400 Saint-Denis
Leadership. André-Maurice Pihouée & Tony Manglou

Réunion Communist Party *(Parti Communiste Réunionnaise,* PCR), founded as an autonomous party in 1959 by the departmental branch of the French Communist Party, disavowed pro-Soviet orthodoxy of metropolitan party, has consistently been the leading left-wing electoral force in Réunion, supporting the successful Socialist Party (PS) candidate for general council president in 1994; returned one of Réunion's five National Assembly deputies in 1993 and three in 1997; allied with the PS and some conservative elements in the *Rassemblement* for the 1998 regional council elections, it slipped from nine to seven seats, but Vergès (also a metropolitan senator) became council president. In 2002, the party slipped back from three to two Assembly deputies, Huguette Bello and Claude Hoarau.
Address. 21bis rue de l'Est, Saint-Denis
Leadership. Paul Vergès & Elie Hoarau

Socialist Party (*Parti Socialiste,* PS), departmental federation of the metropolitan Socialist Party, supports retention of departmental status, consistently allied with the stronger Réunion Communist Party (PCR) against the departmental right, Payet being elected general council president in 1994 with PCR support; returned one of Réunion's five National Assembly deputies in 1993, 1997 and 2002; won six seats in March 1998 regional council elections, allied with the PCR and some conservative elements in the *Rassemblement.*
Address. 85 rue d'Après, Saint-Denis
Leadership. Jean-Claude Fruteau & Christophe Payet

OVERSEAS TERRITORIES AND COLLECTIVITIES

The French overseas territories (*territoires d'outremer,* TOM), namely French Polynesia, the French Southern and Antarctic Territories (with no permanent population), New Caledonia and the Wallis & Futuna Islands, are regarded as integral parts of the French Republic under present arrangements, the three with permanent populations electing representatives to the National Assembly and Senate in Paris and also participating in French elections to the European Parliament. They differ from the overseas departments in that their representative body is the territorial assembly (*assemblée territoriale*) elected by universal adult suffrage) and that they have a greater, although varying, degree of internal autonomy. Also covered below are the two French overseas territorial collectivities (*collectivités territoriales*), namely Mayotte and St Pierre & Miquelon, whose status is explained in the relevant introductions.

French Polynesia

French Polynesia (*capital*: Papeete, Tahiti; *population*: 220,000) consists of some 120 South Pacific islands, including Tahiti, which became a French protectorate in 1847 and a colony in 1860, with the other island groups being annexed later in the 19th century. The territory includes the former French nuclear testing site of Mururoa Atoll. Elections to the 49-member territorial assembly on May 7, 2001, resulted in the People's Front/Rally for the Republic winning 29 seats, the Liberation Front of Polynesia 13 and New Star 7.

Liberation Front of Polynesia (*Tavini Huiraatira/Front de Libération de la Polynésie*, FLP), main pro-independence movement, won four seats in 1991 assembly elections, advancing strongly to 10 in May 1996 and to 13 in May 2001, but remaining in opposition.
Leadership. Oscar Temaru

New Land (*Ai'a Api*), centrist pro-autonomy party founded in 1982, was briefly in territorial government with the People's Front in 1991, having taken third place in that year's territorial elections; retained five seats in 1996 territorial elections, party leader Émile Vernaudon being elected to the French National Assembly in mid-1997 with support from the People's Front; failed to win representation in May 2001 territorial elections.
Address. BP 11055, Mahina, Tahiti
Leadership. Émile Vernaudon

New Star (*Fe'tia Api*), won one seat in May 1996 territorial assembly elections, improving to seven in May 2001.
Leadership. Boris Léontieff

People's Front (*Tahoeraa Huiraatira*, TH), territorial branch of the metropolitan Union for a Popular Movement (UMP), founded in 1971 as a merger of various groups; under assorted names led the territorial government through most of the 1970s and early 1980s, in opposition from 1986, but returned to office under Gaston Flosse on winning a plurality in 1991, first with the support of New Land and then backed by the Autonomous Patriotic Party, whose leader became president of the territorial assembly. Flosse survived a 1992 conviction for illegal use of authority, being re-elected to the French National Assembly in 1993 and in 1998 to the Senate. The TH gained overall majorities in the May 1996 and May 2001 territorial elections, so that Flosse remained head of government into the 21st century, despite a further conviction for corruption in November 1999. In 2002, both National Assembly seats were returned to the UMP candidates.
Address. BP 471, Papeete, Tahiti
Leadership. Gaston Flosse (president)

Mayotte

The Indian Ocean island of Mayotte or Mahoré (*capital*: Dzaoudzi; *population*: 132,000) has been a French possession since the mid-19th century, remaining such when the other Comoro Islands declared independence from France in 1975. In two referendums in 1976 its mainly Christian population opted for maintenance of the French connection rather than incorporation into the Muslim-dominated Comoros, being granted the special status of "territorial collectivity" pending possible elevation to that of a French overseas department. The island's representative body is its 19-member general council. In the 2004 elections, the results were: Union for a Popular Movement 9, Mahoré Departmentalist

Movement 6, Republican and Citizens Movement 2 Mahoré People's Movement 1, others 1.

Mahoré People's Movement (*Mouvement Populaire Mahorais,* MPM), led by Younoussa Bamana (president of the Mayotte general council) and Marcel Henry (member of the French Senate), articulated majority resistance to incorporation into a Comoro state in the mid-1970s, favouring permanent overseas departmental status; once dominant in the local general council, although the party's 1994 overall majority was reduced to a plurality in March 1997 by-elections.
Leadership. Younoussa Bamana & Marcel Henry

Mahoré Union for a Popular Movement (*Union Mahoraise pour une Mouvement Populaire,* UMP), local federation of the conservative metropolitan party, favouring departmental status, rose to five seats in the general council in March 1997 by-elections. In 2002, the National Assembly seat was won by the leader, Mansour Kamardine.
Leadership. Mansour Kamardine

New Caledonia

The New Caledonia archipelago of Pacific islands (*capital*: Nouméa; *population*: 200,000) has been a French possession since 1853. In recent years local politics have been dominated by a demand for the severance of the French connection by groups representing indigenous Melanesians (Kanaks), forming about 45% of the population, and the equally insistent demand of French and other settler groups that French status should be retained. Under complex and frequently changing arrangements instituted to accommodate local aspirations, there are currently three autonomous provincial assemblies (North, South and Loyalty Islands), whose members make up an overall territorial congress. In a November 1998 referendum New Caledonian voters gave 71.9% approval to an accord between the French government and the main territorial parties providing for a gradual transfer of powers to local bodies and for a referendum on independence within 15 to 20 years.

Elections on May 9, 1999, resulted in the 54 seats in the territorial congress becoming distributed as follows: Rally for Caledonia in the Republic (now UMP) 16, Future Together coalition (separatist) 16, Kanak Socialist National Liberation Front 8, Caledonian Union 7, National Front 4, Union of Pro-independence Co-ordinating Committees 1, Kanak Socialist Liberation 1, Union for Caldonian Renewal 1.

Kanak Socialist National Liberation Front (*Front de Libération Nationale Kanak Socialiste,* FLNKS), established in 1984 by radical elements of a pre-existing Independence Front, including the Caledonian Union (UC) and Kanak Liberation Party (PALIKA); prominent in pro-independence agitation in late 1980s and early 1990s, it helped to secure the restoration of New Caledonia to UN list of non-self-governing territories in 1986. The Front accepted the 1988 proposals of Socialist government in Paris for New Caledonia to be divided into three autonomous regions (two dominated by Kanaks), but the assassination in 1989 of then FLNKS leader Jean-Marie Tjibaou and his deputy by a Kanak militant demonstrated the perils of compromise. The FLNKS won pluralities in the North and Loyalty Islands provinces in the 1995 elections, but the dominance of the Rally for Caledonia in the Republic (RPCR) in the populous South province confined the FLNKS to second place in the territorial congress. It gave quaified support to the 1998 Nouméa devolution accord and again took a strong second place in the May 1999 territorial elections, opting to join a coalition government headed by the RPCR.

Leadership. Déwé Gorodey, Rock Wamytan & Paul Neaoutyine

Union for a Popular Movement (*Union pour un Mouvement Populaire*, UMP), territorial section of the conservative metropolitan Union for a Popular Movement, allied with local branches of component parties of centre-right Union for French Democracy, represents both *caldoches* (established settlers) and *métros* (recent immigrants), favours retention of French status, has consistently been the leading electoral force, providing not only the territorial congress president but also the islands' representatives in the French National Assembly and Senate. It remained dominant in the May 1999 territorial congress elections, assembling majority support for the election of Jean Leques (RPCR) as New Caledonia's first President under the 1998 devolution accord. Leques resigned in March 2001, however, and was succeeded the following month by Pierre Frogier at the head of a coalition which again included the pro-independence Kanak Socialist National Liberation Front (FLNKS) as well as the Federation of Pro-independence Co-ordinating Committees (FCCI). In 2002, both National Assembly candidates, Frogier and Jacques Lafleur, were from the UMP.

Address. BP 306, Nouméa
Leadership. Pierre Frogier

St Pierre & Miquelon

St Pierre & Miquelon consists of eight islands off the Canadian Newfoundland coast (*capital*: Saint-Pierre; *population*: 6,750) that have been French possessions since the 17th century and have a population of French stock. Their elevation in 1976 from the status of overseas territory to that of overseas department generated a local campaign for reversion to territorial status with special elements, leading to legislation in 1984 converting the islands into an overseas territorial collectivity with effect from June 1985. Under these arrangements the islands' 19-member general council is the principal representative body, its members also serving as the territorial assembly. Elections to the general council on March 19 and 26, 2000, resulted in the Socialist Party list winning 12 seats, the Union for French Democracy list 5 and the Cape of the Future list 2.

Cape of the Future (*Cap sur l'Avenir*), local branch of the metropolitan Left Radical Party (PRG), won only two seats in the 2000 general council elections, although it took 34% of the first-round vote.

Leadership. Annick Girardi

Socialist Party (*Parti Socialiste*, PS), local section of the metropolitan Socialist Party, for long the majority party in the general council, led the successful campaign against departmental status. In March 1994 its St Pierre & Miquelon 2000 list in St Pierre and the allied Future Miquelon (*Miquelon Avenir*) list led by Jean de Lizarraga won only four general council/territorial assembly seats and went into opposition. It returned to power in the March 2000 elections using the designation Together to Build (*Ensemble pour Construire*), winning 12 of the 19 seats with 37% of the first-round vote.

Address. 2 rue Sœur Césarine, 97500 St Pierre & Miquelon
Leadership. Marc Plantagenest & Karine Claireaux

Union for French Democracy (*Union pour la Démocratie Française*, UDF), local section of centre-right metropolitan

formation. For long overshadowed electorally by the local Socialist Party, it turned the tables in March 1994 with its Archipelago Tomorrow (*Archipel Demain*) list in St Pierre, which together with the allied Miquelon Objectives (*Objectifs Miquelonnais*) list won 15 of the 19 council/assembly seats; elected president of the council, leader Gérard Crignon resigned in June 1996 and was succeeded by Bernard Le Soavec, defined politically as "various right". In the 2000 elections Archipelago Tomorrow, now also designated Forward St Pierre (*En Avant St Pierre*, retained only five seats with 29% of the first-round vote. The UDF has held the islands' National Assembly seat since 1986, Grignon being the deputy. With its consolidation with the UMP in 2002, Grignon retained the seat in 2002.

Leadership. Gérard Grignon

Union for a Popular Movement (*Union pour un Mouvement Populaire*, UMP), local section of conservative metropolitan formation, participated as RPR in 1994 in the victorious Archipelago Tomorrow coalition, which lost power in 2000. Reux retained the islands' seat in French Senate in 1998.

Leadership. Victor Reux

Wallis & Futuna Islands

Situated in the Pacific Ocean north of Fiji and west of Western Samoa, the Wallis & Futuna Islands (*capital*: Mata-Utu; *population*: 15,000) became a French protectorate in 1842 but were never formally annexed. The islands are governed by a French administrator assisted by a 20-member territorial assembly elected by universal adult suffrage for a five-year term. There are also three traditional kingships, of Wallis, Sigave and Alo, exercising limited local powers. Assembly elections on March 10, 2002, resulted in the Rally for the Republic (RPR-UMP) – Voice of Wallis and Futuna People coalition holding 13 seats and The Socialist – Wallis and Futuna People's Union coalition 7.

Gabon

Capital: Libreville
Population: 1,300,000

The Gabonese Republic achieved independence from France in 1960. Executive power is vested in the President, who is elected for a seven-year term and who appoints the Prime Minister and the Council of Ministers. Legislative power is vested in the bicameral parliament, which comprises the 120-member National Assembly (*Assemblée Nationale*) with a term of five years and the 91-member Senate (*Sénat*) which is elected for a six-year term in single member constituencies by local and departmental councillors. The Gabonese Democratic Party (PDG) was the only legal political party from 1968 to 1990, when a national conference in March-April approved the introduction of a pluralist system and opposition parties were legalized.

In multi-party legislative elections held in September-November 1990 the PDG retained an overall majority in the National Assembly, although seven opposition parties gained representation. The results of the elections in five constituencies were subsequently annulled, and by-elections were held in March 1991 resulting in a redistribution of seats mainly in favour of the ruling party.

The re-election of Omar Bongo as President for the

fourth time in December 1993 was disputed by the opposition and resulted in months of political unrest. An agreement between the government and opposition was negotiated in Paris in September 1994 whereby a transitional coalition government was to be installed, with local government elections scheduled to take place in 12 months and legislative elections six months later; also, the electoral code was to be revised. In October 1994 a new government was appointed in which six portfolios were allocated to opposition parties. In a referendum in July 1995, voters overwhelmingly approved the full implementation of the constitutional changes envisaged in the Paris Accords. Municipal elections were held in October 1996 in which the PDG gained a majority, although the opposition parties did well in Gabon's economic capital, Port-Gentil, and northern cities. The polling dates were rescheduled several times for the legislative elections in 1996 owing to organizational difficulties, such as the failure to revise electoral registers in time. Following two rounds of voting in December the PDG maintained its absolute majority with a total of 85 seats. In Assembly elections held in December 2001 the PDG retained its large majority, winning 88 seats, while the opposition Rally of Woodcutters came second with only eight seats. Some opposition parties boycotted the poll after complaining that the authorities had deliberately manipulated the voters' registers.

In April 1997 the legislature passed a constitutional amendment extending the presidential term from five to seven years and creating the position of Vice-President to be appointed by the Head of State. Further constitutional amendments were approved in July 2003 to allow Bongo to stand for re-election an unlimited number of times. In the presidential elections in December 1998 President Bongo had been re-elected in a single round of voting with 66.6% of the vote against a divided opposition of eight candidates. Although opposition discontent was high as the parties claimed intimidation and alleged electoral malpractice, in contrast to 1993 there was no serious civil disorder following the election.

Circle of Liberal Reformers
Cercle des Liberaux Reformateurs (CLR)
Address. c/o Assemblée Nationale, Libreville
Leadership. Gen. Jean-Boniface Assele (president)
The CLR was formed in late 1992 by a breakaway faction of three members (including Gen. Assele, a former minister) of the ruling Gabonese Democratic Party (PDG). It secured two seats in the National Assembly elections in 1996 and managed to retain both seats in the next elections held in December 2001.

Gabonese Democratic Party
Parti Démocratique Gabonais (PDG)
Address. BP 268, Libreville
Telephone. (241) 703121
Fax. (241) 703146
Leadership. Omar Bongo; Simplice Guedet Manzela (secretary-general)
Founded by Omar Bongo in 1968, the PDG was the ruling and sole legal party until early 1990, when a national political conference, convened in the light of growing pressure for democratization and widespread unrest, resulted in the acceptance by the President of a multi-party system. In the legislative elections in the latter part of 1990, the PDG won a majority with 63 seats (subsequently increased to 66 seats following the by-elections in March 1991). In December 1993 Bongo was re-elected as President, despite opposition claims of irregulari-

ties, with just over 51% of the vote. In the December 1996 National Assembly elections the PDG increased its majority by winning 85 seats, although some of its candidates had been defeated by opposition mayors in several major cities in the municipal elections a few months earlier. The party again increased its majority in the next Assembly elections held in December 2001, winning 88 seats.

President Bongo was re-elected for a fifth consecutive term of office in 1998 and has been head of state since 1967.

Gabonese Progress Party
Parti Gabonais du Progrès (PGP)
Address. c/o Assemblée Nationale, Libreville
Leadership. Pierre-Louis Agondjo-Okawe (president); Anselme Nzoghe (secretary-general)
Established as an opposition party in early 1990, the PGP won 18 seats in the National Assembly in the legislative elections later that year – a total subsequently increased to 19 following the March 1991 by-elections. Party leader Pierre-Louis Agondjo-Okawe contested the presidential election in December 1993 but, despite achieving third place, gained less than 5% of the votes cast. In December 1996, the PGP came second in the National Assembly elections, although its total number of seats was halved. The party managed to win only three seats in Assembly elections held in December 2001.

The PGP is a consultative member of the Socialist International.

Rally of Woodcutters
Rassemblement des Bûcherons
Address. c/o Assemblée Nationale, Libreville
Leadership. Fr Paul M'Ba Abessole (leader); Vincent Moulengui Boukosso (secretary-general)
The party name was adopted in February 1991 by what had been the Woodcutters (*Bûcherons*) faction of the Movement for National Regeneration (MORENA) in an effort to more clearly distinguish itself from the parent organization (the original rump of which later joined the African Forum for Reconstruction). The formation emerged from the 1990 legislative elections as the largest single opposition party, initially with 20 of the 120 seats. Despite its success, the party accused the government of electoral fraud and called for the holding of fresh elections under international supervision. The party boycotted the March 1991 by-elections that led to a reduction in its representation to 17 seats.

In the December 1993 presidential election Fr M'Ba Abessole was the runner-up to President Bongo, securing 26.5% of the votes cast – a result disputed by the opposition on the grounds of alleged electoral malpractice by the government. He subsequently successfully united the main opposition parties into an alliance, the High Council of the Resistance (*Haut Conseil de la Résistance*, HCR).

In the 1996 municipal elections, the party secured a majority of the seats in Libreville (where M'Ba Abessole was elected mayor) but was returned with only seven seats in the legislative elections. Before the 1998 presidential election, divisions within the leadership led to a split in the party and the expulsion of its secretary general Pierre-André Kombila Koumba. He was elected to lead a dissident faction within the party and stood as a rival presidential candidate taking fourth place with less than 2% of the vote. M'Ba Abessole, as the official candidate, came third in the election with 13.4% of the vote. In the December 2001 Assembly elections the party was easily defeated by President Bongo's Gabonese Democratic Party, winning only eight seats, while nonetheless remaining the second largest party in the legislature. Kombila Koumba's rival faction managed to win one seat in the Assembly.

The Woodcutters are associated with the International Democrat Union through the Democrat Union of Africa.

Republican and Democratic Alliance
Alliance Démocratique et Républicaine (ADERE)

Address. c/o Assemblée Nationale, Libreville

Leadership. Mboumbou Ngoma (president); Didjob Divungui-Di-N'Dingue (secretary-general)

Party secretary-general Divungui-Di-N'Dingue was an unsuccessful candidate in the 1993 presidential election. ADERE secured one seat in the 1996 National Assembly polling and increased its strength to three in the next election held in December 2001. Divungui-Di-N'Dingue was appointed to the new position of Vice-President in 1997; he was required to deputize for President Bongo, but with no power of succession.

Social Democratic Party
Parti Social-Démocrate (PSD)

Address. c/o Assemblée Nationale, Libreville

Leadership. Pierre Claver Maganga-Moussavou (leader)

The PSD was formed in 1991. The party leader, who is an economist and former minister, contested the December 1993 presidential election, achieving fourth place but attracting less than 4% of the votes cast. In the December 1998 election he came fifth polling less than 1% of the vote. The party won one seat in the National Assembly elections held in December 2001.

Other Parties

African Forum for Reconstruction (*Forum Africain pour la Réconstruction*, FAR), created in early 1992 by an alliance of the following three formations: the Movement for National Regeneration–Originals (*Mouvement de Redressement National*, MORENA-*Originels*), the original MORENA faction which won seven seats in the 1990 legislative elections; the Gabonese Socialist Union (*Union Socialiste Gabonais*, USG), led by Serge Mba Bekale, which initially won four seats in the 1990 elections but subsequently lost one in the March 1991 by-elections; and the Gabonese Socialist Party (*Parti Socialiste Gabonais*, PSG), an extra-parliamentary party. MORENA had been set up in 1981 in clandestine opposition to the then single-party Bongo regime. By early 1990 the party had given rise to dissident factions, the most important of which was what later became the Rally of Woodcutters. In the December 1993 presidential elections, PSG leader Léon Mboyebi polled less than 2% of the votes cast. In the 1996 National Assembly elections, the USG won two seats and the Movement for National Regeneration–Originals one seat. The party failed to win any seats in the 2001 Assembly elections.

Common Movement for Development (*Mouvement Commun pour le Développment*, MCD). The MCD won one seat in National Assembly elections held in December 2001.
Address. c/o Assemblée Nationale, Libreville

Congress for Democracy and Justice (*Congrès pour la Démocratie et la Justice,* CJD), secured one seat in the 1996 National Assembly elections, but failed to win a seat in the 2001 poll.
Leadership. Jules Bourdes Ogouliguende (president)

Circle for Renovation and Progress (*Cercle pour le Renouveau et le Progrès,* CRP), obtained one seat in the 1990 and 1996 National Assembly elections, but failed to gain representation in 2001.

Gabonese People's Union (*Union du Peuple Gabonais*, UPG), founded in 1989 in France as an opposition party whose leader, Pierre Mamboundou, was allowed to return from exile in November 1993 but was prevented from con-testing the presidential elections the following month. The party secured a single seat in the 1996 elections to the National Assembly. Mamboundou was in second place in the 1998 presidential election with 16.5% of the vote; he represented an alliance of five smaller opposition parties, the High Council of the Resistance, which was originally launched by Fr Paul M'ba Abessole of the Rally of Woodcutters against President Bongo in the aftermath of the 1993 election. The party failed to win a seat in the 2001 Assembly elections.
Leadership. Pierre Mamboundou (chairman)

Movement for African Development (*Mouvement Africain de Développment*, MAD)
This small party won one seat in National Assembly elections held in December 2001.
Address. c/o Assemblée Nationale, Libreville

Rally for Democracy and Progress (*Rassemblement pour la Démocratie et le Progrès*, RDP), secured one seat in the 1996 National Assembly elections, but failed to win any seats in 2001.
Leadership. Pierre Emboni (president)

The Gambia

Capital: Banjul
Population: 1,522,700 (2003E)

Gambia achieved independence from Britain in 1965 and became a republic in 1970. Under the 1970 constitution, executive power was vested in the President, since 1977 elected by universal suffrage for a five-year term. Legislative power was vested in a unicameral 50-member House of Representatives, comprising 36 members directly for a five-year term, five indirectly elected chiefs, eight non-voting members and the Attorney-General. In July 1994 Sir Dawda Kairaba Jawara, then President of the Republic and leader of the ruling People's Progressive Party (PPP), was overthrown in a bloodless coup by young army officers led by Capt. Yahya Jammeh, who became head of state. An Armed Forces Provisional Ruling Council (AFRPC) was established, the constitution suspended, the House of Representatives dissolved and all political activity banned.

A new constitution was approved in a referendum held in August 1996, after which the members of the AFRPC retired from the armed forces and Yahya Jammeh announced his intention to stand for the presidency as the candidate of a newly formed Alliance for Patriotic Reorientation and Construction (APRC). The PPP was banned from contesting the forthcoming presidential and legislative elections, as were the two other parties that had held seats in the pre-coup parliament, while all holders of elective office in the 30 years preceding the 1994 coup were declared ineligible to stand in the elections. Yahya Jammeh (one of four candidates to stand) won the September 1996 presidential election with 55.7% of the vote and was inaugurated for a five-year term as President in the following month.

As the former, the new constitution, which took full effect only after the presidential elections in January 1997, provided for a five-year term for the President, elected by absolute majority. The new unicameral National Assembly comprised 49 seats, 45 of which are elected in single member constituencies upon plurality vote and four appointed directly by the President. The Assembly is required to select its speaker and deputy speaker from among the latter group. In January 1997 the APRC won 33 of the 45 elected seats in the first elections to the National Assembly. Of the remaining elective seats 7 were won by the United Democratic Party (UDP), two by the National Reconciliation Party (NRP), one by the People's Democratic Organization for Independence and Socialism (PDOIS) and two by independent candidates.

The second presidential elections, held on Oct. 18, 2001, were won again by Jammeh, securing 53% of the votes cast, followed by the UDP candidate Ousainou Darboe with 32.1%, Hammat Bah (NRP) with 7.7%, Sherriff Dibba (NCP) with 3.4% and Sedia Jatta (PDOIS) with 3.2%. However, serious democratic deficiencies concerning the electoral regulations and increasingly authoritarian tendencies of the APRC regime had become more pronounced. The obvious disadvantages and harassment of opposition candidates as well as shortcomings in the work of the so-called Independent Electoral Commission led the main opposition party, the UDP, to boycott the parliamentary elections on Jan.17, 2002. As a result the APRC won 45 out of the 49 seats (being unopposed in 33 constituencies) and secured an overall dominance in the National Assembly. As one seat was won by the NRP and two seats by PDOIS, the elected opposition held only three seats.

Alliance for Patriotic Reorientation and Construction (APRC)

Address. GAMSTAR Building, Banjul
Leadership. Yahya Jammeh (chairman)
The APRC was formed in 1996 to support Yahya Jammeh's campaign in the forthcoming election to restore a civilian presidency; the leader of the 1994 military coup had previously been associated with the July 22 Movement (officially a non-political organization which was dissolved only in 1999). The presidential election held in 1996 was won by Jammeh with 55.7% of the vote after a campaign in which the three other candidates suffered many obvious disadvantages (including lack of coverage by the state-owned media). In National Assembly elections in 1997, the APRC (the only party with the means to stand in all 45 constituencies) won 33 seats, five of them unopposed, with 52% of the national vote. In 2001 Jammeh won the presidency for the second time with a 53% of the votes cast. The authoritarian tendencies of the APRC regime had reinforced during their first mandate though and provoked the UDP's boycott of the parliamentary elections in 2002 resulting in an overall dominance of the ruling party, which took 45 of the 49 seats.

National Reconciliation Party (NRP)

Leadership. Hammat N.K. Bah
The NRP was founded in 1996 as a liberal party. Its leader, Hammat Bah, came third in the presidential election of Sept. 26, 1996, with 5.5% of the vote. The NRP won two National Assembly seats, with 2% of the national vote, in the legislative elections of Jan. 2, 1997, having fielded candidates in five constituencies. In the presidential elections in 2001 Bah came in third with 7.7% of the votes cast, but the NRP could only hold one parliamentary seat in the 2002 elections.

People's Democratic Organization for Independence and Socialism (PDOIS)

Leadership. Halifa Sallah, Sam Sarr, Sedia Jatta (leaders)
The PDOIS, a radical socialist grouping, was formed in 1986 and has put up candidates for parliamentary elections since 1987, gaining legislative representation in 1997. Sidia Jatta, who had been an unsuccessful presidential candidate in 1992, came fourth in the September 1996 presidential election, with 2.8% of the vote. The PDOIS won one National Assembly seat in the January 1997 legislative elections, having contested 17 constituencies and won 8% of the total national vote; in 2002 PDOIS secured two seats in the National Assembly, having presented candidates in 15 constituencies.

United Democratic Party (UDP)

Address. 16 Ecowas Ave., Banjul
Telephone. (220) 227442
Fax. (220) 223894
Email. info@udpgambia.org
Website. www.udpgambia.org
Leadership. Col. (retd) Sam Sillah (president); Ousainou Darboe (leader)
The UDP was formed in 1996 by a prominent human rights lawyer, Ousainou Darboe, whose associates included a number of former members of pre-1994 parliamentary parties. Darboe was the runner-up in the September 1996 presidential election, winning 35.8% of the vote. UDP candidates stood in 34 constituencies in the January 1997 National Assembly elections, in which the party won 7 seats with 34% of the total national vote. In the presidential elections in 2001 Darboe gained 32.7% of the votes cast. The UDP boycotted the 2002 parliamentary elections claiming that the Independent Electoral Comission allows voting in any area of choice thereby producing massive transfers of ruling party supporters.

The UDP is associated with the International Democrat Union through the Democrat Union of Africa.

Other Parties

Gambia People's Party (GPP), a party launched by the former Vice President Hassan Musa Camara and a group of other defectors from the People's Progressive Party in 1985 to oppose President Jawara in the 1987 elections. The party could not gain parliamentary representation although it secured 14.7% of the votes cast, its leader finishing a distant third in the presidential vote. In the 1992 elections the party secured two parliamentary seats with only 5.5% of the votes cast, but did not present a presidential candidate. After the coup of 1994 the GPP was banned and eventually dissolved.

National Convention Party (NCP), formed in 1975 by the former Vice President and co-founder of the PPP, Sherrif Dibba, and took part in parliamentary and presidential elections from 1977 until 1992, usually finishing in second place. In the 1992 elections the party won 6 legislative seats, and its candidate came second in the presidential poll with 22% of the votes cast. After the coup of 1994 the NCP was banned. Sherrif Dibba, however, stood in the presidential elections in 2001, finishing fourth with 3.4% of the votes cast and being appointed to the National Assembly and elected as speaker of parliament in 2002.

People's Democratic Party (PDP), launched in 1991 by defectors from the NCP and advocating agricultural self-sufficiency, mass education and development of the country's infrastructure. Its president, Dr. Momodou Lamin Bojang, was an unsuccessful candidate in the 1992 presidential election.

People's Progressive Party (PPP), founded in 1958 under British colonial rule. The moderate centre-left PPP held a dominant position as the ruling party between independence in 1965 and July 1994. In the legislative and presidential elections in April 1992 the party won 25 of the 36 directly elected seats in the House of Representatives and its then leader, Sir Dawda Kairaba Jawara, was elected for a sixth term of office with over 58% of the votes cast. After the 1994 military coup Jawara fled the country and the PPP was banned.

United Party (UP), founded in 1952 as a party representing the economic and administrative colonial elite interests. It lost its predominant position with the appearance of the PPP and the introduction of universal suffrage under colonial rule. The UP was the main opposition party until 1977 when it was superseded from its second position by the NCP.

Georgia

Capital: Tbilisi
Population: 5,000,000 (2000E)

The Republic of Georgia replaced the Georgian Soviet Socialist Republic in August 1990 and declared independence from the USSR in April 1991, achieving full sovereignty on the demise of the USSR in December 1991, although it did not join the Commonwealth of Independent States (CIS) until March 1994. A new constitution promulgated in October 1995 renamed the country Georgia and provided for an executive President, who is directly elected for a five-year term (once renewable) by universal adult suffrage and who appoints and presides over a Council of Ministers. The *Sak'art'velos Parlamenti* (Parliament of Georgia), elected for a four-year term, has 235 members, with 150 seats elected by proportional representation and 74 in single-seat constituencies. Eleven members represent displaced persons from the separatist region of Abkhazia. The system of proportional representation subject to a 7% threshold was established in advance of the 1999 parliamentary elections, after 11 parties and blocs had surpassed the previous 5% barrier in the 1995 elections.

In legislative elections on Oct. 31 and Nov. 14, 1999, the Citizens' Union of Georgia (SMK) won 132 seats (with 41.7% of the proportional vote), the All-Georgian Union for Revival 58 (25.2%), Industry Will Save Georgia 15 (7.1%), the Labour Party 2 (6.7%) and independents 16. In addition, 12 Abkhazia deputies elected in 1992 continued to sit in the legislature. In presidential elections held on April 9, 2000, Eduard Shevardnadze of the Citizens' Union of Georgia was re-elected for a third term with the support of 79.8% of those voting.

The legislative elections of Nov. 2, 2003, triggered a series of events with ramifications for the presidential elections and the whole political spectrum of the country. The lack of political will by governmental authorities to organize a genuine democratic election process resulted in irregularities and fraud, leading to a political crisis, street protests, and the resignation of President Shevardnadze on Nov. 23. The former Speaker of Parliament, Nino Burdjanadze, became interim President and called extraordinary presidential elections, which were held on Jan. 4, 2004. Mikhail Saakashvili, joint candidate of the National Movement and the United Democrats, was elected President with 96.2% of votes.

On Nov. 25, 2003, the Supreme Court annulled the results of the proportional component of the Nov. 2 ballot and the Parliament elected in November 1999 was reconvened. On Jan. 4, 2004, four re-runs and 11

second round majoritarian elections were held. On March 28, the proportional component of the elections was repeated, together with two majoritarian contests (in Bolnisi and Chiatura districts). The repeat proportional elections were held in a substantially changed governmental structure. On Feb. 6, the outgoing Parliament passed constitutional amendments that increased the power of the executive, established the post of Prime Minister, and gave the President discretionary powers to dissolve parliament and retain the government even in cases of a parliamentary vote of no-confidence.

The developments at the end of 2003 and beginning of 2004 changed the political environment dramatically. The Citizens' Union of Georgia, the former ruling party, disappeared from the political scene. The National Movement and the Burdjanadze-Democrats that led the November events, known as the Rose Revolution, consolidated their executive power and joined forces. In the final results of the parliamentary elections announced on April 18, the National Movement–Democrats got 66.24% of the proportional vote and a total of 153 parliamentary seats (135 proportional and 18 constituency seats). The Bloc "Rightist Opposition–Industrialists, New Rights" came a distant second with 7.56% of the proportional vote and 23 parliamentary seats (15 proportional and 8 majoritarian). The other five parties – the Labour Party, Political Movement "Freedom", Union of Democratic Revival, Bloc "National Democratic Party–Traditionalists", and Bloc "Jumper Patiashvili–Political Union Ertoba" – did not surmount the 7% threshold in the proportional ballot. In the majoritarian component of the elections, independent candidates won 21 seats, For a New Georgia 19, Georgian Labour Party 3, and Union of Democratic Revival 6. The remaining 11 seats went to MPs elected in Abkhazia in 1992 representing the displaced persons from the separatist region.

For a New Georgia

For a New Georgia was created as an electoral bloc in April 2003 in the run-up to the parliamentary elections. It brought together several pro-Shevardnadze supporters, including the Citizens' Union of Georgia, which was traditionally the former President's main power base. The bloc also comprised the Socialist Party headed by former parliament deputy speaker Vakhtang Rcheulishvili; and the newly-created Silk Road Party headed by Georgian Railways director and long-time Shevardnadze associate, Akaki Chkhaidze. The National Democratic Party of Georgia (NDP), headed by Irina Sarishvili-Chanturia, also joined the bloc.

Contrary to expectations based on opinion surveys, For a New Georgia ranked first in the Nov. 2 ballot with 21.32% of the votes. Following Shevardnadze's forced resignation, charges of corruption were brought against some key figures from the bloc.

In the new Parliament, 19 MPs out of 74 elected in the single-mandate constituencies were endorsed by the now defunct bloc For a New Georgia.

Industry Will Save Georgia (ISG)
Mretsveloba Gadaarchens Sakartvelos
Leadership. Giorgi Topadze (chairman)
The pro-business Industry Will Save Georgia (ISG) was launched in advance of the 1999 parliamentary elections by brewery owner Giorgi Topadze, who maintained that government taxation policies were damaging Georgian business and forcing dependence of foreign aid. He called for tax reductions and import controls until a stable economy was established. Allied in the elections with the ultra-nationalist

Georgia First movement and the Movement for Georgian Statehood, the ISG won 15 seats with a 7.1% vote share. Its group of deputies adopted the name Entrepreneurs and opted to steer a middle course between opposition and supporting the government of Citizens' Union of Georgia.

In 2003, during the street protests triggered by the flawed Nov. 2 parliamentary ballot, Giorgi Topadze convened a joint press briefing with the leaders of the Revival Union and the Labour Party accusing the independent Rustavi 2 broadcasting company of triggering confrontation in the country and calling for its boycotting. Shortly before the repeat parliamentary elections on March 28, 2004, ISG entered into coalition with the New Rights Party forming the "Rightist Opposition–Industrialists, New Rights", which garnered 7.6% of votes.

Labour Party
Sakartvelos Leoboristuli (Shromis) Partia (SLP)
Leadership. Shalva Natelashvili (chairman)

The Labour Party was founded in 1995 with a strong socialist stance advocating free health care, education and social services as well as nationalization of strategically important facilities. It did unexpectedly well in local elections in 1998, winning 9% of votes. In the October-November 1999 parliamentary elections, however, the party just failed to surmount the 7% barrier to proportional representation but won two constituency seats. It claimed that its failure in the proportional balloting was due to vote-rigging by the ruling Citizens' Union of Georgia. In February 2000 the Labour Party joined the new "Freedom and Democracy" bloc of some 25 mainly extra-parliamentary opposition parties, which urged a boycott of the April 2000 presidential elections.

Campaigning under the slogan "Dismantling Shevardnadze's Regime" in the local elections of June 2, 2002, the Labour Party, led by Shalva Natelashvili, emerged as one of the two leading parties alongside Mikhail Saakashvili's National Movement. In Tbilisi, the Labour Party won 25% of the vote. In a surprise move, Nathelashvili offered a partnership to Saakashvili by proposing to support him as chairman of the Tbilisi city council. In 2003, however, the Labour Party declined the National Movement's proposal to have a single list for the upcoming parliamentary elections – discounting Mikhail Saakashvili and his party as a true opposition to then President Eduard Shevardnadze.

In October 2003, Shalva Natelashvili officially announced his plans to run for the presidency in the 2005 elections. The official results of the parliamentary elections of Nov. 2, 2003, placed the Labour Party in fourth position with 12.04% of votes. In the repeat elections of March 28, 2004, the party could not surmount the 7% barrier in the proportionate vote but won three constituency seats. The Labour Party's election platform supported the creation of a two-chamber parliament, the restriction of presidential powers, and nationalization of important facilities.

Before the Rose Revolution Shalva Natelashvili was one of the most popular politicians in Georgia. The November events, however, drove him into radical opposition to the National Movement–Democrats and its leaders, as a result of which many Labour Party activists withdrew their membership. In December 2003, Natelashvili called for a boycott of the extraordinary presidential elections and refused to recognize the ballot as legitimate. Following the March 28 parliamentary ballot, the Labour Party leader and some supporters held a rally outside the Central Election Commission in Tbilisi to protest against what they claimed had been "widespread vote rigging". A group of Labour Party activists launched a hunger strike demanding cancellation of the election results. On April 25, 2004, the Supreme Court of Georgia rejected the appeal for annulment of the elections lodged by the Labour Party, Natelashvili stating afterwards that he would appeal the decision to the European Court of Human Rights in Strasbourg.

National Democratic Party (NDP)
Leadership. Bachuki Kardava (chairman)

The National Democratic Party (NDP), descended from a pre-Soviet era party of the same name and re-established in 1988 as a pro-independence grouping with a Christian democratic orientation, was one of the most influential political groups in Georgia in the early and mid-1990s. The NDP won 32.6% of the vote in the 1990 republican elections; after independence, however, it took only 12 seats in the 1992 parliamentary elections. Having initially supported Shevardnadze's assumption of power in March 1992, the NDP became critical of his policy of rapprochement with Moscow and also opposed Georgian accession to the Commonwealth of Independent States (CIS) in March 1994.

In December 1994 NDP leader Georgi Chanturia was assassinated when gunmen opened fire on his car in Tbilisi. Members of a militant group, known as the *Mkhedrioni*, were prosecuted for the killing. Chanturia's wife, Irina Sarishvili-Chanturia (a former Deputy Prime Minister), was seriously injured in the attack, but recovered sufficiently to assume leadership of the NDP. In the November 1995 legislative elections the NDP came in second place, winning 7.9% of the proportional vote and 31 seats. In January 1996 the NDP deputies failed in their bid to block ratification of the 1994 friendship treaty with Russia.

For the 1999 parliamentary elections, the NDP established the National Democratic Alliance bloc with the Republican Party and the National Party of Entrepreneurs, but its "Third Way" list won only 4.5% of the proportional vote and no seats. In the 2002 local elections, NDP got barely 2% of votes.

In April 2003, the NDP joined the newly established election bloc "For a New Georgia", chaired by then President Shevardnadze. The decision came as a surprise as a year earlier NDP had held consultations with some major opposition parties – the United Democrats, National Movement, New Rights and others – to form an opposition alliance. The alignment of NDP with the pro-Shevardnadze coalition was seen as a step dictated by mere pragmatism in light of the NDP's failure at previous elections. During the November 2003 events, the NDP leader Irina Sarishvili-Chanturia, also acting as spokesperson of the pro-presidential election bloc, declared her readiness to leave the bloc in case the government yielded "to the opposition's pressure." Soon after, the National Democratic Party dismissed her from the leadership position she had held for a decade.

In December 2003, the NDP forged a coalition with the Union of Georgian Traditionalists aiming to have a strong rightist movement for the March 28 repeat parliamentary ballot. The bloc "National Democratic Party – Traditionalists", however, fared poorly with only 2.55% of votes and no constituency seat.

The NDP has been affiliated to the Christian Democrat International since 1993.

National Movement–Democrats (NMD)
Natshionakhuri Modraoba–Democrathebi
Leadership. Mikhail Saakashvili

The National Movement–Democrats emerged as a major political force and the ruling coalition in the aftermath of the flawed November 2003 elections and the resultant civil unrest, known as the Rose Revolution. The party was established on Feb. 4, 2004, uniting President Saakashvili's United National Movement, Prime Minister Zurab Zhvania's United Democrats, and supporters of parliamentary Speaker Nino Burdjanadze. The National Movement–Democrats candidates list for the March 28 elections was basically composed of representatives of those three political parties.

Both Saakashvili and Zhvania were formerly members of Shevardnadze's Citizens' Union of Georgia (SMK) and were known to be radical reformers within Shevardnadze's power base. Both politicians left the SMK in 2001. Saakashvili resigned from the post of Minister of Justice in the government of President Shevardnadze and founded the United National Movement as a moderately nationalist party favouring radical reform of the Georgian state. Zhvania broke from the SMK and resigned as parliamentary Speaker in October 2001 during street protests demanding changes in the country's leadership. In June 2002, Zhvania launched a new party of his own, the United Democrats.

At the beginning of 2003, Saakashvili and Zhvania announced plans to forge a broad opposition alliance for the parliamentary elections. Those plans were viewed as too ambitious in view of the two leaders' differences. Zhvania's United Democrats was considered more moderate in comparison with the more radical United National Movement. In June 2003, parliamentary Speaker Burdjanadze announced plans to found her own political movement. On Aug. 18, Zhvania launched his plan to align with Burdjanaze's political group and on Aug. 21 the creation of a new opposition formation to be known as Burdjanaze-Democrats was formally announced.

In the officially announced results of the Nov. 2 elections, Saakashvili's National Movement was listed third with 18.08% of the votes, while Burdjanadze-Democrats came fifth with 8.79%. Saakashvili, Zhvania and Burdjanadze contested the results and spearheaded mass protests that culminated in the forced resignation of President Shevardnadze on Nov. 23. Within days, opposition leaders aligned behind the single candidacy of Mikhail Saakashvili for the extraordinary presidential elections on Jan. 4, 2004, which he won by an overwhelming majority.

The National Movement–Democrats won 153 seats in the 235-seat Parliament – 135 seats in the proportional ballot and 18 constituency seats. Zurab Zhvania was appointed to the newly created post of Prime Minister, and Nino Burdjanadze resumed her post of parliamentary Speaker.

New Rights Party
Akhali Memarjveneebi
Leadership. David Gamkrelidze
The New Rights Party is led by one of the leading Georgian businessmen, David Gamkrelidze, the head and founder of Aldagi, an insurance company that grew to be one of Georgia's biggest businesses. The leadership also included another successful businessman, Levan Gachechladze, an exporter of Georgian wine and spirits. The party had the support of many of Georgia's well-established businessmen and was one of the few parties to take a strictly centre-right stance on policy issues. On foreign issues, it was strongly pro-Western in its rhetoric. On domestic issues, the party called for a flat tax and other economic reforms.

In the Nov. 2, 2003, elections, New Rights cleared the 7% barrier narrowly coming sixth. For the March 28 repeat elections, the party entered into coalition with Industry Will Save Georgia under the name "Rightist Oppostition – Industrialists, New Rights".

Republican Party
Leadership. Davit Berdzenishvili (chairman)
Website: www.republic.org.ge
Founded illegally in the Soviet period, the Republican Party has had a long history as an opposition force since 1978. In the first multi-party elections in 1990, the party won 3 seats in the Georgian Supreme Soviet and in the summer of 1991 formed the opposition parliamentary faction "Democratic Centre" along with representatives of the Popular Front. In

the 1992 parliamentary elections, the Republican Party won 6 seats and together with Democratic Choice for Georgia formed a 10-member parliamentary faction under the name Republicans. Attempts in 1994 at unifying with two other political organizations – Popular Front and Charter-91 – failed. In 1999, ahead of the parliamentary elections, the Republican Party joined forces with the National Democratic Party of Georgia and the National Party of Entrepreneurs and founded the National Democratic Alliance bloc, known as the "Third Way". The bloc failed to surmount the 7% electoral threshold.

Ahead of the 2003 parliamentary elections, the Republican Party joined Saakashvili's National Movement in the newly established opposition alliance. It subsequently won 6 parliamentary seats on the National Movement–Democrats faction ticket. Relations between the Republican Party and Saakashvili's National Movement quickly deteriorated when in May 2004 the Republican Party's chairman, Davit Berdzenishvili, a native Adjarian, announced his plans to run for the position of mayor of the Adjarian capital, Batumi. Following a decision of the Interim Council prohibiting running for local elections if the candidate holds a seat in the Georgian parliament, Berdzenishvili had to give up his plans. Nothwithstanding their political partnership with the ruling National Movement in the Georgian parliament, the Republican Party ran separately in the snap local Adjarian elections of June 20, 2004, and acted as the main opposition to Saakashvili–Victorious Adjara and to the Adjarian Interim Council. The party cleared the 7% barrier, winning 2 seats in the 30-member Adjarian parliament. Davit Berdzenishvili accused the authorities of vote rigging and fraud, referring to his party's popularity in the region. In 1991, the Republican Party had won 20 seats in the elections for the Supreme Soviet of Adjara Autonomous Republic.

The elections in Adjara precipitated the rift between the Republican Party and Saakashvili's ruling alliance. On June 30, four out of the six Republican parliamentarians, including the party's chairman Berdzenishvili, announced their plans to leave the National Movement–Democrats faction, joining the "out-of-faction" group of parliamentarians. In September 2004, the Republican Party parliamentarians criticized President Saakashvili and the government for conducting military operations in the breakaway region of South Ossetia.

Rightist Opposition–Industrialists, New Rights
Memarjvene Opozicia
Emerging with 23 parliamentary seats from the March 2004 repeat elections, the "Rightist Opposition–Industrialists, New Rights" became the biggest faction in opposition to the National Movement–Democrats. It was composed of two political parties – the New Rights Party and Industry Will Save Georgia – that had formed an electoral bloc just before the March 28 elections. Their popularity had significantly decreased after the leaders of the two parties distanced themselves from the November Rose Revolution.

The political platform of the Rightist Opposition was actually a compilation of the similar programmes of the two constituent parties, focusing on constitutional reforms, adoption of new tax system and protection of business. The issue of local self-governance was also on their agenda and they announced their plans to lobby for adoption of a law which would secure election of provincial governors. The Rightist Opposition also proposed creation of a common trade area in the South Caucasian region and expounded the view that implementation of economic projects with the breakaway regions of Abkhazia and South Ossetia would be a more effective way to restore the country's territorial integrity.

Union of Georgian Traditionalists
Kartvel Traditsionalistta Kavshiri (KTK)

Leadership. Akaki Asatiani (chairman)

The Union of Georgian Traditionalists is one of the oldest political parties in the country. Founded by Georgian emigrants in 1942, it was restored in summer 1990 and officially registered in 1992. Advocating the restoration of the Georgian monarchy, the Union of Georgian Traditionalists won seven seats in the 1992 parliamentary elections. It failed to clear the 5% proportional threshold then in force in the 1995 elections (winning 4.2% of the vote), but had two constituency-based deputies. In July 1999 the party joined the opposition "Batumi Alliance" headed by the All-Georgian Union for Revival (SSAK), securing representation within the bloc in the October–November 1999 parliamentary elections.

For the parliamentary elections on Nov. 2, 2003, the Union of Georgian Traditionalists formed a bloc with the Burdjanadze-Democrats and played a leading role in the Rose Revolution. The party, however, opposed the nomination of Mikhail Saakashvili as candidate for the 2004 extraordinary presidential election and the party's chairman Akaki Asatiani withdrew his support from Nino Burdjanadze and Zurab Zhvania and split from the coalition. In December 2003, the Union of Georgian Traditionalists entered into a rightist coalition with the National Democratic Party (NDP). For the March 28 repeat parliamentary ballot, the NDP–Traditionalists bloc campaigned on an election platform focused on the country's administrative arrangements, liberalization of taxes, Euro-Atlantic structures, reformation of the armed forces and Georgia's withdrawal from the Commonwealth of Independent States (CIS). The bloc, however, could not secure any seats in the new Parliament.

ABKHAZIA

Armed conflict between Georgia and Abkhaz separatists took on serious proportions in 1992-93. On Nov. 26, 1994, the Abkhaz regional government declared Abkhazia independent and since then, the breakaway region has maintained de facto independence.

The Abkhaz Parliament (People's Assembly) has 35 members elected for a five-year term in single-seat constituencies. The last parliamentary elections were held on March 2, 2002. They were declared illegitimate by Georgia as well as by the UN Observer Mission in Georgia (UNOMIG), the OSCE, EU, and Council of Europe. The main Abkhaz opposition party *Aitaira* (Revival) boycotted the elections due to alledged irregularities and breaches of the region's election code. The Republican Party of Vladislav Ardzinba, the Communist Party and the People's Democratic Party of Abkhazia ran in the elections

Vladislav Ardzinba was inaugurated president by the Abkhaz parliament in November 1994 and re-elected in 1999. On July 14, 2004, Abkhazia's parliament announced its decision to hold presidential elections on Oct. 3 as the term of office of the incumbent president was to expire. The 1999 Abkhazia election code defines Abkhazian ethnicity and fluency in Abkhaz language as eligibility criteria for the presidential candidate. The election code was further amended in May 2004, barring from running for the presidency persons who had not lived in Abkhazia in the last five years.

The candidates' registration process was launched on August 3. As a signal of the end of the Ardzinba era, the registration featured a variety of candidates: former Prime Minister Anri Jergenia, Prime Minister Raul Khajimba, Abkhazia's Chernomorenergo power company chairman Sergei Bagapsh, People's Party leader Yakub Lakoba, and Vice President Valerii Arshba. The latter subsequently withdrew. Former Interior Minister and leader of political movement *Aitaria* Alexander Ankvab was denied registration on grounds for failing to meet the residency and language requirements defined in the 1999 Abkhazia election code. In September, the Abkhaz Supreme Court upheld the decision of the Central Election Commission.

Raul Khajimba and Sergei Bagapsh were the main contenders for the presidency. Incumbent Abkhaz president Ardzinba threw his support behind Raul Khajimba, who also enjoyed the approval of the Russian President Vladimir Putin. Sergei Bagapsh had the support of the Abkhaz opposition movements *Amtsakhara* and *United Abkhazia.* Following Ankvab's elimination as a candidate, the opposition movement *Aitaria* and Ankvab himself joined the Bagapsh support group.

In the Oct. 3 elections, Sergei Bagapsh won nearly 48 percent of the vote, while Raul Khajimba followed second with 38.5 percent. The latter subsequently accused his main contender of vote rigging, particularly in the southern region of Gali with predominantly ethnic Georgian population, and called for a renewed countrywide vote. Abkhazia's Central Election Commission, however, ordered October 17 rerun of the elections only in the Gali region. Though partial rerun is not foreseen under the Abkhaz constitution, the decision was primarily political aimed at defusing mounting tensions in the separatist region. Five days after the elections, the incumbent Abkhaz president Ardzinba dismissed Raul Khajimba from his post of prime minister. The appointed successor, Nodar Khashba, is a co-founder of *United Abkhazia,* which is one of the three political movements supporting Sergei Bagapsh.

ADJARA

Adjara was the only case of a South Caucasus autonomous region not involved in armed conflict with its central government after the collapse of the Soviet Union. It had never represented a direct threat to Georgia's territorial integrity due to the fact that the Adjarian authorities and in particular Aslan Abashidze, former chairman of the Supreme Council of the Republic of Adjara, focused their attention on achieving de facto independence without insisting on legalizing this status. In April 2000, a provision was added to the Georgian Constitution specifying that the status of the Autonomous Republic of Adjara would be determined by a constitutional law. By June 2004, there was no clear legal basis for determining the scope of the autonomy of Adjara, while the region was practically outside the jurisdiction of central authorities.

The changes in the political landscape in Georgia in November 2003 had lasting ramifications for the situation in Adjara. In the pre-election campaign, the National Movement's leader Mikhail Saakashvili aspired to win the votes of the region's population, who were believed to be subject to intimidation by pro-government local officials. In October, some 500 members of National Movement tried to stage a rally outside the compound of Aslan Abashidze calling for his resignation. Clashes occurred between Saakashvili supporters on one side and regional law enforcement officers and Abashidze political loyalists, on the other.

Abashidze's party, the Union of Democratic Revival, was placed second nationally with 18.84% of votes in the officially announced results of the Nov. 2 parliamentary ballot. Election results also claimed that turnout in Adjara was 97% with 96.7% of those voting for the Union of Democratic Revival. After the November events, Abashidze denounced the new leadership of the country as "illegitimate" and said that the power transition occurred in violation of the constitution. Polling stations were opened in Adjara for the Jan. 4, 2004, presidential ballot, but the Union of Democratic Revival decided to boycott the elections. In the March 28 repeat parliamentary ballot, Abashidze's party failed to overcome the 7% threshold. The Central Election Commission (CEC) decided to cancel the results in two Adjarian election districts, Khulo and Kobuleti, and set April 18 for repeat elections. Polling stations, however, were not opened and the repeat ballot could not take place. The final vote tally, officially adopted by the CEC on April 18, did not include the votes of 60,000 people from the Khulo and Kobuleti districts.

The situation in Adjara was the priority issue for the new Georgian parliament when convening on April 21. Abashidze was confronted with mounting protests and tension in the region escalated rapidly. On May 2, his supporters blew up bridges and severed railways connecting Adjara with the rest of Georgia. Mediation efforts by the Russian Secretary of the National Security Council, Igor Ivanov, led to Abashidze's peaceful resignation. He fled for Russia on May 6, receiving security guarantees from the Georgian authorities. The Union of Democratic Revival ceased its activities.

Following Abashidze's ouster, President Saakashvili disbanded the two-chamber local Parliament and imposed direct presidential rule. A 20-member Interim Council, chaired by Levan Varshalomidze, was appointed to govern Adjara for the period preceding snap local elections. On May 31, four members of the Interim Council resigned in protest against amendments to the autonomous republic's election law barring Georgian parliamentary deputies from contesting the ballot for a new Adjar legislature.

Local legislative elections for a 30-seat Supreme Council (18 MPs elected through proportional party lists and 12 MPs through single-mandate constituencies) in the Adjara Autonomous Republic were scheduled for June 20, 2004. Nine political parties and one election bloc took part in the contest. A new group was set up under the name of "Saakashvili–Victorious Adjara" made up of members of the ruling National Movement-Democrat party and Saakashvili's supporters. The New Rights Party demanded postponement of local elections in Adjara and subsequently refused to participate in the polls. Its coalition partner Industry Will Save Georgia ran separately. The Republican Party, which entered into coalition with the National Movement for the March 28 repeat ballot and was a political partner to the National Movement–Democrats party in the Georgian Parliament, decided to ran separately, acting as the main opposition to Saakashvili's supporters and the Interim Council in Adjara.

As expected, "Saakashvili – Victorious Adjara" had a landslide victory with 72.1% in the proportional ballot and winning all 12 single-mandate constituencies. The Republican Party, which charged the authorities with attempted vote rigging, garnered 13.5% support. The other eight parties competing failed to surmount the 7% threshold. As a result, Victorious Adjara occupied 28 of the 30 seats in the Supreme Council; the Republican Party occupied the remaining two seats. The new Adjarian Supreme Council convened on July 20 and elected Mikhail Makharadze as its chairman. The new cabinet was approved on July 30 with 23 votes in favour and 2 Republican Party votes against. Levan Varshalomidze became Adjarian Prime Minister.

Following local elections and consolidation of the ruling National Movement–Democrats within Adjara, the central government moved to increase its control over the autonomous region and to set up the legal basis of its territorial-administrative status. On June 25, the Georgian Parliament approved a law on Adjara's powers on first reading by 173 votes to 9. The opposition New Rights parliamentary faction and the Republican Party, a close political party of the National Movement–Democrats party until the June 2004 local elections in Adjara, opposed the draft law.

The Constitutional Law on the Status of the Autonomous Republic of Adjara was introduced in conformity with Article 3, paragraph of Georgia's constitution, but some opponents criticized it for increasing direct presidential rule and for limiting the scope of the region's autonomy. The Council of Europe's expert body on constitutional affairs, the European Commission for Democracy through Law (known as the Venice Commission), discussed the draft law at its 59th Plenary Session on June 18-19 recommending the amendment of some provisions, mainly those related to the increased power of the central government over the affairs of the autonomous region. Opponents from the Rightist opposition and the Republican Party criticized ruling politicians for adopting the law without taking into account most of the Venice Commission recommendations.

SOUTH OSSETIA

Since 1992, the central Georgian government has had only minimal contact with the secessionist leadership of South Ossetia. In May 1999, South Ossetia held parliamentary elections. Four out of 34 parliamentary seats were reserved for ethnic Georgian deputies. They remained vacant, however, as the local Georgian population boycotted the poll.

In a referendum held on April 8, 2001, voters in South Ossetia approved a new constitution that narrowed eligibility for the post of the republic's President, designated Russian a state language together with Ossetian and provided for the official use of Georgian in districts where Georgians form the majority of the population. The Georgian community boycotted the referendum, in which 23,540 of an estimated 45,000 voters participated.

On Nov. 18, 2001, South Ossetia held presidential elections which Georgia and the international community declared illegal. Eduard Kokoev (Kokoyty), a businessman and a Russian citizen, was elected as President.

On May 23, 2004, South Ossetia held its fourth parliamentary elections since 1992. According to the official results of the polls, the ruling party, Unity (*Edinstvo*), which is backed by the *de facto* President of South Ossetia Eduard Kokoev, gained most of the mandates in the 34-seat parliament. The Communist Party of South Ossetia also secured several seats in the legislature. The four seats in the parliament which are allocated for ethnic Georgians living in the region once again remain vacant, as Georgians in South Ossetia continue to boycott these elections.

Germany

Capital: Berlin
Population: 82,000,000 (2004E)

The Federal Republic of Germany (FRG) was established in 1949 in the three Western zones of post-World War II occupation (US, British, and French), achieving full sovereignty in May 1955. The FRG's Basic Law (constitution) defined it as "a democratic and social federal state" with a bicameral parliament consisting of (i) a first chamber (*Bundestag*) directly elected for a four-year term by universal adult suffrage, and (ii) a second chamber (*Bundesrat*) indirectly constituted by representatives of the legislatures of the FRG's constituent states (*Länder*). Executive power was vested in the federal government headed by a Chancellor elected by the *Bundestag*, while the largely ceremonial President (head of state) is elected for a five-year term by a Federal Assembly (*Bundesversammlung*) made up of the *Bundestag* deputies plus an equal number of delegates nominated by the *Länder* parliaments. The reunification of Germany in October 1990 was achieved by the FRG's absorption of the five eastern *Länder* (Brandenberg, Mecklenburg-West Pomerania, Saxony, Saxony-Anhalt and Thuringia) of the former Soviet-occupied and Communist-ruled German Democratic Republic, and also of Berlin (previously under four-power administration). The post-1990 FRG thus consists of 16 *Länder*, with a federal structure still governed by the 1949 Basic Law, under which each *Land* has a parliament exercising substantial powers in the economic and social fields. The FRG was a founder member of what is now the European Union, its membership being extended to the five eastern *Länder* at reunification. Germany elects 99 members of the European Parliament.

The *Bundestag* is formed by a combination of direct elections from 304 single-member constituencies and the proportional allocation of a theoretically equal number of seats to party lists according to their share of the vote. Proportional seats are only allocated to parties winning at least 5% of the national vote or to those returning three deputies directly in any one electoral district (i.e. *Land*). In the 2002 *Bundestag* elections the 304 directly-elected seats were supplemented by 299 proportional seats (for a total complement of 603), the 5 additional "supra-proportional" mandates being required to achieve overall proportionality.

In 1954 Germany became the first West European country to introduce direct public funding of political parties. Under legislation enacted in July 1967, political parties are defined as being a constitutionally necessary element of a free democratic order and as contributing to the formation of the national political will, by influencing public opinion, encouraging participation in public life and training citizens for public office. On these grounds, state funding is granted to political parties or independent candidates obtaining at least 0.5% of the national party-list vote or 10% in any electoral district, payable retrospectively in the next electoral period. Under an amendment to the 1967 law effective from January 1994, parties and independent candidates are entitled to annual payments for each vote received in federal, state and European Parliament elections, now at a rate of €0.85 up to 4 million votes and €0.70 for each additional vote above that figure. They are also allocated €0.38 to match every €1 that they receive from members' contributions or donations, although the total amount of state aid may not exceed a party's income from such sources in the previous year. In 2003 the global sum available in state aid to parties was capped at just under €132 million (about $159 million), with the parties' share being calculated in proportion to their entitlement if the above rules had been fully applied, so that the Social Democratic Party of Germany obtained €47,650,607 (about $57 million) and the Christian Democratic Union €43,896,706 (about $53 million). Separate state aid is paid to foundations associated with the main parties, although such bodies must maintain their organizational independence and not use such funding for party political purposes.

Elections to the *Bundestag* on Sept. 22, 2002 yielded the following results: Social Democratic Party of Germany (SPD) 251 seats (38.5% of the vote), Christian Democratic Union (CDU)/Christian Social Union (CSU) 248 (38.5%), Alliance 90/The Greens 55 (8.6%), Free Democratic Party (FDP) 47 (7.42%), Party of Democratic Socialism (PDS) 2 (4.0%). The

government is headed by Chancellor Gerhard Schröder of the SPD. The President is Horst Kohler.

Each of the 16 *Länder* has its own parliament (*Landtag*, or *Bürgerschaft* in the case of Bremen and Hamburg), elected for a four- or five-year term, the most recent results being as follows:

Baden-Württemberg (March 25, 2001) – CDU 63, SPD 45, FDP 10, Greens 10

Bavaria (Sept. 21, 2003) – CSU 124, SPD 41, Greens 15

Berlin (Oct. 21, 2001) – SPD 44, CDU 35, PDS 33, FDP 15, Greens 14

Brandenburg (Sept. 5, 1999) – SPD 37, CDU 25, PDS 22, German People's Union 5

Bremen (May 25, 2003) – SPD 40, CDU 29, Greens 12, German People's Union 1

Hamburg (Feb. 29, 2004) – SPD 41, CDU 63, Greens 17

Hesse (Feb. 2, 2002) – CDU 56, SPD 33, Greens 12, FDP 9

Lower Saxony (March 1, 1998) – CDU, 91, SPD 63, Greens 15, FDP 14

Mecklenburg-West Pomerania (Sept. 22, 2002) – SPD 33, CDU 25, PDS 13

North Rhine–Westphalia (May 14, 2000) – SPD 102, CDU 88, FDP 24, Greens 17

Rhineland-Palatinate (March 25, 2001) – SPD 49, CDU 38, FDP 8, Greens 6

Saarland (Sept. 5, 1999) – CDU 26, SPD 25

Saxony (Sept. 19, 1999) – CDU 76, PDS 30, SPD 14

Saxony-Anhalt (April 21, 2002) – CDU 48, SPD 25, PDS 25, FDP 17

Schleswig-Holstein (Feb. 27, 2000) – SPD 41, CDU 33, FDP 7, Greens 5, South Schleswig Voters' Union 3

Thuringia (June 13, 2004) – CDU 45, PDS 28, SPD 15

The European Parliament elections held on June 13, 2004, resulted in the following outcome: Christian Democratic Union – 36.5% of the vote – 40 seats (-3); Social Democratic Party – 21.5% of the vote – 23 seats (-10); Alliance 90/The Greens – 11.9% of the vote – 13 seats (+6); Christian Social Union – 8% of the vote – 9 seats (-1); Party of Democratic Socialism – 6.1% of the vote – 7 seats (+1); Free Democratic Party – 6.1% of the vote – 7 Seats (+7). In the new European Parliament Germany has 99 seats. The turnout in the elections was 43%.

Alliance 90/The Greens
Bündnis 90/Die Grünen

Address. Platz vor dem Neuen Tor 1, 10115 Berlin
Telephone. (49–30) 284–420
Fax. (49–30) 2844–2210
Email. info@gruene.de
Website. www.gruene-partei.de
Leadership. Angelika Beer and Reinhard Bütikofer (co-chairpersons); Katrin Göring-Eckardt and Krista Sager (parliamentary group leaders); Steffi Lemke (general secretary)
The Greens first emerged in West Germany in the 1970s at state and local level. A number of these disparate groups came together at a Frankfurt conference in March 1979 to form the Alternative Political Union, The Greens (*Sonstige Politische Vereinigung, Die Grünen*), which was given a federal structure under the rubric The Greens at a Karlsruhe congress in January 1980. A programme adopted in March 1980 called for a worldwide ban on nuclear energy and on chemical and biological weapons, the non-deployment of nuclear missiles in Europe, unilateral disarmament by West Germany, the dismantling of NATO and the Warsaw Pact,

and the creation of a demilitarized zone in Europe. It also advocated the dismantling of large economic concerns into smaller units, a 35-hour week and recognition of the absolute right of workers to withdraw their labor.

Having taken only 1.5% of the vote in the 1980 federal elections, the Greens broke through to representation in 1983, winning 5.6% and 27 lower house seats. They progressed to 8.2% in the 1984 European Parliament elections and to 8.3% in the 1987 federal elections, winning 42 seats. Prominent in the Greens' rise was Petra Kelly, whose charismatic leadership attracted national publicity and acclaim. However, opposition within the party to "personality politics" contributed to her departure from the joint leadership in April 1984. (Some years later, in October 1992, Kelly and her partner, former army general turned pacifist Gert Bastian, were found dead in their Bonn apartment; according to the German police, Kelly had been shot by Bastian, who had then killed himself.)

Divisions also surfaced between the Greens' "realist" wing (*Realos*), favouring co-operation with the Social Democratic Party of Germany (SPD), and the "fundamentalists" (*Fundis*), who rejected any compromises with other formations. In December 1985 the "realist" Greens of Hesse joined a coalition government with the SPD (the first such experience for both parties), but this collapsed in February 1987 after the Green environment minister, Joschka Fischer, had unsuccessfully demanded that the state government should halt plutonium processing at a plant near Frankfurt. The Hesse experience strengthened the "fundamentalist" wing at the Greens' annual congress in May 1987, when it obtained eight of the party's 11 executive seats. By 1989, however, the *Realos* had regained the initiative, in alliance with a "Fresh Start" (*Aufbruch*) group led by Antje Vollmer which had sought to mediate between the contending factions.

In late 1989 a Green Party (*Grüne Partei*) was launched in East Germany, being at that stage opposed to German reunification. It joined with the Independent Women's League (*Unabhängige Frauenbund*) in contesting the March 1990 *Volkskammer* elections, winning 2.2% of the vote and eight seats. Unwilling to join forces with the West German Greens, the eastern Greens instead joined Alliance 90, which had been founded in February 1990 by a number of East German grass-roots organizations, including the New Forum (*Neues Forum*) and Democracy Now (*Demokratie Jetzt*), on a platform urging "restructuring" of the GDR along democratic socialist lines, rather than German unification or the importation of capitalism. In the all-German *Bundestag* elections of December 1990 Alliance 90 secured eight seats by surmounting the 5% threshold in the former GDR, even though its overall national vote was only 1.2%. In contrast, the western Greens, with an overall 3.9% share, failed to retain representation.

With German reunification a fact, the western Greens and Alliance 90 gradually resolved their differences, until parallel congresses in Hanover in January 1993 voted to unite under the official name Alliance 90 but with the suffix "The Greens" being retained for identification purposes. The merger was formalized at a Leipzig congress in May 1983. The Greens' Mannheim congress in February 1994 opted in principle for a "red-green" coalition with the Social Democrats at federal level, although without modifying policies (such as opposition to NATO membership) that were unacceptable to the SPD leadership. In the June 1994 European Parliament elections the Green list took third place with a 10.1% vote share, winning 12 of the 99 German seats. In the October 1994 *Bundestag* elections the Greens achieved a further federal advance, to 7.3% and 49 seats. The new parliamentary arithmetic precluded a coalition with the SPD, but the Green presence was acknowledged by the elec-

tion of a Green deputy (Antje Vollmer) as one of the *Bundestag*'s four vice-presidents.

In 1995 the Greens registered significant advances in *Länder* elections in Hesse (February), North Rhine–Westphalia and Bremen (May) and Berlin (October), winning a vote share of 10–13% in the four contests. At a Green party conference in Bremen in December 1995, a majority of delegates endorsed the party's traditional opposition to any external military role for Germany, although an unprecedented 38% backed a motion by Joschka Fischer (by now a leading Green deputy in the *Bundestag*) to the effect that German troops could be deployed on UN peacekeeping missions. Further divisions were in evidence at the Greens' March 1998 congress, where delegates responded to Fischer's appeal for "discipline and realism" by calling for Germany's withdrawal from the NATO-led peacekeeping force in Bosnia and by adopting a raft of radical proposals, including the trebling of the price of petrol over a 10-year period.

Ousted from the Saxony-Anhalt parliament in April 1998, the Greens also lost ground in the federal elections in September, slipping to 6.7% of the vote and 47 seats. It nevertheless entered into Germany's first "red-green" federal coalition (in which Fischer became Foreign Minister and Vice-Chancellor, Jürgen Trittin Environment Minister and Andrea Fischer Health Minister), on the basis of a pact with the SPD which included commitments to "ecological tax reform" and withdrawal from nuclear power generation. Strains quickly appeared in the coalition, notably over the SPD's insistence on a 20-year time-span for the phasing-out of nuclear plants. A Green congress in Leipzig in December 1998 approved the lifting of the party ban on members holding both public and party offices and set up a 30-member council to defuse internal policy disputes. But it rebuffed a proposal that the Greens should have a recognized chairperson, so that Fischer's aim of establishing a "normal" organizational structure for the party remained unrealized at that stage. On the other hand, at Fischer's urging, a special Green conference in Bielefeld in May 1999 defeated by 444 votes to 318 a proposal from the party's pacifist wing that the Green ministers should not support the NATO military action against Yugoslavia over Kosovo, thus effectively backing the deployment of German troops outside the NATO area.

In the June 1999 European Parliament elections the Greens fell back to 6.4% of the vote, losing five of their 12 seats. They also lost ground in a series of state elections in 1999-2000, being eliminated from the Saarland parliament in September 1999 and losing ground in the Schleswig-Holstein state elections in February 2000 and in North Rhine–Westphalia in May. The following month a party conference in Münster at last opted for a leadership structure akin to those of other parties, electing Renate Künast and Fritz Kuhn as co-chairpersons. In January 2001 Künast was elevated to the federal government as Minister of Consumer Protection, Nutrition and Agriculture, amidst the onset of "mad cow disease" (BSE) in Germany. She and the Greens got some credit for articulating public concern about BSE, but the bad election results continued in March 2001, when the Green vote fell from 12% to 7.7% in Baden-Württemberg and from 7% to 5.2% in Rhineland-Palatinate.

The Greens' electoral problems in 2000-01 were related to activists' disenchantment with compromises made by the party in government, notably its agreement to the resumption of German nuclear waste transportation. Also of concern within the party was the content of a federal government agreement to phase out nuclear power generation in Germany by 2021. Although the accord was hailed by Green ministers as the most dramatic abandonment of nuclear power by any major country, many in the party disliked the long phasing-out period and feared that the agreement might never be implemented. Among the wider electorate, the Greens were damaged in early 2001 by revelations about Fischer's youthful career as a militant street-fighter in Frankfurt in the 1970s, not so much by the facts of his radical past but more by his admission that he had not been honest about it. Nevertheless, Fischer retained sufficient authority, both within the party and the country as whole, to enable him to oversee a major change in Germany's defence and foreign policy posture following the terrorist attacks in the USA of Sept. 11, 2001 – with *Bundeswehr* troops being stationed in Afghanistan and elsewhere as part of the US-led "war on terror".

The *Bundestag* elections of Sept. 22, 2002, proved to be a triumph for the Greens. The party secured 8.6% of the vote, up by 1.9% on 1998, and secured 55 seats in the *Bundestag* (up from 47). In addition, the party also won its first ever direct mandate in the inner-city constituency of Berlin-Friedrichshain-Kreuzberg-Prenzlauer Berg-Ost. Ironically for a party that had started off explicitly rejecting the oligarchical structures of traditional parties, the Greens' slick and often very funny election campaign was highly focused on Joschka Fischer. The Greens' success enabled the return to power of the SPD-led "red-green" coalition after the 2002 elections. As of mid-2004 the Greens continued to participate in a national-level coalition government with the SPD as well as in state-level coalition governments with the SPD in North Rhine–Westphalia and Schleswig-Holstein. The party polled 11.9% of the vote in the European Parliament elections of June 2004.

With an official membership of about 46,000, the German Greens are affiliated to the European Federation of Green Parties. The party's 13 representatives in the European Parliament are members of the Greens/European Free Alliance group.

Christian Democratic Union
Christlich-Demokratische Union (CDU)

Address. Klingelhöferstrasse 8, 10785 Berlin
Telephone. (49–30) 220–700
Fax. (49–30) 220–70111
Email. info@cdu.de
Website. www.cdu.de
Leadership. Angela Merkel (chairperson and parliamentary group leader); Laurenz Meyer (secretary-general)

The moderate conservative CDU was established in October 1950 as a federal organization uniting autonomous groups of Christian Democrats (both Catholic and Protestant) which had re-emerged in all parts of Germany after World War II, descended in part from the Centre Party founded in the 19th century and prominent in the pre-Hitler Wiemar Republic. Following a strong showing in the first *Länder* elections held in West Germany in 1947, an alliance of these groups, including the Christian Social Union (CSU) of Bavaria, had become the strongest element in the first *Bundestag* elections in 1949 under the leadership of Konrad Adenauer, who became the first West German Chancellor. On the formation of the CDU in 1950, the CSU remained a separate though allied party in Bavaria, and has generally been regarded as the more right-wing of the two.

The CDU remained in government until 1969, presiding over the blossoming of the "German economic miracle" under the successive chancellorships of Adenauer (until 1963), Ludwig Erhard (1963–66) and Kurt-Georg Kiesinger (until 1969). From 1959, moreover, Heinrich Lübke of the CDU served two five-year terms in the federal presidency. During this period the CDU/CSU tandem was in coalition with the Free Democratic Party (FDP) until 1957, governed with an absolute *Bundestag* majority until 1961, returned to a coalition with the FDP in 1961–66 and then formed a "grand coalition" with the Social Democratic Party of Germany (SPD). Having slipped to 46.1% in the 1969 elections, the CDU/CSU went into opposition to an SPD/FDP coalition that was to endure until 1982. The CDU/CSU share of the vote fell to 44.9% in 1972, rose to 48.6% in 1976 and then fell to 44.5% in 1980, when a joint electoral list was headed by Franz-Josef Strauss of the CSU, who had threatened a rupture with the CDU unless he was accepted as the alliance's Chancellor-candidate. Meanwhile, Karl Carstens of the CDU had been elected President of West Germany in May 1979.

The FDP's desertion of the SPD-led coalition in October 1982 enabled the CDU/CSU to form a new government with the FDP under the leadership of Helmut Kohl. In *Bundestag* elections in March 1983 the CDU advanced strongly to 38.2% and 191 seats (and the CSU also gained ground), so that the CDU/CSU/FDP coalition continued in office. In May 1984 Richard von Weizsäcker of the CDU, a former mayor of West Berlin, was elected to succeed Carstens as President. In the January 1987 lower house elections the CDU declined to 34.5% and 174 seats (and the CSU also lost ground), but gains by the FDP enabled Kohl to continue as Chancellor with the same coalition partners. Criticism of Kohl's leadership surfaced at the CDU's congress of November 1987, when he was re-elected chairman (as the only candidate) by his lowest-ever number of delegates' votes. In the June 1989 European Parliament elections the CDU slipped to 29.5% of the national vote.

Confidence in Kohl's leadership was restored by his performance as government leader through the process of German reunification in 1990, after which his position in the CDU was unassailable. In the all-German elections of December 1990 the CDU won 36.7% of the vote overall and took 268 seats in the enlarged 662-member *Bundestag*. Although the combined CDU/CSU share of the vote was the lowest since 1949, an SPD decline enabled Kohl to form a further CDU/CSU/FDP coalition. In the 1990 contest the CDU was confirmed as the strongest party in the eastern *Länder*, although it later lost ground because the Kohl government was blamed for the problems of economic transition. As a dedicated pro-European party, the CDU strongly supported German ratification of the Maastricht Treaty on European union (which was finally completed in October 1993); it also backed moves to amend the German constitution so that German forces could be deployed on UN-approved peacekeeping missions outside the NATO area. In May 1994 Roman Herzog of the CDU was elected President, while in the following month's European Parliament elections the CDU registered 32.0% of the vote, winning 39 of the 99 German seats.

In the October 1994 *Bundestag* elections the CDU slipped to 34.2% and 244 seats (out of 672), sufficient to underpin a further CDU/CSU/FDP coalition under the continued chancellorship of Kohl (who was re-elected CDU chairman in November 1994 with over 94% of delegates' votes at a special congress). However, CDU setbacks in *Länder* elections in 1993–94 meant that the SPD established a majority in the indirectly-elected *Bundesrat* (federal upper house). Further setbacks followed in state elections, but Kohl nevertheless announced in April 1997 that he would stand for a fifth term as Chancellor. He was confirmed as the CDU (and CSU) candidate at a party congress in October 1997, when he at last designated CDU/CSU parliamentary leader Wolfgang Schäuble as his preferred successor.

The September 1998 *Bundestag* elections produced a widely-predicted defeat for Kohl and the CDU, whose vote share fell sharply to 28.2% and seat total to 198, with the result that it went into opposition after 17 years of continuous power. In November 1998 Kohl was succeeded as CDU chairman by Schäuble, who was elected unopposed. In the June 1999 European Parliament elections the CDU advanced strongly to 39.3% of the vote and 43 of the 99 German seats. State elections in 1999 also produced some notable successes for the CDU, as the party orchestrated a nationwide campaign against government plans to abolish Germany's 100-year-old law restricting the right of citizenship to those with German blood.

The CDU was tainted from late 1999 by a major funding scandal surrounding its receipt under Kohl's leadership of large secret donations, apparently in return for favors granted by the CDU-led government. Criminal and parliamentary investigations were launched into such illegal funding, the tentacles of which spread to several CDU state parties. One much-publicized allegation was that the CDU's 1994 election campaign had been largely financed by a "commission" from the French Elf-Aquitaine oil company (then state-owned), paid on the orders of President François Mitterrand (a close friend of Kohl's) for assistance in Elf's purchase of an East German oil refinery. Kohl admitted that the CDU had operated a secret slush fund under his leadership, but denied any personal corruption and also doggedly refused to name contributors to the fund, saying that he had given his word of honor to keep them secret.

Accepting responsibility for mishandling the scandal, Schäuble resigned as CDU chairman in February 2000 and was succeeded in April by secretary-general Angela Merkel, a Protestant from East Germany who had been an active Communist in her youth. Meanwhile, the CDU had been punished in state elections in Schleswig-Holstein, losing ground in a contest it had been expected to win. Merkel set about repairing the party's image but quickly came into conflict with her successor as secretary-general (and effectively deputy leader), Ruprecht Polenz. The ousting of Polenz in October 2000 and his replacement by Laurenz Meyer appeared to strengthen Merkel, although the following month both she and Schäuble were fiercely criticized by Kohl in his memoirs for trying to discredit him. The CDU was also accused of being racist for proposing in November 2000 that immigrants should accept Germany's "guiding culture" (*Leitkultur*) by learning German and embracing German traditions and law, including equality for women.

The funding scandal rumbled on in early 2001, amidst complex court battles over fines imposed on the CDU by the *Bundestag* Speaker for its past financial transgressions. In February 2001 Kohl agreed to a deal with the public prosecutors under which he paid a DM300,000 fine in return for the dropping of criminal investigations against him. But he continued to face a slow-moving parliamentary inquiry, and in May 2001 criminal charges were filed against former CDU Interior Minister Manfred Kanther and two others for alleged financial improprieties in Hesse.

In 2002 the CDU (along with its Bavarian sister-party the CSU) fought the September *Bundestag* elections with Bavarian Edmund Stoiber as their joint Chancellor-candidate. The choice of Stoiber – a stiff and rather old-fashioned individual who had made a name for himself whilst minister-president of Bavaria as being a robust conservative – was seen as a setback for Merkel. In the event Stoiber failed to unseat incumbent SPD Chancellor Gerhard Schröder, although the combined CDU/CSU finished in a dead heat with the SPD – each having a 38.5% share of the vote. Since then Merkel has taken a more dominant role within both the CDU and the combined CDU/CSU parliamentary faction, where she is faction leader.

Since the 2002 *Bundestag* elections the CDU has established a formidable opinion poll lead over the SPD of anything up to 20%. Popular support for the CDU is also reflected in its strength at the state level, where it participates in government in 10 out of 15 states (not including Bavaria), in 8 of which it governs alone or is the senior coalition partner. In addition, the extent of the CDU's state-level power base

gives its effective control of the parliamentary second chamber (*Bundesrat*). It also polled 44.5% of the vote in the European Parliament Elections of June 2004, coming first and giving it 40 of the 99 German seats.

With an official membership of 635,000, the CDU is a member of the Christian Democrat International and the International Democrat Union. Its European Parliament representatives sit in the European People's Party/European Democrats group.

Christian Social Union
Christlich-Soziale Union (CSU)

Address. Franz-Josef-Strauss-Haus, Nymphenburger Strasse 64-66, 80335 Munich
Telephone. (49–89) 1243–0
Fax. (49–89) 1243–299
Email. info@csu-bayern.de
Website. www.csu.de
Leadership. Edmund Stoiber (chairman); Michael Glos (federal parliamentary group leader); Joachim Hermann (Bavarian parliamentary group leader); Markus Söder (general secretary)

The CSU was established in Bavaria in January 1946 by various Catholic and Protestant political groups with the aim of rebuilding the economy on the basis of private initiative, property ownership, and the restoration of the rule of law in a federal Germany. Led by Josef Müller, it won an absolute majority in the first Bavarian *Landtag* elections in December 1946 (with 52.3% of the vote), although the emergence of the separatist Bavaria Party in the 1950 elections ate into CSU support, obliging it to form a coalition with the state Social Democratic Party of Germany (SPD). The CSU continued to exist as a separate political party despite the formation of the Christian Democratic Union (CDU) in October 1950, and it was agreed that the CSU would be the CDU's sister party in Bavaria and that neither would oppose the other at elections. While both parties have espoused essentially the same policies, the CSU is generally reckoned to be more conservative than the CDU. It is also relatively less "pro-European" than the CDU leadership and in the 1990s the CSU opposed Germany's participation in the euro currency area.

The post-war CSU/SPD coalition in Bavaria lasted until 1954, when the CSU went into opposition to a four-party government headed by the SPD. Under the leadership of Hanns Seidel, the CSU returned to office in 1957 at the head of a three-party coalition and in 1962 regained an absolute majority in the Bavarian *Landtag*, which it has held ever since. Seidel was succeeded as CSU leader by Franz-Josef Strauss in 1961 and as Bavarian minister-president by Alfons Goppel, who held office from 1962 until 1978. Strauss became the CSU's dominant figure in the CDU-led federal government, serving as Defence Minister from 1956 until being forced to resign in 1963 over the *Spiegel* affair. He returned to government as Finance Minister in the 1966–69 "grand coalition" between the CDU, the CSU and the SPD, but in 1978 opted to become head of the CSU government of Bavaria. Strauss was the unsuccessful CDU/CSU candidate for the chancellorship in the 1980 *Bundestag* elections, in which the CSU vote slipped to 10.3% (from 10.6% in 1976) and its seat total to 52.

Having been in federal opposition since 1969, the CSU returned to government in 1982 as part of a coalition headed by the CDU and including the Free Democratic Party (FDP). In the 1983 *Bundestag* elections that confirmed the coalition in power the CSU improved to 10.6% and 53 seats, although two CSU deputies later departed to join the far-right Republicans. In the 1987 elections the CSU slipped to 9.8% and 49 seats but continued its participation in the federal government. Strauss died in October 1988 and was succeeded as CSU leader by Theo Waigel and as Bavarian minister-president by Max Streibl. In the June 1989 European Parliament elections the CSU list took 8.2% of the overall West German vote. In Bavarian state elections in October 1990 the CSU maintained its absolute majority, winning 54.9% of the vote and 127 of the 204 seats.

As Germany moved towards reunification in 1990 the German Social Union (DSU) was set up in the re-established eastern *Länder* as a would-be sister party of the CSU. However, in the all-German *Bundestag* elections of December 1990 the DSU made minimal impact, while the percentage vote of the Bavaria-based CSU inevitably fell, to 7.1% (8.8% in western Germany), yielding 51 seats out of 662 and enabling the CSU to continue as part of the federal coalition. In the June 1994 European Parliament elections the CSU list took 6.8% and eight of the 99 German seats, while in the Bavarian *Landtag* elections of September 1994 the party won its customary overall majority, although its seat total slipped to 120 and its vote share to 52.8%. The party therefore suffered little from a corruption scandal which had caused the resignation of Streibl as Bavarian minister-president in May 1993 and his replacement by Edmund Stoiber.

The CSU improved its vote share slightly to 7.3% in the October 1994 *Bundestag* elections (although its representation fell to 50 seats) and obtained three portfolios in the re-formed CDU/CSU/FDP federal coalition. In February 1998 it suffered a major defeat when a Bavarian referendum yielded an overwhelming majority in favor of abolition of the state's second chamber, despite CSU advice to the contrary.

The party shared in the federal coalition's defeat in September 1998, slipping to 6.7% of the national vote and to 47 *Bundestag* seats, but retained its overall majority in that month's Bavarian state elections, winning 123 seats on a vote share of 52.9%. Having announced his resignation after the elections, Waigel was succeeded as CSU chairman by Stoiber in January 1999. Stoiber was then chosen to be the joint CDU/CSU chancellor-candidate to challenge Gerhard Schröder in the 2002 *Bundestag* elections. The notoriously stiff and old-fashioned Stoiber failed to unseat the more relaxed and populist Schröder, although the CSU did particularly well in the elections, polling 9% of the national vote. Since the 2002 elections Edmund Stoiber has continued to play a major role in national politics and maintains a healthy rivalry with CDU leader Angela Merkel. The CSU did very well in the June 13, 2004, elections to the European Parliament, polling 57.4% of the vote in Bavaria and taking 9 seats.

With an official membership of around 180,000, the CSU is affiliated to the Christian Democrat International and the International Democrat Union. Its representatives in the European Parliament sit in the European People's Party/European Democrats group.

Free Democratic Party–The Liberals
Freie Demokratische Partei (FDP)–Die Liberalen
Address. Thomas-Dehler-Haus, Reinhardtstrasse 14, 10117 Berlin
Telephone. (49–30) 284–9580
Fax. (49–30) 2849–5822
Email. fdp-point@fdp.de
Website. www.fdp.de
Leadership. Guido Westerwelle (chairman); Wolfgang Gerhardt (parliamentary group leader); Hans-Jürgen Beerfeltz (secretary-general)

Strongly based in the farming community, the centrist and secular FDP was founded in December 1948 at a conference in Heppenheim (near Heidelberg) as a fusion of various liberal and democratic *Länder* organizations descended from the German State Party (*Deutsche Staatspartei*) and the more right-wing German People's Party (*Deutsche Volkspartei*,

DVP) of the Weimar Republic (1918–33), and more distantly from the People's Party (*Volkspartei*) founded in 1866. The DVP had been revived in Baden-Württemberg in 1945 under the leadership of Reinhold Maier (who became the state's first premier and was later FDP leader in 1957–60) and Theodor Heuss (who became the first FDP leader and was then West Germany's first President, from 1949 until 1959). An attempt in 1947 to create an all-German liberal party had foundered on the opposition of the East German Communists to the participation of the Berlin-based Liberal Democratic Party (LDP), whose enforced support for socialism impelled prominent members, notably Hans-Dietrich Genscher, to flee to the West to join the FDP.

The FDP secured representation in the first West German *Bundestag* elected in 1949, with an 11.9% vote share, and joined a coalition government headed by what became the Christian Democratic Union (CDU) and also including the Bavarian Christian Social Union (CSU). It slipped to 9.5% in the 1953 elections and was in opposition in 1956–61, declining further to 7.7% of the vote in the 1957 federal elections. A major advance in 1961, to 12.8% of the vote, brought the party back to office in a new coalition with the CDU/CSU that lasted until 1966, when the FDP again went into opposition, this time to a "grand coalition" of the CDU/CSU and the Social Democratic Party of Germany (SPD). Having declined to 9.5% in the 1965 elections, FDP fell back sharply to 5.8% in 1969, but nevertheless joined a centre-left coalition with the SPD. Having succeeded Erich Mende as FDP chairman in 1968, Walter Scheel served as Vice-Chancellor and Foreign Minister from 1969 until being elected West German President in 1974. During this period opposition within the party to the government's *Ostpolitik* caused several FDP deputies, including Mende, to desert to the opposition Christian Democrats. Scheel was succeeded in his party and government posts by Genscher, under whose leadership the FDP slipped to 7.9% in the 1976 elections (from 8.4% in 1972), before recovering to 10.6% in 1980.

The SPD/FDP federal coalition finally collapsed in September 1982 when the Free Democratic ministers resigned rather than accept the proposed 1983 budget deficit. The following month the party switched to the right and joined a coalition with the CDU/CSU, which caused internal dissension and the exit of some FDP left-wingers. The party slumped to 6.9% in the 1983 federal elections and failed to secure representation in the 1984 European Parliament contest, its problems including the steady decline of its traditional farming constituency. The election of Martin Bangemann as FDP chairman in 1985 in succession to Genscher (who nevertheless remained Foreign Minister) resulted in the party taking a more conservative tack, on which basis it revived to 9.1% in the 1987 *Bundestag* elections and continued its coalition with the CDU/CSU. In 1988 Bangemann opted to become a European commissioner and was succeeded as FDP chairman by Count Otto Lambsdorff, who won a tight party election despite having been forced to resign from the government in 1984 after being convicted of illegal party financing activities. Having recovered some ground in state elections in the late 1980s, the FDP regained representation in the European Parliament in 1989 (winning 5.6% of the German vote).

On the collapse of Communist rule in East Germany, an eastern FDP sister party was formally established in February 1990. In the East German elections of March 1990 this party was part of the League of Free Democrats (together with the Communist-era LDP under new leadership and the German Forum Party), which took a 5.3% vote share. On the reunification of Germany in October 1990 these eastern elements were effectively merged into the western FDP, enabling the party to make a major advance in the all-German *Bundestag* elections in December 1990, to 11.0% of the overall vote and 79 seats out of 662. Maintaining its federal coalition with the CDU/CSU, the FDP showed electoral buoyancy in 1991 but encountered new difficulties following Genscher's resignation from the government in April 1992, as highlighted by the enforced resignation in January 1993 of the FDP Vice-Chancellor and Economics Minister, Jürgen Möllemann, over a corruption scandal.

In June 1993 Genscher's successor as Foreign Minister, Klaus Kinkel, replaced Lambsdorff as FDP chairman, but he failed to halt a series of electoral failures at state level, while the party slumped to 4.1% in the June 1994 Euro-elections and thus failed to win any seats. Kinkel obtained a reprieve when the FDP unexpectedly retained a *Bundestag* presence in the October 1994 federal elections, winning 47 out of 672 seats on a 6.9% vote share. Despite previous strains over issues such as overseas German troop deployment (which the FDP opposed), the party opted to continue the federal coalition with the CDU/CSU and was rewarded with further electoral failures in Bremen and North Rhine–Westphalia in May 1995, whereupon Kinkel vacated the FDP leadership while remaining Foreign Minister. Elected as his successor at a special party congress in June 1995, Wolfgang Gerhardt distanced himself from Chancellor Kohl on various policy issues, but a further FDP failure in Berlin elections in October 1995 served to intensify internal divisions on the party's future course. In December 1995 the FDP Justice Minister, Sabine Leutheusser-Schnarrenberger, resigned after her party colleagues had backed a government plan to institute electronic surveillance of suspected criminals.

After relaunching itself with a more right-wing orientation in January 1996, the FDP polled strongly in state elections in Baden-Württemberg, Rhineland-Palatinate and Schleswig-Holstein in March, winning representation in all three contests. A party congress in June 1996 confirmed the shift to the right, adopting a new programme which placed less emphasis on civil liberties than previous texts. The FDP shared in the defeat of the ruling coalition in the September 1998 federal elections, slipping to 6.3% of the vote and 43 seats.

In opposition, the FDP again failed to secure European representation in June 1999, winning only 3.0% of the national vote, and also fared moderately in state elections in 1999. It gained ground in Schleswig-Holstein in February 2000 and then had a major success in North Rhine–Westphalia in May, returning to the state parliament with 9.8% of the vote. Nevertheless, increasing criticism of Gerhardt resulted in his resignation as party chairman in January 2001 and his replacement by Guido Westerwelle, Gerhardt becoming parliamentary group leader. Hitherto FDP secretary-general, Westerwelle quickly announced the termination of the party's longstanding centre-right alignment with the CDU, declaring that the FDP would contest the 2002 federal elections "on its own" with its options open. The FDP polled 7.4% of the national vote in the 2002 elections and gained 47 seats in the *Bundestag* (up from 43 in the previous parliament). However the party's campaign was overshadowed by a political row over what were seen by many as anti-Semitic comments made in campaign literature in the state of North Rhine–Westphalia by local grandee and nationally-renowned member of the *Bundestag* (MdB), Jürgen Möllemann. The "Möllemann row" would end in tragedy the following year when, on June 5, 2003, Möllemann – a keen parachutist – was killed when he became separated from his parachute during a routine jump.

The FDP has a mixed record of success at the state level and is not represented in 6 out of 16 legislatures. In July 2004 the FDP held office as a junior coalition partner to the CDU in Baden-Württemberg, Saxony-Anhalt, and Lower Saxony. In the June 13, 2004, elections to the European Parliament it polled 6.1% of the national vote and won 7 seats in the European Parliament.

Having an official membership of around 67,000, the FDP is a member party of the Liberal International and of the European Liberal, Democratic and Reformist Party (ELDR).

German People's Union
Deutsche Volksunion (DVU)

Address. Postfach 600464, 81204 Munich
Telephone. (49–89) 896–0850
Fax. (49-89) 834–1534
Email. info@dvu.net
Website. www.dvu.net
Leadership. Gerhard Frey (chairman)

The extreme right-wing DVU claims not to be a neo-fascist party but has been prominent in anti-foreigner and anti-immigration agitation, contending that the majority of Germans want a "racially pure" country. In 1987 Frey launched a DVU/List D movement (the D signifying *Deutschland*) as an electoral alliance which included elements of the National Democratic Party of Germany and which won one seat in the Bremen state elections of September 1987. In January 1990 the DVU participated in the creation of the German Social Union in East Germany, although with minimal lasting electoral impact. Following unification the DVU increased its Bremen representation to six seats in 1991 (with 6.2% of the vote) and also won six seats in Schleswig-Holstein in 1992 (with 6.3%).

The DVU backed the unsuccessful Republicans in the October 1994 federal elections in the wake of reports that the two groups might overcome their longstanding rivalry for the far-right vote. In the May 1995 Bremen elections the DVU declined to 2.5% and lost its representation in the state assembly. It also failed to retain any seats in the Schleswig-Holstein state election on March 1996, taking only 4.3% of the vote. It had more success in the depressed eastern state of Saxony-Anhalt in April 1998, producing the best post-war performance for a far-right party by winning 12.9% of the vote and 16 of the 116 seats.

The DVU obtained only 1.2% of the vote standing in its own right in the September 1998 federal elections; but it returned to the Bremen state parliament in June 1999, winning only 3% of the vote but being awarded one seat because its vote in Bremerhaven was 6%. In September 1999 it returned five members in elections in Brandenburg, giving it representation in three state parliaments. It did not campaign during the 2002 *Bundestag* elections or the 2004 European Parliament elections but, as of July 2004, the party planned to fight two state elections in September 2004, in Brandenburg and Saxony. In July 2004 the DVU has 5 representatives in the Brandenburg state parliament and 1 representative in Bremen.

Law and Order Offensive Party
Partei Rechtsstaatlicher Offensive (PRO)

Address. Gotenstraße 12, 20097 Hamburg
Telephone. (49–40) 2442-300
Fax. (49–40) 2442-300
Email. geschaeftsstelle@offensive-hamburg.de
Leadership. Markus Wagner (chairman); Wolfgang Jabbusch (first deputy chairman)

The populist PRO was launched in July 2000 by Ronald Schill, a former Hamburg judge who had achieved notoriety for his robust views on law and order, which included support for the death penalty and the castration of sex offenders. Known in the press as the "black sheriff" or "judge merciless" for handing down severe sentences for relatively minor offences, Schill had been dismissed from the Hamburg bench in 1997 for advocating the restoration of capital punishment for "bestial" murders and contract killings. As leader of the new PRO, he accused the government then in power in Hamburg of failing to deal with the city's spiraling crime rate, claiming that it was ten times higher than that of Munich and closely related to the recent influx of large numbers of immigrants.

The PRO's campaign for the September 2001 elections in Hamburg was boosted by the discovery that three of the suspected perpetrators of the terrorist attacks on the USA on Sept. 11 had lived for a time in Hamburg, whose authorities were accused by Schill of having provided "the best conditions for their work". The results showed that in its first electoral contest the PRO had won 19.4% of the vote and 25 of the 121 seats in the Hamburg parliament, drawing votes in particular from previous supporters of the far-right German People's Union (DVU). After the elections the PRO joined a coalition with the Christian Democratic Union and the Free Democratic Party which ended 44 years of government by the Social Democratic Party of Germany in Hamburg. Schill became the state interior minister. There then followed a period of relative success for what had become known as the "Schill party", in which the PRO polled 4.5% in state elections in Saxony-Anhalt in April 2002 and 4.4% in May 2003 in Bremen. It also fought the 2002 *Bundestag* elections but failed to make an impact, getting less than 1% of the vote.

In August 2003 Schill was sacked as interior minister following a scandal in which it was alleged that he had tried to blackmail the mayor, Ole von Beust, to stop him dismissing one of Schill's senior aides. As a result of this scandal, Schill left the PRO and claimed that he had now withdrawn from politics. Since Schill's departure the PRO has failed to make any impact on politics in Germany. It maintains party organizations in all the German states, but in state elections has only managed to poll a fraction of its previous support, and even in Hamburg it only managed 0.4% in the state elections of February 2004.

National Democratic Party of Germany
National-demokratische Partei Deutschlands (NPD)

Address. Postfach 840157, D-12531 Berlin

Website www.npd.de

Leadership. Udo Voigt (chairman), Ulrich Eigenfeld (general secretary)

The NPD was founded in Hannover in 1964 as result of the collapse of the ultra-conservative German Reich Party. It enjoyed some prominence during the economic downturn of the mid-1960s but even then failed to scale the 5% electoral hurdle in the 1965 *Bundestag* elections. During the 1970s and 1980s, the NPD operated on the fringe of the German party systems, often in alliance with the DVU. However, in the 1990s the party underwent a process of radicalization and adopted a new strategy that included extra-parliamentary action and developing close links with the Skinhead scene and other neo-Nazi milieus. As a result, the SPD-Green federal government tried unsuccessfully to ban the party. In April 1995 then leader Günter Deckert received a prison sentence for incitement to racial hatred and other offences. The party won 0.3% of the vote in the 1998 federal elections and 0.4% in 1999 Euro-elections, becoming the most prominent far-right formation. In July 2004 the NPD was not represented in any state parliaments in Germany.

Party of Democratic Socialism
Partei der Demokratischen Sozialismus (PDS)

Address. Kleine Alexanderstrasse 28, 10178 Berlin

Telephone. (49–30) 240–090

Fax. (49–30) 241–1046

Email. bundesgeschaeftsstelle@pds-online.de

Website. Sozialisten.de/sozialisten/aktuell/index.htm

Leadership. Lothar Bisky (chairperson); Roland Kutzmutz (general secretary)

The PDS was established under its present name in February 1990 amid the collapse of Communist rule in East Germany,

being descended from the former ruling Socialist Unity Party of Germany (*Sozialistische Einheitspartei Deutschlands*, SED), although it sought to throw off this provenance by espousing a commitment to multi-party democracy. The SED itself had been created in April 1946 as an enforced merger of the East German Social Democratic Party of Germany (SPD) with the dominant Soviet-backed Communist Party of Germany (*Kommunistische Partei Deutschlands*, KPD). The KPD had been founded in December 1918 by the left-wing minority of the SPD and other leftist elements and had played an important opposition role in the inter-war Weimar Republic, usually in conflict with the SPD, until being outlawed on the advent to power of Hitler's Nazi regime in 1933. During the Third Reich many German Communists had taken refuge in Moscow, returning to Germany at the end of World War II to assume power in the eastern Soviet-occupied zone.

In what became the German Democratic Republic (GDR), the SED was effectively the sole ruling party for over four decades, operating through the familiar device of a National Front that included four other "democratic" parties supportive of socialism, namely the Christian Democratic Union, the Democratic Farmers' Party, the Liberal Democratic Party and the National Democratic Party. Walter Ulbricht was elected SED leader in 1950, in which year several leading party members were expelled in the wake of Yugoslavia's break with the Cominform; other were purged in consequence of the major anti-government uprising in East Berlin in 1953. Some of these expellees were rehabilitated in 1956, but further purges followed the Hungarian Uprising later that year. Economic difficulties and the nationalization of agriculture served to increase the exodus of East Germans to the West, to staunch which the authorities erected the Berlin Wall in 1961, extending it along the entire length of the border with West Germany. In August 1968 East German troops participated in the Soviet-led military intervention that crushed the "Prague Spring" in Czechoslovakia.

In May 1971 Ulbricht was replaced as SED leader by Erich Honecker, under whom East Germany normalized its relations with West Germany in 1972 and became a UN member in 1974. In the 1980s Honecker maintained a rigid orthodoxy, showing no enthusiasm for the post-1985 reform policies of Mikhail Gorbachev in the USSR. In 1989, however, a rising tide of protest and renewed flight of East German citizens to the West via Hungary resulted in Honecker being replaced in October by Egon Krenz, who himself resigned in December after the historic opening of the Berlin Wall on Nov. 9 had unleashed irresistible pressure for change. Later in December an emergency SED congress abandoned Marxism, added the suffix "Party of Democratic Socialism" to the party's name and elected Gregor Gysi as chairman. A government of "national responsibility" appointed in February 1990 contained a minority of Communists for the first time in East Germany's history, although Hans Modrow of the SED-PDS retained the premiership. Having dropped the SED component from its name, the PDS polled better than expected in multi-party elections in March 1990 (winning 16.4% of the vote), assisted by the personal standing of Modrow. It nevertheless went into opposition to a broad coalition of parties committed to German reunification.

In the all-German *Bundestag* elections of December 1990 the PDS won only 2.4% of the overall vote but scored 11.1% in the eastern *Länder* and was therefore allocated 17 of the 662 seats by virtue of the separate application of the 5% threshold rule to the two parts of Germany. Thereafter the PDS suffered from a tide of disclosures about the evils of the former SED regime, but retained a substantial following among easterners disadvantaged by rapid economic and social change. In February 1993 Gysi was succeeded as PDS chairman by Lothar Bisky, under whom the party polled strongly in elections in the eastern *Länder* in 1993–94. Although the PDS failed to win representation in the June 1994 Euro-elections, in the October 1994 federal elections it increased its national vote share to 4.4% and its eastern share to around 18%, being allocated 30 *Bundestag* seats from the proportional pool by virtue of having returned three candidates in a single electoral district (Berlin).

In January 1995 a PDS congress voted in favor of a "left-wing democratic" programme and voted down the party's Stalinist faction led by Sarah Wagenknecht. In June 1995 the PDS received a financial boost when an independent commission agreed that it could retain a proportion of the former SED's assets. In Berlin legislative elections in October 1995 the PDS advanced to 14.6% of the vote (giving it 34 of the 206 seats), mainly at the expense of the SPD. Whereas the SPD's then leader, Rudolf Scharping, had consistently rejected any co-operation with the PDS, his successor elected in November 1995, Oskar Lafontaine, envisaged building a broad progressive front, including the PDS, to challenge the Kohl government in the next federal elections. The PDS was the only major party to oppose the proposed merger of Berlin and Brandenburg, which voters of the latter rejected in a referendum in May 1996.

Having polled strongly in Saxony-Anhalt in April 1998 (winning 19.6% and 25 seats), the PDS for the first time surmounted the national 5% barrier in the September 1998 federal elections, winning 5.1% of the vote and 36 seats. In simultaneous state elections in Mecklenburg–West Pomerania, moreover, the PDS advanced to 25.5% and 20 seats, on the strength of which it entered government for the first time in the new Germany, as junior coalition partner to the SPD. Having become a supporter of European integration, the PDS entered the European Parliament for the first time in June 1999, winning a 5.8% vote share and six seats. It then registered major advances in eastern state elections, benefiting from the unpopularity of the SPD-led federal coalition and continuing high unemployment in eastern Germany. In polling in Thuringia and Saxony in September 1999 it pushed the SPD into third place by taking, respectively, 21.4% and 22.2% of the vote. In the Berlin elections in October 1999 the PDS won 17.7% and 33 seats. The party was also strengthened in the *Bundestag* by the defection of a left-wing SPD deputy in late 1999, with the result that PDS representation increased to 37 seats. In June 2004 the PDS was a participant in state-level government in coalition with the SPD in two states: Mecklenburg-Western Pomerania and Berlin.

Despite a generational renewal of the PDS leadership in October 2000 and the adoption of a new strategy document in April 2001, the party did badly in the 2002 *Bundestag* elections. With only 4% of the vote, the party failed to scale the 5% barrier to party list representation and thus are only represented by two directly-elected MdBs. It also means that the PDS is no longer an official parliamentary faction in the *Bundestag* and thus do not have access to the parliamentary resources they enjoyed previously. Nevertheless, in the June 13, 2004, European Parliament elections the PDS polled an impressive 6.1% of the national vote and won 7 seats in the European Parliament.

The PDS members of the European Parliament sit in the European United Left/Nordic Green Left group. The party has an official membership of 70,805.

The Republicans
Die Republikaner

Address. Postfach 87 02 10, D-13162 Berlin
Telephone. (49–1805) 737-000
Fax. (49–49) 737-111
Email. info@rep.de
Website. www2.rep.de

Leadership. Rolf Schlierer (federal chairman)

The far-right anti-immigration Republicans were established as a party in November 1983 by two former *Bundestag* deputies of the Bavarian Christian Social Union (CSU) who had criticized the alleged dictatorial style of the then CSU leader, Franz Josef Strauss, particularly as regards the latter's involvement in developing relations with East Germany in contravention of CSU policy. Standing for German reunification, lower business taxes and restrictions on foreigners, the new party was also joined by the small Citizens' Party (*Bürgerpartei*) of Baden-Württemberg. Having won only 3% in their first electoral contest, for the Bavarian *Landtag* in 1986, the Republicans did not contest the 1987 federal elections. Under the leadership of former SS officer Franz Schönhuber, however, the party won 7.5% and 11 seats in the January 1989 Berlin legislative elections. It also did well in the June 1989 European Parliament elections, winning 7.1% and six seats (on a platform of opposition to European integration).

Amid the progression to reunification in 1990, the Republicans' electoral appeal waned. They obtained less than 2% in state elections in North Rhine-Westphalia and Lower Saxony in May 1990, whereupon Schönhuber was briefly ousted from the party chairmanship, recovering the post in July. In the December 1990 all-German elections the party managed only 2.1% (and no seats), while in simultaneous polling it lost its representation in Berlin, falling to 3.1%. The party made a comeback in the Baden-Württemberg state elections in April 1992, winning 10.9% of the vote and 15 seats. In May 1993, moreover, it secured *Bundestag* representation for the first time when it was joined by a right-wing deputy of the Christian Democratic Union (CDU), Rudolf Krause. In June 1994, however, it failed to retain its European Parliament seats (falling to a 3.9% vote share), while in the October 1994 *Bundestag* elections the Republicans won only 1.9% (and no seats). Prior to the federal polling Schönhuber was again deposed as leader, officially because of an unauthorized meeting with the leader of the German People's Union, but also because of his negative media image.

In state elections in March 1996, the Republicans again polled strongly in Baden-Württemberg, winning 9.1% and 14 seats, while in Rhineland-Palatinate they improved to 3.5%, without gaining representation. In the September 1998 federal elections, however, the Republicans managed only 1.8% of the vote, subsequently falling back to 1.7% in the June 1999 European Parliament elections. In March 2001 the party lost its representation in Baden-Württemberg, slumping to only 4.4% of the vote. As of July 2004 the Republicans have no representatives in state parliaments in Germany.

In the 2002 *Bundestag* elections the Republicans polled 280,735 votes and in the 2004 European Parliament elections the party polled 485, 691 votes or 1.9% of votes cast.

Social Democratic Party of Germany
Sozialdemokratische Partei Deutschlands (SPD)

Address. Willy-Brandt-Haus, Wilhelmstrasse 140, 10963 Berlin
Telephone. (49–30) 259–910
Fax. (49–30) 2599–1720
Email. parteivorstand@spd.de
Website. www.spd.de

Leadership. Franz Münterfering (chairman and parliamentary group leader)); Kurt Beck, Wolfgang Clement, Wolfgang Thierse and Ute Voigt (deputy chairpersons); Klaus-Uwe Benneter (secretary-general)

The origins of the SPD lie in the reformist General Association of German Workers (*Allgemeiner Deutscher Arbeiterverein*, ADA) founded by Ferdinand Lassalle in 1863 and the Social Democratic Labour Party (*Sozialdemokratische Arbeiterpartei*, SDAP) founded by the Marxists Wilhelm Liebknecht and August Bebel in 1869. In 1875 these two forerunners merged to form the Socialist Labour Party of Germany (*Sozialistische Arbeiterpartei Deutschlands*, SAPD), which was outlawed from 1878 under Chancellor Bismarck's anti-socialist laws. Re-legalized in 1890, the SAPD became the SPD at the 1891 Erfurt congress, when the party reaffirmed its Marxist belief in inevitable socialist revolution, although in practice it was already following the reformist line advocated by Eduard Bernstein. Representing the rapidly expanding industrial working class and benefiting from universal male suffrage, the SAPD became the largest party in the *Reichstag* in 1912, although it played no part in Germany's unrepresentative government before 1914.

Ideological divisions within the SPD were intensified by World War I, during which the party split into a "majority" reformist wing supportive of the German war effort and the anti-war "Independent Social Democrats" led by Liebknecht and Rosa Luxemburg. Most of the latter faction joined the Communist Party of Germany founded in December 1918, while the main SPD became a key supporter of the post-war Weimar Republic, of which party leader Friedrich Ebert was the first Chancellor and the first President (from 1919 to 1925). SPD participation in most Weimar coalition governments was accompanied by theoretical criticism of capitalism, notably in the Heidelberg Programme of 1925, but thereafter the party was identified as a defender of the status quo against Soviet-backed Bolshevism on the left and the rising tide of fascism on the right. In the July 1932 elections the SPD was overtaken as the largest party by Hitler's National Socialist German Workers' Party (the Nazis), the latter winning 37.4% and the SPD 24.3%. In further elections in November 1932 the Nazis fell back to 33.2% and the SPD to 20.7%, while the Communists increased from 14.3% to 17%. Nevertheless, Hitler was appointed Chancellor in January 1933 and was granted emergency powers following the burning of the *Reichstag* the following month. In new elections in March 1933 the Nazis won 43.9% against 18.3% for the SPD and 12.1% for the Communists, whereupon an enabling act approved by the non-Nazi centre-right parties (but not by the SPD) gave Hitler absolute power to ban his political opponents, including the SPD.

After World War II the SPD was re-established in both the Western and the Soviet occupation zones, headed in the former by Kurt Schumacher and in the latter by Otto Grotewohl. The East German SPD was quickly constrained to merge with the Communists in the Socialist Unity Party of Germany (SED), founded in April 1946. In the first elections to the West German *Bundestag* in August 1949 the SPD came a close second to the Christian Democrats, with a 29.2% vote share, and was the principal opposition party until 1966, under the leadership of Schumacher until his death in 1952, then of Erich Ollenhauer and from 1958 of Willy Brandt (the mayor of West Berlin). During this opposition phase, the SPD's federal vote slipped to 28.8% in 1953 but then rose steadily, to 31.8% in 1957, 36.2% in 1961 and 39.3% in 1965. Faced with the evidence of West Germany's economic miracle of the 1950s, the SPD in 1959 adopted its celebrated Godesberg Programme, which jettisoned Marxist theory, embraced private ownership within the context of an equitable social order and industrial co-determination (*Mitbestimmung*), and reversed the party's previous opposition to NATO and the European Community.

In October 1966 the SPD entered a West German federal government for the first time, in a coalition headed by the Christian Democratic Union (CDU) and the Bavarian Christian Social Union (CSU). Brandt became Vice-Chancellor and Foreign Minister, in which capacity he pursued an *Ostpolitik* seeking normalization of relations with the Communist-ruled East European states, including East Germany. In March 1969 Gustav Heinemann became West Germany's first SPD President, elected with the backing of the Free Democratic Party (FDP). In the September 1969 federal elections the SPD at last broke the 40% barrier, winning 42.7% of the vote and forming a centre-left coalition with the FDP. Brandt became West German Chancellor and led the SPD to a further advance in the 1972 *Bundestag* elections, to a post-war high of 45.8% of the vote. Brandt continued as head of an SPD/FDP coalition until 1974, when the discovery that a close aide was an East German spy forced him to resign. He was succeeded as Chancellor by Helmut Schmidt (although Brandt remained SPD chairperson) and the SPD/FDP coalition under Schmidt's leadership continued in power through the 1976 and 1980 federal elections, in which the SPD vote was 42.6% and 42.9% respectively.

The SPD/FDP government finally collapsed in September 1982, when the FDP withdrew and opted to join a coalition headed by the CDU/CSU. The SPD remained in opposition after the March 1983 and January 1987 *Bundestag* elections, in which its support fell back to 38.2% and 37.0% respectively, eroded in particular by the advancing Greens. Brandt finally resigned as SPD chairman in March 1987, when the party objected to his appointment of a non-SPD Greek lady as his spokesperson. He was succeeded by Hans-Jochen Vogel, a prominent SPD moderate, who launched a major reappraisal of the party's basic policy programme, although without achieving a definitive resolution of the vexed question of whether the SPD should formally commit to a future federal coalition with the Greens. In the latter context, however, the "red–green" coalition formed in 1985 between the SPD and the Greens in the state of Hesse set a trend of co-operation between the SPD and what was later named the Alliance 90/The Greens.

The sudden collapse of East European communism from late 1989 caught the opposition SPD on the back foot, with the result that it tended to follow in the wake of events leading to German reunification in October 1990. Launched in October 1989, an East German SPD led by Ibrahim Böhme won 21.9% of the vote in multi-party elections in March 1990 and joined an eastern "grand coalition" government. Böhme quickly resigned on being found to have been a Stasi agent and was succeeded by Markus Meckel (then East German Foreign Minister), who was himself replaced by Wolfgang Thierse in June 1990. In September 1990 the East and West German SPDs were merged, but the party found it difficult to recover its pre-war strength in the east. Oskar Lafontaine was the SPD's Chancellor-candidate in the December 1990 all-German *Bundestag* elections, in which the party won only 33.5% of the overall vote (35.7% in the western *Länder*, 24.3% in the east), which yielded 239 of the 662 seats.

The SPD therefore continued in opposition and Vogel immediately resigned as SPD chairman, being succeeded by Björn Engholm, then premier of Schleswig-Holstein. In November 1992 a special SPD conference endorsed a leadership recommendation that the party should give qualified backing to government-proposed constitutional amendments which would end the automatic right of entry to asylum-seekers and would allow German forces to be deployed outside the NATO area on UN-approved peacekeeping missions. Damaged by the revival of an old political scandal, Engholm resigned as SPD leader in May 1993 and was succeeded by Rudolf Scharping (then premier of Rhineland-Palatinate). In the June 1994 European Parliament elections the SPD slipped to 32.2% of the vote (from 37.3% in 1989) and won 40 of the 99 German seats. Scharping then led the SPD to its fourth successive federal election defeat in October 1994, although its share of the vote improved to 36.4% and its representation in the *Bundestag* rose to 252 seats out of 672. Concurrent SPD advances at state level gave it a majority in the *Bundesrat* (upper house), although in May 1995 the party lost ground in North Rhine-Westphalia and Bremen, and in October went down to a heavy defeat in Berlin (once an SPD stronghold).

In November 1995 an SPD conference in Mannheim elected Oskar Lafontaine (then premier of Saarland) as SPD chairman in succession to Scharping, who remained the SPD leader in the *Bundestag*. Located ideologically on the SPD left, Lafontaine had opposed the Maastricht Treaty on European union, on the grounds that it contained inadequate provisions for real political union, and was also an advocate of a political alliance between the SPD, the Greens and the (ex-communist) Party of Democratic Socialism (PDS). He took the SPD into a stance of opposition to any speedy adoption of a single European currency and to the automatic granting of citizenship to ethnic German immigrants from Russia. The party suffered further setbacks in three state elections in March 1996 and also lost ground in Hamburg in September 1997.

In March 1998 the SPD executive elected Gerhard Schröder, an ideological pragmatist who had just won a third term as minister-president of Lower Saxony, as the party's Chancellor-candidate in preference to Lafontaine, who continued as party chairman. Gains for the SPD in Saxony-Anhalt in April were followed by a significant advance in the September 1998 federal elections, in which the SPD vote increased to 40.9% and its *Bundestag* representation to 298 seats. The following month Schröder formed an historic "red-green" federal coalition with the Greens, on the basis of a government programme setting the fight against unemployment as the main priority and also including Green objectives such as an "ecological tax reform" and the phasing-out of nuclear power generation.

SPD-Green strains quickly developed on the nuclear and other issues, but more damage was done to the government by divisions between Schröder and Finance Minister Lafontaine, the former advocating a "New Middle" (*Neue Mitte*) course, the latter preferring a traditional social democratic line. In March 1999 Lafontaine resigned from the government and also as SPD chairman, following a major disagreement with the Chancellor, who was elected as SPD party leader in April. The following month Johannes Rau (former SPD minister-president of North Rhine-Westphalia) was elected as President of Germany by 690 votes in the 1,338-member Federal Assembly. He served in that post until July 1, 2004.

In European Parliament elections in June 1999 the SPD slipped to 30.7% of the vote, losing seven of its 40 seats. Amid growing public disquiet about the federal government's performance, state elections in September–October 1999 saw the SPD being relegated to third place in Saxony and Thuringia, being ousted from power in Saarland and losing ground in Brandenburg and Berlin. The losses meant that the SPD-led federal government commanded only 26 out of 69 votes in the *Bundesrat* (the upper legislative house representing the states).

The SPD's negative electoral trend was reversed in Schleswig-Holstein in February 2000, partly because of the funding scandal then besetting the CDU. It also remained dominant in North Rhine–Westphalia in May, although its vote share fell by over 3%. Despite much criticism of SPD ministers over the outbreak of "mad cow disease" (BSE) in Germany in November 2000 and darkening economic clouds, the SPD continued its electoral recovery in Baden-Württemberg and Rhineland–Palatinate in March 2001, its 8% advance in the former being attributed to glamorous state SPD leader Ute Vogt, who at 36 was the youngest lead candidate of any major party in modern German history. In June 2001, moreover, the CDU-SPD coalition in Berlin was replaced by one led by the SPD and including the Greens, dependent on the external support of the PDS. The new SPD

mayor of Berlin, Klaus Wowereit, became the first prominent German politician to announce that he was a homosexual.

The 2002 *Bundestag* elections saw the SPD returned to power as senior partner in a "red-green" coalition with the Greens. Nevertheless, the SPD's own vote share compared with the previous election fell from 40.9% to 38.5%. In addition the SPD also picked up four "overhang seats" (*Überhangmandate*), which are apportioned after the election on a territorial basis. The 2002 *Bundestag* elections highlighted some worrying trends for the SPD. The party's vote fell by 4% in western Germany, although this was cancelled out to some extent by picking up 4.6% in the east. It also lost 5% amongst male and (its core) working class voters. These voters appear to have gone straight across to the CDU (which gained 6% and 8% in these respective categories of voters).

Despite returning to government, the SPD has in recent years seen a major hemorrhaging of support, with opinion polls consistently putting the party up to 20% behind the CDU/CSU. This drop in support in the polls was also evident in the 2004 European Parliament elections, in which it polled a disastrous 21.5% (down 9.2% on 1999) and in the state parliament elections in Thuringia on the same day in which it polled 14.5% (down 4.0%).

As of July 2004 the SPD no longer had sole control in any state government. It was a participant in government in 7 of the states, as the senior partner in coalition with either the CDU (Bremen, Brandenburg), Greens (Saxony-Anhalt, North Rhine-Westphalia), the PDS (Mecklenburg-Western Pomerania, Berlin) or FDP (Rhineland Palatinate)

With an official membership of 650,798, the SPD is a member party of the Socialist International. Its European Parliament representatives sit in the Party of European Socialists group.

Other Parties

Some 80 other parties are officially registered in Germany. The following is a selection of those parties that have obtained some degree of support in recent federal, state or European Parliament elections.

Animal Rights Party (*Tierschutzpartei*, TP), won 0.3% in 1998 federal elections and 0.7% in 1999 Euro-elections.
Address. Fritz-Schumacher-Weg 111, 60488 Frankfurt
Telephone. (49–69) 768096-59
Fax. (49–69) 768096-63
Website. www.tierschutzpartei.de
Leadership. Jürgen Gerlach

Bavaria Party (*Bayernpartei*, BP), founded in 1946 to seek the restoration of an independent Bavarian state, represented in the *Bundestag* in 1949-53 (but not since) and influential in the Bavarian *Landtag* until the mid-1960s.
Address. Unter Weidenstrasse 14, 81543 Munich
Telephone. (49–89) 651–8051
Fax. (49–89) 654–259
Email. bayernpart@aol.com
Leadership. Dorn Hubert (chairman)

Car-Drivers' Party of Germany (*Autofahrer Partei Deutschlands*, APD)
Address. Emilstrasse 71A, 44869 Bochum
Telephone/Fax. (49–30) 69536971
Email. autofahrerpartei@aol.com
Website. www.autofahrerpartei.de
Leadership. Dr E. Hörber (chairman)

Christian Middle (*Christliche Mitte*, CM), won 0.2% in 1994 European elections, falling to 0.1% in 1999.
Address. Lippstädter Strasse 42, 59329 Liesborn

Telephone. (49–2523) 8388
Fax. (49–2523) 6138
Email. christliche-mitte@t-online.de
Leadership. Adelgunde Menelsacker

German Communist Party (*Deutsche Kommunistische Partei*, DKP), founded in West Germany in 1969 some 13 years after the banning of its predecessor, for long led by Herbert Mies, had close links with the then ruling Socialist Unity Party of East Germany, but lost any impetus on the collapse of the East German regime in 1989; Mies resigned in October 1989 and was replaced by a four-member council at the party's 10th congress in March 1990; won negligible vote in 1994 and 1998 federal elections.
Address. Hoffnungstrasse 18, 45127 Essen
Telephone. (49–201) 1778-890
Fax. (49–201) 1778-829
Email. dkp.pv@t-online.de

The Greys (*Die Grauen*), also known as the Grey Panthers, formerly a pensioners' group within the West German Greens, became a separate party in mid-1989 to represent the interests of older citizens; won 0.8% of the federal vote in 1990, 0.5% in 1994 and 0.3% in 1998, recovering to 0.4% in 1999 Euro-elections.
Address. Postfach 2000 665, D-42206 Wuppertal
Telephone. (49–202) 280–700
Fax. (49–202) 280–7070
Email. info@die-grauen.de
Leadership. Trude Unruh

Islamic Party of Germany (*Islamische Partei Deutschlands*, IPD), based in Germany's Muslim immigrant communities.
Address. Bereiteranger 11, 81541 Munich
Telephone. (49–89) 6511–5190
Fax. (49–89) 6511–5195
Email. ipd_info@fireball.de
Leadership. Sulaiman Hani

Marxist-Leninist Party of Germany (*Marxistisch-Leninistische Partei Deutschlands*, MLPD), Maoist formation whose belief in Marxist-Leninist precepts has survived their collapse in European countries where they were once practiced.
Address. Kostrasse 8, 45899 Gelsenkirchen
Telephone. (49–209) 951–940
Fax. (49–209) 951–9460
Email. mlpd_zk@compuserve.com
Website. www.mlpd.de
Leadership. Stefan Engel

South Schleswig Voters' Union (*Südschleswigscher Wählerverband*, SSW/*Sydslesvig Vaelgerforening*, SSV). The SSW was founded in 1948 to represent the ethnic Danish minority in the northern state of Schleswig-Holstein and has a current membership of 4,500. Enjoying exemption from the 5% threshold rule in state elections, the party won one seat in the 1992 Schleswig-Holstein elections with 1.9% of the vote, increasing to two seats in 1996 with 2.5%. It made further progress in the February 2000 elections, receiving 60,367 votes (4.1%) and being allocated three of the 89 seats in the state legislature.
Address. Norderstraße 74, D-24939 Flensburg
Telephone. (49–461) 1440–8300
Fax. (49–461) 1440–8303
Email. info@ssw-sh.de
Website. www.ssw-sh.de
Leadership. Gerda Eichhorn (chairperson); Anke Spoorendonk (parliamentary group leader); Dieter Lenz (secretary-general)

Ghana

Capital: Accra
Population: 19,533,500 (2000E)

Political parties have had a chequered history in Ghana because of political instability, which has plagued Ghanaian politics since independence in 1957 from Britain. Since the overthrow of the country's first President, Kwame Nkrumah, in 1966, Ghana has experienced several long periods of military rule, the military being in power in 1966-69, 1972-79 and 1981-92. This instability has created a sense of incapacity among political parties in performing their roles effectively in the areas of representation, integration, recruitment and training, making government accountable and organizing opposition. However, in recent years, with elections having been held in 1992, 1996 and 2000, parties have increasingly been able to develop these roles.

The Provisional National Defence Council (PNDC), which was in power from December 1981, relinquished power in January 1993 under a civilian constitution approved in a referendum in April 1992. The ban on the operation of political associations imposed in 1982 was lifted in May 1992. Presidential and legislative elections were held in November and December 1992 respectively, as a prelude to the inauguration of the Fourth Republic in January 1993. Flt.-Lt. (rtd.) Jerry Rawlings, who had come to power as a result of a coup in December 1981, was elected President with over 58% of the votes cast. His National Democratic Congress (NDC) also won an overwhelming victory in the simultaneous legislative polls, which were boycotted by the opposition parties.

In December 1996 Rawlings was re-elected President with 57% of the votes cast, while the NDC won 133 of the 200 parliamentary seats in the same month's legislative elections. Having served two four-year terms, Rawlings was ineligible to stand in the December 2000 presidential election, which was won by John Kufuor of the New Patriotic Party (NPP) with 57% in the second round, while the NDC candidate, Vice-President John Atta Mills, won 43%. The NPP won 100 seats in the December 2000 legislative elections, as against 92 for the NDC; of the remaining seats, three were won by the People's National Convention (PNC), one by the Convention People's Party (CPP) and four by independents.

The 1992 Constitution and the Political Parties Act (Act 574), 2000, make provision for political parties to promote internal democracy. Article 55 (5) of the 1992 Constitution stipulates that: "The internal organization of a political party shall conform to democratic principles and its actions and purposes shall not contravene or be inconsistent with this Constitution or any other law". Similarly, Section 9(a) of the Political Parties Act, 2000, enjoins the Electoral Commission not to register a political party unless: "The internal organization of the party conforms with democratic principles and its actions and purposes are not contrary to or inconsistent with the Constitution".

In the election of executive officers of the parties, the Political Parties Act provides that these executive officers be elected by members of the party. The Act has made it mandatory for the Electoral Commission (EC) to supervise the election of national, regional and constituency executive officers of the political parties. This has been regarded by some as an unwelcome intrusion into the affairs of political parties by the state. However, it is doubtful whether the supervision of intra-party elections by the EC has improved the internal democracy within the parties. In practice, despite parties' formally democratic organization, power tends to be concentrated in the hands of a small group of party leaders. The structure of Ghanaian parties is generally centralized and the mass membership has little say on issues such as party policy. The formal accountability of party leaders to rank and file activists through mechanisms such as party congresses is often imperfectly achieved in practice due to the domination which leaders often exert over their parties. Most of the parties in Ghana seem to be involved in "machine politics", in which party bosses control their parties through patronage and the distribution of favours.

The lack of internal democracy seems to have undermined the stability, cohesion and peace of some of the political parties, especially the National Democratic Congress (NDC), with factionalism, open disagreement and rivalry the outcome. In addition, non-adherence to internal democratic principles has stalled moves to re-unite the Nkrumahist parties (such as the Convention People's Party and the People's National Convention) because one or two leaders do not wish to go through the democratic selection process to fulfill their ambition of becoming a presidential candidate. In some cases, apparently better qualified candidates are pressured to withdraw from intra-party elections in favour of candidates close to party leaders and party leaderships are controlled by those who have funded the party.

One other feature of Ghanaian political parties is the creation of alliances which are formed to contest elections but which are not sustained because of fundamental differences between the parties. In the 1996 elections, for instance, two alliances were formed. They were the Progressive Alliance – made up of the totally dominant National Democratic Congress (NDC) and two smaller parties, the Every Ghanaian Living Everywhere (EGLE) and Democratic People's Party (DPP) – and the Progressive Alliance, which consisted of the New Patriotic Party (NPP) and a faction of the Nkrumahist parties, the People's Convention Party (an amalgam of the People's Heritage Party, National Independence Party and a section of the National Convention Party, which all separately fought the 1992 presidential elections). For the 2004 elections, there is the Great Coalition, comprising the People's National Convention (PNC), EGLE and Great Consolidated Popular Party (GCPP). The inability to sustain these alliances has led some commentators to describe them as "unholy marriages".

State funding of political parties has been advocated as a way of promoting a level playing field. Indeed, there is a consensus among the political parties in favour of public financing of their activities. On the other hand, some people also believe that state funding if not carefully handled can be a drain on the national treasury and a reflection of the behaviour of a cartel interested in promoting a sectarian agenda, instead of a national one. It is also feared that state funding can also degenerate into a social welfare scheme for unemployed politicians.

Convention People's Party (CPP)
Address. 60 Mango Tree Avenue, Asylum Down, POB 10939, Accra-North
Telephone. (+233-21) 227763
Leadership. Edmund Delle (chairman); Nii Noi Duwuona

(general secretary)
The name Convention People's Party – associated historically with the late Kwame Nkrumah, Ghana's first President – was adopted prior to the 2000 election campaign by the party hitherto known as the People's Convention Party (PCP). The PCP was itself formed in 1998 through the merger of the National Independence Party (NIP) and People's Heritage Party (PHP), which together had won five seats in the 1996 parliamentary elections, and the National Convention Party (NCP), which had ceased to serve as junior coalition partner of the then ruling National Democratic Congress in 1995 and had been refused permission to contest the 1996 elections on the grounds that it had not followed correct nomination procedures.

Having fielded 35 candidates, the CPP won one seat in the December 2000 parliamentary elections. Its presidential candidate, George Hagan, was placed fourth with 1.8% of the first-round vote. One contentious issue that has divided members of the party is whether it has the capacity to make an impression in the 2004 presidential elections. Consequently, some people are of the opinion that the party should only concentrate on the parliamentary elections. The party has elected a businessman, Francis Aggudey, as its presidential candidate.

National Democratic Congress (NDC)
Address. 641/4 Ringway Close, Kokomlemle, POB 5825, Accra-North
Telephone. (+233-21) 224905
Website. www.ndc.org.gh
Leadership. Jerry John Rawlings (founder); Obed Asamoah (chairman); Josiah Aryeh (general secretary)
The NDC was launched formally in June 1992, following the legalization of political parties, as a coalition of pro-government organizations. Opposition groups charged the NDC with intimidation during the presidential election in November 1992, won by Flt.-Lt. Rawlings, and staged a boycott of the legislative elections the following month. Consequently, the NDC won 189 of the 200 parliamentary seats, with another nine seats going to its electoral allies (among which the National Convention Party became a junior coalition partner of the NDC until 1995). In 1996 Rawlings was re-elected President with a virtually unchanged share of the vote, but the NDC's parliamentary strength was reduced to 133 seats after a campaign contested by the opposition parties. The post of "life chairman" of the NDC was created for Rawlings at a party congress in December 1998.

In December 2000 Rawlings was ineligible to stand for re-election as President, having served two terms, and abided by the constitution. The incumbent Vice-President, John Atta Mills, stood for election as NDC presidential candidate but was defeated by John Kufuor of the New Patriotic Party (NPP). The NDC (92 seats) was also defeated by the NPP (100 seats) in the simultaneous parliamentary election. Out of office, the party is disunited and cash-strapped and has faced problems regrouping to contest the 2004 elections.

New Patriotic Party (NPP)
Address. C912/2 Duade Street, Kokomlemle, POB 3456, Accra-North, Accra
Telephone. (+233-21) 227951
Fax. (+233-21) 224418
Email. npp@africaonline.com.gh
Website. www.nppghana.com
Leadership. John Kufuor (leader); Harona Esseku (chairman); Daniel Botwe (general secretary)
The NPP announced its formation in June 1992, advocating the protection of human rights and the strengthening of democracy. Its candidate in the November 1992 presidential

election, Albert Adu Boahen, was the closest challenger to Jerry Rawlings of the National Democratic Congress (NDC), polling just over 30% of the votes cast. The NPP boycotted the December 1992 legislative elections. In December 1996 the NPP's John Kufuor (whose candidacy was also supported by the People's Convention Party) won 39.8% of the vote in the presidential election, while the NPP won 60 seats in the parliamentary elections.

In the December 2000 presidential election, Kufuor defeated John Atta Mills, the NDC candidate, his share of the vote rising from 48.3% in the first-round ballot to 57% in the second round. In simultaneous parliamentary elections the NPP increased its strength to 100 seats (half the membership of the House). President Kufuor, who had accused the NDC of inefficient management of the public sector, was committed to enlarging the role of the private sector as part of a programme of free-market reforms.

The NPP is associated with the International Democrat Union through the Democrat Union of Africa.

People's National Convention (PNC)

Address. Kokomlemle, near Sadisco, POB 7795, Accra
Telephone. (+233-21) 236389)
Leadership. Edward Mahama (leader); John F. Edwin (chairman); Scotts Pwamang (general secretary)

The PNC was founded in 1992 by former President Hilla Limann, who came third in that year's presidential election. The PNC won one seat in the 1996 parliamentary election and three seats in the December 2000 election. Its presidential candidate, Edward Mahama, received 3% of the vote in 1996 and 2.5% in 2000. He has formed the Great Coalition, comprising the PNC, EGLE and Great Consolidated Popular Party (GCPP) to contest the 2004 elections. Even though he supported the NPP candidate in the 2000 presidential run-off, he has been one of the most outspoken critics of the NPP government.

Other Parties

Democratic People's Party (DPP), founded in 1992. The DPP supported the National Democratic Congress (NDC) candidate in the 1992, 1996 and 2000 presidential elections. It is affiliated to the NDC through the Progressive Alliance. The party has split because some members were uncomfortable with its alliance with the NDC. The leadership and founding of the party is a subject of contention between lawyer T. Ward-Brew, who claimed that he formed the party, and Daniel Markin, who is now generally recognized as the chairman and leader of the party. Because of the split, the party has no current leadership and survives only as a remnant.

Every Ghanaian Living Everywhere (EGLE) Party, evolved from a pro-Rawlings organization, the Eagle Club, formed in 1991, and won one seat in the 1992 legislative elections. EGLE supported the National Democratic Congress (NDC) candidate in the 1992, 1996 and 2000 presidential elections. It is affiliated to the NDC through the Progressive Alliance. Its chairman, Owurako Amofa, who used to be a Deputy Minister in the NDC government, has been living in the USA for over five years as a result of differences between him and Rawlings. The party is almost dead.
Address. Kokomlemle, POB 1859, Accra
Telephone. (+233-21) 231873
Leadership. Owurako Amofa (chairman); Sam Pee Yalley (general secretary)

Great Consolidated People's Party (GCPP), formed in 1996 by Dan Lartey, who is popularly known as "Mr Domestication" because of his insistence on self-reliance in economic issues. Lartey contested the December 2000 pres-

idential election, winning 1% of the first-round vote. For the 2004 elections, the party has entered into an alliance with the PNC and a breakaway faction of the DPP.
Address. Citadel House, POB 3077, Accra.
Telephone. 233-21-229721
Leadership. Dan Lartey (chairman); Nicholas Mensah (general secretary)

National Reform Party (NRP), founded in 1999 by former members of the National Democratic Congress (NDC), who broke away because of lack of internal party democracy. Its candidate at the 2000 presidential election, Augustus Goosie Tanoh, won 1.2% of the first-round vote. The party is in a state of disarray because of lack of funds. Originally, it wanted to form an alliance with the CPP but it withdrew because it did not agree with some of the conditions set by the CPP.
Address. 31 Mango Tree Avenue, Asylum Down, POB 19403, Accra North, Accra
Telephone. (+233-21) 228578
Leadership. Peter Kpordugbe (chairman); Kyeretwie Opoku (general secretary)

United Ghana Movement (UGM), founded in 1996 by a breakaway group from the NPP led Charles Wireko-Brobbey, who became the UGM presidential candidate in the 2000 elections but came last with 0.3% of the first-round vote. The NPP government appointed Wireko-Brobbey as Chief Executive Officer of the Volta River Authority (VRA). The party has been dormant since the 2000 elections and the party is seen as a one-man party revolving around Wireko-Brobbey.
Address. 1 North Ridge Crescent, Accra
Telephone. (+233-21) 225581
Fax. (+233-21) 231390
Email. info@ugmghana.org
Leadership. Nii Armah Tagoe (chairman); Eric Dutenya Kwabla (general secretary)

Greece

Capital: Athens
Population: 11,100,200 (2003)

Officially called the Hellenic Republic, Greece is a parliamentary democracy with a largely ceremonial President as head of state, elected by the parliament for a five-year term. Predominant executive power resides in the Prime Minister and members of the Cabinet, who must enjoy the confidence of the 300-member unicameral Parliament (*Vouli*). The latter is elected for a four-year term by universal adult suffrage under a system of proportional representation based on electoral constituencies returning between one and 42 deputies depending on their population size. The electoral law of 1990 which is still in use was designed to secure a parliamentary majority for whichever party came first-past-the-post and it introduced a 3% threshold for representation. In the 2001 constitutional revision, some changes were made to the framework affecting electoral law application. The next national elections will be conducted under a new, more proportional electoral system (voted in early 2004). Voting is compulsory for citizens aged 18 years and over (unless they are ill or incapacitated).

State financing of political parties dates from 1984 and is currently regulated by a 1996 law providing for ordinary and electoral funding. Ordinary funding is allocated annually and from 1998 has been equivalent to 1.02% of annual state revenue (reduced in that year by 15% from the previous proportion), while electoral funding is allocated in years of national and/or European Parliament elections and is currently equivalent to 0.425% of annual state revenue. Parties are also eligible for financial aid equivalent to 0.085% of state revenue for their research and educational activities. Of the available funds, 85% is allocated to parties or coalitions represented in the Greek Parliament in proportion to their share of the vote, 5% in equal shares to parties or coalitions which obtain representation in the European Parliament and 10% in equal shares between parties or coalitions presenting candidates in 70% of constituencies and obtaining at least 3% of the national vote.

Parliamentary elections held on March 7, 2004, resulted as follows: New Democracy (ND) 165 seats (with 45.37% of the vote), Pan-Hellenic Socialist Movement (PASOK) 117 seats (40.55%), Communist Party of Greece (KKE) 12 seats (5.89%), Coalition of the Radical Left–Unitary Ticket 6 seats (3.26%).

The European Parliament elections held on June 13, 2004 resulted in the following outcome: New Democracy 43.0% of the vote, 11 seats (+2); PASOK 34.0%, 8 seats (-1); KKE 9.5%, 3 seats; Coalition of the Left and Progress (*Synaspismos*) 4.2%, 1 seat (-1); Popular Orthodox Rally (LAOS) 4.1% of the vote, 1 seat (+1); Others 5.2% of the vote, 2 seats. The turnout in the elections was 63%, well above the EU average.

Coalition of the Left and Progress
Synaspismos tis Aristeras kai tis Proodou

Address. Plateia Eleftherias 1, 10553 Athens
Telephone. (0030–210) 337–8400
Fax. (0030–210) 321–9914
Email. intrelations@syn.gr
Website. www.syn.gr
Leadership. Nicos Constantopoulos (president).

Synaspismos was formed in 1989 as an alliance between the orthodox Communist Party of Greece (KKE), the Greek Left Party (*Elleniki Aristera*, EAR) and a number of minor leftist formations. The EAR had been launched in April 1987 by the majority wing of the KKE Interior (*esoterikou*), itself founded in 1968 by resident Communists opposed to the pro-Soviet orthodoxy of the exiled leadership of the KKE. Following the downfall of the dictatorship in 1974, KKE Interior became part of the United Democratic Left (EDA) – the party that represented the Greek left before 1967 when KKE was illegal – which made an electoral alliance with KKE. This coalition, the United left, had won eight seats in the November 1974 elections. In 1977 the Alliance of Progressive and Left Forces had won two seats, but in 1981 KKE Interior failed to win representation, before regaining one seat in 1985, when its share of the vote was 1.8%. In the 1984 European Parliament elections the KKE Interior had again won one seat, on a 3.4% vote share. EAR was dissolved in June 1992.

Reuniting many of the Greek Communist factions, *Synaspismos* polled strongly in the June 1989 national elections, winning 28 seats out of 300 and 13.1% of the vote. It was the highest percentage for the left in a post-junta election. In concurrent European Parliament elections a *Synaspismos* list won four of the 24 Greek seats with 14.3% of the vote. However, *Synaspismos* formed a short-lived coalition government with the conservative New Democracy (ND). It was the first post-war entry of a communist party in government, but the move did not pay off electorally in the November 1989 elections; the party suffered a considerable setback falling to 21 seats and 11.0% of the vote. Because of the political stalemate following this election, an "ecoumeniki" – an all-party

government, was formed in 1990 under Xenophon Zolotas, ex-governor of the Bank of Greece. Reversing its erstwhile policy of collaboration with the ND, *Synaspismos* decided to cooperate with Pan-Hellenic Socialist Movement (PASOK) in all the single-member districts, though the issue of the cooperation with PASOK always generated rank-and-file unrest. The alliance slipped again in the April 1990 elections, to 19 seats and 10.2% of the vote. The upshot was that in February 1991 the orthodox faction regained control of the KKE, which in June 1991 withdrew from *Synaspismos*. The following month the communist reformer Maria Damanaki was elected *Synaspismos* chair, replacing Harilaos Florakis. *Synaspismos* failed to win parliamentary representation (on a 2.9% vote share) in the October 1993 general election. Damanaki thereupon resigned as *Synaspismos* leader and Nicos Constantopoulos was elected president in 1993. In the June 1994 European Parliament elections *Synaspismos* recovered to 6.3% (only narrowly behind the KKE) and took two of the 25 Greek seats.

Synaspismos returned to the Greek parliament in the September 1996 elections, winning 5.1% of the vote and 10 seats. In opposition to a further PASOK government, *Synaspismos* polled strongly in local elections in October 1998. In the June 1999 European Parliament elections it again won two seats, on a 5.2% vote share. But the party slipped to 3.2% of the vote in the April 2000 parliamentary elections, being reduced to six seats. In the March 2004 general election Nicos Constantopoulos headed the **Coalition of the Radical Left–Unitary Ticket**, an electoral alliance between various formations of the left which were against the war in Iraq and neo-liberal globalization: *Synaspismos* – now renamed Coalition of the Left, Ecology and Social Movements; the Renovating Communist and Ecological Left (AKOA); the Movement for the Union of Action of the Left (KEDA); and the Internationalist Workers Left (DEA). It maintained almost the same percentage as in the previous election.

The *Synaspismos* members of the European Parliament sit in the European United Left/Nordic Green left group, as do the KKE representatives. The party is a member of the New European Left Forum (NELF).

Communist Party of Greece
Kommounistiko Komma Elladas (KKE)

Address. Leoforos Irakliou 145, 14231 Athens
Telephone. (0030–210) 259–2111
Fax. (0030–210) 259–2298
Email. cpg@kke.gr
Website. www.kke.gr
Leadership. Aleka Papariga (general secretary)

KKE is directly descended from the Socialist Workers' Party of Greece (SEKE) founded in November 1918, which joined the Communist International (Comintern) in 1924 and changed its name to KKE. The party secured its first parliamentary representation in 1926 and in 1936 held the balance of power between the Monarchists and the Liberals. During World War II popular resistance to the occupying Axis powers was organized by the Communists in the National Liberation Front (EAM) and the guerrilla Greek People's Liberation Army (ELAS), which gained control of the countryside. The KKE was officially banned in July 1947. After the defeat of its armed forces in the Civil War (1947-49), its leadership and thousands of its members fled to Communist-ruled countries.

In 1967-74 the KKE took a leading role in the opposition to the Greek military junta, but factional conflict not only within the exiled party but also between it and Communist forces in Greece culminated in a decision by the latter in February 1968 to form an independent "interior" KKE. The KKE's support for the Soviet-led suppression of the

Czechoslovak "Prague Spring" later in 1968 and the gravitation of the KKE Interior towards reformist Eurocommunism served to widen the ideological gap between the two factions. Accused of prime responsibility for the split, the KKE leader, Constantine Kolliyannis, was replaced by Harilaos Florakis in 1973.

Legalized after the fall of the military regime in September 1974, the KKE contested the November 1974 elections as part of the EDA, winning five of the EDA's eights seats. Standing on its own in subsequent elections, the KKE advanced to 11 seats in 1977 (with 9.4% of the vote) and to 13 in 1981 (10.9%), when it also secured three of the 24 Greek seats in the European Parliament (with a 12.8% vote share). The KKE had adopted a critical attitude towards PASOK, accusing it of betraying its election promises, notably its pledge to take Greece out of the European Community and NATO.

Concurrently, the party's rigid pro-Moscow orthodoxy, which included support for the Soviet intervention in Afghanistan, caused some internal dissension and defections. In the 1984 European elections, the KKE vote slipped to 11.6% (although it again won three seats), while in the June 1985 national elections it achieved 9.9% of the vote and 12 seats. In the October 1986 municipal elections the KKE withheld crucial second-round support from PASOK candidates, thus ensuring their defeat in Athens, Piraeus and Salonika (the three largest cities).

The KKE subsequently participated in the Coalition of the Left and Progress (*Synaspismos*). The party remained in *Synaspismos* for the April 1990 elections, in which the alliance fell back to 19 seats and 10.2% of the vote. However, the 13th KKE congress in February 1991 resulted in the party's orthodox wing narrowly gaining control and in the election as general secretary of Aleka Papariga, who in June 1991 took the party out of *Synaspismos*. It experienced further internal turmoil, involving the departure of various elements that preferred the reformist line of *Synaspismos*. KKE presented an anti-European Community, anti-NATO and anti-American image. In the October 1993 elections, however, the KKE retained appreciable support, winning 4.5% of the vote and nine seats. In the June 1994 European elections the KKE advanced to 6.3%, taking two of the 25 Greek seats. In the September 1996 general elections the KKE advanced to 5.6% of the vote and 11 seats, remaining in opposition to a further PASOK administration. In the June 1999 European Parliament elections the KKE won an additional seat on the strength of a vote share of 8.7%. In the April 2000 national elections, the party virtually retained its position, again winning 11 seats, this time with 5.5% of the vote. In the March 2004 national elections it won 12 seats and 5.89% of the vote.

The three KKE representatives in the European Parliament sit in the European United Left/Nordic Green left group, as do the *Synaspismos* representatives.

New Democracy
Nea Dimokratia (ND)

Address. Rigillis 18, 10674 Athens
Telephone. (0030–210) 729071–79
Fax. (0030–210) 725–491
Email. valinak@otenet.gr
Website. www.nd.gr
Leadership. Kostas Karamanlis (president).

The conservative ND was founded in October 1974 by Constantine Karamanlis, who had been Prime Minister in 1956–63 as leader of the National Radical Union (ERE) and had opposed the colonels' regime of 1967–74 from exile in Paris. The new party won an absolute majority in the November 1974 elections, securing 220 of the 300 seats on a 54.37% vote share. A referendum was conducted on Dec.8

of that same year which resulted in a decisive vote against the monarchy and the return of the King (69.18% opting for a Presidential Republic). The new constitution of the Third Greek Republic was voted in October 1975. ND was confirmed in power in the November 1977 elections, although it slipped to 172 seats and 41.8% of the vote, with Karamanlis continuing as Prime Minister until being elected President of the Republic in May 1980, when he was succeeded as government and party leader by George Rallis. In January 1981 a key ND policy aim was achieved when Greece became a member of the European Community, but in the October 1981 elections the party was heavily defeated by the Pan-Hellenic Socialist Movement (PASOK), retaining only 115 seats and 35.9% of the vote.

In the wake of ND's 1981 defeat Rallis was replaced by conservative Evangelos Averoff-Tossizza, but the latter resigned in August 1984 following the ND's poor showing in the European Parliament elections two months earlier. He was succeeded by Constantine Mitsotakis, who led ND to another election defeat in June 1985, although it improved to 126 seats and 40.8% of the vote. Mitsotakis's leadership then came under strong criticism from nationalist elements led by Kostis Stephanopoulos, who in September 1985 broke away to form the Democratic Renewal Party (DIANA). Mitsotakis reasserted his authority at a February 1986 ND congress, when liberal policy theses were adopted, and in October 1986 the party made significant gains in municipal elections, taking control from PASOK in the three largest cities (Athens, Piraeus and Salonkia).

ND won a relative majority of 145 seats in the June 1989 general elections, the parliamentary arithmetic obliging it to form a temporary coalition with the Coalition of the Left and Progress (*Synaspismos*). Another election in November 1989 produced another stalemate, with ND representation edging up to 148 seats (on a 46.2% vote share), so that a temporary three-party coalition of ND, PASOK and *Synaspismos* representatives plus non-party technocrats was formed. Yet more general elections in April 1990 gave ND exactly half the seats (150) with 46.9% of the vote, so that Mitsotakis was able to form a single-party government with the external support of the single DIANA deputy. The New Democracy government under Mitsotakis tried to implement a moderate neo-liberal programme whose major objective was to stabilize the ailing economy. In May 1990 Karamanlis was elected for the second time President of the Republic, following the ND's proposal.

Amid a deteriorating economic situation, the Mitsotakis government experienced growing internal rifts in 1992–93, culminating in the formation of the breakaway Political Spring (POLAN) in June 1993 by Antonis Samaras, who as Foreign Minister advocated a hard line of not accepting the name "Macedonia" or any label that would include the term "Macedonia" as the official name of the new state, the Former Yugoslav Republic of Macedonia, while Mitsotakis represented a more compromising position. POLAN attracted three other ND deputies into defection, so that the government lost its narrow parliamentary majority. Mitsotakis resigned in September 1993, precipitating early elections in October, in which ND was heavily defeated by PASOK, falling to 111 seats and 39.3% of the vote. Mitsotakis immediately resigned as ND leader and was succeeded by Miltiades Evert, who resigned from the ND government in October 1991 for criticizing its free-market policies. ND took second place in the June 1994 European Parliament elections, winning 32.7% of the vote and nine of the 25 Greek seats. In October 1994 the ND candidate registered a notable victory in the Athens mayoral contest, while remaining much weaker than PASOK in local government.

In March 1995 the ND candidate, Athanasios Tsaldaris, failed to secure parliamentary election as President. The winning candidate whom PASOK supported, Kostis Stephanopoulos, had disbanded his DIANA party, following a debacle in the 1994 election for the European Parliament. In Ferbruary 2000 Stephanopoulos was re-elected, this time with ND votes as well, and he enjoyed high popularity.

In the September 1996 general elections the ND failed to fulfill expectations that it would oust the PASOK government, winning only 108 seats and 38.2% of the vote. Evert secured re-election in October but in March 1997 he was replaced by Kostas Karamanlis – the nephew of Constantine Karamanlis – who at 40 became the youngest ever leader of a major Greek political party. His election was seen as drastic action by a party fearing marginalization and concerned at having lost business community support to PASOK.

Under new leadership, the ND made a strong showing in the October 1998 local elections, retaining the mayorships of Athens and Salonika, although it was potentially weakened by the launching in May 1999 of the Liberals by a former ND deputy. The ND won 36.0% of the vote in the June 1999 European Parliament elections, thus overtaking PASOK, although its representation remained at nine seats. In the April 2000 national elections, the party narrowly failed to oust PASOK from power, advancing to 42.7% of the vote and 125 seats. ND convincingly won the general elections of March 2004 with a vote share of 47% and 165 seats. Antonis Samaras, who had in 1996 lost the parliamentary representation enjoyed after the elections of October 1993 (when his party had won 10 seats with a vote share of 4.9%), backed ND's electoral campaign.

With an official membership of 400,000, ND is a member party of the Christian Democrat International, the International Democrat Union and the European Democrat Union. Its members of the European Parliament sit in the European People's Party/European Democrats group.

Pan-Hellenic Socialist Movement
Panellenio Sosialistiko Kinema (PASOK)

Address. Charilaou Tricoupi 50, 10680 Athens
Telephone. (0030–210) 368–4037
Fax. (0030–210) 368–4042
Email. pasok@pasok.gr
Website. www.pasok.gr
Leadership. George Papandreou (president).
PASOK was founded in 1974 by Andreas Papandreou. Having worked in the USA as an economics professor, Papandreou had returned to Greece in 1959 and had held ministerial office in pre-1967 Centre Union governments headed by his father George. Briefly imprisoned after the 1967 colonels' coup, he had been allowed to go into exile and in 1968 had founded the Pan-Hellenic Liberation Movement (PAK), becoming convinced of the need for an unequivocally socialist party that would follow a "third road" distinct from West European social democracy and East European communism. PASOK was originally committed to the socialization of key economic sectors and also to withdrawal from the then European Community (EC) and NATO.

PASOK emerged from the November 1974 elections as the third strongest party, with 12 of 300 seats and 13.6% of the vote. In the November 1977 elections it became the strongest opposition party, with 93 seats and 25.3%, and in October 1981 it won an absolute majority of 170 seats (with 48.1% of the vote) and formed its first government under Papandreou's premiership. PASOK's victory was accompanied by the confirmation ot the tripartite structure of the Greek party system which would last until the early 1990s.

Four years later, in June 1985, PASOK was returned for a second term, although with its representation reduced to 161 seats on a 45.8% vote share. Meanwhile, PASOK nominated its own presidential candidate, Christos Sartzetakis, a prominent judge, who was eventually elected President in March

1985, with the help of the votes of the communist MPs. The decision not to support Karamanlis's candidacy was accompanied by a minor revision of the constitution concerning the powers of the President. In office, PASOK experienced considerable internal divisions over the government's foreign and economic policies, including a new five-year agreement signed in September 1983 allowing US bases to remain in Greece, the dropping of opposition to EC and NATO membership, and the introduction of an economic austerity programme in 1985. Various critics of the leadership were expelled from PASOK in the 1980s and a number of breakaway groups were formed, although none had any enduring impact. In the October 1986 municipal elections PASOK suffered sharp reverses, losing the three largest cities to the conservative New Democracy (ND), although it remained by far the strongest party at local level.

In the June 1989 parliamentary elections PASOK was damaged by the Koskotas affair, involving financial malpractice in the Bank of Crete. The party's representation slumped to 125 seats (on a 39.2% vote share) and it went into opposition to a temporary coalition between ND and the Coalition of the Left and Progress (*Synaspismos*). Further elections in November 1989 produced another statemate, with PASOK improving slightly to 128 seats and 40.7% of the vote, well behind ND. Meanwhile, Papandreou had been indicted on corruption charges arising from the Koskotas affair. Greece's third general elections in less than a year, held in April 1990, broke the deadlock, with PASOK slipping to 123 seats and 38.6% and going into opposition to a ND government.

Continuing divisions within PASOK were highlighted during its second congress in September 1990, when Papandreou's nominee for the new post of party general secretary, Akis Tsochatzopoulos, was approved by a bare onevote majority. Papandreou nevertheless remained unchallenged as PASOK leader, and in January 1992 was finally acquitted of the various corruption charges against him. In the October 1993 elections PASOK stood on a manifesto which jettisoned much of the populist rhetoric of the 1980s and supported EC and NATO membership and good relations with the USA. It won an overall majority of 170 seats (on a 46.9% vote share) and returned to government with Papandreou once again Prime Minister. The new government embarked on a policy to stabilize the economy and to lead the country towards the targets defined by the Maastricht treaty. In the June 1994 European Parliament elections PASOK headed the poll, winning 37.6% of the vote and 10 of the 25 Greek seats. In October 1994 PASOK maintained its dominance in local elections, although losing the Athens mayoral contest to an ND candidate.

As Karamanlis' second term as President of the Republic expired, PASOK, with the help of the votes of *Politiki Anixi* (Political Spring), supported the candidacy of Kostis Stefanopoulos – a former leading member of the ND party and leader until 1994 of the small and relatively unsuccessful DIANA party. In March 1995 the parliament elected Stefanopoulos as President of the Republic. At the end of 1995 Papandreou fell seriously ill. He eventually resigned in January 1996 and was succeeded as PASOK political leader and Prime Minister by Kostas Simitis, who defeated acting Prime Minister Apostolos Tsokhatzopoulos in a runoff ballot of PASOK's parliamentary group by 86 votes to 75. Simitis had resigned from the government in September 1995 in protest against alleged sabotage of his reform plans by the PASOK hierarchy. Following the death of Papandreou on June 22, 1996, Simitis prevailed over strong internal opposition by securing election to the PASOK presidency at a special party congress at the end of the month.

Simitis consolidated his position in the September 1996 general elections, rather unexpectedly securing a further mandate for PASOK, which won 162 seats on a 41.5% vote share. Having lost ground in the October 1998 local elections, PASOK was relegated to second place in the June 1999 European Parliament elections, obtaining only 32.9% of the vote and nine seats. The party nevertheless narrowly retained power in the April 2000 national elections, winning 158 seats with 43.8% of the vote. However, it lost the elections of March 2004, winning 117 seats with 40.5% of the vote. Andreas Andrianopoulos, a former ND deputy, and Stephanos Manos, an ex-ND minister, who had launched a new party, The Liberals, in April 1999, were elected as list MPs on the PASOK ticket.

PASOK is a member party of the Socialist International. Its representatives in the European Parliament sit in the Party of European Socialists group.

Other Parties

Democratic Social Movement
Dimokratiko Kinoniko Kinima (DIKKI)
Address. Odos Xalkokondili 9, 10677 Athens
Telephone. (30–1) 380–1712
Fax. (30–1) 383–9047
Email. dikki@otenet.gr
Website. www.dikki.gr
Leadership. Dimitris Tsovolas (president)
DIKKI originated in 1995 in a breakaway from the ruling Pan-Hellenic Socialist Movement (PASOK) opposed in particular to the government's policy of participating in closer European Union integration and of preparing Greece for membership of the single European currency by austerity measures. DIKKI capitalized on the anti-Maastricht climate together with the KKE. In the September 1996 general elections DIKKI achieved 4.4% of the popular vote and won nine parliamentary seats.

In the June 1999 European Parliament elections, DIKKI advanced to 6.8%, taking two of the 25 Greek seats, who sat in the European United Left/Nordic Green Left group. But it failed to repeat this success in the April 2000 national elections, winning only 2.7% of the vote and therefore failing to retain representation. In the March 2004 elections DIKKI received 1.79% of the vote and no parliamentary representation.

Popular Orthodox Rally
Laikos Orthodoxos Synagermo (LAOS)
Address. Vas. Constantinou & Eratosthenous 1, 11635 Athens
Telephone. (0030–210) 7522700
Email. Laos@otenet.gr
Website. www.karatzaferis.gr
Leadership. George Karatzaferis (president)
Launched in September 2000 by George Karatzaferis, a former ND deputy, the party appeared as a right-wing populist party, designating itself also as the defender of national and Orthodox Christian values. LAOS secured 13.6% of the total vote in the local authority election of October 2002 and received 2.19% and no parliamentary representation in the national elections of March 2004. In the June 2004 elections to the European Parliament it took 4.1% of the vote and won one seat.

Grenada

Capital: St George's
Population: 89,500 (2003E)

A former British dependency, Grenada became a fully independent member of the Commonwealth in 1974.

In 1979 the elected Grenada United Labour Party (GULP) government, headed by Sir Eric Gairy, was overthrown in a coup staged by the Marxist New Jewel Movement. This established a People's Revolutionary Government under the leadership of Maurice Bishop. Factional conflict within the regime led to the murder of Bishop in October 1983, prompting US-Caribbean military intervention. Following this the New National Party (NNP) came to power at a general election in December 1984, and a phased withdrawal of US forces was completed by June 1985. The NNP has retained power ever since, except for a period at the beginning of the 1990s.

The head of state is the British sovereign, represented by a Governor-General. The head of government is the Prime Minister. Parliament comprises a 13-member Senate and a 15-member House of Representatives. Simple majorities in single-member constituencies elect members of the House of Representatives on the Westminster model for five-year terms. Senators are appointed by the Governor-General: seven are appointed on the advice of the Prime Minister; three on the advice of the Leader of the Opposition; and three on the advice of the Prime Minister after the Prime Minister has consulted organizations or interests which he believes should be represented.

Politics tend to be fractious with a history of fluid allegiances and short-lived personality-based political formations. In a general election held on Nov. 27, 2003, the New National Party (NNP) of Prime Minister Keith Mitchell retained power for an unprecedented third term in office. However, the NNP won only eight of the 15 parliamentary seats with 49.9% of the vote, compared to all 15 in the previous general election. The National Democratic Congress won the remaining seven seats and 45.1% of the votes. One assembly member who had left the NNP in 2000 to become the leader of the opposition lost his seat.

Grenada United Labour Party (GULP)
Address. Springs PO, St George's
Telephone. (+1-473) 440-0097
Leadership. Gloria Payne Banfield (leader)
The conservative GULP was formed in 1950, held office for periods in the colonial era, and led Grenada to independence in 1974, with its leader Eric Gairy becoming Prime Minister. Gairy was overthrown by the New Jewel Movement coup in 1979 and went into exile, returning in 1984 following the US-led intervention. Efforts to re-establish the GULP as a significant force were unsuccessful, however, and it won only two seats at elections in 1995 and none in 1999. Gairy died in 1997 and the party was subsequently beset by factional divisions, with former Deputy Prime Minister Hubert Prudhomme and prominent lawyer Jerry Seales leading opposing factions. Despite the party's failure to win a seat in the 1999 election, the party gained a voice in parliament after Michael Baptiste, formerly NNP Minister for Agriculture, crossed the floor of the House in June 2000. Baptiste joined the GULP and became leader of the opposition and the GULP by default. In February 2003, however, the GULP elected Gloria Payne Banfield as its new leader in readiness for the expected general election. She was the first woman to lead a political party in the country.

In an attempt to strengthen the opposition, particularly outside parliament, the GULP established a loose coalition with the Maurice Bishop Patriotic Movement (MBPM) and the Democratic Labour Party (DLP) known as the United Labour Platform (ULP). However, few positive developments came from this new grouping, partly due to the lack of a unifying figure at its head, and also because there was marked scepticism within each group about the viability of the political alliance. Indeed, when the general election came in November 2003 the GULP put forward its own list of candidates, while the MBPM and the DLP did not participate in the election. The weak position of the GULP was illustrated by the fact that the party failed to win a single seat, gaining only 3.2% of the vote; Michael Baptiste lost his place in the House of Representatives.

National Democratic Congress (NDC)

Address. Woolwich Road, St. George's
Email. votendc@grenada.gd
Website. www.votendc.com
Leadership. Tillman Thomas (leader); Peter David (general secretary)

The centrist NDC was launched in 1987 by former New National Party (NNP) minister George Brizan. Brizan's successor as leader, Nicholas Brathwaite, became Prime Minister after the 1990 election. Brizan returned to replace Brathwaite as NDC leader in 1994 and as Prime Minister in February 1995. In the June 1995 general election the party retained only five seats and moved into opposition. In the January 1999 election it took 24.9% of the vote, but lost all its seats. Brizan subsequently stepped down as party leader and was reported to have accepted a job as adviser to the victorious NNP. In October 2000 Tillman Thomas was elected party leader, but in May 2001 his deputy, Livingstone Nelson, resigned saying that the party was not being forceful enough in opposing the NNP. Thomas and the NDC were in a difficult position, however, as the party had no presence in the House of Representatives. In the build-up to the November 2003 general election the NDC undertook an effective campaign against the incumbent NNP, and won seven of the 15 parliamentary seats. Thomas secured a seat in the new parliament, thus strengthening the opposition's coherence and role in the legislature.

New National Party (NNP)

Address. PO Box 393, Lucas Street, St George's
Telephone. (1-473) 440-1875
Fax. (1-473) 440-1876
Email. nnphouse1@caribsurf.com
Leadership. Keith Mitchell (leader)

The NNP was created in August 1984 by the merger of the conservative Grenada National Party (GNP), led by Herbert Blaize; the centrist National Democratic Party (NDP), formed earlier in 1984 and then led by George Brizan; and the right-wing Grenada Democratic Movement (GDM), dating from 1983 and led by Francis Alexis. The GNP, which had been set up in 1956, held a majority of the elective seats in the colonial legislature from 1957 to 1961 and from 1962 to 1967, when Blaize was Chief Minister. In the December 1984 general election the NNP won 14 of the 15 seats, and Blaize became Prime Minister. However, the party subsequently suffered internal divisions and in April 1987 Brizan and Alexis left the government and moved into opposition. In January 1989 Keith Mitchell defeated Prime Minister Blaize for the party leadership, prompting the latter to form his own National Party (Blaize died in office in December 1989).

The NNP won only two seats in the 1990 general election but came to power in the June 1995 election, when it won eight seats. The NNP lost its majority in Parliament as a result of the resignation in November 1998 of Foreign Minister Raphael Fletcher, precipitating an early general election in January 1999. Capitalizing on buoyant economic conditions and falling unemployment, the Mitchell government went on to win a sweeping victory, taking 62% of the vote and winning all 15 seats. Economic issues, including high unemployment, a worsening fiscal deficit, and growing labour unrest, dominated the NNP's second term in office. However, the government was credited with improving the country's infrastructure, particularly with regard to health services. In the general election held on Nov. 27, 2003, the NNP suffered a dramatic decline in parliamentary representation, losing seven of its 15 seats. Nevertheless, the party won the remaining eight seats to gain an unprecedented third consecutive term in office. However, in two of those seats the NNP only gained victory by margins of less than 12 votes. Prime Minister Mitchell recognized the closeness of the election in his acceptance speech by stating: "We will work with the opposition. We will consult with the opposition on important national issues. We will listen to the opposition, because we accept the fact that the opposition represents the view of a significant proportion of the population".

The NNP is an associate member of the International Democrat Union and a member of its regional organization, the Caribbean Democrat Union.

Guatemala

Capital: Guatemala City
Population: 11,237,196 (2002 census)

Guatemala's modern political history has been highly unstable. Guatemala enjoyed democratic government for ten years after 1944, but in 1954 the United States sponsored the overthrow of an elected reformist government led by Col. Jacobo Arbenz. Three separate constitutions have been promulgated since then, but for much of the period the country was under direct or disguised military rule. There have been four successful military coups (1957, 1963, 1982 and 1983) and two failed coups (in May and December 1988). In 1960, encouraged by the example of the Cuban revolution, insurgency broke out, but was brutally crushed with the loss of more than 6,000 civilian lives. By the end of the 1970s political and socio-economic exclusion fomented the emergence of a united guerrilla front to challenge the monopoly on power held by a small ruling class and the military. This was put down with extreme violence. In all, some 200,000 people were killed during 36 years of armed conflict, over 90% civilians at the hands of the armed forces. After militarily defeating the guerrilla forces and forcibly pacifying the countryside, the military returned the country to elected rule through a guided transition between 1984 and 1986. In 1986 a civilian President was elected from a narrow spectrum of right and centre-right parties. A new constitution was approved in 1986. Peace talks aimed at national reconciliation, the expansion of democracy, the ending of gross human rights abuses and demilitarization began between the government, moderate sections of the army and the guerrillas in the late 1980s, but were not finalized until December 1996, following the intervention of the United Nations in 1994 as arbiter of the talks. Under an agreement signed in 1996 the guerrilla front was converted into a legal political party and contested the 1999 elections.

Under the 1986 constitution, the Republic of Guatemala has a unicameral Congress (*Congreso de la República*) elected for a four-year term. In 2003 the number of congressional deputies was increased to 158, 127 of whom are directly elected and 31 chosen by party list on a proportional representation basis. Executive authority resides in the President, who is also elected for a four-year term and may not be re-elected. If in a presidential election none of the candidates secures an absolute majority, a second round between the two leading candidates takes place. The President is assisted by a Vice-President and an appointed Cabinet. Voting is compulsory for those 18 years of age and older who can read and write but is optional for illiterates from the same age group. Non-voting is punishable by a small fine, although this is rarely enforced. The police and military personnel on active duty are not allowed to vote.

On Jan. 14, 2004, Oscar Berger Perdomo of the Great National Alliance (GANA) took office as President. He had led the ballot in the first round of presidential elections held on Nov. 9, 2003, with 34.3% of the vote and was elected in the second round on Dec. 28 with 54.1% against 45.8% for Alvaro Colóm Caballeros of the National Union of Hope (UNE). Elections to the unicameral Congress on Nov. 9, 2003, resulted in a hung parliament – the GANA won 47 seats, the Guatemalan Republican Front (FRG) 43, the UNE 32 and the National Advancement Party (PAN) 17, with the remaining seats divided between the Unionist Party (PU) 7, New National Alliance (ANN) 6, the Guatemalan National Revolutionary Unity (URNG) 2, the Democratic Union (UD) 2, the Guatemalan Christian Democratic Party (DCG) 1, and the Authentic Integral Development (DIA) 1.

Great National Alliance
Gran Alianza Nacional (GANA)
Address. 7ª Avenida 10-40, zona 9, Guatemala City
Telephone. (502) 331-0121/ 332-4516/ 331-0144
Email. gana@ganaconoscarberger2003
Website. http://www.ganaconoscarberger2003.org/
Leadership. Oscar Berger Perdomo (presidential candidate 2003); Eduardo Stein Barillas (vice-presidential candidate)

The Great National Alliance was formed in May 2003, following divisions which beset the National Advancement Party (PAN) after the latter lost the 1999 presidential elections to the Guatemalan Republican Front (FRG). The GANA alliance comprised three smaller parties – the Patriotic Party (*Partido Patriotico*, PP), the Reform Movement (*Movimiento Reformador*, MR), and the Party of National Solidarity (*Partido de Solidaridad Nacional*, PSN). However, none of these parties were consolidated or large groupings and in practice they simply served as the legal vehicle for the dissaffected former wing of the PAN led by Oscar Berger to contest the presidency.

The PP was set up in June 2000 by a group of individuals who coalesced around retired General Otto Pérez Molina, formerly on the reformist wing of the military which supported the 1996 peace accords. It was legally registered in June 2002. The MR was originally the Guatemalan Labour Party (*Partido Laborista Guatemalteco*, PLG). The PLG was established in 1991 but did not contest the 1995 or 1999 elections and so retained its legal inscription. In July 2002 the party changed its named to the Reform Movement. Former president of the Chamber of Commerce, Jorge Briz Abularach, was predicted to run for the presidency on the MR slate, but Briz instead joined the GANA alliance in 2003 and ran for mayor of Guatemala City on the GANA ticket. (After Oscar Berger's electoral victory in December 2003 Briz was named Foreign Secretary.) The PSN was registered in August 2002 by businessman Ricardo Castillo Sinibaldi with the aim of contesting the presidency in 2003. However, Sinibaldi and the PSN subsequently joined the GANA alliance.

Prior to his victory in the 2003 presidential elections Berger, who had previously twice been elected mayor of

Guatemala City for the PAN, had lost the 1999 presidential elections to Alfonso Portillo of the FRG, polling only 31.7% of the second round vote. In 2003 he won internal primary elections in the PAN for the presidential nomination, but was blocked by party general secretary Leonel López Rodas and subsequently left the PAN, together with his supporters, to set up GANA. Berger secured the support of the powerful business sector, who had been at loggerheads with the FRG government and were anxious to see a pro-private sector candidate returned to the presidency. He won the second round of presidential elections held on Dec. 28, 2003, on the GANA ticket with 54.1% of the vote. GANA returned 47 deputies to congress in the November 2003 congressional elections.

Guatemalan Republican Front
Frente Republicano Guatemalteco (FRG)
Address. 3 Calle 5–50, zona 1, Guatemala City
Telephone. (502) 238–2756
Website. www.frg.org.gt
Leadership. Efraín Ríos Montt (general secretary)
The authoritarian right-wing FRG was formed in 1988 as a vehicle for former President Gen. (retd.) Efraín Ríos Montt, who had staged a military coup in 1982, assumed dictatorial powers and fought a vicious counter-insurgency campaign before himself being ousted in 1983. The FRG was a key participant in the 1990 "No Sell-Out Platform" (*Plataforma No Venta,* PNV) alliance which included the Democratic Institutionalist Party (PID) and the National Unity Front (FUN), both now defunct. The alliance was de-registered after the 1990 poll on the ground that former heads of state who had participated in coups were banned from running for the presidency. The FRG was similarly affected by this ban, but in the 1994 legislative contest staged an impressive recovery, winning 32 of the available seats, a result which gained Ríos Montt the presidency of Congress. The former President's wife, Teresa Sosa de Ríos, was initially chosen as the FRG's 1995 presidential election candidate but, on being barred on constitutional grounds, was replaced by Alfonso Portillo Cabrera, a populist and former Christian Democrat who secured 22.1% in the first round but was defeated in the run-off in January 1996, while the FRG won 21 seats in the legislative elections and control of 47 municipalities.

As the principal opposition to the post-1996 administration of the National Advancement Party (PAN), the FRG benefited from doubts about the peace agreement ending 36 years of civil war and also from deteriorating economic and social conditions. In the November-December 1999 elections, Portillo swept to a convincing victory in the presidential contest, winning 47.8% in the first round and 68.3% in the runoff against Oscar Berger of the PAN. In the concurrent congressional elections the FRG won an absolute majority of 63 of the 113 seats. Ríos Montt served as head of congress throughout the 1999-2004 term.

The FRG administration was criticized for widespread corruption and abuses, weakening government accountability mechanisms and presiding over a worsening security and human rights situation. In 2003 the executive manipulated elections of Constitutional Court justices and the Court subsequently overturned the constitutional ban on Ríos Montt running for president. However, Ríos Montt had long been accused of responsibility for gross violations of human rights that occurred under his dictatorial rule in 1982-83 and he proved a highly controversial candidate. In the event he came a poor third in the November 2003 first round of presidential elections, taking 19.3% of the vote. However, the FRG remains an important political force and is one of the few political parties to have remained relatively cohesive since its inception, despite its electoral defeats. In November 2003 it gained 43 of the total 158 congressional seats and around half of the country's 331 municipal governments.

National Advancement Party
Partido de Avanzada Nacional (PAN)

Address. 7 Av. 10–38, zona 9, Guatemala City
Telephone. (502) 331-9906
Email. info@pan.org.gt
Website. www.pan.org.gt/
Leadership. Leonel López Rodas (presidential candidate 2003 and general secretary)

Founded in 1989, the centre-right PAN continues to be a significant force in Guatemalan politics, although it was severely weakened by internal divisions and defections following its defeat in the November 1999 presidential elections. The party's founder, Alvaro Arzú Irigoyen, gained his reputation as an efficient administrator during his years as mayor of Guatemala City (1985-90). He resigned from the mayoral post to contest the 1990 presidential elections (with support from the business community and the US government), coming fourth in the first round with 17.3% of the vote, whilst the PAN obtained 12 seats in concurrent congressional elections. A PAN member, Oscar Berger Perdomo, was elected mayor of Guatemala City with 34% of the vote.

Having given second-round support to the victorious 1990 presidential candidate, Jorge Serrano Elías of the Solidarity Action Movement (MAS), Arzú was named as Foreign Minister in the new government and the PAN was also given the communications, transport and public works portfolios. However, following Serrano's marginalization of Arzú from peace talks with the Guatemalan National Revolutionary Unity (URNG) guerrillas held in Mexico in May 1991, Arzú resigned as Foreign Minister in September 1991 in protest at Serrano's decision to establish diplomatic relations with Belize, sovereignty over which had long been claimed by Guatemala. Following the removal of Serrano in June 1993 after his unsuccessful attempt to close down Congress, PAN representatives were included in new national unity government appointed to serve until fresh elections could be held. In congressional elections in August 1994 the PAN was runner-up to the FRG, winning 24 seats to the FRG's 32. It turned the tables in the November 1995 elections, however, by obtaining an overall majority of 43 seats in Congress, while Arzú headed the first-round presidential poll with 36.6% and went on to defeat the FRG candidate in the run-off contest in January 1996 with 51.2% of the vote.

President Arzú moved quickly to sign a definitive peace agreement ending the civil war, overriding reservations from the authoritarian right and military hardliners. But his administration gradually lost popular support, as it failed to make much impact on intractable economic and social problems. The outcome was defeat for the PAN in the November 1999 elections, in which its presidential candidate, Oscar Berger, came a poor second to the FRG contender (with only 31.7% of the second-round vote) and the party's representation in an enlarged Congress was reduced to 37 seats out of 113. Divisions within the party ensued: the faction led by former president Alvaro Arzú abandoned the party to set up the Unionist Party (PU) in 2000 after Arzú lost the post of general secretary to Leonel López Rodas. Divisions within the PAN reached a peak in May 2003 after primary elections which designated former Guatemala City mayor and PAN 1999 presidential candidate Oscar Berger as the PAN's presidential candidate. Following conflicts between Berger and López Rodas and their supporters over nominations for the 2003 congressional and municipal elections, Berger and his faction left the party to form the GANA alliance, which went on to win the November 2003 presidential elections. Leonel López Rodas came fourth in the first round of the presidential elections with 8.4% of the vote. The PAN returned 17 deputies to congress in November 2003.

National Union of Hope
Unidad Nacional de Esperanza (UNE)

Address. 2ª avenida 5-11 zona 9
Telephone.(502) 232-4685/ 251-1892
Leadership. Alvaro Colóm Caballeros (general secretary)

The centrist UNE is one of the newest parties in Guatemala. Its general secretary Alvaro Colóm was Vice-Minister of Economy for six months during the administration of Jorge Serrano Elias (1990-93) and during the governments of Serrano Elias, Ramiro de León Carpio (1994-95) and Alvaro Arzú (1996-2000) held the post of executive director of the National Peace Fund (*Fondo Nacional para la Paz*, FONA-PAZ). In 1999 Colóm ran for the presidency for an electoral alliance, the New National Alliance (ANN), formed by the Guatemalan National Revolutionary Unity (URNG) and the Authentic Integral Development (DIA), coming third in the first round with 12.3% of the votes cast. UNE was founded in 2000, when Alvaro Colóm and his supporters left the ANN and in January 2001 the UNE established itself as a significant opposition force in Congress, including one former ANN deputy and another 13 from other parties. UNE was registered by the Supreme Electoral Tribunal in September 2002 and Colóm, who ran an energetic populist campaign, went on to win second place in the November 2003 presidential elections, with a vote of 26.4%. In the second round run-off on Dec. 28, 2003, Colóm polled a respectable 45.8% against 54.1% for Oscar Berger of the GANA alliance. The UNE is the third largest party in congress, having gained 32 seats in the November 2003 congressional elections.

Other Parties

Authentic Integral Development (*Desarrollo Integral Auténtico*, DIA), a centre-left party set up in 1990 and legally registered in 1994. It first ran candidates for office in the 1995 general elections, but failed to secure any seats in congress or the minimum percentage of votes required by the electoral law and was deregistered. It was re-registered by the Supreme Electoral Tribunal in 1999 and ran in an alliance with the Guatemalan National Revolutionary Unity (URNG) in the 1999 elections. The alliance between the URNG and the DIA dissolved after the 1999 elections and in the 2003 elections the DIA ran alone and gained one seat in congress.
Address. 12 Calle 2–18, zona 1, Guatemala City
Fax. (502) 232–8044
Leadership. Jose Luis Ortega Torres (general secretary)

Democratic Union (*Union Democrática*, UD), launched prior to the 1994 general elections and which campaigned on a platform of being a party with no historical baggage. However, it won only one congressional seat, which it retained at the 1995 and 1999 elections. In 1995 its presidential candidate, José Chea, won 3.5% of the votes cast. In 1999 the party ran in association with the Green Organization (LOV), but their joint candidate for the presidency, José Enrique Asturias Rudeke, obtained only 1.1% of the vote. The UD returned two deputies to congress in the November 2003 elections.
Address. 1a calle 18-83 zona 15, Guatemala City
Telephone. (502) 369-7074
Leadership. Rodolfo Ernesto Paiz Andrade (general secretary)

Guatemalan Christian Democratic Party (*Democracia Cristiana Guatemalteca*, DCG), founded in August 1955 and a centre-right party which, despite its reformist rhetoric, has been decidedly conservative when in office. The party came out of an anti-communist tradition and was founded with the help of the Roman Catholic Church in the belief that a Christian approach to politics would prevent the left coming to power. The DCG's initial policy was to oppose violence and promote social justice through direct church assistance, while at the same time closing ranks with the now disappeared right-wing National Liberation Movement (MLN). These internal contradictions came to a head during the regime of Col. Enrique Peralta Azurdia (1963-66), when an anti-communist faction accepted 10 seats in Congress while the majority of the party campaigned in opposition for basic social welfare and army reforms. After the expulsion of the right-wing faction, the DCG gained considerable support from students, trade unionists and rural communities during the unrest and repression of the 1960s. Following attacks by right-wing paramilitaries and the murder of several of its leaders, the DCG went underground in June 1980 but re-emerged for the 1982 election campaign as a partner of the National Renewal Party (PNR) in the National Opposition Union (UNO). The alliance won three seats in Congress and the PNR presidential candidate came third with 15.6%. The DCG initially supported the 1982 coup led by Efraín Ríos Montt, who promised to put an end to violence and corruption, but distanced itself from the regime when it became an open dictatorship.

Widely seen as the party least involved in repression and corruption and the one most likely to promote social reforms, the DCG won the most seats (20 out of 88) in the 1984 Constituent Assembly elections heralding a return to civilian rule. This paved the way for the party's resounding victory in the late 1985 elections, in which Marco Vinicio Cerezo Arévalo was elected President and the DCG secured a majority in Congress. The Cerezo government disappointed many of its original supporters by pursuing conservative policies. It nevertheless experienced three coup attempts and a number of coup plots by the extreme right and sections of the army between 1987 and 1989. For the November 1990 elections the DCG attempted to restore its progressive image by forging an alliance with the Democratic Convergence (DC), but the deteriorating economy and allegations of corruption against party leaders strengthened general disillusionment. The party mustered only 27 seats in the November 1990 congressional elections, while Alfonso Portillo, who was unable to campaign because of illness, came third in the presidential contest with 17.3% of the votes. In the 1994 congressional elections, moreover, the party's representation fell to 13 seats (out of a total of 80). After the party joined a National Front alliance with the Union of the National Centre (UCN) and the Social Democratic Party (PSD) in April 1995, a number of disgruntled DCG deputies – led by future President Alfonso Portillo – resigned their party membership and set up an independent bloc in Congress. In the November 1995 congressional elections the rump DCG's representation fell to three seats, of which only two were retained in November 1999 (including one seat for ex-president Vinicio Cerezo), when the DCG failed to field a presidential candidate.

In 2003 two presidential candidates for the DCG resigned in succession and the party subsequently nominated Jacobo Arbenz Villanova as its candidate, who polled 1.6% in the first round of presidential elections in November 2003. The DCG gained only one seat in the November 2003 congressional elections.

Address. Av. Elena 20-66 Zona 3, Guatemala City
Telephone. (502) 238-4988
Leadership. Marco Vinicio Cerezo Arévalo (general secretary)

Guatemalan National Revolutionary Unity (*Unidad Revolucionaria Nacional Guatemalteca*, URNG), founded in 1979 as an umbrella organization of the various left-wing guerrilla groups in order to present a unified front against

army offensives. The framework for a central military command was set up in early 1982, but until the late 1980s the individual member groups continued to operate separately. The new period of civilian rule that began in 1986 encouraged the guerrillas to seek an agreement that would allow the URNG to enter the political mainstream. Semi-official peace talks with the National Reconciliation Commission (CNR), made up of representatives from Guatemalan political parties and of "notable citizens", started in Norway in March 1990 and resulted in the Oslo Accords, which set a rough timetable for formal peace negotiations. A major breakthrough came in talks in Mexico City in April 1991, attended for the first time by representatives of the Guatemalan armed forces. Three months later a framework peace agreement was agreed, although a definitive peace accord and an end to armed hostilities was not achieved until Dec. 29, 1996.

In 1995, for the first time in its history, the URNG urged Guatemalans to participate in national elections, tacitly supporting the newly founded centre-left (and now defunct) New Guatemala Democratic Front (*Frente Democrático Nueva Guatemala*, FDNG), which included a number of small parties and social movement activists. Following the 1996 peace settlement the URNG became a political party, legally registering in December 1998. In the 1999 elections the URNG ran jointly with Authentic Integral Development (DIA) in the New National Alliance (ANN). The DIA-URNG candidate for the presidency, Alvaro Colóm, came third with 12.3% of the votes cast, while the alliance obtained a modest nine seats in Congress. However, the URNG was then beset by internal division and some elements, led by former guerrilla commander Jorge Soto, left the party to set up the New Alliance Nation (ANN) as a separate party. Another former guerrilla commander, Rodrigo Asturias, contested the presidency for the URNG in the 2003 presidential elections and received 2.6% of the votes in the first presidential round in November 2003. The URNG gained 2 seats in the 2003 congressional elections.

Address. 11 Av. 11–56 zona 2, Guatemala City
Telephone. (1502–2) 254–05–72, 334–28–08/09
Website. www.urng.org.gt
Leadership. Alba Estela Maldonado (general secretary)

New National Alliance (*Alianza Nueva Nación*, ANN), has its origins in the electoral alliance formed in 1999 between the URNG and the DIA as a vehicle for the former guerrilla forces and in the remnants of the centre-left electoral front the New Guatemala Democratic Front (FDNG, now defunct), which contested the 1995 elections. In the 1999 congressional elections the alliance gained 9 seats. It was registered as a political party in 2003, by which time it had split from the URNG following divisions between former guerrilla commanders. The ANN did not field a presidential candidate in 2003, but contested the congressional elections and won gained 6 seats in November 2003. Amongst its deputies are former guerrilla commander Jorge Soto and Nineth Montenegro, a human rights activist who has campaigned vigorously to increase the accountability of the armed forces.

Address. 15 avenida 5-60, zona 1, Guatemala City
Telephone. (502)-251-2514
Leadership. Alfonso Bauer Paiz (general secretary, resigned 2003); Jorge Soto (acting general secretary)

Unionist Party (*Partido Unionista*, PU), formed in 2000, when a faction of the National Advancement Party (PAN) led by former President and party general secretary Alvaro Arzú lost the party leadership elections to Leonel López Rodas. Together with his followers in Congress, Arzú set up the PU, taking 16 of the 37 deputies elected for the PAN in 1999. The PU suffered internal divisions when Arzú's choice

for party general secretary, Gustavo Porras Castejón (formerly head of the government team in the peace negotiations during the Arzú government) lost the leadership of the party to the conservative former PAN mayor of Guatemala City, Fritz García Gallont. García Gallont stood for the presidency on the PU ticket on 9 November 2003, gaining 3% of the vote. The PU elected 7 deputies in the November 2003 congressional elections and in municipal elections, also held in November 2003, Alvaro Arzú was elected mayor of Guatemala City on the PU ticket.

Address. 5a Avenida 5-11, zona 9, Guatemala City

Telephone. (502) 331-7468

Leadership. Fritz García-Gallont Bischof (general secretary)

Guinea-Bissau

Capital: Bissau
Population: 1,286,000 (2000E)

The Republic of Guinea-Bissau achieved independence from Portugal in 1974 with the African Party for the Independence of Guinea and Cape Verde (PAIGC) becoming the ruling party. Its first President, Luis Cabral, was overthrown in a coup in 1980 by Brig.-Gen. João Bernardo Vieira. The PAIGC continued to be the sole ruling party after the 1980 coup, although the Cape Verde branch broke away from the Guinea-Bissau branch in 1981. In a constitution adopted in 1984 Guinea-Bissau was declared to be an anti-colonial and anti-imperialist republic and a state of revolutionary national democracy, with the PAIGC as the leading force in society and in the state. In January 1991 the PAIGC formally approved the introduction of multi-party democracy, and in May legislation legalizing political activity by opposition parties was adopted. The first political parties were recognized in November 1991. The revised constitution provided for the direct election of the President and a National People's Assembly (Assembleia Nacional Popular).

Multi-party legislative elections took place in July 1994, resulting in victory for the PAIGC, which secured an absolute majority of seats. In presidential elections, which were conducted over two rounds in July and August 1994, President Vieira returned to office, with just over 52% of the vote in the second ballot.

In June 1998 an army rebellion led by Gen. Ansumane Mané (who had been dismissed as chief of staff the previous February) plunged the country into crisis. Troops from neighbouring Senegal and Guinea were called in to help the forces loyal to President Vieira. Following prolonged fighting and efforts at mediation, a peace accord was reached on Nov. 1, 1998. This provided for the withdrawal of foreign troops, the deployment of a West African ceasefire monitoring group and the holding of elections. Following a further outbreak of hostilities, a new government of national unity, led by Francisco Fadul, was sworn in Feb. 20, 1999. However, on May 7, President Vieira was ousted from power by the rebel military junta led by Gen. Mané. National People's Assembly president Malam Bacai Sanhá was appointed acting President of the Republic pending fresh elections, and the government of national unity remained in office. Vieira was allowed to leave the country in June for medical treatment abroad and exile in Portugal.

Presidential and legislative elections were held on Nov. 28, 1999. The presidential poll required a second round of voting on Jan. 16, 2000, resulting in a victory (with 72% of the votes) for Kumba Ialá (Yalla) of the Social Renewal Party (PRS) over Malam Bacai Sanhá of the PAIGC. In the National People's Assembly elections, the PRS emerged as the largest party with 38 seats, while the Guinea-Bissau Resistance–Bafatá Movement (RGB-MB) won 28, the PAIGC 24 and other parties 12. The PRS formed a coalition government with the RGB. Caetano Intchamá, former Minister of the Interior of the National Unity Government, was choosen as Prime Minister. In November 2000, Gen. Mané refused to recognize military promotions by the President and the introduction of military symbols similar to those of the PRS. He publicly cancelled the promotions, putting some military officers under house arrest and assuming the post of Supreme Commander of the Armed Forces, a presidential power. Mané was killed in the armed confrontations that followed, in what was considered a failed attempt to take power. As part of the same process, several leaders of the opposition parties were arrested, accused of being the mentors of this attempt, until the pressure of the international community led to their release some days later. The incident reinforced the President's personal power and extended the supremacy of the Balanta, one of the country major ethnic groups, in the Armed Forces.

In January 2001, the RGB abandoned the coalition government alleging that ministerial changes carried out by Kumba Ialá did not respect a previous agreement. In March, the PRS decided to replace Caetano Intchamá on the basis that his health required permanent healthcare abroad, which was incompatible with his duties as Prime Minister. To replace him they put forward Artur Sanhá, the secretary-general of the PRS, to the displeasure of the President. After threatening his party with the dissolution of the National Assembly, Ialá asked Faustino Imbali, a sociologist and researcher of the National Institute of Studies and Research, to form a PRS government. He recruited several ministers from minor opposition parties and induced a number of members of parliament of the PAIGC and RGB to approve the government programmme and budget. In December 2001, however, Imbali was dismissed by the President, who accused Imbali of embezzling 2.5 million euros donated by Libya and Nigeria.

To replace him Kumba Ialá chose an activist from the PRS, Alamara Nhassé, formerly Minister of the Interior in Imbali's government, but their relationship deteriorated against a background of economic stagnation. In November 2002, Kumba Ialá dissolved parliament in response to moves to approve a constitutional amendment limiting presidential powers. The dissolution of the Assembly was followed by the appointment of a caretaker government (the fourth government in three years) led by Mário Pires, a co-founder of the PRS and secretary-general of the Presidency. Elections were set for February 2003, then postponed to April, later to July and finally to October. The continuous delays were justified by the lack of financial resources to conduct the electoral census.

On Sept. 14, 2003, the military staged a coup, placing the President and the Prime Minister under house arrest. Two days later Kumba Ialá formally resigned. The coup was strongly condemned by Nigeria and Senegal, but many other countries just expressed a slight protest and, in certain cases, even sympathy for the motivations behind the coup. In reality, the coup was just a matter of replacing the President, since there were no visible changes in the restricted circle of people that held power and had supported him. Artur Sanhá, the secretary-general of the PRS, was installed as Prime Minister of the new caretaker government, despite the wave of protests that his nomination caused in Bissau.

The presidency was entrusted to Henrique Rosa, an entrepreneur close to the Catholic Church. His name was welcomed by the majority of the political class. The new caretaker government was appointed to rule the country until the legislative elections. A National Council of Transition was created to control the government's actions and acted as a provisional parliament; it was made up of 25 senior officers from the armed forces, 23 politicians representing each party that signed the Transition Pact, and eight important representatives of civil society.

On March 28, 2004, legislative elections took place, with 16 political formations standing for election. In most areas of the country the elections took place without much uproar, but in Bissau the disorganization affected greatly the electoral process. Many voters were unable to vote as a result of generalized confusion and delays in the delivery of voting papers. Some of them, discontented and fearing the possibility of fraud, caused disturbances in the streets. On March 30, a new voting session was held for the voters who had not been able to vote on March 28. Despite all the disorganization of the process, an international observer mission considered the elections to have been free, fair and transparent.

The days following the election were tense as the PRS, the party in power, and the caretaker Prime Minister, Arthur Sanhá, alleged fraud and refused to recognize the PAIGC's victory. Their position was supported by some military chiefs, especially those of Balanta origin who were traditionally close to the PRS. Diplomatic pressure was exerted by the United Nations, the Economic Community Of West African States (ECOWAS) and countries with larger diplomatic representation in the country, such as Portugal and France, to bring about a resolution. Finally, on April 4, the National Electoral Commission announced provisional results that gave 35 seats to the PAIGC, 35 to the PRS, 17 to the United Social Democratic Party (PUSD), 2 to the Electoral Union (UE) and 1 to the United Popular Alliance (APU), a result subsequently confirmed by the Supreme Court. On May 12, 2004, the PAIGC formed the new Guinean government.

On Oct. 6, 2004, a mutiny took the lives of army commanders General Seabra and Domingos Barros and forced several other military officers to take shelter in the foreign diplomatic missions. The soldiers declared that their action was because of wage arrears and not a coup attempt. Nevertheless, they are trying to impose Tagma Na Wai, an old and illiterate general, as the army leader. He and his followers have close ties with the PRS, which might endanger the transition process.

African Party for the Independence of Guinea and Cape Verde
Partido Africano da Independência da Guiné e Cabo Verde (PAIGC)
Address. CP 106, Bissau
Website. www.rgb-guinebissau.org
Leadership. Carlos Domingos Gomes (president)
The PAIGC was founded in 1956 and engaged in armed struggle against Portuguese colonial rule from the early 1960s. From independence in 1974 it was the sole and ruling party. It had been initially a joint Guinea-Bissau and Cape

Verde organization with a bi-national leadership but the Cape Verde branch broke away from the mainland organization following the November 1980 coup in Guinea-Bissau. While retaining a leftist stance, the PAIGC at the beginning of the 1990s endorsed the establishment of a new multi-party system. In legislative elections in July 1994 the PAIGC won 62 of the 100 seats in the National People's Assembly, with 46% of the votes cast. The simultaneous presidential polls produced no outright winner in the first round but incumbent President Vieira was returned in the second round run-off against the Social Renewal Party candidate in August.

In June 1998 the authority of the PAIGC government was challenged by an army rebellion. Troops from neighbouring Senegal and Guinea were called to help the forces loyal to President Vieira. Despite ceasefires and mediation efforts, the ensuing year-long civil war led to Vieira's overthrow in May 1999 by the rebel military junta. National People's Assembly president Malam Bacai Sanhá was appointed acting President of the Republic pending fresh elections, and the government of national unity which had been appointed the previous February remained in office. Vieira was allowed to leave the country in June for medical treatment abroad. In September 1999 he was expelled from the PAIGC and Francisco Benante assumed the party presidency.

In legislative elections held on Nov. 28, 1999, the PAIGC won only 24 of the 102 National People's Assembly seats, while in the second round of presidential elections on Jan. 16, 2000, PAIGC candidate Malam Bacai Sanhá lost decisively to Kumba Ialá of the Social Renewal Party (PRS). The party was strongly penalized by the electors in the urban areas, especially in Bissau, and it could only keep a good score among the Mandigas and Beafadas, due to the influence of Gen. Ansumane Mané and Malam Bacai Sanhá, who have, respectively, those ethnic origins.

In January 2002, the PAIGC carried out its IV Extraordinary Convention, also called the Reconciliation Convention because several important militants who had been expelled (as a consequence of the defeat of their party faction in the 1998 military conflict) were readmitted. The election for the presidency of the party was won by Carlos Domingos Gomes, with 48% of the votes against 26% for Aristides Gomes. The PAIGC was reorganized and became again one of the most important parties in the country.

In the March 2004 elections, the PAIGC ran a well-resourced campaign that resulted in victory. It won back a substantial part of the electorate that had been lost in the 1999 elections, especially in Bissau, in the Bijagós islands, in the eastern side of the country and notably in the territory of the Papel ethnic group, where it scored a heavy victory. The PAIGC took 33.88% of the vote nationally, winning 45 seats in the National Assembly and forming the new government.

Electoral Union
União Eleitoral (EU)
Leadership. Joaquim Baldé
The Electoral Union, also popularly known as the *partido da vaca* (party of the cow), is a coalition of four parties: the Social Democratic Party, the Renewal and Progress Party, the Socialist Democratic Party for Guinean Salvation and the Guinea-Bissau League for Ecological Protection. All these parties are ruled by leaders with the Baldé surname, which among the Fula population is associated with the traditional legitimacy for the exercise of power. This fact led to accusations, by other parties, that the UE was nothing but a Fula party trying to promote the ethnic vote.

In the March 2004 elections, the Electoral Union got 18,354 votes (4.28%), electing two members to the National Assembly.

Guinea-Bissau Resistance–Bafatá Movement
Resistência da Guiné-Bissau–Movimento Bafatá (RGB-MB)

Website. www.rgb-guinebissau.org
Leadership. Salvador Tchongo

Founded in Portugal in 1986 and legalized in December 1991, the party came second to the ruling African Party for the Independence of Guinea and Cape Verde in the 1994 legislative elections, winning 19 seats. Before the 1999 poll, the RGB held its party convention. Hélder Vaz was elected president but the other candidate, Salvador Tchongo, refused to recognize him, claiming that the results were fraudulent. As a consequence, the party split in two and Tchongo supporters declared the convention outcome null and void. In the November 1999 elections, the RCB-MB won about 70,000 votes, electing 28 members of parliament and becoming the second largest party in the National People's Assembly. Its candidate in the presidential election held at the same time was eliminated after the first ballot, taking third place with 8.2% of the votes. The party's best results were obtain in urban areas, especially in the city of Bissau, where it got the majority of the seats in the National Assembly, and also in the eastern part of the country, among the Fula population, where it traditionally held some influence.

The RGB-MB formed a coalition government with the Social Renewal Party which lasted a year. In January 2002, the RGB-MB abandoned the coalition and joined the opposition. Later that year, in September 2002, the Supreme Court endorsed Salvador Tchongo's claims and removed Hélder Vaz from the presidency of the party. Vaz tried to ignore the judicial decision, declaring that it was a presidential manipulation of the courts, and staged a party convention in October 2002. The convention was held in a tense atmosphere with the sessions being interrupted several times by police intervention.

Salvador Tchongo held his rival congress in December. His faction was the only one accepted in the electoral process, forcing Hélder Vaz and his supporters to look for another "shelter party". After negotiations with many parties they came to an agreement with the Democratic Convergence Party, the Front of Struggle for the Liberation of Guinea, the Social Democratic Front and the Democratic Front to form the United Platform coalition.

The RGB-MB of Salvador Tchongo failed to elect any members to the National Assembly in the March 2004 elections. It got only 7,900 votes (1.8%), joining the extensive list of small parties without parliamentary representation.

Social Renewal Party
Partido para a Renovação Social (PRS)

Leadership. Alberto Nan Beia
Address. Assembleia Nacional Popular, CP 219 – Bissau

The PRS was set up in January 1992 by defectors from the Social Democratic Front, and was legalized the following October. In the 1994 legislative elections it secured 12 seats in the National People's Assembly. Having come second to President Vieira in the first round of the presidential poll, party leader Ialá was narrowly defeated in the second round run-off with nearly 48% of the votes, despite being endorsed by all opposition parties.

Following the military overthrow of Vieira's regime, presidential and legislative elections were held in November 1999. The electoral campaign of the Social Renewal Party was conduct for several months with long term stays in each village, so that the militants could take part in the day-by-day life of the Balanta populations. As a result, the Balanta, who are predominant in several major constituencies, voted massively for this party and for its presidential candidate. The party emerged as the largest single party in the National People's Assembly with 38 of the 102 seats, and Kumba Ialá

headed the first ballot of the presidential poll with almost 39% of the votes. In the second round of voting, in January 2000, Ialá decisively beat the PAIGC candidate and was nominated as President of the Republic in February. He resigned as PRS chairman in May 2000. However, he continued to interfere with the life of the party, even announcing, in 2003, that he would campaign for the PRS.

Since it took power, the party has experienced strong internal conflicts. The PRS was founded by a heterogeneous group of activists, but the decisive influence of the Balanta ethnic group in gaining power has dictated its predominance over the non-Balantas. At the same time, a certain rivalry is noticeable between the so-called Balantas of the North, from the area of Bula to which Kumba Ialá belongs, and those of the South, who support Alamara Nhassé and Arthur Sanhá.

In January 2002, the party convention was controversial. Despite the fact that all the doors were locked with chains, some candidates claimed the results were fraudulent. The election was won by Alamara Nhassé. He resigned the leadership of the party after being dismissed as Prime Minister, Alberto Nan Beia being designated to replace him. After the dismissal of President Kumba Ialá the party became divided between his supporters and those of Sanhá. The latter was in charge of the caretaker government.

In the 2004 elections the PRS was confident of victory. It had ample financial resouces to support the electoral campaign and it managed to get a limited release from his house arrest for former President Kumba Ialá, to appear at political party events in several major cities of the country. The PRS was able to elect some members of parliament in the eastern parts of the country, a region disputed by all the parties, but it was in the Balanta territory, where it has larger influence, that the party got its best results.

Although it obtained about 114,000 votes (26.5%), choosing 35 members for the National Assembly, it strongly disputed PAIGC's victory, slowing for days the announcement of the results. Only on April 24 did the PRS formally recognize the results and congratulate the PAIGC on their victory.

United Platform-Bad luck leave Guinea-Bissau
Plataforma Unida–Mufunessa Larga Guiné (PU)

In its initial form the United Platform was intended to be a broad coalition to stand against the excessive political interference of the President of the Republic. The number of parties (about 10) rapidly started to decrease because of the lack of consensus among parties and due to changes in political circumstances. In its last configuration the Platform was formed by the Party of Democratic Convergence, the Democratic Front, the Front of Struggle for the Liberation of Guinea, the Social Democratic Front and the Hélder Vaz faction of Guinea-Bissau Resistance (RGB).

Despite being considered to be one of the major political forces, it was the great loser in the March 2004 elections. In spite of having ample financial resources for its campaign, it proved unable to elect any member to the National Assembly. It got nearly 21,000 votes (4.83%), but they were far too dispersed throughout the country to win a single seat. The defeat was particularly harsh in Bissau where in the 1999 elections the RGB of Hélder Vaz, one of the leaders of the Platform, had been the most popular party in the city.

United Popular Alliance
Aliança Popular Unida (APU)

The Socialist Alliance led by Fernando Gomes and the Guinean Popular Party led by João Tátis Sá forms this coalition. The reason for the alliance was the electoral score obtained by both leaders as independent candidates in the presidential elections of 1999 when the sum of their votes was close to 50,000, nearly 15 % of the total vote. For the 2004 elections alliance was expected to have some support among two of the leading ethnic groups in the country – Manjacos and Papel – and also on the Bijagós islands. However, the coalition got only about 5 800 votes (1.36%). A determining factor in this failure was the absence of Tátis Sá who remained in Lisbon and he did not participate in the campaign. The potential electorate of the Papel ethnic group that had massively voted in Tátis Sá in the 1999 elections, ended up voting in the PAIGC. The Popular Alliance only won the support of some of the Manjaco population, which elected Fernando Gomes in electoral district 20, region of Cachéu.

United Social Democratic Party
Partido Unido Social Democrático (PUSD)
Website. www.pusd.gb.com
Leadership. Francisco José Fadul

PUSD was formed by a splinter group of the Social Democratic Front in July 1999. Its then leader, Vitor Saúde Maria, had earlier been a Prime Minister under the Vieira regime until March 1984 when he left the ruling African Party for the Independence of Guinea and Cape Verde. The party won no seats in the National People's Assembly in 1994, and its candidate secured only 2% of the votes in the presidential election.

On Dec. 18, 2002, at a convention held in Bissau, the activists of the PUSD chose Francisco José Fadul as president of the party. He had ruled the country from the end of the military conflict to the 1999 elections, and had been forced into exile in Portugal after the death of General Ansumane Mané. His return to the country and his joining the PUSD gave a new breath to this small party. He gave it a national dimension and an importance that it did not have before. In the March 2004 elections, apparently with lesser financial resources for the campaign that its main rivals, the PUSD managed to be placed third. The party won its votes mainly in Bissau and in the eastern regions of the country. It got about 75,000 votes (17.6%), electing 17 members of the National Assembly. Negotiations to form government or to sign a political agreement with the PAIGC were inconclusive. As a consequence some militants started contesting the leadership of Francisco Fadul. In August 2004, eight important militants were expelled from the party, becoming independent MP's. The PUSD parliamentary group is now reduced to 9 seats.

Other Parties

Democratic Alliance (*Aliança Democrática*, AD), formed by the Party of Democratic Convergence and the Democratic Front, both led by the Mandinga brothers. The coalition got 17,500 votes in the legislative elections of 1999, winning three seats in the National People's Assembly. Its zone of electoral influence is in the eastern Islamic regions of the country. For the 2004 elections the Democratic Alliance joined the United Platform.
Leadership. Victor Fernando Mandinga

Democratic Front (*Frente Democrática*, FD), the first party to be legalized in Guinea, in 1991, by Aristides Menezes. The party participated in the first multi-party elections as part of the coalition Union for Change. In 1999, the party ran in the Democratic Alliance in alliance with the Party of Democratic Convergence and in the 2004 elections joined the United Platform.
Leadership. Jorge Mandinga

Front of Struggle for the Liberation of Guinea (*Frente da Luta para a Libertação da Guiné*, FLING), a movement which originated as a contemporary of the PAIGC but was never able to lead a guerrilla war against the colonial army and, consequently, was not involved in the negotiations which delivered power to the PAIGC. After independence it was harassed and disbanded by the PAIGC, remaining active only in exile in Senegal. After the political opening it was legalized in its present form in May 1992. FLING won a single seat in the 1994 legislative elections; its leader contested the presidential elections but achieved less than 3% of the first ballot vote.

In the 1999 elections, the FLING got about 7,000 votes (2% of the total), mainly in the region of Cachéu, where the Manjaco ethnic group gives some support to the party. The voting was not enough to keep the seat it held in the National Assembly. The current party president explained this result in terms of the bad influence of François Kankoila Mendy – the historic leader dismissed at the last convention – who appealed to supporters not to vote for the FLING. To participate in the 2004 electoral process the FLING joined the United Platform electoral coalition.
Leadership. José Catengul Mendes

Guinea-Bissau League for Ecological Protection (*Liga da Guiné-Bissau para a Protecção Ecológica*, LIPE), presents itself as an environmentalist party. It was founded in 1993 and the majority of its support is in electoral district number 2 in the south-east part of the country, especially in the Quebo region in which the Fula ethnic group is predominant. Party leader Bubacar Rachid Djaló has prestige in this region because he belongs to an important line of Islamic dignitaries. After the elections he collaborated closely with the President Kumba Ialá, becoming one of his personal Council members. Recently his authority was contested and the party is being run until the next convention by an interim President, Mustafá Baldé. Meanwhile, the LIPE joined the Electoral Union to run in the 2004 elections.
Leadership. Mamadú Mustafá Baldé

Guinean Civic Forum–Social Democracy (*Fórum Cívico Guineense–Social Democracia*, FCG-SD) in 1999 got less than 1% of the votes. The Forum is the only Guinean party led by a woman, the lawyer Antonieta Rosa Gomes, who also ran in the presidential elections. The party has more the characteristics of a women's rights activist movement than those of a political party though most of its small total of votes (3,262) came in the east, in the Islamic regions of the country. The 2004 party results were also irrelevant.
Leadership. Antonieta Rosa Gomes

Guinean Democratic Movement (*Movimento Democrático Guineense*, MDG), established on Feb. 14, 2003. Its leader, Silvester Alves, is a lawyer who was Minister in the National Unity Government in 1999. With the removal of Kumba Ialá he became the spokesman of the Ad Hoc Commission, which was created to negotiate with the military the post-coup political order.
Website. www.mdg-guinebissau.org
Leadership. Silvestre Alves

Guinean Democratic Party (*Partido Democrático Guineense*, PDG). Manuel Cá was the spokesman of Kumba Ialá's candidature for the Presidency of the Republic in 2000. After the election they followed different paths and, in April 2001, he founded the Guinean Democratic Party, which was legalized by the Supreme Court in 2002.
Leadership. Manuel Cá

Guinean Popular Party (*Partido Popular Guineense*, PPG). In 1999, João Tátis Sá, a doctor living in Portugal, presented himself as a candidate in the presidential elections. He got around 24,000 votes, coming fifth, but in the territory of the Papel ethnic group, to which he belongs, he polled well, taking as much as 61% of the vote in Quinhamel, the heart of

the Papel territory. After the election, he went on to create a party, which was legalized in April 2000. In the 2004 legislative elections the Guinean Popular Party participated in the coalition United Popular Alliance.
Leadership. João Tátis Sá

National Union for Democracy and Progress (*União Nacional para a Democracia e o Progresso*, UNDP), formed in April 1998 by Abubacar Baldé, a militant of the PAIGC and former Minister of the Interior in the time of Nino Vieira. The party was set up shortly before the beginning of the military conflict of 1998. As it mainly brought together elements of the Fula ethnic group, it was accused of being a tribal project (the same designation can be found, in other West African countries, in parties with that ethnic connotation). Others saw in the UNDP, at the time, a satellite party of the PAIGC aimed at weakening the opposition in the legislative elections, which if it had not been for the military conflict would probably have been been held in that same year.

Standing in the first round of the November 1999 presidential elections, Abubacar Baldé took sixth place with 5.4% of the votes. In the legislative polling at the same time, the UNDP secured one National People's Assembly seat. Its electoral support came mainly from the area of Sonaco, in the east of the country where the Fula population is dominant.

In the 2004 elections the UNDP collected only 5,815 votes (1.18%) and did not elect any member to the National Assembly. Its president, Abubacar Baldé, was one of the politicians who most strongly disputed the results, claiming electoral fraud.
Leadership. Abubacar Baldé

National Unity Party (*Partido da Unidade Nacional*, PUN), set up on July 26, 2001, by Idrissa Djaló, a young entrepreneur. The PUN has obtained some media attention, assuming positions that are becoming popular among the new generation of African politicians, such as revitalizing traditional institutions of power capable of adapting the modern state to the African reality. However, in the March 2004 elections the party only got 6,260 votes (1.46% of the vote), quite dispersed throughout the country, without gathering the sufficient number in any electoral district to be able to elect any member to the National Assembly.
Leadership. Idrissa Djaló

Party of Democratic Convergence (*Partido da Convergência Democrática*, PCD) in 1994 was presented by the media and by some political analysts as a party of young and dynamic technocrats, and a serious candidate for victory in the polls. However, this preference was not shown at the ballot boxes and the PCD got only 5.3% of the votes and no seats; also its presidential candidate obtained fourth place in the first ballot of the presidential election. For the 1999 elections, the PDC joined the Democratic Front, forming the Democratic Alliance, which nowadays is part of the coalition United Platform.
Leadership. Victor Fernando Mandinga

Party of the People Manifest (*Partido Manifesto do Povo*, PMP). Faustino Imbali was a presidential candidate in 1999 for the Guinea-Bissau Resistance–Bafatá and for the Democratic Alliance. He presented his *Manifesto* in Medina do Boé, a mythical place of the foundation of Guinea-Bissau, announcing his intention to run in the presidential elections. He got only 30,000 votes, coming third. However, his score was much lower than that obtained by the two parties that had supported him. Faustino was part of the first PRS government and was Prime Minister of the second, between January and November 2001.
Leadership. Faustino Imbali

Renewal and Progress Party (*Partido de Renovação e Progresso*, PRP), set up in 1997 after its president, Mamadú Uri Baldé, abandoned the LIPE, the party for which he was elected member of the National Assembly in 1994. In the 1999 elections both the RPP and its leader, who was a presidential candidate, won below 1% of the votes. In the 2004 elections the PRP was part of the coalition Electoral Union.
Leadership. Mamadú Uri Baldé

Social Democratic Front (*Frente Democrática Social*, FDS), among the first groups to emerge openly in opposition to the Vieira regime, and the first to announce its formation as an opposition party. It was legalized in December 1991. Party leader Barbosa had been one of the founders of the PAIGC, but was subsequently purged and imprisoned before being formally amnestied in 1987. For this reason, in the first multi-party elections the motto of the campaign of his party was: *Barbosa e nô Mandela*, that is to say, "Barbosa is our Mandela".

Factional strife within the FDS has led to several defections by members to launch other groups, including the United Social Democratic Party and the Social Renewal Party. In the November 1999 legislative elections, the FDS won one seat in the National People's Assembly, elected in the area of Quinhamel. In that constituency the ethnic group Papel is predominant and Rafael Barbosa has that ethnic backgroud. In January 2003, the FDS joined the United Platform coalition.
Leadership. Rafael Barbosa

Social Democratic Party (*Partido Social Democrático*, PSD), formed by dissidents from the Guinea-Bissau Resistance–Bafatá Movement. The split was harmful to the RGB in the 1999 elections, since the PSD got about 20,000 votes and won three seats in the National People's Assembly. Its President, Joaquim Baldé, was also a candidate in the presidential elections, but won only 12,000 votes. In January 2003 the PSD joined the Electoral Union.
Leadership. Joaquim Baldé

Socialist Alliance of Guinea-Bissau (*Aliança Socialista da Guiné-Bissau*, ASG), formed in May 2000 by Fernando Gomes, a former chairman of the national human rights league. He ran for President of the Republic and despite having no party support he was the fourth most successful candidate, with about 26,000 votes. He got his best results in the region of Cachéu, among the Manjaco ethnic group to which he belongs, and in the Bijagós islands, where he was born. The Socialist Alliance joined the Guinean Popular Party to form the coalition United Popular Alliance to run for the 2004 legislative elections.
Leadership. Fernando Gomes

Socialist Democratic Party (*Partido Democrático Socialista*, PDS)
Leadership. João Seco Mamadú Mané

Socialist Democratic Party for Guinean Salvation (*Partido Socialista Democrático para a Salvação Guineense*, PSDSG)
*Leadership.*Serifo Baldé

Socialist Party (*Partido Socialista*, PS), legalized in 1992 with the return of its leader Cirilo Rodrigues, a dissident of the FLING, to Guinea-Bissau after a long exile in France. In 1999, he was not a candidate.
Leadership. Cirilo Rodrigues

Solidarity and Labour Party (*Partido da Solidariedade e Trabalho*, PST)
Leadership. Incuba Injai

Union for Change (*União para a Mudança*, UM), set up as an opposition coalition to contest the July 1994 elections. It won six seats in the National People's Assembly but its presidential candidate, Bubakar Djalo, attracted less than 3% of the votes in the first ballot. Reconstituted in 1995, the UM comprises the Democratic Front, the Democratic Party of Progress, the Party of Renovation and Development, the Social Democratic Front and the United Democratic Movement. In the November 1999 elections the UM got 28,000 votes, winning three seats in the National People's Assembly, i.e. three less than in the previous legislature. One of the reasons that were pointed to justify the loss of seats was the accusation of the RGB and PRS that the UM was a party of mestizos, an argument that weakened its position before the Guinean electorate, normally sensitive to this issue.

In 2004, the UM got about 8,600 votes (2.01% of the total) and failed to elect a single member to the parliament.
Leadership. Amine Michel Saad (president)

Guinea

Capital: Conakry
Population: 7,700,000 (2002E)

The Republic of Guinea gained independence from France in 1958. The first President, Ahmed Sekou Touré, dominated the political stage for the next quarter of a century, pursuing a policy of socialist revolution and internal suppression. After his death in March 1984, the armed forces staged a coup, forming a Military Committee for National Recovery (CMRN) under the leadership of Maj.-Gen. Lansana Conté. The 1982 constitution was suspended after the takeover, as was the Democratic Party of Guinea, which had been the ruling and sole legal political party. A new constitution was approved by referendum in December 1990; in early 1991 the CMRN was dissolved and a mixed military and civilian Transitional Committee of National Recovery was set up as the country's legislative body. In April 1992 legislation providing for the legalization of political parties came into effect.

President Conté was confirmed in office in December 1993 in the country's first multiparty elections, and five years later he won his second five-year mandate by a larger majority, taking some 56% of the vote. Another new constitution was approved by referendum in November 2001, although the opposition boycotted the vote. The new constitution removed the limitation of a presidential mandate to two terms in office, allowing President Conté to stand for re-election. It also extended the presidential term from five to seven years and lifted an age limit of 70 for presidential candidates, which would have barred Conté from standing for re-election upon the expiry of his term in December 2003. In the presidential election held on Dec. 21, 2003, Conté was re-elected with 95.6% of the vote, with opposition parties boycotting the election.

In legislative elections in June 1995, the Party of Unity and Progress (PUP), led by President Conté, won a majority of seats in the new 114-member National Assembly. The next elections were delayed until June 2002, partly because of opposition requests for a postponement, but also due to unrest in neighbouring Sierra Leone and Liberia which had spilled over into Guinea. When the National Assembly elections were eventually held the PUP increased its majority, winning 85 of the 114 seats, 14 more than in 1995. However, of the parties competing in the elec-

tion, only three were opposition groups, namely the Union for Progress and Renewal and the Union for the Progress of Guinea, which together won 23 seats, and the Guinean People's Party, which did not win any seats. Other opposition parties boycotted the elections.

Democratic Party of Guinea–African Democratic Rally
Parti Démocratique de Guinée–Rassemblement
Démocratique Africain (PDG-RDA)
Leadership. Ismael Mohamed Gassim Gushein
President Touré's former ruling Democratic Party of Guinea, which had been dissolved in 1984, was revived in 1992 as the PDG-RDA. Following the 1993 presidential election, in which the PDG-RDA leader, Ismael Mohamed Gassim Gushein, secured less than 1% of the vote, the party split, with dissidents forming the Democratic Party of Guinea (PDG-AST) under the leadership of Marcel Cros. Each faction won one National Assembly seat in the 1995 legislative elections. In the Assembly elections held in June 2002 the PDG-RDA won three seats. The party broadly supported the government of President Conté.

Party of Unity and Progress
Parti de l'Unité et le Progrès (PUP)
Leadership. Maj.-Gen. Lansana Conté (leader)
Acting as the core of an informal coalition supporting the ruling regime, the PUP nominated Maj.-Gen. Conté as its candidate for the December 1993 presidential poll, in which he won nearly 52% of the votes cast. In December 1998 Conté won his second five-year presidential term, securing about 56% of the vote. Following changes to the constitution approved by referendum in November 2001, allowing him to stand again for election, Conté went on to win a third term in December 2003 with 95.6% of the votes cast and opposition parties boycotting the poll. In the 1995 legislative elections the PUP won an absolute majority with 71 seats and in the next elections held in June 2002 the party retained its majority, winning 85 seats.

Rally of the Guinean People
Rassemblement du Peuple Guinéen (RPG)
Leadership. Alpha Condé, Tidiane Cisse (leaders)
The RPG leader, Alpha Condé, had been a prominent exiled opponent of former President Touré and the subsequent military regime until his eventual return to Guinea in May 1991. The RPG was one of the first parties registered under the new parties law in 1992. In the December 1993 presidential election, Condé took second place with a 19.5% share of the vote. In the 1995 legislative elections, the RPG won the most seats among the opposition parties with 19. Condé again contested the presidential elections in December 1998, but achieved only third place with 16.6% of the vote. He was arrested and detained after the poll, and eventually sentenced in September 2000 to five years' imprisonment, in what was widely criticized as a show trial. In May 2001 he was unexpectedly released.

In May 2002 the RPG played an instrumental role in the formation of a new opposition alliance, the Republican Front for Democratic Change (FRAD), created by parties which were opposed to participation in the June 2002 legislative elections. Accordingly, the RPG boycotted the poll.

The RPG is a consultative member of the Socialist International.

Republican Front for Democratic Change
Front Républicain pour l'Alternance Démocratique
(FRAD)
This opposition alliance was formed in May 2002 by parties which opposed participation in the forthcoming legislative election. Members included the Rally of the Guinean People

(RPG), the Union of Republican Forces (UFR) and the Djama Party. In early November 2003 the alliance announced that it would boycott the presidential elections scheduled for late December, because it did not expect the poll to be free and fair.

Union for the New Republic
Union pour la Nouvelle République (UNR)
Leadership. Mamadou Boye Ba (leader)
Party leader and presidential candidate, Mamadou Boye Ba, took third place in the December 1993 ballot with just over 13% of the vote. The UNR won nine seats in the 1995 elections to the National Assembly. In September 1998 the UNR absorbed the Party of Renewal and Progress (*Parti pour le Renouveau et le Progrès*, PRP) led by Siradiou Diallo, which had won nine seats in the 1995 legislative elections. Mamadou Boye Ba stood in the December 1998 presidential elections as the joint candidate, coming second with 24.6% of the vote. Unlike a number of other opposition parties, the UNR contested the June 2002 legislative elections, winning 20 seats, thereby becoming the second largest party in the National Assembly, behind the ruling Party of Unity and Progress. Mamadou Boye Ba took 4.4% of the vote in the December 2003 presidential elections which were generally boycotted by the opposition parties.

Union for the Progress of Guinea
Union pour le Progrès de Guinée (UPG)
Leadership. Jean-Marie Dore (leader)
One of only three opposition parties to contest the June 2002 legislative elections, the UPG managed to win three National Assembly seats. The party leader, Jean-Marie Dore, contested the 1993 and 1998 presidential elections but with minimal impact. In mid-November 2003 Dore was reportedly indicted on a charge of insulting President Conté, an offence carrying a prison sentence.

Union of Republican Forces
Union de forces républicaines (UFR)
Leadership. Sidia Toure (leader)
Opposition party led by a former Prime Minister (1996-99). The UFR is a member of the Republican Front for Democratic Change (FRAD), created by parties which were opposed to participation in the June 2002 legislative elections.

Other Parties

Djama Party (*Parti Djama*), secured one seat in the National Assembly poll in 1995. The party is a member of the Republican Front for Democratic Change (FRAD), created by parties which were opposed to participation in the June 2002 legislative elections.
Leadership. Mohamed Mansour Kaba

Guinean People's Party (*Parti du Peuple de Guinée,* PPG), contested the December 1998 presidential elections, but party leader Tolno won less than 1% of the vote to claim fifth place. The PPG contested the June 2002 legislative elections, but did not win any seats.
Leadership. Charles Pascal Tolno

National Alliance for Progress (*Alliance nationale pour le Progrès*, ANP), a small pro-government party which won two seats in National Assembly elections held in June 2002.

Party of Unity and Development (*Parti d'Unité et de Développement*, PUD), a small pro-government party which won one seat in National Assembly elections held in June 2002.

Guyana

Capital: Georgetown
Population: 702,000 (2003E)

Guyana (formerly British Guiana) became independent in 1966 and the Co-operative Republic of Guyana was formally proclaimed within the Commonwealth in 1970. Under the 1980 constitution, the 65-member unicameral National Assembly, elected for five years by universal suffrage, holds legislative power. The President and his government hold executive power. The President appoints a First Vice-President and Prime Minister (who must be an elected member of the National Assembly) and a Cabinet that may include non-elected members and is collectively responsible to the legislature.

The victory of the incumbent People's Progressive Party/Civic (PPP/C) in the December 1997 general elections gave rise to a major political crisis, as the opposition People's National Congress (PNC) disputed their validity amidst violent conflict between supporters of the mainly Indo-Guyanese PPP/C and the predominantly Afro-Caribbean PNC. In January 1998 the two sides signed the CARICOM-brokered Herdmanston Accord, which succeeded in restoring an uneasy peace, although the PNC continued its legal challenge to the elections. Under the accord, a widely representative commission drew up proposals resulting in the passage of the Constitution (Amendment) Act 2000 establishing a permanent Elections Commission to be responsible for the fair conduct of elections. Also passed was the Elections Laws (Amendment) Act 2000, under which 25 of the 65 Assembly members would be elected in 10 geographical regions and the other 40 "national top-up" seats would be allocated proportionally to party lists, headed by the presidential candidate of each party, according to their percentage share of the national vote. Under the legislation, at least a third of the candidates on party lists must be women.

In new elections held on March 19, 2001, which were declared transparent and fair by a number of local and international observers, the PPP/C headed the poll with 52.9% of the vote, so that incumbent President Bharrat Jagdeo was re-elected with the party taking 34 of the Assembly seats. The PNC-Reform obtained 41.8% of the vote and 27 seats and three small parties the remaining four seats.

People's National Congress/Reform (PNC/R)
Address. Congress Place, Sophia, Georgetown
Telephone. (0592) 2257850
Fax. (0592) 2256055
Email. pnc@guyana-pnc.org
Website. www.guyanapnc.org
Leadership. Robert Corbin (leader); Oscar E. Clarke (general secretary)
Forbes Burnham, formerly chairman of the People's Progressive Party (PPP), founded the PNC in 1957 following an open split with PPP leader Cheddi Jagan. The PNC was the main opposition party after the 1957 and 1961 elections, but in 1964, after a change in the electoral system, it joined The United Force (TUF) in a coalition government that led British Guiana to independence in 1966. Drawing most of its support from the African-descended population, the party won all elections until 1992, although these contests were widely regarded as rigged in the party's favour.

The PNC initially followed a moderate socialist line with

emphasis on co-operative principles, before taking a swing to the left in the 1970s and early 1980s. It adopted a more pragmatic approach under the leadership of Hugh Desmond Hoyte, who took over the country's presidency and the party leadership on Burnham's death in 1985. The party experienced severe internal divisions prior to the 1992 elections, in which it lost power to the PPP, winning 27 Assembly seats with 43.6% of the vote. In 1994 a new party constitution was adopted which ceased to refer to the PNC as a socialist movement.

The PNC was also declared the loser of the December 1997 general elections, in which it took 26 Assembly seats and 35% of the vote. The party staged protests against the outcome and there were violent disturbances and attacks on Indian-owned businesses. Tension was reduced by CARICOM mediation but the PNC continued its legal challenge to the election outcome, securing High Court rulings in January 2001 that it had been illegitimate, although the judge also found that she had no powers to remove the President or his government from office.

Meanwhile, in December 2000 the PNC had formed an alliance with the Reform Group, a political interest group led by Jerome Khan and Stanley Ming and drawing its membership from younger professionals and the business class and with an international network in the Guyanese diaspora. Also including the People's Unity Party (PUP) led by Peter Ramsaroop, the alliance took the name PNC/Reform, the letters of the suffix denoting its main policy principles as follows: R – racial harmony, religious tolerance, rebirth and renewal; E – economic revitalization, prosperity and sustainability; F – financial integrity, financial transparency and vision; O – one people, one nation, one destiny; R – rule of law; M – multiculturalism, multi-ethnicism and modernization.

Contesting the March 2001 general elections as a unitary party under Hoyte's leadership, the PNC/R achieved an increased vote share of 41.8% but failed to unseat the ruling PPP/C, its representation in the new Assembly being 27 seats (14 national and 13 geographical). In the immediate aftermath of the election, Hoyte began a process of dialogue with President Jagdeo in an attempt to overcome the deep-seated mistrust between the country's main political-ethnic groupings. There was a hope that if regular political consultations could be undertaken, the defeated side in the election would remain engaged and retain confidence in the governing process. However, the contacts between the two men ended in acrimony in March 2002, with Hoyte expressing dissatisfaction over the government's alleged failure to implement decisions reached in the dialogue process. The breakdown in discussions was doubly grave because the National Assembly had not met since October 2001.

A serious political crisis then resulted, the clearest manifestation of which came on July 3, 2002, when anti-government protesters attacked the presidential complex in Georgetown. Two people were shot dead by the police, while shops and cars were set on fire by rioters. PNC/R leaders condemned the violence, while insisting the grievances of the protesters were genuine. However, the governing PPP/C accused the PNC/R of being centrally involved in the violence, and of launching an unprecedented attempt "to assassinate the President and remove the elected government from office". A way out of the stand-off presented itself after the sudden death of Desmond Hoyte in December 2002. Hoyte's replacement as PNC/R leader, Robert Corbin, made clear that he was prepared to engage the government in constructive talks. As a consequence in February 2003 the PNC/R ended its long-standing boycott of parliament, while in May an agreement was signed between Corbin and Jagdeo creating a number of bipartisan committees to deal with a variety of political, economic and social issues. However, tensions between the opposition and the PPP/C government remained high, and in late March 2004 the PNC/R ended its involve-

ment in the constructive engagement process and instituted a "selective and gradual" withdrawal from parliamentary activities. Corbin stated that full parliamentary relations would not be re-established until the government launched an enquiry into the alleged links between Home Affairs Minister Ronald Gajraj and an extra-judicial hit squad.

People's Progressive Party/Civic (PPP/Civic)

Address. Freedom House, 41 Robb Street, Georgetown
Telephone. (0592) 2272095
Fax. (0592) 2272096
Email. pr@ppp-civic.org
Website. www.ppp-civic.org
Leadership. Bharrat Jagdeo (leader); Sam Hinds (Prime Minister); Donald Ramotar (general secretary)

The left-wing PPP, which was formed by Cheddi Jagan in 1950 from an earlier Political Affairs Committee, started as an anti-colonial party speaking for the lower social classes. It has since drawn its support mainly from the majority ethnic Asian-Indian community. In 1957 the PPP gained an absolute majority in the Assembly and Jagan became the first Chief Minister. In 1961, when the British authorities had conceded internal autonomy, the party again won a majority and Jagan was appointed Prime Minister. In the 1964 elections, held under a British-imposed proportional representation system, the PPP won the most votes but less than half of the Assembly seats, thereby losing power to the coalition headed by the People's National Congress (PNC).

In 1969 the PPP began its formal transformation into a Marxist–Leninist party, Jagan being designated to the new post of "general secretary", which he retained until his death in 1997. After boycotting the National Assembly for over a year in protest at the rigged 1973 elections, the PPP in mid-1975 offered the PNC government its "critical support" in light of the PNC's perceived move towards a socialist path. The party nevertheless denounced the further election victories of the PNC in 1980 and 1985 as fraudulent. Following the collapse of communism in Europe, in 1990 the PPP effectively abandoned its previous Marxist-Leninist line and instead declared its support for a market-oriented economy based on collaboration between the state, private and co-operative sectors.

Prior to the delayed general elections eventually held in October 1992, the PPP became the PPP/Civic, having sought to broaden its appeal by bringing together the Civic group of prominent non-party people from various ethnic and ideological backgrounds. The strategy was successful, in that the party returned to power with 52.3% of the vote and 35 Assembly seats. Cheddi Jagan was accordingly sworn in for a five-year term as President and a PPP/C government was installed.

Cheddi Jagan died in office in March 1997 and was succeeded temporarily by the Prime Minister and Vice-President, Sam Hinds, who quickly stood down to allow his predecessor's widow, Janet Jagan, to become President. An American by origin and active in the party since its inception, Janet Jagan led the PPP/C in the general elections held in December 1997, in which the party was again declared the winner with 48% of the vote and 36 Assembly seats, amidst claims of widespread fraud. Janet Jagan stepped down in August 1999 on grounds of ill-health and was succeeded as President by Bharrat Jagdeo, hitherto Second Vice-President. In the March 2001 elections the PPP/C retained power, winning 52.9% of the vote and 34 Assembly seats (23 national and 11 geographical). Amidst yet another major confrontation with what was now the PNC/Reform, President Jagdeo appointed a new PPP/C-dominated government headed by Sam Hinds and including a representative of The United Force (TUF).

The ability of the PPP/C to govern was seriously hindered by the political crisis precipitated by the fallout between Jagdeo and Hoyte in March 2002, the long-standing PNC/R boycott of parliament, and subsequent periodic opposition walkouts. In addition, a long-standing dispute with the Guyana Teachers' Union and an increasing number of violent crimes and kidnappings in the country damaged the administration's standing. Indeed the government was directly implicated in the violence in January 2004 when PPP/C Home Affairs Minister Ronald Gajraj was accused of having links with members of the extra-judicial "Phantom Squad", which had been blamed for a number of execution-style killings. Although Gajraj denied the allegations and President Jagdeo publicly backed his minister, the United States and Canadian governments revoked Gajraj's visa. The British government and Amnesty International also called on the Guyanese government to thoroughly investigate the allegations.

Other Parties

Guyana Action Party–Working People's Alliance (GAP-WPA), formed in the mid-1970s as an alliance of left-wing groups that included the African Society for Cultural Relations with Independent Africa (ASCRIA), Indian Political Revolutionary Associates (IPRA), *Ratoon* (a student group) and the Working People's Vanguard Party (which left before the WPA constituted itself as a political party in 1979). In 1980 one of its leaders, Walter Rodney, was killed by a bomb explosion, an incident blamed in some quarters on supporters of the ruling People's National Congress (PNC). Having boycotted the 1980 elections, the WPA won one seat in 1985 and two in 1992. The WPA contested the 1997 elections jointly with the Guyana Labour Party in the Alliance for Guyana, which won one Assembly seat.

For the March 2001 general elections the WPA formed a joint list with the Guyana Action Party (GAP), which seeks to represent the country's marginalized Amerindian and other hinterland communities. It was agreed that the GAP would field a presidential candidate (Paul Hardy), while the WPA would field a prime ministerial candidate (Rupert Roopnaraine). Having campaigned for a government of national unity, the GAP-WPA alliance came in third position with 2.4% of the vote and two Assembly seats. The WPA is a consultative member of the Socialist International.

Address. Rodney House, 80 Croal Street, Georgetown
Telephone. (0592) 2253679
Fax. (0592) 2253679
Website. www.saxakali.com/wpa
Leadership. Paul Hardy (leader, GAP); Rupert Roopnaraine (leader, WPA)

Guyana Democratic Party (GDP) formed in 1997 by Asgar Ally, who had been Finance Minister in the 1992-97 administration of the People's Progressive Party/Civic (PPP/C). Capitalist in orientation, the party promised to give entrepreneurs confidence to invest in Guyana as well as to develop the infrastructure of the country in order to encourage capital inflows into areas such as manufacturing, tourism and agriculture. The party won one Assembly seat in 1997 but none in 2001, when its share of the vote was 0.34%.

Address. (0592) 2261119
Fax. (0592) 2256894
Leadership. Asgar Ally (leader)

Justice For All Party (JFAP) founded by TV channel owner and campaigning broadcaster C.N. Sharma, and claiming to speak for the poor and marginalized. Contesting the 2001 elections only in the Georgetown region on a platform of lowering the cost of living and reducing ethnic problems, it took 0.71% of the vote and no seats.

Address. 73 Robb & Wellington Streets, Lacytown, Georgetown
Telephone. (0592) 2265462
Fax. (0592) 2273050
Email. sharma@guyana.net.gy
Leadership. Chandra Narine Sharma (leader)

Rise, Organize and Rebuild (ROAR), founded in January 1999 in West Coast Demerara to protest against the murder of 30 people of Indian descent during the previous year and also in response to what the party's leadership perceived to have been silence following anti-Indian riots in January 1998. Despite this genesis, the movement evolved into a political party claiming to be national with the aim of creating a multi-ethnic society. Campaigning on a platform of social and economic improvements, equal opportunities in the civil service, judiciary, police and army, and an end to corruption and ethnic divisions, the party won 0.9% of the vote in the March 2001 elections and was allocated one National Assembly seat.

Address. 186 Parafield, Leonora, West Coast Demerara, PO Box 101409, Georgetown
Telephone. (0592) 2682452
Email. guyroar@hotmail.com
Leadership. Ravindra Dev (leader)

The United Force (TUF) is a conservative party formed in 1961. Advocating racial integration and a mixed economy, it has historically drawn much of its support from the white, Amerindian and other minority communities. The party joined a coalition government with the People's National Congress (PNC) in 1964 but withdrew in 1968 in protest at the enfranchisement of the many emigrant Guyanese. In the first post-independence elections in 1968, TUF won four Assembly seats. It failed to win any seats in the 1973 election but was credited with two seats in both the 1980 and 1985 polls. TUF retained only one Assembly seat in the 1992, 1997 and 2001 elections, winning 0.7% of the vote in the last contest. The party's leader was nevertheless appointed to the new government formed by the People's Progressive Party/Civic, being allocated the trade, tourism and industry portfolio.

Address. 96 Robb & New Garden Streets, Georgetown
Telephone. (0592) 2262596
Fax. (0592) 2252973
Email. manzoornadir@yahoo.com
Leadership. Manzoor Nadir (leader)

Haiti

Capital: Port-au-Prince
Population: 7,528,000 (2003E)

The Republic of Haiti became independent from France in 1804. Between 1957 and 1986 its rulers were President for Life François "Papa Doc" Duvalier and, from 1971, his son Jean-Claude. The latter years of Jean-Claude "Baby Doc" Duvalier's rule were marked by prolonged popular unrest, and he fled abroad in February 1986. A new constitution, which was drawn up in late 1986 and overwhelmingly approved in a referendum in March 1987, provided for a bicameral legislature made up of a 27-member Senate (*Sénat*) and a Chamber of Deputies (*Chambre des Deputés*) of at least 70 members (currently 83). Repeated military intervention, however, prevented the creation of stable civilian government.

Jean-Bertrand Aristide was elected as President for

the first time in 1990, but was toppled by a violent military coup in 1991, the result of which was reversed by a US military intervention in 1994. Aristide then handed over power to his elected successor, René Préval, in 1996. However, Aristide won the next presidential election, held on Nov. 26, 2000, with 91.8% of the vote and was inaugurated in February 2001. Such a resounding victory was attained in part because the opposition Democratic Convergence (CD) boycotted the election in protest at the results of disputed legislative elections held earlier in 2000. Elections to the Chamber of Deputies and partial elections to the Senate were held in three stages during 2000, resulting in an overwhelming victory for Aristide's Lavalas Family (FL) movement. However, mistakes were made in calculating the results, and there were calls to undertake a recount in a number of disputed seats. The victorious FL refused to sanction a review, which precipitated a political crisis with the CD refusing to recognize the legitimacy of either the President or the parliament. The impasse exacerbated an already tense political and social situation in the country.

Though the Organization for American States (OAS) helped facilitate a meeting between President Aristide and the opposition Democratic Convergence in June 2002, little progress was made towards ending the worsening public security situation. The major issues of disagreement between the two sides focussed on the status of the still disputed 2000 parliamentary elections, President Aristide's unwillingness to prosecute those responsible for the acts of violence immediately after an alleged opposition attack on the presidential palace in December 2001, and his reluctance to provide financial compensation to the victims. Without a proper political dialogue the tensions within society became more acute during 2002 and 2003. A series of protest marches held by opposition and student groups on the one hand, and pro-Aristide elements on the other, resulted in violence. Towards the end of 2003 there was an upsurge in the number of protests, fuelled by the murder of gang leader Amiot Metayer in September, with the opposition implicating Aristide in the killing. Between September 2003 and January 2004 at least fifty people were killed during demonstrations. The social instability was exacerbated by political uncertainty after the mandates of many members of parliament expired because of the failure to hold new elections. The result was that President Aristide was forced to rule by decree from mid-January.

The unrest and associated violence that increased in intensity during the autumn and winter of 2003-04 was just the prelude to a much more organized armed uprising that was launched on Feb. 5, 2004. Guy Philippe, a former police chief who fled to the Dominican Republic after being accused by the Haitian authorities of trying to organize a coup in 2002, led the uprising, which began in the northwestern town of Gonaïves and spread quickly south. The rebel force, only around 200 strong, met little resistance, and within three weeks had control of most of the country. In light of this, President Aristide had little choice but to leave Haiti, although he subsequently accused US Marines of kidnapping him and forcing him out of Haiti and the presidency. The claim was denied by the US government, but the Caribbean Community (CARICOM) called for a United Nations-led investigation into Aristide's fall from power. Following the month-long uprising that left more than 130 dead and the departure of Aristide on Feb. 29,

2004, a UN-backed force of US Marines, French soldiers and Chilean troops entered the country in an attempt to stabilize the situation. In May the UN Security Council agreed to establish a new multinational mission consisting of 8,000 troops and police to replace the US-led force from June 1.

On the political front an interim government was installed after Aristide's departure. On March 8, Haiti's Chief Justice, Alexandre Boniface, was sworn in as acting President; a former Foreign Minister, Gerald Latortue, was chosen to replace the FL's Yvon Neptune as Prime Minister to oversee a broadly based transitional government. The government consisted of 13 ministers, none of whom were affiliated to any political party. In early April, meanwhile, the government reached an agreement with political and civil society actors concerning the transition period. The so-called "Consensus on Political Transition", supported by a broadly based Provisional Electoral Council (although excluding Aristide's Lavalas party), set out a procedure to enable elections to be held in Haiti by the end of 2005.

Despite some progress in stabilizing Haiti's political situation, social unrest continued. The leader of the armed uprising, Guy Philippe, promised that his followers would disarm after Aristide was defeated. However, there was little tangible sign of disarmament in the aftermath of the coup. Furthermore, Philippe made clear his preference for the re-establishment of Haiti's discredited armed forces that had been disbanded by Aristide in 1995. Many supporters of the FL movement, meanwhile, encouraged by Aristide's contention that he was forcibly removed from office, undertook a number of attacks against opponents of the former President. The consequence was that many parts of the country remained in a state of lawlessness.

Christian National Movement
Mouvement Chrétien National (Mochrena)
Address. 7, angle rue Jacob et Mon Repos 36, Carrefour
Telephone. (509) 401-3120
Leadership. Luc Mésadieu and Gilbert N. Léger (co-leaders)
Also known as the Christian Movement to Build a New Haiti (*Mouvement Chrétien pour Bâtir une Nouvelle Haïti*) and dating from 1991, Mochrena won three seats in the 2000 elections to the Chamber of Deputies, making it the largest party in the Chamber after the ruling Lavalas Family.

Democratic Convergence
Convergence Démocratique (CD)
Address. 101, Ave Lamartinière (Bois Verna), Port-au-Prince
Leadership. Paul Evans
Democratic Convergence is a loose coalition of 15 opposition parties and groups, which held together despite disagreements over strategy. In particular divisions were apparent between hard-liners who hoped to force Aristide from office, and those who would have been satisfied with winning concessions to strengthen democracy. At the beginning of 2001, CD demanded that the disputed 2000 legislative and presidential elections should be re-run, while threatening to establish a provisional government of national unity if fresh elections were not held. In response the FL government warned that it would not tolerate challenges to its authority. Attempts by the Organization of American States (OAS) to end the political stalemate were unsuccessful. The OAS put forward Resolution 822 in September 2002 for the establishment of a Provisional Electoral Council – representing all elements of the political spectrum – to arrange elections to replace members of parliament who were elected in the disputed elections of 2000. However, the lack of trust between

Aristide and CD prevented the formation of the Council. CD argued that its failure to cooperate was due to the fact that any elections held in the current political climate would not be fair.

In order to keep up the pressure against President Aristide, CD organized a number of anti-government demonstrations in November and December 2002, followed by a further protest in early January 2003. The latter demonstration, however, turned violent after CD supporters were attacked by a group of FL sympathizers. CD was so chastened by the experience that it moderated its anti-government actions. The group was further constrained by its lack of widespread popular support and a strategy that went no further than perpetuating the existing political stalemate. In the lead-up to the violent overthrow of Aristide, members of CD made it clear that they did not support the armed rebels, but called on Aristide to voluntarily stand down as President. In the aftermath of the coup CD were given a place on the "Council of Sages" that had the task of selecting a new Prime Minister and government. However, members of CD were subsequently left out of the government. Despite being unhappy at this exclusion, CD agreed to accept the legitimacy of the interim government, and subsequently joined the Provisional Electoral Council.

The coalition includes leading figures from the Confederation of Democratic Unity, Organization of Struggling People, the Consultation Group and the Progressive Democratic and National Reunion.

Group of 184

Leadership. Andre Apaid (coordinator)

This umbrella group, originally comprising 184 civil society and business organizations, was established in early 2003 and replaced Democratic Convergence (CD) as the main source of opposition to President Aristide's regime. The group shared a similar position to that of the CD, believing that free and fair elections were impossible under the Aristide government. In order to get its message across, the Group of 184 organised a series of public meetings, billed as the "Caravan of Hope", in a number of provincial towns across Haiti. A more significant action on the part of the group came on Nov. 14, 2003, when it organized a large anti-government demonstration outside the National Palace in Port-au-Prince, calling for the replacement of the Aristide government with a provisional administration. However, as with previous CD protests, supporters of Aristide and his FL movement attacked the march, leaving eight people injured. Despite the risks the Group of 184 continued to organise demonstrations and was a key actor in two successful general strikes held in Haiti in December 2003 and January 2004. Like CD, however, the Group of 184 were keen to distance themselves from the violence that led to the overthrow of Aristide in late February 2004. Representatives of the private sector and civil society associated with the Group of 184 were subsequently invited to participate on the "Council of Sages" to oversee the appointment of a new government for Haiti. The government that was chosen subsequently included Bernard Gousse, an active member of the Group of 184, as Minister of Justice and Public Security.

Lavalas Family (FL)
Fanmi Lavalas

Leadership. Yvon Neptune
Address. Boulevard 15 Octobre, Tabarre, Port-au-Prince
Telephone. (509) 256-7208

The pro-Aristide, centrist Lavalas (variously translated as "waterfall", "flood" or "avalanche") Family emerged in the late 1990s when the Lavalas Political Organization (OPL) split into two main factions. The division had its roots in the presidency of René Préval. Soon after his inauguration as

President in February 1996, Préval saw his support base within the OPL erode, as he failed to push ahead with his main policy objective, a market-based restructuring of the economy. Resistance to Préval's reforms came from within the OPL, including Aristide himself. Aristide's criticism of Préval resulted in the split of the OPL into two new, and opposing, political entities, the Lavalas Family (headed by Aristide) and the Organization of Struggling People, headed by the former OPL leader Gérard Pierre-Charles. Despite the split, Aristide's faction emerged victorious from the 2000 legislative elections, winning all but a few seats in both houses. Aristide went on to an overwhelming victory in the presidential election held in November 2000 and replaced Préval as President in February 2001.

The flawed nature of the election results, however, undermined the authority and power of President Aristide and his FL movement. This in turn led to an increase in civil disruption and disunity. The most serious incident prior to the eventual overthrow of Aristide in February 2004 came on Dec. 17, 2001, when armed men wearing the uniform of the disbanded Haitian army stormed and briefly held the National Palace in Port-au-Prince before it was retaken by police in a battle that left four dead. The FL government accused the opposition of conspiring with the disbanded army to overthrow the government and there was a wave of revenge attacks by Aristide's supporters, who burned down the homes of opposition figures. The situation remained tense during 2002 and 2003, with a series of protest marches held by opposition and student groups on the one hand, and pro-Aristide elements on the other, often resulting in violence.

Despite the continuing poor security situation in the country President Aristide retained a considerable amount of support, helped in no small measure by the dispensing of government patronage. However, demonstrations during the last three months of 2003 became ever more violent, particularly in the rural cities of Cap Haitien and Gonaïves. In protest at the FL's role in the violence Education Minister Marie-Carmelle Paul Austin and Haitian Ambassador to the Dominican Republic, Guy Alexandre, resigned from their positions. International pressure for an end to the violence also increased, with both the Caribbean Community (CARICOM) and the US government calling on Aristide to hold new legislative elections and address the worsening security situation. When the final armed insurrection was launched Aristide's position as President became untenable, and on Feb. 29, 2004, he left the country for the Central African Republic.

Despite Aristide's departure, the FL movement retained a key role in Haitian politics, and as a consequence an FL representative, Lesly Voltaire, was appointed to the Tripartite Group to oversee the process of choosing an interim government. However, the eventual government of Gerald Latortue did not include any FL members. In response, former FL Prime Minister Yvon Neptune warned that the exclusion of FL representatives would polarise the country. In addition, FL declined to participate in the Provisional Electoral Council, claiming that the new administration was failing to safeguard the human rights and personal security of party members.

The process of reconciliation was not assisted when the deposed Aristide refused to accept defeat. In the aftermath of the coup, Aristide claimed that he was still the constitutional President of Haiti, and declared that he supported peaceful resistance. His supporters in Haiti meanwhile undertook a number of revenge attacks on anti-Aristide demonstrators. The most serious example came on March 7 when Aristide supporters attacked a march by opponents of the former President, resulting in the deaths of six people. Aristide's continuing influence over the FL movement was illustrated further by his arrival in Jamaica three weeks after the coup, which signalled his intention to remain close to Haiti at a time of great political uncertainty for the country.

Open the Gates Party
Parti Louvri Barye (PLB)
Address. c/o Chambre des Deputés, Port-au-Prince
Leadership. François Pierre-Louis (secretary-general)
The PLB was formed in 1992 as a pro-Aristide party, its co-founder Matine Remilien being killed shortly afterwards after being arrested by the military for fly-posting photographs of Aristide. In the 2000 legislative elections, the party won two seats in the Chamber of Deputies and one seat in the Senate.

Organization of Struggling People
Organisation de Peuple en Lutte (OPL)
Address. Rue Lamartinière no 105, Bois Verna, Port-au-Prince
Telephone. (509) 245-4214
Fax. (509) 245-4534
Email. scastor@haitiworld.com
Website. http://www.oplpeople.com/home.html
Leadership. Gérard Pierre-Charles
The OPL emerged from a split within the pro-Aristide Lavalas Political Organization (OPL) in the late 1990s. At this time Aristide himself created the Lavalas Family, whilst his erstwhile supporter, and OPL leader, Gérard Pierre-Charles, formed the Organization of Struggling People, which retained the OPL acronym. The OPL contested the 2000 legislative elections as the main opposition party, but managed to win only one seat in the Chamber of Deputies. In late 2000 the OPL united with other opposition groups in the Democratic Convergence to press for an annulment of the election results.

The OPL has observer status in the Socialist International.

Other Parties and Alliances

Confederation of Democratic Unity (*Kovansyon Inite Demokratik,* KID) is an opposition grouping opposed to the rule of Aristide and the Lavalas Family.
Address. 14, Rue Camille Leon, Port-au-Prince
Telephone. (509) 245-0185
Leadership. Paul Evans

Consultation Group is a member of the opposition Democratic Convergence that pressed for the annulment of the 2000 legislative and presidential elections. Leading members include Paul Evans, Victor Benoît and Fred Biutus.

Grandans Resistance Coordination (*Koodinasyon Resistans Grandans*) won one seat in the Chamber of Deputies during the 2000 elections.
Leadership. Joachim Samedi

Mobilization for National Development (*Mobilisation pour le Développment National,* MDN), a centre-right party founded in 1986 and claiming to be the country's first legal political party; latterly opposed to Aristide and the Lavalas Family.
Address. 33 Rue Bonne Foi, Boite Postale 2497, Port-au-Prince
Telephone. (509) 222-3829
Website. www.mdnhaiti.org
Leadership. Hubert de Ronceray (president). Max Carre (secretary-general)

Movement for the Installation of Democracy in Haiti (*Mouvement pour l'Instauration de la Démocratie en Haïti,* MIDH), centre-right party founded in 1986 by Marc Bazin, who had briefly served as Finance Minister in a Duvalier cabinet. The party opposed the ruling Lavalas Family in recent years.
Address. 114 Ave. Jean Paul II, Port-au-Prince
Telephone. (509) 245-8377
Leadership. Marc Bazin (leader)

Party of the National Congress of Democratic Movements (*Pati Kongre Nasyonal Mouvman Demokratik Yo,* KONAKOM), a social democratic party founded in 1987 by delegates from an array of political groups, trade unions, peasant and student organizations, and human rights associations. The party is a member of the opposition Consultation Group and is a full member of the Socialist International.
Address. 101 Bois Verna, Port-au-Prince
Telephone. (509) 245-6228
Leadership. Victor Benoît (general secretary)

Progressive Democratic and National Rally (*Rassemblement Démocratique Progressiste et National,* RDPN), Christian democratic party, a member of the opposition Democratic Convergence which pressed for the annulment of the 2000 legislative and presidential elections. The RDPN is a member of the Christian Democrat International and of the Christian Democratic Organization of America.
Address. 234 Route de Delmas, BP 1199, Port-au-Prince
Telephone. (509) 246-3313
Leadership. Leslie Manigat (secretary-general)

Revolutionary Progressive Nationalist Party (*Parti Nationaliste Progressiste Révolutionnaire,* PANPRA) is a social democratic party formed in 1986, and a member of the Socialist International.
Leadership. Serge Gilles (leader)

Space of Concerted Action (*Espace de Concertation*)
Address. c/o Chambre des Deputés, Port-au-Prince
Founded in 1999, this party won two seats in the Chamber of Deputies during the 2000 elections.

Honduras

Capital: Tegucigalpa
Population: 6,823,500 (2004E)

The Republic of Honduras gained its independence from Spain in 1821 and was a member of the United Provinces of Central America until 1838. The country was ruled by the conservative National Party of Honduras (PNH) from 1933 to 1957, a period which also marked the political ascendancy of the army. In an interlude of civilian government, a series of moderate social and political reforms were introduced by the Liberal Party of Honduras (PLH), in office from 1957 to 1963, which included a programme of land reform and the establishment of a state social security system. The military then ruled from 1963 to 1980, except for a short period under the PNH government of 1971-72, before the PLH returned to power in 1980 although with the military still wielding great influence. The PLH won the presidential election of 1985, which saw the first peaceful transfer of power between civilian Presidents in more than thirty years. Four years later the PLH lost power to the PNH again in peaceful circumstances.

The 1990s were dominated by the PLH, winning the 1993 and 1997 presidential and congressional elections. However, in elections held in 2001 the PLH lost both the presidency and control of Congress. In presidential elections held on Nov. 25, 2001, Ricardo Maduro of the PNH emerged as the winner with 52.2% of the vote. In simultaneous congressional elections the PNH won 61 seats (with 46.5% of the vote), the PLH 55 (40.8%), the National Innovation and Unity Party-Social Democracy 4 (4.6%), the Democratic Unification Party 5 (4.5%), and the Christian Democratic Party of Honduras 3 (3.7%).

Under its 1982 constitution, Honduras has a unicameral National Congress (*Congreso Nacional*) and executive power rests with the President, who is elected for a four-year non-renewable term by a simple majority of votes. The 128-member National Congress is elected for a four-year term on the basis of proportional representation, voting being compulsory for those aged between 18 and 60. In regard to the military, its autonomy and power has diminished since the 1980s, and now poses little threat to civilian rule. An important reform came in 1999 when President Carlos Flores conducted a full-scale purge of the military leadership, replacing several top officers with his own allies from among the junior officer corps.

Christian Democratic Party of Honduras
Partido Demócrata Cristiano de Honduras (PDCH)
Address. Colonia San Carlos, 2da. Av. Atrás de los Castaños No.204, AP 1387, Tegucigalpa DC
Telephone. (504) 323-139
Fax. (504) 326-060
Leadership. Juan Ramon Valazquez Nazzar
Founded in 1980, the PDCH is a Christian democratic party with both progressive and conservative wings. The party has not fared well in presidential and legislative elections, receiving less than 2% in presidential races and no more than 3 seats in the Assembly. It has not, however, been without political significance, joining with other parties in the 1980s in promoting Honduran neutrality in regional conflicts. In the early 1990s, moreover, a member of the PDCH served in the government of the National Party of Honduras (PNH) as Head of the National Agrarian Institute, an agency in charge of agrarian reform. Further, from 2001 the PDCH supported the PNH administration of President Maduro, allowing a number of important economic measures to be passed. In May 2002, for example, the PDCH helped the President to gain majority backing for controversial budget measures to meet IMF requirements for structural and fiscal reform. However, by 2003 the PDCH had become wary of supporting the government's increasingly unpopular economic policies.

The party is a member of the Christian Democrat International and the Christian Democrat Organization of America.

Democratic Unification Party
Partido de Unificación Democrática (PUD)
Address. c/o Congreso Nacional, Palacio Legislativo, AP 595, Tegucigalpa
Leadership. Cesar David Adolfo Ham Pena
The PUD was launched in 1993 as the political wing of a number of former elements of the *Movimiento Revolucionario Hondureño* (MRH), a clandestine guerrilla alliance. The MRH was itself formed in 1983 as an umbrella organization in an attempt to co-ordinate the efforts of the militant left. The aim was a force under one command to conduct a guerrilla war and to play an active part in the event of a regionalization of the Central America crisis. Founding members included the Communist Party of Honduras, the Social Action Party of Honduras, the Central American Workers' Revolutionary Party (PRTC), the Lorenzo Zelaya Popular Revolutionary Forces (FPR-LZ, founded by students at the National Autonomous University in 1980-81), the Revolutionary Unity Movement (MUR), the Cinchonero Popular Liberation Movement (MPL Cinchoneros) and the

Morazanista Front for the Liberation of Honduras (FMLH).

As tensions eased throughout the region, all member groups of the MRH (originally known as the *Directorio Nacional Unificado-Movimiento de Unidad Revolucionario*, DNU-MUR) took advantage of a general amnesty in June 1991, although some rebels made it known that they intended to continue fighting. The group was banned from democratic participation until 1997, when its presidential candidate won 1.2% of the vote and the party's 2.6% of the popular vote ensured one seat in the National Congress. In the following elections held in 2001 the party once again performed badly in the presidential contest, but its representation in Congress increased to 5 seats (with 4.5% of the vote). Although officially against the economic reform policies of President Maduro, the PUD was not uniform in its opposition. In April 2003, for example, a dissident member of the party backed the government's controversial tax measures, allowing the legislation to pass with the narrowest of majorities.

Liberal Party of Honduras
Partido Liberal de Honduras (PLH)
Address. Col. Miramontes, Atrás del Supermercado, 'La Colonia' no. 1, Tegucigalpa DC
Telephone. (504) 320-520
Fax. (504) 320-797
Leadership. Roberto Micheletti Bain
Founded in 1890 and therefore the country's oldest party, the PLH has both conservative and progressive wings, both of which have tended to be conservative in office. In recent times, the party held power from 1957-63 before being deposed by the military, an experience that did not prevent it, in 1980, from being the main force in an interim government under the then military President Gen. Policarpo Paz Garcia. Since 1970 the PLH has been, in effect, a coalition of disparate tendencies, each with its own leadership and structure, overlaying the traditional divide between the conservative rural and the more reformist urban wings of the party.

The PLH won elections in November 1981, gaining an absolute majority in the legislature. Its leader from 1979, Roberto Suazo Córdova, a pro-US right-winger and head of the conservative *rodista* faction of the party, was installed as President in January 1982, formally ending 18 years of almost uninterrupted military rule, although the armed forces retained extensive legal and de facto powers. In January 1983 the PLH almost lost its legislative majority when Suazo Córdova's *rodistas* clashed with the Popular Liberal Alliance (ALIPO) faction of the party, led by the brothers Carlos Roberto Reina and Jorge Arturo Reina, who were subsequently driven out and in February 1984 established the Revolutionary Democratic Liberal Movement (MLDR or M-Lider). The *rodistas* in turn split in 1985, with competing factions backing Oscar Mejía Arellano and José Azcona del Hoyo for the presidency. Azcona had resigned from Suazo Córdova's government in 1983 and subsequently accused the regime of corruption.

Azcona won the presidency in November 1985 in alliance with ALIPO, having agreed a power-sharing national unity pact with the National Party of Honduras (PNH), the second since 1971, giving the PNH two cabinet posts and control of the Supreme Court and other important political and administrative posts. While President Azcona's government was preoccupied with issues arising from the Nicaraguan conflict, not least the presence in the country of some 20,000 US-backed right-wing *contra* rebels, a battle for the PLH presidential nomination ensued, which was eventually won in December 1988 by Carlos Flores Facussé, a former minister in the Suazo Córdova government who had forged a surprise alliance with the dissident M-Lider. Although Flores lost the 1989 presidential election, the party received two posts in the new PNH cabinet.

The Liberals dominated the 1990s. Carlos Reina won handsomely in the presidential elections of 1993 against former Supreme Court president Oswaldo Ramos of the PNH, while in legislative balloting the Liberals defeated the Nationalists by 71 seats to 55. In the November 1997 presidential elections Flores was again the PLH candidate and was elected with 52.7% of the vote, while the Liberals also won 67 National Congress seats to the National Party's 55. During the presidency of Flores the PLH dealt with a number of potentially devastating shocks, including Hurricane Mitch, a drought, and an escalation of tensions with Nicaragua. Despite the government's perceived competence, the PLH's chances of re-election were undermined by a growing fear among voters about the rise in violent street crime. In addition, in-fighting between the conservative and progressive factions within the PLH prior to the 2001 elections damaged the party's chances of victory. Indeed, the PLH lost the presidency by a margin of 8%, and won just 41% of the vote in the congressional elections, leaving it with 55 seats, a net loss of 12. After the defeat the PLH attempted to thwart the new government's economic policy initiatives, and exploit the public's growing disillusionment with President Maduro's rule.

The PLH is a full member of the Liberal International.

National Innovation and Unity Party–Social Democracy
Partido de Innovación Nacional y Unidad–Social Democrácia (PINU-SD)
Address. AP 105, 29 Avenida de Comayagüela 912, Tegucigalpa
Telephone. (504) 371-357
Leadership. Olban Valladares Ordoñéz
Founded in 1970 the PINU describes itself as social democratic in orientation. The party, whose support comes mainly from professionals and some rural workers' groups, was not afforded legal recognition until 1978. In 1981 it secured only 2.5% of the vote and three of the 82 seats in the National Assembly, one of which was won by Lulin Mendez, the first *campesino* (peasant) leader ever to sit in the legislature. It has enjoyed mixed fortunes since, faring relatively well in the 2001 elections, in which party leader Olban Valladares Ordoñéz received 1.5% of the vote to finish third in the presidential race, while the party secured four seats in the National Congress. Although PINU-SD held a sufficient number of seats to provide the National Party of Honduras (PNH) with a majority in the legislature, the party's ideological roots prevented it from supporting the government's liberal economic reforms.

National Party of Honduras
Partido Nacional de Honduras (PNH)
Address. Paseo Obelisco, Camayagüela MDC, AP 3300, Tegucigalpa
Telephone. (504) 323-066
Fax. (504) 385-275
Leadership. Jose Celin Discua Elvir
Founded in 1923, the PNH is by tradition a conservative party which now promotes neo-liberal economic measures. Historically the party of large landowners, it has also been closely identified with the military. The PNH held power from 1933 to 1957, including under the dictatorship of Gen. Tiburcio Carías Andino (1939-49), and in 1971-72 and 1985-87, when it participated with the Liberal Party of Honduras (PLH) in short-lived national unity governments.

The PNH, like the PLH, comprises various factions, including the Movement for Nationalist Democratization (MDN), the Movement for Unity and Change (MUC) and the Nationalist Labour Tendency (TNL). The PLH government of 1981-85 encouraged PNH infighting by using the then PLH-dominated Supreme Court and the National Electoral Tribunal (TEN) to support the pro-government MUC in its claim to control the party. This decision was reversed in 1985 by the military, which supported the accession to power of the newly created MONARCA faction led by Rafael Leonardo Callejas. MONARCA won all 63 of the PNH's 134 seats in the 1985 general election, and as part of the subsequent national unity government, in which it held the foreign affairs and labour portfolios, forced the PLH to give it control of the Supreme Court, the TEN and an important role in the administration of the legislature.

Callejas was the unopposed PNH candidate in the 1989 presidential elections, which he won comfortably. On taking office, his government restored relations with the IMF and other creditors and implemented a package of IMF-approved neo-liberal economic measures. These included the wholesale dismissal of thousands of public sector workers (many of whom were PLH supporters), the privatization of state-owned agencies, the abolition of price controls on basic essentials and the devaluation of the currency. The measures caused widespread social unrest throughout 1990-91, despite Callejas' periodic promises to increase social sector spending. Anti-government protest was increasingly repressed by the security forces, leading to international protests at the high level of systematic human rights abuses.

The PNH lost the 1993 presidential elections under the candidature of former Supreme Court president Oswaldo Ramos Soto. Following this defeat, internal divisions within the party intensified, so that by the end of 1995 there were eight distinct factions, the most important being the *Oswaldista* and *Roma* movements. Such disunity partially explained why the 1997 PNH presidential candidate, Alba Nora Gúnera, was so easily defeated (42.7% to 52.8%) by her PLH opponent. The party nevertheless maintained a substantial presence in the National Congress, winning 55 seats with 41.6% of the vote.

In the run-up to the November 2001 elections, Ricardo Maduro of the *Movimiento Arriba Honduras* faction was eventually, after some debate about his eligibility, chosen as the party's nominee for the presidency. Once nominated Maduro campaigned strongly on a "zero-tolerance" anti-crime platform, a stance that was given force by voters' knowledge that Maduro's son had been murdered in April 1997 during an apparent kidnapping attempt. With high expectations on the part of the electorate Maduro won the presidency, and the PNH gained a plurality, although not a majority of seats in the Congress. Maduro took immediate steps to make good on his campaign pledge, declaring a "war on crime" just days after his inauguration in January 2002. Further, the President committed his government to pursue the structural reforms and fiscal measures necessary to gain debt relief assistance from the IMF. The resulting budgetary package provoked heated debate in the legislature, but was passed in May 2002 with the support of the Christian Democratic Party of Honduras (PDCH). The President similarly relied on the support of the PDCH and a dissident member of the Democratic Unification Party (PUD) to win majority backing for a controversial package of tax measures in April 2003. However, by the middle of 2003, the president's parliamentary allies grew reluctant to support the government's increasingly unpopular economic policies, and even some members of the PNH announced that they would reject further economic retrenchment. There was also increasing civil unrest across Honduras in opposition to the IMF backed reforms. In August 2003, for example, thousands of public sector workers, including teachers and doctors, marched on Tegucigalpa in protest. Despite such pressures the government agreed a debt relief arrangement with the IMF in February 2004, which committed the administration to continue with its tough economic reform programme. However, the ongoing unrest within the PNH and the legislature, the growing anger of the population, and Honduras' reputation for public sector corruption and inefficiency called into question the President's ability to satisfy the demands of the IMF and maintain the economic reform programme.

The government was placed under further pressure by continuing lawlessness, despite Maduro's election commitment to crackdown on crime. In 2003 the government passed anti-gang legislation, but the high number of violent crimes, kidnappings and murders continued. Later in 2003, the US ambassador to Honduras warned that the country was in danger of becoming a "drug state", while in March 2004 the Attorney General charged 51 police and military officers in connection with the killing of over 100 inmates in the El Porvenir prison the previous April. The massacre was believed to have been a revenge killing by death squads against drug gang members in jail.

In an attempt to mollify the growing unrest within Honduras Maduro established the "Great National Dialogue" with the aim of bringing together members of civil society to address issues of concern. However, a number of the participants criticized the process as nothing more than a "talking shop", claiming that it was designed merely to channel public discontent away from the government.

The party is a member of the International Democrat Union, the Christian Democrat International and the Christian Democrat Organization of America.

Hungary

Capital: Budapest
Population: 10,032,375 (2004E)

After four decades of communist rule in the People's Republic of Hungary, in January 1989 the National Assembly legalized freedom of assembly and association. A month later the then ruling Hungarian Socialist Workers' Party (MSMP) approved the formation of independent parties, some of which had begun organizing on an informal basis the previous year. In September formal sanction was given to multi-party participation in national elections, the People's Republic giving way the following month to the revived Hungarian Republic. The President as head of state is indirectly elected for a five-year term by the unicameral National Assembly (*Országgyülés*), which is elected for a four-year term by universal adult suffrage in two rounds of voting, its 386 members including eight providing ethnic minority representation. The complex electoral system involves the election of 176 deputies from single-member constituencies, 152 from 20 multi-member constituencies by a form of proportional representation of parties which obtain at least 5% of the vote, and 58 from national party lists to ensure overall proportional representation. Hungarian parties receive central budget funding for their election campaign expenses, proportionally to the number of candidates presented.

The Assembly elections of May 10 and 24, 1998, resulted as follows: Federation of Young Democrats–Hungarian Civic Party (FIDESz-MPP) 147 seats (with 38.3% of the vote), Hungarian Socialist Party (MSzP) 134 (34.7%), Independent Party of Smallholders, Agrarian Workers and Citizens (FKgP) 48 (12.4%), Alliance of Free Democrats (SzDSz) 24 (6.2%), Hungarian Democratic Forum (MDF) 18 (4.4%), Hungarian Justice and Life Party (MIEP) 14 (3.6%), others 1.

In parliamentary elections held on April 7 and 21, 2002, twenty-four parties and coalitions took part. In a turnout of 70.53% (the first round) and 73.51% (second round) the following results were obtained: the joint list of FIDESz-MPP and MDF won 48.70% of the vote and 188 seats, of which FIDESz-MPP took 164 seats and MDF 24; MSzP won 46.11% of the vote and 178 seats; the SzDSz won 4.92% of the vote and 20 seats. No seats were won by the MIEP with 4.4% of the vote, the Alliance for Hungary–Centre Party (3.9%), Workers' Party (2.8%) or FKgP (0.8%).

The 2002 elections were the most closely contested in Hungary since the first post-communist parliamentary ballot in March and April 1990, and resulted in the Socialists forming a coalition government with the Free Democrats, with whom they were in government between 1994 and 1998. The centre-left coalition (led by Peter Medgyessy until August 2004 when he was succeeded as Prime Minster by Ferenc Gyurcsany) had a majority of only 10. Hungary's National Electoral Committee had to postpone for ten days the announcement of the final results after a series of appeals. The Supreme Court rejected all 25 applications challenging the vote, mostly concerning the way the so-called fragmentary votes were calculated, thus closing all legal avenues to reverse the outcome and the final results were announced on May 5. The announcement, however, did not stop the opposition challenging the outcome. Demonstrations continued for several weeks and in July 2002 protesters calling for a recount brought the city centre of Budapest to a standstill for five hours in the first major civil disobedience action in the capital for a decade.

On April 12, 2003, Hungarian voters in a referendum approved the country's proposed accession to the European Union. In a turnout of 45.62%, the "yes" vote was 83.76%, and "no" vote 16.24%. Hungary formally became a member of the EU on May 1, 2004, and held its first European Parliament elections on June 13, 2004. In a turnout of 38.47% FIDESz-MPP won 47.4% of the votes and gained 12 of the country's 24 seats. The Hungarian Socialist Party took 34.3% of the vote and 9 seats; the Alliance of Free Democrats 7.7% of the vote and 2 seats; the Hungarian Democratic Forum 5.3% of the vote and 1 seat; others 5.2% of the vote and no seats. The parties' election campaigns focused on domestic issues such as the country's economic performance, charges of corruption, and the health service, rather than European affairs. As a result of the Hungarian elections, in which a 30-year-old Roma was elected, Europe's 5 million strong Roma community will for the first time be represented in the European Parliament.

Alliance for Hungary–Centre Party
Összefogás Magyarországért Centrum
Website. www.centrum-part.hu
Leadership. Mihállyal Kupa
Founded on Nov. 23, 2001, the party adopted its present name on Dec. 21, 2001. It was established as an umbrella organization for the purpose of contesting the April 2002 parliamentary elections and comprised the following independent parties and organizations: Hungarian Democratic People's Party (*Magyar Demokrata Néppárt*), Christian-Democratic People's Party (*Kereszténydemokrata Néppárt*), HOME Third Way Hungarian Association (*Harmadik Oldal Magyarországért Egyesület*), Green Democrats (*Zöld Demokraták*), and the Green Line Movement (*Zöld Szalag Mozgalom*). In the 2002 elections the Alliance for Hungary-Centre Party secured 3.9% of the vote, but no seats in the legislature.

Alliance of Free Democrats
Szabad Demokraták Szövetsége (SzDSz)

Address. 6 Mérleg utca, 1051 Budapest V
Telephone. (36–1) 117–6911
Fax. (36–1) 118–7944
Email. intldept@mail.datanet.hu
Website. www.szdsz.hu
Leadership. Gábor Kuncze (president); István Szent-Ivanyi (parliamentary group leader); András Keszthelyi (chief of staff); Csaba Szabady (managing director)

The centrist SzDSz began life in March 1988 as the Network of Free Initiatives, representing the centre-left "urban" rather than the "populist" strand in the opposition, many of its members being lapsed Marxists. The grouping was reorganized as a political party in November 1988 and held its first general assembly in March 1989. It won 91 Assembly seats in 1990 on a vote share of 21.4%, becoming the leading opposition party of the post-communist era. Factional strife between "pragmatists" and "ideologues" appeared to be healed in November 1992 by the election of Iván Peto as party president.

Despite hopes of a major breakthrough, the party slipped to 70 seats in the May 1994 Assembly elections, its first-round voting share falling to 19.8%. It opted to join a centre-left coalition with the Hungarian Socialist Party (MSzP), its presidential nominee, Arpád Göncz, being elected President of Hungary by the Assembly in June 1995. Tarnished by corruption allegations, Peto resigned as SzDSz president in April 1997 and was succeeded the following month by Gábor Kuncze, then Interior Minister and Deputy Prime Minister.

The SzDSz was the biggest loser in the defeat of the government parties in the May 1998 Assembly elections, falling to 24 seats (with only 6.2% of the vote) and going into opposition. Kuncze was quickly replaced as party president by Bálint Magyar, who was in turn replaced in December 2000 by Gábor Demszky, the mayor of Budapest. However, Demszky resigned in June 2001, on the grounds that he had not been supported in his efforts to establish an independent liberal line for the party. Gábor Kuncze returned to the leadership and quickly entered into a mutual support pact with the MSzP for the April 2002 parliamentary elections. During the parliamentary election campaign the party focused heavily on reforming Hungary's decrepit health service. It won 4.92% of the vote and secured 20 seats in the legislature, becoming a junior coalition partner of the Socialists. The party won two seats in the June 2004 European Parliament elections.

The SzDSz is affiliated to the Liberal International.

Federation of Young Democrats–Hungarian Civic Party
Fiatal Demokraták Szövetsége–Magyar Polgári Párt (FIDESz-MPP)

Address. 28 Lenday utca, 1062 Budapest VI
Telephonr. (36–1) 269–5353
Fax. (36–1) 269–5343
Email. sajto@fidesz.hu
Website. www.fidesz.hu
Leadership. Viktor Orbán (president); Zoltán Pokorni (vice-president); Pal Schmitt (vice-president)

Then known simply as the Federation of Young Democrats, this moderate right-wing grouping came in fifth place in the 1990 Assembly elections, winning only 20 of 378 elective seats on a 7.0% vote share, although later that year it won elections for mayor in nine of the country's largest cities. In the May 1994 general elections, its national representation declined further to 20 seats and it remained an opposition party. A 35-year upper age limit on membership was abandoned in April 1993, paving the way for the adoption of the FIDESz-MPP designation two years later.

The FIDESz-MPP was strengthened in 1997 and early 1998 by its absorption of part of the Christian Democratic People's Party (KDNP). Benefiting from public disenchantment with the ruling coalition headed by the Hungarian Socialist Party (MSzP), the FIDESz-MPP achieved a major advance in the May 1998 Assembly elections, winning 147 seats on a 38.3% vote share. As chairman of the largest party, Viktor Orbán unexpectedly opted to form a right-wing coalition with the Independent Party of Smallholders, Agrarian Workers and Citizens (FKgP) and the Hungarian Democratic Forum (MDF), the FIDESz-MPP being allocated 12 of the 17 ministerial posts. The new government took Hungary into NATO in March 1999 and set accession to the European Union as its key objective.

In January 2000 a FIDESz congress decided to divide the party chairmanship from the premiership and elected Secret Services Minister László Kövér to the party post. However, having come under criticism for his aggressive style, Kövér stood down in March 2001 and was replaced by Zoltán Pokorni, the Education Minister. The party then entered into talks with the MDF on forming an alliance in the next parliamentary elections. The combined list with the MDF took 188 seats in the April 2002 parliamentary elections, of which the FIDESz share was 164 seats, but the Socialists (who had won 178 seats) went on to form a government with the support of the Alliance of Free Democrats. On July 3, 2002, Pokorni resigned from both his party and parliamentary posts, after finding out that his father had worked as a police informer under the communist regime.

Having previously been an affiliate of the Liberal International, FIDESz in September 2000 opted to join the Christian Democrat International by becoming an associate member of the European People's Party. It is also affiliated to the European Democrat Union.

Hungarian Democratic Forum
Magyar Demokrata Fórum (MDF)

Address. 3 Bem József tér., 1027 Budapest II
Telephone (36–1) 212–4601
Fax. (36–1) 156–8522
Email. kulugy@freemail.c3.hu
Website. www.mdf.hu
Leadership. Ibolya David (chairperson)

A centre-right party of populist/nationalist orientation, the MDF was founded in September 1988 with the avowed purpose of "building a bridge between the state and society". It held its first national conference in Budapest in March 1989, when it demanded that Hungary should again become "an independent democratic country of European culture". In the April 1990 Assembly election the party won a plurality of 165 of 378 elective seats, on a first-round vote of 24.7%. The result was an MDF-led coalition headed by József Antall, also including the Christian Democratic People's Party (KDNP) and the Independent Party of Smallholders, Agrarian Workers and Citizens (FKgP).

In January 1993 Antall survived a challenge to his MDF leadership from the party's nationalist right, led by István Csurka. In early June Csurka and three parliamentary colleagues were expelled from the party, promptly forming the Hungarian Justice and Life Party. Antall died in December 1993 and was succeeded, on a temporary basis, by Sandor Lezsák, who was named chairman of the MDF executive committee in February 1994, after resigning from the party chairmanship in favour of the then Defence Minister, Lajos Für.

The May 1994 Assembly elections delivered a major rebuff to the MDF, which slumped to 37 seats on a vote share of only 11.7% and went into opposition. As a result, Lezsák withdrew completely from the leadership at the beginning of June, being succeeded by former Finance Minister Iván Szabo as parliamentary leader. On being confirmed as MDF chairman in September, Für ruled out a merger with the KDNP "for the time being". Various problems contributed to

Für's decision early in 1996 to vacate the leadership, which returned to Lezsák, who faced major opposition within the party. An anti-Lezsák group immediately formed the breakaway Hungarian Democratic People's Party, the rump MDF being reduced to some 20 Assembly members.

Notwithstanding an alliance with the Federation of Young Democrats–Hungarian Civic Party (FIDESz-MPP) in the May 1998 elections, the MDF declined further to 18 seats and 4.4% of the vote. It was nevertheless included in the new three-party right-wing coalition government headed by the FIDESz-MPP and including the FKgP. In January 1999 Lezsák was finally ousted as MDF leader by Ibolya David, the Justice Minister, who in February 2000 launched the "Right Hand of Peace 2000" alliance of assorted right-wing groups with the aim of recovering lost support for the MDF. In mid-2001 the MDF entered into negotiations with the FIDESz-MPP on a mutual support pact for the 2002 parliamentary elections. In the April 2002 parliamentary elections the party secured 24 seats in the legislature.

The MDF is affiliated to both the International Democrat Union and the Christian Democrat International, being also an associate member of the European People's Party.

Hungarian Justice and Life Party
Magyar Igazság es Elet Párt (MIEP)

Address. 3 Akadémia utca, 1054 Budapest V
Telephone. (36–1) 268–5199
Fax. (36–1) 268–5197
Email. istvan.csurka@miep.parlament.hu
Website. www.miep.hu
Leadership. István Csurka (chairman)

The extreme right-wing MIEP was launched in June 1993 by dissidents of the then ruling Hungarian Democratic Forum (MDF) after István Csurka had unsuccessfully challenged József Antall for the MDF leadership. Openly anti-semitic, the party contends that national revival is being thwarted by a "Jewish–Bolshevik–liberal conspiracy" and advocates the restoration of Hungary's pre-1914 borders, starting with the annexation of the majority ethnic Hungarian province of Vojvodina in Yugoslavia. The party's original Assembly contingent of about 10 deputies fell to none when it secured only 1.6% of the vote in the May 1994 Assembly elections. It regained representation in the May 1998 elections, winning 14 seats with 3.6% of the vote.

Alone among the parliamentary parties, the MIEP in February 1999 voted against Hungary's accession to NATO. In September 2000 Csurka demanded that a referendum should be held before Hungary joined the European Union. In speeches in mid-2001, Csurka declared the MIEP's willingness to join a "genuinely right-wing" government with the Federation of Young Democrats–Hungarian Civic Party (FIDESz-MPP) after the 2002 parliamentary elections.

In the April 2002 parliamentary elections the party won 4.37% of the vote, but failed to secure representation in the legislature.

Hungarian Socialist Party
Magyar Szocialista Párt (MSzP)

Address. 26 Köztársaság tér., 1081 Budapest
Telephone. (36–1) 210–0068
Fax. (36–1) 210–0011
Email. info@mszp.hu
Website. www.mszp.hu
Leadership. László Kovács (chairman); Katalin Szili (deputy chairperson); Sándor Nagy (parliamentary group leader); György Jánosi (chairman of national board)

The MSP is the successor to the former ruling (Communist) Hungarian Socialist Workers' Party (MSMP), which had been created under an earlier designation by the June 1948 merger of Hungary's Communist and Social Democratic par-

ties. The original Hungarian Communist Party was founded in November 1918 and took a leading role in the short-lived Republic of Councils (soviets) declared in Hungary in March 1919, its leading activists going underground during the succeeding "White Terror" and Horthy dictatorship. Many prominent Communists took refuge in Moscow, and towards the end of World War II (during which Hungary was allied to the Axis powers) the entry into Hungary of Soviet forces was followed by the establishment of a provisional government comprising Communists, Smallholders, Social Democrats and the National Peasant Party. Although the Smallholders obtained an absolute majority (57%) in elections held in November 1945, the coalition was continued, with a Communist as Interior Minister. Two years later, in the elections of August 1947, the Communists emerged as the strongest single party with 22% of the vote), ahead of the Smallholders, while the combined share of the Communists, Social Democrats and National Peasant Party was 45%. Under the leadership of Mátyás Rákosi, the Communists then effectively eliminated their coalition partners as independent political forces and in June 1948 the Social Democratic Party was merged with the Communist Party to form the Hungarian Workers' Party (HWP), many Social Democrats who opposed the merger going into exile.

In elections held in May 1949 the HWP presented an unopposed joint list with four other parties called the People's Independence Front (PIF); of the 402 elective seats in parliament, over 70% were allotted to the HWP. In August 1949 a new constitution was adopted similar to those of other East European "people's democracies". In the elections of May 1953 the HWP was the only party to be mentioned in the manifesto of the PIF, which in October 1954 was replaced by the broader-based Patriotic People's Front (*Hazafiás Népfront*). Meanwhile, former Social Democrats had been gradually eliminated from the HWP leadership and purges were conducted by the Rakosi "Muscovites" against the "home Communists", notably László Rajk, who was executed in October 1949 after a show trial, and János Kádár, who spent several years in prison.

Following Stalin's death in March 1953, Rakosi resigned from the premiership (although continuing as party leader), in which post he was succeeded in July 1953 by Imre Nagy. He embarked on a "new course" economic policy involving the halting of compulsory collectivization, greater emphasis on the production of consumer goods, the release of political prisoners and greater cultural freedom. However, in early 1955 the HWP central committee condemned the new policies as "right-wing" and "opportunist", with the result that Nagy was removed from the premiership and dismissed from his party posts in April 1955.

Following Nikita Khrushchev's denunciation of Stalin at the 20th congress of the Soviet Communist Party in February 1956, Rakosi was obliged to resign from the Hungarian party leadership in July 1956. Thereafter, widespread opposition built up to Rakosi's successor, Ernö Gerö (another hard-liner), culminating in the reappointment of Nagy to the premiership in October 1956 amid violent clashes between Hungarian demonstrators and Soviet forces, which were then withdrawn from the country. Nagy announced a new programme, including free elections, Hungary's withdrawal from the Warsaw Pact and a policy of permanent neutrality, and formed a national coalition administration including non-Communist representatives.

Gerö was succeeded as party secretary by Kádár, who initially supported Nagy's programme but who in early November 1956 formed an alternative "revolutionary workers' and peasants' government". At the invitation of the latter, Soviet forces then returned in strength and crushed Hungarian resistance over several days of heavy fighting. Nagy and his associates were executed as traitors and Kádár was confirmed as leader of the party, which was reconstituted as the Hungarian Socialist Workers' Party (MSzWP). After a period of severe reprisals, Kádár instituted a policy of reconciliation and limited liberalization, which was only partly tarnished by Hungary's participation in the Soviet-led intervention in Czechoslovakia in 1968.

Economic, social and cultural liberalization was followed in 1983 by a partial democratization of the political process, involving in particular a choice of candidates in national and local elections, although still within a framework of MSzWP supremacy. These and other Hungarian initiatives were specifically acknowledged by the new post-1985 Soviet Communist Party leadership as having furnished some guidelines for the Soviet Union's own reform programme under Mikhail Gorbachev.

As communist rule began to collapse in Eastern Europe, an extraordinary party congress of the MSzMP in October 1989 renounced Marxism in favour of democratic socialism, adopted its current name and appointed Rezsö Nyers to the newly-created post of presidium chairman. Chosen to succeed Nyers in May 1990, Gyula Horn led the party to an overall majority in the May 1994 Assembly elections, with a tally of 209 seats on a 32.6% vote share. Nevertheless, mainly for purposes of international respectability, Horn brought the centrist Alliance of Free Democrats (SzDSz) into a new coalition.

Speedily becoming unpopular for its economic austerity measures, the MSzP-led government was also troubled by various corruption scandals and by deep dissension within the party. In the May 1998 Assembly elections, it fell back to second place with 134 seats, although its share of the vote increased slightly to 34.7%. The party went into opposition and in September 1998 Horn was succeeded as chairman by former Foreign Minister László Kovács.

MSzP deputies backed the entry of Hungary into NATO in March 1999 and also formed part of the consensus in favour of accession to the European Union. A party congress in October 1999 resolved that at least 20% of MSzP elected bodies must be under 35 and/or women. The next party congress in November 2000 re-elected Kovács as chairman and elected Katalin Szili to the new post of deputy chairman, while in December Sándor Nagy succeeded Kovács as MSzP parliamentary group leader. In mid-2001 the MSzP entered into a mutual support pact with the SzDSz for the 2002 parliamentary elections, for which it nominated former Finance Minister Peter Medgyessy as its prime ministerial candidate. In the April 2002 parliamentary elections the party won 178 out of 386 seats on a 46.11% share of the vote and went on to form a coalition government with the Alliance of Free Democrats. During the election campaign the party focused heavily on free market-oriented policies, but also promised an increase in social benefits and public sector wages and tax cuts. Peter Medgyessy became the Prime Minister in May 2002. However, his premiership was blighted by scandals. Shortly after the elections, in June 2002, Medgyessy admitted that he had worked as a counter-espionage agent in the finance ministry between 1978 and 1982. However, he denied ever having collaborated with the KGB and maintained that worked to steer Hungary toward IMF membership without Moscow's knowledge.

Since the elections support has plummeted for the Socialist Party-led coalition as spending promises, one of which boosted public sector wages by 50%, have given way to the harsh reality of strict budget controls. The government embarked on spending cuts to bring the country's budget deficit and inflation rates closer to those in the European Union in order that Hungary might join the eurozone in 2010. Peter Medgyessy resigned in August 2004 following a row with the coalition partners over a government reshuffle. He was succeeded by Ferenc Gyurcsany, the Sports Minister, a business tycoon and one of Hungary's richest men.

With a membership of 35,000, the MSzP is a full member party of the Socialist International and an associate member of the Party of European Socialists.

Independent Party of Smallholders, Agrarian Workers and Citizens
Független Kisgazda, Földmunkas és Polgári Párt (FKgP)

Address. 24 Belgrád rakpárt, 1056 Budapest V
Telephone. (36–1) 318–2855
Fax. (36–1) 318–1824
Email. fkgpczp@matavnet.hu
Website. www.fkgp.hu
Leadership. Miklos Reti (chairman)

Advocating the return of collectivized land to former owners, the FKgP was founded in November 1989 as a revival of the party which had emerged as the best supported in Hungary's first post-war election in 1945. Deep internal divisions on the desirability and extent of reparations for property lost during the Communist era came to a head in December 1989. A group of dissidents led by Imre Boros resigned from the FKgP to form the National Smallholders' and Bourgeois Party, which developed no taste for life on the outside and rejoined the parent party in August 1991. Meanwhile, the FKgP had won 44 seats and 11.7% of the vote in the 1990 Assembly elections and had joined a centre-right coalition government headed the Hungarian Democratic Forum (MDF).

In February 1992 FKgP leader József Torgyán announced that the party was withdrawing from the government coalition because the MDF had denied it an opportunity to influence policy. This decision was accompanied by the expulsion of 33 of the FKgP's 45 Assembly deputies, who launched the United Smallholders' Party–Historical Section (EKP-TT) in order to support the MDF-led Antall government. In the May 1994 general elections the rump party recovered somewhat by winning 26 seats on an 8.9% vote share. It then experienced a surge in popular support in the polls, as expressions of extreme nationalist sentiment emanated from Torgyán.

The party then became embroiled in fierce conflict over government moves to produce a new constitution to replace the much-amended communist-era text. One FKgP proposal was that the President should be directly elected, with enhanced powers, on the expiry of the five-year term of Arpád Göncz of the Alliance of Free Democrats (SzDSz) in August 1995. Seeking to force a referendum, the FKP collected well over the number required for a popular consultation, but the then ruling Hungarian Socialist Party (MSzP) contended that such a change would generate political instability. As a consequence of a split in the MDF in March 1996, the FKgP became the largest single opposition party in the Assembly, although it was weakened in late 1997, another split resulting in the formation of the New Federation.

Allied with the rump Christian Democratic People's Party (KDNP) in the May 1998 Assembly elections, the FKgP advanced strongly to 48 seats (with 13.2% of the vote) and joined the subsequent centre-right government headed by the Federation of Young Democrats–Hungarian Civic Party (FIDESz-MPP). By late 2000, however, the party was again beset by chronic internal dissension, centring on hostility to Torgyán's continued leadership and allegations that he had been guilty of various improprieties as Agriculture Minister since 1998. Torgyán resigned from the government in February 2001, but stubbornly refused to vacate the FKgP leadership, despite a stream of defections and the formation of at least three alternative Freeholders' parties. A special congress in Cegled in May re-elected Torgyán as chairman, but dissidents in Budapest simultaneously elected Zsolt Lanyi to the same position. Torgyán was then expelled from the FKgP parliamentary group, but promptly obtained a court ruling that the expulsion was illegal. In June 2001, claiming that his enemies wanted to assassinate him, Torgyán also obtained a Supreme Court ruling that he was still the legal FKgP chairman. The following month two recent FKgP breakaway factions joined with the older EKP-TT to announce that a new Freeholders' party would be formed if Torgyán had not resigned by September 2001. On May 4, 2002, the party's National Council stripped Torgyán of the chairmanship of the FKgP.

In the April 2002 parliamentary elections the party won 0.75% of the vote and failed to secure representation in the legislature. It likewise failed to win a seat in the European Parliament in the June 2004 elections,

The FKgP is affiliated to the Christian Democrat International, an associate member of the European People's Party and a member of the European Democrat Union.

Other Parties

Agrarian Union (*Agrárszövetsége,* ASz), founded in December 1989 as a merger of leftist agrarian groups opposed to the land privatization policies of the Independent Party of Smallholders, Agrarian Workers and Citizens (FKgP). It was allocated one Assembly seat in May 1994 on the basis of a 2.1% vote share; contested 1998 elections in alliance with Hungarian Socialist Party.
Address. 10 Arany János u., Budapest V
Telephone. (36–1) 131–0953
Fax. (36–1) 111–2663
Leadership. Jozsef Solymosy (chairman)

Alliance for Eastern Hungary, launched in early 2000 by two deputies, one previously of the Federation of Young Democrats–Hungarian Civic Party (FIDESz–MPP) and the other of the Hungarian Justice and Life Party (MIEP), to promote the interests of the "neglected" population of the eastern party of the country.
Leadership. Sándor Cseh & Attila Szábo

Christian Democratic People's Party (*Keresztény-demokrata Néppárt,* KDNP), centre-right formation claiming to be a revival of the Popular Democratic Party, the leading opposition formation in the immediate post-World War II period. The party won 21 Assembly seats in 1990 on a 6.5% vote share, joining a three-party coalition government headed by the Hungarian Democratic Forum (MDF). Avoiding the MDF's rout in the 1994 elections, the KDNP improved to 22 seats with 7.1% of the vote, but was subsequently weakened by the defections. In July 1997 ten members of its parliamentary faction quit the group for the Federation of Young Democrats–Hungarian Civic Party (FIDESz–MPP), and the party lost parliamentary faction status. Prior to the 1998 parliamentary elections the party announced that in some electoral districts, it would support the candidates of the far-right Hungarian Justice and Life Party and in one district the candidate of the National Association for Hungary – an extreme nationalist group known for its ant-semitic views. The rump KDNP won only 2.6% in the 1998 elections and no seats. In June 2001 György Giczy, who led the party since 1965, resigned as party chairman after the party's National Board voted "to open up toward moderate right-wing forces." On June 9, 2001, Tivadar Bartók was elected the party's chairman. In the 2002 elections the party competed as part of the Alliance for Hungary, which failed to win a seat.
Address. 5 Nagy Jenö u., 1126 Budapest XII
Telephone. (36–1) 201–8389
Fax. (36–1) 202–0405
Email. btivadar@freemail.hu
Website. www.kdnp.hu
Leadership. Tivadar Bartók (chairman)

Green Democrats (*Zöld Demoktraták,* ZD). The roots of the Hungarian Green movement go back to the beginning of the 1980s. The first attempt to establish an NGO was in 1984, when the Danube Circle (*Duna Kör*) tried to disseminate secret information on a plan for damming the Danube in Czechoslovakia and in Hungary. The Greens took only 0.4% of the vote in 1990. The party was established in 1993 from various NGOs as the Green Alternative and in the 1994 elections attracted 0.62% of the vote. It changed its name to the present one in the summer of 2000. In the 2002 elections the party competed as part of the Alliance for Hungary, which failed to win a seat. Member of the European Federation of Green Parties.
Address. 29 Vadász utca, 1053 Budapest
Telephone/Fax. (36-1) 353-0100
Email. zd@zd.hu
Leadership. György Droppa and Istvan Teszler (co-chairmen)

Hungarian Democratic People's Party (*Magyar Demokrata Néppárt,* MDNP), launched in March 1996 by Iván Szabo after he had been rebuffed in a challenge for the presidency of the Hungarian Democratic Forum, of which he was then leader in the National Assembly. The new party attracted over a dozen centre-leaning MDF deputies, but none were re-elected on the MDNP ticket in 1998. In April 2001 the MDNP resolved to form an alliance with the Liberal Citizens' Alliance, also known as the Entrepreneurs' Party. In the 2002 elections the party competed as part of the Alliance for Hungary, which failed to win a seat.
Leadership. Erzsebet Pusztai (chairwoman)

Hungarian Independence Party (*Magyar Függetlenség Pártja,* MFP), right-wing formation launched in April 1989 as a revival of a post-war group of the same name.
Address. 97 Arany János utca, 7400 Kaposvár
Leadership. Tibor Hornyak

Hungarian People's Party (*Magyar Néppárt,* MNP), centrist grouping founded in 1989 as successor to pre-war National Peasant Party (*Nemzeti Parasztpárt,* NPP), which title it uses as a suffix; won less than 1% of the vote in 1990 and failed to present any candidates in 1994 and 1998.
Address. 61 Baross utca, 1082 Budapest VIII
Leadership. János Marton

Hungarian Romany Alliance, formed in June 2001 for the 2002 parliamentary elections by the Roma Unity Party, the Roma Party in Hungary, the Interest Association of Gypsy Organizations in Hungary and the Hungarian Roma Civil Rights Movement.
Leadership. Pal Ruva

Hungarian Social Democratic Party (*Magyarországi Szociáldemokrata Párt,* MSzDP), revival of the party forced to merge with Hungary's Communist Party in 1948; split in 1989 into "historic" and "renewal" wings, reunited in October 1993; secured less than 1% in the 1994 and 1998 general elections; a consultative member of the Socialist International whereas the (ex-communist) Hungarian Socialist Party is a full member.
Address. 76 Dohány u., 1074 Budapest VII
Leadership. Tibor Sztankovánszki (acting president), Sándor Bácskai (secretary general)

Hungarian Welfare Alliance (*Magyar Népjóleti Szövetség,* MNSz), extreme right-wing grouping led by a Hungarian-born Australian citizen, successor to the World National Party for People's Power (VNP).
Leadership. Albert Szabo (chairman)

Liberal Citizens' Alliance (*Liberális Polgári Szövetség,* LPSz), launched in 1989 as the Entrepreneurs' Party to promote a market economy and low taxation for the country's emerging entrepreneurs. It adopted its present name in June 1990 but failed to secure representation in the 1990 elections. It was credited with one constituency seat in 1994 and none in 1998. In April 2001 the LPSz resolved to form an alliance with the Hungarian Democratic People's Party.
Leadership. József Ekes (chairman)

Lungo Drom Nationwide Gipsy Community of Interest and Civic Federation (*Lungo Drom Országos Cigány Érdekvédelmi és Polgári Szövetség*), the largest Roma organization in Hungary. The federation has three members in parliament and several representatives on local council. In the April 2002 parliamentary elections the organization was part of the FIDESz-MPP coalition.

National Democratic Party (*Nemzeti Demokrata Párt,* NDP), small radical right-wing formation.
Leadership. Vincze János (chairman)
Email. ndp@mail.datanet.hu
Website. www.datanet.hu/ndp

New Federation (*Uj Szöevetség,* USz), founded in late 1997 by a splinter group of the Independent Party of Smallholders, Agrarian Workers and Citizens (FKgP) opposed to the leadership of József Törgyán; failed to win representation in 1998 elections.
Leadership. Agnes Nagy Maczo (chairperson)

Party of the Republic (*Köztársaság Párt,* KP), founded in 1992 on the initiative of János Palotas, a colourful entrepreneur who had been elected to the Assembly in 1990 as a candidate of the Hungarian Democratic Forum (MDF) but had quickly become alienated from that party. The KP won only 2.5% of the national vote in the May 1994 Assembly elections, but was allocated one seat by virtue of a local alliance with the MDF.
Address. 8 Szentkirály utca, 1088 Budapest VIII
Telephone. (36–1) 138–3744
Fax. (36–1) 138–4642
Leadership. János Palotas (chairman)

United Smallholders' Party–Historical Section (*Egyesült Kisgazda Párt–Töténelmi Tagozat, EKP-TT*), launched as a result of the February 1992 decision of the leadership of the Independent Party of Smallholders, Agrarian Workers and Citizens (FKgP) to leave the government coalition, this move being opposed by three-quarters of the 44 FKgP Assembly deputies. Claiming to represent continuity with established FKgP policies, the EKP-TT remained a part of the then ruling coalition headed by the Hungarian Democratic Forum, but failed to secure representation in 1994, 1998 or 2002.
Address. 34 Jókai utca, 1065 Budapest VI
Telephone. (36–1) 132–2900
Leadership. János Szabo (chairman)

Workers' Party (*Munkáspárt,* MP), derived from pro-reform decisions taken at the October 1989 congress of the then ruling Hungarian Socialist Workers' Party (MSzMP), when hardline Communists opposed to conversion into the Hungarian Socialist Party launched the "János Kádár Society" as the "legal heir" to the MSzMP. Using the MSzMP title, it won only 3.7% in 1990 (and no seats). Having adopted the present name prior to the 1994 election, it slipped to 3.3%. It recovered to 4.1% in 1998, but still won no seats. It campaigned against Hungary's membership of NATO and took a similar view on the country's accession to the EU. In the April 2002 parliamentary elections the party won 2.16% of the vote, but failed to secure representation in the legislature.
Address. 61 Baross utca, 1082 Budapest
Telephone. (36–1) 334–2721
Email. hir@hungary.cc
Website. www.munkaspart.hu
Leadership. Gyula Thürmer (chairman)

Iceland

Capital: Reykjavík
Population: 293,966 (2004E)

The Republic of Iceland was established in 1944 (having previously been a Danish possession), with a democratic parliamentary system of government. Under the 1944 constitution as amended, the President is directly elected as head of state for a four-year term (renewable without restriction), although real executive power resides in the cabinet headed by the Prime Minister. Legislative authority is vested in the unicameral parliament (*Althing*) of 63 members, also elected for four years (subject to dissolution) by a mixed system of proportional and direct representation. The *Althing* divides itself by election into an Upper House (*Efri Deild*) of a third of its members and a Lower House (*Nedri Deild*) of the remaining two-thirds.

Vigdís Finnbogadóttir was elected President in 1980 and held that office for successive terms until deciding not to run for re-election in 1996. She was succeeded by Olafur Ragnar Grímsson, former chairman of the People's Alliance, who won the election with 41% of the vote. By agreement of the parties, Grímsson was reinstalled for a second term as President on Aug. 1, 2000, without an election. However, presidential elections did take place in 2004 (June 24). On this occasion Grímsson was re-elected with 85.6% of the vote. He faced two opponents, Baldur Ágústsson (a businessman) and Ásthór Magnússon (a peace activist), who received 12.3% and 1.1% of the vote, respectively.

Icelandic parties are eligible for subventions from state funds, to finance research on political questions, in proportion to the number of *Althing* seats held plus one. In 2001 the total available was IKr46.7 million (about $460,000), of which, for example, the Independence Party received IKr17.8 million. Furthermore, parties holding seats in the *Althing* are also eligible for state funds to finance their general operations in proportion to votes received at the last parliamentary election. In 2001 the total paid out in this category was IKr164 million (about $1.6 million), of which, for example, the Progressive Party received IKr30.3 million.

Recent survey research indicates that the social bases of the Icelandic parties have been eroded to a considerable extent. Whereas there used to be relatively strong ties between social class and voting, this is no longer the case. This is particularly apparent in the traditional working-class parties, which no longer manage between them to obtain even one-third of the working-class vote. All parties now have a rather diffuse social base, and class voting in Iceland has grown far weaker than in other Nordic countries. While social class has weakened as a predictor of voting behaviour, some other factors have grown in importance. Residents of the urban southwest are far more likely to vote for the Independence Party, the Social Democrats and the Women's Alliance. Regional voters, on the other hand, tend to support the Progressives and the People's Alliance to a greater extent than voters in the Reykjavík area.

No party since 1944, when Iceland gained independence from Denmark, has won enough votes to win a majority of seats and form a government on its own. Parties traditionally form a coalition.

Elections to the *Althing* on May 8, 1999, resulted as follows: Independence Party 26 seats (with 40.7% of the vote), Social Democratic Alliance (*Samfylkingin*, consisting of the People's Alliance, the Social Democratic Party and the Women's Alliance) 17 (26.8%), Progressive Party 12 (18.4%), Left–Green Alliance 6 (9.1%), Liberal Party 2 (4.2%).

In elections to the *Althing* held on May 10, 2003, the Independence Party won 33.7% of the vote and took 22 seats; the Social Democratic Alliance 31.0% and 20 seats; the Progressive Party 17.7% and 12 seats; the Left-Green Alliance 8.8% and 5 seats; the Liberal Party 7.4% and 4 seats; and the New Force Party (*Nýtt Alf*) 1.0% and no seats. Incumbent Prime Minister David Oddsson of the Independence Party formed a coalition government with the Progressive Party, with a narrow majority in the parliament.

Independence Party (IP)
Sjálfstædisflokkurinn
Address. Háaleitisbraut 1, 105 Reykjavík
Telephone. (354) 515–1700
Fax. (354) 515–1717
Email. xd@xd.is
Website. www.xd.is
Leadership. Davíd Oddsson (chairman); Geir H. Haarde (vice-chairman); Sigrídur Anna Thórdardóttir (parliamentary group leader); Kjartan Gunnarsson (secretary-general)
The IP is a liberal conservative party, advocating Iceland's continued membership of NATO and the retention of the existing US military base in Iceland. It was established in 1929 by a merger of conservative and liberal groups favouring Iceland's independence from Denmark (achieved in 1944). Having consistently been the strongest party in the *Althing* (although never with an absolute majority), it has taken part in numerous coalition govemments: with the Social Democratic Party (SDP) and a Communist-led left-wing front in 1944–46; with the Progressive Party (PP) and the SDP in 1947–49; with the PP in 1950–56; with the SDP in 1959–71; and with the PP in 1974–78 and 1983–87. Meanwhile, in 1980–83 dissident IP deputies had participated in a coalition with the PP and the People's Alliance (PA).

In the April 1987 elections the IP suffered a major setback (principally because of the impact of a breakaway Citizens' Party), winning only 27.2% of the vote and 18 of 63 seats (as against 38.7% and 23 of 60 seats in 1983). It nevertheless continued in government at the head of a "grand coalition" with the PP and the SDP, with the IP leader, Thorsteinn Pálsson, becoming at 39 Iceland's youngest-ever Prime Minister.

Pálsson stepped down as Prime Minister in September 1988 because of a dispute over economic policy, being succeeded as party chairman in March 1991 by Davíd Oddsson, who formed a government following an election in which the IP consolidated its position as the largest party, rising from 18 to 26 seats. Only one of these was lost in the 1995 election, in which the IP took 37.1% of the vote. However, because of losses by its SDP coalition partner, it opted to form a new centre-right coalition with the PP in order to ensure parliamentary stability and majority government.

Despite vociferous opposition from the left-wing parties, especially after the PA, the SDP and the Women's Alliance

formed an electoral front in mid-1998, the IP-led government gained credit for strong economic growth and low inflation in the May 1999 parliamentary elections. The IP itself advanced to 26 seats and 40.7% of the vote, so that Oddsson was able to form a new centre-right coalition with the PP. Oddsson – a one-time journalist, actor and playwright – established strong economic credentials and has been able to oversee the privatization of industry during his long premiership. In the May 10, 2003, elections the party won 22 seats with 33.7% of the vote, continuing in government with Oddsson as Prime Minister.

The IP is affiliated to the International Democrat Union and the European Democrat Party.

Left-Green Alliance
Vinstrihreyfing-Grænt Frambod
Address. Suðurgötu 3, Box 175, 121 Reykjavík
Telephone. +354 552-8872
Email. vg@vg.is
Website. www.vg.is
Leadership. Steingrímur Sigfússon (chairman); Ögmundur Jónasson (parliamentary group leader)
The Left-Green Alliance was launched in 1998 by factions of the People's Alliance (PA) and the Women's Alliance opposed to the creation by those parties of the United Left (*Samfylkingin*) alliance. The party focuses on more traditional socialist values and environmentalism. It opposes participation in military organizations such as NATO and the US-led invasions of Iraq and Afghanistan. It also rejects participation in the European Union and emphasizes simple, bilateral treaties concerning trade and co-operation. The party supports and wants to strengthen the participation in organizations such as the United Nations, the European Council and the Nordic Council.

In the May 1999 parliamentary elections the Left–Green Alliance helped to ensure the defeat of *Samfylkingin* by winning six seats with 9.1% share of the vote. In the May 2003 elections it secured 5 seats with 8.8% of the vote. In 2004 it claimed a membership of 1,200.

Liberal Party (LP)
Frjáslyndi Flokkurin
Address. Einimelur 9, 107 Reykjavík
Telephone. (354) 562–4515
Fax. (354) 563–0780
Email. xf@xf.is
Website. www.xf.is
Leadership. Sverrir Hemannsson (chairman); Gudjón A. Kristinsson (parliamentary group leader)
The LP was established in 1998 by Sverrir Hemannson, a former director of the National Bank of Iceland and a former government minister associated with the Independence Party. In the May 1999 parliamentary elections it won two seats with 4.2% of the vote. By mid-2001 the party had some 4,000 members. In the May 10, 2003, parliamentary elections voter support increased to 7.4%, which gave the party 4 seats in the *Althing*. The party supports Iceland's membership of NATO but it is firmly opposed to the US invasion of Iraq. It also rejects membership of the EU.

Progressive Party (PP)
Framsóknarflokkurinn
Address. Hverfisgata 33, 101 Reykjavík
Telephone. (354) 540–4300
Fax. (354) 540–4301
Email. framsokn@framsokn.is
Website. www.framsokn.is
Leadership. Halldór Ásgrímsson (leader); Siv Fridleifsdóttir (chairperson); Kristinn H. Gunnarsson (parliamentary group leader); Arni Magnusson (secretary-general)

The PP's principal aim is to safeguard the Icelandic nation's economic and cultural independence on the basis of a democratic and parliamentary system, with emphasis on the freedom of the individual. The party also stands for basing the national economy on private initiative, with state intervention remaining exceptional. The party has favoured Iceland's continued membership of NATO but has called for the withdrawal of NATO forces from the country.

The party was established in 1916 to represent farming and fishing interests and the co-operative movement in these sectors. Historically often the second largest party in the *Althing,* the PP has taken part in various coalition governments: with the Independence Party (IP) and the Social Democratic Party (SDP) in 1946-49; with the IP in 1950–56; with the SDP and the People's Alliance (PA) in 1956–58; with the PA and the Union of Liberals and Leftists in 1971–74; with the IP in 1974–78; with the SDP and the PA in 1978–79; with the PA and dissident IP members in 1980–83; with the IP in 1983-87; with the IP and the SDP in 1987–91; and with the IP since 1995.

The 1983–87 period of coalition with the IP resulted in both parties losing ground in the April 1987 elections, in which the PP slipped from 14 to 13 seats, although its share of the vote increased from 8.5% to 18.9%. Three months later the PP entered a "grand coalition" headed by the IP and also including the Social Democrats. Upon the resignation of the IP Prime Minister in September 1988, then PP leader Steingrímur Hermannsson formed a new government which included the IP and the SDP.

The PP went into opposition following the election of April 1991, at which its parliamentary representation was unchanged. It returned to government after the 1995 contest, in which it advanced to 23.3% of the vote, as the junior partner in a centre-right coalition with the IP.

In the May 10, 2003, elections it won 12 seats with 17.7% of the vote and continued as a junior partner in a coalition government with the IP. Its leader became Prime Minister on Sept. 15, 2004.

The PP has a current membership of 8,150 and is a member party of the Liberal International.

Social Democratic Alliance (SDA)
Samfylkingin

Address. Austurstr–ti 14, 101 Reykjavík
Telephone. (354) 551–1660
Fax. (354) 563–0745
Email. bgs@althingi.is
Website. www.samfylking.is
Leadership. Össur Skarphédinsson (chairman); Margret Frímannsdóttir (vice-chairperson); Bryndís Hlödversdóttir (parliamentary group leader); Björgvin G. Sigurdsson (secretary-general)

The SDA was launched in mid-1998 initially as an electoral front of the People's Alliance (*Althydubandalagid*), the Social Democratic Party (*Althduflokkurinn*) and the Women's Alliance (*Samtök um Kvennalista*) and was converted into a unitary party in May 2000 following the defeat of the front in the May 1999 parliamentary elections. This was an attempt to unify the entire centre-left of Icelandic politics into one party to become a counter-balance to the right-wing Independence Party. The attempt, however, failed as a group of *Althingi* representatives who did not approve of the agenda this new party was to follow founded the Left-Green Alliance. In the May 2003 parliamentary elections the SDA campaigned on social issues including welfare, health and housing, which some Icelandic voters saw as neglected by long-serving Prime Minister David Oddsson. Following the elections, in which the Alliance secured 20 seats with 31.0% of the vote, it kept its status as the second political force in the country. The party's leader at that time, the

charismatic mayor of Reykjavik, Ingiborg Solrun Gisladottir, lost her own Parliamentary seat to a Progressive Party candidate and had to abandon her bid to become the first female Prime Minister.

The **People's Alliance (PA)** had its origins in the formation of the Communist Party of Iceland in 1930 following a split in the Social Democratic Party (SDP). Having joined the Comintern, the Icelandic Communists first obtained representation in the *Althing* in 1937 (with three seats). Although a proposal for reunification was rejected by the SDP in 1938, left-wing Social Democrats joined with the Communists to form the United People's Party–Socialist Party (SA–SF), which left the Comintern and in 1942 won seven parliamentary seats. When Iceland became independent in 1944, the SA–SF entered a coalition government with the SDP and Independence Party (IP), but withdrew in 1946 mainly over its opposition to a US military presence in Iceland.

For the 1956 elections, the SA–SF combined with the small National Defence Party and a left-wing faction of the SDP to form the People's Alliance, which won eight seats and joined a coalition with the SDP and the Progressive Party (PP) which lasted until 1958. Having been essentially an electoral alliance, the PA converted itself into a single political party in 1968, whereupon the non-Marxist section broke away to form the (now defunct) Union of Liberals and Leftists, claiming that the PA had become "the Communist Party under another name". At the same time, the PA denounced the Soviet-led military intervention in Czechoslovakia and thereafter adopted a "Eurocommunist" orientation. Strongly based in the trade union movement, it described itself as a party of "leftists who want to defend and strengthen the independence of the Iceland people, protect the interests of the working class, and ensure progress at all levels in the country on the basis of democratic socialism and co-operation". It also advocated Iceland's withdrawal from NATO and the closure of the US military base.

After winning 10 seats in the 1971 elections, the PA joined a coalition with the PP and the Union of Liberals and Leftists, which resigned in 1974. The PA won 14 seats in the 1978 elections and formed a coalition with the PP and the SDP. After new elections the following year, in which its representation fell to 11 seats, the party entered a coalition with the PP and dissident IP members early in 1980. However, it fell back to 10 seats in 1983 and went into opposition. In the April 1987 elections the PA was for the first time overtaken in terms of votes and representation by the SDP and remained in opposition.

The PA's representation in the *Althing* rose to nine seats in 1991, this level being maintained in 1995 on a slightly reduced vote share of 14.3%. The party remained in opposition through both elections, being active in the opposition to government economic austerity measures. Former Finance Minister Ólafur Ragnar Grímsson vacated the PA leadership in late 1995 in order to stand for the Icelandic presidency, to which in June 1996 he was elected by a comfortable relative majority over three other candidates.

Founded in 1916 by the trade unions, the **Social Democratic Party (SDP)** became organizationally independent in 1940 but was weakened by the defection of its left-wing faction to the Communist-dominated United People's Party-Socialist Party (later the PA). Over the following three decades the SDP remained the fourth strongest party in a stable four-party system, usually polling around 15% in general elections, and participated in five coalition governments, the longest-lived being one with the Independence Party (IP) in 1959–71; it also briefly formed a minority SDP government in 1958–59.

Amid decreasing political stability in the 1970s and early 1980s, the SDP experienced shifting fortunes and was mostly in opposition, although it participated in a centre-left coalition in 1978–79 and then formed another interim minority government. Competition from short-lived alternative social democratic parties resulted in electoral setbacks for the SDP, notably in 1983 when the impact of a left-wing dissident Social Democratic Federation reduced the SDP to only six seats and 11.7% of the vote.

Under the new leadership of Jón Baldvin Hannibalsson, however, the SDP was reinvigorated, as well as strengthened by the return of most of the Federation dissidents in 1986. In the April 1987 elections its share of the vote increased to 15.2% and its representation to 10 seats (out of 63), giving it the status of third-strongest party, ahead of the PA for the first time. The SDP thereupon entered a "grand coalition" headed by the IP and also including the Progressive Party (PP).

The SDP retained 10 seats in the 1991 elections, after which it joined a coalition with the IP. Internal party unrest over government austerity measures culminated in June 1994 in an unsuccessful challenge to the leadership of Hannibalsson (then Foreign Minister) by his deputy, Jóhanna Sigurdardottir (then Social Affairs Ministers), who promptly formed the breakaway People's Movement (PM). In the 1995 *Althing* elections the SDP fell back to fourth place, winning only 11.4% of the vote (and going into opposition), directly damaged by the PM's garnering of an impressive 7.2% vote share and four seats under the campaigning name "Awakening of the Nation".

The **Women's Alliance (WA)** had been launched in March 1983 as an explicitly feminist party, believing the improvement of the condition of women to be "imperative" and also that "the experience, values and perspectives of women are urgently needed to influence the decision-making processes of our society". Rejecting classification on the left/right spectrum and boasting a collective and rotating leadership the Alliance also advocated decentralization of local and national government, the transfer of economic and administrative power to the people, an end to the arms race and the abolition of all military alliances.

Possibly given additional credibility by the fact that Iceland elected a woman President in 1980, the WA was successful in its first general election contest in April 1983, winning 5.5% of the vote and three of the 60 *Althing* seats. It made further significant progress in the April 1987 elections, when it took 10.1% of the vote and doubled its representation to six seats (out of 63). In post-election coalition negotiations with other parties, the WA refused to compromise on its policy principles and accordingly remained in opposition.

The WA fell back to five seats in the 1991 *Althing* elections, remaining in opposition. More evidence of the ebbing of the feminist tide came in the 1995 elections, when the WA slipped further to three seats on a 4.9% vote share, apparently losing support to the new People's Movement under the charismatic female leadership of Jóhanna Sigurdardottir, formerly deputy leader of the Social Democratic Party (SDP). In the June 1996 presidential election, however, WA candidate Gudrun Agnarsdottir won an impressive 26% of the vote.

In the post-1995 parliament, the SDP, PM, PA and WA deputies found themselves co-operating closely in opposition to the centre-right government of the IP and the PP. In due course Sigurdardottir and her followers returned to the SDP fold and were influential in the SDP's decision to enter the SDA, its first-ever formal alliance with the PA. The WA also joined, overcoming its previous resistance to left/right labels. The policy compromises involved in alliance agreement resulted in significant factions of both the PA and the WA defecting to the Left–Green Alliance.

To secure the alliance, the PA moderated its opposition to NATO membership and the US military presence in Iceland, while the pro-European SDP agreed that a *Samfylkingin* government would not seek to join the EU in the next parliamentary term. Instead, the focus would be on improving the social services and introducing family-friendly measures. However, policy differences between the component formations were exposed in the run-up to the May 1999 parliamentary elections, in which the alliance won only 17 seats and 26.8% of the vote, well below the aggregate performance of its component parties in 1995. The alliance therefore remained in opposition to a further centre-right coalition of the IP and the PP, a position that continued after the 2003 elections.

The SDA inherited the SDP's full membership of the Socialist International.

Other Parties

Several very small parties include the following: **Citizen's Party** (*Borgaraflokkurinn*), **Communist Party** (*Kommúnistaflokkurinn*), **Consolidation Party** (*Flicker framfarasinna*), **Home Rule Party** *Heimastjórnarflokkurinn*), **Humanist Party** (*Húmanistaflokkurinn*), **Natural Law Party** (*Nátturulagaflokkur Íslands*), **The old Independence Party** (*Sjálfstæðisflokkurinn eldri*), **Socialist Association** (*Sósialistafélagið*).

India

Capital: New Delhi
Population: 1,000,027,000 (2001E)

The Republic of India gained independence from the United Kingdom in 1947, when the sub-continent was divided into the new states of India and Pakistan. It is a secular and democratic republic, comprising 28 self-governing states and seven union territories. The head of state is the President, who is elected for a five-year term by an electoral college consisting of elected members of the upper and lower houses of parliament (respectively the *Rajya Sabha* and the *Lok Sabha*) and of state legislative assemblies. The President appoints a Prime Minister (the head of government) and, on the latter's advice, a Council of Ministers, all of whom are responsible to parliament. Most of the 245 members of the *Rajya Sabha* are indirectly elected by the state assemblies (one-third being replaced every two years), while all but two of the 545 members of the *Lok Sabha* are directly elected for a five-year term by universal adult suffrage. The remaining two members are appointed by the President to represent the Anglo-Indian community. Legislative responsibility is divided between the Union and the states, the former possessing exclusive powers to make laws in the realm of foreign affairs, defence, citizenship and overseas trade.

At the general election of April-May 1996, the Hindu nationalist *Bharatiya Janata* Party (BJP) was returned with the largest number of seats (161) and invited by the President to form a government. However, it experienced great difficulty in securing coalition partners and lasted only 13 days. The Indian National Congress (INC) – Congress (I) also having tried and failed to form an administration, the mantle of government eventually fell upon a United Front (UF) consisting of a loose alliance of 13 broadly leftist and regional organizations dominated by three national parties, namely the *Janata Dal* (JD), the Communist Party of India–Marxist (CPI-M) and the Communist Party of India (CPI). It also included the All-India Forward Bloc, the All-India Indira Congress–*Tiwari*, the Assam People's Council, the Dravidian Progressive Federation (DMK), the Karnataka Congress Party, the *Madhya Pradesh Vikas*

Congress, the *Maharastrawadi Gomantak*, the Revolutionary Socialist Party, the *Samajwadi* Party, the *Tamil Maanila* Congress and the *Telugu Desam* Party–*Naidu*. Altogether, the UF could still only amass about 180 seats and was kept in office by the support of Congress (I) from the back benches. It elected as its first leader (who then became Prime Minister) H.D. Deve Gowda of the JD. But, within a year, he was ousted by pressure from the Congress (I) in favour of I.K. Gujral, also from the JD. In December 1997, the Congress (I) entirely withdrew its support and the UF government fell.

At the general election of March 1998, the BJP was again returned as the largest single party in the *Lok Sabha* (with 180 seats) and this time succeeded in constructing a coalition government under the leadership of Prime Minister Atal Behari Vajpayee. Its principal sources of support were the *Samata* Party, the *Shiv Sena*, the All-India Dravidian Progressive Federation (AIADMK), the All-India *Trinamool* Congress and the *Telugu Desam* Party–*Naidu*. However, its overall majority was always small and, in April 1999 following the withdrawal of the AIADMK, it fell. The Congress (I) then attempted, but again failed, to put together another coalition. To spare the country the costs of a second general election within a year (and a third within three), President K.R. Narayanan made use of a constitutional provision putting parliament into recess and allowing Vajpayee's cabinet to continue as an interim administration for six months.

In preparation for the next general election, which was held in October 1999, the BJP drew its would-be coalition partners into a National Democratic Alliance (NDA), which presented a collective identity at the polls while allowing each of its constituent parties also to stand in its own right. In comparison to Vajpayee's 1998-99 coalition, the AIADMK was replaced by its local rival in Tamil Nadu politics, the Dravidian Progressive Federation (DMK) and included several fractions of the JD which, in common with the former UF, was then breaking apart. In all, 24 parties stood at the election under the NDA's banner. The BJP was, again, returned as the largest single party in the *Lok Sabha* with 182 seats. But, with the experience of the NDA behind him, Vajpayee had little difficulty in forming a more substantial coalition government. At the time of its taking office, this government commanded an overall majority of about 30 seats. Thereafter, the size of the majority waxed and waned as coalition partners came, went, and returned.

Meanwhile, the opposition to it further fragmented. Congress (I) suffered a disastrous result at the 1996 election, losing nearly half its seats and returning only 140 members. After that, and in spite of the efforts of the new leader Sonia Gandhi to revive it, it experienced further splits and decline. In 1998, it won only 119 seats and, in 1999, just 112. Its attempts to coordinate the general opposition to the BJP also failed and exacerbated tensions with the remnants of the UF. But the UF parties, themselves, faired little better, with the JD breaking apart into a series of separate, and frequently hostile, parties based on regional and personal connections. Although the communist parties retained their own regional followings, their impact on national politics has weakened and, in 2001, the CPI-M even temporarily lost its accredited status as a "national" party with the Election Commission of India. There are still, despite the fact that some of the regional parties are active in several states, only six parties that the Election Commission classes as national: the INC-

Congress (I), the BJP, the CPI, the CPI-M, the Nationalist Congress Party (NCP) and the Bahujan Samaj Party (BSP).

The BJP and its allies lost ground to Congress in state assembly elections in February 2002 and February 2003, leaving the western state of Gujarat as the only major state still controlled by the BJP. The BJP's landslide victory in Gujarat in December 2002 was carried on a wave of local Hindu nationalist sentiment in the aftermath of anti-Muslim pogroms earlier in the year that were widely thought to have been connived in by incumbent chief minister Narendra Modi's administration. However, the tide turned for the BJP in the state assembly elections of December 2003, largely because of two factors: a buoyant economy and a tentative but steady thaw in relations with Pakistan since April 2003, resulting from a personal initiative by Vajpayee. The BJP ousted Congress administrations in three of the five states for which there were polls.

National elections were not due until October 2004, but in January Vajpayee announced his intention to bring them forward, and on the Prime Minister's recommendation President A.P.J. Abdul Kalam dissolved the 13th *Lok Sabha* on Feb. 6, 2004. The Election Commission divided the elections into four major phases, on April 20 (with Tripura's vote moved to April 22), April 26, May 5 and May 10, with counting scheduled for May 13. For the first time in Indian electoral history all votes were cast using electronic voting machines. Turnout was 57.86%, compared with 59.99% in 1999. Against all expectations and the projections based on early exit polls the BJP suffered a defeat that stunned political commentators, with Congress (I) gaining the largest number of seats in the 14th *Lok Sabha*. Vajpayee swiftly and gracefully conceded defeat, saying that although the results were a reverse for the BJP they constituted a victory for India's democracy. Analysts concluded that Congress (I)'s championing of the rural poor, left behind in the high-tech economic boom that had largely benefited urban centres such as Mumbai (Bombay), Hyderabad and Chennai (Madras), had been a decisive factor in the party's resurgence. It also seemed that many voters had rallied to Sonia Gandhi's defence of India's secular traditions and rejected the excesses of Hindu nationalism. That the avowedly leftist parties also made significant gains appeared to confirm the significance of both these factors. Gandhi then renounced the post of Prime Minister, saying that she had campaigned for the party, not out of personal ambition. On May 22, 2004, Manmohan Singh was sworn in as Prime Minister of the first INC-led government since 1996, heading a coalition named the United Progressive Alliance (UPA).

All-India Dravidian Progressive Federation
All-India Anna Dravida Munnetra Kazhagam (AIADMK)

Address. 226 Awai Shanmugam Salai, Royapet, Chennai (Madras) 600014

Tel. 044-8132266, 8130787

Fax. 044-8133510

Email. aiadmkho@aiadmkindia.org

Leadership. Jayalalitha Jayaram (leader)

The AIADMK, which reflects Tamil nationalist sentiment, was formed in 1972 by a breakaway faction of the Dravidian Progressive Federation (DMK), and became one of the dominant regional parties in Tamil Nadu state from 1977. It held power in the state from 1977 to 1989 and from 1991 to 1996 and was re-elected in 2001. Its principal regional rival, the

DMK, held power in the interim. The party's leader, former film star Jayalalitha Jayaram, is a highly controversial figure and was banned from standing in the 2001 regional elections following convictions for corruption. Nonetheless, her party swept the polls in a landslide victory and she was appointed chief minister. By the end of 2003 Jayalalitha's corruption convictions had been quashed and she had been acquitted of almost all other corruption charges filed against her.

In Union politics, the AIADMK has shifted in alliance between the *Bharatiya Janata* Party (whose coalition government it supported in 1998-99) and the Indian National Congress–Congress (I) with which it was allied by 2001. Over the next two years the AIADMK moved back into a relationship with the BJP, until in January 2004 Jayalalitha announced that the party would form a partnership with the BJP in the forthcoming general election, although declining to say whether it would join the National Democratic Alliance (NDA). In the October 1999 general election, the AIADMK won 10 seats to the *Lok Sabha* (all in Tamil Nadu), but the party performed disastrously in the April-May 2004 general election, losing all its seats in the *Lok Sabha* to the resurgent DMK and the other Tamil regional parties. As of May 2004, the AIADMK held nine seats in the *Rajya Sabha*.

All-India Trinamool Congress (AITC)
Address. 30-B, Harish Chatterjee Street, Calcutta 600026
Email. gbasu@trinamool.org
Website. www.trinamool.org
Leadership. Mamata Banerjee (chairperson)
The Trinamool Congress originated in 1997 as a break away from the West Bengal organization of the Indian National Congress–Congress (I) under the leadership of Mamata Banerjee and in opposition to the local alliance of the Congress (I) with Communists. It was renamed as the All-India Trinamool Congress in 1998 although predominantly based in West Bengal. It won seven seats in the *Lok Sabha* at the 1998 general election and eight in 1999 (all of them in West Bengal). The AITC supported the ruling federal coalition governments headed by the *Bharatiya Janata* Party (BJP) from 1998 with the influential but mercurial Banerjee serving as Railways Minister; however, the party resigned from the federal government and re-formed an alliance with the Congress (I) to fight the West Bengal state legislature elections in May 2001. It in turn resigned from this alliance and re-joined the National Democratic Alliance (NDA) in August 2001. Banerjee returned to the Union Cabinet in September 2003 as Minister without Portfolio and in January 2004 she was appointed Minister of Coal and Mines, a post she had previously rejected. The AITC suffered from its participation in the NDA in the April-May 2004 general election, winning only one seat in its heartland of West Bengal and one in Meghalaya. As at May 2004, the AITC held one seat in the *Rajya Sabha*.

Bahujan Samaj Party (BSP)
Address. 12 Gurudwara, Rakabganj Road, New Delhi 110001
Website. www.dalitstan.org/bahujan
Leadership. Kanshi Ram and Mayawati Kumari (leaders)
The BSP represents India's low caste Dalits (formerly Harijans or "untouchables"). Following the 1993 state elections in Uttar Pradesh, the party joined a governing coalition led by the *Samajwadi* Party. It then withdrew from the coalition in June 1995 and formed a new government itself, with the aid of opposition parties. However, on the resignation of the BSP chief minister in October 1995, President's rule was imposed in the state. After the restoration of the State Assembly in 1996, it formed brief administrations supported by the *Bharatiya Janata* Party (BJP). However, it did not

support the BJP-led federal coalition government and sat on the opposition benches. In the October 1999 general election, it won 14 seats (all of them from Uttar Pradesh) in the *Lok Sabha*.

Following state assembly elections in Uttar Pradesh in February 2002 in which the BJP lost control of the state, a BSP-BJP coalition formed a government in May, with the charismatic Mayawati as chief minister. The uneasy coalition, dogged by allegations directed at Mayawati of corruption, extravagant spending and chaotic administration, finally collapsed in August 2003. The BSP is also represented in the Punjab and Madhya Pradesh legislative assemblies. In the April-May 2004 general election the BSP won 19 seats in the *Lok Sabha*, and as at May 2004 it held 5 *Rajya Sabha* seats.

Bharatiya Janata Party (BJP)
(Indian People's Party)
Address. 11 Ashoka Road, New Delhi 110001
Email. bjpco@bjp.org
Website. www.bjp.org
Leadership. Atal Behari Vajpayee (parliamentary leader and former Prime Minister); Venkaiah Naidu (president); Pramod Mahajan (general secretary)
The *Bharatiya Janata* ("Indian People's") Party (BJP) was formed in 1980 as a breakaway group from the *Janata* Party, establishing itself as a radical, right-wing Hindu nationalist organization influenced by the Hindu social-cultural organization the *Rashtriya Swayamsevak Sangh* (RSS, Association of National Volunteers), of which it was effectively the political wing. Its influence as a national party rose dramatically in the 1989 general election, when it won 88 *Lok Sabha* seats (compared with only two in 1984), becoming the third largest party. Having increased its legislative representation to 119 seats in 1991, it became the main opposition to the Indian National Congress–Congress (I) government. It was associated in this period with many actions by militant Hindus opposed to Muslim influence and establishments in the "Hindu belt" of central-northern India.

The most significant of these associations was the BJP's close involvement in the campaign of agitation that started in 1984 for the building of a temple to the Hindu god Rama (or Ram) on the site of the Babri mosque in the town of Ayodhya in the northern state of Uttar Pradesh. Some Hindus, notably the membership of the RSS and of the *Vishwa Hindu Parishad* (VHP, World Council of Hindus) believed that the mosque had been built on the site of an earlier temple to Rama destroyed by Muslims in the 16th century. In December 1992 a mob of Hindu militants destroyed the Babri mosque, unleashing India's worst communal violence since Partition. A number of leading BJP politicians, including L.K. Advani, later Home Affairs Minister (from 1998) and Deputy Prime Minister (from 2002), faced charges of conspiracy and incitement in connection with the razing of the mosque, but by 2004 none of these charges had come to trial, and those against Advani had been dropped in September 2003. However, because of unresolved competing legal claims on ownership of the site, and despite the recurrent pledges of the BJP, the Rama temple remained unbuilt.

In the April-May 1996 general election the BJP emerged for the first time as the largest single party, largely through exploitation of the "Ayodhya factor", winning at least 161 seats and commanding the support of about another 35 *Lok Sabha* deputies from other parties. In mid-May party leader Vajpayee was invited to form a new BJP minority federal government (including *Shiv Sena* representation); however, his administration could not muster sufficient parliamentary support to secure a vote of confidence, with the result that his government resigned after only 13 days in office. But, following the March 1998 election in which it was again returned as the largest single party (with 180 seats), the party did succeed in cobbling together a coalition government under Vajpayee's leadership with the support of a number of smaller regional parties. In April 1999, this coalition was defeated in parliament but subsequently stayed in office for a full six months as an interim government before a new general election was held. Prior to the October 1999 election, the party built a series of electoral alliances with other parties and stood as part of a National Democratic Alliance (NDA). The NDA was victorious (with the BJP winning 182 seats in a total of 19 states and territories) and Vajpayee reconstructed his coalition government on its basis.

In national office the BJP moderated its earlier extreme Hindu nationalism (*Hindutva*) and also aligned itself with a continuation of the policies of gradual economic liberalization adopted but largely unfulfilled by the previous Congress Party administration. By the April-May 2004 general election the cadre-based BJP had become the most modern, efficient political organization in the country, employing information technology to market the party and slick media campaigns. It was also able to draw on the considerable resources, in terms both of personnel and finance, of the RSS. The BJP also attempted – despite its record on Ayodhya and the 2002 massacres of Muslims in western Gujarat state that the local BJP administration had signally failed to prevent – to portray itself as a non-sectarian party and to appeal to Muslim and low-caste *Dalit* voters. However, predictions of another BJP-led NDA majority were confounded, with the BJP's own share of seats in the *Lok Sabha* falling to 138. As of May 2004 the BJP also held 46 seats in the *Rajya Sabha*. There was speculation that in opposition the party would turn away from the face of moderation represented by Vajpayee and revert to the pursuit of a hardline *Hindutva* agenda.

Biju Janata Dal (BJD)

Address. Naveen Nivas, Aerodrome Gate, Bhubaneswar 751009, Orissa
Leadership. Naveen Patnaik (president)
The majority section of the *Janata Dal* (JD) in Orissa, organized around long-time Orissa chief minister Biju Patnaik. Having broken away from the main JD it won nine seats in the *Lok Sabha* in 1998 and 10 in 1999. It supported the 1998-99 federal coalition government headed by the *Bharatiya Janata* Party (BJP) and was a founder member of the National Democratic Alliance; currently it is the ruling party in Orissa state. In the April-May 2004 general election it won 11 seats in the *Lok Sabha*, and in simultaneous elections to the 147-seat Orissa state assembly the BJD secured 61 seats, ensuring its continued governance with its ally the BJP (32 seats). As at May 2004 the BJD also held three seats in the *Rajya Sabha*.

Communist Party of India (CPI)

Address. Ajoy Bhavan, 15 Kotla Marg, New Delhi 110002
Telephone. (91–11) 323-5546
Fax. (91–11) 323-5543
Email. Cpi@cpofindia.org
Website. www.cpofindia.org
Leadership. A.B. Bardhan (general secretary)
Founded in 1925, the CPI split in 1964 when the rival Communist Party of India–Marxist (CPI–M) was formed. From the end of the 1970s the CPI maintained a policy of opposition to the political dominance of the Indian National Congress–Congress (I), working closely with the CPI–M and other left-wing parties. In the general election of April-May 1996 the CPI won 12 seats in the *Lok Sabha* (compared with 13 in 1991) and became an important component within the United Front (UF) government (1996-98). However, it fared badly in the 1998 and 1999 general elections, winning nine seats at the first and only four at the second (three of them in West Bengal). In the April-May 2004 general election it shared in the unexpected resurgence of the left and won 10 seats in the *Lok Sabha*. As of May 2004 the party also held two seats in the *Rajya Sabha* and participated in the Left Front coalition governing in West Bengal. After the 2004 general election the CPM, together with the CPI–M and the All India Forward Bloc (AIFB), announced that its would not join a Congress (I) coalition, but would support the government from the back benches.

Communist Party of India–Marxist (CPI-M)

Address. A.K. Gopalan Bhavan, 27–29 Bhai Vir Singh Marg (Gole Market), New Delhi 110001
Telephone. (91–11) 334–4918
Fax. (91–11) 374–7483
Email. Cpim@vsnl.com
Website. www.cpim.org
Leadership. Harkishan Singh Surjit (general secretary)
The CPI–M was created in 1964 by dissident members of the Communist Party of India (CPI) favouring a more radical leftist line. Originally pro-Chinese, the party declared its independence of China in 1968. Although claiming to be a national party, the CPI–M's main support has traditionally come from West Bengal, Kerala and Tripura. This distinctly regional bias in 2001 led the Election Commission of India to de-recognize it as a national party. In the 1996 general election the CPI–M secured 32 seats in the *Lok Sabha* (having won 35 in 1991) and supported the United Front (UF) alliance government (1996-98) from the back benches. In the 1999 general elections the party won 32 seats, of which 21 were in West Bengal and eight in Kerala, but found itself in opposition to the ruling coalition led by the *Bharatiya Janata* Party. In state assembly elections in May 2001, the CPI–M retained power (as part of the Left Front government) in West Bengal but lost it (as part of a defeated leftist coalition) in Kerala. In the April-May 2004 general election it became the third largest party in the *Lok Sabha*, winning 43 seats, its largest ever representation in the federal parliament. As at May 2004, it also held 12 seats in the *Rajya Sabha*. After the general election the party joined the CPM and other leftist parties in announcing that it would not join an Indian National Congress (INC)–Congress (I) coalition, but would support it from the back benches.

Dravidian Progressive Federation
Dravida Munnetra Kazhagam (DMK)

Address. Anna Arivalayam 268–269, Anna Salai, Teynampet, Chennai (Madras) 600018, Tamil Nadu
Website. www.thedmk.org
Leadership. Muthuvel Karunanidhi (president)
A Tamil nationalist and anti-Brahmin party founded in 1949, the DMK urges full autonomy for the state of Tamil Nadu within the Indian Union and opposes the retention of Hindi as an official language. In 1977 it lost power in Tamil Nadu to the All-India Dravidian Progressive Federation (AIADMK), which had earlier broken away from the parent party. The rump DMK was briefly returned as the ruling party from 1989 until 1991, but after a period of President's rule its AIADMK rival was swept back to power with a large majority in the state legislature. Assisted by various government scandals and a split in the Tamil Nadu Indian National Congress–Congress (I) which produced the pro-DMK *Tamil Maanila* Congress, the DMK turned the tables in the 1996 state elections, winning 172 seats and forming a government on May 13 under veteran leader Muthuvel Karunanidhi. But it was then swept out of power again in May 2001 when the AIADMK secured a landslide victory.

Having won no seats in the *Lok Sabha* in the 1991 general election, the DMK returned 17 representatives from Tamil Nadu constituencies in the April-May 1996 national poll and joined the United Front federal government (1996-98). In the 1998 general election, it won six seats and sat with the opposition to the ruling coalition led by the *Bharatiya Janata* Party (BJP). However, for the general election of October 1999, it joined the National Democratic Alliance (NDA) led by the BJP and, on winning 12 seats, became a key member of the new BJP-led coalition. On Dec. 20, 2003, Karunanidhi announced that the DMK was withdrawing from the NDA in protest against the BJP's support in Tamil Nadu for the AIADMK, and that its two ministers would resign from the Union Cabinet. The DMK announced on Jan. 3, 2004, in anticipation of a general election, the formation of a "progressive front" in Tamil Nadu, including Congress (I) and the Communist Party of India–Marxist (CPI–M). In the April-May 2004 general election the DMK increased its representation in the *Lok Sabha* to 16 seats. As of May 2004, the DMK also held seven seats in the *Rajya Sabha*. Three DMK Cabinet ministers and four ministers of state were appointed to the new Congress (I)-led United Progressive Alliance (UPA) government formed after the election, although there was a delay of a few days in swearing these in as the party objected that it had not received its promised allocation of portfolios. The problem was resolved when the Shipping portfolio was added to those of Road Transport and Highways for Cabinet minister T.R. Baalu, and Minister of State Palani Manickam was moved to Finance.

Indian National Congress (INC)–Congress (I)

Address. 24 Akbar Road, New Delhi 110001
Telephone. (91–11) 301–9606
Fax. (91–11) 301–7701
Leadership. Sonia Gandhi (president)

The Indian National Congress (INC), dating from 1885 and traditionally committed to democracy, socialism and secularism, has been India's ruling formation for most of the period since it led India to independence in 1947 under Jawaharlal (Pandit) Nehru. In 1969, three years after Nehru's daughter, Indira Gandhi, had acceded to the leadership, the party split into two groups when an anti-Gandhi conservative faction – the Indian National Congress–Organization (INC-O) – became India's first recognized opposition party. Having aroused widespread opposition by governing under emergency powers from 1975, the Congress government was defeated in the March 1977 general elections, going into opposition for the first time since independence. Further splits resulted in Gandhi forming the mainstream Congress (I), which returned to power with an overwhelming majority in the elections of early 1980. Her new government's more pro-market orientation contributed to the formation of the breakaway Indian National Congress (Socialist) in 1981. In July 1981 the Supreme Court ruled that Congress (I) was the authentic heir of the historic Congress party, although the Congress (I) designation continued in universal usage.

Indira Gandhi was assassinated by Sikh militants in October 1984 and was succeeded as Prime Minister and party leader by her son, Rajiv Gandhi. Rajiv led the party to a convincing general election victory in 1984-85. However, substantial opposition to his leadership subsequently developed, leading to expulsions and resignations from the party, including the exit of V.P. Singh, who in 1987 formed the *Jan Morcha* anti-corruption movement which heralded the establishment of the opposition *Janata Dal*. As a result of the November 1989 general elections, Congress (I) was forced into opposition by a National Front alliance dominated by *Janata Dal*.

During the next election campaign, Rajiv was assassinated by Sri Lankan Tamil militants in May 1991, but Congress (I) regained power and formed a government under the premiership of the party's new president, P.V. Narasimha Rao. By early 1996, however, Rao's administration was deeply unpopular, its political standing having been badly damaged by alleged involvement in the country's largest corruption scandal and by related ministerial resignations. In the April-May 1996 elections Congress (I) returned only 140 members to the *Lok Sabha*, representing a loss of nearly half of its previous representation. Having manoeuvred to deny a parliamentary vote of confidence to the minority government formed in May by its principal electoral rival, the *Bharatiya Janata* Party (BJP), Congress (I) gave its tacit support to the United Front administration inaugurated in June. However, early in 1998 it withdrew this support, precipitating a general election in which its *Lok Sabha* base contracted further (to 119 seats).

A consequence of this election was the emergence of Sonia Gandhi (the Italian-born widow of Rajiv Gandhi) as the party's new leader. In April 1999, she helped to bring down the ruling BJP-led coalition but was unable to form an alternative coalition government under her own leadership. Further splits within the party followed (leading to the formation of the Nationalist Congress Party) and, at the October 1999 general election, its representation was further reduced to 112 seats. Its support base remained the most geographically spread of Indian parties, however, and Congress (I) maintained a vigorous presence in the local politics of many of the states, where governments or coalitions under its leadership alternated in power with those headed either by the BJP and its coalition partners or by erstwhile United Front parties. As of August 2001, Congress (I) held or shared power in eleven states.

Congress (I) appeared to be staging a revival in 2002-03, making significant gains from the BJP in state assembly elections. However, the momentum seemed to have been lost by December 2003, when the BJP unseated Congress (I) administrations in three state elections. Despite Sonia Gandhi's growth in stature as a leader of the parliamentary opposition, she continued to be dogged by the question of her foreign origin, which had been used as a weapon against her by the BJP and other Indian nationalists ever since she was persuaded to take the helm of the party. During its campaign for the April-May 2004 legislative elections, the BJP proposed introducing a law barring anyone of foreign birth from holding any of the high offices of state. Other critics claimed that she had done too little to revitalize the party in terms of its policies, its organization and its membership, and that she was isolated from the party at large by a small clique of senior Congress officials. Sonia's son Rahul Gandhi stood for his father's old seat of Amethi in the 2004 election, despite previous lack of political experience, in what was seen as an attempt to attract younger voters. However, many analysts maintained that the principal weakness of Congress (I) was its reliance on the "dynastic" appeal of the Nehru-Gandhi family, arguing that this was now demographically irrelevant because there were now many millions of voters too young to remember a government headed by a Gandhi.

Congress (I) fought the election on two broad issues: the preservation of India's secular constitution and identity against the forces of Hindu nationalist sectarianism associated with the BJP; and the charge that the economic growth for which the BJP claimed credit had concentrated wealth in the middle classes and further impoverished the rural population. Sonia Gandhi's nationwide campaigning on these themes resulted in a startling upset in the 2004 general election, with Congress (I) emerging as the largest party in the *Lok Sabha*, winning 145 seats and poised to form a government. It also as of May 2004 held 67 *Rajya Sabha* seats.

Congress (I) also swept to a dramatic victory with a large majority in the simultaneous state assembly election in Andhra Pradesh, winning 186 seats and humbling the incumbent *Telugu Desam* Party (TDP), a significant member of the outgoing National Democratic Alliance (NDA) federal coalition. In the state elections in Karnataka, however, the incumbent Congress (I) saw its share of the 224 seats fall from 133 to 65, with the BJP in first place with 79.

Sonia Gandhi began negotiations to enlarge the Congress (I)-led alliance, which held 217 seats, to command a majority in the *Lok Sabha*. However, after several days and a second meeting with President A. P. J. Abdul Kalam, she announced to an India already stunned by the Congress victory that she would not serve as Prime Minister. Despite the entreaties of many in her party, who attributed its revival in large part to Gandhi's leadership, she stood firm in her decision and nominated Manmohan Singh as Prime Minister, the first Sikh and first non-Hindu to hold that office. Singh was a former Finance Minister who had in the early 1990s laid the basis of the liberalizing economic reforms further developed by successive BJP-led governments. As soon as the election result was known sections of the BJP had resumed their virulent campaign unabated against Sonia Gandhi's foreign origin, and analysts speculated that her renunciation came from a recognition that the running sore of this issue would undermine a Congress government; also that her children Rahul and Priyanka feared for her safety. However, since 1999 and during the campaign, Sonia Gandhi had never explicitly laid claim to the premiership, saying always that the party would decide. Gandhi remained president of the party and it was thought that she would retain influence on the conduct of government. In the new United Progressive Alliance (UPA) coalition government the Congress (I) held 18 Cabinet posts, including the key positions of Finance, Defence, Home Affairs and External Affairs. Although Singh and most of the government was sworn in on May 22 there was a delay before the whole Cabinet could be sworn in while the dissatisfaction of electoral ally the Dravidian Progressive Foundation (DMK, *Dravida Munnetra Kazhagam*) with its allocation of portfolios was accommodated.

Janata Dal–United (JDU)

Address. 7 Jantar Mantar Road, New Delhi 110001
Leadership. George Fernandes (president)
The *Janata Dal* ("People's Party") was formed in 1988 as a merger of the *Jan Morcha* ("Popular Front") dissident faction of the Indian National Congress–Congress (I), the *Lok Dal* and other outgrowths of the old *Janata* Party. It advocated non-alignment, the eradication of poverty, unemployment and wide disparities in wealth, and protection of minorities. The JD contested the 1989 general election as the dominant component of an opposition National Front, winning 141 of the Front's 144 seats. With the support of the *Bharatiya Janata* Party (BJP) and the communist parties, the National Front formed a fragile new government, ousting Congress (I) from power.

A split in the JD in late 1990 resulted in the creation of the breakaway *Janata Dal* (S), which subsequently evolved into the *Samajwadi* Party. This instability led to an early general election in 1991, in which the official JD won only 55 *Lok Sabha* seats and Congress (I) was returned to power. A further party split in 1994 saw the establishment of a separate parliamentary group, which subsequently adopted the *Samata* Party designation.

For the April-May 1996 general elections the JD was the largest constituent in a leftist United Front (UF), but was itself reduced to some 45 seats in the *Lok Sabha*. Following the elections, the Front commanded the support of about 180 lower house deputies, so that it was eventually able to form a new government under the premiership of H.D. Deve Gowda of the JD. In 1997, Gowda was replaced by I.K. Gujral, also of the JD. But the UF government fell early in December 1997, when the Congress (I) withdrew its back bench support and, subsequently, the JD suffered further disintegration. Breakaway factions include the *Janata Dal*–Secular (JD-S), *Biju Janata Dal* (Orissa), the *Rashtriya Janata Dal* (Bihar) and the *Lok Jan Shakti Party* (Karnataka). The rump of the JD – now called the *Janata Dal*–United (JDU) – secured six *Lok Sabha* seats in the 1999 general election. In October 2003 the JDU merged with the *Samata* Party, with Samata's George Fernandes taking over as president of the enlarged JDU. In the April-May 2004 general election the merged JD–U won eight seats, compared with the 20 held by the two separate parties in the previous *Lok Sabha*. As of May 2004 the merged party also held two seats in the *Rajya Sabha*.

Janata Dal is an observer member of the Socialist International

Marumalarchi Dravidian Progressive Federation
Marumalarchi Dravida Munnetra Kazhagam (MDMK)

Address. "Thayagam", No. 141, Rukmani Lakshmi Pathi Salai, Egmore, Chennai (Madras) 600008, Tamil Nadu
Leadership. Thiru Vaiko (president)
This is a breakaway faction of the Tamil Nadu Dravidian Progressive Federation (DMK). It allied with the All-India Dravidian Progressive Federation (AIADMK) for the 1998 general election, winning three seats in the *Lok Sabha* and supporting the federal coalition government headed by the *Bharatiya Janata* Party (BJP). It broke with the AIADMK to join the DMK for the 1999 general election where it stood as part of the National Democratic Alliance (NDA) and won four seats (all in Tamil Nadu); it left the DMK to stand independently in the 2001 Tamil Nadu state elections. Following the example of the DMK earlier in the month, on Dec. 30, 2003, the MDMK announced that it was withdrawing from the NDA. For both parties the motivation appeared less disagreement with national policies than resentment at BJP support in the state for the ruling AIADMK. In the April-May 2004 general election the MDMK won all four seats that it contested, participating in the trouncing of AIDMK.

National Democratic Alliance (NDA)

A loose cross-party "front", the NDA was formed in June 1999 around the core of the multi-party coalition, headed by the *Bharatiya Janata* Party (BJP), which had provided the federal government between March 1998 and April 1999. Its purpose was to offer a coherent platform for the general election of October 1999. Its principal constituents, besides the BJP, were: the *Telugu Desam* Party (TDP), the Dravidian Progressive Federation (DMK), the *Shiv Sena*, the *Biju Janata Dal* (BJD), the All-India *Trinamool* Congress (AITC), the *Shiromani Akali Dal* (SAD), the *Lok Shakti* Party and the *Samata* Party. In all, 24 parties stood under the NDA banner and were successful, gaining an overall majority of about 30 seats in the *Lok Sabha* and forming a new federal government under the leadership of Atal Behari Vajpayee of the BJP. The NDA gave the BJP a broad base that, despite policy differences, personal ructions and occasional defections, enabled it to complete a full term and to choose what seemed the most advantageous moment for the 2004 general election. Yet the presence of significant secular parties in the coalition, such as the TDP, the *Samata* Party and the AITC, also had the effect of reining in the more extreme elements of the Hindu nationalist agenda of which the BJP and *Shiv Sena* were the principal advocates. In the April-May 2004 general election the NDA's share of seats fell to 185, losing power to the Indian National Congress (INC)–Congress (I) and its allies.

Nationalist Congress Party (NCP)

Address. 10 Bishambhar Das Marg, New Delhi 110001
Leadership. Sharad Pawar (president)
The NCP broke away from the main Indian National Congress–Congress (I) in 1999 under the direction of Sharad

Pawar and Purno Sangma in protest at the party leadership of Sonia Gandhi. It has its main base in Pawar's home state of Maharashtra where it took six of the eight *Lok Sabha* seats it won in the 1999 general election. It tried to revive the non-Congress (I) forces of opposition, especially in association with the *Samajwadi* Party; however, the NCP was forced to re-ally with the Congress (I) in Maharashtra in order to form a coalition government to displace the previously ruling combine of *Shiv Sena* and the *Bharatiya Janata* Party.

In January 2004 the NCP split into two factions, each claiming to hold the title to the party's name and symbols. The faction led by Pawar decided to enter an electoral alliance with Congress (I) in the forthcoming (April-May) general election. A breakaway faction led by Sangma allied itself with the National Democratic Alliance (NDA) led by the BJP as part of the regional North-East People's Forum. The NCP won nine *Lok Sabha* seats in the April-May 2004 general election. Pawar was awarded the Cabinet portfolio of Agriculture in the United Progressive Alliance (UPA) coalition government formed by Congress (I) after the election, and the new government also included one minister of state and one minister of state with independent charge. As of May 2004, the NCP also held two seats in the *Rajya Sabha*.

Pattali Makkal Katchi (PMK)

Address. 63, Nattu Muthu Naiken Street, Vanniya Teynampet, Chennai (Madras) 60001
Leadership. S. Ramadoss
This is a party of the large Vanniya caste which is prominent in north Tamil Nadu; vigorously led by Dr S. Ramdoss, the PMK broke its long term association with the Dravidian Progressive Federation (DMK) to stand independently at the 1998 general election where it won three seats in the *Lok Sabha* and joined the federal coalition government headed by the *Bharatiya Janata* Party (BJP) in association with the All India Dravidian Progressive Party (AIADMK). It broke its connection to the AIADMK when the latter resigned from the federal government and re-aligned itself with the DMK for the 1999 general election, joining the National Democratic Alliance (NDA) and winning five *Lok Sabha* seats (all in Tamil Nadu); however, it deserted the DMK again to stand independently at the Tamil Nadu state legislature elections of May 2001.

In January 2004 the PMK announced its withdrawal from the NDA, saying that it would join the "progressive front" in Tamil Nadu announced by the DMK. In the April-May 2004 general election the PMK contested and won six seats in the *Lok Sabha*. In the United Progressive Alliance (UPA) government formed by the Indian National Congress (INC)–Congress (I) after the election the PMK was awarded one Cabinet post and one post of minister of state.

Rashtriya Janata Dal (RJD)

Address. 2 Moti Lal Nehru Place, Akbar Road, New Delhi 110011
Leadership. Laloo Prasad Yadav
This is a breakaway faction of the *Janata Dal* (JD) formed in 1998 around erstwhile JD leader Laloo Prasad Yadav and having its main base in Bihar. The breakaway was fomented by Yadav's indictment for corruption and subsequent forced resignation as Bihar chief minister; however, the party then installed his wife, Rabri Devi, in his place and continued to govern the state. It was generally recognized that Yadav himself continued to exercise power behind the scenes. In the 1998 general election, the RJD won 17 seats in the *Lok Sabha* and, in 1999, seven (all in Bihar). As of May 2004, it held 8 seats in the *Rajya Sabha*. In the April-May 2004 general election, running as an ally of Indian National Congress (INC)–Congress (I), the RJD won 21 seats in the *Lok Sabha*. In the United Progressive Alliance (UPA) government

formed after the election and led by the INC the RJD was allocated two Cabinet posts, including the important Railways portfolio for Yadav, five for ministers of state and one for minister of state with independent charge.

Revolutionary Socialist Party (RSP)

Address. 37 Ripon Street (Muzaffar Ahmed Sarani), Calcutta 700016, West Bengal
Leadership. T.J Chandrachoodan (general secretary)
In the general elections of April-May 1996 the Marxist–Leninist RSP won five seats in the *Lok Sabha*, all from West Bengal, as part of the United Front (UF) alliance, but did not join the subsequent UF government. At both the 1998 and 1999 elections, its representation was reduced to three seats (all from West Bengal). As of May 2004, it held four seats in the *Rajya Sabha* and enjoyed representation in a number of state legislative assemblies, including West Bengal, Tripura and Kerala. The RSP retained its three West Bengal seats in the *Lok Sabha* in the general election of April-May 2004.

Samajwadi Party (SP)

Address. 18 Copernicus Lane, New Delhi 110001
Leadership. Mulayam Singh Yadav (leader)
Inaugurated at a convention in 1992, the *Samajwadi* (Socialist) Party, whose strength lies in Uttar Pradesh although it has contested elections in some other states, derives from a dissident faction of the *Janata Dal* (JD). Following the 1993 state elections in Uttar Pradesh, the SP formed a governing coalition with the *Bahujan Samaj* Party (BSP). However, the coalition collapsed in June 1995 and President's rule was imposed in the state the following October pending fresh elections. In the general elections of April-May 1996 the SP won 17 *Lok Sabha* seats and was allocated the defence portfolio in the new administration. Since the 1998 and 1999 elections, where it won 20 and 26 seats respectively (all of them from Uttar Pradesh), it has taken a leading role on the opposition benches. However, its relations with other opposition parties (most notably the Indian National Congress–Congress (I) and the BSP) have been fraught. At the end of August 2003 Yadav became chief minister of Uttar Pradesh, heading an SP-led alliance, following the collapse of a BSP – Bharatiya Janata Party (BJP) coalition. As of May 2004, it held nine seats in the *Rajya Sabha*. In the April-May 2004 general election the SP won 36 seats, all but one of them in Uttar Pradesh.

Samata Party

Address. 220 Vitthalbhai Patel House, Rafi Marg, New Delhi 110001
Leadership. George Fernandes (president)
The *Samata* ("Equality") Party derived from a factional split in the *Janata Dal* (JD) in early 1994, its president being a veteran socialist and trade union leader. The new grouping contested the general elections of April-May 1996, winning six *Lok Sabha* seats in the state of Bihar, but surprisingly was not part of the victorious United Front alliance. Following the 1998 election, when it won 12 seats, the party joined the ruling coalition headed by the *Bharatiya Janata* Party (BJP) and party leader George Fernandes accepted the defence portfolio. In the 1999 election, the *Samata* Party stood as a member of National Democratic Alliance headed by the BJP. It again won 12 *Lok Sabha* seats and Fernandes resumed as Defence Minister although, in March 2001, he was obliged to resign following a defence contracts scandal (being re-appointed in October 2001). As of August 2001, the *Samata* Party held one *Rajya Sabha* seat. In October 2003 *Samata* merged with the remnant *Janata Dal*–United (JDU) party, Fernandes becoming president of the new merged party, which took the name of the JDU.

Shiromani Akali Dal (SAD)

Address. House No. 256, Sector 9-C, Chandigarh
Leadership. Prakash Singh Badal (president)
The SAD is the main political organization of India's Sikh community, which is concentrated in Punjab. In support of its demands for Sikh self-determination, the SAD became increasingly militant in the early 1980s and has since been subject to factional rivalry and division. In the general elections of April-May 1996 the party won eight of Punjab's 13 *Lok Sabha* seats. In the 1998 elections, it again won eight seats and supported the ruling coalition led by the *Bharatiya Janata* Party (BJP). Perhaps as a result, it suffered severely in the elections of October 1999 and was reduced to two seats. Badal was chief minister in Punjab state 1997-2002, when the SAD was defeated in state assembly elections by the Congress (I) party. In the *Rajya Sabha*, the party as of May 2004 held two seats. Despite the reverse in the fortunes of the BJP in the April-May 2004 general election, the poll saw a resurgence for the SAD, which won eight *Lok Sabha* seats.

Shiv Sena
(Shivaji's Army)

Address. Shivsena Bhavan, Gadkari Chowk, Dadar, Bombay 400028
Website. www.shivsena.org
Leadership. Bal Thackeray (president)
Founded in 1967 and based in Maharashtra state, *Shiv Sena* is a right-wing Hindu communalist party allied to the *Bharatiya Janata* Party (BJP) at state government and federal parliamentary levels. In the general elections of April-May 1996 the party won 15 seats in the *Lok Sabha* and supported the subsequent short-lived BJP federal administration. In the 1998 election, its representation was reduced to six seats but it became part of the ruling BJP-led coalition government. In the 1999 election, it recovered to 15 seats (all in Maharashtra) as part of the victorious BJP-led National Democratic Alliance. Between 1995 and 2000, it governed Maharashtra state in alliance with the BJP, when it was replaced by a Congress (I)-led coalition. Its leader, Bal Thackeray, was originally a firebrand journalist. He was investigated in 1993 for incitement of communal Hindu-Muslim violence in 1992-93, but charges were never filed. In 2000 an attempt by the new Maharashtra administration to prosecute him failed because the alleged offences now fell outside the statute of limitations. In the April-May 2004 general election *Shiv Sena* was reduced to 12 seats in the *Lok Sabha*. As of May 2004 *Shiv Sena* held five seats in the *Rajya Sabha*.

Telugu Desam Party (TDP)

Address. Telugu Desam Party Office, NTR Bhawan, Road No. 2, Banjara Hills, Hyderabad 500033, Andhra Pradesh
Website. www.tdparty.org
Leadership. N. Chandrababu Naidu (president)
Founded in 1982 as an Andhra Pradesh-based leftist party by N.T. Rama Rao, the TDP was the ruling party in the state from 1983 to 1989. In 1994 it regained power from the Indian National Congress–Congress (I) in a convincing victory in the state elections, Rao becoming chief minister again. Political divisions within the party resulted in a split in 1995 between those state assembly deputies supporting Rao and those supporting Chandrababu Naidu (Rao's son-in-law). In August Rao resigned the premiership and was replaced by Naidu in September. On Rao's death in January 1996, leadership of his faction was taken over by his wife, Lakshmi Parvati. In the general election of April-May 1996, the TDP–Naidu faction won 16 seats in the *Lok Sabha* (and the Parvati faction none), being allocated four posts in the subsequent United Front federal government formed in June 1996. At the 1998 general election, the party (over which Naidu had by now established firm leadership) won 12 seats

and supported the BJP-led federal government from the back benches. In the 1999 election, the TDP not only triumphed by winning 29 seats (all in Andhra Pradesh) but, in simultaneous polls to the state legislative assembly, was returned to government with an enhanced majority. For the general election, it remained allied to the BJP as part of the National Democratic Alliance (NDA) but, once again, refused to accept portfolios in the NDA's new federal government.

Party leader Chandrababu Naidu has established a reputation as one of the principal proponents of liberal economic reform in India and as the chief minister of one of the country's most economically-dynamic states, where the "cyber-revolution" has been particularly strong. Perhaps the biggest shock of the April-May 2004 general election and simultaneous Andhra Pradesh state election was the eclipse of the TDP. The party retained only five seats in the *Lok Sabha* and in Andhra Pradesh it was routed by Congress (I), winning only 45 seats in the 294-seat assembly. As of May 2004, the TDP held 8 seats in the *Rajya Sabha*.

United Front (UF)

Address. c/o *Lok Sabha*, New Delhi 110001
Officially called the National Front–Left Front for the April-May 1996 general elections, the UF consisted of a loose alliance of 13 broadly leftist and regional organizations dominated by three national parties, namely the *Janata Dal* (JD), the Communist Party of India–Marxist (CPI-M) and the Communist Party of India (CPI). It also included the All-India Forward Bloc, the All-India Indira Congress–*Tiwari*, the Assam People's Council, the Dravidian Progressive Federation (DMK), the Karnataka Congress Party, the *Madhya Pradesh Vikas* Congress, the *Maharastrawadi Gomantak*, the Revolutionary Socialist Party, the *Samajwadi* Party, the *Tamil Maanila* Congress and the *Telugu Desam* Party–*Naidu*.

Upon the demise of the short-lived post-election government of the *Bharatiya Janata* Party at the end of May 1996, the UF parties, with the support of about 180 members in the *Lok Sabha* and the acquiescence of the Indian National Congress–Congress (I) deputies, formed a new federal administration under the premiership of Deve Gowda (JD) which won a parliamentary vote of confidence the following month. The CPI–M opted not to take ministerial portfolios, while continuing to be a member of the Front, which advocated the preservation of national unity, social and economic equality, and commitment to secularism and federalism. However, after its government fell early in 1998 when the Congress Party withdrew its support, the UF fell apart. Most its constituent parties faired badly in the elections of 1998 and 1999 and many of them suffered internal splits.

United Progressive Alliance (UPA)

The UPA was the coalition formed by the Indian National Congress (INC)–Congress (I) party after the April-May 2004 general election in which it supplanted the *Bharatiya Janata* Party (BJP) as the largest party in the *Lok Sabha* with 145 seats. A number of parties rallied round Congress (I) and its allies after the election in an "anti-BJP" movement, committed to secularism and the reining in of the BJP's market-driven economic policies The left-wing parties, together holding 61 seats, pledged support from the back benches, guaranteeing the new government a majority in the *Lok Sabha*. The UPA government formed in May 2004 included ministers from the *Rashtriya Janata Dal* (RJD), the Dravidian Progressive Federation (DMK), the Nationalist Congress Party (NCP), the *Pattali Makkal Katchi* (PMK), the *Jharkhand Mukti Morcha* (JMM), the *Telenganu Rashtra Samithi* (TRS), the Lok Janshakti Party (LJP), and the Indian Union Muslim League (IUML). The UPA produced a Common Minimum Programme (CMP) that included the protection of social harmony, investment in health, education and rural infrastructure. It pledged the continuance of the peace initiative with Pakistan begun by the previous government. In the economic field the CMP was committed to economic growth and further foreign investment and reforms, but in a way that benefited the rural majority as well as the urban elite. The CMP ruled out privatizations of state-owned banks and profitable state-owned companies.

Other Parties

India has a great profusion of political parties, many of them regional. The following have had an impact at state or national level.

All-India Forward Bloc (AIFB), was founded in 1939 by Subhas Chandra Bhose after his resignation from the Indian National Congress (INC). It is based mainly in West Bengal, where it is a constituent of the Left Front state administration led by the Communist Party of India-Marxist. In the general election of October 1999 the party won two *Lok Sabha* seats (both in West Bengal) but it is without a seat in the *Rajya Sabha*. The AIFB won three seats in the April-May 2004 general election, all in West Bengal.
Address. 28 Gurudwara Rakab Ganj Road, New Delhi 110001
Leadership. Debabrata Biswas (general secretary)

All-India Majlis-e-Ittehadul Muslimeen (AIMIM), a Muslim-based party led by Sultan Salahuddin Owaisi that secured representation in the *Lok Sabha* in a 1994 by-election; declared its support for the United Front central government inaugurated in June 1996; retained its single seat in the 1998, 1999 and 2004 general elections.

Assam People's Council (*Asom Gana Parishad,* AGP), won power in Assam in 1985, the year of its foundation. However, in 1989 the federal government imposed President's rule in the state as a result of the activities of separatist groups. The party was subsequently defeated by the Indian National Congress–Congress (I) in fresh state elections in 1991. It emerged from the April-May 1996 general election with five *Lok Sabha* seats (having won only two in 1991) and obtained two ministerial posts in the United Front national government inaugurated in June 1996. In simultaneous state elections, an AGP-led alliance secured a majority in the Assam legislative assembly, regaining power from Congress (I). However, it failed to retain any of its *Lok Sabha* seats at the 1998 and 1999 general elections and, in May 2001, lost power to Congress (I) in the state. The AGP won two *Lok Sabha* seats in the April-May 2004 general election and holds two seats in the *Rajya Sabha*.
Address. Gopinath Bordoloi Road, Guwahati 781001, Assam
Leadership. Prafulla Kumar Mahanta (president)

Autonomous State Demand Committee (ASDC), secured representation in the *Lok Sabha* in a 1994 by-election and retained it in the 1996 and 1998 general elections; however, was defeated in 1999.
Address. Head Quarter-Diphu, Karbi Anglong 782460, Assam
Leadership. Jayanta Rongpi (general secretary)

Bharatiya Navshakti Party (BNP), won one *Lok Sabha* seat in the April-May 2004 general election.

Communist Party of India (Marxist-Leninist) Liberation (CPI–ML), founded in 1969 by revolutionaries expelled from the Communist Party of India–Marxist (CPI–M), with which it then engaged in a bitter and bloody struggle, particularly in West Bengal. Retains Marxist-Leninist positions advocating a "revolutionary democratic front". Failed to gain national representation until it won a single *Lok Sabha* seat

at the 1999 general election, which it then lost in the April-May 2004 general election.
Address. U-90, Shakarpur, Delhi 110 092
Telephone. (91–11) 222–1067
Fax. (91–11) 221 8248
Website. www.cpiml.org

Haryana Vikas Party (HVP), returned three *Lok Sabha* members from Haryana constituencies in April–May 1996 and supported the short-lived government of the *Bharatiya Janata* Party; suffered internal split in 1997 and returned just one member to the *Lok Sabha* at the 1998 and 1999 general elections. However, it lost this seat in the general election of April-May 2004, but as of May 2004 it held one seat in the *Rajya Sabha*.
Address. Kothi No. 36/22, Sonipat Road, Rohtak, Haryana
Leadership. Bansi Lal (president)

Hill State People's Democratic Party (HSPDP), advocating the preservation of the distinct identity of the tribal peoples of Meghalaya state and the protection of their interests within the Indian Union; without a seat in the *Lok Sabha*.
Address. Kench's Trace, Laban, Shillong 793004, Meghalaya
Leadership. H.S. Lyngdoh (president)

Himachal Vikas Congress, state party in Himachal Pradesh that held one seat in the *Lok Sabha* following the 1999 elections, but lost it in the general election of April-May 2004.
Address. Samkhetar Bazar, Mandi 175001, Himachal Pradesh
Leadership. Sukh Ram (president)

Indian Federal Democratic Party (IFDP), won one *Lok Sabha* seat in the April-May 2004 general election.

Indian National Lok Dal, won five seats in the *Lok Sabha* in 1999 elections, but lost them all in the April-May 2004 general election. However, as of May 2004 the party still held four seats in the *Rajya Sabha*.
Address. 100 Lodhi Estate, New Delhi
Leadership. Om Prakash Chautala (president)

Indian Union Muslim League (IUML), a remnant of the pre-independence Muslim League, aiming to represent the interests of the Muslim ethnic and religious minority; has attracted support mainly in southern India, particularly in Kerala state. The IUML won one seat in the *Lok Sabha* in the April-May 2004 general election, and was awarded the post of Minister of State for External Affairs in the United Progressive Alliance (UPA) government formed by the Indian National Congress (INC)–Congress (I) party.

Jammu and Kashmir National Conference (JKNC), a state-based party, founded by Sheikh Mohammed Abdullah, opposed to Hindu communalism and advocating the maintenance of Jammu and Kashmir's status as an integral part of the Indian Union but with internal autonomy and self-government. It was the dominant party in Kashmir for most of the period from independence until 1990, when communal violence led to the imposition of President's rule in the state. Constitutional government was restored in 1996 with the JKNC winning a majority of seats and forming a government in the State Legislative Assembly although on the basis of a tiny voter turnout. The new chief minister was Farooq Abdullah, Sheikh Mohammed's son, who had been JKNC president since 1980. The party won three *Lok Sabha* seats at the 1998 general election and four at the 1999 polls. It supported the federal coalition governments led by the *Bharatiya Janata* Party (BJP) after both elections but withdrew its backing in 2000 following a dispute over Kashmir policy. Farooq Abdullah handed over presidency of the party to his son Omar, a federal minister, in June 2002. In October 2002 state elections the JKNC lost its majority to the People's Democratic Party (PDP), largely because of the perceived failure of its policies on ending the separatist insurgency. In the April-May 2004 general election the JKNC held only two of its four *Lok Sabha* seats. As of May 2004, the party held one *Rajya Sabha* seat.

Address. Sher-e-Kashmir Bhavan, Residency Road, Jammu; Nawai Subh Complex, Zero Bridge, Srinagar (Jammu & Kashmir)

Leadership. Omar Abdullah; Farooq Abdullah (president)

Jammu and Kashmir People's Democratic Party (JKPDP), a Kashmiri party that came to power after the October 2002 state assembly elections in Jammu and Kashmir in coalition with Congress (I) and the Jammu and Kashmir National Panthers (JKNP) party, breaking the long-standing domination of electoral politics in the state by the Jammu and Kashmir National Conference (JKNC). The JKPDP won one seat in the *Lok Sabha* in the April-May 2004 general election. As of May 2004 the party also held one seat in the *Rajya Sabha*.

Leadership. Mufti Mohammed Sayeed; Mehbooba Mufti (president)

Janata Dal–Secular (JD–S), a breakaway faction of the Janata Dal–United (JD–U) party led by former Prime Minister H.D. Deve Gowda (1996-97). The JD–S won three *Lok Sabha* seats in the April-May 2004 general election, and 58 seats in the simultaneous Karnataka state assembly election.

Address. 5 Safdarjung Lane, New Delhi 110003

Leadership. H.D. Deve Gowda

Janata Party (JP), in power at the federal level from March 1977 until January 1980, after which it fragmented and the rump party's influence declined. It is currently unrepresented in the *Lok Sabha*.

Address. AB-13, Mathura Road, New Delhi 110001

Leadership. Subramanian Swamy (president)

Jharkhand Mukti Morcha (JMM), founded in 1980 to represent the interests of the tribal people of the state of Bihar, where it won about 5% of the seats in the 1995 legislative assembly; also represented in the Orissa state assembly. It won a handful of seats in 1996 general elections to the *Lok Sabha* but lost them at the 1998 and 1999 polls. Nonetheless, JMM pressure was significant in achieving the creation of a new Jharkhand regional state – carved out of Bihar and Orissa – in 2000, where it currently heads a coalition government. In the April-May 2004 general election the JMM won five seats in the *Lok Sabha*, out of the 14 allocated to the state. JMM leader Shibu Soren was awarded the Steel portfolio in the Cabinet of the United Progressive Alliance (UPA) government formed after the election by the Indian National Congress (INC)–Congress (I) party. As at May 2004, the JMM was unrepresented in the *Rajya Sabha*.

Address. Bariatu Road, Ranchi 834008, Jharkhand

Leadership. Shibu Soren (president)

Karnataka Congress Party (KCP), an autonomous state party that won one *Lok Sabha* seat in 1996 as part of the United Front coalition, but subsequently lost it.

Kerala Congress (KC), a participant in the Left Democratic Front coalition government, headed by the Communist Party of India–Marxist (CPI–M), which came to power in Kerala in May 1996 following state elections but was defeated in 2001. However, the KC won one *Lok Sabha* seat in the 1998 general election and retained it in 1999, while a breakaway faction (the Kerala Congress–M) also won a seat in 1999. In the April-May 2004 general election the KC held its seat. As of August 2001, the KC held one *Rajya Sabha* seat.

Address. State Committee Office, Near Star Theatre Junction, Kottayam South, Kerala

Leadership. P.J. Joseph (chairman)

Kerala Congress–M, a breakaway from the Kerala Congress; won one seat in 1999 elections to the *Lok Sabha*, losing it, however, in the April-May 2004 general election.

Address. State Committee Office, Near Fire Station, Kottayam, Kerala

Leadership. C.F. Thomas (chairman)

Lok Janshakti Party (LJP), led by Ram Vilas Paswan, formerly of the *Janata Dal* (JD). Paswan served as a Cabinet minister in the *Bharatiya Janata* Party (BJP)-led National Democratic Alliance (NDA) administrations 1998-2002, resigning in protest against the Union government's failure to act against the BJP government in Gujarat state, which had failed to prevent anti-Muslim pogroms. The LJP won four *Lok Sabha* seats in the April-May 2004 general election. Paswan was awarded the Cabinet post of Chemicals and Fertilizers in the United Progressive Alliance (UPA) government formed after the election by the Indian National Congress (INC)–Congress (I) party.

Lok Shakti, broke away from the Karnataka cadre of the *Janata Dal* (JD) under the leadership of R.K. Hegde in 1998; won three seats in the *Lok Sabha* at the 1998 general election and supported the federal coalition government led by the *Bharatiya Janata* Party with Hegde serving as Commerce Minister. Hegde led a section of the party into the Janata Dal (United) and National Democratic Alliance in July 1999 and won four seats at the 1999 election. The residual *Lok Shakti* was de-recognized as a state party in Karnataka and Nagaland by the Election Commission in September 2000.

Loktantrik Jan Samata Party (LJSP), won one *Lok Sabha* seat in the April-May 2004 general election.

Madhya Pradesh Vikas Congress (MPVC), formed early in 1996 by Madhya Pradesh dissidents of the Indian National Congress–Congress (I), won two lower house seats in the subsequent general elections, declared support for the United Front government inaugurated in June 1996, but was defeated in 1998, 1999 and 2004.

Maharashtrawadi Gomantak Party (MGP), a Hindu-dominated party that has long competed for control of the Goan legislative assembly with the Indian National Congress–Congress (I). Won one *Lok Sabha* seat in 1996 as part of the United Front coalition but was unsuccessful in 1998 and 1999 elections.

Address. c/o Baban A. Naik, "Anant" Dada Vaidya Road, Panaji 403001, Goa

Leadership. Surendra Sirsat (president)

Manipur People's Party (MPP), a state level party that holds no seats in the *Lok Sabha*.

Address. People's Road, Imphal 795001, Manipur

Manipur State Congress Party (MSCP), broke away from the Indian National Congress–Congress (I) in 1997; won one *Lok Sabha* seat at the 1998 general election and retained it in 1999.

Address. Babupara, Imphal 795001, Manipur

Mizo National Front (MNF), legalized in 1986 (upon the conferment of statehood on Mizoram), having earlier waged

an underground campaign for national self-determination. It came to power in the first state assembly elections in 1987, and has remained in government since then, either alone or in coalition with Congress (I) or with other regional parties. In the December 2003 state elections the MNF won a majority of seats. In the April-May 2004 general election the MNF won its first seat in the *Lok Sabha*. As of May 2004 the party also held one seat in the *Rajya Sabha*.
Address. General Headquarters, Zarkawt, Aizwal, Mizoram
Leadership. Zoramthanga (president)

Nagaland People's Front (NPF), led by former state chief minister and moderate Naga nationalist Vizol, formerly of the United Democratic Front (UDF). The NPF gained power in the Nagaland state assembly elections in February 2003 as the lead party in the Democratic Alliance of Nagaland (DAN) coalition. In the April-May 2004 general election the NPF won its first seat in the *Lok Sabha*. As of May 2004 the party also held one seat in the *Rajya Sabha*.
Address. NST Opposite, Kohima 797001, Nagaland
Leadership. Vizol (president)

National Loktantrik Party (NLP), won one *Lok Sabha* seat in the April-May 2004 general election.

Peasants' and Workers' Party of India (PWPI), a Marxist party led by Dajiba Desai, operates primarily in the state of Maharashtra. The PWPI won one *Lok Sabha* seat in the 1998 general election, retaining it in 1999 but losing it in the general election of April-May 2004.

Rashtriya Lok Dal (RLD), won three seats in the April-May 2004 general election, all in Uttar Pradesh.
Address. 12 Tughlak Road, New Delhi 110011
Leadership. Ajit Singh (president)

Republican Party of India (RPI), committed to the egalitarian aims and objectives set out in the preamble to the 1950 Indian constitution; won four *Lok Sabha* seats at the 1998 general election but lost them all in 1999. The party won a single seat in the April-May 2004 general election.
Address. Satpuda, Malabar Hill, Bombay
Leadership. R.S. Gavai (president)

Samajwadi Janata Party (Rashtriya) (SJP–R), won one *Lok Sabha* seat in the April-May 2004 general election.

Sikkim Democratic Front (SDF), a moderate regionalist party that became the ruling party in Sikkim in December 1994. In the April-May 1996 general election the party won Sikkim's single *Lok Sabha* seat, which it retained in the 1998, 1999 and 2004 elections. As of May 2004 the SDF also held one seat in the *Rajya Sabha*. In October 1999 SDF leader Pawan Kumar Chamling won a second successive term as Sikkim chief minister. In the simultaneous Sikkim state assembly election in 2004 the SDF won 31 out of the 32 seats.
Address. Upper Deorali, Gongtok, East Sikkim
Email. Sdf@sikkim.org
Website. www.sikkiminfo.com
Leadership. Pawan Kumar Chamling (president)

Sikkim Revolutionary Forum (*Sikkim Sangram Parishad, SSP*), lost its majority in the Sikkim legislature to the Sikkim Democratic Front (SDF) in state elections in December 1994. In the April-May 1996 general election the party also lost Sikkim's single *Lok Sabha* seat to the SDF.
Address. Sangram Bhavan, Jewan Theeng Marg, Gangtok, Sikkim
Leadership. Nar Bahadur Bhandari (president)

Tamil Maanila Congress (TMC)
Address. Satyamurthy Bhavan, General Platters Road, Madras 600002, Tamil Nadu
Leadership. G.K. Vasan (leader)
The TMC is a breakaway faction of the Indian National Congress–Congress (I) in Tamil Nadu. Its leaders were formally expelled from the parent party in April 1996, prior to the general election in which the TMC secured 20 of Tamil Nadu's 39 seats in the *Lok Sabha*. At state level it was allied with the victorious Dravidian Progressive Federation (DMK), winning 39 legislative assembly seats in its own right. The party was a leading component of the United Front federal government inaugurated in June 1996, being awarded the finance portfolio and four other posts in the new administration. However, it faired poorly in the 1998 election, when it was reduced to three seats, and even worse in the 1999 election, when it failed to win any seats. It also broke its alliance with the DMK, when the latter moved to support the National Democratic Alliance headed by the *Bharatiya Janata* Party in 1999, and re-allied with the All-India Dravidian Progressive Federation (AIADMK).

Telangana Rashtra Samithi (TRS). Led by a former senior official of the Andhra Pradesh Telugu Desam Party (TDP), the TRS began campaigning in 2003 for a separate state in the Telangana region in southern Andhra Pradesh, a status the region had enjoyed from 1948 to 1956. In the April-May 2004 general election the TRS won five seats in the *Lok Sabha*, and took third place in the simultaneous state assembly election in Andhra Pradesh with 26 seats. Following the election the TRS joined the United Progressive Alliance (UPA) coalition formed by the Indian National Congress (INC)–Congress (I) party, and was awarded one Cabinet post and one of minister of state in the new government. Initially TRS leader K. Chandrashekar Rao was allocated the Shipping portfolio, but relinquished this to become Cabinet Minister without portfolio when the rival claims of the Dravidian Progressive Federation (DMK) were accommodated.
Leadership. K. Chandrashekar Rao.

Indonesia

Capital: Jakarta
Population: 218,835,461 (2004E)

The nationalist leaders of Indonesia, which comprises approximately 17,506 islands, proclaimed the independence of the Republic of Indonesia on Aug. 17, 1945, but this was largely unrecognized until December 1949 when sovereignty was transferred from the Netherlands East Indies. Following a brief period as a federation, Indonesia became a unitary state in 1950. It has the largest Muslim population in the world, but is not an Islamic state. The principle of *Pancasila*, enjoining monotheism, humanitarianism, national unity, democracy by consensus and social justice, was enshrined in the 1945 provisional constitution. Despite constitutional and regime changes and attempts by various means to replace it with an Islamic basis over the following fifty years, the *Pancasila* remains the philosophical basis of the state. After the transfer of sovereignty, a new liberal but provisional constitution was adopted and a period of parliamentary politics ensued.

The first national election, held in 1955, was Indonesia's only free and fair election before 1999, but it was unable to deliver stable and effective government. Although dozens of parties contested the election, four emerged with approximately 78% of the vote and of seats in the elected parliament. In order of size, these were the Indonesian Nationalist Party (PNI), the *Masyumi*, the *Nahdlatul Ulama* (NU) and the Indonesian Communist Party (PKI). As the largest party gained a mere 22% of the vote, governments could only be formed through coalitions negotiated by the parties. This was a disappointment, because horse-trading for cabinet positions and the fragility of coalition governments had been features of parliamentary politics from the outset which it had been hoped the election might cure. Moreover, the election campaign had sharpened disagreement over whether Islam or the *Pancasila* should be the basis of the state. This continued with the election in 1955 of a Constituent Assembly whose task was to formulate a permanent constitution. Because two of the big four parties were based on Islam (*Masyumi* and NU) and the other two were not, the two-thirds majority of the Constituent Assembly required for a decision on this question was bound to be difficult, if not impossible, to achieve.

Meanwhile, democratic politics faced other serious challenges. First, there was the armed movement to establish an Islamic State of Indonesia which had been launched in West Java even before the 1949 transfer of sovereignty, and was joined in the 1950s by rebellions in Aceh and South Sulawesi. This challenge to the *Pancasila*-based Republic of Indonesia was ultimately suppressed by military force in the early 1960s. Secondly, in 1956 and 1957 regional rebellions broke out in several parts of Sumatra and Sulawesi. The Sumatran rebel leaders were mostly local military officers expressing regional grievances with Jakarta, and they later joined forces with prominent members of the *Masyumi* and Indonesian Socialist Party (PSI) to proclaim a Revolutionary Government of the Republic of Indonesia (PRRI). Together with a parallel movement in Sulawesi (*Permesta*), they received covert backing from the United States.

As the regional rebellions developed, the central leadership of the Indonesian army persuaded President Sukarno to proclaim martial law in March 1957 to deal with the crisis. At the same time, the elected cabinet resigned and a working cabinet under a non-party Prime Minister was appointed. From this point the influence of the political parties declined, whereas martial law increased the power of the army. The third major challenge was the determination of President Sukarno to abandon the experiment of liberal democracy. With the support of the army leaders and others who yearned for a return to the spirit of the Indonesian revolution of 1945-49, in July 1959 he re-enacted by presidential decree a return to the authoritarian constitution of 1945, thereby instituting a nationalistic new regime, supposedly based on indigenous values, which he called "guided democracy". The dissolution of the elected parliament, its replacement by an appointed legislature, the "simplification" of the party system by reducing the number of parties to ten, the banning of the *Masyumi*, and the failure to hold elections were evidence that the regime was more guided than democratic. Sukarno nonetheless needed the mass support of the remaining political parties to counter the power of the army. This was particularly true of the "progressive revolutionary forces" of the PKI and the radical wing of the PNI.

The uneasy alliance between the army leaders and the President came to an end after the "abortive coup" of October 1965 in which six army generals were killed. The army held the PKI responsible, and in the following months perhaps as many as half a million PKI members and sympathizers were massacred and many others were interned without trial for a long period. Sukarno was gradually sidelined and replaced as president by Gen. Suharto, who established a military-backed "New Order" regime which lasted until 1998. The New Order regime, unlike its predecessor, held regular legislative elections (in 1971, 1977, 1982, 1987, 1992, and 1997) but they were heavily stage-managed. The government further simplified the party system in January 1973 when the nine surviving parties were reduced through forced mergers into the United Development Party (PPP) and the Indonesian Democracy Party (PDI). Both parties were repeatedly manipulated by government agents, and neither of them could compete effectively with Golkar, the government's electoral vehicle, which consistently achieved more than 60% of the votes cast in these elections. The government permitted no other political parties, and made the *Pancasila* the sole ideological basis for the parties and other organizations. The authoritarian 1945 constitution, which remained in force without amendment throughout the New Order period, together with *Pancasila* indoctrination courses, severely limited the scope of permissible political debate.

The constitution provided for a national parliament (*Dewan Perwakilan Rakyat*, DPR) and regional parliaments (*Dewan Perwakilan Rakyat Daerah*, DPRD) at both the provincial and district levels, which were elected simultaneously every five years. Military and police officers were appointed to the DPR and DPRDs. The members of the DPR then constituted themselves as members of the Consultative Assembly (*Majelis Permusyawaratan Rakyat*, MPR) together with as many appointed members representing the regions and "special groups" in society. The MPR then elected the President and Vice-President for the next five years, and laid down general guidelines for government policy. These processes were largely a rubber stamp for President Suharto, who was invariably re-elected unopposed.

Indonesian society became increasingly urban, better educated and more sophisticated under Suharto, but his regime was brought down by the 1997 Asian financial crisis, which served as a catalyst for pent-up popular discontent over his authoritarian rule and the corruption associated with his family. Suharto was replaced in May 1998 by his Vice-President, B.J. Habibie, who quickly lifted restrictions on the formation of political parties and called elections to the DPR for June 1999. Whereas under Suharto there had been only three approved political formations, some 150 parties now sought registration and 48 were approved to present candidates because they met the requirement of having branches in at least half the districts of at least one-third of the 27 (effectively 26) provinces/special regions. Under amendments introduced in 1999, the number of MPR members who were not also DPR members was reduced from 500 to 200, comprising government appointees, delegates of the regional assemblies and representatives of parties and groups (appointed in proportion to their elective seats in the DPR). At the same time, the number of appointed military members was reduced from 75 to 38 in the 500-member DPR.

The outcome of the 1999 election was a legislature quite different from its predecessors under Suharto. As in 1955, no one party gained anywhere near a majority of seats. There was a hotly contested and unprecedented election in the MPR for the positions of

President and Vice-President which was covered live on television, but the real action was done in backroom deals. Habibie, the incumbent President, withdrew his candidature after being held to account by the MPR for a recent bank scandal and the loss of East Timor. (Indonesia had forcibly annexed the former Portuguese colony in 1976, but never fully succeeded in suppressing East Timorese resistance. In a referendum in August 1999 the East Timorese voted overwhelmingly for independence – see under East Timor.)

Abdurrahman Wahid was elected President, although his National Awakening Party (PKB) had secured only about 10% of the seats in the elected DPR. This left him vulnerable to attack, however, and he was dismissed from office less than two years into his five-year term after an impeachment process in the legislature. His Vice-President, Megawati Sukarnoputri, whose Indonesian Democracy Party–Struggle (PDI-P) had secured about one third of the seats in the DPR, replaced him in July 2001. This dismissal of a President who had lost the confidence of the parliament reflected a wider trend, aided by several amendments of the constitution by the MPR, toward strengthening the powers of the parliament at the expense of the executive. Other amendments cut across this apparent reversion to a parliamentary system, most notably weakening the powers of the MPR. In particular, a constitutional amendment provided for the direct election of the President and Vice-President, running as a team. A 2003 law stipulated that such teams had to be nominated by one or more political parties which had obtained at least 15% of the seats in the DPR or 20% of the valid votes cast in the election for the DPR, but the candidates themselves did not have to be party members. To win the election, a team was required to win at least 50% of the votes and 20% in at least half the provinces. The law provided that if no team met the criteria in the July 5, 2004, presidential elections, there would be a run-off election on Sept. 20, 2004, between the top two teams.

The requirements for parties to participate in the 2004 legislative elections were more stringent than in 1999. Of the parties that contested the 1999 elections, only those that won at least 2% of the seats in the DPR or 3% in DPRDs at the provincial or district levels in half the provinces and half the districts could contest the 2004 election. Only six of the parties which contested the 1999 elections met this requirement for 2004. However, parties that failed to meet these criteria were permitted to merge with other parties or to dissolve themselves and form new parties provided that they met the new, tougher criteria laid down in the 2003 general election law, under which parties needed to have "full leadership" in at least two-thirds of the districts of at least two-thirds of the provinces/special regions and had to meet minimum membership requirements. The outcome was that only 24 of the 50 legally registered parties qualified to contest the election in 2004 (half as many as in 1999). All 550 members of the DPR are now elected, but although there are no longer any appointed military or police members, the influence of the military is still important.

The polls on April 5, 2004, were not only for the national DPR and DPRDs. A new Regional Representatives Council (DPD) was elected, which together with the DPR will form the new-style MPR. Whereas the elections for the DPR and DPRDs were between parties, candidates for the DPD had to be individuals who were not affiliated to parties. Each of the 32 provinces, whatever its size, has four representatives who had to meet residential criteria in the province for which they were elected. The powers of the DPD are largely advisory and supervisory.

The results of the polling on April 5, 2004, showed that 17 parties obtained representation (7 of them with less than 10 seats each). The largest parties were Golkar Party 128 seats (21.6% of the vote), Indonesian Democracy Party–Struggle (PDI-P) 109 (18.5%), United Development Party (PPP) 58 (8.2%), Democrat Party 57 (7.5%), National Mandate Party (PAN) 52 (6.4%), National Awakening Party (PKB) 52 (10.6%), Prosperous Justice Party (PKS) 45 (7.3%), Reform Star Party 13 (2.4%), Prosperous Peace Party 12 (2.1%), and Crescent Star Party (PBB) 11 (2.6%).

The first round of the direct presidential election on July 5, 2004, ended inconclusively, necessitating a run-off election in September involving the two front runners. The first round polling was led by Susilo Bambang Yudhoyono of the Democrat Party, a former general and Security Minister under Megawati Sukarnoputri, with President Megawati Sukarnoputri in second place and a former head of the armed forces, Gen. Wiranto, backed by Golkar, coming third. The second round, held on Sept. 20, resulted in a conclusive victory for Yudhoyono, who took 61% of the ballot.

Crescent Star Party
Partai Bulan Bintang (PBB)
Address. Jl. Raya Pasar Minggu KM 18 No. 1 B Jakarta Selatan
Telephone. (62-21) 799-2375
Fax. (62–21) 310–6739
Website. www.pbb-online.org
Leadership. Yusril Ihza Mahendra (chairman)
Founded in July 1998, the Islamic-based PBB claims to be the successor to the *Masyumi* Party, which was the second largest party in the 1955 elections but was later banned under the Sukarno and Suharto regimes. It is one of the more conservative Islamic parties and wants a state "based on Islamic principles", without acknowledging *Pancasila*. It accepts the need for parliamentary activity and advocates extensive decentralization. Its chairman, Yusril Ihza Mahendra, was an unsuccessful candidate for President in 1999, but later became Minister of Justice and Human Rights in the cabinet of Megawati Sukarnoputri. Its main support is in the outer islands, especially among urban Muslims. Although it increased its share of votes cast in 2004 (2.6%) as compared to 1999 (1.8%), it won fewer seats (11 instead of 14) and its ranking dropped from sixth to tenth.

Democrat Party
Partai Demokrat
Address. Jl. Jend. A. Yani Patra II No. 12 Jakarta Pusat 10510
Telephone. (62-21) 4755254
Fax. (62-21) 4754959
Leadership. Prof. Dr. Subur Budhisantoso (chairman); Susilo Bambang Yudhoyono (President of Indonesia)
The *Pancasila*-based Democrat Party is a new party, formed in September 2001 under the chairmanship of a University of Indonesia professor. It performed impressively in its first election campaign in 2004, winning 57 seats with 7.5% of the votes cast. Much of its success was due to the appeal of its presidential candidate, retired general Susilo Bambang Yudhoyono (popularly known as SBY), who led the polls in the July 2004 first round of voting for Indonesia's first directly elected President and then went on to win the run-off contest in September.

Golkar Party
Partai Golongan Karya (Golkar)
Address. Jalan Anggrek Nelly Murni, No. 11A Slipi, Jakarta

Barat 11480
Telephone. (62–21) 530–2222/5481746
Fax. (62-21) 530-3380
Website. www.partai-golkar.or.id
Leadership. Akbar Tanjung (chairman)

Originally formed in October 1964, Golkar became a military and government-sponsored amalgamation of groups representing farmers, fishermen and the professions, and including members of the Indonesian armed forces. It was the dominant political force under Suharto's military regime, for which it provided a civilian basis, expounding the *Pancasila* philosophy. His fall was an enormous challenge. In July 1998 Golkar removed him as leader and issued an apology for wrongdoings in the past. The organization then repositioned itself as a secular-nationalist party under the name Golkar Party, although this alienated Suharto loyalists. It remained the party with the most resources, although since Suharto's fall its offices round the country have frequently been ransacked. In the 1999 elections it won 120 seats, with most of its support coming from the outer islands. This made it the second largest party, and Akbar Tanjung became Speaker of the legislature. Golkar representatives helped to elect Abdurahman Wahid of the National Awakening Party as President in October 1999, albeit after considerable hesitation. As President Wahid's support declined, Golkar representatives were active in urging impeachment.

In February 2004 the Indonesian Supreme Court quashed a three-year prison sentence for corruption imposed on Akbar Tanjung by a lower court in September 2002. Golkar won most seats (128) in the 2004 DPR elections, slightly increasing its support from 20.9% to 21.6% of the vote. In April 2004, Golkar chose as its presidential candidate Gen. Wiranto, a former Defence Minister under Suharto who had in 2003 been indicted by UN prosecutors in East Timor on charges of having had "command responsibility" for deaths in East Timor in 1999. Golkar officials believed that Wiranto would have broader public appeal as a candidate than Akbar Tanjung; Wiranto came only third, however, in the July 2004 presidential election first round, therefore not qualifying for the September run-off.

Indonesian Democracy Party–Struggle
Partai Demokrasi Indonesia (PDI–P)

Address. Jl. Raya Pasar Minggu - Lenteng Agung No. 99, Jakarta Selatan
Telephone. (62–21) 780–6020/6032
Fax. (62–21) 780–2824
Website. www.pdiperjuangan.org
Leadership. Megawati Sukarnoputri (chairperson)

The PDI–P, a *Pancasila*-based party, is derived from the Indonesian Democracy Party (PDI), itself founded in January 1973 as a merger of three nationalist and two Christian-based parties as part of the Suharto government's move to consolidate the party system. As one of the three parties authorized in that era, the PDI advocated the restoration of full civilian rule but remained largely supportive of the Suharto regime, usually obtaining around 15% of the electoral vote. The PDI in 1994 chose Megawati Sukarnoputri (the daughter of former President Sukarno) as its leader. When Suharto prevented her re-election in 1996, she formed the rival PDI–P, thus marginalizing the old PDI. Strong in all 26 provinces, the PDI–P called for the restoration of trust in officials, the market and the judicial system. In the late 1990s Megawati was very robust in defending the integrity of Indonesia and enjoyed support amongst the military. Part of the party's image remained that of being closer to "Christian" than to Muslim values.

Although the PDI–P won most seats (154) in the 1999 legislative elections, Megawati failed to be elected President by the Consultative Assembly, amidst grumblings from Muslims that a woman should not hold the post. Instead she accepted the vice-presidency. For the first year she loyally supported President Wahid of the National Awakening Party, but relations gradually deteriorated, so that the PDI-P supported his impeachment. She became President in August 2001, but her popularity then waned. In the 2004 legislative elections, the PDI-P was forced to yield first place to Golkar, winning 109 seats, with its support falling from 33.7% to 18.5% of the vote. In the subsequent first round of the presidential elections Megawati came second, and in the September run-off she came a poor second to Susilo Bambang Yudhoyono, taking only 39% of the vote.

National Awakening Party
Partai Kebangkitan Bangsa (PKB)

Address. Jl. Kalibata Timur No. 12 Jakarta Selatan
Telephone. (62–21) 7919–0920
Fax. (62–21) 7919–3486
Email. lpp-pkb@yahoogroups.com
Website. www.kebangkitanbangsa.org
Leadership. Alwi Abdurrahman Shihab (chairman)

Formed in July 1998, this party is effectively led by Abdurahman Wahid (popularly known as Gus Dur) and so is close to the largest Muslim organization, the *Nahdlatul Ulama* (NU), of which he is the head. Having 30 million members, the NU is associated with more conservative Sunni values and is especially strong in Java, but is moderate, committed to the principles of democracy, and (albeit with some qualification) accepts *Pancasila* as the basis of authority in Indonesia. It also accepts the importance of the Chinese community for the Indonesian economy.

Its chief appeal being for national reconciliation, the PKB won 51 seats in the June 1999 elections, making it the fourth party in the new legislature. Skilful manoeuvring with the other parties led to Wahid's election as President in October 1999. As President, Wahid attempted to accommodate the separatist movements in various parts of the country that came to the fore after Suharto's fall. However, his eccentric and sometimes aloof style of governing increasingly undermined his support and in August 2001 the Assembly succeeded at the second attempt in impeaching him for corruption. He was replaced by Vice-President Megawati Sukarnoputri, the leader of the Indonesian Democracy Party–Struggle. The PKB was weakened by a split between supporters of the former chairman Matori Abdul Jalil and supporters of Abdurrahman Wahid. Matori left the PKB and in August 2003 he founded the Glory of Democracy Party (PKD) but it did not qualify to contest the 2004 elections. Although in the 2004 legislative elections the PKB slightly increased the number of seats won (52), its ranking in the parliament dropped to equal fifth, and its share of the votes cast dropped markedly from 17.4% to 10.6%.

National Mandate Party
Partai Amanat Nasional (PAN)

Address. Jl. Tebet Timur Raya No. 51-52 Jakarta 12820
Telephone. (62–21) 7279–4535
Fax. (62–21) 726–8695
Website. www.amanat.org
Leadership. Amien Rais (chairman)

Founded in April 1998, PAN accepts *Pancasila* principles as the sole basis of the Indonesian state. Party leader Amien Rais has a doctorate in political science from the University of Chicago and was a strident and courageous opponent of the Suharto regime. Until 1998 he chaired the *Muhammadiyah*, the second largest Muslim organization with 28 million members, which vigorously advocates Islamic values in society but also supports modernization. At its formation, the national leadership of PAN was explicitly non-religious and included many Christian and secular activists, but over time the party has lost some of that support.

The party's economic policy has a nationalist orientation, although in the 1999 elections Rais tried to present himself as moderate and liberal. His party did less well than expected, winning only 35 seats, but he negotiated his election as Speaker of the Consultative Assembly and played a crucial role in the successful impeachment of President Wahid in August 2001. In the 2004 legislative elections, PAN improved its position by winning 52 seats, but its share of votes cast fell from 7.3% to 6.4%.

Prosperous Justice Party
Partai Keadilan Sejahtera (PKS)

Address. Jalan Mampang Prapatan Raya No.98 D–E–F, Jakarta Selatan
Telephone. (62–21) 799–5425
Fax. (62–21) 799–5433
Email. partai@pk-sejahtera.org
Website. www.pk-sejahtera.org
Leadership. Dr. H. M. Hidayat Nur Wahid (chairman)
The Prosperous Justice Party was founded in April 2002 and replaced the Justice Party (PK), founded in July 1998, which had contested the 1999 legislative elections. Like its predecessor, it is based on Islam, seeking to appeal to educated young Muslims, especially women, and advocating morality above capitalism and materialism. Like the new Democrat Party, its anti-corruption stance proved very attractive to voters in the 2004 legislative elections, in which it gained 45 seats with 7.3% of the votes cast (as compared to 6 seats with 1.3% of the vote for the PK in 1999). It has earned a reputation for honesty and sticking to its principles.

Prosperous Peace Party
Partai Damai Sejahtera (PDS)

Address. Jl. Rukan Artha Gading Niaga Blok B No. 10 Kelapa Gading Jakarta Utara
Telephone. (62-21) 45850517
Fax. (62-21) 45850518
Email. berita@partaidamaisejahtera.com
Website. www.partaidamaisejahtera.com
Leadership. Ruyandi Mustika Hutasoit (chairman)
Founded in October 2001, the PDS advocates *Pancasila* and has its base of support among Christians; its campaigning is moralistic and religious in tone. In the 2004 elections, it won 12 seats with 2.1% of the vote.

Reform Star Party
Partai Bintang Reformasi (PBR)

Address. Jl. Radio IV No. 5 Kramat Pela, Kebayoran Baru
Telephone. (62-21) 7220903
Fax. (62-21) 7220903
Leadership. Zainuddin MZ (chairman)
The Islamic-based PBR was founded in January 2002, under the name PPP *Reformasi*, in opposition to the United Development Party (PPP). It took on the name Reform Star Party (PBR) in April 2003, and represents a merger between the New Indonesia Party, the Indonesian *Ummat Muslimin* Party, the Indonesian Muslim Awakening Party, and the Indonesian Republic Party. In the 2004 legislative election, it won 13 seats with 2.4% of the votes cast.

United Development Party
Partai Persatuan Pembangunan (PPP)

Address. Jalan Diponegoro 60, Jakarta Pusat 10310
Telephone. (62–21) 336338
Fax. (62-21) 7817341
Email. dpp@ppp.or.id
Website. www.ppp.or.id
Leadership. Hamzah Haz (chairman)
The PPP, like the Indonesian Democracy Party (PDI), was

created in January 1973 as a result of the Suharto regime's pressure on political organizations to "simplify" the party system. Four Islamic parties merged initially to form the party, although the *Nahdlatul Ulama* (NU) faction withdrew in 1984, after which support for the PPP fell considerably. After the departure of Suharto in 1998, however, the party recovered support as a moderate reformist Islamic party. Whilst President Suharto had required it to accept *Pancasila* as the basis of state authority, it has since revived its demands that government policy should always conform to the principles of Islam, calling for more benefits to be given to the people and for economic democracy.

Despite the alignment of the NU with the new National Awakening Party (PKB), the PPP did surprisingly well in the 1999 elections, becoming the third-largest party in the legislature with 58 seats (including 19 obtained from vote-sharing arrangements with five small Islamic parties). It maintained this position in 2004, winning the same number of seats, but its share of the vote declined from 10.7% to 8.2%. When Megawati Sukarnoputri replaced President Wahid in August 2001, the PPP leader Hamzah Haz became Vice-President. A number of disaffected members of the PPP defected to form the new Reform Star Party (PBR) in 2002.

Other Parties

Concern for the Nation Functional Party (*Partai Karya Peduli Bangsa*, PKPB), a *Pancasila*-based party founded in September 2002 by Suharto loyalists, former military and Golkar people unhappy with Golkar under Akbar Tanjung. Wanted to nominate Suharto's eldest daughter, Siti Hardijanti "Tutut" Rukmana, as presidential candidate, but only won two seats in the 2004 DPR elections.
Address. Jl. Cimandiri No. 30 Raden Saleh Cikini Jakarta Pusat
Telephone. (62-21) 31927421
Fax. (62-21) 31937417
Leadership. R. Hartono (chairman)

Freedom Party (*Partai Merdeka*), founded by Adi Sasono in October 2002 and emphasizing family principles and mutual assistance based on *Pancasila*. It failed to win a seat in the 2004 elections.
Address. Jl. Majapahit Kav. 26H Jakarta Pusat 10160
Telephone. (62-21) 3861464
Fax. (62-21) 3861465
Email. info@partaimerdeka.or.id
Website. www.partaimerdeka.or.id
Leadership. Adi Sasono (chairman)

Independence Bull National Party (*Partai Nasional Banteng Kemerdekaan*, PNBK), founded in July 2002 by Eros Djarot, former speechwriter for Megawati Sukarnoputri, with the name Bung Karno Nationalist Party (PNBK) and with Marhaenisme Bung Karno as its basis. The party name was not permitted because of its use of the name of a person (former President Sukarno), so in January 2003 it was changed to Independence Bull National Party (also PNBK). It won one seat in the 2004 elections.
Address. Jl. Penjernihan I No. 50 Jakarta Utara 10210
Telephone. (62-21) 5739550/5739551
Fax. (62-21) 5739519
Leadership. Eros Djarot (chairman)

Indonesian Nahdlatul Community Unity Party (*Partai Persatuan Nahdlatul Ummah Indonesia*, PNUI), based on Islam and the successor to *Partai Nahdlatul Ummat* (PNU), which won three seats in the 1999 elections. Competing with the National Awakening Party (PKB) for the support of members of the *Nahdlatul Ulama*, it failed to win a seat in the 2004 elections.

Address. Jl. Cipinang Cempedak IV No. I Jatinegara Jakarta Timur 13340

Telephone. (62–21) 857-1736

Fax. (62–21) 421–2701

Leadership. KH. Syukron Ma'mun (chairman)

Indonesian National Party Marhaenism (*Partai Nasional Indonesia*, PNI *Marhaenisme*), founded in May 2002 by Sukarno's daughter Sukmawati Sukarnoputri as successor to PNI Supeni, claiming to be a continuation of the PNI of Sukarno founded in 1927 and having Marhaenisme Bung Karno as its basis. It won one seat in the 2004 elections.

Address. Jl. Cikoko 15 Pancoran Jakarta Selatan 12770

Telephone. (62-21) 8971241

Fax: (62-21) 7900489

Leadership. Diah Mutiara Sukmawati Sukarnoputri (chairman)

Indonesian Unity Party (*Partai Sarikat Indonesia*, PSI), a *Pancasila*-based party founded in December 2002 as the result of a coalition of seven parties which had contested the 1999 elections: People's Sovereignty Party (PDR), Marhaenist National Front Party, PNI *Massa Marhaenis*, Indonesian Unity in Diversity Party (PBI), Democratic Catholic Party (PKD), Unity Party (PP) and Independence Vanguard Party (IPKI). It failed to win a seat in the 2004 elections.

Address. Jl. Ampera Raya No. 65 Cilandak Jakarta Selatan

Telephone. (62-21) 78847138

Fax. (62-21) 7800106

Email. dppsi@indosat.net.id

Website. www.psi.online.or.id

Leadership. Rahardjo Tjakraningrat

Justice and Unity Party of Indonesia (*Partai Keadilan dan Persatuan Indonesia*, PKPI), a *Pancasila*-based party founded in September 2002, replacing the similarly named Justice and Unity Party (PKP) which had been founded in December 1998 by a number of disillusioned former officials and officers of the Suharto regime after its founder, Edi Sudrajat, a former general, had failed to become the Golkar Party leader following Suharto's fall. The PKP won six seats in the 1999 elections, but its successor won only one seat in the 2004 elections.

Address. Jalan Raya Cilandak KKO No.32, Jakarta Selatan 12560

Telephone. (62–21) 780–7653/7656

Fax. (62–21) 780–7657

Web. www.pkp.or.id

Leadership. Edi Sudrajat (chairman)

New Indonesia Alliance Party (*Partai Perhimpunan Indonesia Baru*, PPIB), founded in September 2002 by Dr Syahrir (a well-known University of Indonesia economist) on the basis of an organization called the New Indonesia Association (PIB), focusing on economic reform programs and anti-corruption. It failed to win a seat in the 2004 elections.

Address. Jl. Teuku Cik Ditiro No. 31 Jakarta 10310

Telephone. (62-21) 3108057

Fax. (62-21) 3108058

Leadership. Dr. Syahrir (chairman)

Pancasila Patriots' Party (*Partai Patriot Pancasila*), founded in June 2001, is the electoral vehicle for the Pancasila Youth (*Pemuda Pancasila*, PP), notorious as a *preman* (hoodlum) organization. Although organizationally separate, they have the same leaders. Long loyal supporters of Suharto, PP members are dissatisfied with the new Golkar

Party. The party failed to win a seat in the 2004 elections.

Address. Gedung Tri Tangguh Lt. 3 Jl. Haji Samali No. 31 Kalibata Jakarta Selatan 12740

Telephone. (62-21) 7900477

Fax. (62-21) 7900478

Leadership. Yapto Sulistio Soerjosoemarno (chairman)

Pioneers' Party (*Partai Pelopor*), founded August 2002 by Rachmawati Sukarnoputri (daughter of Sukarno), is a Sukarnoist party with its roots in the old PNI Marhaenist Youth Movement (*Gerakan Pemuda Marhaenis*, GPM) and rivalry between Rachmawati and her sister Megawati. It won two seats in the 2004 elections.

Address. Jl. K H. Syafei A 22, Gudang Peluru, Tebet – Jakarta Selatan

Telephone. (62-21) 8299112

Fax. (62-21) 8301469

Website. www.partaipelopor.or.id *and* www.rachmawati.com

Leadership. Rachmawati Sukarnoputri (chairman)

Regional United Party (*Partai Persatuan Daerah*, PPD), founded November 2002 to represent regional interests in the legislature and adhering to *Pancasila*. Based on the Regional Fraction in the old MPR, its founders doubted the adequacy of the new Regional Representatives Council (DPD) as a replacement. It failed to win a seat in the 2004 elections.

Address. Jl. Dr. Satrio C-4 No. 18 Jakarta Selatan 12940

Telephone. (62-21) 5205764

Fax. (62-21) 5273249

Leadership. Oesman Sapta (chairman)

Social Democratic Labour Party (*Partai Buruh Sosial Demokrat*, PBSD), founded in May 2001 by Muchtar Pakpahan, who led the National Labour Party (*Partai Buruh Nasional*, PBN) in the 1999 DPR election, and having a basis in *Pancasila* and the 1945 constitution. The party's support base is in the trade union federation *Serikat Buruh Sejahtera Indonesia* (SBSI) which he also leads. The SBSI originally supported the PDI under the leadership of Megawati, but they fell out and a new party was formed. It failed to win a seat in the 2004 elections.

Address. Jl. Kramat Raya No. 91A Jakarta Pusat

Telephone. (62-21) 3154092

Fax. (62-21) 3909834

Leadership. Muchtar Pakpahan (chairman)

United Democratic Nationhood Party (*Partai Persatuan Demokrasi Kebangsaan*, PPDK), a *Pancasila*-based party founded July 2002 by intellectuals including Prof. Ryaas Rasyid (a former Minister of Home Affairs). It has taken up issues of regional autonomy and representation of women in the parliament, and won 5 seats in the 2004 elections.

Address. Jl. Ampera No. 99 Jakarta Selatan 12560

Telephone. (62-21) 7807432

Fax. (62-21) 7817341

Leadership. Prof. Dr. Ryaas Rasyid (chairman)

Upholders of Indonesian Democracy Party (*Partai Penegak Demokrasi Indonesia*, PPDI), founded in January 2003 and with *Pancasila* as its basis, is the successor of the old Indonesian Democracy Party (PDI), itself the rump of the PDI created under government pressure in 1973. Nationalist in orientation, the PPDI opposes privatization of state corporations. It won one seat in the 2004 elections.

Address. Jl. RE Martadinata Kompl. Rukan Permata Blok E-1 Ancol, Jakarta Utara

Telephone. (021) 6456215

Fax. (021) 6456216

Leadership. Dimmy Haryanto (chairman)

Iran

Capital: Tehran
Population: 68,278,826 (July 2003 est.)

The Islamic Republic of Iran was proclaimed in 1979 after the overthrow of the monarchy. The country's supreme leader is the *Vali-ye Faqih* (Supreme Jurisprudent), who is chosen by the Assembly of Experts (*Majlis-e Khobregan*), a popularly-elected body of 86 clerics. Iran's first supreme leader – Ayatollah Ruhollah Khomeini – died in June 1989 and was succeeded by Ayatollah Ali Khamenei. The president and the legislature (*Majlis-e Shora-ye Islami*) are elected by universal suffrage every four years. The supreme leader can overrule the executive and legislative branches. The Guardians' Council (*Shora-yi Negahbandan-i Mashrutiyat*), a body of six clerics appointed by the supreme leader and six jurists nominated by the head of the judiciary (who is appointed by the supreme leader), must vet proposed legislation for its compatability with Islamic law and the constitution. The Guardians' Council also is tasked with supervising elections and vetting candidates for elected office. The 38-member Expediency Council (*Shora-ye Tashkhis-e Maslehat-e Nezam*) adjudicates when the legislature and the Guardians' Council cannot reach a compromise on disputed legislation.

Article 26 of Iran's 1979 constitution permits the "formation of parties, societies, political or professional associations, as well as religious societies, whether Islamic or pertaining to one of the recognized religious minorities... provided they do not violate the principles of independence, freedom, national unity, the criteria of Islam, or the basis of the Islamic Republic". A Parties Law passed in September 1981 specifies what a political party is and defines the conditions under which it can operate, and it makes the formation of a party dependent on getting a permit from the Interior Ministry. Article 10 of the Parties Law states that a commission (the Article 10 Commission) comprising one Interior Ministry official, two parliamentarians, and two representatives of the judiciary, will issue party permits and dissolve parties acting illegally. The Parties Law was not really implemented, however, until late 1988, when the Interior Ministry submitted to parliamentary pressure, and almost thirty organizations applied for permits in the following months.

Iran went from being a single-party state under the monarchy to having close to 100 political parties in the months immediately following the 1979 Islamic revolution. As the clerical revolutionary leadership consolidated its position it went after the more secular of these parties. The emergence of the Islamic Republic Party (IRP) and the Mujahedin of the Islamic Revolution Organization (MIRO) can be viewed in this context. Indeed, the IRP was established just 10 days after the collapse of Mohammad Reza Pahlavi's regime, and its main task was to rally supporters of *Velayat-i Faqih* (Rule of the Supreme Jurisprudent) in an organization that had a clerical leadership. The need for these two parties died out as the opposition organizations disappeared, and they also suffered from internal ideological disputes and political competetion; the MIRO disbanded in October 1986 and the IRP in May-June 1987.

Some political organizations were allowed to exist even though they did not meet all the legal requirements (e.g. the Society for the Defence of the Values

of the Islamic Revolution, which was created shortly before the 1997 presidential election to support the candidacy of Hojatoleslam Mohammad Mohammadi-Reyshahri and which was not heard from during the next presidential election). Contradictory statements by government officials about the need for a permit confused the issue even more.

Parties took off after the May 1997 election of a new President, Hojatoleslam Mohammad Khatami, who was an advocate of their role in civil society, and a House of Parties was established in 2000 to create some sort of legal framework for party activities and to minimize differences between the parties. More than 100 licensed political organizations currently exist although this number is deceptive because many of these organizations – such as the Center for Graduates from the Indian Subcontinent or the Islamic Association of Veterinarians – have no real political role. Moreover, individuals can be members of several organizations. In elections, furthermore, the parties do not field candidates. Rather, each party publishes a list of candidates that it backs. Yet the different parties in a faction rarely back the same list of candidates.

In the run-up to the February 2000 and 2004 parliamentary elections the parties could be divided into two factions. The reformist faction is identified as the 2nd of Khordad Front and is named after the date of President Khatami's election on May 23, 1997. It consists of centrists and Islamic leftists who promote social and political liberalization as well as economic revitalization through economic restructuring; there are differences within this faction over the desirable extent of political and social liberalization and also over economic issues. Reformist organizations include the Executives of Construction, Islamic Iran Participation Front, Islamic Iran Solidarity Party, Islamic Labour Party, Militant Clerics Association, MIRO, and Office for Strengthening Unity.

The conservative faction's main focus is to halt the political reforms promoted by the reformists while defending the objectives of the revolution; the conservatives also oppose the spreading of Western influence in Iran and sociocultural liberalization. There are differences within this faction, too. Some hardliners favor violence against the reformists, while some traditionalists oppose liberalization but also oppose violence. More pragmatic conservatives acknowledge the need for some reform so the country can operate in the modern world and to mollify the Iranian public. This faction is united in its belief in the *velayat-i faqih*. The main conservative organizations are the *Ansar-e Hezbullah*, the Islamic Coalition Party, and the Tehran Militant Clergy Association.

The fluidity of Iranian politics also makes it possible to identify three factions – fundamentalists, pragmatists, and reformists. The fundamentalists include the Tehran Militant Clergy Association, the Islamic Coalition Party, and some minor groups. The pragmatists – the Executives of Construction and the Party of Moderation and Development (*Hezb-e Etedal va Toseh*) – are identified with former President Hashemi-Rafsanjani and side with the fundamentalists or the reformists on an issue-by-issue basis. The reformists include the Militant Clerics Association, Islamic Iran Participation Front, Islamic Iran Solidarity Party, and the MIRO.

The Guardians' Council disqualified some 44% of the prospective candidates for the February 2004 parliamentary elections. Among those it disqualified were some 80 incumbent legislators, as well as many former legislators. The reformists staged a futile protest and threatened to boycott the election. The boycott did not take place, but only 51% of the electorate voted, compared to 69% four years earlier. Conservatives dominated the election, winning about 200 out of 290 seats. Individuals connected with the conservative Islamic Iran Developers' Council (*Etelaf-i Abadgaran-i Iran-i Islami*) won all 30 Tehran seats in the legislature.

President Khatami's second term is due to end in 2005.

Ansar-e Hezbullah

Leadership. Masud Dehnamaki

Backed by Guardians' Council secretary Ayatollah Ahmad Jannati, this organization serves as the conservatives' enforcer by attacking pro-reform public speakers and government officials. It also clashes with student demonstrators.

Executives of Construction
Kargozaran-e Sazandegi

Leadership. Mohammad Hashemi-Bahramani

Ten serving cabinet ministers, four vice-presidents, the governor of the Central Bank of Iran, and the mayor of Tehran created the Servants of Construction (*Khedmatgozaran-i Sazandegi*) in 1996 to support then-President Ali Akbar Hashemi-Rafsanjani. This reformist/pragmatist party was renamed the Executives of Construction after the cabinet ministers withdrew due to legal prohibitions on executive involvement in parliamentary elections.

Islamic Coalition Party (ICP)
Hezb-e Motalefeh-ye Eslami

Leadership. Mohammad Nabi Habibi (secretary-general)

Known as the Islamic Colaition Society until January 2004, this very conservative group was formed in 1963 as a coalition of local Islamic clubs, conservative bazaar merchants, and clerics. The ICP reduced its activities after 1979 and many members joined the Islamic Republic Party (IRP). The ICP resumed its activities after the IRP's dissolution in the late 1980s.

Islamic Iran Developers' Council
Etelaf-i Abadgaran-i Iran-i Islami

This group, which is not registered as a party, appeared before the February 2003 municipal council elections; it subsequently won control of 14 of the 15 council seats in Tehran. In the February 2004 parliamentary election candidates associated with this group won all 30 Tehran seats. The speaker in the seventh parliament, Gholam-Ali Haddad-Adel, is associated with the Developers Council.

Islamic Iran Participation Front
Jebhe-ye Mosharekat-e Islami-ye Iran

Leadership. Mohammad Reza Khatami (secretary-general)

The creation of this reformist organization was announced in September 1998 as a partnership between former members of the Executives of Construction, members of the MIRO, and former student activists. It was created to back President Khatami and continues to be one of the leading reformist parties. Leading members include Abbas Abdi, Said Hajjarian, and Mustafa Tajzadeh.

Islamic Iran Solidarity Party
Hezb-e Hambastegi-ye Iran-e Eslami

Leadership. Ebrahim Asqarzadeh (secretary-general)

Created in 1999-2000, this reformist party backed Asqarzadeh's 2001 presidential bid. Prominent members include Rasht parliamentary representative Elias Hazrati and Khavaf & Rashtkhar parliamentary representative Gholam Heidar Ebrahim Bay-Salami.

Islamic Labour Party
Hezb-e Eslami-ye Kar

Leadership. Ali-Reza Mahjoub

This reformist party was created in February 1999 by individuals who were part of the Workers' House (*Khaneh-ye Kargar*) that had supported Khatami's presidential bid. Its initial platform was protecting workers' rights. Parliamentarian Soheila Jelodarzadeh, a founding member, is an advocate of women's issues. Other prominent members are former Labour Minister Abol-Qasem Sarhadi-Zadeh, former Labour Minister Hussein Kamali, and Rasht parliamentary representative Elias Hazrati.

Militant Clerics Association (MRM)
Majma-ye Ruhaniyun-e Mobarez

Leadership. Hojatoleslam Mehdi Mahdavi-Karrubi (secretary-general)

This group broke away from the original Tehran Militant Clergy Association in 1988, and it is now considered the left-leaning, pro-reform clergy association. Many of its candidates were barred from competing in the 1992 parliamentary election so it did not back candidates for the 1996 parliamentary election. It resumed its activities in October 1996. Prominent members of this group are Hojatoleslam Mohammad Khatami, Hojatoleslam Mohammad Asqar Musavi-Khoeniha, and Hojatoleslam Ali-Akbar Mohtashami-Pur.

Mujahedin of the Islamic Revolution Organization (MIRO)
Sazeman-e Mojahedin Enqelab-e Eslami

Leadership. Mohammad Salamati

This reformist group emerged shortly after the Islamic revolution when several underground anti-monarchy organizations merged. It dissolved in the early 1980s but re-emerged in the late 1990s; some of its members served in the Islamic Revolution Guards Corps. Among those responsible for its revival are former Minister of Heavy Industry Behzad Nabavi-Tabrizi, former Deputy Interior Minister Mustafa Tajzadeh, parliamentarian Mohsen Armin, Professor Hashem Aghajari, and former Tehran council member Said Hajjarian.

Office for Strengthening Unity
Daftar-e Tahkim-e Vahdat (DTV)

Leadership. Mohammad Mehdi Ahmadi, Reza Amidi, Mohammad Jabedi, Ghassem Khajehzadeh, Mehdi Mojahedi, Hadi Panahi, Arsh Pur-Nemat, Ahmad Al-e Shahi, Mohammad Mehdi Tabatabai (central council members)

The DTV is a national organization of Islamist university students that supported Khatami's presidential bid in 1997 and reformist parliamentary candidates in 2000. The organization underwent splits over tactical and ideological issues, and in January–February 2002 the existence of two wings within the DTV was formally recognized. The majority wing, known as the "Neshast-e Allameh," is radicalized by the slow pace of reform and believes that student groups should be independent critics of the system. The minority wing, known as the "Neshast-e Shiraz," is more conservative; it prefers to continue operating within the political system and is supportive of the 2nd of Khordad Front. A reuniting reportedly took place at the DTV Central Council elections in May 2004, with the selection of a leadership well past student age.

Party of Moderation and Development
Hezb-e Etedal va Toseh

Leadership. Mohammad Baqer Nobakht (secretary-general)

More than 30 of the parliamentarians elected in February 2000 were identified as members of this centre-right party. It declared its support for President Khatami's reform program, and it has held frequent meetings with Expediency Council chairman Ayatollah Ali-Akbar Hashemi-Rafsanjani. It backed a number of conservative and ultimately victorious candidates in the February 2004 parliamentary elections.

Tehran Militant Clergy Association (JRM)
Jameh-ye Ruhaniyat-e Mobarez-e Tehran

Leadership. Ayatollah Mohammad-Reza Mahdavi-Kani
This conservative group's creation predates the Islamic revolution. Members favour a market economy, and are very conservative culturally. Prominent members include Ayatollahs Ali-Akbar Hashemi-Rafsanjani and Ahmad Jannati, as well as Hojatoleslam Hassan Rohani. This group has not obtained a party permit.

Iraq

Capital: Baghdad
Population: 22,680,000 (2000E)

"Operation Iraqi Freedom", a US-led invasion of Iraq to remove Saddam Hussein and the Ba'ath Party from power, commenced on March 19, 2003. By May, coalition forces had arrived in Baghdad and the 35-year old dictatorship had been consigned to history. The structures of the Iraqi state collapsed and the vacuum was filled first by the Office of Reconstruction and Humanitarian Assistance and then by the Coalition Provisional Authority (CPA) under the leadership of L. Paul Bremer. Saddam himself was not located and arrested until December 2003.

The transition from Ba'ath rule has not proved to be a straightforward task. Certain assumptions made by the USA before Saddam was overthrown proved to be flawed when operating on the ground in Iraq. The first of these – that Iraqis would overwhelmingly welcome the occupying forces – failed to materialise, resulting in an insurgency developing in the early period following the overthrow of the regime, and continuing unabated in 2004. The second of these – that Iraqis would unify under a sense of Iraqi nationalism – ran into problems as a the Shi'a of the south flocked to religious leaders, and the Kurds in the north embraced a vociferous Kurdish nationalism. To understand the political and societal forces unleashed in Iraq with Saddam's removal, it is necessary to highlight pertinent areas of Iraq's history.

The modern state of Iraq was pieced together from the remnants of the Ottoman Empire after its defeat in World War I. The Arab-dominated provinces of Baghdad and Basra were assigned to British tutelage by the San Remo Conference of 1920. To govern the new territory, the British turned to the Hashemite Emir Faisal – a prominent Arab figure but not an Iraqi. The final aggregation of territory occurred in 1925 when the League of Nations officially recognized the northernmost province of Kurdish-dominated Mosul as part of the Iraqi state. Faisal remained King until his death in 1933, but failed to amalgamate Iraq's disparate communities into a coherent nation. Meanwhile, the British occupation of the country was universally opposed. Faisal was succeeded by his son, Ghazi. Iraq then suffered the first in a series of military coups involving extra-constitutional transfers of power. Ghazi died, in suspicious circumstances, in 1939 to be succeeded by his young son, Faisal II, and his protecting uncle Abdul Illah.

The failure of the monarchy to establish its legitimacy with Iraqis resulted in it being violently over-

thrown by the Free Officers' Coup of 1958, led by Brig. Gen Abdul Karim Qassem. Faisal and Abdul Illah were both killed, and the Republic of Iraq was declared. Qassem, however, was to suffer the same fate as Faisal only five years later. One of the groups used by Qassem to come to power, the Ba'ath Party, succeeded in gaining the support of the officer corps of the army. In 1963, the Ba'ath and their military allies overthrew Qassem's regime and executed him. A National Council of the Revolutionary Command (NCRC) was established, headed by General Abdel Salam Arif. Within months, the army had usurped the Ba'ath Party from their partnership, leaving the military in sole power.

The Kurds, until this time, had been in a steady state of low-level rebellion against the central government. However, from 1961, the Kurds openly rebelled with the onset of the "Kurdish Revolution" under the leadership of Mulla Mustafa Barzani. The rebellion would continue on and off until 1991 and the establishment of an autonomous Kurdish entity in the north of the country. From 1961, the notion of Iraq being a solely Arab state was called into question by the existence of this sizeable Kurdish revolt.

The Ba'ath Party returned in 1968, again with a military alliance. This time, however, new Ba'athist leaders including Saddam Hussein ensured that the army would not repeat their deception of five years before. Saddam successfully orchestrated the exile of the leading military figures in the coup, Colonels Da'ud and Nayif, and then strategically placed his Tikriti clansmen into positions of power. As Prime Minister, the Tikriti Gen. Hassan al-Bakr supported his distant kinsman Saddam and he was appointed Deputy Chairman of the Revolution's Command Council (RCC) – second only to Bakr himself. However, Saddam accumulated power and influence quickly and succeeded in becoming the real power in Iraq within a matter of years. Recognizing the need to consolidate power in Baghdad, Saddam needed to placate the ever-troublesome Kurds. In 1970, the March Manifesto was signed with Barzani, guaranteeing a certain degree of autonomy to the Kurds. However, the agreement was never implemented and the Kurds were again rebelling by 1974. The regime's targeting of the Shi'a was altogether more systematic. Following clashes with Shi'a religious groups in 1969 (and principally *Al-Da'wa*), the regime actively targeted Shi'a leaders and passed anti-*Da'wa* legislation. With this coercion, the regime deployed a significant amount of patronage to win over secular Shi'a. This carrot and stick approach came to symbolise Saddam's strategy of manipulating Iraq's communal differences for his own agenda.

By mid-1979, Saddam had succeeded in becoming the most powerful man in Iraq. He persuaded Bakr to stand down, obliging him to turn over the reins of power. The Islamic Revolution in Iraq occurred in 1979, and Ayatollah Khomeini called upon Iraq's Shi'a majority to overthrow the secular and Sunni-dominated Ba'ath regime. After a period of mounting tension, in September 1980 Saddam invaded Iran. The following decade witnessed the twentieth century's last great war with hundreds of thousands on both sides being killed, and with both economies, although especially that of Iraq, being crippled by its effects. After initial swift advances, the invasion ran out of steam as Iran mobilized its larger population to fight back. Finding itself threatened on many fronts, Saddam's regime became increasingly brutal. Following the alliance of Kurdish *peshmerga* with Iran, Saddam launched chemical offensives against Kurdish population centres (the *Anfal* Campaign) in 1987, culminating in the gassing of the city of Halabja in 1988, killing 5,000. The Shi'a similarly suffered chemical attacks and the delicate marshland ecosystem was drained to prevent its expanses being used by Shi'a rebels and/or Iranian military forces. The war ended as a stalemate, but with Saddam desperate to resolve the economic problems generated by the war.

By 1989, Iraqi debts stood at around US$100 billion, with a great deal owed to the Gulf monarchies. Kuwait refused to allow Iraq to relinquish its debt, and succeeded in angering Saddam further by persisting in exceeding its OPEC agreed output quota, thereby driving the price of oil down. On Aug. 2, 1990, Iraq troops crossed into Kuwait and occupied the country. The USA mobilized the UN to pass Resolution 678 in November authorizing members states to use "all necessary means" to evict Iraq from Kuwait if Iraq did not withdraw by Jan. 15, 1991. When this withdrawal did not take place, on Jan. 17 "Operation Desert Storm" was launched by the US-led coalition, wiping out most of Iraq's achievements in socio-economic infrastructure since 19790. Kuwait was liberated and a ceasefire was declared on Feb. 28. Iraq was in open disarray. The Shi'a, following US President George Bush's call for them to overthrow Saddam, rebelled in the south of the country. The Kurds soon followed. Saddam lost control of 15 out of 18 of Iraq's provinces. However, the regime remained firm in the centre and, critically, stronger than the rebelling forces. With US tacit support, Saddam turned his military against the increasingly Iran-influenced southern rebellion, before turning on the Kurds with characteristically brutal efficiency. The Shi'a were crushed, followed quickly by the Kurds, who were forced into the mountains as refugees. Saddam had regained control of the state, but had effectively lost control of the economy as the UN imposed Resolution 687, placing Iraq under comprehensive sanctions and established the UN Special Commission (UNSCOM) to dismantle Iraq's weapons of mass destruction (WMD) programme.

The sanctions regime, while comprehensive, failed to target Saddam's ruling elite. Instead, Saddam manipulated the Iraqi economy in order to preserve his own position, at the expense of the population at large. The Iraqi people, therefore, were oppressed by their own government, but also placed under immense pressure from the constraints posed by the international community. In the north of Iraq, the Kurds benefited from the imposition of a "no-fly zone", and carved out an autonomous entity, with the tacit acceptance of Saddam himself who was in any case unable to adequately garrison the north. The Kurds, again suffering from the sanctions regime, and sanctions imposed by Saddam, began to generate revenue by opening smuggling channels into Turkey and Iran, with Saddam himself becoming dependent on the Kurds in order to smuggle oil out of Iraq. Elections were held in Kurdistan in 1992, creating a Kurdistan National Assembly (KNA) and Kurdistan Regional Government (KRG). After several rounds of fighting between the Kurdistan Democratic Party (KDP) and Patriotic Union of Kurdistan (PUK), the political situation in Kurdistan stabilized from 1997 under US pressure, with the KDP and PUK controlling separate areas of Kurdistan.

Although still in undisputed power outside Kurdistan, Saddam had to find some way to improve the economy of the country. He did so by accepting UN Resolution 986 in 1996, allowing Iraq to export oil worth US$2 billion every six months, with the revenue to be spent on products to meet essential civilian needs. The programme was subsequently expanded to US$5.2 billion. Under the sanctions regime and the "oil-for-food" programme, a two-tier Iraqi economy emerged. A new class of extremely wealthy individuals was created by the black market, while the vast majority of the population continued to exist in poverty. The resilience of Saddam's regime in the 1990s (surviving two major coup attempts orchestrated by the Iraqi National Congress and the Iraqi National Accord) led to the US Congress passing the Iraqi Liberation Act in 1998, authorizing nearly US$100 million in funding for groups intending to overthrow Saddam. With this act passed, Saddam had little incentive to deal with UNSCOM. When UNSCOM head Richard Butler refused to certify that Iraq had destroyed its WMD, Saddam refused further cooperation. UNSCOM was withdrawn, never to return, and in December 1998 the UK and USA launched "Operation Desert Fox" – a feeble aerial campaign that achieved little significant result.

With the inauguration of President George W. Bush in January 2001, it seemed to be the case the Iraq was not a US foreign policy concern. Elected on a minimalist foreign policy agenda, Bush seemed to be the opposite to Bill Clinton, who had pursued an active foreign policy. However, the new administration included a right-wing group advocating action in the Middle East, and Iraq in particular, in order to introduce US-style democracy to the region. These neo-conservatives would gain powerful prominence in the aftermath of September 11.

Following the September 11 attacks, Iraq was identified quickly by neo-conservative hawks (including Vice President Richard Cheney and Deputy Secretary of Defence Paul Wolfowitz) as a target. After Afghanistan and its Taliban regime had been eliminated, Bush's gaze turned to his father's old foe Saddam. After a series of inspections by the newly appointed UN Monitoring and Verification Committee (UNMOVIC, UNSCOM's replacement), and failure to achieve a consensus in the UN Security Council, the Bush administration issued a 48-hour deadline on March 19, 2003, for Saddam to leave Iraq. Shortly after the expiration of the deadline, "Operation Iraqi Freedom" began with the explicit intent of changing the regime in Iraq.

The interim governance of Iraq has been fraught with instability and difficulty. The tenure of the CPA proved to be problematic as it faced widespread rejection in Iraq of its legitimacy. The CPA moved quickly to create an Iraqi Governing Council (IGC), composed of what was considered to be every major political group in Iraq. However, the IGC was dominated by returning exiled politicians and tended to fracture into distinct Shi'a, Kurdish and Sunni groupings. Within this structure, the Kurds and the Shi'a enjoyed most authority, leaving the previously powerful Sunni marginalized. With the Sunni without a representative voice in the governance of the state, the development of an insurgency in the Sunni strongholds in the centre of the country was only a matter of time. In the south, a Shi'a resurgence under the leadership of religious leaders likewise threatened to change the identity of the Iraqi state from being Sunni-dominated to Shi'a-dominated, and the Kurds in the north maintained their autonomous region and demanded for it to be enshrined in a future constitution.

The CPA and IGC signed an agreement on Nov. 15, 2003, providing for a transfer of sovereignty to an Iraqi administration to take place on June 30, 2004, following the selection of a Transitional National Authority (TNA). In March 2004 a temporary constitution (temporary administrative law) was agreed with the IGC to cover the period from the transfer of sovereignty until the adoption of a permanent constitution. The temporary constitution envisaged a federal structure for Iraq with a high degree of autonomy for the Kurdish region. On June 1, 2004, an Iraqi caretaker government was appointed, shaped by conflicting pressures from the USA, the IGC and UN. It was headed by Iyad Allawi (a Shi'a and the favoured candidate of the IGC) as Prime Minister-designate and with Sheikh Ghazi al-Yawar (a Sunni) in the ceremonial role of President, with the IGC being dissolved. Although the formal transfer of sovereignty from the CPA took place in late June (a few days ahead of schedule), to the interim government headed by Allawi, it occurred against a background of continued insurgency in parts of the country and with no early prospect of a withdrawal of the 160,000 US and other occupying forces. In August 2004 a UN-sponsored national conference was held to form a 100-seat assembly intended to pave the way for popular elections to a National Assembly in January 2005 and the formation of a transitional government in February 2005. This in turn was intended to lead to the adoption of a new permanent constitution, a general election in November 2005 and the the formation of a permanent government in December 2005. However, with numerous cities outside effective government or US control, it was suggested by Iraqi and US officials that the January 2005 elections might not take place in all areas of the country.

There is only a tenuous development of formal political parties in Iraq, but the following political and quasi-political formations have been of recent significance.

Action Party for the Independence of Kurdistan (*Parti Kari Sarbakhoy Kurdistan*, PKSK), a splinter from the Iraqi Communist Party, initially allied itself to both the PKK and the PUK. However, relations with the PUK deteriorated after the murder of the PKSK leader, Muhammad Halleq, on Nov. 2, 1995. Thereafter the PKSK aligned itself more closely to the KDP. Its leader, Yusif Hanna Yusif, known as Abu Hikmat, serves as a minister in the cabinet of the KDP in Irbil, but it remains a small faction dependent upon the patronage of the KDP.
Leadership. Yusif Hanna Yusif
Website. www.pksk.org

Al-Da'wa al-Islamiya (The Call of Islam). The *Da'wa* Party has the longest pedigree of all Shi'a political factions. It was formally established in 1968, but was based on the Association of Najaf Ulama (clergy), which began in 1958. *Da'wa/Ulama* fiercely opposed atheism, secularism and communism. It was supported by senior Shi'a ayatollahs from the holy southern cities of Najaf and Karbala, notably Muhsin al-Hakim (al-Tabataba'i) and his son, and subsequently leader of SCIRI, Mohammed Bakr al-Hakim. Its longtime spiritual leader was the venerated Ayatollah Sayyid Muhammad Bakr al-Sadr and its "operational leader" was Sheikh Arif al-Basri. In March 1980 Baghdad made affiliation with the party liable to death; Ayatollah Muhammad Bakr al-Sadr and his sister, Bint al-Huda, were murdered by the Saddam regime on April 9, 1980. *Al-Da'wa* renamed its military wing *Shahid al-Sadr* (The Martyr al-Sadr). Mohammed Sadiq al-Sadr, a pupil of Bakr al-Sadr, succeeded his mentor as *Al-Da'wa* spiritual leader. Unlike many other Shi'a clerics, including the Hakim brothers of SCIRI, he remained in Iraq until he, too, was killed by Saddam agents, in 1999.

Al-Da'wa joined the Iraqi National Congress umbrella group in its own capacity, in 1992. It participated in the INC-

organized October 1992 assembly in Salaheddin, in autonomous Kurdish northern Iraq. However, *Al-Da'wa* left the INC partially in 1993, and fully in May 1995, citing its opposition to the INC's plans for a federal Iraq. *Al-Daw'a* technically has belonged to the Shi'a umbrella group, SCIRI. However, in practice its ideology and strategy have diverged considerably from the latter, and *Al-Daw'a* currently operates separately from SCIRI. *Al-Da'wa* joined the Coalition of Iraqi National Forces upon its launch in July 2002. Like other CINF members, *Al-Da'wa* opposed US plans to invade Iraq, and favoured overthrow of the Ba'ath regime without "outside interference". Nonetheless, an *Al-Da'wa*-affiliated leader of the Shi'a *Ahlul Bayt* World Assembly (ABWA) was appointed to the 65-member US-backed Follow-up and Arrangement Committee. *Al-Da'wa* leaders, Dr Ja'afari and the influential Tehran-based ideologue, Muhammad Baqir al-Nasiri, returned to Iraq after the fall of Saddam Hussein in April 2003. *Al-Da'wa* boycotted the first round of post-war opposition conferences, but participated in the second. Dr Ja'afari accepted a seat on the eventual Governing Council of Iraq, and served as its first chairman, in August 2003. He subsequently became deputy President in the interim government formed in June 2004 and *Al-Da'wa* emphasized the importance of the January 2005 elections proceeding as scheduled.
Leadership. Dr Ibrahim al-Ja'afari (spokesperson for collective leadership)
Website. www.daawaparty.com

Al-Khoei Foundation. An influential body, with headquarters in London and centres in the USA, the Foundation was created in honour of the teachings of Grand Ayatollah Abdul Qasim al-Khoei, regarded as the most senior Shi'a cleric in the world during his lifetime. But the murder in Iraq of his son and Foundation leader, Sayyid Abdul Majid al-Khoei, in April 2003, shocked the group and naturally eroded its potency in the short term. Abdul Majid's younger brothers, including Yusuf al-Khoei, continue to run the Foundation in London but its future role in Iraqi politics remains unclear. Meanwhile, one Shi'a cleric affiliated to the Foundation, Mohammed Bahr al-Ulloom, joined the Governing Council, but resigned his seat in protest at the lack of security that he said led to the assassination of Ayatollah al-Hakim in late August. The imam's son, Ibrahim Mohammad Bahr al-Ulloum, was appointed as Iraq's oil minister in the IGC.
Leadership. Yusuf al-Khoei
Website. www.alkhoeifoundation.com

Ansar al-Islam, formerly known as *Jund al-Islam* (Army of Islam), a title it still employs from time to time, the *Ansar al-Islam* (Supporters of Islam) began as an offshoot of the Islamic Movement of Iraqi Kurdistan (IMIK) in 1998. The *Jund al-Islam* later merged with a group called *al-Tawhid* (Unity), led by Mullah Abdul Ghani Bazazi, and then with *Hezi Du Soran* (Soran Second Force, a military wing of the IMIK) to form the *Ansar al-Islam*. *Ansar's* chief foes are the PUK, as they contest the same territory (north-eastern Kurdistan, near the Iranian border), but also targets the KDP and parties representing religious minorities. The movement was blamed for several bomb attacks and murders in the PUK-controlled region of Sulaymaniyah and Irbil from 1998 onwards. Its attacks intensified in 2002-03, reputedly at the behest of the Saddam government. In early 2002, *Ansar* succeeded in assassinating the KDP head of Irbil, Franso Hariri, and narrowly missed the PUK's Prime Minister Dr Barham Saleh later in the year. During the 2003 war, *Ansar* bore the brunt of concerted attacks by US forces and Kurdish fighters, who moved into the group's former stronghold. After the war it appeared that *Ansar* had regrouped near the eastern border with Iran, sometimes taking refuge over the border. The bombing of the KDP and PUK headquarters in Irbil in February

2004, killing over 100 people including some of the most prominent members of the KDP, suggests that *Ansar* still maintains a well-organized presence in Iraqi Kurdistan.

Leadership. Najmuddin (Najim al-Din) Faraj, better known as Mullah Krekaar

Arab Ba'ath Socialist Party: Iraqi Command (ABSP-IC), founded in 1963 as a breakaway from the parent Arab Ba'ath Socialist Party, the ABSP-IC is based in Syria and led by Fawzi al-Rawi. During the 1960s this offshoot benefited from the split between the official Iraqi and Syrian "regional commands" of the Ba'ath (i.e. governing parties in Baghdad and Damascus), with each branch claiming that it represented the authentic ideology. Michel Aflaq, who founded the Ba'ath in Syria in the 1940s, as an authoritarian, pan-Arab and quasi-fascist group, moved to Iraq after an internal putsch in Syria.

The ABSP-IC lacked a military capability and hoped for a revolt within Iraq's existing power structure, rather than popular uprising or foreign intervention, to achieve change. While condemning the personality cult that developed under Saddam, and declaring itself in favour of political pluralism, it acquiesced in the totalitarian expressions of Assad dynasty Ba'athism in Syria. It has an ageing leadership and more recent dissident Ba'athists and military leaders have associated with groups like the Iraqi National Accord (INA) and Free Officers' Movement (FOM).

Assyrian Democratic Movement (ZOWAA), was founded on April 12, 1979, in Iraq as "a democratic, national and patriotic organization to defend our people and their legitimate rights". Under Saddam ZOWAA was the pre-eminent Assyrian opposition group. Though committed to "self-determination", for Chaldeans, Assyrians and Syriacs alike, ZOWAA has co-operated with other Kurdish and Arab opposition groups since the mid-1980s. The ZOWAA leader, Younadam Youssef Kanna, spent several terms in Iraqi jails for his activities, and then two decades in political exile within Iraq. ZOWAA accounts for most of the five seats in the Kurdistan National Assembly reserved for Christians. After Saddam's demise Kanna proclaimed: "An empire of terrorists has collapsed". On July 13, 2003, he was appointed as the sole Assyrian Christian member of the 25-member post-Saddam Governing Council.

Leadership. Younadam Youssef Kanna (secretary-general)
Website. www.zowaa.org

Ba'ath Arab Socialist Party
Hizb al-Baath al-Arabi al-Ishtiraki
Until 2003 the ruling party, the Ba'ath (Renaissance) offically stood for secular pan-Arabism, socialism, anti-imperialism and anti-Zionism. It was theoretically a regional party of which the Iraqi party was one "regional command", others being in Lebanon and Syria. Founded originally in Syria in the latter part of the 1940s, the Ba'ath held power in Iraq from July 1968 and was banned after the US invasion of 2003. Thereafter Ba'ath party members were excluded from participation in political life and national administration by the occupying power, a position that proved increasingly untenable in the face of the rise of Islamist and other groups previously kept under control by the Ba'ath regime. The effective abandonment of the programme of "de-Ba'athification" was signalled with the inclusion in the June 2004 provisional government of figures with a Ba'athist past, while a process of re-hiring of former Ba'athist administrators was also underway. However, the party remains banned.

Badr Brigade, regarded as the military wing of the Supreme Council of the Islamic Revolution of Iraq (SCIRI), the Badr Brigade has an estimated 8,000-10,000 men under arms. It

was set up in 1983 with the express purpose of combating Iraqi troops in the south of the country. Badr refers to the pivotal battle in early Muslim history fought near Medina. The majority of Badr Brigade members are Iraqi Shi'a who were expelled to Iran during the early days of the Iran-Iraq war. Others are deserters from the Iraqi army, or politicized clerical students. In the 1991 Gulf War the Badr Brigade briefly captured Najaf, on the Euphrates, but in March 1991 Saddam's forces crushed the Shi'a rebellion; escapees rejoined the Brigade in Iran. The Badr Brigade is reportedly officered by members of Iran's *Pasdaran* (Revolutionary Guards). As with other militias it has continued in existence post-invasion in the face of lack of central government authority.

Constitutional Monarchy Movement, the CMM is committed to restoring constitutional monarchy to Iraq. The party's leader. Sharif Ali Bin Al-Hussein, is a scion of the Hashemite family (second cousin of the late King Faisal II) that was ousted from power in 1958. In 1999 Sharif Ali joined Ahmed Chalabi's Iraqi National Congress, and joined the INC's ruling triumvirate. Though pro-Western, he has criticized American inability to understand the centrality of tribal bonds in Iraqi politics. While himself a Sunni, Sharif Ali is married to a member of a prominent Shiite family from Karbala. He favours the adoption of a monarchy, possibly along British lines, following a free national referendum that would restore the constitution of 1925. The CMM stresses the importance of Kurdish-Arab unity as the basis for a democratic Iraqi state.

Leadership. Sharif Ali Bin Al-Hussein
Website. www.iraqcmm.org

Democratic Alliance of Kurdistan (DAK), set up on Oct. 13, 1996, as a protest against KDP co-operation with the Iraqi authorities, the DAK comprised the PUK, Iraqi Toilers' Party, Democratic Movement, Socialist Democratic Kurdistan and the Conservative Party of Kurdistan. The DAK is known as *Hawpaymani Demoqrati Kurdistan* in Kurdish.

Free Officers' Movement (FOM), created in 1996, was reported before the 2003 war as being in favour of a three-pronged infantry assault on Baghdad from Kurdish Iraq, Kuwait and Jordan, without the use of US ground troops. The FOM signed a confederation agreement with the Assyrian National Congress on June 15, 2002, presumably in a bid to broaden its support base. The principal figure in the group is Brig. Gen. Najib al-Salihi, a former Republican Guard officer. That same month, Salihi and fellow former officers, Tawfiq al-Yassir (Iraqi navy) and Brig. Saad al-Obaidi (army), agreed on a "Covenant of Honour", which called for a demilitarized Iraq and pluralist civilian rule. The FOM is connected to the Iraqi Independent Alliance, and Najib Salihi, the leader of the FOM, is a member of the 15-man military council of the Coalition of Iraqi National Forces.

Leadership. Brig. Gen. Najib al-Salihi

Hawza, technically a non-political body, the Najaf-headquartered *hawza 'ilmiya*, is the supreme religious council for Iraqi Shia. Though literally meaning "territory of learning", the *hawza* also provides social and religious services for its community. After the Khomeini revolution, some of its students felt compelled to leave Najaf for the seminary in Qom, Iran. Under Saddam, the *hawza* had to play a cautious game, preserving its congregants' rights and helping distribute UN food-for-oil. Since April 2003 the *hawza* has carried out post-war welfare and economic assistance, and can operate without constant surveillance by the *mukhabarat* (security police). By the same token, it has been drawn into the political turmoil typifying post-Saddam Iraq. Grand Ayatollah Ali al-Sistani heads the council and is generally regarded as the leading

Shi'a spiritual authority in the country and to many Shi'a outside Iraq. As such, he now occupies a position of unprecedented political influence in post-Saddam Iraq and has generally sought to ensure Shi'a representation in the emerging political process (insisting on the importance of early elections) while working to bring an end to violent confrontations between Shi'a groups and the occupying forces, including brokering in August 2004 an end to the siege by US forces of Najaf where Muqtada al-Sadr had raised rebellion.

Leadership. Grand Ayatollah Ali al-Sistani

Higher Muslim Council, the Council is one of the few known Sunni organizations that espouses an Islamic government, while disavowing any attempt to "swap one form of tyranny [i.e. Saddam] for another, like in Iran".

Independent Iraqis for Democracy (IID). Adnan Pachachi, a former Iraqi foreign minister and ambassador to the UN who left Iraq after the 1968 coup, founded the Democratic Centrist Tendency (DCT) in 2000. To some extent, it followed the principles of the old National Democratic Party, founded in the 1940s, but which disbanded after the Ba'ath coup of 1968. On March 29, 2003, Pachachi effectively relaunched the DCT as the Independent Iraqis for Democracy (IID) at a meeting of more than 300 Iraqi exiles in London when he said that a US military postwar administration was "in no way acceptable" and called for a "provisional administration of the UN and Iraqi technocrats". He describes his group as "liberal independents". Pachachi's group was somewhat dwarfed by the INC, INA and other more established coalitions. Pachachi declined Dr Chalabi's invitation to join the INC in February 2003. He also was offered a place on the leadership council of the inclusive Follow-up and Arrangement Committee (FUAC) but declined to take up this post. Though the IID claims high level support in the Gulf, it does not enjoy mass followings in Iraq itself. Pachachi led Iraq's first post-Saddam delegation to the UN General Assembly in September 2003. However, in June 2004 he withdrew his candidacy for President in the new interim government, saying he had been unfairly portrayed as a US stooge.

Leadership. Adnan Pachachi (secretary-general)

Iraqi Communist Party (ICP), founded in 1934, the pro-Soviet ICP – known as *al-Hizb al-Shuyu'i al-Iraqi* in Arabic – enjoyed a substantial popular following, particularly among educated Kurds. The party was not formally legalized until 1973 when it was admitted to the National Progressive Patriotic Front (NPF). The ICP left the NPF again in March 1979 and transferred most of its operations to Kurdistan. As a consequence of the party's long nurtured relations with Kurdish autonomists, the ICP suffered massive repression after the collapse of the Kurdish uprising in 1975. On Nov. 12, 1980, the ICP joined six other parties in a National Democratic and Pan-Arab Front dedicated to overthrowing Saddam Hussein. It supported Iran in the war and looked to Syria as an ally. Following the 1987-88 *Anfal* campaign against the Kurds, the ICP was forced to move to Syria. The collapse of the USSR in 1991 led the ICP to dilute its Marxist-Leninist ideology. After 1991 the ICP joined the JACIO anti-Saddam umbrella coalition. On June 23, 2002, the ICP joined the Coalition of Iraqi National Forces as a senior partner and took up a position opposed to US military intervention in Iraq while accepting that pragmatically this might be necessary to unseat Saddam. The party has been supportive of the post-war efforts to reconstruct Iraq, participating in the IGC.

Leadership. Hamid Majid Mousa (central committee secretary)

Website. www.iraqcp.org

Iraqi Democratic Liberation Movement, a mainly tribal Arab party led by the wealthy Jebouri (or Jaburi) family, the IDLM it is said to enjoy good links with the PUK and KDP, but engages in little activity in northern Iraq.

Iraqi Islamic Party, this party is one of very few Sunni religious opposition groups. It is led by Iyad al-Samara'i who after some arguments joined as one of the 65 members of the Follow-up and Arrangement Committee (FUAC) at the December 2002 London meeting of opposition groups. Samara'i had objected strongly to what he saw as dominance by the Shiite SCIRI and negation of Sunni views. Mohsen Abdel Hamid, a prolific author on the Koran, represented the IIP on the Governing Council. The IIP is the Iraqi branch of the region-wide Muslim Brotherhood, and it may be associated too with the Higher Muslim Council.

Leadership. Iyad al-Samara'i
Website. www.iraqi.com

Iraqi Kurdistan Front (IKF), this ad hoc alliance of seven Kurdish groups apparently co-ordinated *peshmerga* activity against Iraqi forces in 1991. Its members were the Kurdistan Democratic Party (KDP), Patriotic Union of Kurdistan (PUK), Kurdish Hizbollah (led by Sheikh Muhammad Kaled), Kurdistan People's Democratic Party, Kurdistan Socialist Party (led by Rasoul Marmand), Assyrian Democratic Party and the Revolutionary Proletariat Kurdistan Party. After the failure of the 1991 uprising and the KIF's suspension of talks with Baghdad in January 1992, the KIF has largely fallen into abeyance as an independent group. However, its structure may serve as the template for a revived umbrella grouping since the apparent KDP-PUK rapprochement of 2002.

Iraqi National Accord (INA), consisting mainly of Sunni defectors from the Iraqi armed forces, Ba'ath and intelligence network, the INA (*Harakat Wifaq al-Watani*) was created in 1990 at the instigation of the Saudi secret services, and reputedly also Kuwait. In late 1996 the CIA began reorganizing the weakened INA as a counterweight to the INC, which they suspected of disunity and lack of military preparedness. In the late Saddam period the INA had offices in Dahuk, Sulaymaniyah, Zakhu, Salahuddin and Irbil, all within Iraq's Kurdish autonomous region. The INA was the only "national movement" within the Group of Six opposition formations. When constituted as the Group of Four, it formed a powerful counterweight to the INC; the INA brought a crucial Sunni component to the Kurdish one (represented by the PUK and KDP) and the Shi'a (represented by SCIRI). INA leader Iyad Allawi (himself a Shi'a) took a seat on the 25-member Governing Council after June 2003, making him one of the most prominent politicians in post-Saddam Iraq. Another INA member, Nuri Badran, was appointed Interior Minister. Allawi was subsequently appointed Prime Minister of the interim government formed in June 2004.

Leadership. Iyad Allawi
Website. www.wifaq.com

Iraqi National Alliance, this exiled opposition group was established in 1990, and advocated "democracy and pluralism" in Iraq, though not the ouster of Saddam Hussein. Its first major congress was held in Sweden in June 1992. Constituent groups have included the Arab Baath Socialist Party (pro-Syrian wing), Socialist Unity Party (Nasserite), Arab Labour Party, Arab Socialist Movement (offshoot of the Arab Nationalists' Movement), Kurdish Islamic Army, Kurdistan Peace Party, various independents, and what was called the "patriotic current" in the Iraqi Communist Party. Some critics suggested that the Alliance was a front or a pseudo-opposition at best.

Leadership. Abdul Jabbar al-Kubeisi

Iraqi National Congress (INC). The INC began in 1992, with origins in a group known as the Joint Action Committee of the Iraqi Opposition (JACIO), which supported the Kurdish and Shi'a uprisings of 1991. From the outset the INC received CIA support and the INC was a wide coalition, including the Kurdish KDP and PUK, secularists and Islamists, although subject to splits. Dr Ahmed Chalabi was selected as its president. A Shiite, he left Iraq in 1956, moving to Lebanon and later Jordan, where he established the Petra Bank. Chalabi is wanted in Jordan on charges of fraud and of causing the kingdom's currency collapse of 1989. He was convicted in absentia and sentenced to 22 years in jail but has rejected the charges as politically motivated.

In 1995 the INC launched an insurrection to oust Saddam Hussein. After it failed, the INC blamed the USA for withdrawing support at the last minute. In August 1996 Iraqi troops and the KDP attacked the PUK, and also INC bases in northern Iraq, killing 200 supporters and forcing thousands to flee. Iraqi forces ransacked INC offices in Irbil and Salahuddin and captured and interrogated many INC personnel. This eroded INC unity and made Irbil an unsafe location for its headquarters, which moved to London. Chalabi himself settled in the UK and became a British citizen. A chastened INC had to reconsider its relations with the KDP, as well as its rival and the INC's more faithful friend, the PUK.

Chalabi redirected his attention to lobbying in Washington. In 1997 he promoted the establishment of Indict, an organization dedicated to bringing to international justice the top 12 Iraqi officials. He helped draft and realize the 1998 Iraq Liberation Act passed by the US Congress on Sept. 29, 1998. This Act institutionalized the INC as the main US conduit for supporting political change in Iraq, and authorized the passage of nearly $100 million to facilitate activities. In March 1999 the INC sought to rebuild itself by electing a provisional seven-member leadership, in Windsor, UK. However, Kurdish groups soon left, followed by Communists, SCIRI, INA and others. Chalabi was actively favoured by Washington neo-conservatives grouped around the Defence Department, but reportedly mistrusted by the State Department and CIA, which instead favoured Allawi's Iraqi National Accord. Likewise Kurdish groups (albeit technically part of the INC) felt that Chalabi made the USA favour the INC with funds, and deny them access to sums released by the Iraq Liberation Act.

In the run-up to the US invasion Chalabi's name was often cited as the potential head of a post-Saddam government and Chalabi became acting chairman of the provisional Governing Council. However, Chalabi faced suspicion in Iraq as a US puppet and was criticized in the West for having given inaccurate information to the US government concerning Saddam's weapons programmes as well as for pressing the policy of root-and-branch de-Ba'athification by the CPA and dissolution of the Iraqi army, which had come to seem misguided. Relations with the USA cooled and in April 2004 Chalabi described Paul Bremer's decision to moderate the de-Ba'athification policy as "like allowing Nazis into the German government immediately after World War II". In May 2004 the US government cut off its financial support for the INC. Chalabi's influence rapidly faded and he was not a member of the broad-based interim government formed in June 2004.
Leadership. Dr Ahmed Chalabi
Website. www.inc.org.uk

Iraqi National Movement (INM), known as the Iraqi National Liberal Movement, is a Sunni-dominated group that split off from the Iraqi National Congress (INC) in late 2000. Falal al-Naqib, formerly of the INM, was appointed Interior Minister in the interim government in June 2004.
Leadership. Maj-Gen Hasan al-Naqib (secretary-general)

Iraqi Turkoman Front (ITF), a coalition of six major Turkoman groups and numerous minor ones, the ITF was established in April 1995 and is backed by the Turkish government. The ITF desires a major role in the future governance of Kirkuk and Irbil, oil-rich centres of northern Iraq, which it identifies as Turkoman territory. This stance has led to conflict with the Kurdistan Democratic Party (KDP), which also covets these areas. Opposed to the Saddam regime, the Front nonetheless had qualms over the turmoil that might result from a possible US invasion. The ITF opposes the creation of a Kurdish state in northern Iraq, especially one that may adopt Kirkuk as its capital. The Front maintains headquarters in Irbil.
Leader. San'an Ahmad Agha
Website. www.turkmencephesi.org

Islamic Action Organization (IAO), founded in 1965 in Karbala by the late Ayatollah Muhammad al Shirazi, the IAO developed under Shirazi's nephew and current leader, Ayatollah Muhammad Hadi al-Mudarrasi, into a clandestine group during the 1970s. The IAO was inspired by the Iranian example, and members received military training in Lebanon. From its Tehran base, the IAO attempted an armed revolt in Iraq. It was affiliated to Islamic Amal and was also a member of SCIRI and later the INC. Mudarrasi returned to Karbala soon after Saddam's fall in April 2003. He immediately set up two religious seminaries in the town, and cast himself as a moderate Iraqi nationalist who sought gradual, democratic enactment of Islamic mores. He also desires amicable relations with the West, wishes to build a new *hawza* university, and assiduously nurtures ecumenical ties with Sunni groups both in Iraq and outside.
Leadership. Ayatollah Muhammad Hadi al-Mudarrasi

Islamic Movement of Iraqi Kurdistan (IMIK), was formed in 1986 during the Iran-Iraq war, with Iranian sponsorship and under the leadership of Sheikh Uthman Abd al-Aziz. The Sheikh declared in a January 1994 interview with Kanal-6 television that IMIK sought to establish an Islamic state "like Iran" in northern Iraq. That same year Kurdish officials reported that IMIK had set up a joint military base with Iran's Revolutionary Guard in IMIK-controlled areas. Despite these strong Iranian links, there seems to be no proof that IMIK actually adheres to Shiite Islam. IMIK has adopted numerous names over time. Many Kurdish religious factions began life as IMIK breakaways, such as the Kurdistan Islamic Group. In 1998, Sheikh Uthman was elevated to the position of 'Spiritual Guide', allowing his younger brother Mulla Ali Abd al-Aziz to assume leadership of the party. In 1999 IMIK merged with another armed group, the Islamic *Al-Nahdah* (Renaissance) Movement of Mulla Sadiq Abd al-Aziz (another brother), to form the Islamic Unity Movement in Kurdistan. However, it resumed its original name after a split in 2001. By 2002 IMIK was calling itself the Islamic League. In recent years IMIK, which has several hundred militiamen, has been eclipsed in its Halabja stronghold by another, more radical Kurdish Islamist group, *Ansar al-Islam*.
Leadership. Mulla Ali Abd al-Aziz

Kurdish Workers' Party (PKK), now known as KADEK. Led by Osman Ocalan after the capture of his brother Abdullah, the PKK is a Turkish-based movement but has also had bases in northern Iraq, where it has variously allied or come into conflict with indigenous Kurdish groupings. Following the Gulf War of 1991 and the establishment of de facto Kurdish autonomy in northern Iraq, Iraqi Kurds proved more concerned with preserving that autonomy than furthering the PKK's maximalist goal of a Kurdistan uniting Kurds throughout the region. In the 1990s the Kurdistan Democratic Party (KDP), in cahoots with Turkey, attacked

PKK forces based in KDP-controlled autonomous areas. In March 1996 the PKK apparently spawned a local group called the Kurdistan National Democratic Union (YNDK). This offshoot soon split into pro-PKK/PUK and pro-KDP factions. In 1997 the PKK stepped up attacks on civilians in Kurdish-controlled areas, especially members of the Assyrian community who backed the KDP. In October 2000 the PKK also clashed with the PUK in the Qandil Range. Following the 2003 war, Turkey sought the disbandment of PKK bases in northern Iraq in exchange for support for the US-led occupation, although the PKK has largely desisted from attacks in Turkey since the capture of its leader, Abdullah Ocalan, in 1999.

Kurdistan Conservative Party (KCP), known as *Parti Parezgarani Kurdistan* in Kurdish, and *Hizb al-Muhafidhin al-Kurdistani* in Arabic, the KCP established itself in early 1992 as a clan-based entity strongly affiliated to the Surchi tribe. After 1996 its relations with the KDP deteriorated, and it has accordingly since then operated mainly in PUK-controlled territory.

Kurdistan Democratic Party (KDP) (*Parti Democrata Kurdistana* (Kurdish) *Al-Hizb ad-Dimuqraati al-Kurd* (Arabic)); founded in 1946, the KDP remains the strongest Iraqi Kurdish party. It was founded by Mullah Mustafa Barzani, who epitomized the struggle for Kurdish autonomy in Iraq for over 30 years. The death of Mullah Barzani in exile in the United States on March 1, 1979, prompted a power struggle within the KDP, with his son Masoud, born in 1946, emerging as the dominant figure. In the Kurdish elections, held in May 1992, the KDP and PUK emerged as the two dominant groups opposing the Iraqi government. After the hung result of the election, they agreed to split the assembly's 105-member assembly with 50 for each party, the remainder being reserved for Assyrians.

In 1994 fighting broke out between the KDP and the PUK leading to a split in parliament. The KDP-controlled parliament in Irbil became headed by Nechervan Idris Barzani, a nephew of the KDP leader, Masoud Barzani, when he took over the post as deputy Prime Minister in 1996. The KDP and the PUK eventually mended their differences with a peace deal in September 1998, stipulating the limited goal of Kurdish autonomy within a democratic post-Saddam Iraqi republic. Their rapprochement appeared cemented by the first joint session in eight years of the Kurdistan National Assembly, in October 2002. The KDP and PUK have continued to co-operate in taking common positions in defence of the high degree of Kurdish autonomy envisaged by the interim constitution, which has come under attack by some Arab groups in Iraq and also by Turkey.

While Masoud Barzani represented the KDP on the 25-member interim Governing Council, which was instituted on July 13, 2003, another KDP member, Hoshyar Zebari, became Iraq's Foreign Minister. Zebari remained Foreign Minister in the interim government formed in June 2004. Rowsch Shaways, the speaker of the Kurdish regional parliament and KDP member, became one of the two vice-presidents in the interim government.

Leadership. Masoud Barzani (president)
Website. www.kdp.pp.se

Kurdistan Islamic Group (KIG), affiliated to IMIK, the Kurdistan Islamic Group is a comparatively moderate Islamist grouping, led by Mulla Ali Bapir. The KIG was founded in 2001 as a breakaway from the Islamic Unity Movement in Kurdistan. The PUK apparently approved of the KIG running its welfare and social services in PUK-controlled territory. In October 2002 Bapir reversed his earlier policy, and announced the creation of an armed militia. The

BBC reported that the KIG probably has ties with *Al-Tawhid* (Unity), which had attacked KDP forces in the Soran region. US forces arrested Mulla Ali after the invasion of Iraq. He remains imprisoned.
Leadership. Mulla Ali Bapir

Movement for Democratic Change in Iraq, launched by the Iraqi Kurdish politician Hussain Sinjari in March 2002. Earlier he had founded the Iraq Institute for Democracy, funded by the US National Endowment for Democracy. Hussain Sinjari was deported in March 1974 after the Baghdadi authorities demolished his family home. He was Minister of Municipalities in Iraq's autonomous Kurdish region until 1999. His movement has little popular support within Iraq and acts more as an NGO promoting democratic rights rather than a political party.
Leadership. Hussain Sinjari

Mujahidin-e Khalq, this organization of dissident Iranians was based in southern Iraq and backed by Saddam. In March 2003 there were reports that the *Mujahidin-e Khalq* were joining forces with pro-Saddam Iraqis in opposing US troops fighting in southern Iraq.
Leadership. Massoud Rajavi

National Democratic Party (NDP), once active in the 1940s, the NDP experienced an unexpected revival after Saddam's fall as a Sunni alternative to the Ba'ath. Its leader, Naseer al-Chaderchi, tooka seat on the Governing Council as one of only five Sunni representatives; a Shi'a NDP member, Abdel Amir Abbud Rahima, became agriculture minister while a Sunni NDP member, Hisham Abderrahman Shibli, became justice minister.
Leadership. Naseer al-Chaderchi

Patriotic Union of Kurdistan (PUK)
The PUK was formed by former KDP members Ibrahim Ahmad and Jalal Talabani after the collapse of the 1974-75 Kurdish revolt, as a merger of the Kurdistan National Party, the Socialist Movement of Kurdistan and the Association of Marxist-Leninists of Kurdistan. Like the KDP, the PUK officially supports autonomy for Kurds within a "unified democratic Iraq". However, its stance has been more overtly leftist and less traditionalist than that of the KDP. Since 1991 the PUK has run its own Kurdistan Regional Government in Sulaymaniyah. The rival KDP-run zone has its headquarters in Irbil, and clashes between the two groups led to a virtual civil war from 1994-98. On Jan. 21, 2001, Barham Salih, formerly PUK and Kurdistan Regional Government representative to North America for ten years, became Prime Minister of the PUK-run authority and assembly. In October 2002 the PUK and the KDP convened the first joint session of the Kurdistan national assembly in eight years. Barham Salih used the opportunity to openly call for "regime change" in Baghdad. The PUK joined the KDP and other Kurdish factions in June 1992, to establish the Iraqi National Congress (INC), yet Jalal Talabani liked to distinguish between the "opposition of the trenches and the opposition of the hotels". He generally enjoys good relations with a range of disparate nations: Iran, Saudi Arabia, the USA and Turkey. After the fall of Saddam, Jalal Talabani represented the PUK on Iraq's Interim Governing Council, with PUK members Mohammad Tufik Rahim and Latif Rashid also serving as ministers for Industry and Mines, and Water Resources, respectively. Barham Salih, Prime Minister of the PUK administration in Sulaymaniyah, became Deputy Prime Minister responsible for national security in the interim Iraqi government appointed in June 2004.
Leadership. Jalal Talabani
Website. www.puk.org

Sadriyyun ("Partisans of al-Sadr") have enjoyed a meteoric rise since the end of the 2003 war. Their leader, Muqtada al-Sadr, is the son of the revered Ayatollah Mohammed Sadiq al-Sadr, killed by Saddam's forces in 1999. In April 2003 the group organized the first major anti-US demonstration after the US victory. The *Sadriyyun* proved virulently opposed to US forces and to all groups deemed as too pro-Western. In mid-July 2003 Muqtada al-Sadr damned the Interim Governing Council as being full of "non-believers", and threatened to set up his own alternative body. Some members of SCIRI blamed Muqtada al-Sadr's followers for the murder of the SCIRI leader, Ayatollah Mohammed Bakr al-Hakim, on Aug. 29, 2003, outside the Imam Ali Mosque in Najaf. *Sadriyyun* rejected the accusations and Saddam loyalists or Saudi Wahhabists were also seen as possible culprits. His supporters have also been accused of killing Abdul Majid al-Khoei on April 10.

Sadriyyun's stronghold lies in Sadr City – formerly Saddam City – a poor neighbourhood in Baghdad that houses approximately two million Shia, where it has recruited among disaffected young men. Thus *Sadriyyun* arguably reflects a sociological phenomenon – the mass migration of Shi'a from the south to the capital over past decades. Since the 2003 war its supporters have destroyed numerous Christian-controlled liquor shops in Baghdad and established vigilante "protection" forces in the city. In April 2004 Muqtada al-Sadr's forces took up arms; they seized control of the Imam Ali mosque in Najaf, culminating in a three-week siege by US forces in August which ended with an agreement brokered by the highest Shia cleric, Ali al-Sistani, under which Muqtada al-Sadr's forces were allowed to withdraw. Sadr City was also the scene of intense fighting between US forces and Muqtada al-Sadr's *Jaysh al-Mahdi* militia in the summer of 2004. Muqtada al-Sadr refused to participate in the national conference called in August 2004 and as of October 2004 Badr City was still part-controlled by his militia, with a delicate ceasefire with US forces in place. However, there were also some indications that Muqtada al-Sadr might be prepared to join the political process.

Leadership. Muqtada al-Sadr (leader); Ayatollah Sayyid Qadhim al-Ha'iri (spiritual leader)

Supreme Council of the Islamic Revolution of Iraq (SCIRI), also known as the Supreme Assembly of the Islamic Revolution of Iraq (SAIRI), or simply the *Majlis*, this conglomerate organization of Shi'a Islamic parties was founded on Nov. 17, 1982, by Ayatollah Mohammed Bakr al-Hakim. SCIRI technically consists of several groups, including the Movement of the Iraqi *Mujaheddin,* the Islamic Movement in Iraq, *Jund al-Imam,* the Islamic Movement for the Kurds, *Al-Daw'a al-Islamiya,* the Islamic Action Organization and the Islamic Scholars' Organization. Some of these groups have distanced themselves from SCIRI, generally on grounds of its close ties to Tehran, notably *Daw'a.* SCIRI's 70-member assembly consists of members of the six constituent groups, and several influential individual Shiite clerics. A breakaway faction of SCIRI called the Iraqi Islamic Forces Union, led by Abu-Haydar al-Asadi and others, was formed in 2002 when it seemed that SCIRI was about to ally itself with the USA. Mohammad Jassem Khodayyir, who divides his allegiance between *Daw'a* and SCIRI, became Iraq's new immigration minister in the IGC. Another SCIRI affiliate, Ali Faek al-Ghadban, became minister for youth and sports. Bayan Baqer Sulagh, a Shi'a Turkoman and SCIRI member, became minister for the crucial postwar portfolio of reconstruction and housing. Ayatollah Mohammed Bakr al-Hakim was assassinated at the Imam Ali mosque in Najaf in August 2003. He was succeeded by this younger brother Ayatollah Abd al-Aziz al-Hakim.

Leadership. Ayatollah Abd al-Aziz al-Hakim

Tribal Council for *Diwan*, this is the collective name for 11 Shi'a tribes of south and central Iraq, comprising the areas of Diania, Middle Ferat, Samawa, Nassiriyah and Basra. Generally, the USA felt more comfortable dealing with the Council than with SCIRI, as the Council is free of the strong Iranian ties of the latter, better known group. After Saddam's fall, British forces in Basra entrusted power to a local council in Basra headed by a tribal leader, Sheikh Mozahem al-Tamimi, a respected scholar, sometime theologian and former army general. Ten of the council's 24 members were also tribal sheikhs. However, this experiment in transition to local rule prompted fierce protests on April 14. Demonstrators accused tribes of being paid stooges of the Ba'ath regime. They also called the sheikhs "backward" (Tamimi himself being a notable exception) and demanded that they submit to the authority of Ayatollah Ali al-Sistani's *hawza*

Turkoman National Association (TNA). Founded in November 2002, the TNA is an umbrella organization encompassing the Turkoman Cultural Association, Turkoman Brotherhood Party, Turkoman National Liberation Party, Iraqi Turkoman Union Party and Kurdistan Turkoman Democratic Party. In contrast to the Iraqi Turkoman Front, the TNA appears to enjoy better relations with Masoud Barzani's KDP. A TNA member and head of the Turkoman Cultural Association, Jawdat Najjar, is a minister in the KDP-led regional government.

Worker Communist Party of Iraq (WCPI), A more doctrinaire Marxist grouping than the Iraqi Communist Party, the WCPI was founded by Mansoor Hekmat and held its first congress in July 1994. The WCPI is based in Kurdistan, and although the party considers Kurdish autonomy as regression into non-progressive nationalism it demands a referendum on the issue of Kurdish autonomy so that "the people of Kurdistan control their own destiny". It equally regards political Islam as atavistic. Currently led by Rebwar Ahmed, who succeeded Hekmat after his death in 2001. In 2003 it launched ferocious verbal assaults on and arranged large demonstrations against the US "annihilation war" against Iraq.

Leadership. Rebwar Ahmed (secretary)

Website. www.wpiraq.org

Ireland

Capital: Dublin
Population: 3,978,900 (2003)

The Irish Free State was established by a treaty signed in 1921 and ratified by the British and Irish parliaments in 1922, the whole of Ireland having hitherto been under British rule. The Free State was created in the 26 counties of the south and not in the six counties of Northern Ireland, where there was a majority in favour of continued British rule. In 1937, however, Ireland adopted a constitution expressly stating that it applied to the whole of Ireland, and which was therefore seen as containing an implicit territorial claim to the six counties of Northern Ireland under British sovereignty. The Republic of Ireland was declared in 1949. Following the signature of the Good Friday Agreement on Northern Ireland in April 1998, constitutional amendments approved by referendum in the Republic on May 22, 1998, formally enshrined the principle of popular consent to any change in the status of the North. These amendments were promulgated on Dec. 2, 1999, on the establishment of a power-sharing executive in the North and the inauguration of a consultative North-South Ministerial Council (see United Kingdom, Northern Ireland, chapter).

The Irish parliament (*Oireachtas*) consists of (i) the President (*Uachtarán na hÉireann*) directly elected for a seven-year term (once renewable); (ii) a 166-member lower house (*Dáil Éireann*) whose members (TDs) are elected by universal adult suffrage for a five-year term; and (iii) a 60-member indirectly-elected Senate (*Seanad*), including 11 prime ministerial appointees, with power to delay, but not to veto, lower house legislation. The cabinet, which is responsible to the *Dáil*, is headed by a Prime Minister (*Taoiseach*), who is the leader of the majority party or coalition. Members of the *Dáil* are elected by the single transferable vote (STV) version of proportional representation, from multi-member constituencies. In 1973 Ireland joined what became the European Union. It elects 13 members of the European Parliament, a figure reduced for the 2004 European Parliament elections from the former number of 15.

Under legislation governing the remuneration of public representatives as revised in 2004, leaders of parties with one or more elected representative in the *Dáil* or Senate receive annual payments from state funds at a rate of between IR£54,864 and IR£21,950 per deputy and between IR£35,874 and IR£17,937 per senator, the rate tapering the more representatives a party has. These amounts, which are for parliamentary activities such as research, policy formation, training and administration, are reduced by a third for parties in government as regards the *Dáil* but not the *Seanad* part of the allowance. Under the 1997 Electoral Act there is a separate scheme under which registered parties receiving over 2% of first-preference votes in a general election share IR£1 million proportionately to the size of their vote. In addition, parties' election expenses are reimbursed by the state up to a maximum of IR£5,000 for each candidate who receives at least a quarter of the quota of votes required for election at any stage of the count.

Elections to the *Dáil* in May 2002 resulted as follows: *Fianna Fáil* 81 seats (with 41.5% of first-preference votes), *Fine Gael* 31(22.5%), Labour Party 21 (10.8%), Progressive Democrats 8 (4.0%), Green Party 6 (3.8%), *Sinn Féin* 5 (6.5%); Socialist Party 1; independents 13. In presidential elections held on Oct. 30, 1997, Mary McAleese (*Fianna Fáil*) was elected for a seven-year term with 45.2% of the vote in the first count and 58.7% in the second.

Ireland is one of the most enthusiastic EU members – a Eurobarometer poll in February 2004 gave the EU a 75% satisfaction rating. Since it joined the EU in 1973, Ireland has risen to become the second wealthiest country in Europe, in terms of GDP per head. Ireland has 13 seats in the European Parliament. The elections to the European Parliament held in June 2004 resulted in the following outcome: *Fianna Fáil* 29.5% of the vote and 4 seats (-2); *Fine Gael* 27.8% of the vote and 5 seats (+1); Independents 16.8% of the vote and 2 seats (-); Labour Party 10.6% of the vote and 1 seat (no change); *Sinn Féin* 4.8% of the vote and 1 seat (+1); Green Party 4.3% of the vote and no seats (-2). The turnout in the elections was 59.7%, somewhat above the EU average.

Fianna Fáil

Address. 65-66 Lower Mount Street, Dublin 2
Telephone. (353–1) 676–1551
Fax. (353–1) 678–5690
Email. fiannafail@iol.ie
Website. www.fiannafail.ie

Leadership. Bertie Ahern (president); Seamus Kirk (parliamentary party chairman); Seán Dorgan (general secretary)

Fianna Fáil has always been the more republican of the two leading Irish political parties, but hard to classify in European ideological terms – traditionally rather conservative on social policy, less so on economic policy and strongly defending Irish neutrality in foreign policy. It has steadily evolved, however, into a pragmatic broad-based party of the centre-right with support across the Irish geographical and social spectrum (including both urban working-class voters and smaller farmers and trades people in rural areas) as old civil war political divisions have gradually faded. *Fianna Fáil* has been the largest Irish political party since its first victory in the 1932 elections, and has been in power either on its own or in coalition for over 50 of the 80 or so years since independence. Until 1989 all Irish governments consisted either of single party *Fianna Fáil* governments or multi-party coalitions against it. In 1989 it entered into a coalition government for the first time, and subsequent *Fianna Fáil*-led governments have all been coalitions.

Fianna Fáil (literally "Soldiers of Destiny" but officially known in English as the Republican Party) was founded in 1926 by Éamon de Valera. He was the sole surviving leader of the 1916 rebellion against British rule as well as the leading opponent of the 1921 treaty with Britain which led to the creation of the Irish Free State in the 26 counties (i.e. without the six counties of the North). It boycotted the Free State *Dáil* (because of a required oath of allegiance to the British monarchy) until 1927; in 1932 it came to power in general elections. De Valera then became Prime Minister (and was President of Ireland from 1959 until his death in 1973).

Fianna Fáil remained in government until 1948, introducing the constitution of 1937 and maintaining neutrality during World War II. The party was again in power in 1951–54 and in 1957–73. In 1959 Seán Lemass succeeded De Valera as Prime Minister and Ireland began a period of rapid economic growth. Jack Lynch became Prime Minister in 1966 and in 1970 his government was hit by allegations that there was gun-running to Northern Ireland (where intercommunal conflict had broken out in the late 1960s) by some of the party's leading figures, including Charles Haughey. *Fianna Fáil* lost power in 1973 but regained it in 1977 by winning 84 seats and an absolute majority in the *Dáil*. Upon Lynch's retirement in 1979 Charles Haughey became party leader and Prime Minister, having overcome the fall-out from the arms trial in 1970 (in which he was acquitted). *Fianna Fáil* lost power in 1981 but again held it for one short and troubled term of office in 1982. It was then in opposition until 1987 when it won 81 seats (with 44.1% of the vote), and Haughey returned as Prime Minister.

In the June 1989 elections *Fianna Fáil* parliamentary strength was reduced to 77 seats. The subsequent serious political impasse was resolved by Haughey agreeing the following month to the inclusion of the Progressive Democrats (PDs) in *Fianna Fáil's* first-ever experience of coalition government. Subsequently, the FF deputy leader and Defence Minister, Brian Lenihan, began as favourite to win the November 1990 presidential election, but was then defeated by Mary Robinson, the nominee of the Labour Party.

Haughey finally bowed out in January 1992, being succeeded as *Fianna Fáil* leader and therefore as Prime Minister by his old party adversary, Albert Reynolds. In November 1992 the party experienced its poorest election result since World War II (its *Dáil* representation falling to 68 seats and its first-preference vote to 39.1%), but Reynolds managed to persuade the Labour Party to enter into a majority coalition. Less than two years later, however, the coalition collapsed and *Fianna Fáil* then went into opposition to a three-party coalition headed by *Fine Gael*, although it remained the largest parliamentary party under the new leadership of Bertie Ahern.

Fianna Fáil returned to power after the June 1997 elections, in which it recovered to 77 *Dáil* seats, while improving only marginally, to 39.3%, in first-preference votes. As incoming *Prime Minister*, Ahern formed a minority coalition with the Progressive Democrats (PDs), his government being dependent on independents for a parliamentary majority. He quickly lost his Foreign Minister, Ray Burke, who resigned in October 1997 after being named in a financial corruption case. In the same month, however, *Fianna Fáil* candidate Mary McAleese was elected Irish President with 58.7% of the vote on the second count.

Ahern played a major role in the conclusion of the Good Friday Agreement in Northern Ireland in April 1998 and the following month successfully recommended resultant constitutional revisions to Republic voters, involving formal acceptance that Irish unity could only be achieved by consent of the people north and south of the border. At the same time, the Ahern government secured popular endorsement for the EU's Amsterdam treaty.

In spite of ongoing judicial tribunals into corruption allegations in Irish business and politics, the government continued to get credit for the country's rapidly expanding economy and also benefited from weaknesses and divisions in the opposition parties. It had a setback when Irish voters in June 2001 rejected its recommendation that the EU's Nice treaty should be ratified, but the outcome was later reversed in a second referendum. In the general election of May 2002 *Fianna Fáil* won 81 seats on 41.5% of the vote, and was close to an absolute majority, but subsequently entered into a new coalition with the Progressive Democrats, with Bertie Ahern again confirmed as Prime Minister. In the 2004 European elections *Fianna Fáil* lost 2 seats, ending with fewer seats than *Fine Gael*, although at 29.5% of the first preference vote they still had the higher vote share.

The *Fianna Fáil* members in the European Parliament have never sat in one of the two major groups and currently sit in the Union for a Europe of Nations group.

Fine Gael

Address. 51 Upper Mount Street, Dub
Telephone (353–1) 619–8444
Fax. (353–1) 662–5046
Email. finegael@finegael.com
Website. www.finegael.i.e
Leadership. Enda Kenny (leader); Richard Bruton (deputy leader); Tom Hayes (chairperson of parliamentary party; Tom Curran (general secretary)

Fine Gael (literally "Tribe of the Gael"), is the successor of *Cumann na nGaedheal* ("Society of the Gaels"), the party that was created by those supporting the 1921 treaty with Britain that led to the creation of the Irish Free State in the 26 counties of the south of Ireland (i.e. without the six counties of Northern Ireland), including Michael Collins and Arthur Griffith, and that had then won the subsequent civil war between pro and anti-treaty forces. *Cumann na nGaedheal* was set up in 1923 with W.T. Cosgrave as party president. It remained the largest Irish party until 1932, and provided the government of the Irish Free State, with W.T. Cosgrave as Prime Minister. *Cumann na nGaedheal* lost power in 1932 and in 1933 merged with the Centre Party and the fascist Blueshirt Movement of Gen. Eoin O'Duffy to form the new party of *Fine Gael*. Since this date *Fine Gael* has never been the largest Irish party, but it has remained, albeit with considerable fluctuations in its support, the second largest party, and is the only party other than *Fianna Fáil* to have provided Irish Prime Ministers. Unlike *Fianna Fáil*, it has never managed to rule on its own, but only as the largest party in broader-based coalitions.

Irish civil war divisions lasted a long time, and pro-treaty supporters and their descendants provided a historic base for *Fine Gael* support, which only gradually grew weaker over time. Broadly-speaking *Fine Gael* has remained a party of the centre-right, but its support has spanned the spectrum from rural conservatives to urban liberals. It has been weaker than *Fianna Fáil* among urban working class voters and small farmers and shopkeepers, but traditionally stronger among big farmers and in the wealthier suburban constituencies. It has been generally more conservative on economic and budgetary issues than *Fianna Fáil* and in recent years also somewhat more socially liberal, being involved in efforts to make Irish society more pluralistic. While less republican than *Fianna Fáil*, policy differences between the two parties on such issues as Irish unification and neutrality have been more ones of emphasis than of substance (indeed it was a *Fine Gael*-led coalition that established the Irish Republic in 1949).

Fine Gael was out of power for 16 years from 1932 to 1948, and by 1944 had been reduced to only 30 seats in the *Dáil*. In 1948, however, *Fine Gael* returned to government at the head of a five-party coalition government, with John A. Costello as Prime Minister (although the party leader remained the long-serving Richard Mulcahy). Losing power in 1951 (largely because of conflict over the "Mother and Child scheme" for free health care and education) *Fine Gael* again led a coalition government from 1954-57, with Costello having a second term as Prime Minister.

From 1957-73 *Fine Gael* had another lengthy spell in opposition. Mulcahy was replaced as party leader by John Dillon, who was himself later succeeded by Liam Cosgrave, son of W.T. Cosgrave. In the mid-1960s a group of young *Fine Gael* politicians (notably Declan Costello and Garrett Fitzgerald) tried to lead the party in a more liberal direction, with the adoption of a new programme referring to the "Just Society". From 1973-77 Liam Cosgrave was Prime Minister at the head of another coalition, but suffered a severe defeat in 1977, after which Cosgrave resigned as leader and was succeeded by Garrett Fitzgerald. The appointment of Charles Haughey as *Fianna Fáil* leader began a long period of intense rivalry and alternation in power between the two men, with Fitgerald as Prime Minister for a short term in 1981-82 and then for a much longer period from the end of 1982 to 1987. In the February 1987 elections, however, *Fine Gael* was reduced to 27.1% of the vote and 51 *Dáil* seats (from 37.3% and 70 seats in November 1982), resulting in the resignation of FitzGerald. The new *Fine Gael* leader, Alan Dukes, maintained the party's strong commitment to the 1985 Anglo-Irish Agreement whereby the Republic's government recognized the partition of Ireland but secured a consultative role in the administration of the North.

In the June 1989 elections *Fine Gael* increased its parliamentary representation to 55, but remained in opposition. In November 1990 Dukes resigned as party leader and was replaced by his more right-leaning deputy, John Bruton. In the November 1992 *Dáil* elections *Fine Gael* slumped to 45 seats and 24.5% of first-preference votes, its worst showing since 1948. Nevertheless, a political crisis in late 1994 resulted in the resignation of the *Fianna Fáil* Prime Minister and enabled Bruton to form a three-party coalition government with Labour and the Democratic Left. In the June 1997 *Dáil* elections *Fine Gael* recovered to 54 seats and 27.9% of first-preference votes but went into opposition to a centre-right coalition headed by *Fianna Fáil*. Opposition to Bruton's continued leadership mounted in 2000, culminating in his defeat in a confidence vote in the parliamentary party in January 2001. He was succeeded the following month by the instigator of the vote, former Justice Minister Michael Noonan. Continued economic prosperity in Ireland, combined with a perception of ineffective *Fine Gael* opposition to the Ahern government, helped to contribute to a disastrous performance by *Fine Gael* in the 2002 elections, with the party only obtaining 31 seats on 22.5% of the vote. Noonan then resigned, and was replaced by Enda Kenny. The party appeared to be in a fragile position but it then fared very well in the 2004 European elections, polling 27.8% of the vote and winning 5 seats, one more than *Fianna Fáil*.

Fine Gael is affiliated to the Christian Democrat International. Its members in the European Parliament sit in the European People's Party/European Democrats group.

Green Party
Comhaontas Glas
Address. 5A Upper Fownes Street, Dublin 2
Telephone. (353–1) 679–0012
Fax. (353–1) 679–7168
Email. info@greenparty.ie
Website. www.greenparty.ie
Leadership. Trevor Sargent (party leader); Mary White (deputy leader); John Gormley (party chairman); Terence McDonough (national coordinator); Stiofan Nutty (general secretary)

The Green Party is part of the family of European Green parties and its support base has gradually increased after unpromising beginnings, as Irish politics has become less dominated by the old civil war parties and as Ireland's rapid economic growth has been accompanied by increasing land use and environmental problems. The Green Party advocates stronger environmental policies, better conservation of resources, enhanced public transport and the need for truly sustainable development at national and world level. It also calls for the development of a more open, democratic and decentralized political and economic culture in Ireland. Most of its support is in urban areas, with 5 of its 6 members of the *Dáil* elected in the Dublin conurbation and the sixth in the city of Cork.

The party was established as the Ecology Party of Ireland (EPI) in December 1981 with support from what became the UK Green Party and from members of anti-nuclear and environmental protection groups in Ireland. It first put up candidates in the November 1982 elections, but only won 0.2% of the national vote. It became the Green Alliance in 1983 and elected its first local councillor in 1984 (in Killarney). Subsequent internal arguments as to whether it should be a political movement or become a proper political party were resolved in favour of the latter, and it changed its name to the Green Party in 1987.

The party won its first *Dáil* seat in the June 1989 election, when Roger Garland was elected. He lost his seat in 1992 but this was offset by Trevor Sargent's victory elsewhere in Dublin. It then did well in the June 1994 European Parliament elections, winning two of Ireland's 15 seats with 7.9% of the vote. The party improved to two seats in the June 1997 national elections (taking 2.8% of first-preference votes), one of its successful *Dáil* candidates, John Gormley, having in 1994 become Dublin's first Green lord mayor. The Greens retained their two seats in the June 1999 European Parliament elections, although the party's vote share slipped to 6.7%. The party was restructured after disappointing local election results in 1999. Whilst supporting Irish membership of the European Union, the Greens were prominent in the successful opposition to Ireland's ratification of the EU's Nice treaty in a first referendum held on this issue in June 2001. The party's objections focused on a perceived threat of the creation of an unaccountable EU super-state under the treaty that would undercut Irish democracy and neutrality. Trevor Sargent was chosen as leader in 2001, and the party did well in the 2002 national elections, winning 4 additional seats (all at *Fine Gael*'s expense) and ending up with 6 seats on 3.8% of the vote. It lost, however, both of its seats in the European Parliament in the 2004 European elections.

The Green Party is affiliated to the European Federation of Green Parties. Its former representatives in the European Parliament sat in the Greens/European Free Alliance group.

Labour Party
Páirtí Lucht Oibre
Address. 17 Ely Place, Dublin 2
Telephone. (353–1) 678–4700
Fax. (353–1) 661–2640
Email. head_office@labour.ie
Website www.labour.ie
Leadership. Pat Rabbitte (leader); Liz McManus (deputy leader); Willie Pearse (chairperson of parliamentary party); Mike Allen (general secretary)

The Labour Party is a party of social democratic orientation that has traditionally been the main left-of-centre party in Ireland, advocating a fairer society and greater social justice, improved public services, more open and accountable government as well as solidarity and sustainable development at world level. It has been only the third Irish party in terms of votes, and has thus had a smaller support base than most of its sister parties in other European countries. It has suffered, in particular, from Ireland's historical lack of industrialization and of large-scale urban development outside Dublin, as well as the long-standing dominance of civil war divisions in Irish politics, meaning that competition between the two main centre-right parties has been of greater weight than more familiar left-right divisions. Labour has had its most significant support base in Dublin itself, and in other cities, and has been weak in rural Ireland, although a number of (sometimes not very left-wing) Labour politicians have been elected in heavily rural constituencies because of their local implantation and personal qualities.

Labour has never provided an Irish Prime Minister but has provided several Deputy Prime Ministers, having taken part in seven coalition governments, on six occasions in *Fine Gael*-led coalitions against *Fianna Fáil* and on one occasion with *Fianna Fáil*. Labour has now merged with another left-wing party, the Democratic Left Party and is hoping that this, sharp economic disparities between successful and less-successful people in Irish society and the weakening of the old civil war divisions will help to reinforce its support. It has considerable competition from several smaller parties, however, and the merged party was unable to make any real gains in the 2002 general election.

The Labour Party was founded as the political wing of the Irish trade union movement. Its founding date is often claimed to be 1912, and with James Connolly and James Larkin as key early figures, but it did not take firm organizational form until after Independence when it elected 17 members on 22% of the vote in the 1922 elections. It was then the main opposition party in the *Dáil* of the Irish Free State in 1922–27 (but only because *Fianna Fáil* refused to take their seats) but its electoral position later steadily weakened. It became an independent entity from the Irish Trades Union Congress in 1930, although some of the individual trade unions continued to be affiliated to the party. It supported the *Fianna Fáil* minority government under Éamon de Valera in 1932–33 and also supported De Valera when he constituted *Fianna Fáil* governments in 1933 and 1937, but afterwards moved into full opposition. The party subsequently participated in anti-*Fianna Fáil* coalition governments in 1948–51 with four other parties, in 1954–57 with *Fine Gael* and a farmers' party, and with *Fine Gael* alone in 1973–77, 1981–82 and 1982–87, providing the *Tánaiste* (Deputy Prime Minister) in these governments. William Norton was the party leader from 1932-60 and Brendan Corish from 1960-77. Another long-serving leader was Dick Spring from 1982-97.

A Labour conference decided in 1986 to end its participation in coalitions, which had been consistently opposed by its left wing and which had coincided with a steady loss of electoral support (from 17% in 1969 to 9.1% in 1982 and to 6.5% in 1987). The party accordingly withdrew from government in early 1987 in opposition to proposed cuts in the health budget, thus precipitating general elections in which it dropped to 12 seats (from 16 in 1982). Labour's recovery began at the June 1989 elections, when it increased its *Dáil* representation from 12 to 15 seats. The following year it joined with the Workers' Party in backing the successful presidential candidacy of Mary Robinson, who had twice been a Labour parliamentary candidate but was no longer a party member.

In the November 1992 elections Labour achieved its best election result to date, more than doubling its *Dáil* representation to 33 seats (from 19.3% of first-preference votes) after a campaign focusing on the shortcomings of the *Fianna Fáil* government. Nevertheless, in January 1993 the party entered into a coalition with *Fianna Fáil*, which collapsed in November 1994. The party then switched and joined a three-party coalition along with *Fine Gael* and the small Democratic Left party.

The Labour Party was punished in the June 1997 national elections, being reduced to 17 seats and 10.4% of first-preference votes and going into opposition. In October 1997 Labour candidate Adi Roche came a poor fourth in the presidential election, with only 6.9% of the vote. The following month Spring resigned as Labour leader and was succeeded by Ruairí Quinn, hitherto deputy leader.

Seeking to strengthen its political base, the Labour Party in January 1999 merged with the Democratic Left (DL) Party, whose leader became president of the combined party, while Quinn was confirmed as leader. The DL had been launched by a reformist faction of the Marxist Workers' Party in 1992 and had won four seats in that year's *Dáil* elections, retaining them in 1997. The new Labour Party's representation in the lower chamber was therefore 21 seats. Nevertheless, the enlarged party fared badly in the June 1999 European Parliament elections, taking only 8.8% of the vote, although retaining its single seat in Dublin.

The combined party won a disappointing total of 21 seats on 10.8% of the vote in the May 2002 national elections and remained in opposition. Quinn resigned as leader and was succeeded by Pat Rabbitte, who had come from the much smaller Democratic Left component of the merged party, as did Liz McManus, the new deputy leader. In the 2004 European elections the party retained its seat in Dublin, and only narrowly missed winning a further seat in the new East constituency.

The Labour Party is a member of the Socialist International. Its member of the European Parliament sits in the Party of European Socialists group.

Progressive Democrats (PDs)
An Partí Daonlathaoh
Address. 25 South Frederick Street, Dublin 2
Telephone. (353–1) 679–4399
Fax. (353–1) 679–4757
Email. info@progressivedemocrats.ie
Website. www.progressivedemocrats.ie
Leadership. Mary Harney (parliamentary leader); John Higgins (general secretary)

The PDs are a centre-right party of liberal orientation, both in the economic and social sense. They have continued to advocate reduced taxation and tight controls on public expenditure and the promotion of greater enterprise and competition in the Irish economy as well as a more open and pluralistic Irish society. On Northern Ireland they have called for unity by consent and lent strong support to the Anglo-Irish peace process. The party was founded in December 1985 under the leadership of former cabinet minister Desmond O'Malley following a split with *Fianna Fáil* leader Charles Haughey in which four of the party's TDs broke away. As with the SDP-Liberal Alliance within the UK the PDs claimed that they were

"breaking the mould" of traditional Irish politics and offering a fresh alternative to the tired main two parties. The PDs campaigned mainly for fiscal responsibility, to which end they supported what they regarded as "essential and balanced" measures by successive governments, while opposing those seen as "ill-thought-out and unjust". In its first electoral test in February 1987, the party secured 11.8% of the vote and 14 seats in the *Dáil*, thus displacing the Labour Party as the third strongest parliamentary formation.

The PDs then experienced a loss of momentum, falling to only six seats on 6% of the vote at the 1989 national election, although they polled 11.9% in the simultaneous European Parliament elections, and their first general secretary, Pat Cox, topped the poll in the Munster Euro-constituency. After the election the party opted to join a coalition government headed by *Fianna Fáil,* and with the PDs having three ministers. Their withdrawal three years later precipitated the fall of the government and the November 1992 *Dáil* elections, in which PD representation rose to 10 seats, but the party went into opposition. O'Malley resigned as PD leader in October 1993 and was succeeded by Mary Harney, who thus became the first woman to lead a significant Irish party. Her unsuccessful rival, MEP and TD Pat Cox, left the party in 1994 and was re-elected as an independent MEP at the PDs' expense in the Euro elections of that year.

In the June 1997 national elections the PDs slumped to only four seats but opted to join a coalition led by *Fianna Fáil* in which Mary Harney becoming Ireland's first-ever woman Deputy Prime Minister and the party also had two other junior ministerial posts. In the June 1999 European Parliament elections the PDs failed to gain representation, with Cox again being re-elected and going on to be European Parliament President from 2002-04.

In the May 2002 national elections the PDs only got 4% of the vote but effective vote management led to them doubling their seats in the *Dáil* from 4 to 8. They subsequently entered into a new coalition with *Fianna Fáil*, with Mary Harney again as Deputy Prime Minister and with the party having one other full minister and two junior ministers.

Sinn Féin (SF)
Address. 44 Parnell Square, Dublin 1
Telephone. (353–1) 872–6100
Fax. (353–1) 873–3441
Email. sfadmin@eircom.net
Website. www.sinnfein.ie
Leadership. Gerry Adams (president); Mitchel McLaughlin (chairperson); Robbie Smyth (general secretary)

Sinn Féin (literally "Ourselves Alone") is a party of republican, nationalist orientation whose main emphasis has been on rapid achievement of Irish unity, the end of the British presence in Northern Ireland and the creation of a democratic, socialist republic. Generally seen as the political partner of the Irish Republican Army (IRA), it has been regarded with deep suspicion by most other parties (and notably by the Protestant parties in Northern Ireland). *Sinn Féin* has now proclaimed itself to be in favour of the peace process and was a signatory of the 1998 Good Friday Agreement, and has taken part in recent Northern Ireland power-sharing governments (see UK, Northern Ireland section). From its main political base in Northern Ireland, *Sinn Féin* has become increasingly successful in the Irish Republic as well, not least because of the reputation it has developed for providing strong constituency services. It is the only party with growing parliamentary representation on both sides of the border.

The party has inherited the name of the pre-independence nationalist grouping founded in 1905 by Arthur Griffith and which subsequently led Ireland to independence. *Sinn Féin* then split over the issue of whether to support the 1921 treaty, and its anti-treaty wing under Éamon de Valera supported the IRA in a subsequent civil war with Free State forces and continued to use the *Sinn Féin* name in the 1923 general elections. De Valera left *Sinn Féin* in 1926 over the issue of whether to enter the Free State parliament and went on to form *Fianna Fáil*, following which *Sinn Féin* was left on the margins of Irish politics, supporting IRA campaigns conducted mainly in Britain and on the Northern border. *Sinn Féin* won (but did not take up) four seats in the *Dáil* in 1957 but lost them in 1961.

The movement split in 1969-70, the left wing evolving into the Workers' Party, while the nationalist faction became known as Provisional *Sinn Féin* and had as its military wing the Provisional IRA ("the Provos"). By the 1980s *Sinn Féin* had become involved in community and electoral politics in the South, winning some local council seats, although not in the *Dáil*. In 1986 the party ended its policy of non-participation in the *Dáil*. The policy change initially proved to be unsuccessful, since *Sinn Féin* won no seats in the 1987, 1989 or 1992 Irish general elections. In the June 1997 contest, however, it won 2.5% of first-preference votes overall, and returned one member to the *Dáil,* who became th*e* first elected *Sinn Féin* member to actually take up his seat. In the June 1999 European Parliament elections *Sinn Féin* doubled its vote share to 6.3%, but failed to win a seat.

Whilst supporting Irish membership of the European Union, *Sinn Féin* was prominent in the successful opposition to Ireland's ratification of the EU's Nice treaty in a referendum held in June 2001. Its objections focused on a perceived threat to Irish neutrality under the treaty and the possibility that Ireland might be drawn into military alliance with the United Kingdom along with other large countries within a new European superstate.

In the May 2002 general elections *Sinn Féin* put up 37 candidates (up from only 15 in 1997) and its share of the vote went up to 6.5%, with the party winning 5 seats in the *Dáil*. It polled particularly well among working class voters, in Dublin, where it gained two seats, and in border counties, where it elected another two members. Its fifth representative was elected in north Kerry, with its residual republican tradition. In the 2004 European elections it again polled well, winning a seat in the Dublin constituency in addition to the seat it won in Northern Ireland. Its members in the European Parliament sit in the GUE-Nordic Green Alliance Group.

Socialist Party (SP)

Address. 141 Thomas Street, Dublin 8
Telephone. (353–1) 677–2686
Email. info@socialistparty.net
Website. www.socialistparty.net
Leadership. Joe Higgins (leader)
A left-wing party which contends that Labour has sold out working-class Irish people. Its candidates make a pledge to only accept the average wage of an Irish worker. It has been prominent in local community campaigns, notably against water and rubbish charges, in which latter campaign its two most prominent leaders were jailed in 2003. The party's main support is in working class parts of Dublin, where most of its parliamentary candidates have stood, and where Joe Higgins, its leader and only *Dáil* member, was first elected in 1997 and re-elected in 2002. In the May 2002 elections it put up 6 parliamentary candidates in all.

Other Parties

Christian Solidarity Party (*Comhar Críostaí*, CSP). This conservative Christian party is dedicated "to the causes of Life, the Family and the Community" and advocates, inter alia, repeal of the possibility for divorce in Ireland. It was founded in 1994; it fielded eight candidates in the 1997 elections and 23 in 2002, far more than any of the other small parties, although it had scant electoral success.
Address. 73 Deerpark Road, Mount Merrion, County Dublin
Telephone. (353–1) 210
Email. Info@comharcriostai.org

Communist Party of Ireland (CPI). Founded in 1921 by Roddy Connolly as an all-Ireland party and re-established in 1933. It split during the World War II over a 1941 decision to suspend activities in the Republic and the reunification of its southern and northern elements took place only in 1970. The party was staunchly pro-Soviet right up to the demise of the USSR (though it harboured a reformist minority). It has never won a *Dáil* seat and has only limited industrial influence.
Address. 43 East Essex Street, Dublin 2
Telephone/Fax. (353–1) 671–1943
Leadership. Eugene McCartan (general secretary)

Socialist Workers' Party (SWP). This leftist anti-capitalist and anti-globalization formation rejects what it sees as the revisionism of the Labour Party. It nominated four candidates in the 1997 elections, and seven in 2002, but won a minuscule vote wherever it stood – it obtained most votes in one of Ireland's most middle-class constituencies.
Address. PO Box 1648, Dublin 8
Telephone. (353–1) 872–2682
Email. swp@clubi.ie
Website. www.clubi.ie/swp

The Workers' Party (WP, *Pairtí na nOibrí*). The party participates in both Irish and Northern Ireland elections and advocates a united democratic socialist Irish republic to overcome narrow sectarian divisions It has also campaigned against successive European Union treaties, arguing that they would erode Irish neutrality and lead to an undemocratic and unaccountable Europe. The party claims descent from the historic *Sinn Féin*. Following the 1969-70 split producing the Official IRA/*Sinn Féin* and the Provisionals, the former disbanded as an active military organization and from 1971 pursued a parliamentary strategy. Renamed *Sinn Féin–The Workers' Party* from 1977, it adopted its present name in 1982. It returned one *Dáil* member in 1981 and then gained four seats in 1987, and seven in 1989. In 1992 six of these deputies, including leader Proinsías de Rossa, resigned after their proposal to abandon Leninism in favour of democratic socialism had been narrowly rejected at a party conference, and went on to create a new party, Democratic Left (now merged into the Labour Party). The rump WP failed to secure parliamentary representation in the 1992, 1997 and 2002 national elections, nominating seven candidates in the latter (mainly in Dublin) but only winning a small share of votes.
Address. 23 Hill Street, Dublin 1
Telephone. (353–1) 874–0716
Fax. (353–1) 874–8702
Email. wpi@indigo.ie
Website. www.workers-party.org
Leadership. John Lowry (general secretary); Seán Garland (president)

Israel

Capital: Jerusalem (not recognized by UN)
Population: 6,600,000 (Oct 2003E)

The State of Israel declared its independence in 1948, following the end of the British mandate to administer what was then Palestine. The existence of numerous parties within a proportional representation system has meant that no one party has ever secured an overall parliamentary majority. In consequence, the country has been governed by a succession of coalitions. Israel's unicameral 120-seat parliament (*Knesset*) is elected for a maximum term of four years, although several early elections have been called in recent years. The *Knesset* in turn elects the President (a largely ceremonial role) as the constitutional head of state for a five-year renewable term.

Constitutional changes enacted in 1992 provided for the direct election of the Prime Minister (the head of government) with effect from the 1996 general elections. Voters therefore had two ballots, one for the prime ministerial contest and the other for the party election. A two-thirds *Knesset* majority was now required to remove a Prime Minister. In early 2001 the *Knesset* overturned this system, and reverted to the original single poll system.

In elections on May 29, 1996, Binyamin Netanyahu (*Likud*) won the prime ministerial contest with 50.4% of the vote against 49.5% for Shimon Peres of the Israel Labour Party (ILP). Simultaneous elections to the 14th *Knesset* resulted in the ILP winning 34 seats and *Likud* 32. Remaining seats were shared between nine smaller parties. Despite *Likud*'s poor *Knesset* tally, Netanyahu's direct mandate empowered him to head a *Likud*-led coalition government.

A successful vote of no confidence led to new parliamentary and prime ministerial elections on May 17, 1999. Ehud Barak, the new leader of the ILP, defeated Netanyahu in the prime ministerial polls, taking 56% of the votes cast. In the *Knesset* elections, results were as follows: the ILP (competing as One Israel) won 26 seats, *Likud* 19, *Shas* 17, and *Meretz* 10. In addition, *Yisrael Ba'aliya*, *Shinui* and the Centre Party won 6 each, the National Religious Party, United Torah Judaism and the United Arab List (*Ra'am*), 5 each; National Union and *Yisrael Beitenu*, 4 each; the Democratic Front for Peace and Equality (*Hadash*) 3; and *Balad* (National Democratic Assembly) and One Nation (*Am Ehad*), 2 each. Barak headed a broad-based ILP-led government, and the *Likud* went into opposition.

But the failure of the Oslo peace process, the crumbling of the governing coalition and outbreak of a second Palestinian *intifada* in September 2000 prompted the resignation of Prime Minister Ehud Barak in December 2000. New prime ministerial elections were held on Feb. 6, 2001, in which Ariel Sharon, leader of the *Likud*, defeated the incumbent Barak by 62.4% to 37.6%. No simultaneous *Knesset* elections were held. Sharon subsequently led a "government of national unity", including *Likud*, the ILP, and several other parties. *Meretz* headed the opposition.

The coalition collapsed when the ILP withdrew in late 2002, and Prime Minister Sharon called for new elections. These were held on Jan. 28, 2003. By this stage, Israel had abandoned separate polls for Prime Minister and the *Knesset*, and reverted to the pre-1996 single-poll form of parliamentary elections. Results were as follows: *Likud* 38, ILP (no longer competing as One Israel) 19, *Shinui* 15, *Shas* 11, National Union 7, *Meretz* 6, National Religious Party 6, United Torah Judaism 5, the Democratic Front for Peace and Equality 3, One Nation 3, *Balad* 3, *Yisrael B'Aliyah* 2, and United Arab List 2.

Overall, right of centre parties scored a clear victory, winning a majority of seats. After the elections, *Yisrael B'Aliyah* dissolved itself and joined the *Likud*, which raised its final tally to 40 and thus more than doubled its representation in the *Knesset*. The mainly Sephardi-backed *Shas* party suffered a major reverse.

Inasmuch as *Shas* is a religious party, its collapse reflected the general fall in the overall vote for explicitly orthodox Jewish parties. In relative terms, the secular *Shinui* experienced the greatest triumph.

However, only 68.5% of the electorate voted – the lowest turnout in Israeli history. In particular there was a substantial stayaway, if not outright boycott, by Arab voters, reflecting their disillusion with the political system. Israeli Arabs (or Palestinians of Israel, as many now prefer to be called) constitute up to a fifth of Israel's population; in the last few decades they have tended to vote in high proportions, splitting their vote between predominantly Arab and more mainstream Zionist parties.

Reuven Rivlin of *Likud* became *Knesset* Speaker and Mohammed Barakeh of *Hadash*, Deputy Speaker. Eventually the *Likud* formed a narrow coalition with right-wing parties and the centrist *Shinui*, while the ILP took over from *Meretz* as the chief opposition party.. There it was joined by *Shas*, which found itself, after post-election horse-trading, outside a governing coalition. As of 2004, the big issues of the day are the efficacy of the "security fence" built by Israel in the West Bank; attitudes towards the US-backed Road Map for Peace with Palestinians; Ariel Sharon's proposals for "unilateral withdrawal" from the occupied territories; corruption allegations involving the Sharon family; cutbacks to religious agencies; widening poverty; and the *intifada*-hit economy, where a belated and timid recovery since 2002 must still contend with the highest unemployment rate since 1992.

Note. For political movements in the Gaza Strip and West Bank, see separate section on Palestinian Entity.

Balad
National Democratic Assembly

Website. www.balad.org

Leadership. Azmi Bishara (leader)

Formed in 1996, its acronym, *Balad*, means "homeland" in Arabic; the full Arabic name of the party is *Al Tahammu al-Watani al-Dimuqrati*. The party won five seats in elections that year, when it ran jointly with the Democratic Front for Peace and Equality. In 1999 party leader Azmi Bishara, a Christian Palestinian citizen of Israel and a former professor of philosophy, became the first Arab to offer himself as a candidate in Israeli prime ministerial elections. Shortly before polling day, however, he withdrew his candidacy after negotiations with the eventual winner, Israel Labour Party leader Ehud Barak. The party subsequently won two seats in the *Knesset* poll, this time not in alliance with the DFPE. It demands that Israel redefine itself as a state of all its citizens, rather than a Jewish state, and also seeks a measure of "cultural autonomy" for its Arab citizens.

In June 2001 Bishara was indicted for allegedly incendiary anti-Israeli remarks made on a visit to Damascus. On Dec. 21, 2002, and responding to requests from right-wing Israeli politicians and the nation's General Security Services, Israel's Attorney-General sought to disqualify *Balad* prior to the January 2003 elections. Israel's Central Electoral Commission bore out the attorney-general's ruling. However, on Jan. 9, 2003, Israel's Supreme Court considered a plea on *Balad's* behalf – and on behalf of other Arab politicians so affected – and agreed to overturn the earlier ruling. *Balad* subsequently contested the 2003 elections and returned three seats.

Democratic Front for Peace and Equality
Hadash

Address. PO Box 26205, 3 Rehov Hashikma, Tel Aviv

Telephone. (972–3) 827492

Leadership. Mohammed Barakeh (general secretary)

The largely Arab-supported *Hadash* party was established in its present form prior to the 1987 elections, its main component being the pro-Soviet New Communist Party (variously known as *Rakah* or *Maki*). *Hadash* – an acronym that spells the Hebrew word for "new" – has always maintained close ties with the Palestine Liberation Organization, despite an official ban on such relations prior to 1993. It won three seats in the 1992 elections, subsequently lending its support to, though not officially joining, Rabin's Israel Labour Party-led coalition. In 1996 *Hadash* gained five *Knesset* seats, running on a joint ticket with *Balad*.

In 1999 its tally declined to three seats, to the benefit of the United Arab List. In 2003 *Hadash* ran in tandem with another mainly Arab-supported party, *Ta'al*, and returned three seats (originally set at four, but amended after retallying of the vote count). Mohammed Barakeh, a Communist and chairman of the Jewish-Arab Campus Movement, leads *Hadash* in its current incarnation, as he has for several years. However, the *Hadash Knesset* member Dr Ahmad Tibi is probably better known in Israel, partly as he was formerly consultant on Israeli Arabs (or Palestinians of Israel) to PLO chief, Yasser Arafat.

Meir Vilner, the veteran former Communist leader and last surviving signatory of Israel's Declaration of Independence of May 1948, died in 2003. Another prominent Jewish member of *Hadash* was Tamar Gozansky, though she, too, stepped aside to make room for new *Knesset* members. In early 2004, *Hadash* leader Barakeh was the Deputy Speaker of the *Knesset*.

Israel Labour Party (ILP)
Mifleget Avoda Hayisraelit

Address. PO Box 3263, Tel Aviv 69302
Telephone. (972–3) 527–2315
Fax. (972–3) 527–1744
Leadership. Shimon Peres (acting chairman); Ofer Pines-Paz (secretary-general)
Website. http://www.havoda.org.il/eng/platform.asp

The ILP is a Zionist and democratic socialist party, which supports territorial compromise as a means of achieving peace with Israel's Arab neighbours. In 1965 the *Mapai* Labour Party (the mainstay of coalition governments since 1948, and the vehicle of Israel's founding Prime Minister David Ben-Gurion) joined other factions to form the *Ma'arakh* Alignment. The ILP itself was formally established in 1968 through a merger of *Ma'arakh* and two other factions from the general Labour Zionist stream, *Rafi* and *Achdut Ha'avoda*. Its unbroken hold on power ended with the electoral defeat of 1977. The party remained in opposition to *Likud*-led coalitions. The ILP absorbed two smaller factions in 1984: the Independent Liberals and Ezer Weizman's *Yahad*, which was created in March 1984, but contrary to predictions won only three seats in that year's elections.

After the 1984 elections, neither of the main opposing political blocs, ILP or *Likud*, commanded a parliamentary majority. The ILP thereupon became a partner in a "rotating premiership" national unity coalition with *Likud*. Shimon Peres, the ILP leader after 1977, become Prime Minister in 1984-6, and Foreign Minister in 1986-8. Following the 1988 elections the ILP formed another national unity coalition with *Likud*, but this collapsed in 1990, and the ILP went into opposition.

In February 1992 the former Labour Prime Minister, Yitzhak Rabin, regained the party leadership from Shimon Peres. In *Knesset* elections in June the ILP emerged as the largest party with 44 seats, and Rabin became Prime Minister. He led the subsequent ILP-dominated government which negotiated the historic peace agreement between Israel and the Palestine Liberation Organization in September 1993, until his assassination by a right-wing Jewish fanatic in November

1995. He was succeeded as party chair and Prime Minister by Peres, who continued the Middle East peace process. In April 1996 an ILP convention accepted the principle of creating a Palestinian state. In elections the following month, however, Peres narrowly lost the prime ministerial contest to the *Likud* leader. In the separate *Knesset* poll the ILP slumped to 34 seats and went into opposition, although it remained the largest single party in the assembly.

Shimon Peres remained ILP chairman and Leader of the Opposition, until he was replaced by Ehud Barak, a former military Chief of Staff, regarded as a protégé of the late Rabin, in June 1997. Shortly before the elections of 1999, the ILP created and headed a new alliance called One Israel, which also included the mainly Sephardi faction, *Gesher*, and a moderate religious Zionist faction, *Meimad*. Barak defeated *Likud* leader Netanyahu in the prime ministerial polls, receiving 56% of the votes cast. In the accompanying *Knesset* elections, however, One Israel won just 26 seats (of which 23 belonged to the ILP). This constituted 11 fewer seats than it had won in 1996.

Barak formed a broad coalition government that included *Meretz* and two religious groups, the National Religious Party and *Shas*. Barak fulfilled his promise to withdraw Israeli troops from southern Lebanon (achieved in May 2000). However, his administration was blighted by infighting between *Shas* and *Meretz*, hopes of peace with Syria were dashed, and negotiations with the Palestinians at Camp David collapsed in July 2000, leading to the outbreak of a second *intifada* in September. Faced with crumbling support, Barak called for new elections. *Knesset* members vetoed holding a parliamentary poll, and Barak was further undermined by a bid to unseat him by former party leader, Shimon Peres. Meanwhile, *Gesher* had left One Nation in August 2000. That same month the *Likud*'s nominee, the internationally little known Moshe Katsav, beat Shimon Peres in a *Knesset* election to choose Israel's new State President. By now One Israel had effectively disbanded and the ILP recreated itself in its old guise, although the presidential election upset augured ill for the party.

On Feb. 6, 2001, in prime ministerial elections, Barak lost badly to Ariel Sharon, who set up an ILP-*Likud*-dominated "national coalition government". After initial confusion, Barak resigned and handed over temporary party leadership to Shimon Peres, who in March became Ariel Sharon's Foreign Minister. That same month the ILP's Binyamin Ben-Eliezer was appointed Defence Minister. Within the ILP, former *Knesset* Speaker Avraham Burg defeated Ben-Eliezer in a September 2001 internal party primary vote for a new leader to replace Peres. However, the result was disputed amidst allegations of vote-rigging in Druze Arab districts, and in subsequent polls in December, Ben-Eliezer was elected the new ILP leader. The Iraqi-born Ben-Eliezer (whom many still call Fuad, his given Arabic first name) was the first Israeli Jew of Mizrachi or Sephardi (Oriental) origin to lead of one of the country's two major parties. A former senior army commander, military governor of the West Bank, and deputy Prime Minister under the Barak administration since 1999, he was first elected to the *Knesset* in 1984, for *Yahad*. Ben-Eliezer joined the ILP with fellow *Yahad Knesset* members, and over time built a reputation as a pillar of the party's more conservative wing.

Meanwhile tensions had grown within Israel's coalition government between the ILP and *Likud* over how to deal with the persistent Palestinian *intifada*. The ILP favoured keeping channels open to the Palestinian Authority, and welcomed the US Mitchell and Tenet peace plans, whereas Sharon stressed the need to "defeat terror" before talks could recommence. In late December 2001 Sharon openly scorned a bold peace plan forged by Shimon Peres and the Speaker of the Palestinian Legislative Council, Ahmed Qurei.

Ben-Eliezer and Peres wanted to keep the ILP within the *Likud*-led coalition, while most ILP front-benchers increasingly preferred pulling out. By March 2002 even Peres was regretting having joined the "unity government". Prominent former liberal ILP ministers, Haim Ramon, Yossi Beilin and Avraham Burg, all refused places in a coalition cabinet alongside *Likud* figures. In July Ben-Eliezer, having six months earlier rejected a policy of "restraint", presented his own plan for a diplomatic resolution with the Palestinians, having discussed his ideas with Egyptian President Hosni Mubarak. He had already begun to order the dismantling of certain settlements; but Sharon rejected his plans as premature. A final crisis, sparked by ILP opposition to alleged misappropriation of budget funds for the construction of settlements, led Ben-Eliezer to withdraw the ILP from the government in October 2002.

Within two weeks of having done so, however, Ben-Eliezer faced a leadership challenge in internal party primaries. Ben-Eliezer's chief rivals, Avraham Burg and Haim Ramon, threw their weight behind the candidacy of Amram Mitzna. A former IDF general and a major figure in Israel's war in Lebanon, between 1982-5, and the first *intifada*, 1987-91, Mitzna had been mayor of the mixed Jewish-Arab port of Haifa for more than a decade. He won support from business figures and his determined pro-peace stance brought an endorsement from a leading Palestinian politician, Bassam Abu Sharif, as well as an invitation to discuss peace plans with President Mubarak.

Mitzna went on to win the ILP primaries by a large margin on Nov. 19, 2002. Soon afterwards Sharon called for early elections, and Mitzna had barely three months to establish himself nationally. Despite reports of massive graft within the ruling *Likud*, he and his ILP lost the general elections of Jan. 28, 2003. The number of ILP seats fell from 26 to 19, while *Likud* more than doubled its tally, finally emerging with 40. Both *Likud* and *Shinui* gained seats at the ILP's expense.

Mitzna had campaigned for unilateral Israeli withdrawal from the Gaza Strip and renewed negotiations with the Palestinian Authority. He was praised for his integrity, yet failed to capitalize on *Likud*'s internal woes or the deleterious state of the Israeli economy. Mitzna was little known amongst the estimated 900,000 immigrants who arrived in Israel from the former Soviet Union after 1989. In particular, Mitzna could not convince the electorate that he would achieve a higher level of security than the incumbent Sharon, whose record in stopping terrorism was, on paper at least, the worst in Israeli history. Instead, voters blamed the *intifada* on the ILP, as they felt it arose out of the ILP's "naïve and dangerous" Oslo peace policies. Veteran Israeli columnist Yossi Klein Halevi called Mitzna "an anachronism from another more ideological Israel".

Immediately after the elections Mitzna negotiated briefly with the victorious Sharon about joining another "government of national unity". But realizing that *Likud* would never agree to his conditions, he rebuffed Sharon's invitation, saying Sharon intended for ILP to "again serve as a figleaf to his failed policy". Mitzna subsequently welcomed the opportunity to rebuild the ILP's ideological clarity while leading the official opposition. On May 4, 2003, however, Mitzna resigned as ILP leader, citing lack of support within his party. Fearing yet another divisive leadership contest, the ILP named the veteran Shimon Peres as its new "interim leader".

Ofer Pines-Paz is the established ILP secretary-general and *Knesset* faction leader, offering a much needed sense of continuity to his troubled party. In December 2002 he announced that the ILP was willing to give up the Israeli claim on East Jerusalem, in favour of its Arab residents, especially if that would lead to the world recognizing "the Jewish part as the eternal capital of Israel". A year later he demanded that the Health Minister resign after statistics revealed that one-third of Israelis lived below the poverty line.

Israeli commentators have called the ILP a shadow of its former self: financially bereft ($4.8m in debt, and losing an additional $265,000 a month), it is unable to attract younger voters, and lacks clear ideology or strategy. Nonetheless, from its position in opposition, the ILP enthusiastically backs the US Road Map for Peace, and is slowly attempting to build an alternative and coherent social and economic plan to challenge the *Likud*. Mitzna, Burg and other ILP figures were intimately involved in drafting the alternative peace plan, known as the Geneva Accords, officially launched in December 2003; although the ILP *per se* did not formally adopt this plan. On Feb. 3, 2004, 61% of ILP officials voted to support Shimon Peres, now 80, as party leader until December 2005.

The ILP is a member party of the Socialist International.

Likud

Address. 38 Rehov King George, Tel Aviv 61231
Telephone. (972–3) 563–0666
Fax. (972–3) 528–2901
Website. http://www.herut.org.il/english/
Leadership. Ariel Sharon (leader)

Its title meaning "consolidation" or "unity", *Likud* is identified with the claim to indivisible sovereignty over the whole of the biblical Land of Israel (including the West Bank and Gaza). Economically, its constituent groups favour a liberal and free enterprise philosophy. The bloc was formed in 1973, under the leadership of Menachem Begin, and with outside help from Ariel Sharon, as a parliamentary alliance between *Herut* (Freedom) and other smaller groups. *Herut* had led opposition to Labour governments since 1948, in its latter years within the *Gahal* bloc. *Herut*'s own origins lay in the Revisionist Zionist trend after 1920, and the *Irgun Zvai Leumi* and *Lehi* (Stern Gang) militias/terror outfits of the immediate pre-state period. Smaller groups that joined *Likud* included the Liberal Party of Israel, *La'am* (For the Nation) grouping, and *Ahdut Ha-Avodah*, a territorialist and security-conscious Labour Zionist faction. On coming to power in 1977, *Likud* was joined by Sharon's small *Shlomzion* group; two further groups were absorbed prior to the 1988 elections.

The *Likud*-dominated governments of 1977–84, first under Begin and then under Yitzhak Shamir, saw an historic peace agreement signed with Egypt (and the return of Sinai captured by Israel in 1967) and the Israeli invasion of Lebanon in 1982. Having reached an all-time high of 48 seats in 1981, *Likud* fell back to 41 seats in the 1984 elections and was obliged to enter into a "rotating premiership" arrangement with the Israel Labour Party (ILP). This national unity coalition was continued after a further *Likud* decline in the 1988 poll (to 39 seats), until finally breaking down in 1990. The subsequent Shamir government survived with the help of small right-wing parties. This factor probably hastened *Likud*'s electoral defeat in June 1992, when its representation fell to 32 seats.

In March 1993 the youthful and telegenic Binyamin Netanyahu was elected leader of *Likud* in succession to Shamir. His acrimonious relationship with his leadership rival, David Levi, led to a split in early 1996. Levi formed the *Gesher* party, though it later rejoined an electoral alliance with *Likud* and *Tzomet*. Backed by all of the secular and religious right, Netanyahu narrowly defeated Peres in the May 1996 direct elections for the premiership, although in the simultaneous *Knesset* contest *Likud* and its allies remained at 32 seats. Netanyahu formed a coalition which included representatives of *Shas*, the National Religious Party, *Yisrael Ba-Aliya* and Third Way.

The new administration vowed to "slow down" the Oslo peace process, but in time Netanyahu had to acknowledge it as a *fait accompli*. He weathered Palestinian unrest in 1996, signed an accord on Hebron in 1998, and the Wye River Agreement in 1999. But senior *Likud* figures accused him of secrecy, procrastination, fraud, divisiveness and remoteness, and began to resign from his cabinet.

In the May 1999 elections, Netanyahu was beaten by ILP leader Ehud Barak, by a margin of 56.08% to 43.92%. *Likud* polled just 14.14% of the popular vote in the parliamentary poll, and dropped 11 seats to 19, putting it just two seats ahead of the third-placed party, *Shas*. Netanyahu immediately resigned as leader of *Likud*, and was replaced by the former general and outgoing Foreign Minister, Ariel Sharon. Although initially regarded as a spent force and caretaker leader, Sharon succeeded in rebuilding *Likud*'s damaged party institutions. His controversial visit to Jerusalem's Temple Mount in late September 2000 was widely blamed for igniting the second Palestinian uprising. He then rebuffed a return bid by Netanyahu, led opposition to Barak's failing policies and defeated him convincingly at prime ministerial polls the following February. Subsequently *Likud* and the ILP led a broad-based coalition government, with the greatest number of ministers in Israel's history.

However, disagreements over security policy, and in particular, the ILP's objections to a suspicious budgetary allocation to West Bank settlements, prompted the ILP to leave the coalition in late 2002. *Likud* succeeded in winning resultant national parliamentary elections on Jan. 28, 2003, by an impressive margin. After absorbing the two members of Natan Sharansky's *Yisrael B'Aliyah* party, *Likud*'s seats tally in the Knesset totalled 40, more than double its previous representation of 19. One new *Likud* representative was Omri Sharon, son of the Prime Minister and in 2001 unofficial negotiator with the Palestinians.

Yisrael Ba-aliya (Immigration and Israel) was founded as a political lobby in 1992 for Israel's then 900,000-strong Russian and Soviet Jewish immigrant community. It was led by Natan Sharansky, a former Soviet dissident and political prisoner who had immigrated to Israel under a Soviet-Western exchange of 1986. In June 1995 he launched *Yisrael Ba-aliya* as a party in its own right, advocating higher government priority for the absorption of immigrants, and limited Palestinian autonomy. It won seven seats in the May 1996 *Knesset* elections and won two portfolios in the subsequent *Likud*-led coalition government. Sharansky, who enjoyed a high international profile, became Industry and Trade Minister; his deputy leader, Yuli Edelstein, became Absorption Minister. The party fell to six seats in 1999, with some voters deserting to a rival party, *Yisrael Beitenu*. Sharansky's party stayed in the Israel Labour Party-led coalition after 1999, and the *Likud*-led coalition after 2001, in which he served as Deputy Prime Minister. After *Yisrael Ba-aliya*'s representation fell to just two in 2003, reflecting a general move away from "ethnically based" smaller parties, Sharansky dissolved the party within the *Likud*. He is currently Minister for Jerusalem Affairs, although he is no longer a *Knesset* member.

Despite *Likud*'s electoral success in 2003, the party was not free of problems. Scandal broke out after the Dec. 8, 2002, *Likud* convention that chose candidates for their electoral slate, when it emerged that several candidates won their seats using "vote-buying" amongst delegates, in operations that evidently involved underworld criminals. Earlier in 2002, large ideological schisms had emerged after the *Likud* Central Committee, backed by Netanyahu, and against the wishes of Prime Minister Sharon, voted to veto the creation of a Palestinian state anywhere in "Judea and Samaria" (i.e. the West Bank, or occupied territories).

By the same token, Sharon's eventual acceptance in May 2003 of the US-backed Road Map for Peace, which entailed the creation of an independent state of Palestine, exacerbat-

ed existing divisions in the party. Ariel Sharon's decision to dismantle several "outpost settlements", and to evacuate 7,000-12,000 Jewish settlers from Gaza altogether (as announced in January 2004) prompted fierce opposition from the pro-settler wing of the party, now in alliance with smaller, right-wing factions, like the National Union and the National Religious Party. Likewise, many *Likud* MPs disliked the idea of the ILP joining a post-election coalition government, whereas Sharon was in favour. In the event, the badly defeated ILP, then under the leadership of Amram Mitzna, decided to go into opposition. Ariel Sharon, once regarded as the champion of the hardline wing of his party, now appears considerably more willing to compromise than many of his front-benchers. His December 2003 proclamation of a "unilateral disengagement plan", his earlier use of the taboo expression "occupation", and his February 2004 call for the dismantling of 17 settlements in Gaza, have upset many of his colleagues. Moreover, Sharon and his two sons have been caught up in a bribery and embezzlement scandal that has yet to be resolved. It involves accusations of ties to questionable schemes concocted by David Appel, a property developer known as a major *Likud* financier and behind-the-scenes 'kingmaker'.

Tensions have thus mounted over speculation as to who would succeed Prime Minister Sharon as party leader. Judging from statements made, the two main challenges (though as yet covert) come from former Prime Minister and current Finance Minister Netanyahu, adopting a stance to the right of Sharon, and Ehud Olmert, former Mayor of Jerusalem and currently Vice Prime Minister and Minister of Trade and Industry, nominally to the left of Sharon. Since late 2003 Olmert has shocked many *Likud* ideologues by speaking openly of the need to dismantle most settlements, and the end of dreams of a "Greater Israel". Another *Likud* leader who falls within the "pragmatic moderate" camp is Moroccan-born Meir Sheetrit, a former Finance Minister. Currently in the background is former senior minister and one of *Likud*'s "young princes" (i.e. scion of one of its founding families), Dan Meridor, once co-leader of the *Likud* breakaway Centre Party, but who is currently not a *Knesset* member.

Education, Culture and Sport Minister Limor Livnat has been mentioned as a possible outside candidate. Formerly a close ally of Netanyahu's, she has evidently moved from a strict ideological vantage point towards acceptance of the need to compromise in relations with Palestinians and USA. Shaul Mofaz, Israel's Iranian-born Chief of Staff during the first two years of the 2000 intifada, and currently Defence Minister, is cited as a potential successor, although he is not a *Knesset* member and commands no obvious faction within the *Likud* apparatus. Another who stood in the last internal party leadership elections in 2002 was Moshe Feiglin, who heads a faction that expresses the views of committed ideological religious settlers, called *Manhigut Yehudit* (Jewish Leadership). He once led the radical *Zo Artzeinu* group, which in turn was linked by analysts to the even more extreme *Kach*. Feiglin is not a *Knesset* member, but is said by some to represent a focus for internal party opposition, if a massive dismantling of settlements, enforced by US edict, leads to a party crisis.

More mainstream supporters of *Likud*'s conservative core are Tzachi Hanegbi, Minister of Internal Security, Uzi Landau, minister in the Prime Minister's Office, and Yisrael Katz, Minister of Agriculture. Katz also wields considerable influence as the President of the *Likud* Party Convention. He clashed with Olmert in late 2003, when he announced that Israel would double the number of Jewish settlements on the Golan Heights. This was not official *Likud* policy, and damaged chances of reviving peace talks with Syria, hopes for which rose after an initiative by Syrian President Bashar al-

Assad. Israel's current Foreign Minister is the long-serving *Likud Knesset* member and Tunisian-born Silvan Shalom; he is not regarded as a rival to Sharon as he appears loyal and lacks a large support base in the party rank-and-file. Most of the *Likud* supports Sharon on the issue of the "security fence", although its changing route is raising concerns about how it may safeguard settlements left outside.

Meretz

Address. c/o Knesset, Jerusalem
Website. www.meretz.org.il
Leadership. Yosi Sarid (acting leader)
Meretz (meaning "vitality" or "power") was formed in early 1992 as an alliance of three parties of the left. Two of these are the Civil Rights and Peace Movement (*Ratz*) led by Shulamit Aloni (a former member of the Israel Labour Party) and *Shinui* (Change). The third, possibly dominant, component consists of the United Workers' Party (*Mapam*), a socialist Zionist bloc with strong support in the Kibbutz movement. Originally founded in 1948, *Mapam* was subsumed within the Israel Labour Party (ILP) from 1969 until 1984, when it left the alignment, objecting to ILP participation in a coalition government with *Likud*.

The *Meretz* alliance stands for civil rights, equal status for women, electoral reform and religious pluralism. It also advocates a phased peace settlement with the Palestinians and Israel's Arab neighbours by way of interim agreements, and was the first Zionist party to accept the idea of a Palestinian state. In the 1992 *Knesset* elections *Meretz* secured 12 seats and thereafter served as a coalition partner in an ILP-led government. In February 1996 Yosi Sarid, then Environment Minister, ousted Aloni as *Meretz* leader. The formation's representation slipped to nine seats in the May 1996 elections, after which it went into opposition and bitterly criticized Prime Minister Netanyahu's record in implementing the peace process.

Meretz gained 10 seats in the 1999 elections, making it the fourth largest party. One of its new representatives was the first Arab woman in the *Knesset*. *Meretz* joined a broad coalition led by the ILP, which was now constituted as One Israel. Following the election of Ariel Sharon as Prime Minister in February 2001, and the ILP's decision to join a coalition government with *Likud*, *Meretz* became the chief party of opposition.

In the January 2003 elections Meretz suffered from a general right-wing voting trend and returned only six seats. Party leader Yossi Sarid resigned, which prompted a dispute about succession, with the long-standing Iraqi-born *Meretz Knesset* member, Ran Cohen, being the first to officially offer his candidacy. Others in the party mooted a collective leadership. Complicating the issue was a plan to recreate the party in tandem with the *Shahar* movement, led by former Justice Minister and ILP member, Yossi Beilin. This prospective new social democratic party was to be called *Yahad* ("Unity" or "Together" in Hebrew); an earlier suggested acronym, *Ya'ad* ("Target" in Hebrew) was discarded because of linguistic confusion with the Russian for "poison".

Yossi Beilin, who nominally joined *Meretz* just before the 2003 poll, but failed to get elected to the *Knesset*, hoped to become the leader of the new composite party, in preference to Ran Cohen. Senior *Meretz* Knesset member Naomi Chazan, who enjoys good relations with liberal Diaspora Jews, helped formulate the new party's constitution. Meanwhile, many *Meretz* members – in particular Beilin – were intimately involved in negotiating and launching a joint Israeli-Palestinian peace plan, known as the Geneva Accords, after the Swiss city where it was signed in December 2003.

Meretz inherited *Mapam*'s membership of the Socialist International.

National Religious Party (NRP)
Hamiflaga Hadatit Leumit
Mafdal

Address. 166 Ibn Gavirol Street, Kastel Building, Tel Aviv
Telephone. (972–3) 544–2151
Fax. (972–3) 546–8942
Leadership. Efraim Eitam (leader); Yitzhak Levy (chairman)
The NRP was founded in 1956 and favours adherence to Jewish religion and tradition, although in a more accommodating way than the ultra-orthodox parties. Unlike United Torah Judaism, and to a lesser extent *Shas*, the NRP enthusiastically supports military service for its members. Before 1967 noted for its moderation in foreign policy, after the 1973 war especially it has opposed plans to trade territories for peace with the Palestinians.

Having participated in governments headed by the Israel Labour Party up to 1977, the party was represented in *Likud*-led coalitions from 1986. During this period its young guard was closely associated with the pro-settler *Gush Emunim* lobby. The NRP went into opposition following the June 1992 elections, in which it secured six *Knesset* seats, but returned to government (with two portfolios) after increasing its representation to nine seats in May 1996. Under Netanyahu it fought repeated battles with *Shas* for influence and control over the Religious Ministry purse strings. In 1999 its tally of seats fell to five. Factors seen as involved in this decline included the death of its charismatic former chief, Zevulun Hammer, in February 1998, and the desertion of religious Sephardic voters to *Shas*. The Moroccan-born Rabbi Yitzhak Levy replaced Hammer as party leader, and was also Education Minister.

The NRP served under Barak, though Levy and its other ministers began resigning in June 2000. Then it surprised many by choosing to oppose Ariel Sharon in March 2001. Efraim "Effie" Eitam, formerly the most senior IDF officer from a religious background, though born and raised on a very secular kibbutz, replaced Yitzhak Levy as party leader in April 2002. He is known for his uncompromising stance on peace with the Palestinians. Despite a general rightward trend in voting during the January 2003 poll, the NRP returned six seats, just one more than in 1999. The NRP entered the government, having worked out an agreement with the anti-religious *Shinui* fellow partner. Eitam is currently Israel's Housing and Construction Minister; another NRP representative, Zevulun Orlev, serves as Minister for Labour and Social Welfare, while Yitzhak Levy (who nominally remains NRP Chairman) is a Deputy Minister in the Prime Minister's Office.

National Union (NU)
Ha-Ichud Ha-Leumi

Address. c/o Knesset, Jerusalem
Leadership. Benyamin Elon (leader)
The National Union was founded in 1996 and won four seats in the 1999 elections. A coalition of four far-right wing parties, two of its seats went to members of *Moledet* (Homeland), a mainly secular ultra-Zionist party founded in 1992 and led for many years by Gen. Rechavam Ze'evi. A third seat gained in 1999 went to Binyamin Begin, son of former Prime Minister Menachem Begin, and head of *Herut Ha-Hadasha* (or "New *Herut*", a breakaway from *Likud*). Begin's colleague was another *Likud* rebel, Michael Steiner. *Tekumah* (Rebirth) formed the third component of the union.

After 2001 the NU absorbed a fourth party, **Yisrael Beitenu** ("Our Israel"). Founded in 1999, *Yisrael Beitenu* was a largely secular right-wing party backed by immigrants from the former Soviet Union, that ran on a joint ticket with the NU. Its leader and dominant personality was Avigdor Lieberman, formerly director-general of the office of Prime Minister Binyamin Netanyahu. The party criticized Israel's legal system, and won four seats in its first elections, eating into support from its main rival, *Yisrael Ba-Aliya*.

NU leader Ze'evi was assassinated by members of the Popular Front for the Liberation of Palestine (PFLP) on Oct. 17, 2001. Benyamin "Benny" Elon, a former leading light in the radical religious-Zionist *Gush Emunim* settler movement, assumed the party leadership after fending off a challenge from Rechavam Ze'evi's son.

Reflecting Israel's rightward voting trend, the NU increased its *Knesset* representation to seven after the January 2003 elections. Since then it has virulently opposed negotiations with Palestinians. The NU also objects to territorial compromise on the Golan Heights, opposes potential peace talks with Syria, and vows to prevent the dismantling of settlements, as announced by Prime Minister Sharon in late 2003.

In February 2004 the party vowed to leave the coalition if Sharon's disengagement plan became law; and on Feb. 16, 2004, many NU *Knesset* members abstained from three opposition no-confidence motions against the Sharon government, when party leaders granted them the right to vote freely.   Benny Elon first entered the *Knesset* as a member for *Moledet* in 1996, and is currently Israel's Tourism Minister. Romanian-born Zvi Hendel is Deputy Educaton Minister. Though no longer a *Knesset* member, Avigdor Lieberman currently serves as Minister of Transport.

One Nation

Leadership. Amir Peretz (leader)

An offshoot of the Israel Labour Party, led by Amir Peretz, former head of the *Histadrut* labour confederation, it espouses a stronger socialist policy than the ILP, and since January 2003 has had three *Knesset* seats, having won two in the previous elections in 1999. The party gained popular support from its role as the locus for populist opposition to the tight budgetary policies of Finance Minister Binyamin Netanyahu, especially after 2002. The party also encouraged widespread strikes, necessitating involved negotiations between Netanyahu and Peretz to reach a resolution. In late 2003 One Nation sort to merge with the ILP, but on terms that would afford Peretz and his supporters considerably more power. Some ILP members feel that One Nation's message could reinvigorate the ILP, particularly among working class voters. They further contend that an ILP-One Nation union could restore to Labour the social agenda that they contend has been neglected for too long. By contrast, detractors of Peretz within the ILP feel that he represents an antiquated socialism that the ILP had wisely abandoned in the 1980s, and which ultimately would damage ILP electoral fortunes in the future.

Shas (Sephardi Torah Guardians)
Shomrei Torah Sephardim

Address. Beit Abodi, Rehov Hahida, Bene Baraq
Telephone. (972–3) 579776
Leadership. Eliyahu Yishai (chairman); Rabbi Ovadiah Yosef (spiritual leader)

Shas is an ultra-orthodox religious party, formed in 1984 as a splinter group from *Agudat Yisrael* (which later became part of the United Torah Judaism). The acronym *Shas* stands for Shephardi Torah Guardians, yet also traditionally denotes "six books of the *mishna*", or *talmud* (Jewish Oral Law). The party derives most of its support from members of Israel's large Mizrachi or Sephardi (Oriental Jewish) community. In that respect it follows in the footsteps of the *Tami* (Traditional Movement of Israel) Mizrachi party, but was more successful at the polls, winning four seats in 1984 and six in 1988. Just prior to the 1992 legislative elections, Rabbi Ovadiah Yosef, former Sephardic Chief Rabbi of Israel, displaced Rabbi Eliezer Menachem Shach as spiritual leader of the party. This was regarded as a sign of renewed Oriental

Jewish confidence. (Shach was head of the Ashkenazi Lithuanian *yeshiva*, or seminary, network.)

Shas retained its six seats in the 1992 elections and, although previously allied with the right-wing bloc in the *Knesset*, it joined the coalition formed by the Israel Labour Party and *Meretz* in July of that year. Based on the talmudic principle of *pikuah nefesh* (preservation of life) Rabbi Yosef ordered *Shas* members to accept the necessity of territorial compromise in order to achieve peace with Palestinians. *Shas* withdrew from government in September 1993 after a clash over educational policy with the secular *Meretz*. This move undermined the government as it strove to negotiate the difficult Oslo peace process. *Shas* announced its formal return to opposition status in February 1995. The party increased its representation to 10 seats in the May 1996 elections and was subsequently allocated two portfolios in the new government headed by *Likud*.

Analysts suggested that many secular voters opted for *Shas* for reasons of ethnic pride or resentment at an Ashkenazi-dominated polity, rather than for purely religious reasons. Its political genius and *Knesset* leader, Aryeh Deri, served a prison sentence for corruption – a *cause célèbre* that animated *Shas* voters, who accused the politico-legal establishment of anti-Sephardi bias. All *Shas* MKs are male and obey the political edicts of a Council of Sages. Critics say the party's *El Ha-Ma'ayan* (Back to the Wellsprings) school and social network, largely for poorer Sephardim, acts like a state within a state. Its welfare policies filled a vacuum left by the ILP and *Likud*, who appeared to have abandoned their social agendas. *Shas* also has support from some traditionally minded Arab voters.

In 1999 *Shas* increased its representation to 17 seats (just two short of *Likud*). This impressive result made *Shas* Israel's third largest party and confounded predictions that it had reached its maximum strength. *Shas* deserted its alliance with *Likud* to serve under the victorious Ehud Barak. It garnered several important ministerial positions, but clashed again with *Meretz* over educational policy, *Meretz* favouring greater secularization and opposing *Shas* demands for a separate budget to fund its *El Ha-Ma'ayan* network.

By July 2000 these antipathies, and wariness over the extent of Barak's willingness to compromise for peace with Palestinians, led *Shas* ministers to withdraw their support from Barak. Deri, who in 1992 had been charged with taking bribes, had already resigned as minister in 1993, after which Eliyahu Yishai took over as *Knesset* leader. Indicted in 1999, Deri went to prison in September 2000 and was released after serving half his sentence in June 2002. In December 2000 *Shas* members of the *Knesset* voted against a bill that would have led to new parliamentary elections. After March 2001 it joined the newly formed Sharon government and held key social portfolios. But in May 2002 Sharon fired *Shas* ministers for opposing his proposed emergency economic package. *Shas* eventually left the government and went into opposition, prompting a crisis that ultimately resulted in Sharon calling early early elections.

The January 2003 general elections stopped the inexorable upward movement of *Shas*, when its tally of seats fell from 17 to 11. The reverse is ascribed to numerous factors. First, the abandonment of the post-1996 split polling system mitigated against "special interest" parties (though the theory fails to explain the success of *Shinui*). Second, the release from prison of Aryeh Deri exacerbated enmity between his supporters and those of the party's incumbent *Knesset* leader, Yishai. Third, inopportune anti-Arab and anti-Ashkenazi remarks by Rabbi Yosef may have cost the party votes. Fourth, supporters of the aged kabbalist and rival to Rabbi Yosef, Rabbi Yitzhak Kaduri, left the party and formed the breakaway *Ahavat Yisrael* ("Love for Israel"). Although this new group failed to win any seats, it may have eroded the traditional *Shas* voting base. Fifth, former *Likud* supporters who had supported *Shas* now reverted to *Likud* under the perceived strong leadership of Ariel Sharon. And sixth, *Shas* failed to capitalize on a growing revolt against *Likud* budget cuts, led by the unemployed, poorer voters and single mothers, many of them of Sephardi origin.

After the 2003 elections *Shas* negotiated with *Likud* about the possibility of joining the government. However, a schism soon opened between *Shas* and the victorious secular *Shinui*. Ultimately Sharon accepted *Shinui* in partnership with the National Religious Party (NRP), but not *Shas*. The latter accused *Shinui* of anti-Sephardi racism, given that they were prepared to compromise with the mainly Ashkenazi NRP, despite its religious element. *Shas* duly went into opposition.

Shinui

Address. 100 Hashmona'im Street, Tel Aviv
Telephone. (972–3) 5620118
Email. shinui@shinui.org.il
Website. www.shinui.org.il
Leadership. Yosef "Tommy" Lapid (leader)
Shinui ("change") claims to be Israel's only truly liberal party. Founded in 1974, and subject to numerous splits and mergers, it advocated free enterprise, and under Amnon Rubinstein formed one of the constituent groups of *Meretz*. One *Knesset* representative, Avraham Poraz, defected after 1996 to recreate an independent *Shinui*. Then in 1999 Tommy Lapid, a Holocaust survivor and notoriously acidic television interrogator, took over the party and increased its seat tally to six. This "new" *Shinui* had one main aim – strident opposition to orthodox fundamentalism. Although hitherto regarded as left-wing, *Shinui* proved sceptical about chances for peace with Palestinians. Unlike fellow secularists in *Meretz*, it refused to serve alongside the religious *Shas* in the Ehud Barak administration of 1999-2001.

Shinui enjoyed a considerable rise in support in the January 2003 polls, increasing its tally of seats from six to 15. Its success was attributed to various factors. One was widespread anger at ultra-Orthodox Jews and their perceived parasitism vis à vis state funds, as well as their refusal to serve in defence forces, at a time when Israel was under attack from terror. Another factor was the way *Shinui* offered a new home for former Labour supporters, disgruntled at divisions in their party, but unwilling to support *Likud*. *Shinui* is also thought to have attracted some former *Meretz* voters whose views on peace had hardened since the onset of the new Palestinian *intifada* after October 2000, as well as secular immigrants from the former Soviet Union, who had lost their political homes with the decline and disappearance of two mainly Russian parties. Opponents of *Shinui* call it a party of the comfortable Ashkenazi middle classes – only one of its 15 Knesset members, Ehud Ratzabi, is of Sephardi origin.

After considerable political horse-trading, *Shinui* agreed to join a *Likud*-led government in February 2003, despite the presence in the coalition of certain religious parties. Many unresolved tensions remain, not least over *Shinui*'s insistence – formally accepted by *Likud* – that Israel abolish its Religious Affairs Ministry. In the ensuing months, Tommy Lapid and *Shinui* supported the Sharon government's plan for a "security fence", but disputed its route; *Shinui* also appeared to pressurize Sharon to be more receptive to the US-backed Road Map for Peace, and has encouraged Sharon's "unilateral disengagement" plan, in the teeth of opposition from right-wing coalition parties. On economic matters, *Shinui* broadly supports free enterprize and the stringent budgetary policies of Finance Minister Netanyahu. *Shinui* is also determined to streamline national infrastructure, especially municipalities. By late 2003 this policy had led to fierce public protests by Druze Arabs, angry that their villages were being forced to merge.

Shinui members are well represented in the cabinet: Tommy Lapid is currently Israel's Deputy Prime Minister and Minister of Justice, Joseph Paritzky is Minister of Infrastructure, Yehudit Na'or is Minister of the Environment, Avraham Poraz is Minister of Internal Affairs, Eliezer Sandberg is Minister of Science and Technology, and Russian-born Victor Brailovsky is Deputy Minister of Internal Affairs.

Shinui is a member of the Liberal International.

United Arab List (UAL)
Ra'am

Address. c/o Knesset, Jerusalem
Leadership. Abdul Malik Dahamshe
The UAL was created in early 1996 as a coalition between the leftist Arab Democratic Party (ADP), itself founded in 1988 by Abd al-Wahab Darawshah, and the Islamic Movement of Israel, whose radical wing is affiliated with *Hamas*. *Ra'am* is committed to a Palestinian state with east Jerusalem as its capital, the dismantling of Jewish settlements in the occupied territories, and civil equality between Arab and Jewish citizens of Israel. The UAL won four seats in the 1996 *Knesset* elections (the ADP having won two *Knesset* seats in 1992) and five in 1999, making it the largest non-Zionist and Arab-backed party in Israel.

However, it fell back to two seats as a result of the January 2003 elections, when its popular vote tally declined from 114,000 in 1999 to 65,000, reflecting a major realignment of Arab voters. One of its main losers was Salman Abu Ahmed, a representative of the southern wing of the Islamic Movement, who had hoped to win a seat as number three on the UAL list. Abu Ahmed blamed the creation of a breakaway faction by former UAL member, Hashem Mahameed; it won only 20,000 votes, but nonetheless siphoned away support from the UAL. Furthermore, in late 2002 one UAL *Knesset* member with Islamic Movement affiliations, Tawfiq Khatib, had left the UAL *Knesset* faction to give his support to the leftist Zionist *Meretz* party. Khatib ascribed the UAL failure to party leader Dahamshe's policy of favouring on his list Arabs from the Galilee, northern Israel, at the expense of candidates from the so-called Little Triangle area around Nazareth. Triangle voters, said Khatib, "punished" the UAL for this mistake; added to which, the UAL suffered from a general boycott by nearly 40% of Arab voters, who felt frustrated at the establishment's "broken promises".

United Torah Judaism (UTJ)
Yahdut Hatorah

Address. c/o Knesset, Jerusalem
Leadership. Ya'akov Litzman, Rabbi Avraham Ravitz (leaders)
United Torah Judaism was formed before the 1992 elections as a coalition of the ultra-orthodox *Agudat Yisrael* (Israelite Association, originally established in 1912) and *Degel Hatorah* (Flag of the Torah), together with two smaller formations (*Poale Agudat Yisrael* and *Moria*). *Agudat* members include rabbis of the two main Ashkenazi *Haredi* (ultra-Orthodox) trends – *Hassidim* (righteous ones) and *Mitnagedim* (opponents [of the *Hassidim*]) also known as the Lithuanian *yeshiva* (seminary) trend.

Chief Lithuanian school Rabbi Menachem Eliezer Shach created *Degel Hatorah* out of a schism within *Agudat* Yisrael, alongside his other creation, the Mizrachi or Sephardi *Shas* party. The latter enjoyed extraordinary political success, and broke away from Shach's control; by contrast, *Degel Hatorah* had only a few Knesset members, and was reabsorbed within UTJ. By and large, Sephardi Jews are not represented in UTJ. When in government, the UTJ tends to dissuade members from becoming full ministers, denoting a certain agnosticism regarding its relations to the state.

The UTJ won four seats in 1992 and again in 1996, and five seats in 1999. Its policy is described as non- or even anti-Zionist, rendering it distinct from the National Religious Party. However, in recent years it has appeared lukewarm about the Oslo peace process. Former leader Meir Porush opposed the creation of a Palestinian state. UTJ opposes conscription of *haredim* (ultra-orthodox Jews) and the admission to Israel of Jews from non-orthodox communities. The UTJ joined Ehud Barak's One Israel/ILP-led coalition, but departed after six months in September 1999, in protest at the "desecration of the Sabbath" when the government transported a giant turbine on a Saturday.

The UTJ was part of the 2001-03 Sharon government, and UTJ party leader Ya'akov Litzman was also Chair of the Knesset Finance Committee in 2002. The UTJ, like *Shas*, opposed Sharon's emergency economic regulations, which it feared would damage large families and the traditionally poorer Orthodox voter. Consequently Sharon fired his two UTJ deputy ministers in May 2002. In the 2003 general elections the UTJ returned five seats – no change on 1999 – and received 4.3% of all votes cast. The UTJ went into opposition, from where it criticized government legislation. In June 2003 UTJ legislators opposed a bill to deny citizenship to Palestinians who married Israelis. Even so, the party retained and even improved its potency at local level: on June 4, 2003, a UTJ candidate, Uri Lupoliansky, defeated independent Nir Barkat by 51.62% to 42.73% of the vote to become Jerusalem's first *haredi* mayor. Hoping to assuage worried secular residents, he promised "I will wave the flag of patience and tolerance".

Other Parties

A Different Israel (*Yisrael Acheret*) led by Itai Ben-Horin and Boaz Rol was created in late 2002, but failed to gain enough votes to clear the threshold and win a seat in the *Knesset* in 2003, despite initial optimism. It grew out of the students' Awakening Movement, and combined centrist views with an anarchistic rejection of all other political parties.

Ahavat Yisrael (*Love for Israel*) was founded before the 2003 elections as an offshoot of *Shas*. Little distinguished from its parent in terms of ideology; *Ahavat* rather expressed anger at *Shas* for its treatment of its former parliamentary leader, Aryeh Deri, on his release from prison. It also represented supporters of the mystical Rabbi Yitzhak Kaduri and his rivalry with *Shas* spiritual leader, Rabbi Ovadia Yosef. The party was set up by Kaduri's son and grandson; at least one sitting *Shas* representative stood for the new entity. Yet despite the novelty of the centenarian Kaduri campaigning in a plexiglass popemobile-like vehicle, the party failed to pass the necessary voting threshold to win a seat.

Centre Party, founded prior to the 1996 elections by a former mayor of Tel Aviv, Roni Milo, on an anti-orthodox platform. He was joined by prominent deserters from *Likud*, including the moderate pro-peace Dan Meridor and former Defence Minister Yitzhak Mordechai, who became party leader, but withdrew his candidacy for the prime ministerial elections as support began to wane. The party won six seats in the 1999 *Knesset* elections, but failed in its promise to "break the mould" in Israeli politics. Many members returned to their former parties and in 2001, Meridor led remaining party members back into *Likud* and the Sharon government.

Gesher, or "bridge", began as a faction within *Likud* in 1993. It became a separate party in February 1996, headed by the Moroccan-born David Levi, a former *Likud* Foreign Minister who was defeated by Binyamin Netanyahu in a leadership contest in 1993. *Gesher* drew support from Sephardim (Oriental Jews), backed major social programmes, and contested the May 1996 *Knesset* elections in alliance with *Likud* and *Tzomet*. But in 1998 Levi clashed with Netanyahu and again led *Gesher* MKs out of *Likud*. Prior to the 1999 Knesset elections, Gesher joined One Israel. It gained two seats, out of a total alliance tally of 25. In August 2000 *Gesher* broke with the Israel Labour Party concerning concessions over Jerusalem. In 2001 it rejoined *Likud*.

Green Leaf Party (*Aleh Yarok*), favours the legalization of cannabis. Regarded initially as a joke party, it actually drew many protest voters, and in 2003 received 37,855 ballots, or 1% of all votes tallied. It thus came within 7,000 votes of winning a seat in the *Knesset*, outstripping support for 12 other minority parties (including established entities, like the Greens, *Herut* and *Tzomet*). Dan Goldenblatt is one of its leaders.

Islamic Movement of Israel, founded in the early 1980s by Sheikh Abdallah Nimr Darwish, a former Marxist who embraced Islam while in prison on unrest charges. The IMI initially contested only Arab municipal elections, winning six in 1989, and increasing its tally in 1993 and 1998. The movement also runs extensive welfare services in the often impoverished Arab sector. At Darwish's insistence, the IMI fielded candidates in national elections; two members, Abdel Malik Dahamshe and Tawfiq Khatib, were elected on a joint ticket with the Arab Democratic Party, in 1996 and again in 1999 (see United Arab List). Like its ideological partner in Egypt, the Muslim Brotherhood, the IMI does not stand entirely in its own right.

Darwish, based in in Kafr Qasm, has moderated his earlier views, eschews ideas of Islamic rule over all of present day Israel, and co-operates with state institutions. By contrast, a more radical "northern faction" has gained ground of late and dislikes the idea of relations with the "Zionist state", including sitting in the *Knesset*. This faction is led by Sheikh Ra'ed Salah and Kamal Khatib. Since the outbreak of the 2000 *intifada*, right-wing Israeli politicians have accused the IMI of treason and of aiding terror attacks in Israel, in cahoots with *Hamas*. Certainly the IMI has campaigned on the emotional and symbolic issue of "protecting the Al Aqsa Mosque". In 2003 only Dahamshe was returned to the *Knesset*, within the United Arab List, of which he is leader. Threats to ban the IMI have so far not been realized.

Kach ("Thus"), a right-wing religious nationalist and racist party founded by US Jew Rabbi Meir Kahane, who was assassinated in New York in 1990. The party wants to expel all Arabs from Israel and the occupied territories, and eradicate Israeli democracy in favour of a Jewish theocracy. *Kach* was banned in 1994 after one follower massacred Muslim worshipers in Hebron. It still operates clandestinely, especially in certain Jewish settlements. Yigal Amir, assassin of Prime Minister Yitzhak Rabin, belonged to a group affiliated with *Kach,* called *Eyal*. It is unclear who *Kach*'s current leader is, although the name of Noam Federman is often mentioned. Former *Kach* leader Baruch Marzel now leads the National Jewish Front. *Kach* is associated with extremist offshoots like *Ateret Ha-Cohenim* (Crown of the Priests), Temple Mount Faithful, *Zo Artzeinu* (This is Our Land) and Committee for Safety on the Roads. There has been talk of a revived group, "New *Kach*", with strong support in extremist US circles.

Kahane Lives (*Kahane Chai*), a right-wing religious nationalist party named after Rabbi Meir Kahane. It split from *Kach* after Kahane's assassination in 1990, and was led by

Rabbi Binyamin Zeev Kahane (son of the late leader). The party advocates the expulsion of all Arabs from Israel and the occupied territories. It was banned in 1994, along with *Kach*. In December 2000 Palestinian gunmen killed the younger Rabbi Kahane during the second *intifada*.

Meimad, a moderate religious Zionist grouping, won no seats in 1992 or 1996, but won a single seat within the One Israel list in 1999. Its leader since 1996 and sole representative, the Danish-born Rabbi Michael Melchior, was Minister for Diaspora Affairs after 1999 and Deputy Foreign Minister in 2001. He resigned from the government in 2002 along with the ILP, and contested the 2003 elections on a joint slate with the ILP. Melchior has also been deeply involved with the Alexandria Initiative, an interfaith initiative where his chief Christian and Muslim colleagues are, respectively, former Archbishop of Canterbury, George Carey, and Sheikh Muhammad Sayid Tantawi, Imam of Al Azhar, Cairo.

National Jewish Front, founded in late 2003, advocates mass transfer of Palestinians. Its leader is Baruch Marzel, formerly a leading figure in *Kach*. He was offered number two slot on the electoral list for the revived *Herut* party of Michael Kleiner, which broke away from its pact with the National Union; but *Herut* failed to win a seat in 2003.

One Israel (*Yisrael Ehad*) was formed in 1999 as an electoral union between the Israel Labour Party (ILP), *Gesher* and *Meimad*. The ILP was the dominant partner, and the ILP leader, Prime Minister Ehud Barak, became its head. One Israel's *Knesset* seats were allocated as follows: 23 for the ILP, 2 for *Gesher* and 1 for *Meimad*. Following Barak's electoral defeat in 2001, the union effectively came asunder. *Gesher* returned to its original home in the *Likud*, while the ILP reconstituted itself in its former, more familiar guise.

Progressive List for Peace (PLP), a Jewish–Arab movement dating from the early 1980s and led by Muhammad Miari; it lost its small *Knesset* representation in 1992.

Third Way (*Derech Hashlishi*), founded and led by former war hero, Avigdor Kahalani. An offshoot of the Israel Labour Party, it opposed Israeli withdrawal from the Golan Heights (envisaged as likely in the advent of a peace treaty with Syria). The Third Way won four seats in 1996, when a Syrian deal seemed possible; it joined the *Likud*-led government, but failed to win a seat in 1999, and has since largely faded away.

Tzomet, meaning "crossroads", a right-wing, nationalist secular group that won eight *Knesset* seats in 1992. But it suffered repeated splits and failed to win a seat in 1999, or in 2003, when it amassed little over 2,000 votes.

Italy

Capital: Rome
Population: 57,888,245 (Dec 2003)

Under its 1948 constitution, Italy is "a democratic republic founded on work", with a system of parliamentary democracy. The head of state is the President, who is elected for a seven-year term by an electoral college of the two houses of parliament (plus delegates named by the regional assemblies) and who appoints the Prime Minister and, on the latter's recommendation, other ministers. The President has the power to dissolve parliament at any time except in the last six months of its full term. Legislative authority is vested in two chambers with equal powers: (i) the 315-member Senate (*Senato della Repubblica*), whose members are elected for five-year terms on a regional basis; (ii) the 630-member Chamber of Deputies (*Camera dei Deputati*), which is also elected for five-year terms. Presidents may appoint up to 5 life senators during their mandates, and every President, at the end of their term, automatically becomes a life senator. Twenty-nine life senators have been appointed during the Republic, of whom three currently remain in service (Giulio Andreotti, Rita Levi-Montalcini and Emilio Colombo). Nine former Presidents have become life senators, of whom two remain in service (Franceso Cossiga and Oscar Luigi Scalfaro). Under electoral system modifications approved by referendum in April 1993, proportional representation gave way to a mixed majoritarian/proportional system for both houses. In the case of the Chamber, 475 of its 630 members are elected by plurality voting in constituencies and the other 155 by a system of proportional representation, subject to a requirement that at least 4% of the national vote must be won to obtain seats. A founder member of what is now the European Union, Italy elected, in the June 2004 European elections, 78 members of the European Parliament.

Italian parties were made eligible for state financial subventions in 1974, a measure confirmed after a referendum on the issue in 1978 produced a 56.4% majority in favour. The provision was abolished in a referendum in 1993 on a wave of popular revulsion against the party system. A new law passed in the same year introduced a system based on the reimbursement of campaign spending to candidates instead of subsidies to parties. However, the bankruptcy of many parties by the late 1990s led to a further change in 1997, when tax payers were allowed to contribute four of every 1,000 lire of their tax payments to a generic party fund. This too was unsuccessful: in its first six months of operation only 0.5% of tax payers agreed to contribute. This led to a new law, passed in 1999, by which parties receive 4,000 lire for each vote they receive, effectively contradicting the 1993 referendum result.

The established post-war party system underwent a dramatic transformation in the early 1990s following the exposure of political corruption that had operated on a massive scale through most of the major national parties. This exposure, combined with other factors (the collapse of communism in central and eastern Europe; the demands of European integration and the Maastricht Treaty; the rise of protest movements), led to the organizational and electoral collapse of the existing governing parties, and the emergence of new parties and alliances – although there has also been a large element of rebranding and recycling. A key change has occurred through bipolarisation of the party system and the emergence of two blocs – the centre-left Olive Tree and the centre-right House of Freedoms – in place of the old system based on the permanent dominance of a centrist party (Christian Democracy) and its allies.

The general election of May 13, 2001, resulted in a distribtion of Chamber seats as follows: House of Freedoms 368 seats (with 49.4% of the proportional vote), Olive Tree 242 (35.0%), Communist Refoundation Party (PRC) 11 (5.0%), South Tyrol People's Party (SVP) 8, others 1. In the simultaneous Senate elections, the House of Freedoms won 177 seats (42.5%), the Olive Tree 125 (38.7%), the SVP 5 (0.9%), PRC 3 (5.0%), European Democracy 2 (3.2%), Italy of Values 1, Autonomous Lombardy Alliance 1, Valdostan Union 1.

Party Coalitions

House of Freedoms
Casa delle Libertà
Address. c/o Camera dei Deputati, Piazza Montecitorio, 00186 Rome
Email. info@casadelleliberta.net
Website. www.casadelleliberta.net
Leader. Silvio Berlusconi

The *Casa delle Libertà* was the campaigning title adopted for the May 2001 parliamentary elections by the right-wing parties previously linked in the Freedom Alliance (*Polo delle Libertà*, PL). The main participating parties were *Forza Italia* (FI), the National Alliance (AN), the Northern League (LN), the New Italian Socialist Party (NPSI), the Christian Democratic Centre (CCD) and the United Christian Democrats (CDU). The CCD and the CDU were joined in an alliance called the White Flower, and after the elections formed the Union of Christian Democrats and Democrats of the Centre (UDC)

The PL had been formed for the March 1994 general elections, winning a 43% vote share and coming to power under the premiership of Silvio Berlusconi. The alliance quickly experienced dissension, which resulted in the exit of the LN in December 1994. This brought about the collapse of the PL government, and its replacement by a "technocratic" government under the leadership of Berlusconi's former Treasury Minister, Lamberto Dini. Minus the LN, the PL alliance otherwise remained largely in place for the April 1996 general elections, although it was beset by continuing divisions. Although the PL's overall share of the proportional vote rose to some 44%, about 10% higher than that obtained by the centre-left Olive Tree (*Ulivo*) parties, the latter obtained a relative majority of seats, thus keeping the PL parties in opposition to several governments dominated by the Democrats of the Left.

Campaigning on a pledge to "revolutionize" Italy's governmental system, the *Casa delle Libertà* swept to a decisive victory in the May 2001 elections, winning 368 out of 630 seats in the Chamber (with 49.6% of the proportional vote) and 177 of the 315 elective Senate seats. The following month Berlusconi was sworn in for his second term as Prime Minister, forming Italy's 59th government since World War II. It included, at the outset, nine FI ministers, five from the AN, three from the LN, two Christian Democrats and five independents.

Olive Tree Alliance
Ulivo
Address. P.zza SS. Apostoli 55, 00187 Rome
Telephone. +39 06 696 881
Email. scrivi@perlulivo.it
Website. www.ulivo.it
Leader. Francesco Rutelli

The centre-left *Ulivo* alliance dates from July 1995, when a Rome conference of the main centre-left parties endorsed economics professor Romano Prodi, then of the liberal wing of the Christian Democratic Italian Popular Party (PPI) and later leader of the Democrats, as their standard-bearer in the forthcoming general election. In April 1996, the *Ulivo* parties won 34.8% of the Chamber proportional vote, fewer than the right-wing Freedom Alliance, but secured a relative majority of 284 of the 475 Chamber seats distributed according to the plurality formula. Prodi accordingly formed a minority government, staffed by the parties of the Olive Tree Alliance but dependent on the external support of Communist Refoundation (PRC).

The Prodi administration succeeded in winning the agreement of the other EU member states to Italy's inclusion among the first wave of countries to adopt the euro (from 1

Jan. 1999), but attempts to reform the Constitution through the Parliamentary Commission for Constitutional Reform (the so-called *Bicamerale*) made little progress in the face of right-wing opposition. The government's room for manoeuvre also suffered from its dependence on the PRC, the withdrawal of whose support caused the ousting of Prodi in October 1998. Prodi's was followed by three further centre-left governments, one headed by the leader of the Democrats of the Left (DS), D'Alema, and one by the ex-Socialist and former Prime Minister (1992-93) Giuliano Amato (whose government took office following D'Alema's resignation in the wake of the April 2000 regional elections, which had resulted in set-backs for the centre-left).

In October 2000 the *Ulivo* parties endorsed Francesco Rutelli, the popular mayor of Rome, as the coalition's prime ministerial candidate. Rutelli had entered politics in 1983 as a member of the Radical Party and had later joined the Green Federation, before switching to the Democrats in 1999. His own power base within the *Ulivo* was the centrist *Margherita* alliance, embracing the Democrats, the PPI, Italian Renewal (RI) and the Democratic Union for Europe (UDeuR). But the more left-wing DS remained dominant in the *Ulivo*, which also included the Sunflower alliance (of the Greens and the Italian Democratic Socialists) as well as the PdCI and a faction of the regional South Tyrol People's Party (SVP).

The *Ulivo* was defeated at the hands of the right-wing House of Freedoms alliance in the May 2001 parliamentary elections, winning only 242 of the 630 Chamber seats (with 35% of the proportional vote) and 125 of the 315 seats in the Senate (with 38.7%). However the centre-left took some consolation from its success in retaining control of Rome, Turin and Naples in mayoral elections held at the same time, and from the fact that its defeat owed more to the centre-right's more effective system of electoral alliances than it did to significant shifts in the distribution of voting support between the two coalitions.

For the June 2004 elections to the European Parliament, the DS, the *Margherita* and the SDI (together with a smaller group, the European Republicans – *Repubblicani europei*) formed, in contrast with the parties of the centre-right, a single list of candidates under the umbrella heading "United in the Olive Tree" (*Uniti nell'Ulivo*), through which they obtained 31.1% of the vote and 25 seats.

National Parties

Communist Refoundation
Partito della Rifondazione Comunista (PRC)
Address. Viale Policlinico 131, 00161 Rome
Telephone. + 39 06 441 821
Fax. +39 06 441 82286
Email. esteri.prc@rifondazione.it
Website. www.rifondazione.it
Leadership. Fausto Bertinotti (secretary-general); Francesco Giordano (Chamber group leader); Luigi Malabarba (Senate group leader)

PRC came into being in February 1991 at a meeting of members of the Italian Communist Party (PCI) opposed to the preference of the majority in favour of the party's transformation into a non-communist party with a new name: the Democratic Party of the Left (PDS), renamed the Democrats of the Left (DS) in 1998. After legal proceedings, PRC was awarded the right to use the traditional hammer and sickle symbol of the PCI and was formally launched at a Rome conference in May 1991. Having won 5.6% of the vote in the 1992 general elections, the PRC advanced to 6.0% in 1994, when it was part of the left-wing Progressive Alliance (AP) headed by the PDS. Subsequently distancing itself from the AP, the PRC contested the June 1994 European Parliament elections on a joint list with other ex-PCI elements, winning

6.1% of the vote and five seats, while the April–May 1995 regional elections yielded an 8.4% vote share.

In June 1995 the PRC was weakened by the defection of 14 of its 35 lower house deputies in protest at the alleged "isolationism" of the party leadership, the defectors becoming the Unitary Communists (*Comunisti Unitari*), most of whom later joined the DS. Undeterred, the rump of the PRC contested the April 1996 parliamentary elections independently and increased its vote share to 8.6%, which restored its Chamber representation to 35 seats. Although it had, by mutual agreement, remained outside the centre-left Olive Tree alliance, the PRC opted to give qualified parliamentary backing to the Olive Tree minority government of Romano Prodi.

After the PRC had polled strongly in local elections in April–May 1997, persistent strains over the PRC's opposition to government economic policies eventually resulted in the collapse of the Prodi government in October 1998 and its replacement by a majority coalition headed by the DS. Now deprived of its leverage in parliament, the PRC was also weakened by the concurrent launching of the Party of Italian Communists (PdCI) under the leadership of Armando Cossutta, until then president of the PRC.

In the May 2001 parliamentary elections the PRC polled 5% of the proportional vote, taking 11 Chamber seats and three in the Senate, and in the June 2004 European elections 6.1% and five seats. Its representatives in the European Parliament sit in the European United Left/Nordic Green Left group and the party is also a member of the New European Left Forum (NELF).

Daisy
Margherita

Address. Via Sant'Andrea delle Fratte 16, 00187 Rome
Telephone. +39 06 695 321
Fax. +39 06 695 3253
Email. sede@margheritaonline.it
Website. www.margheritaonline.it/
Leaders. Francesco Rutelli (president); Pierluigi Castagnetti (Chamber group leader); Willer Bordon (Senate group leader)

Originally formed as an alliance of four parties – the Italian Popular Party, the Democrats, Italian Renewal (RI) and the Democratic Union for Europe (UDeuR) – *Margherita* was the name given by these parties to the joint list of candidates they fielded for the proportionally distributed seats at the time of the 2001 general election.

The Italian Popular Party (PPI) had been the name chosen by one of the Christian Democrats' (DC's) two "successor parties" when the DC, beset by corruption scandals, had split in January 1994. For long Italy's dominant formation, the DC was consistently returned as the largest parliamentary party until the 1990s. For the general election of 1994, the PPI had formed a centrist alliance with Antonio Segni's "Pact for National Renewal", called the "Pact for Italy", but then, having had confirmation from this experience that centre-placed candidacies, outside one or other of the two main coalitions, were likely to be unproductive given the nature of the electoral system, its anti-Berlusconi wing decided to join the emerging *Ulivo* coalition, while a more right-leaning faction joined the Freedom Alliance as the United Christian Democrats (CDU).

The Democrats had been launched in February 1999 by Romano Prodi in the wake of the collapse of his government the previous October. Seeing themselves as a secular, centre-left, reformist party firmly committed to the consolidation of majoritarian democracy and a bipolar future, the Democrats' *raison d'être* was to campaign for a strengthening of the *Ulivo* and of its authority *vis-à-vis* its constituent parties. Groupings backing the new party included the anti-Mafia Network Movement for Democracy (*La Rete*); the Italy of Values movement formed by Antonio Di Pietro following his exit from the Prodi government in November 1996 in contentious circumstances, and the Hundred Cities for a New Italy (*Centocittà per un Italia Nuova*) movement of mayors, environmentalists and voluntary groups. For the 1999 European elections, a joint list put forward by the Democrats and *La Rete* won seven of Italy's 87 seats with 7.7% of the vote.

Italian Renewal was the political grouping that had been established in February 1996 by ex-Prime Minister Lamberto Dini, when, having been Treasury Minister in the first Berlusconi government in 1994, he decided to carry on his political career under the aegis of the *Ulivo*. Describing itself, at its founding, as a "new, moderate and reformist political formation of the centre", RI's ideological heritage, like that of the PPI and the UdeuR (see separate entry), was essentially that of Christian Democracy.

The *Margherita*'s leader in the 2001 campaign was the Democrats' leader, Francesco Rutelli, who also headed the overall *Ulivo* coalition. Although the *Ulivo* was defeated, the *Margherita* polled well, winning 14.5% of the proportional vote in the Chamber elections. It had 84 members in the new Chamber and 41 in the Senate.

The list's success gave Rutelli the impetus he needed to attempt a merger of the *Margherita*'s four components into a single party. The congress that was designed formally to ratify the merger of these components was finally scheduled for March 22-24, 2002, but, largely owing to uncertainties about the project within the individual parties, it did not represent the emergence of an unambiguously unitary actor. The UDeuR refused, at their congress between March 15-17, to merge with the new formation at all. Meanwhile, the structure of the new formation was such as to allow parties such as the PPI to continue to exist as cultural associations affiliated to the new formation. In June 2002, UDeuR deputies and senators completed the break with the new formation when they walked out of the *Margherita*'s groups in the two chambers of Parliament apparently because of a dispute over the amount of money due to the UDeuR under the laws providing for the public funding of political parties.

For the June 2004 elections, the *Margherita* formed part of the Olive Tree Alliance's single list which obtained 31.1% of the vote and 25 of Italy's 87 seats in the European Parliament.

Democratic Union for Europe–Popular Alliance
Unione Democratica per l'Europa–Alleanza Popolare (UDeuR)

Address. Largo Arenula, 34, 00186 Rome
Telephone. +39 06 684 241
Email. info@alleanza-popolare.it
Website. www.udeur.org
Leadership. Clemente Mastella (political secretary); Mino Martinazzoli (president)

The UDeuR began life as the centre-right Democratic Union for the Republic (UDR), which was launched in February 1998 by Francesco Cossiga, who had been elected President of Italy in 1985 as candidate of the Christian Democratic Party. The UDR initiative had been taken with the aim of restructuring party competition through the creation of a new social democratic pole on the left and a new liberal democratic pole on the right. To do this, it was necessary to exclude the right-wing National Alliance (AN) from government formation, isolate the left and attract dissident parliamentarians belonging to both of the two main coalitions in the construction of a party that would become *Forza Italia's* (FI's) main ally.

The project had some initial success. Within days of its birth it had gained the support of 51 parliamentarians and provoked major splits within the Christian Democratic Centre (CCD) and the United Christian Democrats (CDU), whose dissidents thereby distanced themselves from the Freedom Alliance of conservative parties. In October 1998 it managed to bring about the creation of a centre-left government independent of the PRC. However, in December 1999, it broke up over the formation of a second centre-left government. Some, under Clemente Mastella (a former DC leader who in 1994 had helped to found the CCD) joined the government as the UdeuR. Others, notably CDU leader Rocco Buttiglione, returned to the centre-right Freedom Alliance.

The UDeuR remained within the Olive Tree alliance for the May 2001 parliamentary elections, fielding, with the PPI, the Democrats and Italian Renewal, a joint list of candidates, called the *Margherita* (Daisy), for the Chamber proportional seats. It therefore shared in the centre-left's defeat. In March 2002, it decided against joining the other three parties in the formal merger that turned the *Margherita* into a fully-fledged political party, and in June of that year it abandoned the *Margherita*'s groups in the Chamber and Senate in protest at the way it felt it had been treated over the share-out of funds made available under the laws providing for the public funding of political parties. Adopting the title Popular Alliance–Democratic Union for Europe, in the June 2004 European elections, the party polled 1.3% of the votes and obtained one seat. The UDeuR member of the European Parliament sits in the European People's Party/European Democrats group.

Democrats of the Left
Democratici di Sinistra (DS)

Address. Via Palermo 12, 00184 Rome
Telephone. +39 06 480 231; + 39 06 671 11
Email. posta@democraticidisinistra.it
Website. www.dsonline.it
Leadership. Piero Fassino (secretary general); Massimo D'Alema (president); Luciano Violante (Chamber group leader); Gavino Angius (Senate group leader)

The DS is directly descended, organizationally, from the Italian Communist Party (*Partito Comunista Italiano*, PCI), which voted at an extraordinary congress held in March 1990 to abandon its traditional name. Adoption of the new name, "Democratic Party of the Left" (PDS), followed in February 1991, at a final congress of the PCI. A further change came in February 1998, when the party "absorbed" the Unitary Communists (*Comunisti Unitari*) who had defected from the Communist Refoundation Party in 1995, together with Spini's *Laburisti* (ex-PSI), Carniti's *Cristiano-sociali* (ex-Christian Democrats) and Bogi's left Republicans.

Formed as the result of a split in the Italian Socialist Party at its 1921 Livorno congress, the PCI went underground during the Mussolini period, its then leader, Palmiro Togliatti, escaping to Moscow, where he worked for the Comintern until his return to Italy in 1944. In the early 1940s the PCI played a leading role in the struggle against the Fascist regime and the German Nazi occupation forces. Under Togliatti's leadership the PCI participated in the early post-war coalition governments from 1944, before being expelled from the governing coalition in May 1947. The party played a leading role, through its representatives in the Constituent Assembly, in the drafting of the post-war Constitution, which came into force on Jan.1, 1948. Following the decisive election victory of the Christian Democrats in April 1948 the PCI took the road of democratic opposition and subsequently became the largest and most influential non-ruling Communist party in Europe. Throughout the post-war period the PCI was Italy's second largest party (after the Christian Democrats) in terms of both votes and seats in parliament.

From 1975 the PCI governed a large number of regions, provinces and municipalities (particularly in the "red belt" of Emilia-Romagna, Umbria and Tuscany), usually in coalition with other left-wing parties. At national level, the PCI's

demands to be admitted to government were resisted. However, following the sharp increase in its vote in June 1976 (to over 34%) successive Christian Democrat-led governments accepted its parliamentary support, initially through abstention and subsequently, from March 1978, on the basis of its inclusion in the official parliamentary majority. The PCI withdrew from this arrangement in January 1979 and reverted to a position of full opposition. In the elections of that year its vote share fell to 30.4%.

In 1980 the PCI adopted a new "democratic alternative" strategy based on a sought-after alliance with the Socialists – but the latter remained committed to centre-left coalitions. In the 1983 general elections the PCI again lost ground, winning 198 seats and 29.9% of the vote, although in the June 1984 European Parliament elections it emerged as the largest party, winning 33.3%, largely as the result of a wave of popular sympathy for its leader, Enrico Berlinguer, who died as the result of a stroke suffered just a few days before polling day. In November 1984, under its new leader, Alessandro Natta, the party was strengthened by the absorption of the Party of Proletarian Unity for Communism (originally founded in 972). However, it lost ground in the May 1985 regional and local elections (surrendering Rome to the Christian Democrats) and suffered a further setback in the June 1987 general elections, when its Chamber representation fell to 177 seats and its share of the vote to 26.6%.

In June 1988 Natta was succeeded as leader by Achille Occhetto, who promised a "new course" for Italian communism. This process turned out to be the abandonment of much of the traditional party line and was accelerated by the collapse of the communist regimes in central and eastern Europe. Occhetto proposed in the Autumn of 1989 the transformation of the PCI into a non-communist party of the left, which he achieved in February 1991 through the birth of the PDS. This development witnessed a split in the party and the simultaneous birth of Communist Refoundation. The new party experienced a further decline in its vote as compared to that of its predecessor, securing only 16.1% at the general election of 1992. It advanced to 20.4% in March 1994, although it failed to make the hoped-for breakthrough to political power as the leading member of the left-wing Progressive Alliance. In the June 1994 European Parliament election its support slipped to 19.1% and 16 seats. This setback precipitated the resignation of Occhetto as general secretary and his replacement by Massimo D'Alema.

In July 1995 the PDS took the momentous decision to enter the centre-left Olive Tree alliance (*Ulivo*), which registered a major victory in the April 1996 parliamentary elections. The PDS secured 21.1% of the vote and 156 seats in its own right, and obtained nine posts in the new centre-left government under Romano Prodi.

The launch of the DS, at a conference held in Florence in February 1998, was envisaged as a means of creating a new democratic socialist party as an alternative to the idea of a centre-left "Democratic Party" (viewed with sympathy by those around Walter Weltroni in the PDS) which would bring together the components of the *Ulivo* within one organization.

D'Alema and the DS were the main political beneficiaries of the collapse of the Prodi government in October 1998, the DS leader becoming Prime Minister of a new centre-left coalition. Following his assumption of the office of Prime Minister, D'Alema was succeeded as DS national secretary by former Deputy Prime Minister Walter Veltroni. The DS slipped to 17.4% of the vote and 15 seats at the June 1999 European Parliament election. It also shared in the centre-left's heavy defeat in regional elections in April 2000, which resulted in D'Alema's replacement as Prime Minister by Giuliano Amato as the leader of a further centre-left government in which the DS remained dominant. In October 2000, the DS supported the selection of Francesco Rutelli, then mayor of Rome and a member of the centrist Democrats, as the *Ulivo*'s standard-bearer for the May 2001 parliamentary elections. The party shared in the *Ulivo*'s defeat by the right-wing House of Freedoms, its own share of the proportional vote in the Chamber elections slipping to 16.6%. The DS group in the new Chamber had 136 members and its Senate group 65 members.

A consolation for the DS was its success in electing Walter Veltroni as mayor of Rome, also in May 2001, in succession to Francesco Rutelli. Veltroni resigned as DS national secretary on 1 June and was replaced by Piero Fassino. Fassino's political outlook is close to that of Massimo D'Alema, who was elected to the presidency of the party. For the June 2004 elections, the Democrats formed part of the Olive Tree Alliance's single list which obtained 31.1% of the vote and 25 seats.

DS representatives in the European Parliament sit as members of the Party of European Socialists, the party having been admitted to the Socialist International in 1992.

Forza Italia (FI)

Address. Via dell'Umiltà 36, 00100 Rome
Telephone. +39 06 673 11
Fax. +39 06 599 41315
Email. lettere@forza-italia.it
Website. www.forza-italia.it
Leadership. Silvio Berlusconi (president); Elio Vito (Chamber group leader); Renato Giuseppe Schifani (Senate group leader); Claudio Scajola (national co-ordinator)
Launched in January 1994, FI's name by design recalls the shouts of Italian football supporters when urging on their national team, and is thus variously translated into English as "Go Italy!" or "Come on Italy!". The party was created by Silvio Berlusconi, Italy's most powerful media tycoon (and owner of the leading Milan football club), whose aim was to prevent an electoral victory by the former communist party, the Democratic Party of the Left (PDS), later renamed Democrats of the Left (DS). To this end, it organized the right-wing Freedom Alliance (PL), which at the March 1994 election secured 366 seats and an absolute majority in the Chamber of Deputies, thus going on to form the new government.

In the June 1994 European Parliament elections the PL won a narrow majority of 44 of Italy's 87 seats, 27 of which were taken by FI on a vote share of 30.6%. However, growing strains between the coalition parties culminated in the collapse of the Berlusconi government in December 1994 as a result of the withdrawal of the Northern League (LN). In the April 1996 general elections FI remained at 21% within a reduced PL alliance and the centre-left Olive Tree alliance came to power.

In opposition, FI was damaged by court proceedings against Berlusconi, while the PL was weakened in February 1998 by defections to what became the Democratic Union for Europe (UDeuR). Nevertheless, in April 1998 Berlusconi was formally elected FI president, while in June 1998 the party achieved wider respectability by being accepted as a member of the European People's Party group in the European Parliament, having previously been part of the Union for a Europe of Nations group. Although Berlsuconi faced a wide range of criminal proceedings, his acquittal in March 1999 on a tax fraud charge helped FI to head the poll at the June 1999 European Parliament election, when it took 25.2% of the vote and 22 seats.

For the May 2001 parliamentary elections the PL became the House of Freedoms, under the leadership of Berlusconi, who promised that an FI-led government would introduce large tax cuts, higher minimum pensions, lower unemployment, more public works and better policing of urban areas. Despite still having charges pending against him, Berlusconi achieved a decisive victory, the alliance winning 368 of the

630 Chamber seats and 177 seats in the Senate. FI took 29.4% of the Chamber proportional vote, its group in the new Chamber having 178 members, its Senate group 82. The following month Berlusconi was sworn in for his second term as Prime Minister, forming Italy's 59th government since World War II. In the June 2004 European elections, FI dropped to 21% of the vote and 16 seats.

FI representatives in the European Parliament sit in the European People's Party/European Democrats group. FI is also a member of the European Democratic Union.

Green Federation
Federazione dei Verdi

Address. Via Salandra 6, 00187 Rome
Telephone. +39 06 420 3061
Fax. +39 06 420 04600
Email. federazione@verdi.it
Website. www.verdi.it
Leadership. Grazia Francescato (president); Stefano Bocco (Chamber group leader)
The Italian Greens were founded as a national electoral movement at a constituent assembly held in Florence in December 1984. The formation won some 1.8% of the vote overall in regional and local elections in May 1985, when it was backed by the Radical Party, and made a significant breakthrough in the July 1987 general elections, winning 2.5% of the vote and returning 13 Chamber deputies and one member of the Senate.

The Greens improved further in 1992, winning four Senate and 16 Chamber seats on a vote share of 2.8%. For the 1994 general elections the Greens joined the Progressive Alliance, headed by what later became the Democrats of the Left (DS), their vote share slipping to 2.7%. In a recovery in the June 1994 European Parliament elections, the Greens won three seats on a 3.2% vote share. Joining the centre-left Olive Tree alliance for the April 1996 parliamentary elections, the Greens won 2.5% of the proportional vote and had the satisfaction of seeing party member Edo Ronchi appointed Environment Minister in the new Olive Tree government. He was joined by Laura Balbo as Equal Opportunities Minister when a new coalition was formed in October 1998 under the leadership of the DS.

Damaged by the rival appeal of the Emma Bonino List (Radical Party) in the June 1999 European elections, the Greens slipped to 1.8% of the vote and two seats. In January 2000 a party conference in Chianciano established a more formal leadership structure, electing Grazia Francescato as president. For the May 2001 parliamentary elections the Greens joined with the Italian Democratic Socialists to field, for the proportionally distributed Chamber seats, a joint list of candidates that took as its name "the Sunflower" (*Il Girasole*). This formation shared in the Olive Tree's heavy defeat, winning only 2.2% of the proportional vote in the Chamber elections, and it broke up shortly afterwards. The Greens emerged from the election with seven deputies in the new Chamber and 10 members in the new Senate. In the June 2004 European elections they won 2.5% of the vote and two seats.

The Italian Greens are members of the European Federation of Green Parties. The party's representatives in the European Parliament sit as part of the Greens/European Free Alliance group.

Italian Democratic Socialists
Socialisti Democratici Italiani (SDI)

Address. Piazza San Lorenzo in Lucina 26, 00186 Rome
Telephone. +39 06 687 8688
Fax. +39 683 07659
Email. socialisti@sdionline.it
Website. www.sdionline.it
Leadership. Enrico Boselli (president); Roberto Villetti and

Gianfranco Schietroma (vice-presidents)

The SDI resulted from the merger in 1998 of the Italian Socialists (SI), a designation adopted by the historic Italian Socialist Party (*Partito Socialista Italiano*, PSI) in 1994, and the Italian Democratic Socialist Party (*Partito Socialista Democratico Italiano*, PSDI), which itself had derived from a left–right split in the PSI in 1947.

Founded in 1892, the PSI had first split at its Livorno congress in 1921 when a pro-Bolshevik group broke away to form the Italian Communist Party (Democrats of the Left, DS). At the Rome congress in January 1947 Giuseppe Saragat's right-wing PSI faction, opposed to the majority Pietro Nenni wing's policy of alliance with the Communists, broke away to form the Workers' Socialist Party (PSLI), which in 1952 merged with other factions to become the PSDI. Whereas the Democratic Socialists took part in successive coalitions in 1947-63 headed by the Christian Democrats, the rump PSI remained in opposition, its Chamber representation rising to 87 seats in 1963.

Following the 1963 "opening to the left", the PSI repeatedly co-operated with the dominant Christian Democrats, either by joining coalition governments or by giving external support. The PSI and PSDI signed a reunification agreement in 1966, a combined PSI/PSDI list called the Unified Socialist Party (*Partito Socialista Unificato*, PSU). The new party polled disappointingly, however, in the 1968 national elections, and the two parties re-established their separate identities, although both usually continued to be part of the centre-left majority. Having resigned from the Fanfani government, the PSI advanced from 62 to 73 seats in the June 1983 Chamber elections, with the result that party leader Bettino Craxi formed Italy's first-ever Socialist-led government, based on a coalition with the Christian Democrats, the PSDI and two other parties.

The Craxi administration lasted an unprecedented four years, eventually resigning in March 1987. In the June 1987 elections the PSI gained further ground, obtaining 94 seats and 14.3% of the vote, subsequently joining a further five-party coalition headed by the Christian Democrats and including the PSDI (which declined from 23 to 17 seats and 3%). In the April 1992 elections the PSI slipped to 92 seats and 13.6% of the popular vote, but remained in the government coalition, as did the PSDI, which had won 17 seats and 2.7%.

Craxi then came under judicial investigation on numerous charges of financial corruption and illegal party funding, with the consequence that he resigned as PSI leader in February 1993, having served 17 years in the post. In the wake of charges against many other PSI representatives, the party slumped to 2.2% in the March 1994 Chamber elections, in which the PSDI failed to win any Chamber seats at all. Some PSI elements contested the elections under the banner of the Democratic Alliance, doing the same in the European Parliament elections in June 1994, in which the PSI and PSDI managed only one seat each. The following month Craxi received a long prison sentence, and still faced other charges, along with several dozen other former PSI officials. Craxi, however, never went to prison because he moved to Tunisia before the verdict and later later died there.

Seeking to recover its former constituency, the PSI transformed itself into the SI in November 1994, with a number of Craxi supporters leaving the party to establish a Federation of Democratic Socialists (FDS), which would later provide the basis for the launch of the New Italian Socialist Party (NPSI). In the April 1996 parliamentary elections the SI and the PSDI were both components of the victorious Olive Tree coalition, in close alliance with the new Italian Renewal formation. Reunification of the SI and PSDI was finally accomplished in February 1998 when the two came together with Intini's Socialist Party to create a single organization, the SDI, of sufficient weight to enable it to engage profitably with D'Alema's Democratic Party of the Left (PDS, subsequently Democrats of the Left, DS). The SDI went on to obtain one portfolio in the government formed in October 1998 by D'Alema.

In the June 1999 European elections the SDI won only two seats with 2.1% of the vote. For the May 2001 parliamentary elections the SDI fielded, with the Greens, a joint list of candidates called the Sunflower (*Il Girasole*). The list shared in the Olive Tree's heavy defeat, winning only 2.2% of the proportional vote in the Chamber elections. The SDI elected nine deputies to the new Chamber, and the Sunflower broke up shortly afterwards. In the June 2004 European elections, the SDI formed part of the Olive Tree Alliance's single list, which obtained 31.1% of the vote and 25 seats.

SDI representatives in the European Parliament sit as members of the Party of European Socialists. The SDI inherited the Socialist International membership held by both the PSI and the PSDI.

Italian Radicals
Radicali Italiani

Address. Via di Torre Argentina 76, 00186 Rome

Telephone. +39 06 689 791

Fax. +39 06 880 5396

Email. lcoscioni@virgilio.it

Website. www.radicali.it

Leadership. Luca Coscioni (president); Daniele Capezzone (secretary)

The Radical Party (PR) was founded in December 1955 on a platform of non-violence, anti-militarism, human and civil rights, and the construction of a "socialist and democratic society". It has also campaigned for women's and homosexual rights, against nuclear energy and against "extermination by famine" in the Third World. Originally formed by a left-wing faction of the Italian Liberal Party, the PR sponsored the legalization of divorce in 1970 and subsequently campaigned against the use of the referendum instrument to reverse the measure. It successfully supported legislation on conscientious objection, the lowering of the age of majority to 18 years, more liberal laws on drugs offences and family relations, and the partial legalization of abortion. The Radicals were the first Italian party to have a female secretary (in 1977–78).

Having obtained four Chamber seats in 1976, the Radicals achieved a significant success in the 1979 elections, in which they won 18 seats in the Chamber and two in the Senate. After slipping to 11 Chamber seats in 1983, the party advanced to 13 in 1987, its new deputies including Ilona Staller, a Hungarian-born pornographic film actress better known as Cicciolina. In January 1988 a Radical congress in Bologna decided that the party would not take part in any future Italian elections.

Meanwhile, in November 1979 the then PR secretary-general, Jean Fabre (a French national), had been sentenced by a Paris court to a month in prison for evading conscription. More serious was the 30-year prison sentence passed in 1984 on a PR deputy, Antonio Negri, following his conviction for complicity in terrorist acts, although he and seven others were acquitted in January 1986 of being "moral leaders" of extremist groups such as the Red Brigades.

Marco Pannella's return to leadership of the Radicals in 1992 served to end the electoral non-participation policy and also shifted the party to the right. Contesting the March 1994 elections as part of the Freedom Alliance headed by *Forza Italia*, the Radicals presented a "Pannella List" but won no seats in its own right. Running as "Pannella Reformers" in the June 1994 European Parliament elections, it won two seats with a 2.1% vote share.

The Radicals again presented a "Pannella List" in the June 1996 national elections, failing to win representation in the Chamber (with 1.9% of the proportional vote) but returning one member to the Senate. They contested the June 1999 European elections as the "Emma Bonino List" which, headed by the popular former European commissioner, secured 8.5% of the national vote and seven of Italy's 87 seats. One of those elected was Pannella, who in November 1999 was given a four-month prison sentence for distributing marijuana to draw attention to what he called "the absurdity of the law [outlawing the drug]".

The Radicals remained independent of the main alliances in the May 2001 parliamentary elections, presenting a "Pannella-Bonino List" which won 2.3% of the vote for the Chamber and 2% of the Senate election vote, but no seats in either case. During the campaign Bonino staged a six-day hunger strike in protest against media bias and the non-coverage of smaller parties. In the June 2004 European elections, the party campaigned as the Emma Bonino List, obtaining 2.3% of the vote and two seats.

The Radical/Bonino representatives in the European Parliament are among the "non-attached" contingent. The Radicals have spawned the Transnational Radical Party, with members in 43 countries.

Italian Republican Party
Partito Repubblicano Italiano (PRI)
Address. Corso Vittorio Emanuele II 326, 00186 Rome
Telephone. +39 06 683 4037
Fax. +39 06 654 2990
Email. ufficiostampapri@yahoo.it
Website. www.pri.it
Leadership. Francesco Nucara (national co-ordinator)
Founded as such in 1894, the PRI has its origins in the 1831 association, *Giovine Italia* (Young Italy), which, as a grouping of republicans, fought under the leadership of Giuseppe Mazzini, for national unity and independence. The PRI was dissolved by the Fascist regime and reconstituted in 1943, taking part in the Resistance. Under the republican constitution introduced in January 1948 the PRI was a partner in numerous coalition governments led by Christian Democrats from 1948 to 1981.

In June 1981 the then PRI leader, Giovanni Spadolini, became the first non-Christian Democrat to head an Italian government since the war, forming a five-party centre-left Cabinet which lasted until November 1982. Thereafter the PRI continued its participation in centre-left coalitions until going into opposition in April 1991.

A PRI member, Antonio Maccanico, accepted the post of Cabinet Secretary in the Ciampi government formed in May 1993, although the party itself remained in opposition. Having won 4.4% of the national vote in 1992, the PRI contested the March 1994 poll as a member of the Democratic Alliance (AD), and thus also of the broader Progressive Alliance (AP). In the June 1994 European balloting a specifically PRI list secured 0.7% of the vote, its one seat going to Giorgio La Malfa. Having resigned the party leadership in 1988 and been reinstated in January 1994, La Malfa again resigned in October 1994 and was again reinstated in March 1995.

The PRI contested the April 1996 general elections within Maccanico's new (and short-lived) Democratic Union, and therefore as part of the victorious Olive Tree alliance of centre-left parties. In the resultant Prodi coalition government Maccanico became Minister of Posts and Telecommunications, but was not reappointed when Prodi gave way in October 1998 to a more left-leaning coalition headed by the Democrats of the Left (DS).

The PRI contested the June 1999 European elections on a joint list with the Federation of Italian Liberals which obtained 0.5% of the vote and one seat. This was taken by PRI member Luciana Sbarbati, who in the European Parliament sat as a member of the European Liberal,

Democratic and Reformist group. At the forty-second party congress held in Bari in January 2001, a majority concluded that the time had come to end the party's association with the centre left – with the result that it contested the general election that year as part of the House of Freedoms. Following the election, Francesco Nucara became Undersecretary of State at the Ministry of the Environment and Giorgio La Malfa, president of the Chamber of Deputies' Finance Commission. In July 2001, La Malfa resigned as party secretary. For the June 2004 European elections, the party allied itself with the maverick, Vittorio Sgarbi, campaigning under the title "PRI I Liberal Sgarbi". The result was 0.7% of the vote and no seats.

Italy of Values
Italia dei Valori (IdV)
Address. Via dei Prefetti, 17, 00186 Rome
Telephone. +39 06 684 0721
Fax. +39 06 681 32711
Email. italiadeivalori@antoniodipietro.it
Website. www.antoniodipietro.it
Leader. Antonio Di Pietro (president)
IdV was launched in 1999 by Antonio Di Pietro, who as a magistrate in Milan, had achieved fame in the early 1990s for his "clean hands" anti-corruption investigations which had helped to bring down Italy's old business and political elite. He had joined the Olive Tree government in May 1996 as Public Works Minister but had resigned six months later in protest against the launching of an investigation – later ruled to be illegitimate – into his own alleged corruption. In November 1997 he had been elected to the Senate in a by-election, standing with the support of the Democrats of the Left (DS), but had gravitated to the Democrats after forming IdV, being elected to the European Parliament in June 1999 on the Democrats' list.

Contesting the May 2001 parliamentary elections independently as the *Lista di Pietro Italia dei Valori*, the party won 3.9% of the proportional vote for the Chamber (and no seats) and 3.4% in the Senate contest, which yielded one upper house seat (whose holder however defected to *Forza Italia* as soon as the new parliament met). In the run-up to the June 2004 European elections, Di Pietro formed an alliance with former PCI/PDS leader Achille Occhetto, and campaigned under the name *Società Civile Di Pietro Occhetto Italia dei Valori*. This was an attempt to harness the support of the grass roots movements hostile to the centre left because of its inadequacies, to the more centrist supporters of Di Pietro. However, the experiment was a failure, the alliance obtaining a mere 2.1% of the vote and two seats.

Di Pietro's can fairly be described as a populist party, one that conceives of itself as a formation which, above all others in Italy, seeks to defend the ordinary, honest citizen against illegality, corrupt government and uncertainty about impartial application of the law.

In the European Parliament Di Pietro sits in the European Liberal, Democratic and Reformist (ELDR) group, to which the IdV was formally admitted in December 2000.

Liberal Democratic Party (Segni Scognamiglio Pact)
Partito dei Liberaldemocratici (Patto Segni Scognamiglio)
Address. Via Belsiana 100, 00187 Rome
Telephone. +39 06 678 6240
Fax. +39 06 678 9890
Email. info@ilpatto.it
Website. www.ilpatto.it
Leadership. Mario Segni (secretary); Carlo Scognamiglio (president)
Founded on June 21, 2003, the Liberal Democratic Party is the most recent attempt by former Christian Democratic

(DC) dissident Mario Segni to create a strong political force distinguishable both from the centre-left and centre-right alliances. Having left the DC, Segni launched, for the March 1994 general elections, the Pact for National Renewal (popularly known as the "Segni Pact", PS), drawing in the Italian Popular Party (PPI) to assume the dominant role. Having received only 4.6% of the national vote on that occasion, the PS fell back to 3.3% in the June 1994 European Parliament elections, in which it won three seats.

Segni was an initial supporter of the centre-left Olive Tree alliance in 1995, but withdrew before the April 1996 general elections, which his party did not contest. He then launched a grass-roots movement for political reform (*Comitati di base per la Costituente*, COBAC), calling for the election of a constituent assembly to write a new constitution. In the June 1999 European elections the PS was allied with the right-wing National Alliance (AN), their joint list winning 10.3% of the vote and nine of Italy's 87 seats (including a seat for Segni himself).

Seeing itself as a centre-right formation wishing to strengthen the bi-polar character of the party system, the Liberal Democratic Party nevertheless opposes the Berlusconi government, wishing to build a centre right that it regards as "truly liberal and democratic". For the June 2004 European Parliament elections, it campaigned under the name of the Segni Scognamiglio Pact. (Having begun his career as a professor of Economics, Carlo Scognamiglio was elected to Parliament as a centre-right candidate in March 1994 and appointed to the post of President of the Senate shortly thereafter. He was Minister of Defence between October 1998 and December 1999.) The European elections were a disappointment, resulting in a dismal 0.5% of the vote and no seats.

Liberty of Action (Social Alternative with Alessandra Mussolini List) (LAM)
Libertà di azione (Alternativa sociale con Alessandra Mussolini)

Address. Viale Regina Margherita, 239, 00198 Rome
Telephone. +39 06 442 51916
Fax. +39 06 454 42757
Email. infor@libertadiazione.it
Website. www.libertadiazione.net
Leader. Alessandra Mussolini (secretary)

Liberty of Action was formed in advance of the June 2004 European elections, following the departure of Benito Mussolini's granddaughter, Alessandra Mussolini, from the National Alliance over leader Gianfranco Fini's policy of establishing a clean break with the Fascist heritage. In the European elections the party campaigned under the name "Social Alternative with Alessandra Mussolini", obtaining 1.2% of the vote and a single seat.

National Alliance
Alleanza Nazionale (AN)

Address. Via della Scrofa 39, 00186 Rome
Telephone. +39 06 688 03014
Fax. +39 06 654 8256
Email. internet@alleanzanazionale.it
Website. www.alleanzanazionale.it
Leadership. Gianfranco Fini (president); Gianfranco Anedda (Chamber group leader); Domenico Nania (Senate group leader)

The right-wing AN is the direct descendant of the post-war Italian Social Movement (MSI), which was founded in 1946 as a successor to the outlawed Fascist Party of the late dictator Benito Mussolini. The MSI first contested parliamentary elections in 1948, winning six seats in the Chamber of Deputies. Between 1953 and 972 its representation in the Chamber fluctuated between 29 and 24 members. It contest-

ed the 972 general elections in an alliance (*Destra Nazionale,* DN) with the Italian Democratic Party of Monarchical Unity, the joint list winning 56 seats in the Chamber. The two parties formally merged as the MSI-DN in January 1973, but in the 1976 elections the new party obtained only 35 seats in the Chamber.

The MSI-DN did not rule out the use of violence in its activities, and its extremist members were involved in numerous clashes, which were not approved by the party as a whole. In December 1976 a total of 26 MSI-DN parliamentarians (17 deputies and nine senators) broke away from the party to form a group known as *Democrazia Nazionale* (DN), which was led by Ernesto De Marzio. It repudiated all fascist tendencies and announced that it would support the Christian Democrats. However, in the 1979 elections this group won no seats, while the rump MSI-DN retained 30 seats in the Chamber of Deputies.

In the 1983 elections the party made significant gains both at national and at regional and provincial level, gaining 42 seats in the Chamber of Deputies (with 6.8% of the vote). In the June 1987 elections, however, it slipped back to 35 seats (5.9% of the vote). The party's veteran leader, Giorgio Almirante (who had been a member of Mussolini's government), retired in December 1987 and was succeeded by Gianfranco Fini, regarded as a representative of the young, "new face" of the party. Meanwhile, the party had decided in October 1987 to mount an active campaign in South Tyrol/Bolzano in support of the Italian speaking minority and against the political aspirations of the German-speaking majority.

In the 1992 parliamentary elections the MSI-DN slipped to 34 Chamber seats and 5.4% of the vote, one of the party's successful candidates in Naples being Alessandra Mussolini, grand-daughter of the former dictator. It then sought to capitalize on the massive corruption scandals that engulfed the the Christian Democrats and their governing allies. The AN designation was used by the MSI-DN from January 1994 as part of a strategy to attract support from former Christian Democrats and other right-wing groups, including Italian monarchists, and the party joined the Freedom Alliance (PL) of conservative parties headed by Silvio Berlusconi's new *Forza Italia* party, becoming the leading force in the PL's southern arm, designated the Alliance for Good Government (*Polo del Buon Governo*). In the March 1994 elections the AN advanced strongly to 13.5% of the proportional vote as part of the PL, its support being concentrated (as that of the MSI before it had been) in the South. Six AN ministers were included in the Berlusconi government appointed in May 1994. In the following month's European Parliament elections the AN won 12.5% of the vote and 11 seats.

The party's first post-war experience of national office ended with the collapse of the Berlusconi government in December 1994. The following month the AN title was officially adopted at a Rome congress which also decided to delete most references to fascism in basic AN policy documents. Thereafter party spokespersons became even more insistent in rejecting the "neo-fascist" label commonly appended by the media and others, especially since a hardline minority, which saw no discredit in the term "fascist", had in the meantime broken away to form what became the Tricolour Flame-Social Movement (MS-FT).

The regional elections of April–May 1995 showed a modest increase in the AN vote to 14.1%, which rose appreciably to 15.7% in the April 1996 general elections, for which the AN remained within the PL alliance, winning 91 Chamber seats in its own right. In the 1996 contest Fini added to his reputation as a keen debater and effective campaigner, rather overshadowing Berlusconi. In opposition to a centre-left Olive Tree government, the AN in March 1998 relaunched itself as a "modern, open right-wing party" in which fascist ideology was said to have no place, adopting the ladybird as its new logo. In the June 1999 European elections the AN was allied with the Segni Pact, but the joint list secured only 10.3% of the vote and nine seats.

In the May 2001 parliamentary elections the AN remained in the right-wing alliance, now called the House of Freedoms, participating in its victory. The AN took 12% of the Chamber proportional vote, its group in the new lower house having 99 members, its Senate group 45. The following month five AN ministers were appointed to the second Berlusconi government, including Fini as Deputy Prime Minister.

In the June 2004 European elections, the party obtained 11.5% of the vote and 9 seats. The AN's representatives in the European Parliament sit in the Union for a Europe of Nations group.

New Italian Socialist Party
Nuovo Partito Socialista Italiano (NPSI)

Address. Via di Torre Argentina, 47, 00186 Rome
Telephone. +39 06 676 08389
Fax. +39 06 676 08943
Email. socialisti@socialisti.net
Website. www.socialisti.net
Leadership. Bobo Craxi (national secretary); Gianni De Michelis (secretary); Claudio Martelli (secretary)

The NPSI was formed prior to the May 2001 parliamentary elections by a dissident faction of the Italian Democratic Socialists (SDI) which rejected the SDI's participation in the centre-left Olive Tree alliance, and its shedding of former leader Bettino Craxi's heritage. As part of the right-wing House of Freedoms alliance, the NPSI contributed 0.9% to its 49.4% share of the proportional vote for the Chamber, securing three seats in the lower house. In the June 2004 European elections the party campaigned under the designation "United Socialists for Europe" and won 2% of the vote and two seats.

Northern League
Lega Nord (LN)

Address. Via Arbe 63, 20125 Milan
Telephone. +39 02 607 0379
Fax. +39 02 668 02766
Email. info@leganord.org
Website. www.leganord.org
Leadership. Umberto Bossi (federal secretary); Stefano Stefani (federal president); Alessandro Ce' (Chamber group leader); Francesco Moro (Senate group leader)

The Northern League (LN) "for the independence of Padania" originated in February 1991 as a federation of the Lombardy League (*Lega Lombarda*, LL) and fraternal parties in Emilia-Romagna, Liguria, Piedmont, Tuscany and Venice. The LL had been launched in 1979, named after a 12th-century federation of northern Italian cities. It had achieved prominence in the 1980s as the most conspicuous of several regional groups to challenge the authority of the government in Rome, in particular its use of public revenues from the rich north to aid the impoverished south. Adopting the same stance, the LN called at its foundation for a move to a federal system with substantial regional autonomy in most areas except defence and foreign policy. Later, the LN took as its objective the full independence of what it called "Padania" (which it took to consist of the regions of Emilia-Romagna, Friuli-Venezia Giulia, Liguria, Lombardy, Marche, Piedmont, Sudtirol-Alto Adige, Tuscany, Trentino, Umbria, Valle d'Aosta, and Veneto). Party leaders subsequently denied that the LN's attitude to southern Italians was tantamount to racism but made no apology for the League's advocacy of a strong anti-immigration policy, including resolute action against illegal immigrants and against criminality in immigrant communities.

Having won 8.7% of the national vote and 55 Chamber

seats in the 1992 elections, the LN made political capital out of popular disgust over the bribery and corruption scandals engulfing Italy's political establishment, winning a record 40% of the vote in the Milan mayoral election of June 1993. For the March 1994 parliamentary elections the LN was part of the victorious right-wing Freedom Alliance (PL), winning 8.4% of the national vote and joining a PL government headed by Silvio Berlusconi of *Forza Italia*. In June 1994 the LN won six European Parliament seats on a 6.6% vote share.

In December 1994 the LN brought about the collapse of the Berlusconi government by withdrawing from it, fearful as it was of the consequences of the alliance with the media tycoon and *Forza Italia* for its own visibility and separate identity. Contesting the April 1996 general elections independently, the LN increased its share of the national vote to 10.1%, taking 59 Chamber seats, and became the strongest single party in northern Italy. In opposition to the resultant centre-left Olive Tree government in Rome, the League convened a "parliament" in Mantua in May 1996, and announced the creation of a "Committee for the Liberation of Padania" to act as a "provisional government". However, such schemes received a rebuff in local elections the following month, when the LN polled poorly throughout "Padania" and managed only third place in Mantua, seat of its "parliament". Bossi also came under criticism from moderates within the LN, responding in August 1996 by expelling their leader, former Chamber president Irene Pivetti.

Also in August 1996, Bossi came under pressure from local investigating magistrates, who asked for revocation of his parliamentary immunity so that he could face charges of inciting political violence at LN rallies in the north. Contending that he was not answerable to judges of "colonial Italy", Bossi in September 1996 led a three-day march along the River Po culminating in a Venice rally and the declaration of the independent "Republic of Padania". An accompanying "transitional constitution" provided that the declaration would not come into effect for up to 12 months, during which the LN "provisional government" would negotiate a "treaty of agreed separation" with the Rome government. Bossi announced at the same time that a "national guard" would be set up to protect "Padania's interests". The reaction of government in Rome was to take such activities for the publicity stunts that they were, announcing that it would "not be troubled by political projects that have no roots in the past and no future", whilst police raided the NL headquarters in Milan to search for evidence of the party's alleged unconstitutional activities.

The third LN congress in February 1997 featured some moderation of the party's demand for speedy independence, with Bossi now calling for "consensual secession". Local elections in April-May 1997 were disappointing for the LN and an unofficial referendum organized by the party on May 25, when 99% of participants were said to have supported independence for "Padania", was dismissed by the government as yet another political stunt. Despite this, in October 1997 the LN proceeded to organize "elections" for a 200-member "constituent assembly of the Republic of Padania". The body held its inaugural meeting in November, when the guests included Russian nationalist leader Vladimir Zhirinovsky of the Liberal Democratic Party of Russia.

In January 1998 a Bergamo court gave Bossi a one-year prison sentence and fined him 170 million lire after he was convicted of inciting criminal acts at an LN rally in 1995. In July 1998, moreover, Bossi and another LN leader were given suspended sentences of seven and eight months respectively for offences committed in a clash with police in 1996. In the June 1999 European elections the LN slipped to 4.5% of the national vote and from six seats to four.

Bossi and Berlusconi achieved sufficient resolution of their differences in 2000 for the LN to re-join the coalition of the centre right, now called the House of Freedoms. In November 2000 Bossi derided claims by the centre-left that the return of the LN to government would provoke a crisis with the European Union akin to the one caused by the advent of the Freedom Party of Austria to power in Vienna. In the May 2001 parliamentary elections the LN participated in a centre-right victory, although its contribution to the alliance's 45.4% vote share in the Chamber elections was only 3.9%. Having 30 members in the new Chamber and 17 in the Senate, the LN was allocated three portfolios in the second Berlusconi government. In March 2004, Bossi suffered a severe stroke and was hospitalized, throwing the leadership of the party into doubt.

In the June 2004 European elections the LN secured 5.0% of the vote and 4 seats. The LN's representatives in the European Parliament are not attached to any political group.

Party of Italian Communists
Partito dei Comunisti Italiani (PdCI)

Address. Piazza Augusto Imperatore, 32, 00186 Rome
Telephone. +39 06 686 271
Fax. +39 06 686 27230
Email. direzionenazionale@comunisti-italiani.it
Website. www.comunisti-italiani.it
Leadership. Oliviero Diliberto (secretary general); Armando Cossutta (president)

The PdCI was formally launched in October 1998 under the leadership of Armando Cossutta, until then president of Communist Refoundation (PRC). Its creation was prompted by a division within the PRC over whether or not the Prodi government should continue to be supported, especially as this amounted to a change of policy between congresses. The new party brought together elements deriving from the former Italian Communist Party (PCI) who had not agreed with the PCI's transformation into the Democratic Party of the Left (PDS) but who also opposed the "unreconstructed" line of the PRC. On its formation, the PdCI joined the new centre-left government headed by Massimo D'Alema of the DS, receiving two cabinet portfolios.

In the June 1999 European Parliament elections the PdCI won two of Italy's 87 seats with a vote share of 2.0%. It remained within the Olive Tree fold for the May 2001 parliamentary elections, thereby sharing in the defeat of the centre-left by the right-wing House of Freedoms alliance. With a vote share of 1.7%, the PdCI obtained 10 seats in the new Chamber.

In the June 2004 European elections, the party obtained 2.4% of the vote and two seats. The two PdCI representatives in the European Parliament sit as members of the European United Left/Nordic Green Left group.

Social Idea Movement with Rauti (SIM)
Movimento Idea Sociale con Rauti

Website. http://misconrauti.org
Leadership. Pino Rauti (president); Giuseppe Incardona (secretary)

The *Movimento idea sociale* was formed by Pino Rauti following his expulsion in 2003 from the Social Movement–Tricolour Flame (MS-FT), which he had led since its creation following a split from the Italian Social Movement (MSI) when it became the National Alliance (AN) in 1995. In the June 2004 European elections, the SIM obtained 0.1% of the vote and no seats.

Social Movement–Tricolour Flame
Movimento Sociale–Fiamma Tricolore (MS-FT)

Address. Via Simone De Saint Bon 89, 00195 Rome
Telephone. +39 06 370 1756
Fax. +39 06 372 0376
Email. fiamma@msifiammatric.it

Website. www.msifiammatric.it
Leadership. Luca Romagnoli (national secretary); Fabrizio Taranto (vice secretary)

The MS-FT originated in the opposition of a minority pro-fascism faction of the former Italian Social Movement–National Right (MSI-DN), led by Pino Rauti, to the party's decision in January 1995 to convert itself into the National Alliance (AN). Having made little impact in the 1996 general elections (although its intervention may have delivered to the centre left several seats that might otherwise have gone to the centre right), the splinter group adopted the "Tricolour Flame" logo and won one of Italy's 87 seats in the June 1999 European elections, receiving 1.6% of the vote. In the May 2001 parliamentary elections, the MS-FT won around 1% of the proportional vote, electing Luigi Caruso to the Senate. Rauti's leadership proved to be controversial, resulting in defections and a split in the party, and his expulsion in 2003 to set up an alternative movement, the Social Idea Movement with Rauti.

At the June 2004 European Parliament election, the MS-FT obtained 0.7% of the vote and one seat. Its representative is a member of the "non-attached" group.

Union of Christian Democrats and Democrats of the Centre (UDC)
Unione dei Democratici Cristiani e Democratici di Centro

Address. c/o Camera dei Deputati, Piazza Montecitorio, 00186 Rome
Email. info@udc-camera.it
Website. www.udc-camera.it
Leadership. Luca Volonté (president); Marco Follini (secretary)

The *Unione dei Democratici Cristiani e Democratici di Centro* (UDC), also known as the *Unione Democristiana di Centro* (Christian Democratic Union of the Centre) was formed after the 2001 elections and brought together into a single political entity: the Centre Christian Democrats (CCD), the Christian Democratic Union (CDU), and European Democracy (DE).

The CCD was established by a right-wing group of the former ruling Christian Democratic Party (DC) when its majority wing became the Italian Popular Party (PPI) in January 1994, and the CDU was launched in July 1995 by a right-wing group of the PPI that favoured participation in the Freedom Alliance (PL) rather than the centre-left Olive Tree alliance. The two parties contested the proportional section of the April 1996 elections in close cooperation, their joint list securing 5.8% of the vote. Some in the CCD broke with the PL in February 1998, aligning themselves with the new Democratic Union for the Republic (UDR) led by former President Francesco Cossiga, which in October 1998 joined the centre-left Olive Tree (*Ulivo*) government headed by the Democrats of the Left. For the 2001 parliamentary elections, the CCD again fielded a joint list of candidates with the CDU for the proportionally distributed Chamber seats – this time under the name, *Biancofiore* (White Flower). The *Biancofiore* won 3.2% of the proportional vote in the elections to the Chamber of Deputies, electing 40 members to the lower house and 29 to the Senate. European Democracy (DE) was formed in the run-up to the 2001 elections by Sergio d'Antoni, former general secretary of the (mainly Christain Democrat-oriented) CISL trade union confederation. A centrist, Christian Democratic force, its most famous adherent was Giulio Andreotti. DE contested the elections independently, winning 2.4% of the proportional vote for the Chamber (and no seats) and 3.2% in the Senate contest, which yielded two seats.

The merger of these three groups into a single political entity represents progress towards the achievement of a continuing aspiration of many centrists in Italian politics: the reconstruction of a *grande centro* (a significant centrist party) that can re-occupy the political space created by the collapse of Christian Democracy and, through expansion and absorption of other political parties, establish political dominance along the lines of the old DC. In the June 2004 European elections, however, the UDC obtained only 5.9% of the vote and five seats.

Regional Parties

Autonomous Lombardy Alliance (*Alleanza Lombardia Autonoma*, ALA). Seeks to articulate aspirations to self-government in Italy's border regions in the Alps; includes the Lombard Alpine League (*Lega Alpina Lombarda*, LAL), which won one Senate seat in March 1994 and 0.3% of the vote in the June 1994 European elections. In the May 2001 parliamentary elections the ALA won one Senate seat. In the June 2004 European elections, it won 0.5% of the vote and no seats.

Emilia and Romagna Freedom (*Libertà Emilia & Rumagna*, LER). Founded in 1999 as successor to Emilian Freedom/Emilia Nation (*Libertà Emiliana/Nazione Emilia*), itself dating from a 1994 breakaway by an Emilian faction of the Northern League opposed to the latter's participation in the Freedom Alliance; a centre-left liberal formation, the LER seeks self-government for Emilia-Romagna within a European Union of historic regions. The LER is a member of the Democratic Party of the Peoples of Europe–European Free Alliance, as a part of which it contested the 2004 European elections.
Address. Corso Vallisneri 17v, 42019 Scandiano, Reggio Emilia
Telephone/Fax. +39 0522 981 254
Email. lacittavalenti@libero.it
Website. utenti.tripod.it/libertaemiliana
Leadership. Manuela Pilosio (president); Farouk Ramadan (co-ordinator)

For Trieste (*Per Trieste*). Founded in opposition to the 1975 Osimo Treaty settling the Trieste territorial dispute between Italy and the then Yugoslavia, *Per Trieste* is an autonomist group advocating special status for Trieste within the special statute region of Friuli–Venezia Giulia.
Leadership. Manlio Cecovini

North-Eastern Union (*Unione Nord-Est*). An organization that aims to achieve: a merger of the regions of Veneto, Friuli and Trentino in accordance with the objectives of the Agnelli Foundation; the establishment of 12 autonomous regions; a federal and decentralized Italy, founded on the principle of subsidiarity, with greater powers for the municipalities and the provinces.
Address. Via Rella 1/4, 17100 Savona
Telephone. +39 0198 485 032
Fax. +39 0198 487 352
Email. unionenordest@libero.it
Website. www.unionenordest.it

Romagna Autonomy Movement (*Movimento per l'Autonomia della Romagna,* MAR). Founded in 1991, MAR campaigns for the achievment of regional status for the Romagna area of central Italy.
Address. Via Valsalva 8, 47100 Forlì
Email. mar@regionromagna.org
Website. www.regioneromagna.org/
Leadership. Lorenzo Cappelli and Stefano Servadei

Sardinian Action Party (*Partito Sardo d'Azione*, PsdA). Favours autonomy for the island of Sardinia; took four Chamber seats in 1996 elections as part of the Olive Tree alliance; strongly represented in Sardinian regional council; member of Democratic Party of the Peoples of Europe–European Free Alliance.
Address. Via Roma 231, 09100 Cagliari
Telephone. +39 070 657 599
Fax. +39 070 657 779
Email. psdaz@sol.dada.it
Website. www.psdaz-ichnos.com/

Sicilian Action Party (*Partito Siciliano d'Azione*). Born from the amalgamation of a number of Sicilian autonomist movements in April 1998, the party seeks the full implementation of Sicily's regional statute.
Address. Via Malta 10, 93100 Caltanissetta
Telephone. +39 095 722 6025
Fax. +39 095 722 6975
Email. rsgrois@tin.it
Website. utenti.lycos.it/partitosiciliano/
Leadership. Nino Italico Amico

South Tyrol People's Party (*Südtiroler Volkspartei*, SVP). Christian democratic party of the German-speaking population of Bolzano/Bozen province (South Tyrol). From 1948 onwards it consistently held three seats in the Italian Chamber of Deputies, and from 1979 one seat in the European Parliament. The party's struggle for equal rights for the German-speaking and Ladin-speaking population of South Tyrol led to Austro-Italian agreements on the status of the province in 1969–71 and a new statute for the Trentino–Alto Adige region in 1971. The SVP became the strongest party in the South Tyrol *Landtag* and the second strongest in the regional council of Trentino–Alto Adige, winning 22 seats out of 70 in November 1983. Normally securing representation in the Rome parliament thereafter, the SVP again won one seat in the June 1994 European Parliament elections. For the April 1996 general elections the SVP was part of the victorious centre-left Olive Tree alliance. For the 2001 general elections it again fielded candidates under the banner of the *Ulivo*, as a result of which it succeeded in electing eight members to the Chamber of Deputies. The SVP is affiliated to the European Democrat Union. In the June 2004 European elections it won 0.5% of the vote and no seats.
Address. Brennerstrasse 7/A, 39100 Bozen/Bolzano
Telephone +39 0471 304 000
Fax. +39 0471 981 473
Email. info@svpartei.org
Website. www.svpartei.org
Leadership. Siegfried Brugger (president); Luis Durnwalder (provincial government head); Thomas Widmann (general secretary)

Southern League (*Lega Sud, Ausonia*). Supports political independence for the south of Italy.
Email. vestuto@legasud.it
Website. www.legasud.it
Leadership. Gianfranco Vestuto (secretary)

Two Sicilies (*Due Sicilie*). Movement seeking autonomy for the area once covered by the Kingdom of the Two Sicilies and the creation of a "new Europe" based on historic regions.
Email. info@duesicilie.org
Website. www.duesicilie.org

Union for South Tyrol (*Union für Südtirol*, UfS). Deriving from the radical Fatherland Union (*Heimatbund*), UfS advocates a South Tyrol "free state" able to opt for union with Austria. It has challenged the regional dominance of the

South Tyrol People's Party in seeking enhanced rights for the German-speaking majority. It is a member of Democratic Party of the Peoples of Europe–European Free Alliance.
Address. Garibaldistrasse 6, 39100 Bozen/Bolzano
Teephone. +39 0471 975 696
Fax. +39 0471 978 559
Email. union@unionfs.com
Website. www.unionfs.com
Leadership. Eva Klotz & Andreas Pöder

Valdostan Union (*Union Valdôtaine/Unione Valdostana*, UV). A pro-autonomy grouping founded in 1945 to further the interests of the French-speaking minority in the special statute region of Val d'Aosta, the UV has been represented in the regional assembly since 1959. The general election of 2001 produced one senator for the party. It campaigned in the June 2004 European elections under the name "Federalismo in Europa–Federalisme en Europe", receiving 0.1% of the vote and no seats.
Address. Ave des Maquisards, 11100 Aoste
Telephone. +39 0165 235 181
Fax. +39 0165 364 289
Email. siegecentral@unionvaldotaine.org
Website. www.unionvaldotaine.org
Leadership. Manuela Zublena (president)

Venetian Republic League (*Liga Veneta Repubblica*). Also known as Venetians of Europe (*Veneti d'Europa*), the *Liga Veneta* seeks the restoration of the historic Republic of Venice (which fell in 1797) within a region-based European Union. It has representation in the Veneto regional council.
Address. c/o Consiglio Regionale Veneto, Venice
Email. info@venetarepubblica.org
Website. www.venetarepubblica.org
Leadership. Ettore Beggiato

Other Parties

Christian Democracy (*Democrazia Cristiana*, DC), a party founded with the intention of replicating the most dominant political party in the post-war Republic, Christian Democracy. It has a mutually hostile relationship with the Union of Christian Democrats and Democrats of the Centre (UDC). It campaigned in the June 2004 European elections under the name "Paese Nuovo" and received 0.2% of the votes and no seats.
Address. Piazza del Gesù, 00186 Rome.
Telephone. +39 06 699 1313
Fax. +39 06 697 88315
Email. democraziacristiana@democraziacristiana.net
Website. www.democraziacristiana.it/
Leadership. Giuseppe Pizza (political secretary general); Mariano Coco and Aniello di Vuolo (vice-secretaries)

Fascism and Liberty Movement (*Movimento Fascismo e Libertà*, MFL), a far-right grouping founded in 1991.
Address. Piazza Chiaradia 9, 20100 Milan
Telephone. +39 02 568 14233
Fax. +39 02 568 15402
Email. info@fascismoeliberta.it
Website. www.fascismoeliberta.it
Leadership. Giuseppe Martorana (national secretary)

Italian Marxist-Leninist Party (*Partito Marxista-Leninista Italiano*, PMLI). Maoist formation founded in 1977 from earlier grouping dating from 1969; advocates abstention in all elections.
Address. Via Gioberti 101, 50121 Florence
Telephone/Fax. +39 055 234 7272
Email. pmli.cc@tiscalinet.it

Website. www.pmli.it
Leadership. Giovanni Scuderi (general secretary)

Italian Monarchist Movement (*Movimento Monarchico Italiano*, MMI). Seeks the restoration of the monarchy to cement national unity and territorial integrity; opposed to all regional separatism. The MMI backed the parliamentary moves which in 2003 ended the constitutional ban on Prince Victor Emanuel (son of Italy's last king, who reigned for 27 days in 1946) setting foot on Italian soil.
Address. Via G. B. Belzoni 52, 35100 Padova
Telephone. +39 049 654 507
Fax. +39 049 654 507
Email. segreteriammi@libero.it
Website. www.monarchici.org
Leader. Alberto Claut (national secretary)

Monarchist Alliance (*Alleanza Monarchica*, AM), an umbrella organization for a number of pro-monarchy groupings.
Address. Via Mercanti 30/C, 10121 Turin
Telephone. +39 011 540 720
Email. info@alleanza-monarchica.com
Website. www.geocities.com/anmitaly

National Front (*Fronte Nazionale*, FN), a radical right-wing formation modelled on the National Front of France.
Email. info@frontenazionale.org
Website. www.frontenazionale.it
Leadership. Adriano Tilgher (national secretary)

No Euro, launched in 2003, the organization calls for a referendum to take Italy out of the euro currency zone, which it regards as responsible for high prices and unemployment. It presented candidates in the June 2004 European elections and received 0.2% of the vote and no seats.
Address. Via S. Donato, 55, 10155, Turin.
Telephone. +39 328 926 6466
Email. info@noeuro.it
Website. www.noeuro.it

Pensioners' Party (*Partito Pensionati*, PP). Created to oppose any reduction in Italy's generous pension provisions, especially for civil servants; won 0.7% and one seat in the June 1999 European elections, and in the June 2004 European elections 1.1% of the vote and one seat. The representative affiliates himself to the European People's Party/European Democrats group.
Address. Via Emilia Ovest 3, 29010 Alseno, PC
Telephone. +39 339 833 0022
Email. info@partitopensionati.it
Website. www.partitopensionati.it
Leadership. Carlo Fatuzzo (national secretary); Lino Miserotti (national organizer

Jamaica

Capital: Kingston
Population: 2,700,000 (2003E)

A former British dependency, Jamaica became a fully independent member of the Commonwealth in 1962. The head of state is the British sovereign, represented by a Governor-General. The head of government is the Prime Minister, who is formally appointed by the Governor-General. There is a bicameral parliament. The House of Representatives has 60 members, who are elected on the Westminster model for five-year terms by simple majority in single seat constituencies. The Senate has 21 members, of whom 13 are normally appointed on the advice of the Prime Minister and eight on that of the Leader of the Opposition.

The Jamaica Labour Party (JLP) and the People's National Party (PNP) have dominated Jamaican politics since the first elections under adult suffrage in 1944, with no third party ever establishing a substantial position. The PNP has been in power since 1989, being re-elected most recently on Oct. 16, 2002, and thus gaining a historic fourth consecutive term in office. The PNP won 52.2% of the vote and 34 seats in the House, while the JLP gained 47.2% of the vote and 26 seats.

There is a long-standing tradition of rival armed gangs, especially in Kingston, supporting the two main parties and deriving patronage from them, with some neighbourhoods in Kingston being virtual "no go" areas for political opponents. Much of the violence in recent years, however, has been connected to criminal activities, drugs and territorial disputes between groups, rather than being specifically political in nature. During the 2002 election campaign some 80 murders were committed, although this number was down on previous campaigns. The decline was partly attributable to a code of conduct signed in June 2002 between the two party leaders. The code called on the parties not to encourage violence in political activities, to avoid procuring and distributing weapons or ammunition, and to avoid forcing people to declare their political affiliations.

Jamaica Labour Party (JLP)

Address. 20 Belmont Road, Kingston 5
Telephone. (1-876) 754-7213
Fax. (1-876) 754-7214
Email. info@thejlp.com
Website. www.thejlp.org
Leadership. Edward Seaga (leader); Ken Baugh (general secretary)
The JLP is a conservative party with a free market orientation. Founded in 1943 by Alexander Bustamante as the political wing of the Bustamante Industrial Trade Union (BITU), the JLP was the ruling party from 1944 to 1955 and from 1962 (when it led Jamaica to independence) to 972. The 1970s saw a sharp polarization in Jamaican politics, with the People's National Party (PNP), in government from 972, adopting leftist policies that were bitterly opposed by the JLP. Political violence in the run-up to the 1980 election, in which the JLP won back power, resulted in several hundred deaths.

From 1980 JLP Prime Minister Edward Seaga reversed the PNP's previous programme of state control of the economy. He also improved relations with the United States, severing diplomatic ties with Cuba in October 1981 and backing the US-led intervention in Grenada in October 1983. In December 1983 the JLP won all 60 parliamentary seats after the PNP boycotted the elections. The JLP lost office in 1989, however, and has since been in opposition.

Notwithstanding four successive general election defeats, Seaga has survived as party leader (a position he has held since 1974) despite periods of internal dissension. The most serious case came in October 1995 when Bruce Golding, the former chairman of the JLP, established a new political party, the National Democratic Movement (NDM). However, in September 2002 Golding returned to the JLP fold, and was subsequently re-installed as party chairman. After the 2002 general election defeat Seaga came under pressure to resign, but his position was bolstered by the JLP's good performance in local elections on June 19, 2003. The party won 12 of the 13 parish councils, and 126 of the 227 council seats that were being contested. However, in August 2003 the position of Seaga as leader again came under scrutiny, after a company that he owned was placed into voluntary liquidation; in November 2003 two of Seaga's trusted and long serving deputies lost their posts in internal elections to candidates representing a new generation of JLP politicians. In an attempt to bolster his position an emergency meeting of JLP parliamentarians was convened on Jan. 13, 2004, and a vote of confidence in Seaga's leadership was held. Although 17 of the 21 JLP MPs that voted supported Seaga, his position was still not entirely secure. Members of the youth arm of the JLP – Young Jamaica – remained critical of Seaga's continuing presence as leader.

The JLP is a member of the Caribbean Democrat Union, a regional organization of the International Democrat Union.

People's National Party (PNP)

Address. 89 Old Hope Road, Kingston 6
Telephone. (1-876) 927-7520
Fax. (1-876) 927-4389
Email. webmaster@pnpjamaica.com
Website. www.pnpjamaica.com
Leadership. Percival J. Patterson (leader); Maxine Henry Wilson (general secretary)
Norman Manley, who led the party until 1969, founded the PNP in 1938. It first held office, in the pre-independence period, from 1955-62. Norman Manley was succeeded by his son, Michael Manley, who became Prime Minister following the PNP's first post-independence electoral success in February 972. The subsequent Manley government adopted radical socialist policies, nationalizing key enterprises and building ties with Cuba. According to the Jamaica Labour Party (JLP) the 1970s saw a "wave of terror" against its supporters, including wholesale "partisan cleansing" of JLP neighbourhoods by gangs linked to the PNP. JLP officials were detained under emergency powers in the run-up to the 1976 election in which the PNP retained power. The run-up to the 1980 elections, against a background of economic crisis, was marked by widespread violence and loss of life, and the PNP was defeated 51-9 by the JLP.

The PNP boycotted elections in December 1983, but then returned to power (winning 45-15) in February 1989, Manley abandoning the PNP's 1970s policies and instead continuing the programme of market deregulation and privatization adopted by the JLP. Manley stood down as leader for health reasons in March 1992 and was succeeded by Percival J. Patterson, under whom the party won 52 of the 60 House seats in elections in March 1993.

Despite economic contraction in 1996-97, high unemployment, a series of scandals, and rampant drug-related crime giving Jamaica one of the highest murder rates in the world, the PNP was re-elected with 50 seats in December 1997. A similar set of issues affected the PNP during its third term, but once again the party did enough to retain power in the succeeding general election of October 2002. The PNP's new term in office began in difficult circumstances with a worsening economic situation, an upsurge in crime affecting the tourism sector, and a series of political initiatives meeting strong parliamentary and public opposition. The public's frustration with the government was illustrated in the local elections of June 2003, when the PNP suffered a heavy defeat at the hands of the JLP. In an attempt to re-energize the PNP a new faction emerged in January 2004, the New Foundation Group, which attempted to reform the party's organizational structure. The group's plan, outlined in a document entitled "The Campaign for Transformation" called for a separation of powers within the party, so that the same individuals could not hold official positions both within the party and the government.

The PNP is an affiliate of the Socialist International.

Other Parties

National Democratic Movement (NDM), founded by Bruce Golding in October 1995 following his resignation as chairman of the Jamaica Labour Party. The NDM called for sweeping reform of Jamaican society and politics, pledging to tackle issues such as corruption in government and public contracts, police brutality and paramilitarism, judicial inefficiency, rotten prisons and bureaucratic negligence. It won no seats in the 1997 general election, however. Golding stood down as leader after a poor by-election result in March 2001, and was replaced by one of his vice-presidents, Hyacinth Bennett. In September 2002 Golding rejoined the JLP. In the October 2002 general election and the June 2003 local elections the NDM, in tandem with the Jamaica National Alliance for Unity (NJA), put forward a slate of candidates. However, the NDM/NJA won only a very small number of votes and no seats.

Address. NDM House, 3 Easton Avenue, Kingston 5

Japan

Capital: Tokyo
Population: 127.6 million (2003)

Under its constitution adopted in 1947, Japan is a constitutional monarchy with the hereditary Emperor as "symbol of the State and of the unity of the people, deriving his position from the will of the people with whom resides sovereign power". (The fact that the Emperor was not designated "Head of State" has met objections from some conservatives.) Legislative authority is vested in a popularly elected bicameral Parliament (National Diet, *Kokkai*), composed of (i) an upper House of Councillors (*Sangiin*), and (ii) a lower House of Representatives (*Shugiin*). The lower house has much greater powers than the upper, in practice supplying the Prime Minister and the bulk of the cabinet, but the upper house has some blocking power over ordinary bills, exclusive of the budget, treaties and designation of the Prime Minister.

The 247 members of the upper house are elected for six years, half being due for re-election every three years. The lower house currently consists of 480 members elected for up to four years, 300 from single-member constituencies and 180 by proportional representation from party lists in 11 regional districts. The single-member constituencies for the lower house were introduced under legislation enacted in 1994 with the aim of reducing the prevalence of "money politics" in election campaign funding. Under the previous system all members had been elected in multi-member electoral districts (but with no vote transferability), with resultant competition not only between parties but also between candidates from the same party. Electoral success was therefore heavily dependent on a candidate's personal constituency machine (*koenkai*) and ability to attract funding. These machines, however, still exist under the new electoral system, and may even have been strengthened.

Under the new legislation, corporate and other private donations to individual politicians for electoral purposes were banned, and provision made for annual state subsidies to be paid to individual parties according to their parliamentary representation and percentage share of the vote in the most recent election.

The Liberal Democratic Party (LDP) was in office from its formation in 1955 until 1993, when, under-mined by a series of scandals and splits, it lost control of the lower house for the first time and gave way to a coalition of seven non-LDP parties. In June 1994, however, the LDP returned to power in an unlikely coalition with the Socialists, and in January 1996 regained the prime ministership. From 1994 onwards the LDP has been much the largest party in coalition governments of shifting composition. Its current (2004) coalition partner is the New Komeito, which has close links with the Buddhist sect *Soka Gakkai*. Much the largest party of opposition is the Democratic Party (*Minshuto*), founded in 1996, which has improved its performance at every general election since its formation.

Elections to the House of Representatives in November 2003 resulted as follows: LDP 237, Democratic Party 177, Komeito 34, Japan Communist Party (JCP) 9, Social Democratic Party (SDP) 6, New Conservative Party 4, Independents' Group 1, Liberal League 1, unaffiliated 11. The performance of the Democratic Party was boosted by its very recent merger with the Liberal Party led by the radical conservative Ichiro Ozawa, and the New Conservative Party merged with the LDP after the elections. Given the disastrous performance of the JCP and SDP, the trend appeared to be away from the extreme fragmentation of the 1990s towards a party system based on two major parties. This in turn appeared to relate to the greater stability of government that had gradually emerged since Junichiro Koizumi became LDP president and thus Prime Minister in April 2001. The July 2004 election for half the seats in the upper house reinforced the trend towards a balanced two-party system, with the Democratic Party winning 51 seats and the LDP 49.

Democratic Party of Japan (DPJ)
Minshuto

Address. 1-11-1 Nagata-cho, Chiyoda-ku, Tokyo 100-0014
Telephone. (81-3) 3595 9960
Fax. (81-3) 3595 7318
Email. dpjenews@dpj.or.jp
Website. www.dpj.or.jp
Leadership. Katsuya Okada (president); Hirohisa Fujii (secretary-general)

The DPJ was founded in September 1996 (and won 52 lower house seats in the October elections), principally by a breakaway section of the Social Democratic Party (SDP) and members of the New Party Harbinger (*Shinto Sakigake*). The party was relaunched early in 1998, following the collapse of the three-year-old New Frontier Party (NFP, *Shinshinto*) of Ichiro Ozawa. Several factions of the NFP joined the DPJ at that time, nearly doubling its parliamentary representation, and in lower house general elections of June 2000, the DPJ won 127 out of 480 seats.

The two principal leaders of the DPJ were Yukio Hatoyama (who came from a famous dynasty of conservative politicians) and Naoto Kan, a moderate progressive relying for much of his support on citizens' movements. Each of them spent periods at the head of the party, initially sharing the top position between them. Coming from sharply different backgrounds, they often clashed on policy. Hatoyama was leader from September 1999 until he was forced to resign in December 2002 and was replaced by Kan, under whose leadership the DPJ increased its seat total to 177 in the November 2003 lower house general elections. Shortly before these elections, the DPJ absorbed the small but significant Liberal Party (*Jiyuto*) led by Ozawa. In May 2004, however, Kan had to resign for non-payment of compulsory pension contributions, a fault that also prevented Ozawa from replacing him as leader. Instead, the new leader was Katsuya Okada, a figure far less well known to the electorate.

The DPJ sought to appeal to younger voters, and strongly attacked "bureaucratic-led protection and uniformity". It sought to combine free market forces with welfare provision, thus revealing a significant debt to New Labour in Britain. On defence, however, it combined contrasting influences, and struggled to produce a coherent policy.

Japan Communist Party (JCP)
Nihon Kyosanto

Address. 4-26-27 Sendagaya, Shibuya-ku, Tokyo 151-8586
Telephone. (81-3) 3403 6111
Fax. (81-3) 5474 8358
Email. info@jcp.or.jp
Website. www.jcp.or.jp
Leadership. Tetsuzo Fuwa (central committee chair); Kazuo Shii (executive committee chair)

Founded in 1922 but not legalized until 1945, the JCP gained a considerable following after the Second World War as a rare grouping that had opposed the Emperor-system. In 1950, however, its attempts to satisfy Moscow's criticism of its "softness" alienated most of its erstwhile supporters, and it was a negligible political force until a resurgence began in the 1960s. During that decade it successively broke with the USSR and the People's Republic of China, thus presenting itself as a democratic party independent of external influences. Its best electoral performance was 39 seats out of 511 in the lower house general elections of 1979.

During the 1970s and 1980s the JCP could usually muster 9 or 10 per cent of the total vote, but with the collapse of the Soviet Union, its support started to decline. It enjoyed a brief resurgence in the late 1990s, when it attracted votes from the declining Social Democratic Party, but in the lower house general elections of 2000 its total of seats fell to 20 and in the 2003 elections to nine. Its refusal to contemplate coalition arrangements with other parties probably gained it some protest votes in the 1990s, but the long term effects of the 1994 electoral system ultimately hurt the party, even in its urban heartlands.

Liberal Democratic Party
Jiyuminshuto, Jiminto

Address. 1-11-23 Nagata cho, Chiyoda-ku, Tokyo 100-8910
Telephone. (81-3) 3581 6211
Fax. (81-3) 3503 4180
Email. LDP@hq.jimin.or.jp
Website. www.jimin.or.jp
Leadership. Junichiro Koizumi (president); Tsutomu Takebe (secretary general)

The conservative LDP is a unique party in the Japanese context, having been in power continuously from its foundation in 1955 until August 1993, and again (though now normally as the leading party in a coalition) from June 1994. It is embedded in a ruling structure embracing also the government ministries and key interest groups. The LDP is traditionally pro-business, but also highly protective of agriculture, rural areas being represented disproportionately in parliament. Within it factions (*habatsu*) based on individuals have been a crucial element, acting as funding channels and as power brokers influencing the composition of cabinet and party offices. With the 1994 reform of the lower house electoral system, however, factions have become rather less important, and the current Prime Minister, Junichiro Koizumi, has been able to form cabinets with less concern for factional demands than his predecessors. The party has also contained a number of policy "tribes"(*zoku*), consisting of LDP parliamentarians able to dominate specific policy making areas in conjunction with government officials and representatives of interest groups. The complex committee system of the LDP has considerable policy-making power and on occasion has blocked initiatives by the Prime Minister and cabinet.

The LDP lost office in August 1993 following the defection of Ichiro Ozawa's followers (and others). During the nine months before it returned to power in a coalition with the Social Democratic Party and the New Party Harbinger, affiliated members of parliament, starved of the oxygen of power, were defecting in considerable numbers. In retrospect, it appears that the party was lucky to survive this experience. From 1994 it governed in coalition with a shifting set of smaller parties. After regaining the prime ministership from the Social Democratic Party in January 1996, the LDP was led successively by Ryutaro Hashimoto (1996-98), Keizo Obuchi (1998-2000), Yoshiro Mori (2000-01) and Junichiro Koizumi (2001 to the present), each of them also occupying the post of Prime Minister.

The choice of Koizumi in April 2001 marked a break from the past in two senses. Firstly, he easily won primary elections for party leader among local LDP branches, which were deeply concerned about the party's electoral slide under his unpopular predecessor, Mori. Secondly, he was able to defy factional demands in the construction of his first cabinet, and proclaimed far-reaching reforms of the Japanese political economy. Even though the extent and effectiveness of his reforms is a matter of controversy, he has brought a greater stability to the party than his predecessors were able to manage. In part this is because of the coalition arrangements between the LDP and the New Komeito, which involves electoral pacts in key constituencies.

New Komeito

Address. 17 Minami motomachi, Shinjuku-ku, Tokyo 160-0012
Telephone. (81-3) 5562 7111
Fax. (81-3) 3353 9746
Email. info@komei.or.jp
Website. www.komei.or.jp
Leadership. Takenori Kanzaki (chief representative), Tetsuzo Fuyushiba (secretary-general)

The original Komeito had been established in 1964 by the *Soka Gakkai* sect of Buddhism, with a tightly articulated hierarchical organization and a centrist ideology. In 1970 it was forced to loosen its links with the *Soka Gakkai*, following criticism of its attempt to prevent publication of a book criticizing the group. It entered government for the first time with the formation of the non-LDP government of Morihiro Hosokawa in August 1993. When the New Frontier Party (NFP, *Shinshinto*) was formed in December 1994, the Komeito merged with it, but retained a position of "half in, half out" throughout the three-year existence of that party. After the NFP collapsed in December 1997, the old Komeito eventually reconstituted itself as *Shinto heiwa* (New Party Peace), and later as New Komeito (in Japanese, simply *Komeito*).

In October 1999 New Komeito joined the LDP-led coalition government of Keizo Obuchi, where (under him and his successors) it has remained ever since. After the third coalition member, the New Conservative Party, merged with the LDP late in 2003, the New Komeito became the LDP's sole coalition partner. Its adherence to the coalition is now essential to maintain LDP stability in government, and the two parties' cooperation is cemented through a series of local electoral pacts, whereby candidates of the one party stand down in favour of candidates of the other. As of May 2004 the New Komeito has 34 seats in the lower house and 23 seats in the upper.

Social Democratic Party (SDP)
Shakai Minshuto

Address. 1-8-1 Nagata cho, Chiyoda-ku, Tokyo 100-8909
Telephone. (81-3) 3580 1171
Leadership. Mizuho Fukushima (chair)

Founded in 1945, the party was known in English until 1991 and in Japanese until 1996 as the Japan Socialist Party (JSP).

It was briefly in power in 1947-48 as part of a broad coalition but therefore was perpetually in opposition until 1993. The 1950s were extremely turbulent for it, culminating in the protests against revision of the Japan-US Security Treaty in 1959-60 – a movement in which the JSP was heavily involved. In 1964 the party adopted a radical party platform ("The Road to Socialism in Japan") with a substantial Marxist underpinning. This platform was revised early in 1986, eliminating most of the Marxist language in favour of democratic socialism on the West European model. After the party was badly defeated in the lower house elections of July 1986, Takako Doi was elected party leader, becoming the first woman to head a Japanese political party. Through her own charisma, a "madonna policy" of promoting women as parliamentary candidates and championing women's issues, as well as a forthright insistence that "what is wrong is wrong", she led her party to victory over the LDP in the half upper house elections of July 1989. This success was short-lived, however, and electoral trends throughout the 1990s were remorselessly downhill.

In the July 1993 lower house elections the party's representation fell from 136 to 70 seats, but it remained the largest formation in the non-LDP Hosokawa coalition government that followed from August. When, in April-May 1994, Ichiro Ozawa tried to form a new party excluding the Socialists, they made their peace with the LDP, enabling it to return to power under a Socialist Prime Minister, Tomiichi Murayama. Murayama overturned some of the party's deepest principles by accepting the constitutionality of the Self-Defence Forces and the Japan-US Security Treaty, among other things.

Murayama resigned as Prime Minister in January 1996 and was replaced by the LDP leader, although his party the same month endorsed its change of name to Social Democratic Party and adopted a new platform accepting social democratic aims. In September 1996 the SDP split down the middle, with its right wing joining the newly formed Democratic Party. The rump party won a mere 15 seats in the lower house elections of October 1996, increased these to 19 in the elections of June 2000, but emerged from the November 2003 elections with only six seats. Following this defeat, Takako Doi, who had returned to head to party in 1996 (having resigned in 1991), resigned again and was succeeded as chair by Mizuho Fukushima.

Other Parties

Independents' Group (*Mushozoku no kai*), a small group of former LDP parliamentarians who split from the LDP in the mid-1990s. The group won five lower house seats in 2000 and since 1998 has held four seats in the upper house, but in the November 2003 lower house elections only one member was elected.
Address. 3-1 Kioi cho, Chiyoda-ku, Tokyo 102-0094

Liberal League (*Jiyu rengo*), founded in December 1995, its platform focusing on medical and welfare issues, reducing the size of central government and developing a foreign policy more independent of the US. Its chairman is Dr Torao Tokuda, a medical doctor with an intense interest in medical issues and social welfare.
Address. House of Representatives, 1-7-1 Nagata cho, Chiyoda-ku, Tokyo 100 8960
Website. www.jiyuren.or.jp
Leadership. Torao Tokuda

New Socialist Party (*Shinshakaito*), founded in March 1996 by a left-wing faction of the Social Democratic Party opposed to its abandonment of traditional causes relating to peace. It lost its small parliamentary representation in the 1996 and 1998 elections for the lower and upper houses

respectively, and failed to re-gain it in subsequent elections. It remains, however, quite active.
Address. 6th floor, Sanken Building, 4-3-7 Hatchobori, Chuo-ku, Tokyo 104-0032
Email. honbu@sinsyakai.or.jp
Website. www.sinsyakai.or.jp
Leadership. Tatsukuni Komori (chair)

Jordan

Capital: Amman
Population: 5,500,000 (UN est., 2003)

The Hashemite Kingdom of Jordan attained independence in 1946. It is a constitutional monarchy in which the King, as head of state, appoints a Prime Minister, who in turn selects a Council of Ministers, or cabinet, in consultation with the monarch. The Council is responsible to the bicameral National Assembly (*Majlis al-Umma*). This comprises the 110-member lower House of Representatives (*Majlis al-Nuwwab*), which is meant to be elected for a four-year term in single-seat constituencies, and the upper House of Notables (*Majlis al-Ayaan*), or Senate, whose 40 members are appointed by the King.

Technically, the lower house is entitled to dismiss cabinet ministers and enact or block legislation against the King's will. In practice the Royal Household and Senate still wield considerable power. King Abdullah II ibn Hussein has said that Jordan first needs to strengthen institutions, and improve the economy, social welfare and the "way the government does business" before it can envisage adopting a British or Belgian-style "figurehead monarchy".

In April 1992 King Hussein ibn Talal formally abolished all martial law provisions introduced after the 1967 Arab-Israeli War (in which Israel had occupied the West Bank of the Jordan). In July 1992 legislation was passed lifting the ban on political parties and some 26 parties were registered by 1997, with a rationalization in June 1997, when nine centrist parties united as the National Constitutional Party. Under current regulations, parties are not allowed to receive funding from abroad and are required to undertake to work within the constitution.

The first parliamentary elections in 22 years were held in November 1989. Multi-party elections to the House of Representatives were held on Nov. 8, 1993. With the exception of the Islamic Action Front (IAF), most political parties had a low profile in the elections and the majority of candidates elected were independents. Indeed, the percentage of MPs having party affiliations dropped from 42% in the 11th House to 20% in 1993. The IAF boycotted the polls of Nov. 4, 1997, leading non-partisans to outnumber party MPs by 75 to just five. Turnout was 45.45%. Tensions between Islamists and the Royal House have yet to fully heal more than six years later.

Following the death of King Hussein, his eldest son was sworn in as King Abdullah II on Feb. 7, 1999. Both houses of parliament pledged their loyalty to the new monarch, despite some perturbation over the fact that the King's British mother was born a Christian. (Although she converted to Islam, the constitution technically insists that both the monarch's parents must be Muslim by birth.) Abdullah's wife, Queen Rania, is a Palestinian, which is considered an asset as half the kingdom's population is Palestinian by origin.

Constitutional debate continued about electoral reform, with the government favouring the present first-past-the-post system and opposition forces preferring proportional representation. Municipal elections held on July 14, 1999, resulted in gains for the Islamist tendency. In April 2001 King Abdullah used his royal prerogative to extend the term of the lower house by two years, elections having been due later in the year. On June 16 the King dissolved the Assembly, thus paving the way in theory for new elections. A new draft electoral law appeared shortly thereafter, endorsing the creation of another 24 seats. The existing demarcation of 80 seats was said to favor tribal rural areas over the largely Palestinian-populated cities. The government seemed to promise to put the new constituencies in densely populated areas. However, civil rights organizations argued the opposite, saying that the new seats were being created in the traditionally pro-regime south and west instead. Subsequently a further six seats were created, to be reserved for women candidates. The Jordanian authorities also ordered that the remaining 104 seats should be allocated as follows: 92 seats would go to Muslim candidates, nine to Christians, and three to Circassians, an ethnic group that originates in the north Caucasus, but has lived in Jordan for more than a century. Finally, the minimum voting age was lowered from 19 to 18.

Reportedly King Abdullah feared an electoral backlash as a result of anger about the new *Intifada* that broke out in September 2000 in neighbouring Israel and the occupied territories. He feared that it might spill over the border. The King also worried that Jordan's ailing economy might spark unrest, and on Oct. 6, 2000, he banned public protests. Parliament was disbanded in June 2001, after which Prime Minister Ali Abul Ragheb began "governing by fiat". Between June 2001 and June 2003, Jordan passed 184 "temporary laws", including restrictions on mass gatherings, punishments for criticism of friendly nations, prison terms for journalists who chide the governnment, bans on civil servants signing petitions, and so on. (By contrast, Jordan had passed only 60 such temporary laws in the entire period 1930-99.) Moreover, King Abdullah's policy of "Jordan First", promoted since 2001, alarmed Jordanians of Palestinian origin, though the King insists that it implies inclusiveness of all citizens.

Oft-postponed elections to the *Majlis al-Nuwwab* were eventually held on June 17, 2003. A 58.9% turnout was recorded, of an electorate estimated to number 2,840,000. Significantly, this time the IAF did contest the polls. Non-partisans, including many tribal figures, dominated the polls and a clear majority of those elected were considered supporters of the King. Only two parties returned candidates: the IAF, with 17 seats on 10.4% of the votes cast; and the Jordan Socialist Arab Rebirth Party, or *Baath*, with one seat. In all, 801 candidates contested seats, including a record 55 women, one of whom was the first female to do so from the normally ultra-conservative bedouin community.

Ali Abul Ragheb remained Prime Minister and presided over the opening of the World Economic Forum near Amman shortly after the election. Seen as a technocrat who turned the kingdom into an open market with close ties to the USA and the West, Abul Ragheb reshuffled his cabinet at least six times. But faced with accusations of curbing public freedoms and of doing too little to fight corruption, he resigned on Oct. 20, 2003 – despite having received an overwhelming vote of confidence at an extraordinary session of the new parliament, on Aug. 14, 2003. His successor was Faisal al-Fayez, a Royal Court minister from the Skhour tribe.

On Dec. 1, 2003, King Abdullah II addressed the first ordinary sitting of the new assembly, and called on Jordan to make radical changes so as to become "a modern, democratic country". In a speech which surprised many with its candour and realism, he concentrated on domestic problems – such as the burden of $7bn of foreign debt – and sought to promote Jordan as "a civilized model for tolerance, freedom of thought, creativity and excellence". He specifically called for more involvement by women and young people in government. Some interpreted the speech as a response to US President Bush's recent call for the flowering of democracy in the Middle East. Others saw it as a warning to Muslim Brothers and other Islamists, that Jordan would concentrate on internal affairs before tackling ambitious "regional agendas". Furthermore, the King's earlier interview with the *Financial Times,* after the June 2003 elections, appeared to contradict his democratic sentiments. He said then that he would not choose ministers from parliament, as they spent too much time "ingratiating themselves with their representatives so they can get elected next time round". For the present, parliament is meant to review each of the temporary laws passed since it was disbanded in 2001, and reverse them where it feels it necessary.

Arab Islamic Democratic Movement
Haraki al-Arabiyya al-Islamiyya al-Dimaqrati (Du'a)
Leadership. Yusuf Abu Bakr (secretary-general)
The party is a liberal Islamist grouping, highly critical of the Islamic Action Front's "regressive" interpretation of the Koran. It aims to reinforce the relationship between Muslims and Christians, and includes women and Christians on its executive committee. It won no seats in 1997 or 2003.

Communist Party of Jordan
Hizb al-Shuyu'i al-Urduni
Address. Umm Utheina, Dammam Street, Amman
Leadership. Munir Hamarinah (secretary-general)
Founded in 1948 but banned since 1957, the Communist Party applied for legal status in October 1992. Authorization was initially denied, but granted in early 1993 on the condition that the phraseology of party philosophy was amended to agree with constitutional stipulations. The organization stands for Arab nationalism combined with Marxist-Leninist ideology. It won no seats in 1997 or 2003. In 1998 some CPJ members broke away to form the Jordanian Communist Workers' Party (*Hizb al-Shaghghilah al-Shuyu'iyah al-Urduni*).

Freedom Party
Hizb al-Huriyya
Leadership. Fawaz Hamid al-Zou'bi
Zou'bi, a former member of the Communist Party of Jordan, was reported to be trying to combine in his party a combination of "Marxist ideology with Islamic tradition and nationalist thinking". His party was legalized in February 1993. In 2002 it was reported that Zou'bi was the secretary-general of the "Jordanian Progressive Party", suggesting that the party may have reverted to its older name, "Jordanian Party for Progress" and Zou'bi was subsequently serving as Jordan's Minister of Administrative Development, and also of Information Technology.

Future Party
Hizb al-Mustaqbal
Address. Al-Jaheth Street, Building No 66, Amman
Leadership. Jamal Rifa'i
Recognized in late 1992, this conservative pan-Arab party is a strong proponent of Palestinian rights and opposed normaliza-

tion of relations with Israel. In the 1993 elections it won one seat in the House of Representatives, though none in 1997. Its venerated former secretary-general Suliman Arrar died in 1998. The party joined the Popular Participation Bloc in May 1999, prior to municipal elections in July.

Islamic Action Front (IAF)
Jabhat al-'Amal al-Islami
Address. Amman, Abdali district, Building no. 6
Leadership. Hamza Mansour (secretary-general)
The IAF, a broad-based Islamic coalition but dominated by the Muslim Brotherhood, was formed and registered in late 1992. It advocates the establishment of a *sharia*-based Islamic state, with the retention of the monarchy, and says it advocates the equal rights of women with men. The Front is generally perceived as hostile to peace talks with Israel. More extreme members blame Israel and Jews for spreading corruption in Jordan. Sometimes IAF members are co-opted into government, but always hold domestic portfolios, never foreign policy. Their pragmatism in office has often surprised critics.

Generally, the IAF fulfills the role of an opposition. Although critical of foreign influence in Jordan, it has an understanding with Jordan's Royal Family. The IAF supports national institutions as long as the Hashemites – who are regarded as descended from the Prophet Mohammed – adhere to Islamic values. In the November 1993 elections to the House of Representatives, the IAF emerged as by far the largest single party with 16 seats. In municipal elections in July 1995, however, the IAF was heavily defeated as traditional tribal leaders won majorities in most constituencies.

Abdel Latif Arabiyat replaced the veteran moderate, Ishaq Farhan, a former Minister of Education and Islamic *Awqaf* (Endowments), as party leader in the late 1990s. Hamza Mansour is now the IAF secretary-general, though Arabiyat still remains president of the IAF *Shura* (Council). Abdul Majid al-Zuneibat, leader of the Muslim Brotherhood, increasingly speaks on the IAF's behalf. One of the IAF's main spokesmen is Jamil Abu-Bakr, who in 2004 led a vocal campaign against the launch of a pro-US television station in the Middle East, *Al-Hurra*. Likewise, Mona Abu Dabbus appears to be prominent amongst IAF women members; she led large protests against the new headscarf regulations for schools in France, which became a symbolic *cause célèbre* for many Muslims in the Middle East.

The party boycotted the 1997 elections, citing "discriminatory" electoral laws. Others suggested that the IAF feared losing support (the number of Islamist MPs having fallen from 28 in 1989 to 17 in 1993), resented the ineffectiveness of parliament, or deliberately sought to undermine the legitimacy of Jordan's nascent democratic institutions. Sources within the IAF expressed regret that they had failed to enter the Popular Participation Bloc, a 13-party opposition bloc formed in May 1999.

Nonetheless, the IAF did contest municipal elections in July 1999, and scored particularly well in urban areas with high Palestinian populations, like Zarka, Irbid and Ruseifeh. Some 80% of declared IAF candidates won seats, tapping popular unease with Jordan's economic and social malaise. More than half of IAF members who campaigned as independents won seats. Government sources took some comfort from the low turnout, and the IAF's poorer showing in the capital, Amman. Jordan's expulsion of leaders of the Palestinian Islamist *Hamas* movement in November 1999 appeared to engender a split within the Muslim Brotherhood's leading *shura* council, which unsettled the IAF.

Generally, King Abdullah II has appeared less accomodating towards Islamists than his late father, King Hussein. Apart from his stricter line against *Hamas* sympathizers in the Kingdom, he has sought to crush "extremists", like

Jordanian cells of *Al-Qaeda*, especially after reports of planned attacks on tourist sites over the millennium celebrations, and after the 9/11 attacks on the USA. The IAF has thus taken some pains to avoid undermining the legitimacy of the Hashemite Monarchy. At the same time, it has voiced anger against Israeli policies after the outbreak of the Al Aqsa *Intifada* in neighbouring Israel and the territories, from late 2000 till the present.

The IAF won 17 seats in the 2003 general elections to the National Assembly, making it by far the largest single party bloc in the legislature (only one other party returned a single MP). The IAF's achievement was substantial, in light of the fact that it only fielded 30 candidates, although the total share of the vote won by Islamists (the IAF and independents) was only about 20%. The IAF had objected to rules that forced female voters to remove their veils before male election monitors.

Jordanian Arab Democratic Party (JADP)
Hizb al-Arabi al-Dimaqrati al-Urduni
Leadership. Muniz Razzaz (secretary-general)
Most members of the leftist JADP are former *Baath*-ists and pan-Arabists. The party was recognized in July 1993 and gained two seats in the House of Representatives the following November. The two elected members subsequently joined a broadly leftist parliamentary bloc of leftists, known as the Progressive Democratic Coalition. It holds no seats currently.

Jordanian Arab Socialist Baath Party (JASBP)
Hizb al-Baath al-Arabi al-Ishtiraki al-Urduni
Leadership. Taysir Salameh Homsi (secretary-general)
Initially denied legal status because of apparent ties with its Iraqi counterpart, the party, which originally split from the pro-Syrian Progressive Arab Resurrection (*Baath*) Party in 1970, was legalized in January 1993, following assurances of its independence and a change of name from the *Baath* Arab Socialist Party in Jordan to the JASBP. Its ideology is described variously as extreme leftist or Arab nationalist. One member was returned to the House of Representatives in the 1993 elections, one in the 1997 elections, and again it gained a single seat in the June 2003 elections.

Jordanian People's Democratic Party
Hizb al-Shaab al-Dimaqrati (Hashd)
Leadership. Salim al-Nahhas (secretary-general)
Website. www.hashd-ahali.org.jo
The leftist *Hashd* was set up in 1989 by the Jordanian wing of the Democratic Front for the Liberation of Palestine, a component of the Palestine Liberation Organization (PLO). It was recognized in January 1993 after initial concerns over its independence, and won one seat in the elections the following November. In 1999 the *Hashd* joined the 13-party opposition Popular Participation Bloc. It is not represented in the legislature elected in 2003.

Jordanian Peace Party
Leadership. Dr Shaher Khreis (secretary-general)
Created in June 1996 as a faction supporting improved relations with the former enemy, Israel, the Peace Party failed to win seats in 1997 or 2003.

Jordanian Pledge Party
Al-Ahd
Leadership. Khaldoun al-Nasser (secretary-general)
Recognized in December 1992, the party supported political pluralism, democracy and a free market economy, and emphasized a clear distinction between the Jordanian and Palestinian political entities. Two members were elected to the House of Representatives in 1993. Afterwards, Pledge aligned itself

with a group of independent deputies in a National Action Front. In 1997 then-leader of *Al-Ahd*, Abd al-Hadi al-Majali, dissolved the party into the National Constitutional Party. The party appears to have re-emerged as an independent entity, with Khaldoun al-Nasser as secretary-general.

Jordanian Progressive Democratic Party
Hizb al-Taqaddumi al-Dimaqrati al-Urduni
Address. c/o Majlis al-Nuwwab, Amman
Leadership. Ali Abd al-Aziz Amer (secretary-general)
The party was originally formed as a merger of three leftist groups – the Jordanian Democratic Party, the Jordanian Party for Progress, under Fawaz Hamid Zou'bi (which later withdrew, and was known as the Freedom Party) and the Palestinian Communist Labour Party Organization. It was the first leftist socialist party to attain legal status (in mid-January 1993), and secured one seat in the November 1993 elections. The secretary-general and several other party figures are former members of the Palestinian National Council, as well as of the Democratic Front for the Liberation of Palestine.

Jordanian Socialist Democratic Party (JSDP)
Hizb al-Dimaqrati al-Ishtiraki al-Urduni
Leadership. Isa Madanat (secretary-general)
Established by former members of the Communist Party of Jordan, the leftist JSDP achieved legal status in January 1993 despite refusing a government request to delete the word "socialism" from its party platform. In 1997 the party lost its one member elected in 1993.

National Constitutional Party (NCP)
Address. c/o Majlis al-Nuwwab, Amman
Leadership. Abd al-Hadi al-Majali (president)
The NCP was created as a merger between nine centrist parties in 1997, and is in effect a successor to the Jordanian Pledge Party, *Hizb al-Ahd al-Urduni*, which was also formerly led by al-Majali. One of the prime movers behind the alignment was Prof. Abd al-Salam al-Majali, a relative of the Pledge Party leader and the then Prime Minister of Jordan.

The NCP also incorporated the Jordanian National Alliance Party (JNA, or *Hizb al-Tajammu al-Watani*) led by Mijhem Haditha al-Khreisha, Popular Unionist Party (*Hizb al-Wihda al-Shabiyya*) led by Talal Haroun Ismail al-Ramahi, the Progress and Justice Party (*Hizb al-Taqaddumi wa al-Adl*) led by Mohammed Ali Farid al-Sa'ad, and Reawakening Party (*Hizb Al-Yaqtha*) led by Abdul Raouf Rawabdeh. Other parties included the United Arab Democratic Party (*Hizb al-Wahdawi al-Arabi al-Dimaqrati* also known as The Promise, *Al-Wa'd*) led by Anis Muasher, the Homeland Party (*Hizb al-Watan*) led by Hakam Khair, the Jordanian Arab People's Party led by Abdul Khaleq Shatat, and the Jordanian United Popular Movement Party (*Hizb al-Wihda al-Shabiyya al-Dimaqrati al-Urduni*) led by Musa al-Ma'aytah.

The larger 1997 merger broadened the identity of the resultant NCP. For instance, the JNA (with four members elected in 1993) added strength amongst southern tribal leaders, and *Wa'd* advocated the need to attract foreign investment. Meanwhile the Jordanian Popular Movement Party, which represented Jordanian supporters of the Popular Front for the Liberation of Palestine, brought a leftist hue to the otherwise conservative coalition.

In the 1997 elections, the NCP became the largest single party in the *Majlis*, although with only two MPs (the same tally as Pledge had held on its own in 1993). One member of the NCP, Abdul Raouf Rawabdeh, formerly head of the Reawakening Party (*Al-Yaqtha*) was appointed Prime Minister of Jordan in March 1999 by the newly appointed King. By 2003, it appeared that certain constituent parties were operating separately once more, these including the Jordanian Pledge Party and Reawakening Party.

Popular Participation Bloc
An alliance of 13 opposition leftist, *Baath*-ist and pan-Arab parties. Created in May 1999, shortly after King Abdullah II came to power, it tried but failed to incorporate members of the Islamic Action Front, after much negotiation. The following parties joined the Bloc: Jordanian People's Democratic Party (*Hashd*), Arab *Baath* Party for Progress, the Jordanian Arab *Baath* Socialist Party, the Communist Party of Jordan, the Arab Land Party, Future Party (*al-Mustaqbal*), Progressive Party, the National Democratic Movement, National Action Party (*Al Haq*, led by Mohammed Zou'bi), the Arab Constitutional Front (led by Milhem Tell or Tall; also referred to as Mahdi al-Tall), the Popular Unity Party, *Al Ansar* (led by Mohammed al-Majali), and the Jordan Liberal Party, *Al-Ahrar* (led by Ahmad Zou'bi). Of these parties, only the Arab Land Party held a seat in the assembly following the 1997 elections. Its secretary-general is Dr Muhammad al-'Oran.

Progressive Arab Resurrection (Baath) Party (PARP)
Hizb al-Baath al-Arabi al-Taqaddumi
Founded in 1951, the PARP is one of Jordan's earliest parties, though it was banned for many years. The PARP suffered a split in 1970, from which arose the pro-Iraqi party currently known as the Jordanian Arab Socialist Baath Party (JASBP). The PARP maintains a pro-Syrian stance, which given Jordan's traditional bias towards Iraq, and its fear of its northern neighbour, Syria, may explain the mistrust in which it is held by Jordan's political establishment.

Reawakening Party
Al-Yaqatha
Leadership. Abdul Raouf Rawabdeh (secretary-general)
The centrist Reawakening Party gained two seats in the Nov. 8, 1993, elections to the House of Representatives, and in 1997 joined the coalition of nine parties, represented by the National Constitutional Party (NCP). Its veteran liberal leader, Rawabdeh, though, resigned from the NCP in early 1999. Since then it appears that the Reawakening Party has recovered its separate identity, again under Rawabdeh as secretary-general.

Rawabdeh himself has served in three sittings of the house, representing the constituency of Irbid for his party. He also has held five ministerial portfolios, including a stint as Foreign Minister when he greatly improved Jordan's ties to Gulf states. He spearheaded economic reforms as Prime Minister during 1996-97, and in March 1999 was reappointed Prime Minister, succeeding Fayez Tarawneh. Opinion polls at the time suggested that the famously blunt and occasionally confrontational politician enjoyed high approval ratings. King Abdullah II ordered Rawabdeh to combat nepotism, corruption and public sector incompetence, and pursue modernization and peace with Israel. Rawabdeh's period in office proved problematic, however; bold economic ventures were repeatedly postponed, and at least three ministers resigned in anger. Rawabdeh himself resigned on June 18, 2000, after 44 mainly centrist MPs, including Lower House Speaker Abdul-Hadi Majali, had petitioned the King in April, criticizing Rawabdeh's confrontational and obstructive style regarding domestic affairs. Rawabdeh's party failed to win a seat in the 2003 elections.

Other Parties

Arab Baath Party for Progress (*Hizb al-Baath al-Arabi al-Taqaddumi*), a leftist and pro-Syrian grouping legalized in April 1993, led by Mahmud al-Ma'aytah.

348

Arab Democratic Front, created on Sept. 30, 2000, by two former Prime Ministers of Jordan, Ahmed Ubaydat and Tahir Masri. It favors bolstering Jordan's civil society and democratic institutions, and appears to have received Royal sanction to pursue pan-Arab ties. Ubaydat became head of the Senate in April 2001.

Arab Land Party, once part of the Popular Participation Bloc, the ALP appears to be operating independently again. Its secretary-general is Mohammad Awran.

Constitutional Jordanian Front Party. Also known as the Arab Constitutional Front, and once part of the Popular Participation Bloc, the ALP appears to be operating independently again. Its secretary-general is Milhem Tell.

Green Party of Jordan (*Hizb Khudr*), founded in 2000 and led by secretary-general, Mohammad Batayneh.

Jordanian Arab Dawn Party, licensed on Nov. 29, 1999.

Jordanian Arab Partisans' Party (*Hizb al-Ansar al-Arabi al-Urduni*), led by Muhammed Faysal al-Majali, legalized in December 1995.

Jordanian Democratic Left Party (*Hizb al-Yasar al-Dimuqrati*) arose out of the 1995 merger of four leftist parties. Its secretary-general is Musa al-Ma'aytah. At one stage the party was a constituent member of the National Constitutional Party.

Jordanian Democratic Popular Unity Party (*Hizb al-Wihda al-Shabiyya al-Dimaqrati al-Urduni*) is led by secretary-general, Sa'id Dhiyab Ali Mustafa. Apparently also known as the Jordanian United Popular Movement Party, this radical leftist group was founded in 1990 and has links to the Popular Front for the Liberation of Palestine (PFLP). The party may also be connected to the Jordanian Democratic Left Party.

Muslim Centre Party, founded by Bassam Emoush in July 2001. Many of its members are former ministers and deputies, including moderate dissidents from the Muslim Brotherhood and Islamic Action Front. Emoush himself had been forced to leave the Brotherhood because he flouted a boycott and stood in elections in 1997.

Nation Party (*Hizb al-Umma*), led by secretary-general, Ahmad al-Hanandeh.

National Action Front Party (*Hizb Jabhat al-'Amal al-Qawmi* – though best known by its acronym, *Haqq*, "Truth"), founded as a leftist pan-Arab movement in 1993, and led by secretary-general, Muhammad al-Zou'bi.

New Generations Party, led by Zahi Kasim, licensed in October 2000.

Pan-Arab Democratic Movement, led by secretary-general Mahmoud al-Nuwayhi.

Party of the Popular Democratic National Movement, a small party that is Arab nationalist in orientation, and has ties with Libya.

Right of Jordanian Citizens' Movement, led by Yacoub Suleiman, secretary-general.

Kazakhstan

Capital: Astana
Population: 15,000,000 (2001E)

A constituent republic of the USSR for over half a century, Kazakhstan was one of the last group of Soviet republics to declare independence, on Dec. 16, 1991, on the eve of the demise of the Soviet Union. Later that month Kazakhstan joined the newly formed Commonwealth of Independent States. Nationwide, though uncontested, presidential elections were held in the immediate aftermath of independence. Nursultan Nazarbayev (formerly First Party Secretary of the Communist Party of Kazakhstan), won a landslide victory; he was confirmed in office for a five-year term. The first post-Soviet constitution was adopted in January 1993 and subsequently underwent several modifications. In 1995 the presidential term was extended by referendum until 2000. A new constitution was approved by referendum on Aug. 30, 1995. This provided for an executive President with substantial authority, popularly elected for a five-year term, with powers to appoint the Prime Minister and other ministers, and likewise to dissolve the legislature.

Further constitutional changes were introduced in October 1998. These included the abolition of the maximum age limit for presidential candidates (formerly set at 65 years of age); extension of the term of office of the elected President to seven years; extension of the term of office of deputies from four to six years; and removal of the need to have a minimum of 50% of the electorate participating in the poll. At the same time, a decree was issued confirming that presidential elections would be brought forward to January 1999 (a year earlier than required by law). Although these elections were contested, Nursultan Nazarbayev was again the winner, gaining 79.78% of the vote; there was strong international criticism of the election proceedings, which were felt to have been overly biased in favour of the incumbent President. In June 2000 a bill was passed granting Nazarbayev extraordinary powers and privileges after the expiry in 2006 of his current term of office; opposition leaders sharply criticized this move, on the ground that it amounted to life presidency. In 2003 it was confirmed that Nazarbayev would stand for re-election in 2006. According to the constitution, a person may not be elected President more than twice in succession. However, Nazarbayev is deemed eligible to run again since he was first elected to office after the collapse of the Soviet Union but before the adoption of the new constitution. In 1995 his tenure was extended by referendum, not by election. Thus, were he to win the vote in 2006, technically this would count as his second term.

The supreme legislative body is the bicameral *Kenges*, consisting of a Senate (*Senat*) of 39 members (32 elected by local government bodies and seven appointed by the President) and a 77-member Assembly (*Majlis*) directly elected on the basis of a mixed system of 67 single-seat constituencies and 10 "national list" seats decided by proportional representation for parties. Ten parties took part in *Majlis* elections on Oct. 10 and 24, 1999, the conduct of which was strongly criticized by the OSCE's Office for Democratic Institutions and Human Rights (ODIHR) for mismanagement and obstruction on the part of the authorities. The ODIHR's final report published in January 2000 gave the results as follows: Fatherland Party (*Otan*) 24 seats (with 30.9% of the national list vote), Civic Party 11 (11.2%),

Communist Party of Kazakhstan 3 (17.8%), Agrarian Party 3 (12.6%), People's Congress of Kazakhstan 1 (2.8%), Republican People's Party of Kazakhstan 1, pro-government independents 20, non-party "business" 10, others/unknown 4.

In June 2002, a new law on political parties was passed, which stipulated that in order to be registered (a necessary precondition for legal political activity), a party should have branches in each of the country's regions and a minimum of 700 members in each branch (a total of 50,000 members instead of 3,000, as previously). Some of the opposition existing parties were denied registration, while others did not attempt to seek re-registration (see party entries below). As of mid-2004 there were 12 parties, almost all pro-government and pro-President, that satisfied the new criteria and thus qualified for registration. The next round of parliamentary elections was held, as scheduled, on Sept. 19, 2004. In the main cities an electronic voting system was introduced; elsewhere the traditional system of voting in person was retained. Only 56% of the 8.5 million electorate turned out to vote. Results for party list seats and 45 single-mandate constituencies were announced on Sept. 23, but in 22 single-mandate constituencies a second round of run-off elections was held on Oct. 3. The final results showed that, as anticipated, the presidential Fatherland Party (*Otan*) gained a large majority, winning 42 of the 77 seats (7 party-list and 35 single-mandate); the pro-presidential Agrarian-Civic bloc won 11 seats (one party-list), and *Asar* (Mutual Help), a new party headed by the President's eldest daughter, Dariga Nazarbayeva, 4 seats (one party-list). The centrist *Ak Zhol* (Bright Path) was the only (mildly) oppositional party to win a party-list seat; the pro-presidential Democratic Party of Kazakhstan won one single-mandate seat, while 18 single-mandate seats were won by independents. The electoral proceedings were criticized by opposition activists and several foreign observers, including the OSCE.

Agrarian Party (AP)

Address. c/o Kenges, Astana
Leadership. Romin Madinov
The AP was founded in Astana in January 1999 with the aim of providing support for Kazakhs engaged in agricultural production, grouping workers' unions and agricultural co-operatives. Generally centrist and supportive of President Nazarbayev, the party won three seats in the October 1999 *Majlis* elections, being officially credited with 12.6% of the national list vote. It re-registered in 2003; reported membership: 102,000 (Sept. 2004). In the September 2004 parliamentary election it formed a tactical bloc with the Civic Party.

Ak Zhol (White Way)

Address. c/o Kenges, Astana
Leadership. Bulat Abylov, A. Baimenov, Uraz Jandosov (co-founders); co-chairmen include A. Sarsenbayev and L. Zhulanova.
The founding convention was held in March 2002, on the initiative of several members of the Political Council of the movement Democratic Choice of Kazakhstan. Democratic in orientation, its program includes calls for decentralization of power, independence of the media and an intensification of the fight against corruption. It claims to be an opposition party, but it is seen by some as an alternative to more openly pro-government parties. Others claim that it was a shrewd manoeuvre to split the Democratic Choice of Kazakhstan. The party registered in April 2002, re-registered Dec. 12, 2002; reported membership: 147,000 (Sept. 2004).

Asar (Mutual Help)

Address. c/o Kenges, Astana
Leadership. Dariga Nazarbayeva
The party, which is led by President Nazarbayev's daughter, aims to be inclusive and draws its membership from a broad social and demographic base. It supports the policies of President Nazarbayev and calls for the creation of a state that has a strong economy and a well-developed civil society. Founded in October 2003, it was registered Dec. 19, 2003; reported membership: 177,000 (Sept. 2004).

Auyl (Village)

Address. c/o Kenges, Astana
Leadership. G. Kaliyev
Founded in January 2000, and first registered in March that year, the party aims to strengthen state support for the agrarian sector and to protect the interests of agricultural workers. It also calls for the democratization of society and the implementation of market reforms. Re-registered April 2003; reported membership: 125,000 (Sept. 2004).

Civic Party (CP)

Address. c/o Kenges, Astana
Leadership. Rahmet Mukyshev (chairman); Azat Peruashev (first secretary)
Founded in November 1998, this is a pro-presidential party, with a base among workers in the metallurgy industry. The CP ran an energetic, high-profile campaign during the October 1999 *Majlis* elections, nominating some 30 candidates. Nine of these were successful in constituency contests and two were elected in the proportional section (with 11.2% of the national list vote), so that the party became the second strongest in the new legislature. Re-registered January 10, 2003; reported membership: 160,000 (Sept. 2004). In the September 2004 parliamentary election it formed a tactical bloc with the Agrarian party.

Communist Party of Kazakhstan
Kommunisticheskaya Partiya Kazakhstana (KPK)

Address. c/o Kenges, Astana
Leadership. Serikbolsyn Abdildin (chairman)
The KPK was maintained in being when a faction of the old ruling party opposed its conversion into the Socialist Party of Kazakhstan in September 1991; it eventually achieved legal registration in March 1994. The party advocated close economic ties with other ex-Soviet republics, retention of state ownership of strategic sectors of the economy, universal welfare provision and equality of ethnic groups. The KPK won two seats in the parliamentary elections of late 1995–early 1996.

By the late 1990s the party was broadly social democratic in orientation and represented the main opposition to the government. In the January 1999 presidential elections, party leader Serikbolsyn Abdildin was runner-up to the incumbent, winning 11.7% of the vote. In the October 1999 *Majlis* elections the KPK nominated over 20 candidates, two of whom were elected to national list seats and one in a constituency contest. Official sources gave its share of the popular vote as 17.8%, but independent exit polls estimated that it had won around 28%, more than any other party.

The party was re-registered in March 2003; in early 2004, a splinter group was formed, the Communist People's Party of Kazakhstan (see below). This weakened the KPK, yet it still reported a membership of 70,000 (Sept. 2004). For the September 2004 parliamentary elections it formed a tactical bloc with DCK (see below).

Communist People's Party of Kazakhstan (CPPK)

Leadership. Vladislav Kosarev.
Split from the KPK in early 2004; registered as separate party June 21, 2004. Reported membership: 55,000 (Sept. 2004).

Democratic Choice of Kazakhstan (DCK)

Leadership. Galimzhan Zhakiyanov, Nurzhan Subkhanberdin, Asylbek Kozhakhmetov.

The DCK was first created in late 2001, when a number of politicians joined forces to create a new opposition bloc. In March 2002, two of its founding members, Mukhtar Ablyazov (Minster of Energy, Trade and Industry 1998-99) and Galimzhan Zhakiyanov (former Governor of Pavlodar Province) were arrested, and subsequently imprisoned, on charges relating to abuse of power and corruption. However, the DCK survived these and other, more covert, attempts to undermine its leadership and in February 2004 held its founding convention as a fully fledged political party. It claimed to have collected 58,000 signatures of support, sufficient to secure registration. This was duly granted on May 4, 2004. Reported membership: 87,000 (Sept. 2004). For the September 2004 parliamentary elections it formed a tactical bloc with KPK (see above).

Democratic Party of Kazakhstan

Leadership: Maksut Narikbaev.

Founded in early July 2004; registered July 14, 2004. Draws its support mainly from academics, lawyers and other professionals. Reported membership: 60,108 (Sept. 2004).

Fatherland Party
Otan

Address. c/o Kenges, Astana

Leadership. Collective leadership includes A. Ermegiyayev, Zh. Tuyakbai and A. Pavlov.

The *Otan* party was founded in Almaty in March 1999 by presidential supporters, espousing a social democratic stance. The chairmanship was first offered to President Nazarbayev, but he declined on constitutional grounds; the post was then offered to former Prime Minister Sergei Tereshchenko, who accepted. The new party incorporated a number of other organizations, including the People's Unity Party of Kazakhstan (SNEK), the Kazakhstan 20-30 Movement and the Democratic Movement of Kazakhstan. It rapidly became the dominant party in the country, closely associated with the government and all levels of the administration.

In the October 1999 parliamentary elections, *Otan* fielded the largest number of candidates (some 60 in all) and won the largest number of seats, 20 in constituency contests and four in the national list section. Its share of the proportional vote was officially given as 30.9%, but independent exit polls put its true vote much lower. Re-registered Jan. 10, 2003; reported membership: 312,000 (Sept. 2004).

Party of Patriots of Kazakhstan

Address. c/o Kenges, Astana

Leadership. Gani Kasymov (chairman)

Founded in July 2000, this party was given almost immediate provisional registration, then fully registered in August 2001. It aims to promote the "spiritual and cultural rebirth of society" and to create conditions for economic growth and the alleviation of social problems. It is generally regarded as pro-presidential in outlook. Re-registered March 2003; reported membership: 132,000 (Sept. 2004).

People's Congress of Kazakhstan
Narodnyi Kongress Kazakhstana (NKK)

Address. c/o Kenges, Astana

Leadership. Olzhas Suleymenov (chairman)

The NKK was founded in October 1991, deriving from a well-supported anti-nuclear movement and smaller intellectual groups; it included ecological and internationalist aims in its platform. The party initially appeared to have the backing of President Nazarbayev, and so attracted support in the state bureaucracy. Gravitating to opposition, the party won nine seats in the 1994 election. In August 1995 its chairman was appointed as Kazakhstan's ambassador to Italy. It subsequently lost much of its popular support. In the October 1999 *Majlis* elections, it fielded four candidates, one of whom was elected. The party has not re-registered post-2002.

Republican People's Party of Kazakhstan
Respublikanskoye Narodnoye Partiya Kazakhstana (RNPK)

Address. c/o Kenges, Astana

Leadership. Akezhan Kazhegeldin (chairman)

Founded in early 1999 by former Prime Minister Akezhan Kazhegeldin as an opposition party, the RNPK espoused a platform that included such aims as the building of a law-based society, a socially oriented market economy and the observance of civic freedom and human rights. The party suffered severe harassment from government officials. It was allowed to participate in the October 1999 *Majlis* elections, but withdrew its candidates from the party list section on the eve of the election, on the grounds that its leader had been denied registration. It did contest eight constituency seats, winning one. The party has not re-registered post-2002.

Rukhaniyat (Spirituality)

Address. c/o Kenges, Astana

Leadership. A. Jaganova

Rukhaniyat is the successor to the Kazakhstan Revival Party. Originally a minor pro-presidential group, it was transformed into a nation-wide political party in April 2003. It draws its support from intellectuals and from repatriated ethnic Kazakhs. It remains pro-presidential in orientation; in particular, it emphasizes the need for inter-ethnic accord and spiritual and moral revival. Registered Oct. 30, 2003; reported membership: 75,000 (Sept. 2004).

Other Groupings

Alash National Freedom Party (*Partiya Natsionalynoi Svobody Alash*), founded on the eve of independence and named after a legendary founder of the Kazakh nation. An extreme xenophobic, Islamist grouping, it enjoyed a brief period of popular support in the early 1990s, but was later marginalized. It subsequently revived in a more moderate form and fielded two candidates in the October 1999 *Majlis* elections, without success. Refused re-registration in 2003. *Leadership*. Sabet-Kazy Akatay

Alliance for the Unity and Salvation of the Ethnic Peoples of Kazakhstan, founded in April 2000, with the intention of promoting ethnic harmony. *Leadership*. Zhaksibay Bazilbayev

Association of Russian and Slavic Organizations, representing the interests of the Slav population and sometimes forming a tactical alliance with the Republican People's Party of Kazakhstan known as the Republican Bloc.

Citizen Democratic Party (*Azamat*), founded in April 1996 as an opposition alliance that called for a government of "honest and competent" people. It was the first opposition formation and included eminent public figures from the bureaucracy and the intelligentsia. By 1998 it was close to disintegration, but was relaunched as a political party, moderately oppositional in character, in April 1999. It nominated some 30 candidates in the October 1999 *Majlis* elections, but did not win any seats. Did not seek re-registration post-2002. *Leadership*. Murat Auezov and Galym Abylsiitov (chairmen)

December National Democratic Party (*Natsionalnaya Demokraticheskaya Partiya–Jeltogsan*, NDP-*Jeltoqsan*), founded in 1990 as a pro-independence movement, named after the month of anti-government riots in the capital in 1986 (in the Soviet era). A nationalist movement, *Jeltoqsan* advocates close links with Turkey and Iran, and in 1992 announced the sending of party volunteers to assist Azerbaijan in its conflict with Armenia. In 1995 its leader was prominent in the opposition to the presidential constitution adopted in August.

Freedom Civil Movement of Kazakhstan (*Grazhdanskoye Dvizhenie Kazakhstana–Azat*, GDK-*Azat*), nationalist formation founded in 1990 to promote Kazakhstan's independence, but soon losing ground to other political forces. In October 1992 it joined with the December National Democratic Party and the Republican Party of Kazakhstan to form the Republican Party *Azat*, but the merger quickly broke down over policy and personal differences. By the late 1990s it was moribund.
Leadership. Mikhail Isinaliyev

Generation (*Pokoleniye*), movement seeking to represent the interests of pensioners; sometimes forms alliances with other political parties such as the Citizen Democratic Party (*Azamat*).
Leadership. Irina Savostina

Kazakhstan Revival Party, founded in 1995, this small pro-presidential party nominated 10 candidates in the October 1999 elections to the *Majlis*, but failed to win any seats. Not re-registered post-2002.

My Kazakhstan, founded in September 2001 under the leadership of a nephew of President Nazarbayev.
Leadership. Qayrat Satybaldy

Orleu Movement, opposition movement founded in February 1999, sometimes loosely allied with the Republican People's Party of Kazakhstan in the Republican Bloc. It failed to qualify for participation in the October 1999 *Majlis* elections.
Leadership. Seydahmet Kuttykadam

Republican Party of Labour, small centrist party, formed on the basis of the Republican Engineering Academy. It fielded six candidates in the October 1999 *Majlis* elections, but failed to win any seats.

Republican People's Slavic Movement–Harmony (*Respublikanskoye Obshestvennoye Slavyanskoye Dvizhenie–Lad*), founded in mid-1993, becoming the largest ethnic Russian movement in Kazakhstan, also drawing support from other Russian-speaking groups such as Tatars, Germans and Koreans. Advocating close relations with Russia, dual citizenship for ethnic Russians and equal status for the Russian language, it won four seats in the 1994 elections but did not participate in the October 1999 contest.

Russian Centre (*Rossiiskyi Tsentrum*), grouping based in the ethnic Russian community, denied registration for the 1995 elections.

Socialist Party of Kazakhstan (*Sotsialisticheskaya Partiya Kazakhstana*, SPK), formed a month after the abortive hard-line coup in Moscow in August 1991 as would-be successor to the then ruling Communist Party of Kazakhstan (KPK), adopting a programme of political pluralism and cautious economic reform. President Nazarbayev (the former first party secretary of the KPK) withdrew from the SPK in December 1991 and subsequently launched the People's Unity Party of Kazakhstan (SNEK) as the government party (see Fatherland Party). The SPK then took on the role of an opposition party. It won eight seats in the 1994 legislative elections but was not credited with any in December 1995. In April 1996 SPK leader Petr Svoik, a former head of the State Committee on Prices and Anti-Monopoly Measures, became a co-chairman of the new Citizen Democratic Party (*Azamat*), although the SPK retained its individual identity. It sought to contest the October 1999 parliamentary elections, but was deemed ineligible on the grounds that Svoik formed part of the leadership of a different party, namely *Azamat*. Did not seek re-registration post-2002.
Leadership. Petr Svoik (chairman)

Kenya

Capital: Nairobi
Population: 32,500,000 (2004 est.)

Kenya achieved independence from the United Kingdom in 1963 and was proclaimed a republic the following year. In 1969 the ruling Kenya African National Union (KANU) became effectively the sole legal party, a *de facto* status that turned *de jure* in 1982 and even triggered a failed coup attempt. It was not until December 1991 that President Daniel arap Moi, facing increased internal and external pressures, approved constitutional amendments to re-establish a multi-party system.

The central legislative authority is the unicameral National Assembly, with 210 directly elected representatives, 12 nominated members and two ex officio members (the Speaker and the Attorney General). It has a maximum term of five years. Executive power is vested in the President and to a much lesser extent the Vice-President and the Cabinet. Both the Vice-President and the Cabinet are appointed by the President, who is elected for a five-year term by universal suffrage. The winning presidential candidate must receive besides the majority of votes at least 25% of the votes cast in at least five of Kenya's eight provinces. A new constitution has been under discussion since 2000 and will probably introduce the position of Prime Minister. By February 2004, 53 political parties had been registered, including various previously banned parties such as the *Saba Saba Asili* of Kenneth Matiba and the United Democratic Movement (UDM) of Kipruto arap Kirwa.

The presidential election held on Dec. 27, 2002, marked the dawn of a new era. Daniel arap Moi, Kenya's second President, who had ruled for five successive terms from 1978 onwards, did not stand because he was obliged by the Constitution to step down. His preferred successor and KANU candidate, Uhuru Kenyatta, a son of Kenya's first President, Jomo Kenyatta, lost the election to Mwai Kibaki, the National Rainbow Coalition (NARC) candidate. Kibaki won the presidency with 62.3% of the votes cast, ahead of Kenyatta (31.2%), Simon Nyachae (Forum for the Restoration of Democracy for the People, FORD-People, 5.9%), James Orengo (Social Democratic Party, SDP, 0.4%) and Waweru Ng'ethe (*Chama Cha Umma* Party, CCU, with 0.2%).

In the parliamentary elections, 34 political parties contested the 210 seats, which were distributed as follows: NARC 125, KANU 64, FORD-People 14, Forum for the Restoration of Democracy–Asili (FORD-Asili) 2,

Safina 2, *Sisi kwa Sisi* 2, and *Shirikisho* Party of Kenya (SPK) 1. Nine women MPs were elected. The party distribution of the 12 nominated Assembly seats was as follows: NARC 7, KANU 4 and FORD-People 1. The number of women parliamentarians now stands at 17.

Chama Cha Umma Party (CCU)

Address. P.O. Box 55814, Nairobi
Telephone. +254 (0) 20 240225
Leadership. David Waweru Ng'ethe (chairman and political leader); Geoffrey Wamalwa (secretary-general); Muturi Gitau (organizing secretary); Eunice Nganga (treasurer)
Chama Cha Umma (Party of the People) was registered on Feb. 15, 1999. In the 2002 elections the CCU fielded 11, all unsuccessful, parliamentary candidates and its leader Ng'ethe, an educationalist, ran in the presidential race as well. In 1997, as UMMA Patriotic Party of Kenya candidate, he won 3,543 votes (0.06%) as compared to 10,038 in 2002 (0.2%). Like the SDP's James Orengo, Ng'ethe also failed to win a parliamentary seat. The party's agenda primarily sought to promote traditional African cultures and, for example, to abandon English as the national language and promote Kiswahili instead.

Democratic Party (DP)

Address. PO Box 53695, Nairobi
Telephone. +254 (0) 20 573595
Email. dpkenya@wananchi.net
Website. www.dp-kenya.org
Leadership. Mwai Kibaki (chairman); Joseph Munyao (general secretary); Calista Mwatela (treasurer)
The DP emerged at the beginning of 1992 with the departure from the ruling party of dissatisfied Kenya African National Union members to join the opposition. Its leader, Mwai Kibaki, who had been a longstanding government figure until his resignation in December 1991, attacked widespread official corruption and declared the new party's commitment to democracy, open government and free enterprise. In the December 1992 elections, which the opposition denounced as rigged and fraudulent, Kibaki won third place in the presidential election with almost 20% of the votes cast, while DP candidates secured 23 seats in the National Assembly.

In the December 1997 presidential election, Kibaki was the runner-up with 31.5% of the vote. The High Court dismissed a subsequent petition by Kibaki challenging the validity of the election results. The DP won 39 seats in the December 1997 legislative elections, making it the largest opposition party in the National Assembly. The DP, together with FORD-Kenya and the National Party of Kenya, acted as the "Big Three" who led the formation of the National Alliance (Party) of Kenya (NAK) and ultimately NARC, which won the 2002 elections. The DP's Mwai Kibaki became NARC's frontrunner for the presidency, which he won in a landslide victory over KANU's candidate Uhuru Kenyatta.

Forum for the Restoration of Democracy–Asili (FORD-Asili)

Address. PO Box 72595, Nairobi
Telephone. +254 (0) 733 764698
Leadership. George Nthenge (chairman); Martin Shikuku (secretary-general); A.N. Kathangu (acting secretary-general); Isaac Dahir (treasurer)
FORD was established by prominent opposition politicians in August 1991 and attracted immediate government hostility. The most high-profile figure at that stage was Oginga Odinga, a Vice-President of Kenya in the 1960s and a former member of the ruling Kenya African National Union (KANU). The government's repressive response to the FORD pro-democracy campaign drew international condemnation, threatening Kenya's relations with crucial aid

donors. The party was registered immediately following the regime's acceptance of multi-partyism at the end of 1991. From mid-1992, however, FORD was weakened by mounting internal divisions and rivalry over the selection of the party's presidential election candidate, which resulted in a split into two opposing factions – FORD-Asili under Kenneth Matiba and FORD-Kenya led by Odinga – that were registered as separate political parties in October 1992.

In the December 1992 elections, in which the party claimed that gross irregularities had taken place, Matiba finished second to President Moi with 26% of the vote, while FORD-Asili candidates won 31 seats in the National Assembly (although one representative subsequently defected to KANU in June 1993). Divisions within FORD-Asili emerged in November 1994 when the party's national executive committee reportedly suspended Matiba for six months. Further internal turmoil ensued, with new party officers appointed in March 1996 failing to obtain support from their predecessors. Matiba subsequently formed a separate party, FORD-People.

In the December 1997 presidential election, Martin Shikuku received less than 1% of the vote, while FORD-Asili won only one seat in the legislative elections that were held simultaneously. In 2002 the internal friction further deepened when one section led by acting organizing secretary Wanguhu Ng'ang'a joined NARC while the Martin Shikuku faction decided to try their own luck. They fielded 41 candidates for parliament and won only two seats through popular politicians who had defected from other parties after the nominations – in Tharaka, a candidate who had defected from KANU, and in Kitui South a candidate who had been rejected initially by the NARC headquarters, were declared the winners.

Forum for the Restoration of Democracy–Kenya (FORD-Kenya)

Address. PO Box 57449, Nairobi
Telephone. +254 (0) 20 570361
Leadership. Musikari Kombo (chairman); John Munyes (secretary-general); Ramogi Ochieng Oneko (treasurer)
FORD-Kenya was one of the two main rival elements to emerge from the original FORD opposition movement. The party was registered in October 1992, initially under the leadership of Oginga Odinga, who managed to achieve fourth place in the December 1992 presidential election with almost 17.5% of the votes cast. In the simultaneous legislative elections, FORD-Kenya tied for second place with FORD-Asili, winning 31 National Assembly seats each. FORD-Kenya subsequently joined an opposition alliance to challenge the validity of the election results. In June 1993 Odinga assumed the leadership of the official opposition in the National Assembly. However, he died in January the following year and was succeeded as chairman of FORD-Kenya by Kijana Wamalwa, previously the party's vice-president.

In June 1995 secretary-general Munyua Waiyaki renounced his party membership, subsequently joining the United Patriotic Party of Kenya. At the end of November 1995 it was reported that Wamalwa had been ousted as chairman of FORD-Kenya by Raila Odinga (one of the late leader's sons), which reflected the factional rivalries within the party. However, the following month the High Court confirmed Wamalwa as party chairman, restraining Odinga from taking over as leader. Odinga subsequently joined the National Development Party (NDP).

In the December 1997 presidential election Wamalwa came fourth, with 8.4% of the vote. Despite a weak campaign, Wamalwa retained a substantial level of support in almost all the Luhya districts. In the legislative elections held at the same time, FORD-Kenya won 17 assembly seats, which put it behind the NDP (21 seats) but substantially ahead of FORD-Asili (one seat) and its offshoot FORD-People (3 seats).

Soon after the 1997 elections, FORD-Kenya, like the NDP, seemed to team up with KANU. However, unlike the NDP, the link did not develop into a strong bond, and eventually FORD-Kenya MPs voted with the opposition. The decision to remain in opposition and Wamalwa's attempts to unite it paid off when, after the 2002 elections, Wamalwa became Vice-President. However, his health had been causing concern for a long time and after a one-month stay in a London hospital he died on Aug. 23, 2003, at the age of 61. He had served as Kenya's second-in-command for only eight months. The party leadership was subsequently contested by three candidates, with Musikari Kombo emerging as the winner on Oct. 25, 2003. In the following months, FORD-Kenya, dismayed at having lost the vice-presidency to the Liberal Democratic Party (LDP), positioned itself more independently within the NARC entity, contesting the merging of the original NARC parties into one.

Forum for the Restoration of Democracy for the People (FORD-People)

Address. Nairobi P.O. Box 8380, 00200 Nairobi
Telephone. +254 (0) 20 2737015/2737945
E-mail. fordpeople2002@yahoo.com
Leadership. Simon Nyachae (political leader); Kimani wa Nyoike (chairman); Mwandawiro Mghanga (secretary-general)

FORD-People was founded in October 1997 by Kimani wa Nyoki, a former leader of the Forum for the Restoration of Democracy-Asili, following a split in that party between Matiba and the secretary-general, Martin Shikuku. Matiba then boycotted the 1997 elections. However Kimani wa Nyoike decided to run in both the presidential and parliamentary elections. Lacking charisma and without Matiba's financial backing wa Nyoike won a mere 0.1% of the presidential vote and came only second in the Kipipiri parliamentary elections. FORD-People won three seats in the December 1997 legislative elections (Kinangop, Kangema and Mathioya constituencies in Central Province). FORD-People's future looked even bleaker after Matiba dropped the party for *Saba Saba Asili* and at least two of its MPs were about to switch allegiance to the Democratic Party (DP).

The defection of KANU rebel Simon Nyachae in June 2001, however, gave the party a new and wealthy leader. After falling out with the ruling KANU party, Nyachae had been looking for an existing party for some time. After failing to link with the *Shirikisho* Party of Kenya or another smaller party, he settled for FORD-People. Nyachae had strong support in Kisii Nyanza and through his past KANU links had good contacts in Coast and North Eastern Provinces and parts of Eastern and Rift Valley Provinces. Close to the time of the elections, FORD-People entered into an electoral pact – the Kenya People's Coalition – that incorporated the *Safina* party of Paul Muite and Farah Maalim and the National Labour Party (NLP) headed by labour union activist and former DP parliamentarian Kennedy Kiliku. In the end, the NLP fielded 17, all unsuccessful, candidates alongside FORD-People. The NLP had initially been rumoured to be ripe for a takeover by Nyachae – as were the UDM, *Shirikisho* and the Labour Party Democracy – but disagreements over the inclusion of Ngilu's NPK, favoured by Kiliku, is said to have blocked the move. In the end, the NLP fielded candidates alongside FORD-People, and Kiliku openly campaigned for Kibaki, as did Paul Muite (*Safina*).

The Rainbow Coalition had also signed a memorandum of understanding with the People's Coalition but at the last moment decided to join the National Alliance of Kenya (NAK). Liberal Democratic Party (LDP) officials' preference for Kibaki over Nyachae was a major blow to Nyachae's ambitions to become the sole presidential candidate for a united opposition. Talks about a "Super Alliance" between NAK, the

People's Coalition and the Rainbow Coalition (LDP) collapsed by late October 2002 when Nyachae pulled out due to disagreements over their method of selecting a single presidential candidate for the opposition. Nyachae was accused of being a lone ranger after refusing to join the Super Alliance. In the presidential election Simon Nyachae came third with a total of 345,378 votes (6%), almost three-quarters of which came from Kisii. FORD-People fielded 186 parliamentary candidates and gained 14 seats, mostly (10) in the Kisii region together with Mutito (Eastern), Kinango, Wudanyi (Coast), and Baringo East (Rift Valley).

After the elections a split in the party developed between wa Nyoike and Nyachae over the nomination of Kipkalia Kones to parliament, which did not go down well with the party chairman who had designs on this seat himself. The matter ended up in court and Kones emerged as the winner. In March 2003, however, wa Nyoike announced the suspension of party leader Simon Nyachae, a move that in fact never happened. Nyoike transferred the party offices and left with all the files. Another reason for wrangling in the party was the alleged misappropriation of the nomination fees collected from aspiring candidates. In October 2003 wa Nyoike went back to court to try to force the Electoral Commission (ECK) to nominate him as a parliamentary candidate. The two factions were reconciled in December 2003, only to be back in court over the challenged nomination of Kones by April 2004. A High Court decision revoked his nomination but the Court of Appeal decided on a status quo solution whereby Kones would remain in parliament until the case was heard.

FORD-People had formed a new collaborative pact with KANU by December 2003: the Coalition of National Unity (CNU). KANU supported Nyachae as CNU chairman, with Uhuru Kenyatta, as his deputy until the CNU could hold elections. It could possibly become another major block in Kenyan politics, in particular if dissatisfied factions from within NARC join forces. It remains to be seen if this new initiative will take off seriously.

Kenya African National Union (KANU)

Address. PO Box 72394, Nairobi
Telephone. +254 (0) 20 315946
Email. info@kanu-kenya.org
Website. www.kanu-kenya.org
Leadership. Uhuru Kenyatta (political leader and acting chairman), Julius Sunkuli (acting secretary-general); Yusuf Haji (treasurer)

KANU was established in 1960 espousing centralized government, "African socialism" and racial harmony. It was the ruling party from 1964, and between 1982 and 1991 its status as the sole legal political organisation was embodied in the Constitution. Daniel arap Moi succeeded Jomo Kenyatta as President and party leader in 1978. In December 1990, following President Moi's lead, KANU delegates voted to retain the one-party system. However, the sustained pro-democracy campaign and international pressure for reform made this position increasingly untenable and, in December 1991, the party endorsed Moi's abrupt decision to introduce multi-partyism. KANU subsequently suffered a number of defections to newly established opposition parties.

In the December 1992 elections, Moi retained the presidency with just over 36% of the votes cast, the opposition vote having been split between the leaders of three opposition parties. In the legislative elections, KANU faced strong opposition attacks on government corruption. The party retained power with 100 of the National Assembly seats, although many sitting KANU members were defeated, including 15 cabinet ministers.

In December 1997 Moi was re-elected President with 40.6% of the vote, while KANU won 107 seats in the National Assembly, where it was subsequently supported by the National Development Party (NDP). Its leader, Raila Odinga, had finished third in the 1997 presidential election, receiving over 11% of the vote. In the simultaneous legislative elections, the NDP also placed third, winning 21 seats in the National Assembly. Odinga subsequently aligned the NDP with the KANU. As a reward for collaborating, the NDP had Job Omino elected as deputy speaker in parliament. In June 2001 the NDP's policy of "co-operation" with the government moved closer to full coalition (although this term was not used) when Odinga and another NDP member were appointed to senior ministerial office. Two other NDP members became assistant ministers, while virtually all of the party's backbenchers moved to sit alongside the KANU members of the National Assembly. In March 2002, and after long negotiations, the NDP decided to dissolve itself and merge with KANU to form the New KANU. This move made political observers conclude that the ruling party was assured of victory in 2002.

However, it had become obvious soon after the 1997 elections that the main political battle in the country was not taking place within the National Assembly but in government over President Moi's succession. The rift between KANU-A and KANU-B leaders quickly resurfaced even though the latter had been humiliated by the electorate and the initial non-reappointment of Prof George Saitoti as Vice-President. In April 1998, the first cracks appeared when Finance Minister Simon Nyachae boldly predicted, in front of the opposition, the diplomatic community and three-quarters of KANU MPs, that the Kenyan government would soon go bankrupt and that corruption was rampant within its ranks.

By appointing Uhuru Kenyatta as KANU's candidate for the presidency, Moi gave the final blow that led to the party losing the 2002 elections, ending its 40-year rule of the country. In spite of fielding the highest number of candidates (209), only 64 KANU candidates were elected to parliament in 2002. Uhuru Kenyatta got 1,828,914 votes. Following his defeat, Uhuru Kenyatta tried to re-organize the party. Former President Moi also formally stepped down as party chairman in September 2003. Former Finance Minister Chris Okemo, the organizing secretary Nicholas Biwott, vice-chairman Noah Ngala and nominated MP Mutula Kilonzo, among others, challenged Uhuru's leadership when they indicated their interest in the KANU chairmanship. Former Vice-President Musalia Mudavadi did not seek to become the party's flag bearer and joined NARC on an LDP ticket in November 2003. Soon after, Uhuru launched "the KANU return to power campaign". The KANU party elections that had been scheduled for Jan. 10, 2004, were cancelled. The new alliance with FORD-People and the party leadership issue appear to have split KANU into at least two camps; those supporting Uhuru and others backing powerful Rift Valley KANU MPs such as Nicholas Biwott, Gideon Moi and Julius Sunkuli. In February 2004, MP John Serut of Mt Elgon defected from KANU, later telling his constituents that KANU was dead and that he intended to join a party within the ruling NARC coalition ahead of the next general election. In April 2004 Uhuru was appointed acting chairman without a real contest for the position taking place, something that did not go down well with fellow contenders. This move was seen to be a scheme to revitalise the party and lock out some of the old guard who were regarded as a "burden" when it came to reforming the party. KANU also warmed up relations with their former colleagues in LDP and together they moved some motions in parliament to block the government.

Liberal Democratic Party (LDP)

Address. P.O. Box 78810 Nairobi
Telephone. +254 (0) 20 4441746/4448065
Leadership. Lawrence Gumbe (chairman); Mumbi Ng'aru

(secretary-general); Hussein Sharriff (treasurer); David Musila (acting chairman); Joseph Kamotho (acting secretary-general)

The LDP was formed in 1999 with the assistance of minority-interest activists of Asian extraction. It remained a little-known party until it agreed to host a group of former KANU leaders who had protested against former President Moi's decision to handpick Uhuru Kenyatta as the KANU presidential candidate. These leaders – Raila Odinga, Kalonzo Musyoka, George Saitoti, Moody Awori, Joseph Kamotho – established a pressure group called the Rainbow Alliance on Aug. 14, 2002. They officially abandoned the ruling party on Oct. 14, the day Uhuru Kenyatta was nominated as KANU's presidential candidate; a memorandum of understanding had been signed with the former LDP chairman Dennis Kodhe on Sept. 18 but the union was not unveiled until Oct. 14. Initially LDP (Rainbow) had sought an arrangement with the National People's Coalition of FORD–People, *Safina* and the National Labour Party, but soon decided to team up with the National Alliance (Party) of Kenya (NAK).

The enormous task of setting up a political party – unifying former National Development Party, NDP, and disgruntled KANU politicians while at the same time joining another coalition party (NARC) – is clearly reflected in the problems that emerged over the signing of the memorandum of understanding between the LDP and NAK in the confusion over the party's organisation. The original chairman, Dennis Kodhe, was thought to have handed over to Job Omino, whose position was taken over by David Musila after his death in January 2004. However, according to official Registrar of Societies documents and confirmation by the Electoral Commission of Kenya in February 2004, Lawrence Gumbe and Mumbi Ng'aru are the party's official chairman and secretary-general, respectively. After the death of Kijana Wamalwa, the LDP's Moody Awori obtained the position of vice-president. LDP also saw Mudavadi re-unite with his Rainbow Coalition partners after defecting from KANU. Within NARC relationships with the DP and the NPK in particular were not all that cordial, in spite of several meetings to discuss the problems. From early 2004 onwards LDP issued many threats to walk out of the coalition. On several occasions LDP politicians teamed up with their former KANU brethren to block government policy.

National Rainbow Coalition (NARC)

Address. P.O Box 5751 00200, Nairobi
Telephone. +254 (0)20 571506
Website. www.narc-kenya.org
Leadership. Mwai Kibaki (political leader) Charity Ngilu (chairman); Fidelis Nguli (secretary-general) Peter Malonza (treasurer) Titus Mbathi (acting chairman) Burudi Nabwera (acting secretary-general)

The National Rainbow Coalition (NARC) was formed on Oct. 14, 2002, and brought together 15 groups. A cluster of 12 political parties (DP, FORD-Kenya, National Party of Kenya, FORD-Asili, *Saba Saba Asili*, SPARK, Labour Party of Kenya, United Democratic Movement, SDP, KENDA, Federal Party of Kenya, Mazingira Green Party) formed the National Alliance (Party) of Kenya (NAK) in February 2002. It was joined by the Liberal Democratic Party (LDP) on Oct. 14, a small dormant party taken over by members of the Rainbow Alliance, a dissident faction of the New KANU that united former NDP politicians and disgruntled KANU members. There are also two civil-society organizations – the National Convention Executive Council (NCEC) and the Progressive People's Forum (PPF). This union brought together the four runners-up in the 1997 election: Mwai Kibaki (DP), Kijana Wamalwa (FORD-Kenya), Charity Ngilu (NPK) and Raila Odinga (LDP). In 1997 their combined vote (3,566,716 or almost 58% of the vote) far out-stripped KANU's score of 2,500,320 (40%). In addition, they were able to count on massive support for NARC in at least five populous key regions of the country (i.e. Central, Western, Eastern and Nyanza Provinces and Nairobi). Other prominent NARC supporters were expected to deliver votes in Rift Valley (Saitoti) and Coast (Balala) Provinces.

It took a long time for the opposition to realize that disunity would be a major obstacle to electoral victory. Two important steps were taken to achieve such unity. First, talks between Mwai Kibaki, Kijana Wamalwa and Charity Ngilu began seriously under the heading of the National Alliance for Change (NAC) in 2001, which ultimately resulted in the National Alliance (Party) of Kenya (NAK). Some seven months later the Rainbow Coalition revolted within KANU and eventually broke away. Under the leadership of Raila Odinga, the faction initially sought unity with the FORD-People of Simon Nyachae and *Safina*'s Paul Muite and their Kenya People's Coalition (KPC) before proceeding to join forces with NAK. The proposed Super Alliance between KPC, NAK and the Rainbow Coalition failed to materialize after Raila Odinga hinted during a public rally that Mwai Kibaki would be the best person to lead this opposition alliance. The Swahili phrase *Kibaki anatosha* ("Kibaki is fit to lead") sealed this unity that had eluded the opposition since 1991.

The original parties did not disappear within NAK or NARC. For the 2002 elections they agreed to hold nominations under the NARC umbrella instead of organizing single presidential, parliamentary and civic nominations as separate parties. To avoid the risk of not being allowed to register, NPK became NAK in June 2002 and in October 2002 NAK became NARC. As a result, the officially registered NARC officials are still those of NPK. A memorandum of understanding was signed between the LDP and NAK that advocated a 50-50 power-sharing arrangement between the two parties. The NARC parties were expected to be dissolved after the 2002 elections to pave the way for a single ruling party. After the 2002 elections however, the LDP argued that the agreement was not being fulfilled and delayed unification. The LDP argues that NARC is a coalition of NAK and itself, while NAK claims that NARC is legally a single party as all the government MPs came to power through it. Disagreements between NAK and LDP parliamentarians over the new constitutional proposals are also a major issue, with the latter striving for a strong prime-ministerial position for its *de facto* leader Raila Odinga. NAK members feel that such a position would undermine the power of President Kibaki. In a counter move, the NPK's Charity Ngilu was put forward as a possible candidate for the position of prime minister should a new constitution provide for the office. Opinions differ whether NARC should be a coalition party (LDP, FORD-Kenya, Labour Party of Kenya), a coalition allowing for dual membership (DP, Ford-Asili, UDM, SPARK, *Saba Saba Asili*, Mazingira Green Party) or an individual membership party (NPK, SDP). Attempts by both insiders and outsiders, e.g. religious leaders, to solve these internal frictions had met with failure as of mid-2004. Instead, President Kibaki established a government of national unity when KANU and FORD-People MPs joined his Cabinet in June 2004.

Safina

Address. PO Box 47122, Nairobi.
Telephone. +254 (0) 20 2730630
Leadership. Paul Muite (political leader); Juma Kiplenge (secretary-general); John Icharia (treasurer)
In May 1995 the internationally recognized conservationist and palaeontologist, Richard Leakey, announced that he was joining Paul Muite and other members of the *Mwangaza* ("Enlightenment") Trust (the charitable status of which had

been revoked by the government in January 1995) in the formation of a new opposition party. The following month the party name – *Safina* ("Noah's Ark") – was announced and an application for registration was made. Despite not being registered until Nov. 26, 1997, *Safina* won five seats in the following month's National Assembly elections after campaigning on an anti-corruption and pro-human rights platform. In July 1999 Leakey was appointed head of the civil service and secretary to the Cabinet (with responsibility for fighting corruption) but resigned from this post in March 2001. In October 1998 he had been replaced as the *Safina*-nominated parliamentarian/candidate by Josephine Sinyo. Mwandawiro Mghanga, who had replaced Leakey as secretary general, handed in his resignation on Oct. 31, 1999, barely one year after taking up this position. Mghanga, a former student leader, mentioned frustration from the party ranks and a lack of spirit in *Safina* as the main cause for his decision. *Safina* suffered another blow when two MPs from North Eastern Province, Adan Keynan and Elias Barre Shill, dumped *Safina* for KANU. Both had moved to *Safina* after they had lost in the 1997 KANU parliamentary nominations. In 2002 they ran on a KANU and a NARC ticket respectively but both lost.

In the run-up to the 2002 election, the party was split between a Muite and Kiplenge camp endorsing Mwai Kibaki as presidential candidate and Farah Maalim (*Safina*'s chairman) who supported the FORD-People's candidate Simon Nyachae. *Safina* fielded 59 parliamentary candidates of whom only two won seats. Paul Muite retained his 1997 Kabete seat in Central Province though with a reduced majority. Muite's reputation had suffered from his association with Kamlesh Pattni in the Goldenberg scandal, whereby the latter was said to have offered money to Muite. Peter Munya, after losing the NARC nomination, claimed the Tigania East seat for *Safina* in Eastern Province. Farah Maalim lost the Lagdera seat on a FORD-People ticket. *Safina* seemed to have lost its momentum and members have been decamping en masse to join NARC. In July 2003 Paul Muite said that *Safina* had decided to support NARC and would consider joining it. The close ties with NARC, in particular its NAK section, were also exemplified when Paul Muite was voted in as the chairman of the Parliamentary Select Committee on Constitutional Review in favour of Raila Odinga. In July 2004, though, a combined effort by LDP and KANU politicians resulted in the chairmanship position being taken over by William Ruto of KANU.

Shirikisho Party of Kenya (SPK)

Address. P.O. Box 70421 Nairobi; PO Box 90469, Mombasa
Telephone. +254 (0) 722 430973
Leadership. Mashengu wa Mwachofi (acting chairman); Yusuf Aboubakar (secretary-general); Mwakio Ndau (treasurer)
The *Shirikisho* Party of Kenya (SPK), based in Kenya's Coast Province, won one seat in the December 1997 legislative elections. It has advocated a federal system of government in Kenya (*shirikisho* or "federation"). In parliament it has mainly addressed issues affecting the coastal region and above all its Mijikenda people, such as the alleged privatization of the Kenya Ports Authority and the fraudulent sale of the Kenya Cashew Nut Factory. The party was embroiled in a series of leadership disputes in 1998-99. It fielded 17 candidates in 2002. Harrison Garama Kombe won the Magarini seat in Coast Province after having failed in 1992 and 1997 on PICK and KNC tickets, respectively. *Shirikisho*'s former leader, Suleiman Shakombo, retained his Likoni seat for NARC after initially defecting to KANU in April 2002. *Shirikisho*'s new leader, Mashengu wa Mwachofi, came only third in the constituency of Mwatate. Towards the end of 2003, various *Shirikisho* officials confirmed that they were holding talks with the LDP about forming a possible alliance.

Sisi kwa Sisi Party of Kenya (SKSPK)

Address. P.O. Box 54335 – 00200, Nairobi
Telephone. +254 (0)7 22 723808/769267
Leadership. Zakayo Munyi Karimi (chairman), Adan Wachu Chachole (secretary-general), Mohammed Shebwana Mohammed (treasurer)

The *Sisi kwa Sisi* Party of Kenya ("We with Us") was registered on June 21, 2000, and fielded just 11 parliamentary candidates in the 2002 elections. It won two seats (Juja and Kangundo) with politicians who had defected from NARC and KANU after failing to acquire nomination by these parties. In Kangundo, a first-timer, Moffat Maitha (a teachers' trade unionist), was banking on the support of teachers and won with 26% of the votes, defeating 13 other contenders. In Juja, businessman William Kabongo gained almost 43% of the votes, beating 10 rivals, among them the KANU's outgoing MP Stephen Ndicho who had been favoured by KANU headquarters in spite of losing the party primaries to Kabongo, who won with a landslide vote. Both candidates had bribed voters or security personnel during the KANU primary but Ndicho's links with KANU won him the nomination.

Kabongo's popularity seems to stem from development projects (schools) he supported in the area. The youth factor was also important: his youthfulness and the use of *benga* songs with new and challenging lines sung by popular singers linked to Kabongo's night clubs located along the Kenyan coast seem to have played a decisive role in winning the votes of young Kenyans. Even in early 2003 *Mungiki* sect members indicated they would support the *Sisi kwa Sisi* Party for the presidency. Political observers have suggested that *Sisi kwa Sisi* might be "bought" in the future by national politicians like Kenyatta and transformed into a youth movement for the poor in an attempt to challenge the incumbent Mwa Kibaki's emphasis on investors and the old. Yet soon after the elections both Maitha and Kabongo announced they were on the government's side and voted with it. However, during the run-up to the Naivasha by-election in April 2003, supporters of the *Sisi kwa Sisi* clashed with supporters of the NARC candidate Kihara. The *Sisi kwa Sisi* candidate (Amario) and the party's (then) chairman Rukenya Kabugua and treasurer Zakayo Karimi were arrested.

Social Democratic Party (SDP)

Address. PO Box 21770, Nairobi
Telephone. +254 (0) 2603090/ +254 (0) 722 844896
Leadership. James Orengo (chairman and political leader); Apollo Njonjo (secretary-general); Pheroze Nowrojee (treasurer)

Founded in 1992, the SDP won 15 seats in the December 1997 National Assembly elections. Peter Anyang Nyong'o, who had lost his parliamentary bid, was nominated to parliament. Its (woman) presidential candidate, Charity Ngilu, came fifth with 7.8% of the vote. From 2001, disputes in the party led to it splitting into three factions, each headed by one of the three key officials – Charity Ngilu, Peter Anyang Nyong'o and Apollo Njonjo. Ngilu left the party after a clause was introduced in the party's constitution that required its presidential candidate to be a university graduate, a condition that technically barred her from the top position. She defected to the National Party of Kenya (NPK). The Njonjo faction teamed up with James Orengo, who had defected from FORD-Kenya, while Anyang Nyong'o joined the NARC coalition and stepped down as a presidential candidate. The Orengo faction openly sought to be linked with NARC, but in vain. The Electoral Commission (ECK) recognized the Orengo faction as the legitimate SDP representative and the party subsequently fielded its own parliamentary candidates and presidential hopeful. This split further weakened the party that had already lost a number of SDP parliamentarians during the late 1990s, mainly to KANU

(Kiminza, Ndicho, Murathe, Muiruri). The 2002 elections were fought by 96 SDP candidates and resulted in the SDP losing all of its 16 seats in parliament. James Orengo won 24,537 votes, a meagre 0.4% of the total, and ended in fourth place in the presidential race. Only Beth Mugo, Charity Ngilu, Peter Kaindi, John Katuku and Peter Anyang Nyong'o on a NARC ticket and Patrick Muiruri on a KANU ticket made it back to parliament.

Kiribati

Capital: Tarawa
Population: 80,000 (2000E)

Kiribati (the former UK protectorate of the Gilbert Islands) became an independent republic in 1979. Under the constitution, legislative power is vested in a unicameral 41-seat House of Assembly (*Maneaba ni Maungatabu*). This consists of 39 popularly elected members, one nominated representative of the displaced Banaban community (resident since the 1950s in Fiji because of the environmental degradation of their island by phosphate mining), and the Attorney General (as an ex-officio member, unless already elected). An executive President (the *Beretitenti*), who is popularly elected from amongst members of the Assembly, governs with the assistance of an appointed Cabinet and is empowered to dissolve the Assembly and to call general elections. Both President and Assembly serve a four-year term.

Traditionally there have been no formally organized political parties in Kiribati. In recent elections, however, loose associations have been formed in response to specific issues or in support of particular individuals. In Assembly elections held on Sept. 23 and 30, 1998, two such groupings, the *Maneaban Te Mauri* (MTM) and the *Boutokaan Te Kouaua* (BK), secured 14 and 11 seats respectively, the other 14 elective seats being won by independents. Presidential elections held on Nov. 27, 1998, resulted in the re-election of Teburoro Tito of the MTM with 52.3% of the vote. Tito's third term in 2003 lasted for only a few months after losing a vote of no confidence in parliament. He was replaced by Anote Tong of the BK. Anote Tong's rival for the presidency was his brother Harry Tong, an ally of Tito. The results of the July 4, 2003, presidential elections were as follows: Anote Tong (BK) 47.4%; Harry Tong (MTM) 43.5%; and Banuera Berina (*Maurin Kiribati Pati*) 9.1%. Legislative elections held in May 2003, resulted in the MTM holding 24 seats, the BK 16 and the Banabas (who live in Fiji) 1.

Boutokaan Te Kouaua (BK)

Address. c/o Maneaba ni Maungatabu, Tarawa
Leadership. Anote Tong

Rendered as "Pillars of Truth" or "Supporters of Truth", the BK grouping came second in the 1998 and 2003 legislative elections, with leader Anote Tong winning the 2003 presidential election.

Maneaban Te Mauri (MTM)

Address. c/o Maneaba ni Maungatabu, Tarawa
Leadership. Teburoro Tito

Its title being variously translated as "Protect the Maneaba", "Blessings of the Meeting House" or simply "Good Luck", the MTM emerged in the mid-1990s as the supporting group of President Teburoro Tito. Tito had been elected in 1994 with the backing of a Protestant-oriented Christian Democratic Party

(CDP), defeating incumbent Teatao Teannaki, whose supporters were grouped in the National Progressive Party (NPD). The CDP subsequently coalesced with the NPD to become the MTM, which won 14 of the 39 elective seats in the September 1998 Assembly elections and backed Tito's successful re-election bid two months later. The party lost the presidency in 2003 but remained the largest formation in the legislature.

North Korea

Capital: Pyongyang
Population: 22,082,000 (2000E)

Liberated in 1945 from Japanese colonial rule, the Korean peninsula was occupied by Soviet troops in the north and by US forces in the south. In 1948 separate states were established on either side of the 38th parallel (the north becoming the Democratic People's Republic of Korea, commonly known as North Korea), each of which reflected the ideology of its respective superpower and each of which claimed jurisdiction over the entire peninsula. In 1950 the communist North invaded the South and was resisted by US-led United Nations forces. The Korean War was ended by an armistice in 1953, with the ceasefire line (which became the new *de facto* border) straddling the 38th parallel.

Under North Korea's 972 constitution as amended in 1998, the highest state organ is the unicameral Supreme People's Assembly (SPA), whose 687 members are elected every five years, while the SPA Presidium acts for the SPA between its full sessions. The highest executive body, elected by the SPA, is the 10-member National Defence Committee (NDC), whose chairman holds "the highest office of the state", although the chairman of the SPA Presidium represents the state on formal occasions and receives the credentials of foreign emissaries. The SPA also elects the Prime Minister and Cabinet.

Actual political control is exercised by the communist Korean Workers' Party (KWP), which was dominated by Kim Il Sung, as KWP general secretary and head of state, until his death in July 1994. Also known as the "Great Leader", Kim was the object of an extravagant personality cult and spent his last two decades in power preparing the way for the succession of his son, Kim Jong Il (known as the "Dear Leader"). More than three years after his father's death, Kim Jong Il was in October 1997 formally named as KWP general secretary. In September 1998 he was re-elected chairman of the NDC and thus as de facto head of state under the 1998 constitutional amendments.

Elections to the SPA were last held on Aug. 3, 2003, from a single list of KWP or KWP-approved candidates.

Korean Workers' Party (KWP)
Chosun No-dong Dang
Address. c/o Supreme People's Assembly, Pyongyang
Leadership. Kim Jong Il (general secretary)
Originating at the end of World War II, the KWP became the sole ruling force in the Democratic People's Republic of Korea established in 1948 and has since maintained control of all political activity within the state. Under Kim Il Sung's undisputed leadership, the party adhered to the concept of *Juche* (variously defined as involving political independence, economic self-reliance and national self-defence) as the ideological foundation for North Korean communism.

Having in 1961 again recognized the Communist Party of the Soviet Union as the "vanguard of the world communist movement", the KWP moved to a pro-Chinese line from 1963 and later to an independent stance on the ideological competition between Moscow and Beijing. The sixth KWP congress in Pyongyang in October 1980 resulted in the election of a five-member politburo presidium as the party's new supreme body. No congress has been held since then (and three of the five presidium members have died and one has been dismissed without being replaced).

The rapid post-1989 collapse of communism in Eastern Europe and of the Soviet Union itself in 1991 did not appear to shake the KWP's certainty about its right to rule. With communist regimes becoming an endangered species, the KWP inevitably drew closer to China. But there was no inclination in Pyongyang to follow the Chinese lead in combining communist rule with economic liberalization, and little sympathy in Beijing for North Korea's problems. The result was that North Korea remained in isolated backwardness, amidst increasing economic hardship for its people.

The death of Kim Il Sung in July 1994 generated much external expectation that the forces of political reform would be unleashed in North Korea. In the event, nothing changed in the system of KWP rule, at least on the surface. Long groomed for the succession to his father, Kim Jong Il was at last named as KWP general secretary in October 1997 and a year later was confirmed as head of state. Constitutional amendments introduced in 1998 provided for a very limited move to a market economy, without appreciable effect as the country descended into famine conditions in the late 1990s. In June 2000 Kim Jong Il received the South Korean President in Pyongyang for the first North-South talks since 1948; but there was no sign of any North Korean readiness to abandon its one-party system or to move towards Korean reunification.

Approved Formations

In North Korea's system of one-party rule, the Democratic Front for the Reunification of the Fatherland is an umbrella body for the ruling Korean Workers' Party (KWP) and two minor political parties (below), together with several mass working people's organizations.

Chondoist Chongu Party
Chondogyo Chong-u-dang
Leadership. Yu Mi Yong (chairwoman)
Descended from an anti-Japanese religious nationalist movement of the pre-war period, this party enjoyed a measure of independence until the Korean War, following which it became a subservient appendage of the ruling KWP. It is officially composed of former Buddhist believers.

Korean Social Democratic Party (KSDP)
Choson Sahoeminj-u-dang
Leadership. Kim Pyong Sik (chairman)
Founded as the Democratic Party in 1945, the KSDP initially attracted substantial middle-class and peasant support until its original leaders either fled to the South or were liquidated in 1946. Since then it has been under the effective control of the KWP.

South Korea

Capital: Seoul
Population: 47,470,969 (2000E)

Liberated in 1945 from Japanese colonial rule, the south of the Korean peninsula was occupied by United States troops and the north by Soviet forces. In 1948 separate states were established on either side of the

38th parallel (the south becoming the Republic of Korea), each reflecting the ideology of its respective protecting power and each claiming jurisdiction over the entire peninsula. In 1950 South Korea was invaded by the communist North, but was saved from defeat by US-led United Nations military intervention. The Korean War was ended by an armistice in 1953, with the ceasefire line (which became the *de facto* border) straddling the 38th parallel.

There were frequent constitutional revisions as South Korea evolved through five republics between 1948 and 1987, brief experiments with democracy being invariably undermined by military intervention in the political process. The Sixth Republic was proclaimed in February 1988, following a revision of the constitution the previous October after massive popular unrest. Under this instrument, executive power is held by the President, who is popularly elected for a single five-year term and who governs with the assistance of an appointed State Council (Cabinet) led by a Prime Minister. Legislative authority rests with a unicameral National Assembly (*Kuk Hoe*), serving a four-year term. The number of Assembly seats was reduced from 299 to 273 for the 2000 elections (227 being filled by constituency-based direct election and 46 on the basis of proportional representation) but restored to 299 for the 2004 elections.

In presidential elections held on Dec. 18, 1997, amidst a major economic and financial crisis, longstanding opposition figure Kim Dae Jung, running as candidate of the National Congress for New Politics (NCNP), won a narrow victory with 40.3% of the vote against 38.7% for Lee Hoi Chang of the Grand National Party (GNP). In January 2000 the NCNP was renamed the Millennium Democratic Party (MDP). In elections to the National Assembly on April 13, 2000, the GNP won 133 seats (with 39.0% of the vote), the MDP 115 (35.9%), the United Liberal Democrats (ULD) 17 (9.8%), the Democratic People's Party (DPP) 2 (3.7%), the New Korea Party of Hope 1 (0.4%) and independents 5.

Presidential elections on Dec. 19, 2002, resulted in victory for Roh Moo Hyun of the MDP (taking 48.9% of the vote), who defeated the conservative candidate, Lee Hoi Chang of the GNP (46.6%), on a platform calling for domestic reform and continued improvement of relations with North Korea. On March 12, 2004, following protracted conflict between the opposition parties and the President, the outgoing conservative-dominated parliament voted to impeach Roh Moo Hyun on charges of election violations, corruption and economic mismanagement, this resulting in his suspension from office and replacement on an acting basis by the Prime Minister, Goh Kun.

On April 15, 2004, however, the newly formed Uri Party, associated with the President, swept to victory in the general elections, taking 152 of the 299 National Assembly seats – the result being widely seen as a referendum on the impeachment charges and as marking a further shift away from the right-wing authoritarian establishment of the past. The GNP came second with 121 seats, the Democratic Labour Party third with 10, the MDP was decimated to 9 seats, the ULD declined to 4 seats, and others/non-partisans took 3. The Constitutional Court subsequently dismissed the impeachment case against the President on May 14, 2004, rejecting the charges of corruption and economic mismanagement and although upholding a charge of illegal electioneering, holding it insufficiently serious to warrant impeachment. Roh was restored to office with immediate effect.

Grand National Party (GNP)
Hannara Dang

Address. 17-7 Yoido-dong, Yongdeungpo-ku, Seoul 150–874
Telephone. (82-2) 3786–3371
Fax. (82–2) 3786–3610
Email. jylsej@yahoo.com
Website. www.hannara.or.kr
Leadership. Park Geun Hye (leader)

The GNP was created in December 1997 as a merger of the New Korea Party (NKP) and the Democratic Party (DP) to back the presidential candidacy of Lee Hoi Chang in the elections of that month.

The NKP was the successor to the Democratic Liberal Party (DLP), which had been launched in 1990 as a merger of then President Roh Tae Woo's Democratic Justice Party with Kim Jong Pil's New Democratic Republican Party and Kim Young Sam's Reunification Democratic Party. As the DLP candidate, Kim Young Sam had been elected President in December 1992 with about 42% of the vote. In early 1995, after a dispute with President Kim, Kim Jong Pil had resigned as DLP chairman, subsequently forming the United Liberal Democrats (ULD). The DLP's change of name to NKP in December 1995 had been seen as an attempted break with the legacy of corruption that had enveloped former senior party figures. It had yielded some benefit in the April 1996 legislative elections, in which the NKP had consolidated its position as substantially the largest party with 139 seats out of 299.

The DP had been launched in 1990 mainly by dissident members of the Reunification Democratic Party opposed to the creation of the DLP and in September 1991 had absorbed the New Democratic Party led by Kim Dae Jung, who was the unsuccessful DP candidate in the 1992 presidential elections. The DP had then been the principal opposition party until September 1995, when a majority of its Assembly members had defected to Kim Dae Jung's new National Congress for New Politics (NCNP), later renamed the Millennium Democratic Party (MDP). In the 1996 Assembly elections the rump DP had retained only 15 seats

The NKP-DP merger to create the GNP on the eve of the December 1997 presidential elections was an attempt to counter an earlier split in the NKP arising from the selection of Lee Hoi Chang as the NKP candidate. The selection had for the first time been made in open voting at a party convention (rather than by presidential nomination), but the losing contender, Rhee In Je, had refused to accept the decision and had formed the breakaway New People's Party (NPP) to support his own presidential campaign. In the event, this split enabled NCNP candidate Kim Dae Jung to win the contest with 40.3% of the vote against 38.7% for Lee Hoi Chang and 19.2% for Rhee.

The GNP formed the main opposition to the post-1998 administration of Kim Dae Jung, which made the customary use of incumbency in power to consolidate its support in the Assembly at the expense of the GNP. In the April 2000 Assembly elections, however, the GNP retained its status as the largest party by winning 133 of the 273 seats. It made further gains in by-elections thereafter, gaining control of parliament in 2002 as a result, but the 67-year old Lee Hoi Chang, again the GNP candidate, went down to a narrow defeat in the December 2002 presidential elections. Thereafter the party was damaged by revelations that it had received heavy secret financial backing from the *chaebol* business conglomerates, reinforcing its image as a party associated with the ruling establishment, and it courted unpopularity for its role in bringing about the impeachment of the President on March 12, 2004, on apparently partisan political grounds.

On March 23, against a background of predictions that the party faced a heavy defeat in the April parliamentary elections, the GNP elected Park Geun Hye, the daughter of Park Chung Hee (who led an authoritarian regime from 1961 until his assassination in 1979, and whose name was still widely revered among conservative voters), as its new leader. She promised to save the party by changing its image from that of a "corrupt party with vested interests". In the event, the GNP's losses in the April elections were not as severe as it had feared, the party losing control to the pro-presidential Uri Party but retaining 121 seats, compared with the 137 it held immediately prior to the election.

The GNP is a member party of the International Democrat Union.

Millennium Democratic Party (MDP)
Minju Dang
Address. Kisan Building, 15 Yeoeuido-dong, Youngdeungpo-ku, Seoul 150–101
Telephone. (82–2) 784–7007
Fax. (82–2) 784–8095
Email. minjoo@minjoo.or.kr
Website. www.minjoo.or.kr
Leadership. Han Hwa Gap (chairman)
The MDP was launched in January 2000 as successor to the National Congress for New Politics (NCNP) to support the administration of President Kim Dae Jung, who had been elected as the NCNP candidate in December 1997.

The NCNP had been inaugurated in September 1995 following Kim Dae Jung's return to politics. He had been a major opposition figure in the 1980s, but had been defeated in the 1992 presidential elections by Kim Young Sam (Grand National Party, GNP) as candidate of the Democratic Party (DP). The new NCNP had attracted sufficient DP defectors to become the largest opposition group in the Assembly but had won only 79 seats out of 299 in the 1996 elections and had thus remained in opposition. In the December 1997 presidential elections, however, Kim Dae Jung won with 40.3% of the vote against 38.7% for the GNP candidate and 19.2% for Rhee In Je of the New People's Party (NPP), a GNP splinter group.

Inaugurated in February 1998, Kim Dae Jung formed a coalition government between the NCNP and the United Liberal Democrats (ULD), with a ULD Prime Minister, also drawing sufficient support from the NPP and GNP defectors to ensure a working Assembly majority. On the launching of the new MDP in January 2000, Rhee was appointed as its campaign manager, thus apparently obtaining a base for another presidential bid in 2002. Despite the name change and the benefits of presidential incumbency, the MDP failed to become the largest party in the April 2000 Assembly elections, in which its representation rose to 115 seats out of 273. The renewal of the MDP-ULD coalition strengthened the government's Assembly position, which was further improved when the Democratic People's Party joined the government in April 2001. Kim Dae Jung won the Nobel peace prize in 2000 in recognition of his "sunshine policy" of engagement with North Korea but this policy faltered thereafter and by 2001 his popular approval ratings had slumped from 70% and above in his early period of office to only 25%.

During 2001 the MDP experienced a series of by-election defeats, to the benefit of the conservative Grand National Party; this intensified factional infighting and led to Kim Dae Jung resigning the leadership of the party in November 2001 in an effort to build a broader basis of parliamentary support. In May 2002 Kim Dae Jung resigned from the MDP, apologizing for a series of corruption scandals involving his sons and close aides and stating that he would concentrate on state affairs ahead of the December 2002 presidential elections (in which, under the constitutional provision for only one presidential term, he was unable to stand).

The MDP candidate in the presidential elections, the relatively little-known 56-year-old human rights lawyer Roh Moo Hyun, scored a narrow victory. Roh campaigned on a basis of reducing the power of the family-owned industrial conglomerates (*chaebol*) which dominate the South Korean economy and continuing the "sunshine policy" of engagement with the North, which emphasized dialogue rather than isolating the North. Roh also appeared to capitalise on anti-US sentiment among younger voters and said he would not "kowtow" to the USA – Roh winning easily among younger voters while his conservative opponent scored more heavily with older age groups. In office, however, he moderated his position in respect of the USA (also committing South Korean forces to Iraq), while his domestic agenda was log-jammed by opposition dominance in the legislature. Meanwhile the "sunshine policy" attracted criticism as a result of allegations that North Korean participation in the historic North-South summit in June 2000 had been bought by secret payments by the South Korean government channelled via the Hyundai business group.

In September 2003 a group of President Roh's supporters in the legislature broke away from the MDP, going on to form the Uri Party. Roh resigned from the MDP to become nominally independent but was seen as closely associated with the Uri Party – the MDP's response being to join the GNP in voting his impeachment in March 2004. This proved an unsuccessful strategy, however, much of the previous MDP electoral support shifting to the Uri Party in the April 2004 elections, and the MDP being reduced to a rump of only nine legislators.

United Liberal Democrats (ULD)
Jayu Minju Yonmaeng
Address. Insan Building, 103-4 Shinsoo-dong, Seoul 121–110
Telephone. (82–2) 701–3355
Fax. (82–2) 707–1637
Email. jamin@jamin.or.kr
Website. www.jamin.or.kr
Leadership. Kim Hak Won (president)
The conservative ULD was established in March 1995 by Kim Jong Pil and other defectors from the then ruling Democratic Liberal Party. Kim Jong Pil had been a conspirator in the 1961 coup which led to the era of military rule under Gen. Park Chung Hee (1961-79), in which Kim Jong Pil (related to Park by marriage) was heavily involved, serving at times both as Prime Minister and head of intelligence.

Having its chief regional base is Chungchong province, it became the third largest party with 50 seats in the April 1996 Assembly elections. In December 1997 the ULD backed the successful presidential candidacy of Kim Dae Jung of what later became the Millennium Democratic Party (MDP) on the understanding that South Korea would move to a more parliamentary system and that Kim Jong Pil would be appointed Prime Minister.

Kim Jong Pil resigned the premiership at the beginning of 2000 and in February took the ULD out of the government in preparation for the April 2000 Assembly elections. It suffered a serious setback, however, winning only 17 seats, whereupon Kim Jong Pil resigned as ULD chairman. He was replaced by Lee Han Dong, who took the ULD back into coalition with the MDP and was appointed Prime Minister in August 2000. The ULD remained committed to a more parliamentary form of government, but neither the MDP nor the main opposition GNP showed any enthusiasm for the idea.

Kim Jong Pil retired from political life in April 2004, having lost his seat in parliament in the general election, at which the ULD declined to only four seats.

Uri Party

Leadership. Roh Moo Hyun (national President)

The Uri Party was formed following the defection from the Millennium Democratic Party in September 2003 of a minority group of MDP legislators dissatisfied with the level of support the party was giving to President Roh. It adopted the name "Our Party", or Uri Party as it is generally known, in Ocober 2003. Although Roh was not formally a party member at this stage, he also left the MDP and the party was regarded as a presidential vehicle. The impeachment of the President by the opposition-dominated legislature in the run-up to the April 2004 parliamentary elections (on charges including illegal campaigning for the Uri Party, when as President he was required to remain neutral), proved widely unpopular with public opinion, to the advantage of the Uri Party, which portrayed the impeachment as a "parliamentary coup" by a corrupt political establishment.

Prior to the election the party had a parliamentary base of 49 legislators, but in the elections it became the largest party in parliament with 152 of the 299 seats. The party adopted a liberal-progressive stance in the election campaign. It represented itself as offering a generational break with the past, then leader Chung Dong Young causing controversy during the election campaign by advising older people to stay at home and rest on polling day. It also sought to build a national base whereas the GNP was traditionally strongest in the more developed south-east and the MDP was based in the less prosperous south-west. However, the party leadership also affirmed its commitment to the military alliance with the USA and sought to allay investor fears of a shift to the left, saying it would combat corruption.

In May 2004 Chung Dong Young was succeeded as leader by Shin Ki Nam, a former human rights lawyer, and President Roh (whose impeachment had been overturned by the Constitutional Court on May 14, restoring him to office) officially joined the party on May 20. In August 2004, however, Shin Ki Nam resigned as party leader after revelations that his father had collaborated with the Japanese colonial occupiers. The resignation was a consequence of an investigation into Korean modern history initiated by President Roh that critics believed had been intended primarily to uncover past connections of individuals linked with the Grand National Party and other conservative establishment groups.

Other Parties

Democratic Labour Party (DLP), founded in January 2000 on an anti-capitalist and pro-unification platform, its president having won 1.2% of the vote in the 1997 presidential elections as "People's Victory 21" candidate. The DLP also took 1.2% in the 2000 Assembly elections and the party leader, Kwon Young Ghil, took 3.9% of the vote in the 2002 presidential elections. In the April 2004 elections the party secured parliamentary representation for the first time, taking 10 seats.
Email. jjagal@yahoo.co.kr
Website. www.kdlp.org
Leadership. Kim Hye Kyung (president)

Democratic People's Party (DPP, *Minkook Dang*). The DPP was formed in February 2000 by dissident Assembly members of the opposition Grand National Party (GNP) associated with former President Kim Young Sam (1993–98) and aggrieved that they had been excluded from the GNP list of candidates for the April 2000 elections. Also including defectors from the ruling Millennium Democratic Party, the new party retained only two seats in the Assembly elections. Following the appointment of DPP leader Kim Yoon Hwan as Minister of Foreign Affairs and Trade in March 2001, the DPP opted for formal membership of the MDP-led government coalition. It is no longer represented in parliament.

Kuwait

Capital: Kuwait City
Population: 2,420,000 (2003E) (including 1.5m non-Kuwaiti citizens)

Kuwait is an hereditary monarchy governed by the Amir, who is chosen by and from the royal family. He appoints the Prime Minister and the Council of Ministers. The 1962 constitution provides for an elected legislature, and in 1963 Kuwait became the first Gulf country to hold elections. Successive polls followed in 1967, 1971 and 1975. Following unrest, the National Assembly was suspended between 1976 and 1981. New elections were held in 1981 and 1985, but the Assembly was dissolved in 1986. Thereafter Amir Jabir al-Sabah ruled by decree without reference to any legislative body until 1990, when a National Council (partly elected and partly appointed) was created. In August 1990 Kuwait was in vaded and occupied by Iraq, which declared the emirate its 19th province.

Following Kuwait's liberation from Iraqi annexation by US-led coalition forces in the Gulf War, a new National Assembly (*Majlis al-Umma*) superseded the old Council in 1992. The Assembly has some veto rights and consists of 50 members elected for a four-year term by direct (but very restricted) adult male suffrage and 25 appointed by the Amir. Only Kuwaiti males over 21 and citizens naturalized for 20 years are eligible to vote.

No political parties as such have been authorized in Kuwait and Assembly candidates stand as independents. Nevertheless, several political "tendencies" have functioned since the October 1992 Assembly elections, some in opposition to the government. Article 29A of the 1962 Kuwait Constitution stipulates that "all people are equal in human dignity and in public rights and duties before the law"; however, a law passed the same year restricts the vote to men. To highlight this contradiction, a Kuwaiti brought a legal test case to declare that the exclusion of his wife's name from the electoral role was illegal. In January 2001 the Constitutional Court rejected his case.

Amir Jabir Al Sabah had earlier tried to overturn this constitutional impediment, in a country where in other respects women enjoy greater freedoms than in most Gulf states. On May 16, 1999, the Amir passed a decree specifying that women would have the vote and be eligible for public office from 2003. However, the Assembly rejected the decree in November 1999; a similar proposal presented by Assembly members was defeated by 32 votes to 30 in November 2000. So the changes have yet to be implemented as decreed.

The 1992 Assembly elections produced Kuwait's first legislative opposition majority, encompassing liberal and Islamist groupings. The next Assembly balloting in October 1996 resulted in pro-government members becoming the largest single bloc, although opposition groups continued to be strong. Assembly members can initiate legislation, and question or express lack of confidence in individual ministers. Tensions between the opposition and the government, headed by Crown Prince Saad al-Abdullah Al Sabah since 1978, culminated in the dissolution of the Assembly in May 1999 when the government was threatened with defeat in a no-confidence vote.

Early elections on July 3, 1999, resulted in a strong showing for liberal and Islamist opposition candidates. Islamists won 20 seats, liberals 16 (though estimates of the number in this loose category varied), and government supporters, 13. A new government was formed, also headed by Crown Prince Saad and dominated by members of the Al-Sabah royal family. However, it adopted many changes that seemed to heed opposition criticism of government economic and social policy. Curiously, MPs had rejected the Amir's decrees on economic liberalization and nationality, but re-introduced them as parliamentary legislation. Further major ministerial changes were made in a new government formed by Crown Prince Saad in February 2001.

New elections were held on July 5, 2003, with a turnout estimated at 80% of eligible voters – although only 136,715 men were qualified to vote out of a local population of 898,000, with women entirely barred from voting or running for political office. Within those limits, the polls were broadly considered to be free and fair, notwithstanding certain reports of "vote-buying" by both the government and opposition. All candidates were formally deemed "non-partisan", although one reputable source reported that Islamist sympathizers won 21 of the 50 seats, government supporters 14, liberals 3, and otherwise unaffiliated non-partisans 12. Another source put the Islamist tally at 17 and pro-government MPs at 20.

Clearly liberals were the chief losers in 2003, their defeat being blamed variously on overly close associations with the government, and anger at the recent US-led war in neighbouring Iraq. Liberals had called for a directly elected Prime Minister. The number of independent Shia Islamists fell from six to five, and two prominent Shia opposition figures, Adnan Abdul-Samad and Abdul-Mohsen Jamal, both lost their seats. The new assembly included 24 new MPs.

Tribal confederations organize primaries, and agree to vote for certain candidates. These candidates are usually closely aligned with either the government or the Islamists, but their main goal is the protection of tribal interests. All Kuwaiti Islamists go to great lengths to disassociate themselves from foreign backers. The Islamists tend also to be better organized and more vocal than their secular counterparts.

Islamic Constitutional Movement (*Al-Haraka Al-Dusturiya*), a moderate Sunni Muslim grouping enjoying support from merchants and professionals, and deriving influence from *diwaniyat*, private weekly meetings held in the homes of prominent families. Having gained representation in the 1992 Assembly elections, the grouping returned four adherents in 1996 and five in 1999. It has usually formed part of the opposition to the government. In 2003 elections the ICM lost support, and returned only two MPs. One prominent figure, Nasser al-Saneh, held his seat, though another, Mubarak al-Duwailah, lost his. Although evidently affiliated to the conservative Muslim Brotherhood, the ICM does support political rights for women, based on an interpretation of Islamic law.
Leadership. Ismael al-Shatti and Tareq Suweidan.

Islamic National Coalition, drawing support from the Shia community, who make up about a quarter of the Kuwaiti population, although many Shias run for election as independents.

Islamic Popular Movement, a small conservative Sunni Muslim faction, also known as the *Salafiyoun* (roughly "founding fathers"); three members were elected to the Assembly in 1996, two in 1999 and two again in 2003.

Islamic Popular Scientific Movement, a breakaway from the *Salafiyoun*, returned one member in both the 1996 and the

1999 Assembly elections. They fared better in 2003, returning three MPs, including the hardliner, Waleed al-Tabtabai.

Kuwait Democratic Forum (*Minbar al-Dimuqrati al-Kuwayti*), a loose pro-reform grouping which encompasses secular liberals and pan-Arabist Nasserists. It has been represented in the Assembly since 1992, two members being elected in 1996 and three in 1999. All three of these MPs – the veteran Abdullah al-Naibari, Ahmed al-Rubie and Mishari al-Osaimi – lost their seats in 2003, leaving the KDF without representation.
Leadership. Yousef Naser Salah al-Shaiji.

Kyrgyzstan

Capital: Bishkek
Population: 4,800,000 (2001E)

Having been a constituent republic of the USSR since December 1936, the independent Republic of Kyrgyzstan was proclaimed in August 1991; it became a sovereign member of the Commonwealth of Independent States in December 1991. Under the post-Soviet constitution of May 1993, as amended significantly by referendum in February 1996, the President is popularly elected for a five-year term and appoints and dismisses the Prime Minister (subject to parliamentary endorsement). The Soviet-era unicameral legislature was replaced in 1995 by a bicameral Supreme Council (*Zhorgorku Kenesh*), consisting of (i) a Legislative Assembly (*Myizam Chygaruu Jyiyny*) of 60 members directly elected for a five-year term, 45 in single-member constituencies and 15 from national party lists on a proportional basis subject to a 5% threshold; and (ii) a People's Representative Assembly (*El Okuldor Jyiyny*) of 45 members, also directly elected for a five-year term from single-member constituencies.

Legislative elections held on Feb. 20 and March 12, 2000, were contested by 11 of the 27 registered parties (most of the prominent opposition formations being barred on minor technicalities), although a large majority of the 420 candidates for the two chambers stood as independents. The conduct of the elections was strongly criticized by the OSCE's Office for Democratic Institutions and Human Rights (ODIHR) as unfair to opposition parties and there were many allegations of vote falsification. Confused and disputed results indicated that the vast majority of successful constituency candidates were non-partisans. The allocation of the 15 national list seats in the Legislative Assembly was as follows: Party of Communists of Kyrgyzstan (PKK) 5 (with 27.7% of the vote), Union of Democratic Forces (SDS) 4 (18.6%), Democratic Party of the Women of Kyrgyzstan 2 (12.7%), Political Party of War Veterans in Afghanistan 2 (8.0%), Socialist Party–Fatherland (*Ata-Meken*) 1 (6.5%), My Country Political Party (*Moya Strana*) 1 (5.0%). Of these, the PKK, the SDS, *Ata-Meken* and *Moya Strana* also won constituency seats, as did the Agrarian Labour Party of Kyrgyzstan, the People's Party and the Progressive-Democratic Party of Free Kyrgyzstan. As of mid-2004, 43 political parties had secured registration, most of these being very small. The next parliamentary elections are scheduled for February 2005. By that time a new unicameral system is due to have been introduced.

In July 1998 the Constitutional Court ruled that President Askar Akayev, who had been re-elected for a five-year term with around 72% of the vote in December 1995, was eligible to stand again in 2000, rejecting the opinion of many opposition leaders that this would amount to seeking a third term, which was not permitted under the constitution. Akayev was duly re-elected on Oct. 29, 2000, gaining 74.4% of the vote against five other candidates. Several nominees were excluded on technicalities, such as allegedly failing the obligatory Kyrgyz language test. There were again allegations of widespread ballot-rigging from Kyrgyz commentators as well as international observers. The next presidential elections are scheduled for late 2005.

Agrarian Labour Party of Kyrgyzstan
Agrarno-Trudovnaya Partiya Kyrgyzstana (ATPK)
Address. 120 Kievskaya Street, Bishkek
Telephone. (996–3312) 215508
Leadership. Usun Sydykov (chairman)
The ATPK was founded in June 1995 to represent agro-industrial workers. In the February 2000 parliamentary elections it gained 2.5% of the vote and so failed to win any national list seats. However, it won at least one of the constituency contests. In March 2001 the ATPK became a component of a newly-formed People's Patriotic Movement of nine opposition parties.

Democratic Movement of Kyrgyzstan
Demokraticheskoye Dvizhenie Kyrgystana (DDK)
Address. 205 Abdymomunova Street, Bishkek
Telephone. (996–3312) 277205
Leadership. Jypar Jeksheyev (chairman)
Founded in May 1990, the DDK originally served as an umbrella for a number of pro-democracy and pro-independence groups, including the Mutual Help Movement (*Ashar*), Truth (*Aqi*) and the Osh Region Union (*Osh Aymaghi*). Following Kyrgyzstan's declaration of independence from the Soviet Union in August 1991, several components broke away to launch independent formations, leaving the rump DDK with a more nationalist identity. The DDK backed the election of Askar Akayev to the presidency in October 1991, but later withdrew its support because it opposed his policies of equal rights for all ethnic groups. The DDK formally constituted itself as a political party in June 1993.

Although enjoying considerable popular support, the DDK was excluded from the February 2000 parliamentary elections on the grounds of alleged irregularities in its congress earlier that year.

Democratic Party of the Women of Kyrgyzstan
Demokraticheskaya Partiya Zhenshchin Kyrgyzstana (PDZK)
Address. 145 Baitik Batyr Street, Bishkek
Telephone. (996–3312) 271681
Leadership. Tokon A. Shailiyeva (chairperson)
Founded in 1994 to encourage the participation of women in politics, the PDZK won the third largest share of the popular vote in the February 2000 parliamentary elections, gaining 12.7% and securing two seats. In August 2000, however, the Bishkek city court ruled that the party should forfeit these seats on the grounds of technical irregularities.

Dignity
Ar-Namys
Address. 60 Isanova Street, Bishkek
Leadership. Feliks Kulov (chairman)
The moderate centrist *Ar-Namys* was founded in autumn 1999 by former Vice-President Feliks Kulov, a former mayor of Bishkek, and quickly established itself as the main opposition party. It was harassed by the government in the run-up to the February 2000 parliamentary elections, which it was not allowed to contest because it had existed for less than a year. The leadership therefore took the decision to merge, at least temporarily, with the Democratic Movement of Kyrgyzstan (DDK). However, the DDK was also excluded from the elections, so that Kulov stood as an independent in a constituency contest. Although he headed the poll in the first round, he was defeated in the run-off in contested circumstances.

Quickly arrested, Kulov was tried on charges of abuse of authority when he was National Security Minister in 1997-98. Although he was acquitted in August 2000, the case was reopened by the authorities, who in January 2001 secured Kulov's conviction and sentencing to seven years' imprisonment. Meanwhile, *Ar-Namys* had backed the unsuccessful candidate of the Socialist Party–Fatherland in the October 2000 presidential elections, on the understanding that if he had won Kulov would have become Prime Minister.

In February 2001 further charges were brought against Kulov, who was now in prison, related to his tenure of a regional governorship in 1995. The following month *Ar-Namys* became a leading component of a newly-formed People's Patriotic Movement of nine opposition parties.

My Country Political Party
Politicheskaya Partiya Moya Strana (MS)
Address. 110 Tynystanova Street, Bishkek
Leadership. Almazbek Ismankulov (chairman)
Moya Strana was founded in January 1999 as a party broadly supportive of President Akayev. It contested the February 2000 parliamentary elections, winning 5.0% of the popular vote and securing one national list seat and at least three constituency seats.

Party of Communists of Kyrgyzstan
Partiya Kommunistov Kyrgyzstana (PKK)
Address. 31-6 Erkindik Blvd., Bishkek
Telephone. (996–3312) 225685
Leadership. Absamat Masaliyev (first secretary)
The PKK was launched in June 1992 as the successor to the former ruling Kyrgyz Communist Party, which had been disbanded in August 1991. Registered in September 1992, the PKK attracted significant support and won representation in the February 1995 general elections. In 1999, amidst accusations of corruption and nepotism, the PKK experienced an internal split; this resulted in the formation of a small splinter group, the Communist Party of Kyrgyzstan. Nevertheless, in the February 2000 parliamentary elections the PKK won more votes than any other party (27.7%), securing five national list seats and at least one constituency seat. In March 2001 the PKK became a component of a newly-formed People's Patriotic Movement of nine opposition parties.

People's Party
El (Bei Becharalai)
Address. 63 Razzakova Street, Bishkek
Telephone. (996–3312) 264984
Leadership. Melis Eshimanov (chairman)
This party was formed in 1995 to represent disaffected intellectuals and students and by 2000 had become one of the largest opposition formations in Kyrgyzstan. The party was denied registration for the national list section of the February 2000 parliamentary elections and several of its nominees for constituency seats, including the then party chairman, Daniyar Usenov, were excluded from participation on administrative technicalities. However, at least two candidates associated with the party were successful in constituency contests. In March 2001 El became a component of a newly-formed People's Patriotic Movement of nine opposition parties.

Political Party of War Veterans in Afghanistan
Politicheskaya Partiya Veteranov Vojny v Afganistane (PPVVA)

Address. 4/A Chui pr., Bishkek
Leadership. A.D. Tashtanbekov (chairman)
Previously called the Democratic Party of Economic Unity, the PPVVA has an even longer full title encompassing an aspiration to represent veterans from other conflicts apart from Afghanistan. Classified as a "pro-presidential" party, it won 8.0% of the popular vote and two national list seats in the February 2000 parliamentary elections.

Progressive-Democratic Party of Free Kyrgyzstan
Progressivno-Demokraticheskaya Partiya Erkin Kyrgyzstan (ErK)

Address. 205 Kirova Street, Bishkek
Telephone. (996–3312) 277107
Leadership. Bakir Uulu Tursunbai (chairman)
The ErK (an acronym meaning "Will") was founded in 1991 as a splinter group of the Democratic Movement of Kyrgyzstan on a platform of moderate nationalism and support for a liberal market economy. It was weakened in 1992 by the secession of the more nationalist *Ata-Meken* group (Socialist Party–Fatherland), after which its attempts to build a pro-democracy alliance made little progress. The party has suffered frequent harassment from the government. In 1996 its founder, Topchubek Turgunaliyev (a former rector of the Bishkek Humanities University), was charged with defaming the honour of the President and imprisoned for four years (whereupon Amnesty International adopted him as a prisoner of conscience). He was released in November 1998 on parole.

ErK contested the February 2000 elections, in which it took 4.2% of the proportional vote and therefore failed to win national list representation, although at least one ErK candidate was successful in the constituency contests. The party was further weakened in May 2000 by the formation of the breakaway Freedom party under Turgunaliyev's leadership.

Socialist Party–Fatherland
Socialisticheskaya Partiya Ata-Meken

Address. 64 Erkindik Blvd., Bishkek
Telephone. (996–3312) 271779
Leadership. Omurbek Tekebayev (chairman)
Ata-Meken was founded in 1992 by a splinter nationalist faction of the Progressive-Democratic Party of Free Kyrgyzstan. In the February 2000 parliamentary elections it gained 6.5% of the proportional vote and was allocated one national list seat, while at least one *Ata-Meken* candidate won a constituency seat. In the October 2000 presidential elections party leader Omurbek Tekebayev came second to the incumbent with 13.9% of the vote, having received backing from Honour (*Ar-Namys*) and other opposition parties. In March 2001 *Ata-Meken* became a leading component of a newly-formed People's Patriotic Movement of nine opposition parties.

Union of Democratic Forces
Soyuz Demokraticheskikh Sil (SDS)

Address. c/o Zhorgorku Kenesh, Bishkek
Leadership. J. Ibrahimov (leader)
Strongly pro-presidential in orientation, the SDS is a coalition comprising the Birimdik Party, the Economic Revival Party, the Justice Party and the Social Democratic Party of Kyrgyzstan; it came second to the Party of Communists of Kyrgyzstan in the February 2000 parliamentary elections, winning 18.6% of the vote and gaining four national list seats. It also won some eight constituency seats.

Other Parties

Agrarian Party of Kyrgyzstan, founded in 1993. In the February parliamentary 2000 elections it formed alliances with smaller parties and gained 2.4% of the vote but no seats.
Address. 96 Kievskaya Street, Bishkek
Leadership. Erkin Aliyev (chairman)

Banner National Revival Party (*Partiya Natsionalnogo Vozrozhdeniya Asaba*), named after a Kyrgyz military banner and launched in November 1991 by a nationalist faction of the Democratic Movement of Kyrgyzstan, In the February 2000 parliamentary elections it gained 1.5% of the vote but no seats.
Address. 26 Chui pr., Bishkek
Leadership. Chaprashty Bazarbayev (chairman)

Communist Party of Kyrgyzstan (*Kommunist Partiya Kyrgyzstana*, KPK), formed in August 1999 by a dissident faction of the Party of Communists of Kyrgyzstan (PKK) which claimed that the PKK leader had failed to combat corruption.
Address. 241/12 Panfilova Street, Bishkek
Leadership. Klara Ajibekova (chairperson)

Freedom (*Erkindik*), founded in May 2000 by a splinter group of the Progressive-Democratic Party of Free Kyrgyzstan (ErK). In September 2000 the new party's chairman (the original founder of ErK) received a 16-year prison sentence (later reduced to 10 years) on being convicted of the "ideological leadership" of an assassination plot against President Akayev. He was granted clemency in September 2001.
Address. 115 Chamgarak Street, Bishkek
Leadership. Topchubek Turgunaliyev (chairman)

Justice (*Adilet*), also known as the Kyrgyzstan Republican Party, founded in November 1999 by leading scholars and political activists, including former Prime Minister Apas Jumagulov. Its aims are to promote "constructive cooperation" with other parties, a more equal distribution of power among state institutions and the development of the business sector. It formed part of the Union of Democratic Forces in the 2000 parliamentary elections (see above).
Leadership. Chingiz Aitmatov (chairman)

Party of Spiritual Renaissance (*Manas-El*), advocating the unity of the Kyrgyz people, won 1.5% of the vote in the February 2000 elections.
Address. 4 Balyk-Kumar Street, Orto-Sai
Leadership. O.V. Zubkov (chairman)

Laos

Capital: Viang Chan (Vientiane)
Population: 5,100,000 (2000E)

The Lao People's Democratic Republic (LPDR) was proclaimed on Dec. 20, 1975, bringing to an end the six-century-old Lao monarchy and installing in its place a communist regime modeled on those of the Soviet Union and the Democratic Republic of Vietnam. The victory of the Lao revolutionary movement (the *Pathet Lao*) climaxed a "30-year struggle" waged first against French colonialism, then against the government of the independent Kingdom of Laos. The structure of the new regime comprised the President (the head of state), the Council of Ministers presided over by the Prime Minister, and the Supreme People's Assembly (SPA), nominally the supreme lawmaking body, but in reality little more than a rubber-stamp parliament for legislation already decided upon by the leadership of the Lao People's Revolutionary Party (LPRP). All political power is exercised by the LPRP, the sole legal political organization.

The original Supreme People's Assembly was a nominated body and the first elections for the SPA were not held until 1989. The first task of the newly-elected 79-member SPA was to ratify the constitution of the LPDR, which was eventually promulgated in August 1991. Under its terms, the SPA was renamed the National Assembly (*Sapha Heng Xat*). The constitution spelled out the powers of the President, the government and the National Assembly. The only mention of the LPRP is in Article 1, which defines Laos as a "people's democratic state" under the leadership of the LPRP, as the "leading nucleus" of the political system. Members of the National Assembly are elected for five-year terms by all Lao citizens over the age of 18 years. The Assembly in turn elects the President, who appoints, with the endorsement of the National Assembly, the Prime Minister and ministers forming the government (also normally for a five-year period).

New elections for an expanded 85-member National Assembly were held under the terms of the new constitution on Dec. 20, 1992. All 154 candidates who contested the election had been approved by the Lao Front for National Construction (LFNC), the broad umbrella organization of regional, social and even religious groups that in 1979 succeeded the Lao Patriotic Front (LPF). The LFNC is organized at the local, regional, provincial and national levels and is theoretically open to all Lao, party and non-party members alike. Its three principal tasks are to unify all ethnic groups, raise political consciousness, and mobilize the people to develop the national economy. Like the LPF before it, the LFNC remains under the close control of the LPRP.

The first President of the LPDR was Prince Souphanouvong. In August 1991, for reasons of ill-health, he was replaced by Kaison Phomvihan, who was concurrently leader of the LPRP. When Kaison died in November 1992, Nouhak Phoumsavan became state President. Nouhak retired in 1998 to make way for Gen. Khamtai Siphandon, who like Kaison added the state presidency to the presidency of the LPRP.

The most recent elections took place in February 2002, for 109 seats in an enlarged National Assembly. Of the 166 candidates, all vetted by the LFNC, only one was not a member of the LPRP. This candidate, who has long had close ties with the LPRP, was duly elected. Voting was, in accordance with the electoral law, for a slate of candidates within 18 multi-member constituencies representing 16 provinces, one "special zone" (Xaisombun) and one municipality (Viang Chan). Members elected represented the three broad ethnic groups in the country: ethnic Lao and upland Tai, Austroasiatic-speaking tribal minorities and Hmong-Mien and Sino-Tibetan speakers from northern Laos. Overall members were better educated, and more women were elected. At its first sitting, the National Assembly re-endorsed Gen. Khamtai Siphandon as state President, Gen. Choummali Xainyason as Vice-President, and Bounnyang Vorachit (who had replaced Gen Sisavat Keobounphan a year before) as Prime Minister presiding over a slightly reshuffled ministry.

Lao People's Revolutionary Party (LPRP)
Phak Paxaxon Pativat Lao

Address. PO Box 662, Viang Chan

Telephone. (856–21) 413515

Fax. (856–21) 413513

Leadership. Gen. Khamtai Siphandon (president); Gen. Saman Vignaket, Gen. Choummali Xainyason, Thongsing Thammavong, Bounnyang Vorachit, Gen. Sisavat Keobounphanh, Gen. Asang Laoly, Bouasone Bouphavanh, Thongloun Sisoulith & Maj.-Gen. Douangchay Phichit. (The other member of the politburo, Gen. Osakan Thammatheva, died in 2002.)

The LPRP traces its origins back to the Indochinese Communist Party (ICP), founded in 1930 by Ho Chi Minh. The first two Lao members joined in 1935, but in 1951 the ICP was wound up to make way for national parties in Vietnam, Cambodia and Laos. A small nucleus of Lao communists formed the Lao People's Party (LPP) in March 1955, renamed the LPRP at its second party congress in 972. By that time the party's membership had climbed to around 21,000. Throughout the "30-year struggle", successively the clandestine ICP, LPP and LPRP constituted the leading force directing the Lao Patriotic Front (LPF) and the Lao revolutionary movement (*Pathet Lao*). On three occasions (in 1957, 1962 and 1973) the LPF entered into coalition government with moderate neutralist and right-wing parties, until such time as the LPRP was able to rule alone. Upon its seizure of power in 1975, all other political parties were banned.

The LPRP has a structure similar to other communist parties. From its founding the party was led by its secretary-general, Kaison Phomvihan. At the fifth party congress in 1991, the secretary-general was re-designated president of the party. Upon Kaison's death in November 1992, Khamtai Siphandon became party president. The party leader presides over a political bureau (politburo) of between seven and 11 members elected by the central committee, whose membership has doubled in size from the original 27 to the present 53 members. Until its abolition in 1991, a small secretariat ran the day-to-day business of the party. Since then this task has been handled by the office of the party president and by the politburo.

The LPRP is poorly represented in the more remote of the country's 11,500 villages, but has cells in all district towns and provincial capitals. It is also well represented in the Lao People's Army and in the bureaucracy. The party is organized on the basis of democratic centralism, with lower levels electing representatives to higher levels. Every five years the party elects representatives from throughout the country to the party congress. The central committee and political bureau are elected at the party congress, from among representatives to the congress.

At the sixth party congress in March 1996, the Lao People's Army powerfully increased its representation on the central committee, and especially on the politburo. Of the nine politburo members, six were serving or former generals and one was a former colonel. Gen. Sisavath Keobounphan was appointed as the country's first Vice-President. This strong military presence was maintained at the seventh party congress held in March 2001, when army representation on the politburo was increased to eight out of eleven members.

The congress brought together 452 delegates representing around 105,000 members, figures indicating continued increase in party membership from one congress to the next. The Central Committee of the party was increased from 49 to 53 members (one has since died), including for the first time all provincial governors, the military head of the Xaisombun special zone, and the mayor of Viang Chan, a move designed to reinforce central party control at a time when economic decentralization was being encouraged.

Dissident Groups

Since the seizure of power by the Lao People's Revolutionary Party and declaration of the Lao People's Democratic Republic in December 1975, various organizations have been formed by anti-communist Lao who fled abroad. Some of these were short-lived; all supported more or less ineffective guerrilla operations mounted out of Thailand (and briefly China in the early 1980s). Broadly speaking, guerrilla operations fell into two groups. In northern Laos members of the Hmong ethnic minority who had previously been recruited to fight the US Central Intelligence Agency's "secret war" kept up their opposition to the new regime; while in the south guerrilla operations were mounted from Thailand by ethnic Lao. In 1980 dissident groups formed the **United National Front for the Liberation of the Lao People**, though cooperation between Lao and Hmong was never close.

By the late 1980s, as Thai policy towards Laos changed from antagonism to economic co-operation, Thai authorities withdrew their support for Lao resistance movements. Resolution of the problem of Cambodia in the early 1990s, and particularly the return of Sihanouk as King, gave the Lao diaspora (primarily located in the United States, France, Australia and Canada) renewed hope for international support for restoration of the Lao monarchy. Ineffective armed opposition largely gave way to political agitation. A broad political front was formed called the **Movement for Democracy in Laos (MDL)**, later known as the **Lao Democratic Party**. This competed with another organization, the **Lao United League for Democracy**. Both organizations supported a conference held in Seattle in September 1997, which formed the Assembly of Lao Representatives Abroad to support the claim of Prince Soulivong Savang to the Lao throne. The Prince is the eldest son of the former Crown Prince of Laos, Vong Savang, who died under *Pathet Lao* imprisonment in 1980.

Not all expatriate Lao support the prince, however, and not all favour peaceful political struggle. The Hmong in particular have kept up armed opposition to the Lao regime. After a number of small bombings and an attack on a border post in southern Laos in 2000, Hmong and ethnic Lao resistance groups announced formation of a new Lao Liberation Alliance, of which little has been heard since. None of these various dissident organizations has ever seriously threatened the authoritarian control of the Lao People's Revolutionary Party, which has consistently repressed even the slightest sign of internal dissent.

Latvia

Capital: Riga
Population: 2,306,306 (2004E)

Latvia proclaimed its independence in 1920. In June 1940, under the Hitler-Stalin pact, Soviet troops invaded the country and in August it was incorporated into the Soviet Union. Latvia declared its independence on Aug. 21, 1991, in the midst of the unsuccessful August 1991 coup in Moscow and subsequently (July 6, 1993) restored its 1922 Constitution. This confirms the Republic as a parliamentary democracy in which the sovereign power of the people is exercised through a unicameral Parliament (*Saeima*). The 100 members of the *Saeima* are elected from five electoral districts for a four-year term by universal, equal, direct, secret and non-compulsory suffrage of those aged 18 and over, on the basis of proportional representation but subject to

at least 5% of the vote being obtained by a party. The President, elected by the *Saeima* by absolute majority for four years, is the head of state and appoints, subject to parliamentary approval, the Prime Minister (head of government), whose task it is to form the Cabinet of Ministers (government), again subject to *Saeima* consent.

The first post-1991 free elections were held on June 5-6, 1993 in which more than twenty political parties or coalitions contended for seats in the *Saeima*. Latvia's Way, a centrist coalition founded three months before the election, won the largest number of seats – thirty-six. It succeeded in uniting a wide range of prominent advocates of democratization, a free-market economy, and closer cooperation among the Baltic states. The Latvian National Independence Movement, which was further to the right on the political spectrum, won 15 seats; the moderate-left Harmony for Latvia, which took a liberal stance on the controversial issue of citizenship, won 13 seats; and the centre-right Latvian Farmers' Union won 12 seats. Four smaller groups – *Ravnopraviye*, the Fatherland and Freedom Union, the Christian Democratic Union, and the Democratic Centre Party (subsequently renamed the Democratic Party) – won fewer than 10 seats each. The Popular Front of Latvia, despite its large following before independence, fell short of the 4% threshold required for representation.

The post-election period was characterized by struggle over a set of issues left by four decades of Soviet domination. It included many political problems rooted in the process of state-building, the presence of Soviet troops, the question of citizenship, the incipient reprivatization of collectivized land and property and the pace and direction of the de-sovietization. The Latvian parliament was deeply divided over these issues and these divisions brought forward parliamentary elections.

The Sept. 30-Oct. 1, 1995, elections produced a deeply fragmented parliament with nine parties represented – the largest party commanding only 18 of 100 seats. Attempts to form right-of-centre and leftist governments failed. After seven weeks of negotiations a broad but fractious coalition government of six of the nine parties was voted into office under Prime Minister Andris Skele, a widely popular, nonpartisan businessman. In the summer of 1997 the Latvian government was thrown into deep crisis when it was revealed that Cabinet ministers and two-thirds of parliamentarians appeared to violate the 1966 anti-corruption law, which bars senior officials from holding positions in private business. Under pressure from Skele, several ministers subsequently resigned or were fired. However, after months of increasing hostility between Skele and leading coalition politicians, the coalition parties demanded, and received, the Prime Minister's resignation on July 28, 1997. A new government survived until the next parliamentary elections on Oct. 3, 1998.

These elections produced the following results: People's Party (TP) 24 seats (with 21.2% of the vote), Latvia's Way (LC) 21 (18.1%), Fatherland and Freedom–Latvian National Conservative Party (TB-LNNK) 17 (14.7%), National Harmony Party 16 (14.1%), Latvian Social Democratic Union (LSDA) 14 (12.8%), New Party (JP) 8 (7.3%). These elections led to the consolidation of Latvia's party structure with only six parties obtaining seats in the *Saeima*. Though the election represented a victory for the centre-right, personality conflicts and scandals within the two largest right-of-centre parties, Latvia's Way and the People's Party, hindered the effective functioning of the government. Two shaky governments collapsed in less than a year: Prime Minister Vilis Kristopans resigned in July 1999 and his successor, Andris Skele, was forced to quit in April 2000. In May 2000, a compromise candidate, Andris Berzins, became the Prime Minister. His four-party coalition government lasted until the next elections in 2002.

On June 17, 1999, the *Saeima* elected Vaira Vike-Freiberga, with no party affiliation, to the presidency. Though born in Riga in 1937 she grew up abroad, becoming an academic in Canada and returning to Latvia in 1998 to lead the Institute of Latvia, an organization devoted to promoting Latvia abroad. Vike-Freiberga was re-elected for another four years with 88 votes for and 6 against on June 20, 2003.

Elections to the *Saeima* on Oct. 5, 2002, resulted as follows: New Era took 26 seats (with 23.9% of the vote); For Human Rights in a United Latvia (PCTVL, an alliance including the National Harmony Party) 25 (18.9%); People's Party (TP) 20 (16.7%); Latvia's First Party 10 (9.6%); Alliance of the Greens and Farmers' Union 12 (9.5%); TB-LNNK 7 (5.4%).

The success of the New Era party, formed only a few months before the election by Einars Repse, the former head of the Central Bank, was widely attributed to the party leader's personal charisma and reputation for honesty. Three of the six parties winning seats and 67 of the 100 deputies were newly elected. However, this would appear a continuation of the established pattern of post-Soviet Latvian politics. Each of the previous elections, after 1991, was won by a party formed less than one year before the poll and at least half of all parliamentary deputies have lost their seats. Indeed, each victorious party since 1995 can be characterized as moderately nationalist, promising sweeping reforms and rapid economic development. The ethnic and gender composition of parliament remained much the same in 2002, with ethnic Latvians (79 out of 100) and men (82 out of 100) still dominant.

After weeks of wrangling, on Nov. 7, 2002, a coalition government, led by Einars Repse and his New Era party was formed. It included Latvia's First Party, the Greens and the Farmers' Union and Fatherland and Freedom (TB-LNNK). Repse's cabinet included a large number of young ministers, with several in their early 30s and the oldest minister, Foreign Minister Sandra Kalniete, being just 49. The youthful and perhaps inexperienced government collapsed, after months of squabbling, on Feb. 5, 2004. Subsequently the President named Indulis Emsis, a deputy leader of the Alliance of the Greens and Farmers' Union and former Environment Minister, as the new Prime Minister. He formed a minority centre-right coalition with the People's Party and Latvia's First Party.

Latvia became a a member of the EU on May 1, 2004 (following endorsement in a national referendum in which some 67% voted in favour of membership). It held its first European Parliament elections on June 12, 2004, sixteen parties competing. In a turnout of 41.23% the TB-LNNK won 29.8% of the votes and gained 4 of the country's 9 seats; the New Era party took 19.7% of the vote and 2 seats; For Human Rights in a United Latvia 10.7% of the vote and 1 seat; People's Party 6.7% of the vote and 1 seat; Latvia's Way 6.5% of the vote and 1 seat. Four parties narrowly missed the 5% threshold – the Latvian Social Democratic Workers' Party 4.8%, National Harmony Party 4.8%, Alliance of the Greens and Farmers' Union 4.3%, and Latvia's First Party 3.3%. The elections were a major defeat for the coalition government

in power, as the three coalition parties together won only 14.2% of the popular vote. The People's Party was the only coalition party to win a seat.

Alliance of the Greens and Farmers' Union
Established before the 2002 parliamentary elections the alliance consists of two political parties, the Latvian Farmers' Union and Latvian Green Party (see entries). During the November 2002 parliamentary election campaign it ran on an ideologically amorphous agenda and won 9.5% of the vote and secured 12 out of 100 seats in the *Seima*. In February 2004 Indulis Emsis, the leader of the Green Party, became Prime Minister of a minority centre-right government. In the June 2004 European elections, the Alliance took only 4.3% of the vote, failing to win a seat.

Fatherland and Freedom–Latvian National Conservative Party
Tevzemei un Brvibai–Latvijas Nacionala Konservativa Partija (TB–LNNK)
Address. Kaleju iela 10, Riga 1050
Telephone. (371) 708–7273
Fax. (371) 708–7268
Email. tb@tb.lv
Website. www.tb.lv
Leadership. Maris Grinblats (chairman); Vladimirs Makarovs & Janis Straume (deputy chairmen); Vents Balodis (*Saeima* group chairman); Juris Saratovs (secretary-general)
The right-wing TB–LNNK was formed in June 1997 as a merger of the TB and the LNNK, intended to consolidate popular support for the right. However, some LNNK members rejected the merger and defected to the new Latvian National Reform Party.

Of the two components, the TB was itself an alliance of several groups of the far right, reportedly in contact with right-wing extremists in Germany, and was viewed as being descended from the party of the *Waffen SS* at the time of the German occupation during World War II. The TB won 5.4% of the vote and six seats in the 1993 parliamentary elections, this tally rising to 11.9% and 14 seats in the 1995 elections. It thus became the strongest single party within the National Bloc alliance of conservative parties founded in September 1994. After the TB leader, Maris Grinblats, had tried and failed to build a viable coalition government, the party joined a broad centre-right coalition headed by a non-party Prime Minister, with Grinblats becoming a Deputy Prime Minister and Education Minister.

The LNNK was founded in 1988 as the Latvian National Independence Movement (*Latvijas Nacionala Neatkaribas Kustiba*, LNNK), retaining the LNNK abbreviation when it became the Latvian National Conservative Party in June 1994. Ultra-nationalist and anti-Russian, the party wanted welfare benefits to be limited to ethnic Latvians and that no more than 25% of non-Latvians should be accorded Latvian citizenship. In the 1993 general elections the party won 15 seats on a 13.6% vote share; but its image was tarnished by association with the campaign rhetoric of a far-right party member of German origin, Joahims Zigerists, who was later expelled from the LNNK and formed the Popular Movement for Latvia–Zigerists Party. On the President's invitation, Andrejs Krastins (then the LNNK associate chairman) attempted to form a right-wing government in August 1994, but was rebuffed by the *Saeima*. The LNNK was also a member of the opposition National Bloc launched in September 1994. However, for the autumn 1995 parliamentary elections it formed an unlikely alliance with the Latvian Green Party, winning eight seats on a 6.3% vote share. It subsequently joined a broad centre-right coalition government under a non-party Prime Minister, in which Krastins (by now LNNK chairman) became a Deputy Prime Minister and Defence Minister.

Immediately after the TB–LNNK merger, the party in August 1997 successfully nominated Guntars Krasts as Prime Minister of a reconstituted centre-right coalition. In the October 1998 parliamentary elections, however, the TB–LNNK won only 17 of the 100 seats on a 14.7% vote share, well below the combined vote of the component parties in 1995. The party also failed to get popular endorsement in a simultaneous referendum for its attempt to block recent legislation liberalizing Latvia's naturalization laws. It nevertheless joined a new centre-right coalition headed by Latvia's Way (LC), continuing in government when the People's Party obtained the premiership in July 1999 and also when it reverted to the LC in April 2000.

In the November 2002 parliamentary election the TB–LNNK won 5.4% of the vote and secured 7 out of 100 seats in the *Seima*. During the June 2004 election campaign for the European Parliament it strongly promoted Latvia's national interests and was an opponent of a federal Europe. It won 29% of the vote and 4 of Latvia's 9 seats.

For Human Rights in United Latvia
Par Cilveka Tiesibam Vienota Latvija (PCTVL)
Address. Ul. Dzirnavu 102a, Riga 1050
Telephone. +371 728 8883
Email. info@lzapchel.lv
Website. www.pctvl.lv
Leadership. Janis Jurkans (leader)
This alliance of several political parties emphasizes issues important to the Russian-speaking community. It was established in May 1998 ahead of the October parliamentary elections by the National Harmony Party (TSP), the Equal Rights Party (commonly known as Equality), and Latvian Socialist Party (LSP), all of which were mainly supported by Russian-speaking voters. A survey of citizens made by the Baltic Social Sciences Institute prior to the election revealed that over 80% of its supporters were non-Latvians. The alliance, however, failed to secure registration in time to run under that label and its candidates therefore stood under the TSP banner, winning 14.1% of the vote and 16 out of the 100 seats and becoming the largest component of the opposition to the subsequent centre-right coalition. In the municipal elections in 2001 the PCTVL won 13 out of 60 seats in Riga city council and a member, Sergejs Dolgopolovs, became the deputy mayor of Riga.

In the Oct. 5, 2002, *Saeima* elections the PCTVL won 18.9% of the vote and secured 25 seats – the only leftist party to make it into parliament. The PCTVL partially broke up in 2003. The TSP was the first to leave the alliance and the LSP followed half a year later. Riga's deputy-mayor Sergejs Dolgopolovs also left the alliance planning to start a new political party. The remnant of PCTVL has only 6 members in the Latvian parliament but, according to public opinion polls, is more popular than any of the parties that left the alliance. PCTVL supports a federal Europe, with a "common economical and political space from Lisbon to Vladivostok". It has also proposed the creation of a Europe-wide party of ethnic Russians. In the June 2004 European Parliament elections one of Latvia's seats was won by the PCTVL, by Tatyana Zhdanok, previously prominent as a leader of the Latvian Communist Party and the anti-independence movement in Latvia in the early 1990s. In the parliament she affiliated with the Greens/European Free Alliance grouping in the European Parliament.

Latvia's First Party
Latvijas Pirma Partija (LPP)
Website. www.lpp.lv
Leadership. Eriks Jekabsons (chairman)
The party was founded by Eriks Jekabsons, a Lutheran pastor and former kickboxer, and took 10 seats in the 2002 elec-

tions. The party's withdrawal in Jan. 28, 2004, from the coalition government led by Prime Minister Einars Repse led to its collapse. The LPP subsequently joined the coalition government of Prime Minister Indulis Emsis. In the June 2004 European Parliament elections it took 3.3% of the vote and failed to win a seat.

Latvia's Way
Latvijas Cels (LC)
Address. Jauniela iela 25-29, Riga 1050
Telephone. (371) 722–4162
Fax. (371) 782–1121
Email. lc@lc.lv
Website. www.lc.lv
Leadership. Andris Berzins (leader); Andrejs Pantelejevs (chairman); Kristiana Libane (*Saeima* group chairperson)
The LC originated as an association of well-known pro-independence personalities, sponsored by the World Federation of Free Latvians and the influential Club 21 network, who came together prior to the 1993 parliamentary elections. Although evincing a centre-right political stance and a liberal-conservative socio-economic approach, the party was viewed by many Latvians as rooted in the ways of the Soviet era because of the earlier careers of many of its leading members. Nevertheless, its pivotal parliamentary position enabled it to lead successive post-independence coalition governments, its 32.4% vote share in 1993 making it the largest party in the *Saeima*, with 36 seats.

Paying the democratic penalty for government incumbency in difficult times, the LC slumped to 17 seats and 14.6% in the 1995 elections, although it continued in government in a broad centre-right coalition in which the *Saimnieks* Democratic Party (Latvian Democratic Party) had the dominant position, with Maris Gailis of the LC becoming a Deputy Prime Minister and Environment and Regional Development Minister.

In the October 1998 elections the LC recovered somewhat to 21 seats and 18.1% of the vote, so that the LC's Vilis Kristopans became Prime Minister of a new centre-right coalition government. In July 1999 the LC surrendered the premiership to the People's Party but recovered it in April 2000 in the person of Andris Berzins, the mayor of Riga, who became head of Latvia's ninth government in a decade of independence. In the Oct. 5, 2002 *Seima* elections the party failed to reach the 5% threshold needed to enter parliament but it won one seat, with 6.5% of the vote, in the June 2004 European elections

The LC is a member party of the Liberal International.

Latvian Democratic Party
Latvijas Demokratiska Partija (LDP)
Address. Maza Monetu iela 3, Riga 1050
Telephone. (371) 728–7739
Fax. (371) 728–8211
Email. ldp@ldp.lv
Website. www.ldp.lv
Leadership. Andris Ameriks (chairman)
The LDP is descended from the pre-war Democratic Centre Party (*Demokratiska Centra Partija*, DCP), which was relaunched in 1992 and won five seats on a 4.8% vote share in 1993. The DCP subsequently became the Democratic Party before merging with another group in 1994 under the *Saimnieks* Democratic Party (DPS) label, a Latvian term denoting a traditional source of authority (usually rendered in English as "Master"). Taking a pro-market position on economic issues and exhibiting a moderate nationalist policy orientation, *Saimnieks* became the largest single party with 15.1% of the vote and 19 seats in the 1995 general elections. After an attempt by party chairman Ziedonis Cevers to form a coalition including the far-right Popular Movement

for Latvia–Zigerists Party had been thwarted by presidential opposition, *Saimnieks* settled for participation, as the strongest party, in a broad centre-right coalition headed by a non-party Prime Minister.

Subsequent tensions between *Saimnieks* and its coalition partners were apparent in the party's decision to nominate Ilga Kreituse (DPS Speaker of the *Saeima*) as its presidential candidate in 1996, in opposition to incumbent Guntis Ulmanis of the Latvian Farmers' Union. In the parliamentary voting in June 1996, Kreituse was runner-up with 25 votes. The following month *Saimnieks* was strengthened by an agreement that it would absorb the small Republican Party (led by Andris Plotnieks) and by the decision of two deputies of the National Harmony Party (TSP) to defect to its ranks. But it was weakened in early 1997 by a row over the irregular funding practices of then Finance Minister Aivars Kreituss, who was expelled from the party and who launched the rival Labour Party. Shortly afterwards *Saimnieks* lost more adherents to the new Latvian National Reform Party.

Saimnieks withdrew from the government coalition in April 1998, but was still punished in the October 1998 parliamentary elections, its vote share slumping to 1.6%, so that it failed to retain representation. Cevers thereupon resigned as chairman and in December 1999 the party opted to drop the *Saimnieks* label and to become simply the Latvian Democratic Party (LDP). It is not represented in the parliament elected in 2002.

Latvian Farmers' Union
Latvijas Zemnieku Savieniba (LZS)

Address. 2 Republikas laukums, Riga 1010
Telephone. (371) 732–7163
Leadership. Augusts Brigmanis (chairman)

This is the modern descendant of a similarly-named organization founded in 1917 and prominent in the inter-war period and then banned in 1934. The party is primarily devoted to defending rural interests, taking a somewhat conservative position on the nationality issue. It won 12 seats in the June 1993 general elections (with 10.6% of the vote), following which Guntis Ulmanis (a former chairman of the Latvian Supreme Soviet) was the successful LZS candidate in the July parliamentary election of a new President. For the autumn 1995 elections the LZS entered into alliance with the Latvian Christian Democratic Union and the Democratic Party of Latgale, winning eight seats on a 6.3% vote share. It subsequently joined a broad centre-right coalition government under a non-party Prime Minister and in June 1996 Ulmanis was re-elected President with the backing of most of the coalition parties, serving until mid-1999. In the 1998 parliamentary elections the LZS slumped to 2.5% of the vote, ceasing to be represented. In the 2002 elections, however, its alliance with the Latvian Green Party won 12 seats and it subsequently entered government.

Latvian Green Party
Latvijas Zala Partija (LZP)

Address. Kalnciemaiela 30, Riga 1046
Telephone. (371) 761–2626
Fax. (371) 761–4927
Leadership. Indulis Emsis (chairman)

Founded in 1990, but captured only 1.2% of the vote and no seats in the 1993 election, although a Green became Minister of State for the Environment in the new government headed by Latvia's Way. The Greens also obtained representation at junior ministerial level in the broad centre-right coalition government formed after the 1995 elections, which it had contested in alliance with the Latvian National Conservative Party. The Greens contested the 1998 elections in alliance with the Labour Party and the Latvian Christian Democratic Union, their 2.3% vote share yielding no seats. In 2002, in

contrast, the party joined the Alliance of the Greens and Farmers' Union, which won 12 seats. The party chairman Indulis Emsis became Prime Minister in February 2004.

Latvian Social Democratic Workers' Party
Latvijas Socialdemokratiska Stradnieku Partija (LSDSP)

Address. Bruninieku iela 29–31, Riga 1001
Telephone. (371) 227–4039
Fax. (371) 227–7319
Email. lsdsp@lis.lv
Website. www.lsdsp.lv
Leadership: Dainis Ivans (chairman)

Having been Latvia's leading party in the 1920s, the LSDSP was re-established in 1989 after 50 years' existence in exile. It fared badly in early post-independence elections, not least because social democratic forces were split. In October 1997 it joined with the (ex-communist) Latvian Social Democratic Party (LSDP) to launch the Latvian Social Democratic Union (LSDA), which in the October 1998 elections advanced strongly to 14 seats on a 12.8% vote share. In February 1999 the LSDA undertook to give qualified support to the incumbent centre-right coalition headed by Latvia's Way. In May 1999 the LSDA components opted for collective reversion to the historic LSDSP designation. The party had some sucesses in the 2001 local elections when one of its members became the mayor of Riga. In the 2002 parliamentary elections, however, it secured only 4% of the vote and failed to pass the 5% threshold to secure seats in the parliament.

The LSDSP is a member party of the Socialist International.

Latvian Socialist Party
Latvijas Socialistiska Partija (LSP)

Address. Burtnieku iela 23, Riga 1006
Telephone. (371) 755–5535
Fax. (371) 755–5535
Website. www.vide.lv/lsp
Leadership. Alfreds Rubiks (chairman)

The LSP was created in 1994 as successor to the Equal Rights Party (commonly known as Equality), which had been founded in 1993 to represent the interests of the non-Latvian population and had advocated the adoption of Russian as Latvia's second official language. At the time of the June 1993 general elections, the party's most prominent figure, Alfreds Rubiks (a former member of the Politburo of the USSR Communist Party), was in prison awaiting trial for supporting the abortive August 1991 coup by hardliners in Moscow. The party won seven seats on a 5.8% vote share, although Rubik's credentials as an elected deputy were rejected by the new *Saeima*.

In July 1995 Rubiks was sentenced to eight years' imprisonment for conspiring to overthrow the government in 1991. He was nevertheless placed at the head of the candidates' list of the new LSP for the autumn 1995 elections, in which the party won five seats on a 5.6% vote share. Still in prison, Rubiks was a candidate in the June 1996 *Saeima* elections for a new President, receiving five votes. Following his release in late 1997, he was elected chairman of the LSP, shortly after the party's five deputies had formed a parliamentary alliance with the National Harmony Party (TSP).

For the October 1998 elections the LSP joined an alliance with the TSP and two ethnic Russian groupings called "For Human Rights in a United Latvia", but it failed to secure registration in time to run under that label. The alliance's candidates therefore stood under the TSP banner, the grouping winning 16 seats on a 14.1% vote share and becoming the largest component of the opposition to the succeeding centre-right coalition. The LSP itself took four seats. The party contested the Oct. 5, 2002, *Saeima* elections as a member of the For Human Rights in a United Latvia (PCTVL) alliance and won 5 out of 100 seats. In 2003, however, it left the PCTVL.

National Harmony Party
Tautas Saskanas Partija (TSP)
Address. Lacplesaiela 60, Riga 1010
Telephone (371) 728–9913
Fax. (371) 728–1619
Email. tsp@saeima.lv
Website.www.tsp.lv
Leadership. Janis Jurkans (chairman and parliamentary leader)

The TSP was formed by the residue of the Harmony for Latvia–Rebirth (*Saskana Latvijai–Atdzimana*) grouping following a split in 1994 which led to the creation of the now defunct Political Union of Economists. From its beginning the party was popular with ethnically Russian voters, due to its very moderate positions on citizenship and language issues. Unlike the other parties popular with Russians, it also had a considerable number of ethnic Latvians in its leadership and sought to bridge the gap between the two communities. It won six seats on a 5.6% vote share in the autumn 1995 elections, on a platform advocating harmony between Latvians and non-Latvians with guaranteed rights for minorities. In July 1996 the TSP *Saeima* contingent was reduced to four (one below the number required for official recognition as a group) by the decision of two members to join the *Saimnieks* Democratic Party (see Latvian Democratic Party). However, it was strengthened in September 1997 by a parliamentary alliance with the five-strong Latvian Socialist Party (LSP) group led by Alfreds Rubiks, who had been leader of the Soviet-era Latvian Communist Party.

For the October 1998 elections the TSP created an alliance called "For Equal Rights in a United Latvia", which included the LSP and two ethnic Russian groupings, but failed to secure registration in time to run under that label. The alliance's candidates therefore stood under the TSP banner, winning 16 seats on a 14.1% vote share and becoming the largest component of the opposition to the succeeding centre-right coalition.

By late 2000 serious divisions had developed within the TSP-led alliance over the LSP's advocacy of civil disobedience by ethnic Russians against language law regulations. The TSP contested the Oct. 5, 2002, *Saeima* elections as a member of the For Human Rights in a United Latvia (PCTVL) alliance, which won 25 seats, but left the PCTVL in 2003. In the June 2004 European elections the TSP, running separately, won only 4.8% of the vote and failed to win a seat.

New Christian Party
Jauna Kristigo Partija (JKP)
Address. c/o Saeima, 11 Jekaba, Riga 1811
Email. tatjanaj@saeima.lv
Leadership. Guntis Dislers (chairman); Ingrida Udre (*Saeima* group chairperson)

The centre-left JKP was founded as the New Party (JP) in March 1998 and renamed in January 2001. Popular composer Raimond Pauls was principal founder and first chairman of the JP, which drew support from the upwardly-mobile young for its pro-market, pro-Western policies combined with an inclusive approach to ethnic Russians (provided they learnt Latvian). In the October 1998 parliamentary elections, however, the JP won only eight of the 100 seats (with 7.3% of the vote), being upstaged by the even newer People's Party (TP). It nevertheless became the most junior partner in a centre-right coalition government headed by Latvia's Way.

In February 2001 the JP withdrew from the government, claiming that it had failed to honour pledges to introduce new laws on pensions and property taxes. The following month the JP transformed itself into the JKP, with clergyman Guntis Dislers as chairman, in what was seen as a move to attract support from existing Christian democratic parties. The party is unrepresented in parliament following the 2002 elections.

New Era
Jaunais Laiks
Address. Jekaba kazarmas, Torna iela 4 - 3b, Riga 1050
Website. www@jaunaislaiks.lv
Leadership. Einars Repse (president)

The party was formed in January 2002 by Einars Repse, former head of Latvia's Central Bank. He took over the Central Bank at the age of 30 and steered the country's economy through the tricky post-Soviet years. Repse managed the replacement of the Russian rouble by a stable national currency, the lat, seen as marking the beginning of Latvia's economic revival. During the 2002 parliamentary election campaign the party made the fight against corruption and mismanagement central parts of its programme. The New Era programme also included conservative reforms in health care and education, such as replacing government-funded higher education by student grants. In the Oct. 5, 2002, *Seima* elections the party emerged as the biggest with 23.9% of the vote and secured 26 seats in the parliament. The impressive performance was attributed to Repse's personal charisma and reputation for honesty. The party became the principal partner in a right-wing coalition government that included Latvia's First Party, the Greens and the Farmers' Union and the TB-LNNK. The coalition collapsed on Feb. 5, 2004, after months of internal disagreements. In the June 2004 European elections, New Era won 2 seats with 10.7% of the vote.

People's Party
Tautas Partija (TP)
Address. c/o Saeima, 11 Jekaba, Riga 1811
Telephone. (371) 708–7222
Fax. (371) 708–7289
Email. tautpart@saeima.lv
Website. www.tautaspartija.lv
Leadership. Atis Slakteris (chairman)

The centre-right TP was officially launched in May 1998 by Andris Skele, a former businessman who had been non-party Prime Minister in 1995–97 attempting to lead a series of fractious centre-right coalitions. Advocating family values and national regeneration in the October 1998 parliamentary elections, the TP emerged as narrowly the largest party, winning 24 of the 100 seats on a 21.2% vote share. It nevertheless went into opposition to a coalition headed by Latvia's Way (LC), until July 1999, when Skele returned to the premiership at the head of majority centre-right coalition. Skele was forced to resign in April 2000 over a paedophilia scandal (later being cleared of allegations against him personally), whereupon the TP again became a junior partner in a coalition headed by the LC. In the Oct. 5, 2002, *Seima* elections the party emerged with 20 seats and 16.7% of the vote Andris Skele, who had been chairman of the party since its foundation, retired from active politics in 2002 and was replaced in the post by Atis Slakteris. In the June 2004 European elections the TP took 6.7% of the vote and won 1 seat

The TP is an associate member of the European People's Party.

Popular Movement for Latvia–Zigerists Party
Tautas Kustiba Latvijai–Zigerists Partija (TKL-ZP)
Address. Gertrudes iela 64, Riga
Telephone. (371) 721–6762
Leadership. Joahims Zigerists (chairman)

The radical right-wing TKL–ZP, commonly referred to as

Latvijai, was founded in 1995 by Joahims Zigerists, who had been elected to the *Saeima* in 1993 as a candidate of the Latvian National Conservative Party (LNNK) (see Fatherland and Freedom) but had later been expelled from the LNNK after a court conviction in Germany for incitement to racial hatred. Zigerists had been born and brought up in Germany (as Joachim Siegerist) but claimed Latvian nationality through his father, an ethnic German who had fled from Latvia as the Red Army approached at the end of World War II. In August 1995 Zigerists was expelled from the *Saeima* for poor attendance and was also barred from standing in the autumn 1995 general elections because of his inability to speak much Latvian. His party nevertheless took an impressive third place, winning 14.9% of the vote and 16 *Saeima* seats. A post-election move by the *Saimnieks* Democratic Party to draw the TKL–ZP into a government coalition was successfully resisted by President Ulmanis.

In *Saeima* elections for the state presidency in June 1996, the TKL–ZP candidate, Imants Liepa, took third place with 14 votes. In the same month the TKL–ZP parliamentary group was weakened by the departure of six deputies on the grounds that the party had become "undemocratic". Further defections followed. In the October 1998 parliamentary elections the party won only 1.7% of the vote and therefore no seats and it similarly failed to secure representation in 2002.

Other Parties

Christian People's Party (*Kristigo Tautas Partija*, KTP), formed in February 1996 as successor to the residue of the Latvian Popular Front (*Latvijas Tautas Fronte*, LTF), which had led Latvia's independence campaign but had failed to win seats in the 1993 and 1995 elections.
Leadership. Uldis Augstkalns

Labour Party (*Darba Partija*, DP), launched in March 1997 by Aivars Kreituss and his wife Ilga after he had been expelled from the Saimnieks Democratic Party (Latvian Democratic Party) and she had resigned, thereby quickly losing the speakership of the Saeima. Favouring retention of a state economic role, the DP contested the 1999 elections in alliance with the Latvian Christian Democratic Union and the Latvian Green Party, their vote share of only 2.3% yielding no seats.
Leadership. Aivars Kreituss (chairman)

Latvian Christian Democratic Union (*Latvijas Kristigo Demokratu Savieniba,* LKDS), founded in March 1991 and descended from pre-World War II parties of similar orientation that had substantial parliamentary representation. Having won six seats and 5% of the vote in 1993, the LKDS was allied with the Latvian Farmers' Union in the autumn 1995 elections, in which the alliance took eight seats and 6.3% of the vote, subsequently participating in government at junior level. In the 1998 elections the LKDS was allied with the Labour Party and the Latvian Green Party, the alliance winning 2.3% of the vote. The LKDS is affiliated to the Christian Democrat International.
Address. 28 Jekabaiela, Riga 1811
Telephone. (371) 732–3534
Fax. (371) 783–0333
Leadership. Talavs Jundzis (chairman)

Latvian National Reform Party (*Latvijas Nacionala Reformu Partija*, LNRP), launched in mid-1997 by then EU Affairs Minister Aleksandrs Kirsteins, hitherto a member of Fatherland and Freedom–Latvian National Conservative Party, with the aim of accelerating Latvia's preparations for EU and NATO membership. It failed to make any impact in the 1998 elections.

Leadership. Aleksandrs Kirsteins (chairman)

Latvian Unity Party (*Latvijas Vienibas Partija*, LVP), established in 1994 by a group of orthodox Communists opposed to rapid economic and social change. Its 7.1% and eight seats in the 1995 parliamentary elections gave it a pivotal role in the formation of a broadly conservative coalition. Appointed a Deputy Prime Minister and Agriculture Minister, LVP leader Alberis Kauls lasted only eight months, being forced to resign in May 1996 over his persistent criticism of the coalition's agricultural policy and being replaced by LVP deputy leader Roberts Dilba. The party failed to win representation in 1998.
Leadership. Alberis Kauls (chairman)

National Power Unity (*Nacionala Speka Savieniba*), is a nationalist party founded in 2003 by Aigars Prusis and and Viktors Birze on the basis of the human rights group Helsinki-86.

Lebanon

Capital: Beirut
Population: 4,079,000 (2000)

The Republic of Lebanon gained independence from France in 1944. A "National Covenant", agreed in 1943, determined that power should be allocated between the country's main religious communities on the basis of their relative numerical strength according to a (disputed) 1932 census. The President is by convention a Maronite Christian, the Prime Minister a Sunni Muslim and the Speaker of the unicameral National Assembly (*Majlis al-Umma/Assemblée Nationale*) a Shia Muslim. Between 1975 and 1990 civil war caused immense damage to Lebanon. Rooted in traditional inter-communal rivalries and exacerbated by foreign political and military interventions, the conflict undermined central government authority and enhanced the power of contending militias and paramilitary factions.

Constitutional amendments were approved in September 1990, within the framework of the 1989 Taif Accord. Designed to restore civil peace, the Accord upgraded the executive powers of the (Sunni) Prime Minister and the Cabinet, gave greater powers to the (Shia) Speaker, and reduced the powers of the (Maronite) President. A 1992 electoral law added 20 seats in the National Assembly, to achieve equal representation of Christian and Muslim communities, rather than the previous ratio of 6:5 in favour of the Christians. Few Palestinians are Lebanese citizens and accordingly, although they make up about 10% of the population, they are barred from national politics.

The subsequent return of relative peace to most of Lebanon, with a strong Syrian military presence and the disarming of militia groups, enabled general elections to be held for the first time in 20 years. Several militias reconstituted themselves as political parties. However, communal allegiances tended to persist, despite calls for national unity.

Voting for the 128-member Assembly was conducted in stages between August and October 1992. Thirty-four seats were reserved for Maronite Christians (despite the Christian parties' boycott), 27 for Sunnis and 27 for Shias. Remaining seats were shared among smaller religious denominations (Greek Orthodox, Greek Catholics, Druzes, Armenian Orthodox, Armenian Catholics,

Alaouites and Protestants). Most Christian parties refused to participate, so Syrian nominees made up the numbers. New elections were held in 1996 and again in 2000. Meanwhile, Lebanon held local elections for the first time in 35 years, in 1998. However, polling did not take place in the south, where fighting still simmered between *Hizballah* and Israel's allies.

The National Assembly elected Elias Hrawi as President for a six-year term in November 1989, artificially extended by two years in 1995. In November 1998, former army chief Emile Lahoud replaced him as president. Greater power, though, resided in the construction magnate, Rafiq Hariri, who took office as Prime Minister in 1992.

Lebanese political parties maintain their independent structure, but at election time they reformulate themselves as electoral blocs or lists divided by region. (The six electoral districts or *muhafazat* were originally North Lebanon, Beirut, Mount Lebanon, Beka', Nabatiyya and South Lebanon; some were later subdivided, resulting in the current 14 *muhafazat*). This approach, overseen by Syria, forces politicians to draw support from outside their usual ethno-religious support base. The correlation between parties and lists is not distinct and anti-Syrian dissidents charge that both "government" and "opposition" blocs are dominated by Damascus.

Given the weakness of political parties, powerful figures tend to command the allegiance of looser blocs of MPs. After he took office in 1992, Prime Minister Hariri counted on the loyalty of up to 40 MPs and the Speaker, Nabi Berri, on some 25 MPs. Together, Hrawi, Hariri and Berri were referred to as "the troika". More Christians participated in the 1996 elections, but many still accused Syria of bribing voters, rigging lists and manipulating constituency boundaries to divide Christian power bases.

In 1998 Hariri lost power to Salem al-Hoss amidst economic turmoil and allegations of corruption; but he was re-elected Prime Minister after assembly elections, the third since the end of the civil war, were held on August 27 and September 3, 2000. Hariri's list defeated Hoss's in Beirut by a margin of nearly four to one. He also scored gains in the central Mount Lebanon district. The election was the first held in the southern region since the end of civil war, following Israel's withdrawal in March 2000. A *Hizballah-Amal* alliance scored well here. Interior Minister Michel al-Murr both supervised the poll and ran the government election campaign. Some independent observers claimed that Syria, in particular military intelligence chief, Gen. Ghazi Kenaan, had massaged the election results, especially by redrawing constituency boundaries, slanting the media and enfranchising many thousands of newly naturalized Lebanese who had recently arrived from Syria. For his part, Murr praised opposition gains as signs of political transparency.

The departure of Israeli troops from southern Lebanon in March 2000 had revived hopes of unifying the country and developing the long neglected south. Israel's unilateral withdrawal also prompted calls for 20,000-35,000 Syrian troops to leave the rest of Lebanon, as their *raison d'être* for staying – defence against Israel – now looked questionable. Individual politicians have cited UN Resolution 520 in their support, as well as the terms of the 1989 Ta'if Accords, which Syria itself framed.

The next legislative election is scheduled for 2005, and jostling for position has already started, with clashes reported especially in the south between the rival *Amal* and *Hizballah* groups.

Lists that participated in the 2000 elections

The following lists won seats in the 2000 elections to the 128-member National Assembly, in addition to which 20 non-partisans were elected.

Resistance and Development, formed mainly by the rival Shia parties, *Hizballah* and *Amal,* and led by Nabi Berri; it took 23 seats in 2000 and forms the largest bloc in the Assembly. *Hizballah*'s attempt to run independently in 1996 were reportedly quashed by Syrian fiat. Syria apparently strives for parity on the list between the two rival parties, and ensured that no more than nine *Hizballah* seats were returned. In 2000 the bloc dominated the polls in South Lebanon and Nabatieh.

Al-Karamah (Dignity), a combination of three electoral lists in Beirut, allied with Rafiq Hariri, it won 18 out of 19 possible seats, thus displacing rival lists led by sitting Prime Minister Salim al-Hoss. 106 out of 128 Assembly members subsequently supported a new Hariri administration.

Baalbeck-Hermel al Ii'tilafiah (Baalbeck-Hermel Coalition), the Progressive Socialist Party leader Walid Jumblatt led this bloc, also backed by *Hizballah*. It won nine out of 10 allocated seats in this mostly Shia area.

Al Jabhar Al Nidal Al Watani (National Defence Front, JNW), took 8 seats. Former Speaker Hussein Husseini and former Prime Minister Omar Karami are prominent members of this opposition front.

Wahdal al Jabal (Mountain Union, WJ), won 7 seats.

Ii'tilafiah (Coalition), contesting a northern district dominated by the anti-Syrian Christian Samir Geagea, this list won 6 out of 11 seats.

Al-Karal (Decision), took 6 seats in West Beka'.

Al Kitla Al Chaabi-Elias Shaft (People's Front-Elias Shaft), took 5 seats.

Al Wifah Al Matni (Metn Accord, WM), this list represents the Interior Minister Michel Murr and took 5 seats. Even so, the WM did not enjoy a clean sweep, as leading dissident and WM opponent, Nassib Lahoud, also won a seat.

Al Karamah wah Tajdid (Dignity and Renewal, KT), led by Suleiman Franjieh and Najib Mikati, this list won 5 seats, eating into support for Omar Karami in his Tripoli and Zaghorta fiefdom.

Al Karal al Chaabi (Popular Decision), this list headed by Fouad Turk staged an opposition upset in Zahle, taking 3 seats.

Al Wifac wal Tajdid (Consensus and Renewal), based in the Baabda-Aley district of Mount Lebanon, led by Wajdi Mrad and Talal Arslan, Druze rival to the Progressive Socialist Party's Walid Jumblatt; took 3 seats. *Hizballah* lent its support to this regional list, which was established with the aid of Syrian officials. Elie Hobeika of Waad was initially on the list, but dropped due to *Hizballah* objections, and ran as an independent "sign-in" candidate.

Al Irada al Chaabia (Popular Will), took 3 seats.

Al Karamah al Wataniyah (National Dignity), took 2 seats, supporting Omar Karami in Tripoli and Zaghorta.

Al Tawafoc al Watani (National Understanding), won 1 seat.

Al Kitla al Chaabi-Fouad el Turk (People's Front – Fouad Turk, KC-T), won 1 seat.

Lubnan (Lebanon), won 1 seat.

Al Huriya (Freedom), won 1 seat

Political Parties

Amal

Leadership. Nabi Berri

Amal ("Hope") was founded by Imam Musa Sadr, a charismatic Iranian-educated Shia preacher, as a political adjunct to his Movement of the Downtrodden. The party challenged the corrupt patronage networks of the traditional feudal lords, or *zu'ama*. Nabi Berri assumed the leadership after Imam Sadr "disappeared" in Libya in 1978. Although a part of the Muslim leftist and Palestinian Alliance in the post-1975 civil war, *Amal* subsequently focused more on its own Shia constituents, and clashed during the 1980s with other Muslims, Palestinians, Druze and the Christian right. Increasingly the leadership aligned itself with Syria. It also adopted a more secular orientation, and fought for the Shia turf with its religiously zealous rival, the Iranian-backed *Hizballah*.

Following legislative elections in which *Amal* made an impressive showing in the south, Berri was elected as Speaker of the National Assembly on Oct. 20, 1992, and has remained Speaker ever since. He also controls the Council of the South, which is responsible for the mixed Shia/Christian south of Lebanon. However, critics claim that he has neglected the area and turned a blind eye to corruption. Contesting the 2000 elections together with the rival *Hizballah*, *Amal* helped secure their joint Resistance and Development Bloc a solid 23-seat presence in the National Assembly. Analysts suggest that Syria has long sought to maintain parity in this bloc between its preferred protégé, *Amal*, and the originally Iranian backed *Hizballah*.

Baath Arab Socialist Party (BASP)
Hizb al-Baath al-Arabi al-Ishtiraki

Leadership. Abd al-Majid Rafii (secretary-general of pro-Iraqi wing); Abdullah al-Amin (secretary-general of pro-Syrian wing)

Originally established as the Lebanese regional command of the pan-Arab *Baath* ("Renaissance"), the BASP soon split into competing pro-Iraqi and pro-Syrian factions. Neither wing enjoys the strength of the party in Syria or in Iraq under Saddam. After civil war began in 1975 the BASP joined the left-wing National Movement, and in 1984 joined a new Muslim leftist National Democratic Front. The pro-Syrian wing eclipsed the pro-Iraqi element, thanks in part to the presence of Syrian forces in Lebanon.

Hizballah

Leadership. Sheikh Sa'id Hassan Nasrallah (secretary-general); Sheikh Naim Qassem (deputy secretary-general)

Hizballah (or *Hezbollah*), meaning "Party of God" in Arabic, began as a militant, pro-Iranian Shia Muslim group in 1982, opposed to both Israel and the West. Tributary groups included the Lebanese branch of the Iraqi Shia *Al-Da'wa* movement (many *Hizballah* clerics being educated in seminaries in Najaf and Karbala), Iranian *Pasdaran* (Revolutionary Guards) and a radical breakaway from *Amal* called Islamic *Amal*. Affiliated groups were involved in numerous kidnappings, suicide bombings and other violence. In the 1980s *Hizballah* fought against its pro-Syrian and more secular Shia rival, *Amal*. Allied groups launched suicide bombings against US and European multi-national forces in October 1983 that encouraged their departure from Lebanon in 1984. Meanwhile *Hizballah's* armed wing, *Al Moqawama al Islamia* (The Islamic Resistance), fought Israel and her allies, the South Lebanese Army (SLA). A cross-border strike by Israeli forces in February 1992 killed *Hizballah* secretary-general, Abbas Musawi.

Hizballah survived a massive Israeli attack called Operation Grapes of Wrath in April 1996, and was forced to negotiate indirectly with the old enemy. Sporadic fighting continued regardless and eventually Israeli forces were persuaded to vacate their "southern security zone" in March 2000. This was hailed as a victory for Lebanon as a whole and *Hizballah* in particular. However, the triumph raised questions over whether *Hizballah* would now at last disarm, as other militias had done. Also, its evident reluctance to surrender control of the south to the National Army, and its pledge to prosecute defeated SLA officers for treason, worried Beirut.

Beyond the battle zone, *Hizballah* grew into a more broad-based, populist group. Enjoying generous sponsorship from its Iranian supporters, its widespread health and welfare facilities operated as alternatives to Lebanon's still weak state institutions, especially in its three strongholds: the south, Beka' Valley (its original stronghold) and West Beirut.

Musawi's death exacerbated an internal power struggle, with the more pragmatic Sheikh Hassan Nasrallah triumphing over Hassan Tufayli to become secretary-general in 1992. In the same year Tufayli set up a breakaway group known as the Movement (or Revolt) of the Hungry, which clashed with *Hizballah*. Tufayli's support derived from Shia farmers in the Beka' Valley, destitute after Beirut outlawed their cultivation of hashish and other narcotics. Tufayli claimed to have remained true to the original *Hizballah* idea of setting up an Islamic state on an Iranian model in Lebanon. However, the death of Ayatollah Khomeini in 1989 undermined his stance, and led to *Hizballah's* more accommodating attitude towards non-Shia Lebanese and national institutions. When Tufayli's group raided a *Hizballah* religious school in 1998, this set off a confrontation with the Lebanese Army. Since then the Syrians appear to be protecting Tufayli in his home town of Britel, even though his "criminal renegades", as described in the press, had been the target of a manhunt only months earlier. Analysts suggest that Syria uses his group as a counterweight to *Hizballah*. Disaffected *Hizballah* militiamen joined Tufayli's group in Beka'; in April 1999 his men overran a *Hizballah* arms depot near Baalbek. Yet Tufayli supporters failed to win much support against the parent party in the 2000 elections in Baalbek, after initial reports that Syria wanted them to run against *Hizballah* candidates.

Sheikh Mohammed Fadlallah has remained *Hizballah's* spiritual mentor throughout. *Hizballah* also began building alliances with Christian groups, partly allaying earlier fears that it was seeking to institute an Islamic *shari'a* state over all of Lebanon. While not supporting the Taif Accord, the group accepted it as a "bridge to a internal peace" and non-sectarianism. *Hizballah* first participated as a political party in the 1992 elections, contributing, with *Amal,* to a significant Shia representation in the National Assembly. This was after Damascus warned *Hizballah* against forming a coalition with traditional Shia politicians opposed to Syrian "occupation", like former Parliamentary Speaker Kamel al-Asaad and various Communists and independents.

The two parties, *Hizballah* and *Amal*, contested the 1996 elections jointly, as the Resistance and Development Bloc; in 2000, the Bloc won 23 seats in the National Assembly, of which nine belonged to *Hizballah*. *Hizballah* had originally requested the right to have 14 seats. However, *Hizballah* claimed it lost its seats in Baabda and Beirut through Syrian-engineered electoral fraud; and in municipal elections in the strongly Shia southern suburbs of Beirut *Hizballah* scored a landslide victory in 1998.

Hariri began criticizing *Hizballah* for increasing cross-border raids against Israel after 1998. However, *Hizballah*'s national prestige rose after Israel's departure in 2000, and Nasrallah was unanimously re-elected leader in August 2001. Notwithstanding his pragmatic reputation, Nasrallah probably remains an ally of Iran's spiritual leader, Ayatollah Khamenei. He was also embarrassed at Tufayli's accusations that he was neglecting his poorer constituency.

Increasingly Prime Minister Hariri has grown irritated at *Hizballah*'s sniping at Israelis around the disputed Shebaa Farms area, even though cross-border violence is considerably reduced on the pre-2000 period. Many Lebanese – including numerous Shias – reportedly dislike the continuing disruption that *Hizballah*'s actions are causing to the southern region's economy. They also feel uncomfortable that Syria has allowed *Hizballah* troops to patrol national borders with Israel, instead of divisions of the Lebanese Army.

It appears that *Hizballah*'s once pivotal ties with Iran have lessened; today it derives more income from expatriate Lebanese than from Tehran's coffers; while Syria still appears to control *Hizballah*'s ability to act. Since March 2001 *Hizballah* has vocally supported Syria's right to stay in Lebanon, contrary to calls from Maronite clergy, Druze politicians and leading newspapers. In November 2001 the Lebanese authorities refused US requests to freeze *Hizballah* assets, after the Sept. 11 attacks in the USA.

In May 2003 US Secretary of State Colin Powell specifically asked Syrian President Bashar al-Assad to stop sponsoring *Hizballah* in Lebanon; *Hizballah* rejected Powell's "dictations". In January 2004, after many months of intensive intermediatory negotiations through the offices of Germany, *Hizballah* and Israel agreed to an historic deal. Several hundred *Hizballah* members and Palestinian militants, who were imprisoned in Israel, were exchanged for the return of a kidnapped Israeli businessman and the bodies of three Israeli soldiers killed in action. Also in early 2004, Palestinian security officials confirmed that *Hizballah* had funded Palestinian groups, like the Al Aqsa Martyrs Brigade, and encouraged specific suicide bombings of Israelis.

Lebanese Forces Party (LFP)
Website. www.lebanese-forces.org

The Lebanese Forces (LFP) began as a wing of the Phalangist militia, but under the leadership of Samir Geagea constituted itself as a party in its own right in 1990, opposed to the Taif Accord. In March 1994 the government proscribed the LFP. Geagea was arrested the following month in connection with the assassination in 1990 of Dany Chamoun, leader of the National Liberal Party, and was sentenced to life imprisonment in June 1995. In 1998 some 300 LFP officials won seats in municipal elections, and in 1999 the LFP in the "diaspora" established a temporary political council under Dr. Joseph Gebeily. Geagea's *Ii'tilafiah* (Coalition) electoral list won six seats in a northern district in 2000 elections.

National Bloc
Kutla Al-Wataniyah
Leadership. Carlos Edde

A conservative Maronite Christian party founded in 1943 by a former President, Emile Edde, the National Bloc opposed basic changes in Lebanon's traditional power structure, seeking to exclude the military from politics. It was one of the few political movements not to run a militia during the civil war. Raymond Edde led the Bloc from 1949 until his death in Parisian exile in 2000. His nephew and successor, Carlos Edde, advocates more "co-ordination" with Syria, and backed Jumblatt's list in the Chouf during the 2000 elections.

National Liberal Party
Hizb al-Ahrar al Watani
Parti National Libéral (PNL)
Address. rue du Liban, Beirut
Leadership. Dory Chamoun

Founded in 1958 by Camille Chamoun at the end of his term as President of Lebanon, the PNL lost ascendancy among Maronite Christians to its Phalangist Party rivals in the late 1970s. Having assumed the party leadership from his father in the mid-1980s, Dany Chamoun was assassinated in 1990 (for which murder the then Phalangist militia leader was convicted in June 1995). He was succeeded by his brother, Dory, in May 1991. The party has pressed for the withdrawal of Syrian forces from the country and argues that a federal system is the only way to preserve a single Lebanese state. The PNL boycotted the polls in 1992, 1996 and 2000. Its leaders often gather support amongst expatriate Lebanese communities in the USA and Australia, where Joseph H. Touma is the PNL commissioner.

Phalangist Party
Kata'eb
Leadership. Georges Saade (party president)

The Phalangist Party is a right-wing, originally quasi-fascist Maronite Christian organization, founded in 1936 by Pierre Gemayel. He dominated its affairs until his death in 1984. Gemayel was succeeded as party leader by his vice-president, Elie Karameh, who was replaced by the present leader in 1986. From the early 1970s the party built up militias to counter the growing strength and militancy of Lebanese Muslim leftists and Palestinian groups. Phalangists spearheaded the Christian side in clashes leading to the outbreak of civil war in 1975 and, following subsequent rivalry with the National Liberal Party (PLN), emerged at the end of the decade as the dominant Christian formation. From 1982 to 1988 the Phalangists' pro-American leader Amin Gemayel was Lebanon's President, having assumed office after the assassination in September 1982 of his brother, Bashir Gemayel.

Amin Gemayel fashioned a peace treaty with Israel in 1983, though Syrian pressure led the Lebanese parliament to abrogate the agreement a year later. Phalangist militias, sometimes operating independently of the party command, continued to fight others over the next five years. Georges Saade helped negotiate the Taif Accord on national reconciliation in 1989, resulting in the breakaway of Samir Geagea's Lebanese Forces Party. However, the party backed the Maronite Christian boycott of the 1992 elections, demanding that Syrian troops withdraw from Lebanon before it would contest seats. It participated in 1996 polls, but cried foul when it lost out to Syrian-backed candidates. Over objections from Amin Gemayel, Phalangist politbureau member Rashad Selameh allied his faction of the party to the Phalange's former enemies in the Syrian Social Nationalist Party when contesting Metn in 2000. Amin Gemayel's son, Pierre, won a seat. Conversely, the anti-Phalange Maronite politician and Agriculture Minister, Suleiman Franjieh, also won a seat on the Dignity and Renewal List, in the north.

Overall, the Phalange has lost status since the early 1980s; Maronite power, such as it is, resides more in the institution of the church under Patriarch Sfeir, and the presidency under Elias Hrawi and then Gen. Lahoud.

Progressive Socialist Party (PSP)
Hizb al-Taqaddumi al-Ishtiraki
Parti Socialiste Progressiste (PSP)
Address. PO Box 11–2893–1107–2120, Beirut
Telephone. (961–1) 303455
Fax. (961–1) 301231
Email. secretary@psp.org.lb
Website. www.psp.org.lb
Leadership. Walid Jumblatt (president); Sharif Fayad (general secretary)

Founded in 1949, the PSP draws most support from the Druze, a Muslim sub-sect, and advocates democratic socialism. Following the outbreak of civil war in 1975, the PSP helped create the National Movement of Muslim leftists and Palestinians against the Phalangists and other right-wing Christian formations. Walid Jumblatt assumed the leadership on the assassination of his father Kamal in 1977. He has fended off threats from the rival Arslan family. The PSP fought against the Israeli invasions of 1978 and 1982. It then consolidated control of the Chouf Mountains, the Druze heartland. It created a separate civil administration there, yet never fulfilled its threat to secede from Lebanon altogether.

The PSP also became increasingly hostile to the Shia *Amal* movement, with which PSP forces engaged in heavy fighting in 1987. The party participated in the 1992 National Assembly elections (in which Druze candidates achieved eight seats), and subsequent elections in 1996 and 2000. Walid Jumblatt's Baalbeck-Hermel Coalition cross-party electoral list includes both PSP and *Hizballah* candidates, and won nine seats in the 2000 elections. Syria, it is said, initially backed Jumblatt and his PSP. But they later switched to backing his Druze rivals from the Arslan clan, and tried to persuade Christian voters to support the latter.

Jumblatt himself has served as a minister in successive governments, and was responsible for repatriating refugees uprooted by the 16-year civil war. In 2001 Jumblatt marked a new departure by forging a joint Druze-Christian front against Syrian "occupation" with the Maronite Patriarch, Nasrallah Butros Sfeir. In February 2004 he told a BBC interviewer that he intended to call for a referendum on the issue. Jumblatt belongs to an opposition grouping known as the Qornet Shehwan Gathering, within which his stance on Syria has attracted support from the powerful MP from Jbeil, Fares Soueid.

The PSP is a member party of the Socialist International.

Other Groupings

Ahbash (officially, the Society of Islamic Philanthropic Projects) is a quasi-political Sufi grouping popular amongst Sunnis, but regarded as a Syrian front by foes.

Free National Current (FNC) (*Al-Tayyar al Watani*), represents supporters of the popular Gen. Michel Aoun, who acted as Prime Minister until ousted by the Syrians in 1990 and is currently in exile in Paris. In his absence, Nadim Lteif acts as the FNC's national co-ordinator. The FNC took part in municipal elections in 1998, but boycotted the 2000 assembly elections, alleging that Syria was "flagrantly imposing its alliances…to guarantee the election of a subjugated parliament". Since April 2000 the FNC has organized street demonstrations in Lebanon against the Syrian troop presence. It claims support across sectarian divisions, favours a national unity government, and appears to enjoy support amongst expatriate Lebanese communities. It appears that the FNC is the same as the Free Patriotic Movement.
Website. www.tayyar.org

Islamic Unification Movement (*Tawhid Islami*), a Sunni Muslim group with a religious orientation, formed in Tripoli in 1982, led by Sheikh Said Shaban until his death in 1998.

Lebanese Christian Democratic Union (*Union Chrétienne Démocrate Libanaise,* UCDL), a member of the Christian Democrat International.
Address. 23 Benoit Barakat Street, Jabre Building 3rd Floor, Badaro, Beirut
Telephone. (961–1 386444
Fax. (961–1) 383 583
Email. george@lawjabre.com
Leadership. GeorgeJabre

Lebanese Communist Party (*Hizb Al-Shuyui Al-Lubnani*), dates from 1924 but was legalized only in 1970; primarily Christian during the first 50 years of its existence (drawing support from the Greek Orthodox community in particular), the party participated in leftist Muslim fronts in the post-1975 civil war, although it often clashed with the Shia *Amal* movement; party secretary-general Faruq Dahruj narrowly failed to win a seat in West Beka' in the 2000 elections.
Address. POB 633, rue Al-Hout, Beirut
Website. www.communistparty-lb.org
Leadership. Faruq Dahruj (secretary-general)

Kornet Shehwan Gathering, a mainly Christian group opposed to Syrian "occupation" of Lebanon. The Druze politician, Walid Jumblatt of the Progressive Socialist Party, has leant it his support. In late October 2002 Beirut banned protests by the Gathering, against plans to shut down the Murr television station, which is owned by the Murr family (see *Al Wifah Al Matni* - Metn Accord).

South Lebanon Army, organized in 1978 in the wake of Israel's limited incursion, and expanded in 1982. Regarded as Israel's proxy army, it consisted of mainly Christian Lebanese officers, like its leader, Anton Lahad, and mixed Shia and Christian footsoldiers. Israel wanted the SLA to be integrated into the national Lebanese Army in any peace deal, a plea Beirut always rejected. Established Christian parties also shunned ties with the SLA after 1983, despite rumours that the SLA desired a political future. The SLA fought *Hizballah* for nearly 18 years in the south, but collapsed when Israel unilaterally withdrew in early 2000, after which SLA members sought refuge in Israel.

Syrian Social Nationalist Party (*Parti Socialiste Nationaliste Syrien,* PSNS), organized in 1932 and banned between 1962 and 1969. Led by Dawoud Baz, it advocates a "Greater Syria" embracing Lebanon, Syria, Iraq, Jordan and Palestine. It contested the Metn area in the 2000 elections on a list alongside former enemies, the Phalangists.
Website. www.ssnp.com

Waad Party, formed in 1991 by breakaway members of the Lebanese Forces militia and led by Elie Hobeika, a Syrian loyalist and ex-minister, formerly allied to Israel. Hobeika was accused of carrying out the Sabra and Chatilla massacre of 1982. In 1996 his list carried the constituency of South Metn, amidst allegations of ballot-stuffing. In early 2000 legal proceedings opened that implicated Hobeika, a former Electricity Minister, in assassination attempts on leading politicians, including on Salem al-Hoss in 1984. Hobeika himself was assassinated by unknown assailants on Jan. 24, 2002. Some Lebanese blamed an Israeli conspiracy, others suggested aggrieved Palestinians took their revenge, and least one local anti-Syrian group claimed responsibility. Two other *Waad* leaders, Jean Ghanem and Michael Nassar, were killed in the same month.

Lesotho

Capital: Maseru
Population: 2,208,000 (2002E)

The Kingdom of Lesotho became an independent constitutional monarchy in 1966. Between 1970, when the constitution was suspended after the ruling Basotho National Party (BNP) lost the country's second general election but retained power, and the beginning of 1986, the country was ruled by a Council of Ministers headed by Chief Leabua Jonathan, and the power of the King was considerably eroded. In January 1986 the armed forces staged a bloodless coup, executive and legislative powers being conferred upon the King, although a Military Council became the effective ruling body. In March 1986 all political activity was banned. In March 1990 the chairman of the Military Council seized all executive and legislative powers from King Moshoeshoe II, who was removed from the throne and went into exile. His son was placed on the throne by the military government in his stead as Letsie III.

Following changes in the military leadership in April 1991 a new constitution was adopted, providing for the re-establishment of a bicameral parliament consisting of a directly-elected 65 member National Assembly and a Senate made up of chiefs and nominated members. Executive power is vested in the Prime Minister, as leader of the majority parliamentary party, and the Cabinet appointed by the Prime Minister. In Westminster-style, plurality multi-party elections held in March 1993 the Basotho Congress Party (BCP) won all the seats in the National Assembly in a contest which was adjudged free and fair by independent observers. The following month the BCP leader, Ntsu Mokhehle, was sworn in as Prime Minister and the Military Council was dissolved.

In August 1994 King Letsie III suspended the constitution, dissolving the National Assembly and dismissing the BCP government, and attempted to install a non-elected provisional council. However, following vigorous diplomatic intervention by South Africa and other regional powers, he then agreed to restore the elected government in September. Subsequently, following Letsie's voluntary abdication, Moshoeshoe II was restored to the throne in January 1995, only to be killed in a car accident in January 1996. Letsie III then returned to the throne, having given a formal undertaking not to involve the monarchy in politics.

In 1997, following Mokhehle's loss of control of his party's organizational structures outside parliament, the ageing Prime Minister and 37 other members of the National Assembly resigned from the BCP and formed a new party, the Lesotho Congress for Democracy (LCD), which immediately became the party of government.

For the next legislative elections, on May 23, 1998, the voting age was lowered from 21 to 18 years and the number of seats in the National Assembly was increased to 80, elected from single-member constituencies. The LCD, with 60.7% of the vote, won 79 seats, while the Basotho National Party, with 24.5%, won only one seat. Despite this highly imbalanced result, independent electoral observers again deemed the election to have been free and fair. None the less, the outcome led to bitter protests by the opposition parties, and in September 1998 the government invited the South African Development Community (SADC) to despatch troops into Lesotho to counter a perceived danger of a "creeping" coup by the military (which had long been aligned with the BNP). Troops from South Africa and Botswana, acting on behalf of SADC, thereupon entered the country and imposed their control over the military, although not before opposition supporters had burned down numerous buildings belonging to the government or which had South African connections.

In December 1998 a multi-party Interim Political Authority, backed by expert international mediators, was set up to draft a new electoral system for Lesotho and in particular to address opposition calls for the introduction of an element of proportional representation. After difficult and extended deliberations, agreement was reached upon the introduction of a Mixed Member Proportional electoral system, under which all existing 80 constituency seats, elected by the plurality system, were retained, but were now joined by 40 new compensatory seats to be elected by a national list system of proportional representation. A general election using the new system was conducted in May 2002, which whilst returning the LCD to power, simultaneously provided for proportionate representation of some nine opposition parties.

Basotho Congress Party (BCP)

Address. POB 111, Maseru
Leadership. Ntsukunyane Mphanya (leader)
The BCP was formed as a pan-Africanist, radical nationalist party in the early 1950s. It led government after winning the first general election of 1960 (when a 40-member National Council was indirectly elected by district councils), but subsequently lost narrowly to the conservative BNP in the pre-independence general election (when 65 constituency MPs were elected directly from single member constituencies) in 1965. Subsequently, its refusal to co-operate with the government of Chief Jonathan following the suspension of the 1970 constitution led to a factional divide. One wing of the party, led by Gerard Ramoreboli, accepted seats in an appointed interim National Assembly. In contrast, the main branch, led from exile in Botswana by party founder Ntsu Mokhehle, continued to oppose the Jonathan regime, notably by the formation of the Lesotho Liberation Army (LLA), which from 1979 launched numerous armed attacks on pro-government targets. Because the LLA had to launch these attacks from South African territory, it was almost inevitably drawn into an awkward collaboration with South African security services. However, the latter effectively terminated the LLA's operations in 1983 after pressure from Pretoria had coerced Jonathan into clamping down on the African National Congress, which South Africa claimed was using bases in Lesotho to make assaults across the border .

Mokhehle was allowed by the Military Council to return to Lesotho in 1989. The BCP won a landslide victory in the multi-party elections in March 1993, securing all 65 seats in the National Assembly, with Mokhehle assuming power as Prime Minister. However, in June 1997, after a long period of bitter rivalry between different factions of the party, Mokhehle resigned from the BCP and formed the Lesotho Congress for Democracy, which with the backing of 37 other members of the National Assembly, immediately became the new ruling party. Molapo Qhobela, who had been dismissed from Mokhehle's Cabinet in May 1996, was elected as the new leader of the BCP and thus became the leader of the official opposition in the National Assembly.

In the general election of May 1998 the BCP failed to win any seats. Further factional struggles followed, with Qhobela losing out to T'seliso Makhakhe in leadership tussles in the run up to the 2002 election, and subsequently leaving the party to form the Basutoland African Congress (the original name of the BCP in the 1950s). The BCP won only 3 of the compensatory, PR seats in the 2002 election, following which Makhahke resigned, to be replaced by Ntsukunyane Mphanya.

Basotho National Party (BNP)
Address. POB 124, Maseru
Leadership. Justin Metsing Lekhanya (leader)
The BNP was founded in the late 1950s as the Basutoland National Party (changing its name at independence in 1966) by Chief Leabua Jonathan, who was Prime Minister from 1965 until the military coup in January 1986. During his premiership Chief Jonathan wrested executive control from the King, suspending the 1970 constitution and increasing his power over the country. Following the overthrow of the BNP government, supporters of Chief Jonathan (who died in 1987) were barred from political activity. With the legalization of political parties in May 1991, the BNP re-emerged as one of the two leading parties under the leadership of the former military leader, Major General Justin Lekhanya. None the less, although it won nearly 23% of the popular vote in the general election of 1993, it failed to win a single seat. This was overwhelmingly a result of the relatively uniform distribution of support between the minority BNP and majority BCP in every constituency. However, the BNP prescribed its defeat to electoral malpractice by its opponent.

In the May 1998 general elections the BNP received 24.5% of the total vote but was again seriously underrepresented in parliament, winning only one seat in the National Assembly. The BNP subsequently led a campaign for the introduction of full proportional representation, modelled on the system currently used in neighbouring South Africa. It eventually agreed to a compromise in terms of the Mixed Member Proportional system adopted for the general election of May 2002, in which it again won no constituency seats but secured 21 out of the 40 compensatory seats.

The BNP is associated with the International Democrat Union through its membership of the Democrat Union of Africa.

Lesotho Congress for Democracy (LCD)
Address. c/o National Assembly, PO Box 190, Maseru 100
Leadership. Bethuel Pakalitha Mosisili (leader).
The LCD was formed in June 1997 by Lesotho's then Prime Minister, Ntsu Mokhehle, when he resigned from the Basotho Congress Party (BCP). He chose to retain his seat in the National Assembly (as did 37 other sitting BCP members who joined the LCD) and the LCD became the party of government for the remainder of the current legislative term. In February 1998 Mokhehle was succeeded as LCD leader by Pakalitha Mosisili, who led the party to victory in the May 1998 general election, when it gained 60.7% of the vote and won 79 of the 80 seats in an enlarged National Assembly. As Prime Minister, Mosisili came under intense international as well as domestic pressure to hold fresh elections under a more representative voting system, and he agreed in December 1998 to the establishment of an Interim Political Authority to oversee arrangements for the next elections. The LCD opposed the introduction of a national list, proportional representation electoral system, as was favoured by various opposition parties, but eventually agreed to the compromise represented by the adoption of MMP, under which the 80 constituency seats would be complemented by the addition of 40 compensatory seats elected by proportional representation.

In the May 2002 general election, the LCD won 77 out of the 78 constituency contests conducted on general election day, and subsequently followed up by by-election victories in the two constituencies where elections had been postponed owing to the deaths of participating candidates. However, because it had already exceeded its quota of seats as prescribed by MMP, it was awarded none of the compensatory seats, even though it had won 54.9% of the votes under PR.

Other Parties

Basutoland African Congress (BAC), formed in 2001 as a breakaway from the Basutoland Congress Party by the latter's former leader Molapo Qhobela. Won 3 of the compensatory seats in the 2002 general election.
Address. c/o National Assembly, PO Box 190, Maseru 100.
Leadership: Molapo Qhobela (leader)

Communist Party of Lesotho (CPL), set up in the early 1960s, operating legally until it was banned in 1970. This ban was only partially lifted in 1984, and not until 1992 did the party begin operating in the open. The CPL has drawn its support mainly from Basotho migrant workers in South Africa.
Address. POB 441, Maseru
Leadership. Mokhafisi Kena (secretary-general)

Kopanang Basotho Party (KBP), launched in 1992 to campaign against what it terms repressive and discriminatory laws against women in Lesotho.
Address. Lithoteng Private Centre, PB 133, Maseru
Leadership. N. P. Mosala (leader)

Lesotho People's Congress (LCP), formed as a breakaway from the Lesotho Congress for Democracy (LCD) by former Deputy Prime Minister Kelebone Maope in October 2001. He took 27 of the LCD's sitting MPs with him, but the party managed to gain only 4 PR seats in the 2002 general election.
Address. c/o National Assembly, PO Box 190, Maseru 100

Lesotho Workers' Party (LWP), was formed by trade unionists prior to the 2002 general election, in which it won one of the compensatory seats.
Address. c/o National Assembly, PO Box 190, Maseru 100.
Leadership. Billy Macaefa (leader)

Marematlou Freedom Party (MFP), formed in 1962 from a merger of the Basutoland Freedom Party (itself a breakaway from the Basutoland Congress Party) and the royalist Marematlou Party. Took 16.5% of the popular vote in both the 1965 and 1970 elections, but was thereafter squeezed by the BNP and BCP in political appeal, and was unable to take more than 1.5% of the vote in the three elections of 1993, 1998 and 2002. It gained one compensatory seat in the National Assembly in 2002.
Address. c/o National Assembly, PO Box 190, Maseru 100
Leadership. Vincent Malebo

National Independence Party (NIP), originally formed as a breakaway from the Basotho National Party. Gained a tiny proportion of the popular vote in 1993 and 1998, but secured 5.5% of the PR vote in 2002 (and hence 5 seats), largely because its symbol of a bird closely resembled that of the Lesotho Congress for Democracy.
Address. c/o National Assembly, PO Box 190, Maseru 100
Leadership. A. Manyeli

National Progressive Party (PNP), established in 1995 following a split in the Basotho National Party. It gained one PR seat in the 2002 election.
Address: c/o National Assembly, PO Box 190, Maseru 100.
Leadership. Chief Peete Nkoebe Peete (leader)

Popular Front for Democracy (PFD), formed in May 1991 by progressive trade unionists, civil society activists and left leaning academics on socialist platform. Took a tiny proportion of the popular vote in both the 1993 and 1998 elections, but gained 1.3% of the PR vote and hence one seat in the National Assembly in 2002.

Address. c/o National Assembly, PO Box 190, Maseru 100
Leader. L. Rakuoane

Liberia

Capital: Monrovia
Population: 3,300,000

The Republic of Liberia, an independent state from 1847, was founded by freed black slaves from the USA. In September 1990 Gen. Samuel Kanyon Doe, who had seized power in a military coup in 1980 and had been elected President in 1985, was deposed and killed as rival rebel groups struggled with government forces for control. The Economic Community of West African States (ECOWAS), which had sent a peacekeeping force to Liberia in August 1990, backed the nomination of Amos Sawyer as Interim President, and in January 1991 an Interim Government of National Unity (IGNU) was appointed. Civil war continued, however.

In July 1993 a UN-sponsored peace agreement was signed by the IGNU, the National Patriotic Front of Liberia (NPFL) and the United Liberation Movement for Democracy in Liberia (ULIMO). It provided for a ceasefire, the encampment of troops and the formation of a transitional civilian administration. A five-member Council of State and 35-member Transitional Legislative Assembly were installed in March 1994, while the National Transitional Government met for the first time two months later. As a result of further peace talks involving all the main factions, it was agreed in December 1994 that a new Council of State should be appointed which would hand over to an elected government on Jan. 1, 1996, following multiparty elections in November 1995. However, negotiations on the composition of the Council were stalled until August 1995 when a new peace accord was brokered. In September the Council was inaugurated, a new 16-member transitional government was formed and elections were rescheduled for August 1996. However, further fighting erupted in Monrovia in April 1996, and it was not until February 1997 that ECOWAS was able to announce a new target election date of May 1997. The main faction leaders, having formally disbanded their military organizations (some of which were reconstituted as political parties), resigned from the Council of State in order to stand for the presidency.

After further delay, elections were finally held in July 1997. The former NPFL leader, Charles Taylor, standing as the candidate of the National Patriotic Party (NPP), won over 75% of the votes cast in a 13-way contest for the presidency. Under Liberia's 1986 constitution, the President is elected for a six-year term of office (renewable once) as head of state, head of executive government and commander-in-chief of the armed forces. President Taylor assumed office in August 1997. Legislative elections were held in July 1997, for a 64-member House of Representatives (term of office six years) and a 26-member Senate (term of office nine years). The NPP won a large majority in both chambers.

By mid-2003, however, rebel forces of the Liberians United for Democracy (LURD) and the Movement for Democracy in Liberia (MODEL) had closed in on Monrovia and President Taylor – who had been indicted for war crimes by UN prosecutors in Sierra Leone –

came under intense international pressure to agree to resign. Taylor stood down as President on Aug. 11 in favour of Moses Blah, the Vice President, and took up an offer of refuge in Nigeria. Shortly afterwards, Blah's government and leaders of LURD, MODEL and the unarmed opposition signed an ECOWAS-brokered peace agreement. Under the terms of the agreement, Gyude Bryant, a little known businessman and leader of the small Liberian Action Party (LAP), was installed as chairman of a transitional government of national unity, which was intended to hand power to an elected administration by January 2006.

All Liberia Coalition Party (ALCOP)
Leadership. Lusinee Kamara (leader)
The ALCOP was founded in 1997 by elements of the former armed faction ULIMO-K (the wing of the United Liberation Movement of Liberia for Democracy led by Alhaji G.V. Kromah). Alhaji Kromah won 4% of the vote in the 1997 presidential election. In the legislative elections ALCOP won three seats in the House of Representatives and two seats in the Senate. Alhaji Kromah left the country in 1998 after his dismissal as head of a national reconciliation commission. The party was a signatory to the peace agreement signed in August 2003 that established an interim government ahead of elections scheduled to be held in late 2005. The party's leader, Lusinee Kamara, was appointed as Finance Minister in the interim administration formed in October 2003.

Equal Rights Party (ERP)
The party was a signatory to the peace agreement signed in August 2003.

Free Democratic Party of Liberia (FDPL)
Leadership. Sarh Ciaph Gbollie (national chairman)
The FDPL contested the 1997 legislative elections and its presidential candidate received 0.3% of the vote. The party was a signatory to the peace agreement signed in August 2003.

Labour Party (LP)
Leadership. Rev. R. Reuben C. J. Forte (chairman); Pero M. K. Kerkula (secretary general)
The LP was a signatory to the peace agreement signed in August 2003.

Liberia National Union (LINU)
Leadership. Jonathan K. Weedor (chairman)
The LINU contested the 1997 legislative elections and its presidential candidate received 1% of the vote. The LINU was a signatory to the peace agreement signed in August 2003.

Liberian Action Party (LAP)
Leadership. Gyude Bryant (leader)
Founded in 1984, the LAP fought the 1997 elections as part of the Alliance of Political Parties, comprising also the Liberian Unification Party. The Alliance won two seats in the House of Representatives, while its joint candidate received 2.6% of the vote in the presidential election. The LAP was a signatory to the peace agreement signed in August 2003 and the party's leader, Gyude Bryant, was appointed as chairman of the interim administration formed under the terms of the peace agreement.

Liberian People's Party (LPP)
Leadership. Togba-Nah Tipoteh (leader)
Formed in 1984 by former members of the Movement for Justice in Africa, the LPP won one seat in the House of Representatives in July 1997. Its leader received 1.6% of the vote in the presidential election. The LPP was a signatory to the peace agreement signed in August 2003.

Liberian Unification Party (LUP)

Email. lkpargoi@hotmail.com
Website. www.lupliberia.org
Leadership. Joseph Merchant (national chairman); J. Dallamah Sulonteh (secretary general)
Formed in 1984, the LUP fought the 1997 elections as part of the Alliance of Political Parties, comprising also the Liberian Action Party (LAP). The LUP was a signatory to the peace agreement signed in August 2003 and former Senate President Charles Walker Brumskine was seen as the likely LUP candidate in the presidential elections.

Liberians United for Reconciliation and Democracy (LURD)

Leadership. Sekou Damante Konneh (chairman)
The rebel LURD began fighting against the government of President Charles Taylor in the country's north-western Lofa County in 2000. The group was reportedly supported by the regime of President Lansana Conté in Guinea. Fighting alongside the smaller Movement for Democracy in Liberia (MODEL), in August 2003 LURD forced Taylor to flee Liberia. Shortly afterwards, LURD was one of a number of groups and parties that signed the peace accord establishing an interim administration which was intended to hand power to an elected administration by January 2006. The new administration included five LURD members.

Movement for Democracy in Liberia (MODEL)

Leadership. Thomas Nimely Yaha (leader)
The rebel Movement for Democracy in Liberia (MODEL) surfaced in early 2003 in the south-east of the country as a breakaway faction of the Liberians United for Reconciliation and Democracy (LURD). MODEL was dominated by the Krahn ethnic group of the late President Samuel Kanyon Doe and was reportedly supported by the government of President Laurent Gbagbo of Côte d'Ivoire. After months of heavy fighting, MODEL and LURD managed to force President Charles Taylor to flee Liberia in August 2003. Shortly afterwards, MODEL was one of a number of parties to a peace accord that established an interim administration which was intended to hand power to an elected administration by January 2006. The new administration included five MODEL members, including the group's leader, Thomas Nimely, as Foreign Minister.

National Democratic Party of Liberia (NDPL)

Leadership. Isaac Dakinah (leader)
The NDPL was founded in 1997 by members of the former armed faction, the Liberia Peace Council. In the July 1997 elections the NDPL received 1.3% of the presidential vote and won no seats in the legislature. The NDPL was a signatory to the peace agreement signed in August 2003.

National Patriotic Party (NPP)

Leadership. Cyril Allen (chairman)
The NPP was founded in 1997 by members of the former armed faction, the National Patriotic Front of Liberia (NPFL), whose leader, Charles Taylor, had launched the armed rebellion that led to the collapse of the Doe regime in September 1990 and embroiled the country in protracted civil war. Charles Taylor won the 1997 presidential election with 75.3% of the vote, while the NPP won 49 of the 64 seats in the House of Representatives and 21 of the 26 seats in the Senate. Following months of intense fighting between government forces and rebels of the Liberians United for Democracy (LURD) and the Movement for Democracy in Liberia (MODEL), Taylor – who had been indicted for war crimes by the Special Court for Sierra Leone – fled the country in August 2003. The NPP was a signatory to the peace agreement signed shortly after Taylor's departure that established an interim government ahead of elections scheduled to be held in late 2005.

National Reformation Party (NRP)

Leadership. Martin Sherif (leader)
The NRP contested the 1997 legislative elections, but failed to win a seat. Its presidential candidate and leader, Martin Sherif, received 0.5% of the vote in the accompanying presidential poll. The NRP was a signatory to the peace agreement signed in August 2003.

New Democratic Alternative for Liberia Movement (New Deal Movement)

Address. 107 Randall Street, Monrovia
Website. www.newdealmovement.com
Leadership. Nigbah Wiaplah (national chairman); Kerkula Foeday (secretary general)
The New Deal Movement was launched in January 2000 with a radical anti-corruption programme and it was legally registered in July 2002. The party was a signatory to the peace agreement signed in August 2003.

People's Democratic Party of Liberia (PDPL)

Leadership. George T. Washington
The PDPL contested the 1997 legislative elections, but failed to win a seat. Its presidential candidate and leader, George T. Washington, received 0.5% of the vote in the accompanying presidential poll. The PDPL was a signatory to the peace agreement signed in August 2003.

People's Progressive Party (PPP)

Leadership. Chea Cheapoo (chairman)
The PPP contested the 1997 legislative elections and its presidential candidate received 0.3% of the vote. The PPP was a signatory to the peace agreement signed in August 2003.

Reformation Alliance Party (RAP)

Leadership. Henry Boimah Fainbulleh (chairman)
The RAP contested the 1997 legislative elections and its presidential candidate received 0.3% of the vote. The party was a signatory to the peace agreement signed in August 2003.

True Whig Party (TWP)

Leadership. Rudolph E. Sherman (chairman)
From independence in 1847 until the Doe coup of 1980, Liberia was a one-party state ruled by the Americo-Liberian dominated True Whig Party. The party was a signatory to the peace agreement signed in August 2003.

United People's Party (UPP)

Leadership. Wesley Johnson (chairman)
The UPP was founded in 1984 by former members of the Progressive People's Party (in opposition prior to the 1980 military coup). It won two seats in the House of Representatives in July 1997, when its candidate received 2.5% of the vote in the presidential election. The UPP was a signatory to the peace agreement signed in August 2003 and in October 2003 the chairman of the UPP, Wesley Johnson, was sworn in as vice chairman of the country's interim administration.

Unity Party (UP)

Leadership. Charles Clarke (leader)
Founded in 1984, the Unity Party was the runner-up in the July 1997 elections, winning seven seats in the House of Representatives and three seats in the Senate. Its presidential candidate, Ellen Johnson Sirleaf (a senior official of a United Nations Agency), received 9.6% of the vote in the presidential election. The UP was a signatory to the peace agreement signed in August 2003.

Libya

Capital: Tripoli
Population: 5,410,000 (2003)

Libya achieved independence in 1951 under a monarchy which was subsequently overthrown in 1969 by a military coup led by Col. Moamer al-Kadhafi. Kadhafi himself is referred to as "the leader of the revolution", and sometimes also as head of state and chairman of parliament. Yet while he wields considerable power, technically he holds no official post. Initially the regime modelled itself on the Free Officers' Movement that took over Egypt in 1952; Kadhafi's cohorts even called themselves Free Officers. Executive authority resided in a Revolutionary Command Council (RCC) and Kadhafi encouraged the creation of a single party, the Arab Socialist Union (ASU or *Al-Ittihad al-Ishtiraki al-Arabi*; again, the name of Nasser's party in Egypt). The ASU's first national congress took place on March 28, 1972.

However, moves towards a proper party structure were superseded when the March 2, 1977, constitution of the Socialist People's Libyan Arab *Jamahiriyah* was introduced. *Jamahiriyah* is a neologism modelled on the Arabic for "republic", and broadly means "people's power". Officially the constitution vests authority in the Libyan people, with local "basic people's congresses" forming an indirect electoral base for a legislature called the General People's Congress (GPC) – in Arabic, *Mu'tammar al-sha'ab al 'amm*. In his famous "Green Book", Kadhafi argued that parties and factions undermined true democracy, and that only his system gave sovereignty to the individual, in consonance with the Islamic principle of *shura* – consultation. In practice, however, Kadhafi has sought to crush all opposition to his personal rule, and many analysts describe Libya as a thinly disguised military dictatorship.

The GPC consists of about 2,700 representatives of basic people's congresses; since 1992 Zintani Muhammad az-Zintani has been its secretary-general. The legislature is serviced by a secretariat, which succeeded the RCC. This secretariat in turn appoints the General People's Committee, which is broadly equivalent to a Council of Ministers. Since 2000 Secretary-General Mubarak Abdullah al-Shamikh has presided over the Committee; Shokri Ghanem holds the position of Prime Minister.

There are no legal political parties, which were officially banned in 1971, and no opposition groups have been allowed to operate legally within the country. Nonetheless, numerous dissident groups have emerged amongst Libyans in exile. In December 2003, Kadhafi surprised the world when he announced that Libya was willing to surrender its weapons of mass destruction, and intended to re-enter the community of nations. It remains to be seen whether in the light of this *volte-face*, Western powers will demand that Libya adopt multi-party democracy, as they have called for in Iraq and other Middle Eastern countries.

Military and other domestic opposition

Since assuming power in 1969, Kadhafi has experienced numerous challenges to his authority stemming from the army that brought him to power. Many officers feared that building a *Jamahiriyah* implied a reduction in their own status. In August 1975 a former RCC member, Omar al-Muhaishi, launched a radio station in Egypt denouncing the Kadhafi regime. In 1984 some 70 senior military officers were forced to resign, apparently over their political discontents; six air force personnel deserted to Egypt in March 1987. Since late 1993 Kadhafi's longtime deputy and ideological partner turned rival, Maj. Abdesasalem Jalloud, has been marginalized after expressing political differences. Another close colleague and defence commander, Khoueldi Hamidi, found himself at odds with the leader in 1995. Military officers criticized (usually in secret) Kadhafi's repeated and invariably unsuccessful military ventures in Chad.

His championing of African unity since 1999 has upset many Libyans, forcing the leader to rely more heavily on his own clan for support. That same year unrest broke out over unresolved social issues and 100 died in the ensuing violence. Major unrest began in the early 1970s with a revolt by a Libyan students' movement that demanded a freer democracy. Initial dialogue with Kadhafi descended into mass arrests and some public executions. A major furore erupted in 1976 at Benghazi University over students who refused to join the ASU; in April 1984 two student leaders were hanged, resulting in retaliatory attacks on pro-Kadhafi "revolutionary committees".

Other societal sectors have also from time to time provided sources of opposition. These include Muslim clerics and traditional tribal confederations. In October 1993 two of Libya's three largest tribes, the Warfalla and Magarha, became increasingly critical of Kadhafi's rule. Some Libyan nationalists have objected to Kadhafi's repeated bids to merge Libya with neighbouring countries. Allegations of economic mismanagement and over-centralization have also fueled protest. For instance, dissidents claim Libya depends too much on oil (discovered in 1959 and nationalized in 1970) despite attampts to diversify into agriculture and industrial production. Oil receipts, it is said, have not filtered down to ordinary people, while salaries have been deliberately suppressed.

Islamist opposition

In the 1990s, there was an upsurge of Islamist opposition to the Kadhafi regime. Such opposition remains fragmented and has suffered at the hands of the regime's security apparatus. The Islamic Liberation Party (*Hizb at-Tahrir* – the Libyan branch appears to have been established in July 1980; otherwise see under Jordan) and the Muslim Brotherhood (*Ikhwan al-Muslimin* – see under Egypt) have both caused the regime much anxiety. The ILP's platform attacks the paralysis and corruption of the state and advocates a progressive agenda of equitable redistribution of wealth. Ultimately it seeks the restoration of a Muslim Caliphate, covering many nations. The party's endorsement of armed resistance and its successful recruitment of students from the universities and military academies has made it an important source of opposition. In 1973 Kadhafi specifically listed the Muslim Brotherhood, alongside Baathists and others, as a social evil. Although long prosecuted by the regime, the Brotherhood has also experienced a revival of late.

Often regarded as more militant are groups whose memberships include Libyan veterans of the Afghan war. Disenchanted with limited economic prospects, these groups include the Islamic Martyrs' Movement, The Fighting Islamic Group (*Aj-jamaa Al-islamiya Al-mokatila*, which revealed its constitution in 1991) and the Libyan Islamic Group (*Aj-jamaa Al-islamiya*

Libya, established in 1979). Another movement that may fall into the same category is the Islamic Movement Libya (*Al-haraka Al-islamiya Libya*) established in May 1980. On Sept. 24, 2001, in the wake of the Sept. 11 attacks on the USA, the Bush administration froze the assets of the Fighting Group; thereafter Kadhafi ordered his intelligence agents to co-operate with the CIA and other US agencies.

The former Libyan monarchy derived its legitimacy from the indigenous Sannusi Muslim order, a *sufi* and Sunni movement which had led the battle against former Italian colonizers. Many of the official *ulama* (Muslim clergy) still adhere to Sannusi doctrines. They have rejected as "un-Islamic" Kadhafi's Third Universal Theory, which includes the abolition of money and private property (including, by extension, the *waqf,* or Muslim religious endowments). Libya's grand mufti openly critized sequestration of private property in 1977. Clerics also lambasted Kadhafi for calling into question central tenets of normative Islam, like the pilgrimage to Mecca. They rejected Kadhafi's presumption to indulge in *ijtihad* (theological rationalizing), a task for which they said he lacks credentials; they charged his Green Book with undermining *sharia* (Islamic law); and they opposed Kadhafi's decision in 1977 to alter the Muslim calendar. In February 1978 Kadhafi accused the *ulama* of siding with the upper classes, and of interfering in the regime's socialist policies. In 1969 the leader had forbidden *ulama* from issuing fatwas (religious decrees); in an apparent bid to reclaim the support of "moderate" clerics, he reversed this edict and restored their rights in 1994.

Increasingly, more militant Islamists appear to have come under the sway of the *Salafi* movement, and have spurned the Sannusi tradition. *Salafi* signifies a return to the fundaments of the founding fathers of the Muslim faith. In its extreme variant the *Salafi* movement has connections with the global *Al-Qaeda* group. That said, there are disputes over the extent of logistical connections between the Salafists and *Al-Qaeda.* Islamist violence grew especially intense in the latter half of the 1990s, particularly in central and eastern Libya, where there were reports of frequent clashes between the security forces and Islamists. Some analysts suggest that unrest was exacerbated by similar occurences across the border, in Algeria. Kadhafi is known to bitterly oppose the *Al-Qaeda* leader, Osama Bin Laden; he alleges that *Al-Qaeda* has tried to assassinate him on several occasions, and in 2001 he tacitly approved the US-led "war on terrorism".

Exile organizations

Due to internal strictures, most opposition groups have had their headquarters outside Libya, particularly in Sudan and Egypt. Since the late 1970s, Libyans in exile, especially students, have formed numerous political bodies and unions; and the Kadhafi government became notorious for physically liquidating many of these foreign-based foes, who included former ambassadors, businessmen and students (some 20 opponents were killed overseas between 1980 and 1987). Certain of these groups have in turn been linked to assassinations of Libyan officials abroad and are thought to have received sponsorship from foreign governments, including from Iraq under Saddam.

National Front for the Salvation of Libya (NFSL), the main expatriate opposition to the Kadhafi regime. Known in Arabic as *Aj-jabha Al-wataniya Li-inqad Libya,* the NFSL

was formed in Sudan in on Oct. 7, 1981, and its party magazine is *Al-Inqad.* The Front aims to end Kadhafi's rule and establish "a constitutional and democratically elected government in Libya". It operates out of Egypt and the USA, and also has members in the UK. Protests by NFSL in 1984 led to the incident outside the Libyan Embassy in London, when a woman police officer, Yvonne Fletcher, was shot and killed by gunfire that emanated from the building. The UK held the Libyan government responsible, and the incident cast a pall on UK-Libyan relations for the next two decades.

A NFSL attack on Kadhafi's Bab al Aziziyah headquarters on May 8, 1984, led to a major crackdown in Libya, including about 2,000 arrests, televised trials and the hanging of eight leading NFSL members. At the time there were rumours of support from the American intelligence agency, the CIA, and a joint US State Department/Egyptian venture in support of the NFSL. The Front suffered when the Nimeiry regime was toppled in Libya in 1985 and his successors expelled the movement. As of March 2004 Ibrahim Sahad was its secretary-general, Mouftah al-Tayar his deputy, and Dr. Suleiman Abdalla, chairman of its National Congress.
Website. www.nfsl-libya.com

Liechtenstein

Capital: Vaduz
Population: 33,436 (2004E)

The Principality of Liechtenstein, which dates its origins to the Middle Ages, is an hereditary constitutional monarchy in the male line. The Imperial Principality of Liechtenstein was established in 1719 and it became a sovereign state in 1806. Under its constitution of 1921, the Prince (currently Prince Hans-Adam II von und zu Liechtenstein) exercises legislative power jointly with a unicameral Diet (*Landtag*) of 25 members, who are elected every four years by universal adult suffrage under a proportional representation system. The elections take place in two constituencies – the Upper Country election district elects 15 members to the *Landtag,* the Lower Country election district elects 10. The government consists of the Chief of Government – the leader of the majority party in the Diet, and four Councillors. They are appointed by the Reigning Prince on recommendation of the Parliament. The two electoral areas of the country, the highlands and the lowlands, are entitled to at least two members of the government, and their respective deputies must come from the same area.

From 1938 to 1997, Liechtenstein had a distinctive government system. Until recent years, only two parties were represented in the Parliament: the Patriotic (or Fatherland) Union (*Vaterländische Union,* VU) and the Progressive Citizens' Party (*Fortschrittliche Bürgerpartei,* FBPL). The party winning the majority in Parliament also provided the majority of ministers. The minority party acted as the opposition in Parliament and as the junior coalition partner in the government. This Liechtenstein form of coalition government came to an end in April 1997. From 1997 to 2001, the VU was solely responsible for government business and provided all Ministers. Since 2001, all Ministers have been from the FBPL. The minority parties counterbalance the government as opposition parties in Parliament and in parliamentary committees.

Having been introduced for most local elections in 1977, female suffrage at national level was narrowly approved by referendum in July 1984 (of male voters), the first elections in which women could vote being held in February 1986.

In *Landtag* elections on Feb. 9 and 11, 2001, the FBPL won 13 seats (with 49.9% of the vote), the VU won 11 (41.3%) and the Free List 1 (8.8%). Having been in opposition since 1997, the FBPL formed a new government on April 5, 2001.

The Liechtenstein electorate on March 16, 2003, endorsed Prince Hans-Adam II's proposal for a revision of the Liechtenstein constitution with 64.3% of votes. Prior to the vote, the Prince indicated that he and the reigning family would to go into exile at his palace in Vienna if the revised constitution failed to be adopted. Before the vote, he had already possessed more power than any other European monarch. The Prince now has the power to dissolve Parliament and appoint an interim government, rule by emergency decree, dismiss individual members of the government, and veto any parliamentary legislation by not signing the bill within six months. Without the approval of the reigning prince, no further constitutional amendments can be adopted, except in the case of a referendum abolishing the royal house. Finally, the Prince now has the final say on the appointment of judges, and the State Court loses its key competence to mediate between the government and the Prince on constitutional matters. The Council of Europe, of which Liechtenstein is a member, decided to investigate "whether one can speak of a pluralistic democracy following the constitutional changes that occurred in March 2003". In August 2004 Prince Hans-Adam handed over government responsibilities to his son, Prince Alois, while remaining head of state.

Free List
Freie Liste (FL)
Address. Im Bretscha 4, Postfach 177, 9494 Schaan
Email. fliste@lie-net.li
Website. www.freieliste.li
Leadership. Dr Pepo Frick, Elisabeth Tellenbach-Frick, Adolf Ritter (executive members)
The environmentalist and social democratic FL was formed prior to the 1986 elections, in which it mounted the first third-party challenge to the then ruling coalition parties since 1974 but narrowly failed to secure the 8% vote share necessary for parliamentary representation. The FL again fell short in 1989, in part because 3.2% of the vote went to a new Liechtenstein Non-Party List (which quickly became defunct). Its breakthrough came in the February 1993 elections, when it won two seats, although it was reduced to one in the second 1993 elections in October. The FL again won two seats in the 1997 elections, becoming a vigorous critic of the VU government in the next parliamentary term. In the 2001 elections, however, the party fell back to one seat. The FL is concerned with envirormntal protection and aims to achieve more participation in all areas of life and consistent equal rights of men and women. It is engaged on behalf of immigrants and refugees and demands fair trade with economically weaker countries.

The FL has links with the European Federation of Green Parties.

Patriotic Union
Vaterländischen Union (VU)
Address. Fürst-Franz-Josef-Strasse 13, 9490 Vaduz
Telephone. (1423) 236–1616
Fax. (141–75) 236–1617
Email. gs@vu-online.li
Website. www.vu-online.li
Leadership. Heinz Frommelt (chairman); Peter Kranz (general secretary)
Also refered to in English as the Fatherland Union, the VU is considered the more liberal of the two major parties. It favours a constitutional monarchy, democracy and social progress. It was founded at the end of World War I as the People's Party (*Volkspartei*, VP), which attracted substantial working-class support (particularly among returning emigrant workers) for its programme of economic union with Switzerland and a constitution according rights to the people. After winning a majority in the 1918 elections, the party formed the government in 1918-28 and implemented many of the aforementioned policies.

In 1936 the VP merged with the *Heimatdienst* movement to create the VU, which served as the junior coalition partner of the Progressive Citizens' Party in Liechtenstein (FBPL) from 1938 to 1970, when it became the senior partner. It lost its coalition seniority to the FBPL in 1974 but regained it in 1978, holding the government leadership until the elections of February 1993, when the FBPL gained the advantage. However, unprecedented second elections the same year re-established the VU as the leading government party under the premiership of Mario Frick.

The VU again won 13 of the 25 *Landtag* seats in early 1997 elections, whereas the FBPL lost one and opted to end the 39-year-old coalition, going into opposition to a VU government headed by Frick. The VU was therefore solely accountable for subsequent difficulties, including the naming of Liechtenstein as a "harmful tax haven" by the OECD and strains with Prince Hans-Adam over his demand for constitutional changes to give more power to the citizenry, which the VU saw as an increase in royal prerogatives at the expense of parliament. The party paid the price in the February 2001 elections, retaining only 11 *Landtag* seats and going into opposition to a majority government of the FBPL.

The VU is a member party of the European section of the International Democrat Union (as is the FBPL).

Progressive Citizens' Party in Liechtenstein
Fortschrittliche Bürgerpartei in Liechtenstein (FBPL)
Address. Aeulestrasse 56, 9490 Vaduz
Telephone. (1423) 237–7940
Fax. (1423) 237–7949
Email. marcus.vogt@fbp.li
Website. www.fbpl.li
Leadership. Johannes Matt (president); Elmar Kindle (vice-president); Rony Uehle (vice-president)
Founded in 1918 as the conservative Citizens' Party (*Bürgerpartei*), what subsequently became the FBPL held a majority of Diet seats from 1928 to 1970 and in 1974-78 and therefore headed the government in those periods. From 1938 it participated with the Patriotic Union (VU) in long-serving government coalitions, being the junior partner in 1970-74 and from 1978 until it regained the premiership in the elections of February 1993. However, the incoming FBPL Chief of Government, Markus Büchel, quickly alienated his own party and in September 1993 lost a confidence vote tabled by the FBPL itself. Further general elections in October, in which the FBPL list was headed by Josef Biedermann, reduced the FBPL to junior status in the ruling coalition.

In the 1997 *Landtag* elections the FBPL lost one of its 11 seats and unexpectedly decided to go into opposition to the VU, thus ending Europe's longest-lasting coalition government. Its reward in the February 2001 elections was a major advance (by local standards) from 10 to 13 seats with just short of half the popular vote. The FBPL accordingly formed a new single-party government under the premiership of Otmar Hasler.

The FBPL is a member party of the European section of the International Democrat Union (as is the VU).

Lithuania

Capital: Vilnius
Population: 3,462,553 (2003)

The Republic of Lithuania was independent from the end of World War I until it was incorporated into the Soviet Union in August 1940. In 1989 the Lithuanian parliament voted to declare the Soviet annexation illegal. In the elections held in 1990 the nationalist movement *Sajudis* won the majority of seats in the parliament and its leader Vytautas Lansbergis was elected President. The republic declared its independence on March 11, 1990. Following the failed August 1991 coup against President Mikhail Gorbachev in Moscow, the USSR recognized Lithuania's indepdence on Sept. 6, 1991. Lithuania adopted its present constitution on Oct. 25, 1992. The constitution provides for an executive President who is directly elected for a five-year term and who appoints the Prime Minister and other ministers, subject to parliamentary approval. Legislative authority is vested in a Parliament (*Seimas*) of 141 members serving a four-year term, of whom 71 are elected from constituencies by majority voting and 70 by proportional representation. Under changes to the electoral law given parliamentary approval in June 1996, the threshold for obtaining proportional seats was raised from 4% to 5% (and previous concessions on the threshold rule for minority parties were abolished), while voters became entitled to record a preference for individual candidates on party lists.

Lithuania has a highly fractious party political scene. Under legislation enacted in 1999, Lithuanian parties become eligible for annual state funding if they receive at least 3% of the vote in the most recent national and/or local elections. Allocated in proportion to representation and support obtained, the total sum available is set at a ceiling of 0.1% of budgeted government expenditure each year.

In presidential elections held in two rounds on Dec. 21, 1997, and Jan. 4, 1998, an independent candidate endorsed by the Homeland Union–Lithuanian Conservatives (TS–LK), Valdas Adamkus, was elected with 50.3% of the second-round vote, against 49.7% for left-wing candidate Arturas Paulauskas. Parliamentary elections on Oct. 8, 2000, resulted in the Brazauskas Social Democratic Coalition, consisting mainly of the Lithuanian Democratic Labour Party (LDDP) and the Lithuanian Social Democratic Party (LSDP), winning 51 seats (with 31.1% of the vote), the Lithuanian Liberal Union (LLS) 34 (17.3%), the New Union–Social Liberals (NS–SL) 29 (19.6%), the TS–LK 9 (8.6%), the Lithuanian Peasants' Party 4 (4.1%), the Lithuanian Christian Democratic Party 2 (3.1%), the Lithuanian Centre Union (LCS) 2 (3.1%) and the Lithuanian Polish Union 2 (1.9%), with five other lists obtaining one seat each and three independents being elected.

The first outcome of the October 2000 parliamentary elections was a coalition government headed by the LLS and including the NS–SL and the LCS. In January 2001 the LDDP and LSDP merged under the historic LSDP title. Following the collapse of the LLS-led government in June 2001, a coalition of the LSDP and the NS–SL was installed in July.

In presidential elections held in two rounds on Dec. 22, 2002, and Jan. 5, 2003, Rolandas Paksas, former mayor of Vilnius and twice Prime Minister, endorsed by the Liberal Democratic Party, was unexpectedly elected with 54.7% of the second-round vote, against 45.3% for independent candidate Valdas Adamkus. Paksas, an accomplished stunt pilot, fought a flamboyantly populist campaign, including flying his single-seater propeller aircraft with two others underneath a low bridge.

During 2003-04 Lithuanian politics was dominated by a series of political scandals centred on President Paksas. Following a report delivered by the Lithuanian internal security services to a parliamentary commission in October 2003 and damaging press stories about his alleged connections with criminals, the *Seimas* launched an investigation. The investigation committee reported at the beginning of December 2003 that the President was responsible for leaks of sensitive information and had allowed Almax, a public relations company suspected of links to Russian intelligence, to influence his decisions. The parliamentary committee also confirmed an earlier report by Lithuanian secret service which found links between Paksas's office and alleged criminals. On Dec. 18, 2003, the *Seimas* started impeachment proceedings against the President when an impeachment petition signed by 86 of the 141 members was approved by the parliament. The impeachment papers accused Paksas of posing a threat to national security, leaking state secrets, illegally influencing private firms, handling conflicts of interest improperly, obstructing the work of state institutions and allowing aides to abuse their offices. Paksas wavered between denying the charges and conceding that he had been blackmailed into committing unlawful acts. In March 2004 Lithuania's Constitutional Court found that the President had "grossly violated the constitution". On April 6, 2004, the *Seimas* voted by a two-thirds majority to remove Paksas from the presidency on the grounds that he had unlawfully granted Lithuanian citizenship to Yuri Borisov, a Russian businessman who financed his election campaign, and had divulged official secrets (informed Borisov about a police investigation into his activities) and exerted unlawful influence on a highway privatization programme in favour of his friends. Paksas became the first modern European head of state to be impeached. In accordance with the constitution Arturas Paulauskas, speaker of the Lithuanian parliament, became President of the republic, until new presidential elections were held.

Despite the impeachment the Lithuanian Liberal Democratic Party on April 18, 2004, nominated Paksas as its candidate in the new presidential elections. However, the Constitutional Court on May 25, 2004, barred Paksas for life from holding senior state posts. The Court also ruled that an "impeached president under the constitution can never again be elected president".

In presidential elections held in two rounds on June 13 and 27, 2004, Valdas Adamkus (Independent) was elected with 51.87% of the second-round vote, against 46.69% for Kazimira Danute Prunskiene candidate of the Farmers' Party–The Party for New Democracy (LVP-NDP).

Lithuania held a referendum on membership of the European Union on May 10-11, 2003, with 91% voting in favour. It joined the EU on May 1, 2004, and held its first European Parliament elections on June 13, 2004 (in parallel with the first round of presidential elections). In a turnout of 48.38% the recently formed Labour Party won 30.16% of the votes and gained 5 of the country's 13 seats. Other seats were won by the Democratic Labour Party of Lithuania (5); Lithuanian Social Democratic Party 2; Homeland

Union–Lithuanian Conservatives, Union of Lithuanian Political Prisoners and Deportees, Christian Democrats 2; Liberal and Centre Union 2; Union of Farmers and New Democracy Party 1; Liberal Democratic Party 1.

In the *Seimas* elections held on Oct. 10 and 24, 2004, the newly formed Labour Party, led by the populist Russian-born millionaire Viktor Uspaskich, secured 28.4% of the vote and 39 seats in the 141-seat parliament. The electoral alliance For a Working Lithuania received 20.7% of the vote, giving the Lithuanian Social Democratic Party 20 seats and the New Union–Social Liberals 11. The Homeland Union secured 14.6% of the vote and 25 seats; the Order and Justice electoral coalition (Liberal Democratic Party and Lithuanian People's Union for a Fair Lithuania) 11.4% and 10; the Liberal and Centre Union 9.1% and 18; the Union of Farmers and New Democratic parties (Lithuanian Peasants' Party and New Democratic Party) 6.6% and 10; Election Action of Lithuania's Poles 3.8% and 2; and non-partisans 6. Following the elections the Labour Party joined a coalition government with the Social Democrats and Social Liberals

Homeland Union–Lithuanian Conservatives
Tevynes Sajunga–Lietuvos Konservatoriai (TS-LK)

Address. 15 Gedimino pr., Vilnius 2000
Telephone. (370–2) 396450
Fax. (370–2) 396450
Email. rupetr@lrs.lt
Website. www.tslk.lt
Leadership. Andrius Kubilis (chairman); Jurgis Razma (executive secretary)

The centre-right TS–LK was launched in May 1993 as successor to the remnants of the Lithuanian Reform Movement (*Sajudis*), which had spearheaded Lithuania's independence campaign. Under the leadership of Vytautas Landsbergis, the broadly-based *Sajudis* had been the leading formation in the 1990 elections, but in the face of economic adversity had suffered a heavy defeat in 1992, winning only 20% of the popular vote. Boosted by the unpopularity of the post-1992 left-wing government, the TS–LK won an overall majority of 70 seats in the 1996 parliamentary elections, opting to form a centre-right coalition with the Lithuanian Christian Democrats (LKD) and the Lithuanian Centre Union (LCS) under the premiership of Gediminas Vagnorius. However, in direct presidential elections in late 1997 and early 1998, Landsbergis came a poor third in the first round with only 15.7%, following which the TS–LK backed the narrow second-round winner, Valdas Adamkus (non-party).

In May 1999 Vagnorius was succeeded as Prime Minister by Rolandas Paksas, then the TS–LK mayor of Vilnius, but growing divisions between the coalition partners resulted in his replacement in October 1999 by Andrius Kubilius. Splits within the TS–LK followed, including the defection of Paksas to the Lithuanian Liberal Union and the formation of the Moderate Conservative Union by Vagnorius. In the parliamentary elections of October 2000 the rump party was reduced to nine seats and went into opposition.

In the June 2004 elections to the European Parliament it gained 12.58% of votes and returned two MEPs, one of whom is Vytautas Landsbergis.

The TS–LK is a member of the European Democrat Union and European People's Party.

Labour Party
Darbo Partija (DP)

Address. Lukiskiug. 5, Vilnius
Telephone. (370–5) 2107152
Fax. (370–5) 2107153
Email. info@darbopartija.lt
Website. www. darbopartija.lt
Leadership. Viktor Uspaskich (chairperson); Anastas Bosas (vice-chairman); Viktoras Muntianas (vice-chairman); Zilvinas Padaiga (vice-chairman)

The party was founded on Oct. 20, 2003, by a Russian-born self-made business millionaire Viktor Uspaskich (Viktoras Uspaskikh), who is the head of corporate giant Vikonda with its strong ties to Russian c ompanies. The programme adopted by the 812 delegates who attended the founding congress calls for replacing the current mixed parliamentary election system with single-mandate election districts based on a majority vote. The party also seeks to abolish counties and introduce the direct election of mayors. In its first electoral test, the June 2004 elections to the European Parliament, the DP was by far the most successful party, gaining 30.16% of the vote and returning 5 MEPs. In the European Parliament it joined the group of the Alliance of Liberals and Democrats for Europe. It followed this success by heading the polls in the *Seimas* elections in October 2004, taking 39 of the 141 seats and joining a coalition government.

Liberal and Centre Union
Liberaluir centro sajunga (LiCS)

Address. Vilniaus g. 22/1, Vilnius 01119
Telephone. (370–2) 231 3264
Fax. (370–2) 261 9363
Email. info@lics.lt
Website. www.lics.lt
Leadership. Arturas Zuokas (chairperson); Kestutis Glaveckas (deputy chairperson); Vytautas Bogusis (deputy chairperson)

The party was formed in 2003 by a merger of the Lithuanian Liberal Union, the Lithuanian Centre Union and the Modern Christian-Democratic Union. In the June 2004 elections to the European Parliament it gained 11.23% of votes and returned two MEPs, and took 18 seats in the Seimas elected in October 2004. The party is a member of the Liberal International.

Lithuanian Christian Democrats
Lietuvos Krikscionys Demokratai (LKD)

Address. Pylimo 36/2, Vilnius 2001
Telephone. (370–5) 2626126
Fax. (370–5) 2127387
Email. lkdp@takas.lt
Website. www.lkdp.lt
Leadership. Valentinas Stundys (chairman); Algirdas Saudargas & Ignas Vegele (deputy chairmen); Cicilionis Nerijus (treasurer and executive secretary)

The LKD programme stresses the importance of the family and its values as a base for Lithuanian society. It also underscores that Lithuania depends on the Christian culture of Western Europe. The party aims to struggle for social justice and peaceful dialogue and the promotion of Christian values in society. It sees Lithuania as a member of developing Europe while cherishing its own original culture and way of life.

The LKD came into being in May 2001 as a merger of the Lithuanian Christian Democratic Party (LKDP) and the Lithuanian Christian Democratic Union (LKDU), healing a split dating from 1992 in an attempt to restore Christian Democratic electoral fortunes.

The LKDP had been launched in 1989 as the revival of a pre-Soviet party dating from 1905, adopting a classic Christian democratic programme advocating a social market economy and Lithuanian membership of Western institutions. The breakaway LKDU was formed prior to the 1992 parliamentary elections, in which the LKDP came third with 18 seats and 12.2% of the vote, achieved in co-operation with *Sajudis* (later the Homeland Union–Lithuanian Conservatives, TS–LK) and other groups, while the LKDU won one seat. Both parties were in opposition until the 1996 elections, in which the LKDP fell back to 16 seats and 10% of the vote but became the second-largest party, while the LKDU retained its single mandate. The LKDP then joined a centre-right coalition government headed by the TS–LK. In the 1997 presidential elections the LKDU leader, Kazys Bobelis, came fifth with 4% of the vote.

Tensions in coalition relations from mid-1999 were accompanied by further factional strife in LKDP ranks, resulting in the formation of the Modern Christian Democratic Union (MKDS). In the October 2000 parliamentary elections the rump LKDP slumped to two seats and 3.1% of the vote, going into opposition, while the LKDU and the MKDS won one seat each.

The reunification of the LKDP and LKDU was achieved at a joint conference in Vilnius in May 2001, with Bobelis being elected chairman of the new KDS and former LKDP leader Algirdas Saudargas becoming one of two deputy chairmen. A small faction of the LKDP led by Alfonsas Svarinskas declined to join the merged party. Bobelis was subsequently replaced by Valentinas Stundys.

The LKD is a member of the Christian Democrat International and an associate member of the European People's Party.

Lithuanian Green Movement
Lietuvos zaliuju judejimas
Address. A/D 160, 44002 Kaunas
Telephone. (370 37) 324 241
Fax. (370 37) 324 201
Email. zalieji@zalieji.lt
Website. www.zalieji.lt
The Lithuanian Green Movement (LGM) was established by national environmental clubs, groups and activists in 1988. LGM coordinates the activities and exchanges information between some 500 members all over Lithuania.

The LGM is a member of Friends of the Earth International, Coalition Clean Baltic, Central Eastern Europe Bankwatch Network, Foundation for Environmental Education, and International Network for Sustainable Energy.

Lithuanian Liberal Democratic Party
Lietuvos Liberaldemokratu Partija (LLP)
The party was formed on Jan. 22, 2002, by former Prime Minister Rolandas Paksas and ten other deputies who left the Lithuanian Liberal Union (LLS). Its programme is almost identical to that of the LLS, but with a greater emphasis on governance, social policy, and rural issues. On March 9, 2002, the party held its founding congress, and elected Paksas as party chair and parliamentary deputy Henrikas Zukauskas as first deputy chair. Following his election as the President of Lithuania, Paksas relinquished in January 2004 the party post and was replaced as acting chairman by Valentinas Mazuronis. The party backed Paksas during the subsequent impeachment procedures against him. In the June 2004 elections to the European Parliament it received 6.83% of votes and elected one MEP.

Lithuanian Liberal Union
Lietuvos Liberalu Sajunga (LLS)
Address. Vilniaus g. 22/1, Vilnius 2600
Telephone. (370–2) 313264
Fax. (370–2) 791910
Email. lls@lls.lt
Website. www.lls.lt
Leadership. Eugenijus Gentvilas (chairman)
The LLS was founded in November 1990 by pro-independ-

ence activists at Vilnius University and elsewhere. It failed to gain representation in the 1992 elections and won only one seat in 1996, but in December 1999 was greatly strengthened by the adhesion of a breakaway faction of the Homeland Union–Lithuanian Conservatives (TS–LK) led by former Prime Minister Rolandas Paksas, who became LLS chairman.

In the October 2000 parliamentary elections the LLS achieved a major advance, to 34 seats on a 17.3% vote share. Paksas was therefore able to form a centrist majority coalition government embracing the LLS, the New Union–Social Liberals and the Lithuanian Centre Union (LCS). In June 2001, however, the government collapsed over differences on privatization policy and the LLS went into opposition to a government headed by the Lithuanian Social Democratic Party. Paksas resigned as LLS chairman in September 2001 and on Dec. 21, 2001, together with ten other LLS deputies formally left the party and formed the Liberal Democratic Party (LDP). The party split again in 2003 when a majority of its members joined the Liberal Democratic Party and Liberal the Liberal and Centre Union.

The LLS is a member of the Liberal International.

Lithuanian Peasants' Party
Lietuvos Valstieciu Partija (LVP)
Address. Blindziu 17, Vilnius 2000
Telephone. (370–2) 725268
Leadership. Ramunas Karbauskis (chairman)
Dating from 1905 and revived in 1990 as Lithuania's principal agrarian party, the LVP adopted its present name in 1994. Having won one seat in the 1996 legislative elections, the party polled strongly in local elections in March 2000, before advancing to four national seats (with 4.1% of the vote) in the October 2000 elections.

Lithuanian Polish Union
Lietuvos Lenku Sajunga (LLS)
Address. 40 Didzioji, Vilnius 2001
Telephone. (370–2) 223388
Leadership. Valdemar Tomasevski (chairman)
Founded in 1992 to represent Lithuania's ethnic Poles (about 8% of the total population), the LLS seeks the "national rebirth" of Lithuanian Poles through the promotion of Polish education but stresses its commitment to the Lithuanian state. Having won four *Seimas* seats in 1992 with a 2.1% vote share, it contested subsequent elections as the Lithuanian Poles' Electoral Action (LLRA), falling to one seat in 1996 but recovering to two in October 2000 with 1.9% of the vote.

Lithuanian Social Democratic Party
Lietuvos Socialdemokratu Partija (LSDP)
Address. Barboros Radvilaites 1, Vilnius 2000
Telephone/Fax. (370–2) 615420
Email. gekirk@lrs.lt
Website. www.lsdp.lt
Leadership. Algirdas Brazauskas (chairman)
The LSDP is directly descended from the original LSDP founded in 1896 and was relaunched in January 2001 as a merger of the (ex-communist) Lithuanian Democratic Labour Party (LDDP) and the post-independence LSDP.

Prominent in the inter-war period of independence, the LSDP was revived in 1989 with a social democratic platform on the West European model. Having formed part of the broad pro-independence movement under the umbrella of *Sajudis* (later the Homeland Union–Lithuanian Conservatives), the party contested the 1992 parliamentary elections independently, winning eight seats with 5.9% of the vote) and subsequently forming part of the parliamentary opposition to the ruling LDDP. The LDDP had been launched in December 1990 by a pro-reform and pro-independence faction of the Lithuanian Communist Party (LCP) following a constitutional revision revoking its monopoly of power (the LCP being banned in August 1991 and its property confiscated). It had registered an unexpected victory in the 1992 parliamentary elections, winning an overall majority of seats with 42.6% of the vote on a platform of gradual transition to a market economy. The LDDP leader, Algirdas Brazauskas, was accordingly elected chairman of the *Seimas* and thus head of state, in which capacity he received popular endorsement in presidential elections in February 1993.

Damaged by government financial scandals and internal feuding, the LDDP was heavily defeated in the October 1996 parliamentary elections, retaining only 12 seats and 10% of the vote, whereas the LSDP advanced to 12 seats and 7%. The LSDP candidate, Vytenis Andriukaitis, came fourth with 5.7% of the vote in the first round of presidential elections in December 1997. However, the LSDP and the LDDP mounted increasingly effective joint opposition to the post-1996 centre-right government headed by the Homeland Union–Lithuanian Conservatives (TS–LK) and contested the October 2000 parliamentary elections within the "Brazauskas Social Democratic Coalition", which also included the small New Democracy Party (NDP) and the Lithuanian Russian Union (LRS). The alliance became substantially the largest bloc, winning 51 of the 141 seats with 31.1% of the vote.

Outmanoeuvred in the subsequent inter-party negotiations, the LSDP and LDDP went into opposition to a centrist coalition government headed by the Lithuanian Liberal Union (LLS). The two parties formally merged at a Vilnius congress in January 2001, Brazauskas being elected chairman of the unified party, which adopted the historic LSDP name to signify the reunification of the Lithuanian left after 80 years of division. Following the collapse of the government coalition in June 2001, the LSDP came to power in July, with Brazauskas becoming Prime Minister of a new majority coalition with the New Union–Social Liberals.

In the June 2004 elections to the European Parliament it gained 14.43% of votes and returned two MEPs and in the October 2004 *Seimas* elections took 20 seats.

The LSDP is a member of the Socialist International.

New Union–Social Liberals
Naujoji Sajunga–Socialliberalai (NS-SL)

Address. Gedimino av. 10/1, Vilnius 2000
Telephone. (370–5) 2107 600
Fax. (370–5) 2107 602
Email. centras@nsajunga.lt
Website. www.nsajunga.lt
Leadership. Arturas Paulauskas (chairman)
The centrist NS-SL was launched in April 1998 by Arturas Paulauskas, a former public prosecutor who, standing as an independent, had narrowly lost the presidential elections in December 1997 and February 1998, taking a commanding lead in the first round with 44.7% but narrowly losing in the second to the candidate backed by the Homeland Union–Lithuanian Conservatives. The NS–SL polled strongly in its first parliamentary elections in October 2000, winning 28 seats on a 19.6% vote share. NS–SL leader Arturas Paulauskas was elected president of the new *Seimas* and the party became a leading component of the resultant centrist coalition headed by the Lithuanian Liberal Union (LLS). It continued in government on the formation in July 2001 of a centre-left coalition headed by the Lithuanian Social Democratic Party (LSDP). In 2004 the party claimed membership of 5.000 and 60 branches throughout the country. It won 11 seats in the October 2004 *Seimas* elections, when it was allied with the LSDP.

The party is member of the Liberal International, European Liberal Democrat and Reform political group (ELDR).

Peasants' and New Democratic Party Union
Valstieciuir Naujosios demokratijos partiju sajungos (VNDS)

Address. Gedimino pr. 24, Vilnius 2000
Telephone. (370–5) 210822
Fax. (370–5) 210821
Email. info@vnds.lt
Website. www. vnds.lt/
Leadership. Kazimira Prunskiene (president)
The origins of the VNDS go back to the centre-left New Democracy Party (NDP) and its leader, Kazimira Danute Prunskiene. She became Prime Minister in 1990–91 as Lithuania regained its independence, having then been a member of the Lithuanian Communist Party. After leaving office, she had rejected a Supreme Court ruling of 1992 that in the Soviet era she had collaborated with the KGB as head of the Lithuanian Women's Association. Elected to the *Seimas* in 1996 as candidate of the Lithuanian Women's Party (LMP), she was re-elected in 2000 for the NDP, which won two seats within the alliance headed by what became the Lithuanian Social Democratic Party.

At an extraordinary congress held in Vilnius on Dec. 15, 2002, the New Democracy Party (NDP) and the Peasants' Party (VP) merged creating the Peasants' and New Democracy Union. NDP leader and former Prime Minister Prunskiene was elected head of the new party, with VP chairman Ramunas Karbauskis as her first deputy chairman. The congress also elected two deputy chairmen from each party. In the June 2004 elections to the European Parliament the VNDS received 7.41% of votes and elected one MEP.

Union of Lithuanian Political Prisoners and Deportees
Lietuvos politiniu kaliniu ir tremtiniu sajunga (LPKTS)

Address. Laisves al. 39, Kaunas 3000
Telephone. (8-37) 32 32 14
Fax. (8-37) 32 07 49
Email. tretinys@takas.lt
Website. www. lpkts.lt
Leadership. Povilas Jakucionis (chairman)
During the period of national revival in 1988 former political prisoners of Soviet concentration camps and Siberian deportees were the first to organize outside communist state control. On July 30, 1988, they formed the Deportees' Club. Subsequently the organization renamed itself as the Union of Lithuanian Political Prisoners and Deportees. The LPKTS has 60 branches throughout Lithuania and 50,000 members and takes part in elections of all levels. The main goal of the activities of the Union is securing theindependence of Lithuania, and other tasks include restitution of the historical truth about the resistance to occupation. The Union attaches priority to cultural events and has built many monuments to Lithuanian partisans.

Other Parties

Lithuanian Freedom Union (*Lietuvos Laisves Sajunga*, LLS), right-wing formation which won one seat in the 2000 parliamentary elections with 1.3% of the vote.
Leadership. Vytautas Sustauskas

Lithuanian National Party (*Lietuviu Nacionaline Partija*, LNP), right-wing formation which won one parliamentary seat in 1996 under the "Young Lithuania" (*Jaunoji Lietuva*, JL) banner and retained it in 2000 in the Young Lithuania–New Nationalists (*Naujuju Tautininku*, NT)–Political Prisoners' Union (*Politiniu Kaliniu Sajunga*, PKS) alliance, which took 1.2% of the vote.
Leadership. Stanislovas Buskevicius

Lithuanian National Union (*Lietuviu Tautininku Sajunga,* LTS), right-wing party launched in April 1989 as a revival of a leading inter-war party of the same name. The LTS 1992 election list, which incorporated the Lithuanian Independence Party, won four seats, but the party was reduced to one seat in 1996 and none in 2000, when its vote share was 0.9%.
Leadership. Rimantas Smetona

Lithuanian People's Union (*Lietuvos Liaudies Sajunga,* LLS), contested the 2000 parliamentary election under the slogan "For a Fair Lithuania", obtaining 1.5% of the vote but no seats. In 2004 contested with the Liberal Democratic Party in the Order and Justice electoral coalition.
Leadership. Julius Veselka

Lithuanian Russian Union (*Lietuvos Rusu Sajunga, LRS*), party representing the Russian minority, whose leader was elected to the *Seimas* in 2000 within the alliance headed by what became the unified Lithuanian Social Democratic Party.
Leadership. Sergejus Dmitrijevas

Lithuanian Social Democracy Party 2000 (*Lietuvos Partija Socialdemokratija 2000,* SD-2000), founded in opposition to the alliance between the Lithuanian Social Democratic Party and the (ex-communist) Lithuanian Democratic Labour Party; won 0.5% of the vote in the 2000 elections.
Leadership. Rimantas Dagys

Moderate Conservative Union (*Nuosaikiuju Konservatoriu Sajunga,* NKS), splinter group of the Homeland Union–Lithuanian Conservatives, won one seat in the 2000 *Seimas* elections with 2% of the vote.
Leadership. Gediminas Vagnorius (chairman)

Luxembourg

Capital: Luxembourg-Ville
Population: 462,690 (2004E)

Fully independent since 1867, the Grand Duchy of Luxembourg is, under its 1868 constitution as amended, a constitutional hereditary monarchy in which the head of state (the Grand-Duke, since October 2000, Henri) exercises executive power through a government headed by a Prime Minister and accountable to the unicameral Chamber of Deputies (*Chambre des Députés*). The members of the 60-seat Chamber of Deputies are elected for a five-year term by citizens aged 18 and over (voting being compulsory). A system of proportional representation is based on four electoral districts, in which each voter has the same number of votes as there are seats and may cast them all for a single party list or may select candidates of more than one party. For the national and European elections, the allocation of seats is done by the Hagenbasch-Bischoff method. There is also an advisory Council of State, whose 21 members are appointed for life, seven directly by the Grand Duke and the other 14 by him on the recommendation of the Council itself or of the Chamber of Deputies. Luxembourg is a founder member of what became the European Union and elects six members of the European Parliament.

Since political parties in Luxembourg do not have a legal personality, there is no law providing for state funding of parties. However, groups represented in the Chamber of Deputies receive subsidies from public funds according to their size for the purposes of financing their parliamentary activities. Parties also have the benefit of certain free postal services during election campaigns.

Elections to the Chamber on June 13, 2004, resulted as follows: Christian Social People's Party 24 seats (with 36.11% of the vote), Luxembourg Socialist Workers' Party 14 (23.37%), Democratic Party 10 (16.5%), The Greens 7 (11.58%), Action Committee for Democracy and Social Justice 5 (9.95%). The Left (1.9%), Communist Party of Luxembourg (0.92%), and Luxembourg Freedom Party (0.12%) failed to win seats.

At the same time Luxembourg's electorate also voted for the contry's six representatives in the European Parliament. In a turnout of 90% – the second highest in the EU – the elections gave the following results: Christian Social People's Party 37.1% of the vote and 3 seats; Luxembourg Socialist Workers' Party 22.0% and 1 seat; The Greens 15.0% and 1 seat; Democratic Party 14.9% and 1 seat.

Action Committee for Democracy and Social Justice
Aktiounskomitee fir Demokratie a Gerechtegkeet (ADR)
Comité d'Action pour la Démocratie et la Justice Sociale
Address. 9, rue de la Loge L-1945 Luxembourg
Telephone. (352) 463–742
Fax. (352) 463–745
Email. adr@chd.lu
Website. www.adr.lu
Leadership. Robert Mehlen (president); Fernand Greisen (secretary-general); Gaston Gibéryen (Chamber group chairman)
The ADR was launched in March 1987 as the "Five-Sixths Action Committee" to campaign for universal entitlement to pensions worth five-sixths of final salary. Benefiting from the increasing number of pensioners on electoral rolls, the right-leaning formation won four Chamber seats in the 1989 elections and five in 1994. In the June 1999 elections it increased its representation to seven seats, with a 10.5% share of the vote. However, it failed to gain representation in simultaneous elections for the European Parliament, in which it won 8.99% of the vote. In the June 2004 elections, it declined to five seats in the Chamber of Deputies, while also losing two of its seats in the European Parliament. During the campaign, the ADR opposed the application of Turkey for EU membership and also immigration from outside the European Union.

The party in 2003 became a member of Union for a Europe of the Nations in the European Parliament.

Christian Social People's Party
Chrëschtlech-Sozial Vollekspartei (CSV)
Parti Chrétien Social (PCS)
Address. 4 rue de l'Eau, BP 826, L-2018 Luxembourg
Telephone. (352) 225–731
Fax. (352) 472–716
Email. csv@csv.lu
Website. www.csv.lu
Leadership. François Biltgen (president); Michel Wolter (Chamber group chairman); Jean-Louis Schiltz (general secretary)
Committed to the promotion of "a policy of solidarity and social progress under the guidance of Christian and humanist principles" and the preservation of the constitutional status quo, the CSV has long been Luxembourg's strongest party, drawing its support from the conservative middle class, civil servants, Catholic workers and the farming com-

munity. The party is a keen proponent of European economic and monetary union via the European Union (EU), with the proviso that Luxembourg's special banking secrecy laws must be maintained against any EU encroachment. Founded as the *Parti de la Droite*, the CSV adopted its present name in December 1944. Since 1919 the party has taken part to coalition governments with various other parties and has supplied Prime Ministers as follows: Émile Reuter (1919–25), Joseph Bech (1926–37), Pierre Dupong (1937–53), Joseph Bech (1953–58), Pierre Frieden (1958–59), Pierre Werner (1959–74 and 1979–84), Jacques Santer (1984–94) and Jean-Claude Juncker (since 1995). This sequence was interrupted when, in 1974, after an unsatisfactory electoral result, though still the first party in the country, the CSV decided to go in opposition. A coalition government between the liberals and the socialists, led by the liberal Gaston Thorn, former president of the European Commission, was created.

The party formed a coalition with the Luxembourg Socialist Workers' Party (LSAP) following the June 1984 elections, prior to which it had been in coalition with the Democratic Party. Its share of the vote in June 1984 was 34.9%, while in simultaneous elections to the European Parliament it retained three of Luxembourg's six seats. In the June 1994 elections the CSV's Chamber representation fell back to 21 seats (with 31.4% of the vote), while in simultaneous European elections it lost one of its three seats. Having formed another coalition with the LSAP, CSV Prime Minister Jacques Santer was unexpectedly appointed president of the European Commission from January 1995, being succeeded as head of the Luxembourg government and CSV leader by Juncker, hitherto Finance Minister.

In the June 1999 elections the CSV slipped further to 19 seats (and 30.1% of the vote) but remained the biggest Chamber party, so that Juncker was able to form a new coalition government, this time with the DP. In simultaneous European elections, the CSV again won two of Luxembourg's six seats, with a vote share of 31.7%. One of the CSV seats was taken by Santer, who had resigned as European Commission president in March 1999, together with his fellow commissioners, after an inquiry set up by the European Parliament had found evidence of corruption and fraud in the Commission.

After ten years of uninterrupted economic growth (the best in the EU), the elections in 2004 gave a solid victory for Prime Minister Jean-Claude Juncker. The party increased to 24 seats in the national parliament and gained one extra seat at the European Parliament. Among the actions of the outgoing government that may have been of influence in the election were the adoption of a new status for civil servants (civil servants representing almost 40% of all voters), pensions reform, and the declaration of the Prime Minister in 2002 in favour of dual nationality (almost 41% of the resident population of the Grand Duchy being foreigners, 85% of them from elsewhere in the European Union).

The CSV is a member of the European People's Party and the International Democrat Union. Its three representatives in the European Parliament sit in the European People's Party/European Democrats group.

Democratic Party
Demokratesch Partei (DP)
Parti Démocratique Libéral (PDL)

Address. 40, rue du Curé, L-1368 Luxembourg
Telephone. (352) 221 418 41
Fax. (352) 471-007
Email. dp@dp.lu
Website. www.dp.lu
Leadership. Lydie Polfer (president); Henri Grethen (secretary-general and Chamber group chairman)

Dating from the origins of parliamentary democracy in Luxembourg in the 1840s, the DP became an established party in the 19th century with the name *Ligue libérale*, unsuccessfully resisting the introduction of universal suffrage and as a consequence suffering a major defeat in 1919. After a process of adaptation, the party became one of the three major national parties represented in the post-1945 Chamber, taking part in many coalition governments: in the national unity administration of 1945–47; in coalition with the Christian Social People's Party (CSV) in 1947–51 (when the PD was known as the *Groupement Patriotique et Démocratique*) and in 1959–64 and 1968–74; with the Luxembourg Socialist Workers' Party (LSAP) in 1974–79; and with the CSV again in 1979–84. The liberal-socialist coalition abolished the death penalty, voted a law which legalized divorce and abortion, authorized the 40-hour working week and a fifth week of paid holiday and created (1977) a new process of institutionalized consultation between government, employers and trade unions called the Tripartite Co-ordination Committee. This committee was founded as a means of dealing with the economic crisis, and the most important achievement in this tripartite context was to enable the reorganization of the steel industry (which from 1975 to 1982 lost almost 18,000 jobs) on a consensual basis. Today, the Tripartite is considered as the base of the Luxembourg social model.

In the June 1984 elections the DP slipped to 14 seats (and from 21.3% to 18.7% of the vote) and went into opposition to a coalition of the CSV and LSAP. At the same time, it retained one of Luxembourg's six seats in the European Parliament. The DP remained in opposition after the 1989 elections, in which it fell back to 11 seats, and also after 1994 elections, in which it improved its performance to 12 seats, taking 18.9% of the vote. It retained its European Parliament seat on both occasions.

By Luxembourg standards the June 1999 elections brought a breakthrough for the DP, to the status of second-strongest Chamber party with 15 seats, from a 22.4% vote share. It accordingly returned to government after 15 years in opposition, taking half of the portfolios in a new coalition headed by the CSV, with Lydie Polfer of the DP becoming Deputy Prime Minister. In the simultaneous European elections, the DP retained its single seat with a 20.5% vote share.

In the outgoing government, the liberal party persuaded the CSV to prepare a bill for unmarried and homosexual couples, similar to the French civil contract called "pacs". The party also influenced the adoption of a new status for civil servants and supported fiscal reforms aimed at a balanced budget and reducing the tax burden on companies. However, in the June 2004 elections the party did poorly, losing five seats in the Chamber and its share of the vote in the European Parliament election falling to 14.87% as against 20.4% in 1999.

The DP is affiliated to the Liberal International, its member of the European Parliament sitting in the European Liberal, Democratic and Reformist group.

The Greens
Déi Gréng
Les Verts

Address. 31, Grand'rue L-1661 Luxembourg
Telephone. (352) 463–7401
Fax. (352) 463–741
Email. greng@greng.lu
Website. www.greng.lu
Leadership. Henri Kox and Viviane Loschetter (spokespersons); François Bausch (Chamber group chairman)

The organized Greens date from June 1983, when a number of individuals and groups, including former Socialists, founded the Green Alternative (*Di Gréng Alternativ/Parti Vert Alternatif*, GAP/PVA). The new party won two seats and

5.2% of the vote in the June 1984 national elections, while in European Parliament elections the same month it achieved 6.1% without winning representation. In accordance with the rotation principle established by the German Greens (Alliance 90/The Greens Party), the party's two elected deputies were replaced by alternates half way through the parliamentary term. The GAP/PVA again won two seats in the 1989 elections, before making a major advance in the 1994 contest, to five seats. Concurrent elections to the European Parliament were contested jointly with the less radical Green Ecologist Initiative List (*Gréng Lëscht Ekologesch Initiativ/Initiative Vert Écologiste*, GLEI/IVE), the alliance achieving 10.9% of the vote and one of the Grand Duchy's six seats.

A long-contemplated merger between the GAP/PVA and most of the GLEI/IVE was eventually consummated in advance of the June 1999 elections, although the Greens' then representative in the European Parliament launched the separate Green and Liberal Alliance (*Gréng a Liberal Allianz*, GaL). Led by Jup Weber, this new formation wanted to become a centrist ecology party and became a member of the European radical alliance group. The GaL failed to gain representation in the June 1999 elections, winning only 1.1% of the vote for the Chamber and 1.8% in the European contest. After, this bitter defeat the party was dissolved. In contrast the Greens retained five seats, although their vote share slipped to 9.1%. In the simultaneous European elections the Greens took 10.7% of the vote and again won one seat, the party's representative joining the Greens/European Free Alliance group.

However, to break the Greens' isolation in the Luxembourg political system, François Bausch, the most prominent ecologist leader, sought to transform the party, on the lines conceived by Jup Weber with GaL, into a centrist ecology formation. During the 1999-2004 legistature, the ecologist party supported the government's liberal reform agenda both in the economic and political spheres and backed the promotion of the Luxembourg finance sector. In June 2004, the party gained two additional seats in the national elections, taking it to seven, and increased its share of the vote to 15.2% (against 10.1% in 1999) in the European Parliament elections, although not gaining an extra seat.

The party is a member of the European Federation of Green Parties.

Luxembourg Socialist Workers' Party
Lëtzebuerger Sozialistesch Arbechterpartei (LSAP)
Parti Ouvrier Socialiste Luxembourgeois (POSL)
Address. 16 rue de Crécy, L-1364 Luxembourg
Telephone. (352) 455–991
Fax. (352) 456–575
Email. info@lsap.lu
Website. www.lsap.lu
Leadership. Jean Asselborn (president); Lucien Lux (secretary-general); Ben Fayot (Chamber group chairman)
Founded in 1902 as the Luxembourg Social Democratic Party, the party made little initial progress because of the qualified franchise. After a minority broke away in 1921 to form the Communist Party of Luxembourg, the party first took part in government from the end of 1937, after which the Socialist ministers laid the basis for modern social legislation. During the Nazi occupation the party was dissolved, but after World War II it re-emerged under its present name and took part in a government of national union until 1947, when it returned to opposition. Following renewed government participation in 1951–59 and 1964–68, the party was defeated in the 1968 legislative elections, after which it was temporarily weakened by the formation of the breakaway Social Democratic Party (which later became defunct).

A reconstructed LSAP made gains in the 1974 elections,

after which it joined a coalition government with the Democratic Party (DP). It returned to opposition after losing ground in the June 1979 elections, but returned to government (in coalition with the Christian Social People's Party, CSV) after making a major advance in the June 1984 national elections, in which it rose from 14 to 21 seats and from 24.3 to 33.6% of the vote. In European Parliament elections the same month the LSAP retained two of the six Luxembourg seats. The LSAP won 18 seats (25.5% of the vote) in a smaller Chamber in 1989 and slipped to 17 (24.8%) in 1994, retaining two European Parliament seats on both occasions and continuing as the junior coalition partner. The LSAP was the principal loser in the June 1999 elections, falling to third place in the Chamber of Deputies behind the CSV and the DP, winning only 13 seats on a slightly reduced vote share of 24.3%. In simultaneous European elections, the LSAP retained two seats with 23.6% of the vote. At the last elections in 2004, the LSAP became the second largest party in the Chamber (although gaining only one extra seat) and joined a coalition with the CSV. In the European elections, the Socialists' support declined slightly, to 22.9% against 23.4% in 1999, and they lost their second seat in the European Parliament.

The LSAP is a member party of the Socialist International, its representative in the European Parliament being a member of the Party of European Socialists group.

Other Parties

Communist Party of Luxembourg (*Kommunistesch Partei vu Letzeburg*, KPL/*Parti Communiste Luxembourgeois*, PCL). Formed as a result of a split in the Luxembourg Socialist Workers' Party (LSAP) at the 1921 Differdange congress. It first obtained a Chamber seat in 1934 but the result was annulled by the Chamber majority (though a proposal to ban the party was defeated in a referendum in 1937). The party was represented in the Chamber from 1945, its number of seats fluctuating between three in 1954–64 and six in 1968–74, and declining to two in 1979. It took part in the national unity government of 1945–47, after which it went into opposition, but co-operated with the LSAP at local level. In June 1979 elections the KPL obtained 5.8% of the vote (compared with 10.4% in 1974), while in 1984 its share fell to 5.0%. The KPL's representation fell to a single seat in the 1989 elections, while the death in 1990 of veteran leader René Urbany (son of the party's previous leader) was a further blow. Having in 1994 experienced its first post-war failure to win Chamber representation, the party did not contest the 1999 elections directly, instead backing the Left list, which won one seat. In December 2003, it decided to compete alone in the national and European elections scheduled for June 2004, accusing the Left of betraying the communist and revolutionary heritage and forgetting the working class. The KPL failed to win a seat in the national or European parliaments, taking 0.92% and 1.17% of the vote, respectively. With the Left movement, it was the only Luxembourg political party that presented foreign candidates on the European list. The party survives largely because its newspaper *Zeitung vum lëtzebuerger Vollek* receives funds from the government in order to maintain ideological pluralism in the press in Luxembourg.
Address. 2, Rue Astrid L-1143 Luxembourg
Telephone. (352) 446-066-1
Email. info@zlv.lu
Website. http://www.zlv.lu/
Leadership. Aly Ruckert (president)

The Left (*Déi Lénk, La Gauche*). This grouping was launched prior to the June 1999 elections by leftist groups and individuals and with the backing of the Communist

Party of Luxembourg, which had failed to win parliamentary representation in 1994. The new formation secured 3.3% of the vote and won one Chamber seat, while taking only 2.8% of the vote in the simultaneous European Parliament elections. During 2003 the electoral alliance fractured, with the new socialist wing, the anti-globalization movement and the communist renovators aiming to attract socialist and ecologist supporters disaffected with their own parties. The Left wishes to become a new radical left party without any direct reference to communist ideology. The former leaders of the Communist Party of Luxembourg rejected this new strategy and left the coalition. In the June 2004 elections the Left lost its seat in the Chamber of Deputies and its share of the vote in the European contest delined to 1.68%. The Left is an "observer member" in the Party of the European Left.

Address. 8 rue Notre Dame, L-2240 Luxembourg

Telephone. (352) 2620–2072

Fax. (352) 2620–2073

Email. sekretariat@dei-lenk.lu

Website. www.dei-lenk.lu

Leadership. Serge Urbany (former Chamber deputy); David Wagner (national secretary)

Luxembourg Freedom Party (*Fräi Partei Lëtzebuerg*, FPL/*Parti de la Liberté au Luxembourg*, FLP). Populist movement advocating lower state expenditure and balanced development between social classes and regions. The party only presented candidates in the North electoral district in 2004, winning 0.12% of the vote in the 2004 national elections. It did not present any candidates in the European contest. After this bitter defeat the party was dissolved.

Macedonia

Capital: Skopje
Population: 2,000,000 (2003E)

Modern Macedonia came into existence in 1945 as one of the six constitutive republics of Socialist Federated Republic of Yugoslavia (SFRY). When Yugoslavia disintegrated in the second half of 1991, Macedonia chose to assert its own independence rather than remain in a truncated Yugoslav state likely to be dominated by Serbia without the counterbalancing influences of Croatia and Slovenia. Macedonia declared independence on Nov. 21, 1991, and today is a democratic multiparty state. The President is elected for a term of five years by popular vote, while the unicameral Assembly (*Sobranie*) is comprised of 120 members. According to new electoral laws adopted in June 2002 (the Law on Election of Members of Parliament of 2002, the Law on the Voter List, and the Law on Election Districts) the parliamentarians are elected for a four-year term by those aged 18 and over, in six electoral districts. Each district has about 275,000 voters and elects 20 members by proportional representation subject to a 5% threshold. The political system is semi-presidential akin to the French model.

The peaceful transformation of Macedonian society in the early 1990s was preceded by an uneasy period of democratic consolidation. The combination of Greek diplomatic pressure and the economic embargo imposed on Macedonia (1992-95), and the difficulties stemming from observation of UN sanctions against the Federal Republic of Yugoslavia, significantly impaired Macedonian democratic stabilization efforts. Due to Greek objections the admission of Macedonia to membership in the United Nations in April 1993 required the

new member to be "provisionally referred to for all purposes within the United Nations as 'the former Yugoslav Republic of Macedonia' pending settlement of the difference that has arisen over the name of the State." Although the reference to the Yugoslav past was to be used within the UN as a result of Greek pressure, other international institutions have continued to refer to Macedonia as the "former Yugoslav republic". Despite recent warming of relations between Skopje and Athens, Greek approval of Macedonia remains absent. Besides the "name issue", during the democratization period inter-ethnic relations and the question of minority rights were at the forefront of the political issues on the domestic agenda. Following civil conflict in early and mid 2001, involving unrest among the Albanian minority, and the signing of the Ohrid Framework Agreement, Macedonia made a number of amendments to the constitution that clarified the position of the national minorities in the legal system.

Macedonia's fourth post-independence parliamentary elections were held on Sept. 15, 2002. The elections were conducted in accordance with OSCE commitments and international standards for democratic elections. Out of the registered 1,664,296 voters, 1,216,339 or 73%, came out to vote on election day. The winners, the coalition "Together For Macedonia" comprising the Social Democratic Union of Macedonia (SDSM), the Liberal Democratic Party (LDP), and a number of smaller parties representing the ethnic minorities in the country won 60 seats, while their main opponents, the coalition between the Internal Macedonian Revolutionary Organization–Democratic Party for Macedonian National Unity (VMRO–DMPNE) and the Liberal Party (LP), won 33 seats. The Macedonian Albanian parties won 26 seats, the Democratic Union for Integration (DUI) 16, the Democratic Party of Albanians (DPA) 7, the Party for Democratic Prosperity (PDP) 2, and the National Democratic Party (NDP) and Socialist Party of Macedonia took one each. In total 14 parties were represented in the new Parliament. The new government was effectively a coalition between the parties that made up "Together For Macedonia" and DUI, the Prime Minister being the leader of the SDSM, Branko Crvenkovski.

On Feb. 26, 2004, President Boris Trajkovski died in a plane crash. Extraordinary presidential elections were held on the 14th and 28th of April 2004. The turnout was 54% and Branko Crvenkovski was elected President in the second-round ballot with 42.47% of the vote. His main rival, the presidential candidate of VMRO-DPMNE, Sasko Kedev, gained 34.07% of the votes.

Democratic Party of Albanians
Demokratska Partija na Albancite (DPA)

Address. Marsal Tito 2, Tetovo 44000

Telephone. (389–44) 31534

Email. arben@pdsh.org

Website. www.pdsh.org

Leadership. Arben Xhaferi (chairman); Menduh Thachi (deputy chairman)

The Democratic Party of Albanians (DPA in Macedonian or PDPSh in Albanian) is one of several parties representing Macedonian Albanians (who comprise about 23% of the population according to the 1994 census). The party's origins hail to events in 1993 when a struggle developed for the control of Party for Democratic Prosperity (PDP) as a young generation of politicians favoring a radical agenda rose to eminence. PDP radicals, led by Arben Xhaferi and Menduh Thaci, complained strongly that the party, as part of the ruling coalition, made too many compromises which undermined ethnic Albanian interests, and initially argued for a separate Albanian state in Macedonia. At a national congress held by the PDP on Feb. 12, 1994, the party officially splintered into two factions, the moderate faction still supporting active participation in the political system. The radical faction founded a new party, PDP-A (Party of Democratic Prosperity of Albanians) which later registered in the courts as the DPA. Being in power in the period 1998-2002, DPA lost the intra-Albanian political contest in the 2002 elections to the newly formed Democratic Union for Intergration (DUI) led by Ali Ahmeti, winning only 7 to DUI's 16 seats.

Democratic Union for Integration
Demokratska Unija za Integracija (DUI)

Address. Shaban Bajrami 5
Telephone. (389–2) 2634955
Leadership. Ali Ahmeti (president); Agron Buhxaku & Teuta Arifi (vice-presidents)

The Democratic Union for Integration is the successor to the National Liberation Army which fought in Macedonia in early and mid-2001 under the leadership of Ali Ahmeti. Having secured constitutional reform and amnesty for his fighters Ahmeti made a leap into legitimate political activities. Although in the spring of 2002 he toyed with the idea of becoming a "coordinator" of the existing Macedonian Albanian political parties, thus achieving the status of an informal leader of this population's political structures, Ahmeti concentrated on founding a political party in the summer of 2002. Together with his former fighting associates, and co-opting various members of the Macedonian Albanian intelligentsia, Ahmeti founded the Democratic Union for Integration, (DUI in Macedonian and BDI in Albanian) on June 5 in Tetovo. In his inaugural speech, delivered beneath a large Albanian flag in Tetovo's "Palace of Culture", Ahmeti emphasized that the DUI is founded on the principle of equality, rather than discrimination, and promised to work for peace while repudiating the use of violent methods. In the parliamentary elections on Sept. 15 the DUI managed to win most of the votes of the Macedonian Albanian community and secure 16 seats in the Macedonian parliament. Following lengthy and tense negotiations DUI entered the coalition government of Branko Crvenkovski, leader of the Social Democratic Alliance of Macedonia, the third partner being the small but influential Liberal Democratic Party of Macedonia.

Internal Macedonian Revolutionary
Organization–Democratic Party for Macedonian
National Unity
Vnatresna Makedonska Revolucionerna
Organizacija–Demokratska Partija za Makedonsko
Nacionalno Edinstvo (VMRO–DPMNE)

Address. Macedonia 17A, 1000 Skopje
Telephone. (389–2) 3124244
Fax. (389–2) 3124336
Email. info@vmro-dpmne.org.mk
Website. www.vmro-dpmne.org.mk
Leadership. Nikola Gruevski (president); Ganka Samoilovska-Cvetanova (vice-president)

VMRO-DPMNE is a right-wing party named after the historic clandestine organization that fought for the liberation of Macedonia from Ottoman Turkish rule. Supported by Macedonian emigrants and by such eminent Macedonian dissidents as Dragan Bogdanovski and Goran Jakovlevski, the party was founded in late June 1990. While in the early 1990s VMRO-DPMNE had a more nationalist outlook, failing to win the parliamentary elections in 1990 and 1994, as well as the presidential elections in 1994, it changed rhetoric on the eve of the 1998 vote, allying with a new pro-business party Democratic Alternative (DA). The alliance emerged as a clear

winner, with 59 of the 120 seats, allowing Ljupco Georgievski to form a coalition government including DA and DPA.

Despite trailing in the first round of the presidential elections in 1999, the candidate of VMRO–DPMNE, Boris Trajkovski, was elected with 52.9% of the second round vote. Wavering between the harsh nationalist vocabulary of the former Minister of Interior Ljube Boshkovski and the more moderate pragmatic tones of the Finance Minister Nikola Gruevski the party lost the 2002 elections (winning only 29 seats), after which the charismatic leader Georgievski stepped down from all party functions.

Liberal Democratic Party
Liberalno-Demokratskata Partija (LDP)

Address. Partizanski odredi 89, 1000 Skopje
Telephone. (389–2) 3063675
Fax. (389–2) 3063099
Email. contact@ldp.org.mk
Website. www.ldp.org.mk
Leadership. Risto Penov (president); Jovan Manasievski & Angelka Peeva-Laurenchikj (vice-presidents); Vlado Popovski (secretary)

The Liberal Democratic Party (LDP) was created in January 1997 as a merger of the Liberal Party of Macedonia (LPM) led by Stojan Andov and the Democratic Party (DP) led by Petar Goshev. In 2000 a number of party members from the "liberal" wing decided to quit the LDP and (re-)found the Liberal Party of Macedonia. The party has a pro-reform market orientation and is particularly strong in the capital city, where LDP's Risto Penov has been repeatedly elected as the mayor. Goshev, the leader of the DP and subsequently the LDP, resigned after the party's poor results in the 1998 parliamentary elections In March 1999 Goshev was succeed by Penov, an economist. In the 2002 parliamentary elections the LDP won 13 seats in coalition with SDSM and a number of smaller parties.

The LDP, which has an official membership of 35,000, is affiliated to the Liberal International.

Liberal Party of Macedonia
Liberalnata Partija na Makedonija (LPM)

Address. c/o Sobranje, Oktomvri 11, 91000 Skopje
Website. www.liberalna.org.mk
Leadership. Stojan Andov (president); Ljupcho Meshkov & Sasho Bogdanovski (vice-presidents)

Led by former Yugoslav diplomat and career politician Stojan Andov, the Liberal Party of Macedonia (LPM) was originally founded in 1989 as the Alliance of Reform Forces of Macedonia (SRSM), then an affiliate of Ante Markovic's Alliance of Yugoslav Reform Forces (SRSJ). The LPM in the early 1990s closely cooperated with the Social Democrats and was included in the coalition governments until 1996. Following the split with the SDSM, and being in the opposition to the government, in early 1997, the LPM merged with Goshev's DP, founding the LDP. Following the dismal performance of LDP presidential candidate Stojan Andov in the elections in 1999, when he was relegated to fifth place with only 11.2% of the first-round vote, and losing elections for the LDP presidency, Andov and his followers re-established the LPM in 2000. The LPM gave external support to the centre-right government headed by the VMRO-DPMNE and for a short period of time was a coalition partner. In the 2002 elections LPM won 5 seats in a coalition with VMRO-DPMNE.

Party for Democratic Prosperity
Partija za Demokratski Prosperitet (PDP)

Address. 62 Karaorman, 44000 Tetovo
Telephone. (389–44) 25709
Leadership. Abdurahman Aliti (chairman)

The Party for Democratic Prosperity (PDP) was in the 1990s

the main party of Macedonian Albanians. The PDP, together with a smaller ethnic Albanian National Democratic Party (NDP) joined a coalition government headed by the Social Democratic Alliance of Macedonia (SDSM) in 1992. Following turbulent events in Macedonia in 1993 and 1994 the PDP underwent a split in between moderates and nationalists. In the 1994 elections the PDP won only 10 seats but still remained a member of the government headed by the SDSM. The coalition government with SDSM proved unstable, and the PDP protested against numerous governmental laws and actions, even boycotting parliamentary sessions for a period of time in 1995. Although in the 1998 elections the PDP ran on a joint list with DPA winning 14 seats it did not enter the government led by VMRO-DPMNE, although the DPA did. After the poor showing of their candidate in the presidential elections in 1999, Muhamed Halili winning only 4.4% of the first-round vote against Muharem Hexipi from PDA who obtained 14.9%, PDP had an even worse showing in the 2002 parliamentary elections, winning only 2 seats.

Social Democratic Alliance of Macedonia
Socijaldemokratski Sojuz na Makedonija (SDSM)
Address. Bihachka 8, 1000 Skopje
Telephone. (389–2) 3221-371
Fax. (389–2) 3221-071
Email. contact@sdsm.org.mk
Website. www.sdsm.org.mk
Leadership. Branko Crvenkovski (president); Vlado Buchkovski, Ilinka Mitreva, Nikola Popovski (vice-presidents)
The Social Democratic Alliance of Macedonia (SDSM) is successor to the former ruling Alliance of Communists of Macedonia (SKM). Reformed by then party leader Petar Gosgev in 1989, SKM changed its name into SKM-PDP adding "Party of Democratic Change" (*Partija za Demokratska Preobrazba*, PDP) to its title. Led by a young and reform minded generation of politicians, SKM-PDP came a close second in the 1990 parliamentary elections, with 31 seats. Following the fall of the "government of experts", SKM-PDP now renamed the SDSM, headed a coalition government from 1992 till 1998. Their nominee, Kiro Gligorov, was elected head of state by the parliament in January 1991, and reelected in the direct presidential elections in 1994. Due to numerous corruption scandals and unpopular foreign policy moves, SDSM lost power in the parliamentary elections of late 1998, winning only 29 seats. The defeat was confirmed when in the 1999 a presidential election, the SDSM candidate Tito Petkovski, was defeated in the second round by the VMRO-DPMNE nominee, Boris Trajkovski.

In the 2002 elections SDSM together with the Liberal Democratic Party and other smaller parties convincingly won the elections winning 42 seats. The new coalition government has included the DUI.

Socialist Party of Macedonia
Socijalistika Partija na Makedonija (SPM)
Address. Ilindenska bb, 1000 Skopje
Telephone. (389–2) 3228–015
Fax. (389–2) 3220–025
Leadership. Ljubisav Ivanov (president); Todor Kalamatiev, Petar Ilievski, Branko Petkovski, Milan Hristovski, Sasho Vasilevski (vice-presidents)
The Socialist Party of Macedonia (SPM) is the successor to the Socialist Alliance–Socialist Party of Macedonia, registered in the courts in September 1990. After winning 4 seats in the 1990 elections, the SPM joined the SDSM-led coalition government, remaining a member until the 1998 elections. The party faired very poorly in the 1998 elections, securing only two seats. Many blame the decline on the decreasing popularity of the aging president Ljubisav Ivanov, and the some-

what rural background of the party leadership, which proved unappealing to the majority of young and urban voters. The party won only one seat in the 2002 elections.

Other Parties

Democratic Party of Turks in Macedonia (*Demokratska Partija na Turcite vo Makedonija*, DPTM), draws its votes from the 77,000 strong Macedonian Turkish community. It won one seat in the 2002 elections in coalition with SDSM and LDP.
Leadership. Erdogan Sarach

Democratic League of Bosniaks (*Demokratska Liga na Boshnjacite*), a party representing the interests of the Bosniaks/Muslims in Macedonia. It won one seat in the 2002 elections in coalition with SDSM and LDP.
Leadership. Rafet Muminovic

Democratic Party of Serbs (*Demokratska Partija na Srbite*), a party representing the interests of the Serbs in Macedonia. It won one seat in the 2002 elections in coalition with SDSM and LDP.
Leadership. Ivan Stoiljkovic

People's Democratic Party (*Narodna Demokratska Partija*, NDP) is a radical Albanian minority party once part of PDP but now an independent organization; it won one parliamentary seat in the 2002 elections.

United Party of the Roms of Macedonia (*Obedineta Partija na Romite od Makedonija*, OPRM), representing Macedonia's Roms, won one seat in the 2002 elections in coalition with SDSM and LDP
Leadership. Nevdzhet Mustafa

Madagascar

Capital: Antananarivo
Population: 16,400,000

The Republic of Madagascar became fully independent from France in 1960. Post-independence politics were dominated by President Philibert Tsiranana and his Malagasy Social Democratic Party until 1972, when the military took control. In 1975 Didier Ratsiraka assumed the presidency, his regime retaining power until a new multi-party constitution heralded a decisive opposition victory in presidential and legislative elections in 1993. The constitution, which had been approved by national referendum in August 1992, was amended and also endorsed by referendum in March 1998. The amendments strengthened presidential powers and introduced provincial autonomy. The President, directly elected as head of state for a five-year term, appoints the Prime Minister and Council of Ministers. The bicameral legislature consists of (i) the Senate (*Sénat*) as the upper house, two-thirds of whose 90 members are indirectly elected by an electoral college representing the autonomous provinces and a third nominated by the President; and (ii) the National Assembly (*Assemblée Nationale*), whose 150 members are directly elected for a four-year term from 82 single-member and 34 dual-member constituencies.

Presidential elections in November 1992 and February 1993 resulted in Albert Zafy, representing an alliance of opposition forces launched in 1991, defeating the incumbent President Ratsiraka, taking nearly

67% of the vote in the second round. In legislative elections in June 1993 political groupings supporting President Zafy secured a majority in the National Assembly with over 70 of the 138 seats contested. The following three years were characterized by a series of power struggles between the President and the Assembly, leading in September 1996 to Zafy's impeachment. In subsequent presidential elections held in November and December 1996, Zafy was narrowly defeated by Ratsiraka, who took 50.7% of the second-round vote. President Ratsiraka consolidated his position in 1998 with the strengthening of presidential powers in a constitutional referendum held in March. In National Assembly elections in May 1998 Ratsiraka's Association for the Rebirth of Madagascar (AREMA) won 63 of the 150 seats and predominantly pro-Ratsiraka independent candidates 32.

Serious unrest erupted in the aftermath of the disputed presidential election of December 2001 which resulted in the opposition candidate, Marc Ravalomanana, coming in first place but short of an outright victory over the incumbent Ratsiraka. After a series of massive street protests Ravalomanana, the mayor of Antananarivo and a successful businessman, proclaimed himself President in February 2002 and formed a government. With Ravalomanana in control of the capital, Ratsiraka re-located his own government to his stronghold of Toamasina on the east coast and a low-level civil war ensued which ended in July 2002 when Ratsiraka fled the country and forces loyal to Ravalomanana gained control of the whole island. Whilst the war was underway the High Constitutional Court had in April confirmed Ravalomanana's victory in the presidential poll and he had been officially sworn in as President in May.

Elections to an enlarged 160-member National Assembly held in December 2002 resulted in an overwhelming victory for a coalition of parties supporting President Ravalomanana, mainly the I Love Madagascar party (103 seats) and the National Union (22 seats). The previously ruling AREMA, founded and led by Ratsiraka, was routed, winning only three seats.

Association for the Rebirth of Madagascar
Association pour la Rénaissance de Madagascar (AREMA)
Andry sy Riana Enti-Manavotra an'i Madagasikara (AREMA)

Address. c/o Assemblée Nationale, Antananarivo
Leadership. Pierrot Rajaonarivelo (national secretary)
Launched by Didier Ratsiraka in 1976 (and also known variously as the Vanguard of the Malagasy Revolution and the Vanguard for Economic and Social Recovery), AREMA was the dominant element of a coalition front, known as the National Front for the Defence of the Revolution (FNDR), within which all political formations were required to conduct their activity. From March 1990, however, participation in the FNDR ceased to be obligatory for political parties. In elections in 1993, Ratsiraka lost the presidency to Albert Zafy and AREMA lost its dominance in the National Assembly.

Ratsiraka made a come-back in 1996, being re-elected to the presidency, while AREMA emerged from the 1998 Assembly elections as by far the largest single party with 63 of the 150 seats, with some 60 of the other seats being won by pro-Ratsiraka parties or independents. In indirect Senate elections in March 2001 AREMA took 49 of the 60 elective seats.

In the aftermath of the disputed presidential election of December 2001 the country was effectively divided into sup-

porters of Ratsiraka and AREMA, on the one hand, and opposition candidate, Marc Ravalomanana, on the other. The country was plunged into civil war which ended in July 2002 when Ratsiraka fled the country and forces loyal to Ravalomanana gained control of the whole island. Adding insult to injury the national secretary of AREMA, Pierrot Rajaonarivelo, immediately announced his recognition of Ravalomanana's government and offered to be part of a government of national unity. For the December 2002 legislative elections AREMA was split; one faction called for a boycott of the poll, while another faction put forward 94 candidates. Despite suffering a massive defeat and winning only three seats, AREMA remained the main opposition party to President Ravalomanana.

Economic Liberalism and Democratic Action for National Reconstruction
Libéralisme Economique et Action Démocratique pour la Reconstruction Nationale (LEADER–Fanilo)

Address. c/o Assemblée Nationale, Antananarivo
Leadership. Herizo Razafimahaleo
Founded in 1993 as a pro-Ratsiraka party, LEADER–Fanilo returned 13 deputies to the National Assembly in the 1993 elections. Party leader Razafimahaleo came third in the first round of the 1996 presidential elections with 15.1% of the vote. In the May 1998 legislative elections, the party won 16 seats to become the second largest party in the Assembly. The party has opposed the presidency of Marc Ravalomanana and managed to win only one seat in the December 2002 Assembly elections.

I Love Madagascar
Tiako I Madagasikara (TIM)

Address. c/o Assemblée Nationale
Leadership. Solofonantenaina Razoarimihaja (national president); Jacques Sylla (general secretary)
The TIM was originally formed as a group that supported Marc Ravalomanana's candidacy for mayor of Antananarivo during the municipal elections in 1999. When Ravalomanana presented himself as a candidate for the presidential elections in 2001, the group became a fully-fledged political party. In the elections to the 160-member National Assembly held in December 2002 the party was the main component of a pro-Ravalomanana coalition, which opposed the previously-ruling Association for the Rebirth of Madagascar (AREMA) and also included the National Union. The TIM won an overwhelming victory, gaining 103 of the 160 seats contested. The party's general-secretary, Jacques Sylla, had served as Prime Minister since February 2002.

Movement for the Progress of Madagascar
Mouvement pour le Progrès de Madagascar
Mpitolona ho'amin'ny Fanjakan'ny Madinika (MFM)

Address. c/o Assemblée Nationale, Antananarivo
Leadership. Manandafy Rakotonirina
The MFN was formed by radical students in 1972 as the *Parti luttant pour le puovoir des Prolétaires* (the Party Fighting for Power to the Proletariat), originally with radical left-wing credentials but latterly with an increasingly liberal outlook. A significant opposition group by the end of the 1980s, it was the second largest party in the National Assembly following legislative elections in 1989. Party leader Rakotonirina, who stood as a first-round presidential candidate in November 1992 (taking third place with just over 10% of the vote) supported the victorious Albert Zafy in the second round. However, following the June 1993 legislative elections, in which it won 15 Assembly seats, the party went into opposition. In the May 1998 Assembly polling, the MFM's representation fell to three seats. The MFM presented 101 candidates for the 2002 legislative elec-

tion, but managed to win only two seats. The party is in opposition to the government led by the pro-Ravalomanana I Love Madagascar (TIM).

National Union
Firaisankinam-Pirenena (FP)
Address. c/o Assemblée Nationale, Antananarivo

This pro-Ravalomanana party was created in early 2002 and contested the National Assembly elections held at the end of that year, winning 22 seats to make it the second largest party in the legislature after the I Love Madagascar (TIM) party.

Renewal of the Social-Democratic Party
Rénaissance du Parti Social-Démocratique (RPSD)
Address. c/o Assemblée Nationale

Formed by members of the Social Democratic Party (*Parti Social Democratique*, PSD) which dominated the political scene during the first republic. The party presented 62 candidates for the December 2002 legislative elections and won four seats. The RPSD supports the Ravalomanana government.

Union of Popular Forces
Herim-Bahoaka Mitambatra (HBM)
Address. c/o Assemblée Nationale

Formed in the aftermath of the disputed December 2001 presidential election, the party presented 74 candidates in the December 2002 legislative election and won one seat. The party supports President Ravalomanana.

Other Parties

Action and Reflection Group for the Development of Madagascar (*Groupe de Réflexion et d'Action pour le Développement de Madagascar, GRAD/Iloafo*), an anti-Ratsiraka party, the GRAD/*Iloafo* won a single seat in both the 1993 and the 1998 Assembly elections, but failed to win a seat in the December 2002 elections.
Leadership. Tovananahary Rabetsitonta

Action, Truth, Development and Harmony (*Asa, Fahamarinana, Fampandrosoana, Arind*, AFFA)
AFFA was established in the early 1990s by Albert Zafy (President between 1993-96) in opposition to President Ratsiraka and his Association for the Rebirth of Madagascar (AREMA). In the May 1998 elections AFFA won six seats in the National Assembly. Zafy opposed the presidency of Marc Ravalomanana and was one of the promoters of the so-called "Front du Refus" that tried to organize a boycott of the December 2002 National Assembly elections. Despite Zafy's call for a boycott, a small number of AFFA candidates stood in the elections, but none were successful.
Leadership. Albert Zafy

Confederation of Civil Societies for Development–Fihaonana (*Confédération des Societés pour le Développement–Fihaonana*), a pro-Zafy formation which won eight seats in the 1993 legislative elections, but fell to a single seat in 1998 and failed to win any seats in the December 2002 elections.
Leadership. Guy Razanamasy

Congress Party for Madagascar Independence-Renewal (*Antoky Kongresy Fahaleonvantenani Madagaskar*, AKFM–Fanavaozana), launched by a breakaway faction of the left-wing Congress Party for Madagascar Independence (AKFM) in 1989. A pro-Zafy group, it took five seats in the 1993 legislative elections, while the pro-Ratsiraka AKFM rump won none. Leader Rev. Richard Andriamanjato took

fifth place, with 4.9% of the vote, in the first round of the 1996 presidential elections. In the 1998 Assembly elections, the AKFM–*Fanavaozana* won three seats, but failed to win any seats in the December 2002 election.
Leadership. Rev. Richard Andriamanjato

Judged by One's Work (*Ny Asa Vita no Ifampitsanara*, AVI), promoting human rights and hard work, was founded in 1997 and secured 14 seats in the May 1998 legislative elections to become the third largest party in the National Assembly. Party leader Norbert Ratsirahonana had earlier gained 10.1% of the first-round vote in the 1996 presidential elections. The party failed to win a seat in the December 2002 legislative elections.
Leadership. Norbert Ratsirahonana

Make Madagascar Dynamic (*Madagasikara Vanona no Asandratra*, MAVANA) was founded in 2002 in the far south of the island. It presented 50 candidates for the December 2002 National Assembly elections, but failed to win a seat. In the elections MAVANA candidates neither supported nor opposed the presidency of Marc Ravalomanana.
Leadership. Louisette Raharimalala

Party Uniting Common Efforts (*Antoko Miombon' Ezaka*, AME), formed after the political crisis in early 2002, the party presented 40 candidates for the December 2002 National Assembly elections but failed to win a seat. The party supports President Ravalomanana.
Leadership. Gen. (retd) Désiré Ramakavelo

Rally for Socialism and Democracy (*Rassemblement pour le Socialisme et la Démocratie*, RPSD), whose leader Evariste Marson came fourth in the first round of the presidential elections in November 1992 with 4.6% of the vote. The party switched allegiance to the winner, Albert Zafy, in the second round, but later, having won eight National Assembly seats in the June 1993 elections, went into opposition. In the May 1998 Assembly elections the RPSD increased its representation to 11 seats. However, the party failed to win any seats in the December 2002 Assembly elections.
Leadership. Evariste Marson

Malawi

Capital: Lilongwe
Population: 10,385,850 (2000E)

The former British protectorate of Nyasaland achieved independence as Malawi in 1964, becoming a one-party republic under a new constitution two years later. The authoritarian regime of President Hastings Banda and his Malawi Congress Party (MCP) retained power until widespread popular protest in the early 1990s led to constitutional amendments introducing multi-party democracy in 1993. An interim constitution, drafted by a National Consultative Council and approved in May 1994, provided for a directly elected executive President and a 177-member National Assembly, both serving five-year terms. The constitution was formally promulgated in May 1995 at the end of its review period. The size of the Assembly, which is elected from single-member constituencies by universal suffrage in a first-past-the-post electoral system, was increased to 193 members in 1999. A constitutional provision for the creation of an indirectly elected Senate as an upper chamber was repealed by the required two-thirds majority of the Assembly in January 2001. More importantly, efforts to enable President Bakili Muluzi, (first elected 1994 and reelected 1999), to possibly serve a third term after the elections due in 2004 proved unsuccessful, when moves to change the Constitution failed to gain two-thirds majorities in 2000 and 2001. Subject to legal contestation has also been Section 65 of the Constitution that provides for the loss of parliamentary seats when MPs "cross the floor" and join another political party or an organization which is "political in nature".

Multi-party legislative and presidential elections in May 1994 resulted in victory for the United Democratic Front (UDF) and its leader, Bakili Muluzi, whose government initially included representatives of other former opposition parties. In presidential elections held on June 15, 1999, Muluzi was re-elected, winning 51.4% of the vote in a five-way contest. In simultaneous elections for the National Assembly, the UDF won 93 seats (with 47.3% of the vote), the MCP 66 (33.8%), the Alliance for Democracy (AFORD) 29 (10.6%) and independents 4. The four independent MPs were all former UDF members who decided to vote with the UDF in the Assembly, thus giving that party a slim working majority. Following the correction of polling results, floor crossing, the return of most of the independents to the UDF and several by-elections, the UDF was able to consolidate its somewhat precarious absolute majority in the National Assembly to 101 of 193 MPs in 2000. In early 2001, however, five deputies left for the newly founded UDF-offshoot National Democratic Alliance (NDA) of former cabinet minister Brown Mpinganjira. Stripped of its majority Muluzi and the UDF had to rely on a faction of the MCP until AFORD's president Chihana joined government as a second Vice-President, provoking severe unrest in his party. Months before the general elections planned for 2004 the three major parties were confronted with major problems of defections and factionalism. Efforts to unite the opposition proved partly successful when six smaller parties signed a memorandum of understanding for an electoral alliance named the *Mgwirizano* (Chichewa for "unity") coalition in January 2004.

Considerable disenchantment with party politics in general resulted in a low turnout of 59.4% and 40 independents winning seats in the National Assembly in the general elections in May 2004. The UDF's poor performance in government reduced its seat share to 50 MPs, coming in only second after the MCP with 57 seats. *Mgwirizano* secured 25 seats, the NDA eight seats and AFORD only six seats. However, Bingu Wa Mutharika won the presidential race with 35% of the vote, ahead of MCP's John Tembo with 27.5% of the votes cast. Subsequently, Bingu and the UDF managed to secure a working majority in the National Assembly by coopting independents and opposition parties. Once again, personal interest and lack of principles proved to be the major drive behind Malawian politics when former *Mgwirizano* members MGODE and Chakuamba's RP as well as Mpinginjira's NDA joined the government in June 2004.

Alliance for Democracy (AFORD)

Address. Private Bag 28, Lilongwe
Telephone. (265) 743166
Fax. (265) 743170
Leadership. Chakufwa Chihana (president)
AFORD was launched in September 1992 to secure democratic reforms in Malawi. Later that year the government declared membership of the group illegal, and its leader was subsequently imprisoned until mid-1993, when the party was legalized. In March 1993 AFORD absorbed the membership of the former Malawi Freedom Movement, an organization founded by Orton Chirwa, who had been a minister in the Banda regime in the 1970s before being arrested and imprisoned for treason in 1981.

In the multi-party legislative elections in May 1994, AFORD won 36 seats, almost exlusively in the Northern region. In the presidential poll, Chakufwa Chihana came third with 18.6% of the votes cast. Subsequent talks to bring AFORD into the coalition government led by the UDF broke down, and in June 1994 the party declared that it had signed a memorandum of understanding with the defeated MCP. However, in September 1994, Chihana and five other AFORD politicians joined the cabinet, and the party's alliance with the MCP was terminated the following January.

In July 1995 AFORD's ties with the UDF were strengthened by the signature of a formal coalition agreement. In May 1996 Chihana resigned as Second Vice-President and Minister of Irrigation in order to spend more time on party work, and in June 1996 AFORD terminated the coalition agreement. Several AFORD ministers who refused to resign from the Cabinet were dismissed from AFORD's national executive. They remained in the Cabinet as independent members of the Assembly, rejecting demands from AFORD and the MCP that they should resign their Assembly seats and seek formal re-election as independents.

AFORD contested the June 1999 presidential and legislative elections in alliance with the MCP. Chihana was the vice-presidential running-mate of the MCP candidate, who came second in the election. AFORD won 29 Assembly seats (all but one in the northern region) and subsequently cooperated with the MCP (66 seats) in mounting an ultimately unsuccessful legal challenge to the election results in certain constituencies won by the UDF. Chihana's sudden move to align with the UDF in 2002 and to join Muluzi's government in April 2003 resulted in the formation of a dissident group named Genuine-AFORD (GAFORD) by half of AFORD's MPs, accusing Chihana of violating party congress decisions. After attempts at reconciliation failed, GAFORD was renamed the Movement for Genuine Democractic Change (MGODE), officially launched in early October 2003. The split proved to be a disaster for AFORD, which gained only six seats in the parliamentary elections 2004. However, the party managed to stay as a minor coalition partner in the newly formed government of Bingu Wa Mathurika.

Malawi Congress Party (MCP)

Address. Private Bag 388, Lilongwe 3
Telephone. (265) 783322
Leadership. John Tembo (president)
Under the leadership of Hastings Banda, the traditionalist and conservative MCP was the sole legal party from 1966 until 1993, when multi-party democracy was introduced in the wake of growing popular demands for political reform. The MCP lost power in May 1994, coming second in the Assembly elections with 56 seats, while Dr Banda was defeated in the presidential election by the UDF candidate, winning only 33.6% of the vote.

An alliance between the MCP and AFORD, which had been announced in June 1994, was ended by AFORD in January 1995. However, a subsequent coalition agreement between AFORD and the UDF (now the effective party of government) was short-lived, and AFORD entered into a new alliance with the MCP. In the campaign for the June 1999 elections, the MCP accused the UDF government of abetting corruption and failing to deliver on its economic and social promises. In the presidential contest, MCP president Gwanda Chakuamba was runner-up with 44.3% of the vote, while the MCP won 66 Assembly seats (most of them in the central region) and became the official opposition to the UDF government, supported by AFORD.

After two MCP deputies had defected to the UDF in May 2000, opposing factions of the MCP organized rival party conventions in August 2000. One re-elected Chakuamba as party president, while the other elected John Tembo (the former MCP vice-president) to the same post. Litigation to resolve the leadership issue resulted in a court ruling that Chakuamba remained the legal party president. Pending an appeal, Tembo organized a meeting in Lilongwe in June 2001 at which 37 of the 41 MCP district chairmen called on Chakuamba to stand down and declared their support for Tembo. The turmoil continued with a bitter legal battle and violence between supporters of the two factions during 2002 and 2003. In November and December 2002, Tembo was suspended from the National Assembly and lost his right to run for both parliamentary and presidential elections for the following seven years due to "contempt of court" in connection with the party congress in 2001. After an acrimonious party congress in Lilongwe in April 2003 where the party's headquarters went up in flames, the Chakuamba and Tembo factions succeeded in coming to terms with each other at a congress held only weeks later. Chakuamba accepted the election of Tembo to the post of party president and contented himself with the post of MCP vice-president. The reconciliation proved to be superficial only, after Tembo's suspension from the National Assembly was overturned by the Supreme Court of Appeals in late 2003. Chakuamba announced on Jan. 7, 2004, that he was leaving the party to form the Republican Party (RP) stripping MCP of its southern electoral base. The Republican Party signed a memorandum of understanding for an electoral alliance in January 2004 whereas the MCP refused to do so. MCP came first in the parliamentary elections in May 2004 securing 57 seats, whereas presidential candidate Tembo lost with 27.5% to the winning contender Bingu. MCP has since then been the principal opposition party.

The MCP is associated with the International Democrat Union through its membership of the Democrat Union of Africa.

United Democratic Front (UDF)

Address. PO Box 5946, Limbe
Telephone. (265) 651275
Fax. (265) 645725
Email. udf@malawi.net
Website. www.udf.malawi.net
Leadership. Bakili Muluzi (party chairman)

The UDF was formed in 1992 by former officials of the MCP to campaign for a multi-party democracy, and emerged from the elections in May 1994 as the leading political force. The party won 85 Assembly seats and party leader Bakili Muluzi secured the presidency with 47.3% of the votes cast. UDF members predominated in subsequent governments, a coalition agreement with the AFORD proving to be short-lived. As the ruling party, the UDF claimed to be promoting human rights after the repression of the Banda era and to be working for economic improvement in the face of harsh global conditions.

In the June 1999 elections President Muluzi was returned to office with an absolute majority (51.4%), an outcome that was unsuccessfully challenged in court by the MCP and AFORD. The UDF narrowly failed to win an overall majority in the National Assembly, but with a final tally of 94 of the 193 seats (80% of them in the southern region) was able to form a minority UDF government with the support of independent members.

During 2000 UDF party unity came under increasing strain, while the Muluzi government became subject to allegations of economic mismanagement, corruption and nepotism. In November 2000 President Muluzi dismissed several senior ministers, one of whom, Brown Mpinganjira, was subsequently acquitted of corruption charges. Claiming that his dismissal had been politically motivated, Mpinganjira announced in early 2001 the establishment of a "pressure group" called the National Democratic Alliance (NDA), which gained some support from disaffected UDF Assembly members, who left the governing party to sit as independents. The new pressure group was strongly opposed to President Muluzi's reported intention to seek re-election for a third presidential term. The UDF government responded by securing the passage in June 2001 of a law specifying that the seat of any Assembly member defecting to another party would be declared vacant. The unsuccessful efforts of Muluzi for a third term in 2002 and early 2003 prompted Muluzi to promote former United Party (UP) presidential candidate Bingu wa Mutharika as his successor as a presidential candidate in the 2004 elections. At the UDF party congress on Aug. 7-10, 2003, Bingu wa Mutharika was elected party presidential candidate, while Muluzi moved to the newly created supreme post of party chairman. The fast advancement of the newcomer Bingu prompted further dissatisfaction within the UDF's ranks, resulting in numerous defections and expulsions. In January 2004, Vice-President Justin Malewezi left the UDF for the small opposition party People's Progressive Movement (PPM). As a result, the UDF lost half of its seats in the parliamentary elections in May 2004 and was reduced to 50 seats. However, Bingu Wa Mathurika won the presidential race with 35% of the vote. Due to a broad coalition being formed some weeks after the elections, the UDF managed to stay in power.

The UDF is a member party of the Liberal International.

Other Parties

The 1999 and 2004 parliamentary elections were unsuccessfully contested by a number of parties, of which three also presented presidential candidates.

Christian Democratic Party (CDP), registered in Feb. 1995 and renamed Social Democratic Party (SDP) on Feb. 18, 1996. The SDP contested unsuccessfully the 1999 parliamentary elections.

Congress for National Unity (CONU), registered in March 1998, received 0.51% of the vote in the 1999 presidential election for its candidate, Daniel Nkhumbwe. The CONU failed to win seats in the parliamentary elections in 1999 but contested more successfully in 2004 by securing one seat.

Forum Party (FP), registered in November 1997. The FP did not contest the 1999 elections.

Labour Party, registered in May 1997 with George Nathaniel Gama as party president, but did not participate in the 1999 elections.

Malawi Democratic Party (MDP), performed poorly in the 1994 elections, attracting less than 1% in both the legislative and presidential contests. In 1999 the party's presidential candidate, Kamulepo Kalua, came third with 1.43% of the vote. In January 2004 the MDP signed a memorandum of understanding to form an electoral alliance named *Mgwirizano* for the pending elections in 2004. The MDP did not win any seats in the parliamentary elections in 1999 and 2004 respectively.

Malawi Democratic Union (MDU), registered as a political party in October 1993. The MDU gathered only 323 votes in the 1994 elections (0.0% of the vote). Similarly, the MDU failed to win any seat in 1999 and 2004. Malawi Forum For Unity and Development (Mafunde), registered in June 2002 with George Nnensa as chairman. Mafunde helped form the *Mgwirizano* electoral alliance in January 2004 but failed to win a seat in the subsequent elections in May.

Malawi Freedom Party (MFP), registered in January 1996 with Suleman Ishmail Shuwah as party president. The MPF did not contest the 1999 elections.

Malawi National Democratic Party (MNDP), registered as a political party in August 1993. In the 1994 elections the MDP attracted only 0.1% of the vote and no seat. The MNDP participated unsuccessfully in the 1999 elections.

Mgwirizano Coalition, was launched in January 2004 when a memorandum of understanding was signed with a number of pposition parties, namely Malawi Democratic Party (MPD), Malawi Forum For Unity and Development (Mafunde), National Unity Party (NUP), People's Transformation Party (PETRA), PPM, and the Republican Party (RP). Shortly afterwards, MGODE joined the alliance. Originally, the major reason to form the coalition was to unseat the UDF government by uniting opposition forces. However, due to personal rivalries for the position of presidential candidate, *Mgwirizano* failed to attract more support, especially from the MCP and NDA. It finally agreed on RP's Chakuamba and PPM's Aleke Banda as presidential candidate and running mate respectively. *Mgwirizano* secured 25 seats altogether in the 2004 elections and its presidential and vice-presidential candidate were awarded with 24.5% of the votes cast. However, the coalition proved to be shortlived when RP and MGODE left for government posts in June 2004.

Movement for Genuine Democratic Change (MGODE), was launched by 16 former AFORD MPs in early October 2003, Goeffrey Du Mhango becoming interim chairman. The breakaway resulted from grievances over AFORD president Chihana's unilateral move to align with the UDF in violation of party congress decisions in 2002, Chihana joining the unity government of President Muluzi in April 2003. Five AFORD MPs led by Greene Mwamondwe, now MOGDE spokesman, formed a grouping called Genuine AFORD (GAFORD); they were suspended from the National Assembly by the parliamentary speaker on Aug. 5, 2003, but continued to sit in parliament ahead of their cases being subject to judicial review. GAFORD members decided to register as a political party but were stopped by the Supreme Court, which granted an injunction sought by AFORD claiming that the two names were too similar and would confuse voters. Originally, Mwamwonde announced that the party would be called Genuine Alliance for Democratic Change (GADC) before the party adopted its present name. MGODE announced in late January 2004 it would join the *Mgwirizano* electoral opposition alliance formed the same month. However, MGODE gained only three seats in the May 2004 elections. Despite the bitter split from AFORD over that party's support for the UDF, MGODE surprisingly joined the government in June 2004.

National Democratic Alliance (NDA), was formed as a pressure group in January 2001 by Brown Mpinganjira and three other former UDF deputies. Mpinganjira had been sacked as a cabinet minister by Muluzi in late 2000, officially because of corruption allegations, but apparently also due to his opposition to Muluzi's third term bid and his own ambitions.. In order to avoid the loss of the parliamentary seats of the five former UDF MPs under the disputed constitutional provisions (section 65), the NDA was hesitant to register as a fully-fledged political party until June 2003. Subsequently, the Speaker of Parliament declared their seats vacant but the sus-

pension was provisionally overturned by an injunction only days later. Mpinganjira commands strong support in the Mulanje region (South) and was therefore feared by the UDF. The NDA and Mpingajira faced several attempts to hinder its activity by the UDF and government, including violence by UDF radicals and trumped up charges of treason and murder. The NDA refused to join the opposition coalition *Mgwirizano* formed in January 2004 and won eight seats in the elections in May 2004. Mpinganjira gathered a disappointing 8.4% of the votes cast in the presidential race. Only two weeks after the new government was formed, Mpinganjira surprisingly announced that the NDA would join the government, prompting protest by five newly elected MPs.

National Independent Party (NIP), registered in December 1999 as a political party but was cancelled on Nov. 6, 2000.

National Patriotic Front (NPF), registered in May 1995. The NPF unsuccessfully contested the 1999 parliamentary elections in a handful consituencies.

National Solidarity Movement, registered in February 1999 but did not participate in the elections the same year.

National Unity Party (NUP), registered in August 1995. The NUP unsuccessfully contested the 1999 elections. The NUP helped form the opposition electoral alliance *Mgwirizano* in January 2004 but unsuccessfully contested the elections in May.

New Dawn for Africa, registered in February 2003 rather as a briefcase party by UDF and Muluzi sympathizers in order to confuse Brown Mpinganjira's plan to launch a party with an identical acronym – the National Democratic Alliance.

Pamodzi Freedom Party (PFP), registered in June 2002 with Rainsford Chigandala Ndiwo as party president.

People's Democratic Party (PDP), registered in October 1996 with Rolf R. Patel as party chairman but did not participate in the 1999 elections.

People's Progressive Movement (PPM), launched in March 2003 by the former chairman of the chamber of commerce, Jimmy Koreia-Mpatsa. The PPM commands the support of the former cabinet minister and founding member of the UDF, Aleke Banda, who owns *The Nation*, one of Malawi's two main daily newspapers. Banda became party president at a party congress in 2003. Justin Malewezi, the country's Vice-President, who had left the ruling UDF party the same month, became vice-president. The PPM took part in launching the electoral opposition alliance *Mgwirizano* in January 2004. Former Vice-President Justin Malewezi's membership in PPM was shortlived as he decided to run for President as an independent candidate. He came in last with 2% of the votes cast. Aleke Banda became running mate of the alliance's presidential candidate Chakuamba in the 2004 elections, coming in third. The PPM won six seats in the National Assembly.

People's Transformation Party (PETRA), registered on Dec. 12, 2002, with Kamuzu Chibambo as interim chairman. PETRA took part in launching the electoral opposition alliance *Mgwirizano* in January 2004 and managed to secure one seat in the May 2004 elections under the coalition's umbrella.

Sapitwa National Democratic Party (SNDP), registered in October 1997. Several SNDP candidates unsuccessfully ran for some of the constituencies in the 1999 Parliamentary elections.

Congress for the the Second Republic of Malawi (CSR), registered in February 1994. The CSR participated in the 1994 parliamentary elections but failed to win any seat in the National Assembly. The CSR did not contest the balloting in 1999.

United Front for Multiparty Democracy (UFMD), founded in July 1993. The UFDM failed to win seats in the 1994 (0.3% of the popular vote) and did not contest the 1999 elections.

United Party (UP), founded in 1997. The UP candidate in the 1999 presidential election, Bingu wa Mutharika, received 0.46% of the vote. After the return of (later winning presidential canididate) Bingu Wa Mutharika to the UDF in 2002, the party was offically cancelled on Feb. 8, 2002.

Republican Party (RP), an offshoot of the MCP. Former MCP party president and presidential candidate Chakuamba announced he would leave the MCP on Jan. 7, 2004, to form the "Republican Party", stripping MCP of its southern electoral base. The Republican Party signed a memorandum of understanding for an electoral alliance in January 2004 and contested the general elections within the *Mgwirizano* coalition. RP gained 15 seats of 25 seats for the coalition in the May 2004 elections. Chakuamba running as the coalitions's presidential candidate came in third with 24.5% of the votes cast. Largely greeted with incredulity was Chakuamba's sudden move to join an alliance with the UDF, accepting three cabinet posts in June 2004.

Malaysia

Capital: Kuala Lumpur
Population: 23,000,000 (2003E)

The Federation of Malaysia consists of the 11 states of Peninsular Malaysia and the two states of Sarawak and Sabah situated on the northern coast of the island of Kalimantan (Borneo). It gained independence from Britain in 1957, subsequently merging with the self-governing state of Singapore and the former British crown colonies of Sarawak and Sabah in 1963. Singapore was ousted from the federation two years later. Malaysia's constitution specifies a federal system of government under an elective constitutional monarchy. The nine hereditary Malay rulers of Peninsular Malaysia (but not the heads of the states of Malacca, Penang, Sarawak and Sabah) elect a Supreme Head of State (*Yang di-Pertuan Agong*) every five years from among their own number. The *Yang di-Pertuan Agong* gives royal consent to miniersterial appoitments recommended by the Prime Minister. The bicameral legislature consists of an appointed Senate (*Dewan Negara*) and a fully elected House of Representatives (*Dewan Rakyat*). Each state has its own constitution and a unicameral state assembly which shares power with the federal parliament.

The major political force in Malaysia is the National Front (*Barisan Nasional*, BN), at present a coalition of 14 parties that represents the country's major ethnic groups (Malay, Chinese, and Indian), as well as smaller indigenous groups in East Malaysia. In elections to the House of Representatives in March 2004, the BN coalition, dominated by the United Malays National Organization (UMNO), was returned to power with 198 seats out of 219 seats. Twenty seats won by the opposition were distributed as follows: Democratic Action Party (DAP) 12, Pan-Malaysian Islamic Party (PAS) 7, People's Justice Party (PKN) 1. An independent candidate won one seat in East Malaysia. In concurrent elections for 12 state assemblies, the BN won 11, the PAS 1.

National Front
Barisan Nasional (BN)
Address. Suite 1 & 2, 8th Floor, Menara Dato' Onn, World Trade Center, Jalan Tun Ismail, 50480 Kuala Lumpur
Telephone. (603) 26920384
Fax. (603) 26934743
Email. info@bn.org.my
Website. www.bn.org.my
Leadership. Tan Sri Khalil Yaacob (secretary-general).
The BN is the governing multi-ethnic coalition in Malaysia, currently comprising 14 parties (each described below). Launched in 1973, the BN superseded the earlier Alliance Party, which had been founded in 1952 and held power from independence in 1957. The BN contests state and federal elections as a single political body, with candidates of the constituent parties agreeing not to stand against each other. It has remained in power since its foundation, winning a majority of seats in 10 consecutive general elections.

National Front Parties

Liberal Democratic Party (LDP)
Parti Liberal Demokratik
Address. Level 2, Lot 1, Jasaga Bldg., Leboh Dua, PO Box 1125, 90712 Sandakan, Sabah.
Telephone. (6089) 271888, 241681
Fax. (6089) 288278
Leadership. Datuk Chong Kah Kiet (president)
The LDP is an ethnic Chinese-dominated party based in Sabah. It joined the federal National Front (BN) in 1991 and won three state seats in the 2004 election.

Malaysian Chinese Association (MCA)
Persatuan China Malaysia
Address. Wisma MCA, 8th Floor, 163 Jalan Ampang, PO Box 10626, 50720 Kuala Lumpur
Telephone. (603) 2618044, 2619918
Fax. (603) 2635715
Email. info@mca.org.my
Website. www.mca.org.my
Leadership. Dato' Seri Ong Ka Ting (president)
The MCA was formed in 1949 to support the interests of the Chinese community in Malaysia, though it was most closely associated with Chinese business interests. It joined the Alliance in the early 1950s, through briefly withdrew in 1969 after it was abandoned in elections by most Chinese voters. The MCA later joined the BN and while it remains a "junior" partner to the United Malays National Organization (UMNO), it is regarded as the second most powerful party in the 14-member coaltion.

In the 1995 elections the MCA increased its parliamentary representation from 18 to 30 seats. It retained 29 seats in the 1999 elections, thereby helping to offset the UMNO's decline. However, with its subordinate status necessitating policy compromises, the MCA has continued to experience serious factional tensions. In May 2000, the MCA president, Ling Liong Sik, resigned as federal Transport Minister amidst complaints that the party had obtained an insufficient number of senior ministerial posts after the 1999 elections. He was succeeded as MCA president by Ong Ka Ting in 2003 through arrangements that appeared to be mediated by Prime Minister Mahathir. The MCA won 31 parliamentary seats and 76 state seats in the 2004 election.

Malaysian Indian Congress (MIC)
Kongres India Se-Malaysia

Address. Menara Manickavasagam, 6th Floor 1 Jalan Rahmat, Off Jalan Tun Ismail, 50350 Kuala Lumpur
Telephone. (603) 4424377
Fax. (603) 4427236
Email. michq@mic.org.my
Website. www.mic.org
Leadership. Dato Seri S. Samy Vellu (president)
The MIC, founded in the mid-1940s, is the main representative of the ethnic Indian community in Malaysia. It joined the Alliance party in the mid-1950s and has remained a steadfast member of the BN ever since. Although Malaysia's Indian community forms a majority in none of the country's electoral constituencies, the MIC was allocated nine seats to contest in the 2004 federal elections and won all of them. It also won 19 state seats.

Malaysian People's Movement Party
Parti Gerakan Rakyat Malaysia (PGRM, Gerakan)

Address. Menara PGRM, No. 8, Jalan Pudu Hulu, Cheras, 56100 Kuala Lumpur
Telephone. (603) 9876868
Fax. (603) 9878866
Email. pgrmhq@pgrmhq.po.my
Website. www.gerakan.org.my
Leadership. Dato Seri Dr Lim Keng Yaik (president)
Founded in 1968 and mainly based in Penang, *Gerakan* is a social democratic party that attracts most of its support from Chinese intellectuals and the middle class, competing directly for that constituency with the opposition Democratic Action Party. Unlike other National Front (BN) parties, however, it claims to be non-communal in its membership, recruitment and ideology. The party won ten parliamentary seats and 30 state seats in the 2004 election.

People's Progressive Party (PPP)

Address. 27–29A Jalan Maharajalela, 50150 Kuala Lumpur
Telephone. (603) 2441922, 2442043
Fax. (603) 2442041
Website. www.jaring.my/ppp
Leadership. Datuk M. Kayveas (president)
Founded in the mid-1950s and centred in Ipoh, the nominally left-wing PPP was originally based in the local Chinese community but today draws most of its support from lower-caste Indians. Although a member of the National Front (BN) since the mid-1970s, it did not hold a federal lower house seat for many years. The party won one parliamentary seat in the 2004 election.

Sabah Progressive Party (SAPP)
Parti Maju Sabah

Address. Level 2, Lot 23, Bornion Centre, Luyang, 88300 Kota Kinabalu, Sabah
Telephone. (6088) 242107
Fax. (6088) 248188
Email. sapp@po.jaring.my
Website. www.sapp.org.my
Leadership. Datuk Yong Teck Lee (leader)
The SAPP was set up in 1994 as a breakaway group from the Sabah United Party, being a predominantly ethnic Chinese party within the National Front (BN). In 1996 its leader, Yong Teck Lee, was appointed Sabah chief minister under the state BN's two-year rotational scheme. The SAPP won two parliamentary seats and four state seats in the 2004 election.

Sabah United Party
Parti Bersatu Sabah (PBS)

Address. Block M, Lot 4, 2nd & 3rd Floor, Donggongan Newtownship, Penamapng, Sabah
Telephone. (6088) 8714891
Fax. (6088) 8718067
Email. pbshq@pbs-sabah.org
Website. www.pbs-sabah.org
Leadership. Datuk Joseph Pairin Kitingan (president)
The PBS was founded in 1985 by dissidents from the Sabah People's Union (*Berjaya*) and won a majority of state assembly seats that year, drawing most of its support from non-Muslim indigenous groups. The PBS was admitted to the federal National Front (BN) in 1986, but its relations with the dominant United Malays National Organization (UMNO) remained strained. Just days before the 1990 federal elections the PBS withdrew from the BN and went into the opposition, prompting the UMNO to set up its Sabah branch. The PBS suffered damaging defections in early 1994, forcing it to relinquish the state government to the BN. The party contested the 1999 federal elections as an opposition party, winning three parliamentary seats. It has since gained reentry to the BN and won four parliamentary seats and 13 state seats in the 2004 election.

Sarawak Progressive Democratic Party
Parti Demokratik Progresif Sarawak (SPDP)

Address. Lot 4319-4320, Blok 27, KNLD, Jalan Stapok, Sungai Maong, Kuching, 93250 Sarawak
Telephone. (6082) 311180
Fax. (6082) 311190
Leadership. Datuk William Mawan anak Ikom (president)
The SPDP grew out of the Sarawak National Party (SNAP), one of the oldest parties in the BN and winner of four parliamentary seats in the 1999 election. SNAP was deregistered in late 2002 over its failure to resolve leadership tensions, though won a stay of execution from the Court of Appeals. Elements within the SNAP formed the SPDP in order to remain in the BN. Like its predecessor, the SPDP is supported largely by the Iban population (ethnic Dayaks) of Sarawak, though officially maintains a multi-ethnic orientation. The SPDP won four parliamentary seats in the 2004 election.

Sarawak Native People's Party
Parti Bansa Dayak Sarawak (PBDS)

Address. No. 622, Jalan Kedandi, Tabuan Jaya, PO Box 2148, 93742 Kuching, Sarawak
Telephone. (6082) 365240, 366701
Fax. (6082) 363734
Leadership. Daniel Tajem (president)
The PBDS was set up in 1983 by a breakaway group of the Sarawak National Party (SNAP). The following year it was accepted as a National Front (BN) partner and formed a state coalition government with the SNAP, the United Traditional Bumiputra Party, and the Sarawak United People's Party. In 1987, having been dismissed from the state (but not the federal) BN coalition, the PBDS emerged from state elections as the largest single party with 15 seats. However, its presence in state politics was sharply eroded in subsequent elections. The PBDS rejoined the BN in 1994. In the 1999 federal elections, the party won six lower house seats. The party has since grown factionalized, with its longtime leader, Telecommunications Minister Leo Moggie, resigning as president. Factions have crystallized around the current party president and the Information Minister, summoning intervention from the Registrar of Societies and the party's exclusion from BN Supreme Council meetings. The PBDS won 6 parliamentary seats in the 2004 election.

Sarawak United People's Party (SUPP)
Parti Rakyat Bersatu Sarawak

Address. 7 Jalan Tan Sri Datuk Ong Kee Hui, PO Box 454, 93710 Kuching, Sarawak
Telephone. (6082) 246999

Fax. (6082) 256510
Email. supp@po.jaring.my
Website. www.sarawak.com.my/supp/
Leadership. Datuk Amar George Chan Hong Nam (president)
The traditionally Chinese-based SUPP is a member not only of the ruling National Front (BN) at the federal level but also of the Sarawak BN, as part of which it has gained significant representation in the state assembly. The SUPP won six parliamentary seats in the 2004 election.

United Malays National Organization (UMNO)
Pertubuhan Kebangsaan Melayu Bersatu

Address. Menara Dato' Onn, 38th Floor, Putra World Trade Center, Jalan Tun Dr Ismail, 50480 Kuala Lumpur
Telephone. (603) 4429511
Fax. (603) 4412358
Email. info@umno.org.my
Website. www.umno.org.my
Leadership. Dato' Seri Abdullah Ahmad Badawi (president); Dato' Seri Najib Tun Razak (deputy president); Dato' Seri Mohd Radzi Sheikh Ahma (secretary-general)
Founded in 1946, the UMNO mostly draws its support from the majority Malay community, but supports the right of all Malaysians to participate in the political, economic, and cultural life of the nation. The party has been the dominant political organization since independence in 1957, and it is the leading component of the ruling National Front (BN). It was led from 1981 by Mahathir Mohamad, who succeeded Datuk Hussein bin Onn as UMNO president and Prime Minister.

Following an economic recession in the mid-1980s, the UMNO experienced intense internal conflict, with Prime Minister Mahathir only narrowly defeating a challenge for the party presidency by one of his key ministers, Tengku Razaleigh Hamzah. The intra-party strife culminated in 1988 in the organization of the "New" UMNO (UMNO *Baru*) by the pro-Mahathir faction, while Razaleigh and his dissident supporters formed the rival "Spirit of '46" party. Despite this period of discord, Mahathir led the UMNO (under its original name) to another federal election success in 1990, and he was subsequently reconfirmed as party president.

In the 1995 federal elections, the UMNO secured 88 of the BN's 162 seats in the House of Representatives. The rival "Spirit of '46" was dissolved in the following year. In the wake of the East Asian economic crisis of 1997-98, fierce rivalry erupted between Mahathir and his heir-apparent, Anwar Ibrahim, who was dismissed as Deputy Prime Minister and Finance Minister in September 1998. Anwar was then arrested on various criminal charges widely seen as politically inspired, resulting in April 1999 in his receiving a nine-year prison sentence for corruption and a further six-year term in August 2000 for sexual misconduct. Anwar's wife responded by launching the opposition National Justice Party (PKN) in April 1999.

That the Anwar affair had damaged the UMNO among its Malay constituency was confirmed by the 1999 federal elections. Although the BN retained a clear majority, the UMNO fell from 88 to 71 seats, less than the total representation gained by its coalition partners. It was also defeated by the Pan-Malaysian Islamic Party (PAS) in concurrent state elections in Kelantan and Terengganu. Nevertheless, Mahathir was re-elected as UMNO president in May 2000 (a putative challenge by veteran rival Razaleigh Hamzah having come to nothing), while in November 2000 the UMNO supreme council successfully resisted grass-roots calls for more internal party democracy.

Pressure on Mahathir intensified in June 2001 when his long-standing ally, Daim Zainuddin, resigned as Finance Minister and UMNO treasurer following allegations of impropriety. Mahathir himself resigned in October 2003. He was succeeded as Prime Minister by his deputy Abdullah Ahmad Badawi, then as UMNO president by Abdullah in 2004. The UMNO won 109 parliamentary seats and 302 state seats in the 2004 election. In September 2004 Anwar Ibrahim was released from jail after his conviction for sexual misconduct was overturned in Malaysia's highest court, but he remained barred from participating in politics until 2008 after the court upheld his conviction for abuse of power.

United Pasok Momogun Kadazandusun Organization (UPKO)

Address. c/o Sabah State Assembly, Kota Kinabalu
Telephone. (6088) 718182
Web. www.upko.org.my
Leadership. Datuk Bernard Dompok
The UPKO was formed from the Sabah Democratic Party, which in turn had been organized by defectors from the Sabah United Party (PBS) in 1994. It draws support from non-Muslim indigenous groups in Sabah, complementing the appeal of the United Malays National Organization (UMNO) to indigenous Muslims. The UPKO leader, Bernard Dompok, served as Sabah's chief minister in 1998-2000 under the unique two-year rotational scheme operated by the National Front (BN). The UPKO won four parliamentary seats and five state seats in the 2004 election.

United Sabah People's Party
Parti Bersatu Rakyat Sabah (PBRS)

Address. PO Box 20148, Luyang, 88761 Kota Kinabalu, Sabah
Telephone. (6088) 269282, 263282
Fax. (6088) 269282
Leadership. Datuk Joseph Kurup (leader)
The PBRS was formed in 1994 by a breakaway faction of the Sabah United Party and is a member of the ruling National Front (BN). Like the United Pasok Momogun Kadazandusun Organization (UPKO), it draws support from non-Muslim indigenous groups within Sabah. The PBRS won one parliametary seat and one state seat in the 2004 election.

United Traditional Bumiputra Party
Parti Pesaka Bumiputra Bersatu (PBB)

Address. Lot 401, Jalan Bako, PO Box 1953, 93400 Kuching, Sarawak
Telephone. (6082) 448299, 448292
Fax. (6082) 448294
Leadership. Tan Sri Datuk Patinggi Amar Haji Abdul Taib Mahmud (president)
A member of the federal BN, the PBB is also the dominant partner in the ruling state BN coalition in Sarawak, together with the Sarawak United People's Party and the Sarawak Native People's Party. The PBB won 11 parliamentary seats in the 2004 election. The Sarawak state election was not held concurrently.

Main Opposition Parties

Democratic Action Party (DAP)
Parti Tindakan Demokratik

Address. 24 Jalan 20/9, 46300 Petaling Jaya, Selangor
Telephone. (60–3) 7957–8022
Fax. (60–3) 7957–5718
Email. dap.malaysia@pobox.com
Website. www.malaysia.net/dap
Leadership. Lim Guan Eng (secretary-general); Karpal Singh (chairman).
The DAP was founded in 1966 as the Malaysian offshoot of the People's Action Party (PAP) of Singapore. It is a predominantly Chinese party with a democratic socialist orientation and is a member of the Socialist International.

Contesting its first general elections in May 1969 in alliance with the Malaysian People's Movement Party

(*Gerakan*), it made a political breakthrough for non-Malays, winning 13 federal and 31 state assembly seats. However, this success precipitated a wave of serious communal violence and the detention of leading DAP members, including then leader Lim Kit Siang. Thereafter the DAP's activities were circumscribed by various internal security measures. It nevertheless remained the main opposition party at the national level during the 1970s and 1980s, although its representation in the House of Representatives dropped sharply in the April 1995 federal elections from 20 seats to nine.

In the 1999 federal elections, the DAP co-operated with the Pan-Malaysian Islamic Party (PAS) under the umbrella of the Alternative Front (*Barisan Alternatif*, BA). However, many Chinese were fearful of the PAS commitment to an Islamic state, with the result that the DAP won only 10 parliamentary seats, while the PAS advanced to 27 seats and replaced the DAP as the main opposition party. Having lost his own parliamentary seat, Lim Kit Siang was succeeded as DAP secretary-general by Kerk Kim Hock, assuming a more ceremonial role as party president.

Growing strains in the DAP's alliance with the PAS came to a head over the massive terrorist attack on the USA of Sept. 11, 2001. After the PAS called publicly for *jihad* in order to opposed US-led retaliation in Afghanistan, the DAP formally withdrew from the BA and reiterated its commitment to a secular Malaysia. The DAP won 12 parliamentary seats and 15 state seats in the 2004 election. Lim Guan Eng was elected DAP secretary general in 2004.

People's Justice Party
Parti Keadilan Rakyat (PKR)

Address. No. 101 & 201, Block A, Pusat Dagangan Phileo Damansara II, No. 15, Jalan 16/11, off Jalan Damansara, 46350 Petaling Jaya, Selangor
Telephone. (603) 7954–0469
Fax. (603) 7954–0419
Leadership. Datin Wan Azizah Wan Ismail (president); Syed Husin Ali (deputy president)
The PKR resulted from a proposed merger, undertaken over a two-year period, between two parties, the National Justice Party (*Parti Keadilan Nasional*) and the People's Party of Malaysia (*Parti Rakyat Malaysia*, PRM). *Keadilan* was launched in April 1999 by Wan Azizah Wan Ismail following the prosecution of her husband, former Deputy Prime Minister Anwar Ibrahim, and his expulsion from the ruling United Malays National Organization (UMNO). The party began as a pressure group geared principally to winning Anwar's release, but evolved quickly into a political party bridging the gulf between the Pan-Malaysian Islamic Party (PAS) and the Democratic Action Party (DAP) within the opposition Alternative Front (*Barisan Alternatif*, BA). Officially non-communal but drawing most of its support from middle-class Malays, *Keadilan* failed to make the hoped-for impact in the 1999 federal elections. Although Wan Azizah successfully defended her husband's seat in Penang, her party won only five seats in total. The PKR won only one parliamentary seat in the 2004 election.

Though undergoing several name changes, the People's Party of Malaysia traced its roots to the early post-War period. Its leftist orientations softened in reformist aims over time, and it appealed mostly for support among progressive middle-class Malays. However, because it remained unable for many years to gain representation in parliament, the PRM functioned more as an civil society organization, advocating political reform. During the 1999 general election, it was a member of the Alternative Front.

In August 2003, *Keadilan* and the PRM announced that they had completed their merger, giving rise to the People's Justice Party (PKR). Wan Azizah of *Keadilan* was chosen as PKR president, and the leader of PRM, Husin Ali, was made

deputy. They are supported by a 62-member transitional team. However, in September 2003, their application for formal registration was rejected by the Registrar of Societies on technical grounds. The PKR has mounted an appeal.

Pan-Malaysian Islamic Party
Parti Islam SeMalaysia (PAS)

Address. Markaz Tarbiyyah PAS Pusat, Lorong Haji Hassan, off Jalan Batu Geliga, Taman Melawar, 68100 Batu Caves, Selangor
Telephone. (603) 61899296
Fax. (603) 61869618
Email. webmaster@parti-pas.org
Website. www.partipas.org/
Leadership. Abdul Hadi Awang (president); Datuk Haji Nik Abdul Aziz Nik Mat (spiritual leader); Nasharuddin Mat Isa (secretary-general)
Founded in the early 1950s, the revivalist PAS seeks the establishment of an Islamic state and society. It joined the ruling National Front (BN) in 1973, but returned to opposition four years later. Contesting the 1990 and 1995 elections as part of the Muslim Unity Movement (formed in 1989 as a loose opposition alliance), the PAS won seven seats in the federal House of Representatives on both occasions. In the 1990 state assembly elections, the party won control of Kelantan, its stronghold, enabling Datuk Haji Nik Abdul Aziz Nik Mat to form a PAS government in coalition with the "Spirit of '46" splinter group of the United Malays National Organization (UMNO).

For the 1999 elections, PAS joined a more deeply integrated opposition coalition called the Alternative Front (*Barisan Alternatif*, BA), including the Democratic Action Party (DAP) and the National Justice Party (PKN). The PAS won more than half of the popular Malay vote, hence greatly increasing its representation in the federal parliament to 27 seats. It also retained control of Kelantan and won enough seats to form a new state government in Terengganu under the chief ministership of Datuk Haji Abdul Hadi Awang. As a result of the elections, the PAS president, Datuk Fadzil Noor, became leader of the opposition in the federal parliament.

In June 2001 Lolo Mohamad Ghazali became the first woman to be elected to the PAS central committee. In September 2001, however, the PAS reaction to the terrorist attacks on New York and Washington, particularly calls by Nik Abdul Aziz Nik Mat for *jihad* against any US-led retaliation in Afghanistan, prompted the DAP to withdraw from the BA. In 2002, Fadzil Noor died and was succeeded as acting party president by Hadi Awang. At the PAS general assembly in September 2003, Hadi Awang was returned to the presidency unopposed. PAS won only seven parliamentary seats and 36 state seats in the 2004 election, narrowly retaining control of Kelantan, but losing in Terengganu.

Sarawak National Party
Parti Kebangsaan Sarawak (SNAP)

Address. Lot 3-4-5 Mei-jun Bldg., No. 1, Rubber Rd. PO Box 2960, 93758 Kuching, Sarawak
Phone. (6082) 254244
Fax. (6082) 253562
Leadership. Edwin Dundang (president)
Supported largely by the Iban population (ethnic Dayaks) of Sarawak, the SNAP was formed in 1961 and was one of the first parties to join the BN. Under the leadership of James Wong, the party won four parliamentary seats in the 1999 federal election. The party divided in leadership rivalries in 2002, leading to the party's deregisration and the emergence of the Sarawak Progressive Democratic Party. SNAP is currently appealing its deregistration, but has meanwhile been denied its parliamentary seats and membership in the BN.

Maldives

Capital: Malé
Population: 310,000 (2002E)

There are no political parties in the Republic of Maldives, a former British protectorate until independence in 1965 with the status of a sultanate outside the Commonwealth. In 1968 the Sultan was deposed following a referendum and the Maldives became a republic, rejoining the Commonwealth partially in 1982 and fully in 1985. There is a 50-member legislature (the People's *Majlis*), 42 members of which are elected for five years, with the remaining eight appointed by the President. The People's *Majlis* designates the President for a five-year term, but the action must be confirmed by popular referendum. The President appoints, and presides over, the Cabinet.

President Maumoun Abdul Gayoom first took office in 1978. His re-election for a fifth term was confirmed in October 1998 after he won an overwhelming majority of votes cast in a national referendum. There had been speculation that the new constitution which took effect from Jan. 1, 1998, would allow the formation of political parties, but the only electoral change that it introduced was a provision for multiple candidates in the *Majlis*'s election of the President. Non-party elections to the People's *Majlis* were held in November 1999. In a ballot on Sept. 25, 2003, the People's *Majlis* voted unanimously to nominate Gayoom, 64, for a sixth presidential term; on this occasion three other candidates stood against him. The nomination was endorsed on Oct. 17 by more than 90% of the votes in a referendum, with a turnout of over 77%.

The election of Gayoom by the *Majlis* in September 2003 came only days after riots in the streets of Malé as police and troops suppressed the Maldives' first ever public demonstrations against the government, following prison disturbances in which up to four prisoners were killed by guards. Gayoom blamed "criminal elements" for the riots, but critics said that the unrest was an expression of popular anger against human rights abuses perpetrated by the police. A report in July 2003 by the London-based human rights group Amnesty Inter-national had accused the government of arbitrary detention of opponents and the systematic suppression of dissent.

Mali

Capital: Bamako
Population: 10,700,000 (2000E)

The former colony of French Sudan achieved independence in association with Senegal as the Federation of Mali in June 1960. The Federation was dissolved only two months later in August 1960 when Senegal withdrew. French Sudan then adopted the title of the Republic of Mali. From 1960 onwards, the country was ruled as a one party state under the Sudanese Union–African Democratic Convention (*Union Soudanaise–Rassemblement Démocratique Africaine*, US-RDA), headed by President Modibo Keita. Following a coup in 1968, the country was ruled until 1991 by a Military Committee for National Liberation (*Comité Militaire de Libération Nationale*, CMLN) with Gen. Moussa Traoré as executive President, head of state and government, and (from 1979) secretary-

general of the sole legal political party, the Mali People's Democratic Union (*Union Démocratique du Peuple Malien*, UDPM). On March 26, 1991, the regime was overthrown in a coup and replaced by a transitional military civilian administration, the Transition Committee for the Salvation of the People (*Comité Transitoire pour le Salut du Peuple*, CTSP), headed by Lieutenant-Colonel Amadou Toumani Touré.

A new constitution establishing multi-party rule was approved in a referendum in January 1992. It provides for a directly elected executive President, with a five-year term of office, and a National Assembly (*Assemblée Nationale*) of 129 members (13 of whom represent the interests of Malians resident abroad), who also serve for five years. In January 1997, a new Electoral Code was adopted which, inter alia, raised the number of National Assembly seats to 147, with 13 extra seats resereved to represent the interests of Malians abroad (hence 147 seats are open for elections in Mali). A proposition for constitutional reform, changing about 122 paragraphs of the constitution, was approved by the National Assembly in July 2000, with the modification that Mali's parliamentary structure would remain unicameral. The new constitution can, however, only be amended by a national referendum, which has so far been postponed.

The Malian landscape of political parties is extremely dense and fractured, as it is centred around political personalities rather than ideologies or programmes. A fluctuating number of around 60 parties exists, these having importance at local level at least, which merge or split along diverging or common interests and which often form coalitions to obtain majorities in local councils or the national parliament.

In multi-party legislative elections held over two rounds in July and August 1997 the Alliance for Democracy in Mali (*Alliance pour la Démocratie au Mali*, ADEMA), in power since 1992, secured an overwhelming majority in the National Assembly. (A first round of polling had taken place in April, but the results of this vote had been annulled by the Constitutional Court because of "serious irregularities".) The elections were characterized by a low turnout in both rounds of voting and by violence in which at least two people were killed. Presidential elections held in May 1997 resulted in the re-election of incumbent President Alpha Oumar Konare, the leader of ADEMA.

The presidential elections were boycotted by a coalition of small opposition parties, the Opposition Coalition (*Coalition d'Opposition*, COPPO, not to be mistaken for the political party COPP), headed by Almamy Sylla, leader of the Rally for Democracy and Progress (*Rassemblement pour la Démocratie et le Progrès*, RDP). The COPPO had less strength in parliament (where it held no seats) than on the streets of the capital Bamako, where it organized a number of riots. The party leaders were all arrested in the aftermath of the elections and faced charges relating to violent incidents reported during the election campaign.

President Konare did not present himself at the 2002 presidential elections as the constitution allows for only two terms in office. He was succeeded by former CTSP leader and independent presidential candidate Amadou Toumani Touré, who defeated his last remaining rivals, Soumaïla Cissé and Ibrahim Boubacar Keita, in two rounds on April 28 and May 12, 2002. In the last round he defeated Cissé with 65.01% of the vote. Ibrahim Boubaker Keita, already defeated in the first round, left ADEMA in 2002 as not he, but Soumaïla Cissé was made the party's presidential candidate. Keita then formed his own party, the Rally for Mali (*Rassemblement pour le Mali*, RPM), which coalesced with other parties under the name Hope 2002 (*Espoir 2002*).

The National Assembly elections of July 2002 did not result in any party obtaining a majority although the *Espoir* 2002 coalition headed by Keita's RPM gained a small majority over the ADEMA-led coalition Alliance for the Republic and Democracy (*Alliance pour la République et la Démocratie*, ARD) with 66 seats (46 for PRM) against 59 (45 for ADEMA). The party coalition Alliance Alternative and Change (*Alliance Alternance et Changement*, ACC), linked to party-independent President Touré gained 10 seats, while 6 seats were taken by independent candidates (despite this being against the electoral code). In two electoral contests, Sikasso and Tin Essako, the results were annuled due to fraud, leaving 8 seats in parliament open. The partial elections of October 2002 over these seats brought victory to the ADEMA-led ARD coalition. Mali's current cabinet is headed by party-independent Prime Minister Ousmani Issoufi Maiga, who replaced equally party-independent Mohamed Ahmed ag Hamani (in office since 2002) in May 2004.

On May 30, 2004, communal elections were held. The turnout of 43.05% of 5,595,450 registered voters is amongst the highest in recent years. The elections showed a general regaining of strength for ADEMA, which won a country wide average of 28% of the votes. ADEMA was followed with 14% of the votes by the new party Union for the Republic and Democracy (*Union pour la République et la Démocratie*, URD), headed by former ADEMA presidential candidate Soumaïla Cissé. Ibrahim Boubakar Keita's RPM came third with 13%.

African Solidarity for Democracy and Independence
Solidarité africaine pour la démocratie et l'indépendance (SADI)
Telephone. (223) 248782
Leadership. Oumar Mariko
SADI is headed by the former leader of the Malian Student association AEEM, which initiated the protests of 1991 leading to the downfall of the Traoré regime. Since then, the AEEM itself (Mariko having left) has gained some notoriety in disrupting Malian educational life through long-term strikes. In the 2002 National Assembly elections, SADI won 6 seats. It is independent from the major party coalitions.

Alliance for Democracy in Mali–African Party for Solidarity and Justice
Alliance pour la Démocratie au Mali–Parti Africain pour la Solidarité et la Justice (ADEMA–PASJ)
Address. BP 1791, Bamako
Leadership. Dioncounda Traoré (president)
Originally an alliance of six exiled opposition parties, ADEMA was a principal element in the pro-democracy campaign launched in 1990 against the Moussa Traoré regime and was represented in the Transition Committee (CTSP) set up after the March 1991 coup. It transformed itself into a political party in May 1991, at which moment a number of its constituent parties left the coalition. In March-April 1992 it gained control of the legislature in multi-party elections and former ADEMA leader Konare won the presidential ballot. In the 1997 legislative elections ADEMA won 129 of the 147 seats in the National Assembly. In the May 1997 presidential election Konare was re-elected with 95.9% of the votes cast, which rendered a second round of the election unnecessary. However, Konare's victory was achieved in the face of an almost total boycott of the poll by other candidates. For the 2002 presidential elections, conflict broke out over the issue of

who should be the party's candidate between leading members Ibrahim Boubacar Keita, the then acting Prime Minister Mande Sidibi and Soumaïla Cissé. Cissé won the primaries with Keita leaving the party. Both Cissé and Keita lost in the presidential elections to independent candidate Touré. In the legislative elections of July 2002, ADEMA was defeated by Keita's Rally for Mali (RPM), ADEMA winning only 45 seats. The ADEMA-led party coalition Aliance for the Republic and Democracy (ARD) holds 59 seats.

ADEMA is a full member of the Socialist International.

Democratic Bloc for African Integration
Bloc Démocratique pour l'Intégration Africaine (BDIA)
Address. Missira, Rue du RDA Porte N° 41 - Bamako PO box E1413 - Bamako
Leadership. Yousouf Traoré
A hive off from the US-RDA (with which it still seems to share an address), the BDIA now forms part of the ACC coalition supporting President Touré.

Malian Party for Social Progress
Parti Malien pour le Progrès Social (PMPS)
Telephone. (223) 22.06.65
Leadership. Moriba Samake
A party of regional importance in Segu, the PMPS forms part of the ACC coalition supporting President Touré.

Movement for African Independence, Renascence and Integration
Mouvement pour l'Indépendance, la Renaissance et l'Intégration Africaine (MIRIA)
Address. Bolibana, Rue 417 Porte N° 66 - Bamako
Leadership. Mamadou Lamine Traoré
Founded in 1994 as a split off from ADEMA, MIRIA now forms part of the ACC coalition supporting President Touré.

National Congress for Democratic Initiative–Party for the Development of the Country
Congrès Nationale d'Initiative Démocratique–Faso Yiriwa Ton (CNID–FYT)
Address. BPO box 2572 - Bamako
Telephone. (223) 214275
Fax. (223) 228321
Email. cnid@cefib.com
Leadership. Mountaga Tall (president)
Together with ADEMA, CNID headed the opposition movement against the Traoré regime in the late 1980s and early 1990s. It was represented in the CTSP and formed the major opposition party to ADEMA during and after the 1992 elections. The party has its stronghold in Segu, one of Mali's largest cities, in which CNID leader Tall's family has played an important political role since the early 19th century. In the 2002 elections, CNID gained 12 seats in parliament. It is part of the Hope 2002 coalition.

Rally for Mali
Rassemblement pour le Mali (RPM)
Address. Hippodrome, Rue 228 Porte N° 1164 - Bamako
Telephone. (223) 21 69 40
Fax. (223) 21 69 56
Email. rpm@timbagga.com.ml
Leadership. Ibrahim Boubakar Keita (president)
The RPM was created by former Prime Minister and prominent ADEMA figure, Ibrahim Boubakar Keita, after he was not selected as ADEMA's candidate for the 2002 presidential elections. One of Mali's most prominent politicians, Keita came out second in the 2002 elections. His party gained 46 seats of a total of 147 in the elections for the National Assembly in July 2002, which made it the biggest party in the Asembly, ahead of ADEMA with 45 seats. The party coalition Hope 2002, head-

ed by the PRM, holds 66 seats in the National Assembly of which Keita was elected President in September 2002.

Sudanese Union–African Democratic Rally
Union Soudanaise–Rassemblement Démocratique Africain (US-RDA)

Address. Missira, Rue du RDA Porte N° 41 - Bamako PO box E1413 - Bamako
Telephone. (223) 21 45 22
Leadership. Mamadou Gologo

The former ruling single party, banished in 1968 by the CMLN, joined the ADEMA coalition in 1990 to leave it again in May 1991. The US-RDA reconstituted itself in 1991, under the leadership of the former Minister of Information under Modibo Keita, Mamadou Gologo. During and after the 1997 elections, the US-RDA formed part of the radical opposition coalition COPPO. In the 2002 elections, the US-RDA, after an internal split leading to the creation of the Party for Independence, Democracy and Solidarity (*Parti de l'Indépendance, la Démocratie et la Solidarité*, PIDS), joined in the party coalition Alliance Alternative and Change (ACC) supporting Amadou Toumani Touré, which gained in total 10 seats in the National Assembly.

Union for the Republic and Democracy
Union pour la République et la Démocratie (URD)

Address. Niaréla, rue 268, porte 45, Bamako
Leadership. Younoussi Touré

Created in June 2003 by former ADEMA presidential candidate Soumaïla Cissé and former ADEMA member and Prime Minister Younoussi Touré. Touré has affirmed that the URD supports the secularism of the Malian state, and that it is against "wild liberalism". The party came second in the 2004 communal elections.

Malta

Capital: Valletta
Population: 388,867 (2003)

Malta gained its independence from Britain in 1964 and became a member of the Commonwealth. It declared itself a Republic in 1974. Its 1964 constitution, amended in 1974, defines Malta as a parliamentary democracy, with a President elected for a five-year term by the legislature. Executive power resides in the Cabinet headed by the Prime Minister, chosen from and responsible to the unicameral House of Representatives of 65 members elected for a five-year term (subject to dissolution) by universal suffrage of those aged 18 and over. Members are returned from 13 five-seat electoral divisions by a voting system based on proportional representation and the single transferable vote. A 1987 constitutional amendment specifies that a party winning a majority of the valid votes cast is awarded "bonus" seats if such are needed to give it a one seat parliamentary majority. Another amendment adopted at the same time, also by agreement between the two main parties, gave constitutional force to Malta's status as a neutral state.

In elections to the House of Representatives held in April 2003 the Nationalist Party (NP) won 35 seats (51.79% of valid votes cast) while the Malta Labour Party (MLP) won 30 (47.51%). This result was a replica of the 1998 election in which the NP won 35 seats (51.81%) and the MLP 30 (46.97%).

In July 1990 Malta applied for EU membership and joined on May 1, 2004, following the successful outcome of a referendum held in March 2003. In June 2004

the NP was thrashed in the elections to the European Parliament electing 2 seats (39.76% of the vote) to the MLP's 3 (48.42%). Traditional Nationalist voters shifted allegiance to *Alternattiva Demokratika* (AD), but its share of the vote at 9.33% was not enough to win a seat.

Malta Labour Party (MLP)
Partit tal-Haddiema

Address. Centru Nazzjonali Laburista, Triq Milend, Hamrun HMR 02
Telephone. (356) 21249900
Fax. (356) 21244204
Email. mlp@mlp.org.mt
Website. www.mlp.org.mt
Leadership. Alfred Sant (leader); Charles Mangion (deputy leader for parliamentary affairs); Michael Falzon (deputy leader for party affairs); Stefan Zrinzo Azzopardi (president); Jason Micallef (secretary-general)

The MLP was founded in 1920 as a trade union party and played a prominent role in the 1921–30 period of internal self-government. In the first elections to a Maltese Legislative Assembly, held in October 1947 under a new constitution restoring internal self-government, the MLP led by Paul Boffa won 24 of the 40 seats. A government formed by Boffa held office until September 1950. The MLP split in 1949. In the 1950 elections, the (moderate) Independent Labour Party headed by Boffa gained 11 seats. In 1951 as the Malta Workers' Party it won 7, and then three in 1953, whereafter it contested no further elections.

The MLP regained a majority of seats (23 out of 40) in the Assembly in 1955 and remained in power under Dom Mintoff until 1958, when his government resigned over a dispute with Britain concerning Malta's constitutional future. Mintoff had sought integration with Britain. In the 1962 general election the MLP gained only 16 out of 42 parliamentary seats, after the Roman Catholic Church hierarchy had called on the electorate not to vote Labour. It was returned to power in 1971 (under Mintoff's leadership) when it won 28 of the 55 seats in the House of Representatives. In May 1978 the party was officially amalgamated with the General Workers' Union but the two separated again in the mid-1990s.

In the 1976 election the MLP won 34 out of 65 seats and did the same in the 1981 election but with fewer votes than the Nationalist Party (NP). After a constitutional crisis, during which the Nationalists boycotted the House of Representatives for 15 months, the constitution was amended so that a party winning a majority of votes would if necessary gain additional seats to enable it to govern. This happened in the 1987 elections, when the MLP retained 34 seats to the NP's 31, but since the latter won 50.9% of the votes it was allocated four additional seats. Labour thus went into opposition under Karmenu Mifsud Bonnici (who had succeeded Mintoff in December 1984).

The MLP's decline (to 46.5% of the vote) continued in the 1992 general elections. Mifsud Bonnici was replaced by Alfred Sant as party leader. The latter initiated a modernization of Labour's programme and organization (also completing a new party headquarters), while maintaining the party's policy of neutrality in international relations and opposition to membership of the European Union (EU).

The MLP returned to power under Sant's leadership in early elections in October 1996, winning 50.7% of the vote and thus being allocated a one-seat overall majority of 35 seats. The new Labour government immediately withdrew Malta from NATO's Partnership for Peace (agreed by the previous NP government) and suspended the EU membership application. Responding to a worsening public deficit in 1997, the government introduced spending cuts and austerity measures which provoked fierce trade union opposition and caused Mintoff, still a member of the House, to bring down the government. An election called in September 1998 saw the MLP decisively defeated (winning 30 seats and 47% of the vote). The MLP vigorously opposed the NP government's opening of fast-track negotiations for EU accession in 1999. The party refused to recognize the March 2003 referendum result in which just under 53% voted in favour of EU membership. In the election held in April 2003 the MLP lost again. Alfred Sant survived a leadership challenge and the party began to change its EU policy. It subsequently joined the Party of European Socialists (PES) and contested the elections to the European Parliament in June 2004 winning 3 of the 5 seats allocated to Malta. Internal divisions on Europe simmer under the surface with Mintoff and Mifsud Bonnici still campaigning against the EU.

The MLP is a member party of the Socialist International.

Nationalist Party (NP)
Partit Nazzjonalista (PN)
Address. Dar Centrali, Triq Herbert Ganado, Pietà
Telephone. (356) 21243641
Fax: (356) 21243640
Email. jsaliba@pn.org.mt
Website. www.pn.org.mt
Leadership. Lawrence Gonzi (leader); Tonio Borg (deputy leader); Joe Saliba (secretary-general); Victor Scerri (president)

Dating from 1880, the NP has its origins in the wave of nationalism which swept Europe in the 19th century and it fought successfully for Malta's self-government and later independence. Between 1887 and 1903, when Malta had representative government, the party held all elective seats in the Council of Government. After a period of colonial rule representative government was reintroduced in 1921 and the party held a majority of seats until 1927, when the Constitutional Party and the Malta Labour Party (MLP) formed an alliance. When the NP regained a majority in 1933, the self-government constitution was revoked.

During World War II several leaders of the party were detained or exiled without a fair trial, but from 1950 to 1955 the party was in government in coalition with Boffa's Workers' Party. It won a parliamentary majority in 1962 and again in 1966 under the leadership of George Borg Olivier, who was Prime Minister from 1962 to 1971. In 1964 Malta gained independence.

The party was narrowly defeated by the MLP in 1971 and again in 1976. In the elections of December 1981 the party gained 50.9% of the vote but only a minority of seats in the House of Representatives. The party subsequently conducted a civil disobedience campaign and boycotted sessions of the House until March 1983. Following the 1987 constitutional amendments ensuring that the party with the majority of valid votes enjoyed a majority of seats, the NP obtained a majority in May 1987 and formed a government under Edward Fenech Adami. In 1990 Malta applied to join the European Union.

The NP increased its majority in the February 1992 general elections. The NP government's main priority was to expedite Malta's application to join the European Union. It also joined NATO's Partnership for Peace programme (1995), while pledging to uphold neutrality. However, Fenech Adami unwisely called early elections in October 1996 and the MLP regained a narrow 35–34 ascendancy in the House of Representatives.

The Labour government's chronic problems resulted in another election being held in September 1998, when Fenech Adami led the NP back to power with a decisive 51.8% vote share and a 35–30 majority in the House. In 1999 Malta embarked upon fast-track negotiations for EU accession, undertaking to hold a referendum on membership when the negotiations were completed. The referendum, the first to be

held from among the 10 prospective member states, was held in March 2003 and 53% voted in favour of EU membership. Constrained to call a snap election after the MLP refused to acknowledge the referendum result, the NP again emerged victorious with 35 seats and 51.79% of the vote. A day after the election result was announced Fenech Adami and Foreign Minister Joe Borg flew to Athens to sign the Treaty of Accession, which was subsequently also ratified by the House of Representatives with the MLP voting against.

On Feb. 7, 2004, Fenech Adami relinquished the leadership of the NP and his deputy Lawrence Gonzi was elected to replace him. Gonzi became Prime Minister on March 23, 2004. In the elections to the European Parliament held in June 2004 the NP secured only 39.76% of the votes and 2 seats to the MLP's 48.42% and 3 seats. Traditional NP voters deserted the party to *Alternattiva Demokratika*, which won 9.33% of the vote.

The NP is affiliated to the Christian Democrat International and is a member of the European People's Party. It is also a member of the International Democrat Union.

Other Parties

Communist Party of Malta (*Partit Komunista Malti*, PKM), founded in 1969 as an orthodox pro-Soviet party by former members of the Malta Labour Party, to which it gave unofficial support in the Mintoff era by not contesting elections. The party fielded a candidate in each of 12 of the 13 electoral divisions in the 1987 election but secured only minimal support. It did not contest subsequent elections.
Leadership. Anthony Vassallo (general secretary)

Democratic Alternative
Alternattiva Demokratika (AD)
Address. AD The Green Party, Triq Manwel Dimech, Sliema
Telephone. (0356) 21314040
Fax. (0356) 21314046
Website. www.alternattiva.org.mt
Email. info@alternattiva.org.mt
Leadership. Harry Vassallo (chairman); Mario Mallia (deputy chairman); Stephen Cachia (secretary general); Mark Causson (administrative secretary general)
Alternattiva Demokratika is an environmentalist party formed in October 1989 prior to the 1992 elections, in which it obtained 1.7% of the vote and no seats. After slipping to 1.5% in 1996, it contested the 1998 elections on a joint list with the Social Justice Alliance which took 1.2% of the vote. In the 2003 election it obtained 0.68%. AD came out in support of EU membership in the March 2003 referendum and in the June 2004 European elections it won 9.33% of the vote, though this was not sufficient to win a seat. AD belongs to the European Federation of Green Parties and Arnold Cassola, a member of the party, is secretary general to the Greens in the European Parliament.

Social Justice Alliance (*Alleanza Gustizzja Socjali*, AGS), a progressive grouping which contested the 1998 elections on a joint list with *Alternattiva Demokratika*. It has since been dissolved.

Marshall Islands

Capital: Dalap-Uliga-Darrit (Majuro)
Population: 57,000 (2000E)

The Marshall Islands consist of a double chain of atolls in the Pacific region of Micronesia. From 1947, as part of the UN Trust Territory of the Pacific, they were administered by the United States. In 1979 a new constitution was adopted, and in 1982 the Republic of the Marshall Islands signed a compact of free association (implemented in 1986) under which the United States recognized the territory as a fully sovereign and independent state, while retaining authority in regard to defence. In December 1990 the UN Security Council approved the termination of the Trusteeship in relation to the Marshall Islands, and the country joined the UN the following year.

The Marshall Islands have a 12-member Council of Chiefs (the *Iroij*), composed of traditional leaders, with consultative authority on matters relating to custom. Legislative authority resides in a 33-member legislature (the *Nitijela*), which is elected for four years and which chooses a President from among its members. The President is both head of state and head of government and appoints the Cabinet.

President Amata Kabua was returned to office for a fifth successive term in November 1995, having been chosen by members of the new *Nitijela* elected earlier that month. Following his death in December 1996, he was succeeded by his cousin, Imata Kabua. In the traditional absence of political parties, presidential and opposition forces were at that stage aligned in loose informal groupings. However, further elections to the *Nitijela* on Nov. 22, 1999, marked the emergence of the country's first recognizable party, the United Democratic Party (UDP), which won 18 of the 33 seats and in January 2000 secured the election of Kessai Note to replace Imata Kabua as President.

United Democratic Party (UDP)

Address. c/o Nitijela, Dalap-Uliga-Darrit, Majuro Atoll
Leadership. Kessai Note

The UDP emerged from the *Ralik-Ratak* grouping formed in 1991 under the leadership of Tony DeBrum in opposition to President Amata Kabua, whose own supporters were associated with the Our Islands (*Ailin Kein Ad*) movement chaired by the President. Following the 1995 elections to the *Nitijela*, its newly-elected Speaker, Kessai Note, became the leader of anti-Kabua forces and stood unsuccessfully for the presidency following Amata Kabua's death in December 1996. In the November 1999 elections to the *Nitijela*, Note's supporters adopted the UDP designation and became the majority grouping with 18 seats. The resultant election of Note as President in January 2000 was the first time that a sitting government had been voted out of office since the Marshall Islands became independent. The UDP remained the sole but loose party grouping in legislative elections in November 2003.

Mauritania

Capital: Nouakchott
Population: 2,920,000 (2003E)

The Islamic Republic of Mauritania achieved independence from France in 1960 as a one party state under the Mauritanian People's Party. Following a military coup in 1978, the constitution was suspended and the legislature and former government and ruling party were dissolved. The Military Council of National Salvation (CMSN), headed from Dec. 12, 1984, by the Armed Forces Chief of Staff Col. Moaouia Ould Sid' Ahmed Taya, ruled until 1992.

Mauritania was affected to some degree by the movement to greater political pluralism apparent in much of Africa in the early 1990s. In July 1991 a new constitution was approved, providing for the election of a President by universal suffrage for a six-year term and for the appointment of a Prime Minister, broadly along French lines. Legislative power was vested in an 81-member National Assembly (*Assemblée Nationale* or *Al Jamiya al-Wataniyah*) directly elected in single-seat constituencies for five years. A 56-member Senate (*Majlis al-Shuyukh*) consists of three senators elected by Mauritanians abroad; the remaining 53 are elected indirectly, by municipal councillors, for a six-year term, with a rolling one-third re-elected every three years. At the same time the CMSN approved legislation that allowed for the formation of political parties. Daddah's People's Party survived until 1992, though no longer operates.

Taya's Democratic and Social Republican Party (PRDS) won an overwhelming victory in multi-party elections in March 1992; Taya had also won the presidential election in January 1992. Further legislative elections were held over two rounds in October 1996, with the PRDS taking 71 of the seats in the National Assembly. Other seats were taken by non-partisans with Action for Change (AC) winning the only seat won by any party opposed to the government. However, following allegations of electoral fraud by the Union of Democratic Forces (UFD), the second round was largely boycotted by opposition parties. The PRDS also maintained control of the Senate when indirect elections were held in April 2000. The PRDS took 52 of the 56 seats, with one other held by an independent and three representing Mauritanians abroad.

Multi-party presidential elections were held in late 1997 when President Taya was returned to office for a further term with more than 90% of the votes cast, defeating four other candidates. National Assembly elections were held in October 2001. Generally considered fair and transparent, the polls saw opposition parties make significant gains, particularly in urban areas. Support for the PRDS fell to 64 seats, while opposition parties collectively won 17 seats. Senatorial elections on April 12, 2002, resulted in a Senate membership of 54 seats for the PRDS, and one each for the RFD and UNDD.

President Taya survived a violent coup attempt by rebel soldiers in June 2003. The attempt was apparently sparked by dissatisfaction with his authoritarian rule, with his crackdown on Islamist foes earlier in the year, and with Mauritania's ties to the West and Israel (in 1999 Mauritania having become the third member of the Arab League, after Egypt and Jordan, to recognize Israel). Anti-Taya forces included Islamists, some possibly affiliated to *Al-Qaeda*; sacked and disgruntled military officers; and Baathist associates of the ousted Iraqi dictator, Saddam Hussein, some of whom evidently fled to Mauritania after their defeat at American hands in April 2003.

Taya appointed a new Prime Minister, Sighair Ould M'Bareck, in July 2003. He was re-elected President on Nov. 7, 2003, with 67% of the vote; overall voter turnout was 60.8%. The unsuccessful candidates were Mohamed Khouna Ould Haidallah who won 18.7% of the vote; Ahmed Ould Daddah of the UFD (6.9%); and Messaoud Ould Boulkheir of the AC (5.0%). Again, opposition forces alleged electoral fraud by Taya's allies. Haidallah was Mauritania's leader before Taya, a former ally of his, seized power in 1984. Although Haidallah represented no named party, clearly the regime felt threatened, as it arrested him on the eve of the election, and accused his supporters, both Islamists and liberal reformers, of planning a coup if he lost. Haidallah was re-arrested after the poll. The elections were also the first in Arab history to field a female presidential candidate, Aicha Mint Jeddane. The daughter of nomads, unable to read or write, she campaigned for women's rights but polled few votes.

Action for Change
Action pour Changement (AC)
Address. c/o Assemblée Nationale, Nouakchottt
Leadership. Messaoud Ould Boulkheir
Formed in August 1995, the AC did not join the opposition boycott of the 1996 National Assembly elections and secured one seat, the only seat taken by a party other than the Democratic and Social Republican Party. The AC champions the rights of former slaves, called *haratin*, and black Africans, two groups which have felt excluded by the so-called "white Moors" or Arabized Mauritanians who have traditionally ruled Mauritania. The AC claims that slavery is still practiced, even though it was officially outlawed in 1981. In October 2001 the party gained 5.5% of votes cast in legislative elections, and won four seats. Although the AC was banned in January 2002, its leader, Boulkheir, became the first descendant of *haratin* to stand for the office of head of state in the November 2003 presidential elections.

Democratic and Social Republican Party
Parti Républicain Démocratique et Social (PRDS)
Address. c/o Assemblée Nationale, Nouakchottt
The centre-left PRDS was formed following the legalization of multi-partyism in 1991 as a vehicle for Moaouia Ould Sid' Ahmed Taya, who had headed the ruling military council since 1984. It won 67 of the 79 seats in elections to the new National Assembly in March 1992, although critics alleged that the poll was flawed, as all soldiers were commanded to vote for the PRDS. The party retained power in October 1996 elections when it won 71 seats; and it maintained an overwhelming majority in the indirectly elected Senate after success in the inaugural election of 1992. Support for the PRDS fell slightly in the October 2001 polls, to 64 seats, garnering 51% of all votes cast. Though the PRDS seats tally greatly outnumbered the total for opposition parties – 17 seats – it did reflect dissatisfaction with the President's policies and the allegedly authoritarian nature of his rule.

Taya's flagging popularity revived in June 2002 when he secured for Mauritania $1.1 billion in debt relief; this followed a new law to encourage foreign investment, in December 2001, and plans to exploit offshore oil. The failure of the June 2003 coup attempt suggests that the rebels were not universally popular; and Taya's success in the November 2003 presidential polls also bolstered the PRDS. Clearly, the 67% of the vote he received in 2003 contrasted favourably with the 51% his party achieved in 2001 legislative elections; although the comparison may be misleading, given the different nature of the polls, and also given allegations of pre-poll malpractice and state media bias.

Mauritanian Renewal Party
Parti Mauritanien pour le Rénouvellement (PMR)
Leadership. Moulaye al-Hassan Ould Jeydid (leader)
Registered in 1991, the centrist PMR failed to secure any electoral success in the 1996 lower house elections. Jeydid stood as a candidate in the 1997 presidential election and finished in third place with less than 1% of the vote.

National Union for Democracy and Development (UNDD)
Leadership. Tidjane Koita
The UNDD won a single seat in 2002 senatorial elections, though did not appear to contest the 2001 legislative elections.

National Vanguard Party
Parti Nationale de l'Avant-Garde (PNAG)
Leadership. Khattri Ould Jiddou
Legalized in late 1991, the PNAG failed to secure any seats in the 1996 National Assembly election. In December 1997, however, PNAG leader Jiddou was appointed to the government as Minister of Culture and Islamic Orientation.

Rally for Democracy and National Unity
Rassemblement pour la Démocratie et l'Unité Nationale (RDUN)
Leadership. Ahmed Mokhtar Sidi Baba (leader)
The centre-right RDUN failed to win any seats in the first round of the 1996 legislative elections and subsequently joined other parties in boycotting the second round. In the October 2001 polls it took second place after the ruling PRDS, winning three seats on an impressive 9.6% of the vote.

Socialist and Democratic Popular Union
Union Populaire Socialiste et Démocratique (UPSD)
Leadership. Mohammed Mahmoud Ould Mah (leader)
Legalized in 1991, the UPSD contested the December 1997 presidential election, but party leader, Ould Mah, came fourth in the poll with only 0.7 per cent of the votes cast. The party had boycotted the October 1996 legislative elections. The UPSD has been linked to the Iraqi wing of the pan-Arab *Baath* party; some accused its members of involvement in the abortive June 2003 coup attempt. President Taya had earlier enjoyed good relations with Baghdad, but these deteriorated after 1999.

Umina Party
Leadership. Ould Sidi Yayia (leader)
An influential Islamic fundamentalist organization, Umina was formed in 1991 but was prevented from registering as a political party because of the constitutional ban on parties based on religion. Islamists were said to be behind the abortive coup attempt of June 2003, shortly after 32 of their leaders were charged with "plotting against the constitutional order".

Union for Democracy and Progress
Union pour la Démocratie et le Progrès (UDP)
Leadership. Hamdi Ould Mouknass (president)
The UDP was legalized in 1993, its ranks reportedly including former prominent members of the Union of Democratic Forces. In October 2001 the UDP won three seats on 8.1% of the vote.

Union of Democratic Forces
Union des Forces Démocratiques (UFD)
Leadership. Ahmed Ould Daddah (leader)
Legalized in October 1991 and generally considered the strongest opposition formation, the UFD organized the boycott of the October 1996 legislative elections. Its leader, Ahmed Ould Daddah, is the half-brother of Mauritania's first president, Moktar Ould Daddah, who was deposed in a military coup in 1978 after his army's poor showing against Algerian-supported Polisario rebels in Western Sahara. The former President went into exile in Paris, where he died in October 2003. He had declined invitations to re-enter politics in 1992; presumably supporters of his now defunct Mauritanian People's Party shifted their support to Ahmed Daddah's UFD. The latter Daddah has himself been arrested on numerous occasions.

The UFD-instigated 1996 boycott followed the publication of results from the first round of voting in which the Democratic and Social Republican Party (PRDS) had secured 61 seats. UFD leader Daddah accused the government of tampering with the voters' register to exclude opposition supporters and called on all parties to boycott the second round of voting. It appears that the UFD boycotted the 2001 legislative elections, too, although Daddah stood for president in November 2003, polling 6.9% of the vote. The UFD – also sometimes referred to as the Rally for Democratic Forces – also won a single seat in the 2002 senatorial indirect elections.

Other Parties

In April 2001 the Interior Ministry legalized six new political parties. They were the **Mauritanian Liberal Democrats**, led by Mustapha Ould Lemrabet; the **Third Generation**, led by Lebat Ould Jeh; the **Democratic Alliance**, led by Mohammed Ould Taleb Othman; the **Mauritanian Labour Party**, led by Mohammed Hafid Ould Denna; the **New Mauritanian Renewal Party**, led by Atiq Ould Attia and the **Alliance for Justice and Democracy**, led by Kabeh Abdoulaye. None of these parties appears to have registered significant results in the October 2001 legislative elections.

Mauritius

Capital: Port Louis
Population: 1,200,000

A former British colony, Mauritius achieved independence in 1968. The British monarch remained as head of state until the country became a republic in March 1992. The post of President is a largely ceremonial role, executive power being vested in the Prime Minister, who is leader of the majority parliamentary party. The President, elected for a five-year term by the National Assembly, appoints the Council of Ministers on the recommendation of the Prime Minister. There is a unicameral National Assembly, 62 of whose members are elected by universal adult suffrage for a term of five years from single-member constituencies, while up to eight additional seats are allocated by the independent Electoral Supervisory Commission under a "best loser" system.

General elections in September 2000 were won by an alliance led by the Mauritian Militant Movement (MMM) and the Militant Socialist Movement (MSM), which took 54 of the 60 Mauritius elective seats with 51.7% of the vote. The six remaining seats and 36.6% of the vote went to an alliance led by the Labour Party and the Xavier-Luc Duval Militant Movement (PMXD), while the Organization of the People of Rodrigues (OPR) retained the two Rodrigues elective seats. Four "best loser" seats were allocated to the MSM/MMM alliance, two to the Labour/PMXD alliance (one of these to the PMXD leader, who had failed to retain his elective seat) and two to the Rodrigues Movement. Minor parties within the MSM/MMM alliance included the Republican Movement and the rump of the Mauritian Social Democratic Party, each of which won one elective seat.

Cassam Uteem (a former MMM minister) was elected President of Mauritius by the National Assembly in June 1992 and re-elected in June 1997. Uteem resigned as President in February 2002 following his refusal to promulgate an anti-terrorism bill that had been passed by the National Assembly. Uteem was replaced by Karl Offman who was in turn replaced in October 2003 by the MSM's Sir Anerood Jugnauth, who had recently been replaced as Prime Minister by the MMM's Paul Bérenger.

Labour Party
Parti Travailliste

Address. 7 Guy Rozement Square, Port Louis
Telephone. (+230) 212 6691
Fax. (+230) 670 0720
Email. labour@intnet.mu
Website. www.labour.intnet.mu
Leadership. Navinchandra Ramgoolam (leader); Sarat Dutt Lallah (secretary general)
The Labour Party led Mauritius to independence in 1968 under the premiership of Sir Seewoosagur Ramgoolam but lost all of its elective seats in 1982. Recovering some ground in the 1983 contest, it was a constituent of the subsequent governing coalitions led by the Militant Socialist Movement (MSM). In September 1990 it moved into opposition as a consequence of an electoral alliance forged between the MSM and the Mauritian Militant Movement (MMM) to promote constitutional measures that would allow Mauritius to become a republic. The Labour Party contested the 1991 general election in an opposition alliance with the Mauritian Social Democratic Party (PMSD), but won only a handful of seats.

In April 1994 the Labour Party signed an electoral pact with the MMM, and in the December 1995 general election this alliance defeated the ruling coalition, taking all the elective seats for the main island. Labour leader Navinchandra Ramgoolam (son of Sir Seewoosagur) was sworn in as the country's new Prime Minister at the end of December. He stated that his Labour/MMM coalition government would continue the pro-market economic policies of its predecessor but with more emphasis on equal opportunities and welfare for the poor.

Holding 35 seats, the Labour Party governed alone after the ending of its coalition with the MMM in 1997, although in September 1999 it backed the successful by-election campaign of Charles Gaëtan Xavier-Luc Duval , who had formed the Mauritian Party of Xavier-Luc Duval (PMXD) breakaway faction of the PMSD and who joined the government the following month. The September 2000 general election was called against a background of corruption scandals involving Labour Party ministers. It resulted in the defeat (by an MSM/MMM alliance) of Labour and its current electoral allies, which retained only six elective and two "best loser" seats in the new National Assembly.

The Labour Party is a full member of the Socialist International.

Mauritian Militant Movement
Mouvement Militant Mauricien (MMM)

Address. 21 Poudrière Street, Port Louis
Telephone. (+230) 212 6553
Fax. (+230) 208 9939
Leadership. Paul Bérenger (leader); Ahmed Jeewah (chairman); Ivan Collendavelloo (general secretary)
The socialist MMM was founded in 1969 with a substantial trade union following. Briefly in government from 1982, the party split in 1983 when the then MMM president and Prime Minister, Sir Aneerood Jugnauth, was expelled from the party and thereupon formed the Militant Socialist Movement (MSM). In the 1991 general election an alliance of the MMM, the MSM and the Democratic Labour Movement won a large parliamentary majority, and the MMM gained substantial representation in the new coalition government which transformed the country into a republic in 1992. Disputes between the MMM and the MSM during 1993 led to the dismissal of the MMM leader, Paul Bérenger, from the Council of Ministers and the subsequent departure, in mid-1994, of the pro-coalition faction within the party to form the Mauritian Militant Renaissance. In April 1994 the MMM signed an electoral pact with the Labour Party, and in the

December 1995 general election this alliance ousted the ruling coalition.

In June 1997 Bérenger was dismissed from the Labour government led by Navinchandra Ramgoolam, of whose policies he had become an increasingly outspoken critic, after which he took the MMM into opposition for the remainder of the current parliament. The MMM entered into an "informal" alliance with the MSM in February 1999, subsequently concluding a detailed agreement in August 2000 when a general election was called. Pursuant to this agreement, the substantial MSM/MMM victory in September 2000 was followed by Bérenger's appointment as Deputy Prime Minister in the government formed by Sir Aneerood Jugnauth, who had given an undertaking to relinquish the premiership in Bérenger's favour in 2003. Accordingly, in September of that year Bérenger replaced Jugnauth as Prime Minister and he appointed a new Cabinet the following month. Jugnauth took on the largely ceremonial post of President.

Mauritian Social Democratic Party
Parti Mauricien Social-Démocrate (PMSD)

Address. c/o National Assembly, Port Louis
Leadership. Maurice Allet (leader); Hervé Duval (honorary president); Mamade Kodabaccus (secretary general)

The conservative PMSD originated in the pre-independence period, mainly representing the French-speaking and Creole middle classes. Under the leadership of Sir Gaëtan Duval, the party increased its representation to 23 seats in 1967 and took part in the 1969–73 national unity government led by the Labour Party, with Duval as External Affairs Minister. Its departure in December 1973 was because of Labour opposition to Duval's policy of dialogue with South Africa. The PMSD was again in coalition with Labour in 1976–82, while from 1983 until 1988 it was a junior member of coalition headed by the alliance of Labour and the Militant Socialist Movement (MSM).

Although the PMSD fought the 1991 election in an opposition alliance with Labour, it agreed to enter the governing coalition led by the MSM in February 1995, one of its ministerial appointees being Sir Gaëtan Duval's son, Charles Gaëtan Xavier-Luc Duval, who had succeeded his father as PMSD party leader. Opposition to this move from within the party led to Xavier-Luc Duval's departure from the government and the subsequent reversion to his father of the party leadership. Tarred by the government's unpopularity and despite standing as the "Gaëtan Duval Party", the PMSD failed to win an elective seat in the December 1995 contest, although Sir Gaëtan was awarded the party's "best loser" seat.

On Sir Gaëtan Duval's death in May 1996, his brother, Hervé Duval, took over the party leadership and became its representative in the National Assembly. The leadership was subsequently regained by Xavier-Luc Duval as the party became increasingly polarized into a faction loyal to him and a faction loyal to his uncle, who claimed to represent the so-called "true blue" traditions of the party. The Hervé Duval faction came to be identified with the designation PMSD (and therefore effectively with the full party name), while Xavier-Luc began to use the designation PMXD, standing for the Xavier-Luc Duval Mauritian Party, notably in political situations where there was direct confrontation between the two factions. Hervé Duval was elected leader of the PMSD at a congress organized by his faction in January 1999, but stepped down in favour of Maurice Allet later in the year. This faction of the PMSD fought the 2000 election as an ally of the MSM/MMM, its only successful candidate being Maurice Allet. Allet was confirmed unopposed as leader at the next party congress in May 2001, the party executive having refused to allow the nomination of Ghislaine Henry (sister of Hervé Duval), who was seen as an advocate of reunification with the PMXD.

Militant Socialist Movement
Mouvement Socialiste Militant (MSM)

Address. Sun Trust Building, 31 Edith Cavell Street, Port Louis
Telephone. (+230) 212 8787
Fax. (+230) 208 9517
Website. www.msmsun.com
Leadership. Sir Aneerood Jugnauth (leader); Joe Lesjondard (president); Nando Bohde (secretary)

Formed in 1983 by Sir Aneerood Jugnauth, following his expulsion from the Mauritian Militant Movement, the MSM was the dominant party in subsequent coalition governments until the general election in December 1995 when, in alliance with the Mauritian Militant Renaissance, it failed to retain any seats in the National Assembly. In 1999 the MSM prepared the ground for a long-term alliance with the MMM, and in September 2000 (having returned to power as the head of an MSM/MMM coalition) Sir Aneerood Jugnauth appointed the MMM leader, Paul Bérenger, as his Deputy Prime Minister on the understanding that Bérenger would take over the premiership after three years. Accordingly, in September 2003 Bérenger replaced Jugnauth as Prime Minister and the latter was appointed to the largely ceremonial post of President.

Organization of the People of Rodrigues
Organisation du Peuple Rodriguais (OPR)

Address. c/o National Assembly, Port Louis
Leadership. Louis Serge Clair (leader)

Representing the interests of the people of the island of Rodrigues, the OPR has consistently held the two elective seats for Rodrigues in the National Assembly and has been included in most post-independence government coalitions.

Xavier-Luc Duval Mauritian Party
Parti Mauricien Xavier-Luc Duval (PMXD)

Address. c/o National Assembly, Port Louis
Leadership. Charles Gaëtan Xavier-Luc Duval

The designation PMXD came into use in the late 1990s to distinguish the faction of the Mauritian Social Democratic Party (PMSD) led by Xavier-Luc Duval following a rift within that party. He won a parliamentary by-election as PMXD candidate in October 1999, subsequently serving as a minister in the Labour Party government of Navinchandra Ramgoolam. The PMXD fought the September 2000 general election as an ally of the Labour Party, but failed to win any elective seats. Its leader was, however, allocated a "best loser" seat in the new Assembly.

Other Parties

Democratic Union of Mauritius, member of the Christian Democrat and People's Parties International; unrepresented in the legislature.
Address. 105 Chancery House, Port Louis
Telephone. (+230) 212 0252
Fax. (+230) 212 8799
Leadership. Guy Ollivry (president); Rossind Bowwarbe (secretary general)

Hizbullah, an Islamic fundamentalist formation that obtained sufficient support in the December 1995 elections to be awarded one "best loser" seat.
Leadership. Cehl Mohamed Fakeemeeah (leader)

Mauritian Militant Socialist Movement (*Mouvement Militant Socialiste Mauricien*), supported the Labour Party in the 2000 general election campaign, but failed to win any seats.
Leadership. Madun Dulloo (leader)

Rally for Reform (*Rassemblement pour la Réforme*, RPR), supported the Labour Party in the 2000 general election campaign, but failed to win any seats.
Leadership. Sheila Bappoo (leader)

Republican Movement (*Mouvement Républicain*), founded in 1996 and won one seat in the 2000 general election, having given its support to the winning MMM/MSM alliance. In May 2001 the party instructed its sole Assembly member, deputy leader Sunil Dowarkasing, to switch his support from the ruling coalition to the official opposition.
Leadership. Rama Valayden (leader)

Rodrigues Movement (*Mouvement Rodriguais*), founded in 1992 to represent the interests of Rodrigues island, competing with the Organization of the People of Rodrigues; was allocated two "best loser" seats in the National Assembly following the 1995 and 2000 general elections.
Leadership. Nicholas Von Mally (leader)

Socialist Workers' Party (*Parti Socialiste Ouvrier*, PSO), founded in 1997 with a Marxist-Leninist programme.
Leadership. Didier Edmond (general secretary)

Mexico

Capital: Mexico City
Population: 104,959,104 (2004E)

Mexico achieved independence from Spain in 1821. The iron rule of Porfirio Díaz, President from 1876 to 1911 (known as the *Porfiriato*), except for the period 1880-84, ended the political instability of earlier years but precipitated the violent revolution of 1910–20 which produced such leaders as Emiliano Zapata and Francisco "Pancho" Villa. From 1929 one party, renamed the Institutional Revolutionary Party (PRI) in 1946, inherited the mantle of the revolution and held power until 2000.

Under the 1917 constitution (as amended) a bicameral Congress is made up of a 128-member Senate, elected every six years (two directly from each state plus two chosen by proportional representation), and a 500-member federal Chamber of Deputies (half elected by majority vote for territorial constituencies, half chosen by proportional representation). Executive power rests with the President, who appoints a Cabinet. State governors, state legislators and the head of the Federal District are elected directly. As with national elections, state governors are elected under a single ballot system whereas legislators are elected under proportional representation.

The President is elected for a six-year term, known as the *sexenio,* as are the senators. The 500 deputies are elected every three years. Each state is administered by a governor, who is elected for a six-year term. All elections, both national and state, are held on the basis of universal adult suffrage, and are overseen by an independent Federal Electoral Institute (IFE). All Mexican citizens 18 years of age and older are required to vote, although the law is rarely enforced.

The PRI finally lost its tenure of power when Vicente Fox Quesada, as the candidate of a coalition of parties whose main component was the conservative National Action Party (PAN), defeated Francisco Labastida Ochoa of the PRI in the July 2000 presidential election by a margin of 42.5% to 36.1%. The candidate of the leftist Party of the Democratic Revolution

(PRD), Cuauhtémoc Cárdenas, was in third place, taking 16.6%. This outcome came at the end of a long period in which the PRI's share of the vote in presidential elections had been in decline, falling from 95% in 1976 to 74% in 1982, 51% in 1988, and 50% in 1994. One factor in this decline is that elections have become increasingly fair and vigorously contested with the PRI and PAN competing as the two main parties.

Legislative elections in July 2000 left no party in overall control. Competing as part of the Alliance for Change formed for the election, the PAN took 218 seats in the Chamber of Deputies, with its junior partner in the Alliance, the Green Ecologist Party of Mexico (PVEM) taking 5 seats. The PRI, standing independently, won 209 seats, while the Alliance for Mexico, a coalition of left-leaning parties, took 68 seats; of these 53 were won by the Party of the Democratic Revolution (PRD), nine by the Labour Party (PT) and two each by the Convergence for Democracy (CD), the Socialist Alliance Party (PAS) and the Nationalist Society Party (PSN). The Senate contests resulted as follows: PRI 60 seats, PAN 46, PRD 15, PVEM 5, PT 1, CD 1. Eleven registered parties contested the mid-term elections of 2003 but discontent was shown by the fact that only 41.8% of registered voters took part and of those 957,410 spoilt their ballots. The PRI in alliance with the PVEM increased its standing in the Chamber of Deputies to 222 seats to 151 for the PAN and 95 for the PRD; the remainder were divided among PVEM supporters not allied with the PRI 17, PT 6 and Convergencia 5.

Institutional Revolutionary Party
Partido Revolucionario lnstitucional (PRI)
Address. Insurgentes Norte 59, Colonia Buenavista, Delegación Cuauhtémoc, 06359 México DF
Tel. (55) 57 29 56 00
Fax. (55) 57 29 96 57
Website. www.pri.org.mx
Leadership. Roberto Madrazo Pintado (president); Elba Esther Gordillo Morales (secretary-general)
The PRI was founded in 1929 as the National Revolutionary Party. It was renamed the Party of the Mexican Revolution in 1938 before becoming the Institutional Revolutionary Party (PRI) in 1946. The party inherited a populist and symbolic tradition from the 1910–20 Mexican Revolution which gave it room to manoeuvre in practice, uniting disparate political tendencies from socialism and social democracy through to right-wing conservatism. Its current belief in a market-led economy and the conservatism of its foreign policy, points to a clear move to the right.

Of the many PRI Presidents, the most radical and most influential was probably Gen. Lázaro Cárdenas (1934-40). His re-organization of the party led to it becoming a huge network for social control and patronage, incorporating labour and peasant unions and popular organizations for civil servants, professional groups and the army. Cárdenas nationalized the oil industry in 1938 and introduced significant land reforms through the *ejido* common land system.

The authoritarian face of the party was shown most forcibly during the presidencies of Gustavo Díaz Ordaz (1964-70) and Luis Echeverría Alvárez (1970-76), when student unrest was violently repressed. Rhetorically Díaz Ordaz was associated with the right and Echeverría with the left, but they were both repressive Presidents. President José López Portillo (1976-82) headed another authoritarian regime but in foreign policy it supported the 1979 Nicaraguan revolution and permitted the legalization of several left-wing parties.

President Miguel de la Madrid (1982-88), from the right

of the party, had to deal with the severe economic consequences of a debt crisis that hit all of Latin America in 1982. He adopted some ambitious market-oriented reforms. Internal unrest also surfaced within the PRI as dissidents in the Critical Current faction (*Corriente Crítica*) and the Movement for Democratic Change (*Movimiento por el Cambio Democrático*, MCD) objected to the lack of internal democracy and the continuation of the *dedazo* system whereby the President hand-picked election candidates and delegates to the PRI's national assembly.

The 1988 election victory of President Carlos Salinas de Gortari, by the smallest margin in the PRI's history, was one of the most controversial ever, opposition leaders being united in their claims that the PRI had been involved in widespread fraud. In the past, there had not been enough democratic competition to make fraud necessary, but by 1988 there were the first signs of competitive democracy taking root. In July 1989 the PRI conceded victory to the National Action Party candidate in the governorship election in Baja California, its first electoral defeat in 60 years.

The Salinas administration set out to improve the country's image and continue with the policy of market-oriented reform and gradual democratization. Salinas initiated an ambitious programme to deregulate and liberalize the economy and privatize the state sector, most notably re-privatizing state banks nationalized in 1982. Negotiations were also begun in 1990 to conclude a North American Free Trade Agreement (NAFTA) with the USA and Canada. Mexico's entry into the NAFTA in January 1994 became the centre piece of the government's strategy to modernize the country and extricate it from a decade of debt-ridden stagnation.

In 1994 Salinas chose Donaldo Colosio to be his replacement, much to the disappointment of Manuel Camacho Solís who had expected the nomination (and went on to found the Party of the Democratic Centre). However, Colosio was murdered in March 1994, and Ernesto Zedillo Ponce de Leon, who had been Education Minister under Salinas, was nominated in his place. Zedillo was elected to the presidency in August 1994, and pledged to continue with the Salinas government's policies. However in December 1994 financial crisis returned as the Mexican government bungled a devaluation and once more nearly defaulted on its debts. This contributed to PRI unpopularity, and the party lost control of the Chamber of Deputies in the mid-term 1997 elections.

Zedillo gave up the right to choose his own successor as presidential candidate, and instead organized a primary election within the party. The two main candidates for the nomination were Francisco Labastida Ochoa and Roberto Madrazo Pintado. Labastida won the nomination but in the July 2000 presidential election went down to defeat at the hands of Vicente Fox of the National Action Party. In the July 2000 legislative elections, the PRI came second (with 209 seats) to the PAN (218), while remaining in first place in the Senate (although without an overall majority), with 60 seats to the 46 held by the PAN. Since 2000 the policy of allowing party activists to choose the main candidates has continued although with some significant local variations, and the party has shown considerable resilience, winning over a significant number of Green votes and securing 36.46% of the vote and 222 seats in the Chamber of Deputies in 2003.

The PRI is a consultative member of the Socialist International.

National Action Party
Partido Acción Nacional (PAN)
Address. Av. Coyoacán No 1546, Col. Del Valle, Del. Benito Juárez, México D.F.
Telephone. (55) 52 00 40 00
Email. pan@pan.org.mx

Website. www.pan.org.mex
Leadership. Vicente Fox Quesada (President of Mexico); Luis Felipe Bravo Mena (president of the party)
Founded in 1939, the PAN is a conservative social Christian party. It has close associations with the Roman Catholic Church, and also with some of the business community.

Since its founding, the party has been the major opposition grouping and has stood against the Institutional Revolutionary Party (PRI) in congressional elections since 1943 and most presidential elections since 1952. Internal disputes prevented it from presenting a presidential candidate in 1976. Its fortunes have been on a slowly rising trend since 1982.

Together with the Authentic Party of the Mexican Revolution (PARM), the PAN was long regarded as a fairly benign opposition permitted to win a limited number of seats in order to give a pluralist credibility to a monolithic system dominated by the PRI. However, the bank nationalization of 1982 led to the PAN taking a much more militantly oppositional line than it had earlier. During 1984-86, PAN supporters accused the PRI of blatant electoral fraud and were involved in numerous and occasionally violent protests, mainly in the relatively prosperous northern states from which the party drew much of its support. In July 1989, the party inflicted the first electoral defeat on the PRI in 60 years when the PAN candidate won the governorship of the state of Baja California Norte. In the August 1991 congressional elections, however, the PAN's representation in the Congress was cut from 102 to 89 seats.

In the August 1994 presidential election, the PAN came second to the PRI with 25.9% of the popular vote whilst also taking the party's chamber representation above its 1991 level by winning 119 seats. It also took 25 seats in the newly enlarged Senate.

In July 1997 the PAN increased its number of deputies to 121 and together with the Party of the Democratic Revolution (PRD) were able to deny the PRI overall control of the Senate. The PAN continued to perform generally well in state governorship elections after 1997 despite surprisingly losing the governorship of Chihuahua in 1998. Ahead of the 2000 elections, it nominated businessman Vicente Fox Quesada as its presidential candidate although Fox ran at the head of an alliance ("Alliance for Change") that included the Greens (PVEM) and some minor parties. He ended PRI control of the presidency and the party also won more seats (218) in the Chamber of Deputies than did the PRI (209), although the PAN with 46 seats remained in second place in the Senate. Its main base is in the Bajio and the North, though in recent years it has had unexpected successes elsewhere, e.g. in the isthmian state of Campeche. However owing to Fox's failure to propitiate his PVEM allies, at the mid-term elections of 2003, though the party secured 30.64% of the vote, it lost 54 seats and, with only 151 seats left, faced serious difficulties in continuing its legislative programme.

The PAN is a member of the Christian Democrat International.

Party of the Democratic Revolution
Partido de la Revolución Democrática (PRD)
Address. Centro de Cómputo PRD, Durango 338, Col Roma, CP 06700, Mexico DF
Website. www.cen-prd.org.mx
Leadership. Leonel Godoy Rangel (president); Cuauhtémoc Cárdenas Solórzano (presidential candidate)
The PRD originated from a split in the Institutional Revolutionary Party (PRI) that developed during 1986-87 over the free market policies being followed by the government. Cuauhtémoc Cárdenas, the son of former President Lázaro Cárdenas (1934-40) and the leader of the Democratic

Current faction within the PRI, was expelled from the party in 1987. He then brought together several parties to form an electoral coalition, the National Democratic Front (*Frente Democrático Nacional*, FDN), to back his candidacy in the July 1988 presidential election. These included the Authentic Party of the Mexican Revolution (PARM), the Popular Socialist Party (PPS), the Mexican Socialist Party (PMS), the right-wing Mexican Democratic Party (PDM) and the Socialist Workers' Party (*Partido Socialista de los Trabajadores*, PST).

The FDN claimed that the subsequent PRI victory was a "massive fraud", Cárdenas contending that he had won a clear majority. The FDN parties, however, still managed to stun the PRI by taking over 31% of the vote and receiving between them a total of 139 seats in the Congress owing to a low direct vote being boosted by seats awarded by proportional representation.

Of the FDN parties, only the PMS merged into the newly-formed PRD in October 1988 and the FDN itself became effectively defunct. The PRD emerged as the most important party on the left, with a few minor fringe parties continuing to operate independently.

The PRD never again reached the high point that it achieved in 1988, although it did continue to maintain an electoral presence of some significance. In the August 1994 presidential elections, Cárdenas received 16.6% of the vote while PRD representation in the Chamber rose to 71 seats and to eight in the enlarged Senate. It then benefited from the economic recession that hit Mexico during 1995-97 by winning the first ever elections for the mayoralty of Mexico City and by winning enough seats in elections for the Senate to be able, in alliance with the National Action Party (PAN), to deny an automatic majority to the PRI.

In the 2000 presidential election Cárdenas, backed by the Alliance for Mexico (involving mainly the PRD but also some minor parties), took 16.6% of the vote. In the legislative elections the PRD won 53 seats in the Chamber of Deputies and 15 in the Senate, maintaining its position as the third force in Mexican politics, and in 2003, profiting from the general dissatisfaction with the government, it further increased its number of Deputies to 95, though obtaining only 17.66% of the vote. Andrés Manuel López Obrador, who succeeded Cárdenas as Mayor of Mexico City, led the party to an impressive victory in the capital in 2003, winning an absolute majority of the Federal District legislature and 13 of the city's 16 delegaciones

The PRD is a full member party of the Socialist International.

Other Parties

In addition to the following national parties there are also a number of purely local political parties that occasionally contest local and regional elections, usually as a flag of convenience for a well-known individual.

Authentic Party of the Mexican Revolution (*Partido Auténtico de la Revolución Mexicana*, PARM) was founded in 1954. It is led by Porfirio Muñoz Ledo, who withdrew his candidacy in the 2000 presidential election to support Vicente Fox of the National Action Party. Notwithstanding this move, he still received 0.4% of the vote. Although the PARM is very weak, and has no seats in the Congress, Porfirio Muñoz Ledo remains a well-known figure on the Mexican political scene.
Website. www.parm.org.mx

Democratic Convergence (*Partido de Convergencia por la Democracia*, DC), founded in 1999. It formed part of the left-leaning coalition led by the Party of the Democratic

Revolution in the 2000 elections and won two seats in the Chamber of Deputies, increased to 5 in 2003.
Address. Louisiana 113, Col. Napoles, CP 03810 Mexico DF
Telephone. (52) 55 43 85 57
Leadership. Dante Delgado Ranauro (president)

Green Ecologist Party of Mexico (*Partido Verde Ecologista de Mexico*, PVEM), entered the political arena in 1987; its 1994 presidential candidate obtained 0.9% of the vote. In the 2000 elections it competed as part of the Alliance for Change led by the National Action Party and won five seats in the Chamber of Deputies, but in 2003 many of its state parties switched their alliance to the PRI and its strength in the Chamber rose to 17.
Address. Medicina No. 74 esq. AV. Copilco - Universidad, Deleg. Coyoacán, CP 04360 Mexico DF and Loma Bonita No. 18, Col.Lomas Altas, C.P. 11950, México, DF
Telephone/Fax. 52 57 01 88, 52 57 01 56
Website. www.pvem.org.mx
Leadership. Sen. Jorge Emilio González Martínez (president)

Labour Party (*Partido del Trabajo*, PT), founded before the 1991 congressional elections; in 2000 it ran as part of the Alliance for Mexico led by the Party of the Democratic Revolution, and won nine seats in the Chamber of Deputies, retaining 6 after the 2003 elections.
Address. Cuauhtémoc 47, Colonia Roma, CP 06700, Mexico DF
Telephone. (52) 55 25 84 19
Email. pt@pt.org.mx
Website. www.pt.org.mx

Nationalist Society Party (*Partido de la Sociedad Nacionalista*, PSN), founded in 1999 and joined the Alliance for Mexico coalition led by the Party of the Democratic Revolution in the 2000 elections, in which it won two seats in the Chamber of Deputies.
Address. Adolfo Priento 428, Col. Del Valle, CP 03100 Mexico DF
Website. www.psn.org.mx

Party of the Democratic Centre (*Partido de Centro Democrático*, PCD) was founded by Manuel Camacho Solís for whom it served as a personal vehicle; Camacho was a close ally of Salinas, but left the Institutional Revolutionary Party in 1994 in disappointment at not being selected for the presidential nomination. He ran for President in 2000 and received 0.6% of the vote. The PCD failed to win a seat in Congress.

Popular Socialist Party (*Partido Popular Socialista*, PPS), a left-wing party founded in 1948 by the labour organizer Vicente Lombardo Toledano; pro-Cuban, but tolerated by the PRI during its period of ascendancy.
Email. ppsm@ppsdemexico.org
Website. www.ppsdemexico.org
Telephone. (55) 56 72 20 57

Social Alliance Party (*Partido Alianza Social*, PAS), founded in 1999 and joined the Alliance for Mexico coalition led by the Party of the Democratic Revolution in the 2000 elections, in which it won two seats in the Chamber of Deputies.
Address. Edison 89, Col. Tabacalera, CP 06030 Mexico DF
Telephone. (52) 55 66 53 61
Website. www.pas.org.mx

Social Democracy (*Democracia Social*, DS), is largely the personal vehicle of a widely-respected Mexican politician, Gilberto Rincón Gallardo. He is associated with the left and was formerly a senior figure in the Mexican Socialist Party (PMS). In 2000 he won 1.6% of the presidential vote, but his party failed to secure any congressional representation.

Federated States of Micronesia

Capital: Palikir
Population: 118,000 (2000E)

The Federated States of Micronesia (FSM), consisting of more than 600 islands, occupies the archipelago of the Caroline Islands in the western Pacific Ocean. From 1947, as part of the UN Trust Territory of the Pacific, they were administered by the United States. In 1979 a new constitution was adopted, and in 1982 the FSM signed a compact of free association (implemented in 1986) under which the United States recognized the territory as a fully sovereign and independent state, while retaining authority in regard to defence. In December 1990 the UN Security Council approved the termination of the Trusteeship in relation to the FSM, and the republic joined the UN the following year.

The four constituent states of the FSM are the island groups of Chuuk (formerly Truk), Kosrae, Pohnpei and Yap, each of which have elected governors and legislatures. Federal authority is vested in a President who is elected by the unicameral federal Congress from among its members together with a Vice-President. The Congress has 14 senators, of whom four "at large" members (one from each state) are elected for a four-year term and the other 10 for a two-year term. There are no formal political parties in the FSM.

Following congressional elections on March 2, 1999, Leo Falcam was elected President on May 12, 1999, in succession to Jacob Nena. Further congressional elections were held on March 6, 2001. In 2003 Joseph Urusemal was elected President.

Moldova

Capital: Chisinau
Population: 4,446,455 (2004E)

The land currently constituting the Republic of Moldova has only been an independent state since 1991. Various parts of the territory had historically fallen under the jurisdiction of the Russian and Ottoman empires, before the Bessarabian territory was incorporated in "Greater Romania" after the First World War. The current territory was brought together in 1940, when the Ribbentrop-Molotov Pact resulted in the Soviet annexation of Bessarabia – giving rise to the formation of the Soviet Socialist Republic of Moldova. Fifty years on, as the central control of Moscow over the peripheral republics of the Soviet Union weakened, Moldova followed the lead of the Baltic republics by declaring independence in May 1991.

Following Chisinau's declaration of independence a separatist movement (assisted by Russian military forces in the region), declared independence for the east bank region of the Dniester River – originally termed the Transdniester Moldovan Soviet Socialist Republic, and after October 1991 the Transdniester Modovan Republic or Dniester Moldovan Republic

(DMR). The DMR has consolidated de facto autonomy, with continuing Russian support. Efforts to create a federal structure have so far proved unsuccessful.

The official language of Moldova is "Moldovan" (which is, in essence, identical to Romanian), although there are a number of significantly-sized minority language groups. The ethnic breakdown is Moldovan /Romanian 64%, Ukrainian 14%, Russian 13%, Gagauz (Turkic-Christian) 3.5%, Bulgarian 2%, other 3%.

Under its 1994 constitution, the Republic of Moldova is governed through what is essentially a presidential system. However, a constitutional amendment in July 2000 saw the roles of the legislature and executive become intertwined. The President is now elected by the unicameral parliament for a four-year term, following national parliamentary elections, which are also held on a four-yearly basis. Underneath the President is a Prime Minister, who is selected in consultation with the parliament. After the nomination, the Prime Minister-designate then presents a cabinet and policy programme before the parliament, which must then endorse the proposed platform for the apppointments to be ratified. The parliament elected the Communist Party chair, Vladimir Voronin, as President in April 2001; Vasile Tarlev has been Prime Minister also since April 2001.

The political party scene in Moldova remains somewhat volatile, with a plethora of small parties joining to form broad-reaching alliances, which are reorganized and redefined periodically. The Communist Party of the Moldovan Republic is an exception to this trend; its strong, centralized organizational structure is arguably a contributing factor to its current dominance of the national parliament.

The most recent national elections were held on Feb. 25, 2001. The Communist Party took 49.9% of the vote, was awarded 71 of the 101 seats in parliament, and has since formed a government led by Prime Minister Tarlev. With 13.4 % of the vote in 2001, the Braghis Alliance (now reformed as the "Our Moldova" Alliance) took 19 seats, and the Christian Democratic People's Party received 11 seats for its 8.2% share of the vote. No other parties passed the 6% threshold required to gain a seat allocation in the parliament. However, the Party of Revival and Accord, with 5.7%, and the Democratic Party of Moldova, with 5.1%, came near. The next set of parliamentary elections are scheduled for early in 2005.

Christian Democratic People's Party
Partidul Popular Crestin-Democrat (PPCD)
Address. str. N. Iorga nr. 5, Chisinau, 2009
Telephone. (373-2) 23-45-47, 23-86-66, 23-86-35
Fax. (373-2) 23-44-80
Email. magic@cni.md
Website. http://ppcd.dnt.md
Leadership. Iurie Rosca (president); Ion Neagu (secretary-general)
The centre-right PPCD was founded in 1992 as the Christian Democratic People's Front (FPCD – itself the successor of the pan-Romanian wing of the Popular Front of Moldova). The Front had led the push for Moldovan independence in 1990, and was the dominant political organization at the time of the collapse of Soviet rule. Calling Moldova by the historic name of "Bessarabia," the FPCD saw independence as the first step towards the "sacred goal" of reunification with Romania. Despite a strong and highly visible presence during the early years of independence, the FPCD was victim to the defeat of pro-Romanian factions in the elections of February 1994, taking only nine seats and a vote-share of 7.5%.

Having backed the unsuccessful re-election bid of Mircea Snegur in the presidential elections of 1996, the FPCD then became a founding member of the Democratic Convention of Moldova (CDM), a coalition which also included Snegur's Party of Revival and Accord of Moldova (PRCM). In the March 1998 legislative elections, the CDM won 26 seats, with 19.2% of the vote, but was outpolled by the revived Communist Party of the Moldovan Republic (PCRM). Neverthelss, fear of a return to communist rule meant that the CDM and other centre-right groupings were able to form a coalition government, which included the FPCD.

The FPCD broke with the CDM and the centre-right coalition in March 1999, when it joined the PCRM in voting against the installation of Ion Sturza as Prime Minister. Then in opposition, the FPCD changed its name to the Christian Democratic People's Party (PPCD) in December 1999.

The renamed party also adopted a new programme, which called for "integration within a Europe of nations and the fulfilment of national unity" (in contrast to the earlier position of "the national unity of all Romanians in Romania and Moldova"). This pro-European stance is reflected in the party's logo, which features the stars and colours of the European Union. Central to the party's current platform is a vociferous anti-communist line, and a rejection of movements towards closer ties with Russia.

In the parliamentary elections of February 2001, in which the PCRM obtained a landslide majority, the PPCD was one of only two other parties to gain representation, winning 11 seats with 8.3% of the vote.

The PCD is a member of the Christian Democrat International.

Communist Party of the Moldovan Republic
Partidul Comunistilor din Republica Moldova (PCRM)

Address. 118 M. Dosoftei str., Chisinau
Telephone. (373-2) 23-36-73, 24-94-41, 24-83-84
Email. info@pcrm.md
Website. www.pcrm.md
Leadership. Vladimir Voronin (chairman); Victor Stepaniuk (parliamentary group chairman)

The Soviet-era Communist Party was formally banned in August 1991. However, a reborn Communist Party of the Moldovan Republic (PCRM) was then introduced and allowed to legally register in 1994. Once legalized, the party quickly attracted defectors from other organizations, and formed a coalition named the Popular Patriotic Forces Front, in support of Vladimir Voronin's candidacy in the 1996 presidential elections. With 10.3% of the vote, Voronin ran third in the first round of elections. The PCRM then backed the victorious Petru Lucinschi in the second round – a strategy which saw the Communists rewarded with two ministerial posts in the resultant coalition government.

In March 1998 the PCRM ran in its first national parliamentary elections, on a platform that advocated "the rebirth of a socialist society." A strong organizational base, and public disenchantment with economic reforms, saw the PCRM emerge from the elections as the strongest single party, with 40 seats and 30.1% of the vote. Nevertheless, the Communists were still forced into opposition, against a broad-reaching, centre-right coalition government. Following one of a series of subsequent government crises, Voronin was nominated by President Lucinschi to take the postion of Prime Minister, in late 1999. The deal fell through, however, when Voronin failed to obtain sufficient parliamentary support.

The PCRM was able to exact revenge in the parliamentary elections of February 2001, winning a landslide victory with 71 of the 101 seats and 49.9% of the vote. The party then took advantage of new constitutional provisions, which provided for election of the President by parliament. As a result, Voronin was elected President of Moldova in April

2001. To contrast with Voronin's "establishment" image, the party opted for an independent businessman, Vasile Tarlev, as Prime Minister. Tarlev headed a government dominated by the PCRM; one which remains committed to a strong state role in the economy and the re-establishment of close ties with Russia. Shortly after the 2001 elections Voronin was re-elected PCRM chairman, after the Constitutional Court had ruled that the posts of President and party chair were not incompatible.

The PCRM remains the only overtly communist party to have been elected to power in the states of the former Soviet Union.

"Our Moldova" Alliance Party
Partidul Alianta "Moldova Noastra"

Address. mun. Chisinau, str. Puskin nr. 62 (A)
Telephone. (373-2) 54-85-38, 27-18-37, 54-85-28
Email. vitalia@ch.moldpac.md , oleg_esanu@rambler.ru
Leadership. Dumitru Braghis (Social Democratic Alliance – *Aliantei Social-Democrate din Moldova*); Veaceslav Untila (Liberal Party – *Partidului Liberal*), Serafim Urechean (Independents' Alliance of Moldova – *Aliantei Independentilor din Republica Moldova*) (co-chairs)

The self-described "social-liberal" alliance "Our Moldova" was formed on July 19, 2003, in view of the local elections to follow. The alliance, which describes itself as largely "centre-left," is an amalgamation of further coalitions; namely, the Social Democratic Alliance, the Liberal Party, and the Independents' Alliance of Moldova.

Although formally under co-chairmanship, Dumitru Braghis is the most prominent of the alliance's leaders. Braghis was Prime Minister from December 1999 until the elections of 2001, and remains chair of the Social Democratic Alliance. In February 2001, he led a forerunner to "Our Moldova" (the "Braghis Alliance", BA) in national parliamentary elections. However, the BA ran a distant second to the PCRM, winning only 19 of the 101 seats and 13.4% of the vote. The BA then rejected a PCRM proposal to join a new coalition government, and declared that it would prefer to advocate its policies from the perspective of a loyal opposition.

Members of the Braghis Alliance included the New Force Social-Political Movement (*Miscarea Social-Politica Forta Noua*, MSPFN), the Hope Movement of Professionals (*Miscarea Profesionistilor Speranta-Nadejda*), the Centrist Union of Moldova (*Uniunea Centrista din Moldova*, UCM), the Social Democratic Party (*Partidul Democratiei Sociale Furnica*, PDSF), the Socialist Party of Moldova (*Partidul Socialist din Moldova*, PSM) and the Labour Union (*Uniunea Muncii*, UM).

A constituent of "Our Moldova," the Liberal Party was formed in March 2003, following a merger between the Party of Rebirth and Reconciliation of Moldova, the National Peasant Christian Democratic Party and the Social Liberal Union "Force of Moldova". Representing the right wing of the "Our Moldova" Alliance, the Liberal Party presents itself as a neo-liberal conglomerate.

The Independents' Alliance of Moldova is led by the Serafim Urechean, Mayor of Chisinau, and is a loose coalition. It does not adhere to any strict ideological platform, choosing instead to describe itself as a "democratically oriented socio-political movement."

Other Parties

Democratic Agrarian Party of Moldova (*Partidul Democrat Agrar din Moldova, PDAM*).
Address. mun. Chisinau, str. Teatrului no. 15
Telephone. (373-2) 22-22-74, 22-60-50, 22-81-40
The PDAM was founded in 1991 by Soviet-era agrarian

forces. Favouring continued Moldovan independence in combination with participation in CIS economic structures, it won a narrow overall parliamentary majority in 1994, with 43.2% of the popular vote. However, a series of splits and new parties formations followed, and the PDAM took only 1.2% of the vote in 2001. The party is currently chaired by Anatol Popusoi.

Democratic Party of Moldova (*Partidul Democrat din Moldova*, PDM).
Address. 32 Tighina str, Chisinau, MD 2001
Telephone. (373-2) 27-82-29, 27-82-52
Fax. (373-2) 27-82-30
Led by Dumitru Diacov, the PDM ran fifth in the 2001 elections, with 5.1% of the vote. The group is essentially a social democratic party, and can be traced back to the formation of a "pro-Lucinschi" bloc, which was a group of centrists who aimed at supporting the presidential candidacy of Petru Lucinschi. The party formally changed its name to the current form in 2000.

"New Force" Social Movement (*Miscarea social-politica "Forta Noua"*)
Address. mun. Chisinau, str. Bernardazzi nr. 64
Telephone. (373-2) 22-22-97, 22-66-04, 23-32-14
Leadership. Valeriu Plesca

Party of Reform (*Partidul Reformei*)
Address. mun. Chisinau, str. Bucuresti, no. 87
Tel./Fax. (373-2) 23-26-89, 22-80-97
Leadership. Mihai Ghimpu

Social Democratic Party of Moldova (*Partidul Social Democrat din Moldova*, PSDM).
Address. Chisinau, str. Causeni nr. 1, of. 36
Tel. (373-2) 27-67-85, 23-77-74, 21-73-73
Fax. (373-2) 21-25-83
Email. oazu_nantoi@moldovacc.md
Website. http://psdm.usam.md
Currently under the leadership of Ion Musuc, the PSDM is one of the earliest and longest lasting parties in Moldova. First established in May 1990, the PSDM's initial policy push was for the creation of a Moldovan Soviet Socialist Republic, independent of the Soviet Union. Despite its "early mover" advantage, the PSDM has not been a substantial, independent player in Moldovan politics – particularly since internal turmoil undermined the party's structure in the mid-1990s. With 2.5% of the national vote in 2001, the PSDM failed to pass the 6% threshold for gaining seats.

DNIESTR MOLDOVAN REPUBLIC

The separatist government of the Dniestr Moldovan Republic (DMR), which exercises *de facto* control of Moldova east of the Dniestr river (a geographical region known Transnistria), is a dictatorship with a poor human rights record. The DMR remains autonomous, although the international community has refused to recognize its claims to independence. A 1999 treaty signed between Moldova and Ukraine saw the latter assure Moldova's territorial integrity. Nevertheless, the DMR maintains is own flag, anthem, and currency. Its constitution was amended in June 2000, shifting the DMR to a presidential system, in which the executive presides over the government, or Council of Ministers. Despite the veneer of democracy that regime portrays, the rights of free assembly and association are not respected.

The DMR has its own President, Igor Smirnov (since 1991), and 43-member Council of Peoples'

Deputies. In the last presidential elections, held on Dec. 9, 2001, Smirnov received 81.9% of the vote. Elections to the Council of Peoples' Deputies were held on Dec 10, 2000. These elections were not generally considered to be either free or fair. Parties and opposition publications were banned just before the elections.

While the Communist Party of Moldova operates as a formal (and the only) opposition party in the DMR, its influence is limited.

Bloc of Patriotic Forces. The party of power in the DMR. The bloc has been under the leadership of Igor Smirnov (President of DMR) since its inception, in 1990. Bloc member, Grigori Marakusa, was "re-elected" chair of the Supreme Soviet in 2000 – a position he has also held since 1990.

Monaco

Capital: Monaco-Ville
Population: 32,270 (2004E)

The Principality of Monaco is a hereditary constitutional monarchy dating from the 13th century in which constitutional limitations on the monarch's powers have been in force since 1911. Under a treaty signed in 1918 the French Republic provides limited protection over Monaco. The treaty establishes that Monegasque policy is aligned with French political, military and economic interests. Since then, the relations between the sovereign states of France and Monaco have been further defined in the Treaty of 1945 and the Agreement of 1963. A new revised treaty is expected to enter into force in 2004. Under the terms of the new treaty France would assist Monaco in joining the Council of Europe as a full member, and would upgrade its representation in Monaco from consulate general to that of an embassy; permit, for the first time, other countries to accredit ambassadors to Monaco; and formally recognize the succession scheme set out in the 1962 constitution, which extends eligibility to the Prince's daughters and other family members.

The 1962 constitution of Monaco vests executive authority in the Prince – since 1949, Rainier III - who governs through a Minister of State selected from a list of three French civil servants submitted by the French government, assisted by government councillors and palace personnel. Legislative authority is vested in the Prince and the National Council (*Conseil National*) of 24 members, who are elected by citizens aged 21 and over for a five-year term. Sixteen members are elected by majority system and eight by proportional representation. There are no formal political parties in Monaco, although informal groupings have been formed to contest recent elections. In National Council elections on Feb. 1 and 8, 1998, the National and Democratic Union (UND) won all seats. In the Feb 9, 2003, elections to the National Council, the electoral alliance Union for Monaco (*Union pour Monaco*) won 58.5 % of the vote and 21 of the 24 seats, while the National and Democratic Union (*Union Nationale et Démocratique*, UND) secured 41.5% of the vote and 3 seats.

National and Democratic Union (*Union Nationale et Démocratique*, UND), formed in 1962 as a merger of the National Union of Independents (*Union Nationale des Indépendants*) and the National Democratic Entente (*Entente*

Nationale Démocratique). It won all 18 National Council seats in the elections of 1968, 1978, 1983 and 1988, before being superseded by more politically focused lists in 1993. In 1998 it again won all 18 seats, but in 2003 won only three.

Union for Monaco (*Union pour Monaco*, UM) is a political platform between the National Union for the Future of Monaco (*Union Nationale pour l'Avenir de Monaco*, UNAM) and Rally for the Monegasque family (*Rassemblement pour la famille monégasque*, RFM).

Mongolia

Capital: Ulan Bator
Population: 2,382,500 (2000)

Mongolia was, prior to January 1992, called the Mongolian People's Republic (MPR). The MPR had been proclaimed in the Constitution adopted in November 1924 by the first Great *Hural* (national assembly), following the decision of the (communist) Mongolian People's Revolutionary Party (MPRP) to pursue "non-capitalist development", making the country the first Soviet satellite.

The collapse of communist regimes abroad and the growth of the popular democratic movement at home forced the old MPRP leaders out of office in March 1990 and obliged the new ones to give up the MPRP's monopoly of power. In April the People's Great *Hural* voted to remove from the preamble of the 1960 Constitution the passage defining the MPRP's role as the "guiding and directing force of society and the state". In May it passed a law legalizing political parties, and amended the 1960 Constitution to institute the post of President and set up a 50-member standing legislature called the State Little *Hural*. The MPRP, having secured victory in the first multi-party elections in July 1990, was awarded 31 seats in the State Little *Hural* on the basis of proportional representation.

In February 1992 a new constitution entered into force, emphasizing human and civil rights and permitting all forms of ownership. It proclaimed Mongolia an independent sovereign republic with a directly elected legislature and directly elected President. The members of the unicameral 76-seat Mongolian Great *Hural* are elected for a four-year term by all citizens over 18 years of age. The majority party in the Great *Hural* nominates the Prime Minister (the head of government), whose appointment is supported by the President and approved by the Great *Hural*. The Prime Minister nominates his Cabinet, whose members are approved by the Great *Hural* individually.

The Great *Hural* elections on June 28, 1992 were won by the MPRP with 71 seats. Four years later, however, elections on June 30, 1996, resulted in the defeat of the MPRP by the Mongolian National Democratic Party (MNDP) and Mongolian Social Democratic Party (MSDP), whose Democratic Alliance won 50 seats, but left the MPRP with sufficient seats to prevent the Democratic Alliance forming a quorum. At the next elections on July 2, 2000, the MPRP returned to power, winning 72 of the 76 seats in the *Hural*. Three parties (the newly formed Civil Will Party, the MNDP and the Mongolian Democratic New Socialist Party, MDNSP) won one seat each with the remaining seat going to a non-partisan. In December 2000 several opposition parties, including the MNDP and the MSDP, merged to form the Democratic Party.

The first direct presidential election was held on June 6, 1993, resulting in victory for the incumbent, Punsalmaagiyn Ochirbat, who received 57.8% of the vote, defeating the MPRP candidate, Lodongiyn Tudev. Ochirbat had been elected President by the People's Great *Hural* in 1990 as a representative of the ruling MPRP, but was rejected by the MPRP in April 1993 and adopted by the opposition. In the second presidential election, held on May 18, 1997, President Ochirbat was beaten by the MPRP candidate, Natsagiyn Bagabandi, who received 60.8% of the vote.

The third presidential election, held on May 20, 2001, resulted in victory for President Bagabandi, who took 57.9% of the vote. Radnaasumbereliyn Gonchigdorj, standing for the Democratic Party, took 36.6% of the vote and Luvsandambyn Dashnyam, candidate of the Civil Will Party, 3.6%.

For the parliamentary elections of June 27, 2004, the ruling MPRP was opposed by a coalition of three opposition parties, the Motherland Democratic Coalition, comprising the Democratic Party (DP), the MDNSP and the Civil Will Party (CWP). The coalition allocated seats to be fought in the election on the basis of 51 to the DP, 20 to the MDNSP and 5 to the CWP. The MPRP's parliamentary strength was reduced to 36, while the coalition took 34 seats; one seat was won by the Mongolian Republican Party leader while others were won by non-partisans or disputed. After two months of deadlock, the coalition parties and the MPRP in August 2004 went on to form a "grand coalition government", with Tsakhiagiyn Elbegdorj of the Democratic Party becoming Prime Minister.

As of mid-2004 there were reported to be some 20 political parties in Mongolia and the 2004 election was contested by 10 parties, including the three in the Motherland Democratic Coalition. The handover of power at successive elections has been contrasted with the rigidity seen elsewhere in inner Asia.

Civil Will Party (CWP)
Address. Post Office Box 49, Ulan Bator 13
Telephone. (976–11) 312649
Fax. (976–11) 328243
Leadership. Sanjaasurengiyn Oyuun (president)
The Civil Will Party (alternatively known by variations including Civic Will Party, Civil Courage Party, Citizens' Will Party, Civil Will-Republican Party) was created in March 2000 by dissident Mongolian Great *Hural* members of the Mongolian National Democratic Party, led by Sanjaasurengiyn Oyuun, sister of Sanjaasurengiyn Zorig, the Minister of Infrastructure Development murdered in 1998, one of the founders of Mongolia's democracy movement. Oyuun was the CWP's only member of the Mongolian Great *Hural* elected in July 2000. In November 2000 the For Mongolia Party and the Regional Development Party merged with the party, whose May 2001 presidential candidate, Luvsandambyn Dashnyam, took 3.6% of the vote. For the June 2004 elections, the party competed as part of the Motherland Democratic Coalition.

Democratic Party (DP)
Address. Chingisiyn Orgon Choloo 1, Ulan Bator
Telephone. (976–11) 324221
Fax. (976–11) 325170
Email. mndp@mongol.net
Website. www.demparty.mn
Leadership. Dambyn Dorligjav (chairman)
The DP was created in December 2000 on the amalgamation of five parties, the Mongolian National Democratic Party (MNDP), Mongolian Social Democratic Party (MSDP),

Mongolian Democratic Party (MDP), Mongolian Democratic Renewal Party (MDRP), and the Mongolian Believers' Democratic Party (MBDP). The DP National Advisory Council comprises two members representing each of the 76 Mongolian Great *Hural* constituencies, plus former party leaders and prime ministers, and has standing committees on policy issues similar to those of the Great *Hural*. The DP had only two members in the Mongolian Great *Hural* elected in July 2000: ex-Prime Minister Janlavyn Narantsatsralt, who stood for the MNDP, and Lamjavyn Gundalay, who was an independent but joined the DP. Radnaasumbereliyn Gonchigdorj, the DP's presidential candidate in May 2001, came second with 36.6% of the vote. In the June 2004 elections the DP competed as part of the Motherland Democratic Coalition, which took 34 of the 76 seats in the Great *Hural*. The post-election deadlock was ended with the formation of a coalition government, including both the MPRP and the Motherland Democratic Coalition parties. Tsakhiagiyn Elbegdorj of the DP became Prime Minister, a position he had previously held for a period in 1998.

The DP is an associate member of the International Democrat Union.

Mongolian Democratic New Socialist Party (MDNSP)

Address. Post Office Box 44, Ulan Bator 49
Telephone. (976–11) 453176
Fax. (976–11) 453178
Leadership. Badarchiyn Erdenebat (chairman)
The MDNSP was founded in December 1998 by Badarchiyn Erdenebat, a businessman, founder of the Erel company. Erdenebat was the party's only member of the Mongolian Great *Hural* elected in July 2000. After the election, the MDNSP tended to support the Mongolian People's Revolutionary Party, backing its nominee for the 2001 presidential election. However, it formed part of the Motherland Democratic Coalition for the 2004 elections.

Mongolian People's Revolutionary Party (MPRP)

Address. Baga Toyruu 37, Ulan Bator 11
Telephone. (976–11) 323245
Fax. (976–11) 320368
Website. www.mprp.mn
Leadership. Nambaryn Enhbayar (chairman)
Founded in 1921 as the Mongolian People's Party, the MPRP was the country's only authorized political formation from 1924 until 1990. During that time it was organized along communist lines with a tightly centralized structure, its policies reflecting its close links with the Comintern and Soviet Communist Party. In March 1990, the ruling MPRP Politburo headed by Jambyn Batmonh were replaced by new leaders headed by the former trade union chairman Gombojavyn Ochirbat. In April an extraordinary MPRP congress approved separation of the powers of party and state, and the first multi-party elections were held in July, which the MPRP won.

Following the adoption of the country's new Constitution in February 1992, the MPRP adopted a new programme in which it redefined itself as a parliamentary party standing for national democracy and pledged to implement the Constitution. Aiming for continuity, it abandoned "outdated" Marxist-Leninist concepts, but promised to build "humane socialism" in Mongolia. On this basis it won the multi-party elections of June 1992. The party lost office in the elections of June 1996 but returned to power in July 2000, winning 72 of the 76 seats in the Great *Hural*. Former party chairman Natsagiyn Bagabandi was elected President of Mongolia in 1997 and re-elected in May 2001.

The party chairman, Nambaryn Enhbayar, an avowed admirer of the "third way" policies of British Prime Minister Tony Blair, served as Prime Minister from 2000 until the 2004 elections, when the MPRP unexpectedly slumped to 36 seats (although remaining the largest party), with 46.5% of the vote. The MPRP initially refused to accept the results of the polls and boycotted parliament, but in August 2004 agreed to form a coalition government with a Democratic Party Prime Minister. Nambaryn Enhbayar became Speaker of Parliament.

The MPRP has observer status with the Socialist International.

Other Parties

Mongolian Green Party, organized in 1990 as the political wing of the Mongolian Alliance of Greens. For the July 2000 election the party was in an unsuccessful alliance with the Civil Will Party, and in January 2001 its chairman, Davaagiyn Basandorj, signed a long-term electoral cooperation agreement with the Democratic Party. The party stood independently in the 2004 elections but did not win a seat.

Mongolian Republican Party, formed in 1997 on the basis of the Mongolian Capitalists' Party under the chairmanship of Bazarsadyn Jargalsayhan, a businessman, founder of the Buyan company. Having failed to win any seats in the July 2000 election, in 2002 the party was reported as having merged with the Civil Will Party, but in the 2004 elections Jargalsayhan won a seat under the Republican Party banner on a platform calling for reform of the financial system and the extension of home ownership.

Morocco

Capital: Rabat
Population: 31,689,265 (July 2003E)

The Kingdom of Morocco was established in 1957 (the former French and Spanish protectorates having joined together as an independent sultanate the previous year). It became a constitutional monarchy under the 1962 constitution, with the Prime Minister and Cabinet appointed by the King. Mohammed VI ascended the throne in July 1999, following the death of his father, King Hassan II.

A national referendum held in September 1996 approved constitutional amendments providing for freedom of expression and press, and the introduction of a bicameral legislature. This latter institution comprises a 325-member Assembly of Representatives (*Majlis al-Nuwab*), the lower house, elected for a five year term by popular vote in multi-seat constituencies; and a 270-member Assembly of Councillors (*Majlis al-Mustasharin*), elected for a nine year term by local councils (162 seats), professional chambers (91 seats) and wage-earners (27 seats).

Elections to the Assembly of Representatives were held in November 1997. The opposition left-nationalist *Koutla* group of parties won 102 of the 325 seats, of which 57 went to the country's largest left-wing party, the Socialist Union of Popular Forces (USFP). The nationalist Independence Party (*Istiqlal*), the other major *Koutla* partner, won 32 seats, compared with the 51 that it had held in the outgoing legislature. The pro-government, right-wing, *Wifaq* grouping secured 100 seats, of which a half were won by the Constitutional Union (UC). A number of centre parties won 97 seats between them. Opposition forces alleged widespread fraud and vote-rigging.

Indirect elections were held to the Assembly of Councillors in December 1997. The pro-government *Wifaq* bloc and the centre parties emerged as clear winners, gaining a total of 166 seats. The opposition left-nationalist *Koutla* bloc won only 44 seats. In early 1998 Abderrahmane el-Yousifi, veteran leader of the USFP, was appointed as the new Prime Minister. Described as Morocco's first "opposition-led" government, Yousifi's Cabinet comprised ministers from the *Koutla* bloc (the USFP, *Istiqlal*, and the Party of Renewal and Progress), centre parties (the National Rally of Independents and the National Popular Movement), the Front of Democratic Forces, the Socialist Democratic Party (PSD) and a number of independents.

Elections to the Assembly of Councillors were held on Sept. 15, 2000. Elections to the Chamber of Representatives were held on Sept. 27, 2002, and saw a 51.6% turnout. The USA and France praised the election for being more fair and transparent than the previous 1997 poll. In all, 26 parties vied for election, of which 22 won seats. The USFP retained its first place, albeit with a reduced tally of 50 seats. Next-placed were *Istiqlal* with 48 seats; Justice and Development (PJD) with 43; and National Rally (RNI) 41. Three conservative parties took fifth, sixth and seventh place respectively: the Popular Movement (MP) with 27, the National Popular Movement (MNP) 18, and Constitutional Movement (UC) 16.

Prior to the elections, womens' associations got the political establishment to accept the notion of a 10% quota reserved for women, determined at 30 seats. In the event, 34 women were elected, by stark contrast with the 1997 poll, when only two female MPs won seats. Egypt's *Al Ahram* newspaper reported this as a "major first in the Arab world". Another notable feature of the 2002 elections was the dramatic emergence of the moderate Islamist PJD as chief opposition. However, the PJD was evidently embarrassed by the suicide attacks by Islamist extremists in May 2003, which saw 45 die in Casablanca. This explains the reticence of Islamist parties to participate in Morocco's municipal elections in September 2003: the PJD put up only 3% of the candidates and contested only 18% of the 23,689 local constituencies.

These elections were considered a victory for the two largest mainstream parties. *Istiqlal* came slightly ahead of the USFP, winning 3,890 seats to the latter's 3,373. Between them, the USFP and Istiqlal won 30% of the seats. On Dec. 10, 2002, King Mohammed VI had reduced the lower voting age from 20 to 18, so the number of newly registered electors reached 1.5 million. In all 122,069 candidates ran for local councils, of whom 31% were aged 34 or less. For the first time Moroccans elected councils for the country's six big cities, Casablanca, Fez, Marrakesh, Rabat, Salé and Tangiers. The Interior Minister, Mostapha Sahel, hailed the election as "an important step in the democratization of the country". However, the turnout, estimated at 54% of the 14.6 million registered voters, was well down on the 75.1% of the previous local elections, held in June 1997. A total of 127 women were elected in these local polls – more than the 83 elected in 1997, but still a small percentage of the 6,024 women who stood for election.

Driss Jettou, a non-party appointee, business-minded technocrat, and until then Interior Minister, had replaced Yousifi as Prime Minister on Oct. 9, 2002. His government includes a woman minister, Yasima Baddu. Following the bombings in Casablanca, his government began a rapid programme of improving amenities, electrification and transport links in urban shanty towns, from which many of the bombers came, including Sidi Moumen in Casablanca itself. According to one analysis, it was fear of the growth of the Islamist Justice Party that led to Jettou's decision to postpone local and chambers of commerce elections from June to September 2003.

In July 2003 King Mohammed VI explicitly warned Moroccans that "there is no place for political parties that monopolise Islam… or use it as a springboard for ambitions of rule". Apart from the battle against terrorism, and the conditions which arguably contribute to the phenomenon, the government is also concerned about inherited economic disparities, evidenced in statistics from 2000 showing that more than half the population was illiterate (and 70% of women), two-thirds had no access to drinking water, 87% lacked electricity and 93% enjoyed no medical care.

Other issues include women's rights, illegal immigration and curbing the power of the *makhzen*, the clique that traditionally surrounds the throne and apparently still takes the major decisions. The government is also trying to meet demands for Berber cultural recognition; estimates suggest that Berbers constitute at least 30% of the population, yet feel sidelined by Arabic speakers.

Action Party
Parti de l'Action (PA)
Address. 113 Avenue Allal ben Abdellah, Rabat
Telephone. (212–7) 206661
Leadership. Mohammed el-Idrissi (national secretary)
This is a liberal party, formed in 1974 to advocate democracy and progress. The PA contested the 1997 legislative elections, winning two seats in the lower house and 13 seats in the upper house. The party did not join the ruling coalition formed in 1998, and appeared not to have won any seats in 2002.

Constitutional Union
Union Constitutionelle (UC)
Address. 158 Avenue des FAR, Casablanca
Telephone. (212–2) 313630
Fax. (212–2) 441141
Leadership. Mohammed Abied (interim leader)
Founded in 1983 and supporting the constitutional status quo, the centre-right UC became the dominant element in the government coalition formed after the 1984 elections, participating in the National Entente of pro-government parties. Its president was Maati Bouabid, a former Prime Minister. In the 1993 parliamentary elections the party's representation in the legislature fell significantly to 54 seats. The UC contested the 1997 elections as the main member of the pro-government, right-wing *Wifaq* group. It secured 50 seats in the lower chamber and took third place with 28 seats in the upper chamber. After the elections the UC became the main opposition party. It won 16 seats (two held by women) in the 2002 House of Representatives elections, and 4.92% of the popular vote. The UC won just over 4% of the seats and popular vote in the House of Councillors elections in 2003. Its relative decline may be ascribed to it being outflanked by Islamists amongst conservative voters, and the recent favour shown by the monarchy towards the socialist USFP.

Democratic and Social Movement
Mouvement Démocratique et Social (MDS)
Address. 471 Avenue Mohamed V, Rabat
Telephone. (212–7) 709110

Leadership. Mahmoud Archane (secretary-general)
Formed in 1996, the centrist MDS performed well in the 1997 elections, winning 32 seats in the lower house and 33 seats in the upper house, the *Majlis al-Mustashirin*. In the latter poll the MDS took second place to the National Rally of Independents. The party did not join the coalition government led by Abderrahmane el-Yousifi, leader of the Socialist Union of Popular Forces (USFP), and is a member of the opposition. Since 1997 its fortunes appear to have waned, as it won only seven seats in the 2002 House of Representatives elections. MDS member Abdesammad Archane was elected president of the provincial council of Khémisset in the September 2003 local polls.

Democratic Party for Independence
Parti Démocratique pour l'Indépendance (PDI)

Address. c/o Chambre des Représentants, B.P. 432, Rabat
Leadership. Thami el-Ouazzani (leader)
Established in the 1940s, this small party won nine seats in 1993, and contested the 1997 legislative elections, winning one seat in the lower house and four seats in the upper house. The party was not a member of the ruling coalition. In the September 2002 election for the House of Representatives, the PDI won two seats and 0.62% of the popular vote. Its fortunes declined somewhat in local elections a year later, when it won 96 seats and 0.42% of the popular vote.

Democratic Union
Union Démocratique (UD)

Leadership. Bouazza Ikken (leader)
The UD won 10 seats in the September 2002 House of Representatives elections, and 3.08% of the popular vote, taking 11th place. It markedly improved its performance in the October 2003 Assembly of Councillors elections, taking fifth place, with 90% of its candidates winning their seats. In all, the UD won 1,515 seats and 6.6% of the popular vote. The UD is a central player in a bloc of parties, known as the Popular Movement, which also includes the MP, MNP and UDS. There was talk of formalizing the bloc into an electoral federation, especially at the local or municipal level. Ikken is determined to highlight the needs of the estimated 53% of Moroccans who are still illiterate.

Front of Democratic Forces
Parti du Front des Forces Démocratiques (FFD)

Address. 13 Bld Tarik Ibnou Ziad, Rabat
Telephone. (212–7) 661623
Leadership. Thami Khyari (secretary-general)
Formed in 1997, the FFD contested the legislative elections held at the end of that year, winning nine seats in the Assembly of Representatives (the lower house) and 12 seats in the Assembly of Councillors (the upper house). The FFD subsequently joined the ruling coalition headed by Abderrahmane el-Yousifi, leader of the Socialist Union of Popular Forces (USFP), and the party secretary general (Thami Khyari) has served as Minister Delegate for Fisheries and Minister of Health. The FFD won 12 seats (two held by women) in the 2002 House of Representatives elections, and 3.69% of the popular vote.

Independence Party
Parti de l'Istiqlal (Istiqlal)

Address. 4 Avenue Ibn Toumert, Bab El Had, Rabat
Telephone. (212–7) 730951
Fax. (212–7) 725354
Leadership. Abbas El Fassi (secretary-general)
The party was founded in 1943 and was the leading political force prior to Moroccan independence. Originally nationalist in orientation, and a firm supporter of the monarchy, it has adopted a reformist and critical stance, stressing the need for better living standards and equal rights for all Moroccans. It also takes the strongest pan-Arabist stance of all major parties.

A member of the left-nationalist *Koutla* group of parties, *Istiqlal* won 50 seats in elections to the Assembly of Representatives elections in 1993. In subsequent elections in November 1997 it won 32 seats; and 21 seats in indirect elections to the upper house (the Assembly of Councillors) held the following month. This latter disappointing result suggested a partial switch in support away from the *Istiqlal* by the monarchy. The party nonetheless joined the coalition government formed in early 1998 by Socialist Union of Popular Forces (USFP) leader Abderrahmane el-Yousifi.

The party took second place to the USFP in the 2002 House of Representatives elections, with 48 seats (two less than the USFP) and 14.77% of the popular vote. Four of the 48 are women. One successful candidate, a lawyer, Yasima Baddu, was subsequently appointed as Morocco's first female full minister. Her portfolio, Minister of Family Affairs, is new, and represents an attempt to address the hitherto neglected concerns of women and children. Meanwhile, Abass El Fassi had replaced Mohammed Boucetta as party secretary-general.

Istiqlal narrowly squeezed out its rival, the USFP, to take first place in the September 2003 local elections. It won 16.96% of the seats, or 3,890, to the USPF's 14.7%. In these polls the *Istiqlal* candidate, Mohammed El Yamani, was elected as president of the prefectoral council of Fes, Mohammed El Mrani was elected president of the provincial council of Taza, Mohammed Larbi Benchlika was elected president of the municipal council of Kelaât Sraghna, and Abdelaziz Abba was elected president of the communal council of Boujdour. The party's French language newspaper is called *L'Opinion*.

Justice and Charity Group
Jama'at al-'Adl wal-Ihsan

Leadership. Sheikh Abdessalam Yassin (spiritual leader)
Al-'Adl is a growing force in Moroccan politics, although it appears wary of participating in the mainstream. Currently the party is banned. Its venerated spiritual leader, Sheikh Abdessalam Yassin, was only released after ten years in prison in May 1999. An Islamist movement, it boycotted the 2002 House of Representatives elections, by contrast with the more centrist religious party, the Justice and Development Party. *Al-'Adl* is best known for its extensive welfare infrastructure for Morocco's poor.

The group is on record as opposing the existence of political parties, and denying the Islamic legitimacy of Morocco's Alawite monarchy (which claims descent from the House of the Prophet Mohammed). On both these issues, *Al-'Adl* stands at variance with the Justice and Development Party; although in most other respects their ideologies seem virtually indistinguishable. Yassin was particularly antigonistic towards the late King Hassan, whom he accused of gross corruption and of skewing his policies according to the bidding of the *makhzen*, or traditional cronies. He has spoken more affectionately about Hassan's son and successor, Mohammed VI, whom he dubs "Prince Charming". Yassin's group made much capital over its opposition to government plans to reform the status of Moroccan women. In foreign matters, Yassin showed some sympathy for the global Islamist movement, including its more militant branch, responsible for the Sept. 11 atrocities in the USA. Since the May 2003 bombings in Casablanca, however, the group has tried to distance itself from terrorism. Yassin remains militantly anti-Zionist and has spoken out against Moroccan Jews who are close to the monarchy; the group organized the largest demonstrations in the Middle East against Israeli actions during the Al Aqsa Intifada.

Justice and Development Party
Hizb al-Adala wal-Tanmiyya
Parti du Justice et Développement (PJD)
Address. 352 Bld Mohamed V, Rabat
Telephone. (212–7) 734601
Leadership. Dr Abdelkarim Khatib (secretary-general); Mustapha Rashid (president); Saad Eddine Othmani (deputy secretary-general)
Formed in 1999 as a breakaway from, and effectively a successor to, the Constitutional and Democratic Popular Movement (*Mouvement Populaire Constitutionnel et Démocratique*, or MPCD), the PJD supports a polity based on sharia (traditional Muslim law), and advocates a total ban on alcohol, gender segregated beaches and the establishment of Islamic banking. The PJD took third place in the September 2002 legislative polls with 43 seats, and almost 13% of the popular vote. This was its first election in its new incarnation. The PJD trebled the previous MPCD tally and became the chief opposition force in the kingdom.

The moderate Islamist MPCD was formed in the late 1960s as a breakaway group from the Popular Movement. In the 1997 legislative elections the party won nine seats in the lower chamber, the Assembly of Representatives. Its total was later reported as 14 (possibly the result of defections to the MPCD from other parties). The MPCD did not join the coalition government led by Abderrahmane el-Yousifi, leader of the Socialist Union of Popular Forces (USFP), and became a member of the opposition. In May 1999 MPCD member Abdelilah Ben Kirane won a seat in the Assembly of Representatives in a by-election at Sale, near the capital, Rabat. Ben Kirane defeated the candidate of the USFP, the dominant member of the ruling coalition. Ben Kirane was regarded as a firebrand from Morocco's Islamist youth movement in the 1970s, and his victory sent shock waves through the political establishment. He subsequently left to form the much more successful PJD.

In its new guise, the PJD had already made its presence felt on Dec. 12, 1999, when it helped to lead mass demonstrations against government plans to changes women's status. Hence some liberals were surprised when the PJD fielded numerous female candidates; indeed, four of its 42 elected representatives in 2002 were women. Independent observers suggested that the PJD would have gained more seats had there not been tampering with results at the counting stage of the elections. According to Ben Kirane, the PJD was prepared to enter a conservative *Istiqlal*-led government, but their antipathy towards the USFP's socialist ethos led to them becoming the head of the opposition. Rejecting claims that the PJD was extremist, Ben Kirane added that: "We do not want to apply what is inapplicable. We merely want to protect what is there".

The PJD did considerably worse in municipal and local elections, held in late 2003; it was loath to contest many seats, and this was ascribed to its wariness after it was condemned – quite unfairly, it felt – following the suicide bombings in Casablanca that May. Explaining the PJD's caution, its deputy secretary-general Othmani said: "It's a political decision because of the huge fears that an Islamist reference now sparks here and abroad. May 16 has confused things [regarding] the perception of Islamists. We don't want Morocco to become like Algeria".

The PJD contested only 18% of the 23,689 local constituencies, and put up just 3% of all candidates. Overall, it took 11th place out of 26 parties with a tally of only 593, or 2.6% of the total seats available. The party concentrated its forces on Morocco's six largest cities, where many of its typically younger and poorer voters live. Significantly, perhaps, it took a close third place to the two big parties in the first-ever council elections in Casablanca.

National Democratic Party
Parti National Démocrate (PND)
Address. 18 rue de Tunis, Hassan, Rabat
Telephone. (212–7) 732127
Fax. (212–7) 720170
Leadership. Abdallah Kadiri (secretary-general)
The PND, established in 1981 by disaffected members of the National Rally of Independents, was one of the smaller parties in the centre-right coalition government formed after the 1984 parliamentary elections. As a National Entente party, it maintained its legislative representation in the 1993 elections, winning 24 seats. The PND contested the 1997 elections as a member of the pro-government, right-wing *Wifaq* group (alongside the Constitutional Union and the Popular Movement) and secured 10 seats in the lower chamber and 21 seats in the upper chamber. After the elections the PND became an opposition party. The PND, which is principally based in rural areas, won 12 seats (two held by women) and 3.69% of the popular vote in the 2002 House of Representatives elections. By the end of 2003 Abdallah Kadiri had replaced Mohammed Arsalane al-Jadidi as the party's secretary general.

National Popular Movement
Mouvement National Populaire (MNP)
Address. Avenue Imam Malik, Rue El Madani Belhoussni, Souissi Rabat
Telephone. (212–7) 753623
Fax. (212–7) 759761
Leadership. Mahjoubi Aherdane (leader)
The National Popular Movement was set up in 1991 by Mahjoubi Aherdane, former leader of the Popular Movement. Contesting the 1993 elections as a National Entente party, the MNP won 25 seats in the legislature. In the 1997 legislative elections, the party won 19 seats in the lower house and 15 seats in the upper house. The party is considered conservative in its views. It joined the coalition government of Abderrahmane el-Yousifi formed in early 1998 and was given a small number of portfolios. In the 2002 House of Representatives elections the MNP won 18 seats (two held by women) and 5.54% of the popular vote. MNP member Abdelkebir Berkia was re-elected president of the region Rabat-Salé-Zemmour-Zaër in September 2003 local elections, in which the MNP improved its stature, gaining 1,406 seats and 6.13% of the popular vote.

National Rally of Independents
Rassemblement National des Indépendants (RNI)
Address. 6, Rue Laos, Avenue Hassan II, Rabat
Telephone. (212–7) 721420
Fax. (212–7) 733824
Leadership. Ahmed Osman (president)
Essentially a political vehicle for the late King Hassan, the royalist RNI was established in 1978 to give cohesion to the group of independents which was then numerically dominant in the legislature. Its leader and founder was then Prime Minister Ahmed Osman; he still leads the party today. Even after a number of independents had defected to the National Democratic Party in 1981, the RNI emerged as the second strongest party after the 1984 legislative elections, continuing its government participation. Its parliamentary representation fell to 41 seats in the 1993 elections, but in elections to the House of Representatives (the lower house of the newly-created bicameral legislature) held in November 1997, the party won 46 seats. The RNI emerged as the largest party (with 42 seats) in the new second chamber, the House of Representatives, indirectly elected in December 1997. In early 1998 the party joined the coalition government led by Abderrahmane el-Yousifi, leader of the Socialist Union of Popular Forces.

The RNI, now considered a centre-left party, took fourth place in the 2002 House of Representatives elections with 41 seats (four held by women) and 12.62% of the popular vote. It rose to third place in the September 2003 local elections, winning 10.97% of the available seats. RNI member Taeib Rhafes was elected president of the Eastern Region in the 2003 local elections; another RNI member, Omar Bouaida, was re-elected president of the council for the region Guelmim-Smara, and Ali El Mziliqui was voted president of the provincial council of Tantan.

Organization of Democratic and Popular Action
Organisation de l' Action Démocratique et Populaire (OADP)

Address. 29 Avenue Lalla Yacout, Appt No 1, BP 15797, Casablanca

Telephone/Fax. (212–2) 278442

Leadership. Ait Idder Mohamed Ben Said (secretary-general)
The left-wing OADP was formed in 1983. Although the party contested the 1997 legislative elections as a member of the left-nationalist *Koutla* group, winning four seats in the lower assembly, the House of Representatives, it did not join the coalition government led by Abderrahmane el-Yousifi, leader of the Socialist Union of Popular Forces. The OADP backed radical leftist domestic policies, though supports Morocco's claim to Western Sahara. It does not appear to have been active of late.

Party of Renewal and Progress
Parti du Renouveau et du Progrès (PRP)

Address. 4 Rue ibn Zakour, Quartier des Oranges, Rabat

Telephone. (212–7) 208672

Fax. (212–7) 208674

Leadership. Ismail Alaoui (secretary-general)
Recognized in 1974 (as the Party of Progress and Socialism, until it changed its name in 1994), the party was the successor to the banned Moroccan Communist Party. It advocates nationalization and democracy as part of its left-wing orientation, and joined in the formation of the opposition Democratic Bloc in 1992. It draws most support from urban centres and disaffected youth. The party contested the 1997 legislative elections as part of the left-nationalist *Koutla* group (alongside the Socialist Union of Popular Forces (USPF), the Independence Party and the Organization of Democratic and Popular Action) and gained nine seats in the lower house and seven seats in the upper house. In early 1998 the party joined the coalition government led by Abderrahmane el-Yousifi, leader of the USPF. The PRP leader, Ismail Alaoui – who had replaced Ali Yata, was appointed as Minister of National Education; he was shifted to Agriculture in a reshuffle carried out in September 2000.

The party won 11 seats (two held by women) in the 2002 House of Representatives elections, and 3.38% of the popular vote. Its fortunes improved slightly a year later, when the PRP won 1,207 municipal seats on more than 5% of the popular vote. According to some sources it campaigned under its pre-1994 name in both the 2002 and 2003 polls. The prominent feminist, Nouzha Skalli Benis, is affiliated to the PRP.

Popular Movement
Mouvement Populaire (MP)

Address. 66 Rue Patrice Lumumba, Rabat

Telephone. (212–7) 767320

Fax. (212–7) 767537

Leadership. Mohammed Laensar (secretary-general)
The centre-right MP was set up in 1957, its support coming principally from the Berber population. It has been a participant in government coalitions from the early 1960s. The party's founder, Mahjoubi Aherdane, was ousted as MP secretary general in 1986 and later set up the breakaway National Popular Movement. Contesting the 1997 elections as a member of the right-wing *Wifaq* bloc, the MP secured 40 seats in the Assembly of Representatives (the lower house) and 27 seats in the Assembly of Councillors (the upper house). The MP did not join the coalition government formed after the elections and is a member of the opposition. It subsequently won 27 seats (two held by women) in the 2002 Assembly of Representatives elections, and 8.31% of the popular vote.

Berber issues are rising to the fore under the Mohammed VI monarchy, especially amongst the Amazigh, speakers of the Tamazight language. Amazigh activists issued a "Berber Manifesto" in March 2000, in response to which the king issued a royal decree, on Oct. 17, 2001, promising a "Royal Institute of Berber Culture". Ultimately this body may help introduce Berber languages and cultures into school curricula. Matters are complicated by the phenomenon of Islamists and religious conservatives – themselves an increasingly vocal public sector – who express hostility towards Berbers, seeing ancient Berber patrimony as somehow "anti-Islamic".

According to one source, the MP had split into three groups (see under Democratic Union). The MP itself took fourth place in the September 2003 local elections, with 2,248 seats, on 9.8% of the popular vote. The total percentage of seats taken by parties regarded as belonging to the broader Popular Movement bloc amounted to an impressive 22% of all available seats.

Reform and Development
Parti de Réforme et Développement (PRD)

Leadership. Abderrahmane El Cohen (leader)
Formed in June 2001 by former members of the National Rally of Independents, it is led by Abderrahmane El Cohen, of Jewish origin, and won three seats in the September 2002 elections. Shortly afterwards the party, which enjoys most support in the rural and more sparsely populated Moroccan south, launched its own Arab language newspaper.

Socialist Democratic Party
Parti Socialiste Démocratique (PSD)

Address. 43 Rue Abou Fariss Al Marini, Rabat

Telephone. (212–7) 208571

Fax. (212–7) 208573

Leadership. Aissa Ouardighi (secretary-general)
Founded in 1996, the PSD contested the 1997 legislative elections and won five seats in the Assembly of Representatives (the lower house) and four seats in the Assembly of Councillors (the upper house). In early 1998 the PSD joined the ruling coalition headed by Abderrahmane el-Yousifi, leader of the Socialist Union of Popular Forces (USFP). The PSD won six seats in the 2002 House of Representatives elections and 1.85% of the popular vote.

Socialist Union of Popular Forces
Union Socialiste des Forces Populaires (USFP)

Address. 17 rue Oued Souss, Agdal, Rabat

Telephone. (212–7) 773902

Fax. (212–7) 773901

Website. www.usfp.ma

Leadership. Abderrahmane el-Yousifi (first secretary); Mohammed el-Yazghi (deputy first secretary).
Originally the Rabat section of the National Union of Popular Forces, and temporarily suspended by the government in 1973, the party was formed separately with its current name the following year. The social democratic USFP has close links with the Democratic Confederation of Labour (CDT) trade union centre. The USFP fought elections to the Assembly of Representatives (the lower house of the bicameral legislature) held in November 1997 as part of the opposition left-nationalist *Koutla* group of parties. The *Koutla*

parties won 102 of the 325 seats, of which 57 went to the USFP. However, in indirect elections to the upper house (the Assembly of Councillors) held the following month, the USFP won only 16 of the 270 seats.

On Feb. 4, 1998, the veteran Tangiers-born lawyer and USFP leader, Abderrahmane el-Yousifi, was appointed Prime Minister at the head of a coalition government that included many USFP members. Yousifi had been imprisoned in 1959 for allegedly taking part in a plot against then Crown Prince Hassan. Sentenced to death in absentia – he lived in exile in Paris for many years during the 1970s – he received a royal pardon in 1980 and was allowed to return to Morocco. Yousifi replaced the long-serving Abderrahim Bouabid as the USFP first secretary on Jan. 8, 1992.

In power, he stressed the need to improve jail conditions and facilitate a freer press. He also drew attention to the "darker chapters" of Morocco's past history, sought to reform the administration and streamline tax collection, and attempted to renegotiate debts into investments via numerous visits to Spain, France and other Western countries. Yousifi committed his government to build low-income housing, to introduce a "national pact for employment" (at least a quarter of the population is unemployed), and to find a solution to the dispute over Western Sahara.

After Mohammed VI came to power, in 1999, Yousifi accelerated his plans to free detainees and welcome back exiles, most notably the veteran Marxist Abraham Sefarty and the family of the late Mehdi Ben Barka, who had been assassinated in Paris by Moroccan security agents during the 1960s. The King and Yousifi agreed to limit the wide and often draconian powers of Morocco's Interior Ministry, to the extent of ousting the powerful Interior Minister Driss Basri in November 1999. Yousifi also partly succeeded in reforming electoral and labour laws, assisted by his Finance Minister and the head of the USFP parliamentary faction, Fathallah Oualalou.

Even so, there were limits to Yousifi's willingness to reform, as evidenced by his temporary banning of three weekly papers for publishing an old letter that implicated opposition politicians (including Yousifi) in an abortive coup attempt against King Hassan II in the early 1970s. The centrepiece of Yousifi's legislation was to have been his "Plan of Action for Women's Integration and Development". It sought to reform the *Mudawwana*, or Code of Personal Status, based on Maliki Sunni Muslim law. The plan envisaged raising the age of marriage for girls; granting women a voice in divorce courts; giving women the right to half their husband's property after divorce; and cancelling guardianship and polygamy customs. However, on March 13, 2000, a massive public demonstration against the plan by Islamist groups – notably the Justice and Charity Group, and the Justice and Development Party – ensured that it was shelved.

One of Yousifi's last major acts was agreeing to the drafting of the terms to a US-Morocco Free Trade Agreement, in April 2002. Critics, though, chided Yousifi for not addressing with more vigour issues like rural poverty and inadequate education. He was also hampered by a cabinet that had to encompass seven ideologically diverse parties and by the power of the King, who personally controlled the key portfolios of justice, interior, foreign affairs, religious matters and defence.

Elections to the House of Representatives, held on Sept. 27, 2002, saw the USFP retain its first place, albeit with a reduced tally of 50 seats and 15.38% of the popular vote. Five of the 50 are women. In September 2003, however, the USFP's chief rival within the *Koutla* Bloc, the *Istiqlal* (Independence Party) narrowly overtook the USFP to take first place in municipal elections. *Istiqlal* won 16.96% of the seats to the USPF's 3,373, or 14.7 %.

Meanwhile, King Mohammed VI had replaced Yousifi with the non-party affiliated Driss Jettou as Prime Minister in October 2002. To some this represented a deliberate demotion of the USFP's national role. USFP representatives were nonetheless still represented in the cabinet; and one woman member, Nezha Chekrouni, a professor of linguistics from Meknes, was appointed a junior minister mandated to deal with the problems of Moroccans living abroad.

The USPF is an affiliate of the Socialist International; it projects an image of being like European social democratic parties, and enjoys support from organized labour, urban areas and youth groups.

Other Parties

In order of seats attained in the 2002 House of Representatives elections, are the following smaller parties, with seats tally in brackets: *Parti Al Ahd*, known as *Al Ahd* (Unity), led by its chairman, Najib El Ouazzani (5); *Alliance des Libertés* (Alliance of Liberties) ADL, led by Ali Belhaj (4); *Parti de la Gauche Socialiste Unifiée* (Party of the Unified Socialist Left) GSU, led by Mohammed Ben Said Ait Idder (3); *Parti Marocain Libéral* (Moroccan Liberal Party) PML, led by Mohammed Ziane (3); *Forces Citoyennes* (Citizens' Forces) FC, led by Abderrahman Lahjouji (2); *Parti de l'Environnement et du Développement* (Environment and Development Party) PED, led by Ahmed el-Alami (2); *Parti Démocratique et de l'Indépendance* (Democratic Party of Independence) PDI, led by Abdelwahed Maach (2); and *Parti du Congrès National Ittihadi* (National Congress Party *Ittihadi*–United) CNI, led by Abdelmajid Bouzoubaa (1).

In February 2004 it was announced that the Moroccan "extreme left" had organized itself in a bloc dubbed the G5. It consisted of the GSU (listed above); *Ennahj Addimocrati*, led by Abdellah El Harif; the Party of the Democratic and Socialist Vanguard (PADS, an offshoot of the Socialist Union of Popular Forces), led by Ahmed Benjelloun; the CNI (listed above); and Fidelity to Democracy. Analysts predicted that the front may develop into a single political party in the medium term, although certain political differences may be difficult to overcome. For instance, *Ennajh Addimocrati* still argues for "self-determination for the Saharawis", while the four other groups back a "political solution which does not question Moroccan sovereignty over the Sahara".

A number of other parties did not receive any seats in the 2002 legislative elections. These include: the Citizens' Initiatives for Development, led by Mohammed Benhamou; the National Union of Popular Forces, or UNFP, led by Abdellah Ibrahim – from which the Socialist Union of Socialist Forces broke away; the Party of Renewal and Equity, or PRE, led by Chakir Achabar; the Social Centre Party, or PSC, led by Lahcen Madih; and the Liberal Progressive Party, or PLP, led by Aknoush Ahmadou Belhaj, which backs individual freedoms and free enterprize.

In addition, a number of labour unions and other economic associations act as political pressure groups. Seats are reserved for trade unionists in elections to the House of Councillors; on Dec. 5, 1997, they won 27 out of the 270 seats. These groups include the Democratic Confederation of Labour, or CDT, led by Noubir Amaoui; the General Union of Moroccan Workers, or UGTM, led by Abderrazzak Afilal; the Moroccan Employers' Association, or CGEM, led by Hassan Chami; the National Labour Union of Morocco, or UNMT, led by Abdelslam Maati; and the Union of Moroccan Workers, or UMT, led by Mahjoub Benseddik.

Mozambique

Capital: Maputo
Population: 19,105,000 (2000E)

The Republic of Mozambique gained independence from Portugal in June 1975 after a 10-year armed struggle by the Front for the Liberation of Mozambique (FRELIMO). A one-party system was established with FRELIMO as the sole legal party, but a continuing rebellion was waged against the regime by the anti-communist Mozambique National Resistance (RENAMO). After FRELIMO had in 1989 abandoned Marxist-Leninist ideology in favour of democratic socialism, the following year a new constitution came into effect heralding a multi-party system, direct elections and a free market economy. Under the constitution, the President was to be elected by universal adult suffrage for a five-year period, and might be re-elected on only two consecutive occasions. Legislative authority was to be vested in the Assembly of the Republic (*Assembléia da República*), similarly elected for a five-year term.

Negotiations between the FRELIMO government and RENAMO to end the protracted civil war culminated in the signing of a peace accord in October 1992. Because of delays in the implementation of the peace plan, presidential and legislative elections did not take place until October 1994. These resulted in victory for incumbent President Joaquim Chissano and for FRELIMO, which won 129 of the 250 seats in the Assembly, against 112 for RENAMO and nine for the Democratic Union. Eleven of the 14 groups contesting the Assembly elections failed to win representation.

The presidential election held on Dec. 3–5, 1999, was won by the FRELIMO incumbent, Joaquim Chissano, who received 52.3% of the votes, as against 47.7% for the RENAMO leader, Afonso Dhlakama, whose candidacy was supported by an alliance of RENAMO with a group of opposition parties styled RENAMO–Electoral Union (RENAMO–UE). The RENAMO–UE alliance also presented a joint list of candidates in the December 1999 legislative election, in which FRELIMO won 133 Assembly seats with 48.5% of the vote, while RENAMO-UE won the remaining 117 seats with 38.8% of the vote. The validity of the 1999 election results (strongly challenged by RENAMO) was upheld by the Mozambique Supreme Court and by international monitors. Opposition members took up their seats in the new Assembly but boycotted its proceedings to protest against the election results. The RENAMO–UE coalition continued to function as a single opposition bloc, within which RENAMO itself reportedly had 99 seats and its junior partners 18 seats.

Municipal elections for 33 localities were held on Nov. 19, 2003, the first to have the participation of RENAMO, which had boycotted the previous ones. FRELIMO won 28 municipalities, RENAMO 4, mainly coastal cities, and the two parties shared one municipality. There was some controversy over the results, with accusations of electoral fraud (especially in Beira). Presidential and legislative elections were next due by end 2004.

Democratic Renewal Party
Partido Renovador Democrático (PRD)
Address. c/o União Eleitoral, Assembléia da República, CP 1516, Maputo
Leadership. Maneca Daniel (president)

The PRD obtained legal status in 1994. It won no seats in that year's legislative elections. It fought the 1999 elections as part of the RENAMO-UE alliance, led by the main opposition party, Mozambique National Resistance (RENAMO).

Front for the Liberation of Mozambique
Frente de Libertação de Moçambique (FRELIMO)
Address. Rua Pereira do Lago 3, Maputo
Telephone. (258–1) 490181
Leadership. Joaquim Chissano (president)

FRELIMO was founded in 1962 by the merger of three nationalist organizations. It fought against Portuguese rule from 1964 until 1974, when agreement on independence was reached, thereafter assuming the status of the sole legal party until 1990. Although initially committed to a Marxist-Leninist ideology, FRELIMO abandoned the doctrine in 1989 (subsequently embracing democratic socialism), at the same time calling for a negotiated settlement with the Mozambique National Resistance (RENAMO), against which it had been fighting a protracted civil war. In the October 1994 elections, consequent upon the peace process dating from the 1992 accord, FRELIMO retained power. President Chissano won the presidential election with 53% of the votes cast, while the party secured 129 of the 250 seats in the Assembly of the Republic. In December 1999 Chissano was re-elected with a virtually unchanged share of the vote (52.3%), while the party increased its representation in the Assembly to 133 seats.

FRELIMO is a full member party of the Socialist International.

Independent Alliance of Mozambique
Aliança Independente de Moçambique (ALIMO)
Address. c/o União Eleitoral, Assembléia da República, CP 1516, Maputo
Leadership. Ernesto Sergio (secretary-general)

Founded in 1998, ALIMO fought the 1999 elections as part of the RENAMO-UE alliance, led by the main opposition party Mozambique National Resistance (RENAMO).

Mozambique National Movement
Movimento Nacionalista Moçambicano (MONAMO)
Address. Av Mao Tse Tung 230, 1st Floor, Maputo
Telephone. (258–1) 422781
Leadership. Maximo Dias (secretary-general)

The social democratic MONAMO, founded in 1992, fought the 1999 elections as part of the RENAMO-UE alliance, led by the main opposition party Mozambique National Resistance (RENAMO).

Mozambique National Resistance
Resistência Nacional de Moçambique (RENAMO)
Address. Av Ahmed Sekou Toure 657, Maputo
Telephone. (258–1) 422617
Leadership. Afonso Dhlakama (president); João Alexandre (secretary-general)

Reportedly with foreign support, RENAMO was in military conflict with the Front for the Liberation of Mozambique (FRELIMO) government from 1976 until the peace process launched by the October 1992 accord. It registered as a political party in August 1994, and was the principal opponent and the runner-up to FRELIMO in the elections the following October. Afonso Dhlakama was the closest contender after FRELIMO's Chissano for the presidency, winning almost 34% of the vote, while RENAMO candidates secured 112 seats in the Assembly of the Republic.

RENAMO fought the December 1999 presidential and legislative elections in an alliance (RENAMO–UE) with eight small parties. Dhlakama (as the sole opposition candidate) won 47.7% of the vote for the presidency, to which

FRELIMO's Joaquim Chissano was re-elected. The REN-AMO–UE alliance won 117 seats in the Assembly, of which 99 were reportedly allocated to RENAMO and 18 to its allies. The outcome of the 1999 elections was strongly contested by RENAMO, which threatened to set up "parallel governments" in the six provinces where RENAMO–UE had won a majority of the votes cast. Following violent clashes between police and opposition supporters in the previous month, Dhlakama met with President Chissano in December 2000 (their first meeting since the elections) to discuss ways of reducing political tensions.

RENAMO is a member party of the Chrtistian Democrat International.

National Convention Party
Partido de Convenção Nacional, PCN
Address. c/o União Eleitoral, Assembléia da República, CP 1516, Maputo
Leadership. Lutero Simango (chairman); Gabriel Mabunda (secretary-general)
The PCN, which obtained legal status in 1992, favours free-market economics, support for agriculture and respect for human rights. Having failed to win any seats in the 1994 Assembly elections, it fought the 1999 elections as part of the RENAMO–UE alliance, led by the main opposition party Mozambique National Resistance (RENAMO).

National Unity Party
Partido de Unidade Nacional (PUN)
Address. c/o União Eleitoral, Assembléia da República, CP 1516, Maputo
Formed in 1995 and registered in 1997, the PUN fought the 1999 elections as part of the RENAMO–UE alliance, led by the main opposition party Mozambique National Resistance (RENAMO).

Patriotic Action Front
Frente de Ação Patriotica (FAP)
Address. c/o União Eleitoral, Assembléia da República, CP 1516, Maputo
Leadership. João Palaço (president); Raul da Conceição (secretary-general)
Founded in 1991, the FAP fought the 1999 elections as part of the RENAMO–UE alliance, led by the main opposition party Mozambique National Resistance (RENAMO).

Popular Party of Mozambique
Partido Popular de Moçambique (PPM)
Address. c/o União Eleitoral, Assembléia da República, CP 1516, Maputo
The PPM fought the 1999 elections as part of the RENAMO–UE alliance, led by the main opposition party Mozambique National Resistance (RENAMO).

United Front of Mozambique
Frente Unida de Moçambique (FUMO)
Address. Av Mao Tse-tung 230, Maputo
Leadership. José Samo Gudo (secretary-general)
In the 1994 elections FUMO (which won no seats) advocated the defence of human rights, the privatization of all state-owned companies, a market economy and denationalization of land. The party fought the 1999 elections as part of the RENAMO–UE alliance, led by the main opposition party Mozambique National Resistance (RENAMO).

Other Parties

Democratic Liberal Party of Mozambique (*Partido Democrático Liberal de Moçambique*, PADELIMO), founded in 1998. PADELIMO failed to win any seats in the 1999 Assembly elections, in which it received less than 1% of the vote.
Leadership. Joaquim José Nyota (president)

Democratic Party of Mozambique (*Partido Democrático de Moçambique*, PADEMO), legally recognized in June 1993 and strongly federalist in outlook, PADEMO secured less than 1% of the vote in the 1994 Assembly elections, while its candidate in the presidential contest was a distant third. It fought the 1999 Assembly elections as part of the Mozambique Opposition Union (UMO) coalition, which received 1.5% of the vote and failed to win any seats.
Leadership. Wehia Ripua (president)

Green Party of Mozambique (*Partido Verde de Moçambique*, PVM), founded in 1997.
Leadership. Armando Sapembe

Independent Party of Mozambique (*Partido Independente de Moçambique*, PIMO), an Islamically oriented party, founded in 1994, which gives priority in its policies to moral education and peace, land privatization and job creation for demobilized soldiers. It won just over 1% of the vote in both the presidential and legislative polls in 1994 and less than 1% in the 1999 legislative elections.
Leadership. Yaqub Sibindy (president)

Labour Party (*Partido Trabalhista*, PT), formed in 1993. Decentralist and mildly socialist, the party came last in the 1994 legislative elections. It received 2.7% of the vote and won no seats in the 1999 elections.
Leadership. Miguel Mabote (president)

Liberal and Democratic Party of Mozambique (*Partido Liberal e Democrático de Moçambique*, PALMO), founded in 1990. PALMO has been particularly critical of what it regards as the economic domination of the country by the non-indigenous population. The party fought the 1994 Assembly elections as a coalition member of the Democratic Union, which won nine seats. In the 1999 Assembly elections PALMO received 2.47% of the vote and won no seats.
Leadership. Martins Bilal (chairman); Antonio Muedo (secretary-general)

Mozambican National Union (*União Nacional Moçambicana*, UNAMO), formed in 1987 by a breakaway faction of the Mozambique National Resistance (REN-AMO). A federalist and social democratic organization, it was the first opposition party to be granted legal status. It won no seats in the 1994 legislative elections, while its presidential candidate received less than 3% of the vote. It fought the 1999 Assembly elections as part of the Mozambique Opposition Union (UMO) coalition, which received 1.5% of the vote and failed to win any seats.
Leadership. Carlos Reis (president)

National Democratic Party (*Partido Nacional Democrático*, PANADE), legalized in 1993. Supports a market economy, better education and training, and incentives to private investment. It contested the 1994 Assembly elections as a coalition member of the Democratic Union, which won nine seats. In the 1999 Assembly elections the Democratic Union (now comprising PANADE and the National Party of Mozambique) received 1.48% of the vote and won no seats.
Leadership. Jose Massinga (leader)

National Party of Mozambique (*Partido Nacional de Moçambique*, PANAMO), joined with the Liberal and Democratic Party of Mozambique and the National Democratic Party (PANADE) to contest the 1994 elections

as a constituent of the Democratic Union alliance, which won nine seats. In the 1999 elections the Democratic Union (now comprising only PANAMO and PANADE) received 1.48% of the vote and won no seats.
Leadership. Marcos Juma (president)

National Workers' and Peasants' Party (*Partido Nacional dos Operários e Camponêses*, PANAOC), founded in 1998. In the 1999 elections it received less than 1% of the vote and won no seats
Leadership. Armando Gil Sueia

Progressive Liberal Party of Mozambique (*Partido de Progresso Liberal de Moçambique*, PPLM), founded in 1993, received less than 1% of the vote and won no seats in the 1999 Assembly elections.
Leadership. Neves Pinto Serrano

Social, Liberal and Democratic Party (*Partido Social, Liberal e Democrático*, SOL), formed by a breakaway faction of the Liberal and Democratic Party of Mozambique and legally recognized in 1993, SOL campaigned on a platform of equality, a market economy and decentralization, taking fifth place in the 1994 Assembly elections with nearly 1.7% of the vote but no seats. In the 1999 elections it received 2% of the vote and won no seats.
Leadership. Casimiro Nhamithambo (president)

Myanmar (Burma)

Capital: Yangon (Rangoon)
Population: 50,600,000 (2001E)

The Union of Myanmar (formally the Union of Burma) achieved independence from the United Kingdom in 1948, with a Westminster-style parliamentary democracy. The government was led by a broad-based coalition, the Anti-Fascist People's Freedom League (AFPFL), until a military coup in 1962. The Revolutionary Council, led by General Ne Win, established a socialist state and banned all political parties except for the newly formed Burma Socialist Program Party (BSPP). Initially established as a cadre party, the BSPP was expanded into a mass organization, controlled by retired military officers, and took over state leadership from the Revolutionary Council in 1974. In July 1988, economic strife and political demonstrations led to the announcement by Ne Win, then chairman of the BSPP, that multi-party elections would be held. This failed to appease political dissent, and on Sept. 18, 1988, a military coup brought the State Law and Order Restoration Council (SLORC) to power.

SLORC maintained that it was a transitional body and it allowed political parties to register and campaign for an election held on May 27, 1990. Over 200 parties were registered and 93 contested the election. However, when the main opposition party, the National League for Democracy (NLD), won around 60% of the vote, SLORC refused to let a parliament convene. It has since maintained that the purpose of the election was to elect delegates to draft a new constitution at a National Convention, which was formed in January 1993. Only seven of the political parties (but including the NLD) that won seats in the election were invited to take part. Other participants included members of former insurgent organizations that had reached ceasefire agreements with the government, and representatives of

social groups chosen by SLORC. Some of the participants denounced the National Convention as a sham, and it made little progress by the time it went into recess in 1996. The process of drafting a constitution, according to official sources, is being continued by the National Convention Convening Committee (NCCC).

In May 2004, the National Convention was re-convened by the SPDC to resume writing the country's new constitution. Proceedings were conducted in closed sessions and very little progress towards agreement on a new constitution was announced. The convention went into recess in July without any notification on when it would resume.

Although the NLD and some other parties have not been de-registered, their operations have been severely restricted and many members have been imprisoned for attempting to carry out political activities. The repression eased somewhat after the NLD and the State Peace and Development Council (SPDC), as the re-organized SLORC was renamed in 1997, entered into confidence-building talks in October 2000. The United Nations commissioned two representatives, one the Special Rapporteur on Human Rights Paulo Pinheiro, and the other the Secretary-General's Special Rapporteur Razali Ismail, to mediate between the NLD and SPDC. Razali's success in this venture was not notable despite consistent efforts. The government-coordinated attacks on the NLD in May 2003 ended what some believed was a gradual shift to a more open political system, and political mobilization was again curtailed.

Since 1989, eighteen insurgent organizations have reached ceasefire agreements with the government, and remain as political entities in their areas with varying degrees of autonomy. Many of these have distinct political and military wings, such as the Kachin Independence Organization (KIO), that provide services to "liberated zones" within Myanmar, refugee constituents, and Internally Displaced Peoples (IDPs). Six of the ceasefire groups attended the National Convention in May 2004, but issued a statement calling for changes to the rules governing the participation of delegates and their freedom to voice dissenting opinions. The SPDC refused permission for their statement to be raised in the convention.

Democratic Party for a New Society (DPNS)
Leadership. Aung Moe Zaw (chairman); Aung Thu Nyein (vice-chairman); Zaw Nai Oo (general secretary)
Formed in October 1988, the DPNS was originally a leftist-oriented party that appealed to students and youth. It widened its support base to a purported 250,000 members and 120 branches nationwide before the 1990 election. Allied to the NLD, the DPNS decided not to contest the election and risk splitting votes. Following the election, the party was banned in November 1991. The leadership had already moved to the "liberated zones" of the Thai-Burma border where they regrouped to become an advocacy organization. It now operates predominantly in Thailand as a research and advocacy party with strong links to other umbrella organizations. It calls for a democratic Burma and would likely contest free elections in the future.
Email. hq@dpns.org
Website. www.dpns.org

National League for Democracy (NLD)
Address. 97B West Shwegondine Road, Bahan Township, Yangon
Leadership. U Aung Shwe (chairman); Daw Aung San Suu Kyi (general secretary); U Tin Oo (vice-chairman)

The NLD was formed soon after the September 1988 military coup as a broad-based coalition to unite the opposition. Daw Aung San Suu Kyi, the daughter of the father of Burmese independence, became general secretary and figurehead of the NLD. Both she and party chairman U Tin Oo were placed under house arrest in July 1989 but in transitional elections in May 1990 the NLD won 392 of the 485 contested seats. The result proved meaningless as the SLORC arrested NLD leaders and failed to convene a Constituent Assembly. In October 1991 Suu Kyi was awarded the Nobel Peace Prize. During 1991-92 the regime took steps to annul the election of numerous NLD Assembly members and to effect the expulsion of Suu Kyi from the party.

From January 1993 the NLD participated in a National Convention, formed to draft a new constitution. In March 1995 U Tin Oo was released from prison and in July 1995, in the face of international pressure, the regime unexpectedly freed Suu Kyi from house arrest and she was reinstated as the general secretary of the NLD in October 1995. In November 1995 the NLD withdrew from the National Convention and was formally expelled for non-attendance. In an effort to highlight the military's continued refusal to convene the parliament elected in 1990 (although many of the elected MPs were imprisoned, in exile or deceased), the NLD formed a ten-member Committee Representing the People's Parliament, in September 1998. The party survived despite long periods of house arrest of its leaders, imprisonment of many members, and the shutting down of many of its offices. This repression slightly eased after the NLD and the regime entered into confidence-building talks in October 2000. By September 2001, over 200 political prisoners had been released, and several NLD party offices in Yangon permitted to reopen.

This liberalization was further strengthened by the release of Suu Kyi in May 2002. A government spokesman promised "a new page" in the country's history. The NLD leadership embarked upon several tours around the country to reopen party offices and shore up supporters. The authorities and USDA (see below) members harassed the touring groups, but the NLD drew thousands of spectators in key urban areas and small rural towns. On the eighth trip in late May 2003, the NLD motorcade was attacked by hundreds of armed protesters and a violent confrontation ensued. The NLD leadership was arrested and taken to undisclosed locations. The SPDC claimed four people had been killed in the attack, although exiled groups citing witnesses claimed over seventy killed and hundreds wounded. The SPDC closed all NLD offices in the country and arrested scores of activists in what was clearly a concerted attempt to rollback the activities of the party and end the pressure to engage the opposition in multiparty talks.

Due to restrictions on the operating regulations at the National Convention, and the continued detention of key NLD leaders, including Daw Aung San Suu Kyi, the party voted not to attend the convention in May 2004.

National Unity Party (NUP)
Leadership. U Than Kyaw (chairman)
The National Unity Party was formed as a successor to the former ruling Burma Socialist Program Party (BSPP) to contest the 1990 election. It inherited the former party lists, and was given considerable government backing and extra privileges in the election campaign, but won only ten seats. During the 1990s the NUP faded into obscurity and its future role was uncertain. In an interview in mid-2001, a senior member of the NUP, Khin Maung Gyi, stated that the party had two million members and 800,000 "supporters", and maintained offices around the country. In 2002, a report to the UN General Assembly noted that the NUP was still permitted to engage in political organization and the distribution of party materials and publications, activities which other legal parties are largely restricted from carrying out. Khin Maung Gyi claimed that the Myanmar army is still "needed in national politics", which illustrates the continuing close relationship between the regime and the party. There is also a National Unity Party of Myanmar, which was the original name of the United Wa State Party, a former Communist Party ethnic group aligned to the SPDC.

Shan Nationalities League for Democracy (SNLD)
Leadership. U Khun Tun Oo (chairman)
Formed to unite Shan ethnic nationalities within a democratic system, the SNLD won 23 seats in Shan State, in the northeast of the country during the 1990 elections. This was the second largest number of elected representatives after the NLD. One elected MP, Sai Hla Pay, won the highest share of the vote in the entire election, 91.45%. The SNLD argues for a reformed Union, converting the seven ethnic states and seven administrative divisions into just eight ethnic states. Its guiding principles are "Democracy, Unity, Human Rights, Internal Peace, Development, Free Enterprise and Equality." The SNLD is a member of the Committee Representing the People's Parliament (CRPP) and cooperates with other political parties to end military rule in Myanmar.

The SNLD is also a target for regular government harassment. In February 2003, the Joint Secretary General-1 of the SNLD, Sai Nood (aka Sai Nyunt Lwin), was arrested and detained for three months for distributing anti-government literature. There are tensions too with its larger partner, the NLD. Criticism of the NLD's refusal to alert the SNLD to Suu Kyi's planned trips to Shan State was met with mistrust by much of the executive of the party. While there were legitimate security concerns for this, one Shan politician reportedly called it a "breach of diplomacy", and illustrates the continuing distrust many ethnic parties have of the Burman-dominated NLD.

The SNLD also has the nominal support of all the Shan insurgent groups. Two of the ceasefire groups, the Shan State Army-North (SSA-N) and the Shan State National Army (SSNA), together with the SNLD, formed the Joint Action Committee to represent the interests of "above-ground" organizations. The other main political grouping is the Restoration Council of Shan State (RCSS), which is technically comprised of the three members of the Joint Action Committee, plus the Shan State Army-South (SSA-S), which continues to fight the central government. Recent policy changes by the RCSS mean it now largely mirrors the SNLD in its call for a Union of eight ethnic states.

Other Parties

The following ethnically based parties participated in the National Convention, but have not had an active role to play since the last meeting in 1996: Khami National Solidarity Organization (KNSO); Lahu National Development Party (LNDP); Shan State Kokang Democratic Party (SSKDP); Union Pa-O National Organization (UPNO) Mon National Democratic Front (MNDF).

Other Political Organizations

Committee Representing the People's Parliament (CRPP), formed in September 1998 to pressure the SPDC into convening the 1990 elected parliament. The CRPP has thirteen representatives, nine from the NLD and four representing other political parties, the Arakan League for Democracy (ALD), Mon National Democracy Front (MNDF), Shan National League for Democracy (SNLD), and the Zomi National Congress (ZNC). Two other parties joined the five extant members in late 2002, the Party for

National Democracy (PND) and National Democratic Party for Human Rights (NDPHR). The CRPP is constituted of sub-committees that represent broad portfolios to be instituted in a democratic transition. While it has nominal support from other opposition groups in and outside of Myanmar, the SPDC has curtailed the activities of the CRPP and ignores their calls for convening the parliament.

Leadership. U Aung Shwe (chairman); U Tin Oo (deputy chairman)

National Coalition Government of the Union of Burma (NCGUB), formed by elected MPs who fled to the Thai-Burmese border in 1990 as a government-in-exile. It was formed within an umbrella organization, the National Council of the Union of Burma, which was an alliance of armed ethnic organizations, the National Democratic Front, and the Democratic Alliance of Burma. However, these alliances have been weakened as some of the groups entered ceasefire agreements with the government, and following the capture by government forces of the headquarters at Manerplaw in 1995. The NCGUB's primary role is advocacy in international organizations such as the United Nations General Assembly.

Leadership. Dr Sein Win ("prime minister")
Address. NCGUB Information Office, 815 15th Street, NW, Suite 910, Washington DC 20005, USA
Telephone. (1–202) 393–7342
Fax. (1–202) 393–7343
Email. ncgub@ncgub.net
Website. www.ncgub.net

National Council of the Union of Burma (NCUB) formed in August 1992 as an umbrella organization of a range of pro-democracy groups in exile. Its members are the National Democratic Front (NDF), Democratic Alliance of Burma (DAB), National League for Democracy–Liberated Area (NLD-LA), and the Members of Parliament Union (MPU). Essentially an advocacy organization, the NCUB seeks to formulate common policies of smaller organizations and the political positions of armed groups. The NCUB is a coalition that works to overcome internecine conflicts within the pro-democracy movement. Its structure consists of a presidium, a secretariat, advisors and six working committees.

Leadership. Bo Mya (presidium president); Aung Moe Zoe (secretariat general secretary)
Address. PO Box 29, Huamark Post Office, Bangkok Thailand 10243

Union Solidarity and Development Association (USDA), formed in September 1993 as a mass social organization to promote national unity. Its five objectives mirror those of the SPDC as "non-disintegration of the Union, non-disintegration of national solidarity, perpetuation of sovereignty, promotion and vitalization of national honor, and emergence of a peaceful, prosperous and modern Union." It is hierarchically structured, with an executive committee at the top and associations parallel to each level of government. At last count these included 16 state and division associations, 63 district level associations, 320 township-level associations, and 14,865 village-tract associations. The Association claimed in 1999 that it had 12 million members. Many receive paramilitary training and assorted "nation building" tasks.

Often compared by observers to Indonesia's Golkar, it offers the only path other than the military for social mobility, and membership is vital to promotion in the civil service and to educational opportunities. Members are groomed for leadership in political, economic and social fields, and are obliged to show support for the government in staged mass rallies that denounce the NLD, US sanctions and Thai interference in the civil war. In economic sanctions imposed by the United States in mid-2003, USDA executive members were prohibited from obtaining visas to the USA.

The militant wing of this organization attacked an NLD motorcade in Yangon in November 1996, slightly injuring one of the leaders and narrowly missing Daw Aung San Suu Kyi. The NLD leader later characterized the USDA as akin to "Nazi Brown Shirts". USDA groups were prominent in staging anti-NLD demonstrations in 2002-03, and they played a leading role in the attack on the NLD in late May 2003.

Leadership. President Than Shwe (patron); U Than Aung (secretary-general)
Address. 455-457 New University Avenue Rd., Yangon
Telephone. 545 131

Namibia

Capital: Windhoek
Population: 1,771,000 (2000E)

Originally under German colonial rule, Namibia came under South African control in 1915. South Africa's mandate to rule the territory was terminated by the United Nations in 1966, but it continued its occupation until final agreement was reached at the end of 1988 on the implementation of a UN-sponsored independence plan, resulting in the country's independence in March 1990. Under the 1990 multi-party constitution, executive power is vested in the President and the Cabinet. The President, as head of state and government, is directly elected by universal adult suffrage, and must receive more than 50% of the votes cast. One person may not hold the office of President for more than two five-year terms. The legislature consists of the National Assembly and the National Council. The National Assembly, with a five-year mandate, has 72 members elected by a proportional representation electoral system and up to six non-voting members nominated by the President. The indirectly-elected and mainly advisory National Council, consisting of two members from each region, has a six-year term of office.

Party politics were already shaped by the elections for the Constituent Assembly in late 1989 when the the South West Africa People's Organization of Namibia (SWAPO) won 56.9% of the seats, Sam Nujoma (the SWAPO leader) thereafter being elected President by the Assembly's members. The first post-independence presidential and legislative elections were held on Dec. 7-8, 1994, returning the incumbent President Nujoma for a second term and SWAPO winning 53 seats (with 73.9% of the votes cast) in the National Assembly (this being a sufficiently large majority to pass constitutional amendment bills). In 1998 the constitution was amended to permit the current incumbent to stand for a third five-year presidential term (as an exceptional case). Following regional council elections held in December 1998, SWAPO increased its representation in the 26-member National Council from 19 to 22 members. Voting for the presidency and the National Assembly took place on Nov. 30 and Dec. 1, 1999. President Nujoma was re-elected with 76.8% of the vote in a four-way presidential contest, while SWAPO won 55 of the elective Assembly seats with 76.1% of the vote. Despite fears Nujoma would seek another term in office, in May 2004 a special SWAPO party congress nominated cabinet minister Hifikepunye Pohamba as the party's candidate for the upcoming elections in late 2004.

Congress of Democrats (CoD)

Address. PO Box 40905, Ausspannplatz, Windhoek
Telephone. (264–61) 256954
Fax. (264–61) 256980
Email. codemo@mweb.com.na
Website. www.cod.org.na
Leadership. Benjamin Ulenga (leader); Ignatius Nkotongo Shixwameni (secretary-general)

The CoD was formed in March 1999 by a former senior official of the SWAPO, Benjamin Ulenga, who had resigned his post as Namibian high commissioner in London in protest against SWAPO's 1998 decision to amend the constitution to allow President Nujoma to stand for a third term of office. The CoD's campaign against various aspects of Nujoma's record in office prompted several government policy initiatives in 1999 to address the problems of certain aggrieved groups (notably unemployed ex-combatants). In the November–December 1999 elections, Ulenga was runner-up to Nujoma in the presidential contest, winning 10.5% of the vote, while the CoD won 7 elective seats in the National Assembly with 9.9% of the vote. Observers agreed that the CoD's support at the election came not from former SWAPO voters but from opposition voters who had previously supported the Democratic Turnhalle Alliance of Namibia (DTA), the official opposition party in the previous Assembly. Although the CoD won a slightly higher share of the popular vote in the 1999 Assembly elections, the DTA (which also won 7 seats) entered into a coalition with the United Democratic Front (UDF) to form the official opposition in the new Assembly.

Democratic Turnhalle Alliance of Namibia (DTA)

Address. PO Box 173, Windhoek
Telephone. (264–61) 238530
Fax. (264–61) 226494
Website. www.democratafrica.org/namibia/dta
Leadership. Katuutire Kaura (president); Johan de Waal (chairman)

Founded in 1977 as a multiracial coalition, the DTA was the majority political formation in the South African-appointed transitional government prior to independence and was supported by South Africa. Following Constituent Assembly elections in 1989 (organized under the UN-sponsored independence plan) it became the main opposition grouping with 28.6% of the votes cast and 41 seats. Having been revamped as a single party in November 1991, the DTA contested the legislative and presidential elections in 1994, focusing on the issues of unemployment, rising crime and corruption. In the presidential poll, the DTA candidate, Mishake Muyongo, came second to incumbent President Nujoma of the SWAPO with 23.08% of the votes cast. In the National Assembly elections the party secured 15 seats with a 20.8% vote share, trailing SWAPO by a considerable margin. Muyongo went on to form the secessionist Caprivi Liberation Army (CLA) that took up arms in August 1999 in the Caprivi strip. Being prosecuted for high treason, Muyongo was subsequently expelled from his party and went into exile.

In the 1999 elections, the DTA candidate, Katuutire Kaura, came third in the presidential contest, with 9.6% of the vote, while the party won 7 Assembly seats with 9.5% of the vote. In April 2000 the DTA entered into a coalition with the UDF to form the official opposition in the National Assembly. In August and September 2003 the exclusively white-supported Republican Party (RP) and the Herero-based National Unity Democratic Organization (NUDO), both constituent parties of the DTA, pulled out, dealing a heavy blow to the party's chances in the elections due in late 2004.

The DTA is an associate member of the International Democrat Union and a member of its regional associate, the Democrat Union of Africa.

Monitor Action Group (MAG)

Address. PO Box 80808, Olympia, Windhoek
Leadership. Kosie Pretorius

The MAG, set up during 1994 by the former leader of the predominantly white Action Christian National (ACN), defines itself as a pressure group for "principle politics" rather than a political party as such. It aims to promote "a Christian outlook and standpoint" and advocates the removal of the "secular concept" from the Namibian constitution. In the elections to the National Assembly in December 1994 the MAG won a single seat, which it retained in the 1999 elections.

South West Africa People's Organization of Namibia (SWAPO)

Address. PO Box 1071, Windhoek
Telephone. (264–61) 238364
Fax. (264–61) 232368
Website. www.swapo.org.na
Leadership. Hifikepunye Pohamba (president); Ngarikutuke Tjirange (secretary general)

SWAPO was established in 1958 as the Ovamboland People's Organization, adopting its present name in 1960. It was the principal liberation movement in the pre-independence period, having launched an armed struggle in 1966. From 1973 it was recognized by the UN General Assembly as "the authentic representative of the people of Namibia". In the pre-independence Constituent Assembly elections in 1989, SWAPO won a majority of seats. In February 1990 the Assembly adopted the new constitution and elected SWAPO leader Sam Nujoma to be Namibia's first President. Following independence, SWAPO formed the government, advocating national reconciliation, economic development, and an improvement in the basic conditions of life for the majority.

In December 1991 SWAPO held its first congress since its inception. The party's constitution and political programme were amended to transform SWAPO from a liberation movement into a mass political party. In the December 1994 elections Nujoma retained the presidency, winning just over 76% of the vote, while SWAPO candidates secured 53 of the 72 elective seats in the National Assembly. This was a sufficient majority to amend the constitution in 1998 to allow Nujoma to stand for a third presidential term (as an exceptional case). Nujoma was re-elected President in December 1999 with 76.8% of the vote, while SWAPO won 55 elective Assembly seats with 76.1% of the vote. In November 2001, Nujoma declared that he would not seek to stand for a fourth term as national President. At the third SWAPO party congress in August 2002, Nujoma retained his post as party president, but indicated he would step down and possibly then adopt a newly created post of party chairman at an extraordinary party congress set for May 2004. Candidates to succeed him both as national and party president were the newly elected vice-president Hifikepunye Pohamba (a former general secretary), Foreign Minister Theo Ben Gurirab (who replaced Prime Minister Hage Geingob in a sudden move shortly after the party congress), and the new Foreign Minister, Hidipo Hamutenya. In May 2004, Hifikepunye Pohamba was elected SWAPO presidential candidate for general elections in a SWAPO special party congress thus leaving little doubt who will be Namibia's future President.

United Democratic Front (UDF)

Address. POB 20037, Windhoek
Telephone. (264–61) 230683
Fax. (264–61) 237175
Leadership. Justus Garoeb (president); Eric Biwa (national chairman)

Founded as a centrist alliance of eight ethnic parties, the UDF won four seats in the 1989 Constituent Assembly elections, subsequently reorganizing itself as a unitary party in October 1993. Although in third place in the December 1994 legislative poll, the party attracted only 2.7% of the vote and won only two National Assembly seats. In the 1999 elections it retained two Assembly seats (with 2.9% of the vote), while its presidential candidate received the lowest share of the vote (3%). In April 2000 the UDF went into coalition with the DTA to form the official opposition in the National Assembly.

Other Parties

Democratic Coalition of Namibia (DCN), founded in 1994 as a coalition of the National Patriotic Front (NPF), the German Union, and the South West African National Union (SWANU, withdrew in November 1994.) The DCN gained one seat in the 1994 legislative elections (0.8% of the votes cast) but failed to do so in 1999 (0.3% of the votes cast).

Federal Convention of Namibia (FCN), founded in 1988 and contested the 1989 elections for the Constituent Assembly, winning one seat that was filled by a member of its constituent party, the National Patriotic Party (NPP). However, in 1994 and 1999 the FCN failed to win any seat in the legislative elections, gaining 0.2% and 0.1% of the votes cast respectively.

National Unity Democratic Organization (NUDO), formerly a constituent part of the DTA, from which it pulled out in September 2003. As the main reason for this decision chairman and paramount Herero Chief Riruako, named the unwillingness of the DTA leadership to support Herero interests, apparently including legal cases against the German government and companies for war atrocities and genocide during the Herero uprising in 1904 under colonial rule. NUDO held its first congress as an independent party after independence in early January 2004.
Leadership. Kuaima Riruako (chairman)

South West African National Union (SWANU), founded in 1959 and contested the 1989 elections for the Constituent Assembly as part of the Nambia National Front (NNF). In 1994, the SWANU joined the DCN but withdrew before the elections and failed to win any seats (0.5% of the votes cast). In 1999 SWANU again unsuccessfully contested the legislative elections together with WRP (0.3% of the votes cast).

Workers' Revolutionary Party (WRP), founded 1989, and part of the UDF in the 1989 elections for the Constitutent Assembly that won four seats (none of them filled by a WRP candidate, however). In 1994 it participated without success in the parliamentary elections, taking only 0.2% of the votes cast. In 1999 the WRP, this time in coalition with the SWANU, performed poorly again with only 0.3% of the votes cast.

Nauru

Capital: Domaneab
Population: 11,500 (2000E)

Nauru achieved independence in 1968, having previously been a UN Trust Territory administered by Australia. Under the constitution, legislative power is vested in an 18-member unicameral Parliament, directly elected for up to three years, which selects a President from among its members. The President, who is head of state, governs with the assistance of an appointed Cabinet.

Nauru's first President, Hammer DeRoburt, dominated the island's politics until 1989, when he was succeeded by Bernard Dowiyogo, who served six mostly consecutive terms until being replaced by René Harris in March 2001. The political process tends to operate on family rather than party lines, although members of the legislature have from time to time grouped themselves into informal parties. Supporters of Dowiyogo (who died in March 2003) were identified as the Democratic Party and those of Harris as the Nauru Party. Nauru, facing economic crisis due to depletion of its phosphate resources and mismanagement of the income they generated, has experienced political turmoil leading to constant changes in government. In 1997 Nauru had four different Presidents in as many months. Between 1997 and 1998 Kinza Godfrey was President, followed by Harris in 1999. Harris was President from 1999 to 2000 and again from 2001 to 2003. He lost power briefly in 2003 and then assumed the presidency again in August 2003 for the fourth time. In 2003 alone Nauru had seven changes in the presidency and in 2004 Ludwig Scotty became President.

Nepal

Capital: Kathmandu
Population: 24,179,000 (2002E)

Following the overthrow of the ruling Rana family in a popular revolt in 1950, the King of Nepal resumed an active political role. In 1959 the country's first constitution was promulgated and a parliament was elected. However, at the end of the following year the King dissolved parliament and dismissed the government. All political parties were banned in 1961 and for the next 30 years Nepal experienced direct rule by the monarchy, although a tiered, party-less system of *panchayat* (council) democracy was introduced under a new constitution in 1962.

In February 1990 a series of peaceful demonstrations in support of the restoration of democracy and human rights escalated into full-scale confrontation with the government. The following April the ban on political parties was rescinded, restrictions on the press lifted and constitutional reform promised. A new constitution guaranteeing parliamentary government and a constitutional monarchy was proclaimed in November 1990. It provides for a bicameral legislature comprising a popularly-elected 205-member House of Representatives (*Pratinidhi Sabha*) and a National Council (*Rashtriya Sabha*) of 60 members, of whom 10 are nominees of the King, 35 are elected by the House of Representatives and 15 are elected by an electoral college.

The first multi-party general election was held in May 1991 and resulted in a victory for the Nepali Congress Party (NCP). In further elections on Nov. 15, 1994, the United Communist Party of Nepal–Marxist-Leninist (UCPN) became the largest party with 88 seats against 83 for the NCP, with the National Democratic Party (RPP) winning 20, the Nepal Workers' and Peasants' Party (NWPP) 4, the Nepal Sadbhavana Party (Nepal Goodwill Council, NSP) 3 and independents 7. The UCPN leader, Man Mohan Adhikari, was accordingly sworn in as the country's first communist Prime Minister at the end of the month.

A political crisis arose in June 1995 when Adhikari recommended the dissolution of parliament by King Birendra and a fresh general election, apparently to avoid losing an imminent vote of no confidence. The Prime Minister's decision, and his appointment as head of a caretaker government pending elections scheduled for November, were challenged by opposition parties which, in August, won a ruling from the Supreme Court reinstating the existing parliament. In September Adhikari resigned after losing a parliamentary vote of no confidence and was replaced as Prime Minister by Sher Bahadur Deuba of the NCP. A new coalition government led by the NCP and including the RPP and the NSP then took office.

However, Deuba's government fell in March 1997 to be replaced by one headed by Lokendra Bahadur Chand of the RPP, who split his party and formed a coalition with the NCP, the NSP and also the UCPN. But, in October 1997, Chand was forced to resign after losing a no-confidence motion in the *Pratinidhi Sabha*. He was replaced as Prime Minister by Surya Bahadur Thapa, who headed the other faction of the RPP and drew support from the NCP and the NSP. However, this combination also proved short-lived. In March 1998, the UCPN split, leaving the NCP as the largest party in parliament. In April 1998, NCP leader Girija Prasad Koirala was invited to take office at the head of a minority administration, which lasted only until December when Koirala was re-appointed to head a coalition government between the NCP and the majority faction of the UCPN.

A new general election in May 1999 finally changed the awkward composition of the previous *Pratinidhi Sabha*. The NCP was returned with 111 of the 205 seats and formed a majority government under Krishna Prasad Bhattarai, who was a rival of Koirala for the party's leadership. The rump of the main UCPN won 68 seats, while the new communist breakaway group, the Communist Party of Nepal–Marxist-Leninist (CPN-ML), failed to win any. The RPP (Thapa) took 11 seats and the RPP (Chand) was left seatless. The NSP gained 5 seats, as did the National People's Front (RJM), which had stood in the original 1991 election but had split in 1993. However, Bhattarai's government lasted only until March 2000 when it was overthrown by an internal coup inside the NCP, restoring Koirala to the party leadership and the Prime Minister's office. But Koirala, himself, faced mounting party dissidence, having to reshuffle his cabinet no fewer than 9 times in 15 months, and eventually fell victim to the circumstances surrounding the assassination of King Birendra in June 2001. In July, he was replaced as Prime Minister of the NCP government by Sher Bahadur Deuba.

Meanwhile, from 1993, dissident factions within the old United People's Front (SJN), which had played a pivotal role in the 1990 campaign for democracy, had begun to contemplate armed resistance to the constitutional state. A "Maoist" strategy was put into force in 1996, which was strengthened in 1998 when many former members of the (now-split) UCPN became attracted to it. Maoist guerrilla groups, of which the most prominent is the Nepal Communist Party–Maoist (NCP-M), led by "Comrade Prachanda" (the *nom de guerre* of Pushpa Kamal Dahal), now effectively control considerable stretches of rural territory where the writ of the government does not run.

Deuba's priority was to find a way of ending the escalating Maoist insurgency, his first act as Prime Minister being to offer on July 23 a ceasefire, which was immediately reciprocated by Comrade Prachanda. Government negotiators held three rounds of peace talks with the CPN-M between August and November, but these foundered on the Maoists' demands for the dissolution of the constitution, the appointment of an interim government and the establishment of a constituent assembly (although Prachanda did set aside his initial demand for the abolition of the monarchy). In response to a major military offensive launched by the Maoists following the breakdown of the talks King Gyanendra declared a state of emergency on Nov. 26, promulgating anti-terrorist measures including the suspension of civil liberties and press freedom. Additionally Gyanendra authorized for the first time the full mobilization of the Royal Nepalese Army (RNA) against the rebels. Subsequently political life has been dominated by what has become effectively a full-scale civil war, severely hampering the implementation of a programme of land and caste reforms, anti-corruption and women's rights measures introduced by Deuba in October 2001 with the intention of removing the conditions that fuelled support for the rebellion.

The *Pratinidhi Sabha* on Feb. 21, 2002, backed Deuba's three-month extension of the state of emergency with the necessary two-thirds majority. Despite urging the government to reopen negotiations with the CPN-M, the UCPN supported the measure in exchange for pledges to establish an anti-corruption commission and introduce constitutional reforms to ensure free elections. However, Deuba failed to introduce a constitutional bill before the end of the parliamentary session on April 17. Deuba was coming under increasing pressure from a faction in the NCP led by his long-standing rival Koirala, which made it unlikely that the government would secure a further extension of the state of emergency when it expired on May 25. On Deuba's recommendation King Gyanendra on May 22 dissolved the *Pratinidhi Sabha*, setting Nov. 13 as the date for fresh elections. Three of Deuba's Cabinet resigned in protest against the dissolution and the NCP disciplinary committee, dominated by Koirala's supporters, voted on May 26 to expel Deuba from the party. As the dispute between the two factions grew more acrimonious the party formally split in late June and in September Deuba's faction registered as a new party [see below]. On Oct. 4 Gyanendra, invoking article 127 of the 1990 constitution, sacked Deuba's government for "incompetence" and Deuba's request for a one-year postponement of the elections scheduled for Nov. 13, made because of the deteriorating security situation of the escalating Maoist insurgency, and specifically because the CPN-M had called for a general strike on Nov. 11-13. It was the first dismissal of an elected government by a king since the end of absolute monarchy in 1990. After inconclusive, separate talks with six political parties the King on Nov. 11 recalled Lokendra Bahadur Chand as Prime Minister. Chand formed a government composed largely of career civil servants and professionals rather than elected politicians. This was rejected from the outset by all the major political parties except the RPP and even described as a "puppet government".

At a meeting on Jan. 22, 2003, the NCP, the UCPN, the People's Front Nepal (PFN) and the NWPP declared Gyanendra's dismissal of Deuba's government unconstitutional and launched a campaign of peaceful protests. Meanwhile there was a surprise announcement on Jan. 29 of a truce between government forces and the Maoist rebels, in preparation for the resumption of peace talks. Although Gyanendra and Chand made repeated overtures towards the parties to draw them into participation in the government and involvement in the peace process, these were rebuffed. By February even the RPP boycotted an all-party meeting called by Chand. On May 4 five major parties – now including the NSP-Ananda Devi faction – made a joint declaration committing themselves to reversing the "unconstitutional royal steps", restoring the House of Representatives and re-establishing "the sovereignty of the people". The declaration also founded the Joint People's Movement (JPM), which committed the five parties to a co-ordinated movement of peaceful protest intended to bring about a return to democratic government. Almost daily demonstrations against the government in Kathmandu, organized by the JPM and backed by the student movement, resulted in the resignation on May 30 of Chand. On the previous day police had prevented the JPM from entering the Parliament building to reconvene the *Pratinidhi Sabha*. The JPM proposed Madhav Kumar Nepal, general secretary of the UCPN, as its candidate for Prime Minister, but on June 4 King Gyanendra appointed Surya Bahadur Thapa, leader of the other faction of the RPP. After Koirala and M.K. Nepal rebuffed Thapa's invitation to join his government, the new Prime Minister on June 11 appointed a small Cabinet drawn from the RPP, but retaining most of the portfolios himself, suggesting that he still hoped to broaden his administration. The JPM, however, called for his resignation and the formation of an all-party government.

Meanwhile, the government and the Maoist CPN-M held three rounds of peace talks in April, May and August 2003, during which time the ceasefire between the two sides largely held. The third round collapsed when the government refused the CPN-M demand for elections to a constitutional assembly, resulting in a declaration by Comrade Prachanda on Aug. 27 that both talks and ceasefire were at an end. The next few months were marked by escalating violence, with almost daily clashes between the army and the guerrillas and many civilian casualties. A Nepalese human rights group estimated in October that around 1,000 people had been killed since the end of the ceasefire. It was estimated that over 8,000 people had been killed since the start of the insurgency in 1996; of these at least 5,400 had died since the breakdown of Deuba's peace talks in November 2001. Although the parties of the JPM had refused to participate in the negotiations by Chand's and Thapa's governments with the CPN-M, they had themselves held talks with the Maoists since March. The danger for any Prime Minister appointed by the King was that as the political statemate continued the positions of the JPM and the CPN-M would converge in a common strain of republicanism, with the Maoists appearing to gain legitimacy in contrast with Gyanendra's interventions in government, widely portrayed as autocratic and unconstitutional.

National Democratic Party
Rashtriya Prajatantra Party (RPP)
Address. c/o House of Representatives, Kathmandu
Telephone. (977-1) 223044, 223089 (Chand); 437057, 437058 (Thapa)
Leadership. Lokendra Bahadur Chand, Surya Bahadur Thapa (leaders); Pashupati Shumshere J.B. Rana (president); Khem Raj Pandit (joint secretary-general)
The right-wing, monarchist RPP is composed of two principal factions, led by former Prime Ministers Chand and Thapa respectively. In the November 1994 elections the

party secured 20 seats in the House of Representatives, joining the NCP-led coalition government which replaced the communist administration in September 1995. But, in March 1997, Chand bid for the prime ministership himself, seeking to draw the communists into a new coalition. This precipitated a deeper split in the RPP and, in October 1997 he was displaced in office by Thapa at the head of a new coalition excluding the communists. However, this government was also short-lived and fell in March 1998. At the 1999 general election, the two factions stood independently, the Thapa group winning 14 seats in the *Pratinidhi Sabha* and the Chand group none. Yet it was to Chand that King Gyanendra first turned to head a government in October 2002 after he had dismissed the Sher Bahadur Deuba administration. When Gyanendra replaced Chand with Thapa in June 2003, the RPP split into "ghovernment" and "party" factions, the latter calling for Thapa to resign.

National People's Front (NPF)
Rashtriya Janata Morcha (RJM)
Address. Mahabouda, Kathmandu
Telephone. (977-1) 224226
Formerly the National People's Council (*Rashtriya Janata Parishad*, RJP), formed in 1992 by Maitrika Prasad Koirala and Kirti Nidhi Dista, both former Prime Ministers seeking a non-radical alternative to the Nepali Congress Party. In the 1999 general election, as the Rashtriya Janata Morcha, RJM, it won five seats in *Pratinidhi Sabha* (House of Representatives).

Nepal Goodwill Council
Nepal Sadhbhavana Parishad (NSP)
Address. Tripureshwor, Kathmandu
Telephone. (977-1) 228419
Leadership. Gajendra Narayan Singh (president); Hridayesh Tripathi (general secretary)
This small party promotes the rights of the Madhesiya Indian community of the Terai region of Nepal. In November 1994 it won three seats in the elections to the House of Representatives. Its president was awarded a portfolio in the NCP-led coalition government formed in September 1995. It also supported a series of subsequent coalition governments and, in the 1999 general election, won five seats.

Nepal Workers' and Peasants' Party (NWPP)
Nepal Mazdoor Kisan Party (NMKP)
Address. Golmadi, Bakhtapur
Telephone. (977-1) 610974, 610026
Leadership. Narayan Man Bijukchhe (chairman)
The formerly pro-Chinese communist NWPP moderated its policies and now advocates a mixed economy, winning four seats in the House of Representatives in the 1994 elections but only one in 1999, with 0.6% of the vote.

Nepali Congress Party (NCP)
Address. Central Office, Teku, Kathmandu
Telephone. (977–1) 227748
Fax. (977–1) 227747
Email. ncparty@mos.com.np
Website. www.nepalicongress.org.np
Leadership. Girija Prasad Koirala (president); Sushil Koirala (general secretary); Sher Bahadur Deuba (president, NCP-D)
Founded in the late 1940s as Nepal's wing of the Indian National Congress, with a socialist but pro-monarchist orientation, the NCP came to government in 1959 but was ejected by the monarch a year later and banned along with other political parties from 1961. Over the following two decades many NCP activists were detained or restricted, while the exiled leadership campaigned for the restoration of democracy. The party achieved a measure of official accept-

ance through the 1980s, although various moves to reach a political accord with the King were inconclusive amid periodic repressive action by the authorities.

Following the widespread popular agitation that began in early 1990, the NCP president was appointed by the King to lead a coalition government pending multi-party elections in May 1991, in which the NCP won an overall majority of 110 seats. In further elections to the House of Representatives in November 1994 (brought about by a vote of no confidence in the NCP government), the party won only 83 of the 205 seats and relinquished power to the United Communist Party of Nepal (UCPN). However, following the resignation of the UCPN administration in September 1995, the NCP formed a new coalition under the premiership of Sher Dahadur Deuba. This was displaced in March 1997 by two short-lived coalitions led by the National Democratic Party (RPP) in which the NCP participated. From March 1998 to May 1999, the NCP headed a series of minority and coalition governments under the leadership of Girija Prasad Koirala. At the May 1999 general election, the party won 110 of the 205 seats in the House of Representatives and, to July 2001, had formed three successive majority governments: first, under Krishna Prasad Bhattarai, then under Koirala and then under Deuba again. Internecine feuds between these three leaders has been a dominant feature of the party since the restoration of full democracy in 1991.

The struggle between the Deuba and Koirala factions came to a head in May 2002 when the NCP disciplinary committee voted to expel Deuba from the party. In retaliation, Deuba's faction held a "general convention" on June 16-19 at which his supporters voted to expel Koirala and elected Deuba party president. Koirala's supporters, who denounced these proceedings as illegal, had already filed a petition asking the Supreme Court to declare Deuba's dissolution in May of the *Pratinidhi Sabha* unconstitutional. The Supreme Court rejected this petition on Aug. 6. However, on Sept. 17 the Election Commission recognized Koirala's majority faction as the legitimate holder of the party title, resulting in the registration by Deuba's supporters on Sept. 23 of a new party, the Nepali Congress Party–Democratic (NCP-D). The two factions remained separate to December 2003, despite King Gyanendra's dismissal of Deuba's government, although by the end of the year there was some evidence of attempts at reconciliation and co-operation between the two factions.

The NCP is a member party of the Socialist International.

United Communist Party of Nepal–Marxist-Leninist (UCPN)

Address. POB 5471, Kathmandu.
Telephone. (977–1) 223639
Leadership. Madhav Kumar Nepal (general secretary)
The UCPN was formed in early 1991 by the merger of the Marxist and Marxist-Leninist factions of the Communist Party of Nepal. In the May 1991 elections it won the second highest number of seats (69) in the House of Representatives, thereby becoming the official opposition. Although the party was left short of a workable majority in the November 1994 elections (from which it emerged as the largest party with 88 seats), the UCPN leader, Man Mohan Adhikari, was invited to form a new government. However, his controversial efforts to maintain his administration ended with his resignation as Prime Minister in September 1995 and the party's return to opposition status. Between March and October 1997, the party supported the coalition government led by Lokendra Bahadur Chand of the National Democratic Party (RPP). But this precipitated a major split in March 1998 when the Communist Party of Nepal–Marxist-Leninist (CPN) left the main branch of the party. The widely respected Adhikari died in April 1999,

shortly before the general election of in May that year, in which the UCPN won 68 seats and the CPN, although polling 6.4% of the vote, none. The UCPN on Feb. 15, 2002, formally reabsorbed the CPN.

United People's Front–Nepal (Sanyunkta Janamorcha Nepal–SJN),

a leftist movement which participated in the campaign for democracy in 1990 and won nine seats in the *Pratinidhi Sabha* at the 1991 election. However, it split in 1993 over the issue of whether to work within the constitution or to raise armed resistance against it. A small group has continued to follow the parliamentary path and won one seat at the 1999 election. But the majority faction, informed by leading ideologue Babu Ram Bhattarai, has gravitated towards the insurrectionist politics of the Communist Party of Nepal–Maoist. The SJN, also known as the People's Front Nepal (PFN) in January 2003 joined the Joint People's Movement (JPM) of political parties campaigning for the restoration of Parliament and rejecting the government appointed by King Gyanendra as unconstitutional.

Underground Party

Communist Party of Nepal–Maoist (CPN-M),

an underground communist faction led by "Comrade Prachanda" (Pushpa Kamal Dahal) which is organizing an armed insurrection against the state, with the primary object of abolishing the monarchy. By November 2002 the CPN-M was thought to control about a third of Nepal's 75 districts, especially remote western districts such as Rukum, Rolpa, Jumla, Gorkha and Dang, but also, increasingly, in central and eastern Nepal. The Maoists establish a parallel administration at village level in the districts they dominate, imposing their own taxes. It was reported in August 1999 that the CPN-M had begun to organize elections to village development committees in Rukum district, while preventing officially elected members of committees from carrying out their duties. Following the breakdown of peace talks with the government in August 2003 the CPN-M further developed political structures in the areas under its control. In January 2004 the party's politburo announced the creation of several "autonomous provincial regional people's governments", saying that in these areas activity by other political parties was banned until further notice.

The US State Department on Oct. 31, 2003, banned the CPN-M as a terrorist organization that threatened the security of the USA, freezing any financial assets under US jurisdiction. The USA also banned the party's aliases of the United Revolutionary People's Council (URPC) and the People's Liberation Army of Nepal (PLAN). Prachandra had recently announced a shift of policy from sabotaging government infrastructure to targeting US-backed organizations.
Leadership. Comrade Prachanda (Pushpa Kamal Dahal) (general secretary); Babu Ram Bhattarai (chief ideologue and negotiator); Krishna Bahadur Mahara

Netherlands

Capital: Amsterdam
Population: 16,318,199 (2004E)

The Kingdom of the Netherlands (consisting of the Netherlands in Europe and the Caribbean territories of Aruba and the Netherlands Antilles) is a constitutional and hereditary monarchy whose two non-European parts enjoy full autonomy in internal affairs (see next section). Under its 1815 constitution as amended, the Netherlands in Europe has a multi-party parliamentary system of government employing proportional representation to reflect the country's religious and social diversity. Executive authority is exercised on behalf of the monarch by a Prime Minister and other ministers, who are accountable to the States-General (Staten-Generaal). The latter consists of (i) the 75-member First Chamber (Eerste Kamer) elected by the members of the country's 12 provincial councils for a four-year term; and (ii) the 150-member Second Chamber (Tweede Kamer), also elected for a four-term but by universal suffrage of those aged 18 and over by a system of "pure" proportional representation with no minimum percentage threshold requirement. A founder member of what is now the European Union, the Netherlands elects 27 (previously 31) members of the European Parliament.

While political parties in the Netherlands have traditionally relied on members' subscriptions and donations, since 1972 state funding has been available for policy research and educational foundations attached to parties represented in the Second Chamber. Parties also receive certain concessions to defray expenses during election campaigns, including a limited amount of free media access.

Elections to the Second Chamber on Jan. 22, 2003, resulted as follows: Christian Democratic Appeal 44 (with 28.6% of the vote), Labour Party 42 seats (27.3%), People's Party for Freedom and Democracy 28 (17.9%), Socialist Party 9 (6.3%), List Pim Fortuyn 8 (5.7%), Green Left 8 (5.1%), Democrats 66 6 (4.1%), Christian Union 3 (2.1%), Reformed Political Party 2 (1.6%).

The Netherlands has 27 seats in the new European Parliament (EP). In the elections to the EP held on June 10, 2004, the ruling centre-right parties, the Christian Democratic Appeal and the People's Party for Freeedom and Democracy, polled comparatively poorly, receiving 24.4% of the vote and 7 seats (-2) and 13.2% of the vote and 4 seats, (-2), respectively. One of the main reasons for the decline in their electoral suport was believed to be the growing discomfort of the voters with the government's support for the war in Iraq. A new anti-war party, Transparent Europe, picked up 7.3% of the vote and two seats. The opposition Labour Party secured 23.6% of the vote and 7 seats (+1). Other results were as follows: Green Left 7.4% and 2 seats (-2); Socialist Party 7.0% and 2 seats (+1); Christian Union-Reformed Political Party 5.9% and 2 seats (-1); Democrats '66 4.2% of the vote and 1 seat (-1). The turnout in the elections was 39.1%.

Christian Democratic Appeal
Christen-Democratisch Appèl (CDA)

Address. Dr Kuyperstraat 5, 2514 BA The Hague
Telephone. +31-(0)70-342–4814
Fax. +31-(0)70-364–3417
Email. cda@bureau.cda.nl
Website. www.cda.nl
Leadership. Marja van Bijsterveldt (chair); Maxime Verhagen (parliamentary leader).
The right-of-centre Christian-inspired CDA was founded in April 1975 as a federation of (i) the Anti-Revolutionary Party (*Anti-Revolutionaire Partij,* ARP) founded in 1878 by Abraham Kuyper; (ii) the Christian Historic Union (*Christelijk Historische Unie,* CHU) established by ARP dissidents in 1908; and (iii) the Catholic People's Party (*Katholieke Volkspartij,* KVP) dating from 1928 and renamed in 1945. The new CDA formation represented an attempt by these confessional parties to reverse the steady decline in their vote since 1945. The CDA was constituted as

a unified party in October 1980, after a five-year preparatory phase. It gained 49 seats in the Second Chamber in 1977, 47 in 1981 and 45 in 1982.

From 1977 the CDA headed several coalition governments: with the People's Party for Freedom and Democracy (VVD) until September 1981, with the Labour Party and the Democrats 66 (D66) until May 1982, with D66 only until November 1982, and with the VVD after that under Ruud Lubbers. Having slipped from 48 to 45 Second Chamber seats in the September 1982 elections, the CDA subsequently experienced some internal dissension over the government's economic and defence policies. Nevertheless, in May 1986 it staged a sharp recovery, to 54 seats, and continued in government with the VVD.

The CDA retained 54 seats in the 1989 Second Chamber elections (with 35.3% of the vote), after which it formed a centre-left coalition with the PvdA, under the continued premiership of Lubbers, who became the Netherlands' longest-serving post-war Prime Minister. In advance of the May 1994 election, however, Lubbers announced his retirement from Dutch politics, with the result that the CDA campaigned under the new leadership of Elco Brinkman, amid difficult economic and social conditions. The outcome was that the party suffered its worst-ever electoral defeat, losing a third of its 1989 support and slumping to 22.2% and 34 seats, three less than the PvdA. The CDA recovered somewhat in the June 1994 European Parliament elections, to 30.8%, which yielded 10 of the 31 Dutch seats; nevertheless, Brinkman resigned as CDA leader in August 1994, as the party went into opposition to a PvdA-led coalition.

The CDA lost even more ground in the May 1998 general elections, winning only 18.4% of the vote for the Second Chamber and falling to 29 seats. It therefore remained in opposition to another PvdA-led coalition. In the June 1999 European elections the party slipped to 26.9% of the national vote, losing one of the 10 seats it held previously. Jaap de Hoop Scheffer resigned as party leader in parliament at the end of September 2001 saying he lacked support from party leaders for him to head the 2002 election campaign. Under the leadership of his successor, Jan Peter Balkenende, the party made a strong comeback in the May 2002 elections, securing 27.9% of the vote and 43 seats in the Second Chamber. As a result a coalition government led by Prime Minister Balkenende was formed with the CDA, the VVD and the List Pim Fortuyn (LPF, the party established by Pim Fortuyn who was murdered nine days before the elections, which had won 26 seats). However, the ongoing leadership struggle which plagued the LPF after the loss of its founder eventually led to the downfall of this coalition government on Oct. 16, 2002. In January 2003 early general elections were held in which the CDA sustained its 2002 election success, securing 28.6% of the votes, resulting in a further increase in CDA seats from 43 to 44. This made a second coalition government under Balkenende possible, this time with the VVD and D66, and without the LPF which had suffered a loss of 18 seats. In the June 2004 European elections, the CDA lost two of its nine seats.

The CDA is a member of the Christian Democrat International. Its representatives in the European Parliament sit in the European People's Party/European Democrats group.

Christian Union
Christen Unie (CU)

Address. PO Box 439, 3800AK, Apeldoorn
Telephone. +31-(0) 33-422 69 69
Fax. +31-(0)33-422 69 68
Email. bureau@christenunie.nl
Website. www.christenunie.nl/
Leadership. Thijs van Daalen (chair); André Rouvoet (parliamentary party leader)

The CU was founded in 2000, as a merger between the Reformational Political Federation (RPF) and Reformed Political Association (GPV).

Founded in March 1975, the **Reformational Political Federation** sought a reformation of political and social life in accordance with the Bible and Calvinistic tradition and creed. The party was formed by the National Evangelical Association, dissenters from the Anti-Revolutionary Party (ARP) and the Associations of Reformed (Calvinist) Voters. It won two seats in the Second Chamber in 1981 and again in 1982, when it also obtained 10 seats in provincial elections and about 100 in municipal elections. In 1986 it was reduced to one seat, which it retained in 1989, but trebled this tally in May 1994 on a 1.8% vote share. For the following month's European Parliament elections the RPF presented a joint list with the Reformed Political Association (GPV) and the Reformed Political Party (SGP), which took a 7.8% vote share and elected two members (neither from the RPF). The RPF improved to 2.0% in the May 1998 national elections, retaining three Second Chamber seats. In the June 1999 European Parliament elections it again presented a joint list with the GPV and SGP, which improved to 8.7% of the vote and three seats, one of which went to the RPF. All three representatives joined the Europe of Democracies and Diversities group.

On its creation in April 1948, the founders of the **Reformed Political Association** (GPV) claimed to represent the continuation of the ideas of the Dutch national Calvinists of the 16th and 17th centuries, but on the basis of recognition of the separation of church and state and of spiritual and fundamental freedoms. Before World War II the Anti-Revolutionary Party had claimed to represent these ideas, but the founders of the GPV objected to the "partly liberal and partly socialistic" tendencies which they believed to be developing in that party. Having won one Second Chamber seat in 1986, the GPV recovered to two seats in 1989 and retained them in the 1994 and 1998 elections, with 1.3% of the vote in each contest. In the 1994 and 1999 European Parliament elections the GPV presented a joint list with the Reformational Political Federation (RPF) and the Reformed Political Party (SGP), which took 7.8% of the vote and two seats in 1994, rising to 8.7% and three seats in 1999, one for each constituent party. All three representatives joined the Europe of Democracies and Diversities group.

Under the leadership of André Rouvoet, who prior to the merger of the RPF and GPV had been a member of Parliament for the RPF, the Christian Union secured 2.5% of the votes and 4 seats in the Second Chamber in the May 2002 elections. In the early elections of January 2003 the Party secured only 2.1% of the votes and 3 seats.

With the establishment of a CU-SGP Europe coalition, the tradition of RPF, GPV and SGP joint participation in European Parliament elections has been continued. It lost one seat, taking its total to two, in the June 2004 European elections.

Democrats 66
Democraten 66 (D66)

Address. PO Box 660, 2501 CR The Hague
Telephone. +31–(0)70 356–6066
Fax. +31–(0)70 364–1917
Email. info@d66.nl
Website. www.d66.nl
Leadership; Alexander Pechtold (chair); Boris Dittrich (parliamentary leader)

D66 was founded in 1966 as a left-of-centre progressive non-socialist party with "a commitment to change inspired by a sense of responsibility for the future", favouring pragmatism over ideology and strongly libertarian in inclination. Long-term leader Hans van Mierlo recorded that both liber-

alism and socialism were sources of inspiration for D66, both movements having "taken responsibility for a part of the whole truth" but then having erected their part into "the whole truth", so that false antitheses had been engendered, such as liberty against equality, individual against community and the free market against state control.

D66 won seven seats in the Second Chamber in 1967 and 11 in 1971, but only six seats in 1973 and eight in 1977. In 1981 the party increased its electoral support significantly, gaining over 11% of the vote and 17 seats in the Second Chamber. A downward trend reappeared in 1982, when the party was reduced to six seats. However, in May 1986 it recovered to nine seats and 6.1 % of the votes. D66 has usually regarded the Labour Party (PvdA) as its most obvious partner for participation in government. It took part in a coalition government with the PvdA (and three other parties) in 1973-77, but subsequently joined in coalition with the Christian Democratic Appeal (CDA) in 1982. This experience of government was seen as contributing to the party's setback in the September 1982 elections, in light of which Jan Terlouw resigned as leader and was eventually replaced by his predecessor, Hans van Mierlo.

D66's lower house representation rose from nine seats in 1986 to 12 in 1989, the latter tally being doubled to 24 in a major advance in May 1994 on a vote share of 15.5%, on the basis of which the party joined a coalition government with the PvdA and the People's Party for Freedom and Democracy (VVD). In the June 1994 European Parliament elections D66 slipped back to 11.7%, taking four of the 31 Dutch seats. A key condition of D66 participation in the government was that the constitution should be amended to make provision for "corrective referendums" in which parliamentary legislation on some subjects could be overturned by the people. After VVD ministers had opposed the proposal and Labour had expressed doubts, the version given cabinet approval in October 1995 excluded more subjects from referendum correction than D66 had originally proposed.

The May 1998 general elections delivered a major setback to D66, which slumped to 9.0% of the vote and 14 seats. The party nevertheless joined a further coalition with the PvdA and VVD. The November 1998 D66 conference in Gouda adopted a proposal by a group of young activists called "Upheaval" (*Opschudding*) that the party should officially identify itself as a "social liberal" formation, a committee being set up to draft a new mission statement to that effect. In the June 1999 European elections the D66 vote was halved, to 5.8%, and its representation reduced from four to two seats. The party suffered further electoral setbacks in the May 2002 elections when it only secured 5.1% of the votes and 7 seats, and again in the January 2003 elections when it only secured 4.1% of the votes and 6 seats in the Second Chamber. It also lost one of its two seats in the June 2004 elections for the European Parliament.

With an official membership of 12,000, D66 is a member party of the Liberal International. Its representatives in the European Parliament sit in the European Liberal, Democratic and Reformist group.

Green Left
GroenLinks (GL)

Address. PO Box 8008, 3503 RA Utrecht
Telephone. +31–(0)30 239–9900
Fax. +31–(0)30 230–0342
Email. info@groenlinks.nl
Website. www.groenlinks.nl
Leadership. Herman Meijer (chair); Femke Halsema (parliamentary leader)

The GL was founded prior to the 1989 Second Chamber elections as an alliance of the Evangelical People's Party (*Evangelische Volkspartij*, EVP), the Radical Political Party

(*Politieke Partij Radikalen*, PPR), the Pacifist Socialist Party (*Pacifistisch Socialistische Partij*, PSP) and the Communist Party of the Netherlands (*Communistische Partij van Nederland*, CPN). It became a unitary party in 1991, when each of its constituent groups voted to disband.

Of the component parties, the EVP had been formed in 1978 and had held one seat in the 1982-86 Second Chamber. The PPR had been founded in 1968 by a left-wing faction of the Catholic People's Party (later the mainstay of the Christian Democratic Appeal), had won seven seats in 1972 and had participated in a centre-left coalition in 1973–77. The PSP had dated from 1957 and had won between one and four seats in subsequent elections. The CPN had been founded in 1918 by left-wing Social Democrats, had held 10 seats in the post-1945 Second Chamber but had steadily declined to zero representation in 1986.

Having won six seats and 4.1% of the vote in its first general election contest in 1989, the GL slipped to five seats and 3.5% in May 1994. In the following month's European Parliament elections it recovered slightly to 3.7%, retaining one of the two seats it had won in 1989. It registered major gains in the May 1998 national elections, more than doubling its vote share to 7.3% and its Second Chamber representation to 11 seats. It continued its advance in the June 1999 European elections, winning 11.9% of the vote and four seats. However, the party lost ground slightly in the May 2002 elections, despite the effort by then party leader Paul Rosemuller to take on the controversial leader of the LPF, Pim Fortuyn, in a television debate in the lead up to these elections. The party secured 7.0% of the votes and 10 seats in the Second Chamber. The fall of the first Balkenende-led CDA, VVD and LPF coalition government in October 2002 eventually led to the calling of early elections in January 2003. It was now up to Femke Halsema, who succeeded Paul Rosemuller as parliamentary party leader in December 2002, to lead the party through these elections. Despite her efforts the party suffered another decline in these elections, securing 5.1% of the votes and 8 seats in the Second Chamber, and it also lost two if its four seats in the European Parliament elections of June 2004.

With an official membership of 14,000, the GL is affiliated to the European Federation of Green Parties. Its representatives in the European Parliament sit in the Greens/European Free Alliance group.

Labour Party
Partij van de Arbeid (PvdA)
Address. Herengracht 54, 1000 BH Amsterdam
Telephone. +31–(0)20 551–2155
Fax. +31–(0)20 551–2250
Email. pvda@pvda.nl
Website. www.pvda.nl
Leadership. Ruud Koole (chair); Wouter Bos (parliamentary party leader)

The PvdA was founded in 1946 as the post-war successor to the Social Democratic Workers' Party, founded in 1894 by P.J. Troelstra and other dissidents of the Social Democratic Union (created by F.D. Nieuwenhuis in 1881). From its establishment in 1946 as a broader-based party including many former Liberals, the PvdA engaged in the reconstruction of the Netherlands after the German occupation. Its leader, Willem Drees, was Prime Minister of a Labour-Catholic coalition government from 1948 to 1958, whereafter the PvdA was in opposition for 15 years – except briefly in 1965–66, when it took part in a coalition government with the Catholic People's Party (KVP) and the Anti-Revolutionary Party (ARP). The PvdA was weakened in 1970 by a right-wing breakaway by followers of Dr Willem Drees (son of the former Prime Minister), who formed the Democratic Socialists 1970 (DS-70) party. Although DS-70 gained eight seats in the 1971 elec-

tions, thereafter its representation declined and the party was dissolved in January 1983.

In 1971 and 1972 the PvdA contested elections on a joint programme with the Democrats 66 (D66) and the Radical Political Party, and in 1973 it formed a coalition government with these parties and also the KVP and the ARP, with the then PvdA leader, Joop den Uyl, becoming Prime Minister. This was the first Dutch government with a left-wing majority of ministers. However, after the 1977 elections, in which the PvdA increased its seats in the Second Chamber from 43 to 53, the party went into opposition to a centre-right government led by the Christian Democratic Appeal (CDA). From September 1981 to May 1982 the party took part in a coalition government with the CDA and D66. The PvdA was then in opposition, despite achieving a significant advance in the May 1986 Second Chamber elections, from 47 to 52 seats. Following those elections, Wim Kok (hitherto leader of the Netherlands Trade Union Confederation) became PvdA leader in succession to den Uyl (who died in December 1987).

Although it fell back to 49 seats on a 31.9% vote share, the PvdA returned to government after the 1989 elections, as junior coalition partner to the CDA. In August 1991 Marjanne Sint resigned as PvdA chairperson because of the party's acceptance of cuts in the state social security system, introduced by the CDA–PvdA coalition. In the May 1994 lower house elections the PvdA slipped again, to 24.0% and 37 seats, but overtook the CDA as the largest party and therefore became the senior partner in a new three-party coalition, this time with the People's Party for Freedom and Democracy (PVV) and D66. In the June 1994 elections to the European Parliament, support for Labour declined further, to 22.9%, giving it eight of the Netherlands' 31 seats.

Helped by the popularity of Prime Minister Kok, the PvdA staged a major recovery in the May 1998 general elections, winning 45 seats on a 29.0% vote share. Kok accordingly formed a further coalition with the PVV and D66. In the June 1999 European elections, however, the PvdA declined to 20.1% of the vote, its representation falling from eight to six seats.

In August 2001 Kok announced that he would not be a candidate for the premiership after the general elections due in May 2002 and would stand down from the PvdA leadership in advance of the elections. It was up to his designated successor, former party leader Ad Melkert, to lead the party through the May 2002 elections. However, the election results proved disastrous, the party securing only 15.1% of the votes and 23 seats in the Second Chamber. This in turn led to Ad Melkert's decision to step down as party leader. Under the leadership of his successor, Wouter Bos, the PvdA made a formidable comeback in the early elections of January 2003, securing 27.3% of the votes and 42 seats in the Second Chamber. It continued this success in the June 2004 European Parliament elections when it gained one seat, increasing its total to seven.

With an official membership of 60,000, the PvdA is a member party of the Socialist International. Its European Parliament representatives sit in the Party of European Socialists group.

List Pim Fortuyn
Lijst Pim Fortuyn (LPF)
Address. Albert Plesmanweg 43m, 3088GB Rotterdam
Telephone. +31-(0)10-7891140
Fax. +31-(0)10-7891141
Email. Info@lijstpimfortuyn.nl
Website. www.lijstpimfortuyn.nl
Leadership. Ton van Dillen (chair); Mat Herben (parliamentary party leader)

Established in February 2002 by Professor Dr Pim Fortuyn, the LPF's main aim was the reform of Dutch politics and public administration, which, in the eyes of its founder suffered from too much bureaucracy, too much top-down regulation, too much leniency with regards to the enforcement of existing laws, and a lack of vision as to how contemporary issues of multiculturalism should be addressed. His openness regarding his extravagant personal life and his ability to shock an audience with what were seen by many as controversial statements on issues such as religion and multiculturalism, ensured that Fortuyn never failed to attract the attention of the media. Rather than positioning itself along traditional left-right lines, the party profiled itself as a reformist and secular formation whose *raison d'être* was the shaking up of an unresponsive Dutch public administration and government.

Pim Fortuyn was assassinated on May 6, 2002, nine days before the national elections, precipitating a phase that would be characterised by immediate electoral success on the one hand, and subsequent decline and internal turmoil on the other. After consultation with the LPF leadership, Prime Minister Balkenende decided to let the elections go ahead, and the LPF, which had never before participated in national elections, secured 17% of the vote and 26 seats in the Second Chamber. Having become the second largest party, the LPF now occupied a pivotal position in the process of forming a new coalition government. A new centre-right government was eventually formed with the CDA, LPF and VVD, which ended an era of eight years of centre-left government. However, soon after the formation of this new coalition government, the LPF, having lost its undisputed leader, was gripped by internal strife and allegations of corruption. The ongoing disputes between two of the LPF cabinet ministers, Bomhoff and Heinsbroek, eventually led to the downfall of the government on Oct. 16, 2002. In the resultant January 2003 elections, the LPF suffered a dramatic decline, securing only 5.7% of the votes and 8 seats in the Second Chamber. The result of these elections, which were generally much more in line with traditional voting patterns, was that the LPF was reduced to the fifth largest party, losing its pivotal position in the formation of a new coalition government. What emerged was indeed a coalition, led by Jan Peter Balkenende, with CDA, VVD and D66, but without the LPF. In August 2004 a dispute between the party's members of Parliament and the party leadership led to a schism in the party. At present a court case is pending with regards to the question which of the two sections will be entitled to continue under the name LPF.

People's Party for Freedom and Democracy
Volkspartij voor Vrijheid en Democratie (VVD)

Address. Koninginnegracht 57, PO Box 30836, 2500 GL The Hague
Telephone. +31–(0)70 361–3061
Fax. +31–(0)70 360–8276
Email. alg.sec@vvd.nl
Website. www.vvd.nl
Leadership. Bas Eenhoorn (chair); Jozias van Aartsen (parliamentary leader)
Founded in 1948, the VVD is descended from the group of Liberals led by J.R. Thorbecke who inspired the introduction of constitutional rule in 1848. Organized as the Liberal Union from 1885, the Dutch Liberals (like their counterparts elsewhere in Europe) lost influence as the move to universal suffrage produced increasing electoral competition on the left, with the result that after World War II many Liberals joined the new Labour Party. However, other Liberal elements under the leadership of P.J. Oud founded the VVD, which remained in opposition to Labour–Catholic coalitions until 1959, when an electoral advance enabled the party to join a coalition with the Catholics.

After languishing electorally in the 1960s, the VVD made steady advances in the 1970s under the leadership of Hans Wiegel, winning 28 seats in the Second Chamber in 1977 and joining a coalition headed by the new Christian Democratic Appeal (CDA). Reduced to 26 seats in 1981, the VVD went into opposition, but under the new leadership of Ed Nijpels made a big advance to 36 seats the following year and joined a further coalition with the CDA. This was continued after the 1986 elections, although the VVD slipped back to 27 seats and from 23.1 to 17.4% of the vote.

Under the leadership of Joris Voorhoeve, the VVD lost ground once again in the 1989 elections, resulting in the party going into opposition for the first time since 1982. In the May 1994 contest, however, the VVD, now under the leadership of Frits Bolkestein, made a major advance by Dutch standards, from 14.6 to 19.9% of the vote, while the June European Parliament elections gave it a 17.9% tally and six of the 31 Dutch seats. In August 1994 the VVD, returned to government, joining a coalition with the PvdA and Democrats 66 (D66). In provincial elections in March 1995 the VVD struck a popular chord with its tough policy prescriptions on immigration and asylum seekers, overtaking the CDA as the strongest party at provincial level and therefore increasing its representation in the First Chamber to 23 seats. Within the national government, VVD ministers urged cuts in government spending to reduce the deficit to the Maastricht criterion for participation in a single European currency, thereby coming into conflict with the PvdA, which preferred to raise taxes.

In the May 1998 national elections the VVD, now led by Henri Frans (Hans) Dijkstal, overtook the CDA as the second-strongest party, winning 24.7% of the vote and 38 Second Chamber seats and subsequently joining a further coalition with the PvdA and D66. In the June 1999 European elections, moreover, it advanced to 19.7% and retained six seats. However, the VVD dropped to 15.5% of the vote and 24 seats in the elections of May 2002. The VVD became nevertheless a coalition partner in the first Balkenende government, together with the CDA and newcomer LPF. When early elections were called in January 2003, the party was led by Gerrit Zalm, who also served as Minister of Finance in the government. Under his leadership the party recovered slightly, securing 17.9% of the vote and 28 seats in the Second Chamber. Having retained its position of third largest party, the VVD was able to negotiate a new term in government in a CDA, VVD, D66 centre-right government. Zalm continued his roles as Minister of Finance and Deputy Prime Minister in this new government, while Jozias van Aartsen became the party's new parliamentary leader. The June 2004 European Parliament elections proved a setback for the VVD, as for the other government parties, it losing two of its six seats.

The VVD is a member of the Liberal International. Its European Parliament representatives sit in the European Liberal, Democratic and Reformist group.

Reformed Political Party
Staatkundig Gereformeerde Partij (SGP)

Address. Laan van Meerdervoort 165, 2517 AZ The Hague
Telephone. +31–(0)70 345–6226
Fax. +31–(0)70 365–5959
Email. partijbureau@sgp.nl
Website. www.sgp.nl
Leadership. Rev. D. Heemskerk (chair); Bastiaan Johannis (Bas) van der Vlies (parliamentary leader)
Founded in 1918, the right-wing Calvinist SGP bases its political and social outlook on its interpretation of the Bible. The SGP, which has been led by van der Vlies since 1986, advocates strong law enforcement, including the use of the death penalty, and is opposed to supranational government on the grounds that it would expose the Netherlands to corrupting influences. It has consistently attracted somewhat under 2% of

the vote, which gave it three Second Chamber seats through the 1980s, slipping to two in May 1994 on a vote share of 1.7%. For the following month's European Parliament elections the SGP presented a joint list with the Reformed Political Association (GPV) and the Reformational Political Federation (RPF), which took a 7.8% vote share and two seats (one for the SGP and one for the GPV).

The SGP improved to 1.8% of the vote in the May 1998 national elections, sufficient to increase its Second Chamber representation to three seats. In the June 1999 European Parliament elections it again presented a joint list with the GPV and RPF, which improved to 8.7% of the vote and three seats, one of which went to the SGP. All three representatives joined the Europe of Democracies and Diversities group. In the national elections of May 2002 the party secured 1.7% of the vote and 2 seats in the Second Chamber while it secured 1.6% of the vote and 2 seats in the early national elections of January 2003. The SGP has an official membership of approximately 25,500.

In the June 2004 European Parliament elections the SGP competed on a joint list with the Christian Union (the successor to the GPV and RPF), the list losing one of its three seats.

Socialist Party
Socialistische Partij (SP)
Address. Vijverhofstraat 65, 3032 SC Rotterdam
Telephone. +31–(0)10 243–5555
Fax. +31–(0)10 243–5566
Email. sp@sp.nl
Website. www.sp.nl
Leadership. Jan Marijnissen (chair and parliamentary leader).
The left-wing SP derives from a Maxist-Leninist party founded in 1971 and has latterly obtained electoral support from former adherents of the Communist Party of the Netherlands, which disbanded in 1991 to become part of the Green Left. The SP increased its vote share from 0.4% in 1989 to 1.3% in the May 1994 Second Chamber elections, returning two deputies.

Contending in the May 1998 elections that the incumbent coalition led by the Labour Party had done little to alleviate poverty and had allowed wealth differentials to grow, the SP almost trebled its vote, to 3.5%, and won five Second Chamber seats. It registered a further advance in the June 1999 European Parliament elections, taking 5.0% of the vote and winning its first seat. Its representative joined the European United Left/Nordic Green Left group. The upwards trend which the party had seen in the 1998 elections continued in the national elections of May 2002, when it secured a remarkable 5.9% of the vote and 9 seats in the Second Chamber. This electoral success was maintained, and even slightly increased in the the early national elections of January 2003 when the SP secured 6.3% of the vote and 9 seats in the Second Chamber. It also gained an additional seat in the June 2004 elections to the European Parliament. The party has an official membership of approximately 27,000.

Other Parties

Centre Democrats (*Centrumdemocraten*, CD), radical right-wing party created in 1986 by the majority "moderate" wing of the Centre Party (CP). Established on an anti-immigration platform mainly by former members of the ultranationalist Dutch People's Union (NVU), the CP had succeeded in attracting significant support among white working-class voters in inner city areas with heavy immigrant concentrations. In the 1982 Second Chamber elections it had obtained over 68,000 votes (0.8%) and one seat, while in the 1984 local elections it won 10% of the vote in Rotterdam and eight seats on the city council. Violent incidents occurred at several CP meetings prior to the May 1986 Second Chamber elections, in which the party failed to secure representation. Eight days before polling the CP had been declared bankrupt by a Dutch court after failing to pay a fine of 50,000 guilders imposed for forgery of election nominations. Re-emerging as the CD, the party regained one Second Chamber seat in 1989 and advanced to three seats in May 1994, winning 2.5% of the vote. It slumped to 0.6% in May 1998 and failed to win a seat and is now dissolved.

The Conservatives.nl (*Conservatieven.nl*), promoting the ideas of murdered political leader Pim Fortuyn. The Conservative.nl formation was founded in 2002 by former List Pim Fortuyn (LPF) member Winnie de Jong, after she had been forced to step down as an MP by fellow LPF members. The party secured less than 0.1% of the vote in the January 2003 national elections and failed to secure a seat in the Second Chamber.
Telephone. +31-(0)70-3185850
Fax. +31-(0)70-3185889
Email. info@deconservatieven.nl
Website. www.deconservatieven.nl
Leadership. Winnie de Jong

Dutch Middle Class Party (*Nederlandse Middenstands Partij*, NMP), conservative formation founded in 1970, but having no electoral impact .
Address. PO Box 2087, 8203AB Lelystad
Telephone/Fax: +31-(0)320-281412
Email. info@nmp.nl
Website. www.sdnl.nl/nmp.htm
Leadership. Jos Bron

European Party (*Europese Partij*, EP), founded in 1998 to advocate "global subsidiarity" and "democratic European governance" for its citizens and to oppose the "wasteful bureaucracy" of the present European Union.
Address. PO Box 136, 2501 CC The Hague
Telephone. +31–(0)10 213–6218
Email. r.nieuwenkamp@minocw.nl
Website. http://www.europesepartij.nl
Leadership. Kees Nieuwenkamp & Roel Nieuwenkamp

Frisian National Party (*Fryske Nasjonale Partij*, FNP), founded in 1962 to seek autonomy for the northern province of Friesland within a federal Europe; affiliated to Democratic Party of the Peoples of Europe–European Free Alliance.
Address. Obrechtstrjitte 32, 8916 EN Ljouwert
Telephone. +31–58 213–1422
Fax. +31–58 213–1420
Email. fnp.ynfo@fnp.nl
Website. www.fnp.nl/
Leadership. Cees van der Meulen (chair)

The Greens (*De Groenen*), founded in 1984 as a conservative church-oriented environmentalist party, opposed to leftist radicalism of Green Left; won one upper house seat in March 1995 but failed to gain lower house representation in 1994 or 1998, its vote share in the latter contest being 0.2%; member of European Federation of Green Parties.
Address. PO Box 1251, 3500 BG Utrecht
Telephone. +31-(0)71-5762027
Email. info@degroenen.nl
Website. www.degroenen.nl
Leadership. Jacques de Coo

List Emile Ratelband, party that promotes citizen participation and consultation using the internet. Founded in

December 2002 by Emile Ratelband, after a failed attempt to become political leader of Liveable Netherlands (LN). In the national elections of January 2003, Ratelband, who had gained celebrity status in the Netherlands with his extravagant media and communications training programmes and his flamboyant lifestyle, managed to secure 0.1% of the vote and no seat in the Second Chamber.
Email. info@lijstratelband.nl
Website. www.lijstratelband.nl
Leadership. Emile Ratelband

List Veldhoen, promoting a hardline approach to immigration issues; obtained less than 0.1% of the vote in the 2003 elections.
Telephone. +31-(0)10-4131800
Email. lijstveldhoen@unetmail.nl
Website. www.lijstveldhoen.freeler.nl
Leadership. J. Veldhoen

Liveable Netherlands (*Leefbaar Nederland*, LN), pro-law enforcement, citizen participation and democratic reform; founded in 1999. Won 1.6% of the vote in 2002 national elections and 2 seats in the Second Chamber, but with only 0.4% of the vote in the early national elections of January 2003 the party is no longer entitled to a seat in the Second Chamber.
Address. PO Box 18581, 2502 EN The Hague
Email. info@leefbaar.nl
Website. www.leefbaar.nl
Leader. Fred Teeven

Netherlands Mobile (*Nederland Mobiel*), conservative pro-motorist party founded in 1997, won 0.5% in 1998 lower house elections.
Address. PO Box 5795, 3008 AT Rotterdam
Telephone. +31-(0)6-53673404
Fax. +31-(0)111483583
Email. croos@publishnet.nl
Website. www.nederland-mobiel.nl
Leadership. Hans Grashoff (chair)

New Dutch Communist Party (*Nieuwe Communistische Partij Nederland*, NCPN). Founded in 1992 after the Dutch Communist Party (*Communistische Partij Nederland*, CPN) had merged with Green Left (*Groen Links*, GL). The party did not participate in the May 2002 national elections. However, it did participate in the January 2003 national elections, securing 0.1% of the vote and no seat in the Second Chamber.
Address. Haarlemmerweg 177, 1051 LB, Amsterdam
Telephone. +31–(0)20-682–5019
Fax. +31–(0)20-682–8276
Email. manifest@wanadoo.nl
Website. www.ncpn.nl

Party of the Animals (*Partij voor de Dieren*, PvdDieren). Animal rights party which in January 2003 participated for the first time in national elections. It obtained 0.5% of the vote, but failed to secure a seat in the Second Chamber.
Address. PO-box 92082, 1090AB Amsterdam
Telephone. +31-(0)20-4631211)
Email. info@partijvoordedieren.nl
Website. www.partijvoordedieren.nl
Leader. Marianne Thieme

Party of the Future (*Partij voor de Toekomst*, PvdT), won 0.5% of the vote in the January 2003 national elections.
Address. p/a Marconilaan 72, 5621 AB, Eindhoven
Website. www.partijvdtoekomst.nl
Leader. Johan Vlemminx

Progressive Integration Party (*Vooruitstrevende Integratie Partij*, VIP). Multiculturalist, anti-discrimination party; in January 2003 participated in national elections for the first time, obtaining less than 0.1% of the vote.
Address. Muzenplein 58, 2511 GD, Den Haag.
Telephone. +31-(0)70-3627151
Fax. +31-(0)70-3453432
Website. www.integratiepartij.nl
Leader. Ranesh Dhalganjansing

Reform and Democracy Alliance (*Alliantie Vernieuwing en Democratie*, AVD) Promoting the ideas of murdered political leader Pim Fortuyn; in January 2003 participated for the first time in general national elections, securing less than 0.1% of the vote and failing to secure a seat in the Second Chamber.
Email. info@avd-web.nl
Website. www.avd-web.nl
Leader. IJsbrand van der Krieke

Socialist Workers' Party (*Socialistische Arbeiders Partij*, SAP). Internationalist Trotskyist formation founded in 1983 as the continuation of the International Communist Association (*Internationaal Kommunistenbond*, IKB), a union of different smaller communist groups. Since the early 1990s, a section of the party operates under the name SAP-rebel.
Address. Postbus 2096, 3000 CB Rotterdam
Telephone. +31-(0)20-6259272
Website. www.grenzeloos.org/sap/
Email: redactie@grenzeloos.org
Leadership. H.E.W. Lindelauff

Sustainable Netherlands, (*Duurzaam Nederland*, DN). Party that promotes protection of the environment and better communication between government and citizens. Founded in December 2002 as a spin-off from Liveable Netherlands (LN); secured 0.1% of the vote and no seat in the Second Chamber in the 2002 and 2003 national elections.
Telephone. +31-(0)10-2653621
Fax. +31-(0)10-4664078
Email. info@duurzaamnederland.nl
Website. www.duurzaamnederland.nl
Leadership. Manuel Kneepkens (chair); Dr. Seyfi Özgüzel (political leader)

Transparent Europe (*Europa Transparant*, ET), founded in 2004 by former European commissioner Paul van Buitenen who lost his job as a commissioner after he went public with the details of financial fraud and corruption in the European Commission under Jacques Santer. As a result all twenty commissioners decided to step down in spring 1999. Transparent Europe is a single issue party aimed at promoting transparency and the reduction of corruption and cronyism. The party secured two seats in the European Parliament elections of 2004.
Address. Corkstraat 46, 3047AC, Rotterdam
Telephone. +31–(0)10 208–5925
Email. contact@europatransparant.nl
Website. www.europatransparant.nl
Leadership. Paul van Buitenen

NETHERLANDS DEPENDENCIES

The Kingdom of the Netherlands incorporates two Caribbean territories which became Dutch possessions in the 17th century, namely Aruba and the Netherlands Antilles, both of which exercise full autonomy in domestic affairs and have flourishing multi-party systems. Unlike those in French dependencies in the same region, political parties in Aruba and the Netherlands Antilles have little direct connection with or derivation from metropolitan parties.

Aruba

Capital: Oranjestad
Population: 71,000 (2003E)

Located off the north-east coast of Venezuela, the island of Aruba was part of the Netherlands Antilles until it secured self-government (*status aparte*) on Jan. 1, 1986. It has an appointed Governor representing the Dutch sovereign and a 21-member legislature (*Staten*) elected for a four-year term, to which the Prime Minister and Council of Ministers are accountable for their executive authority (which excludes external relations and defence). Elections to the *Staten* on Sept. 28, 2001, resulted as follows: People's Electoral Movement 12 seats (with 52.4% of the vote), Aruban People's Party 6 (26.7%), Aruban Patriotic Party 2 (9.6%), Aruban Liberal Organization 1 (5.7%).

Aruban Liberal Organization
Organisacion Liberal Arubano (OLA)
Address. c/o Staten, Oranjestad
Leadership. Glenbert F. Croes
Founded in 1991, the moderate OLA won two seats in the 1994 elections and joined a coalition headed by the Aruban People's Party (AVP). It withdrew from the government in September 1997 but again won only two seats in the resultant December 1997 elections and re-joined the AVP in office. It fell back to one seat in the September 2001 elections and went into opposition.

Aruban Patriotic Party
Partido Patriótico Arubano (PPA)
Address. c/o Staten, Oranjestad
Leadership. Benedict (Benny) J.M. Nisbett
The PPA was founded in 1949 and later became an anti-independence grouping. It won two seats in the 1985 elections and joined an Aruban home rule government headed by the Aruban People's Party (1986–89) and then a coalition headed by People's Electoral Movement (1989–93). It was reduced to one seat in the 1993 elections and was unrepresented in 1994–2001, but returned to the *Staten* in September 2001 with two seats.

Aruban People's Party
Arubaanse Volkspartij (AVP)
Address. Ave Alo Tromp 57, Oranjestad
Telephone. (297) 26326
Fax. (297) 37870
Leadership. Jan Henrik (Henny) A. Eman (leader); Robertico Croes (chairman); Mito Croes (secretary-general)
The AVP was founded by Henny Eman in 1942 and long advocated separation from Netherlands Antilles (but not full independence). On the achievement of home rule in 1986, Eman became Prime Minister of Aruba. It was in opposition from 1989 until 1994 when it formed a coalition with Aruban Liberal Organization (OLA).

The AVP/OLA coalition collapsed in acrimony in September 1997, but was revived after the December elections, in which the AVP retained 10 seats. This government almost served its full term, but was defeated by the People's Electoral Movement (MEP) in elections in September 2001, with the AVP retaining only six seats.

The AVP is affiliated to the Christian Democrat International and the Christian Democrat Organization of America.

People's Electoral Movement
Movimento Electoral di Pueblo (MEP)
Address. Santa Cruz 74D, Oranjestad
Telephone. (297) 854495
Fax. (297) 850768
Email. mep@setarnet.aw
Leadership. Nelson Orlando Oduber (chairman)
The MEP was founded in 1971 by Gilberto (Betico) François Croes and became the leading advocate of Aruba's separation from Netherlands Antilles and eventual full independence, not least so that Aruba would have full benefit from offshore oil reserves. In opposition on the achievement of separate status in 1986, the MEP returned to power after the 1989 elections under Nelson Oduber, who became head of a coalition government which included the Aruban Patriotic Party. The MEP then backtracked on the aim of full independence in 1996, instead accepting continued Dutch sovereignty. The government collapsed in 1994, causing new elections in which the MEP took second place (with nine of 21 seats) and went into opposition to a coalition headed by the Aruban People's Party.

The MEP remained at nine seats in the December 1997 elections and continued in opposition. In September 2001, however, Oduber led it back to power with an absolute majority of 12 seats.

The MEP is a member party of the Socialist International.

Other Parties

National Democratic Action (*Acción Democratico Nacional*, ADN). Founded in 1985 and a member of the first post-separation coalition in 1986–89 headed by the Aruban People's Party. It was in a coalition headed by the People's Electoral Movement in 1989–94, meanwhile winning only one seat in the 1993 elections, which it lost in 1994. The ADN took 2.4% of the vote in 1997 and 1.1% in 2001, but failed to secure a seat in the *Staten*.
Leadership. Pedro Pablo Kelly

Netherlands Antilles

Capital: Willemstad (Curaçao)
Population: 216,000 (2003E)

Consisting of the Caribbean islands of Curaçao, Bonaire, St Maarten, St Eustatius (or Statia) and Saba, the Netherlands Antilles have an appointed Governor representing the Dutch sovereign and a 22-member legislature (*Staten*), to which the Prime Minister and Council of Ministers are responsible. The *Staten* members are elected for a four-year term subject to dissolution, 14 from Curaçao, three each from Bonaire and St Maarten and one each from St Eustatius and Saba. In a referendum in St Maarten in June 2000, nearly 70% of voters approved proposals for St Maarten to leave the Netherlands Antilles and to become an autonomous territory within the Kingdom of the Netherlands.

Producing the customary wide distribution of seats between the parties, most of which exist in one island only, elections to the *Staten* on Jan. 18, 2002, resulted as follows: Workers' Liberation Front of the 30th May 5 seats (with 23.0% of the vote), Restructured Antilles

Party (PAR) 4 (20.6%), National People's Party (PNP) 3 (13.4%), Labour Party People's Crusade (PLKP) 2 (12.1%), Democratic Party-St Martin (DP-SM) 2 (5.5%), Bonaire Patriotic Union (UPB) 2 (3.6%), Democratic Party-Bonaire (DP-B) 1 (2.6%), Democratic Party St. Eustatius (DP-SE) 1 (0.5%), Windwards Islands People's Movement (WIPM) 1 (0.5%), National Alliance (NA) 1 (4.8%). The current coalition government consists of FOL, PNP, PLKP, PDB, and WIPM, and is led by Prime Minister Mirna Louisa Godett, the political leader of the FOL.

Bonaire Patriotic Union
Unión Patriótico Bonairano (UPB)
Address. Kaya Hulanda 26, Kralendijk, Bonaire
Telephone. +599–(0)7175330
Leadership. Ramon Booi
The UPB has been represented in the *Staten* since 1977, and won 2 seats in the January 2002 elections. The party is affiliated to the Christian Democrat International and the Christian Democrat Organization of America.

Democratic Party–Bonaire (DP-B)
Partido Democratico Bonairano (PDB)
Address. Kaya E.B. St. Jago, PO Box 294, Kralendijk, Bonaire
Telephone. +599 (0)7176758
Leadership. Laurenso A. (Jopie) Abraham (leader)
The centrist DP-B was founded in 1954 as an autonomous island party linked with other Antilles Democratic parties. The DP-B retained two *Staten* seats in the January 1998 elections and joined the government eventually formed by the National People's Party (PNP), with party leader Jopie Abraham becoming Second Deputy Prime Minister. He lost that status (but retained his ministerial portfolios) when the PAR regained the premiership in November 1999. In the *Staten* elections of January 2002 the party only secured 2.6% of the vote, leaving it with only one seat. The PDB is part of the current FOL, PNP, PLKP, PDB, WIPM coalition government.

Democratic Party–St Eustatius
Democratische Party–St Eustatius (DP-SE)
Leadership. Julian Woodley
This was the dominant party on mainly Catholic St Eustatius until 1998, when it lost the island's single *Staten* seat to the St Eustatius Alliance (SEA). It was also defeated by the SEA in the May 1999 island council elections, retaining only two of the five seats. The party secured 0.5% of the vote and 1 seat in the January 2002 *Staten* election.

Democratic Party–St Martin
Democratische Partij–Sint Maarten (DP–SM)
Address. PO Box 414, Philipsburg, St Maarten
Leadership. Sarah Wescott-Williams
The centrist DP–SM is based in the English-speaking community of St Maarten and has participated in successive Antilles governments, as well as usually having strong representation in the St Maarten council. Having two *Staten* seats in 1990, the party was weakened thereafter by splits and corruption allegations against its then leaders and was reduced to one seat in 1994. Under the new leadership of Sarah Wescott-Williams, the DP–SM recovered to two seats in 1998 and held two portfolios in the 1998-99 Antilles government headed by the National People's Party (PNR).

In elections to the St Maarten council in May 1999 the DP–SM won seven of the 11 seats and formed the territory's first-ever non-coalition government. In a referendum in June 2000 the government secured nearly 70% backing for its proposal that St Maarten should leave the Netherlands Antilles and become an autonomous territory within the

Kingdom of the Netherlands. The party managed to hold on to its two seats in the *Staten* in the January 2002 elections. The party was initially part of a FOL, DP-SM, PNP, PLKP, PDB, WIPM coalition government, but withdrew from it in August 2003.

Labour Party People's Crusade
Partido Laboral Krusada Popular (PLKP)
Address. Schouwburgweg 44, Willemstad, Curaçao
Telephone. +599–(0)9 737–0644
Fax. +599–(0)9 737–0831
Website. www.cur.net/krusado
Leadership. Errol A. Cova (leader)
The Curaçao-based PLKP was launched in 1997 with trade union backing and won three *Staten* seats its first elections in January 1998, opting to join a six-party centre-left government headed by the National People's Party (PNP). The party also polled strongly in Curaçao council elections in May 1999, winning four seats. In the January 2002 *Staten* elections the party secured only 12.1% of the vote, leaving it with only 2 seats. The party became nevertheless part of the current FOL, PNP, PLKP, PDB, WIPM coalition government.

National Alliance (NA)
The National Alliance is a cooperative union of two St Maarten based parties, the St Maarten Patriotic Alliance and the National Progressive Party, two opposition parties which have been overshadowed in recent years by the more powerful DP-SM, the main St. Maarten based party. In the January 2002 elections, the National Alliance secured 4.8% of the vote and 1 seat in the *Staten*.

National People's Party
Partido Nashonal di Pueblo (PNP)
Address. Penstraat 24, Willemstad, Curaçao
Telephone. +599–(0)9 462–3544
Fax. +599–(0)9 461–4491
Email. scamelia@pnp.an
Leadership. Suzanne (Suzi) Camelia-Römer (leader); Dudley Lucia (secretary-general)
Founded in 1948, the Christian democratic Curaçao-based PNP provided the Netherlands Antilles' first woman Prime Minister in 1984–85, when a coalition was headed by then leader Maria Liberia-Peters. She returned to the premiership in 1988 but resigned over the defeat in a November 1993 referendum of the PNP's proposal that Curaçao should seek Aruba-style separate status. The party was reduced from seven to three *Staten* seats in 1994 elections, being outpolled by the new Restructured Antilles Party (PAR). The PNP again won three *Staten* seats in the January 1998 elections, following which new leader Suzi Camelia-Römer eventually became Prime Minister of a six-party coalition. This collapsed in November 1999, whereupon Camelia-Römer became Deputy Prime Minister with responsibility for economic policy in a new coalition headed by the PAR. Meanwhile, in elections to the Curaçao council in May 1999, the PNP had advanced from four seats to five. The party maintained its position in the *Staten*, securing 13.4% of the vote and 3 seats, in the January 2002 elections and is part of the current FOL, PNP, PLKP, PDB, and WIPM coalition government. The PNP is affiliated to the Christian Democrat International and the Christian Democrat Organization of America.

New Antilles Movement
Movimentu Antiá Nobo (MAN)
Address. Landhuis Morgenster, Willemstad, Curaçao
Telephone. +599–(0)9 468–4781
Leadership. Kenneth Gijsbertha (leader)
The Curaçao-based centre-left MAN was founded in the

1970s by a non-Marxist faction of the Workers' Liberation Front of May 30. Under the leadership of Dominico F. Martina it headed Antilles coalition governments in 1982–84 and 1985–88 but was reduced to two *Staten* seats in 1990. It again won two seats in 1994, when it joined a coalition headed by the Restructured Antilles Party (PAR), but went into opposition after failing to improve on its two-seat tally in 1998. The MAN has participated in several recent Curaçao governments, although its representation in the island's council fell from six seats to two in May 1999. This downward trend continued in the January 2002 *Staten* elections when the party, obtaining only 3.0% of the vote, failed to secure a seat.

The MAN is a member party of the Socialist International.

Restructured Antilles Party
Partido Antiá Restrukturá (PAR)
Address. Fokkerweg 26/3, Willemstad, Curaçao
Telephone. +599–(0)9-465–2566
Fax. +599–(0)9-465–2622
Leadership. Miguel A. Pourier (president); Pedro J. Atacho (secretary-general)
The Christian social Curaçao-based PAR was founded in 1993 and became the leading Antilles party in the 1994 elections with eight seats, so that Miguel Pourier became Prime Minister of a government coalition with five other parties. It slumped to four seats in the January 1998 *Staten* elections, leaving it as still the largest single party but unable to form a new majority coalition. It therefore went into opposition to a government headed by the National People's Party (PNP), until a crisis in November 1999 enabled Pourier to regain the premiership at the head of a broad-based coalition. Meanwhile, in Curaçao council elections in May 1999, the PAR had slipped from six to five seats, although it had remained the largest single party. Although the Party managed to maintain its position in the *Staten*, securing 20.6% of the vote and 4 seats in the January 2002 elections, it failed to become part of the new coalition government.

Windward Islands People's Movement (WIPM)
Address. The Level 211, Av. Windwardside, Saba
Telephone. +599–(0)4 2244
Leadership. Will Johnston (president)
Based in mainly English-speaking and Catholic Saba and St Eustatius (Statia). It was the dominant party in Saba until 1995 and has won Saba's single *Staten* seat in the last five general elections. It returned to power in Saba in the May 1999 council elections, winning four of the five seats. The WIPM retained Saba's single seat in the *Staten* in the January 2002 elections, after which the party became part of the FOL, DP-SM, PNP, PLKP, PDB, WIPM coalition government. The party is affiliated to the Christian Democrat International and the Christian Democrat Organization of America.

Workers' Liberation Front of May 30
Frente Obrero Liberashon 30 di Mei (FOL)
Address. Mayaguanaweg 16, Willemstad, Curaçao
Telephone. +599–(0)9 461–8105
Email. agodett@fol.an
Leadership. Mirna Louisa Godett (leader)
The Curaçao-based pro-independence FOL was founded in 1969 and held one *Staten* seat in 1985–90. Having moderated its original Marxist ideology, it regained representation in 1998, winning two seats in alliance with the Independent Social (*Soshal Independiente*) grouping formed by dissidents of the National People's Party (PNP). The party then opted to join a six-party government headed by the PNP. The FOL won four Curaçao council seats in May 1999. Under the leadership of Mirna Louisa Godett, the party managed to

secure a remarkable 23% of the vote and an increase from 2 to 5 seats in the January 2002 *Staten* elections. This resulted in the formation of a FOL, DPSM, PNP, PLKP, PDB, WIPM coalition government, led by FOL leader Godett as Prime Minister.

New Zealand

Capital: Wellington
Population: 4,061,000 (2004)

New Zealand is a constitutional monarchy in which the British monarch is sovereign and the Governor-General exercises the powers of appointed representative. The unicameral parliament has 120 members, seven of whom represent Maori territorial units, and is elected for three years. Although the Prime Minister and cabinet are at the apex of the political system, parliament is the ultimate source of democratic accountability. As a result, the tenure of any government is dependent upon its ability to retain the confidence of parliament.

From the 1930s New Zealand politics had a two party character with the conservative National Party and the Labour Party alternating in government. Even when the two-party vote dropped, plurality voting effectively ensured that the two major parties maintained a stranglehold on parliamentary and executive power. Beginning in the late 1970s, electoral support for the two major parties began to decline, from an average of 95% in the post-World War II period to 70% in 1993. The radical economic and welfare policies of successive Labour (1984-90) and National (1990-93) governments provoked deep divisions within party ranks and brought about the formation of a number of splinter parties. By 1992 a five-party Alliance had emerged, mostly from the left flank of Labour, and in 1993 the New Zealand First party was formed from the populist and nationalist wing of the National Party. The gradual transition to a more fragmented multi-party system was completed by the electorate's decision, which took effect in 1996, to replace the plurality voting system with proportional representation.

As the result of a general election on July 27, 2002, a total of seven parties held seats in the new parliament, as follows: New Zealand Labour Party 52 (with 41.3% of the vote), New Zealand National Party 27 (20.9%), New Zealand First Party 13 (10.4 %), ACT New Zealand 9 (7.1%), Green Party of Aotearoa 9 (7.0%), United Future New Zealand 8 (6.7%), and the Progressive Party 2 (1.7%). The Labour Party subsequently formed a minority coalition government with the Progressive Party. Since the Alliance (1.3%) failed to meet the 5% electoral theshhold, it lost its entitlement to parliamentary seats. In 2004, a Labour minister, Tariana Turia, resigned from Labour and formed a new party, the Maori Party.

ACT New Zealand
Address. PO Box 99651, Newmarket, Auckland
Telephone. (64–4) 523–0470
Fax. (64–9) 523–0472
Email. info@voteact.org.nz
Website. www.act.org.nz
Leadership. Rodney Hide (leader); Catherine Judd (president); Val Wild (chief executive)
The ACT Party was formed in 1994 as the political instrument of a right-wing pressure group, the Association of Consumers

and Taxpayers. Its founding leader, Roger Douglas, was Labour's Minister of Finance during the 1980s. ACT's core beliefs include the maximization of "individual freedom and choice, personal responsibility, respect for the rule of law, and the protection of the life, liberty and property of each and every citizen". At various times it has advocated the abolition of personal income tax, fewer MPs and ministers, and the introduction of a voucher system for health and education. At the 1996 election the party won 6.1% of the vote and eight seats. Between 1998 and 1999 its support was crucial to the survival of the minority New Zealand National Party government. It is an extremely well funded party, with substantial business donations, and appeals to tactical voters who view the small party as an integral part of any future centre-right coalition. In 1999 it won 7% of the vote and nine parliamentary seats, also winning nine in 2002.

Green Party of Aotearoa (New Zealand)
Address. PO Box 11 652, Wellington
Fax. (64-4) 801–5104
Email. greenparty@greens.org.nz
Website. www.greens.org.nz
Leadership. Jeanette Fitzsimons and Rod Donald (co-leaders); Karen Davis and Paul de Spa (co-convenors); Ken Spagnolo (general secretary)
The Green Party's precursor, the Values Party, was formed in 1972. Values contested several elections, with little electoral success, before evolving into an environmental pressure group. In late 1989 the Values Party was officially disbanded. This left the way open in 1990 for the creation of the Green Party. Although its focus was the environment, the new party adopted the same post-materialist or "quality-of-life" issues that had characterised Values. In recent years, for example, the party has been a vocal critic of economic globalization, genetically modified plants and food, and the logging of native forests.

Only months after its formation, the Greens attracted 7% of the vote at the 1990 election. As a member of the third party grouping The Alliance, the party had three MPs elected at the 1996 election. However, tensions over policy priorities and organizational strategies, together with a growing confidence that the Greens had the electoral potential to go it alone, caused a break with the third party grouping in early 1999. It is the only parliamentary party to disclose its membership figures (2,800) and has relations with federations of green parties worldwide. It won nine seats, with 7.0% of the vote, in the 2002 elections.

New Zealand First Party
Address. Private Box 1574, Wellington
Telephone. (64–4) 471-9292
Fax. (64–4) 472-7751
Email. nzfirst@parliament.govt.nz
Website. www.nzfirst.org.nz
Leadership. Winston Peters (leader); Doug Woolerton (president); Graham Harding (secretary general)
New Zealand First was established in 1993 as the political vehicle of a prominent Maori politician, Winston Peters. The former New Zealand National Party MP's criticism of that party's neo-liberal agenda led to his dismissal from cabinet in 1991 and expulsion from the party caucus the following year. New Zealand First made its mark as a populist movement, adopting strong nationalistic policies on such issues as immigration and foreign investment. At the 1993 election it received 8.4% of the vote nationwide. Following the 1996 election, in which its 13.4% share of the vote gave it the balance of power, New Zealand First formed a coalition with its former National Party adversary. On the collapse of the coalition in 1998, nine of New Zealand First's 17 MPs broke away from the party and continued to support the govern-

ment. At the 1999 election New Zealand First received only 4.3% of the vote and five parliamentary seats, but in 2002 it improved to 10.4%, taking 13 seats.

New Zealand Labour Party
Address. PO Box 784, Wellington
Telephone. (64–4) 384–7649
Fax. (64–4) 384–8060
Email. labour.party@parliament.govt.nz
Website. www.labour.org.nz
Leadership. Helen Clark (leader); Mike Williams (president); Mike Smith (general secretary)
The Labour Party is the oldest of New Zealand's political parties, having been formed in 1916. During its first period in office from 1935-49 it introduced legislation creating a comprehensive welfare state. From 1949-84 the party was in opposition to the New Zealand National Party other than for terms in 1957-60 and 1972-75. During a second significant period of reform, between 1984 and 1990, under Prime Minister David Lange, Labour faced the consequences of deep-seated economic stagnation caused in good measure by loss of traditional markets for the agricultural commodities that were the bedrock of the economy. The new Labour programme reversed previous socialist and protectionist policies and instead included a commitment to economic deregulation, the ending of subsidies to the manufacturing and agricultural sectors, privatization of state-owned assets, encouragement of multi-national investment, and a more targeted system of welfare. Paradoxically it also introduced a system of compulsory trade union membership of a sort not seen in any other Western country. Whilst pursuing a largely neo-conservative economic agenda, Labour adopted a liberal position on such social issues as homosexual law reform and pay equity for women. Internationally, Labour's most prominent initiative was its ban on nuclear-powered and armed ships, a decision that led to the cancellation of New Zealand's ANZUS defence treaty with the United States.

Labour's economic reforms sparked conflict between the party's left and right wings, both in government and in the wider party. In 1989, following a public disagreement between the Finance Minister, Roger Douglas, and the Prime Minister, David Lange, over the cabinet's decision to introduce a flat 23% rate of income tax, Lange tendered his resignation. The following year, a group of Labour activists broke away to form a new left-wing party, which they named New Labour. Despite having had three Prime Ministers in as many years (Lange 1984-89; Geoffrey Palmer 1989-90; and Mike Moore 1990), Labour was unable to stem the growing tide of defections. At the 1990 election the National Party was returned to power with a landslide majority.

Following Labour's 1993 election defeat, its second in succession, Helen Clark replaced Moore as party leader. Despite its modest 28% share of the vote at the 1996 election, Labour was widely expected to lead the first coalition government under proportional representation. Instead, the third party holding the balance of power (New Zealand First) surprised almost everyone, including its own supporters, by choosing to go into government with its former adversary, National. During the next three years, the Labour leader established the basis for a workable coalition arrangement with the Alliance. In the November 1999 election Labour emerged as the largest party with 49 seats and it then formed a minority government with the Alliance (which had won 10 seats), the Alliance being given four seats in the 20-seat cabinet. Under Clark's prime ministership, Labour attempted to broaden its appeal as the party of "middle New Zealand" by pursuing a "Third Way" agenda based on a commitment to conservative economic principles, individual responsibility, and moderate social welfare reform. At the same time it criticized "excesses" in neo-liberalism and market deregulation under the previous National administration. Following the 2002 election, when it came first with 41.3% of the vote and 52 seats, the party formed a minority coalition with the two-person Progressive Party. The United Future Party's eight MPs promised the new government confidence and supply for the next three-year term.

The Labour Party is a member party of the Socialist International.

New Zealand National Party

Address. PO Box 1155, Wellington
Telephone. (64–4) 472–5211
Fax. (64–4) 478–1622
Email. hq@national.org.nz
Web. www.national.org.nz
Leadership. Don Brash (leader); Judy Kirk (president); Steven Joyce (general manager)

The National Party was a product of the merger of two conservative parties, Reform and United, in 1936. In fulfilment of the claim implicit in its title of representing the interests of all major segments of the New Zealand community, for most of the post-war period National was the party of government (1949-57; 1960-72; 1975-84; 1990-99). As a pragmatic party of a mildly conservative hue, the early National Party was able to persuade voters that in an era of plentiful job opportunities and high living standards it was the party best equipped to provide a balance between the goals of individual liberty, free enterprise, and welfare.

When National returned to power in 1990, Prime Minister Jim Bolger and Finance Minister Ruth Richardson intensified the process of economic liberalization begun by the New Zealand Labour Party while in office from 1984 in response to the country's worsening economic position. National carried out deregulation of the labour market (scrapping the system of compulsory trade union membership enacted by Labour in 1984), sharp reductions in government spending, and repayment of overseas debt through such methods as the selective privatization of state-owned assets. The impact of these policies resulted in an attrition of party members, especially those on fixed retirement incomes. In 1992 two National MPs defected to form an anti-free-market party, which later joined the Alliance, and the following year a former National cabinet minister and Maori MP, Winston Peters, established the New Zealand First Party.

Following National's modest but nonetheless winning performance at the 1993 election (when it took 35% of the vote, compared with 34.7% for Labour and a combined total of 30.3% for the minor parties), the Prime Minister signalled a return to a more moderate policy agenda. The success of the 1993 electoral referendum, together with the precariousness of his one-seat parliamentary majority, prompted Bolger to introduce a number of changes, including relieving Richardson of her finance portfolio, suspending several key privatization plans, and introducing a more measured and gradual approach to welfare reform. Following yet more defections from National's parliamentary ranks, Bolger entered into a coalition arrangement with a new centre party, the United Party, in February 1996. Although National lost further ground at the 1996 election, declining to a 33.8% share of the vote, New Zealand First's decision to go into coalition with the National Party provided National with its third successive term in government.

The National/New Zealand First coalition was unpopular from the time of its formation, even among the two parties' own voters. At the end of 1997, Jenny Shipley replaced Bolger as Prime Minister, a move intended to strengthen National's hand in its dealings with New Zealand First. The following year Shipley expelled Peters, who was the Deputy Prime Minister and Treasurer, from the cabinet. Although National was able to retain power with the help of the ACT

Party and a small group of minor party defectors, notably from New Zealand First, it trailed Labour in the opinion polls from the time of the coalition's break-up. In the November 1999 election its share of the vote (30.5%) plummeted to its lowest since National was established in 1936. After the election, Shipley was replaced as leader by Bill English. The party's new record low vote at the 2002 election resulted in a move to replace English as leader. In October 2003, the party replaced him with Dr Don Brash, a previous Governor of the Reserve Bank and first-term MP.

The National Party is a member of the International Democrat Union and the Asia-Pacific Democrat Union

United Future New Zealand

Address. PO Box 13–236, Wellington
Telephone. (64-4) 471–9410
Fax. (64–4) 499–7266
Email. peter.dunne@parliament.govt.nz
Web. www.united.nz.org.nz
Leadership. Peter Dunne (leader); Anthony Walton (deputy leader); Ian Tulloch (president); Murray Smith (general secretary)

The party was formed as the United Party in 1995 with the defection of seven MPs from the New Zealand National Party and the New Zealand Labour Party. As a centre party, it propped up the National government by taking a seat in cabinet in the final months leading up to the 1996 election. Although it received less than 1% of the vote at both the 1996 and 1999 elections, it was able to retain one seat by virtue of Peter Dunne's victory in the affluent Wellington constituency of Ohariu-Belmont. In 2000 the party merged with a Christian party, Future New Zealand, to become United Future New Zealand. After the 2002 election, when it emerged with eight seats, it made a "confidence and supply" agreement with the Labour minority government.

NEW ZEALAND'S ASSOCIATED TERRITORIES

Cook Islands

The Cook Islands, with a population of some 20,000, became a self-governing territory in free association with New Zealand in August 1965. Although New Zealand takes responsibility for foreign affairs and defence, it acts in consultation with the Cook Islands government. The head of state is the British monarch, and the parliament is a unicameral body of 25 members. At elections in June 1999, the Democratic Alliance Party took 11 seats, the Cook Islands Party 10 and the New Alliance Party 4. The Cook Islands Party, which had been in government for ten years under the premiership of Geoffrey A. Henry, was replaced by a coalition of its two rivals.

Other Territories

New Zealand's other associated territories include **Niue**, with a population of 2,500. Since 1974 Niue has had self-government in free association with New Zealand. There is a local Assembly but the political system is not based on formal party organizations. The **Ross Dependency**, in Antarctica, has no permanent population. In **Tokelau**, which has a population of 1,500, executive authority is exercised by an administrator appointed by New Zealand; the territory's national representative body is the General *Fono*, but there are no political parties.

Nicaragua

Capital: Managua
Population: 5,360,000 (2004E)

The Republic of Nicaragua achieved independence in 1838 but was subject to US military intervention in 1912-25 and 1927-33. The country was subsequently left in the control of the Somoza family until the overthrow of the right-wing dictatorship of Gen. Anastasio Somoza Debayle by a popular revolutionary movement, the Sandinista National Liberation Front (*Frente Sandinista de Liberación Nacional*, FSLN) in 1979. The FSLN introduced a number of far-reaching economic and social reforms despite attempts by conservative groups and US-backed right-wing *contra* rebels to destabilize the government. The FSLN won the presidential and legislative elections in 1984, the first to be held in the country since 1974, but lost subsequent elections in 1990, 1996 and 2001.

War fatigue among the population and a decade of economic austerity were instrumental factors in the FSLN's unexpected and heavy electoral defeat in 1990. Although the FSLN remained the country's largest party, a right-wing alliance, the National Opposition Union (UNO), won on a platform that promised to end the civil war, promote national reconciliation and attract foreign aid and investment. Arnoldo Alemàn Lacayo, the candidate of the Liberal Alliance (AL, the main opposition to the FSLN) won the next presidential election in 1996. The AL also won the legislative poll held at the same time. With the support of other conservatives, the Alliance patched together an absolute majority in the legislature.

In the most recent elections held in November 2001, the Constitutional Liberal Party (PLC) (formerly the largest member of the AL) won the presidency and a majority in the National Assembly. However, a subsequent power struggle between President Enrique Bolaños Geyer and his predecessor, Alemàn, led to a formal split within the PLC. This meant that Bolaños no longer had a majority in the Assembly, which led to an extended period of legislative paralysis.

Under the 1987 constitution, executive power rests with the President, who is head of state and commander-in-chief of the Defence and Security Forces and governs with the assistance of a Vice President and an appointed Cabinet. Amendments to the constitution approved in 1995 reduced the presidential term from six to five years and barred the President from serving more than two consecutive terms. A unicameral National Assembly is made up of 90 representatives (each with an alternative representative), who are directly elected for a five-year term by a system of proportional representation. Additional seats (currently three) are allotted to losing presidential candidates who have obtained the required national quotient to be elected to the Assembly.

Further constitutional reforms were enacted in January 2000, which saw the PLC and FSLN sign a pact that allotted the two parties control of the Electoral Council, the Supreme Court and the audit office. The pact also reduced the extent of party competition by making it much more difficult for smaller parties to register themselves, and so become eligible to participate in the electoral process. Further, it was agreed that the percentage of votes required to elect a President without the need for a run-off should be reduced from 45% of the total to 35%. The reforms

were an attempt by the PLC and FSLN to secure their own political futures, while reducing the influence of smaller parties in Nicaraguan politics.

Conservative Party of Nicaragua
Partido Conservador de Nicaragua (PCN)
Address. Costado Sur de la Diplotienda, Managua
Leadership. Mario Rappaccioli
The PCN was formed in 1992 when the Democratic Conservative Party of Nicaragua (PCDN) entered into a merger with the much smaller Conservative Social Party (PSC) and the Conservative Party of Labour (PCL). (Launched in 1979, the PCDN had been a right-wing party formed by three factions of the traditional Conservative Party, which had been the main legal opposition during the Somoza era.) In the presidential election held in 1996 the PCN's candidate, Noel José Vidaurre, finished fourth, winning just over 2% of the vote. The party won three National Assembly seats in legislative elections contested at the same time. In the build up to the 2001 elections the PCN leadership made an unsuccessful attempt to forge a "grand alliance" of political parties opposed to the pact between the Constitutional Liberal Party (PLC) and the Sandinista National Liberation Front (FSLN) agreed in January 2000. In the elections that followed the PCN's presidential candidate, Alberto Saborío, finished a distant third with 1.4% of the vote, while the party won two seats in the legislature. In May 2004, in an attempt to strengthen the party's position, the PCN negotiated a formal alliance with the rump of the PLC loyal to President Bolaños. The Alliance for the Republic (APRE) was established to present an alternative to the dominant pro-Alemàn PLC faction and the FSLN in the November municipal elections.

Constitutional Liberal Party
Partido Liberal Constitucionalista de Nicaragua (PLC)
Address. Apartado Postal 4569, Managua
Telephone. (505-2) 781754
Fax. (505-2) 781800
The PLC is the principal rival to the Sandinista National Liberation Front and headed the government from 1996. Formed in 1968, the PLC gained parliamentary representation for the first time in 1990 as part of the victorious National Opposition Union (UNO) alliance. In 1994 the PLC created a new coalition, the Liberal Alliance (AL), to support the presidential bid of the party's leader, Arnoldo Alemàn Lacayo. Alemàn won the 1996 election, and the AL, dominated by the PLC, also gained control of the legislature. During his tenure in office Alemàn gained credit for improving the armed forces and eradicating landmines, but was widely criticized for leading a corrupt and authoritarian administration.

Prior to the 2001 presidential and parliamentary elections the PLC decided to contest the elections in its own name. The AL was dissolved, but the PLC retained the backing of a number of small centre-right parties, including the Nicaraguan Resistance Party (PRN) (the political vehicle of the *contras*) and the Nicaraguan Christian Path (CCN). The PLC's presidential candidate, Enrique Bolaños Geyer, won a convincing victory over his Sandinista National Liberation Front (FSLN) challenger, while the party also gained a solid majority in the National Assembly. Former President Alemàn, meanwhile, used his influence to gain the presidency of the legislature, hoping to use the position as a launch pad for recapturing the presidency in 2006. However, Alemàn did not survive in his position for long.

After assuming the presidency Bolaños undertook an anti-corruption crusade that targeted several members of his own party, most notably the former President. In the power struggle that resulted, most PLC members backed Alemàn.

However, Bolaños had sufficient support in the National Assembly, after forming an ad hoc alliance with the FSLN, to strip Alemàn of his immunity from prosecution. Alemàn was subsequently charged with embezzling $100 million in public funds. In addition, Bolaños also relied on the FSLN to ensure the enactment of IMF-sponsored tax reform measures. The backlash against Bolaños for acting with the Sandinistas and against the former President was severe. In early August 2002, the PLC leadership announced that it had ceased to recognize Bolaños as its political leader, and later that month a majority of the parliamentary party joined the opposition benches. In early 2003, the party voted to formally sever its ties to the President. Bolaños then formed a separate faction, Liberal Unity, which was represented in the National Assembly by nine members of the divided PLC.

In October 2003, Alemàn, who was in prison awaiting trial, entrusted to his wife, María Fernanda Flores, the leadership of the PLC for the period of his imprisonment and trial. Many in the PLC leadership resented the move, believing that Flores was preparing the ground to secure the party's nomination for the 2006 presidential election in the event of her husband's conviction. Three members of the party's executive resigned their posts in protest. Alemàn was subsequently convicted on Dec. 7 on charges of fraud, money laundering and theft of state funds. The former President was fined US$17 million and sentenced to 20 years' imprisonment. However, the court ruled that Alemàn could serve the sentence under house arrest, due to his ill health.

After the conviction it was expected that the pro-Alemàn faction of the PLC would temper its opposition to President Bolaños and seek a rapprochement. However, hostility towards the President within the PLC did not moderate, and Alemàn maintained his grip on the party. Further, the Sandinistas ended their ad hoc relationship with the government, which resulted in legislative paralysis in February 2004. Bolaños appeared incapable of imposing his authority on the situation, and the growing impression was of a lame duck government. However, in May 2004 President Bolaños gave his backing to a new electoral alliance, the Alliance for the Republic (APRE), to fight the November municipal elections. The grouping consisted of six parties, including pro-government PLC members and the Conservative Party of Nicaragua (PCN). It was hoped that the alliance would block the advances of the Sandinistas and regain supporters loyal to former president Alemàn.

The PLC is a member of the Liberal International.

Nicaraguan Christian Path
Camino Cristiano Nicaragüense (CCN)
Address. c/o Asamblea Nacional, Managua
Leadership. Guillermo Osorno
The Christian, right-wing CCN won 3.7% of the vote and four National Assembly seats in the 1996 legislative elections. The party's candidate in the 1996 presidential elections, Guillermo Osorno, finished a distant third, winning some 4% of the vote. In the 2001 parliamentary elections the CCN won four seats in alliance with the Constitutional Liberal Party (PLC). However, in May 2004 the CCN leader, Osorno, renounced his entente with the PLC in the legislature. Osorno wanted to re-affirm the party's identity, in light of the emergence of a rival evangelical party, the Christian Alternative (AC).

Nicaraguan Resistance Party
Partido de la Resistencia Nicaragüense (PRN)
Address. Optica Nicaragüense, 100 varas al Lago, Managua
Telephone. (505-2) 668098
Leadership. Salvador Talavera
Former *contra* commanders formed the PRN in late 1992. In the 1996 legislative elections the party managed to win 1.2%

of the vote and one seat in the National Assembly. In the 2001 parliamentary elections the PRN gained representation in parliament through an alliance with the Constitutional Liberal Party (PLC).

Sandinista National Liberation Front
Frente Sandinista de Liberación Nacional (FSLN)
Address. Costado Oeste, Parque El Calmen, Managua
Telephone. (505-2) 660845
Fax. (505-2) 661560
Website. www.fsln-nicaragua.com
Leadership. Daniel Ortega Saavedra (secretary-general)
The FSLN was founded in 1961 and is named after the national hero Agusto César Sandino. It was founded by a small group of intellectuals, including former Nicaraguan Socialist Party (PSN) member Carlos Fonseca Amador and Tomás Borge Martínez, and began guerrilla activity against the US-backed Somoza regime in 1963. After suffering a series of defeats, it abandoned all military activity from 1970 to the end of 1974.

Fonseca, the FSLN's leading theoretician, was killed in 1976, and after 1975 disagreements on strategy split the movement into three factions. The Protracted People's War (GPP) group, led by Borge, favoured the creation of "liberated zones" on the Chinese and Vietnamese model, which would provide bases from which to attack towns. The Proletarian Tendency (PT), led by Jaime Wheelock, maintained that the FSLN should concentrate on winning the support of the urban working class. The "third way" group (*terceristas*), led by Daniel Ortega Saavedra, advocated a combination of an armed offensive and broad political alliances with other opposition organizations, which would lead to a general insurrection. A synthesis of all three strategies was finally agreed upon but with the *terceristas* the dominant tendency, and in March 1979 a national directorate was formed, consisting of the three main leaders of each faction. After intensified fighting, the Somoza regime was overthrown in the popular revolution of July 1979.

The FSLN's decisive role in the overthrow of the Somoza dictatorship inevitably made it the dominant political force after the revolution, although it shared power initially with anti-Somoza forces in the FSLN-led Patriotic Revolutionary Front (FPR) and with elements of the conservative middle class, in the Council of State. This Council was superseded in 1984 when Daniel Ortega was elected President and the FSLN secured a clear majority in a new National Assembly.

Half the national budget came to be devoted to the war against US-backed right-wing *contra* rebels who had initiated in 1981 a guerrilla war to destabilize the government. US trade and investment embargoes led to greater reliance on Soviet-bloc aid until 1987, when the Soviet Union began to scale down its oil supplies. In 1987, the emphatic opposition of the FSLN to direct negotiations with the *contras* was modified when it welcomed peace plans devised by the Contadora group and by President Arias of Costa Rica, which took shape in the Guatemala region peace accords. The Sandinistas made major concessions to their critics in the hope of achieving peace, including an end to the state of emergency, a readiness to talk to the *contras*, an amnesty of prisoners and an end to bans on the media. In December 1989, the FSLN signed a regional agreement calling for the demobilization of the Salvadoran guerrillas in the expectation that other governments would finally act to dismantle *contra* camps in Honduras.

After their surprise defeat in the 1990 presidential and legislative elections, the Sandinistas vowed to defend the "fundamental conquests of the revolution", such as nationalization of banks and foreign trade, state farms and the rights and freedoms contained in the 1987 constitution. After the elections, however, the FSLN lost both its discipline and unity. Grass-root members became increasingly alienated from the leadership, which was criticized for collaborating too much with the Chamorro government in the name of a responsible opposition. This gulf deepened when the leadership interposed itself between the centre-right government and the mass Sandinista organizations during strikes in 1990 against cuts in jobs and services. Accusations that the FSLN leadership had personally benefited from laws allowing for the disposal of state property and land before the Sandinistas relinquished power (known locally as the *pinata* after a children's game where everyone rushes to grab what they can) also left their mark on rank-and-file supporters. However, when right wing parties in the National Assembly in June 1991 repealed the laws that had also given land to *campesinos* (peasants), all 39 FSLN delegates withdrew from the Assembly indefinitely. Sandinista mass organizations rallied to their defence and in September President Chamorro partially vetoed the Assembly's decision.

Following an extraordinary party congress in May 1994, three distinct factions emerged within the FSLN: an "orthodox" faction headed by Ortega; a moderate "renewalist" faction headed by former Nicaraguan Vice President Sergio Ramírez Mercado; and a centrist "unity" grouping headed by Henry Ruiz Hernández. At the congress, the Ortega faction proved victorious, although Ramírez gained for himself the role of Ortega's alternate. Ortega ousted Ramírez from this post in September 1994 but the FSLN delegation then elected a moderate, Dora María Téllez, as its new leader. In early 1995 the disagreement came to a head with Ramírez, Téllez and 75% of the Sandinista legislative delegation withdrawing from the FSLN to form a new party, the Sandinista Renewal Movement (MRS).

In the presidential election of October 1996, Arnoldo Alemàn Lacayo, candidate of the Liberal Alliance (AL), heavily defeated Ortega. Ortega polled some 38% of the vote, against 51% for Alemàn. The FSLN also lost out to the AL in the accompanying legislative poll, winning 37 seats against 42 for the AL. Importantly, however, the FSLN did manage to fend off the threat from the MRS, which won only one seat. Following the election, the FSLN staged protests in Managua against alleged electoral irregularities, but the results stood and the Sandinistas remained in opposition.

Despite facing charges (later dropped) of sexually abusing his stepdaughter, Ortega was able to exploit the general hostility among the Sandinistas toward President Alemàn to reaffirm his position as head of the party and to secure its nomination for the presidential election in 2001. However, he suffered his third consecutive defeat, losing by a margin of 14%. In the National Assembly elections the FSLN performed disappointingly, gaining only an additional seat, bringing its total to 38.

In the aftermath of the election, pressure grew within the party for Ortega to make way for a new leader who was not burdened by a revolutionary past. Nevertheless, at a March 2002 party congress that FSLN dissidents criticized for its lack of democratic participation, Ortega was re-elected as the party's secretary-general for another four years. In July 2003, Ortega took a big step towards political rehabilitation by publicly apologizing for the revolutionary government's treatment of the Catholic Church, which wields significant political influence. Meanwhile the serious split within the governing Constitutional Liberal Party (PLC) enhanced the FSLN's legislative power, and strengthened Ortega's standing in the country and the party.

The FSLN is a member party of the Socialist International.

Niger

Capital: Niamey
Population: 10,080,000 (2000E)

The Republic of Niger attained independence from France in 1960 under the leadership of President Hamani Diori's Nigerien Progressive Party (*Parti Progressiste Nigérien*, PPN). Following a coup in 1974, the military took control and set up a Supreme Military Council, under Lt.-Col. Seyni Kountché, which ruled the country for the next 15 years. After Kountché's death in 1987, the Council appointed Brig. Ali Saïbou as his successor. The National Movement for a Society in Development–*Nassara* (*Mouvement National pour une Société de Développement*, MNSD–*Nassara*) was formed as the sole legal political party in August 1988 with Saïbou as its chairman. In May 1989 Saïbou was named as head of the country's new ruling body, a joint military-civilian Higher Council for National Orientation, which superseded the Supreme Military Council. A national conference held between July and November 1991 under the presidency of André Salifou suspended the constitution, took over executive authority from Saïbou and then appointed a transitional Prime Minister. In a referendum in December 1992, voters approved a new multi-party constitution. This provided for a directly elected President with a five-year term (once renewable) and for a similarly elected 83-member National Assembly (*Assemblée Nationale*), also with a five-year mandate. The party landscape in Niger is characterized by some stability in the number of parties and in its leaders, contesting each other in varying alliances during elections, punctuated by two coups d'état.

Parliamentary elections on Feb. 14, 1993, led to a victory of the Alliance of Forces for Change (*Alliance des Forces du Changement*, AFC) headed by Mahamadou Issoufou, who was installed as Prime Minister on April 17. On March 27, 1993, AFC candidate Mahamane Ousmane was elected as President, defeating MNSD candidate Colonel Mamadou Tanja. Power struggles within the government culminated in a coup d'état on Jan. 27, 1996, by Colonel Ibrahim Mainassare Barré who, after the adoption of a new constitution and the lifting of a ban on political parties, was himself elected as President on July 7, 1996, with 52.22% of the votes. These elections were widely declared fraudulent. Barré remained in place, despite protests from the opposition parties, united in two party coalitions – the Front for the Restoration and Defence of Democracy (*Front pour la Restauration et la Défense de la Démocratie*, FRDD), and the Alliance of Democratic and Social Forces (*Alliance des Forces Démocratiques et Sociales*, AFDS).

On April 9, 1999, Mainassare Barré was murdered. Prime Minister Ibrahim Hassane Mayaki dissolved the National Assembly. On April 11, the head of the Presidential Guard, Maj. Daouda Mallam Wanké, assumed power as head of the National Reconciliation Council (*Conseil de Réconciliation Nationale*, CRN) with Mayaki remaining Prime Minister of an FRDD and AFDS coalition cabinet. In July 1999 a new constitution introducing a balance of powers between the President, Prime Minister and legislature was approved by popular referendum, and promulgated shortly thereafter.

Multi-party legislative and presidential elections held in October and November 1999 were won by the

MNSD. Final results gave an absolute majority to the MNSD in combination with its ally the Democratic and Social Convention *Rahama* (*Convention Démocratique et Social*, CDS–*Rahama*), which obtained 38 and 17 seats respectively. An alliance of opposition parties, the Coordination of Democratic Forces (*Coordination des Forces Démocratiques*, CFD), led by the centre-left Niger Party for Democracy and Socialism *Tarayya* (*Parti Nigérien pour la Démocratie et le Socialisme*, PNDS-*Tarayya*) secured the remaining 28 seats. The presidential race was won by the MNSD candidate Col. (ret.) Mamadou Tanja, who defeated former Prime Minister Mahamadou Issoufou of the PNDS. Wanké relinquished power in December 1999 and Tanja was sworn in as President for a five-year term, appointing the MNSD's Amadou Hama as Prime Minister.

In July and August 2002, Tanja was confronted with an army mutiny over arrears in pay and living conditions in the garrisons of Diffa, N'Gourti and N'Guigmi, which he declared a rebellion against the state and which was subsequently suppressed by loyal units. In July 2003, Tanja used the MNSD's majority in the National Assembly to change the electoral code, abolishing the requirement for the National Election Council to be presided over by a magistrate and the requirement for Ministers to leave office when standing for election. Opposition parties boycotted the parliamentary session voting these changes and took the issue to the Constitutional Court, which annuled the changes.

Communal elections planned for spring 2004, after the completion of adminstrative decentralization and the creation of communes, were postponed.

Democratic and Social Convention–Rahama
Convention Démocratique et Social–Rahama (CDS)

Address. c/o Assemblée Nationale, BP 12234, Place de la Concertation, Niamey

Leadership. Mahamane Ousmane (leader)

A former member party of the Alliance of Forces for Change (AFC) coalition, the CDS–*Rahama* won 22 seats in the February 1993 legislative elections, and party leader Ousmane secured the presidency of the country in March 1993 (he was, however, overthrow in a military coup in 1996). In the January 1995 National Assembly elections the party increased its number of seats to 24. However, other AFC parties did not secure sufficient additional seats to retain the coalition's majority over the National Movement for a Society of Development–*Nassara* (MNSD) and its allies. In the legislative elections of October 1999 the CDS–*Rahama* secured the second largest share of seats in the National Assembly with 17 legislators elected, and entered into an informal coalition with the MNSD. In the first round of voting in the October 1999 presidential elections Ousmane was placed third, with only a 0.2% margin between himself and Niger Party for Democracy and Socialism–*Tarayya* (PNDS) candidate Mahamadou Issoufou.

National Movement for a Society of Development–Nassara
Mouvement National pour une Société de Développement (MNSD)

Address. c/o Assemblée Nationale, BP 12234, Place de la Concertation, Niamey

Leadership. Mamadou Tanja (chairman); Hama Amadou (secretary general)

The MNSD was formed by the military regime in 1988 as the sole legal political party. Although the MNSD won 29 seats in the February 1993 legislative elections the formation of the Alliance of Forces for Change (AFC) coalition relegat-

ed it to minority status. In the January 1995 elections the MNSD again won 29 seats, securing, with other opposition parties, a three-seat majority over AFC members. In October 1999 the MNSD secured the largest share of seats in the National Assembly, with some 38 legislators elected, and became the senior partner in an informal ruling coalition with the Democratic and Social Convention–*Rahama*. In the presidential election also held in late 1999, the MNDS leader Mamadou Tanja secured 59.9% of the vote and defeated former Prime Minister Issoufou of the Niger Party for Democracy and Socialism–*Tarayya*.

Niger Alliance for Democracy and Social Progress–Zaman Lahiya
Alliance Nigérienne pour la Démocratie et le Progrès Social–Zaman Lahiya (ANDPS-Zaman Lahiya)

Address. c/o Assemblée Nationale, BP 12234, Place de la Concertation, Niamey

Leadership. Moumouni Djermakoye (leader)

A former member of the Alliance of Forces for Change (AFC) coalition the ANDPS–*Zaman Lahiya* won 11 seats in the 1993 legislative elections but its representation fell to nine seats in the 1995 elections. In the legislative elections of October 1999 the ANDPS–*Zaman Lahiya* secured four seats in the National Assembly.

Niger Party for Democracy and Socialism–Tarayya
Parti Nigérien pour la Démocratie et le Socialisme (PNDS)

Address. c/o Assemblée Nationale, BP 12234, Place de la Concertation, Niamey

Leadership. Mahamadou Issoufou (secretary general)

PNDS secretary general Issoufou was appointed Prime Minister after elections in early 1993, holding the post until September 1994, when the party withdrew from the ruling Alliance of Forces for Change. This move led to early legislative elections in January 1995, in which the party took third place with 12 seats. In the legislative elections of October 1999 the centre-left PNDS secured 16 seats in the National Assembly and formed the main opposition to the National Movement for a Society of Development–*Nassara* (MNSD). In the second round of voting in the presidential election in November 1999 Issoufou polled 40.1% of the vote, but was defeated by the MNSD candidate, Mamadou Tanja.

The PNDS is a consultative member of the Socialist International.

Rally for Democracy and Progress–Djamaa
Rassemblement pour la Démocratie et le Progrès (RDP–Djamaa)

Address. c/o Assemblée Nationale, BP 12234, Place de la Concertation, Niamey

The RDP–*Djamaa* was the largest political force in the defunct Convergence for the Republic (CPR), a 15-member grouping of political parties formed in August 1998 to support President Mainassara. In the legislative elections of October 1999 the RDP–*Djamaa* secured eight seats in the National Assembly.

Nigeria

Capital: Abuja
Population: 132,800,000 (2002E)

Nigeria attained independence from the UK in 1960, becoming a federal republic within the Commonwealth in 1963. A series of coups have punctuated the post-independence politics of the country, resulting in long periods of military rule. A lengthy and often delayed process of transition from military to civilian rule was interrupted when the military regime of Gen. Ibrahim Babangida annulled the July 1993 presidential elections, which were widely believed to have been won by centre-left candidate Moshood Abiola. In November 1993 Defence Minister Gen. Sani Abacha seized power, signed a decree establishing a new military junta, the Provisional Ruling Council, and declared the restoration of the 1979 constitution, although most of its provisions remained in abeyance during a transitional period. Abacha, who intended to stand himself as the sole candidate in presidential elections, died suddenly in June 1998 and he was succeeded as head of state by Gen. Abdulsalam Abubakar. Abubakar's pledge to continue with Abacha's programme prompted protests by the United Action for Democracy (UAD), an alliance of 22 pro-democracy and human rights organizations formed in 1997 to put pressure on Abacha to step down and allow a transitional government of national unity to oversee the restoration of elected institutions. The protests prompted Abubakar to release the detained 1993 election candidate Moshood Abiola, whose subsequent death prompted violent anti-government demonstrations. Gen. Abubakar then abandoned the Abacha programme and adopted a new timetable for a return to civilian rule by May 1999. Municipal council elections were held in late 1998 in which three parties received sufficiently large shares of the vote (and a sufficiently wide geographical spread of their vote) to qualify for registration to contest the forthcoming state and federal elections.

Elections to the country's 36 state legislatures were held in January 1999, after which two of the three registered parties, the All Nigeria People's Party (ANPP) and the Alliance for Democracy (AD), agreed to mount a joint campaign in the federal elections. The presidential election, held in February 1999, was won by the People's Democratic Party (PDP) candidate, Gen. (retd) Olusegun Obasanjo, who easily defeated Olu Falae, the joint candidate of the AD and the ANPP. President Obasanjo was inaugurated in May 1999, bringing into effect a federal constitution broadly based on the 1979 constitution (drawn up when Obasanjo had presided over a previous transition to civilian rule). The President is head of state, chief executive of the federation and commander-in-chief of the federal armed forces. The presidential term is four years, and the successful candidate is required to win at least 25% of the popular vote in at least two-thirds of the states of the federation. In presidential elections held in April 2003, Obasanjo was re-elected for a second term, easily defeating his main challenger, the ANPP's Gen. Muhammed Buhari.

The President and both houses of the bicameral legislature, the National Assembly, are directly elected by universal adult suffrage, with a voting age of 18. In National Assembly elections held in February 1999, the party shares of the 360 seats in the lower chamber, the House of Representatives, were PDP 221, ANPP 70 and AD 69, while the 109 seats in the upper house, the Senate, were distributed PDP 67, ANPP 23 and AD 19. The term of both houses of the federal legislature is four years. A total of 24 new political parties were officially registered in December 2002, bringing the total number of political parties in the country to 30. However, the creation of the new parties had little impact on the results of the legislative elections held in April 2003, the three main parties again dominating. In the contest for the House of Representatives the PDP won 198 seats, against 83 for the ANPP, 30 for the AD and seven for four other smaller parties. In the Senate poll, the PDP won 72 seats, the ANPP 28 and the AD five.

All Nigeria People's Party (ANPP)

Address. Plot 274, Central Area, Behind NICON Plaza, Abuja

Leadership. Alhaji Attahiru D. Bafarawa (chairman)

The ANPP was established in 1998 by a number of groupings which had formerly participated in the Abacha regime's programme for the reintroduction of civilian rule. In the January 1999 state elections its best results were achieved in central and some northern areas of Nigeria. In a development that was subsequently revealed to be rooted in factional rivalries over the selection of a candidate from within the ANPP, the party agreed to support the presidential candidate of the Alliance for Democracy (AD) in the February 1999 federal elections. The presidential election was won by the candidate of the People's Democratic Party (PDP), while in the legislative elections the ANPP was the runner-up to the PDP in terms of the overall number of seats won. In the aftermath of the elections the organizers of the ANPP's presidential candidate selection process came under fierce criticism from rival factions of the party. This conflict was resolved in December 1999 by the holding (on the initiative of the ANPP's state governors and National Assembly members) of a party convention which elected a new national leadership acceptable to all sections of the party.

The party selected Gen. Muhammed Buhari, a former military ruler from 1983 to 1985, as its candidate for the April 2003 presidential election. The contest between Buhari and incumbent President Olusegun Obasanjo mirrored the country's north-south religious divide, with the former being a Muslim for the north and the latter a Christian from the south-east. The incumbent won, gaining over 60% of the vote, against some 32% for Buhari. In the legislative elections, also held in April, the ANPP was the only serious challenger to Obasanjo's PDP, winning 83 seats in the House of Representatives (against 198 for the PDP) and 28 seats in the Senate (72 for the PDP). In May a court rejected an attempt to block Obasanjo's inauguration by Buhari, who had claimed that the presidential poll had been marred by vote rigging.

All Progressive Grand Alliance (APGA)

Address. House No. 4, Road 116 Gwarinpa Housing Estate, Abuja

Leadership. Chief Chekwas Okorie (chairman)

Emeka Odumegwu-Ojukwu contested the April 2003 presidential election and won 3.29% of the vote. In elections to the House of Representatives also held in April the party won 1.36% of the vote and two seats; in the accompanying elections to the Senate, the party won 1.48% of the vote, but failed to win a seat.

Alliance for Democracy (AD)

Address. Abeokuta Street, Area 8 Garki, Abuja

Telephone. (234–9) 2345463

Email. info@alliancefordemocracy.org

Website. www.afrikontakt.com/alliance

Leadership. Rival factions led by Alhaji Adamu Ahmed Abdulkadir (national chairman) and Chief Mochael Koleosho (national chairman)

Founded in late 1998, the AD was the most radical of the three parties that won registration to contest the Nigerian elections of January and February 1999. Many of its founders had previously been associated with the National Democratic Coalition (NADECO), a grouping of human rights activists, civilian politicians and retired military officers which was formed in May 1994 to campaign for the resignation of the Abacha regime and a rapid return to democratic government.

After the state election results of Jan. 9, 1999, confirmed the AD's position as the strongest party in the south-western part of Nigeria, the AD agreed to ally itself with the All Nigeria People's Party (ANPP, whose best results were in other areas) in the forthcoming federal election campaign. The AD's Olu Falae was selected as the alliance's joint presidential candidate, with the ANPP's Umaru Shinkafi as his running mate for the vice-presidency. The AD won one fewer seats than the ANPP in the legislative elections of Feb. 20, 1999, but the overall winner of these elections was the People's Democratic Party (PDP), which gained an absolute majority of seats in each chamber. The presidential election of February 1999 was also decisively won by the PDP candidate, with 62.8% of the vote, compared with 37.2% for Falae. Alhaji Adamu Ahmed Abdulkadir was elected national chairman of the AD at a party convention held on Nov. 1, 2000, in the presence of observers from the independent national electoral commission. The electoral commission rejected as illegitimate a rival AD meeting's election of Yusuf Mamman to the same post (which he had previously held on an interim basis).

The party did not contest the April 2003 presidential election, instead backing the candidacy of incumbent President Obasanjo. The AD contested the legislative elections also held in April, finishing a distant third in both houses behind the PDP and the ANPP. In July Abdulkadir was replaced as the AD's national chairman by his deputy, Chief Mochael Koleosho, and he took up the post of special adviser (on manufacturing and the private sector) to President Obasanjo. However, in mid-December Abdulkadir and his supporters within the party – including the faction led by Yusuf Mamman – claimed that he never resigned as national chairman, but had merely "vacated" the post temporarily and would now resume the leadership. The party appeared to be on the verge of a serious division into two factions led by Abdulkadir and Koleosho.

National Democratic Party (NDP)
Address. Plot 495, Bangui Street, Off Ademola Adetokunboh C, Abuja
Leadership. Alhaj Abo Fari (chairman)
Ike Omar Sanda Nwachukwu contested the April 2003 presidential election, winning only 0.34% of the vote. In elections to the House of Representatives also held in April the NDP won 1.92% of the vote and one seat; in the accompanying elections to the Senate, the party won 1.58% of the vote, but failed to win a seat.

People's Democratic Party (PDP)
Address. c/o House of Representatives, PMB 141, Abuja
Leadership. Chief Audu Ogbeh (national chairman)
The PDP was founded in August 1998 by a broad range of political interest groups, represented principally by 34 former senior political figures who had come forward earlier in 1998 to challenge the legality of Sani Abacha's bid to secure the civilian presidency of Nigeria. At least nine established groupings were brought into the new party as it sought to build a nationwide presence. In the January 1998 state elections the PDP's only area of significant weakness was the south-west (where the Alliance for Democracy predominated), while in parts of northern and central Nigeria the PDP was challenged with some success by the All Nigeria People's Party (ANPP). The PDP's candidate for the federal presidency, Gen. (retd) Olusegun Obasanjo, a native of the south-west, was a former detainee of the Abacha regime and a strong supporter of Nigerian federalism. In February 1999 Obasanjo was elected President with 62.8% of the vote,

defeating the joint candidate of the two other parties, while the PDP won substantial majorities in the Senate and House of Representatives. This did not, however, guarantee the easy passage of legislation supported by the President, as the broadly-based and ideologically unfocused PDP proved to be notably lacking in party discipline. Barnabas Gemade, elected party national chairman in November 1999, faced dissent from several sections of the membership, and in mid-2001 his unsuccessful rival in the chairmanship election, Sunday Awoniyi, was one of five members of the board of trustees to be expelled from the PDP for "anti-party activities". Also expelled were three national executive committee members who had taken legal action to challenge their earlier suspension from office. Chief Audu Ogbeh replaced Gemade as party national chairman in November 2001.

In the April 2003 presidential election, incumbent President Obasanjo faced a serious challenge from another former military ruler, the ANPP's Gen. Muhammed Buhari. In the event, Obasanjo easily defeated Buhari, winning over 60% of the vote, against some 32% for the challenger. Buhari accused Obasanjo and the PDP of electoral fraud, but failed to persuade the courts to support his allegations. In elections also held in April, the PDP managed to maintain comfortable majorities in the House of Representatives and the Senate.

People's Redemption Party (PRP)
Address. City Plaza, Plot 596 (2nd Floor), Ahmadu Bello Way, Abuja
Telephone. (234-9) 4139441; 5234160
Leadership. Abdulkadir Balarabe Musa (chairman)
This is an offshoot of the old Northern Elements Progressive Union/People's Redemption Party founded by the late Alhaji Muhammed Aminu Kano in the late 1970s. Party chairman Abdulkadir Balarabe Musa contested the April 2003 presidential election, but managed to win only 0.26% of the vote. In elections to the House of Representatives also held in April the party won 0.76% of the vote and one seat; in the accompanying elections to the Senate, the party won 0.71% of the vote, but failed to win a seat.

People's Salvation Party (PSP)
Address. Plot 769, Panama Street, Maitama, Abuja
Telephone. (234-9) 4139441; 5234160
Leadership. Alhaj Lawal Maiturare (chairman)
The PSP contested the April 2003 legislative elections, winning 0.33% of the vote (and one seat) in the contest for the House of Representatives and 0.40% of the vote (but no seat) in the Senate.

United Nigeria People's Party (UNPP)
Address. Plot 1467, Safana Close, Off Zaria Street, Garki I, Abuja
Leadership. Saleh Jambo (chairman)
Jim Nwobodo Ifeanyichukwu, an incumbent senator from Enugu state, contested the April 2003 presidential election on behalf of the UNPP (formerly the United Nigeria Democratic Party, UNDP), but only managed to win 0.43% of the vote. In elections to the House of Representatives also held in April the party won 2.75% of the vote and two seats; in the accompanying elections to the Senate, the party won 2.72% of the vote, but failed to win a seat.

Other Parties

African Renaissance Party (ARP), contested the April 2003 presidential and legislative elections with little success. The party's candidate in the presidential poll, Alhaji Yahaya G. K. Ezemue, won only 0.03% of the vote; the party won the same small share of the vote in the contest for the House of Representatives and the Senate and no seats.

All People's Liberation Party (APLP), contested the April 2003 presidential and legislative elections. The party's candidate in the presidential poll, Chief Emmanuel Osita Okereke, won 0.07% of the vote; the party won 0.04% of the vote in the contest for the House of Representatives and 0.05% in the vote for the Senate, and no seats in either chamber.
Address. Plot 1159 Lake Chad Crescent, Along Lake Chad Gues, Abuja
Telephone. (234-9) 3155340
Leadership. Alhaji Umar Mohammed (chairman)

Better Nigeria Progressive Party (BNPP), contested the April 2003 presidential and legislative elections with minimal success, winning only 0.02% of the vote (and no seats) in the legislative contest. The party's candidate for the presidency, Godwill Ifeanyichukwu Nnaji, won only 0.02% of the vote.
Address. 12, Crescent, House 12, Kado, Abuja
Telephone. (234-9) 2346662; 5212154
Leadership. Alhaji Bashir Maidugu (chairman)

Community Party of Nigeria (CPN), contested the April 2003 legislative elections, but managed to win only 0.02% of the vote in the contest for the House of Representatives and 0.03% in the Senate.
Address. Plot 1139, Thomas Sankara Street, Asokoro, Abuja
Telephone. (234-9) 3116045
Leadership. Musari Bukar Sani (chairman)

Democratic Alternative (DA), contested the April 2003 presidential poll and its candidate, party chairman Antonio Abayomi Ferreira, won 0.02% of the vote. The party failed to win any seats in the legislative election also held in April, winning 0.02% of the vote in the contest for the House of Representatives and the Senate.
Address. Ben Sima House, Suite B2 Off Aguiyi Ironsi Street, Abuja
Telephone. (234-9) 3013320
Leadership. Antonio Abayomi Ferreira (chairman)

Green Party of Nigeria (GPN), contested the April 2003 legislative elections, but failed to win a seat, gaining only 0.01% of the vote in the contest for the House of Representatives and 0.02% in the Senate.
Address. 25 Niamey Street, Wuse Zone 2, Abuja, Abuja
Leadership. Olisa Agbakoba (chairman)

Justice Party (JP), is led by Chief Ralph Obioha, a former activist with the National Democratic Coalition (NADECO). The party endorsed the Rev. Christopher Okotie as its candidate for the April 2003 presidential elections. Okotie, pastor of the Lagos-based charismatic church, Household of God, had initially made his formal bid for the country's presidency on the platform of the National Democratic Party (NDP), but came second at the party's nomination convention. In the election, Okotie won 0.30% of the vote. The party failed to a win a seat in the legislative elections also held in April 2003, gaining 0.09% of the vote in the contest for the House of Representatives and 0.10% in the Senate.
Address. 379 Nouckchott Street, Wuse, Zone 1, Abuja
Telephone. (234-9) 330384
Leadership. Chief Ralph Obioha (chairman)

Liberal Democratic Party of Nigeria (LDPN), contested the April 2003 presidential poll but its candidate, Christopher Pere Ajuwa, won only 0.01% of the vote. The party failed to win any seats in the legislative election also held in April, winning 0.02% of the vote in the contest for both houses.
Address. Suite 114 Banex Plaza, P.O. Box 8978, Abuja
Telephone. (234-9) 4136674; 3154331; 3234338
Leadership. Chief Felix Modebelu (chairman)

Masses Movement of Nigeria (MMN), contested the April 2003 presidential poll but its candidate, Mojisola Adekunle Obasanjo, won only 0.01% of the vote. The party failed to win any seats in the legislative election also held in April, winning 0.01% of the vote in the contest for both houses.
Address. Obafemi Awolowo Way, Along Utako Express Way, Jabi, Abuja
Telephone. (234-9) 4926313; 3178131
Leadership. Maj. (retd) Isola Adekunle Obasanjo (chairman)

Movement for Democracy and Justice (MDJ), contested the April 2003 presidential poll but its candidate, Alhaji Mohammed Dikko Yusuf, won only 0.05% of the vote. The party failed to win any seats in the legislative election also held in April, winning 0.04% of the vote in the contest for the House of Representatives and 0.02% in the Senate.
Address. Plot 750 Aminu Kano Crescent, Banex Plaza, Abuja
Leadership. Alhaji Kalli al-Gazali (chairman)

National Action Council (NAC), contested the April 2003 presidential poll but its candidate, party chairman Agoro Olapade, won only 0.01% of the vote. The party failed to win any seats in the legislative election also held in April, winning 0.02% of the vote in the contest for both chambers.
Address. 2A Niger Street, Sani Abacha Housing Estate, Abuja
Leadership. Agoro Olapade (chairman)

National Conscience Party (NCP), declares itself as "people-focused, people-centered, people-oriented, and people-propelled" and as a "party for poor people". Its chairman, Chief Gani Fawehinmi, contested the April 2003 presidential poll and won 0.41% of the vote. The party failed to win any seats in the legislative election also held in April, winning 0.48% of the vote in the contest for the House of Representatives and 0.51% in the Senate.
Address. 18 Lake City Avenue, Phase 1, Low Cost Housing Est, Abuja
Leadership. Chief Gani Fawehinmi (chairman)

National Mass Movement of Nigeria (NMMN), contested the April 2003 legislative elections, but managed to win only 0.01% of the vote in the contest for the House of Representatives and the Senate and no seats.
Address. Plot 547 Kautiala Link off Ademola Adetokunbo St, Abuja
Leadership. Alhaji Zanna Bukar Mandara (chairman)

National Reformation Party (NRP), contested the April 2003 legislative elections, but managed to win only 0.05% of the vote in the contest for the House of Representatives and the Senate and no seats.
Address. BS207-8 Banex Plana, Plot 750, Aminu Kano Crescent, Abuja
Leadership. Chief Anthony Enahoro (chairman)

New Democrats (ND), failed to win any seats in the legislative election held in April 2003, winning 0.07% of the vote in the contest for the House of Representatives and 0.05% in the Senate.
Address. Phase 1, Street B, House 24, Gwagwalada, Abuja FCT, Abuja
Leadership. Isa Odidi (chairman)

New Nigeria People's Party (NNPP), contested the April 2003 presidential poll but its candidate, Kalu Idika Kalu, won only 0.06% of the vote. The party failed to win any seats in the legislative election also held in April, winning 0.03% of the vote in the contest for the House of Representatives and 0.04% in the Senate.

Address. Plot 515 Usuma Close by Usuma Street, Off Gana St., Abuja

Leadership. B.O. Aniebonam (chairman)

Nigeria Advance Party (NAP), contested the April 2003 presidential poll but its candidate, party chairman Olatunji Braithwaite, won only 0.02% of the vote. The party failed to win any seats in the legislative election also held in April, winning 0.02% of the vote in the contest for the House of Representatives and 0.03% in the Senate.

Address. Plot 120, Karu Federal Housing Road, Opposite Cust, Abuja

Leadership. Olatunji Braithwaite (chairman)

Nigerian People's Congress (NPC), failed to win any seats in the legislative election held in April 2003, winning 0.04% of the vote in the contest for the House of Representatives and the Senate.

Address. Plot 503, Abogo Largema Street, Central Business D, Abuja

Telephone. (234-9) 5232041; 5232080

Leadership. Alhaji M. I. Atta (chairman)

Party for Social Democracy (PSD), failed to win any seats in the legislative election held in April 2003, winning 0.04% of the vote in the contest for the House of Representatives and the Senate.

Address. 1st Floor, Labour House, Central Business District, Abuja

Telephone. (234-9) 2343345

Leadership. O.Z. Ejiofor (chairman)

People's Mandate Party (PMP), contested the April 2003 presidential poll and its candidate, party chairman Arthur Nwankwo, won 0.15% of the vote. The party failed to win any seats in the legislative election also held in April, winning 0.10% of the vote in the contest for the House of Representatives and 0.17% in the Senate.

Address. Plot 159, Koforidua Street, Wuse Zone 2, Abuja

Leadership. Arthur Nwankwo (chairman)

Progressive Action Congress (PAC), contested the April 2003 presidential poll and its candidate, Sarah N. Jibril, won 0.40% of the vote. The party failed to win any seats in the legislative election also held in April, winning 0.47% of the vote in the contest for the House of Representatives and 0.49% in the Senate.

Address. Plot 1921, Dalaba Street, Wuse Zone 5, Abuja

Telephone. (234-9) 6704168

Leadership. Chief A.C. Nwodo (chairman)

United Democratic Party (UDP), failed to win any seats in the legislative election held in April 2003, winning 0.04% of the vote in the contest for the House of Representatives and 0.05% in the Senate.

Norway

Capital: Oslo
Population: 4,574,560 (2004E)

Norway achieved independence from Sweden in 1905 on the basis of the 1814 Eidsvold Convention. This provides for a constitutional and hereditary monarchy, with the monarch exercising authority through a Council of State (government) headed by a Prime Minister. The monarch has, since the introduction of parliamentary democracy in 1884, only had symbolic power, while real power rests with the Prime Minister and his or her cabinet. The government is accountable to the legislature (*Storting*) of 165 members, who are elected for a four-year term by universal suffrage of citizens aged 18 and over on the basis of proportional representation in 19 electoral districts. The *Storting* divides itself by election into an upper house (*Lagting*) of a quarter of its members and a lower house (*Odelsting*) of the remaining three-quarters, with each house being required to consider and vote on legislative proposals. In the event of a disagreement between the houses, a bill requires approval by a majority of two-thirds of the *Storting* as a whole. An important feature of the constitution is that the *Storting* cannot be dissolved between elections and that any vacancies are filled from party lists rather than by-elections. If the government falls on a vote of no confidence, the leader of the opposition party holding the highest number of seats is asked to form a new government.

Norwegian political parties receive funds from the public purse in proportion to their electoral support, to be used in connection with their political education work and parliamentary activities. The total amount allocated in 2000 was NOK230,899,000 (about US$26 million), of which some 80% was received by party organizations and the balance by party groups in the *Storting*.

Parliamentary elections on Sept. 10, 2001, resulted as follows: Norwegian Labour Party 43 seats (with 24.3% of the vote), Conservative Party 38 (21.2%), Progress Party 26 (14.6%), Socialist Left Party 23 (12.5%), Christian People's Party 22 (12.4%), Centre Party 10 (5.6%), Liberal Party 2 (3.9%), Coastal Party 1 (1.7%). On Oct. 17, 2001, Jens Stoltenberg (Labour) stood down as Prime Minister to allow the formation of a minority right-of-centre coalition government under Kjell Magne Bondevik comprising Bondevik's Christian People's Party, the Conservative Party and the Liberals and which the Progress Party said it would support.

Centre Party
Senterpartiet (SP)

Address. PB 6734, St Olavs plass, 0130 Oslo

Telephone. (47) 2298–9600

Fax. (47) 2220–6915

website. www.senterpartiet.no

Email. epost@senterpartiet.no

Leadership. Åslaug Haga (leader); Lars Peder Brekk (first deputy leader); Liv Signe Navarsete (second deputy leader); Marit Arnstad (parliamentary leader); Dagfinn Sundsbø (secretary-general).

Originating from the farmers' trade organization, the party was founded in 1920 as the Agrarian Party with the object of gaining greater political and parliamentary influence for those working in rural occupations and raising them to the level of other occupations. Since 1931, when the tight co-operation with the farmers' trade organization was ended, the party has been more independent, changing its name to Centre Party in 1959, thus emphasizing its position between the right-wing and left-wing parties.

In 1931–33 the party formed a minority government. After unsuccessful efforts to work with the Conservative and Liberal parties, the party, in 1935, entered into a "crisis compromise" with the Norwegian Labour Party (DNA), which was then in power for 30 years. In 1963 the party entered into a brief minority coalition with other non-socialist parties; from 1965 to 1971 it headed a majority non-socialist government; and in 1972–73 it participated in a minority government with the Liberal Party (*Venstre*) and the Christian People's Party (KrF).

The SP was in opposition to minority Labour governments from 1973 to September 1981, when it gave its general support to a minority Conservative Party administration. In June 1983 it entered a majority three-party centre-right government headed by the Conservatives, which continued until, in May 1986, it was replaced by a further minority Labour administration. Meanwhile, the SP had won 12 seats and 6.7% of the vote in the September 1985 elections, as against its earlier high-point of 20 seats and 11% in 1973.

Having slipped from 12 to 11 seats in the 1989 elections (on a 6.5% vote share), the SP joined another centre-right coalition headed by the Conservatives but withdrew in October 1990 in protest against government policy towards the European Union. As the leading partner in the coalition, the Conservative Party, had membership in the European Union as its aim, the Centre Party dropped out. This caused the coalition's collapse and the formation of a minority Labour government in November 1990 to which the SP gave qualified parliamentary support. Campaigning on a strongly anti-EU platform, the SP made major gains in the September 1993 elections, overtaking the Conservatives by increasing its representation to 32 seats on a 16.7% vote share (an all-time high). It subsequently played a prominent role in the successful "no" campaign in the November 1994 referendum on EU accession.

With the EU issue temporarily resolved, the SP slumped to 11 seats and 7.9% of the vote in the September 1997 elections, but was nevertheless included in a minority government with the KrF and *Venstre*. This government resigned in March 2000 after losing a vote of confidence and was replaced by a minority Labour administration. In the September 2001 elections the SP slipped further to 10 seats and 5.6% of the vote.

Christian People's Party
Kristelig Folkeparti (KrF)

Address. Øvre Slottsgate 18–20, 0105 Oslo
Telephone. (47) 2310–2800
Fax. (47) 2310–2810
Email. krf@krf.no
Website. www.krf.no
Leadership. Dagfinn Høybråten (leader); Dagrun Eriksen (first deputy leader); Knut Arild Hareide (second deputy leader); Jon Lilletun (parliamentary leader); Inger Helene Venås (secretary-general).

Founded in 1933 as a regional non-socialist Christian-oriented formation, the KrF returned its first member to the *Storting* in 1933, followed by two in 1936, and became formally established at national level by 1939. Having won eight seats in 1945, it steadily increased its parliamentary representation, winning 22 seats in 1977 and thus becoming the country's third strongest party (although in 1981 it retained only 15 seats). It took part in majority coalition governments in 1965-71 (with the Conservative, Liberal and Centre parties) and in a minority coalition government with the Centre and Liberal parties in 1972–73 under the premiership of Lars Korvald of the KrF. The Korvald government came to power as a result of the Labour government's resignation after the "no" vote in the 1972 referendum on joining the European Community (now EU). In June 1983 it entered a centre-right government with the Conservatives and the Centre Party, but went into opposition in May 1986 to a minority administration of the Norwegian Labour Party. In the September 1985 elections the party had won 16 seats and 8.3% of the vote, retaining its position as the third strongest formation.

The KrF fell back to 14 seats in the 1989 elections (8.5%), after which it joined a centre-right coalition with the Conservative and Centre parties that lasted only a year. It fell again to 13 seats (7.9%) in the September 1993 contest, its advocacy of the popular cause of opposition to EU membership doing it little good, as non-socialist voters who were strongly engaged in the struggle against EU-membership opted for the Centre Party.

The KrF advanced strongly to 25 seats and a vote share of 13.7% in the September 1997 elections, as a result of which Kjell Magne Bondevik of the KrF was appointed Prime Minister of a government which included the Centre and Liberal parties but which commanded only 42 of the 165 *Storting* seats. The strains of office induced depression in Bondevik, who took a month's sick leave in September 1998. He soldiered on until March 2000, when his government lost a confidence vote on its opposition to two new gas-fired power stations and was replaced by a minority Labour administration. In the September 2001 elections the KrF slipped to fourth place with 22 seats and 12.4% of the vote, failing to benefit from a big swing against Labour. However, on Oct. 17, Labour Prime Minister Jens Stoltenberg stood down and Bondevik returned to office as leader of a right-of-centre coalition.

The KrF is a member of the Christian Democrat International and an observer member of the European People's Party.

Coastal Party
Kystpartiet (KP)

Address. c/o Stortinget, Karl Johansgt. 22, 0026 Oslo
Website. www.kystpartiet.no
Leadership. Steinar Bastesen (chairman)

The KP was founded to represent the interests of the whaling industry and fishermen in northern Norway, with particular reference to the continuing international hostility to whaling as practiced by Norway. The party broke through to parliamentary representation in the September 1997 elections, when its chairman won a *Storting* seat in Nordland county with 0.4% of the national vote. It retained the seat in the September 2001 elections, increasing its national vote share to 1.7%.

Conservative Party
Høyre (H)

Address. Stortingsgaten 20, PB 1536 Vika, 0117 Oslo
Telephone. (47) 2282–9000
Fax. (47) 2282–9080
Email. hoyre@hoyre.no
Website. www.hoyre.no
Leadership. Erna Solberg (leader); Per-Kristian Foss (first deputy leader); Jan Tore Sanner (second deputy leader) Oddvar Nilsen (parliamentary leader); Trond R. Hole (secretary-general)

Since its foundation in 1884 the Conservative Party has participated in many governments, most of them coalitions with other non-socialist parties. Having commanded half of the electorate in its early days, the party declined to around 20% in the years before World War II, since when its support has fluctuated from well under 20% to around 30%. On the basis of the substantial gains in the September 1981 elections, then Conservative leader Kåre Willoch formed a one-party minority administration, which was transformed into a three-party government in June 1983 when the Centre and Christian People's parties accepted cabinet membership. However, this government fell in April 1986 and was replaced by a minority administration of the Norwegian Labour Party. In August 1986 Willoch was succeeded as party leader by Rolf Presthus, but the latter died unexpectedly in January 1988 and was succeeded by Jan. P. Syse.

Although the party's representation declined to 37 seats in 1989 (on a 22.2% vote share), Syse succeeded in forming a minority centre-right coalition with the Centre and Christian People's parties. This collapsed a year later upon the withdrawal of the Centre Party as a result of disagreement on the question about membership in the European Union, giving way to another minority Labour government.

In the September 1993 *Storting* elections the Conservatives slumped to 28 seats (and 16.9%), being damaged by their strong advocacy of Norwegian membership of the EU. The party accordingly remained in opposition under the new leadership of Jan Petersen.

The party's decline continued in the 1997 elections, to an all-time low of 14.3% and 23 seats. In the September 2001 contest, however, the unpopularity of the incumbent Labour government enabled the Conservatives to recover to 38 seats (the second largest tally) and 21.2% of the vote. In October a new government was formed with Kjell Magne Bondevik of the Christian People's Party returning as Prime Minister while the Conservatives took the key portfolios of foreign affairs (Jan Petersen) and finance (Per-Kristian Foss).

The Conservative Party is affiliated to the International Democrat Union and is an associate member of the European People's Party.

Liberal Party
Venstre (V)

Address. Møllergt. 16, 0179 Oslo
Telephone. (47) 2240–4350
Fax. (47) 2240–4351
Email. venstre@venstre.no
Website. www.venstre.no
Leadership. Lars Sponheim (leader); Trine Skei Grande (first deputy leader and parliamentary leader); Olaf Thommessen (second deputy leader); Geir Rune Nyhus (secretary-general)

Founded in 1884, *Venstre* held 23 seats in the *Storting* in 1936, but its parliamentary representation after World War II was consistently lower, its 21 seats in 1949 being reduced to 14 by 1961, though rising to 18 in 1965. Of its 13 members elected in 1969, a majority supported the projected entry of Norway into what is today the European Union. After entry had been rejected in the referendum of September 1972, the anti-membership minority participated in a coalition government with the Christian People's and Centre parties, while the pro-European Liberals formed the breakaway Liberal People's Party (DLF).

The rump *Venstre* was thus left with only four seats in the *Storting,* this number being reduced to two in September 1973. It retained two seats in 1977 and 1981, but failed to secure representation in 1985, when its share of the vote fell to 3.1%. In June 1988 the DLF rejoined the parent party, which nevertheless failed to regain *Storting* representation in 1989, when its vote share was 3.2%.

A partial Liberal comeback began in the September 1993 elections, in which the party took one seat with 3.6% of the vote. It continued in the September 1997 legislative polling, which yielded six seats (with 4.5% of the vote) and resulted in the party joining a minority government with the Christian People's and Centre parties. However, following the collapse of this government in March 2000, *Venstre* fell back to two seats and 3.9% in the September 2001 parliamentary elections. It subsequently joined the right-of-centre coalition government formed by Christian People's Party leader Kjell Magne Bondevik.

Venstre is a member of the Liberal International.

Norwegian Labour Party
Det Norske Arbeiderparti (DNA)

Address. PB 8734 Youngstorget, 0028 Oslo
Telephone. (47) 2294–0600
Fax. (47) 2294–0601
Email. dna@dna.no
Website. www.dna.no
Leadership. Jens Stoltenberg (party leader and parliamentary leader); Hill-Marta Solberg (deputy leader); Martin Kolberg (secretary general)

Descended from a rural socialist movement of the mid-19th century, the DNA was established in 1887 amid a rapid growth of urban trade unionism in the 1880s. In 1904 the party won four seats in the *Storting* and by 1915 it had 62,000 members and the support of over 30% of the electorate. In 1918 the party leadership was taken over by the left wing, largely under the influence of the Russian revolution, but disagreements ensued over whether to join the Third International (Comintern). In 1921 anti-Bolshevik dissenters formed the Social Democratic Party, while the Communist Party was formed in 1923 by part of the Labour left. In 1927, however, a reunified Labour Party (including the Social Democrats and some Communists) obtained 36.8% of the electoral vote, thus becoming the strongest party.

After a short-lived first Labour minority government in 1927, the party won 40% of the vote in 1933 and two years later formed its second government. Under the German occupation during World War II the party was illegal and its leaders went into exile or were sent to German concentration camps. At the end of the war Labour leader Einar Gerhardsen formed a broad coalition government, but in October 1945 Labour obtained a parliamentary majority and remained in office until 1965 except for a brief interval in 1963. The party was again in power from 1971 to 1972, when the government headed by Trygve Bratteli resigned on being defeated in a referendum which rejected Norway's membership of what is now the European Union (EU).

During the 1973–81 period the party formed a series of minority governments, but went into opposition following a setback in the September 1981 elections. However, the Conservative-led non-socialist coalition collapsed in April 1986 and was replaced by a further minority Labour government under Gro Harlem Brundtland. Meanwhile, the DNA had won 71 seats and 40.8% of the vote in September 1985, an improvement on its 37.1% share in 1981 but significantly below the levels regularly obtained up to 1969. The DNA went in opposition after the September 1989 elections, in which it lost eight seats. A year later, however, Brundtland formed her third minority government, with the parliamentary backing of the Centre Party.

In November 1992, following the death of her son, Brundtland resigned the DNA chairmanship, while continuing as Prime Minister. Her successor in the party post was Thorbjørn Jagland, hitherto general secretary. In the September 1993 elections Labour rose to 67 seats on a 36.9% vote share, so that Brundtland formed her fourth minority government. In June 1994 delegates at a special party conference decided by a two-to-one majority to support Norwegian accession to EU in the forthcoming national referendum, although substantial rank-and-file opposition to membership contributed to the decisive 52.2% "no" vote in November 1994. Unlike her Labour predecessor in 1972, and despite having strongly advocated a "yes" vote, Brundtland did not resign over an acknowledged major defeat. Instead, she stressed the need for continuity and for negotiations to clarify Norway's relationship with the EU as a non-member.

Brundtland eventually vacated the premiership in October 1996, being succeeded by Jagland, who was quickly beset by several scandals involving senior Labour figures. In the September 1997 elections the DNA fell back to 65 seats and 35.1%, whereupon Jagland honoured his pre-election pledge not to continue as Prime Minister if Labour lost ground compared to the previous national election. Nominally in opposition over the next two-and-a-half years to a minority coalition headed by the Christian People's Party, the DNA exerted substantial external influence on the government's budgetary and other policies.

In February 2000 Jagland was replaced as DNA parliamentary leader by Jens Stoltenberg, a former Minister of

Finance, who the following month moved to bring down the government and to become, at 41, Norway's youngest-ever Prime Minister, heading yet another minority Labour administration. Despite being compared to Tony Blair of the Labour Party in Britain, Stoltenberg had even less success than Jagland in the popularity stakes, amidst mounting public opposition to high taxation combined with deteriorating public services. In the September 2001 elections Labour lost support both to the centre-right and to the Socialist Left Party, slumping to an 80-year low of 24.4% and 43 seats. In the aftermath of the election Stoltenberg stood down as Prime Minister on Oct. 17 and a right-of-centre government took office.

The DNA is a member party of the Socialist International.

Progress Party
Fremskrittspartiet (FrP)
Address. PB 8903 Youngstorget, 0028 Oslo
Telephone. (47) 2313–5400
Fax. (47) 2242–5401
Email. frp@frp.no
Website. www.frp.no
Leadership. Carl Ivar Hagen (chairman and parliamentary leader); Siv Jensen (first deputy leader); John I. Alvheim (second deputy leader); Geir Mo (secretary-general)

The right-wing populist FrP was established in April 1973 as Anders Lange's Party for a Strong Reduction in Taxation and Public Intervention, its founder being a well-known dog-kennel owner who had become a national celebrity as a result of his political comments in a dog-breeding magazine. Following Lange's death in 1974, the party took its present name in January 1977. Having never exceeded four *Storting* seats in previous contests, the FrP became the third strongest parliamentary party in the 1989 elections, winning 22 seats and 13.0% of the vote, but was excluded from the resultant government formed by the traditional centre-right parties.

In the 1993 elections the FrP experienced a major reverse, winning only 10 seats and 6.3% of the vote. It recovered strongly in 1997, becoming the second-strongest parliamentary party, although with small margins, after the Norwegian Labour Party with 25 seats and a 15.3% vote share. It nevertheless continued to be treated as a pariah by the other centre-right parties, notwithstanding some calls in the Conservative Party in particular for it to be accepted as a potential coalition partner. During the next parliamentary term the FrP, in opposition to successive centrist and Labour minority governments, was by early 2001 heading polls of voting intentions. However, the party was damaged by the enforced resignation in February 2001 of deputy leader and heir apparent Terje Søeviknes over rape allegations. In the September 2001 elections, although the FrP improved from 25 to 26 seats, its vote slipped to 14.7% and it fell back to third place behind Labour and the resurgent Conservatives. It said it would support the new coalition government formed in October 2001 by the Christian People's, Conservative and Liberal parties.

Socialist Left Party
Sosialistisk Venstreparti (SV)
Address. Storgata 45, 0185 Oslo
Telephone. (47) 2193–3300
Fax. (47) 2193–3301
Email. post@sv.no
Website. www.sv.no
Leadership. Kristin Halvorsen (leader); Øystein Djupedal & Henriette Westhrin (deputy leaders); Bård Vegar Solhjell (secretary)

The SV was founded in March 1975 as the unitary successor to the Socialist Electoral Alliance, linking the Communist Party of Norway, the Socialist People's Party and the Left Social Democratic Organization. The Socialist Electoral Alliance was a result of a cooperation among those who worked against Norwegian membership in the European Community (EC, later the EU) during the 1972 referendum campaign. In the 1973 elections the Alliance had won 16 seats in the *Storting* (with 11.2% of the vote) on a strongly socialist economic and social platform which also included opposition to Norwegian membership of NATO and the EC. On the conversion of the Alliance into the SV, the Communist Party decided not to merge into the new party.

The SV won only two seats in the 1977 parliamentary elections, but progressed to four seats in 1981 and to six in 1985. It made a major advance in 1989, to 17 seats on a vote share of 10.1%, but fell back to 13 seats (7.9%) in 1993. It subsequently played a prominent part in the successful campaign against Norwegian accession to the EU, but got no reward in the 1997 parliamentary elections, in which it declined further to nine seats and 6.0 % of the vote.

The unpopularity of the minority government of the Norwegian Labour Party formed in March 2000 yielded substantial benefit to the SV in the September 2001 elections, in which the party increased its representation to 23 seats from a vote share of 12.5%.

Other Parties

Communist Party of Norway (*Norges Kommunistiske Parti, NKP*), founded in 1923 by left-wing faction of the Norwegian Labour Party (DNA); was influential during and after World War II, winning 11 parliamentary seats in 1945, but declining in the 1950s and ceasing to be represented from 1961. In 1973 the party joined the Socialist Election Alliance, which won 16 seats in that year's elections, but it rejected joining the successor Socialist Left Party. Having polled 0.2% in 1985, the NKP was allied with the Red Electoral Alliance in 1989 without success and did not contest the 1993 elections. It polled 0.1% in 1997 and presented no candidates in 2001.
Address. Helgesens gt. 21, 0553 Oslo
Telephone. (47) 2271–6044
Fax. (47) 2271–7907
Email. nkp@nkp.no
Website. www.nkp.no
Leadership. Zafer Gözet (leader)

Green Party of Norway (*Miljøpartiet de Grønne*), founded in October 1988 from earlier groups, has won some local representation but none nationally, in part because environmental issues are promoted by major formations, notably the Socialist Left Party; affiliated to the European Federation of Green Parties.
Address. PB 9124 Grønland, 0133 Oslo
Telephone. (47) 2242–9758
Fax. (47) 2266–0122
Email. gronne@gronne.no
Website. www.gronne.no
Leadership. Trude Malthe Thomassen (female spokesperson); Brynmor Evans (male spokesperson)

Pensioners' Party (*Pensjonistpartiet, Pp*), founded in 1985 and active in the pensioners' cause in recent elections, polling 0.7% in 2001.
Address. Landstads gt. 30, 3210 Sandefjord
Telephone. (47) 3346–7319
Website. www.pensjonistpartiet.no
Leadership. Turid Sveen Aase (leader)

Red Electoral Alliance (*Rød Valgallianse, RV*), derived from the electoral front of the (Maoist) Workers' Communist Party (founded in 1972), later attracted independent socialists. It was allied with the Communist Party of Norway in the

1989 elections, failing to make an impact. Standing on its own in 1993 it won one seat (on a 1.1% vote share), but lost it in 1997 even though it vote increased to 1.7%. It polled 1.2% in 2001 without regaining representation.

Address. 27 Osterhausgt., 0183 Oslo

Telephone. (47) 2298–9050

Fax. (47) 2298–9055

Email. rv@rv.no

Website. www.rv.no

Leadership. Torstein Dahle

Oman

Capital: Muscat
Population: 2,713,462 note: includes 527,078 non-nationals (July 2002 est.)

Oman is a hereditary state, ruled by the Al Bu-Said dynasty since 1741. In 1970, Qaboos bin Said Al Bu-Said ousted his father and has ruled as Sultan ever since. The Sultan is both the chief of state and head of government. On Nov. 6, 1996, he issued a royal decree which, among other things, clarified the royal succession and established a bicameral legislature.

The bicameral *Majlis* consists of a 48-seat upper chamber (*Majlis al-Dawla*) and an 83-seat lower chamber (*Majlis Al-Shura*). The upper chamber is appointed by the monarch and the lower is elected by limited suffrage for three-year term. Both chambers have only advisory powers, however, with the members of the lower house having some limited powers to propose legislation. In both chambers, the Sultan has the final decision.

There are no political parties in Oman. Suffrage in the elections of 2000 was limited to approximately 175,000 Omanis, chosen by the government to vote for the *Majlis Al-Shura*. Two women were elected for the first time to the *Majlis Al-Shura* and about 100,000 people voted.

Pakistan

Capital: Islamabad
Population: 149,163,000 (mid-2002E)

The Islamic Republic of Pakistan was proclaimed in March 1956, Pakistan having been granted independence as a Commonwealth dominion following the partition of the British Indian Empire in August 1947. The constitution promulgated in 1973 provided for a parliamentary system with a bicameral federal legislature (*Majlis-e-Shoora*) consisting of a 237-member National Assembly, to serve a five-year term and in which 217 seats (207 Muslim and 10 non-Muslim) were directly elected and 20 reserved for women, and an 87-member upper house (Senate), half of whose members were elected every three years for a six-year term. The President, who is elected by the federal legislature for a (renewable) term of five years, is empowered under the constitution to dismiss the Prime Minister and dissolve parliament. In practice military governments have largely dominated the political stage since independence.

Gen. Zia ul-Haq came to power in a coup in 1977 in which he overthrew the Pakistan People's Party (PPP) government of Zulfiqar Ali Bhutto. Zia was killed in an air crash in August 1988 and subsequent elections resulted in victory for the PPP with Bhutto's daughter, Benazir Bhutto, becoming Prime Minister. Her government was dismissed by President Ghulam Ishaq Khan in August 1990. Fresh elections in October 1990 resulted in victory for the right-wing Islamic Democratic Alliance (IDA) headed by Mian Mohammad Nawaz Sharif, who formed a coalition administration. Subsequently, the IDA fell into disarray, and political paralysis led to the resignations of both President Khan and Prime Minister Nawaz Sharif in July 1993. As a result of further National Assembly elections held on Oct. 9, 1993, the PPP returned to power as the largest single party.

The new PPP government led by Prime Minister Benazir Bhutto survived until Nov. 5, 1996, when it was dismissed by President Farooq Leghari. The country was facing multiple economic, political, judicial and constitutional crises amidst widespread allegations of corruption against her cabinet and the Bhutto family, especially Benazir's husband, Asif Ali Zardari. In new elections held in February 1997, the Pakistan Muslim League-Nawaz (PML-N), led by Nawaz Sharif, took power, winning 135 seats in the National Assembly. The PPP, in considerable disarray and suffering public opprobrium, took just 19 seats. Of the other parties, the *Muhajir* National Movement (MQM-A) strengthened its position winning 12 seats and the *Awami* National Party (ANP) took 9. Among the Islamist groups, the Assembly of Islamic Clergy (JUI) increased its representation to two seats but the Pakistan Islamic Assembly (JI) and Assembly of Pakistani Clergy (JUP) boycotted the polls. A major feature of the election was the very low level of voter turn out (28%), which considerably qualified the scale of Nawaz Sharif's triumph.

In provincial elections held at the same time, the PML-N also swept the board in Punjab winning 211 out of 231 seats, and, in Sindh, it took 15 seats which, in association with the 28 won by the MQM-A, enabled it to displace the dominance of the PPP, which captured only 36 seats. In North-West Frontier Province, the ANP, with 31 seats, closely matched the PML-N's 33, and in Baluchistan, the regionalist Baluchistan National Party (BNP) (10 seats) did well alongside the Islamist JUI (7 seats).

Nawaz Sharif formed a new government and attempted to use his dominant position in the National Assembly to concentrate power in his own hands, first, over his party and, second, over the other institutions of the state. This provoked further splits within the PML and led to a series of constitutional crises involving the Supreme Court, the office of the President and, finally, the army. In October 1999, after being forced by international pressure to withdraw support for an army-backed guerrilla incursion into Indian-held Kashmir, he attempted to remove the Commander-in-Chief of the Armed Forces, General Pervez Musharraf, but was instead overthrown himself in a military coup. Musharraf then suspended the constitution in order to impose direct military rule. In 2000, his coup was ratified by the Supreme Court on the understanding that it was temporary and that he would restore a democratic constitution by October 2002. Responding to this understanding, in April–May 2001 Musharraf organized elections to local councils and municipalities but on a basis which prohibited the operation of political parties. In July 2001, he also declared himself President for three years and dissolved the National Assembly, the Senate and the provincial assemblies (all of which had been in recess since October 1999) with a view to restructuring them for new elections to be held within the specified time period.

Musharraf held a referendum on April 30, 2002, that secured the extension of his term of office by a further five years, until 2007. The plebiscite also asked whether voters supported his policies of economic reform and of fighting extremism. The official figures found that 97.7% of the 43.9 million votes cast (a turnout of 56%) endorsed the extension of Musharraf's presidency. The Alliance to Restore Democracy (ARD) coalition of opposition parties, which had urged a boycott of the vote, claimed, however, that the result was produced by massive electoral fraud. This view was supported by the independent Human Rights Commission of Pakistan, which cited ballot-box stuffing, multiple voting, compulsory voting for government employees, and the fact that the electoral register had been suspended. EU observers and international commentators also found the referendum to be deeply flawed, with the result that what was designed as an exercise in legitimizing Musharraf's government appeared to be a parody of the democratic process.

Before holding national elections in October 2002 Musharraf announced on Aug. 21 a number of constitutional amendments under the umbrella of the Legal Framework Order (LFO). These included the expansion of the National Assembly to 342 seats, including 60 seats reserved for women (allocated on the basis of proportional representation) and 10 reserved for non-Muslim minorities. Musharraf also reintroduced the joint electoral register; previously minority groups had been registered on separate electoral rolls, able to vote only for candidates from their own minorities. The voting age was lowered to 18. A requirement that candidates for both the National Assembly and the provincial assemblies should hold a university degree would later lead to challenges to some results, and occasional re-run elections. The government claimed that this law would reduce the dominance of Pakistani politics by feudal landowning families. However, it not only disqualified a number of candidates from the mainstream secular parties who had sat in previous Assemblies, but also appeared to be weighted against many Islamist candidates whose qualifications were obtained from *madrassas* (Islamic seminaries), which were in most cases not regarded as equivalent to university degrees. The LFO also disqualified any candidate who had a "criminal or corrupt record" and limited any federal or provincial prime minister to two terms. Both these measures were seen as designed to exclude both the self-exiled Bhutto – who had been convicted on a 1994 corruption charge – and Sharif – who had been convicted in April 2000 of hijacking and terrorism, but released from life imprisonment into exile in Saudi Arabia in December – from ever holding office again. Bhutto had been out of the country when she was convicted in absentia of corruption in April 1999, and had remained in exile.

The most contentious parts of the LFO related to the increased powers that it gave the presidency and the apparent integration of the armed forces into the political structure. Musharraf would continue both as President and as chief-of-staff of the army, holding in this dual role the chairmanship of a National Security Council (NSC) that would include the other chiefs of the armed services in addition to the Prime Minister, provincial chief ministers, the head of the parliamentary opposition and the speakers of both houses of the legislature. The role of the NSC was described as being that of a "forum for consultation on strategic matters". The LFO restored to the President the power – removed by Sharif – to dissolve the National Assembly. Constitutional amendments abandoned since an earlier draft of the LFO included the power of the President to dismiss the Cabinet, and the reduction of the terms of the National Assembly and the provincial assemblies from five years to four and of the Senate's term from six years to four. Many of the measures in the LFO, especially Musharraf's retention of his army position and the creation of the NSC, were strongly opposed by the PML and the PPP and most other political parties, which saw them as a means to perpetuate the role of the armed forces in politics. Musharraf himself, who insisted that he was trying to build a "sustainable democracy" in place of the "sham democracy" of Pakistan's past, said that the army needed to be given a place in the system in order to pre-empt the possibility of a military coup.

In the National Assembly elections of Oct. 10, 2002, held four years after Musharraf's coup, the deadline stipulated by the ruling of the Supreme Court, and the first held since February 1997, the largest party in the 342-seat Assembly was the pro-Musharraf PML faction Pakistan Muslim League–*Qaid-i-Azam* (PML-QA) with 77 seats, followed by the pro-Bhutto principal PPP faction the Pakistan People's Party–Parliamentarians (PPP-P) with 63 seats. The pro-Sharif Pakistan Muslim League–Nawaz (PML-N) won only 14 seats. However, the major surprise was the success of the alliance of six conservative Muslim parties, the *Mutiha Majlis-i-Amal* (MMA), which emerged as the third-largest bloc with 53 seats. In the allocation of seats for women and minorities according to proportional representation the PML–QA was boosted to 99 seats, the PPP-P to 78 and the MMA to 63.

A team of election monitors from the EU concluded that the electoral process had been "seriously flawed", less through irregularities in the count than in the use of official resources, including state-run television coverage and state funding, to aid campaigning by the PML-QA and the MMA, contrasting with restrictions imposed on campaigning by other parties opposed to Musharraf's rule, especially the PPP-P and the PML-N. Commonwealth observers concurred with this verdict, and the suspension of Pakistan from the Commonwealth was maintained on the grounds that the country's return to democracy had been incomplete. Analysts concluded that despite the opposition of the Islamist MMA to Musharraf's support for the US-led campaign in Afghanistan and the "war on terrorism", and to his avowed vision of a secular and non-sectarian Pakistan, the President felt more threatened by the intransigent hostility to his personal rule, and to the continuing influence of the military in political life, of the two main secular parties. Islamist parties had traditionally been partners of military governments in Pakistan. The religious parties' electoral success in October 2002 was in sharp contrast to their negligible impact in the 1993 and 1997 elections. Although the advance of the MMA was achieved largely by the exploitation of the geographically concentrated Pashtun vote, it was nevertheless widely seen as a radical departure in Pakistani politics. According to the Pakistan Election Commission turnout in the federal election was 41.8%.

In simultaneous elections on Oct. 10 to provincial assemblies the MMA won 48 seats in the 99-seat assembly of the largely ethnic Pashtun North-West Frontier Province (NWFP), where there was considerable sympathy for the fellow-Pashtun Taliban regime in Afghanistan ousted by the USA. The MMA formed a government with the help of allies. In neighbouring Baluchistan province the MMA, with 14 seats, formed the largest group in the 48-seat assembly, forming a coalition government with the PML-QA; again, the MMA relied largely on the Pashtun vote. However, the MMA won only a handful of seats in the more urbanized and populous Sind and Punjab provinces. In Sind the PPP-P was the largest party, with in the 130-member assembly with 51 seats, followed by the regional MQM with 31. In Punjab the PML-QA came close to a majority in the 297-member assembly with 128 seats, followed by the PPP-P with 53 and the PML-N with 40.

After protracted negotiations on forming a government between the major parties the National Assembly on Nov. 21 elected Zafarullah Khan Jamali of the PML-QA, a former chief minister of Baluchistan, as Prime Minister. Jamali secured a narrow majority with 172 votes, ahead of Maulana Fazlur Rehman of the MMA with 86 votes and Shah Mahmood Qureshi of the PPP-P with 70 votes. Musharraf had suspended a law banning legislators from changing parties, with the result that both the PML-QA's current strength of 121 seats and Jamali's majority were sustained by such defections – largely from the PPP-P – and by the recruitment of Independents. The PPP-P was reduced to 61 seats. Jamali on Nov. 23 formed a government dominated by the PML-QA, with some portfolios being held by PPP-P defectors. Jamali fulfilled a constitutional requirement on Dec. 30 by securing 188 votes to win a confidence motion in the National Assembly. Elections were held on Feb. 25, 2003, to the 100-seat Senate, the upper house of the federal legislature. The provincial legislatures elected 88 members, while the Federally Administered Tribal Areas (FATA) elected eight and the federal capital, Islamabad, elected four. The PML-QA won the most seats, 31, followed by the MMA with 17 and the PPP-P with 11.

The operation of the National Assembly was paralyzed for more than a year by an opposition alliance of the PPP-P, the PML-N (with the other ARD parties) and the MMA, who despite their disparate objectives and ideologies presented a united front in their opposition to the powers Musharraf had awarded himself under the LFO, in particular his dual role as President and chief of army staff. Very little parliamentary business was concluded apart from the budget, which was eventually passed during an opposition boycott of the chamber. Finally, after negotiations with the MMA, Musharraf announced on Dec. 24 that he would step down as army chief at the end of 2004. Within days the MMA joined pro-government legislators in voting through approval of the provisions of the LFO as the 17th Amendment of the 1973 constitution.

Alliance for the Restoration of Democracy (ARD)
Leadership. Javed Hashmi (president) (PML-N); Makhdoom Amin Fahim (chairman) (PPP-P)
The ARD is an alliance of 15 parties founded in November 2000 by the veteran politician Nawabzada Nasrullah Khan in reaction against Musharraf's military dictatorship. Nasrullah Khan, leader of the small Pakistan Democratic Party (PDP), was skilled at forging political alliances, and had organized opposition movements against previous periods of military rule, under Gen. Mohammad Zia ul-Haq and President Gen. Ayub Khan, and against corruption and autocratic tendencies

in civilian governments. As ARD chairman he succeeded not only in bridging the bitter rivalry between Bhutto's secular Pakistan People's Party (PPP) and Sharif's Pakistan Muslim League (PML), but also in enlisting the partial co-operation of the *Mutahida Majlis-e-Amal* (MMA–United Council for Action), an alliance of six Islamist parties (which, however, remained outside the ARD). Nazrullah Khan died in September 2003, and on Oct. 8 the ARD leadership elected his successors, creating a new position of president to balance the two major components of the alliance, the PPP–Parliamentarians and the PML–Nawaz group.

Awami National Party (ANP)
Leadership. Asfandyar Wali Khan (president)
The ANP was formed in 1986, as a successor to the reformist National Awami Party (NAP) by merger of a number of left-wing groups including the National Democratic Party (NDP). Having won six National Assembly seats in the 1990 elections, the ANP secured only three in the October 1993 polls. The party held one ministerial appointment in the Pakistan People's Party (PPP)-led government. In the general election of February 1997, now in alliance with the Pakistan Muslim League–Nawaz (PPP-N) it increased its representation to nine seats in the National Assembly and 31 in its regional stronghold in the North-West Frontier Province (NWFP) assembly. In the October 2002 elections the secular ANP suffered for its support for the military overthrow of the Taliban government in Afghanistan and lost all its seats in the National Assembly, while shrinking to eight seats in the NWFP assembly. The party won two seats in the February 2003 elections to the federal Senate.

Islami Tehrik Pakistan (ITP)
Leadership. Syed Sajjad Naqvi
The ITP is the one Shia Muslim component of the *Mutahida Majlis-e-Amal* (MMA) alliance of Islamist parties. Although the MMA claimed its National Assembly seats collectively in the October 2002 elections, it is reported that no ITP candidate was successful.

Jamaat-e-Islami Pakistan (Pakistan Islamic Assembly, JI)
Address. Mansura, Multan Road, Lahore
Telephone. (92–42) 5419520-24
Fax. (92–42) 5419505
Email. amir@ji.org.pk
Website. www.jamaat.org
Leadership. Qazi Hussain Ahmed (president); Syed Munawar Hasan Qayyim (secretary-general)
The JI (or JIP) is a Sunni Islamist party founded in 1941 by the Islamic scholar Abdul A'ala Maududi. The JI provided the major political support to the Islamicization policy followed by the military government led by Gen. Zia-ul-Haq (1978-88). It participated in the formation of the Islamic Democratic Alliance (IDA) in 1988 and in the 1990 elections won eight National Assembly seats. However, in May 1992 the party withdrew from the IDA, alleging that the alliance had failed to implement the process of Islamicization that had been part of its election manifesto. In 1993 it was instrumental in launching the Pakistan Islamic Front (PIF), which contested the October 1993 elections and won three National Assembly seats. It endorsed the presidential dismissal of the Pakistan People's Party government and dissolution of the National Assembly in 1996 but boycotted the general election of 1997.

In October 2001 the JI organized protests against US military action in Afghanistan with leader Qazi Hussain Ahmad predicting that Gen. Musharraf's continued support for the USA would lead to his downfall and the installation of an Islamic regime in Pakistan. Numerous JI activists were reported to have been arrested. As part of the *Mutahida Majlis-e-Amal* (MMA) the party won 17 seats in the National Assembly elections of October 2002, regaining some ground in Sindh province lost to the *Mutahida Qaumi Mahaz* (MQM) in the 1980s. Based largely on the urban intellectual, professional and business classes the JI is foremost amongst the religious parties in organizational, financial and media skills, and has indeed been described as the best organized political party in Pakistan. In terms of Sunni orthodoxy the JI is midway between the Deobandi and Barelvi sects and to some degree espouses the notion of Islamic unity by exploring contacts with Shia groups.

Jamiat Ahle Hadith (JAH)

Leadership. Sajid Mir (leader)

A party representing followers of the puritanical Saudi Arabian Wahhabi tradition, the JAH is a member of the Islamist alliance the *Mutahida Majlis-e-Amal*, but its candidates won no seats in the October 2002 elections to the National Assembly.

Jamiat Ulema-e-Islam (JUI, Assembly of Islamic Clergy)

Leadership. Maulana Fazlur Rehman (JUI-F faction); Sami-ul-Haq (JUI-S faction)

Both factions of the JUI, a Sunni Islamist formation, are adherents of the fundamentalist Deobandi Sunni tradition originating in the northern Indian state of Uttar Pradesh in 1867. Founded in 1945 in support of the establishment of Pakistan as a state guided by Islamic principles, the JUI early espoused the concept of *jihad* (holy war) and formed a close association with the military government of Gen. Zia-ul-Haq (1978-88). The party won six National Assembly seats in the 1990 elections, failed to retain any in 1993 but won back two in 1997; it also won seven seats in the Baluchistan provincial assembly and one in the North-West Frontier Province (NWFP) assembly in 1997. These predominantly ethnically Pashtun provinces constitute the JUI's chief power base.

The party split into two factions in 1990 when Rehman formed a short-lived alliance of convenience with the Pakistan People's Party (PPP), but they are divided on personal rather than ideological lines. The JUI has been closely involved with the conservative religious-political movements in Afghanistan, both the anti-Soviet Mujahideen rebellion and its successor the Taliban movement. It has also been an advocate of the militant Islamic separatist groups fighting Indian rule in the northern state of Jammu and Kashmir. Following the commencement of US-led hostilities against the Taliban regime in October 2001 the JUI organized demonstrations hostile to the Musharraf government's pro-US position. Both the JUI-F and the JUI-S fought the October 2002 elections as part of the six-party Islamist alliance the *Mutahida Majlis-e-Amal* (MMA), the JUI-F becoming the largest party in the MMA with 41 seats and the JUI-S winning two.

Jamiat Ulema-e-Pakistan (JUP, Assembly of Pakistani Clergy)

The JUP is a moderate Sunni Muslim formation in the *Mutahida Majlis-e-Amal* (MMA) alliance of Islamist parties. It represents the inclusive Barelvi tradition that embraces the roles of the sufis and hereditary saints, and is thus the antithesis of the puritanical Deobandi tradition. The JUP was represented in the Sharif coalition government following the October 1990 elections; it failed to gain representation in 1993 and boycotted the polls in 1997. In the October 2002 elections the JUP gained one seat in the National Assembly as part of the MMA. Although the party had declined since its prominence in the 1970s and 1980s, being based largely in Karachi and Hyderabad in Sind province, its leader Maulana Shah Ahmed Noorani Siddiqui,

who died on Dec. 11, 2003, aged 77, was an influential figure whose integrity was widely respected. An intellectual and widely-travelled cleric who spoke several languages, he was a member of the committee that drafted Pakistan's 1973 constitution and a consistent opponent both of military rule and political corruption.

Mutahida Majlis-e-Amal (United Council for Action, MMA)

Leadership. Qazi Hussain Ahmed (interim president)

The MMA was formed in January 2002 by six Islamist parties drawn from membership of the Pak-Afghan Defence Council, a grouping established in October 2002 of 26 religious parties opposed to the US military campaign to oust the Taliban government in Afghanistan and to Musharraf's alliance of Pakistan with the USA's war against terrorism. The Council's campaign against the war in Afghanistan failed to arouse sufficient popular support, and the formation of the MMA saw a change of focus to domestic politics. Its membership comprises disparate and even opposed strands of Islam, even including one minority Shia party. The component parties of the MMA are *Jamaat-e-Islami Pakistan* (JI), the two factions of *Jamiat Ulema-e-Islam* (JUI-F and JUI-S), *Jamiat Ulema-e-Pakistan* (JUP), *Jamiat-e-Ahle Hadith* (JAH) and *Islami Tehrik Pakistan* (ITP).

The MMA collectively won 53 seats in the October 2002 general election, this being increased to 67 with the award of reserved seats for women and minorities. In the simultaneous elections for provincial assemblies it gained an absolute majority in North-West Frontier Province (NWFP) and the largest number of seats in Baluchistan. The MMA does not disclose a breakdown of seats by party, and figures quoted for individual parties reflect independent estimates. The death on Dec. 11 of MMA president Maulana Shah Ahmed Noorani Siddiqui, also leader of the JUP, was described as a major setback for the MMA.

Mutahida Qaumi Mahaz (United National Movement, MQM)

Leadership. Altaf Hussain (leader of main faction)

Address. Nine Zero, 494/8 Azizabad, Federal B Area, Karachi

Telephone. 92 21 6313690, 6329131, 6329900

Fax. 92 21 6329955

Email. mqm@mqm.org (MQM International Secretariat, UK)

Founded in 1978 as *the Mojahir Qaumi Mahaz*, the MQM changed its name on July 26, 1997, in an attempt to broaden its political base. The party was originally formed to champion the ethnic identity and interests of Urdu-speaking Muslim migrants to Pakistan (*Mojahirs*), who came mostly from India at the time of partition, as the "fifth nationality" of the country. Its political base lies almost entirely in Sind province, especially in Karachi, the provincial capital and Pakistan's largest city. The party won 15 seats in the National Assembly elections in 1990 and was represented in the Sharif coalition government until its withdrawal in mid-1992. Divided into two main factions, the MQM did not contest the National Assembly in the 1993 elections, but retained substantial support in the Sind province assembly poll. MQM militants and the government held talks during 1995 in an attempt to end serious fighting and civil disorder in areas of Sindh, especially in Karachi. Little progress was made, however, and the death toll in 1995 approached 2,000. Renewed violence in December 1995 followed the discovery on the outskirts of Karachi of the bullet-riddled bodies of two relatives of the main MQM leader, Altaf Hussain. By then the MQM was split into at least two factions. However, the fall of Benazir Bhutto's government in November 1996 revived its fortunes, especially those of the MQM-A led by

Altaf Hussain. At the general election of February 1997, it won 12 seats in the National Assembly and 28 in the Sindh provincial assembly. By contrast, the other faction, MQM-Haqiqi, which was widely seen as a creature of the army and secret service, did poorly. The MQM-A used its strengthened assembly positions to pursue a policy of co-operation with the Pakistan Muslim League–Nawaz government of Prime Minister Nawaz Sharif until its fall in October 1999. In the October 2002 elections the MQM won 13 seats in the National Assembly and 31 seats in the Sind provincial assembly. A breakaway faction, the Mojahir Qaumi Movement Pakistan (MQMP), secured one seat in the National Assembly and one seat in the Sind assembly.

National Alliance
Leadership. Ghulam Mustafa Jatoi (leader)
The National Alliance comprises six small pro-Musharraf parties including Jatoi's National People's Party (NPP) , the Sind Democratic Alliance and the Millat Party, the latter founded by former President Farooq Leghari (1993-97), who had resigned in a constitutional confrontation with Prime Minister Nawaz Sharif. In the October 2002 elections, after the award of women's and minorities' seats, the National Alliance held 16 seats in the National Assembly. No party breakdown of this total was available.

Pakistan Muslim League (PML)
Leadership. Javed Hashmi (acting president of Nawaz group); Mian Azhar (leader of *Quaid-i-Azam* or Like-Minded group)
The PML was established in 1962 as the successor to the pre-independence All-India Muslim League. It has long been beset by factional rivalries and divisions. By 1995, the PML-N (Nawaz group) was the largest factional element, headed by former Prime Minister Nawaz Sharif, who had been instrumental in the formation of the Islamic Democratic Alliance, which had won the 1990 federal elections. Following the October 1993 elections, in which it secured 73 National Assembly seats, the PML-N formed the core of the parliamentary opposition to the Pakistan People's Party (PPP) administration. The PML-J (Junejo group), headed by Hamid Nasir Chattha and named after former Prime Minister Mohammed Khan Junejo (who died in 1993), won six seats in the 1993 federal polling and joined the PPP-led government in coalition. By contrast, in the 1997 elections the PML-N won 135 National Assembly seats and formed a new government under Nawaz Sharif, while the PML-J failed to retain a single seat and was reduced to a representation of just five members across the provincial assemblies of Punjab, North-West Frontier Province and Baluchistan.

In 1998 a faction of the PML-J opted to return to the fold, merging with the PML-N. However, the PML-N itself then began to split: first, in reaction to Nawaz Sharif's attempts to impose a personal dictatorship and, subsequently, following Sharif's displacement by a military coup. A PML-Q (*Quaid-i-Azam*), or PML-LM (Like-Minded) group, emerged in early 2001 under the leadership of Mian Azhar to offer broad support to General Musharraf's new government. Since Nawaz Sharif's trial, conviction and exile, effective leadership of the PML-N has passed to Javed Hashmi as acting president. The party formed an unlikely partnership with its bitter rival the PPP in the 15-party Alliance to Restore Democracy (ARD). In the October 2002 elections the PML-QA, dubbed the "King's party", emerged as the dominant faction, effectively eclipsing the PML-N, even in Nawaz Sharif's electoral homeland of Punjab. Of the other factions of the party the Pakistan Muslim League–Functional (PML-F) secured five seats in the National Assembly, the PML-J won three seats, the PML-Zia won two seats and the PML-Jinnah won one seat. On Oct. 30, 2003, PML-N acting pres-

ident Javed Hashmi was arrested and later charged with inciting mutiny after displaying at a press conference letters, allegedly written by junior army officers, critical of President Musharraf.

Pakistan People's Party (PPP)
Address. Zardari House-8, Street 19, Sector F-8/2, Islamabad
Email. ppp@comsats.net.pk
Website. www.ppp.org.pk
Leadership. Benazir Bhutto (life chairperson); Makhdoom Amin Fahim (acting president); Jahangir Badar (general secretary); Aftab Ahmed Sherpao (PPP-S); Ghinva Bhutto (PPP-SB)
The PPP was formed in 1967, advocating Islamic socialism, democracy and a non-aligned foreign policy. A PPP government was overthrown in a coup in 1977 led by Gen. Zia ul-Haq and the party's founder, Zulfiqar Ali Bhutto, was executed in 1979 by the military regime. The party leadership was then assumed by his widow, Begum Nasrat, and by his daughter, Benazir. In the November 1988 National Assembly elections, held after Gen. Zia's death in a plane crash, the PPP became the largest single party (although without an overall majority) and Benazir Bhutto was designated Prime Minister. The party lost power with the dismissal of her government in August 1990, after which, in elections the following October, its legislative strength was more than halved. In 1992 the party formally abandoned its previous state socialist programme in favour of building a social market economy. The party returned to power in the October 1993 elections, winning 89 of 206 contested National Assembly seats and assuming control (by April 1994) of three of the country's four provincial assemblies. In a presidential election in November 1993, the federal parliamentary deputies elected Farooq Leghari, the PPP nominee.

In December 1993 the PPP hierarchy ousted the Prime Minister's mother as party co-chair, reflecting the estrangement between Benazir and both her mother and her brother, Murtaza Bhutto, who announced the formation of a breakaway left-wing faction of the PPP, the PPP-SB, in March 1995. However, Murtaza was assassinated in 1996 and although his wife attempted to sustain his faction it did poorly at the elections of 1997, winning only one seat in the National Assembly and two in the Sindh provincial assembly. Meanwhile, following the dismissal of Benazir Bhutto's government by President Leghari in November 1996, the main PPP also went into decline. In the 1997 elections, it retained only 19 of the 98 National Assembly seats that it had won in 1993 and saw its representation in the Sindh provincial assembly reduced to a minority 36 seats. After her indictment for corruption later in 1997, Benazir Bhutto also left the country and subsequently has attempted to maintain her leadership from abroad. Following press speculation that the Musharraf government was negotiating with senior PPP officials for the party to drop Bhutto as leader, she announced in early September 2001 that she intended to lead the party in the elections promised for 2002.

Following the terrorist attacks in the USA of Sept. 11, 2001, the PPP called on the Musharraf government to distance itself from the Taliban regime in Afghanistan and create a government of national consensus. The party was initially cautiously supportive of Musharraf's re-alignment of Pakistan with the USA in the war to overthrow the Taliban and of his pronouncements against religious fundamentalism and sectarian violence. However, it has come to see his military-backed government as essentially undemocratic and opposes the sweeping powers he has awarded himself in the Legal Framework Order (LFO). The PPP reinvented itself in August 2002, to comply with new electoral regulations, as the PPP–Parliamentarians for the October elections, in which it staged a revival, winning a total of 78 seats, although some were subsequently lost by defection to the Musharraf-backing Pakistan Muslim League–*Qaid-i-Azam* (PML-QA). In the October 2002 elections a breakaway faction of the PPP led by Aftab Ahmed Sherpao (who had been expelled from the party by Benazir Bhutto in 1999), called the Pakistan People's Party–Sherpao (PPP-S) won two seats in the National Assembly. The PPP-S campaigned in alliance with the PML-QA, and Sherpao himself was rewarded with a post in Zafarullah Khan Jamali's Cabinet. The PPP-SB also won two seats in the National Assembly.

The PPP is a consultative member of the Socialist International, although it has largely abandoned its former socialist aspirations and no longer offers a programme of social reform.

Other Parties

Baluchistan National Party (BNP), a regionalist party that won three seats in the February 1997 National Assembly elections. In the October 2002 elections it retained only one seat in the National Assembly and was relegated to third place in the Baluchistan provincial assembly with two seats. The party was founded in 1996 under the leadership of Sardar Ataullah Mengal.

Islami Jamhoori Mahaz (IJM), won four seats in October 1993 Assembly elections but retained none of them in February 1997.

Jamhoori Wattan Party (JWP), won two seats in October 1993 Assembly elections, which it retained in 1997 when it also won eight seats in the Baluchistian provincial assembly. It retained only one seat in the National Assembly in the October 2002 elections and was reduced to three seats in the Baluchistan assembly.
Leadership. Nawab Akbar Bugti

Millat-e-Islamia (MI), founded by Maulana Azam Tariq, leader of the extremist Sunni fundamentalist group *Sipah-e-Sahaba Pakistan* (SSP), after the latter was banned by Musharraf's government in January 2002 because of its violent sectarian campaign against Shia Muslims. Tariq won a seat in the October 2002 elections while still in prison. He was assassinated on Oct. 6, 2003, in Islamabad, responsibility being claimed by a previously unknown Shia group.

National People's Party (NPP), formed in 1986 by a breakaway faction from the Pakistan People's Party (PPP), the NPP was a member of the Sharif coalition government from 1990 until its expulsion in March 1992. It won one seat in both the 1993 and 1997 elections, and fought the October 2002 elections as part of the National Alliance.
Leadership. Ghulam Mustafa Jatoi (chair)

Pakhtoon Khawa Milli Awami Party (PKMAP), largely representing Pashtuns in Baluchistan, won three seats for Baluchistan in October 1993 Assembly elections; failed to retain any of them in February 1997 but took two seats in the North-West Frontier Province assembly. It failed to take any National Assembly seats in October 2002.
Leadership. Mehmood Achakzai

Pakistan Awami Tehrik (PAT), an orthodox religious party founded in 1989 by Maulana Muhammad Tahir-ul Qadri, a former ally of the Pakistan Muslim League–Nawaz (PML-N), won one seat in the October 2002 elections to the National Assembly after electoral failure in 1990, 1993 and 1997. PAT was denied membership of the Islamist alliance *Mutahida Majlis-e-Amal* because it was seen as supporting

Musharraf's policy of opposing religious militancy. The PAT's literature condemns the "feudal" element in Pakistan's polity, commits itself to the elimination of poverty, social injustice, exploitation and corruption, supports democracy, devolution, an independent judiciary and fundamental human rights including gender equality and religious freedom.
Address. 365-M Model Town, Lahore
Telephone. (92) 42 5169111-4
Fax. (92) 42 5169114, 5168184
Email. ForeignAffairs@PAT.com.pk

Pakistan Democratic Party (PDP), won no seats in the October 2002 elections to the National Assembly. Its leader, Nawabzada Nasrullah Khan, an influential veteran politician who had organized alliances against military governments since the rule of Gen. Mohammed Ayub Khan, was disqualified from standing by his lack of a university degree. Nawabzada Nasrullah Khan was also the founder and president of the Alliance for the Restoration of Democracy (ARD). He died in September 2003, being succeeded as leader of the PDP by his son Nawabzada Mansoor Ahmed Khan.

Pakistan Shia Political Party (PSPP), won one seat in the October 2002 elections to the National Assembly.

Pakistan Tehrik-e-Insaaf (PTI, Movement for Justice), founded in April 1996 by Imran Khan, the former Pakistan cricket captain, who declared that its aim was to "bring about a change in the country by demanding justice, honesty, decency and self-respect". The PTI is committed to accelerated economic growth and the development of a welfare state. Imran's party proved a failure at the polls of February 1997, winning no seats in either the National Assembly or the Punjab provincial assembly. In the October 2002 elections Imran himself won the party's sole seat in the National Assembly.
Leadership. Imran Khan (chairman)
Address. Central Secretariat, 66 Bazar Road, G-6/4, Islamabad
Email. pti@isb.comsats.net.pk

Sind National Front (SNF), led by Mumtaz Ali Bhutto (an uncle of the former Prime Minister), advocating broad autonomy for the four provinces of Pakistan; won one seat in the Sind provincial assembly in 1997. It currently functions as part of the National Alliance. It promotes an egalitarian society and a federalism entailing deeper autonomy for the four provinces.

Palau

Capital: Koror
Population: 17,500 (2000E)

The Republic of Palau (also known as Belau) consists of a chain of islands and islets in the western Pacific Ocean. From 1947, as part of the UN Trust Territory of the Pacific, they were administered by the United States. At the beginning of 1981 a popularly approved constitution came into force which prohibited the stationing of US nuclear weapons and the storage of nuclear waste in Palau. However, the following year Palau and the United States signed a compact of free association under which the USA granted internal sovereignty and economic aid in return for continuing control of Palau's defence. From 1983 onwards, a succession of referendums to override the constitutional ban on the transit and storage of nuclear materials and enable the compact to come into effect failed to gain the required 75% majority. In 1992 the approval requirement was lowered to that of a simple majority, and in a referendum the following year the compact was accepted. On Oct. 1, 1994, Palau became a sovereign and independent state, and the UN Trust Territory of the Pacific was terminated.

Under the 1981 constitution, executive authority is vested in a President, who is directly elected for a four-year term. Legislative authority is exercised by the National Congress (*Olbiil era Kelulau*), a bicameral body consisting of a 16-member House of Delegates (one member from each of Palau's constituent states) and a 14-member Senate. The constitution also provides for a Council of Chiefs to advise the President on matters relating to tribal laws and customs. There are no formal political parties, although two broad tendencies emerged during the pre-independence constitutional dispute, namely the Coalition for Open, Honest and Just Government, which opposed the compact of free association, and the *Ta Belau* Party, which defended it. More recently an opposition Palau National Party has been formed.

In the presidential election of Nov. 7, 2000, the incumbent Vice-President, Tommy Remengesau, was elected with 52% of the vote against 46% for Peter Sugiyama. Senator Sandra Pierantozzi became Vice-President.

Palestinian Entity

Government centre: Ramallah and Gaza City
Population: 2,783,084 (1997)

Of the Arab territories captured by Israel in the Six-Day War of 1967, the Gaza Strip, the West Bank and East Jerusalem contained a substantial Palestinian Arab population. The Palestine Liberation Organization (PLO), founded in 1964, subsequently led resistance to Israeli occupation and increasing Jewish settlement of these areas. Following the *intifada* revolt, which began in December 1987, a peace process started in October 1991, which indirectly resulted (via secret talks in Oslo) in a declaration of principles (DOP) on interim Palestinian self-rule, in September 1993. The PLO now agreed to renounce terrorism and recognize Israel's right to exist within secure borders. For its part, Israel recognized the PLO as "the legitimate representative of the Palestinian people". The DOP also established a timetable for progress towards a final settlement.

By early 1996, the Israeli military had withdrawn from most of the Gaza Strip and most Arab towns and villages in the West Bank, though Jewish settlements remained under Israeli military protection. The accord also transferred many powers to a PLO-dominated Palestine National Authority (PNA) and mandated elections for an 88-member Palestinian Legislative Council (PLC) and for a President. On Jan. 20, 1996, over 750,000 voters out of an electorate of 1,013,235 participated in these dual ballot elections. Turnout was estimated at 88% in Gaza and 70% in the West Bank. PLO chairman, Yasser Arafat, was returned as President by an overwhelming majority against another candidate, Samiha Khalil (Democratic Front). The

PNA Basic Law allows for a President to be elected to a five-year term; he is not subject to votes of no-confidence, and can select a cabinet of up to 26 ministries, though this cabinet must consist of at least 80% of elected members of the PLC. As chief executive, the President has the power to initiate legislation and promulgate laws passed by the PLC.

Arafat's *Fatah* grouping and allies (mainly independent candidates) won a decisive majority in the Palestinian Council, and PLO factions began developing into political movements. One UNDP report said that while independents won 60% of the vote, they received only 40% of seats. Palestinian critics spoke of a circumscribed choice of eligible candidates: instead of genuine party officials, many representatives were Tunis era bureaucrats, or agents of *hamulas* (extended tribal families) and local notables. However, "rejectionist" groups both within and outside the PLO refused to take part, notably the Islamic Resistance Movement (*Hamas*). Since the inauguration of the PLC, opposition forces have alleged that Arafat's government was ignoring the assembly, by taking unilateral decisions without consulting the body, tolerating corruption, not involving the PLC in negotiations with Israel, and failing to push through a Basic Law (preparatory to a full constitution).

The right took power in Israel in May 1996 and initially halted Israeli withdrawal from the West Bank. Labour's victory in Israel's 1999 elections suggested that the peace process might resume. However, the collapse of talks on "final status issues" at Camp David in the USA, in July 2000, increased popular Palestinian frustration, and a new *intifada* (uprising) erupted in October 2000. Israeli politicians – notably after February 2001, new Prime Minister Ariel Sharon – accused Arafat of fomenting revolt, and retaliated against PNA institutions. Citing continued violence and political confusion as an impediment, Arafat repeatedly postponed new elections to the PLC, which ought have been held by 2000.

Currently, the PNA and Israel have formally signed the US-backed Road Map for Peace, which entails, *inter alia*, major Palestinian reforms, cessation of violence, to be followed by Palestinian elections and "interim statehood" for Palestine in 2005. Implementation of the Road Map has been delayed by a combination of ongoing violence and disagreements with Israel, not least over Israel's construction of a "security fence" that cuts into West Bank territory. Nonetheless, Arafat agreed to the institution of a newly empowered Palestinian Prime Minister. Both holders of this portfolio to date have come from *Fatah*.

Tentative security talks recommenced between Israeli and Palestinian officials in November 2003, encouraged in part through Israeli Prime Minister Sharon's talk of "unilateral disengagement", especially in Gaza. Even so, Israel's erection of the barrier in the West Bank has become a major grievance for Palestinians, prompting suspicions of Israel's real aims. And the PNA's evident failure to prevent terror attacks has bolstered the Israeli right-wing in their opposition to dismantling settlements, or resuming peace talks.

Formally at least, the PLO persists as an organization representing Palestinians in the "diaspora". Its legislative body is the Palestinian National Council (PNC) which as of 1997 had 669 members. In theory these include the 88 PLC members. The PLO Executive Committee is the PLO's executive organ and consists of 18 members elected by the PNC. Yasser

Arafat was Chairman of the PLO, in addition to being *ra'is* (President) of the PNA, until his death in November 2004.

Al-Fatah

Website. www.fateh.net

Al-Fatah (the reverse acronym of the Arabic for Palestine Liberation Movement, and meaning Conquest) was established in 1959 and is the core component of the PLO. Some date its formal foundation as 1964. It has always been primarily nationalist in orientation, and eschewed the Marxist accretions of other Palestinian factions. *Fatah* leader Yasser Arafat was elected PLO chairman in 1969, and then remained the dominant political figure on the Palestinian stage. Despite resistance from "rejectionist" PLO factions, in 1988 he and *Fatah* (and in turn the PLO) adopted at a meeting of the Palestine National Council the Algiers Declaration, which nominally declared Palestinian independence. It also appeared to abandon earlier support for armed battle against and replacement of Israel by a "single, democratic secular state" over all of "historical Palestine", in favour of a "two-state solution".

Arafat began negotiations with Israel that led, in 1993, to mutual recognition and the start of Palestinian self-rule in the occupied territories. Yet there was opposition within *Fatah*; Secretary-General Farouk Qadummi, called the PLO "foreign minister" since 1988, boycotted the November 1993 ratifying meeting of the *Fatah* Revolutionary Council, along with half its members. Qadummi remains in exile, choosing not to return to Palestinian soil.

Arafat and other *Fatah* figures, however, did return from exile in 1994, after which *Fatah* regained support in the former *Hamas* stronghold of Gaza. Zakariya al-Agha became head of its local *Fatah* Higher Command. In the 1996 PLC elections, *Fatah* candidates won 55 of the 86 seats, and "independent *Fatah*" candidates won between 7 and 12. Arafat was elected to the Council's presidency with 88.1% of the popular vote. No further elections have been held.

Since 1993, schisms have developed between indigenous *Fatah* activists, mostly veterans of the 1987-91 *intifada*, and *Fatah* leaders who were formerly exiled in Tunis. Likewise, various *Fatah*-affiliated police and paramilitary groups have grown in strength, while Arafat poured water on attempts to "democratize" the party. The outbreak of the Al Aqsa *intifada* in October 2000 resulted in new status for the grassroots *Fatah* faction called *Tanzim*, under its young putative leader, once spoken of as head of *Fatah* in the West Bank, Marwan Barghouti. Husayn al-Shaykh was appointed secretary general of the *Fatah* Higher Committee in the West Bank after Barghouti's capture by Israel in April 2002. *Fatah* was also linked to a more militant entity called the Al Aqsa Martyrs Brigade. PLC Speaker Ahmed Qurei (Abu Ala), was effectively the Council's *Fatah* faction leader.

Israel effectively reoccupied much of the area allocated to the PNA in Spring 2002, in Operation Defensive Shield. Arafat himself was corralled in his *Muqata* presidential residence in Ramallah, and refused permission to leave. On June 24, 2002, US President Bush asked that Palestinians get the chance to vote out leaders "tainted by terrorism" – a phrase generally interpreted to mean Arafat himself. Dissent amongst Arafat's *Fatah* colleagues has grown, including within his cabinet. One minister, Nabil Amr, resigned in protest at Arafat's resistance to internal reforms. Responding to criticism, Arafat ordered another *Fatah* figure, Foreign Minister Nabil Shaath, to develop a proper constitution. Shaath was also involved in negotiations with *Hamas* about a possible ceasefire and rapprochement with the PNA. Conversely, the perception of US and Israeli "persecution" of Arafat served to raise his profile amongst ordinary Palestinians, as a martyr-hero.

Following the official acceptance by the PNA and Israel of the US-backed Road Map for Peace, in early 2003, Arafat accepted the appointment of a newly empowered Palestinian Prime Minister. Both holders of the post to date have been veteran *Fatah* members: Mahmoud Abbas (Abu Mazen) was the first, but he resigned in September 2003, citing lack of support from both Israel and Arafat.

Abbas was regarded as number two to Arafat within *Fatah*; an ideological heavyweight, and founder member of *Fatah*, he seemed prepared to shelve earlier demands for an immediate return of Palestinian refugees. He also sought to curb militias, so as to attain peace with Israel. Abbas was born in Safad in 1935, became a refugee, and worked in Syria and Qatar. Since 1977 he has advocated a two-state solution, in consort with Israeli leftists, a stance frowned upon at the time by the PLO. After returning to Palestinian soil in July 1995 he headed the Palestinian Electoral Commission during 1996-2002. In November 2002 he strongly criticized the direction of the armed *intifada*. Abbas appointed Gazan security chief Mahmoud Dahlan as PNA security minister. Dahlan was born as a refugee, had earlier cracked down on the *Hamas* military wing, and was favoured by Israel and the USA. In June 2003 Dahlan had apparently negotiated terms for an Israeli military withdrawal from Gaza with Amos Gilad, Israeli military co-ordinator in the territories. When this deal failed, probably stymied by Arafat, Dahlan withdrew from the PNA in anger.

Abbas's successor as prime minister was Ahmed Qurei (Abu Ala). Long before he became Speaker of the PLC, Qurei had been associated with the Muslim Brotherhood (see Egypt), then became a founding member of *Fatah* in 1964, and created and ran the *Samed* industrial and investment fund that bankrolled the PLO. He had also been a key negotiator at Oslo during 1992-93; yet in Israel's view, he was too loyal to Arafat.

Qurei effectively took office in November 2003, though problems persisted regarding the remit of his authority. At first he presided over a scaled-down eight-member "emergency cabinet". He wanted to fill the post of Interior Minister with a decisive figure who could tackle the difficult task of dismantling armed militias, as per the Road Map, and suggested overall PNA security chief, Nasser Youssef. But Arafat, it appeared, once again thwarted a Prime Minister's efforts when he insisted that his acolyte, Hakam Balawi, fill the post. After a long lull, a massive suicide bombing on Aug. 21, 2003, led Israel to suspend tentative talks with Qurei.

On Nov. 12, 2003, the PLC endorsed the new cabinet by 48-12 with five abstentions. A notable inclusion in the Qurei cabinet was Jibril Rajoub, previously head of Preventive Security in the West Bank, and once referred to as *Fatah* leader in the region. Rajoub had been forced from office after allegedly failing to counter Israeli incursions in 2002; his reinclusion thus represented a political renaissance of sorts. The USA was reportedly especially pleased at the retention of Salam Fayyad, a *Fatah* figure widely respected as an efficient and honest PNA finance minister.

One figure whose fortunes revived under Abu Ala is Dr Sa'eb Erekat, appointed Negotiations Minister, who was earlier credited for his work in preparing voters for the 1996 PLC elections. From his stronghold in Jericho, this former *intifada* participant and veteran of peace talks with Israel has kept relative calm in his locale. He also leads Palestinian arguments against the "security fence" or wall that Israel is currently building.

Opinion polls suggest that *Fatah* has been losing popular support to *Hamas* and other movements; armed anarchy has reportedly overwhelmed many Palestinian cities. In February 2004, up to 400 *Fatah* members publicly resigned in protest at alleged corruption, maladministration, lack of financial transparency and abuse of democratic procedures by the *Fatah* establishment. Defending Arafat against their charges was Amin Maqboul, *Fatah's* current acting secretary-general in the West Bank.

On Feb. 26, 2004, *Fatah's* Revolutionary Council, a 130-member key decision-making body, met for the first time in three years. Yasser Arafat promised a push for peace with Israel, plus fresh leadership elections to "bring new blood into Fatah based on democratic principles." Internal party polls for *Fatah* Central Committee posts are meant to be held every five years, though the last such election took place 15 years ago. Most Council members reportedly demanded elections to replace the elite that has surrounded Arafat for decades. Abbas Zaki, a PNC *Fatah* representative, even warned of dissolving the PNA altogether if reforms were not fulfilled.

Al-Fatah is a consultative member of the Socialist International.

Democratic Front for the Liberation of Palestine (DFLP)

Leadership. Nayif Hawatmeh
Website. www.alhourriah.org/dflp
Formed in 1969 as a Marxist splinter from the Popular Front for the Liberation of Palestine. It was known for various acts of terrorism within Israel during the 1970s and 1980s, including the killing of 27 Israelis at a school in Ma'a lot, northern Israel in 1974. The DFLP was active during the first *intifada*. Paradoxically, the DFLP was also one of the first movements to consider a two-state solution, and to open secret talks with Israelis. In 1991 the DFLP split after the Madrid peace conference, with the creation of the Palestinian Democratic Union. After 1993, its main faction under the Jordanian-born Nayif Hawatmeh has opposed the peace accords with Israel, although other DFLP members participate in the PNA. The movement is said to have 500 active members, mainly in Lebanon, Syria and the Palestinian territories.

Samiha Khalil, the veteran women's rights and welfare worker on the West Bank, who was the sole opposition candidate to run against Yasser Arafat for the PNA presidency on Jan. 20, 1996, was affiliated with DFLP groups. She lost the election, receiving 11% of the vote, and subsequently died. In August 1999 the DFLP was co-ordinating policy lines with the PLO, and possibly as a result was expelled from the Damascus 10 anti-Oslo front.

Hamas (Islamic Resistance Movement)

Website. www.palestine-info.com/hamas
A vehemently anti-Israeli, Islamic fundamentalist movement in the occupied territories which rose to prominence in 1988. Its origins lay in the conservative *Mujama* association, apparently a Gazan offshoot of Egypt's Muslim Brotherhood; during the 1970s Israel often encouraged *Mujama* as a counterweight to secular PLO nationalists.

Opposed to mainstream PLO groups, and particularly popular in Gaza, *Hamas* objected to the 1993 Oslo Accords, and thus did not field any official candidates in the 1996 Palestinian Council elections, although five *Hamas*-affiliated members won seats, and one, Imad Faluji, is a PNA cabinet minister. The party's spiritual leader, Sheikh Ahmed Yassin, was released from an Israeli jail in October 1997, after a botched attempted assassination by Israeli agents on external *Hamas* politbureau leader, Khaled Mish'al, in Amman, Jordan. In November 1999 Jordan expelled other leaders of the *Hamas* political wing, Moussa Abu Marzouk and Ibrahim Ghawshah, to Qatar.

In Gaza and the West Bank, *Hamas* social welfare and medical facilities rival those of the PNA. Its military wing, the *Izzat-Din al-Qassem* Brigades, has taken credit for many

terror attacks in Israel. A spate of *Hamas* bombings in early 1996 turned Israelis against Prime Minister Peres, and led indirectly to his defeat in that year's elections. *Hamas*, the PFLP, Islamic Jihad and eight other groups had coalesced into an anti-Oslo front in Damascus by 1994.

Though curbed by the PNA, *Hamas* (which means "zeal") enjoys renewed support as the Al Aqsa *intifada* has radicalised opinions. Its mode of suicide bombings against civilians have been imitated by other organizations. In retaliation, Israeli military units have assassinated many *Hamas* leaders, including on Nov. 24, 2001, Mahmoud Abu Hanoud, head of its military wing, in Gaza; and on July 23, 2002, his successor, Saleh Shehadeh. Increasingly it has targeted political and even comparatively "moderate" figures, like Ismail Abu Shenab, killed in 2003; and in June, an attempt on *Hamas* number two, Abdel Aziz Rantisi.

Following extensive negotiations hosted by Egypt, in mid-2003 *Hamas* agreed to institute a *hudna*, or temporary ceasefire, in its battle against Israel. However, after a lull, a *Hamas* bombing that killed 21 Israelis in Haifa on Aug. 21 (the first such action by *Hamas* to use a female suicidal operative), led to Israeli units firing at a leader of *Hamas* political wing, Mahmoud al-Zahar, and Sheikh Yassin himself, both in early September 2003, wounding but not killing them. Yet Israel continued targetting leaders it accused of directing terror attacks. The *hudna* now appears to be over, although certain comments by Sheikh Yassin have been interpreted to imply *de facto* acceptance of Israel, and a willingness to become involved in PNA politics.

Hamas has been placed on the US list of banned foreign terror organizations; and the EU, which formerly regarded only the *Hamas* military wing as "terrorist", since 2002 extended this categorization to the movement as a whole. Nonetheless, a network of Islamic charities from the Gulf to Muslim communities in the USA and UK siphons funds to *Hamas*. There are also reported financial ties between *Hamas* and Iran and assistance from *Hizballah*. Israel particularly fears *Hamas* acquisition of mortars and missiles, often via tunnels that cross the Egyptian border at Rafah, on the southern border of the Gaza Strip. *Hamas* has rebuffed various *Fatah* attempts to integrate the movement into the PNA structure. Some say it hopes to replace the PNA altogether, and build an Islamic Palestine over all of Israel and the territories (though in reality its military capability is limited to terror, not armed conquest).

Palestine People's Party (PPP)

Website. www.palpeople.org
Formed in 1982 as the Palestine Communist Party, assuming its present name in 1991, after the collapse of the Soviet Union and its adoption of the policy of mixed economy. The PPP backed the 1993 Israel–PLO peace accord, having long supported a two-state solution based on UN 242 (and originally also UNGA 181). It only joined the PNA in 1996, after that year's elections, and officially withdrew in 1998. Dr Haidar Abd al-Shafi, the independent PLC representative who received the highest personal vote of all candidates, used to have Communist affiliations.

The party is well organized in the West Bank, especially round the town of Salfit near Nablus, though it has a small membership. The PPP has firm links with Israeli Communists which date back to the united workers' front of Jews and Arabs in British Mandatory Palestine in the 1920s. West Bank Communists have operated via a number of organizations: the National Liberation League since 1943, the Jordanian Communist Party after 1951, Democratic Youth Organization since 1954, and the Palestinian National Front since 1973. The PPP is traditionally strong in the media: its official organs are *al-Watan* and *al-Tali'a*, though it also ran the popular West Bank newspaper, *al-Fajr*.

The PPP lost its leader, Bashir Barghouti, in September 2000; his successor, Suleiman Najjab, died in August 2001. Mustafa Barghouti was regarded as PPP secretary-general after internal party elections in October 1998; though after he set up the pro-democracy Palestinian National Initiative, in June 2002, it appears he may have left his post in the PPP. Other leading PPP figures are the veteran Na'im al-Ashhab, who still intercedes with Israeli Communists; PNA Labour Minister since 2002, Ghasan al-Khatib; and the economist and erstwhile advisor to Arafat, Samir Abdullah. PPP member Hasan Asfur was a key diplomat in the negotiations in Oslo, was elected as an independent for Khan Yunis in Gaza in 1996, and was a PNA minister until 2002. Hana Amira currently holds the PPP seat on the PLO Executive Committee.

Palestine Popular Struggle Front (PPSF)

An offshoot of the Popular Front for the Liberation of Palestine, founded in the West Bank before 1967. Led by Samir Ghawsha, it was sponsored in turns by Egypt, Libya and Syria, and has since split into factions with its mainstream endorsing the 1993 Israel–PLO peace accord. Ahmad Majdalani belongs to this tendency and currently works in the PNA International and Arab Affairs Department. An anti-Oslo group is based in Damascus and led by Khalid Abd al-Majid.

Palestinian Democratic Union (PDU)
Fida

Website. www.fida-palestine.org
Leadership. Yasser Abed-Rabbo; Salih Ra'fat (secretary-general)

The PDU, also known by its Arabic acronym, *Fida* (sacrifice), was created in 1991 by members of the Democratic Front for the Liberation of Palestine. It dropped the strict Marxist tenets of the DFLP, and supported the September 1993 Declaration of Principles between the PLO and Israel. Its leader, Yasser Abed-Rabbo, has at various stages served as a key ministerial ally of PNA President Yasser Arafat.

FIDA participated in the 1996 PLC elections and won a single PLC seat. It may also enjoy support amongst certain elected independents. Abed-Rabbo was the chief Palestinian architect of the late 2003 Geneva Accords, an unofficial programme for resolving final status issues between the PNA and Israel, which he co-devised with the prominent left-wing Israeli politician, Yossi Beilin, and numerous other figures from Israel and Palestine.

Popular Front for the Liberation of Palestine (PFLP)

Website. www.pflp-pal.org
Leadership. Ahmad Saadat

Established in 1967 by members of the Arab National Movement (founded in 1951) and other factions. Its ideology combines Marxism with pan-Arabism, and it endorsed hijackings and terrorism in the early 1970s. Led by the charismatic Georges Habash, the PFLP grew into the second largest PLO faction after *Fatah*, despite suffering numerous defections. Its hitherto dormant West Bank branch acquired new status during the 1987-91 *intifada*.

The PFLP returned to the PLO fold and endorsed the "two-state solution" of the Palestine National Council's Algiers Declaration in 1988. However, it subsequently led a ten-member Damascus-based "Rejection Front" that condemned the peace accord of September 1993 and officially boycotted the Palestine Authority's first indigenous elections, in January 1996, despite qualms from local leader, Riyad Malki and the election of PFLP-affiliated independents.

In 1999 some PFLP leaders were allowed to return to the West Bank, including PFLP deputy leader, Abu Ali Mustafa (born Mustafa Zibri). In July 2000 he was elected as

Habash's successor, after which the PFLP left the Damascus 10 anti-Oslo coalition and on Oct. 30 that year, released a new "political initiative", clarifying policy on future Palestinian independence. Israeli forces assassinated Mustafa on Aug. 27, 2001, following several car bombings attributed to the PFLP in Jerusalem. The PFLP retaliated in October 2001, when members of its militia, now renamed the Abu Ali Mustafa Brigades, shot dead an Israeli minister, Rechavam Ze'evi. After this event the PNA arrested several PFLP figures. Overall, the PFLP has lost support amongst radicals to the Islamic movement, *Hamas*. The PFLP's new secretary-general since October 2001 is Ahmad Saadat, a former mathematics teacher in Ramallah whom Israel had detained seven times previously. He defeated his chief rival, Abdul Rahim Mallouh, by a two-to-one margin of votes within the PFLP central committee.

On Jan. 16, 2002, PNA authorities detained Saadat without charge in a Jericho prison facility, following a compromise agreement with the USA, UK and Israel. The Palestinian High Court ordered Saadat's release in mid-2002, but the PNA executive refuses to accede. In February 2004, following Israeli "retaliatory raids" in Gaza, Saadat called for joint action with other Palestinian factions, under the auspices of the PNA, to launch "painful strikes against the usurping Zionist entity in all areas of historical Palestine" (i.e. including in pre-1967 borders Israel).

Other Groups

Arab Liberation Front (ALF), an Iraqi-backed group that in 1995 split between "rejectionists" and those favouring the peace process. In October 2002 Israel captured its secretary-general, Rakad Salem, partly on charges of distributing $12.5m in Iraqi funds to families of 'martyrs' of the current *intifada*. The new leader of the ALF appears to be Ibrahim al-Zanin.

Islamic Jihad (*Al-Jihad al-Islami*), militant fundamentalist and anti-Israeli group, responsible for suicide bombing attacks on Israeli military and civilian targets in the 1990s, opposed to the Israel–PLO peace process. Founded in the late 1970s by the Hebronite sheikh, Asad al-Tamimi, the group enjoys less mass support than fellow Islamic radicals, *Hamas*. Its secretary-general, Fathi Shqaqi, was shot dead in Malta in October 1995 by Israeli agents. His successor is the Damascus-based Ramadan Abdallah Shalah. Islamic Jihad has been very active in sending suicide attacks against Israeli civilians during the Al Aqsa Intifada, and many of its leaders have been assassinated by Israeli squads. As of January 2003, its leadership rejected the PLO as representing Palestinians; yet operatives often co-operate with the more militant *Fatah* forces, and, unlike *Hamas*, two Jihad leaders actually hold seats on the 124-member PLO Central Council. Furthermore, by early 2004 many *Fatah* cadres in the northern West Bank had reportedly defected to Islamic Jihad, thereby reviving the fortunes of a faction that was once considered marginal.

Palestine Liberation Front (PLF), originally Iraqi-backed, it later split into various factions (some affiliated to *Fatah*). The PLF was associated with terrorist attacks, notably the *Achille Lauro* hijacking in 1985; reported to be more united in the early 1990s. Its leader is Muhammad Zaydan, better known as Abul Abbas, and captured by US forces in Baghdad after the 2003 war. West Bank and Gaza PLF branches appear much weaker than those in Lebanon.

Popular Front for the Liberation of Palestine–General Command, a militant offshoot of the main PFLP led by Ahmed Jibril. It maintains support in Lebanon, but less so in

PNA-ruled areas. With Jibril increasingly taking a lower profile, deputy secretary-general Talal Naji is said to be the group's effective leader.

Revolutionary Council of Fatah (better known as the Abu Nidal Group), an anti-Arafat guerrilla organization responsible for numerous terrorist incidents around the world over the last 20 years. The RCF murdered many PLO representatives in capitals throughout Europe and the Middle East, as well as Lebanese and Jordanian diplomats. Once backed by Libya, it later accepted funds and guidance from Syria, possibly Egypt, and finally Iraq. Its leader was Sabri Banna, better known by his nomme du guerre of Abu Nidal. He took refuge in many Arab capitals: Tripoli in Libya, Damascus in Syria, and lastly Baghdad in Iraq, where he reportedly killed himself in August 2002. Though much reduced in strength and influence, it persists under a leadership which currently includes Ali al-Farra.

Revolutionary Palestinian Communist Party (RPCP), led by Abdullah Arabi Awwad, founded in the late 1980s by a faction of the Palestine Communist Party, which in turn became the Palestine People's Party. The RPCP supported the first *intifada,* later criticized the Israel-PLO peace process and enjoys some Syrian support.

Tanzim, meaning "organization", represents many grassroots *Fatah* supporters in the West Bank; under Marwan Barghouti it has played a prominent part in fomenting the Al Aqsa *intifada.* Some say *Tanzim* was set up by *Fatah* in 1995 to match the militias of *Hamas* and Islamic Jihad. The group absorbed *Fatah*-affiliated groups of militant youths from the 1987-91 era, like the *Shabiba* and Fatah *Hawks.* Before 2000 there were reports friction between *Tanzim* and the official PNA security force, with the latter seen as protecting the "Tunis set", older *Fatah* figures who returned from exile in 1994-96. On Jan. 16, 2002, Israeli units assassinated a senior *Tanzim* leader in Tulkarm, Ra'ed Karmi. This incident prompted a large escalation in attacks on Israel, and Israeli retaliations which soon developed into Operation Defensive Shield (effective reoccupation of Palestinian cities).

Senior *Tanzim* leader Barghouti was a student veteran of the first *intifada,* an early advocate of the 1993 peace deal with Israel, a familiar intercessor with centre-left Israelis, and co-founder of the Copenhagen Peace Movement around 1998. He was elected to a PLC seat for Ramallah in 1996, but while spoken of as effective leader of *Fatah* in the West Bank, he received no official PNA position commensurate with his obvious popularity. In September 1997 he condemned bombings in Jerusalem, and said that those behind the attacks were "trying to destroy the peace process".

Israeli security forces arrested Barghouti in April 2002; he is currently facing trial on charges of aiding and abetting terrorism. The Israeli newspaper *Ha'aretz* said that Israel felt Barghouti had "turned *Tanzim* from a civic guard into a terror machine". Advocates of his capture say that in the first weeks of the 2000 intifada, Barghouti deliberately flouted Arafat's calls to cease attacks on civilians. Many Palestinians, however, see him as a maligned hero.

On April 13, 2002, Israel captured Nasr Awis, the *Tanzim* commander in Nablus regarded as Barghouti's deputy. He was convicted on Jan. 5, 2003 of 14 counts of murder, conspiracy, and other charges involving the deaths of scores of Israelis. Israeli sources have linked *Tanzim* to the Al Aqsa Martyrs Brigade, and say the *Tanzim* still collects funds from the PNA; conversely, senior *Tamzim* figures were involved in negotiations towards the Geneva Accords peace accords. According to certain reports, *Tanzim* had agreed to a full ceasefire, negotiated over two months and described in a detailed communique, in June 2002, but called it off after

Israel killed *Hamas* military leader, Saleh Shehadeh. It was also reported that from his prison cell Barghouti had helped to clinch the *hudna* (temporary truce) declared by *Hamas,* Islamic Jihad, Al Aqsa Martyr Brigades and the *Tanzim* in 2003. Formally at least, Barghouti – and so possibly by extension, the *Tanzim* as a whole – accepts a two-state solution, and not the elimination of Israel.

Panama

Capital: Panama City
Population: 3,000,463 (2004E)

The Republic of Panama seceded from Colombia in 1903 and immediately ceded in perpetuity to the United States the right to construct an inter-oceanic canal. Until 1979 the Canal Zone was US sovereign territory and the rest of the country essentially a protectorate of the United States. Internal politics, punctuated by military intervention, were turbulent and elected governments were overthrown in 1941, 1949, 1951 and 1968, usually after disputed elections. There were serious constitutional crises in 1918, 1948 and 1955. In 1968 a reforming military government seized power, led by Omar Torrijos Herrera. In the 1972 and 1978 elections to the then National Assembly of Community Representatives, no candidate was allowed to represent a political party. Meanwhile the Torrijos government negotiated the Panama Canal Treaties of 1977 by which the USA relinquished its claims (with control of the Canal passing to Panama on Dec. 31, 1999).

Constitutional reforms adopted in April 1983 established a unicameral Legislative Assembly consisting of 67 members. Executive power rests with the President, assisted by two Vice Presidents, elected for a term of five years. The President appoints a Cabinet and numerous other officials including the president of the Panama Canal Commission. Panama has historically had a highly fragmented party system, characterized by the importance of personalities and family ties. One person, Arnulfo Arias Madrid, dominated Panamanian politics from his first election as President in 1940 until his death in 1988, balancing, not always successfully, opposition to US hegemony with political realism. De-registration of parties in Panamanian politics occurs at the comparatively high cut-off point of 5% of the vote. Those parties that fail to gain this minimum level of support in an election providing legislative representation are subsequently banned from the electoral process. The number of parties represented fell from 13 in the 1994 elections to 9 in 1999 and 7 in 2004. All adult citizens over the age of 18 can vote and voting is compulsory.

A tentative return to democratic government in the early 1980s was overshadowed by the presence of the National Guard, whose commander, Gen. Manuel Antonio Noriega Moreno, effectively ruled the country. Nicolás Ardito Barletta of the Democratic Revolutionary Party (PRD), the winner of the May 1984 presidential election, was initially favoured by the military and his election campaign was supported by a centre-right coalition of six parties led by the now defunct National Democratic Union (UNADE). He was forced to resign by the military in September 1985 when he announced that he would investigate charges that Noriega had ordered the killing of a political opponent, Hugo Spadafora. Barletta's successor, Eric Arturo Delvalle, was in turn forced to flee the country after an abortive attempt to dismiss Noriega but still claimed to be president from exile. An interim President, Manuel Solís Palma, was then appointed by the military. Domestic and international pressure, especially from the USA, for the removal of Noriega, who had also been implicated in drug smuggling, continued to mount. His attempt to deny the Civic Opposition Democratic Alliance (ADOC) victory in the May 1989 presidential and legislative elections, by annulling the result, led to rapidly deteriorating relations with the United States culminating in a US military invasion in December. The results of the May 1989 elections, which had been held in safe keeping by the Roman Catholic Church, were then declared valid on Dec. 27 though they were incomplete and covered only 64% of voters. Guillermo Endara Galimany was duly sworn in as "constitutional President" to head a democratic government of reconstruction and national reconciliation, which, however, was not a success. Endara's austerity policies were highly unpopular and not only did Panama receive negligible compensation from the USA for the damage done by the invasion but it also suffered from the effect of the US anti-narcotics campaign.

Ernesto Pérez Balladares of the PRD won the presidential elections held on May 8, 1994, with 33.3% of the vote. In simultaneous legislative elections, the PRD emerged as the largest single party, with 21 out of 72 seats. Pérez Balladares took office on Sept. 1, including in his Cabinet independents and members of the Arnulfista Party (PA) and Christian Democratic Party (PDC).

In elections held in May 1999 parties competed in three groupings. The New Nation (*Nueva Nación*, NN) group won the most seats (42), these being taken by the Democratic Revolutionary Party (PRD) 34, the Solidarity Party (PS) 4 and the National Liberal Party (PLN) 4. In second place, the Union for Panama (*Unión por Panamá*, UPP) won 24 seats, shared by the Arnulfista Party (PA) 18, the Nationalist Republican Liberal Movement (MOLIRENA) 3, Democratic Change (CD) 2 and the National Renewal Movement (Morena) 1. The Opposition Action alliance (*Acción Opositora*, AO) took 6 seats, won by the Christian Democratic Party (PDC) 5 and the Civic Renewal Party (PRC) 1. Simultaneous presidential elections were won by the candidate of the Union for Panama, Arnulfista Party (PA) leader Mireya Elisa Moscoso Rodríguez de Gruber, who took 44.9% of the votes.

In presidential elections held on May 2, 2004, the runner-up in 1999, Martín Torrijos Espino of the PRD, with 47.4% of the vote, defeated Guillermo Endara of *Solidaridad* with 30.9%, José Miguel Alemán of the PA (16.4%) and Alberto Vallarino Clement of Democratic Change (5.3%). In the concurrent leguislative elections the results were: PRD 41, PA 17, PS 9, Molirena 4, CD 3, PLN 3, Popular Party (PP) 1. The government is formed by the PRD and the PP.

Arnulfista Party
Partido Arnulfista (PA)

Address. Avda. Perú y Calle 38E N° 37–41, Apartado 9610, Zona 4, Panamá
Telephone. (507) 227–1267
Fax. (507) 217–2645
Leadership. Mireya Elisa Moscoso Rodríguez de Gruber (president); Carlos Raul Piad (secretary-general)
Founded in 1990 and with a registered membership in January 2001 of 150,100, the PA is now the main right-wing party in Panama. It was established by a faction of the now defunct Authentic *Panameñista* Party (*Partido Panameñista Auténtico*, PPA) led by the late veteran politician Arnulfo

Arias Madrid. Arias was President of Panama in 1940–41, 1949–51 and for an eleven-day period in 1968 as the successful candidate of the five-party Opposition National Union (UNO) before being deposed in a coup d'état. The PPA itself had been launched in 1984 as the "authentic" *Panameñista* party, as distinct from a rival *Panameñista* Party (PP) set up against Arias' wishes by Alonso Pinzón and Luis Suarez to contest the 1980 legislative elections.

The PPA, along with the Nationalist Republican Liberal Movement (MOLIRENA) and the Christian Democratic Party (PDC), joined the Civic Opposition Democratic Alliance (ADOC) to back Arias's fifth presidential campaign in 1984 against the military's choice, Nicolas Ardito Barletta of the National Democratic Union (UNADE), whose victory the ADOC later claimed was fraudulent. The opposition also refused to accept the official results giving ADOC only 27 of the 67 seats in the Legislative Assembly.

The PPA, which gradually lost the leadership of the ADOC to the PDC, itself split in August 1988 following Arias's death. One faction, again taking the party's original name (PP) and willing to collaborate with the military-backed regime, nominated Hildebrando Nicosia as their candidate in the May 1989 presidential elections. The other faction, however, received ADOC's endorsement of its presidential candidate, Guillermo Endara Gallimany. Endara was judged to have won the election, despite the result being annulled by the military, and was sworn in as president on a US marine base immediately before the US invasion of December 1989. To confirm a break with the past, Endara's supporters then established the PA, which was legalized in May 1990.

The ruling ADOC coalition government weathered massive public opposition to its October 1990 austerity policies only to face sustained protests by the trade unions, especially public sector workers, in the new year. Internal divisions and evidence of official corruption and drug-related scandals, some involving Endara's own law firm, severely damaged Endara's reputation. In April 1991, he dismissed five PDC cabinet ministers whom he accused of "disloyalty and arrogance", leaving the *Arnulfistas* without an assured majority in the Legislative Assembly. The PDC had 28 seats to the 16, seven and four respectively of the remaining ADOC members, MOLIRENA, the AP and the PLA.

Endara was also increasingly accused of sacrificing national sovereignty by being subservient to the US government, especially in his harsh public criticism of Cuba and most controversially in agreeing to the radical reform of the country's banking secrecy laws in July 1991, which critics said would do little to stop drug trafficking and money laundering but would drain the country of foreign exchange. Critics, led by the PDC, also accused the government of fomenting military coup scares in order to keep the country in a perpetual state of emergency. This, they alleged, allowed state security forces more effectively to quell opposition protest. Endara was also blamed for not pressing the US government for adequate compensation for the civilian victims of the December 1989 military invasion, and for not placing imprisoned military associates of Noriega on trial. In September 1991 Endara's choice for Legislative Assembly president was defeated when Marco Ameglio, a PLA member, aligned himself with the opposition.

The widow of former President Arias Madrid, Mireya Elisa Moscoso Rodríguez de Gruber, stood as the party's presidential candidate in the 1994 elections, which she lost to the Democratic Revolutionary Party (PRD) candidate, Ernesto Pérez Balladares. In May 1999, however, as candidate of the Union for Panama, she gained 44.9% of the votes cast in a three-way contest. It fell to her therefore to be the President who formally received the Canal from former President Jimmy Carter of the United States who said: "Take it, it's yours". With the new Nation grouping the largest in

Congress, she was not able to count on a congressional majority between September 2000 and September 2002, and when she tried to push through reform of the tax and social welfare system, she continued to encounter stiff resistance from business interests and from the opposition PRD and was forced to drop proposals to reform income and corporation tax. In the May 2004 elections its presidential candidate was defeated and its representation in the Legislative Assembly fell to 17.

Democratic Change
Partido Cambio Democrático (CD)
Address. Parque Lefevre, Plaza Carolina, arriba de la Juguetería del Super 99, Panamá
Telephone. (507) 217–2643
Fax. (507) 217–2645
Leadership. Ricardo Martinelli Berrocal (president); Roberto Ortiz (secretary general)
Alternatively called the Democratic Party (PD), the CD campaigned in 1999 as part of the successful Union for Panama coalition and gained two seats in the Legislative Assembly. It first registered in 1998 and its registered membership in January 2001 was 47,671. In the May 2004 elections it increased its legislative representation to three.

Democratic Revolutionary Party
Partido Revolucionario Democrático (PRD)
Address. Calle 42 Bella Vista, entre Avda. Perú y Avda. Cuba, bajando por el teatro Bella Vista, Zona 9, Panamá
Telephone. (507) 225–1050, 225–5525
Fax. (507) 225–1802
Email. secreprd@sinfo.net
Leadership. Hugo H. Guiraud (president); Martín Torrijos Espino (secretary-general); Ernesto Pérez Balladares (former President)
The PRD was originally dedicated to the nationalist revolutionary beliefs of Gen. Omar Torrijos Herrera, Commander-in-Chief of the National Guard, who had led a coup in October 1968. Torrijos campaigned against imperialism and the oligarchy and in favour of national independence. The Torrijos years (1968–79) included land re-distribution, the creation of a non-party National Assembly of Community Representatives in 1972 to replace a dissolved National Assembly, and the signing, in 1977, of the Panama Canal Treaties. The party subsequently in the 1980s became a vehicle for Gen. Manuel Noriega and after his fall was characterized by its critics as the mainstay of the right-wing Noriega tradition.

Formally created in 1979 by Torrijos supporters, who included businessmen, Christian Democrats and Marxists, the party retained its progressive-populist image until the death of Torrijos in an air crash in July 1981. The military continued the tradition of Torrijos, albeit manipulating political power from the right of the political spectrum. By the time of the May 1984 presidential and legislative elections, the PRD-led National Democratic Union (UNADE) coalition was a tool of the military and was duly declared the clear winner despite evidence of widespread fraud. The lack of PRD political autonomy was amply demonstrated when the UNADE President Nicolas Ardito Barletta was forced to stand down by the military in 1985 after indicating his intention of investigating allegations that Noriega was implicated in the murder of an opposition candidate, Hugo Spadafora. Well-publicized allegations in 1985–88 of Noriega's involvement in murders, drug-dealing, money-laundering, gun-running and espionage for and against the United States did not deflect PRD support for the military.

The party was a member of the Coalition of National Liberation (COLINA) alliance in the May 1989 presidential and legislative alliance and served as apologists for

Noriega's annulment of the result until the US military invasion in December. Subsequently, in pursuit of a popular grass-roots base, it allied itself with domestic groups demonstrating for adequate compensation from the US government for civilians killed and property destroyed during the invasion. It backed popular protests against corruption in the government and against its austerity policies. In July it opposed government moves to abolish the army, stating that it was needed to guarantee the security of the Panama Canal, and also spearheaded opposition to US demands that Panama's banking secrecy laws be repealed to assist in the detection of drug traffickers and money launderers.

In early 1990 a new group of PRD leaders emerged, distancing themselves from General Noriega and declaring themselves for democracy. In the elections of 1994 the PRD finally took power with a plurality of 31 seats in the legislature and victory for Ernesto Pérez Balladares in the presidential contest. In 1999 as part of the New Nation coalition its presidential candidate, Martín Torrijos Espino, obtained 37.6% of the vote but was defeated by Mireya Moscoso de Gruber of the *Arnulfista Party*. However the coalition gained 57.7% of the vote in the legislative elections and the PRD increased its legislative representation to 34, making it the largest party.

In the May 2004 elections Torrijos was elected President and the PRD became the largest party in the Legislative Assembly with 41 seats, giving it an absolute majority. With a registered membership of 326,705 in 2003 the PRD is an observer member of the Socialist International.

National Liberal Party
Partido Liberal Nacional (PLN)
Address. Vía Fernández de Córdoba, Vista Hermosa, Plaza Córdoba, antigua Ersa, Local 6–7, Panamá
Telephone. (507) 229–7523
Fax. (507) 229–7524
Email. pln@sinfo.net
Internet. www.sinfo.net/liberal-nacional
Leadership. Viola Icaza de García (president); Ricardo Anguizola (executive secretary)
The PLN was founded in 1979 and is broadly liberal. It campaigned as part of the New Nation coalition at the 1999 elections and won 4 seats in the Legislative Assembly, reduced to 3 in the May 2004 elections. The PLN's registered membership was 64,896 in January 2001 and it is an observer member of the Liberal International.

Nationalist Republican Liberal Movement
Movimiento Liberal Republicano Nacionalista (MOLIRENA)
Address. Calle Venezuela, Bella Vista, Casa N° 5, entre Calle 50 y Vía España (Antiguo Restaurante La Casona), Apartado 7468, Panamá 5
Telephone. (507) 213–5928
Fax. (507) 265–6004
Email. molirena@hotmail.com
Internet. www.sinfo.net/molirena
Leadership. Jesús L. Rojas (president); Arturo Vallarino (secretary-general)
Founded in October 1981, MOLIRENA is a right-wing libertarian party that preaches the principles of a free market. The party was established by breakaway groups of the now defunct Third Nationalist Party (TPN), Republican Party (PR) and the Liberal Party (PL). Opposed to the military's hold on the country, it joined the Opposition Democratic Alliance (ADO) to contest the 1984 presidential and legislative elections and thereafter supported the campaign of the National Civic Crusade for the removal of the Commander of the Defence forces, Gen. Manuel Noriega. The party was a member of the Opposition Civic Democratic Alliance (ADOC) denied power by Noriega following the presidential

and legislative elections of May 1989. Once the ADOC was installed in power following the US military invasion in December, the party received 15 seats in the Legislative Assembly. The party backed the government's IMF-approved economic austerity programme and proposals for the wholesale privatization of the state sector, including, most controversially, social welfare agencies. The party suffered as a result of the unpopularity of these policies, its representation falling from 15 to 5 seats in 1994. In 1999 the party campaigned as part of the successful Union for Panama coalition. Its candidate, Arturo Ulises Vallarino Bartuano was elected First Vice President but the party won only 3 seats in the Legislative Assembly, which it increased to 4 in May 2004. It had a registered membership of 57,890 in January 2001.

Popular Party
Partido Popular (PP)
Address. Avda. Perú (frente Plaza Porras), Edf. María No. 55, Apdo. 6322, Zona 5, Panamá
Telephone. (507) 227–3204
Fax. (507) 227–3944
Email. pdcpanama@cwpanama.net
Leadership. Rubén Arosemena Valdés (president); José Domingo Torres (secretary-general)

Founded as the **Christian Democratic Party** or *Partido Demócrata Cristiano* (PDC) in 1960, this centre-right party had its origins in the student National Civic Union (1957–1960), where the tradition of European Christian democratic parties was assimilated. Middle-class professionals, intellectuals and students swelled its ranks but the Federation of Christian Workers (FTC) was also an early affiliate. The PDC contested the 1964 and 1968 presidential elections without much success. During the period when party politics were effectively banned by the Torrijos government (1968–78), the party reorganized itself, winning 20% of the vote in the 1980 legislative elections and taking 19 of the 56 seats in the newly formed National Legislative Council (the other 37 being filled by nominees of a nonparty National Assembly of Community Representatives established in 1972). In 1984, the PDC was part of the Civic Opposition Democratic Alliance (ADOC) which lost the presidential and legislative elections following suspected widespread fraud by the military.

During 1987, the PDC became increasingly involved in confrontations with the government, openly campaigning through strikes (supported mainly by businesses rather than trade unions) and street demonstrations (which were violently suppressed) for the resignation and removal of Gen. Manuel Noriega, who was accused of drug trafficking, electoral fraud, corruption and murder. The PDC was again part of the ADOC electoral alliance in May 1989 which supported the presidential candidacy of Guillermo Endara of the Arnulfista Party, and, after the official ratification of the results following the US military invasion in December, Ricardo Arias Calderón became First Vice-President and the PDC the largest party in the Legislative Assembly with 28 of the 67 seats. Its subsequent withdrawal from the ADOC coalition government in April 1991, when Endara dismissed five PDC cabinet ministers, caused a political crisis. This followed months of in-fighting during which Arias Calderón had publicly described Endara's economic programme, which advocated severe austerity measures and the privatization of state enterprises, as "senseless". Although Arias Calderón was stripped of his Interior and Justice Ministry post he won the May 1989 presidential election annulled by Noriega.

In succeeding months, the PDC became the leader of the opposition, to such an extent that it was exerting strong influence within such organizations as the Civic Crusade, an organization from which Endara had drawn his strongest support and which in June called for a plebiscite to decide on the desirability of Endara remaining in office. In September 1991, the PDC was judged firmly to have secured its political influence on parliamentary committees as a direct result of facilitating the victory of a dissident PLA candidate in the election of a new president of the Legislative Assembly.

Arias Calderón resigned the Vice Presidency in December 1992 in a move designed to distance himself from President Endara in the run-up to the May 1994 presidential election. However, the party managed to gain only one seat in the legislative elections. In the 1999 presidential election its candidate, Alberto Vallarino Clement, ran a distant third with 17.5% of the poll but as part of Opposition Action the PDC won 5 legislative seats. It has since changed its name to the Popular Party (PP). It obtained only one seat in the May 2004 elections, despite winning some 6% of the vote, but forms part of the ruling Patria Nueva coalition supporting President Martín Torrijos.

With a registered membership in January 2001 of 51,627 the PP is a full member of the Christian Democrat International.

Solidarity Party
Partido Solidaridad (PS)
Address. Edif. Maheli, Avda. Ramón Arias, esq. con la Via Transistémica, Panamá
Telephone. (507) 261-2966
Fax. (507) 261-5083
Leadership. Samuel Lewis Galinda (president); Jorge Ricardo Fabrega (secretary-general)

Founded and registered in 1993 the PS won two Assembly seats in the May 1994 polls. In 1999 it ran as part of the New Nation coalition and increased its representation in the Assembly to 4. In the May 2004 elections it ran separately and increased its representation to 9. Its registered membership was 33,458 in January 2001.

Other Parties

Authentic Liberal Party (*Partido Liberal Auténtico*, PLA), originated as a breakaway from the National Liberal Party in 1987; it held two seats as a result of the 1994 legislative elections but lost both of them and its registration in 1999.
Leadership. Arnulfo Escalona Riós (president)

Civic Renewal Party (*Partido Renovación Civilista*, PRC*)*. Registered in 1992 shortly after the 1991 elections, the PRC is an anti-military grouping which succeeded in winning three legislative seats in the 1994 elections. In the 1999 legislative elections it ran as part of Opposition Action (AO) with the Christian Democratic Party, and secured one seat, but lost its registration.
Address. 1a/Of.4 Edif. Casa Oceánica, Avda. Aquilino de la Guardia, Panamá
Telephone. (507) 263–8971
Fax. (507) 263–8975
Leadership. Serguei de la Rosa; Tomás Herrera (president): Carlos Harris (secretary-general)

Independent Democratic Union (*Union Democrática Independiente*, UDI). The UDI won one seat in the 1994 legislative elections but lost both its representation and its registration in 1999.
Leadership. Jacinto Cárdenas

Labour Party (*Partido Laborista*, PALA). PALA was founded in September 1982 by Azael Vargas to establish a strong party on the extreme right. It won one seat in the 1994 legislative elections but is currently unrepresented.

Liberal Party (*Partido Liberal*), won one seat in the 1994 legislative elections but is currently unrepresented and unregistered, despite contesting the 1999 elections as part of Opposition Action.

Motherland Movement (*Movimiento Papa Egoro/Tierra Madre*), an unusual party that rapidly grew from inauspicious beginnings in November 1991 to being the third placed grouping in the 1994 presidential elections and has since collapsed. The party's founder was the film star, singer and sometime lawyer, Rubén Blades, who in both 1992 and 1993 was quoted in opinion polls as being the favourite for the presidency in 1994. Blades, however, found it hard to shake off the rumours that his nomination in 1993 was no more than a stunt to advance his career, especially in the United States. After the May 1994 elections, in which his party won 6 seats in the Legislative Assembly, Blades returned to California to resume his show business career, leaving the party to its current leader Fernando Manfredo. The party contested the 1999 elections as part of the New Nation coalition but lost all its seats and its registration.

National Renewal Movement (*Movimiento de Renovación Nacional*, MORENA). Founded and registered in 1993, MORENA gained one legislative seat in the 1994 elections. In the 1999 elections it campaigned as part of the successful Union for Panama coalition for the presidency and retained its one seat in the Legislative Assembly, but lost its registration and has since dissolved.
Leadership. Joaquín José Vallarino Cox (president); Demetrio Decerega (secretary-general)

Republican Liberal Party (*Partido Liberal Republicano, Libre,* PLR). Libre won two seats in the 1994 legislative elections, but lost both seats and its registration in 1999.

Papua New Guinea

Capital: Port Moresby
Population: 5,130,000 (2000 census)

Papua New Guinea has an essentially Westminster-style parliamentary system with a unicameral legislature which elects a Prime Minister, the head of government, who appoints the National Executive Council (cabinet). The head of state is the British sovereign, represented by a locally nominated Governor-General. The National Parliament comprises 109 members, 89 elected from single-member constituencies and twenty elected to represent the nineteen provinces and National Capital District, so that each voter elects two members, one constituency and one provincial. Up till 2002 all were elected under a first-past-the-post voting system, but from 2002 Papua New Guinea has switched to a limited preferential system; voters are required to express a preference for at least three candidates. Members are elected for a five-year term.

Every government since independence from Australia in 1975 has been a coalition. Coalitions tend to emerge only after elections have been completed, and have proved fluid. Constitutional provision is made for votes of no confidence in the government, from eighteen months after an election until twelve months before a new election, and up till 2002 every parliament had seen a mid-term change of government.

Parties mostly revolve around personalities, and lack both clear ideological differentiation and mass bases. New parties are continuously being created – especially on the eve of elections – and often prove short-lived. Since the 1970s almost every major political party has

at some stage been in coalition with every other. Also, since the pre-independence election of 1972 the number of candidates contesting elections has increased steadily, notwithstanding a substantial increase in candidate fees, to an average per constituency of 26 in 2002. The proportion of candidates standing as independents has also increased. In an attempt to strengthen the party system, in late 2000 the Papua New Guinea parliament passed an Organic Law on the Integrity of Political Parties and Candidates (OLIPPC), which provides for the registration and public funding of parties (on the basis of the number of MPs), and sanctions (including loss of seat) against MPs who change party affiliation during the life of the parliament.

Before the 2002 national elections 43 parties had registered with the registrar for political parties, though many of these had very small memberships and on the eve of polling a number had not provided the registrar with the required list of candidates. In the event, with "failed elections" declared in six seats, 24 parties were represented in the new parliament: the National Alliance (NA) with 19 members, People's Democratic Movement (PDM) 13, People's Progress Party (PPP) 8, *Pangu Pati* 6, People's Action Party (PAP) 5, People's Labour Party 4, nine parties with 2 or 3 members and another nine with one member each. Seventeen candidates were elected as independents. By December 2003 the number of parties had been reduced, through amalgamations, to 18. As leader of the National Alliance, Sir Michael Somare – the country's Prime Minister at independence – was invited to form a government, and became Prime Minister. The PDM, which in 1999 had become the first party in Papua New Guinea's political history to hold an absolute majority in the National Parliament, joined the opposition, subsequently changing its name to Papua New Guinea Party (PNGP).

The 18 parties listed by the registrar of political parties as at December 2003 were: Advance Papua New Guinea Party, Christian Democratic Party, National Alliance, *Pangu Pati*, Melanesian Alliance, Papua New Guinea Labour Party, Papua New Guinea National Party, People's Action Party, Papua New Guinea Party, People's Labour Party, People's National Congress, PPP, United Party, United Resources Party, Pipol First Party, Papua New Guinea First Party, Papua New Guinea Revival Party, and Pan Melanesian Congress.

Melanesian Alliance (MA)
Leadership. Sir Moi Avei (leader)
The Melanesian Alliance had its origins in a group established within the Constitutional Planning Committee (CPC) by CPC deputy chairman John Momis and member John Kaputin, and Bernard Narokobi, who in 1997 became speaker of the National Parliament. The MA is a progressive party, with a strong base in the New Guinea Islands Region and links to the Catholic Church.

National Alliance (NA)
Leadership. Sir Michael Somare (leader)
Formed by Sir Michael Somare before the 1997 elections, the NA comprised the Melanesian Alliance (MA), Stephen Pokawin of the Movement for Greater Autonomy, and some *Pangu* supporters and progressive independents. In the elections of 1997, the NA (including the MA) gained 11 seats and looked likely to form a government. But the NA failed to get the numbers when Bill Skate, who had promised support, reneged and took his People's National Congress (PNC) into a rival grouping and gained the Prime Ministership. In 2001 Somare was dropped from the Morauta government's cabinet

and moved to the opposition, but other NA members remained with the government. The following year it emerged with the largest number of seats in the National Parliament and Somare returned as Prime Minister.

Pangu Pati

Leadership. Chris Haiveta (leader)

Pangu is one of Papua New Guinea's first significant parties, forming a coalition government after the elections of 1972 and leading the country to independence in 1975. Its former parliamentary leader, Sir Michael Somare, was Papua New Guinea's first Prime Minister. The party subsequently suffered three major splits. In 1985 Paias Wingti left to form the People's Democratic Movement (PDM), and in 1986 Anthony Siaguru broke away to form the League for National Advancement. Ten years later, Somare, then a member of a coalition government headed by Sir Julius Chan (People's Progress Party, PPP), opposed legislation which fundamentally changed the country's provincial government system and was dropped from cabinet. He subsequently founded the National Alliance. From about this time, *Pangu* was weakened by internal differences. In 1997 *Pangu*, under the leadership of Chris Haiveta, joined Skate in the coalition government, and Haiveta was for a while deputy Prime Minister. But Skate and Haiveta later had differences and when in 1999 Skate dropped Haiveta from the cabinet *Pangu* withdrew from the coalition, subsequently backing the PDM in a move to oust Skate. In mid 2000, *Pangu* was the third largest component of the coalition government, behind PDM and the Papua New Guinea First Party. Also in 2000 Somare's membership of *Pangu* was terminated, further deepening the rifts within the party. In 2002 the party secured only six seats.

(Papua New Guinea) National Party (NP)

Leadership. Melchior Pep (leader)

The Papua New Guinea National Party (originally the New Guinea National Party) was formed in 1971 in the New Guinea highlands, largely as a reaction to the conservative political advocacy of the United Party. It was once described as "the highlands equivalent of *Pangu*". The NP was a member of the governing coalition in the 1972-77 parliament, but after its leader and deputy leader were dropped from cabinet in 1976 the party split and virtually collapsed. Two years later the party was revived under colourful NP politician Iambakey Okuk, who became leader of the parliamentary opposition, and in 1980 deputy Prime Minister. The party split again in 1985 and in 1987 following the death of Okuk. It was revived in the 1990s under the leadership of another highlands politician, Paul Pora, but in the 1997 elections secured only one seat. In May 2001 it was re-launched in the highlands and in the 2002 elections won three seats (though Pora failed to gain re-election).

People's Action Party (PAP)

Leadership. Moses Maladina (leader)

In 1981 a Papua Action Party was formed as a regional party, drawing on Papuan separatist sentiments. It was aligned with the National Party. Around the same time, former Papua New Guinea Defence Force commander, Ted Diro, a Papuan, stood successfully in the 1982 elections, in association with several candidates, mostly Papuans, who formed an "Independent Group". In 1982 Diro became opposition leader before stepping down in favour of National Party leader Okuk. The People's Action Party was founded shortly before the 1987 elections, with Diro as leader and strong support from Papua (including members of the Papua Action Party and the Independent Group). It gained six seats in 1987 and double that number in 1992, becoming the third largest parliamentary party; it also broadened its regional

support base. In 1997 it secured 4.6% of the vote and five seats, and in 2002 retained five seats, with significant support in the highlands.

Papua New Guinea Party (PNGP), formerly People's Democratic Movement (PDM)

Address. P.O. Box 37, Jacksons Airport, NCD, Papua New Guinea.

Telephone. (+675) 323 3744

Leadership. Sir Mekere Morauta (leader); Thomas Negints (acting convenor); Agonia Tamarua (acting secretary)

The PDM was formed by a breakaway from *Pangu Pati* in 1985, led by prominent highlander member Paias Wingti. Wingti subsequently became Prime Minister, following a vote of no confidence. The Wingti-led coalition was returned to office in the election of 1987 but was itself removed in mid-term in 1988. After the 1992 election Wingti again became Prime Minister, heading a coalition dominated by PDM, PPP and LNA, but in 1994, having resigned and sought re-election as Prime Minister (in a move to avoid a vote of no confidence) he was removed as Prime Minister by a Supreme Court ruling, and in 1997 lost his seat. Following the 1997 elections, the PDM was initially in opposition, but led a challenge to Prime Minister Skate and in 1999 became the major partner in a coalition headed by Sir Mekere Morauta, who became parliamentary leader of the PDM in 1998. Following the passage of the Organic Law on the Integrity of Political Parties and Candidates (OLIPPC), in 2001 a number of members switched allegiance to the PDM, giving it an absolute majority in parliament. The 2002 elections, however, saw a shift away from the PDM, which won only 13 seats. Morauta became leader of the opposition. In 2003 the party changed its name to Papua New Guinea Party. Wingti, having gained re-election, was listed as independent.

People's National Congress (PNC)

Leadership. Peter O'Neill (leader)

Formed prior to the 1997 elections, principally as the electoral vehicle for National Capital member Bill Skate, the PNC gained six seats in 1997 (all in Papuan electorates). Skate emerged as Prime Minister in a coalition government but lost office in 1999. In 2002 the party won only two seats but by December 2003 claimed the allegiance of 10 MPs.

People's Progress Party (PPP)

Leadership. Sir Julius Chan (leader); Andrew Baing (parliamentary party leader)

The PPP is one of the country's oldest and most successful parties, and remains a major player. It is generally regarded as having a pro-business orientation. Its leader, Sir Julius Chan, was deputy Prime Minister in the first post-independence government and has twice been Prime Minister, but lost his seat in 1997 after his government attempted to employ mercenaries to end a rebellion on the island of Bougainville. In the 2002 elections the PPP won eight seats. Allan Marat subsequently became deputy Prime Minister, but his position as parliamentary leader was successfully challenged by Andrew Baing.

Pipol First Party (PFP)

Leadership. Luther Wenge (leader)

PFP was formed prior to the 2002 national elections and won two seats in that election.

United Party (UP)

Leadership. Bire Kimisopa (leader)

The UP was founded, initially as the Combined Political Associations (Compass), in 1970. Its political base was in the highlands, and its principal platform was opposition to a rapid movement to independence. In the pre-independence elections of 1972 it gained more seats than any other party but was outmanoeuvred in the formation of coalitions and became the leading opposition party. Subsequently it lost support and in 1978 split, with a number of its members joining the National Party. It remains as a minor party (having gained three seats in the 2002 elections), still predominantly highlands-based, and has been a junior partner in several governing coalitions.

Other Parties

Advance Papua New Guinea Party (APP). The party emerged on the eve of the 1997 elections, and its parliamentary party leader, John Pundari, subsequently played a crucial role in the moves which brought down the Skate government and installed Sir Mekere Morauta as Prime Minister. In May 2001 Pundari announced that the 13-member, predominantly highlander, APP was merging its name and identity with the governing PDM. Soon after, however, Bonny Igime, who had been secretary general of the APP, proclaimed himself "caretaker" of the party, which, he said, would contest the 2002 elections. In 2002 it won one seat.

Christian Democratic Party (CDP), launched in 1995 "with the vision to provide Christian Leadership in all levels of government". It gained one seat in the elections of 1997 and three seats in 2002.
Leadership. Dilu Goma (chairman); Tota Bun (parliamentary leader)

League for National Advancement (LNA). The LNA (initially known as the Pangu Independent Group) was formed as a breakaway from the *Pangu Pati* in 1986, by leading *Pangu* members Anthony Siaguru, Barry Holloway and John Nilkare. Although Siaguru failed to gain re-election in 1987, the LNA enjoyed modest electoral success, and was a member of governing coalitions, until 1997, when it faded out.

Movement for Greater Autonomy (MGA). Formed prior to the 1997 elections by former Manus Province governor, Stephen Pokawin, who had been an outspoken opponent of changes to the provincial government system in 1995, the MGA drew support from the New Guinea Islands Region. Pokawin was elected in 1997, when he and the MGA joined the ÕNational Alliance, but he lost his seat in 2002.
Leadership. Stephen Pokawin (leader)

Papua New Guinea Labour Party (PNGLP), launched in August 2001 in Port Moresby by PNG Trade Union Congress general secretary John Paska, as the latest of a series of union-linked parties, none of which has had significant electoral success.
Leadership. Dr Bob Danaya (president)

People's Labour Party (PLP). Launched in the highlands in July 2001 by controversial Madang businessman and politician, Peter Yama, the PLP won four seats in the 2002 elections.
Leadership. Peter Yama (leader)

United Resources Party (URP), created amongst mostly highlander MPs during the 1997-2002 parliament, but by 2001 weakened by defections to the PDM. It endorsed candidates in 2002 and in December 2003, having attracted several independents, claimed nine MPs.
Leadership. Tim Neville (leader)

Paraguay

Capital: Asunción
Population: 5,200,000 (2002C)

Paraguay was in 1811 the first Latin American country to achieve independence from Spain. Its first constitution was introduced in 1844 in order to legitimize the power of Carlos Antonio López, one of the three consecutive dictators to rule Paraguay up to the end of the War of the Triple Alliance or National Epic (*Epopeya Nacional*) in 1870, in which Paraguay's population was halved. Political forces subsequently developed into the *Colorado* and Liberal parties, which have dominated Paraguayan politics since 1876. A three-year period of military rule, albeit by reformist officers, followed the 1932-37 Chaco War with Bolivia. A new constitution introduced in 1940 failed to bring about needed changes and, after a succession of unstable governments, Gen. Alfredo Stroessner took power in a military coup in 1954.

During Stroessner's 35-year rule (the *stronato*) Paraguay was under a permanent state of siege and all constitutional rights and civil liberties were suspended. The country's economic and political structure was nonetheless stabilized and its infrastructure greatly modernized. Stroessner was declared the winner of all eight elections, which were held at five-year intervals. He was overthrown on Feb. 3, 1989, in a "palace coup" led by his son-in-law Gen. Andrés Rodríguez, who was sworn in immediately as interim President. The subsequent presidential and congressional elections on May 1, 1989, in which Rodríguez and the *Colorado* Party won a sweeping victory, were considered to have been relatively free and open by international observers. Election to membership of the Group of Rio in October 1990 and entry in March 1991 into the Southern Common Market (MERCOSUR), with Argentina, Brazil and Uruguay, did much to restore the country's international credibility. The *Colorado* Party (ANR-PC) has remained the leading party since the restoration of democratic institutions with the Authentic Radical Liberal Party (PLRA) the principal party of opposition.

Under the 1992 constitution, which curtailed his previously extensive powers, executive power is vested in the President, who is directly elected by simple plurality for a non-renewable five-year term and who governs with the assistance of the Council of Ministers, which he appoints. Legislative authority is vested in the bicameral National Congress, consisting of a 45-member Senate and 80-member Chamber of Deputies, directly elected by proportional representation for five-year terms. Voting is compulsory for all men and women of 18 years of age and older. Women have been able to vote since 1958.

Presidential and legislative elections were held in May 1998, with the PLRA and National Encounter (EN, now PEN) allying in the Democratic Alliance (AD). The contest for the Chamber of Deputies resulted in the ANR-PC taking 45 seats, the PLRA 27 and EN 8. In the Senate contest the ANR–PC took 24 seats, the PLRA 13, the EN 7 and the White Party (*Partido Blanco*) 1. In the concurrent presidential elections Raúl Alberto Cubas Grau (ANR-PC), with 55.4% of the votes cast, defeated Domingo Laíno (PLRA-EN) with 43.9%. Following the assassination of his Vice President, Luís María Argaña, however, in which he was widely seen as implicated, Cubas fled the country in March 1999. He was succeeded as President by the President of the Senate, Luís González Macchi, and a special election held on Aug. 13, 2000, to choose a new Vice President.

In elections held on April 27, 2003, Óscar Nicanor Duarte Frutos (ANR-PC) obtained 37.1% of the vote and was elected President for the term 2003-08. In concurrent congressional elections the ANR-PC remained the largest party with 16 seats (out of 45) in the Senate and 37 (out of 80) in the Chamber of Deputies.

Authentic Radical Liberal Party
Partido Liberal Radical Auténtico (PLRA)
Address. Mariscal López 435, 1750 Asunción
Telephone. (595–21) 24–4867
Fax. (595–21) 20–4867
Leadership. Julio César Ramón ('Yoyito') Franco Gómez (Vice President of the Republic and president); Domingo Isabelino Laíno Figueredo (founder and 1998 presidential candidate)
This centrist party is a descendant of the Liberal Party (PL), founded in 1887, which dominated Paraguayan politics from 1904 to 1936. It was founded in 1978 by Domingo Laíno, and has been the second party in Paraguayan politics since that time. The party was a founder member of the National Agreement (*Acuerdo Nacional*, AN), a coalition of four opposition parties with the aim of pressing for democratization and respect for human rights under the Stroessner regime. The PLRA was denied legal status and boycotted all elections and organized anti-government rallies.

The PLRA was legalized on March 8, 1989, a month after the military coup that overthrew Stroessner. In the May 1989 elections Laíno stood as the PLRA presidential candidate and the party came second in both the presidential and the congressional contests, although its share of the vote was far smaller than that of the ruling National Republican Association–*Colorado* Party. This pattern was repeated in the 1991 Constituent Assembly elections and the 1993 and 1998 elections. In 1998, the party (running in alliance with National Encounter (EN)) won 27 seats in the Chamber of Deputies and 13 in the Senate, while Laíno came second, with 43.9% of the vote, in the presidential contest. In the 2000 special vice presidential election the PLRA candidate, Julio César Franco, won a narrow victory, taking 49.64% of the votes cast to 48.82% for the ANR-PC candidate, Félix Argaña, brother of the assassinated Vice President. In the 2003 presidential election Franco ran second to the ANR-PC candidate, Oscar Nicanor Duarte Frutos, but remained Vice President, while the PRLA won 12 seats in the Senate and 21 in the Chamber of Deputies.

The PLRA is a member party of the Liberal International.

Dear Fatherland Movement
Movimiento Patria Querida (MPQ)
Leadership. Pedro Nicolás Maráa Fadul Niella (2003 presidential candidate)
Centre-right populist movement with ill-defined ideology founded in 2002 to contest the 2003 elections, in which it obtained 8 seats in the Senate and 10 in the Chamber of Deputies. Its presidential candidate, Pedro Nicolas Fadul Niella, came third with 21.3% of the vote.

National Encounter Party
Partido Encuentro Nacional (PEN)
Address. Senador Long 370, esq. Del Maestro, Asunción
Telephone. (595–21) 61–0699, 61–0701
Fax. (595–21) 61–0699
Leadership. Guillermo Caballero Vargas (leader)
PEN (formerly known simply as *Encuentro nacional*, EN) was founded in 1992 as an electoral vehicle for Guillermo

Caballero Vargas, who took 23.14% of the votes in the 1993 presidential contest while his party won eight seats in each house and entered into opposition with the Authentic Radical Liberal Party (PLRA). As the Democratic Alliance (*Alianza Democrática*, AD), the PEN and PLRA jointly contested the 1998 election, when the PEN won 7 seats in the Senate and 8 in the Chamber of Deputies. However in the 2003 legislative elections the PEN, running separately, failed to win any seats in either house.

National Republican Association–Colorado Party
Asociación Nacional Republicana–Partido Colorado (ANR-PC)
Address. 25 de Mayo 842, Calle Tacuary, Asunción
Telephone. (595–21) 44–4137, 49–8669
Fax. (595–21) 44–4210
Email. anr@uninet.com.py
Leadership. Oscar Nicanor Duarte Frutos (President of the Republic)
The right-wing *Colorado* ("Red") Party was founded in 1887 and has been a major force in Paraguayan politics ever since. It originated in a conservative faction created by Gen. Bernardino Caballero (President of Paraguay 1882–91) and it took its name from the faction's red banners.

The *Colorado*s were in power from 1887 until 1904 when the Liberals took power in a popular uprising. They remained in opposition to Liberal governments until the brief *Febrerista* interlude in 1936-37 and the sudden death in an accident of the war hero Marshal José Félix Estigarribia in 1940. They opposed the pro-Axis regime of Higinio Moríngo, until a *Colorado/Febrerista* Revolutionary Party (PRF) coalition government was installed in 1946 after the USA put pressure on the regime to oust fascist sympathizers. A series of coups and fraudulent elections followed, the PRF were edged out and the *Colorado*s were the only legal party between 1947 and 1963.

The military coup of May 5, 1954, marked the beginning of Gen. Alfredo Stroessner's 35-year dictatorship. Then an army commander, he was officially elected President in July 1954. In 1956 Stroessner re-organized the party after exiling his main *Colorado* rival, Epifanio Méndez Fleitas. The 1958 elections were, like all six later elections held under his rule, completely stage-managed. To give a semblance of democracy, after 1963 selected opposition parties or acceptable fractions of parties were permitted to take part (and even win some seats in Congress from 1968 onwards). The manipulated results invariably showed overwhelming support for Stroessner, despite the reality of exile, arrests, long prison sentences and torture being meted out to his political opponents. However after 1979 an extra-parliamentary opposition, the National Agreement (*Acuerdo Nacional*) emerged, made up of the Authentic Radical Liberal Party (PLRA), the *Febrerista* Revolutionary Party (PRF), Christian Democratic Party (PDC) and the Popular *Colorado* Movement (*Movimiento Popular Colorado*, MOPOCO), an anti-Stroessner faction of the *Colorado*s.

The violent coup of Feb. 3, 1989 which toppled Stroessner took place shortly before his former close ally and son-in-law, Andrés Rodríguez, was due to be transferred from his top army position of First Army Commander to the passive role of Defence Minister. Rodríguez, as interim President, legalized most opposition parties and called a general election for May 1, 1989. As the *Colorado*'s presidential candidate, Rodríguez won 78.18% of the valid vote and the party polled 72.8% of the vote in the congressional elections. Under the then Constitution, however, the winning party automatically gained two-thirds of the seats in Congress. Promising that he would hold elections in 1993 and not stand for a second term, Rodríguez was sworn in on May 15, 1989, and retained his interim Cabinet.

The ensuing power struggle between the "traditionalists" and the newly formed "democratic" wing led, however to a severe rift in the party. A *Colorado* Party convention, dominated by "traditionalists", went ahead in early December 1989 despite a court injunction brought by the "democratic" faction, led by Blas Riquelme, and said to be supported by Rodríguez. This was followed on Dec. 11, 1989, by the resignation of the whole Cabinet. The leader of the "traditionalists", the Foreign Minister Dr José María Argaña, was dismissed in mid-August 1990 after making a defiant public statement that the *Colorado*s would never give up power.

At an extraordinary *Colorado* convention in February 1993 the military-backed Juan Carlos Wasmosy defeated Argaña for the party's presidential nomination. Following this rejection, Argaña campaigned against Wasmosy in the May 1993 general elections. Following the elections (won by Wasmosy), Argaña set up a new break-away party called the National Reconciliation Movement (*Movimiento Reconciliación Nacional*, MRN), which formed a rival legislative block with the PLRA and EN. In late 1994 three generals accused Wasmosy of vote-rigging and officially called for his impeachment. This clash between the *Colorado* Party and the military continued into 1995 with General Lino César Oviedo Silva emerging as the leader of the fight against Wasmosy. A new party faction was launched, fuelled by Oviedo, which began making overtures to the exiled Albert Stroessner, son of the former dictator, thus prompting the possibility of a new *stronista* faction within the *Colorado* party. In April 1996, however, Oviedo and his supporters attempted to launch a coup, which was defeated after the Organization of American States (OAS) had made it clear it would not be recognized.

Although imprisoned, Oviedo was chosen as the *Colorado* candidate for the presidency in 1998. Legally barred from running, he was then replaced by his proposed running mate, Raúl Cubas Grau, who was elected in May 1998 in an election generally regarded as free and fair. On taking office, Cubas commuted Oviedo's sentence and ordered his release. In March 1999 Vice President Luís María Argaña was assassinated and it was widely believed that this was the result of a conspiracy between Cubas and Oviedo. After several days of mounting crisis, with widespread strikes and demonstrations and impeachment pending in Congress, Cubas fled to Brazil, where he was given political asylum. He was succeeded as President by the President of the Senate, Luís González Macchi, who formed a government of national unity. In a special election held on Aug. 13, 2000, to choose a new Vice President the Colorado candidate, Félix Argaña, the brother of the assassinated Vice President, was narrowly defeated by the PLRA candidate.

The presidential election of Apr. 27, 2003, gave victory to the ANR-PC candidate, Oscar Nicanor Duarte Frutos. In the concurrent congressional elections the party obtained 16 seats in the 45-member Senate and 37 seats in the 80-member Chamber of Deputies.

National Union of Concerned Citizens
Union Nacional de Ciudadanos Eticos (UNACE)
Leadership. Guillermo Sánchez Guffanti (2003 presidential candidate)

This is a nationalist breakaway faction of the ruling ANR-PC, founded in September 2002 and associated with the dissident former General Lino César Oviedo Silva, currently in exile in Brazil. It obtained 7 seats in the Senate and 10 in the Chamber of Deputies in the 2003 legislative elections. Its presidential candidate, Guillermo Sánchez Gufffanti, came fourth with 13.5% of the vote.

Party for a Country in Solidarity
Partido Pais Solidario
This is a democratic socialist party. It obtained 2 seats in the Senate and 2 in the Chamber of Deputies in the 2003 elections.

Other Parties

Christian Democratic Party (*Partido Demócrata Cristiano*, PDC), founded in 1960 but was illegal until following the February 1989 coup which toppled Stroessner; won one seat in the Chamber in the 1989 and 1991 elections but has been unrepresented since 1993; affiliated to the Christian Democrat International.
Leadership. Prof. Dr. Jeronimo Irala Burgos (president), Dr Luis M. Andrada Nogues (general secretary).
Address. Colón 871, Casilla 1318, Asunción
Telephone. (595–21) 42–0434
Fax. (595–21) 42-3539
Email. icm@infonet.com.py

Constitution for All (*Constitución Para Todos*, CPT), founded in 1991 with support from within the Church and the CUT and CNT trade union confederations; grew out of Asunción for All (*Asunción para Todos,* APT), a progressive movement led by Carlos Filizzola, a former president of the Association of Physicians, which won the May 1991 municipal elections in the capital; took 16 seats in the 1991 Constituent Assembly elections, but failed to win a seat in the 1993 or 1998 elections. In 1998 Filizzola ran as vice presidential candidate on the Democratic Alliance ticket with Domingo Laíno of the Authentic Radical Liberal Party.
Leadership. Carlos Alberto Filizzola Pallares

Febrerista Revolutionary Party (*Partido Revolucionario Febrerista,* PRF), originated among the junior ranks of the armed forces, who carried out a radical nationalist coup of Feb. 17, 1936, which inspired the party's name. Founded in 1951, the party called anti-government protests against the dictatorship in the mid-1980s. It failed to win a seat in the 1993, 1998 and 2003 legislative elections. It is a member party of the Socialist International.
Address. Casa del Pueblo, Manduvira 552, Asunción
Telephone. (595–21) 49–4041
Fax. (595–21) 49–3995
Email. partyce@mixmail.com
Leadership. Carlos María Liubetic (president); Ricardo Estigarribia Velásquez (secretary-general)

Humanist Party (*Partido Humanista,* PH). Party candidate Ricardo Buman, polled 1.54% of the vote in the vice presidential elections of Aug. 13, 2000.
Address. Rca. de Colombia 1260, esq. Rojas Silva y Capitán Fayol, Asunción
Telephone. (595–21) 21–3211
Fax. (595–21) 21–3211
Email. ph@humanista,org.py

Peru

Capital: Lima
Population: 27,544,305 (2004E)

The Republic of Peru achieved independence from Spain in 1826, and until 1979 periods of civilian government alternated with long periods of military rule. Under the 1993 constitution executive power is vested in a President, who is directly elected for a five-year term and is eligible for re-election. The President governs with the assistance of a Prime Minister and an appointed Council of Ministers. Legislative authority is vested in a unicameral 120 member National Congress elected for a five-year term from a single national list. Voting is compulsory from the ages of 18 to 70.

Alberto Keinya Fujimori, of Change 90 (*Cambio 90*), was elected as President in June 1990. Fujimori staged a presidential coup (*autogolpe*), with the support of the military, in April 1992, when he dissolved the legislature and suspended the constitution. He survived an abortive counter-coup put down by loyal forces in November 1992 and a new constitution was approved by referendum in October 1993. Fujimori was a comfortable victor in presidential elections held in April 1995, becoming the first incumbent in the country's history to be re-elected for a consecutive term. His ruling New Majority–Change 90 (NM–C90) alliance also secured a majority in Congress by winning the simultaneous legislative elections.

In December 1999 Fujimori announced that he would run as the presidential candidate of the Peru 2000 alliance in the forthcoming elections. The opposition launched a legal challenge to Fujimori's candidacy on the grounds that the constitution barred a third term. However, the national election board declared that because the constitution was last amended in 1993, Fujimori had in fact stood for election only once under the current constitution and was, therefore, eligible for a further term. In May 2000 Fujimori won a comfortable victory, his opponent, Alejandro Toledo, having decided to boycott a run-off poll because of the widespread view that it would not be conducted fairly. In simultaneous elections to the Congress, Fujimori's Peru 2000 alliance lost its absolute majority. In July 2000 Fujimori was sworn in for a third presidential term amid threats of international isolation and uproar on the streets of the capital, Lima. However, in a dramatic development, Fujimori made a televised announcement in September 2000 in which he stated that he intended to step down and call an election in which he would not be a candidate. Two months later, in a development that stunned the country, Fujimori (the son of Japanese immigrants) fled to Japan and announced his resignation as President from a Tokyo hotel.

In fresh presidential elections held in April and June 2001, Toledo, backed by his centrist Peru Possible (PP) party, took 53.1% of the vote in a run-off victory over Alan García of the populist left-of-centre Peruvian *Aprista* Party (APRA). In legislative elections held in April 2001, Toledo's PP emerged as the largest single party, with 45 seats (from 26.3% of the vote), while APRA took 26 seats and nine other parties shared the remaining seats.

Independent Moralizing Front
Frente Independiente Moralizador (FIM)

Address. c/o Congreso de la República, Plaza Bolivar S/N, Lima 1
Leadership. Luis Fernando Olivera Vega
The FIM was launched in 1990 by Fernando Olivera, a former investigator for the State Prosecutor's Office who had pursued former President Alan García of the Peruvian *Aprista* Party on corruption charges. The party has adopted a consistent anti-corruption stance and support for it and its leader has grown over the years. In the 2001 presidential election, Olivera finished fourth, gaining just under 10% of the vote. The party won 12 seats in the accompanying legislative elections, making it one of only four parties to achieve double figures, and became a junior partner in the ruling PP coalition.

National Unity
Unidad Nacional (UN)

Address. c/o Congreso de la República, Plaza Bolivar S/N, Lima 1

Leadership. Lourdes Celmira Rosario Flores Nano (2001 presidential candidate)
The centre-right National Unity electoral alliance was created as a vehicle for the presidential ambitions of Lourdes Flores Nano, who had led the Popular Christian Party (*Partido Popular Cristiano*, PPC) for a number of years. In the first round of the 2001 presidential election (held in April), Flores finished in third place having secured 24.3% of the vote, narrowly missing the run off. In the legislative elections (also in April), the UN emerged as the third strongest party, winning almost 14% of the vote and 17 seats in the 120-member Congress.

Peru 2000

A four-party coalition formed in 1999 to support President Alberto Keinya Fujimori in his bid to win a third presidential term. It included Change 90 (*Cambio 90*), the grouping originally founded in 1989 to help Fujimori's presidential aspirations, and the New Majority (*Nueva Mayoría*), formed by Fujimori in the early 1990s. Following the creation of Peru 2000, the main opposition parties mounted an unsuccessful legal challenge to Fujimori's candidacy on the ground that he was running for a third term, barred by the constitution. In the May 2000 elections the Peru 2000 parties took 51 seats and Fujimori was re-elected, but he subsequently resigned and fled the country amid widespread discontent. With the departure of Fujimori, the Peru 2000 alliance collapsed. Two of the member parties – Change 90 and New Majority – contested the 2001 legislative election on a joint ticket, but were soundly defeated, winning only four seats in the Congress.

Peru Possible
Perú Posible (PP)

Address. Bajada Balta 131 Oficina 11, Miraflores, Lima
Telephone. (51–1) 447–4413
Website. www.peruposible.org.pe
Leadership. Alejandro Toledo Manrique (President of the Republic)
Peru Possible was formed in 1994 by Alejandro Toledo, an American Indian who had risen from poverty to become a business-school professor and World Bank official. Toledo contested the presidency in 1995 as the candidate of the (now defunct) Democratic Co-ordinating Movement–Peru Viable Nation (Code), winning just over 3% of the vote and finishing well behind President Fujimori and three other candidates. However, by the time of the 2000 elections, Toledo and the PP posed the main challenge to Fujimori. In a highly charged atmosphere, Fujimori and Toledo went through to a second round of voting in the presidential election, but the latter boycotted the poll after accusing the incumbent President of electoral malpractice and Fujimori won a third consecutive term. In the legislative elections held in April 2000, Fujimori's Peru 2000 party lost its absolute majority in Congress with the PP becoming the largest opposition force, with 28 seats in the 120-member Congress.

In November 2000 Fujimori resigned the presidency and fled the country, forcing a new round of elections in 2001. In the first round of the presidential election in April Toledo secured over 36% of the vote in the first round (against 26% for Alan García of the Peruvian *Aprista* Party, APRA). In the second round of voting held in June, Toledo defeated García, taking 53.1% of the vote and becoming the first Peruvian President of indigenous ancestry. In the April 2001 legislative elections, the PP had emerged as the strongest party, winning 45 seats, against 26 for APRA and 17 for the National Unity Party, and attracted support from a number of smaller parties.

Peruvian Aprista Party
Partido Aprista Peruano (APRA) (also known as *Alianza Popular Revolucionaria Americana*)
Address. Avenida Alfonso Ugarte 1012, Lima
Telephone. (51–1) 440–6886
Fax. (51–1) 445–2986
Website. www.apra.org.pe
Leadership. Alan Gabriel Ludwig García Pérez (president and 2001 presidential candidate); Jorge del Castillo Gálvez, Mauricio Mulder Bedoya (secretaries-general).

APRA has historically been the leading centre-left force in Peruvian politics. APRA started as a continent-wide anti-imperialist movement formed in 1924 by Victor Raúl Haya de la Torre, a Peruvian Marxist in exile in Mexico. Its original purpose was to unite Latin America politically, obtain joint control of the Panama Canal and gain social control of land and industry. The Peruvian branch of APRA, the Peruvian *Aprista* Party (PAP), was founded in 1930 when Haya returned to Peru. As it became the sole surviving *Aprista* party, the PAP was and is commonly referred to as APRA.

Alan García took over as secretary general in 1982 and led the party to victory in the April 1985 elections, thereby becoming the first *Aprista* to be elected President, and the youngest Peruvian ever to hold the office. García's principal election promise was to halt the country's economic decline by devoting no more than 10% of export earnings to service the huge foreign debt. In an attempt to address widespread and escalating guerrilla activity, he set up a Peace Commission. In June 1986, however, García ordered the quelling of mutinies in three different prisons, staged mainly by Shining Path guerrillas, as a result of which an estimated 254 guerrillas were killed by the security forces. All the members of the Peace Commission resigned in protest. In addition, accusations that the government was using the right-wing Commando Rodrigo Franco death squads to intimidate left-wing opponents dented APRA's liberal image.

In the 1990 elections, APRA won only 16 senatorial seats and 49 seats in the Chamber of Deputies. Its presidential candidate and secretary general Luís Alvaro Castro, was beaten into third place in the presidential contest and the party backed Alberto Keinya Fujimori of Change 90, the victor, in the run-off.

In the aftermath of Fujimori's April 1992 presidential coup, García went into hiding from where he called for popular resistance to restore democratic rule. In early 1993, an extradition request made to Colombia to hand over the exiled García was rejected. Following attempts by García to obtain Colombian citizenship, he was stripped of the position of secretary general of APRA and a new leadership was installed. The internal strife and unpopularity of the party led to its candidate, Mercedes Cabanillas, achieving a dismal 5% of the presidential vote in April 1995 while in 1996 García was convicted in absentia on corruption charges.

In the 2000 elections the party again performed badly. APRA's candidate in the presidential poll, Abel Salinas Eyzaguirre, was eliminated in the first round of voting after gaining just over 1% of the vote and in the legislative elections the party gained only just over 5% of the total vote, having failed to compete effectively with either Peru 2000 or Peru Possible (PP).

The catalyst for the party's revival occurred in early 2001 when García returned to Peru from Colombia and announced his intention to contest the April presidential election. After his return, the Supreme Court lifted all arrest warrants against him, following an earlier ruling of the Inter-American Court on Human Rights that his 1996 conviction was spent under a statute of limitations. The subsequent performance of García was impressive, but he still failed to defeat the PP candidate, Alejandro Toledo, who won by a margin of 53% to 47% in a second round of voting held in June. In the legislative elections, APRA also did well but again the party failed to overtake the PP, winning 20% of the popular vote and 26 seats. However, in November 2002 the party made substantial gains in the elections for provincial governorships and won a majority of the mayoral contests across the country to emerge as the strongest force in Peruvian politics.

APRA is a full member party of the Socialist International.

Popular Action
Acción Popular (AP)
Address. Paseo Colon 218, Lima
Telephone. (51–1) 423–4177
Email. webmaster@accionpopular.org.pe
Website. www.accionpopular.org.pe
Leadership. Victor Andres Garcia Belaunde (presidential candidate); Valentin Paniagua (president); Javier Diaz Orihuela (secretary general)

The right-wing AP was founded by Fernando Belaunde Terry in 1956 and is a strong proponent of free-market policies. Belaunde Terry was among prominent politicians opposed to Fujimori's April 1992 army-backed presidential coup. The party has made little headway in recent years. In the April 2001 elections it won three seats and became a junior partner in the ruling PP coalition.

Union for Peru
Unión por el Perú (UPP)
Address. c/o Congreso de la República, Plaza Bolivar S/N, Lima 1
Website. www.unionporelperu.org
Leadership. Javier Pérez de Cuellar (honorary president)

The independent social democratic UPP was founded in 1994 by the former UN Secretary-General, Javier Pérez de Cuellar. In the 1995 presidential election, incumbent President Alberto Fujimori easily defeated Pérez de Cuellar, who finished second but only managed to win some 22% of the vote. The UPP emerged as the main opposition party to the pro-Fujimori alliance in the legislature, but only with 17 seats. In the 2000 presidential election, the party's candidate, Maximo San Roman, won less than 0.4% of the vote. The party did not field a candidate in the 2001 presidential poll, but won six seats in the legislature and is a junior partner in the ruling PP coalition.

We Are Peru
Partido Democrático Somos Perú (SP)
Address. Avenida Arequipa 3990, Miraflores, Lima
Telephone. (51–1) 221-5921
Email. postmaster@somosperu.org.pe
Website. www.somosperu.org.pe
Leadership. Alberto Andrade Carmona (leader)

This party was formed in 1998 by Alberto Andrade, the populist mayor of Lima, who converted his *Somos Lima* (We Are Lima) Movement into *Somos Perú* (We Are Peru). The party competed in the municipal elections of 1998 and won control of Lima and various other provinces and districts. In the 2000 presidential election, however, Andrade failed to make an impact, finishing a distant third behind incumbent President Fujimori and Alejandro Toledo of the Peru Possible party. Andrade did not compete in the 2001 presidential poll, but in the legislative elections the SP won four seats and became a junior partner in the ruling PP coalition.

Other Parties

All For Victory (*Todos por la Victoria*, TV), won one seat in the April 2001 elections.

Andean Renaissance (*Renacimiento Andino*, RA), won only one seat in the 2001 congressional elections. Its presidential candidate, Ciro Alfredo Gálvez Herrera, fared even worse, gaining less than 1% of the votes cast. RA became a junior partner in the ruling PP coalition.

Christian Democrat Union (*Union Demócrata Cristiano*, UDC), is a member party of the Christian Democrat International but is unrepresented in Congress.
Address. Avenida España 321, Lima
Email. sluti@lullitec.com.pe
Leadership. Julio Luque Tijero (president)

Christian People's Party (*Partido Popular Cristiano*, PPC), is a member party of the Christian Democrat International.
Address. Avenida Alfonso Ugarte 1484, Lima
Email. aflores@congreso.go.be
Leadership. Antero Flores Araoz (president)

People's Solution (*Solución Popular*, SP), won one seat in the April 2001 congressional elections.

Project Country (*Proyecto Pais*, PrP), took 1.6% of the vote but no seats in the April 2001 elections.

Philippines

Capital: Manila
Population: 86,242,000 (2004 est.)

The Republic of the Philippines became an independent state in 1946. From its previous colonial ruler, the United States, it inherited a democratic system with two dominant parties, the *Nacionalista* Party and the Liberal Party. In 1972 the then President, Ferdinand Marcos, suspended the constitution and declared martial law. Political parties were for a time illegal; subsequently politics was dominated by President Marcos's *Kilusang Bagong Lipunan* (New Society Movement, KBL). In 1986, facing mounting opposition, Marcos called a snap election which precipitated the "People Power revolution", and Corazon Aquino, widow of assassinated opposition leader Benigno Aquino, was installed as President. A new constitution was passed by plebiscite in 1987 and elections were held in that year for the bicameral legislature, and for provincial and local offices.

The constitution provides for a House of Representatives of not more than 250 members, 20% of whom are to be elected from a party-list of organizations, approved by the Commission on Elections, representing marginalized and under-represented sectors (the introduction of the party-list system was intended to help prevent a return to the pattern of pre-Marcos "traditional politics"). Other members of the lower house are elected from single-member constituencies for a three-year term, with a limit of three terms. The party-list system was not fully implemented until 1998 (prior to this sectoral representatives were nominated by groups and appointed by the President). As at July 2004 the House comprised 236 members, including 24 party-list members. There is a 24-member Senate. Senators are elected directly for a six-year term (with a limit of two terms), half of them being elected every three years. Executive authority rests with the President, directly elected for a single six-year term, and a Vice President, elected separately.

Expectations in some circles of a return to a dominant two-party system after 1986 were not borne out. The Liberal and *Nacionalista* parties re-emerged, but as relatively minor parties (though the Liberal Party has been gaining support). The KBL suffered a massive decline. For the most part, parties revolve around key personalities and allegiance is fluid. New groupings appear before each election and have frequently disappeared before the next – in 2001 alone, 162 parties and organizations applied for party-list registration. Virtually all political leaders since 1986 have been associated with two or more parties or coalitions.

President Aquino did not identify with a political party; however in 1987 Congress was dominated by successful candidates who identified with Aquino. In 1988 her supporters formed a coalition, *Laban ng Demokratikong Pilipino*, LDP), to support the candidature of pro-Aquino candidates. In elections in 1992, LDP emerged as the most successful group, though its presidential candidate failed after President Aquino had endorsed former Philippines National Police chief, Fidel Ramos. Ramos, who had been a member of LDP, formed a new party, *Partido Lakas–Tao* (*Lakas*), and, campaigning in alliance with the National Union of Christian Democrats (NUCD) and United Muslim Democrats of the Philippines (UMDP), was elected President. In 1992 *Lakas*-NUCD-UMDP gained less than 24% of the presidential vote, only two Senate seats, and about a fifth of the seats in the lower house. By 1994, however, *Lakas*-NUCD-UMDP had gained through defections from other parties (especially the LDP) and in 1995, in alliance with LDP, won a substantial majority in the lower house and nine of the twelve Senate seats being contested.

In the presidential elections of 1998, *Lakas*-NUCD-UMDP's candidate lost to Joseph Estrada, whose party, *Partido ng Masang Pilipino* (PMP, Party of the Philippine Masses) formed a coalition with LDP and the Nationalist People's Coalition (NPC) – the *Laban ng Makabayan Masang Pilipino* (LAMMP). Three years later, Estrada was accused of corruption and as a result of impeachment proceedings and popular pressure he vacated the presidency and was replaced by Vice President Gloria Macapagal-Arroyo, the daughter of a former President, who had stood in 1998 as the *Lakas*-NUCD-UMDP's vice presidential candidate. The elections in 2001 were seen by many as a test of strength between the supporters, respectively, of Macapagal-Arroyo and Estrada. The pro-Macapagal-Arroyo People Power Coalition (PPC) included *Lakas*-NUCD, the Liberal Party, *Partido Demokratikong Pilipino*, *Aksyon Demokratiko*, *Partido ng Demokratikong Reporma–Lapiang Manggagawa*, and Promdi; the pro-Estrada coalition, *Puwersa ng Masa* (Power of the Masses), comprised the three elements of LAMMP plus the People's Reform Party. The outcome was a victory for the PPC, consolidating the position of *Lakas*-NUCD-UMDP. The party-list vote also saw the emergence of significant support for the Left, with the CPP-aligned *Bayan Muna* topping the party-list vote and another leftist group, *Akbayan!* also polling well.

Macapagal-Arroyo (who had said in December 2002 that she would not run in 2004 because her candidacy would be divisive) contested the presidential election in May 2004 as leader of the renamed *Lakas*-CMD (Christian Muslim Democrats), which, with the LP, the *Nacionalista* Party and the People's Reform Party, formed the *Koalisyon ng Katapatan at Karanasan para sa Kinabukasan* (K-4, Coalition of Truth and Experience for Tomorrow). Macapagal's main opponent was Ferdinand Poe Jr, a movie actor without previous political experience and without party attachment. Poe was supported by the *Koalisyon ng Nagkakaisang Pilipino* (KNP, Coalition of United Filipinos), a group dominated by the PMP and LDP. The NPC initially supported the opposition but some NPC members later gave their backing to the K-4. A third presidential candidate was former police chief Senator Panfilo Lacson, a member of the LDP whose candidacy caused a split in the LDP, with one faction backing Poe and another Lacson. Another coalition, *Alyansa Pag-asa* (Alliance of Hope), consisting of former PPC members *Aksyon Demokratiko*, *Reporma* and Promdi, backed the candidature of Raul Roco, but broke up as Roco's health deteriorated.

In the event, President Macapagal-Arroyo was elected by a fairly narrow margin over Poe, taking 40% of the vote to his 36.5% amid allegations of vote rigging by Poe's supporters; 8 of the 12 Senate candidates put forward by the K-4 were elected, and K-4 candidates won almost 70% of the seats in the House of Representatives. Twenty-four party-list candidates from 16 organizations were elected, with *Bayan Muna* again getting the strongest support. The 2004 elections were hailed by many as consolidating the political party system, which, however, remains highly personalistic and fluid.

Kilusang Bagong Lipunan (New Society Movement, KBL)

The KBL was founded by President Marcos in 1978, initially as an umbrella organization which recruited Marcos supporters from both the NP and LP. It went into decline following the demise of Marcos in 1986, but survives, principally as a political vehicle for the political careers of the Marcos family.

Laban ng Demokratikong Pilipino (Fight of Democratic Filipinos, LDP)

Leadership. Edgardo Angara (party president)
Established in 1988 by President Aquino's brother Jose Cojuangco, through a merger of the *Laban* wing of PDP-*Laban* and *Lakas ng Bansa* (People Power, a party of Aquino supporters formed in 1987) as an electoral vehicle for pro-Aquino politicians. From 1988 to 1992 it was in effect the government party, though President Aquino declined to be a member of a party. The LDP did well in the Congressional and local elections in 1992 but its presidential candidate, Ramon Mitra, lost out to Fidel Ramos and the party was subsequently weakened by defections. In the 1995 elections it campaigned in alliance with *Lakas*-NUCD-UMDP, and polled well. However it split in August 1995. In 1998 the LDP was part of LAMMP, and in 2001 it joined the *Puwersa ng Masa* coalition which lost out to the pro Macapagal-Arroyo PPC.

In the 2004 presidential election the LDP formed the main opposition to President Macapagal-Arroyo and the *Lakas*-CMD party. However the candidacy of Senator Panfilo Lacson, a member of the LDP, caused a split in the party. Lacson was backed by the party's general secretary, Agapito "Butz" Aquino. Party president Edgardo Angara, however, gave his endorsement to Ferdinand Poe. The two factions sought a ruling from the Commission on Elections as to which candidate had LDP endorsement; the Commission's decision was to recognize two "parties" – the LDP-Angara Wing and the LDP-Aquino Wing. Lacson subsequently resigned from the party.

Laban ng Makabayan Masang Pilipino (Fight of the Patriotic Filipino Masses) (LAMMP)

Leadership. Joseph Estrada (titular head); Edgardo Angara (president)

Coalition formed prior to the 1998 elections, comprising Joseph Estrada's *Partido ng Masang Pilipino* (PMP), NPC and *Laban*.

Lakas-CMD

Leadership. Jose de Venecia (party president)
Partido Lakas-Tao (People Power Party) was formed by Fidel Ramos in 1992 after he failed to gain the LDP's presidential nomination. In the 1992 elections *Lakas* entered into alliance with the National Union of Christian Democrats (NUCD), headed by Raul Manglapus, and the United Muslim Democrats of the Philippines (a Mindanao-Sulu based party). After Ramos became President in 1992 *Lakas* gained by defections from other parties (principally the LDP) and in 1995 emerged as the dominant group in Congress. In 1998 the *Lakas*-NUCD-UMDP presidential candidate, de Venecia, lost out to Joseph Estrada, but the coalition's vice presidential candidate, Gloria Macapagal-Arroyo, was successful. *Lakas* also polled well in Congressional and local elections, but in the months following the elections support drifted across to Estrada's LAMMP. When impeachment proceedings against Estrada began in 2000, much of this support began flowing back to *Lakas*-NUCD, and in the elections of 2001 *Lakas*-NUCD gained a clear parliamentary majority. Before the 2004 elections *Lakas*'s partner changed its name to Christian Muslim Democrats (CMD). In early 2004, also, party president (and Philippines Vice President) Teofista Guingona split from the party, forming a new political organization, the *Bangon Pilipinas* (Philippines Arise) Movement. Backed by a coalition including *Lakas*-CMD, Macapagal-Arroyo was re-elected as President in May 2004.

Liberal Party (LP)

Leadership. Florencio Abad (party president); Franklin Drilon (chairman); Benigno Aquino III (secretary-general)
Address. J&T Building 3894 Ramon Magsaysay Blvd., Sta Mesa, Manila
Telephone. (63-2) 716 8187
Fax. (63-2) 716 8210
Email. liberal@tri-sys.com
Website. www.liberalparty.ph
A remnant of pre-Marcos politics, having been formed as a breakaway from the *Nacionalista* Party in 1945. Revived in the 1980s as part of the traditional political opposition to Ferdinand Marcos, the LP polled well in 1987, under the leadership of Jovito Salonga, who became Senate president; however it suffered from internal factionalism. In 2001 the LP was a minor but significant player in the PPC and in 2004 was a member of the winning K-4 coalition.

Nacionalista Party (NP)

The older of the two dominant pre-martial-law parties, the NP was established in 1907. Ferdinand Marcos was elected as the *Nacionalista* Party candidate in 1965. In the "snap election" of 1986 NP leader Salvador Laurel stood with Corazon Aquino, but in 1992 the party split over the nomination of its presidential candidate, with major factions led by Laurel, Juan Ponce Enrile and Eduardo Cojuangco (the latter forming the NPC). It survives as a minor party.

Nationalist People's Coalition (NPC)

Leadership. Frisco San Juan (party president); Faustino Dy (chairman); Eduardo Cojuangco (chairman emeritus)
Formed in 1992 by former Marcos crony Eduardo Cojuangco, as a centre-right coalition. It derives much of its support from politicians who split from the *Nacionalista* Party and the KBL. In the 1992 presidential contest Cojuangco received 18% of the vote (compared with Ramos's 24%) and the NPC polled strongly in the

Congressional elections. It subsequently became part of a "rainbow coalition" with *Lakas*-NUCD-UMDP. In 2001 it was part of the pro-Estrada *Puwersa ng Masa* coalition, and became the second largest party in the Congress. In 2004 there was talk of Cojuangco standing again for President, and seeking the *Lakas*-CMD nomination if Macapagal-Arroyo did not contest. When Macapagal-Arroyo announced that she would stand, the NPC aligned itself with the opposition, though some NPC members identified with *Lakas*.

PDP-Laban

Leadership. Jejomar Binay (party president); Aquilino Pimentel (chairman)
Email. mail@pdp-laban.com
Website. www.pdp-laban.com
The PDP-Laban was formed in 1982 as a merger of the *Partido Demokratikong Pilipino* (PDP), a broadly social democrat/Christian democrat grouping formed during the martial law years with strong support in Mindanao, and the *Lakas ng Bayan* (National Struggle) (*Laban*) party founded by Marcos opposition leader and former LP candidate Benigno Aquino. In 1988 PDP-*Laban* joined with *Lakas ng Bansa* and recruited some former supporters from the KBL, but a faction of PDP-*Laban*, led by Aquilino Pimentel and regarded as more progressive than the faction led by President Aquino's brother Jose Cojuangco, opposed the merger and has continued to operate as a separate political group. In 1992 Pimentel stood as vice presidential candidate with the LP's Salonga, but in 1998 stood for the Senate on the LAMMP list. By 2004 PDP-*Laban* had become a minor player.

People's Reform Party (PRP)

Leadership. Miriam Defensor-Santiago
The PRP is one of several effectively one-person parties. It was formed in 1991 as a vehicle for the presidential bid of Miriam Defensor-Santiago. Santiago finished second in the 1992 presidential race, with 20% of the vote, behind Fidel Ramos (24%). In 1995 she was elected to the Senate, but failed in a re-election bid in 2001, in which she was aligned with the *Puwersa ng Masa*. In 2004 Defensor-Santiago initially affiliated with the KNP but after a falling-out with the coalition leadership shifted allegiance to the K-4.

Other Parties

Akbyan! (Citizens' Action Party). Formed in 1998, as a coalition of progressive groups including *Buklurang Sosyalista sa Isip at Gawa* (BISIG), *Siglaya*, *Pandayan*, the Institute for Popular Democracy, the Institute for Politics and Governance, and the Alliance of Progressive Labor. In 2001 *Akbayan!* polled well in the party-list vote. Became a member of the Socialist International in 2003.
Address. 14 Mapagkumbaba St., Sikatuna Village, Quezon City
Telephone. (+63-2) 433 6933/6831
Fax. (+63-2) 925 2936
Email. secretariat@surfshop.net
Website. www.akbayan.org

Aksyon Demokratiko (Democratic Action), formed in 1997 by Senator Raul Roco, after he failed to secure the *Laban* nomination for the presidential contest. In 2001 *Aksyon* was part of the PPC. In 2004 Roco stood for the presidency, heading the *Alyansa Pag-asa*, but lost support when he had to go overseas mid-campaign for medical treatment.
Leadership. Raul Roco
Address. 16th Floor Strata 2000 Building, Emerald Ave., Ortigas Centre, Pasig City 1600

Telephone. (+63-2) 638 5381
Fax. (+63-2) 634 3073
Email. rroco@starnet.net.ph
Website. www.raulroco.com/Aksyon

Alayon. A Visayan regional party founded in Cebu in 2000 by Senator John Osmeña and drawing membership primarily from former Estrada supporters.
Leadership. John Osmeña (president)

Bagong Lakas ng Nueva Ecija (Balane). A regional party, dominated by the Joson clan of the province of Nueva Ecija.

Bayan Muna (Nation First), emerged on the Left prior to the 2001 elections to contest the party-list vote. It topped the poll in 2001 and repeated this performance in 2004, securing the maximum possible three party-list members on both occasions.
Address. No 1 Matagag cnr.Maaralin Sts. Central District, Quezon City
Telephone. (63-2) 921 3499
Fax. (63-2) 921 3473
Email. bmhq@info.com.ph
Leadership. Satur Ocampo (chairman)

Bileg Party, a regional party of Ilocos Sur, backed by Governor Luis Singson.
Leadership. Luis Singson

Communist Party of the Philippines (CPP). Founded in 1968 as the Communist Party of the Philippines–Marxist-Leninist–Mao Tse Tung Thought, as a Maoist breakaway from the *Partido Komunista ng Pilipinas* (PKP). (The PKP, founded in 1930 was for most of its existence an illegal organization. It followed a pro-Soviet orientation and by the 1970s was a largely spent force.) Under the leadership of Jose Maria Sison, the CPP formed a National Democratic Front (now based in the Netherlands), and from 1969 carried on an armed insurgency through its military wing, the New People's Army. In 1985 the NDF/CPP boycotted the elections which led to the downfall of President Marcos, and subsequently went through a long process of self-examination. A leftist *Partido ng Bayan* (National Party) contested the 1987 elections, with only modest success. In 2001 and 2004 the CPP-aligned *Bayan Muna* topped the party-list poll. The NPA remains active in some villages, reportedly having more than 10,000 guerrillas in 2002, and in 2001 assassinated two congressmen. Sison remains in exile in the Netherlands.
Leadership. Jose Maria Sison

Partido ng Demokratikong Reporma (Democratic Reform Party, Reporma). Formed by former Defence Secretary Renato de Villa before the 1998 elections, after he lost the *Lakas* party's presidential nomination to Jose de Venecia. In 2001 *Reporma* was part of the PPC, and in 2004 a member of *Alyansa Pag-asa*.
Leadership. Renato de Villa

Partido ng Masang Pilipino (Party of the Filipino Masses, PMP). Formed in 1997 as the political vehicle for then Vice President Joseph Estrada's bid for the presidency, it was initially aligned with NPC and LDP in the LAMMP coalition, and was part of the *Puwersa ng Masa* coalition in 2001. By 2004 it had become a minor player.
Leadership. Horacio Morales (party president)

Probinsya Muna Development Initiatives (Promdi). Formed in 1997 by Cebu Governor and Ramos advisor Emilio Osmeña, as a vehicle for his presidential bid in 1998, Promdi draws on regional resentment in the Visayas and

Mindanao towards the political dominance of Manila (*promdi* is a slang term for someone "from the provinces"). In 2001 Promdi was part of the PPC and in 2004 a member of *Alyansa Pag-asa*.
Leadership. Emilio Osmeña.

United Negros Alliance (UNA). A regional party of Negros province supporting the interests of Eduardo Cojuangco, and aligned in 2001 with the PPC.
Leadership. Eduardo Cojuangco.

Poland

Capital: Warsaw
Population: 38,626,349 (2004E)

Communist rule effectively collapsed in Poland after the June 4, 1989, semi-democratic elections that brought to power the first non-communist government in Eastern Europe since the 1940s, led by Tadeusz Mazowiecki. Subsequently Poland embarked on a process of political, economic and social transformation aiming at first the introduction, and later the consolidation of democracy, a market economy, and re-direction of the country's foreign policy with the specific aim of joining NATO and membership of the European Union. The country became a member of NATO on March 12, 1999 and of the EU on May 1, 2004.

In 1997 a new constitution was approved in a nationwide referendum. Under the constitution the President (Head of State) is popularly elected for five-year term. He appoints the Prime Minister subject to parliamentary approval. Legislative authority is vested in a bicameral National Assembly (*Zgromadzenie Narodowe*) elected by universal adult suffrage for a four-year term. The upper chamber, the Senate (*Senat*) comprises 100 members, of whom 94 are returned from 47 two-member provinces and three each from the provinces based on Warsaw and Katowice. The lower house, the *Sejm*, is composed of 460 deputies elected by a system of proportional representation that requires party lists (except those representing ethnic minority communities) to obtain at least 5% (8% for coalitions of parties) of the vote. The threshold rule was introduced because the parliamentary elections of October 1991 had produced a highly fragmented *Sejm* in which 29 parties or groups had obtained representation.

The first round of presidential elections on Oct. 8, 2000, resulted in outright victory for the incumbent candidate of the Democratic Left Alliance (*Sojusz Lewicy Demokratycznej* – SLD), Aleksander Kwasniewski, with 53.9% of the vote. Eleven other candidates stood in these elections. His closest rival, Andrzej Olechowski, only summoned 17.3% of the votes.

Elections to the *Sejm* on Sept. 23, 2001, on a turnout of 45%, resulted in a coalition of the Democratic Left Alliance (SLD) and the Union of Labour (*Unia Pracy* – UP) winning 219 seats (with 41.3% of the vote), the Citizens' Platform (*Platforma Obywatelska* – PO) 63 (12.7%), Self-Defence (*Samoobrona*) 53 (10.0%), Law and Justice (*Prawo i Sprawieliwosc* – PiS) 47 (9.8%), the Polish Peasant Party (*Polskie Stronnictwo Ludowe* – PSL) 42 (8.8%) and League of Polish Families (*Liga Polskich Rodzin* – LPR) 34 (7.7%), with one seat being taken by the German minority. In simultaneous Senate elections the SLD-UP coalition won 75 of the 100 seats. The result saw a shift of power away from the right-wing Solidarity Alliance government (AWS) elected in

1997, back to the former communist SLD, which had been in power in 1993-97. The party, however, failed to gain an overall majority in the *Sejm*. At the same time older formations – including the Solidarity bloc – failed to surmount the 5% threshold for entry into parliament.

Leszek Miller, leader of the SLD, became Prime Minister in a coalition government with the Polish Peasant Party (PSL) and the small left-wing Union of Labour. He inherited from the previous right-wing government a legacy of soaring unemployment and looming financial crisis, but promised to lead Poland into the European Union and put the country's economy back on track. Following earlier tensions, the coalition collapsed on March 1, 2003, when Miller ejected the PSL from the government after the party voted in parliament against government tax proposals. The departure of the PSL left the Miller government with only 212 seats in the 460-seat *Sejm*.

Following the collapse of the coalition the Polish government was in perpetual crisis. Miller led a minority administration damaged by factional battles, financial scandals, and an inability to tackle Poland's biggest economic challenge – high unemployment of 20%. The unemployment rates that have grown continually in the last few years hit hardest at young people; one third of all unemployed are less than 30 years old. In January 2004, in an attempt to shore his government's dwindling support Miller replaced the Finance Minister, who was blamed for failing to revive Poland's floundering effort at privatizing state-owned companies, and reshuffled other posts in the cabinet. But these changes did not forestall a further decline in his government's support and in fact accentuated internal party disintegration. On March 25, 2004, 22 of the 192 SLD members of the *Sejm*, led by Marek Borowski, the speaker of the lower house, declared their decision to break away and form a new party – the Social Democracy of Poland (SDPL). Leszek Miller announced his resignation the following day with effect from May 2 – the day after Poland formally joined the European Union.

Following Miller's departure President Kwasniewski asked Marek Belka, former Finance Minister and official in the US-led administration in Iraq, to form the new government. Belka failed to secure a parliamentary vote of confidence on May 15, with 262 votes against his government and 188 in favour. However, despite the lack of parliamentary approval he was again nominated by the President and remained in a caretaker capacity for almost two months, thus accentuating the political crisis. The political stalemate halted work on key fiscal reforms. While trying to secure parliamentary approval for Belka's government, Kwasniewski and the ruling SLD elite sought to prevent the holding of parliamentary elections in August 2004 – a year ahead of the scheduled parliamentary poll. Early elections could have resulted in substantial gains for the populist Self-Defence Party. Finally on June 24 Marek Belka won a parliamentary confidence vote, bringing to a close months of political instability. Belka's victory, by a 236-215 vote of deputies, averted snap elections and gave the deeply unpopular ruling left a chance to regroup and win back popularity badly damaged by the previous cabinet. As a concession to win support the new Prime Minister promised to call another confidence vote in October 2004 to ensure he still had a mandate. Belka has sought to distance his government from party political interests by appointing independent figures – some of whom are even linked to opposition groups – to government positions, though this has worsened his relations with the SLD, the main government party, and could make it more difficult to push controversial legislation through parliament.

On June 13, 2004, Poles took part in their first elections to the European Parliament. Eight political parties cleared the 5% threshold, thus being able to claim some of the 54 seats ascribed to Poland. The turnout in the elections of 20.42% was the second lowest in the EU, after Slovakia. The elections resulted in a heavy defeat for the governing coalition. The final outcome was as follows: Citizens' Platform, 24.1% of the vote – 15 seats; League of Polish Families, 15.2% – 10 seats; Law and Justice, 12.7% – 7 seats; Self-Defence, 10.8% – 6 seats; Democratic Left Alliance–Union of Labour, 9.3% – 5 seats; Freedom Union, 7.3% – 4 seats; Polish Peasant Party, 6.3% – 4 seats; Social Democracy of Poland, 5.3% – 3 seats; Others (twelve parties) 8.3%.

Citizens' Platform
Platforma Obywatelska (PO)
Address. ul Andersa 21 Warsaw 00 159
Telephone. +48 22 635 78 79
Fax. + 48 22 635 76 41
Website. www.platforma.org
Leadership. Donald Tusk (chairman); Jan Maria Rokita (chairman of parliamentary group)

The centrist strongly pro-EU PO was launched on Jan. 19, 2001 by Maciej Plazynski, Speaker of the *Sejm* and hitherto a member of the then ruling Solidarity Electoral Action (AWS), supported by such luminaries as Donald Tusk, Deputy Speaker of the Senate and hitherto a member of the Freedom Union (UW), and independent politician Andrzej Olechowski, who had come second in the 2000 presidential election with 17.3% of the vote. Declaring its basic aim as being to prevent the Democratic Left Alliance (SLD) from regaining power in the forthcoming parliamentary elections, the new formation quickly attracted substantial support from within both the UW and the AWS.

In the September 2001 parliamentary elections the PO failed to prevent an SLD victory, but came a creditable second with 63 of the 460 lower house seats. In the simultaneous upper house elections the PO formed part of the five-party Senate 2001 Bloc, which won 16 seats. Citizens' Platform is the only party in Poland which has chosen candidates for parliament using a pre-election process.

Citizens' Platform proposes: flat tax rates of 15%, and 15% VAT; higher education reform, with equal rights for private and public universities; that more spending should be done by local government, less by central government; privatization and demonopolization; direct elections of mayors and governors; private health care; majoritarian parliamentary elections; labour law reform; narrowing the privileges of trade unions; giving the National Bank of Poland full control over monetary policy; and reduction in the number of MP in the *Sejm* from 460 to 230, and depriving them of parliamentary immunity. The party scored highly in opinion polls throughout 2003-04. The rise in its popularity is in part the effect of Jan Maria Rokita's participation in the *Sejm*'s Special Inquiry Commission where he managed to uncover many irregularities in the post-communist SLD-run cabinet.

Citizens' Platform was the leader in the 2004 elections to the European Parliament, with 24.1% of the votes, taking 15 of the 54 seats reserved for Poland in the EP.

Democratic Left Alliance
Sojusz Lewicy Demokratycznej (SLD)
Address. ul. Rozbrat 44A, Warsaw 00-419
Telephone. +48 22 621–0341
Fax. +48 22 621–6657

Email. bsz@sld.org.pl
Website. www.sld.org.pl
Leadership. Krzysztof Janik (chairman); Jozef Oleksy (deputy chairman); Jerzy Szmajdzinski (deputy chairman); Katarzyna Piekarska (deputy chairman); Grzegorz Napieralski (deputy chairman); Marek Dyduch (secretary-general)

The SLD was created on April 15, 1991, prior to parliamentary elections that year, as an alliance of Social Democracy of the Polish Republic (SRP) and the All-Poland Trade Unions' Federation (OPZZ). The SRP had been founded in January 1990 upon the dissolution of the former ruling (Communist) Polish United Workers' Party (PZPR), of which it was the organizational successor, although with democratic socialism replacing its previous Marxism–Leninism. The OPZZ derived from the official trade union federation of the communist era.

The PZPR had been created in 1948 as an enforced merger of the Polish Workers' Party (successor to the Polish Communist Party established in 1918) and the Polish Socialist Party. It had then been in power through four decades of Soviet-decreed one-party rule, featuring a renunciation of Stalinism and some liberalization under Wladyslaw Gomulka (1956–70) and further reforms under Edward Gierek (1970–80), although the regime had remained essentially authoritarian and loyal to Moscow. PZPR rule had therefore come under severe challenge in the 1980s from the Solidarity free trade union movement led by Lech Walesa, which in June 1989 had made a virtual clean sweep of unreserved seats in partially democratic elections. Constitutional amendments in December 1989 had deleted reference to the PZDR's "leading role" and the goal of socialism, following which the PZPR had transformed itself into the SRP.

The SRP's communist-era organizational strength enabled the SLD alliance to win 60 lower house seats in the October 1991 elections on a 12% vote share. Its deputies faced considerable hostility in the new legislature, but the SLD image improved rapidly as transition to a market economy took a social toll and the ruling centre-right parties became increasingly fragmented. In the September 1993 parliamentary elections the SLD became the largest formation in the *Sejm*, winning 171 seats with 20.4% of the vote. Despite its seniority, the SRP opted to accept participation in a coalition headed by the Polish Peasant Party (PSL), being conscious of its need to prove its democratic credentials. The PSL held the premiership until February 1995, when Jozef Oleksy of the SLD/SRP took the post, amid chronic strains between the government and President Lech Walesa, who used his power of veto on a series of measures adopted by parliament.

The SLD candidate in the November 1995 presidential elections was the then SRP leader, Aleksander Kwasniewski, who headed the first-round polling with 35.1% of the vote and defeated Walesa in the second with 51.7%, supported by over 30 other groupings. In February 1996 Oleksy was replaced as Prime Minister by Wlodzimierz Cimoszewicz of the SLD. In the September 1997 parliamentary elections the SLD increased its share of the vote to 27.1%, but its lower house representation fell to 164 seats, well below the total achieved by the new centre-right Solidarity Electoral Action (AWS). The SLD therefore went in opposition, taking some consolation from a strong performance in local elections in October 1998.

Having supported Poland's accession to the North Atlantic Treaty Organization (NATO) in March 1999, the SLD formally established itself as a unitary party two months later. At the first congress of the new SLD in December 1999, former Interior Minister Leszek Miller was elected chairman and the party undertook to support pro-market reforms. The party also reiterated its strong support for Polish accession to the European Union. Benefiting from the unpopularity of the AWS-led government, the SLD secured the re-election of Kwasniewski in presidential elections in October 2000 in which he won 53.9% in the first round.

The SLD contested the September 2001 parliamentary elections in alliance with the Union of Labour (UP). Their joint ticket secured 219 of the 460 seats and an overall Senate majority of 75 out of 100 seats. During the electoral campaign the party vowed to abolish the Senate, criticizing it as a useless and expensive cog in the legislative process. However, having won three-quarters of the seats in the upper-house it quickly dropped the idea. Leszek Miller became Prime Minister of a coalition government comprising SLD, UP and PSL. The coalition collapsed in March 2003.

During 2003-04 the party was battered by corruption scandals, high unemployment and accusations that it had abandoned its left-wing roots by supporting economically liberal politics. As the party's leader, Miller accepted the need for the SLD to distance itself from its roots as the successor to the communist party, but many rank-and-file members proved reluctant to make the same ideological journey. In a sign of the depth of the SLD's troubles, about 70,000 members quit or were removed during 2003 when the party undertook an internal screening of its membership, leaving only 80,000 members. By 2004 the party had suffered a dramatic decline in popular support with a drop from 30% to just below 10% in the opinion polls. The Miller government failed to get to grips with Poland's stagnating economy and was running a budget deficit at around 5-6%. Miller's position became untenable after Marek Borowski, speaker of the *Sejm*, led 22 rebel deputies to form a breakaway party – the Social Democracy of Poland (SDPL).

In the June 2004 elections to the European Parliament the SLD received 9% of the votes, giving it 5 of the 54 seats reserved for Poland in the EP. The SLD is a full member of the Socialist International.

Freedom Union
Unia Wolnosci (UW)
Address. ul. Marszalkowska 77–79, Warsaw 00024
Telephone. +48 22 827 5047
Fax. +48 22 827 7851
Email. uw@uw.org.pl
Website. www.uw.org.pl
Leadership. Wladyslaw Frasyniuk (chairman)
The UW was founded on March 24, 1994 as a merger of the Democratic Union (UD) and the smaller Liberal Democratic Congress (KLD). Both these parties had roots in the Solidarity movement. The new formation declared itself to be strongly of the democratic social centre, favouring market-oriented reforms but urging sensitivity to resultant social problems.

Of the UW components, the pro-privatization KLD had been founded in 1990 under the leadership of journalist Donald Tusk and had won 37 seats in 1991, but had failed to reach the 5% threshold for representation in the 1993 elections. The UD had been created in 1990 to support the presidential candidacy of then Prime Minister Tadeusz Mazowiecki (unsuccessfully) and had been identified with the "shock therapy" economic programme of then Finance Minister Leszek Balcerowicz, although it had called for more consideration to be given to its social consequences. In the October 1991 parliamentary elections the UD had won 62 seats on a 12.3% vote share, gaining the small distinction of having more seats than any of the other 28 parties with representation. Its then leader, Bronislaw Geremek, had tried and failed to form a government, so that the UD had become the main opposition to the 1991–92 government headed by

the Democratic Left Alliance (SLD). Upon its fall in June 1992, Hanna Suchocka of the UD had formed a seven-party coalition, becoming Poland's first female Prime Minister; but her government had fallen in May 1993. In the September 1993 parliamentary elections the UD had improved its representation to 74 seats under the new leadership of Balcerowicz, but had slipped to 10.6% of the vote and third place in the parliamentary order, becoming the principal opposition to an SLD-dominated government.

The candidate of the merged UW in the 1995 presidential elections was Jacek Kuron, who achieved third place in the first round with 9.2% of the vote. In the September 1997 parliamentary elections the UW won 13.4% and 60 seats and decided, somewhat reluctantly, to join a centre-right coalition headed by Solidarity Electoral Action (AWS) in which Balcerowicz returned to the Finance Ministry and Geremek became Foreign Minister. Both ministers won international praise, Geremek for supervising Poland's admission to NATO in 1999 and both for advancing Poland's aspiration to join the European Union. However, opposition to Balcerowicz's further economic reform plans on the populist wing of the AWS resulted in the UW leaving the government in June 2000. The UW did not present a candidate in the October 2000 presidential election.

Following Balcerowicz's appointment as president of the Polish Central Bank in December 2000, Geremek resumed the UW chairmanship. In January 2001 the UW was weakened when Tusk and other prominent centrist politicians formed the Citizens' Platform (PO), which was joined by a substantial number of UW members. The rump UW accordingly failed to retain any seats in the September 2001 lower house elections, winning only 3.1% of the vote, although in simultaneous upper house elections it retained representation within the five-party Senate 2001 Bloc, which won 16 seats. Soon after the elections Geremek resigned as UW chairman and was replaced by Wladyslaw Frasyniuk.

Surprisingly, due to extremely low voter turnout, the party managed to cross the required 5% threshold in the 2004 European Parliament elections, reciving 7% votes and 4 of 54 seats reserved for Poland in the EP.

The UW is a member of the European Liberal, Democrat and Reform Party and an associate member of the European People's Party.

Law and Justice
Prawo i Sprawieliwosc (PiS)
Address. ul. Nowogrodzka 85/86 , Warsaw 02 018
Email. biuro.organizacyjne@pis.org.pl
Telephone. +48 22 621 5035
Fax. +48 22 621 6767
Webside. www.pis.org.pl
Leadership. Lech Kaczynski (chairman); Ludwik Dorn (vice-president, chairman of the parliamentary group)
This centre-right formation was launched in April 2001 by Lech Kaczynski (a former Justice Minister) and his twin brother Jaroslaw Kaczynski, who had been close associates of Lech Walesa before and during the latter's presidency (1990–95). Declaring its opposition to the incumbent Solidarity Electoral Action (AWS) government, the PiS effectively succeeded the Centre Alliance (*Porozumienie Centrum*, PC), which had been allied with the AWS in the 1997 parliamentary elections.

The PC had been founded in 1990 as an attempt to create a Polish version of the German Christian Democratic Union, i.e. a broad-based Christian-oriented party of the centre-right. It had backed the presidential candidacy of Walesa and had subsequently became the core component of the Centre Citizens' Alliance (POC), which had won 44 *Sejm* seats (with 8.7% of the vote) in the October 1991 parliamentary elections, becoming the fourth largest grouping and providing the Prime Minister (Jan Olszewski) of the subsequent centre-right government. Following the collapse of the latter in June 1992, a PC congress had voted to expel Olszewski and other elements (later regrouped in the Movement for the Reconstruction of Poland). After agreeing to join the seven-party government formed in July 1992 by Hanna Suchocka of the Democratic Union (later the Freedom Union), the PC had unexpectedly withdrawn its support later in the year to become part of the "soft" opposition. Having narrowly failed to retain representation in the September 1993 elections (winning only 4.4% of the vote), the PC had supported Walesa's unsuccessful re-election bid in November 1995 before becoming part of the victorious AWS bloc in the 1997 elections.

Drawing support previously given to the AWS, the new PiS polled strongly in the September 2001 parliamentary elections on an anti-corruption platform, winning 47 lower house seats with 9.8% of the vote. In the simultaneous upper house elections the PiS was part of the five-party Senate 2001 Bloc, which won 16 seats.

The party proposes the establishment of an anti-corruption agency, reform of the police system, amending the Constitution to end the system of two centres of executive power, the establishment of a national guard, far reaching reform of the secret service, changes to the justice department, amendments to the penal proceedings code and the penal code in order to facilitate and accelerate the punishment of criminals, and to increase government spending on health and education.

The PC was an affiliate of the Christian Democrat International and of the International Democrat Union.

League of Polish Families
Liga Polskich Rodzin (LPR)
Address. ul. Hoza 9, Warsaw 00-528
Telephone. +48–22 622-3648
Fax. +48–22 622-3138
Website. www.lpr.pl/
Leadership. Roman Giertych (president of the Congress); Marek Kotlinowski (chairman of the Main Board); Zygmunt Wrzodak (chairman of the Political Board); Sylwester Chruszcz (vice chairman); Bogdan Pek (vice chairman); Robert Srak (vice chairman); Wojciech Wierzejski (treasurer)

The radical Catholic LPR was formed in April 2001 in advance of the September 2001 parliamentary elections by ten small groups and parties that stood little chance of getting into parliament on their own, on a platform of opposition to Polish membership of the European Union because of its liberal abortion laws. The group's platform was pure right-wing populism – staunchly Catholic and strongly nationalistic – and it appealed to the most conservative and xenophobic parts of Polish society. It also advocated close alliance with the USA to protect Poland from domination by either Germany or Russia. Attracting rural voters who had previously supported Solidarity Electoral Action (AWS), the LPR entered the *Sejm* at its first attempt, winning 34 seats with 7.7% of the vote, and also securing two Senate seats.

Since 2001 the LPR has grown in strength becoming, by the time of the June 2004 European elections, the second most popular political party. The League has a strongly clerical streak to it, and has established a close association with the conservative and controversial Catholic radio station, Radio Maryja, which is based in Torun and run by a cleric who has been criticized by the hierarchy of the Roman Catholic Church in Poland. The League denounces the EU as a vehicle for German domination, and looks forward to amiable relations with the UK Independence Party. "We would like to see the European Union disintegrate," explained Maciej Giertych, one of its successful candidates in the European Parliament elections, in which the LPR secured 15.92% of the vote and won 10 of the 54 seats allocated to Poland.

Movement for the Reconstruction of Poland
Ruch Odbudowy Polski
Address. ul. Piekna 22 lok. 7, Warsaw 00 - 549
Telephone. +48 22 625 32 82
Fax. +48 22 625 32 82
Email. biuro@rop.sky.pl
Website. www.rop.sky.pl
Leadership. Jan Olszewski (chairman); Seweryn Jaworski (vice chairman); Wincenty Pawlaczyk (vice chairman); Eugenia Multanska (secretary); Dariusz Cieslak (treasurer)

The ROP was launched by former Prime Minister Jan Olszewski on a strongly pro-market platform following his respectable fourth place (with 6.9% of the vote) in the first round of the November 1995 presidential elections. Then identified with the Centre Alliance (PC), Olszewski had become Prime Minister in the wake of the 1991 parliamentary elections, heading a centre-right coalition which had eventually fallen in June 1992 in acrimonious circumstances related to the government's proposal to publish lists of communist-era collaborators. Expelled from the PC, Olszewski had become leader of the more right-wing Movement for the Republic (RdR) but had been replaced in December 1993 following the general defeat of pro-market formations in the September 1993 parliamentary elections, although in April 1994 he had become honorary chairman of a deeply divided RdR.

The ROP won only six lower house seats (from 5.6% of the vote) and five Senate seats in the September 1997 parliamentary elections, thereafter becoming part of the ruling Solidarity Electoral Action (AWS) bloc. In the September 2001 elections much of AWS/ROP support switched to new centre-right formations such as Law and Justice (successor to the PC), so that the ROP shared in the AWS failure to retain any lower house seats. In the simultaneous upper house elections, however, the ROP retained representation within the five-party Senate 2001 Bloc, which won 16 seats.

Polish Peasant Party
Polskie Stronnictwo Ludowe (PSL)
Address. 4 ul. Grzybowska, Warsaw 00131
Telephone. (48–22) 206020
Email. bpras@psl.org.pl
Website. www.psl.org.pl
Leadership. Janusz Wojciechowski (chairman)

The PSL was founded in 1945 by Stanislaw Mikolajczyk after the leadership of the historic Peasant Party (founded in Galicia in 1895) had opted for close co-operation with the Communists. In November 1949, after Mikolajczyk had been ousted by leftist PSL members, the two groups merged as the United Peasant Party (ZSL), which became part of the Communist-dominated National Unity Front. The ZSL was thus committed to the goal of transforming Poland into a socialist society, although private peasant ownership of land was guaranteed by the Communist regime from 1956 and by constitutional guarantee from 1983. ZSL members were consistently included in the government and other state bodies under Communist rule. In 1987 the party backed a government programme for the democratization of political life and introduction of market mechanisms, while supporting the maintenance of the existing power structure.

In August 1989 a group of rural activists revived the PSL on the basis of its 1946 programme, becoming known as the Polish Peasant Party–Wilnanov (PSL–W). The following month the ZSL was included in the new Solidarity-led coalition government and in November relaunched itself as the Reborn Polish Peasant Party (PSL–O). Six months later, in May 1990, the PSL–O, PSL–W and some members of Rural Solidarity held a unification congress to constitute the present PSL, which aimed to establish itself as the "third force" in Polish politics. In September 1990 the PSL withdrew its support from the Solidarity-led government. The then PSL leader, Roman Bartoszcze, received 7.2% of the vote in the first round of presidential elections in November 1990.

In June 1991 Bartoszcze was replaced as PSL leader by Waldemar Pawlak, who restored unity to the party and led it to a creditable 8.7% of the vote and 48 seats in the October 1991 *Sejm* elections, in which it headed a Programmatic Alliance list. Although it broadly supported the subsequent centre-right government, the PSL opposed its proposal to release secret police files to expose informers of the communist era. This issue brought down the government in June 1992, whereupon Pawlak was endorsed by the *Sejm* as the new Prime Minister, but was unable to form a government.

Benefiting from rural disenchantment with economic "shock therapy", the PSL polled strongly in the September 1993 parliamentary elections, becoming the second largest party with 132 seats in the *Sejm* on an overall vote share of 15.4% (and a historically high 46% of the peasant vote). It then opted to join a coalition government with the Democratic Left Alliance (SLD), which agreed that Pawlak should be Prime Minister in light of doubts about the SLD's political ancestry in the previous regime. The new coalition displayed tensions almost from the start, notably over government appointments, and in November 1994 the PSL deputy president was dismissed as chairman of the *Sejm*'s privatization committee on the grounds that he had tried to block or slow down the sell-off of state enterprises. It also came into protracted conflict with President Walesa and the latter's concepts of presidential government, the eventual result being Pawlak's resignation in February 1995 and the appointment of an SRP Prime Minister, although the SRP/SLD coalition was maintained. In the November 1995 presidential elections Pawlak received a modest 4.3% of the first-round vote.

The PSL's government participation came to an end at the September 1997 parliamentary elections, in which its vote share slumped to 7.3% and its *Sejm* representation to 27 seats. The following month Pawlak was replaced as party chairman by former Agriculture Minister Jaroslaw Kalinowski, a representative of the PSL's conservative Christian democratic wing which favoured tariff protection for Polish farmers. Over the next two years the PSL was weakened by the formation of at least two breakaway peasant parties, although in the October 2000 presidential election Kalinowski did better than his predecessor, winning 6% of the first-round vote.

The PSL further improved its position in the September 2001 parliamentary elections, winning 42 lower house seats on an 8.8% vote share, and also electing seven candidates to the Senate.

In September 2004 the PSL claimed membership of 120,000 and had organized a campaign to pull Polish troops out of Iraq.

Self-Defence
Samoobrona

Address. Aleje Jerozolimskie 30, Warsaw 00 024
Telephone. +48 22 625 04 72
Fax. +48 22 625 07 77
Email. samoobrona@samoobrona.org.pl
Website. www.samoobrona.org.pl
Leadership. Andrzej Lepper

Self-Defence first emerged as a new radical populist peasant trade union organization, formed in January 1992, as a consequence of earlier demonstrations and hunger strikes outside parliament in October-November on behalf of peasant debtors struggling with repayments. It continued to attract attention through the use of French-style road blockade protests and the occupation of the Ministry of Agriculture in April 1992. In the 1993 parliamentary elections it secured 2.78% of the vote but failed to enter the *Sejm*. In 1995 its leader, Andrzej Lepper, ran for President and gained 1.32% of the vote. The former collective farm director became a wild card of Polish politics by rising to public prominence in 2000 through media-seeking public actions that led to violent clashes between him, his supporters and the police.

Standing in the October 2000 presidential elections, Lepper came fifth with 3.1% of the vote. The party was formally launched in mid-2001 in opposition to Polish accession to the European Union, claiming that Poland's attempts to prepare for membership were already impoverishing Polish farmers. In the September 2001 parliamentary elections the *Samoobrona* list achieved a remarkable 10% vote share, which made it the third strongest group in the *Sejm* with 53 seats. For good measure, it also won three Senate seats. Following the elections Lepper became a deputy speaker of the lower house of parliament; however, after outrageous behaviour and violations of political *savoir-vivre* he was dismissed. The party has also marked its presence in the *Sejm* by unconventional disruptive behavior. Among their numerous exploits have been such diverse incidents as using their own loudspeakers or claiming that the largest opposition party, Citizens' Platform, met with members of the Taliban in Klewki (a small village near Olsztyn) to sell them anthrax. Several *Samoobrona* members of parliament are subject to criminal investigations on charges including forgery, tax evasion, insurance fraud, and hooliganism. Parliamentary immunity has allowed most to avoid prosecution. Lepper alone has faced more than 100 criminal charges. The website of the *Sejm* contains details of seven parliamentary investigations into his un-parliamentary behaviour.

Even following the September elections the party resorted to direct action. Self-Defence supporters, led by Lepper, dumped manure outside the Ministry of Agriculture and occupied the building; the party's MPs drove official limousines to a Warsaw rail junction and poured imported German grain on the railway tracks. However, the party enjoys large popular support, despite being very much a one-man-show. It calls for vastly increased government spending, a guaranteed minimum of 900 zlotys ($235) a month in social support, tax rises to 50% for high salaried personnel, a slowing of privatization, and the spending of the Central Bank's currency reserves. The party also wants to turn Poland towards markets in the former Soviet Union. According to Lepper "self-defence is not just about defending yourself... it is also about going on the attack". *Samobrona* opposes Poland's membership of the EU in general and the terms on which it acceeded in particular. In the June 2004 elections to the European Parliament it won 10.8% of the vote and 6 seats.

Social Democracy of Poland
Socjaldemokracja Polska (SDPL)

Address. ul. Bernardynska 14a, Warsaw 02 904
Telephone. +48 22 885 57 69
Fax. +48 22 840 60 08
Email. sdpl@onrt.pl
Website. www.socjaldemokracjapolska.org.pl
Leadership. Marek Borowski

The party was founded in April 2004 after 22 members of the ruling Democratic Left Alliance (SLD), including the speaker of the lower house of the Polish parliament, Marek Borowski, broke away from the party. As its founding members the party lists the names of 32 MPs and six Senators. In the European Parliament elections in June 2004 it secured three seats. Opinion polls carried out in September 2004 suggested it enjoyed the support of 9% of the electorate. Its name should not be confused with a former party, Social Democracy of the Republic of Poland – SdRP.

Solidarity Electoral Action
Akcja Wyborcza Solidarnosc (AWS)
Address. c/o Zgromadzente Narodowe, Warsaw 00902
Telephone. (48–22) 694–1934
Fax. (48–22) 694–1943
Website. www.aws.org.pl
Leadership. Jerzy Buzek (chairman)

The centre-right multi-party AWS is descended indirectly from the Solidarity independent trade union movement responsible for accelerating the demise of European communism in the 1980s under the leadership of Lech Walesa. Having been disowned by Walesa after his election as President in 1990, the Solidarity political wing had played a minor role in the early 1990s, failing to win *Sejm* representation in 1993. Following Walesa's narrow failure to secure re-election in 1995, a Solidarity congress in June 1996 resolved to form the AWS as a broad alliance to challenge the incumbent government dominated by the Democratic Left Alliance (SLD). Chaired by Solidarity leader Marian Krzaklewski, the new grouping attracted some 35 existing formations to its banner, notably the Christian National Union (ZChN), the Centre Alliance (PC), the Conservative Peasant Party (SKL), the Christian Democratic Labour Party (ChDSP) and the Christian Democratic Party (PChD).

Attracting substantial rural support, the AWS led the polling in the September 1997 parliamentary elections, winning 201 of the 460 lower house seats with 33.8% of the vote, well ahead of the SLD. It therefore formed a coalition government with the liberal Freedom Union (UW) under the premiership of Jerzy Buzek, while Krzaklewski became chairman of the AWS parliamentary group. At the end of 1997 about half of the AWS deputies formed the AWS Social Movement (AWS–RS), also under Krzaklewski's chairmanship, in a move to create a unitary party; the other half, however, preferred to remain affiliated to AWS component parties. In September 1998 Krzaklewski was re-elected leader of the Solidarity trade union at a congress which resolved that senior union and party posts could not be held by the same person. Accordingly, Krzaklewski was succeeded by Buzek as AWS–RS chairman in January 1999, although he remained chairman of the AWS parliamentary group.

Growing tensions in the coalition government culminated in the withdrawal of the UW in June 2000, leaving Buzek as head of a minority AWS government with eroding parliamentary and popular support. In the October 2000 presidential elections Krzaklewski came a poor third with only 15.6% of the vote, the SLD candidate being elected outright in the first round. In a bid to revive centre-right fortunes in advance of the forthcoming parliamentary elections, Buzek in January 2001, as chairman of the AWS–RS, took over the leadership of the overall AWS from Krzaklewski, who had been under further attack since his presidential election defeat. However, Buzek's efforts to create a more cohesive AWS bloc were rebuffed by the SKL (which in March 2001 withdrew from the AWS and aligned itself with the new Citizens' Platform), while the PC component mostly joined the new Law and Justice grouping. In May 2001, moreover, the Solidarity trade union federation formally withdrew from the AWS bloc.

In considerable disarray, what remained of the AWS adopted the suffix "of the Right" for the September 2001 parliamentary elections, only to experience widely forecast decimation. The grouping obtained only 5.6% of the vote and so failed to win any lower house seats, while in the simultaneous upper house elections it retained slender representation only by forming part of the five-party Senate 2001 Bloc, which won 16 seats.

The AWS is an associate member of the European People's Party.

Union of Labour
Unia Pracy (UP)
Address. 4 ul. Nowogrodzka, Warsaw 00513
Telephone. +48 22 628 5859
Fax. +48 22 625 6776
Email. biuro@uniapracy.org.pl
Website. www.uniapracy.org.pl
Leadership. Izabela Jaruga-Nowacka (chairperson)

The social democratic UP was founded in June 1992 as a merger of two small parliamentary groupings of Solidarity provenance, namely Labour Solidarity (SP), led by Ryszard Bulgaj, Aleksander Malachowski and Karol Modzelewski, and the Democratic Social Movement (RDS), led by Zbigniew Bulgaj and Wojciech Borowik, plus elements of the divided Polish Socialist Party (PPS) and the Great Poland Social Democratic Union. Its first leader was Ryszard Bugaj, a former underground Solidarity leader who had previously been prominent in the Democratic Action Civil Movement (ROAD) – later part of the Democratic Union, which became the Freedom Union – and had been an articulate critic of the economic "shock therapy" policies of the immediate post-communist period. Bugaj left the party in 1998.

Despite the paucity of its resources, the UP achieved an impressive 7.3% of the vote in the September 1993 parliamentary elections, winning 41 *Sejm* seats and becoming the main left-wing opposition to the new government dominated by the Democratic Left Alliance (SDL). It nevertheless suffered from a general swing to the right in the September 1997 parliamentary elections, slipping below the then applicable 5% barrier, and in 1998 lost several prominent members to the Freedom Union and other parties. Under the leadership of Marek Pol (2001-04) the rump UP responded by opting for a left-wing course and presenting a joint list with the SDL in the September 2001 parliamentary elections. In the contest the party won 16 seats in the *Sejm* and seven in the Senate.

The UP is a full member of the Socialist International.

Other Parties

Ancestral Home (*Dom Ojczysty*), a small party and part of the electoral alliance of the League of Polish Families. In 2004 it had four members of the *Sejm*.

Catholic-National Movement (*Ruch Katolicko-Narodowy*, RKN), a small party forming part of the electoral alliance of the League of Polish Families. In 2004 it had five members of the *Sejm*.
Website. http://rkn.kluby.sejm.pl
Leadership. Antoni Macierewicz (chairman)

Communist Party of Poland (*Komunistyczna Partia Polski*), a very small Marxist-Leninist party based on the Silesian town of Dabrowa Gornicza.
Email. kontakt@kompol.org
Website. www.kompol.org

Conservative-People's Party (*Stronnictwo Konserwatywno-Ludowe*, SKL), a small conservative party – part of the electoral alliance with Citizens' Platform. Following the departure of several of its MPs, including its former leader, Jan Rokita, who joined the Platform, the SKL had only two members of the *Sejm* in 2004.
Leadership. Artur Balasz (chairman); Irenesz Niewiarowski (chairman of parliamentary group)

Green Party (*Zieloni*), founded on Sept. 7, 2003, by several NGO groups concerned with ecological, human rights, feminist issues and national and sexual minorities.

Website. www.zieloni.org.pl
Leadership. Magdalena Mosiewicz, Jacek Bozek (co-chairpersons)

Polish Agreement (*Porozumienie Polskie*), a small party and part of the electoral alliance of the League of Polish Families. In 2004 it had three members of the *Sejm*.
Leadership. Jan Lopuszanski

Silesian Autonomy Movement (*Ruch Autonomii Slaska*, RAS), a regionalist party advocating autonomy for the Silesian region within the European Union. Its ultimate goal is to regain the autonomy Silesia briefly enjoyed when Poland was restored after World War I.

In 2002, the autonomy movement made headlines by achieving official recognition of the Silesian nationality, specifically the right to be listed in the national census conducted that year. The RAS claims that more than a million people "of Silesian nationality" live in Upper Silesia. RAS candidates during the 2001 parliamentary elections stood as part of the Citizens' Platform, but received only minimal support.
Address. Plac Wolnosci 7, 44-200 Rybnik
Telephone. +48 32 423 7822
Fax. +48 32 423 7822
Email. biuro.ras@RASlaska.org
Website. www.raslaska.org
Leadership. Jerzy Gorzelik (chairman); Jerzy Bogacki (vice chairman); Leon Swaczyna (treasurer)

Union of Political Realism (*Unia Polityki Realnej*), formed on Nov. 14, 1987, as an underground movement, Real Politics Movement (*Ruch Polityki Realnej*), it emerged in 1989. In the 1991 parliamentary elections it won 2.25% of the vote and three seats. It improved its performance to 3.18% in 1993, but failed to cross the threshold for parliamentary representation. Its significance has been declining ever since. In 2004 it had one member of the *Sejm*.
Leadership. Stanislaw Wojtera

Portugal

Capital: Lisbon
Population: 10,524,145 (2004E)

Under Portugal's 1976 constitution as amended, legislative authority is vested in the unicameral Assembly of the Republic (*Assembléia da República*), currently consisting of 230 members elected for a four-year term (subject to dissolution) by universal adult suffrage of those aged 18 and over according to a system of proportional representation in multi-member constituencies. The head of state is the President, who is popularly elected for a five-year term (once renewable) by absolute majority, a failure to achieve which in a first round of voting requires the two leading candidates to contest a second round. The President appoints the Prime Minister, who selects his or her ministerial team, all subject to approval by the Assembly. There is also a Supreme Council of National Defence, a 13-member Constitutional Court and an advisory Council of State chaired by the President. Portugal joined what became the European Union on Jan. 1, 1986, and since 2004 elects 24 members of the European Parliament

Portuguese political parties and parliamentary groups are eligible for annual subsidies from public funds, on the following basis: (i) a sum equivalent to 1/225th of the minimum national salary is payable on each vote obtained at the most recent Assembly elections; (ii) a sum equivalent to four times the minimum salary, plus one-third of the minimum national salary multiplied by the number of deputies in an Assembly group, is payable to defray deputies' secretarial costs.

Elections to the Assembly on March 17, 2002, resulted as follows: Social Democratic Party (PSD) 105 (with 40.21% of the vote); Socialist Party (PS) 96 (37.79%); Popular Party (PP) 14 (8.71%); Portuguese Communist Party–Ecologist Party The Greens (PCP-PEV) 12 (6.94%); Left Bloc (BE) 3 (2.74%). In a presidential election on Jan. 14, 2001, Jorge Sampaio (PS) was re-elected for a second five-year term with 55.8% of the vote.

Portugal has 24 seats in the new European Parliament. The elections to the EP held on June 13, 2004, resulted in the Socialist Party winning 46.4% of the vote and 12 seats, while nine seats (34.6% of the vote) were taken by the list Advance Portugal! of right-of-centre parties. The Communist Party took two seats (9.5%) and the Left Bloc one seat (5.1%).

Ecologist Party The Greens
Partido Ecologista Os Verdes (PEV)
Address. Rua da Boa Vista,n°83,3°Dto,1200-066 Lisbon
Telephone. (351–21) 396,02 91/396 03 08
Fax. (351–21) 396 04 24
Email. osverdes@mail.telepac.pt
Website.www.osverdes.pt
Leadership. Isabel Castro, Alfonso Luz (spokespersons)
The left-leaning PEV joined the Communist-dominated United Democratic Coalition (CDU) prior to the 1987 Assembly elections, obtaining representation in that and subsequent contests. In the March 2002 elections it again ran in alliance with the Portuguese Communist Party (PCP) and the PEV took two of the 12 Assembly seats won by the PCP-PEV coalition, as the CDU had become. It has a youth movement branch called *Ecolojovem*. The party is affiliated to the European Federation of Green Parties.

Left Bloc
Bloco do Esquerda (BE)
Address. Rua de S. Bento 698–1°, 1250–223 Lisbon
Telephone. (351–21) 388–5034
Fax. (351–21) 388–5035
Email. udp@esoterica.pt
Website. www.bloco.org
Leadership. Luís Fazenda, Francisco Louca, Miguel Portas
The BE was formed for the 1999 elections by three far-left parties, namely the Marxist–Leninist Popular Democratic Union (*União Democrática Popular*, UDP), the Trotskyist Revolutionary Socialist Party (*Partido Socialista Revolucionario*, PSR) and Politics XXI (*Politica XXI*).

In the June 1999 European Parliament elections the alliance took 1.8% of the vote and no seats. Standing on a platform of opposition to the "anti-working class" policies of the incumbent Socialist Party government, the alliance won 2.74% of the vote and two Assembly seats in the March 2002 national elections, while in the January 2001 presidential election Fernando Rosas of the BE took 3% of the vote. It won one seat in the June 2004 European Parliament elections, with 5.1% of the vote.

Popular Party (Democratic Social Centre-Popular Party)
Partido Popular (PP or CDS-PP)

Address. Largo Adelino Amaro da Costa 5, 1146-063 Lisbon
Telephone. (351–21) 886–9730
Fax. (351–21) 886–0454
Email. Sede-nacional@partidopopular.pt
Website. www.partido-popular.pt
Leadership. Paulo Portas (president)

Advocating a social market economy, the conservative Christian democratic PP was established in 1974 as the Democratic Social Centre (*Centro Democrático Social*, CDS). It quickly began using the suffix "Popular Party" (or People's Party) to distinguish itself from the main Social Democratic Party (PSD), being formally known as the CDS–PP until opting for the shorter PP title in the 1990s (although the CDS-PP designation persists).

The CDS was founded on the basis of an earlier Manifesto Association (*Associação Programa*) formed by Prof. Diogo Freitas do Amaral, who had been a member of the Council of State under the quasi-fascist Salazarist regime overthrown in 1974. The CDS was attacked by left-wing groups in 1974–75. In the April 1975 constituent elections, in which it allied with the Christian Democrats, it won 16 of the 250 seats. In 1976 it became the largest party in the new Assembly, with 15.9% of the vote and 42 of the 263 seats. The CDS joined a government headed by the Socialist Party (PS) in January–July 1978, but fought the 1979 and 1980 elections as part of the victorious Democratic Alliance, led by the PSD; Freitas do Amaral became Deputy Prime Minister in the ensuing coalition government.

The coalition ended in April 1983 and the CDS, standing alone, won only 12.4% and 30 seats in that month's Assembly elections; it then elected a new leader, Dr Francisco António Lucas Pires. In 1985 the CDS declined further, to 9.8% and 22 seats. The leadership of the CDS passed in 1985 to a former Salazarist minister, Prof. Adriano Alves Moreira. Freitas do Amaral, endorsed by the CDS and PSD, narrowly lost the second round of the 1986 presidential elections to Mário Soares of the PS. The CDS continued to decline, securing only 4.4% and four seats in the 1987 Assembly elections, and Freitas do Amaral was re-elected leader at a congress in January 1988.

What was now known as the PP won only five Assembly seats in the 1991 elections (again with a 4.4% vote share), after which Freitas do Amaral finally resigned the party leadership and was succeeded by Manuel Monteiro. In the European Parliament elections of June 1994, the party regained support, winning three of Portugal's 25 seats on a 12.5% vote share. This European success did not moderate the party's deep reservations about Portuguese membership of the European Union, which struck something of a chord with voters in the October 1995 Assembly elections, when the PP advanced to 9.1% of the vote and 15 seats.

Internal divisions in the PP from September 1996 eventually resulted in Monteiro being succeeded as leader by Paulo Portas. After an attempted alliance with the PSD had collapsed in March 1999, the PP contested the June 1999 European elections on its own, slipping to 8.2% of the vote and two seats. The party also lost ground in the October 1999 Assembly elections, winning a vote share of 8.3% and 15 seats. In the March 2002 elections the PP was able to secure a vote share of 8.71 % and 14 seats and strengthen the position of third largest party ahead of the Communist–Greens coalition. After one-month of negotiations the PP formed a coalition with the PSD as the senior partner. Three PP members became part of the Durão Barroso government, with Paulo Portas becoming Deputy Prime Minister and Minister of Defence. In the June 2004 European Parliament elections, competing in alliance with

the PSD in the coalition Advance Portugal! (*Forca Portugal*), the party retained its two seats.

The PP is an affiliate of the International Democrat Union. Its two European Parliament members sit in the European People's Party group. In 2001, the PP had a membership of 32,571.

Portuguese Communist Party
Partido Comunista Português (PCP)

Address. Rua Soeiro Pereira Gomes 3, 1600 Lisbon
Telephone. (351–21) 781–3800
Fax. (351–21) 796–9126
Email. pcp.dep@mail.telepac.pt
Website. www.pcp.pt
Leadership. Carlos Carvalhas (secretary-general); Bernardino Soares (parliamentary leader)

The PCP was founded in March 1921 by the pro-Bolshevik wing of the Socialist Party (PS) and was banned from May 1926 until April 1974. Its leader from the 1940s was Alvaro Barreirinhas Cunhal, a charismatic Stalinist who was imprisoned throughout the 1950s and was then in exile until 1974. The PCP took part in interim governments between May 1974 and July 1976. In April 1975 it won 30 seats (out of 250) in constituent elections, with 12.5% of the vote; in April 1976 it won 40 seats in the Assembly, with 14.6%, but in June its presidential candidate took only 7.6%. From 1979 to 1986 the PCP was in an electoral front – the Popular Unity Alliance (APU) – with the small Portuguese Democratic Movement (MDP/CDE). The PCP itself won 44 seats in the Assembly in 1979, 39 in 1980 and 44 in 1983. In 1985 the APU won 15.4% and 38 seats, almost all for the PCP. In the 1986 presidential elections the PCP at first backed Dr Francisco Salgado Zenha, but in the second round it reluctantly endorsed Mário Soares of the PS.

In the 1987 elections the PCP formed a new front, the United Democratic Coalition (CDU), along with a minority section of the MDP known as the Democratic Intervention (ID), some independent left-wingers and the Ecologist Party The Greens (PEV). The CDU secured 31 seats with 12.1% of the vote, but the PCP-led parliamentary bloc rose from fourth to third place as a result of the eclipse of the Democratic Renewal Party (PRD); it also retained its three seats in Portugal's first direct elections to the European Parliament held simultaneously. In early 1988 the PCP experienced internal divisions as it prepared for a congress, some members calling for "democratization" and the Cunhal leadership insisting on maintaining rigid pro-Soviet orthodoxy.

In the event, the 12th PCP congress in December 1988 showed some awareness of developments in the Soviet Union by making a formal commitment to freedom of the press and multi-party politics, the CDU being rewarded in the June 1989 European Parliament elections with four seats and 14.4% of the vote. Yet even as communism was collapsing all over Eastern Europe in 1989–90, the PCP majority maintained a hardline view of events, showing no sympathy with the popular aspirations to multi-party democracy. The electoral consequence was that the PCP-dominated CDU fell back to 17 seats (8.8% of the vote) in the 1991 elections and to 15 seats (8.6%) in October 1995. In between, the CDU slipped to three seats and an 11.2% vote share in the June 1994 European elections.

The June 1999 European elections brought a further reverse for the CDU, to 10.3% of the vote and two seats. In the October 1999 Assembly elections, however, the CDU reversed its long decline, winning 9.0% of the vote and 17 seats, of which the PCP took 15 and the PEV two. The PCP candidate in the January 2001 presidential election was António Simões de Abreu, who took 5.1% of the vote. During 2001 and 2002 a number of members voiced dissent about the leadership, leading to further divisions inside the party.

One major point was the demand to organize a party conference, so that such divisions and the strategy of the party could be discussed. The repercussions of this division led to the worst ever election result for the Communist-led coalition in the March 2002 elections, the PCP-PEV alliance, as the CDU had become, taking 6.94% of the vote and 12 seats – 10 seats for the PCP and two for the PEV. In the June 2004 European elections the CDU got 9.1 % and 2 seats.

The PCP-PEV representatives in the European Parliament sit in the European United Left/Nordic Green Left group. In 2001, the PCP had a membership of 131,000.

Social Democratic Party
Partido Social Democrata (PSD)

Address. Rua de São Caetano 9, 1296 Lisbon
Telephone. (351–21) 395–2140
Fax. (351–21) 397–6967
Email. psd@psd.pt
Website. www.psd.pt
Leadership. Pedro Santana Lopes (president); Miguel Relvas (secretary-general); Guilherme Silva (president of the parliamentary group)

Centre-right rather than social democratic in orientation, the PSD was founded in May 1974 as the Popular Democratic Party (*Partido Popular Democrático*, PPD) and adopted the PSD label in 1976, when the Portuguese political scene created by the 1974 revolution was heavily tilted to the left. The party took part in five of the first six provisional governments established after the April 1974 revolution. It was in opposition in June–September 1975 and in 1976–79; it supported the election of Gen. António Ramalho Eanes as President in 1976. It was the second largest party in the April 1975 constituent elections, with 27% of the vote, and in the April 1976 legislative elections, in which it took 24%.

Having supported the non-party government of November 1978–June 1979, the PSD fought the 1979 elections along with the Democratic Social Centre (CDS, later the Popular Party, PP) as the Democratic Alliance, winning 79 seats for itself. The then PSD leader (and party co-founder), Dr Francisco Sa Carneiro, became Prime Minister and continued in office after fresh elections in October 1980, in which PSD representation increased to 82 seats. Sa Carneiro died in December 1980 at the age of 46 and was succeeded by Dr Francisco Pinto Balsemão, also a co-founder of the PSD, who brought the Popular Monarchist Party (PPM) into the coalition in September 1981. The PSD held 75 seats in the April 1983 elections, which it fought alone, and in June it joined the Socialist Party (PS) in a new coalition government, with a new PSD leader, former Prime Minister (1978-79) Carlos Mota Pinto, as Deputy Prime Minister.

In October 1985 the PSD increased its vote share to 29.9% and won 88 seats – the largest bloc – in the Assembly, allowing it to form a minority government under Aníbal Cavaco Silva, who had been elected party leader in May 1985. He subsequently strengthened his control over the party and after the presidential elections of 1986, in which the PSD endorsed the losing CDS candidate, he opposed all suggestions of alliance with other parties. On April 3, 1987, his government lost a vote of confidence concerning the integration of Portugal into what became the European Union. In early elections in July 1987 the PSD greatly increased its vote, to 50.2% and 148 seats, giving it an absolute majority (the first in the Assembly since 1974). In simultaneous elections to the European Parliament, the nine PSD members appointed in January 1986 were replaced by 10 popularly-elected PSD members (from the total of 24 Portuguese representatives). In August 1987 Cavaco Silva was reappointed Prime Minister of an almost wholly PSD government.

The PSD retained governmental office in the October 1991 parliamentary elections, although with a slightly reduced majority of 135 of 230 seats on a 50.4% vote share. In the June 1994 European Parliament elections the party fell to 34.4%, taking only nine of the 25 Portuguese seats. This result and the PSD's negative opinion poll ratings impelled Cavaco Silva to resign from the party leadership in January 1995, although he remained Prime Minister until the October elections to prepare for a presidential challenge. Under the new leadership of Joaquim Fernando Nogueira, the PSD lost the October contest, although its retention of 88 seats on a 34% vote share was a better performance than many had predicted. Cavaco Silva's presidential ambitions were also thwarted by the swing of the political pendulum to the left. Standing as the PSD candidate in January 1996, he was defeated by the Socialist candidate in the first voting round, winning only 46.2% of the vote. The PSD's somewhat drastic response to these twin setbacks was to elect a new leader, namely Marcelo Rebelo de Sousa, a popular media pundit who had never held ministerial office.

Rebelo de Sousa lasted as PSD leader until March 1999, when the acrimonious collapse of plans for an alliance with the PP precipitated his resignation. He was succeeded by José Manuel Durão Barroso, under whom the PSD retained nine European Parliament seats in June 1999 (on a reduced vote share of 31.1%). In the October 1999 national elections the PSD slipped to 81 Assembly seats on a vote share of 32.3%. The PSD candidate in the January 2001 presidential election, Joaquim Martíns Ferreira do Amaral, was defeated by the Socialist incumbent with 34.5% of the vote. Due to the deteriorating budgetary and economic situation throughout 2001, Durão Barroso put the Guterres government under considerable pressure. It led to the resignation of Prime Minister Guterres after the defeat of the Socialist Party in the local elections. The call for new elections in March 2002 by President Jorge Sampaio led to the victory of the PSD under the leadership of Durão Barroso. The PSD got a 40.21% share of the vote and 105 seats. In the June 2004 European elections the PSD entered a coalition with the CDS-PP called Advance Portugal! (*Forca Portugal*) and achieved just 33.3 % and 9 seats. In July 2004 Durão Barroso became president of the European Commission and resigned as Prime Minister. He was succeeded by Pedro Santana Lopes as Prime Minister and president of the party.

The PSD is affiliated to the International Democrat Union and the Christian Democrat International. Its European Parliament representatives belong to the European People's Party/European Democrats group. The PSD has a membership of about 100,000.

Socialist Party
Partido Socialista (PS)

Address. Largo do Rato 2, 1269–143 Lisbon
Telephone. (351–21) 382–2021
Fax. (351–21) 382–2023
Email. info@ps.pt
Website. www.ps.pt
Leadership. José Socrates (general secretary); António Almeida Santos (president); António José Seguro (parliamentary group chairman)

Originally founded in 1875, the early Portuguese Socialist Party was a member of the Second International and played a minor role in the first period of democratic government in Portugal (1910–26). Forced underground during the period of the fascistic "New State" (1928–74), Socialists were active in various democratic movements. In 1964 Dr Mario Alberto Nobre Lopes Soares and others formed Portuguese Socialist Action (*Accão Socialista Portuguesa*, ASP), which led to the revival of the Socialist Party (PS) among exiles in West Germany in April 1973.

Soares was repeatedly arrested and banished from Portugal, but the April 1974 revolution permitted his return and the PS took part in the coalition government formed in May 1974. In April 1975 the party won 116 of the 250 seats in a Constituent Assembly which drew up a constitution aspiring to a "transition to socialism", although in July-September the PS was excluded from the government, along with other parties except the Portuguese Communist Party (PCP). In April 1976 the PS won 35% of the vote and 107 of the 263 seats in the new Assembly. In June it supported the successful presidential candidate, Gen. António Ramalho Eanes, who in July appointed Soares as Prime Minister of a minority PS government including independents and military men. That was followed in January-July 1978 by a coalition, also led by Soares, of the PS and the Democratic Social Centre (CDS, later the Popular Party, PP). The PS subsequently supported a government of independents formed in October 1978.

The PS later suffered numerous defections, was decisively defeated in the 1979 Assembly elections, and went into opposition. In June 1980 it formed the Republican and Socialist Front (*Frente Republicana e Socialista,* FRS) electoral coalition with the (now defunct) Independent Social Democratic Action party (ASDI) and the Left Union for a Socialist Democracy (UEDS, formed in 1978 by António Lopes Cardoso, a former PS Agriculture Minister). The FRS won 74 seats in the October 1980 Assembly elections. Reforms in 1981 (since reversed) increased the power of the PS general secretary, leading to dissent within the party. In the April 1983 elections the PS obtained 36.2% of the valid vote and 101 (out of 250) seats; it then formed a coalition government with the Social Democratic Party (PSD). In 1985 that government lost a vote of confidence and in the ensuing elections the PS fell to 20.7% and 57 seats, being excluded from the minority government formed by the PSD. In February 1986, however, Soares was elected as the country's first civilian President in over 50 years, whereupon he resigned his PS posts. His 1986 opponents included two former PS ministers – Maria de Lourdes Pintasilgo, backed by the Popular Democratic Union (UDP) and Dr Francisco Salgado Zenha, backed by the PCP.

The sixth PS congress in June 1986 elected Manuel Vitor Ribeiro Constâncio (a former Finance Minister and central bank governor, regarded as a pragmatic left-winger) as party leader. It also significantly moderated the party's programme and altered its structure. A minority faction developed around Dr Jaime Gama, a former Foreign Minister close to Soares, but he was later reconciled with the leadership, whereafter the *Soaristas* (who wanted more active opposition to the PSD, including co-operation with the Communists) were led by the President's son, João Soares. Elections in July 1987 gave the PS 22.3% of the vote and 60 seats, so that it remained the leading opposition party; it also held its six European Parliament seats, which were subject to direct election for the first time. The October 1991 parliamentary elections resulted in the PS advancing to 72 seats (on a 30% vote share), but the party remained in opposition, with its leadership passing in February 1992 from Jorge Sampaio to António Guterres, a young technocrat with a non-ideological approach to politics. The party achieved an all-time high national vote in the December 1993 local elections and again outpolled the ruling PSD in the June 1994 European Parliament elections, in which its vote share was 34.9% and its seat tally 10 of the 25 allocated to Portugal.

In the October 1995 Assembly elections Guterres led the PS back to governmental office, albeit in a narrow minority position in terms of strict parliamentary arithmetic, its seat tally being 112 out of 230 (on a 43.9% vote share). The new minority PS government, which was expected to obtain the external support of the United Democratic Coalition on most key issues, announced a programme of accelerated privatiza-tion of state enterprises, combined with introduction of a guaranteed minimum wage, social and educational improvements and regional devolution for mainland Portugal. In January 1996 Socialist political authority was consolidated when PS presidential candidate Sampaio (who had become mayor of Lisbon) was elected to the top state post with a commanding 53.8% of the first-round vote.

The PS polled strongly in local elections in December 1997 and also in the June 1999 European Parliament elections, in which it advanced to 43.1% of the national vote and 12 seats. In the October 1999 national elections the PS retained power, winning exactly half of the 230 Assembly seats with a 44.1% vote share. In January 2001 Sampaio was re-elected for a second presidential term with 55.8% of the vote. During 2001 and 2002, however, the Guterres government was losing the capacity to control the economy and the budget. There also strong signs of weariness apparent in Guterres and the government after six years in power. All this contributed to a deterioration of the image of the government and the resignation of António Guterres after the local elections at the end of 2001. He was hastily replaced by one of the former ministers of the Guterres government, Eduardo Ferro Rodrigues. In the March 2002 elections, the PS declined sharply to 37.79% of the vote and 96 seats, although it remained strong enough to deny the PSD, which took 105 of the 230 seats, an absolute majority. Ferro Rodrigues was duly elected leader at a party conference in November 2002 and introduced a strategy to overcome the crisis after the departure of Guterres. In the June 2004 European Parliament elections, the PS retained its 12 seats.

After the appointment of Durão Barroso to president of the European Commission, Ferro Rodrigues started a campaign for new elections. The appointment of Santana Lopes by President Sampaio was regarded by Ferro Rodrigues as a defeat of this campaign and he, consequently, resigned. A new party leader, José Socrates, was duly elected with 80.1% of votes in September 2004.

The PS is a member of the Socialist International, of which Guterres became president in 1999. Its representatives in the European Parliament sit in the Party of European Socialists group. The party had a membership of 60,000 in 2002.

Other Parties

Communist Party of Portuguese Workers (*Partido Comunista dos Trabalhadores Portugueses*, PCTP), a Maoist faction which won a 0.9% vote share in the June 1999 European Parliament elections. Its leader obtained 1.6% in the January 2001 presidential election, standing as the candidate of the PCTP and the Portuguese Proletarian Revolutionary Movement (MRPP). In the legislative elections of March 2002 it received a 0.66 % share of the vote.
Leadership. António Garcia Pereira

Movement of the Earth Party (*Movimento do Partido da Terra,* MPT), an ecological party founded in the late 1990s and advocating sustainable development and a renewal of the Portuguese political system. It was able to create a small network comprising different cities in Portugal. It achieved 0.28% of the vote in the March 2002 legislative elections.
Address. Aven. Eng. Arantes Oliveira nº11/1A, 1900-221 Lisbon
Telephone. (351) 21 84 38 021
Fax. (351) 21 84 38029.
Email. mpt.terra@ clix.pt
Website. www.mpt.pt.
Leadership. Goncalo Ribeiro Teles (president); Paulo Trancoso (secretary-general)

National Solidarity Party (*Partido Solidariedade Nacional*, PSN), pensioners' party founded in 1990, won one Assembly seat on 1991, but none in 1995 or 1999; obtained 0.3% in the June 1999 European Parliament elections. Afterwards, it disappeared completely from the political scene.
Leadership. Manuel Sergio

Popular Monarchist Party (*Partido Popular Monárquico*, PPM), pro-market monarchist formation, won six Assembly seats in 1980, but none in subsequent elections; took 0.5% in the June 1999 European Parliament elections. The party received 0.23 % in the March 2002 national elections
Leadership. Gonçalo Ribeiro Telles & Augusto Ferreira do Amaral

Workers' Party of Socialist Unity (*Partido Operário de Unidade Socialista*, POUS), Trotskyist cell formed in 1979 by Socialist Party dissidents; won 0.2% in June 1999 European Parliament elections.
Address. Rua de Santo António Glórian n°52B, cave C, 1250-217 Lisbon
Email. pous@sapo.pt.

Qatar

Capital: Doha
Population: 793,341 (July 2002 est.)

The State of Qatar is a traditional monarchy that has been ruled by the Al Thani family since the nineteenth century. Previously a British protectorate, it became an independent state on Sept. 3, 1971. The current Amir is Hamad bin Khalifa Al Thani who, when the crown prince, ousted his father, Amir Khalifa bin Hamad Al Thani, in a bloodless coup on June 27, 1995. A provisional constitution was enacted on April 19, 1972, but there is no parliament and no elections have been held since. There is, however, a 35-member Advisory Council (*Shoura*). Women have the right to vote and some ran as candidates for the Central Municipal Council, but none were elected. A committee was appointed in June 1999 by the Amir to draw up a new constitution with provision for a national elected legislature. The Amir reiterated in his remarks to the committee members that he expects their efforts to lead to the establishment of an elected parliamentary body.

Political parties or pressure groups remain banned and no open opposition is tolerated. The government severely limits freedom of assembly, does not allow political demonstrations and severely limits freedom of association. The government does not allow political parties or membership in international professional organizations critical of the government or of any other Arab government. Private social, sports, trade, professional, and cultural societies must be registered with the government and the security forces monitor the activities of such groups.

Romania

Capital: Bucharest
Population: 22,355,550 (2004E)

Following the declaration of a communist "People's Republic" in 1947, Nicolae Ceausescu came to power in 1965. As a result of his willingness to resist the influence of Moscow, Ceausescu initially won wide respect in the West. However, the increasingly draconian leadership he showed in the 1980s led to disdain (albeit covert) for Ceausescu on his home soil, culminating in the revolution of December 1989. After revolt spread east from the Transylvanian city of Timisoara, the leader and his wife were tracked down, arrested and summarily executed on Christmas Day 1989.

A rapidly-formed collection of supposedly "reform-minded" ex-Communists – under the banner of the National Salvation Front (FSN) – proclaimed the right to lead an interim government. The group then ran in the first set of elections, in May 1990, and was able to dominate due to its monopoly of resources. The current PSD government, and incumbent President, Ion Iliescu, trace their roots to the FSN.

Under the constitution adopted on December 8, 1991, Romania has a semi-presidential system of government, akin to the arrangement operating in the French Fifth Republic. The President, as Head of State, and the Prime Minister, as Head of Government, share executive functions. In practice however, the presidency was the primary locus of power until around 2002, when Iliescu began to shift control to his hand-picked Prime Minister, Adrian Nastase. As Iliescu draws towards the end of his second full term as President at the end of 2004 (the maximum allowed under the constitution), this transferral of responsibility to Nastase is seen as preparation for Nastase's own candidacy for the presidency.

The President is elected by popular vote for a four-year term. The Prime Minister is appointed by the President, but should retain the confidence of parliament. The parliament is bicameral, consisting of the 140-member Senate (*Senat*) and the 345-member Chamber of Deputies (*Camera Deputatilor*). The legislature is populated through proportional representation, with elections every four years. To gain seats in either house, individual parties must pass a 5% threshold of the national vote; two-party alliances require 8%; the figure is 9% for three-party alliances and 10% for groupings of four parties or more. For minority groups, 19 Chamber seats were allocated in the 2000 elections – one seat for each of the recognized minority parties (with the exception of the Hungarian Democratic Union of Romania (UDMR), which easily passed the threshold).

The 1996 Political Parties Law allows for state subsidies for parties, to a maximum amount of 0.04% of budgeted government revenue. Under the 2001 budget, the total sum available in subsidies to parties was 58 billion lei (around US$1.7 million).

Electoral contests since 1992 have produced successive major swings of the political pendulum. After their domination of post-transition Romanian politics, Ion Iliescu's largely leftist government was replaced in November 1996 by a coalition of the centre-right, headed by the Christian Democratic/National Peasants' Party (PNT-CD). Completing the "two turnover" test, the PNT-CD was then itself heavily defeated by Iliescu's renamed Romanian Social Democratic Party, in both the parliamentary and presidential elections of November 2000. Elections to the Chamber of Deputies resulted in the Social Democratic Pole – an alliance of the Romanian Social Democratic Party (PSDR), the Party of Social Democracy in Romania (PDSR) and the Humanist Party of Romania (PUR) – winning 155 seats (with 36.6% of the vote). The PSDR and PDSR then merged into the Social Democratic Party (PSD) in June 2001.

The Greater Romania Party (PRM) came in second, with 84 seats (19.5%). The Democratic Party (PD) was awarded 31 seats for a 7.0% share of the vote, the National Liberal Party (PLN) 30 (6.9%) and the UDMR, 27 (6.8%). The remaining 19 seats were allocated to the 19 ethnic minority parties. In simultaneous Senate elections the Social Democratic Pole parties won 65 seats, the PRM 37, the PD 13, the PLN 13 and the UDMR 12.

In presidential elections on Nov. 26 and Dec. 10, 2000, Ion Iliescu of the PDSR (who had previously been President in 1990-96) won in the second round with 66.8% of the vote, defeating Corneliu Vadim Tudor of the nationalist/populist PRM.

Elections are next scheduled for late in 2004.

National Peasant Party–Christian Democrat
Partidul National Taranesc–Cretin Democrat (PNT-CD)

Address. 34 bd. Carol I, sector 2, Bucharest 7000

Telephone. (40–1) 312–0603

Fax. (40–1) 312–3436

Email. contact@pntcd.ro

Website. www.pntcd.ro

Leadership. Victor Ciorbea (chairman); Ion Diaconescu (honorary chairman); Teodor Morariu (secretary-general)

The orgins of the PNT-CD can be traced back to the National Peasant Party (PNT), founded in 1869, which played a significant role in Romania's partially democratic inter-war period, but was banned by the Communists in 1947. Revived in December 1989 under veteran leader Ion Puiu, the party refused to co-operate with the post-communist National Salvation Front (FSN) because of the large number of former Communists within FSN ranks. Prior to the May 1990 elections, the bulk of the "historic" PNT opted to merge with a younger group, of Christian Democratic orientation, under the chairmanship of Corneliu Coposu – another veteran peasant leader, who had served 17 years in prison under the Communist regime before becoming Prime Minister in its final phase. The result of the merger was the current PNT-CD. Today, the party is generally centre-right, favouring a full market economy and the accession of Romania to the European Union.

Lacking resources and access to public media (due to the National Salvation Front's dominance thereof) the PNT-CD only won 12 Chamber seats in the elections of 1990. However, as a leading component of the centre-right Democratic Convention of Romania (CDR), the PNT-CD advanced to 42 seats in September 1992, when it also won 21 Senate seats. Coposu died in November 1995 and was succeeded by Ion Diaconescu, who led the PNT-CD and the CDR to a plurality win in the November 1996 elections. At this time, the CDR candidate, Emil Constantinescu, was also elected President, with 54.4% of the second-round vote. As the dominant coalition partner, PNT-CD won 88 of the CDR's 122 Chamber seats. Victor Ciorbea, of the PNT-CD, became Prime Minister of a centre-right coalition, which included the Democratic Party (PD), the National Liberal Party (PNL) and the Hungarian Democratic Union of Romania (UDMR). Interparty feuding resulted in the replacement of Ciorbea by Radu Vasile (also of the PNT-CD) in March 1998.

Following his loss of the Prime Minister's role, Ciorbea defected and founded the breakaway Christian Democratic National Alliance (ANCD) in April 1999. Meanwhile, the PNT-CD-led government descended into disarray amidst accelerating economic and social deterioration. In August 2000 the PNT-CD and four other parties re-launched the CDR, but in the November elections the so-called "CDR 2000" and its allies failed to surmount the threshold for representation. The PNT-CD's presidential candidate, Constantin Mugur Isarescu, came a poor fourth, with only 9.5% of the first-round vote.

In January 2001 Diaconescu was replaced as PNT-CD chairman by former Education Minister, Andrei Marga, who quickly succeeded in bringing Ciorbea's ANCD (also now without parliamentary representation) back into the party. However, the re-election of Ciorbea as chairman of the PNT-CD national committee in June 2001 prompted Marga to resign as party chairman the following month, complaining that he had been thwarted in his attempts to bring corrupt, former PNT-CD ministers to book. In August 2001, a dissident faction of Marga supporters, including former deputy chairman Vasile Lupu, held a rival congress which elected Lupu as chairman.

Following a series of mergers and splits, a number of splinter parties have emerged from the PNT-CD. Former President Emil Constantinescu now leads the Popular Action Party (AP) and Vasile Lupu is president of the Popular Christian Party (PPC). These two parties are loosely affliated.

The PNT-CD is a member of the Christian Democrat International and an associate member of the European People's Party, as well as an affiliate of the European Democrat Union.

Democratic Party
Partidul Democrat (PD)

Address. 1 allea Modrogan, sector 1, 71274 Bucharest

Telephone. (40–1) 230–1332

Fax. (40–1) 230–1332

Email. office@pd.ro

Website. www.pd.ro

Leadership. Traian Basescu (chairman); Alexandru Sassu (Chamber group leader); Marian Viorel Pana (Senate group leader); Mihai Stanisoara (executive secretary)

The PD is one of the derivative parties of the National Salvation Front (FSN). Having taken on a party identity in February 1990, the FSN had a landslide victory in the May elections, winning 66.3% of the vote and 263 Chamber seats. FSN leader Ion Iliescu was elected President with 85.1% of the vote. Iliescu then vacated the FSN leadership (in compliance with a law barring the head of state from serving as the leader of a political party) and the Front became divided between those favouring rapid economic liberalization and those supporting the President's more cautious approach. In March 1991, the first FSN national conference approved a radical free-market reform programme presented by then Prime Minister Petre Roman. The latter vacated the premiership in October 1991 and was re-elected FSN leader in March 1992. With these movements, the Iliescu faction broke away to form the Democratic National Salvation Front (which later became the Social Democracy Party of Romania, which, in turn, became the Social Democratic Party).

The FSN candidate (backed by the more right-leaning members of the ealier group), Caius Dragomir, came a poor fourth in the autumn 1992 presidential election, winning only 4.8% of the first-round vote. The party fared better in the concurrent parliamentary elections, winning 43 Chamber and 18 Senate seats on a vote share of over 10%. The following year it adopted the name of "Democratic Party." The PD contested the November 1996 elections within the Social Democratic Union (USD) alliance – which it formed with the Romanian Social Democratic Party. Roman came in third at the presidential poll, with 20.5% of the vote, and the PD won 43 Chamber seats its own right. The PD then joined the subsequent coalition government, headed by the centre-right Christian Democratic National Peasants' Party (PNT-CD). The PD then left the coalition briefly in February 1998, but rejoined two months later, when Radu Vasile replaced Victor Ciorbea as Prime Minister. Despite this reconciliation, the PD continued to have strained relations with the other coalition parties during the remainder of the government's term.

Given its willingness to join in coalition with right-leaning parties, the alliance between the Social Democrats and the PD collapsed, and so the PD contested the November-December 2000 elections on its own. Damaged by its membership of a deeply unpopular outgoing government, the PD suffered. Roman sank to sixth place, with less than 3% of the vote in the first round of the presidential contest. The party then backed Iliescu in his second-round victory over the leader of the far-right Greater Romania Party. In the parliamentary elections, the PD was reduced to 31 Chamber seats, with 7% of the vote, and to 13 Senate seats. It thereafter gave qualified external support to a minority government headed by what became the Social Democratic Party (PSD).

A post-election internal power struggle culminated in Roman being ousted from the PD chairmanship of an extraordinary party convention in May 2001, and replaced by the popular mayor of Bucharest, Traian Basescu. A declaration adopted by the party convention stated that the PD favoured "a market economy but not a market society." Roman showed his displeasure by resigning as PD leader in the Senate, while some of his supporters left the PD parliamentary caucus. The PD leadership responded by negotiating the absorption of the small National Alliance Party led by Virgil Magureanu, following the latter's separation from the Romanian National Unity Party (PUNR). Magureanu expressed confidence that the PD would assimilate the PD's nationalist doctrines.

In September 2003, the PD and the National Liberal Party (PNL) allied in preparation for the 2004 elections – going by the name *Alianta Dreptate si Adevar*, "Justice and Truth." After the withdrawl of PNL presidential candidate, Theodor Stolojan, just weeks before the elections, PD leader and Mayor of Bucharest, Traian Basescu, was put forward as the Alliance's presidential nominee.

The PD was admitted to membership of the Socialist International in November 1999.

Greater Romania Party
Partidul România Mare (PRM)
Address. str. Georges Clemenceau nr.8-10, sector 1 Bucuresti
Telephone. (40) 213130967
Fax. (40) 213126182
Email. prm@prm.org.ro
Website. www.prm.org.ro
Leadership. Corneliu Vadim Tudor (chairman); Augustin Lucian Bolcas (Chamber group leader); Gheorghe Funar (executive secretary)
Registered in June 1991, the PRM is the political wing of the extreme nationalist Greater Romania movement, which advocates strong government in pursuit of Romanian nationalist interests, including the recovery of Romanian-populated territories lost during World War II. Often accused of anti-semitism, the party also sees merit in the "patriotic achievements" of the Ceausescu regime.

Formally, the party identifies itself as being of the centre-left, from a socio-eocnomic perspective, and centre-right, from a socio-political perspective. Thus, by combining socialist economic platforms with populist nationalist rhetoric, the PRM attempts to appeal to a broad cross-section of the electorate. This, indeed, proved to be the case in the 2000 elections, when the party's leader, Corneliu Vadim Tudor, was able to take 28.3% of the vote (second place) in the first round of the presidential race, and the PRM was the second largest vote winner in the parliamentary elections.

This success built on foundations the party had laid in the early 1990s, when the PRM had won 16 Chamber and six Senate seats in the 1992 elections (with a vote share of 3.9%). The PRM then became one of the so-called

"Pentagon" parties, giving external support to the government of the Social Democracy Party of Romania (PDSR). In 1995, Tudor repeatedly urged the government to ban the Hungarian Democratic Union of Romania (UDMR), which he accused of planning a Yugoslav-style dismemberment of Romania. This polemic combined with other differences to result in the PRM withdrawing its support from the government in October 1995.

Tudor encountered problems in April 1996, when the Senate voted to withdraw his parliamentary immunity. This step exposed the PRM's leader to a range of legal actions, including some related to his extremist political views. Also in April 1996, a PRM congress endorsed a programme of action for the party in government. Proposed measures which again included banning the UDMR and placing restrictions on foreign investment in Romania. In September 1996, the PRM absorbed the small Romanian Party for a New Society (PRNS) which had been led by Gen. Victor Voichita. Despite this merger, the party only enjoyed small gains in the November 1996 elections, with Tudor coming in fifth in the presidential polling (4.7% of the vote) and the party taking 19 Chamber seats with 4.5%.

In late 1998 the PRM was strengthened when it was joined by Gheorghe Funar, the former leader of the far-right Romanian National Unity Party (PUNR). Further consolidation occurred in mid-1999, when the party absorbed Dorin Lazar Maior's Democratic Forces Party (PFD). This far-right consolidation combined with a general disenchantment at the social ramifications associated with the reforms of 1997-2000, to boost support for the PRM in the November–December 2000 elections. Placing second in the initial round of presidential elections, Tudor then went on to the run-off race. He took 33.2% of the second round vote, against the victorious Ion Iliescu of (what became) the Social Democratic Party (PSD). In the parliamentary contest, the PRM became the second largest party, taking 84 of the 346 Chamber seats on a vote share of 19.5%.

In 2001 the PRM mounted vigorous opposition to a bill granting certain language rights to ethnic Hungarians and other minorities and renewed its campaign to get the UDMR outlawed because of its alleged treachery. It also accused the PSD government of not properly opposing new Hungarian legislation which accorded special status to Hungarian minorities in neighbouring countries, including Romania.

Humanist Party of Romania
Partidul Umanist din România (PUR)
Address. 118 calea Victoriei, etaj 5, Bucharest
Telephone. (40–1) 212 9547
Fax. (40–1) 212 5301
Email. pur@itcnet.ro
Website. www.pur.ro
Leadership. Dan Voiculescu (chairman); Bogdan Pascu (first vice-president); Codrut Seres (secretary-general)
The PUR was founded in December 1991 as a social liberal formation, which aimed to build post-communist democracy and civil society. It obtained strong local representation in municipal elections in June 1996, but failed to win seats in the national parliamentary elections of November 1996. For the November 2000 elections the PUR joined the left-wing Social Democratic Pole, which mainly consisted of what would later becme the Social Democratic Party (PSD). Under the auspices of the Pole, the party was able to win six Chamber seats, and four in the Senate, and formed part of the resulting minority government. However, in August 2003, the PUR opted out of the coalition, due to both ideological and personal splits between the PUR and the PSD.

Now describing itself as the party of the SME business class, the PUR places itself "to the left of the PNL and to the right of the PSD."

Hungarian Democratic Union of Romania
Uniunea Democrata Maghiara din România (UDMR)
Romániai Magyar Demokraták Szövetsége (RMDSz)
Address. 8 str. Avram Iancu, sector 2, PO Box 34-26, Bucharest
Telephone. (40–1) 314–6849
Fax. (40–1) 314–4356
Email. elhivbuk@rmdsz.rdsnet.ro
Website. www.rmdsz.ro
Leadership. Béla Markó (chairman); Csaba Takács (executive chairman); Bishop László Tőkes (honorary chairman); Atilla Kelemen (Chamber group leader); Károly Szabó (Senate group leader)

The UDMR is the principal political vehicle of Romania's ethnic Hungarian minority. The party registered in January 1990, with the aim of furthering ethnic Hungarian rights within the framework of a democratic Romania. It took 7.2% of the vote in the May 1990 parliamentary elections, winning 29 Chamber and 12 Senate seats, so that it became the largest single opposition formation. Despite being affiliated to the centre-right Democratic Convention of Romania (CDR), the UDMR contested the September 1992 elections separately, winning 7.5% of the vote and 27 Chamber seats, while again returning 12 senators.

Following the resignation of Géza Domokos as UDMR chairman, the moderate Béla Markó was elected as his successor at a party congress in January 1993, after the more radical Bishop László Tőkes (hero of anti-Ceausescu protest actions in Timisoara at the outset of the Romanian revolution in 1989) had withdrawn his candidacy and accepted appointment as honorary chairman. The same congress called on the government to assist with the preservation of Hungarian language and culture, while calling for self-administration of majority Hungarian districts – rather than the full autonomy urged by some radicals.

In 1996, the UDMR came under increasingly fierce attacks from the extreme nationalist Greater Romania Party (PRM), which called openly for the UDMR to be banned. For the November 1996 presidential election, the UDMR candidate was Senator György Frunda, who came in fourth with 6% of the first-round vote. In the simultaneous parliamentary elections, the UDMR slipped to 25 seats with 6.6% of the vote. It then opted to join a coalition government headed by the CDR, despite suggestions the previous year by a CDR spokesperson that the UDMR was an extreme nationalist party.

While in coalition, frequent strains developed with CDR parties over Hungarian language rights. Still, the UDMR's government participation survived until the November–December 2000 elections, in which Frunda came fifth in the presidential contest, with 6.2% of the vote. In the parliamentary contest, the UDMR improved slightly to 27 seats – again taking 6.8% of the vote. Thereafter, the Union gave qualified external support to a minority government under the Social Democratic Party (PSD), on the understanding that legislation would be enacted granting more language rights to ethnic Hungarians. In 2001, the UDMR came under renewed attack from the PRM, this time for supporting Hungary's new legislation giving special status to ethnic Hungarians abroad. There was also internal UDMR dissent over its backing for the PSD government.

In 2003, the UDMR reaffirmed its cooperative arrangement with the ruling PSD, indicating that the two parties "will permanently cooperate" on policy matters at both the national and regional levels. Given the UDMR's willingness to go into coalition with the government party of the day – be they centre-left or centre-right – the notion of a "permanent cooperation" should be seen as somewhat contingent on the performance of the PSD.

The UDMR is a member of the European Democrat Union and the Christian Democrat International and an associate member of the European People's Party.

National Liberal Party
Partidul National Liberal (PNL)
Address. 86 bd. Aviatorilor, sector 1, 71299 Bucharest
Telephone. (40–1) 231–0795
Fax. (40–1) 231–0796
Email. secretargeneral@pnl.ro
Website. www.pnl.ro
Leadership. Theodor Stolojan (chairman); Mihai Voicu (secretary-general)

Dating from 1848 and founded as a party in 1875, the centre-right PNL suspended operations in 1947, so as not to expose members to Communist persecution, and was revived in January 1990. The party took third place in the May 1990 elections, winning 29 Chamber seats on a 6.4% vote share and 10 Senate seats, but was weakened by internal divisions that produced the breakaway Liberal Union. The PNL was a then a founding member of the Democratic Convention of Romania (CDR), but withdrew in April 1992 because of policy differences with other coalition members.

A PNL congress in February 1993 approved a merger with the New Liberal Party and elected Mircea Ionescu-Quintus as chairman. This appointment, however, was contested by the outgoing leader, Radu Campeanu, who had been the PNL candidate in the 1990 presidential elections. A Bucharest court chose to reinstate Campeanu in early 1994, but Ionescu-Quintus showed that he had majority support among party members. Merger with the New Liberals was finalized in May 1995, when the PNL also absorbed a faction of the Civic Alliance Party. It thus regained parliamentary representation of about a dozen deputies, although they were technically classified as independents.

As the party's name suggests, its focus is on a centre-right promotion of individual liberty – social, economic and political. A feature of the early PNL programme was the call for the restoration to the Romanian throne of the exiled King Mihai, who had been deposed by the Communists in 1947. In 1992, the former monarch declined nomination as the PNL presidential candidate, having briefly visited Romania in April that year (but later being twice barred from entry). Complications ensued for Mihai's claim to the throne when a Romanian court ruled in October 1995 that the first son of his father, the pre-war Carol II, was the rightful heir.

The PNL rejoined the CDR for the November 1996 elections, backing the successful presidential candidacy of Emil Constantinescu (CDR), and winning 25 Chamber seats under the CDR banner. The party became a component of the resultant CDR-led coalition government and was strengthened in February 1998 by absorbing the Civic Alliance Party (PAC). Nevertheless, frequent strains between the PNL and other CDR components were accompanied by internal divisions and defections, notably over the choice of a presidential candidate for 2000. In the event, the PNL contested the November–December 2000 elections outside the CDR and therefore escaped the obliteration suffered by the latter. The party's presidential candidate, Theodor Stolojan, came third in the first round with 11.8% of the vote, while in the parliamentary elections, the PNL advanced to 30 Chamber seats on a vote share of 6.9% and also won 13 Senate seats. A breakaway PNL list headed by former leader Radu Câmpeanu took only 1.4% of the vote.

In December 2000 the PNL agreed to give qualified external support to a minority government of what became the Social Democratic Party (PSD). Opposition to this arrangement was strongly expressed at a PNL congress in February 2001, which elected former Deputy Premier and Justice Minister Valeriu Stoica as party chairman in succession to Ionescu-Quintus. In May 2001 Stoica announced the abrogation of the agreement with the PSD, claiming that the government had failed to bring forward economic and political reforms.

In September 2001 the PNL further announced that it would merge with the Alliance for Romania (ApR). Former Presidential candidate, Stolojan, was elected leader of the PNL and initiated moves towards a further alliance with the Democratic Party, in preparation for the 2004 elections. The alliance was named *Dreptate si Adevar*, "Justice and Truth" in January 2004. Stolojan was to be the Alliance's candidate in the November 2004 elections, but was forced to withdraw from the race just weeks before the poll, due to health concerns. PD leader, Traian Basescu was then put forward as the Alliance's nominee.

The PLN is a member of the Liberal International.

Party of Romanian National Unity
Partidul Unitatii Natiunii Romane (PUNR)

Address. bulevardul Carol nr. 17, sector 2, Bucharest
Telephone. (40–21) 313-5375; 313-4644
Website. www.punr.ro
Leadership. Mircea Chelaru (president), Valeriu Tabara (first vice-president), Ioan Curtean de Hondol (secretary general)
Although the party has retained it its acronym of PUNR, the recent, very subtle name change – from the earlier Romanian National Unity Party – reflects minor structural changes that the right-wing, nationalist party has undergone in the past two years

The party began, in March 1990, as the political arm of the nationalist "Romanian Hearth" (*Vatra Romaneasca*) social movement, which aimed to recover the "greater Romania" borders of the inter-war period, and was strongly opposed to any special recognition of the rights of Romania's ethnic Hungarian minority.

Running on this platform, the party was fifth-placed in the September 1992 parliamentary elections, winning 30 Chamber and 14 Senate seats, on a vote share of some 8%. In August 1994, it opted to join the "red-brown" government coalition headed by the Social Democracy Party of Romania (PDSR). In mid-1995, serious coalition tensions arose when the PUNR demanded the foreign affairs portfolio and asserted that too many concessions were being made by Romania in its quest for better relations with Hungary. However, after the PDSR had threatened to either continue as a minority government or to bring about an early election, the PUNR moderated its position and remained in the ruling alliance.

Underlying differences remained, however, and were sharpened in October 1995 by the decisions of the Socialist Party of Labour and the fellow far-right Greater Romania Party (PRM) to withdraw external support from the government. The dismissal of the PUNR Communications Minister in January 1996 caused a new crisis, and led to PUNR's March announcement that it was definitely leaving the government. Although the group was again persuaded to change its mind, the PUNR had, by then, become an opposition party in all but ministerial status. An important factor at play was the party's desire to establish an independent image in the run up to the elections scheduled for November 1996. The PUNR was particularly concerned not to be outflanked on the nationalist right by the PRM.

In the latter context, the PUNR's then leader and presidential candidate, Gheorghe Funar, became a vocal critic of a draft treaty with Hungary tabled by the government in mid-1996, contending that its provisions on the rights of Romania's Hungarian minority amounted to a "national betrayal". One such outburst in early September 1996, in which Funar made a fierce personal attack on President Iliescu (or the PDSR), finally brought matters to a head, with the PUNR being ejected from the government by the Prime Minister. Despite its drive towards independent recognition,

the party performed poorly in the November 1996 elections, being out-polled by the PRM in both the presidential contest (in which Funar came sixth with only 3.2%) and parliamentary polls; the PUNR slumped to 18 Chamber and seven Senate seats.

A period of intense internal feuding ensued, in which Funar was ousted as chairman in February 1997 (and later expelled from the party) and replaced by Valeriu Tabara. In early 1998 Funar's supporters mustered a majority in the party's national council and restored him to the leadership, but the courts ruled that Tabara remained chairman. Funar then attempted to launch his own party, but failed to secure official registration, whereupon he threw in his lot with the PRM.

For the November 2000 parliamentary elections, the rump PUNR joined with the Romanian National Party (PNR) to form the National Alliance Party (PAN), but the PAN list secured only 1.4% of the vote and no seats. This failure provoked further feuding which culminated in the PUNR re-establishing itself as an independent party in June 2001 and the rump PAN opting for an unlikely merger with the centre-left Democratic Party.

At the party congress of May 2002, the subtle name change was adopted – as a symbol of the "fresh start" that party members wished to make, in the wake of several years of internal turmoil. In addition to Mircea Chelaru being elected party chair, a new party statute was also adopted at this summit, although the central, nationalist tenets of the party have been retained.

Social Democratic Party
Partidul Social Democrat (PSD)

Address. Ion Ionescu de la Brad no.1 Street, Bucharest
Telephone. (40–21) 202-7300
Fax. (40–21) 260-7387
Email. psd@psd.ro, comunicare@psd.ro
Website. www.psd.ro
Leadership. Adrian Nastase (chairman); Alexandru Athanasiu (chairman of national council)
Although its roots can be traced back to the immediate post-revolutionary period and the National Salvation Front (FSN) which quickly grabbed power at that time, the PSD was created in June 2001 as a merger of the Social Democracy Party of Romania (PDSR) and the smaller Romanian Social Democratic Party (PSDR), which had won a plurality in the 2000 elections under the guise of the "Social Democratic Pole alliance." Parties of the alliance had taken office as a minority government in wake of those elections.

The PDSR was launched in 1993 – itself the product of a merger between the Democratic National Salvation Front (FSND), the Romanian Socialist Democratic Party and the Republican Party. The new party formation provided a political base for President Ion Iliescu, who had held second-level elite positions during the Ceausescu era. The FSND had come into being in March 1992, when a group of pro-Iliescu deputies of the FSN had withdrawn from the parent party. Carrying with it the advantages of incumbency, the FSND then won a relative majority of seats in both houses of parliament in the September 1992 elections and backed Iliescu's successful re-election bid in the concurrent presidential contest. In 1993, the renamed PDSR was born – and defined itself as a social democratic, popular and national party supporting transition to a market economy on the basis of social responsibility.

Having formed a minority government as a result of the 1992 elections, the PDSR had entered into a coalition with the right-wing Romanian National Unity Party (PUNR) in August 1994, with external support also coming from the more radically nationalist Greater Romania Party (PRM) and the neo-communist Socialist Party of Labour (PSM). By mid-1995, however, serious differences had developed within the so-called "red-brown" government parties. As a result, the PRM and the PSM withdrew their support in late 1995, while the PUNR was ejected from the government in September 1996.

Meanwhile, in January 1996, the Romanian Social Democratic Party (PSDR, not to be confused with the PDSR) formed an alliance with the Democratic Party (PD), which was itself a splinter group of the original FSN. With a population keen for the pace of reforms to increase, the November 1996 elections saw Iliescu fail to secure re-election as President, and he was defeated in the second round by 54.4% to 45.9% by CDR candidate Emil Constantinescu. In the parliamentary contest, the PDSR won only 91 Chamber seats, with 21.5% of the vote, and went into opposition.

While the ideologically similar Romanian Social Democratic Party (PSDR) had taken its ten seats into the CDR's coalition government, it withdrew from government in September 2000, and abandoned its alliance with the PD to form the Social Democratic Pole with the PDSR and the Humanist Party of Romania (PUR).

In the November-December 2000 elections, Iliescu regained the presidency as the Pole candidate, winning 66.8% of the second-round vote against a challenge by the PRM leader, Corneliu Vadim Tudor. In the parliamentary contest, the Pole parties won a total of 155 of the 346 Chamber seats (and 36.6% of the vote), of which the PDSR obtained 142, the PSDR a disappointing seven and the PUR four. The Pole parties formed a minority government under the premiership of Adrian Nastase. Qualified pledges of support for the government were given by the PD, the National Liberal Party (PLN) and the Hungarian Democratic Union of Romania.

In January 2001 Nastase was elected chairman of the PDSR in succession to Iliescu (who was disqualified from party affiliation during his presidential term). The party then embarked upon negotiations for a formal merger with the PSDR, which came to fruition in June 2001, with Nastase being elected chairman of the unified PSD. Former PSDR leader Alexandru Athanasiu was made chairman of the PSD national council.

The PSD now claims a fairly standard social democratic position on issues, although there is a recognition of the ongoing need for privatization of industry in the Romanian economy. The party's support for European integration has also increased in recent years. The party remains the dominant force in Romanian politics, and is expected to take the largest share of the 2004 vote. With Ion Iliescu ineligible for a further term as President, it appears that current PSD chair and Romanian Premier, Adrian Nastase, is being groomed as the PSD candidate for the presidency.

The PSD did not inherit the PSDR's membership of the Socialist International (SI), due to doubts over the PDSR's democratic credentials. Rather, the PSD was given "permanent guest" status, pending further evaluation. Accession to the SI remains a stated goal of the PSD.

Ethnic Minority Parties

The 19 formations listed below were each allocated one Chamber seat in the November 2000 parliamentary elections.

Albanian League of Romania (*Liga Albanezilor din România*, LAR)
Leadership. Oana Manolescu

Armenian Union of Romania (*Uniunea Armenilor din România*, UAR)
Leadership. Varujan Pambuccian

Bulgarian Union of the Banat–Romania (*Uniunea Bulgara din Banat-România*, UBBR)
Leadership. Petru Mirciov

Croatian Union of Romania (*Uniunea Croatilor din România*, UCR)
Leadership. Mihai Radan

Cultural Union of Ruthenians of Romania (*Uniunea Culturala a Rutenilor din România*, UCRR)
Leadership. Gheorghe Firczak

Democratic Union of Tatar Turkish-Muslims of Romania (*Uniunea Democrata a Tatarilor Turco-Musulmani din România*, UDTTMR)
Leadership. Negiat Sali

Democratic Union of Slovaks and Czechs of Romania (*Uniunea Democratica a Slovacilor si Cehilor din România*, UDSCR)
Leadership. Ana Florea

German Democratic Forum of Romania (*Forumul Democrat al Germanilor din Romania*, FDGR)
Leadership. Eberhard-Wolfgang Wittstock

Greek Union of Romania (*Uniunea Elena din Romania*, UER)
Leadership. Sotiris Fotopolos

Italian Community of Romania (*Comunitatea Italiana din Romania*, CIR)
Leadership. Ileana Stana-Ionescu

Jewish Community Federation of Romania (*Federatia Comunitatilor Evreiesti din România*, FCER)
Leadership. Dorel Dorian

Lipova Russian Community of Romania (*Comunitatea Rusilor Lipoveni din România*, CRLR)
Leadership. Miron Ignat

Polish Union of Romania (*Uniunea Polonezilor din România*, UPR)
Leadership. Ghervazen Longher

Roma Party (*Partida Romilor*, PR)
Leadership. Nicolae Paun

Serbian Union of Romania (*Uniunea Sarbilor din România*, USR)
Leadership. Slavomir Gvozdenovici

Slav Macedonian Association of Romania (*Asociatia Macedonenilor Slavi din România*, AMSR)
Leadership. Vasile Ioan Savu

Turkish Democratic Union of Romania (*Uniunea Democrata Turca din România*, UDTR)
Leadership. Metin Cerchez

Ukrainian Union of Romania (*Uniunea Ucrainienilor din România*, UUR)
Leadership. Stefan Tcaciuc

General Union of Ethnic Associations of Romania (*Uniunea Generala a Asociatiilor Etniei Hutule din România*, UGAEHR)

Other Parties

Among well over 100 other registered parties in Romania, those listed below featured unsuccessfully in the 2000 elections.

Alliance for Romania (*Alianta pentru România*, ApR), formed in mid-1997 by dissidents of the Social Democracy Party of Romania (later the Social Democratic Party), being backed by about a dozen deputies and two senators. None were re-elected on the ApR ticket in the November 2000 elections, the party winning only 4.1% of the vote. In September 2001 the ApR agreed to merge with the National Liberal Party in mid-2002.

Leadership. Teodor Melescanu (chairman)

Christian Democratic National Alliance (*Alianta Nationala Crestin Democrata,* ANCD), a coalition of group-ings of Christian orientation which formed part of the defeated Democratic Convention of Romania 2000 alliance in the November 2000 parliamentary elections. The group includes the Hungarian Christian Party of Romania (RMKDM) led by Kálmán Kelemen.

Ecologist Federation of Romania (*Federatia Ecologista din România*, FER), the latest of various manifestations of the Green movement in Romania, which obtained five Chamber seats in the 1996 elections. In 2000 the FER was part of the defeated Democratic Convention of Romania 2000 alliance.

Union of Right-Wing Forces (*Uniunea Fortelor de Dreapta*, UFD), an amalgam of various groups which formed part of the defeated Democratic Convention of Romania 2000 alliance in the 2000 elections.

Website. www.ufd.ro

Russia

Capital: Moscow
Population: 145,164,000 (2002 census)

The Russian Federation was formerly the Russian Soviet Federative Socialist Republic (RSFSR), the largest constituent republic of the USSR, and became a sovereign member of the Commonwealth of Independent States in December 1991. Approved by a national vote in December 1993, its present constitution defines Russia as a democratic federation headed by an executive President, directly elected for a four-year term (once renewable consecutively), who guides the domes-tic and foreign policy of the state, serves as command-er-in-chief of the armed forces and nominates the Prime Minister and other ministers, subject to approval by the legislature. The latter body is the bicameral Federal Assembly (*Federal'noe Sobranie*), consisting of (i) the upper Federation Council (*Sovet Federatsii*) of 178 members, to which each of the Federation's 89 territori-al entities sends two representatives; and (ii) the lower State Duma (*Gosudarstvennaya Duma*) of 450 mem-bers elected for a four-year term. From 1993 to 2003, half were returned by proportional representation from party lists obtaining at least 5% of the vote and the other half from single-member constituencies on the basis of plurality voting. (The two halves of the election were unconnected in terms of seat distribution.) In September 2004, as part of a package of reforms introduced in the wake of a series of major terrorist attacks, President Putin announced a proposal that State Duma elections should henceforth take place solely on the basis of a proportional system, on the premise of "strengthening the political system of the country".

The President is the dominant actor in the Russian political system. If the State Duma passes a vote of no confidence in the government twice within three months, the President can announce the resignation of the government or, alternatively, the dissolution of the State Duma itself. Similarly, the President must appoint the Prime Minister and dissolve the State Duma if the latter rejects his nominees for the post three times in a row. A presidential veto on legislation can only be reversed by a two-thirds majority in both chambers of the Federal Assembly. The President can issue decrees if these do not contradict the Constitution or federal law. The strict formal separa-tion of powers between the executive and the legisla-ture is emphasized by the fact that deputies of the State Duma are banned under article 97.3 of the Constitution from holding government office, although in 2004 a restriction on cabinet ministers being party members was lifted. The Federal Assembly can impeach the President, but the proce-dure is complicated: it requires an indictment of trea-son or high crime from the Supreme Court, a two-thirds majority in both houses, and a ruling from the Constitutional Court.

From 1995 onwards, regional governors were elect-ed directly by the electorate in their regions. In September 2004, Putin proposed ending this system in favour of direct presidential nomination of governors.

Elections to the State Duma on Dec. 7, 2003, pro-duced the following results: United Russia 223 seats (120 in the party list section, with 37.6% of the vote, and 103 through single-member district constituen-cies); Communist Party of the Russian Federation 52 (40 party list, with 12.6% of the vote, and 12 single-member district); Liberal Democratic Party of Russia 36 (all from party list, with 11.5% of the vote); Motherland 37 (29 party list, with 9.0% of the vote, and 8 single-member district). The People's Party won 17 single-member district seats despite obtaining just 1.2% of the vote in the party list section. When the parliament convened, the United Russia faction had swollen to over 300 deputies with the co-option of a large number of members elected from single-member districts. Inter-factional movement has been common-place in post-communist Russia, and election results do not necessarily reflect the composition of the par-liament exactly. Similarly, there has been considerable fluidity in party formation and dissolution since the early 1990s.

Vladimir Putin succeeded Boris Yeltsin as President when the latter resigned on Dec. 31, 1999, and subse-quently won in the first round of the March 2000 pres-idential election against 10 other candidates with 52.9% of the vote. He was re-elected for a second term in March 2004 against five other candidates, winning 71.3% of the vote.

In order to register with the Ministry of Justice, the July 2001 Law on Political Parties requires Russian parties to have 10,000 members, with branches of no fewer than 100 members in at least half the constituent subjects of the Russian Federation (although at the time of writing a bill is being examined in the State Duma which would increase these minimum figures). Only registered parties may participate in the party list section of State Duma elections (although an approved list of public organizations can participate with politi-cal parties in electoral blocs). At the outset of the 2003 campaign, 44 parties were properly registered and entitled to participate, compared with 139 organiza-tions in 1999 under the previous legislation. (The number which competed – 26 in 1999 and 23 in 2003 – was hardly reduced, however.) Limits are placed on individual and corporate financial contributions to parties, which are eligible for state financial assistance in proportion to their electoral support if they obtain at least 3% of the vote or 12 single-member district seats.

Agrarian Party of Russia
Agrarnaya Partiya Rossii (APR)

Address. B. Golovin per. 20, str. 1, Moscow
Telephone. (+7–095) 207 9951 (central office); (+7-095) 207-9885 (press office)
Email. press@agroparty.ru
Website. www.agroparty.ru
Leadership. Vladimir Plotnikov

The APR was founded in February 1993 to provide political representation for collective and state farmers, as well as for agro-industrial workers and managers, initially on a platform opposed to the introduction of a free market in land. Its predominantly conservative constituent organizations included the Agrarian Union of Russia (*Agrarnyi Soyuz Rossii*, ASR) led by Vasilii Starodubtsev, which had held its inaugural congress in June 1990. APR spokesmen made a point of stressing that the APR was not the agrarian branch of the Communist Party of the Russian Federation (KPRF). In policy terms the two parties shared much common ground, notably a conviction that the free-market programme of the Yeltsin administration was damaging Russia.

The APR took fourth place in the December 1993 State Duma elections, winning 8.0% of the popular vote and 33 seats (which increased to 55 in the Duma with the addition of single-member district deputies elected on other platforms). The party aligned itself with the KPRF/nationalist opposition in the new parliament, even though the Agriculture Minister in a more conservative Yeltsin administration was identified with the APR. In the December 1995 parliamentary elections, the APR received only 4.8% of the party list vote and thus did not qualify for proportional seats. However, it won 20 seats in the constituency section of the ballot, and with the assistance of the KPRF, which "lent" it the extra deputies required, was able to form an Agrarian faction in the State Duma.

The APR backed the unsuccessful candidacy of the KPRF leader in the mid-1996 presidential elections and subsequently, without great enthusiasm, joined the new KPRF-inspired Popular-Patriotic Union of Russia. An APR congress in April 1997 adopted a new policy platform accepting the privatization of state-owned land in some circumstances and generally moving to a more centrist stance.

The APR did not run as an independent entity in the December 1999 State Duma elections, but allied itself with the Fatherland-All Russia (OVR) movement headed by former Prime Minister Evgenii Primakov and Moscow Mayor Yurii Luzhkov (United Russia). This decision split the party, and the deputy chairman, Nikolai Kharitonov, co-operated instead with the Communist Party and subsequently led the Agricultural-Industrial faction in the Duma.

In January 2001 the party chairman Mikhail Lapshin reverted to the APR's original line by calling for a moratorium on the buying and selling of land that had been owned by the state. Lapshin himself was elected head of the Altai Republic in January 2002. In May 2003 the party removed from its leadership Kharitonov and Aleksei Gordeev, the Russian agriculture minister.

The Agrarian Party ran independently in the 2003 State Duma election, winning 3.6% of the vote. Although this fell short of the 5% barrier necessary for representation, two single-member district deputies were elected under its auspices.

Lapshin lost the leadership of the party at an acrimonious XII congress in April 2004. His replacement, Vladimir Plotnikov, sits in the United Russia faction in the State Duma, and announced in October 2004 that the Agrarians

would henceforth seek "a course of constructive co-operation with the authorities".

Communist Party of the Russian Federation
Kommunisticheskaya Partiya Rossiiskoi Federatisii (KPRF)

Address. M. Sukharevskii per. 3, 103051 Moscow
Telephone. (+7–095) 928 3373
Website. www.kprf.ru
Leadership. Gennadii Zyuganov

The Communist Party of the Russian Federation (KPRF) considers itself the official successor to the former ruling Communist Party of the Soviet Union (KPSS). Its roots lie in the Russian branch of the latter, formed within the KPSS in June 1990 but banned through the decrees of Russian President Boris Yeltsin in late 1991. In November 1992 the Constitutional Court ruled that, whilst Yeltsin's ban on the party at the national level was legal, local branches still had the right to undertake their activities. Many (but not all) of the splinter left-wing groups which had emerged in the interim consolidated into the KPRF, which was re-established under the chairmanship of Gennadii Zyuganov in February 1993 at a "revival/unification" congress near Moscow.

The KPSS was directly descended from Lenin's majority (Bolshevik) wing of the Russian Social Democratic Labour Party, itself established in 1898, which at the party's second congress held in London in 1903 out-voted the minority (Menshevik) wing on Lenin's proposal that in existing Russian conditions the party must become a tightly-disciplined vanguard of professional revolutionaries. In 1912 the Bolshevik wing established itself as a separate formation, which became a legal party in Russia following the overthrow of the Tsar in February 1917 and which in October 1917 seized power from the Mensheviks. The party changed its name to Russian Communist Party (Bolsheviks) in 1918, to All-Union Communist Party (Bolsheviks) in 1925 and to the KPSS designation in 1952.

Following Lenin's death in January 1924, Joseph Stalin (who had become general secretary of the central committee in April 1922) took control over the party and government. He proceeded to eliminate all actual and potential rivals on the right and left of the party, notably Leon Trotsky (the architect of the Communist victory in the post-revolution civil war), who was expelled from the party in November 1927, exiled in January 1929 and finally murdered by Stalin's agent in his Mexican home in August 1940.

The Stalin era was characterized by rapid industrialization and the forcible collectivization of agriculture (the latter involving the virtual elimination of the land-owning peasants, or *kulaks,* as a class). Between 1928 and 1938 total industrial output almost quadrupled, although agricultural output fell as millions of animals and tonnes of grain were destroyed in the process. The assassination in December 1934 of the head of the Leningrad branch of the party, Sergei Kirov, was one of the triggers of the great purges of the late 1930s, in which almost the entire generation of party activists formerly associated with Lenin was killed or exiled, some (such as Bukharin and Zinoviev) after managed "show trials". In December 1936 a new constitution was promulgated under which the Communist Party was enshrined as the leading force in the state.

After the interval provided by the August 1939 Nazi–Soviet Pact, the German invasion of the Soviet Union in June 1941 coincided with Stalin's assumption for the first time of formal government responsibilities as Prime Minister and supreme commander of the Soviet armed forces. The eventual victory of the Red Army and its penetration into Eastern Europe led to the establishment of Soviet-aligned Communist regimes in a number of states and the beginning of the Cold War era. During the post-war period Stalin remained in absolute control of the party and state apparatus and mounted further purges of suspected opponents.

Immediately after Stalin's death in March 1953 moves were initiated to reverse the Stalinist system and the cult of his personality. Stalin's secret police chief, Lavrenti Beria, was executed and Stalin's designated successor, Georgii Malenkov, was ousted immediately from the party leadership by Nikita Khrushchev and replaced as Prime Minister by Nikolai Bulganin in February 1955. Under Khrushchev's leadership, the KPSS in 1955 re-established relations with the Yugoslav Communists (hitherto regarded as right-wing deviationists), and, in his celebrated "secret" speech to the 20th Party congress in February 1956, Khrushchev denounced the Stalinist terror and cult of personality.

Khrushchev's denunciation of Stalin triggered serious challenges to the Communist regimes in Poland and also in Hungary, where orthodox Communist rule was re-established by Soviet military intervention in November 1956. In March 1958 Khrushchev added the premiership to his party leadership, but growing doubts within the KPSS hierarchy about his policies and leadership style culminated in his removal from the party and government leadership in October 1964, in which posts he was succeeded by Leonid Brezhnev and Alexei Kosygin respectively.

Under Brezhnev's leadership the cautious liberalization policy of the Khrushchev era was largely halted or reversed. Although the Soviet government pursued a policy of detente with the West, its refusal to countenance deviation from Communist orthodoxy was demonstrated by the Soviet-led intervention in Czechoslovakia in 1968, following which Brezhnev enunciated his doctrine that Communist countries were entitled to intervene in other Communist countries if the preservation of socialism was deemed to be threatened. Having established a position of complete authority as party leader, Brezhnev was elected USSR head of state in June 1977.

The Brezhnev era was essentially a period of conservatism and stagnation. Following his death in November 1982 he was succeeded by former KGB chief Yurii Andropov, who died in February 1984. His successor, Konstantin Chernenko, lasted less than a year in office before he too died. The party then opted for the relatively young Mikhail Gorbachev (54), who embarked upon a reform programme that was ultimately to lead to the demise of the Soviet Union.

Gorbachev's policies of economic and social *perestroika* ("restructuring"), informational *glasnost'* ("openness") and political *demokratizatsiya* (democratization), allowed a more open discourse to develop. In the forms presented at the April 1985 plenary meeting of the KPSS central committee, and the 1986 XVII Party congress, these programmes were conceived initially as a means of increasing responsibility and attacking the ossified bureaucratic planned economy, but ultimately the reforms took on a momentum unforeseen by Gorbachev at the outset.

Differences within the KPSS leadership over the desirable pace of reform were demonstrated by the dismissal of Boris Yeltsin as first secretary of the Moscow party committee in November 1987, as a direct consequence of a speech by him to the KPSS central committee the previous month in which he had accused other senior leaders of frustrating the *perestroika* process and had also criticized aspects of the current leadership style. Formerly a close associate of Gorbachev, Yeltsin was dropped from alternate membership of the KPSS political bureau in February 1988.

Despite considerable obstacles and an electoral system designed to favour the KPSS, voters' clubs and citizens' committees succeeded in the selection and election of a small minority of reform-minded individuals in the March 1989 USSR Congress of People's Deputies election. Among them was Yeltsin, who was at this stage still a member of the party but had been excluded from the list of candidates nominated for the party's reserved hundred seats. However, it was not until March 1990 that article 6 of the 1977 Soviet Constitution, which rendered the KPSS the "leading and guiding force of Soviet society", was altered to allow the legal existence of alternatives.

Meanwhile, Gorbachev had succeeded Andrei Gromyko as USSR head of state in October 1988, and in March 1990 persuaded the Congress of People's Deputies to elect him to a new executive presidency of the USSR. By this time, as the economic crisis continued to deepen, he was caught between radical reformers and hardline conservatives. Following a March 1991 referendum on the continuation of the USSR, Gorbachev's proposed new Union Treaty, envisaging an association of "sovereign" republics with extensive powers of self-government, was the final straw for his hardline conservative opponents, and in August 1991 they attempted to assume power in Moscow while Gorbachev was on holiday. The coup attempt quickly crumbled, not least because of the rallying opposition displayed by Yeltsin; but it served to accelerate the unravelling of the Soviet system. In a country ruled for over seventy years by the Communist Party alone, Yeltsin used the opportunity to sign decrees suspending the party's activities on Russian soil (under a presidential decree issued on Nov. 6, 1991, the party's assets were declared state property), and Gorbachev resigned as general secretary when it became apparent that the coup had been led by hardline elements of the party's "inner circle". Just four months later – on Dec. 25, 1991, by which time many of the union republics had declared independence or sovereignty, and the leaders of the three Slavic republics had formed the Commonwealth of Independent States (CIS) – Gorbachev also resigned as Soviet President, since the USSR had effectively ceased to exist.

The leadership of the revived KPRF elected at the February 1993 congress was headed by Gennadii Zyuganov, a former Soviet apparatchik who had been co-chair of the National Salvation Front formed in October 1992 by Communists and Russian nationalists who deplored the passing of the perceived glories of the Soviet era. The KPRF was thus placed in uneasy spiritual alliance with the non-Communist nationalist right in opposition to the reformist forces of the centre in governmental power in Moscow, in particular to the Yeltsin presidency. The manifest negative effects of economic transition, including rampant crime and spiralling unemployment and inflation, provided the KPRF with powerful ammunition in its unaccustomed role as a party seeking electoral support in a multi-party system. In the State Duma elections of December 1993 it took third place with 48 seats and 12.4% of the proportional vote, thereafter becoming the principal focus of opposition to the Yeltsin administration.

In the mid- to late 1990s, the KPRF was the most successful party in federal and regional elections, although the marginal role of the State Duma and its exclusion from the federal government meant that electoral success did not necessarily translate into major political influence. Using the slogan "For our Soviet motherland", it contested the December 1995 State Duma elections on a platform promising the restoration of "social justice" and became the largest party with 157 seats. Some 99 of these came from its 22.3% share of the vote in the proportional half of the contest. Remaining in opposition (although welcoming a more conservative government orientation), the KPRF presented Zyuganov as its candidate for the mid-1996 presidential election, on a platform condemning the devastation of Russia's industrial base by IMF-dictated policies and promising to restore economic sovereignty. He came a close second to Yeltsin in the first round of voting on June 16, winning 32.0% compared with the incumbent President's

35.3%, but lost in the second round, gaining 40.3% to Yeltsin's 55.8%. The KPRF thereupon initiated the creation in mid-1996 of the Popular–Patriotic Union of Russia (*Narodno-Patrioticheskii Soyuz Rossii*, NPSR), which was designed to rally all anti-Yeltsin forces, although Zyuganov insisted, shortly before being elected as its leader, that it was not a Communist front organization.

In the late 1990s the KPRF sought to distance itself from the nationalist right, while continuing to espouse a form of Russian nationalism harking back to the Soviet era. The party urged a return to centralized government and the transfer of presidential powers to the government and the legislature, as well as the creation of a "Slavic union" of Russia, Ukraine and Belarus, arguing that only a KPRF government could resurrect Russia's status as a great power. Although its total representation in the Duma fell to 113 seats following the December 1999 State Duma election (more parties crossed the 5% barrier in the party list vote than in 1995, reducing the advantage of the largest organizations), its share of the vote increased marginally to 24.3% and it remained the largest single party.

Since then the influence of the KPRF has waned as a result of internal crises and exogenous changes in the Russian political system. In presidential elections in March 2000, Zyuganov was again the KPRF candidate but was defeated heavily by Putin in the first round, receiving only 29.2% of the vote. In the December 2003 State Duma contest, battered by a sustained assault from the state media and a weak campaign, the KPRF had its worst federal election result for a decade, winning just 12.6% of the vote in the party list and only a handful of single-member district seats. When the State Duma convened for the first time in late December 2003, the KPRF faction remained the second largest, but numbered 52 deputies compared with 300 for the dominant United Russia group. Zyuganov did not contest the 2004 presidential election, but the party nominated Nikolai Kharitonov, the leader of the Agricultural-Industrial faction in the 1999-2003 State Duma (see Agrarian Party of Russia), who came second to Vladimir Putin with 13.7% of the vote.

For the KPRF, an increasing problem has been that Putin's strategy of strengthening the state, and his emphasis on protecting the national interests of Russia, have echoes of its own rhetoric, neutralizing its distinctive message. Moreover, tensions between the main ideological groupings within the party have become more explicit, and the Kremlin has made concerted efforts to exacerbate these. In the spring of 2002 a number of high-ranking members of the party – including the then State Duma speaker Gennadii Seleznev, who had been second on the KPRF's party list in 1999 – were expelled from its ranks over an incident triggered by their failure to resign their Duma posts in protest at a pre-emptive strike by the parliament's pro-presidential majority, which had removed the KPRF from most of its committee chairmanships. The formation shortly before the 2003 State Duma election of the Motherland bloc, headed by another leading member of the KPRF State Duma faction, Sergei Glaz'ev, and the tacit assistance rendered to it by the Kremlin, proved another major blow to the party's fortunes.

In the wake of the electoral defeats of 2003-04, challenges to Zyuganov's leadership became more overt, particularly from Gennadii Semigin, chairman of the executive committee of the Popular–Patriotic Union of Russia, who was expelled from the party in May 2004. The internal party schism manifested itself dramatically on July 3, 2004, when two meetings were held in Moscow simultaneously, each claiming to be the official X congress of the party. One re-elected Zyuganov to the post of party chairman; the other replaced him with the governor of Ivanovo province, Vladimir Tikhonov, and elected a new Central Committee. The Ministry of Justice examined the documents submitted by both groups, and ruled in August 2004 that the "Zyuganovite" congress had been the legitimate one.

Liberal Democratic Party of Russia
Liberalno–Demokraticheskaya Partiya Rossii (LDPR)

Address. Lukov per. 9, 103045 Moscow

Telephone. (+7-095) 925 0715/924 0869 (Central Apparatus); 292 1195 (Zhirinovsky)

Fax. (+7-095) 928 0869

Email. pressldpr@duma.gov.ru

Website. www.ldpr.ru

Leadership. Vladimir Zhirinovsky

The LDPR is led by (and essentially the party of) the flamboyant nationalist Vladimir Zhirinovsky. It held its first congress on March 31, 1990, and initially was called the Liberal Democratic Party of the Soviet Union (LDPSU). Zhirinovsky came third, attracting 6.2 million votes (7.8%), in the 1991 presidential election on an openly xenophobic platform with racist and anti-Semitic overtones. Among his more extravagant proposals was one for a Russian re-conquest of Finland (which had been part of the Tsarist empire until World War I). The LDPR supported the August 1991 coup attempt. The party was technically banned in August 1992 on the grounds that it had falsified its membership records. However, it was allowed to contest the December 1993 parliamentary elections, in which it became the second strongest State Duma party with 64 seats and actually headed the proportional voting with 22.9% of the national poll.

Subsequently the LDPR lost momentum, its support roughly halving with every subsequent election as its leader made increasingly bizarre utterances and was shunned by other politicians close to him in the ideological spectrum. In the December 1995 State Duma elections the LDPR took second place on the party list and won a total of 51 seats, but slumped to 11.2% of the proportional vote. In the 1996 presidential elections, moreover, Zhirinovsky came fifth in the first round, with only 5.7% of the vote.

Because of irregularities in its paperwork, the party was denied registration for the December 1999 State Duma elections, which it therefore contested as "Zhirinovsky's Bloc". In a further major setback, the formation slumped to 17 seats and 6% of the proportional vote. Worse followed in the March 2000 presidential elections, in which the LDPR leader came a distant fifth with only 2.7% of the vote.

In the December 2003 State Duma election, however, the LDPR increased its vote for the first time in a decade, coming third in the party list with 11.5% of the vote and increasing its representation to 36 seats. Zhirinovsky declined to participate in the 2004 presidential election personally. Instead, the party nominated Oleg Malyshkin, once Zhirinovsky's chief bodyguard, as its candidate. Malyshkin came fifth out of the six candidates, winning just 2.0% of the vote.

The party's name is highly misleading: it does not advocate liberalism, but rather imperialism, nationalism, and protectionism. Zhirinovsky has been prodigious in his output of ideological pamphlets and, amongst other infamous pronouncements, he has advocated the expansion of Russia's borders to the point where "the Indian Ocean washes the shores of Russia". He styles himself as an opposition politician, although the LDPR often votes with the establishment. Indeed, Zhirinovsky is sometimes viewed as a "kite flyer" for more senior politicians, to test public opinion prior to the announcement of a new proposal. Bills put forward by the party often have an extremist or flippant nature (such as a proposal in October 2000 to legalize polygamy as a means of solving the country's demographic crisis), which arguably is aimed at maintaining this anti-system image whilst masking the close relationship between the LDPR and pro-government forces.

Motherland–People's Patriotic Union
Rodina–Narodno-Patrioticheskii Soyuz

Address. c/o State Duma, Okhotny Ryad 1, 103265 Moscow
Email. info@rodina-nps.ru
Website. www.rodina-nps.ru
Leadership. Dmitrii Rogozin

Rodina began as an electoral bloc formed around Sergei Glaz'ev and Dmitrii Rogozin. From 1992-93 Glaz'ev was the Minister for External Economic Affairs, and was elected in December 1993 to the State Duma on the party list of the Democratic Party of Russia (DPR). He headed the State Duma economic committee in the first (1993-95) convocation. He failed to win representation in the second State Duma, but was closely linked with Aleksandr Lebed's presidential campaign in 1996, and through this connection was appointed to the Security Council as head of the economic security administration when Yeltsin briefly appointed Lebed' secretary of the Security Council. In 1999 he returned to the Duma on the KPRF list, although not formally a member of the party. His increasing profile was given a further boost in September 2002 when he came a respectable third in the Krasnoyarsk gubernatorial election. Rogozin, a founder and former leader of the Congress of Russian Communities, headed the Duma Committee on International Affairs in the third convocation.

The *Rodina* bloc was formed in September 2003 to unite leftist and "patriotic" parties for the December 2003 State Duma election. In addition to the Party of Russian Regions (PRR), which Glaz'ev and Rogozin headed, approximately thirty other minor organizations were included in the bloc – but not the KPRF. There were suggestions that the formation of *Rodina* was part of a Kremlin plan to split the leftist vote and thus draw support from the Communists, rumours which Glaz'ev appeared to confirm in various media interviews a few months after the election.

The election result was highly favourable for *Rodina*: it came fourth in the party list, winning 9.0% of the vote and gaining a total of 37 seats.

Glaz'ev was appointed chairman of the parliamentary faction, but splits between the bloc's co-leaders became apparent shortly after the State Duma election. Glaz'ev decided to participate in the presidential election without the bloc's approval, and in late January 2004, in the absence of Rogozin, he attempted to appropriate the bloc's name to found a new public organization with himself as leader. For this and other alleged violations, he was expelled from the PRR in February 2004, and replaced by Rogozin as head of the *Rodina* parliamentary faction in early March. The renamed party elected Rogozin as its sole chairman in July 2004. *Rodina* is broadly loyal to Putin, although it has on occasion been critical of the government.

Union of Rightist Forces
Soyuz Pravykh Sil (SPS)

Address. Ul. M. Andronevskaya 15, 109544 Moscow
Telephone. (+7-095) 278 9518 (International Department)
Website. www.sps.ru

The pro-market SPS was launched prior to the December 1999 State Duma elections as an alliance of parties and groups broadly descended, through many complex changes of name and alignment, from those which had supported the "shock therapy" economic policies of the early 1990s, notably Egor Gaidar's Russia's Democratic Choice (DVR). These formations had lost influence in the more conservative later years of the presidency of Boris Yeltsin, with whom Gaidar had broken irrevocably in 1996, and had been widely blamed for the deterioration and corruption engendered by the early rush to a market economy.

DVR was originally founded in November 1993 as Russia's Choice (VR), deriving from the Bloc of Reformist Forces–Russia's Choice (BRVR) created five months earlier by a group of radical pro-market reformers which had included Gaidar. The BRVR had itself derived from the pro-Yeltsin Democratic Choice (DV) bloc created by a large number of centre-right groups in July 1992. The new VR grouping was part of an attempt to provide a stable political framework for centre-right reformist forces hitherto operating under a host of different and constantly changing party or alliance labels. It became the largest parliamentary grouping in the December 1993 State Duma elections, winning 70 seats and 15.5% of the national vote in the party list section. But strong advances by anti-reform parties resulted in Gaidar and most other radical reformers being dropped from the government. (Gaidar had already lost his post as Prime Minister in December 1992.) In April 1994, in securing Gaidar's signature of his "treaty on civil accord", President Yeltsin expressed a desire for close co-operation with the VR bloc, while explaining that he could not, as head of state, become an actual member.

In June 1994 VR formally established itself as a political party, adding "Democratic" to its title, to become DVR. Thereafter, DVR criticism of the slow pace of economic reform under the government of Viktor Chernomyrdin continued despite the promotion of Anatoly Chubais (then of DVR) to the rank of First Deputy Prime Minister in November 1994. In March 1995 DVR withdrew support from President Yeltsin in protest against the Russian military action in Chechnya. Two months later Chubais announced that he was suspending his DVR membership and giving his support to Chernomyrdin's new Our Home is Russia (NDR) formation (see United Russia). The centre-right's incorrigible addiction to new nomenclature was displayed again in June 1995 when DVR launched the United Democrats (OD) as its electoral bloc, including over 20 ethnic minority groups. The December 1995 elections proved dismal for the DVR/OD, which slumped to 3.9% of the national vote and thus won no proportional seats, although it did win single-member representation in nine constituencies. The Yeltsin administration's shift to an even more conservative posture as a result of the electoral verdict caused Egor Gaidar to resign from the Presidential Advisory Council in January 1996 in what he described as a "final and irrevocable" breach with Yeltsin. In the same month Chubais was dismissed from the government for disregarding presidential instructions. In June-July 1996 most DVR elements nevertheless backed President Yeltsin's successful re-election bid, although some preferred the candidacy of Grigorii Yavlinsky of Yabloko.

Gaidar and DVR then embarked upon yet another attempt to create a centre-right bloc, launching in late 1998 the Just Cause (*Pravoe Delo*, PD) alliance, partly in response to the murder in St Petersburg of Galina Starovoitova, a DVR State Duma deputy and prominent human rights campaigner. However, the unwillingness of the other major centre-right formations to join the PD initiative eventually persuaded DVR to become part of SPS on its creation in 1999, together with smaller organizations such as Boris Nemtsov's "Young Russia"; Irina Khakamada's "Common Cause"; the "New Force" movement, headed by another former Prime Minister, Sergei Kirienko; and "Voice of Russia", led by Samara governor Konstantin Titov.

SPS won 29 State Duma seats in the December 1999 elections, with 8.5% of the proportional vote. It subsequently gave broad support to the new presidency of Vladimir Putin, while maintaining its distance from the main pro-Putin Unity Inter-Regional Movement (see United Russia). In May 2000 the SPS alliance formally constituted itself as a national organization and in May 2001 held a constituent congress in Moscow at which Boris Nemtsov was elected chairman and Gaidar one of five co-chairmen. At this point the constituent movements dissolved themselves.

Subsequently it held another "founding" congress to reconstitute itself as a political party in accordance with the 2001 Law on Political Parties. SPS was accepted as a member of the International Democrat Union in succession to DVR.

Despite tentative attempts at co-operation with the other main liberal party, Yabloko, no formal merger between the two took place, and SPS contested the 2003 State Duma election on its own platform. Chubais played a highly visible role in the campaign, placed third on its party list after Nemtsov and Khakamada. The election result was a significant setback: the party's support more than halved compared with 1999 to just under 4.0% of the vote, which meant that it missed out on the distribution of seats from the party list. Although a handful of SPS deputies were elected in single-member districts, none of the party's leaders won representation to the State Duma, and most took on other projects in early 2004.

The party spent most of 2004 in a state of deep introspection. Khakamada parted company from SPS in March 2004 after it refused to support her presidential election campaign (she came fourth with 3.8% of the vote), and announced that she would be forming her own organization. SPS held a congress in late June 2004, but took no substantial decisions on its most pressing question – who should be its new leader. A leadership election was scheduled for late 2004.

United Russia
Edinaya Rossiya
Address. Bannyi per. 3, corp. A, 129110 Moscow
Telephone. (+7-095) 786 8678
Fax. (+7-095) 975 3078
Website. www.edinros.ru
Leadership. Boris Gryzlov

United Russia is the latest – and by far the most successful – incarnation of the "party of power" in Russia. It is directly descended from three previous contenders for that title.

Following the 1998 economic crisis, the mayor of Moscow, Yurii Luzhkov, became increasingly active in federal-level politics. In December of that year, he founded the Fatherland (*Otechestvo*) movement, amalgamating several leftist opposition movements with the support of some prominent regional governors and ex-government officials. In the course of 1999 Luzhkov gradually distanced himself from the Kremlin, to which he had previously been loyal but by which he was now perceived as a threat. His coalition was broadened by an alliance with the regionally-based All Russia (*Vsya Rossiya*) movement in August 1999, forming the Fatherland-All Russia (*Otechestvo-Vsya Rossiya*, OVR) bloc. Crucially, the popular former Prime Minister Evgenii Primakov was persuaded to lead the movement, which was by then considered the pre-election favourite.

By this time, the Kremlin perceived the threat from the movement, and a hastily-formed alternative "party of power" – the Unity Inter-Regional Movement (*Edinstvo*) – was created, formally headed by the Minister for Emergency Affairs, Sergei Shoigu. From the Kremlin's perspective, it was essential that Primakov's presidential ambitions be curtailed. Moreover, it was perceived that the existing "party of power" – Our Home is Russia (*Nash Dom–Rossiya*, NDR), headed by former Prime Minister Viktor Chernomyrdin – had little chance of success, and a successful campaign for a pro-Kremlin bloc would serve the purpose both of giving the "establishment" presidential candidate (the then virtually unknown Vladimir Putin) some momentum whilst simultaneously ensuring a more loyal Duma than had been the case in the 1995-99 sitting.

Despite its late start and weak infrastructure, *Edinstvo* won 22.3% of the party list vote, within less than two percentage points of the victorious CPRF. By contrast, a combination of poor organization, the unexpected rise of Putin,

and sustained media bombardment in the state media meant that OVR obtained just 13.3% and came a distant third. NDR picked up 7 constituency seats, but its nationwide vote slumped to a mere 1.2% (compared with 10.1% in 1995).

Primakov's chances of winning the 2000 presidential election were damaged severely, and Putin's momentum was greatly increased. As Prime Minister he had remained above the mudslinging of the election campaign but benefited from the success of what was perceived unofficially as "his" party. When Yeltsin resigned early and Primakov decided not to put forward his candidature, Putin's success was virtually guaranteed, and the acting President won in the first round with 52.9% of the vote, backed (but not nominated) by *Edinstvo* and also by a wide range of prominent Russian politicians, including, belatedly, Luzhkov.

Following its 1999 success and Putin's election as President in March 2000, *Edinstvo* began almost immediately to consolidate its structure and transform the movement into a party, which culminated in its first congress on May 27, 2000. In February 2001 the remains of NDR were incorporated, and on Dec. 1, 2001, a formal merger took place with *Otechestvo* and *Vsya Rossiya* to form a new political party – United Russia (*Edinaya Rossiya*, ER).

2002 saw increasing co-operation between the four pro-Putin factions in the State Duma, which together held a majority, and increasing co-option of regional elites to the ER cause. Despite the fact that article 10.3 of the 2001 Law on Political Parties forbids state officials (such as ministers and governors) from using their offices to promote a party or being linked with party decisions, most of the senior leadership fell into these categories, using various loopholes to avoid contravening the law. (For instance, party chairman Boris Gryzlov, the Interior Minister, was not technically a member of the organization.)

In the 2003 State Duma election, bolstered by substantial administrative resources, favourable and extensive media coverage, and the explicit backing of Vladimir Putin (the President attended ER's September 2003 pre-election congress and the party used the slogan "Together with the President" on its campaigning materials), ER won close to an absolute majority of seats in the parliament (223), and took 37.6% of the party list vote – three times more than its nearest rival, the KPRF. None of the 29 regional governors included on the party list actually took up his seat. When the State Duma met, the co-option of various unattached deputies had swelled the ER faction to over 300 – a constitutional (2/3) majority. Gryzlov, who had been the *Edinstvo* faction's leader in the previous Duma before relinquishing his seat to become the Minister of the Interior, was elected speaker of the parliament by an overwhelming majority (352 of 437 votes).

Since the election, the ER faction has dominated the legislature, passing a number of substantial procedural reforms to bolster its position within the parliament (such as enabling Gryzlov simultaneously to be head of the faction and speaker of the Duma), and supporting the legislative agenda of the Russian government and the initiatives of President Putin. Its voting strength means that virtually all legislation supported by the political elite can be passed with a minimum of delay.

Yabloko
Address. Ul. Novyi Arbat 21, floor 18, 119992 Moscow
Telephone. (+7-095) 202 8072
Website. www.yabloko.ru
Leadership. Grigorii Yavlinsky

Yabloko was launched in October 1993 as the Yavlinsky–Boldyrev–Lukin Bloc by Grigorii Yavlinsky, Yuri Boldyrev and Vladimir Lukin, who supported transition to a market economy but strongly opposed the "shock therapy" then being administered by the Yeltsin administration.

Yavlinsky was a well-known economist, Boldyrev a scientist and Lukin a former ambassador to the United States. The title "Yabloko" came from an amalgamation of the first letters of their surnames, but is coincidentally the Russian word for "apple", which has become the party symbol. The organization has positioned itself as a democratic opposition party, in opposition to the Yeltsin regime and critical of Putin's. Its main electoral appeal has been to the urban intelligentsia.

Having won 23 seats and 7.9% of the proportional vote in the December 1993 elections, Yabloko was one of the few State Duma groups which declined to sign the April 1994 "civic accord treaty" between the government and most political groupings, on the grounds that the initiative contravened constitutional provisions. Yabloko also condemned the Russian military operation in Chechnya launched in December 1994.

In the December 1995 State Duma elections, Yabloko took a creditable fourth place, winning 45 seats on a proportional vote share of 6.9%. Its candidate in the 1996 presidential election was Yavlinsky, who came fourth in the first round with 7.3% and gave qualified support to incumbent Boris Yeltsin in the second. The party nevertheless opposed many aspects of the new government's economic policy, drawing particular support from older professionals. In the December 1999 State Duma elections, Yabloko fell back to 20 seats with 5.9% of the proportional vote, while Yavlinsky came third (with 5.8%) in the March 2000 presidential election won by Vladimir Putin. Yabloko thereafter adopted a stance of "constructive opposition" to the Putin administration.

Between 2000 and 2003, discussions took place about an alliance between Yabloko and the Union of Right Forces (SPS), providing initially for the presentation of joint candidates in forthcoming elections and possibly leading to a full merger. However, although there was some co-ordination between the two parties, it proved impossible to find enough common ground for a more comprehensive alliance, and Yabloko entered the 2003 State Duma campaign on its own platform. The December 2003 election result was a significant setback for the party. Its 2.6 million votes translated into just 4.3% of the vote, failing for the first time to pass the 5% barrier necessary for representation. The party boycotted the 2004 presidential election.

Yabloko, having previously enjoyed observer status, became a full member of the Liberal International (LI) in 2002. The LI awarded its 2004 Prize for Freedom to Yavlinsky for his opposition to the Chechen war.

Other Parties

As of Aug. 25, 2004, there were 44 political parties registered with the Ministry of Justice. The Dec. 7, 2003, State Duma election witnessed the participation of a total of 23 parties and electoral blocs, some of which included more than one registered party. In addition to the parties listed above, the following parties gained over 1% in the party list section of the 2003 State Duma election.

People's Party of the Russian Federation (*Narodnaya Partiya Rossiiskoi Federatsii*, NPRF), was created on the basis of the People's Deputy (*Narodnyi Deputat*, ND) faction in the State Duma, and registered as a party in October 2001. The ND faction was formed by single-member district deputies, mainly elected independently of parties in the 1999 State Duma election. In the third (1999-2003) State Duma it allied itself with the other pro-presidential centrist factions. As expected, given its heritage, it did considerably better in the constituency ballot than the party list in the 2003 State Duma election, winning 17 seats in the Duma despite polling only 1.2% of the vote nationwide. On the basis of its single-member district results, it qualified for state funding. The

party's deputies sit in the United Russia faction in the State Duma. In April 2004 Gennadii Raikov, leader since the party's foundation in 2001, was replaced by Gennadii Gudkov.
Leadership. Gennadii Gudkov
Website. www.narod-party.ru

Russian Party of Life (*Rossiiskaya Partiya Zhizni*, RPZh), registered with the Ministry of Justice in September 2002, is headed by the speaker of the Federation Council, Sergei Mironov. It fought the 2003 State Duma election together with the Party of Russian Rebirth (*Partiya Vozrozhdeniya Rossii*, PVR), headed by the then speaker of the State Duma, Gennadii Seleznev, who had been expelled from the Communist Party (KPRF) in 2002. The electoral bloc of the two parliamentary speakers won 1.1 million votes in the party list section, which amounted to 1.9% of the vote.
Website. http://www.rpvita.ru/
Leadership. Sergei Mironov (chairman)

Russian Party of Pensioners (*Rossiiskaya Partiya Pensionerov*, RPP), founded in late 1997 to promote the interests of pensioners. The party re-registered under the new electoral legislation in May 2002, and fought the 2003 State Duma election in a bloc with the Party of Social Justice (*Partiya Sotsial'noi Spravedlivosti*, PSS). The bloc won 3.1% of the vote, thereby qualifying for state funding. In February 2004, Sergei Atroshenko was replaced as chairman of the RPP by Valerii Gartung.
Leadership. Valerii Gartung

Unity (*Edinenie*) (not to be confused with *Edinstvo*, the main original constituent part of the dominant United Russia party), was registered in September 2002 and had an eclectic programme of contradictory values for the 2003 State Duma campaign. It won 1.2% of the vote, perhaps aided by appearing first on the ballot paper and having a name not dissimilar to the winning party.
Leadership. Konstantin Petrov.

Rwanda

Capital: Kigali
Population: 8,200,000 (2002E)

The Republic of Rwanda achieved independence from Belgium in 1962. Following a military coup led by Gen. Juvénal Habyarimana in 1973, the Hutu-dominated regime created the National Republican Movement for Democracy and Development (MRNDD), which remained the sole legal political party until the adoption of a multi-party constitution in 1991. By then a rebellion had been launched by the predominantly Tutsi Rwandan Patriotic Front (FPR), with which the government signed the Arusha Accord of August 1993 providing for the establishment of interim institutions in a transition period leading to multi-party elections. However, delays in the deployment of a UN observer force and divisions within various political parties led to the repeated postponement of the start of the transition period.

The fragile peace process ended abruptly in April 1994 when President Habyarimana was killed in a plane crash and mass violence of genocidal proportions ensued. Although generally presented as an ethnic conflict between the majority Hutu and minority Tutsi, the violence was also politically-motivated, in that supporters of the Habyarimana regime sought to eliminate all opposition, Tutsi and Hutu. The violence prompted the resumption of the rebellion by the FPR which, by July 1994, claimed military victory. In the same month Pasteur Bizimungu, a senior FPR figure, was inaugurated as President for a five-year term and the composition of a new government of national unity was announced. Posts in the Council of Ministers were assigned to the FPR, the Republican Democratic Movement, the Liberal Party, the Social Democratic Party and the Christian Democratic Party. The new administration declared its intention to honour the terms of the 1993 Arusha Accord within the context of an extended period of transition (to June 1999). However, the MRNDD and the Coalition for the Defence of the Republic (CDR) were excluded from participation in the government.

A 70-member Transitional National Assembly was inaugurated in December 1994 (without benefit of election). In May 1995 the Assembly adopted a new constitution which brought together elements of the 1991 constitution, the 1993 Arusha Accord, the FPR's victory declaration of July 1994 and a protocol of understanding signed in November 1994 by political parties not implicated in the earlier massacres.

In June 1999 the Transitional National Assembly was extended for a further four years. President Bizimungu resigned in March 2000; he was succeeded in April by Maj.-Gen. Paul Kagame who was elected in a special parliamentary vote. Kagame, the (Tutsi) FPR military chief, had formerly been Vice-President and Minister of National Defence. A new constitution was approved overwhelmingly in a referendum held in May 2003. The new constitution provided for a President and a bicameral legislature. Kagame, candidate of the FPR, won a landslide victory in the presidential elections held in August 2003. Kagame easily defeated two Hutu candidates, who both stood as independents, Faustin Twagiramungu of the Republican Democratic Movement (MDR) and Jean Nepomucene Nayinzira of the Christian Democratic Party (CDR).

Elections to the lower house, the Chamber of Deputies, were held on Sept. 29-Oct. 2 and resulted in a landslide victory for the FPR and its four coalition allies – the CDR, the Islamic Democratic Party, the Rwandan Socialist Party (PSR) and the Rwandan People's Democratic Union (UDPR) – which together won 40 of the 53 contested seats in the 80-member Chamber. The two mainly Hutu opposition parties – the Social Democratic Party (PSD) and the Liberal Party (PL) – together won 13 seats. A total of 24 seats were reserved for women's representatives, two seats for representatives of the National Youth Council and one seat for representatives of the Federation of the Association of the Disabled.

Christian Democratic Party
Parti Démocratique Chrétien (PDC)
Leadership. Jean-Nepomuscene Nayinzira
The PDC was established in 1990 by Jean-Nepomuscene Nayinzira, a Hutu. In the wake of the 1994 genocide, Nayinzira spent six years in government alongside the Rwandan Patriotic Front (FPR). He was removed from the Transitional National Assembly in 2002 for "immoral behaviour", an event he dismissed as "manoeuvring by the FPR, which doesn't like my independent way of thinking." In the August 2003 presidential elections Nayinzira was one of two challengers to FPR leader and incumbent President Paul Kagame. Nayinzira managed to win just over 1% of the vote. The PDC contested the Sept. 29-Oct. 1, 2003, elections to the newly-created Chamber of Deputies, the lower house of

the bicameral legislature, as part of a FPR-led coalition. The party won three seats.

Coalition for the Defence of the Republic
Coalition pour la Défense de la République (CDR)
The CDR was formed in 1992, drawing support from uncompromising Hutu groups. In the mass violence between April and June 1994, its unofficial militia (*Impuza Mugambi*, or "Single-Minded Ones") was reported to have taken a leading role in the slaughter of Tutsis and moderate Hutus. CDR participation in the transitional government and legislature was subsequently proscribed by the new administration led by the Rwandan Patriotic Front.

Islamic Democratic Party
Parti Démocratique Islamique (PDI)
Leadership. Andre Bumaya
The PDI contested the Sept. 29-Oct. 1, 2003, elections to the newly-created Chamber of Deputies, the lower house of the bicameral legislature, as part of a coalition led by the Rwandan Patriotic Front (FPR). The party won two seats.

Liberal Party
Parti Libéral (PL)
Leadership. Pie Mugabo; Enock Kabera; Prosper Mugiraneza
The PL was formed in 1991 but split into two factions during late 1993 and early 1994, one faction joining the coalition government installed by the Rwandan Patriotic Front (FPR) following its military victory in July 1994. The PDC contested the Sept. 29-Oct. 1, 2003, elections to the newly-created Chamber of Deputies, the lower house of the bicameral legislature, and won over 10% of the vote and six seats. In the presidential poll held in August 2003, the PL had supported the FPR candidate and eventual winner, Paul Kagame.

National Republican Movement for Democracy and Development
Mouvement Républicain National pour la Démocratie et le Développement (MRNDD)
The MRNDD (known as the National Revolutionary Movement for Democracy until 1991) was founded in 1975 by Gen. Juvénal Habyarimana as a single national party embracing both military and civilian elements. Of Catholic orientation, it remained the sole legal party until the promulgation of legislation authorizing the formation of political parties in June 1991. The party retained a strong presence in subsequent coalition governments, ensuring President Habyarimana's continuing powerful influence. In the carnage that followed the President's death in April 1994, the MRNDD's large unofficial militia (*Interahamwe*, or "Those Who Stand Together") was reported to be extensively involved in Hutu atrocities. The party was consequently excluded from the transitional government formed in July 1994 following the defeat of government forces by the Rwandan Patriotic Front. The *Interahamwe* remain active militarily in the volatile eastern region of the Democratic Republic of the Congo.

Republican Democratic Movement
Mouvement Démocratique Républicain (MDR)
Leadership. Faustin Twagiramungu (chairman)
The current MDR, legalized in July 1991, stems from the Hutu *Parmehutu*-MDR which was the dominant party until 1973 when it was banned by the Habyarimana regime. The MDR led the campaign in late 1991 for the creation of a provisional government of all parties to manage the transition to pluralism and, from April 1992, headed successive coalition governments. The party was a signatory of the August 1993

Arusha Accord with the then rebel Rwandan Patriotic Front (FPR), and Faustin Twagiramungu (on the anti-Habyarimana wing of the party) became the agreed nominee of the pro-democracy parties for the premiership in the envisaged transitional government. Many MDR members were subsequently victims of Hutu extremism in the atrocities perpetrated from April 1994. Twagiramungu was appointed Prime Minister in the FPR-dominated administration formed in July 1994. However, in August 1995, he was dismissed by President Bizimungu and replaced by Pierre-Celestin Rwigyema. Twagiramungu fled into exile in Belgium. Rwigyema served as Prime Minister until his resignation in February 2000, and was replaced by Bernard Makuza, also of the MDR, the following month.

In April 2003 the Transitional National Assembly, the legislature, voted to dissolve the MDR after accusing it of propagating "divisive" ideology. Forty-seven individuals were named in the report, including two government ministers, five deputies in the Assembly, three high-ranking military officers and an ambassador. Apparently fearing for their safety, two of the high-ranking military officers named in the report, former Minister of Defence, Brig.-Gen. Emmanuel Habyarimana and the army representative to the Assembly, Lt-Col Balthazar Ndengeyinka, had fled to Uganda in late March. In June party leader Twagiramungu returned to Rwanda from exile in Belgium in order to compete in the forthcoming presidential election. In the poll, held in August, Twagiramungu was easily defeated by incumbent President Paul Kagame of the FDR, winning less than 4% of the vote. Twagiramungu ran as an independent. In October Kagame reappointed Bernard Makuza as Prime Minister. Despite the banning of the MDR, Makuza had remained publicly loyal to Kagame.

Rwandan Patriotic Front
Front Patriotique Rwandais (FPR)
Leadership. Maj.-Gen. Paul Kagame (chairman); Charles Muligande (secretary-general)
The largely Tutsi FPR launched an insurgency from Uganda against the Habyarimana regime in October 1990. By 1992, in the light of extensive territorial gains by the FPR in northern Rwanda, the government was obliged to enter into negotiations which, a year later in August 1993, culminated in the signing of the Arusha Accord. The peace process was shattered in April 1994 by the massacres of Tutsis and moderate Hutus which followed the death of President Habyarimana, as a consequence of which the FPR, under the command of Kagame, renewed the military offensive that brought it to power three months later.

Pasteur Bizimungu, who had become national President in July 1994, resigned in March 2000. He was replaced the following month by Kagame, who had previously served as Vice-President and Minister of National Defence. Kagame was the first Tutsi President since Rwanda gained independence in 1962. Kagame won a landslide victory in presidential elections held in August 2003, easily defeating his two Hutu challengers. In elections to the newly-established Chamber of Deputies held on Sept. 29-Oct. 2, 2003, the FPR and its four coalition allies – the Christian Democratic Party, the Islamic Democratic Party, the Rwandan Socialist Party and the Rwandan People's Democratic Union – won a landslide victory, gaining 40 of the 53 contested seats.

Rwandan People's Democratic Union
Union Démocratique du People Rwandais (UDPR)
Leadership. Adrien Rangira
The UDPR contested the Sept. 29-Oct. 1, 2003, elections to the newly-created Chamber of Deputies, the lower house of the bicameral legislature, as part of a coalition led by the Rwandan Patriotic Front (FPR). The party won one seat.

Rwandan Socialist Party
Parti Socialiste Rwandais (PSR)
Leadership. Medard Rutijanwa
The PSR contested the Sept. 29-Oct. 1, 2003, elections to the newly-created Chamber of Deputies, the lower house of the bicameral legislature, as part of a coalition led by the Rwandan Patriotic Front (FPR). The party won a single seat.

Social Democratic Party
Parti Social–Démocrate (PSD)
Leadership. Vincent Biruta
The Hutu PSD was one of the first three opposition parties to be recognized under the 1991 constitution, and participated in government coalitions from April 1992. The party's president and vice-president were both killed in the mass violence which erupted in 1994, their bodies being discovered and identified in February 1995. The PSD contested the Sept. 29-Oct. 1, 2003, elections to the newly-created Chamber of Deputies, the lower house of the bicameral legislature, and won over 12% of the vote and seven seats.

Other Parties

Party for Progress and Concord (*Parti pour le Progrès et la Concorde*, PPC), contested the Sept. 29-Oct. 1, 2003, elections to the newly-created Chamber of Deputies, but failed to win the necessary 5% of the vote required to be allocated a seat.

St. Christopher and Nevis

Capital: Basseterre (St. Kitts)
Population: 39,000 (2003E)

The former British dependency of Saint Christopher (St. Kitts) and Nevis has been an independent member of the Commonwealth since 1983. The head of state is the British sovereign, represented by a Governor-General, who is appointed on the recommendation of the Prime Minister, the head of government. The unicameral federal Parliament or National Assembly, which has a five-year mandate, consists of 11 elected members together with three appointed senators (nominated by the Governor-General on the advice of the government and the opposition). It also includes the Speaker (elected by the members) and the Attorney General, either of who may or may not be elected members.

The strength of separatist sentiment in the island of Nevis (which has a population of just over 10,000) was acknowledged in the independence constitution under which Nevis was granted considerable local autonomy, including its own Assembly, executive and Premier (parallel structures do not exist in St. Kitts). The constitution also granted Nevis the right to secede subject to various conditions. In August 1998 a referendum resulted in 62% of Nevisians voting for independence, but this fell short of the two-thirds majority required under the constitution.

In St. Kitts there are two political parties, the St. Kitts-Nevis Labour Party (SKNLP) and the People's Action Movement (PAM), while the two parties in Nevis are the Concerned Citizens' Movement (CCM) and the Nevis Reformation Party (NRP). In federal elections on March 6, 2000, Labour (in office since 1995) won a further five-year term, taking all eight elected seats on St. Kitts. The CCM took two of the three seats in Nevis and the NRP the third. The CCM forms the local administration in Nevis, where elections were last held in 2001.

Concerned Citizens' Movement (CCM)
Address. Golden Rock, Gingerland, Nevis
Telephone. (1-869) 469-2736
Leadership. Vance Amory (leader)
The Nevis-based CCM has held a majority in the local Nevis Assembly since 1992. In federal elections it won two of the three Nevis seats in each of the elections of 1993, 1995 and 2000. The CCM urged a vote for secession from St. Kitts at a referendum in August 1998 but this proposal narrowly failed to win the required two-thirds majority. Since then little progress has been made regarding constitutional reform, and as a consequence the option of independence is once again on the agenda. An indication of this came in February 2003, when the CCM together with the Nevis Reformation Party (NRP), announced that they would no longer participate in future federal elections and would campaign for full autonomy from St. Kitts. At a meeting of the Nevis Island Assembly, on June 23, 2003, which approved the island's attempts to seek independence, Premier Amory stated that the people of Nevis wanted to assume "full responsibility for their destiny, politically, economically, socially and in every way possible". Further, in August, under Section 113 of the federal constitution, the Nevis government presented a draft constitution for the island. Despite a small population the CCM believes that the many thousands of offshore businesses operating from Nevis provide a basis for economic independence from St. Kitts. The opponents of secession, meanwhile, maintain that independence would effectively hand over control of the island to money launderers and drug cartels.

Nevis Reformation Party (NRP)
Address. Government Road, Charlestown, Nevis
Telephone. (1-869) 469-0630
Leadership. Joseph Parry (leader)
The NRP was formed in 1970, advocating the separation of Nevis from St. Kitts. In 1980, having retained two National Assembly seats, the party formed a coalition government with the People's Action Movement, which in 1983 oversaw the independence of St. Kitts and Nevis as a federation with considerable local autonomy for Nevis. In the 1990s the Concerned Citizens' Movement (CCM) displaced the NRP as the major party on Nevis, with the NRP retaining only one National Assembly seat in each of the 1993, 1995 and 2000 elections. In the 1998 referendum on independence for Nevis the NRP opposed secession, party leader Joseph Parry warning that Nevis lacked the human and economic resources to sustain itself as an independent nation. However, the party has since reversed its position after becoming disillusioned with the lack of progress towards greater autonomy for the island and fearful of losing the political initiative to the CCM.

The NRP is a member of the Caribbean Democrat Union, a regional organization of the International Democrat Union.

People's Action Movement (PAM)
Address. Lockhart Street, Basseterre
Telephone. (1-869) 465-9335
Leadership. Lindsay Grant (leader)
The centre-right PAM was formed in 1965. In 1979 Dr. Kennedy Simmonds became (in a by-election) the first person ever elected on the island of St. Kitts who was not from the Labour Party. Campaigning in the 1980 elections on a platform of early independence, the party won three of the (then) nine elective seats, which with the two seats won by the Nevis Reformation Party (NRP) allowed it to form a coalition government.

The coalition led St. Kitts-Nevis to independence in

1983, and Simmonds became the country's first Prime Minister. The PAM remained in government through the 1984 and 1989 elections. In the 1993 elections, although finishing second in the popular vote and returning only four of the 11 National Assembly members, the PAM retained office as a minority government with the support of the NRP. As a result of political instability and civil disorder, together with allegations of government corruption and links with organized crime, an early election was called for July 1995, in which the party lost all but one seat and was forced into opposition. In the 2000 elections the PAM campaigned on a platform that argued the ruling Labour Party had failed to revive the sugar industry or tackle the country's external debt, and had allowed organized crime and drug racketeering to flourish, but it won no seats. The PAM alleged that the result was flawed because of electoral fraud arising from improper voter registration and bribery, and criticized the government for failing to invite a Commonwealth observer group to monitor the election. After the election Kennedy Simmonds stepped down as leader and was replaced by Lindsay Grant. Grant's effectiveness as opposition leader has been hindered, however, by the PAM's lack of representation in the National Assembly.

The PAM is a member of the Caribbean Democrat Union, a regional organization of the International Democrat Union.

St. Kitts-Nevis Labour Party (SKNLP)
Address. Masses House, Church Street, Basseterre
Telephone. (1-869) 465-2229
Email. labourleads@caribsurf.com
Website. www.sknlabourparty.org
Leadership. Denzil L. Douglas (political leader); Timothy Harris (chairman)
Originating in 1932 as the St. Kitts Workers' League, the Labour Party had a majority in the legislature in every election from the introduction of adult suffrage in 1952 until 1980. Having lost power in the 1980 elections to a coalition of the People's Action Movement (PAM) and the Nevis Reformation Party (NRP), Labour opposed what it regarded as the disproportionate amount of power given to Nevis by the independence constitution of 1983. Denzil Douglas became party leader in 1989. Elections in November 1993 resulted in both the PAM and the Labour Party winning four seats (although Labour won 54.5% of the vote in St. Kitts compared with the 41.7% won by the PAM), with PAM continuing in office with the support of the NRP. Labour and its supporters then agitated for early fresh elections with political instability and violence resulting; a state of emergency was declared for ten days in December 1993 because of disturbances and in 1994 there was further unrest with Labour boycotting the Assembly.

In November 1994 the political parties and civic groups reached agreement to hold early general elections. When these took place in July 1995 Labour won seven of the eight seats in St. Kitts and returned to power. In 1998 US magazine *Newsweek* charged that the 1995 Labour campaign had been in part financed by Charles "Little Nut" Miller, wanted in the United States on drug trafficking charges. Efforts by the US authorities to extradite Miller, who had substantial business interests in St. Kitts and was widely seen as above the law, failed until the eve of the March 2000 election when (after a Cabinet decision) he was arrested and handed over to US law enforcement officials. The action, described by Douglas as being taken to eradicate the threat to foreign investment posed by intimidation and blackmail, was seen as bolstering the government's popularity. Labour went on to retain power, taking all eight seats in St. Kitts. Labour's 2000 election programme pledged an inclusive society and poverty eradication as priorities, "zero tolerance" for crime, full employment and never to re-introduce personal income tax.

The government's second term has been defined to a large extent by the ongoing dispute over the nature of the St. Kitts-Nevis relationship. The SKNLP is opposed to full autonomy for Nevis but supports a new constitutional relationship that would mean that the federal government retains responsibility for only external affairs, national security and the judiciary. However, the deep antipathy between the SKNLP and the Nevis governing administration has made it very difficult to reach a settlement on constitutional reform.

The Labour Party is a consultative member of the Socialist International.

St. Lucia

Capital: Castries
Population: 162,000 (2003E)

Saint Lucia gained independence from the United Kingdom in 1979, remaining within the Commonwealth. The head of state is the British sovereign, represented by a Governor-General. The head of government is the Prime Minister. There is a bicameral parliament consisting of an appointed 11-member Senate and a 17-member House of Assembly. Assembly members are elected on the Westminster model for five-year terms on the basis of first past the post in single-seat constituencies. Senators are appointed by the Governor-General, six on the advice of the Prime Minister, three on the advice of the Leader of the Opposition and two at the discretion of the Governor-General after consulting religious, economic and social bodies.

The St. Lucia Labour Party (SLP) retained power when in elections on Dec. 3, 2001, it won 14 of the 17 Assembly seats, taking 54.2% of the vote. The remaining seats were won by the United Workers' Party (UWP), which gained 36.6% of the vote.

St. Lucia Labour Party (SLP)

Address. Tom Walcott Building, PO Box 427, Jeremie Street, Castries
Telephone. (1-758) 458-2096
Email. slp@candw.lc
Website. www.slp.org.lc
Leadership. Kenny D. Anthony (leader)
The centre-left SLP originated in the late 1940s as the political arm of the St. Lucia Workers' Cooperative Union, a trade union. It won the first elections held under universal adult suffrage in 1951 and formed the administration in the then colony until 1964. Other than in the period 1979-82 it was thereafter continuously in opposition to the governing United Workers' Party (UWP) until the elections of May 1997 when, led by former law lecturer Kenny Anthony, it took 16 of the 17 Assembly seats. It came to office on a platform promising "people centred" government, economic development and improved health care and education, while capitalizing on allegations of corruption and scandal surrounding the outgoing UWP government.

Despite a worsening economic situation in the build up to the general election in December 2001, and the defection of George Odlum, former SLP Foreign Affairs Minister, to the National Alliance (NA), the SLP retained power with another large parliamentary majority. The SLP was helped by a fractious and deeply divided opposition. One issue that strained the unity of the SLP in the new parliament was that of abortion. In November 2003 a vote was taken in the House of Assembly on a new criminal code bill, which contained an amendment to the abortion act legalizing the practice in special circumstances. Although the measure was passed, Home Affairs and Gender Relations Minister Sarah Flood-Beaubrun voted against the bill, and accused her cabinet colleagues of being "pro-abortionists", "child killers", and "murderers". In response Prime Minister Anthony sacked Flood-Beaubrun for breaking the rules of collective responsibility and for her insulting behaviour towards fellow cabinet members. In turn, Flood-Beaubrun resigned from the SLP in March 2004, becoming an independent member of the House.

The SLP is a consultative member of the Socialist International.

United Workers' Party (UWP)

Address. 1 Riverside Road, Castries
Telephone. (1-758) 452-3438
Email. uwp@iname.com
Website. www.geocities.com/capitolhill/8393
Leadership. Marcus Nicholas (parliamentary leader); Vaughan Lewis (party leader)
The conservative UWP was formed in 1964 and under the leadership of John Compton ruled from 1964 until 1979, when it was decisively beaten in the first post-independence election. It returned to power in May 1982 and then remained in government until 1997. In April 1996 Compton was succeeded as party leader and Prime Minister by Vaughan Lewis, under whom the UWP slumped to defeat in the May 1997 elections, taking only one seat. Morella Joseph was elected party leader in October 2000 following Lewis's resignation, becoming the first woman party leader in St. Lucia. In May 2001 she also became the vice-president of the anti-SLP National Alliance (NA). However, the UWP's involvement in the NA lasted only until October, when the party announced that it would contest the forthcoming general election alone.

At the election the UWP slightly improved its parliamentary standing, but only managed to win three seats. Further, both UWP leader Morella Joseph and former leader and Prime Minister Vaughan Lewis failed to win seats in the newly constituted House of Assembly. The lack of an experienced leader and serious divisions within the UWP damaged further the opposition's effectiveness. The first UWP leader in the new parliament, Marius Wilson, was replaced in February 2003 after criticism of his poor performance. Wilson's successor Arsene James, however, soon developed a reputation for being easily intimidated by the ruling SLP. The situation was aggravated further by Wilson's strong criticism of the UWP and his decision to leave the party and become an independent MP. The instability within the parliamentary party continued in March 2004, when the third of the party's MPs, Marcus Nicholas replaced James as parliamentary leader. Nicholas gained the leadership with the support of Marius Wilson, but without consulting the UWP party leadership or his constituency branch. Once sworn in, Nicholas strongly criticized the leadership of Vaughan Lewis, who had been reappointed party head after the 2001 election, and attempted to replace the party's three existing members of the Senate with his own supporters. In retaliation, the UWP hierarchy suspended Nicholas' membership of the party in April and undertook disciplinary action against him. The result was that the UWP's position in both the House of Assembly and Senate was seriously undermined.

The UWP is a member of the Caribbean Democrat Union, a regional organization of the International Democrat Union.

Other Parties

Committee for Meaningful Change and Reconstruction emerged from the defunct National Alliance (NA) in early 2004. The NA was originally set up in Spring 2001 as an umbrella group for opponents of the St. Lucia Labour Party (SLP) government in preparation for the forthcoming general election, promising to establish a "national unity government". Its three co-leaders were George Odlum, dismissed as the SLP government's Foreign Affairs Minister on March 29, 2001, because of reports of his involvement in the formation of the Alliance, Sir John Compton, former UWP leader and Prime Minister, and the then UWP leader Morella Joseph. In May 2001 Odlum was named NA political leader, with Compton and Joseph as president and vice-president respectively. However, the UWP left the NA after only six months, a move precipitated by a serious falling out between Odlum and Compton over the leadership of the party. Odlum chose to retain the name National Alliance, but at the general election held in December 2001 the party failed to win a single parliamentary seat, gaining only 3.5% of the vote. The defeat brought to an end the party's attempts to establish itself as a viable third force within St. Lucian politics. However, members of the NA established subsequently a new political organization, known as the Committee for Meaningful Change and Reconstruction, to promote the ideals of George Odlum.

National Development Movement (NDM) was formed in February 2004 under the leadership of Ausbert D'Auvergne, a former senior public servant and aide to former St. Lucia Prime Minister and UWP leader John Compton. D'Auvergne claimed that the party was established to address the growing problems of crime and the spiritual and moral decay within society.

St. Vincent and the Grenadines

Capital: Kingstown
Population: 117,000 (2003E)

A former British dependency, Saint Vincent and the Grenadines became fully independent within the Commonwealth in 1979. The head of state is the British sovereign, represented by a Governor-General. The head of government is the Prime Minister. The unicameral House of Assembly, which serves a term of office of up to five years, comprises six appointed Senators (four nominated by the government and two by the opposition) and 15 representatives elected on the first past the post system in single member constituencies.

The conservative New Democratic Party (NDP) of Sir James F. Mitchell won four successive elections in 1984, 1989, 1994 and 1998. In the June 1998 election, however, the opposition social democratic Unity Labour Party (ULP), although winning only seven seats to the NDP's eight, took 55% of the vote to the NDP's 45%. The ULP demanded fresh elections and a period of unrest culminated in Prime Minister Mitchell, in the Grand Beach Accord of May 2000, agreeing to hold a further general election by the end of March 2001. In the run-up to the elections, which were held on March 28, 2001, the three contesting party leaders signed a code of conduct agreeing equal access to the media and not to incite or encourage violence. The elections, which were monitored by Commonwealth observers at the government's request, resulted in victory for the ULP. The ULP won 12 of the 15 elected seats, with 56.7% of the vote, while the NDP took the remaining three seats with 40.7% of the vote.

New Democratic Party (NDP)
Address. Democrat House, PO Box 1300, Kingstown
Telephone. (1-784) 457-2647
Email. ndp@caribsurf.com
Leadership. Arnhim Eustace (leader)
James Mitchell founded the conservative NDP in 1975, advocating political unity in the East Caribbean, social development and free enterprise. In 1984 the NDP formed the government for the first time, with Prime Minister Mitchell then winning three further successive elections (in 1989, 1994 and 1998). In the 1998 election, however, although the NDP took eight seats to the Unity Labour Party's seven, it won fewer votes. The ULP demanded fresh elections and tensions climaxed in April-May 2000 in work stoppages, road blockades and demonstrations against plans to provide improved benefits for parliamentarians. Mitchell refused to resign, warning of the damage being done to the country's reputation by the instability, but in the Grand Beach Accord, brokered by heads of other Caribbean states in May 2000, he agreed to hold elections two years ahead of schedule. In October 2000 Mitchell stood down as Prime Minister and was replaced by his Finance Minister, economist Arnhim Eustace.

In the run-up to the March 2001 elections Eustace warned that failing to re-elect the NDP with an increased majority would jeopardize foreign investment and he promised to accelerate restructuring of the economy, which had been damaged by the decline of exports of bananas, the principal commodity. However, the NDP lost office, retaining only three seats. Since the election the party has found it difficult to turn its fortunes around, despite a growing number of problems facing the government. In frustration at its lack of political influence the NDP held an "alternative parliament" in March 2004. Citing discrimination and the lack of opportunity to participate in parliamentary debate, NDP leader Eustace stated "it is the first time in the history of our country that one has found it necessary to have an alternative parliament".

The NDP is an associate member of the International Democrat Union (IDU) and a member of the IDU's regional organizations, the Americas Democrat Union and the Caribbean Democrat Union.

Unity Labour Party (ULP)
Address. Beachmount, Kingstown
Telephone. (1-784) 457-2761
Fax. (1-784) 456-2811
Email. headquarters@ulpsvg.com
Leadership. Ralph E. Gonsalves (political leader)
The centre-left ULP was established in September 1994 by the merger of the moderate social democratic St. Vincent Labour Party (SVLP) and the more left-wing Movement for National Unity (MNU), founded in 1982 by lawyer Ralph Gonsalves. The SVLP was in power from 1967-84 and led the country to independence in 1979. The conservative New Democratic Party then won a string of election victories in 1984, 1989, 1994 and 1998. Gonsalves succeeded the ULP's first leader, Vincent Beache, in December 1998. The ULP disputed the result of the 1998 elections (which the NDP won by one seat) and was behind subsequent anti-government demonstrations that forced the government to accept early elections. Gonsalves then led the ULP to victory in the March 2001 election, when it won 12 seats with 56.7% of the vote.

On taking office Gonsalves pledged to clean up St. Vincent's offshore financial sector, which had attracted criticism from the OECD's Financial Action Task Force (FATF). The government instituted a series of legislative acts to tighten the regulation of the sector and in June 2003 the country was removed from the FATF's list of non-cooperative countries. Despite the government's success on this front, its reputation was tarnished by a number of scandals during 2003. A series of corruption charges were levelled against the government, while the ULP also came under pressure for its alleged links with the marijuana trade. The latter claim was particularly serious, as it undermined the government's stated commitment to address the issue of drug cultivation and the growing problem of violent crime associated with the trafficking of cocaine. In spite of these problems Prime Minister Gonsalves retained his popularity.

The ULP is a consultative member of the Socialist International.

Other Parties

People's Progressive Movement (PPM) founded by Ormiston (Ken) Boyea, a former leading figure in the Unity Labour Party, in 2000. It won only 2.6% of the vote and no seats in the March 2001 election.

Samoa

Capital: Apia
Population: 168,000 (2000E)

Administered by New Zealand after World War I (in later years with self-government), Western Samoa achieved full independence in 1962 and opted for the shortened name Samoa in 1997. The head of state acts as a constitutional monarch with the power to dissolve the unicameral 49-member legislative assembly (the *Fono*) and to appoint a Prime Minister upon its recommendation. The *Fono* is elected by universal adult suffrage for up to five years, although the right to stand for election remains confined to members of the *Matai* (elected clan leaders).

In general elections on March 2, 2001, the ruling Human Rights Protection Party (HRPP) won 23 seats against 13 for the Samoan National Development Party, while 13 independents were elected. On March 16 the leader of the HRPP and incumbent Premier, Tuilaepa Sailele Malielegaoi, was re-elected by members of the *Fono*.

Human Rights Protection Party (HRPP)
Address. POB 3898, Apia
Leadership. Tuilaepa Sailele Malielegaoi (leader)
The HRPP was founded in 1979 as Western Samoa's first formal political party. Having won 22 parliamentary seats in the 1982 general elections, the party won an overall majority in 1985. However, subsequent defections brought down the government headed by Tofilau Eti Alesana at the end of that year. Tofilau Eti formed a new HRPP administration following the 1988 election, and the party's majority was enhanced in polling in 1991. In the 1996 elections, the HRPP won 24 of the 49 seats but quickly drew in enough independent deputies to retain a comfortable overall majority.

Tofilau Eti resigned for health reasons in November 1998 and was succeeded by his deputy, Tuilaepa Sailele Malielegaoi. Campaigning for elections to the *Fono* in March 2001 featured opposition allegations of corruption against the government and a demand, rejected by the Prime Minister, that the franchise and the right to stand in elections should be extended to Samoans resident abroad. In the event, the HRPP lost ground slightly, winning 23 seats, but again used its control of the levers of government to attract sufficient independents to ensure a continued majority.

In the wake of the elections the HRPP moved to appease its critics by setting up an electoral commission, but failed to convince the opposition that it would be independent. In August 2001 three HRPP ministers appeared in court on charges of bribery in the recent elections.

Samoan National Development Party (SNDP)
Address c/o Fono, Apia
Leadership. Tupua Tamasese Efi (leader)
The SNDP was created following the 1988 elections as an alliance of independents and Christian Democratic Party (CDP) members. The CDP had been formed by Tupua Tamasese Efi prior to the February 1985 general election and, in January 1986, had entered into a coalition government with a dissident faction of the Human Rights Protection Party (HRPP). SNDP was constituted following the 1988 elections, which saw the return to power of the HRPP.

The SNDP remained the principal opposition party through the 1990s. In the campaign for the March 2001 elections the party accused the HRPP government of corruption, notably by selling Samoan passports to Chinese and Taiwanese nationals and in its management of Polynesian Airlines, the national carrier. However, the SNDP made only limited progress at the polls, returning 13 members of the *Fono*, and remained in opposition.

Other Parties

Samoa Democratic Party (SDP), formed in 1993 by a previously independent deputy in the *Fono* who objected to the extension of the legislature's term from three to five years without popular endorsement in a referendum.
Leadership. Le Tagaloa Pita

Samoa Labour Party (SLP), launched in 1994 by Toleapaialii Toesulusulu Siueva, a hotel owner who accused the ruling Human Rights Protection Party of corruption. He won a seat in the 1996 elections but resigned after being accused of bribery.
Leadership. Toleapaialii Toesulusulu Siueva

Samoa Liberal Party (SLP), established in early 1994 mainly by dissidents of the ruling Human Rights Protection Party opposed to the introduction of value-added tax.
Leadership. Nonumalo Leulumoega Sofara

Samoa National Party (SNP), established in January 2001, but unsuccessful in the March elections.

Samoans For Tomorrow (SFT), founded in 1998 and subsequently prominent in popular opposition to the ruling Human Rights Protection Party.
Leadership. Tuifa'asisina Meaole Keil

San Marino

Capital: San Marino
Population: 26,266 (2004)

The Most Serene Republic of San Marino, which traces its independent history back to 301 AD and its constitution to 1600, is a parliamentary democracy with a flourishing multi-party system. Legislative power is vested in the 60-member Grand and General Council (*Consiglio Grande e Generale*), which is directly elected by a system of proportional representation by citizens aged 18 and over, serving a five-year term subject to dissolution. A 10-member Congress of State (*Congresso di Stato*), or government, is elected by the Council for the duration of its term. Two members of the Council are designated for six-month terms as executive Captains Regent (*Capitani Reggenti*), one representing the city of San Marino and the other the countryside. An interval of three months must elapse before a councillor can be re-elected as a Captain Regent.

Early elections to the Grand and General Council on June 10, 2001, resulted as follows: Christian Democratic Party of San Marino 25 seats (with 41.4% of the vote), Socialist Party of San Marino 15 (24.2%), Party of Democrats 12 (20.8%), Popular Alliance of San Marino Democrats for the Republic 5 (8.2%), Communist Refoundation 2 (3.4%), San Marino National Alliance 1 (1.9%).

Christian Democratic Party of San Marino
Partito Democratico Cristiano Sammarinese (PDCS)
Address. via delle Scalette 6, 47890 Repubblica di San Marino
Tel. +378 0549 991 193
Fax. +378 0549 992 694
Email. pdcs@omniway.sm
Website. www.pdcs.sm
Leadership. Giovanni Lonfernini (political secretary); Pier Marino Mularoni (Council group leader); Ernesto Benedettini (president)
Founded in 1948, the PDCS was in opposition to a left-wing coalition until 1957, following which it headed centre-left coalitions until 1978. The party achieved narrow pluralities in successive Council elections, winning 25 seats in 1974, 26 in both 1978 and 1983 and 27 in 1988. The PDCS returned to power in July 1986, when the left-wing government collapsed and was replaced by San Marino's (and Europe's) first-ever coalition between Christian Democrats and Communists. This lasted until February 1992, when the PDCS opted to form a coalition with the Socialist Party of San Marino (PSS).

The Christian Democrats retained their Council dominance in the 1993 and 1998 elections, albeit with slightly reduced representation of 26 and 25 seats respectively, and continued to govern in coalition with the PSS. In early elections in June 2001 the party again won 25 seats, opting this time to broaden the ruling coalition to include both the PSS and the Party of Democrats.

The PDCS is affiliated to the Christian Democrat International.

Party of Democrats
Partito dei Democratici (PdD)
Address. via Sentier Rosso 1, 47890 Repubblica di San Marino
Tel. +378 0541 991 199
Email. info@democratici.sm
Website. www.democratici.sm
Leadership. Claudio Felici (secretary-general); Emma Rossi (president)
The PdD was founded in April 1990 as the Progressive Democratic Party (PDP), which was the successor to the San Marino Communist Party (PCS) in line with similar conversions to democratic socialism on the part of communist parties elsewhere in Europe. Founded in 1941, the PCS had been an orthodox pro-Soviet party after World War II and had been in government with the San Marino Socialist Party (PSS) until 1957 and again from 1978 until 1986, when the coalition had collapsed in 1986 amid differences over foreign and domestic issues. It had been replaced by the first-ever coalition of the PCS and the San Marino Christian Democratic Party (PDCS). PCS representation in the Council had risen to 18 at the May 1988 elections, although its conversion into the PDP in 1990 resulted in two of its councillors joining the breakaway Communist Refoundation.

The new PDP was forced into opposition in February 1992, when the PDCS decided that the PSS was a more suitable partner, and won only 11 seats in both the 1993 and the 1998 elections, remaining in opposition to a PDCS–PSS coalition. Having changed its name to the PdD, the party improved to 12 seats in the June 2001 elections and agreed to join a three-party "grand coalition" with the PDCS and PSS.

Popular Alliance of San Marino Democrats for the Republic (APDSR)
Alleanza Popolare dei Democratici Sammarinesi per la Repubblica
Address. 26 via Ca' Bartoletto, Cailungo, 47890 Repubblica di San Marino
Tel. +378 0549 907 080
Fax. +378 0549 907 082
Email. info@alleanzapopolare.net/
Website. www.alleanzapopolare.net/
Leadership. Roberto Giorgetti (coordinator)
The centrist APDSR was founded before the May 1993 Council elections, in which it took fourth place behind the three main parties, winning four seats on a platform advocating constitutional and institutional reform. It improved to six seats in 1998 but fell back to five in 2001.

Socialist Party of San Marino
Partito Socialista Sammarinese (PSS)
Address. via G. Ordelaffi 46, Borgo Maggiore, 47031 Repubblica di San Marino
Tel. +378 0549 902 016
Fax. +378 0549 906 438
Website. www.pss.sm
Leadership. Mauro Chiaruzzi (secretary-general); Alberto Cecchetti (president)
The PSS was in coalition government with the Communists from 1945 until 1957 and then in opposition until 1973, when it entered a coalition with the Christian Democratic Party of San Marino (PDCS). Throughout this period the Socialists were a distant second to the PDCS in successive Council elections, winning eight seats in 1974 against 25 for the PDCS. The PDCS-PSS coalition continued until November 1977, when the Socialists withdrew because of economic policy differences. The party retained eight Council seats in the 1978 elections, thereafter entering a left-wing coalition with the Communists and the Unitarian Socialists (PSU) which continued after the 1983 elections, in which the PSS advanced to nine seats. The left-wing coalition collapsed in mid-1986, when the PSS went into formal opposition for the first time since World War II. In 1990 the PSU (which had been formed in 1975 by a left-wing faction of the Independent Social Democrats, themselves originally a right-wing splinter of the Socialist Party) merged with the PSS.

The PSS revived its coalition with the PDCS in February 1992, continuing it after the May 1993 elections, when it advanced to 14 seats, and after those of May 1998, in which it retained 14 seats. In the early elections of June 2001 the party advanced to 15 seats, thereafter becoming part of a three-party coalition led by the PDCS and including the Party of Democrats.

The PSS is affiliated to the Socialist International.

Other Parties

Communist Refoundation (*Rifondazione Comunista*, RC). Founded in 1990 by a minority Marxist-Leninist faction of the San Marino Communist Party which declined to accept the conversion of the latter into the democratic socialist Progressive Democratic Party in April 1990 (Party of Democrats). RC won two Council seats in May 1993, retaining them in October 1998 and June 2001.

Address. Via Ca' dei Lunghi , 70/A, Borgo Maggiore, 47893 Repubblica di San Marino
Tel./Fax +378 0549 906 682
Email. rcs@omniway.sm
Website. www.rifondazionecomunista-rsm.org/
Leadership. Ivan Foschi

San Marino National Alliance (*Alleanza Nazionale Sammarinese*, ANS). New, right-wing formation which won a single seat in the June 2001 Council elections.
Telephone. +378 0549 907 801
Fax. +378 0549 987 280
Website. www.alleanzanazionalersm.sm/
Leadership. Glauco Sansovini

São Tomé and Príncipe

Capital: São Tomé
Population: 160,000 (2000E)

The Democratic Republic of São Tomé and Príncipe achieved full independence from Portugal in 1975. There was only one legal political party – the Movement for the Liberation of São Tomé and Príncipe–Social Democratic Party (MLSTP-PSD) – until August 1990, when a new constitution providing for a multi-party democratic system was approved by referendum. Under the constitution, executive power is vested in a directly-elected President who may serve for a maximum of two consecutive five-year terms. Legislative power is vested in a 55-member National Assembly (*Assembléia Nacional*) with a maximum four-year term. A regional government looks after the affairs of the island of Príncipe, which assumed autonomous status in April 1995.

Presidential elections in March 1991 were won by independent candidate Miguel Trovoada, who was supported by the Democratic Convergence Party–Reflection Group (PCD-GR), which had defeated the ruling party in the first multi-party legislative elections two months earlier. Further legislative elections in October 1994 resulted in the MLSTP-PSD winning a plurality of 27 seats and regaining governmental power. In August 1995 a group of young army officers temporarily seized power in a bloodless coup. However, following mediation by Angolan representatives, the President and civilian government were restored to office.

In further presidential elections on June 30 and July 21, 1996, incumbent Miguel Trovoada (Independent Democratic Action, ADI) was re-elected in the second round with 52.7% of the vote. Another brief military takeover by young army officers followed in August, but President Trovoada was restored to power on Aug. 22. Eight political parties contested the National Assembly elections held on Nov. 8, 1998, which returned the MLSTP-PSD to power with 31 seats and an outright majority. The ADI and PCD-GR won 16 and 8 seats respectively, and were the only opposition parties to secure representation.

In a presidential election held on July 29, 2001, ADI candidate Fradique de Menezes won in the first round by polling 56.3% of the vote; his closest rival, former President Manuel Pinto da Costa of the MLSTP-PSD, gained 38.7%.

Legislative elections were held on March 3, 2002. The MLSTP gained 39.6% of the vote and 24 seats in the National Assembly; the PCD-GR running with the Democratic Movement Force for Change followed closely, polling 39.4% of the vote and getting 23 seats; the UE–Kedadji Coalition (Independent Democratic Action and other small parties) won 16.2% of the vote and 8 seats.

On July 16, 2003, Major Fernando Pereira "Cobo" seized power in a coup for eight days, while President Fradique de Menezes was on a private visit to Nigeria. After negotiations, the President returned to the country.

Democratic Convergence Party–Reflection Group
Partido de Convergencia Democrática–Grupo de Reflexão (PCD-GR)
Address. c/o Assembléia Nacional, São Tomé
Leadership. Aldo Bandeira (president)
Initially an underground opposition movement, the PCD-GR formally came into existence following the constitutional changes in 1990. In the January 1991 legislative elections the party won a majority with just over 54% of the votes cast, and in March it supported the successful presidential candidacy of Miguel Trovoada. Relations between the PCD-GR and the President subsequently deteriorated, as did the party's popularity, culminating in defeat in the legislative elections in October 1994, in which its representation in the National Assembly fell from 33 to 14.

Having supported a no-confidence motion against the government and signed an agreement which provided for the formation of a nine-member coalition with the Movement for the Liberation of São Tomé and Príncipe–Social Democratic Party (MLSTP-PSD), three members of the PCD-GR were appointed to the new administration formed in October 1996. However, the party came third in the 1998 legislative elections, declining to 8 seats (with just 16% of the vote). In the 2002 elections the party ran with the Democratic Movement Force for Change and came second with 39.4% of the vote and 23 seats.

Democratic Movement Force for Change
Movimento Democrático Força de Mudança (MDFM)
Address. c/o Assembléia Nacional, São Tomé
Leadership. Fradique de Menezes (president); Tome Vera Cruz (secretary-general)
This party was formed by President Fradique de Menezes and some of his supporters and ran for the first time in the 2002 elections with the PCD-GR, coming second with 39.4% of the vote and 23 seats.

Independent Democratic Action
Acção Democrática Independente (ADI)
Address. c/o Assembléia Nacional, São Tomé
Leadership. Carlos Agostinho das Neves
Founded in 1992 under the leadership of an adviser to President Trovoada, the centrist ADI won 14 of the 55 seats in the National Assembly in the 1994 elections, making it the joint runner-up with the Democratic Convergence Party–Reflection Group. In January 1996 the ADI accepted representation in a government of national unity headed by the Movement for the Liberation of São Tomé and Príncipe–Social Democratic Party (MLSTP-PSD). Trovoada was re-elected President in the second round of voting in July, having come a poor second in the first round with only 25% of the vote. The party refused to participate in the next MLSTP-PSD coalition government formed in October 1996 with the Democratic Convergence Party–Reflection Group (PCD-GR). In the 1998 legislative elections, the ADI came second (increasing its representation by two seats), although it complained of irregularities in the elections.

President Trovoada stepped down after the two five-year terms permitted under the constitution, and in the presidential elections in July 2001 ADI candidate Fradique de Menezes, a businessman, was elected in the first round with 56.3% of the vote. In the 2002 elections the ADI formed a coalition with the other small parties, the UE–Kedadji Coalition, and came third with 16.2% of the vote, securing 8 seats.

Movement for the Liberation of São Tomé and Príncipe–Social Democratic Party
Movimento de Libertação de São Tomé e Príncipe–Partido Social Democrata (MLSTP–PSD)

Address. c/o Assembléia Nacional, São Tomé
Leadership. Manuel Pinto da Costa (president); Carlos Alberto da Graça (secretary-general)

The leftist MLSTP was formed in the early 1970s and became the driving force in the campaign against Portuguese rule. After independence it maintained its position as the sole legal political organization until the adoption of multi-partyism in 1990, at which point the Social Democratic Party designation was added to its title and the longstanding leader and former President, Manuel Pinto da Costa, stood down. The party was defeated by the Democratic Convergence Party–Reflection Group (PCD-GR) in the January 1991 legislative elections and did not endorse any candidates in the presidential poll the following March. However, in the October 1994 legislative elections, the MLSTP-PSD was returned to power winning 27 of the seats in the 55-member National Assembly. The party's secretary-general, Carlos Alberto da Graça, was appointed Prime Minister of a Cabinet largely composed of MLSTP-PSD members. In December 1995, however, he was replaced by his party deputy, Armindo Vaz de Almeida, who formed a national unity government also including the Independent Democratic Alliance (ADI) and the extra-parliamentary Opposition Democratic Coalition. The MLSTP-PSD candidate in the mid-1996 presidential elections was da Costa, who headed the field in the first round with 40% of the vote but lost to the incumbent in the second round, when he received 47.3%.

The De Almeida government was dissolved after its defeat in a confidence motion in September 1996. President Trovoada refused to appoint the party's first choice of Prime Minister and Raúl Wagner da Conceição Bragança Neto was appointed to form a nine-member coalition government with the PCD-GR and one independent in October 1996. (De Almeida was expelled from the party in December, accused of corruption.)

Following an extraordinary party congress in May 1998, the party approved new statutes providing for: the creation of the position of party president, to which Pinto da Costa was elected; three vice-presidential appointments; and the enlargement of the national council from 95 to 120 members. The party held power securing a further four parliamentary seats (with over 50% of the vote) in the 1998 elections. Guilherme Posser da Costa was appointed Prime Minister, but his first nominations for the Council of Ministers were rejected by the President.

The power struggle between government and President has blocked decisions on important political and economic issues. In the July 2001 presidential elections, Pinto da Costa stood for the MLSTP but was beaten in the first round of voting by the ADI candidate backed by the outgoing President.

Saudi Arabia

Capital: Riyadh
Population: 23,513,330 – includes 5,360,526 non-nationals (July 2002 est.)

Saudi Arabia is an hereditary monarchy, ruled by the Al-Saud dynasty. The current royal family are the descendants of King Abdul-Aziz ibn Saud, who in 1902 captured Riyadh and embarked on a 30-year campaign to unify the Arabian Peninsula. The current King and Prime Minister (since June 1982) is Fahd bin Abdul-Aziz Al-Saud. The Crown Prince and First Deputy Prime Minister is Abdullah bin Abdul-Aziz Al-Saud (brother to the monarch and heir to the throne).

In 1992 a written constitution and a bill of rights were adopted. Since 1993 the Saudi Kingdom has been divided into 13 administrative districts that are administered by appointed governors and assemblies of local notables. In larger cities, municipal governments are appointed by local leaders, and towns and villages are governed by councils of elders. The constitution is based on *Shari'a* (Islamic law) and it is a principle that new legislation must be in accordance with *Shari'a* law. The government strictly limits freedom of association. It prohibits the establishment of political parties or any type of opposition group. By its power to license associations, the Government ensures that groups conform to public policy. There are no formal democratic institutions, and only a few citizens have a voice in the choice of leaders or in changing the political system. In August 2004 it was announced that municipal-level elections (for half of municipal council members, the others remaining appointed) would be held in early 2005 (no municipal elections having been held since the 1960s); however, in October it was announced that women would not be able to participate in the elections.

The King's powers are limited because he must observe the *Shari'a* and other Saudi traditions. He also must retain a consensus of the Saudi royal family, religious leaders (*ulema*), and other important elements in Saudi society. The leading members of the royal family choose the King from among themselves with the subsequent approval of the *ulema*.

Senegal

Capital: Dakar
Population: 9,987,000 (2000E)

Senegal was under French rule until it achieved independence in federation with Mali in June 1960. The federation was dissolved in August 1960 when Senegal withdrew. The following month the Republic of Senegal was proclaimed. President Léopold Sedar Senghor progressively monopolised political life, and Senegal became a de facto single-party state in 1966. But during the late 1970s, Senghor progressively liberalized the political sphere, a process which was carried further by Abdou Diouf, who took over when Senghor decided to step out of politics in 1980.

Under the constitution (most recently amended in 2001), executive power is vested in the President, who is directly elected by universal suffrage for a five-year term. The President, as head of state and head of government, appoints the Prime Minister, who appoints the Council of Ministers in consultation with the President. Legislative power is vested in the 120-member National Assembly (*Asssemblée Nationale*), which is also directly elected for a five-year term.

In presidential elections on Feb. 21, 1993, President Abdou Diouf of the Senegal Socialist Party (PSS) won his third term of office (extended from five to seven years following a constitutional amendment in 1991), with 58.4% of the votes cast. In Assembly elections on

May 9, 1993, the PSS obtained 84 seats, the Senegalese Democratic Party (PDS) 27 and four minor parties or alliances the other nine seats. In March 1998 the National Assembly voted to increase the number of its deputies from 120 to 140. At the following elections held on May 24, 1998, the PSS won 93 of the 140 seats, with the PDS again in second place with 23.

In January 1999 elections were held for the newly-established Senate; 45 of the 60 senators were elected by the National Assembly and local, municipal and regional councillors (and all were returned for the PSS), with 12 appointed by the President and three elected by Senegalese living abroad. Eight candidates stood in the presidential elections held on Feb. 27, 2000. After a second round on March 19, Abdoulaye Wade of the PDS with 58.5% of the vote beat the PSS incumbent Diouf (who took 41.5% of the vote). Diouf had led after the first round but lost after five of the six candidates who dropped out after the first round gave their support to Wade, so ending 40 years of uninterrupted socialist rule.

In a referendum on Jan. 7, 2001, an amended constitution was approved by over 90% of voters. It provided for the dissolution of the Senate, the reduction of the number of deputies in the National Assembly from 140 to 120 members, and the limiting of the presidential term from seven to five years – a measure not applicable to Wade's first term. It also gave the President power to dissolve the Assembly without the agreement of a two-thirds majority. Early legislative elections were held on April 29, 2001, in which the *Sopi* ("Change") coalition, led by President Wade's PDS, won a landslide victory over the former ruling party, taking 89 of the 120 seats. Mame Madior Boye, who had been appointed as Senegal's first woman Prime Minister in March 2001, was re-appointed in May. The local elections in May 2002 hinted to a progressive weakening of the presidential coalition's electoral hegemony: the PDS and its allies won 9 of the 11 regions, 40 of the 110 municipal councils and 250 of the 320 rural councils. In November 2002, Boye was replaced by Idrissa Seck, the assistant national secretary of the PDS and cabinet director of President Wade. Amidst growing political turmoil over poor governance, Seck resigned in August 2003, only to be confirmed by Wade a few days later; in this episode, contrary to expectations, Wade and Seck failed to bring new parties into the cabinet and stop the continuing shrinking of their coalition, the *Cap 21* (i.e. Cape 21st century). Conversely, the Permanent Structure for Coordination (*Cadre Permanent de Concertation*, CPC), a loose coalition of opposition parties, has kept growing since its constitution in May 2001. In April 2004, Wade finally dismissed Seck, replacing him with Macky Sall, hitherto Minister of the Interior; on that occcasion, the URD left the CPC for the *Cap 21*, and its leader Djibo Ka entered the government. A minor reshuffle happened in July 2004, allowing for the entry in the cabinet of Ousmane Ngom, the leader of a former PDS splinter party, now allied with Wade.

Senegal hosts a vast majority of Muslims (95% according to the 1988 census) most of whom are related to various Sufi brotherhoods. There long were close relationships between the leaders of these brotherhoods, the marabouts, and the state, colonial and postcolonial, but these links have been slackening since the 1980s, thus opening the door for a more direct and less univocal intervention of Islamic leaders in politics. Over the past few years in consequence, although confessional parties have long been officially forbidden by the Constitution, Senegal has had a growing number of parties with barely hidden Islamic identities, particularly since 2000. Often controlled by leading marabouts, these parties have moderate agendas.

And Jëf/African Party for Democracy and Socialism
And Jëf/Parti Africain pour la Démocratie et le Socialisme (AJ/PADS)
Address. BP 12136, Dakar
Telephone. (221) 825–7267
Fax. (221) 823–5860
Website. www.ajpads.org
Leadership. Landing Savané (secretary-general)
The progressive and pan-Africanist AJ/PADS was formed in 1991 by a merger of the And-Jëf-Revolutionary Movement for the New Democracy with three other left-wing groups. The party's leader, Landing Savané, took third place in the February 1993 presidential election but gained less than 3% of the votes cast. In May 1993 the party contested the legislative elections in an alliance with the National Democratic Rally and the Convention of Democrats and Patriots, which was called *Jappoo Liggeeyal* (Let Us Unite) and which won three National Assembly seats (and 4.9% of the vote). In February 1994 Savané and the leader of the Senegalese Democratic Party (PDS) were arrested and charged with provoking anti-government riots; all charges were dropped later in the year. The party won four seats in the 1998 National Assembly polling, and contested the Senate elections the following year in a coalition which included the Independence and Labour Party (PIT), although it failed to gain representation.

Throughout the years of PS rule, AJ/PADS was the only significant opposition party to refuse to join the government. Savané backed the successful candidature of Abdoulaye Wade for the presidential election in 2000 and was appointed Minister for Industry and Mines in the new government. The AJ/PADS ran on its own for the 2001 Assembly elections, retained two of its seats with 4% of the vote and has remained a member of Wade's coalition; Savané's ministry has since been reorganized and now covers Industry and Handicraft.

Alliance of Progressive Forces
Alliance des Forces du Progrès (AFP)
Address. BP 5825, Dakar Fann
Telephone. (221) 825–1488
Fax. (221) 825–7770
Email. admin@afp-senegal.org
Website. www.afp-senegal.org
Leadership. Moustapha Niasse (secretary-general)
The AFP was formed in June 1999 by a dissident faction of the Senegal Socialist Party (PSS) led by Moustapha Niasse, a former Minister of Foreign Affairs and close associate of President Senghor, subsequently turned to wealthy businessman. Niasse stood in the first round of the presidential election in 2000, coming third with 16.8% of the vote, and then transferred his support to Abdoulaye Wade in the run-off. Appointed Prime Minister in the subsequent new government, he was dismissed in March 2001 following his decision to contest the legislative elections the following month as leader of the AFP. The party came second in the polling, winning 11 seats, and plays a leading role in the CPC.

Democratic League–Labour Party Movement
Ligue Démocratique-Mouvement pour le Parti du Travail (LD–MPT)
Address. BP 10172, Dakar Liberté
Fax. (221) 827-4300
Email. ldmpt@metissacana.sn
Leadership. Abdoulaye Bathily (secretary-general)
The LD–MPT originated as a Marxist party in 1981. Increasingly critical of the Diouf administration, party leader

Bathily took part to the opposition *Sopi* alliance in 1988 and launched a campaign in 1990 for a "non-Diouf unity government". Bathily's presidential candidacy in February 1993 attracted only 2.4% of the votes cast, although the party secured three seats in the National Assembly elections the following May. Bathily was a Minister responsible for the environment from 1993 to 1998. The LD–MPT retained its Assembly seats in the 1998 elections with nearly 4% of the vote. In March 1999 it joined a left-wing coalition to back the Senegalese Democratic Party (PDS) candidate in the presidential election and Bathily was appointed Minister for energy and water in the subsequent new government. In the 2001 Assembly elections the party joined the PDS-led *Sopi* coalition, which won a landslide victory with 89 seats. Bathily subsequently left his ministry, to be replaced by other LD-MPT Ministers; the LD-MPT has retained two ministers in the cabinet since then – Seydou Sy Sall and Yéro Deh.

Independence and Labour Party
Parti de l'Indépendance et du Travail (PIT)
Address. BP 5612, Dakar Fann
Telephone. (221) 827-2907
Fax. (221) 820-9000
Website. www.pit-senegal.com
Leadership. Amath Dansokho (secretary-general)
The left-wing PIT, very influential in the trade-union milieu, was officially registered in 1981. Party leader Dansokho served in the Diouf government from 1991-95, and the PIT supported Aboud Diouf during the 1993 presidential election. It nevertheless allied with the Senegalese Democratic Party (PDS) to back the victorious PDS candidate in the 2000 presidential election. Dansokho was appointed Minister for urban planning in the new government, but he was sacked in November 2000. The party retained its single seat in the 2001 legislative polling. Dansokho is the national convener of the opposition coalition CPC.

Senegal Socialist Party
Parti Socialiste Sénégalais (PSS)
Address. BP 12010, Dakar
Telephone. (221) 824-7432
Fax. (221) 825-8054
Email. ps@telecomplus.sn
Website. www1.telecomplus.sn/ps
Leadership. Ousmane Tanor Dieng (executive secretary)
Founded in 1958 but descended from pre-war socialist movements in French West Africa, the democratic socialist PSS was the ruling party in Senegal from independence in 1960 to 2000. It adopted its present name at the end of 1976, before which change it had been called the Senegalese Progressive Union (UPS). Although it was in effect the country's only legal party between 1966 and 1974 under the presidency of its founder, Léopold Sedar Senghor, the constitution continued to guarantee a plurality of political parties and in 1974 the Senegalese Democratic Party (PDS) was officially recognized as an opposition party. A three-party system, introduced in 1976, was later extended to allow a multiplicity of parties. Abdou Diouf assumed the leadership of the PSS in 1981, after which new agricultural and industrial policies, intended to give a greater role to the private sector, were adopted.

The PSS dominated all Senegalese elections until 2000. Having retained the Presidency of the Republic in 1993, Diouf was elected to the new post of party chairman in 1996 and a new position of executive secretary was also created. During 1997 there were rumours of serious divisions within the PSS over Diouf's choice of Ousmane Tanor Dieng as his presumptive heir; a dissident group, led by Djibo Kâ, which had begun a campaign for party reform broke away in 1998 prior to the legislative elections that year. However, the PSS secured 93 of the 140 seats in the National Assembly and all the elected seats to the newly created Senate in 1999.

Diouf narrowly won the first round of the presidential elections in 2000 (with 41% of the vote) but lost the second round to the PDS candidate, Abdoulaye Wade, who was backed by the major opposition parties. Diouf subsequently left the PSS, and Ousmane Tanor Dieng assumed full command. Weakened by further defections, the PSS lost out badly in the 2001 legislative elections, winning only ten seats with 17% of the vote. The PSS belongs to the anti-Wade CPC coalition.

The party is a member of the Socialist International

Senegalese Democratic Party
Parti Démocratique Sénégalais (PDS)
Address. Boulevard Dial Diop, immeuble Serigne Mourtada Mbacké – Dakar
Telephone. (221) 823-5027 / 654-4778
Fax. (221) 823-9402
Website. www.sopionline.com
Leadership. Abdoulaye Wade (secretary-general)
Founded in 1974, the liberal democratic PDS was required by a constitutional amendment of March 1976 to adopt a formal political position to the right of the government party (in a three-party system which was later expanded to cover further parties). In successive legislative elections from 1970 until 2001, it was runner-up to, but some distance behind, the Senegal Socialist Party (PSS). In presidential elections until 2000, party leader Wade was similarly placed.

Although the PDS was the major element in the growing opposition movement at the end of the 1980s, the party was persuaded by early 1991 (like the Independence and Labour Party, PIT) to accept the government's offer of participation in a coalition administration. This continued until October 1992, when Wade and the other PDS members in the government resigned their posts. In May 1994 charges against Wade for his alleged role in the assassination of a member of the Constitutional Court in May 1993 were dismissed. Other charges, linked to anti-government rioting in February 1994, were similarly dropped later in the year. In March 1995 the PDS resumed its participation in the PSS-dominated coalition government, being assigned five portfolios.

In February 1998 Wade lodged an appeal to overturn legislation to enlarge the National Assembly and withdrew the party from government in March to prepare for the legislative elections scheduled for May. At the elections, however, the PDS secured only 23 seats with less than 20% of the vote.

Returning from a year in exile, Wade formed an alliance with the African Party for Democracy and Socialism (AJPADS), the PIT and the Democratic League–Labour Movement (LD–MPT) in 1999 and he was nominated as their joint candidate for the presidential elections in 2000. Enjoying the support of almost all opposition parties, Wade won a substantial victory over Diouf with 58.5% of the vote in the second round and negotiated the new constitution by referendum which enabled him to dissolve the PSS-dominated parliament. Under the name of *Sopi* ("Change"), a PDS-led coalition won 89 seats, giving it a commanding majority, in the new National Assembly. In November 2002, Idrissa Seck, second-in-command of the party, became Prime Minister; he resigned in August 2003, but was confirmed as PM by President Wade. Uneasy relationships between Seck and Wade finally resulted in the former's replacement as a PM by Macky Sall, another important PDS figure, in April 2004; a number of pro-Seck PDS ministers left the government at the same time.

From 2001 onwards, the PDS has managed to incorporate a number of splinter parties that had progressively formed while the PDS was in opposition – Ousmane Ngom's Senegalese Liberal Party (*Parti Libéral Sénégalais*, PLS),

Serigne Diop's Senegalese Democratic Party–Renovation (*Parti Démocratique Sénégalais–Rénovation*, PDS-R), and Jean-Paul Dias' *Bloc des Centristes Gaïndé* (BCG "Lion") have all returned to their mother-party, the PDS. Significant numbers of ex-PSS figures, as well as a number of other small parties, such as that of Mbaye-Jacques Diop, the former PSS mayor of Rufisque, the Party for Progress and Citizenship (*Parti pour le Progrès et la Citoyenneté*, PPC), or Samba Diouldé Thiam's Party of Rebirth and Citizenship (*Parti de la Renaissance et de la Citoyenneté*, PRC), have also joined the PDS since 2000.

The PDS is a member of the Liberal International.

Union for Democratic Renewal
Union pour le Renouveau Démocratique (URD)
Address. c/o Assemblée Nationale
Telephone. (221) 820-5598 / 825-4144
Leadership. Djibo Leyti Kâ (secretary-general)
Founded in April 1998 by former PSS Minister Kâ, hostile to the leadership of Ousmane Tanor Dieng over the PSS, the URD obtained 11 seats in the 1998 legislative elections. Kâ came fourth in the first round (with 7% of the vote) of the presidential elections in 2000 and was the only opposition member to support incumbent President Diouf in the run-off. In the 2001 Assembly elections the URD preserved only three of its seats, with just under 4% of the vote. The URD belonged to the anti-Wade CPC coalition, but finally rallied the PDS coalition in April 2004, and Kâ took over the ministry for the maritime economy.

Other Parties

African Party of Independence (*Parti africain de l'indépendance*, PAI). A Marxist-Leninist party founded in 1957, legalized in 1976. Now led by Majhmout Diop. While it supported Wade in the second round of the presidential election of 2000, the PAI subsequently opposed Wade's constitutional reforms and joined the CPC.

Alliance Jëf Jël, formerly the centrist Alliance for Progress and Justice (*Alliance pour le Progrès et la Justice*), its name was changed to its present style in 2000. Led by Talla Sylla, a former student leader, the Alliance won one seat in the 2001 National Assembly elections. The Alliance came to the forefront of Senegalese politics in October 2003 when, following the release by Sylla of a tape of anti-Wade songs, he was brutally attacked in the streets of Dakar by people rumoured to be connected to President Wade's kins. Alliance Jëf Jël is a member of the anti-Wade CPC coalition.

Citizen Movement for a Development Democracy (*Mouvement des Citoyens pour une Démocratie de Développement*, MDC). Created shortly prior to the 2000 election under the leadership of Ousseynou Fall, the MDC earned 1.1% of the votes on the first round and rallied to Wade on the second round.

Convention of Democrats and Patriots/Garab gi (*Convention des Démocrates et des Patriotes/Garab gi*, CDP), founded in 1992 by academic and former Diouf Minister Iba Der Thiam; he took 1.2% of the vote in the first round of the 2000 presidential poll, and backed the PDS-led coalition in the 2001 Assembly elections. Iba Der Thiam acts as the national convener of the pro-Wade coalition *Cap 21*.

Front for Socialism and Democracy/Benno Jubël (*Front pour le socialisme et la démocratie/Benno Jubël*, FSD/BJ). Formed in 1996 by Cheikh Ablaye Dièye, a minor marabout of the Muridiyya brotherhood; Dièye was elected MP in 1998, he ran for the 2000 presidential election, won 1% of the votes on the first round and rallied to Wade on the second round. Following his death in 2002, the FSD/BJ was revived by his son Cheikh Bamba Dièye.

Movement for Socialism and Unity (*Mouvement pour le Socialisme et l'Unité*, MSU). A left-wing party, created in 1981 by Mamadou Dia, a former Prime Minister of President Senghor. Now led by Mouhamadou Bamba Ndiaye; backed the PDS-led *Sopi* list in the 2001 legislative elections, but subsequently withdrew its support from Wade and joined the anti-Wade CPC coalition.

National Democratic Rally (*Rassemblement National Démocratique*, RND), a party created in in 1976 by the leftist and panafricanist academic Cheikh Anta Diop; it backed Wade in 2000 and won one seat in the 2001 Assembly elections. Its present leader, Madior Diouf, was briefly a Minister in the cabinet Niasse formed after Wade's election, but he quickly left. The RND is now a member of the anti-Wade CPC coalition.

Party of Truth for Development (*Parti de la Vérité pour le Développement*, PVD). The PVD was founded in February 2004 by Cheikh Modou Kara Mbacké, a junior marabout of the Muridiyya. Modou Kara Mbacké is the leader of a youth group, the World Movement for the Unicity of God (*Mouvement mondial pour l'unicité de Dieu*, MMUD) and a popular and controversial figure among the Senegalese youth; Talla Sylla of Alliance Jëf Jël is considered to be a disciple of his.

Party for Unity and Union (*Parti pour l'Unité et le Rassemblement*, PUR), formed in 1998 by a leading marabout from the Tijaniyya Sufi brotherhood, Serigne Mustapha Sy. The son of Cheikh Tidiane Sy, a major marabout and ephemeral leader of a Muslim party in late colonial Senegal, Sy had formed a Tijani youth movement, the *Moustarchidines wa Moustarchidaty*. Sy had initially supported Diouf, but allied to Wade in 1993 with such fierceness that violent clashes pitted his *Moustarchidines* against the police. Sy was condemned to a brief term of prison. Thereafter, he had progressively drawn closer to Abdou Diouf, whom his father supported during the 2000 election.

Rally of the Ecologists of Senegal–the Greens (*Rassemblement des Ecologistes du Sénégal–Les Verts*, RES). An ecologist party created in 1999, which has taken over from another rather moribund green party created in 1992. Led by Ousmane Sow Huchard. The Greens carry very little electoral weight, except for a few local councils in the suburbs of Dakar.

Union for Democratic Renewal–Front for Alternance (*Union pour le Renouveau Démocratique–Front pour l'Alternance*, URD-FAL), formed in 2000 as a pro-Wade splinter from URD, when Kâ decided to back Diouf during the second round of the presidential elections, it has maintained its allegiance to Wade but is critical of the PDS; it is led by executive secretary Mahmoud Saleh and belongs to the CPC. Saleh was condemned to a six-month jail-term in July 2004, following an altercation with a penitentiary guard during a visit to an imprisoned journalist.

Other Muslim parties include Serigne Mamoune Niasse's **Rally for the People** (*Rassemblement du peuple*, RP), Ahmed Khalifa Niasse's **Front of Patriotic Alliances** (*Front des Alliances Patriotiques*, FAP) and Mbaye Niang's **Movement for Reform towards Social Development** (*Mouvement de la Réforme pour le Développement Social*, MRDS).

Serbia and Montenegro

Capital: Belgrade
Population: 10,700,000 (2000E)

The one-party regime of the former League of Communists of Yugoslavia (LCY) collapsed in 1989–90, heralding the break-up of the Yugoslav federation established in 1945. Four of the former constituent republics (Slovenia, Croatia, Bosnia and Herzegovina, and Macedonia) seceded during 1991–92. The remaining two republics of Serbia and Montenegro declared themselves the Federal Republic of Yugoslavia (FRY) in April 1992. Within the Serbian Republic, meanwhile, the overwhelmingly ethnic Albanian province of Kosovo and the province of Vojvodina, with a substantial Hungarian minority, had lost the autonomous status that they had enjoyed under LCY rule.

Montenegro developed a high degree of autonomy within the FRY from 1997, openly aspiring to independence from 1999-2000 onwards, although the issue was divisive within Montenegro. In Montenegro, the Democratic Party of Socialists (DPS), successor to the League of Communists, has been dominant since 1990. It has won every election, even after the break-away of the Socialist People's Party (SNP) in 1997 over the issue of relations with Serbia and the Milosevic government. The wish for a looser relationship was reflected in the transformation of the FRY into the State Union of Serbia and Montenegro in 2003. As a result of this, both republics are represented in a 126-member unicameral parliament, with 35 deputies to be elected in Montenegro and 91 in Serbia. The deputies are to be elected directly in both republics. However, for the first two years, the deputies were indirectly elected by the assemblies of the two constituent republics and the previous Federal Assembly.

Within the state union most powers reside in the two constituent republics (except defence, foreign affairs, foreign economic relations and human rights), with the much larger Serbian Republic dominating. The unicameral Serbian and Montenegrin National Assemblies (of 250 and 75 members respectively) are themselves directly elected for four-year terms and each republic has its own directly-elected President, who appoints the republican Prime Minister subject to Assembly approval.

The FRY was dominated from its creation by the Socialist Party of Serbia (SPS), successor to the Serbian branch of the LCY and led by Slobodan Milosevic, who was President of Serbia in 1989–97 and President of the FRY from July 1997 to October 2000. The SPS and its allies remained dominant in legislative elections in November 1996, but from early 1998 the Milosevic regime faced insurrection by separatists in Kosovo and mounting international concern over escalating violence between ethnic Albanians and Serbian security forces. In March 1999 forces under the command of the North Atlantic Treaty Organization (NATO) launched a bombing campaign against Serbian government targets, forcing the withdrawal of Serbian forces from Kosovo, which was placed under interim UN administration. Although UN Resolution 1244, adopted by the Security Council on June 10, 1999, formally reaffirmed the sovereignty and territorial integrity of the FRY, since that time Kosovo has been a de facto UN protectorate and no early resolution of its final status seems likely.

Although most Serbs had backed Milosevic's resistance to NATO's demands over Kosovo, support for the regime and its increasingly authoritarian policies dwindled. Early federal elections were called after the enactment in July 2000 of federal constitutional amendments providing for direct presidential elections and thus enabling Milosevic (who had been elected by the Federal Assembly in 1997) to seek re-election. Despite widespread intimidation and ballot-rigging by Milosevic's supporters, the federal presidential elections on Sept. 24, 2000, were generally believed to have produced an outright first-round victory for the candidate of the multi-party Democratic Opposition of Serbia (DOS), Vojislav Kostunica. Prevarication by the government, which at first insisted that a second round of voting was needed and then sought to annul the elections, provoked massive popular protest, which in early October forced Milosevic to vacate the presidency in favour of Kostunica. Equally flawed elections to the federal Chamber of Citizens also held on Sept. 24, 2000, resulted in the DOS alliance being credited with 58 seats, an alliance of the SPS and the Yugoslav United Left 44, the Socialist People's Party of Montenegro (SNP) 28, the Serbian Radical Party (SRS) 5, the Serbian People's Party of Montenegro 2 and the Union of Vojvodina's Hungarians 1. The Democratic Party of Socialists of Montenegro (DPS), the republic's main ruling party, boycotted both federal elections.

Freer and fairer elections to the Serbian Assembly on Dec. 23, 2000, resulted in the DOS alliance winning 176 seats, the SPS 37, the SRS 23 and the SSJ 14. Elections to the Montenegrin Assembly on April 22, 2001, resulted in a pro-independence alliance headed by the DPS winning 35 seats, an anti-independence alliance headed by the SNP 33, the LSCG 8 and Albanian parties 3. Early parliamentary elections on Oct. 22, 2002 resulted in DPS and SDP gaining 39 seats, SNP, SNS and NS 30 and LSCG 4 seats. Two seats were won by two Albanian minority parties.

Early elections to the Serbian Assembly were held on Dec. 28, 2003, after the DOS government failed to secure a parliamentary majority. The elections were generally considered to be free and fair. In the elections the SRS gained 82 seats, Democratic Party of Serbia (DSS) 53, Democratic Party (DS) 37, G17plus 34, a coalition of the Serbian Renewal Movement (SPO) and New Serbia (NS) 23, and SPS 21.

In presidential elections in Serbia in June 2004, the candidate of the Democratic Party (DS), Boris Tadic, won 53.5% of the vote in the second round. His opponent was the candidate of the Serbian Radical Party (SRS), Tomislav Nikolic, who took 45.1%. The consolidation of the party scene continued in local elections in October 2004 with the Democratic Party and the Radical Party dominating.

Christian Democratic Party of Serbia
Demohriscanska Stranka Srbije (DHSS)

Address. Hadzi Nikole Zivkovica 2-II, 11000 Belgrade
Telephone. (381-11) 303-22-72
Fax. (381–11) 184–568
Email. office@dhss.org.yu
Website. www.dhss.org.yu
Leadership. Vladan Batic (chairman)

The party is a breakaway from the Democratic Party of Serbia. The DHSS was part of the victorious Democratic Opposition of Serbia (DOS) alliance in the late 2000 federal and Serbian elections, party leader Vladan Batic being appointed Justice Minister in the Serbian government. The party advocates an independent Serbia and reintroduction of a constitutional monarchy. The party failed to enter the Serbian parliament in the 2003 elections, gaining only 1.1% of the vote. In October 2000 the DHSS was admitted as an observer member of the Christian Democrat International.

Civic Alliance of Serbia
Gradjanski Savez Srbije (GSS)
Address. Dusana Bogdanovica 10, 11000 Belgrade
Telephone. (381–11) 344 34 81, 344 22 61
Fax. (381–11) 434 244
Email. gss@gradjanskisavez.org.yu
Website. www.gradjanskisavez.org.yu
Leadership. Goran Svilanovic (chairman)
The liberal GSS was founded in 1992 by peace campaigner Vesna Pesic, who was elected to the Serbian Assembly in 1993 within the DEPOS opposition coalition. It subsequently joined the *Zajedno* ("Together") alliance with the Democratic Party (DS) and the Serbian Renewal Movement (SPO), which won 22 lower house seats in the November 1996 federal elections, but boycotted the Serbian Assembly elections in September 1997 in protest against media manipulation by the Milosevic regime. In late 1998 the GSS joined a new opposition grouping called the Alliance for Change, which formed the core of the anti-Milosevic Democratic Opposition of Serbia (DOS) alliance launched in January 2000, by which time Pesic had been succeeded as GSS leader by Goran Svilanovic. When the DOS alliance came to power in October 2000, Svilanovic was appointed Foreign Minister in the federal government. Other members held ministerial posts in the Serbian government. The party ran on the electoral list of the Democratic Party (DS) in the Serbian parliamentary elections in December 2003.

Coalition List for Sanjak
Koalicija Lista za Sandzak (LzS)
Address. P.O. Box 102, Marsala Tita 2A, 36300 Novi Pazar
Telephone. (381-20) 313 032
Fax. (381-20) 313 033
Email. bncs@EUnet.yu
Website. www.sandzak.co.yu/lista.html
Leadership. Sulejman Ugljanin (president)
The coalition incorporates four smaller Bosniak (Bosnian Muslim) parties and the dominant Party of Democratic Action under the leadership of Sulejman Ugljanin. Founded in 1990 as a sister party of the leading Bosniak party with the same name in Bosnia, the party sought to represent the interests of the Bosniak minority in the Sanjak. The coalition advocates territorial autonomy/regionalism for Sanjak. The coalition has been represented in the Serbian parliament, entering in December 2003 with two members on the list of the Democratic Party. The party is furthermore dominant in the municipalities along the Montenegrin border, where most Bosniaks of Serbia live.

Democratic Alternative
Demokratska Alternativa (DA)
Address. Beogradska 39, I sprat, 11000 Belgrade
Telephone. (381–11) 3231 523, 3235 313, 3235 749
Fax. (381–11) 334–3192
Email. da@da.org.yu
Website. www.da.org.yu
Leadership. Nebojsa Covic (chairman)
The DA was established by the former mayor of Belgrade and member of the Socialist Party of Serbia Nebojsa Covic in 1997. It formed part of the victorious Democratic Opposition of Serbia (DOS) alliance in the late 2000 federal and Serbian elections, party leader Covic being appointed a Deputy Prime Minister in the new Serbian republican government, responsible for Southern Serbia and Kosovo. The

party ran independently in the Serbian parliamentary elections in 2003 and failed to enter parliament, receiving only 2.1% of the vote. The party merged with the Social Democratic Party (SDP) in autumn 2004.

Democratic Centre
Demokratski Centar (DC)
Address. Terazije 3/II, 11000 Belgrade
Telephone. (381–11) 322–9925
Fax. (381–11) 322–3321
Email. dcentar@infosky.net
Website. www.dc.org.yu
Leadership. Dragoljub Micunovic (chairman)
The DC was formed in 1996 by a moderate splinter group of the Democratic Party (DS) aspiring to "maintain the original spirit" of the DS. It formed part of the victorious Democratic Opposition of Serbia (DOS) alliance in the late 2000 federal and Serbian elections. The chairman was elected president of the Federal parliament. Micunovic ran as candidate for Democratic Opposition of Serbia (DOS) in failed Serbian presidential elections in November 2003. The party ran on the electoral list of the Democratic Party (DS) in the Serbian parliamentary elections 2003. A merger with the Democratic Party (DS) has been planned.

Democratic Opposition of Serbia
Demokratska Opozicija Srbije (DOS)
The DOS was launched in early 2000 in the wake of the 1999 Kosovo crisis as a broad-based alliance of parties and groups seeking the removal of Slobodan Milosevic from power and an end to the dominance of his Socialist Party of Serbia (SPS). The alliance eventually embraced 19 parties and organizations, including the moderate Democratic Party (DS) and the conservative-nationalist Democratic Party of Serbia (DSS); the liberal Civic Alliance of Serbia (GSS); the pro-business New Democracy (ND); the centrist Christian Democratic Party of Serbia, Democratic Centre and Movement for a Democratic Serbia; the centre-left Social Democratic Union and Social Democracy; the regional League for Sumadia–Sumadia Coalition; the Union of Vojvodina's Hungarians and three other parties representing ethnic Hungarians; the ethnic Albanian Party of Democratic Action (PDA); the Serb Resistance Movement–Democratic Movement (of Serbs in Kosovo); and the Association of Free and Independent Trade Unions (ASNS).

The DOS candidate for the September 2000 federal presidential elections was Vojislav Kostunica of the DSS, regarded as the most right-wing of the alliance components. Despite widespread intimidation and vote-rigging, Kostunica was widely believed to have obtained an outright first-round victory over Milosevic. Attempts by the regime to resist the democratic verdict prompted a DOS-orchestrated national uprising, which forced Milosevic to hand over power in early October. Concurrent (and equally flawed) federal parliamentary elections resulted officially in the DOS alliance winning 58 of the 138 lower house seats.

Inaugurated as federal President, Kostunica appointed Zoran Zizic of the Socialist People's Party of Montenegro (SNP) as federal Prime Minister, heading a government which consisted mainly of DOS ministers. In elections to the Serbian Assembly in December 2000, the DOS alliance displayed its real popular strength by winning 176 of the 250 seats with 65.8% of the valid vote. A new Serbian government appointed in January 2001 was headed by DS leader Zoran Djindjic and included representatives of all of the main DOS components. Despite being in government, the alliance continued to use the DOS appellation pending a possible decision to adopt a more appropriate title and/or to create a unitary movement from the component formations, which in the meantime all maintained their individual identities.

Western pressure and the threat to withhold economic aid quickly persuaded Djindjic's Serbian government not only to arrest Milosevic but also to hand him over to the tribunal at The Hague in late June 2001. This action, on which Kostunica complained that he had not been consulted, provoked serious strains in the DOS alliance, with the DSS taking their parliamentary deputies out of the DOS caucus in late July. While DOS continued to govern until after early parliamentary elections in December 2003, its majority in parliament continued to dwindle with parties and deputies leaving the party. With the Social Democratic Party leaving the coalition in November 2003, DOS lost its parliamentary majority. The coalition was dissolved prior to the elections and most parties ran independently.

Democratic Party
Demokratska Stranka (DS)
Address. Krunska 69, 11000 Belgrade
Telephone. (381–11) 344–3003
Fax. (381–11) 344–2946
Email. info@ds.org.yu
Website. www.ds.org.yu
Leadership. Boris Tadic (chairman)
The right-wing DS was founded in 1990 as Serbia's first opposition party under the leadership of prominent academic Dragoljub Micunovic, adopting a nationalistic programme and advocating Serbian intervention in support of Serb separatists in Bosnia and Herzegovina. Weakened by the defection of its nationalist wing to form the Democratic Party of Serbia (DSS), the DS won five lower house seats in the December 1992 federal elections. It advanced to 29 seats in the Serbian Assembly elections in December 1993 and subsequently joined a coalition government headed by Slobodan Milosevic's Socialist Party of Serbia (SPS), hoping to reform the system from within. In January 1994 Micunovic was succeeded as DS chairman by Zoran Djindjic, then mayor of Belgrade.

The DS reverted to opposition in 1996, joining the *Zajedno* ("Together") alliance with the DSS, the Serbian Renewal Movement (SPO) and the Civic Alliance of Serbia, which won only 22 lower house seats in the November 1996 federal elections. The alliance collapsed in mid-1997 when Djindjic refused to back the SPO leader as opposition candidate for the Serbian presidency, whereupon the SPO retaliated by helping to eject the DS leader from the Belgrade mayorship. The DS then boycotted the Serbian Assembly elections in September 1997 in protest against media manipulation by the Milosevic regime.

In late 1998 the DS joined a new opposition grouping called the Alliance for Change, which formed the core of the anti-Milosevic Democratic Opposition of Serbia (DOS) alliance launched in January 2000. The eventual victory of the DOS candidate in the September 2000 federal presidential elections resulted in DS representatives joining the federal government. Moreover, following a landslide DOS victory in Serbian Assembly elections in December 2000, Djindjic was appointed Prime Minister of the Serbian government in January 2001.

Whereas the DOS election platform had ruled out handing over indicted Yugoslav war criminals such as Milosevic to the international tribunal at The Hague, Djindjic quickly pushed through a Serbian government decree authorizing co-operation with the tribunal, thereby attracting criticism from the more nationalist DOS components that he was bowing to Western economic blackmail. After the assassination of Djindjic on March 12, 2003, by individuals linked to organized crime and the red berets (a special police unit linked to war crimes in Croatia, Bosnia and Kosovo and Milosevic's pretorian guard), the party entered a temporary leadership crisis. Headed by Zoran Zivkovic, the successor to Djindjic

as Prime Minister, and Boris Tadic, the Minister of Defence, the party was unable to hold the DOS coalition together and struggled amidst a number of corruption scandals. Boris Tadic took control of the party in the run-up to parliamentary elections in December 2003 and formally took over as chairman in February 2004. In the parliamentary elections, the party received 12.6% of the vote (37 of 250 seats), making it the third largest party in parliament. The party chairman Boris Tadic won the presidential elections in Serbia in June 2004 with 53.5% of the vote in the second round.

Democratic Party of Serbia
Demokratska Stranka Srbije (DSS)
Address. Pariska 13, 11000 Belgrade
Telephone. (381–11) 3204-719
Fax. (381–11) 3204-743
Email. info@dss.org.yu
Website. www.dss.org.yu
Leadership. Vojislav Kostunica (chairman)
The DSS was founded in 1992 by a nationalist faction of the Democratic Party (DS) and contested the December 1992 federal elections as part of the DEPOS opposition alliance, which won 20 lower house seats. In the December 1993 Serbian Assembly elections, the DSS won seven seats in its own right, remaining in opposition. It subsequently joined the *Zajedno* ("Together") alliance with the DS, the Serbian Renewal Movement (SPO) and the Civic Alliance of Serbia, which won 22 lower house seats in the November 1996 federal elections, but ran independently in local elections, where *Zajedno* was able to win key towns and municipalities. The party boycotted the Serbian Assembly elections in September 1997 in protest against media manipulation by the Milosevic regime.

DSS leader Vojislav Kostunica became the DOS candidate in the September 2000 federal presidential elections, winning an outright majority in the first round according to independent estimates and eventually being installed as President in early October. Following a landslide DOS victory in Serbian Assembly elections in December 2000, the DSS was represented by two ministers in the resultant Serbian government headed by the DS leader. Before the elections in 2000, the DSS had been considered a small party with limited influence outside Belgrade. Only after the electoral victory of Kostunica did the DSS emerge as one of the strongest parties in Serbia.

The coming to power of the DOS and Kostunica was welcomed by the international community, although the new President declared that his administration would be nationalist in orientation, notably in that it would resist any move to detach Kosovo from Serbia and would not co-operate with the international war crimes tribunal at The Hague in its pursuit of Yugoslavs indicted for alleged crimes, including Milosevic. He also came out strongly in favour of maintenance of Serbia's federation with Montenegro and against the latter's moves towards independence.

The Serbian government's decision in June 2001 to extradite Milosevic to the war crimes tribunal at The Hague provoked serious strains between the DSS and the DS. Although the DOS alliance survived, Kostunica took the DSS out of the Serbian government in 2001, claiming that it was already compromised by corruption. The party subsequently opposed the DOS coalition. Kostunica ran against the DOS candidate Miroljub Labus in presidential elections in September–October 2002. While he gained most votes in the elections, low turn-out invalidated the results. In early parliamentary elections in December 2003, the DSS emerged as the second-largest party with 18% of the vote (53 seats), forming a coalition with G17plus, SPO, and NS and supported by SPS. Kostunica was elected Prime Minister of Serbia in March 2004.

G17Plus

Address. Trg Republika 5, 11000 Belgrade
Telephone. (381–11) 3344-930
Fax. (381–11) 3344-930
Website. www.g17plus.org.yu
Leadership. Miroljub Labus (chairman)

Founded as an NGO of economic experts in 1997, the grouping emerged as a key player in opposition to the SPS-led government of Slobodan Milosevic. It authored the economic programme for DOS and took key positions in the Yugoslav government after 2000. In November 2002, the chairman of G17plus and the Deputy Prime Minister of Yugoslavia, Miroljub Labus, ran unsuccessfully as DOS candidate in presidential elections against Vojislav Kostunica. The NGO subsequently transformed into a political party, increasingly opposing the DS-led government. The party endorsed a liberal economic programme and portrayed itself as reformist. All G17plus members, inasmuch as they joined the party from the NGO, left government. In the parliamentary election in December 2003, the party gained 11.7% of the vote (34 seats) and subsequently joined in government with the DSS with three ministers and the post of Deputy Prime Minister.

League of Social Democrats of Vojvodina
Liga Socialdemokrata Vojvodina (LSV)

Address. Trg Mladenaca 10, Novi Sad
Telephone. (381-21) 422-192
Email. office@lsv.org.yu
Website. www.lsv.org.yu
Leadership. Nenad Canak (chairman)

The LSV, founded in 1990, has been the main regionalist party of Vojvodina. The party opposed the Milosevic government and its nationalist policies. While cooperating with other opposition parties, it had uneasy relations with parties seated in Belgrade due to their opposition to restoring autonomy to Vojvodina. The party joined DOS in 2000 and achieved represention in the Serbian and Vojvodina governments. In Vojvodina the party gained key posts, including that of president of the Vojvodina assembly, held by Nenad Canak. The party joined a Hungarian and a Bosniak minority party in the coalition of tolerance for the Serbian parliamentary elections in December 2003, but failed to gain a seat. The party won seven seats in coalition with other regionalist parties in the September/October 2004 regional elections in Vojvodina.

Liberals of Serbia
Liberali Srbije (LS)

Address. Krunska 76, 11000 Belgrade
Telephone. (381–11) 444–0677
Fax. (381–11) 444–9778
Website. www.liberali-srbije.org.yu
Leadership. Dusan Mihajlovic (chairman)

The New Democracy (ND) party was established in 1990 as the successor to the official youth organization of the communist era, subsequently attracting support in the business community. Claiming to be both social democratic and liberal, the party contested the 1992 federal and 1993 Serbian Assembly elections as part of the DEPOS opposition alliance, but in February 1994 deserted DEPOS to join the Serbian government led by the Socialist Party of Serbia (SPS). It remained allied with the SPS in the 1996 federal and 1997 Serbian elections (winning five seats in the latter contest), but in 1998 joined what became the anti-Milosevic Democratic Opposition of Serbia (DOS) alliance. It therefore participated in the DOS victories in the elections of late 2000, with ND leader Dusan Mihailovic becoming Minister of the Interior in the new Serbian government appointed in January 2001. The party was renamed Liberals of Serbia in 2003 and gained

observer status with the Liberal International. In the parliamentary elections in December 2003, the party failed to enter parliament, gaining only 0.7% of the vote.

Movement "Force of Serbia"
Pokret Snaga Srbije (PSS)

Email. srbija@snagasrbije.org
Website. www.snagasrbije.com
Leadership. Bogoljub Karic (president)

The party was formed by the controversial businessman Bogoljub Karic, who gained 19.3% of the vote (taking third place) in the Serbian presidential elections in June 2004. Modelled on Silvio Berlusconi's *Forza Italia*, the party has received support from the companies controlled by Karic and runs on a platform of economic populism and European integration. The party has been able to establish itself as a relevant political party during the presidential and local elections in 2004.

New Serbia
Nova Srbija (NS)

Address. Obilicev Venac 4/I, 11000 Belgrade
Telephone. (381–11) 3284-766
Fax. (381–11) 3284-681
Email. info@nova-srbija.org.yu
Website. www.nova-srbija.org.yu
Leadership. Velimir Ilic

The NS was formed by the mayor of Cacak, Velimir Ilic, as a breakaway from the Serbian Renewal Movement (SPO) in 1998. The party favors the introduction of the monarchy and endorses a conservative-nationalist platform. The NS joined the victorious Democratic Opposition of Serbia (DOS) alliance in the late 2000 federal and Serbian elections, party chairman Velimir Ilic being appointed a Deputy Prime Minister. His party formed a pre-election coalition with the Serbian Renewal Movement (SPO) in November 2003 and joined the government in March 2003, with Ilic taking a ministerial portfolio.

Sandzak Democratic Party
Sandzacka Demokratska Partija (SDP)

Address. Postanski fah 101, 36300 Novi Pazar
Telephone. (381–20) 311–454
Leadership. Rasim Ljajic (chairman)

The moderate Bosnik SDP split from the more nationalist SDA in 1997. Under the new leadership of Rasim Ljajic, the party joined the anti-Milosevic Democratic Opposition of Serbia (DOS) alliance and therefore participated in the DOS victories in the elections of late 2000, Ljajic becoming Minister of National and Ethnic Communities in the federal government. The party failed to enter parliament in Serbia in December 2003 after forming an unsuccessful pre-election coalition with the LSV and the SVM.

Serbian Radical Party
Srpska Radikalna Stranka (SRS)

Address. Trg Pobede 3, 11080 Zemun
Telephone. (381–11) 3164 –621
Email. gensek@srs.org.yu
Website. www.srs.org.yu
Leadership. Vojislav Seselj (president); Tomislav Nikolic (deputy & acting president)

Founded in 1991, the SRS has been the most extreme party in mainstream Serbian politics, espousing an ultra-nationalist programme and advocating the creation of a Greater Serbia. The party won 34 federal lower house seats in December 1992 and subsequently co-operated with the dominant Socialist Party of Serbia (SPS) until September 1993. Its representation in the Serbian Assembly was almost halved to 39 seats in December 1993, following which the party disbanded its paramilitary wing (named after the Chetniks of the World War II resistance), which had been accused of atrocities in Serb separatist campaigns elsewhere in former Yugoslavia. In the November 1996 federal elections SRS lower house representation fell to 16 seats on a 17.9% vote share. In the September 1997 Serbian Assembly elections, however, the SRS advanced strongly to 82 seats and 29.3% of the vote and in March 1998 was included in a Serbian coalition government headed by the SPS. Meanwhile, SRS leader Vojislav Seselj had stood in the protracted Serbian presidential elections in late 1997, his victory in the first contest being annulled because of a low turnout, following which his losing vote share against the SPS candidate in the second was 40%. The following year, the SRS joined the Serbian government.

The SRS strongly backed President Milosevic's intransigence in the 1998-99 Kosovo crisis, and opposed the withdrawal of Serbian forces from Kosovo in June 1999. The party remained part of the ruling coalition and in June 2000 forced the withdrawal of a controversial new "anti-terrorism" bill seen as intended to curb any opposition to the Milosevic regime. The party opted to run Tomislav Nikolic in the September 2000 federal presidential elections, but only obtained around 6% of the first-round vote. In the post-election crisis surrounding Milosevic's initial reluctance to accept his defeat by Vojislav Kostunica of the Democratic Opposition of Serbia (DOS), a crucial factor was Seselj's endorsement of Kostunica's claim of victory. Having won only five lower house seats in the simultaneous federal parliamentary elections, the SRS slumped to 23 seats (and 8.5% of the vote) in Serbian Assembly elections in December 2000.

Having been indicted at the international war crimes tribunal for alleged participation in ethnic cleansing in Croatia in 1991-92, Seselj voluntarily surrendered in January 2003. Tomislav Nikolic has been the acting president since and won 46.9% of the vote in the first round of (repeated) presidential elections in November 2003, which were annulled due to low turn-out. In parliamentary elections in December 2003, the SRS won 27.7% of the vote and gained the largest number of seats (82 of 250) in the Serbian parliament. It was, however, unable to form a coalition in the absence of any partners. Its renewed success has rested largely on dissatisfaction with the reforms since 2000 and its use of populism and nationalism.

Serbian Renewal Movement
Srpski Pokret Obnove (SPO)
Address. Knez Mihailova 48, 11000 Belgrade
Telephone. (381–11) 635-281
Fax. (381–11) 628-170
Email. info@spo.org.yu
Website. www.spo.org.yu.
Leadership. Vuk Draskovic (chairman)
The nationalist SPO was formed in 1990 as a merger of four previous nationalist groups and led by the charismatic writer Vuk Draskovic. Orginally radically nationalist, the party moderated its position in 1992, opposing the war in Bosnia. The party became the lynchpin of the DEPOS opposition alliance in the 1992 and 1993 elections, in which the DEPOS parties won 20 federal lower house seats and 45 seats in the Serbian Assembly. The SPO subsequently joined the *Zajedno* ("Together") alliance with the Democratic Party (DS), the Democratic Party of Serbia (DSS) and the Civic Alliance of Serbia (GSS), which won 22 lower house seats in the November 1996 federal elections. After the break-up of *Zajedno,* the SPO was the only moderate opposition party to contest the Serbian presidential and parliamentary elections in late 1997, Draskovic coming third in the former contest with 15.4% of the first-round vote and the party winning 45 seats and 20% of the vote in the latter.

In January 1999 Draskovic took the SPO into the federal government headed by the Socialist Party of Serbia (SPS), becoming a Deputy Prime Minister. Three months later the party was dismissed by the SPS over policy differences on Kosovo. The SPO failed to join DOS and in the September 2000 federal presidential elections which ousted Milosevic from power, SPO candidate Vojislav Mihajlovic obtained only about 3% of the vote, while the party failed to obtain representation in either the federal lower house or the Serbian Assembly, winning 4% of the vote in the latter elections. After lacking parliamentary representation for three years, in 2003 the party re-entered parliament in coalition with New Serbia (NS), gaining 7.8% of the vote. The party subsequently joined the government with Vuk Draskovic taking office as Foreign Minister of Serbia and Montenegro in April 2004.

Social Democratic Party
Socialdemokratska Partija (SDP)
Address. Ruzveltova 45, 11000 Belgrade
Telephone. (381-11) 3290-293
Fax. (381-11) 768 156
Email. office@sdp.org.yu
Website. www.sdp.org.yu
Leadership. Nebojsa Covic (chairman)
The SDP was established in 2002 as a merger of the Social Democratic Union (SDU) and Social Democracy (SD). The party positions itself on the centre-left and has been pursuing a moderate policy in regard to national minorities and other marginalized groups. As a merger of two members of DOS, it held one ministerial position and initially remained in the coalition. After the SDU left the party in 2003, the party allied itself with G17plus and withdrew its support for the DOS, resulting in early elections. It attained three seats in parliament on the election list of G17plus and joined the government in March 2004, obtaining one ministerial portfolio. The Democratic Alternative merged with the party and its chaiman Nebojsa Covic became the new party president.

Social Democratic Union
Socijaldemokratska Unija (SDU)
Address. Masarikova 5, 11000 Belgrade
Telephone. (381–11) 3061-394
Fax. (381–11) 3061-394
Email. info@sdu.org.yu
Website. www.sdu.org.yu
Leadership. Zarko Korac (chairman)
Founded in May 1996 by a social democratic splinter group of the Civic Alliance of Serbia, the SDU opposed the policies of the Milosevic regime in Kosovo in 1998-99 and called for full Yugoslav co-operation with the war crimes tribunal at The Hague. It formed part of the victorious Democratic Opposition of Serbia (DOS) alliance in the late 2000 federal and Serbian elections, following which party leader Zarko Korac was appointed a Deputy Prime Minister in the Serbian republican government. The party subsequently merged with Social Democracy to form the Social Democratic Party in 2002. The joint party fell apart with most of the original SDU leaving the party in 2003. The party ran on the list of the Democratic Party in the December 2003 elections and is represented in parliament with one deputy.

Socialist Party of Serbia
Socijalisticka Partija Srbije (SPS)
Address. Studentski trg 15, 11000 Belgrade
Telephone. (381–11) 3012-343
Fax. (381–11) 3119-343
Email. info@sps.org.yu
Website. www.sps-bg.org.yu
Leadership. Slobodan Milosevic (chairman); Ivica Dacic (president of the main committee)

The SPS was created in July 1990 by the merging of the Serbian wings of the former ruling League of Communists of Yugoslavia (LCY) and the associated Socialist Alliance of the Working People, with Milosevic (who had become leader of the Serbian LCY in 1986 and Serbian President in 1989) as its chairman. While acknowledging its origins in the communist-era ruling structure, the SPS officially subscribed to democratic socialism, favouring a continuing state economic role and preservation of the social security system. In reality, the SPS became the political vehicle for the hardline Serbian nationalist policies of Milosevic in the regional conflicts of the 1990s and for an increasingly repressive response to domestic opposition.

Having won an overwhelming majority in the Serbian Assembly in December 1990 (when Milosevic was re-elected Serbian President with 65% of the vote), the SPS obtained a narrow lower house majority in the May 1992 federal elections. The imposition of UN sanctions from mid-1992 resulted in reduced popular support for the SPS, which lost its overall majorities in the federal lower house and the Serbian Assembly in December 1992, although it remained the largest single party in both and Milosevic was re-elected President of Serbia with 56% of the vote. In further Serbian elections in December 1993, the SPS increased its lower house representation from 101 to 123 seats out of 250, subsequently forming a government with the New Democracy (ND) party.

Milosevic's reluctant acceptance of the November 1995 Dayton peace agreement for Bosnia and Herzegovina brought him into conflict with ultra-hardliners within the SPS, several of whom defected or were expelled. In federal elections in November 1996 a Joint List alliance of the SPS, the Yugoslav United Left (JUL) led by Milosevic's wife, and the ND won 64 of the 138 lower house seats, so that the SPS continued to dominate the federal government. In simultaneous local elections, however, opposition parties captured Belgrade and most other Serbian cities – results which the government-controlled courts tried to annul but which Milosevic eventually accepted in the face of mass popular protests and strikes.

Being constitutionally barred from a third term as Serbian President, Milosevic was in July 1997 elected as federal President by the Federal Assembly, under the then prevailing system of indirect election. Serbian Assembly elections in September 1997 resulted in the SPS/JUL/NS alliance winning 110 seats, the outcome being a coalition government of the SPS, the JUL and the ultra-nationalist Serbian Radical Party (SRS) under the continued premiership of Mirko Marjanovic. In protracted Serbian presidential elections in late 1997, SPS candidate Milan Milutinovic was eventually returned with 59% of the vote, in balloting regarded as deeply flawed by international observers.

The Kosovo crisis of 1998–99 and the eventual bombardment of Serbia by NATO initially appeared to strengthen Milosevic and the SPS politically. However, following the withdrawal of Serbian forces from Kosovo in June 1999 and the indictment of Milosevic for alleged war crimes, growing popular pressure for a change of government was orchestrated by what became the Democratic Opposition of Serbia (DOS). Milosevic and his coterie resisted the pressure, the President being re-elected to the SPS chairmanship unopposed in February 2000 and telling a party congress that the Kosovo conflict had been "a struggle for freedom and independence". In July 2000, moreover, Milosevic secured the enactment of constitutional amendments providing for the direct election of the federal President, which meant that the ban on a second federal presidential term no longer applied.

However, in balloting in September 2000 intimidation and vote-rigging by Milosevic's supporters failed to prevent what observers regarded as an outright victory for the DOS

candidate in the first round, with Milosevic's vote being estimated at little more than 37%. After last-ditch attempts by the regime to resist the verdict had provoked a massive popular uprising, Milosevic eventually surrendered the federal presidency in early October. In simultaneous federal parliamentary elections, themselves marred by irregularities, the SPS/JUL alliance declined to 44 lower house seats out of 138. Three months later Serbian Assembly elections in December revealed the true state of opinion by reducing the SPS/JUL to only 37 of the 250 seats and 14% of the vote.

At the beginning of April 2001, Milosevic was arrested at his Belgrade home and charged with misappropriation of funds and other abuses as President. The following month Serbian President Milutinovic, whose signature was one of those on the arrest warrant for Milosevic, resigned from his SPS leadership posts. Worse was to follow for Milosevic, because the new Serbian government headed by Zoran Djindjic of the Democratic Party, contrary to the DOS election pledge that those charged with war crimes should be tried in Yugoslavia, in late June 2001 unexpectedly handed Milosevic over to the international war crimes tribunal at The Hague. Milosevic has sought to direct the party from The Hague, but relations have been increasingly strained, as Milosevic failed to endorse certain SPS policies, including the choice for candidate in the 2002 (failed) presidential elections. In the parliamentary elections in December 2003, SPS only gained 7.4% of the vote (21 seats), making it the smallest parliamentary party.

Union of Vojvodina's Hungarians
Savez Vojvodjanskih Madjara (SVM)
Vajdasagi Magyar Szovetsege (VMSz)

Address. Age Mamuzica 13/II, 24000 Subotica
Telephone. (381–24) 553–801
Email. office@vmsz.org.yu
Website. www.vmsz.org.yu
Leadership. Jozsef Kasza (chairman)

The SVM/VMSz was launched in mid-1994, effectively succeeding the Democratic Community of Vojvodina Hungarians (DZVM). Campaigning for the restoration of autonomy to Vojvodina (which had been abolished by the Milosevic regime), the formation won three federal parliamentary seats in 1996 and four in the Serbian Assembly in 1997. In early 2000 the SVM/VMSz joined the multi-party Democratic Opposition of Serbia (DOS), in which three ethnic Hungarian formations had separate membership status, namely the Reform Democratic Party of Vojvodina (*Reformska Demokratska Stranka Vojvodine*, RDSV) led by Miodrag Isakov, the League of Social Democrats of Vojvodina (*Liga Socijaldemokrata Vojvodine*, LSV) led by Nenad Canak and the Vojvodina Coalition (*Koalicija Vojvodina*, KV) led by Dragan Veselinov.

As well as participating in the victory of the DOS alliance in the late 2000 federal and Serbian elections, the SVM/VMSz also won one federal lower house in its own right. SVM/VMSz leader Jozsef Kasza was appointed a Deputy Prime Minister in the government of Serbia. The party, together with the SDP of Rasim Ljajic and the LSV formed a pre-election coalition which failed to gain seats in parliament, gathering only 4% of the vote.

KOSOVO

The 1998–99 Kosovo crisis and the aftermath of UN administration stimulated even greater proliferation of already numerous political parties in the province, particularly those based in the majority ethnic Albanian population. A total of 26 lists (several being alliances of individual parties) were registered for elections to a new 120-member Kosovo Assembly in November

2001. The four groupings covered below (three ethnic Albanian and one Serb) emerged as the leading formations in their respective communities.

Alliance for the Future of Kosovo
Aleanca për Ardhmërinë e Kosovës (AAK)

Address. Bulevardi i Dëshmorëve 49, Pristina

Telephone. (381 38) 548 322

Leadership. Ramush Haradinaj (chairman)

One of the three main ethnic Albanian formations in Kosovo, the AAK was created in the aftermath of the 1998-99 crisis as an alliance of various pro-independence groupings, mostly emerging from the Kosovo Liberation Army (UÇK). While not differing substantially from other parties in its demand for independence, it is seen as being more radical than the Democratic League of Kosovo (LDK) and the Democratic Party of Kosovo (PDK). In the parliamentary elections in 2001, the party received 7.8% of the vote (8 of 120 seats).

Democratic League of Kosovo
Lidhja Demokratike e Kosovës (LDK)

Address. Kompleksi "Qafa", Pristina

Telephone. (381–38) 242 242

Fax. (381–38) 245 305

Email. ldk@ldk-kosova.org

Website. www.ldk-kosova.org

Leadership. Ibrahim Rugova (chairman)

Advocating independence for Kosovo, the LDK was launched in 1990 when the Belgrade government ended the province's autonomous status, thus provoking widespread ethnic Albanian protest against Serb rule. Calling for a negotiated settlement and officially opposing armed struggle, the LDK won a majority of seats in provincial assembly elections organized by Albanians in May 1992, following which Rugova was declared "President of Kosovo". However, the elections were declared illegal by the Serbian and federal authorities and the assembly was prevented from holding its inaugural session. Subsequent Serbian and federal elections were boycotted by the LDK.

Although Rugova and the LDK won large majorities in further presidential and assembly elections organized illegally in Kosovo in March 1998, he and his party appeared to be marginalized as conflict in the province intensified and the Kosovo Liberation Army (UÇK) emerged as the fighting arm of Albanian separatism. Rugova continued to support a negotiated settlement, attracting criticism from ethnic Albanians when he appeared on television with President Slobodan Milosevic in April 1999 (possibly under duress), soon after the start of the NATO bombardment of Serbia. He was also criticized for spending the rest of the conflict in Italy.

Following the withdrawal of Serb forces from Kosovo in June 1999 and Rugova's return a month later, the LDK recovered its status as the principal political representative of Kosovar Albanians. In August 1999 it joined the Kosovo Transitional Council set up by the new UN administration, thereafter working with the UN to promote inter-ethnic peace and reconciliation. In the parliamentary elections the LDK won an overwhelming majority of 46.2% (47 seats), but due to the electoral system was forced to enter a coaltion. Rugova was elected as president of Kosovo in early 2002.

The LDK is a member of the Christian Democrat International.

Democratic Party of Kosovo
Partia Demokratike e Kosovës (PDK)

Address. Nene Teresa, Pristina

Telephone. (381-38) 548-161

Leadership. Hashim Thaci (chairman)

The PDK was founded in the wake of the 1998-99 Kosovo crisis as the party political manifestation of the militant sep-aratist Kosovo Liberation Army (UÇK), in which Hashim Thaci had been "head of the political directorate". Standing for immediate independence for Kosovo, the PDK was heavily outpolled in municipal elections in October 2000 by the more moderate (but also pro-independence) Democratic League of Kosovo (LDK), winning 27% of the vote and taking control in six of the 30 municipalities at issue. In the parliamentary elections in 2001, the party consolidated its position as second-largest party by gaining 25.5% of the vote and 26 seats. It joined a grand-coaltion government, with Bajram Rexhepi of the PDK taking office as Prime Minister.

Return Coalition
Koalicija "Povratak" (KP)

Leadership. Dragisa Krstovic (head of the parliamentary group)

The KP was created by ethnic Serb parties and groups closely associated with the Democratic Opposition of Serbia (DOS). The coalition demanded that Serbs who had fled or been forcibly expelled from Kosovo during the 1998-99 hostilities should be guaranteed safe return to their homes and that Kosovo should remain under Serbian/Yugoslav sovereignty. The alliance received the backing of the DOS government in Belgrade. In the parliamentary elections in October 2001, the party received 10.9% of the vote and 22 seats (10 are set-aside seats for Serbs), gaining one ministerial post and a member of the Kosovo Assembly presidency. The coalition has been reluctant to fully cooperate with Kosovo institutions and has not been able to engage in any substantive cooperation with Albanian parties. As a coalition it has been fragile and subject to political developments in Serbia.

MONTENEGRO

Democratic Alliance of Montenegro
Demokratski Savez Crne Gore (DSCG)

Address. Kuvendi Komunal, Ulcinj

Telephone. (381-85) 411-026

Email. dscg@skupstina.mn.yu

Leadership. Mehmet Bardahi (chairman)

One of two major parties representing the 6% ethnic Albanian component of Montenegro's population, the DSCG obtained one of the five Assembly seats (2002: four) reserved for ethnic minorities in the May 1998, April 2001 and October 2002 Montenegrin elections.

Democratic Party of Socialists of Montenegro
Demokratska Partija Socijalista Crne Gore (DPS)

Address. Jovana Tomasevica bb, 81000 Podgorica

Telephone. (381–81) 243–952

Fax. (381–81) 243–347

Email. webmaster@dps.cg.yu

Website. www.dps.cg.yu

Leadership. Milo Djukanovic (chairman)

The DPS is the successor to the League of Communists of Montenegro, which changed its name in 1991, and was in favour of the federation with Serbia until the late 1990s, thereafter moving to a pro-independence stance. The party obtained an overall majority in the Montenegrin Assembly in December 1992, also winning 17 lower house seats in simultaneous federal elections and joining a coalition government led by the Socialist Party of Serbia (SPS) of Slobodan Milosevic. The following month the then DPS leader, Momir Bulatovic, was elected President of Montenegro. The DPS retained its Montenegrin Assembly majority in November 1996, when it also advanced to 20 federal lower house seats.

Increasing internal opposition to Bulatovic for his pro-federation stance culminated in October 1997 in his narrow defeat by Prime Minister Milo Djukanovic in Montenegrin presidential elections in which both stood as DPS candidates.

Djukanovic also became undisputed DPS chairman, while Bulatovic launched the breakaway Socialist People's Party of Montenegro (SNP). Advocating greater independence for Montenegro, the DPS contested the May 1998 Montenegrin Assembly elections as leader of the "For a Better Life" alliance, which included the People's Party of Montenegro (NS) and the Social Democratic Party of Montenegro (SDP) and which won 42 out of 78 seats and therefore formed a new government with Filip Vujanovic as Prime Minister.

Relations between the DPS and the Milosevic regime deteriorated during the 1998–99 Kosovo crisis, when the Montenegrin government received strong Western backing for a proposed loose "association" with Serbia. When Milosevic enacted constitutional amendments in July 2000 which were seen as reducing Montenegrin powers in the federation, the DPS came out in favour of full separation and boycotted the September 2000 federal elections, in which Milosevic and the SPS were defeated by the Democratic Opposition of Serbia (DOS). In Montenegro the consequence was that the NS withdrew from the ruling coalition, leaving the DPS and the SDP without a majority.

In early Montenegrin Assembly elections in April 2001 the DPS headed an alliance of pro-independence parties called "Victory for Montenegro", including the SDP and indirectly the Democratic Union of Albanians. The alliance emerged as the largest bloc with 36 of the 77 seats (and 42% of the vote) in a close result in which the overall pro-separation vote was only 5,000 higher than that against. Lacking an overall majority and failing to reach a coalition agreement with the pro-independence Liberal Alliance of Montenegro (LSCG), the DPS-led bloc opted to form a minority government (with LSCG external support). After agreeing with the Serbian government on forming a new state union in 2002, the DPS lost support from the LSCG and early elections were held. In the elections, the DPS gained, together with the junior SDP, 47.7% of the vote and 39 seats in parliament, enabling it to govern with an additional coalition partner. Subsequently, Djukanovic exchanged the post of President for that of Prime Minister, with Filip Vujanovic of the DPS succeeding him after two rounds of presidential elections, which had failed due to low turn-out. The government agreed on the creation of a state union of Serbia and Montenegro in February 2003, but continues to advocate independence for Montenegro.

Democratic Union of Albanians (DUA)

Address. Kuvendi Komunal, Ulcinj
Telephone. (381-85) 412-757
Email. dua@skupstina.mn.yu
Leadership. Ferhat Dinosa (president)
Based in Montenegro's ethnic Albanian population (about 6% of the total), the DUA obtained representation in the 1996 and 1998 republican Assembly elections. In the April 2001 and October 2002 elections it obtained one of the five (four in 2002) seats reserved for ethnic minorities and became part of the government headed by the Democratic Party of Socialists of Montenegro, in which Gezim Hajdinaga was appointed Minister for the Protection of National Minorities.

Liberal Alliance of Montenegro
Liberalni Savez Crne Gore (LSCG)

Address. Ulica Ilije Milacica 101, 81000 Podgorica
Telephone. (381–81) 624-213
Fax. (381–81) 623–509
Email. lscg.info@cg.yu
Website. www.lscg.cg.yu
Leadership. Miodrag Zivkovic (leader); Vesna Perovic (chairperson)
Strongly in favour of the withdrawal of Montenegro from the

Yugoslav federation, the LSCG was founded in 1990 and gained third place in the December 1992 Montenegrin Assembly elections by winning 13 seats. The party contested the November 1996 elections within the People's Unity alliance with the People's Party of Montenegro, which won 19 Montenegrin seats and eight in the federal lower house. Reverting to independent status for the next Montenegrin elections in May 1998, it won five seats on a platform of secession from the Yugoslav federation.

Following the fall of the Milosevic regime in Belgrade in late 2000, the LSCG contested the April 2001 Montenegrin Assembly elections outside the pro-independence alliance led by the Democratic Party of Socialists of Montenegro (DPS), because it doubted that the DPS was deeply committed to separation. The narrowness of the result between the pro-independence and pro-federation sides left the LSCG, which won six seats from 7.9% of the vote, able to give the DPS-led bloc an overall majority. However, coalition talks foundered on the LSCG's demand for additional seats in the Assembly, whereupon the party pledged external support to a DPS-led minority government which promised to hold an independence referendum in March 2002. The party withdrew support from the government in 2002 over its support for a state union with Serbia (under EU pressure), triggering early elections. The LSCG obtained 5.7% of the vote and four members in parliament. In forming a technical coalition with the pro-Serb opposition SNP, the LSCG placed a higher priority on a change of government than the goal of Montenegrin independence.

The LSCG is a member party of the Liberal International.

People's Party
Narodna Stranka (NS)

Address. Vasa Raickovica bb, Podgorica
Telephone. (381-81) 238-715
Fax. (381-81) 238 717
Email. narodna@cg.yu
Website. www.narodnastranka.cg.yu
Leadership. Dragan Soc (chairman)
Advocating the maintenance of federal ties with Serbia, the NS won 14 seats in the Montenegrin assembly elections and four seats in the federal Chamber of Citizens in 1992. In the 1996 elections an unlikely alliance between the NS and the pro-separation Liberal Alliance of Montenegro won 19 Montenegrin seats and eight in the federal lower house. For the May 1998 Montenegrin elections the NS was part of the victorious "For a Better Life" alliance headed by the Democratic Party of Socialists of Montenegro (DPS) and including the Social Democratic Party of Montenegro (SDP), winning seven seats itself and joining a three-party coalition government.

The NS withdrew from the Montenegrin government in late 2000 when its two coalition partners adopted a platform calling for Montenegro's relationship with Serbia to be redefined as a union of two independent states which should each receive international recognition. In early Montenegrin elections in April 2001 and again in October 2002 the NS was a component of the anti-separation bloc headed by the Socialist People's Party of Montenegro (SNP), which was defeated by the pro-independence bloc led by the DPS.

Serbian People's Party of Montenegro
Srpska Narodna Stranka Crne Gore (SNS)

Address. Bulevar Lenjina 10, Podgorica
Telephone. (381-81) 225-317
Email. sns@skupstina.mn.yu
Website. www.sns.cg.yu
Leadership. Andrej Mandic (president)
The SNS is a breakaway from the People's Party (NS), endorsing a more radical pro-Serb platform. The SNP won

two federal lower house seats in the disputed September 2000 elections, on a platform of opposition to the separation of Montenegro and Serbia. In the April 2001 and October 2002 Montenegrin Assembly elections it was part of the defeated anti-independence alliance headed by the Socialist People's Party of Montenegro.

Social Democratic Party of Montenegro
Socijaldemokratska Partija Crne Gore (SDP)

Address. Jovana Tomasevica bb, Podgorica
Telephone. (381-81) 248-648
Email. sdp@skupstina.mn.yu
Website. www.sdp.cg.yu
Leadership. Ranko Krivokapic (chairman)

The SDP was created in June 1993 from a merger of the Social Democratic Reform Party and the Socialist Party of Montenegro. Having won one federal lower house seat in 1996, the SDP contested the May 1998 Montenegrin Assembly elections in alliance principally with the Democratic Party of Socialists of Montenegro (DPS), winning five seats and becoming a member of the subsequent republican government. In the April 2001 Montenegrin elections the party was part of the pro-independence "Victory for Montenegro" alliance headed by the DPS, whose narrow plurality resulted in the formation of a minority government in which then SDP chairman Zarko Rakocevic became a Deputy Prime Minister and one other SDP minister was appointed. In view of his government participation, Rakocevic was succeeded as party chairman by Ranko Krivokapic in October 2001. The party continued to remain the junior partner of the DPS, holding several ministerial posts and the presidency of parliament.

The SDP is a consultative member of the Socialist International.

Socialist People's Party of Montenegro
Socijalisticka Narodna Partija Crne Gore (SNP)

Address. Address: "13 Jula" No 49, Podgorica
Telephone. (381 81) 272-421
Fax. (381 81) 272-420
Email. admin@snp.cg.yu
Website. www.snp.cg.yu
Leadership. Predrag Bulatovic (chairman)

The pro-federation SNP was launched in early 1998 by a breakaway faction of the Democratic Party of Socialists of Montenegro (DPS) led by Momir Bulatovic, following his narrow defeat by an anti-federation DPS candidate in Montenegrin presidential elections of October 1997. The SNP drew on substantial pro-federation opinion to take second place in the May 1998 Montenegrin Assembly elections, winning 29 of the 78 seats with 36% of the vote. Shortly before the elections, Momir Bulatovic had been appointed federal Prime Minister by President Slobodan Milosevic of the Socialist Party of Serbia (SPS), charged with maintaining the federation at a time of national crisis over the status of Kosovo.

The SNP maintained its pro-federation stance in the September 2000 federal elections, in which Milosevic and the SPS were defeated by the Democratic Opposition of Serbia (DOS). The dubious official results of a contest boycotted by the DPS gave the SNP 28 of the 138 lower house seats, following which the new federal President, Vojislav Kostunica, appointed Zoran Zizic of the SNP as federal Prime Minister (in accordance with the rule that if the President was from Serbia the Prime Minister must be from Montenegro). The luckless Momir Bulatovic was then ousted from the chairmanship of his new party, being succeeded in February 2001 by Predrag Bulatovic (no relation), who was more aligned with the new government in Belgrade.

In early elections to the Montenegrin Assembly in April 2001 the SNP headed the "Together for Yugoslavia" pro-fed-eration alliance (including the People's Party of Montenegro and the Serbian People's Party of Montenegro). The alliance lost very narrowly, winning 33 of the 77 seats with 40.6% of the vote, and therefore contended that the resultant minority DPS-led government had no mandate for independence. The party continued to be a partner in the Yugoslav government until February 2003, when the newly established state union of Serbia and Montenegro resulted in renewed participation of the DPS in the institution and a coalition with the Serbian government, ousting the SNP from the coalition at the federal level. In October 2002, the SNP and its coalition partners were defeated, gaining only 37.8% of the votes and 30 seats. The party subsequently boycotted parliament over the media dominance of the ruling DPS. As the core of the Montenegrin opposition, the party continues to support close links with Serbia and generally more conservative and anti-reformist policies.

Seychelles

Capital: Victoria (on Mahé)
Population: 84,000

The Republic of Seychelles achieved independence from the UK in June 1976. President James Mancham, who at that time led the Seychelles Democratic Party, was ousted in a coup in 1977 by France-Albert René. René established a one-party state with the Seychelles People's Progressive Front (SPPF) as the sole legal party. Pressure for democratic reform was resisted until December 1991, when the leftist SPPF endorsed a return to political pluralism. A new constitution, drafted by an elected constitutional commission, was approved in a popular referendum in June 1993. It provided for the simultaneous direct election for five-year terms of the President and unicameral National Assembly (with 11 of the Assembly's 33 seats allocated on a proportional basis to parties obtaining at least 9% of the total votes cast). In 1996 the constitution was amended to redefine the composition of the National Assembly as 25 directly elective seats and a maximum of 10 proportionally allocated seats. The President may hold office for a maximum of three consecutive terms.

Multi-party Assembly elections in July 1993 and March 1998 resulted in overwhelming victory for the SPPF. However, in elections held in December 2002 the main opposition party, the centrist Seychelles National Party (SNP), managed to win 11 seats, with 42.6% of the vote, against 23 seats for the SPPF, with 54.3% of the vote. The conservative Democratic Party (DP), which had managed to win one seat in the 1998 poll, failed to win a seat with 3.1% of the vote.

President René was re-elected as sole candidate in polling in 1979, 1984 and 1989 and retained the presidency despite challenges in 1993 and 1998. René called further presidential elections two years ahead of time for Aug. 31-Sept. 2, 2001 (following a constitutional amendment in May 2000 relating to consecutive executive mandates). He was re-elected, but with a significantly reduced share of the vote (54%) than in 1998, and there were widespread opposition claims of government cheating. In February 2004 René announced his intention to retire and in mid-April he handed over the presidency to James Michel, hitherto Vice President and secretary-general of the SPPF.

Democratic Party (DP)

Address. POB 169, Mont Fleuri, Mahé
Telephone. (248) 224916
Fax. (248) 224302
Leadership. Sir James Mancham (leader); Daniel Belle (secretary-general)

The DP was registered in March 1992 as a revival of the former Social Democratic Party, which had been effectively dissolved following the declaration of a one-party state in the late 1970s. Party leader and former President of the Republic, Sir James Mancham, returned from exile in April 1992. In July 1992 the DP won eight of the 22 seats on the constitutional commission elected to draft a new constitution. In multi-party presidential elections held the following July, Mancham was runner-up to incumbent President René of the Seychelles People's Progressive Front (SPPF), taking 36.7% of the vote. At the same time, in elections to the National Assembly, the DP obtained four seats allocated on a proportional basis. The DP adopted a policy of "reconciliation" with the SPPF in the aftermath of the 1993 elections, and in late 1997 rejected an invitation from the United Opposition (as the Seychelles National Party was then known) to form an alliance at the 1998 elections. In these elections Mancham (with 13.8% of the vote) took third place in the presidential election and lost his seat in the National Assembly (where the DP won only one seat). The party did not contest the 2001 presidential election. The DP did, however, contest the December 2002 National Assembly elections but failed to win any seats having gained only 3.1% of the vote.

The DP is associated with the International Democrat Union through the Democrat Union of Africa.

Seychelles National Party (SNP)

Address. PO Box 81, Arpent Vert, Mont Fleuri, Mahé
Telephone. (248) 224124
Fax. (248) 225151
Email. Snp2003@hotmail.com
Website. www.seychelles.net/snp/
Leadership. Wavel Ramkalawan (leader); Roger Mancienne (secretary)

Seychelles National Party is the name adopted in July 1998 by the United Opposition. This had been formed in 1995 through the merger of three parties (Seychelles Party, National Alliance Party and Seychelles National Movement) which had contested the 1993 elections as a coalition, winning one proportionally allocated Assembly seat and receiving less than 4% of the vote in the presidential election. In the March 1998 legislative elections the party won three Assembly seats with 26.1% of the vote, while its leader was runner-up in the simultaneous presidential election, winning 19.5% of the vote. In an early presidential election held on Aug. 31–Sept. 2, 2001, Ramkalawan made a substantial advance, taking 44.9% of the vote, but was again defeated by incumbent President René. Ramkalawan's subsequent complaints that there had been vote rigging, including intimidation, bribery and under-age voting, were rejected by the Elections Commissioner. The party made further progress in the December 2002 National Assembly elections, winning 42.6% of the vote and 11 seats.

The SNP is an observer member of the Liberal International.

Seychelles People's Progressive Front (SPPF)
Front Populaire Progressiste des Seychelles (FPPS)

Address. PO Box 91, Victoria
Telephone. (248) 224455
Fax. (248) 225351
Leadership. France-Albert René (president); James Michel (secretary-general)

Founded in 1964 as the left-of-centre Seychelles People's United Party, the SPPF adopted its present name in 1978, a successful coup having been staged the previous year by party leader René, who was then Prime Minister. René assumed the presidency of the Republic and the SPPF became the sole legal party until December 1991, when the ban on political activity by other parties was suspended. In elections to the constitutional commission in July 1992, the SPPF won the majority of the votes cast and was awarded 14 of the 22 seats on the commission. In the presidential and legislative elections in July 1993, René and the SPPF won an emphatic victory. René retained the presidency with almost 59.5% of the vote, while the party won 28 seats (22 of them directly elected) in the National Assembly. In March 1998 President René was re-elected with 66.7% of the vote, while the SPPF won 30 seats in the National Assembly.

René called further presidential elections two years ahead of time, on Aug. 31–Sept. 2, 2001, citing the need to demonstrate political stability to investors concerned about the country's economic difficulties. He was re-elected, but with a significantly reduced share of the vote (54.2%) compared with 1998. In National Assembly elections held in December 2002 the SPPF faced a serious challenge from the Seychelles National Party (SNP), but managed to retain its majority, winning 54.3% of the vote and 23 of the 34 seats.

In February 2004 René announced that he intended to retire during 2004 and hand over power to James Michel, Vice President, Minister of Finance and Economic Planning, Information Technology, and Communications and secretary general of the SPPF. Accordingly, in mid-April, René, at the age of 68, stepped down and handed over the presidency to Michel, aged 60. Michel said that his priorities would be ensuring stability and improving the Seychellian economy through dialogue with the private sector. René retained the presidency of the SPPF.

Sierra Leone

Capital: Freetown
Population: 5,200,000 (2002E)

The Republic of Sierra Leone achieved independence from the UK in 1961, originally as a constitutional monarchy. In 1971 a republican constitution was adopted and Siaka Stevens, leader of the All People's Congress (APC), became President. The APC was declared the sole legal party in 1978, and the country remained a one-party state until a referendum in 1991 endorsed the introduction of multiparty politics. General elections were arranged for the following year, but the process was curtailed in April 1992 by a military coup led by Capt. Valentine Strasser. In 1993 the Strasser regime announced the adoption of a transitional programme envisaging a return to civilian government in early 1996 following multiparty elections. Towards this end, in April 1995 Strasser lifted the ban on political activity. However, this development took place against a background of intensifying rebel activity by the Revolutionary United Front (RUF).

In January 1996 Strasser was deposed by Brig Julius Maada Bio. Nevertheless, legislative and presidential elections went ahead as planned in February 1996 under the provisions of the 1991 constitution (which had been suspended since the Strasser coup). This provided for a unicameral legislature with 12 indirectly elected members and 68 members directly elected for a five-year term. Executive power was vested in a directly elected President, who could serve for no more than two five-year terms. In voting for the presidency, no candidate won an absolute majority, but in a run-off ballot held in March 1996, Ahmed Tejan Kabbah of the Sierra Leone People's Party (SLPP) – which had won the most number of seats in the legislative elections – was elected with almost 60% of the vote. In May 1997, however, President Kabbah was deposed in a military coup led by Maj. Johnny Paul Koroma, who formed a junta, suspended the 1991 constitution and banned political activity.

In March 1998 President Kabbah was restored to office and the civilian government institutions were formally reinstated. A further round of armed conflict, in which the RUF forces were backed by former supporters of the Koroma junta, led to a ceasefire agreement between the RUF and the Kabbah government in May 1999. A peace accord was signed in July 1999 under which the RUF pledged to disarm and reconstitute itself as a political organization, with an entitlement to representation in a proposed government of national unity. The RUF was duly registered as a political party (the Revolutionary United Front Party, RUFP) in November 1999, but it failed to fulfil its disarmament pledges and in early 2000 the peace process collapsed and there was a fresh cycle of brutal armed conflict before the RUF signed another ceasefire agreement with the Kabbah government in November 2000. The disarmament process ended in January 2002 and in May presidential and legislative elections were held, resulting in an overwhelming victory for incumbent President Kabbah and his SLPP.

All People's Congress (APC)

Address. 137H Fourah Bay Road, Freetown, Sierra Leone
Website. /www.new-apc.org
Leadership. Ernest Bai Koroma (leader)
Established in 1960 by Siaka Stevens (who died in 1988), the leftist APC was the dominant party from 1968 and the sole authorized political formation between 1978 and 1991. In the 1996 legislative elections the party came in fourth place with less than 6% of the vote and only five seats. In the presidential poll the APC candidate finished fifth. The party performed much better in the next elections held in May 2002. In the presidential poll, party leader Ernest Bai Koroma finished second, winning over 22% of the vote. In the legislative elections, the party again finished second, wining 27 seats, mainly in the north and the west of the country, against 83 seats for the ruling Sierra Leone People's Party (SLPP).

Peace and Liberation Party (PLP)

Leadership. Lt-Col (retd) Johnny Paul Koroma (leader)
The PLP was formed by former military leader Lt-Col (retd) Johnny Paul Koroma to contest the May 2002 presidential and legislative elections. Koroma had led a coup against President Kabbah in May 1997 and had ruled as chairman of the Armed Forces Revolutionary Council (AFRC) until Kabbah's restoration in March 1998. He had chaired the Commission for the Consolidation of Peace from 1999 until 2001, having retired from the military in 2000. In the May 2002 presidential poll, Koroma managed to win only 3% of the vote and the PLP won two seats in the legislature.

Revolutionary United Front Party (RUFP)

Leadership. Alimamy Pallo Bangura (secretary general)
The Revolutionary United Front (RUF) engaged in armed conflict with the government from 1991 and was linked to the National Patriotic Front of Liberia (which subsequently evolved into Liberia's former ruling National Patriotic Party). Some RUF leaders were appointed to the Armed Forces Revolutionary Council which held power in Sierra

Leone from May 1997 to February 1998. In July 1999 the RUF signed an agreement with the restored civilian government of President Kabbah to disarm and reform itself into a political organization, but fresh fighting soon erupted. However, the signing of another ceasefire agreement by the RUF and the government in Abuja (the Nigerian capital) in November 2000 heralded the beginning of a peace process that resulted in the RUF's eventual disarmament (in January 2002) and its transformation into a political party, the Revolutionary United Front Party (RUFP).

In presidential elections held in May 2002 (and won by Kabbah) the RUFP secretary general, former academic Alimamy Pallo Bangura, won only 1.7% of the vote. The party failed to win a single seat in legislative elections held at the same time, despite fielding 203 candidates in all of the country's 14 electoral districts. Despite the RUF's transformation into a political party, RUF fighters continued to be accused of launching attacks in Guinea at the behest of their chief backer, former President Charles Taylor of Liberia.

Sierra Leone People's Party (SLPP)

Address. 29 Rawdon Street, Freetown
Telephone. (232–22) 228222
Website. www.slpp.ws
Leadership. Ahmad Tejan Kabbah (leader); Solomon Berewa (deputy leader); Sama S. Banya (national chairman); Prince A. Harding (national secretary general)
The SLPP was the dominant party at independence and the party of government until 1967. It was then banned in 1978 but resurfaced in 1991 under the leadership of Salia Jusu-Sheriff. In the February 1996 elections the party won the largest share of the votes in both the legislative and presidential polls (36.1% and 35.8% respectively), securing 27 seats in the legislature. The SLPP's presidential candidate, Ahmad Tejan Kabbah, won the second round run-off in March against his nearest rival from the United National People's Party (UNPP), taking almost 60% of the vote. In May 1997 Kabbah was deposed in a military coup, but he was restored to office less than a year later amidst continuing armed conflict with the Revolutionary United Front. Kabbah was returned to power in presidential elections held in May 2002, winning over 70% of the vote. In simultaneous legislative elections, the SLPP won a total of 83 of the 112 elective seats in the National Assembly, giving it an absolute majority.

United National People's Party (UNPP)

Address. Sierra Leone Parliament, Freetown
Leadership. John Karefa-Smart (leader); Haja Memuna Conteh (secretary general)
The UNPP was runner-up to the SLPP in the 1996 elections, winning almost 22% of the vote and 17 seats in the legislative poll and over 40% of the vote in the final round of the presidential contest. Party leader Karefa-Smart contested the May 2002 presidential poll, but managed to win only 1% of the vote. The UNPP fielded 155 candidates in simultaneous legislative elections, but failed to win a seat.

Other Parties

Citizens United for Peace and Progress (CUPP), whose presidential candidate Raymond Bamidele Thompson won less than 1% of the vote in the May 2002 presidential election. It put forward no candidates in the accompanying legislative elections.

Grand Alliance Party (GAP), whose presidential candidate Raymond Kamara – a former member of the United National People's Party – won less than 1% of the vote in the May 2002 presidential election. The party fielded 84 candidates in the accompanying legislative elections, but failed to win a seat.

Movement for Progress (MOP), whose presidential candidate Zainab Hawa Bangura – a former National Co-ordinator of the civil society group Campaign for Good Governance – won less than 1% of the vote in the May 2002 presidential election. The party fielded 33 candidates in the accompanying legislative elections, but failed to win a seat.

National Democratic Alliance (NDA), fielded 32 candidates in the May 2002 legislative election, but failed to win a seat.

Young People's Party (YPP), led by Sylvia Blyden, fielded 71 candidates in the May 2002 legislative election, but failed to win a seat. In the accompanying presidential poll, YPP candidate Andrew Duramani Turay won less than 1% of the vote.

People's Democratic Party (PDP), led by Osman Kamara, supported the candidacy of President Kabbah in the May 2002 presidential elections. The party fielded 208 candidates in the accompanying legislative election, but failed to win a single seat.

Singapore

Capital: Singapore City
Population: 4,000,000 (2000)

Singapore achieved internal self-rule from the United Kingdom in 1959, and four years later joined the Federation of Malaysia. On leaving the federation in 1965, Singapore became an independent sovereign state.

Singapore is a republic with a parliamentary system based on the Westminster model in which the Prime Minister is head of government. The constitution provides for a President who is the head of state. Prior to 1991, the President was appointed by Parliament and held a largely ceremonial role. Following constitutional amendments that year, an elected presidency was created, with wider powers of veto and oversight of government activities. Presidential candidates are first vetted by a Presidential Elections Committee, and in the first elections on Aug. 28, 1993, Ong Teng Cheong of the People's Action Party (PAP) became Singapore's first directly elected President. The current President, Sellapa Rama Nathan, was declared President-elect on Nomination Day when he was the sole candidate approved by the Committee. He was sworn in on Sept. 1, 1999.

Parliament is a unicameral chamber currently comprising 84 Members of Parliament (MPs) elected by universal adult suffrage for five years and ten appointed members. In the last general election held on Nov. 3, 2001, the PAP (which has held a majority continuously since 1959) won 82 of the 84 elective seats taking 75.3% of the vote in the 29 contested seats. The PAP was unopposed in 55 seats. The Singapore People's Party (SPP) and the Workers' Party (WP) took one seat each. Most MPs were elected from 14 wards, each with five or six seats, the party winning the ward taking all the seats, a system seen as favouring the PAP. Only nine MPs were elected from single-seat wards.

People's Action Party (PAP)
Address. Blk 57B, New Upper Changi Road, #01–1402, PCF Building, Singapore 463057
Telephone. (65) 6244–4600
Fax. (65) 6243–0114
Email. paphq@pap.org.sg
Website. www.pap.org.sg
Leadership. Goh Chok Tong (secretary-general)
The PAP, founded as a radical socialist party in 1954, has been Singapore's ruling party since 1959. After the defection of its more militant members to form the Socialist Front (*Barisan Sosialis*) in 1961, the PAP leadership effectively transformed the party into a moderate, anti-communist organization, supporting a pragmatic socialist programme emphasizing economic development and social welfare. Despite its overwhelming legislative dominance, the PAP's share of the total vote fell steadily from 1980 (down to 61% in 1991). However, the January 1997 election results showed the party raising its share of the total vote to 65% and recapturing two of the four seats previously lost to the opposition. In the November 2001 elections it further improved its vote share to over 75%. The party had emphasized the need to retain continuity in government in the face of Singapore's worst recession since the 1960s.

Until the end of 1992, the party's secretary-general (i.e. leader) was Lee Kuan Yew, who was also Prime Minister from 1959 to 1990. Lee remained a senior figure in the party and in the government led by his successor, Goh Chok Tong, who held the prime ministership up to Aug. 12, 2004. Goh stepped down that day and handed over the office to Lee's eldest son, Lee Hsien Loong. Both Goh and the elder Lee retain influential roles within the current government, holding the titles Senior Minister and Minister Mentor, respectively.

Singapore People's Party (SPP)
Address. Blk 108, Potong Pasir Avenue 1, #01-496, Singapore 350108
Telephone. (65) 6858-5771
Fax. (65) 6220-2426
Email. feedback@spp.org.sg
Website. www.spp.org.sg
Leadership. Chiam See Tong (secretary-general)
Formed largely by defecting Singapore Democratic Party (SDP) members in 1993, the SPP is similarly liberal and centrist in its tendencies. It has, however, adopted a less confrontational approach to the ruling People's Action Party, thereby cultivating an image of a more moderate and responsible opposition. In its first electoral effort in the 1997 elections, it fielded three candidates, including Chiam See Tong, who had earlier defected from the SDP. Chiam was the only successful candidate, delivering the SPP a single seat in parliament.

In June 2001, the SPP formed the Singapore Democratic Alliance with three other smaller opposition parties (the Singapore Justice Party, National Solidarity Party and Singapore Malays National Organization) to contest the next general elections. In the November 2001 elections Chiam See Tong retained his seat for the SPP, but the alliance had no other successes.

Workers' Party (WP)
Address. 411B Jalan Besar Road, Singapore 209014
Telephone. (65) 6298-4765
Fax. (65) 6454-4404
Email. wp@wp.org.sg
Website. www.wp.org.sg
Leadership. Low Thia Khiang (secretary-general)
The WP, originally founded in 1957, was revived by its previous secretary-general, J. B. Jeyaretnam, in 1971. The party

advocates the establishment of a democratic socialist government, with a constitution guaranteeing fundamental citizens' rights. In a by-election in 1981, Jeyaretnam became the first opposition member of Parliament since 1968, although he forfeited the seat in 1986 following a controversial conviction. In 1988, the WP merged with the left-wing Socialist Front (*Barisan Sosialis*), which had been established by People's Action Party dissidents in 1961, and with the Singapore United Front (dating from 1973). Although the party won no seats in the 1988 legislative elections, it attracted nearly 17% of the total votes cast. In the 1991 poll, the WP contested 13 seats, won one and gained over 14% of the total vote. This performance was repeated in the 1997 elections, when it won one of 14 seats contested and again received more than 14% of total votes. It retained its single seat in the November 2001 elections.

Other Parties

According to the Registrar of Societies, there are 21 other registered political parties in Singapore. A number of these exist in name only: party activities are minimal and they have not contested general elections for some time. Some others lie dormant in the intervals between elections, springing to life once these are called and fielding a token number of candidates. Only a few parties have an active and ongoing political programme. The listing below only includes parties that have contested recent elections and/or have an active programme of political activity.

Democratic Progressive Party (DPP), a small and somewhat obscure party founded in 1973 which is unrepresented in parliament. In the 1999 presidential election, leader Tan Soo Phuan was one of two candidates that sought, and was denied, a Certificate of Eligibility to run for President by the Presidential Elections Committee. In the absence of any other contenders, Sellapa Rama Nathan was subsequently declared President-elect. The party fielded two candidates in the 2001 general elections, both of whom were unsuccessful.
Leadership. Tan Soo Phuan

National Solidarity Party (NSP), centrist party formed in 1987 by mainly young professionals. The party seeks to broaden popular political participation in Singapore, while functioning as a credible opposition providing checks and balances against the ruling People's Action Party. It contested three constituencies in the 1997 elections and, although failing to win a parliamentary seat, attracted over 6% of total votes cast. The NSP is one of four opposition parties that are members of the Singapore Democratic Alliance launched in June 2001. Competing under that banner, none of its candidates were returned in the general election held that year.
Address. Hong Lim Complex, Blk 531 Upper Cross Street, #03–30, Singapore 050531
Telephone. (65) 6536–6388
Fax. (65) 6532–6598
Email. nspnsp@singnet.com.sg
Website. www.nsp-singapore.org
Leadership. Yip Yew Weng (president); Steve Chia (secretary-general)

Singapore Democratic Party (SDP), a liberal and centrist party founded in 1980 by Chiam See Tong in an attempt to create a credible opposition to the ruling People's Action Party (PAP). In the 1991 elections, the SDP was the most successful of the opposition parties, winning three of the nine parliamentary seats it contested (Chiam See Tong retaining the seat he had held since 1984). In June 1993, Chiam resigned as secretary-general of the party, apparently as the result of an internal power struggle, and later joined

the Singapore People's Party just prior to the 1997 elections. Under the leadership of his successor, Chee Soon Juan, the SDP adopted a more aggressive and vocal stance against the PAP. In the 1997 elections, the SDP contested 12 seats. It lost in all, but received more than 10% of total votes. It again failed to win a seat in the 2001 elections.
Address. 1357A Serangoon Road, Singapore 328240
Telephone. (65) 6398-1675
Fax. (65) 6398-1675
Email. speakup@singaporedemocrats.org
Website. www.singaporedemocrat.org
Leadership. Chee Soon Juan (secretary-general)

Singapore Justice Party (SJP), established in 1972 but has yet to win any parliamentary representation. The party joined the Singapore Democratic Alliance formed in June 2001 to contest the general election that year.

Singapore Malays National Organization (*Pertubohan Kebangsaan Melayu Singapura*, PKMS), founded as an affiliate of the United Malays National Organization in Malaysia in the early 1950s, assuming its present title in 1967. It seeks to advance the rights of Malays in Singapore, to safeguard and promote Islam, and to encourage racial harmony. Together with three other parties, it joined the Singapore Democratic Alliance to contest the 2001 general election, but has so far failed to gain parliamentary representation.
Address. 218F Changi Rd, #04-00, PKMS Bldg., Singapore 419737
Telephone. (65) 6345–5275
Fax. (65) 6345–8724
Email. pkms_melayu@pacific.net.sg
Website. www.geocities.com/pkms218/
Leadership. Mohammed Rahizan Yaacob (secretary-general)

Slovakia

Capital: Bratislava
Population: 5,380,000 (2002E)

The independent Slovak Republic came into being on Jan. 1, 1993, upon the dissolution of the Czechoslovakia which had been proclaimed in October 1918 as one of the successor states of the Austro-Hungarian Empire. Czechoslovakia was originally a unitary state, which had been transformed into a federation during the communist-era regime, which ended in November 1989. Slovakia's constitution, adopted in September 1992, vests supreme legislative authority in the unicameral National Council of the Slovak Republic (*Narodna rada Slovenskej republiky*) consisting of 150 members, who are elected for a four-year term by citizens aged 18 and over. Elections are by a system of proportional representation under which single parties must obtain at least 5% of the national vote to be allocated seats. Alliances of two or three parties must obtain 7% and four and more parties 10%. The head of state is the President, who under a 1999 constitutional amendment is directly elected for a five-year term (renewable once) and who appoints the Prime Minister subject to approval by the National Council.

In presidential elections on May 15 and 29, 1999, Rudolf Schuster of the Party of Civic Understanding was elected with 57.2% of the second-round vote, defeating Vladimir Meciar of the HZDS (42.8%). In presidential elections on April 3 and 17, 2004, Ivan

Gasparovic of the Movement for a Democracy (HZD) and former leading politician of the HZDS was elected with 59.9% of the second-round vote, defeating Vladimir Meciar of the HZDS (40.1%).

National Council elections on Sept. 20–21, 2002, resulted as follows: Movement for a Democratic Slovakia (HZDS, now People's Party–Movement for a Democratic Slovakia, LS-HZDS) 36 seats (with 19.5% of the vote); Slovak Democratic and Christian Union (SDKU) 28 (15.1%); Direction 25 (13.5%); Hungarian Coalition Party (SMK) 20 (11.2%); Christian Democratic Movement (KDH) 15 (8.3%); New Civic Alliance (ANO) 13 (8.0%); Communist Party of Slovakia (KSS) 11 (6.3%).

Slovakia joined the European Union in 2004 and elects 14 members of the European Parliament. The June 2004 European election resulted as follows: SDKU 3 seats (with 17.1% of the vote); LS-HZDS 3 seats (17%); Direction 3 seats (16.9%); KDH 3 seats (16.2%); SMK 2 seats (13.2%).

Christian Democratic Movement
Krestansko–demokraticke hnutie (KDH)

Address. Zabotova 2, 81104 Bratislava
Telephone. (+421–2) 524 92 5416
Fax. (+421–2) 52496313
Email. kdhba@isternet.sk
Website. www.kdh.sk
Leadership. Pavol Hrusovsky (chairman); Pavol Minarik (vice-chairman and parliamentary group leader)

The party was founded in February 1990 under the leadership of communist-era Catholic dissident Jan Carnogursky. The conservative KDH follows in both the tradition of Slovak political Catholicism from the first half of the 20th century (when the father of Jan Carnogursky was an active politician) and of Western European Christian democracy. It began to co-operate with the Czech Christian Democrats but presented its own list in Slovakia for the 1990 National Council elections, coming in second place with 31 seats and 19.2% of the vote. The KDH opted to join a coalition headed by the winner of that election – the pro-democratic movement Public Against Violence (VPN) and two small parties, the Hungarian Independent Initiative (MNI) and the Democratic Party (DS). Jan Carnogursky became Prime Minister of Slovakia following the break up of the VPN and dismissal of Vladimir Meciar (VPN) in April 1991.

Shortly before the elections in June 1992, a strong radical nationalistic group in the KDH headed by Jan Klepac broke away, but in the National Council elections obtained only 3% of the vote and later joined the Slovak National Party (SNS). The KDH fell back to 18 seats with 8.9% of the vote in the 1992 National Council elections and the party went into opposition. The KDH returned to government in March 1994, after the second dismissal of Prime Minister Vladimir Meciar of the HZDS, as part of a broad coalition led by Prime Minister Jozef Moravcik (Democratic Union). KDH went into opposition again after the autumn 1994 parliamentary elections. In that contest it was allied with the non-party Standing Conference of the Civic Institute, the combined list taking a credible 10.1% vote share and 17 seats. The KDH subsequently rebuffed suggestions that it should join a government coalition with the winning HZDS.

The KDH participated in creating the anti-Meciar five-party electoral alliance, the Slovak Democratic Coalition (SDK), in summer 1997, in which it represented the biggest component. But internally the alliance was deeply divided between two clearly identifiable factions: one headed by KDH chairman Carnogursky and the other led by the SDK leader Mikulas Dzurinda. The Carnogursky wing wanted to maintain the independent identity of the KDH and emphasized its Christian-conservative character. On the other hand, the Dzurinda wing aspired to convert the SDK into a fully integrated single party having a broad centre-right profile. Before parliamentary elections in 1998, the SDK had to transform itself into an "election party" because of new electoral rules specifying that each party of an alliance must surmount the 5% threshold to obtain representation (this rule being applied only in that particular election). In the September 1998 elections, the component parties, including the KDH, delegated their representatives to the list of the "election party" SDK and supported it. Following the elections, in which the SDK won 42 seats and 26.3% of the vote and narrowly failed to outpoll the HZDS, Mikulas Dzurinda formed a broad right-left coalition government with the Party of the Democratic Left (SDL), the Party of Civic Understanding (SOP) and the Hungarian Coalition Party (SMK). The KDH was a part of the coalition, which secured the election of Rudolf Schuster (SOP) as President in May 1999.

During 1998-99, the Carnogursky wing resisted Dzurinda's moves to convert the SDK into an integrated single party and sought to keep KDH's separate identity. In April 1999, the KDH congress barred SDK members from holding posts in the KDH (at that time Slovak rules allowing for dual party membership). The conflict ended in January 2000, when Mikulas Dzurinda announced the foundation of new political party, the Slovak Democratic and Christian Union (SDKU). Subsequently around one-quarter of the KDH's 30,000 members left the party, mainly joining the SDKU. In October 2000, Carnogursky was succeeded as party chairman by Pavol Hrusovsky. The following month the KDH deputies signalled the party's intention to keep its separate identity by withdrawing from the SDK parliamentary caucus and forming a separate group (comprising 9 members). At the same time the KDH became formally the fifth member of Dzurinda's government coalition.

Before the parliamentary elections in September 2002, the KDH refused the appeal of the SDKU to create an election coalition. Considering the party's former divisions, the KDH result – 15 seats and 8.3% of the vote – appeared quite respectable, most of its electoral support coming from traditional Catholic believers. After the elections, the KDH became a member of a centre-right government coalition led by Dzurinda's SDKU (the KDH having three ministers). KDH supported the entry of Slovakia to NATO and the European Union, although its former leader Carnogursky argued strongly against the EU in conformity with his eurosceptic position. In the June 2004 European elections the party obtained an exceptional 16.2% of the vote and three seats, confirming the ability of the party to bring out its supporters (voter turnout being only 17%).

The KDH is a member of the European People's Party, a full member of the International Democrat Union and observer member of the Christian Democrat and People's Party International. In 2003 the party claimed a membership of about 20,000.

Communist Party of Slovakia
Komunisticka strana Slovenska (KSS)

Address. Hattalova 12A, 831 03 Bratislava
Telephone. (+421-2) 44372540
Fax. (+421-2) 44372540
Email. sekr@kss.sk
Website. www.kss.sk
Leadership. Jozef Sevc (chairman of KSS central committee); Ladislav Jaca (general secretary)

The former Communist Party of Slovakia (branch of the Communist Party of Czechoslovakia) in 1990 transformed itself into the Party of the Democratic Left (SDL) with a social democratic programmme. The SDL abandoned

Marxism-Leninism and distanced itself from the former communist regime. A new communist formation in Slovakia appeared in 1991, when two orthodox communist groups separated from SDL and formed the Communist Party of Slovakia '91 (*Komunisticka strana Slovenska '91*, KSS '91) and the Association of Slovak Communists (*Zvaz komunistov Slovenska,* ZKS). In the National Council elections 1992, representatives of KSS '91 were on the list of the ZKS, but this list obtained only 0.8 % of the vote.

In August 1992, both communist formations joined together and formed the new Communist Party of Slovakia (KSS) and Vladimir Dado was elected the first chairman of KSS Central Committee. The KSS defined itself as a successor of the Communist Party of Slovakia and Communist Party of Czechoslovakia before 1989 and as a Marxist-Leninist formation, opposed to the market economy and supporting central planning. It described the political development after 1989 as the worst era of Slovak modern history.

The KSS obtained only 2.7% of the vote in the 1994 elections and 2.8% of the vote in 1998. Subsequent to the elections it elected Jozef Sevc as the new chairman of its central committee. In the presidential elections of 1999, KSS candidate Juraj Lazarcik obtained only 0.15% of the vote in the first round. The surprising success of KSS – 6.3% of the vote and 11 seats – in the parliamentary elections in September 2002 was a result of the strong protest support which the party obtained in East Slovakia – the poorest part of country with declining living standards. In the June 2004 European elections, however, the party obtained only 4.54% of the vote and failed to win a seat. The KSS had opposed Slovakia's entry to the EU (and also to NATO).

In 2003 the party claimed a membership of about 22,000. The KSS is a member of the Party of the European Left.

Direction
Smer

Address. Sumracna 27, 821 02 Bratislava
Telephone. (+421-2) 43426297
Fax. (+421-2) 43426297
Email. tajomnik@strana-smer.sk
Website. www.strana-smer.sk
Leadership. Robert Fico (chairman)
Registered in November 1999 and formally established in December 1999 (first congress) by former first vice-chairman of the ex-communist Party of the Democratic Left (SDL) and very popular politician, Robert Fico. This populist formation was sharply critical of the social impact of the policies of Dzurinda's broad government coalition (1998–2002). It favours the abolition of proportional representation to reduce party fragmentation (and introduced proposals for establishing the mix or first past the post election system). It also advocates a tougher approach to Roma (Gypsies), including the restriction of welfare benefits to the first three children per family. The movement supports NATO and EU membership. The key political slogan has been "order, justice and stability". During its December 2001 congress, Direction presented itself as a party of Tony Blair's "third way" and stated that it belongs to the Western European social democratic left. From 2000 to mid-2002, Direction obtained between 15-20% in public opinion polls of voting intentions, and the key party figure, Fico, was the most popular Slovak politician.

However, in the parliamentary elections in September 2002, Direction surprisingly took only third place with 13.5% of the vote and 25 seats and remained in opposition. The prime reason for this result was its overly confrontational and aggressive election campaign and also the fact that Direction, although distancing itself from Meciar's Movement for a Democratic Slovakia, failed to allay suspicions that it might create a government coalition with

Meciar's HZDS. Most of the Direction voters were former voters of the Party of the Democratic Left and the Party of Civic Understanding (SOP). After the 2002 elections, Direction called for other parties to join it to integrate the Slovak left. In March 2003, the SOP responded to this call and joined Direction. During 2003, Direction was in first place, obtaining 25-35% support, in public opinion polls of voting intentions but in the June 2004 European elections the party obtained only 16.9% of the vote and three seats. In these elections the SDL, the Social Democratic Party of Slovakia (SDSS) and the Green Party in Slovakia (SZS) were on the Direction list, one of the three seats going to the SDL. All three representatives sit in the Party of European Socialists group. In 2003 Direction claimed a membership of about 6,500.

Hungarian Coalition Party
Strana madarskej koalicie (SMK)
Magyar Koalicio Partja (MKP)

Address. Cajakova 8, 811 05 Bratislava
Telephone. (+421-2) 524 97 684
Fax. (+421-2) 524 95 791
Email. smk@smk.sk
Website. www.mkp.sk
Leadership. Bela Bugar (chairman); Arpad Duka Zolyomi (vice-chairman); Gyula Bardos (parliamentary group leader)
The SMK represents the Hungarian community in Slovakia (approximately half a million ethnic Hungarians) and is committed to defending their rights. It was founded in June 1998 as a result of the unification of three Hungarian political groups into a single party: the Hungarian Christian Democratic Movement (*Madarske krestansko demokraticke hnutie*, MKDH), the Coexistence (*Egyutteles-Spoluzitie*) and the Hungarian Civic Party (*Madarska obcianska strana*, MOS).

These three political parties emerged before the first democratic elections in 1990. The liberal MOS (originally named the Hungarian Independent Initiative, MNI) had secured representation in 1990 on the pro-democracy Public Against Violence (VPN) list and worked in government from 1990 to 1992 (one government vice-chairman). In the elections of 1992, it failed (taking only 2.3% of the vote). The nationalistic Coexistence and the Christian-conservative and pro-market MKDH created an electoral coalition in the elections of 1990 (obtaining 8.6 % of the vote and 14 seats) and 1992 (7.4% of the vote and 14 seats) and they were in opposition. In 1994, both parties gave parliamentary support to Jozef Moravcik's government but were not directly a part of it.

Before the 1994 elections all three Hungarians parties created a joint election coalition named the Hungarian coalition (MK) which won 10.2% of the vote and 17 seats. After the elections, MK was in opposition and it came into increasing conflict with the policies of the government of the Movement for a Democratic Slovakia (HZDS), which intended to impose an exclusively Slovak concept of national identity.

The reason for the formation of the SMK in 1998 as a single party was new electoral rules (applied only in that election) specifying that each component of an alliance must surmount the 5% threshold to obtain representation. The SMK defined itself as a right-of-centre formation based on Christian democratic, liberal-conservative values and fully supported the entry of Slovakia into the EU and NATO. The party originally created two party platforms – Christian-conservative (comprising former members of the MKDH and Coexistence) and Civic-liberal (former members of the MOS). Later, the SMK congress abolished them to eliminate coalition elements in the party.

In the September 1998 parliamentary elections, the SMK lost ground slightly compared with the aggregate results of the component parties in 1994, returning 15 deputies on a vote share of 9.1%. It opted to join a broad left-right coalition government headed by the Slovak Democratic Coalition (SDK), receiving three ministerial portfolios and a promise that more ethnic Hungarian rights would be enacted. Inevitably disappointed by the slow progress on that front, the SMK on several occasions threatened to leave the coalition, notably in August 2001, when the SMK executive committee voted unanimously for withdrawal. As in previous crises, however, the party was persuaded to remain in the government by new promises from the other coalition parties. Another reason for staying in the government was strong foreign pressure (EU, NATO) to prevent the collapse of Dzurinda's government.

In the September 2002 elections, the SMK won 11.16 % of the vote and 20 seats. This improvement on 1998 was the result of heavy turnout by the Hungarian minority. Following the 2002 parliamentary elections, the SMK joined the new Dzurinda right-of-centre coalition government and obtained four portfolios. The chairman of SMK, Bela Bugar, was elected vice-president of the National Council. In the June 2004 European elections the party obtained 13.2% of the vote and two seats.

The SMK is a member of the European People's Party and the International Democrat Union as well as an observer member of the Christian Democrat and People's Party International. In 2003, the party claimed a membership of 11,000.

New Civic Alliance
Aliancia noveho obcana (ANO)

Address. Drobneho 27, 841 01 Bratislava
Telephone. (+421-2) 692 029 19
Fax. (+421-2) 692 029 20
Email. ano@ano-aliancia.sk
Website. www.ano-aliancia.sk
Leadership. Pavol Rusko (chairman); Lubomir Lintner (first vice-chairman)

This centre-liberal formation was founded by a part-owner and director of private television station "Markiza", Pavol Rusko, in May 2001. Besides Rusko, the leadership of ANO includes a few well-known personalities from the sports, cultural and economic fields. In the September 2002 elections the Alliance received strong and prominent support from television "Markiza", the influential radio "Okey" and the *Narodna obroda* newspaper (parts of Rusko's financial group). The Alliance secured 8% of the vote and 15 seats. After the elections ANO became a member of the right-of-centre Dzurinda government coalition and acquired three ministerial portfolios.

In spring 2003, the ANO tried to bring about liberalization of the abortion law, which caused hostility from the Christian Democratic Movement and led to a brief crisis in the government coalition. In August 2003, there emerged a personal conflict between Pavol Rusko and ANO's Economics Minister, Robert Nemcsics, whereupon Nemcsics resigned and Rusko became the new Economics Minister. Nemcsics (as a deputy) and one other deputy left ANO and this, together with the departure of Ivan Simko's Free Forum (SF) from the Slovak Democratic and Christian Union (SDKU), caused the government coalition's support to drop to under half the total of 150 deputies.

In the June 2004 European elections the party obtained only 4.6% of the vote and failed to win a seat. In 2003 the party claimed a membership of about 6,000.

The ANO is a member of the European Liberal, Democratic and Reform Party and an observer member of the Liberal International.

People's Party–Movement for a Democratic Slovakia
Ludova strana–Hnutie za demokraticke Slovensko
(LS–HZDS)

Address. Tomasikova 32/A, 830 00 Bratislava
Telephone. (+421-2) 48 220 209
Fax. (+421-2) 48 220 229
Email. webmaster@hzds.sk
Website. www.hzds.sk
Leadership. Vladimir Meciar (chairman); Tibor Cabaj (parliamentary group leader); Frantisek Blanarik (general secretary)

The centrist-populist Movement for a Democratic Slovakia (HZDS) emerged in March 1991 as a result of a conflict in the leadership of the pro-democracy movement Public Against Violence (VPN). Prime Minister of Slovakia (then still part of Czechoslovakia) Vladimir Meciar founded a platform "For a Democratic Slovakia" inside VPN. A month later, Meciar was dismissed as Prime Minister and founded the HZDS. The HZDS was registered in May 1991 and Meciar was elected the chairman at a party congress in June 1991.

The newly formed HZDS defined itself with an explicitly nationalist appeal and argued in favour of a diluted form of federalism providing greater protection for Slovak economic and political interests than was contemplated in Prague. The HZDS quickly confirmed that it was Slovakia's leading political formation, winning 74 of the 150 Slovak National Council seats (37.3% of the vote) in the June 1992 elections. Restored to the premiership, Meciar at first resisted Czech insistence that either the federation should have real authority at government level or the two parts should separate. By late 1992, however, he had embraced the latter option, leading Slovakia to sovereignty on Jan. 1, 1993. After the elections of 1992, HZDS formed a government which had the parliamentary support of the radical right-wing Slovak National Party (SNS) (its chairman Ludovit Cernak taking the Defence portfolio) and the ex-communist Party of the Democratic Left (SDL).

The Meciar government of independent Slovakia quickly came under attack for its perceived authoritarian tendencies. Besides, the HZDS connected different political streams (radical nationalist, social democrats, liberals etc.) resulting quickly in conflicts. Policy and personal clashes precipitated a series of defections from the HZDS in 1993–94. A first splinter group (of eight deputies), headed by Milan Knazko, who had been dismissed as Minister of Foreign Affairs, left HZDS in March 1993 and formed the Alliance of Democrats of Slovakia. At the same time, the SNS and SDL stopped support for the government, because Meciar did not want to create formally a coalition government and to give up several ministerial portfolios in their favour. In October 1993, Meciar had to accept a coalition with the SNS, which obtained three ministerial portfolios. However, divisions within the HZDS led to the breakaway of another group of deputies – who in February 1994 created the Realistic Political Alternative headed by Jozef Moravcik, Knazko's successor in the Foreign Minister portfolio – and to Meciar's defeat on a no-confidence motion and reluctant resignation in March 1994. Being in opposition to a new coalition government headed by Jozef Moravcik (Democratic Union, uniting the Alliance of Democrats of Slovakia and the Realistic Political Alternative), the HZDS remained the country's strongest formation based on Meciar's charisma.

Allied in the autumn 1994 elections with the small Agrarian Party of Slovakia, the HZDS won a decisive plurality of 61 seats (on a 35% vote share) and became the leading partner in a "red-brown" government coalition with the SNS and the radical left-wing Slovak Workers' Front (ZRS). The time between the elections of 1994 and 1998 was filled by a sharp confrontation between the government and parliamentary opposition when effective checks on executive power were made impossible. The HZDS completely took control over public service electronic media. To prevent another split, such as had happened in 1993-94, and to discipline its parliamentary caucus, the HZDS took the unconstitutional step, using its parliamentary majority (HZDS, SNS, ZRS), of relieving deputy Frantisek Gaulieder of his mandate because he had announced he was leaving the HZDS.

The HZDS also revived the earlier conflict between Meciar and President Michal Kovac, who had been elected by the legislature in February 1993 as candidate of the HZDS but who had subsequently distanced himself from the movement as he became embattled with the Prime Minister on a series of issues. The tension stepped up in March 1995 when the President refused at first to sign a bill transferring overall control of the security services from the head of state to the government. However, Kovac had to sign the measure the following month when the National Council had readopted it. The HZDS called for his resignation and tried several times to dismiss him in Parliament, but did not succeed in finding the necessary support of a three-fifths majority of deputies.

The confrontation between Meciar and Kovac remained unresolved in 1996–97, with the HZDS government blocking opposition moves for a referendum on a proposal that the President should be directly elected. When the opposition succeed in getting a referendum in May 1997 (concerned with, as well as the direct election of the President, the entry of Slovakia to NATO), Minister of the Interior Gustav Krajci of the HZDS held up the distribution of ballot papers concerning the direct election of the President. Subsequently, the Central Referendum Commission declared the referendum to be invalid. As Kovac's five-year term came to an end, the legislature failed in several votes to produce the required three-fifths majority for a successor, so that in March 1998 Meciar, as Prime Minister, assumed important presidential functions (the rest being taken by then parliamentary chairman Ivan Gasparovic – HZDS).

Before the elections of 1998, the HZDS was joined by the New Agrarian Party (formed by the Agrarian Party of Slovakia and another small agrarian organization – the Farmers Movement of Slovakia, HPS) and by the small Party of Entrepreneurs and Tradesmen. In the National Council elections in September 1998, the HZDS narrowly remained the largest party, but slumped to 43 seats on a 27% vote share and went into opposition to a right-left coalition led by the Slovak Democratic Coalition (SDK). Following this the new National Council had in January 1999 adopted a constitutional amendment providing for direct presidential elections, Meciar emerging from post-election seclusion to run as the HZDS candidate. However, in the elections in May 1999 he was defeated in the second round by the government coalition nominee on a 57.2% to 42.8% split.

In March 2000 Meciar was re-elected HZDS chairman by a party congress which also approved the conversion of the HZDS into a formal political party with the suffix "People's Party" (new party abbreviation HZDS-LS), signifying a shift to a less nationalistic stance, and the party declared its full support for membership in the European Union and NATO. The congress also agreed to a re-registration of members, which caused their rapid decrease – in 1998 the HZDS declared it had 70,000 members and since 2000 it has reported about a half of the previous number.

In April 2000 Meciar was arrested and fined for refusing to testify on the murky affair of the kidnapping of President Kovac's son in 1995 at the height of the HZDS leader's dispute with the President. The HZDS-LS then succeeded in collecting sufficient signatures to force a referendum on its proposal that early parliamentary elections should be held. However, only 20% of the electorate voted when the consul-

tation was held in November 2000, so that the result had no validity. During the period 2001–02, HZDS-LS tried to demonstrate a change in its profile, ending its opposition co-operation in with the radical-nationalist SNS and fully supporting the entry of Slovakia to NATO and EU. Nevertheless, because of international political reasons, it still remained unacceptable as a potential partner of coalition government. This was shown after parliamentary elections in September 2002, when HZDS-LS won again, but a new right-centre government was established without it.

The HZDS-LS election result in 2002 – 19.5% of the vote and 36 seats – was the weakest in party history. It was influenced by continual splitting caused by disagreement with leader Meciar and his policies. Already, after the elections of 1998, the party had been left by deputy Ivan Mjartan, who established his own political party, the Centre, but it stayed marginal. In April 2002, HZDS-LS was left by another deputy, Jozef Kalman, who established a new party – the Left Bloc – which obtained only 0.22% of votes in the 2002 election. In the same month, the HZDS-LS congress under Meciar's instruction expunged from the ballot for the 2002 elections some prominent politicians including the number two in the party, Ivan Gasparovic. Subsequently, Gasparovic established a new political organization – the Movement for a Democracy (HZD), which gained 3.3% of the vote in the 2002 elections, weakening the HZDS-LS result. The splitting in HZDS-LS continued after the elections. In January 2003 a group of eleven deputies headed by vice-chair Vojtech Tkac left the party – again because of disagreement with the chairman's policy – and established the People's Alliance (LU).

In June 2003, the HZDS-LS congress changed the name of the party to People's Party–Movement for a Democratic Slovakia (LS-HZDS) and re-elected Meciar as chairman (there was no other candidate). As of 2003 the LS-HZDS claimed a membership of about 45,000. In the April 2004 presidential elections Meciar was defeated in the second round by Gasparovic on a 59.9% to 40.1% vote. In the June 2004 European elections the party obtained 17% of the vote and three seats.

Slovak Democratic and Christian Union
Slovenska demokraticka a krestanska unia (SDKU)

Address. Ruzinovska 28, 827 35 Bratislava
Telephone. (+421-2) 4341410205
Fax. (+421-2) 4341 4106
Email. sdk@sdk.sk
Website. www.sdkuonline.sk
Leadership. Mikulas Dzurinda (chairman); Milan Hort (parliamentary group leader)

The SDKU is a successor formation of the Slovak Democratic Coalition (SDK), which was founded in June 1997 as a broad electoral alliance of five different parties then in opposition, namely the right-centre Christian Democratic Movement (KDH), the conservative-liberal Democratic Party (DS), the liberal-centre Democratic Union (DU), the left-wing Social Democratic Party of Slovakia (SDSS) and the ecological Green Party in Slovakia (SZS). The goal of SDK was to unite fragmentary anti-Meciar opposition, to win the parliamentary elections in 1998 and to push Meciar's Movement for a Democratic Slovakia (HZDS) out of power. The vice-chairman of KDH, Mikulas Dzurinda, became the leader of SDK.

Before the elections in 1998, the SDK had to transform into an "election party" because of new electoral rules specifying that each party in an alliance must surmount the 5% threshold to obtain representation (this rule was applied only in this election). Membership of the SDK comprised 150 members (candidates for deputies) from five foundation parties that did not stand separately in the elections but supported the SDK. Inside the new party there appeared five political formations which joined together members of the foundation parties.

In the September 1998 parliamentary elections, the SDK narrowly failed to overtake the ruling HZDS, winning 42 of the 150 seats with 26.3% of the vote. Nevertheless, on the basis of a pre-election agreement, Dzurinda was able to form a majority coalition government, which included the ex-communist Party of the Democratic Left (SDL), the Party of Civic Understanding (SOP) and the Hungarian Coalition Party (SMK), on a programme of accelerated pro-market reform and accession to the European Union and NATO. In direct presidential elections in May 1999, the SDK officially backed the successful candidacy of Rudolf Schuster of the SOP.

Between 1998 and 2000, relationships between the "election party" SDK and the five foundation parties, which were not officially components of the government coalition, were characterized by permanent tension and disputes. The SDK leadership headed by Dzurinda disagreed with a return to the original electoral coalition whereas, on the contrary, representatives of the foundation parties rejected his proposal for a full integration with the SDK and for the formation of a single party. In January 2000, Prime Minister Dzurinda and eleven other leaders of the SDK announced the creation of a new political party, the Slovak Democratic and Christian Union (SDKU) as the effective successor of the SDK. The main idea was to strengthen the centre-right of the divided Slovak political spectrum through a process of integrating smaller political parties into a larger one and thus repeat the success of SDK.

The SDKU was registered in February 2000. In November 2000, its founding congress elected Dzurinda as party leader. To maintain governmental stability the SDK formally existed until the 2002 elections. About half the SDK deputies and eight of the nine SDK ministers joined the SDKU. Furthermore, in summer 2000, the Democratic Union and the small formation Union of Businessmen and Tradesmen joined the SDKU. Also, many KDH members and some members of the DS, SDSS and SZS joined the SDKU. The SDKU declared itself a centre-right formation embracing Christian democratic and liberal-conservative values, fully supporting the entry of Slovakia to the EU and NATO. There appeared two institutionalized inner platforms inside the SDKU – the Christian democratic and the Liberal. Before the September 2002 elections, SDKU unsuccessfully called for the formation of a right-wing electoral block (orientated to the KDH). It partly succeeded with the DS, which abandoned its election candidacy and asked its voters to vote for the SDKU shortly before election (for this, the DS obtained one ministerial portfolio after the elections). In the elections, the SDKU obtained quite a good result – 28 seats and 15.1% of the vote – enabling it to become leader of the centre-right government coalition with the KDH, SMK and the New Civic Alliance (ANO) with a tight parliamentary majority (78 seats from 150). It had five ministerial portfolios (one of them DS) plus the prime ministerial position (Dzurinda). In 2003, there was a big dispute concerning Jan Mojzis, the head of the National Security Authority, who lost Dzurinda's confidence and was dismissed. This dismissal was not supported by the Minister of Defence and SDKU vice-chairman, Ivan Simko. Subsequently, Dzurinda dismissed Simko. In November 2003, Simko, another vice-chairman, Zuzana Martinakova, and several deputies left the SDKU and created a new party – the Free Forum (SF).

In the April 2004 presidential elections SDKU candidate Eduard Kukan was defeated (with only 22.09% of the vote) in the first round by Ivan Gasparovic and Vladimir Meciar. In the June 2004 European elections the party obtained 17.1% of the vote and three seats. SDKU claim a membership of about 7,000 (2003).

The SDKU is a member of the European People's Party.

Other Parties

Democratic Party (*Demokraticka strana*, DS), a liberal-conservative formation, descended from a party of the same name founded in 1944 but suspended in 1948 when the Communists came to power. Revived in 1989, the DS joined the Slovak government in 1990 but failed to win representation in the 1992 elections. Although the party absorbed several small centre-right groupings in 1993-94, a joint list of the DS and the Party of Entrepreneurs and Tradesmen won only 3.4% of the vote and no seats in the autumn 1994 parliamentary elections. For the September 1998 parliamentary elections the DS supported by the Slovak Democratic Coalition (SDK), obtaining six deputies on the SDK list. In December 2000 five the DS deputies withdrew from the SDK parliamentary caucus, though they were too few to form their own group. This step provoked the resignation from the party of Deputy Prime Minister Ivan Miklos (who remained in the government and later joined the Slovak Democratic and Christian Union, SDKU).

In January 2001 a DS congress first elected deputy chairman Frantisek Sebej, a right-conservative, as chairman and Ludovit Kanik, a liberal-pragmatic, as a vice-chairman. When Sebej immediately handed back the post on the grounds that he could not work with Kanik, the congress elected Kanik as chairman. Sebej and his group left the DS and created their own party – the Civic Conservative Party, which obtained only 0.3% of the vote in elections in September 2002. Shortly before the elections, the DS made an agreement with the SDKU over electoral support and did not present its own list. For this, the DS chairman Kanik was given a ministerial portfolio in Dzurinda's government after the elections.
Leadership. Ludovit Kanik (chairman)

Green Party in Slovakia (*Strana zelenych na Slovensku*, SZS), ecological formation founded in January 1990, arguing that the creation of a market economy was not an end in itself but rather the means of improving the quality of life. It won six seats in the National Council in 1990. In 1991 a group which disagreed with the party aim to change Czechoslovakia into a confederation separated, and the SZS lost all its parliamentary seats in the elections in 1992, regaining two in 1994, when it was part of the left Common Choice (SV) alliance headed by the Party of the Democratic Left (SDL). In 1998 the SZS was part of the Slovak Democratic Coalition, which thereafter headed the government. In the election of 2002, the party gained only 1.0% of the vote. The SZS is a member of the European Green Party/European Federation of Green Parties.
Leadership. Jozef Pokorny (chairman)

Party of the Democratic Left (*Strana demokratickej lavice*, SDL), ex-communist left-wing formation created by the transformation of the Slovak Communists into a social democratic formation. In January 1991, it accepted the present-day name Party of the Democratic Left (SDL), while a dissident orthodox communist minority left the party and later renovated the Communist Party of Slovakia (KSS). In June 1992 SDL won 29 seats on a 14.7% vote share in the National Council elections; in 1994 it was a component of Jozef Moravcik's coalition government, but after the autumn 1994 elections, the SDL fell back to 13 seats. Its election coalition called the Common Choice (SV), created by three small left-wing parties – the Social Democratic Party of Slovakia (SDSS), Green Party in Slovakia (SZS) and the Farmers Movement of Slovakia (HPS) – obtained only 10.4% of the vote in these elections. The SDL rejected Meciar's HZDS's offer to share in government and stayed in opposition until 1998.

In the September 1998 elections the SDL advanced to 23

seats on a 14.7% vote share and then joined a broad Dzurinda coalition government. As a result of a 1999 party crisis, in September 1999 popular vice-chair Robert Fico left the party and formed Direction. At the beginning of 2002, the party was left by a "moderate" group headed by former SDL chairman Peter Weiss and former vice-chairman Milan Ftacnik, who criticized the party's shift to the left and formed the Social Democratic Alternative (SDA). However, the SDA obtained only 1.8% of the vote in the elections of 2002. For those elections, the SDL created a common list with the Social Democratic Party of Slovakia (SDSS) and the Party of Civic Understanding (SOP), but won only 1.4 % of the vote. In 1998, the party had about 23,000 members, by 2003 only 10,000. In the June 2004 European elections the SDL was on the Direction list (one of three seats of this list going to the SDL). The SDL is a member party of the Socialist International and the Party of European Socialists.

Leadership. Lubomir Petrak (chairman)

People's Alliance (*Ludova unia*, LU), established as an independent party in May 2003; it separated from the People's Party–Movement for a Democratic Slovakia (LS-HZDS), and had eleven deputies in the parliament. The party distanced itself from the authoritarian style of HZDS leader V. Meciar. The LU is an affiliated member of the Union for a Europe of Nations.

Leadership. Vojtech Tkac (chairman)

Slovak National Party (*Slovenska narodna strana*, SNS), a radical nationalistic party founded in March 1990, its programme calling for the assertion of Slovak rights and the revival of national pride and patriotism. Opposed to Slovak NATO and EU membership. It obtained 13.9% of the vote in the 1990 National Council elections, but only 7.9% (and nine seats) in the June 1992 contest. It joined a coalition with the dominant Movement for a Democratic Slovakia (HZDS) from October 1993 to March 1994. In February 1994 the SNS was weakened by a split involving the defection of the party's "moderate" wing led by the then chairman, Ludovit Cernak. Cernak's group founded the National Democratic Party–New Alternative which later joined the Democratic Union. In the autumn 1994 elections, the SNS took only 5.4% of the vote (and nine seats), being nevertheless awarded two portfolios in a new HZDS-led coalition.

Before the elections in September 1998, the SNS was joined by two small formations – the Christian-social Union, which separated from the Christian Democratic Movement (KDH) in 1992, and the Slovak Green Alternative. In these elections the SNS advanced to 14 seats with 9.1% of the vote but went into opposition to a right-left coalition government headed by the Slovak Democratic Coalition (SDK). In September 1999, then chairman Jan Slota was ousted as SNS chairman by a party congress, being succeeded the following month by Anna Malikova (then vice-chairman). During the following two years, there proceeded a fight between wings represented by the new and former leaders of the party. Besides personal clashes, Malikova called for a "moderate conservative" shift of the SNS; on the contrary, Slota wanted to maintain the radical nationalistic position. In September 2001, Slota's wing separated and formed the Real Slovak National Party (*Prava Slovenska narodna strana*, PSNS). In the elections of 2002, the SNS obtained only 3.3% of the vote and the PSNS 3.7% of the vote. In May 2003, both parties re-unified.

Leadership. Jan Slota (chairman); Anna Malikova (vice-chairman)

Slovak Workers' Front (*Zdruzenie robotnikov Slovenska*, ZRS), established as an independent party in April 1994, having previously been a trade union component of the Party of the Democratic Left. Standing on a radical left-wing platform urging protection of workers' rights and neutrality, it obtained 7.3% and 13 seats in the 1994 elections, opting to join a coalition government headed by the Movement for a Democratic Slovakia. Internal division and disillusion of former voters contributed to the party's failure to win any seats in 1998, when its vote slumped to 1.3%. In the September 2002 elections, the party obtained only 0.5% of the vote.

Leadership. Jan Luptak (chairman)

Social Democratic Party of Slovakia (*Socialnodemokraticka strana Slovenska*, SDSS), derives from the historic Czechoslovak Social Democratic Party, which was forcibly merged with the Communist Party in 1948. The party was re-launched in February 1990. The Slovak social democrats quickly asserted its separate identity. The left-wing SDSS failed in the National Council elections of 1990 and 1992. In elections in 1994, the SDSS was a component of the left-wing election coalition Common Choice (SV), which was headed by the Party of the Democratic Left (SDL), enabling it to obtain 2 seats. Similarly, joining the Slovak Democratic Coalition (SDK), the party obtained 4 seats in the SDK parliamentary caucus as a result of the 1998 elections.

By 2000 divisions within the SDK had impelled the SDSS into "parallel" negotiations on a possible union with the SDL and Party of Civic Understanding (SOP) and in the elections of 2002, representatives of the SDSS were on the SDL list; however it gained only 1.4% of the vote. During its existence the SDSS has experienced repeated internal clashes caused by relationships with other political formations (HZDS, SDL, SDK, Direction), leading to party fragmentation and the departure of several groups. After 1998, the SDSS came into deep internal crisis caused by its participation in the SDK, which weakened the connection between the party and its voters. In the June 2004 European elections, the representative of the SDSS was on the Direction list, the party having already in May 2004 reached agreement with the Direction about unification.

The SDSS is a member of the Socialist International and the Party of the European Socialists.

Leadership. Jaroslav Volf (chairman)

Slovenia

Capital: Ljubljana
Population: 1,964,036 (2002 census)

Having been a constituent republic of the Communist-ruled Socialist Federal Republic of Yugoslavia since World War II, Slovenia declared independence in June 1991 on the basis of a referendum held in December 1990. Its Constitution adopted in December 1991 provides for a multi-party democracy, in which the largely ceremonial President is directly elected for a five-year term and for a maximum of two consecutive terms, and the head of government is the President of the Government (Prime Minister), who is elected by the National Assembly (upon a proposal by the President, following consultation with the leaders of National Assembly groups). The National Assembly may also terminate the office of the President of the Government and ministers.

The legislature is a bicameral body, consisting of (i) the upper National Council (*Drzavni svet*) – a representative body of social, economic, professional and local interests – whose 40 indirectly elected members serve a five-year term, 22 being local representatives and 18 elected by socio-economic interest groups; and (ii) the lower National Assembly (*Drzavni zbor*) whose 90 members are directly elected for a four-year term. Members of the National Assembly are elected by proportional representation from party lists that have obtained 4% of the vote at the national level (before the October 2000 elections, the threshold had been 3%). There are eight electoral units in Slovenia, each electing 11 members of parliament. In addition, one seat is reserved for Slovenia's Hungarian community and one for the Italian national community, each forming a special electoral unit in which an MP is elected on the basis of the first-past-the-post system.

In a second round of presidential elections on Dec. 1, 2002, Dr Janez Drnovsek, the candidate of the Liberal Democracy of Slovenia and a former President of the Government, was elected for a first five-year term with 56.5% of the vote. He is only the second person to have become the President of Slovenia, after Milan Kucan, a reformed Communist, had won all previous elections.

In the most recent general elections to the National Assembly, held on Oct. 3, 2004, only seven political parties passed the 4% threshold and entered parliament. The elections were marked by the lowest turnout in the history of Slovenian parliamentary democracy with only 60.6% of the electorate (as opposed to 70.1% in 2000) casting their vote. The elections brought victory to the (centre) right political parties. With just 22.8% of the vote and 23 seats, the Liberal Democracy of Slovenia, the leading political party in the past 12 years, lost 11 seats to become the second strongest party in the National Assembly after the Slovenian Democratic Party (29 seats, based on 29.1% of the vote). The United List of Social Democrats won 10 seats (10.2%), the New Slovenia–Christian People's Party 9 (9.1%), the Slovenian People's Party 7 (6.8%), the Slovenian National Party 6 (6.3%), and the Democratic Party of Pensioners of Slovenia 4 (4%). The newly elected National Assembly is presided over by France Cukjati (Slovenian Democratic Party).

On June 13, 2004, Slovenians elected seven Members of the European Parliament (MEPs) for the first time. The turnout was only 28.3%. Slovenia's MEPs are directly elected from party lists by proportional representation and for the European elections there is only one electoral unit in Slovenia. The New Slovenia–Christian People's Party won two seats (with 23.5% of the vote), as did a joint list by the Liberal Democracy of Slovenia and the Democratic Party of Pensioners of Slovenia (21.9% of the vote), and the Slovenian Democratic Party (17.7%). The United List of Social Democrats won the remaining seat with 14.2% of the vote. Three out of seven elected MEPs are women, following an intensive campaign by non-governmental and civil society groups that led to the adoption of a special law, requiring that party lists be based on equal representation of men and women (with a minimum of 40%, or three candidates, being of one gender; and with at least one candidate of either gender being placed to the upper part of every party list). No such requirement is in place for the elections to the National Assembly, where the proportion of women has been one of the lowest in Europe, with 11 women elected to the National Assembly in 2004.

Democratic Party of Pensioners of Slovenia
Demokraticna stranka upokojencev Slovenije (DeSUS)
Address. Cankarjevo nabrezje 7, 1000 Ljubljana
Telephone. (+386-1) 4397350, (+386-31) 364045 (mobile)
Fax. (+386-1) 4314113
Email. desus@siol.net

Website. www.desus.si
Leadership. Anton Rous (president); Franc Znidarsic (National Assembly group leader); Pavel Brglez (secretary-general)
The Democratic Party of Pensioners of Slovenia was formed in early 1990, with a view to enabling the ever-growing elderly population of Slovenia to participate in decision-making processes that concern both questions of the elderly and the future of the country. It has been particularly active with respect to matters of social policy (especially pension and health security). DeSUS was part of the (ex-communist) United List of Social Democrats (ZLSD) in the 1992 parliamentary elections, but contested those of 1996 independently, winning five seats with 4.3% of the vote. It then joined a coalition government headed by the Liberal Democracy of Slovenia (LDS), successfully opposing proposals for the privatization of the pensions system. In the October 2000 parliamentary elections, the party slipped to four seats (while improving to 5.2% of the vote), but was included in a new ruling coalition headed by the LDS and also including the ZLSD and the Slovenian People's Party (SLS+SKD). In the October 2004 elections, the party retained four seats, but only barely made it into the parliament (winning just 4.04% of the vote). The DeSUS contested the June 2004 European elections with the LDS, but its candidate, listed fourth on the joint party list, failed to win a seat.

Liberal Democracy of Slovenia
Liberalna demokracija Slovenije (LDS)
Address. Trg Republike 3, 1000 Ljubljana
Telephone. (+386-1) 2312659, (+386-1) 2000310
Fax. (+386-1) 4256150, (+386-1) 2000317
Email. lds@lds.si
Website. www.lds.si
Leadership. Anton Rop (president and National Assembly group leader); Peter Jamnikar (secretary-general)
The centre-left and secular LDS was founded in 1994 as a merger of the ruling Liberal Democratic Party (LDS), itself derived from the communist-era Association of the Socialist Youth of Slovenia (ZSMS) and established in 1990, and three small formations: (i) a moderate faction of the Democratic Party of Slovenia; (ii) the Greens – Ecological-Social Party; and (iii) the Socialist Party of Slovenia (SSS), which was derived from the communist-era front organization.

The former LDS had come down the list of parties winning seats in the first multi-party elections in April 1990 in what was then still Yugoslavia. Following the declaration of independence in 1991, the LDS leader, Dr Janez Drnovsek, became the President of the Government in April 1992, heading a centre-left coalition government, committed to privatization of the economy. After the first post-independence elections in December 1992, the LDS became the strongest party in the National Assembly, winning 23.5% of the vote and 22 seats. Drnovsek formed a new government that included the Slovenian Christian Democrats (SKD, later the Slovenian People's Party, SLS+SKD), the United List of Social Democrats (ZLSD, then the United List) and the Social Democratic Party of Slovenia (SDSS, later Slovenian Democratic Party – SDS).

The launching of the new LDS in March 1994 coincided with the exit of the SDS (then SDSS) from the ruling coalition in acrimonious circumstances, followed by the ZLSD in January 1996. The LDS nevertheless retained power until the November 1996 general elections, when it remained the largest party, with 25 seats and 27% vote share. The following month Drnovsek narrowly secured re-election as Prime Minister on the basis of a coalition that included the ZLSD on the left and the far-right Slovenian National Party (SNS). In February 1997, however, he succeeded in forming a more stable coalition which included the Slovenian People's Party

(SLS) and the Democratic Party of Pensioners of Slovenia (DeSUS).

In presidential elections in November 1997 the LDS candidate, Dr Bogomir Kovac, came a distant seventh with only 2.7% of the vote. Mounting strains in the coalition culminated in the withdrawal of the SLS in April 2000 and Drnovsek's resignation after he had lost a confidence vote. In June 2000, the SLS+SKD and the Slovenian Democratic Party (SDS, then still called the Social Democratic Party) formed a coalition until the following general elections in October 2000. In the intervening four months, this right-wing coalition, having succeeded a decade of LDS-led governments, posted its political supporters to all major political positions and to some prominent state-owned companies, thus upsetting a conservative Slovenian public and a large proportion of the centre (left) electorate. Drnovsek and the LDS obtained revenge in parliamentary elections in October 2000, when the LDS won a record 36.3% of votes and 34 seats in the National Assembly. Drnovsek again proceeded to form a broad-based centre-left coalition, which included the SLS+SKD, the ZLSD and the DeSUS. Before the presidential elections in December 2002, Drnovsek stepped down as the LDS president and as the President of the Government, and was subsequently elected President of the Republic.

His successor to both posts, Anton Rop, headed the same coalition between late 2002 and the 2004 elections. Although the opposition tried hard to expose alleged corruption in Slovenia under the LDS-led governments, the LDS remained the strongest political party in public opinion polls until 2004, mainly due to the inablity of the opposition to present a credible economic and socio-political programme that would appeal to the voters in the centre (or centre-left) of the political spectrum. In early 2004, however, public opinion polls briefly showed the LDS level-pegging with the Slovenian Democratic Party (SDS), due to the right-wing stand of the SDS with respect to the question of the so-called "erased persons" (i.e. some 18,000 people who had been erased from the registry of permanent residents of Slovenia in the early 1990s and hence were not eligible to obtain Slovenian citizenship automatically). This problem has only been known to the public for some two years, and the government has so far failed to address it adequately.

The June 2004 European elections again alarmed the LDS as it got a lower share of the vote than the opposition New Slovenia–Christian People's Party. The LDS and its ally DeSUS obtained only two seats in the European Parliament, although they had openly expected three. The inefficient legal system, several alleged corruption scandals (many of them related to the privatization process) and the loss of jobs, but also the perceived arrogance with which the LDS answered such allegations and explained some other less popular policies (e.g. the reform of the health system), were generally seen as the major reasons for the growing discontent with the government in mid-2004. The October 2004 elections clearly confirmed the trend of the LDS losing touch with the electorate. Not only did the party lose 11 seats in the National Assembly (winning merely 23 seats, based on 22.8% of the vote), but it also became only the second strongest party in Parliament. Following the practice according to which the leader of the strongest party is asked by the President of Slovenia to form the government, the LDS will not be entrusted to form a coalition government for the first time in 12 years.

The LDS is a member of the Liberal International. Its two MEPs sit in the ELDR group in the European Parliament.

New Slovenia–Christian People's Party
Nova Slovenija–Krscanska ljudska stranka (NSi)
Address. Cankarjeva cesta 11, 1000 Ljubljana
Telephone. (+386-1) 2416650
Fax. (+386-1) 2416670

Email. tajnistvo@nsi.si
Website. www.nsi.si
Leadership. Dr Andrej Bajuk (president and National Assembly group leader); Anton Kokalj (secretary-general)
The NSi was launched prior to the October 2000 National Assembly elections, by the then Prime Minister and vice president of the Slovenian People's Party (SLS+SKD), Dr Andrej Bajuk, who hoped that the new party would help to maintain him in office. Born in Slovenia in the 1940s and having then emigrated with his family to Argentina during World War II, Bajuk was lured to Slovenia in 2000 from his Paris-based job at the Inter-American Development Bank to become the President of the Government as a unknown politician in Slovenia. Bajuk became Prime Minister in June 2000, following the fall of the government headed by the Liberal Democracy of Slovenia (LDS). The coalition government led by Bajuk was composed of his SLS+SKD and the Slovenian Democratic Party (SDS, then still called the Social Democratic Party). The following month, he responded to the National Assembly's rejection of his proposal for the abandonment of proportional representation by leaving the SLS+SKD (which had voted against such a change) and announcing the creation of the NSi.

At the launching congress of the new party, held in Ljubljana in August 2000, Bajuk became its first president. The NSi formation attracted support from some prominent politicians, especially members of the Slovenian Christian Democrats (SKD) who had opposed the SKD's merger with the SLS. However, in the October 2000 parliamentary elections, the NSi obtained only eight seats and 8.6% of the vote and went in opposition, with Bajuk thus having headed the shortest-lived administration since independence.

The NSi won the largest share of the vote in the European elections in June 2004, and two seats in the European Parliament. This result raised the party's expectations for the general elections in October 2004, although the European result was probably affected by the extremely low turnout (just over 28%) and especially by its popular MEP candidate, Lojze Peterle (former SKD president and the President of the Government between 1990 and 1992), who received the highest number of preferential votes among all the candidates of all party lists.

The NSi contested the October 2004 elections independently, though as a member of the Coalition Slovenia (with the Slovenian Democratic Party). The party came fourth, winning 9 seats (based on 9.1% of the vote), and Bajuk openly expressed his disappointment with the result. The NSi and the SDS together won only 38 seats (out of the 90 MPs) and will have to form the new government with at least one other party. With just 9 MPs, as opposed to the SDS's 29, the NSi has come out of the elections as the weaker of the two parties in the Coalition Slovenia – the result that the party clearly had not expected after the European elections in June 2004.

The NSi is a member of the European People's Party. Its two MEPs have joined the EPP-ED group in the European Parliament.

Party of Slovenian Youth
Stranka mladih Slovenije (SMS)
Address. Rimska cesta 8, 1000 Ljubljana
Telephone. (+386-1) 4211400
Fax. (+386-1) 4211401
Email. info@sms.si
Website. www.sms.si
Leadership. Dominik S. Cernjak (president); Joze Vozelj (secretary-general)
The SMS was launched in 1999 as an ecologically oriented formation believing that the established parties did not properly represent young people. In its first National Assembly elections in October 2000, the SMS unexpectedly entered

parliament, winning 4.3% of the vote and being allocated four seats in the National Assembly. Since then, however, the party has suffered from allegations that its president, Dominik S. Cernjak, misused his position to gain public funds. Furthermore, following disagreements as to how the party should be run, particularly in preparation for the European elections, the then leader of the SMS National Assembly group, Igor Stemberger, resigned and renounced his party membership, together with the deputy president of the SMS, Tadej Slapnik. Stemberger and Slapnik joined a popular journalist (from TV Slovenia), Franci Kek, to form a new party – called Active Slovenia (*Aktivna Slovenija*; AI) – in March 2004. (In the meantime, the AI has failed to enter the National Assembly, although it won 3% of the vote nationally in the October 2004 general elections.) Amidst its internal problems and with a new political party competing for the same part of the electorate (the youth vote), the SMS focused on the June 2004 European elections. To the astonishment of many (including some SMS members), the SMS attracted Alenka Paulin, formerly a prominent member of the Slovenian Democratic Party (SDS), to join the party and head the SMS party list in the June 2004 European elections. The result was nonetheless a disappointing eighth place, with a mere 2.3% of the vote. In the October 2004 National Assembly elections the party lost all its seats, winning just 2.1% of the vote nationally.

Slovenian Democratic Party
Slovenska demokratska stranka (SDS)

Address. Komenskega ulica 11, 1000 Ljubljana
Telephone. (+386-1) 4345450
Fax. (+386-1) 4345452
Email. tajnistvo@sds.si
Website. www.sds.si
Leadership. Janez Jansa (president); Bogomir Zamernik (National Assembly group leader); Dusan Strnad (secretary-general)

Since September 2003, the party has been known as the Slovenian Democratic Party, replacing the older name of Social Democratic Party (previously Social Democratic Party of Slovenia, SDSS), but keeping the same acronym (SDS). The party associates the membership and the legal inheritance of the former Social Democratic Union of Slovenia and the Slovenian Democratic Union – two powerful parties of the former DEMOS coalition which, after the defeat of the communist regime in the 1990 elections, carried out the democratization of Slovenia and led the quest for Slovenian independence and international recognition. The Slovenian Democratic Union was founded in January, and the Social Democratic Union in February, 1989.

The SDS seeks to be the authentic Slovenian party of European social democracy but has been obliged to compete for the left-wing vote with the organisationally powerful United List of Social Democrats (ZLSD). Some of its policies (such as that with respect to the so-called "erased persons") have been more reminiscent of right-wing political views, rather than of modern democratic views.

In the presidential elections in December 1992, the party's candidate took only 0.6% of the vote, but it won 3.3% and 4 seats in the National Assembly in the simultaneous parliamentary elections. The party subsequently participated in the coalition government headed by the Liberal Democracy of Slovenia (LDS). In 1993, the SDS Defence Minister and party leader, Janez Jansa, became enmeshed in an arms-trading scandal, which led indirectly to his dismissal in March 1994, whereupon the SDS joined the parliamentary opposition. The SDS contested the November 1996 parliamentary elections as part of the Slovenian Spring (SP) alliance with the Slovenian People's Party (SLS) and the Slovenian Christian Democrats (SKD), making a break-

through by winning 16 seats and 16.1% vote share. It continued in opposition, making little impact in the November 1997 presidential elections but contributing to the fall of the LDS-led coalition in April 2000 and becoming part of the SLS+SKD-led coalition formed in June 2000. In the October 2000 parliamentary elections, the SDS fell back to 14 seats (15.8% of the vote) and was not included in the new LDS-led coalition.

In the presidential elections in December 2002, the SDS supported Barbara Brezigar, who ran as an independent candidate, but failed to win the post in the second round of the presidential elections, gaining 43.5% of the vote.

The SDS rise in the opinion polls by early 2004 was widely attributed to its right-wing stand with respect to the question of the "erased persons". Later, the party's general election campaign moved away from such extreme issues thereby arguably winning over a part of the electorate in the centre. Together with the New Slovenia—Christian People's Party (NSi), the SDS formed a coalition (*Koalicija Slovenija* – Coalition Slovenia) to contest the October 2004 general elections. Coalition Slovenia failed to win a majority in parliament (the NSi and SDS together winning 38 seats) but the SDS came out of the elections as the strongest party, taking 29 seats (based on 29.1% of the vote), or 15 seats more than in 2000. Its president, Jansa, is likely to become the Prime Minister of what will be the first (centre) right coalition government (with a brief exception of the government led by NSi's Bajuk in 2000) in 12 years.

The SDS won two seats (with 17.7% of the vote) in the European Parliament in the June 2004 European elections.

The SDS was an observer member of the Socialist International until 1996, when it was replaced as the Socialist International's Slovenian affiliate by the United List of Social Democrats. Instead, the party has become an associate member of the European People's Party. Its two MEPs have joined the EPP-ED group in the European Parliament.

Slovenian National Party
Slovenska nacionalna stranka (SNS)

Address. Tivolska 13, p.p. 2922, 1001 Ljubljana
Telephone. (+386-1) 2529020, (+386-41) 610281 (mobile)
Fax. (+386-1) 2529022
Email. info@sns.si
Website. www.sns.si
Leadership. Zmago Jelincic Plemeniti (president and National Assembly group leader); Misa Glazar (secretary-general)

Founded in 1991, the SNS is an extreme right-wing formation advocating a militarily strong Slovenia, revival of the Slovenes' cultural heritage and protection of the family as the basic unit of society. It is also strongly opposed to any consideration being given to Italian and Croatian irredentist claims on Slovenian territory or property, and more recently, it opposes any solution, proposed by the Slovenian Government, to the border issue between Slovenia and Croatia, claiming that those solutions are all contrary to Slovenian national interests.

The party won 10% of the vote and 12 seats in the National Assembly in December 1992 but became deeply divided in 1993 after it became known that the party leader, Zmago Jelincic, had served as a federal Yugoslav agent. Reports that leading members of the party were listed in security service files as informers in the communist era also affected its credibility. As a result of these and other embarrassments, five SNS deputies formed an independent Assembly group that became the core of the breakaway Slovenian National Right.

The rump SNS slumped to only four seats in the National Assembly and 3.2% of the vote in the November 1996 parliamentary elections. It was then brought into a mixed coalition government headed by Liberal Democracy of Slovenia (LDS), but reverted to opposition status when the LDS found a larger partner in February 1997. In the October 2000 parliamentary elections, the SNS improved slightly to 4.4% of the vote but again won only four seats. As part of the opposition (2000-04), the SNS called (unsuccessfully) for a special session of the National Assembly on the situation of the Slovenian minority in Austria, and it was particularly critical of the government's approach to the question of the so-called erased persons – the SNS objecting to any grant of citizenship to these people. It was also very critical of the government's policies towards the Roma population (numbering some 10,000). It criticized any attempt by the government to resolve the border issues with Croatia, spoke against Slovenia's proposed membership in the EU and then criticized Slovenia's approach to entering the EU as being ill-prepared. However, with Slovenian accession to the EU a reality, the SNS participated in the European elections in June 2004; it failed to win a seat and came sixth with 5% of the vote.

In the general elections of October 2004, the SNS won 6.3% of the vote and 6 seats in the National Assembly (2 more than in 2000). Jelincic Plemeniti – whose *persona* has been the key to the party's popular appeal – expressed his willingness to enter the new coalition government, and his personal ambition to become the new Minister of Culture.

Slovenian People's Party
Slovenska ljudska stranka (SLS)

Address. Beethovnova ulica 4, 1000 Ljubljana
Telephone. (+386-1) 2418802, (+386-1) 2418820
Fax. (+386-1) 2511741
Email. tajnistvo@sls.si
Website. www.sls.si
Leadership. Janez Podobnik (president); Jakob Presecnik (National Assembly group leader); Ales Vehar (secretary-general)

The centre-right Slovenian People's Party (SLS) has changed its name several times. Identifying its antecedents in the late-19th century Catholic/populist party of the same name, the SLS was founded in May 1988 as the Slovenian Peasant League (*Slovenska kmecka zveza*, SKZ) which was, in January 1990, renamed as the Slovenian Peasant League–People's Party (*Slovenska kmecka zveza—Ljudska stranka*) when it was also registered as a political party. The party entered the National Assembly in 1990 as a member of the victorious DEMOS coalition. The party was renamed again in June 1992, when it became the Slovenian People's Party (*Slovenska ljudska stranka*, SLS). In the December 1992 national elections, the SLS then won 10 seats in the National Assembly (based on 8.7% of the vote). In the following general elections in 1996, the SLS advanced to 19 seats and 19.4% vote share.

The SLS+SKD Slovenian People's Party was launched in April 2000 as a merger of the Slovenian People's Party (SLS) and the Slovenian Christian Democrats (SKD), adoppting the name of the former but retaining both acronyms. The SKD was founded in March 1990 by a group of "non-clerical Catholic intellectuals" advocating the full sovereignty of Slovenia, gradual transition to a market economy and integration into European institutions, especially the European Union. After the April 1990 first democratic elections (in which it ran as a member of the winning DEMOS coalition), its president, Lojze Peterle, became the Prime Minister and led Slovenia to the achievement of full independence in 1991. He retained the post despite the break-up of DEMOS at the end of 1991, but was then forced to resign in Spring 1992 (due to a no-confidence vote). In the December 1992 National Assembly elections, the SKD won 15 seats (based

on 14.5% of the vote), and joined a new centre-left coalition headed by what became the Liberal Democracy of Slovenia (LDS). Strains in the SKD's relations with the LDS sharpened in 1994, leading to Peterle's resignation in September in protest against the induction of an LDS president of the National Assembly. The SKD remained a government party, but renewed coalition tensions in 1996 were highlighted by the support given by the SKD deputies to a motion of no confidence in the LDS Foreign Minister in May.

The SLS and the SKD contested the November 1996 parliamentary elections within the Slovenian Spring (SP) alliance. Following an election campaign calling for honesty and integrity, the SLS advanced to 19 seats, whereas the SKD won a disappointing 10 seats in the National Assembly. The SLS then deserted the SP alliance and joined a coalition government headed by the LDS, whereas the SKD went in opposition. In the November 1997 presidential elections, Janez Podobnik of the SLS came a poor second to the incumbent, Milan Kucan (independent), winning only 18.4% of the vote, while the joint nominee of the SKD and the Slovenian Democratic Party (SDS), Jozef Bernik, came third, with 9.4% of the vote. Strains in the SLS's relations with the LDS culminated in April 2000, when the party withdrew from the government, thus causing the coalition government to fall. In June 2000, it was replaced by the SLS+SKD coalition (joined by the SDS) under the premiership of Dr Andrej Bajuk. The new Prime Minister promptly left the SLS+SKD to launch a new political party, the New Slovenia–Christian People's Party.

The rump SLS+SKD obtained a disappointing result in the October 2000 parliamentary elections when it won 9 seats in the National Assembly, based on 9.5% of the vote, but subsequently joined the new government coalition headed by the LDS, which also included the United List of Social Democrats (ZLSD) and the Democratic Party of Pensioners of Slovenia (DeSUS). The SLS+SKD party congress in January 2002 decided to rename the party again, as the Slovenian People's Party (SLS). The SLS had no candidate in the presidential elections in December 2002, but offered its support to a candidate who only came fourth.

The SLS left the government in April 2004, following a disagreement with the government's policy with respect to the "erased persons". The party participated in the June 2004 European elections, but failed to win a seat in the European Parliament. This came as a huge shock and disappointment both for its first-listed candidate, Franc But, former Minister for Agriculture (until the SLS left the governing coalition in April 2004) and former president of the SLS, and for the party itself since it only received 8.4% of the vote. Following this setback, the party then fought the October 2004 general election by appealing to traditional values and exploiting the Slovenian-Croatian border issue (which resulted in the detention of a group of SLS members, including the SLS president Podobnik, by the Croatian police). However, the electorate did not respond favourably: the party slipped to fifth place at the polls, winning just 7 seats and 6.8% of the vote, and Podobnik failed to be elected to the National Assembly.

The SLS+SKD inherited the SKD's affiliation to the Christian Democrat International and associate membership of the European People's Party, as well as its membership of the European Democrat Union. In the meantime, the SLS has become a full member of the European People's Party.

United List of Social Democrats
Zdruzena lista socialnih demokratov (ZLSD)

Address. Levstikova 15, 1000 Ljubljana
Telephone. (+386–1) 425–4222, (+386–41) 774–488 (mobile)
Fax. (+386–1) 251–5855
Email. press@zlsd.si

Website. www.zlsd.si

Leadership. Borut Pahor (president); Miran Potrc (National Assembly group leader); Dusan Kumer (secretary-general)

The United List (*Zdruzena lista, ZL*) was created prior to the December 1992 elections as an alliance of formations deriving from the former ruling League of Communists and its front organization, including the Democratic Party of Pensioners of Slovenia (DeSUS), the Social Democratic Union (SDU), the Workers' Party of Slovenia and the Party of Democratic Reform (SDR, which had taken first place in the first multi-party elections in Slovenia in 1990, but with only 17.3% of the vote had gone into opposition). The ZLSD emerged in April 1993. In May 1993 a unification congress was held in Ljubljana at which bodies and the leadership of the new party were elected. The congress elected Janez Kocijancic as the president of the new party.

In the 1992 elections, this electoral coalition of socially oriented left-centre parties came third, winning 13.6% of the vote or 14 seats in the National Assembly. The United List (ZL) joined the so-called big coalition of what became the Liberal Democracy of Slovenia (LDS) and the Slovenian Christian Democrats (SKD). The coalition was headed by the LDS. The ZLSD held four ministerial positions (for economic affairs; labour, family and social affairs; science and technology; and culture). The ZLSD lasted as a coalition partner until January 1996, when the LDS Prime Minister's move to dismiss one of its four ministers caused the party to withdraw from the government (due to disagreement with the government's policies on pensions and social affairs). In September 1996, the ZLSD became a full member of the Socialist International as the only left political party from Slovenia, replacing the conservative-leaning Social Democratic Party of Slovenia (SDS). But the decision of the DeSUS to re-establish itself as an autonomous party weakened the ZLSD in the November 1996 parliamentary elections, the party representation falling to 9% of the vote and winning only nine seats in the National Assembly.

The ZLSD advanced to eleven seats and 12.1% in the October 2000 elections, opting thereafter to join a coalition government headed by the LDS and also including the Slovenian People's Party (SLS+SKD) and the DeSUS. The ZLSD was assigned ministerial positions covering the areas of labour, family and social affairs; internal affairs; and culture.

In the June 2004 European elections, the ZLSD won one seat in the European Parliament. Controversially, its president, Borut Pahor (also the then president of the National Assembly), was elected by preferential votes as the seventh-listed candidate. The ZLSD first put Pahor on the top of its list, creating speculation about discontent within the party with the present leadership; Pahor subsequently announced he would run, but not as the party's front-runner. Following his election to the EP, he quickly dismissed the idea he would not accept the MEP post. In the general elections in October 2004, the ZLSD came third, with 10.2% of the vote, taking 10 seats in the National Assembly. It was not immediately clear whether the party would join the opposition.

In addition to its full membership in the Socialist International, the ZLSD also became a full member of the Party of European Socialists (PES) in May 2003. Its MEP has joined the PES group in the European Parliament.

Other Parties

Slovenia is Ours (*Slovenija je nasa*, SJN) was formed in Spring 2004, declaring itself as an independent party in the centre of the political specturum. Its president is Boris Popovic, a controversial mayor of Koper (who had been held in custody for alleged misuse of his post), and the party aims to offer support to all independent mayors and small independent political parties across Slovenia. The party failed to win a seat in the June 2004 European elections, but obtained the highest percentage vote among the non-parliamentary parties (4.1%); it failed to enter parliament in the October 2004 general elections when it won only 2.6% of the vote.

Address. Gortanov trg 15, 6000 Koper

Telephone. (+386–5) 627–8158

Fax. (+386–5) 627–8159

Email. info@slovenijajenasa.com

Website. www.sjn.si

Leadership. Boris Popovic (president), Janez Sodrznik (secretary-general)

Solomon Islands

Capital: Honiara (Guadalcanal)
Population: 418,000 (2000E)

The Solomon Islands achieved internal self-government in 1976 and became independent in July 1978. The head of state is the British sovereign represented by a Governor-General. Legislative authority is vested in a unicameral National Parliament, the 50 members of which are popularly elected from single-member constituencies for up to four years. The Prime Minister (who is elected by members of Parliament from among their number) and an appointed Cabinet exercise executive power and are responsible to Parliament.

Government composition since independence has been determined by an extremely fluid party structure and constantly shifting coalitions. Parliamentary elections on Aug. 6, 1997, resulted in the Group for National Unity and Reconciliation (GNUR) led by incumbent Prime Minister Solomon Mamaloni winning command of 24 seats but losing power to the multi-party Solomon Islands Alliance for Change (SIAC), which mustered 26 seats and installed Bartholomew Ulufa'alu as Prime Minister. From mid-1999 inter-ethnic conflict between the indigenous inhabitants of Guadalcanal (Isatabu) and settlers from the neighbouring island of Malaita escalated into virtual civil war, fought between the paramilitary Isatabu Freedom Movement (IFM) and the Malaita Eagles Force (MEF). In June 2000 Ulufa'alu was briefly taken prisoner by the MEF and resigned shortly after his release, whereupon a government of "national unity, reconciliation and peace" was installed. The new Prime Minister was Manasseh Sogavare, who had become leader of the opposition People's Progressive Party (successor to the GNUR) following Mamaloni's death in January 2000. A peace agreement between the rival militias was reached under Australian auspices in October 2000, resulting in limited disarmament.

Elections held on Dec. 5, 2001, resulted as follows: People's Alliance Party (PAP) 20; Association of Independent Members (AIM) 13; Solomon Islands Alliance for Change (SIAC) 12; People's Progressive Party (PPP) 3; Labour Party (LP) 1. Sir Allan Kemakeza of the PAP became Prime Minister heading a government coalition between the PAP and AIM, the latter consisting largely of independent politicians who came together in a loose alliance. Following further unrest, an Australian-led peacekeeping force of troops and police was sent to the Solomon Islands in July 2003 at the request of the Kemakeza government and the situation has since been stable.

People's Alliance Party (PAP)

Address. c/o National Parliament, Honiara
Leadership. Allan Kemakeza

The PAP is currently the dominant party in the ruling coalition with the Association of Independent Members. The party was formed in 1979 just prior to the first independent general elections. It was a merger between the PPP and the Rural Alliance Party (RAP). Solomon Mamaloni became its leader and used the PAP as political platform for political dominance in the 1980s. Mamaloni won the election in 1989 but there were moves within the PAP to oust him as a result of allegations of corruption in the logging sector. He then sacked those opposed to his leadership and he secured the support of independent politicians to form the Group for National Unity and Reconstruiction (GNUR). In the process he ditched leadership of the PAP.

The PAP later joined hands with other political groups to form the National Front for Progress (NFP) for the purpose of toppling Mamaloni. Although the GNUR under Mamaloni won the elections in 1993 with 21 seats, the anti-Mamaloni alliance, which included the PAP, later formed the government, this collapsing in October 1994. This resulted in the re-emergence of Mamaloni as Prime Minister of a broad coalition government.

The PAP's political fate has been largely determined by the highly fluid nature of Solomons Islands politics. Most governments have been based on coalitions and as certain groups withdrew their support, power would also shift. The PAP has been either part of the government or opposition, depending on the shift in the political support. Like most Solomon Islands political parties, it does not have a coherent political ideology as such.

During the 2001 election, it won more seats than any other polical party. This provided it with the platform to seek partnership with willing political groups. The current leader of the PAP is Allan Kemakeza, the Prime Minister.

People's Progressive Party (PPP)

Address. c/o National Parliament, Honiara
Leadership. Manasseh Sogavare

The PPP was originally founded under British rule by Solomon Mamaloni, who served as Chief Minister in 1974-76 and as Prime Minister in 1981-84, 1989-93 and 1994-97, during which his party went through numerous name and composition changes. The PPP title was revived on Mamaloni's death in January 2000 as a tribute to him.

Following independence, Mamaloni in 1979 merged the PPP with the Rural Alliance Party to form the People's Alliance Party (PAP), which provided his power-base in the 1980s. Having regained the premiership in 1989, Mamaloni in October 1990 resigned as PAP leader to lead a broader-based government, the components of which were organized as the Group for National Unity and Reconstruction (GNUR) in the May 1993 elections. Under Mamaloni's leadership the GNUR secured the most seats, winning 21, but an alliance of anti-Mamaloni parties and independents formed a new administration, which remained in power until losing its slim majority in October 1994. The following month Mamaloni resumed the post of Prime Minister.

Mamaloni's fourth and last premiership proved to be the most controversial, as his government repealed or relaxed many of the regulations introduced by the previous government to conserve forestry resources. It also attracted opposition charges of general economic incompetence and political corruption. In the August 1997 elections for a Parliament enlarged from 47 to 50 members, the GNUR grouping (which was also known as the National Unity and Reconciliation Progressive Party) again won a plurality of 21 seats, and was backed by three independents. But the anti-Mamaloni Solomon Islands Alliance for Change (SIAC)

mustered 26 seats and was able to form a government.

In opposition, Mamaloni adopted the designation Coalition for National Advancement (CNA) for his followers. His successor when he died in January 2000 was former Finance Minister Manasseh Sogavare, whose adoption of the historic PPP rubric coincided with rising inter-ethnic conflict on Guadalcanal. Sogavare denied government claims that the PPP was involved in fomenting the indigenous unrest, which led directly to the government's resignation in June 2000. Sogavare was the political beneficiary, being installed as Prime Minister of a national unity government committed to national reconciliation and including some SIAC representatives.

Solomon Islands Alliance for Change (SIAC)

Address. c/o National Parliament, Honiara
Leadership. Bartholomew Ulufa'alu

The SIAC was formed prior to the 1997 elections by the disparate forces opposed to the government headed by Solomon Mamaloni, then leader of the Group for National Unity and Reconciliation (GNUR), which later became the People's Progressive Party (PPP). The alliance was effectively the successor to the National Coalition Partners (NCP) combination which had ousted Mamaloni after the 1993 elections and installed a government led by Francis Billy Hilly, who had survived until October 1994, when Mamaloni had returned to power.

The SIAC formations included (i) the Solomon Islands Liberal Party led by Bartholomew Ulufa'alu, which had been founded in 1976 as the National Democratic Party and had participated in the 1981-84 Mamaloni government; (ii) the National Action Party of the Solomon Islands led by Francis Saemala; (iii) the People's Alliance Party led by Sir David Kausimae, originally established in 1979 under the leadership of Mamaloni, who had deserted the party in 1990; (iv) the Solomon Islands United Party led by Ezekiel Alebua, which had been founded by Sir Peter Kenilorea (the first post-independence Prime Minister) and had been the senior partner in the 1984-89 coalition government; and (v) the Solomon Islands Labour Party led by Joses Tuhanuku, which dated from 1988.

Castigating the Mamaloni government for its alleged corruption and subservience to foreign logging companies, the SIAC parties emerged from the 1997 elections commanding 26 of the 50 Assembly seats and so were able to install Ulufa'alu as Prime Minister. From mid-1999, however, his government was powerless to prevent a descent into virtual civil war between the indigenous population of Guadalcanal and immigrants from Malaita. Though himself a Malaitese, Ulufa'alu was in June 2000 abducted and held captive by Malaitese guerrillas for five days, in what proved to be tantamount to an armed coup. Emerging from captivity, Ulufa'alu tendered his resignation as demanded and was replaced by Manasseh Sogavare of the PPP, with some SIAC figures joining the new government. In June 2001 Ulufa'alu filed a somewhat belated suit challenging the legality of the Sogavare government.

Other Parties

Labour Party, formed by the trade unions led by Joses Tuhanuku in 1988. The idea was to introduce class-based politics to break the traditional kin-based system. They won two seats during the 1989 election. The Labour Party has always been a disciplined but minority party whose support is largely urban based. At the moment it has only one representative in parliament.

Somalia

Capital: Mogadishu
Population: 7,488, 773 (2003 est.)

The Republic of Somalia was formed by the unification of the British Somaliland Protectorate and the former Italian Trust territory of Somalia at independence in July 1960. Initially, the country was ruled by a Western-style parliamentary regime. But the viability of this political system was challenged by separate colonial experiences, clan differences, economic inequities and a complex electoral system of Italian-style proportional representation. The degeneration of Somalia's democracy was epitomized by the general election of March 26, 1969, when 1,002 candidates, representing 62 political parties, contested 123 seats. The resultant victory of the ruling Somali Youth League (SYL) with an overwhelming majority left a bitter legacy of discontent. Opposition groups charged that the SYL government were guilty of electoral fraud and intimidation.

In October 1969, Major General Mohammed Siyad Barre, commander of the Armed Forces, seized power in a military coup. The constitution was suspended, parliament was dissolved and all political parties, except the Somali Revolutionary Socialist Party (SRSP) led by General Siyad, were declared illegal. In July 1974, President Siyad signed a Treaty of Friendship and Co-operation with the Soviet Union. Three years later, with the help of Soviet arms, Somalia attempted to seize the Ogaden region of Ethiopia, but was defeated thanks to Soviet and Cuban backing for Ethiopia, which had declared itself socialist in the mid-1970s. As an upshot, President Siyad ended his strategic partnership with Moscow and switched sides in the Cold War. In August 1980, an agreement was concluded that gave US forces access to military facilites in Somalia.

However, the demise of the Cold War in the late 1980s undermined the life-support system that sustained President Siyad's dictatorship. In 1989, the US Congress, citing human rights violations by Siyad's regime in northern Somalia, forced the Bush administration to suspend its military and economic aid programme to Mogadishu. By January 1991, Siyad was overthrown in an armed rebellion led by the United Somali Congress (USC). But instead of heralding a return to the 1961 consitution, the ousting of Siyad accelerated the disintegration of the Somali state.

The leaders of the victorious USC became absorbed in a bloody power struggle that spread chaos and starvation throughout southern Somalia. Meanwhile, in the north-west area that had formerly constituted the British Somaliland Protectorate, Somali National Movement (SNM) insurgents, confronted with the disorder of the south, declared unilateral independence from Somalia in May 1991. While the "Republic of Somaliland" failed to achieve any international recognition, it did manage to largely avoid the turmoil of the rest of Somalia.

In 1992, constant civil war and drought combined to produce a catastrophic famine killing an estimated 300,000 Somalis. A large-scale humanitarian intervention was the world's response with a US-led UN Task Force (UNITAF) authorized to create a secure environment for the distribution of food aid. But the operation did not live up to expectations. Reluctant to engage in the process of political reconstruction, the US-UN force became embroiled in hostilities with the most formidable of the Somali warlords, General Mohamed Farah Aidid. The confrontation effectively ended the UN operation and led to the withdrawal of UN troops in March 1995.

Many of the conditions that led to the UN/US intervention in Somalia still persist in 2004. Somalia has been without an internationally recognized functioning government for more than 13 years. Various clan-based groups have unsuccessfully tried to impose their control over the country. In mid-June 1995 factions allied with Gen. Aidid elected him President of the country, and the appointment of a Cabinet was subsequently announced. On Gen. Aidid's death shortly thereafter, his supporters elected his son, Hussein Aidid, to succeed him as "interim President". In January 1997 representatives of 26 anti-Aidid factions established a 41-member National Salvation Council.

At the same time, since 1991 there have been at least 14 regional efforts at national reconciliation in Somalia; to date, none has been successful. In the mid-1990s, Ethiopia hosted several Somali peace conferences and initiated talks at the Ethiopian city of Sodere, which generated some measure of agreement between competing armed factions. The governments of Egypt, Yemen, Kenya, and Italy have also tried to bring the Somali factions together. In 1997, the Organization of African Unity (OAU) and the Intergovernmental Authority (IGAD) gave Ethiopia the mandate to promote Somali reconciliation.

In 2000, Djibouti hosted a major reconciliation conference that in August resulted in the creation of the Transitional National Government, with a three-year mandate. A 245-member transitional national assembly, in which seats were allocated after detailed negotiations between representatives of different Somali clans, was inaugurated and went on to elect Abdulkasim Salat Hassan, a former minister under President Siyad, as President of Somalia. His interim national government established a presence in Mogadishu from mid-October 2000 but remained highly vulnerable to continuing outbreaks of faction fighting and was unable to extend its control beyond 25% of the capital.

In October 2002, Kenya organized a further reconciliation effort under IGAD auspices. The Nairobi-led peace talks brought together all armed Somali factions and were expected to be concluded within two months. But the talks dragged on and have so far cost $7 million provided by the European Union, individual EU member states and the Arab League. Interim Somali President Abdulkassim Salat Hassan, whose delegation walked out of the peace talks in November 2003, was only persuaded to rejoin them after the personal intervention of Uganda's President Yoweri Museveni. The main stumbling block has been over the number of members of parliament to be chosen by each group.

Nevertheless, mediators at the Nairobi talks claimed in late January 2004 that a "breakthough" had been achieved. After considerable international pressure, all the Somali factions apparently agreed to the establishment of a federal system of government with a parliament of 275 members, selected by warlords and traditional elders. On Sept. 2, 2004, the inaugural meeting of Somalia's new parliament was held. But it remains to be seen whether this development will actually end the anarchy in Somalia. A number of similar accords have already been signed since 1991, each stillborn.

The Somali factions, especially those led by warlords, either lack the political will to support the restoration of effective central government or lack the capacity to deliver on such agreements. The lack of a regional consensus on Somalia also hinders the peace process. The Djibouti government has never hidden its support for the TNG. On the other hand, it is no secret that Ethiopia actively supports factions that oppose the transitional government. At present, therefore, it is still difficult to envisage in the near future the return of a functioning party system in Somalia.

SOMALILAND

The example of Somaliland (with a population of some 2-3 million) does show that political reconstruction is possible. Although not recognized by any government, Somaliland has gradually restored order and governance in very difficult circumstances. In 1998, the area of Puntland in the northeast of Somalia also declared itself autonomous and currently disputes its border with Somaliland. Despite this development, Somaliland has persevered with the process of rebuilding. In 2001, 98% of voters opted in a free and fair election for a new constitution that boldly made the case for independence. Somaliland then had internationally monitored, local council elections in 2002 and a free and fair presidential election in April 2003. The presidential election was significant because the ruling UDUB party, led by President Dahir Rayale Kahin, won by only 217 votes out of almost 500,000 cast. The opposition KULMIYE party challenged the count, but eventually accepted the result.

South Africa

Capital: Pretoria (administrative), Cape Town (legislative), Bloemfontein (Judicial)
Population: 44,819,778 (2001 census)

The Republic of South Africa was established in 1961, evolving from the Union of South Africa which had been formed in 1910 and achieved independence as a Dominion from the United Kingdom in 1931. The National Party (NP), which was the ruling party from 1948 until May 1994, pioneered the system of apartheid under which the population was divided into four different racial categories (Whites, Coloureds, Indians and Africans), each entitled to varying degrees of political, social and economic rights. In practice, the system maintained the supremacy of the minority white (particularly Afrikaner) population.

In the face of domestic and international pressure, the NP government in 1989 indicated a preparedness to negotiate an end to apartheid, the following year lifting restrictive measures against the African National Congress (ANC) and other proscribed organizations. Multi-party negotiations began in December 1991 and resulted in the adoption in November 1993 of an interim constitution, under which South Africa's first non-racial, multi-party legislative elections took place on April 26-29, 1994. These resulted in a decisive victory for the ANC, which had been in the forefront of the struggle against the apartheid regime. In May 1994 the ANC leader, Nelson Mandela, was elected President of the Republic by the National Assembly (lower house of parliament), and a transitional government of national unity, composed of the three largest parties (ANC, NP and Inkatha Freedom Party) assumed office. The two houses of parliament sat jointly as a Constituent Assembly to draft a permanent constitu-

tion, which entered into force in February 1997. The NP subsequently left the ruling coalition to reforge its identity as a party of opposition.

The 1997 constitution provides for a bicameral parliament comprising a National Assembly of 400 members, popularly elected by universal adult suffrage (200 from national party lists and 200 from regional party lists) under a system of proportional representation, and a 90-seat National Council of Provinces, appointed by the members of the elected legislatures of the nine South African provinces. Any vacancy occurring in the national or provincial assemblies in the period between general elections is filled by the "next-in-line" candidate on the same party list. The President, who is head of state and head of the executive, is elected by the National Assembly from among its members, thereafter ceasing to be a member, although retaining speaking rights. No person may serve more than two presidential terms.

A general election held on June 2, 1999, produced an increased ANC majority in the National Assembly, where the distribution of seats among the larger parties was ANC 266, Democratic Party (DP) 38, Inkatha Freedom Party 34, New National Party (NNP, successor to the NP) 28 and United Democratic Movement 14. Nine small parties accounted for the remaining 20 seats. The Democratic Party formed the official opposition in the new Assembly, while the Inkatha Freedom Party concluded a coalition agreement with the ANC. Thabo Mbeki (who had succeeded Nelson Mandela as ANC party president at the end of 1997) was elected President of South Africa by the new Assembly and was formally inaugurated in office on June 16, 1999.

In June 2000, the DP and NNP sought to consolidate the opposition by forming the Democratic Alliance (DA), although – because the constitution prevented elected representatives crossing to other political parties – their members continued to sit in national and provincial assemblies as members of their original parties. However, philosophical and organizational differences led to the collapse of the arrangement in November 2001, when the NNP leadership pulled out of the DA and opted, once more, to work in cooperation with the ANC at national, provincial and local government levels. The re-arrangement of coalitions which this implied (notably the DA's loss of control over the Western Cape provincial government to the NNP-ANC) was facilitated by controversial legislation passed in mid-2002. This amended a constitutional bar on floor-crossing at all levels of government, to provide for a mechanism whereby representatives of parties would be able to cross to another party (so long as such crossing involved at least 10% of the party's representatives) during two pre-determined periods per annum. Following a 2003 Constitutional Court judgement which ruled that the legislation was constitutional (following challenge by the United Democratic Movement which argued that it defeated the intent of the proportional representation electoral system), the ANC emerged as the net beneficiary, achieving a two-thirds majority in parliament as it absorbed members from opposition parties. Whilst enabling unhappy members of the NNP to cross back to the DA, an unintended outcome of the legislation was the creation of six completely new small political parties by members of the opposition (at both national and provincial level) who defected from established parties. Three of these parties now appeared in parliament.

The floor-crossings of 2003 did nothing to halt the

NNP's demise, and following the April 2004 general election, in which the former ruling party was reduced to just 7 seats in the National Assembly, party leader Marthinus van Schalkwyk joined the government and announced his intention to join the ANC at the first opportunity. His announcement effectively represented the death of the NNP, all of whose MPs are expected to cross over to the ANC in parliament at the first opportunity provided for by the law.

African Christian Democratic Party (ACDP)

Address. PO Box 2417, Durbanville 7551
Telephone. (27–21) 461–2048
Fax. (27–21) 462–5394
Website. www.acdp.org.za
Leadership. Kenneth Meshoe (president); Louis Green (deputy president)
The ACDP won two National Assembly seats in the April 1994 elections, having campaigned for the social and economic transformation of the country based on a "moral, judicial and ethical system, open market economics and direct democracy". It won 6 seats in the 1999 National Assembly elections and secured an extra seat in parliament in 2003 when an MP defected from the DA. It retained 6 seats in the election of 2004.

African National Congress (ANC)

Address. 54 Sauer Street, Johannesburg 2001; POB 61884, Marshalltown 2107
Telephone. (27–11) 376–1000
Fax. (27–11) 376–1134
Email. anchq@anc.org.za
Website. www.anc.org.za
Leadership. Thabo Mbeki (president); Jacob Zuma (vice-president); Kgalema Motlanthe (secretary-general); Patrick Lekota (national chairman)
Founded in 1912, the ANC became the leading black formation in South Africa. It was banned by the apartheid regime from 1960 to 1990, its most prominent figures being imprisoned (in particular, Nelson Mandela and Walter Sisulu) or exiled. From the late 1970s, as ANC guerrilla attacks within the country escalated, the South African armed forces increased counter-insurgency operations against the liberation movement's camps in neighbouring states.

While emphasizing that it was prepared for an armed seizure of power in order to establish a non-racial political system, the ANC indicated that this position did not preclude a negotiated transition to democracy. ANC proposals, set out in 1989, argued that negotiations would only be possible in a free political climate. Having released Walter Sisulu from detention in October of that year, the National Party (NP) government then released Mandela in February 1990 and legalized all previously banned organizations. The ANC began the transformation from liberation movement to political party, suspending its armed struggle and engaging in constitutional talks with the government.

Substantive multi-party negotiations on a future constitution took place from 1991 to 1993, although the process was frequently threatened by escalating political violence, for which the ANC blamed the Inkatha Freedom Party (IFP) and members of the state security forces.

Although the ANC had replaced its commitment to comprehensive nationalization with an emphasis on a mixed economy, the organization announced a radical plan in January 1994 to end the economic and social inequities of the apartheid era. This Reconstruction and Development Programme gave priority to housing, education, health improvement and economic growth. Subsequently, the RDP was subordinated to a Growth, Employment and Redistribution strategy which placed emphasis upon tight

fiscal control, export-oriented growth and the attraction of foreign investment.

The non-racial, multi-party legislative elections in April 1994 resulted in an overwhelming victory for the ANC, which secured 252 National Assembly seats with 62.6% of the vote and took control of seven of the nine provincial assemblies. The following month Nelson Mandela became President of the Republic. The new Cabinet was dominated by the ANC, but also included members of the NP and the IFP. (The NP, later renamed the New National Party, withdrew from the government in 1996.)

Thabo Mbeki succeeded Walter Sisulu as ANC vice-president in December 1994, subsequently becoming president of the ANC in succession to Nelson Mandela in December 1997. With the support of the South African Communist Party (SACP) and the Congress of South African Trade Unions (COSATU), Mbeki led the ANC to victory in the June 1999 general election, when it won 66.4% of the vote and 266 seats in the National Assembly, as well as gaining control of seven out of the nine provinces (the exception being KwaZulu-Natal, where it served as a junior partner in a ruling coalition with the IFP, and the Western Cape, where it formed the opposition to a coalition forged by the DP and NNP). Having been elected President of South Africa by the National Assembly, he appointed a Cabinet which included three members of the IFP. President Mbeki's government came under strong pressure from its SACP and trade union allies for its perceived conservatism on economic policy issues, while Mbeki himself attracted much national and international criticism for his controversial views on South Africa's HIV/AIDS crisis. In nationwide municipal elections in December 2000 the ANC's share of the total vote was about 59%, a fall of over 7% compared with the 1999 general election.

The re-establishment of the ANC's coalition with the NNP in 2002 led to the appointment of two members of the latter as junior ministers, and subsequently, following the passage of the floor-crossing legislation, to NNP leader Marthinus van Schalkwyk becoming Premier of the Western Cape, even though the ANC had increased its membership of the provincial assembly, largely at the expense of the NNP. Overall, the ANC was the overwhelming beneficiary of the floor-crossing legislation, attracting some nine opposition MPs into its ranks for a total of 275 members in the National Assembly, as well as its securing extra seats in the Eastern Cape (2), KwaZulu-Natal (1) and Western Cape (4) provincial assemblies. It also gained control over an extra 13 municipalities for a total of 242 out of 284 municipalities ruled by the ANC.

The ANC's dominance of the electoral arena was confirmed and extended by the general election of 2004 when – albeit in a lower poll – it secured nearly 70% of the votes cast and 279 seats in the National Assembly. Meanwhile, although failing to secure outright majorities in both the Western Cape and KwaZulu-Natal, it was able to form ANC-led majority governments, and hence to achieve its goal of establishing political control over all nine provinces.

Afrikaner Unity Movement
Afrikaner Eenheidsbeweging (AEB)

Address. PO Box 5460, Pretoria
Telephone. (27–12) 329–1220
Fax. (27–12) 329–1229
Website. www.aeb.org.za
The AEB, a right-wing Afrikaner movement, won one National Assembly seat in the June 1999 general election. Following a challenge by conservatives to his attempt to take the party in a non-racial direction, its one MP defected to form the *Nasionale Aksie*/National Action party in 2003. The AEB was absorbed into the Freedom Front in September 2003.

Azanian People's Organization (AZAPO)

Address. PO Box 4230, Johannesburg 2000
Telephone. (27–11) 336–3556
Fax. (27–11) 333–6681
Website. www.azapo.org.za
Leadership. Mosibudi Mangena (president)

The AZAPO is a black consciousness movement that was launched in 1978. Its leader, Mosibudi Mangena, had been imprisoned on Robben Island for five years from 1973. AZAPO rejected constitutional negotiations with the white minority government and declared its opposition to the April 1994 elections. It excludes white members. AZAPO registered to contest the June 1999 general election, in which Mangena won the party's sole seat in the National Assembly. In January 2001 Mangena became Deputy Minister of Education. In 2003 it entered talks with the UDM with a view to electoral cooperation, but retained its independence during the 2004 general election, as a result of which it retained its single seat.

Democratic Alliance (DA)

Address. PO Box 1698, Cape Town 8000
Telephone. (27–21) 461–5833
Fax. (27–21) 461–5329
Email. info@da.org.za
Website. www.da.org.za
Leadership. Tony Leon (leader); Joe Seremane (chairperson); Greg Krumbock (national executive director)

The DA was formed in June 2000 through the merger of the Democratic Party (DP, which won 38 seats in the National Assembly in 1999) and the formerly ruling New National Party (NNP, which won 28 seats in the 1999 National Assembly elections).

The predominantly white DP had been formed in 1989 (by the merger of the Progressive Federal Party and two other smaller parties in the whites-only National Assembly), advocating the establishment of a democratic, non-racial society by peaceful means. It traced its own origins back to the formation in 1959 of the Progressive Party, whose MP Helen Suzman was for 13 years the sole anti-apartheid campaigner in the South African parliament. In the April 1994 elections, the DP had taken fifth place, winning seven seats in the newly democratic parliament with just 1.7% of the votes cast. However, as a result of vigorous opposition and campaigning, the DP secured second placing in the June 1999 general election, with 9.5% of the vote and 38 seats, and its leader, Tony Leon, became the Leader of the Opposition, greatly to the chagrin of the formerly ruling NNP. The decision by the DP and NNP to merge into the DA was therefore taken against a background of historical bitterness and tension between the coalescing parties.

At the formation of the DA, DP leader Tony Leon became leader, with NNP leader Marthinus van Schalkwyk as his Deputy. The aim of the new party was "to consolidate the support of opposition voters in South Africa based on common values for a better South Africa for all its citizens". The values in question were broadly liberal ones, long held by the DP (the senior partner in the merged party) but rather more recently adopted by the NNP (formerly the National Party). The DA's primary electoral challenge was to attract black votes away from the ruling African National Congress (which sought to portray the DA as the party of the white opposition in South Africa). In December 2000 the DA stood as a merged party in nationwide municipal elections, fielding candidates of all races (over half of them black) and receiving 23% of the total vote, compared with the 16.4% combined share of the DP and the NNP at the June 1999 general election. The new party won control of the Cape Town "megacity" administration.

South African electoral law prevented the Democratic Alliance from registering as a merged party in the current National Assembly, with the consequence that the DP and the NNP continued to be represented as separate parties. Unless there was an early change in the law to facilitate mergers of sitting parties, the DP and the NNP did not intend to disband until the end of the Assembly's term in 2004, at which point the DA would be registered in their place to contest the next general election. In the meantime, a merged party structure was put in place at national and provincial levels, the composition of each DA committee being determined on the basis of votes received by the DP and NNP at the June 1999 elections. The DP accordingly became the dominant component of the DA at national level and in seven of South Africa's nine provinces.

The NNP had joined with the DP to put a halt to what appeared to be its historic plunge into obscurity. However, the newly formed coalition was from the beginning stressed by differences between NNP conservatives and DP liberals. Consequently, it was not long before resentment within the NNP at alleged marginalization by their former rivals led to the decision by its leadership to leave the DA and to re-establish the coalition with the ANC in November 2001. Whilst this initially weakened the DA in parliament (where the combined parties had paraded 66 MPs), defections from the NNP back to the DA following the floor-crossing legislation left it with a total of 46 seats (an increase of 8 over those secured at the election of 1999). However, floor crossings at the provincial level meant that it lost control of the Western Cape (which it had previously ruled in coalition with the NNP) and of 22 (out of a total of 40) DA ruled municipalities around the country.

The NNP's weakness and its close relationship with the ANC left the field clear to the DA as the major party of opposition in the 2004 general election. Under the leadership of Tony Leon it mounted a vigorous offensive which attracted many former supporters of the NNP, and as a result it increased its number of seats in the National Assembly from 38 to 50. However, the DA remains vulnerable to the charge that it remains overwhelmingly dependent upon the support of whites.

The DA is a consitituent member party of the Liberal International.

Federal Alliance (FA)

Address. PO Box 767, Saxonwold 2132
Telephone. (27–11) 486 0783
Fax. (27–11) 486 3508
Email. media@federalalliance.org.za
Website. www.federalalliance.org.za
Leadership. Louis Luyt (leader)

The Federal Alliance, established in September 1998 by Louis Luyt, a wealthy businessman and former president of South Africa's Rugby Football Union, won two seats in the National Assembly at the June 1999 general election. It subsequently concluded a parliamentary co-operation agreement with the United Democratic Movement (UDM) whereby FA members may attend UDM caucus meetings. In June 2000, prior to the merger between the Democratic Party (DP) and the New National Party, the FA reached an electoral pact with the DP to field joint candidates in the 2000 municipal elections. (The DP subsequently contested these elections through the Democratic Alliance, which retained the FA's support under the electoral pact.)

Freedom Front
Vryheidsfront (VF)

Address. POB 74693, Lynnwood Ridge 0040, Pretoria
Telephone. (27–12) 322–7141
Fax. (27–12) 322–7144
Website. www.vryheidsfront.co.za

Leadership. Pieter Mulder (leader)

The VF was launched by General Constandt Viljoen in March 1994 following a rift in the right-wing Afrikaner People's Front (linking groups opposed to black majority rule) over the issue of participation in the forthcoming April elections. Viljoen opted to register the new party in order to promote the objective of a confederal South Africa based on the right of self-determination for Afrikaners and all other groups. The VF was the only white far-right party to contest the elections, in which it secured nine National Assembly seats with almost 2.2% of the vote. In the 1999 general election the VF won three seats with 0.8% of the vote. As of late 2003, it held a total of 4 seats in 4 different provincial legislatures. New leader Pieter Mulder announced that it had absorbed the Conservative Party and Afrikaner *Eenheidsbeweging* in September 2003. The FF won 4 seats in the 2004 general election.

Independent Democrats

Address. PO Box 912, Cape Town, 8000
Telephone. (27) 21 448 6899
Fax. (27) 448 6883
Leadership. Patricia de Lille (leader); Prof Themba Sono (deputy leader)

Formed by Patricia de Lille after her defection from the PAC, the party stands for a mixed, open economy with strong social security; accountable, effective government based on democratic principles; and for closing the poverty gap and redressing social ills such as HIV/AIDS and unemployment. It promised to contest elections nationally and in all provinces in the 2004 elections. In the event, it secured a total of 7 seats which, although a creditable first showing, was regarded as disappointing by its supporters.

Inkatha Freedom Party (IFP)

Address. POB 4432, Durban 4000
Telephone. (27–21) 403 2996
Fax. (27–31) 301 0279 or 21 403 3266
Website. www.ifp.org.za
Leadership. Chief Mangosuthu Buthelezi (leader); Zakhele Khumalo (secretary-general)

Formed originally as a cultural liberation movement (*Inkatha Ya Ka Zulu*) in the 1920s and revived by Chief Mangosutho Buthelezi in 1975, Inkatha played an ambiguous role under apartheid, serving as both the ruling party of the KwaZulu ethnic homeland yet seeking to rival the ANC as the principal party of liberation. After the unbanning of the ANC and other organisations in 1990, the movement, renamed the Inkatha Freedom Party (IFP), was re-constituted as a multi-racial political party, although it remains a predominantly Zulu organization with its power base in KwaZulu/Natal. Hostility between the IFP and the Afican National Congress (which accused the IFP of being an ally of the white minority regime) engendered serious political violence, particularly in the early 1990s, and major differences over constitutional and other issues continued to cause friction for some years.

Having belatedly agreed to participate in the April 1994 elections, the IFP took third place with 43 National Assembly seats and about 10.5% of the votes cast. The party was awarded three portfolios in the ensuing ANC-dominated Cabinet. It also secured a bare majority of seats in the KwaZulu/Natal provincial assembly, thereby assuming the leading role in the coalition with the ANC which operated at provincial level. However, the disaffection of the IFP and its Zulu supporters continued, centring on the demand for separate status for KwaZulu/Natal. In April 1995 IFP members withdrew from the Constituent Assembly charged with the drafting a permanent constitution.

During the latter part of the Mandela presidency relations between the IFP and the ANC improved considerably, thanks largely to the efforts of Deputy President Thabo Mbeki. In the 1999 general election the IFP won 34 National Assembly seats with 8.6% of the vote and entered into a new coalition agreement with the ANC. Chief Buthelezi (one of three IFP cabinet ministers) continued to hold the home affairs portfolio. The IFP continued as the senior partner in its ruling coalition with the ANC in KwaZulu-Natal, although its hold was to be shaken by the defection of two provincial members of legislature to the ANC during the floor-crossing saga in 2003. Although the ANC now became the largest party in the provincial assembly, the IFP retained the premiership by threatening a major political crisis in the province most prone to political violence.

In the lead up to the general election of 2004, the IFP announced a working relationship with the DA, increasing speculation that it would terminate its coalition with the ANC. In the event, this did nothing to prevent the further erosion of the IFP's support. It was reduced to 28 seats in the National Assembly (down from 34 in 1999), and came second to the ANC in the provincial election in Kwazulu-Natal. Strains between President Mbeki and Chief Buthelezi led to the latter being excluded from the new cabinet, and the IFP refusing the invitations made to two prominent party members to accept deputy ministerships. Without remaining representation in the national government, the IFP was also reduced to being the junior partner in the government of Kwazulu-Natal, which was now headed by the ANC.

Minority Front

Address. 76 Trisula Avenue, Arena Park 4037
Telephone. (27–31) 404–1993
Fax. (27–31) 404–9059
Leadership. Amichand Rajbansi (leader)

The Minority Front, based in Durban and supported mainly by the Indian community, won no seats in the 1994 national elections and one National Assembly seat in the June 1999 general election. It formed a political alliance with the African National Congress in June 1999.

National Action
Nasionale Aksie

Leadership. Cassie Aucamp.

Formed in June 2002, and secured the defection of Cassie Aucamp from the Afrikaner *Eenheidsbeweging* in 2003. Stands for Christian principles, and minority rights. Has attracted support from Afrikaners (especially youth). Based principally in Guateng, Limpopo, and North West provinces.

New National Party (NNP)

Address. PO Box 1698, Cape Town
Telephone. (27–21) 461–5833
Fax. (27–21) 461–5329
Email. info@natweb.co.za
Website. www.natweb.co.za
Leadership. Marthinus van Schalwyk (national leader)

The name New National Party was adopted by the former National Party (NP) prior to the 1999 general election. The Afrikaner nationalist NP had come to power in 1948, and was the instigator of the system of apartheid in South Africa which was maintained repressively until the end of the 1980s. At that point the party, under the new leadership of F.W. de Klerk, abandoned its defence of apartheid in favour of reform of the political system, although it continued to advocate the constitutional protection of minority rights.

Following his inauguration as State President in 1989, de Klerk implemented a number of dramatic measures, including the release of political prisoners and the legalization of banned organizations, as a prelude to substantive constitutional negotiations with anti-apartheid groups. South Africa's white population voted in support of continuing the reform process in a referendum in March 1992, after which de Klerk declared "today we have closed the book on apartheid".

In the multi-party elections in April 1994 the NP was runner-up to the ANC, winning 82 National Assembly seats with just over 20% of the votes cast. The party also won a majority of seats in the Western Cape regional assembly. De Klerk was subsequently named as one of two Executive Deputy Presidents in the new Mandela administration, which also included several other NP ministers. However, the NP withdrew from the Government of National Unity in June 1996, following the conclusions of negotiations concerning the new, "final" constitution.

Having lost control of the government in the wake of the advent of majority rule, the party was faced with the need to chart a new role. The lead was taken by Roelf Meyer, who had played a key role on the part of the NP government during the constitutional negotiation process and who now took up the new post of NP secretary-general in February 1996. Meyer's proposals for radical restructuring were rejected by the party, prompting his resignation from the NP. He later co-founded the United Democratic Movement.

Meyer's successor as NP secretary-general, Marthinus van Schalkwyk, became party leader after de Klerk's resignation in August 1997. Renamed the NNP, the party won only 6.9% of the vote and 28 National Assembly seats in the June 1999 general election, after which it was superseded as the official national opposition party by the Democratic Party (DP). In Western Cape province, the NNP and the DP formed a coalition government after the June 1999 provincial election.

In June 2000 the NNP responded to coaxings from the leadership of the DP (which had been attracting increasing numbers of former NNP members) to negotiate a merger agreement. Van Schalkwyk agreed to become deputy leader of a new Democratic Alliance led by the DP's Tony Leon, although the NNP and the DP did not immediately disband their separate party organizations.

NNP resentment of DP domination of the DA led to the party's withdrawal from the arrangement in November 2001, and the re-establishment of a working relationship with the ANC. However, this overturning of alliances provoked considerable discord within the party. Gerald Morkel, opposed to the renewal of linkages with the ANC, was ousted as Premier of the Western Cape in November 2001, following which Peter Marais took his place as head of a new NNP-ANC provincial government. Marais was subsequently replaced as Premier by van Schalkwyk himself in late 2002 following his involvement in a funding scandal.

The renewal of the NNP's coalition with the ANC had reestablished its access to government, and 22 municipal councils peviously controlled by the DA fell to the ANC-NNP coalition as a result of the floor-crossings of late 2002. Overall, however, the floor crossings weakened the NNP significantly: its seats in the National Assembly were reduced from 27 to 18 and in the Western Cape provincial assembly from 17 to 10 (van Schalwyk hanging on to his premiership only by grace of the ANC). Similarly, although some 340 municipal councillors crossed back to the NNP from the DA, 51 also crossed to the ANC (whereas the NNP had taken some 612 councillors into the DA at the time of merger).

Following the reduction of the NNP's representation in the National Assembly to just 7 seats in the general election of 2004, its leader Marthinus van Schalkwyk anounced that he would cross the floor to the ANC at the first opportunity, taking his supporters in parliament with him. This represented the effective end of the party of apartheid.

The NNP was an associate member of the International Democrat Union and a member party of its regional organization, the Democrat Union of Africa.

Pan-Africanist Congress of Azania (PAC)

Address. Box 13412, The Tramshed 0126
Telephone. (27–12) 320–6243
Fax. (27–12) 320–1509
Email. azania@icon.co.za
Website. www.paca.org.za
Leadership. Motsoko Pheko (president); Mofihli Likotsi (secretary-general)

The PAC was formed in 1959 by a breakaway faction of the ANC and advocated the establishment of a democratic society through African, and not multi-racial, organizations. It rejected multi-racial co-operation on the grounds that it was a means of safeguarding white interests. Like the ANC, the PAC was banned by the apartheid regime between 1960 and 1990. Having announced in January 1994 that it was abandoning armed struggle, and claiming to be the authentic voice of the black population, the PAC registered for the April elections, in which it secured 1.25% of the vote and five National Assembly seats. In the June 1999 general election it won 0.7% of the vote and three National Assembly seats. Patricia de Lille, the party's most high profile MP, defected from the party in 2003 and founded a new party, the Independent Democrats. The party was racked by internal battles throughout 2003 which were not resolved by the disputed election of Motsoko Pheko to the leadership. The party regained its three seats in the 2004 general election, but offered no indication to contradict commentary that it was slowly dying.

South African Communist Party (SACP)

Address. PO Box 1027, Johannesburg 2000
Telephone. (27–11) 339–3633
Fax. (27–11) 339–4244
Email. sacp@wn.apc.org
Website. www.sapc.org.za
Leadership. Charles Nqakula (national chairman); Blade Nzimande (secretary-general)

The Communist Party of South Africa was formed in 1921 and re-founded as the SACP in 1953. Banned until 1990, it has long co-operated closely with the African National Congress (ANC), some senior appointments within which have been held by SACP members. SACP candidates were included on the ANC list for the April 1994 elections after which the then party chairman, Joe Slovo (who died in January 1995), was appointed to President Mandela's new administration. In the 1999 general election the SACP called on its members to vote for the ANC (as did the Congress of South African Trade Unions, the third component of the "tripartite alliance"). Despite differences over economic strategy with the government, the SACP renewed its support for the ANC in the run up to the 2004 elections.

United Christian Democratic Party (UCDP)

Address. PO Box 3010, Mafikeng
Telephone. (27–18) 381–5691
Fax. (27–18) 381–5603
Leadership. Lucas Mangope (leader)

The UCDP was registered to contest the June 1999 elections by Lucas Mangope, the former president of the "independent homeland" of Bophuthatswana (whose government had been overthrown by an uprising in March 1994). Drawing many of its officials from the leadership of Mangope's former Bophuthatswana Democratic Party, the UCDP won three seats in the National Assembly in 1999, while at provincial level it became the official opposition party in the legislature of the North West province (largely corresponding to the former Bophuthatswana). In January 2000 the UCDP concluded a co-operation agreement with the Democratic Party.

The UCDP retained three seats in the general election of 2004.

United Democratic Movement (UDM)

Address. PO Box 26290, Arcadia 0007
Telephone. (27–12) 321–0010
Fax. (27–12) 321–0014
Email. info@udm.org.za
Website. www.udm.org.za
Leadership. Bantu Holomisa (president).

The UDM, which claimed to have a membership "directly corresponding to the demographic composition of South Africa", was co-founded in September 1997 by Bantu Holomisa and Roelf Meyer. Holomisa, a former head of government (1987-94) in the "independent homeland" of Transkei, had been dismissed as a deputy minister in Nelson Mandela's government of national unity and expelled from the African National Congress after making corruption allegations against another ANC minister in testimony to South Africa's truth and reconciliation commission. Meyer, a former secretary-general of the National Party, had been obliged to resign from the NP after the party's rejection of his call for it to disband and/or undergo radical restructuring following its withdrawal from the government of national unity in 1996. In 1998 Holomisa became president, and Meyer deputy president, of the UDM, which won 14 National Assembly seats in the June 1999 general election. The UDM subsequently concluded a parliamentary co-operation agreement with the Federal Alliance. In January 2000 Roelf Meyer resigned from his parliamentary seat and his UDM position, stating that he was retiring from politics. The position of UDM deputy president was left vacant, reflecting a lack of agreement between different sections of the party over the selection of a successor. The UDM gained control of the Sabata Dalindyebo Municipality (Umtata, the capital of the former Transkei homeland) in the muncipal elections of 2000.

The UDM's unsuccessful challenge to the floor-crossing legislation in the Constitutional Court in 2002 proved costly, as subsequently 10 of its 14 MPs defected to the ANC. It also lost 2 of its 9 provincial representatives in the Eastern Cape and its sole representative in the Western Cape to the ANC. These reflected wider rifts within the party revolving around claims about poor leadership, mismanagement and corruption.

The representation of the UDM was reduced to nine seats in the general election of 2004.

Other Parties

At the end of 2003 there were some 131 organizations registered as political parties with the Independent Electoral Commission. Other parties of some recent significance include:

Christian Democratic Party, an Afrikaner-led group calling for a government based on Christian values.
Address PO Box 6134, Westgate, 1734
Telephone. (27-11) 679 2155
Fax. (27-11 679 2155.
Website. www.christiandemocraticparty.org.za
Leadership. Revd. Theunis Botha & Revd. Rudi du Plooy

Conservative Party of South Africa (*Konsertwatiewe Party van Suid-Afrika*), launched in 1982 by former National Party members who rejected any constitutional moves towards power-sharing with the non-white population. The party was runner-up to the National Party at the elections in 1987 and 1989. It unsuccessfully urged white voters to reject the reform process in the March 1992 referendum, thereafter insisting on the right to self-determination including the possibility of a white homeland. The party did not register to contest elections held in the 1990s. The party merged itself into the Freedom Front in September 2003.

The Green Party of South Africa, formerly known as the Government by the People Green Party, contested the 1999 general election but won no seats in the National Assembly.
Address. PO Box 114, Noordhoek.
Telephone. (27-21) 789 1391
Fax. (27-21) 789 1143
Email. info@greenparty.org.za
Website. www.greenparty.org.za
Leadership. Judy Sole (founder)

New Labour Party, formed by Peter Marais after he was ousted as NNP Premier of the Western Cape. Aimed at representing the interests of the coloured population on the Cape Flats and elsewhere in the Western Cape; may receive support from some revivalist pastors.
Address. 3 Vegesig Street, Schoongesight, Durbanville, 7550
Telephone. (27 21) 487 1808
Fax. (27-21) 487 1810
Leadership. Peter Marais

Reconstituted National Party (*Herstigte Nasionale Party,* HNP), founded in 1969 by extreme right-wing former members of the National Party. The HNP, advocating "Christian nationalism" and strict apartheid, briefly held one parliamentary seat (following a by-election) between 1985 and 1987. It opposed the constitutional reform process and did not register to contest elections held in the 1990s.
Address. PO Box 1888, Pretoria 0001
Telephone. (27–12) 342–3410
Fax. (27–12) 342–3417
Email. info@hnp.org.za
Website. www.hnp.org.za

Socialist Party of Azania (SOPA), contested the 1999 general election but won no seats in the National Assembly.

Spain

Capital: Madrid
Population: 40,900,000 (2001E)

The Kingdom of Spain's 1978 constitution rescinded the "fundamental principles" and organic legislation under which General Franco had ruled as Chief of State until his death in 1975 and inaugurated an hereditary constitutional monarchy. Executive power is exercised by the Prime Minister and the Council of Ministers nominally appointed by the King but collectively responsible to the legislature, in which they must command majority support. Legislative authority is vested in the bicameral *Cortes Generales*, both houses of which are elected for four-year terms (subject to dissolution) by universal adult suffrage of those aged 18 and over. The upper Senate (*Senado*) has had 259 members since the 2000 elections, of whom 208 were directly elected and 51 designated by 17 autonomous regional legislatures. The lower Congress of Deputies (*Congreso de los Diputados*) consists of 350 deputies elected from party lists by province-based proportional representation, with each of the 50 provinces being entitled to a minimum of three deputies. Spain joined what became the European Union on Jan. 1, 1986, and elects 54 members of the European Parliament.

Pursuant to the constitutional description of political parties as the expression of pluralism and an essential instrument of political participation, subsidies are available from state funds for parties represented in the Congress of Deputies, in proportion to the number of seats and votes obtained at the most recent general elections. Parties are also eligible for state subsidies to defray election campaign expenses, again in proportion to representation obtained, and to certain benefits during campaigns, such as free advertising space in the media. A separate channel of public subsidy is the entitlement of parliamentary groups in the national and regional legislatures to financial assistance according to their number of members.

The March 14, 2004, legislative elections were overshadowed by a wave of terrorist bombings in Madrid on March 11 that resulted in heavy loss of life. Prior to March 11 opinion polls predicted a clear absolute majority for the governing People's Party (PP). However, statements by the government unambiguously attributing the bombings to the Basque separatist group ETA (in conflict with evidence that pointed to the involvement of Islamic fundamentalists) were perceived by sections of the public as being a strategy of misinformation. In particular, blaming ETA appeared to be an attempt to deflect the electorate's attention from the highly unpopular decision by the PP government to send Spanish troops to Iraq. The consequence was a collapse of the PP vote and the victory of the Socialists of the PSOE.

The elections to the Congress of Deputies on March 14, 2004, resulted as follows: Spanish Socialist Workers' Party 164 seats (with 42.64 % of the vote); People's Party 148 (37.64%); Convergence and Union 10 (3.24.%); Republican Left of Catalonia 8 (2.54%); Basque Nationalist Party 7 (1.63 %); United Left (led by the Communist Party of Spain) 5 (4.96%); Canarian Coalition 3 (0.86 %); Galician Nationalist Bloc 2 (0.8 %); Aragonese Union 1 (0.37 %); Basque Solidarity 1 (0.32%); Navarran Party 1 (0.24%).

Spain held elections to the European Parliament on June 13, 2004. In a turnout of 45.94% (down from 77% for the general election in March) the elections produced the following results: Spanish Socialist Workers' Party won 43.30% of the votes and gained 25 (+1) of the country's 54 seats; People's Party 41.30%, 24 seats (-3); Peoples of Europe coalition (Convergence and Union, Basque Nationalist Party, Galician Nationalist Bloc) 5.17%, 2 seats (-3); Green Left coalition (United Left, United and Alternative Left) 4.16%, 2 seats; Europe of the Peoples coalition (Republican Left of Catalonia and others) 2.49%, 1 seat.

Communist Party of Spain
Partido Comunista de España (PCE)
Address. Calle Toronga 27, 28043 Madrid
Telephone. (34–91) 300–4969
Fax. (34–91) 300–4744
Email. internacional@pce.es
Website. www.pce.es
Leadership. Francisco Frutos (secretary-general)
The PCE was founded in April 1920 by dissident members of the youth wing of the Spanish Socialist Workers' Party (PSOE) who wished to join the Third (Communist) International and who united in November 1921 with the *Partido Comunista Obrero Español* (PCOE), formed by further defections from the PSOE. The PCE held its first congress in 1922 but was forced underground by the Primo de Rivera dictatorship and had only 800 members by 1929. The party formed part of the republican Popular Front from January 1936, winning 17 seats in the Congress in that year. During the Francoist uprising the PCE policy was "victory first, then revolution", in contrast to the Trotskyists and anarcho-syndicalists. Under the subsequent Franco regime, the PCE was active in the clandestine resistance, its general sec-

retaries (in exile) being Dolores Ibárruri Gómez ("*La Pasionaria*") in 1942–60 and Santiago Carrillo Solares from 1960 (when Ibárruri was appointed honorary president of the party). Undergoing various splits during the 1960s, the PCE developed links with the Italian Communist Party (PCI), sharing the latter's opposition to Moscow's leadership and the 1968 Czechoslovakia intervention, and its support for co-operation with other democratic parties.

In July 1974 the exiled PCE leadership joined other anti-Franco parties in the *Junta Democrática*, which in March 1976 joined the Socialist-led Democratic Platform to form the Democratic Co-ordination. Legalized in April 1977, when it had some 200,000 members, the PCE supported the restoration of a constitutional monarchy and won 20 seats in the Congress of Deputies elected in June 1977 (and three in the Senate). The ninth (1978) PCE congress was the first to be held in Spain for 46 years. The party's congressional strength increased to 23 in the elections of March 1979, but it became internally divided between two large and broadly Euro-communist factions and two smaller and broadly pro-Soviet factions. The weakened party was reduced to 4.1% of the vote and four deputies in the October 1982 elections, whereupon Carrillo resigned and was succeeded as PCE secretary-general (in November) by a more committed Euro-communist, Gerardo Iglesias Argüelles.

In local elections in May 1983 the PCE vote recovered to 7.9%, but in the following months it suffered a series of splits, mainly between "*gerardistas*" favouring a broad left alliance and "*carrillistas*" opposed to such a strategy. In March 1985 Carrillo was forced out of the PCE leadership, his supporters being purged from the central committee. In April 1986 the PCE was a founder-member of the United Left (IU), which secured 4.6% of the vote and seven lower house seats in the June general elections. The then deputy general secretary, Enrique Curiel, resigned in December 1987, and Iglesias himself resigned in February 1988 after losing the support of the large Madrid, Catalan and Andalusian sections. Later that month the 12th PCE congress elected Julio Anguita (a former mayor of Córdoba) as his successor. Meanwhile, the PCE had become involved in sporadic efforts to reunify the Spanish communist movement following the establishment by Ignacio Gallego of the People's Communist Party of Spain (PCPE) and by Carrillo of what became the Workers' Party of Spain (PTE).

PCE president Dolores Ibárruri died in November 1989, whereafter the PCE continued its "broad left" strategy in the 1993, 1996 and 2000 elections, deriving some benefit in 1996 from the troubles of the then ruling PSOE and the broadly conservative policies of the González government, but falling back sharply in 2000. At the 15th PCE congress in December 1998, Anguita was succeeded as secretary-general by Francisco Frutos. Frutos became also the coordinator general of United Left before and after the 2000 March elections. Frutos formed a pre-electoral coalition with the PSOE to defeat the PP, but this led to the loss of half of the previous share of the vote. Following the March 2000 elections, Frutos was successfully challenged by Gaspar Llamazares as leader of the United Left coalition, nevertheless the former remained secretary general of the PCE. In the March 2004 elections the United Left took 5 seats, with 4.96% of the vote, compared with the 8 seats won in 2000.

Popular Party
Partido Popular (PP)
Address. Génova 13, 28004 Madrid
Telephone. (34–91) 557–7300
Fax. (34–91) 308–4618
Email. oipp@pp.es
Website. www.pp.es
Leadership. José María Aznar López (president); Luis de

Grandes Pascual (Congress spokesman); Esteban González Pons (Senate spokesman); Javier Arenas Bocanegra (secretary-general)

The moderate conservative PP was established in its present form in January 1989 as successor to the Popular Alliance (*Alianza Popular*, AP), which been created in October 1976 as a distinctly right-wing grouping embracing the dominant political forces of the Franco era. The AP had been formed as a coalition of seven right-wing and centre-right parties: *Reforma Democrática* (RD), led by a former Francoist minister Manuel Fraga Iribarne; *Acción Regional* (AR), led by Laureano López Rodó; *Acción Democrática Española* (ADE), formed in 1976 and led by Federico Silva Muñoz; *Democracia Social* (DS), led by Licinio de la Fuente; *Unión del Pueblo Español* (UDPE), led by Cruz Martínez Esteruelas; *Unión Nacional Española* (UNE), led by Gonzalo Fernández de la Mora, and *Unión Social Popular* (USP), led by Enrique Thomas de Carranza. In March 1977 five of these parties merged as a single organization named the *Partido Unido de Alianza Popular* (PUAP) led by Fraga Iribarne as secretary-general. The two non-participating parties were the ADE and the UNE, both led by former Francoist ministers, but they remained in alliance with the PUAP until late 1979.

In the June 1977 general elections the AP, then widely regarded as a Francoist grouping, won 8.2% of the vote, giving it 16 seats in the Congress of Deputies and two in the Senate. Divided over whether to endorse the 1978 constitution (which Fraga Iribarne in the event supported), the AP lost support. In the March 1979 general elections the Democratic Coalition which it had formed with other right-wing groups, including *Acción Ciudadana Liberal*, the *Partido Popular de Cataluña*, *Renovación Española* (RE) and the Popular Democratic Party (PDP), won only 6% of the vote, giving it nine seats in the Congress and three in the Senate. At the 1979 and 1980 party congresses, the AP leadership moved the party, with some difficulty, towards a mainstream conservative orientation, a leading advocate of which was Fraga Iribarne, who was elected AP president in 1979. In mid-1980 the AP merged with the PDP and RE; the combined party, projecting a moderate image (and denouncing the 1981 coup attempt), doubled its membership in 1981–82.

The Galician elections of October 1981 enabled the AP to form a minority government in that region, where it secured a majority in 1983 by recruiting members of the by then dissolved Union of the Democratic Centre (UCD). Meanwhile, in the national parliamentary elections of October 1982 the AP-led bloc won 26.6% of the vote and 106 seats in the lower chamber (and 54 in the upper), so eclipsing the UCD and becoming the main opposition formation. From 1983 the AP led a regional and national electoral alliance, the Popular Coalition (*Coalición Popular*, CP), including the PDP, the Liberal Union (UL) and regional formations such as the Union of the Navarrese People (UPN), the Aragonese Party and the Valencian Union. The CP came under severe strain following the June 1986 general elections, in which it secured 26% of the vote and 105 seats in the lower house (and 63 in the Senate). In July 1986 the PDP broke away. In December, after an electoral rout in the Basque Country, Fraga resigned as AP president. In January 1987 the national AP broke with the Liberal Party (PL, as the UL had become) although the AP-PL alliance remained in existence in some regions. The 8th AP congress, in February 1987, installed a new youthful party leadership headed by Antonio Hernández Mancha, who had been AP leader in Andalusía. During 1987 the AP contested elections at various levels, securing 231 seats in autonomous parliaments, over 13,000 local council seats and 17 seats in the European Parliament (for which its list was led by Fraga Iribarne). However, by late 1987 defections resulting from chronic internal infighting had reduced the party's strength in the national Congress of Deputies to 67.

The conversion of the AP into the PP at a party congress in January 1989 reflected the wish of most AP currents to present a moderate conservative alternative to the ruling Spanish Socialist Workers' Party (PSOE) and to eschew any remaining identification with the Franco era. The congress was preceded by a power struggle between Hernández and Fraga Iribarne, the latter having been persuaded by supporters that he should try to regain the leadership. In the event, Hernández opted out of the contest shortly before the congress, so that Fraga Iribarne resumed the leadership of a more united party, which subsequently made particular efforts to build alliances with regional conservative parties. In the October 1989 general elections it advanced marginally to 106 seats and 30.3% of the vote, but remained far behind the PSOE. In December 1989 the PP won an absolute majority in the Galician assembly, whereupon Fraga Iribarne became regional president, being succeeded as PP leader by José María Aznar López.

In the early 1990s the PP was not immune from scandals concerning irregular party financing, of the type affecting most of Latin Europe; but it remained relatively untarnished compared with the ruling PSOE. In general elections in June 1993 the party increased its Chamber representation to 141 seats and its vote share to 34.8%, less than four points behind the PSOE. Continuing in opposition, the PP registered major victories in the October 1993 Galician regional election and in the June 1994 European Parliament elections, on the latter occasion overtaking the PSOE by winning 40.6% of the vote and 28 of the 64 seats. Further advances followed in regional and local elections in May 1995, although in actual voting the PP failed to match its large opinion poll lead over the PSOE. Aznar's public standing was boosted by a car-bomb assassination attempt against him in Madrid in April 1995.

In early general elections in March 1996 the PP at last overtook the PSOE as the largest Chamber party, but its 156 seats (from 38.9% of the vote) left it well short of an overall majority. Aznar was accordingly obliged to form a minority government, which received qualified pledges of external support from the Catalan Convergence and Union (CiU), the Basque Nationalist Party (PNV) and the Canarian Coalition (CC) in return for concessions to their regional agendas. His government programme promised urgent economic austerity measures to achieve the "national objective" of meeting the Maastricht treaty criteria for participation in a single European currency. The PNV withdrew its support from the PP government in September 1997, without affecting its ability to survive. The PNV withdrawal was confirmed in June 1999 following municipal and regional elections in which the PP maintained its status as the leading political formation, retaining control in nine of the 13 autonomous regions where elections were held. In simultaneous European Parliament elections the PP slipped to 39.8% of the national vote and 27 seats.

Economic progress related to the discipline required for joining the euro boosted the PP's popularity in the run-up to the March 2000 parliamentary elections, the party also being assisted by a public desire for continuity following the ending of the Basque separatist ETA's ceasefire in December 1999. The results showed that the party had secured an historic overall majority of 183 lower house seats on a 44.6% vote share as well as an overall majority of 150 seats in the Senate. The new Aznar government therefore had the unfettered authority to enact long-discussed legislation, including a tough new immigration bill and the standardization of the teaching of humanities throughout Spain's regions. Although it no longer needed their votes, the PP again negotiated external support agreements with the CiU and the CC, but made no attempt to establish a new accord with the PNV.

After José María Aznar announced that he would step down as Prime Minister before the legislative elections of March 2004, several candidates sought to become his successor. A decision was only taken in the autumn of 2003, when Aznar presented the Galician Mariano Rajoy as his successor. The party remained quite disciplined during the second Aznar period in office. In 2002, it agreed a pact for the reform of the judiciary with the PSOE and adopted a tougher line against Basque terrorism, including the banning of the political arm of ETA, *Herri Batasuna*, in which the government was supported by the PSOE. This bipartisan position of the two main parties led to even more polarization between the Basque nationalists (including the moderate PNV) and Madrid. Aznar's support for US President George W. Bush in the Iraq war in 2003 led to major divisions in Spanish society, which was overwhelmingly against the intervention. Nonetheless, opinion polls in the run-up to the 2004 legislative elections suggested that the PP would get an absolute majority. The Madrid bombings three days before the elections, and the widely disbelieved claims by top government officials that the bombings were the work of ETA, led to a reversed result in which the PP became the runner up and the PSOE was able to win the elections. The PP took 37.64% of the vote and 148 seats.

The PP is affiliated to the Christian Democrat International and the International Democrat Union. Its representatives in the European Parliament (in which it holds 24 seats following the June 2004 European elections) sit in the European People's Party/European Democrats group. It has a membership of 620,000.

Spanish Socialist Workers' Party
Partido Socialista Obrero Español (PSOE)

Address. Ferraz 68–70, Madrid 28008
Telephone. (34–91) 582–0444
Fax. (34–91) 582–0525
Email. internacional@psoe.es
Website. www.psoe.es
Leadership. José Luis Rodríguez Zapatero (secretary-general); Jesús Caldera Sánchez-Capitán (Congress spokesman); Juan José Laborda Martín (Senate spokesman)
Of social democratic orientation, the PSOE seeks a fairer and more united society based on social, economic and political democracy. It supports Spanish membership of the European Union (EU) and of the Atlantic Alliance, having opposed the latter until 1986. It defined itself as Marxist in 1976, but since 1979 has regarded Marxism as merely an analytical tool. It defends divorce and the decriminalization of abortion in certain circumstances.

Originally founded in 1879 from socialist groups in Madrid and Guadalajara, the PSOE held its first congress in 1888 and became a leading party of the Second International. It was allied with the Republicans from 1909, as a result of which its founder, Pablo Iglesias, was elected to the Congress of Deputies in 1910. The party had some 40,000 members when its left wing broke away in 1920–21 to form the Communist Party of Spain (PCE). The PSOE doubled its membership during the 1920s and returned about one third of the deputies in the Congress in 1931. It played an important role in the history of the Spanish Republic until the end of the Civil War in 1939, when it was banned by the Franco regime. The exiled leadership, based in Toulouse (France), refused to ally with other anti-Franco forces, but a more radical internally-based "*renovador*" faction began to organize in the late 1960s. The internal section gained control at a congress in Paris in 1972, and in 1974 it elected Felipe González as first secretary (although a rival "*historico*" faction survived in France and evolved into the Socialist

Action Party). Both the PSOE and various regional socialist parties experienced rapid growth in Spain at about this time, partly due to the death of Franco.

In June 1975 the PSOE joined other non-Communist opposition parties in the *Plataforma Democrática* alliance, which in March 1976 merged with the PCE-led *Junta Democrática*. The latter had been created in 1974 and included the Popular Socialist Party (*Partido Socialista Popular*, PSP), which had been formed in 1967 as the *Partido Socialista del Interior* (PSI). The PSOE was also a component of the even broader *Coordinación Democrática*, which negotiated with the post-Franco government for the restoration of civil and political rights, regional autonomy and popular consultation on the future form of government. During 1976 the PSOE formed the *Federación de Partidos Socialistas* along with groups such as the Party of Socialists of Catalonia (PSC), *Convergencia Socialista Madrileña*, the *Partit Socialiste des Illes*, the *Partido Socialista Bilzarrea* and the Aragonese and Galician Socialist parties.

In December 1976 the PSOE, the largest socialist group with about 75,000 members, held its first congress inside Spain for 44 years, the venue being in Madrid. It was formally legalized on Feb. 17, 1977, along with a number of other parties. The PSOE participated in the June 1977 general elections together with the PSC and the Basque Socialist Party (PSE–PSOE), winning a total of 118 seats in the Congress of Deputies and 47 in the Senate. In February 1978 the PSC formally affiliated to the national party, as the PSC–PSOE, and in April the PSOE absorbed the PSP, which had six deputies and four senators. The Aragonese and Galician parties were similarly absorbed in May and July 1978. In the March 1979 general elections the PSOE, with its Basque and Catalan affiliates, won 121 seats in the Congress and 68 in the Senate, therefore remaining in opposition. At a centennial congress in May 1979 González unexpectedly stepped down as party leader after a majority of delegates refused to abandon a doctrinal commitment to Marxism. His control was re-established during a special congress in late September 1979, the hard-liners being defeated by a 10 to 1 majority.

The PSOE made further gains in the October 1982 general elections, in which it won 48.7% of the vote (passing the 10 million mark for the first time) and gained an absolute majority in both chambers (with 202 of the 350 deputies and 34 of the 208 senators). A PSOE government was formed on Dec. 1, with González as Prime Minister; it subsequently negotiated Spain's entry into what became the European Union (EU) with effect from Jan. 1, 1986. In January 1983 the PSOE absorbed the Democratic Action Party (*Partido de Acción Demócrata*, PAD), which had been formed in March 1982 by centre-left defectors from the then ruling Union of the Democratic Centre (UCD). In 1985 the PSOE experienced serious internal divisions over the government's pro-NATO policy, which ran counter to the party's longstanding rejection of participation in any military alliance. The issue was resolved by a referendum of March 1986 which delivered a majority in favour of NATO membership on certain conditions, including reduction of the US military presence in Spain.

The PSOE retained power in the June 1986 general elections with a reduced vote share of 43.4% but a renewed majority of 184 lower house seats and 124 in the Senate. It thereafter pursued what were generally seen as moderate and somewhat conservative policies, particularly in the economic sphere. The PSOE's narrow loss of an overall majority in the October 1989 general elections (in which it slipped to 175 seats in the lower house on a 39.6% vote share) was attributed in part to internal divisions, highlighted by the prior emergence of the dissident Socialist Democracy splinter group and by the defection of a substantial PSOE group to the United Left (IU). In the early 1990s the PSOE's standing was damaged further by a series of financial scandals involving prominent party figures, combined with familiar left/right tensions. At the 32nd PSOE congress in November 1990 the left-leaning Deputy Prime Minister and deputy party leader, Alfonso Guerra, was able to block a move by the party's right to strengthen its base in leadership bodies. However, a corruption scandal involving his brother compelled Guerra to resign from the government in January 1991; although he remained deputy leader of the party, the PSOE right became increasingly dominant thereafter.

In early general elections in June 1993 the party retained a narrow relative majority of 159 Chamber seats (on a 38.7% vote share), sufficient for González to form a minority government with regional party support. Held amid further disclosures about irregular party financing, the 33rd PSOE congress in March 1994 resulted in the transfer of the party's controversial organization secretary, José María ("Txiki") Benegas, to another post. In the June 1994 European Parliament elections PSOE support slumped to 31.1%, so that the party took only 22 of the 64 Spanish seats, while in simultaneous regional elections the PSOE lost overall control of its stronghold of Andalusia. Further setbacks followed in Basque Country elections in October 1994 and in regional/municipal polling in May 1995, although the PSOE retained control of Madrid and Barcelona.

The tide of corruption and security scandals rose inexorably through 1995, with the CESID phone-tapping disclosures in June, causing the small Catalan Convergence and Union party to withdraw its external support from the PSOE government the following month. The eventual upshot was another early general election in March 1996 in which the PSOE finally lost power, although the margin of its defeat was less wide than many had predicted: it retained 141 seats with 37.5% of the vote, only slightly down on its 1993 showing and only 1.5% behind the Popular Party, which was therefore obliged to form a minority government.

González finally vacated the PSOE leadership at the 34th party congress in Madrid in June 1997, being succeeded by Joaquín Almunia Amann, an uncharismatic Basque politician. On Almunia's proposal the first-ever "primary" elections were held in April 1998 to choose the party's prime ministerial candidate, the unexpected victor being not Almunia but articulate former minister Josep Borrell Fontelles. An uneasy dual leadership ensued, until Borrell resigned as Prime Minister-candidate in May 1999 over a controversial financial investment by his now-estranged wife in the 1980s. In the June 1999 European Parliament elections the PSOE presented a joint list with the Democratic Party of the New Left (PDNI), advancing to 35.3% of the vote and 24 of the 64 Spanish seats. The following month Almunia was elected unopposed as the PSOE candidate for Prime Minister.

In the run-up to the March 20000 parliamentary elections the PSOE entered into a ground-breaking agreement to cooperate with the Communist-led IU in the contest, although at IU insistence the pact to present joint lists extended only to the Senate elections. In the event, both parties fared badly, with the PSOE falling to 125 lower house seats and 34.1% of the vote, while the combined efforts of the parties yielded only 69 Senate seats. Almunia immediately resigned as PSOE leader and was replaced at the 35th party congress in July 2000 by 39-year-old José Luis Rodríguez Zapatero, a Castilean lawyer, who embarked upon a rejuvenation of the party's leadership bodies and the renewal and modernization of the party. He also sought to modernise the ideological foundations of the party by moving it towards the centre. Zapatero cooperated with the PP government to introduce major reforms in the judiciary, in the fight against terrorism and the enhancement of Spain's position in the European Union. Simultaneously, he was at the forefront of the active protest movement against the support of Spain for the Iraq war. The party campaigned in 2004 on a promise of recalling Spanish troops from Iraq. Although most opinion polls indicated that the PSOE would lose the 2004 legislative elections, the bombings in Madrid on March 11, and the PP government's response, profoundly influenced the result and led to a strong absolute majority for the PSOE. The PSOE secured 43.6% of votes and 164 seats. In the June 2004 European Parliament elections the PSOE substantially increased its share of the vote compared with 1999 (to 43.30%), enabling it to increase its total of seats by one to 25 despite the reduction in the overall Spanish contingent to 54.

The PSOE is a member party of the Socialist International and its European Parliament representatives sit in the Party of European Socialists group. The PSOE has 200,000 members.

United Left
Izquierda Unida (IU)
Address. Olimpo 35, 28043 Madrid
Telephone. (34–91) 300–3233
Fax. (34–91) 388–0405
Email. org.federal@izquierda-unida.es
Website. www.izquierda-unida.es
Leadership. Gaspar Llamazares (secretary)

The radical left-wing (mainly Marxist) IU was founded in April 1986 as an electoral alliance, its first president being the then PCE leader, Gerardo Iglesias. The IU originally consisted of the Communist Party of Spain (PCE), the Socialist Action Party (PASOC), the Peoples' Communist Party of Spain (PCPE), the Progressive Federation (FP) and the Communist Union of Spain (UCE). It was expanded in 1988–89 to include the Republican Left (IR) and the Unitarian Candidature of Workers (*Candidatura Unitaria de Trabajadores*, CUT), led by Juan Manuel Sánchez Gordillo. Later temporary participants included the Carlist Party, the Humanist Party (PH) and the Unity of the Valencian People (UPV).

In the June 1986 general elections the IU won seven seats in the Congress of Deputies and none in the Senate. The FP left the IU in late 1987, partly as a result of the unilateral decision of the PCE to sign a parliamentary accord against political violence without consulting the other IU parties. In December 1987 the IU leadership adopted a strategy seeking to make the IU a permanent rather than *ad hoc* alliance, and to broaden its base during 1988 beyond the member parties to incorporate independent left-wingers and pressure groups. In the October 1989 general elections the IU increased its lower house representation to 18 seats (on a 9.1% vote share) and also won one Senate seat.

Proposals for a formal merger between the IU parties caused dissension in 1991–92, the outcome being that component formations retained their autonomous identity. In the June 1993 general elections the IU made only marginal headway, again winning 18 lower house seats but with 9.6% of the vote. It fared substantially better in the June 1994 European Parliament elections, obtaining nine of the 64 Spanish seats on a 13.5% vote share. In simultaneous regional elections in Andalusia, it won 19.2% of the vote. In the March 1996 general elections the IU derived some benefit from the defeat of the Spanish Socialist Workers' Party (PSOE), winning 10.6% of the national vote and 21 lower house seats (although none in the Senate). However, the June 1999 European elections brought a sharp reverse for the IU, to only 5.8% of the vote and four seats.

In February 2000 the IU concluded its first-ever electoral pact with the PSOE, but covering only the forthcoming Senate elections and not those to the Congress of Deputies. The results of the polling the following month showed a slump in IU support, to 5.5% of the vote, which yielded only eight seats. Veteran IU secretary Julio Anguita González immediately resigned and was succeeded by Gaspar Llamazares. Thereafter, the IU was a vehement opponent of the policies of the Aznar government. It was involved in several protest movements and was supportive of the nationalist cause in the Basque Country. The party had also to slim down after the catastrophic electoral results, which led to a considerable reduction of the state subsidies, their main source of income. The legislative elections of 2004 confirmed the declining trend of the IU vote. The IU received 4.96% of the vote and 5 seats and was surpassed by the Catalan regionalist parties CiU and ERC and the Basque PNV in terms of seats

The IU representatives in the European Parliament sit in the European United Left/Nordic Green Left group. The IU has an official membership of 68,000.

Other National Parties

Alliance for National Union (*Alianza por l'Unión Nacional*, AUN), radical far-right formation seeking the preservation of the unity of the Spanish state and a halt to immigration.
Address. c/ibiza n°37, bajo-centro-izquierda, 28009 Madrid
Telephone. (+34) 91 504 37 91
Leadership. Ricardo Saenz de Ynestrillas

Carlist Party (*Partido Carlista*, PC), formed in 1934, a left-wing group which arose from a 19th-century Catholic monarchist movement; strongest in the north of Spain; the Carlists turned against the Franco regime after 1939 and many of its leaders were exiled; in the post-Franco era it became a component of the United Left alliance. It got 0.01% of the vote in March 2000 elections
Address. c/Sagasta 7, 28004 Madrid
Telephone. (+34) 91 591 40 29
Fax. (+34) 91 319 39 85
Email. partidocarlista@partidocarlista.com
Website. www.partidocarlista.com

Centrist Union (*Unión Centrista*, UC), launched in early 1995 by elements that included former members of the Democratic and Social Centre (*Centro Democrático y Social*, CDS), which had been founded prior to the 1982 elections by Adolfo Suárez González, who had vacated the leadership of the Union of the Democratic Centre (*Unión de Centro Democrático*, UCD) on resigning as Prime Minister in January 1981 and had been rebuffed when he tried to regain the party leadership in July 1982; allied regionally and locally with the Popular Party (PP) and an affiliate of the Liberal International, the CDS had won 14 lower house seats and five European Parliament seats in 1989, although the resignation of Suárez González in September 1991 had heralded virtual extinction in the 1993 national and 1994 European elections; the new UC fared little better in the 1996 general elections.
Address. Jorge Juan 30, 28001 Madrid
Leadership. Fernando García Fructuoso

Feminist Party of Spain (*Partido Feminista de España*, PFE), founded in 1979, aiming to spread the gospel of women's liberation at the political and social levels, but not making much headway in Catholic and socially conservative Spain.
Address. Magdalena 29/1A, 28012 Madrid

The Greens (*Los Verdes*), confederation resulting from ecologist conferences in Tenerife in May 1983 and in Malaga in June 1984, legally registered in November 1984, inaugurated at a congress in Barcelona in February 1985; the resultant Green Alternative (*Alternativa Verde*) electoral alliance won

less than 1% of the vote in the 1986 general elections, and subsequent assorted electoral variants (sometimes simultaneous and competing) made no further progress, although the movement has gained some representation at local level and won 1.4% in the June 1999 European Parliament elections. It got 0.31 % of the vote in the March 2000 legislative elections
Address. c/Juan de Ocana, 28 931 Mostoles (Madrid).
Telephone. (+34) 91 61 38 300
Email. Organizacion@verdes.es
Website. www.verdes.es

Humanist Party of Spain (*Partido Humanista de España*, PHE), formed in 1984, a member of the United Left electoral coalition (IU) in the 1986 general elections, subsequently independent. It promotes a non-violent approach to politics based on the respect of human dignity. It got 0.08 % of the vote in the March 2000 legislative elections
Website. www.mdnh.org
Leadership. Rafael de la Rubia

Liberal Party (*Partido Liberal*, PL), founded in 1977, absorbed the small Liberal Union (*Unión Liberal*, UL) in 1985, closely allied with the Popular Party from 1989, although retaining independent party status.

National Democracy (*Democracia Nacional*, DN), right-wing formation founded in 1995.
Website. www.democracianacional.org
Leadership. José Luis Perez

National Front (*Frente Nacional*, FN), far-right party founded in October 1986 aiming to rally Francoist forces against the then ruling Spanish Socialist Workers' Party.

Republican Left (*Izquierda Republicana*, IR), left-wing formation dating from 1934, became a component of the United Left (IU) in 1988.

Socialist Action Party (*Partido de Acción Socialista*, PASOC), founded in January 1983 by left-wing socialists who regarded the then ruling Spanish Socialist Workers' Party (PSOE) as having betrayed the working class; succeeded the PSOE *Histórico*, which arose from the 1974 split between the *renovadores* ("renewal") group based inside Spain (led by Felipe González) and the *historicos* loyal to the exiled leadership of Rodolfo Llopis; having absorbed some even smaller socialist formations, PASOC was a founder member of the United Left alliance in 1986, through which it gained representation at national, regional and European levels.

Socialist Democracy (*Democracia Socialista*, DS), founded in 1990 by a left-wing dissident faction of the then ruling Spanish Socialist Workers' Party.

Spanish Falange (*Falange Española de las* JONS), residual survival of the ruling formation of the Franco era, won one lower house seat in 1979 in a National Union (*Unión Nacional*) with other neo-fascist groups; other far-right formations appeared to supersede the Falange in the 1980s, notably the National Front; in the 1990s it sought to articulate right-wing sentiment among those damaged by free-market government policies. It got 0.06 % of the vote in the March 2000 elections.

Revolutionary Workers' Party (*Partido Obrero Revolucionario*, POR), Trotskyist formation founded in 1974.

Regional Parties

As the leading national formations, the Popular Party (PP),

Spanish Socialist Workers' Party (PSOE) and United Left (IU) are organized in most of Spain's autonomous regions, either under their own name or in alliance with autonomous regional parties. There are also many regional parties without national affiliation.

ANDALUSIA

Regional assembly elections in 2000, resulted as follows: PSOE 52 seats, PP 46, a joint list of the IU 6, Andalusian Party 5.

Andalusian Party
Partido Andalucista (PA)
Address. Av. San Francisco Javier 24, Edificio Seville 1/9A-2, 41005 Seville
Telephone. (34–95) 422–6855
Fax. (34–95) 421–0446
Email. pa-secretaria@p-andalucista.org
Website. www.p-andalucista.org
Leadership. Alejandro Rojas-Marcos de la Viesca (president); Antonio Ortega García (secretary-general)
The PA was founded in 1976 (as the Socialist Party of Andalusia) on a progressive nationalist platform, seeking self-determination for Andalusia on terms more concessionary than those of the 1981 autonomy statute. Legalized in 1977, the party fought the 1979 general elections on a moderate regionalist manifesto, securing five seats in the Congress of Deputies (which it failed to hold in 1982). It won two seats in the Catalan assembly in March 1980 and three seats in the Andalusian assembly in May 1982 (with 5.4% of the vote). The party adopted its present name at its fifth congress in February 1984. In the 1986 Andalusian elections it was reduced to two seats, but it slightly raised its vote in the 1987 local elections.

The PA regained national representation in 1989, winning two lower house seats, and advanced strongly to 10 seats in the Andalusian regional assembly in 1990. However, it lost its national seats in 1993 and fell back to three regional seats in 1994. In the 1996 contests the PA again failed at national level, while improving to four seats in the Andalusian assembly. It contested the June 1999 European elections as part of the European Coalition (*Coalición Europea*, CE) of regional parties, winning one of the CE's two seats, its representative sitting in the Greens/European Free Alliance group. In March 2000 the party regained national representation, winning one lower house seat with 0.9% of the vote, but failing to hold its seat in 2004.

ARAGON

Regional assembly elections on May 28, 2003, resulted as follows: PSOE 27, PP 22 Aragonese Party 8, Aragonese Union 9, IU 1.

Aragonese Party
Partido Aragonés (PAR)
Address. Coso 87, 50001 Zaragoza, Aragon
Telephone. (34–976) 200–616
Fax. (34–976) 200–987
Website. www.partidoaragones.es
Leadership. José Angel Biel (president)
Officially called the Aragonese Regionalist Party (*Partido Aragonés Regionalista*) until 1990, the PAR was founded in January 1978 to campaign for greatly increased internal autonomy for the provinces of Aragon within the Spanish state. Having its main strength in Zaragoza, it secured one of the region's 13 seats in the national lower house in 1977, retaining it in 1979. In the 1982 general elections the PAR was allied with the conservative Popular Alliance (later the

Popular Party) and lost its seat. It became the third-largest bloc in the regional assembly in the May 1983 elections, which gave it 13 seats. Standing alone in the 1986 national elections, it regained a lower house seat. After the 1987 regional elections, which produced no overall majority, the then PAR president, Hipólito Gómez de las Roces, was elected regional premier. The party retained its one national seat in 1989 and 1993, but lost it in 1996 (despite being allied with the PP). In the interim, it won 14 seats in the regional assembly in March 1995. It contested the June 1999 European elections as part of the European Coalition (*Coalición Europea*, CE) of regional parties, failing to win representation.

Aragonese Union (*Chunta Aragonesista,* ChA), of socialist and ecological orientation, advanced from two to five seats in June 1999 regional elections in Aragon and won one national lower house seat in March 2000; claims 2,000 members. In the 2004 legislative elections the Aragonese Union won 0.37% of the vote and 1 seat.
Address. c/ Conde de Aranda 14/16/1°, 50003 Zaragoza
Telephone. (34–97) 628–4242
Fax. (34–97) 628–1311
Email. sedenacional@chunta.com
Website. www.chunta.com
Leadership. Bizén Fuster Santaliestra (chairman); José Antonio Acero (secretary-general)

ASTURIAS

Regional assembly elections on May 28, 2003, resulted as follows: PSOE 22 seats, PP 19, IU 4.

BALEARIC ISLANDS

Regional assembly elections on May 28, 2003, resulted as follows: PP 30 seats, PSOE 15, Socialist Party of Majorca–Nationalists of Majorca 5, Majorcan Union 3, IU 2, Other 5.

Majorcan Union
Unió Mallorquina (UM)
Address. Av. de Joan March 1/3/3, 07004 Palma de Mallorca
Telephone. (34–971) 726–336
Fax. (34–971) 728–116
Email. Um@unio-mallorquina.com
Website. www.unio-mallorquina.com
Leadership. M. Antonia Munar Riutort (secretary-general)
The regionalist UM has a centrist political orientation. It won six of the 52 regional assembly seats in 1983, so that it held the balance of power between the PP and the PSOE. By 1995 it had slipped to only two seats, recovering to three in June 1999. On the latter occasion it contested the European elections as part of the Nationalist Coalition/Europe of the Peoples (*Coalición Nacionalista/Europa de los Pueblos*) alliance, without winning representation.

The UM became an observer member of the Liberal International in 2000.

Socialist Party of Majorca–Nationalists of Majorca
(*Partit Socialista de Mallorca–Nacionalistes de Mallorca,* PSM-NM), left-oriented nationalist formation, won six out of 59 regional assembly seats in 1995, falling to five in 1999. It was able to retain 5 seats in the May 2003 autonomous community elections.
Address. c/Isidoro Antillón 9, baixos, 07006-Ciutat de Mallorca, Iles Balears
Telephone. (+34) 971775252
Fax. +971 77 48 48
Email. mallorca@psm-entesa.org

BASQUE COUNTRY (EUSKADI)

Regional assembly elections on May 13, 2001, resulted as follows: Basque Nationalist Party/Basque Solidarity alliance 33 seats, PP 19, Basque Socialist Party-Basque Left 13, We Basques 7, IU 3.

Basque Nationalist Party
Partido Nacionalista Vasco (PNV)
Euzko Alderdi Jeltzalea (EAJ)

Address. Ibáñez de Bilbao 16, 48001 Bilbao, Euzkadi
Telephone. (34–94) 403 94 00
Fax. (34–94) 403 94 12
Email. ebb@eaj-pnv.com
Website. www.eaj-pnv.com
Leadership. Juan José Ibarretxe Markuartu (*lehendakari* of Basque government); Xabier Arzallus Antía (president); Ricardo Ansotegui (secretary)

Dating from 1895, the Christian democratic PNV stands for an internally autonomous Basque region (including Navarra) within Spain and is opposed to the terrorist campaign for independence waged by the Basque Homeland and Liberty (*Euzkadi ta Azkatasuna*, ETA), although it favours dialogue with the ETA political wing. It opposes unrestrained capitalism and supports a mixed economy.

The PNV developed from the Basque Catholic traditionalist movement led by its founder, Sabino Arana y Goiri. It returned seven deputies to the Spanish *Cortes* in 1918, 12 in 1933 and nine in 1936, succeeding in the latter year in establishing an autonomous Basque government under José Antonio Aguirre. Allied with the republican regime in the Spanish civil war, its leadership was forced into exile by Gen. Franco's victory, and the party was suppressed throughout the Franco era. Aguirre died in 1960 and the Basque "government in exile" nominated Jesus María de Leizaola to succeed him as *lendakari* (president of the Basque government).

In the 1977 Spanish general elections the PNV won seven seats in the Congress of Deputies and eight in the Senate; its representatives abstained in the parliamentary vote on the 1978 constitution, and its supporters were among the 56% of voters in Guipúzcoa and Vizcaya (the two largest Basque provinces) who abstained in the ensuing referendum. It lost one of its seats in Congress in 1979, but in that year's elections to the Basque general junta the PNV won 73 of the 171 seats in the two main provinces, whereupon de Leizaola returned from France, ending the 43-year-old "government in exile". In the March 1980 elections to the new Basque parliament it won 37.6% of the vote and 25 of the 60 seats. The then PNV leader, Carlos Garaikoetxea, became *lendakari* of the autonomous Basque government in April 1980.

In 1982 the PNV secured eight seats in the Spanish Congress and nine in the Senate. In the February 1984 Basque elections it won 42% of the vote and 32 of the 75 seats. Garaikoetxea was forced to resign due to intra-party disputes in December 1984, and in February 1985 was succeeded as party leader by Xabier Arzallus and as *lendakari* by José Antonio Ardanza Garro, a PNV member, who agreed a "pact of government" with the Basque Socialist Party (later the Basque Socialist Party–Basque Left, PSE–EE). In June 1986 the PNV's representation in the *Cortes* fell to six seats in the lower chamber and seven in the upper. The party split in September, with supporters of Garaikoetxea leaving to form Basque Solidarity (EA). In the Basque elections of November 1986 the PNV held only 17 of its seats and was again obliged to govern in coalition with the PSE (which won fewer votes but more seats than the PNV).

In January and March 1989 the PNV organized huge demonstrations in Bilbao calling upon separatist militants to end their armed struggle. However, subsequent efforts to form an electoral alliance with the EA and the Basque Left (EE) failed, with the result that in October 1989 the PNV's national representation fell to five Congress and four Senate seats, although it was confirmed as the largest party in the 1990 Basque parliament elections, with 22 seats. The PNV again won five lower house seats in the 1993 general elections, after which the PNV usually gave external support to the PSOE minority government. In the June 1994 European Parliament election the PNV headed a regional list which won 2.8% of the vote and two seats, one of which was taken by a PNV candidate. In regional elections in October 1994, the PNV won 22 of the 75 Basque parliament seats and formed a coalition with the Basque Socialist Party–Basque Left (PSE–EE).

In the March 1996 national elections the PNV retained five lower house seats and improved from three to four in the Senate. The following month it joined with the Catalan Convergence and Union and the Canarian Coalition in undertaking to give external parliamentary support to a minority Popular Party (PP) government, in exchange for certain concessions to its regionalist agenda. Having withdrawn its backing for the PP national government in September 1997, the PNV fell out with the PSE-EE in the regional government in June 1998. In the October 1998 Basque regional elections, held a month after ETA had declared a ceasefire, the PNV slipped to 21 seats under the new leadership of Juan José Ibarretxe Markuartu. It nevertheless became the leading party in the region's first-ever wholly nationalist coalition, including the EA and, controversially, ETA's political wing, We Basques (EH). In the June 1999 European elections the PNV was part of the Nationalist Coalition/Europe of the Peoples (*Coalición Nacionalista/Europa de los Pueblos*) regional alliance, winning one seat.

ETA's return to violence in December 1999 appeared to strengthen the appeal of the PNV, which advanced to seven lower house seats and six in the Senate in the March 2000 national elections. In early regional elections in May 2001, moreover, a joint PNV–EA list won a commanding 33 seats (out of 75) and 43% of the vote in a high turnout, with the PNV taking 25 seats. It therefore claimed that the public supported its policy of dialogue with ETA and that the PP government in Madrid had failed in its efforts to tarnish the party with association with terrorism. Ruling out any further co-operation with the EH while ETA violence continued, Ibarretxe formed a minority coalition with the EA and the Basque United Left (which had won three seats). In the 2004 national elections it won 1.63% of the vote and 7 seats.

The PNV's European Parliament representative sits in the Greens/European Free Alliance group. The party was for many years a member of the Christian Democrat International, but in 2000 it was expelled on the proposal of the PP because of its advocacy of dialogue with ETA.

Basque Socialist Party–Basque Left
Partido Socialista de Euskadi–Euskadiko Ezkerra (PSE-EE)

Address. Plaza de San José 3, Bilbao 9, Euzkadi
Telephone. (34–94) 424–1606
Leadership. José María (Txiki) Benegas (president); Nicolás Redondo Terreros (secretary-general)

The PSE–EE was created in March 1993 when the PSE (the autonomous Basque federation of the Spanish Socialist Workers' Party, PSOE) merged with the smaller and more radical EE. The merged party continued with the PSE's pro-autonomy line, whereas the Marxist EE had previously been committed to independence for the Basque provinces. That the latter was able to accept the PSE's stance for the merged party was in part because its militant pro-independence wing rejected the merger and broke away to maintain the Basque Left (EuE) in being as an independent formation.

Founded in 1977, the PSE won seven seats in the Congress of Deputies in 1977, and five in 1979. It was in an autonomist pact until late 1979, when it parted company with the Basque Nationalist Party (PNV) over the latter's insistence on the necessity of including Navarra in the Basque autonomy statute. However, having won eight lower house seats in the 1982 national elections, the PSE from early 1985 agreed to support a PNV administration. In June 1986, for the first time, the PSE–PSOE won more seats in the Congress than any other party in the region, with seven deputies to the PNV's six, although the Socialist vote in the three provinces of the Basque autonomous region was the lowest anywhere in Spain, at around 25%. In November 1986, after a split in the PNV, the PSE was confirmed as the largest single party, winning 19 of the 75 seats in elections to the Basque parliament. Early in 1987 the PSE joined a coalition administration with the PNV, with a PSE member Jesus Eguiguren, being elected president of the parliament. In the 1990 Basque elections the PSE slipped to 16 seats.

The EE had been launched in 1976 as a pro-independence electoral alliance which had as its main component the Basque Revolutionary Party (*Euskal Iraultzarako Alderdia*, EIA), which had been formed by supporters of Mario Onaindía Machiondo, then a political prisoner, as a non-violent Marxist offshoot of the *Politico-Militar* faction of the terrorist group, Basque Nation and Liberty (ETA). Onaindía was secretary-general of the EE for some ten years after its foundation. In June 1977 the EE secured one seat in each chamber of the Spanish parliament, both EE representatives subsequently voting against the 1978 constitution because of its limited provisions for Basque autonomy. The party lost its Senate seat in 1979, but in the 1980 elections to the Basque parliament the EE won 9.7% of the vote and six seats (out of 60). The EIA dissolved itself in mid-1981, and the EE was reorganized shortly afterwards, incorporating Roberto Lertxundi Baraffano's faction of the Basque Communist Party (EPK). It was relaunched in March 1982, as the Basque Left–Left for Socialism alliance (EE–IS), and retained its Congress seat in October. A radical nationalist faction, the New Left (*Nueva Izquierda*), led by José Ignacio Múgica Arregui, broke away from the EE later in 1982; *Ezkerra Marxista*, a similar tendency formed in October 1983, sought to remain within the EE, but the leadership declared its intention to purge any dissident groups. The EE held its six Basque parliament seats in 1984, following which Onaindía resigned as general secretary in January 1985. In 1986 the EE won a second seat in the Congress, and nine in the Basque parliament. In the 1990 Basque elections the EE tally was again six seats.

The merged PSE–EE did not aggregate the two parties' previous electoral support, winning only 12 seats in the 1994 Basque parliament elections, although it joined a regional coalition headed by the PNV. In the October 1998 Basque elections the PSE–EE advanced to 14 seats, thereafter becoming part of the regional opposition. It fell back to 13 seats in May 2001, continuing in opposition after talks on joining a coalition with the PNV had come to nothing.

Basque Solidarity
Eusko Alkartasuna (EA)

Address. Camino de Portuetxe 23/1°, 20009 Donostia-San Sebastián
Telephone. (34–943) 020–130
Fax. (34–943) 020–132
Email. prentsa@euskoalkartasuna.org
Website. www.euskoalkartasuna.org
Leadership. Begoña Errazti Esnal (president); Gorka Knörr Borras (secretary-general)

The EA is a radical nationalist (pro-independence), pacifist and social democratic movement, which rejects revolutionary nationalism. Its ideological determinants have included the anti-communist *Bultzagilleak* group from Guipúzcoa, the traditional nationalists known as *sabinianos* after early nationalist leader Sabino Arana and the *abertzales* or patriots. The party was founded in September 1986 as the Basque Patriots (*Eusko Abertzaleak*) by a breakaway faction of the Basque Nationalist Party (PNV) led by Carlos Garaikoetxea, who as then PNV leader had been *lendakari* (president of the Basque government) in 1980-84. The split precipitated early elections to the Basque parliament in November, when the EA won 14 seats against 17 for the parent party. Its first congress in April 1987 showed that it then had the support of several hundred mayors and local councillors.

In January 1987 the EA agreed a joint programme for government with the Basque Left (EE/EuE), this document later applying to the EA's relations with the radical EuE following the main EE's decision to create the Basque Socialist Party–Basque Left. In June 1987 the EA contested European Parliament elections as part of the autonomist Europe of the People's Coalition (EPC), with Garaikoetxea winning a seat. In November the EA declined to sign an inter-party Basque accord against terrorism paralleling that signed by parties in the Spanish parliament; the EA stated that the accord did not address the fundamental issues of self-determination and national reintegration. It slipped to nine seats in the 1990 Basque parliament elections and to eight in 1994, but retained its single national lower house seat in the March 1996 elections on a joint list with the EuE.

The EA won only six seats in the October 1998 Basque regional elections but joined a minority coalition with the PNV and We Basques, the first to be formed entirely by nationalist parties. In the June 1999 European elections it was part of the Nationalist Coalition/Europe of the Peoples (*Coalición Nacionalista/Europa de los Pueblos*) alliance, winning one seat, whose holder joined Greens/European Free Alliance group. Under the new leadership of Begoña Errazti Esnal, the EA retained its single national seat in March 2000 and recovered to eight seats in Basque regional elections in May 2001, standing on a joint list with the PNV. It was allocated three portfolios in the resultant PNV-led government. The EA secured 0.32% of the vote and 1 seat in the last legislative elections in 2004.

The EA is a member of the Democratic Party of the Peoples of Europe–European Free Alliance.

We Basques
Euskal Herritarrok (EH)

Address. Astarioa 8/3°, 48001 Bilbao, Euzkadi
Telephone. (34–943) 424–0799
Fax. (34–943) 423–5932
Leadership. Arnaldo Otegi

The EH was launched in 1998 as successor to United People (*Herri Batasuna*, HB) following action against the latter by the Spanish authorities. A Marxist-oriented Basque nationalist formation, HB/EH has called for the withdrawal of "occupation forces", i.e. the Spanish military and police, and negotiations leading to the complete independence of Euzkadi. It is regarded as the closest of the main parties to the illegal terrorist group Basque Nation and Liberty (*Euzkadi ta Askatasuna*, ETA).

HB was founded in 1978 as an alliance of two legal Basque nationalist groups, the social democratic Basque Nationalist Action (*Accion Nacionalista Vasca*, ANV), formed in 1930, and the Basque Socialist Party (*Euskal Socialista Biltzarrea*, ESB), formed in 1976, with two illegal groups, the People's Revolutionary Socialist Party (HASI) and the Patriotic Workers' Revolutionary Party (LAIA). HASI and LAIA had formed the *Koordinadora Abertzale*

Sozialista (KAS), which functioned in effect as the political wing of the main ETA faction, ETA *Militar*, and the KAS manifesto was adopted more or less in full by HB.

HB contested Basque and Spanish elections from 1979, when it won three seats (which it refused to occupy) in the Spanish Congress of Deputies, one in the Senate and a total of 48 seats (out of 248) in the provincial assemblies of Guipúzcoa, Vizcaya and Navarra. In October 1979 HB called for abstention in the referendum on the creation of an autonomous Basque region excluding Navarra; in a 59% turnout the draft statute was supported by some 90.3% of voters. In March 1980 HB won 16.3% of the vote and 11 of the 60 seats in elections to the new Basque parliament, although it refused to take up its seats in assemblies above the level of *ayuntamientos* (local councils). Although it lost one of its Congress seats in the elections of October 1982, albeit with an increased vote, it won 12 seats (out of 75) in the Basque parliamentary elections of February 1984. Also in 1984 it won a High Court ruling obliging the Interior Ministry to recognize it as a party despite its alleged links with ETA.

In 1986 HB secured five seats in the Spanish Congress, one in the Senate and 13 in the Basque parliament. In February 1987 HB (unsuccessfully) nominated one of its leaders, Juan Carlos Yoldi (then in prison charged with ETA activities), as its candidate for *lendakari* (Basque premier). Also in early 1987 HB called for the formulation of a joint nationalist strategy with the Basque Nationalist Party (PNV) and Basque Solidarity (EA). In June 1987 an HB candidate was elected to the European Parliament (with 1.7% of the national vote). In January 1988 HB was the only one of the seven parties represented in the Basque parliament which was not invited to sign a pact against terrorism.

In the 1989 national elections HB lost one lower house seat and surprised observers by announcing that it would occupy its four remaining seats, ending a decade-long boycott of representation at that level. However, on the eve of the opening of parliament, HB deputy-elect Josh Muguruza was killed and HB leader Iñaki Esnaola wounded in an attack apparently carried out by right-wing terrorists. Later, the remaining HB deputies were expelled for refusing to pledge allegiance to the constitution. HB won two Congress seats and one in the Senate in the 1993 national elections, while the October 1994 Basque parliament balloting yielded 11 seats (two less than in 1990). Meanwhile, HB had lost its European Parliament seat in June 1994, its share of the national vote falling to 0.97%. In the 1996 national elections the HB again won two lower house seats.

In December 1997 the entire 23-member HB leadership received seven-year prison terms for "collaborating with an armed band" (i.e. ETA). A new leadership was elected in February 1998, following which the party opted to change its name to *Euskal Herritarrok* (EH) and to take its seats in the regional parliament. In the October 1998 Basque elections EH improved to 14 seats, whereupon the party took the historic step of joining a minority regional government headed by the PNV and including the EA. In the June 1999 European Parliament elections the EH regained a seat with a 1.5% national vote share, its representative becoming one of the non-attached members. The following month the old HB leadership was released from prison.

ETA's decision to call off a 14-month truce in December 1999 damaged the EH in terms of electoral support. Having failed to win any seats in the March 2000 national elections, it slumped to only seven seats (with 10% of the vote) in the Basque regional elections in May 2001, following which it went into opposition to a PNV-led coalition. Shortly before the summer 2002, the Cortes decided to declare EH/HB and all related political groups illegal. Both the PP and PSOE were supportive of this measure, due to the continuing ter-rorist acts of violence perpetrated by ETA. HB/EH was not allowed to take part in the municipal elections of May 28, 2003.

Other Parties

Alavan Unity (*Unidad Alavesa*, UA), a Popular Party splinter group founded in 1989, campaigning for recognition of the rights of the province of Alava within the Basque Country. It won three seats in the 1990 Basque parliament elections, five in 1994 and two in 1998.
Leadership. Pablo Mosquera Mata (president), Enriqueta Benito Bengara(secretary-general)
Email.ua@unidadalavesa.es

Basque Left (*Euskal Ezkerra*, EuE), formed by militant pro-independence elements of the previous Basque Left grouping who rejected the 1993 merger with the Basque federation of the Spanish Socialist Workers' Party to create the Basque Socialist Party–Basque Left. In the March 1996 national elections the EuE presented a joint list with Basque Solidarity, returning one deputy to the lower house, but the alliance was not sustained in subsequent national and regional elections.
Address. Jardines 5/1°, 48005 Bilbao, Euzkadi
Leadership. Xabier Gurrutxaga (secretary-general)

CANARY ISLANDS

Regional assembly elections on May 23, 2003, resulted as follows: Canarian Coalition 22 seats, PSOE 18, PP 17, Other 3.

Canarian Coalition
Coalición Canaria (CC)
Address. Galcerán 7–9, 38003 Santa Cruz de Tenerife
Telephone. (+34) 922 279 702
Fax. (+34) 922 280 957
Leadership. Paulino Rivero (president)
Website. www.coalicioncanaria.es
The broadly centrist CC was created prior to the 1993 general elections by the following parties: (i) the Canarian Independent Groupings (*Agrupaciones Independientes de Canarias*, AIC) led by Manuel Hermoso Rojas and Paulino Rivero; (ii) the Canarian Independent Centre (*Centro Canario Independiente*, CCI) led by Lorenzo Olarte Cullén; (iii) the Canarian Initiative/Left (*Iniciativa/Izquierda Canaria*, ICAN) led by José Mendoza Cabrero and José Carlos Mauricio Rodríguez; and (iv) the Majorca Assembly (*Asamblea Majorera*, AM) led by José Miguel Barragan Cabrera.

Of these components, the AIC was formed in 1985 as an alliance of Hermoso's *Agrupación Tinerfeña Independiente* (ATI) of Santa Cruz de Tenerife with the *Agrupación Palmera Independiente* (API) of Las Palmas and the *Agrupación Gomera Independiente* (AGI) of Tenerife. In the June 1986 general elections the AIC won about 60,000 votes, securing one seat in the Congress of Deputies and two in the Senate. The AIC retained one lower house seat in the 1989 general elections and was subsequently the only party to support Prime Minister González's re-election apart from his own Spanish Socialist Workers' Party (PSOE). In the 1991 Canaries regional elections the AIC, with 16 seats, took second place behind the PSOE and the AIC candidate, Manuel Hermoso Rojas, was elected to the island presidency with support from the ICAN (five seats), the AM (two) and other parties.

In the 1993 national elections the CC returned four deputies and six senators, who subsequently gave qualified support to the minority PSOE government. In June 1994 the

CC captured one seat in elections to the European Parliament. In September 1994 the CC-led regional government lost its narrow majority when the Canarian Nationalist Party (PNC) left the alliance. In the May 1995 regional elections the CC obtained a plurality of 21 assembly seats out of 60 and continued to lead the islands' government. In the March 1996 national elections the CC retained four lower house seats but won only two of the directly elected Senate seats. It thereupon pledged qualified external support for a minority government of the centre-right Popular Party (PP).

The CC increased its regional representation to 25 seats in June 1999, thus retaining leadership of the islands' government. In simultaneous European elections the CC was part of the European Coalition (*Coalición Europea*) of moderate regional parties, winning one seat. In the March 2000 national elections the CC again won four lower house seats and increased its representation in the Senate to five seats. Although the PP now had an absolute majority, it again concluded an external support agreement with the CC. It received 0.86% of the vote and 3 seats in the 2004 legislative elections.

The CC's representative in the European Parliament sits in the European Liberal, Democratic and Reformist group.

Other Parties

Canarian Nationalist Party (*Partido Nacionalista Canario*, PNC), was original component of Canarian Coalition, but withdrew in 1994, winning four seats in 1995 Canaries regional elections.
Address. Sagasta 92, 35008 Las Palmas de Gran Canaria
Telephone/Fax. (34–928) 221–736
Leadership. Pablo Betancor Betancor & José Luis Alamo Suárez

Hierro Independent Grouping (*Agrupación Herreña Independiente*, AHI), won one regional assembly seat in 1995 and two in 1999.
Address. La Constitución 4, 38900 Valverde, El Hierro, Santa Cruz de Tenerife
Telephone. (34–922) 551–34
Fax. (34–922) 551–224
Leadership. Tomás Padrón Hernández

Lanzarote Independents' Party (*Partido de Independientes de Lazarote*, PIL), returned one candidate to the Senate in the March 2000 national elections.
Leadership. Juan Pedro Hernández Rodríguez

National Congress of the Canaries (*Congreso Nacional de Canarias*, CNC), pro-independence group founded in 1986, favours leaving the EU and joining the OAU.
Address. Avda 3 de Mayo 81, 1° y 2°, Santa Cruz de Tenerife
Telephone/Fax. (34–922) 283–353
Leadership. Antoni Cubillo Ferreira

CANTABRIA

Regional assembly elections on May 28, 2003, resulted as follows: PP 18 seats, PSOE 13, Regionalist Party of Cantabria 8.

Regionalist Party of Cantabria (*Partido Regionalista Cántabro*, PRC), centre-right formation which obtained two of the 35 seats in the May 1983 elections to the regional parliament; by the June 1999 elections it had improved to six seats out of 39.
Leadership. Migel Angel Revilla
Website. www.prc.es

Union for the Progress of Cantabria (*Unión para el Progreso de Cantabria*, UPCA), conservative formation, contested the 1991 regional elections on the Popular Party (PP) list, winning 15 of that list's 21 seats (out of 39). In June 1993, however, the UPCA president of the regional government, Juan Hormaechea Cázon, broke with the PP, with the result that his party was reduced to seven seats in the May 1995 regional elections and lost the government presidency.

CASTILLA Y LEON

Regional assembly elections on May 28, 2003, resulted as follows: PP 48 seats, PSOE 30, Union of the León People 1, IU 1, others 1.

Union of the León People (*Unión del Pueblo Leonés, UPL*), separatist formation that won two seats (out of 84) in the 1995 regional elections, rising to three in 1999, but falling to one in 2003.
Website. www.uniondelpuebloleones.com

CASTILLA–LA MANCHA

Regional assembly elections on May 28, 2003, resulted as follows: PSOE 29 seats, PP 18.

CATALONIA

Regional assembly elections on Oct. 17, 1999, resulted as follows: Convergence and Union 56 seats, Party of Socialists of Catalonia 52, PP 12, Republican Left of Catalonia 12, Initiative for Catalonia/Greens 3.

Convergence and Union
Convergència i Unió (CiU)
Address. Valencia 231, 08007 Barcelona, Catalunya
Telephone. (34–93) 487–0111
Fax. (34–93) 215–8428
Email. gpc.ciu@convergencia.org
Website. www.convergencia-i-unio.org
Leadership. Artur Más i Gavarró (secretary general); Xavier Trias i Vidal de Llobatera (Congress spokesman)
The pro-autonomy CiU was founded in 1979 as an alliance of the Democratic Convergence of Catalonia (*Convergència Democràtica de Catalunya*, CDC) and the Democratic Union of Catalonia (*Unió Democràtica de Catalunya*, UDC), and later absorbed the small Catalan Democratic Left Party (*Esquerra Democràtica de Catalunya*, EDC). The CDC and UDC had contested the 1977 general elections as part of a Democratic Pact (*Pacte Democràtic*), which obtained 11 seats in the Congress of Deputies (and voted for the 1978 constitution). In the 1979 elections the CiU won eight seats in the Congress and one in the Senate. In elections to the new Catalan parliament in March 1980 the CiU displaced the Party of Socialists of Catalonia (PSC) as the region's main political force, winning 28% of the vote and 43 of the 135 seats. Pujol was elected premier of the *Generalitat* (the Catalan administration) and formed a coalition with the local affiliate of the Union of the Democratic Centre, then the ruling party in Madrid, and a number of independents. In the October 1982 general elections the CiU increased its representation in the Spanish Congress to 12 members (and nine in the Senate). In the April 1984 Catalan elections the CiU won 46.8% of the vote and 72 seats, enabling it to form a majority administration.

In the 1986 national elections the CiU returned 18 deputies and eight senators, thus becoming the fourth-largest party in the Spanish parliament. It was allied with the new liberal Democratic Reformist Party (PRD), which failed to win any seats, their joint candidate for Prime Minister having been Miquel Roca Junyent, the CiU parliamentary leader who had formed the PRD and was regarded as the national leader of the reformist–liberal bloc. The CiU obtained three seats in the 1987 European Parliament elections. In March 1992 the CiU confirmed its regional dominance by winning 71 of the 135 seats in the Catalan assembly, while national elections in June 1993 yielded 17 lower house and 14 Senate seats, on a vote share of nearly 5%. The party thereafter gave qualified parliamentary support to the minority government of the Spanish Socialist Workers' Party (PSOE). In June 1994 the CiU retained three seats in the European Parliament elections with 4.7% of the vote.

The travails of the PSOE government in 1994–95 encouraged the CiU to attach more autonomist conditions to its continued support, beyond the original demand for greater transfer of tax receipts to the Catalan government. After much confusion, the CESID phone-tapping scandal of mid-1995 finally impelled the CiU into formal opposition and support for new general elections. This switch enabled the party to maintain its ascendancy in regional elections in Catalonia in November 1995, although it fell back to 60 seats (out of 135). Held in March 1996, early national elections resulted in the CiU slipping to 16 lower house and eight Senate seats, with 4.6% of the overall vote. After protracted negotiations, the CiU agreed to give external support to a minority government of the anti-regionalization Popular Party (PP), which in return was obliged to swallow a dose of further devolution and to express admiration for Catalan culture. Featuring a doubling (to 30%) of tax receipt transfers from Madrid to Barcelona (and to the other autonomous regions), the deal with the PP was approved by the CiU executive in late April 1996 by 188 votes to 20 with 21 abstentions.

The CiU retained three seats in the June 1999 European elections (two for the CDC and one for the UDC), with 4.4% of the vote. In regional elections in October 1999 the CiU's long dominance came under serious challenge from the PSC, but the party just managed to remain the largest party with 56 seats (though with only 37.7% of the vote against 37.9% for the PSC). Pujol was therefore able to form a further minority administration. In the March 2000 national elections the CiU declined further to 15 lower house seats (with 4.2% of the vote), while retaining eight Senate seats. Although the PP now had an absolute majority, it again concluded an external support agreement with the CiU. In spite of several political scandals related to alleged abuse of power and misappropriation of funds as in the Pallerols case, Jordi Pujol was able to hold on to the presidency of the *generalitat* with the regional parliamentary support of the PP. He retired at the end of the legislature and was replaced by Artur Mas. In the regional elections of November 2003, the CiU was ousted from the regional government by the PSC. The CiU secured 3.24% of the vote and 10 seats in the 2004 national elections.

Of the CiU components, the UDC is affiliated to the Christian Democrat International and its representative in the European Parliament sits in the European People's Party/European Democrats group. The two CDC representatives sit in the European Liberal, Democratic and Reformist group.

Initiative for Catalonia–Greens
Iniciativa per Catalunya–Verts (IC-V)
Address. Ciutat 7, 08002 Barcelona, Catalunya
Telephone. (34–93) 301–0612
Fax. (34–93) 412–4252
Email. iniciativa@ic-v.org
Website. www.ic-v.org
Leadership. Joan Saura (president)
The IC was launched in 1986 as an alliance of Communist and other left-wing formations in Catalonia, headed by the Unified Socialist Party of Catalonia (*Partit Socialista Unificat de Catalunya*, PSUC) led by Ribó Massó and also including the Party of Communists of Catalonia (*Partit dels Comunistes de Catalunya*, PCC) and the Union of Left Nationalists (*Entesa des Nacionalistes d'Esquerra*, ENE).

Founded in 1936 by the merger of four left-wing groups, the PSUC took part in the government of Catalonia until 1939, when it was forced underground by the Francoist victory. Legalized again in 1976, it became a member of the provisional government of Catalonia. In the 1980 elections to the new Catalan parliament the PSUC obtained 19% of the vote and 25 of the 135 seats; but in the 1984 elections it was reduced to six seats and 5.8% of the vote. In the June 1986 national elections the PSUC retained the single seat in the Congress of Deputies which it had won in 1982 (as against eight won in 1979 and 1977).

Contesting the 1992 regional and 1993 national elections as effectively the Catalan version of the national United Left, the IC made little impact. For the November 1995 regional elections it formed an alliance with the Catalan Greens (*Els Verds*), their joint list obtaining 11 of the 135 seats. It maintained the alliance in the October 1999 regional elections but also gave tactical support to the Party of Socialists of Catalonia and confined its own effort to Barcelona, with the result that its representation fell to three seats. In the March 2000 national elections a joint IC–Green list won a single lower house seat.

Party of Socialists of Catalonia
Partit dels Socialistes de Catalunya (PSC)
Address. Calle Nicaragua 75–77, 08029 Barcelona, Catalunya
Telephone. (34–93) 495–5400
Fax. (34–3) 495–5435
Email. psc@psc.es
Website. www.psc.es
Leadership. Pasqual Maragall (president); Narcís Serra (first secretary)
The PSC is affiliated to, but not formally part of, the Spanish Socialist Workers' Party (PSOE), pursuing similar economic and social policies but seeking the transformation of the current autonomist constitution into a federal one. The present party was founded in July 1978 as a merger of three pre-existing socialist formations, including the Catalan branch of the PSOE. After winning 15 lower house seats in the 1977 national elections, the following year the PSC affiliated to the PSOE, contesting subsequent national elections as a federation of the Spanish party.

In the 1979 general elections the PSC returned 17 lower house deputies, but was defeated by the centrist Convergence and Union (CiU) alliance in the 1980 elections to the Catalan parliament, obtaining 33 of the 135 seats. In the 1982 national elections the PSC won an absolute majority (25) of the Catalan seats in the lower house. In the 1984 Catalan elections it obtained 30% of the vote and 41 seats, while in the 1986 national elections it fell back to 21 seats but remained ahead of other Catalan parties. The same pattern of ascendancy in national contests and inferiority at regional level was apparent in subsequent elections. In the November 1995 Catalan elections the PSC won 34 seats (against 39 in 1992), again coming a distant second to the CiU.

In June 1999 three PSC members were elected to the European Parliament on the PSOE list. In the October 1999 regional elections the PSC mounted a strong challenge against the CiU, on a platform of less strident Catalan nationalism and greater accommodation with the rest of Spain. It outpolled the CiU in popular vote terms (37.9% to 37.7%) and increased its representation to 52 seats, but narrowly failed to become the leading party and so remained in opposition. Pasqual Maragall continued vigorous opposition to the presidency of Pujol throughout the regional legislature (1999-2003). Pascual Maragall's PSC then won the regional elections of November 2003 and formed a coalition government with ERC.

Republican Left of Catalonia
Esquerra Republicana de Catalunya (ERC)
Address. c/ Villarroel 45 ent., 08011 Barcelona, Catalonia
Telephone. (34–93) 453–6005
Fax. (34–93) 323–7122
Email. info@esquerra.org
Website. www.esquerra.org
Leadership. Josep Lluís Carod-Rovira (secretary-general and parliamentary leader); Jordí Carbonell (president)

Dating from 1931, the ERC was the majority party in the Catalan parliament of 1932 but was forced underground during the Franco era. Re-legalized in 1977, it adopted a moderate left-wing economic programme, also advocating Catalan self-determination and defining languages other than Catalan as foreign. It contested the June 1977 national elections along with the *Partido del Trabajo de España*, other groups and independent candidates in an alliance, the *Esquerra de Catalunya–Front Electoral Democràtic*, and elected one deputy. In 1979 the ERC allied with the *Front Nacional de Catalunya*, and won one seat each in the Spanish Congress of Deputies and the Senate. In elections for the new Catalan parliament in March 1980 the ERC gained 9% of the vote and 14 of the 135 seats. In the October 1982 Spanish elections it held its single seat in the Congress, and in the Catalan elections in April 1984 it won 4.4% and its strength was reduced to five members.

The ERC divided during the 1980s between a liberal wing, which favoured participation in the Catalan *Generalitat* (government), and the left, which favoured an independent line. The 15th (1985) ERC congress elected the liberal Joan Hortalà i Arau (the Catalan industry minister) as the party's leader, succeeding the more nationalistic Heribert Barrera i Costa. The 1986 elections deprived the ERC of its representation in the Madrid parliament, but in 1987 the party was part of the Europe of the Peoples Coalition (CEP) that secured a seat in the European Parliament (this being retained in 1989 but lost in 1994).

In 1991 the ERC absorbed the radical separatist Free Land (*Terre Lliure*) movement, the consequences being a switch from a pro-federalism line to advocacy of outright independence for Catalonia. The ERC retained its single seat in the national lower house in the 1993, 1996 and 2000 elections. In Catalonia it won 11 of 135 regional parliament seats in 1992, rising to 13 in November 1995. The ERC was part of the Nationalist Coalition/Europe of the Peoples (*Coalición Nacionalista/Europa de los Pueblos*) of regional parties in the June 1999 European elections, though it failed to win one of the Coalition's two seats.

In the October 1999 regional elections the ERC slipped to 12 seats on a vote share of 8.7%. However, the ERC was able to make important gains in the local elections of May 28, 2003 and this continued when in the national elections of March 2004 the ERC secured 2.54% of the vote and 8 seats.

Having some 5,000 members, the ERC is a member of the Democratic Party of the Peoples of Europe–European Free Alliance.

Other Party

Liberty and Democracy (*Libertat i Democracia,* LiD), the small centrist LiD has made little electoral impact, although it has been a member of the Liberal International since 1975.

EXTREMADURA

Regional elections on May 28, 2003, resulted as follows: PSOE 36 seats, PP 26, IU 3.

GALICIA

Regional elections on Oct. 21, 2001, resulted as follows: PP 41, Galician Nationalist Bloc 17, Party of Galician Socialists 17.

Galician Nationalist Bloc
Bloque Nacionalista Galego (BNG)
Address. Avda Rodríquez de Viguri, Bloque 3 Baixo, 15703 Santiago de Compostela, Galicia
Telephone. (34–981) 555–850
Fax. (34–981) 555–851
Email. beiras@bng-galiza.org
Website. www.bng-galiza.org
Leadership. Xosé Manuel Beiras (secretary-general)

Founded in 1983, the BNG advocates greater autonomy for Galicia and moderate left-wing economic policies. In 1991 it absorbed the more centrist Galician National Party (*Partido Nacionalista Galego*, PNG) led by Pablo González Mariñas, which had been formed in 1986 by a progressive faction of the Galician Coalition. The BNG's regional electoral support rose steadily, from five seats in 1989, 13 in 1993 and 18 in October 1997. Meanwhile, it had won two lower house seats in the 1996 national elections. Having taken one seat in the June 1999 European elections (with 1.7% of the national vote), the BNG improved its national lower house representation to three seats in March 2000 but lost one of its regional seats in October 2001. In the national elections of March 2004, the BNG secured 0.8% and 2 seats.

The BNG's representative in the European Parliament sits in the Greens/European Free Alliance group.

Party of Galician Socialists
Partido dos Socialistas de Galicia (PSdG)
Address. Pino 1–9, 15704 Santiago de Compostela
Telephone. (34–981) 589–622
Leadership. Emilio Pérez Touriño (secretary-general)

The PSdG is the autonomous regional federation of the Spanish Socialist Workers' Party (PSOE). Although it increased its representation in the Galician parliament from 17 seats to 22 in 1985, control of the Xunta passed to what became the Popular Party (PP). The PSdG re-established control in 1987, but went into opposition to the PP after the 1989 regional elections, despite advancing to 28 seats. It slumped to 19 seats in the 1993 regional elections and continued in opposition, falling further to 15 seats in October 1997, when it was allied with the regional United Left–Galiciian Left (*Esquerda Unida–Esquerda Galega*, EU-EG) and the Greens. In the October 2001 regional elections the PSdG recovered to 17 seats.

MADRID

Regional elections on May 28, 2003, resulted as follows: PP 55 seats, PSOE 47, IU 9.

MURCIA

Regional elections on May 28, 2003, resulted as follows: PP 28 seats, PSOE 16, IU 1.

NAVARRE

Regional elections on May 28, 2003, resulted as follows: Union of the Navarrese People 23 seats, Socialist Party of Navarra 11, Nationalist Basque Party 4.

Socialist Party of Navarra
Partido Socialista de Navarra (PSN)
Address. c/o Regional Assembly, Pamplona, Navarra
Leadership. Víctor Manuel Arbeloa (president); Juan José Lizarbe (secretary-general)
The PSN is the regional federation of the Spanish Socialist Workers' Party (PSOE). Formed in 1975 as the *Federación Socialista de Navarra*, it was integrated into the PSOE in 1982, although it retained its own identity and structure. Having won 19 of the 50 regional seats in 1991, the PSN was in opposition to the Union of the Navarrese People until the 1995 elections, in which it fell back to 11 seats but nevertheless secured the election of Javier Otano as regional premier by virtue of support from other parties. It again won 11 seats in the 1999 and 2003 regional elections.

Union of the Navarrese People
Union del Pueblo Navarro (UPN)
Address. Plaza Príncipe de Viana 1/4°, 31002 Pamplona, Navarra
Telephone. (34–948) 223 402
Fax. (34–948) 210–810
Email. info@upn.org
Leadership. Miguel Sanz Sesma (president); Albert Catalán Higueras (secretary-general)
Founded in 1979, the conservative and Christian democratic UPN won a single seat in the Congress of Deputies in 1979 but lost it in 1982. In the 1982 and 1986 national elections the UPN allied with the right-wing Popular Alliance, precursor of the Popular Party (PP); it also co-operated with the Popular Democratic Party (PDP) and the Liberal Union (UL), now the Liberal Party. In the 1983 Navarra regional elections the UPN (then led by Javier Gomara) won 13 of the 50 seats, increasing to 14 in 1987 and to a plurality of 20 in 1991, when its candidate Juan Cruz Alli Aranguren was elected president of the regional government. It slipped to 17 seats in 1995 and went into opposition to a coalition headed by the Socialist Party of Navarra but won 22 seats in 1999.

LA RIOJA

Regional assembly elections on May 28, 2003, resulted as follows: PP 17 seats, PSOE 14, Rioja Party 2.

Rioja Party
Partido Riojano (PR)
Address. Portales 17/1°, 26001 Logroño, La Rioja
Telephone. (34–941) 238–199
Fax. (34–941) 254–396
Leadership. Miguel González de Legarra (president); Alejandro Fernandez de la Pradilla Ochoa (secretary-general)
This small regionalist grouping has attempted, with little success, to challenge the dominance in the Rioja region of the national parties (mainly the PP and the PSOE, the latter organized locally as the *Partido Socialista de La Rioja*). It has usually returned two candidates in regional elections.

VALENCIA

Regional elections on May 28, 2003, resulted as follows: PP 48 seats, Socialist Party of Valencia 36, Unity of the Valencian People 5.

Socialist Party of Valencia
Partido Socialista del País Valenciano (PSPV)
Address. Almirante 3, 46003 Valencia
Leadership. Antonio García Miralles (president); Antoni Asunción (secretary-general)
The PSPV is the autonomous Valencian wing of the Spanish Socialist Workers' Party (PSOE) and was the dominant Valencian party in regional and national elections of the 1980s and early 1990s. In the 1995, 1999 and 2003 regional elections, however, it came a poor second to the Popular Party.

Unity of the Valencian People
Unitat del Poble Valencià (UPV)
Leadership. Pere Mayor Penadés (chairman)
The UPV was founded in 1982 by two regionalist parties as a "democratic, left nationalist, egalitarian, ecologist and pacifist" formation; in alliance with the United Left, it won two regional seats in 1987, failed to win representation in 1995 and advanced to five seats in 1999.

CEUTA AND MELILLA

Under legislation approved in September 1994, the North African enclaves of Ceuta and Melilla acquired full autonomous status as regions of Spain. Political life in both possessions was dominated until recently by local branches of metropolitan formations, notably the Popular Party (PP) and the Spanish Socialist Workers' Party (PSOE). However, elections on May 28, 2003, in Ceuta resulted in the newly-founded Independent Liberal Group (GIL) winning 12 seats, against eight for the PP, two for the PSOE and three for others, while in Melilla the GIL won seven seats, the Coalition for Melilla five, the PP five, the PSOE two and others six.

Independent Liberal Group (*Grupo Independiente Liberal,* GIL), led by the mayor of the mainland city of Marbella, won pluralities in both Ceuta and Melilla in June 1999, on a platform of closer integration of the enclaves with mainland Spain.
Leadership. Jesús Gil (secretary-general)

Initiative for Ceuta (*Iniciativa por Ceuta, IC*), leftist grouping formed in December 1990, based in the Muslim community and named after the Initiative for Catalonia.

Progress and Future of Ceuta (*Progreso y Futuro de Ceuta, PFC*), supports continued Spanish status, won six Ceuta assembly seats in 1995, its leader being elected government president with support from other parties.

Coalition for Melilla (*Coalición por Melilla, CpM*), won five seats in 1999 and 2003 elections.

Union of the Melilla People (*Unión del Pueblo Melillense, UPM*), right-wing formation founded in 1985.

Sri Lanka

Capital: Colombo
Population: 18,500,000 (2001E)

Ceylon gained its independence from the United Kingdom in 1948, and in 1972 was redesignated the Republic of Sri Lanka. Under the present constitution, promulgated in 1978, its name was changed again to the Democratic Socialist Republic of Sri Lanka, and a presidential form of government was adopted. The President, who is directly elected by universal suffrage for a six-year term, has the power to appoint or dismiss members of the Cabinet, including the Prime Minister, and to dissolve Parliament. The unicameral Parliament has 225 members, directly elected for a period of six years under a system of proportional representation first introduced in 1989.

In a general election held on Aug. 16, 1994, the United National Party (UNP), in power since 1977, was defeated by a left-wing coalition, the People's Alliance, which emerged as the largest grouping. Chandrika Bandaranaike Kumaratunga was sworn in as Prime Minister of a coalition government dominated by her Sri Lanka Freedom Party (SLFP), and including the Lanka Equal Society Party (LSSP), the Democratic United National Front (DUNF), the Sri Lanka Muslim Congress (SLMC), the Communist Party of Sri Lanka (CPSL) and later, the Ceylon Workers' Congress (CWC).

On Nov. 12, 1994, Kumaratunga was elected President with 62.3% of the popular vote, being succeeded as Prime Minister by her mother, Sirimavo Bandaranaike. Kumaratunga's first term in office was dominated by the civil war against the Liberation Tigers of Tamil Ealam (LTTE) and, after her peace strategy based on constitutional reform was blocked in Parliament, she called an early presidential election in December 1999. This confirmed her in office but with a proportion (51%) of the vote sufficiently reduced for her not to consider calling early parliamentary elections as well. Kumaratunga's new devolutionary constitution was withdrawn in July 2000 when the UNP and moderate Tamil parties withdrew their support and senior Buddhist monks rejected it as threatening the Sinhala ascendancy. When Parliament completed its six-year term, a general election was held on Oct. 11, 2000. Kumaratunga's People's Alliance was returned again as the largest grouping with 107 seats in the 225-member House. To secure a majority for her government, Kumaratunga had to include new elements in her ruling coalition – specifically, the National Unity Alliance (which was part of the SLMC) and the Eelam People's Democratic Party (EPDP) – and expand her cabinet to 44 members (or almost a sixth of the total House). But bitter faction fighting soon broke out within the new government and, in June 2001, the SLMC withdrew its support. Faced with a no-confidence motion, Kumaratunga utilized her presidential prerogative to suspend Parliament for up to 60 days. When the House re-convened on Sept. 3, Kumaratunga revealed that she had obtained backbench support from the Marxist Sinhala ultra-nationalist People's Liberation Front (*Janatha Vimukthi Peramuna*, JVP), to sustain the government. However, further defections from the ruling coalition followed and, on Oct. 11, 2001, she dissolved Parliament and called a new general election for December.

In the elections held on Dec. 5 Kumaratunga's People's Alliance was swept out of power by the UNP and its allies, its representation in Parliament falling to 77 seats, with 37.19% of the vote. The UNP was the largest party in the new Parliament, winning 109 seats with 45.62% of the vote. Together with its allies, the Tamil National Alliance (TNA, 15 seats) group of parties and the Sri Lanka Muslim Congress (SLMC, five seats), it held 129 seats and formed a United National Front (UNF) government on Dec. 12 under UNP leader Prime Minister Ranil Wickremasinghe. The election was reported to be one of the bloodiest in Sri Lanka's history, with 43 people killed during the campaign and 17 on election day itself. The independent Centre for Monitoring Election Violence (CMEV) reported that polling was "severely marred by widespread incidents of violence, rigging and other electoral malpractices".

The result meant that for the first time since Sri Lanka had adopted a presidential system the President found herself heading a government composed of her opponents. Effectively Wickremasinghe now became head of government, assuming powers that had been largely nominal when Kumaratunga had ruled in partnership with a People's Alliance Prime Minister. Kumaratunga with great reluctance handed over her own portfolios of Defence and Finance. The first fruit of this change was the establishment of a reciprocal four-week truce with the separatist LTTE from Dec. 24, renewed in January 2002. With the assistance of Norwegian diplomacy both sides on Feb. 22 signed an indefinite, internationally-monitored ceasefire. Kumaratunga's failure to bring to an end the escalating war against the LTTE – which had caused some 64,500 deaths since 1983 – either through military victory or negotiations, was thought to have been a major factor in the People's Alliance's defeat in the December 2001 elections. Despite occasional breaches of the ceasefire and numerous political obstacles Wickremasinghe's government opened a first round of direct peace negotiations with the LTTE in September 2002, in the same month temporarily lifting the ban on the LTTE so that it could take part in the talks. Kumaratunga, sidelined by the peace process, repeatedly criticized as excessive concessions made by the government's negotiators to the LTTE and more than once threatened to dismiss the government, to dissolve Parliament and also to intervene in her capacity as head of the armed forces. Wickremasinghe meanwhile prepared legislation to curb presidential powers, but in October the Supreme Court ruled that the bill, because of its provisions for constitutional change, required not only a two-thirds majority in Parliament but endorsement in a popular referendum. Neither would be possible without the support of the People's Alliance, which was unlikely to vote to reduce the powers of its own President.

The uneasy cohabitation between Kumaratunga and Wickremasinghe was further threatened in February 2003 when the People's Alliance formed a partnership with the extremist Sinhala JVP, which took a hard line against proposals for Tamil autonomy and was strongly opposed to any concessions to the LTTE. After six rounds of negotiations and despite substantial progress the LTTE in April 2003 suspended its participation in peace talks while still maintaining its commitment to the ceasefire. With the peace process stalled it was reported in September that the People's Alliance had proposed establishing a national government with the UNP and its allies. The alliance with the JVP had apparently foundered on the latter's intransigent rejection of most aspects of the negotiations with the LTTE. The government had accepted in principle the solution of a federal structure for Sri Lanka, but any legislation enacting such constitutional change would again require the support of the People's Alliance to achieve the necessary two-thirds majority in Parliament.

Following the publication a few days earlier of the LTTE's proposals for an interim settlement (see below), Kumaratunga on Nov. 4, 2003, executed what amounted to a coup against her own government. Taking advanrtage of Wickremasinghe's absence in the USA for trade negotiations, the President dismissed the Ministers of Defence, Interior and Information – taking over the portfolios herself – and suspended Parliament until Nov. 19. Kumaratunga, who justified these steps as being "in the national interest...to prevent further deterioration of the security situation in the country", also declared a short-lived state of emergency and took control of the state-owned media. She had effectively taken control of the security apparatus and so of the implementation of the peace process. On his return from the USA Wickremasinghe, who had accused her of bringing Sri Lanka to the verge of "chaos and anarchy", held two meetings with Kumaratunga and suggested that she take over personal responsibility for the peace process, whilst the President called for the establishment of a government of national unity including her own PA. The US State Department, which had backed Wickremasinghe's negotiations with the LTTE, warned that Kumaratunga's actions threatened the peace process and urged the two rivals to co-operate. The second meeting between President and Prime Minister on Nov. 18 ended with agreement to establish a committee to devise new arrangements for cohabitation in government, but this failed to produce concrete results.

On Jan. 13, 2004, the political crisis deepened when Kumaratunga announced that she was entitled to hold office as President until December 2006, not December 2005 as expected. This claim was made firstly on the ground that she had called the December 1999 election a year before the end of her previous six-year term, and secondly because she claimed that in 2000 she had undergone a second, private investiture. The legality of this move was regarded as debatable. In February Kumaratunga attempted to break the deadlock with Wickremasinghe by calling legislative elections for April 2, reportedly against the advice of international donors led by the USA, Japan and the EU, who warned her that the polarizing effect of the elections could jeopardize the peace process with the LTTE. The donors had pledged some US$4.5 billion of aid for the reconstruction of Sri Lanka, on condition that the peace talks, suspended since April 2003, were resumed and concrete progress was made towards a final settlement. The SLFP had already in January 2004 made an electoral alliance with the JVP, the United People's Freedom Alliance (UPFA), a partnership that made the prospect of further negotiations with the LTTE problematic, given the JVP's antipathy towards proposals for Tamil autonomy.

There were fears that the election process itself might plunge Sri Lanka into chaos, especially when a seriously rift emerged in the ranks of the LTTE in March (see below), but although five people were killed during the election campaign, the level of violence was much lower than that during the 2001 election. In a high turnout of about 75% of voters the the UPFA emerged as the biggest bloc in the new 225-member Parliament, with 45.6% of the vote and 105 seats against 82 seats for the UNF, eight seats short of a majority. It was reported that the EPDP'S single MP would support a UPFA government, and negotiations began with the CWC, which had run under the banner of the UNF. Analysts said that despite Wickremasinghe's success in achieving an enduring ceasefire with the LTTE, and the consequent beginnings of an economic revival, his economic policies were generally unpopular, especially cuts in agricultural subsidies and provision for the poor, whilst allegations of corruption attached to his government.

Kumaratunga on April 6, 2004, swore in veteran former SLFP minister Mahinda Rajapakse, 58, leader of the opposition in the last Parliament, as Prime Minister, although the JVP, and, reportedly, Kumaratunga herself, were said to have initially favoured former Foreign Minister Lakshman

Kadirgamar for the post. It was noted that the elections left Parliament highly polarized, with a reported 40 seats for the Marxist Sinhala-nationalist JVP, increased representation for the TNA, and unexpected success for a new right-wing Sinhala Buddhist supremacist party, the *Jathika Hela Urumaya* (JHU, National Heritage Party). When the new Parliament met on April 22 the government suffered an immediate reverse when former Justice Minister W.J.M. Lokubandara of the UNP was elected Speaker by 110 votes, against 109 votes for Kumaratunga's candidate, after the first vote had been tied. Several JHU legislators, who had proposed their own candidate, abstained from voting. The Speaker's role was important in controlling Parliament's legislative agenda.

Ceylon Workers' Congress (CWC)

Address. 72 Ananda Coomaraswamy Mawatha, Colombo 07
Telephone. (94-1) 574-524-28
Leadership. Arumugam Thondaman (president)
The CWC is both a trade union (with its main strength being among Tamil workers of Indian origin on tea plantations) and a political party, seen as representing the community of Indian descent. It has held the rural development portfolio in the government since 1978 through changes of administration. It has long been split into two factions. The dominant faction contested the general elections of 1994 and 2000 as part of the People's Alliance (PA) and was represented in government. But a dissident faction stood, on both occasions, under the United National Party (UNP) banner. After the December 2001 election CWC president Arumugam Thondaman joined the United National Front (UNF) government led by the UNP with the Housing and Plantation Infrastructure portfolio. In the April 2004 general election the CWC ran under the UNP/UNF banner. The Department of Elections published no breakdown of the UNP/UNF's 82 seats, but it was reported that the CWC won seven seats and also that Thondaman was considering supporting a government formed by the PA's successor grouping, the United People's Freedom Alliance (UPFA).

Communist Party of Sri Lanka (CPSL)

Address. 91 Dr N.M. Perera Mawatha, Colombo 08
Telephone. (94-1) 688942
Fax. (94-1) 691610
Leadership. D.E.W. Gunasekara (secretary)
Formerly a Soviet-oriented party, founded in 943. It has consistently advocated the nationalization of banks, agricultural estates and industry. The CPSL was instrumental in forming the short-lived United Left Front (UFL) in 1977 with the SLFP and the LSSP and later in the formation of the left-wing People's Alliance (PA) in 1994. Following the victory of the People's Alliance in the 1994 elections, the party secured one Cabinet portfolio in the government led by the Sri Lanka Freedom Party and retained it after the 2000 election. The CPSL fought the December 2001 elections as part of the People's Alliance. The CPSL contended the April 2004 elections as part of the PA's successor grouping, the United People's Freedom Alliance (UPFA), winning only one seat.

Democratic People's Liberation Front (DPLF)

Address. c/o Parliament, Colombo; (secretary) 16 Haig Road, Bambalapitiya, Colombo 04
Telephone. (94-1) 586289
Leadership. Dharmalingam Sithadthan (leader); S. Sathananthan (secretary)
The DPLF is the political wing of the Tamil separatist People's Liberation Organization of Tamil Eelam (PLOTE), and has operated as a national political party since 1988. In the 1994 legislative elections it secured three parliamentary

seats but lost them in the 2000 election. The party secured one seat in the December 2001 general election but lost it in the April 2004 election.

Democratic United National Front (DUNF)
Address. 60 1st Lane, Rawathawatte, Moratuwa
Telephone. (94-1) 645566
Fax. (94-1) 645566
Leadership. Ariyawansha Dissanayake (general secretary)
The DUNF was formed in 1992 by a dissident group of United National Party (UNP) politicians. Following the electoral victory of the People's Alliance in the 1994 legislative polling, the party joined the coalition administration headed by the Sri Lanka Freedom Party and continued to support it in both the 2000 and December 2001 elections.

Eelam People's Democratic Party (EPDP)
Address. 121 Park Road, Colombo 05
Telephone. (94-1) 584961
Fax. (94-1) 503467
Leadership. Douglas Devananda (general secretary)
Formed in 1995 and formerly the Eelavar Democratic Front (EDF, 1988-94), the EPDP is a Tamil regionalist party, nine members of which secured parliamentary seats as independents from Jaffna in the 1994 legislative elections. By 1998 the EPDP had earned the enmity of the separatist Liberation Tigers of Tamil Eelam (LTTE) by defying the latter's call to boycott elections. At the 2000 election, it won four seats and joined the People's Alliance (PA) coalition government headed by the Sri Lanka Freedom Party (SLFP). However, the EPDP fought the December 2001 elections independently of the PA and secured two seats in Parliament. After the April 2004 election, which it also contested independently, winning one seat with 0.27% of the vote, Devananda indicated that he would support a government formed by the PA's successor grouping, the United People's Freedom Alliance (UPFA). Devananda was rewarded with a Cabinet post in the new government.

Janatha Vimukthi Peramuna (JVP, People's Liberation Front)
Address. 198/19, Panchikawattha Road, Colombo 10
Telephone. (94–1) 345594
Fax. (94–1) 725619
Email. contact@jvpsrilanka.com
Website. www.jvpsrilanka.com
Leadership. Somawansa Amarasinghe (leader); M. Tilvin Silva (general secretary); Wimal Weerawansha (propaganda secretary).
A Sinhalese-based Marxist party with a continuing pro-Chinese orientation, the People's Liberation Front (JVP) was founded in 1965 in opposition to the participation of other left-wing parties in the Bandaranaike government. In 1971, it attempted to overthrow the government and again, in the late 1980s, sought to raise insurrection, after which it was severely repressed (with many supporters killed) and legally proscribed. However, it was rehabilitated after the victory of the People's Alliance in 1994 and, adopting a constitutionalist strategy, stood at the October 2000 general election, winning 10 seats in parliament. In September 2001, it briefly offered back-bench support to the coalition government led by the Sri Lanka Freedom Party, keeping it in office for an additional month, citing efforts to destabilize the country by the "murderous" United National Party (which it blamed for past massacres of JVP supporters), imperialists, and Tamil separatist forces. The JVP won 16 parliamentary seats in the December 2001 general election.

For the April 2, 2004, election the JVP joined forces with President Kumaratunga's Sri Lankan Freedom Party (SLFP) to form the United People's Freedom Alliance (UPFA),

which won a total of 105 seats in the new Parliament. Although the Department of Elections gave no breakdown of the total it was reported that the JVP had increased its representation to 40 seats. Kumaratunga awarded the JVP four Cabinet posts and four deputy ministerial posts, but not the influential River Basin Development portfolio that the party had set its sights on. In protest the JVP ministers boycotted the April 10 oath-taking ceremony at the President's House, but after negotiations resulting in an unspecified compromise the JVP on April 28 allowed its four Cabinet ministers to be sworn in for the portfolios of Cultural Affairs and National Heritage, Small and Rural Industries, Fisheries and Aquatic Resources, and Agriculture, Livestock, Land and Irrigation.

Lanka Equal Society Party
Lanka Sama Samaja Party (LSSP)
Address. 457 Union Place, Colombo 2
Telephone. (94-1) 596903
Leadership. Batty Weerakoon (secretary)
The LSSP originated in the 1930s and has been a rare example worldwide of a Trotskyist party with significant political influence, participating in left-wing governments from 1964. Upon the defeat of the United National Party by the People's Alliance (PA) in the August 1994 parliamentary elections, the LSSP leader joined the new coalition government headed by the Sri Lanka Freedom Party and continued to support it at the 2000 election. The LSSP contested the December 2001 elections as part of the People's Alliance. It also contested the April 2004 general election under the banner of the PA's successor grouping, the United People's Freedom Alliance (UPFA), but won no seats.

People's Alliance (PA)
Address. 121 Wijerama Mawatha, Colombo 07
Telephone. (94-1) 868917
Fax. (94-1) 868915
Leadership. Chandrika Bandaranaike Kumaratunga (leader); D.M. Jayarathna (secretary)
The People's Alliance was formed in 1993 as a coalition of left-wing groups dominated by the Sri Lanka Freedom Party (SLFP). In the 1994 legislative elections it secured 105 of the 225 seats, subsequently forming a new administration with the parliamentary support of moderate Tamil parties and the Sri Lanka Muslim Congress (SLMC). In November 1994 Kumaratunga won the presidential election as the People's Alliance candidate, with 62.3% of the popular vote. She retained the presidency in December 1999 with 51% of the vote and led the Alliance to victory in the October 2000 general election where it secured 107 parliamentary seats. In the December 2001 election, precipitated by the defection from the coalition of the SLMC and others, the People's Alliance won only 77 seats. The PA was superseded for the April 2004 election by the **United People's Freedom Alliance (UPFA),** consisting largely of the SLFP and the *Janatha Vimukthi Peramuna* (JVP). The UPFA won 105 seats with 45.6% of the vote, eight short of a parliamentary majority.

Sri Lanka Freedom Party (SLFP)
Address. 301 T.B. Jayah Mawatha, Colombo 10
Telephone. (94–1) 696289, 692384
Website. www.slfp.lk
Leadership. Chandrika Bandaranaike Kumaratunga (leader); Maithripala Sirisena (general secretary)
Founded in 1951, the SLFP campaigned for the attainment of republican status for Sri Lanka prior to adoption of the 1972 constitution. With a democratic socialist orientation, the party advocated a non-aligned foreign policy, industrial development in both the state and private sectors, and safeguards for national minorities. One family has led the party

throughout its history. S.W.R.D. Bandaranaike (originally a leading figure in the United National Party (UNP), historically the country's other major party) was the party's founder and first Prime Minister from 1956 until his assassination in September 1959. His widow, Sirimavo Bandaranaike, in 1960 became the world's first woman Prime Minister (when the Prime Minister was head of government), holding this post until 1965 and again from 1970-77. Following the party's return to power after 17 years in the August 1994 elections, she was again Prime Minister (the post by now being reduced in importance by the introduction of a semi-presidential system) from November 1994 until her death in October 2000. Chandrika Bandaranaike Kumaratunga, the daughter of S.W.R.D. and Sirimavo, was Prime Minister from August-November 1994, becoming the elected President in November 1994.

The party slumped to defeat in the 1977 elections, when it won only eight seats. During the 1980s it faced periodic harassment from the ruling UNP including Sirimavo's expulsion from parliament and detention. In August 1994, however, the SLFP returned to power heading the People's Alliance coalition, which emerged as the largest parliamentary grouping in the legislative elections with 49% of the vote. The party formed a new government under the premiership of Chandrika Kumaratunga, who was subsequently elected President of the Republic in direct balloting in November. As President she sought reconciliation with Tamil separatists in the face of entrenched opposition and violence from hardliners in both the Tamil and majority Sinhalese communities. Kumaratunga retained the presidency at the December 1999 election and led the People's Alliance to another victory in the October 2000 general election, where it won 48% of the vote and formed another coalition government. However, in October 2001, following defections from the People's Alliance coalition, Kumaratunga called new elections for December 2001. Losing these elections to the UNP and its allies the SLFP became the principal opposition party.

In January 2004 the SLFP formed an electoral pact with the Marxist and Sinhala nationalist People's Liberation Front (*Janata Vimukthi Peramuna*, JVP), dubbed the United People's Freedom Alliance (UPFA). Kumaratunga herself did not attend the inauguration ceremony for the UPFA. The JVP had been widely held responsible for the assassination of her husband Vijaya in 1984. In the April 2, 2004, election the UPFA won 105 seats, of which the SLFP's share was reported to be just over 60. The SLFP held 29 of the 35 Cabinet posts in Kumaratunga's new government.

Sri Lanka Muslim Congress (SLMC)

Address. Sama Mandiraya, 53 Vauxhall Lane, Colombo 02
Telephone. (94-1) 431711
Website. www.slmc.org
Leadership. Rauf Hakeem (leader of majority section); M. Hafrath (secretary)
The SLMC was formed under the leadership of M.H.M. Ashraff in 1981 to represent the Tamil-speaking Muslim population of the Eastern province and was organized as an all-island party in 1986. In the August 1994 elections the party won six parliamentary seats in its own right and three on the People's Alliance national list, with Ashraff securing a post in the new coalition Cabinet headed by the Sri Lanka Freedom Party (SLFP). Immediately before his death in a helicopter crash in September 2000 SLMC leader Ashraff said that he intended the associated National Unity Alliance (NUA), of which he was convenor, to be a separate political party. In 2001 the SLMC/NUA (which in practice were indivisible) split into a majority faction backing Rauf Hakeem while three of the 11 SLMC/NUA MPs elected in October 2000 backed Ashraff's widow, Ferial Ashraff, who in February 2001 joined the government as Minister of Eastern

Rehabilitation and Reconstruction. In June 2001 President Kumaratunga dismissed Hakeem from the government, precipitating a withdrawal of support for the government by his supporters and, after internal party pressure, those of Ashraff. Ashraff resigned her Cabinet post but said she would continue to support the President.

The SLMC won five seats in the December 2001 general election as an ally of the United National Party (UNP). The separatist Liberation Tigers of Tamil Eelam (LTTE) in April 2002 agreed that the SLMC should be a party to forthcoming peace talks with the government (which eventually began in September). About 100,000 Muslims had been expelled from the Tamil-majority northern areas, including the Jaffna peninsula, in the early 1990s. For the April 2, 2004, election the SLMC did not join President Kumaratunga's United People's Freedom Alliance (UFPA), which contained the virulently anti-Tamil and anti-Muslim *Janatha Vimukthi Peramuna* (JVP), but running independently won five seats in Parliament with 2.02% of the vote. Ferial Ashraff was given a Cabinet post in the new SLFP-led government.

Tamil National Alliance (TNA)
Illankai Tamil Arasu Kachchi

The Tamil National Alliance was formed in 2001 by the All-Ceylon Tamil Congress (ACTC), the Eelam People's Revolutionary Liberation Front (EPRLF), the Tamil Eelam Liberation Organization (TELO) and the Tamil United Liberation Front (TULF), contesting the December 2001 elections in alliance with the United National Party (UNP) – which had promised peace talks with the separatist Liberation Tigers of Tamil Eelam (LTTE) – as part of the United National Front, winning 15 seats. When President Kumaratunga called legislative elections for April 2004 the LTTE, which had previously maintained a policy of attempting to extinguish alternative political voices for its Tamil constituency, advised Tamils to vote for the TNA. In the election the TNA increased its representation to 22 seats with 6.84% of the vote. It was reported that before the new Parliament sat, LTTE leader Vellupillai Prabhakaran met and briefed the TNA MPs, with the implication that he regarded them as the LTTE's representatives in the legislature.

Tamil United Liberation Front (TULF)

Address. 30/1B Alwis Place, Colombo 03
Telephone. (94-1) 503831
Leadership. Murugesu Sivasithamraram (president); R. Sampanthan (secretary)
The moderate TULF was formed in 1976 by a number of Tamil groups. It aims to establish a Tamil homeland (Tamil Eelam) in north-eastern Sri Lanka with the right of self-determination. In the August 1994 elections, its parliamentary representation fell from 10 to five seats, which it retained in the 2000 general election. It fought the December 2001 general election as part of the four-party Tamil National Alliance (TNA) in electoral alliance with the United National Party (UNP), which had pledged negotiations with the separatist militant Liberation Tigers of Tamil Eelam (LTTE). The Department of Elections published no breakdown of the TNA results, but it was reported that the TULF won all of its 15 seats.

The TULF has long been a target of the LTTE. In May 1998 Sarojini Yogeswaran, a TULF member and the newly elected major of Jaffna (the first for 14 years), was shot dead by a group allied to the LTTE because she refused the LTTE's demand that she step down from the post. Her successor was killed by a bomb in September 1998 and a TULF party secretary assassinated in December. Neelan Tiruchelvam, a TULF legislator and internationally respected human rights campaigner, was killed by an LTTE suicide bomber in July 1999. Tiruchelvam was an architect of

President Kumaratunga's proposals for constitutional reform that were abandoned in July 2000. The TULF contested the April 2, 2004, general election as part of the Tamil National Alliance (TNA).

United National Party (UNP)

Address. Sirikotha, 400 Kotte Road, Sri Jayawardenepura
Telephone. (94–11) 2865374-75
Fax. (94–11) 2865347
Email. info@unplanka.org
Website. www.unplanka.org/unp
Leadership. Ranil Wickremasinghe (leader); Malik Samarawickrama (chairman); Senarath Kapukotuwa (general secretary)

The conservative UNP, with the Sri Lanka Freedom Party historically one of the country's two leading parties, was founded in 947. Although principally based on the support of Sri Lanka's Sinhalese majority it has generally adopted a moderate stance on communal issues. It advocates the development of the country though free markets and inter-communal co-operation. It formed the government from 947-56 and again from 1965-70. In 1977 it secured a landslide victory under J. R. Jayawardene (who became the country's first executive President under the Constitution adopted in 1978) and then held office for 17 years. In 1989 Jayawardene was succeeded as President by Ranasinghe Premadasa, but he was assassinated on May 1, 1993.

The party lost power in August 1994 when it secured only 94 of the 225 seats in Parliament. In the presidential election of November 1994 the replacement UNP contender, Srima Dissanayake (whose husband Gamini Dissanayake had been the party's candidate prior to his assassination in October), came second with 35.9% of the vote. In the presidential election of December 1999, Ranil Wickremasinghe, who became party leader in November 1994, stood in his own right and was defeated, taking 42% of the vote. At the general election in October 2000, the UNP won 89 seats and remained in opposition.

In the December 2001 general election the UNP was the largest party, winning 109 seats, and Wickremasinghe became Prime Minister leading a United National Front (UNF) coalition. Wickremasinghe had defeated President Kumaratunga's People's Alliance largely through promising a war-weary electorate peace talks with the militant separatist Liberation Tigers of Tamil Eelam (LTTE). Despite successfully negotiating in February 2002 an enduring ceasefire with the LTTE, Wickremasinghe's government was hampered by a constant and escalating feud with President Kumaratunga, culminating when Kumaratunga called new parliamentary elections for April 2004. The UNP/UNF representation fell to 82 seats with 37.83% of the vote, second to Kumaratunga's United People's Freedom Alliance (UPFA). It appeared that voters supported Kumaratunga's criticism that Wickremasinghe had made too many concessions in negotiations with the LTTE and that they had rejected the UNP's pro-free market economic policies.

The UNP claims 1.4 million members and is a member party of the International Democrat Union.

Other Parties and Separatist Organizations

All Ceylon Tamil Congress (ACTC). Founded in 1944, it is regarded as the first organization to campaign for a separate Tamil state. Under the People's Alliance governments 1994-2001 the ACTC was accused of supporting the militant separatist Liberation Tigers of Tamil Eelam (LTTE). The party's general secretary G.C.K. Ponnambalam, a 1982 presidential candidate, was shot dead on Jan. 5, 2000, in Colombo, responsibility being claimed by an organization calling itself the National Front Against Tigers. It contested the December 2001 general election as a member of the four-party Tamil National Alliance (TNA). It also contested the April 2004 elections as part of the TNA.

Leadership. Nalliah Kumuraguruparan (general secretary)
Address. 15 Queens Road, Colombo 03
Telephone. (94-1) 581677, 586232

Eelam People's Revolutionary Liberation Front (EPRLF), formerly a militant separatist group and a rival to the Liberation Tigers of Tamil Eelam (LTTE). Backed by India as a political vehicle for Tamil aspirations, especially through the presence of the Indian peacekeeping Force (IPKF – 1987-90), the EPRLF won a majority of seats in 1988 in the newly created North-East Provincial Council. However, India retreated from its initial support for Tamil independence, affirming, before it withdrew the IPKF in late March 1990, the unity of Sri Lanka. The Indian withdrawal left the EPRLF exposed to the military superiority of the LTTE, and its then leader Annamalai Varatharaja Perumal went into exile in India with other senior officials. Although the LTTE then took effective control of much of the North-East the EPRLF continued to survive as a political party. It contested the December 2001 general election as a member of the four-party Tamil National Alliance (TNA). Senior EPRLF leader Thambirajah Subathran was shot dead on June 14, 2002, in Jaffna by an unidentified sniper; it was thought that he was killed on the orders of the LTTE. Subathran was the most prominent of some 30 politicians from other Tamil groups assassinated since the beginning of the ceasefire between the LTTE and government forces, which suggested that the LTTE's policy was still to eliminate all Tamil political alternatives to itself, despite its recently professed adherence to a multi-party polity. The EPRLF also contested the April 2004 elections under the banner of the TNA.

Leadership. Suresh Premachandran
Address. 85/9 Pokkuna Road, Hendala, Wattala

Jathika Hela Urumaya (JHU, National Heritage Party), was originally named the *Sihala Urumaya* (SU), a right-wing Sinhalese nationalist organization founded in 2000, initially led by S.L. Gunasekere, which won one seat in parliament at the 2000 general election. However, the seat then fell vacant when Gunasekere, a Christian, was forced to resign from the SU by its Buddhist majority. In March 2004 the party was relaunched as the JHU, controversially announcing that it was fielding 280 Buddhist monks in the April general election. It claimed that Buddhism, the religion of at least 70% of Sri Lankans, was under threat as the state religion and promised that the JHU would create a "righteous state". The party is opposed to any concessions to Tamil autonomy, promises a law against "unethical" conversions by Christian evangelists and to revoke the "privileges" granted to the Hindu, Muslim and Christian minorities. The JHU also campaigned against the perceived corruption and inefficiency of the two main parties, the Sri Lankan Freedom Party (SLFP) and the United National Party (UNP), accusing them of making Sri Lanka a haven of terrorism and international crime. To the surprise of most political analysts the JHU received 5.97% of the vote in the April 2, 2004, general election, winning nine seats. It was reported that the party's support was concentrated in urban, middle-class areas. The JHU immediately announced that it would not join any coalition but would remain neutral, voting only on the merits of particular issues.

Leadership. Ven. Ellawa Medhanana Thera (president); Thilak Karunaratne (secretary); Ven. Uduwe Dhammaloka
Address. 655 Elvitigala Mawatha, Colombo 05
Telephone. (94-1) 501412, 596821
Fax. (94-1) 075-344801
Website. www.jathikahelaurumaya.org

Liberal Party, closely aligned with Sri Lanka Freedom Party and a member of the Liberal International.
Address. 88/1 Rosmead Place, Colombo 7
Telephone. (94–1) 691589, 580565
Fax. (94-1) 580565
Leadership. Rajiva Wijesinha (president); Kamal Nissanka (secretary)

Liberation Tigers of Tamil Eelam (LTTE), the Tamil Tigers, the largest and most hardline of the militant Tamil separatist groups, has been fighting Sri Lankan forces for control of the Tamil majority areas in the north and east of the country since 1983. A major government offensive at the end of 1995 succeeded in capturing the main LTTE stronghold of Jaffna city but broke down in the northern mainland; in 1999, the LTTE struck back re-capturing much of the lost ground – although not Jaffna city – and restoring a military stalemate with the government. From 1999 several attempts were made to broker peace negotiations under Norwegian auspices, but without success until the election in December 2001 of a UNP-led government under Prime Minister Ranil Wickremasinghe that had campaigned on a pledge to bring the conflict to an end.

The new government's efforts led to an indefinite and internationally monitored ceasefire signed in February 2002 under Norwegian supervision, and six rounds of negotiations, again with the participation of Norwegian diplomacy. During the negotiations the LTTE indicated that they were prepared to forgo their goal of a fully independent Tamil state in exchange for a form of federal autonomy, but rejected proposals by the government on the form of an interim administration in the North-East. The LTTE suspended participation in the talks in April 2003, ostensibly because of its exclusion from a preliminary meeting in the USA earlier in the month to discuss foreign aid for Sri Lanka, although some analysts thought that this was a ploy to win further concessions from the government. The LTTE also boycotted in June an international donor conference for Sri Lanka held in Japan. Nevertheless, despite occasional ceasefire violations on both sides the peace continued to hold until on Nov. 1 the LTTE published its first detailed set on proposals for a settlement to the conflict. These centred on the establishment of an Interim Self-Governing Authority (ISGA) for all the northern and eastern districts claimed by the LTTE. The ISGA, which would have a majority of LTTE members, would have plenary administrative, legal and financial powers in the North-East, including the control of foreign aid funds, land, marine and offshore resources. The LTTE proposed that the interim arrangement should continue pending the conclusion of a permanent settlement. If, however, no final settlement had been reached in four years, further negotiations should be entered into to renew the interim agreement. Critics saw the LTTE's plan as essentially a demand for independence under another name, and its publication appeared to precipitate President Kumaratunga's move on Nov. 4, 2003, to take control of the government and suspend Parliament. During the ensuing political crisis in Colombo the LTTE refrained from taking sides in the power struggle, merely announcing that negotiations would remain suspended until the political situation "in the South" was resolved. The Norwegian negotiators led by Deputy Foreign Minister Vidar Helgesen later in the month announced that they were temporarily withdrawing from Sri Lanka until the government's position on the peace process became clear. In February 2004, following President Kumaratunga's announcement of legislative elections on April 2, the LTTE advised Tamils to vote for members of the four-party Tamil National Alliance (TNA), which went on to win 22 seats in the election.

In March 2004 the LTTE, an organization renowned for its tight discipline and intolerance of internal dissent, suffered the first serious division in its ranks when "Col Karuna" (*nom de guerre* of V. Muralitharan), a senior commander and leader of some 6,000 of the LTTE's fighters in the eastern district of Batticaloa, announced that he was seceding from the LTTE, complaining of its domination by a northern Tamil leadership. His bid for a separate ceasefire with the government was rejected, and the LTTE issued a veiled death threat against Karuna. Although the increased tension in the north-eastern Tamil areas did not materially disrupt the general election, two pro-Karuna candidates were shot dead. Within a week of the elections fighting broke out between the two LTTE factions, with Karuna's breakaway forces quickly capitulating.
Leadership. Vellupillai Prabhakaran (leader); Anton Balasingham (chief political adviser and negotiator)
Website. www.eelam.com

Muslim United Liberation Front (MULF), active nationally since 1988, has focused on preserving a Muslim presence in the Tamil-dominated North, whence some 100,000 Muslims were expelled in the early 1990s. It has had no success in national or provincial council elections.
Address. 34 Hulftsdorp Street, Colombo 12
Telephone. (94-1) 501198
Leadership. Muheer Rahuman (secretary)

Sinhalese Freedom Front (*Singhalaye Nithahas Peramun,* SNP), led by Arya Sena Tera, a Buddhist-centred nationalist group launched in 1994.

Tamil Eelam Liberation Organization (TELO), formed in April 1984 from a merger of three existing militant Tamil separatist groups, was almost wiped out by the Liberation Tigers of Tamil Eelam (LTTE) in 1986. The TELO stood in the 2000 general election in Northern province and won three seats in parliament. It contested both the December 2001 and April 2004 general elections as a member of the four-party Tamil National Alliance (TNA).
Address. C.28, MPs' Quarters, Madiwela, Kotte, Sri Jayawardenapura
Telephone. (94-1) 585620
Fax. (94-1) 585620
Leadership. S. Vinothalingam

Up-Country People's Front (UCPF), a breakaway party from the Ceylon Workers' Congress (CWC), it also represents Tamils of Indian origin working in the central tea plantations. In the April 2004 general election the UCPF won its first seat in the national Parliament, with 0.54% of the vote.

Sudan

Capital: Khartoum
Population: 32,400,000 (2002E)

The Republic of Sudan has, since its establishment in 1956, experienced political instability, north-south division and civil war. At the end of the 1990s the population included up to 4,000,000 displaced people, of whom an estimated 2,600,000 were in government-controlled areas of the country. A period of transitional military rule followed the coup of 1985 in which the army seized power from President Jaafar al-Nemery, who had himself come to power in a coup in 1969 and established a one-party state. Power was transferred to a civilian regime in May 1986, and for three years a series of coalition governments held office, with Sadiq al-Mahdi as the most prominent political figure (as he had been in civilian administrations prior to the Nemery coup). In June 1989, another military coup installed a Revolutionary Command Council (RCC) led by Lt.-Gen. Omar Hassan Ahmad al-Bashir. In October 1993 the RCC dissolved itself and named Bashir as President of a new civilian government which included most ministers from the outgoing administration. Elections were held on a non-party basis in March 1996 for 265 of the 275 elective seats in a 400-seat National Assembly (unicameral legislature) with a term of four years. Hassan al-Turabi, the then secretary-general of the National Islamic Front (NIF, a fundamentalist party with close links to successive Bashir governments) was unanimously elected president (Speaker) of the new legislature. Omar al-Bashir was elected to a five-year term as President of Sudan in March 1996, winning 75.5% of the vote in a contest with 40 other candidates.

A new constitution, approved by the National Assembly and endorsed by a referendum, came into force in July 1998. Organized political activity, banned since the 1989 coup, resumed in November 1998, the first approvals of party registration applications being announced in early 1999 (although the most important opposition parties remained in exile). The NIF evolved into the National Congress (NC) party, with President Bashir as its president and Hassan al-Turabi as its secretary-general. Relations between the two men deteriorated progressively during the second half of 1999, which also brought a reopening of contacts between Bashir and Sadiq al-Mahdi, the exiled leader of the *Umma* Party (one of the two major parties which, together with the NIF, had dominated Sudanese politics before the 1989 coup). In December 1999 President Bashir suspended the National Assembly before it could vote on a bill (supported by Turabi) to reduce the powers of the President. The Assembly was dissolved in February 2000, and in June 2000 Turabi (who had been suspended as secretary-general of the NC) set up a Popular National Congress (PNC) party in opposition to Bashir. Sudan's 1998 law on political associations (widely criticized for imposing restrictive registration requirements) was replaced in March 2000 by a more liberal political organizations act which the government said was designed "to open doors for national dialogue that could provide peaceful solutions to the country's problems".

Presidential and legislative elections held from Dec. 13 to 23, 2000, were boycotted by the PNC and other principal opposition parties (including the *Umma* Party, whose leadership had returned from exile between April and November 2000). In a five-way presidential contest President Bashir was re-elected with 86.5% of the vote; the runner-up, with 9.6% of the vote, was former President Nemery, who had returned to Khartoum under an amnesty granted in May 2000. The National Assembly elected in December 2000 had 360 members, of whom 270 were directly elected by universal adult suffrage (with a voting age of 17 years) and 90 were indirectly elected to represent women, university graduates and trade unions. Voting did not take place in three southern states under rebel control. The NC won a total of 355 Assembly seats (112 of them unopposed) with the five remaining seats going to independent candidates.

In June 2002 the government entered into peace talks in Kenya with southern-based rebels of the Sudan People's Liberation Movement/Army (SPLM/A). Despite various setbacks the two sides had by early 2004 made progress towards reaching a full and comprehensive peace agreement to end Africa's longest-running war which had been underway for over 20 years.

Democratic Unionist Party (DUP)
Leadership. Mohammed Osman al-Mirghani (leader)
The DUP, formed in 1968 through the merger of two long-established parties, is a largely secularist Islamic centre party, supported primarily by the *Khatmiya* sect. In November 1988 (while participating in a government of national unity led by the *Umma* Party) the DUP played a leading role in opening peace talks with the rebel Sudan People's Liberation Movement. After the 1989 military coup the DUP leader, Osman al-Mirghani, went into exile and aligned the party with the National Democratic Alliance (NDA), of which he became chairman in 1995. It was in his capacity as NDA chairman that Mirghani held talks with President Bashir in Eritrea in September 2000 (this being their first meeting since the 1989 coup). A statement issued after the meeting recorded the two sides' "determination to bring about a quick end" to Sudan's civil war and to strive to create "suitable conditions for voluntary unity between the north and the south".

However, Mirghani did not announce any plans to return to Sudan or to end the DUP's participation in the NDA (whereas the *Umma* Party leader, who had broken with the NDA in March 2000, was about to return to Sudan). Mirghani advised his followers to boycott the presidential and legislative elections held in December 2000, and in February 2001 a DUP spokesman praised the *Umma* Party for refusing an offer to participate in the Bashir Cabinet. Not all DUP members supported Mirghani's insistence that the DUP should maintain its stance as a party in exile. Siddiq al-Hindi, a former deputy Prime Minister of Sudan, returned to the country in 1997 to establish an internal faction of the DUP (sometimes known as the "DUP General Secretariat") with himself as chairman. In February 2001 Hindi and two other members of his internal DUP faction accepted ministerial portfolios in the Bashir Cabinet.

Muslim Brotherhood
Leadership. Habir Nur al-Din
The Muslim Brotherhood was a main focus of Islamic fundamentalism in Sudan until the mid-1980s, when its dominant faction leader, Hassan al-Turabi, set up a separate National Islamic Front which later evolved into the National Congress (NC). Another splinter group – the Muslim Brothers – was led by Sadig Abdallah Abdel Magid. After Turabi's departure the Brotherhood took little active part in Sudanese politics. In February 2001 a member of the Brotherhood, Isam Ahmed al-Bashir (described as a moderate Muslim scholar and staunch advocate of national reconciliation), joined the government as Minister for Religious Guidance and Endowments.

National Congress (NC)
Address. c/o National Assembly, Omdurman
Leadership. Lt.-Gen. Omar Hassan Ahmad al-Bashir (president); Ibrahim Ahmed Omar (secretary-general)
The NC was founded in 1999, having evolved out of the National Islamic Front (NIF), an Islamic fundamentalist party established in the mid-1980s which had become a de facto government party under the Bashir regime. The secretary-general of the NIF, Hassan al-Turabi, became the first secretary-general of the NC but was suspended from that office in May 2000 (together with the other members of the party's national secretariat and its regional leaders) after he had called on party members to ignore Lt.-Gen. Bashir's announcement of a meeting to launch his presidential re-

election campaign. Turabi subsequently left the NC to found the Popular National Congress, which participated in an opposition boycott of the presidential and legislative elections held in December 2000. In these elections President Bashir was re-elected with 86.5% of the vote, while the NC won 355 of the 360 seats in the National Assembly (112 of them unopposed).

National Democratic Alliance (NDA)
Leadership. Moulana al-Sayed Mohammed Osman al-Mirghani) (president of Leadership Council); Gen. Abd-al-Rahman Saeed (vice-president of Leadership Council); Fagan Amom (secretary-general of executive bureau)

The NDA was formed in the immediate aftermath of the June 1989 military coup as a coalition which linked, somewhat awkwardly, a disparate group of opponents of the Bashir regime, including the Sudan People's Liberation Movement/Army (SPLM/A) and a number of Muslim-based parties, many of which not only supported the imposition of Islamic shari'a law on the south, but had also opposed southern autonomy or secession prior to the coup. Members also included Sudan's two main centrist parties, the Democratic Unionist Party (DUP) and the *Umma* Party (UP); several smaller, more radical parties (the Communist Party of Sudan and the Arab Ba'ath Socialist Party); the General Council of the Trade Unions Federations (trade union activity having been banned in the post-coup ban on political activities); and political representatives of various small armed rebel groups operating in southern Sudan, including the Beja Congress and the Sudan Alliance Forces (SAF). Over 95% of the NDA combatants are provided by the SPLM's military wing, the Sudan People's Liberation Army (SPLA), and the SPLM/A's leader, John Garang, sits on the NDA's Leadership Council as representative of the Unified Military Command of the NDA. The NDA has its headquarters in Asmara, the capital city of Eritrea, together with branch offices at Cairo, Nairobi, Washington and London.

Since 1995 the NDA has been led by Osman al-Mirghani, the exiled leader of the DUP. Mubarak al-Mirghani, a senior member of the UP, was suspended as NDA secretary general in late 1999 after the UP leader, Sadiq al-Mahdi, held secret peace talks with President Bashir without first consulting other NDA members. The talks resulted in the signing of the so-called "Call of the Homeland" accord by the UP and the government, following mediation by the government of Djibouti. Mubarak al-Murghani resigned as secretary-general in March 2000 when the UP withdrew from the NDA and shortly thereafter he returned from exile to Khartoum, as did UP leader Mahdi in November 2000.

Osman al-Mirghani held a round of "exploratory" talks with President Bashir in Eritrea in September 2000. A few months later the government arrested the NDA's then secretary-general, Joseph Okelo, and other members of the NDA's Khartoum secretariat on charges including espionage and plotting armed opposition to the government.

In early December 2003 the NDA and the Sudanese government signed in Saudi Arabia an accord supporting the ongoing negotiations between the government and the SPLM/A and calling for a new democratic Sudan benefiting all political parties. The agreement was signed by NDA leader Osman al-Mirghani and the powerful Sudanese First Vice President, Ali Osman Muhammed Taha, who was leading the government delegation in the Kenyan peace talks with the SPLM/A. The agreement was signed after al-Mirghani had complained that northern opposition parties had been excluded from the direct negotiations between the SPLA and the government in Kenya. After the signing of the agreement, Taha said that the peace process was "spacious enough to include everyone." Al-Mirghani was quoted as saying that it was a "great day on which the nation is unified around the peace issue" and that "the road for returning home has now been paved."

Popular National Congress (PNC)
Leadership. Hassan Abdallah al-Turabi

The National Islamic Front, formed by Hassan al-Turabi (a leading Islamic theoretician and former member of the Muslim Brotherhood) to contest the April 1986 general election, was reconstituted in 1999 as the National Congress (NC) under the leadership of President Bashir, setting the scene for a power struggle which culminated in Turabi's departure from the NC in June 2000 to set up the PNC. The new party was formally registered in September 2000 but boycotted the December 2000 elections, in which the NC was the only party to win seats in the National Assembly, while President Bashir was re-elected to office by a massive margin. In February 2001 the PNC signed a "memorandum of understanding" with the Sudan People's Liberation Movement (SPLM), reportedly calling for "an escalation of popular and peaceful resistance against the government". According to the authorities, the PNC had claimed that it had a "sacred duty to overthrow the government", and its contacts with the SPLM (whose military wing had been engaged in armed rebellion in southern Sudan since 1983) represented a conspiracy to overthrow the government. Turabi and three other PNC officials were detained on conspiracy charges in February 2001. A PNC spokesman said in April 2001 that the party had no intention of rescinding its accord with the SPLM.

President Bashir was quoted as saying in May 2001 that the government would "never allow" Turabi to return to politics. However, in October 2003 – and in the context of ongoing peace talks between the government and the SPLM – Turabi was freed from house arrest. At a press conference held after his release, he called for "unity among the Sudanese people through dialogue and entrenchment of freedoms".

Sudan People's Liberation Movement/Army (SPLM/A)
Leadership. Col. John Garang (chairman and commander-in-chief); James Wani Igga (secretary-general)

The SPLM is the political wing of the Sudan People's Liberation Army (SPLA, formed in 1983), the principal armed rebel force in southern Sudan. The SPLM/A was one of the founder members of the National Democratic Alliance (NDA) set up after the military coup of 1989 to provide a joint forum for a wide range of opponents of the Bashir regime (including mainstream political parties). The broad political objective of the SPLM/A has been represented as a form of self-determination for the south within the framework of a secular Sudanese state, and its leaders have denied accusations that it has a "hidden agenda" involving the secession of the south to form a separate state. After the December 2000 elections there was an intensification of national and international efforts to negotiate a peaceful solution to the conflict in Sudan. In addition to maintaining close links with its partners in the NDA, the SPLM concluded a controversial accord with the Popular National Congress in February 2001, while in May 2001 Col. Garang held talks with the leader of the *Umma* Party (which had withdrawn from the NDA in March 2000), who urged him to declare a ceasefire to prepare the way for talks between the government and all the opposition groups in Sudan.

In late July 2002 President Bashir held his first face-to-face meeting with Col. Garang in the Ugandan capital, Kampala, one week after government officials and SPLM/A leaders had agreed on a framework for talks to end the civil war. The meeting between Bashir and Garang followed five weeks of intensive talks in the Kenyan town of Machakos, under the auspices of the regional Inter-Governmental

Authority on Development (IGAD), in which both sides agreed to enter into negotiations to end the war. The framework Machakos protocol called for Sudan's constitution to be rewritten so that Islamic sharia law would not be applied to non-Muslims in the south. It also calls for a referendum to be held in six years' time to determine whether the south should remain a part of Sudan or gain its independence. The Machakos protocol set out only the broad outlines of a peace agreement so that talks on specific areas of dispute continued during 2003 and into 2004. In September 2003, after talks at the Kenyan lakeside resort of Naivasha, the two sides signed an agreement on security arrangements and in January 2004 agreement was reached on wealth-sharing, thereby removing a key obstacle to a full accord. The main remaining obstacles to a comprehensive peace settlement were the composition of a transitional administration and the fate of three disputed areas in central Sudan – the Nuba mountains, the southern Blue Nile and Abyei. In another important development, a SPLM delegation had visited Khartoum in December 2003 for talks with government officials. It was the first time in 20 years that a SPLM delegation had been allowed to visit the capital.

Umma Party (UP)

Leadership. Sadiq al-Mahdi (leader); Omar Nur al-Dayem (secretary-general)

The UP is a largely secularist Islamic centre party, supported primarily by the Ansar sect. Led by Sadiq al-Madhi (Prime Minister of Sudan in 1966-67 and 1986-89), the UP operated from exile in Eritrea in the latter part of the 1990s, allying itself with other exiled political organizations (and with armed opponents of the Bashir regime) through its membership of the National Democratic Alliance (NDA). In late November 1999 Mahdi held talks with President Bashir in Djibouti, resulting in the signature of a declaration (envisaging the holding of a referendum on key issues within four years) which was rejected by other NDA members. The UP suspended contacts with the NDA's external leadership in March 2000, whereupon the Bashir government released the UP's Khartoum premises (confiscated in 1989) in preparation for the return to Sudan of 30 leading UP officials in the following month. Sadiq al-Mahdi himself returned to Khartoum in November 2000. The UP did not contest the December 2000 elections (joining an opposition boycott to protest at the holding of elections while a state of emergency remained in force), nor did it accept an offer of ministerial representation in the Cabinet appointed in February 2001. However, Mahdi did play an active role in the first half of 2001 in the search for a peaceful solution to the conflict in Sudan, travelling abroad to attend meetings organized by various mediators between rival Sudanese factions.

Other Parties

Alliance of the People's Working Forces, formed as a platform for a future presidential election bid by Jaafar al-Nemery (president of Sudan from 1969 to 1985) on his return from exile in May 1999 after being granted an amnesty by the Bashir Government. When the presidential election took place in December 2000, Nemery received only 9.6% of the vote, compared with 86.5% for the incumbent, President Bashir. (The remaining 3.9% of the vote went to three previously unknown independent candidates.)
Leadership. Jaafar al-Nemery

Arab Ba'ath Socialist Party, one of the constituent parties of the National Democratic Alliance.

Beja Congress, one of the constituent parties of the National Democratic Alliance. The Beja Congress effectively controls a swathe of eastern Sudan centred around Garoura and Hamshkoraib and populated by some 3 million Beja tribespeople.
Leadership. Amin Shingrai

Federal Democratic Alliance, one of the constituent parties of the National Democratic Alliance.

Free Lions Association, one of the constituent parties of the National Democratic Alliance.

Free Sudanese National Party, officially registered in April 1999.
Leadership. Philip Abbas

Islamic-Christian Solidarity, small party based in Khartoum and founded by Hatim Abdullah az-Zaki Husayn

Islamic Revival Movement, small party based in Khartoum and founded by Siddiq al-Haj as-Siddiq.

Islamic Umma Party, officially registered in April 1999. Despite the similar name, this party is completely separate and independent of the *Umma* Party.
Leadership. Wali al-Din al-Hadi al-Mahdi

Legitimate Command of the Sudanese Armed Forces, formed by dissident military officers and part of the National Democratic Alliance. Its members are normally military or ex-military officers of some rank.
Leadership. Lt-Gen. Abd al-Rahman Sa'id

Movement of the New Sudanese Forces, small group formed in the mid-1990s by members of the Sudan Communist Party.

National Alliance for Salvation, group of professional associations, trade unions and political parties founded in 1985.

National Democratic Party, formed in early 2002 by the merger of three left-wing parties, the Union of Nationalistic Forces, the Sudan Communist Party, and the National Solidarity Party.

Nile Valley Conference, small party based in Khartoum and founded by Lt Gen. (retd) Umar Zaruq.

Popular Masses' Alliance, small party based in Khartoum and founded by Faysal Muhahhamd Husayn.

Socialist Popular Party, based in Khartoum and founded by Sayyid Khalifah Idris Habbani.

Southern Sudanese Political Association, based in Juba and the largest southern party, it advocates unity of the Southern Region.

Sudan African National Union, southern-based party, supports continuation of regional rule.

Sudan Federal Democratic Alliance, small group launched in London in 1994 by former *Umma* Party politician, Ahmed Ibrahim Diraige. Liberal democrat in outlook.

Sudanese African Congress, small Juba-based party.

Sudanese African People's Congress, small Juba-based party.

Sudanese Central Movement, based in Khartoum and founded by Muhammad Abu al-Qasim Haj Hamad.

Sudanese Green Party, environmental party, based in Khartoum and founded by Zakaraia Bashir Imam.

Sudanese National Party, one of the constituent parties of the National Democratic Alliance.
Leadership. Hasan al-Mahi

United Democratic Salvation Front, registered in January 1999 to represent various former southern Sudanese rebel factions which had concluded a peace agreement with the government in 1997 (and had participated in government since 1998).
Leadership. Maj.-Gen. Elijah Hon Top (chairman)

United Sudan National Party (USNP), formed in December 2002 to represent the Nuba people, who had largely been on the political periphery, aligning themselves neither to the government in the north or the rebel forces in the south. The USNP was formed by a merger of parties representing the Nuba Mountain region, such as the Sudan National Party (SNP), the Sudan National Party-Collective Leadership and the Free Sudan National Party (FSNP).

Union of Sudan African Parties, one of the constituent parties of the National Democratic Alliance.

Suriname

Capital: Paramaribo
Population: 435,000 (2003E)

Formerly Dutch Guiana, the Republic of Suriname achieved complete independence from the Netherlands in 1975. In 1980 the constitution was suspended and the legislature dissolved following the overthrow of the elected government and the formation of a military junta, the National Military Council (NMR). Behind a democratic façade real power remained with Lt-Col Désiré "Desi" Bouterse, commander-in-chief of the army until his resignation in 1992.

Under a new constitution approved in a national referendum in 1987, ultimate authority rests with a 51-member National Assembly, elected for a five-year term, while executive authority rests with the President (elected by the National Assembly) as head of state, head of government, head of the armed forces, chair of the Council of State and of the Security Council which, in the event of "war, state of siege or exceptional circumstances to be determined by law", assumes all government functions. The President is assisted by a Vice-President, who is also elected by the National Assembly, and a Cabinet appointed by the President and responsible to the Assembly. Constitutional amendments, unanimously approved by the National Assembly in 1992, restricted the role of the army to national defence and combating "organized subversion". Serving members of the armed forces were restricted from holding representative political office but not denied personal involvement in political activity.

Former President Ronald Venetiaan's opposition four-party coalition, the New Front for Democracy (NF), won elections to the National Assembly held in May 2000, taking 32 of the 51 seats. The NF easily defeated its closest rival, the Millennium Combination, an alliance of the National Democratic

Party (NDP), led by Bouterse, and two smaller parties, which took 10 seats. The Democratic National Platform 2000 (DNP 2000), headed by outgoing President Jules Wijdenbosch, came third, suffering a resounding defeat in taking only 3 seats. President Wijdenbosch had called the general election a year earlier to quell street demonstrations demanding his resignation after the economy collapsed and a series of resignations from his Cabinet had left him with a minority in the National Assembly.

In August 2000, Ronald Venetiaan was sworn in as the new President of the country, after being elected by a two-thirds majority of National Assembly members.

Democratic Alternative
Democratisch Alternatief
Address. c/o National Assembly, Paramaribo.
Leader. S.D. Ramkhelawan
This offshoot of the Democratic Alternative '91 contested the May 2000 general election as a member of the Millennium Combination coalition.

Democratic Alternative '91
Democratisch Alternatief '91 (DA '91)
Address. c/o National Assembly, Paramaribo
Email. info@da91.sr
Website. www.da91.sr
Leadership. Winston Jessurun (president)
Formed in 1991 as an anti-military, centre-left coalition consisting of the Alternative Forum (AF) and Brotherhood and Unity in Politics (BEP), DA '91 has campaigned for the constitutional exclusion of the military from involvement in the political process. The party contested the May 2000 general election, gaining over 6% of the vote and two seats in the legislature.

Democratic National Platform 2000
Democratisch Nationaal Platform 2000 (DNP 2000)
Leader. Errol Alibux
Following calls for his resignation after the virtual collapse of the economy, President Jules Wijdenbosch called an early general election in May 2000 and formed the DNP 2000 to contest the poll. Wijdenbosch had hitherto been a member of the National Democratic Party. The DNP 2000 performed poorly in the elections, winning only 10% of the vote and three seats in the legislature. Wijdenbosch was subsequently replaced as President by Ronald Venetiaan, leader of the New Front for Democracy coalition. At present the party is led by Errol Alibux.

Millennium Combination
Millennium Combinatie (MC)
Leader. Désiré (Dési) Bouterse
The MC was created to contest the May 2000 general election. Dominated by the National Democratic Party (NDP) of former military strongman Désiré Bouterse, the MC also includes the Democratic Alternative (DA) and the Party for National Unity and Harmony (KTPI). In the May election the MC won only 10 seats, being easily defeated by the New Front for Democracy alliance.

National Democratic Party
Nationale Democratische Partij (NDP)
Address. c/o National Assembly, Paramaribo
Telephone. +597 (0) 499–183
Fax. +597 (0) 432–174
Email. ndp@cq-link.sr
Leadership. Lt.-Col. Désiré Bouterse (leader)
Founded in 1987, the NDP is a right-wing party, which is backed by the Suriname military. The NDP was formed by

Standvaste, the 25 February Movement, under Lt.-Col. Désiré Bouterse, and has played a major role in the country's political life, vying for power with the multi-ethnic, centre-left New Front for Democracy (NF). Prior to the May 2000 general election the NDP aligned itself with two smaller parties to form the Millennium Combination but this took only 10 seats in the election.

New Front for Democracy and Development
Nieuwe Front voor Democratie (NF)

Address. c/o National Assembly, Paramaribo
Leadership. Ronald Venetiaan (leader)
Founded in 1987 as a coalition of Indian, Javanese and mixed-race ethnic groups, the NF alliance won a decisive victory in the May 2000 general election. The NF leader, Ronald Venetiaan, was elected as President shortly thereafter. The four components of the NF are Venetiaan's National Party of Suriname (NPS), the Progressive Reform Party (VHP), the *Pertjajah Luhur* (PL) and the Suriname Labour Party (SPA).

The NF had its origins in the Front for Democracy and Development (*Front voor Demokratie en Onnvikkeling*, FDO) led by former President Henck Arron (toppled by the Bouterse-led army in 1980). In November 1987 the FDO won the election with an overwhelming 85% of the vote. Following the December 1990 military coup, dissident groups, critical of the NF's failure to curb military influence, left in March 1991 to form the Democratic Alternative 1991 (DA' 91). The NF had its ranks swelled by the Suriname Labour Party (SLA), who joined shortly before the May 1991 general election which it convincingly won, taking 30 seats and over 54% of the vote. The NF won 24 out of the 51 National Assembly seats in the 1996 general election It subsequently disintegrated, to the benefit of the National Democratic Party, but managed to put a halt to divisive infighting ahead of the 2000 elections.

National Party of Suriname
Nationale Partij Suriname (NPS)

Address. Wanicastraat 77, Paramaribo
Telephone. +597 (0)477–302
Fax. +597 (0)475–796
Email. nps@sr.net
Website. www.nps.sr
Leadership. Ronald Venetiaan (leader)
Founded in 1946, the Creole-based NPS is a mainstay of the ruling coalition, the New Front for Democracy (NF). Led by Ronald Venetiaan, the party won 14 of the 32 seats taken by the NF in the May 2000 general election, thereby becoming the largest single party in the National Assembly and Venetiian subsequently becoming President.

Party of Unity and Harmony
Kerukanan Tulodo Pranatan Ingil (KTPI)

Address. Weidestraat, Paramaribo
Leader. Willy Soemita
Founded in 1947, the party has been the traditional protector and promoter of the interests of the ethnic Indonesian community and has switched its political allegiances to further this end. The party was a founder member of the New Front for Democracy (NF) in the late 1980s, but, prior to the May 2000 general election it joined forces with former military leader Désiré Bouterse in his Millennium Combination. The coalition performed poorly, winning only 10 seats in the legislature.

Pertjajah Luhur (PL)

Address. c/o National Assembly, Paramaribo
Leader. Paul Somohardjo
The PL is the Javan-based member of the ruling coalition, the New Front for Democracy (NF). The party won seven National Assembly seats in elections held in May 2000.

Political Wing of the FAL
Politieke Vlevgel Van de FAL (PVF)

Address. c/o National Assembly, Paramaribo
Leadership. Joewan Sital
The PVF won 4.1% of the vote and two legislative seats in the May 2000 general election.

Progressive Reform Party
Vooruuitstrevende Hervormings Partij (VHP)

Address. c/o National Assembly, Paramaribo
Website. www.parbo.com/vhp
Leadership. Jagernath Lachmon (chairman)
Founded in 1949 (with several changes of name thereafter and also styled the *Verenigde Hervormings Partij*), the VHP is the leading left-wing party, a Hindustani-based grouping that stresses Suriname's cultural diversity and need for co-existence. It has alternated in opposition and as part of governing coalitions. In the 1996 elections it won nine seats but subsequently suffered five defections and joined the opposition. A founder member of the New Front for Democracy (NF), the party won nine National Assembly seats in elections held in May 2000 that resulted in victory for the NF coalition.

Progressive Workers' and Farm Labourers' Union
Progressieve Arbeiders en Landbouwers Unie (PALU)

Address. c/o National Assembly, Paramaribo
Leadership. Iwan Krolus
Founded in the late 1970s, the PALO is a nominally socialist party that supported the Bouterse regime (1980-87) and in the May 2000 general election won only one seat.

Suriname Labour Party
Suriname Partij voor Arbeid (SPA)

Address. c/o National Assembly, Paramaribo
Leader. Fred Derby
The SPA, whose membership is predominantly Creole, is a member of the ruling coalition, the New Front for Democracy (NF). The party won two National Assembly seats in elections held in May 2000. The party has links with the C-47 trade union.

Other Parties

Basic Party for Renewal and Democracy (*Basispartij voor Vernieuwing en Democratie*, BVD), with a predominantly Hindustani-based membership; gained 3.2% of the vote in the May 2000 general election, but no seats.
Leader. Tjan Gobardhan

Democrats of the 21st Century (*Democraten van de 21ste Eeue*, D21), founded in March 2000 and which gained 1.3% of the vote but no seats in the May 2000 general election.
Leader. Soewarto Moestadja

General Liberation and Development Party (*Algemene Bevrijdings–en Ontwikkelingsparkj*, ABOP), which secured 1.7% of the vote but no seats in the May 2000 general election. It is led by Ronnie Brunswijk, who in the 1980s led a small force of Maroon or Bush Negroes (*boschneger*) in armed insurrection against the Bouterse regime.

National Party for Leadership and Development (*Nationale Partij voor Leiderschap en Ontwikkeling*, NPLO), led by O. Wangsabesari, was founded in March 2000 and secured 1% of the vote but no seats in the May 2000 general election.

Naya Kadan (New Choice, NK), which secured 2.4% of the vote in the May 2000 general election, but failed to win a seat.
Leader. Indra Djawalapersad

Party for Democracy & Development Through Unity (*Partij voor Democratie & Ontwikkeling door Eenheid*, DOE), led by Monique Essed-Fernandes; secured 2.5% of the vote, but no seats in the May 2000 general election.

Pendawa Lima (PL), led by Raymond Sapoen, a Javanese-based party which secured 1% of the vote but no seats in the May 2000 general election.

Progressive People's Party of Suriname (*Progressieve Surinaamse Volkspartij*, PSV).
The PSV was founded in 1946 and resumed activities in 1987 after a long period of inactivity. PSV is a member of the Christian Democrat International and of the Christian Democrat Organization of America.
Address. Keizerstraat 122, PO Box 195, Paramaribo
Telephone. +597 (0) 472–979
Fax. +597 (0) 410–555
Leadership. Eugene Wong Loi Sing (president); S. E. Van Dal (secretary general)

Renewed Progressive Party (*Hernieuwde Progressieve Partij*, HPP). Founded in the 1970s and social democratic in orientation, the HPP won 2.5% of the vote in the May 2000 general election, but failed to win representation in the legislature.
Leader. Harry Kisoensingh
Email. hpp@cq-link.sr
Website. www.cq-link.sr/hpp

Swaziland

Capital: Mbabane (administrative);
Lobamba (legislative)
Population: 1,100,000 (2002E)

The Kingdom of Swaziland achieved full independence from the United Kingdom in 1968. The country is ruled by a King (*Ngwenyama* or Paramount Chief) whose succession is governed by Swazi law and custom. The present King, Mswati III, acceded to the throne in 1986. Under the 1978 constitution considerable executive power is vested in the King and is exercised by a Cabinet appointed by him. The bicameral Parliament consists of a Senate and a House of Assembly, with limited powers. The House of Assembly has 65 members, 55 of whom were directly elected for the first time in September–October 1993 (on a non-party basis), with voters electing one representative from each of the *Tinkhundla* (tribal assemblies). A further 10 members are appointed by the King. There are 30 members of the Senate, 20 of whom are nominated by the King and 10 elected by the House of Assembly.

Party political activity, banned in 1973, was formally prohibited under the 1978 constitution. However, following indications that the constitution might be revised, a number of political associations re-emerged during the 1990s. The Constitutional Review Commission, established in 1996, submitted a private report to the King in mid-2001. Some of the key recommendations of the report were that the absolute monarchy should continue in its current form and that political parties should remain banned, although provision should be made for a bill of rights. In late 2001 the King announced the appointment of a team to draft a new constitution. Non-party National Assembly elections were held in October 2003. A total of five women were appointed to the Assembly by King Mswati; no women had been members of the outgoing Assembly. Royal loyalists won most of the Assembly seats as pro-democracy groups boycotted the poll.

Confederation for Full Democracy in Swaziland, formed in 1992 as an alliance of organizations advocating democratic reform, including the People's United Democratic Movement and the Swaziland Youth Congress.

Imbokodvo National Movement (INM), founded in 1964, a traditionalist and royalist organization, but also advocates policies of development and the elimination of illiteracy.

Ngwane National Liberatory Congress (NNLC), founded in 1962 as a result of a split in the Swaziland Progressive Party; seeks an extension of democratic freedoms and universal suffrage. The NNLC competed in the October 2003 legislative elections, ignoring the call for a boycott issued by the Swaziland Democratic Alliance. The party's president, former Prime Minister Obed Dlamini, was elected as a member of the new Assembly.
Leadership. Obed Dlamini (president)

People's United Democratic Movement (PUDEMO), emerged in the 1980s, circulating pamphlets critical of the King, thus attracting official hostility and suppression; campaigns for electoral reform, multi-party democracy and limits on the power of the monarchy. In January 2003 PUDEMO published its manifesto in the form of a New Year's message, calling for the repeal of the 1973 royal decree that banned parties and activity in opposition to royal rule. PUDEMO, it said, would "lead all the oppressed and democracy-seeing forces," in the country.
Leadership. Mario Masuku (president); Bong'nkhosi Dlamini (secretary-general)

Swaziland Coalition of Concerned Civic Organisations (SCCCO), an alliance of teachers, workers, employers, churches and activists formed in early 2003 and which called on the government to address urgently the "disastrous state of affairs" in the country.

Swaziland Democratic Alliance (SDA), pro-democratic umbrella group composed of banned political parties and human rights, civil and labour groups. In September 2003 the SDA began the process of drafting an "alternative constitution" to counter the government draft. The alliance called for a boycott of the October 2003 legislative elections.

Swaziland National Front (SWANAFRO)
Leadership. Elmond Shongwe (president)

Swaziland Progressive Party (SPP), founded in 1929 as the Swazi Progressive Association, adopted present title in 1960, after which it suffered from factional divisions and defections.
Leadership. J.J. Nquku (president)

Swaziland United Front (SUF), founded in 1962 following a split within the Swaziland Progressive Party.
Leadership. Matsapa Shongwe

Swaziland Youth Congress (SWAYOCO), a constituent of the Confederation for Full Democracy in Swaziland.
Leadership. Bongani Masuku (president)

Sweden

Capital: Stockholm
Population: 8,975,199 (2003)

The Kingdom of Sweden is a parliamentary democracy in which the monarch has purely ceremonial functions as head of state. There is a Cabinet headed by a Prime Minister and responsible to a unicameral Parliament (*Riksdag*) of 349 members elected for a four-year term by universal adult suffrage of citizens above the age of 18 years under a system of proportional representation, with 310 seats being filled in 28 multi-member constituencies and the remaining 39 allocated to parties according to a complex formula. A party must obtain 4% of the national vote to qualify for a seat. Sweden joined what became the European Union on Jan. 1, 1995.

Since 1966 state subsidies have been paid to political parties which have at least one representative in the *Riksdag* or have obtained at least 2.5% of the national vote in either of the two most recent elections, with an additional "secretariat subsidy" being available for parties achieving 4% or more of the vote. The amount of the subsidies is related to party representation or voting strength, but "secretariat subsidies" are higher for opposition parties than for those in the government. Similar arrangements apply at the level of regional and local government.

The parliamentary elections held on Sept. 15, 2002, gave the following results: Swedish Social Democratic Labour Party 144 seats (with 39.8% of the vote), Moderate Party 55 (15.2%), Liberal People's Party 48 (13.3%), Christian Democrats 33 (9.1%), Left Party 30 (8.3%), Centre Party 22 (6.1%), Green Ecology Party 17 (4.6%).

On Sept. 14, 2003, a referendum was held on joining the European Monetary Union. A large majority of 55.9% voted against joining, while 42% voted in favour, with the remaining voting blank or casting invalid ballots.

In the June 13, 2004, elections to the European Parliament, even fewer people voted than in the referendum. Only 37.8% voted, making it the lowest turn-out of any country excluding the newest members from Central and Eastern Europe. The Social Democrats remained the largest party with 24.7% of the votes (5 seats), with the Moderate Party receiving 18.2% (4 seats), the Left Party 12.8% (2 seats), the Centre Party 6.3% (1 seat), the Green Ecology Party 5.9% (1 seat) and the Christian Democrats 5.7% (1 seat). The big surprise was the June List, which ran a coalition of candidates from all political parties who are opposed to federalism within the EU. The coalition received 14.4% of the vote (3 seats), making it the third largest Swedish formation in the European Parliament.

Centre Party
Centerpartiet (CP)
Address. Bergsgatan 7B, PO Box 22107, 104 22 Stockholm
Telephone. (46–8) 617–3800
Fax. (46–8) 652–6440
Email. centerpartiet@centerpartiet.se
Website. www.centerpartiet.se
Leadership. Maud Olofsson (chair); Agne Hansson (parliamentary group leader); Jöran Hägglund (secretary-general)
The Centre Party works for a decentralized society with a social market economy, with all parts of the country having an equal chance to develop; for the protection of the environ-

ment; and for the use of technology not only for material welfare but also for mental well-being. The party is strongly opposed to the development of nuclear energy.

The party was founded in 1910 as the Farmers' Union Party to represent the population in rural areas but now has both rural and urban support. It first gained parliamentary representation in 1917 and formed its first government in June 1936. From October 1936 it co-operated in government with the Swedish Social Democratic Labour Party (SAP), and in 1939–45 in a national coalition government. In 1951–57 the party was again a partner with the SAP in a coalition government, at the end of which it changed its name to Centre Party–Farmers' Union Party (1957), shortening this to Centre Party a year later.

In 1976–78 the CP headed a three-party non-socialist government including also the Liberal People's (FP) and Moderate (MSP) parties, this coalition, led by Thorbjörn Fälldin, being re-established after the September 1979 elections. In elections to the *Riksdag* in September 1982 the CP obtained 15.5% of the valid votes and 56 (out of 349) seats and went into opposition. In the September 1985 elections, which it contested jointly with the Christian Democratic Community Party (KdS), the CP slipped to 12.4% and 44 seats (including one Christian Democrat) and continued in opposition. In view of this setback Fälldin resigned the party leadership in December 1985, having come under sharp criticism for his opposition to a rapprochement with the SAP, the party's traditional allies. He was replaced by Karin Söder (who became Sweden's first female party leader), but she resigned in January 1987 for health reasons and was succeeded by Olof Johansson.

The CP's decline continued in the 1988 and 1991 elections, to 42 and 31 seats respectively, but after the latter contest the party entered a centre-right coalition headed by the MSP. In June 1994 its participation was shaken by the resignation of party chairman Johansson as Environment Minister, in opposition to the controversial Öresund Sound bridge project. In the September 1994 parliamentary elections the CP was further reduced to 27 seats (on a vote share of 7.7%) and again went into opposition. The CP supported Swedish accession to the European Union (EU), while advocating non-participation in a single European currency or in any EU defence co-operation. In Sweden's first direct elections to the European Parliament in September 1995, the CP won two of the 22 seats on a 7.2% vote share.

In April 1998 Olof Johansson was succeeded as CP leader by Lennart Daléus, who led the party to a further defeat in the September 1998 general elections, when its vote fell to 5.1% and its representation to only 18 seats. In the June 1999 European elections the CP vote slipped to 6.0%, giving the party only one seat. After his electoral defeats, Daléus left politics to become head of the Scandinavian section of Greenpeace. Maud Olofsson replaced him in 2001 and contributed to the party's slight increase in support of 1.1% in the September 2002 general elections.

The CP's representative in the European Parliament sits in the European Liberal, Democratic and Reformist group.

Christian Democrats
Kristdemokraterna (Kd)
Address. Malargatan 7, PO Box 451, 101 26 Stockholm
Telephone. (46–8) 723–2550
Fax. (46–8) 723–2510
Email. brev.till@kristdemokrat.se
Website. www.kristdemokrat.se
Leadership. Alf Svensson (chair); Stefan Attefall (parliamentary group chairman); Urban Svensson (secretary-general)
The Kd has described itself as "the third alternative in Sweden, where all [other] parties are socialistic or non-socialistic". It propagates "a new way of life" and concen-

trates on social problems, calling for a review of the abortion law among other things. It also opposes the development of nuclear energy. The party was founded in 1964 and obtained some 78,000 votes in its first general election in 1964. By 1982 this total had increased to 103,820 (1.9%). Having thus failed to pass the 4% barrier to representation in the *Riksdag*, in September 1985 it entered into an electoral pact with the Centre Party, winning some 2.6% of the vote in its own right and being allocated one of the Centre Party's 44 seats (Alf Svensson becoming the party's first representative in the *Riksdag*). Meanwhile, the party had established a significant local government presence, with almost 300 elected councillors by the mid-1980s.

Originally called the Christian Democratic Assembly (*Kristen Demokratisk Samling*), the party changed its name to the Christian Democratic Community Party (*Kristdemokratiska Samhällspartiet*, KdS) in 1987, when it also adopted a new programme. The KdS failed to secure representation in the 1988 parliamentary elections, but again came back strongly three years later, winning 26 *Riksdag* seats in 1991 (with 7.1% of the vote) and becoming a member of a centre-right coalition government. It slipped back in the 1994 contest, only just clearing the 4% barrier and winning 15 seats. It thereupon went into opposition to a minority government of the Swedish Social Democratic Labour Party. The KdS was strongly in favour of Swedish accession to the EU in 1995.

In 1996 the party once again changed its name, this time to the Christian Democrats (*Kristdemokraterna*). Campaigning on a platform of family values and opposition to sleaze, the KdS registered a record advance in the September 1998 general elections, winning 42 seats on a vote share of 11.8%. It remained in opposition and lost impetus by the time of the June 1999 European elections, in which it won two seats and 7.6% of the vote. In the September 2002 general elections, the party fell to 33 seats and 9.1% of the vote.

The Kd is affiliated to the Christian Democrat International. Its representatives in the European Parliament sit in the European People's Party/European Democrats group.

Green Ecology Party
Miljöpartiet de Gröna

Address. PO Box 12660, 112 93, Stockholm
Telephone. (46–8) 208–050
Fax. (46–8) 201–577
Email. ursula@mp.se
Website. www.mp.se
Leadership. Maria Wetterstrand & Peter Eriksson (spokespersons); Mikael Johansson (parliamentary group leader); Håkan Wåhlstedt (secretary)

Founded in September 1981, the party has developed a mainstream environmentalist programme based on "fourfold solidarity" with (i) animals, nature and the eco-system, (ii) future generations, (iii) the people of the world and (iv) the people of Sweden. It advocates enhanced international co-operation on environmental issues, human rights, cultural development, disarmament and peace, and favours the establishment of an international court on environmental matters. It also demands a halt to all exports of weapons from Sweden and the subordination of free trade to environmental requirements and labour conditions, "so that the environment, poor people and individuals are not exploited by the wealthy". Unlike most other EU Green parties, it is opposed to EU membership on the grounds that it is damaging for Sweden, and has called for a referendum to be held on withdrawal.

In the 1982 and 1985 general elections the party fell well short of the 4% vote minimum required for representation in the *Riksdag*, not least because the major parties, particularly the Left Party and the Centre Party, had incorporated a strong environmentalist strand in their platforms. On the other hand, it succeeded in obtaining representation in over 30% of local councils by 1988, in which year it became the first new party to enter the *Riksdag* for 70 years, winning 20 seats on a 5.5% vote share. It slumped to 3.4% in 1991 and so failed to gain representation; but in 1994 it recovered strongly to 5.0% and 18 *Riksdag* seats, thereafter giving qualified external support to the minority government of the SAP.

Opposed to Sweden's accession to the EU, the Greens were prominent in the "no" campaign for the November 1994 referendum on EU membership, finishing on the losing side. The party nevertheless polled strongly in Sweden's first direct elections to the European Parliament in September 1995 winning four seats on a vote share of 17.2%. In the September 1998 general elections, however, the party slipped to 4.5% and 16 seats, thereafter giving external support to a further minority SAP government. In the June 1999 European elections the Greens were reduced to two seats, with a 9.5% vote share. In the 2002 general election its support remained rather stable compared to the previous general election, as the party obtained 4.6% of the votes and 17 seats. It continued to support the Social Democratic minority government after the elections, but only after engaging in tough, drawn-out negotiations with the SAP. At one point, the Social Democrats even broke off negotiations with the Greens, as the Greens engaged in parallel negotiations with the centre-right parties. Once the Centre Party broke off its negotiations with the Greens, the environmentalists re-entered negotiations with the SAP and reached an agreement, although they were unable to achieve their goal of obtaining ministerial posts. In the 2003 referendum, the Greens were extremely active in opposing Sweden joining the EMU.

The Greens are affiliated to the European Federation of Green Parties. The party's representatives in the European Parliament are members of the Greens/European Free Alliance group.

Left Party
Vänsterpartiet (VP)

Address. Kungsgatan 84, PO Box 12660, 112 93 Stockholm
Telephone. (46–8) 654–0820
Fax. (46–8) 653–2385
Email. orjan.svedberg@vansterpartiet.se
Website. www.vansterpartiet.se
Leadership. Ulla Hoffmann (chair); Lars Bäckström (parliamentary group leader); Pernilla Zethraeus (secretary-general)

The VP is the latter-day successor to the historic Swedish Communist Party, which was founded as early as May 1917 under the name Left Social Democratic Party by the revolutionary wing of the Swedish Social Democratic Labour Party (SAP). It changed its name to Communist Party in 1921, having joined the Communist International (Comintern), to which it belonged until that organization's dissolution in 1943. In the post-1945 era, the party at first displayed pro-Soviet orthodoxy but in the 1960s embarked upon a revisionist course in line with "Euro-communist" prescriptions. To signify the party's aim of becoming "a forum for the whole socialist left", the new designation Left Party – Communists (*Vänsterpartiet – Kommunisterna*, VPK) was adopted in 1967. This decision, combined with attendant policy evolution, generated much dissension within the party prior to the withdrawal of an orthodox faction in early 1977 to form the Communist Workers' Party. The suffix "Communists" was dropped from the party's title by a congress decision of May 1990.

The party has been represented in the *Riksdag* since its foundation, and for long periods minority SAP governments have relied on its support. In both the 1979 and 1982 general elections what was then the VPK obtained 20 seats and 5.6% of the valid votes, while in September 1985 it slipped to 5.4% and 19 seats (out of 349); but a concurrent SAP decline meant that VPK voting strength became crucial to the SAP government's survival in the late 1980s. The renamed VP won 16 seats in the 1991 general elections (on a vote share of 4.5%), thereafter going into full opposition to a centre-right coalition government. In a general swing to the left in September 1994, the VP achieved the party's best result since 1948, winning 6.2% of the vote and 22 seats.

The VP campaigned vigorously against Sweden's accession to the European Union (the only parliamentary party to do so), but was on the losing side in the November 1994 referendum. In Sweden's first direct elections to the European Parliament in September 1995 the VP won three seats on a 12.9% vote share. In September 1997 party leader Gudrun Schyman announced that she was taking leave of absence for the latest round in her long public struggle against alcoholism. She returned to lead the party to a record result in the September 1998 general elections, in which the VP vote, boosted by disaffected SAP supporters, climbed to 11.9% and its representation to 43 seats. It thereafter gave external support to a further SAP minority government and maintained its forward impetus in the June 1999 European elections, in which it again won three seats with an increased vote share of 15.8%.

In the September 2002 general elections, however, the party lost some steam and declined to 8.3% of the votes, giving it 30 seats, despite an extremely strong showing by Schyman in the nationally televized electoral debates. After the elections, it agreed to continue supporting a minority SAP goverment. Unlike the Greens, it never demanded ministerial positions. In 2003 Schyman resigned after being accused of filing incorrect tax returns during several years. Ulla Hoffmann took over as a temporary chair, until a permanent leader could be found. At the time of writing, party veteran Lars Ohly is the strongest candidate, having been nominated by the party electoral committee.

In September 2000 the VP warmly welcomed Denmark's referendum decision not to join the single European currency, contending that it strengthened the case for Sweden remaining a non-participant. The party also campaigned strongly again Sweden joining the EMU in the 2003 referendum.

The party's representatives in the European Parliament sit in the European United Left/Nordic Green Left group.

Liberal People's Party
Folkpartiet Liberalerna (FPL)

Address. Drottninggatan 97/1tr, PO Box 6508, 113 83 Stockholm
Telephone. (46–8) 5091–1600
Fax. (46–8) 5091–1660
Email. info@liberal.se
Website. www.folkpartiet.se
Leadership. Lars Leijonborg (chair); Bo Könberg (parliamentary group leader); Johan Pehrson (secretary-general)

Although the present party dates from 1934, organized liberalism began in Sweden at the end of the 19th century with the objectives of social justice, universal suffrage and equality. After World War I a coalition government with the Swedish Social Democratic Labour Party (SAP), led by a Liberal Prime Minister, completed the process of democratization. At the same time, the introduction of universal suffrage reduced the party's influence, while between 1923 and 1934 the party was split over the issue of alcohol prohibition. Nevertheless, it formed governments in 1926–28 and 1930–32 and it took part in the national government during World War II.

In 1948 the party became the second strongest in the then lower chamber of the *Riksdag*, with 57 seats, but by 1968 its representation had declined to 34. In the unicameral *Riksdag* established in January 1971 the party won 58 seats in 1970, but only 34 in 1973 and 39 in 1976. It then took part in the

first non-socialist government to be formed in Sweden for 44 years in coalition with the Centre and Moderate (Conservative) parties. The collapse of this coalition in October 1978 over the nuclear issue was followed by a year of minority Liberal rule under Ola Ullsten; but as a result of the September 1979 elections the three-party non-socialist coalition was re-established. However, the Conservatives left this government in 1981 after disagreements on taxation, and the Liberal and Centre parties formed a minority government until the September 1982 elections brought the Social Democrats back to power. In those elections the Liberal vote dropped to 5.9% and its representation to 21 seats.

The FPL staged a significant recovery in the September 1985 elections, winning 14.2% of the vote and 51 seats, but remaining in opposition. It fell back to 44 seats to 1988 (12.2%) and to 33 in 1991 (9.1%), when it joined a four-party centre-right coalition. Another setback followed in the September 1994 elections, which yielded only 7.2% and 26 seats, after which the party reverted to opposition status and party leader Bengt Westerberg gave way to Maria Leissner. The FPL was strongly in favour of Swedish accession to the EU in January 1995, but in Sweden's first direct elections to the European Parliament in September 1995 it managed only 4.8% of the vote and one seat.

Elected party leader in March 1997, Lars Leijonborg led the FPL to a further defeat in the September 1998 general elections, in which the party fell back to 4.7% of the vote and 17 seats. In the June 1999 European elections, however, the FPL recovered strongly to 13.9% of the vote, which gave it three seats. As the party continued to slip in the polls, discussions began about replacing Leijonborg. However, the party's fortunes radically changed when it played on anti-immigrant feelings by demanding that immigrants take a language test in order to become Swedish citizens. Suddenly, the party's support skyrocketed and in the 2002 general elections it reached 13.3% and 48 seats. Despite the party's increased support, it was unable to persuade a majority of voters to vote "yes" in the referendum held in September 2003 on joining the EMU.

The FPL is a member of the Liberal International. Its representatives in the European Parliament sit in the European Liberal, Democratic and Reformist group.

Moderate Party
Moderata Samlingspartiet (MSP)

Address. PO Box 1243, SE–111 82 Stockholm
Telephone. (46–8) 676–8000
Fax. (46–8) 216–123
Email. info@moderat.se
Website. www.moderat.se
Leadership. Fredrik Reinfeldt (chair); Mikael Odenberg (parliamentary group leader); Sven Otto Littorin (secretary-general)

The MSP combines a conservative heritage with liberal market ideas to advocate a moderate, anti-socialist policy in favour of a free-market economy and individual freedom of choice. The party was originally founded in 1904 as the political expression of better-off peasants and the emerging industrial bourgeoisie. It participated in coalitions or formed minority governments several times before 1932, after which the Swedish Social Democratic Labour Party (SAP) was in almost uninterrupted power for 44 years (though during World War II all democratic parties took part in the government). The party increased its support during the 1950s, winning more than 20% of the vote in the 1958 general elections. It declined in subsequent contests, obtaining only 11.6% in the 1970 elections, prior to which it changed its name from Right Party to Moderate Party (its preferred English translation, although the Swedish means something like "Moderate Alliance Party").

Later the party advanced again, gaining 15.6% of the vote in the 1976 elections whereupon it entered the first non-socialist coalition for 40 years (with the Centre and Liberal parties). This was dissolved in October 1978 but re-established after the September 1979 elections, in which the party made a significant advance, to 20.3% and 73 seats. It withdrew from the coalition in May 1981 amid disagreements over fiscal policy, although it generally gave external support to the government thereafter. In the elections of September 1982 the party gained further support (23.6% of the vote and 86 seats) and thus became the dominant non-socialist party in Sweden, although the Social Democrats were returned to power as a minority government. In the September 1985 elections the MSP slipped to 21.3% and 76 seats (out of 349) and continued in opposition. In light of this setback, Ulf Adelsohn resigned as party chairman in June 1986 and was succeeded by Carl Bildt (son-in-law of Adelsohn's immediate predecessor, Gösta Bohman).

A further decline in 1988 (to 18.3% and 66 seats) was followed by recovery in 1991 to 21.9% and 80 seats, enabling Bildt to form a four-party centre-right coalition with the Centre, Christian Democratic Community and Liberal People's parties. In the September 1994 elections the MSP again won 80 seats (and a slightly higher 22.4% vote share), but a general swing to the left resulted in a minority SAP government. Two months later the MSP warmly welcomed the referendum decision in favour of EU membership. Released of the burdens of government, Bildt accepted appointment as the EU's chief mediator in former Yugoslavia, while retaining the less taxing post of MSP chairman. In Sweden's first direct elections to the European Parliament in September 1995 the MSP took five of the 22 seats with a vote share of 23.2%.

Despite the unpopularity of the SAP government, the MSP failed to make major inroads in the September 1998 general elections, winning 82 seats on a slightly higher vote of 22.9%. Remaining in opposition, the party also registered a lacklustre performance in the June 1999 European elections, retaining five seats but on a reduced vote share of 20.7%. In August 1999 Bildt was succeeded as party leader by Bo Lundgren, a former MSP Finance Minister. However, he was considered a weak and uninspiring leader and was encouraged to resign after the party's electoral debacle in September 2002, in which it lost 27 seats, while only receiving 15.2% of the votes and 55 seats in parliament. After the election, many party members, especially the leaders of the party's youth organization, demanded a thorough rejuvenation of the party's leadership. As a result, younger members took over all of the party's important positions, including the chairmanship. The new party chair, Fredrik Reinfeldt, was in his 30s.

The MSP has 85,000 members and is affiliated to the Christian Democrat International, the International Democrat Union and the European Democrat Union. Its members of the European Parliament sit in the European People's Party/European Democrats group.

Swedish Social Democratic Labour Party
Sveriges Socialdemokratiska Arbetareparti (SAP)

Address. Socialdemokraterna, Sveavägen 68, 105 60 Stockholm
Telephone. (46–8) 700–2600
Fax. (46–8) 219–331
Email. sap.international@sap.se
Website. www.sap.se
Leadership. Göran Persson (chairman); Brit Bohlin (parliamentary group leader); Lars Stjernkvist (general secretary)
The SAP seeks "to transform society in such a way that the right of decision over production and its distribution is placed in the hands of the entire nation"; to replace "a social order based on classes" by "a community of people in part-

nership on a basis of liberty and equality"; to maintain "Sweden's non-alignment and neutrality in war"; and to work for "world peace on the basis of self-determination for every nation, of social and economic justice, of détente and disarmament and of international co-operation". The party has shown majority support for Sweden's participation in the European Union (EU) and joining the European Monetary Union (EMU), though a significant SAP minority is opposed to further EU integration.

Founded in April 1889, the party sent its first member to the *Riksdag* in 1896, namely Hjalmar Branting, who, after serving as Minister of Finance in 1917–18, became Prime Minister in Sweden's first Social Democratic government in 1920; he was Prime Minister again in 1921–23 and in 1924–25. The share of national vote gained by the party in elections rose from 28.5% in 1911 to 53.8% in 1940, whereafter it declined to 46.7% in 1944 and remained more or less stable until 1968, when it rose to 50.1%. In the four succeeding elections the SAP share fell to 42.9% in 1976, rose slightly to 43.3% in 1979 and to 45.6% in 1982, but slipped to 45.1% in September 1985, when it won 159 seats in the *Riksdag* (out of 349).

Except for a short interval in 1936, the party was in office from 1932 to 1976, in coalition with the Centre Party between 1936 and 1939 and between 1951 and 1957, in a four-party coalition during World War II, and at other times as a minority party requiring the support of one or more other parties on important issues. The party's 44 years of virtually uninterrupted power established the record for continuous governmental power by a social democratic party, and also resulted in Sweden becoming what was widely regarded as a model social democracy. In over 100 years of existence, the SAP has had only six leaders, namely Hjalmar Branting, Per-Albin Hansson, Tage Erlander, Olof Palme, Ingvar Carlsson and Göran Persson (since March 1996). Carlsson succeeded to the party leadership and premiership following the (still unexplained) assassination of Palme on a Stockholm street on Feb. 28, 1986.

Having formed a minority government since 1982, the SAP went into opposition after the September 1991 elections, when its share of the vote fell from 43.2% in 1988 to 37.6% and its representation from 156 seats to 138. It recovered in a general swing to the left in the September 1994 elections, bringing it 45.3% of the vote and 161 seats and enabling it to form another minority government under Carlsson. For the November 1994 referendum on EU membership, the official government and party line was to favour a "yes" vote but the extent of anti-EU opinion within SAP ranks compelled the leadership to allow the contrary case to be made within the party. In both the 1994 general elections and the September 1995 European Parliament polling anti-EU candidates were included on the SAP lists. The result on the latter occasion was that three of the seven Social Democrats elected (on a vote share of only 28%) were "Eurosceptic" to a greater or lesser extent.

Meanwhile, Carlsson had surprised the political world by announcing in August 1995 that he intended to stand down as party leader and Prime Minister the following March, marking the 10th anniversary of his elevation. The initial favourite to succeed him was Deputy Prime Minister Mona Sahlin but disclosures about irregularities in her financial affairs forced her not only to withdraw from the leadership race but also to resign from the government. Instead, the succession went to the Finance Minister, Göran Persson, who was elected SAP chairman unopposed at a special party congress on March 15, 1996, and appointed Prime Minister two days later.

The Persson government came under pressure in 1997–98 for sticking to unpopular economic retrenchment policies. In the September 1998 general elections the SAP recorded its worst result for 70 years, winning only 36.4% of the vote and

131 seats. It nevertheless continued as a minority government, with the external support of the Left Party and the Green Ecology Party. In the June 1999 European elections the SAP slipped to 26.0% of the vote, winning only six seats.

An SAP congress in March 2000 voted by 234 to 133 to make participation in the single European currency official party policy, coupled with a stipulation that approval in a referendum would be required before Sweden adopted the euro. However, although strongly supported by Persson, euro membership was opposed by several ministers and by a substantial section of the SAP rank-and-file. When Denmark voted against euro membership in September 2000, Persson contended that it had been "purely a Danish decision" but SAP opponents of the euro saw it as strengthening their case.

In November 2000 Persson opened another debate within the SAP by proposing that Sweden should abandon its 100-year-old policy of neutrality, arguing that the end of the Cold War had rendered it irrelevant. Although he said that Sweden should remain non-aligned and should not join NATO, his proposal sparked immediate contention within the party, which would be required to revise its commitment to neutrality before an SAP government could act on the proposal. As that debate continued, Persson disclosed in August 2001 that after the 2002 elections an SAP government would begin evaluating whether to recommend euro membership in a referendum. He expressed confidence that, provided the January 2002 change-over to the euro in other EU states went well, Sweden would approve participation and would join in 2005.

In the general elections in September 2002 the party made a moderate political comeback, increasing its share of the vote from 36.4% to 39.8%. Once again it was able to form a minority goverment by reaching an agremment with the Greens and Left Party. However, 2003 proved a heavy year for Prime Minister Persson. First, the Foreign Minister, Anna Lindh, was murdered on Sept. 11. She was one of the country's most popular politicians and was slated to replace Persson as party leader before the next elections. Merely three days later, Swedish voters rejected EMU in a national referendum, despite Persson's intensive campaigning in favour of joining.

Having an official membership of 152,462, the SAP is a member party of the Socialist International. Its European Parliament representatives are members of the Party of European Socialists group.

Other Parties

Alliance Party (*Allianspartiet*, AP), centrist formation; won 58 votes in 2002 general election.
Address. Wemmenhögsgatan 23, 231 45 Trelleborg
Telephone/Fax. (46–410) 40904
Email. jlm-trbg@algonet.se
Website. www.allianspartiet.se
Leadership. Jerry Larsson (chairman)

Communist Party of Marxist–Leninists (Revolutionaries)
(*Kommunistiska Partiet Marxist-Leninisterna (Revolution-ärerna)*, KPML(r)), founded in 1970 as a pro-Albanian party originally; has contested elections with minimal national support, although it elected 11 local councillors in 1998, including 6 in Karlshamn, which made it the third largest party in that town.
Address. PO Box 31187, 400 32 Göteborg
Telephone. (46–31) 122–631
Fax. (46–31) 244–464
Email. kpmlr@kpmlr.o.se
Website. www.kpmlr.se
Leadership. Anders Carlsson (chair)

European Labour Party (*Europeiska Arbertarpartiet*, EAP), won 163 votes in 2002 general election.

Address. PO Box 11918, 161 11 Bromma
Leadership. Tore Fredin (chairman)

New Democracy (*NyDemokrati*, NyD), founded in February 1990 on a populist platform of massive tax cuts, abolition of the welfare state, stringent curbs on immigration, opposition to EU membership and cheaper alcohol. It caused a sensation in the 1991 general elections, winning 24 *Riksdag* seats with a vote share of 6.7%. For most of the subsequent parliamentary term it gave often vital external voting support to the centre-right minority government. In March 1994, however, the resignation of its controversial leader, Count Ian Wachmeister (sometimes labelled "the crazy count"), assisted a reorientation which resulted in the party joining the opposition. Having lost its early momentum, New Democracy fell well short of the 4% barrier to representation in the 1994 elections, taking only 1.2% of the vote; it failed again in 1998, winning only 8,297 votes. In 2002 it fell further to a mere 106 votes. The party has gone bankrupt and its homepage does not currently list a leader.
Website. www.nydemokrati.se

New Progress (*Ny Framtid*), won 9,337 votes in 2002 general election.
Address. PO Box 84, 565 22 Mullsjö
Telephone. (46–392) 31500
Fax. (46–392) 12610
Email. feedback@nyframtid.com
Leadership. Sune Lyxell

Socialist Justice Party (*Rättvisepartiet Socialisterna*, RS), Trotskyist formation founded in 1997, claims to be biggest Trotskyist party in Scandinavia, affiliated to Committee for a Workers' International; won 1,519 votes in 2002 general election. In Umeå it elected one candidate to the city council.
Website. www.socialisterna.org/rs
Email. rs@socialisterna.org

Socialist Party (*Socialistiska Partiet*, SP), a Trotskyist grouping founded in 1953 as the Communist Workers' League by dissidents of the main Communist Party (later the Left Party); took its present name in 1982; has contested elections but with minimal support (winning only 3,213 votes in 2002). It elected a member to the city council in Köping.
Address. PO Box 6087, 102 32 Stockholm
Telephone. (46–8) 310–850
Fax. (46–8) 441–4575
Email. sp@internationalen.se
Website. www.internationalen.se/sp

Stockholm Party (*Stockholmspartiet*), aiming to promote the interests of Sweden's capital city. From 1998-2002 it supported a centre-right government in Stockholm.
Address. Kungsgatan 37/2tr, 111 56 Stockholm.
Telephone. (46–8) 219–959
Fax. (46–8) 219–279
Email. kontakt@stockholmspartiet.se
Website. www.stockholmpartiet.se

Swedish Communist Party (*Sveriges Kommunistiska Parti*, SKP), founded in 1977 as the Communist Workers' Party by a pro-Soviet faction of what later became the Left Party, renamed in 1979; unrepresented nationally since 1979, it contested the 2002 elections as simply "Communists" and received 1,182 votes.
Address. PO Box 1566, 171 29 Solna
Telephone. (46–8) 735–8640
Fax. (46–8) 735–7902
Email. skp@skp.se
Website. www.skp.se

Swedish Democrats (*Sverigedemokraterna,* SD), radical right-wing formation opposed to immigration and multiculturalism; claiming 5,000 members, it increased its votes by nearly four-fold in the 2002 elections, receiving 76,300 votes and electing a total of 49 city councillors in 29 cities.
Address. PO Box 20085, 104 60 Stockholm
Telephone. (46–8) 641–2011
Fax. (46–8) 643–9260
Email. kansli@sverigedemokraterna.se
Website. www.sverigedemokraterna.se
Leadership. Mikael Jansson (chairman)

Swedish Pensioners' Interests Party (*Sveriges Pensionärers Intresseparti,* SPI), won 37,573 votes in 2002 general election and elected 73 local councillors in 42 towns.
Address. PO Box 5187, 200 72 Malmö
Website. www.spipartiet.org/
Telephone. (46-40) 91 88 37
Fax. (46-40) 91 88 38
Leadership. Nils-Olof Anderson (chair)

Switzerland

Capital: Bern
Population: 7,364,100 (2004E)

The Swiss Confederation, which first secured its indepedence in 1315, has a unique system of government.

The bicameral Federal Assembly, *Bundesver-samm-lung* or *Assemblée Fédérale* is elected by citizens above the age of 18. It comprises (i) a Council of States (*Ständerat* or *Conseil des États*) consisting of two members for each of 20 cantons and one for each of six half-cantons, elected by respective constituencies in of each of the cantons or half-cantons; (ii) a 200-member National Council (*Nationalrat* or *Conseil National*) elected for a four-year term under a system of proportional representation by the electorate in each of the cantons and half-cantons. The 20 cantons and six half-cantons have to be represented by at least one member. In cantons where there is only one deputy the proportional representation remains purely theoretical and the system is *de facto* majoritarian. In all cantons and half-cantons the elections to the National Council are conducted under a list system with proportional representation, with voters being able to cast preferential votes; in all but one canton and one half-canton a simple majority system applies for elections to the Council of States. Members of both houses serve for four years.

The collective Head of State, the Federal Council (*Bundesrat* or *Conseil Fédéral*), is a collegial body of seven members. The President of the *Bundesrat*, who is also the President of the Confederation, is elected, together with a Vice-President (who shall be the next President) for a one-year term by the two Houses of Parliament, which also elect the members of the government for a four-year term.

The Swiss system of government provides for a unique system of referenda and initiatives through which the electorate may challenge any law voted by the federal parliament, making Switzerland a semi-direct democracy. Constitutional amendments may be enacted as a result of an initiative supported by at least 100,000 voters and either containing a draft amendment or proposing the substance of an amendment and leaving the drafting to Parliament. A referendum may be held on a matter already approved by Parliament. Constitutional amendments and the most important international treaties are subject to approval by popular vote and by the cantons in a "compulsory referendum". A national "facultative referendum" may be held on other matters of general validity (but not on the budget) already approved by Parliament if, within 90 days of parliamentary adoption, 50,000 voters or eight cantons request a vote on the specific act or decree.

While there is no state financial support for party organizations, parliamentary groups receive a basic payment of SwF90,000 per annum plus SwF16,500 per member.

Elections to the National Council on Oct. 19, 2003, resulted as follows: Swiss People's Party (SVP) 55 (26.6%), Social Democratic Party of Switzerland 52 seats (with 23.3% of the vote), Radical Democratic Party of Switzerland 36 (17.3%), Christian Democratic People's Party of Switzerland 28 (14.4%), Green Party 13 (7.4%), Liberal Party of Switzerland 4 (2.2%), Evangelical People's Party 3 (2.3%), Federal Democratic Union 2 (1.3%), Swiss Party of Labour 2 (0.7%), Swiss Democrats 1 (1.0%), Left Alliance 1 (0.5%), *Solidarités* 1 (0.5%), Christian Social Party 1 (0.4%), Ticino League 1 (0.4%). The outcome was a break in the relative stability of the long-standing political equilibrium called the "magic formula", which had remained intact until 2003, when it was called into question as a result of the polarization of Swiss politics – the rise in support for the Swiss People's Party and Social Democratic Party, and a loss of public support for the centre parties (Radical Democratic Party, Christian Democratic People's Party and the Liberals). The federal elections of October 2003 also confirmed a shift to the right. This was clearly in evidence during the re-election of the Federal Council on Dec. 10, 2003, when one of the two Christian Democrat representatives was replaced by a Swiss People's Party candidate to reflect that party's share of the electoral vote. Opinion remains divided as to whether this is the death knell for the "magic formula" or simply a condition of an otherwise stable system.

The current political confrontation has become tougher, more chaotic and unpredictable. As a result all four governmental parties have instituted smaller and lighter management teams capable of reacting more quickly to developments and challenges. The goal is to keep a clear political profile. Another result of the increased polarization has been a certain lack of confidence of the eletorate in the Federal Council. For many years, the electorate has voted according to the recommendations of the government. In 2004 however, in votes which took place on February 8 and May 16, all five proposals by the Federal Council were rejected.

Christian Democratic People's Party of Switzerland
Christlichdemokratische Volkspartei der Schweiz (CVP)
Parti Démocrate–Chrétien Suisse (PDC)
Partito Popolare Democratico Svizzero (PPD)
Partida Cristiandemocratica dalla Svizra (PCD)
Address. Klaraweg 6, Postfach 5835, 3001 Bern
Telephone. (41–31) 357–3333
Fax. (41–31) 352–2430
Email. info@cvp.ch
Website. www.cvp.ch
Leadership. Doris Leuthard (president); Bruno Frick (vice president); Dominique de Buman (vice president); Jean-Michel Cina (parliamentary leader)
The CVP is a mainstream Christian democratic party, advocating the encouragement of family life, a social market economy, peace in independence and freedom (i.e. maintenance of the country's armed forces) and solidarity with the

Third World poor. The party was founded in 1912 as the Swiss Conservative Party (*Parti Conservateur Suisse*), following the establishment of national (i.e. not cantonal) parties by the Social Democrats in 1882 and the Radicals in 1894 and a call for the creation of a Swiss Catholic party. By adopting the name Conservative Party, the founders emphasized the political rather than the denominational character of the new party, which was joined by representatives of Christian trade union groups in denominationally-mixed cantons. Having in 1957 become the *Parti Conservateur Chrétien–Social Suisse*, the party took its present name in 1970, becoming a party organized at federal level and no longer a union of cantonal parties.

The party has had two representatives in the seven-member federal government since 1959, although its share of the national vote has declined in recent elections. It was the strongest party in the *Nationalrat* between 1975 and 1983, falling to third place in the latter year but recovering to second place in 1987, with 42 seats and 20% of the vote. It fell back to third place in 1991, with 36 seats and 18.3% of the vote, and slipped further in 1995 to 34 seats and 17.0%. The party then sought to develop new policies for the 21st century, based on its view that Switzerland's destiny was to join the European Union. However, in the October 1999 parliamentary elections the party became the smallest of the four coalition parties with 15.8% of the vote, even though it made a one-seat gain to 35. In the October 2003 elections the party remained in fourth place, declining to 14.4% of the vote and 28 seats.

The party congress held in Bern on Sept. 19, 2004, sought ways to halt the party's collapse following the October 2003 elections. In addition to electing a new leadership the congress also approved the CVP charter which defines its priorities as the economy, family and social security. Its goal is to be more "visible" and "credible" and closer to the electorate. According to the new president, the party has an "historic opportunity" to become a "third way" in a political landscape marked by a polarization between left and right. In concrete terms, its first objective will be to fight against youth unemployment.

The CVS is a member party of the Christian Democrat International, an associate member of the European People's Party and a member of the European Democrat Union.

Christian Social Party
Christlichsoziale Partei (CSP)
Parti Chrétien–Social (PCS)
Partito Cristiano–Sociale (PCS)
Address. Bruneggweg 4, 8002 Zurich
Telephone. (41–1) 201–1941
Fax. (41–1) 201–2114
Email. bloch.suess@bluewin.ch
Website. www.csp-pcs.ch
Leadership. Monika Bloch Süss (chairperson); Marlies Schafer-Jungo (secretary)
The small CSP stands on the progressive wing of Christian democracy, advocating that governments have important social responsibilities to which resources must be allocated. The party won one *Nationalrat* seat in the October 1995 general elections and retained it in 1999 and 2003, its elected member joining the Green Party parliamentary group. The classical electorate of this party are the Christian trade unions. Its only MP, Hugo Fasel, is the president of the Swiss Confederation of Christian Trade Unions.

Evangelical People's Party
Evangelische Volkspartei (EVP)
Parti Évangelique (PEV)
Partito Evangelico (PEV)
Address. Josefstrasse 32, 8005 Zurich
Telephone. (41–1) 272–7100

Fax. (41–1) 272–1437
Email. info@evppev.ch
Website. www.evppev.ch
Leadership. Ruedi Äschbacher (chairman); Joel Blunier (general secretary)
Founded in 1919, the EVP is a centrist party based on Protestant precepts, advocating a social market economy, avoidance of damage to the environment, a restructuring of agriculture, land reform, strict control of traffic, civilian service for conscientious objectors and a halt to the construction of nuclear power stations. First represented in the *Nationalrat* in 1919, the party has maintained a small but consistent presence in the post-war era, winning three seats in 1991 (with 1.9% of the vote), slipping to two seats in 1995 (with 1.8%) but recovering to three seats (again with 1.8%) in 1999. In the *Nationalrat* the EVP has been closely aligned with the Independents' Alliance. In 2003, the EVP retained its three seats and increased its share of the vote to 2.3%, its highest share ever.

The EVP is affiliated to the Christian Democrat International.

Federal Democratic Union
Eidgenössisch–Demokratische Union (EDU)
Union Démocratique Fédérale (UDF)
Unione Democratica Federale (UDF)
Address. Postfach, 3601 Thun
Telephone. (41–33) 222–3637
Fax. (41–33) 222–3744
Email. info@edu-udf.ch
Website. www.edu-udf.ch
Leadership. Hans Moser (chairman)
The EDU was founded in 1975 on a policy platform deriving from a conservative and fundamentalist Protestant interpretation of the Bible. The party was established by Max Wahl and other members of the (now defunct) Swiss Republican Movement, which had itself been created in 1971 by James Schwarzenbach, who had previously founded what later became the Swiss Democrats. Advocating restrictions on the permanent settlement of foreigners in Switzerland, the EDU won four *Nationalrat* seats in 1975 and one in 1983. It failed to win representation in the 1987 general elections, but obtained one seat in 1991, which it retained in 1995 and increased to three in 1999.

The EDU was the only small right-wing party able in the 2003 elections to maintain the level of electoral support it had reached in 1999. Many of the supporters of these parties, who come mostly from the religious movements in the valleys of the canton of Bern, have instead switched their support to the SVP/UDC.

Green Party–Greens
Grüne Partei–Grüne
Parti Écologiste–Les Verts
Partida Ecologista–I Verdi
Address. Waisenhausplatz 21, 3011 Bern
Telephone. (41–31) 312–6660
Fax. (41–31) 312–6662
Email. gruene@gruene.ch
Website. www.gruene.ch
Leadership. Ruth Genner (chairman); Ueli Leuenberger (vice-chairman); Cécile Bühlmann (parliamentary leader); Hubert Zurkinden (general secretary)
The mainstream environmentalist GPS was founded in May 1983 as the Federation of Green Parties of Switzerland, embracing nine groupings, among them the *Groupement pour l'Environnement* in the canton of Vaud (which had gained one seat in the *Nationalrat* in 1979), the *Parti Écologique* of Geneva, the *Mouvement pour l'Environnement* of Neuchâtel, the Green Party of Zurich and the Green Party of North-West

Switzerland. In the 1983 general elections the federated party obtained 2.9% of the vote and three seats in the *Nationalrat*. After it had been joined by further groups, it changed its name to Green Party in 1985. Thereafter the Greens operated both as a federal party and as a collection of cantonal groups, which were free to make their own electoral alliances.

In the October 1987 federal elections the GPS obtained nine seats in the *Nationalrat* (and 4.8% of the vote), rather less than had been expected in view of public alarm over recent chemical pollution of the Rhine and also over the Chernobyl nuclear disaster in the then Soviet Union. Part of the reason was that some pro-ecology voting support went to the Progressive Organizations of Switzerland, which included left-oriented Greens (but later became inactive). The mainstream GPS made a substantial advance in the 1991 elections, to 14 seats and 6.1% of the vote.

The tide of environmental concern had receded by the time of the October 1995 federal elections, in which the Greens fell back to nine seats on a 5% vote share. Four years later the party achieved precisely the same result, despite campaigning jointly with the left-leaning Green Alliance, although its parliamentary group was increased to 10 by the adhesion of the Christian Social Party representative. Thereafter the Greens were active with the Social Democratic Party of Switzerland in demanding that Swiss defence expenditure should be reduced by a third over 10 years (a proposal to that effect being decisively defeated in a referendum in November 2000).

Along with the Swiss People's Party, the Greens proved the other significant winners in the 2003 elections, taking 13 seats. As a result, they are clearly the most important non-governmental party. At the beginning of July 2004, however, old disputes led to the splitting of the Greens of Zurich into two parties and the creation of the new Green-Liberal party of the canton of Zurich (*Grün-liberale Partei des Kantons Zürich*, GliZ) around Martin Bäumle and Verena Diener. The latter believe that the Greens have become too fundamentalist and scorn liberal and "realistic" principles (especially since the activist Balthasar Glättli was elected to the co-chairmanship of the cantonal party instead of Martin Bäumle).

The Swiss Greens are members of the European Federation of Green Parties.

Liberal Party of Switzerland
Liberale Partei der Schweiz (LPS)
Parti Libéral Suisse (PLS)
Partito Liberale Svizzero (PLS)
Address. Spitalgasse 32, Postfach 7107, 3001 Bern
Telephone. (41–31) 311–6404
Fax. (41–31) 312–5474
Email. info@liberal.ch
Website. www.liberal.ch
Leadership. Claude Ruey (chairman); Christophe Berdat (central secretary)
The LPS stands for "the maintenance of federalism and of the market economy and the guaranteeing of individual freedom and responsibility, without ignoring the need for solidarity and the necessity of the functions of the state". It also calls for protection of the individual, the maintenance of an efficient defence force and of "armed neutrality", cooperation with the Third World, improvement of the quality of life, the use of natural gas and nuclear power as an alternative to oil, and freedom of information (but with state control over radio and television frequencies).

Descended from the liberal movement of the late 19th century, the LPS is based in the four mainly Protestant cantons of Geneva, Vaud, Neuchâtel and Basel-Stadt, where the party maintained an independent identity as liberals in other cantons were absorbed into the Radical Democratic and Christian Democratic People's parties. The party took its present name in 1977, having previously been the Liberal Democratic Union of Switzerland.

In the 1983 general elections the LPS retained eight *Nationalrat* seats on the basis of 2.8% of the vote, advancing in 1987 to nine seats (although with 2.7% of the vote). A further advance in 1991 to 10 seats and 3.0% was followed by a decline to seven seats and 2.7% of the vote in October 1995 and to six seats (2.2%) in October 1999. In the October 2003 elections the party secured 2.2% of the votes and four seats. It currently lacks a leader of its representation in parliament as the four LPS MPs resulting from 2003 elections are not enough to form a group - they have joined the Radical Group. On many issues in the few cantons where it has a presence the LPS plays the role of right-wing opposition.

The LPS is a member of the Liberal International.

Radical Democratic Party of Switzerland
Freisinnig–Demokratische Partei der Schweiz (FDP)
Parti Radical–Démocratique Suisse (PRD)
Partito Liberale–Radicale Svizzero (PLR)
Address. Neuengasse 20, Postfach 6136, 3001 Bern
Telephone. (41–31) 320–3535
Fax. (41–31) 320–3500
Email. gs@fdp-prd.ch
Website. www.fdp.ch
Leadership. Léonard Bender (vice-chairman); Fulvio Pelli (parliamentary leader); Guido Schommer (secretary-general).
The FDP claims to be "the founder of modern Switzerland" in that "after a confrontation with conservative forces in 1848 it laid the foundations for the Swiss federal state as it exists today". A Radical Democratic group was first established in the Federal Assembly in 1878, 16 years before the establishment of the party as such in 1894. The introduction of proportional representation in 1919 diminished the party's influence in the *Nationalrat*, but it held a dominant position in the federal government until 1959. In that year it formed a coalition with the Social Democratic Party, the Christian Democratic People's Party and the Agrarians (later the Swiss People's Party), which has been maintained ever since.

The 1983 general elections resulted in the FDP becoming the country's strongest party, with 23.4% of the vote and 54 of the 200 *Nationalrat* seats. It remained so in 1987, with 51 seats and 22.9% of the vote, and in 1991, despite slipping to 44 seats and 21.0%. In the October 1995 elections, however, it yielded first place to the Social Democrats, despite improving marginally to 45 seats on a lower vote share of 20.2%. In October 1999 it slipped to third place, with 43 seats and 19.9% of the vote.

The scandal of the Swissair bankruptcy – many administrators of the airline were Radicals – and the outrageous cost of the national fair Expo.02, widely supported by Radicals, has made of the party a symbol of easy money and lack of responsibility in public management. This contributed to the party's declining fortunes in the October 2003 elections during which it secured 17.3% of the vote and won 36 seats – the worst result since 1919. Mark Sutter, one of the FDP's most liberal politicians, lost his seat, marking the party's shift to the right. Rolf Schweiger resigned as party chairman in November 2004.

The FDP is a member of the Liberal International.

Social Democratic Party of Switzerland
Sozialdemokratische Partei der Schweiz (SPS)
Parti Socialiste Suisse (PSS)
Partito Socialista Svizzero (PSS)
Address. Spitalgasse 34, Postfach 7876, 3001 Bern
Telephone. (41–31) 329–6969
Fax. (41–31) 329–6970
Email. info@spschweiz.ch
Website. www.sp-ps.ch

Leadership. Hans-Jürg Fehr (chairman); Hildegard Fässler (parliamentary leader); Reto Gamma (general secretary)

Founded as a federal party in 1888, the SPS quickly became a powerful political force in the country, particularly after the introduction of proportional representation in 1919. In the post-1945 period it regularly obtained about 25% of the total vote and since 1959 has held two of the seven seats in a four-party coalition government also including the Radical Democratic (FDP), Christian Democratic People's (CVP) and Swiss People's (SVP) parties. During the 1970s "new left" elements were in the ascendancy within the party, which accordingly adopted more radical policies (although with little effect on governmental action). However, at a congress held in Lugano in November 1982 a new programme of basic principles was adopted by a large majority, confirming the reformist, social democratic character of the party and thus representing a defeat for the left wing, which had argued for a socialist programme based on the concept of self-management.

In the 1983 general elections the SPS was outpolled by the FDP for the first time for 58 years, being reduced to 22.8% of the vote and 47 of the 200 *Nationalrat* seats as against 24.4% and 51 seats in 1979. Thereafter opposition within the SPS to continued participation in the federal coalition government came to a head when the party's nomination of female left-winger Lillian Uchtenhagen for a ministerial post failed to secure the support of the other coalition parties. However, a recommendation from the executive in favour of withdrawal from the government was effectively rejected by an emergency party congress in Bern in February 1984 by 773 votes to 511.

The SPS contested the 1987 general elections on a platform including ecological objectives; it lost six lower house seats, polling only 18.4% of the vote and obtaining the party's lowest representation (41 seats) since 1919. In the canton of St Gallen the SPS held its two seats in alliance with a Green List for People, Animals and the Environment (*Grüne Liste für Mensch, Tier und Umwelt*). The 1991 federal elections were also bad for the SPS, which languished on 18.5% of the vote, although the canton-based voting system gave it three additional seats, for a total of 44.

Demonstrating its commitment to women's equality by having a rule that at least one-third of its election candidates must be women, in 1993 the SPS again became exercised by the resistance of its coalition partners to female ministerial participation when its nomination of Christiane Brunner was rejected, apparently because of her unorthodox life style and outspoken feminism. The SPS promptly nominated another woman, Ruth Dreifuss, and warned that it would leave the coalition if she too were blackballed. The result was that Dreifuss was elected to the government, becoming Interior Minister.

Benefiting from a swing to the left in the October 1995 general elections, the SPS recovered its position as the premier party, advancing to 54 seats in the *Nationalrat* on a vote share of 21.8%. It retained the leading position in the October 1999 elections with 51 seats and 22.5%, although it was narrowly outpolled in terms of the popular vote by the SVP. In the new *Nationalrat*, the SPS group was joined by the single representative of the Left Alliance. In the subsequent government formation, the SPS successfully resisted SVP demands for an additional seat on the seven-member Federal Council, but failed in its attempt to have the SVP ejected from the ruling coalition.

Internal dissension contributed to the resignation of Ursula Koch, who represented the "fundamentalist" wing, from the SPS chairmanship in April 2000. She was succeeded in October 2000 by Brunner, representing the "pragmatic" wing. The following month the SPS, alone among the four coalition parties, supported a referendum proposal that Swiss defence expenditure should be reduced by a third over 10 years, expressing disappointment at the decisive rejection given by the voters.

In the 2003 elections, the SPS achieved a slight progression for the fourth election in succession, compensating slowly for its losses of the 1980s – its vote share of 23.3% representing its best result since 1979. The SPS achieved notable successes with the popular rejection of a law aiming at the liberalization of the electricity market in 2002 and of a tax measure reducing taxes on the wealthy in 2004.

The SPS is a member of the Socialist International

Swiss Democrats
Schweizer Demokraten (SD)
Démocrates Suisses (SD)
Democratici Svizzeri (DS)
Address. Postfach 8116, 3001 Bern
Telephone. (41–31) 974–2010
Fax. (41–31) 974–2011
Email. sd-ds@bluewin.ch
Website. www.schweizer-demokraten.ch
Leadership. Rudolf Keller (chairman); Bernhard Hess (secretary)

The party was founded in 1961 as the National Action Against Foreign Infiltration of People and Homeland (*Nationale Aktion Gegen Überfremdung von Volk und Heimat*), which was later shortened to National Action for People and Homeland (*Nationale Aktion für Volk und Heimat*) and abbreviated to National Action (NA). It called for strict curbs on immigration, an end to the "misuse" of the right to asylum and measures to limit the sale of property to foreigners. It also advocated "the protection of the natural environment, full employment of the Swiss population, political independence, and security, law and order in liberty".

In 1968 the NA launched a campaign for setting a ceiling on the proportion of foreigners resident in Switzerland and initiated a national referendum to that end, which was defeated by a slight majority in June 1970. Although the government subsequently issued certain restrictive regulations on foreign residents the NA continued its campaign and launched another initiative, which was also rejected by a majority of citizens in 1974. Following an increase in the number of naturalizations, the NA undertook a further initiative together with one demanding the submission of all future treaties with foreign countries to a referendum. The Federal Council thereupon drafted a counter-proposal which was approved in a referendum in March 1977. In 1981 the NA asked for a referendum on a proposed bill relaxing some of the existing restrictions on foreign workers, and in a referendum in June 1982 this bill was rejected by a large majority.

In the 1967 elections to the *Nationalrat* the NA won one seat for its founder, James Schwarzenbach, who left the NA in 1970 and later founded the (now defunct) Swiss Republican Movement. In the 1971 *Nationalrat* elections the NA won four seats (while the Swiss Republican Movement obtained seven). By October 1979 the NA's representation had fallen to two but in the 1983 elections it rose again to four seats, after the party had contested the elections on a joint list with the Swiss Republican Movement which obtained 3.5% of the vote. In August 1985 Hans Zwicky (who was then president of the NA) asserted that there was no connection between the NA and the newly formed National Socialist Party.

Despite scoring some local election successes in the mid-1980s, in the general elections of October 1987 the NA lost one of its four seats in the *Nationalrat* and obtained only 2.9% of the vote. The new SD title was adopted prior to the 1991 federal elections, in which the party rose to five seats, having presented a joint list with the Ticino League which took 3.4% of the vote. Standing alone, it dropped back to three seats and

3.1% in the October 1995 elections and to only one seat and 1.8% in October 1999. The SD was subsequently prominent in the campaign for a constitutional limit of 18% on the proportion of foreigners in the Swiss population, which was heavily defeated in a national referendum in September 2000. In the 2003 elections, when it retained its single seat, its vote share of 1.0% was the worst in the history of the party.

Swiss Party of Labour
Parti Suisse du Travail (PdT)
Partei der Arbeit der Schweiz (PAS)
Partito Svizzero del Lavoro (PSL)

Address. Rue du Vieux-Billard 25, CP 232, 1211 Geneve 8
Telephone. (41–22) 322–2290
Fax. (41–22) 322–2295
Email. pst-pda@bluemail.ch or abringolf@vtx.ch_
Website. www.pst.ch *or* www.pda.ch
Leadership. Alain Bringolf (chairman); Anjuska Weil (chairperson of the programme committee); Sonia Crivelli (chairperson of the central committee)

The PST was founded in October 1944 by members of the pre-war Communist Party (formed in 1921 but banned in 1939) and left-wing socialists who had been expelled or had resigned from the Social Democratic Party of Switzerland. The party is organized in a dozen cantons, in particular in Geneva, Vaud, Neuchâtel and Basel (all predominantly French-speaking) and in Italian-speaking Ticino. Formerly an orthodox pro-Soviet party, the PST converted to democratic socialism on the demise of the USSR in 1991. Its reward in the 1991 elections was a tripling of its *Nationalrat* representation from one to three seats, which it retained in 1995 with 1.2% of the vote. In October 1999, however, it fell back to two seats and 1%.

The PST, which is present primarily in French-speaking Switzerland, and its close ally the movement *Solidarités* (Sol.), together managed 1.2% of the vote in the Ocotober 2003 elections, the PST itself taking 0.7% and retaining its two seats.

Swiss People's Party
Schweizerische Volkspartei (SVP)
Union Démocratique du Centre (UDC)
Unione Democratica di Centro (UDC)
Uniun Democratica dal Center (UDC)

Address. Brückfeldstrasse 18, 3000 Bern 26
Telephone. (41–31) 300–5858
Fax. (41–31) 300–5859
Email. gs@svp.ch
Website. www.svp.ch
Leadership. Ueli Maurer (chairman); Caspar Baader (parliamentary leader); Gregor Rutz (general secretary)

The right-wing populist SVP was founded in its present form in 1971 as successor to (i) the Farmers', Traders' and Citizens' (i.e. Agrarian) Party, which had been formed in Zurich in 1917 and in Bern in 1918, and which was joined by the artisans and former Conservative Liberals of the canton of Bern in 1921, becoming a government party in 1929; and (ii) the former Swiss Democratic Party (founded in 1942), which had its origins in the Democratic Party established in the canton of Zurich in 1867, the Democratic and Workers' Party set up in the canton of Glarus in 1890 and the Democratic Party founded in Grisons in 1942. Since the 1971 union, the SVP has continued to hold the one seat in the federal government which the Agrarian Party had held since 1959 in coalition with the Radical Democratic, Social Democratic and Christian Democratic People's parties.

In the 1983 general elections the SVP retained 23 seats in the *Nationalrat* on the basis of 11.1% of the vote. In the 1987 contest the party obtained 25 seats on a slightly reduced vote share, which it increased to 11.9% in 1991 while still win-

ning 25 seats. The October 1995 elections brought something of a breakthrough by Swiss standards, to 14.9% of the vote and 29 seats, only five less than the Christian Democrats (which held two government posts). The SVP's success in 1995 was attributed in particular to its participation, alone among the coalition parties, in the successful campaign against Swiss membership of the European Economic Area and its consistent opposition to accession to the European Union. Also important was the party's articulation of growing public concern about immigration and the number of foreign workers in Switzerland.

Building on this populist platform, the SVP scored a major victory in the October 1999 parliamentary elections, winning more votes than any other party, although the peculiarities of the electoral system gave it second representative place with 44 seats. Despite now being stronger than two of the other three coalition parties, the SVP's demand for equal representation in the government was successfully resisted, especially by the Social Democrats. The SVP was subsequently prominent in the campaign that resulted in March 2001 in a decisive referendum decision against opening negotiations on EU membership.

The strong progress of the SVP in the 1990s continued in the 2003 election. With 26.6% of the votes it has clearly become the strongest party in the country, it now also having the largest number of seats (55). The more than doubling of the party's electoral support since 1991 is the more striking in that for 50 years previously the party had had a stable proportion of about 10%-12% of the votes, consistently remaining the fourth and smallest governmental party. It is generally considered that the charismatic leadership of multimillionaire Christoph Blocher has boosted the party's fortunes and support. As a result of the SVP's strong performance Christoph Blocher was elected to the Federal Council on Dec. 10, 2003, at the expense of the Christian Democrats, finally giving the SVP two seats on the Council and shifting the governmental balance to the right.

Ticino League
Lega dei Ticinesi (LdT)

Address. Via Monte Boglia 7, CP 2311, 6901 Lugano
Telephone. (41–91) 971–3033
Fax. (41–91) 972–7492
Website. www.legaticinesi.com
Leadership. Giuliano Bignasca (chairman); Mauro Malandra & Guido Quadri (secretaries)

Based exclusively in the Italian-speaking canton of Ticino, the LdT combines right-wing economic and social policy prescriptions with advocacy of greater autonomy for Ticino within the confederation. It won two *Nationalrat* seats in 1991 on a joint list with the equally right-ring Swiss Democrats. Standing on its own, it retained only one seat in the October 1995 contest, improving to two in October 1999 with 0.9% of the vote. In October 2003 with 0.4% of the votes, the Lega secured the worst result in its history, declining again to one seat.

Other Parties

Freedom Party of Switzerland (*Freiheits Partei der Schweiz*, FPS), better known as the Automobile or Car Party, the name under which it was launched in March 1985 to represent motorists' "rights", to support the construction of motorways and the provision of parking facilities in towns, and to oppose increases in car tax or a levy on vehicles using motorways. More broadly, the party espouses free enterprise and anti-state precepts, akin to those of the conservative wing of the Radical Democratic Party (of which its first leader, Michael Dreher, had been a member). The FPS title was adopted in 1994, by which time the party was combining concern for the interests of motorists with a demand for curbs on immigration. Having won two *Nationalrat* seats at its first election in 1987 (with 2.6% of the vote), the party advanced strongly to eight seats on a 5.1% vote share in 1991, but fell back to seven seats and 4.0% in 1995. In October 1999 it failed to gain representation, taking only 0.9% of the vote. In October 2003 it secured only 0.2% of the vote.

Website. www.freiheits-partei.ch
Leadership. Jürg Scherrer (president)

Green Alliance (*Grünes Bundnis*, GB / *Alliance Verte et Sociale*, AVeS / *Alleanza Verde e Sociale*, AVeS), left-wing ecologist grouping which urges the eventual abolition of the Swiss Army. It established a presence in the Lucerne cantonal parliament, before contesting the 1987 general elections on a joint list with the (now inactive) Progressive Organizations of Switzerland (POCH), winning four seats and 3.5% of the vote. (The last section of POCH dissolved in 1993). Having failed to gain representation in 1991 and 1995, it overcame its original hostility to the mainstream Green Party by presenting joint lists with the latter in 1999, winning one of the Greens' nine seats. Green Allliance is a member of the Green Party, and leader Franziska Teuscher sits in the Green Parliamentary Group.

The GB is a member of the European Federation of Green Parties.

Address. Neubrückstrasse 17, 3012 Bern
Telephone. (41–31) 301–8209
Fax. (41–31) 302–8878
Email. info@gbbern.ch
Website. www.gb-aves.ch or www.gbbern.ch
Leadership. Franziska Teuscher (*Nationalrat* member); Jacqueline Morgenegg (secretary)

Independents' Alliance (*Landesring der Unabhängigen* (LdU)/*Alliance des Indépendants* (AdI)). The LdU was founded in 1936 to represent the interests of socially responsible citizens and consumers outside the conventional party framework. In the post-war era, operating very much like a conventional party, the formation achieved significant *Nationalrat* representation, of 10 seats between 1951 and 1967, when its tally rose to 16. Thereafter it was in steady decline, in part because of the emergence of the Green Party of Switzerland and other formations representing particular interests. Having won five seats from 2.8% of the vote in 1991, the LdU fell to three seats (1.8%) in 1995 and to one seat (0.7%) in October 1999. A few weeks after 1999 elections, the AdI broke up.

Left Alliance/Solidarités (*Alliance de Gauche*), left-wing alternative movement advocating a "new citizenship" and rights for foreign workers, opposing gender discrimination and social exclusion; standing as *Solidarités*, it won one *Nationalrat* seat in Geneva in October 1999, its member joining the group of the Social Democratic Party of Switzerland. In the 2003 elections one seat each was won in the name of the Left Alliance and *Solidarités*.

Address. CP 2089, 1211 Geneva
Telephone. (41–22) 740–0740
Fax. (41–22) 740–0887
Email. info@solidarites.ch
Website. www.solidarites.ch
Leadership. Christian Grobet

National Socialist Party (*Nationalsozialistische Partei*, NSP), radical right-wing party founded in 1985 by a faction of what became the Swiss Democrats "to improve the image of national socialism" and to combat "over-population by foreigners".
Leadership. Ernst Meister

Ticino Socialist Party (*Partito Socialista, Sezione Ticinese*), left-wing socialist grouping based in the Italian-speaking canton of Ticino, founded in 1988 as the Unitarian Socialist Party (PSU), which was a merger of the Autonomous Socialist Party with a section of the smaller Community of Ticinese Socialists (CST).
Leadership. Anna Biscossa

Women Do Politics! (*Frauen Macht Politik!*, FraP!), seeking to change what it regards as ingrained resistance to female participation within established Swiss parties by persuading more women to become involved in politics. It established a bridgehead in the October 1995 elections, winning one *Nationalrat* seat, but lost it in 1999. The FraP dissolved before the 2003 elections, because its only MP, Christine Goll, had joined the Social Democratic Party (SPS).

Syria

Capital: Damascus
Population: 17,586,000 (2003 E)

The Syrian Arab Republic is, under its 1973 constitution, a "socialist popular democracy". It has an executive President, who is secretary-general of the *Ba'ath* Arab Socialist Party (BASP) and also chairman of the National Progressive Front (*al-Jubha al-Wataniyya al-Taqaddumiyya*, NPF), embracing the country's legal parties. These are the BASP, the Arab Socialist Party (ASP), the Arab Socialist Union (ASU), the Socialist Unionist Democratic Party (SUDP), the Socialist Unionist Movement (SUM), and the Syrian Communist Party (SCP). Legislative authority rests with the unicameral People's Assembly (*al-Majlis al-Sha'ab*), which is elected for a four-year term by universal adult suffrage of citizens over the age of 18 years and under a simple-majority system in multi-member constituencies. The assembly has 250 seats, of which the BASP is guaranteed at least half as part of 167 seats allotted to the NPF, with the remaining 83 seats going to independent deputies.

Parliamentary elections held on March 2-3, 2003, returned 135 deputies for the BASP, and 32 for other members of the NPF. The previously banned Syrian Social Nationalist Party (SSNP) won four independent seats, with the remaining 79 going to formally unaffiliated deputies.

Largely due to a law promulgated in 2002, which imposed mandatory retirement for public servants at the age of 65, the 2003 elections replaced 178 serving deputies while returning 125 deputies under the age of 50. Only 63.5% of eligible voters participated in the elections, compared to 82% in the 1998 elections. Five non-NPF parties urged their supporters to boycott the elections. While these parties are technically illegal, their existence has been tolerated by the leadership under President Bashar al-Assad, and several independent deputies are known to be informally affiliated with them.

The President is elected every seven years in a nation-wide referendum after nomination as sole candidate by the People's Assembly on the recommendation of the BASP. In a referendum held on July 10, 2000, Bashar al-Assad was confirmed as President following the death the previous month of his father, Hafez al-Assad, who had served as President since 1971. The President appoints the Vice-Presidents and the Council of Ministers.

Following the appointment of Bashar al-Assad, a period of liberalized political dialogue accompanied a programme of economic and social reform. Concerns within the staunchly secular BASP leadership about the pace and direction of political reform, especially the practical dilemma of legalizing secular political parties while maintaining a ban on the Muslim Brotherhood, the primary underground opposition organization, halted political liberalization and was accompanied by arrests of several outspoken oppositionists. In June 2004, the authorities reiterated their intention to create a more inclusive party system, while at the same time restating the ban on party activities outside the framework of the NPF.

Arab Socialist Party (ASP)
Hizb al-Ishtiraki al-Arabi
Address. c/o Majlis al-Sha'ab, Damascus
Leadership. Abd al-Ghani Qannut
The party has taken part in government since 1970, normally being allocated one ministerial post. It has been represented in the People's Assembly since 1973 as part of the NPF structure, obtaining six seats in the 1994, 1998 and 2003 elections. It is anti-Egyptian and seeks a revival of free competition among political parties.

Arab Socialist Union (ASU)
Ittihad al-Ishtiraki al-Arabi
Address. c/o Majlis al-Sha'ab, Damascus
Leadership. Jamal al-Atassi
The party is "Nasserite," subscribing to the socialist ideals of the former Egyptian President Gamal Abdel Nasser. It has been represented in every People's Assembly, as part of the NPF, and took seven seats in the 1994, 1998 and 2003 elections.

Ba'ath Arab Socialist Party
Hizb al-Ba'ath al-Arabi al-Ishtiraki
Address. PB 9389, Damascus
Leadership. Bashar al-Assad (secretary-general, chairman of the National Progressive Front); Abdallah al-Ahmar (assistant secretary-general)
Website. www.albaath.com (*al-Ba'ath* Newspaper, organ of the BASP)
The BASP espouses secular pan-Arabism, anti-imperialism, anti-Zionism and socialism. It is historically (but now only theoretically) a regional party of which the Syrian "branch" is a "regional command", the others being the Iraqi and Lebanese commands. This ideological regionalism continues to have a profound effect on Syrian foreign policy.

Founded by Michel Aflaq in Syria in 1947, the *Ba'ath* Party absorbed the Syrian Arab Socialist Party in December 1953 and assumed its current name. The party was behind the March 1963 coup (the month after its involvement in a coup in Iraq) and has held office in Syria ever since. Following an internal crisis in 1966, the party expelled the "rightist" wing headed by Aflaq, who fled to Iraq. The Iraqi *Ba'ath* returned to power in 1968, having been ousted at the end of 1963, but the theoretical unity of the party was not restored. Instead, the Syrian and Iraqi branches became fierce enemies, both sides sponsoring violent action against the other.

Hafez al-Assad's group within the BASP seized power in late 1970 and he maintained his dominance of the Syrian political scene until his death in 2000. The BASP has consistently dominated the NPF, which it formed as an umbrella group in 1972 to provide a framework for putting forward approved lists of candidates for legislative elections. In the 1994, 1998 and 2003 elections, 135 BASP candidates were returned. Following the death of his father, Bashar al-Assad took over as BASP secretary-general and NPF chairman.

Syrian Social Nationalist Party
Hizb al-Suri al-Qawmi al-Ijtimai
Leadership. Jubran Urayji
Websites. www.ssnp.com; www.alqawmi.com
Established by Antun Saada in 1932, the party began as a secret society opposing French colonial rule and seeking to unify "greater Syria," encompassing what is today Syria, Lebanon, Palestine/Israel, and Jordan. Saada was executed for treason by the Lebanese authorities in June 1949, and the party was suppressed by the Syrian military authorities in 1955. It remained active primarily in Lebanon and subscribes to many of the BASP's principles. Following the appointment of Bashar al-Assad, the SSNP was given increasing public space, culminating in its participation in the 2003 elections, when it won four seats.

Socialist Unionist Democratic Party
Hizb al-Dimuqrati al-Tawdhidi al-Ishtiraki
Address. c/o Majlis al-Sha'ab, Damascus
Leadership. Ahmad al-Assad
The party first appeared as one of the constituent parts of the NPF at the legislative elections held in May 1990. It took four seats in the 1994, 1998 and 2003 elections.

Socialist Unionist Movement
Haraka al-Tawhidiyah al-Ishtiraki-yah
Address. c/o Majlis al-Sha'ab, Damascus
Leadership. Sami Sufan
The party proclaims "Nasserite" socialist ideals. It has been represented in government since 1967, and is also represented in the People's Assembly through its membership of the NPF, obtaining seven seats in the 1994, 1998 and 2003 elections.

Syrian Communist Party (SCP)
Hizb al-Shuyui al-Suri
Address. c/o Majlis al-Sha'ab, Damascus
Leadership. Yusuf Faysal
Founded in 1925 (as part of a joint Communist Party of Syria and Lebanon until 1958), the SCP is generally regarded as the largest Communist Party in the Arab world, and was pro-Soviet in orientation until the collapse of the Soviet bloc. It is technically illegal, but is permitted to operate openly and has been represented in the cabinet since 1966. The SCP is a part of the NPF framework, taking eight seats in the 1994, 1998 and 2003 elections.

Taiwan

Capital: Taipei
Population: 22,191,087 (2000E)

The government of Taiwan (Formosa) is derived from that which ruled the Chinese mainland prior to the 1949 communist revolution and the establishment of the People's Republic of China (PRC). The Taiwan government continues to be called the Republic of China, though it abandoned claims to the mainland in 1991. Martial law, imposed in 1949, was lifted in 1987, this decision opening the way for the legalization of opposition parties. Since a constitutional revision in 2000 the National Assembly (*Kuomin Tahui*) confines itself largely to constitutional matters, whilst other legislation is the preserve of the elective Legislative *Yuan* (*Lifa Yuan*, LY).

Elections in December 1991 for 325 seats in the new National Assembly resulted in the Nationalist Party (*Kuomintang* or KMT), which had ruled the island since 1949, winning 254, the Democratic Progressive Party

(DPP) 66, the National Democratic Independent Political Alliance 3 and independents 2. In elections to the 164-member LY in 1995, however, the KMT achieved only a narrow majority, winning 85 seats, against 54 for the DPP, 21 for the New Party and 4 for independents. For the December 1998 LY election the number of seats was increased to 225, with 41 elected from national lists including 8 for Overseas Chinese. The KMT confirmed their supremacy, winning 123, whilst the DPP won only 70, and the New Party 11. By April 2000 91 parties had registered with the government, but only four had representatives in the LY.

Constitutional reforms approved in July 1994 provided for the direct election of the executive President (previously elected by the National Assembly). In March 1996 the incumbent, President Lee Teng-hui of the KMT, was re-elected with 54% of the votes cast despite strident military threats from the PRC. In 2000, however, rivalry between two potential candidates from the KMT, Lien Chan and James Soong, led to the latter standing at the head of his own People First Party (PFP). This, combined with increasing public exasperation over corruption scandals, let in Chen Shui-bian as the first President from the DPP, with Soong second and Lien an embarrassing third.

The DPP consolidated this success in the Dec. 1, 2001, legislative elections, taking 87 of the 225 seats in the LY, with 36.6% of the vote, while the KMT declined to 68 seats (31.3%). Other parties gaining seats were the PFP (46), Taiwan Solidarity Union (13), New Party (1), and Green Party Taiwan (1), with 9 non-partisans also elected. The elections gave the opposition parties a narrow majority in the legislature, with the PFP allying with the KMT.

The presidential election held on March 20, 2004, was again contested by Chen Shui-bian for the DPP and Lien Chan for the KMT, with James Soong, the leader of the PFP, this time contesting as Lien's running mate in an effort to unite the opposition. The election proved intensely controversial. President Chen was slightly wounded (along with his deputy, Annette Lu) in an apparent assassination attempt on March 19. Some DPP supporters attributed the shootings to the KMT and Beijing; the KMT, however, alleged that the assassination attempt could have been a hoax, arranged by Lien in a last-minute attempt to win public sympathy and tilt the result of a tight contest in which the rival candidates were locked neck-to-neck in the opinion polls. In the balloting, Chen gained only a fractional advantage (50.1% to 49.9%) over Lien Chan, triggering allegations of electoral fraud and demands for a recount from the KMT and its allies. Chen was inaugurated for a second term in May 2004 but the opposition continued with legal challenges.

Democratic Progressive Party (DPP)
Minchu Chinpu Tang
Address. 10th Fl, 30 Pei ping E. Road, Taipei 100
Telephone. (886–2) 2392–9989
Fax. (886–2) 2393–0342
Email. dpp@dpp.org.tw
Website. www.dpp.org.tw
Leadership. Chen Shui-bian (chairman)
The DPP was formed in 1986 (although the restrictions of martial law still applied at that time) by a dissident movement (*Tangwai*, meaning "outside the party"), which had been set up to promote multi-party democracy. Its base support comes from the "Taiwanese", i.e. those born on the island, and they are more concentrated in the south. Accorded legal status in 1989, the party was identified with

the call for an independent sovereign Taiwan and abandoning the concept of unification with the mainland.

During the 1990s it gradually increased its share of seats in the Legislative *Yuan*, from 21 in 1989 to 70 in 1998, but it never seemed likely to overtake the ruling Nationalist Party (KMT). It seemed trapped in a strategy of appealing for Taiwanese independence that was not enough to win majority support. In the March 1996 presidential election the party's candidate, Peng Ming-min, came second with 21% of the vote. In March 2000, however, a split within the KMT ranks allowed Chen Shui-bian to win with 39%, though he had to cohabit with a KMT-dominated Legislative *Yuan*. In the December 2001 legislative elections the DPP proved able to build on Chen's presidential victory, emerging as the leading party with 87 of the 225 seats in the LY, 19 more than the KMT.

Chen had a reputation as an advocate of independence and his election challenged the Taipei-Beijing consensus that Taiwan's status would not change other than through ultimate unification with the mainland. In February 2000, on the eve of the Taiwanese elections, the Beijing government issued a White Paper underlining its position of "peaceful reunification, and one country, two systems". While not commiting itself to never using force, Beijing's emphasis was on the development of cross-Straits trade and other contacts and a negotiated reunification, with a settlement modelled on that achieved for Hong Kong. In his inaugural address in May 2000 President Chen pledged that he would not declare Taiwan independent or change the name of the country provided Beijing did not seek to use force, and the benefits of the studied bilateral ambiguity over Taiwan's position were demonstrated when, in choreographed moves, China joined the World Trade Organization in December 2001 and Taiwan joined the following month, under the designation "Separate Customs Territory of Taiwan, Penghu, Kinmen and Matsu". Cross-strait relations remained delicate, however, with Beijing not disguising its suspicion of Chen's intentions, and Chen in August 2002 raising the prospect of a referendum on Taiwanese independence – China responding that it would "never tolerate" an independent Taiwan. In the event, in the face of opposition in the legislature and internationally (including from the USA), Chen's referendum proposals as eventually finalized in January 2004 were anodyne and innocuous, not raising the possibility of independence or a change of name; in the resultant popular referendum in March they in any case failed because of inadequate turnout. Notwithstanding some heightening of his rhetoric in the campaign for the presidential elections in March 2004, in his second inaugural address, in May 2004, Chen adopted a conciliatory tone in regard to Beijing, saying he would seek to reform the island's constitution without opening the issues of sovereignty or territory and would not take unilateral steps in respect of those issues. In practice Chen's government had focused resources on electorally popular areas like education and welfare, with defence spending having dropped to just over 2% of the GDP.

The DPP has observer status in the Liberal International.

Nationalist Party
Kuomintang (KMT)
Address. 9th Floor, 11 Chung Shan South Road, Taipei
Telephone. (886–2) 2343–4847
Fax. (886–2) 2343–4850
Website. www.kmt.org.tw
Leadership. Lien Chan (chairman); Lin Fong-cheng (secretary-general)
Dating from 1894, the *Kuomintang*, or KMT, was dominant at all levels of government from the proclamation of the Republic of China in 1949 until the 2000 presidential election. Its platform is still based on the "three principles of the

people" (nationalism, democracy and social well-being) originally enunciated by Sun Yat-sen, the party's founder. Organizationally it was modelled on Leninist Bolshevism until recently. The loser in the Chinese civil war, until the 1990s it still aspired to return to the mainland, but now it has effectively reconciled itself to a future on Taiwan. Over the decades people born on the island came to displace those born on the mainland within the leading ranks of the party. This was symbolized by Lee Teng-hui, who succeeded Chiang Ching-kuo as President of Taiwan and leader of the party in 1988. Later, in 1998, he launched the concept of the "New Taiwanese" as a call for national unity.

Once competitive party elections were allowed, the KMT's supremacy gradually declined. It was hit from without by increasing allegations of corruption and from within by suspicions that Lee Teng-hui was moving towards a position favouring Taiwanese independence. In 1993 members of a younger and more reform-minded New KMT Alliance faction within the party defected to form the New Party (NP). In 1995 two conservative KMT vice-chairs who favoured closer ties with China were expelled for aligning themselves with the NP.

Nevertheless Lee Teng-hui won Taiwan's first direct presidential election in March 1996, drawing 54% of the total vote. The KMT also remained the leading party in the Legislative *Yuan* as a result of the December 1998 elections, when it took 123 seats. For the March 2000 presidential election, however, the Vice-President, Lien Chan, and a former secretary general of the KMT, James Soong, both sought the party nomination, Lee being constitutionally barred. Lien won the nomination but Soong refused to withdraw, forming the People First Party (PFP). In the election the candidate of the opposition Democratic Progressive Party (DPP) came first, while Soong pushed Lien into third place, taking 37% of the vote to Lien's 23%. In the recriminations that followed, Lee was forced to step down early as KMT chair, being replaced by Lien.

After the victory of the DPP in March 2000, a re-registration of KMT party members showed 2.5 million instead of 3.5 million. Politicians with a mainland background made a come-back in the KMT under Lien and the party expanded its contacts with the People's Republic of China and the Communist Party of China. Where Lee advocated that cross-Straits relations be handled on the basis of full equality, Lien floated the concept of a confederation with the PRC. Partly in protest against these moves, Lee set up the Taiwan Solidarity Alliance in August 2001 and expressed support for President Chen Shui-bian. In the December 2001 elections the KMT lost its first place in the legislature, falling back to 68 seats, but Lien Chan rejected President Chen's call for the KMT to participate in a "National Stabilization Alliance". Since the formation of a DPP government under President Chen, the KMT, somewhat paradoxically, has become the party clearly most favoured by Beijing, with many KMT legislators visiting Beijing in the period since Chen's election.

In the March 2004 presidential election Lien Chan was again the KMT candidate and this time the party avoided the split that had proved disastrous in 2000 – instead James Soong contested as Lien Chan's running mate. The election was extremely close, and Lien was declared to have lost by only 29,000 votes – leading the KMT to mobilize its supporters in mass demonstrations to demand a recount. In May 2004 the central standing committee of the KMT voted to seek unification with two KMT splinters, the New Party and the People First Party, in an effort to consolidate the opposition to the DPP ahead of the next legislative elections in December 2004.

The KMT is an affiliate of the International Democrat Union.

New Party (NP)
Hsin Tang
Address. 4th Floor, 65 Kuangfu Nanlu, Taipei 105
Telephone. (886–2) 2756–2222
Fax. (886–2) 2756–5555
Website. www.np.org.tw
Leadership. Chou Yang-sun (chair)
The New Party was set up in mid-1993 by dissident Nationalist Party (KMT) members in the Legislative *Yuan* and merged later that year with the China Social Democratic Party (which had broken away from the Democratic Progressive Party (DPP) in 1991). The party advocates a "one China" policy while supporting the concept of direct talks with the mainland communist government. In the December 1995 elections the NP's representation in the Legislative *Yuan* rose to 21, making it the third largest formation. In the March 1996 presidential election the NP-backed candidate was former KMT vice-chair Lin Yang-kang, who came third with 15% of the popular vote. In 1998, however, its representation in the Legislative *Yuan* fell to 11 seats and its candidate in the 2000 presidential election only polled 0.13% of the votes after urging voters to support James Soong. In the December 2001 legislative elections it experienced a further decline, taking only 2.9% of the vote and being reduced to one seat. In May 2004 it was announced that the party had been invited to join merger talks between the KMT and People First Party.

People First Party (PFP)
Ch'in Min Tang
Email. webservice@pfp.org.tw
Website. www.pfp.org.tw
Leadership. James Soong (chairman); Tsai Chung-hsiung (secretary general)
The party was initially formed as a vehicle to support the 2000 presidential campaign of James Soong, a former secretary general of the Nationalist Party (KMT). His success in coming came second with 37% of the vote encouraged him to turn it into a regular party, attracting a number of defections by KMT legislators. In the December 2001 legislative elections, the party emerged as a significant third force, taking 46 seats on a 20.3% share of the vote in a campaign in which it declared itself the party of small government. Many PFP legislators were considered as speaking for the "mainlanders" who came to Taiwan in 1949. The party remained close to KMT thinking and in the March 2004 presidential elections Soong was KMT candidate Lien Chan's running mate – Soong being seen as adding an element of charisma lacking in Lien – with the ticket only narrowly losing. In May 2004 it was announced that Soong and Lien would form a committee to plan a merger of the PFP with the KMT.

Taiwan Solidarity Union (TSU)
Website. www.taiwanunion.com
Leadership. Huang chu-wen (chairman)
The TSU was formed in August 2001 by a breakaway group of KMT supporters loyal to former President Lee Teng-hui (who had moved increasingly towards a pro-independence outlook) and represented the first time that a party had included the name Taiwan in its title. Its declared aim was to "mobilize those who favour stability and a middle course" by working with the DPP. Lee himself gave public support to the new party and was stripped of his KMT membership. Twenty former KMT members stood for the TSU in the December 2001 legislative elections, with the new party taking 13 seats on an 8.5% share of the vote. In September 2003, Lee stated that the time had come for the country to officially change its name to Taiwan from the "unrealistic" Republic of China, stating: "the time was not ripe when I was President. Now, time is running out".

Other Parties

Green Party–Taiwan, seeing itself as part of the worldwide Green movement and formed in 1996. It scored a small electoral success in the December 2001 legislative elections when it gained 0.5% of the vote and one seat.

Website. http://gptaiwan.yam.org.tw

Tajikistan

Capital: Dushanbe
Population: 6,500,000 (2001E)

The Soviet Socialist Republic of Tajikistan declared independence from the USSR in September 1991 as the Republic of Tajikistan, which became a sovereign member of the Commonwealth of Independent States (CIS) in December 1991. The post-Soviet constitution adopted by referendum in November 1994 established an executive presidency, with the President as head of state, chief executive and commander-in-chief, being popularly elected for a five-year term (once renewable consecutively) and having the authority to appoint and dismiss the Prime Minister and other ministers, subject to approval by the legislature.

The Soviet-era Communist establishment remained in power in independent Tajikistan until civil war erupted in mid-1992, when allied pro-democracy and Islamic parties briefly took control, before being driven into opposition and armed insurgency by the resurgent Communists. Five years of bitter internal conflict followed, until on June 27, 1997, a peace agreement was concluded in Moscow between the Tajikistan government and the United Tajik Opposition (UTO) providing for UTO participation in government and the legalization of opposition parties. Implementation of the agreement proved slow and difficult, however, as disaffected Islamic groups and others continued their armed struggle.

As provided for under the Moscow agreement, important changes to the constitution were adopted by referendum in September 1999. These included the extension of the presidential term of office to seven years and the reform of the Supreme Assembly, introducing a bicameral system in place of the unicameral Soviet-era body. The highest legislative body remains the Supreme Assembly (*Majlisi Oli*). The lower Chamber of Representatives (*Majlisi Namoyandagon*) has 63 members, elected by universal adult suffrage on the basis of a mixed voting system of constituency seats (41) and proportional representation of parties (22 seats) subject to a threshold of 5% of the national vote. The upper National Chamber (*Majlisi Milli*) has 33 members, 25 elected by members of the provincial governments and eight appointed by the President. Both houses hold office for five-year terms.

Having been returned to office in November 1994 as interim incumbent, President Imomali Rakhmonov of the People's Democratic Party of Tajikistan (HDKT) was re-elected with a landslide 96.97% of the vote in presidential elections on Nov. 6, 1999. In June 2003, the constitution was amended by referendum; some fifty changes were introduced, including the extension of the number of presidential terms that could be served consecutively by a single individual. This cleared the way for President Rakhmonov to stand again in the next election, scheduled for 2006.

For elections to the newly-established Chamber of Representatives on Feb. 27 and March 12, 2000, six parties satisfied the requirements for registration and hence were allowed to nominate candidates. According to results published in May 2000 by the OSCE's Office for Democratic Institutions and Human Rights (ODIHR), the HDKT won 36 seats (with 63.4% of the proportional vote), the Communist Party of Tajikistan 13 (20.4%) and the Islamic Renaissance Party 2 (6.8%), the remaining 12 seats being won by independents or not decided. Elections to the National Chamber were also held in March 2000. The next elections for the upper and lower Chambers are scheduled for 2005. In preparation for this, in April 2004 three opposition parties formed a coalition. Called "For fair and transparent elections in Tajikistan", the new bloc comprises the Islamic Renaissance Party, the Social Democratic Party (Justice and Development Party) and the Socialist Party.

Communist Party of Tajikistan (CPT)

Address. c/o Supreme Assembly, Dushanbe
Leadership. Shodi Shabdollov (first secretary)

Having been the ruling (and only legal) party since 1924 as the republican branch of the Communist Party of the Soviet Union, the CPT entered the era of independence still very much in charge in conservative Tajikistan, with a substantial genuine membership concentrated in areas of high ethnic Uzbek or Russian population such as the northern industrial region of Khodjent (formerly Leninabad). Twelve days after Tajikistan's declaration of independence, a CPT congress voted on Sept. 21, 1991, to convert the party into the Tajik Socialist Party, with a democratic socialist orientation. In response to immediate mass protests, a presidential decree of Sept. 22 banned the party and nationalized its assets. One day after that, the Communist-dominated Supreme Soviet voted to rescind the prohibition, triggering further popular protests which resulted in the ban being confirmed on Oct. 2. However, the direct election of Communist Rakhman Nabiyev to the presidency in November 1991 with 58% of the popular vote resulted in the ban being officially lifted in January 1992; thereafter the party resumed activities under the CPT title, while maintaining its new commitment to democratic socialist principles.

The onset of civil conflict in 1992 ranged the Communist-era establishment against the allied forces of the Islamic and pro-democracy opposition, with the establishment emerging victorious, as indicated by the accession of Imomali Rakhmonov to the presidency in November 1992. The Supreme Court's decision in June 1993 to ban the four leading opposition parties served to confirm the CPT in its resumed role as effectively the ruling formation. Several new parties were launched in 1993-94, the most significant of which was the pro-presidential People's Democratic Party of Tajikistan (HDKT). Some observers initially regarded the HDKT as part of the CPT network, but the two parties soon diverged. When Rakhmonov formally opted for the HDKT in March 1998, the CPT effectively became part of the secular opposition.

The continuing strength of the CPT's countrywide organization was apparent in the February–March 2000 parliamentary elections, in which the party won over 20% of the national vote and 13 lower house seats, as well as four seats in the indirectly-elected upper house. In March 2001 the CPT announced that 1,200 people had applied to join the party in 2000, bringing its membership to 65,000.

Democratic Party of Tajikistan (DPT)

Address. c/o Supreme Assembly, Dushanbe
Leadership. Mahmadruzi Iskandarov (chairman)

The strongly anti-Communist DPT was launched in 1990 on a platform advocating Tajik sovereignty, the introduction of a market economy and a cultural revival. Its candidate in the October 1991 presidential election was Davlat Khudonazarov, who came a creditable second on the strength of an alliance with the Islamic Renaissance Party (IRP) against the ruling establishment of the Communist Party of Tajikistan. The DPT was prominent in the "government of national reconciliation" of May–November 1992, but the reassertion of Communist authority in late 1992 forced it into armed resistance. It was one of four opposition parties banned by the Supreme Court in June 1993, amid escalating internal conflict ranging pro-democracy and Islamic forces against the government. Peace talks resulting in a notional cease-fire agreement in September 1994 failed to bring the DPT and other opposition parties into the elections of late 1994 and early 1995.

Divisions between the moderate and hard-line wings of the DPT led to an open split in June 1995, when Shodmon Yusuf was deposed from the leadership but refused to recognize the election of Jumaboy Niyazov as his successor. Claiming to be the authentic DPT leader, Yusuf came to an agreement with the government under which his faction of the party, the DPT–Tehran, was re-legalized in July, whereas the Niyazov faction, the DPT–Almaty, entered into a formal opposition alliance with the IRP. Yusuf later fell out with the government and sought political asylum in Austria.

The DPT–Almaty was re-registered in August 1999, whereas in November that year the DPT–Tehran was denied registration because it had essentially the same name as a registered party. In the run-up to the February-March 2000 parliamentary elections the DPT–Almaty itself became seriously divided between supporters of new chairman Mahmadruzi Iskandarov (a former Emergency Situations Minister) and Niyazov's faction, which criticized Iskandarov for being too accommodating to the government. In the elections the DPT–Almaty obtained only 3.5% of the vote, thus failing to qualify for proportional representation seats. In February 2001 Niyazov initiated moves for a reconciliation of the DPT–Almaty factions, whereas the former DPT–Tehran in May 2001 re-launched itself as the Development Party.

Islamic Renaissance Party (IRP)
Nahzati Islomi Tojikistan
Address. c/o Supreme Assembly, Dushanbe
Leadership. Sayed Abdullo Nuri (leader); Mohieddin Kabiri (deputy leader); Muhammad Sharif Himatzada (chairman)
The IRP was founded in June 1990 as the Tajik branch of a network of Islamic parties that emerged in the last phase of the USSR. Based in the rural population, the IRP has declared its long-term objective to be the conversion of Tajikistan into an Islamic republic, although it rejects the label "Islamic fundamentalist". The party was refused permission to hold its founding congress in Dushanbe in October 1990 and was subsequently proscribed by the presidium of the then Tajikistan Supreme Soviet. It nevertheless took an active part in organizing the mass protests that followed the Dushanbe government's support for the attempted coup by hard-liners in Moscow in August 1991. Legalized in October 1991, the IRP supported the unsuccessful presidential candidacy of Davlat Khudonazarov of the Democratic Party of Tajikistan in October 1991.

The IRP was again banned in June 1993, along with three other opposition parties, and became a leading component of the insurgent Islamic Revival Movement, which in 1996 was renamed the United Tajik Opposition (UTO). The IRP's then deputy leader, Ali Akbar Turajonzoda, had been Tajikistan's chief *kazi* (senior Muslim cleric) until February 1993; thereafter he acted as an opposition spokesman in peace negotiations with the government. Their failure to produce political agreement resulted in an IRP boycott of the presidential and

legislative elections of late 1994 and early 1995. The IRP leader, as chairman of the UTO, then entered into "inter-Tajik" peace talks under the auspices of Iran, Russia and the UN, with support from the OSCE, the USA and neighbouring states such as Uzbekistan and Pakistan. Armed conflict between government troops and UTO forces continued intermittently in 1995-96, but on June 27, 1997, after eight rounds of negotiations, a "general agreement on the establishment of peace and national accord" was signed by President Rakhmonov and Nuri in Moscow, in the presence of President Yeltsin of Russia and senior representatives of the UN and other supporters of the peace process. Under the agreement, UTO representatives were subsequently appointed to the government, although full reconciliation proved to be a slow process.

The IRP was officially re-registered in August 1999 and put forward government minister Davlat Usmon as its candidate for the presidential elections in October. Although he withdrew at the last moment, his name remained on ballot papers and attracted 2% of the vote, as incumbent President Rakhmonov was re-elected with a massive majority that was dismissed as fraudulent by the IRP. The IRP was allowed to contest the February–March 2000 parliamentary elections, winning two seats in the lower house with 6.8% of the proportional vote. At an IRP congress in December 1999, Nuri affirmed that the party would observe the constraint of Tajikistan's constitution in its efforts to create an Islamic state.

People's Democratic Party of Tajikistan
Hizbi Demokrati Khalkii Tojikston (HDKT)
Address. c/o Supreme Assembly, Dushanbe
Leadership. Imomali Rakhmonov (chairman)
Initially launched in August 1993 in the wake of the banning of the main opposition parties two months previously, the People's Party of Tajikistan (PPT) – renamed the People's Democratic Party of Tajikistan (HDKT) in June 1997 – was formally constituted in April 1994, apparently as a product of the ruling establishment's wish to demonstrate the multi-party character of the new Tajikistan. Reports that the new party was intended as a successor to the Communist Party of Tajikistan (CPT) proved to be premature, as the CPT remained in being on its own account. In the 1995 parliamentary elections the PPT was credited with winning five seats in the 181-member Supreme Assembly.

Having become the HDKT, the party rapidly became the dominant formation in Tajikistan, with a membership of some 20,000 by 1998. President Rakhmonov formally joined the party in March 1998 and was elected as its chairman the following month. He was therefore the HDKT candidate in the November 1999 presidential elections, his 97% vote in which was regarded as highly suspect by the opposition. The HDKT also dominated the February–March 2000 parliamentary elections, winning 36 of the 63 lower house seats with 63.4% of the proportional vote. The party also won a majority of the seats in the March 2000 indirect elections to the upper house.

Other Parties

Agrarian Party of Tajikistan, founded in 1998, but banned in September 1999 and so did not contest the 2000 parliamentary elections.
Leadership. Hikmatullo Nasriddinov (chairman)

Badakhshan Ruby Movement (*Lali Badakhshan*), founded in the late 1980s to represent the distinctive Pamiri (Ismaili Muslim) people of Gorny-Badakhshan; it originally demanded full autonomy, to which end it joined the opposition alliance headed by the Democratic and Islamic Renaissance parties in armed struggle against the Dushanbe government and was banned in June 1993. The ban was lifted in August 1999, but the party was unsuccessful in the 2000 parliamentary elections.

Leadership. Atobek Amirbek (chairman)

Civil Patriotic Party of Tajikistan Unity (*Soyuz*), founded in 1994; banned in April 1999 and so did not contest the 2000 parliamentary elections.

Leadership. Bobohan Mahmadov (chairman)

Development Party (*Taraqqiyot*), founded as a "constructive opposition" formation in May 2001 by the former "Tehran faction" of the Democratic Party of Tajikistan (DPT), aspiring to reunite the various currents of the DPT.

Leadership. Sulton Quvvatov (chairman).

Justice and Development Party, founded in 1998 and registered in February 1999; did not contest the 2000 parliamentary elections. Also known as the Social Democratic Party.

Leadership. Rahmatullo Zoirov (chairman)

Justice Party (*Adolatho*), founded in 1995; contested the 2000 parliamentary elections, winning only 1.4% of the vote and no seats; suspended for six months in January 2001 for contravening the electoral law and banned outright in August.

Leadership. Abdurahmon Karimov (secretary-general)

National Movement (*Jumbish*), founded in February, favouring integration with CIS, denied registration in April 1999, and so did not contest 2000 parliamentary elections.

Leadership. Hakim Muhabbatov (chairman)

Rebirth Movement (*Rastokhez*), founded in 1990 as a nationalist/religious movement advocating the revival of Tajik culture and traditions; participated in the anti-communist, pro-independence agitation of 1990–91 and in the "government of national reconciliation" of May–November 1992, prior to being banned in June 1993. The ban was lifted in August 1999 but the party did not contest the 2000 parliamentary elections.

Socialist Party of Tajikistan, founded in 1996 and based in the Leninabad region; its first leader, Safarali Kenjayev, was murdered in April 1999 and succeeded by his son; contested the 2000 parliamentary elections but took only 1.2% of the vote.

Leadership. Sherali Kenjayev (chairman)

Tajikistan Party of Political and Economic Renewal, founded in 1993 as a pro-market formation, credited with winning one seat in the 1995 elections. Then leader Mukhtor Boboyev was murdered in northern Tajikistan by unknown gunmen; the party was suspended in April 1999 owing to administrative irregularities and did not contest the 2000 elections.

Leadership. Vali Babayev (chairman)

Tanzania

Capital: Dodoma
Population: 34,568,609 (2002)

The United Republic of Tanzania was established in 1964, when the newly independent states of Tanganyika and Zanzibar merged. Under the constitution, executive power is vested in the President of the United Republic, who is elected by direct popular vote for a five-year term, renewable once only. Legislative

power is exercised by the National Assembly, which serves a five-year term. It comprises 232 members directly elected from single seat constituencies, 37 women nominated by the President, and five seats reserved for members of the Zanzibar House of Representatives. Zanzibar's internal administration provides for a popularly elected President and House of Representatives. In December 1994 a constitutional amendment was introduced ending the convention that the President of Zanzibar would automatically serve as a Vice-President of the United Republic.

The ruling Revolutionary Party of Tanzania (*Chama Cha Mapinduzi*, CCM) was the sole legal political party until 1992. Multi-party presidential and legislative elections were held throughout Tanzania in October-November 1995 resulting in victory in the presidential election to the CCM candidate, Benjamin Mkapa, with 61.8% of the vote, while the CCM also gained an overwhelming majority in the legislature. Zanzibar also held elections for its own president and legislature in October 1995. The CCM's incumbent presidential candidate, Salmin Amour, was narrowly re-elected with 50.2% of the votes cast, while in the House of Representatives the party secured 26 of the 50 elective seats, the other 24 going to the Zanzibar-based Civic United Front (CUF).

In 2000 Zanzibar held its internal elections at the same time as the Tanzanian national presidential and legislative elections. Polling took place throughout Tanzania on Oct. 29, 2000, with re-runs in 16 of the 50 Zanzibar constituencies on Nov. 5. The conduct of the October elections throughout Zanzibar was strongly criticized by international observers, and the 16 re-runs (in constituencies containing 42% of Zanzibar's electorate) were boycotted by opposition parties, which called for fresh elections in all 50 Zanzibar constituencies. Benjamin Mkapa was re-elected President of Tanzania, having received 71.7% of the national vote in a four-way contest, while the CCM's candidate for the presidency of Zanzibar, Amani Abeid Karume, was elected with 67% of the local vote in a two-way contest with Seif Shariff Hamad of the CUF. The elections to the Tanzanian legislature resulted in the CCM holding 202 seats, the CUF 17, the Party for Democracy and Progress (CHADEMA) 4, the Tanzania Labour Party (TLP) 4, the United Democratic Party (UDP) 2, and the National Convention for Construction & Reform–Mageuzi (NCCR-M) 1.

In the Zanzibar House of Representatives, the CCM won 34 of the elective seats, the remaining 16 seats going to the CUF. In April 2001 CUF members of the National Assembly and the Zanzibar House of Representatives, who had boycotted their respective legislatures in protest at the conduct of the 2000 elections in Zanzibar, were declared to have forfeited their seats because they had committed technical breaches of parliamentary standing orders. This action followed the introduction of legislation to extend from 90 days to two years the maximum period for holding by-elections to fill vacant seats in the National Assembly and the Zanzibar House of Representatives. After extended negotiations between the CCM and CUF a reconciliation accord (*muafaka*) allowed by-elections for the 17 seats in May 2003. The CUF won 11 seats, while six were won by the CCM under dubious circumstances – six CUF candidates being disqualified on questionable grounds after the nomination process was closed. At the same time, all 15 by-elections for the Union parliament were won by the CUF. These by-elections had become necessary because CUF MPs had lost their seats after boycotting parliament to protest the irregularities in the elections on Zanzibar in 2000.

As of June 2004 16 political parties were registered at the Electoral Commission.

Civic United Front (CUF)
Chama Cha Wananchi
Address. Mtendeni Street, PO Box 3637, Zanzibar
Telephone. (255–54) 237446
Fax. (255–54) 237445
Leadership. Ibrahim Haruna Lipumba (chairman); Shaaban Khamis Mloo (vice-chairman); Seif Shariff Hamad (secretary general)

The mainly Zanzibar-based CUF was formed in 1992 through the merger of *Kamahuru* (a Zanzibar-based pro-democracy pressure group) and the Civic Movement (a mainland-based human-rights organization). In the 1995 Tanzanian presidential election the CUF candidate, Ibrahim Lipumba, took third place with 6.4% of the votes cast, while in the National Assembly elections the party won 24 of the directly-elected seats and was allocated three of the nominated women's seats. In the Zanzibar presidential poll, the CUF's Seif Shariff Hamad was narrowly beaten into second place, having secured 49.8% of the vote, while the CUF won 24 of the 52 elective seats in the Zanzibar House of Representatives. The authorities in Zanzibar arrested 18 members of the CUF (including members of the House of Representatives) in late 1997 and early 1998 on charges of "plotting to destabilize Zanzibar". They were held in detention for the remainder of President Amour's term of office but were released as part of an amnesty to mark his successor's inauguration in November 2000.

The 2000 elections, which were described by Commonwealth observers as "falling far short of minimum standards", resulted in the CUF holding 15 seats in the National Assembly and 17 in the Zanzibar House of Representatives. Ibrahim Lipumba was runner-up in the national presidential election, with 16.3% of the vote, while Said Shariff Said came second with 33% of the vote in the Zanzibar presidential election. Having called for re-runs of the 2000 elections in all 50 Zanzibar constituencies, the CUF boycotted the re-runs that were held in 16 of the constituencies. Not all CUF MPs supported the boycott of the Union parliament in 2000; in January 2001 a splinter group registered itself as a separate party under the name Forum for the Restoration of Democracy (FORD).

The CUF has had observer status with the Liberal International since 1997.

Party for Democracy and Development
Chama Cha Demokrasia na Maendeleo (CHADEMA)
Address. PO Box 5330, Dar es Salaam
Telephone. (255–22) 2668866
Website. www.democratafrica.org/tanzania/chadema
Leadership. Bob N. Makani (chairman); Aman Walid Kabourou (secretary general)

CHADEMA was registered in 1993, advocating democracy and social development. It has a broadly right-of-centre pro-business orientation. It took four seats in the 2000 National Assembly elections.

The party is associated with the International Democrat Union through the Democrat Union of Africa.

Revolutionary Party of Tanzania
Chama Cha Mapinduzi (CCM)
Address. PO Box 50, Dodoma
Telephone. (255–61) 2282
Website. www.ccm.or.tz
Leadership. Benjamin Mkapa (leader); Philip J. Mangula (secretary general)

The CCM was formally launched in 1977 upon the merger of the Tanganyika African National Union (TANU) with the Afro-*Shirazi* Party (ASP) of Zanzibar. Since the adoption of a one-party constitution in 1965, TANU had been the sole party of mainland Tanzania and the ASP the sole party of Zanzibar. Under President Julius Nyerere, the party had pursued a policy of socialism and self-reliance. However, Ali Hassan Mwinyi, who succeeded Nyerere as President of Tanzania in 1985 and as CCM chairman in 1990, implemented free-market reforms and economic liberalization. In February 1992 an extraordinary national conference of the CCM unanimously endorsed the introduction of a multi-party system, reflecting developments in much of Africa at that time.

In July 1995 Benjamin Mkapa was selected in succession to Mwinyi as presidential candidate for the CCM. The party reasserted its political dominance in the multi-party elections in October–November 1995, retaining the presidency and achieving an overwhelming majority in the National Assembly, although its victories in the Zanzibar polls were much narrower. The 2000 elections further increased the CCM's dominance, Mkapa being re-elected Tanzanian President with 71.7% of the vote and Amani Abeid Karume winning the Zanzibar presidency with 67% of the vote. The CCM held 244 seats in the National Assembly and 33 of the 50 elective seats in the Zanzibar House of Representatives.

Tanzania Labour Party (TLP)
Address. PO Box 7273, Dar es Salaam
Telephone. 00255-022-2443237
Leadership. Augustine Mrema (chairman); Harold Jaffer (secretary general)

The TLP, founded by Leo Herman Lwekamwa and registered 1993, gained representation in the National Assembly in April 1999 through the defection to it of a faction of the National Convention for Construction and Reform–*Mageuzi* led by Augustine Mrema. In the 2000 elections Mrema came third (with 7.8% of the vote) in the contest for the Tanzanian presidency, while the TLP won 3 seats in the National Assembly. In April 2001 Leo Herman Lwekamwa (a vice-chairman of the TLP) and 29 other TLP members claimed to have removed Mrema from the party chairmanship. In the following month Mrema contested this claim, stating that his opponents had "abdicated their membership of the party".

United Democratic Party (UDP)
Address. PO Box 5918, Dar-es-Salaam
Telephone. (255–22) 2628131
Leadership. Amani J Nzugile (chairman); Mussa Hussein (secretary general)

In the 2000 elections the UDP presidential candidate, John Cheyo, former leader of UDP, took fourth place in the Tanzanian presidential election with 4.2% of the vote, while the UDP won two seats in the National Assembly. The party has had observer status with the Liberal International since 1996.

Other Parties

National Convention for Construction and Reform–Mageuzi (NCCR-M), registered 1993; in the 1995 elections its presidential candidate Augustine Mrema (who had resigned from the ruling Revolutionary Party of Tanzania in March 1995) took second place with almost 28% of the vote and the party gained 19 seats; the party subsequently split with a majority faction led by Mrema defecting to the Tanzania Labour Party. Having been seriously undermined by this development, the NCCR-M won only one seat in the 2000 elections.
Address. PO Box 5316, Dar es Salaam
Leadership. James F. Mbatia (chairman); Mwaiseje S. Polisya (secretary-general)

National League for Democracy (NLD), registered in 1993. In June 1999 the NLD chairman became chairman of an umbrella organization linking six opposition parties with no representation in the National Assembly.
Address. PO Box 352, Dar es Salaam
Leadership. Emmanuel Makaidi (chairman)

Thailand

Capital: Bangkok
Population: 64,340,000 (2004 E)

The Kingdom of Thailand is the only south-east Asian country not to have been colonized by a European power. Modern Thailand came into being in 1932 when a civilian-military group carried out a coup replacing the country's absolute monarchy with a system modelled on European constitutional monarchies. From 1938 to 1979 military rule prevailed, interspersed with short periods of democratic government. Since 1979 an elected parliament has prevailed, interrupted only by a coup in February 1991 and a period of military rule before democratic procedures were restored after mass street demonstrations in May 1992.

In reaction to this most recent military intervention, a popular movement demanded a new constitution, which was finally approved by parliament in August 1997. It confirmed Thailand as a parliamentary democracy in which the Prime Minister and the Cabinet appointed by the Prime Minister must have the confidence of the elected legislature. The National Assembly (*Ratha Sapha*) consists of a House of Representatives (*Sapha Phu Thaen Ratsadorn*) and Senate (*Wuthi Sapha*), both elected by universal adult suffrage at 18 years and above. The 200 senators, who must not be members of political parties, are returned by territorial constituencies. The 500-member lower house has 400 MPs elected by single-member territorial constituencies and 100 returned from party lists which secure at least 5% of valid votes. All MPs must be members of a registered political party. The Cabinet is restricted to 25 persons. MPs chosen as ministers must resign their seats.

The first elections under the new constitution, supervised by an independent Election Commission, were held for the Senate in March–June 2000 and for the House of Representatives on Jan. 6, 2001. The results of the polling for the House (after re-runs in several constituencies where malpractice was found by the Election Commission) were as follows: Thais Love Thais (*Thai Rak Thai*) 248 seats, Democrat Party 128, Thai Nation Party (*Chart Thai*) 41, New Aspiration Party 36, National Development Party (*Chart Pattana*) 29, Liberal Democratic Party (*Seri Tham*) 14, Citizens' Party (*Ratsadorn*) 2, Social Action Party 1, Thai Motherland Party 1. In February 2001 *Seri Tham* merged into the *Thai Rak Thai*.

Citizens' Party
Phak Ratsadorn
Address. c/o Sapha Phu Thaen Ratsadorn, Bangkok 10300
Leadership. Somboon Rahong (chairman)
Originally formed in 1986 by elements with military links, *Ratsardorn* became moribund in the mid-1990s but was revived in 1999 as a vehicle for a small group of old politicians found unacceptable by other parties. The party won only two seats in the 2001 elections, so that its future again came into question.

Democrat Party (DP)
Phak Prachathiphat
Address. 67 Setsiri Road, Samsen Nai, Phaythai, Bangkok 10400
Telephone. (66–2) 270–1683
Fax. (66–2) 279–6086
Email. webmaster@democrat.or.th
Website. www.democrat.or.th
Leadership. Banyat Bantadtan (leader)
Established in 1946, the liberal DP is Thailand's oldest political party. Having won by far the largest number of legislative seats in 1986, the party split in 1988, in which year it experienced a dramatic fall in electoral support, becoming a party of the southern region. However, Chuan Leekpai subsequently re-established a Bangkok following by recruiting several technocrats and new young politicians. On this base, the DP became the "party of government" through the 1990s, heading the ruling coalition from September 1992 until May 1995. Having increased its representation to 86 seats (out of 391) in July 1995, it returned to power in November 1997 without a new election, after the New Aspiration-led government had collapsed in the face of urban demonstrations.

The post-1997 DP-led government headed by Chuan Leekpai lost popularity through its association with the IMF programme to manage Thailand's 1997-98 financial crisis. It was again reduced to a southern regional party at the January 2001 elections, in which it won 128 seats (out of 500), becoming the leading opposition party. In April 2003 the party elected Banyat Bantadtan, a 61-year old party veteran and former Deputy Prime Minister, as leader.

National Development Party
Phak Chart Patthana (CP)
Address. 10 Soi Phaholyothin 3, Phyathai, Bangkok 10400
Telephone. (66–2) 279–3104
Fax. (66–2) 279–4284
Website. www.chartpattana.or.th
Leadership. Korn Dabbaransi (leader)
Launched in mid-1992 by Chatichai Choonhavan following his defection from the Thai Nation Party (*Chart Thai*), the CP won 50–60 seats in the elections of 1992, 1995 and 1996, serving as a junior partner in all the subsequent coalition governments, including that led by the Democrat Party from late 1997. After Chatichai's death in 1998, the party leadership passed to his nephew. At the January 2001 polls, the party won 28 seats and Korn Dabbaransi subsequently joined the government as a Deputy Prime Minister.

New Aspiration Party (NAP)
Phak Khwam Wang Mai
Address. 310 Soi Ruamchit, Nakhornchaisri Road, Dusit, Bangkok 10300
Telephone. (66–2) 243–5000
Fax. (66–2) 241–2280
Website. www.nap.or.th
Leadership. Gen. Chavalit Yongchaiyut (leader)
The NAP was set up in 1990 as a vehicle for the political ambitions of its leader, a former army commander and self-styled "soldier for democracy". Despite his background, Chavalit was strongly critical of the military's intervention in national politics in 1991-92. The NAP won 51 seats at the September 1992 elections, and joined the ruling coalition until December 1994, when it withdrew. In July 1995 the party won 57 seats and joined the government led by the Thai Nation Party (*Chart Thai*). After the opposition mounted two no-confidence debates against this coalition, Chavalit pressured the *Chart Thai* Prime Minister into resigning in September 1996. Attracting many *Chart Thai* defectors, the NAP emerged as the largest party with 125 seats (out of 391)

at the November 1996 polls, whereupon Chavalit formed a coalition government.

The Chavalit government failed to manage the onset of Thailand's financial crisis in mid-1997 and was driven from power by pressure from the IMF, army and business leaders and by white-collar street demonstrations. In 1998 the small Mass Party (*Phak Muan Chon*) merged into the NAP, but the party was weakened when a major faction defected to the new Thais Love Thais Party (*Thai Rak Thai*). The rump NAP won only 36 seats (out of 500) at the January 2001 elections, but became a junior partner in the resultant governing coalition.

Social Action Party (SAP)
Phak Kit Sangkhom
Address. 126 Soi Ongkarak, Nakhon Chaisi Road, Dusit, Bangkok 10300
Telephone. (66–2) 243–0100
Fax. (66–2) 243–3224
Website. www.sap.or.th
Leadership. Bunphan Khaewattana (leader)
The SAP was formed in 1974 by a conservative faction of the Democrat Party (DP) led by Kukrit Pramoj. It became the largest parliamentary party in 1979 and again in 1983. In 1991 the leadership passed to Montri Pongpanich, following which the SAP joined coalition governments in 1992 (briefly), 1995 and 1996. The party split in November 1997, some members joining the DP-led coalition. It declined further after Montri's death in 1998. At the January 2001 polls it won only one seat.

Thai Motherland Party
Phak Thin Thai
This party was formed in 2000 by the outgoing Bangkok mayor, Bhichai Rattakul. It campaigned on an environmental platform in the January 2001 parliamentary elections, but won only a single seat. The party was dissolved by the Election Commission in 2002.

Thai Nation Party
Phak Chart Thai
Address. 325/74–76 Lukluang Road, Dusit, Bangkok 10300
Telephone. (66–2) 280–7054
Fax. (66–2) 282–4003
Website. www.chartthai.or.th
Leadership. Banharn Silpa-Archa (leader)
Established in the mid-1970s by a right-wing, pro-business group of retired military officers, *Chart Thai* rose in the late 1980s by attracting the new generation of "godfather" provincial politicians. It won the most seats in the 1988 elections, and headed the coalition later thrown out by a military coup in February 1991. In 1992 party leader Chatichai Choonhavan defected to form the National Development Party (*Chart Pattana*), and the original ex-military group was supplanted by provincial notables such as the new leader, Banharn Silpa-Archa.

In the July 1995 elections *Chart Thai* emerged as the largest legislative party, increasing its representation from 77 to 92 seats and forming a new seven-party coalition administration. The coalition collapsed in September 1996 after two no-confidence debates had detailed charges of corruption and maladministration against Banharn and several other ministers. Many members defected. At the polls in November 1996, the party was reduced to 39 seats (out of 393), although it participated in subsequent ruling coalitions.

For the 2001 election, *Chart Thai* brought in some new faces and proclaimed a programme of rural reform, but won only 41 seats (out of 500), mostly in a few isolated areas of the central and north-eastern regions, and only narrowly surmounted the 5% threshold for party-list seats. Nevertheless, the party was invited to join the subsequent coalition headed by the Thais Love Thais Party.

Thais Love Thais Party
Phak Thai Rak Thai (TRT)
Address. 237/2 Ratchawithi Road, Chitlada, Dusit, Bangkok 10300
Telephone. (66–2) 668–2000
Fax. (66–2) 668–6000
Email. spokesman@thairakthai.or.th
Website. www.thairakthai.or.th
Leadership. Thaksin Shinawatra (leader)
Launched in July 1998 by Thaksin Shinawatra, who became one of Thailand's richest entrepreneurs in the early 1990s from telecommunications concessions. In the early 1990s, Thaksin joined the Moral Force Party (*Palang Dharma*) and briefly served as Foreign Minister and Deputy Prime Minister. The TRT was launched to capture the soft nationalism generated in reaction to the IMF's perceived botched management of the 1997-98 financial crisis. With an initial slogan of "think new, act new", Thaksin attracted many old activists as well as intellectuals and new political aspirants. He also welcomed the defection of a large faction of old-style politicians from the crumbling New Aspiration Party (NAP).

To contest the 2001 polls, Thaksin announced a programme of financial reforms and rural uplift, investing part of his considerable fortune in grassroots political organization and American-style campaign techniques – all innovations in Thai political life. The party swept to an overall majority of 248 seats and Thaksin became Prime Minister of a coalition government which included the NAP and the Thai Nation Party (*Chart Thai*). Immediately after the elections the TRT absorbed the small Liberal Democratic Party (*Seri Tham*, ST), which had won 14 seats in north-eastern Thailand.

In June 2001 Thaksin appeared before the Constitutional Court on charges (filed by the anti-corruption commission shortly before the January elections) that he had made false asset declarations while in government in the 1990s.

Other Parties

Moral Force Party (*Palang Dharma*), formed in 1988 by the then governor of Bangkok, Chamlong Sirimaung, as a vehicle to enter national politics; declined after 1992 when Chamlong withdrew into community work. The party was subsequently led by Thaksin Shinawatra, who went on to establish the Thais Love Thais party. The party failed to win any seats at the 2001 national elections, but remained active in Bangkok municipal politics.
Address. 445/15 Soi Ramkhaeng 39, Wangthonglang, Bangkapi, Bangkok 10310
Telephone. (66–2) 718–5626
Leadership. Chaiwat Sinsuwong (leader)

Solidarity Party (*Phak Ekkaphap*), formed in 1989 from the merger of four opposition parties (*Ruam Thai*, Community Action, Progressive Party and *Prachachon*), briefly acceded to the governing coalition prior to the 1991 military coup. In the 1992, 1995 and 1996 general elections the party won eight seats, but failed to win any in 2001.

Thai Citizens' Party (*Prachakorn Thai*, PT), formed in 1979 a vehicle for the right-wing populist, Samak Sundaravej. The party split in 1997, while Samak resigned from parliament and was elected mayor of Bangkok in 2000. The party failed to win representation in the January 2001 legislative elections.
Address. 9/250 Soi Ladprao 55, Lardrap Road, Bangkapi, Bangkok 10310
Telephone. (66–2) 559–0008
Leadership. Samak Sundaravej (leader)

Togo

Capital: Lomé
Population: 5,020,000 (2000E)

The Republic of Togo gained full independence in 1960, having previously been administered by France as a United Nations Trust Territory. In 1967 the present head of state, Gen. Gnassingbé Eyadéma, seized power in a bloodless coup and assumed the title of President. Existing political parties were banned, and in 1969 the Rally of the Togolese People (RPT) was established as the ruling and sole legal party. By early 1991 Eyadéma was facing increasing opposition pressure for the introduction of multi-party democracy, and he agreed to the holding of a National Conference, in July and August of that year, to determine the political future. The Conference set up a transitional High Council of the Republic which subsequently engaged in a power struggle with President Eyadéma. Amid the continuing political tension, a multi-party constitution was given approval in a referendum in September 1992. This vested executive power in the President and legislative power in an 81-member National Assembly (*Assemblée Nationale*), both directly elected for five-year terms of office.

Togo's first multi-party presidential elections in August 1993 resulted in victory for the incumbent Eyadéma, although the contest was marked by the absence of any serious challengers and accusations of electoral malpractice. In legislative elections in February 1994, the opposition Action Committee for Renewal (CAR) and Togolese Union for Democracy (UTD) won 36 and 7 Assembly seats respectively (although the results in three constituencies were subsequently declared invalid by the Supreme Court), while the ruling RPT took 35 seats.

In further presidential elections held on June 21, 1998, Eyadéma was re-elected with 52% of the vote. Opposition groups claimed irregularities and international observers expressed doubts about the credibility of the results. The legislative elections held on March 21, 1999, which returned the RPT to power, were boycotted by the major opposition parties, which claimed that their concerns over the earlier disputed presidential polling had not been resolved. In July 1999, the European Union brokered the Lomé Framework Agreement, by which the opposition parties entered into negotiations with the President to establish an independent electoral commission and prepare for a new round of legislative elections.

On the occasion of the Oct. 27, 2002, Assembly elections, the opposition parties, citing irregularities in the organization of the elections, formed a front and organized a boycott which was largely observed by the opposition group. The RPT gained 72 seats out of 81 and eight seats were shared by four parties regarded as satellite parties of the RPT: the Rally for the Strengthening of Democracy and Development (RSDD), the Union for Democracy and Social Progress (UDPS), JUVENTO, and the Movement of Believers in Equality and Peace (MOCEP). The last seat was won by an independent candidate called Kokou Kakaki.

Eyadéma was re-elected, with 57.2% of the vote, in presidential elections on June 1, 2003.

Action Committee for Renewal
Comité d'Action pour la Renouveau (CAR)
Leadership. Yao Agboyibo (leader)

Part of an opposition coalition with the Togolese Union for Democracy (UTD), the CAR boycotted the presidential election in August 1993 but participated in the legislative balloting in February 1994. Initially the party gained the highest number of seats, with 36, although this was subsequently reduced to 34 by a controversial Supreme Court decision that prompted a CAR boycott of the new National Assembly. In the light of the election results, the CAR/UTD coalition declared in March 1994 that CAR leader Agboyibo had been selected for appointment as the new Prime Minister. However, President Eyadéma refused to endorse this, and in April he appointed the UDT leader, Edem Kodjo, as Prime Minister in a move which fractured the unity of the CAR/UTD coalition. The CAR rejected the appointment, continuing to assert that the new Prime Minister should come from within its own ranks, and boycotted the Assembly for a period.

As the party's presidential candidate in the June 1998 election, Agboyibo came third with 9.6% of the vote. Following further claims of irregularities in that election the CAR boycotted the National Assembly elections held in 1999 and refused to serve in the new administration. The party boycotted the Oct. 27, 2002, Assembly elections claiming that the organization of the elections was marred by irregularities. In the June 2003 presidential elections, Agboyibo came third, with 5.2% of the vote.

Co-ordination of New Forces
Co-ordination des Forces Nouvelles (CFN)
Leadership. Joseph Kokou Koffigoh (president)

The CFN was formed in 1993, comprising six political organizations and led by the (then) Prime Minister, Koffigoh. He resigned as premier in March 1994, following the legislative elections the previous month in which the CFN won one seat. The party stood in the March 1999 legislative elections but failed to secure representation and boycotted the 2002 Assembly elections.

Patriotic Pan-African Convergence
Convergence Patriotique Panafricaine (CPP)
Leadership. Edem Kodjo (president)

Launched in 1999, the party was a merger of the Togolese Union for Democracy (UTD), the Party of Action for Democracy (*Parti d'Action pour la Démocratie*, PAD) led by Francis Ekoh, the Party of Democrats for Unity (*Parti des Démocrates pour l'Unité*, PDU) and the Union for Democracy and Solidarity (*Union pour la Démocratie et la Solidarité*, UDS) headed by Antoine Foly. The party joined the opposition boycott of the October 2002 Assembly elections; standing as the party's candidate in the June 2003 presidential elections, Kodjo was credited with only 1.0% of the vote.

Rally of the Togolese People
Rassemblement du Peuple Togolais (RPT)
Address. Place de l'Indépendance, BP 1208, Lomé
Telephone. (228) 212018
Leadership. Gen. Gnassingbé Eyadéma (president)

The RPT was established in 1969 under the sponsorship of President Eyadéma, and ruled on a single-party basis until its constitutional mandate was abrogated in 1991 by the National Conference. The Conference, convened in response to increasing opposition to the regime, set up a transitional High Council of the Republic and a serious power struggle subsequently developed between this body and Eyadéma.

In presidential elections held in August 1993, which were boycotted by the main opposition parties, Eyadéma was confirmed in office with about 96.5% of the votes cast, although voter turnout was extremely low. In January 1994 an attempt was made on the President's life; the government alleged that the Union of Forces for Change (UFC), with Ghanaian sup-

591

port, was responsible. In legislative elections in February 1994, the RPT took only 35 National Assembly seats, leaving it without a majority. President Eyadéma subsequently split the opposition ranks by appointing the leader of the Togolese Union for Democracy (UTD) as the new Prime Minister and RPT members secured key portfolios in a coalition Cabinet. The RPT gained a parliamentary majority by winning three by-elections held in August 1996; following this, Kwassi Klutse, the former Minister of Planning, was appointed Prime Minister of a new government of mainly Eyadéma supporters, since the main opposition parties refused to serve.

Early returns suggested that Eyadéma might lose the presidential elections in June 1998. Voting was suspended and, once the head of Togo's electoral commission resigned, the Minister of the Interior declared Eyadéma the winner without resuming the count. The government survived a vote of no confidence in September 1998 and went on to win the legislative elections in March 1999 without the outcome of the presidential elections being resolved. Condemned by the opposition, the RPT stood virtually unopposed, winning 79 seats in the new National Assembly (the remaining two seats going to independent candidates). Koffi Eugene Adoboli, a former United Nations official, was appointed as the new Prime Minister in May 1999. Following a Constitutional Court ruling that the Minister of the Interior had violated the electoral code and EU mediation with the opposition, Eyadéma pledged to stand down at the next presidential election due in 2003. In August 2000, Kodjo Agbéyomè, the president of the National Assembly, was appointed Prime Minister.

In the Oct. 27, 2002, Assembly elections, which were generally boycotted by the opposition, the RPT won 72 seats out of 81. Reversing his earlier pledge to stand down in 2003, Eyadéma stood again for President in June 2003, being re-elected with 57.2% of the vote.

Togolese Union for Democracy
Union Togolaise pour la Démocratie (UTD)

In alliance with the Action Committee for Renewal (CAR), the UTD boycotted the presidential polls in 1993 but participated in the National Assembly elections in February 1994. The party secured seven seats initially, although the election of one UTD member was subsequently invalidated. Having refused to appoint the CAR leader as the new Prime Minister, President Eyadéma chose UTD leader Edem Kodjo in April 1994 to head a new government drawn heavily from the President's Rally of the Togolese People. Kodjo's acceptance caused a breach in relations between the UTD and the CAR. The UTD left the government in 1996. In 1999 it boycotted the National Assembly elections and merged with the newly formed Patriotic Pan-African Convergence (CPP).

Union of Forces for Change
Union des Forces du Changement (UFC)

Email. contact@ufc-togo.com
Website. www.ufc-togo.com
Leadership. Gilchrist Olympio; Jean-Pierre Fabre (secretary-general).

Initially a coalition of anti-Eyadéma organizations under Olympio, the UFC was launched as a social democratic party in 1993. Having been exiled in Ghana with other Togolese dissidents, Olympio's candidature for the 1993 presidential election was disallowed on a legal technicality. Following government allegations that he was involved in an attack on the President in 1994 (which he denied), the UFC boycotted the legislative elections that year.

Olympio returned from exile to stand as the party presidential candidate in 1998. Although early voting figures suggested that he was ahead of President Eyadéma, once voting was suspended Olympio was declared to have come second with 34% of the vote. The UFC staged demonstrations, claiming that that the results were fraudulent, and boycotted the National Assembly elections in 1999. The party joined the opposition boycott of the 2002 Assembly elections. Its candidate in the June 2003 presidential elections, Emmanuel Bob Akitani, came second with 34.1% of the vote.

Other Parties

Democratic Convention of African Peoples (*Convention Démocratique des Peuples Africains,* CDPA), one of the earliest identifiable opposition movements to emerge under the Eyadéma regime at the end of the 1980s. Party leader Gnininvi took fifth place in the presidential elections held in 1998 with less than 1% of the vote and the party joined the opposition boycott of the October 2002 Assembly elections. The CDPA has consultative status with the Socialist International.
Leadership. Leopold Mensan Gnininvi.

JUVENTO, allied with the government, won two seats in the October 2002 elections.

Movement of Believers in Equality and Peace (*Mouvement des Croyants pour l'Egalité et la Paix,* MOCEP), a pro-government party that won one seat in the October 2002 elections.

Party for Democracy and Renewal (*Parti pour la Démocratie et le Renouveau,* PDR), launched in 1991. Party leader Ayewa came fourth in the presidential election in 1998 with only 3% of the vote and the party joined the opposition boycott of the October 2002 Assembly elections
Leadership. Zarifou Ayewa.

Rally for the Strengthening of Democracy and Development (*Rassemblement pour le soutien de la Démocratie et du Développement,* RSDD), a pro-government formation led by Harry Olympio, a former Minister of Human Rights in the Eyadéma government, which won three seats in the October 2002 Assembly elections.

Union for Democracy and Social Progress (*Union pour la Démocratie et le Progrès,* UDPS), a satellite of the ruling RPT, won two seats in the October 2002 elections.

Union of Independent Liberals (*Union des Libéraux Indépendants,* ULI), launched by Jacques Amouzou, who contested the 1993 presidential election but came a very distant second to Gen. Eyadéma with 1.87% of the vote. Amouzou took sixth place in the presidential elections in 1998 with less than 1% of the vote and the party joined the opposition boycott of the October 2002 Assembly elections.
Leadership. Jacques Amouzou.

Tonga

Capital: Nuku'alofa (Tongapatu)
Population: 100,000 (2000E)

The Kingdom of Tonga, an independent constitutional monarchy within the Commonwealth, was a British Protected State for 70 years prior to achieving full independence in 1970. The Tongan sovereign is head of state and exercises executive power in conjunction with an appointed 11-member Privy Council which functions as a Cabinet. The 30-member unicameral Legislative Assembly consists of the King, Privy Council, nine nobles elected by the country's 33 hereditary peers, and nine popularly elected representatives. In recent years this system has faced an increasingly determined challenge from a pro-democracy movement, members of which in 1994 founded a formal organization, initially called the People's Party and later the Human Rights and Democracy Movement (HRDM). In the March 12, 1999, election, candidates associated with the HRDM won five of the nine seats open to popular vote, while in the March 6-7, 2002, election the HRDM won seven seats.

Trinidad and Tobago

Capital: Port of Spain
Population: 1,104,000 (2003E)

Trinidad and Tobago gained independence from the United Kingdom in 1962 and became a republic in 1976. Under the 1976 constitution the head of state is the President, who is elected for a five-year term by a parliamentary electoral college. The head of government is the Prime Minister. There is a bicameral parliament. The House of Representatives has 36 members (34 from Trinidad, two from Tobago), elected for five-year terms in single seat constituencies. The Senate has 31 members appointed by the President: of these, 16 are appointed on the advice of the Prime Minister, six on that of the Leader of the Opposition, and nine at the President's own discretion to represent economic, social and community organizations. Tobago, the smaller of the country's two main constituent islands with a population of only 50,000, enjoys a measure of internal self-government. Its House of Assembly, established in 1980 and given extended powers in 1996, has 15 members (12 directly elected and three chosen by the majority party), who serve four-year terms.

In a general election to the House of Representatives held on Oct. 7, 2002, the People's National Movement (PNM), led by Patrick Manning, broke a political deadlock in effect since the tied elections in 2001, winning 20 of the 36 seats. The opposition United National Congress (UNC) won the remaining 16 seats. The political impasse had followed the elections in December 2001, when the UNC refused to accept the President's decision to appoint Manning as Prime Minister, after each party had won 18 seats in the House of Representatives.

Elections to the local Tobago House of Assembly were held most recently on Jan. 29, 2001, and resulted in the PNM winning 8 of the 12 elected seats with the National Alliance for Reconstruction (NAR), previously the dominant party in Tobago, taking four.

There is a distinct racial element to support for the two main parties, which intensifies at election time. The PNM is backed mainly by the African-descended population whereas the UNC's main strength is among people of East Indian descent, the two communities each constituting about 40% of the population with the balance being mainly of mixed race.

National Alliance for Reconstruction (NAR)
Address. 37 Victoria Square, Port of Spain/Robinson and Main Streets, Scarborough, Tobago
Telephone. (1-868) 627-6163 (Port of Spain)/(1-868) 639-

4431 (Tobago)
Email. ttnar@yahoo.com
Leadership. Hochoy Charles (leader in Tobago); Abdool Wahab (chairman)
The NAR was formed in February 1986 as a "rainbow coalition" of opposition parties aiming to unite support between the African and Indian communities and adopting the slogan "One Love". Although the NAR, under the leadership of Arthur N.R. Robinson, won a landslide victory in the 1986 general election, taking 33 of the 36 seats, it subsequently broke apart against a background of worsening economic conditions, with dissidents forming the United National Congress (UNC) in 1989. Since 1991 the NAR has held seats only in Tobago (Robinson's home island), although following the 1995 general election it held the balance of power and supported the formation of a UNC-led government in exchange for a Cabinet seat for Robinson and increased autonomy for Tobago. In the following general election in December 2000 the NAR retained its one Tobago seat, but lost its place in government after the UNC won an outright parliamentary majority. Tensions have since emerged between party supporters in the two islands of Trinidad and Tobago, and this has helped to undermine the NAR's standing amongst the electorate. In the general elections of 2001 and 2002 the party was unable to maintain its presence in the House of Representatives. In addition, in the January 2001 elections for the Tobago House of Assembly the NAR, which had dominated the Assembly since its creation in 1980, lost its majority to the PNM, which took 8 of the 12 elected seats to four for the NAR.

Former NAR Prime Minister Arthur Robinson was national President (head of state) between 1997 and 2003.

People's National Movement (PNM)
Address. Balisier House, Tranquility Street, Port of Spain
Telephone. (1-868) 625-1533
Email. pnm@carib-link.net
Leadership. Patrick Manning (political leader); Martin R. Joseph (general secretary)
The centre-right PNM has traditionally derived its main support from Trinidadians of African descent. It won every election in Trinidad and Tobago from its formation in 1956 until 1986. The party's founder, Eric Williams, Chief Minister under colonial rule from 1956, became the first Prime Minister on independence in 1962 and died in office on March 29, 1981. In December 1986 the party lost a general election for the first time, being heavily defeated by the newly formed National Alliance for Reconstruction (NAR). George Chambers, who had assumed the leadership on the death in 1981 of the party's founder, lost his seat in the election and resigned as party leader, being replaced by Patrick Manning. The PNM returned to office at the 1991 general election, winning 21 seats, but went into opposition again after the November 1995 election when it and the United National Congress (UNC) each won 17 seats and the UNC went on to form a government with NAR support. The PNM remained in opposition after the December 2000 election, when it won 16 of the 36 seats.

However, the PNM's fortunes changed dramatically after a serious split developed within the UNC during 2001. Three dissident UNC MPs agreed to form an alliance with the PNM, thus ending the UNC's majority in Parliament. The consequence was that the government was forced to dissolve the House of Representatives on Oct. 13, 2001, and call new elections. When the general election was held on Dec. 10, 2001, the PNM and UNC each won 18 seats. After much discussion between the two parties and President Arthur Robinson, the PNM's Patrick Manning was chosen as Prime Minister, and was sworn in on Dec. 24. However, no sooner had the Prime Minister begun to appoint his cabinet than the

UNC questioned the legitimacy of the government and blocked all parliamentary business.

The political stalemate came to a head with the PNM's failure to elect a parliamentary Speaker on Aug. 28, 2002, after the UNC blocked the PNM's candidate. Without a Speaker, the government was unable to present a budget that was required for the new financial year beginning in November. Further, the legitimacy of the PNM government was coming under growing criticism, as parliament had met only twice since the December 2001 general election. The only option was to call another election, which was held on Oct. 7, 2002. The outcome was a victory for the PNM, gaining 20 of the 36 seats. Since the election the PNM has come under increasing pressure to act against rising crime, and in particular the growing number of murders and kidnappings for ransom across the country.

In January 2001 the PNM gained control of the Tobago House of Assembly for the first time, winning eight of the 12 seats. On July 14, 2003, the party made significant gains in local government elections winning 83 of the 126 seats available, and nine out of the 14 Municipal and Regional Corporations. Local government representation had previously been divided equally between the PNM and UNC.

United National Congress (UNC)

Address. Rienzi Complex, 78-81 Southern Main Road, Couva
Telephone. (1-868) 636 8145
Email. unc@tstt.net.tt
Website. www.unc.org.tt
Leadership. Basdeo Panday (leader); Fazal Karim (general secretary)

The UNC has its base in the East Indian-descended 40% of the population and its leader, Basdeo Panday, was the country's first Prime Minister of Indian extraction. In 1975, Panday, then (and until 1995) president of the All Trinidad Sugar and General Workers' Trade Union (ATS/GWTU), formed the United Labour Front (ULF). In the 1976 elections the ULF won 10 of the 36 House seats on a platform that included worker participation, nationalization of key enterprises and land reform. The ULF subsequently participated in the National Alliance for Reconstruction (NAR), which won the 1986 general election. Panday was expelled from the NAR in 1988 and in 1989 with other former ULF members formed the UNC. The UNC won 13 seats in the 1991 elections and then in 1995 won 17, enabling it to form the government with the support of the weakened NAR.

In office from 1995 the UNC pursued similar policies of economic restructuring and encouragement of foreign investment as had the preceding People's National Movement (PNM) government. It also benefited from the rise in the world price of oil, hydrocarbons being the bulwark of the economy. In the December 2000 election the UNC retained power, winning 19 seats. The government ran on its record in creating jobs and tackling the country's problems of violent crime and drug trafficking. However, the campaign was dominated by racial tension and PNM claims that the UNC was engaged in systematic electoral fraud, targeted particularly on five marginal seats (all of which the UNC won). In response to charges by PNM leader Patrick Manning that the election would be "stolen", Panday invited a Commonwealth Observer Group to monitor the polling, but the conclusion of its small team of observers that the elections were fair had little impact on the domestic controversy.

However, the controversy over the general election of December 2000 was soon to be superseded by divisions in the UNC, which led to new elections twelve months later. In the summer of 2001, a new faction within the governing UNC was established, named "Team Unity". The group –

consisting of four cabinet ministers, led by Attorney General Ramesh Maharaj – was highly critical of the Prime Minister's handling of a number of corruption allegations against the government. The acrimony between the UNC and Team Unity worsened to such an extent that three dissident MPs agreed to form a political alliance with the opposition PNM, thus ending the UNC's majority in Parliament. After Parliament was dissolved the PNM made clear that the alliance with the three dissidents would not extend to the general election, so attention turned to the battle for control of the UNC. In the end, a court ruling decided that the UNC faction led by Basdeo Panday should retain the party name and symbol and supply the party's list of candidates for the general election. This was an important decision, as when the general election was held on Dec. 10, 2001, the UNC won 18 seats, while Team Unity did not win any after gaining only 2.5% of the vote.

Despite the UNC's victory over Team Unity, the party lost ground to the PNM, with each party winning 18 parliamentary seats. To break the political deadlock President Arthur Robinson chose PNM's Patrick Manning as Prime Minister. Although, it seemed at first that the UNC had accepted the decision, the party soon began to question the legitimacy of the government and subsequently blocked all parliamentary business in protest. The UNC's campaign was successful as Prime Minister Manning was forced to call new elections. However, continuing allegations of corruption against the UNC damaged the party's standing during the build up to the new vote. The result of the October 2002 election saw the party lose two seats compared to the election ten months earlier, thus giving the PNM a working majority in parliament. Since the election the UNC has been destabilized by the extra-parliamentary activities of Ramesh Maharaj and his newly formed National Team Unity. Furthermore, the UNC's effectiveness in opposition has been hindered by the uncertainty over Panday's position as leader. In November 2003, Panday announced that he would stand down from the role in January 2004, but he later rescinded his resignation and agreed to continue as party leader.

In January 2001 the UNC contested the local elections to the House of Assembly in Tobago (which has only a small Asian community) for the first time, but failed to win a seat. In the July 2003 local elections, the party lost heavily to the PNM.

The UNC is an affiliate of the Christian Democrat International.

Other Parties

Citizens' Alliance (CA) is a newly established party based in Trinidad, calling for a fresh approach to politics based on the full participation of civil society. More particularly the party wants to introduce greater transparency and accountability into the political process, with more equitable policies and better constituency representation. The Citizens' Alliance nominated candidates for the October 2002 general election, but won only 1% of the vote and no parliamentary seats.
Address. 2 Gray Street, St Clair, Port of Spain
Telephone. (1-868) 622-1881
Fax. (1-868) 628-3553
Email: citizensal@wow.net
Website. www.citizensalliance.org.tt
Leadership. Wendell Mottley (leader)

National Team Unity (NTU) was formed from the "Team Unity" faction that broke away from the UNC in 2001. Former Attorney General and UNC cabinet member, Ramesh Maharaj, leads the party. Originally Team Unity was a group within the ruling UNC government consisting **of** four cabinet ministers, led by Ramesh Maharaj, which was highly critical of the Prime Minister's handling of a number of corruption allegations against the government. The acrimony between the UNC and Team Unity worsened to such an extent that on Oct. 1, 2001, Prime Minister Panday sacked Maharaj, precipitating the resignation of two other cabinet ministers. The three dissident MPs then formed an alliance with the opposition People's National Movement (PNM), thus ending the UNC's majority in Parliament. After Parliament was dissolved the PNM made clear that the alliance with the three dissidents would not extend to the general election. In an attempt to strengthen the group's position the Team Unity faction claimed that they had the right to adopt the party name and symbol of the UNC, and the party's list of candidates for the general election. However, a court ruled against Team Unity, allowing Basdeo Panday's faction to retain control of the UNC. The consequence was that when the general election was held on Dec. 10, Team Unity gained only 2.5% of the vote and no seats in parliament.

The faction again faired badly in the October 2002 election, but under Maharaj's leadership has since regrouped to form NTU. In an attempt to bolster the new party Maharaj tried to lure a number of senior UNC figures into the fold, precipitating fears on the part of Basdeo Panday that such activity might split the UNC. Despite this, Maharaj, who is of Indian descent, retains strong support from within certain sections of the UNC, and some even see him as a possible replacement for Panday as UNC leader. However, others in the UNC suggest they would leave the party if Maharaj returned, believing that he was the cause of their electoral defeats in 2001 and 2002.
Leadership. Ramesh Maharaj (leader)

People's Empowerment Party (PEP), based in Tobago and led by lawyer Deborah Moore-Miggins, a former NAR member, was founded in December 1999. It put forward candidates without success in the two Tobago constituencies in the December 2000 national elections and in the January 2001 Tobago House of Assembly elections.
Address. Miggins Chamber, Young Street, Scarborough, Tobago
Telephone. (1-868) 649-3175
Leadership. Richard Alfred (general secretary)

Tunisia

Capital: Tunis
Population: 9,974,722 (2004E)

The Republic of Tunisia was declared in 1957, a year after the country achieved independence from France with the end of the protectorate and the abolition of the monarchy. Characterized by a strong presidential regime under Habib Bourguiba and the domination of one party – the Neo-Destour Party, known from the mid-1960s as the Destourian Socialist Party (*Parti Socialiste Destourien*, PSD) – the new republic modelled its 1959 constitution on the French system where the President was elected every five years and appointed the Prime Minister and the government. The unicameral Chamber of Deputies (*Al Majlis al-Nuwab/Chambre des Députés*) was also elected for a five-year term by universal suffrage (with a minimum voting age of 20). Despite the definition of strong social policies (education, development, status of women, etc.), progress towards democracy was slow and opposition parties were banned. In 1975, Bourguiba proclaimed himself "President-for-life". In October 1987, Bourguiba appointed Zine El Abidine

Ben Ali as the new Prime Minister. One month later, the old President was deposed and replaced by Ben Ali. The new President promised various reforms in favour of political pluralism and human rights crystallized by the signing of the "National Pact" with the opposition parties. The Chamber also voted to limit the number of presidential mandates to three five-year terms and fixed an age limit.

Renamed as the Democratic Constitutional Rally (RCD), the ruling party still dominated the political scene at the 1989 and 1994 elections. In the 1994 presidential elections, Ben Ali was officially stated to have been re-elected with over 99% of the votes cast. In simultaneous elections for the Chamber of Deputies, the RCD won all 144 seats contested in the traditional first-past-the-post district list system. Four of the six legal opposition parties (Islamist parties were excluded from the ballot) shared the remaining 19 seats reserved under a new system for parties which did not secure a majority of the constituencies.

The 1998 electoral reform increased the number of seats in the Chamber of Deputies from 163 to 182 and guaranteed 20% of the seats to opposition parties (34 seats) according to the proportion of votes received nationally by each party. The result of the October 1999 legislative and presidential elections did not provoke a political upheaval. Ben Ali was re-elected with 99.4% of the vote and his parties won 148 seats at the Chamber of Deputies.

On May 26, 2002, the first referendum in the history of the country was organized with the purpose of reforming the Constitution. In addition to general articles guaranteeing human rights and individual liberties, the text consisted of major amendments concerning the nature and the duration of the presidential mandate: it ended the limit on the number of terms, increased the age limit from 70 to 75, and gave lifetime immunity to the President for decisions taken in office. The changes were approved by 99.52% of those who voted, opening the way for Ben Ali to serve two further terms. The RCD was expected to remain the main political force after elections in October 2004.

Congress for the Republic
Congrès pour la République (CPR)
Website. www.tunisie2004.net, www.cprtunisie.com
Leadership. Moncef Marzouki
Founded in 2001 by Marzouki, who is currently living in France, the CPR has sought to mobilize international public opinion before the 2004 elections in favour of political alternatives for Tunisia.

Democratic Constitutional Rally
Rassemblement Constitutionnel Démocratique (RCD)
Address. blvd 9 Avril 1938, Tunis
Telephone. (216–1) 560393
Fax. (216–1) 569143
Email. info@rcd.tn
Website. www.rcd.tn
Leadership. Zine El Abidine Ben Ali (chairman); Hamed Karoui (deputy chairman); Abderrahim Zouari (secretary-general)
Founded in 1934 as the Neo-Destour Party – a breakaway group from the old Destour (Constitution) Party – the organization led the movement for independence and for a republic, adopting in effect a single party framework between 1963 and the early 1980s. The party used the name Destourian Socialist Party from 1964 to 1988. The change to its present name at the end of that period was intended to reflect a greater political openness under President Ben Ali.

The RCD has a moderate left-wing republican orientation. At a congress held in July 1993 it confirmed its commitment to free-market economic policies and its opposition to Islamic fundamentalist militancy. Despite the controlled and limited multi-partyism implemented since 1991, the RCD has retained its monopoly of power. It won 144 of the 163 seats in the Chamber of Deputies in the 1994 elections against nominal opposition from six parties, and took 148 seats (all the seats other than those reserved for opposition parties) with 91.6% of the vote in the 1999 polling. In the 1999 presidential elections Ben Ali won 99.4% of the vote standing against two opposition candidates, and the party is expected to remain the main actor on the Tunisian political scene.

The RCD is a member party of the Socialist International.

Democratic Socialist Movement
Mouvement des Démocrates Socialistes (MDS)
Address. c/o Chambre des Députés, Tunis
Leadership. Ismail Boulahya (secretary-general)
Legally registered in 1983, the MDS was originally organized in 1977 by a number of former cabinet members from the ruling party who sought greater political liberalization in Tunisia. The MDS boycotted legislative elections in 1986, following the arrest and disqualification of its leader Ahmed Mestiri from running for legislative office, and failed to secure representation in the 1989 poll, after which Mestiri resigned as secretary-general. The party also boycotted municipal elections in June 1990 in protest against the failure of democratization efforts in the country.

In March 1994 the MDS supported Zine El Abidine Ben Ali for re-election as President but challenged the ruling Democratic Constitutional Rally in the national legislative balloting. Although no MDS candidates were successful on their own, 10 subsequently entered the Chamber of Deputies under the new electoral arrangement guaranteeing the opposition a minimal number of seats. The MDS gained 13 seats in the 1999 elections under electoral reforms which increased the number of seats guaranteed to opposition parties. The former leader of the party, Mohamed al Mouadda was charged in 2001 after planning to form a political pact with the Islamist party *Al Nahda* (banned from several electoral campaigns).

Liberal Social Party
Parti Social Libéral (PSL)
Address. 38 rue Gandhi, 1001 Tunis
Telephone. (216–1) 712-54928
Fax. (216–1) 983-44659
Leadership. Mounir Beji (president); Hosni Lahmar (vice-president)
Advocating liberal social and political policies and economic reforms, the PSL was officially recognized as a legal party in September 1988 under the name of the Social Party for Progress (*Parti Social pour le Progrès*, PSP). The party assumed its present name in October 1994. The party was allotted two seats in the Chamber of Deputies following the 1999 legislative elections. It has been an observer member of the Liberal International since 1997 and releases a newspaper called *El Oufok*.

Popular Unity Party
Parti de l'Unité Populaire (PUP)
Address. 7 rue d'Autriche, 1002 Tunis
Telephone. (216–1) 289678
Fax. (216–1) 796031
Leadership. Muhammad Bouchire (leader)
The PUP evolved out of a factional conflict within the Popular Unity Movement over the issue of participation in the 1981 legislative elections. It was officially recognized in

1983 as a legal organization and is a leftist party. The party failed to win legislative representation in the elections in 1989, but secured two of the 19 seats proportionally allocated in the Chamber of Deputies to opposition parties in March 1994. In October 1999 Muhammad Belhadj Amor stood as the party candidate in the presidential elections, coming second but with only 0.3% of the vote. The party was allocated seven seats in the Chamber of Deputies following the legislative elections held at the same time. It releases the periodical *Al-Wihda*.

Renewal Movement
Mouvement de la Rénovation–Ettajdid (MR)
Address. 6 Rue Metouia, 1000 Tunis
Leadership. Mohamed Harmel (secretary-general); Mohamed Ali el Halouani (chairman)
Formerly the Tunisian Communist Party (PCT), the MR adopted its new name at an April 1993 congress when it was announced that Marxism had been abandoned as official party doctrine. The PCT had been banned in 1963, regaining legality in 1981. In 1986 it boycotted the legislative elections because it was debarred from presenting a "Democratic Alliance" list with the then illegal Progressive Socialist Rally. The party was critical of the government's emphasis on free-market economic policies but initially welcomed President Ben Ali's political liberalization measures in the late 1980s. However, it subsequently became disillusioned over the lack of progress on full democratization, boycotting the June 1990 municipal elections, having earlier failed to win any seats in the 1989 national legislative poll. No MR candidates were successful in the 1994 elections, although four party members were subsequently seated in the Chamber of Deputies under the new electoral arrangement established for opposition parties. Following the 1999 polling, the party was allotted five legislative seats.

Unionist Democratic Union
Union Démocratique Unioniste (UDU)
Address. c/o Chambre des Députés, Tunis
Leadership. Abderrahmane Tlili (secretary-general)
Legalized in November 1988, the UDU is led by a former member of the Democratic Constitutional Rally who resigned from the ruling party to promote the unification of various Arab nationalist tendencies in Tunisia. Under the proportional arrangement for opposition parties, three UDU members were seated in the Chamber of Deputies following the March 1994 elections. Tlili stood as the party candidate in the 1999 presidential elections, taking third place with 0.2% of the vote. Seven party members were allocated seats in the Chamber following the legislative polling.

Illegal Groups

Communist Workers' Party (*Parti des Travailleurs Communistes,* PTC), an unrecognized splinter group of the former Tunisian Communist Party founded in 1986.
Leadership. Hamma Hammani

National Arab Rally (*Rassemblement National Arabe,* RNA), banned following its launch in 1981; the organization advocates unity among Arab countries.
Leadership. Bashir Assad

Popular Unity Movement (*Mouvement de l'Unité Populaire,* MUP), formed in 1973 by Ahmed Ben Salah, a former minister who fell out of favour with President Habib Bourguiba and who directed the party from exile. The movement reorganized itself as a political party in 1978 but was unable to gain legal recognition. In 1981 Ben Salah was excluded from a government amnesty and he urged the party not to participate in national elections in that year. This caused a split between his supporters and the faction which broke away to form the Popular Union Party. Although Ben Salah returned to Tunisia in 1988, the government refused to restore his civil rights, thereby preventing his participation in national elections. The MUP is a consultative member of the Socialist International.

Renaissance Party (*Hizb al-Naḥda/Parti de la Renaissance*), formed in 1981 as the Islamic Tendency Movement (*Mouvement de la Tendance Islamique*, MTI) by fundamentalists inspired by the 1979 Iranian revolution, and renamed in 1989. MTI adherents were harassed under the Bourguiba regime, and although President Ben Ali initially adopted a more conciliatory approach, the movement was denied legal status on the grounds that it remained religion-based. Despite the party's denials of any complicity in violent or revolutionary activity, the government labelled it a terrorist organization in the early 1990s and took repressive action against it, including sentencing its leader in exile to life imprisonment. Some of its members have seen their families sent to jail. The organization has become largely inactive inside Tunisia itself since the crackdown in the early 1990s and the group's founder Ghanouchi emains in exile.
Leadership. Rachid al-Ghanouchi (leader)

Turkey

Capital: Ankara
Population: 67,700,000 (2001)

Under its (fourth) constitution, approved by referendum in November 1982 and amended repeatedly since then, Turkey is a democratic secular state in which legislative authority is vested in a unicameral Grand National Assembly (*Turkiye Buyuk Millet Meclisi*), currently of 550 members, who are elected by universal suffrage for a maximum five-year term by a system of proportional representation in 81 provinces, treated as multi-member constituencies. Under the electoral law in force in 2004, a political party must win at least 10% of the national poll to qualify for representation in the Assembly. This threshold may be lowered in the course of the harmonization process with the European Union, a process which has already led to a reduction of the powers of the National Security Council (NSC) and, generally, of the role of the military in Turkish politics.

The development of Turkish political parties has been interrupted by two military coups, in 1960 and 1980. The first led to the dissolution of the ruling Democrat Party (DP), and the second to the closure of all the political parties, some of which reappeared later under new names to compete with new parties established after 1980. In addition, parties have on several occasions been dissolved by the courts for infringing the ban on ethnic, secessionist and religious parties. Recent constitutional amendments have made it more difficult to ban political parties. There were in 2004 some fifty registered political parties in Turkey. However, most of them exist only in name and cannot fulfil the legal requirement of putting up candidates in at least half the provinces, a condition for participation in general elections. One reason for the proliferation of political parties is that leaders dominate party organizations. Rivals unable to oust them often choose to quit and form their own breakaway parties. The competition between new parties established after the 1980

coup and old parties revived under new names, appealing to the same constituencies, has reinforced the tendency for personal rivalry between leading politicians to dominate political debate.

The multiplicity of parties and frequent changes in their names can obscure strong elements of continuity in Turkish party politics. While voters are fickle in their support for specific parties (or rather specific politicians), the division of the electorate into two broad camps has evolved only gradually since the first free elections in 1950. The main division is between supporters of the state as established by the republic's founder, Mustafa Kemal Ataturk, in the 1920s and 1930s, and critics of the establishment. The first camp, usually labelled centre-left, relies on the votes of state employees in the civil service, the armed forces, education, state enterprises, etc., as well as on people fearful of domination by the Sunni Muslim majority – the secularized elite and the minority heterodox Alevi community. In politics, the centre-left has been represented mainly by the Republican People's Party (CHP), founded by Ataturk in 1923, which has resumed its old name after many changes and splits following the 1980 coup. Parties to the left of CHP (Socialists, Communists, etc.) have been electorally insignificant. The centre-left has never won an absolute majority since 1950.

The CHP gave birth to the Democratic Left Party (DSP), when the CHP leader Bulent Ecevit resumed his political career after 1980, while refusing to make common cause with the mass of CHP supporters who came together in the Social Democracy Party (SODEP) led by Professor Erdal Inonu, son of Ismet Inonu, the second president of the republic (whom Ecevit had displaced in the leadership of CHP in 1972). Later, SODEP merged with the Populist Party (HP), sponsored by the military, and was renamed Social Democrat Populist Party (SHP), reverting to the name CHP when Erdal Inonu resigned from the leadership. It then suffered a number of splits, the most serious when former Ankara mayor and Foreign Minister Murat Karayalcin quit and formed the Social Democratic People's Party (reviving the acronym SHP). Two other prominent CHP supporters also broke away and formed phantom parties: the Independent Republic Party (BCP), under another former Foreign Minister, Professor Mumtaz Soysal, and the Republican Democracy Party, led by Yekta Gungor Ozden, former president of the constitutional court. Ecevit's DSP also gave birth to two small breakaway parties: the New Turkey Party (YTP), led by former Foreign Minister Ismail Cem, and the Socialist Democratic Party (TDP), formed by Sema Piskinsut, formerly chair of the parliamentary human rights committee. Ecevit retired in July 2004 and was replaced by Zeki Sezer. In October 2004, YTP merged with CHP.

The second broad camp, usually called centre-right, groups economic liberals and social conservatives, who are broadly loyal to Ataturk's reforms, but wish for a stronger say in, and a diminution of the role of, the civil and military bureaucracy of the state. It first won power in 1950 under the banner of the Democrat Party (DP), which was carried forward by the Justice Party (AP), under Suleyman Demirel, then the Motherland Party (ANAP), formed by Turgut Ozal, and later both by the Motherland Party and the True Path Party (DYP, a re-incarnation of AP), and finally by the Justice and Development Party (AKP), led by Recep Tayyip Erdogan.

Parties further to the right have had much more

impact than in the case of the far left. These far-right parties divide into nationalists and Islamists. The most notable nationalist leader was Alpaslan Turkes, a member of the military junta in 1960, whose Nationalist Action Party (MHP), a partner in two coalition governments formed by the AP leader Suleyman Demirel in the late 1970s, was revived after the 1980 coup. Turkes was succeeded by Devlet Bahceli, who served in the coalition government of Bulent Ecevit between 1999 and 2002. MHP has given birth to a number of small breakaway parties: the Great Unity Party (BBP) under Muhsin Yazicioglu and the Nation Party (MP) under Aykut Edibali.

The founder of the political Islamist movement in Turkey is Professor Necmettin Erbakan, whose National Order Party (MNP), National Salvation Party (MSP) and Welfare Party (RP), were all banned by the constitutional court. Erbakan entered into coalitions under both Ecevit and Demirel in the 1970s, and led a coalition government with the DYP between 1996 and 1997, when he was eased out of office by the secularists spearheaded by the military. When RP was banned, its members regrouped in the Virtue Party (FP), under Erbakan's lieutenant, Recai Kutan. When FP was banned in turn, the Islamists split between conservatives and modernizers. The conservatives formed the Felicity Party (SP), while the modernizers found a new leader in Recep Tayyip Erdogan who set up the Justice and Development Party (AKP) and, moving it to the centre-right, won an absolute majority in the 2002 elections.

The ban on ethnic parties has not prevented Kurdish nationalists from forming parties, both legal and illegal. The main illegal Kurdish nationalist party was the Kurdish Workers' Party (PKK), of Marxist-Leninist inspiration, which led an insurgency in south-eastern Turkey between 1984 and 1999, when its leader Abdullah Ocalan was snatched from Nairobi by Turkish commandos. PKK later changed its name to Kurdistan Democratic Congress (KADEK and then KONGRA-GEL) and split into factions. Kurdish nationalists were also active under the legal cover of theoretically non-ethnic parties: first, the People's Labour Party (HEP), then the Democracy Party (DEP), some of whose members were elected to parliament on the list of the centre-left SHP, but then broke away and revived their old party. DEP was banned by the constitutional court and its MPs (among them Leyla Zana, wife of the former mayor of Diyarbakir, the chief city of the Kurdish-inhabited area) were convicted of collusion with the PKK and imprisoned. In June 2004 they were freed, pending retrial. DEP was replaced by the People's Democracy Party (HADEP), which was also banned, and reappeared under the name of the Democratic People's Party (DEHAP).

In the early elections held in November 2002, only two parties managed to exceed the threshold of 10% of the national poll: the newly formed Justice and Development Party (AKP), which won an absolute majority of 362 seats on 34% of the poll, and the oldest party, the Republican People's Party (CHP) with 177 seats and 19% of the poll. Subsequently, an independent, Mehmet Agar, was elected leader of the centre-right True Path Party (DYP), which he represented in parliament, where he was joined by three other MPs. In October 2004 the distribution of seats in the Grand National Assembly was as follows: AKP 368, CHP 171, DYP 4, independents 6.

Of formerly important parties, Ecevit's DSP and ANAP, now led by Nesrin Nas (replacing Mesut Yilmaz who had served as Foreign Minister, Prime Minister and deputy Prime Minister), appear to be in terminal decline.

Democratic People's Party
Demokratik Halk Partisi (DEHAP)
Address. Ruzgarli Mah. Soydaslar Sok. 4/6 Ulus/Ankara
Website. www.dehap.tk
Leader. Mahmut Ihsan Ozgen
DEHAP is the successor of HEP (People's Labour Party), DEP (Democracy Party) and HADEP (People's Democracy Party), as a legal vehicle for radical Kurdish nationalism. Its predecessors were accused of being front organizations for the PKK (Kurdish Workers' Party) militants who waged an armed struggle against the Turkish authorities from bases in Syria, Iraq, etc. between 1984 and 1999, and which were consequently banned by the constitutional court. As essentially (although not officially) an ethnic party, DEHAP has little support outside the main Kurdish-inhabited areas and can, therefore, hope to cross the 10% barrier only if it joins forces with a national party. DEP had fought the 1991 elections on the ticket of the centre-left (old) SHP, led at the time by Erdal Inonu. But its deputies resigned from SHP a few months after the election. Its successor HADEP did well in the local government elections in south-eastern Turkey, receiving just over a million votes and winning control of the main cities in the area. But in the 1999 general elections its nationwide share of the poll was below 5% and it did not enter parliament. DEHAP did better in 2002 with over 6%, but again did not gain any seats in the Assembly. In the 2004 local government elections DEHAP joined forces with the (new) SHP (led by Murat Karayalcin) and with other left-wing groups. The combined share of the poll of the coalition amounted to only 5% nationwide, and Kurdish nationalists lost control of some of the councils they had captured earlier. Dissensions in the ranks of radical Kurdish nationalists explain the reverse. An independent was elected mayor of Diyarbakir, the chief city of south-eastern Turkey, which had earlier been controlled by HADEP. After the capture of the PKK leader Abdullah Ocalan, his organization splintered, and so did his sympathizers operating legally in Turkey. The PKK successor organizations (KADEK, then KONGRA-GEL) announced that they would resume the armed struggle, first in December 2003 then in June 2004.

DEHAP, which is pressing for cultural rights (and eventually political minority rights) for the Kurds, is theoretically committed to a peaceful solution of the Kurdish problem, while maintaining links with radical Kurdish nationalist organizations outside Turkey and keeping its own radical image (its website is decorated with pictures of Marx and Lenin). In view of the factionalism endemic in Kurdish society, DEHAP is bound to be challenged on its home ground, but if Turkey abides by EU standards, Kurdish nationalism will continue to find expression in political parties with a strong regional, if not national, presence.

Felicity Party
Saadet Partisi (SP)
Address. Ziyabey Cad. 2. Sok. No:15 Balgat/Ankara
Telephone. (90-312) 284 88 00
Website. www.sp.org.tr
Leadership. Recai Kutan
The SP was founded on July 20, 2001, and led by Recai Kutan as a proxy for Necmettin Erbakan whose (Islamist) Welfare Party (RP) had been dissolved by the constitutional court. Erbakan was elected to the leadership in May 2003, but his position was insecure in view of a conviction for having secreted away the funds of the RP, and the leadership reverted to Recai Kutan. In the 2002 elections, SP received

only 2.5% of the national vote, as most Islamists rallied to Erdogan's AKP. In the local government elections in March 2004, the SP share of the vote rose only slightly to 4%. Nevertheless, it remains a contender for the Islamist constituency (which has usually accounted for at least 10% of the electorate), should the coalition of Islamists, centre-right conservatives and economic liberals forged by Erdogan within AKP fall apart, as a similar coalition assembled by Turgut Ozal gradually dissolved when Ozal was replaced by Mesut Yilmaz in the leadership of ANAP. In 2004 SP was the only significant political party opposed to Turkey's EU membership, reverting to the position defended by Erbakan until his brief tenure of office in 1996-97.

Justice and Development Party
Adalet ve Kalkinma Partisi (AKP)

Address. Ceyhun Atif Cad. No: 202 Balgat/Ankara
Website. www.akparti.org.tr
Leadership. Recep Tayyip Erdogan (leader and Prime Minister)

The AK Parti (the acronym AK translates as "white" or "pure") was founded in 2001 by a group of modernizers in the ranks of the Virtue Party (*Fazilet Partisi*/FP) of Islamic inspiration. Chief among them was Recep Tayyip Erdogan, who had been elected mayor of Istanbul in 1994 at the age of forty, and was deprived of his office and served four months in prison in 1998 for reciting a poem which summoned the faithful to battle. Although Erdogan's conviction disqualified him from political office, he led the party in the run-up to the early general elections in November 2002. Describing the party's stance as "democratic conservative", and repudiating the label "Islamic", Erdogan profited from the unpopularity of the incumbent coalition government which was blamed for the sharp drop in living standards in the wake of a financial crisis the previous year. When AKP won an absolute majority in the elections, it secured parliamentary approval for a constitutional amendment which removed Erdogan's disqualification. Between November 2002 and March 2003, when Erdogan won a by-election and entered parliament, the office of Prime Minister was filled by the party's deputy leader, Abdullah Gul, while a third founding member, Bulent Arinc, became speaker of parliament.

As he waited for office, Erdogan toured Western capitals in an effort to secure a date for the commencement of accession negotiations with the EU. (In December 2003, the EU Council of Ministers decided that talks would begin without delay if the Commission reported a year later that Turkey had met the criteria for membership.) As the Iraq war drew near, Erdogan allowed his members of parliament a free vote on a government motion to permit US troops to transit through Turkish territory. The motion was lost on March 1, 2003, and when Erdogan became Prime Minister on March 14 (with Abdullah Gul as his Foreign Minister) he had to cope with adverse US reaction, while pushing forward domestic reforms and demonstrating Turkey's willingness to find a solution to the Cyprus problem. He was successful in all three fields: the US was pleased by the decision taken by the Turkish parliament in October 2003 to send peacekeepers to Iraq (a decision which had no effect since the Iraqis opposed the presence of Turkish troops); Turkey agreed to a referendum in Cyprus on the unification plan presented by UN secretary general Kofi Annan, and won praise when the plan was endorsed by Turkish Cypriots on April 24, 2004, but rejected by the Greek Cypriots; and the last batch of constitutional amendments designed to meet EU requirements was passed in May 2004. The AKP government continued to implement the economic recovery programme agreed with the IMF in 2001, and, as the economy improved, it was able to make gains in the local government elections on March 28, 2004, when its share of the poll rose to 42% and it won

control of such opposition strongholds as Gaziantep in the south-east and Antalya in the south, while strengthening its hold on the town councils of Istanbul and Ankara.

Nationalist Action Party
Milliyetci Hareket Partisi (MHP)

Address. Karanfil Sokak No: 69 Bakanliklar/Ankara
Telephone. (90-312) 417 50 60
Website. www.mhp.org.tr
Leadership: Devlet Bahceli

Founded in 1969, MHP represents a tradition of ethnic Turkish nationalism, which stresses links with the Turkic peoples in the former Soviet Union and in western China, and which finds supporters particularly in central Anatolia, in areas of tension between Turks and Kurds and Sunnis and Alevis (Turkish heterodox Shiites). The MHP youth organization, known officially as "Hearths of Idealists" and unofficially as "Grey Woves", was actively involved in street violence in the 1970s.

After the death of its founder and Great Leader (*Basbug*), Alpaslan Turkes, who had served as deputy Prime Minister in Suleyman Demirel's "Nationalist Front" coalition governments in 1975-78, MHP achieved its best results in 1999, when it won 129 seats on 18% of the national poll, under the leadership of Devlet Bahceli. Bahceli served as deputy Prime Minister in Ecevit's coalition government in 1999-2002, when he objected to some of the reforms (such as the abolition of the death penalty) enacted in order to meet EU membership criteria. Sharing in the unpopularity of the government in the wake of the 2001 economic crisis, MHP saw its share of the poll drop to 8% in the 2002 elections. However, it reached 10% in the 2004 local government elections. It thus stands a chance of re-entering parliament where it has usually had a presence. MHP is theoretically in favour of EU membership, but objects to the recognition of cultural rights for the Kurds and to any concessions in Cyprus.

Republican People's Party
Cumhuriyet Halk Partisi (CHP)

Address. Cevre Sok. No: 38 Cankaya/Ankara
Telephone. (90-312) 468 59 69
Website. www.chp.org.tr
Leadership. Deniz Baykal

Founded by Ataturk in 1923 and in power without interruption until 1950, and then intermittently as a partner in coalition governments between 1961 and 1996, the CHP saw its share of the poll fall below the 10% threshold in the 1999 elections and was therefore denied representation in parliament for the first time in its history. Its leader, Deniz Baykal, thereupon resigned only to resume control a few months later. The party's absence from the unpopular coalition government formed by its former leader, Bulent Ecevit, who had formed the rival Democratic Left Party/DSP, allowed CHP to raise its share of the vote to 19% and to return to parliament in 2002. It was also strengthened by the support of Kemal Dervis, the former World Bank Vice-President who had negotiated the stabilization programme with the IMF. However, as Baykal refused to countenance moves to reunite the centre-left, while failing to present a coherent alternative to the AKP government, the CHP share of the vote dropped marginally to 18% in the local elections in March 2004. Dervis resigned his party posts, and a campaign developed to oust Baykal from the leadership. But in October 2004 his position improved as the left-wing splinter New Turkey Party/YTP decided to merge with CHP.

The traditional ideology of CHP – secularist, interventionist in the economy, and nationalist in foreign policy – still commends itself to a sizable minority of voters. But since Ecevit broke with the party, it has lacked leaders capable of appealing to a larger constituency. Strongest in the more prosperous western provinces, it is seen as the party of the secularist elite, whose expectations it nevertheless fails to satisfy. Its future electoral fortunes depend on the emergence of a leader willing and capable of reuniting the traditional centre-left/social-democratic/statist constituency, which averaged 35% of the electorate between 1950 and 1980. In 1999, CHP (under Deniz Baykal) and DSP (under Bulent Ecevit) together polled 31% but in 2002 the combined share of the poll of the centre-left fell to 22%.

True Path Party
Dogru Yol Partisi (DYP)

Address. Selanik Cad. No: 40 Kizilay/Ankara
Telephone. (90-312) 417 59 64 – 417 22 41
Website. www.dyp.org.tr
Leadership. Mehmet Agar

The DYP was founded in 1983 and was led by proxies for Suleyman Demirel, who assumed the leadership in 1987 when the ban on pre-1980 politicians was lifted. Designed as a reincarnation of the Justice Party (AP), which was dissolved by the military in 1980, DYP tried to regain its constituency which had been appropriated by Turgut Ozal's Motherland Party (ANAP). In 1987, DYP polled 19% of the vote against ANAP's 35% cent. In 1991 it overtook ANAP (led by Mesut Yilmaz after Ozal's election to the presidency), with 26% against 23%, and Demirel became Prime Minister at the head of a centre-right/centre-left coalition with SHP (led by Erdal Inonu). In 1993, Turgut Ozal died and Demirel was elected President of the Republic. He was succeeded as Prime Minister and DYP leader by Tansu Ciller, an academic economist who became Turkey's first woman Prime Minister. Her tenure of office witnessed an economic crisis in 1994, the intensification of counter-insurgency operations against Kurdish secessionists, and the conclusion of a customs union with the EU, which came into force on Jan. 1, 1996.

As the DYP-CHP coalition broke down, early elections were held in November 1995, in which the DYP share of the poll fell to 19%. Ciller tried first to team up with Mesut Yilmaz, whose ANAP was marginally more successful, but they disagreed after a few months, and on June 28, 1996, she formed a coalition with Necmettin Erbakan's (Islamist) Welfare Party (*Refah Partisi*/RP), which had emerged as the single strongest party in parliament (with 158 seats won on 21% of the total poll, against DYP's 135 seats). The RP-DYP coalition, in which Erbakan was Prime Minister (the first Islamist to hold this post in the republic's history) and Ciller deputy Prime Minister and Foreign Minister, lost its majority when a number of DYP deputies broke away and formed the Democratic Turkey Party (DTP) in response to pressure by the military, and on June 30, 1997, Erbakan resigned and was replaced by Mesut Yilmaz at the head of a secularist coalition. In 1999 the DYP share of the poll fell to 11% and its total of parliamentary seats to 135.

In the 2002 elections, which Ciller fought as leader of the opposition, the DYP won 9.5% of the vote, and was denied representation in parliament as it was marginally below the 10% barrier. Tansu Ciller thereupon resigned the party leadership, and was replaced by Mehmet Agar, a former police chief who had been elected to parliament as an independent. As ANAP had slipped even lower to 5% of the poll, DYP was best placed among the old parties to reclaim the centre-right constituency from AKP, should the latter suffer a reverse. In the 2004 local government elections DYP received nearly 10% of all votes cast.

Other Parties

Among the some 50 legally established and currently active parties, the following have had particular impact in recent years.

Democratic Left Party (*Demokratik Sol Partisi*, DSP). Following the secular and republican principles enunciated by Kemal Ataturk, the DSP was founded in 1984 mainly by former members of the CHP, which until it was banned following the October 1980 military coup had been led by Bulent Ecevit, who had served two terms as Prime Minister in the 1970s. It was formally established as a party under the chairmanship of Rahsan Ecevit, wife of the former Prime Minister, who himself remained subject to a 10-year political ban under transitional provisions of the 1982 constitution. Following a September 1987 referendum decision in favour of lifting the ban, Bulent Ecevit was elected chairman of the DSP, with his wife becoming his deputy. The party was one of the most important of the 1990s, forming the government in coalition with other parties at times and Ecevit again serving as Prime Minister. In the 1999 general elections the DSP was the largest party taking 136 seats from 22.3% of the vote. However, it failed to reach the 10% threshold for parliamentary representation in 2002 and is now a marginal force.

Address. Maresal Fevzi Cakmak cad. 17, Besevler, Ankara
Telephone. (90-312) 212 49 50
Email. info@dsp.org.tr
Website. www.dsp.org.tr
Leadership. Zeki Sezer

Motherland Party (*Anavatan Partisi*, ANAP). Founded in May 1983 by Turgut Ozal, the conservative and nationalist ANAP aspired to occupy the political ground held by the pre-1980 Justice Party. In the November 1983 Assembly elections it won an absolute majority (212 of the 400 seats) against two other parties, whereupon Ozal became Prime Minister. It retained its overall majority in the 1987 elections, but (now led by Mesut Yilmaz) was defeated in the October 1991 elections, its Assembly representation slumping from 275 to 115 seats (out of 450), on a vote share of 24%. The party then experienced factional fighting and lost its founder and supreme leader when (now President) Ozal died of a heart attack in April 1993. Following the Dember 1995 elections ANAP formed a coalition government with the DYP in March 1996, with Yilmaz taking first turn as Prime Minister. He had only three months in the top political job, however, before the collapse of the coalition, when ANAP again found itself in opposition, this time to a coalition of the RP and the DYP. The collapse of the RP/DYP government in June 1997 brought Yilmaz back to the premiership, heading a coalition with the Democratic Left Party (DSP) and the small Democratic Turkey Party. This government collapsed in November 1998. In the April 1999 elections ANAP declined to 86 seats and 13.3% of the vote and accepted the status of junior partner in a three-party coalition headed by the DSP and also including the ultra-nationalist Nationalist Action Party. However, in the November 2002 elections ANAP failed to reach the 10% threshold, and it is consequently unrepresented in parliament.

Address. 13 cad. 3, Balgat, Ankara
Telephone. (90-312) 286 5000
Email. anavatan@anap.org.tr
Website. www.anap.org.tr
Leader. Nesrin Nas

Young Party (*Genc Parti*, GP), formed in July 2002 by the controversial Uzan family of entrepreneurs, and won a remarkable 7% of the national poll in the November 2002 elections (although below the 10% threshold for parliamentary representation). Arrest warrants have been issued for members of the family charged with fraud.

Address. Cetin Emec Bulvari Oguzlar Mah. 55. Sok. No: 3 06520 Cankaya/Ankara
Leader. Cem Uzan

Turkmenistan

Capital: Ashkhabad
Population: 5,100,000 (2001E)

The Turkmen Soviet Socialist Republic declared independence from the USSR in October 1991 as the Republic of Turkmenistan. It became a sovereign member of the Commonwealth of Independent States (CIS) in December 1991. A new constitution was adopted in May 1992, providing for an executive President as head of state and government. Legislative authority is vested in the 50-member Assembly (*Majlis*), elected by popular vote for a five-year term. A non-legislative People's Council (*Khalk Maslakhaty*) is the supreme representative and supervisory body, consisting of 50 directly elected members as well as the 50 *Majlis* deputies, the members of the Council of Ministers, 10 appointed regional representatives and other senior executive and judicial officials. The Communist Party of Turkmenistan was transformed into the Democratic Party of Turkmenistan (DPT) on the eve of the demise of the USSR.

A presidential election on June 21, 1992, resulted in incumbent head of state Saparmurad Niyazov (former First Secretary of the Communist Party of Turkmenistan) being elected unopposed. In a referendum on Jan. 15, 1994, almost unanimous approval was given to a proposal that Niyazov's term of office be extended until January 1999, so that he was not required to seek re-election in 1997. On Dec. 28, 1999, moreover, the *Majlis* voted unanimously in favour of a recommendation by the People's Council that there should be no limit to Niyazov's term of office. As of 2004 this ruling was still in force.

Although the 1992 constitution allows for multi-partyism, the DPT remains the only party with legal status, attempts to create opposition formations having quickly withered. Elections to the *Majlis* on Dec. 11, 1994, and Dec. 12, 1999, accordingly endorsed the DPT as the sole legislative party, although on the latter occasion the 50 seats were contested by 102 DPT candidates. After the December 1999 elections, President Niyazov ruled out the legalization of other parties for at least a decade. The next elections to the *Majlis* are scheduled for late 2004.

Democratic Party of Turkmenistan (DPT)

Address. 28 Gogolya Street, 744014 Ashkhabad 14
Telephone. (7–3632) 251212
Leadership. Saparmurad Niyazov (chairman)
The DPT was founded in November 1991 as in effect the successor to the former ruling Communist Party (CP) of the Turkmen SSR, which had been suspended immediately after the attempted coup by hardliners in Moscow in August 1991 and was officially dissolved by decision of its 25th congress on Dec 16, 1991. At its inauguration, the DPT distanced itself from its predecessor's "mistakes" but declared itself to be the country's "mother party", dominating all political activity but seeking to engender a "loyal" political opposition. In succeeding years very little of the latter made its presence felt, as the DPT maintained a grip on power every bit as firm as that exercised by its predecessor.

In February 1992 President Niyazov gave an outline of his version of a multi-party system in Turkmenistan, suggesting that former CP officials and supporters in rural areas should set up a peasant party, and that everyone else should join the DPT. In a further pronouncement in December 1993, the President said that a peasants' party would be granted official registration as the first step towards a multi-party system. In the event, however, registration was not granted.

As the only legal party, the DPT retained its legislative monopoly in elections to the *Majlis* in December 1994 and December 1999. Amidst a burgeoning cult of personality surrounding the former general turned politician, Niyazov was in December 1999 effectively confirmed as having life tenure of the presidency, without need of re-election. In February 2001 Niyazov said that the next presidential elections would be held in 2010 and confirmed that no other parties would be legalized until then.

Tuvalu

Capital: Fongafale (Funafuti atoll)
Population: 10,000 (2000E)

Tuvalu, formerly the Ellice Islands, became a fully independent country in 1978. The head of state is the British sovereign, represented by a Governor-General. Legislative authority is vested in a unicameral Parliament (*Parlamene o Tuvalu*) of 13 members, 12 of whom are popularly elected for up to four years. Executive power is exercised by a Cabinet drawn from, and answerable to, Parliament, and headed by a Prime Minister elected by Parliament.

There are no political parties in Tuvalu, where members of Parliament tend to be aligned with the leading political personalities. The most recent election, fought on a non-partisan basis in July 2002, resulted in Saufatu Sopoanga becoming Prime Minister.

Uganda

Capital: Kampala
Population: 24,600,000 (2000E)

Uganda became an independent state in 1962 after some 70 years of British rule, a republic being instituted in 1967. In 1971 President Milton Obote and his Uganda People's Congress (UPC) regime were deposed by Idi Amin Dada, whose military government was in turn overthrown in 1979 following internal rebellion and military intervention by Tanzania. General elections were held the following year in which Obote and the UPC were returned to power. The current President, Yoweri Museveni, assumed power in January 1986 as leader of the National Resistance Movement (NRM). The NRM had waged a guerrilla war since 1981, firstly against the Obote government and subsequently against the military regime which deposed Obote in July 1985.

Although political activity is banned, political parties are permitted to exist and the main traditional groupings, the UPC and the Democratic Party, have been represented in the NRM-dominated government. In 1993 the government published a draft constitution. The following year a Constituent Assembly was elected, on a non-party basis, to debate, amend and enact the new constitution. Having extended the NRM's term of office in November 1994, the Assembly voted in June 1995 to retain the current system of non-party government. The constitution came into effect in October 1995, after which the Constituent Assembly was disbanded.

In non-party presidential and legislative elections on May 9 and June 27, 1996, respectively, President

Museveni was victorious in the former with 74.2% of the vote, while the latter resulted in presidential supporters winning a majority in the new 276-seat unicameral National Parliament. On June 29, 2000, the continuation of the existing non-party political system (known officially as the Movement system) was approved by 90.7% of the vote in a national referendum, with only 9.3% of voters favouring a return to a multi-party system. However, opposition forces boycotted the referendum and there was a turnout of only 47.2%. On June 25, 2004, the Constitutional Court issued a ruling that effectively nullified the referendum, stating that the National Parliament had enacted a bill adopting the results of the referendum in contravention of established procedures. President Museveni rejected the ruling and the government lodged an appeal.

President Museveni was re-elected with 69.3% of the vote in a presidential election held on March 12, 2001. Col. Kizza Besigye, the runner-up (with 27.8% of the vote) and candidate of the informal Reform Agenda, claimed that the conduct of the election had been "massively fraudulent". Besigye, a former NRM colleague of Museveni, had accused the incumbent President of heading a corrupt and nepotistic administration. There were four other candidates in the election.

Democratic Party (DP)

Address. PO Box 458, Kampala

Telephone. (256–41) 344155

Email. ssemo2@swiftuganda.com

Website. www.framework.co.za/dua/uganda/dp

Leadership. Paul Ssemogerere (president general); Byanyima Boniface (chairman)

The DP was founded in 1954, attracting strong Roman Catholic support in southern Uganda. Having been banned from the late 1960s, it became the main opposition party to the Uganda People's Congress (UPC) following the parliamentary elections held in December 1980. After the assumption of power by the National Resistance Movement (NRM) in 1986, the DP was represented in the coalition government under President Museveni. Party leader Ssemogerere, who had continued to campaign against NRM dominance and against the regime's refusal to move more quickly to a multi-party system, resigned his post as Second Deputy Prime Minister and Minister of Public Service in June 1995, announcing that he would contest planned presidential elections as the DP candidate. In the event, under the October 1995 constitution party labels were barred in the May 1996 presidential elections, in which Ssemogerere came a poor second to the incumbent with only 23.7% of the vote. Factors damaging his cause reportedly included his gravitation to an alliance with the unpopular Milton Obote's UPC and his reluctance to make outright condemnation of the militant anti-government Lord's Resistance Army. In the March 2001 presidential election Ssemogerere urged DP members to vote for Kizza Besigye, who was seen as the strongest challenger to Museveni.

The DP is affiliated to the Christian Democrat International and the Democrat Union of Africa.

Forum for Democratic Change (FDC)

Leadership. Sam Njuba, Augustine Ruzindana, Eliphas Kahuku Karuhanga Chaapa (leaders of governing council)

The FDC was formed in August 2004 by the merger of various opposition groups, including the Reform Agenda, the Parliamentary Advocacy Forum and the National Democratic Forum. It was reported that several MPs affiliated to the Democratic Party and the Uganda People's Congress had also joined the FDC.

National Resistance Movement (NRM)

Address. c/o Parliamentary Buildings, PO Box 7178, Kampala

Leadership. Yoweri Museveni (interim chairman); Al Hajji Moses Kigongo (first vice chairman); Bidandi Ssali (second vice chairman)

The NRM was founded in early 1981 as the political wing of the guerrilla National Resistance Army in opposition to the Obote government. The armed struggle had been launched when the political party formed by Museveni in mid-1980 (the Uganda Patriotic Movement) was deemed to have won only one seat in the December 1980 legislative elections. The NRM assumed power in early 1986, ousting the short-lived military regime which had deposed Obote, and has since been the dominant force within government.

The NRM was only officially registered in May 2003, with Al Hajji Moses Kigongo as interim chairman. President Museveni could not participate in the interim executive because of being barred by the law as a serving officer of the armed forces. Museveni retired from the army in April 2004 and four months later was elected to replace Kisongo as the party's interim chairman. Paul Ssemogerere, leader of the Democratic Party, said that Museveni's election as NRM interim chairman was "part of ongoing schemes to entrench himself in power" and "a prelude to the third [presidential] term."

Reform Agenda (RA)

Leadership. Col. Kizza Besigye (in exile); Betty Kamya (spokesperson)

The informal Reform Agenda spearheaded the candidacy of Col. Kizza Besigye in the March 2001 presidential election. Besigye, a former member of the ruling National Resistance Movement (NRM), won almost 28% of the vote, but was defeated by incumbent President Museveni of the NRM. After reports that he had been harassed by the security forces, Besigye fled to the USA in August 2001 and has since remained in exile. In August 2004 the RA joined with other opposition groups to form the Forum for Democratic Change.

Uganda Patriotic Movement (UPM)

Leadership. Jaberi Ssali (secretary-general)

Co-founded by Yoweri Museveni in 1980, the UPM controversially won only a single seat in the December 1980 legislative elections, prompting a subsequent guerrilla struggle against the Obote government. Having dissolved upon Museveni's formation of the National Resistance Movement, the UPM re-emerged after the NRM took control in 1986 and several of its members were accorded ministerial positions.

Uganda People's Congress (UPC)

Address. PO Box 1951, Kampala

Website. www.upcparty.net

Leadership. Milton Obote (leader in exile); James Rwanyarare (national leader)

The UPC is a mainly Protestant formation, with a socialist-based philosophy, dating from 1960. It led the country to independence in 1962 under Milton Obote and was the ruling party until overthrown in 1971. The UPC returned to power, after the ousting of Idi Amin, with a disputed victory in the December 1980 elections. Obote was again overthrown by the military in 1985, but UPC adherents were included within the broad-based government established by Museveni after the National Resistance Movement assumed power in early 1986. Friction has persisted between the government and Obote loyalists, and a number of UPC offshoots have reportedly taken up armed resistance to the Museveni government. In May 1999 Museveni announced that Obote would be permitted to return to Uganda, if he so wished, under the terms of a current amnesty for all exiles. Obote chose to remain in exile and to urge his supporters to oppose

Museveni. In the non-party presidential election of March 12, 2001, Aggrey Awari, an MP who was a member of the UPC, was placed third with 1.4% of the vote.

Other Parties

Conservative Party
Leadership. Joshua S. Mayanja-Nkangi (leader); Ken Lukyamuzi (secretary-general)

Justice Forum, whose leader Mayanja stood in the 1996 and 2001 presidential elections, winning 2.1% and 1.0% of the vote, respectively.
Leadership. Muhammad Kibirige Mayanja (leader)

National Democrats Forum (NDF). Party leader Chaapa stood in the 2001 presidential election, winning only 0.1% of the vote. The NDF joined with other groups in August 2004 to form the Forum for Democratic Change.
Leadership. Eliphas Kahuku Karuhanga Chaapa (leader)

National Progressive Movement (NPM). Formed in April 2004, the party was subsequently linked with the political ambitions of David Pulkol, the former director-general of the External Security Organisation (ESO).
Leadership. Mary Komunte (national chairperson); Arthur Kwesiga (vice-chairperson); Fred Kakooza (secretary-general)

Parliamentary Advocacy Forum (PAFO), an opposition group which merged with other groups in August 2004 to form the Forum for Democratic Change.
Leadership. Augustine Ruzindana (leader)

Ukraine

Capital: Kyiv (Kiev)
Population: 48,457,000 (2001)

The Ukrainian Soviet Socialist Republic declared independence from the USSR in August 1991 as Ukraine, which became a sovereign member of the Commonwealth of Independent States (CIS) in December 1991. A new constitution adopted in June 1996 defines Ukraine as a democratic pluralist state and recognizes the right to private ownership of property, including land. It vests substantial powers in the executive President, who is directly elected for a five-year term and who nominates the Prime Minister and other members of the government, for approval by the legislature. Legislative authority is vested in a Supreme Council (*Verkhovna Rada*) of 450 members, who are elected for a four-year term by universal adult suffrage. Under an amendment to the Electoral Law adopted in October 1997, half of the Supreme Council deputies are elected by majority vote in single-member constituencies and the other 225 from party lists by proportional representation subject to a threshold of 4% of the national vote.

Elections to the Supreme Council on March 29, 1998, resulted in 445 of the 450 seats being validly filled, as follows: Communist Party of Ukraine (KPU) 121 seats (with 24.7% of the proportional vote), Popular Movement of Ukraine (*Rukh*) 46 (9.4%), a joint list of the Socialist Party of Ukraine and the Peasants' Party of Ukraine 34 (8.6%), Popular Democratic Party 28 (5.0%), *Hromada* All-Ukrainian Association 24 (4.7%), Green Party of Ukraine 19 (5.4%), Social Democratic Party of Ukraine–United 17 (2.9%), Progressive

Socialist Party 16 (2.5%), Agrarian Party of Ukraine 9 (3.7%), National Front 5 (2.7%), Party of Reforms and Order 3 (3.1%), Forward Ukraine! 2 (1.7%), Christian Democratic Party of Ukraine 2 (1.3%), Party of Regional Revival 2 (0.9%), six other parties or alliances 6, independents 111. Most of the independents joined parliamentary groups set up by the main parties, with the result that the centre-right factions commanded an overall majority, although the composition and names of the groups changed continually in the post-1998 parliamentary term.

In presidential elections on Oct. 31 and Nov. 14, 1999, incumbent Leonid Kuchma, standing without party affiliation, was re-elected for a second term with 56.3% of the valid second-round vote against 37.8% for the KPU candidate.

In a referendum on April 16, 2000, President Kuchma obtained overwhelming popular approval for proposed constitutional amendments providing for a bicameral parliament, a reduction in the size of the Supreme Council from 450 to 300 members, reduced parliamentary immunity from prosecution and enhanced presidential powers of dissolution. Meanwhile a new Electoral Law adopted by the Supreme Council in January 2001, under which all seats would be allocated by proportional representation, was vetoed by President Kuchma in March, following which the Council in May 2001 failed to master the two-thirds majority needed to override the veto. Only in October 2001 did the parliament adopt a new election law, subsequently signed by President Kuchma, that retained the mixed principle of 50% MPs elected directly and 50% on party lists.

The parliamentary elections held on March 31, 2002, resulted in the following allocation of seats: pro-presidential bloc "For a United Ukraine" 102, reformist bloc of former Prime Minister Viktor Yuschenko "Our Ukraine" 111, Communist Party 66, Social Democratic Party (United) 31, centre-right Bloc of Yuliya Tymoshenko (Fatherland) 23, Socialist Party 22, and 93 independents.

Out of 33 blocs and parties participating in the 2002 elections, 27 did not pass the 4% threshold of the national vote and did not make it into the *Verkhovna Rada*. As a result of political regrouping, however, the pro-presidential faction "For a United Ukraine" increased to 175 MPs by the end of 2002; it then fragmented into a number of party blocs but together with other groups and factions formed an unstable majority with the United Social Democrats. All opposition factions lost a number of MPs to the pro-presidential majority under "informal" political pressure and by January 2004 had the following number of seats: "Our Ukraine" 102, Communist Party 59, Socialist Party 20, Bloc Tymoshenko 19.

The work of the *Verkhovna Rada* was blocked in December 2003 by the opposition parties protesting against attempts by the pro-presidential majority, with the cooperation of the Communists, to get through a constitutional reform allowing election of the President by the parliament as opposed to a direct vote based on universal suffrage in a secret ballot.

A law "On political parties in Ukraine" adopted by parliament on April 5, 2001, specified that only all-Ukrainian political organizations that participate in elections (at least once in a decade), have representations (offices) in two-thirds of the regions of Ukraine, and with at least 10,000 initial supporters, could be registered as parties. Following the 2002 parliamentary elections, the Ukrainian justice department initiated in March 2003 a review of all parties and 46 parties were found to have irregularities in their registration documents by September 2003. The Highest Court of Ukraine considered violations of the law in the documents of 37 parties and annulled the registration of 31 parties by January 2004, reducing the list of registered parties to 96. On Nov. 7, 2003, the President of Ukraine submitted to the parliament proposed amendments to the law on political parties that would allow cancelling the registration of parties that did not achieve parliamentary representation within a decade

Agrarian Party of Ukraine
Ahrarna Partiya Ukrainy (APU)
Address. 6a Reytarska St., Kyiv
Telephone. 0038 044 4640190
Fax. 0038 044 4640587
Leadership. Mykhaylo Hladiy (chairman)
Favouring the de-collectivization of the agricultural sector, the APU was launched in 1996 as an alternative to the pro-collectivization Peasants' Party of Ukraine (SelPU). Backed by the presidency of Leonid Kuchma, the party obtained some support in the agriculture bureaucracy. Led by Kateryna Vashchuk in the 1998 parliamentary elections, the APU failed to achieve the 4% proportional threshold but won nine constituency seats.

Under the new leadership of Mykhaylo Hladiy, the APU in July 2001 joined a "pro-presidential" bloc, later designated "For a United Ukraine", with the People's Democratic Party, the Labour Party of Ukraine (Together) and the Party of Regional Revival of Ukraine, with the aim of creating "a powerful democratic force of centrist orientation". After the 2002 election victory of "For a United Ukraine" the APU resisted moves to weld the bloc into a single political party and created a separate fraction with 16 MPs led by Kateryna Vashchuk. The APU supported Prime Minister Yanukovych as presidential candidate in 2004.

Communist Party of Ukraine
Komunistychna Partiya Ukrainy (KPU)
Address. 7 Borysohlibska St., Kyiv 04070
Telephone. (380–44) 416–5487
Fax. (380–44) 416-31-37
Website. www.kpu.kiev.ua
Leadership. Petro Symonenko (first secretary)
The Soviet-era KPU was formally banned in August 1991, but a campaign for its revival began as early as the summer of 1992, culminating in two restoration congresses in Donetsk in March and June 1993. The party claims to be the "legal successor" to the Soviet-era KPU, but avoided declaring the June congress to be the "29th" in the party's history and has been unable to claim former KPU property. The party was officially registered in October 1993, the day after President Yeltsin's troops bombarded the White House in Moscow. Unlike other "successor" parties in Eastern Europe, the KPU remains aggressively anti-capitalist and anti-nationalist. It stands for the restoration of state control over the economy, and for some kind of confederative union between Ukraine and Russia. The KPU's populist nostalgia rapidly gained it support in economically troubled industrial areas of eastern Ukraine, especially in the Donbas, where party leader Petro Symonenko had been second secretary of the Donetsk party under the Soviet regime).

In the mid-1994 presidential elections the KPU gave crucial backing to Leonid Kuchma, then of the Inter-Regional Bloc for Reform, in his successful challenge to the incumbent. In the parliamentary elections that began in March 1994, the KPU emerged as substantially the largest single party, with an initial total of 90 seats (nearly all in eastern and southern Ukraine). The party thus became the fulcrum

of potential further conflict between the eastern and western regions of Ukraine. In 1995–96 the KPU put up determined resistance to the new "presidential" constitution favoured by President Kuchma, claiming in February 1996 to have collected 2.5 million signatures in support of a referendum on the issues at stake. However, following the final adoption of the new text in June 1996 (without a referendum), the party leadership announced that it would no longer question the constitution's legitimacy, but would instead mount a campaign for early presidential and parliamentary elections, combined with mass industrial action in protest against government economic policy.

The KPU confirmed its position as the largest party in the March 1998 parliamentary elections, advancing to 121 seats on a vote share of 24.7% and subsequently being joined by some independent deputies. Standing for the KPU in the autumn 1999 presidential elections, Symonenko came second to Kuchma in the first round with 22.2% of the vote and lost to the incumbent in the second, receiving 37.8% on the strength of backing from other left-wing parties. The KPU leader complained that the polling had been rigged, as did international observers. In March 2000 the KPU's headquarters in Kyiv were briefly occupied by nationalist militants, who accused the party of promoting the colonization of Ukraine by Russia.

In the major crisis which overtook the Kuchma administration in early 2001 over allegations that he had been involved in the murder of a journalist, the KPU claimed credit for securing the dismissal of "pro-American" Prime Minister Viktor Yushchenko in April and declared itself ready to form a government. At a May Day rally Symonenko asserted that "nationalists and oligarchic capitalists", assisted by the West, were seeking to divide Ukraine into three parts and to detach the country from "fraternal Slavic peoples". Earlier in the year the KPU had signed a co-operation agreement with the Communist Party of the Russian Federation and declared its support for Ukrainian membership of the Belarus-Russia Union.

Following the terrorist attacks on the USA in September 2001, the KPU condemned the US-led military action against Afghanistan as "unleashing a new world war". Calling for Ukraine to declare neutrality and non-alignment, the party castigated the Kuchma administration for granting US military planes the right to use Ukrainian airspace. The KPU was likewise against Ukrainian participation in the US-led coalition forces in Iraq and voted against the Ukrainian peace-keeping mission in Liberia in 2003.

Despite earlier talks with other opposition parties to unite against the "regime" of President Kuchma, the KPU joined with the pro-presidential majority in proposing a constitutional reform in 2004 that would allow parliament to elect the President. The KPU has been widely accused of being the "official opposition" party in a virtual party politics played by the pro-presidential clans to keep President Kuchma in power. The KPU nominated its leader as its presidential candidate in 2004.

Fatherland
Batkivschchyna
Address. Room 916, 26 Lesi Ukrainky Ave, Kyiv, 01133
Telephone. 0038 044 2944221
Website. http://fatherland.freeservers.com
Leadership. Yuliya Tymoshenko (chairperson)
The moderate conservative Fatherland was launched in March 1999 by a faction of the *Hromada* All-Ukrainian Association after *Hromada* leader Pavlo Lazarenko had fled to the USA to escape charges of financial corruption when he was Prime Minister in 1996-97. The new party was joined by 23 Supreme Council deputies, 19 of them former *Hromada* members. In January 2000 Fatherland leader

Yuliya Tymoshenko was appointed Deputy Prime Minister and given charge of the energy sector. In August 2000 her husband was among several state energy officials arrested on embezzlement charges and was later also accused of paying large bribes to Lazarenko when he was Prime Minister.

Tymoshenko herself was then charged with corruption when she had been a state energy official and was dismissed from the government in January 2001, whereupon Fatherland joined the parliamentary opposition to President Kuchma, who was concurrently under intense pressure to resign over his alleged involvement in the murder of a journalist. The arrest of Tymoshenko in mid-February 2001 was condemned by Fatherland as punishment for her anti-Kuchma stance and her attempts to reform the energy sector. She was released and re-arrested in March, before being re-released by decision of the Supreme Court in April 2001. Under hospital treatment for a stomach ulcer through these machinations, Tymoshenko on her re-release called for Kuchma to be removed by constitutional procedures. She subsequently dismissed as "cheap provocation" the filing of bribery charges against her by military prosecutors in Russia.

In July 2001 Tymoshenko announced the creation of the anti-Kuchma "National Salvation Forum", within which it was envisaged that Fatherland would contest the 2002 elections in an alliance of centre-right parties including the Christian Democratic Party of Ukraine, the Social Democratic Party of Ukraine, the Ukrainian Republican Party and the Ukrainian Conservative Republican Party. The following month the Forum was joined by the Confederation of Free Trade Unions of Ukraine. Fatherland (as the Bloc of Yuliya Tymoshenko) actively participated as an opposition party in the 2002 election and won 23 seats in the *Verkhovna Rada*. However, due to political pressure the Fatherland fraction was reduced to 19 by 2004. Fatherland actively supported Viktor Yuschenko as presidential candidate in 2004.

Party of Industrialists and Entrepreneurs of Ukraine (PIEU)
Partiya promyslovtsiv ta pidpryiemtsiv Ukrayiny
Address. 11 Shota Rustavelli Str., Kyiv – 01023
Telephone. 0038 044 2343707
Fax. 0038 044 235 82 58
Leadership. Anatoliy Kinakh
Registered by former Prime Minister Anatoliy Kinakh in March 2000, the party was formed on the basis of the Ukrainian Union of Industrialists and Entrepreneurs active since the early 1990s. The UUIE united the directors of big, initially state-owned enterprises and was briefly led by Leonid Kuchma before he became President in 1994. Anatoliy Kinakh became head of the UUIE in 1997 and worked as vice-Prime Minister in charge of the economy from August 1999 to January 2000. After his dismissal he formed the Party of Industrialists and Entrepreneurs of Ukraine (PIEU) in February 2000 and was nominated as Prime Minister in March 2001. After being dismissed in November 2002 Kinakh and the PIEU joined the coalition of pro-presidential parties in the parliamentary elections of March 2002 and formed a faction with Labour Ukraine in June 2002. PIEU has 6 MPs in the faction including former Minister of Economy Vasyl Gureyev. Anatoliy Kinakh remained the president of the Ukrainian Union of Industrialists and Entrepreneurs, which includes the Ukrainian Federation of Employers and the Ukrainian Agrarian Confederation. The PIEU nominated Kinakh as its presidential candidate in 2004.

Party "Labour Ukraine"
Politychna Partiya "Trudova Ukrayina"
Address. 4 Shovkovychna Str., Kyiv – 01021
Teephone. 00 38 044 2298903

Website. www.trud.org.ua
Leadership. Sergiy Tihipko
Political party "Labour Ukraine" was registered in June 2000 and united six public organizations under the leadership of a powerful business and political grouping in the Ukrainian parliament that had formed the "Labour Ukraine" fraction in April 1999. The parliamentary lobby included the wealthiest Ukrainian entrepreneur and President's son-in-law Viktor Pinchuk, ex-minister and industrialist Ihor Sharov, and ex-Ukrainian Security Service (SBU) officer turned powerful businessman, Andriy Derkach. Andriy Derkach, apart from being the self-declared godson of Leonid Kuchma is also the son of the former head of the SBU, Leonid Derkach, and sponsor of a pro-Russian political coalition "To Europe with Russia".

Ihor Sharov became head of the party after initial leader Mykhaylo Syrota left, and quickly turned the "Labour Ukraine" fraction into the second largest in the parliament with 46 members. The party congress in autumn 2000, however, elected ex-Minister of Economy Sergiy Tihipko as its leader, who proclaimed the "labour" ideology of "Labour Ukraine". The party controlled four parliamentary committees and had a number of ministers in the government associated with the party. Despite its "labour" rhetoric Labour Ukraine is a coalition of self-sufficient "oligarchs" with the support of the law enforcement agencies such as the SBU.

Labour Ukraine joined the pro-presidential coalition "For a United Ukraine" during the parliamentary election campaign in 2002. "For a United Ukraine" formed a majority with a number of independent MPs and disintegrated into factions among which Labour Ukraine formed one with the Party of Industrialists and Entrepreneurs (42 members). Labour Ukraine controlled two parliamentary committees (foreign affairs and finance) while Sergiy Tihipko is the Head of National Bank of Ukraine. As a result of a symbolic coalition between the government and the parliament, Labour Ukraine, as a part of the parliamentary majority, nominated the Minister of Economy and Minister of Industrial Policy in the government of Viktor Yanukovych. There are 17 ex-ministers or deputy-ministers within the parliamentary fraction of Labour Ukraine. Labour Ukraine has initiated a number of political projects in support of President Leonid Kuchma whose popularity plummeted after the "cassette scandal", linking him to a murder of a journalist.

Labour Ukraine supported Prime Minister Yanukovych as presidential candidate in 2004.

Party of Reforms and Order
Partiya Reformy i Poryadok (PRiP)
Address. 2 Tymiriazivska St., Kyiv 01014
Telephone. 0038044 2014115
Fax. 0038044 2014117
Website. www.reformy.org
Leadership. Viktor Pynzenyk (chairman)
The PRiP was launched in advance of the 1998 parliamentary elections by a group of economic reformers led by former Deputy Prime Minister Viktor Pynzenyk, who had resigned from the Kuchma administration in April 1997 in protest against the slow pace of reform. As originally conceived, the "reforms" component of the party's platform was to be represented by Pynzenyk, while Supreme Council committee chairman Hryhoriy Omelchenko was to supply a "law and order" dimension. In the event, Omelchenko opted to join Forward Ukraine, and later Ukraininian People's Party "Sobor". In the 1998 polling the PRiP unexpectedly failed to achieve the 4% minimum in the proportional section (winning 3.1%) and returned only three candidates in the constituency contests.

In political manoeuvring for the 2002 parliamentary elections, the PRiP in July 2001 joined the "Our Ukraine" bloc led by former Prime Minister Viktor Yushchenko and also including both factions of the Popular Movement of Ukraine (*Rukh*), and hence gained representation in the *Verkhovna Rada*. PRiP actively supported Viktor Yuschenko as presidential candidate in 2004 and promoted the idea of creating a single party "Our Ukraine".

Party of the Regions
Partiya Regioniv

Address. Apt 5, 3 Kudriavska Str., Kyiv - 04053
Telephone. 0038 044 212 55 70
Fax. 0038 044 1225583
Website. www.partyofregions.org.ua
Leadership. Viktor Yanukovych

The Party of the Regions was registered in March 2001 after four other parties joined its predecessor – the Party of Regional Revival of Ukraine (PRVU). The PRVU was founded in November 1997 by Volodymyr Rybak, the mayor of Donetsk, with the declared aim of protecting the socio-economic interests of the regions and promoting regional autonomy. It won only 0.9% of the proportional vote in the March 1998 parliamentary elections, but elected two candidates in constituency contests. The PRVU supported Leonid Kuchma in the 1999 presidential elections. The new Party of the Regions aquired a powerful political lobby in the parliament and elected a new leader – the head of the State Tax Inspectorate, Mykola Azarov. The party was modelled on the Russian pro-presidential political bloc "Yedinstvo" and incorporated the industrialist lobby from Donbas including ex-Prime Minister Yuhym Zviagilski, Donetsk mayor Volodymyr Rybak, Regional governor Viktor Yanukovych and one of the most powerful Donetsk "oligarchs" – Rinat Akhmetov.

The Party of the Regions created a parliamentary faction "Regions of Ukraine" that included 24 members and established its presence in all regions of Ukraine with some help from the state tax authority and its head Mykola Azarov. The Party of the Regions joined the pro-presidential bloc "For a United Ukraine" in the March 2002 parliamentary elections and formed a new faction "Regions of Ukraine" with a satellite group "European choice" (67 members). After a political compromise Viktor Yanukovych was approved as Prime Minister in April 2003 and immediately elected as head of the Party of the Regions with a clear view to the presidential contest in late 2004. With the head of the party as Prime Minister and ex-head of the party Mykola Azarov as vice-Prime Minister and Minister of Finance, the Party of the Regions also controls a number of key govermental ministries such energy and fuel, and is one of the main political, financial and administrative forces in the country – i.e. one of the so-called "parties of power". Despite the past criminal convictions of Viktor Yanukovych and the murky origins of the wealth amassed by the involved "oligarchs", the party was hopeful and indeed well positioned to win the presidential elections in October 2004.

Popular Democratic Party
Narodno-Demokratychna Partiya (NDP)

Address. 107 Antonovycha St., Kyiv 03150
Telephone. (0038 044) 252–8418
Fax. (0038 044) 2528420
Website. www.ndp.org.ua
Leadership. Valeriy Pustovoytenko (chairman)

The pro-market NDP was formed in mid-1996 as a merger of several small centrist groupings, notably the Democratic Revival Party of Ukraine (PDVU), which had won four parliamentary seats in 1994, and New Wave (NK), which had also won four. From July 1997 to November 1999 the NDP provided the Prime Minister in the person of Valeriy Pustovoytenko. In the March 1998 parliamentary elections

the NDP advanced to 28 seats on a proportional vote share of 5% and became part of the centre-right parliamentary majority giving qualified backing to governments appointed by President Kuchma, whom the party supported in his successful re-election bid in 1999.

In September 2000 the NDP parliamentary group chairman, Oleksandr Karpov, was elected head of the centre-right pro-government majority in the Supreme Council. The NDP joined the "For a United Ukraine" bloc in 2002 parliamentary elections securing 6 seats on the party list and 8 in local constituencies. NDP supported Prime Minister Yanukovych as presidential candidate in 2004.

Popular Movement of Ukraine
Narodnyi Rukh Ukrainy (NRU)

Address. 33 Honchara St., Kyiv 01034
Telephone. (0038 044) 2359430
Fax. (0038 044) 246–4759
Email. mail@rukhpress-center.kiev.ua
Website. www.nru.org.ua
Leadership. Borys Tarasyuk

The first attempt to unite all Ukrainian opposition groups in a "popular front" modelled on similar groups in the Baltic republics was crushed by the authorities in the summer of 1988. The second attempt brought in moderate elements from the Communist Party of Ukraine (KPU) and the Writers' Union of Ukraine over the winter of 1988–89, and resulted in the publication of a draft manifesto in February 1989. At that stage, *Rukh* (Ukrainian for "movement") still accepted the leading role of the KPU and refrained from any direct mention of Ukrainian independence. This pattern was largely confirmed by the movement's first congress in September 1989, which elected the writer Ivan Drach as leader. The autumn of 1989 also brought the resignation of the KPU's veteran conservative leader, Volodymyr Shcherbytskiy, and the beginning of the campaign for republican elections, which allowed *Rukh* to expand its influence. *Rukh*'s high-water mark came in March 1990, when the movement's front organization, the Democratic Bloc, won 27% of the seats in the elections to the Ukrainian parliament.

Thereafter, *Rukh* lost its status as the sole opposition group. Other political parties began to appear, and *Rukh* fell increasingly under the control of its nationalist wing. The various elections and referendums of 1991 showed no advance on *Rukh*'s 1990 position, and the movement effectively split at its third congress in February-March 1992, with the more nationalist wing leaving to found the Congress of National Democratic Forces in August 1992. Vyacheslav Chornovil was left in charge of a rump *Rukh*, which formally turned itself into a political party under his leadership at its fourth congress in December 1992.

Under Chornovil's leadership, *Rukh* took a centre-right line on most questions, supporting market reforms and a liberal democratic state united around territorial rather than ethnic patriotism, but also advocating strong national defence and Ukraine's departure from the Commonwealth of Independent States (CIS). On this platform, it won 20 seats in its own right in the 1994 elections and subsequently attracted half a dozen independent deputies into its parliamentary group. The party subsequently strongly opposed the successful KPU-backed presidential candidacy of Leonid Kuchma, whom Chornovil described as Ukraine's "most dangerous enemy".

Declaring itself to be in favour of Ukrainian membership of the European Union and NATO, *Rukh* sought to rally anti-left forces for the March 1998 parliamentary elections. Benefiting from its substantial following in western Ukraine, *Rukh* emerged as the second largest party (though far behind the KPU), winning 46 seats on a vote share of 9.4%. It then became part of a highly fluid parliamentary majority defined by its opposition to the left and broadly supportive of Kuchma-appointed governments, although critical of Kuchma himself.

Festering divisions within *Rukh* became critical in February 1999 when Chornovil was ousted from the party chairmanship and replaced by Yuriy Kostenko. Chornovil and his supporters thereupon established another version of *Rukh*, of which Hennadiy Udovenko became leader following Chornovil's death in a car crash in March. Both Kostenko and Udovenko were candidates in the autumn 1999 presidential elections, but won only 2.2% and 1.2% of the first-round vote respectively. With hostility between the two factions growing, a third *Rukh* faction was formed in November 2000 under the leadership of Bohdan Boyko with the aim of "reuniting" the other two. Such efforts resulted in a joint announcement by Kostenko and Udovenko in September 2001 that their factions would reunite under the umbrella of the "Our Ukraine" bloc led by former Prime Minister Viktor Yushchenko. However, after the 2002 parliamentary elections Kostenko's party (UNR) formed with the Democratic Party of Ukraine a new party – the Ukrainian People's Party (UNP). NRU, UNP and the Party of Reforms and Order form the backbone of the "Our Ukraine" reformist political bloc led by Viktor Yuschenko.

Social Democratic Party of Ukraine–United
Sotsial-Demokratychna Partiya Ukrainy–Obyednana (SDPU-O)

Address. 18 Ivana Franka St., Kyiv
Telephone. (0038 044) 5361571
Fax. (0038 044) 5361578
Email. sdpuo@org.ukr.net
Website. www.sdpu.org.ua
Leadership. Viktor Medvedchuk (chairman)
A Ukrainian social democratic movement first emerged in 1988, when various all-USSR groups became active in the republic. In 1989–90 the Ukrainian groups cut their ties with fraternal organizations in the rest of the USSR, organizing a founding congress in May 1990. However, the congress resulted in an immediate split, with the moderates, who supported Ukrainian sovereignty and German-style social democracy, forming the Social Democratic Party of Ukraine (SDPU) and the more left-wing faction the SDPU–O. After the SDPU won only two seats in the 1994 elections and the SDPU–O none, a reunification attempt was made but broke down in late 1997.

In the 1998 parliamentary elections, most social democratic forces, including former President Leonid Kravchuk and former Prime Minister Yevgeniy Marchuk, swung behind the SDPU–O, but the party won only 17 seats and just over 4% of the proportional vote. In the 1999 presidential elections, SDPU–O candidate Vasyl Onopenko took only 0.5% of the first-round vote, in part because Marchuk, running without party attribution, obtained 8.1%. Thereafter, the SDPU–O parliamentary group became part of a fluid pro-government centre-right majority, of which Kravchuk was the leader until September 2000.

By the end of the 1990s SDPU-O completely transformed and became social democratic only in its rhetoric. The founder of the party, Vasyl Onopenko, was ousted after a failed presidential bid in 1999. A successful businessman, Viktor Medvedchuk, with the support of the Kyiv business lobby, transformed SDPU-O into the exemplary party of the "oligarchs", with alleged mafia links and a strong political lobby. Vasyl Onopenko formed an alternative and marginal Ukrainian Social Democratic Party, while Marchuk briefly supported the Social Democratic Union led by Sergiy Peresunko. SDPU-O, however, became by far the most powerful "social democratic" force with control of major media outlets and especially TV channels.

Heavy domination of the Ukrainian electronic media and affluent financial support did not allow SDPU-O, however, to win more than 6.27% of the national vote in the 2002 parliamentary elections. This was due to the negative public image of its leader Viktor Medvedchuk, associated with aggressive business tactics and "black" PR. The political fortunes of the SDPU-O leader seemed to rocket as his fraction in the *Verkhovna Rada* became the key to creation of a pro-presidential majority. Political agreement among pro-Kuchma forces elevated Medvedchuk to the position of head of presidential administration, giving him enormous though extra-constitutional powers. SDPU-O formally supported Prime Minister Yanukovych as presidential candidate in 2004.

Socialist Party of Ukraine
Sotsialistychna Partiya Ukrainy (SPU)

Address. 45 Vorovskogo St., Kyiv - 01054
Telephone. (0038 044) 2168882
Email. press@socinfo.kiev.ua
Website. www.socinfo.kiev.ua
Leadership. Oleksandr Moroz (chairman)
The SPU was the first would-be successor to the Soviet-era Communist Party of Ukraine (KPU), being formed only two months after the August 1991 coup attempt in Moscow under the leadership of Oleksandr Moroz, the former KPU chairman of the Ukrainian legislature. Moroz steered the SPU away from open nostalgia for the old system, but in 1992–94 adopted a populist position, attacking the "introduction of capitalism" and the "growth of national-fascism" in Ukraine. He also called for the reintroduction of state direction of the economy, price controls and "socially just privatization". In the sphere of external policy, the party has advocated closer economic and political ties with Russia and the other CIS states (its more radical members supporting a restored USSR). Unlike the revived KPU, however, the SPU was generally reconciled to the fact of Ukrainian independence.

In June 1993 the SPU formed an alliance called "Working Ukraine" with the Peasants' Party of Ukraine (SelPU) and smaller left-wing groups, in close co-operation of the KPU, although the latter did not join. The SPU claimed the support of 38 deputies in the Ukrainian parliament in 1992–93 while it enjoyed the advantage of being the only organized leftist successor to the KPU. Its pre-eminence on the left disappeared with the rise of the restored KPU in 1993–94, but it nevertheless won 15 seats in the 1994 elections, after which Moroz was elected chairman of the Ukrainian parliament. By mid-1994 the SPU controlled a parliamentary faction of 25 deputies. In early 1996, however, the party was weakened by a split resulting in the formation of the Progressive Socialist Party (PSP).

The SPU contested the 1998 parliamentary elections in an alliance with the SelPU called "For the Truth, For the People, For Ukraine", their joint list winning 34 seats with 8.6% of the proportional vote. Plans for a joint presidential candidate of the alliance and other left-leaning parties foundered in the run-up to the 1999 contest, with the result that Moroz stood for the SPU and came third with 11.3% of the first-round vote. In the second round the SPU supported KPU leader Petro Symonenko, who was defeated by incumbent Leonid Kuchma. In early 2000 the SPU was prominent in ultimately abortive left-wing attempts to prevent the ousting of Council president Oleksandr Tkachenko (SelPU) by the centre-majority, whose action was described by Moroz as tantamount to a coup d'état.

Moroz and the SPU also took a leading role in the major political crisis which developed from late 2000 over President Kuchma's alleged role in the murder of a journalist. After being sued for slander by Kuchma's chief of staff for revealing apparent presidential involvement in the affair,

Moroz described the crisis as "a turning-point" in Ukraine's national history. In May 2001 the SPU initiated moves for a national referendum in which voters would be asked to approve the removal of the President. In May 2001 Moroz announced that the SPU would contest the 2002 parliamentary elections in alliance with at least four other left-wing parties. Despite strong political confrontation with pro-presidential parties, the SPU won 6.87% of the national vote in 2002 and managed to get 22 seats in the parliament. SPU nominated its leader as presidential candidate in 2004.

Other Parties and Alliances

The following selection from other registered parties in Ukraine focuses on those which contested the March 2002 parliamentary elections, either on their own or within blocs, or are of other particular interest.

All-Ukrainian Association Hromada (*Vseukrayinske Obyednannya Hromada*). The free-market *Hromada* ("Community") party was re-launched in late 1997 under the leadership of Pavlo Lazarenko, who had been dismissed as Prime Minister by President Leonid Kuchma some months earlier because of corruption allegations against him. Based in Dnipropetrovsk, the party became part of the anti-Kuchma opposition and won 24 seats in the 1998 parliamentary elections (with a vote share of 4.7%), subsequently attracting about 20 independent deputies into its parliamentary group. In February 1999, however, Lazarenko fled to the USA after the Supreme Council had removed his immunity from prosecution, whereupon a substantial section of *Hromada* broke away to form the Fatherland grouping. Since late 2000 Lazarenko has been in custody in the USA facing money-laundering charges. *Hromada* did not participate in the 2002 parliamentary elections.
Address. 1 Laboratornyi provulok, Kyiv 01133
Telephone. (0038–044) 2528857
Fax. 0038 044 2528857
Website. http://www.hromada.kiev.ua
Leadership. Pavlo Lazarenko (chairman), Anatoliy Moskalenko

All-Ukrainian Political Bloc "Women for future" ("*Zhinky za maybutnie*" *Vseukrayinske politychne obyednannia*). The bloc was only registered in March 2001 but secured 2.11% of the national vote in March 2002, allegedly due to unofficial support from the presidential administration. Its registered leader is Valentyna Dovzhenko, but the organization was widely associated with Liudmyla Kuchma, the wife of President Kuchma.

Christian Democratic Party of Ukraine (*Khrystyiansko-Demokratychna Partiya Ukrainy*, KhDPU). The KhDPU was founded in June 1992 by a moderate splinter group of the more nationalistic Ukrainian Christian Democratic Party (UKhDP). The KhDPU won two seats in the 1994 parliamentary elections, one in Transcarpathia and the other in Odessa. It retained two constituency seats in 1998, although it won only 1.3% of the proportional vote. The KhDPU did not feature on the party list in parliamentary elections in 2002. Party leader Zhuravskyi was appointed First Deputy Minister of Science and Education in August 2003.
Address. 1/2a Baseyna St., Kyiv
Telephone. (00380–44) 235–3996
Leadership. Vitaly Zhuravskyi (chairman)

Forward Ukraine! (*Vpered Ukrayino!*). Adapting the name of a Russian formation of the mid-1990s, Forward Ukraine! was launched for the 1998 elections as an alliance of (i) the Christian Popular Union Party (*Partiya Khrystyyan-*

sko–Narodnyi Soyuz, PKNS) led by Volodymyr Stretovych; and (ii) the Ukrainian Christian Democratic Party (*Ukrainska Khrystyyansko–Demokratychna Partiya*, UKhDP). Plans for a broader electoral front to include the Party of Reforms and Order came to nothing, with the result that Forward Ukraine! scored only 1.7% of the proportional vote and won only two constituency seats in 1998.

Based in the Uniate Catholic population of Galicia, the nationalist UKhDP had been founded in 1990 but had been weakened by a 1992 schism with its more moderate Orthodox wing, which broke away to form the Christian Democratic Party of Ukraine. The PKNS is an observer member of the Christian Democrat International.

Forward Ukraine joined the political bloc of Viktor Yuschenko "Our Ukraine" in the 2002 parliamentary election and supported the idea of creating a single party on the basis of this bloc after the elections.
Address. 10/17 Velyka Zhytomyrska St., Kyiv 01025
Telephone. (00380–44) 2125462
Fax. (00380–44) 228–0461
Leadership. Viktor Musiyaka

Green Party of Ukraine (*Partiya Zelenykh Ukrainy*, PZU). The PZU was created in 1990 by environmentalist groups which had emerged in the wake of the 1986 Chernobyl nuclear accident, its platform urging government action on the huge environmental problems faced by Ukraine arising from Soviet-era industrialization. It had early links with the Communist Party of Ukraine (KPU) and generally supported the presidency of Leonid Kravchuk (1991–94), but has been more critical of the successor administration of Leonid Kuchma. Having failed to achieve representation in 1994, the PZU won 19 seats in the 1998 legislative elections on a vote share of 5.4%, becoming part of a fluctuating parliamentary majority defined by its opposition to the KPU-led left. That success, however, was achieved at the price of the Greens accepting sponsorship by Eastern Ukrainian industrialists involved in highly polluting steel and oil production industries. In the 1999 presidential elections, PZU leader Vitaliy Kononov obtained only 0.3% of the first-round vote, while by mid-2001 the Green parliamentary group had declined to 17 members. Among the "business" members of the Green Party parliament fraction four were under criminal investigation. Although the PSU participated in the parliamentary elections in March 2002 it managed to attract only 1.3% of voters and failed to gain any seats.
Address. 2/16 Chapayeva St., Kyiv 01030
Telephone. (0038 044) 2249103
Fax. (0038 044) 2273016
Email. greenparty@ukrpost.net
Website. www.Greenparty.org.ua
Leadership. Vitaliy Kononov (leader); Oleh Shevchuk (deputy leader and secretary-general)

National Front–National Salvation Forum (*Natsionalnyi Front* (NF)–*Forum Natsionalnoho Poriatunku*). The right-wing nationalist NF was created for the March 1998 parliamentary elections as an alliance of (i) the Congress of Ukrainian Nationalists (*Kongres Ukrainskykh Natsionalistiv*, KUN); (ii) the Ukrainian Republican Party (*Ukrainska Respublikanska Partiya*, URP); and (iii) the Ukrainian Conservative Republican Party (*Ukrainska Konservatyvna Respublikanska Partiya*, UKRP). Their joint list fell well below the 4% barrier in the proportional section (obtaining 2.7%), while in the constituency contests its tally of five seats compared unfavourably with the 17 seats won by the three parties in 1994.

The KUN was established in October 1992 by the émigré Organization of Ukrainian Nationalists (OUN) and quickly absorbed other rightist groups. Its programme advocates a strong nation state, independent in all respects from Russia, and withdrawal from the Commonwealth of Independent States (CIS). Economically, the KUN has veered between the strongly pro-capitalist orientation of its émigré members and a recognition of the need for state protection for the enfeebled Ukrainian economy. In the 1994 elections KUN chairman Slava Stetsko was prevented from standing in a Lviv constituency, but the party had considerable support in western Ukraine, where it elected five deputies in its own name and endorsed several successful non-party candidates. Slava Stetsko was elected an MP from a Western Ukrainian constituency in 1997 and again in 1998. KUN joined the "Our Ukraine" bloc in the parliamentary elections in March 2002.

The URP was the first non-communist political party to be openly formed in Ukraine in modern times (in April 1990), as the direct successor of the Ukrainian Helsinki Union (1988–90), itself a revival of the Ukrainian Helsinki Group (1976–80). The party bases its ideology on the conservative Ukrainian philosopher Viacheslav Lypynskiy and supports "the Ukrainian character of national statehood", while advocating a tolerant approach to ethnic minorities. It stands for resolute national defence, immediate withdrawal from the CIS and a strong, unitary, presidential republic. Economically, the party supports the creation of "a society of property owners" but opposes "socially unjust privatization".

The URP became the best-organized nationalist party in the early 1990s, but was weakened by the formation in June 1992 of the breakaway UKRP by a radical right-wing faction led by deputy chairman Stepan Khmara. The UKRP adopted a vigorously anti-Russian line and, unlike the URP, strongly opposed any compromise with former Communists such as Leonid Kravchuk (President until July 1994), whom Khmara had accused of being a "traitor" to Ukrainian national interests. Khmara also advocated a nuclear Ukraine and support for ethnic Ukrainians in neighbouring Russian territories. Despite fielding 130 candidates, the URP performed poorly in the 1994 elections, winning only 11 seats. Its then chairman, Mykhailo Horyn, was defeated by Khmara in Lviv, although that was the UKRP's only success. Following defeat in the 1998 parliamentary elections the URP declared its intention to unite with the Ukrainian Christian Democratic Party (UKhDP) and the Ukrainian People's Party "Sobor". In combination with the Ukrainian Social Democratic Party, UKRP and "Fatherland" these six parties created the "National Salvation Forum" in July 2001 that later turned into the political "Bloc of Yuliya Tymoshenko". After Khmara's UKRP merged into "Fatherland" and UKhDP into URP, the Ukrainian Republican Party joined the Ukrainian People's Party "Sobor" creating URP "Sobor" led by Anatoliy Matvienko since April 2002.

Address. 111/21 Kreshchatyk Street, Kyiv
Telephone. (+38 044) 229–2425
Leadership. Olexiy Ivchenko (KUN chairman); Levko Lukyanenko (URP chairman); Stepan Khmara (UKRP chairman), Anatoliy Matviyenko (URP Sobor).

Peasants' Party of Ukraine (*Selianska Partiya Ukrainy*, SelPU). The roots of the SelPU lie in the rural organizations of the former ruling Communist Party of Ukraine (KPU), which first established the Peasants' Union of Ukraine in September 1990 and then the SelPU in January 1992. While collective farm chairmen and heads of agro-industries usually preferred to remain "non-party" publicly, in practice many supported the SelPU, which emerged as a powerful force maintaining the flow of subsidies to the agricultural sector and obstructing plans for land privatization. In alliance with the KPU and the Socialist Party of Ukraine (SPU), the SelPU polled strongly in the 1994 parliamentary elections,

winning 19 seats in conservative rural areas. In the Supreme Council elected in 1998, it became the dominant component of the Rural Ukraine faction.

The SelPU contested the 1998 parliamentary elections in an alliance with the SPU called "For the Truth, For the People, For Ukraine", winning about a third of the joint list's 34 seats (with 8.6% of the vote). A prominent SelPU member, Oleksandr Tkachenko, was elected chairman of the new Supreme Council and became a prospective candidate in the 1999 presidential elections, until withdrawing in favour of the KPU leader, Petro Symonenko, and backing his unsuccessful bid. In a lengthy political crisis in early 2000, during which two competing legislatures were sitting at one stage, Tkachenko was ousted from the Council presidency by the centre-right majority.

The 2002 parliamentary elections brought only 0.37% of national support (and no seats) to the party that is mostly associated now with the personality and wealth of Serhiy Dovhan, famous for his extensive network of distilleries and vodka brands. Tkachenko, however, was elected to parliament on the Communist Party list.
Address. 17 Starovokzalna St., Kyiv 01032
Telephone. 0038 044 2463842
Fax. 0038 044 2463843
Leadership. Serhiy Dovhan (chairman)

Political Party "Yabluko". *Yabluko* was registered in November 1999 and formed a faction (15 members) in the parliament under the leadership of Mykhaylo Brodskyi. Modelled on the Russian *Yabloko* it claims to be a liberal party, with a motto "For a rich and free Ukraine" that reflects the wealth and business orientation of its leader and many other business-oriented members. Brodskyi was the owner of the popular tabloid *Kievskiye Vedomosti* and has broad economic interests. Sometimes *Yabluko* is referred to as another "oligarch" party; however, after it achieved only 1.15% of the national vote in the March 2002 parliamentary election, failing to gain any sits in the *Verkhovna Rada*, *Yabluko* claims to be an opposition party. *Yabluko* nominated its leader as presidential candidate in 2004 despite claiming earlier support to Viktor Yuschenko's "Our Ukraine" political bloc in the 2004 presidential elections.
Address. Office 1, 33 Liuteranska Str., Kyiv – 01024
Telephone. 0038 044 2935671
Fax. 0038 044 2936200
Website. www.yabluko.org.ua
Leadership. Mykhaylo Brodskyi; Viktor Chaika

Progressive Socialist Party (*Prohresyvna Sotsialistychna Partiya*, PSP). The leftist PSP was launched in 1996 by a dissident faction of the Socialist Party of Ukraine (SPU). Under the leadership of Nataliya Vitrenko, the party called for a return to "the radiant past" of the Soviet era, opposed privatization of "national security enterprises" and advocated closer links with Russia and Belarus. The PSP just achieved the 4% threshold in the March 1998 parliamentary elections, winning 16 seats and becoming part of the left-wing parliamentary opposition headed by the Communist Party of Ukraine (KPU).

Standing for the PSP in the 1999 presidential elections, Vitrenko came a creditable fourth, winning 11% of the first-round vote. In July 2001 she announced that the PSP would contest the 2002 parliamentary elections as "an independent political force". However, the political bloc of marginal parties named "Bloc of Natalia Vitrenko" won only 3.22% of the national vote in 2002 and failed to get any parliamentary seats. There was widespread speculation that the bloc was supported by the government to divert left-wing voters from supporting the Socialist Party of Olexander Moroz, who strongly opposed the President of Ukraine, presenting in the parliament damaging audio-recordings that connected Leonid Kuchma to the murder of a journalist. In 2004 the PSP signed an agreement with the right-wing Russian parliamentary bloc "Rodina". PSP nominated its leader as presidential candidate in 2004.

Address. 15 Kominternu St., Kyiv – 01032
Telephone. 0038 044 2917460, 2464722
Leadership. Nataliya Vitrenko (chairperson)

Ukrainian National Assembly (*Ukrainska Natsionalna Asambleya,* UNA). The Ukrainian National Assembly, an ultra-nationalist formation, was founded initially as the Inter-Party Assembly in June 1990 by a group of allegedly right-wing activists on the basis of an ideological mixture of Ukrainian civic nationalism, extreme populism and some sort of Buddhist rhetoric. The UNA, however, became popular among some inhabitants of Western Ukraine who viewed the Assembly as an alternative to the corrupt administration of the old Soviet *nomenklatura* and unreformed Communists dominating the parliament. The UNA managed to secure 3 seats in the Ukrainian parliament in June 1994. 15 members of UNA were detained in Kyiv during a clash with police who attempted to block a funeral procession from entering the Cathedral complex in July 1995. The Justice Department of Ukraine, however, cancelled the UNA's registration on an unrelated legal pretext and a number of UNA members were detained and arrested. Those arrests, however, did not result in further criminal prosecutions and the UNA re-registered with the Department of Justice in September 1997. The party has participated since then in local as well national elections, but has decreased in popularity and won only 0.4% of the 1998 national vote and 0.04% in 2002. The UNA is better known for its more active paramilitary wing – the UNSO. Its involvment in anti-presidential demonstrations in March 2001 led to mass arrests and 15 convictions. The party experienced division when Andriy Shkil (MP with Fatherland) was formally dismissed in April 2002 as head of the organization. The Ministry of Justice registered Eduard Kovalenko as the new head; however, part of the organization supports Andriy Shkil. UNA supported Bohdan Boyko (*Rukh za yednist*) as presidential candidate in 2004.

Address. Room 92, 132 Velyka Vasylkivska Str., Kyiv
Telephone. 0038 044 2692445
Fax. 0038 044 2692445
Website. www.una-unso.org
Leadership. Eduard Kovalenko &Andriy Shkil (lead rival factions)

United Arab Emirates

Capital: Abu Dhabi
Population: 2,445,989

On July 18, 1971, rulers of six emirates (Abu Dhabi, Dubai, Al Fujayrah, Ash Shariqah, Ajman, and Umm al Qaywayn), known as the Trucial Coast states, ratified the provisional constitution of the United Arab Emirates (UAE). This union went into effect on Dec. 2, 1971. Ras Al-Khaymah, the seventh emirate, joined the union in February 1972.

The executive branch consists of the Supreme Council of Rulers (SCU), the Council of Ministers (the cabinet), and the presidency. The SCU consists of the rulers of the seven hereditary emirates; it elects from among its members a President and a Vice President, who serve for a term of five years. Zayid bin Sultan Al-Nuhayyan (ruler of Abu Dhabi since August 1966) had been the President of the federation since its creation

until his death in November 2004. Decisions of the SCU require the approval of at least five members, including the rulers of Abu Dhabi and Dubai.

The UAE has no political parties. There is talk of steps toward democratic government, but nothing concrete has emerged. The rulers hold power on the basis of their dynastic position and their legitimacy in a system of tribal consensus. Rapid modernization, enormous strides in education, and the influx of a large foreign population have changed the face of the society but have not fundamentally altered this traditional political system.

United Kingdom

Capital: London
Population: (including N. Ireland): 59,500,000 (2000E)

The United Kingdom of Great Britain and Northern Ireland is a hereditary constitutional monarchy in which the monarch, as head of state, has numerous specific responsibilities. The supreme legislative authority is Parliament, consisting of (i) a 659-member House of Commons, with a life of not more than five years, directly elected under a simple-majority system in single-member constituencies, the right to vote being held by British subjects (and citizens of any Commonwealth member country or the Republic of Ireland resident in the United Kingdom) above the age of 18 years, and (ii) a House of Lords, the upper house. Under a reform enacted in November 1999 the majority hereditary component of the House of Lords was abolished and a 670-member "interim chamber" (of 578 life peers, bishops and law lords plus 92 ex-hereditaries elected by their peers) was set up pending definitive reform of the upper chamber – although in March 2004 plans to further reform the Lords were abandoned for the duration of the present parliament, in the absence of prospective agreement on how this should be done. The government is headed by the Prime Minister who is leader of the party which commands a majority in the House of Commons. The UK joined what became the European Union on Jan. 1, 1973, and as from 2004 elects 78 members of the European Parliament.

Opposition parties in the House of Commons receive financial assistance from state funds to assist them in fulfilling their parliamentary duties, the subsidies being known as "Short money", after the minister (Edward Short) who first introduced the arrangement in 1975, with funding based on the number of seats held and votes won. Since 1996 a similar scheme of state financial assistance has operated for non-government parties in the House of Lords, known as "Cranborne money" after the then leader of the upper chamber, Lord Cranborne. The 2000 Political Parties, Elections and Referendums Act, implementing most of the recommendations of the Neill Committee report on political funding published in 1998, banned parties from accepting financial donations from foreign sources and laid down disclosure and other rules for donations from domestic sources and for campaign expenditure. It also provided for the creation of an Electoral Commission charged with ensuring compliance with the new rules and with maintaining a register of political parties.

In general elections to the House of Commons in May 1997 the Labour Party ended 18 years of

Conservative rule by winning an overwhelming majority. Further elections on June 7, 2001, confirmed Labour in power with a similar majority, the results being as follows: Labour Party 412 seats (with 42.0% of the vote), Conservatives 166 (32.7%), Liberal Democrats 52 (18.8%), Ulster Unionist Party* 6, Democratic Unionist Party* 5, Scottish National Party (SNP) 5, *Plaid Cymru* 4, *Sinn Féin** 4, Social Democratic and Labour Party* 3, Independent Kidderminster Hospital and Health Concern 1, Speaker 1.

Under devolution legislation enacted in 1998, a 129-member Scottish Parliament and a 60-member Welsh Assembly were elected on May 6, 1999, by a combination of single-member constituency voting and proportional representation of party lists. The second elections to the Scottish Parliament held on May 1, 2003, resulted as follows (with change on 1999): Labour 50 (-6), SNP 27 (-8), Conservatives 18 (no change), Liberal Democrats 17 (no change), Greens 7 (+6), Scottish Socialist Party 6 (+5), others 4 (+3). The second elections to the Welsh Assembly (also on May 1, 2003) resulted in Labour winning exactly half (30) of the seats, two up on 1999. *Plaid Cymru* won 12 (-5); the Conservative Party 11 (+2); Liberal Democrats 6 (no change), and one independent was elected. The Scottish Parliament possesses broader powers than the Welsh Assembly, which may not adopt primary legislation or raise taxes.

The June 2004 elections to the European Parliament resulted in the following distribution of seats: Conservative Party 27; Labour Party 19; Liberal Democrats 12; United Kingdom Independence Party 12; Green Party 2; Scottish National Party 2; *Plaid Cymru* 1; Democratic Unionist Party 1, Ulster Unionist Party 1, *Sinn Féin* 1.
*Northern Ireland party: see separate section below.

Conservative and Unionist Party
Address. Conservative Central Office, 25 Victoria Street, London, SW1H 0DL
Telephone. (+44–20) 7222–9000
Website. www.conservatives.com
Leadership. Michael Howard (leader); Michael Ancram (deputy leader); Dr Liam Fox & Lord Maurice Saatchi (co-chairmen)
Founded in the 1830s, the Conservative Party was the most successful British party of the twentieth century. Officially the Conservative and Unionist Party, it is now almost exclusively referred to as the Conservative Party, reflecting the changed relationship with unionist political currents in Northern Ireland since the 1970s. It regards freedom of the individual under the rule of law as its guiding principle. It believes that political arrangements should be so designed as to give people "the maximum degree of control over their own lives, whilst restricting the role of government so that the state exists for the benefit of the individual and not vice versa". The party stands for wider ownership of property and wealth and for lower taxes on earnings, and is strongly committed to the free enterprise system. Believing in the maintenance of the United Kingdom, it opposed the devolution of power to Scotland and Wales (though now participating fully in the devolved assemblies); it is also opposed to the introduction of proportional representation for House of Commons elections. The party is pledged to the maintenance of strong defence and regards the concept of deterrence as central to the nation's nuclear and conventional defence capability. It favours Britain's continued membership of a European Union of nation states and opposes any further transfer of sovereignty to the EU, though the degree to which Britain should participate in the EU project has been perhaps the most divisive issue within the party in recent years.

The Conservatives trace their history back to the 17th and 18th century, but the modern party was formed by Sir Robert Peel, who established the first Conservative government in 1834, shortly before which the term "Conservative" was first used as opposed to "Tory" (a term of Irish origins applied to members of the political grouping which from 1679 opposed Whig attempts to exclude the future James II from the succession to the throne). The party assumed its present official name in 1912 when it was formally joined by the Liberal Unionists (former Liberals who opposed home rule for Ireland and had supported the Conservative Party since 1886). During World War I the party took part in a coalition government. It was returned to power in 1922 and remained in government for most of the inter-war years (from 1931 as the dominant party in a National government) and in the World War II all-party coalition (under Winston Churchill from May 1940 to July 1945).

In the post-war era the Conservative Party has been led by Churchill (1940–55), Anthony Eden (1955–57), Harold Macmillan (1957–63), Sir Alec Douglas-Home (1963–65), Edward Heath, the first leader elected by Conservative MPs (1965–75), Margaret Thatcher (1975–90), John Major (1990–97), William Hague (1997–2001), Iain Duncan Smith, the first leader to be elected by the party membership as well as by MPs (2001–03), and latterly Michael Howard.

After heavily losing the 1945 elections to the Labour Party, the Conservatives were in opposition until 1951 and thereafter in power until 1964. The next Conservative government, under Heath in 1970–74, successfully negotiated Britain's entry into what later became the European Union. Following his 1974 election defeat, Heath was ousted as leader in 1975 by Margaret Thatcher, who in the May 1979 elections became the UK's first woman Prime Minister. The party was confirmed in power with large majorities in June 1983 (benefiting from the successful British military action in 1982 to recover the Falkland Islands from Argentinian occupation) and again in June 1987, although its percentage share of the vote slipped from 43.9% in 1979 to 42.4% in 1983 and to 42.3% in 1987. Thatcher's 1987 victory, with a Commons majority of 102 seats, made her the first British Prime Minister in modern history to win three consecutive terms in office.

Under the Thatcher premiership the Conservatives pursued radical right-wing social and economic policies, with the party's moderate "one nation" wing being increasingly marginalized (and referred to dismissively by the Thatcherites as "wets"). Major reforms included stringent curbs on the powers of trade unions, the promotion of individual choice and market mechanisms within the welfare state structure, the sale of council houses to their tenants and the privatization of many industries and companies previously under public ownership. Her government also cut income tax rates to pre-war levels (although without appreciably reducing the proportion of GDP spent by the state) and presided over an economic boom in the late 1980s, when for a while there was an actual surplus in government finances. During her third term, however, an attempt to reform the financing of local government so that all residents paid a "community charge" provoked large-scale opposition to what was dubbed a "poll tax". There were also deepening divisions within Conservative ranks over British membership of an EU that was constantly expanding its competences, which many Conservatives saw as eroding the national sovereignty of member states.

Thatcher, rhetorically at least, positioned herself on the Eurosceptic wing of the party, delivering a celebrated speech in Bruges (Belgium) in September 1988 in which she categorically rejected schemes for a federal European state.

However, a series of by-election defeats in 1989–90 weakened her position, which was fatally undermined by the proEuropean Sir Geoffrey Howe, who delivered a blistering critique of her stewardship following his exit from the government in November 1990. The speech precipitated an immediate leadership challenge by the pro-European former Defence Minister, Michael Heseltine, who obtained enough first-round votes to force a second round, whereupon Thatcher resigned in the face of almost certain defeat. Two other contenders then entered the lists, including the Chancellor of the Exchequer, John Major, who was regarded as the Thatcherite candidate and for that reason was elected in the second-round ballot by a comfortable margin.

Becoming at 47 Britain's youngest 20th-century Prime Minister, Major quickly jettisoned his predecessor's more controversial policies (which he had staunchly supported), including the "poll tax". The Conservatives fought the April 1992 election on a somewhat more centrist platform of further privatization (including British Rail and the coal mines), financial accountability in the National Health Service (NHS) and freedom of choice in the state education sector. In the sphere of economic policy, they contended that the recession into which Britain had descended in the early 1990s would become much worse under a Labour government. Assisted by public doubts as to the prime ministerial calibre of Labour leader Neil Kinnock, the Conservatives won an almost unprecedented fourth term, although by the much narrower margin of 336 seats out of 651 (from an aggregate vote of 14.1 million, representing a 41.9% share).

Also almost unprecedented was the massive post-election slump in the Conservative government's public standing, as evidenced by disastrous local election results in 1993 and 1994 and the more damaging loss of several hitherto safe Conservative parliamentary seats to the Liberal Democrats. Contributory factors included Britain's humiliating enforced exit from the European exchange rate mechanism in September 1992, representing a traumatic collapse of government economic policy (but not generating any immediate ministerial resignations) and leading to a ramp of additional taxation in direct breach of the party's election pledge to reduce taxes. Also damaging were internal Conservative divisions over Europe, evidenced in protracted resistance to ratification of the 1991 Maastricht Treaty creating the EU (despite the much-trumpeted opt-outs negotiated for Britain by Major), and a never-ending series of "sex and sleaze" scandals featuring prominent Conservatives.

In June 1994 the Conservatives fared badly in elections for the European Parliament, falling from 34 to 18 seats (out of 87) with only 26.8% of the vote and losing several seats in the Conservative heartland of southern England. Further by-election and local election disasters in late 1994 and early 1995, with Labour now the main beneficiary, fuelled increasing Conservative criticism of Major's leadership. In June 1995 the Prime Minister unexpectedly confronted his critics, when he announced his resignation as party leader (although not as Prime Minister) to force a leadership election in which he requested his critics to "put up or shut up". Only one Conservative dared to "put up", namely Welsh Secretary John Redwood, representing the Eurosceptic right wing of the party. Major was duly re-elected with the support of 218 of the 329 Conservative MPs and therefore continued as Prime Minister, immediately elevating Heseltine to "number two" in the government as reward for his crucial support during the leadership contest.

Major's leadership election victory had no impact on the historically low opinion poll ratings being accorded to the Conservative Party, which kept losing by-elections no matter how "safe" the seat. It also, unusually, suffered defections from the parliamentary party, one to Labour in September 1995, another to the Liberal Democrats at the end of the year

and a third who eventually opted for the Liberal Democrats. Yet another by-election defeat in April 1996 reduced the government's overall theoretical majority in the Commons to one and another local election disaster in May all but eliminated the Conservative Party from local government. The following month internal party dissension over Europe intensified when 74 Conservative back-benchers voted in favour of an early referendum on whether Britain should surrender further sovereignty to the EU.

The Conservatives were decimated in the May 1997 general elections, retaining only 165 seats on a vote share of 31.5%, their worst result of the 20th century, which left the party without representation in Scotland and Wales. Major immediately resigned as leader and was succeeded by William Hague, who at 36 became the party's youngest leader for over 200 years. Inheritor of the "Thatcherite" mantle, Hague quickly came into conflict with the party's proEuropean wing, as he moved to oppose UK participation in the single European currency (euro). On the eve of the Conservative conference of October 1998 Hague secured 84% endorsement from party members for the proposition that a Conservative government would not join the euro during the lifetime of the next parliament. Nevertheless, infighting on the issue continued, with Heseltine and former Chancellor Kenneth Clarke to the fore in insisting that the party should not rule out participation in the single currency.

The Conservatives showed signs of recovery in the May 1999 local elections, displacing the Liberal Democrats as the second strongest party in local government. The party also secured representation in the new legislatures of Scotland and Wales elected in that month, though they were in opposition in both. In June 1999 the Conservatives were the main victors in European Parliament elections, winning 36 of the 87 UK seats on a vote share of 35.8% despite a powerful performance by the anti-EU UK Independence Party. However, the party continued to be dogged by internal division and controversy, notably when its candidate for the new post of mayor of London, Lord (Jeffrey) Archer of Weston-superMare, was forced to withdraw in November 1999 over allegations that he had suborned a potential witness in a 1987 libel trial. In the same month the return to the Commons of former Defence Secretary Michael Portillo in a London byelection served to increase the pressure on Hague, though Portillo pledged that he would be loyal. Portillo was rewarded for his loyalty by being appointed shadow Chancellor in February 2000, whereupon he immediately abandoned the Conservatives' opposition to the national minimum wage and the independence of the Bank of England. In September 2000 the Labour government's disarray in the face of fuel price protests which paralysed the country resulted in the Conservatives taking the lead in opinion polls, but only briefly. Conservative by-election results continued to be poor. As his party returned to a distant second place behind Labour in the polls, Hague continued to be undermined internally by divisions on Europe and by behind-the-scenes criticism of his leadership. Also damaging was the preferment of perjury and other charges against Archer (who was later convicted and sent to prison for four years), it being recalled that Hague had publicly endorsed him for the London mayoralty despite warnings about his probity.

In his campaign for the June 2001 parliamentary elections Hague tried to bring the European currency issue to the fore, claiming that it was the last chance to "save the pound" because a further Labour government would join the euro. He also sought to make capital from the failings of the government's political asylum policy, pledging that a Conservative government would introduce detention for all applicants while their cases were assessed and would speedily deport those refused asylum. But such policies seemed to fall on deaf ears. The results showed that the Conservatives had suffered another heavy defeat, making a net gain of only one seat (to 166) and increasing their share of the vote by only 1.2% (to 32.7%).

Hague immediately resigned as party leader, acknowledging that he had failed to attract popular support. Five candidates came forward for a leadership election, which under new rules introduced by Hague involved voting by Conservative MPs to narrow the field to two, who were then submitted for election by the 330,000 individual party members. In the MPs' stage the three candidates eliminated were Portillo (who had begun as the favourite), former party chairman Michael Ancram and former junior minister David Davis. The two who went forward were defence spokesman Iain Duncan Smith from the Eurosceptic right and former Chancellor Kenneth Clarke from the pro-EU wing of the party, who had unsuccessfully sought the leadership in 1997.

The membership stage of the contest in August-September 2001 featured intense personal acrimony and controversy. Hague and Baroness Thatcher endorsed Duncan Smith, whereas Clarke was backed by Major, who launched a fierce attack on Duncan Smith and Thatcher for disloyalty to his 1990–97 government. Other party figures weighed into a level of vituperation seen as unprecedented in the party's history as Clarke depicted himself as the candidate of "one nation" conservatism and assailed Duncan Smith for being a right-wing "hanger and flogger".

Declared in September 2001, the result of the membership ballot was a decisive victory for Duncan Smith with 61% of some 255,000 votes cast. Himself without ministerial experience, the new leader appointed a front-bench team dominated by opponents of euro participation, including Ancram as shadow Foreign Secretary and deputy party leader, Michael Howard (a former Home Secretary) as shadow Chancellor and Oliver Letwin as shadow Home Secretary. The party chairmanship was entrusted to Davis. Seeking to repair damage done during the leadership contest, Hague and Davis decreed that the right-wing Monday Club, which advocated voluntary repatriation of immigrants, was no longer an acceptable pressure-group within the party.

Hopes that Duncan Smith might stabilize and revitalize the party were soon disappointed. He sacked Davis as party chairman in July 2003, replacing him with Theresa May, and faced continual and highly publicised unrest within the party machinery at Conservative Central Office. His own description of himself as "the quiet man" of British politics was underscored by his failure to make any sort of impression on the electorate and lacklustre performances in the House of Commons and he faced mounting plotting within a fractious party. This culminated in his ouster when on Oct. 29, 2003, he lost a vote of confidence by the parliamentary party by 90 votes to 75. Seemingly anxious not to refer the issue back to the party membership in the country – the constituency that gave Duncan Smith victory in the 2001 leadership election – the party's MPs rapidly rallied around Michael Howard as a consensus choice, potential rivals such as Ken Clarke and David Davis stood aside, and Howard assumed the leadership by acclamation of the parliamentary party without any vote in the larger party. It was a remarkable change of fortune for Howard, who had enjoyed little public popularity when a minister in the Major government, had come last in the 1997 Conservative leadership contest, and was widely associated in the public mind with the comment made by his former junior minister, Ann Widdecombe, that there was "something of the night about him".

Howard quickly announced a trimmed down shadow cabinet: Theresa May was removed as party chairman (although she was given the enironment and transport portfolio) and replaced by two co-chairmen – Liam Fox and Lord (Maurice) Saatchi (who had coined the 1979 winning campaign slogan "Labour isn't working") – while David Davis, whose decision not to run for party leader had eased Howard's way into the job, became shadow Home Secretary. Michael Portillo declined a position in the shadow cabinet and subsequently announced he would leave parliament at the next general election. In addition Howard announced the creation of an advisory council including Kenneth Clarke and John Major and the last two party leaders, and Tory MPs were hopeful that Howard was set to give the party revived and decisive leadership.

However, although Howard spoke of the need to recapture centre-ground voters, his own political background as a right-winger, the instincts of most of the opposition Front Bench, and much of the pressure from the party in the country pulled in the direction of consolidating on the right-wing. This was exacerbated by the perceived need to silence the siren voice of the UK Independence Party (UKIP), which was gaining increasing support on the party's right with its emphasis on issues such as opposition to the European Union and immigration. This concern mounted after UKIP won 12 seats in the European Parliament in the June 2004 elections. In September 2004 Howard brought leading Eurosceptic John Redwood back into the shadow cabinet and in October he told the party conference that a Conservative government would "bring powers back from Brussels to Britain". In the country, the party struggled with declining grass-roots membership, exacerbating an uneasy financial dependence on a few big individual backers in the business community, and with its loss of influence at local government level, where it had been totally eclipsed in many cities in which it had managed to hold onto strong positions in previous periods of Labour government in the 1960s and 1970s. Although the Conservatives came first on a low turnout in the June 2004 European elections, taking 27 seats, the party's performance in local elections and by-elections in 2004 was not such as to suggest any likely resurgence on the scale needed to topple Labour's huge majority at Westminster. Rhetorical bravado from the party leaders notwithstanding, there seemed to be a fatalistic acceptance in sections of the party that the next election, most likely in 2005, would be their third defeat in a row.

The Conservative Party is a founder member of the International Democrat Union. Its representatives in the European Parliament sit in the European People's Party/European Democrats group (consisting mainly of Christian Democrats).

Green Party of England and Wales (GPEW)

Address. 1A Waterlow Road, Archway, London, N19 5NJ
Telephone. (+44–20) 7272–4474
Fax. (+44–20) 7272–6653
Email. office@greenparty.org.uk
Website. www.greenparty.org.uk
Leadership. Caroline Lucas & Keith Taylor (principal speakers)

The Green Party propagates policies which are based on the principle that people must live in harmony with nature within the limitations of the earth's finite supply of resources. Its aims include unilateral disarmament, a ban on all nuclear as well as chemical and biological weapons, an end to Britain's involvement in NATO, an end to nuclear power generation, material security through a Basic National Income scheme, land reform, decentralization, proportional representation and increased aid for third-world countries in the form of grants not loans. The Scottish Green Party is organizationally separate from the GPEW.

The party was founded in 1973 as the Ecology Party, which nominated 54 candidates for the 1979 general elections, All of them lost their deposits and gained an average of only 1.2% of the vote in the contested constituencies, the party's best results being 2.8% in two. In the 1983 general elections Ecologists contested 109 seats, the highest vote for any candidate being 2.9%. In September 1985 the party changed its name to Green Party, which in the 1987 general elections fielded 133 candidates, the highest vote obtained by any of them being 3.7%. Meanwhile, the party had elected its first two local councillors in the district elections of May 1986, when its candidates averaged 6% in the wards which it contested.

The Greens seemed to make a breakthrough when they obtained 2.3 million votes (15% of the total) in the June 1989 European Parliament elections in Britain (but no seats). However, internal divisions between the moderates and a radical wing weakened the party in the early 1990s. It was also damaged when well-known television sports commentator David Icke, a party member, announced in 1991 that he was the new messiah sent to save mankind (and also left himself open to charges of anti-semitism in a new book). The party obtained only 171,927 votes (0.5%) in the April 1992 general elections, when all 253 Green candidates lost their deposits. Four months later Sara Parkin resigned as leader, stating that because of perpetual infighting "the Green Party has become a liability to green politics". Britain's other best-known environmentalist, Jonathon Porritt, also distanced himself from the party, becoming an adviser on green issues to the Prince of Wales.

The Greens staged a minor recovery in the June 1994 European Parliament elections, winning 3.1% of the vote (but again no seats). In the May 1997 general elections, however, the Greens' 95 candidates all lost their deposits in amassing an aggregate vote of 63,991 (0.2%). Two years later the Scottish Parliament elections of May 1999 yielded better fortune, with the Scottish Greens winning 3.6% of the vote and returning the first Green candidate ever to be elected in a major UK poll. In the June 1999 European elections, moreover, the Greens won two seats from a national vote share of 6.3%.

In November 1999 the party obtained formal Westminster representation for the first time when Lord Beaumont of Whitley, hitherto a Liberal Democrat life peer, crossed the floor in the House of Lords. In May 2000, moreover, the Greens won three of the 25 seats on the new Greater London Assembly (with 11.1% of the proportional vote), one of its elected members being given the environment portfolio in the new mayoral administration of Ken Livingstone. However, the June 2001 general elections produced the familiar universal failure for the Greens' 145 candidates, although their share of a much-reduced national vote rose to 0.6%. In the June 2004 European Parliament elections the Greens held on to their two seats.

With an official membership of 5,000, the GPEW is affiliated to the European Federation of Green Parties. Its representatives in the European Parliament sit in the Greens/European Free Alliance group.

Labour Party

Address. 16 Old Queen Street, London, SW1H 9HP
Telephone. 08705 900 200
Email. info@new.labour.org.uk
Website. www.labour.org.uk
Leadership. Tony Blair (leader); John Prescott (deputy leader); Ian McCartney (chairman); Matt Carter (general secretary)

The party was founded in 1900 as the Labour Representation Committee at a conference held in London attended by representatives of the trade unions, the Independent Labour Party, the Fabian Society and other socialist societies, having been convened as a result of a decision by the Trades Union Congress (TUC) to seek improved representation of the labour movement in parliament. Later in 1900 two Labour members were elected to parliament. The name of the Committee was changed to Labour Party in 1906, when there were 29 Labour members in the House of Commons. The first (minority) Labour government was in office from January to November 1924 and the second from June 1929 to August 1931, both under the premiership of Ramsay MacDonald, although MacDonald then headed a National government from which the bulk of the Labour Party dissociated itself.

Labour joined an all-party coalition during World War II and won an overwhelming victory in the 1945 general elections under the leadership of Clement Attlee (party leader from 1933 to 1955). His government carried out many social and economic reforms, among them the creation of the National Health Service (NHS), remaining in office until 1951. After 13 years in opposition (for part of which the party was led by Hugh Gaitskell), Labour was narrowly returned to power in 1964 under the leadership of Harold Wilson, who consolidated Labour's majority over the Conservative Party in further elections in 1966. Wilson's goal of social modernization made little progress and his government became increasingly troubled. Nevertheless, Labour's defeat by the Conservatives in the 1970 elections was unexpected.

In March 1974 Wilson returned to office as head of a minority administration after Labour had become the largest single parliamentary party in elections the previous month. The party subsequently achieved a narrow overall majority in further elections in October 1974. In a referendum in June 1975 the Labour government secured approval for its recommendation that Britain should remain a member of the European Community, despite the party being predominantly anti-European in those days. Wilson unexpectedly vacated the leadership in March 1976 and was succeeded by James Callaghan, who was obliged to enter into a parliamentary pact with the small Liberal Party (later the Liberal Democrats) after Labour's majority had been eroded by by-election losses. The Callaghan government became increasingly embroiled in disputes with militant public sector unions, culminating in the 1978–79 "winter of discontent", in which civil society seemed to have broken down. In the May 1979 general elections the Labour Party suffered a decisive defeat at the hands of Margaret Thatcher's Conservative Party and was then in opposition for the next 18 years.

Labour's 1979 election defeat resulted in the party's left wing gaining the ascendancy. Personifying Labour's "old left", Michael Foot succeeded Callaghan as leader in 1980 and sought to unify the party on the basis of radical policy commitments and opposition to membership of the European Community. The response of leading right-wingers was the formation in March 1981 of the breakaway Social Democratic Party (later mostly subsumed into what became the Liberal Democrats). In the June 1983 elections, Labour went down to a further heavy defeat, its 27.6% vote share being the party's lowest since 1918. Foot quickly resigned and a party conference in October 1983 elected another left-winger, Neil Kinnock (then 41), as the party's youngest-ever leader.

Kinnock failed to mount a credible challenge to the Thatcher government, being shackled by his own left-wing provenance and the influence of the hard left within the party. In June 1987 Labour suffered its third general election defeat in a row, albeit with the consolation of having reversed its electoral decline by increasing its share of the vote to 31.6% and its seat total to 229 (out of 650). Kinnock responded by initiating a major revision of Labour policies in key areas, featuring abandonment of the party's commitment to unilateral nuclear disarmament and of its opposition to UK membership of the European Community, for which the party quickly became a great enthusiast at the same time as much of the Conservative Party became increasingly Eurosceptic. Labour also moved towards acceptance of the market economy (subject to "regulation" in the general interest), while remaining opposed to privatization. At the same time, Kinnock launched a major drive to cleanse the Labour Party of hard-left "entryists" of the Militant Tendency.

Nevertheless, Labour was again defeated by the Conservatives in the April 1992 elections, although its total of 271 seats and 11.6 million votes (34.4%) represented a significant improvement. Kinnock resigned immediately after the contest and was succeeded by John Smith, a pro-European Scottish lawyer on Labour's moderate wing. Smith continued with the modernization programme, securing the adoption of "one member one vote" (OMOV) arrangements for the selection of Labour candidates and leadership elections, and led Labour to major advances in the 1993 and 1994 local elections. Smith died of a heart attack in May 1994 and was succeeded in July, under the new voting arrangements, by another "modernizing" and pro-European lawyer, Tony Blair (41). Meanwhile, under the interim leadership of Margaret Beckett, Labour had won a decisive victory in the June 1994 European Parliament elections, taking 62 of the 87 UK seats with 42.7% of the vote and for the first time in recent memory breaking through in hitherto "safe" Conservative areas in southern and central England.

In a symbolic revision of Labour's constitution initiated by Blair, a special party conference in April 1995 approved the abandonment of the party's 77-year-old clause 4 commitment to "the common ownership of the means of production, distribution and exchange". It was replaced by a general statement of democratic socialist aims and values asserting that the party seeks "a dynamic economy, serving the public interest, in which the enterprise of the market and the rigour of competition are joined with the forces of partnership and co-operation to produce the wealth the nation needs and the opportunity for all to work and prosper". In another significant policy shift, the Blair leadership in June 1996 announced that plans for the creation of directly-elected assemblies in Scotland and Wales would be submitted to referendums in each country before the necessary legislation was introduced by a Labour government at Westminster.

Blair led the party to a landslide victory in the May 1997 general elections, achieving a national swing from Conservative to Labour of 10.6%. The party won 418 of the 659 seats (with a vote share of 44.4%), giving it the largest parliamentary majority since 1945. The new Labour cabinet included John Prescott as Deputy Prime Minister and Secretary of State for Environment, Transport and the Regions, as well as Gordon Brown as Chancellor of the Exchequer, Jack Straw as Home Secretary and Robin Cook as Foreign and Commonwealth Secretary. Scottish and Welsh devolution bills were introduced and enacted in 1998, elections to the new legislatures in May 1999 producing Labour pluralities of 56 seats out of 129 in Scotland and 28 out of 60 in Wales. Accordingly, Labour formed a coalition with the Liberal Democrats in Scotland under Donald Dewar as first minister and a minority government in Wales under Alun Michael.

The Blair government was buffeted in 1998 by a series of disclosures involving claims that power and influence under Labour were concentrated in a small group of "Tony's cronies"; it was also accused of "control freakery" and of excessive "spin-doctoring" of the news. In December 1998 close Blair aide Peter Mandelson was forced to resign as Trade and Industry Secretary over a controversial private loan at a preferential rate received from another government minister. In the June 1999 European elections, held for the first time by proportional representation based on regional lists, Labour was out-polled by the Conservatives, winning only 28.0% of the vote and dropping from 62 to 29 seats. Nevertheless, Labour held its own in parliamentary by-elections and remained well ahead of the Conservatives in opinion polls,

assisted by a generally buoyant economy and falling unemployment, so that Blair felt able to restore Mandelson to the cabinet in October 1999 as Northern Ireland Secretary.

The resignation in January 2000 of junior minister Peter Kilfoyle on the grounds that Labour was losing touch with its working-class supporters highlighted growing discontent with the Blair leadership in sections of the party. In Wales, Blair appointee Alun Michael was forced to resign as first secretary in February by a revolt of the Labour Assembly members, his successor being the more independent Rhodri Morgan. More damaging was the strong support in London Labour ranks for the candidacy of left-wing Labour MP Ken Livingstone for the post of mayor in a restored administration for the capital. The Blair leadership used every stratagem to block Livingstone, securing the selection of former Cabinet minister Frank Dobson as the official Labour candidate even though 60% of London party members backed Livingstone. The latter responded by running as an independent (and accepting expulsion from the party) and easily winning the election in May 2000, with Dobson trailing a poor third. In September 2000 the government was caught entirely unprepared by a fuel price protest which brought the country to a standstill for a time. Overhanging such difficulties was the débâcle of London's Millennium Dome, which the government had insisted on building at huge public expense despite being warned that it would be a financial disaster.

In Scotland, the sudden death of Labour first minister Donald Dewar in October 2000 was a blow to a party under increasing challenge from the Scottish National Party, the new first minister, Henry McLeish, being much less popular than his predecessor (and eventually resigning in November 2001). In Wales, Morgan brought the Liberal Democrats into a majority coalition with Labour in October, partly with the aim of achieving greater leverage with the London government in pursuit of Welsh demands. The second enforced resignation of Mandelson in January 2001, this time over his alleged role in a citizenship application by one of the wealthy Hinduja brothers, caused further embarrassment for the government, although many in the party welcomed Mandelson's downfall because of his reputation as the architect of the Blair "modernization" project.

Notwithstanding such difficulties, and the outbreak of a major epidemic of foot-and-mouth disease in February 2001, Labour continued to ride high in the opinion polls, bolstered by a strong economy and the government's reputation for economic competence. The party's manifesto for the general elections eventually held in June 2001 pledged that the economic success of the post-1997 term would be translated in a second term into a major real increases in spending on the NHS, education and public transport. The outcome was a second overwhelming majority for Labour, which won 412 seats (a net loss of only six) and 42% of the vote (down only 2.4 percentage points). However, celebration of an unprecedented full second term for a Labour government was somewhat dampened by a voting turnout of only 59.4%, the lowest since 1918.

Cabinet changes and a government restructuring announced by Blair in the wake of the June 2001 elections were intended to ensure delivery of Labour's core pledge to improve the public services. They included the reallocation of Prescott's departmental responsibilities to other ministers, the demotion of Cook to the leadership of the Commons, the appointment of Straw as Foreign and Commonwealth Secretary and the promotion to the Home Office of David Blunkett, who became the first blind person to hold such a senior office. More controversially, Blair appointed Charles Clarke as chairman of the Labour Party (and Cabinet minister), with the stated objective of ensuring close liaison between government and party.

The Blair second term has proved more fraught with difficulties than the first. A constant source of tension has been the barely disguised aspiration of the Chancellor, Gordon Brown, to succeed Blair – though when, and on what terms, has been less clear. A state of continuous low-level warfare between those in the Blair camp and those in the Brown camp has led to a series of reports of the depth of enmity between the two men, punctuated by unconvincing denials from the principals and their allies. At times Brown has seemingly flirted with the notion of adopting the mantle of "old" Labour, while pulling back from a decisive confrontation – most notably when he reportedly called off his allies in the Commons from voting against the government in a critical vote on higher education funding on Jan. 27, 2004, which Blair won by just five votes. Brown's influence has been seen in the deferral of prospective British entry into the euro currency zone into a distant and hazy future, whereas it was a project for which Blair had shown considerable enthusiasm in his first term.

The Iraqi war, in which British military involvement is second only to that of the USA, led to strains within Labour ranks and divisions in the country as a whole. A Commons vote on March 18, 2003, to approve immediate military action was won by 396 votes to 217, but 139 of the 410 Labour MPs voted against the government. Two prominent party figures, Robin Cook (leader of the Commons) and Clare Short (the International Development Secretary) resigned over the commencement of hostilities (in Cook's case shortly before and in Short's case somewhat after the event). Nor was the disquiet allayed by the rapid overthrow of Saddam. Blair took Britain into the war substantially on the premise that Saddam Hussein possessed weapons of mass destruction (WMD) that posed a threat to the security of the region and even to the UK itself that required urgent action – this claim was the nain conclusion of a dossier of evidence presented to Parliament by Blair on Sept. 24, 2002. However, the government's claims over WMD were rapidly undermined by evidence on the ground in Iraq after the invasion of March 2003 and the issue then became one not of the existence of such weapons but of whether the government had deliberately overstated its case to give a basis for war. A report in a BBC news programme on May 29, 2003, quoting unnamed sources to the effect that Downing Street had "sexed up" the dossier to make the weapons evidence more compelling, led to a protracted and vicious row which resulted in the suicide on July 17, 2003, of a Ministry of Defence WMD expert (David Kelly) after he had been "outed" by the government as the source of the report. This was followed by the resignation (in January 2004) of the director-general (Greg Dyke) and chairman (Gavyn Davies) of the BBC after the publication of a report by Lord Hutton that exonerated the government in the affair of Kelly's death and strongly criticized the BBC. The widespread public scepticism over the conclusions of the Hutton report led the government to set up a second inquiry, headed by Lord (Robin) Butler, with broader terms of reference; this second report, issued in July 2004, proved somewhat more critical of the government without doing it serious damage. By late 2004 Tony Blair's position had evolved in a series of measured steps to one where he had effectively abandoned the justification for the war as being Saddam's weapons of mass destruction, and now rested his case on the benfit to Iraq and the world of the removal of Saddam – a justification he had before the war rejected as invalid. At the September 2004 party conference he acknowledged that the war had led to a decline in public trust in his leadership, but the essentials of government policy in Iraq remained unchanged.

Notwithstanding the more troubled nature of Blair's second term, he remained generally adept at side-stepping potential dangers. Reversing a previous position that was looking increasingly problematic, Blair in April 2004 announced that Britain would hold a referendum on the prospective EU constitutional treaty. He thereby at a stroke deferred controversy over the issue until after the next election while also taking away from the Tories what they had thought to be one of their strongest themes – that Blair was planning to railroad Britain into new constitutional arrangements without reference to the British people. Blair's determination to set the agenda for the next election campaign himself was underscored by his appointment in early September 2004 of Alan Milburn, a close ally who had left government for private interests in June 2003, as his general election campaign coordinator, in what was widely seen as a snub to Gordon Brown. That the point should not be lost, Blair revealed on Sept. 30 that he intended to serve out a full third term before standing down – an intention that, if carried out, was generally regarded as likely to be fatal to Brown's prospects of succeeding him, given the likely emergence of new and younger contenders in the intervening period.

Although Labour, with 19 seats, came a poor second to the Conservatives in the June 2004 European Parliament elections, the result was not seen as likely to indicate the outcome in a British general election, where turnouts are much higher and the issues different. The party's standing in the opinion polls and performance in by-elections in 2004 suggested that, barring a dramatic recovery by the opposition parties, a third term at a general election in 2005 was well within grasp.

The party remains heavily dependent on financial contributions from the trade unions (union donations representing more than half of party income, and its most stable income stream), a situation reinforced by the rapid decline of party membership from a 1997 peak of 407,000 to only 215,000 by the end of 2003, and by the dampening effect on large individual donations of the new requirement for all donations above £5,000 to be declared and restrictions on donations by companies. The appointment of Ian McCartney, seen as an "old Labour" figure popular with the unions, as party chairman (in succession to John Reid) in April 2003 was seen as a gesture to a trade union movement that was restive with the direction of "new" Labour's policies.

The Labour Party is a founder member of the Socialist International. Its representatives in the European Parliament sit in the Party of European Socialists group.

Liberal Democrats
Address. 4 Cowley Street, London, SWIP 3NB
Telephone. (+44–20) 7222–7999
Fax. (+44–20) 7799–2170
Email. info@libdems.org.uk
Website. www.libdems.org.uk
Leadership. Charles Kennedy (leader); Menzies Campbell (deputy leader)

The Liberal Democrats are directly descended from the historic Liberal Party, by way of an alliance and then merger between the latter and the bulk of the new Social Democratic Party, initially under the title Social and Liberal Democrats, which was shortened in late 1989 to Liberal Democrats. The party's federal constitution states that the party "exists to build and defend a fair, free and more equal society, shaped by the values of liberty, justice and community, in which no-one shall be enslaved by poverty, ignorance or conformity". The party is committed to continued British membership of the European Union (EU) and of the North Atlantic Treaty Organization (NATO), while advocating the freezing of Britain's nuclear deterrent capacity at the existing level. It also advocates devolution of power to Scotland, Wales and the English regions, an elected second chamber at Westminster and the introduction of a form of proportional representation. In Northern Ireland its sister party is the Alliance Party.

Of the two components of the Liberal Democrats, the Liberal Party traced its earliest origins to the 17th-century struggle by English Whigs in favour of freedom of conscience and civil rights, which led ultimately to parliament rather than the monarch being accepted as the country's supreme authority. (The Scottish term Whig was applied to those who opposed the succession of James II in 1685 on account of his Catholic sympathies.) The term Liberal Party was first formally used by Lord John Russell in 1839 in letters to Queen Victoria, Liberal governments holding office for over 50 of the 83 years up to 1914. The National Liberal Federation, set up in 1877, was the national political organization and Liberals were the first to produce party manifestos; they also introduced a national system of education, the secret ballot, the foundations of the welfare state and a reform of the House of Lords. During World War I, when the party led a coalition government under David Lloyd-George, it became divided and began to decline, a process accelerated by the rise of the Labour Party on the strength of universal adult suffrage and its trade union base.

Liberals held office in the World War II coalition government, and Sir William Beveridge, a Liberal MP in 1944–45, was the architect of the post-war National Health Service and other welfare state structures created by the Labour government. By now the Liberals' representation in the Commons was tiny, remaining at six seats in the three elections of the 1950s, rising to nine in 1964 and 12 in 1966, and then falling back to six in 1970. In this period the party was led by Clement Davies (1945–56), Jo Grimond (1956–67) and Jeremy Thorpe (1967–76). Under Thorpe's leadership the Liberals obtained over 6 million votes (19.3% of the total) and 14 seats in the February 1974 elections, when Conservative Prime Minister Edward Heath, having narrowly lost his majority, tried and failed to entice them into a coalition. The result was a minority Labour government and further elections in October 1974, in which the Liberals fell back to 5.3 million votes (18.3%) and 13 seats.

Undone by scandal, Thorpe was succeeded in July 1976 by David Steel, who became the first Liberal leader to be elected directly by party members. Steel took the party into the 1977–78 "Lib-Lab pact", under which the Liberals supported the minority Labour government in its pursuit of economic recovery between March 1977 and July 1978. But his hope that the Liberals would thereby acquire a beneficial "governmental" aura was disappointed in the May 1979 elections, in which the party won only 11 seats on a 13.8% vote share.

With the Conservative Party now in power under the radical right-wing leadership of Margaret Thatcher and the Labour Party having moved sharply to the left following its election defeat, the Liberal Party's hopes of presenting a viable centrist alternative appeared to be strengthened in early 1981 when a right-wing Labour faction broke away to form the Social Democratic Party (SDP). In June 1981 the Alliance of the Liberals and the SDP was launched in a joint statement entitled *A Fresh Start for Britain*, in which the two parties agreed not to oppose each other in elections. After winning a number of Commons by-elections on the basis of this agreement, the Alliance contested the June 1983 general elections with an agreed distribution of candidates between the two parties. However, although it garnered 7.8 million votes (25.4% of the total), the yield in seats was only 23, of which the Liberals took 17.

The Alliance was nevertheless maintained and contested the June 1987 elections under the uneasy joint leadership of Steel and former Labour Foreign Secretary David Owen (who had become leader of the SDP immediately after the 1983 elections). However, a further decisive Conservative victory and a partial Labour recovery denied the Alliance its minimum target of securing the balance of power between the two major parties: its aggregate support fell to 22.6%, with the Liberals winning 4.2 million votes (12.8%) and 17 seats and the SDP 3.2 million (9.8%) and five seats.

Three days after the June 1987 elections Steel unexpectedly proposed a "democratic fusion" of the two Alliance parties, a proposal supported with some reservations within his own party but which divided the SDP into pro-merger and anti-merger factions, the latter including Owen and, at that stage, three of the other four SDP MPs. A subsequent ballot of the SDP membership showed a 57.4% majority in favour of merger negotiations, whereupon Owen resigned as SDP leader in August 1987 and launched an anti-merger Campaign for Social Democracy. His successor was Robert Maclennan, a former Labour MP who had joined the SDP on its formation, had initially opposed merger with the Liberals but was now prepared to negotiate in good faith. After both the SDP and Liberal 1987 annual conferences had given overwhelming approval to the concept of a merger, detailed negotiations on the constitution and platform of a unified party took place. After one false start, these resulted in a modified policy document (published in January 1988) and agreement that the new party should be called the Social and Liberal Democrats (and Democrats for short). Later in January 1988 special conferences of the two parties each voted heavily in favour of proceeding to a further ballot of their memberships to secure final approval of the merger plan. Both of these ballots showed large majorities in favour, enabling the new SLD to be formally launched in March 1988, under the joint interim leadership of Steel and Maclennan pending an election for a single leader. This resulted in July 1988 in the election of Paddy Ashdown, who proceeded to rename the merged party the Liberal Democrats. On the declaration of the SDP's final ballot decision in favour of merger, Dr Owen announced the re-launching of the Social Democratic Party as an independent formation. It did not prosper and was dissolved in June 1990.

Ashdown led the Liberal Democrats to some improvement in the April 1992 general elections, when the party won 20 seats and almost 6 million votes (17.9% of those cast) on a platform which included a commitment to a general increase in the basic income tax. By June 1994 its Commons representation had risen to 23 seats on the strength of a series of stunning by-election victories in hitherto "safe" Conservative seats. In the same month the party at last achieved European Parliament representation, winning two of the 87 UK seats, although its share of the national vote fell back to 16.1%. Thereafter the Liberal Democrats were somewhat eclipsed by Tony Blair's "new" Labour Party, which gained ascendancy as the main opposition party, although the Liberal Democrats were boosted to 26 Commons seats by two Conservative defectors in 1995–96.

The response of the Liberal Democrat leadership to the resurgence of Labour was to make increasingly explicit offers of support for a future Labour government in the event that the Liberal Democrats held the balance of power. In the event, the Labour landslide meant that Liberal Democrats did not hold the balance of power after the May 1997 general elections, although thanks to anti-Conservative tactical voting their seat tally rose sharply to 46 (the highest since 1929) on the basis of a reduced vote share of 17.2%. Liberal Democrats thereafter accepted appointment to a special Cabinet committee of the new Labour government concerned with constitutional and electoral reform (later extended to cover other issues); but the party's influence was limited in the face of Labour's large majority and it made no progress on its aim of bringing in proportional representation (PR) for general elections.

A form of PR was introduced for elections to the new devolved legislatures of Scotland and Wales in May 1999, the Liberal Democrats winning 17 Scottish seats (and joining a formal coalition with Labour) and six Welsh seats. Regional PR also operated in the European elections in June 1999, when the Liberal Democrats lifted their seat tally to 10, though on a reduced vote share of 12.7%. Meanwhile, Ashdown had in January 1999 announced his imminent departure as Liberal Democrat leader after 11 years in the post. His successor, elected in August, was Scottish MP and former SDP member Charles Kennedy (39), whose nearest challenger was London MP Simon Hughes. Kennedy pledged that he would seek to build a "strong, independent, progressive" party, while backing the continuation of political co-operation with the Labour government.

In March 2001 Kennedy concluded an agreement with Prime Minister Tony Blair that the forthcoming Labour election manifesto would promise a review of UK electoral systems to establish whether a referendum should be held on the introduction of proportional representation for Westminster elections. The formula kept alive the Liberal Democrats' holy grail of national PR, although party leaders had no illusions about the lack of real Labour support for a change. The Labour pledge did not feature prominently in the Liberal Democrat campaign for the June 2001 general elections, in which the party consolidated its position by winning 52 seats (a net gain of six) and 18.8% of the vote (up 1.6%).

In September 2001 Kennedy withdrew his party from the Cabinet committee in which it had co-operated with Labour since 1997, thereby signalling his intention that the Liberal Democrats would become a genuine party of opposition. Speaking to the annual party conference in Bournemouth later in the month, Kennedy called upon moderate Conservatives and dissident Labour voters to join the Liberal Democrats.

The differences of the Liberals with the government sharpened over the war in Iraq, the Liberals having called for continued efforts to find a resolution through the UN. Kennedy declared himself "delighted" with the outcome of the June 2004 European elections, although the Liberals lost third place in the share of the vote to the UK Independence Party (with the same number of seats – 12), and the party performed well in local elections the same month. The party has more seats in the House of Commons than at any time since the 1920s and has vastly improved its conversion rate of votes into seats under the difficult first past the post system as compared with the 1970s and 1980s. This gives it a strong base in the approach to the next general election, expected in 2005. However, the party faces difficulties in positioning itself for the election. On the one hand, the party has taken positions to the left of the now firmly centrist Labour Party on a variety of issues, and has emerged as the clearest opponent of the war in Iraq, a war which has caused disquiet among many Labour voters. For the Liberals to be able to hold the balance of power in the next parliament, it is essential that Labour's present large majority is dramatically eroded. On the other hand, the practical reality is that the great majority of its top target seats to capture are currently held by Conservatives, implying the need to win over disaffected Conservatives. Kennedy has claimed, however, that local and by-election results in 2004 showed that the party could simultaneously win ground from Labour in its heartlands and from the Tories in theirs.

With an official membership of 90,000, the Liberal Democrats are affiliated to the Liberal International. Their representatives in the European Parliament sit in the European Liberal, Democratic and Reformist group.

Plaid Cymru–The Party of Wales

Address. Ty Gwynfor, 18 Park Grove, Caerdydd/Cardiff, CF10 3BN, Wales
Telephone. (+44–29) 2064–6000
Fax. (+44–29) 2064–6001
Email. post@plaidcymru.org
Website. www.plaidcymru.org
Leadership. Dafydd Iwan (president); Ieuan Wyn Jones (leader in Welsh Assembly)

Founded in August 1925, *Plaid Cymru* seeks self-government for Wales based on socialist principles, Welsh membership of the European Union and restoration of the Welsh language and culture. It has contested all elections to the Westminster parliament since 1945 but remained unrepresented until July 1966, when its then president, Dafydd Elis Thomas, won a by-election at Carmarthen. Although the party lost that seat in 1970, it won two others in the February 1974 elections (Carnarvon and Merioneth) and added the Carmarthen seat in October of that year, for a tally of three. The party also built up significant representation in local government. In light of this performance, the then Labour Party government tabled proposals for an elected Welsh Assembly, but the idea was rejected by Welsh voters in a referendum of March 1979.

In the May 1979 general elections *Plaid Cymru* held the Carnarvon and Merioneth seats but lost Carmarthen to Labour. It retained its two seats in the 1983 elections, winning a total of 125,309 votes. In the June 1987 elections the party again moved up to three Commons seats by winning Ynys Mon in North Wales, although its total vote slipped to 123,595 (7.3% of the Welsh total). The April 1992 general elections yielded the party's best result to date, four of the 32 seats contested being won, including Pembroke North, with an aggregate vote of 148,232 (about 8.5% of the Welsh total). In the June 1994 European Parliament elections, moreover, *Plaid Cymru* advanced to over 17% of the Welsh vote, although without winning any seats.

In the May 1997 general elections *Plaid Cymru* presented 40 candidates, winning four seats with an aggregate vote of 161,030 (9.9% in Wales). It thereafter backed the new Labour government's introduction of a devolved Assembly for Wales and sought to explain the very narrow referendum vote in favour in September 1997 (in a turnout of only 50%) by citing the legislature's lack of tax-raising powers. In the Welsh Assembly elections in May 1999 *Plaid Cymru* made inroads in Labour strongholds in south Wales, taking second place with 17 of the 60 seats on a vote share of 30.5%. In the June 1999 European elections the *Plaid Cymru* share of the vote in Wales leapt forward to 29.6%, giving it representation (two seats) for the first time.

Plaid Cymru Assembly members contributed to the ousting of Labour first secretary Alun Michael in February 2000 and saw the formation of a Labour-Liberal coalition administration in October as confirming the party's status as the only genuine opposition in Wales. In the UK general elections of June 2001 *Plaid Cymru* again won four seats, but its increased popular vote (195,892) represented a significant advance to 14.3% in Wales.

In August 2001 Ieuan Wyn Jones, Westminster MP for Ynys Mon, was elected leader of *Plaid Cymru* in succession to Dafydd Wigley, who had announced his retirement after 10 years in the post. In September 2001 the party's annual conference in Cardiff formally dropped the goal of independence from the *Plaid Cymru* programme, instead setting full membership of a regionalized EU as the party's aim for Wales. The May 2003 elections to the Welsh Assembly were a serious setback for *Plaid Cymru*, the party losing 5 of its previous 17 seats and coming a poor second to Labour, and only one seat ahead of the Conservative Party. Ieuan Wyn Jones resigned as party president a few days later, to be succeeded in that role in September by Dafydd Iwan, a folk singer (though Wyn Jones remained party leader in the Welsh Assembly). Another effect of the loss of Assembly seats was that the party again seemed to restore the goal of eventual Welsh independence to a prominent place in its agenda. In the June 2004 European elections the party lost one of its two seats, being disadvantaged by the reduction in the total of UK seats.

Plaid Cymru is a member of the Democratic Party of the Peoples of Europe–European Free Alliance. It reports a membership of about 10,000. Its representative in the European Parliament sits in the Greens/European Free Alliance group.

Scottish National Party (SNP)

Address. 107 McDonald Rd, Edinburgh, EH7 4NW, Scotland
Telephone. (+44–131) 525–8900
Fax. (+44–131) 525–8901
Email. snp.hq@snp.org
Website. www.snp.org
Leadership. Alex Salmond (leader); Nicola Sturgeon (deputy leader & leader in the Scottish Parliament); Winifred Ewing (president); Alasdair Allan (national secretary)

The SNP's basic aim is Scottish independence within the European Union (EU) and the Commonwealth, while on economic and social questions it identifies itself as "moderate, left-of-centre". The party was founded in 1934 as a merger of the National Party of Scotland and the Scottish Party. It won a House of Commons by-election at Motherwell in April 1945 but lost this seat to the Labour Party in the general elections three months later. Over the next three decades the SNP held only single seats in the House of Commons: Hamilton in 1967-70, Western Isles in 1970–74 and Govan in 1973–74. In the February 1974 elections, however, the party won seven seats with 21.9% of the vote in Scotland, boosted by the discovery of oil in the North Sea and the prospect that an independent Scotland would be financially viable on the basis of oil revenues.

In the October 1974 elections the SNP advanced further to 11 seats with 30.4% of the Scottish vote, whereupon the then Labour government tabled proposals for the creation of a devolved Scottish assembly. But the tide of pro-independence feeling had ebbed somewhat by the time of the March 1979 referendum on the plans, the outcome being that the 52% vote in favour represented only 32.8% of those entitled to vote (the turnout having been 63.7%). Basing itself on an earlier decision that a higher real vote in favour would be required, the UK parliament thereupon refused to set up the assembly. In the May 1979 general elections the SNP lost all but two of its seats, although it still polled 17.2% of the Scottish vote. Both of these seats were retained in the 1983 elections, but the SNP's share of the Scottish vote contracted to 11.8%. In the June 1987 elections the SNP polled 416,873 votes (14% of the Scottish total) and won three parliamentary seats. Immediately prior to the 1987 general elections, the SNP signed an agreement with *Plaid Cymru* (Welsh Nationalists) pledging mutual support in parliament.

By-election successes increased the SNP's representation in the Commons to five seats in the course of the 1987–92 parliament, but the party fell back to three in the April 1992 general elections despite increasing its share of the Scottish vote to 21.5% (629,564 votes), just behind the Conservative Party. The SNP established itself as Scotland's second party (after Labour) in the June 1994 European Parliament elections, obtaining nearly a third of the Scottish vote and winning two Euro-seats (compared with one in 1979). In May 1995, moreover, the party increased its Commons representation to four seats as a result of a by-election victory over the Conservatives in which it took 40% of the vote.

In the May 1997 general elections the SNP increased its representation in the Commons to six seats and its share of the Scottish vote to 22.1%, although in a lower turnout its vote aggregate fell to 621,550. It thereafter opted to work with the incoming Labour government's devolution plan for Scotland, although it fell far short of core SNP aims, and

helped to secure 74% approval for the proposals in a referendum in September 1997. In elections to the new Scottish Parliament in May 1999 the SNP came second behind Labour, winning 35 of the 129 seats with a 27.3% share of the list vote and becoming the principal opposition to a coalition of Labour and the Liberal Democrats. In the June 1999 European elections the SNP again won two seats on a UK vote share of 2.7%.

In March 2000 the SNP published plans for a referendum on independence for Scotland if the party came to power in the 2003 Scottish elections. In July 2000 Alex Salmond unexpectedly announced his decision to vacate the SNP leadership after 10 years in the post. In a leadership ballot three months later John Swinney, who advocated a "gradualist" approach to the goal of independence, easily defeated Alex Neil, a "fundamentalist", by winning 67% of delegates' votes at the party's annual conference in Inverness. Its priority now being the Scottish Parliament, the SNP mounted a low-key campaign for the UK general elections in June 2001. It lost one of its six seats (to the Conservatives) and its share of the Scottish vote fell to 20.1% (464,305).

In the May 2003 elections to the Scottish Parliament the SNP lost 8 seats, declining to 27, well behind Labour (50), and remained in opposition. Among those elected as independents was one of the most well-known SNP figures from earlier years, Margo MacDonald. In September 2003 Swinney comfortably defeated a leadership challenge at the party annual conference. However, internal dissatisfaction with his leadership continued and was exacerbated by the party's performance in the June 2004 European elections (in which the party's share of the vote in Scotland fell by 7.5 percentage points compared with 1999, to 19.7%, well behind Labour, although the SNP retained its two seats). This led to Swinney's resignation as party leader later the same month and the unexpected return to the helm of former leader Alex Salmond, who won a ballot of the party's 8,500 members in August 2004. As an MP at Westminster, Salmond ran on a joint slate with Nicola Sturgeon as his candidate for deputy, Sturgeon being the party leader in the Scottish Parliament.

The SNP is a member of the Democratic Party of the Peoples of Europe–European Free Alliance. Its representatives in the European Parliament sit in the Greens/European Free Alliance group.

UK Independence Party (UKIP)

Address. PO Box 9876, Birmingham, B6 4DN
Telephone. (+44–121) 333-7737
Email. mail@independence.org.uk
Website. www.independence.org.uk
Leadership. Roger Knapman (leader); Mike Nattrass (deputy leader); Petrina Holdsworth (chairman)

UKIP was founded at the London School of Economics in 1993 by Alan Sked to oppose what it regards as the unacceptable surrender of British sovereignty to the European Union (EU). Having contested the 1992 general elections as the Anti-Federalist League (whose 16 candidates all lost their deposits), UKIP fought most UK seats in the 1994 European Parliament elections, winning an overall vote share of 1%. In the May 1997 general elections 193 UKIP candidates took only 0.3% of the vote, all but one losing their deposits. However, the party broke through in the June 1999 European elections (held under a form of proportional representation), winning 7.0% of the national vote and returning three MEPs.

UKIP split in April 2000 when the election of MEP Jeffrey Titford as leader (in succession to Michael Holmes) was seen by a minority faction as confirming the party's drift to the far right. The defectors established the Reform 2000 Party but failed to attract much rank-and-file support. In the June 2001 general elections UKIP fielded 428 candidates (all unsuccessful, although six saved their desposits), who obtained an aggregate of 390,576 votes, representing a 1.5% share.

In the European elections in June 2004, UKIP, benefiting in part from the greater enthusiasm of its supporters for a contest with a low turnout, scored a remarkable 16.8% of the vote, increasing its total of MEPs from three to 12. In the East Midlands, Eastern, South West and South East regions, it came second to the Conservatives, pushing Labour into third place. It stated it would use its new position, in combination with other Eurosceptic parties elsewhere in Europe, to obstruct and delay EU legislation. The new crop of UKIP MEPs included Robert Kilroy-Silk, a former Labour MP who had recently lost his TV chat show following publicity given to perjorative remarks he had made about Arabs; Kilroy-Silk quickly voiced his desire to become party leader himself at the expense of Roger Knapman (a former Conservative government whip who had replaced Titford in October 2002), leading to a highly public wrangle between the two men. A further complication emerged in October 2004 when Paul Sykes, the party's biggest financial supporter, announced he was ending his backing for the party and planned to vote Conservative at the next election.

The UKIP representatives in the European Parliament joined the Independence/Democracy Group of Eurosceptic parties; however, one of the MEPs elected in June 2004 has had the whip withdrawn and is unattached.

Other Parties

There is a large proliferation of parties in Britain, most of only fringe or local interest and with no electoral significance. The following is a selection of some of the parties that have had some national significance or are of other interest.

British National Party (BNP), an extreme right-wing formation standing for "rights for whites", a cessation of non-white immigration, encouragement of the "repatriation" of non-whites and a halt to "multiculturalism" in the UK. The party was founded in 1960 as an alliance of the League of Empire Loyalists, the White Defence League and the National Labour Party. A split in the mid-1960s resulted in the formation of a paramilitary elite corps (named "Spearhead") under the leadership of Colin Jordan and John Tyndall, the rump BNP being one of the founder members of the National Front in 1967. In 1982 the BNP re-emerged as an independent party under Tyndall's leadership, contesting 53 seats in the 1983 general elections (losing 53 deposits) and a smaller number in 1987 (with the same result). Although Tyndall had been sentenced to 12 months' in prison in 1986 for incitement to racial hatred, the party subsequently sought to give a "respectable" face to extreme right-wing politics and to develop contacts with like-minded movements in continental Europe. The 13 BNP candidates all lost their deposits in the 1992 general elections (achieving an aggregate vote of 7,005), but in September 1993 the party won its first local council seat in the east London borough of Tower Hamlets, an area of high Bangladeshi settlement. It lost the seat in the May 1994 local elections, although its overall vote in the borough increased. In the 1997 general elections 57 BNP candidates won 35,832 votes (0.1%), all but three losing their deposits. In June 2001 the BNP's 33 candidates won 47,129 votes (0.2%), five saving their deposits by benefiting from racial tension in northern English constituencies with high Asian populations, notably in Oldham, where BNP chairman Nick Griffin took 16.4%. Under Griffin (leader since 1999) the party has adopted a more sophisticated approach to campaigning and has become the main extreme right party in Britain, campaigning with some minor success in elections to local councils,

primarily in certain depressed industrial towns in northern England. In the June 2004 European elections the party took 4.9% of the vote, but did not win any seats, its effort to appeal to the Eurosceptic vote frustrated by the greater success of the UK Independence Party.

Address. PO Box 287, Waltham Cross, Herts, EN8 8ZU
Telephone. 0870 7576 267
Website. www.bnp.org.uk
Leadership. Nick Griffin (chairman)

Christian People's Alliance (CPA), founded in 1999 by Kenyan Asian businessman Ram Gidoomal as an attempt to create a continental-style Christian democratic party in Britain. In the May 2000 London elections Gidoomal won 2.5% in the mayoral race, ahead of the Green Party and UK Independence Party candidates, while the CPA list took 3.2%, without securing representation.

Address. 7 Storey's Gate, London SW1P 3AT
Telephone. 0845 45 65 478
Email. info@cpalliance.net
Website. www.cpalliance.net
Leadership. Ram Gidoomal (leader)

Communist Party of Britain (CPB), originally founded in 1920, the present party deriving from a 1988 breakaway by a minority faction of the Communist Party of Great Britain (see Socialist Alliance) which opposed the CPGB's espousal of "Euro-communism" and later rejected any theoretical accommodation with the collapse of communism in Eastern Europe. The new CPB is closely aligned with the co-operative which has retained control of *The Morning Star* (once the official daily newspaper of the old CPGB). The party's six candidates in the 2001 elections all lost their deposits.

Address. 94 Camden Rd, London NW1 9EA
Leadership. Robert Griffiths (general secretary)

Co-operative Party, founded in 1917 by the British Co-operative Union (the central body representing British consumer and other co-operatives) in order to secure for the co-operative movement direct representation. The party has been represented in parliament ever since, in alliance with the Labour Party (described as its "sister party") whereby its representatives stand as "Labour and Co-op" candidates. There have been Co-operative members in all Labour governments since 1924 and as of 2004 there were 29 "Labour and Co-operative" MPs (for most purposes, however, simply referred to as Labour MPs). The party has a membership of 8,000.

Address. 77 Weston Street, Lomdon SE1 3SD
Email. p.hunt@party.coop
Website. www.co-op-party.org.uk
Leadership. Gareth Thomas (chair); Peter Hunt (national secretary)

Countryside Party, founded in 2000 "out of a feeling that recognized political parties were at best neglecting or at worst ignoring the feelings of the countryside, and the people who work in the country, or enjoy country sports and the rural way of life". It contested one Scottish seat in June 2001, winning 265 votes. It came seventh in the June 2004 European elections in the South West region, winning 30,824 votes.

Address. The Croft, Sunnyside, Culloden Moor, Inverness, IV2 5EE
Email. cparty@btinternet.com
Website. www.countrysideparty.com
Leadership. James Crawford (leader)

English Democrats Party, launched in 2002 and the successor to the English National Party (founded 1974); opposes

membership of the EU and calls for an English Parliament with powers to equal those of the Scottish Parliament. It competed without electoral success in the June 2004 European Parliament elections, though aggregating 130,056 votes.
Leadership. Robin Tilbrook (leader)

Liberal Party (LP), founded by former Liberal MP Michael Meadowcroft as an attempt to keep the historic LP in existence following the formation in 1989 of what became the Liberal Democrats. The LP obtained 64,744 votes in the 1992 general elections, although only one of its 73 candidates saved his/her deposit. In 1997 its 55 candidates obtained a total of 45,166 votes (0.1%), all but two losing their deposits. Less ambitiously, it contested nine seats in 2001, losing deposits in eight in winning 10,920 votes. Such support as it has is particularly found in the north-west of England, and in the 2004 European Parliament elections it put up a full slate of candidates in the North West region, coming seventh with 96,325 seats.
Address. 402 Hurcott Road, Kidderminster, DY10 2QQ
Website. www.liberal.org.uk
Leadership. Michael Oborski (leader)

Mebyon Kernow (Party for Cornwall), founded in 1951 to campaign for the self-government of Cornwall. By 1960 it claimed to have the active support of three Cornish MPs of other parties, although such people became ineligible for membership following the movement's 1974 decision to contest parliamentary elections itself. It has gained representation in Cornish local government, often under the "independent" label, but has failed at national level, its three candidates in 2001 all losing their deposits in winning 3,199 votes.
Address. Lanhainsworth, Fraddon Hill, St Columb, Cornwall, TR9 6PQ
Email. dickcole@tinyworld.co.uk
Website. www.mebyonkernow.org
Leadership. Dick Cole (leader)

Monster Raving Loony Party (MRLP), Britain's premier "alternative" party, founded in the early 1960s by David ("Screaming Lord") Sutch (a former rock musician). Sutch contested over 40 by-elections before he committed suicide in June 1999, never saving a deposit. Sutch was succeeded by publican Alan ("Howling Lord") Hope. In 2001 its 15 candidates won a total of 6,655 votes.
Address. The Dog and Partridge, 105 Reading Road, Yateley, Hampshire, GU46 7LR
Leadership. Alan Hope (leader)

National Front (NF), far-right formation founded in 1967, seeking the restoration of Britain as an ethnically homogeneous state by means of the "repatriation" of coloured immigrants and their descendants. It also seeks to "liberate" Britain from international ties such as the United Nations, NATO and the European Union, and opposes the international financial system and "big business capitalism", favouring instead small privately-owned enterprises and workers' co-operatives. The NF was founded as a merger of the British National Party (BNP), the League of Empire Loyalists and the Racial Preservation Society. It has nominated candidates in all general elections since its formation, rising to 303 in 1979, but has received only negligible support, although a 1973 by-election in West Bromwich yielded 16% of the vote. In the 1970s NF meetings frequently led to violence, as opponents mounted counter-demonstrations. The right of NF candidates to hire halls for election meetings was upheld by the High Court in November 1982, but many NF marches have been banned under the Public Order Act since then, while some NF leaders have been convicted of "incitement

to racial hatred" under the Race Relations Act. From the mid-1980s the Front sought to improve its image by electing a new generation of university-educated leaders who developed an intellectual basis for the movement (described as "new positivism") and publicly distanced themselves from the violent street activism previously associated with Martin Webster (the NF organizer ousted from the party in 1983–84). Nevertheless, internal divisions continued, leading to a split between a "revolutionary nationalist" group and a "radical nationalist" group in 1986–87, by which time the NF had largely been eclipsed on the far right by the revived BNP. The NF's 14 candidates in the 1992 elections all lost their deposits, obtaining a total of 4,816 votes. In 1997 six NF candidates won 2,716 votes, all losing their deposits and in 2001 five NF candidates also failed, winning 2,484 votes in total.
Address. PO Box 114, Solihull, B91 2UR
Telephone. (+44–121) 246-6838
Website. www.natfront.com
Leadership. Tom Holmes (chairman)

Respect – The Unity Coalition, a left-wing electoral alliance launched in January 2004 and having George Galloway, an MP who had been expelled from the Labour Party, as its leading figure. It has been prominent in opposition to the war in Iraq, seeming to pitch its appeal particularly towards Muslim voters. In the June 2004 European elections it took only 1.7% of the vote nationally, gaining no seats, but in London it polled 4.8%; it followed this comparative success by achieving second place in a by-election in London in September 2004.
Website. www.respectcoalition.org

Revolutionary Communist Party of Britain–Marxist-Leninist (RCPB–ML), leftist grouping founded in 1981. Its eight candidates all lost their deposits in the 1992 general elections, obtaining an aggregate vote of 745 electors. The party did not contest the 1997 and 2001 elections.
Address. 170 Wandsworth Road, London, SW8 2LA
Telephone. (144–20) 7627–0599
Email. office@rcpbml.org.uk
Website. www.rcpbml.org.uk
Leadership. Chris Coleman (national spokesperson)

Scottish Green Party, autonomous environmentalist party in Scotland linked fraternally with the Green Party of England and Wales. Its one successful candidate for the new Scottish Parliament in May 1999 was the first for the Greens in a major UK election. In the 2001 general elections three of the party's four candidates lost their deposits, the aggregate party vote being 4,551. In the May 2003 elections to the Scottish Parliament, however, the party succeeded in electing 7 MSPs.
Address. 3 Lyne Street, Edinburgh EH7 5DN
Telephone. 0870 772 207
Email. info@scottishgreens.org.uk
Website. www.scottishgreens.org.uk
Leadership. Robin Harper (principal speaker)

Scottish Senior Citizens' Unity Party, formed to represent the interests of pensioners in February 2003; its leader, John Swinburne, won a seat in the May 2003 elections to the Scottish Parliament.
Address. The Chapman Building, Fir Park Street, Motherwell, ML1 2QN

Scottish Socialist Party (SSP), left-wing formation in Scotland that has brought together various groups ranging from Labour Party militants to Trotskyists united by opposition to the "revisionism" of Blair's Labour Party. It failed to make an impact in the 1997 general elections (then being known as the Scottish Socialist Alliance), but was joined by Labour MP Dennis Canavan, who won a seat in the Scottish Parliament elections in May 1999 (and whose Westminster seat was regained by Labour in a December 2000 by-election following his expulsion from the party). In the 2001 general elections the 72 SSP candidates were all unsuccessful (62 losing their deposits), mustering an aggregate vote of 72,279 (3.1% in Scotland). However, the party performed strongly in the 2003 elections to the Scottish Parliament, being awarded 6 seats under the additional member system, one of them being taken by party leader Tommy Sheridan. Canavan sits as an independent MSP.

Address. John Maclean Centre, 70 Stanlet Street, Kinning Park, Glasgow, G41 1JB

Website. www.scottishsocialistparty.org

Leadership. Tommy Sheridan (leader); Jim Wallace (leader in Scottish Parliament)

Socialist Alliance, formed prior to the 2001 elections as a broad front of some 15 groupings to the left of the Labour Party, including the Communist Party of Great Britain (CPGB), descended from the "moderate" majority wing of the historic Communist Party by way of the Democratic Left formation of the 1990s; the Socialist Party (SP), led by former Labour MP Dave Nellist; and the Socialist Workers' Party (SWP), founded in 1950 as the International Socialists and known under that name until 1977. The SWP is the largest group involved in the Alliance. The Alliance ran 98 candidates, who won a total of 60,496 votes (0.2%), with only three saving their deposits. The Socialist Alliance has collaborated with former Labour MP George Galloway in the "Respect" coalition, in which the SWP is a major participant.

Socialist Equality Party (SEP), British section of the (Trotskyist) International Committee of the Fourth International, fighting against "the post-Soviet school of falsification which seeks to draw an equals sign between the bloody dictatorship of Stalin and genuine socialism".

Address. PO Box 1306, Sheffield, S9 3UW

Telephone. (+44–114) 243–4212

Email. sep@socialequality.org.uk

Website. www.socialequality.org.uk

Socialist Labour Party (SLP), launched by Arthur Scargill in 1996 to provide a radical left-wing alternative to the "new" Labour Party of Tony Blair. As president of the National Union of Mineworkers, Scargill had led abortive opposition to the policies of the Thatcher government in the 1980s, becoming disenchanted with the line of the Labour leadership. In the 1997 general elections 61 of 64 SLP candidates lost their deposits, the party's aggregate vote being 52,109. In 2001 all but one of the 114 SLP candidates lost their deposits, their aggregate vote being 57,536 (0.2%).

Address. 9 Victoria Road, Barnsley, S. Yorks, S70 2BB

Telephone/Fax. (+44) 1226 770–957

Leadership. Arthur Scargill (chairman)

Socialist Party of Great Britain (SPGB), a Marxist formation founded in 1904 in quest of "a world-wide community based on the common ownership and democratic control of the means of wealth distribution and production". In the course of its long history the SPGB opposed both world wars. Its parliamentary and local election forays have also met with regular lack of success. The SPGB has links with similarly named and orientated parties in a number of other developed countries, together constituting the World Socialist Movement.

Email. enquiries@spgb.org.uk

Website. www.spgb.org.uk

Socialist Workers' Party, Trotskyist formation known until 1977 as the International Socialists; at its peak in the 1970s when it was prominent in the student left, though with negligible industrial influence; remains active with a tradition of sponsoring and working within broader coalitions, from the notably successful Anti-Nazi League in the late 1970s to the current Stop the War and Respect coalitions. It has no electoral significance in England but in Scotland the SWP is organized as a faction within the Scottish Socialist Party, which is represented in the Scottish Parliament.

Address. PO Box 82, London E3 3LH

Telephone. (+44-20) 7538-5821

Website. www.swp.org.uk.

Workers' Revolutionary Party (WRP), far-left formation which rejects "the parliamentary road to socialism" but has contested recent general elections. Descended from the prewar Militant Group, by way of the Workers' International League and the Revolutionary Communist Party (among other earlier formations), the WRP succeeded the Socialist Labour League (founded in 1959) and at first worked inside the Labour Party. The party ran six candidates in the 2001 elections, garnering a total of 607 votes.

Address. BCM Box 747, London, WC1N 3XX

Telephone. (+44–20) 7232–1101

Fax. (+44–20) 7740–2401

Email. info@wrp.org.uk

Website. www.wrp.org.uk

Leadership. Sheila Torrance (general secretary)

Northern Ireland

Capital: Belfast
Population: 1,665,000 (2000E)

Northern Ireland was created in 1921 as an autonomous component of the United Kingdom of Great Britain and Northern Ireland, its territory comprising six counties (four with a Protestant majority) of the historic nine-county Irish province of Ulster. Amid a descent into sectarian violence between Protestants and the Catholic minority and the launching by the Irish Republican Army (IRA) of an armed campaign against British rule, the Northern Ireland parliament was suspended in 1972. For the next 27 years (apart from a brief period in 1974) Northern Ireland was ruled directly from Westminster, the responsible member of the UK Cabinet being the Secretary of State for Northern Ireland. However, the multi-party Good Friday Agreement signed in Belfast on April 10, 1998, provided for the restoration of a Northern Ireland legislature and government (executive) with substantial economic and social powers, the executive to be constituted under power-sharing arrangements giving all major parties representation.

Elections to a new Northern Ireland Assembly were held on June 25, 1998, the 108 seats being filled by the single transferable vote method in 18 six-member constituencies, as follows: Ulster Unionist Party (UUP) 28 seats (with 21.3% of the vote), Social Democratic and Labour Party (SDLP) 24 (22.0%), Democratic Unionist Party (DUP) 20 (18.1%), *Sinn Féin* 18 (17.6%), Alliance Party of Northern Ireland 6 (6.5%), United Kingdom Unionist Party 5 (4.5%), Independent Unionists 3 (3.0%), Progressive Unionist Party 2 (2.5%), Northern Ireland Women's Coalition 2 (1.6%).

A year and a half later, on Dec. 2, 1999, the new power-sharing executive was formally established, whereupon the Irish government promulgated amendments to the Republic's 1937 constitution (approved by referendum on May 22, 1998) formally enshrining the principle of popular consent to any change in the status of the North. Also inaugurated on Dec. 2, 1999, were a consultative North–South Ministerial Council, a re-launched UK-Irish Intergovernmental Council and a "Council of the Isles" (representing the parliaments of the UK, the Irish Republic, Northern Ireland, Scotland, Wales, the Channel Islands and the Isle of Man).

In the UK general elections of June 7, 2001, the 18 Northern Ireland seats (filled by simple majority in single-member constituencies) were distributed as follows: UUP 6 (with 26.8% of the Northern Ireland vote), DUP 5 (22.5%), *Sinn Féin* 4 (21.7%), SDLP 3 (21.0%).

The operation of the power-sharing executive was subject to recurrent crises and it was suspended by the British government for three months in 2000 and twice for brief periods in 2001. In the face of the intended resignation of David Trimble as First Minister, the British government suspended the Northern Ireland Assembly and executive on Oct. 14, 2002, and the bodies have not functioned since that time. Plans for further elections to the Assembly were twice postponed in 2003 in the face of evidence of unravelling support for the Good Friday Agreement (although there was continued general observance of ceasefires). When elections were finally staged on Nov. 26, 2003, they resulted in a sharp polarization of the communities. The DUP emerged as the largest party with 30 seats at the expense of the UUP, which took 27 seats (the DUP further consolidating its position with 3 defections from the UUP in January 2004). *Sinn Féin* in turn, in winning 24 seats displaced the moderate nationalist SDLP (18 seats) as the leading party representing the Catholic community. The results created an impasse which made formation of a power-sharing executive impossible and direct rule from Westminster remained in force.

Alliance Party of Northern Ireland (Alliance/APNI)

Address. 88 University Street, Belfast, BT7 1HE
Telephone. (+44–28) 9032–4274
Fax. (+44–28) 9033–3147
Email. alliance@allianceparty.org
Website. www.allianceparty.org
Leadership. David Ford (leader); Eileen Bell (deputy leader); Stephen Farry (general secretary)

The Alliance Party was founded in April 1970 as a centrist, non-sectarian unionist party, drawing support from the moribund Ulster Liberal Party and the moderate (Faulknerite) Unionist Party of Northern Ireland. It advocates the restoration of a devolved government with the sharing of power between the Catholic and Protestant sections of the community. The party, which has tended to have a mainly Protestant following but Catholic leaders, is generally regarded as a liberal middle-class formation, and is strongly opposed to political violence. It was the only unionist party to support the Anglo-Irish Agreement of November 1985.

Alliance first contested elections in 1973, winning 9.2% of the vote for the Northern Ireland Assembly. In January 1974 it joined a power-sharing executive (provincial government) with Brian Faulkner's faction of the Ulster Unionist Party and with the Social Democratic and Labour Party (SDLP). That executive collapsed in May 1974. In the May 1975 Constitutional Convention elections Alliance obtained 9.8% of the vote, and its support peaked in the 1977 local government elections, when it came third with 14.3%. In the Assembly elections of October 1982 it won 10 of the 78 seats, with 9.3%. In the June 1983 UK general elections Alliance polled 8% of the vote, and in those of June 1987 9.9%.

John Cushnahan, who had succeeded Oliver Napier as party leader in 1984, resigned in October 1987 and was succeeded by John T. Alderdice. In the 1989 local, 1992 general and 1993 local elections the party secured 6%, 8.7% and 7.7% of the vote respectively. It fell to 4.1% in the 1994 European polls but recovered to 6.5% in the 1996 Forum elections. Strongly supportive of the April 1998 Good Friday Agreement, the party again won 6.5% of the vote in the June 1998 Assembly elections, which gave it six seats, insufficient for representation on the new power-sharing executive. Sean Neeson was elected party leader in September 1998 after Lord Alderdice (as he now was) had resigned on his appointment as initial presiding officer (speaker) of the new Assembly. In the June 2001 UK general elections Alliance fielded 10 candidates, who took 3.6% of the Northern Ireland vote without winning a seat. Neeson resigned as party leader in September 2001 to be replaced by David Ford. In the November 2003 Assembly elections the Alliance again took six seats, though its share of the first preference votes declined sharply to 3.7%.

Alliance is a full member of the Liberal International, which it joined in 1991, and of the European Liberal Democratic and Reformist Party (ELDR). It has had close relations, but no organic link, with the Liberal Party in Great Britain, and subsequently with the Liberal Democrats.

Democratic Unionist Party (DUP)

Address. 91 Dundela Avenue, Belfast, BT4 3BU
Telephone. (+44–28) 9047–1155
Fax. (+44–28) 9047–1797
Email. info@dup.org.uk
Website. www.dup.org.uk
Leadership. Rev. Ian Richard Kyle Paisley (leader); Peter Robinson (deputy leader)

The DUP is a loyalist party closely identified with its leader's brand of fundamentalist Protestantism and drawing its main support from the urban working class and small farmers. The DUP is more populist than the Ulster Unionist Party (UUP, formerly OUP). It is vehemently opposed to any involvement of the Dublin government, which it regards as alien and Catholic-controlled, in the administration of the North. It also opposes the European Union, which it has denounced as a Catholic conspiracy, although the party has accepted representation in the European Parliament.

The holder of an honorary doctorate from the Bob Jones University of South Carolina (USA), Paisley founded and leads the Free Presbyterian Church, a fiery sect which provides much of the DUP's core support. He was also founder and leader of the DUP's predecessor, the Protestant Unionist Party (PUP), which was formed in 1969 (by the amalgamation of the Ulster Constitution Defence Committee with Ulster Protestant Action) and which in 1970 won two seats in the Northern Ireland parliament and one in the UK parliament. The DUP was founded in 1971 (then being formally known as the Ulster Democratic Unionist Party, UDUP) and won eight of the 78 seats in the Northern Ireland Assembly in 1973. Paisley was re-elected to the UK House of Commons in February and October 1974, when the DUP and other groups combined as the United Ulster Unionist Council (UUUC). He was re-elected in 1979, when the DUP gained two other seats, and in the same year Paisley was elected to the European Parliament. In 1975–76 the party held 12 of the 46 UUUC seats in the inconclusive Northern Ireland Constitutional Convention.

In the October 1982 elections to a Northern Ireland Assembly the DUP secured 21 of the 78 seats (with 23% of the vote). The DUP's Westminster MPs, re-elected in 1983 (when the party secured 20% of the vote), resigned their seats along with their OUP colleagues in January 1986, forcing by-elections as a form of referendum on the 1985 Anglo-Irish Agreement: all three held their seats, as they did in the June 1987 UK general elections, when the DUP declined to 11.7% (having agreed not to contest any OUP-held seats). Peter Robinson, who had lost prestige in unionist circles by paying a fine imposed for participating in a riot in the Republic of Ireland, resigned after seven years as deputy leader in October 1987, but was re-appointed in early 1988.

In the 1992 UK general elections the DUP increased its vote to 13.1%, retaining its three MPs, and in 1993 it won 17.2% in local elections (down from 17.7% in 1989). After the IRA ceasefire first declared in 1994 and reinstated in 1996, the DUP resolutely opposed any negotiations by political parties or government representatives with *Sinn Féin*. In the 1996 Forum elections it increased its vote to 18.8%, winning 24 of the 110 seats.

The DUP slipped to two seats and a 12.3% vote share in the UK general elections in May 1997. It refused to participate in the negotiations that produced the Good Friday Agreement of April 1998 and claimed that only a minority of Protestants had endorsed it in the referendum held in May 1998. In the June 1998 Assembly elections the DUP won 18.0% of the vote and 20 of the 108 seats, therefore becoming entitled to two posts in the new power-sharing executive. In the June 1999 European elections the DUP again won one seat (heading the Northern Ireland poll with 28.0% of the vote). Having called unsuccessfully for the expulsion of *Sinn Féin* from the peace process, the two DUP ministers (Peter Robinson and Nigel Dodds), took their seats when the executive was eventually inaugurated in December 1999, although they refused to sit in meetings with *Sinn Féin* representatives.

In the June 2001 UK general elections the DUP advanced strongly to five Commons seats and 22.5% of the Northern Ireland vote, its gains being at the expense of the UUP. In October 2001 Paisley and other DUP leaders were entirely unconvinced by the long-delayed start of arms decommissioning by the IRA, but the DUP nonetheless agreed to nominate ministers for the power-sharing executive, allowing the four-party executive to be restored. The DUP's scepticism was shared by a significant proportion of the loyalist electorate, pushing the Ulster Unionist Party leadership into more uncompromising positions and leading to the breakdown of the power-sharing executive in October 2002. When new Assembly elections were finally held in November 2003, the DUP benefited from the general perception in the loyalist community that the British government had failed to secure any further meaningful decommissioning by the IRA, and the DUP came out ahead of the UUP, taking 30 seats and 25.7% of the first preference votes. The outcome entitled the DUP to hold the position of First Minister in the executive and *Sinn Féin* that of Deputy First Minister, and the DUP's opposition to any form of collaboration in government with *Sinn Féin* ensured there was no restoration of the executive. The DUP in January 2004 gained a further three Assembly seats with the defection of Jeffrey Donaldson and two other UUP members, and Donaldson also increased its representation in the House of Commons to six seats.

The single DUP representative in the European Parliament is one of the non-attached members. Paisley, 77, stood down as the party's representative in the EP in the June 2004 elections (having been an MEP continuously since 1979) to concentrate on his role in Northern Ireland; he is also an MP at Westminster.

Northern Ireland Women's Coalition (NIWC)

Address. 50 University Street, Belfast, BT7 1HB
Telephone. (+44–28) 9023–3100
Fax. (+44–28) 9024–0021
Email. info@niwc.org
Website. www.niwc.org
Leadership. Monica McWilliams (leader)

The NIWC began as an ad hoc grouping formed to raise the profile of women's issues in the May 1996 Forum elections and the subsequent discussions. It obtained just over 1% of the vote and its regional-list nominees, Monica McWilliams and Pearl Sagar, were among only 14 women elected to the 110–seat body, in which they frequently protested that their interventions were not taken seriously. Strongly supportive of the April 1998 Good Friday Agreement, the NIWC won two seats and a 1.6% vote share in the June 1998 Assembly elections. In the June 2001 UK elections the NIWC fielded only one candidate, who obtained 2,968 votes and in the November 2003 Assembly elections the party's decline was confirmed, it winning only 0.83% of the first preference votes and losing its two seats.

Progressive Unionist Party (PUP)

Address. 182 Shankill Road, Belfast, BT13 2BH
Telephone. (+44–28) 9032–6233
Fax. (+44–28) 9024–9602
Email. central@pup-ni.org.uk
Website. www.pup-ni.org.uk
Leadership. David Ervine (leader)

Formed in 1977 (succeeding the Volunteer Political Party, VPP), the PUP is the political wing of one of the two largest loyalist paramilitary groupings, namely the Ulster Volunteer Force (UVF), and also speaks for the Red Hand Commando (RHC). Although the UVF has been illegal almost since its formation, the existence of the PUP permitted the British government to engage openly in ministerial-level negotiations with it from late 1994, the declared aim of the government being to secure the disarmament of the loyalist groups. It was widely accepted that the electoral system for the 1996 Forum elections, in which the PUP secured 3.5% of the vote and two seats, was designed to ensure representation for the two parties euphemistically described as "close to the thinking of" the loyalist paramilitaries.

The PUP was strongly supportive of the peace process which resulted in the April 1998 Good Friday Agreement, being regarded as the most left-wing of the unionist parties. In the June 1998 elections to a new Northern Ireland Assembly it won two seats on a vote share of 2.5%. In the June 2001 UK elections its two candidates, both unsuccessful, won 0.6% of the Northern Ireland vote. In January 2003 PUP leader David Ervine stated that the UVF and the Red Hand Commando (which by this time were the only loyalist paramilitary groups formally observing the ceasefire) were breaking off contacts with Gen. John de Chastelain's Independent International Commission on Decommissioning (set up in 1997 to oversee paramilitary disarmament) in view of the exclusion of loyalists from secret negotiations between the British government and *Sinn Féin*/IRA. However, in 2004 the UVF continued to officially observe the ceasefire. In the November 2003 Assembly elections the PUP lost one of its two seats, its share of first preference votes falling to only 1.2%.

Sinn Féin (SF)

Address. 53 Falls Road, Belfast, BT12 4PD
Telephone. (+44–28) 9022–3000
Fax. (+44–28) 9022–3001
Email. sinnfein@iol.ie
Website. www.sinnfein.ie
Leadership. Gerry Adams (president); Martin McGuinness (chief negotiator); Mitchel McLaughlin (chairperson)

Sinn Féin (meaning "ourselves" or "we alone" in Irish) is one of a small number of parties active in both jurisdictions on the island of Ireland (see also entry in Ireland chapter). The Northern membership, which forms a majority within the party, is formally integrated in the all-Ireland structure, although a Northern executive deals with matters specific to what the party calls "the occupied area" or "the six counties".

Founded in 1905 as a nationalist pressure group, *Sinn Féin* in 1918 won 73 of the 105 Irish seats in the UK House of Commons, refusing to take them and instead forming a Constituent Assembly for an independent state in Dublin. After the partition of Ireland in 1922 it was the political wing of the militant republican movement, supporting the periodic guerrilla campaigns of the Irish Republican Army (IRA) against British rule. The main party of the Catholic electorate in the North after 1922 was the Nationalist Party, as *Sinn Féin* candidates stood on a policy of refusing to recognize or participate in any of the three parliaments claiming jurisdiction on the island. In the 1955 Northern Ireland parliamentary elections, however, SF won 150,000 votes (some 56% of the Catholic total). The party was banned in Northern Ireland in 1956 (and remained so until 1973).

A period of left-wing activity from 1967 moved *Sinn Féin* to an overtly socialist position, but communal violence in 1969 led to a resurgence of the traditional nationalist tendency. A split in 1970 led to the creation of a "Provisional" Army Council, which rebuilt the IRA to pursue a military campaign against British rule; the political wing of this more militant faction became known as Provisional *Sinn Féin*, to distinguish it from "Official" *Sinn Féin*. The latter group evolved into the Workers' Party, leaving only one *Sinn Féin* and making redundant the Provisional prefix (which was never formally adopted but is still widely used in the abbreviated "Provos" form).

The Provisional tendency portrayed itself through the 1970s as a classic national liberation movement, adopting Marxist rhetoric for non-American audiences, but in fact having almost no party political activity because of its principle of abstention from the institutions of the "partitionist" states. In the early 1980s, however, the movement was transformed by the emotional reaction and mass demonstrations generated by the hunger strikes of IRA (and other) prisoners, and by the election of abstentionist republican (not, formally, *Sinn Féin*) candidates to the Westminster and Dublin parliaments. *Sinn Féin* capitalized on the hunger strike issue to involve a new generation in its political activities, which broadened to include participation in community issues and contesting local and parliamentary elections. It continued to demand British disengagement from the North and the negotiation of a new all-Ireland framework. In 1981 it won the UK Commons seat which had been held by an IRA volunteer, Bobby Sands, who had died on hunger strike.

In the 1982 elections to the Northern Ireland Assembly, SF candidates secured 10.1% of the vote. In the 1983 UK general elections SF won 13.1% in Northern Ireland (43% of the Catholic vote), with Gerry Adams (who had become national leader of SF in 1983) being the only SF candidate elected (and holding to the abstentionist policy). By late 1987 SF had some 60 seats on local councils in the North, having won its first in 1983. In the UK general elections of June 1987, SF received 11.2% of the vote, with Adams holding his seat in West Belfast. In the 1992 elections, however, he lost it to the Social Democratic and Labour Party (SDLP) and the SF vote slipped to 10%.

From January 1988 *Sinn Féin* had a series of discreet meetings with the SDLP, much to the consternation of the unionist camp, which spoke of a "pan-nationalist pact". The contacts were instrumental in bringing about secret negotiations with the British government in 1991–93, and the announcement of an IRA ceasefire in August 1994. During the ceasefire the party sought to become involved in ministerial-level negotiations with Britain and in all-party talks on a new constitutional framework, but the British government and most unionist parties insisted that substantive talks had

to be preceded by the partial or complete disarmament of the IRA. The IRA resumed its bombings in February 1996, following which *Sinn Féin* continued to press for unconditional inclusion in negotiations. It was bolstered by its increased share of the vote (15.5%) in the June 1996 elections to a consultative Northern Ireland Forum (the proceedings of which SF boycotted because of its continued exclusion from constitutional talks).

Sinn Féin scored a major success in the May 1997 UK elections, returning two candidates (Adams and deputy SF leader Martin McGuinness) and securing 16.1% of the vote. Both declined to swear the oath of allegiance and so were barred from taking up their seats (their attempt to obtain members' facilities at Westminster being rebuffed by Speaker Betty Boothroyd). The reinstatement of the IRA ceasefire in July 1997 and the referral of the arms decommissioning issue to an international commission facilitated the inclusion of *Sinn Féin* in peace talks which yielded the Good Friday Agreement of April 1998. In elections to a new Northern Ireland Assembly in June 1998, SF candidates took 17.6% of the vote, winning 18 of the 108 seats, which entitled the party to two seats on the new power-sharing executive. In the June 1999 European elections the SF vote held up at 17.1%, but the party did not gain representation.

On the eventual implementation of the April 1998 accord in December 1999, McGuinness and Bairbre de Brun became the two SF ministers in the new Northern Ireland executive, responsible respectively for education and health. *Sinn Féin* deplored the reimposition of direct rule in February 2000 and welcomed the restoration of the executive 108 days later. It thereafter accused the Ulster Unionist Party (UUP) of seeking to sabotage the peace process by insisting on IRA arms decommissioning as a condition for its continued participation, arguing that general demilitarization was required, applying also to British forces. In April 2001 McGuinness for the first time acknowledged publicly that he had been an IRA commander in the 1960s. This did not harm *Sinn Féin* in the UK general elections in June, when the party outpolled the SDLP by winning 21.7% of the Northern Ireland vote and doubling its seat tally from two to four.

In October 2001 Adams announced that the *Sinn Féin* leadership had urged the IRA to begin arms decommissioning in the interests of saving the peace process. The confirmation within days that the IRA had responded positively was seen as an historic renunciation of armed struggle by the mainstream republican movement. Most commentators related the decision to the Sept. 11 terrorist attacks on the USA and the resultant US denunciation of all forms of terrorism. However, dissatisfaction with the level, pace and lack of transparency of such disarmament on the part of loyalists and the British and Irish governments increased during 2002 and provided the context for the collapse of the Assembly and power-sharing executive in October. Little changed during 2003, but this did not stand in the way of *Sinn Féin* consolidating its position in its own community in the November 2003 Assembly elections, when it came second to the DUP in its share (23.5%) of the first preference votes and eclipsed the SDLP as the leading Catholic party. Although the outcome of the election ensured the power-sharing executive would not be reformed, the DUP refusing to participate with *Sinn Féin*, an informal track of dialogue nonetheless continued in 2004. SF's premier position in the Catholic community was further underlined when in the June 2004 elections it took the European Parliament seat hitherto held by the SDLP.

While committed to the Good Friday Agreement, SF continues to maintain a studied ambiguity in respect of its relationship to the IRA. In recent years British and Irish government officials have repeatedly suggested that a decisive breakthrough on the issue of IRA arms decommissioning was imminent, without such a breakthrough ever being achieved.

The meaning of symbolic acts of decommissioning by the IRA, undertaken after choreographed requests by *Sinn Féin*, has been variously and very differently interpreted by the parties to the conflict. However, *Sinn Féin* insists that it is committed to a peaceful and democratic resolution of all differences and points to the reality of the cessation of all hostilities against British forces – no British soldier having been killed in Northern Ireland since February 1997. The party's elected MPs at Westminster continue to refuse to take up their seats while making use of office space and receiving expenses.

Sinn Féin has no formal international affiliations, although it corresponds with many overseas socialist parties and nationalist movements. It has a particular affinity with the We Basques (*Eukal Herritarrok*) separatist party in Spain. The party's single Northern Ireland MEP (Bairbre de Brun) is a member of the leftist European United Left/Nordic Green Left (GUE/NGL) group; *Sinn Féin* in the Irish Republic also has one MEP.

Social Democratic and Labour Party (SDLP)
Address. 121 Ormeau Road, Belfast, BT7 1SH
Telephone. (+44–28) 9024–7700
Fax. (+44–28) 9023–6699
Email. sdlp@indigo.ie
Website. www.sdlp.ie
Leadership. Mark Durkan (leader); Alasdair McDonnell (deputy leader)

The nationalist, centre-left SDLP was for three decades until the start of the 21st century the main party of the Catholic minority, and has as its long-term objective the reunification of Ireland by consent; it rejects political violence and seeks co-operation with the Protestant majority. It was for some years the only major party in Northern Ireland committed to the maintenance of the 1985 Anglo–Irish Agreement, and to the institutionalization of the Dublin government's advisory role in respect of Northern affairs; subsequently it became a driving-force in the peace process which led to the Good Friday Agreement of April 1998. There are within the SDLP various currents of opinion committed to greater or lesser degrees to traditional nationalism; the social democratic aspect of its ideology has tended to be understated.

The SDLP grew out of the civil rights agitation of the late 1960s; it was formed in August 1970 by members of the then Northern Ireland Parliament. Two of its founders sat for the Republican Labour Party (including Gerry Fitt, also a Westminster MP, who became leader), one for the Northern Ireland Labour Party, one for the Nationalist Party and three as independents. Having rapidly overtaken the Nationalist Party as the main party of the Catholic community, the SDLP participated with moderate unionist members of the Northern Ireland Assembly in the short-lived power-sharing executive formed in 1974. SDLP candidate John Hume was elected to the European Parliament in 1979, in which year he won the party leadership from Fitt (who left the party, lost his Westminster seat and was later appointed to the UK House of Lords). In the 1982 Assembly elections the SDLP won 14 seats, with 18.8% of the vote, but did not take them up because of the opposition of the unionist parties to power-sharing. Hume entered the UK House of Commons in the 1983 elections, when the SDLP's advantage over the radical republican *Sinn Féin* (SF) fell to 4.5 percentage points (17.9% to 13.4%), although it recovered ground in the Catholic community thereafter.

The SDLP won an additional Westminster seat in the 15 by-elections held in Northern Ireland in early 1987, and a third seat in the 1987 UK general elections, with 21.6% of the vote. In the 1992 UK general elections the party took 23.5% of the Northern Ireland vote and captured a fourth seat, winning back West Belfast from *Sinn Féin*. However, Hume's central role in bringing about the IRA ceasefire of

1994–96 and its reinstatement in July 1997, and in persuading *Sinn Féin* to commit itself publicly to a negotiated settlement, proved of more electoral benefit to *Sinn Féin* than to the SDLP. In the 1996 Forum elections the decline in the SDLP vote (to 21.4%) contributed significantly to the dramatic increase in the *Sinn Féin* vote. In the May 1997 UK general elections the SDLP fell back to three seats, although its share of the Northern Ireland vote improved to 24.1%, eight points ahead of *Sinn Féin*.

Strongly supportive of the April 1998 Good Friday Agreement, the SDLP won 24 of the 108 seats in the new Northern Ireland Assembly elected in June 1998, taking a 22.0% vote share. Hume was the joint recipient, with Ulster Unionist Party (UUP) leader David Trimble, of the 1998 Nobel Peace Prize. He was again elected to the European Parliament in June 1999, the SDLP winning 27.7% of the Northern Ireland vote, well ahead of the UUP. In the new power-sharing executive inaugurated in December 1999, Séamus Mallon became Deputy First Minister and three SDLP ministers were appointed, namely Mark Durkan (finance), Seán Farren (higher education and employment) and Brid Rodgers (agriculture).

Through the repeated crises in the peace process in 2000-01, the SDLP consistently called on the IRA to begin arms decommissioning in advance of the general demilitarization (including by the British government) demanded by *Sinn Féin*. This brought it no reward in the June 2001 UK general elections, in which the SDLP retained three seats but fell back to 21% of the Northern Ireland vote and was overtaken by *Sinn Féin*. In September 2001 Hume announced his retirement as SDLP leader for health reasons (although not as a Westminster MP and MEP) and was succeeded in November by Durkan (41). Durkan became Deputy First Minister in the reformed Northern Ireland executive in November 2001, until this was suspended in October 2002. However, in the November 2003 Assembly elections the SDLP saw its share of the first preference vote fall back sharply to 17.0% and its total of seats fall from 24 to 18, and it lost its first place among the Catholic community to *Sinn Féin*, reflecting the renewed polarization of the two communities. The SDLP has arguably suffered from the perception that the British government has come to regard *Sinn Féin* as the more significant interlocutor on behalf of the nationalist/republican community, not least because it, not the SDLP, is the conduit to the IRA.

The SDLP is a full member of the Socialist International. Its representative in the European Parliament formerly sat in the Party of European Socialists group, but the party lost its seat in the Parliament to *Sinn Féin* in June 2004.

Ulster Unionist Party (UUP)
Address. Cunningham House, 429 Hollywood Rd, Belfast, BT4 2LN
Telephone. (+44–28) 9076–5500
Fax. (+44–28) 9076–9419
Email. uup@uup.org
Website. www.uup.org
Leadership. David Trimble (leader)

Dating from 1905, the UUP has traditionally been the largest party of the (mainly Protestant) unionist majority in Northern Ireland, standing for the maintenance of the union with Great Britain, while also accepting in recent years the need for power-sharing with the Catholic minority and a consultative all-Ireland dimension in the governance of the province. Generally conservative on social and economic issues, the party was closely linked for most of its existence with the British Conservative Party, but those ties were considerably weakened during the early 1970s and were terminated as a result of the Conservative Party's commitment to the 1985 Anglo–Irish Agreement.

The original Unionist Party, which with the semi-secret Orange Order mobilized the Protestant majority in north-eastern Ireland in defence of the union with Britain, was founded in 1905. It was the monolithic ruling party from the creation of Northern Ireland in 1921 (by the partition treaty which gave the rest of the country autonomy within the British Empire) until the prorogation of the regional parliament and the introduction of direct rule from London in 1972. During this period of Protestant unionist hegemony, which was challenged from time to time by upsurges of republican violence, the region was ruled by a parliament and government based at Stormont, although it continued to be represented in the UK legislature at Westminster.

The party fragmented in 1970–73 under pressures arising from the agitation of the Catholic minority for civil rights. The faction informally known as the Official Unionist Party (OUP) was the largest and the most successful in claiming historical continuity with the old Unionist Party, whereas the Democratic Unionist Party (DUP) was the only breakaway party to achieve and retain a significant electoral following. James Molyneaux succeeded Harry West as OUP leader in 1974, and was himself succeeded in September 1995 by David Trimble.

During the 1980s the OUP gradually reasserted the original title of Ulster Unionist Party (although legally constituted as the Ulster Unionist Council, UUC) and consistently won a large proportion of parliamentary and local council seats, sometimes in coalition with other unionist parties. In 1982 it secured 26 of the 78 seats in the Northern Ireland Assembly, with 29.7% of the vote; in 1983 it won 34% and 11 of the 17 Northern Ireland seats in the UK House of Commons (losing one in a subsequent by-election). In June 1987 it won nine Westminster seats, with 37.7% of the vote, holding them in 1992 with a 34.5% vote share. In 1994 it held its European Parliament seat with 23.8% of first-preference votes. In the June 1996 Northern Ireland Forum elections it headed the list of successful parties, winning 30 of the 110 seats on a 24.7% vote share.

In the May 1997 UK general elections the UUP advanced to 10 out of 18 seats, although its share of the Northern Ireland vote slipped to 32.7%. The party was a leading participant in the subsequent multi-party peace negotiations which yielded the Good Friday Agreement of April 1998, although a substantial section of the party persistently opposed accommodation with the nationalist minority on the terms proposed and in particular any dealings with *Sinn Féin*. In the June 1998 elections for a new Northern Ireland Assembly, the UUP headed the poll by winning 28 of the 108 seats, but its share of the vote fell to 21.3% because of defections by anti-agreement unionists. In the June 1999 European elections the UUP slipped further to 17.4% of the Northern Ireland vote, although it retained its single seat. Meanwhile, Trimble was the joint recipient, with Social Democratic and Labour Party leader John Hume, of the 1998 Nobel Peace Prize in recognition of their role in the peace process.

Seeking to preserve unionist support for the April 1998 agreement, Trimble subsequently demanded that arms decommissioning by the IRA must precede the creation of a power-sharing executive containing *Sinn Féin* representatives. His eventual acceptance in November 1999 that decommissioning would follow the establishment of the executive was endorsed by the UUP party council, although with significant minority dissent. Trimble became First Minister of the new executive inaugurated in early December 1999, the other UUP ministers being Sir Reg Empey (enterprise and trade), Sam Foster (environment) and Michael McGimpsey (culture and leisure).

During the protracted crises in the power-sharing arrangements in 2000–01, Trimble was assailed both on the unionist side, for "appeasing" the republicans, and on the republican side, for endangering the peace process by insisting on IRA arms decommissioning. In March 2000 Trimble only narrowly survived a challenge to his UUP leadership by hardliner Martin Smyth, while the following month he attracted fierce unionist criticism for proposing that the UUP should end its institutional links with the Orange Order. In a by-election in September 2000 the OUP suffered the humiliating loss of its "safe" Westminster seat of South Antrim to the DUP.

A month before the UK general elections of June 2001 Trimble announced that he would resign as First Minister at the end of June if arms commissioning had not been delivered. His stance did the UUP little good at the polls, its representation slumping to six seats on a 26.8% share of the Northern Ireland vote, with most of its lost support going to the DUP. Trimble thereupon carried out his resignation threat, forcing the UK government to suspend the power-sharing arrangements. The resultant deadlock was broken in October 2001 by the IRA's decision to put a quantity of weapons "beyond use" under the personal supervision of Gen. de Chastelain Significant sections of Trimble's own party, however, joined the DUP in open scepticism as to the meaningfulness of the IRA's gesture and Trimble was only re-elected as First Minister on Nov. 6 by the expedient of members of the the Alliance Party and Northern Ireland Women's Coalition agreeing to be categorized as "unionists" to achieve the required majority. Despite this the executive continued to function through 2002 until October when police raids on *Sinn Féin* offices seemed to confirm unionist fears that an IRA "spy ring" had been operating within Stormont. In response Trimble resigned as First Minister, but before the resignation could take effect, both the Assembly and the executive were again suspended by the British government on Oct. 14. Rumbling discontent among hardliners in the party was reflected when on June 16, 2003, Trimble only narrowly (by 444 votes to 369) won a vote on a motion put forward in the party's council by Jeffrey Donaldson, an inveterate opponent of the Good Friday Agreement, calling on the party to oppose British government policy on the restoration of power-sharing.

When elections to form a new Assembly were finally held in November 2003, they did so in the absence of any further decisive act of arms decommissioning by the IRA, which the British government had earlier in the year insisted was a precondition for the elections to go ahead. The UUP, as the unionist party closest to the British government, inevitably suffered the consequences. The UUP found itself displaced as the leading unionist party by the hardline DUP, taking 27 seats to the UUP's 30 and its share (22.7%) of first preference votes putting it in third place behind both the DUP and *Sinn Féin*. The resultant impasse made it impossible to reform the executive but Trimble rejected calls led by Donaldson for him to stand down as party leader. Donaldson and two other UUP Assembly members then defected to the DUP in January 2004.

The single UUP representative in the European Parliament is a member of the European People's Party–European Democrats group.

United Kingdom Unionist Party (UKUP)

Address. Parliament Buildings, Stormont, Belfast
Telephone. (+44–28) 9052 1482
Email. info@ukup.org
Website. www.ukup.org
Leadership. Robert McCartney (leader)
Not so much a party as the personal vehicle of McCartney, a leading barrister, the UKUP arose to support his successful bid to succeed the similarly independent-minded unionist Sir James Kilfedder as MP for the affluent constituency of North Down after the latter's death in 1995. McCartney, formerly a leading member of the Campaign for Equal

Citizenship, fought the by-election in June 1995 as an independent "United Kingdom Unionist" candidate on a platform of resolute opposition to the involvement of the Republic in the internal affairs of Northern Ireland. Thus he opposed the Anglo–Irish Agreement of 1985, the Downing Street Declaration issued by the UK and Irish governments in 1993 and the post-1997 peace process which yielded the April 1998 Good Friday Agreement. He is identified with hardline unionism and opposed to the line of the Ulster Unionist Party (UUP), although vigorously rejecting the religious sectarianism associated with others of that tendency.

In the June 1996 Northern Ireland Forum elections, McCartney headed a list which became known as the UKUP, although it was not formally constituted as a party. McCartney was the only UKUP candidate elected to a constituency seat, but two regional-list seats went to the curious UKUP pairing of Conor Cruise O'Brien (a former Foreign Minister in the Dublin government representing the Irish Labour Party and latterly a journalist sympathetic to the Northern unionists) and Cedric Wilson (an inveterate protester against "Dublin interference", formerly a member of the Democratic Unionist Party and subsequently founder of the Northern Ireland Unionist Party). McCartney retained his Westminster seat in the May 1997 UK general elections.

Opposed to the Good Friday Agreement, the UKUP won five seats and 4.5% of the vote in the Northern Ireland Assembly elections in June 1998. The party split thereafter, with all the Assembly members except McCartney himself in January 1999 founding the Northern Ireland Unionist Party. In the UK general elections in June 2001 McCartney narrowly lost the North Down seat to the UUP and in the November 2003 Assembly elections McCartney held on to the one UKUP seat, the party taking 0.82% of the first preference vote.

The UKUP describes itself as a sister party of the London-based anti-EU UK Independence Party.

Other Parties

Conservative Party and Unionist Party, an attempt to extend the British Conservative and Unionist Party to Northern Ireland in the late 1980s, following the breakdown of the Conservatives' long relationship with the Ulster Unionist Party. The party in Northern Ireland has failed to achieve a significant following in terms of membership or electoral support. It has constituency associations in several parts of the region, but has local council representation only in the commuter belt of North Down. Despite securing 5.7% in the 1992 general election, and several council seats in 1993, it won less than 0.5% in the 1996 Forum elections. In the 2001 UK elections its three candidates won 0.3% of the Northern Ireland vote and lost their deposits.
Address. PO Box 537, Belfast BT16 1YF
Website. www.conservativesni.com

Irish Republican Socialist Party (IRSP), a small revolutionary formation founded in 1974 by dissident members of the "Official" republican movement (later the Workers' Party). Damaged by allegations of gangsterism and drug dealing, and by frequent and bloody feuding among members of its armed wing (the Irish National Liberation Army, INLA) and between the INLA and other republican groups, the IRSP has never been numerically significant.
Address. 392 Falls Road, Belfast, BT48 6DH
Website. www.irsm.org/irsp/

Northern Ireland Labour. The British Labour Party has not organized or recruited members in Northern Ireland since partition in the 1920s and in recent decades the closest party ideologically to Labour in the province, the Social Democratic

and Labour Party, has been restricted in its appeal almost entirely to the Cathloic community. An independently constituted non-sectarian Northern Ireland Labour Party, with which the British Labour Party had relations, had no significant electoral support after 1975 – by which time most of its electorate had polarized to the unionist and nationalist parties – ceasing to exist in the 1980s, but other locally organized groups using the name "Labour" but with no connection with the British Labour Party were formed. A single Labour Coalition list was put forward in the 1996 Forum elections, but secured only 0.8% of the vote and disintegrated. A Northern Ireland Labour group was launched in May 1999, but had little impact. In 2003, in the face of pending litigation under human rights legislation, the British Labour Party dropped its ban on residents of Northern Ireland joining the party, but it still does not recruit in the province.

Northern Ireland Unionist Party (NIUP), small unionist formation set up in 1999 by four of the five Assembly members of the United Kingdom Unionist Party opposed to the Good Friday Agreement; its two candidates won 1,794 votes (0.2%) in the 2001 UK elections, both losing their deposits. It lost all its seats in the November 2003 Assembly elections.
Address. 18 Woodford Park, Newtonabbey, BT36 6TJ
Leader. Cedric Wilson

Ulster Democratic Party (UDP), founded in the 1970s (as the Ulster Loyalist Democratic Party, ULDP, dropping the second word in 1992) as a political front for the Ulster Defence Association (UDA). The UDA, the leading loyalist paramilitary group and responsible for many hundreds of murders, mainly of Catholic non-combatants, was eventually declared illegal in 1992; by that time the party had established some distance between itself and the parent organization, presenting itself as quite independent. The UDP contested local government elections, securing a handful of council seats by election or defection, but its main role was as a channel of communication with the UDA and the Protestant underclass which supports it. In that capacity it participated in talks with the British government, some at ministerial level, following the loyalist ceasefire declared in October 1994, four months after that of the IRA. It secured only 2.2% of the poll in the 1996 Forum elections, winning no constituency seats, but was accorded two at-large seats under the formula designed to bring the UDP and its associated party, the PUP, into negotiations. It endorsed the Good Friday Agreement. In October 2001, following a number of incidents, the British government ruled that the UDA could no longer be considered to be observing the ceasefire it had announced in October 1994. On Nov. 28, 2001, it was announced that the UDP had been dissolved, reportedly on the ground that most UDA members no longer supported the Good Friday Agreement.

The Workers' Party (WP), a semi-autonomous Northern section of the Dublin-based WP, a Marxist republican party which arose from the "Official" majority faction which remained loyal to the then leadership of *Sinn Féin* in the 1969–70 split, at which time the Northern section of *Sinn Féin* operated under the name Republican Clubs. The associated armed faction known as the Official IRA wound down its activities during the 1970s and was said to have disbanded in the 1980s. The movement's attempts to develop radical anti-sectarian socialist politics in the North, reflected in its change of name to The Workers' Party–Republican Clubs and its subsequent abandonment of the suffix, were hampered not only by the climate of violence in the 1970s and 1980s but by allegations of gangsterism associated with the Official IRA and by factionalism within the political wing. It is no longer politically significant but still compete in elections. Having won 0.4% of the Northern Ireland vote in the

1997 UK elections, the WP ran six candidates in 2001, winning a total of 2,352 votes (0.3%).

Address. 6 Springfield Road, Belfast, BT12 7AG

Telephone. (+44–28) 9032–8663

Fax. (+44–28) 9033–3475

Email. info@workers-party.org

Website. www.workers-party.org

Leadership. John Lowry (regional secretary)

UK CROWN DEPENDENCIES

The three crown fiefdoms of Jersey and Guernsey (the Channel Islands) and of the Isle of Man are historically distinct from the United Kingdom, although to all intents and purposes they are British territory and accepted as being such by the vast majority of their inhabitants and under international law. Legally, both entities are under the jurisdiction of the crown rather than the Westminster Parliament (in which they are not represented) and neither is part of the European Union *de jure*.

Located in the English Channel off the French coast, the **Channel Islands** (capital: St Helier, Jersey; 2000E population: 150,000), consisting of Jersey and Guernsey with dependencies, have been attached to the crown of England since 1106. Each of the two islands has a Lieutenant-Governor representing the British monarch and a Bailiff (appointed by the crown) as president of each of the States (legislatures) and of the royal courts. Elections to the States are not held on British party political lines, although in Jersey some elected members have represented the Jersey Democratic Movement.

Situated in the Irish Sea between Britain and Ireland, the **Isle of Man** (capital: Douglas; 2000E population: 70,000) has been a dependency of the crown for four centuries, but retaining its own laws administered by the Court of Tynwald, consisting of a Governor (appointed by the crown), an 11-member Legislative Council and the House of Keys, which is a 24-member representative assembly elected for a five-year term by adult suffrage and which elects eight of the Legislative Council members. Elections to the House of Keys have involved candidates without official party attribution, although informal groupings exist.

UK DEPENDENT TERRITORIES

The United Kingdom retains sovereignty over 13 overseas territories, of which three (British Antarctic Territory, British Indian Ocean Territory, and South Georgia and the South Sandwich Islands) have no settled population.

Anguilla

The Caribbean island of Anguilla (population: 10,000) was a British colony from 1650 to 1967, when it became part of the new Associated State of St Christopher/St Kitts–Nevis–Anguilla. However, the Anguillans repudiated government from St Kitts, and in 1969 a British commissioner was installed following a landing by British security forces. In 1976 Anguilla was given a new status and separate constitution, formally becoming a UK dependent territory in 1980. Constitutional amendments introduced in 1982 (and in 1990) provide for a Governor (as the representative of the British sovereign) with wide-ranging powers, an Executive Council and a House of Assembly. The Executive Council consists of the Chief

Minister and three other ministers (appointed by the Governor from among the elected members of the House of Assembly), together with the Deputy Governor and the Attorney-General as ex-officio members. The House of Assembly includes seven representatives elected by universal adult suffrage, two ex-officio members (the Deputy Governor and Attorney-General) and two nominated members.

In general elections on March 3, 2000, an alliance of the Anguilla National Alliance (ANA), led by Osbourne Fleming, and the Anguilla Democratic Party (ADP), led by Victor Banks, came to power by winning, respectively, three seats (with 34.1% of the vote) and one seat (10.8%). The Anguilla United Party (AUP) won two seats (12.1%) and an independent took the remaining seat.

Bermuda

First settled by the British in 1609 and located in the western Atlantic, the crown colony of Bermuda, with a population of 62,000, has enjoyed internal self-government since 1968. The Governor, representing the British sovereign, has responsibility for external affairs, defence, internal security and police. Internal executive authority in most matters is exercised by the Premier and the Cabinet, who are appointed by the Governor but are responsible to the 36-member House of Assembly, which is popularly elected for a five-year term. The Governor also appoints the 11-member Senate, including five on the recommendation of the Premier and three on the advice of the Leader of the Opposition.

In the most recent general elections to the House of Assembly on July 24, 2003, the Progressive Labour Party (PLP) retained power by winning 22 seats with 51.6% of the vote. The conservative multi-racial United Bermuda Party (UBP), which prior to its loss of power to the PLP in the 1998 elections had won eight consecutive general election victories, took 14 seats with 48.0% of the vote. Founded in 1963 (and therefore Bermuda's oldest party) and drawing most of its support from the black population, the left-leaning PLP was the runner-up to the United Bermuda Party (UBP) in successive elections from 1968 to 1993. While favouring an end to British sovereignty, the party urged its supporters to abstain in the August 1995 referendum on the principle of independence, which was rejected by a 58.8% majority. Since then the PLP has regarded independence as a long-term goal rather than an immediate objective. The PLP government is pledged to enhancing Bermuda's attractiveness to foreign companies and to maintaining its existing favourable tax regime.

British Virgin Islands

Located in the Caribbean and under British rule since 1672, the 60 or so islands comprising the British Virgin Islands are a crown colony, with an appointed Governor representing the British sovereign. The population is 18,500. Under the present constitution, which took effect from 1977, the Governor is responsible for defence, internal security, external affairs and the civil service. The Legislative Council consists of a Speaker, chosen from outside the Council, one ex-officio member (the Attorney-General) and 13 directly elected members, representing nine constituency seats and four territory-wide ("at large") seats. The Executive Council, chaired by the Governor, has one ex-officio member (the Attorney-General) and four ministers (including a Chief Minister) drawn from the elected members of Legislative Council.

In Legislative Council elections on June 16, 2003, the National Democratic Party (NDP), founded in 1998, gained power for the first time, taking 8 of the directly elected 13 seats, while the Virgin Islands Party (VIP), which had hitherto dominated political life, took the remaining five.

Cayman Islands

Under British rule from 1670, the Caribbean Cayman Islands were governed from Jamaica until its independence in 1962, when the islands opted to remain under the British crown. They have a population of 28,000. The constitution provides for a Governor, Executive Council and Legislative Assembly. The Governor represents the British sovereign and is responsible for external affairs, defence, internal security and the civil service. The Executive Council, chaired by the Governor, consists of three official members (Chief Secretary, Financial Secretary and Attorney-General) and five other members elected by the Legislative Assembly from their own number. The Assembly includes the three official members of the Executive Council and 15 directly elected members.

Elections to the Legislative Assembly have been contested by loose groupings or "teams" of candidates, as well as by independents, but all candidates have been committed to the economic development of the islands and the maintenance of colonial status. The most recent general elections were held on Nov. 8, 2000. Following the elections a group of members constituted themselves as the United Democratic Party to form a government.

Falkland Islands

Situated in the South Atlantic and with a population of 2,200, the Falklands Islands have been under continuous British rule since 1833, except for a brief period in 1982 when Argentina (which calls them Las Malvinas) asserted its claim to sovereignty by military occupation in early April but surrendered to British forces in June. Under the 1985 constitution, the Falkland Islands and their former dependencies (South Georgia and the South Sandwich Islands) are administered by a Governor representing the British monarch. The Governor presides over an Executive Council with two other (non-voting) ex officio members and three elected by and from the Legislative Council. The latter body has two (non-voting) ex officio members and eight elected by universal adult suffrage. Decisions of the Executive Council are subject to veto by the Governor and the British Foreign Secretary.

All candidates elected to the Legislative Council in both 1997 and 2001 stood as independents favouring the maintenance of British status and avoidance of unnecessary contact with Argentina until the latter abandoned its claim to sovereignty.

Gibraltar

Located on the southern tip of the Iberian Peninsula, Gibraltar became a British possession under the 1713 Treaty of Utrecht. It has a population of 34,000. Under its 1969 constitution, the dependency has a crown-appointed Governor exercising executive authority, a Gibraltar Council under a Chief Minister and a House of Assembly of two ex-officio and 15 elected members

serving a four-year term. The franchise is held by British subjects and citizens of the Republic of Ireland resident in Gibraltar for at least six months prior to registration as voters. Each voter has the right to vote for up to eight candidates, which is the maximum number that any one party can present in Assembly elections.

In elections to the House of Assembly held on Nov. 28, 2003, the Gibraltar Social Democrats retained power by taking the maximum eight of the elective seats, an alliance of the Gibraltar Socialist Labour Party and the Liberal Party being allocated the remaining seven – an identical result to the previous elections in 2000.

A major issue in these and earlier elections was the Spanish claim to sovereignty over Gibraltar and the local response to ongoing UK–Spanish negotiations seeking to resolve the dispute. Following the acceleration of discussions between the British and Spanish governments in 2001-02 with the apparent objective of reaching agreement on a form of dual sovereignty, the Gibraltar government in November 2002 staged a locally organized referendum in which almost 99% of Gibraltarians (on a turnout of 88%) rejected any sharing of sovereignty with Spain. Although the UK government stated the referendum had no legal weight, no substantive progress in the talks was reported thereafter.

The **Gibraltar Social Democrats (GSD)**, led by Peter Caruana, was launched in 1989 as a centre–right party advocating that the government should participate in the ongoing UK–Spanish negotiations on Gibraltar, thus differing sharply from the boycott policy of the then ruling Gibraltar Socialist Labour Party (GSLP). The GSD first came into office in 1996, taking the maximum possible eight seats, and it and Caruana have been in government since then. The new Chief Minister took a higher profile in ongoing UK–Spanish exchanges on the territorial issue, while remaining firmly opposed to any concessions to Spain's claim to sovereignty. In the February 2000 elections Caruana led the GSD to a second term, with an impressive 58.3% share of the popular vote. The Caruana government boycotted resumed UK-Spanish talks on the future of Gibraltar, and in November 2002 secured overwhelming rejection in a referendum of any sharing of sovereignty with Spain.

The **Gibraltar Socialist Labour Party (GSLP)** was founded in 1976 (originally as the Gibraltar Democratic Movement) with the aim of "the creation of a socialist decolonized Gibraltar based on the application of self-determination", so that it vigorously opposed Spain's claim to Gibraltar as well as the 1984 UK–Spanish Brussels agreement providing for negotiations on the sovereignty issue. The GSLP finally came to power in the March 1988 Assembly elections, when it won eight seats and approaching 60% of the popular vote. As Gibraltar's new Chief Minister, Joe Bossano reiterated his party's election pledge that a GSLP government would not participate in the negotiating process initiated under the 1984 Brussels agreement. The GSLP was confirmed in power in the January 1992 elections, retaining the maximum permissible eight seats but with a vote share of over 70%.

Economic and other difficulties during Bossano's second term, including lack of any progress on the GSLP's self-determination aim, resulted in a seepage of popular support, amidst worsening relations with London over the rise of drug-trafficking and money-laundering in Gibraltar. In the May 1996 elections the GSLP was soundly defeated by the Gibraltar Social Democrats (GSD), winning seven of the 15 elective seats on a greatly reduced popular vote of 39%. The popularity of the GSD government impelled the GSLP to contest the February 2000 Assembly elections in alliance with the newly organized Liberal Party, with only negligible results in terms of the popular vote. Of the seven seats allocated to the alliance, the GSLP took five, a pattern exactly repeated when the two parties again competed in the 2003 elections in alliance.

The **Liberal Party** was launched in 1998 as successor to the Gibraltar National Party (GNP), which had been founded in December 1991 to promote the idea of self-determination for Gibraltar from a centre-right perspective. Despite rising from 5% of the vote in 1992 to 13% in 1996, the GNP had remained without representation. For the February 2000 Assembly elections the new Liberal Party formed an alliance with the Gibraltar Socialist Labour Party (GSLP), being allocated two of the seven seats won by the joint list and becoming part of the parliamentary opposition to the ruling Gibraltar Social Democrats. It remained in opposition following the 2003 elections. The Liberal Party is a member of the Liberal International and the European Liberals, Democrats and Reformists (ELDR).

Montserrat

The Caribbean island of Montserrat formed part of the British federal colony of the Leeward Islands from 1871 until 1956, when it became a separate dependent territory. Under the 1960 constitution as amended, Montserrat has a Governor who represents the British sovereign and is responsible for defence, internal security and external affairs (including, from 1989, regulation of the "offshore" financial sector in response to a banking scandal). The Legislative Council consists of the Speaker, nine elected representatives, two official members (the Attorney-General and Financial Secretary) and two nominated members. Executive authority in most internal matters is exercised by a seven-member Executive Council, presided over by the Governor and including the Attorney-General, Financial Secretary and four ministers (including the Chief Minister) drawn from the Legislative Council.

The massive eruption of the Soufrière Hills volcano in June 1997 severely disrupted economic and political life, leading directly to the resignation of the government in face of protest against its handling of the crisis. By the end of 1997 about three-quarters of the previous population of some 12,500 had fled from the island. Some returned as reconstruction was put in hand, but regular minor eruptions in subsequent years prevented a return to anything like normalcy.

In general elections on April 2, 2001, the New People's Liberation Movement won seven seats (against two for the National Progressive Party) and thus returned to power after a decade in opposition.

Pitcairn Islands

Britain's only remaining Pacific dependency, Pitcairn Island was settled in 1790 by the mutineers of *The Bounty* and became an official British possession in 1887, together with three nearby uninhabited islands. Under the 1940 constitution, the Governor (since 1970 the UK High Commissioner in New Zealand) represents the British monarch. An Island Magistrate elected every three years presides over the Island Court and the Island Council of 10 members, five of whom are elected annually. There is no party activity among Pitcairn's small and dwindling population of a few dozen.

St Helena and Dependencies

Situated in the South Atlantic, St Helena, which has a population of 6,500, was governed by the British East India Company from 1673 and brought under the con-

trol of the crown in 1834. The constitution in force since 1989, applying to St Helena and its dependencies of Ascension Island and the Tristan da Cunha island group, provides for a crown-appointed Governor and Commander-in-Chief, who presides over an Executive Council, which includes five members selected from among their number by a popularly-elected Legislative Council of 12 members. Elections to the latter in the 1970s and early 1980s were contested on a party basis reflecting differing views on the constitutional future of the islands. More recently, however, there has been no party activity, the most recent elections, in 1997 and 2001, being conducted on a non-partisan basis.

Turks and Caicos Islands

A Jamaican dependency from 1873 until 1959, the Turks and Caicos Islands became a separate British colony in 1962, following Jamaican independence. The population is 14,500. From 1965 the islands were administratively associated with the Bahamas, until Bahamian independence in 1973. Under the 1976 constitution as amended, executive power is vested in the Governor, who represents the British sovereign and is responsible for external affairs, defence and internal security. The Governor presides over the Executive Council, which includes ministers appointed from among the elected members of the Legislative Council and also ex-officio members. The Legislative Council is made up of the Speaker, three nominated members, the ex-officio members of the Executive Council and 13 directly-elected representatives.

In general elections to the Legislative Council on April 24, 2003, the **People's Democratic Movement (PDM)** retained power by winning 7 seats against 6 for the Progressive National Party. The PDM was founded in the mid-1970s, favouring internal self-government and eventual independence for the islands. The party won the first elections held under the 1976 constitution, but then went into opposition following defeat in 1980 on an explicitly pro-independence manifesto. Having overwhelmingly won the 1988 elections, and then lost to the Progressive National Party in 1991, the PDM returned to power in the January 1995 poll, winning further victories in 1999 and 2003.

The Progressive National Party is committed to continued dependent status for the islands. It was the ruling party from 1980 until the suspension of ministerial government and its replacement by a nominated executive headed by the Governor in 1986. This followed a period of domestic political tension in the islands and investigations by a commission of inquiry into political and administrative malpractices. At the 1988 elections, preceding the islands' return to constitutional rule, the PNP suffered a heavy defeat by the People's Democratic Movement. Having been returned to power in 1991, the party retained only four seats in the January 1995 elections and again went into opposition.

United States of America

Capital: Washington DC
Population: 288,000,000 (2004)

The United States of America has under the "separation of powers" laid down in its founding Constitution three branches of national government, the executive, the legislative and the judicial. The President is the head of the executive branch and is elected for a four-year term (for a maximum of two terms): the President nominates Cabinet officers, the heads of government agencies, and federal judges, subject to confirmation (not automatically or always accorded) by the Senate. The legislative branch is Congress, comprising the House of Representatives and the Senate, whose members are elected on a first past the post basis. The 435 members of the House are elected for two-year terms and represent districts of approximately equal population. The composition of the Senate reflects the federal character of the Union, with each of the 50 states having two Senators, elected for six-year terms (with one-third of the Senate standing for re-election every two years). This has the effect that rural states with small populations are comparatively over-represented in the Senate, an imbalance reflected in its somewhat more conservative composition. The judicial branch has at its apex the US Supreme Court. The nine Supreme Court justices are nominated by the President, and their appointments ratified by the Senate, but once appointed enjoy lifetime tenure with considerable powers to strike down and interpret legislation on the basis of a judicial reading of the Constitution. Parallel systems (with small variations) prevail in the 50 states of the Union, in which elected Governors head the executive branch: the degree of autonomy enjoyed by the individual states is constantly under debate, but in general has declined steadily over the past two centuries.

Under the separation of powers the President, although the nation's chief executive, does not necessarily command a majority in either House of Congress. A tradition of bi-partisan agreement underpins the effective functioning of government: when this breaks down over controversial issues and the President cannot win the support of Congress, deadlock may ensue. Equally, although the President does not control the initiation of legislation, he does have powers of veto to override the wishes of Congress. To a degree unaccustomed in many parliamentary systems, therefore, the enactment of legislation is often disrupted. The President may not in the event of an impasse dissolve Congress to call elections (legislators sitting for fixed terms), nor may the Congress vote out a President other than in the extreme circumstance of impeachment and conviction.

Two parties, the Democrats and the Republicans, have dominated the American political landscape (both nationally and at state level) since the middle of the nineteenth century. While numerous third-party challengers have appeared over the years none has come close to threatening the hegemony of the two main parties, which have also enjoyed overall a remarkable parity in terms of office-holding. The parity between the two parties in the national popular vote has been notably pronounced in recent years, although there is great disparity state by state.

Neither of the main parties has an accepted single political leader. Presidential candidates are selected as the outcome of a vigorously contested (other than in the case of incumbent Presidents seeking re-nomination) process of primary elections, state by state, taking place over several months and culminating in a nominating convention, and the presidential nomination is sometimes won by an individual who emerges from comparative obscurity. Traditionally presidential aspirants have often built a successful run for their party's nomination from a base in state rather than national politics, with four of the last five Presidents having been former state

Governors who had never sat in Congress. Similarly, Presidents select their Cabinet members from a disparate constituency (sometimes including individuals with a non-partisan background), rather than from among a coherent party leadership. It is in consequence difficult to ascribe a clear policy programme to the major US parties in the way that is possible in the majority of developed democratic countries that have straightforward leadership structures and national policy-making processes. At the same time party loyalties and machines tend to be notably strong and cases of politicians in the main parties switching allegiance are rare: only seven US Senators have switched parties since World War II. In addition, when a party holds the presidency, the President generally sets a course and defines the image for the party in the country as a whole regardless of the party's internal divisions; it is in the nominating process, and when a party does not hold the White House, that the lack of a single leader is most apparent.

Campaign finance has been a matter of controversy since the Watergate affair of 1972–74 included revelations of large-scale donations by wealthy individuals to the re-election campaign of President Richard M. Nixon. Following Nixon's resignation in August 1974 in the face of a threatened vote of impeachment, Congress enacted comprehensive legislation, aimed at increasing transparency in election financing by limiting both campaign contributions and expenditures. The legislation also provided for public financing of presidential campaigns and established an independent commission to administer the legislation. In 1976, however, citing the first Amendment to the Constitution, which guarantees freedom of expression and association, the Supreme Court threw out the imposition of spending limits in federal elections, other than in the case of presidential candidates who voluntarily accepted public funding. Other aspects of the 1974 legislation were upheld, however, leaving a situation where, in broad terms, campaign contributions were limited (and subject to disclosure) but spending was not. At federal level (elections for the presidency and Congress) the amount an individual could donate to a candidate during a campaign remained fixed at $1,000 from 1974 until 2002. In addition an individual could contribute $5,000 per year to a political action committee and $20,000 per year to a political party.

The significance of the distinction between campaign contributions and expenditures was illustrated in 1992 when billionaire H. Ross Perot took 18.9% of the vote in the presidential election on the basis of a campaign funded mainly from his own personal fortune. In contrast other third-party initiatives have been severely hampered by the need, without strong grass-roots organization, to raise donations in relatively small amounts.

Campaign finance reform assumed renewed prominence in 2000 when it was put onto the agenda by Sen. John McCain (Arizona) in his (unsuccessful) campaign to win the Republican presidential nomination. Particular attention was focused on so-called "soft money", unregulated payments to political parties, nominally for general promotional purposes rather than to support individual candidates, by corporations and individuals. An estimated $500 million in soft money was raised by the two major parties for the 2000 elections, split fairly evenly between the parties, compared with $477 million raised by the Republicans and $270 million raised by the Democrats in (regulated) "hard money". The outcome was the eventual passage in 2002 of the Bipartisan Campaign Reform Act or McCain-Feingold law (McCain's co-sponsor being Wisconsin Democratic Senator Russ Feingold) banning soft money contributions to national parties but raising ceilings on hard money contributions to candidates and parties. This law took effect immediately after the November 2002 mid-term elections. On Dec. 10, 2003, the US Supreme Court by 5-4 upheld the McCain-Feingold law, although the majority opinion observed: "We are under no illusion that [the law] will be the last congressional statement on the matter. Money, like water, will always find an outlet". The legislation doubled to $2,000 per election the ceiling on individual donations per candidate per campaign (with primaries and general elections counting separately). Estimates suggested that $4bn in donations flowed into the 2004 election campaigns, overwhelmingly from individual donations, of which $1.2bn was for the presidential contest.

Parties that win more than 5% of the vote in federal elections are entitled to financial subsidies in the next election. In the 2000 election campaign George W. Bush (Republican) and Al Gore (Democrat) each received $67.6m. in federal funding. In the primaries Gore also received matching funding although Bush declined this in order not to face limits on his spending. In the 2004 campaign Bush again did not take up federal matching funds and this example was also followed by John Kerry.

Following three terms of Republican Presidents (Ronald Reagan 1981-89 and George Bush 1989-93), Bill Clinton won two successive terms for the Democrats (1993–2001). The presidential election held on Nov. 7, 2000, resulted in extreme controversy arising from the closeness of the vote between the two main candidates. According to official results later compiled by the Federal Election Commission based on state reports, the total of votes won by the leading candidates were (in descending order): Al Gore (Democrat) 50,992,335 (48.38%); George W. Bush (Republican) 50,455,156 (47.87%); Ralph Nader (Green candidate) 2,882,897 (2.74%); Patrick J. Buchanan (Reform Party) 448,892 (0.42%); Harry Browne (Libertarian Party) 384,429 (0.36%). No other candidate gained more than 100,000 votes. Total turnout at 105,396,641 was only just over 51%, although this was more than two percentage points higher than in 1996. The number of votes given to the various third-party candidates in 2000 was widely seen as having been depressed by the much anticipated closeness of the vote between Bush and Gore. The 2000 election was the third in a row in which the victorious candidate had taken less than 50% of the popular vote.

It became clear in the immediate aftermath of voting that Gore would narrowly win the popular vote. However, the President is not elected directly but by an Electoral College to which each state sends delegates who by law or convention vote en bloc for the candidate who won the popular vote in their state. The number of Electoral College seats per state is determined on the basis of the combined representation of each state in the Senate and the House of Representatives which means (given that each state has two Senators) it has a small bias in favour of the less populated rural states, where Bush had run comparatively strongly. Attention quickly focused particularly on the exceptionally close race in Florida, which controlled a decisive number (25) of Electoral College votes, all of which would go to the candidate declared the victor in the state. The controversy was exacerbated by the fact that the state Governor, Jeb Bush, was the Republican candidate's brother. On Nov. 8, the Florida Division of Elections reported that Bush had beaten Gore by 2,909,135 votes to 2,907,351, and there then followed a period in which the Democratic campaign sought manual recounts in a series of counties where disputes existed over the reliability of the count, while the Republican campaign resisted such recounts. Over several weeks there was a series of court-ordered partial recounts against a background of suits and counter-suits in state and federal courts brought by the two main parties and others. The controversy was marked by conflicting judgements in both state and federal courts and focused in particular on the issue of whether voter intent could be determined in the case of ballots that had been imperfectly perforated by the voting machines, although broader issues of ballot access also surfaced. On Dec. 8 the Florida Supreme Court (with a Democratic-appointed majority) ordered a lower state court to hand count 9,000 disputed ballots in Miami-Dade County. On Dec. 12, however, the US Supreme Court voted in effect to overrule the Florida Supreme Court, end the counting, and leave Florida's electoral votes with Bush. While the issues decided were nominally largely technical in character, relating to the feasibility of staging an accurate re-count with each ballot assessed equally, the split in the Court was unambiguously ideological, with the five most conservative judges (all Republican appointees) voting to block the recount process altogether, two centre-ground justices taking a middle position that there were serious problems with the recount process but that these potentially could be rectified if more time were allowed, and the two most liberal justices dissenting entirely. While Justice John Paul Stevens, for the liberal wing, declared that the decision would cost "the nation's confidence in the judge as an impartial guardian of the rule of law", the majority decision was immediately accepted by Gore as marking the end of the controversy. The Electoral College went on to award 271 college votes (from 30 states) to Bush while Gore took 266 (from 20 states and the District of Columbia).

The November 2000 congressional elections were also extremely close. In the elections to the House the two parties took an almost identical share of the vote but the Republicans retained a reduced majority, holding 221 seats to the Democrats' 212 (with two seats going to independents). The Senate races resulted in the Democrats and Republicans each holding 50 seats, but with the Republicans retaining effective control by virtue of the casting vote of the Vice-President. This was the first time since 1954 that the Republicans had simultaneously controlled the presidency and both Houses of Congress. In May 2001, however, the defection of a Republican senator to become an independent handed control of the Senate, and the key positions of chairs of its legislative committees, to the Democrats. The Republicans won back control of the Senate in the November 2002 mid-term elections, with 51 seats to the Democrats' 48 (with one independent), though this was not a workable majority for most legislative purposes. In the House contest, the Republicans further increased their majority, taking 229 seats to the Republicans' 205 and with one independent. Commentators have noted that only a small minority of House seats are now considered competitive at election times, partly as a result of aggressive redrawing of district border lines: in the 2002 elections to the 435 seats in the House of Representatives only four incumbents lost to challengers, 200 contests were won by a margin of more than 40 percentage points, and 80 seats were uncontested.

The 2004 presidential election was contested between Massachusetts Senator John Kerry for the Democrats and George W. Bush. The only other candidacy of potential significance was that of Ralph Nader, whose 2.74% share of the vote in 2000 was widely regarded by Democrats as having fatally tipped the balance against Gore. Nader, who ran as an independent other than being backed by the rump of the Reform Party, finally declared his candidacy on Feb. 22, 2004, ignoring Democrat appeals for him not to stand, stating that he wanted to challenge the duopoly of power in Washington, which was "corporate occupied territory". This time, however, a forlorn Nader lacked grass-roots organization, was spurned by many former activists anxious at all costs to defeat Bush by electing Kerry, and was quickly discounted as a factor in the election.

With opinion polls indicating that Bush and Kerry were running neck-and-neck, both main parties put great efforts into encouraging voter registration among what they saw as their own supporters, while many hundreds of lawyers were put on stand-by to file objections to the way the poll had been conducted. The intensity of the election was reflected in the highest turnout (60%) since the 1960s. In the event, however, the result of the election (held on Nov. 2), although close, was clear cut, Bush this time winning the popular vote by a margin of 51% to 48%, without any benefit from Nader taking any significant number of Kerry votes, and reaching the required total of 270 votes in the Electoral College without controversy (ultimately ending at 286 to 252) – Kerry conceding the day after the election. Only three states voted differently than in 2000: New Hampshire, with only 4 electoral college votes, switched to Kerry, thereby joining all the other New England states, while Bush narrowly took Iowa (7 votes) and New Mexico (5) won by Gore in 2000. However, the general position was that states Bush had narrowly won in 2000 (including Florida) came more firmly into the Bush camp while Kerry failed to make hoped for gains in the Midwest. The pattern of the elections showed a consolidation of the geographical patterns seen in 2000, with the West Coast, upper Midwest and North-East going solidly Democrat in the presidential race while the entire South and interior of the country went Republican. The collapse of Nader's campaign and the lack of any other third-party challenge meant that Bush was the first presidential candidate since 1988 to win an outright majority in the popular vote: overall, third-party candidates took less than 1% of the vote, Nader himself winning some 400,000 votes (0.34%) compared with nearly 2.9 million in 2000.

The congressional elections, held at the same time, also showed Republican gains. The Republicans won 19 of the 34 Senate seats up for election, increasing their margin to 55 to 44 (with one independent). In the House, where all seats were up for election, the Republican advantage increased slightly to 231 seats to 200 (with one independent and three seats not immediately decided). The Republicans retained their advantage in governorships, holding 28 to the Democrats' 21 (with one of the 11 contests not immediately decided). The pattern of control of governorships is not an exact match to voting in presidential elections: the Democrats hold the governorships of a number of states in the South and Midwest/Mountain states, while there are currently Republican governors of major urban states that voted solidly for Kerry in 2004 and Gore in 2000, including California and New York.

Democratic Party

Address. Democratic National Committee, 430 South Capitol Street, SE, Washington, DC 20003
Telephone. (1–202) 863–8000
Website. www.democrats.org
Leadership. Terry McAuliffe (national chair); Harry Reid (Senate minority leader); Nancy Pelosi (House minority leader); John Kerry (2004 presidential candidate)

The Democratic Party may be broadly defined as occupying the centre–left of the US political spectrum. Supportive of a free-market economy, the party also places emphasis on equality of opportunity and civil, labour and minority rights. Like the Republicans, however, the Democrats are a broad coalition and the party embraces individuals who in Europe would affiliate to socialist and radical parties as well as those who are ideologically sympathetic to most Republican positions but have a traditional Democratic allegiance.

The Democratic Party traces its origins back to the late 18th century; it adopted the present name and set up the Democratic National Committee (DNC) in the 1840s, making it one of the longest established political parties in the world. However, much of its contemporary character took shape during the New Deal of the 1930s when, under President Franklin D. Roosevelt (1933–45), it initiated a wide range of spending and welfare programmes to help counter economic depression. Since then the Democrats have been identified as the more liberal of the two main parties, with a greater belief in the role of the federal government in combating poverty and discrimination.

In common with the Republicans, the Democrats do not have a single accepted "leader". When the party holds the presidency, the President is the leading individual voice, but the President does not automatically command the support of all or most of his party in Congress. Leading figures in the party tend to be long-standing members of Congress (especially if they chair key committees), and sometimes state Governors, but there is considerable fluidity without a well-defined leadership group. Holders of major Cabinet offices are not necessarily major figures within the party. It is arguable that no Democratic President since Roosevelt has been able to "lead" his party in the way that characterizes British Prime Ministers or German Chancellors.

Internal ideological conflicts within the party climaxed in the 1960s and early 1970s. Under Presidents John F. Kennedy (1961–63) and Lyndon B. Johnson (1963–69), the party addressed the long-ignored issue of Southern segregation and the denial of civil rights to blacks. Since the Civil War the Republicans, as the party of Lincoln, had been anathema to the (white) South: the region had become known as the "solid South" in its allegiance to the Democrats. However, the impact of Democratic sponsorship of civil rights legislation in Washington was to break up Democratic support in the South. At the same time the party was challenged from a "new left" bitterly opposed to Johnson's prosecution of the war in Vietnam and which found increasing numbers of allies on the liberal wing of the party. The 1968 Democratic convention in Chicago was marked by violent division in the conference hall and on the streets and the Republican candidate for the presidency, Richard M. Nixon, went on to secure election on a platform emphasizing his appeal to the non-radical "silent majority". In 1972 a chaotic Democratic convention nominated George McGovern, who stood far outside what had hitherto been the party mainstream and slumped to defeat by Nixon. In 1974 Nixon was forced to resign over the Watergate scandal (which originated in a 1972 break-in at the DNC offices by individuals linked to the White House). Watergate and the legislation it spawned (including sweeping restrictions on the powers of the President and the CIA) marked the high water mark of radicalism, however. The party's successful nomination of Jimmy Carter (President 1977–81) as its presidential candidate in 1976 marked a quest to recover the ideological centre ground and (as Carter, the Governor of Georgia and a peanut farmer, was very much an "outsider" from the Washington political establishment) to re-connect with the concerns of heartland America. From the end of the 1970s, however, the political agenda was set by the newly energized Republican right-wing and the Republicans went on to hold the presidency, under Ronald Reagan and George Bush, through three terms from 1981-93. The Democrats regained the presidency with the election of Bill Clinton in 1992, and in 1996 Clinton became the first Democratic President to be re-elected since Roosevelt.

The Clinton era confirmed a re-positioning of the party. While substantial parts of the liberal social agenda from the 1960s and 1970s have been absorbed by the mainstream Democratic Party (notably in areas such as the treatment of minorities and personal morality) much of the Republican agenda on issues such as taxation, balanced budgets, and freedom of enterprise has also been accepted. Indeed, although Clinton inherited a $290 billion budget deficit he was able, following several years of rapid growth, to leave office with a considerable budget surplus, something the Republicans had previously made a touchstone for political success but failed to achieve. George W. Bush's victory in the 2000 presidential election was notable in that it came against a background where the Democratic contender, Vice-President Al Gore, could point to a record of several years of sustained economic growth, record employment, low inflation and balanced budgets, positive elements lacking when the Republicans re-captured the presidency in 1980. Among the factors suggested as tipping an extremely close contest to the Republicans were distaste for the air of sleaze and scandal surrounding the second term of the Clinton presidency, Gore's lack of charisma, and his late-campaign rhetoric which seemed to be aimed more at traditional Democratic voters than the undecided.

The party's contemporary hard-core base of support lies particularly among minorities, in the inner cities, in older industrial regions, among organized labour and among public sector workers. Although the Democratic Party is not a socialist party its support base closely resembles that of democratic socialist parties in western Europe. The support of blacks (representing 12% of the population) for the party is now overwhelmingly high – in the 2000 presidential election, only 9% of black voters supported George Bush, compared with nearly 40% for Eisenhower in 1956. The party is also the preferred choice of most Hispanics (also about 12% of the population), with the notable exception of Cuban Americans (2004 seeing the election of the first Cuban-American US Senator, a Florida Republican, Mel Martinez). While the business community tends to be heavily Republican in sympathies, it is the custom for big corporations to fund both of the major parties. The AFL–CIO labour confederation is strongly supportive of the party and assists in organizing grass-roots campaigning: it, however, affiliates fewer than 10% of private sector workers and its main strength is in public services, to which the Democrats show much greater commitment than do the Republicans.

Different currents within the party find a degree of formal organization. Most significant is the Democratic Leadership Council (DLC), spearheading the New Democrat Movement that seeks to transcend "stale left-right debate" and define a "Third Way" in politics. Past chairs of the DLC include former President Bill Clinton and former House minority leader Richard Gephardt. An offshoot of the New Democrat Movement is the New Democrat Coalition, which has 74 members in the House and 20 in the Senate. The left-wing of the party associates in the Congressional Progressive Caucus; it is based in the House of Representatives and includes Dennis Kucinich, Jesse Jackson Jr. and House minority leader Nancy Pelosi. The party's conservative wing in Congress includes adherents of the 36-member Blue Dog Coalition, so-named because their views had been "choked blue" in the party before 1994, and who particularly emphasize fiscal responsibility; it lacks major names, however, and most members come from the South and the West. In 2004 Howard Dean formed Democracy for America with the declared objective of increasing grass-roots participation in the party.

A key consideration for the Democrats is ensuring that they attract support beyond their core constituencies by ensuring balanced tickets that reach out to all sections of the country. Although the Democrats have put up presidential candidates from various parts of the country since Kennedy, the only candidates to win have been from the South (Johnson, Texas, in 1964; Carter, Georgia, in 1976; Clinton, Arkansas, in 1992 and 1996). With the two main parties taking very similar shares of the popular vote in national elections since the mid-1990s, the Democrats (as the Republicans) regard it as essential to maximize their support in the centre ground while also ensuring that they mobilize their core constituency on polling day, objectives that can come into conflict as was witnessed during Al Gore's campaign in 2000. Some commentators suggested that John Kerry's New England background was a negative factor for him in the 2004 elections.

With the election of Bill Clinton in 1992 the party gained simultaneous control of the presidency and both Houses of Congress for the first time since the 1970s. At the congressional mid-term elections of 1994, however, the Democrats suffered a major setback, losing control of the Senate and, more dramatically, losing their majority in the House of Representatives for the first time since 1954. The Republicans' control of Congress subsequently enabled them to frustrate unpalatable aspects of Clinton's legislative programme, even though he secured re-election in 1996, and during his second term Clinton was put on the defensive by the Monica Lewinsky affair. This climaxed in the vote of the (Republican-controlled) House in December 1998 to impeach him (requiring a trial before the Senate). However, despite widespread criticism of Clinton's moral conduct within his own party, the effort to remove him from office never (unlike in the Watergate affair) developed any bi-partisan character, without which (a Senate vote for conviction requiring a 2/3 majority) it was bound to fail, given that there were then 45 Democratic and 55 Republican Senators. When on Feb. 13, 1999, the Senate came to vote on the two articles of impeachment (Article 1, perjury before a grand jury; Article 2, obstruction of justice) all 45 Democrats voted for acquittal on both counts and they were even joined by 10 Republicans on Article 1 and five on Article 2. Despite the heated rhetoric surrounding the Lewinsky affair its lasting impact (in contrast to Watergate) was slight; it resulted in no landmark legislation, and it did not result in any major shift in voting patterns in the 2000 elections, where the parties remained very evenly balanced. In the November 2000 elections the Republicans retained control of the House but with a reduced majority; in the Senate the parties were left in a dead heat (50 seats each) but the Republicans retained control by virtue of the Vice-President's casting vote. However, in May 2001 the defection of a Republican senator (who became an independent) handed the Democrats control of the Senate and the key positions of the chairmanships of its committees.

The conflict surrounding the 2000 presidential election underscored the divergence of approach within the Democratic Party and its character as a coalition. To sections of organized labour, some representatives of minorities, and party liberals with a radical agenda, the effort to prevent a Bush victory had an intense urgency as he was seen as a mouthpiece for unrestrained right-wing politics and the big corporations. To these elements of the party Bush's election victory was irreversibly tainted by his second-place in the popular vote, electoral practices that worked against minorities, and perceived bias in the US Supreme Court decision (swung by a majority of Republican appointees) that had effectively handed him the contest. Centrist Democrats, in contrast, including most in Congress, were disinclined to continue the controversy beyond the Supreme Court decision, putting their emphasis on the need for national reconciliation. This latter approach was cemented by the events of Sept. 11, 2001, with the position of the President as national leader and commander-in-chief, rather than a partisan politician, coming to the fore in the "war on terrorism".

The ascendancy of the Bush administration was underlined by the poor mid-term election results for the Democrats in 2002, when they lost control of the Senate and declined further in the House. Thereafter, however, as the Bush administration seemed progressively less sure in both domestic and foreign affairs, the party began to rebuild at the grass-roots, being notably successful in building a campaign war chest for the 2004 elections. Terry McAuliffe, who became DNC chairman in February 2001, was widely credited with having restored the party's finances with a programme of aggressive fund-raising.

The campaign to win the Democratic presidential nomination in 2004 took place with no clear favourite at the outset (and with 2000 candidate Al Gore having announced in December 2002 that he would not run again). Prior to the primaries getting underway, the front-runner in the opinion polls was Howard Dean, the former Governor of Vermont, who galvanized grass-roots sentiment against the war in Iraq, raising substantial campaign funds from small donations over the internet. Dean was endorsed in December 2003 by Al Gore. However, Dean's emphatic anti-war posture and liberal agenda alarmed many in the party who were uncomfortably reminded of the failed candidacy of George McGovern during the Vietnam War. Once the primaries commenced Dean quickly fell away, and ultimately suspended his campaign on Feb. 18 without having won any of the 18 state contests to that point. The first contest, the Iowa caucuses on Jan. 19, set the pattern, with Senator John Kerry of Massachusetts coming in first and Senator John Edwards of North Carolina running second: thereafter Kerry never looked back, winning a succession of victories in all parts of the country while Edwards demonstrated wide appeal to the party with a number of good second places. Kerry had locked up the nomination by March 11, although it was not until early July that he took the step of announcing his choice of Edwards as his running mate. Though a first-term Senator seen as lacking in national experience, Edwards, a youthful-seeming 51 year-old and a fluent-talking former trial lawyer with a relaxed style, brought a dimension to the campaign that the stiff, gaunt and somewhat patrician Kerry, 60, lacked – as well as, it was hoped, strengthening the ticket in the South.

Kerry's campaign was both buoyed and made difficult by the Iraq issue. His own record as a Vietnam veteran who had been decorated but had come to be a prominent opponent of the war arguably gave him appeal to a wide constituency – nonetheless the Republican campaign, with perhaps surprising success (given that Bush had never served in Vietnam, although of age) attacked Kerry as unable to defend America and Republican groups were behind a series of attacks of varying subtlety on Kerry's own combat record in Vietnam, some of which ultimately came to embarrass the President himself. What Kerry could not offer was an unequivocal statement of his own position on Iraq: he had supported the war at its outset and his efforts to distance himself from its difficult course seemed at times uncomfortable. Republicans alternately sought to stigmatise him as a "flip-flopper" who

shifted his ground with changing circumstances (though Kerry's relatively slight legislative record in 19 years in the Senate gave comparatively little ammunition) and an unreconstructed liberal who could not be trustsed with the nation's future.

While aiming to attract disenchanted centre ground voters away from Bush – with an appeal on issues such as economic insecurity (Bush's record on employment standing poorly against Clinton's, with the new era sometimes described as one of "jobless prosperity") and fears of cuts in social security and public services – the Democrat campaign also focused strongly on mobilizing the core vote. Immense effort was put into voter registration campaigns to ensure blacks and low income groups and other core constituencies turned out in numbers on polling day. By the last stages of the campaign there were bitter recriminations over this strategy, with Republicans alleging widespread fraudulent registration.

While the turnout in the election was the highest since 1968, the Democrats failed to gain the advantage from this that they and most commentators had anticipated. The presidential election was essentially a re-run of 2000, only three states shifting their allegiance, but with Bush gaining a clear margin of victory in the popular vote. The Bush victory was this time sufficiently clear-cut to mean that there was no Democratic challenge in the courts. In the congressional race the Democrats also suffered setbacks: the Senate shifted to 55 Republicans and 44 Democrats (with one independent), while in the House the Republicans also further consolidated their majority. A notable result was the defeat of Senator Tom Daschle of South Dakota, the Senate minority leader – the first party leader in the Senate to be voted out since 1952; Louisiana also elected its first Republican senator since the post-Civil War Reconstruction period. However, the Republican advantage in the Senate was still short of the majority needed to give a clear run to all controversial legislation, while Lincoln Chafee (Rhode Island), a survivor of the Republicans' old liberal wing, had threatened to switch parties if Bush were re-elected.

While nationally the presidential contest was close, the election showed a pronounced geographical pattern. Kerry won all the West Coast states (California, Oregon and Washington) as well as the upper Midwestern states of Minnesota, Wisconsin, Michigan and Illinois and every state in the north-east. In Massachusetts Kerry won by 62% to 37%, in New York by 58% to 40%, in California by 54% to 45%. The demographics of the core Democratic constituency were starkly illustrated by the fact that Kerry won the overwhelmingly black District of Columbia by 90% to 9%. Exit polls indicated that, in terms of religion, Kerry won the Jewish vote (overwhelmingly), the Catholic vote was virtually tied and Kerry lost the Protestant and Evangelical vote (the latter overwhelmingly). Kerry won among union households, first-time voters, gays (overwhelmingly) and those with incomes below $50K but lost among those married with children and all higher-income groups. Despite having a Southern senator as his running mate, Kerry lost every state in the South, including Florida, which most Democrats believed they had in reality won in 2000 but been denied by Republican state electoral officials and the US Supreme Court. Most disappointingly for the Democrats, they failed to win the key Midwest state of Ohio, with 20 Electoral College votes, where hopes had been placed on the possible impact of loss of jobs in the state since Bush came to office; instead Bush took the state 51% to 48%.

The outcome of the election suggested that a period of Democratic introspection on how to broaden their electoral coalition might follow, given that the exceptional effort to bring out the vote had been negated by the strengthening of Republican sentiment in wide swathes of the country away from the major cities and areas with substantial minorities. It seemed unlikely, however, that the party, following its defeat by Bush's "moral majority", would veer to the left in the way it had after defeat by Nixon's "silent majority" in 1968.

The Democratic Party is an observer member of the Christian Democrat International and of the Liberal International.

Republican Party

Address. Republican National Committee, 310 First Street SE, Washington, DC 20003

Telephone. (1–202) 863–8500

Fax. (1–202) 863–8820

Email. info@gop.com

Website. www.rnc.org & www.gop.com

Leadership. Ed Gillespie (national chairman), Ann L. Wagner (co-chairman); Bill Frist (Senate majority leader); Tom DeLay (House majority leader); George W. Bush (President of the United States); Richard Cheney (Vice-President of the United States)

The Republican Party represents the centre-right of the American political spectrum. Ideologically it favours small government and fiscal restraint (although in practice often acting as a party of "big government"), free enterprise and conservative social values. In foreign affairs it has traditionally been somewhat less interventionist than the Democratic Party although the isolationist wing of the party, a significant factor immediately after World War II, has been a marginal force in recent decades.

Informally known as the "Grand Old Party (GOP)", the Republican Party was founded in 1854 by opponents of Southern slavery. In 1860 its candidate, Abraham Lincoln, was elected President with the votes of the northern states, with the subsequent civil war between North and South (1861-65) resulting in victory for the North. The Republicans then held the presidency for all but 16 years in the period through to the election of Democrat Franklin D. Roosevelt in 1932, since when the presidency has been fairly evenly shared between the two main parties. The 1930s New Deal also marked a watershed in that thenceforth the Republicans were far more clearly seen as standing to the right of the Democrats. The once prominent progressive wing of the party largely disintegrated or re-located to the Democrats in this period, although to this day there remains a small and increasingly isolated element of what right-wing Republicans refer to dismissively as "Republicans in name only". In the 1960s the allegiance of much of the once solidly Democratic white vote in the South also shifted to the Republicans in protest at the civil rights legislation of the Kennedy and Johnson presidencies.

In 1968 and 1972 Richard M. Nixon was elected on platforms that promised to speak for the "silent majority" at a time of national strife over Vietnam and race, but he was forced to resign in August 1974 as a consequence of the Watergate scandal. His (unelected) successor, Gerald Ford, seen as representing traditional moderate establishment Republicanism, was defeated in the 1976 election by Jimmy Carter. By this time, however, a "new right", in some respects representing an ideological counter-point to the "new left" that had influenced the Democrats over the past decade, was an increasing force in the party. In 1980, former California Governor Ronald Reagan, with the backing of the new right, captured the party nomination and went on to win successive presidential terms (1981–89). "Reaganism", like Thatcherism in the United Kingdom, gave the nation's main conservative party an ideological dynamic that had been lacking for several decades during which the Democrats had set the agenda for change while the Republicans had fought a rearguard action in favour of the status quo. Reagan's successor (from 1989) George Bush (as Thatcher's successor from 1990, John Major), represented a dilution of the more radical and ideological aspects of Reaganism. In 1992 Bush was defeated for re-election by Bill Clinton, who went on to win a second term in 1996 when he defeated moderate Senator Bob Dole of Kansas. In 2000, however, George W. Bush, the Governor of Texas and son of the former President, recaptured the presidency for the Republicans (with Richard Cheney as his running mate for Vice-President) in an election in which he gained a majority in the Electoral College despite taking a smaller share of the popular vote than the Democratic candidate Al Gore.

In 1994, the Republicans won control of both Houses of Congress, substantially weakening the effectiveness of the Clinton presidency. Congressional powers of investigation were subsequently employed to undermine Clinton, culminating in his impeachment over the Monica Lewinsky affair. However, while the threat to drive Clinton from office was often compared with the process that led to the resignation of Nixon over Watergate, the national mood of contentment and prosperity could not be compared with the febrile and self-doubting atmosphere of the last days of the Vietnam War, when many members of Nixon's own party turned against him. When the Senate came to vote on Feb. 13, 1999, at the end of a trial on the two articles of impeachment (requiring a 2/3 majority for conviction) the 45 Democrats voted en bloc for acquittal on both counts, and they were joined by 10 Republicans on one count and five on the other. The fact that the Republicans voting for acquittal came from the liberal wing of the party, including figures such as Olympia Snowe of Maine and Arlen Specter of Pennsylvania, underscored that the Senate had split on grounds of ideological orientation rather than on the merits of the case. The Senate vote reflected the fact that in the country as a whole, the campaign to bring down Clinton had not built a constituency beyond the ranks of those who had previously been implacably hostile to him in any case.

In November 2000, with the election of George W. Bush as President, the Republicans briefly enjoyed simultaneous control of the presidency and both Houses of Congress for the first time since 1954. However, with the Senate tied 50:50, control in the Senate relied on the exercise of the casting vote of the Vice-President. In May 2001 a hitherto obscure liberal Republican Senator, James Jeffords (Vermont), quit the party, saying he would sit as an independent, and as a consequence the Democrats gained control of the chamber, creating potential difficulties for the Bush agenda on a wide range of issues, including appointments requiring Senate approval.

Since the election of Ronald Reagan in 1980 many of the major political issues have been resolved on terms favoured by the Republicans: balanced budgets have become an orthodoxy, as have tax cuts; commitment to a strong military and foreign policy has been renewed; and the worldwide challenge of communism has collapsed. The most potent issues on the political right now tend to be in the areas of domestic social concern and personal morality, such as opposition to abortion, stem cell research and gun controls, and with a dimension of (Christian) religious fundamentalism that sits uncomfortably with the values of suburban voters central to Republican electoral success. While the "Republican landslide" of 1994 was hailed by the right as representing a decisive victory, the realities of the virtual dead heat nationwide between the two parties in vote share over the following years have driven Republican campaign managers to attempt to win the centre ground while not driving right-wing radicals into third-party activity.

In common with the Democrats, the Republicans do not have a single accepted "leader"; individual members of Congress have considerable autonomous influence and principal Cabinet officers are not necessarily leading members of the party. Different streams within the party find representation within a range of pressure groups. The Republican Leadership Council is an independent group of centrist Republicans, established in 1997 to resist the pressure on the party from an "intolerant vocal minority" and seen as a mirror of the Democratic Leadership Council in its association with the party establishment. The Republican Main Street Partnership, founded in 1998, aims to give voice to the "principled but pragmatic centre" within the party: it emphasizes fiscal conservatism but moderation on social issues and has strong support from numerous leaders of major corporations. The Republican Liberty Caucus represents a libertarian, laissez-faire current. The National Federation of Republican Assemblies (the self-declared "Republican wing of the Republican Party") stands on the right and the agenda is also influenced from the right by non-partisan organizations such as the American Conservative Union and Pat Robertson's Christian Coalition, although the latter is a much diminished force. Leading figures often identified with the religious right include former Attorney General John Ashcroft, former Senate foreign relations committee chairman Jesse Helms and former Senate minority leader Trent Lott.

The November 2002 elections resulted in the Republicans regaining the narrow majority in the Senate (51 of the 100 seats) for the new Congress that they had lost with the defection of James Jeffords to the Democrats in May 2001. However, Trent Lott (Mississippi), the Senate Republican leader, was forced to stand down in December 2002 after comments he had made on Dec. 5 at a celebration of Senator Strom Thurmond's 100th birthday, when he regretted the fact that Thurmond had not won his avowedly segregationist campaign for the presidency in 1948. He was replaced by Bill Frist (Tennessee) but the controversy drew attention to the fact that the 108th Congress, which convened in January 2003, included not a single black Republican. The narrow majority in the Senate meant that much legislation in practice ended up blocked, with the Republicans lacking the 60 seats needed to stop regular filibustering and other stalling devices.

In the states the Republicans scored a notable success in October 2003 with the victory in a special recall election for Governor of California of the movie actor Arnold Schwarzenegger, defeating Democratic incumbent Gray Davis. The party was further encouraged by the capture of Kentucky and Mississippi in the gubernatorial elections of November 2003 (adding to the caputure of Alabama, Georgia and South Carolina in 2002) as a result of which it further consolidated its dominant position in the South – although the Democrats won back Louisiana.

The initial impact of Sept. 11 was to consolidate national support behind the President to almost unprecedented levels. This remained true through the war in Afghanistan and the momentum was sustained through to the seemingly effortless overthrow of Saddam Hussein's regime in March–April 2003, President Bush announcing an end to major combat operations on May 1, 2003, with the loss of only 115 US combat personnel. Bush was less vulnerable than had been Tony Blair in the UK to the progressive confirmation thereafter that Saddam had possessed no weapons of mass destruction, as "regime change", not capturing offensive weapons, had always been the main plank of the Bush case for war. He was vulnerable, however, to the mounting perception that the conflict, whose end he had declared prematurely, was becoming a quagmire from which there was no easy exit. Nor was the domestic scene entirely comforting for Bush, as the economy, although generally robust, had failed to generate new jobs (Bush being the first President since Herbert Hoover in the 1930s to end his term with fewer Americans in jobs than at the start), and his tax cuts which had benefited mainly the wealthy had contributed to record deficits. With Bush unable to bask in his successes, and with all polls predicting an intensely close contest,

the Republican campaign in 2004 became increasingly negative in its attacks on the Democratic contender, John Kerry.

Republican anxiety in the final stages of the 2004 presidential contest was palpable, although there seemed every confidence that the congressional result would be positive. In the event, however, the Republican grass-roots effort to mobilize the vote proved decisive, with Bush widening his margin of victory over 2000. Bush racked up big majorities of the popular vote in a wide swathe of states through the South and Midwest and Mountain regions, including 61% to 38% in his own state of Texas, and most critically stretched his narrow lead in 2000 in swing states such as Florida (which this time he won 52% to 47%); however, he took only two states he had not won in 2000 (while losing one) and the result confirmed that the country was profoundly divided between the periphery (the West Coast and North-East and more urban upper Midwest), on the one hand, all of which went with Kerry, and the South and interior on the other. Demographically, Bush won among men (Kerry among women in general, but not among married women), Protestant and Evangelical Christians (overwhelmingly among the latter) and middle and higher-income groups, and his success seemed to confirm the wisdom of the strategy of the chief Bush campaign strategist, Karl Rove, to focus on mobilizing the core vote on social, moral and religious issues.

It remained to be seen how in practice Bush would interpret his victory and make use of his greater strength in the Senate. While the election had tipped towards the Republicans, it had also illustrated that among Democratic activists antagonism towards a Republican President was greater than at any time since Richard Nixon. Furthermore, while the tightness of the race to the very end threw Bush's victory into relief as a success, it would have been an unparalleled defeat in time of war had Bush actually lost. Furthermore, the mobilization of the Republican right-wing grass-roots of itself potentially created expectations that would be hard to deliver. Of particular concern to many on the evangelical wing of the Republican Party was the future composition of the Supreme Court (eight of whose nine justices were over 65): the composition of the Court, more than that of Congress, held the key to future action on social and moral issues such as abortion, gay marriages, and stem cell research. However, the Republican majority in the Senate was too narrow, and a sufficient number of Senate Republicans too centrist, to ensure that nominees to the Court acceptable to the evangelical wing would command assent from the Senate

The Republican Party is a member of the International Democrat Union.

Other Parties

There are numerous US would-be third parties, particularly at the ideological poles. The most successful in recent years have been the Reform Party, the Libertarian Party and the green movement, now crystallized into the Green Party of the United States; each of these has had some influence on the national political agenda (although none has elected a candidate to Washington). The Democrats and Republicans are dominant throughout the country and there are no important regional parties. The listing below includes relevant minor parties with operations or influence beyond the single-state level as well as continuing parties of particular historical interest.

America First Party, formed by a split of Pat Buchanan supporters from the Reform Party in 2004; a right-wing socially conservative party calling for a radical downsizing of the federal government and with an isolatioist approach to foreign policy (hence opposing the US invasion of Iraq). It gained its first elected local official in March 2004 and in the 2004 presidential contest backed the candidacy of Michael Peroutka of the Constitution Party.

Address. 1630A 30th Street, Boulder, CO 80301

Email. info@americafirstparty.org

Website. www.americafirstparty.org

Leadership. Daniel Jay Charles (national chairman)

American Independent Party, originated in California in 1967 as a vehicle for the third-party presidential aspirations of anti-Washington segregationist Gov. George Wallace of Alabama (who won five Southern states in 1968); claiming to have some 300,000 registered members in California it last fielded a presidential candidate in 1980 and is now affiliated nationally to the right-wing Constitution Party; favours small government, abolition of the Internal Revenue Service, disengagement from NAFTA and the WTO, an "America First" non-interventionist foreign policy and ending abortion rights. It supported Constitution Party candidate Michael Peroutka in the 2004 elections.

Address. 8158 Palm St, Lemon Grove, California 91945

Website. www.aipca.org

Leadership. Nancy Spirkoff (state chairman)

American Party, right-wing formation dating from 1972, advocating an isolationist foreign policy, restrictions on the federal government, and an end to gun controls; has declined since the 1970s and its 2000 presidential aspirant failed to get on the ballot in a single state.

Address. PO Box 612, Tooele, UT 84074

Email. liberty@theamericanparty.org

Website. www.theamericanparty.org

Leadership. Arly Pedersen (national chairman); Diane Templin (2004 presidential candidate)

American Reform Party (ARP), formed in 1997 by a faction of the Reform Party (RP) that had wanted to nominate former Colorado Governor Dick Lamm rather than Ross Perot for President in 1996; subsequently attracted supporters of Minnesota Governor Jesse Ventura and other RP defectors; adopted reformist, centrist programme calling for paying down the national debt, reduced immigration, and economic protectionism, but also advocating continued engagement in international affairs, payment of dues to the UN, universal health care, environmental protection and restoration of diplomatic relations with Cuba. In 2000 joined the loose coalition backing Ralph Nader's presidential bid but has failed to establish much continuing organizational identity.

Website. www.americanreform.org

Leadership. Roy Downing (chairman)

Communist Party–USA (CP–USA), founded in 1919 and historically aligned with the Soviet Union (which subsidized the party's operations); at its peak during the 1930s depression and World War II alliance between the USA and Soviet Union, but of negligible influence since then; retains Marxism-Leninism as its "guiding theory". Last put forward a presidential candidate (who took 36,000 votes) in 1984 and currently emphasizes efforts to build a united front of progressive forces against Republican President Bush and the "ultra-right".

Address. 235 W. 23rd Street, New York, NY 10011

Telephone. (1-212) 989-4994

Website. www.cpusa.org

Leadership. Sam Webb (national chair)

Conservative Party of New York State, founded in 1962 to oppose liberalism and collectivism and has had national influence on the American right; runs its own candidates but more commonly endorses favoured candidates from the major parties; claims 170,000 members.

Address. 486 78th Street, Brooklyn, NY 11209

Email. info@cpnys.org

Website. www.cpnys.org

Constitution Party, founded in 1992 as the US Taypayers' Party (calling for abolition of the US Internal Revenue Service) and adopted present name in 1999. This is a right-wing formation that wants to limit the federal government to activities specifically authorized by the Constitution and has a programme shaped by the concerns of the religious right. Howard Phillips, the party's three-time presidential candidate was a leading figure in the ideological "new right" that influenced the Reagan presidency; he took 98,020 votes (0.09% of the total) in the 2000 presidential election. Its presidential candidate in 2004 was Michael Peroutka who was on the ballot in 36 states; he won 130,986 votes (0.11%), coming fifth.

Address. 23 North Lime Street, Lancaster, Pennsylvania 17602

Telephone. (1–717) 390–1993

Fax. (1–717) 390–5115

Email. info@constitutionparty.com

Website. www.constitutionparty.com

Leadership. Jim Clymer (chairman)

Democratic Socialists of America (DSA), established under its present name in 1983 as a coalition of old-style socialists, New Deal progressives and new left elements, including defectors from the old Socialist Party (which had in 1972 become Social Democrats USA); the principal US affiliate of the Socialist International but an insignificant force in domestic politics; does not put forward its own candidates and generally works within the left-wing of the Democratic Party.

Address. 198 Broadway, Suite 700, New York, NY 10038

Telephone. (1–212) 727–8610

Fax. (1–212) 608–6955

Email. dsa@dsausa.org

Website. www.dsausa.org

Leadership. Horace Small (national director)

Green Party of the United States (GPUS), describing itself as a "confederation of state green parties", the GPUS was founded in July 2001 at a national conference of the Association of State Green Parties (ASGP). It is the larger of the two groups using the Green name (see also Greens/Green Party USA) and nearly all state and local Green organizations affiliate to its national committee. The ASGP had itself been created as a network of state green parties in November 1996 as a development from Ralph Nader's first presidential bid, when he took over 700,000 votes. Its membership overlapped with that of the Greens/Green Party USA although ASGP was sometimes seen as the more moderate wing of the movement. In 2000 the ASGP again endorsed Nader as its presidential candidate (although Nader ran with a far wider constituency of support than just the Green movement, including some former supporters of the Reform Party). Nader was on the ballot in 44 states and took 2,882,897 votes (2.74% of the total) on a platform that emphasized opposition to the "special interests", capitalist globalization and the power of big corporations: his success was widely blamed by Democrats as having brought about Bush's narrow victory. The high national profile the Nader campaign created encouraged the ASGP to launch the GPUS. The agenda defined by GPUS leaders included opposition to global corporate power and the IMF, World Bank and WTO; boycotting the major oil companies to force the Bush administration to re-join the Kyoto accord; demanding universal health care; ending the death penalty, and the expansion of local democracy. The GPUS opposed the military campaign launched against Afghanistan in the wake of the Sept. 11, 2001, terrorist attacks in the USA, calling for "international co-operation" to bring the perpetrators of the Sept. 11 attacks before an international tribunal.

In 2002 the Greens won a seat in the Maine House of Representatives but other success at state or national level has eluded them. As of September 2004, 212 Greens held elective office on city councils and other local bodies in 27 states and the District of Columbia, headed by California with 65. Ralph Nader's decision to run again for President in 2004 was endorsed by some individual Greens, but the party instead at its June 2004 convention adopted its own ticket of David Cobb for President and Pat LaMarche as his running mate. Reflecting the collapse of third-party voting in 2004, the Cobb-LaMarche ticket won only 106,264 votes (0.09%) and came in sixth, with Nader and the Libertarian and Constitution party candidates taking more votes.

Address. PO Box 57065, Washington DC 20037

Telephone. (1–202) 319–7191

Email. info@greenpartyus.org

Website. www.gp.org

The Greens/Green Party USA (G/GPUSA), locally based green groups, focusing on community and environmental issues and inspired by the German Greens, formed the Green Committees of Correspondence in 1984, held their first full delegated congress in 1989, and adopted the present name in 1991. The G/GPUSA, which calls itself an "anti-party party", and is more inclined to direct action than electoral politics, has a small membership base and has been seen as the left-wing of the Green movement in its strongly anti-capitalist orientation compared with the Association of State Green Parties, which in July 2001 founded the Green Party of the United States (GPUS). The G/GPUSA backed Nader's 2000 presidential campaign although Nader did not accept its nomination. The 2001 G/GPUSA convention failed to produce the necessary 2/3 majority for merger into the new GPUS but a sizeable proportion of the membership reportedly joined the new party. The two groups remain distinct but the G/GPUSA is the minor organization.

Address. PO Box 3568, Eureka, CA 95502

Email. info@greenparty.org

Website. www.greenparty.org

Labor Party, held its first constitutional convention in November 1998 with backing from some labour unions; campaigning reflects union agenda on issues such as labour law and health care; it has not recently run candidates for office and has made little progress, with the union movement remaining overwhelmingly committed to Democratic candidates.

Address. PO Box 53177, Washington DC 20009

Telephone. (1–202) 234–5190

Fax. (1–202) 234–5266

Email. lp@thelaborparty.org

Website. www.thelaborparty.org

Libertarian Party (LP), founded in 1971 in Colorado, organized in every state, and among the most significant of the various third parties over the last two decades. It represents a distinctive American ideological stream, rooted in traditions of individualism, hostility to big government, and isolationism in international affairs. The LP believes in shrinking the role of the government, including ending corporate and farm subsidies and the complete withdrawal of the federal government from areas such as health, education and welfare. It promises to reduce government spending to a level where income taxes are unnecessary. It is hostile to government interference in personal conduct, opposing gun control laws, compulsory

wearing of seat belts, laws on under-age drinking and street security cameras. It opposes the government's war on drugs saying that this has undermined civil liberties. In foreign relations it advocates a foreign policy based on non-intervention, peace and free trade. It opposes foreign aid as creating welfare dependence in the recipient countries and US involvement in countries such as Iraq and former Yugoslavia, and believes defence spending should be confined to defending the USA. Following the Sept. 11, 2001, attacks on the USA it reiterated its view that the underlying solution lay in US non-intervention internationally, arguing that Switzerland had never suffered a terrorist attack, and opposed the Patriot Act; a poll of LP members showed, however, that most also supported military action against Osama bin Laden on the ground that it was a response to a direct attack on the USA. The 2004 national platform called for a "return to the historic libertarian tradition of avoiding entangling alliances, abstaining totally from foreign quarrels and imperialist adventures" and the party has called for the withdrawal of US troops from the "doomed mission" in Iraq.

The LP at end 2003 had over 600 elected officials at local level but has no current representation in state legislatures and has never won an election for a seat in the US Congress (although its 1988 presidential candidate, Ron Paul, is now a Republican congressman). In the 2000 elections it put up candidates in 255 of the 435 House districts, winning an aggregate of 1.7 million votes. Its presidential candidates have had little impact. The most successful year was 1980 when Ed Clark won 921,199 votes. In 2000, Harry Browne won 384,429 votes (0.36% of votes cast), representing a decline from 1996 when he gained 485,798 votes. The 2004 election saw a further decline, Michael Badnarik taking only 381,270 votes (0.33%) despite being on the ballot in all but two states, though in a year in which third parties were severely squeezed by the intensity of the Democrat–Republican battle, that was sufficient to put him in fourth place behind Bush, Kerry and Nader.

Address. 2600 Virginia Avenue, NW, Suite 100, Washington DC 20037

Telephone. (1–202) 333–0008

Fax. (1–202) 333–0072

Email. hq@lp.org

Website. www.lp.org

Leadership. Michael Dixon (national chairman); Joe Seehusen (executive director)

Natural Law Party (NLP), founded in 1992 by followers of the Maharishi Mahesh Yogi; sees social and economic problems as a resulting from violations of "natural law"; practical policy positions tend to be centrist or ambiguous with emphasis on achieving "harmony" with natural law as the solution. After the Sept. 11 terrorist attacks called on President Bush to train US troops in the "peace-promoting techniques of transcendental meditation". Unlike most Natural Law parties worldwide has had some perceptible political identity: its leader and presidential candidate, physicist John Hagelin (described as "Minister of Science and Technology of the Global Country of World Peace"), won 110,000 votes in 1996; in 2000 he gained support from a disaffected section of the Reform Party, but polled only 83,555 votes (0.08% of the total). Thereafter Maharishi Mahesh Yogi ceased to fund the party and it was officially wound up at national level in April 2004, Hagelin then continuing as the president of a movement called the "US Peace Government".

Prohibition Party (PP), originating in 1869 it has since then run a presidential candidate in every election; in the late nineteenth and early twentieth century the party had great influence in many states; maintains its historic opposition to the commercial sale of alcohol and emphasizes a conservative moral and social agenda. Earl Dodge, its 2000 presidential candidate, appeared on the ballot only in Colorado, winning 208 votes. The party is now split into factions for and against Dodge.

Reform Party (RPUSA), for a period in the 1990s the ideologically diffuse conservative–populist movement inspired by Texas billionaire H. Ross Perot constituted the most significant third-party challenge for decades. It called for paying down the national debt, balanced budgets, electoral and campaign reform, and opposed the North American Free Trade Agreement (NAFTA) as exporting American jobs.

Perot announced on a TV show in February 1992 that he would run as an independent in that year's presidential election if the citizens would put him on the ballot in all 50 states. An ad hoc grass-roots movement, which coalesced as "United We Stand America" (UWSA), aided by heavy spending on advertising by Perot, propelled him to 18.9% of the vote in the November 1992 election. Perot's expenditure from his personal fortune was estimated at $60 million. Perot was thought to have taken votes disproportionately from the Republican candidate, George Bush, thereby contributing to the victory of Democrat Bill Clinton. Following the election, UWSA continued in existence as a "watchdog group" with chapters in every state. In the 1994 congressional elections, in which the Republicans took control of both Houses, Perot urged his supporters to vote for Republican candidates. In September 1995 Perot announced he would assist UWSA supporters to create a Reform Party to challenge the country's two-party structure. In the 1996 campaign, as Reform Party presidential candidate, Perot had the benefit of federal matching funds because of his success in taking above 5% of the national vote in 1992 but was excluded (unlike in 1992) from the live televised presidential debates; he took less than 9% of the vote.

In November 1998 former professional wrestler Jesse Ventura was elected as Governor of Minnesota on a Reform Party ticket, the first time since 1916 that a candidate from a nationally-organized third party had won a state governorship. In 1999-2000, however, with Perot now remaining aloof from its affairs, the party was split by a series of personality and ideological conflicts, with hostile factions claiming to represent the RP nationally. In February 2000 Ventura resigned from the party calling it "hopelessly dysfunctional" and warning that its likely presidential candidate, former conservative Republican commentator Patrick J. Buchanan, was "an anti-abortion extremist and unrealistic isolationist". The party nonetheless went on to nominate Buchanan at its convention in August 2000, although a minority faction held a rival convention which nominated John Hagelin, the leader of the Natural Law Party, who claimed to be the heir to the Reform Party of Perot. Although the Federal Election Commission awarded Buchanan the $12.6 million in matching federal funding to which the party was eligible based on its 1996 electoral performance, Hagelin's backers succeeded in keeping Buchanan off the ballot in some states. Other former RP supporters, in the American Reform Party, backed Ralph Nader, the most left-wing of the main candidates, while Perot himself ultimately endorsed the Republican candidate, George W. Bush. In the November 2000 presidential election Buchanan won only 0.42% of the vote. The result meant that the party would not attract matching federal campaign funds in the next presidential election. In 2002 Buchanan supporters split away to form the America First Party and many state parties disaffiliated, leaving the rump "official" Reform Party controlled by opponents of Buchanan's "right wing radical agenda". For the 2004 presidential election the party endorsed Ralph Nader (who variously appeared on the ballot in some states as the Reform candidate and in others as an independent), but it had ceased to be a force of any significance, its nation-

al convention in August 2004 being attended only by a few dozen people meeing in a motel. Nader, despite Democratic challenges in many states, got on the ballot in 34 states but attracted only 0.34% of the national vote, having no influence on the outcome in any state.
Address. 420½ South 22nd Avenue, Hattiesburg, MS 3940
Telephone. (1-877) 467-3367
Website. www.reformparty.org
Leadership. Shawn O'Hara (national chair)

Social Democrats USA (SDUSA), claiming descent from the Socialist Party (SP) founded in 1901 that had some influence in the early decades of the 20th century when leader Eugene Debs won nearly one million votes running for President in 1912 and 1920; its 1932 presidential candidate, Norman Thomas, took 896,000 votes but thereafter much of its support moved to the New Deal Democratic Party. In 1972 the party, which stood to the right of the contemporary new left movement, adopted its current name; leftists within the SP subsequently formed the Socialist Party USA. The SDUSA is, with the Democratic Socialists of America, one of the two US member parties of the Socialist International but a minor force in US politics; it is close to the liberal wing of the Democratic Party.
Address. PO Box 18865, Washington DC 20036
Telephone. (1–202) 467–002
Email. info@socialdemocrats.org
Website. www.socialdemocrats.org
Leadership. David Jessup (president)

Socialist Party USA, small radical democratic socialist formation founded in 1973 by left-wingers opposed to the renaming of the original Socialist Party as Social Democrats USA; focuses mainly on local and grass-roots activism but puts forward presidential candidates to raise awareness, its 2000 candidate, David McReynolds, winning 5,602 votes.
Address. 339 Lafayette Street, #303, New York, NY 10012
Telephone/Fax. (1–212) 982–4586
Email. socialistparty@sp-usa.org
Website. www.sp-usa.org
Leadership. Greg Pason (national secretary)

US DEPENDENCIES

The achievement of independence by Palau in October 1994 effectively terminated the US government's administration of the United Nations Trust Territory of the Pacific Islands, the other components of which had either achieved full independence or, in the case of the Northern Marianas, opted for US Commonwealth status on the same basis as Puerto Rico. These two territories are covered below, together with the other US dependencies of significance in the Pacific and the Caribbean.

American Samoa

The South Pacific islands known collectively as American Samoa, with a population of about 67,000, form an unincorporated territory of the United States, administered since 1951 under the US Department of the Interior. Executive authority is vested in a Governor, who is popularly elected for a four-year term. The bicameral legislature (*Fono*) consists of a Senate, whose 18 members are chosen for four-year terms by traditional clan leaders, and a popularly elected 21-member House of Representatives, to which members are normally elected on a non-partisan basis. The territory sends one non-voting delegate to the US House of Representatives, with election to this position contested by the (US) Republican and Democratic parties, as well as by independents; the Democratic candidate was elected in November 2000.

Guam

The Pacific island of Guam, with a population of 157,000, is an unincorporated territory of the United States and is administered under the US Department of the Interior. Executive power is exercised by a Governor popularly elected for a four-year term. The unicameral Guam Legislature has 15 members who are popularly elected for a two-year term. The territory elects one non-voting delegate to the US House of Representatives. Political activity mirrors that on the US mainland and is therefore dominated by the Democratic and Republican parties. The gubernatorial election of November 2002 resulted in the election of the Republican candidate, Felix Camacho, with a 55.2% share of the vote. In the November 2002 legislative elections, the Democrats won 9 seats and the Republicans 6.

Northern Mariana Islands

Originally part of the UN Trust Territory of the Pacific administered by the United States, the Northern Mariana Islands voted to become a US Commonwealth Territory in 1975, following which a new constitution came into effect in 1978. The territory has a population of 75,000. One of two US Commonwealth Territories (the other being Puerto Rico), its inhabitants have US citizenship. The territory does not send a delegate to the US Congress but has a "resident representative" in Washington. Executive authority is held by the Governor, elected by universal adult suffrage for a four-year term. The bicameral legislature consists of a directly elected Senate, with nine members elected for four-year terms, and a House of Representatives, with 18 members elected for two-year terms.

The US Democratic and Republican parties have traditionally dominated political activity. Elections held on Nov. 3, 2001, resulted in victory for the Republicans, with their candidate Juan Nekai Babauta retaining the governorship for the party in a four-way race with 43% of the vote, while the Republicans also retained control of both Houses of the legislature. In the November 2003 legislative elections, however, the Covenant Party came first with 9 seats, the Republicans taking seven, the Democrats one and with one independent being elected. The Covenant Party had been founded in 2001 to challenge the dominance of the US-based parties in the territory, its name referring to the 1975 Covenant under which the islands' constitutional status was established; in the 2001 gubernatorial contest the party's candidate, former Republican House Speaker Benigno R. Fitial, came second with 24% of the vote, while the party also secured minority representation in both legislative Houses.

Puerto Rico

The Caribbean island of Puerto Rico (capital San Juan and with a 2001 population of 3,937,000) was ceded by Spain to the United States as a result of the Spanish–American War of 1898 and has had Commonwealth status since 1952. While this status has been often described as one of "free association" with the USA, the US House of Representatives in 1998 concluded that Puerto Rico was in effect an unincorporated territory that did not meet the US or international definition of free association. Although Puerto Ricans have been US citizens since 1917 they do not have a vote in US congressional or presidential elections and are instead represented in the US Congress by a Resident Commissioner, elected for a four-year term, who may vote on committees but not from the floor. The US President is head of state. The head of government is the Governor, who is elected for a four-year term and assisted by an appointed Cabinet. There is a bicameral Legislative Assembly comprising a Senate and a House of Representatives; both chambers are directly elected for a four-year term, with the majority of seats decided by direct election from single-seat districts.

Two parties, the Popular Democratic Party (PPD) and the New Progressive Party (PNP) have dominated Puerto Rican politics since the late 1960s, alternating in power. The principal political issue in Puerto Rico for several decades has been its constitutional status. The PPD favours continued Commonwealth status and the PNP seeks statehood within the USA. The only other party of any current significance is the Puerto Rican Independence Party (PIP), which favours full independence. In 1967, a plebiscite resulted in 60.4% supporting continued Commonwealth status, 39% statehood within the USA, and 0.6% independence. In November 1993, 48.6% of voters opted for continued Commonwealth status, 46.3% for statehood and 4.4% for independence. A further plebiscite was held on Dec. 13, 1998. However, while the PNP and PIP supported the statehood and independence options on the ballot, respectively, the PPD rejected the terminology for the continuation of Commonwealth status. The result was that votes were cast as follows for the main options: 787,900 (50.3%) for "none of the above" (i.e. the PPD's position); 728,157 (46.5%) for statehood; and 39,838 (2.5%) for independence. The 1998 plebiscite was locally organized and the US Congress while endorsing the principle of self-determination for Puerto Rico had not, however, defined what options it was in practice prepared to accept.

The general election held on Nov. 7, 2000, resulted in a clean sweep of victories for the PPD, which won back control from the PNP. The results were as follows: House of Representatives, PPD 30, PNP 20, PIP 1; Senate, PPD 19, PNP 8, PIP 1. The PPD gubernatorial candidate, Sila María Calderón was likewise victorious (taking 48.6% of the vote, compared with the 45.7% taken by the PNP candidate and 5.2% by the PIP candidate) as was its candidate for Resident Commissioner, Aníbal Acevedo Vilá. Voter turnout, at close to 90%, was markedly higher than in the simultaneous national elections in the USA, where only 51% cast their vote in the presidential election.

Preliminary results for the election held on Nov. 2, 2004, indicated that the PPD had narrowly held on to the governorship, with Aníbal Acevedo Vilá taking 48.4% of the vote, compared with 48.2% for the PNP candidate, Pedro Rosselló. However, the PNP gained a resounding victory in the contests for both House (PNP 32, PPD 18, PIP 1) and Senate (PNP 18, PPD 8, PIP 1) while the PNP candidate for Resident Commissioner, Luis Fortuño, was also elected. As Fortuño was the US Republican Party's national committee man in the USA and Acevedo a Democrat, the result was seen as weakening the influence of the Governor in Washington relative to the Resident Commissioner.

New Progressive Party
Partido Nuevo Progresista (PNP)
Address. PO Box 1992, Fernández Juncos Station, San Juan, PR 00910–1992
Telephone. (1–787) 289–2000

Website. www.pnp.org
Leadership. Pedro Rosselló (leader)
Formed in 1967 as a break-away away from the Popular Democratic Party (PPD), since when it has rivalled the PPD as one of the two major parties. It has won the governorship for five four-year terms (in 1968, 1976, 1980, 1992 and 1996).

The PNP since its formation has advocated statehood for Puerto Rico within the USA. It maintains that Commonwealth status deprives Puerto Ricans of the full opportunities and obligations of their US citizenship. In a plebiscite on the issue held in 1967, 39.0% voted in favour of statehood. In a further plebiscite held in 1993 after the PNP returned to office in 1992 the gap narrowed, with 46.3% voting for statehood. However, a further plebiscite held in December 1998 following an intensive campaign by the PNP, showed that the PNP had been unable to capitalize on its then control of the legislature and governorship, the proportion of the electorate favouring statehood remaining virtually unchanged at 46.5%. The US Congress, while acknowledging the right of self-determination for Puerto Rico, has never indicated that it is prepared to accept Puerto Rico's admission as the 51st state and it is generally considered that there is no majority support for such an option in Congress.

The PNP held comfortable majorities in both House and Senate following the 1992 and 1996 elections, but lost control of both chambers to the PPD in November 2000. Pedro Rosselló won the gubernatorial elections of 1992 and 1996 for the PNP, but in 2000 the PNP candidate, Carlos I. Pesquera, lost to the PPD's Sila María Calderón, while the PNP's candidate for Resident Commissioner, Carlos Romero Barceló (a former Governor) was also defeated. Rosselló was again the party's candidate in the 2004 gubernatorial contest, preliminary results indicating he had been very narrowly defeated, but the PNP won control of both House and Senate, taking 32 of the 51 House seats and 18 of the 27 Senate seats.

Popular Democratic Party
Partido Popular Democrático (PPD)
Address. POB 9065788, San Juan, PR 00906-5788
Telephone. (1-787) 721 2004
Website. www.ppdpr.net
Leadership. Aníbal Acevedo Vilá (president); Anibal Jose Torres (secretary-general)
The PPD was founded in 1938 and was the dominant political formation from 1940 until a split in the party in 1968 resulted in the New Progressive Party (PNP) gaining power, since when the PPD and PNP have alternated in office. The PPD won the first election for Governor in 1948 and then held the governorship until it was captured by the PNP in 1968. Since then the PPD has won the governorship for five four-year terms (in 1972, 1984, 1988, 2000 and 2004).

The PPD has traditionally embraced a wide range of views on social and economic issues, including strongly pro-business and pro-American conservatives and left-liberals who favour greater autonomy from the USA, although the majority tend to identify with the Democratic Party in the USA. In the early years the PPD, while emphasizing social and economic reform, favoured independence, but with the onset of the Cold War in the mid-1940s repudiated this position (with disaffected supporters then joining the Puerto Rican Independence Party, PIP) and then became a framer and consistent defender of the Commonwealth status granted in 1952. Perceived benefits of Commonwealth status include automatic US citizenship, federal tax breaks for investors, welfare benefits paid for by the US taxpayer but exemption of Puerto Ricans from federal taxes, a common market with the USA, and US military defence, while also providing sufficient autonomy to enable Puerto Rico to retain its distinctive Hispanic culture and identity. In successive plebiscites (most recently in December 1998) the electorate has, though in 1993

and 1998 by narrow majorities, rejected the quest for statehood favoured by the PNP. In the 1998 plebiscite, the PPD rejected the terminology adopted, which it said was biased in favour of the statehood option, and backed a vote for "none of the above", which won 50.3% of the ballot.

In the 1992 elections the PPD lost control of both the House and Senate to the PNP and failed to recover any ground in 1996. In November 2000, however, the PPD recovered strongly, capturing both Houses and with its candidates being elected for the posts of Governor and Resident Commissioner. Sila María Calderón (the Mayor of San Juan) became the island's first woman Governor. Aníbal Acevedo Vilá was the party's gubernatorial candidate in 2004, preliminary results indicating he had scored a very narrow victory over the PNP candidate, but the party lost heavily in the contest for Senate and House.

Puerto Rican Independence Party
Partido Independentista Puertorriqueño (PIP)
Address. 963 Ave. Roosevelt, San Juan, PR 00920-2901
Email. pipnacional@independencia.net
Website. www.independencia.net
Leadership. Rubén Berríos Martínez (president)
The democratic socialist PIP was formed in 1946 by defectors opposed to the movement of the ruling Popular Democratic Party (PPD) away from advocacy of independence. The PIP regards the status of Puerto Rico as being that of a colony, and campaigns to achieve "national freedom". The independence issue was at its most potent in the late 1930s through to the early 1950s, with terrorist attacks in both Puerto Rico and the USA and widespread detentions in Puerto Rico, but independence is now favoured by only a small minority (being supported by only 2.5% in the most recent plebiscite, held in December 1998). In the 1992, 1996 and 2000 elections the PIP won one seat in both the House and Senate on each occasion, while its 2000 candidates for Governor and Resident Commissioner took just over and just under 5% of the vote, respectively.

The PIP believes that Puerto Rico's status has fostered a culture of dependence on federal welfare payments and tax reliefs for US investors; it argues that statehood for Puerto Rico (as favoured by the PNP) would inevitably be on second-class basis as its per capita income is only one-third of the US average and it is overwhelmingly Hispanic, with only a minority adequately speaking English; likewise it regards the existing Commonwealth status, as supported by the PPD, as an "outmoded remnant of the Cold War" when the USA was concerned that it should ensure control. The party also rejects "free association" on the model of the Marshall Islands, Micronesia and Palau as a diluted form of independence.

The PIP opposes the "militarization" of Puerto Rico and has waged a campaign of non-violent resistance against the Navy's use of the island of Vieques as a bombing range. Following a mass trespass, party leader Rubén Berríos (a law professor) was tried in May 2001 and sentenced to four months' imprisonment; however, in June 2001, US President George W. Bush said the Navy would halt the bombing on Vieques in "a reasonable period of time", an announcement seen as a gesture to the Hispanic vote. In a referendum held on July 29, 2001, on Vieques nearly 70% voted in favour of the immediate and permanent cessation of Navy bombing. In the 2004 gubernatorial election, Rubén Berríos took only 2.7% of the vote while the PIP won its customary one seat in each of the House and Senate.

The PIP is a member party of the Socialist International.

US Virgin Islands

Located in the Caribbean east of Puerto Rico, the US Virgin Islands were purchased from Denmark and proclaimed US territory in 1917. The group is an unincorporated territory administered under the US Department of the Interior and has a population of some 122,000. Executive authority is vested in a Governor, directly elected for a four-year term, and legislative authority in a unicameral 15-member Senate, popularly elected every two years.

The main parties currently are the US Democratic Party and the local Independent Citizens' Movement (ICM), which was founded as a breakaway from the Democratic Party and has held the governorship for periods since 1974. In the November 2002 elections, the Democratic candidate Charles W. Turnbull won a second term, while the Democrats also retained a majority in the Senate. The islands also send one non-voting delegate (currently a Democrat) to the US House of Representatives.

Uruguay

Capital: Montevideo
Population: 3,400,000 (2002E)

The independence of the Republic of Uruguay was recognized in 1830 after a period in which its territory was the subject of a dispute between Argentina and Brazil. Internal politics were then dominated by the struggle between the liberal *Colorado* (red, PC) and conservative *Blanco* (white – or National, PN) parties, giving rise to civil wars throughout the 19th century. The *Colorados* held power continuously from 1865 to 1958 before giving way to the *Blancos*. The illusion that Uruguay was "the Switzerland of Latin America" was shattered when in 1971 laws curtailing civil liberties were introduced to give the army a free hand in fighting the *Tupamaro* guerrillas. Two years later in 1973 the armed forces took power, dissolving Congress and replacing it with an appointed Council of State. Although by 1976 the military promised a return to democracy, their regime of terror continued, with an estimated 6,000 political opponents imprisoned and subjected to torture, of whom some 900 died.

With an eye on eventually transferring power to a civilian government, the military regime drafted a new constitution meant to ensure the army's say in all national security matters. This was rejected by a plebiscite in November 1980. Amidst mass protests, demonstrations and strikes and an economic crisis, the military finally agreed to elections being held in November 1984, which were won by the *Colorado* candidate, Julio María Sanguinetti. His government was marked by a major controversy over whether an amnesty should be given to all military and police personnel accused of human rights infringements, which was finally approved in a referendum in April 1989. The first fully free elections since the coup were held in November 1989, from which the *Blancos* emerged as the winners, with their leader, Luis Alberto Lacalle Herrera, becoming President.

In November 1994 Sanguinetti was elected President for a second time, then presiding over a coalition government between the *Colorados* and the *Blancos*. In November 1999 Jorge Batlle of the *Colorado* Party was elected President in a run-off against the candidate of the Progressive Encounter – Broad Front (*Encuentro Progresista – Frente Amplio*) (EP–FA), Tabaré Vázquez. Batlle won the second round election with the support of the *Blancos*, taking 54.1% of the vote compared with the 45.9% vote for Vázquez. However, the EP–FA in the legislative elections held on Oct. 31, 1999, emerged as the largest party in Congress. The EP–FA won 12 seats in the Senate, against 10 for the *Colorados*, 7 for the *Blancos* and 1 for the New Space (*Nuevo Espacio*). In the Chamber of Deputies the EP–FA won 40 seats, the *Colorados* 33, the *Blancos* 22 and the New Space 4. President Batlle took office for a five-year term on March 1, 2000, leading a coalition government with the *Blancos*.

Under the 1966 constitution, the Republic has an executive President who is assisted by a Vice-President and an appointed Council of Ministers. Legislative power is vested in a National Congress consisting of a 99-member Chamber of Deputies and a 31-member Senate (30 senators plus the Vice-President, who presides over Senate business but is also permitted to vote). The President and Vice-President are elected for a five-year term by direct universal suffrage on a run-off system. The President cannot be re-elected. Under a constitutional reform passed in 1996, parties must choose their presidential candidates by open primary elections that take place simultaneously for all parties on the last Sunday of April of the year of the presidential election. Senators and deputies are elected by proportional representation for fixed five-year terms. Senators are elected from a national constituency and deputies from the 19 departmental (provincial) sub-divisions. Under Uruguayan electoral law, the electorate votes in congressional elections for factions within each party itself. Parties usually present a large number of lists of candidates for the two chambers of parliament and congressmen represent both their faction and their party. Congressional party discipline necessitates coordination between the party's factions. Provincial (departmental) elections take place in May of the year following the general election. Voting is compulsory for all citizens who are 18 or older.

Christian Democratic Party
Partido Demócrata Cristiano (PDC)
Address. Aquiles Lanza 1318 bis, Montevideo
Telephone and Fax. (598–2) 903-0704
Email. pdc@chasque.apc.org
Website. www.chasque.apc.org/pdc
Leadership. Dr Héctor Lescano (president); Francisco Ottonelli (secretary general)
A centre–left party within the Progressive Encounter alliance (alongside the Broad Front), the PDC was founded in 1962. The party was formed as a successor to the Civic Union of Uruguay, a Catholic party founded in 1872. The majority decision to join the Broad Front in 1971 caused a more conservative section to split away and re-form the Civic Union (UC). Like all Broad Front parties, the PDC was banned after the coup in 1973 but was legalized again in July 1984.

In 1988 the Christian Democrats opposed the inclusion of the former *Tupamaros* guerrillas (by now called the National Liberation Movement) in the Broad Front. Soon afterwards, the party had further disagreements with the more left-wing members of the Front when the candidacy of Hugo Batalla (leader of the Party for the Government of the People, PGP) was not approved for the 1989 presidential elections. The Christian Democrats, together with the PGP and the Civic Union, withdrew from the Broad Front in March 1989 and together formed the New Space alliance, which came fourth in the November 1989 general election. The PDC left the New Space and joined the Progressive Encounter alliance in 1994. The PDC has one deputy in the 2000-05 legislature.

The PDC is an affiliate of the Christian Democrat International.

644

Civic Union
Unión Cívica (UC)
Address. Río Branco 1486, Montevideo
Telephone. (598–2) 900-5535
Email. info@unioncivica.com
Website. www.unioncivica.com
Taking the name of a Catholic formation dating back to 1872, the Civic Union originated as a centre-right faction of the Christian Democratic Party (PDC) that broke away when the PDC joined the Broad Front in 1971. In 1989 it joined the Christian Democrat-led New Space alliance.

Colorado Party
Partido Colorado (PC)
Address. Andrés Martínez Trueba 1271, Montevideo
Telephone. (598–2) 4090180
Website. www.partido-Colorado.org
Leadership. Julio María Sanguinetti Cairolo (*Foro Batllista* faction, President 1985-90 and 1995-2000); Jorge Batlle Ibáñez (*1999 Battlismo Radical* faction, President of the Republic 2000-05)
The *Colorado* party has dominated Uruguayan politics throughout most of the country's history. One of Uruguay's two so-called traditional parties, it is a broad-based, catch-all, centrist political force. It is composed of different organized factions with their own leaders, which compete among themselves. The *Colorados* emerged from the 1836-48 civil war and were named after the red flag of one of the warring factions. The party first came to power in 1865 and governed Uruguay uninterruptedly for 93 years. In the early twentieth century its leader and two-term President José Batlle y Ordóñez (1903-07 and 1911-15), introduced a wide-ranging social welfare system. Since then *Batllismo,* as the party's dominant strand came to be known, became associated with welfarism and industrial development. Having lost a national election for the first time in the twentieth century in 1958, the *Colorados* regained power in the 1966 elections and won again in 1971. In 1973, however, the constitutional government was deposed by the military, which then ruled the country for over a decade.

The November 1984 election, which marked the end of military rule, was won by the *Colorado* party and the leader of its largest faction "Unity and Reform", Julio María Sanguinetti, became the country's President. Sanguinetti's most controversial policy was the *caducidad* ("no punishment") law, granting immunity from prosecution to military and police officers accused of gross human rights violations during the period of military rule from 1973-85. Although widely opposed, mollification of the military was uppermost in the government's mind and an amnesty law (*punto final*) was passed by Congress in December 1986 with the assistance of the National Party (*Blancos*).

The *Colorados* lost the November 1989 elections to the *Blancos* but won the subsequent 1994 (Sanguinetti) and 1999 (Jorge Batlle) presidential elections. However, the party failed to gain a congressional majority of its own in both elections, forcing it to forge a coalition with the *Blancos*. The party is divided between a neo-liberal faction headed by President Batlle and a social democratic one, led by former President Sanguinetti. The party has 10 senators (plus the Vice-President) and 33 deputies in the 2000-05 legislature.

Communist Party of Uruguay
Partido Comunista del Uruguay (PCU)
Address. Rio Negro 1525, 11100 Montevideo
Telephone. (598–2) 903-7171
Fax. (598–2) 901-1050
Email. pcu@i.com.uy
Leadership. Marina Arismendi (secretary-general)
Founded in 1921, the PCU was once a major force in the

Broad Front but is now in decline. Unusually for a Latin American Communist party, the PCU remained legally recognized for 52 years and regularly had candidates elected to Congress. The party has also had a strong representation in the trade union movement throughout its history.

In 1971 the PCU set up the Broad Front (FA) in conjunction with 16 other left-wing and centre-left parties and groups, and in the general election of the same year the Communists won two of the 18 FA seats in the Chamber. As a result of the 1973 military coup, the PCU was banned and fiercely persecuted. The party's secretary-general, Rodney Arismendi, was permitted to go into exile in the Soviet Union in 1975 but many other members were subjected to torture in prison. The PCU continued to be the dominant left-wing force in the Broad Front after the restoration of civilian government. It took a major part in the campaign for a referendum on the *punto final* amnesty law and contributed to the Front's success in the November 1989 general election, in which 21 Broad Front deputies and seven senators were elected. However the fall of the Berlin Wall and the dissolution of the Soviet Union caused divisions and splits within the party, which remained under the control its orthodox faction under the leadership of Arismendi's daughter, Marina. The party has since entered a process of decline but remains a well organized and disciplined political force with influence in the trade union movement. It has one senator in the legislature elected in October 1999.

National Liberation Movement–Tupamaros
Movimiento de Liberación Nacional–Tupamaros (MLN)
Address. Tristan Narvaja 1578, C.P. 11.200, Montevideo
Telephone. (598–2) 409-2298
Fax. (598–2) 409-9957
Email. mln@chasque.apc.org
Website. www.chasquenet/mlnweb
Leadership. José Mujica (secretary-general)
The left-wing MLN has its roots in the guerrilla movement of the 1960s and 1970s. Although it is now committed to democratic politics the movement has never renounced its past. It campaigns for radical economic reforms and represents the more left-wing faction within the Broad Front as part of an alliance known as the Popular Participation Movement (*Movimiento de Participación Popular,* MPP).

The MLN was founded in 1962 by Raúl Sendic Antonaccio as the political wing of the *Tupamaros* guerrilla group (named in honour of the 18th century Peruvian Indian leader Tupac Amaru). It was originally concentrated in rural areas, motivated by the plight of the sugar cane cutters (whom Sendic had helped to organize in strikes of 1961-62) and fought for agrarian reform and rural workers' rights. The group switched its attention to the cities in 1966 and became engaged in armed struggle. Between 1966 and 1972 the *Tupamaros* became one of Latin America's most successful urban guerrilla groups.

Following the army offensive launched against them in 1972, and the ensuing military dictatorship, the MLN was virtually annihilated. On the return to civilian rule, all guerrillas were released in an amnesty in 1985, Sendic announcing that the MLN would now be working within the democratic political system. While piloting MLN towards parliamentary involvement, Sendic founded a movement to promote rural reform but he died shortly afterwards. Although at first excluded from the Broad Front, the MLN was finally permitted to join in late 1988. In May 1989 it obtained legal recognition as a political party.

The MLN has become an influential although minority faction of the Progressive Encounter–Broad Front alliance. As part of the umbrella Movement for Popular Participation (*Movimiento de Participación Popular,* MPP) the MLN has 2 senators and 5 deputies in the legislature elected in October 1999.

National Party
Partido Nacional (PN)–Blancos
Address. Juan Carlos Gómez 1384, Montevideo
Telephone. (598–2) 916–3831
Email. partidonacional@partidonacional.com.uy
Website. www.partidonacional.com.uy
Leadership. Luis Alberto Lacalle Herrera (*Herrerista* faction; president of the party's directorate, President of the Republic 1990-95, presidential candidate 1999); Juan Andrés Ramírez (leader *Desafío Nacional* faction); Alberto Zumarán (secretary general)

Like the other so-called traditional party, the *Colorados*, the PN is a catch-all, centrist party composed of several organized factions. Deriving their name from the white flag of one of the factions in the 1836-48 civil war, the *Blancos* were founded by an alliance of rural chieftains (*caudillos*) and urban elites.

With a mainly rural base of support, the National Party was for a long time the permanent opposition party to the ruling *Colorados* and only fully turned to parliamentary politics after an unsuccessful uprising in 1904. The PN did not win national power in the 20th century until 1958, when it obtained six of the nine seats on the then collective executive, the National Governing Council (CNG). The party retained a majority in this collective executive in the elections of 1962. However, in 1966, when the presidential system was reinstated, the PN lost the elections to the *Colorados*. In the 1970s the party began a process of renewal and adopted a left-of-centre programme that appealed to a more modern, urban constituency. The party leader, Wilson Ferreira Aldunate, won the most votes of any single candidate in the 1971 presidential elections, but lost the election under the aggregate party vote system. He was forced into exile after the 1973 military coup. Other reformist PN members who remained in the country suffered persecution and imprisonment. Ferreira Aldunate was imprisoned by the military for six months to prevent him running for president in the 1984 elections but nonetheless he acknowledged the legitimacy of the victory of the *Colorado* candidate, Julio María Sanguinetti, and gave congressional support to his administration. He seemed certain to be the party's 1989 presidential candidate but died of cancer before the election.

For the presidential elections of November 1989, the party selected Luis Alberto Lacalle Herrera, representing the neo-liberal right-wing, as its candidate. Lacalle won the election although with only 37% of the ballot. The Lacalle government's programme of economic liberalization and austerity measures met with sustained opposition not only from the Inter-Union Workers' Assembly–Workers' National Convention (PIT–CNT) labour confederation, which staged numerous general strikes between 1990 and 1992, but also from sections of the *Colorado* Party and even a faction of the *Blancos*.

In the 1994 elections the *Blancos* lost power to the *Colorados*. Lacalle was again the party's presidential candidate in 1999 but fared poorly, coming a distant third to the Broad Front and *Colorado* parties' candidates. He supported the *Colorado* Party candidate Jorge Batlle in the run-off presidential election. In 1999 the party had its worst-ever electoral result taking only 22% of the national vote, resulting in the party holding 22 seats in the Chamber and 7 in the Senate, behind the Progressive Encounter–Broad Front alliance and the *Colorados*. Since 1995 the *Blancos* have served in governing coalitions with the ruling *Colorados*.

New Space
Nuevo Espacio (NE)
Address. Eduardo Acevedo 1615, 11200 Montevideo
Telephone. (598-2) 402-6989
Email. larosa@adinet.com.uy
Website. www.nuevoespacio.org.uy
Leadership. Rafael Michelini (leader), Héctor Pérez Piera

(president), Edgardo Carvalho (secretary)

This electoral alliance was originally formed by the Christian Democratic Party (PDC), the Party for the Government of the People (PGP) and the Civic Union (UC), after the PDC and PGP left the Broad Front (FA) in March 1989 following disagreements over the presence in it of former *Tupamaro* guerrillas, its policies and the choice of presidential candidate for the forthcoming elections.

The New Space alliance backed the moderate campaign of Hugo Batalla, the leader of the PGP, who came fourth in the November 1989 elections with 8.5% of the national vote. The alliance together won nine seats in the Chamber and two seats in the Senate.

In the run-up to the 1994 elections, the PDC left the alliance to join the Progressive Encounter alliance and the Civic Union withdrew to campaign separately. The PGP in turn split and Batalla left the NE to join the *Colorado* Party as Sanguinetti's vice-presidential candidate. A faction led by congressman Rafael Michelini remained the backbone of the NE and came in fourth in the 1994 election. In 1999 Michelini again came fourth, with only 4.4% of the vote, in the first round of the presidential election while the party won one seat in the Senate and four in the Chamber.

The NE is a consultative member of the Socialist International.

Progressive Encounter–Broad Front
Encuentro Progresista–Frente Amplio (EP-FA)
Address. Colonia 1367, 2o, 11100 Montevideo
Telephone: (598-2) 902-2176
Email. info@epfaprensa.org
Website. www.epfaprensa.org
Leadership. Tabaré Vázquez Batlle (party president, presidential candidate 1994 and 1999); Jorge Brovetto (party vice-president), Rodolfo Nin Noboa (1994 and 1999 vice-presidential candidate)

The Progressive Encounter–Broad Front alliance is a broad alliance of left and left-of-centre political forces, based on the Broad Front originally formed to resist the military government. It is currently formed by 19 different political parties and movements although not all its constituent members have congressional representation. The Front has campaigned vigorously against the government's neo-liberal policies but has lately moderated its own political programme to attract centre ground voters.

Founded in 1971 the original Broad Front (*Frente Amplio*) came to consist of 17 parties of such diverse allegiances as the Christian Democratic Party (PDC), the Uruguayan Socialist Party (PSU) and the Communist Party of Uruguay (PCU) plus various dissident *Colorado* and National (*Blanco*) factions. Internal divisions caused by political differences and over the nomination of a presidential candidate led to a serious split in March 1989 and the formation of the New Space. The Front nevertheless scored considerable success in the November 1989 elections: Líber Seregni, its presidential candidate, came third with 21% of the vote. The Front also won the municipal (departmental) election in the capital Montevideo and came third in the congressional elections with 21 seats in the Chamber and seven seats in the Senate. The Front supported a broad campaign against the *Blanco* government's privatization programme and in Congress voted against proposed austerity measures.

By April 1992 the Socialists had displaced the Communists as the dominant grouping in the FA. In parallel, the influence of the popular mayor of Montevideo, the Socialist Tabaré Vázquez grew. In March 1994 he was declared the alliance's presidential candidate.

In 1994 the original Front fought the election in alliance with a dissident *Blanco* leader, Rodolfo Nin Noboa, forming the present Progressive Encounter–Broad Front alliance

(EP–FA). The EP was formed prior to the 1994 election. It is effectively an electoral appendix of the Broad Front with no political influence of its own. The constituent parties in this left-of-centre alliance are the Broad Front (FA), the Christian Democratic Party (PDC), a dissident National Party (*Blanco*) faction led by Rodolfo Nin Noboa (who was the EP's vice presidential candidate in 1994 and 1999) and several small groups with no electoral weight. In an extremely closely fought contest the EP–FA came third in the 1994 presidential election, with 30.6% of the votes, against 32.3% for the winning *Colorados* and 31.2% for the second-placed *Blancos*. The Front also comfortably retained the government of Montevideo and increased their congressional representation

In the 1999 elections the EP–FA broke the *Blancos'* and *Colorados'* historical domination of Uruguayan politics by effectively becoming Uruguay's leading political force after it gathered 40% of the vote in the first round presidential and congressional elections. Vázquez lost the presidential contest to Jorge Batlle of the *Colorados* in a run-off but the EP–FA became Uruguay's largest formation in the 2000-05 legislature, taking 40 of the 99 Assembly seats, and 12 of the 31 Senate seats, on a 40.1% share of the vote.

Uruguayan Socialist Party
Partido Socialista del Uruguay (PSU)
Address. Casa del Pueblo, Soriano 1218, 11100 Montevideo
Telephone. (598–2) 9013344
Fax. (598–2) 9082548
Email. ps@chasque.apc.org
Website. chasque.apc.org/ps
Leadership. Manuel Laguarda (secretary general)
The PSU was founded in 1910 and reorganized after the majority split away to form the Communist Party (PCU) in 1921. The PSU moved to the left in 1959 and became a founder member of the Broad Front (FA) in 1971. Currently the party is divided between its more orthodox left-wing faction and the social-democrat modernizers. One of its leaders, Tabaré Vázquez, became the first left-wing mayor of Montevideo in the November 1989 elections. Subsequently Vázquez became the president of the Progressive Encounter–Broad Front (EP–FA) and the Front's presidential candidate in the 1994 and 1999 elections. Benefiting from Vázquez's popularity and the decline of the Communists, the PSU has become the largest party within the EP–FA with 4 senators and 14 deputies in the legislature elected in 1999.

The PSU is a member party of the Socialist International.

Uzbekistan

Capital: Tashkent
Population: 5,700,000 (2001E)

The Republic of Uzbekistan declared its independence from the Soviet Union at the end of August 1991 and became a member of the Commonwealth of Independent States (CIS) in December of that year. In direct presidential elections on Dec. 29, 1991, Islam Karimov (who had been elected to the newly established post of President by the then Supreme Soviet in March 1990) was confirmed in office, winning 86% of the vote. A new constitution, adopted in December 1992, provided for a smaller legislature, the 250-member Supreme Assembly (*Oly Majlis*), consisting of 83 directly elected members and 167 indirectly elected by local administrative bodies and various citizens' groups.

Elections to the Supreme Assembly were held for the first time in January 1994–January 1995 and were contested by only two parties, of which the ruling People's Democratic Party (PDP) won a large majority of directly and indirectly elected seats. Five registered parties took part in the next parliamentary elections on Dec. 5 and 19, 1999, and each gained representation. The PDP retained a substantial majority, the second-largest bloc being that of the Self-Sacrifice Party, followed by Progress of the Fatherland. However, since all five parties are supportive of government and presidential policies, there is no opposition as such. In 2002 a constitutional amendment provided for a second chamber, to be established in 2004. Members are to be directly elected.

Meanwhile, in a referendum held in March 1995, the electorate had almost unanimously approved an extension of President Karimov's term of office to the year 2000. In a presidential election held on Jan. 9, 2000, the incumbent was credited with receiving 91.9% of the vote against one other candidate, thus being returned to office for a further five-year term. A referendum held in 2002 confirmed an amendment to the constitution whereby the presidential term of office was extended to seven years. The next presidential election is scheduled for December 2007.

Justice–Social Democratic Party of Uzbekistan
Adolat
Address. c/o Oly Majlis, Tashkent
Leadership. Anwar Jurabayev (first secretary)
Adolat was registered as a political party in February 1995, establishing a parliamentary faction claiming to have the support of nearly 50 deputies in the Supreme Assembly. The party advocates greater social justice and the consolidation of democratic reform. In the December 1999 elections it was credited with 11 seats in its own right, but as after the 1994 polling its faction attracted deputies elected without party affiliation.

Liberal Democratic Party of Uzbekistan (LDPU)
Ozbekiston Liberal-Demokratik Partiyasi
Address. c/o Oly Majlis, Tashkent
Leadership. Qobiljon Toshmatov (chairman)
Founded in October 2003, the LDPU was characterized by President Karimov as filling a gap in the political life of the country. The new party, which has a multi-ethnic membership, aims to support entrepreneurs and businessmen. At its founding congress in November a 104-member Political Council was elected.

National Revival Party
Milli Tiklanish
Address. c/o Oly Majlis, Tashkent
Leadership. Aziz Kayumov (chairman)
Including several prominent Uzbek intellectuals, *Milli Tiklanish* was formed in May 1995 (and registered the following month), favouring democracy and the establishment of a law-based state. It was credited with winning 10 seats in its own right in the December 1999 elections.

People's Democratic Party (PDP)
Khalk Demokratik Partiyasi
Address. c/o Oly Majlis, Tashkent
Leadership. Abdulhafiz Jalalov (first secretary)
The PDP was formed under the leadership of President Karimov in November 1991, as effectively the successor to the Communist Party of Uzbekistan (of which Karimov had been the last Soviet-era first secretary). It has since remained the dominant political force, directly or indirectly. One of only two parties permitted to register for the legislative elections in December 1994 and January 1995, the PDP secured a large majority in the Supreme Assembly. Karimov resigned his position as party leader in June 1996, bowing to the view that it was incompatible with that of head of state.

The PDP was less dominant in the official results of the December 1999 legislative elections, returning 48 candidates under its own label, but was again assured of commanding a majority by virtue of support from other pro-government parties and deputies. To give a semblance of democratic competition to presidential elections in January 2000, party leader Abdulhafiz Jalalov was the nominal PDP candidate against President Karimov. It was reported that Jalalov's only appearance was on election day, when he came out to vote for Karimov.

Progress of the Fatherland
Vatan Tarakkiyoti

Address. c/o Oly Majlis, Tashkent
Leadership. Anwar Yoldashev (chairman)
Progress of the Fatherland, formed in 1992 to advocate the development of a market economy, was supportive of the dominant People's Democratic Party (PDP). It was the only party, other than the PDP, permitted to contest the legislative elections in December 1994 and January 1995, gaining 14 seats in the Supreme Assembly. In the December 1999 elections it advanced to 20 seats. This party subsequently merged with the Self-Sacrifice Party.

Self-Sacrifice Party
Fidokorlor

Address. c/o Oly Majlis, Tashkent
Leadership. Ahtam Tursunov (first secretary)
Established in December 1998, *Fidokorlor* came second in the December 1999 legislative elections, returning 34 deputies under its party label. It subsequently formally nominated President Karimov as candidate in the presidential elections held in January 2000. It later absorbed the Progress of the Fatherland party.

Other Parties

Free Farmers' Party (*Ozod Dehqonlar*), founded in late 2003, aims to represent the interests of the peasants. Its primary goal is to reform the agricultural sector, but it is committed to pursuing a broad agenda of democratization of the state. It is prepared to cooperate with the government, but seeks to limit presidential powers. Its application for official registration has been rejected.

Freedom (*Erk*), opposition party established in 1990 as an offshoot of Unity (*Birlik*). Its leader, Mohammad Salih, was President Karimov's only rival in the December 1991 presidential elections, winning 12% of the vote. After independence *Erk* had a brief period of co-operation with the government. However, relations soon soured and the party was banned in December 1992; many of its activists, including Salih, sought asylum abroad. Several members of *Erk* were allegedly implicated in an assassination attempt on President Karimov in February 1999, Salih being publicly named as one of the organizers; he was subsequently tried and sentenced for terrorism *in absentia*. In June 2003 *Erk* was unexpectedly granted permission to hold a public meeting. However, it continued to experience serious harrassment from the authorities.
Leadership. Mohammad Salih (chairman)

Unity (*Birlik*), a nationalist and secular organization formed in the late 1980s as the first significant non-communist political grouping in Uzbekistan. After independence it was subjected to repressive measures by the Uzbek government and was finally banned in 1992. Several of members, including its leader, sought asylum abroad. In mid-2003, the Uzbek government appeared to be willing to take a more conciliatory approach to opposition parties and *Birlik* was allowed to hold a public meeting to launch its political programme. Abdurahim Polat,

still in self-imposed exile abroad, was elected chairman. Nearly 5,500 people, drawn from all over Uzbekistan, joined the new party. Later, however, *Birlik*'s application for legal registration was rejected without explanation.
Website. www.birlik.net
Leadership. Abdurahim Polat (chairman)

Vanuatu

Capital: Port Vila
Population: 182,000 (2000E)

Vanuatu, the former Anglo-French condominium of the New Hebrides, became an independent republic in July 1980. Legislative authority is vested in a unicameral Parliament, the 52 members of which are elected for four years from 14 multi-member constituencies on the basis of universal adult suffrage. Executive power is exercised by the Prime Minister (who is elected by Parliament from among its members) and by the Council of Ministers, which consists of members of Parliament appointed by the Prime Minister. The President, the republic's head of state, is elected for five years by an electoral college composed of the Parliament and the presidents of the regional councils (local government bodies to which a considerable degree of power is constitutionally devolved).

Elections held in July 2004 resulted in the following distribution of seats: National United Party (NUP) 10; *Vanua'aku Pati* (VP) 8; Union of Moderate Parties (UMP) 7; Vanuatu Republican Party (VRP) 4; Melanesian Progressive Party (MPP) 2; People's Progressive Party (PPP) 4; Green Confederation (GC) 3; National Community Association (NCA) 2; People's Action Party (PAP) 1; *Namagi Aute* (NA) 1; *Nevsem Neparata* (NN) 1; Independents 8. Serge Vohor was elected Prime Minister. As is usually the case in Vanuatu, during the 2004 elections a number of new political parties were formed and won seats. These included the PPP, GC, NCA, PAP, *Namagi Aute* and *Nevsem Neparata*.

Melanesian Progressive Party (MPP)

Address. c/o Parliament, Port Vila
Leadership. Barak Sope (chairman)
The anglophone MPP was formed in mid-1988 by an expelled faction of the *Vanua'aku Pati* (VP) and became part of the opposition Unity Front in the November 1995 general elections. In February 1996 it became part of the coalition which ousted the UMP-NUP government and form a new coalition administration.

The MPP withdrew from government in August 1996 after its leader, Barak Sope, was dismissed from government. The MPP won only 6 seats in the March 1998 election and went into opposition to a coalition government led by the VP. On the collapse of the VP-led government in November 1999, Sope became Prime Minister in a new coalition of the MPP and the UMP but this government was defeated in a confidence vote in April 2001, whereupon the MPP reverted to opposition to a new government headed by the VP. In the 2002 elections the MPP won only 3 seats and this was further reduced to 2 seats in the 2004 elections.

National United Party (NUP)

Address. c/o Parliament, Port Vila
Leadership. Willie Titongoa (chairman)
The NUP was launched in 1991 by former Prime Minister Fr. Walter Lini following his removal as leader of the then ruling *Vanua'aku Pati* (VP). In the December 1991 general

elections the NUP gained 10 parliamentary seats and joined a coalition supporting the premiership of Maxime Carlot Korman of the Union of Moderate Parties (UMP). In August 1993 a majority NUP faction led by Lini withdrew its support from Carlot Korman. In the November 1995 general elections the NUP won 9 seats and, in December, joined a faction of the divided UMP in a new coalition government. This survived only until February 1996, but in October 1996 the NUP joined a new coalition headed by another faction of the UMP and continued in government when the UMP factions were temporarily reunited in May 1997.

In the March 1998 general elections the NUP won 11 seats and; this was reduced to 8 during the 2002 elections but increased to 10 in the 2004 election.

Union of Moderate Parties (UMP)
Union des Partis Modérés (UPM)
Address. PO Box 698, Port Vila
Leadership. Serge Vohor (chairman)
The francophone UMP was formed in 1980 as a coalition of groups opposed to the *Vanua'aku Pati* (VP) government and won the second largest number of seats during the 1983 and the 1987 elections. Following the UMP's success in the December 1991 election, in which it won 19 out of 46 seats, the party joined with the Fr. Walter Lini's National United Party (NUP) to form a coalition under Carlot Korman's premiership. In the November 1995 general elections the UMP won 17 out of 50 seats. In May 1997 a coalition between UMP factions, the NUP and the Melanesian Progressive Party (MPP) was formed but later collapsed in November 1997. In early elections in March 1998 the UMP declined to 12 seats out of 52 and went into opposition to a coalition headed by the VP. In the 2002 elections, the UMP won 15 seats but this was reduced to 7 during the 2004 elections.

Vanua'aku Pati (VP)
Address. c/o Parliament, Port Vila
Leadership. Edward Nipake Natapei (president)
The *Vanua'aku Pati* was established in the early 1970s as the New Hebrides National Party, adopting its present title (which means something like "Party of Our Land") in 1977 and led the country into independence in 1980 and retained power after the 1983 and 1987 elections. As a result conflict and split within the VP, the leader, Lini was ousted and the party lost the December 1991 electionss.

The VP was part of an opposition coalition including MPP and Tan Union after the November 1995 election. In February 1996, however, the UF joined a faction of the divided UMP to oust the UMP-NUP government and form a new coalition administration. In early elections in March 1998 the VP became substantially the largest party by winning 18 of the 52 seats. The VP failed to win a seat in 2002 but came back to win 8 seats during the 2004 elections.

Other Parties

Green Confederation (GC), founded in 2002 by Father Gerard Leynang, a Catholic priest, after breaking away from the NUP. Originally had an inclination towards environmental issues but later came to be dominated by localized political issues. Won 3 seats in the 2004 elections.
Leadership. Moana Carcas

John Frum Movement, based on the southern island of Tanna, won two seats in the March 1998 elections and was part of the 1998-99 government headed by the *Vanua'aku Pati.* Failed to win a seat in the 2004 election.

Namagi Aute, formed in 2002 on the isalnd of Malekula by breakaway members of the UNP and Greens. Won one seat in the 2004 elections.
Leadership. Paul Telukluk

National Community Association (NCA), founded in 2002 as a result of a breakaway from the MPP and mostly consists of people from Tana Island. Closely aligned to the John Frum Movement. Won 2 seats in the 2004 election.
Leadership. Sabi Natonga

Nevsem Neparata, consists of indigenous groups from Erronango Islands in the south. Won one seat in the 2004 election.
*Leadership.*Thomas Nentu

People's Action Party (PAP), formed in 2003 by a group of breakaway politicians from the *Vanua'aku Pati*; won one seat in the 2004 elections.
Leadership. Silas Hakwa

People's Progressive Party (PPP), founded in 2002 after splitting from the MPP and won 4 seats in 2004.
Leadership. Sato Kilman (president)

Vanuatu Republican Party, founded in January 1998 by former Prime Minister Maxime Carlot Korman following his break with the Union of Moderate Parties. He was the new party's only successful candidate in the March 1998 elections but the party won four seats in the 2004 elections.
Leadership. Maxime Carlot Korman (chairman)

Vatican City State (Holy See)

Capital: Vatican City
Population: 921 (citizens)

The Roman Catholic Church is unique among the world's major religions in having an independent and internationally recognized sovereign state. The terms Holy See and the Vatican City State are deployed synonymously in modern usage. In the narrow sense the Holy See means the office of the Pope (the head of the Catholic Church). In the wider sense the Holy See signifies the whole complex of congregations, tribunals, offices, commissions, etc., through which the Pope oversees the government of the Catholic Church. The term Vatican City State specifically refers to the entity created on Feb. 11, 1929, by bilateral treaty between the Holy See and the Kingdom of Italy (the Lateran Treaty), which established Vatican City as an independent state, restored the civil sovereignty of the Pope as a monarch, and compensated the Holy See for loss of the papal states. The Roman Pontiff – the Pope – exercises supreme legislative, executive, and judicial power over the Holy See and the Vatican City State. There are no political parties or political organizations in the Vatican.

Venezuela

Capital: Caracas
Population: 23,500,000 (2000E)

The Republic of Venezuela achieved full independence from Spain in 1830. Sucessive *caudillos* ruled the country until 1945, when Gen. Isaías Medina Angarita was removed by a coup led by progressive army officers and supported by emerging party political organizations. An interim revolutionary junta was established and a new constitution introduced, which provided for the direct election of the President and Congress by universal suffrage. This democratic experiment, known as the *Trienio*, was terminated in 1948 when partisan tensions led to a military coup and the removal of the first democratically elected President, Rómulo Gallegos of the Democratic Action (AD) party, in 1948. A period of repressive military rule under Gen. Marcos Pérez Jiménez, who proclaimed himself President in 1952, alienated all sections of opinion and led the previously antagonistic parties to unite against Jiménez, who was overthrown in 1958 by a popular uprising. The restoration and subsequent consolidation of the democratic system was facilitated by the 1958 Pact of Punto Fijo, devised by the leading parties, AD and the Social Christian Party (COPEI) in conjunction with representatives from the labour and business sector.

AD and COPEI subsequently alternated in office but growing disaffection with the parties combined with their poor record of economic management led to the success of Lt.-Col. Hugo Chávez Frías in the presidential elections of 1998, when he defeated Henrique Salas Römer, an independent endorsed by AD and COPEI. Chávez's inexperienced Fifth Republic Movement (MVR) also performed strongly in the legislative elections, breaking AD and COPEI's traditional monopoly of political representation. Chávez, who had led a failed coup attempt in 1992, campaigned on a platform of radical change that appealed to the socially marginalized. A new constitution, drafted by a Constituent Assembly composed overwhelmingly of supporters of Chávez, was promulgated in December 1999. Serving as the architecture for his radical programme, the constitution permits the President to serve two consecutive six-year terms (the 1961 constitution mandating five-year terms and barring immediate re-election). It also replaced Congress (the bicameral legislature) with a unicameral, 165-member National Assembly, thereby eliminating the Senate (the upper house) and it replaced the Supreme Court and Supreme Electoral Council with the Supreme Justice Tribunal and National Electoral Council respectively.

Underscoring the demise of the traditional parties, Chávez was re-elected in July 2000 for a new six-year term, in a presidential election called under the terms of the new constitution. Elections were also held for the newly-created National Assembly in which the MVR won the largest number of seats (76), but fell short of the absolute two-thirds majority Chávez required to overrule opposition. Owing to their failure to reform, the traditional parties wre inadequately positioned to capitalize on the rising hostility to the Chávez government that emerged forcefully after 2001. Twenty opposition parties, including organizations formerly supportive of the government, subsequently came together in the Democratic Co-ordinator (CD) alliance organization, which campaigned for Chávez to stand down from office. In August 2004, however, Chávez triumphed in a recall referendum on his presidency that was organized by the opposition. The President won 59% of the vote in a contest characterized by an unusually high level of participation (70%).

Democratic Action
Acción Democrática (AD)
Address. Calle los Cedros, Entre Avenida Los Jabillos y Samanes, La Florida, Caracas 1050

Telephone. (58–2) 749855
Leadership. Henry Ramos Allup (president)
Founded in 1936, the nominally social democratic AD was the leading political force after democratization in 1958 until the victory of Chávez in 1998. The party was formed by Rómulo Betancourt under the name of the National Democratic Party (*Partido Democrático Nacional*, PDN) and was registered under its present name in 1941. Its grassroots support came mainly from organized labour. AD developed an unofficial policy of *coincidencia* with COPEI, under which the two parties maintained a minimum consensus on government policy. The party's charismatic and populist leader Carlos Andrés Pérez served as President from 1973 to 1978 and again from 1988 to 1992, the latter term ending with his arrest for corruption. Pérez's dismissal underscored a deeper crisis within the AD party, which was divided throughout the 1990s between factions committed to retaining the organizational and programmatic *status quo* and younger elements that pushed for internal democratization of the party and policy renewal. After expelling the party's long term leader and presidential aspirant, the octogenarian Luis Alfaro Ucero, in 1998, AD backed the independent candidate Salas Römer, in a futile last minute move to prevent the victory of Chávez.

In what was widely regarded as a major setback for the AD and the other much discredited traditional parties, a coalition headed by Chávez's Movement for the Fifth Republic (MVR) virtually matched the performance of the AD in legislative elections held in November 1998. Elections to a Constituent Assembly, charged with formulating a new constitution, were held in July 1999 and in a tactical move designed to delegitimize the process, AD opted not to participate in the election. The decision faciliated a landslide victory by MVR and one month later, the entire leadership of the party, including president Carlos Canache Mata, resigned. Canache was replaced by David Morales Bello, hitherto first vice-president of the party. However, Morales and the party's entire national executive committee resigned in January 2000. Henry Ramos Allup was appointed as the new party president in June, ahead of presidential and legislative elections in July.

The party performed better than expected in the legislative elections, emerging as the second-largest party in the new National Assembly by taking 29 seats in its own right and four in alliance with COPEI. In-fighting within the party continued in the wake of the elections, however. AD entered the CD alliance in 2002, but leading party figures became increasingly disaffected with the umbrella organization and proposals to run joint slates in the regional elections of 2004. The death of Morales Bello in April 2004 prompted a period of introspection for the organization.

The AD is a member party of the Socialist International.

Movement for the Fifth Republic
Movimiento V República (MVR)
Address. Calle Lima, cruce con Av. Libertador, Los Caobos, Caracas
Telephone. (58-2) 7931521
Fax. (58-2) 7829720
Leadership. Hugo Chávez Frías (leader)
The MVR was launched by Lt.-Col. (retd.) Hugo Chávez Frías in July 1997. Chávez, a former paratroop commander who led a failed coup attempt in 1992, had spent two years in prison before being released in 1994 by President Rafael Caldera Rodríguez. Chávez was a populist figure who drew strong support amongst the poor and those disillusioned with traditional politics in Venezuela, which had been dominated for the previous four decades by the Democratic Action (AD) party and the Social Christian Party (COPEI).

During the 1998 election campaign Chávez frightened

the business establishment with his pledges of radical economic and political change; however once in office, his administration followed a largely orthodox economic policy. Chávez was re-elected in July 2000 for a new six-year term, polling close to 60% of the vote in the election called under a new constitution approved by referendum in late 1999. He easily defeated his main challenger and erstwhile comrade-in-arms Fransisco Arias Cárdenas, who had helped him carry out the failed 1992 coup. The July 2000 elections were also called to elect a new 165-member unicameral National Assembly. The MVR won 77 seats in the new Assembly, short of the absolute two-thirds majority required to appoint state officials.

The ruling Patriotic Pole (*Polo Patriótico*) coalition, combining the MVR, Movement Towards Socialism (MAS) and Homeland for All (PPT) parties, began to splinter in 2001 as Chávez assumed an increasingly aggressive stance toward his opponents. Internal divisions within the MVR between civilian and military members further weakened the coherence of the party, which was increasingly displaced by grassroots based Bolivarian Circles (CBs) as a vehicle for electoral and political mobilisation.

The introduction by executive decree in November 2001 of 49 laws intended to roll out the social and economic rights established by the 1999 constitution, led the administration's diverse opponents to unite and push for the removal of the government. In April 2002, sections of the military and civilian opposition captured Chávez and replaced his government with a new administration headed by the president of the leading private sector business association, Fedecámaras, Pedro Carmona. Chávez returned to power two days after the coup following a popular uprising against Carmona and a revolt by constitutionalist elements in the military. The CD and more radical Democratic Bloc (BD) mobilized a fiscally damaging general strike in November 2002 which failed to dislodge Chávez and in 2004, the CD launched a drive to collect over 3.4 million signatures required for a recall referendum on the President. The organizational weaknesses of MVR led Chávez to institute "comandos" or grassroots organizations to mobilize support for the government during the recall referendum campaign. The *comando* Maisanta was instrumental in ensuring a high voter turnout and victory for Chávez in the August 2004 referendum.

Movement Towards Socialism
Movimiento al Socialismo (MAS)

Address. Urb. Las Palmas, Av. Valencia, Qta.Alemar, Caracas
Telephone. (58–2) 782 7309
Fax. (58–2) 782 9720
Leadership. Leopoldi Puchi (leader)

This democratic socialist party was founded in 1971 by the bulk of the membership of the Communist Party of Venezuela (PCV). This followed a split on the revolutionary left in 1970 after the expulsion of PCV leader and former guerrilla leader Teodoro Petkoff Maleo for his open condemnation of the 1968 Soviet invasion of Czechoslovakia and his rejection of both Soviet and Eurocommunist models for the development of Venezuelan socialism. Although the party offered a programmatic alternative to AD and COPEI following its entry into formal politics in 1973, it failed to develop an effective national presence owing to the closed block list system of national voting, which led many MAS sympathizers to consider a vote for the party "wasted". Policy and organizational disputes also weakened the party. Political and administrative decentralization introduced in 1989 allowed MAS to consolidate support at the local level and win control of a number of major states. In 1993, the party formed an alliance with sixteen other parties that backed the *Convergencia* candidate Rafael Caldera in the

presidential elections and following his success, the MAS was rewarded with cabinet posts, including the Planning Ministry. The increasingly neo-liberal drift of the Caldera administration led to tensions within the MAS, with senior party figures withdrawing from the coalition as Caldera's term progressed.

In 1998, the party endorsed Hugo Chávez as their presidential candidate against the recommendations of three prominent MAS leaders who had served as members of Caldera's Cabinet, including Petkoff, who announced the following month that he was resigning his membership of the party that he had co-founded. MAS's organizational experience proved invaluable to the politically immature MVR although the party gained minimally in terms of seats in the Chávez cabinet. The Patiotic Pole (PP) coalition that grouped MVR, MAS and the PPT parties won the most votes in the 1998 legislative elections, with MAS taking almost 9% of the vote and 17 seats in the Chamber of Deputies (the lower chamber). MAS continued to support Chávez in the July 2000 elections. The 21 seats that they won in the new legislature provided Chávez with a solid majority in the assembly (the MVR having won only 77 out of the total 165 seats). In May 2001 the alliance between MAS and the MVR began to disintegrate following an announcement by President Chávez that he was considering the declaration of a state of emergency and the assumption of emergency powers. Disputes over the continued role of the MAS in the PP coalition culminated in the division of the party in 2001. The official MAS party moved into the CD opposition alliance while the United Left (IU) remained loosely allied with the government.

Project Venezuela
Proyecto Venezuela (Proven)

Address. c/o Asamblea Nacional, El Silencio, Caracas 1010
Website. www.proyectovenezuela.org.ve
Leadership. Henrique Salas Römer (leader)

This party was founded in 1998 by former COPEI member Salas Römer, who ran as an independent candidate for the presidency in 1998 with the support of Democratic Action and the Social Christian Party but was defeated by Hugo Chávez. The party evolved from the *Proyecto Carabobo* organization, formed by Salas Römer to contest (succesfully) for the state governorship of Carabobo in 1992 and 1995. *Proyecto Venezuela* won seven National Assembly seats in the July 2000 legislative election but failed to develop into a national political force. The party entered the CD alliance in 2002 but Salas Römer's presidential ambitions served to weaken the movement's organizational unity.

Social Christian Party
Partido Social Cristiano (COPEI)

Address. Erb. El Bosque, Quinta Cuijito, detras Jefe de Camaras, Calle Gloria, Caracas
Telephone. (58–2) 7313393
Fax. (58–2) 7313990
Email. copei@infoline.wtfe.com
Website. www.copei.org
Leadership. Rosana Ordonez (president); Edgar Mora-Contreras (secretary-general)

Founded in 1946, COPEI is a centrist, Christian democratic party although senior figures have been associated with extremist Catholic political organizations. COPEI was founded by Rafael Caldera as the Organizing Committee for Independent Electoral Policy (*Comité de Organización Politica Electoral Independiente*). Alongside the Democratic Action (AD) party, COPEI dominated Venezuelan politics for the four decades prior to the rise of Lt.-Col. Hugo Chávez Frías; however, internal disputes that persisted throughout the 1990s gradually weakened the organization.

COPEI was plunged into deep disarray when Caldera quit the party when his bid for the party's 1993 presidential candidacy was rejected. A number of Caldera loyalists joined him in the *Convergencia* party that he created in 1993 and under which he subsequently won the election. Younger, reform oriented factions defected from the party throughout the 1990s, creating new organizations that include the Justice First (PJ) party.

In the November 1998 legislative elections the party came fourth with little over 10% of the vote and 27 seats in the lower house (down from almost 70 seats a decade earlier). This poor performance was repeated in the July 2000 legislative election when COPEI won only five seats in its own right and four in alliance with the AD. COPEI joined the CD in 2002 and despite its lack of broad based support, leading party figures assumed positions of influence within the alliance.

COPEI is a member party of the Christian Democrat International.

Other Parties

A Homeland for All (*Patria por Todos,* PPT), founded in 1998 by pro-Chávez sections of the Radical Cause (LCR), the PPT played a leading role in the formation of the Patriotic Pole alliance and won one National Assembly seat in the July 2000 legislative election. The weak electoral performance of the party masks a high level of influence within the Chávez government, with *PPTistas* having been appointed to key positions in the state and the cabinet, including the labour, education and energy ministries and the presidency of the state oil company, Petróleos de Venezuela.
Website. www.patriaparatodos.org
Leadership. Pablo Medina (secretary-general)

A New Time (*Un Nuevo Tiempo,* UNT), won three National Assembly seats in the July 2000 legislative election. Was allied to the Fifth Republic Movement (MVR) in the National Assembly and is a member of the *Cambio* (Change) bloc in the National Assembly.

Alliance of Brave People (*Alianza Bravo Pueblo,* ABP), an offshoot of the Democratic Action (AD) party, ABP won one National Assembly seat in the July 2000 legislative election; it is a member of the opposition alliance, the CD.

Communist Party of Venezuela (*Partido Comunista de Venezuela,* PCV), founded in 1931, now a negligible force and unrepresented in the legislature.

First Justice (*Primero Justicia,* PJ), founded in 1992 as a pro-market and pro-decentralization party, PJ won five National Assembly seats in the July 2000 legislative election; comprised largely of a young, technocratic elite, there were high expectations that the party would become a progressive national force. After leading members of the party were implicated in the 2002 coup attempt and the party decided to adopt an uncomprising stance toward the administration of Hugo Chávez thereafter, the influence of the organization began to wane in the CD, which the party joined in 2002.
Website. www.primerojusticia.net and pjelhaltillo@cantv.net

Lapy, a regional party that won three National Assembly seats in the July 2000 legislative election.

National Convergence (*Convergencia Nacional,* CN), launched in 1993 as a (successful) presidential campaign vehicle for Rafael Caldera Rodríguez; won one National Assembly seat in the July 2000 legislative election (for its leader, Juan José Caldera); it is a member of the opposition CD alliance.

National Council of Venezuelan Indians (*Consejo Nacional Indio de Venezuela,* CONIVE), won three National Assembly seats in the July 2000 legislative election; allied to the Movement for the Fifth Republic (MVR) in the legislature.

Organization of Forces in Movement (*Organization Fuerza en Movimiento,* OFM), won one National Assembly seat in the July 2000 legislative election; was allied with the Fifth Republic Movement (MVR).

The Radical Cause (*La Causa Radical,* LCR), has its main support base in the Guayana industrial region and won three National Assembly seats in the July 2000 legislative election; the party split in 1998 when a section of the leadership moved to support Hugo Chávez in the presidential election under the banner of a separate party, the PPT. LCR is a member of the opposition CD alliance.
Leadership. Lucas Matheus (secretary-general)

Solidaridad, formed by Luis Miquilena, a political mentor of Chávez, who occupied a number of senior posts in the cabinet and constituent assembly. Miquilena broke with Chávez in 2001, taking a small number of MVR legislative representatives into his new organization.

Union Party, formed in May 2001 by Francisco Arias Cárdenas, a former governor of Zulia state and a one-time comrade-in-arms of President Chávez, who had finished second to him in the July 2000 presidential election. A member of the opposition CD alliance.

United Multiethnic People of the Amazon (*Pueblos Unidos Multietnicos de Amazonas,* PUAMA), won one National Assembly seat in the July 2000 legislative election and is allied with the Fifth Republic Movement (MVR) in the legislature.

We All Gain All Independent Movement (*Movimiento Independiente Ganamos Todos,* MIGATO), won one National Assembly seat in the July 2000 legislative election; was allied to the Fifth Republic Movement (MVR) in the legislature.

Vietnam

Capital: Hanoi
Population: 80,780,000 (2003)

In 1954 Vietnam was partitioned following protracted Communist-led resistance to French colonial authority. The Socialist Republic of Vietnam (SRV) was proclaimed in July 1976, following the reunification of Vietnam after two decades of warfare between North and South. Effective political power has since been exercised by the Communist Party of Vietnam (CPV).

In 1992 a new state constitution entered into force, which recognized five forms of economic ownership, including private, to provide a legal basis for market-oriented economic reforms. The constitution, however, vested land ownership with the state. The new constitution also declared that the CPV was "the leading force of the state and society". Under the constitution the National Assembly (*Quoc Hoi*), the highest organ of state power, elects the President (from among its own deputies for a five-year term), the Vice-President and the Prime Minister, and ratifies the Prime Minister's nominees for ministerial-level positions in Cabinet.

Elections to the 498-member National Assembly were last held in May 2002. Candidates were nominated by a variety of organizations and approved by the Vietnam Fatherland Front, the CPV-controlled body embracing the country's various mass organizations. In September 2002, the National Assembly elected Tran Duc Luong as President and Phan Van Khai as Prime Minister.

Communist Party of Vietnam (CPV)
Dang Cong San Viet Nam

Address. 1C Hoang Van Thu Street, Hanoi
Telephone. (+84–4) 431472
Email. cpv@hn.vnn.vn
Website. http://www.cpv.org.vn/
Leadership. Nong Duc Manh (secretary-general)

The CPV was founded in February 1930 by Ho Chi Minh. The CPV changed its name to Indochinese Communist Party (ICP) at the request of the Third (Communist) International (or Comintern) when it applied for admission in October 1930. The ICP was officially dissolved in November 1945 but continued to function as an underground organization. In 1951 the ICP re-emerged taking the name Vietnam Workers" Party (VWP); separate communist parties later emerged in Laos and Cambodia. In December 1976, after reunification, the party reverted to its original name, CPV.

Ho Chi Minh (literally, "Ho the seeker of enlightenment") was born in 1890 as Nguyen Tat Thanh in Nghe Tinh province in the central region of what was then French Indo-China. Ho was a founding member of the French Communist Party in 1920 and subsequently worked as an agent of the Comintern in Asia. Simultaneously with the formation of the CPV, a peasant rebellion broke out in Indo-China that then received Communist backing. The CPV was suppressed and Ho was sentenced to death *in absentia* by the French authorities. Colonial policy was changed by the Popular Front government in France and the ICP revived and resumed its public activities.

During World War II, the French colonial authorities in Indo-China, representing the Vichy government, collaborated with Japan. The ICP conducted armed resistance and instigated an unsuccessful uprising in southern Vietnam in 1940. In 1941 Ho was instrumental in forming the League for the Independence of Vietnam, known popularly as the *Viet Minh*. The *Viet Minh* developed its own administrative structure and guerrilla force. *Viet Minh* guerrillas harried the Japanese until the end of the war.

In August 1945, immediately after the Japanese surrender, the *Viet Minh* set up a provisional government in coalition with other nationalist groups. *Viet Minh* forces seized power in Hanoi and across the country. On Sept. 2, 1945, Ho proclaimed Vietnam's independence under the name of the Democratic Republic of Vietnam (DRV). Ho became the Democratic Republic's first President as well as Prime Minister and Foreign Minister.

French colonial forces returned and reasserted their authority in the south. All attempts to negotiate a political settlement between the DRV and the French proved unsuccessful. In late 1946 armed hostilities broke out. This conflict lasted eight years until the French were defeated at the battle of Dien Bien Phu in May 1954. The 1954 Geneva Conference brought an end to hostilities and partitioned Vietnam at the 17th parallel. Ho Chi Minh became both President and Prime Minister of the DRV. Ho relinquished the premiership in 1955 but retained the presidency and chairmanship of the VWP until his death in September 1969.

In 1960, at the VWP's third national congress, the party decided to complete "the national democratic revolution" and to reunify Vietnam. This decision resulted in the initiation of a DRV-supported guerrilla war in the south against the then government of the Republic of Vietnam, backed by the United States. In the mid-1960s the war entered a con-

ventional phase as the United States committed ground troops and initiated an air war over the North. In January 1973 a peace agreement was reached in Paris and the United States withdrew. Hostilities between North and South resumed culminating in a Communist military victory on April 30, 1975, with the capture of Saigon (the capital of the South).

After reunification, the DRV political system became the basis of the SRV. The Provisional Revolutionary Government of the Republic of South Vietnam was formally merged with the DRV. The southern National Front for the Liberation of South Vietnam (founded in 1960) was merged with the Vietnam Fatherland Front (founded in 1955). In 1988 Vietnam formally became a one party state with the dissolution of two minor pro-Communist parties (Vietnam Socialist Party and Vietnam Democratic Party) which had allied themselves with the CPV-led *Viet Minh* in the 1940s. Representatives of these minor parties served in the DRV's National Assembly throughout the Vietnam War.

Commencing with the fourth national party congress in December 1976, the CPV has convened regular national party congresses every five years. Party congresses have the responsibility for amending the party statutes and platform, approving the political report of the party secretary general, selecting the party's national leadership, and adopting long-term socio-economic plans. The fourth congress, for example, approved Vietnam's Second Five-Year Plan (1976-80) that aimed to create "a modern industrial-agricultural structure" on the basis of developing heavy industry, a "great leap" in agriculture and light industrial production.

After the fourth congress, Vietnam experienced a major crisis in its economy at the same time that the *Khmer Rouge* regime in Cambodia stepped up attacks along their border. Vietnam invaded Cambodia in late 1978 and occupied that country before withdrawing in 1989. China attacked Vietnam's northern border provinces in early 1979 in retaliation. Most western and regional states imposed trade and aid sanctions. These developments forced Vietnam into economic and military dependence on the Soviet Union for over a decade.

At the fifth national party congress, held in Hanoi in March 1982, Le Duan, was re-elected CPV general secretary. The congress set two strategic tasks to be accomplished over the next five years: to build socialism and to defend the fatherland. This congress recognized the parlous state of Vietnam's economy, including the lack of sufficient foodstuffs to provide adequate rations, but refrained from undertaking major economic reforms. The congress gave its backing to laying the material and technical basis of socialism and completing the socialist transformation of the south.

Le Duan died in July 1986 and was replaced as party leader by Truong Chinh, who served as caretaker. The sixth national party congress, held in Hanoi in December 1986, is now recognized as a major turning point. Influenced in part by reforms adopted by Mikhail Gorbachev in the Soviet Union, the CPV chose to endorse *doi moi* or renovation. The sixth congress endorsed the abandonment of central planning and the adoption of limited pro-market economic reforms under state direction. By doing so Vietnam was able to extricate itself from a serious socio-economic crisis over the next five years. Party leaders publicly acknowledged their "errors and shortcomings". The congress elected Nguyen Van Linh, a noted reformist, as its next secretary general.

Vietnam's economic reforms were accompanied by calls for political liberalization. The collapse of socialism in Eastern Europe and the disintegration of the Soviet Union resulted in a backlash in Vietnam. Reformist Nguyen Van Linh was replaced as party secretary general by Do Muoi, a cautious conservative party administrator, at the seventh national congress in June 1991. The seventh congress set as its main objective "to emerge from crisis, [and to] stabilize the socio-economic situation." This objective was accomplished and at the party's first mid-term conference in January 1994 priority was now given to the goal of industrialization and modernization. The eighth congress in June 1996 endorsed the objective of becoming a modern and industrial state by the year 2020.

Internal party factionalism at the sixth congress resulted in a leadership compromise. Do Muoi was re-elected as party leader on the proviso that he step down in mid-term. The 1997 Asian Financial Crisis and major peasant demonstrations in Thai Binh province at the end of the year brought the leadership change forward. In December 1997, Le Kha Phieu, a former army political commissar, became CPV secretary general. Le Kha Phieu successfully rode out the financial crisis but otherwise provided lackluster leadership. As the next party congress approached, domestic pressure built up to replace him.

At the ninth congress in April 2001, Phieu was replaced as secretary general by Nong Duc Manh. Nong Duc Manh is a member of the Tay ethnic minority with long service as chairman of the National Assembly's Standing Committee. The ninth congress vowed to continue pursuing the objective of industrialization and modernization with the goal of doubling GDP by 2010. CPV membership stood at 2.4 million.

Western Sahara

Capital: El Aaiún
Population: 800,000 (2003E)

The former Spanish Western Sahara (consisting of Saguia el Hamra and Rio de Oro) was partitioned between Morocco and Mauritania under a 1975 treaty following Spain's decision to withdraw from a region which it had controlled since the 19th century. However, the 1975 partition decision was not accepted by the territory's principal national liberation movement, the Popular Front for the Liberation of Saguia el Hamra and Rio de Oro (Polisario Front). In 1976 the Front proclaimed the Sahrawi Arab Democratic Republic (SADR). However, Morocco extended its sovereignty over the whole territory when Mauritania officially renounced all claims with the Algiers Declaration and ceasefire of Aug. 5, 1979. Morocco stakes its claim to these 267,028 sq km on the basis of the allegiance that Sahrawi tribes traditionally paid to Moroccan monarchs.

The SADR has since been recognized by more than 75 countries, and was admitted to the Organization of African Unity (OAU, now the African Union) in 1982, despite a serious division of opinion among the member states (Morocco then withdrawing from the organization). However, Morocco has continued to exercise de facto control over the territory, building an extensive defensive wall. The population balance has been substantially altered by an influx of Moroccans who now outnumber the indigenous Sahrawis, many of whom have fled as refugees to neighbouring countries.

The protracted and militarily inconclusive (although of recent years largely dormant) conflict between Morocco and the Polisario Front (based in Algeria) has been the subject of United Nations mediation efforts, envisaging the holding of a UN-sponsored referendum to determine the future status of the territory. The UN proposed a plan in 1988, officially accepted by both Morocco and the Polisario. A cease-fire was brokered in 1991, after which the UN Mission for the Referendum in Western Sahara (MINURSO) was set up to facilitate a settlement. In 1997 UN Secretary-General Kofi Annan appointed former US Secretary of State James Baker as his personal envoy to solve the dispute. However, preparations for a referendum have repeatedly stalled over the issue of voter eligibility, as each side accuses the other of falsifying voter registration lists. An additional complicating factor is the discovery of offshore oil, which makes Morocco less keen to surrender control of the territory. Conversely, Polisario has argued that one key objection to SADR independence – its likely economic non-viability – no longer applies.

The MINURSO mandate has been extended *de facto*, although Algeria's continued stipulations on the need for proper UN monitoring and guarantees appears to have pushed Morocco towards rejection of current plans. A 1,500 km wall still divides Western Sahara, keeping the population centres and economic assets under Moroccan control, guarded by 120,000 Moroccan troops and more than a million landmines. Some circles in Rabat are beginning to query the wisdom of this policy, which has hampered Morocco in its desire to play a greater role in pan-African affairs.

Popular Front for the Liberation of Saguia el Hamra and Rio de Oro (Polisario Front)
Frente Popular para la Liberación de Saguia el Hamra y Rio de Oro (Frente Polisario)

Address. BP 10, El-Mouradia, Algiers
Leadership. Mohammed Abdelaziz (secretary-general)
Website. http://www.wsahara.net/sadr.html
http://www.wsahara.net/polisario.html

Formed on May 10, 1973, and committed to pursuing independence for Spanish Sahara, the socialist Polisario Front was initially based in Mauritania, but its political leadership has operated since the mid-1970s from Tindouf, the westernmost town of Algeria. Polisario grew out of the anti-colonial liberation organization, whose full Arabic title was *Harakat Tahrir Saguia El Hamra wa Uad Ed-Dahab*. This guerrilla movement was founded in 1967 by Mohamed Sidi Brahim Bassiri, who was captured by Spanish security forces in June 1970 and never seen again. In later years the Algerian government began diminishing its support for Polisario, and its original military contingent of 10,000 troops appears to have dwindled.

At first Polisario was led by Mustapha Ouali, a former member of the Communist Party of Morocco, though he later broke ranks with the movement. In August 1976, Polisario's third congress elected Mohammed Abdelaziz as its new secretary-general. A congress in 1982 elected Abdelaziz as President of the SADR (necessarily a provisional entity, given the realities of war and exile). Abdelaziz is also considered to be the chief of the Saharawi Popular Liberation Army. Polisario's national secretariat elects the secretary-general for a three-year mandate, and the deputies of a 101-member National Assembly are elected by a general congress. Executive power is vested in the secretary-general and a 13-member government. As of 2003, all members of the SADR cabinet were Polisario members; these included Prime Minister Abdelkader Taleb Oumar and Foreign Minister Mohamed Salem Ould Salek. At its third Congress, Polisario replaced the SADR's previous more decidedly socialist constitution with a new one, which aimed to be "a model of democratic and socialist progressivism, respecting the traditional values of Islam". Polisario says it wishes to see a multiparty democracy emerge after independence.

In a post-Cold War climate much less friendly to liberation movements, the military stalemate and reduced financial and material support from Algeria and Libya caused serious problems for Polisario, which suffered from a stream of defections to Morocco, including SADR foreign minister Brahim Hakim in August 1992. The chief bone of contention between Morocco and Polisario concerns who is eligible to vote in a referendum. Polisario wishes to enfranchise all those who lived in the territory in 1976, plus their descendants. Morocco, by contrast, argues that only current residents may vote; that means disqualifying the many Sahrawi residents who have fled as refugees over the past 28 years, and qualifying those Moroccans whom Rabat encouraged to settle in Western Sahara over the same period. The 1991 ceasefire was to entail a process of "voter identification", although complications and disputes led to the UN suspending this process in May 1996. During 1997-2000, talks yielded progress in the fields of exchanges of POWs, though they stymied over the referendum question. After 1999, Abdelaziz called on the EU to make relations with Morocco conditional on their acceptance of a referendum. He hoped to put pressure on Morocco's new king, Mohammed VI; but his appeals to the EU fell on deaf ears, and he deemed the young monarch to be as "unco-operative" as his late father.

Polisario strongly protested Morocco's awarding of offshore oil exploration deals to foreign companies in 2001. Since then the Polisario government-in-exile has itself signed a rival deal with the Anglo-Australian company, Fusion Oil. Polisario considers that recent UN proposals unfairly favour Morocco, which it accuses of deepening its occupation. For its part, the UN has justified the alleged "dilution" of earlier plans – from Sahrawi independence to the more nebulous option of autonomy – because direct talks between Polisario and Morocco have been so "counter-productive". Polisario rejects Moroccan claims that it is merely an arm of the Algerian security forces, though its dependence on Algeria seems clear. France, in turn, traditionally backs Algeria's stance on the Western Sahara issue.

In 2003 Polisario appeared to buckle before intense international and Algerian pressure, and drop its long-held support for the effectively defunct 1991 Settlement Plan. As a goodwill gesture, Polisario allowed 115 Moroccan prisoners of war to return home in January 2003. The UN and USA responded by demanding that both Morocco and the Polisario Front release the nearly 1,100 remaining Moroccan and 300 Saharawi prisoners of war from their 27-year-long conflict. Polisario's room for manoeuvre has narrowed. Algeria now seeks to realign its interests towards pan-Maghrebi economic liberalization. Moreover, in early 2003 Algeria's still powerful former military chief, Khaled Nezzar, issued statements that implied a rapprochement between "the two brother countries" (i.e. Morocco and Algeria) – possibly at Polisario's expense.

Fears of a resumption of hostilities remain, although many observers believe that Polisario does not have sufficient military and manpower resources to mount a major campaign. Veteran guerrillas are ageing and weapons stock has declined. Polisario officials reported that frustrated camp-dwellers were pressurizing its leadership to resume the armed struggle. Some 160,000 people – representing more than half the Sahrawi people, say some – live in refugee camps run by Polisario on Algerian soil. The camps, particularly the main one, Smarna, 30 km south of Tindouf, are noted for their democratic and egalitarian structure, education services and commitment to equality between the genders, rare in North Africa and the Middle East. Yet Polisario's grip on the camps may be slipping, as younger refugees escape to Spain and elsewhere for work, or to gain further educational qualifications. Meanwhile petty commerce, plus small-scale pilfering, is undermining the former collectivist regime.

Polisario's October 2003 conference in Tifirati (located in "liberated territories") approved the latest plan put forward

by UN Secretary-General Annan for five years of semi-autonomy followed by a referendum.

Closely associated with Polisario is ARSO, *Association de soutien à un référendum libre et régulier au Sahara Occidental*; and also the human rights group, BIRDHSO, the International Bureau for the Respect of Human Rights in Western Sahara. Polisario remains the only major Saharawi opposition force, and it enjoys a measure of international solidarity.

Yemen

Capital: Sana'a
Population: 20,000,000 (2003E)

The Republic of Yemen was established on May 22, 1990, through the unification of the Yemen Arab Republic (North Yemen) and the People's Democratic Republic of Yemen (South Yemen). A referendum held in May 1991 approved the country's new constitution. There had previously been no political parties in North Yemen, while South Yemen had been a one-party state. Unification and political liberalization led to the creation of large number of political groups. At one stage Yemen had up to 22 political parties, although only 12 are currently regarded as truly active entities.

Executive power is held by the President, who is directly elected every seven years and who appoints the Prime Minister and Council of Ministers. Legislative power is vested in a bicameral parliament consisting of the 301-member House of Representatives (*Majlis al-Nuwab*), which is elected for a six-year term, and a second chamber, the 111-member *Shura* Council, appointed by the President.

At elections to the House of Representatives held on April 17, 1993, 80% of the seats were won by the three major parties – the General People's Congress (GPC), the Yemeni *Islah* Party (YIP) and the Yemen Socialist Party (YSP) – which subsequently signed an agreement providing for the creation of a coalition government. Smaller parties won 12 seats, independent candidates 47 and one seat was undeclared. In October 1993 the House elected a five-member Presidential Council, which in turn elected the GPC's leader, Lt.-Gen. Ali Abdullah Salih, as the country's President. Salih had previously been President of the Yemen Arab Republic, a post he had held since assuming power there in 1978.

Mounting tensions between the YSP, with its power base in former South Yemen, and the GPC from the North erupted into full-scale civil war between forces from the two former territories in May 1994. The southern leader and former Vice-President of unified Yemen, Ali Salim al-Bid, proclaimed the formation of the independent Democratic Republic of Yemen (DRY) in the South. In the North, which continued to designate itself the Republic of Yemen, YSP members were dismissed from political office and the armed forces. The DRY forces were defeated by the North in early July 1994 and its leadership fled abroad. In October 1994 the Presidential Council was abolished, President Salih was confirmed in office and a new GPC/YIP coalition, excluding the YSP, was formed.

Twelve parties contested the parliamentary elections held on April 27, 1997, which returned the GPC with the majority (187) of seats. The YIP took 54 seats and independent candidates 55. The YSP boycotted the elections. Salih was re-elected on Sept. 23, 1999, in the country's first direct presidential election. He claimed 96.3% of the vote, although overall turnout was about 66% (and was believed to be less than 10% in the South).

Seven months before the next parliamentary elections were scheduled to be held, parliament voted for a series of significant constitutional amendments, which were put to a referendum on Feb. 20, 2001. About 77% of the electorate voted for the changes which extended the presidential term from five to seven years and the parliamentary mandate from four to six years (rescheduling the next election from 2001 to 2003). The establishment of the *Shura* Council was also approved (this body being appointed in May 2001).

Investigations following the attacks in the USA of Sept. 11, 2001, led to revelations of links between Yemeni radicals and the global *Al-Qaeda* movement of Osama Bin Laden (whose family originated in the Hadhraumat region of Yemen that abuts Saudi Arabia). The resultant crackdown by the Salih administration sparked fears that democratic rights might be curbed, especially following allegations of growing links between elements in the YIP and *Al-Qaeda*. Leaders of four opposition parties, the *Baath*, Nasserites, Islamic *Al-Haq* and Popular Federation, were arrested in March 2003, following bloody clashes between demonstrators and police.

However, parliamentary elections were duly held on April 27, 2003, with turnout officially registered as 76%. The GPC increased its seats tally to 238; the YIP took 46 seats, the YSP 8, the Nasserite Unionist People's Organization 3, and *Baath* 2. Four non-partisans were also elected, a considerable decline on the tally recorded for 1997; according to one interpretation, this indicated greater acceptance of a multi-party system. Chairing the first parliamentary session after the polls, President Salih announced: "There can be no retreat from the democratic choice. Whenever depression overtakes the nation, the Yemeni people again find hope...Democracy is bitter [yet] we must accept it as it is".

Baath Arab Socialist Rebirth Party
Hizb al-Baath al-'Arabi al-Ishtiraki
Address. c/o House of Representatives, Sana'a
Leadership. Dr. Qassim Salaam (leader)
This Yemeni version of the historic pan-Arab *Baath* returned seven successful candidates in the 1993 elections to the House of Representatives. In early 1995 the party was reportedly a constituent of a Democratic Coalition of Opposition. It retained only two seats in the 1997 elections. Although Dr. Salaam was appointed to the new *Shura* Council in 2001, his party joined the Co-ordination Council of Opposition Parties (CCOP). In the 2003 elections the party again returned two seats, on 0.7% of votes cast. Yemeni Baathists are closer to the Iraqi wing of the party than the Syrian wing.

General People's Congress (GPC)
Mutamar al-Shabi al-Am
Address. c/o House of Representatives, Sana'a
Leadership. Ali Abdullah Salih (leader); Abdul-Karim Ali al-Iryani (secretary-general; Sultan Al-Barakani (chairman of the parliamentary party)
The GPC was formed in 1982 in what was then North Yemen (the Yemen Arab Republic, or YAR) as a 1,000-member consultative body rather than a political party. It contested multiparty elections in the YAR in 1988. Lt.-Gen. Salih, the longtime President of the YAR, relinquished his position as secretary-general of the GPC upon assuming the presidency of the unified Republic of Yemen in May 1990. However, he still dominates party business. Since Oct. 3, 1994, another GPC figure, Maj. Gen. Abd al-Rab Mansur al-Hadi, has been Vice President while Salih himself now enjoys the military rank of Field Marshal. Abdul-Karim al-Iryani, who held four top min-

isterial portfolios before becoming Prime Minister in 1980-83 and 1998, has been GPC secretary-general since 1995. He formally left the government in March 2001, on grounds of ill health, though retains his party portfolio and continues to advise President Salih. In March 2003 Iryani led large public protests against the impending US war in Iraq.

With the Yemen Socialist Party (YSP, based in the former South Yemen) the GPC was responsible for guiding the new republic through a transitional period culminating in the 1993 legislative elections. The GPC was the most successful party in these elections, taking 123 seats. It subsequently formed a coalition government with the YSP and the Yemeni *Islah* Party (YIP), and took two seats on the Presidential Council. However, the GPC and the YSP became increasingly estranged, leading to the 1994 civil war. In October 1994, with the southern rebellion quashed, the GPC formed a new coalition government with the YIP, further strengthening its position as the dominant partner in a ministerial reshuffle in June 1995.

The GPC was returned as Yemen's leading party with a substantial majority, taking 187 seats in the 1997 parliamentary elections, and dissolved its post-1994 alliance with the YIP. Opposition parties alleged electoral manipulation, and thus cast doubt on the GPC's assertion that it was becoming a truly national, as opposed to Northern-centred, political party. They also depict the GPC as a manufactured and obedient "party of the President", rather than a genuine mass political party in the conventional sense.

In 1999 President Salih opened up the presidency to directly contested elections, although his only opponent, Najeeb Qahtan Al-Sha'abi, who gained less than 4% of the poll, was a relatively unknown parliamentarian from his own party. In an attempt to appease opposition parties following the result of the referendum in February 2001 extending the presidential and legislative terms, President Salih proposed further amendments to make elections to the presidency more competitive, including reducing the percentage of parliamentary support required for nominations from 10% to 5%. Local municipal elections were also held, coinciding with the referendum. These elections apparently fulfilled a key plank of the GPC platform, to reform Yemeni politics via decentralization of power, but were marked by a measure of pre-poll violence.

Salih appointed Adul-Qader Ba Jamal, as Prime Minister in charge of a new government on April 4, 2001. Born in the Hadhramaut region and formerly a minister in Marxist South Yemen, he was arrested there in 1986, following a a coup attempt against its President, and joined the GPC in 1990. Ba Jamal served as Deputy Prime Minister during 1994-2001. His appointment symbolizes an attempt to "balance the ticket" of the ruling party with a prominent southerner. The GPC also approved the President's strict military measures against Islamist forces. In November 2001 President Salih visited Washington DC, following the attacks of Sept. 11, and pledged Yemen's assistance in the "war on terrorism". In February 2002 Yemen expelled more than 100 foreign Islamic scholars suspected of ties to *Al-Qaeda*.

The GPC adopted a new National Alignment policy in early 2003, which aimed at resisting "all trends trying to damage the social norms and values of Yemeni society". Amongst its new actions was a commitment to curbing corruption and encouraging development in remoter tribal regions, such as the Marib and Sa'adah governorates. As in 1991, the party strongly opposed the US invasion of Iraq in March 2003. The war in Iraq formed a backdrop to the parliamentary elections of April 2003, in which the party increased its seats tally to 238, and claimed 58% of all votes cast.

Nasserite Unionist People's Organization (NUPO)
Al-Tantheem al-Wahdawi al-Sha'bi al-Nasseri
Address. c/o House of Representatives, Sana'a
Leadership. Abul Malek al-Makhlafi

Recognized as a legal party in 1989, the leftist NUPO won three seats in the 1997 parliamentary elections. It subsequently formed a joint parliamentary opposition bloc with the Yemen Socialist Party, Yemeni *Islah* Party and *Baath*. In April 2003 it won just three seats once again, on 1.9% of votes cast. The NUPO has opposed government-backed reforms to the local government laws as a "retreat from democracy, an insult to Yemen and a contradiction of its constitution". It also opposes GPC dominance of parliamentary procedures, lack of clarity regarding the powers of parliament as compared to the *Shura* council, absenteeism by members of parliament, and budgetary emphasis on oil at the expense of other economic spheres.

Yemen Socialist Party (YSP)
Hizb al-Ishtirakiya al-Yamaniya

Leadership. Ali Salih Muqbil (leader); Ali Saleh Obad (secretary-general)

The YSP was formed in 1978 as a Marxist-Leninist "vanguard" party for the People's Democratic Republic of Yemen (South Yemen), and maintained one-party control despite several leadership conflicts until unification with the North in 1990. Upon unification the then YSP secretary-general, Ali Salim al-Bid, was named Vice-President of the new republic, in which the YSP, together with the General People's Congress (GPC) from the North, was charged with the management of the transitional period prior to elections.

Having won 56 seats in the 1993 legislative elections, the YSP was allocated nine cabinet posts in the subsequent coalition government and took two seats on the Presidential Council. However, increasing political tensions resulted from the disparate ideologies of the YSP and the GPC. For instance, the YSP resisted the imposition of the former Northern republic's conservative education system – including the division of genders – over all of a united Yemen. In addition, the collapse of the eastern bloc in 1989, and then the Soviet Union itself, in 1991, had deprived the Marxist YSP of useful international support.

Eventually inter-party rivalry led to the outbreak of civil war in mid-1994 and the short-lived secession of the (southern) Democratic Republic of Yemen. Despite the election of a new party leadership after the civil war, in which the North and GPC triumphed, the YSP was excluded from the new coalition government which was formed in October 1994. The YSP boycotted the 1997 elections, alleging unfairness, and therefore had no parliamentary support to nominate a candidate for the presidential election in 1999. The party opposed the referendum in February 2001, particularly criticizing those amendments giving the President power to dissolve the parliament and to appoint the members of the new *Shura* Council.

The YSP's fourth general conference, held in 2000 without government restriction, voted to elect former members, exiled since 1994, to its central committee. This included individuals sentenced to death or imprisonment for their role in the 1994 civil war. The party joined the Co-ordination Council of Opposition Parties (CCOP) in 2001. That same year it agreed to contest local elections. In December 2002 YSP deputy secretary-general Jarallah Omar was shot dead after giving a speech at the annual general assembly of the rival Yemeni *Islah* Party. An *Islah* party member was arrested. Unlike in 1997, the YSP chose to contest the April 2003 parliamentary elections, though it returned a disappointing eight seats on 3.8% of votes cast.

Yemeni Islah Party (YIP)
Islah

Address. POB 23090, Sana'a

Leadership. Sheikh Abdullah bin Hussein al-Ahmar (leader)

The YIP, also known as the Yemeni Alliance for Reform, was established in September 1990, attracting support from the conservative pro-Saudi population in northern tribal areas. The party campaigned against the new constitution adopted in May 1991 in alliance with several other groups advocating strict adherence to Islamic law. In the 1993 legislative elections the YIP emerged with 62 seats, subsequently assuming six cabinet posts in the coalition government and taking one seat on the Presidential Council. The party leader, Sheikh Ahmar, was also elected speaker of the House of Representatives, a position he has held ever since. Ahmar heads the North's powerful Hashid tribal confederation, to which President Salih and his family also belong.

In the 1994 civil war the YIP strongly supported President Salih and the northern forces. It formed a new coalition with the dominant General People's Congress in the government announced in October 1994, although it lost ground in a ministerial reshuffle in June 1995. The YIP reportedly formed a co-operation agreement with the ruling GPC, winning 54 seats in the 1997 elections and supporting President Salih's nomination for the presidential election in 1999. However, it joined the Co-ordination Council of Opposition Parties (CCOP) in 2001.

Meanwhile, reports grew of radicalism within YIP ranks, which seemed to undermine the leadership of the more ameliordatory Abdullah al-Ahmar. Riyadh dropped its hitherto strong support for the YIP after President Salih patched up relations with Saudi Arabia in mid-2000; consequently, certain elements of the YIP were said to have turned to *Al-Qaeda* as an alternative source of succour. At the YIP's annual general assembly in December 2002, one YIP member shot dead the deputy secretary general of the rival Yemen Socialist Party, Jarallah Omar, who had just finished addressing the gathering.

In April 2003 elections the YIP was again confirmed as the number two party to the dominant GPC, although its number of seats fell slightly to 46, on 22.6% of total votes cast. The YIP alleged electoral rigging in certain constituencies, and accused the GPC of abusing its powers over the security forces to skew the results. Nonetheless, more conservative YIP members took some satisfaction in seeing their ideological rivals, the Socialists, so badly defeated.

Other Parties

Co-ordination Council of Opposition Parties (CCOP), established in 2001, its members seeking full participation in the political process and opposing the constitutional amendments proposed in the February 2001 referendum.

Truth Party (*Al-Haq*), established by Islamic religious scholars in 1991. It secured two seats in the House of Representatives in the 1993 elections which were lost in the 1997 polling.
Leadership. Sheikh Ahmad ash-Shami (secretary-general)

Zambia

Capital: Lusaka
Population: 10,421,000 (2000)

After Zambia gained independence from the United Kingdom in 1964, the next 27 years of its political life were dominated by the republic's first President, Kenneth Kaunda, and the United National Independence Party (UNIP), which was declared the sole legal political organization in 1972. However, in September 1990, in line with developments in much of Africa at that time, the party agreed to the termination of its monopoly on power and to contest elections on a multi-party basis. Accordingly, a new democratic constitution was approved in August 1991, under which executive authority is vested in the President, who is elected by universal adult suffrage for a five-year term (once renewable) at the same time as elections to the 150-member National Assembly. The President appoints a Vice-President and a Cabinet from members of the National Assembly. The constitution also provides for a 27-member consultative House of Chiefs.

Multi-party presidential and legislative elections on Oct. 31, 1991, resulted in a clear victory for Frederick Chiluba and the Movement for Multi-Party Democracy (MMD) over Kaunda and the UNIP. In May 1996 the National Assembly approved a constitutional amendment requiring presidential candidates to be Zambian nationals of Zambian parentage. In protest at this amendment (which effectively prevented Kenneth Kaunda from standing as a candidate) and other electoral issues, the UNIP boycotted Zambia's 1996 elections, as did a number of other opposition parties. The presidential election of Nov. 18, 1996, was won by Chiluba with 72.5% of the vote in a five-way contest. Simultaneous National Assembly elections gave the MMD 131 seats; of the remaining seats, ten were won by independents and nine by candidates of small opposition parties (National Party 5, Agenda for Zambia 2, Zambia Democratic Congress 2). The Zambia Democratic Congress subsequently merged into the Zambia Alliance for Progress.

The third multi-party presidential and legislative elections on Dec. 27, 2001, were hotly contested. The dispute about a third term for Frederick Chiluba had not only fuelled several split-offs from the ruling party MMD, but also broad civil society opposition against a constitutional amendment which would have allowed more than two terms for a President. Chiluba's handpicked MMD candidate for the presidency, Levy P. Mwanawasa, won only by a small margin against his main opponent, Anderson Masoka (United Party for National Development, UPND) with 29.1% of the vote against 27.2%. Also standing were Christon Tembo (Forum for Democracy and Development, FDD) 13.2%; Tilyeni Kaunda (UNIP) 10.1%; Godfrey Miyanda (Heritage Party) 8.1%; Benjamin Mwila (Zambian Republican Party) 4.9%. The results of the presidential elections were regarded as manipulated and were challenged in the courts by the main contenders (a ruling being awaited).

In parliament the MMD lost its absolute majority, but remained the strongest party with 69 seats of the 150 elected members (UPND 49, UNIP 13, FDD 12, Heritage Party 4, Patriotic Front 1, Zambia Republican Party 1, and 1 independent). An additional 8 MPs and the Speaker were nominated by the President increasing the total of MPs to 159. To regain a secure majority in parliament the President appointed several MPs from opposition parties to his cabinet without forming a formal coalition. Not all such MPs from the opposition parties left or were expelled from their parties, and only those who switched to the MMD had to stand in by-elections, which all of them won on the MMD ticket. As a result of a number of by-elections MMD had regained its absolute majority with 76 elected MPs by November 2003.

In June 2003 the Registrar of Societies had 25 political parties registered.

Forum for Democratic Development (FDD)
Address. PO Box 35868, Lusaka
Telephone. (260–1) 225661
Leadership. Lt. Gen. Christon Tembo (president); Ernest Mwansa (general secretary)

The FDD was one of the parties founded in 2001 (being registered in August) over the third term issue. The breakaway group comprised 22 MPs and nine ministers from Chiluba's government. Christon Tembo, a former Vice President (1997-2001) was viewed as a major candidate to become Chiluba's successor in the MMD. As the FDD candidate in the December 2001 presidential contest he came third with 13.2%.

The party is split, since three of its MPs took ministerial posts in Mwanawasa's government. The party leadership tried to expel those MPs from the party who joined the MMD government after 2001, but because of a technicality in the party constitution the MPs were able to challenge the rightfulness of the expulsion in court; a decision is pending. Founded on one issue, the third term, the party is often regarded as being too close to the MMD, although its leadership maintains it is based on issues, not on personalities. The FDD supports decentralization and a truth commission to look into the corruption of the Chiluba government. Of its 12 seats the party won 6 in Lusaka and 5 in Eastern Province.

Heritage Party (HP)
Address. PO Box 51055, Lusaka
Telephone. (260–1) 292370
Leadership. Gen. Godfrey Miyanda (president); E. M. Siwale (general secretary)

As another one issue party the HP was registed in June 2001 as part of the anti-third term campaign. Its president was a minister for education in the last Chiluba government. For development purposes the party propagates the "village concept" which is linked to pre-colonial family settings. The party is not able to maintain a headquarters in Lusaka. In the December 2001 elections the HP won two seats in Lusaka and one each in Eastern and Copperbelt Provinces, and in the latter came in second to the MMD in the overall vote. Two of its four MPs joined the Mwanawasa government, but were not expelled by the party.

Movement for Multi-Party Democracy (MMD)
Address. Private Bag E365, Lusaka
Leadership. Levy P. Mwanawasa (acting president)

The MMD was formed in July 1990 as an informal alliance of groups opposed to the then ruling United National Independence Party, and was granted legal recognition the following December. In February 1991 Frederick Chiluba, the head of the Zambian Congress of Trade Unions, was elected party president. In the elections held in October 1991 the MMD, having focused its campaign on UNIP's poor record of economic management, secured 125 seats in the National Assembly, an overwhelming majority. In the presidential poll Chiluba dislodged Kenneth Kaunda, winning just over 75% of the votes cast.

The MMD government's rigorous IMF-directed economic policies proved unpopular and caused increasing discord within the MMD, as evidenced by the emergence during 1992-93 of new opposition groups, including the National Party (NP), following splits in the ruling party. Further tensions within the MMD led in July 1995 to the expulsion of the party treasurer (who announced the formation of the Zambia Democratic Congress and stood as that party's candidate in the 1996 presidential election, winning 12.5% of the vote compared with 72.5% for Chiluba). In the November 1996 Assembly elections (which were boycotted by UNIP and some of the other opposition parties) the MMD increased its representation to 131 seats. Criticism of Chiluba's record in office intensified during his second presidential term, which included major confrontations with public sector trade unions and widespread arrests of suspects during a five-month state of emergency following an abortive coup attempt in October 1997.

Chiluba's ambitions to have a third term as President caused major splits in the MMD, and many prominent MMD politicians and ministers launched their own parties (FDD, HP, Patriotic Front) in the run-up to the elections of 2001, in which the MMD nonetheless came first in the legislative contest, winning 69 seats, and with its candidate, Levy P. Mwanawasa, winning the presidential contest. Although hand-picked by his predecessor, Mwanawasa tried to establish his own leadership and independence as President by charging Chiluba and his administration with corruption while in office as President of Zambia. This caused a further split within the MMD. Chiluba's supporters organized themselves in the "True Blue" faction to challenge Mwanawasa's leadership. Some of its MPs even voted against the President in a failed impeachment attempt by opposition parties. Many MPs became disgruntled also because of Mwanawasa's lack of patronage towards his own party when he appointed opposition MPs to cabinet posts. The factions within the MMD have an ethnic-regional basis, too; Mwanawasa's major support is among the Lenji and Lamba in Central Province and in the Copperbelt, while the "True Blue" faction is based in Luapula and Northern Province among the Bemba.

The MMD is a member of the Democrat Union of Africa, a regional organization of the International Democrat Union.

Patriotic Front (PF)
Address. PO Box 30885, Lusaka
Leadership. Michael Sata (president); Guy Scott (general secretary)
The party was registered in October 2001 and based on opposition to a third presidential term for Chiluba. It won only one seat in parliament in the December 2001 elections. Its leadership is comprised of ex-MMD ministers; Sata was a minister and national secretary of MMD. The party has some following in Luapula, Northern and Copperbelt Province, and runs only a tiny office in one ot the president's companies; it had no manifesto for the elections, but declares itself to be a "liberal party"; tax reduction is a major issue and sometimes also human rights.

United National Independence Party (UNIP)
Address. PO Box 30302, Lusaka
Telephone. (260–1) 221197
Fax. (260–1) 221327
Leadership. Tilyenji Kaunda (president); Njekwa Anamela (secretary-general)
Dating from 1958, the UNIP under Kenneth Kaunda ruled Zambia from independence in 1964 until 1991, for most of that period as the country's sole legal political organization. In the multi-party elections held in October 1991, Kaunda suffered a resounding defeat, taking only about 25% of the presidential vote, while UNIP candidates secured only 25 of the 150 National Assembly seats in the legislative elections. Kaunda resigned as party leader in January 1992, although he continued to take an active interest in political developments. In March 1993 the Movement for Multi-Party Democracy government accused radical elements within UNIP of plotting a coup with foreign backing.

In June 1994 the UNIP joined six other parties in launching a Zambia Opposition Front. Also in mid-1994, Kaunda announced his intention to return to active politics, being elected UNIP president in June the following year. In October 1995 the government raised questions about Kaunda's nationality, since he had failed to register as a Zambian citizen at independence in 1964 and had retained citizenship of Malawi (his birthplace) until 1970. In May 1996 the constitution was amended to impose a citizenship qualification which effectively prevented Kaunda from standing again as a presidential candidate. UNIP boycotted Zambia's November 1996 presidential and legislative elec-

tions and did not resume electoral participation until 1998, when it won 15% of the seats in municipal elections.

Kenneth Kaunda resigned as UNIP president in March 2000. His son, Tilyenji Kaunda (appointed secretary-general of the party in May 2000), became president of UNIP in April 2001. The party is split into at least two factions; one is in support of the Kaunda family, the other wants to regain electoral appeal without any "Kaunda" at the top of the party. While T. Kaunda wanted to form a formal alliance with Mwanawasa's MMD in 2003, the UNIP central committee decided against it. The party's manifesto is social democratic, but some of its leaders claim it is still a "socialist party". The former ruling party, which won 13 seats in the December 2001 elections, is largely reduced to a regional party in Eastern Province.

United Party for National Development (UPND)
Address. PO Box 33199, Lusaka
Leadership. Anderson Mazoka (president); Logan Shemena (general secretary)
Founded in 1998 by a former senior business executive, the UPND soon proved to be the strongest challenger to the MMD by winning a number of by-elections before the 2001 elections. At the elections UPND emerged as the stongest opposition party, and Anderson Mazoka only marginally lost the race for the presidency – most likely only due to electoral fraud.

The party kept fairly close control of its MPs after the election; it was the only opposition party which immediately expelled all MPs who accepted appointment to a cabinet post or to a governmental commission. It lost, however, all the resultant by-elections, reducing its number of MPs from 49 to 43. It is the only opposition party with none of its MPs participating in the government. The UPND was weakened when Mazoka fell seriously ill for more than half a year in 2003-04. It has its stronghold in Southern Province and it is therefore regarded as a "Tonga party", although it also enjoyed substantial support in Western, Northwestern Province and in Lusaka. UNIP got financial support from liberal parties abroad; during the election campain the party's major issues were agriculture and education.

Zambia Republican Party (ZRP)
Address. PO Box 32129, Lusaka
Leadership. Benjamin Mwila (president); Wynter M. Kabimba (vice-president); Sylvia T. Masebo (secretary general)
The ZRP, registered in August 2000, was launched by dissident members of the ruling Movement for Multi-Party Democracy (MMD) following the expulsion from the MMD of Benjamin Mwila, a former minister who had publicly expressed an ambition to seek the MMD nomination for the presidency in 2001. The ZRP was temporarily merged with the Zambia Alliance for Progress (ZAP), which was itself a merger of several other parties whose members had a political background in UNIP, MMD and UPND. The party won only one seat, in Lusaka, in the 2001 elections and and since then has been torn into two factions, the so-called "Kabimba" and "Mwila" factions. Its only MP, Sylvia T. Masebo, is serving as a cabinet minister in the Mawanawas administration.

Zimbabwe

Capital: Harare
Population: 13,000,000 (2002E)

The white minority regime in Rhodesia, which had declared unilateral independence from the United Kingdom in 1965, ended in 1979 with the adoption of the Lancaster House Agreement. The following year the country gained full independence as the Republic of Zimbabwe. It has since been ruled by the Zimbabwe African National Union–Patriotic Front (ZANU-PF).

An amendment in 1987 to the 1980 pre-independence constitution vested executive power in the President, who is both head of state and head of government, with a six-year mandate. Previously executive authority had been held by the Prime Minister. When the Lancaster House Agreement on the constitution expired in April 1990, the former bicameral legislature set up at independence was replaced by a single-chamber House of Assembly with a six-year term of office and 150 members (120 elective, 10 traditional chiefs, eight provincial governors appointed by the President and 12 other presidential appointees).

Robert Mugabe (ZANU-PF), who had been Prime Minister since independence, was elected President by the House of Assembly in December 1987. In March 1990 he was directly elected to the presidency for the first time, being re-elected for a second six-year term in March 1996 as the sole candidate. In March 2002 Mugabe won a third term in controversial circumstances, when his widely disputed victory was called into question by the main opposition challenger, Morgan Tsvangirai of the Movement for Democratic Change (MDC), and by large sections of the international community. In legislative elections held on June 24–25, 2000, ZANU-PF won 62 of the elective seats with 48.6% of the vote, while Tsvangirai's MDC won 57 seats with 47% of the vote. The remaining elective seat was won by the ZANU-*Ndonga* party. A proposed new constitution for Zimbabwe (the final drafting of which was overseen by ZANU-PF) was rejected in a national referendum held on Feb. 12-13, 2000.

Movement for Democratic Change (MDC)

Address. 6th Floor, Robinson House, Angwa Street/Union Ave., Harare
Telephone. (263–4) 781138
Email. support@mdc.co.zw
Website. www.mdczimbabwe.com
Leadership. Morgan Tsvangirai (president); Welshman Ncube (secretary-general)

The MDC was founded in September 1999 to offer a broad-based alternative to the ZANU-PF party of President Mugabe, which the MDC accused of ruling in an increasingly oppressive manner since its overwhelming victory in the 1995 National Assembly elections. The MDC president, Morgan Tsvangirai (then secretary-general of the Zimbabwe Congress of Trade Unions) was part of a multi-ethnic leadership made up of academics, trade unionists, businessmen, churchmen and human rights activists. Politically centrist, the MDC favoured industrialization, privatization, dialogue with international agencies on Zimbabwe's economic situation, and strict adherence to the rule of law in the land redistribution process in Zimbabwe.

The MDC contested all 120 elective seats in the June 2000 National Assembly elections and won 57 of them, receiving 47% of the recorded vote in what international observers agreed were far from satisfactory polling conditions. A total of 32 MDC supporters were killed during the election campaign, and Tsvangirai himself failed to be elected. The results in 38 constituencies were challenged by the MDC. By early June 2001 three results (including that in the constituency contested by Tsvangirai) had been annulled, while a further three seats had become vacant through deaths of sitting members.

In February 2002 Tsvangirai and two MDC colleagues, party secretary-general Welshman Ncube and MP Renson Gasela, were charged with high treason for their part in an alleged plot to assassinate President Mugabe. The charge, which carried the death penalty, was dismissed by the MDC as a political ploy designed to discredit Tsvangirai ahead of the forthcoming presidential election. Despite the charge, Tsvangirai contested the poll in early March 2002, but was defeated, winning 42% of the vote against some 56% for Mugabe. Tsvangirai immediately called Mugabe's victory into question, claiming that the government had rigged the poll and disenfranchised thousands of MDC supporters. In April the MDC filed a petition with the High Court seeking to overturn the results of the election. At the same time, the party entered into talks with ZANU-PF aimed at ending the political crisis which had engulfed the country in the aftermath of the elections. The talks, sponsored by Nigeria and South Africa, ended in May with little progress having been made.

The trial for treason of Tsvangirai and his two MDC colleagues, Ncube and Gasela, opened in Harare in early February 2003. All three had pleaded not guilty to the charge. The following month the MDC organised a two-day nationwide "mass action" against the Mugabe government, closing a large number of offices and shops. Reports suggested that large numbers of MDC supporters were beaten and arrested by security forces or members of ZANU-PF militias in the weeks following the "mass action". Those arrested included Gibson Sabanda, the MDC vice president, and Paul Themba Nyathi, the party's chief spokesman. (Nyathi had replaced Learnmore Jongwe as the MDC's chief spokesman after Jongwe had in October 2002 died in prison where he had been awaiting trial for allegedly killing his wife the previous month. Tsvangirai had blamed the government for Jongwe's death.)

Following diplomatic intervention by South Africa, Nigeria and Malawi, in May 2003 President Mugabe agreed to resume negotiations with the MDC on resolving the country's deepening political and economic crisis, but only on condition that the MDC drop its legal challenge to Mugabe's victory in the March 2002 election. Tsvangirai insisted that the MDC would press ahead with its challenge, which was formally launched in the High Court in early November 2003. In early June the party organized a week of nationwide strikes and demonstrations. On the final day of the protests (June 6) police arrested Tsvangirai and again charged him with treason, for calling for the violent overthrow of Mugabe. He was released in bail on June 20. In August a High Court judge ruled that the first treason trial against Tsvangirai must proceed, but dismissed the charges against Ncube and Gasela.

The MDC defeated ZANU-PF in local council elections held in cities and towns across the country in early September 2003. The MDC won 137 of the 222 council seats contested in 21 cities and towns. John Houghton, an MDC candidate, became the first white person to win a mayor's seat in Zimbabwe since independence in 1980, defeating ZANU-PF in the northern lakeside resort town of Kariba.

Zimbabwe African National Union–Ndonga (ZANU-Ndonga)

Address. PO Box UA525, Union Avenue, Harare

Rev. Ndabaningi Sithole, the founding president of the Zimbabwe African National Union, broke away from that party in 1977 to form ZANU-*Ndonga*, which he led until his death in 2000. Right-wing in outlook and hostile to the ruling Zimbabwe African National Union-Patriotic Front (ZANU-PF), ZANU-*Ndonga* was the only opposition party to gain parliamentary representation in the April 1995 elections, winning two House of Assembly seats with 6.5% of the vote. In October 1995 Sithole was arrested and charged with conspiracy to assassinate President Mugabe and overthrow the government. His conviction (handed down in 1997) was quashed on appeal. In December 1995 a Sithole lieutenant, Simon Mhlanga, was found guilty of undergoing illegal guerrilla training in Mozambique, the court finding that he was leader of the *Chimwenje* armed dissident movement. In January 1996 the Mozambique government ordered the expulsion of all *Chimwenje* members from its territory. ZANU-*Ndonga* won one seat in the June 2000 elections. Wilson Kumbula had been scheduled to stand as the party's candidate in the March 2002 presidential election, but the party had refused to endorse his candidacy. In the event, Kumbula stood as an independent and received only 1% of the vote.

Zimbabwe African National Union–Patriotic Front (ZANU-PF)

Address. PO Box 4530, Harare
Telephone. (263–4) 750516
Fax. (263–4) 752389
Email. info@zanupf.net
Website. www.zanupf.net
Leadership. Robert Mugabe (president); Joseph Msika (vice-president)

Originally a black nationalist liberation movement, the party was founded in 1963 as the Zimbabwe African National Union (ZANU), a breakaway group from Joshua Nkomo's Zimbabwe African People's Union (ZAPU), which had itself been formed in 1961. In the mid-1970s ZAPU and ZANU organized military wings to conduct guerrilla operations against the white minority regime. In 1976 Mugabe and Nkomo agreed to set up the Patriotic Front alliance with the objective of achieving genuine black majority rule, although in practice ZANU and ZAPU remained separate organizations. The following year Rev. Ndabaningi Sithole broke away from the Mugabe faction of ZANU to form the Zimbabwe African National Union–*Ndonga*.

In the pre-independence elections in 1980 (consequent upon the Lancaster House settlement) and in several subsequent elections, Mugabe's ZANU-PF won substantial parliamentary majorities, culminating in its securing 118 of the 120 elective House of Assembly seats in April 1995. In the first direct presidential election in 1990, Mugabe retained office with 78% of the votes cast. Nkomo's PF–ZAPU was formally incorporated into ZANU-PF in 1989. In 1991 Mugabe announced that he had abandoned plans to introduce a one-party state structure, and the party agreed to delete references to Marxism, Leninism and scientific socialism from its constitution.

Having been nominated as ZANU-PF's candidate in December 1995, Mugabe registered a somewhat hollow triumph in the presidential election of March 1996, the withdrawal of other candidates leaving him effectively unopposed. In a 32% turnout, he was credited with receiving 93% of the votes cast, the residue going to two names that had remained on ballot papers. In February 2000 the electorate rejected (on a 54.6% "no" vote) a proposed new constitution that would have increased the power of the President, weakened civil liberties and redistributed white-owned land. The government nevertheless introduced legislation (passed in April 2000) to amend the existing constitutional provisions on land ownership. Having legalized the compulsory transfer of white-owned land to landless blacks, the authorities made little effort to prevent or punish acts of violence and intimidation by pro-government "war veterans" who carried out forcible seizures of land. Known supporters of the recently formed Movement for Democratic Change (MDC) were among the white farmers attacked (and in some cases killed) by war veterans and suspected ZANU-PF activists in the weeks preceding the June 2000 legislative elections, which also brought an upturn in attacks on black MDC

organizers and supporters. Despite the physical danger facing campaigners in some parts of Zimbabwe, the MDC (with 47% of the vote and 57 seats) drastically reduced the ZANU-PF majority (to 48.6% of the vote and 62 seats).

Mugabe and his ZANU-PF faced a further electoral challenge from the MDC in March 2002, when MDC leader Morgan Tsvangirai ran in the presidential poll. Although Mugabe, aged 78, won the election (gaining 56.2% of the vote, against 42% for Tsvangirai) and was sworn in for a further six-year term, the victory was denounced by the opposition and by many international observers amidst allegations of widespread vote rigging. In his inauguration speech Mugabe insisted that his victory had "dealt a stunning blow to imperialism" and claimed that the West would have only recognized an election won by "their protégé" Tsvangirai. The post-election period was marked by a concerted government crackdown on the opposition, the media and the judiciary and the continuation of the government's controversial "land reform" programme despite critical food shortages and general economic collapse. Rumours concerning Mugabe's deteriorating health led to increased speculation over the question of his successor as President and party leader. Mugabe's favoured successor was reported to be Emmerson Mnangagwa, the Speaker of the House of Assembly. One of the party's two vice presidents, Simon Muzenda, Vice President since December 1987, died in September 2003.

Other Parties

Conservative Alliance of Zimbabwe (CAZ), the name adopted in 1984 by a party founded in 1962 as the Rhodesian Front (a coalition of right-wing white parties) and known from 1981 as the Republican Front. As the Rhodesian Front, it was the party responsible for the 1965 unilateral declaration of independence and the subsequent period of white minority rule. As the CAZ, it ended its whites-only membership policy. With the abolition of reserved white seats in 1987 the CAZ ceased to be represented in the legislature.

National Alliance for Good Governance (NAGG), established by Shakespeare Maya before the March 2002 presidential election. In the poll, Maya, a former executive director of the Harare-based Southern Centre for Energy and Environment, won only 0.4% of the vote.

United Parties (UP), established in 1994 by Bishop Abel Muzorewa, who had briefly been Prime Minister prior to independence. Having boycotted the April 1995 House of Assembly elections, Muzorewa announced his withdrawal from the 1996 presidential election on the grounds that the contest was unfairly weighted in favour of the ruling Zimbabwe African National Union–Patriotic Front. The UP is unrepresented in the legislature elected in 2000.

Zimbabwe African Peoples Union (ZAPU), small Matabeleland-based party led by Agrippa Madlela which emerged from Joshua Nkomo's original ZAPU. In late 2001 the party became divided over the choice of a presidential candidate for the March 2002 presidential poll amid allegations that ZAPU was being bankrolled by the ruling Zimbabwe African National Union–Patriotic Front to destabilize the opposition Movement for Democratic Change (MDC) in Matabeleland. In early 2002 Madlela announced that he would not contest the election and urged his supporters to vote for the MDC leader Morgan Tsvangirai. The move split the party and the former general secretary Paul Siwela contested the poll as an independent, winning only 0.4% of the vote.

APPENDIX A: INTERNATIONAL PARTY ORGANIZATIONS

Centrist Democrat International (Christian Democrat International)

The Centrist Democrat International is the renamed Christian Democrat International (CDI), which was established at a conference in Quito (Ecuador) in November 1982, as successor to the Christian Democratic World Union founded in 1961, with the aim of expanding international co-operation between Christian democratic parties and promoting the formation of new parties. CDI affiliates in Europe are members or associate members of the European People's Party (EPP), which provides the first part of the name of the European Parliament group in which MEPs from these parties and some others sit (see Appendix B). Latin American and Caribbean member parties are grouped in the regional Christian Democratic Organization of America (ODCA), which dates from 1949.

Address. 67 rue d'Arlon, B-1047 Brussels, Belgium
Telephone. (+32–2) 285–4160
Fax. (+32–2) 285–4166
Email. idc@idc–cdi.org
Website. www.idc–cdi.org
Leadership. Antonio López-Iztúriz (executive secretary)

International Democrat Union

The International Democrat Union (IDU) was established in London in June 1983 with the aim of promoting co-operation between conservative and centre-right parties. It has over 80 member parties including, for example, the British Conservative Party, the German Christian Democratic Union and Christian Social Union and the Republican Party in the USA. The IDU currently embraces five regional unions, namely the Americas Democrat Union (ADU), the Asia-Pacific Democrat Union (APDU), the Caribbean Democrat Union (CDU), the Democrat Union of Africa/African Dialogue Group (DUA/ADG) and the European Democrat Union (EDU). Parties can be members of regional unions without being members of the IDU itself.

Address. 100 Pall Mall, St James's, London, SW1Y 5HP, UK
Telephone. (+44–20) 7222–0847
Fax. (+44–20) 7664–8711
Email. rnormington@idu.org
Website. www.idu.org
Leadership. John Howard (chairman); Richard Normington (executive secretary)

Liberal International

The Liberal International (LI) was established in its present form at a conference held in Oxford (England) in April 1947 but traces its origins back to pre-war international co-operation between Liberal parties. LI membership increased only slowly for four decades, but accelerated sharply following the end of communist rule in Eastern Europe and the formation or re-emergence of many liberal parties. LI affiliates in Europe are members of the European Liberal, Democratic and Reformist Party (ELDR) (see Appendix B).

Address. 1 Whitehall Place, London, SW1A 2HD, UK
Telephone. (+44–20) 7839–5905
Fax. (+44–20) 7925–2685
Email. all@liberal–international.org
Website. www.liberal–international.org
Leadership. Annemie Neyts-Uyttebroeck (president); Federica Sabbati (secretary-general)

Socialist International

The present-day Socialist International (SI) dates from 1951 but traces its origins back to the First International (1864–76) and more particularly to the Second International founded in Paris in 1889. Seriously weakened by the outbreak of World War I in 1914, the Second International was irrevocably split by the formation of the Third (Communist) International, or Comintern, in 1919. Four years later, in 1923, the socialist parties which rejected the Soviet revolutionary model established the Labour and Socialist International (LSI), which itself finally collapsed in 1940 when German forces occupied Brussels, where its secretariat was located.

After World War II efforts spearheaded by the British Labour Party to revive a democratic socialist world organization culminated in the foundation of the Socialist International (SI) at a congress held in Frankfurt (Germany) in mid-1951. Originally consisting mainly of European parties, the SI steadily expanded its membership in the Third World, notably after the relaunching of the organization in 1976 under the presidency of Willy Brandt (Social Democratic Party of Germany). A further influx of new members followed the collapse of communism in Europe in 1989–91, many of the new entrants being democratic socialist successors to the former ruling communist parties. In 1992 Brandt was succeeded as SI president by Pierre Mauroy (Socialist Party of France), who was in turn succeeded by António Gutteres (Socialist Party of Portugal) at the SI's 21st congress held in Paris in November 1999 (Gutteres being re-elected at the 22nd congress in October 2003). SI affiliates in Europe are members of the Party of European Socialists (PES), which gives its name to the European Parliament group in which MEPs from these parties and some others sit (see Appendix B).

Address. Maritime House, Old Town, Clapham, London SW4 OJW, UK
Telephone. (+44–20) 7627–4449
Fax. (+44–20) 7720–4448
Email. secretariat@socialistinternational.org
Website. www.socialistinternational.org
Leadership. António Gutteres (president); Luis Ayala (secretary-general)

APPENDIX B: PAN-EUROPEAN POLITICAL GROUPINGS

The European Union's uneven mix of supranationalism and intergovernmentalism has been mirrored by the varying degrees of cooperation that have developed between similarly minded national political parties at European Union level. In a number of cases there have been sufficient political affinities to permit the creation of Europe-wide party federations – the European People's Party (EPP), the Party of European Socialists (PES), the European Liberal, Democratic and Reformist Party (ELDR), the European Green Party and the Democratic Party of the Peoples of Europe–European Free Alliance (DPPE/EFA). These have their own independent structures and secretariats, adopt Europe-wide manifestos for European Parliament elections, seek to hold pre-summits before European Council meetings, and have been exploring other ways of achieving even greater cooperation in the future. In practice their national components are still dominant and their decision-making is still essentially based on consensus rather than on majority voting. Nevertheless they have longer-term aspirations to be become the nuclei of Europe-wide political parties, and this is encouraged by the European Union's Nice Treaty's reference to a European Party Statute. This was later followed up by the European Parliament and Council Regulation (EC) No 2004/2003 of Nov. 4, 2003, on the regulations governing political parties at European level and the rules regarding their funding.

In addition to these, however, there are also seven political groups within the European Parliament. In the case of the five federations mentioned above, their membership is closely related to that of the corresponding political group within the European Parliament but is not necessarily identical. The new ALDE group, for example, not only contains the ELDR parties but a variety of other parties of the centre, including some formerly associated with the EPP. Moreover, the British Conservative Party is not a member of the EPP federation, but its members of the European Parliament are within the EPP-ED group in the European Parliament, a distinction reflected in the different name of the group. Finally, the European Green Party and the European Free Alliance are both within the same political group in the European Parliament.

Besides these, however, there are a number of other political groups within the European Parliament which do not have a corresponding Europe-wide party federation and whose political affinities and degree of voting cohesion tend to be less tight. Regulation 2004/2003 requires a clearer distinction to be made between a European political party and its associated political group within the European Parliament. The text below thus makes a formal separation between its description of the five European party federations and of their corresponding groups within the European Parliament, with their different membership and distinctive features outlined where appropriate. It concludes by listing the other political groups in existence at the beginning of the 2004-09 European Parliament, and just after the set of elections in June 2004 that saw the EP expanding from 626 members in 15 countries to 732 members in 25 countries. For ease of cross-reference, the party names shown in the tables correspond to the English versions used in the country sections of the present volume. It should be noted that in some cases the party name changed after the June 2004 European elections, while in others the list title used in the elections was not the same as the official party name.

EUROPEAN PEOPLE'S PARTY–CHRISTIAN DEMOCRATS (EPP)

(i) European People's Party

Parties of Christian democratic orientation first began to cooperate with each other in the 1920s. After the Second World War cooperation was resumed in the form of a grouping known as Nouvelles Equipes Internationales (NEI), whose constituent Congress was held in Chaudfontaine in Belgium in 1947. In 1965 the NEI was renamed as the European Union of Christian Democrats. In 1976 the statutes for a European People's Party were approved in Luxembourg and the first EPP Congress was then held in 1978. In 1983 the Secretariat of the EUCD in Rome and of the EPP in Brussels were merged (with the combined headquarters located in Brussels), and in 1999 the EUCD was finally incorporated within the EPP. After EU enlargement in May 2004, 20 new parties joined the EPP as full members, and the EPP almost doubled its size in terms of the number of its member parties.

The founding members were essentially all Christian democratic parties with a strong belief in European integration. Over time the EPP has been joined by a number of other parties of the centre-right, such as *Partido Popular* in Spain, *Forza Italia* in Italy, and the Nordic Conservative parties, which are not explicitly Christian democratic parties and which do not always share the European federalist vision of the EPP founding fathers. Membership of the EPP, however, is still not identical with the group of the EPP-ED within the European Parliament.

There are currently 41 parties which are full members of the EPP, 11 observer parties (defined as parties close to the EPP from EU member states or other European countries) and 8 associated parties from countries that have applied to join the European Union. The EPP also has a number of other associated groups, YEPP (the EPP youth organisation), EDS (European Democratic Students), EPP Women, the European Union of Christian Democratic Workers, the SME Union (the EPP organisation dealing with small and medium-sized enterprises) the European Senior Citizens' Union and the European Local and Regional Government Association. Individuals wishing to obtain membership of the EPP may also apply, although "in principle" they should belong to a member party.

The EPP's governing structures are its presidency (president, secretary-general, 10 vice-presidents, treasurer and two honorary presidents), council, political bureau and congress, which is convened every two years. There are also regular EPP summits before European Council meetings, and at which all the top EPP leaders take part. The EPP is also a member of the Christian (now Centrist) Democrat International.

Address. 67 rue d'Arlon, B-1047 Brussels, Belgium
Telephone. (+32-2) 285-4140
Fax. (+32-2) 285-4141
Email. secgen@evppe.be
Website. www.europarl.eu.int/ppe
Leadership. Wilfried Martens (president); Antonio López Istúriz (secretary-general)

Member Parties:
Austria: Austrian People's Party
Belgium: Christian Democrat and Flemish Party; Humanist and Democratic Centre
Cyprus: Democratic Rally of Cyprus (DISY)
Czech Republic: Christian Democratic Union
Denmark: Conservative People's Party; Christian

Democrats
Estonia: Pro Patria (Fatherland) Union; Res Publica
Finland: National Coalition
France: New Union for French Democracy; Union for the Popular Majority
Germany: Christian Democratic Union; Christian Social Union
Greece: New Democracy
Hungary: Alliance of Young Democrats; Hungarian Civic Party (FIDESZ); Hungarian Democratic Forum
Ireland: *Fine Gael*
Italy: *Forza Italia*; Italian Popular Party; Union of Christian Democrats; Union of European Democrats
Latvia: People's Party; New Era
Lithuania: Homeland Union; Lithuanian Christian Democrats
Luxembourg: Christian Social People's Party
Malta: Nationalist Party
Netherlands: Christian Democratic Appeal
Poland: Civic Platform; Solidarity Electoral Action; People's Conservative Party–Movement for a New Poland
Portugal: Social Democratic Party
Slovakia: Christian and Democratic Movement; Slovak Christian and Democratic Union; Hungarian Coalition Party
Slovenia: New Slovenia–Christian People's Party; Slovenian People's Party; Slovenian Democratic Party
Spain: Popular Party; Democratic Union of Catalonia
Sweden: Moderate Party; Christian Democrats

Associated Parties and Movements:
Bulgaria: Banu–People's Union; Union of Democratic Forces
Croatia: Christian Democratic Union
Norway: Hoyre
Romania: Christian Democratic National Peasants Party; Hungarian Democratic Union of Romania
Switzerland: Christian Democrat People's Party; Evangelical People's Party

Observer Parties:
Albania: New Democrat Party; Democratic Party of Albania
Croatia: Croatian Peasants Party, Democrat Centre
Finland: Finnish Christian Democrats
Italy: South Tyrol People's Party
Norway: Christian People's Party
San Marino: San Marino Christian Democrats
Serbia-Montenegro: G17 Plus; Christian Democratic Party of Serbia; Democratic Party of Serbia

(ii) Group of the European People's Party (Christian Democrats) and European Democrats (EPP-ED)

The EPP/ED group dates from June 1953 and was called the Christian Democratic group until 1979. As in the EPP the original Christian democratic core of the group has been diluted in recent years by the adhesion of other centre-right parties. Most of these have also joined the EPP but a notable exception are the British Conservatives who are only in the group and at whose insistence the words "European Democrats" were added to the group's title. The group has provided over half of the presidents of the European Parliament. The 1999 elections resulted in the EPP/ED group becoming substantially the largest in the European Parliament (for the first time since 1975) with 233 members. After the 2004 elections it remained the largest group with 268 members from 44 parties and lists, and was the only political group with representation in all 25 member states of the enlarged European Union.
Address. European Parliament, Rue Wiertz, B-1047 Brussels, Belgium
Telephone. (+32-2) 284-2111
Fax. (+32-2) 230-9793

Email. Epp-ed@europarl.eu.int
Website. www.europarl.eu.int/ppe
Leadership. Hans-Gert Pottering (chairman); Niels Pedersen (secretary-general)

EPP member parties (and no. of MEPs elected in 2004):
Austria: Austrian People's Party (6)
Belgium: Christian Democrat and Flemish Party/New Flemish Alliance (4); Humanist and Democratic Centre (1)
Cyprus: Democratic Rally of Cyprus (DISY) (2)
Czech Republic: Christian Democratic Union (2)
Denmark: Conservative People's Party (1)
Estonia: Pro Patria (Fatherland) Union (1)
Finland: National Coalition (4)
France: Union for the Popular Majority (17)
Germany: Christian Democratic Union (40); Christian Social Union (9)
Greece: New Democracy (11)
Hungary: Alliance of Young Democrats, Hungarian Civic Party (FIDESZ) (12); Hungarian Democratic Forum (1)
Ireland: *Fine Gael* (5)
Italy: *Forza Italia* (16); Union of Christian Democrats (5); Union of European Democrats (1)
Latvia: People's Party (1); New Era (2)
Lithuania: Homeland Union (2)
Luxembourg: Christian Social People's Party (3)
Malta: Nationalist Party (2)
Netherlands: Christian Democratic Appeal (7)
Poland: Civic Platform (15)
Portugal: Social Democratic Party (7)
Slovakia: Christian and Democratic Movement (3); Slovak Christian and Democratic Union (3);
Hungarian Coalition Party (2)
Slovenia: New Slovenia–Christian People's Party (2); Slovenian Democratic Party (2)
Spain: Popular Party (24)
Sweden: Moderate Party (4); Christian Democrats (1)

The following parties and movements are also in the group:
Belgium Christian Social Party (CSP-EVP) (1)
Cyprus: "For Europe" (1)
Czech Republic: Civic Democratic Party (9); Group of Independents–European Democrats (3)
Italy: Pensioners Party (1); South Tyrol People's Party (1)
Poland: Polish People's Party (4)
Portugal: Social Centre Democrats (2)
United Kingdom Conservative Party (27); Ulster Unionist Party (1)

Total: 268 MEPs

PARTY OF EUROPEAN SOCIALISTS

(i) Party of European Socialists (PES)

A Confederation of Socialist Parties of the European Community was first established in 1974. In 1992 this was succeeded by the Party of European Socialists (PES). Containing parties of socialist, social democratic and labour orientation, its main objectives are the promotion of cooperation between its national member parties and the European Parliament group, the development of common policies at EU level, and the adoption of European Parliament election manifestos. It currently consists of 32 member parties from 25 countries, along with 8 associated parties and 5 observer parties. Its supreme body is the PES congress which meets twice every five years. The congress also elects the PES president. In addition the PES has a broader-based presidency (with 33 voting members) as well as a secretariat which is run from Brussels. The PES has a youth wing (ECOSY, European Community Organisation of Socialist Youth) and a women's standing committee. Regular meetings are also held of social-ist party leaders as well as of socialist members of the Council of Ministers. Its current president is Poul Nyrup Rasmussen of Denmark, who narrowly defeated Giuliano Amato of Italy in the April 2004 election to succeed Robin Cook of the United Kingdom, who had been PES president since 2001.

Address. European Parliament, Rue Wiertz, B-1047 Brussels, Belgium
Telephone. (+32-2) 284-2976
Fax. (+32-2) 230-1766
Email. pes@pes.org
Website. www.pes.org
Leadership. Poul Nyrup Rasmussen (president); Philip Cordery (secretary-general)

Member Parties:
Austria: Social Democratic Party of Austria
Belgium: Socialist Party (PS); Socialist Party (SPA-Spirit)
Cyprus: Movement of Social Democrats (KISOS)
Czech Republic: Czech Social Democratic Party
Denmark Social Democratic Party
Estonia: Social Democratic Party
Finland: Finnish Social Democratic Party
France: Socialist Party
Germany: Social Democratic Party of Germany
Greece: Pan-Hellenic Socialist Movement
Hungary: Hungarian Socialist Party; Hungarian Social Democratic Party
Ireland: Labour Party
Italy: Democrats of the Left; Italian Democratic Socialists
Latvia: Latvian Social Democratic Workers Party
Lithuania: Lithuanian Social Democratic Party
Luxembourg: Luxembourg Socialist Workers' Party
Malta: Labour Party
Netherlands: Labour Party
Norway: Norwegian Labour Party
Poland: Union of Labour; Democratic Left Alliance
Portugal: Socialist Party
Slovakia: Party of the Democratic Left; Social Democratic Party of Slovakia
Slovenia: United List of Social Democrats
Spain: Spanish Socialist Workers' Party
Sweden: Social Democratic Labour Party
United Kingdom: Labour Party; Social Democratic and Labour Party

Associated Parties:
Bulgaria: Bulgarian Social Democratic Party; Bulgarian Socialist Party
Croatia: Social Democratic Party of Croatia
Macedonia: Social Democratic Union of Macedonia
Romania: Democratic Party;Social Democratic Party
Switzerland: Swiss Social Democratic Party
Turkey: Republican Peoples Party

Observer Parties:
Andorra: Social Democratic Party
Iceland: Social Democratic Alliance
Israel: Meretz; Labour Party
San Marino: San Marino Socialist Party

(ii) Group of the Party of European Socialists
The PES group dates from June 1953 and was known as the Socialist group until the formation of the PES in 1993. The socialists were the largest group in the European Parliament from the first direct elections in 1979 until 1999, when the collapse of the representation of the British Labour Party (from 62 to 29 members) was among the main reasons for its relegation to the status of second largest group, a status which it retained after the 2004 elections, when it obtained 200 seats. It current-

ly contains 27 parties from 23 member states, not being represented in two of the new member states (Cyprus and Latvia)
Address. European Parliament, Rue Wiertz, B-1047 Brussels, Belgium
Telephone. (+32-2) 284-2111
Fax. (+32-2) 230-6664
Email. pesnet@europarl.eu.int
Website. www.europarl.eu.int/pes
Leadership. Martin Schulz (chairman); David Harley (secretary-general)

PES member parties (and no. of MEPs elected in 2004):
Austria: Social Democratic Party of Austria (7)
Belgium: Socialist Party (PS) (4); Socialist Party/Spirit (SP) (3)
Czech Republic: Czech Social Democratic Party (2)
Denmark: Social Democratic Party (5)
Estonia: Social Democratic Party (3)
Finland: Finnish Social Democratic Party (3)
France: Socialist Party (31)
Germany: Social Democratic Party of Germany (23)
Greece: Pan-Hellenic Socialist Movement (8)
Hungary: Hungarian Socialist Party (9)
Ireland: Labour Party (1)
Italy: Democrats of the Left (12)
Lithuania: Lithuanian Social Democratic Party (2)
Luxembourg: Luxembourg Socialist Workers' Party (1)
Malta: Labour Party (3)
Netherlands: Labour Party (7)
Poland: Democratic Left Alliance (5)
Portugal: Socialist Party (12)
Slovenia: United List of Social Democrats (1)
Spain Spanish Socialist Workers' Party (24)
Sweden: Social Democratic Labour Party (5)
United Kingdom: Labour Party (19)

Others:
Italy: Italian Democratic Socialists (2); Independents (2)
Poland: Polish Social Democracy (3)
Slovakia: Direction (*Smer*) (3)

Total: 200 MEPs

EUROPEAN LIBERAL, DEMOCRATIC AND REFORMIST PARTY (ELDR)

The Liberal International was founded in 1947 but European liberal leaders only started to meet systematically in the early 1970s. In February 1976 the Federation of Liberal and Democratic Parties in the European Community was established. In April 1986 its name was changed to the Federation of Liberal Democratic and Reformist Parties, which in turn in December 1993 became the European Liberal, Democratic and Reformist Party. Its main organs are the ELDR political leaders' meeting, as well as its bureau (with a president, seven vice-presidents and a treasurer), council and congress. It currently has 48 member parties from 31 European countries.
Address. Rue Montoyer 40, B-1000 Brussels, Belgium
Telephone. (+32-2) 284-3169
Fax. (+32-2) 231-1907
Email. eldrparty@europarl.eu.int
Website. www.eldr.org
Leadership. Werner Hoyer (president); Lex Corijn (secretary-general)

Member parties:
Albania: Democratic Alliance
Andorra: Liberal Party
Austria: Liberal Forum
Belgium: Flemish Liberals and Democrats; Liberal

Reformist Party
Bosnia-Herzegovina: Liberal Democratic Party
Bulgaria: Movement Rights and Freedoms; National Movement Simeon II
Croatia: Croatian People's Party; Libra; Croatian Social Party; Liberal Party
Cyprus: United Democrats (UDP)
Czech Republic: Civic Democratic Alliance (ODA); Way of Change (*Cesta Zmeny*)
Denmark: Liberal Party; Radical Liberal Party
Estonia: Estonian Reform Party; Estonian Centre Party
Finland: Centre Party of Finland; Swedish People's Party
Germany: Free Democratic Party
Hungary: Alliance of Free Democrats
Ireland: Progressive Democrats
Italy: Italian Renewal; Italian Republican Party; Italy of Values–Di Pietro Liste; The Democrats; Movement of European Republicans
Latvia: Latvia's Way
Lithuania: Liberal Centre Union; New Union
Luxembourg: Democratic Party
Macedonia: Liberal Party of Macedonia
Netherlands: People's Party for Freedom and Democracy; Democrats 66
Norway: Liberal Party
Poland: Freedom Union
Romania: National Liberal Party
Serbia and Montenegro: Liberals of Serbia; Kosovo Liberal Party
Slovakia: New Civic Alliance (ANO)
Slovenia: Liberal Democrats of Slovenia
Sweden: Centre Party; Liberal People's Party
Switzerland: Radical Party
United Kingdom: Liberal Democrats; Alliance Party of Northern Ireland

Alliance of Liberals and Democrats for Europe (ALDE)
The ALDE group in the European Parliament is the successor to the ELDR group. This dated from the foundation in 1953 of the Liberal group, became the Liberal and Democratic group in 1976 and the ELDR group in 1986. Its size as the third largest European Parliament group had remained relatively stable in recent years, although in the 1999 elections the number of EU countries represented in it fell from 13 to 10. After the 2004 elections, however, it greatly increased in size to 88 members from 31 parties in 19 countries, holding its own in the original 15 states, winning a number of recruits in the new member states and also attracting a number of members from other groups (notably the EPP). Its wider composition to include former EPP and other non-ELDR parties is reflected in the new name of the group, the Alliance of Liberals and Democrats for Europe (ALDE)
Address. European Parliament, Rue Wiertz, B-1047 Brussels, Belgium
Telephone. (+32-2) 284-2111
Fax. (+32-2) 230-2485
Email. eldrgroup@europarl.eu.int
Website. www.eld.europarl.eu.int
Leadership. Graham Watson (chairman); Alexander Beels (secretary-general)

ELDR member parties (and no. of MEPs elected in 2004):
Belgium: Flemish Liberals and Democrats (3); Liberal Reformist Party (2)
Cyprus: United Democrats (UDP) (1)
Denmark: Liberal Party (3); Radical Liberal Party (1)
Estonia: Estonian Reform Party (1); Estonian Centre Party (1)
Finland: Centre Party of Finland (4); Swedish People's Party (1)
Germany: Free Democratic Party (7)

Hungary: Alliance of Free Democrats (2)
Italy: Italy of Values–Di Pietro List (2)
Latvia: Latvia's Way (1)
Lithuania: Liberal Centre Union (2)
Luxembourg: Democratic Party (1)
Netherlands: People's Party for Freedom and Democracy (4); Democrats 66 (1)
Poland: Freedom Union (4)
Slovenia: Liberal Democrats of Slovenia (2)
Sweden: Centre Party (1); Liberal People's Party (2)
United Kingdom: Liberal Democrats (12)

Other parties:
Belgium: Movement of Citizens for Change (MCC) (1)
France: New Union for French Democracy (11)
Ireland: Independent (Marian Harkin) (1)
Italy: Democracy and Liberty–Margherita (7); Movement of European Republicans (1); Bonino List (2)
Lithuania: Labour Party (5)
Spain: Convergence and Union-Democratic Convergence of Catalonia (1); Basque National Party (1)

Total: 88 MEPs

EUROPEAN GREEN PARTY

After national Green parties started to have their first electoral successes in the early 1980s, Green parties from seven European countries got together in 1984 to form the European Coordination of Green Parties. In 1993 this was then turned into the closer-coordinated European Federation of Green Parties. In 2004 it was decided to transform this into a fully-fledged European political party. The European Green Party was thus launched in Rome on Feb. 21, 2004, along with a common campaign platform for the 2004 European Parliament elections. The European Green Party currently has 32 member parties from 29 European countries, and there are also 7 observer parties. (For details of Green party representation in the European Parliament, see under Greens/European Free Alliance, below.)
Address. Rue Wiertz, 2C 85, B-1047 Brussels, Belgium
Telephone. (+32-2) 284-5135
Fax. (+32-2) 284-9135
Email. EFGP@europarl.eu.int
Website. www.europeangreens.org
Leadership. Grazia Francescato & Pekka Haavisto (spokespersons); Arnold Cassola (secretary-general)

Member Parties:
Austria: The Greens
Belgium: Green; Ecolo
Bulgaria: Bulgarian Green Party
Cyprus: Cyprus Green Party
Czech Republic: Green Party
Denmark: The Greens
Estonia: Estonian Greens
Finland: Green Union
France: The Greens
Georgia: Georgia Greens
Germany: Alliance 90/The Greens:
Greece: Ecologists Greens
Hungary: Green Democracy
Ireland: Green Party
Italy: Green Federation
Latvia: Latvian Green Party
Luxembourg: The Greens
Malta: Democratic Alternative
Netherlands: The Greens; Green Left
Norway: Environment Party–The Greens
Portugal: The Greens

Romania: Ecological Federation of Romania
Russia: Interregional Green Party
Slovakia: Slovak Green Party
Spain: The Greens Confederation
Sweden: Environment Party–The Greens
Switzerland: The Greens
Ukraine: Green Party of Ukraine
United Kingdom: Green Party; Scottish Green Party

Observer Parties:
Albania: Greens of Albania
Denmark: Socialist People's Party
Moldova: Ecological Party "Green Alliance" of Moldova
Serbia & Montenegro: Greens of Serbia
Slovenia: Youth Party of Slovenia
Spain: Federation of the Greens–Green Left

EUROPEAN FREE ALLIANCE

The European Free Alliance has existed since 1981 as an association of regionalist and democratic nationalist parties within the European Union which advocate either outright independence and full statehood for their regions or at least greater autonomy and devolution. In 1995 they took on the new name **Democratic Party of the Peoples of Europe–European Free Alliance (DPPE-EFA)** and in 1999 they joined up with the Greens in the European Parliament in the Greens–EFA group. On March 25-26, 2004, they turned themselves into a European political party within the meaning of Regulation 2004/2003. At their founding congress they had 27 member parties and 5 observer parties.
Address. Rue Wiertz, 2C 33, B-1047 Brussels, Belgium
Telephone. (+32-2) 284-3040
Fax. (+32-2) 284-1771
Website. www.efa-dppe.org
Leadership. Nelly Maes (president); Jose Luis Linazasoro (secretary-general)

Member parties:
Belgium: Party of the German-Speaking Belgians; Spirit
France: Savoy Regional Movement; Savoy League; Occitania Party; Breton Democratic Union; Union of the Alsatian People; Party of the Corsican Nation
Greece: Rainbow–Vinozhito (Party of the Macedonians in Greece)
Italy: Emilia and Romagna Freedom; Sardinian Action Party; Slovene Association; Union for South Tyrol; Valdostan Union; League of the Venetian Front
Lithuania: Lithuanian Polish People's Party
Netherlands: Frisian National Party
Poland: Silesian Autonomy Movement
Spain: Andalusian Party; Aragonese Union; Galician National Bloc; Basque Solidarity; Republican Left of Catalonia; Catalan Unity
United Kingdom: *Mebyon Kernow* (Party of Cornwall); *Plaid Cymru*–the Party of Wales; Scottish National Party

Observer parties: Hungarian Federalist Party; Moravian Democratic Party; Basque Nationalist Party; Socialist Party of Mallorca and Menorca; Transylvanian Party.

Greens/European Free Alliance (G/EFA)
The Greens first founded a European Parliament group after the 1989 elections but this remained relatively small until more than doubling its size in the 1999 elections, thanks in part to the adhesion of regionalist parties of the European Free Alliance (EFA). The combined Greens/EFA group included representatives from 12 of the 15 EU countries. They won 42 seats at the 2004 EP elections, having representatives from 12 of the 15 original member states and only winning one seat (an

EFA seat in Latvia) in the 10 new member states.
Address. European Parliament, LEO 2C, Rue Wiertz, B-1047 Brussels, Belgium
Telephone. (+32-2) 284-3045
Fax. (+32-2) 230-7837
Email. jkutten@europarl.eu.int
Website. www.europarl.eu.int/greens
Leadership. Daniel Cohn-Bendit & Monica Frassoni (co-chairpersons); Juan Behrend & Vula Tsetsi (co-secretaries-general); Neil Fergusson (deputy secretary-general and EFA secretary-general)

Green Parties:
Austria: The Greens (2)
Belgium: Ecologist Party (ECOLO) (1); Green (1)
Finland: Green Union (1)
France: The Greens (6)
Germany: Alliance 90–The Greens (13)
Italy: Green Federation (2)
Luxembourg: The Greens (1)
Netherlands: Green Left (2)
Spain: The Greens (1); ICV (1)
Sweden: Green Ecology Party (1)
United Kingdom: Green Party (2)

European Free Alliance Parties (or allies):
Denmark: Socialist People's Party (1)
Latvia: Human Rights in a United Latvia (1)
Spain: Republican Left of Catalonia (1)
UK: Scottish National Party (SNP) (2); *Plaid Cymru*–The Party of Wales (1)

Others:
Transparent Europe (2)

Total: 42 MEPs

European United Left/Nordic Green Left (GUE/NGL)
The GUE/NGL group in the European Parliament dates from the formation of the Communist and Allies Group in October 1973 and has gone through many complex changes, as ex-Communist parties embraced democratic socialism and in some cases joined the Party of European Socialists. The GUE title was adopted after the 1994 European elections, the suffix "Nordic Green Left" being added on the accession of leftist parties from Finland and Sweden following EU enlargement in 1995. The 1999 elections produced an advance for the group, with 42 members elected and with member parties from 10 EU countries. After the 2004 elections they ended up with 41 seats from 18 parties in 14 countries. The parties in the group vary greatly in character, and they have not succeeded in forming a European political party.
Address. European Parliament, Rue Wiertz 45, B-1047 Brussels, Belgium
Telephone. (+32-2) 284-2683
Fax. (+32-2) 230-5582
Email. guewebmaster@europarl.eu.int
Website. www.europarl.eu.int/gue
Leadership. Francis Wurtz (chairman); Maria d'Alimonte (secretary-general)

Member parties (and no. of MEPs elected in 2004):
Cyprus: AKEL (2)
Czech Republic: Czech and Moravian Communist Party (6)
Denmark: People's Movement against the European Union (1)
Finland: Left Alliance (1)
France: French Communist Party and Allies (3)
Germany: Party of Democratic Socialism (7)
Greece: Communist Party of Greece (3); Coalition of the Left and Progress (1)

Ireland: *Sinn Féin* (1)
Italy: Communist Refoundation Party (5); Party of Italian Communists (2)
Netherlands: Socialist Party (2)
Portugal: Portuguese Communist Party (2); Left Bloc (1)
Spain: United Left (1)
Sweden: Left Party (2)
United Kingdom: *Sinn Féin* 1

Total: 41 MEPs

Independence/Democracy Group (IND/DEM)

The Europe of Democracies and Diversities group (EDD) was a new group established in the European Parliament after the 1999 elections and consisting mainly of Eurosceptic parties from four EU countries. The 2004 European elections yielded further gains for such parties, notably in the UK, Poland and Sweden. The EDD Group was then re-constituted and renamed as the Independence/Democracy Group (IND/DEM). It is substantially larger than the old EDD group, and currently has 37 members from 10 countries. Most of these are highly critical of the EU and of further European integration, and the largest component party (United Kingdom Independence Party) would like the UK to leave the EU.
Address. European Parliament, Rue Wiertz, B-1047 Brussels, Belgium
Telephone. (+32-2) 284-2111
Fax. (+32-2) 230-9793
Email. jpbonde@europarl.eu.int
Website. www.europarl.eu.int/groups
Leadership. Jens-Peter Bonde & Nigel Farage (co-chairmen); Claudine Vangrunderbeeck & Herman Verheirstraeten (co-secretaries-general)

Member parties (and no. of MEPs elected in 2004):
Czech Republic: Independents Movement (1)
Denmark: June Movement (1)
France: Movement for France (3)
Greece: Popular Orthodox Rally (LAOS) (1)
Ireland: Independent (Kathy Sinnott) (1)
Italy: Northern League (4)
Netherlands: Reformational Political Federation/Reformed Political Association/Reformed Political Party (2)
Poland: League of Polish Families (10)
Sweden: June List (3)
United Kingdom: UK Independence Party (11)

Total: 37 MEPs

Union for a Europe of Nations (UEN)

The UEN group in the European Parliament was formed after the June 1999 European elections as a successor to earlier Gaullist-dominated groups – although the French Gaullist Rally for the Republic switched to the European People's Party/European Democrats and was replaced by the Eurosceptic Rally for France and the Independence of Europe (RPF-IE), whose leader and former Gaullist Minister, Charles Pasqua, became chairman of the group. Divisions within the RPF-IE subsequently resulted in nine of its 12 MEPs defecting from the UEN group, three joining the Europe of Democracies and Diversities (EDD) group and six opting to sit as Non-Attached Members. After the 2004 elections the UEN managed to survive as a group, but as the smallest of the EP's 7 groups with 27 members from 6 European countries, with almost half of these from the new EU member states.
Address. European Parliament, Rue Wiertz, B-1047 Brussels, Belgium
Telephone. (+32-2) 284-2111
Fax. (+32-2) 230-9793
Email. fwurtz@europarl.eu.int
Website. www.europarl.eu.int/groups
Leadership. Cristiana Muscardini and Brian Crowley (co-chairmen); Frank Barrett (secretary-general)

Member parties:
Denmark: Danish People's Party (1)
Ireland: *Fianna Fáil* (4)
Italy: National Alliance (9)
Latvia: Fatherland and Freedom (4)
Lithuania: Liberal Democrats (1)
Lithuania: Union of Farmers and New Democracy Parties (1)
Poland: Law and Justice (7)

Total: 27 MEPs

Non-Attached Members

Listed below are the parties represented in the 2004-09 European Parliament which are not members of any of the above groups. A number of these are parties of the far right that were unable to form a separate political group. There are currently 29 such members.
Austria: Freedom Movement (1)
Austria: Hans-Peter Martin List (2)
Belgium: Flemish Bloc (3)
Czech Republic: Independent (1)
France: National Front (7)
Italy: Socialist Unity for Europe (2)
Italy: Tricolour Flame (1)
Italy: Social Alternative–Mussolini List (1)
Poland: Self-Defense (6)
Slovakia: Movement for a Democratic Slovakia (3)
UK: Democratic Unionist Party (DUP) 1; one MEP elected as United Kingdom Independence Party

Total: 29 MEPs

INDEX OF PERSONAL AND PARTY NAMES

Note: party page references are to the main entry for each party. Where there are parties of the same name in different countries the country name is given.

A Different Israel 329
A Homeland for All 652
A New Time 652
Aasar, Abdul Moneim El- 193
Aase, Turid Sveen 454
Abacha, Gen. Sani 448-9
Abachi, Sid Áhmed 14
Abad, Florencio 477
Abashidze, Aslan 246-7
Abate Kisho 208
Abba, Abdelaziz 419
Abbas, Mahmoud 462
Abbas, Maldom Baba 118
Abbas, Philip 567
Abd al-Majid, Khalid 464
Abdala Nósseis, Vítor Jorge 85
Abdalla, Dr. Suleiman 381
Abdallah, Mahamat Ali 119
Abdel Karim, Farid 193
Abdel Rahman, Sheikh Omar 194
Abdelaziz, Mohammed 654-5
Abdel-Fatouh, Abdel-Moneim 195
Abdel-Fattah, Nabil 190
Abdenour, Maître Ali Yahia 16
Abderrahman, Ahmed Abdullah 134
Abdi, Abbas 308
Abdic, Fikret 75
Abdildin, Serikbolsyn 350
Abdoulaye, Kabeh 408
Abdul-Aziz ibn Saud, King 510
Abdulkadir, Alhaji Adamu
Ahmed 448-9
Abdullah Ahmad Badawi, Dato'
Seri 400
Abdullah bin Abdul-Aziz Al-Saud, Crown
Prince 510
Abdullah II, King of Jordan 345-8
Abdullah, Farooq 299-300
Abdullah, Omar 300
Abdullah, Samir 464
Abdullah, Sheikh Mohammed 299
Abdul-Samad, Adnan 362
Abed-Rabbo, Yasser 464
Abeille, Patrice 235
Abied, Mohammed 418
Abiola, Moshood 448
Ablyazov, Mukhtar 351
Aboubacar, Ahmed 134
Aboubakar, Yusuf 356
Abraham, Laurenso A. (Jopie) 440
Abu Ahmed, Salman 328
Abu al-Nasr, Hamid 195
Abu Bakr, Yusuf 346
Abu Dabbus, Mona 347
Abu Hamza al-Masri, Sheikh 194
Abu Hanoud, Mahmoud 463
Abu Nidal 465
Abu Saada, Hafez 193
Abu Sharif, Bassam 324
Abu Shenab, Ismail 463
Abubakar, Gen. Abdulsalam 448
Abu-Bakr, Jamil 347
Abul Abbas 464
Abul Ragheb, Ali 346
Abul-Atta, Abdel-Azim 190
Abyadnanaya Grazhdanskaya Partyya
Belarusi 56
Abylov, Bulat 350
Abylsiitov, Galym 351
Acção Democrática Independente 509
Acción Democrática 650
Acción Democrática Nacionalista 71
Acción Democratico Nacional 439
Acción Popular 475
Acción por la República-Nueva Dirigencia
25
Acero, José Antonio 551
Acevedo Vilá, Aníbal 642-3
Achabar, Chakir 422
Achakzai, Mehmood 460
ACT New Zealand 441
Action and Reflection Group for the
Development of Madagascar 394
Action Committee for Democracy and Social
Justice 387

Action Committee for Renewal 591
Action démocratique du Québec 111
Action for Change 407
Action for Meritocracy and Equal
Opportunity Party 107
Action for the Renewal of Chad 119
Action for the Republic-New Direction 25
Action Front for Renewal and Development
66
Action Party (Morocco) 418
Action Party for the Independence of
Kurdistan 311
Action pour Changement 407
Action pour le Renouvellement du Tchad 119
Action Tchadienne pour l'Unité et le
Socialisme 119
Action, Truth, Development and Harmony
394
Adalet ve Kalkinma Partisi 599
Adamec, Ladislav 165
Adami, Lahib 15
Adamkus, Valdas 383-4
Adams, Gerry 320, 624-5
Adams, J.M.G. (Tom) 51
Adams, Sir Grantley 51
Adanlin, Timothée 67
Addad, Hakim 16
Adel, Gholam-Ali Haddad- 308
Adelsohn, Ulf 574
Adenauer, Konrad 250
Adhikari, Man Mohan 429-30, 432
Adilet 364
Adisu Legese 207
Adoboli, Koffi Eugene 592
Adolat 647
Adolatho 587
Advance Papua New Guinea Party 471
Advani, L.K. 293
Aelvoet, Magda 60
Afewerki, Isayas 200-1
Affirmation for a Republic of Equals 25
Afghan Mellat 2
Afghan Nation 2
Afghan Social Democratic Party 2
Afghanistan Independence Party 2
Afifi, Anwar 193
Afilal, Abderrazzak 422
Afirmación para una República Igualitaria 25
Aflaq, Michel 312, 582
African Christian Democratic Party 541
African Democratic Rally 95
African Forum for Reconstruction 241
African Movement for Democracy and
Progress 66
African National Congress 541
African Party for Independence 95
African Party for the Independence of Cape
Verde 113
African Party for the Independence of
Guinea and Cape Verde 270
African Party of Independence (Senegal) 513
African Renaissance Party 449
African Solidarity for Democracy and
Independence 403
Afrikaner Eenheidsbeweging 541
Afrikaner Unity Movement 541
ag Hamani, Mohamed Ahmed 403
Agar, Mehmet 598, 600
Agazade, Igbal 42
Agbakoba, Olisa 450
Agbéyomè, Kodjo 592
Agboyibo, Yao 591
Aggudey, Francis 259
Agha, San'an Ahmad 314
Agha, Zakariya al- 462
Aghajari, Hashem 308
Agnarsdottir, Gudrun 291
Agondjo-Okawe, Pierre-Louis 240
Agonistiko Dimocratico Kinima 157
Agov, Petur 87
Agrarian Labour Party of Kyrgyzstan 363
Agrarian Party (Kazakhstan) 350
Agrarian Party of Albania 5
Agrarian Party of Belarus 55
Agrarian Party of Kyrgyzstan 364

Agrarian Party of Russia 496
Agrarian Party of Tajikistan 586
Agrarian Party of Ukraine 604
Agrarian Union (Hungary) 287
Agrarnaya Partiya Rossii 496
Agrarnaya Partyya Belarusi 55
Agrarno-Trudovnaya Partiya Kyrgyzstana
363
Agrárszövetsége 287
Agricultural Labour Action Party 144
Agripino, José 83
Agrupación Herreña Independiente 555
Aguirre, José Antonio 552
Ágústsson, Baldur 288
Ahadi, Anwar al-Haq 2
Ahavat Yisrael 329
Ahbash 391
Aherdane, Mahjoubi 420-1
Ahern, Bertie 317-8
Ahidjo, Ahmadou 105
Ahmad, Ibrahim 315
Ahmadi, Mohammad Mehdi 308
Ahmadzai, Ahmad Shah 2
Ahmar, Abdallah al- 582
Ahmar, Sheikh Abdullah bin Hussein al 657
Ahmed, Ahmed Ougoureh Kifleh 180
Ahmed, Hamdi 191
Ahmed, Hossam 192
Ahmed, Moudad 50
Ahmed, Qazi Hussain 457-8
Ahmed, Rebwar 316
Ahmedov, Ali 45
Ahmedov, Ramiz 43
Ahmeti, Ali 391
Aho, Esko 212
Ahrarna Partiya Ukrainy 604
Ahtisaari, Martti 213
Ai'a Api 238
Aidid, General Mohamed Farah 539
Aidid, Hussein 539
Aït Ahmed, Hocine 11, 15-6
Ait Idder, Mohammed Ben Said 421-2
Aitmatov, Chingiz 364
Ajanovic, Mirnes 74
Ajibekova, Klara 364
Ajouhu, Ernest Wan 237
Ak Zhol 350
Akatay, Sabet-Kazy 351
Akayev, Askar 362-4
Akbyan! 478
Akcja Wyborcza Solidarnosc 484
Akef, Mohammad Mahdi 195
Akhali Memarjveneebi 245
Akhmetov, Rinat 606
Akin, Kenan 161
Akinci, Mustafa 159-60
Akitani, Emmanuel Bob 592
Akoto, Paul Yao 147
Aksyon Demokratiko 478
Aktiounskomitee fir Demokratie a
Gerechtegkeet 387
Akulliit Partiiat 178
Al Huriya (Lebanon) 373
Al Irada al Chaabia 372
Al Jabhar Al Nidal Al Watani 372
Al Karal al Chaabi 372
Al Karamah al Wataniyah 372
Al Karamah wah Tajdid 372
Al Khalifa, Sheikh Hamad ibn Issa 47
Al Kitla Al Chaabi-Elias Shaft 372
Al Kitla al Chaabi-Fouad el Turk 373
Al Sabah, Amir Jabir 361
Al Takaful 194
Al Tawafoc al Watani 373
Al Ummah 193
Al Wasat 193
Al Wifac wal Tajdid 372
Al Wifah Al Matni 372
Al-Ahd 347
Alami, Ahmed el- 422
Alamo Suárez, José Luis 555
Alaoui, Ismail 421
Alarcón Rivera, Fabián 187, 189
Alash National Freedom Party 351
Alavan Unity 554

669